Weiss Ratings' Guide to Banks and Thrifts

A Quarterly Compilation of Financial Institution Ratings and Analyses

Winter 2004 - 05

Copyright ©2004 by Weiss Ratings, Inc.

P.O. Box 689608
Jupiter, FL 33468-9608
(561) 627-3300

www.WeissRatings.com

Our customer hotline is here to serve you.
Don't hesitate to call us at

(800) 289-9222

This line is open from 8:30 am - 6:00 pm from Monday to Friday,
Eastern Standard Time.

ISSN: 1049-5673
ISBN: 1-58773-132-0

Edition: No. 56, Winter 2004 - 05

Data: June 30, 2004

Raw data source: Board of Governors of the
Federal Reserve System, Washington, D.C.
and Office of Thrift Supervision, Washington, D.C.

Contents

Terms and Conditions

This Document is prepared strictly for the confidential use of our customer(s) and those advising our customers. It has been provided to you at your specific request. This Document is not intended for the direct or indirect solicitation of business. Weiss Ratings, Inc. expressly disclaims any warranty of merchantability or fitness for any particular purpose that may exist with respect to this Document.

The information contained herein has been derived from data furnished by official sources that we deem reliable. However, Weiss Ratings, Inc. has not independently verified the data. The data and information contained herein are, therefore, provided "as is" without warranty of any kind. As such, Weiss Ratings, Inc. makes no warranty, express or implied, or representation as to the accuracy, adequacy or completeness of the information relied upon by it in preparing this Document.

Weiss Ratings, Inc. uses the most current information in its possession during the rating review process. However, in the interim, the institution may have disclosed other information which could have a bearing on the opinions expressed in this Document.
Weiss Ratings, Inc. disclaims any and all liability to any person or entity for any loss or damage caused, in whole or in part, by any error (negligent or otherwise) or other circumstances involved in, resulting from or relating to the procurement, compilation, analysis, interpretation, editing, transcribing, publishing and/or dissemination or transmittal of any information contained herein.

The ratings and other opinions contained in this Document must be construed solely as statements of opinion from Weiss Ratings, Inc., and not statements of fact. Each rating or opinion must be weighed solely as a factor in your choice of an institution and should not be construed as a recommendation to buy, sell or otherwise act with respect to the particular product or company involved.

This Document and the information contained herein is copyrighted by Weiss Ratings, Inc. Any copying, displaying, selling, distributing or otherwise delivering of this information or any part of this Document to any other person, without the express written consent of Weiss Ratings, Inc. except by a reviewer or editor who may quote brief passages in connection with a review or a news story, is prohibited.

Welcome to Weiss Ratings'
Guide to Banks and Thrifts

Most people automatically assume their bank will survive, year after year. However, prudent consumers and professionals realize that in this world of shifting risks, the solvency of financial institutions can't be taken for granted. After all, your bank's failure could have a heavy impact on you in terms of lost time, lost money (in cases of deposits exceeding the federal insurance limit), tied-up deposits, lost credit lines, and the possibility of being shifted to another institution under not-so-friendly terms.

If you are looking for accurate, unbiased ratings and data to help you choose a commercial bank, savings bank, or savings and loan for yourself, your family, your company or your clients, Weiss Ratings' Guide to Banks and Thrifts gives you precisely what you need.

Weiss Ratings' Mission Statement

Weiss Ratings' mission is to empower consumers, professionals, and institutions with high quality advisory information for selecting or monitoring a financial services company or financial investment.

In doing so, Weiss Ratings will adhere to the highest ethical standards by maintaining our independent, unbiased outlook and approach to advising our customers.

Why rely on Weiss?

For more than 30 years, Weiss Ratings, Inc. has been advising people on the safety offered by financial institutions. Our mission is to provide fair, objective ratings to help professionals and consumers alike make educated financial decisions.

At Weiss, integrity is number one. Weiss never takes a penny from rated companies for issuing its ratings. And, we publish the Weiss Safety Ratings without regard for institutions' preferences. Our analysts review and update the Weiss ratings each and every quarter, so you can be sure that the information you receive is accurate and current – providing you with advance warning of financial vulnerability early enough to do something about it.

Other rating agencies focus primarily on a company's current financial solvency and consider only mild economic adversity. Weiss also considers these issues, but in addition, our analysis covers a company's ability to deal with severe economic adversity in terms of a sharp decline in the value of its investments and a drop in the collectibility of its loans.

Our use of more rigorous standards stems from the viewpoint that a financial institution's obligations to its customers should not depend on favorable business conditions. A bank or thrift must be able to honor its loan and deposit commitments in bad times as well as good.

Weiss' rating scale, from A to F, is easy to understand. Only a few outstanding companies receive an A (Excellent) rating, although there are many to choose from within the B (Good) category. A large group falls into the broad average range which receives C (Fair) ratings. Companies that demonstrate marked vulnerabilities receive either D (Weak) or E (Very Weak) ratings. So, there's no numbering system, star counting, or color-coding to keep track of.

The U.S. Government agrees — Weiss' ratings are the best

In a recent study covering the life insurance industry, the United States General Accounting Office (GAO) concluded that Weiss was the most accurate of all five insurance rating agencies studied.

According to the GAO study, Weiss rated more companies than the other agencies, and did so more accurately. In fact, Weiss outperformed A.M. Best 3 to 1 in warning of coming financial troubles – with warning coming an average of eight months earlier than Best's!

You can be confident that the same spirit of independence and consumer advocacy that has produced these excellent results applies to our analysis of the banking industry as well and will continue in the months and years ahead.

Thank you for your trust and purchase of this Guide. If you have any comments, or wish to review other products from Weiss Ratings, please call 1-800-289-9222 or visit www.WeissRatings.com. We look forward to hearing from you.

How to Use This Guide

The purpose of the *Guide to Banks and Thrifts* is to provide consumers, businesses, financial institutions, and municipalities with a reliable source of banking industry ratings and analysis on a timely basis. We realize that the financial safety of a bank or thrift is an important factor to consider when establishing a relationship. The ratings and analysis in this Guide can make that evaluation easier when you are considering:

- a checking, merchant banking, or other transaction account
- an investment in a certificate of deposit or savings account
- a line of credit or commercial loan
- counterparty risk

The rating for a particular company indicates our opinion regarding that company's ability to meet its obligations – not only under current economic conditions, but also during a declining economy or in an environment of increased liquidity demands.

To use this Guide most effectively, we recommend you follow the steps outlined below:

Step 1   To ensure you evaluate the correct company, verify the company's exact name as it was given to you. It is also helpful to ascertain the city and state of the company's main office or headquarters since no two banks with the same name can be headquartered in the same city. Many companies have similar names but are not related to one another, so you will want to make sure the company you look up is really the one you are interested in evaluating.

Step 2   Turn to Section I, the Index of Banks and Thrifts, and locate the company you are evaluating. This section contains all federally-insured commercial banks, savings banks, and savings and loans. It is sorted alphabetically by the name of the company and shows the main office city and state following the name for additional verification.
If you have trouble finding a particular institution or determining which is the right one, consider these possible reasons:

- You may have an incorrect or incomplete institution name. There are often several institutions with the same or very similar names. So, make sure you have the exact name and proper spelling, as well as the city in which it is headquartered.

- You may be looking for a *bank holding company*. If so, try to find the exact name of the main bank in the group and look it up under that name.

Step 3   Once you have located your specific company, the first column after the state shows its current Weiss Safety Rating. Turn to *About the Weiss Safety Ratings* on page 7 for information about what this rating means. If the rating has changed since the last edition of this Guide, a downgrade will be indicated with a down triangle ▼ to the left of the company name; an upgrade will be indicated with an up triangle ▲.

Step 4   Following the current Weiss Safety Rating are two prior ratings for the company based on year-end data from the two previous years. Use this to discern the longer-term direction of the company's overall financial condition.

Step 5   The remainder of Section I provides insight into the areas our analysts reviewed as the basis for assigning the company's rating. These areas include size, capital adequacy, asset quality, profitability, liquidity, and stability. An index within each of these categories represents a composite evaluation of that particular facet of the company's financial condition. Refer to the table on page 8 for an interpretation of which index values are considered strong, good, fair, or weak. In most cases, lower-rated companies will have a low index value in one or more of the indexes shown. Bear in mind, however, that the Weiss Safety Rating is the result of a complex qualitative and quantitative analysis which cannot be reproduced using only the data provided here.

Step 6   If the company you are evaluating is not highly rated and you want to find a bank or thrift with a higher rating, turn to the page in Section II that has your state's name at the top. This section contains those Weiss Recommended Companies (rating of A+, A, A- or B+) that have a branch office in your state. If the main office telephone number provided is not a local telephone call or to determine if a branch of the bank or thrift is near you, consult your local telephone Yellow Pages Directory under "Banks," "Savings Banks," or "Savings and Loan Associations." Here you will find a complete list of the institution's branch locations along with their telephone numbers.

Step 7   Once you've identified a Weiss Recommended Company in your local area, you can then refer back to Section I to analyze it.

Step 8   In order to use the Weiss Safety Ratings most effectively, we strongly recommend you consult the *Important Warnings and Cautions* listed on page 11. These are more than just "standard disclaimers." They are very important factors you should be aware of before using this Guide. If you have any questions regarding the precise meaning of specific terms used in the Guide, refer to the Glossary beginning on page 405.

Step 9   Make sure you stay up to date with the latest information available since the publication of this Guide. For information on how to set up a rating change notification service, acquire follow-up reports, check ratings online or receive a more in-depth analysis of an individual company, call 1-800-289-9222 or visit www.WeissRatings.com.

About the Weiss Safety Ratings

The Weiss Safety Ratings represent a completely independent, unbiased opinion of an institution's financial safety – now, and in the future. The ratings are derived, for the most part, from quarterly financial statements filed with federal regulators. Although we seek to maintain an open line of communication with the companies being rated, we do not grant them the right to influence the ratings or stop their publication.

The Weiss Safety Ratings are assigned by our analysts based on a complex analysis of hundreds of factors that are synthesized into five indexes: capitalization, asset quality, profitability, liquidity and stability. These indexes are then used to arrive at a letter grade rating. A good rating requires consistency across all indexes. A weak score on any one index can result in a low rating, as insolvency can be caused by any one of a number of factors, such as inadequate capital, poor underwriting practices, operating losses, or the failure of an affiliated company.

The primary components of the Weiss Safety Rating are as follows:

- **Capitalization Index** gauges capital adequacy in terms of each institution's cushion to absorb future operating losses under various potential business and economic scenarios as they may impact the company's net interest margin, securities' values, and the collectibility of its loans.

- **Asset Quality Index** measures the quality of the company's past underwriting and investment practices based on the estimated liquidation value of the company's loan and securities portfolios.

- **Profitability Index** measures the soundness of the company's operations and the contribution of profits to the company's financial strength. The profitability index is a composite of five sub-factors: 1) gain or loss on operations; 2) rates of return on assets and equity; 3) management of net interest margin; 4) generation of noninterest-based revenues; and 5) overhead expense management.

- **Liquidity Index** values a company's ability to raise the necessary cash to satisfy creditors and honor depositor withdrawals.

- **Stability Index** integrates a number of sub-factors that affect consistency (or lack thereof) in maintaining financial strength over time. Sub-factors include 1) risk diversification in terms of company size and loan diversification; 2) deterioration of operations as reported in critical asset, liability, income and expense items, such as an increase in loan delinquency rates or a sharp increase in loan originations; 3) years in operation; 4) former problem areas where, despite recent improvement, the company has yet to establish a record of stable performance over a suitable period of time; and 5) relationships with holding companies and affiliates.

Each of these indexes is measured according to the following range of values.

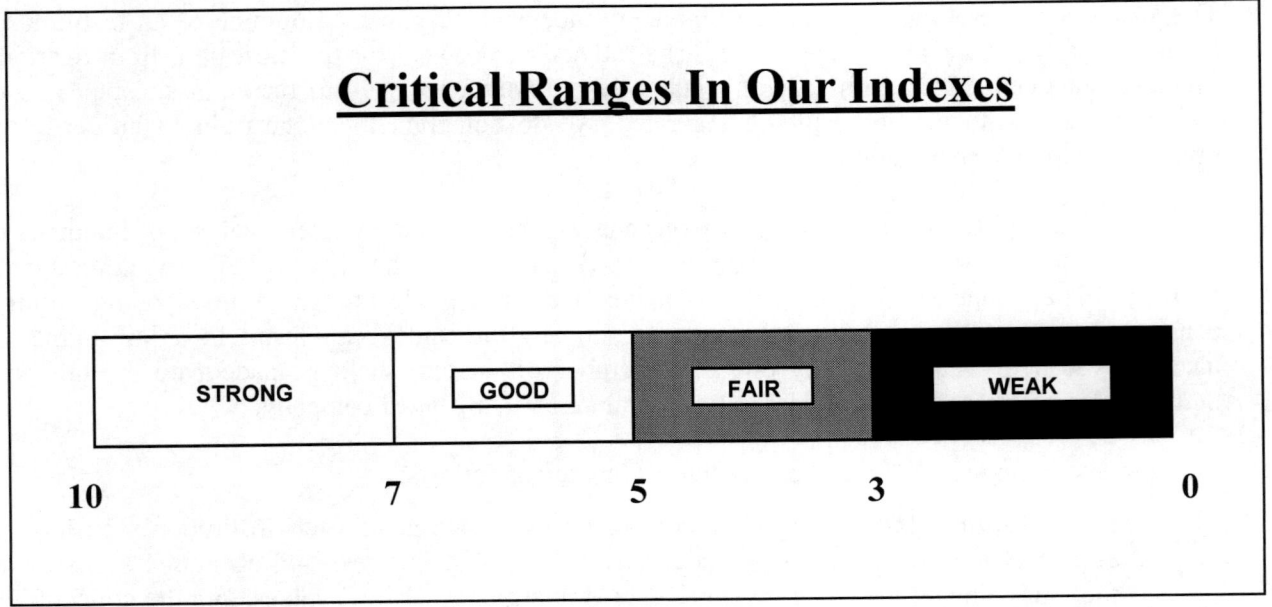

Finally, the indexes are combined to form a composite company rating which is then verified by one of our analysts. The resulting distribution of ratings assigned to all banks and thrifts looks like this:

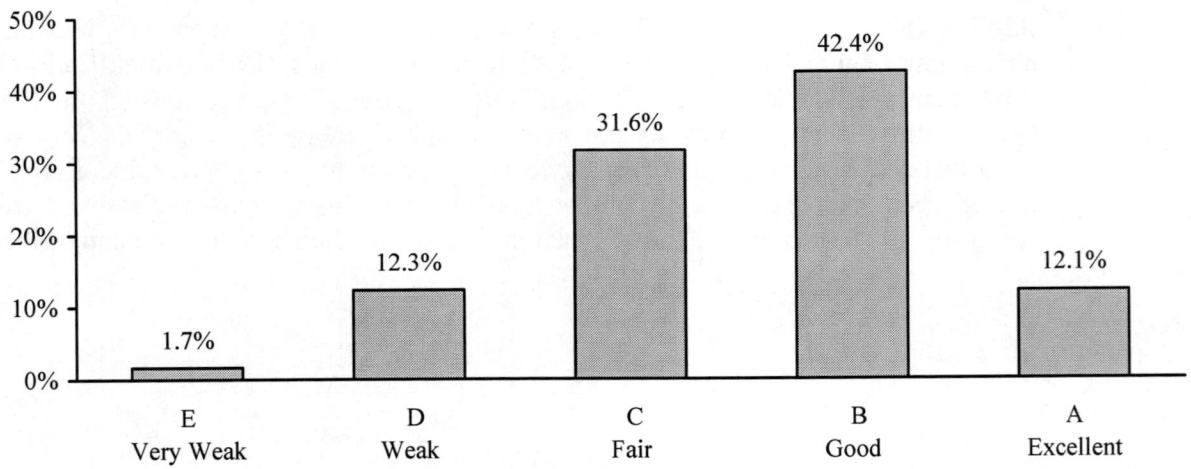

What Our Ratings Mean

A   **Excellent.** The institution offers excellent financial security. It has maintained a conservative stance in its business operations as evidenced by its strong equity base, top-notch asset quality, steady earnings, and high liquidity. While the financial position of any company is subject to change, we believe that this institution has the resources necessary to deal with severe economic conditions.

B   **Good.** The institution offers good financial security and has the resources to deal with a variety of adverse economic conditions. It comfortably exceeds the minimum levels for all of our rating criteria, and is likely to remain healthy for the near future. Nevertheless, in the event of a *severe* recession or major financial crisis, we feel that this assessment should be reviewed to make sure that the company is still maintaining adequate financial strength.

C   **Fair.** The institution offers fair financial security, is currently stable, and will likely remain relatively healthy as long as the economic environment avoids the extremes of inflation or deflation. In a prolonged period of adverse economic or financial conditions, however, we feel this company may encounter difficulties in maintaining its financial stability.

D   **Weak.** The institution currently demonstrates what we consider to be significant weaknesses which could negatively impact depositors or creditors. In an unfavorable economic environment, these weaknesses could be magnified.

E   **Very Weak.** The institution currently demonstrates what we consider to be significant weaknesses and has also failed some of the basic tests that we use to identify fiscal stability. Therefore, even in a favorable economic environment, it is our opinion that depositors or creditors could incur significant risks.

F   **Failed.** The institution has been placed under the custodianship of regulatory authorities. This implies that it will be either liquidated or taken over by another financial institution.

+   **The plus sign** is an indication that the company is at the upper end of the letter grade rating.

-   **The minus sign** is an indication that the company is at the lower end of the letter grade rating.

U   **Unrated Institutions.** The institution is unrated due to insufficient data at the time its rating was updated.

Peer Comparison of Bank/Thrift Safety Ratings

Weiss	Veribanc	Bauer Financial	IDC Financial	Bankrate.com	Lace Financial
A+, A, A-	Green, Three Stars w/ Blue Ribbon recognition	5 stars, 4 stars	201-300	1, Five stars	A+, A
B+, B, B-	Green, Three Stars w/out Blue Ribbon recognition	3 ½ stars	166-200	2, Four stars	B+
C+, C, C-	Green Two Stars, Yellow Two Stars	3 stars	126-165	3, Three stars	B, C+
D+, D, D-	Green one star, Yellow one star, Green no stars	2 stars	76-125	4, Two stars	C, D
E+, E, E-	Yellow no stars, Red no stars	1 star	1-75	5, One star	E

Important Warnings And Cautions

1. **A rating alone cannot tell the whole story.** Please read the explanatory information contained here, in the section introductions and in the appendix. It is provided in order to give you an understanding of our rating philosophy as well as to paint a more complete picture of how we arrive at our opinion of a company's strengths and weaknesses. In addition, please remember that our safety rating is not an end-all measure of an institution's safety. Rather, it should be used as a "flag" of possible troubles, suggesting a need for further research.

2. **Safety ratings shown in this directory were current as of the publication date.** In the meantime, the rating may have been updated based on more recent data. Weiss offers a notification service for ratings changes on companies that you specifiy. For more information call 1-800-289-9222 or visit www.WeissRatings.com.

3. **When deciding to do business with a financial institution, your decision should be based on a wide variety of factors in addition to the Weiss Safety Rating.** These include the institution's pricing of its deposit instruments and loans, the fees you will be charged, the degree to which it can help you meet your long-term planning needs, how these costs/benefits may change over the years, and what other choices are available to you given your current location and financial circumstances.

4. **The Weiss Safety Ratings represent our opinion of a company's insolvency risk.** As such, a high rating means we feel that the company has less chance of running into financial difficulties. A high rating is not a guarantee of solvency nor is a low rating a prediction of insolvency. The Weiss Safety Ratings are not deemed to be a recommendation concerning the purchase or sale of the securities of any bank or thrift that is publicly owned.

5. **All firms that have the same Weiss Safety Rating should be considered to be essentially equal in safety.** This is true regardless of any differences in the underlying numbers which might appear to indicate greater strengths. The Weiss Safety Rating already takes into account a number of lesser factors which, due to space limitations, cannot be included in this publication.

6. **A good rating requires consistency.** If a company is excellent on four indicators and fair on one, the company may receive a fair rating. This requirement is necessary due to the fact that fiscal problems can arise from any *one* of several causes including poor underwriting, inadequate capital resources, or operating losses.

7. **Our rating standards are more conservative than those used by other agencies.** We believe that no one can predict with certainty the economic environment of the near or long-term future. Rather, we assume that various scenarios – from the extremes of double-digit inflation to a severe recession – are within the range of reasonable possibilities over the next one or two decades. To achieve a top rating according to our standards, a company must be adequately prepared for the worst-case reasonable scenario, without impairing its current operations.

8. **We are an independent rating agency and do not depend on the cooperation of the companies we rate**. Our data are derived, for the most part, from quarterly financial statements filed with federal regulators. Although we seek to maintain an open line of communication with the companies being rated, we do not grant them the right to influence the ratings or stop their publication. This policy stems from the fact that this Guide is designed for the protection of our customers.

9. **Inaccuracies in the data issued by the federal regulators could negatively impact the quality of a company's Safety Rating.** While we attempt to find and correct as many data errors as possible, some data errors inevitably slip through. We have no method of intercepting fraudulent or falsified data and must take for granted that all information is reported honestly to the federal regulatory agencies.

10. **Institutions that operate exclusively or primarily as a trust company may have skewed financial information.** Due to the nature of their business, these companies often record high profit levels compared to other more "traditional" banks and thrifts. Trust companies can usually be recognized by the initials "TC" or "& TC" in their names.

11. **The ratios and indexes contained in this edition of the *Guide to Banks and Thrifts* reflect updates to previous editions.** Therefore, comparisons of indexes or ratios between this edition and previous editions may not be appropriate.

12. **This Guide does not cover nonbank affiliates of banking companies.** Although some nonbank companies may be affiliated with the banks and thrifts cited in this Guide, the firms are separate corporations whose financial strength is only partially dependent on the strength of their affiliates.

13. **There are many companies with the same or similar sounding names, despite no affiliation whatsoever.** Therefore, it is important that you have the exact name, city, and state of the institution's headquarters before you begin to research the company in this Guide.

14. **Affiliated companies do not automatically receive the same rating.** We recognize that a troubled institution may expect financial support from its parent or affiliates. The Weiss Safety Ratings reflect our opinion of the measure of support that may become available to a subsidiary bank, if the subsidiary were to experience serious financial difficulties. In the case of a strong parent and a weaker subsidiary, the affiliate relationship will generally result in a higher rating for the subsidiary than it would have on a stand-alone basis. Seldom, however, would the rating be brought up to the level of the parent.

    This treatment is appropriate because we do not assume the parent would have either the resources or the will to "bail out" a troubled subsidiary during a severe economic crisis. Even when there is a binding legal obligation for a parent corporation to honor the obligations of its subsidiary banks, the possibility exists that the subsidiary could be sold and lose its parental support. Therefore, it is quite common for one affiliate to have a higher rating than another. This is another reason why it is especially important that you have the precise name of the company you are evaluating.

15. **This publication does not include foreign banking companies, or their U.S. branches.** Therefore, our evaluation of foreign banking companies is limited to those U.S. chartered domestic banks owned by foreign banking companies. In most cases, the U.S. operations of a foreign banking company are relatively small in relation to the overall size of the company, so you may want to consult other sources as well. In any case, do not be confused by a domestic bank with a name which is the same as – or similar to – that of a foreign banking company. Even if there is an affiliation between the two, we have evaluated the U.S. institution based on its own merits.

Section I

Index of Banks and Thrifts

An analysis of all rated

U.S. Commercial Banks, Savings Banks,

and Savings and Loans.

Institutions are listed in alphabetical order.

Section I Contents

This section contains the Weiss Safety Ratings, key rating factors, and summary financial data for all U.S. federally-insured commercial banks, savings banks, and savings and loans. Companies are sorted in alphabetical order, first by company name, then by city and state.

Left Pages

1. Institution Name	The name under which the institution was chartered. If you cannot find the institution you are interested in, or if you have any doubts regarding the precise name, verify the information with the bank or thrift itself before proceeding. Also, determine the city and state in which the institution is headquartered for confirmation. (See columns 2 and 3.)
2. City	The city in which the institution's headquarters or main office is located. With the adoption of intrastate and interstate branching laws, many institutions operating in your area may actually be headquartered elsewhere. So, don't be surprised if the location cited is not in your particular city.
	Also use this column to confirm that you have located the correct institution. It is possible for two unrelated companies to have the same name if they are headquartered in different cities.
3. State	The state in which the institution's headquarters or main office is located. With the adoption of interstate branching laws, some institutions operating in your area may actually be headquartered in another state.
4. Weiss Safety Rating	The Weiss rating assigned to the institution at the time of publication. Our ratings are designed to distinguish levels of insolvency risk and are measured on a scale from A to F based upon a wide range of factors. Please see page 9 for specific descriptions of each letter grade.
	Highly rated companies are, in our opinion, less likely to experience financial difficulties than lower rated firms. See *About the Weiss Safety Ratings* on page 7 for more information. Also, please be sure to consider the warnings beginning on page 11 regarding the ratings' limitations and the underlying assumptions.
5. Prior Year Weiss Safety Rating	The Weiss rating assigned to the institution based on data from December 31 of the previous year. Compare this rating to the company's current rating to identify any recent changes.
6. Weiss Safety Rating Two Years Prior	The Weiss rating assigned to the institution based on data from December 31 two years ago. Compare this rating to the ratings in the prior columns to identify longer term trends in the company's financial condition.
7. Total Assets	The total of all assets listed on the institution's balance sheet, in millions of dollars. This figure primarily consists of loans, investments (such as municipal and treasury bonds), and fixed assets (such as buildings and other real estate).

Overall size is an important factor which affects the company's ability to diversify risk and avoid vulnerability to a single borrower, industry, or geographic area. Larger institutions are usually, although not always, more diversified and thus less susceptible to a downturn in a particular area. Nevertheless, do not be misled by the general public perception that "bigger is better." Larger institutions are known for their inability to quickly adapt to changes in the marketplace and typically underperform their smaller brethren.

8. **One Year Asset Growth**

The percentage change in total assets over the previous 12 months. Moderate growth is generally a positive since it can reflect the maintenance or expansion of the company's market share, leading to the generation of additional revenues. Excessive growth, however, is generally a sign of trouble as it can indicate a loosening of underwriting practices in order to attract new business.

9. **Commercial Loans/ Total Assets**

The percentage of the institution's asset base invested in loans to businesses. Commercial loans are the traditional bread and butter of commercial banks, although many thrifts have increased their business lending in recent years.

10. **Consumer Loans/ Total Assets**

The percentage of the institution's asset base invested in loans to consumers, including credit cards and home equity loans. Consumer lending has grown rapidly in recent years due to the high interest rates and fees institutions are able to charge. On the down side, consumer loans usually experience higher delinquency and default rates than other loans, negatively impacting earnings down the road.

11. **Home Mortgage Loans/ Total Assets**

The percentage of the institution's asset base invested in residential mortgage loans to consumers, excluding home equity loans. Savings banks and savings and loans have traditionally dominated mortgage lending. Indeed, the S&L charter still requires thrifts to invest a minimum percentage of their assets in mortgages and mortgage-backed securities.

This type of loan typically experiences lower default rates. However, the length of the loan's term can be a subject for concern during periods of rising interest rates.

12. **Securities/ Total Assets**

The percentage of the institution's asset base invested in securities, including U.S. Treasury securities, mortgage-backed securities, and municipal bonds. This does not include securities the institution may be holding on behalf of individual customers.

Although securities are similar to loans in that they represent obligations to pay a debt at some point in the future, they are a more liquid investment than loans and usually present less risk of default. In addition, mortgage-backed securities can present less credit risk than holding mortgage loans themselves due to the diversification of the underlying mortgages.

13. Capitalization Index   An index that measures the adequacy of the institution's capital resources to deal with potentially adverse business and economic situations that could arise. It is based on an evaluation of the company's degree of leverage compared to total assets as well as risk-adjusted assets. See the graph on page 8 for a description of the different critical levels presented in this index.

14. Leverage Ratio   A regulatory ratio defined by the federal banking and thrift regulators as core (tier 1) capital divided by tangible assets. This ratio answers the question: How much does the institution have in stockholders' equity for every dollar of assets? Thus, the Leverage Ratio represents the amount of actual "capital cushion" the institution has to fall back on in times of trouble. We feel that this is the single most important ratio in determining financial strength because it provides the best measure of an institution's ability to withstand losses.

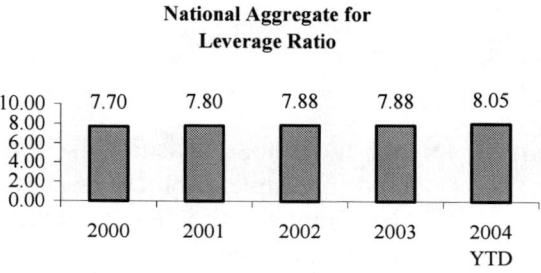

**National Aggregate for
Leverage Ratio**

15. Risk-Based Capital Ratio   A regulatory ratio defined by the federal banking and thrift regulators as total (tier 1 + tier 2) capital divided by risk-weighted assets. This ratio addresses the issue that not all assets present the same level of credit risk to an institution. As such, all assets and certain off-balance sheet commitments are assigned to risk categories based on the level of credit risk they pose and then weighted accordingly to arrive at risk-weighted assets.

For instance, assets with virtually no risk, such as cash and U.S. Treasury securities, are risk-weighted at 0% and therefore, not included in the calculation. Assets with low risk, for example, high quality mortgage-backed securities and state and municipal bonds, are partially weighted at 20%. Those assets possessing moderate risk, such as residential mortgages and state and local revenue bonds, are partially weighted at 50%. And finally, assets considered to possess "normal" or "high" risk, including certain off-balance sheet commitments such as unfunded loans, are risk-weighted at 100%. The summation of these categories of risk-weighted assets results in the figure used in the denominator of this ratio.

Please be aware that not all banks and savings banks are required to report risk-weighted assets as defined by the federal regulators. Consequently, we have estimated this figure when necessary based on estimates used by the regulators themselves.

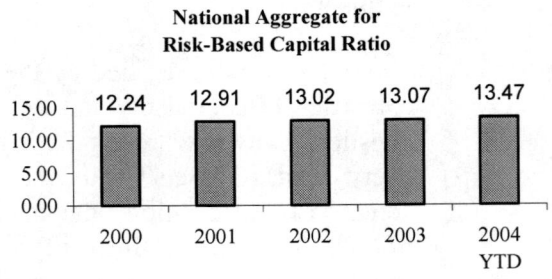

Right Pages

1. Asset Quality Index

An index that measures the quality of the institution's past underwriting and investment practices. It is derived from an evaluation of the company's estimated liquidation value based on nonperforming loans, loan types, and the market value of its securities. See the graph on page 8 for a description of the different critical levels presented in this index.

2. Nonperforming Loans/ Total Loans

The percentage of the institution's loan portfolio which is either past due on its payments by 90 days or more, or no longer accruing interest due to doubtful collectibility. This ratio is affected primarily by the quality of the institution's underwriting practices and the prosperity of the local economies where it is doing business. While only a portion of these loans will actually end up in default, a high ratio here will have several negative consequences including increased loan loss provisions, increased loan collection expenses, and decreased interest revenues.

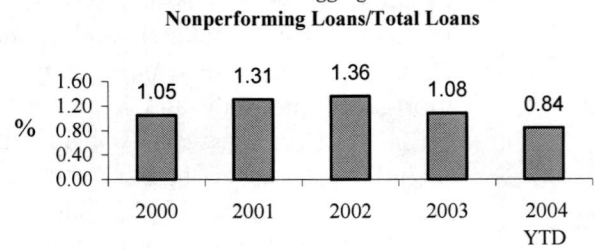

3. Non-performing Loans/ Capital

The percentage of past due 90 days and nonaccruing loans to the company's core (tier 1) capital plus reserve for loan losses. This ratio answers the question: If all of the bank's significantly past due and nonaccruing loans were to go into default, how much would that eat into capital? A large percentage of nonperforming loans signal imprudent lending practices which are a direct threat to the equity of the institution.

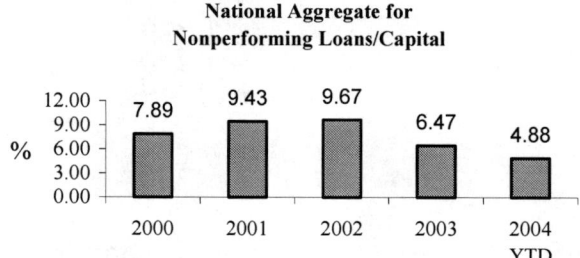

National Aggregate for Nonperforming Loans/Capital

4. Net Charge-offs/ Average Loans

The ratio of foreclosed loans written off the institution's books since the beginning of the year (less previous write-offs that were recovered) as a percentage of average loans for the year. This ratio answers the question: What percentage of the bank's past loans have actually become uncollectible? Past loan charge-off experience is often a very good indication of what can be expected in the future, and high loan charge-off levels are usually an indication of poor underwriting practices.

5. Profitability Index

An index that measures the soundness of the institution's operations and the contribution of profits to the company's financial strength. It is based on five sub-factors: 1) gain or loss on operations; 2) rates of return on assets and equity; 3) management of net interest margin; 4) generation of noninterest-based revenues; and 5) overhead expense management. See the graph on page 8 for a description of the different critical levels presented in this index.

6. Net Income

The year-to-date net profit or loss recorded by the institution, in millions of dollars. This figure includes the company's operating profit (income from lending, investing, and fees less interest and overhead expenses) as well as nonoperating items such as capital gains on the sale of securities, income taxes, and extraordinary items.

7. Return on Assets

The ratio of net income for the year (year-to-date quarterly figures are converted to a 12-month equivalent) as a percentage of average assets for the year. This ratio, known as ROA, is the most commonly used benchmark for bank and thrift profitability since it measures the company's return on investment in a format that is easily comparable with other companies.

Historically speaking, a ratio of 1.0% or greater has been considered good performance. However, this ratio will fluctuate with the prevailing economic times. Also, larger banks tend to have a lower ratio.

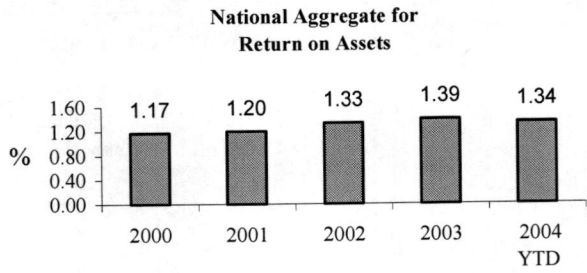

8. Return on Equity

The ratio of net income for the year (year-to-date quarterly figures are converted to a 12-month equivalent) as a percentage of average equity for the year. This ratio, known as ROE, is commonly used by a company's shareholders as a measure of their return on investment. It is not always a good measure of profitability, however, because inadequate equity levels at some institutions can result in unjustly high ROE's.

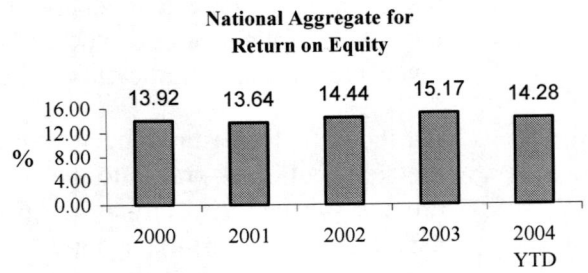

9. Net Interest Spread

The difference between the institution's interest income and interest expense for the year (year-to-date quarterly figures are converted to a 12-month equivalent) as a percentage of its average revenue-generating assets. Since the margin between interest earned and interest paid is generally where the company generates the majority of its income, this figure provides insight into the company's ability to effectively manage interest spreads.

A low Net Interest Spread can be the result of poor loan and deposit pricing, high levels of non-accruing loans, or poor asset/liability management

10. Overhead Efficiency Ratio

Total overhead expenses as a percentage of total revenues net of interest expense. This is a common measure for evaluating an institution's ability to operate efficiently while keeping a handle on overhead expenses like salaries, rent, and other office expenses. A high ratio suggests that the company's overhead expenses are too high in relation to the amount of revenue they are generating and/or supporting. Conversely, a low ratio means good management of overhead expenses which usually results in a strong Return on Assets as well.

11. Liquidity Index

An index that measures the institution's ability to raise the necessary cash to satisfy creditors and honor depositor withdrawals. It is based on an evaluation of the company's short-term liquidity position, including its existing reliance on less stable deposit sources. See the graph on page 8 for a description of the different critical levels presented in this index.

12. Liquidity Ratio

The ratio of short-term liquid assets to deposits and short-term borrowings. This ratio answers the question: How many cents can the institution easily raise in cash to cover each dollar on deposit plus pay off its short-term debts? Due to the nature of the business, it is rare (and not expected) for an established bank to achieve 100% on this ratio. Nevertheless, it serves as a good measure of an institution's liquidity in relation to the rest of the banking industry.

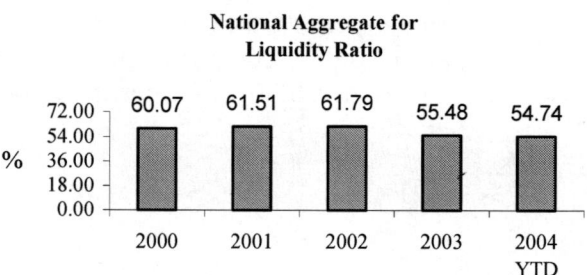

National Aggregate for
Liquidity Ratio

13. Hot Money Ratio

The percentage of the institution's deposit base that is being funded by jumbo CDs and brokered deposits. Jumbo CDs (high-yield certificates of deposit with principal amounts of at least $100,000) and brokered deposits (pooled funds sold by brokers seeking the highest interest rate available) are generally considered less stable (and more costly) and thus less desirable as a source of funds.

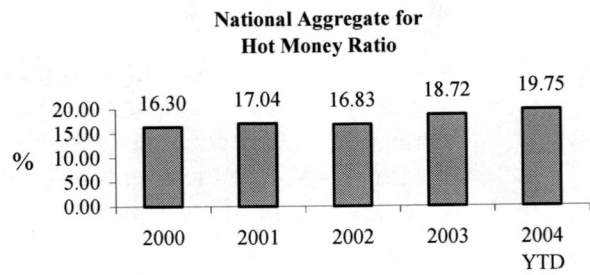

National Aggregate for Hot Money Ratio

14. Stability Index

An index that integrates a number of factors such as 1) risk diversification in terms of company size and loan diversification; 2) deterioration of operations as reported in critical asset, liability, income and expense items, such as an increase in loan delinquency rates or a sharp increase in loan originations; 3) years in operation; 4) former problem areas where, despite recent improvement, the company has yet to establish a record of stable performance over a suitable period of time; and 5) relationships with holding companies and affiliates. See the graph on page 8 for a description of the different critical levels presented in this index.

Name	City	State	Weiss Safety Rating	2003 Weiss Safety Rating	2002 Weiss Safety Rating	Total Assets ($Mil)	One Year Asset Growth	Asset Mix (As a % of Total Assets) Commercial Loans	Consumer Loans	Home Mortgages	Securities	Capitalization Index	Leverage Ratio	Risk-based Capital Ratio
▲ 1ST BANK OF SEA ISLE CITY	SEA ISLE CITY	NJ	C+	C-	C-	189.4	2.79	0.7	0.1	49.3	7.7	4.6	6.6	12.5
▲ 1ST BK	SIDNEY	MT	B+	B	B+	44.9	5.32	12.0	8.2	8.3	0.8	10.0	12.8	19.2
▲ 1ST BK YUMA	YUMA	AZ	C+	D+	D	57.8	22.20	22.0	1.6	8.9	3.5	8.8	12.4	14.0
▼ 1ST CENTENNIAL BK	REDLANDS	CA	B-	B	B-	332.9	42.21	18.8	0.7	1.3	8.3	3.2	8.3	10.1
1ST CENTURY BK NA	LOS ANGELES	CA	D	NR	NR	52.8	N/A	6.5	0.0	0.0	45.8	10.0	59.0	125.0
1ST CHOICE BK	HOUSTON	TX	C+	C+	C+	206.7	9.95	18.9	5.5	6.1	15.3	5.6	7.7	11.4
▲ 1ST COLONIAL NB	COLLINGSWOOD	NJ	C+	C	C	124.7	15.30	9.5	2.3	18.5	33.8	10.0	12.8	21.0
1ST EQT BK NW	BUFFALO GROVE	IL	D	D	NR	28.4	N/A	6.2	0.0	4.4	17.8	10.0	23.1	34.4
1ST EQUITY BANK	SKOKIE	IL	A-	A-	A-	111.9	4.08	8.8	0.2	18.4	6.1	7.2	9.1	12.9
▲ 1ST FINANCIAL BK	OVERLAND PARK	KS	D	E	E	54.1	-12.21	17.3	2.3	10.3	8.6	7.9	10.2	13.3
1ST GEORGIA BANKING CO	FRANKLIN	GA	D	D	NR	137.7	N/A	24.5	9.9	13.5	24.6	10.0	11.6	16.1
▼ 1ST INDEPENDENCE BK	NEW ALBANY	IN	C+	B-	D+	145.4	38.45	7.6	1.2	30.0	1.5	5.1	8.2	11.1
1ST NB OF SOUTH FLORIDA	HOMESTEAD	FL	B-	B-	B	252.4	7.60	2.5	1.3	5.3	38.6	7.0	9.0	14.2
▼ 1ST NB&TC	BRADENTON	FL	C+	B-	B-	304.8	31.35	3.1	1.0	23.8	16.4	2.7	7.8	9.7
1ST REGIONS BK	ANDOVER	MN	B-	B-	D	51.6	34.50	15.0	2.0	4.5	20.7	10.0	15.9	19.6
1ST SECURITY BK OF WA	LYNNWOOD	WA	B-	NR	NR	280.6	N/A	0.0	34.8	42.9	4.2	9.8	10.9	14.9
1ST SERVICE BK	MC LEAN	VA	C+	B-	C-	102.6	40.47	3.0	1.7	81.5	0.0	5.7	7.7	13.8
1ST ST BK	SAGINAW	MI	D	NR	NR	16.5	N/A	0.9	1.6	0.5	24.3	10.0	74.8	89.9
1ST ST BK MASON CITY	MASON CITY	IL	C	C	C	20.3	-6.46	6.1	14.0	20.3	28.8	10.0	11.6	20.8
▲ 1ST UNITED BK	BOCA RATON	FL	E+	E-	D-	140.2	192.90	11.9	2.2	3.0	20.8	10.0	11.0	15.9
1ST UNITED BK	FARIBAULT	MN	B	B	B-	110.0	-4.02	9.2	2.6	12.4	28.3	5.6	7.6	12.5
▲ 21ST CENTURY BK	HAM LAKE	MN	B-	C+	B-	203.3	11.65	8.1	1.5	4.8	7.9	3.9	8.7	10.4
A J SMITH FSB	MIDLOTHIAN	IL	B+	B+	B+	259.5	7.03	0.0	0.2	46.4	23.6	10.0	11.6	23.8
A.G. EDWARDS TRUST CO	ST LOUIS	MO	B+	B+	B+	45.0	9.85	0.0	0.0	0.0	96.5	10.0	91.7	554.5
▼ ABACUS FSB	NEW YORK CITY	NY	A-	A	A-	226.7	-8.96	0.1	0.2	27.6	18.2	10.0	13.5	19.5
ABBEVILLE B&L ST	ABBEVILLE	LA	B+	B+	B+	29.2	-12.85	0.0	1.2	50.0	11.7	10.0	21.0	40.2
▲ ABBEVILLE S&LA SSB	ABBEVILLE	SC	C+	C	C	66.1	0.90	0.2	3.3	52.1	19.8	7.8	9.6	17.0
ABBY BK	ABBOTSFORD	WI	B-	B-	B-	182.1	1.87	4.7	2.2	14.0	16.3	8.2	9.8	13.9
ABINGTON SB	JENKINTOWN	PA	B	B	B+	634.2	7.51	1.5	0.5	37.0	32.5	6.8	8.8	15.2
ACACIA FSB	FALLS CHURCH	VA	B-	B-	C+	934.1	19.66	2.6	0.2	61.4	9.8	6.4	8.4	14.9
▲ ACADEMY BK	LEBANON	TN	B	B-	C+	41.7	7.17	3.3	12.0	17.4	17.3	10.0	12.4	17.3
▲ ACCESS NB	RESTON	VA	B	B-	B-	343.3	16.28	10.1	0.3	35.4	5.8	6.6	9.2	12.2
▼ ACCESSBANK	CLOVIS	NM	B-	B-	C+	277.1	39.74	6.5	7.7	30.2	19.9	3.1	6.0	10.1
ACKLEY ST BK	ACKLEY	IA	B	B	B	91.6	19.71	10.6	1.8	7.3	25.5	6.2	8.5	11.9
▲ ACUITY BANK	TOMAH	WI	C+	C	C+	162.7	0.70	15.0	1.5	20.2	15.9	8.3	9.8	14.2
ADAMS B&TC	OGALLALA	NE	C+	C	C	339.4	23.94	12.2	4.1	9.3	14.5	5.6	8.7	11.5
▼ ADAMS CO-OP BK	ADAMS	MA	B-	B	B-	162.0	2.85	4.2	11.3	59.4	6.2	9.1	10.4	17.0
▲ ADAMS COUNTY B&LC	W UNION	OH	C+	C	C	25.8	-1.48	0.0	0.5	38.0	0.1	10.0	14.3	29.1
ADAMS COUNTY BK	KENESAW	NE	B	B	B	62.9	4.61	7.0	2.3	7.2	6.0	8.1	10.4	13.4
ADAMS COUNTY NB	GETTYSBURG	PA	B	B	A-	892.7	7.08	1.5	1.3	24.4	45.0	5.5	7.5	14.2
ADAMS NB	WASHINGTON	DC	B	B+	A-	238.6	10.12	9.6	0.2	4.2	18.1	8.2	10.4	13.5
▲ ADAMS ST BK	ADAMS	NE	A-	B+	B+	26.1	-0.50	4.4	5.4	19.7	33.6	10.0	25.2	34.0
ADEL BKG CO	ADEL	GA	B+	B+	B+	80.2	13.54	1.1	14.3	8.2	23.0	10.0	11.0	16.5
▲ ADIRONDACK BK	UTICA	NY	C	C-	C-	306.2	15.36	18.0	4.8	20.1	33.4	5.9	7.9	14.0
ADIRONDACK TRUST CO	SARATOGA SPRINGS	NY	A-	A	A	587.9	3.16	13.5	8.2	11.0	31.8	8.9	10.2	18.7
▼ ADRIAN BK	ADRIAN	MO	C+	B-	B-	67.4	1.65	17.7	6.2	21.1	12.4	5.8	8.2	11.6
ADRIAN ST BK	ADRIAN	MN	C+	C+	B-	27.1	4.66	7.4	2.7	10.7	34.6	9.9	10.9	18.3
▲ ADVANCE BK	BALTIMORE	MD	D+	D	C-	75.2	-17.76	5.2	0.7	33.0	15.5	10.0	11.3	21.2
ADVANCE FINANCIAL SVGS BK	WELLSBURG	WV	C	C-	C+	314.9	-0.07	5.3	14.4	37.6	7.7	5.0	7.0	11.4
ADVANTA BK CORP	DRAPER	UT	A-	A-	A-	1,033.7	-35.91	55.5	0.0	0.0	4.8	10.0	26.7	28.2
▲ ADVANTA NB	WILMINGTON	DE	B-	C	D	82.2	-61.26	0.0	0.0	6.3	3.3	10.0	60.7	213.7
▲ ADVANTAGE BK	LOVELAND	CO	B-	B-	C	175.1	43.23	10.2	0.4	4.5	1.6	7.1	11.4	12.6
▲ ADVANTAGE BK	BRANCHBURG	NJ	C+	C	C-	136.4	10.18	13.1	3.0	6.3	13.6	7.6	9.8	13.0
ADVANTAGE BK	CAMBRIDGE	OH	B-	B-	B-	1,056.5	-0.58	1.3	1.2	52.7	11.8	5.2	7.2	12.0
▲ ADVANTAGE BK	SPENCER	OK	C	C-	C	40.4	6.47	6.4	17.9	23.6	22.2	6.9	8.9	14.5
▲ ADVANTAGE COMMUNITY BK	DORCHESTER	WI	D+	D-	E-	74.7	74.34	8.8	3.9	18.1	7.0	7.1	9.1	12.9
▲ ADVANTAGE NB	ELK GROVE VLG	IL	C-	D+	D-	240.2	123.47	22.3	2.6	5.0	19.6	6.1	9.3	11.9
ADVEST TRUST COMPANY	HARTFORD	CT	B-	B-	C+	3.8	-3.60	0.0	0.0	0.0	52.4	10.0	66.2	191.8
AF BK	W JEFFERSON	NC	C+	C+	B-	209.2	10.52	6.0	5.5	42.3	2.1	4.8	8.1	10.9
AFFILIATED BK	BEDFORD	TX	C	C	D+	96.8	32.07	12.4	3.5	4.9	32.9	5.7	7.7	13.6
▲ AFFINITY BK	VENTURA	CA	B	B-	B-	880.0	22.62	0.0	0.0	1.7	15.4	6.3	8.7	11.9
AFFINITY BK OF PA	WYOMISSING	PA	D-	D	NR	87.8	282.53	4.9	0.1	3.0	61.3	7.5	9.3	22.7
AIG FSB	WILMINGTON	DE	B-	B-	B-	1,366.1	45.50	0.0	0.0	41.8	36.9	4.0	6.0	12.7
▲ AIMBANK	LITTLEFIELD	TX	E+	E-	E-	31.3	177.14	12.3	15.4	21.0	10.2	5.7	8.9	11.5

Asset Quality Index	Non-Performing Loans as a % of Total Loans	Non-Performing Loans as a % of Capital	Net Charge-offs Avg Loans	Profitability Index	Net Income ($Mil)	Return on Assets (R.O.A.)	Return on Equity (R.O.E.)	Net Interest Spread	Overhead Efficiency Ratio	Liquidity Index	Liquidity Ratio	Hot Money Ratio	Stability Index
7.2	0.14	1.4	0.00	5.5	0.8	0.92	13.89	3.70	58.3	1.5	35.0	52.9	3.8
5.1	1.54	7.3	0.04	7.4	0.4	1.55	12.04	4.07	67.2	6.5	113.3	12.6	7.3
6.8	0.22	1.5	0.05	3.8	0.3	1.23	9.95	5.14	74.9	2.7	17.9	15.8	1.6
6.4	0.05	0.4	0.09	7.0	1.5	1.02	10.19	7.10	69.9	4.9	66.1	16.3	5.1
10.0	0.00	0.0	0.00	0.0	-2.0	-11.11	-16.40	1.00	1,143.6	9.3	288.3	4.6	0.0
6.3	0.38	3.3	-0.06	6.7	1.2	1.16	15.72	4.27	52.5	2.9	56.4	33.5	3.6
8.9	0.08	0.4	0.00	3.4	0.3	0.41	4.34	3.26	73.2	3.2	33.0	16.9	3.1
7.8	0.00	0.0	0.00	0.0	-0.2	-1.86	-7.18	2.59	138.4	4.3	134.6	43.6	0.0
8.7	0.11	0.9	0.00	6.7	0.9	1.62	17.96	2.88	43.9	5.2	148.8	27.8	6.6
3.3	0.53	2.7	0.31	4.3	0.8	2.80	22.47	3.71	51.8	1.8	32.3	30.6	1.6
8.0	0.00	0.0	0.03	0.0	-0.8	-1.44	-10.20	3.45	100.5	1.5	14.0	24.4	0.0
6.2	0.69	6.1	0.16	3.7	0.2	0.33	3.50	4.04	85.7	0.9	23.3	39.1	4.4
5.5	1.30	6.8	-0.02	4.4	1.1	0.88	9.25	4.48	75.1	3.8	28.4	12.0	5.6
5.6	0.60	5.2	0.00	5.9	1.4	0.94	11.90	4.02	64.3	3.6	22.2	11.7	4.2
5.6	2.21	9.6	0.00	4.2	0.3	1.15	7.29	5.19	67.6	2.5	34.9	22.3	1.4
6.8	0.08	0.6	2.03	4.2	0.5	0.75	6.90	5.22	78.0	5.7	42.7	6.0	3.5
9.1	0.00	0.0	0.03	3.2	0.1	0.14	1.58	2.76	92.1	0.4	6.6	60.0	1.2
9.6	0.00	0.0	0.00	0.0	-0.3	-5.20	-8.48	0.39	977.4	6.2	222.2	24.6	0.0
7.8	0.46	2.2	0.10	4.5	0.1	0.84	7.54	3.01	63.4	4.1	61.9	16.5	2.7
4.5	1.37	5.0	-0.34	0.0	-1.6	-3.40	-24.43	3.63	189.2	5.1	63.1	14.8	0.0
6.7	0.10	0.8	0.07	9.6	1.0	1.95	24.91	3.94	60.3	2.8	51.5	32.3	6.1
7.3	0.03	0.3	0.00	7.4	1.2	1.23	13.79	4.65	52.7	3.3	28.2	14.6	4.6
6.8	1.08	5.7	0.07	4.8	0.7	0.59	4.97	3.40	72.9	1.8	20.6	21.2	6.6
9.8	0.00	0.0	0.00	10.0	3.4	15.19	16.87	4.18	61.4	5.0	500.9	100.0	3.0
6.4	1.16	4.3	0.02	5.4	0.5	0.42	3.01	4.57	88.1	4.5	48.0	14.3	7.6
6.5	2.41	8.0	0.00	6.9	0.2	1.19	5.89	3.96	68.3	8.5	223.4	10.1	6.6
3.5	2.93	19.6	0.08	6.6	0.4	1.29	13.70	3.90	55.2	3.5	74.4	29.1	1.9
4.5	1.03	7.3	-0.04	6.9	1.1	1.26	12.65	3.75	52.1	2.2	16.7	18.0	6.3
9.6	0.01	0.0	0.08	4.3	1.9	0.61	6.96	2.58	66.9	2.9	23.6	15.6	5.4
8.2	0.01	0.1	0.00	5.7	4.2	0.89	10.89	2.48	43.9	0.2	2.8	80.4	4.5
7.7	0.44	2.5	0.11	4.2	0.2	0.81	6.61	4.08	72.3	1.0	13.2	31.7	3.9
6.4	0.53	4.7	0.00	7.5	1.5	0.97	11.88	3.78	85.2	1.2	12.2	28.4	6.1
5.3	0.28	3.1	0.25	6.2	1.1	0.95	9.76	4.22	65.4	1.3	22.8	29.9	4.8
2.7	2.56	17.6	-0.01	5.1	0.4	0.98	10.68	3.52	61.4	2.2	20.8	18.6	5.2
4.1	1.56	11.2	0.33	3.7	0.3	0.36	3.56	2.90	90.7	1.6	25.9	26.4	5.0
5.5	0.38	2.9	0.05	6.0	1.5	1.02	12.37	5.25	70.0	3.1	11.8	13.0	4.4
4.4	1.24	9.4	0.27	4.1	0.5	0.62	5.93	3.92	67.9	4.2	22.8	8.7	5.9
3.2	5.89	23.8	0.00	3.1	0.0	0.31	2.17	3.07	84.8	4.9	50.7	12.3	6.0
6.2	0.36	2.6	-0.02	6.8	0.4	1.25	12.30	3.69	50.6	3.1	30.2	16.2	6.0
5.9	1.29	8.3	0.01	5.2	3.9	0.90	12.01	3.02	65.3	4.5	22.3	6.4	6.0
4.5	0.85	5.5	0.03	9.8	1.8	1.55	15.48	5.20	52.6	3.2	30.7	15.8	7.0
8.6	0.05	0.1	0.00	9.1	0.4	3.17	12.93	4.60	39.2	4.0	42.9	15.3	7.5
7.5	0.54	2.8	0.15	5.7	0.5	1.39	12.20	3.36	64.6	3.4	54.1	21.1	7.3
5.5	0.89	6.5	0.22	3.3	0.8	0.52	6.41	3.87	84.4	5.8	61.5	11.1	2.9
5.5	0.93	4.4	0.00	6.8	3.5	1.17	10.39	4.03	65.0	8.3	177.0	8.8	8.5
2.9	1.85	16.1	0.22	8.8	0.7	2.14	26.07	4.48	48.3	3.8	33.5	14.1	5.1
7.4	0.82	3.9	1.11	3.5	0.1	0.74	6.62	3.73	78.3	5.4	54.0	10.5	4.4
3.1	3.88	19.0	0.05	0.9	0.0	0.05	0.45	4.33	99.6	2.8	43.6	24.2	5.2
3.3	0.92	10.1	0.15	5.0	1.2	0.72	8.36	3.23	59.7	2.0	10.8	18.7	4.9
5.7	3.69	6.6	8.18	10.0	36.3	7.00	26.67	4.73	56.6	3.7	85.6	55.1	9.0
10.0	0.00	0.0	0.00	4.0	0.6	0.97	2.28	0.68	14.4	10.0	714.3	0.0	4.8
7.2	0.00	0.0	0.00	5.4	0.7	0.89	7.70	5.35	66.0	1.9	36.0	32.1	3.4
7.0	0.46	3.5	0.01	3.5	0.4	0.56	5.80	4.12	75.8	2.6	31.4	19.3	5.1
4.8	1.39	13.9	0.15	4.0	2.8	0.54	7.21	2.57	69.4	3.2	25.5	16.8	5.4
3.5	1.70	10.8	1.01	6.3	0.3	1.30	14.26	6.14	77.5	3.8	14.7	10.0	4.5
6.3	0.26	1.7	-0.25	1.8	0.2	0.50	5.35	2.99	75.9	6.7	139.0	14.0	1.8
6.0	0.34	1.5	0.01	2.8	0.6	0.59	3.92	3.24	70.3	3.6	80.8	34.2	3.2
6.6	0.00	0.0	0.00	0.0	0.0	-2.28	-3.22	2.79	105.1	4.0	145.2	100.0	4.4
7.1	0.28	2.9	-0.02	4.2	0.5	0.49	5.77	3.79	77.3	0.9	8.3	31.4	3.4
8.4	0.03	0.2	0.05	6.7	0.5	1.10	14.90	4.13	53.2	0.6	19.5	66.6	3.1
7.2	0.07	0.6	0.02	10.0	13.9	3.27	39.67	4.56	44.4	1.5	13.8	23.4	6.7
10.0	0.00	0.0	0.00	0.0	-0.4	-1.11	-12.88	1.32	163.6	8.6	118.1	0.3	0.0
9.8	0.07	0.5	0.00	6.8	7.5	1.18	19.27	3.87	94.3	5.0	241.5	96.6	4.8
5.8	0.15	0.9	0.21	2.8	0.2	1.08	10.08	4.68	83.4	3.1	31.5	16.5	0.6

| Name | City | State | Weiss Safety Rating | 2003 Weiss Safety Rating | 2002 Weiss Safety Rating | Total Assets ($Mil) | One Year Asset Growth | Asset Mix (As a % of Total Assets) | | | | Capital- ization Index | Leverage Ratio | Risk-based Capital Ratio |
								Comm- ercial Loans	Cons- umer Loans	Home Mort- gages	Secur- ities			
▲ AIR ACADEMY NB	US AIR FORCE ACA	CO	A-	B+	A-	91.0	7.70	10.1	1.4	13.2	11.5	10.0	16.4	26.4
▲ ALABAMA EXCHANGE BK	TUSKEGEE	AL	B	B-	B-	80.1	1.89	8.7	7.2	21.5	40.8	5.4	7.4	16.1
ALABAMA TR BK NA	SYLACAUGA	AL	C+	C+	C+	59.3	37.78	9.2	10.5	9.9	43.1	6.9	8.9	15.9
▼ ALAMANCE NB	GRAHAM	NC	C-	C-	C-	143.7	14.33	13.5	1.7	14.0	24.0	5.8	7.8	13.5
▲ ALAMERICA BK	BIRMINGHAM	AL	B	B	B	62.3	-18.27	15.6	9.7	9.5	32.1	10.0	17.0	25.6
▲ ALAMO BK OF TEXAS	ALAMO	TX	B	B-	B-	273.2	15.53	25.3	6.1	4.9	23.1	6.5	8.5	12.5
ALAMOGORDO FS&LA	ALAMOGORDO	NM	B	B	B	157.6	0.49	1.2	1.7	53.3	21.0	10.0	17.1	33.5
ALAMOSA NB	ALAMOSA	CO	B+	B	B	109.2	-1.63	12.2	14.8	7.5	15.4	6.2	8.2	12.7
ALASKA FIRST B&TC NA	ANCHORAGE	AK	C-	C-	C-	67.8	-1.79	4.7	3.9	6.1	55.9	5.8	7.8	20.1
▲ ALASKA PACIFIC BK	JUNEAU	AK	B-	C+	C+	165.6	5.12	13.1	3.3	33.8	5.7	6.9	8.9	13.0
ALBANY B&TC NA	ALBANY	GA	B-	B-	C+	135.9	6.82	15.2	7.0	22.8	19.1	7.9	9.6	13.9
▲ ALBANY B&TC NA	CHICAGO	IL	A	A-	A-	446.2	5.06	17.7	1.3	2.0	16.5	10.0	12.2	17.6
▲ ALBEMARLE FIRST BK	CHARLOTTESVILLE	VA	D	D-	D-	117.6	19.18	17.0	5.3	22.0	18.1	5.0	7.5	11.0
▲ ALBINA COMMUNITY BK	PORTLAND	OR	C	C	D+	102.5	9.10	10.7	4.0	5.5	14.9	7.4	9.6	12.8
ALBION NB	ALBION	NE	B-	C+	C+	60.2	-0.69	7.6	3.7	2.9	38.5	8.1	9.7	16.8
ALDEN ST BK	ALDEN	KS	D	E+	E-	16.0	4.00	8.5	7.3	18.3	28.2	6.8	8.8	17.4
▲ ALDEN ST BK	ALDEN	MI	D+	D	C-	196.5	6.61	6.9	6.5	30.5	3.4	6.2	8.2	12.3
ALDEN ST BK	ALDEN	NY	B+	B+	B	179.7	-1.26	6.2	3.4	38.3	32.5	10.0	13.7	25.9
▼ ALERUS FINANCIAL NA	GRAND FORKS	ND	B	A-	A-	606.4	18.18	20.7	3.5	11.4	19.8	3.9	7.1	10.5
ALFALFA COUNTY BK	CHEROKEE	OK	C+	C+	C	30.1	-0.14	23.9	3.2	2.7	10.4	8.8	10.3	14.0
▼ ALGONQUIN ST BK	ALGONQUIN	IL	B	A-	A-	144.0	-1.42	0.9	0.5	30.3	38.4	10.0	12.0	31.4
ALIANT BANK	ALEXANDER CITY	AL	B	B	B-	698.0	0.73	11.6	3.9	17.9	16.8	7.6	9.4	13.4
ALL AMERICA BK	OKLAHOMA CITY	OK	D	D	D	54.6	11.98	2.3	8.3	11.0	33.5	4.4	6.4	10.9
ALLAIRE COMMUNITY BK	WALL	NJ	B	B	B+	206.0	21.94	5.8	1.3	14.4	31.4	5.6	7.6	11.5
ALLEGHENY VALLEY BK	PITTSBURGH	PA	A-	A-	A	314.8	5.73	8.9	1.1	19.7	36.0	10.0	11.9	21.1
▲ ALLEGIANCE BK OF NORTH	BALA CYNWYD	PA	C	C-	D-	78.4	24.24	12.9	0.9	24.5	3.4	10.0	12.3	15.0
ALLEGIANCE COMMUNITY BK	TINLEY PARK	IL	C	C	C	66.5	0.63	2.0	1.5	10.6	12.0	7.1	9.3	12.5
▲ ALLEGIANCE COMMUNITY BK	S ORANGE	NJ	C+	C	D+	67.2	28.97	11.5	0.7	11.7	21.1	8.5	10.0	13.9
ALLEGIANT BK	ST LOUIS	MO	C+	B-	B-	2,751.4	15.47	8.7	2.8	11.5	10.7	3.6	8.0	10.3
ALLEN B&TC	HARRISONVILLE	MO	B-	B-	B-	100.5	21.81	18.7	3.3	13.2	23.4	5.4	7.4	11.4
▼ ALLENDALE COUNTY BK	FAIRFAX	SC	E-	E	E+	42.7	-9.10	5.5	22.7	2.7	48.0	5.3	7.3	16.3
ALLIANCE BANK NA	SYRACUSE	NY	B-	B-	B-	857.5	9.75	7.9	14.5	21.1	34.8	5.6	7.6	13.7
ALLIANCE BANKING CO	NEW BUFFALO	MI	C-	C-	D	127.7	-5.57	1.7	5.6	15.3	21.8	6.1	8.1	13.9
▲ ALLIANCE BK	CULVER CITY	CA	B-	C+	C+	345.5	42.09	20.3	0.3	0.8	17.5	7.6	9.4	13.3
ALLIANCE BK	TOPEKA	KS	C+	B-	B-	57.3	24.36	20.1	2.4	16.1	4.6	7.1	10.3	12.5
▲ ALLIANCE BK	NEW ULM	MN	B	B-	B-	385.9	6.53	28.7	5.7	7.1	7.5	4.8	9.7	10.9
ALLIANCE BK	CAPE GIRARDEAU	MO	C-	C	C	101.1	34.11	9.2	9.1	14.7	9.1	2.7	8.4	9.8
▲ ALLIANCE BK	SULPHUR SPRINGS	TX	B-	C+	C	412.8	-3.02	6.7	5.0	22.1	30.1	6.7	8.7	14.7
▲ ALLIANCE BK	MONDOVI	WI	C+	C	C+	119.0	2.21	6.0	5.7	22.4	27.5	6.6	8.6	14.4
ALLIANCE BK CORP	FAIRFAX	VA	C+	C+	C+	484.8	29.25	11.5	1.0	4.2	40.6	8.6	10.0	19.5
▼ ALLIANCE BK OF ARIZONA	PHOENIX	AZ	C	C+	NR	261.4	94.10	13.6	0.2	2.6	28.0	9.9	11.5	14.9
▲ ALLIANCE FSB	NILES	IL	B-	C+	B-	183.2	6.22	0.0	0.0	32.7	29.1	6.4	8.4	19.6
▲ ALLIANCE NB	DALTON	GA	C+	C-	D	92.3	10.99	12.9	7.0	9.9	25.6	7.4	9.3	14.0
▲ ALLIANT BANK	SEDGWICK	KS	D	D-	D	20.0	-13.01	9.7	2.8	6.6	27.7	9.0	10.3	17.6
ALLIANT BK	MADISON	MO	C+	C+	C-	63.1	9.04	15.6	6.8	22.5	13.6	7.2	9.1	14.2
ALLIED BK	MULBERRY	AR	B	B-	C+	126.5	14.13	9.3	8.7	17.1	32.2	5.8	7.8	11.8
▲ ALLIED FIRST BK SB	NAPERVILLE	IL	B-	C+	C	132.0	29.96	3.9	17.6	47.0	5.4	6.3	8.3	12.1
▲ ALLSTATE BK	VERNON HILLS	IL	D+	D	D	954.5	20.77	0.2	0.0	0.3	96.3	10.0	11.6	34.4
ALMA EXCH B&TC	ALMA	GA	B-	B-	B-	76.2	-2.25	18.8	7.2	7.1	10.2	8.2	10.6	13.5
ALMENA ST BK	ALMENA	KS	E-	E-	E-	11.9	-4.89	12.6	9.7	10.7	5.0	3.8	7.5	10.4
▲ ALPHA COMMUNITY BK	TOLUCA	IL	B-	C+	C+	204.6	6.69	17.9	6.0	13.6	30.4	6.7	8.7	13.0
ALPINE BK	GLENWOOD SPRINGS	CO	B+	B+	B+	1,254.1	16.34	5.2	6.2	13.4	8.2	4.8	9.2	10.9
▲ ALPINE BK OF ILLINOIS	ROCKFORD	IL	B-	C+	C	438.2	-0.67	12.4	8.6	10.5	26.6	5.1	7.8	11.1
ALPINE CAP BK	NEW YORK	NY	C+	C+	C+	200.7	37.55	1.9	2.7	14.7	47.1	7.4	9.3	18.3
ALTA VISTA ST BK	ALTA VISTA	KS	D	D	D+	16.1	-4.78	6.1	4.3	12.5	41.5	6.9	8.9	14.6
▲ ALTAMAHA B&TC	UVALDA	GA	B-	C+	C	120.6	5.32	9.4	8.4	22.0	21.0	6.6	8.6	13.3
ALTON BK	ALTON	MO	A-	A-	A-	41.1	6.61	5.3	7.2	19.8	45.8	10.0	15.3	31.5
ALTOONA FIRST SVGS BK	ALTOONA	PA	C+	C+	B	155.0	2.93	2.6	2.6	41.5	17.2	9.5	10.7	17.5
ALTURA ST BK	ALTURA	MN	B+	B+	B+	41.5	0.81	6.9	6.9	20.7	20.7	10.0	11.9	18.3
ALVA ST B&TC	ALVA	OK	D+	D+	C-	162.7	0.27	5.7	4.0	2.7	25.3	10.0	12.7	18.1
AMALGAMATED BK	NEW YORK	NY	C-	C-	C	3,653.1	7.13	5.1	0.3	25.5	55.8	4.5	6.5	14.4
AMALGAMATED BK CHICAGO	CHICAGO	IL	B	B	B+	643.1	8.99	4.9	12.3	2.0	20.6	6.7	8.7	13.8
AMARILLO NB	AMARILLO	TX	A-	A-	A-	1,502.6	5.31	20.5	13.1	9.5	10.7	8.2	9.8	14.6
AMBANK	SILVER CITY	NM	C	C	C+	78.4	12.97	7.7	10.2	12.3	33.3	6.7	8.8	16.9

Asset Quality Index	Non-Performing Loans as a % of Total Loans	Non-Performing Loans as a % of Capital	Net Charge-offs Avg Loans	Profitability Index	Net Income ($Mil)	Return on Assets (R.O.A.)	Return on Equity (R.O.E.)	Net Interest Spread	Overhead Efficiency Ratio	Liquidity Index	Liquidity Ratio	Hot Money Ratio	Stability Index
9.1	0.02	0.1	0.82	9.6	0.7	1.62	9.73	4.07	72.7	6.2	47.4	3.8	8.0
4.9	1.24	7.1	-0.18	9.1	0.6	1.49	19.35	4.60	54.7	3.7	15.6	10.7	6.6
4.3	2.00	11.0	0.04	5.8	0.3	0.98	11.21	4.14	66.1	4.8	47.6	12.3	0.9
3.1	2.96	24.7	0.17	2.8	0.3	0.49	6.33	3.33	81.7	0.6	10.9	44.2	3.0
4.9	0.00	0.0	0.16	8.5	0.6	2.09	11.95	4.66	49.7	0.6	15.3	55.8	3.0
5.7	0.87	6.7	0.64	7.2	1.6	1.23	14.32	5.19	62.7	2.2	9.8	17.5	4.9
9.1	0.18	0.7	0.00	3.8	0.3	0.41	2.41	2.90	74.1	1.4	15.8	26.9	7.7
6.3	0.31	2.4	0.10	9.9	1.4	2.40	29.14	5.00	52.2	3.2	48.0	23.4	6.2
7.9	0.00	0.0	-0.02	3.0	0.2	0.51	6.70	3.58	90.4	5.3	33.5	5.0	2.7
7.5	0.07	0.6	0.04	4.1	0.4	0.52	5.84	4.81	81.9	0.8	9.8	33.5	5.1
6.5	0.03	0.2	0.09	4.7	0.6	0.81	8.48	3.96	72.7	2.2	15.6	17.9	5.5
7.2	0.16	0.9	0.13	6.1	2.1	0.99	7.95	4.30	63.9	3.2	53.0	27.1	7.5
2.6	2.43	18.6	-0.54	0.7	0.0	0.04	0.45	3.68	96.3	2.9	8.2	14.0	2.2
2.6	1.94	13.7	0.63	5.7	0.3	0.58	6.12	5.17	80.5	3.0	37.8	19.3	4.8
3.2	3.17	16.0	0.41	6.0	0.4	1.21	12.48	4.08	61.8	5.1	92.9	17.6	6.1
7.8	0.00	0.0	-0.08	4.0	0.1	1.04	12.46	4.16	81.0	4.8	81.0	16.1	1.4
1.3	3.79	32.8	0.42	6.4	1.1	1.14	13.83	5.21	52.0	5.0	33.6	7.1	4.5
4.2	3.99	16.6	2.06	6.3	1.1	1.18	8.52	4.33	55.4	7.7	101.5	5.8	7.1
8.2	0.03	0.2	-0.21	7.0	3.7	1.28	15.60	4.05	73.6	5.7	47.8	8.0	5.9
4.8	0.55	3.8	2.22	8.5	0.3	2.10	21.04	4.04	43.8	2.8	41.2	24.1	4.8
9.8	0.28	1.0	0.00	3.9	0.5	0.71	5.45	3.41	80.4	7.6	88.9	4.3	8.1
7.2	0.33	2.4	0.11	4.9	3.8	1.09	11.82	3.86	69.6	3.4	39.6	18.1	6.2
6.4	0.22	2.0	0.02	5.2	0.3	1.27	21.21	4.73	76.0	2.1	18.7	18.8	2.4
8.9	0.00	0.0	0.00	5.2	0.9	0.89	12.07	4.49	67.8	3.9	22.4	10.1	5.0
6.0	1.33	6.0	0.71	6.9	2.1	1.37	10.78	4.16	56.7	2.8	14.4	14.7	8.0
7.6	0.00	0.0	0.13	3.1	0.3	0.75	6.53	4.54	76.9	1.1	8.3	28.8	3.6
2.7	3.80	28.3	0.00	3.8	0.2	0.59	6.41	3.15	66.3	4.2	91.4	24.5	4.7
8.7	0.16	1.1	0.02	3.8	0.4	1.09	11.67	3.75	74.5	5.1	41.1	9.9	1.6
2.2	1.54	5.5	0.10	3.9	2.7	0.21	1.48	1.26	76.2	3.3	11.3	12.5	6.6
8.0	0.19	1.6	1.52	5.3	0.3	0.70	9.01	4.42	67.7	2.3	28.3	19.8	4.5
1.8	5.91	25.0	2.59	2.4	0.1	0.36	5.03	4.88	75.2	2.6	40.5	25.8	0.0
4.7	0.81	5.8	0.08	4.7	3.5	0.83	10.68	3.77	73.3	2.0	16.8	19.2	4.6
4.8	0.90	6.6	0.71	1.9	0.1	0.17	2.06	3.84	91.8	4.3	17.8	7.0	2.7
4.4	1.65	11.6	0.38	6.7	1.5	0.95	10.90	4.32	64.1	4.6	48.8	14.2	4.0
6.0	0.52	3.5	-0.01	5.1	0.2	0.87	7.92	4.11	59.0	6.2	85.4	11.0	4.6
5.2	0.68	5.5	0.00	9.5	3.1	1.66	17.22	4.65	47.8	1.1	17.0	30.9	6.7
6.6	0.41	3.9	0.08	3.5	0.3	0.54	6.27	3.64	71.4	3.2	32.2	16.3	4.5
5.3	1.05	6.2	-0.02	4.6	1.9	0.89	9.52	4.13	73.1	4.5	25.4	7.0	4.4
3.3	2.50	16.9	-0.01	6.5	0.9	1.45	16.29	3.74	59.6	4.3	19.1	6.9	6.4
9.4	0.06	0.2	0.03	3.6	1.5	0.68	8.77	2.85	77.4	1.7	34.1	33.3	4.1
8.7	0.00	0.0	0.00	0.9	0.1	0.12	1.24	3.79	83.3	4.2	19.2	7.8	2.8
4.7	0.66	4.8	0.00	4.2	0.6	0.60	5.67	2.58	69.6	2.6	35.7	21.8	5.2
7.9	0.26	1.7	0.22	3.9	0.4	0.94	10.41	3.75	71.7	1.7	12.9	21.4	4.8
1.3	7.99	37.6	0.00	2.4	0.1	0.46	4.42	3.82	85.0	2.5	47.8	25.3	1.5
3.1	2.79	19.2	-0.07	5.5	0.3	0.84	9.01	5.16	74.9	4.7	72.3	16.6	4.1
6.2	0.00	0.0	0.05	8.0	1.3	2.23	22.68	4.29	58.4	1.1	6.7	27.6	5.4
7.7	0.00	0.0	0.25	5.9	0.9	1.35	17.21	3.00	53.1	3.1	20.0	13.8	3.2
9.6	0.00	0.0	0.00	1.0	0.4	0.09	0.71	1.44	91.6	0.3	1.2	59.9	6.7
3.2	1.90	12.7	-0.04	6.1	0.4	1.14	11.28	4.70	61.0	2.0	24.2	20.2	5.5
2.3	0.85	8.1	0.00	4.3	0.1	0.92	12.43	7.17	87.4	2.9	23.2	14.9	0.0
5.5	0.93	6.9	0.05	6.1	1.7	1.61	20.19	3.50	58.1	1.2	10.3	28.1	4.3
8.2	0.02	0.2	0.05	9.8	9.8	1.62	17.88	5.61	59.9	5.3	30.0	8.1	8.4
6.6	0.22	1.6	0.04	4.2	1.5	0.70	8.50	3.43	76.7	4.2	28.6	10.4	5.1
9.5	0.00	0.0	0.00	3.5	0.7	0.78	8.12	2.21	55.4	5.7	152.5	20.8	2.3
5.1	1.98	10.8	-0.22	4.9	0.1	0.88	10.32	4.07	71.5	2.2	39.7	25.0	2.3
4.6	0.94	7.6	0.77	5.0	0.6	0.99	11.78	4.91	65.1	1.7	24.0	24.2	4.1
8.9	0.20	0.6	0.09	7.4	0.3	1.56	10.22	4.50	56.0	2.0	25.5	20.8	7.5
8.9	0.29	1.7	0.02	3.9	0.4	0.58	5.15	3.50	72.4	6.6	82.6	9.9	6.4
5.7	0.80	4.1	-0.04	7.2	0.4	1.77	14.01	4.36	55.6	5.1	65.9	13.6	7.0
0.6	5.87	29.0	0.24	6.1	1.7	2.11	16.80	3.66	44.8	2.4	31.1	20.0	5.3
9.9	0.21	1.6	-0.03	2.2	5.2	0.28	5.52	2.60	87.5	5.0	22.0	4.5	3.6
5.4	1.27	7.5	0.48	4.4	2.1	0.67	8.08	3.49	77.0	7.5	118.3	8.6	4.5
5.7	0.70	4.3	0.33	8.0	13.3	1.85	19.18	4.00	58.9	6.6	62.4	7.8	8.7
3.8	3.04	14.2	0.20	4.5	0.3	0.70	8.00	5.04	77.7	5.3	50.8	10.2	3.5

Name	City	State	Weiss Safety Rating	2003 Weiss Safety Rating	2002 Weiss Safety Rating	Total Assets ($Mil)	One Year Asset Growth	Commercial Loans	Consumer Loans	Home Mortgages	Securities	Capitalization Index	Leverage Ratio	Risk-based Capital Ratio
▼ AMBLER SVG BK	AMBLER	PA	C+	B	NR	207.2	1.00	0.3	0.3	30.3	49.4	6.9	8.9	21.9
AMBOY NB	OLD BRIDGE	NJ	B+	B+	B	2,250.0	2.90	3.2	0.0	18.6	21.7	6.6	9.2	12.2
AMCORE BK NA	ROCKFORD	IL	B-	B-	B-	4,753.8	6.43	9.7	11.0	9.4	25.0	5.6	7.9	11.4
AMERASIA BK	NEW YORK CITY	NY	A-	B+	B	141.5	6.49	5.8	0.1	9.4	6.6	9.1	10.5	14.2
▲ AMERIANA B&TC SB	NEW CASTLE	IN	C-	D+	D+	428.6	-9.06	1.1	1.2	20.1	38.7	7.0	9.0	15.8
▼ AMERIBANK INC	WELCH	WV	D	C-	C-	86.2	12.95	4.4	11.4	19.5	0.7	5.6	7.6	16.1
▲ AMERICA CALIFORNIA BK	SAN FRANCISCO	CA	B-	C-	C-	105.0	-5.61	9.4	0.6	4.2	19.4	10.0	11.3	16.8
AMERICA WEST BK	LAYTON	UT	C+	B-	C+	63.3	20.40	15.5	1.7	3.9	25.7	9.5	10.7	17.5
AMERICAN B&T	WESSINGTON SPRNG	SD	B-	C+	B	160.6	9.16	14.1	6.4	3.7	15.8	4.3	8.3	10.6
AMERICAN B&T WI	CUBA CITY	WI	B-	B-	C+	81.5	9.07	8.6	3.9	7.8	11.8	5.8	7.8	12.0
▲ AMERICAN B&TC	BOWLING GREEN	KY	C-	C-	C-	121.2	42.02	15.7	6.3	18.1	7.8	3.3	7.6	10.2
▲ AMERICAN B&TC	COUSHATTA	LA	D	D-	D-	69.8	2.82	27.5	19.6	12.8	6.2	6.0	8.1	11.8
AMERICAN B&TC	OPELOUSAS	LA	A-	A-	A	97.4	2.19	8.6	5.7	14.6	42.9	10.0	13.9	30.2
AMERICAN B&TC	TULSA	OK	B	B-	B	128.5	3.16	35.0	0.9	2.3	38.9	10.0	11.9	20.6
AMERICAN B&TC	LIVINGSTON	TN	C	C	C-	55.3	4.42	5.5	11.1	22.2	24.9	7.0	9.0	12.6
AMERICAN B&TC NA	DAVENPORT	IA	B-	C+	C+	468.5	4.27	10.0	2.0	10.8	32.3	5.6	7.6	12.0
▲ AMERICAN BK	GENEVA	AL	A	A-	A-	80.1	1.46	12.6	6.2	15.7	37.4	10.0	15.0	25.6
▼ AMERICAN BK	WELSH	LA	C-	C+	C+	52.2	-5.39	12.4	3.9	9.6	16.0	10.0	16.4	27.7
▼ AMERICAN BK	ROCKVILLE	MD	C	C+	B-	252.7	26.50	13.5	8.6	23.0	16.0	4.5	7.0	10.8
AMERICAN BK	ST PAUL	MN	A-	A-	B+	602.6	4.61	12.2	0.6	5.1	5.7	9.2	10.5	14.4
AMERICAN BK	BURR	NE	C+	C+	C+	11.1	2.06	3.2	5.3	12.0	32.1	10.0	13.5	26.3
AMERICAN BK	WAGONER	OK	B	B	B	26.1	-1.69	3.2	10.3	9.0	48.8	10.0	18.4	43.4
AMERICAN BK	ALLENTOWN	PA	C+	C+	C	501.2	6.14	4.1	0.7	15.4	47.2	5.7	7.7	14.2
AMERICAN BK	EAU CLAIRE	WI	B	B	A-	68.3	-7.43	19.8	1.0	11.4	10.2	7.6	10.6	13.0
AMERICAN BK	FOND DU LAC	WI	A	A	A	170.5	-6.78	28.3	0.5	10.3	21.1	10.0	15.7	22.3
AMERICAN BK LAKE CITY	LAKE CITY	MN	B	B+	A-	71.3	11.15	15.9	5.2	8.0	10.5	8.7	12.4	13.9
AMERICAN BK NA	LE MARS	IA	B-	B-	C+	160.8	2.32	13.0	4.7	5.2	10.4	4.6	8.1	10.8
▼ AMERICAN BK NA	CORPUS CHRISTI	TX	C+	B-	B-	581.8	14.74	17.9	3.7	8.1	17.4	3.5	7.2	10.2
▼ AMERICAN BK NA	DALLAS	TX	D	C	C-	26.6	6.56	5.1	48.5	3.2	17.5	5.9	7.9	13.8
AMERICAN BK NA	KELLER	TX	B	B	B	41.6	1.70	4.0	18.3	4.8	37.8	9.4	10.6	18.8
▼ AMERICAN BK NA	WACO	TX	B	B+	B+	266.1	9.42	12.2	4.2	12.0	31.5	6.9	8.9	13.1
AMERICAN BK NORTH	NASHWAUK	MN	B-	B-	B-	400.3	22.67	14.8	5.2	24.9	6.9	5.2	8.1	11.1
AMERICAN BK OF CMRC	PROVO	UT	C+	C+	C+	30.0	0.05	39.3	7.5	0.8	3.1	10.0	11.0	16.1
AMERICAN BK OF COMMERCE	WOLFFORTH	TX	D+	D	E+	436.3	11.87	19.2	4.1	5.1	16.0	3.9	7.4	10.5
▲ AMERICAN BK OF MT	BOZEMAN	MT	B+	B	B	320.8	2.29	13.1	3.1	14.0	3.8	8.1	11.6	13.4
AMERICAN BK OF OK	COLLINSVILLE	OK	C-	C-	C-	53.6	5.29	16.9	16.1	25.8	5.3	4.2	8.2	10.6
AMERICAN BK OF TEXAS	SHERMAN	TX	C+	C+	C	803.6	4.10	11.6	8.4	10.2	20.2	7.5	9.3	13.3
AMERICAN BK TX NA	MARBLE FALLS	TX	C+	C	C+	241.0	60.17	9.0	2.9	12.7	6.2	4.6	8.2	10.8
AMERICAN BK-BAXTER	BAXTER SPRINGS	KS	C+	C+	C	87.5	7.39	7.0	3.1	15.7	7.9	3.8	8.0	10.4
▲ AMERICAN BKG CO	MOULTRIE	GA	B	B-	C+	180.7	2.15	8.6	4.4	10.4	19.8	5.4	7.4	11.6
AMERICAN BUSINESS BK	LOS ANGELES	CA	C+	C+	C+	392.8	12.87	12.1	0.6	0.3	52.7	5.0	7.0	15.4
AMERICAN CHARTERED BK	SCHAUMBURG	IL	C+	C+	C+	1,477.1	24.51	20.3	0.4	5.8	18.5	3.8	8.0	10.4
AMERICAN CITY BK	TULLAHOMA	TN	C+	C+	C+	143.4	20.38	11.0	3.7	11.6	14.9	5.9	8.7	11.7
▲ AMERICAN COMMUNITY B&T	WOODSTOCK	IL	C+	C	D+	309.6	23.97	12.2	0.3	13.9	5.9	8.4	10.7	13.7
AMERICAN COMMUNITY BK	MONROE	NC	D+	D+	C-	285.0	16.30	21.2	8.5	5.4	15.5	3.4	7.7	10.2
AMERICAN COMMUNITY BK	GLEN COVE	NY	C+	C-	D	56.9	10.22	8.9	0.6	1.3	30.3	10.0	12.0	17.6
▲ AMERICAN EAGLE BK	S ELGIN	IL	D+	D-	D	68.8	83.86	5.4	51.3	4.9	6.0	6.3	9.5	12.0
AMERICAN EAGLE SVGS BK	BOOTHWYN	PA	C-	C-	C-	36.4	4.98	0.0	0.1	34.4	56.0	6.9	8.9	20.6
▲ AMERICAN ENTERPRISE BK	BUFFALO GROVE	IL	C-	C-	C-	228.4	13.55	16.6	0.3	7.8	10.0	4.4	8.3	10.7
AMERICAN ENTERPRISE BK OF	JACKSONVILLE	FL	D	NR	NR	29.6	N/A	19.6	5.6	0.8	0.0	10.0	35.2	33.0
▲ AMERICAN EXCHANGE BK	ELMWOOD	NE	B-	C+	C+	31.2	10.31	13.6	4.8	5.8	33.0	10.0	12.2	20.8
AMERICAN EXCHANGE BK	HENRYETTA	OK	B+	B+	A-	60.6	0.34	9.1	9.7	20.6	28.9	10.0	11.7	16.6
AMERICAN EXCHANGE BK	LINDSAY	OK	B	B-	B-	37.1	-5.93	10.3	5.2	14.7	54.4	10.0	11.5	20.6
▲ AMERICAN EXPRESS BK, FSB	SALT LAKE CITY	UT	C-	D	D+	10,934.8	180607.4	53.7	33.3	0.3	0.3	7.3	12.0	12.8
AMERICAN EXPRESS	SALT LAKE CITY	UT	C	C	C	14,020.0	-19.89	0.0	70.9	0.0	7.3	7.0	11.1	12.5
▲ AMERICAN FEDERAL BK	FARGO	ND	B-	C+	C	232.8	-5.33	27.4	3.4	21.2	6.3	5.8	7.8	12.0
▲ AMERICAN FNB	HOUSTON	TX	C+	C	C+	204.8	6.79	17.8	2.2	0.8	11.4	5.5	8.5	11.4
▲ AMERICAN FOUNDERS BK INC	FRANKFORT	KY	B+	B	C-	177.9	62.63	8.4	3.5	25.2	15.6	10.0	15.5	19.8
AMERICAN FSB	HELENA	MT	A-	A-	B	201.2	-0.14	2.4	4.9	28.5	44.4	10.0	11.4	18.9
AMERICAN GATEWAY BK	PORT ALLEN	LA	C	C	C	254.0	12.40	2.0	4.2	17.5	22.7	5.2	7.2	11.5
▲ AMERICAN HEARTLAND B&TC	SUGAR GROVE	IL	C	C-	D	79.4	19.43	10.6	0.6	12.5	16.7	5.8	7.8	11.9
▼ AMERICAN HERITAGE BK	CLOVIS	NM	D-	D	D-	66.1	-12.23	25.0	11.4	13.2	2.3	4.0	7.9	10.5
AMERICAN HERITAGE BK	SAPULPA	OK	B+	B+	B+	458.7	3.83	6.2	7.0	17.3	51.4	7.1	9.1	19.0
AMERICAN HERITAGE NB	LONG PRAIRIE	MN	B+	B+	B	166.1	-7.27	12.5	1.9	4.3	13.6	8.0	9.8	13.4

Asset Quality Index	Non-Performing Loans as a % of Total Loans	as a % of Capital	Net Charge-offs Avg Loans	Profitability Index	Net Income ($Mil)	Return on Assets (R.O.A.)	Return on Equity (R.O.E.)	Net Interest Spread	Overhead Efficiency Ratio	Liquidity Index	Liquidity Ratio	Hot Money Ratio	Stability Index
9.2	0.45	2.0	0.00	3.4	0.8	0.76	8.46	2.46	71.8	6.9	169.0	15.6	2.7
5.7	0.80	5.2	-0.03	9.8	34.9	3.10	34.62	4.01	25.1	7.4	150.8	12.0	9.0
5.6	0.57	4.4	0.44	5.7	24.1	1.05	12.85	3.72	59.9	1.2	8.3	27.3	6.4
7.6	0.00	0.0	-0.13	8.4	0.7	0.95	9.24	4.55	55.5	4.1	75.8	23.8	6.4
3.5	3.11	14.4	0.76	2.0	1.0	0.47	5.09	3.09	83.3	4.4	28.8	8.8	1.0
2.6	3.12	18.4	0.34	2.8	0.0	0.00	0.06	3.51	89.6	4.1	70.2	19.6	2.3
7.2	0.00	0.0	-0.01	3.9	0.6	1.09	9.50	4.50	70.7	3.1	55.0	29.2	3.7
2.8	2.16	14.5	0.01	5.8	0.5	1.53	14.46	4.54	68.9	0.4	8.2	64.9	0.6
5.5	0.29	2.0	-0.01	7.4	1.8	2.27	23.16	5.55	56.5	3.4	15.2	12.1	6.9
6.1	0.20	1.2	0.05	4.3	0.4	1.02	9.29	3.79	69.4	5.3	48.2	9.6	6.8
4.7	0.48	5.1	0.06	5.0	0.5	0.91	12.60	4.03	54.1	1.9	17.3	19.5	0.8
0.5	3.36	26.6	0.16	4.8	0.3	0.80	10.00	5.23	74.3	3.7	57.1	19.4	2.9
8.8	0.26	0.7	0.03	5.6	0.5	0.97	6.84	4.31	73.0	4.4	31.6	10.2	8.3
7.2	1.60	6.8	0.00	4.2	0.5	0.68	5.69	4.28	77.6	3.6	18.1	11.2	6.4
4.8	0.81	5.6	0.11	4.7	0.2	0.81	9.16	3.85	70.2	2.9	65.7	35.3	3.6
7.7	0.30	2.3	0.02	4.0	2.4	1.07	13.63	3.19	74.8	2.9	20.2	14.8	4.5
8.5	0.54	1.9	-0.04	9.1	0.7	1.76	11.43	4.62	45.5	3.4	33.4	15.6	8.4
4.0	1.86	5.3	0.34	7.7	0.3	1.17	6.31	5.04	70.2	7.1	105.9	8.9	3.7
4.0	0.56	5.8	0.10	5.4	1.1	0.92	13.30	3.57	69.6	1.6	36.9	53.5	3.5
6.6	0.13	0.8	-0.02	8.3	6.4	2.21	17.33	4.66	61.4	5.1	45.7	10.8	8.0
6.4	3.16	10.0	0.00	5.0	0.1	1.16	8.87	2.84	55.1	8.8	172.7	4.4	5.1
8.4	0.02	0.0	2.31	4.7	0.1	0.90	4.81	4.85	76.2	5.7	38.3	4.9	6.1
9.4	0.00	0.0	0.00	3.7	1.6	0.63	8.31	2.03	51.3	7.8	127.1	7.6	3.6
6.0	0.28	2.0	-0.01	6.7	0.3	0.86	8.27	4.05	62.7	3.0	12.4	14.0	6.3
8.3	0.00	0.0	0.00	7.2	1.4	1.65	10.04	4.35	52.7	5.1	41.0	9.7	9.2
4.1	1.84	9.4	0.01	10.0	0.9	2.46	16.43	5.29	47.4	1.0	6.9	30.3	8.4
4.2	0.72	6.2	0.36	6.3	1.1	1.41	16.36	3.38	51.0	4.9	60.3	15.5	5.4
5.6	0.39	3.5	0.06	6.1	4.5	1.59	20.51	4.50	71.9	5.2	30.3	4.3	5.8
5.7	0.10	0.6	2.88	7.1	0.1	0.56	6.57	10.92	72.1	6.0	66.8	9.3	2.3
7.6	0.00	0.0	-0.09	3.8	0.1	0.50	4.66	4.62	88.7	2.7	35.9	21.2	5.3
8.4	0.10	0.6	0.16	5.2	1.0	0.83	9.12	3.49	67.2	2.8	40.0	22.5	5.5
5.5	0.37	3.7	0.06	8.4	3.8	1.97	24.52	4.24	50.9	3.8	10.0	9.6	5.4
7.3	0.13	0.7	0.02	3.4	0.1	0.56	4.97	6.40	78.8	6.8	75.5	5.6	5.5
5.0	0.62	5.8	0.15	4.7	1.8	0.83	11.14	4.14	72.6	2.2	32.2	24.3	2.0
6.3	0.05	0.3	0.00	9.1	3.1	1.97	17.14	5.09	57.8	1.8	11.9	19.8	8.1
7.3	0.12	1.2	0.05	5.8	0.3	0.97	12.18	5.50	74.3	2.6	13.0	15.8	0.5
3.9	1.53	9.9	0.06	6.8	4.8	1.20	12.27	4.14	58.6	5.4	57.5	12.4	7.1
3.4	0.66	3.6	0.01	5.7	0.9	0.82	6.69	5.83	74.0	4.0	24.7	9.9	7.2
7.3	0.05	0.5	0.05	7.4	0.8	1.73	22.18	4.48	58.4	2.5	16.3	16.8	5.1
5.7	0.61	5.1	0.02	9.2	1.4	1.44	19.71	4.19	50.8	2.3	30.2	21.2	6.1
9.2	0.00	0.0	-0.03	4.0	1.3	0.68	10.00	3.91	72.5	4.3	37.7	12.7	2.9
5.1	1.19	10.6	0.44	6.0	7.2	1.03	13.17	3.83	52.7	0.9	6.7	31.3	5.7
4.6	0.57	2.3	0.00	2.7	-0.1	-0.09	-0.87	0.57	112.9	3.8	63.1	24.8	5.0
7.5	0.00	0.0	0.00	3.7	1.0	0.69	6.53	3.28	58.5	1.1	27.3	46.6	2.5
4.7	0.88	8.2	0.05	3.6	0.9	0.64	8.78	3.29	71.1	0.7	8.9	38.2	3.4
7.7	0.03	0.1	1.87	3.4	0.1	0.44	3.51	4.81	75.0	3.7	38.6	15.8	2.1
5.7	0.00	0.0	0.18	1.9	0.3	0.97	10.53	3.90	78.0	5.2	89.7	16.4	0.0
8.5	0.37	1.2	0.00	2.5	0.0	0.11	1.00	2.48	93.8	3.8	21.3	10.8	3.8
7.1	0.53	4.7	0.09	3.8	0.7	0.64	8.15	3.05	72.4	2.4	48.9	37.3	2.6
8.4	0.00	0.0	0.00	0.0	-1.4	-15.21	-33.43	0.92	1,247.1	3.7	98.1	34.3	0.0
3.7	4.46	20.0	-0.05	7.2	0.3	1.79	14.78	4.47	59.9	5.3	44.9	9.1	6.8
6.9	0.56	2.6	1.68	5.8	0.4	1.34	11.23	5.42	66.1	4.0	26.4	10.7	6.4
9.0	0.66	1.9	0.11	4.5	0.2	0.96	7.88	4.62	75.8	4.3	30.1	10.4	5.4
5.0	1.22	7.5	4.75	4.5	146.0	7.35	56.63	10.39	46.7	0.5	13.6	83.0	3.5
2.9	1.11	6.5	3.82	10.0	560.7	6.23	56.38	12.87	47.0	0.1	4.6	98.7	8.3
5.6	0.00	0.0	0.07	5.3	0.9	0.75	9.38	3.96	75.7	1.7	4.7	19.5	4.7
5.4	0.06	0.5	0.00	3.7	0.5	0.48	5.59	4.12	74.3	1.7	33.2	33.2	3.7
8.4	0.15	0.8	0.15	5.5	0.9	1.11	7.90	4.03	49.7	1.8	36.9	38.6	4.5
7.7	0.64	2.7	0.07	6.2	0.7	0.90	8.00	3.28	66.5	1.9	10.9	19.0	6.9
4.5	0.56	5.0	0.06	6.8	1.6	1.27	17.60	4.85	64.8	2.5	12.0	16.0	3.1
6.1	0.07	0.6	0.14	3.7	0.3	0.67	8.78	3.49	59.6	0.9	22.6	35.4	1.2
3.3	1.40	11.6	3.75	1.3	-0.1	-0.26	-2.98	4.68	76.4	4.2	96.1	26.0	0.0
8.7	0.18	0.8	0.18	7.1	3.6	1.59	17.14	4.13	62.5	3.8	48.2	17.9	6.1
7.4	0.02	0.1	-0.10	8.0	1.0	1.15	11.87	4.61	59.8	5.7	36.3	3.4	5.5

Name	City	State	Weiss Safety Rating	2003 Weiss Safety Rating	2002 Weiss Safety Rating	Total Assets ($Mil)	One Year Asset Growth	Commercial Loans	Consumer Loans	Home Mortgages	Securities	Capitalization Index	Leverage Ratio	Risk-based Capital Ratio
AMERICAN HOME BK NA	LANCASTER	PA	D	C-	C	164.1	51.49	0.1	0.4	22.8	18.0	7.7	9.5	21.3
AMERICAN HORIZONS BK	MONROE	LA	B-	C+	C-	263.9	7.68	12.7	6.3	19.6	4.6	8.6	10.1	13.8
▲ AMERICAN INTERSTATE BK	ELKHORN	NE	B	B-	B	100.1	35.20	6.6	5.0	7.9	12.0	5.9	9.0	11.7
▲ AMERICAN INVESTMENT BK	SALT LAKE CITY	UT	B	B-	D+	177.7	-34.53	1.3	1.4	0.0	71.5	10.0	48.2	219.6
AMERICAN INVESTORS BANK	EDINA	MN	D	NR	NR	18.5	N/A	0.0	0.0	34.8	0.0	10.0	25.3	27.3
AMERICAN L&SA	HANNIBAL	MO	D+	D+	D+	5.2	-8.98	0.0	1.3	80.2	5.5	10.0	19.8	36.2
AMERICAN MARINE BK	BAINBRIDGE ISLD	WA	B-	C+	C+	320.2	12.08	8.5	2.6	24.8	14.5	8.1	9.8	13.6
▲ AMERICAN METRO BK	CHICAGO	IL	B-	C+	C+	54.7	-0.96	8.1	1.9	19.3	6.3	9.3	10.5	15.6
AMERICAN NATIONAL BK	DENVER	CO	C	C	B	1,339.9	92.09	8.6	2.7	6.0	24.8	6.0	8.0	12.5
AMERICAN NB	OAKLAND PARK	FL	B	B-	B-	142.2	7.10	5.4	0.3	1.1	2.8	6.0	9.1	11.8
AMERICAN NB	HOLSTEIN	IA	C	C	C	168.8	95.49	8.5	3.6	13.8	1.0	3.0	7.9	10.0
▲ AMERICAN NB	OMAHA	NE	B-	C+	C+	994.9	9.53	9.9	34.9	7.1	11.9	3.9	7.8	10.5
▲ AMERICAN NB	PARMA	OH	C+	C-	C-	31.9	1.36	28.9	0.2	0.5	6.5	10.0	23.9	28.8
AMERICAN NB	ARDMORE	OK	B	B	B	125.6	-0.49	4.1	14.3	9.9	28.9	7.4	9.3	15.8
AMERICAN NB	GONZALES	TX	B-	B-	B-	185.1	7.33	7.1	6.5	13.5	15.8	5.5	7.5	12.1
▲ AMERICAN NB	WICHITA FALLS	TX	C+	C	C+	238.6	-0.94	10.6	6.0	11.1	9.0	5.0	7.9	11.0
AMERICAN NB OF BEAVER	BEAVER DAM	WI	B	B+	B+	118.4	-4.79	2.6	3.7	40.1	23.3	7.1	9.1	16.6
AMERICAN NB OF DE KALB	SYCAMORE	IL	C+	C+	C	220.4	-11.25	7.6	8.6	9.8	24.6	9.5	10.7	17.6
AMERICAN NB OF FREMONT	FREMONT	NE	C+	C+	C+	130.5	10.17	16.9	2.8	14.9	16.2	5.7	8.1	11.5
▲ AMERICAN NB OF MN	BAXTER	MN	D+	D-	D-	241.8	0.75	8.2	3.2	17.4	1.3	6.9	11.0	12.4
▲ AMERICAN NB OF MT	MT PLEASANT	TX	C	D+	D-	73.6	2.15	7.1	11.4	29.1	17.9	6.9	9.0	15.9
AMERICAN NB OF ROCK	ROCK SPRINGS	WY	B+	B+	A-	49.9	6.03	9.1	13.6	10.7	28.0	10.0	12.5	24.7
▼ AMERICAN NB OF SIDNEY	SIDNEY	NE	B+	A-	A-	64.9	6.85	19.7	11.1	3.4	44.2	10.0	11.5	20.5
AMERICAN NB TX	TERRELL	TX	B-	B-	C+	1,074.6	3.05	6.1	5.8	9.2	35.5	4.5	6.5	11.4
AMERICAN NB&TC	DANVILLE	VA	A-	A	A+	630.0	-0.11	12.5	2.8	14.9	31.4	9.8	10.9	16.6
▲ AMERICAN NB-FOX CITIES	APPLETON	WI	B	B-	B-	144.6	9.26	34.8	1.4	3.4	12.6	5.1	8.6	11.1
▲ AMERICAN PACIFIC BK	PORTLAND	OR	B+	B	C	120.0	8.02	6.0	3.1	2.8	1.0	9.7	12.0	14.8
AMERICAN PREMIER BK	ARCADIA	CA	D	D	NR	47.5	N/A	11.7	0.0	3.3	5.9	10.0	17.5	30.4
▲ AMERICAN RIVER BK	SACRAMENTO	CA	A-	B+	B+	430.2	50.07	10.0	0.8	2.2	27.7	6.6	8.6	13.0
AMERICAN SAVINGS BANK	MIDDLETOWN	OH	B-	B-	B-	32.1	-1.61	0.0	0.6	59.3	9.0	10.0	21.7	37.7
AMERICAN SECURITY B&TC	HENDERSONVILLE	TN	D	NR	NR	19.3	N/A	2.6	1.7	0.0	15.3	10.0	144.1	201.3
AMERICAN ST B&TC	DICKINSON	ND	B-	B-	B	163.7	9.23	14.8	14.6	2.6	18.6	5.2	8.2	11.1
AMERICAN ST B&TC	WILLISTON	ND	C+	C+	C	195.6	6.88	9.4	12.4	8.1	36.4	4.5	6.5	11.5
▲ AMERICAN ST B&TC NA	GREAT BEND	KS	C+	C-	D-	121.4	15.30	14.1	4.0	4.7	20.8	5.5	8.1	11.4
AMERICAN ST BK	JONESBORO	AR	C-	C-	D+	304.8	28.17	6.7	3.5	23.7	30.2	5.9	7.9	12.7
AMERICAN ST BK	SIOUX CENTER	IA	B-	B-	C+	268.1	4.35	21.5	2.5	2.1	6.7	4.0	8.8	10.5
AMERICAN ST BK	LAWRENCEBURG	IN	D+	D+	D+	69.9	4.62	10.4	5.3	29.8	15.1	5.8	7.8	12.4
AMERICAN ST BK	ERSKINE	MN	B	B	B	19.8	1.22	12.2	8.4	12.3	14.2	10.0	12.6	19.3
▲ AMERICAN ST BK	BROKEN BOW	OK	A	A-	A	47.3	1.34	9.6	4.4	17.1	34.3	10.0	18.7	29.7
▲ AMERICAN ST BK	TULSA	OK	E	E-	E-	10.1	-31.97	8.4	6.4	31.6	12.6	3.6	6.1	10.3
AMERICAN ST BK	OLDHAM	SD	C	C	C+	18.6	-2.39	5.9	4.4	2.8	50.1	10.0	12.7	24.0
AMERICAN ST BK	LUBBOCK	TX	A-	A-	A-	1,726.9	12.68	8.3	3.1	5.7	57.9	7.8	9.5	20.5
AMERICAN ST BK OF GRYGLA	GRYGLA	MN	C+	C+	C+	17.0	11.42	9.0	11.2	15.9	12.5	8.8	10.2	16.5
AMERICAN ST BK OF OLIVIA	OLIVIA	MN	A-	A-	B+	64.1	32.20	13.8	3.8	5.9	0.0	5.7	9.5	11.5
AMERICAN ST BK OF PIERRE	PIERRE	SD	B	B	B	102.0	12.01	19.2	5.8	3.9	21.9	6.8	8.8	13.3
AMERICAN STATE BK	OSCEOLA	IA	B	B	B-	87.9	9.49	19.8	4.5	17.8	22.5	5.1	7.1	11.6
▲ AMERICAN STERLING BK	SUGAR CREEK	MO	B	C+	C	227.6	-16.61	4.9	2.7	33.8	21.3	6.4	8.4	16.9
▲ AMERICAN SVG	FARMINGTON	MN	B	B-	B-	29.5	-14.10	15.4	1.0	16.6	30.8	8.5	10.0	19.9
▼ AMERICAN SVG BK	TRIPOLI	IA	B+	A-	A	39.9	3.38	7.3	1.7	16.4	47.7	10.0	14.4	27.2
▲ AMERICAN SVG BK DANVILLE	DANVILLE	IL	C+	C	C-	49.8	-3.01	0.5	1.6	62.8	19.0	7.7	9.4	20.3
AMERICAN SVGS BK FSB	HONOLULU	HI	B	B-	C+	6,461.9	1.01	4.4	1.3	34.4	43.9	4.9	6.9	15.3
AMERICAN SVGS BK FSB	PORTSMOUTH	OH	B	B	B	165.2	9.61	9.1	2.5	46.1	14.8	7.5	9.3	16.6
AMERICAN SVGS BK OF NJ	BLOOMFIELD	NJ	C+	C+	C+	404.6	8.51	0.3	0.2	58.4	24.3	6.0	8.1	16.7
▲ AMERICAN SVGS FSB	MUNSTER	IN	B-	C+	C	152.8	1.18	3.1	1.7	53.3	3.0	6.7	8.7	15.1
AMERICAN T&SB	DUBUQUE	IA	B-	B-	C+	612.2	-2.69	25.6	4.3	5.7	15.1	4.7	8.1	10.9
AMERICAN T&SB	LOWDEN	IA	B	B	B	33.7	4.34	4.2	1.8	1.3	74.9	10.0	16.7	30.7
AMERICAN T&SB	WHITING	IN	C+	C+	C+	144.3	8.78	2.6	2.0	41.4	36.1	5.1	7.1	15.2
AMERICAN TR BK OF EAST TN	LENOIR CITY	TN	D	NR	NR	25.1	N/A	2.1	1.3	13.3	9.8	10.0	51.6	73.1
AMERICAN TRUST BK	ROSWELL	GA	D	D	NR	47.7	N/A	13.9	0.2	0.6	12.0	10.0	17.0	19.4
▼ AMERICAN UNION S&LA	CHICAGO	IL	E+	D-	D-	8.8	0.35	0.0	0.8	17.7	55.6	6.6	8.6	36.0
▲ AMERICANA COMMUNITY BK	SLEEPY EYE	MN	D-	E-	E-	124.2	8.84	19.4	5.6	5.3	2.6	1.7	7.4	8.7
AMERICANA NB	ALBERT LEA	MN	E-	E-	E-	80.3	-12.75	14.2	1.2	4.1	17.4	4.7	6.7	11.0
AMERICANTRUST FSB	PERU	IN	C-	C-	D+	109.5	9.26	14.8	2.7	28.1	35.3	4.4	6.4	11.8
▲ AMERICANWEST	SPOKANE	WA	C	D+	D	1,085.3	13.73	14.4	2.6	5.4	6.6	3.9	9.2	10.5

Asset Quality Index	Non-Performing Loans as a % of Total Loans	as a % of Capital	Net Charge-offs Avg Loans	Profitability Index	Net Income ($Mil)	Return on Assets (R.O.A.)	Return on Equity (R.O.E.)	Net Interest Spread	Overhead Efficiency Ratio	Liquidity Index	Liquidity Ratio	Hot Money Ratio	Stability Index
6.9	0.71	4.5	0.02	0.9	-0.4	-0.59	-6.03	3.94	102.6	6.9	216.4	18.1	0.0
4.6	0.79	5.8	0.60	6.6	1.7	1.32	13.48	4.68	58.9	2.1	32.6	26.5	4.7
7.0	0.03	0.3	-0.11	10.0	1.6	3.64	44.62	5.66	27.0	3.5	29.0	13.8	6.3
8.2	10.01	0.5	48.99	7.4	12.5	14.50	33.74	10.38	48.4	5.4	502.1	45.1	4.7
9.0	0.00	0.0	0.00	0.0	-0.2	-3.38	-7.00	2.91	147.9	0.5	4.4	38.3	0.0
7.7	0.00	0.0	0.00	2.3	0.0	0.04	0.17	6.14	98.9	3.3	9.6	12.0	3.6
4.6	1.26	8.9	0.15	4.9	1.3	0.81	8.69	4.98	74.9	1.5	15.2	23.8	5.1
5.0	0.92	6.0	-0.09	4.8	0.3	1.12	10.80	4.54	77.1	4.5	89.7	20.0	4.8
2.9	2.49	17.6	0.20	5.6	8.9	1.59	20.85	4.95	74.3	6.5	48.3	6.1	4.2
7.3	0.00	0.0	-0.01	10.0	1.1	1.62	18.64	5.26	51.6	6.6	53.0	3.7	5.6
3.7	0.47	4.8	0.24	8.4	0.9	1.08	13.27	3.58	50.0	5.0	32.8	6.7	5.3
4.4	0.47	4.2	0.26	9.8	12.1	2.47	30.81	4.46	47.7	3.4	35.6	16.5	6.6
2.7	4.29	13.8	0.00	7.9	0.4	2.18	9.12	5.07	68.0	1.5	29.3	31.2	7.1
7.5	0.19	1.1	0.10	7.9	0.8	1.33	14.44	4.52	62.2	4.3	44.8	14.5	5.6
4.7	0.91	6.2	0.08	5.1	0.7	0.83	8.98	4.31	77.0	3.3	45.9	20.7	4.6
3.5	1.22	8.8	0.05	4.9	1.1	0.90	9.88	3.93	77.8	1.8	23.2	21.7	5.3
7.5	0.30	2.2	0.22	6.2	0.8	1.28	14.11	3.98	73.0	3.0	15.1	13.9	6.2
4.7	1.23	6.8	0.37	5.7	0.6	0.55	5.50	3.78	75.0	3.5	51.8	21.9	4.5
5.3	0.34	2.9	0.04	6.0	0.9	1.38	17.40	3.65	61.7	2.0	15.5	19.0	3.1
2.2	1.16	8.5	0.40	7.2	1.6	1.43	13.33	5.98	55.8	2.9	15.0	14.6	4.8
5.0	0.67	4.6	0.36	4.5	0.4	0.96	10.82	4.13	66.4	2.8	42.2	23.9	3.0
5.3	0.80	3.7	0.24	10.0	0.7	2.99	23.70	5.48	45.8	5.0	115.0	21.1	7.5
8.0	0.30	1.1	0.28	5.8	0.3	1.02	9.03	4.06	64.8	5.8	38.8	4.1	6.5
7.4	0.38	2.5	0.18	7.0	6.5	1.20	16.17	5.12	67.5	5.2	37.8	10.7	6.3
5.7	1.02	5.5	0.15	9.1	5.0	1.55	14.10	3.84	51.1	3.6	22.4	11.5	8.7
5.8	0.77	6.7	0.18	8.2	1.0	1.37	16.25	3.67	43.1	0.5	6.2	48.2	5.6
6.5	0.06	0.4	0.17	9.2	0.8	1.47	13.20	5.64	56.8	4.5	97.6	26.2	5.6
9.1	0.00	0.0	0.00	0.0	-1.1	-5.60	-26.89	1.41	409.2	5.6	171.9	25.9	0.0
8.6	0.03	0.2	0.11	9.9	3.2	1.66	18.75	5.27	49.4	4.1	37.8	13.9	6.3
7.6	0.37	1.0	-0.04	3.7	0.1	0.45	2.08	3.68	81.9	3.6	35.1	15.3	5.9
10.0	0.00	0.0	0.00	0.0	-0.7	-8.97	-11.83	0.42	1,757.1	5.5	1,094.5	39.8	0.0
4.3	0.60	4.5	-0.01	9.4	1.3	1.61	17.23	5.14	61.4	3.0	11.1	13.5	6.1
4.4	0.76	6.1	-0.25	7.2	1.5	1.53	22.08	3.96	62.0	4.6	27.7	7.4	5.3
7.4	0.20	1.5	0.01	3.6	0.4	0.66	7.11	3.95	69.0	1.2	8.1	27.2	2.8
7.4	0.38	2.8	0.20	4.7	1.2	0.84	11.67	3.74	67.2	3.1	19.2	13.7	2.3
6.8	0.00	0.0	-0.02	7.4	2.4	1.77	19.77	3.43	57.4	5.3	47.5	10.2	5.9
1.5	3.05	25.6	0.22	4.6	0.3	0.74	9.44	4.81	75.5	2.5	39.0	26.0	2.7
7.1	0.92	4.0	0.00	5.0	0.1	0.58	4.74	3.82	74.9	6.7	103.3	9.4	5.1
5.4	2.75	8.0	0.07	8.7	0.3	1.35	7.05	4.20	51.2	1.1	10.0	28.7	8.4
3.2	1.04	10.0	1.97	0.0	-0.1	-2.52	-42.77	5.73	124.9	3.9	51.8	15.7	0.0
8.7	0.24	0.7	0.00	3.0	0.0	0.45	3.46	3.82	89.2	5.3	32.9	2.5	4.0
8.8	0.53	1.6	0.16	8.0	11.5	1.34	13.02	3.83	57.1	2.4	21.9	18.8	8.4
5.0	0.79	5.2	0.00	8.1	0.2	1.87	18.15	4.48	65.4	5.1	85.1	15.3	4.9
3.8	1.55	13.1	0.48	5.8	0.2	0.74	7.98	4.61	50.2	3.4	30.2	14.6	5.9
4.6	0.73	5.2	0.00	9.6	0.8	1.52	17.56	5.06	56.3	1.4	15.9	26.7	5.6
5.6	0.80	7.0	0.05	8.0	0.7	1.67	22.23	4.15	60.9	2.8	26.3	16.3	5.8
7.0	0.38	2.7	0.49	8.4	1.8	1.59	18.76	3.35	65.0	2.1	43.0	39.1	3.9
4.7	2.81	13.5	0.00	4.1	0.2	1.04	10.46	2.56	53.3	7.0	536.7	17.4	4.7
5.2	2.94	9.7	0.26	7.0	0.3	1.72	11.62	3.48	45.5	5.5	41.3	6.9	8.2
6.1	0.72	5.4	0.09	4.4	0.2	0.77	8.52	3.32	60.0	3.0	27.7	15.8	3.7
8.2	0.11	0.8	0.23	5.7	11.7	0.36	4.34	3.16	64.0	1.4	5.8	23.6	6.8
4.7	0.97	7.4	0.10	7.4	1.1	1.32	13.86	3.83	53.9	3.8	14.0	10.1	6.6
8.3	0.07	0.6	0.00	4.3	1.1	0.57	7.08	2.64	66.2	0.8	10.9	34.2	3.5
4.1	1.11	10.1	0.13	5.2	0.6	0.80	9.19	3.43	67.4	1.4	14.8	26.3	4.3
6.4	0.64	5.2	-0.02	5.4	3.8	1.23	15.20	3.27	68.9	5.4	36.0	5.3	5.9
9.4	0.53	0.6	-3.26	4.3	0.2	0.97	4.78	4.03	74.6	5.3	61.6	12.2	6.5
7.4	0.07	0.5	0.02	3.6	0.3	0.48	6.36	3.50	83.7	3.7	19.7	11.2	4.0
9.0	0.00	0.0	0.00	0.0	-0.6	-7.13	-11.11	1.92	324.2	5.5	635.2	35.9	0.0
7.4	0.00	0.0	0.00	0.0	-0.5	-2.53	-12.43	3.43	140.5	9.4	232.3	4.1	0.0
9.0	0.00	0.0	0.00	1.9	0.0	-0.07	-0.66	4.19	101.8	3.7	29.2	11.2	1.0
5.0	0.28	2.8	0.03	3.2	0.5	0.73	9.48	5.05	81.4	4.6	16.3	4.9	3.0
0.4	5.93	35.5	0.53	1.0	-0.2	-0.42	-5.72	4.24	108.9	2.9	40.5	21.4	0.3
6.8	0.25	2.0	0.10	2.2	0.1	0.21	3.36	2.54	84.6	2.5	53.0	56.9	3.0
2.9	1.34	10.1	1.16	7.6	5.1	0.97	9.44	6.26	59.4	4.1	23.3	11.3	8.8

Name	City	State	Weiss Safety Rating	2003 Weiss Safety Rating	2002 Weiss Safety Rating	Total Assets ($Mil)	One Year Asset Growth	Asset Mix (As a % of Total Assets) Commercial Loans	Consumer Loans	Home Mortgages	Securities	Capitalization Index	Leverage Ratio	Risk-based Capital Ratio
AMERICAS COMMUNITY BK	BLUE SPRINGS	MO	D+	D+	D+	31.5	-1.49	2.3	1.3	25.0	8.6	5.3	7.3	11.7
▲ AMERICASBANK	TOWSON	MD	D-	E-	D-	30.1	6.66	5.3	0.7	20.9	1.1	10.0	17.5	28.8
▲ AMERICAUNITED B&TC USA	SCHAUMBURG	IL	C	C+	B-	199.3	9.71	13.6	0.8	4.1	16.8	6.6	8.6	12.4
AMERICREST BK	OKLAHOMA CITY	OK	C+	C+	C+	682.6	-0.03	19.0	6.0	11.0	2.2	3.9	8.8	10.4
AMERICUS ST BK	AMERICUS	KS	D-	D	D	13.4	12.59	4.8	6.2	24.9	27.7	6.2	8.2	15.0
AMERIFIRST BK	UNION SPRINGS	AL	B-	B-	B-	163.6	5.23	14.3	7.0	12.9	27.6	6.4	8.4	12.6
▲ AMERIKA SAMOA BK	PAGO PAGO	AS	A-	B	C+	78.4	2.62	5.1	31.1	30.3	0.0	10.0	12.0	18.9
AMERIMARK BK	VILLA PARK	IL	C+	C	C-	173.2	31.15	16.1	3.3	5.5	8.5	5.7	9.3	11.5
AMERISERV FINANCIAL BK	JOHNSTOWN	PA	D	D	D	1,171.9	0.95	3.9	2.1	14.4	47.4	6.2	8.2	16.0
AMERISTATE BK	ATOKA	OK	A-	B+	A-	118.8	1.16	2.9	10.4	17.4	34.3	10.0	11.2	20.4
▲ AMES COMMUNITY BK	AMES	IA	C	C-	C-	126.4	25.62	10.9	2.1	5.9	11.5	4.9	8.8	10.9
▲ AMFIRST BK NA	MC COOK	NE	B-	C	C	126.0	15.50	13.4	6.2	7.3	6.1	5.2	9.3	11.2
AMISTAD BK	DEL RIO	TX	C-	C-	C-	14.3	-56.98	8.8	3.9	15.3	7.0	10.0	11.9	17.4
AMORY FS&LA	AMORY	MS	B-	C+	C-	52.9	-4.09	0.0	2.0	77.8	0.0	10.0	11.4	24.5
AMSOUTH BK	BIRMINGHAM	AL	B+	B+	B	48,212.8	10.01	9.0	9.6	13.2	25.1	5.2	7.2	11.1
AMVESCAP NATIONAL TRUST	ATLANTA	GA	B+	B+	B+	155.1	2.49	0.0	0.0	0.0	4.8	5.9	7.9	42.4
▼ ANADARKO B&TC	ANADARKO	OK	B-	B+	A-	70.2	16.14	9.8	7.2	10.2	27.4	7.1	9.1	14.3
▲ ANAHUAC NB	ANAHUAC	TX	D+	D	D-	36.7	-10.40	6.9	13.8	12.2	23.2	6.9	8.9	15.3
ANCHOR BK FARMINGTON NA	FARMINGTON	MN	B-	B-	B-	93.5	8.52	25.1	2.8	12.9	7.7	4.0	8.3	10.5
ANCHOR BK HERITAGE NA	N ST PAUL	MN	B-	B-	B-	230.7	-2.87	26.4	1.7	6.0	15.9	5.1	8.1	11.1
ANCHOR BK NA	WAYZATA	MN	C+	C+	B-	309.0	1.16	16.0	1.6	3.2	30.1	5.1	7.1	11.4
ANCHOR BK ST PAUL	ST PAUL	MN	B-	B-	B-	46.0	-20.55	23.3	4.4	9.2	20.2	9.0	10.3	15.0
ANCHOR BK WEST ST PAUL	W ST PAUL	MN	B-	B-	B-	294.0	7.61	35.7	2.7	7.1	16.5	4.0	8.0	10.5
▲ ANCHOR MSB	ABERDEEN	WA	B-	C	C+	472.8	10.68	1.4	3.4	14.0	23.3	9.4	10.6	15.6
ANCHOR ST BK	ANCHOR	IL	E-	E-	E-	13.9	5.41	4.1	1.9	9.0	41.1	4.8	6.8	11.3
ANCHORBANK FSB	MADISON	WI	B-	B-	B	3,757.3	5.26	4.4	6.8	24.4	8.8	4.6	7.9	10.8
ANDALUSIA COMMUNITY BK	ANDALUSIA	IL	B	B	B	21.8	-5.96	6.0	14.2	25.0	22.6	10.0	16.8	31.7
▼ ANDERSON BK	CINCINNATI	OH	C-	C	C	62.4	22.62	16.7	7.2	29.8	0.8	3.7	8.7	10.4
ANDERSON BROTHERS BK	MULLINS	SC	C	C-	C-	244.6	16.19	11.3	17.5	14.5	21.3	7.2	9.1	13.4
▼ ANDERSON ST BK	ONEIDA	IL	B-	B	B	53.1	5.67	5.7	5.8	8.9	42.6	10.0	17.0	31.1
ANDES ST BK	LAKE ANDES	SD	C+	C+	B-	14.7	-1.65	4.3	4.3	0.5	35.7	10.0	13.3	22.1
ANDOVER BK	ANDOVER	OH	B+	B+	A-	252.2	0.67	1.6	2.9	29.6	44.3	7.4	9.3	19.7
ANDOVER ST BK	ANDOVER	KS	C-	C-	D+	51.1	2.76	2.8	8.3	32.8	20.5	6.8	8.8	15.0
ANDREW JOHNSON BK	GREENEVILLE	TN	B	B	B-	177.0	-3.35	12.1	10.4	49.0	6.3	6.9	8.9	14.9
▲ ANDROSCOGGIN SVGS BK	LEWISTON	ME	B+	C+	C+	482.5	1.60	4.2	10.5	25.4	20.6	8.9	10.3	14.4
ANGELINA SVGS BK FSB	LUFKIN	TX	C	C	C-	43.7	-2.31	2.0	19.0	30.9	13.3	9.0	10.4	21.7
▼ ANN ARBOR COMMERCE BK	ANN ARBOR	MI	C-	C	C	328.5	-0.20	13.0	1.0	17.8	0.1	3.1	7.9	10.0
▲ ANNA NB	ANNA	IL	A	A-	A-	118.6	3.12	4.7	9.8	24.8	34.5	10.0	12.8	23.1
▼ ANNA ST BK	ANNA	IL	B+	A-	A-	59.2	3.56	2.4	6.1	18.4	45.9	10.0	14.8	34.3
ANNANDALE ST BK	ANNANDALE	MN	A-	A-	A-	106.4	3.88	7.2	6.5	26.6	24.8	9.2	10.5	17.0
ANNAPOLIS BKG&TC	ANNAPOLIS	MD	A-	A-	A	458.9	5.41	6.6	4.7	11.7	42.1	7.0	9.0	18.2
ANSON B&TC	WADESBORO	NC	C+	C+	B-	35.6	22.16	5.9	0.9	36.0	12.9	10.0	11.3	17.0
▲ ANTWERP EXCHANGE BK CO	ANTWERP	OH	B-	C+	C	54.3	0.00	2.6	8.0	29.9	36.3	8.0	9.7	19.2
APOLLO TRUST CO	APOLLO	PA	A-	A-	A	124.0	-5.15	5.5	22.0	15.5	37.8	10.0	13.0	22.5
APPALACHIAN COMMUNITY BK	ELLIJAY	GA	C	C-	D+	453.7	13.93	7.0	4.5	15.8	11.7	4.1	7.9	10.6
▼ APPLE BK FOR SVGS	SCARSDALE	NY	B	B+	A-	6,618.6	19.35	0.0	0.6	9.2	63.3	6.3	8.3	31.2
APPLE CREEK BKG CO	APPLE CREEK	OH	C-	C-	C-	73.0	-1.38	1.5	1.9	58.3	9.0	6.1	8.1	15.0
▲ APPLE RIVER ST BK	APPLE RIVER	IL	C+	C	C-	190.6	3.56	17.8	6.1	13.4	39.7	5.4	7.4	13.0
APPLE VALLEY B&TC	CHESHIRE	CT	D	D	D	47.5	15.84	8.3	0.6	3.6	27.3	10.0	12.8	17.7
▲ ARCHER BK	CHICAGO	IL	B	B-	B-	436.6	11.15	1.7	0.3	7.0	31.9	5.2	7.2	11.4
ARCOLA HMSTD SVGS BK	ARCOLA	IL	C-	C-	C-	4.9	1.00	0.0	1.0	12.9	51.7	10.0	16.3	37.7
AREA BK	ROSICLARE	IL	B	B	B	37.9	5.53	3.9	6.9	13.8	63.3	10.0	11.6	26.0
▲ ARGENTINE FEDERAL SVGS	KANSAS CITY	KS	C	C-	C-	55.3	-6.04	0.0	0.8	62.0	24.5	10.0	11.2	23.9
▼ ARIZONA B&T	MESA	AZ	B-	B	NR	55.1	N/A	9.9	1.0	0.7	15.8	10.0	24.7	27.8
▼ ARKANSAS BANKERS BK	LITTLE ROCK	AR	C	C+	B-	241.7	18.95	1.6	0.0	0.4	55.2	6.4	8.4	26.7
ARKANSAS DIAMOND BK	GLENWOOD	AR	B	B-	B-	108.1	-0.04	3.4	8.5	23.9	31.4	8.9	10.3	18.0
▲ ARKANSAS NB	BENTONVILLE	AR	B-	C+	C+	534.8	8.00	7.8	7.9	20.1	9.1	4.1	7.8	10.6
▼ ARKANSAS ST BK	SILOAM SPRINGS	AR	B-	B	A-	170.8	5.96	10.9	4.5	17.0	27.6	10.0	15.5	16.0
▲ ARKANSAS VALLEY ST BK	BROKEN ARROW	OK	A	A-	A-	248.4	9.99	11.2	4.2	10.2	33.5	10.0	13.2	21.2
ARLINGTON BK	UPPER ARLINGTON	OH	B-	C+	C+	170.3	13.24	1.0	0.7	53.2	0.0	6.9	8.9	13.2
ARLINGTON ST BK	ARLINGTON	MN	C-	C	C	54.9	-2.46	10.5	2.0	8.2	38.0	6.8	8.8	16.3
▲ ARMED FORCES BK NA	FORT LEAVENWORTH	KS	A-	B+	A-	548.3	4.04	8.2	2.0	2.0	40.5	8.9	10.3	21.0
▲ ARMED FORCES BK OF CA NA	SAN DIEGO	CA	A-	B	B	15.6	2.50	19.7	0.5	5.8	0.7	10.0	45.2	64.4
▲ ARMSTRONG BK	MUSKOGEE	OK	B-	C+	C+	327.9	15.72	8.1	14.2	15.1	19.1	9.1	10.6	14.3

Asset Quality Index	Non-Performing Loans as a % of Total Loans	as a % of Capital	Net Charge-offs Avg Loans	Profitability Index	Net Income ($Mil)	Return on Assets (R.O.A.)	Return on Equity (R.O.E.)	Net Interest Spread	Overhead Efficiency Ratio	Liquidity Index	Liquidity Ratio	Hot Money Ratio	Stability Index
6.3	0.66	5.9	0.10	4.7	0.2	1.15	15.46	4.36	70.5	4.1	73.8	19.9	2.7
8.5	0.31	1.0	-0.19	0.0	-0.7	-4.67	-32.71	2.40	225.8	7.0	233.1	17.7	3.6
2.3	1.29	9.7	-0.01	7.2	1.2	1.25	14.05	4.23	56.0	0.9	17.3	33.8	5.1
3.6	0.88	7.8	0.27	7.4	4.1	1.22	14.00	4.58	64.6	5.5	56.2	11.4	5.4
3.6	3.19	23.9	0.00	3.8	0.0	0.58	6.88	3.40	79.6	2.9	52.3	22.3	1.7
5.4	0.74	5.6	0.42	5.7	0.8	0.98	11.65	4.15	63.5	0.8	16.1	36.2	5.0
6.8	0.29	1.7	0.26	10.0	0.9	2.36	19.81	8.32	50.1	3.5	42.1	17.6	6.5
4.5	1.05	7.7	0.02	3.8	0.5	0.61	5.81	4.21	70.3	1.2	18.2	29.9	4.6
5.0	2.68	12.4	0.48	0.9	1.2	0.21	2.29	2.68	93.9	3.8	8.4	9.7	5.5
8.3	0.25	1.1	0.04	6.2	1.0	1.72	13.38	4.62	68.8	4.0	50.5	17.6	8.4
6.5	0.01	0.1	-0.03	2.5	0.4	0.58	6.51	3.46	64.6	0.7	13.3	44.1	1.6
7.7	0.13	1.1	0.05	5.3	0.8	1.41	15.39	4.91	69.6	2.0	18.6	19.4	4.3
6.8	0.47	2.3	0.12	5.6	0.1	1.28	11.19	7.47	81.3	3.4	46.7	17.2	2.9
3.7	3.22	22.5	0.00	6.9	0.3	1.12	10.56	3.43	47.0	1.3	29.3	36.0	5.4
6.4	0.48	3.9	0.36	8.3	335.6	1.43	18.74	3.45	54.6	3.5	14.5	11.9	7.3
10.0	0.00	0.0	0.00	9.1	1.6	1.77	23.94	0.58	88.2	5.0	N/A	0.0	4.8
3.3	2.69	15.4	0.36	7.8	0.5	1.57	15.53	5.11	63.4	2.3	29.8	20.4	6.0
6.4	0.01	0.1	1.93	4.9	0.2	1.31	14.24	5.90	75.6	5.0	47.0	11.4	1.5
5.2	0.89	6.7	-0.01	5.1	0.4	0.80	8.13	4.99	71.9	5.0	58.2	13.1	5.6
4.5	1.15	9.6	0.34	5.7	0.9	0.76	9.67	3.93	70.1	3.8	29.9	12.8	4.4
5.4	1.11	8.2	-0.01	4.3	1.1	0.70	10.05	3.58	66.9	6.7	75.8	8.3	4.2
7.3	0.24	1.5	0.08	6.2	0.2	0.82	8.19	4.09	73.1	4.4	28.8	9.2	5.7
7.2	0.22	1.9	0.01	9.8	2.2	1.57	19.70	5.11	57.8	6.2	47.5	4.8	5.2
5.6	0.26	1.6	0.30	4.5	2.5	1.06	10.07	4.25	68.5	1.0	16.7	32.2	5.3
7.6	0.00	0.0	-0.03	1.5	0.0	0.03	0.42	3.03	99.1	2.6	3.8	14.6	0.1
3.9	1.07	10.6	0.21	8.2	20.8	1.12	13.49	3.20	51.2	0.6	6.4	41.1	7.5
5.4	3.42	10.3	0.00	9.4	0.2	1.57	9.29	4.93	59.5	5.5	57.9	8.7	6.7
8.0	0.00	0.0	0.00	3.5	0.2	0.52	5.52	3.32	73.6	2.6	24.1	16.7	4.2
3.1	1.75	12.2	0.64	9.9	2.0	1.70	18.35	6.43	57.1	1.7	16.5	21.3	5.0
7.4	0.65	1.7	1.14	3.5	0.1	0.35	2.01	3.11	67.1	7.4	110.0	7.5	6.1
8.7	0.57	1.5	0.00	4.3	0.1	0.74	5.42	4.17	78.6	6.7	132.6	12.8	5.1
5.4	1.88	9.3	0.07	6.5	1.6	1.25	12.91	4.10	62.7	3.0	20.9	14.7	6.6
5.6	0.53	3.7	0.05	3.9	0.1	0.34	3.69	4.15	88.6	4.9	31.3	7.0	3.0
5.8	0.42	3.2	0.28	6.6	0.8	0.88	9.60	4.79	70.8	3.3	32.0	15.7	5.5
7.1	0.20	1.1	0.11	6.6	3.9	1.63	13.92	3.26	51.1	5.1	31.5	5.9	6.1
7.0	0.07	0.4	0.14	5.8	0.2	0.83	8.07	4.29	74.6	3.3	43.8	19.2	3.9
1.5	2.08	20.6	0.51	8.8	2.1	1.30	16.70	4.43	47.9	3.6	67.8	29.0	5.7
6.8	1.43	6.6	0.28	8.3	0.8	1.42	11.22	4.35	47.1	2.8	25.6	16.3	7.6
6.1	3.14	8.7	0.08	5.0	0.2	0.83	5.68	3.48	65.8	7.0	89.8	6.6	7.2
6.2	0.60	3.7	-0.08	8.8	1.0	1.90	18.29	4.56	58.7	4.9	32.8	7.6	7.7
8.6	0.01	0.0	0.02	10.0	4.5	1.97	21.12	4.81	41.3	7.2	61.2	2.0	8.1
5.6	0.85	4.6	0.02	2.1	0.0	0.04	0.29	3.53	90.2	2.9	12.6	14.3	5.9
5.3	2.61	15.2	0.03	4.8	0.3	0.94	9.70	3.80	67.5	4.3	34.1	11.7	4.8
7.5	0.21	0.7	0.17	5.6	0.7	1.10	8.07	4.28	67.0	5.9	37.3	2.7	7.5
4.4	0.45	4.1	0.05	5.5	2.2	1.01	12.15	4.51	61.1	1.6	24.0	25.1	3.7
9.8	0.18	0.4	-0.04	4.7	23.0	0.72	7.95	1.67	47.5	8.3	280.4	11.0	7.6
6.1	1.03	8.8	0.09	4.5	0.2	0.49	6.08	4.79	80.3	5.2	29.1	4.1	2.3
5.2	0.68	4.9	0.25	5.3	1.4	1.41	19.74	2.87	48.3	6.1	74.2	11.3	3.3
8.9	0.00	0.0	0.00	0.0	-0.2	-0.63	-4.79	3.75	113.8	3.6	49.1	18.3	0.0
5.7	0.35	2.2	-0.01	9.8	3.7	1.73	20.69	5.52	51.7	2.6	32.9	19.8	6.7
9.7	0.00	0.0	0.00	1.3	0.0	-0.49	-2.83	2.85	118.2	3.7	77.4	23.2	4.4
8.9	0.87	2.2	0.00	4.1	0.2	0.96	8.64	3.05	68.6	5.6	40.6	6.3	4.8
9.1	0.52	3.0	0.00	2.6	0.1	0.17	1.52	3.00	93.1	3.6	7.5	10.3	4.6
7.6	0.00	0.0	0.00	0.0	-0.5	-2.31	-8.07	4.91	160.9	4.7	16.0	4.4	4.9
9.9	1.16	1.2	0.00	8.8	1.7	1.50	20.99	3.61	64.2	5.3	38.2	6.9	2.6
5.2	0.92	5.0	0.14	8.6	1.2	2.28	22.56	4.37	52.4	2.3	30.8	21.6	7.0
4.2	0.98	9.4	0.10	9.7	7.9	3.04	36.94	5.27	50.9	0.5	6.0	44.0	6.3
5.2	2.08	8.1	0.25	3.4	0.4	0.51	3.32	3.37	75.4	2.0	24.1	19.9	6.5
7.6	1.07	4.5	0.33	6.9	1.4	1.12	8.41	4.56	61.5	1.3	20.9	29.5	7.7
4.3	1.79	16.3	0.11	9.6	1.3	1.59	18.40	4.12	38.1	5.0	88.5	18.8	7.0
2.9	3.71	19.4	0.01	4.6	0.1	0.50	5.24	3.77	59.4	6.3	99.0	12.1	4.0
9.0	0.03	0.1	0.73	10.0	12.2	4.36	40.92	2.97	50.9	6.7	51.4	2.3	7.9
8.6	0.03	0.0	1.09	5.5	0.1	1.16	2.58	5.83	84.9	5.9	67.8	8.2	7.4
4.0	1.17	7.6	0.21	9.9	2.8	1.81	16.81	5.58	65.4	1.9	10.2	19.0	6.6

Name	City	State	Weiss Safety Rating	2003 Weiss Safety Rating	2002 Weiss Safety Rating	Total Assets ($Mil)	One Year Asset Growth	Commercial Loans	Consumer Loans	Home Mortgages	Securities	Capitalization Index	Leverage Ratio	Risk-based Capital Ratio
▼ ARMSTRONG COUNTY B&LA	FORD CITY	PA	B-	B	B	66.3	1.52	0.0	0.7	44.4	46.9	10.0	15.5	32.6
▲ AROOSTOOK COUNTY FS&LA	CARIBOU	ME	B-	C+	C-	66.5	2.06	1.5	3.9	75.1	0.0	8.5	10.0	18.3
▲ ARP ST BK	ARP	TX	A-	B+	A	121.5	-3.43	3.9	13.9	4.3	68.5	10.0	17.7	39.6
ARROWHEAD BANK	LLANO	TX	B-	B-	B	100.3	0.34	3.3	7.9	4.0	32.6	8.2	9.8	19.0
ARROWHEAD COMMUNITY BK	GLENDALE	AZ	C	C	C	68.0	29.76	13.5	1.3	8.0	0.1	3.0	8.7	10.0
▼ ARTHUR ST BK	UNION	SC	B+	A-	A+	399.1	77.04	29.8	5.7	20.4	14.0	7.4	9.4	12.9
ARTISANS BK	WILMINGTON	DE	C	C+	C	487.0	2.95	6.8	1.2	15.8	12.5	4.5	9.6	10.8
ARUNDEL FSB	BALTIMORE	MD	B	B	B+	350.4	-5.86	0.0	0.2	51.2	42.4	10.0	12.2	35.0
ARVEST BK	FAYETTEVILLE	AR	C+	C+	C+	7,168.3	40.35	8.0	10.1	20.9	14.4	5.2	7.2	11.6
▼ ASCENCIA BK INC	LOUISVILLE	KY	C+	B-	C+	281.5	14.44	3.2	0.3	10.8	15.5	8.3	10.1	13.6
ASHEVILLE SVG BK SSB	ASHEVILLE	NC	B+	B+	B	528.5	8.19	3.7	18.6	37.1	7.8	9.5	10.7	15.2
ASHTON ST BK	ASHTON	IA	B+	B	B	27.0	0.14	4.3	3.1	8.3	36.5	10.0	13.8	23.6
ASHTON ST BK	ASHTON	NE	C+	C	C-	11.0	-2.61	1.9	3.5	1.4	14.5	10.0	11.7	16.6
▲ ASIA BK NA	NEW YORK CITY	NY	A-	B	C+	353.8	5.47	1.6	0.0	3.0	23.5	9.4	10.6	16.1
▼ ASIA-EUROPE-AMERICAS BK	SEATTLE	WA	D+	C-	C+	134.2	-6.99	35.6	0.9	1.2	6.0	8.4	10.0	13.6
ASIAN AMERICAN B&TC	BOSTON	MA	C+	C+	B	125.2	9.98	1.6	0.5	27.7	27.3	10.0	14.1	21.2
ASIAN BK	PHILADELPHIA	PA	D	D-	D-	47.2	5.52	8.2	0.0	0.9	11.4	4.9	8.0	10.9
▲ ASIAN PACIFIC NB	SAN GABRIEL	CA	B-	C+	C	51.6	-6.09	1.2	0.9	1.4	26.3	10.0	13.4	19.2
ASSOCIATED BK CHICAGO	CHICAGO	IL	B-	B-	B-	703.3	-3.08	28.5	1.2	14.4	5.8	5.0	8.8	11.0
ASSOCIATED BK MN NA	MINNEAPOLIS	MN	B-	B-	B-	1,963.0	5.20	19.2	1.4	5.8	13.6	6.2	8.3	11.9
ASSOCIATED BK NA	GREEN BAY	WI	B-	B-	B-	12,965.0	26.44	11.2	4.5	15.5	25.6	4.5	6.5	11.0
ASSOCIATES CAPITAL BK	SALT LAKE CITY	UT	B-	B-	B	359.9	20.39	84.0	0.0	0.2	0.6	10.0	27.0	32.3
ASSURANCE PARTNERS BK	CARMEL	IN	D	D	D	36.8	8.06	7.9	31.7	28.9	7.5	10.0	18.6	27.6
ASTORIA FS&LA	NEW YORK CITY	NY	B	B	B	22,033.0	0.16	0.1	0.1	39.4	37.8	5.1	7.1	14.7
ATASCOSA NB	PLEASANTON	TX	C+	C+	C+	48.1	-5.79	7.6	3.5	5.7	23.8	8.7	10.1	22.7
ATHENS FEDERAL	ATHENS	TN	B-	B-	B-	181.0	1.67	3.6	6.1	31.9	26.6	9.1	10.4	19.1
▼ ATHENS FIRST B&TC	ATHENS	GA	B-	B	B	926.8	6.59	6.9	1.8	18.9	13.1	3.1	7.5	10.0
ATHENS ST BK	ATHENS	IL	B-	B-	B	61.1	-2.47	1.8	8.0	28.4	43.7	8.0	12.5	13.3
▲ ATHOL SVGS BK	ATHOL	MA	B	B-	B	259.6	4.53	2.9	0.5	47.5	24.2	10.0	11.2	20.4
▼ ATHOL-CLINTON CO-OP BK	ATHOL	MA	B-	B	B	85.9	4.92	0.0	1.1	58.3	20.8	9.5	10.7	20.3
ATKINS SVG B&TC	ATKINS	IA	B	B	B-	29.1	4.75	6.7	4.2	8.7	44.6	10.0	11.2	18.5
ATLANTA NB	ATLANTA	IL	C+	C+	C+	43.9	-4.50	4.1	11.1	9.1	53.4	8.6	10.1	21.3
▲ ATLANTIC BK OF NEW YORK	NEW YORK	NY	C+	C	C	3,394.1	10.42	13.8	0.1	1.6	52.4	3.9	5.9	11.0
▲ ATLANTIC CENTRAL BANKERS	CAMP HILL	PA	A-	B-	C	280.2	-6.40	1.3	0.0	0.5	9.7	9.6	10.7	14.7
ATLANTIC COAST FEDERAL	WAYCROSS	GA	C-	C+	B-	580.3	17.94	0.7	10.3	51.8	3.8	4.2	7.2	10.6
▼ ATLANTIC LIBERTY SVGS FA	NEW YORK CITY	NY	B+	B+	C+	179.5	30.52	0.0	0.6	34.9	28.4	9.6	10.8	20.1
ATLANTIC NB	BRUNSWICK	GA	C+	B-	B	138.8	2.83	6.6	2.8	29.8	9.6	6.0	8.0	14.0
ATLANTIC STEWARDSHIP BK	MIDLAND PARK	NJ	B-	B-	B-	401.3	12.73	6.4	1.5	24.7	24.2	5.7	7.7	12.3
ATLAS S&LA	NEW YORK CITY	NY	B+	B+	A-	65.9	-1.38	0.0	0.0	15.8	66.5	10.0	24.1	88.6
ATWATER ST BK	ATWATER	MN	C+	C	C	20.8	0.38	7.2	7.1	21.5	16.2	7.2	9.1	14.0
AUBURN BKG CO	AUBURN	KY	D	D-	E	55.4	0.06	4.2	8.7	21.7	31.6	5.7	7.7	13.7
▲ AUBURN COMMUNITY BK	AUBURN	CA	C+	C-	C+	107.7	19.94	5.2	0.9	1.4	0.0	6.6	9.0	12.2
AUBURN S&LA	AUBURN	ME	D	D	D	57.8	-0.74	3.3	0.7	60.9	12.4	5.0	7.0	11.7
AUBURN ST BK	AUBURN	NE	A-	A-	A-	69.7	5.20	5.2	5.3	22.0	32.3	10.0	18.1	33.2
▲ AUBURNBANK	AUBURN	AL	C+	C	C-	597.9	15.03	7.8	1.9	11.2	48.0	5.7	7.7	15.2
AUDUBON SB	AUDUBON	NJ	C	C	C	150.5	14.63	0.7	0.1	42.5	42.5	5.2	7.2	16.1
▼ AUDUBON ST BK	AUDUBON	IA	C+	B-	B-	62.2	2.27	9.6	5.2	6.4	25.1	4.4	7.1	10.7
▲ AUSTIN BK OF CHICAGO	CHICAGO	IL	B-	C+	C+	223.8	-0.67	3.1	1.4	6.6	29.5	5.8	7.8	11.8
AUSTIN BK TX NA	JACKSONVILLE	TX	B	B	B	623.1	7.27	12.5	12.3	22.9	14.2	7.7	9.5	13.5
AUTO CLUB TRUST FSB	DEARBORN	MI	D	D	D	3.9	-1.84	0.0	0.0	0.0	83.1	10.0	85.7	472.5
▼ AVON CO-OP BK	GEORGETOWN	MA	B	B+	B+	57.7	4.90	0.0	1.2	35.0	49.8	10.0	11.2	28.0
▲ AVON ST BK	AVON	MN	B	B-	C+	101.7	0.67	5.4	7.4	34.2	29.0	8.6	10.0	19.7
AXSYS NB	SIOUX FALLS	SD	B+	B+	B+	20.3	-3.91	0.0	0.0	0.0	0.0	10.0	94.2	453.7
▼ B&L BK	LEXINGTON	MO	B-	B	B	133.9	-5.60	10.0	5.7	32.2	24.1	9.2	10.5	17.8
BAC FLORIDA BK	MIAMI	FL	C+	C+	C+	735.3	13.85	1.0	0.5	55.5	21.8	5.1	7.1	15.4
BACK & MIDDLE RIVER FS&LA	ESSEX	MD	D	D	D	4.4	-1.28	0.0	0.0	64.8	0.0	10.0	14.4	30.5
BADGER ST BK	CASSVILLE	WI	C+	C+	C	82.3	10.42	5.9	4.0	14.6	21.4	5.8	7.8	11.6
▲ BAILEYVILLE ST BK	SENECA	KS	E+	E	E-	23.7	0.67	8.2	5.0	12.3	36.1	6.6	8.6	15.5
▼ BAKER-BOYER NATIONAL	WALLA WALLA	WA	D+	C-	C	381.5	-1.84	11.0	3.8	21.6	25.5	5.9	7.9	12.4
BALBOA T&LA	CHULA VISTA	CA	C	C-	D+	123.1	8.54	0.6	84.7	2.1	0.5	5.7	10.0	11.6
BALCONES BK SSB	SAN MARCOS	TX	B-	B-	B	111.6	-0.58	2.4	1.8	18.4	38.0	5.6	7.6	16.8
BALDWIN ST BK	BALDWIN CITY	KS	B-	B-	B	49.0	-0.78	5.9	15.6	14.2	38.7	10.0	13.2	28.3
BALLINGER NB	BALLINGER	TX	C+	C+	C+	35.4	-7.21	8.7	7.4	5.0	51.0	10.0	12.1	26.5
BALLSTON SPA NB	BALLSTON SPA	NY	C	C	D+	290.7	5.62	4.6	11.0	24.2	40.2	5.6	7.6	15.6

Asset Quality Index	Non-Performing Loans as a % of Total Loans	Non-Performing Loans as a % of Capital	Net Charge-offs Avg Loans	Profitability Index	Net Income ($Mil)	Return on Assets (R.O.A.)	Return on Equity (R.O.E.)	Net Interest Spread	Overhead Efficiency Ratio	Liquidity Index	Liquidity Ratio	Hot Money Ratio	Stability Index
9.6	0.66	2.0	0.00	3.6	0.1	0.32	2.02	1.81	68.7	1.6	9.6	21.7	6.8
5.9	0.50	4.6	0.01	6.0	0.3	1.04	10.63	4.00	60.4	1.3	5.3	24.8	4.5
8.5	0.04	0.1	0.24	5.1	0.7	1.11	6.29	4.24	68.7	2.6	40.8	26.4	7.8
8.2	0.12	0.5	0.11	4.8	0.5	0.89	9.41	3.79	70.2	6.6	69.5	7.9	5.3
7.0	0.00	0.0	-0.02	4.9	0.3	0.86	9.63	5.14	73.7	2.1	31.2	24.4	2.9
5.5	0.62	4.8	0.08	9.4	3.2	1.64	17.31	4.30	58.1	4.7	52.0	14.5	6.9
6.0	0.44	3.4	0.27	2.6	0.8	0.33	3.39	3.81	80.6	4.7	29.6	7.5	5.3
9.2	0.05	0.2	0.00	4.6	1.2	0.69	5.54	2.74	59.8	1.8	12.0	19.8	6.7
3.3	1.27	7.9	0.32	5.6	27.5	0.78	7.79	4.23	77.3	7.3	89.3	7.9	6.5
2.7	2.95	21.7	0.01	4.5	1.1	0.80	7.86	2.89	52.5	4.3	5.6	5.5	5.6
5.2	0.77	6.0	0.56	5.8	2.1	0.83	8.04	3.66	63.2	3.0	21.2	14.6	6.7
8.6	0.05	0.2	-0.03	8.8	0.3	1.99	14.80	3.97	46.4	6.0	42.2	4.1	7.6
5.2	0.86	4.7	-0.05	6.9	0.1	1.33	11.54	4.54	60.8	6.8	121.9	11.2	5.0
6.9	0.32	1.9	0.01	6.6	1.5	0.85	8.06	3.83	63.0	4.5	52.4	15.5	6.2
1.7	6.71	36.9	1.04	4.9	0.6	0.81	8.20	5.14	71.0	2.9	57.7	36.4	3.2
9.3	0.00	0.0	0.00	2.6	0.1	0.17	1.15	4.47	91.2	6.2	47.6	4.7	7.1
5.5	0.00	0.0	0.33	2.9	0.2	0.69	9.04	4.63	83.5	1.8	23.5	22.2	2.3
7.6	0.00	0.0	0.00	3.2	0.1	0.46	3.51	3.46	77.3	3.3	85.3	38.8	6.0
4.6	0.49	4.3	0.63	8.8	4.7	1.35	15.30	4.09	46.4	2.8	9.7	14.3	6.1
3.6	1.59	5.2	0.07	6.1	9.8	1.00	5.79	3.68	55.8	6.6	46.7	4.8	7.6
5.8	0.56	4.6	0.18	9.5	106.5	1.65	23.55	3.67	48.5	3.7	13.7	10.8	6.4
5.2	1.66	4.9	3.93	10.0	12.4	7.06	27.57	13.24	14.2	0.3	15.2	98.7	7.9
6.8	0.05	0.2	-0.16	0.0	-0.4	-2.23	-11.08	2.28	173.5	1.0	25.0	35.8	0.0
8.4	0.20	1.6	0.00	6.4	120.0	1.07	13.60	2.19	37.7	1.4	0.9	22.1	7.4
6.0	3.68	12.0	0.02	4.3	0.2	0.81	8.39	3.05	70.6	6.7	73.3	5.9	3.7
3.7	2.09	11.8	0.24	4.8	0.6	0.70	6.71	3.74	70.3	2.1	36.4	30.5	6.2
4.8	0.55	5.5	0.03	9.5	7.0	1.55	20.76	4.08	44.9	2.8	15.3	15.2	7.2
5.3	2.06	7.6	0.11	6.4	0.4	1.36	11.08	4.02	52.4	4.7	34.1	9.4	5.9
9.7	0.02	0.1	0.00	4.0	1.0	0.75	6.56	3.76	77.5	4.5	32.8	10.1	7.0
5.3	1.91	11.2	0.03	4.2	0.2	0.57	4.90	3.56	73.7	4.3	24.8	7.7	5.9
8.9	0.00	0.0	0.09	5.6	0.2	1.55	13.61	3.38	54.1	6.9	90.6	7.5	5.5
8.2	0.00	0.0	-0.07	3.6	0.2	0.82	7.73	3.30	74.1	4.7	28.9	7.1	4.6
6.3	1.17	6.6	0.15	5.8	15.2	0.94	13.70	3.48	57.0	3.5	11.4	11.3	4.2
7.1	0.24	1.1	0.34	9.1	2.3	1.52	13.34	4.09	47.0	1.7	28.9	28.2	6.8
4.0	0.79	8.7	1.74	4.7	1.7	0.59	7.68	3.42	65.2	1.3	11.4	26.7	1.9
8.1	0.08	0.5	-0.05	5.9	0.7	0.84	7.38	4.14	66.3	1.1	3.7	27.7	5.4
5.4	1.19	8.9	0.02	3.5	0.4	0.56	7.25	2.28	74.2	4.4	61.0	18.3	4.2
7.1	0.57	4.7	0.08	6.0	2.0	0.99	13.20	4.38	64.9	4.2	20.1	7.9	3.8
9.7	0.00	0.0	0.00	4.6	0.1	0.35	1.44	3.39	78.7	4.3	50.6	15.2	6.8
3.4	2.38	16.0	-0.06	5.8	0.2	1.45	16.17	4.54	67.0	5.2	45.9	7.3	4.3
1.9	3.42	24.2	-0.19	6.0	0.5	1.85	22.58	4.11	58.0	1.5	9.7	23.5	1.6
3.6	0.06	0.2	0.02	5.7	0.6	1.11	5.11	5.68	57.1	3.8	31.6	13.2	6.3
8.6	0.00	0.0	0.00	2.6	0.1	0.25	3.55	2.48	85.4	0.6	7.0	40.7	2.3
8.7	0.00	0.0	0.00	7.4	0.5	1.37	7.56	4.11	55.1	5.0	50.5	12.0	7.8
7.4	0.43	2.6	0.12	5.2	3.2	1.05	14.55	2.76	55.8	3.2	44.7	20.1	3.2
9.7	0.04	0.3	0.00	3.4	0.4	0.53	7.45	2.75	67.0	4.0	10.0	8.0	3.2
6.5	0.00	0.0	0.01	8.2	0.5	1.63	20.20	3.67	69.7	4.1	26.9	10.2	6.0
4.0	0.80	6.0	0.03	6.3	1.6	1.39	17.31	4.22	68.3	1.5	24.5	27.0	5.5
4.5	0.71	5.4	0.06	6.1	3.2	1.05	10.59	4.66	73.5	3.0	36.5	19.1	6.1
9.1	0.00	0.0	0.00	0.0	-0.2	-10.02	-11.74	3.79	227.5	5.0	967.3	100.0	0.0
10.0	0.00	0.0	0.00	4.1	0.2	0.61	5.54	3.12	69.7	6.5	207.9	20.5	6.0
5.1	1.12	6.5	0.23	8.7	1.2	2.33	23.54	3.85	37.0	4.7	35.6	9.8	6.5
10.0	0.00	0.0	0.00	9.5	0.5	5.15	5.49	0.91	27.8	5.0	N/A	0.0	1.6
3.1	3.51	21.3	0.18	4.4	0.5	0.72	6.89	2.81	65.0	1.5	27.8	30.5	5.4
5.9	0.71	6.8	-0.01	6.8	3.5	0.97	13.53	4.03	65.0	2.8	55.9	35.5	4.1
8.6	0.00	0.0	0.00	1.3	0.0	0.00	0.00	3.95	101.3	2.1	33.5	20.8	3.3
6.6	0.31	2.4	0.00	6.2	0.6	1.42	18.37	3.13	50.3	3.4	58.4	23.2	4.8
2.2	5.68	32.7	0.03	2.2	0.0	0.23	2.67	3.00	88.6	3.8	35.5	12.5	1.7
1.3	4.52	33.6	0.12	4.7	2.0	1.05	13.06	4.49	69.9	4.1	24.4	9.2	3.3
3.1	0.54	4.3	2.09	9.9	1.0	1.71	17.65	9.69	45.0	7.1	426.2	17.0	5.4
7.3	0.13	0.9	0.00	4.4	0.6	1.01	13.71	3.63	81.1	6.5	69.2	8.2	4.3
5.4	2.00	7.0	-0.12	4.5	0.2	0.99	7.36	3.54	78.3	5.2	55.1	11.6	5.0
4.1	5.45	16.3	0.09	4.5	0.2	0.84	7.06	3.64	82.6	2.8	39.7	22.0	4.5
5.1	0.92	5.7	0.02	3.1	0.6	0.39	4.80	3.89	88.6	3.8	13.5	9.5	3.4

Name	City	State	Weiss Safety Rating	2003 Weiss Safety Rating	2002 Weiss Safety Rating	Total Assets ($Mil)	One Year Asset Growth	Asset Mix (As a % of Total Assets) Commercial Loans	Consumer Loans	Home Mortgages	Securities	Capitalization Index	Leverage Ratio	Risk-based Capital Ratio
BALLY SAVINGS BK	BALLY	PA	C-	C	B-	21.3	10.09	0.0	0.0	40.5	4.0	8.6	10.1	24.6
▼ BALTIC ST BK	BALTIC	OH	C+	B-	B-	23.3	-3.08	1.8	6.2	49.9	23.7	10.0	16.0	16.7
BALTIMORE COUNTY SVGS BK	BALTIMORE	MD	C	C	C	735.7	17.63	2.4	9.5	26.1	43.7	5.1	7.1	14.9
BALTIMORE TRUST CO	SELBYVILLE	DE	A-	A-	A	422.4	19.28	4.1	1.3	18.1	9.4	6.0	8.0	16.8
BANCFIRST	OKLAHOMA CITY	OK	B	B	B	3,001.5	6.53	11.8	9.2	14.1	18.3	5.3	7.3	11.3
BANCO BILBAO VIZCAYA	SAN JUAN	PR	C-	C-	D+	5,376.9	0.40	11.2	20.5	9.2	34.0	4.7	6.7	12.3
BANCO POPULAR DE PR	SAN JUAN	PR	B-	C+	C	22,812.0	-0.12	0.2	0.0	0.0	40.1	5.8	7.8	13.9
BANCO POPULAR NA	ORLANDO	FL	B-	C+		66.3	-18.09	0.0	0.0	12.3	19.3	10.0	31.9	79.6
▲ BANCO POPULAR NORTH	NEW YORK CITY	NY	C+	C	C	7,467.0	24.10	26.1	6.8	12.0	21.6	4.1	7.5	10.5
BANCO SANTANDER PR	SAN JUAN	PR	C-	C-	C-	7,881.1	20.00	9.7	6.5	25.4	30.5	4.6	6.7	11.1
BANCORP BK	WILMINGTON	DE	C	C-	D	503.4	102.41	8.0	0.1	10.9	21.0	10.0	23.9	31.8
BANCORPSOUTH BK	TUPELO	MS	B+	B+	B+	10,668.2	0.83	6.6	4.5	18.2	30.7	6.2	8.3	13.8
BANCROFT ST BK	BANCROFT	WI	C-	C-	D+	54.9	1.46	9.6	5.8	25.6	20.7	5.7	7.7	12.3
BANDERA BK	BANDERA	TX	B+	B+	B	27.8	5.73	10.0	14.9	24.0	6.9	10.0	11.2	16.4
BANGOR SVGS BK	BANGOR	ME	B-	C+	C+	1,795.3	21.00	5.4	24.1	24.0	15.5	4.7	7.4	10.9
▲ BANK	JENNINGS	LA	C-	D+	C-	77.4	10.70	17.4	20.0	20.7	14.1	7.3	9.2	13.6
BANK & TRUST CO	LITCHFIELD	IL	C+	C+	C+	192.5	1.97	12.8	10.3	15.6	29.6	6.0	8.0	13.4
▲ BANK & TRUST SSB	DEL RIO	TX	B+	B	B	256.9	1.11	6.8	5.9	19.1	45.9	7.5	9.3	16.4
BANK 10	BELTON	MO	B-	B-	B-	167.4	17.37	3.6	1.9	11.7	11.0	4.8	8.2	10.9
▲ BANK 1ST	ALBUQUERQUE	NM	C	D	E-	69.5	4.44	16.8	0.2	3.0	18.5	10.0	11.1	16.6
▲ BANK 2	OKLAHOMA CITY	OK	C	D	D-	59.4	60.04	4.1	5.4	21.7	26.1	10.0	13.6	22.5
▲ BANK 21	CARROLLTON	MO	B	B-	C+	49.6	-2.67	5.4	3.3	11.0	29.2	10.0	11.1	16.6
BANK @LANTEC	VIRGINIA BEACH	VA	B+	NR	NR	91.4	N/A	0.0	23.4	16.4	33.5	10.0	15.0	31.0
BANK AT BROADMOOR	COLORADO SPRINGS	CO	B	B	B	110.0	9.87	9.0	4.0	8.1	29.9	5.9	7.9	14.5
BANK BREVARD	MELBOURNE	FL	B-	B-	B-	161.4	16.27	10.9	2.3	11.7	12.2	5.6	7.6	11.4
▲ BANK CALUMET	HAMMOND	IN	A-	B+	B	1,093.3	5.62	12.3	2.5	24.7	29.3	7.9	9.6	14.5
BANK CENTER FIRST	BISMARCK	ND	B	B-	B	216.4	7.83	16.9	6.1	8.8	20.1	4.5	8.2	10.7
BANK FEDERATED ST	KOLONIA	FM	B-	B-	B+	85.8	-3.53	4.6	9.2	0.0	66.2	10.0	14.1	42.9
BANK IA	CLARINDA	IA	B	B-	B-	92.4	0.77	6.3	3.4	11.6	38.6	5.5	7.5	14.2
BANK INDEPENDENT	SHEFFIELD	AL	B-	B-	B-	416.8	2.54	3.2	3.8	30.9	23.5	6.3	8.3	13.5
▲ BANK IOWA	ALTOONA	IA	B	B-	B-	69.9	22.81	3.9	3.3	22.9	27.9	5.3	7.3	12.0
BANK IOWA	DENISON	IA	B	B+	B+	107.2	8.55	7.2	3.6	8.3	33.8	5.5	7.5	12.4
▲ BANK IOWA	OSKALOOSA	IA	B	B-	B-	83.7	0.10	11.6	4.1	18.4	32.5	5.5	7.5	15.2
BANK IOWA	RED OAK	IA	B	B	B-	99.0	0.26	10.6	3.5	13.0	24.3	5.9	7.9	11.7
▼ BANK LEUMI USA	NEW YORK	NY	C+	B-	B	5,490.7	11.91	25.8	0.0	0.1	49.1	4.6	6.6	13.1
BANK MIDWEST MN IOWA NA	FAIRMONT	MN	B-	B-	B-	381.4	2.35	12.7	3.8	15.0	15.1	4.3	7.9	10.7
▲ BANK MIDWEST NA	KANSAS CITY	MO	A-	B	A-	2,626.4	-10.99	6.8	1.4	12.6	20.6	8.3	9.9	13.6
▲ BANK MUTUAL	MILWAUKEE	WI	B+	B	C+	3,049.7	8.39	2.4	3.3	35.2	35.9	10.0	14.9	30.1
BANK NA	MCALESTER	OK	B-	B-	B+	287.4	-4.88	12.4	9.0	20.2	30.5	6.8	8.8	15.4
BANK NORTH	CRIVITZ	WI	B+	B+	B+	93.8	3.36	2.3	3.4	29.5	32.8	10.0	11.3	21.1
BANK NORTHWEST	HAMILTON	MO	C+	C+	C+	65.9	13.27	13.8	5.8	15.2	15.4	4.3	7.4	10.6
BANK OF ABBEVILLE & TRUST	ABBEVILLE	LA	A-	A-	A	122.1	2.52	4.0	5.3	4.9	70.0	10.0	18.4	60.9
BANK OF ADVANCE	ADVANCE	MO	A	A	A	142.7	1.05	6.9	8.0	24.1	28.8	10.0	13.3	19.9
BANK OF AGRICULTURE &	STOCKTON	CA	B-	B-	B-	332.6	11.18	9.1	1.4	1.5	38.8	4.5	6.5	11.4
BANK OF AKRON	AKRON	NY	A	A	A	148.9	2.06	3.1	4.3	22.6	27.6	10.0	13.0	23.1
BANK OF ALABAMA	BIRMINGHAM	AL	C	C	C-	270.4	3.58	9.1	6.6	7.0	22.0	5.9	7.9	11.8
BANK OF ALAMEDA	ALAMEDA	CA	B-	B-	C	194.3	15.34	11.0	1.1	8.1	13.9	6.1	8.4	11.8
BANK OF ALAPAHA	ALAPAHA	GA	B+	B+	A-	78.5	9.50	2.0	14.2	12.5	21.4	9.8	10.9	15.2
▲ BANK OF ALBUQUERQUE NA	ALBUQUERQUE	NM	B-	C+	C+	1,405.1	8.24	9.1	0.8	4.3	0.8	4.6	6.6	17.4
▲ BANK OF ALICE	ALICE	TX	D	D-	D-	144.8	7.18	19.7	9.4	7.8	3.4	6.0	9.2	11.8
BANK OF ALMA	ALMA	WI	A	A	A	155.3	16.07	4.3	3.7	16.0	20.3	10.0	25.6	33.1
BANK OF ALPENA	ALPENA	MI	C-	C-	D	63.1	15.49	37.7	2.2	17.3	16.1	6.5	8.5	13.1
BANK OF AMADOR	JACKSON	CA	A	A	A	129.0	15.72	3.9	0.7	7.1	18.5	10.0	11.7	16.7
BANK OF AMERICA CA NA	SAN FRANCISCO	CA	B	B	B-	1,601.1	1338.02	0.0	0.0	53.4	0.0	6.2	8.2	25.3
BANK OF AMERICA GEORGIA	ATLANTA	GA	B	B	B+	9,342.3	31.93	0.0	0.0	88.6	0.0	5.2	7.2	17.0
BANK OF AMERICA NA	CHARLOTTE	NC	B-	B-	B-	706,888.2	7.72	7.4	5.1	18.0	20.9	4.2	6.2	11.2
▼ BANK OF AMERICA NA USA	PHOENIX	AZ	C	C+	C+	39,355.3	37.07	5.0	94.8	0.0	0.0	7.4	9.7	12.8
BANK OF AMERICA OREGON	PORTLAND	OR	B	B	B	8,214.8	-3.86	0.0	0.0	91.7	0.0	8.9	10.3	21.9
BANK OF AMERICAN FORK	AMERICAN FORK	UT	A	A	A	521.9	-0.35	6.8	2.8	3.0	19.0	10.0	13.8	17.2
BANK OF ANDERSON NA	ANDERSON	SC	B-	B-	B-	136.1	8.09	8.9	1.9	20.9	18.8	4.1	7.0	10.5
BANK OF ANGUILLA	ANGUILLA	MS	D+	D+	D+	83.4	1.58	5.3	7.7	4.4	28.3	10.0	14.3	19.8
BANK OF ANN ARBOR	ANN ARBOR	MI	B-	B-	C	413.5	12.98	13.2	0.8	11.4	22.6	4.7	8.0	10.9
▲ BANK OF AR NA	FAYETTEVILLE	AR	B-	C+	C+	180.2	-6.70	5.8	1.5	4.4	0.6	6.9	8.9	21.1
BANK OF ASH GROVE	ASH GROVE	MO	B	B	B+	81.7	7.81	0.4	4.6	16.2	58.9	10.0	15.4	36.8

Asset Quality Index	Non-Performing Loans as a % of Total Loans	Non-Performing Loans as a % of Capital	Net Charge-offs Avg Loans	Profitability Index	Net Income ($Mil)	Return on Assets (R.O.A.)	Return on Equity (R.O.E.)	Net Interest Spread	Overhead Efficiency Ratio	Liquidity Index	Liquidity Ratio	Hot Money Ratio	Stability Index
6.6	1.22	5.6	0.00	3.8	0.0	0.40	3.90	2.17	60.6	9.0	1,440.9	6.8	3.4
7.6	1.42	5.9	-0.01	4.5	0.1	0.98	6.23	3.96	75.7	3.8	25.7	10.5	5.8
7.2	0.30	2.2	0.20	3.0	0.8	0.22	2.87	2.49	87.0	2.1	32.7	25.7	3.9
7.6	0.00	0.0	-0.05	10.0	3.8	1.96	23.41	4.73	37.7	8.6	159.2	5.1	8.7
6.4	0.40	2.8	0.12	7.1	17.5	1.19	13.95	4.37	64.9	7.3	89.8	8.2	7.2
2.7	2.33	14.1	0.81	4.0	18.0	0.68	7.82	3.38	56.7	1.3	23.4	40.6	4.3
6.5	1.84	10.9	0.72	7.2	179.0	1.58	19.24	4.04	55.5	2.8	9.2	14.8	6.2
7.8	0.06	0.0	-0.11	9.5	3.0	9.58	27.92	2.00	61.4	5.0	534.1	101.0	5.5
4.6	0.88	7.0	0.58	4.1	23.6	0.69	8.04	4.01	66.3	1.4	13.1	26.5	6.0
4.2	1.93	16.7	0.77	3.0	37.2	0.99	14.79	3.05	68.9	0.8	12.6	35.0	3.2
8.8	0.00	0.0	0.01	2.7	1.2	0.59	3.06	3.80	84.9	1.1	27.3	40.9	2.2
6.9	0.47	3.0	0.33	7.1	62.8	1.19	13.16	3.71	62.5	3.2	35.4	21.2	7.3
2.7	3.07	23.3	0.31	4.4	0.2	0.65	8.38	3.70	73.4	4.0	37.4	14.2	4.5
7.7	0.05	0.3	0.03	8.5	0.3	2.01	17.38	6.39	67.7	3.8	41.9	16.2	7.0
6.8	0.14	1.2	0.13	4.3	6.2	0.74	8.46	3.55	70.1	3.2	13.2	13.1	6.0
2.0	1.83	13.4	0.29	6.8	0.4	1.18	12.87	5.14	64.7	2.8	31.0	18.2	4.1
4.4	1.16	8.6	0.05	4.6	0.7	0.74	9.20	3.90	71.1	2.8	15.6	15.1	4.3
7.6	0.63	3.1	-0.02	7.5	1.7	1.31	14.64	3.92	58.1	2.0	26.1	21.5	5.4
8.5	0.08	0.7	0.00	7.5	1.5	1.93	23.59	4.61	63.0	5.7	61.6	11.9	5.6
4.0	2.09	10.4	0.04	2.9	0.2	0.43	3.81	4.31	86.2	3.8	65.8	21.6	2.3
8.6	0.09	0.4	0.08	3.2	0.3	0.89	7.05	5.26	81.1	1.4	31.9	48.2	2.8
7.2	0.70	3.2	-0.22	5.0	0.3	1.36	10.44	4.24	74.0	5.9	59.7	8.2	6.1
7.4	0.15	0.4	0.76	5.3	0.4	1.41	9.43	3.89	90.1	2.6	38.1	24.3	4.2
8.9	0.08	0.5	0.01	5.1	0.7	1.22	14.40	4.28	74.0	6.0	50.2	6.9	5.5
8.1	0.20	1.7	0.00	5.7	0.7	0.87	11.85	3.79	55.1	5.1	58.7	14.3	4.4
8.7	0.32	1.8	0.07	6.4	6.4	1.19	12.83	4.11	61.7	5.9	57.2	11.6	7.7
7.1	0.06	0.3	0.02	5.8	0.9	0.86	7.24	4.56	67.3	5.2	32.8	5.7	6.1
8.0	4.24	4.5	1.06	3.1	0.4	0.84	5.76	3.19	78.3	4.8	103.1	20.8	6.5
6.9	0.01	0.0	-0.04	8.6	0.9	1.98	24.52	4.58	51.7	4.8	37.8	10.2	6.7
4.7	1.01	6.8	0.60	3.9	1.4	0.69	7.87	3.94	78.8	3.4	26.7	13.8	5.2
7.8	0.38	3.0	0.04	5.7	0.4	1.19	16.26	3.56	70.2	4.1	44.1	15.3	5.9
6.6	0.44	2.5	-0.35	5.2	0.5	0.93	9.24	3.18	70.3	3.1	16.9	13.5	7.0
3.9	1.96	13.3	0.09	7.7	0.7	1.68	20.96	3.84	55.2	4.8	30.9	7.4	5.6
7.4	0.13	1.0	-0.12	7.9	0.9	1.81	21.71	4.45	57.6	3.8	23.6	10.9	6.3
8.7	0.41	2.2	0.11	3.6	15.4	0.57	8.18	1.95	64.0	3.6	80.4	55.4	5.4
6.9	0.20	1.5	0.01	6.5	2.9	1.55	16.36	4.06	61.8	6.5	87.0	10.8	6.5
6.2	0.83	4.8	-0.02	6.7	18.4	1.36	13.00	3.22	52.4	6.7	57.0	6.6	7.3
8.0	0.43	1.7	0.02	5.1	13.4	0.87	5.27	2.94	57.8	1.4	3.2	22.8	6.3
3.9	1.90	13.1	0.22	9.6	3.2	2.24	24.99	4.73	58.2	2.2	10.8	17.6	6.6
6.9	0.63	3.1	0.01	5.2	0.5	1.05	8.96	4.44	70.0	2.2	16.9	18.2	7.1
7.6	0.01	0.1	0.05	10.0	0.8	2.61	35.90	4.70	48.6	1.8	16.6	20.3	4.2
7.6	3.81	4.9	0.38	5.6	0.7	1.18	6.68	4.21	62.9	1.7	21.0	24.0	8.5
6.4	1.05	4.8	0.04	9.0	1.1	1.57	11.79	4.97	51.8	2.9	12.3	14.4	8.1
6.6	0.71	5.0	-0.01	7.6	3.0	1.88	26.35	4.91	64.1	4.5	34.3	10.6	4.1
8.9	0.36	1.4	0.01	6.3	0.8	1.04	7.55	4.58	66.2	6.7	66.1	6.1	7.9
3.4	0.95	8.0	0.14	4.1	1.0	0.74	9.54	3.41	65.0	2.4	7.8	16.5	3.3
7.4	0.06	0.5	0.12	7.0	1.0	1.08	12.91	5.22	64.5	4.7	26.1	6.1	4.1
5.8	0.47	2.7	0.41	7.4	0.5	1.23	11.23	4.57	59.9	2.3	31.3	21.8	7.0
9.1	0.51	1.4	0.55	3.8	4.3	0.63	8.28	2.42	65.1	7.5	181.5	13.7	5.4
1.3	2.32	18.7	0.88	7.3	1.3	1.84	19.56	5.43	63.4	1.8	22.5	21.6	5.2
7.1	0.86	2.5	0.05	10.0	2.4	3.16	12.59	5.69	14.7	4.1	10.7	7.3	9.5
5.0	1.02	7.8	0.86	2.9	0.1	0.42	5.09	4.22	67.5	3.8	79.6	27.2	0.0
6.7	0.75	3.8	0.02	9.8	1.0	1.55	12.95	4.78	47.5	6.3	64.6	8.6	8.7
9.9	0.00	0.0	0.00	9.2	5.0	1.64	10.99	3.15	6.2	1.7	33.5	100.0	8.2
9.3	0.16	1.8	0.06	10.0	134.4	2.89	32.37	4.97	6.7	0.1	5.8	100.0	5.0
6.2	0.59	3.8	0.27	7.9	4,897.7	1.46	19.75	3.14	59.9	6.7	71.0	9.1	6.6
1.8	1.68	12.2	4.97	10.0	609.9	3.27	35.22	10.42	18.1	5.0	0.4	0.0	7.0
9.9	0.09	0.7	0.00	9.8	109.3	2.52	21.26	4.41	4.9	0.1	1.9	100.0	6.3
5.8	1.11	5.5	-0.25	9.9	4.3	1.67	12.15	5.99	57.9	5.7	47.3	7.6	10.0
8.2	0.04	0.4	-0.01	4.5	0.5	0.75	11.03	3.44	65.4	1.3	11.7	26.1	4.3
1.1	11.37	45.4	0.74	6.1	0.4	1.05	7.66	4.70	65.4	2.5	16.4	16.4	6.0
8.8	0.12	0.9	0.00	6.6	2.4	1.19	15.11	3.92	65.3	7.8	93.1	3.7	4.3
7.8	0.57	1.7	-0.24	3.8	0.4	0.49	5.82	2.49	73.5	5.3	433.2	58.7	4.8
9.3	0.68	1.5	0.38	4.3	0.3	0.74	4.75	2.96	64.7	4.8	70.2	15.9	7.3

Name	City	State	Weiss Safety Rating	2003 Weiss Safety Rating	2002 Weiss Safety Rating	Total Assets ($Mil)	One Year Asset Growth	Asset Mix (As a % of Total Assets)				Capital- ization Index	Leverage Ratio	Risk-based Capital Ratio
								Comm- ercial Loans	Cons- umer Loans	Home Mort- gages	Secur- ities			
▲ BANK OF ASHEVILLE	ASHEVILLE	NC	B	C+	C	120.3	14.56	15.5	1.3	11.1	19.2	10.0	11.2	16.7
BANK OF ASTORIA	ASTORIA	OR	B-	B-	C+	154.5	6.08	7.0	1.4	1.8	24.7	7.9	9.6	14.4
BANK OF AUGUSTA	AUGUSTA	AR	B-	B-	B-	46.4	-0.63	4.9	7.1	8.4	45.5	10.0	12.7	23.0
BANK OF BAKER	BAKER	MT	C+	C+	C	52.6	20.18	15.5	4.4	4.4	33.9	6.4	8.4	14.2
▲ BANK OF BARTLETT	BARTLETT	TN	C-	D	D	436.0	5.06	5.7	0.8	6.2	37.3	6.0	8.0	12.8
▼ BANK OF BEARDEN	BEARDEN	AR	B+	A-	A-	37.6	21.57	15.3	9.4	15.2	16.3	10.0	18.2	31.5
BANK OF BEAVER CITY	BEAVER	OK	D	D	C-	62.3	8.46	7.7	8.3	10.2	27.0	3.2	6.6	10.1
▲ BANK OF BELEN	BELEN	NM	C+	C	C	106.7	8.84	10.7	6.5	9.9	14.2	7.0	9.0	12.8
BANK OF BELLE GLADE	BELLE GLADE	FL	B	B	B+	45.2	-3.09	6.7	2.8	21.6	38.5	10.0	12.9	27.6
BANK OF BELTON	BELTON	MO	D+	C+	C+	56.2	-6.20	8.7	3.7	7.7	31.6	8.6	10.1	18.1
▼ BANK OF BENNINGTON	BENNINGTON	NE	D+	C-	C-	57.2	-3.26	25.5	3.3	14.7	6.8	5.7	8.8	11.5
BANK OF BENNINGTON	BENNINGTON	VT	C+	C+	C+	182.5	1.04	4.0	0.6	52.1	1.1	6.6	8.6	15.0
▲ BANK OF BENOIT	BENOIT	MS	C-	D+	D	13.9	5.97	7.7	23.7	12.1	13.6	10.0	11.4	22.7
BANK OF BENTON	BENTON	KY	C	C	C	318.0	1.87	5.8	13.7	26.9	30.9	8.4	9.9	16.9
BANK OF BERTRAND	BERTRAND	NE	B	B-	C+	27.8	8.33	6.5	5.6	1.0	28.8	10.0	17.9	26.1
BANK OF BILLINGS	BILLINGS	MO	D	D	D+	31.1	2.68	1.3	3.3	12.1	66.2	5.6	7.6	19.5
BANK OF BIRCH TREE	BIRCH TREE	MO	C	C-	D+	21.9	-3.84	9.6	11.1	29.3	28.3	10.0	13.8	24.3
BANK OF BLEVINS	BLEVINS	AR	B	B	B+	16.0	-11.34	2.5	21.1	25.1	36.6	10.0	13.4	28.4
▼ BANK OF BLOOMSDALE	BLOOMSDALE	MO	B+	A-	A-	145.7	7.03	7.5	4.1	20.6	31.0	5.5	7.5	13.7
BANK OF BLUE VALLEY	OVERLAND PARK	KS	C+	C+	C+	619.2	0.76	17.7	6.7	7.9	13.5	3.3	7.9	10.1
BANK OF BLUFFS	BLUFFS	IL	B	B	B+	49.9	2.42	3.2	9.8	20.9	37.1	10.0	16.3	31.3
▲ BANK OF BOLIVAR	BOLIVAR	MO	C+	C	D+	110.4	3.19	9.7	4.9	27.5	12.3	5.2	7.2	12.6
▲ BANK OF BOLIVAR	BOLIVAR	TN	C+	C-	E-	52.3	0.47	4.0	5.7	19.4	45.2	8.8	10.2	20.9
▲ BANK OF BOLIVAR CTY	SHELBY	MS	D-	E	D-	20.4	-0.96	5.5	7.0	7.9	53.5	6.0	8.0	28.0
▲ BANK OF BONIFAY	BONIFAY	FL	B+	B	B	147.8	27.73	5.7	5.3	27.5	4.3	6.9	10.2	12.4
BANK OF BOTETOURT	BUCHANAN	VA	C+	C+	C+	206.5	10.29	9.6	6.1	16.3	10.3	5.5	8.2	11.4
BANK OF BOURBONNAIS	BOURBONNAIS	IL	C	C	C	52.0	26.21	6.5	0.9	5.7	20.0	5.0	7.3	11.0
▼ BANK OF BRADFORD	BRADFORD	TN	B-	B	B+	39.3	-1.37	1.5	5.5	14.7	46.6	10.0	15.3	43.5
▲ BANK OF BRENHAM NA	BRENHAM	TX	B+	B	B-	36.6	13.68	15.7	11.6	17.5	21.4	10.0	11.9	19.4
BANK OF BREWTON	BREWTON	AL	B+	B+	B+	51.3	-13.68	12.4	7.2	4.7	48.7	10.0	14.7	27.7
BANK OF BRIDGER NA	BRIDGER	MT	B-	C+	C+	143.1	83.78	7.0	4.7	12.9	28.7	6.3	8.3	13.2
BANK OF BRINKLEY	BRINKLEY	AR	A	A	A+	148.6	37.04	4.7	2.2	2.3	63.3	8.3	9.9	24.5
BANK OF BRODHEAD	BRODHEAD	WI	B	B	B	98.2	0.02	3.1	2.5	6.4	48.5	10.0	12.1	23.2
BANK OF	BROOKFIELD	MO	B+	A-	A-	66.5	5.27	1.7	3.5	13.7	46.1	10.0	11.0	23.3
BANK OF BROOKHAVEN	BROOKHAVEN	MS	B	B-	C+	63.4	1.28	28.7	6.8	12.6	22.3	10.0	12.6	17.9
BANK OF BUFFALO	BUFFALO	KY	B	B	B	51.8	7.43	3.8	17.6	32.3	30.5	8.5	10.0	16.8
BANK OF BURLINGTON	BURLINGTON	CO	C+	C+	B-	40.0	-6.94	4.6	1.5	1.1	75.4	5.8	7.8	24.6
BANK OF CADIZ & TR CO	CADIZ	KY	B-	B-	B-	87.2	-0.52	3.8	6.3	32.2	26.7	7.2	9.1	15.6
▲ BANK OF CAIRO & MOBERLY	MOBERLY	MO	B+	B	C	65.4	5.48	9.6	5.2	29.9	17.0	9.6	10.7	17.3
BANK OF CALHOUN CTY	HARDIN	IL	E-	E-	E-	50.0	-10.83	1.7	6.9	29.2	31.9	4.9	6.9	13.9
▲ BANK OF CAMDEN	CAMDEN	SC	C-	D+	D	37.5	32.09	7.3	2.5	26.3	25.2	10.0	13.9	22.5
BANK OF CAMDEN	CAMDEN	TN	A-	A-	A-	146.4	-2.01	1.9	9.6	13.2	54.6	10.0	14.2	24.8
▲ BANK OF CAMILLA	CAMILLA	GA	B-	C-	B-	75.6	-8.70	9.5	8.9	9.1	19.2	10.0	13.5	18.9
BANK OF CANEYVILLE	CANEYVILLE	KY	C-	C-	C	45.6	10.29	4.9	4.2	16.9	51.8	5.9	7.9	19.5
▲ BANK OF CANTON	CANTON	MA	C+	C	C-	560.6	3.07	2.9	0.4	19.3	34.5	6.3	8.3	13.9
BANK OF CARBONDALE	CARBONDALE	IL	B-	B-	B-	137.2	6.54	18.5	3.9	18.1	21.4	6.2	8.2	13.1
BANK OF CASHTON	CASHTON	WI	C	C-	D+	46.7	10.99	22.0	4.2	12.3	17.8	7.4	9.3	12.8
▼ BANK OF CASTILE	CASTILE	NY	B-	B	B	481.7	8.14	17.2	7.9	15.8	19.7	3.6	7.1	10.3
BANK OF CATTARAUGUS	CATTARAUGUS	NY	C-	C	C-	12.5	-0.88	4.2	7.8	49.8	22.0	8.8	10.2	22.2
▲ BANK OF CAVE CITY	CAVE CITY	AR	D+	D	C-	111.4	10.01	2.9	10.4	23.1	24.0	5.5	7.5	14.7
▼ BANK OF CHARLES TOWN	CHARLES TOWN	WV	A-	A	A	225.7	12.31	11.4	7.4	26.6	22.9	8.1	9.7	15.3
▲ BANK OF CHARLOTTE CTY	PHENIX	VA	A	A-	A-	107.1	5.09	9.5	7.0	37.4	17.5	10.0	11.6	17.5
BANK OF CHEROKEE CTY	HULBERT	OK	D+	D+	D+	82.5	9.61	7.9	12.4	21.4	22.5	5.1	7.1	12.1
BANK OF CHESTNUT	CHESTNUT	IL	E-	E-	E-	14.6	-4.77	3.5	9.5	35.0	19.8	6.3	8.3	15.2
BANK OF CHICKAMAUGA	CHICKAMAUGA	GA	A-	A-	A	60.2	-0.78	0.3	8.1	25.2	48.5	10.0	20.4	53.1
BANK OF CLARENDON	MANNING	SC	A	A	A	155.5	9.74	3.4	3.3	18.6	41.2	10.0	11.5	18.0
▲ BANK OF CLARK COUNTY	VANCOUVER	WA	C+	C	C-	195.7	29.23	23.4	2.0	4.6	0.8	5.7	10.3	11.6
▲ BANK OF CLARKE CTY	BERRYVILLE	VA	B+	B	B	371.2	16.17	6.6	8.8	30.0	12.5	6.8	9.0	12.3
▼ BANK OF CLARKS	CLARKS	NE	D-	D	D-	32.6	80.47	10.6	3.4	13.0	7.0	6.7	8.7	12.5
BANK OF CLARKSON	CLARKSON	KY	A-	A-	A-	98.6	0.09	1.8	7.7	27.1	34.9	7.5	9.3	18.3
BANK OF CLEVELAND	CLEVELAND	TN	A-	A-	A-	168.9	9.87	6.8	4.1	25.7	0.3	7.0	9.4	12.5
BANK OF CLOVIS	CLOVIS	NM	C+	C+	C	70.6	11.52	9.7	8.2	10.1	40.5	6.6	8.6	19.4
BANK OF COLORADO	FORT COLLINS	CO	B+	B+	B+	1,029.6	6.32	5.3	2.7	9.4	16.2	5.0	8.0	11.0
▲ BANK OF COLUMBIA	COLUMBIA	KY	A-	B+	B	124.5	7.47	18.7	7.1	20.7	15.8	6.8	8.8	12.7

Asset Quality Index	Non-Performing Loans as a % of Total Loans	Non-Performing Loans as a % of Capital	Net Charge-offs Avg Loans	Profitability Index	Net Income ($Mil)	Return on Assets (R.O.A.)	Return on Equity (R.O.E.)	Net Interest Spread	Overhead Efficiency Ratio	Liquidity Index	Liquidity Ratio	Hot Money Ratio	Stability Index
5.4	1.12	6.0	0.94	4.0	0.3	0.58	5.15	4.31	64.2	5.7	40.4	5.7	4.0
4.3	0.85	5.3	0.33	9.3	1.2	1.59	16.33	5.52	55.0	5.2	31.5	4.9	7.1
4.8	2.83	10.4	0.25	4.9	0.3	1.08	8.81	3.91	64.1	1.5	17.5	25.6	5.3
5.5	0.67	3.8	-0.75	7.6	0.5	1.87	21.32	3.77	47.6	5.9	31.9	0.5	5.7
4.6	1.66	9.5	0.41	2.7	1.0	0.47	5.68	3.64	85.2	4.9	36.6	9.0	2.2
3.7	9.25	25.1	0.06	9.3	0.3	1.81	9.84	4.52	51.2	5.1	107.6	19.4	8.0
6.8	0.16	1.6	0.21	4.9	0.4	1.38	22.13	4.28	66.8	1.7	18.0	21.6	2.3
5.4	0.57	4.5	0.01	5.4	0.4	0.84	10.22	5.43	75.9	4.6	31.8	9.0	4.0
9.1	0.02	0.1	-0.03	3.9	0.1	0.51	4.13	4.20	83.8	5.2	39.3	8.5	5.6
6.5	0.43	1.9	0.58	1.2	-0.2	-0.51	-4.64	3.58	109.2	6.5	50.8	2.2	3.7
2.7	2.06	17.6	0.00	5.5	0.3	0.92	10.41	5.25	66.4	3.1	13.7	13.6	2.8
4.8	0.59	5.3	0.18	3.7	0.4	0.44	5.17	3.30	80.5	1.3	10.8	26.8	4.9
7.1	0.32	1.4	0.27	4.9	0.1	1.40	11.43	4.50	71.6	3.7	90.0	28.4	2.9
2.6	3.07	17.5	0.41	5.4	1.7	1.05	10.60	4.54	68.5	4.1	10.8	7.2	4.6
7.8	0.92	2.9	0.06	5.3	0.1	0.88	5.07	4.04	67.6	7.0	90.9	6.6	6.0
5.3	3.47	14.9	0.61	3.2	0.1	0.62	8.61	3.06	69.8	3.3	4.1	11.4	2.4
6.9	0.00	0.0	1.38	4.6	0.1	0.70	5.12	5.27	79.9	3.8	27.9	10.7	3.9
5.1	2.37	9.2	0.02	3.2	0.1	0.66	4.99	4.48	85.0	4.2	106.4	26.5	6.2
8.5	0.03	0.2	-0.01	9.8	1.9	2.66	34.59	3.89	39.3	2.7	46.3	29.8	6.6
3.6	1.55	13.2	0.13	5.1	1.9	0.62	7.59	3.21	79.0	4.1	55.7	18.2	4.9
7.2	0.93	2.9	0.46	4.7	0.3	1.17	7.19	3.37	65.0	6.0	90.5	12.4	6.6
5.1	0.43	4.5	0.03	5.9	0.6	1.16	16.61	3.60	57.4	2.5	13.7	16.1	3.4
4.0	1.68	6.9	2.03	5.2	0.5	1.81	19.06	5.12	64.9	2.5	10.8	16.2	3.3
8.1	0.42	1.4	-0.07	3.5	0.1	0.73	9.42	3.43	75.4	2.5	43.0	22.0	0.9
5.6	0.40	3.3	0.13	10.0	1.8	2.67	29.31	5.27	55.8	1.4	8.2	23.7	6.9
3.7	1.34	11.5	0.25	6.0	1.1	1.09	12.93	4.69	56.9	4.2	35.0	12.4	4.4
4.8	0.13	1.2	0.00	3.7	0.1	0.55	7.81	3.77	76.0	3.3	55.0	23.3	3.2
9.2	0.06	0.1	-0.04	3.6	0.1	0.54	3.53	2.90	75.3	6.7	164.3	16.2	6.2
7.9	0.39	2.1	0.27	4.2	0.2	1.31	11.08	4.64	65.0	4.7	56.9	14.2	4.7
8.5	0.82	2.1	0.01	6.5	0.3	1.07	7.22	4.69	67.9	4.4	47.0	14.3	5.6
5.5	1.19	7.6	0.05	6.1	0.7	1.09	11.76	4.56	65.9	4.6	44.0	13.0	4.4
8.7	0.16	0.4	0.15	9.8	2.1	2.82	25.51	4.28	35.4	2.0	37.9	33.6	7.2
8.3	0.51	1.8	0.19	4.5	0.4	0.88	7.17	3.52	64.3	4.0	36.6	14.0	6.5
7.9	0.80	3.1	0.05	5.0	0.4	1.11	9.84	3.23	64.3	5.7	38.6	4.7	6.5
8.1	0.00	0.0	0.01	4.8	0.4	1.08	8.92	4.40	74.3	2.7	16.0	15.4	3.3
4.4	1.09	6.4	0.01	10.0	0.8	3.18	30.93	4.79	33.8	2.8	40.8	23.0	7.0
9.8	0.00	0.0	0.00	6.0	0.3	1.31	14.85	3.57	64.4	5.8	73.3	11.5	4.2
7.6	0.26	1.7	0.26	4.5	0.4	0.80	8.41	3.98	69.1	3.1	11.9	13.4	4.7
8.4	0.21	1.3	-0.01	7.6	0.4	1.35	12.52	4.40	58.3	5.0	61.3	13.6	5.5
1.8	4.73	29.8	-0.28	1.0	0.1	0.36	5.25	4.16	90.8	5.4	39.7	7.4	0.0
8.4	0.65	2.9	0.17	2.0	0.1	0.26	1.84	4.16	85.4	1.1	26.9	42.4	0.0
5.9	4.10	9.1	0.05	8.8	1.1	1.49	10.33	4.58	54.7	3.1	43.5	21.2	7.5
3.8	3.06	14.0	0.44	4.2	0.4	0.99	7.26	4.30	72.6	3.3	57.6	23.9	5.4
8.8	0.29	1.3	0.01	5.6	0.3	1.23	16.46	3.52	60.6	4.0	32.1	12.3	2.9
8.5	0.33	2.9	0.00	4.5	1.8	0.65	10.19	3.51	70.7	5.2	48.2	10.9	3.6
3.7	2.13	17.1	0.10	6.9	0.8	1.12	14.26	3.69	53.4	4.9	22.5	3.4	4.6
5.9	0.83	5.8	0.06	4.8	0.3	1.12	12.03	4.42	65.8	2.2	28.9	21.5	3.5
5.3	0.48	4.5	0.45	5.2	2.2	0.90	12.45	4.02	62.7	5.0	58.3	14.4	5.6
5.9	1.25	6.6	0.00	3.3	0.0	0.45	4.05	6.25	92.1	5.4	30.2	0.9	3.4
1.7	2.40	17.7	1.31	4.2	0.3	0.49	6.25	4.11	59.9	1.8	27.0	25.5	4.0
8.0	0.09	0.6	0.02	9.0	1.6	1.44	14.57	4.57	58.1	4.2	16.6	7.5	6.5
8.3	0.24	1.4	0.00	8.2	0.8	1.45	12.45	4.98	53.9	3.6	27.6	12.8	7.2
2.3	2.06	18.6	0.15	5.8	0.4	1.05	14.75	5.15	70.6	1.1	15.6	30.9	3.0
0.9	4.50	31.8	0.53	2.2	0.0	0.54	6.46	4.15	81.9	3.1	37.0	16.2	0.0
7.5	1.82	3.2	0.34	8.6	0.5	1.47	7.15	5.17	56.9	5.5	83.5	14.0	7.6
9.1	0.12	0.6	0.05	8.7	1.1	1.45	12.80	4.21	58.3	3.2	10.8	12.7	8.0
5.8	0.39	3.2	0.09	5.2	0.8	0.93	9.50	4.41	63.7	0.8	17.7	41.6	5.6
8.2	0.09	0.7	0.07	7.0	2.1	1.17	12.87	4.44	65.0	4.7	33.9	9.5	5.4
0.0	5.94	44.3	0.77	5.2	0.1	0.78	9.05	4.75	76.0	4.9	35.2	8.2	3.2
6.7	0.82	4.7	0.00	8.2	0.6	1.27	13.81	3.56	51.9	5.7	59.4	9.4	7.5
6.1	0.26	2.3	0.04	9.9	1.4	1.67	18.33	5.22	54.7	3.5	12.9	11.5	7.5
8.5	0.17	0.7	0.43	4.3	0.3	0.79	8.88	4.35	63.8	4.3	42.3	13.9	1.4
7.2	0.34	2.4	0.00	8.8	6.9	1.36	14.59	4.43	56.9	6.1	77.8	12.8	7.7
6.3	0.33	2.7	0.22	9.7	1.4	2.32	26.26	4.29	47.0	2.8	10.1	14.7	7.2

Name	City	State	Weiss Safety Rating	2003 Weiss Safety Rating	2002 Weiss Safety Rating	Total Assets ($Mil)	One Year Asset Growth	Commercial Loans	Consumer Loans	Home Mortgages	Securities	Capitalization Index	Leverage Ratio	Risk-based Capital Ratio
BANK OF COMMERCE	SARASOTA	FL	C	C	C-	169.9	41.13	13.5	1.6	8.2	13.3	4.2	8.1	10.6
BANK OF COMMERCE	IDAHO FALLS	ID	A+	A+	A+	533.5	3.99	15.1	3.5	7.6	31.2	10.0	15.5	23.8
▲ BANK OF COMMERCE	DOWNERS GROVE	IL	E+	E-	D	60.6	-5.93	19.0	0.5	7.0	0.4	7.3	9.7	12.7
BANK OF COMMERCE	CHANUTE	KS	B-	B-	B-	118.9	1.07	6.7	6.0	15.2	33.9	5.5	7.5	15.4
BANK OF COMMERCE	UDALL	KS	C-	C	C	8.4	5.94	4.0	7.4	2.9	57.6	10.0	12.0	44.0
BANK OF COMMERCE	WHITE CASTLE	LA	B	B+	B+	42.1	-4.76	12.2	4.4	10.2	18.0	10.0	16.7	21.2
BANK OF COMMERCE	GREENWOOD	MS	A	A	A	161.6	7.00	1.6	5.7	21.2	52.8	8.9	10.3	23.1
▲ BANK OF COMMERCE	HENDERSON	NV	B	C+	C	143.0	26.28	27.0	0.4	5.8	19.9	7.8	9.5	13.8
BANK OF COMMERCE	CHELSEA	OK	D+	D	D	118.4	7.53	7.8	8.9	20.8	7.2	4.8	7.8	10.9
BANK OF COMMERCE	CHOUTEAU	OK	B-	B-	B-	32.9	-1.32	4.8	14.9	24.4	17.0	7.5	9.3	15.7
▲ BANK OF COMMERCE	DUNCAN	OK	D+	D	D-	55.5	18.33	23.9	3.7	5.6	9.3	5.1	8.7	11.1
▲ BANK OF COMMERCE	STILWELL	OK	A-	B-	B-	77.4	2.29	12.5	5.6	9.1	37.2	10.0	12.5	22.2
BANK OF COMMERCE	WETUMKA	OK	C+	C+	C+	33.4	122.41	10.4	17.4	19.9	16.6	6.8	8.9	13.2
▲ BANK OF COMMERCE	MCLEAN	TX	C	C-	C-	10.7	-7.87	7.6	1.9	3.2	26.7	10.0	11.4	27.7
▼ BANK OF COMMERCE	RAWLINS	WY	B-	B	B	64.0	4.76	18.7	9.5	11.5	31.6	10.0	11.2	18.5
▲ BANK OF COMMERCE &	WELLINGTON	KS	D+	D	D-	45.8	1.48	7.6	3.5	13.5	28.4	5.1	7.1	14.1
BANK OF COMMERCE &	CROWLEY	LA	B+	B+	A-	282.2	5.00	4.1	2.9	5.4	67.8	10.0	11.9	31.1
▼ BANK OF CORBIN	CORBIN	KY	E	D-	D-	73.7	19.10	18.4	8.1	24.0	6.4	4.7	7.7	10.8
BANK OF CORDELL	CORDELL	OK	D	D-	D	32.2	-3.90	27.7	5.2	8.5	19.1	5.8	7.8	13.8
BANK OF COUSHATTA	COUSHATTA	LA	B+	B	B+	86.5	-1.07	2.1	8.0	15.0	58.8	10.0	13.2	34.3
▼ BANK OF COWETA	NEWNAN	GA	B-	B	B	363.3	11.78	10.9	2.8	11.0	10.4	3.8	7.7	10.4
▲ BANK OF CROCKER	WAYNESVILLE	MO	B	B-	B-	138.8	4.34	5.1	13.1	16.7	23.6	7.7	9.4	14.8
BANK OF CROCKETT	BELLS	TN	B+	B+	B+	98.8	-2.01	8.3	4.4	9.4	38.0	8.0	9.7	17.3
BANK OF CROWLEY	CROWLEY	TX	C+	C+	C+	24.6	-3.85	4.2	14.3	15.1	32.8	7.3	9.2	19.3
▲ BANK OF CURRITUCK	MOYOCK	NC	A	A	A	123.9	-6.78	4.7	3.3	16.8	16.5	10.0	12.4	17.9
BANK OF CUSHING & TRUST	CUSHING	OK	B+	B	B	72.7	-2.36	13.4	9.0	6.6	45.1	10.0	11.8	18.7
BANK OF DADE	TRENTON	GA	C+	C+	B-	77.4	3.42	1.8	6.1	20.5	40.0	4.4	6.4	13.5
▲ BANK OF DADEVILLE	DADEVILLE	AL	B	B-	B-	79.8	6.79	5.6	6.6	22.8	34.3	5.2	7.2	14.1
▲ BANK OF DARDANELLE	DARDANELLE	AR	B-	C+	D	128.2	-0.15	1.8	13.8	30.5	20.7	9.5	10.7	19.9
BANK OF DAWSON	DAWSON	GA	A-	A-	B+	86.3	8.38	4.4	7.7	19.1	36.7	10.0	12.6	24.2
BANK OF DE SOTO NA	DESOTO	TX	B-	B-	C+	115.6	-0.04	8.4	18.9	12.9	8.5	7.0	9.0	15.4
▲ BANK OF DEERFIELD	DEERFIELD	WI	B	B-	C+	55.6	7.25	36.6	3.9	25.1	4.0	7.2	11.0	12.6
▲ BANK OF DELIGHT	DELIGHT	AR	A	A-	A-	76.8	1.30	12.5	9.2	16.4	31.2	10.0	18.1	31.0
▲ BANK OF DELMARVA	SEAFORD	DE	B-	C+	B-	241.3	8.98	8.5	2.1	15.5	29.1	6.3	8.3	13.2
BANK OF DENTON	DENTON	KS	C+	C+	C	9.9	-0.98	3.6	8.2	23.9	36.3	10.0	18.7	41.0
BANK OF DENVER	DENVER	CO	B+	B+	B+	159.0	2.44	6.2	23.5	2.9	20.9	8.5	10.0	14.7
BANK OF DICKSON	DICKSON	TN	A	A	A	160.4	-2.61	2.7	7.0	27.6	39.0	10.0	13.0	25.2
BANK OF DIXON CTY	PONCA	NE	C+	C+	C	50.7	5.61	5.0	7.1	15.7	22.7	8.6	10.0	16.3
BANK OF DONIPHAN	DONIPHAN	NE	C+	C+	C+	70.5	-4.54	8.0	10.5	17.3	13.9	5.7	8.8	11.5
BANK OF DOOLY	VIENNA	GA	A-	A-	A-	61.8	-0.41	6.5	6.1	17.4	13.5	10.0	20.6	29.2
BANK OF DUDLEY	DUDLEY	GA	B-	B-	C+	117.0	2.59	8.6	12.1	14.4	16.6	6.1	8.2	11.8
▼ BANK OF DURANGO	DURANGO	CO	D-	D	E+	45.0	26.50	60.7	3.7	4.1	1.4	2.9	8.4	9.9
BANK OF DWIGHT	DWIGHT	IL	A-	A-	A-	46.1	13.02	19.0	5.3	17.9	48.6	7.4	9.3	19.9
▲ BANK OF DYER	DYER	TN	C	C-	D+	40.0	-20.66	5.5	5.9	18.2	38.9	5.7	7.7	16.9
BANK OF EARLY	BLAKELY	GA	B+	B+	B+	70.6	0.13	13.6	5.5	20.2	18.5	10.0	12.4	16.8
BANK OF EAST ASIA USA NA	NEW YORK	NY	D+	C+	B-	342.1	89.31	5.7	0.1	2.4	12.0	6.6	10.4	12.2
▼ BANK OF EASTERN OREGON	ARLINGTON	OR	C	B-	B-	164.1	102.51	6.1	3.2	2.7	42.0	4.0	6.1	10.5
▲ BANK OF EASTMAN	EASTMAN	GA	C+	C	C-	194.5	7.22	11.8	8.2	16.2	14.9	5.1	7.6	11.1
▲ BANK OF EASTON, A CO-OP	N EASTON	MA	B-	C+	C	86.3	-2.77	0.2	2.1	46.0	28.8	6.5	8.5	17.0
BANK OF EDISON	EDISON	GA	C+	B-	B-	37.5	-2.21	3.8	6.8	17.1	32.6	9.0	10.3	17.2
BANK OF EDMONSON CTY	BROWNSVILLE	KY	A-	A-	B+	151.8	1.27	3.5	6.7	28.6	22.4	10.0	11.6	17.4
BANK OF EDWARDSVILLE	EDWARDSVILLE	IL	B	B	B-	1,027.6	2.25	8.7	2.2	12.3	35.3	7.1	9.0	14.0
▲ BANK OF ELGIN	ELGIN	NE	C-	D+	D+	39.4	-2.43	7.7	2.8	3.2	24.8	5.3	7.3	11.8
BANK OF ELK RIVER	ELK RIVER	MN	C+	C+	C+	285.6	10.94	15.7	10.5	14.3	15.5	4.2	7.9	10.6
BANK OF ELMWOOD	RACINE	WI	C-	D+	D	238.9	-1.79	4.7	4.3	25.4	22.6	5.7	7.7	12.9
BANK OF ENGLAND	ENGLAND	AR	C+	C+	C-	125.9	30.94	13.9	6.5	24.9	13.5	4.1	7.6	10.6
BANK OF ERATH	ERATH	LA	B+	B+	B+	59.7	2.17	18.6	6.9	9.6	46.9	10.0	14.7	24.5
BANK OF ESCONDIDO	ESCONDIDO	CA	C	C	NR	44.5	N/A	16.6	1.9	4.2	0.0	10.0	21.9	30.3
▲ BANK OF ESSEX	TAPPAHANNOCK	VA	B	B-	C	237.1	0.78	8.7	2.8	16.6	22.3	9.7	10.8	15.0
BANK OF EUFAULA	EUFAULA	OK	B	B	B	69.3	-0.57	3.0	7.9	4.2	61.0	10.0	16.5	45.7
BANK OF EUREKA SPRINGS	EUREKA SPRINGS	AR	B+	B+	B+	96.6	3.82	3.9	4.4	23.6	23.1	10.0	11.7	17.6
▲ BANK OF EVANSVILLE NA	EVANSVILLE	IN	C-	D+	D-	147.6	35.26	28.3	0.9	15.8	10.5	6.6	9.5	12.2
BANK OF EVERGREEN	EVERGREEN	AL	D-	D-	D-	39.5	48.37	8.4	7.4	16.5	20.5	5.0	7.0	11.6
▲ BANK OF FAIRFIELD	FAIRFIELD	WA	C	C+	D	103.4	-2.27	9.1	7.9	11.9	5.4	7.6	9.7	13.0

Asset Quality Index	Non-Performing Loans as a % of Total Loans	Non-Performing Loans as a % of Capital	Net Charge-offs Avg Loans	Profitability Index	Net Income ($Mil)	Return on Assets (R.O.A.)	Return on Equity (R.O.E.)	Net Interest Spread	Overhead Efficiency Ratio	Liquidity Index	Liquidity Ratio	Hot Money Ratio	Stability Index
7.2	0.00	0.0	0.02	4.3	0.6	0.75	9.37	3.64	61.9	1.5	10.8	22.8	1.6
8.6	0.04	0.2	0.01	10.0	5.9	2.22	14.66	5.09	33.0	4.5	60.5	17.4	10.0
0.0	3.78	29.8	1.54	2.5	0.1	0.48	5.65	3.56	84.3	1.5	33.6	40.8	0.3
8.8	0.00	0.0	0.01	5.9	0.8	1.36	18.44	3.50	63.0	6.2	105.7	14.4	4.9
9.1	0.34	0.7	0.10	4.1	0.0	0.78	6.52	3.56	78.3	8.2	109.0	0.0	3.7
5.2	1.52	5.6	0.07	5.1	0.2	1.07	6.66	4.42	75.1	5.1	52.3	11.6	7.3
8.9	0.32	1.2	0.02	7.7	1.2	1.54	14.86	3.64	46.5	0.9	6.9	31.2	7.2
7.8	0.28	2.0	0.98	5.3	0.7	1.02	10.62	4.76	62.7	2.0	14.3	19.0	4.9
4.1	0.94	9.0	0.21	5.5	0.6	0.97	12.96	4.70	65.4	2.3	34.9	24.7	1.8
4.3	1.30	8.3	0.61	9.9	0.4	2.21	23.40	6.76	60.9	4.0	57.8	17.7	5.2
6.9	0.00	0.0	-0.01	3.4	0.2	0.81	7.67	4.19	65.8	4.5	100.9	24.4	0.1
5.9	1.88	6.8	0.12	5.6	0.5	1.41	10.35	4.21	66.4	2.8	35.2	19.3	7.9
3.8	1.46	11.0	0.10	8.4	0.2	1.81	20.95	7.87	68.9	4.3	28.0	9.2	4.5
9.4	0.00	0.0	0.00	5.1	0.1	1.15	10.35	4.04	64.8	6.0	165.9	19.4	3.2
4.3	2.85	13.2	1.07	3.9	0.1	0.40	3.78	4.37	70.3	2.8	38.8	21.8	3.8
7.6	0.43	3.0	0.01	5.0	0.3	1.15	16.11	3.96	68.2	5.0	74.4	15.6	2.2
6.8	3.02	7.1	0.39	4.9	1.4	0.96	8.55	3.17	56.3	1.5	28.8	31.1	6.4
1.9	2.78	27.3	0.05	1.6	0.1	0.16	2.08	3.75	85.9	1.8	17.3	20.6	0.0
3.3	1.55	13.1	0.00	4.0	0.2	1.04	13.00	2.65	67.7	3.8	89.1	30.5	2.6
5.4	4.66	11.6	0.75	5.2	0.6	1.32	9.93	3.75	57.4	4.3	97.5	25.9	6.3
5.9	0.21	2.0	0.08	10.0	3.7	2.08	27.78	4.87	37.8	1.1	25.2	33.9	7.1
5.0	0.37	2.5	0.11	5.4	0.8	1.13	11.73	3.91	61.9	2.9	47.7	27.7	5.5
6.8	0.68	3.0	0.10	7.8	0.7	1.40	14.27	4.15	50.4	5.3	48.1	9.5	6.8
7.1	0.38	1.7	-0.12	5.3	0.1	0.96	10.42	5.06	76.5	5.9	42.0	1.7	4.7
6.4	0.55	2.9	0.26	7.0	0.6	0.97	7.78	5.29	69.7	3.9	17.4	9.7	7.9
4.5	3.48	12.0	-0.36	8.8	0.7	1.73	13.32	5.77	63.4	1.6	11.7	22.3	7.5
4.9	1.35	9.9	-0.62	10.0	1.0	2.52	37.45	4.75	50.4	4.5	74.2	18.2	5.3
8.7	0.12	0.9	0.00	10.0	0.9	2.13	30.30	4.72	42.2	3.3	23.8	13.1	6.8
4.2	1.38	6.9	0.45	6.6	0.6	0.96	8.75	4.51	64.2	5.0	61.8	15.5	5.8
6.9	1.38	5.5	-0.08	7.5	0.6	1.37	10.31	4.47	53.8	2.1	33.5	27.5	7.1
3.7	1.32	8.5	0.79	9.6	1.4	2.47	27.70	5.68	52.0	5.5	128.2	19.7	5.6
6.8	0.04	0.3	-0.01	10.0	0.5	1.74	15.66	4.65	55.7	1.8	8.5	19.4	6.3
7.9	1.00	3.0	0.03	7.8	0.6	1.54	8.60	4.23	47.2	4.8	105.5	21.2	8.6
5.1	0.71	5.0	0.34	5.5	1.2	1.01	11.85	4.27	63.0	3.8	15.1	9.9	4.9
5.9	2.79	7.0	-0.08	5.2	0.1	1.17	6.28	3.51	59.6	6.1	54.0	3.8	5.0
6.9	0.09	0.6	0.22	5.4	0.7	0.83	8.10	5.07	74.0	2.4	26.2	18.5	5.7
8.7	0.20	0.8	0.00	6.2	0.9	1.15	8.69	4.25	62.1	3.1	9.7	13.1	7.4
7.0	0.38	2.2	0.11	6.4	0.3	1.39	13.57	4.05	53.4	6.1	88.9	11.7	4.9
4.6	0.55	3.6	0.02	4.3	0.2	0.60	5.74	4.24	83.0	1.3	18.0	28.5	5.5
6.8	0.88	3.1	0.03	10.0	0.7	2.17	10.91	5.26	43.6	2.1	33.1	27.2	8.7
5.8	0.46	3.5	0.25	5.4	0.5	0.92	10.76	4.37	66.9	2.7	41.3	24.9	4.7
4.3	1.40	12.3	0.33	6.6	0.3	1.44	17.65	5.89	60.1	2.3	33.7	24.4	1.7
5.5	1.04	4.6	-0.49	6.1	0.3	1.24	12.66	3.77	51.2	1.6	17.7	24.0	6.0
3.4	3.86	20.2	3.23	0.0	-0.3	-1.20	-16.22	3.92	121.9	3.9	38.3	15.0	2.5
5.2	1.53	8.3	0.09	7.0	0.6	1.60	12.69	4.76	66.8	2.9	15.3	14.6	7.0
5.3	0.04	0.2	0.00	1.8	0.1	0.04	0.32	3.07	97.0	3.2	55.9	29.1	7.0
4.3	1.48	10.0	0.05	3.8	0.4	0.45	6.23	4.17	88.4	2.8	10.9	14.6	3.7
4.2	1.36	11.4	0.36	5.1	1.1	1.23	15.64	4.76	64.5	3.3	54.9	26.2	3.4
9.2	0.01	0.1	0.00	5.1	0.4	0.91	10.93	3.28	60.3	5.5	57.7	10.5	4.1
4.4	1.67	10.1	0.96	4.4	0.2	1.06	10.52	4.42	73.0	2.5	21.6	17.0	4.5
6.1	0.85	5.0	0.04	6.9	1.1	1.42	12.36	4.13	52.9	2.6	38.3	24.6	7.0
6.2	1.24	6.9	-0.07	5.1	5.1	1.00	10.85	3.68	64.3	5.9	43.6	8.2	7.3
6.6	0.13	0.9	-0.41	7.0	0.4	1.86	21.66	4.18	54.7	4.5	30.0	9.2	4.3
5.4	0.48	4.4	0.08	5.9	2.1	1.56	19.96	4.42	64.2	2.6	22.7	17.0	4.6
5.1	0.86	7.2	0.29	3.9	1.1	0.91	12.34	4.19	78.1	3.7	25.3	11.8	2.6
3.2	1.37	13.1	0.11	9.9	0.9	1.63	20.75	5.88	54.6	0.6	4.5	34.6	4.3
8.5	0.41	1.2	-0.47	5.4	0.3	0.95	6.33	4.83	71.8	3.5	24.1	12.4	6.7
8.8	0.00	0.0	0.00	0.0	-0.2	-1.28	-4.96	3.78	133.8	7.8	132.2	7.2	3.4
4.8	1.34	7.7	0.36	5.8	1.4	1.20	10.50	4.62	64.5	3.8	23.1	10.7	5.8
8.6	0.54	0.6	0.53	4.4	0.3	0.83	5.02	3.72	69.2	5.2	61.4	12.4	6.1
5.8	1.78	9.4	0.02	5.8	0.4	0.91	7.83	4.26	71.9	1.4	11.0	24.6	6.3
8.4	0.00	0.0	0.02	2.2	0.3	0.41	4.23	3.28	78.3	0.8	13.7	35.4	1.0
5.6	0.58	4.6	0.09	4.4	0.1	0.66	10.40	4.16	64.0	3.8	68.0	21.4	0.0
2.9	1.80	14.0	0.32	7.4	1.1	2.02	21.31	6.01	60.8	4.0	39.7	14.8	4.1

| Name | City | State | Weiss Safety Rating | 2003 Weiss Safety Rating | 2002 Weiss Safety Rating | Total Assets ($Mil) | One Year Asset Growth | Asset Mix (As a % of Total Assets) | | | | Capital- ization Index | Risk-based | |
								Comm- ercial Loans	Cons- umer Loans	Home Mort- gages	Secur- ities		Leverage Ratio	Capital Ratio
BANK OF FAIRPORT	FAIRPORT	MO	C	C	C-	19.8	2.33	3.6	5.9	16.4	40.6	10.0	11.1	20.2
BANK OF FALL RIVER, A	FALL RIVER	MA	B-	B-	B-	140.2	4.54	8.7	4.6	26.5	11.0	6.6	8.6	12.2
BANK OF FARMINGTON	FARMINGTON	IL	B+	B+	B+	64.9	4.18	4.1	10.6	15.7	38.9	10.0	12.6	22.4
BANK OF FAYETTE COUNTY	MOSCOW	TN	C+	C	D	90.1	17.06	3.3	5.2	23.9	8.6	5.6	8.7	11.5
▲ BANK OF FAYETTEVILLE NA	FAYETTEVILLE	AR	C	C-	C-	309.9	22.61	7.2	2.0	11.6	34.8	6.1	8.1	13.3
BANK OF FINCASTLE	FINCASTLE	VA	A-	A-	B	139.0	3.81	11.6	5.1	19.4	4.3	10.0	13.8	17.2
BANK OF FLORIDA	FORT LAUDERDALE	FL	D-	D-	D-	85.7	80.96	7.8	2.4	20.8	1.8	3.2	7.7	10.1
▲ BANK OF FLORIDA A NA	NAPLES	FL	D	D-	D-	210.3	60.36	14.3	3.6	29.2	1.6	3.7	7.3	10.4
BANK OF FLOYD	FLOYD	VA	B-	B-	B-	178.7	-4.21	2.9	1.5	14.4	22.9	7.4	9.3	15.0
BANK OF FOREST	FOREST	MS	A	A	A	127.6	-1.11	4.4	8.6	11.6	45.6	10.0	12.2	23.1
BANK OF FRANKEWING	FRANKEWING	TN	B+	B	B-	113.7	12.30	14.7	12.8	25.0	12.6	8.5	10.0	14.3
▼ BANK OF FRANKLIN	MEADVILLE	MS	C+	B-	B+	79.9	-2.56	3.4	13.5	13.8	42.5	10.0	14.4	27.5
BANK OF FRANKLIN COUNTY	WASHINGTON	MO	C+	C+	C-	109.0	34.90	4.0	1.9	28.8	27.8	4.9	6.9	11.7
BANK OF FREEBURG	FREEBURG	MO	B+	B+	B+	36.2	6.63	1.7	3.8	28.8	32.2	10.0	13.4	29.8
BANK OF FRIO CANYON	LEAKEY	TX	B-	B-	B	31.8	8.12	4.5	7.3	11.8	28.3	9.0	10.3	20.2
▲ BANK OF GALESVILLE	GALESVILLE	WI	C+	C-	D+	61.8	1.87	12.7	8.7	23.3	15.2	8.6	10.1	13.9
BANK OF GASSAWAY	GASSAWAY	WV	B-	C+	C+	171.1	7.33	4.6	11.4	21.6	38.3	6.4	8.4	18.9
BANK OF GENEVA	GENEVA	IN	B	B	A-	113.4	1.85	2.5	2.8	31.8	26.7	10.0	11.3	21.5
▲ BANK OF GEORGIA	PEACHTREE CITY	GA	C	C	C-	237.7	27.80	5.1	2.6	1.1	13.8	5.0	8.7	11.0
BANK OF GERMANTOWN	GERMANTOWN	KY	C+	C+	C+	23.4	-2.84	7.7	5.7	19.0	21.5	6.5	8.5	14.0
▲ BANK OF GIBSON CITY	GIBSON CITY	IL	C+	D+	C+	60.1	-0.15	5.1	7.7	5.8	49.7	10.0	11.4	22.0
BANK OF GLEASON	GLEASON	TN	A	A-	A-	105.5	-2.21	5.7	10.6	14.1	43.8	10.0	16.2	27.2
BANK OF GLEN BURNIE	GLEN BURNIE	MD	B	B	B	307.9	3.77	1.7	24.2	19.2	33.3	7.6	9.4	15.7
BANK OF GLEN ULLIN	GLEN ULLIN	ND	B+	B+	B+	30.1	8.26	6.7	1.3	1.8	15.9	10.0	12.5	16.2
BANK OF GODFREY	GODFREY	IL	C	C	D-	32.0	8.78	24.5	2.1	31.0	11.8	10.0	13.6	20.6
▲ BANK OF GOOCHLAND NA	GOOCHLAND	VA	D+	C	C+	43.8	97.58	5.2	7.9	6.0	17.1	7.4	9.3	13.6
BANK OF GRAIN VALLEY	GRAIN VALLEY	MO	A	A	A	93.8	-0.03	14.5	1.4	6.0	42.4	10.0	11.8	18.8
BANK OF GRANDIN	GRANDIN	MO	A-	A	A	100.5	3.23	16.2	8.5	8.8	36.8	10.0	13.9	21.5
▼ BANK OF GRANITE	GRANITE FALLS	NC	A-	A	A+	957.1	28.00	22.8	3.5	8.9	15.8	10.0	12.7	16.4
▼ BANK OF GRAVETT	GRAVETTE	AR	B	B+	A-	222.5	20.03	3.0	6.5	21.9	34.5	7.7	9.4	17.4
▲ BANK OF GREELEY	GREELEY	KS	B+	B	B	26.6	-3.02	6.2	7.8	21.5	27.3	10.0	12.9	22.1
BANK OF GREELEYVILLE	GREELEYVILLE	SC	D	D-	D-	45.9	1.88	22.3	14.2	20.8	9.0	6.7	8.7	12.8
▲ BANK OF GREENE COUNTY	CATSKILL	NY	B+	B	B-	276.8	9.52	2.3	1.6	40.5	34.8	7.3	9.2	19.4
▲ BANK OF GREENEVILLE	GREENEVILLE	TN	C	C-	D	91.0	37.27	27.2	6.6	11.1	0.0	5.5	8.5	11.4
BANK OF GREENSBURG	GREENSBURG	LA	B	B+	B+	62.0	-2.14	9.3	8.9	16.9	23.5	10.0	15.3	27.0
BANK OF GUAM	AGANA	GU	C-	C-	C+	730.9	1.38	11.1	10.5	11.8	33.8	6.9	9.0	16.3
BANK OF GUEYDAN	GUEYDAN	LA	A	A	A	74.8	-2.68	1.9	7.3	3.8	71.3	10.0	20.5	56.0
BANK OF HALLS	HALLS	TN	B+	B	B	47.6	0.99	2.6	3.5	13.5	33.5	10.0	12.2	19.2
BANK OF HAMILTON	HAMILTON	ND	B-	B-	B-	13.3	9.45	4.8	7.9	3.8	9.2	10.0	18.4	49.6
BANK OF HAMPTON ROADS	CHESAPEAKE	VA	A	A	A	322.7	6.34	18.3	5.6	4.4	18.9	10.0	12.0	16.3
BANK OF HANCOCK CTY	SPARTA	GA	A-	A-	A-	81.8	9.71	1.9	11.7	28.2	35.3	10.0	16.5	31.6
BANK OF HANOVER & TRUST	HANOVER	PA	B	B	B-	677.7	2.90	11.0	8.9	24.0	25.6	5.9	7.9	12.4
BANK OF HARLAN	HARLAN	KY	B+	A-	A-	119.2	14.75	7.7	7.2	30.6	32.2	9.6	10.8	17.8
▲ BANK OF HARRISBURG	HARRISBURG	AR	B	B-	C+	65.1	1.08	8.4	3.7	16.2	51.9	10.0	12.0	25.6
BANK OF HARTINGTON	HARTINGTON	NE	C+	C+	C-	38.6	-3.93	13.2	5.7	2.5	49.3	8.8	10.2	19.0
BANK OF HAWAII	HONOLULU	HI	B+	B+	A-	9,742.9	1.41	6.3	5.7	21.4	30.9	5.1	7.1	13.8
BANK OF HAYTI	HAYTI	MO	B	B	B+	62.9	-4.71	11.0	21.1	19.5	17.7	10.0	13.3	19.2
▲ BANK OF HAZELTON	HAZELTON	ND	B-	C+	C+	25.0	-2.17	7.6	2.5	2.6	26.5	8.2	9.8	15.9
▲ BANK OF HAZLEHURST	HAZLEHURST	GA	B-	C+	B	78.5	8.21	30.2	16.1	13.5	13.7	7.3	9.2	13.2
BANK OF HEATH SPRINGS	HEATH SPRINGS	SC	C	C+	C+	17.4	1.30	8.8	3.7	6.1	39.4	10.0	30.3	73.4
BANK OF HEMET	RIVERSIDE	CA	B-	B-	B-	326.9	8.54	3.0	0.2	1.5	7.2	4.4	9.0	10.7
BANK OF HERRIN	HERRIN	IL	A-	A-	A-	132.1	-3.60	7.7	5.0	15.0	41.4	9.3	10.5	19.4
▲ BANK OF HIAWASSEE	HIAWASSEE	GA	C	C-	C	256.9	10.86	5.7	4.8	25.9	6.4	6.2	8.8	11.9
BANK OF HILLSBORO	HILLSBORO	MO	B	B	B	43.3	-5.08	1.1	1.8	10.2	34.6	10.0	13.2	19.3
BANK OF HINDMAN	HINDMAN	KY	A	A	A	130.1	2.56	5.2	4.2	11.0	71.7	10.0	14.3	41.7
BANK OF HOLDEN	HOLDEN	MO	C	C-	C-	105.1	-4.45	8.4	5.3	22.3	30.0	6.7	8.7	15.4
BANK OF HOLLAND	HOLLAND	MI	C	C	C-	318.3	21.83	27.9	1.8	11.0	6.4	3.4	8.8	10.2
BANK OF HOLLAND	HOLLAND	NY	B+	B+	B+	59.5	19.18	5.2	3.8	52.2	16.0	10.0	11.0	16.8
▲ BANK OF HOLLY SPRINGS	HOLLY SPRINGS	MS	A	A-	A-	133.7	-1.87	19.6	15.5	17.2	16.8	10.0	13.5	20.7
BANK OF HOLYROOD	HOLYROOD	KS	B-	B-	C+	25.6	8.67	15.9	8.2	19.0	18.7	10.0	11.8	19.2
▼ BANK OF HOUSTON	HOUSTON	MO	C+	B	B	52.7	0.85	4.3	3.0	11.8	17.6	10.0	12.0	20.8
▲ BANK OF HYDRO	HYDRO	OK	D+	D	C-	60.6	-1.40	11.2	9.4	9.1	9.3	4.1	6.8	10.6
BANK OF IBERIA	IBERIA	MO	D	D+	D+	49.4	13.87	6.0	13.7	35.8	12.7	4.5	7.0	10.7
▲ BANK OF IDAHO	IDAHO FALLS	ID	B-	C+	C	175.1	7.13	18.4	4.6	5.3	24.5	6.3	8.3	12.6

Asset Quality Index	Non-Performing Loans		Net Charge-offs Avg Loans	Profitability Index	Net Income ($Mil)	Return on Assets (R.O.A.)	Return on Equity (R.O.E.)	Net Interest Spread	Overhead Efficiency Ratio	Liquidity Index	Liquidity Ratio	Hot Money Ratio	Stability Index
	as a % of Total Loans	as a % of Capital											
4.3	4.18	15.1	0.74	4.1	0.0	0.25	2.22	3.73	85.3	6.8	66.4	1.7	3.4
7.7	0.25	2.0	0.01	4.4	0.4	0.53	6.42	4.19	77.4	4.0	39.4	15.0	4.7
8.2	0.50	2.1	0.13	7.2	0.6	1.69	13.18	4.12	44.3	3.7	13.9	10.4	6.2
7.8	0.12	1.2	0.07	6.1	0.5	1.18	13.76	5.06	63.4	2.5	16.8	16.6	3.8
4.8	1.39	9.1	0.06	4.3	1.0	0.72	10.25	3.72	75.3	3.9	11.1	8.8	2.8
6.5	0.67	3.8	0.16	7.4	0.9	1.34	9.93	4.83	59.2	4.2	24.0	8.4	8.0
7.4	0.00	0.0	0.00	0.0	-0.2	-0.41	-5.05	3.86	94.4	3.7	45.0	17.5	0.0
5.6	0.66	7.9	0.00	1.1	0.3	0.32	4.47	3.31	80.5	0.7	13.1	42.3	2.3
4.0	2.28	14.2	-0.25	7.3	1.3	1.43	15.76	4.10	50.9	5.3	47.1	10.4	5.2
8.1	0.60	2.1	0.05	7.8	1.2	1.93	14.65	4.19	57.1	4.2	57.9	18.2	8.3
7.6	0.12	0.8	0.42	8.5	0.8	1.52	15.46	5.39	54.5	3.4	45.7	19.4	5.6
5.7	2.69	7.0	6.70	2.1	0.0	0.01	0.06	3.95	72.8	5.5	129.9	19.1	5.3
8.9	0.00	0.0	0.04	4.2	0.4	0.72	10.09	3.05	58.1	3.6	30.2	13.7	2.3
9.1	0.05	0.2	0.02	6.0	0.2	1.03	7.92	3.30	49.2	8.1	160.9	8.7	6.2
3.7	3.57	16.2	-0.09	5.5	0.2	0.90	8.71	4.05	66.7	2.9	67.1	37.1	5.5
4.0	1.10	7.9	-0.14	9.7	0.9	2.80	29.31	5.44	58.5	4.0	25.1	10.2	5.7
4.4	1.35	6.6	1.39	5.9	0.6	0.75	9.02	4.47	60.4	4.0	60.0	20.3	5.0
8.1	0.78	4.1	-0.02	5.0	0.6	1.08	9.55	4.10	70.6	3.7	27.8	12.6	7.2
7.3	0.11	0.9	0.08	4.1	0.9	0.82	10.71	4.08	66.5	2.6	52.5	40.7	2.0
4.1	0.58	3.8	2.50	2.4	0.1	0.65	7.47	4.64	72.4	4.7	34.5	6.7	3.7
6.0	1.41	5.2	-0.08	4.1	0.4	1.32	11.55	3.67	58.9	3.1	12.0	13.1	3.4
7.5	1.33	3.8	0.55	9.0	1.1	1.98	12.39	4.85	36.5	3.2	48.9	23.5	7.8
6.1	0.40	2.4	0.14	5.7	1.6	1.08	11.25	4.70	71.5	4.2	15.6	7.6	5.7
7.4	0.00	0.0	0.00	7.5	0.2	1.65	13.17	4.11	55.2	3.8	52.9	17.9	7.0
7.4	0.57	2.0	0.32	1.0	0.0	-0.05	-0.28	2.85	95.6	6.2	153.5	17.8	5.9
7.2	0.00	0.0	0.00	0.0	-0.2	-0.85	-8.76	4.08	105.8	3.7	63.4	20.8	1.3
9.0	0.00	0.0	-0.01	9.3	0.9	2.03	17.41	4.02	48.9	4.5	70.7	17.8	8.4
5.0	2.88	11.4	0.34	9.3	0.7	1.34	9.82	4.17	40.4	3.5	33.7	15.3	8.3
5.2	1.42	7.4	0.35	9.1	6.4	1.34	9.59	4.51	49.1	2.6	33.5	20.1	9.2
3.7	2.82	14.9	0.15	6.7	1.8	1.63	17.43	3.82	47.5	2.0	40.9	40.3	5.8
6.1	1.67	7.6	0.23	7.7	0.3	1.83	14.24	3.85	55.5	5.0	51.1	12.0	7.1
2.7	1.43	11.1	-0.04	5.7	0.3	1.43	16.34	5.12	73.5	4.2	31.4	11.1	2.7
9.2	0.23	1.3	0.03	5.7	1.4	1.06	11.58	4.16	66.7	7.0	60.2	3.2	5.4
3.5	2.99	24.7	-0.01	6.1	0.5	1.19	14.00	5.01	59.4	5.7	75.7	12.2	1.1
4.3	4.54	14.9	0.43	3.8	0.2	0.46	3.07	4.78	82.5	3.4	56.4	22.2	6.4
2.2	4.08	22.3	0.64	4.8	3.0	0.81	9.18	4.83	73.0	3.6	60.2	25.9	4.7
9.0	0.62	0.7	0.14	6.6	0.4	1.12	5.50	2.83	41.0	5.3	146.5	24.1	7.9
8.3	0.24	1.0	0.11	7.1	0.3	1.25	10.61	4.04	59.3	1.6	26.1	27.0	7.5
8.6	2.01	2.5	-0.84	6.8	0.1	1.63	8.93	3.61	40.9	9.2	183.6	3.4	5.0
8.1	0.36	2.0	0.13	6.3	1.8	1.12	9.46	4.45	63.8	4.0	28.2	11.0	8.4
6.0	2.55	8.0	0.17	5.0	0.4	0.86	5.22	4.05	67.0	4.6	74.9	17.8	7.7
8.1	0.07	0.6	0.09	4.0	2.6	0.75	9.18	3.73	76.6	6.5	106.9	12.9	5.5
5.2	1.17	6.0	1.00	6.8	0.7	1.14	10.35	4.88	55.7	4.2	52.9	17.3	7.0
5.0	4.47	13.5	-0.32	5.7	0.5	1.45	12.23	3.57	60.0	1.9	24.3	20.9	6.0
5.8	0.69	3.0	0.04	3.3	0.1	0.44	4.42	3.82	86.5	4.2	16.2	7.3	4.4
8.1	0.32	2.3	0.02	9.9	89.4	1.83	23.56	4.43	56.9	6.5	51.8	6.9	7.0
4.0	1.89	9.6	1.72	8.0	0.4	1.33	10.40	4.91	48.3	1.2	19.6	30.1	6.8
6.6	0.02	0.1	0.00	7.5	0.2	1.69	17.74	4.33	54.7	4.4	72.8	17.0	5.7
3.8	0.50	2.2	0.21	9.5	0.8	2.00	12.84	4.82	60.3	1.7	11.2	20.6	7.2
8.6	3.45	3.3	-0.04	3.4	0.1	0.71	2.38	3.63	79.8	6.2	66.0	5.3	4.9
7.1	0.00	0.0	0.00	9.9	4.3	2.69	30.90	4.79	48.1	4.9	32.0	6.8	5.7
8.9	0.12	0.6	0.04	6.8	0.9	1.34	11.77	3.64	56.3	6.6	49.4	2.8	7.3
2.9	1.84	15.6	0.02	6.9	1.5	1.22	14.29	4.63	61.9	5.0	73.9	16.8	4.6
9.3	0.42	1.3	0.00	4.5	0.2	0.82	6.23	4.09	69.5	7.0	86.0	6.1	5.4
9.6	1.66	2.4	0.07	7.9	0.9	1.44	10.28	3.64	43.1	4.1	75.6	24.4	8.5
4.5	1.54	10.1	0.59	3.9	0.4	0.74	8.50	4.44	66.5	4.9	53.8	14.0	3.2
5.8	0.44	4.2	0.03	4.6	1.2	0.82	9.84	2.76	55.5	0.3	4.7	67.3	4.4
5.4	2.47	14.2	-0.01	5.2	0.2	0.75	6.38	4.51	76.8	6.2	62.6	6.8	6.4
7.1	0.65	3.2	-0.10	8.2	1.1	1.59	12.10	5.57	57.7	2.5	36.4	23.4	7.7
5.8	1.35	7.4	0.05	7.9	0.2	1.74	14.86	3.87	45.9	2.3	36.0	27.1	4.5
2.2	8.06	33.9	-0.08	3.9	0.2	0.77	5.81	3.23	75.2	6.5	80.0	8.6	6.7
7.2	0.05	0.6	0.00	5.1	0.4	1.43	21.19	2.96	54.6	1.7	29.7	29.4	2.7
7.0	0.14	1.5	0.16	4.1	0.2	0.72	10.32	4.50	74.8	3.0	31.1	16.8	1.9
5.1	0.59	4.4	0.05	5.9	0.9	1.04	12.84	4.89	73.8	3.6	11.9	10.8	4.1

Name	City	State	Weiss Safety Rating	2003 Weiss Safety Rating	2002 Weiss Safety Rating	Total Assets ($Mil)	One Year Asset Growth	Asset Mix (As a % of Total Assets)				Capital-ization Index	Leverage Ratio	Risk-based Capital Ratio
								Comm-ercial Loans	Cons-umer Loans	Home Mort-gages	Secur-ities			
BANK OF ILLINOIS IN NORMAL	NORMAL	IL	D+	D+	D+	93.7	4.62	14.7	1.2	14.8	15.4	5.1	7.8	11.1
BANK OF INTERNET USA	SAN DIEGO	CA	B-	B-	C+	404.8	48.17	0.0	0.0	5.4	1.0	5.6	7.8	11.5
BANK OF INVERNESS	INVERNESS	FL	B+	B+	A-	234.8	0.98	0.1	0.4	41.1	39.3	5.4	7.4	18.7
BANK OF JACKSON	JACKSON	TN	B+	B	B	93.0	3.29	6.8	4.5	21.6	15.2	10.0	11.1	15.7
▲ BANK OF JACKSON CTY	GRACEVILLE	FL	E+	E	E	31.1	0.93	4.6	9.7	10.0	19.7	5.6	7.6	12.3
BANK OF JACKSON HOLE	JACKSON	WY	A-	A-	A-	246.0	3.92	17.7	1.3	19.6	0.2	7.5	11.3	12.9
BANK OF JACOMO	BLUE SPRINGS	MO	B	B-	B	248.3	-0.52	8.6	3.6	11.6	12.9	6.5	8.5	12.6
BANK OF JAMESTOWN	JAMESTOWN	KY	A	A	A	136.0	-1.86	3.9	5.9	19.4	49.8	10.0	12.3	24.4
BANK OF JEFFERSON	JEFFERSON	SC	C-	C-	C	16.7	1.76	1.2	21.2	15.6	18.8	10.0	12.5	24.5
BANK OF JENA	JENA	LA	C-	C-	C+	53.4	-3.43	4.2	8.8	16.5	39.4	6.6	8.7	19.7
▲ BANK OF JONES COUNTY	LAUREL	MS	A-	B+	B	124.1	4.18	10.6	6.5	21.2	38.7	8.5	10.0	17.2
BANK OF JUDA	JUDA	WI	B	B	B+	32.2	7.48	4.6	6.5	22.2	25.0	10.0	13.1	19.9
BANK OF KAMPSVILLE	KAMPSVILLE	IL	B-	B-	C+	79.3	1.80	3.7	14.2	23.2	35.5	7.4	9.2	16.3
BANK OF KANSAS	S HUTCHINSON	KS	B-	B-	B-	72.3	2.33	7.3	8.5	19.8	29.5	8.4	9.9	17.3
BANK OF KAUKAUNA	KAUKAUNA	WI	B-	B-	B+	64.9	7.83	24.0	3.6	10.9	6.2	9.9	11.8	14.9
▲ BANK OF KENNEY	KENNEY	IL	C-	D+	D+	4.8	-3.15	3.5	1.9	3.7	13.5	10.0	15.4	23.0
▲ BANK OF KENOSHA	KENOSHA	WI	C-	D+	D-	123.3	33.14	11.9	2.0	20.1	7.6	5.3	8.2	11.2
▼ BANK OF KENTUCKY	CRESTVIEW HILLS	KY	C+	B-	B-	831.8	5.44	15.8	2.4	13.2	6.0	3.2	9.0	10.1
BANK OF KEYSTONE	KEYSTONE	NE	D+	D+	D	29.0	7.36	12.1	3.9	3.4	12.5	6.7	8.7	13.1
▲ BANK OF KILMICHAEL	KILMICHAEL	MS	C+	C-	D	59.8	2.56	13.9	6.9	8.2	41.3	9.4	10.6	17.6
▲ BANK OF KIMBERLING CITY	KIMBERLING CITY	MO	A-	B	B	125.6	-1.87	5.4	5.4	35.9	14.4	9.0	10.4	16.2
BANK OF KIRKSVILLE	KIRKSVILLE	MO	B-	B-	B-	330.3	4.70	8.4	3.5	31.2	32.7	5.3	7.3	15.9
▲ BANK OF KREMLIN	KREMLIN	OK	C+	C-	C-	133.3	3.22	15.7	6.4	6.9	4.3	5.5	9.2	11.4
BANK OF LA FAYETTE	LA FAYETTE	GA	A+	A+	A+	154.8	3.83	3.2	9.9	17.9	51.0	10.0	16.7	44.0
BANK OF LAKE MILLS	LAKE MILLS	WI	D	D	D+	107.7	6.92	5.5	12.1	26.0	12.9	8.0	9.6	13.5
BANK OF LAKE VILLAGE	LAKE VILLAGE	AR	D	D	B-	63.4	-12.09	5.2	1.7	4.5	24.4	7.1	9.0	13.0
BANK OF LANCASTER	KILMARNOCK	VA	C+	C+	B-	301.0	8.01	6.6	3.2	33.2	19.8	3.8	6.6	10.4
▲ BANK OF LANCASTER CTY NA	STRASBURG	PA	B+	B	B-	1,548.6	5.58	20.3	3.2	12.4	18.8	6.3	9.9	11.9
▼ BANK OF LANDISBURG	LANDISBURG	PA	A	A+	A+	184.7	4.53	0.0	1.7	41.0	45.1	10.0	16.5	37.5
BANK OF LAS VEGAS	LAS VEGAS	NM	B	B-	C+	137.3	2.80	6.2	1.7	13.5	25.0	6.5	8.6	13.5
BANK OF LAS VEGAS	LAS VEGAS	NV	C	C	C	49.9	56.01	12.8	0.4	1.9	0.5	10.0	12.2	15.5
BANK OF LAVERNE	LAVERNE	OK	B+	B+	B+	47.9	0.35	5.3	9.2	2.2	50.0	10.0	16.8	36.2
BANK OF LAWRENCE CTY	BRIDGEPORT	IL	C+	C+	C+	26.8	18.80	13.7	2.5	10.4	14.2	10.0	16.8	41.7
▼ BANK OF LEE'S SUMMIT	LEE'S SUMMIT	MO	B+	A-	A	209.6	6.85	4.9	3.4	14.7	12.1	9.2	10.7	14.3
BANK OF LEETON	LEETON	MO	D+	D+	C-	8.8	20.80	6.3	10.9	5.3	5.7	9.3	13.5	14.4
BANK OF LEIGH	LEIGH	NE	D+	D+	D+	20.3	8.87	8.1	7.1	15.8	10.5	6.9	8.9	12.6
▲ BANK OF LENAWEE	ADRIAN	MI	B-	C+	B-	261.5	4.68	8.8	3.8	13.0	8.3	8.4	10.1	13.7
BANK OF LENOX	LENOX	GA	D	D	D-	31.3	-8.13	16.0	14.4	16.8	23.6	7.1	9.0	15.2
▲ BANK OF LINCOLN CITY	FAYETTEVILLE	TN	B-	C	D	78.1	32.94	7.6	8.3	16.0	22.0	10.0	12.6	18.6
BANK OF LINCOLN CTY	ELSBERRY	MO	B+	B+	B+	38.5	1.19	4.4	3.5	24.6	45.2	10.0	12.2	24.6
▼ BANK OF LINCOLNWOOD	LINCOLNWOOD	IL	D+	D+	C-	223.0	1.51	18.1	2.1	5.1	6.3	2.1	7.5	9.1
BANK OF LINDSAY	LINDSAY	NE	D+	D+	D	22.0	-3.94	11.4	2.8	4.5	4.5	7.7	10.8	13.1
BANK OF LITTLE ROCK	LITTLE ROCK	AR	B	B	C	104.7	4.42	15.8	3.1	12.3	26.2	9.1	10.4	16.4
▼ BANK OF LOCUST GROVE	LOCUST GROVE	OK	B	B	A-	27.6	3.92	4.3	18.6	32.9	12.3	9.2	10.5	18.6
▲ BANK OF LODI NA	LODI	CA	C	C	C	323.4	15.61	21.1	0.5	0.5	22.6	3.6	7.0	10.3
BANK OF LOUISA NA	LOUISA	VA	C	NR	NR	14.8	N/A	6.5	2.6	2.1	63.4	10.0	35.9	68.3
▲ BANK OF LOUISIANA	NEW ORLEANS	LA	C-	D+	D+	95.1	-5.69	4.9	18.3	17.6	19.5	7.2	9.2	15.3
BANK OF LOUISIANA	LOUISIANA	MO	C-	C-	C-	47.6	5.06	14.8	4.0	27.3	11.0	7.4	9.2	14.7
BANK OF LUMBER CITY	LUMBER CITY	GA	C	C	C	18.9	5.03	10.8	12.3	20.4	30.9	10.0	18.1	30.2
▲ BANK OF LUXEMBURG	LUXEMBURG	WI	D+	D+	C+	174.5	2.05	36.1	5.9	18.3	6.8	3.2	9.1	10.1
BANK OF MACKS CREEK	MACKS CREEK	MO	D	D	D+	22.1	13.03	9.8	26.2	25.6	9.9	5.8	7.8	11.6
▲ BANK OF MADERA COUNTY	OAKHURST	CA	C	C-	C-	61.9	16.48	18.2	2.1	4.1	0.0	5.2	8.0	11.2
BANK OF MADISON	MADISON	GA	B+	A-	A	154.0	14.15	5.0	4.0	22.5	10.9	8.6	10.1	13.8
BANK OF MADISON	MADISON	NE	C	C	D+	54.5	4.20	9.2	5.5	7.5	31.8	9.5	10.7	17.8
BANK OF MAGNOLIA	MAGNOLIA	KY	C	C+	C	83.1	4.36	3.3	5.8	21.4	34.8	6.4	8.4	14.6
BANK OF MAGNOLIA CO	MAGNOLIA	OH	C+	C+	C+	60.5	1.87	6.6	7.2	23.5	41.9	7.0	9.0	19.5
▲ BANK OF MANSFIELD	MANSFIELD	MO	C+	C	D+	41.9	-4.11	3.0	5.9	32.7	32.4	9.5	10.7	20.3
▲ BANK OF MAPLE PLAIN	MAPLE PLAIN	MN	A-	B+	B	49.9	-8.95	7.1	3.2	18.9	26.9	10.0	12.0	19.4
BANK OF MARIN	CORTE MADERA	CA	B	B	B	691.3	20.36	10.7	10.8	2.5	17.4	5.3	8.9	11.2
▼ BANK OF MARINGOUIN	MARINGOUIN	LA	B	B+	B+	34.3	-0.46	19.7	3.2	20.5	26.0	10.0	12.1	22.3
BANK OF MARION	MARION	IL	B+	B	B-	193.8	-2.98	4.4	8.0	4.8	54.9	8.2	9.8	18.3
BANK OF MARION	MARION	VA	B	B	B	321.0	2.16	5.5	7.4	23.0	35.2	6.3	8.3	14.8
▲ BANK OF MASON	MASON	TN	C	C-	D+	8.0	-19.60	2.2	7.3	8.8	50.5	10.0	12.2	26.4
▲ BANK OF MAUSTON	MAUSTON	WI	B-	C	C-	168.9	-3.35	4.6	5.0	16.8	27.7	9.2	10.7	14.3

Asset Quality Index	Non-Performing Loans as a % of Total Loans	Non-Performing Loans as a % of Capital	Net Charge-offs Avg Loans	Profitability Index	Net Income ($Mil)	Return on Assets (R.O.A.)	Return on Equity (R.O.E.)	Net Interest Spread	Overhead Efficiency Ratio	Liquidity Index	Liquidity Ratio	Hot Money Ratio	Stability Index
3.4	1.56	15.0	0.10	3.6	0.2	0.51	6.73	3.70	79.1	3.5	21.3	12.0	2.5
6.8	0.00	0.0	0.00	5.2	1.5	0.84	10.12	2.10	40.5	2.9	16.0	14.4	2.5
9.4	0.14	0.9	0.00	9.6	2.7	2.32	29.46	4.49	52.1	4.3	29.2	9.7	6.5
8.1	0.18	1.1	0.11	7.0	0.6	1.26	11.36	4.10	49.3	1.8	30.8	28.4	6.6
3.1	2.14	15.6	-0.15	1.4	0.0	0.06	0.83	4.47	105.8	6.3	53.2	4.4	1.4
7.2	0.00	0.0	0.06	8.9	1.6	1.31	11.62	4.60	55.5	1.1	13.0	29.3	8.0
4.7	0.81	2.9	0.08	9.8	2.0	1.58	9.04	4.86	50.6	9.1	197.1	5.7	8.2
7.0	1.28	4.7	1.22	6.9	0.9	1.38	11.63	4.05	57.1	5.2	60.0	13.7	7.6
5.3	1.31	4.7	1.45	4.2	0.1	0.98	8.06	4.90	71.0	6.3	91.3	10.1	3.1
5.0	1.42	6.7	0.41	3.3	0.2	0.62	7.13	4.50	84.9	3.1	45.5	20.8	3.2
8.6	0.06	0.3	0.23	7.2	0.7	1.21	11.60	4.28	54.7	2.5	38.9	26.5	5.9
7.6	0.61	2.9	0.14	5.7	0.2	1.03	7.92	3.48	58.5	3.8	30.1	12.9	6.3
5.0	0.51	2.7	0.37	7.5	0.5	1.24	11.91	3.92	52.7	4.3	39.4	13.3	5.3
7.1	0.62	3.4	-0.01	5.9	0.3	0.88	8.82	4.49	69.6	4.0	77.5	23.6	4.9
4.4	1.05	6.9	0.00	6.1	0.4	1.35	13.54	3.88	62.2	1.7	24.9	24.4	7.1
7.3	0.00	0.0	0.00	4.6	0.0	0.38	2.47	4.30	89.7	5.9	69.4	8.1	3.7
6.7	0.40	3.7	0.00	1.9	0.2	0.31	3.67	3.25	71.1	0.8	16.8	41.1	0.8
5.2	0.48	3.6	0.10	7.9	5.2	1.27	12.49	4.08	55.3	3.4	13.3	11.6	6.9
4.4	1.36	8.9	0.01	4.3	0.1	0.63	7.22	4.09	72.4	6.5	89.3	9.9	2.1
3.4	3.70	15.8	-0.02	3.6	0.2	0.63	5.74	3.45	76.3	3.3	70.2	30.0	4.5
7.8	0.23	1.6	0.01	10.0	1.6	2.53	25.31	4.50	48.9	4.3	24.8	8.1	6.9
7.1	0.36	2.7	-0.01	5.9	2.5	1.49	20.55	2.45	47.3	4.2	56.5	18.2	4.6
3.8	0.43	3.6	0.06	8.3	1.6	2.37	25.87	4.40	49.2	1.6	22.8	26.0	6.5
8.1	1.11	2.6	0.01	8.4	1.2	1.48	9.03	5.12	59.1	4.2	18.5	7.9	8.9
1.0	4.20	32.7	0.49	6.5	0.8	1.52	16.25	3.96	43.2	3.8	13.7	9.7	6.3
0.0	6.84	36.7	7.25	0.9	-1.0	-3.19	-31.63	3.68	114.5	1.3	9.8	25.6	3.8
4.6	0.93	7.8	0.10	4.5	1.1	0.75	9.64	3.88	75.3	5.4	55.0	11.9	4.8
8.1	0.20	1.2	0.09	9.2	13.1	1.71	15.06	5.34	64.3	6.5	44.7	5.0	8.7
8.8	1.49	4.5	0.00	6.8	1.2	1.25	7.52	3.36	47.2	6.0	65.2	10.7	9.1
7.0	0.36	2.5	-0.93	9.6	1.9	2.82	33.55	4.83	51.7	4.0	32.3	12.4	5.1
7.4	0.00	0.0	0.00	1.2	0.0	0.00	0.00	4.86	97.4	7.0	142.0	12.6	2.9
7.8	1.99	4.0	0.22	6.8	0.3	1.22	7.42	4.29	55.6	5.1	66.0	14.0	6.0
9.0	0.00	0.0	0.00	2.5	0.1	0.52	2.96	3.01	80.0	5.0	120.7	22.8	5.7
5.1	0.11	0.4	0.45	9.0	1.3	1.28	6.29	4.90	52.5	4.8	11.2	3.0	8.7
5.4	0.15	0.6	0.06	5.2	0.1	1.02	6.52	5.07	62.6	5.1	57.1	10.5	3.0
3.3	1.65	12.9	0.10	8.6	0.2	2.03	21.12	4.73	55.5	3.1	33.0	15.1	3.0
4.7	0.64	4.7	0.09	8.6	1.7	1.30	12.15	5.24	69.1	2.9	10.4	14.2	6.4
4.4	0.94	5.5	0.17	2.0	0.0	0.16	1.75	4.93	114.5	2.0	28.6	23.9	1.7
8.1	0.17	0.9	0.10	4.5	0.4	1.00	7.91	4.54	61.4	1.6	33.8	38.7	3.3
9.3	0.06	0.2	0.02	6.4	0.3	1.52	12.42	3.84	63.1	3.7	16.3	10.5	6.4
2.1	2.28	22.3	0.00	7.4	1.9	1.65	22.78	4.91	63.8	3.0	31.1	16.9	4.8
4.5	0.52	3.7	0.00	4.1	0.1	0.55	5.19	4.65	83.7	4.0	22.5	9.2	2.5
4.7	1.99	10.4	0.28	7.2	0.6	1.18	11.24	5.55	72.1	3.7	24.3	11.7	5.5
6.8	0.01	0.0	0.23	10.0	0.3	2.27	17.08	7.90	55.4	6.0	57.2	7.3	6.3
4.5	0.75	6.1	0.61	4.9	1.5	0.91	13.04	4.74	72.4	4.4	40.3	13.1	3.6
9.4	0.00	0.0	0.00	0.0	-0.7	-14.35	-30.64	0.71	1,400.0	6.3	354.9	23.3	0.0
2.7	1.95	12.0	0.94	3.4	0.2	0.49	5.41	8.99	87.0	6.6	44.6	0.5	3.0
2.5	2.48	18.6	0.22	5.4	0.2	0.99	10.69	3.67	61.5	5.8	51.5	7.5	5.3
6.1	1.40	4.6	-0.80	5.3	0.1	0.73	3.99	5.75	88.3	2.3	20.7	17.6	4.7
2.4	1.61	13.3	0.27	6.1	0.8	0.95	10.26	4.06	68.4	3.6	30.5	13.8	5.9
5.3	0.42	4.0	0.42	6.7	0.1	1.02	12.87	6.14	65.6	3.8	57.4	17.4	1.8
7.7	0.00	0.0	0.09	5.0	0.4	1.20	15.51	4.80	70.5	4.8	106.8	22.1	3.6
5.6	0.41	3.2	-0.07	9.9	1.2	1.63	16.33	5.11	51.7	1.4	14.8	25.3	7.2
4.5	2.30	9.8	-0.50	4.9	0.2	0.83	7.04	4.03	82.0	3.3	30.5	15.5	3.1
7.1	0.28	1.8	-0.08	2.7	0.1	0.32	3.72	3.41	86.0	4.6	34.9	10.5	4.0
8.8	0.12	0.6	-0.15	4.9	0.3	1.04	10.16	4.36	69.2	5.6	48.6	7.9	4.7
6.2	0.51	2.5	-0.07	4.7	0.2	0.75	6.94	4.84	77.4	3.0	18.5	14.3	3.3
7.5	0.86	4.1	-0.01	8.7	0.6	2.27	19.98	4.38	47.3	6.3	58.7	5.6	6.0
6.8	0.00	0.0	0.03	8.6	4.4	1.31	15.04	4.96	57.0	4.6	31.6	9.0	6.0
5.9	3.24	14.0	0.00	5.8	0.2	1.21	10.05	4.48	75.5	5.9	61.8	9.2	6.4
7.9	0.36	1.4	0.14	6.4	1.3	1.32	13.51	3.80	52.3	3.0	8.1	13.5	6.1
7.9	0.24	1.4	0.19	6.3	1.9	1.20	12.43	4.30	62.1	2.5	22.5	17.4	5.7
8.5	0.98	2.2	0.25	3.5	0.0	0.38	3.33	4.87	94.1	6.6	80.5	6.1	5.5
4.5	1.29	7.5	0.00	8.9	2.5	3.04	29.27	4.79	45.9	4.5	50.9	15.1	6.8

Name	City	State	Weiss Safety Rating	2003 Weiss Safety Rating	2002 Weiss Safety Rating	Total Assets ($Mil)	One Year Asset Growth	Asset Mix (As a % of Total Assets)				Capital- ization Index	Leverage Ratio	Risk-based Capital Ratio
								Comm- ercial Loans	Cons- umer Loans	Home Mort- gages	Secur- ities			
BANK OF MAYSVILLE	MAYSVILLE	KY	A	A	A	110.2	-3.41	1.1	3.5	34.6	32.7	10.0	14.1	26.9
BANK OF MCCREARY COUNTY	WHITLEY CITY	KY	B-	B-	B-	117.8	6.07	3.7	17.7	33.4	19.8	8.6	10.1	16.8
▲ BANK OF MCCRORY	MC CRORY	AR	B+	B	B	66.4	-1.60	4.7	6.0	6.7	40.9	10.0	11.7	21.8
BANK OF MCKENNEY	MC KENNEY	VA	A-	A-	A-	129.0	15.28	6.0	3.2	20.7	13.3	10.0	11.8	16.6
BANK OF MCLOUTH	MC LOUTH	KS	B	B	B+	31.5	1.34	9.2	10.1	10.1	40.1	10.0	17.4	25.8
BANK OF MEAD	MEAD	NE	D	D	D	18.4	-2.52	6.7	6.7	19.8	33.2	6.4	8.4	15.6
▲ BANK OF MILAN	MILAN	TN	E+	E-	E-	48.1	-4.71	2.9	4.0	21.7	40.7	7.5	9.3	17.1
▼ BANK OF MILLBROOK	MILLBROOK	NY	A	A+	A+	132.7	8.96	4.1	8.0	25.9	33.0	10.0	12.9	26.9
BANK OF MILTON	MILTON	WI	C+	C+	C-	42.6	-1.03	12.1	8.2	23.8	11.3	7.5	9.7	12.9
▲ BANK OF MINDEN	MINDENMINES	MO	B	B-	B-	26.8	-5.02	25.0	10.1	22.5	11.0	10.0	13.2	21.3
BANK OF MINGO	NAUGATUCK	WV	B+	B+	B	101.4	4.74	8.8	12.8	23.3	34.4	10.0	11.6	23.1
BANK OF MINTO	MINTO	ND	C+	C+	C+	19.5	0.43	20.0	3.4	0.5	29.4	10.0	11.6	26.6
BANK OF MISSOURI	PERRYVILLE	MO	C+	C	C	373.5	21.57	6.1	11.0	20.9	25.0	3.9	7.2	10.4
BANK OF MODESTO	MODESTO	IL	B-	B-	B-	21.6	1.00	8.1	9.3	9.7	18.2	10.0	13.8	18.5
BANK OF MONROE	UNION	WV	B+	B+	A-	93.9	3.07	6.0	7.0	18.8	44.8	8.6	10.1	20.7
BANK OF MONTGOMERY	MONTGOMERY	IL	B	B	B	37.5	5.51	13.4	3.9	18.0	28.9	10.0	11.9	18.8
BANK OF MONTGOMERY	MONTGOMERY	LA	C+	C	C	74.5	15.82	10.1	13.6	24.2	29.7	7.3	9.2	16.0
▲ BANK OF MONTGOMERY CTY	WELLSVILLE	MO	C	D-	E-	37.9	44.86	17.6	2.9	31.1	7.1	8.3	9.8	14.6
BANK OF MONTICELLO	MONTICELLO	GA	C+	C+	B-	83.4	17.02	24.2	15.7	24.1	12.8	6.0	8.1	13.3
BANK OF MONTICELLO	MONTICELLO	MO	B	B	B	65.5	3.76	5.9	7.5	15.5	27.6	10.0	11.5	15.1
▲ BANK OF MONTICELLO	MONTICELLO	WI	C	D+	D+	62.1	-0.50	9.3	5.5	14.2	12.0	7.8	10.2	13.2
▲ BANK OF MORTON	MORTON	MS	B+	B	B	46.1	0.81	2.9	12.1	24.4	34.5	10.0	13.0	21.3
▲ BANK OF MOUNDVILLE	MOUNDVILLE	AL	D+	D	D	75.9	0.30	10.1	7.9	6.9	53.0	5.8	7.8	15.8
BANK OF MOUNTAIN VIEW	MOUNTAIN VIEW	AR	A+	A+	A+	171.5	6.94	5.0	5.1	15.4	53.7	10.0	15.1	30.4
▲ BANK OF MT HOPE	MT HOPE	WV	B-	C+	C+	70.0	-0.93	8.4	20.1	21.5	25.0	7.5	9.3	16.5
▲ BANK OF NAPLES	NAPLES	FL	C-	C-	D-	87.6	45.54	14.0	3.9	24.7	5.0	4.9	7.4	11.0
BANK OF NASHVILLE	NASHVILLE	TN	B-	B-	C+	631.8	4.07	14.8	2.1	5.0	11.9	3.2	8.8	10.1
▲ BANK OF NAVASOTA NA	NAVASOTA	TX	B	B-	B	69.1	2.18	8.2	17.6	9.9	25.6	10.0	11.1	21.2
▼ BANK OF NEBRASKA	LA VISTA	NE	B+	A-	B+	101.5	2.69	14.1	2.1	9.6	14.4	7.3	10.3	12.8
BANK OF NEW ALBANY	NEW ALBANY	MS	A	A	A+	300.7	2.71	4.0	6.7	26.5	36.4	10.0	13.3	24.6
BANK OF NEW CAMBRIA	NEW CAMBRIA	MO	C+	C+	C	27.9	7.78	2.5	4.7	8.4	28.3	9.3	10.5	16.3
▲ BANK OF NEW CANAAN	NEW CANAAN	CT	D	D-	D	83.0	27.22	1.5	0.3	36.1	14.7	10.0	12.0	19.1
▼ BANK OF NEW CASTLE	NEW CASTLE	DE	C+	B-	B	14.8	0.52	0.0	0.0	0.0	99.7	10.0	96.3	96.6
BANK OF NEW GLARUS	NEW GLARUS	WI	C+	C+	B-	97.1	3.48	7.8	4.4	19.8	19.4	6.1	8.5	11.8
BANK OF NEW MADRID	NEW MADRID	MO	C+	C+	C+	74.7	-7.68	6.5	6.9	18.9	30.2	6.7	8.7	13.9
BANK OF NEW ORLEANS	METAIRIE	LA	B	B	B	243.6	6.25	0.2	2.2	20.5	62.9	10.0	11.0	32.5
BANK OF NEW YORK	NEW YORK	NY	B-	B-	B	94,536.4	-2.02	2.8	0.9	2.1	23.2	3.7	5.7	11.4
▼ BANK OF NEW	NEWARK	DE	B	B	B	577.5	41.13	0.0	25.9	0.9	0.0	7.1	9.1	15.7
BANK OF NEWINGTON	NEWINGTON	GA	B-	B-	B-	66.3	11.18	9.9	5.2	21.5	2.3	7.5	9.4	13.5
▲ BANK OF NEWPORT	NEWPORT	RI	B-	C+	B-	922.8	4.07	2.1	0.3	33.1	42.4	6.8	8.9	15.2
▲ BANK OF NICHOLS HILLS	OKLAHOMA CITY	OK	B	B-	B-	92.4	16.43	22.0	2.6	11.4	4.2	6.4	8.7	12.0
BANK OF NORTH CAROLINA	THOMASVILLE	NC	C+	C+	C+	457.6	38.17	24.2	4.7	14.9	7.2	3.7	8.3	10.4
BANK OF NORTH GEORGIA	ALPHARETTA	GA	B-	B-	B-	1,798.2	11.50	13.2	0.9	6.7	10.7	3.4	9.7	10.2
▼ BANK OF NORTHERN MI	PETOSKEY	MI	C-	C	C-	149.5	15.28	15.3	1.2	15.1	7.3	3.5	8.3	10.2
BANK OF NORTHUMBERLAND	HEATHSVILLE	VA	C+	C+	C	199.7	5.50	8.9	7.4	40.1	17.7	4.2	6.2	13.9
BANK OF NV	LAS VEGAS	NV	C-	D+	D+	208.6	27.74	15.4	0.6	0.4	9.4	5.3	8.5	11.2
BANK OF O'FALLON	O'FALLON	IL	A	A	A+	227.1	-0.82	2.5	3.3	30.0	44.4	10.0	23.2	54.0
BANK OF OAK RIDGE	OAK RIDGE	LA	B-	B-	B-	35.5	0.12	1.0	4.2	0.0	82.9	9.4	10.6	40.0
▲ BANK OF OAK RIDGE	OAK RIDGE	NC	D+	D-	D	113.2	34.29	13.8	3.1	23.0	27.2	10.0	13.0	19.5
BANK OF OAKFIELD	OAKFIELD	WI	C-	D+	D	52.1	-1.51	7.0	6.7	19.6	16.5	6.8	8.8	13.3
BANK OF OCEAN CITY	OCEAN CITY	MD	A	A	A	108.3	10.34	11.9	2.2	10.5	9.3	10.0	13.6	17.6
BANK OF ODESSA	ODESSA	MO	A	A	A	287.1	-2.64	5.8	3.4	14.3	50.6	10.0	18.4	41.8
BANK OF OHIO CTY	DUNDEE	KY	A-	B+	B+	65.3	-1.42	6.6	5.5	20.2	28.2	10.0	12.5	21.2
BANK OF OKLAHOMA NA	TULSA	OK	B-	B-	B-	11,414.7	-0.99	20.4	2.9	7.2	40.5	5.0	7.0	11.6
BANK OF OKOLONA	OKOLONA	MS	D	D+	C	55.8	-7.61	8.6	19.0	18.6	18.9	10.0	15.1	25.4
BANK OF OLD MONROE	OLD MONROE	MO	A-	A-	B+	146.9	9.90	6.4	2.4	14.3	36.7	9.6	10.7	20.2
▲ BANK OF ONTARIO	ONTARIO	WI	D	D-	E	25.8	5.82	6.6	10.0	43.2	8.0	6.4	8.5	13.2
BANK OF ORANGE COUNTY	ORANGE	CA	B+	B	B-	449.9	2.94	13.7	0.8	3.3	1.5	7.2	9.4	12.6
▲ BANK OF ORCHARD	ORCHARD	NE	B-	C+	C+	20.3	1.76	3.2	2.6	0.6	56.8	10.0	11.7	28.2
BANK OF ORRICK	ORRICK	MO	C+	C+	C-	31.2	-1.51	7.3	4.5	20.1	30.3	10.0	13.0	23.8
BANK OF OTTERVILLE	OTTERVILLE	MO	D-	D-	D-	18.1	-2.36	11.9	6.4	17.8	1.7	5.5	7.5	12.5
BANK OF PALATINE	PALATINE	IL	C	C-	B-	62.6	-2.23	2.8	2.0	19.1	26.4	7.4	9.2	22.6
▲ BANK OF PALMER	PALMER	KS	D-	D-	D-	24.0	6.47	1.6	6.1	12.5	36.3	5.3	7.3	13.1
BANK OF PARAGOULD	PARAGOULD	AR	B-	B-	C	96.6	20.32	5.4	7.5	44.5	4.7	9.3	10.6	15.6

Asset Quality Index	Non-Performing Loans as a % of Total Loans	Non-Performing Loans as a % of Capital	Net Charge-offs Avg Loans	Profitability Index	Net Income ($Mil)	Return on Assets (R.O.A.)	Return on Equity (R.O.E.)	Net Interest Spread	Overhead Efficiency Ratio	Liquidity Index	Liquidity Ratio	Hot Money Ratio	Stability Index
8.3	0.37	1.3	0.27	6.6	0.7	1.22	7.49	4.43	64.0	3.1	26.8	15.1	8.6
4.2	0.69	4.4	0.11	9.8	1.3	2.20	21.40	4.83	55.9	4.0	33.0	12.9	7.0
6.8	0.95	4.0	0.45	8.0	0.5	1.35	12.10	3.82	48.2	2.9	16.2	14.8	5.4
8.6	0.26	1.5	-0.01	5.8	0.6	0.93	7.99	4.67	73.0	4.3	36.3	12.3	7.0
8.1	0.28	0.8	0.11	5.1	0.2	1.03	5.74	4.11	65.7	5.9	48.4	5.7	6.3
7.6	0.02	0.1	0.29	5.7	0.1	0.92	11.35	3.80	61.8	4.9	63.9	12.8	2.1
5.0	0.90	4.2	-1.98	2.9	0.3	1.30	13.82	3.76	75.1	3.0	21.8	14.7	0.2
8.7	0.09	0.3	-0.03	7.0	0.6	0.98	7.40	4.18	62.6	5.6	54.9	10.9	8.5
6.3	0.46	3.2	-0.10	7.5	0.2	1.01	10.46	5.26	69.8	4.3	37.7	12.6	4.3
5.8	1.41	7.0	0.99	5.9	0.2	1.11	8.65	4.52	55.0	5.1	67.1	14.1	5.8
5.2	1.51	6.6	1.16	6.7	0.7	1.31	11.30	5.43	59.0	4.4	68.8	19.0	7.0
6.3	2.06	7.7	-0.24	6.7	0.2	1.43	12.65	3.79	61.1	7.3	136.9	10.2	4.8
7.6	0.21	2.0	0.05	7.3	2.3	1.30	19.89	3.94	52.3	1.9	12.1	19.2	3.7
6.8	0.74	3.9	-0.03	8.0	0.2	1.56	11.67	4.43	51.4	4.7	28.9	5.5	5.5
8.5	0.31	1.4	0.01	5.6	0.5	1.03	10.08	3.81	59.5	2.6	40.2	25.5	6.1
7.0	0.97	3.8	-0.01	6.2	0.2	1.09	8.77	4.58	64.7	5.5	89.2	15.1	5.6
7.3	0.19	1.3	0.35	7.6	0.7	1.83	22.20	5.17	66.3	1.7	17.5	21.7	3.8
4.3	1.12	7.0	-0.01	5.9	0.2	1.10	10.22	5.57	59.4	5.7	49.0	7.4	3.7
5.2	0.28	2.2	0.09	5.9	0.4	0.98	11.71	4.23	63.6	4.8	105.7	21.5	4.1
6.4	1.06	5.9	0.09	6.1	0.4	1.33	11.84	3.79	54.2	3.0	48.0	24.4	5.4
4.1	0.57	3.5	0.15	4.5	0.2	0.75	6.74	4.38	72.6	4.9	45.1	11.3	5.3
6.8	1.17	4.6	0.01	8.0	0.5	1.93	14.56	5.19	65.4	3.0	44.5	22.7	7.3
4.0	2.20	11.0	0.37	3.5	0.3	0.73	9.99	3.51	75.4	1.0	17.5	32.2	2.1
8.9	0.71	1.9	0.01	9.6	2.4	2.85	18.48	4.96	35.9	1.3	13.2	26.7	9.2
7.5	0.00	0.0	0.00	7.0	0.4	1.14	12.44	4.42	63.4	3.9	24.1	10.3	4.5
5.6	0.38	3.6	0.29	3.6	0.4	1.02	13.61	3.80	64.0	3.9	38.6	14.8	0.6
5.8	0.22	0.9	0.32	4.3	2.2	0.70	4.00	3.95	65.0	1.0	18.7	32.5	7.7
4.9	1.59	6.2	0.61	7.3	0.5	1.37	12.09	4.72	58.0	5.3	79.6	14.6	5.4
7.2	0.15	1.1	-0.02	7.7	0.8	1.54	14.66	5.06	70.9	3.5	30.6	14.5	6.6
7.0	0.86	3.5	0.22	9.6	2.6	1.77	13.60	4.04	42.2	1.7	13.7	20.8	9.1
8.6	0.03	0.1	0.03	3.5	0.1	0.40	3.74	3.70	84.9	7.0	82.9	5.5	4.6
9.6	0.00	0.0	0.00	0.1	-0.2	-0.37	-3.09	4.05	104.5	4.8	22.9	4.1	0.0
10.0	0.00	0.0	0.00	2.4	0.0	0.14	0.14	1.13	77.2	5.0	2,901.4	100.0	0.0
4.3	1.20	9.5	0.27	3.9	0.3	0.61	7.26	3.96	79.6	3.9	22.6	10.4	4.3
4.9	1.01	7.0	0.16	5.5	0.5	1.30	15.56	4.72	72.5	1.6	11.3	21.2	4.8
9.4	0.21	0.6	-0.02	4.2	0.7	0.59	5.32	2.60	68.9	3.6	25.5	12.1	6.1
5.8	0.88	3.8	0.24	7.0	598.9	1.32	14.45	1.67	68.4	4.9	92.8	21.8	7.8
5.5	0.70	2.4	1.80	9.8	6.9	2.83	32.22	3.93	63.3	7.0	227.1	17.7	6.4
5.8	0.53	4.2	-0.02	8.4	0.6	1.89	20.32	4.91	48.0	1.0	25.7	46.2	4.3
8.8	0.29	1.5	0.00	4.2	3.7	0.81	8.48	3.36	74.4	4.5	12.3	5.3	6.0
7.2	0.34	2.8	-0.51	6.5	0.5	1.11	13.23	4.60	63.2	3.2	38.0	18.3	5.2
5.1	0.64	5.5	0.09	5.0	1.7	0.81	9.24	3.97	67.9	1.1	18.4	31.8	4.7
4.8	0.65	5.3	0.00	8.1	10.7	1.24	13.01	3.67	47.8	4.6	20.8	6.5	7.4
6.3	0.12	1.2	0.12	3.9	0.5	0.63	7.89	3.03	67.1	0.5	5.6	55.6	1.3
4.3	1.12	11.1	-0.03	9.2	1.6	1.58	25.47	4.37	50.5	4.1	33.6	12.5	4.9
3.6	1.48	10.1	0.26	6.8	1.3	1.28	13.00	5.44	57.4	4.5	56.8	16.9	1.7
9.5	0.30	0.6	-0.01	6.1	1.2	1.07	4.66	2.81	42.5	5.4	161.4	27.8	8.7
9.7	0.13	0.1	-0.42	6.0	0.2	1.26	11.21	3.22	38.8	3.5	88.9	36.0	4.7
7.5	1.28	6.3	0.19	1.5	0.1	0.21	1.86	3.51	85.4	1.4	11.7	25.7	1.0
3.0	1.80	13.0	-0.01	6.8	0.3	1.24	14.03	4.50	56.3	4.0	36.3	13.7	3.8
7.3	0.02	0.1	0.00	9.4	0.8	1.51	10.62	5.05	53.7	4.0	16.3	9.0	8.9
6.8	2.43	5.8	0.03	10.0	3.1	2.11	11.62	3.70	22.8	8.6	238.5	9.1	8.9
7.4	1.30	6.2	0.06	9.1	0.8	2.48	19.99	4.79	51.6	5.4	50.0	9.7	7.4
6.5	0.79	5.2	0.28	7.2	69.2	1.23	18.19	2.71	51.5	1.3	18.1	30.0	5.2
0.6	6.72	29.6	0.44	9.8	0.6	2.19	14.02	5.05	47.7	1.4	11.8	24.7	7.8
6.5	1.17	4.7	0.17	6.4	0.8	1.14	10.65	3.61	55.3	6.5	66.7	7.7	6.8
5.3	0.37	3.3	-0.01	6.9	0.2	1.40	16.65	5.33	70.5	2.4	27.2	18.7	2.3
4.5	0.61	2.7	0.00	6.8	0.3	0.15	1.02	5.83	71.3	8.6	174.2	6.8	8.3
9.0	0.15	0.3	-0.37	7.5	0.2	1.52	13.08	3.44	42.3	4.2	39.3	11.3	4.7
5.8	3.29	13.1	-0.04	3.2	0.1	0.67	5.22	4.24	76.4	6.2	61.2	7.0	5.2
4.5	1.10	8.6	0.13	8.3	0.1	0.96	12.79	4.78	50.2	8.0	241.6	12.4	1.3
10.0	0.05	0.2	-0.02	3.0	0.2	0.48	5.22	3.55	85.9	5.2	93.8	17.0	4.4
8.4	0.00	0.0	0.00	3.2	0.1	0.51	6.97	3.26	80.1	3.9	17.3	9.4	1.2
5.6	0.56	4.3	0.12	5.7	0.4	0.94	8.78	4.12	60.8	1.3	14.9	27.5	5.2

Name	City	State	Weiss Safety Rating	2003 Weiss Safety Rating	2002 Weiss Safety Rating	Total Assets ($Mil)	One Year Asset Growth	Asset Mix (As a % of Total Assets) Commercial Loans	Consumer Loans	Home Mortgages	Securities	Capitalization Index	Leverage Ratio	Risk-based Capital Ratio
BANK OF PARSONS	PARSONS	KS	B-	B-	B-	10.2	3.91	1.5	9.3	44.0	11.9	4.9	6.9	15.3
BANK OF PAXTON	PAXTON	NE	C+	C+	C+	21.3	-1.93	10.8	8.3	3.4	19.4	10.0	12.3	17.4
BANK OF PENSACOLA	PENSACOLA	FL	B-	B-	B	793.6	9.61	12.3	1.7	10.4	10.2	3.6	8.1	10.3
BANK OF PERRY	PERRY	GA	C+	C+	C+	114.5	8.88	13.8	3.0	16.8	16.1	3.5	7.3	10.2
BANK OF PERRY CTY	LOBELVILLE	TN	A-	A-	A-	78.5	-3.96	5.8	21.2	29.2	15.2	10.0	16.8	26.3
▼ BANK OF PINE HILL	PINE HILL	AL	C-	C	C	24.7	-3.59	6.8	5.4	15.7	53.0	10.0	11.9	27.7
▼ BANK OF POCAHONTAS	POCAHONTAS	AR	D+	D+	C	118.6	-10.87	16.9	16.6	7.0	33.2	6.8	8.9	16.6
BANK OF PONTIAC	PONTIAC	IL	A-	A-	A-	229.6	2.22	7.9	6.9	28.4	27.1	10.0	13.3	24.5
▲ BANK OF POWHATAN NA	POWHATAN	VA	C	C+	C	61.7	21.89	17.4	4.0	9.9	14.1	10.0	11.3	15.9
BANK OF POYNETTE	POYNETTE	WI	C+	C+	C+	67.5	-1.11	7.6	3.2	24.8	6.8	5.9	7.9	13.0
BANK OF PRAGUE	PRAGUE	NE	C+	C+	C+	14.8	7.69	3.2	5.3	6.5	37.1	10.0	15.6	27.3
▲ BANK OF PRAIRIE DU SAC	PRAIRIE DU SAC	WI	A+	A	A	193.8	4.18	6.5	3.2	11.9	30.9	10.0	15.7	22.6
▲ BANK OF PRESCOTT	PRESCOTT	AR	A-	B+	B+	69.0	2.59	9.9	7.1	17.4	43.2	10.0	12.0	24.9
▲ BANK OF PROTECTION	PROTECTION	KS	C+	C	C-	19.5	1.98	10.1	5.1	6.8	20.1	10.0	12.8	17.0
BANK OF PUTNAM CTY	COOKEVILLE	TN	B	B	B	243.9	7.31	2.3	7.1	23.6	42.7	5.6	7.6	18.9
BANK OF QUAPAW	QUAPAW	OK	B-	B-	B-	8.4	0.76	2.7	9.4	16.7	35.4	9.3	10.6	29.8
▲ BANK OF QUINCY	QUINCY	IL	C	C-	D+	32.6	24.93	8.8	4.5	27.8	1.5	9.4	11.6	14.5
▲ BANK OF RANTOUL	RANTOUL	IL	A	A-	A-	151.5	0.51	17.0	2.8	9.4	33.9	8.0	9.6	16.2
▲ BANK OF RICHMOND NA	RICHMOND	VA	C	C-	D	116.5	14.31	5.9	2.8	4.1	11.6	10.0	12.3	16.3
▲ BANK OF RICHMONDVILLE	RICHMONDVILLE	NY	B-	C+	C+	98.4	1.22	6.7	3.9	30.6	23.1	6.5	8.5	16.3
▲ BANK OF RIDGEWAY	RIDGEWAY	SC	B	B-	B	89.7	-1.62	5.8	8.4	16.3	27.0	6.6	8.6	15.2
BANK OF RINGGOLD	RINGGOLD	LA	B-	B	B+	38.6	2.65	1.8	7.2	10.5	49.8	10.0	20.3	77.5
▼ BANK OF RIO VISTA	RIO VISTA	CA	C+	B	C+	153.6	7.64	10.1	1.1	1.0	42.0	10.0	12.0	18.2
BANK OF RIPLEY	RIPLEY	TN	A-	A-	A-	162.5	2.84	1.2	9.3	18.9	46.1	10.0	14.4	27.9
▲ BANK OF RISON	RISON	AR	B+	B	B	27.7	1.77	11.9	10.6	11.6	29.4	10.0	15.2	30.6
BANK OF ROGERS	ROGERS	AR	C	C	C	119.1	11.55	13.4	7.6	19.3	9.8	3.0	7.8	10.0
BANK OF ROMNEY	ROMNEY	WV	B+	B+	A-	180.2	2.09	3.1	14.0	40.5	19.8	10.0	11.2	17.3
BANK OF ROTHVILLE	ROTHVILLE	MO	C-	D+	D+	41.6	-4.74	4.1	7.2	9.6	35.7	7.2	9.1	17.1
BANK OF SACRAMENTO	SACRAMENTO	CA	C+	C+	C	195.2	22.75	19.0	1.0	0.8	22.1	5.2	8.9	11.2
▲ BANK OF SALEM	SALEM	AR	C	C-	C+	103.7	4.32	7.9	9.7	22.3	13.1	7.0	9.0	13.6
▲ BANK OF SALEM	SALEM	MO	B+	B	B	79.4	-2.18	5.0	7.2	29.0	35.1	8.9	10.3	20.0
▲ BANK OF SALEM	SALEM	OR	A+	A	A	133.5	23.99	3.9	0.5	2.2	12.9	10.0	16.8	20.1
BANK OF SAN JACINTO CTY	COLDSPRING	TX	B	B-	C+	28.3	-0.45	5.9	16.0	34.6	17.4	10.0	12.5	22.2
BANK OF SHOREWOOD	SHOREWOOD	IL	C-	C-	C-	72.6	34.87	8.1	2.4	16.0	20.7	5.3	8.0	11.2
▲ BANK OF SMITHTOWN	SMITHTOWN	NY	B+	B	C+	633.8	25.35	6.4	0.6	8.2	8.8	5.6	8.4	11.5
▲ BANK OF SOPERTON	SOPERTON	GA	C+	C	B-	39.4	-16.10	5.4	5.3	17.1	36.2	9.2	10.4	17.9
BANK OF SOUTH CAROLINA	CHARLESTON	SC	A-	A-	A	194.4	6.20	23.1	3.7	7.8	13.4	8.4	10.3	13.7
▲ BANK OF SOUTHERN CT	NEW HAVEN	CT	C-	D	D	69.4	46.30	23.3	1.3	8.1	16.4	10.0	15.5	20.1
BANK OF SOUTHERN	LA PLATA	MD	A-	A-	A	241.6	2.29	14.0	2.7	5.5	40.2	7.5	9.3	24.8
BANK OF SOUTHSIDE VIRGINIA	CARSON	VA	B	A-	A	421.4	0.42	5.2	11.7	10.0	36.7	9.6	10.7	15.7
▲ BANK OF SPRING VALLEY	SPRING VALLEY	WI	A	A-	A-	54.4	0.72	6.2	5.0	8.2	42.6	10.0	17.2	32.2
▲ BANK OF SPRINGFIELD	SPRINGFIELD	IL	C+	C-	D+	371.3	12.76	17.3	3.8	17.2	1.6	4.0	8.2	10.5
BANK OF ST CROIX	CHRISTIANSTED	VI	C+	C+	B-	88.6	41.72	3.2	0.4	24.5	44.1	5.4	7.4	17.4
BANK OF ST EDWARD	ST EDWARD	NE	A-	A-	A-	34.1	-1.60	3.4	1.3	2.9	41.9	10.0	21.4	26.3
BANK OF ST ELIZABETH	ST ELIZABETH	MO	B+	B+	B	45.5	0.35	5.1	7.5	30.8	13.7	10.0	13.2	22.4
BANK OF ST FRANCISVILLE	ST FRANCISVILLE	LA	C+	C+	C+	49.7	-3.27	10.0	13.4	22.3	21.6	6.5	8.5	14.4
▼ BANK OF ST PETERSBURG	ST PETERSBURG	FL	C-	B	B	125.9	59.41	14.2	1.1	15.2	7.4	10.0	18.4	22.7
▲ BANK OF ST. AUGUSTINE	ST AUGUSTINE	FL	C+	C	C	78.6	27.46	6.9	1.8	32.9	10.7	7.2	9.1	13.9
BANK OF STANLY	ALBEMARLE	NC	C+	C+	B-	242.8	4.75	9.8	4.4	23.0	8.4	5.5	8.4	11.4
▲ BANK OF STAPLETON	STAPLETON	NE	D	D-	D-	15.0	1.21	13.3	7.7	8.8	13.0	7.2	9.2	14.1
BANK OF STAR CITY	STAR CITY	AR	B-	B-	B-	88.4	1.32	17.4	7.6	15.8	25.3	10.0	11.1	16.7
▲ BANK OF STAR VALLEY	AFTON	WY	C+	C-	C	61.0	-4.50	16.3	14.2	5.6	8.6	7.7	9.5	13.9
▲ BANK OF STEINAUER	STEINAUER	NE	D	D	D+	8.4	5.83	5.4	9.3	22.9	36.5	7.3	9.2	16.7
▼ BANK OF STOCKTON	STOCKTON	CA	B	B+	A-	1,700.8	22.43	10.6	18.3	2.7	20.7	4.8	6.8	11.0
BANK OF STRONGHURST	STRONGHURST	IL	B-	B-	B	61.7	-1.55	1.0	2.2	8.6	59.8	10.0	17.9	47.4
▲ BANK OF SULLIVAN	SULLIVAN	MO	B	B-	B-	252.8	6.39	7.2	4.3	35.3	11.2	6.7	8.7	12.7
BANK OF SUN PRAIRIE	SUN PRAIRIE	WI	A	A-	A-	223.3	7.34	20.8	5.6	7.0	0.1	10.0	17.8	21.7
BANK OF SUNSET & TRUST	SUNSET	LA	A-	A-	B+	64.7	2.81	6.4	4.3	14.4	28.4	10.0	15.1	24.3
BANK OF TALLAHASSEE	TALLAHASSEE	FL	D	D	D	41.2	71.21	15.6	2.8	3.7	21.6	10.0	19.4	26.9
BANK OF TALMAGE	TALMAGE	NE	D+	D+	D+	4.1	7.61	3.9	0.9	0.0	26.1	10.0	46.6	80.4
BANK OF TAMPA	TAMPA	FL	C	C	C	696.0	18.49	24.6	4.6	1.9	24.7	2.9	6.9	9.9
BANK OF TAZEWELL CTY	TAZEWELL	VA	B+	B+	B+	307.7	0.88	3.3	4.6	16.0	39.7	7.1	9.0	14.1
BANK OF TENNESSEE	KINGSPORT	TN	B-	B-	C+	440.1	16.70	12.0	2.6	22.1	10.7	5.7	8.9	11.5
▼ BANK OF TERRELL	DAWSON	GA	D+	C-	D+	118.1	0.65	6.2	4.6	12.9	22.6	6.0	8.0	12.5

Asset Quality Index	Non-Performing Loans as a % of Total Loans	Non-Performing Loans as a % of Capital	Net Charge-offs Avg Loans	Profitability Index	Net Income ($Mil)	Return on Assets (R.O.A.)	Return on Equity (R.O.E.)	Net Interest Spread	Overhead Efficiency Ratio	Liquidity Index	Liquidity Ratio	Hot Money Ratio	Stability Index
8.7	0.00	0.0	0.00	4.7	0.1	1.12	16.33	3.54	75.3	5.6	172.7	26.3	4.8
7.6	0.00	0.0	0.00	6.3	0.1	1.13	9.40	4.84	60.8	2.6	54.1	28.0	4.8
4.0	0.78	7.4	0.34	9.5	6.0	1.55	19.35	4.29	36.8	1.0	11.0	30.1	7.1
7.3	0.00	0.0	0.05	6.8	0.9	1.61	21.53	4.53	66.1	1.5	12.5	23.6	4.8
5.5	1.43	5.8	0.23	10.0	1.1	2.66	15.66	5.01	37.2	3.2	49.6	21.2	7.2
6.4	1.62	4.7	0.33	1.1	0.0	-0.05	-0.38	3.25	85.6	4.3	43.3	11.8	4.9
3.0	2.21	10.3	1.44	1.1	-1.0	-1.63	-16.89	3.82	137.8	5.0	53.9	13.3	4.0
6.4	1.16	5.2	0.38	9.9	1.9	1.64	12.15	4.82	43.8	3.8	30.7	13.1	8.4
8.2	0.31	2.0	0.00	4.7	0.3	1.08	10.47	4.56	74.7	3.3	46.7	19.4	2.4
3.0	2.36	18.5	0.24	6.2	0.3	0.89	11.40	4.06	66.2	6.7	85.7	8.1	4.5
8.4	0.54	1.7	-0.03	5.1	0.1	0.80	5.10	4.27	74.2	5.7	52.2	5.9	4.9
7.8	0.61	2.3	0.00	9.8	1.8	1.86	11.66	4.46	43.3	5.0	32.9	6.7	9.8
7.4	0.81	3.0	-0.12	8.6	0.5	1.56	13.46	4.47	50.9	2.4	24.5	17.8	6.7
8.0	0.30	1.5	0.01	6.2	0.1	1.21	9.52	4.76	63.5	2.7	49.6	23.9	4.7
8.8	0.12	0.7	0.33	5.1	1.3	1.06	13.87	3.18	69.3	6.3	131.8	15.7	5.0
5.9	0.00	0.0	-1.00	4.7	0.1	1.28	7.56	4.42	66.9	3.0	59.7	25.2	5.1
6.2	0.00	0.0	0.00	3.7	0.1	0.78	7.82	4.02	78.7	3.7	64.5	21.8	5.4
8.4	0.07	0.3	0.12	9.9	1.7	2.24	20.46	4.78	42.6	4.7	28.2	6.8	7.9
7.4	0.00	0.0	0.05	2.9	0.3	0.52	4.02	3.78	73.6	8.0	151.8	8.6	7.0
4.8	2.13	13.6	0.09	5.8	0.5	1.02	12.35	4.15	60.0	6.8	53.1	0.7	4.7
3.7	0.90	3.0	0.24	4.5	0.3	0.74	4.83	4.09	71.3	4.8	42.9	11.6	7.2
9.1	1.62	1.7	-0.02	3.4	0.1	0.43	2.09	3.03	81.1	6.5	101.4	11.5	6.1
2.4	7.62	28.2	-0.28	6.3	0.9	1.19	10.09	4.68	62.2	3.7	32.6	14.0	6.9
8.0	1.26	3.8	0.08	5.1	0.8	0.94	6.52	4.25	71.9	2.5	35.8	22.8	7.3
7.5	1.12	3.2	0.00	6.4	0.2	1.46	9.64	4.04	61.6	4.3	90.4	22.7	6.9
5.2	0.84	7.9	0.09	8.8	0.8	1.36	17.76	4.92	53.1	1.7	25.0	24.7	4.3
4.5	2.12	13.2	0.34	8.3	1.1	1.23	11.29	4.78	57.0	3.6	22.7	11.6	6.9
5.8	0.89	4.6	0.02	4.1	0.3	1.20	13.23	3.42	73.6	5.3	46.3	9.6	3.2
5.3	0.41	3.0	0.00	5.4	1.0	1.04	11.78	4.37	62.6	2.2	21.8	18.8	4.3
2.7	2.06	16.0	0.11	6.1	0.6	1.08	11.72	4.42	57.3	1.9	20.8	20.0	4.9
8.5	0.26	1.4	0.04	5.7	0.4	1.02	9.90	4.14	62.9	2.6	23.7	17.0	5.3
7.3	0.06	0.3	0.02	10.0	1.5	2.40	13.78	5.92	27.4	5.6	75.8	13.9	9.5
4.4	3.13	16.3	0.17	9.0	0.4	2.71	22.95	6.10	62.0	5.9	41.4	4.6	6.8
7.6	0.45	3.8	0.10	4.2	0.3	0.74	9.95	4.42	76.4	4.1	38.7	14.3	2.4
7.4	0.10	0.9	0.06	9.9	5.0	1.64	19.57	4.51	48.6	5.9	68.9	11.7	6.3
6.2	0.84	3.7	0.17	5.0	0.3	1.42	13.67	4.67	71.3	3.5	50.3	19.0	4.3
8.2	0.18	1.0	0.14	6.2	0.9	0.98	9.47	4.13	72.4	8.8	270.1	8.3	6.7
8.4	0.15	0.6	0.12	2.0	0.2	0.62	4.71	4.81	86.3	4.6	40.9	12.4	0.5
8.7	0.15	0.8	-0.01	9.8	2.5	2.08	21.52	4.47	37.8	8.8	162.6	4.4	8.7
4.0	2.18	8.0	-0.08	10.0	4.8	2.27	18.82	5.43	44.5	7.5	110.3	7.6	8.9
8.1	1.49	3.7	0.10	8.8	0.9	3.16	18.14	3.86	48.1	8.0	112.3	3.4	8.9
5.0	0.43	4.0	0.06	7.0	1.9	1.07	13.17	3.76	58.9	3.8	24.1	10.8	3.7
5.4	2.35	15.1	0.00	7.1	0.8	1.80	26.37	3.90	48.4	4.5	17.6	5.6	4.6
8.3	0.45	1.0	-3.17	10.0	0.8	4.52	20.40	4.96	19.1	4.6	49.3	13.5	7.8
8.3	0.40	2.1	-0.02	8.9	0.6	2.62	19.38	4.33	44.4	5.5	41.7	7.2	7.2
5.4	0.52	3.6	0.22	8.7	0.4	1.35	16.96	5.98	62.8	2.6	11.5	15.4	4.2
7.4	0.06	0.2	0.00	1.2	-1.0	-1.78	-9.37	3.54	124.6	2.7	15.0	15.7	5.9
8.7	0.03	0.3	0.00	6.4	0.6	1.50	19.84	3.78	61.7	0.8	19.2	43.6	4.4
5.1	0.58	5.0	0.19	4.8	1.1	0.90	10.24	4.20	72.1	3.0	15.8	14.1	4.6
0.9	2.58	19.3	-0.09	7.1	0.1	1.56	17.45	5.96	58.5	1.4	6.5	23.8	2.1
3.8	2.83	15.8	0.13	4.9	0.5	1.03	9.54	4.52	63.2	1.8	16.5	20.4	5.5
3.9	1.77	11.3	0.13	6.0	0.4	1.22	13.03	4.35	58.9	5.7	80.4	13.0	3.6
8.4	0.00	0.0	0.13	7.1	0.1	1.53	17.42	4.12	62.0	4.8	7.9	2.1	1.8
4.8	0.74	4.0	0.71	6.9	11.1	1.32	11.96	4.61	66.4	5.3	88.6	18.3	9.0
9.6	0.49	0.8	0.04	3.7	0.2	0.72	4.13	3.17	68.8	7.1	160.9	13.8	7.0
6.3	0.26	2.2	0.11	5.5	0.9	0.74	7.95	4.46	71.6	1.5	11.5	23.2	5.4
7.9	0.26	1.1	0.10	8.8	1.6	1.40	8.08	4.65	54.3	6.2	60.3	8.7	8.0
7.8	1.06	3.7	-0.09	7.1	0.2	0.72	4.74	4.43	76.4	4.6	47.9	13.1	8.3
8.5	0.06	0.2	0.00	0.2	0.0	0.03	0.17	3.47	93.8	2.2	40.0	32.0	0.0
8.8	0.00	0.0	0.00	0.4	0.0	-0.68	-1.46	4.41	116.9	6.2	44.3	0.0	3.0
5.7	0.83	6.9	0.05	4.4	2.4	0.71	10.39	4.39	63.6	6.5	57.5	6.0	3.6
5.6	0.93	4.3	0.52	6.2	1.9	1.25	11.20	4.41	56.6	2.4	26.8	18.8	6.7
4.3	1.29	10.8	0.13	7.9	3.5	1.67	20.70	3.89	61.6	2.2	12.8	17.9	5.1
1.4	5.27	38.3	2.63	3.4	0.6	1.02	12.02	3.59	68.6	3.0	48.2	26.4	3.6

Name	City	State	Weiss Safety Rating	2003 Weiss Safety Rating	2002 Weiss Safety Rating	Total Assets ($Mil)	One Year Asset Growth	Asset Mix (As a % of Total Assets) Commercial Loans	Consumer Loans	Home Mortgages	Securities	Capitalization Index	Leverage Ratio	Risk-based Capital Ratio
▲ BANK OF TESCOTT	TESCOTT	KS	A-	B+	B	153.5	0.67	7.5	4.7	25.0	16.4	10.0	12.0	18.6
BANK OF TEXAS	AUSTIN	TX	C-	C	C+	69.2	11.10	11.3	4.8	7.0	5.3	6.8	8.8	12.5
BANK OF TEXAS	DEVINE	TX	C-	C	C-	45.9	5.69	11.1	8.6	7.8	8.2	10.0	11.4	15.5
BANK OF TEXAS NA	DALLAS	TX	B-	B-	B-	2,863.9	12.61	20.5	2.5	5.9	1.7	5.4	7.4	11.8
BANK OF THAYER	THAYER	MO	C	C	C-	75.8	-3.01	9.4	5.3	19.1	24.3	5.8	7.8	12.8
BANK OF THE BLUEGRASS &	LEXINGTON	KY	A-	A-	A-	177.0	22.08	1.8	1.7	36.2	12.9	7.3	9.2	14.1
BANK OF THE CAROLINAS	MOCKSVILLE	NC	C+	C+	C	243.8	15.61	13.6	1.4	22.5	12.2	7.0	9.2	12.5
▼ BANK OF THE CASCADES	BEND	OR	B-	B	B-	874.9	28.01	18.7	4.5	3.5	4.1	3.6	8.5	10.3
BANK OF THE	NORFOLK	VA	C	C-	C-	324.6	15.52	14.3	3.0	21.8	3.1	4.1	7.9	10.5
BANK OF THE EASTERN	CAMBRIDGE	MD	A-	A-	A-	165.2	10.37	7.0	5.1	24.3	20.1	10.0	11.2	17.0
BANK OF THE HILLS NA	KERRVILLE	TX	B-	B-	B-	235.3	26.16	6.6	4.0	15.2	25.1	5.1	7.1	13.1
BANK OF THE JAMES	LYNCHBURG	VA	B-	B-	C+	161.2	35.34	30.7	1.9	12.6	12.8	4.5	7.7	10.8
BANK OF THE LAKES NA	OWASSO	OK	C	C	C	127.1	3.49	32.9	8.4	11.7	1.1	3.3	8.2	10.1
BANK OF THE MOUNTAINS	W LIBERTY	KY	B-	B-	B-	57.9	16.77	12.5	15.1	34.8	7.9	8.2	9.8	16.0
BANK OF THE ORIENT	SAN FRANCISCO	CA	C+	C+	C	527.0	5.89	7.3	0.4	2.6	13.5	5.5	8.0	11.4
▲ BANK OF THE OZARKS	LITTLE ROCK	AR	A-	B+	B+	1,511.4	26.76	6.4	4.7	15.1	23.9	6.1	8.1	12.0
BANK OF THE PACIFIC	ABERDEEN	WA	B	B+	B+	423.5	50.85	20.6	2.3	7.6	11.5	4.2	7.9	10.6
BANK OF THE PANHANDLE	GUYMON	OK	C+	C	C	75.0	-1.72	6.5	6.6	5.2	42.4	8.5	10.0	19.3
▲ BANK OF THE PRAIRIE	OLATHE	KS	C-	D+	E-	70.4	46.55	17.4	3.7	20.2	7.2	4.1	7.7	10.6
BANK OF THE RIO GRANDE NA	LAS CRUCES	NM	B	B	B	79.5	10.20	27.0	7.6	9.6	9.4	6.9	9.8	12.4
▼ BANK OF THE ROCKIES NA	WHITE SULPHR SPR	MT	D+	C	C-	58.1	3.08	8.6	2.4	10.6	11.3	9.4	10.6	16.3
BANK OF THE SAN JUANS	DURANGO	CO	C	C	C-	86.8	16.51	6.1	2.2	8.2	7.7	3.2	7.8	10.1
BANK OF THE SIERRA	PORTERVILLE	CA	B-	C+	C	930.3	26.82	11.3	5.9	5.8	21.1	6.2	8.4	11.9
BANK OF THE SOUTH	PENSACOLA	FL	A-	A	A	58.7	1.06	0.0	1.5	5.1	74.3	10.0	19.9	99.2
▼ BANK OF THE SOUTH	CRYSTAL SPRINGS	MS	B+	A-	A-	35.0	6.13	16.4	6.9	13.9	20.4	10.0	13.3	21.4
▲ BANK OF THE SOUTH	MT JULIET	TN	C	C-	D	244.1	27.08	7.6	3.8	13.1	17.3	7.2	10.0	12.7
▲ BANK OF THE SOUTHWEST	TEMPE	AZ	D	D-	D+	84.3	9.01	33.2	12.8	5.4	7.2	7.6	9.9	13.0
▲ BANK OF THE SOUTHWEST	ROSWELL	NM	B+	B	C+	115.7	14.39	33.3	16.3	16.0	3.5	6.5	9.1	12.1
▲ BANK OF THE VALLEY	BELLWOOD	NE	C-	D+	D-	31.4	1.52	7.4	5.4	10.2	9.0	7.5	9.3	13.1
BANK OF THE WEST	SAN FRANCISCO	CA	B	B-	B-	30,812.9	10.79	8.7	23.5	11.7	13.4	7.6	9.6	13.0
BANK OF THE WEST	THOMAS	OK	C+	C+	C	102.6	9.23	19.2	3.9	15.9	1.5	4.1	8.2	10.6
▼ BANK OF THE WEST	EL PASO	TX	B+	A-	A-	575.4	11.01	16.3	5.0	2.6	39.3	6.2	8.2	13.7
▲ BANK OF THE WEST	IRVING	TX	B	B-	C+	218.6	1.16	10.8	2.0	3.7	23.7	7.5	9.4	13.9
BANK OF THE WICHITAS	SNYDER	OK	D+	C	B	55.2	7.08	3.3	16.0	12.8	26.9	5.2	7.2	11.2
BANK OF THOMAS CTY	THOMASVILLE	GA	B-	B-	C+	42.2	-13.84	11.5	7.5	17.3	25.7	8.5	10.0	15.7
▲ BANK OF TIOGA	TIOGA	ND	A-	B+	B	51.5	-1.02	6.9	4.1	3.1	48.6	10.0	14.9	30.3
▲ BANK OF TOKYO MITSUBISHI	NEW YORK	NY	A-	B	B-	5,780.9	-2.10	16.6	0.0	0.0	43.0	10.0	13.1	18.9
BANK OF TRAVELERS REST	TRAVELERS REST	SC	B-	B-	C+	295.6	7.86	12.2	6.5	11.4	21.7	6.4	8.4	12.4
▲ BANK OF TRUMANN	TRUMANN	AR	B	C	C	88.9	0.51	4.0	6.0	14.4	44.5	10.0	14.3	27.2
▲ BANK OF TUCSON	TUCSON	AZ	C+	C	C	156.4	7.47	15.8	0.7	1.7	9.5	4.8	7.6	10.9
▲ BANK OF TURTLE LAKE	TURTLE LAKE	ND	C+	C	C-	20.7	4.39	6.9	3.4	2.1	36.4	9.3	10.5	16.8
BANK OF TURTLE LAKE	TURTLE LAKE	WI	B-	B-	B-	59.6	-4.61	5.4	7.0	25.3	34.5	7.7	9.5	20.5
BANK OF TUSCALOOSA	TUSCALOOSA	AL	B-	B-	B	321.2	2.38	25.8	3.6	10.1	10.0	3.5	8.6	10.2
▲ BANK OF UNION	UNION CITY	OK	C+	C-	D+	100.0	2.51	20.8	10.2	16.7	15.3	5.4	7.8	11.3
▲ BANK OF UPSON	THOMASTON	GA	A-	B+	B+	246.8	-0.50	4.4	11.4	15.5	36.1	7.7	9.5	16.2
▲ BANK OF URBANA	URBANA	MO	A-	B+	B	122.9	1.41	4.0	4.2	30.2	30.2	10.0	12.3	20.7
▲ BANK OF UTAH	OGDEN	UT	B	B-	B	544.2	1.44	8.2	1.1	5.1	31.7	6.2	8.2	13.1
BANK OF UTICA	UTICA	NY	B	B	B	962.5	6.13	2.2	0.5	0.8	90.9	5.7	7.7	16.5
BANK OF VENICE	VENICE	FL	D	D	NR	33.7	68.42	5.5	10.2	26.5	7.0	10.0	18.4	22.9
▲ BANK OF VERDEN	VERDEN	OK	B-	C+	C+	20.5	6.87	5.0	12.1	15.8	28.2	10.0	14.1	24.7
BANK OF VERNON	VERNON	AL	C+	C+	C+	106.7	4.08	36.1	6.0	17.2	9.2	6.3	8.8	12.0
▼ BANK OF VERNON	VERNON	TX	C	C+	C+	16.8	-17.07	6.0	4.2	6.0	13.2	10.0	17.8	40.0
▲ BANK OF VERSAILLES	VERSAILLES	MO	A-	B+	B	267.4	8.35	2.1	2.9	56.5	12.0	8.6	10.1	19.3
BANK OF VICI	VICI	OK	C+	C+	C	23.4	3.99	12.1	18.1	9.9	24.2	10.0	12.0	19.0
BANK OF VIRGINIA	MIDLOTHIAN	VA	D	NR	NR	32.9	N/A	11.7	2.0	0.0	27.2	10.0	36.7	56.7
▲ BANK OF VISALIA	VISALIA	CA	B-	C	C	152.8	18.00	16.8	1.2	2.8	18.5	8.0	9.6	13.7
BANK OF WALDRON	WALDRON	AR	A	A	A	92.7	10.38	0.3	8.6	12.6	55.0	10.0	15.3	32.1
BANK OF WALKER CNTY	JASPER	AL	D	NR	NR	18.5	N/A	22.0	6.7	20.6	19.5	10.0	63.7	89.9
BANK OF WALNUT CREEK	WALNUT CREEK	CA	B	B+	A-	481.6	9.41	13.3	0.2	5.0	19.5	5.8	9.0	11.6
BANK OF WALNUT GROVE	WALNUT GROVE	MS	B+	B+	B+	36.8	-1.87	1.0	18.0	14.4	19.6	10.0	14.1	28.7
BANK OF WALTERBORO	WALTERBORO	SC	C-	D+	D+	129.4	6.46	22.0	7.9	6.0	19.1	7.3	9.2	14.3
▲ BANK OF WARRENSBURG	WARRENSBURG	IL	C	C	C-	8.5	-6.34	12.9	9.1	43.0	16.2	10.0	15.5	24.8
BANK OF WASHINGTON	WASHINGTON	MO	A	A	A	366.7	11.25	20.6	2.7	20.9	10.2	10.0	19.2	23.9
▲ BANK OF WASHINGTON	EDMONDS	WA	B	C+	B	111.2	22.73	7.1	2.0	16.3	11.4	7.6	9.8	13.0

Asset Quality Index	Non-Performing Loans as a % of Total Loans	Non-Performing Loans as a % of Capital	Net Charge-offs Avg Loans	Profitability Index	Net Income ($Mil)	Return on Assets (R.O.A.)	Return on Equity (R.O.E.)	Net Interest Spread	Overhead Efficiency Ratio	Liquidity Index	Liquidity Ratio	Hot Money Ratio	Stability Index
5.3	1.39	7.7	0.23	6.5	0.9	1.13	9.42	3.79	52.5	4.6	64.8	17.6	7.1
8.2	0.00	0.0	-0.16	3.4	0.1	0.34	3.89	4.70	83.9	6.4	61.8	5.6	2.8
8.1	0.21	1.1	0.08	1.6	0.0	-0.06	-0.49	4.53	97.0	5.3	63.8	12.4	4.2
5.2	0.59	2.2	0.32	5.1	12.2	0.87	6.90	3.77	64.5	7.0	144.0	13.6	7.2
7.6	0.05	0.4	0.04	3.4	0.2	0.53	7.16	4.14	87.6	2.9	23.0	15.4	3.3
6.7	0.38	3.2	0.36	9.6	1.4	1.63	17.67	4.28	47.5	3.7	37.8	15.5	6.5
5.5	0.79	6.3	0.13	3.6	0.7	0.59	6.36	3.60	69.4	3.2	14.0	13.0	4.5
6.7	0.04	0.4	0.12	10.0	7.4	1.83	21.10	5.75	53.4	5.6	32.2	2.6	6.5
3.4	0.65	6.9	0.00	4.9	1.5	0.97	12.49	4.20	62.2	1.7	11.0	20.4	4.0
5.4	1.46	8.8	-0.07	5.6	0.9	1.10	10.00	3.42	56.3	2.8	38.2	21.7	6.9
8.6	0.02	0.1	0.02	8.9	1.7	1.49	21.32	4.15	50.7	7.1	81.8	6.1	4.0
5.6	0.66	6.1	0.06	5.9	0.8	1.01	13.34	4.39	67.1	5.0	35.7	8.4	4.9
4.9	0.35	3.4	-0.03	5.5	0.5	0.87	10.22	4.37	64.6	2.6	35.7	21.7	4.8
4.3	1.17	8.0	0.12	4.6	0.2	0.57	5.72	5.22	78.7	5.3	58.8	11.6	4.5
5.5	0.45	4.0	0.30	4.0	1.6	0.62	7.97	3.74	76.5	2.0	25.2	20.5	4.1
7.8	0.24	1.9	0.10	10.0	13.8	1.92	23.61	4.79	42.6	0.9	10.9	33.2	7.5
7.5	0.07	0.5	0.01	9.5	3.3	1.70	17.28	5.36	57.3	2.6	22.5	16.9	6.2
4.7	3.47	15.8	0.22	4.2	0.4	1.11	11.29	4.19	64.3	2.6	26.1	17.4	4.1
7.8	0.09	0.8	0.01	4.7	0.3	0.89	11.43	4.24	60.5	2.3	32.1	22.1	3.4
7.8	0.19	1.2	0.04	9.2	0.5	1.40	14.36	5.94	65.0	3.9	34.4	13.8	5.8
1.5	5.03	33.0	0.05	6.2	0.3	0.95	8.69	6.02	65.2	3.5	24.3	12.7	5.9
7.4	0.11	1.1	0.01	5.8	0.4	0.96	12.72	4.80	68.7	5.6	41.1	6.3	3.7
4.5	0.83	5.9	0.23	9.3	6.6	1.54	17.07	5.77	54.9	2.3	24.6	18.7	5.4
10.0	0.00	0.0	0.00	7.0	0.3	0.96	4.88	4.22	65.7	6.8	57.5	2.0	8.4
8.3	0.00	0.0	0.32	6.2	0.2	0.85	6.16	4.17	79.6	4.6	83.3	18.5	7.9
8.0	0.21	1.5	0.12	2.7	0.6	0.55	5.44	3.74	83.4	3.2	55.7	28.4	1.5
4.5	0.68	5.2	0.05	1.0	0.0	0.10	1.15	3.59	93.4	2.8	27.3	17.0	3.8
7.0	0.11	0.9	0.10	10.0	1.5	2.61	30.13	7.05	63.0	4.7	32.8	9.1	6.1
5.6	0.24	1.8	-0.11	5.5	0.2	1.08	12.48	4.51	67.4	2.5	31.5	19.9	2.5
4.9	0.61	2.6	0.20	9.2	200.5	1.34	8.16	4.33	48.1	3.2	27.1	17.5	9.3
5.8	0.57	5.9	0.04	9.8	1.2	2.42	30.05	5.14	48.8	1.3	12.3	26.8	6.4
8.3	0.03	0.2	0.04	8.3	5.5	1.98	23.29	4.18	56.5	2.0	17.2	19.3	6.8
6.6	0.74	4.4	0.04	4.9	1.0	0.92	9.69	4.71	74.4	3.7	23.4	11.5	4.7
1.1	5.25	45.6	0.01	8.5	0.6	2.10	29.96	4.96	63.8	4.5	36.3	11.1	5.3
2.9	3.30	18.5	1.09	4.9	0.2	0.95	10.50	4.23	70.8	1.2	18.9	29.4	4.7
8.8	0.06	0.2	-0.01	7.3	0.6	2.31	15.28	4.00	43.1	4.7	33.3	9.1	6.7
7.8	1.06	2.1	-0.31	7.1	41.6	1.43	10.60	1.28	59.8	5.6	60.8	13.3	8.9
4.2	1.63	12.1	0.15	6.7	1.7	1.14	13.53	3.90	58.6	1.5	27.4	29.9	4.7
7.5	0.72	1.9	-0.02	7.6	0.8	1.71	10.89	4.30	46.1	2.3	12.0	17.0	7.0
7.3	0.45	3.5	0.00	10.0	1.5	1.83	24.78	5.39	46.5	8.8	201.0	7.8	5.9
3.8	2.56	11.8	0.33	4.1	0.1	0.65	6.13	3.77	71.3	4.9	36.6	6.2	5.5
6.4	0.49	2.5	0.14	4.9	0.3	1.07	10.85	3.84	67.1	5.9	64.3	9.6	4.5
4.3	0.99	8.4	0.49	7.2	1.9	1.20	13.71	4.24	52.5	0.6	8.2	39.4	6.6
4.5	0.93	7.7	0.11	8.7	1.1	2.25	28.06	5.00	45.7	2.2	23.7	19.1	3.9
7.6	0.12	0.6	0.17	7.9	1.8	1.43	13.66	4.49	58.7	4.1	22.4	9.0	6.2
5.4	2.23	10.5	0.31	6.2	0.7	1.13	9.24	3.93	58.2	4.5	14.8	5.6	7.5
5.6	0.46	2.8	0.26	7.3	4.3	1.59	18.08	4.28	65.8	5.9	57.1	9.6	7.2
10.0	0.06	0.0	-0.19	7.6	6.9	1.44	17.86	2.66	21.7	7.1	170.3	15.0	5.2
8.3	0.00	0.0	0.00	0.0	-0.2	-1.09	-5.34	3.55	122.2	4.4	82.8	19.5	0.0
6.0	1.55	6.2	0.00	7.8	0.2	2.04	14.33	5.68	63.4	4.3	46.2	12.3	5.6
3.2	1.65	14.8	1.24	4.5	0.4	0.72	8.14	4.48	52.9	1.5	20.7	25.8	4.8
7.9	3.16	5.8	-0.13	2.0	0.0	-0.06	-0.33	3.61	100.3	6.6	175.4	17.0	4.6
6.1	0.60	4.5	0.01	7.4	1.9	1.50	14.91	3.21	37.6	5.7	33.9	2.8	6.0
6.7	0.90	4.2	0.09	7.8	0.2	1.80	15.07	5.49	65.3	4.2	46.0	13.0	3.8
9.6	0.00	0.0	0.00	0.0	-1.1	-10.40	-21.14	1.25	809.6	6.5	440.1	20.1	0.0
5.5	0.45	3.1	-0.03	6.0	0.7	0.98	10.08	4.94	71.7	3.3	27.3	14.3	4.9
8.6	0.63	1.7	0.02	9.5	0.7	1.51	9.95	3.72	37.7	0.9	6.8	30.5	8.8
8.6	0.00	0.0	0.00	0.0	-0.4	-7.02	-10.45	2.88	294.6	5.8	248.8	30.9	0.0
8.1	0.21	1.5	-0.08	5.9	2.1	0.88	9.59	4.94	67.1	8.0	141.0	7.7	5.9
7.7	0.35	1.1	-0.03	5.9	0.2	1.28	9.22	4.11	66.6	5.8	181.8	25.6	5.9
2.2	2.96	18.4	0.26	7.1	0.8	1.24	13.82	4.33	51.9	3.8	62.2	23.5	5.8
3.7	2.87	13.2	-0.03	6.1	0.0	0.94	6.11	5.58	76.3	4.7	19.4	4.5	5.5
8.2	0.49	2.2	0.03	8.1	2.0	1.07	5.69	4.43	57.5	3.3	17.5	12.9	9.1
5.7	0.00	0.0	0.00	7.0	0.7	1.24	12.64	5.40	57.5	1.7	15.2	22.1	6.3

Name	City	State	Weiss Safety Rating	2003 Weiss Safety Rating	2002 Weiss Safety Rating	Total Assets ($Mil)	One Year Asset Growth	Asset Mix (As a % of Total Assets)				Capital-ization Index	Leverage Ratio	Risk-based Capital Ratio
								Comm-ercial Loans	Cons-umer Loans	Home Mort-gages	Secur-ities			
BANK OF WASHTENAW	SALINE	MI	C+	C+	B-	72.9	8.33	23.3	1.3	10.4	0.0	5.6	9.7	11.5
▼ BANK OF WAUKEGAN	WAUKEGAN	IL	D+	B-	C+	663.5	4.63	6.1	0.6	3.9	38.8	6.1	8.1	12.7
▲ BANK OF WAUSAU	WAUSAU	WI	B-	C+	D+	74.9	17.77	10.5	1.3	32.4	10.5	10.0	11.4	16.1
BANK OF WAYNESBORO	WAYNESBORO	TN	A-	A-	A-	93.7	20.23	8.3	14.7	27.8	12.5	9.5	10.7	15.9
BANK OF WEDOWEE	WEDOWEE	AL	D-	D+	C+	170.8	-1.70	4.8	5.2	14.3	44.5	4.6	6.6	12.9
BANK OF WESTERN MA	SPRINGFIELD	MA	B-	B-	B-	569.8	9.43	25.8	0.9	8.2	7.4	3.3	8.3	10.2
▼ BANK OF WESTERN	ELK CITY	OK	D-	D+	D	138.4	87.21	9.6	3.0	5.2	35.1	1.7	6.3	8.7
▼ BANK OF WESTMINSTER	WESTMINSTER	SC	B-	B	B+	29.9	1.86	1.6	19.6	18.2	34.2	10.0	19.7	42.5
▲ BANK OF WESTON	WESTON	MO	C	C-	C-	77.5	1.76	8.2	1.8	28.0	22.4	6.3	8.3	14.6
BANK OF WHITEWATER	WHITEWATER	KS	C-	C-	C-	11.8	2.79	6.8	8.5	17.7	28.9	6.4	8.5	16.2
BANK OF WHITMAN	COLFAX	WA	B-	B-	C	312.5	12.55	15.1	1.8	6.6	1.3	8.4	11.8	13.7
▲ BANK OF WHITTIER NA	WHITTIER	CA	D+	D	D+	26.1	-18.69	7.1	2.8	2.4	3.6	10.0	11.8	25.4
▲ BANK OF WIGGINS	WIGGINS	MS	A-	B+	B	135.6	5.83	8.3	11.9	17.4	32.2	8.1	9.7	17.9
▼ BANK OF WILLIAMSBURG	WILLIAMSBURG	VA	B-	B	B-	76.8	13.20	7.5	3.1	34.8	4.0	5.9	9.2	11.7
▲ BANK OF WILLITS	WILLITS	CA	A+	A	A	107.2	4.30	2.1	1.1	8.2	44.9	10.0	16.1	26.9
BANK OF WILMINGTON	WILMINGTON	NC	B-	B-	C	161.1	41.86	6.6	1.6	8.2	13.3	8.7	11.2	13.9
BANK OF WINNFIELD & TRUST	WINNFIELD	LA	A-	A-	A-	105.8	1.50	7.1	5.6	15.2	44.2	10.0	11.8	25.2
▲ BANK OF WINONA	WINONA	MS	A-	B+	B+	88.9	2.81	2.7	4.8	16.1	37.4	10.0	14.5	23.7
BANK OF WISCONSIN DELLS	WISCONSIN DELLS	WI	C	C+	B	274.2	8.58	12.2	3.6	7.5	14.5	5.6	8.9	11.4
BANK OF WOLCOTT	WOLCOTT	IN	B+	B+	B+	65.3	4.78	11.4	5.5	21.3	22.8	10.0	11.9	17.1
▲ BANK OF WRIGHTSVILLE	WRIGHTSVILLE	GA	C-	D+	C-	68.1	3.94	15.4	8.3	15.5	8.1	9.3	10.6	14.4
▲ BANK OF WYANDOTTE	WYANDOTTE	OK	C-	D+	C-	13.1	0.98	14.6	16.5	17.7	26.1	9.3	10.5	19.2
BANK OF YATES CITY	YATES CITY	IL	C+	C+	C+	40.4	0.61	6.1	6.8	12.8	50.5	9.5	10.6	19.4
▼ BANK OF YAZOO CITY	YAZOO CITY	MS	B-	B	A-	162.2	16.91	7.3	4.8	23.9	20.8	8.8	10.2	14.9
BANK OF YORK	YORK	AL	B+	A-	A-	94.2	8.27	8.7	9.4	11.8	57.2	9.6	10.8	21.5
BANK OF YORK	YORK	SC	A+	A+	A+	136.4	-3.61	6.4	5.6	12.6	13.5	10.0	14.1	23.6
BANK OF YUTAN	YUTAN	NE	C+	C+	C	20.6	-1.34	9.5	7.0	19.7	14.5	10.0	13.5	18.8
BANK OF ZACHARY	ZACHARY	LA	B	B	B	113.0	4.87	4.7	5.0	18.7	46.3	7.8	9.5	22.2
▲ BANK OF ZUMBROTA	ZUMBROTA	MN	A-	B+	B+	105.0	-2.76	13.0	4.8	9.5	24.7	8.5	10.2	13.7
BANK ONE DE NA	WILMINGTON	DE	B	B	B	17,370.6	-2.85	3.0	19.0	0.0	54.3	10.0	14.7	15.0
▼ BANK ONE DEARBORN NA	DEARBORN	MI	C	C+	C+	17.4	-11.38	0.0	0.0	0.0	0.0	10.0	95.5	491.4
▲ BANK ONE NA	CHICAGO	IL	B-	C+	C+	245,783.0	6.35	11.3	2.9	2.7	21.3	4.7	6.7	12.8
BANK ONE NA	COLUMBUS	OH	C	C	C	64,770.0	1.75	7.5	24.0	28.3	0.6	3.8	5.8	11.1
▼ BANK ONE TC NA	COLUMBUS	OH	C+	B-	B	860.5	-61.80	0.0	0.0	0.0	0.0	10.0	32.2	58.2
▲ BANK PLUS	ESTHERVILLE	IA	B-	C+	C+	76.2	-8.35	13.9	6.4	12.0	19.1	7.2	9.2	13.5
BANK RHODE ISLAND	E PROVIDENCE	RI	B-	C+	C+	1,199.4	14.45	10.4	0.2	35.1	22.3	4.8	6.9	10.9
BANK SOUTH	TULSA	OK	C	C	D	93.7	17.14	29.0	5.0	15.1	1.6	7.1	10.0	12.5
▲ BANK STAR	PACIFIC	MO	C+	C	C-	65.5	17.33	6.0	5.7	22.5	30.6	6.4	8.4	14.7
▲ BANK STAR OF THE	STEELE	MO	C+	C	C-	69.3	37.44	7.3	9.4	23.1	26.0	5.8	7.8	12.5
▲ BANK STAR OF THE LEADBELT	PARK HILLS	MO	C+	C	C-	81.1	-0.02	4.7	8.9	39.4	15.7	5.1	7.1	12.0
▲ BANK STAR ONE	FULTON	MO	C+	C	C-	84.1	2.82	10.1	4.8	37.9	20.5	6.4	8.4	14.1
BANK TRUST	MOBILE	AL	B	B+	A-	522.2	93.68	21.8	7.1	10.5	20.0	7.3	9.3	12.7
BANK USA FSB	PHOENIX	AZ	B-	B-	B-	136.1	10.66	4.8	0.3	4.3	15.2	7.1	9.8	12.6
BANK/FIRST CITIZENS BK	CLEVELAND	TN	B	B	B-	383.2	8.75	13.1	5.1	12.7	20.6	5.6	8.0	11.5
▲ BANKANNAPOLIS	ANNAPOLIS	MD	B	B-	C+	267.2	12.11	15.9	8.3	8.7	15.1	6.3	8.8	12.0
BANKATLANTIC	FORT LAUDERDALE	FL	B	B	B-	5,057.7	-1.57	3.5	0.5	34.5	12.5	5.7	7.8	11.6
▲ BANKCDA	COEUR D'ALENE	ID	C	C-	D+	41.4	34.41	24.4	4.3	2.3	15.2	9.1	10.5	14.3
BANKCHAMPAIGN, NA	CHAMPAIGN	IL	C	C-	C	118.6	13.77	14.1	0.9	20.3	28.5	4.8	6.8	11.2
▼ BANKEAST	KNOXVILLE	TN	B-	B	B-	73.0	42.74	9.3	4.4	17.5	20.2	10.0	24.2	32.1
BANKERS BANK OF KANSAS,	WICHITA	KS	C	C-	D+	89.9	21.88	8.3	8.8	0.7	2.9	5.6	8.5	11.4
▲ BANKERS BANK OF KY INC	FRANKFORT	KY	A-	B+	B	48.6	3.58	2.9	0.7	3.6	0.0	10.0	11.3	18.5
BANKERS BANK OF THE WEST	DENVER	CO	B-	B-	B+	360.5	59.33	5.1	0.1	3.9	0.9	5.1	7.1	13.7
BANKERS BANK, NORTHEAST	GLASTONBURY	CT	D+	D+	C	56.2	23.97	0.0	0.0	0.0	43.7	4.3	6.3	45.2
BANKERS BK	ATLANTA	GA	C+	C+	C	1,622.5	29.25	8.3	4.5	0.8	35.0	5.6	7.6	12.8
BANKERS BK	OKLAHOMA CITY	OK	C-	C-	D+	118.8	19.93	4.7	2.2	1.2	5.3	4.8	6.8	13.6
BANKERS BK	MADISON	WI	A	A	A	260.0	39.58	3.6	0.2	1.9	1.9	10.0	13.0	24.4
BANKERS TC NA	DES MOINES	IA	B-	B-	B-	1,593.5	-5.17	15.7	0.5	19.7	24.4	4.7	6.8	10.9
▼ BANKERS TRUST COMPANY	CEDAR RAPIDS	IA	C+	B-	B-	93.3	123.56	16.6	2.0	27.9	17.3	6.9	9.2	12.5
▲ BANKFINANCIAL FSB	OLYMPIA FIELDS	IL	C+	C	C	1,443.3	-0.31	11.6	0.2	18.2	16.9	5.1	7.8	11.1
BANKFIRST	WINTER PARK	FL	C+	C	C-	244.6	28.84	13.3	1.0	4.1	20.0	5.4	7.4	11.5
BANKFIRST	NORFOLK	NE	C+	C+	C-	195.8	-5.03	9.9	2.0	22.6	27.8	5.4	7.4	11.8
▲ BANKFIRST	SIOUX FALLS	SD	C-	D	C-	669.8	-16.02	0.1	65.8	0.2	36.3	10.0	24.4	38.5
▼ BANKFIRST FINANCIAL SVC	MACON	MS	C	C+	C+	365.4	18.57	8.7	5.5	18.0	13.7	3.1	7.5	10.0
BANKHAVEN	HAVEN	KS	C-	C-	C-	33.3	39.88	9.8	7.1	6.5	25.8	7.9	9.6	15.1

Asset Quality Index	Non-Performing Loans as a % of Total Loans	Non-Performing Loans as a % of Capital	Net Charge-offs Avg Loans	Profitability Index	Net Income ($Mil)	Return on Assets (R.O.A.)	Return on Equity (R.O.E.)	Net Interest Spread	Overhead Efficiency Ratio	Liquidity Index	Liquidity Ratio	Hot Money Ratio	Stability Index
5.6	1.05	8.8	0.01	1.2	0.1	0.20	2.08	3.85	92.5	1.8	26.4	24.0	3.3
1.3	5.06	33.4	1.05	4.5	1.7	0.49	5.42	2.81	54.4	0.7	12.5	44.4	6.0
4.4	2.20	14.9	0.09	3.9	0.3	0.70	6.07	4.09	66.0	1.7	12.7	20.9	3.7
6.5	0.17	1.0	0.78	8.6	0.6	1.29	11.89	4.83	53.6	4.0	49.5	16.5	5.9
3.3	3.19	16.9	1.46	0.2	-1.1	-1.32	-20.25	2.66	72.0	3.6	50.6	19.7	1.9
4.8	0.51	4.4	0.00	6.4	2.8	0.99	10.94	4.51	64.4	3.9	19.8	10.0	6.1
5.9	0.59	4.2	0.02	2.5	0.2	0.36	4.97	3.30	90.3	3.8	52.2	19.1	0.3
7.5	1.21	2.6	0.68	2.9	0.0	-0.07	-0.31	4.95	88.0	5.7	56.7	8.9	5.2
8.9	0.02	0.1	-0.47	3.6	0.2	0.52	6.58	3.96	80.6	5.5	34.8	4.6	2.6
5.2	1.20	7.4	0.00	7.2	0.1	1.74	20.74	4.59	64.2	6.6	79.6	5.9	3.7
7.9	0.03	0.2	0.38	7.5	3.1	2.14	19.69	5.95	58.6	0.6	9.1	39.8	4.7
4.6	4.86	12.3	0.00	0.7	0.0	-0.22	-1.92	3.03	106.6	7.3	148.6	11.7	2.8
7.2	0.41	2.2	0.10	7.0	0.8	1.20	12.40	3.84	60.5	2.0	33.5	28.0	6.5
7.6	0.00	0.0	0.03	5.6	0.4	1.00	11.92	4.03	57.2	3.0	9.0	13.2	5.0
9.6	0.12	0.3	0.00	8.1	0.7	1.24	7.52	4.73	58.9	5.8	86.4	14.3	9.2
4.0	0.78	5.4	0.05	3.6	0.5	0.66	5.69	3.79	74.4	2.1	29.5	22.8	5.9
7.8	0.80	2.6	0.01	5.2	0.6	1.03	8.59	3.91	68.3	5.4	63.6	13.4	7.1
7.7	1.14	3.2	0.03	5.6	0.6	1.38	9.51	3.97	62.7	5.0	55.1	12.3	6.5
2.9	1.52	11.9	0.29	9.0	2.1	1.60	17.85	4.48	46.7	2.6	29.7	18.7	6.4
5.0	1.71	9.8	0.54	6.3	0.4	1.06	9.10	4.62	66.3	2.7	13.3	15.4	6.0
3.0	1.47	8.4	0.17	7.8	0.6	1.87	17.50	4.28	56.5	5.0	79.7	16.0	5.7
4.8	0.78	3.7	1.14	3.5	0.1	0.71	6.97	4.50	76.1	4.6	37.3	8.1	2.7
4.8	2.24	8.9	0.55	4.0	0.2	0.95	8.08	3.76	62.7	6.5	62.8	4.9	4.0
6.4	0.30	1.9	0.16	4.0	0.7	0.89	8.54	4.04	81.2	1.9	25.6	22.4	5.5
6.0	1.14	3.5	1.36	5.0	0.3	0.62	5.70	3.28	54.4	1.9	25.8	22.8	5.4
8.6	0.29	1.1	0.22	9.1	1.0	1.38	9.88	4.51	55.3	5.0	54.4	13.5	8.5
2.5	4.50	23.2	-0.18	9.1	0.2	1.60	11.93	4.46	50.3	4.8	38.9	7.7	5.1
5.1	2.23	9.6	0.21	4.6	0.4	0.70	7.45	3.87	76.1	3.1	35.8	18.2	5.5
7.7	0.31	1.9	-0.01	7.7	1.0	1.80	16.87	4.38	59.4	3.4	19.3	12.6	7.2
6.7	1.26	1.3	4.47	10.0	195.9	2.07	11.53	4.90	73.0	2.0	38.7	98.2	5.7
7.7	0.00	0.0	0.00	4.7	0.1	0.83	0.87	1.28	11.5	0.3	0.0	67.3	4.3
6.0	0.67	4.7	0.29	6.7	1,624.0	1.28	18.38	2.25	58.0	7.4	76.5	4.9	4.4
2.8	1.03	14.2	0.69	9.4	606.0	1.85	37.03	4.97	50.0	4.8	9.1	2.8	4.0
8.1	1.03	0.1	0.00	6.5	5.7	3.22	9.51	0.62	90.8	9.0	133.8	0.0	5.0
4.8	0.84	6.1	0.23	6.6	0.5	1.40	15.27	4.59	65.1	3.1	26.8	15.2	4.7
8.4	0.04	0.3	0.02	4.4	4.6	0.81	10.62	3.48	68.5	5.5	25.8	4.0	5.5
3.0	1.85	16.1	-0.07	3.7	0.3	0.62	6.30	4.19	73.2	1.7	16.1	22.1	3.7
7.3	0.22	1.3	0.05	6.5	0.3	1.04	11.17	4.60	63.7	5.6	36.4	4.7	4.0
6.6	0.29	2.2	0.18	7.2	0.3	0.92	11.75	4.75	68.9	1.3	23.2	30.1	4.1
7.3	0.27	2.6	0.06	4.7	0.4	0.89	12.45	4.18	72.7	3.7	22.2	11.2	3.7
5.6	0.73	5.6	0.00	4.5	0.3	0.73	8.46	4.62	77.2	4.2	22.3	8.5	3.7
5.6	0.82	5.1	0.25	7.8	3.2	1.49	15.90	5.20	58.7	2.5	29.8	19.1	6.2
1.9	2.35	15.1	-0.12	5.7	0.4	0.51	4.01	4.07	77.3	0.5	19.0	89.6	6.7
5.1	0.60	4.9	0.07	9.0	3.8	1.98	25.41	4.43	55.1	2.4	20.1	17.6	6.3
8.0	0.01	0.1	0.00	4.9	1.0	0.81	9.29	4.05	69.6	4.0	29.7	11.4	4.7
7.2	0.33	2.9	-0.20	5.1	17.3	0.73	7.04	3.67	79.8	0.6	5.1	44.3	8.1
6.5	0.22	1.4	1.08	1.7	0.1	0.28	2.61	3.81	83.9	5.7	105.9	15.8	1.6
7.3	0.57	5.0	-0.01	3.9	0.4	0.73	10.32	3.65	73.8	2.2	13.3	17.7	3.1
7.6	0.93	1.7	0.39	3.2	-0.4	-1.30	-7.24	1.31	167.5	4.4	129.9	33.4	4.9
7.7	0.03	0.2	0.38	5.4	0.4	0.93	11.96	4.05	76.3	7.0	71.6	3.5	3.1
8.5	0.00	0.0	0.00	8.2	0.3	1.03	8.26	4.86	84.8	6.0	32.7	0.4	7.0
7.4	0.21	1.2	0.01	5.7	1.4	0.76	11.41	3.58	70.6	7.5	60.8	0.0	3.6
10.0	0.00	0.0	0.00	2.8	0.1	0.33	3.23	3.00	94.9	7.5	70.0	0.0	0.0
7.9	0.57	3.8	0.21	4.3	6.1	0.79	11.35	3.09	70.4	2.4	24.5	21.2	3.7
4.3	1.13	6.5	0.00	4.7	0.4	0.75	11.10	3.28	78.5	7.3	56.0	0.1	2.8
7.1	2.03	5.0	-0.01	9.3	1.7	1.62	12.17	2.73	76.6	7.4	75.5	3.0	8.0
8.6	0.13	1.2	0.03	5.1	7.9	0.98	14.57	3.42	65.1	5.3	43.5	11.8	4.7
8.6	0.00	0.0	0.00	0.4	0.0	-0.01	-0.06	3.71	87.9	3.0	27.3	15.7	3.8
6.3	0.61	6.1	-0.04	3.3	2.9	0.40	4.86	3.06	83.5	0.8	6.2	33.1	6.3
7.4	0.49	3.8	0.10	4.4	1.1	0.97	13.26	4.77	80.7	6.4	70.0	9.3	3.5
5.1	0.69	4.1	-0.02	6.4	1.1	1.14	11.86	3.79	62.7	4.1	18.9	8.7	4.8
1.8	4.32	7.3	21.95	9.5	11.7	3.34	14.57	16.38	47.2	7.7	312.5	14.0	8.3
6.1	0.33	3.2	0.26	5.2	1.4	0.82	11.04	3.95	66.6	2.4	33.9	23.4	3.4
3.7	5.53	30.9	0.05	1.9	0.0	0.25	2.36	3.67	94.0	3.8	59.3	19.1	4.1

Name	City	State	Weiss Safety Rating	2003 Weiss Safety Rating	2002 Weiss Safety Rating	Total Assets ($Mil)	One Year Asset Growth	Asset Mix (As a % of Total Assets) Commercial Loans	Consumer Loans	Home Mortgages	Securities	Capitalization Index	Leverage Ratio	Risk-based Capital Ratio
▼ BANKILLINOIS	CHAMPAIGN	IL	B+	A-	A-	741.9	9.46	11.5	3.9	6.9	32.0	5.6	7.9	11.5
▲ BANKIOWA	CEDAR RAPIDS	IA	B-	C+	C+	305.7	1.35	11.7	3.2	13.7	14.1	5.1	8.1	11.1
BANKNORTH NA	PORTLAND	ME	B-	B-	B-	29,277.7	13.86	9.5	7.3	13.5	26.8	4.6	6.6	10.8
BANKORION	ORION	IL	B-	B-	B-	210.2	0.14	8.7	2.1	9.4	37.2	6.4	8.4	16.0
BANKPACIFIC, LTD	HAGATNA	GU	D+	D+	D	83.7	-1.57	16.5	3.1	57.2	0.0	10.0	11.2	20.2
BANKPLUS	BELZONI	MS	A-	B+	B+	1,253.9	6.51	9.4	4.0	14.5	18.9	7.9	9.6	13.5
BANKPLUS FSB	MORTON	IL	C-	C-	C-	320.0	5.07	1.1	1.6	38.6	31.5	4.5	6.5	16.1
BANKSOUTH	DOTHAN	AL	A-	A-	A-	221.9	3.45	11.1	3.1	33.8	8.8	10.0	12.6	17.6
BANKSOUTH	GREENSBORO	GA	B	B	B+	196.0	11.79	7.1	3.4	20.7	3.8	5.8	8.5	11.6
BANKSTAR FINANCIAL	ELKTON	SD	C	C	B-	45.2	11.85	11.1	7.2	12.6	14.7	7.4	9.4	12.8
▲ BANKTENNESSEE	COLLIERVILLE	TN	C-	D+	D+	191.2	3.70	4.8	1.6	16.1	17.8	5.8	7.8	12.9
BANKTRUST	SANTA ROSA BEACH	FL	B-	B-	B	220.7	41.77	8.7	1.0	23.1	5.3	3.4	7.8	10.2
BANKTRUST OF ALABAMA	EUFAULA	AL	B-	B-	B	194.7	17.68	10.8	3.9	7.4	10.0	5.2	9.2	11.1
BANKTRUST OF FLORIDA	WEWAHITCHKA	FL	B	B	B-	52.5	11.17	6.7	6.5	18.8	11.5	7.2	9.2	13.9
BANKUNITED FSB	CORAL GABLES	FL	B-	B-	B-	8,110.9	17.16	1.9	0.3	53.1	31.5	5.2	7.2	15.6
▼ BANKVISTA	SARTELL	MN	D+	C	D-	46.0	31.35	16.4	3.3	13.2	7.0	9.8	12.9	14.8
BANKWEST	CASTLE ROCK	CO	D	D-	E-	63.2	13.48	19.9	1.7	10.0	10.2	7.2	10.8	12.6
BANKWEST	ROCKFORD	MN	C+	C	C	99.7	16.33	16.4	7.5	12.8	1.3	3.4	8.5	10.2
BANKWEST INC.	PIERRE	SD	B-	C+	C+	444.4	12.56	5.8	13.3	6.7	11.7	5.4	9.3	11.3
BANKWEST OF KANSAS	GOODLAND	KS	B	B-	C+	84.6	-8.07	8.3	4.8	6.3	13.0	10.0	12.0	15.6
BANKWEST OF NEVADA	LAS VEGAS	NV	C+	C+	C+	1,547.1	51.30	9.1	0.8	2.4	41.6	3.3	5.8	10.2
BANNER BANKS	BIRNAMWOOD	WI	B+	B+	B+	90.7	5.49	6.7	2.2	13.7	22.1	8.6	10.1	15.7
BANNER BK	WALLA WALLA	WA	C+	C+	C	2,755.2	9.66	12.3	1.3	10.8	23.6	4.9	7.5	11.0
BANNER COUNTY BK	HARRISBURG	NE	D+	D	E+	25.2	12.04	11.5	7.0	1.1	30.0	8.1	9.8	16.5
BANTERRA BK	MARION	IL	B-	B-	B-	954.5	-3.81	9.1	2.7	13.7	31.9	5.9	7.9	11.9
BAR HARBOR BANKING & TC	BAR HARBOR	ME	B	B	B	671.2	22.27	5.1	1.8	31.8	30.6	5.8	7.8	12.6
BAR HARBOR S&LA	BAR HARBOR	ME	C+	C+	C	23.6	20.83	0.0	0.5	81.1	2.0	10.0	16.4	36.2
BARABOO NB	BARABOO	WI	C+	B-	B-	412.5	13.42	21.8	8.6	18.1	6.8	5.3	8.8	11.2
BARDWELL DEPOSIT BK	BARDWELL	KY	D	D-	D	59.1	-5.45	15.5	5.2	15.3	41.7	7.3	9.2	19.3
BARNES BKG CO	KAYSVILLE	UT	B-	B-	C-	556.6	2.89	8.6	2.5	3.2	7.5	10.0	13.8	17.3
BARNSDALL ST BK	BARNSDALL	OK	C+	C+	C	11.4	4.15	8.6	10.7	0.8	66.6	10.0	14.1	30.9
BARRE SVGS BK	BARRE	MA	C-	C-	C-	123.9	-1.29	0.4	1.3	51.5	23.3	9.5	10.6	19.0
BARRINGTON B&TC NA	BARRINGTON	IL	C+	C+	C	635.3	30.00	27.9	4.3	12.9	16.0	5.6	8.5	11.5
BARTLETT FARMERS BK	BARTLETT	OH	C+	C+	C+	43.6	1.04	4.3	5.7	29.3	42.1	6.6	8.7	19.2
BARTONVILLE BK	BARTONVILLE	IL	B	B	B-	79.2	2.53	3.2	6.7	16.1	49.8	7.3	9.2	25.7
▲ BARTOW COUNTY BK	CARTERSVILLE	GA	C	C	C	284.5	2.95	9.9	5.3	15.9	19.8	5.2	7.3	11.2
BARWICK BKG CO	BARWICK	GA	D	D	D+	12.0	6.42	10.8	5.9	7.2	24.1	7.2	9.1	20.4
BASILE ST BK	BASILE	LA	B-	B-	C+	40.0	0.71	11.8	13.4	24.5	19.4	7.3	9.2	16.9
BASIN ST BK	STANFORD	MT	B-	B-	C+	83.6	6.83	15.3	4.0	5.2	14.1	6.3	8.3	12.3
BATH NB	BATH	NY	D+	D+	D+	461.7	-7.54	5.7	7.2	16.2	36.2	6.6	8.6	16.2
▲ BATH ST BK	BATH	IN	C+	C	C	104.4	13.89	4.4	2.9	20.2	13.3	4.6	8.0	10.8
▼ BATH SVGS INSTITUTION	BATH	ME	B-	B+	B	350.2	13.68	3.4	1.3	34.5	24.4	8.0	9.6	17.7
BATTLE CREEK ST BK	BATTLE CREEK	NE	D+	D+	B-	28.6	-7.77	4.6	2.2	7.2	27.6	6.0	8.0	14.2
BAXTER ST BK	BAXTER SPRINGS	KS	B-	B-	B-	26.3	-3.38	15.1	9.4	18.9	20.1	10.0	15.6	24.5
BAY B&TC	PANAMA CITY	FL	B	B+	B+	234.3	15.69	5.5	1.1	9.2	6.7	8.7	10.1	16.1
▲ BAY BK	THEODORE	AL	D	D-	D-	32.0	21.43	7.1	3.9	19.2	16.7	6.8	8.8	12.4
▲ BAY BK	GREEN BAY	WI	B+	B	B-	76.2	8.21	23.7	6.2	24.0	10.0	10.0	11.8	15.5
BAY CITIES BK	TAMPA	FL	C+	C+	C	176.3	33.24	8.9	1.1	2.0	29.5	6.1	8.1	12.1
BAY CITIES NB	REDONDO BEACH	CA	C+	C+	C	255.7	22.60	10.2	0.6	2.1	41.7	4.5	6.5	11.7
▲ BAY FINANCIAL SVGS BK FSB	TAMPA	FL	B	C+	C-	119.5	6.45	0.0	0.0	94.2	0.0	10.0	17.8	35.7
BAY NB	BALTIMORE	MD	D	D-	D-	142.6	16.40	48.8	3.1	14.4	1.6	3.1	8.8	10.0
▲ BAY NET A COMMUNITY BANK	BEL AIR	MD	C-	D	D-	67.7	-5.56	3.2	4.4	17.3	22.8	7.0	9.0	18.8
▲ BAY PORT ST BK	BAY PORT	MI	E	E-	E-	61.0	12.28	9.4	3.5	27.4	2.5	3.9	7.3	10.4
BAY STATE SVGS BK	WORCESTER	MA	B-	B-	B	259.8	6.26	4.0	0.9	34.3	24.5	6.8	8.8	14.2
BAY VIEW FS&LA	MILWAUKEE	WI	B+	B+	B+	83.1	1.62	0.0	0.1	14.5	50.1	10.0	15.2	46.4
▲ BAY-HERMANN-BERGER BK	HERMANN	MO	B+	B	B	42.0	0.68	14.4	3.7	22.8	25.8	5.9	7.9	12.9
BAY-VANGUARD FSB	BALTIMORE	MD	C	C	C	98.0	15.25	0.0	9.9	51.3	10.3	6.1	8.1	15.4
▲ BAYBANK	GLADSTONE	MI	B-	C+	C+	67.6	8.00	6.1	10.2	30.2	12.2	7.8	9.5	13.4
▲ BAYLAKE BK	STURGEON BAY	WI	C	D+	D+	1,005.3	10.40	8.1	1.4	9.5	17.9	3.9	7.8	10.5
BAYONNE COMMUNITY BK	BAYONNE	NJ	B-	B-	C	362.2	58.44	1.3	0.1	14.5	33.4	5.9	7.9	12.2
BAYSIDE BK	MINNETONKA	MN	D-	D-	E	77.8	53.83	1.0	2.9	60.4	3.6	3.9	5.9	10.8
BAYSIDE SAVINGS BANK	PORT ST JOE	FL	D	D	NR	35.8	N/A	0.9	2.1	18.1	10.1	10.0	14.8	25.2
▲ BAYTREE NB&TC	LAKE FOREST	IL	D-	E+	E	149.3	41.15	49.6	1.5	17.6	2.3	4.1	8.6	10.5
BB&T BANKCARD CORP	COLUMBUS	GA	B+	B+	B+	123.0	24.85	11.0	68.4	0.0	0.8	10.0	24.1	26.6

Asset Quality Index	Non-Performing Loans as a % of Total Loans	Non-Performing Loans as a % of Capital	Net Charge-offs Avg Loans	Profitability Index	Net Income ($Mil)	Return on Assets (R.O.A.)	Return on Equity (R.O.E.)	Net Interest Spread	Overhead Efficiency Ratio	Liquidity Index	Liquidity Ratio	Hot Money Ratio	Stability Index
7.2	0.50	3.7	0.14	8.7	4.8	1.33	17.20	3.54	50.9	5.3	43.9	9.1	6.9
6.1	0.27	2.1	0.54	5.2	1.9	1.21	13.15	4.18	70.9	3.7	9.0	9.9	5.0
6.0	0.41	2.2	0.20	8.7	196.6	1.43	13.63	3.85	50.8	4.5	13.6	5.6	9.3
4.9	1.25	7.5	0.01	4.7	1.0	0.96	11.13	3.34	59.5	2.0	26.2	21.8	4.8
0.6	5.50	36.3	0.68	5.1	0.4	0.90	8.24	7.21	82.0	1.1	27.4	47.7	5.0
7.1	0.26	1.8	0.42	8.4	8.5	1.39	14.30	5.14	65.0	3.5	29.4	17.0	7.7
6.2	0.37	3.5	0.02	3.5	0.4	0.28	4.24	2.36	82.3	1.5	4.2	20.6	2.8
8.5	0.13	0.8	-0.09	5.4	1.0	0.90	7.14	3.09	55.5	4.4	30.2	9.4	7.2
5.5	0.72	6.1	0.06	6.3	1.2	1.27	14.64	4.27	65.1	0.8	16.4	42.0	6.7
4.3	0.67	5.0	0.27	4.0	0.3	1.25	13.24	4.30	69.4	5.2	39.6	8.3	3.9
1.5	4.19	34.4	1.07	0.8	0.0	0.02	0.22	3.69	94.5	1.9	28.1	24.1	3.2
5.8	0.05	0.2	0.11	5.3	0.9	0.88	5.10	4.85	65.6	2.6	27.9	17.9	6.9
4.9	0.34	1.2	0.06	4.0	0.8	0.83	4.22	4.35	69.2	2.5	12.3	16.0	6.9
5.4	0.17	0.8	-0.33	4.0	0.2	0.71	5.69	4.33	74.5	4.2	52.9	16.3	5.8
8.0	0.29	2.6	-0.04	4.9	29.7	0.78	10.26	2.06	47.5	0.5	3.5	49.2	5.6
7.2	0.16	1.0	0.09	1.7	0.0	-0.07	-0.48	3.57	86.8	4.8	83.8	17.8	0.0
3.6	1.31	7.1	0.05	0.8	-0.3	-1.17	-8.96	5.65	119.9	1.7	21.8	23.1	1.8
5.2	0.76	7.2	0.04	9.2	1.0	2.13	24.85	5.46	62.6	3.6	15.0	11.2	5.1
7.4	0.11	0.9	0.04	7.7	2.6	1.20	12.83	5.23	72.0	2.3	20.4	17.9	5.1
6.2	0.27	1.5	0.55	5.0	0.4	0.85	6.49	5.15	79.3	2.4	7.4	16.1	5.8
8.9	0.03	0.2	-0.02	7.6	9.0	1.30	24.77	3.88	46.3	5.2	52.5	14.5	4.4
5.5	0.78	4.7	-0.01	8.4	0.9	1.98	19.72	4.40	49.4	4.2	45.3	15.1	7.2
4.5	1.32	9.6	0.10	4.2	10.4	0.77	8.68	3.82	67.8	1.0	14.5	32.6	6.0
1.7	6.73	33.2	-0.08	6.2	0.2	1.53	16.51	4.11	56.2	3.8	61.1	19.7	2.7
5.1	0.83	5.2	0.31	6.4	6.7	1.41	15.12	3.73	61.7	3.8	23.9	10.6	5.6
7.5	0.30	2.2	0.23	4.5	2.5	0.80	10.11	3.46	72.7	4.1	14.8	7.8	5.1
8.2	0.58	2.9	0.00	6.8	0.1	0.98	5.40	3.59	55.8	1.6	7.5	20.6	5.0
3.7	1.22	10.2	0.05	6.9	2.3	1.17	12.59	3.80	54.7	1.6	23.5	25.2	6.0
3.2	2.61	11.7	3.54	0.9	0.0	0.12	1.30	3.10	80.7	2.5	39.0	25.8	1.4
3.5	2.33	11.1	0.90	7.3	2.9	1.05	7.68	4.59	52.1	5.3	98.7	18.4	8.5
8.3	1.69	2.5	0.00	5.1	0.1	1.05	7.50	5.00	75.7	4.7	25.7	5.1	4.4
9.8	0.16	0.9	0.00	1.9	0.2	0.30	2.71	3.51	95.6	5.5	38.3	5.6	6.3
6.8	0.17	1.3	0.01	5.6	3.2	1.09	12.45	3.24	59.4	1.4	18.0	27.5	5.4
5.2	1.93	10.5	0.20	3.4	0.1	0.48	5.43	4.38	86.2	5.5	31.6	3.2	4.3
9.0	0.08	0.3	-0.03	5.0	0.5	1.27	13.56	3.44	63.9	6.4	104.9	12.5	5.7
3.0	1.43	13.2	0.18	6.3	1.5	1.05	14.64	4.13	57.3	1.4	14.9	25.6	3.8
7.9	0.42	1.8	0.00	2.3	0.0	0.18	1.99	2.86	90.7	5.8	128.1	16.9	2.2
4.3	2.41	14.9	0.27	8.9	0.4	1.99	21.14	5.09	62.5	3.2	64.8	29.0	5.4
4.7	0.38	3.3	-0.01	8.4	0.9	2.04	26.00	4.49	53.0	5.4	44.5	8.0	6.2
1.2	3.05	8.8	0.43	5.7	2.4	1.05	6.36	4.10	63.1	4.5	28.5	7.9	5.9
5.1	0.86	7.9	0.02	5.6	0.5	1.03	12.86	3.82	60.4	1.8	16.7	20.9	4.4
8.7	0.20	1.2	0.00	4.6	1.1	0.65	5.91	3.52	77.5	5.6	54.2	10.8	6.2
8.7	0.02	0.1	0.00	3.9	0.1	0.68	8.68	2.91	71.1	6.0	59.0	7.7	2.2
6.4	1.15	4.2	0.12	6.2	0.2	1.48	9.54	5.00	68.1	4.6	33.4	9.6	6.2
8.5	0.29	1.6	-0.03	4.6	1.2	1.06	12.50	3.44	73.2	6.2	67.7	10.2	6.0
6.6	0.02	0.2	0.40	1.2	0.0	0.26	2.40	5.51	90.2	2.8	40.0	22.4	2.1
5.9	0.62	4.1	0.32	9.2	0.6	1.51	13.29	4.43	51.8	1.1	23.0	32.9	5.4
6.7	0.37	2.6	0.00	3.9	0.5	0.62	7.78	3.46	61.1	1.1	20.5	32.0	5.0
8.5	0.00	0.0	0.00	5.4	0.8	0.67	9.17	3.87	68.7	8.9	208.5	7.4	4.1
4.2	3.55	16.7	0.16	8.0	0.6	0.97	5.32	3.26	55.7	0.6	6.4	45.0	7.7
8.0	0.00	0.0	0.01	1.3	0.2	0.34	4.11	3.27	82.1	2.9	17.4	14.5	0.0
8.9	0.19	1.1	0.00	2.5	0.2	0.51	5.59	2.73	76.4	2.2	50.2	52.0	0.5
5.8	0.19	2.1	0.07	2.5	0.1	0.34	4.64	3.78	85.5	4.1	54.2	16.9	0.7
7.4	0.47	3.3	0.05	4.2	0.9	0.74	8.10	4.05	80.5	5.3	45.2	9.5	5.2
8.6	1.67	3.8	0.00	5.1	0.3	0.75	4.95	2.46	50.2	5.4	60.9	11.6	7.4
8.0	0.08	0.6	0.01	5.9	0.3	1.52	18.82	4.42	63.5	3.7	18.3	10.7	5.8
4.3	0.69	6.1	0.15	3.9	0.2	0.53	6.20	3.37	75.8	1.4	25.6	30.1	3.4
4.4	1.27	9.5	0.05	6.4	0.4	1.15	12.05	5.03	67.1	3.3	17.8	12.7	4.8
3.5	1.52	11.8	0.16	5.7	5.1	1.02	12.16	3.89	59.4	1.2	5.3	26.9	5.9
8.3	0.17	1.3	0.21	5.7	1.5	0.88	12.34	4.05	58.7	4.0	12.9	8.6	3.1
5.9	0.44	5.2	0.27	0.6	-0.3	-0.76	-8.08	3.29	129.3	0.9	17.6	34.8	2.0
9.3	0.00	0.0	0.00	0.4	-0.1	-0.44	-2.07	4.05	97.5	3.5	100.9	69.7	0.0
4.9	0.74	7.0	0.01	0.8	0.0	0.02	0.27	4.85	98.4	0.5	6.0	52.5	0.0
5.4	0.31	0.7	3.77	6.9	0.3	0.41	1.45	7.88	60.5	5.1	7.3	0.0	8.6

Name	City	State	Weiss Safety Rating	2003 Weiss Safety Rating	2002 Weiss Safety Rating	Total Assets ($Mil)	One Year Asset Growth	Asset Mix (As a % of Total Assets) Commercial Loans	Consumer Loans	Home Mortgages	Securities	Capitalization Index	Leverage Ratio	Risk-based Capital Ratio
BC NATIONAL BANKS	BUTLER	MO	C+	C	C-	92.4	-2.56	5.3	1.0	20.0	15.0	6.4	8.4	14.0
BCBANK	PHILIPPI	WV	B	B	B	95.2	1.06	4.0	2.4	14.3	43.8	10.0	12.1	21.6
BCPBANK NA	NEWARK	NJ	D-	D-	D-	338.6	43.14	8.6	0.3	20.4	11.6	5.3	7.3	12.3
▼ BEACH BK	MIAMI BEACH	FL	D+	D+	D+	125.6	57.36	15.0	2.4	11.5	24.5	4.7	7.7	10.8
BEACH BUSINESS BK	MANHATTAN BEACH	CA	D	NR	NR	16.9	N/A	3.4	0.0	2.4	0.0	10.0	290.5	189.3
▲ BEACH COMMUNITY BK	FORT WALTON BCH	FL	D+	D	D-	198.6	47.95	11.8	1.8	11.4	16.9	5.0	8.4	11.0
▲ BEACH FIRST NB	MYRTLE BEACH	SC	C	C+	B	195.8	30.69	14.2	3.9	15.3	13.8	4.6	8.2	10.8
▼ BEACON BANK	SHOREWOOD	MN	C-	C+	C+	170.8	5.63	24.4	6.2	3.9	9.2	7.3	10.6	12.8
BEACON FEDERAL	E SYRACUSE	NY	B	B	B-	375.8	33.53	4.5	19.2	45.7	10.5	6.1	8.1	14.0
BEAL BK SSB	PLANO	TX	B	C+	D+	7,012.2	28.17	1.3	0.2	12.7	31.1	10.0	23.7	27.8
BEARDSTOWN SVGS BK	BEARDSTOWN	IL	C	C	C+	52.9	8.57	0.0	5.4	50.7	25.8	7.4	9.2	21.1
BEAUREGARD FSB	DE RIDDER	LA	B+	B+	B+	45.7	9.94	3.9	10.1	43.9	26.4	10.0	17.8	34.3
BEDFORD FSB	BEDFORD	IN	D	D	D	107.4	-5.28	5.0	6.4	57.3	13.1	5.3	7.3	12.7
BEDFORD FSB	BEDFORD	VA	B	B+	A-	285.7	14.21	4.1	1.4	53.1	5.4	8.0	9.7	15.5
BEDFORD LOAN & DEPOSIT BK	BEDFORD	KY	B	B	B+	65.1	7.72	0.9	7.9	42.1	24.6	10.0	11.7	22.4
BELGRADE ST BK	BELGRADE	MO	B-	C+	B-	128.5	3.72	12.2	6.7	23.1	14.5	6.8	8.9	12.3
BELK NB	LAWRENCEVILLE	GA	C-	C+	C+	8.2	-26.08	0.0	25.6	0.0	5.5	10.0	50.5	66.9
BELLEVUE ST BK	BELLEVUE	IA	C+	C	C	51.2	6.62	4.4	12.1	23.6	17.0	8.0	9.6	15.9
BELLS BKG CO	BELLS	TN	B-	B-	B	32.4	-5.69	7.1	6.3	13.5	30.7	10.0	13.5	30.0
BELMONT FS&LA	BELMONT	NC	B	B	B	89.2	-2.35	0.0	0.3	48.8	17.1	10.0	14.9	36.8
BELMONT NB	WHEELING	WV	C	C-	D+	298.2	2.14	4.6	1.6	15.9	32.8	6.3	8.3	13.7
BELMONT SVG BK	BELLAIRE	OH	C+	C+	C+	257.0	3.62	0.0	4.3	17.2	73.9	10.0	11.8	41.1
▼ BELMONT SVGS BK	BELMONT	MA	C-	C+	C+	421.2	-4.98	0.5	0.3	54.8	27.9	7.2	9.1	16.6
BELPRE SVG BK	BELPRE	OH	B-	B-	B-	55.7	7.40	0.0	8.2	54.1	23.4	10.0	11.5	24.1
▲ BELT VALLEY BK	BELT	MT	B-	B	B-	51.1	-0.15	6.2	4.3	12.2	24.3	10.0	11.1	18.6
BELVIDERE NB&TC	BELVIDERE	IL	B-	B-	C+	235.7	-3.75	8.1	4.3	4.6	39.7	7.6	9.4	13.9
BEN FRANKLIN BK OF ILLINOIS	ARLINGTON HGHTS	IL	D+	D	D-	118.9	-8.69	0.9	0.1	47.7	10.7	4.5	6.5	11.7
▲ BENCHMARK BK	AURORA	IL	D+	D-	E	160.3	6.38	23.1	2.1	4.5	18.5	4.6	8.7	10.8
▲ BENCHMARK BK	PLANO	TX	C	C-	C+	98.2	-0.89	34.1	3.8	15.5	0.0	10.0	12.3	15.1
BENCHMARK COMMUNITY	KENBRIDGE	VA	B+	B+	B+	281.5	3.53	11.6	6.4	34.7	10.3	6.8	8.8	13.3
BENDENA ST BK	BENDENA	KS	D+	D+	D+	16.2	0.97	5.5	3.8	12.4	14.4	7.6	9.4	14.6
BENEFICIAL MSB	PHILADELPHIA	PA	B	B	B+	2,264.9	0.95	1.4	21.9	27.8	23.7	10.0	11.5	19.1
BENEFIT BK	FORT SMITH	AR	C+	C+	C	111.4	19.36	13.6	5.5	32.1	0.0	4.8	8.3	10.9
▲ BENJAMIN FRANKLIN SVG BK	FRANKLIN	MA	C+	C	C-	501.8	4.84	1.0	0.4	42.4	22.0	5.6	7.6	12.4
BENNINGTON ST BK	SALINA	KS	B-	B-	B	258.5	4.37	12.4	3.1	17.9	21.7	9.6	10.8	16.2
BENTON BKG CO	BENTON	TN	C	C-	C	93.1	-0.97	15.5	17.9	16.6	9.6	7.8	9.6	13.2
BENTON COUNTY ST BK	BLAIRSTOWN	IA	A-	A-	A-	35.0	0.35	4.9	1.2	20.4	26.9	10.0	13.2	21.3
BENTON ST BK	BENTON	WI	D	D	D-	34.9	4.81	8.1	9.9	29.6	19.8	5.3	7.3	11.2
BEREA NB	BEREA	KY	C+	C+	B-	89.6	-0.82	6.8	7.2	28.5	33.0	9.3	10.5	19.8
BERGEN COMMERCIAL BK	PARAMUS	NJ	C+	C+	C+	258.4	14.10	7.9	0.9	9.1	10.7	3.8	7.5	10.4
BERKSHIRE BK	PITTSFIELD	MA	C	C	C-	1,294.6	15.96	12.1	9.2	17.2	32.7	5.8	7.8	12.5
BERKSHIRE BK	NEW YORK	NY	B	B	B	948.4	24.80	1.2	0.6	16.7	63.8	6.3	8.3	23.8
▲ BERKSHIRE BK	WYOMISSING	PA	C	D	NR	45.5	N/A	1.9	0.5	13.9	52.6	10.0	15.1	32.6
BERLIN CITY BK	BERLIN	NH	C	C	C+	399.4	2.39	4.5	23.3	23.5	10.5	4.9	7.5	10.9
BESSEMER TC	WOODBRIDGE TWP	NJ	A-	A-	A-	452.6	-19.80	0.0	58.5	0.0	25.4	10.0	11.6	16.8
BESSEMER TRUST CO NA	NEW YORK	NY	A-	A-	A-	361.8	-3.51	0.0	27.4	0.0	19.6	10.0	17.7	26.0
BETHEL B&LC	BETHEL	OH	C-	C-	C+	34.5	-5.18	0.0	0.6	36.8	20.4	10.0	14.8	47.0
BEVERLY B&TC NA	CHICAGO	IL	C+	NR	NR	37.2	N/A	50.0	0.9	4.2	14.1	10.0	31.0	28.8
▲ BEVERLY CO-OP BK	BEVERLY	MA	B	B-	C+	164.2	8.72	14.3	0.4	44.8	7.0	7.1	9.1	14.6
BEVERLY NB	BEVERLY	MA	C+	C+	B-	366.6	7.61	11.5	1.8	15.6	33.7	4.8	6.8	12.0
BIDDEFORD SVGS BK	BIDDEFORD	ME	B	B	B-	224.1	1.53	0.9	2.7	56.8	24.7	10.0	11.9	20.7
BIG HORN FSB	GREYBULL	WY	C	C	D+	135.0	-1.89	3.9	6.5	27.6	26.0	7.0	9.0	19.1
BIG LAKE NB	OKEECHOBEE	FL	C	C	C-	250.0	13.57	3.3	4.3	37.7	16.0	4.9	6.9	12.9
BIG SKY WESTERN BK	GALLATIN GATEWAY	MT	B	B	B	223.6	16.04	10.6	2.2	9.1	26.0	4.7	7.7	10.8
▼ BILTMORE BK OF ARIZONA	PHOENIX	AZ	C+	B-	NR	99.6	326.12	25.6	2.6	16.5	1.8	10.0	22.6	21.8
BIPPUS ST BK	HUNTINGTON	IN	C+	C+	C+	89.2	5.08	28.1	3.4	17.1	21.9	5.4	8.3	11.3
▼ BISON ST BK	BISON	KS	D-	D	D+	8.4	0.66	3.9	9.9	20.4	43.6	10.0	12.6	25.7
BITTERROOT VALLEY BK	LOLO	MT	B	B	B	154.3	14.44	13.1	6.4	15.4	1.0	5.0	8.0	11.0
BLACK EARTH ST BK	BLACK EARTH	WI	C	C	D	42.4	0.06	3.4	6.5	21.9	36.0	7.1	9.1	16.8
BLACK MNT CMNTY BK	HENDERSON	NV	C	C	C	102.9	58.10	11.9	0.7	2.0	0.3	3.4	8.3	10.2
BLACK MTN SVG BK SSB	BLACK MOUNTAIN	NC	B-	B-	C+	25.4	-1.67	0.0	0.0	75.1	0.0	10.0	12.3	26.0
BLACK RIVER COUNTRY BK	BLACK RIVER FALL	WI	B	B	B	59.2	-0.13	4.5	6.7	29.5	17.4	10.0	11.2	18.3
BLACKHAWK ST BK	MILAN	IL	B-	B-	C+	590.0	8.13	8.0	2.2	11.9	52.5	5.2	7.2	14.9
▲ BLACKHAWK ST BK	BELOIT	WI	C	C-	C	414.8	21.06	6.6	4.5	20.5	31.2	5.8	7.8	13.5

Asset Quality Index	Non-Performing Loans as a % of Total Loans	as a % of Capital	Net Charge-offs Avg Loans	Profitability Index	Net Income ($Mil)	Return on Assets (R.O.A.)	Return on Equity (R.O.E.)	Net Interest Spread	Overhead Efficiency Ratio	Liquidity Index	Liquidity Ratio	Hot Money Ratio	Stability Index
4.3	1.23	7.1	-0.01	4.4	0.4	0.79	7.68	4.38	75.6	3.9	38.3	14.8	5.2
9.1	0.00	0.0	0.04	3.6	0.3	0.67	5.34	3.39	67.9	4.6	29.3	8.0	6.8
5.1	1.08	6.8	0.00	0.0	-1.7	-1.07	-10.05	3.64	136.9	4.4	85.9	23.6	0.0
3.3	2.31	17.0	0.00	2.6	0.3	0.52	6.53	3.81	83.5	2.0	32.3	27.0	0.1
9.9	0.00	0.0	0.00	0.0	-0.4	-6.12	-8.07	0.42	820.8	7.2	338.3	16.6	0.0
6.3	0.00	0.0	0.04	2.8	0.5	0.59	6.84	3.95	65.5	3.8	19.1	10.5	1.0
5.6	0.78	7.3	0.25	4.4	0.7	0.72	10.04	4.32	63.2	1.3	14.6	26.9	4.0
2.0	3.31	23.0	0.00	5.7	0.7	0.85	7.96	5.01	65.8	1.4	13.4	26.2	5.1
6.5	0.01	0.1	0.14	6.5	1.8	1.04	12.22	3.71	57.1	1.4	2.2	21.4	4.5
4.9	6.63	12.3	0.67	10.0	282.2	8.57	40.97	8.01	18.3	2.2	39.1	72.2	10.0
4.4	1.96	10.8	0.09	3.4	0.1	0.45	4.64	2.84	74.2	9.0	861.6	6.8	4.6
6.7	0.42	1.6	0.01	10.0	0.8	3.59	19.69	5.90	41.4	2.7	51.9	30.0	8.0
5.2	0.58	5.4	-0.02	1.1	0.0	0.00	-0.02	2.59	101.7	0.7	11.4	37.8	2.3
4.3	0.59	5.3	0.00	6.8	1.5	0.98	5.95	3.47	47.7	1.8	10.8	19.4	7.3
6.1	1.50	7.7	0.24	3.6	0.2	0.51	4.32	3.99	81.0	3.5	51.8	19.7	5.9
5.8	0.60	4.7	-0.01	5.2	0.6	0.87	9.73	4.53	72.1	3.5	15.9	11.5	4.4
7.9	0.00	0.0	0.00	3.1	0.0	0.23	0.72	0.36	92.4	2.6	N/A	14.3	4.8
5.1	0.84	5.6	-0.12	7.0	0.3	1.31	13.63	4.22	52.7	4.7	43.6	12.0	3.9
8.9	0.00	0.0	0.15	3.8	0.1	0.65	4.94	3.67	77.3	5.7	125.5	17.6	4.3
8.6	0.00	0.0	0.00	4.0	0.2	0.40	2.45	2.62	74.1	3.3	71.2	30.7	7.3
5.6	1.07	6.0	-0.06	6.2	1.3	0.89	8.64	3.75	73.7	6.2	52.0	6.0	3.1
7.3	3.60	6.4	0.39	3.4	0.7	0.55	4.47	2.49	58.0	6.9	140.6	13.3	5.7
10.0	0.05	0.3	0.01	2.3	0.4	0.17	1.87	2.63	90.8	4.5	49.7	14.8	4.8
7.0	0.76	4.0	0.09	3.6	0.1	0.45	3.58	3.25	72.0	4.8	83.7	17.9	5.8
5.0	2.37	11.9	0.14	4.8	0.2	0.72	6.44	3.61	62.3	7.3	133.6	10.5	5.9
5.3	1.19	6.1	0.01	4.8	1.1	0.91	9.38	3.39	70.8	2.3	33.2	24.3	6.0
8.4	0.00	0.0	0.00	2.3	0.1	0.16	2.49	2.93	90.9	3.0	8.5	13.2	2.1
7.0	0.05	0.4	0.12	3.6	0.8	1.05	12.38	3.56	68.2	2.1	10.7	18.2	2.9
3.0	3.38	22.4	-0.08	6.1	0.5	0.97	8.27	4.97	84.8	4.9	30.0	5.9	6.5
6.0	0.40	3.3	0.06	7.3	1.8	1.23	13.95	4.32	58.0	3.7	29.8	13.2	6.0
7.2	0.00	0.0	-0.02	4.8	0.1	1.57	16.58	3.78	76.6	4.2	63.0	16.2	3.0
7.4	0.24	1.4	0.14	4.0	7.6	0.67	5.86	3.12	70.6	6.0	36.6	5.6	8.6
6.1	0.47	4.6	0.00	5.0	0.5	0.89	10.27	4.11	80.4	0.8	6.6	32.3	5.7
9.0	0.01	0.1	-0.01	3.0	1.0	0.41	5.22	3.16	78.4	6.1	61.3	9.4	3.4
3.5	2.30	13.8	0.02	9.0	2.6	2.04	18.93	3.67	49.5	3.4	39.1	17.5	8.0
2.5	1.82	13.7	0.45	6.4	0.5	1.01	10.65	4.63	67.8	2.9	39.4	21.5	4.8
8.8	0.00	0.0	0.00	9.5	0.3	1.78	12.86	4.45	45.9	2.9	31.1	17.6	7.3
6.2	0.41	3.9	0.18	4.6	0.1	0.71	9.92	4.05	71.9	2.5	17.0	16.7	1.6
6.7	1.01	4.7	1.14	3.1	0.2	0.47	4.41	4.48	77.6	4.2	61.1	17.5	4.6
3.9	0.78	6.4	0.04	7.5	1.4	1.17	15.00	4.03	58.2	7.4	88.4	5.4	4.9
6.8	0.62	4.3	0.13	3.3	5.4	0.86	10.01	3.37	63.1	2.4	15.5	17.3	6.5
8.9	0.16	0.5	-0.02	5.1	3.9	0.84	9.33	2.58	43.6	2.6	28.4	18.2	5.9
9.7	0.00	0.0	0.00	0.0	-0.6	-3.18	-17.15	1.22	227.6	9.9	414.9	0.8	2.5
2.8	1.23	10.4	0.09	4.3	1.6	0.78	8.83	4.03	76.1	4.4	21.5	6.9	5.0
5.7	0.00	0.0	0.00	9.8	5.3	2.10	19.99	2.00	76.7	9.7	179.2	0.0	8.6
6.5	0.00	0.0	0.00	8.0	3.8	1.87	5.80	1.22	92.1	10.0	872.3	0.0	9.0
9.8	0.00	0.0	0.00	1.1	0.0	-0.22	-1.51	1.48	126.7	5.2	71.0	14.3	4.8
8.3	0.00	0.0	0.00	0.0	-0.3	-2.70	-7.40	0.55	452.2	4.9	106.0	19.8	1.2
9.0	0.07	0.6	0.01	4.5	0.5	0.61	6.84	4.56	76.8	4.4	13.1	5.7	4.5
6.2	0.55	4.4	0.40	4.1	1.0	0.59	8.74	3.85	80.6	6.1	43.0	3.7	3.4
9.5	0.00	0.0	0.00	4.5	0.8	0.71	5.96	3.50	69.1	6.2	70.3	10.4	6.9
3.0	2.56	12.3	0.05	3.5	0.2	0.35	3.80	3.18	84.7	3.8	57.5	21.1	5.3
6.6	0.31	2.7	0.09	4.4	0.9	0.71	9.82	3.76	75.7	7.1	78.1	5.7	3.1
5.9	0.42	2.9	0.11	9.8	1.7	1.57	18.38	4.66	45.8	3.9	5.4	8.4	6.5
8.7	0.00	0.0	0.00	0.0	-0.9	-2.22	-9.14	3.72	137.1	6.3	69.6	7.6	3.7
8.3	0.04	0.4	0.02	3.9	0.4	0.80	9.46	3.74	77.8	2.2	10.1	17.8	4.0
2.3	7.34	26.2	-1.13	1.9	0.0	0.35	2.67	4.23	92.7	3.4	22.3	12.4	1.7
5.1	0.66	5.7	0.35	9.4	1.4	1.90	24.13	4.83	55.4	2.6	35.4	21.1	6.0
8.4	0.22	1.4	-0.01	6.6	0.3	1.18	13.64	3.75	54.2	5.6	47.6	7.9	3.3
4.6	0.28	2.1	-0.22	7.3	0.6	1.29	14.38	5.30	58.3	5.9	101.6	15.8	2.9
9.1	0.68	4.4	0.00	3.8	0.1	0.43	3.54	3.54	79.7	1.8	N/A	18.8	5.1
8.5	0.16	0.9	0.14	4.9	0.3	0.88	7.93	3.94	67.6	5.4	62.6	11.7	5.4
5.5	0.93	4.6	0.13	7.3	7.0	2.41	27.29	3.99	47.1	5.3	45.0	9.4	5.3
4.3	1.60	9.1	0.85	3.2	1.1	0.51	5.51	3.60	83.6	3.5	24.3	12.6	3.9

| Name | City | State | Weiss Safety Rating | 2003 Weiss Safety Rating | 2002 Weiss Safety Rating | Total Assets ($Mil) | One Year Asset Growth | Asset Mix (As a % of Total Assets) | | | | Capital-ization Index | Leverage Ratio | Risk-based Capital Ratio |
								Comm-ercial Loans	Cons-umer Loans	Home Mort-gages	Secur-ities			
▲ BLAINE ST BK	BLAINE	MN	**D**	D	D	23.4	-4.49	9.6	23.0	19.4	16.4	**5.2**	7.4	11.2
BLANCO NB	BLANCO	TX	**C+**	C+	C-	114.1	10.39	5.8	14.2	11.2	15.6	**8.0**	10.3	13.3
BLC COMMUNITY BK	LITTLE CHUTE	WI	**A**	A	A-	166.8	16.09	15.1	1.5	18.6	18.0	**9.2**	11.8	14.4
BLENCOE ST BK	BLENCOE	IA	**D+**	D+	C-	21.4	0.45	6.4	7.1	14.7	29.1	**7.8**	9.6	14.2
BLISSFIELD ST BK	BLISSFIELD	MI	**B+**	A-	A-	78.1	-1.86	1.8	4.4	27.3	42.0	**8.5**	10.0	18.5
▲ BLOOMBURG ST BK	BLOOMBURG	TX	**C**	C-	C-	10.9	-3.12	10.9	10.9	9.0	11.9	**9.8**	10.9	18.9
▲ BLOOMFIELD ST BK	BLOOMFIELD	IN	**B-**	C+	C	332.2	12.43	12.3	3.7	20.9	19.5	**6.9**	8.9	13.1
BLOOMINGDALE B&T	BLOOMINGDALE	IL	**B-**	B-	B-	405.9	6.54	36.7	0.1	7.0	12.9	**5.6**	9.1	11.4
BLUE BALL NB	BLUE BALL	PA	**B+**	B	B	1,125.7	8.49	7.2	0.8	12.0	26.2	**5.7**	8.0	11.5
▼ BLUE GRASS FS&LA	PARIS	KY	**B**	B+	A-	31.5	-3.02	0.0	3.2	56.9	19.2	**10.0**	28.2	52.3
BLUE GRASS SVG BK	BLUE GRASS	IA	**A-**	A-	A-	143.9	0.90	5.6	3.7	10.2	57.9	**10.0**	16.6	30.9
BLUE GRASS VALLEY BK	BLUE GRASS	VA	**C**	C-	C-	30.7	4.18	6.0	11.2	32.2	9.8	**8.6**	10.0	15.6
BLUE RIDGE B&TC	INDEPENDENCE	MO	**C+**	B-	B-	445.4	-0.31	11.9	10.4	7.8	19.4	**6.3**	8.7	12.0
▼ BLUE RIDGE BK NA	FLOYD	VA	**D+**	C-	C-	258.4	-4.66	1.8	3.2	6.3	26.8	**5.5**	7.5	14.8
BLUE RIDGE BK OF WALHALLA	WALHALLA	SC	**A-**	A-	A-	58.3	1.42	0.0	3.3	17.5	67.2	**10.0**	15.1	40.9
▲ BLUE RIDGE SVGS BK INC	ASHEVILLE	NC	**C+**	C-	D+	206.0	14.78	0.6	0.6	14.0	4.9	**7.0**	9.0	12.7
BLUESTEM NB	FAIRBURY	IL	**B-**	C+	B-	79.6	-3.17	2.1	3.6	8.0	56.5	**10.0**	15.3	34.1
▲ BMW BK OF NORTH AMERICA	SALT LAKE CITY	UT	**B**	C+	C	1,219.5	6.07	0.0	101.3	0.0	0.8	**6.1**	10.2	11.8
BNC NB	PHOENIX	AZ	**C**	C-	C-	632.6	6.90	10.0	0.9	4.7	41.6	**5.4**	7.4	11.5
▼ BNY WESTERN TC	LOS ANGELES	CA	**B-**	B	B+	354.4	10.97	0.0	0.0	0.0	4.3	**10.0**	44.1	164.0
BOARDWALK BK	LINWOOD	NJ	**B-**	B-	C	268.8	48.69	4.6	0.3	14.2	29.9	**8.8**	10.4	14.0
▼ BODCAW BK	STAMPS	AR	**B+**	A-	A-	73.5	-1.43	1.3	7.9	12.7	63.8	**9.4**	10.6	20.5
▲ BOELUS ST BK	BOELUS	NE	**C+**	C	C	10.5	2.91	2.4	6.3	4.9	3.8	**10.0**	13.2	21.0
BOGOTA SVG BK	BOGOTA	NJ	**A+**	A	A	190.3	-0.67	0.0	0.1	84.0	6.4	**10.0**	15.3	30.7
BOILING SPRINGS SVGS BK	RUTHERFORD	NJ	**B**	B	B	1,087.8	-3.33	0.1	0.1	25.5	35.6	**10.0**	11.7	22.3
▲ BONANZA VALLEY ST BK	BROOTEN	MN	**D+**	D	D-	29.8	11.30	18.2	4.5	8.3	14.4	**5.1**	8.1	11.1
BONDUEL ST BK	BONDUEL	WI	**A-**	A-	A-	44.8	0.79	12.7	4.0	9.8	40.1	**10.0**	21.1	50.0
BONHAM ST BK	BONHAM	TX	**B**	B	B	98.5	2.32	5.8	6.3	18.7	40.3	**8.0**	9.7	18.8
BONNEVILLE BK	PROVO	UT	**B**	B	B	28.6	13.80	22.5	10.2	1.8	3.0	**10.0**	17.8	32.6
BOONE B&TC	BOONE	IA	**A-**	A-	A-	116.1	6.08	6.6	1.9	10.2	41.2	**8.5**	10.0	14.5
▲ BOONE CTY BK	MADISON	WV	**B-**	C+	C+	156.4	-3.47	7.6	3.9	19.0	37.8	**7.3**	9.2	19.6
BOONE CTY NB OF COLUMBIA	COLUMBIA	MO	**B-**	B-	B-	951.5	6.98	9.0	8.3	17.3	28.0	**5.1**	7.1	11.5
▲ BOONE NATIONAL S&LA FA	COLUMBIA	MO	**B-**	C	C+	164.5	11.99	5.7	1.9	34.5	0.3	**6.2**	8.2	12.5
BOONE NB	BURLINGTON	KY	**D+**	D+	D	33.5	-3.22	2.0	5.5	20.8	33.1	**10.0**	12.6	21.4
BOONVILLE FSB	BOONVILLE	IN	**C+**	C+	C	38.2	-3.35	7.8	17.8	38.5	3.0	**10.0**	11.3	20.0
BORDER ST BK	GREENBUSH	MN	**C+**	C+	C	181.4	83.38	19.7	9.7	11.9	11.6	**7.4**	9.3	12.8
BORDER ST BK	INTERNATL FALLS	MN	**C+**	C+	C	33.7	9.78	24.7	6.9	19.7	2.7	**5.4**	8.7	11.3
▲ BORDER TRUST CO	S CHINA	ME	**D+**	D	D-	64.0	-17.44	12.0	12.2	7.4	21.2	**6.6**	8.6	12.8
BOREL PRIVATE B&TC	SAN MATEO	CA	**B-**	B-	B-	647.9	27.82	2.0	0.6	8.8	10.1	**3.5**	8.1	10.3
▼ BORREGO SPRINGS BK NA	BORREGO SPRINGS	CA	**C-**	C	C-	142.5	22.79	10.6	0.4	0.7	15.5	**4.2**	6.2	16.6
BOSQUE COUNTY BK OF	MERIDIAN	TX	**C**	C	C-	61.1	5.87	6.5	19.5	13.8	32.8	**6.3**	8.3	15.5
BOSTON FSB	BURLINGTON	MA	**C**	C+	C+	1,680.9	23.15	1.5	0.3	54.8	17.9	**4.0**	6.0	10.8
BOSTON PRIVATE B&TC	BOSTON	MA	**B-**	B-	B-	1,805.7	21.67	7.2	2.1	39.5	26.1	**4.0**	6.0	10.6
▲ BOSTON TR & INVESTMENT	BOSTON	MA	**C+**	C	C	44.1	2.35	0.2	0.0	0.0	0.0	**10.0**	37.4	61.3
BOUNDARY WATERS BK	ELY	MN	**D+**	C-	C-	81.0	25.68	27.0	2.8	10.5	4.7	**3.7**	7.0	10.4
BOW MILLS B&T	BOW	NH	**C+**	C+	C	118.9	9.77	8.5	2.9	26.8	24.2	**5.0**	7.0	11.7
BOWEN ST BK	BOWEN	IL	**A**	A	A	17.4	2.58	8.9	4.8	12.9	37.6	**10.0**	12.1	19.4
BPD BK	NEW YORK	NY	**B-**	B-	B-	322.6	13.41	2.1	10.9	1.3	44.5	**7.5**	9.3	15.8
BRADFORD BANK	BALTIMORE	MD	**B-**	B-	B	383.2	4.52	3.1	0.4	45.8	24.1	**5.6**	7.6	16.5
BRADFORD NB OF	GREENVILLE	IL	**C+**	C+	B	194.6	3.57	3.1	3.2	13.6	45.8	**6.0**	8.0	15.3
BRADY NB	BRADY	TX	**B**	B	B	64.0	11.38	10.6	6.8	16.3	22.5	**5.9**	7.9	11.9
▲ BRAINERD S&LA FA	BRAINERD	MN	**D+**	D	C-	59.6	-0.02	0.0	4.7	55.8	21.1	**5.0**	7.0	12.0
▲ BRAINTREE CO-OP BK	S BRAINTREE	MA	**C+**	C	C-	183.1	1.61	1.6	1.2	44.7	28.3	**5.3**	7.3	14.5
▼ BRAMBLE SAVINGS BK	MILFORD	OH	**D+**	NR	NR	53.8	N/A	0.0	0.1	62.9	4.8	**7.7**	9.4	17.6
BRANCH B&TC OF VA	RICHMOND	VA	**B**	B	B	21,849.1	78.58	5.5	7.8	10.6	17.3	**5.6**	7.6	13.0
BRANCH BKG&TC	WINSTON-SALEM	NC	**B**	B	B	74,890.2	10.98	8.3	6.7	22.9	17.5	**5.1**	7.1	11.1
BRANCH BKG&TC SC	GREENVILLE	SC	**B**	B	B	6,025.6	5.58	10.1	10.4	12.3	1.2	**5.6**	8.3	11.4
BRAND BKG CO	LAWRENCEVILLE	GA	**B+**	B+	A-	656.3	14.97	6.8	2.6	14.1	18.2	**5.0**	8.2	11.0
BRANSON BK	BRANSON	MO	**C+**	C+	C+	62.6	19.07	55.1	8.4	10.5	10.4	**3.5**	7.8	10.3
BRANTLEY B&TC	BRANTLEY	AL	**B+**	B+	B+	54.7	2.19	9.8	8.9	8.4	55.4	**10.0**	16.2	35.3
▲ BRATTLEBORO S&LA FA	BRATTLEBORO	VT	**C-**	D+	D+	149.5	13.12	1.9	3.3	43.5	0.0	**3.7**	6.4	10.3
BRAZOS NB	RICHWOOD	TX	**B-**	B-	B	12.9	-4.08	2.4	10.6	6.1	47.0	**10.0**	16.6	33.3
BRECKINRIDGE BK	CLOVERPORT	KY	**A-**	A-	A-	30.4	9.48	3.2	12.1	19.4	45.2	**6.1**	8.1	17.9
▼ BREDA SVG BK	BREDA	IA	**C**	C+	C+	23.2	0.34	5.9	1.9	6.6	49.3	**10.0**	22.6	51.4

Asset Quality Index	Non-Performing Loans as a % of Total Loans	Non-Performing Loans as a % of Capital	Net Charge-offs Avg Loans	Profitability Index	Net Income ($Mil)	Return on Assets (R.O.A.)	Return on Equity (R.O.E.)	Net Interest Spread	Overhead Efficiency Ratio	Liquidity Index	Liquidity Ratio	Hot Money Ratio	Stability Index
2.8	1.39	13.7	0.18	7.1	0.2	1.40	18.49	5.90	77.3	4.2	18.3	7.6	2.3
3.9	1.24	8.9	0.86	6.5	0.9	1.55	15.38	6.40	66.9	2.5	35.2	22.3	5.3
7.5	0.42	2.5	0.00	9.2	1.3	1.56	12.21	3.99	43.7	0.7	12.4	40.2	9.4
6.3	0.43	2.7	0.01	4.5	0.1	0.87	8.99	4.32	72.8	4.0	27.0	9.6	3.1
9.1	0.26	1.3	0.01	5.9	0.4	0.92	9.00	4.04	65.0	4.3	22.7	7.4	6.3
8.1	0.00	0.0	0.40	3.9	0.1	0.81	7.59	4.37	78.4	5.8	72.7	9.9	3.1
5.4	0.69	4.7	0.29	5.4	1.9	1.17	12.53	4.01	58.5	3.0	22.5	14.6	4.2
7.6	0.00	0.0	0.85	4.5	1.6	0.82	8.93	3.42	51.2	0.7	12.0	40.2	5.5
8.8	0.12	0.9	0.00	6.8	7.5	1.35	17.12	3.64	59.7	5.7	34.2	6.6	6.8
7.0	2.21	5.4	0.00	7.3	0.2	1.19	4.29	3.82	53.7	1.9	24.6	20.8	6.3
5.8	3.88	9.0	0.86	5.7	0.9	1.24	7.59	2.63	31.2	4.4	63.3	18.3	8.2
3.6	1.42	9.6	0.04	4.6	0.1	0.84	8.48	4.04	64.3	5.3	113.5	18.9	4.6
3.1	3.21	22.8	0.76	3.0	0.8	0.35	3.98	4.27	78.8	5.3	52.7	11.6	4.2
1.5	4.55	31.1	0.02	5.3	1.2	0.88	12.10	3.00	58.9	6.6	80.8	9.8	3.1
9.7	0.41	0.8	0.13	5.3	0.2	0.76	5.14	3.44	71.9	3.8	8.2	9.3	7.2
3.7	0.95	7.7	0.19	10.0	3.2	3.20	37.81	5.03	31.4	1.0	25.3	35.6	6.7
8.4	1.39	2.4	0.02	3.5	0.4	0.96	5.76	3.38	84.7	6.2	68.5	8.6	6.6
5.5	0.18	1.5	0.81	9.5	16.3	2.64	26.53	3.05	32.6	0.2	1.4	77.2	9.8
5.4	0.14	0.5	0.96	4.9	3.3	1.05	9.44	3.44	77.6	1.8	13.0	20.0	3.2
6.5	0.00	0.0	0.00	9.5	9.9	5.74	8.00	0.07	58.9	10.0	1,740.3	0.0	5.0
6.2	0.57	3.3	-0.31	4.0	0.9	0.75	7.33	3.13	62.7	2.7	39.4	24.1	4.8
7.8	0.85	2.1	0.16	5.6	0.4	1.21	10.49	2.97	50.3	2.2	47.0	36.5	7.3
7.1	0.00	0.0	0.00	4.3	0.1	0.91	6.86	2.79	57.8	8.7	307.1	9.0	4.7
10.0	0.07	0.4	0.00	9.3	1.6	1.64	11.01	3.39	28.9	5.8	77.2	13.3	8.9
8.7	0.81	3.5	0.00	4.8	5.1	0.93	7.73	3.46	56.2	5.7	45.6	10.5	8.9
5.7	0.35	2.8	0.18	5.2	0.2	1.55	18.98	4.06	67.4	6.2	55.2	5.3	2.3
9.5	1.28	1.9	-0.08	6.4	0.3	1.35	6.42	3.96	57.5	8.4	182.6	8.6	8.3
5.6	1.19	5.7	0.74	6.7	0.6	1.21	13.03	4.21	58.0	5.1	39.3	8.8	5.2
7.8	1.15	2.7	0.51	5.1	0.1	0.90	5.13	4.94	78.1	7.1	145.4	12.5	4.9
6.6	0.51	2.5	0.04	9.8	1.1	1.83	17.08	4.50	43.7	1.6	12.0	22.2	7.8
5.7	0.31	1.0	-0.09	7.8	1.1	1.33	9.44	3.97	48.9	5.3	39.5	7.9	5.7
5.0	0.79	6.3	0.15	7.8	6.3	1.34	18.18	3.67	57.6	5.4	42.1	8.0	5.4
4.2	0.94	8.8	-0.01	6.7	1.0	1.24	12.97	2.97	76.2	1.1	26.4	37.6	5.9
6.2	1.29	5.6	0.50	0.7	0.0	0.27	2.11	4.06	98.6	6.9	95.0	8.2	0.0
6.9	0.74	4.2	0.07	2.7	0.1	0.30	2.65	3.12	88.1	2.7	42.0	26.2	4.7
3.5	1.42	10.3	0.17	7.9	1.2	1.31	14.53	4.61	62.0	3.3	26.1	13.8	5.0
7.8	0.03	0.2	0.05	9.4	0.3	1.80	21.67	5.40	49.9	2.4	40.5	29.1	3.0
7.9	0.09	0.6	-0.01	3.3	0.3	0.98	11.67	3.80	74.5	3.8	37.5	15.3	2.1
7.4	0.01	0.1	0.00	8.8	3.8	1.25	15.81	4.55	52.7	4.0	81.0	28.3	5.9
4.6	2.48	12.0	0.04	4.6	0.5	0.73	11.44	2.88	88.3	6.3	259.3	22.7	2.7
4.7	0.92	6.0	0.46	6.2	0.5	1.53	17.83	4.52	65.9	2.5	23.9	17.3	3.9
5.8	0.64	7.1	0.04	3.0	2.2	0.26	3.79	2.57	81.6	0.6	4.3	38.7	5.6
9.0	0.11	1.1	0.00	5.2	7.2	0.86	13.41	3.15	66.3	7.5	89.9	6.5	5.2
6.5	0.00	0.0	0.00	0.5	0.0	0.04	0.05	2.66	101.1	10.0	626.8	0.0	7.8
1.9	2.13	17.3	1.53	3.1	-0.6	-1.60	-18.60	3.55	132.2	5.3	73.6	14.1	4.7
8.6	0.14	1.2	-0.02	3.7	0.2	0.41	5.89	4.03	88.8	4.8	22.7	4.6	3.1
3.4	2.83	12.2	1.51	5.5	0.1	0.90	7.25	4.51	74.1	4.1	15.4	7.5	7.8
6.9	1.18	5.4	0.16	3.3	0.4	0.23	2.44	3.57	93.7	1.4	32.2	41.4	4.1
5.6	0.93	8.2	0.00	4.0	1.0	0.52	5.60	2.99	71.1	1.9	19.2	20.2	5.3
8.8	0.26	1.3	0.04	3.9	0.7	0.73	8.35	3.29	70.1	5.9	47.1	6.4	4.6
8.2	0.01	0.1	0.03	7.4	0.6	1.76	23.64	4.49	66.0	1.1	24.4	33.6	5.4
8.3	0.02	0.1	0.08	2.3	0.0	0.05	0.61	3.10	96.8	2.7	33.8	19.5	2.9
8.4	0.46	3.6	-0.01	3.4	0.6	0.65	8.83	3.25	80.5	4.3	23.0	7.8	3.3
2.3	2.71	23.1	0.00	0.2	-0.2	-0.82	-8.98	3.63	109.4	4.2	58.5	17.3	0.0
6.1	0.37	1.3	0.06	5.5	101.2	0.96	6.09	3.11	62.7	7.3	181.8	14.9	8.3
5.1	0.62	4.0	0.32	9.2	593.1	1.67	17.04	3.98	53.6	4.0	37.8	16.9	8.0
5.0	0.62	4.7	0.34	6.6	35.7	1.19	13.57	3.08	50.6	8.0	195.1	12.0	7.3
7.3	0.08	0.7	0.16	7.2	5.5	1.76	21.09	3.90	56.1	3.0	26.8	15.7	7.2
2.8	1.69	16.4	0.12	3.5	0.2	0.56	7.32	3.82	73.6	1.6	23.4	26.2	2.9
7.3	0.99	2.1	0.16	8.7	0.4	1.45	8.74	4.73	47.3	3.8	57.0	18.7	6.3
3.2	0.92	11.5	0.10	4.5	0.5	0.62	9.60	3.64	80.6	1.3	7.8	25.2	3.2
8.7	0.29	0.4	0.00	4.4	0.1	0.88	5.26	3.42	80.3	6.9	113.6	9.8	6.1
4.7	2.00	9.6	0.66	6.4	0.2	1.61	20.27	3.94	50.1	5.9	65.1	9.8	5.9
8.0	0.46	0.8	-0.11	3.0	0.1	0.39	1.72	3.49	86.2	6.5	88.2	7.9	3.9

| Name | City | State | Weiss Safety Rating | 2003 Weiss Safety Rating | 2002 Weiss Safety Rating | Total Assets ($Mil) | One Year Asset Growth | Asset Mix (As a % of Total Assets) | | | | Capital- ization Index | Leverage Ratio | Risk-based Capital Ratio |
								Comm- ercial Loans	Cons- umer Loans	Home Mort- gages	Secur- ities			
BREMEN B&TC	ST LOUIS	MO	C	C+	C+	212.0	17.92	20.8	1.0	11.3	20.1	4.8	8.3	10.9
BREMER BK NA	ALEXANDRIA	MN	B-	B-	B-	481.7	8.47	19.5	10.6	7.6	15.0	4.1	7.8	10.5
BREMER BK NA	BRAINERD	MN	B	B	B-	304.8	18.14	12.2	5.3	11.3	23.7	4.5	7.1	10.8
BREMER BK NA	INTERNATL FALLS	MN	B-	B-	B-	74.2	1.74	8.5	7.0	13.3	45.5	4.7	6.7	12.8
BREMER BK NA	MARSHALL	MN	B-	B-	B-	196.0	3.57	12.7	5.8	7.2	31.2	5.4	7.4	12.2
BREMER BK NA	MOORHEAD	MN	B	B-	B-	550.4	9.76	13.4	7.2	7.6	16.1	5.4	8.6	11.3
BREMER BK NA	S ST PAUL	MN	B-	B-	B-	1,961.4	9.20	16.8	2.8	5.0	13.7	5.4	8.7	11.3
▲ BREMER BK NA	ST CLOUD	MN	B	B-	B-	561.8	15.15	21.1	3.5	4.4	20.6	4.2	7.5	10.6
BREMER BK NA	WILLMAR	MN	B-	B-	B-	227.4	8.54	13.0	9.3	6.2	28.7	3.5	6.6	10.3
BREMER BK NA	GRAND FORKS	ND	B	B	B	618.6	11.90	15.3	12.8	5.5	19.8	4.5	7.0	10.8
BREMER BK NA	MINOT	ND	B-	B-	B-	415.5	2.91	11.7	7.9	5.7	32.3	3.9	6.3	10.5
BREMER BK NA	MENOMONIE	WI	B-	B-	B-	521.5	4.15	5.5	5.9	11.7	29.5	4.5	6.5	11.0
▲ BRENHAM NB	BRENHAM	TX	B+	B	B	167.1	7.05	5.4	2.4	14.5	17.4	7.7	9.5	14.7
▼ BRENTWOOD BK	BETHEL PARK	PA	C+	B-	B-	348.8	3.22	5.2	0.1	31.7	42.2	5.7	7.7	14.8
BRICKWELL COMMUNITY BK	WOODBURY	MN	D	NR	NR	6.9	N/A	0.0	0.0	0.0	0.0	10.0	93.3	303.5
BRICKYARD BK	LINCOLNWOOD	IL	D-	E+	E-	142.5	-6.03	8.5	0.3	9.6	31.0	4.9	6.9	12.6
▲ BRIDGE BK NA	SAN JOSE	CA	C	C-	D	340.4	50.13	20.8	1.0	0.0	11.0	7.4	9.2	12.8
BRIDGE CITY ST BK	BRIDGE CITY	TX	C	C	C-	80.1	-7.28	3.3	8.7	11.3	39.2	6.1	8.2	15.5
▲ BRIDGE COMMUNITY BK	MECHANICSVILLE	IA	C	C-	C+	45.4	3.64	5.9	8.7	13.7	39.3	6.3	8.3	14.7
▲ BRIDGEHAMPTON NB	BRIDGEHAMPTON	NY	A-	B+	B+	557.5	9.55	7.0	1.2	8.2	41.9	6.0	8.0	12.7
BRIDGEVIEW BK GROUP	BRIDGEVIEW	IL	C-	C	D+	1,158.9	13.58	17.0	0.5	8.0	7.7	3.3	7.5	10.1
BRIDGEWATER CO-OP BK	BRIDGEWATER	MA	E-	E+	D-	17.8	3.03	0.0	2.9	34.5	24.7	5.0	7.0	17.0
▼ BRIDGEWATER SVGS BK	RAYNHAM	MA	B-	B-	C+	300.4	15.04	12.7	3.0	22.4	33.3	9.4	10.6	21.4
▲ BRIGHTON BK	BRIGHTON	TN	C	C-	D	51.9	-3.83	12.6	9.6	19.9	11.1	8.6	10.1	14.7
▲ BRIGHTON BK	SALT LAKE CITY	UT	A+	A	A	149.6	-25.70	3.0	1.8	4.0	9.7	10.0	11.6	19.3
BRIGHTON CMRC BK	BRIGHTON	MI	C	C	C	96.0	11.58	7.3	0.6	5.7	0.6	3.2	8.1	10.1
BRILL ST BK	RICE LAKE	WI	C+	C+	B-	47.9	18.34	11.0	7.4	31.3	4.1	5.7	7.7	11.6
▲ BRIMFIELD BK	BRIMFIELD	IL	B-	C+	C+	37.3	-2.21	7.2	6.1	31.1	28.2	9.1	10.4	19.2
BRISTOL BK	CORAL GABLES	FL	D	D-	D-	70.0	17.25	21.0	3.2	24.7	10.4	3.5	7.5	10.2
BRISTOL COUNTY SVGS BK	TAUNTON	MA	A	A	A+	822.7	4.08	5.9	0.3	20.8	40.2	10.0	13.8	23.2
BRITTON & KOONTZ BK NA	NATCHEZ	MS	B	B	B	378.6	10.46	7.7	3.6	22.0	34.2	6.5	8.5	14.2
▲ BROADWAY BK	CHICAGO	IL	B	B-	C+	530.8	11.70	4.9	0.2	4.8	18.7	9.5	10.7	14.9
BROADWAY FEDERAL BK FSB	LOS ANGELES	CA	C+	C+	C+	253.3	17.13	0.0	0.3	11.6	4.9	4.3	7.3	10.6
BROADWAY NB	FORT LEE	NJ	C+	C+	B-	228.7	26.46	6.5	0.0	3.7	21.7	5.3	8.4	11.3
▲ BROADWAY NB	SAN ANTONIO	TX	A	A-	A-	1,345.1	3.91	9.5	3.6	7.6	50.1	8.2	9.8	17.7
BROOKLINE BANK	BROOKLINE	MA	B+	B+	B+	1,447.7	18.61	2.6	22.4	10.3	16.5	10.0	29.8	37.0
▲ BROOKLINE CO-OP BK	BROOKLINE	MA	B+	B	B-	63.8	2.07	0.1	2.3	56.4	6.0	10.0	11.5	20.7
▲ BROOKLYN FSB	NEW YORK CITY	NY	A	A-	A-	318.4	1.60	0.0	0.1	17.8	36.0	10.0	11.2	21.5
BROOKVILLE B&SA	BROOKVILLE	OH	B-	B-	B-	42.8	6.82	0.6	1.2	63.2	19.4	10.0	11.3	28.4
BROOKVILLE NB	BROOKVILLE	OH	B	B	B	82.2	-5.07	5.5	5.2	20.1	42.4	10.0	11.2	28.1
BROTHERHOOD B&TC	KANSAS CITY	KS	C-	C	D+	423.3	5.32	10.5	1.8	2.1	63.6	6.7	8.7	20.9
BROWN COUNTY ST BK	MT STERLING	IL	C+	C+	C+	54.6	0.58	6.2	7.2	19.2	25.6	6.4	8.4	12.7
BROWNSVILLE DEPOSIT BK	BROWNSVILLE	KY	B-	B-	C+	52.6	9.10	4.8	7.9	30.9	6.5	5.9	8.0	11.7
BRUCETON BK	BRUCETON MILLS	WV	B+	B	B-	176.3	7.36	7.3	9.2	39.0	7.4	8.7	10.1	14.7
BRUNING ST BK	BRUNING	NE	A-	B+	B+	109.7	-17.89	3.7	1.0	2.3	37.7	10.0	14.6	23.4
BRUNSWICK B&TC	NEW BRUNSWICK	NJ	A+	A+	A	127.5	2.29	6.2	0.7	10.2	30.5	10.0	18.3	34.2
▲ BRUNSWICK ST BK	BRUNSWICK	NE	B-	C+	C	31.4	1.85	5.7	6.6	2.3	15.8	10.0	13.7	20.8
BRUSH COUNTRY BK	FREER	TX	C	C	C	28.4	-5.59	16.0	27.8	13.6	15.9	6.2	8.2	13.9
▲ BRYAN B&TC	RICHMOND HILL	GA	B-	C+	B	142.7	13.90	7.9	3.5	17.2	10.0	4.8	7.9	10.9
▲ BRYANT ST BK	BRYANT	SD	B	B-	B-	19.0	6.08	4.0	6.6	6.0	23.5	10.0	15.6	24.3
BRYN MAWR TRUST CO	BRYN MAWR	PA	B	B	B	659.7	13.76	11.6	2.2	30.2	4.6	5.1	9.6	11.1
▲ BSB B&TC	BINGHAMTON	NY	B-	C	D+	2,186.1	1.40	6.5	11.5	29.4	31.4	6.2	8.3	13.7
BTC BK	BETHANY	MO	A	A-	A-	149.3	7.28	6.1	4.3	20.8	16.8	10.0	11.4	15.2
BUCKEYE COMMUNITY BK	LORAIN	OH	B-	B-	D	81.5	22.97	21.5	0.6	13.7	13.9	10.0	14.3	19.8
BUCKHEAD CMNTY BK NA	ATLANTA	GA	B-	C+	C	207.9	26.07	14.8	1.3	5.9	25.1	5.4	8.7	11.3
BUCKHOLTS ST BK	BUCKHOLTS	TX	B-	B-	A-	42.1	0.52	5.4	8.3	3.9	35.7	10.0	12.2	28.3
BUCKLEY ST BK	BUCKLEY	IL	B	B	B	33.3	-0.32	8.3	4.2	3.6	21.5	10.0	13.3	21.5
▲ BUCS FEDERAL BANK	OWINGS MILLS	MD	B-	C+	C+	120.4	2.66	3.5	17.4	28.1	17.2	6.7	8.8	12.8
BUENA VISTA NB	CHESTER	IL	A-	A-	A-	95.3	-2.13	6.2	7.4	15.4	49.8	10.0	17.7	37.1
BUFFALO FS&LA	BUFFALO	WY	C-	B-	B	80.5	2.65	7.8	4.2	27.0	14.7	8.9	10.3	15.3
BUFFALO PRAIRIE ST BK	BUFFALO PRAIRIE	IL	B	B	B	40.7	4.94	3.8	1.5	2.1	66.1	10.0	15.0	35.2
BUFFALO RIDGE BK	BEARDSLEY	MN	C	C	C-	29.4	3.25	9.2	5.4	5.1	22.2	6.9	8.9	13.1
▲ BUFFALO SVG BK	BUFFALO	IA	C	D+	E+	37.0	-3.37	14.0	3.0	15.1	49.5	8.4	9.9	21.9
▲ BUILDERS BK	CHICAGO	IL	D	D-	D-	385.5	-7.97	1.8	0.0	3.7	12.3	10.0	13.8	20.0

Asset Quality Index	Non-Performing Loans as a % of Total Loans	as a % of Capital	Net Charge-offs Avg Loans	Profitability Index	Net Income ($Mil)	Return on Assets (R.O.A.)	Return on Equity (R.O.E.)	Net Interest Spread	Overhead Efficiency Ratio	Liquidity Index	Liquidity Ratio	Hot Money Ratio	Stability Index
4.9	1.12	9.1	-0.05	3.2	0.5	0.52	6.00	3.23	70.2	1.6	9.1	21.8	4.5
6.0	0.26	2.3	0.14	7.7	2.7	1.17	15.05	4.14	59.9	4.9	20.8	3.7	6.2
4.7	1.09	9.3	0.01	6.8	1.4	0.96	12.62	3.82	62.0	4.9	28.7	5.4	6.2
7.6	0.02	0.2	-0.02	7.3	0.4	1.15	17.91	3.77	62.6	4.0	62.0	18.9	6.0
5.9	0.45	3.6	0.05	8.3	1.3	1.31	18.24	4.03	57.5	5.8	49.8	8.0	5.8
7.9	0.04	0.4	0.03	7.6	3.3	1.23	14.64	4.03	54.9	4.1	13.6	7.7	6.0
6.2	0.37	2.2	0.12	6.7	9.6	1.00	8.36	4.02	60.3	7.1	55.6	3.4	7.9
8.2	0.11	1.0	0.03	9.3	3.9	1.42	19.52	3.89	48.3	4.6	20.9	5.4	5.7
7.3	0.21	1.9	0.10	7.7	1.4	1.26	19.23	3.87	57.4	5.6	37.9	4.9	5.8
6.4	0.21	1.9	0.02	7.0	3.1	1.05	14.55	3.63	59.2	4.5	27.3	7.9	6.1
4.8	0.95	8.2	0.06	6.8	2.3	1.11	16.49	3.78	60.0	5.5	45.1	8.1	5.8
5.0	0.43	3.2	0.10	7.4	3.2	1.25	15.18	3.79	59.9	5.7	42.4	6.5	6.6
8.6	0.02	0.1	0.22	6.9	1.5	1.83	18.55	4.34	60.3	4.8	40.4	11.3	6.5
8.2	0.37	2.4	0.03	3.5	1.1	0.64	8.31	2.59	70.8	5.1	43.3	10.2	3.8
10.0	0.00	0.0	0.00	0.0	-0.1	-1.85	-1.93	0.04	7,000.0	10.0	2,811.7	0.0	0.0
0.3	9.38	60.0	2.24	2.9	0.6	0.86	12.59	2.21	117.7	4.8	129.8	30.1	2.4
8.4	0.13	0.9	0.16	3.6	1.1	0.68	7.31	4.58	70.3	5.6	48.7	9.0	2.5
4.1	2.18	10.8	0.39	3.5	0.3	0.82	9.96	4.23	78.1	4.7	27.3	6.3	3.8
7.9	0.18	1.2	0.63	5.9	0.3	1.38	16.81	4.26	62.5	4.2	23.3	8.4	3.5
9.0	0.18	1.2	0.02	10.0	5.2	1.94	24.19	4.96	47.3	5.2	36.3	7.2	6.7
2.7	1.67	14.4	0.12	8.0	7.5	1.39	16.39	4.74	52.4	1.6	15.7	23.9	4.9
6.3	0.94	5.9	0.00	2.6	0.0	0.25	3.50	2.78	85.8	9.6	232.2	2.7	0.7
8.8	0.08	0.4	0.00	3.9	0.8	0.58	5.32	3.83	84.7	4.3	7.9	5.9	5.0
4.2	1.50	10.3	0.44	3.0	0.1	0.34	3.39	4.92	82.3	3.5	28.1	13.3	2.7
7.5	0.00	0.0	0.02	10.0	3.2	4.01	35.48	6.15	48.1	9.9	202.7	0.6	8.2
2.9	1.17	10.9	0.00	7.3	0.5	1.07	12.41	4.56	63.3	2.4	44.2	31.0	5.8
4.7	0.65	6.4	0.00	7.1	0.4	1.65	21.77	4.06	55.0	4.5	96.8	21.8	4.6
8.3	0.01	0.1	0.02	4.9	0.2	0.90	8.54	3.84	63.9	3.8	43.6	16.7	4.5
5.3	0.86	7.2	0.15	1.5	0.1	0.20	2.32	3.54	88.1	2.1	44.4	35.5	4.4
9.3	0.21	0.7	0.00	6.7	7.7	1.90	12.16	3.77	61.1	6.7	65.2	6.1	10.0
6.3	0.63	4.0	0.08	4.3	1.4	0.74	8.28	4.15	75.1	1.5	11.0	23.8	4.7
5.6	0.01	0.1	0.00	10.0	12.7	4.77	46.47	6.28	20.8	0.3	5.1	77.1	8.1
7.2	0.03	0.4	0.00	5.6	1.1	0.88	11.92	4.15	67.9	0.5	5.5	43.8	4.0
5.9	0.47	4.1	-0.07	6.7	1.3	1.21	14.81	4.08	56.6	1.2	7.8	26.5	4.1
6.9	1.17	4.4	0.24	7.5	11.2	1.67	16.01	4.38	67.0	7.4	78.5	5.3	9.0
5.9	0.01	0.0	0.05	8.2	7.9	1.13	3.70	3.42	44.3	2.5	39.6	36.3	6.0
9.3	0.04	0.2	0.02	5.4	0.3	0.84	7.38	4.51	68.3	5.7	57.6	9.1	5.1
7.9	0.01	0.0	0.00	7.9	1.8	1.17	10.60	3.61	52.4	1.9	11.2	19.0	7.4
9.3	0.42	2.5	0.00	4.5	0.1	0.67	5.71	3.19	68.5	4.0	11.6	8.0	5.3
8.8	0.77	2.7	0.03	3.6	0.2	0.58	5.16	3.21	70.7	6.9	73.2	4.4	5.9
2.1	8.87	25.6	-0.02	5.8	3.3	1.52	16.11	3.52	62.1	3.1	7.2	12.7	4.4
6.2	0.56	4.0	0.05	5.9	0.3	1.07	13.29	3.04	53.8	1.8	18.3	21.1	5.0
3.3	1.67	15.5	0.06	6.0	0.3	1.13	13.85	4.36	62.7	4.0	25.9	10.2	4.8
7.3	0.11	0.9	0.10	7.6	1.0	1.18	11.73	4.79	64.0	3.3	10.2	12.0	6.2
8.7	0.06	0.2	-0.01	6.3	0.5	0.79	6.12	3.29	48.6	5.2	52.0	12.0	7.4
7.5	1.89	4.7	0.00	8.7	0.7	1.09	5.53	5.32	66.4	5.9	43.4	5.5	9.3
3.6	2.56	10.4	1.07	4.3	0.1	0.70	5.07	4.46	55.9	6.4	65.2	6.2	5.5
3.4	1.21	6.4	0.40	8.6	0.3	2.00	19.05	5.24	62.0	3.9	71.5	22.0	5.3
7.3	0.07	0.7	0.00	8.5	1.0	1.43	17.96	4.09	50.5	1.8	18.1	21.3	6.3
8.3	0.42	1.5	-0.06	8.7	0.7	7.32	52.67	12.40	46.2	6.2	61.7	4.3	6.3
8.3	0.07	0.6	0.03	9.9	5.2	1.66	17.80	4.51	65.6	5.1	31.2	5.4	7.7
4.2	2.57	15.6	0.09	4.3	11.1	1.00	12.35	3.40	55.5	2.2	18.1	18.6	5.9
7.6	0.38	2.4	0.05	9.6	1.2	1.60	13.06	4.29	42.7	4.4	19.8	6.8	8.4
8.5	0.12	0.6	0.11	3.2	0.2	0.55	4.60	3.49	69.0	4.2	44.3	14.9	6.1
7.5	0.00	0.0	-0.02	4.5	0.9	0.95	11.35	4.33	61.6	2.1	15.4	18.3	4.2
8.5	0.25	0.7	0.00	4.4	0.3	1.54	12.60	3.73	63.5	6.3	105.4	13.1	4.2
8.5	0.28	1.0	0.00	4.1	0.2	0.97	7.20	3.15	62.4	9.2	209.4	5.5	5.8
7.2	0.10	0.8	0.18	3.8	0.2	0.38	4.42	3.22	83.1	1.1	9.8	28.5	4.4
8.0	1.85	3.8	0.33	7.2	0.6	1.14	6.57	4.27	61.6	3.9	23.9	10.5	7.6
4.4	1.25	8.4	-0.03	2.2	-0.1	-0.13	-1.22	3.38	102.3	1.7	28.2	27.3	7.4
7.4	2.32	4.3	2.17	4.7	0.2	1.05	6.71	2.97	44.5	5.9	216.3	28.7	5.3
7.2	0.34	2.4	-0.11	7.0	0.3	1.77	20.07	4.62	59.3	3.8	27.1	11.7	4.1
5.4	2.21	7.0	0.03	4.9	0.2	1.30	12.08	3.80	67.1	7.1	161.2	13.8	3.1
0.4	6.02	24.7	0.49	3.6	1.4	0.71	5.05	4.79	76.7	0.9	24.7	49.4	4.9

Name	City	State	Weiss Safety Rating	2003 Weiss Safety Rating	2002 Weiss Safety Rating	Total Assets ($Mil)	One Year Asset Growth	Asset Mix (As a % of Total Assets)				Capital- ization Index	Leverage Ratio	Risk-based Capital Ratio
								Comm- ercial Loans	Cons- umer Loans	Home Mort- gages	Secur- ities			
▼ BULLITT COUNTY BK	SHEPHERDSVILLE	KY	B-	B	B-	156.5	5.60	5.4	3.8	17.3	6.5	6.3	9.1	12.0
BURKE & HERBERT B&TC	ALEXANDRIA	VA	A+	A+	A+	1,260.8	9.65	2.3	1.3	16.5	40.4	9.4	10.6	16.1
BURLING BK	CHICAGO	IL	B+	B+	B+	107.2	-1.22	15.3	0.5	13.3	56.9	7.1	9.1	20.9
BURLINGTON B&T	BURLINGTON	IA	B-	B-	C+	199.6	7.61	14.3	2.5	24.9	24.5	5.4	7.5	11.3
BURT COUNTY ST BK	TEKAMAH	NE	C+	B-	B-	40.8	3.72	10.9	14.2	4.6	24.3	5.7	7.7	12.8
BURTON ST BK	BURTON	TX	B	B+	A-	40.2	-2.02	2.0	7.7	10.2	12.5	10.0	13.6	37.1
BUSEY BK	URBANA	IL	B	B	B	1,469.2	5.31	8.0	4.5	22.4	13.9	4.8	7.4	10.9
BUSEY BK FSB	FORT MYERS	FL	B	B	B	136.6	55.73	4.8	2.1	18.0	4.5	6.7	8.7	12.4
▼ BUSINESS BK	BATON ROUGE	LA	C	C+	C+	163.7	0.63	30.9	1.9	6.3	13.8	3.3	8.0	10.2
▲ BUSINESS BK	MINNETONKA	MN	C	C-	C-	77.6	4.28	32.6	3.4	2.3	27.7	7.8	9.6	13.4
▲ BUSINESS BK	CLAYTON	MO	C	D	D	195.2	107.94	17.4	1.2	19.0	1.7	6.4	10.7	12.1
▼ BUSINESS BK	VIENNA	VA	C+	B-	B	150.0	15.00	8.9	1.9	15.2	14.1	4.0	7.4	10.5
▲ BUSINESS BK FOX RIVER	APPLETON	WI	C	C-	C-	153.7	27.75	34.4	1.4	0.0	6.1	3.5	9.2	10.3
BUSINESS BK OF NV	LAS VEGAS	NV	C+	C+	C	307.0	24.94	9.2	0.3	0.3	17.8	5.0	7.3	11.0
BUSINESS FIRST NB	SANTA BARBARA	CA	B-	B-	B-	94.2	16.91	30.9	3.6	4.5	9.0	10.0	12.6	15.8
▲ BUTLER BK A CO-OP BK	LOWELL	MA	C+	B-	B	115.1	24.12	0.3	0.8	23.0	6.0	4.7	8.2	10.9
BUTTE CMNTY BK	CHICO	CA	B+	B+	B	412.8	12.01	14.9	2.0	10.6	1.1	5.7	8.7	11.5
▲ BUTTE ST BK	BUTTE	NE	D+	D	D+	25.3	7.72	9.1	6.9	5.4	16.6	7.0	9.7	12.5
▼ BYRON BK	BYRON	IL	B-	B+	B+	125.4	-0.15	8.3	3.6	19.5	27.9	7.0	9.0	14.9
▲ BYRON CENTER ST BK	BYRON	MI	B-	C	C-	516.8	-0.64	11.2	5.7	11.8	19.3	8.9	10.5	14.1
▲ BYRON ST BK	BYRON	NE	B-	C	C	24.7	3.47	7.1	6.2	5.1	7.5	10.0	11.8	18.0
C&G SAVINGS BANK	ALTOONA	PA	C	C	C	116.9	2.15	0.0	5.9	56.1	23.9	9.8	10.9	20.2
CABARRUS B&TC	CONCORD	NC	C+	C+	NR	45.0	69.86	15.9	4.5	16.1	9.6	10.0	14.9	18.7
CABOOL ST BK	CABOOL	MO	B-	B-	B	61.7	0.76	5.8	6.3	13.9	32.2	10.0	16.1	28.4
CACHE B&T	GREELEY	CO	D+	D+	D+	105.1	9.09	16.9	3.3	11.7	16.6	6.4	9.1	12.0
CACHE VALLEY BK	LOGAN	UT	C-	C-	C	155.8	0.47	20.1	3.8	9.1	16.1	3.8	8.4	10.4
CACTUS COMMERCE BK AZ BK	GLENDALE	AZ	D	D	NR	13.9	N/A	24.1	2.1	3.4	24.3	10.0	37.6	53.1
CAIRO BKG CO	CAIRO	GA	B-	B-	C+	79.6	-4.13	5.5	4.6	4.6	33.1	5.6	7.6	13.3
▲ CALAIS FS&LA	CALAIS	ME	B	B-	B-	45.2	11.94	4.8	4.6	73.4	4.6	10.0	15.5	26.2
CALDWELL B&TC	COLUMBIA	LA	C+	C+	C-	73.4	3.15	7.6	11.2	20.5	26.4	7.0	9.0	12.9
CALDWELL SAVINGS & LOAN	CALDWELL	OH	C+	C+	C+	42.4	-3.21	0.2	4.3	51.0	22.4	10.0	12.8	29.5
CALDWELL ST BK IN	CALDWELL	KS	B	B	B	29.9	1.66	13.7	5.8	3.8	22.8	10.0	12.0	17.0
CALHOUN COUNTY BK	HAMPTON	AR	B+	B	B-	37.1	-6.39	13.9	8.6	12.2	32.8	10.0	12.1	20.5
CALHOUN COUNTY BK	GRANTSVILLE	WV	C+	C+	C+	86.0	0.64	16.3	14.3	31.3	16.9	7.2	9.1	15.4
CALIFORNIA B&TC	SAN DIEGO	CA	B-	B-	B-	9,682.0	10.07	16.3	1.1	15.0	9.1	4.4	6.4	11.4
▲ CALIFORNIA COMMERCE BK	CENTURY CITY	CA	C+	C	B-	1,902.8	-13.75	0.4	6.1	3.2	12.6	9.2	10.4	16.9
CALIFORNIA COMMUNITY BK	ESCONDIDO	CA	D	D	NR	38.7	N/A	27.8	0.5	1.2	0.0	10.0	28.2	38.1
▲ CALIFORNIA FIRST NB	IRVINE	CA	C+	D+	D	60.1	42.34	0.0	0.0	0.0	1.7	10.0	32.0	36.7
CALIFORNIA NB	LOS ANGELES	CA	B	B	C+	5,181.6	-1.36	0.5	0.4	4.7	20.2	7.8	11.0	13.2
▲ CALIFORNIA OAKS ST BK	THOUSAND OAKS	CA	D-	E-	D-	83.7	-18.44	22.1	2.0	0.8	13.2	5.5	8.0	11.4
▲ CALIFORNIA PACIFIC BK	SAN FRANCISCO	CA	A-	B	B+	85.3	3.59	47.1	0.3	1.2	4.6	10.0	16.6	17.7
CALIFORNIA SVGS BK	SAN FRANCISCO	CA	B-	B	B+	775.3	-3.11	0.0	0.1	18.9	1.2	10.0	12.8	18.4
▼ CALLAWAY BK	FULTON	MO	B	B+	B+	230.8	6.62	11.5	2.9	19.1	22.9	8.3	9.9	15.5
▲ CALNET BUSINESS BANK NA	SACRAMENTO	CA	D	D-	D	112.6	43.62	9.1	0.0	1.1	11.0	6.5	8.8	12.1
CALUMET COUNTY BK	BRILLION	WI	B-	C+	B	60.6	-0.02	18.5	4.0	19.0	28.1	10.0	11.2	18.6
CALVERT B&TC	PRINCE FREDERICK	MD	A-	A-	A	270.0	2.98	7.9	2.9	20.9	36.3	7.4	9.3	19.3
CALVIN B TAYLOR BKG CO	BERLIN	MD	A+	A+	A+	390.4	2.92	4.0	0.6	18.1	39.2	10.0	16.2	39.4
▲ CAMBRIA COUNTY FS&LA	CRESSON	PA	B-	C+	C+	39.6	2.38	2.4	5.2	49.2	22.4	10.0	11.6	23.5
CAMBRIDGE BK	LAKE ZURICH	IL	C	C	D+	277.2	17.90	7.7	1.2	2.5	15.0	3.2	8.3	10.1
▼ CAMBRIDGE ST BK	CAMBRIDGE	MN	C+	B	B-	74.6	-0.72	24.6	0.9	6.3	19.4	9.7	11.1	14.8
CAMBRIDGE ST BK	CAMBRIDGE	WI	C+	C+	C+	72.1	4.67	10.4	5.2	19.4	9.2	3.2	7.0	10.1
CAMBRIDGE SVGS BK	CAMBRIDGE	MA	B-	B-	B-	1,996.2	8.39	2.5	0.1	39.4	27.2	5.2	7.2	11.4
CAMBRIDGE TRUST CO	CAMBRIDGE	MA	B	B+	B+	720.7	7.41	5.3	3.4	17.8	49.2	6.0	8.0	18.0
CAMDEN NB	CAMDEN	AL	B+	B	B+	76.8	5.51	13.8	18.9	16.9	15.6	10.0	11.0	15.7
CAMDEN NB	CAMDEN	ME	B	B	B	938.8	7.45	13.2	1.8	21.6	18.5	5.2	7.2	11.6
CAMELBACK CMNTY BK	PHOENIX	AZ	C	C	C	79.9	-15.19	12.6	1.0	3.9	0.1	6.3	9.8	12.0
▲ CAMERON ST BK	LAKE CHARLES	LA	A-	B+	B+	420.1	14.32	9.6	8.2	14.8	24.8	8.7	10.1	15.7
▼ CAMP GROVE ST BK	CAMP GROVE	IL	C+	B-	B-	13.4	-10.55	0.1	5.1	5.0	39.7	10.0	25.4	49.8
▼ CAMPBELL & FETTER BKRS	KENDALLVILLE	IN	B+	A-	B+	307.5	22.08	6.5	4.0	21.4	59.9	6.8	8.8	21.5
▲ CAMPBELL COUNTY BK	HERREID	SD	A-	B+	B+	60.9	5.59	11.9	1.3	0.0	27.2	10.0	11.1	17.5
CAMPBELLSVILLE NB	CAMPBELLSVILLE	KY	C+	C+	C+	63.9	7.90	1.8	12.6	36.4	11.3	6.5	8.5	13.2
CAMPUS ST BK	CAMPUS	IL	D+	D+	D+	15.4	-3.76	0.0	13.7	31.0	17.6	8.1	9.7	18.2
CANAAN NB	CANAAN	CT	C+	C+	C+	105.6	-1.52	5.8	4.1	17.4	42.3	5.8	7.8	12.7
▲ CANADIAN ST BK	YUKON	OK	C-	D+	D+	71.1	7.63	10.8	6.7	15.1	14.0	5.5	7.5	11.6

Asset Quality Index	Non-Performing Loans as a % of Total Loans	as a % of Capital	Net Charge-offs Avg Loans	Profitability Index	Net Income ($Mil)	Return on Assets (R.O.A.)	Return on Equity (R.O.E.)	Net Interest Spread	Overhead Efficiency Ratio	Liquidity Index	Liquidity Ratio	Hot Money Ratio	Stability Index
2.9	1.31	11.2	0.16	9.4	1.3	1.61	18.09	4.59	44.3	3.4	33.7	16.1	5.9
9.3	0.01	0.0	-0.01	9.6	10.0	1.64	16.27	4.25	43.6	6.5	47.9	5.9	9.6
7.5	1.33	4.7	0.05	5.9	0.5	0.80	8.54	3.43	80.6	5.0	53.3	13.5	6.1
6.8	0.27	2.0	0.28	7.2	1.1	1.12	13.38	3.82	75.3	4.0	17.5	9.2	5.4
3.6	1.84	12.6	1.41	5.2	0.2	1.02	13.21	4.27	51.6	6.1	73.3	10.1	4.6
9.0	0.03	0.1	-0.02	4.2	0.1	0.64	4.53	2.59	63.8	8.6	305.6	9.2	6.1
8.0	0.19	1.7	0.17	8.7	10.2	1.43	17.26	3.67	48.5	6.0	47.2	8.8	7.4
7.3	0.06	0.5	0.01	4.3	0.6	0.94	9.71	4.10	55.8	0.9	23.3	46.8	5.6
5.4	0.34	3.1	0.92	4.2	0.5	0.62	7.68	3.59	62.7	1.9	20.6	20.6	3.8
7.2	0.00	0.0	1.95	2.7	0.1	0.24	2.46	3.95	75.2	0.5	10.2	57.8	1.0
6.6	0.04	0.4	0.10	4.2	0.8	0.93	10.69	3.94	47.4	1.0	16.8	32.9	2.6
7.5	0.00	0.0	-0.05	3.8	0.4	0.53	7.53	4.02	76.4	5.4	47.0	9.4	3.9
6.9	0.07	0.7	0.06	4.8	0.6	0.88	9.74	2.93	45.8	1.3	11.4	26.2	5.2
7.5	0.00	0.0	0.06	5.2	1.4	0.93	12.83	5.07	70.5	4.8	38.6	10.3	3.7
8.1	0.00	0.0	-0.02	2.1	0.2	0.47	3.82	3.72	83.3	2.3	24.2	18.3	5.4
4.5	1.40	13.2	-0.01	8.1	0.6	1.03	12.67	5.41	66.2	1.8	20.8	21.9	5.2
8.3	0.03	0.3	-0.01	9.6	2.8	1.39	15.95	5.40	59.5	7.6	136.7	10.0	5.8
5.7	0.13	0.9	0.09	7.1	0.2	1.95	20.52	4.80	54.9	2.0	24.3	20.3	3.2
4.8	1.20	7.8	0.01	9.5	1.3	2.14	22.76	4.24	50.7	2.1	25.1	19.7	7.1
7.0	0.48	3.0	0.08	4.0	1.7	0.66	6.19	3.34	78.4	2.4	23.1	18.1	6.7
6.2	0.81	4.2	0.35	6.5	0.2	1.87	16.40	3.34	42.9	6.8	137.8	12.6	5.4
6.5	0.88	5.1	0.02	3.0	0.2	0.37	3.42	3.13	81.6	7.0	71.9	5.5	6.2
8.4	0.09	0.4	0.01	0.0	-0.2	-0.99	-6.25	3.60	128.0	0.9	14.3	33.2	2.0
5.5	1.71	5.5	0.02	3.7	0.2	0.67	4.07	4.22	79.6	6.1	63.9	8.2	6.2
8.3	0.03	0.2	-0.12	1.7	0.2	0.34	3.58	3.95	96.5	0.8	13.6	35.7	3.5
2.1	2.53	20.9	1.29	6.4	0.8	1.09	13.04	3.96	54.4	1.3	23.1	29.9	4.7
9.2	0.00	0.0	0.00	0.0	-0.4	-8.71	-17.42	2.84	294.8	8.5	135.4	1.7	0.0
5.4	1.23	7.1	0.00	6.4	0.5	1.14	15.18	3.18	60.7	5.7	57.8	9.4	6.3
7.5	0.33	1.7	0.01	6.2	0.2	1.00	5.96	5.17	62.1	3.2	1.5	11.7	6.3
3.8	2.08	13.1	0.03	6.0	0.6	1.65	18.25	5.02	68.4	2.3	42.7	32.5	4.6
6.4	1.87	8.6	0.17	4.1	0.1	0.49	3.85	3.05	77.0	4.8	34.5	8.9	5.2
8.0	0.08	0.5	0.00	4.2	0.1	0.84	7.06	3.60	75.6	3.5	27.6	13.4	5.5
6.8	0.83	3.6	-0.10	6.8	0.2	1.19	10.25	4.22	54.3	3.2	36.7	17.7	6.5
4.1	1.50	10.4	0.16	3.7	0.2	0.57	6.19	4.44	75.8	4.3	69.5	18.3	4.4
5.8	0.41	2.6	0.09	9.7	70.1	1.48	14.30	4.71	49.2	8.1	154.7	8.9	7.8
4.6	3.21	13.7	1.65	4.6	8.2	0.86	8.38	2.77	63.9	5.5	172.7	30.2	6.1
8.8	0.00	0.0	0.00	0.0	-0.9	-5.61	-17.11	2.88	258.2	5.6	146.3	19.9	0.0
9.4	0.00	0.0	0.00	3.6	0.4	1.29	4.00	5.21	73.6	7.0	364.9	17.4	2.1
4.5	1.45	7.3	-0.01	8.5	33.6	1.30	10.00	4.08	48.7	6.1	177.6	21.3	8.0
8.4	0.11	0.9	-0.31	4.8	0.9	2.06	27.99	5.83	77.7	5.5	27.5	1.0	0.5
8.4	0.00	0.0	-0.22	6.9	0.5	1.07	6.53	3.92	64.1	4.8	128.8	27.1	7.7
7.4	0.02	0.1	0.00	3.2	0.6	0.16	1.30	2.97	89.3	2.0	37.4	32.5	7.6
4.7	1.56	9.9	0.03	6.2	1.2	1.05	10.32	4.72	66.9	3.3	14.6	12.7	6.0
7.6	0.00	0.0	0.00	1.7	0.2	0.44	5.01	4.06	87.5	6.4	67.0	8.3	0.5
4.3	2.46	13.0	0.59	5.2	0.3	1.02	9.05	4.16	67.0	2.8	36.7	19.8	5.6
8.6	0.22	1.2	0.02	10.0	3.2	2.38	24.51	5.09	39.3	8.5	121.2	2.2	8.5
9.5	0.32	0.8	0.00	9.2	2.7	1.41	8.97	3.79	44.6	7.2	83.4	5.9	9.8
8.7	0.00	0.0	0.00	5.3	0.2	0.93	8.19	3.10	62.8	2.0	19.7	19.6	5.3
4.6	0.75	6.4	0.16	7.8	1.8	1.33	15.80	4.43	52.3	3.4	41.0	18.1	3.7
1.6	3.83	23.4	-0.09	6.2	0.6	1.57	14.03	4.27	62.4	5.2	61.2	12.4	7.4
5.6	0.27	2.8	0.25	7.0	0.4	1.15	17.29	3.94	56.8	2.9	49.3	26.5	4.3
9.4	0.05	0.4	0.00	4.2	5.8	0.61	8.09	3.23	70.0	7.4	162.2	13.2	5.9
5.8	1.19	5.4	0.24	5.4	3.5	1.00	11.69	4.28	75.5	8.3	140.8	5.4	5.8
6.7	0.23	1.4	0.14	7.3	0.5	1.39	12.60	4.80	59.7	4.2	60.8	17.3	5.8
5.5	0.56	5.0	0.04	9.3	7.1	1.52	19.79	3.73	44.9	1.5	6.3	21.6	7.2
5.4	0.43	3.0	0.23	4.9	0.2	0.53	5.09	5.58	60.9	3.9	13.3	9.1	4.3
5.8	0.60	3.5	0.11	8.4	2.8	1.32	13.18	5.15	67.7	5.6	71.1	13.7	5.8
8.4	0.00	0.0	0.00	3.7	0.0	0.49	1.91	4.52	88.5	4.7	13.7	3.5	5.8
9.2	0.32	1.4	0.03	6.0	1.5	1.03	11.32	3.23	60.3	2.5	20.6	16.9	5.0
7.3	0.40	2.1	-0.01	8.8	0.5	1.70	15.41	4.55	48.4	2.2	14.5	18.2	6.8
7.3	0.16	1.5	0.08	7.7	0.4	1.34	16.32	4.63	61.7	4.3	20.8	7.2	4.6
4.9	0.90	5.8	-0.09	4.9	0.1	1.13	11.47	3.76	76.5	7.4	154.9	11.1	2.6
6.3	0.48	3.0	0.04	3.9	0.4	0.72	9.32	3.43	73.8	4.4	32.1	10.6	4.3
5.1	0.90	7.5	0.06	5.9	0.3	0.94	12.65	4.46	73.2	3.4	42.7	18.5	2.1

Name	City	State	Weiss Safety Rating	2003 Weiss Safety Rating	2002 Weiss Safety Rating	Total Assets ($Mil)	One Year Asset Growth	Asset Mix (As a % of Total Assets) Commercial Loans	Consumer Loans	Home Mortgages	Securities	Capitalization Index	Leverage Ratio	Risk-based Capital Ratio
▲ CANANDAIGUA NB&TC	CANANDAIGUA	NY	C+	C	C-	914.7	7.14	15.3	14.0	6.2	21.1	5.7	7.9	11.6
CANEY VALLEY NB	CANEY	KS	B	B	B+	43.6	6.68	9.3	6.9	20.6	32.5	8.1	9.7	17.3
CANISTEO S&LA	CANISTEO	NY	D-	D-	D-	5.8	6.50	0.0	5.7	55.9	0.3	9.2	10.5	21.4
CANON NB	CANON CITY	CO	B-	B-	B	170.9	6.62	8.1	2.6	16.0	24.0	6.1	8.1	12.8
▲ CANTON CO-OP BK	CANTON	MA	C+	C	B-	76.7	-3.05	0.0	0.1	28.1	58.9	10.0	15.4	52.2
CANTON ST BK	CANTON	MN	C+	C	D+	26.2	-3.43	11.2	3.2	6.7	23.3	9.4	10.7	14.5
CANTON ST BK	CANTON	MO	D	D+	C+	39.9	1.37	2.3	2.0	18.4	23.8	4.7	6.7	11.4
CANYON COMMUNITY BK NA	TUCSON	AZ	B-	B-	C-	61.4	42.14	18.4	1.9	3.5	19.8	8.3	10.7	13.6
CANYON NB	PALM SPRINGS	CA	B-	B-	C+	183.0	20.46	14.8	2.1	9.5	9.7	5.3	7.3	11.8
▲ CAPAHA BK SB	TAMMS	IL	C	C-	D+	118.1	1.07	13.0	2.8	17.4	6.1	4.6	7.1	10.8
CAPE ANN SVGS BK	GLOUCESTER	MA	B+	A-	A-	352.0	-0.29	0.3	0.6	35.0	40.3	10.0	19.0	44.4
▼ CAPE COD CO-OP BK	YARMOUTH PORT	MA	B	B+	B	384.3	8.88	1.7	0.9	49.4	18.2	7.4	9.3	15.6
CAPE COD FIVE CENTS SB	HARWICH PORT	MA	B	B	B+	1,306.3	5.55	1.7	0.3	40.3	28.7	8.5	10.0	19.0
▲ CAPE SVGS BK	CAPE MAY	NJ	A-	B+	B+	514.5	8.30	1.5	0.2	35.6	20.1	10.0	11.0	18.2
▼ CAPITAL B&TC	NASHVILLE	TN	C	C+	C+	304.9	16.90	8.8	1.9	16.2	19.7	3.9	7.3	10.5
CAPITAL B&TC FSB	BREA	CA	B+	B+	B+	66.0	18.76	0.0	0.0	0.0	88.4	10.0	57.8	281.6
▲ CAPITAL BANK NA	ROCKVILLE	MD	D+	D	D	69.5	54.98	18.7	1.7	8.5	8.9	7.3	10.0	12.8
CAPITAL BK	MONTGOMERY	AL	C	C	C-	30.9	23.70	6.8	0.9	8.0	14.1	10.0	24.7	32.3
CAPITAL BK	LITTLE ROCK	AR	D+	C-	C-	110.0	26.71	11.3	3.8	9.5	57.1	4.9	6.9	14.5
CAPITAL BK	FORT OGLETHORPE	GA	B-	B	B	126.0	41.94	13.0	2.1	16.0	8.1	5.0	8.7	11.0
CAPITAL BK	ST PAUL	MN	B	B+	B+	51.0	9.37	19.3	4.2	2.8	27.3	6.0	8.0	13.2
▲ CAPITAL BK	RALEIGH	NC	C	D+	C+	885.0	-2.62	10.9	1.5	6.6	16.4	5.5	8.6	11.4
▼ CAPITAL BK	JACINTO CITY	TX	B	B+	B+	119.9	0.47	16.0	6.8	9.8	14.4	9.6	11.6	14.7
CAPITAL BK OF TX	CARRIZO SPRINGS	TX	C-	D+	NR	38.9	-8.46	7.2	9.3	7.3	37.3	8.2	9.8	21.1
▲ CAPITAL BK&TC	ALBANY	NY	D-	E-	E-	84.1	-5.36	31.0	0.8	2.4	13.4	7.4	9.4	12.9
CAPITAL CITY BK	TALLAHASSEE	FL	B+	A-	B+	2,024.7	8.51	8.4	11.4	18.8	8.8	5.5	8.4	11.3
CAPITAL CITY BK	TOPEKA	KS	C+	C+	C	362.5	11.57	7.3	3.9	11.6	45.6	5.7	7.7	14.2
▲ CAPITAL COMMUNITY BK	PROVO	UT	C	C-	C+	75.2	-15.46	12.1	2.0	5.2	0.0	7.4	9.3	13.9
CAPITAL CROSSING BK	BOSTON	MA	B-	B-	B	1,193.1	32.24	4.0	0.9	10.5	16.5	10.0	12.8	18.0
▲ CAPITAL ONE BK	GLEN ALLEN	VA	B	B-	C+	26,347.1	30.07	0.0	42.8	0.0	24.6	10.0	11.6	19.0
CAPITAL ONE FSB	MC LEAN	VA	B-	C+	C	13,813.9	12.48	18.3	57.6	0.0	17.8	10.0	14.1	16.7
CAPITAL PACIFIC BK	PORTLAND	OR	D	D	NR	29.3	N/A	38.7	0.3	0.7	8.4	10.0	46.4	56.4
CAPITAL SAVINGS BK SSB	EL PASO	TX	D-	D	D+	45.5	-12.22	5.5	5.5	5.4	16.3	6.6	8.6	12.9
CAPITAL ST BK	CHARLESTON	WV	C+	C+	C+	190.3	17.48	6.4	7.2	15.9	28.3	4.0	7.0	10.5
▼ CAPITALBANK	GREENWOOD	SC	B	B+	B	531.7	32.11	7.2	3.9	26.0	13.5	6.1	8.2	11.8
CAPITOL BK	MADISON	WI	C+	C	D+	112.1	4.70	17.4	1.5	13.1	7.9	5.0	8.5	11.0
▼ CAPITOL CITY B&TC	ATLANTA	GA	D+	C-	B-	159.2	28.77	15.3	4.3	5.0	19.2	4.7	9.6	10.9
▼ CAPITOL FEDERAL SVGS BK	TOPEKA	KS	B	B+	A	8,480.1	-2.15	0.0	0.2	50.5	42.1	9.0	10.4	25.5
▲ CAPITOL NATIONAL BANK	LANSING	MI	C+	C	C	226.1	9.87	26.9	3.0	12.0	0.5	3.5	7.5	10.3
CAPON VALLEY BK	WARDENSVILLE	WV	C+	C+	C+	127.6	-4.34	3.1	23.2	34.1	8.5	5.7	7.7	11.9
CAPSTONE BK	WATSEKA	IL	C	C	C	205.9	-0.12	4.6	2.4	17.7	48.4	4.8	6.8	14.0
▲ CARDINAL BK NA	FAIRFAX	VA	D+	D	D-	805.5	56.03	7.3	1.2	5.3	40.7	9.8	10.8	15.2
▲ CARDINAL ST BK	DURHAM	NC	D	D-	D-	119.0	67.26	6.8	2.4	18.5	1.7	10.0	16.2	19.9
CARDUNAL SVGS BK FSB	W DUNDEE	IL	C-	C-	C-	167.6	-0.51	4.4	1.5	36.0	25.1	4.4	6.4	11.7
▼ CARLINVILLE NB	CARLINVILLE	IL	C	B-	C+	164.5	-5.60	17.3	5.9	7.3	27.8	7.2	9.1	14.0
CARLSBAD NB	CARLSBAD	NM	A-	A-	A-	183.8	5.29	8.9	4.2	16.5	52.4	7.2	9.2	21.0
CARMINE ST BK	CARMINE	TX	B+	B+	B+	32.7	8.94	3.9	18.8	8.5	30.7	10.0	15.1	30.3
CARNEY ST BK	CARNEY	OK	D-	D-	D	15.8	6.99	2.2	9.0	14.8	54.5	6.3	8.3	27.7
CAROLINA B&TC	LAMAR	SC	B	B	B+	254.4	2.32	45.3	8.9	8.4	11.4	8.3	10.0	13.6
CAROLINA BK	GREENSBORO	NC	C+	C+	C	242.7	22.07	15.2	2.7	9.8	12.6	4.1	8.4	10.5
CAROLINA COMMERCE BK	GASTONIA	NC	D	NR	NR	9.4	N/A	0.0	0.0	0.0	0.0	10.0	3,905.3	302.3
CAROLINA COMMERCIAL BK	ALLENDALE	SC	B-	B-	B-	35.9	-2.91	5.8	9.1	4.4	65.8	10.0	12.1	31.7
▲ CAROLINA FIRST BK	GREENVILLE	SC	B-	C+	C	8,953.6	25.63	10.5	3.4	5.7	35.4	5.1	7.1	12.6
CAROLINA FSB	CHARLESTON	SC	C+	C	D+	58.1	2.65	4.6	17.3	34.0	0.0	7.1	9.6	12.6
CAROLINA NB&TC	COLUMBIA	SC	D-	D-	D	89.5	129.37	9.8	3.0	12.2	3.3	5.1	8.7	11.1
▲ CAROLINA TRUST BK	LINCOLNTON	NC	D	D-	D	71.3	19.12	12.5	5.0	16.9	5.9	4.8	8.3	10.9
CARROLL B&T	HUNTINGDON	TN	B	B	A-	151.6	0.88	5.5	18.2	22.3	30.9	9.2	10.4	16.9
CARROLL COUNTY S&LA	CARROLLTON	MO	D	D	D+	23.6	1.48	0.0	0.2	26.2	54.3	7.6	9.4	35.0
CARROLL COUNTY ST BK	CARROLL	IA	B-	B-	B-	156.0	16.21	12.9	2.7	7.2	23.3	7.3	9.8	12.7
CARROLL COUNTY TC	CARROLLTON	MO	A-	A-	A-	81.7	-3.49	6.0	3.1	3.8	53.6	10.0	12.7	21.3
▲ CARROLLTON BK	CARROLLTON	IL	B	B-	C+	420.7	1.17	15.2	2.3	14.5	20.6	6.3	8.3	12.6
▲ CARROLLTON BK	BALTIMORE	MD	C+	C-	C	303.0	-9.66	12.7	0.9	8.7	16.0	8.2	9.8	13.9
▼ CARROLLTON FEDERAL BANK	CARROLLTON	KY	C	B-	B-	34.0	18.83	0.5	9.0	37.9	37.5	10.0	13.9	33.9
▲ CARSON NB OF AUBURN	AUBURN	NE	B	B-	B-	45.5	3.36	5.4	3.6	8.1	46.9	10.0	12.2	21.6

Asset Quality Index	Non-Performing Loans as a % of Total Loans	Non-Performing Loans as a % of Capital	Net Charge-offs Avg Loans	Profitability Index	Net Income ($Mil)	Return on Assets (R.O.A.)	Return on Equity (R.O.E.)	Net Interest Spread	Overhead Efficiency Ratio	Liquidity Index	Liquidity Ratio	Hot Money Ratio	Stability Index
3.3	1.45	11.9	0.14	5.4	4.9	1.09	14.10	4.47	67.2	8.0	123.1	6.0	3.9
8.3	0.00	0.0	0.00	6.4	0.3	1.53	15.56	3.77	55.0	2.2	9.3	17.6	5.7
7.8	0.00	0.0	0.00	2.9	0.0	0.79	7.69	3.42	76.2	3.1	36.2	16.1	2.3
7.4	0.05	0.4	0.28	5.8	0.8	0.93	11.65	4.37	61.3	5.6	70.3	13.4	3.6
10.0	0.00	0.0	0.00	2.9	0.1	0.35	2.35	2.49	79.9	7.3	142.1	10.9	6.8
7.7	0.36	2.3	-0.09	6.7	0.2	1.64	15.65	4.20	61.6	4.3	39.5	13.3	5.0
4.0	1.96	15.3	3.79	3.4	0.2	0.84	11.71	3.03	72.4	2.0	37.1	31.7	2.3
8.4	0.01	0.0	0.00	4.8	0.2	0.83	7.58	5.04	66.6	4.8	13.9	3.5	2.3
7.8	0.01	0.1	0.02	9.0	1.2	1.42	19.36	5.57	56.2	6.0	48.9	6.0	4.5
3.9	1.07	10.3	0.10	4.1	0.4	0.63	8.27	4.11	75.3	3.1	20.9	13.9	3.8
9.7	1.07	2.3	0.01	4.4	1.2	0.66	3.02	2.74	67.5	6.8	156.1	15.4	8.4
8.2	0.27	2.1	0.08	4.8	1.2	0.66	7.07	3.14	67.3	7.1	97.3	8.9	5.6
9.5	0.26	1.5	0.00	4.1	6.3	0.98	9.73	3.04	77.2	6.3	94.3	13.8	8.1
8.4	0.55	3.2	0.00	5.3	2.2	0.86	7.62	4.06	66.7	4.9	28.6	5.6	6.7
4.4	1.07	10.1	0.31	5.3	1.3	0.90	12.40	3.90	60.2	0.9	12.8	33.2	3.6
6.9	0.00	0.0	0.00	10.0	4.5	12.74	25.21	4.28	81.9	0.0	0.8	100.0	3.7
7.3	0.17	1.3	-0.02	1.2	0.1	0.30	2.87	3.70	90.9	2.1	44.6	44.0	3.3
7.4	0.00	0.0	0.00	0.6	0.0	0.15	0.59	3.27	83.2	3.6	32.7	14.4	1.7
7.6	0.81	4.6	-0.01	6.1	0.8	1.46	22.24	4.49	49.6	0.7	9.3	34.1	1.3
5.7	0.49	4.6	0.07	6.6	0.7	1.33	16.09	5.28	68.4	3.4	12.9	11.9	6.0
5.7	1.41	8.8	-0.05	9.2	0.6	2.18	28.54	4.53	56.0	6.2	61.6	6.6	6.4
3.2	1.02	6.7	0.19	3.4	2.5	0.58	5.62	3.25	72.6	2.2	20.2	18.7	4.4
4.2	1.15	6.8	0.87	2.8	0.1	0.18	1.46	4.80	93.4	3.6	22.5	11.9	7.0
7.5	0.00	0.0	0.09	2.7	0.1	0.36	2.89	2.93	87.2	7.4	93.7	4.8	0.2
1.0	5.54	32.1	0.33	0.9	-0.1	-0.15	-1.70	3.85	104.8	3.8	48.5	17.4	1.2
7.4	0.22	1.6	0.23	8.3	11.6	1.19	11.76	4.76	68.7	6.7	57.2	6.8	8.3
6.0	0.90	5.4	0.04	4.4	1.7	0.94	12.26	3.32	67.4	0.8	13.4	35.9	3.4
4.9	0.65	3.4	-0.97	4.1	0.2	0.49	5.71	5.21	87.9	6.1	88.2	11.9	2.9
3.5	2.24	16.4	0.24	9.9	9.5	1.78	20.18	6.40	60.5	1.8	35.1	96.7	7.4
4.7	1.35	5.3	3.43	10.0	571.1	4.44	36.23	5.60	65.0	2.2	43.8	97.3	8.8
3.3	1.23	5.1	7.13	8.2	152.9	2.30	16.02	5.28	46.1	0.7	11.6	44.9	7.7
8.5	0.00	0.0	0.00	0.0	-0.7	-5.66	-10.85	3.78	196.8	8.4	147.7	5.2	0.0
0.9	3.37	27.2	0.16	2.4	0.1	0.34	4.05	4.42	92.4	3.0	67.7	33.2	2.4
4.7	0.66	4.9	0.04	5.1	0.8	0.91	10.75	3.53	56.7	1.5	6.4	22.1	5.0
5.8	0.36	2.5	0.07	6.4	2.6	1.08	10.43	4.35	65.0	2.8	11.1	14.6	6.1
7.0	0.19	1.8	0.03	4.9	0.4	0.82	9.84	3.54	64.9	1.2	26.3	32.7	3.9
1.6	2.15	14.8	0.09	8.3	1.1	1.53	15.67	4.99	64.1	2.5	35.9	23.6	5.8
9.6	0.18	0.9	0.00	4.6	19.1	0.45	4.40	1.35	51.6	2.1	23.0	23.0	7.3
4.5	0.89	8.6	0.21	9.8	1.7	1.54	20.50	5.03	44.9	4.9	66.6	16.5	5.5
4.9	0.21	1.9	0.39	4.9	0.5	0.85	11.02	4.40	65.4	3.2	41.5	19.5	4.2
6.0	0.74	3.8	0.28	3.8	0.9	0.88	10.39	3.33	74.6	4.2	24.5	8.8	4.5
8.9	0.05	0.3	0.06	2.6	1.8	0.51	5.73	2.85	73.1	3.4	52.6	24.0	3.0
7.4	0.02	0.1	0.00	0.2	0.0	0.03	0.29	3.19	90.5	2.3	43.5	33.3	0.0
3.3	1.46	13.5	0.00	3.2	0.2	0.22	3.21	2.72	87.4	0.9	19.8	34.3	3.1
2.6	2.86	16.3	-0.02	9.3	1.4	1.59	15.43	4.50	51.6	4.1	26.7	10.1	5.8
8.7	0.00	0.0	0.12	9.7	2.1	2.28	24.29	3.97	54.7	4.9	60.0	15.3	6.8
7.8	0.45	1.2	0.08	6.5	0.2	1.42	9.20	4.53	60.3	7.4	173.5	13.1	7.2
7.1	1.02	3.5	0.09	3.7	0.1	0.69	8.13	3.59	76.8	4.4	65.0	15.5	1.6
4.9	0.52	3.6	0.06	6.1	1.4	1.09	10.97	4.55	70.6	3.3	31.0	15.7	5.9
7.0	0.17	1.5	0.03	3.6	0.8	0.64	7.57	3.44	67.5	1.3	12.5	26.1	4.2
10.0	0.00	0.0	0.00	0.0	-0.7	-15.36	-16.58	0.00	35,050.0	5.0	661.0	101.0	0.0
6.8	1.46	3.1	0.00	3.5	0.1	0.62	5.08	3.08	77.4	2.6	28.2	17.9	5.2
4.8	1.14	6.4	0.42	6.1	52.7	1.21	13.65	3.22	49.3	1.8	20.7	24.6	6.2
6.8	0.10	0.9	0.09	5.3	0.3	0.87	8.97	4.79	76.0	0.8	4.5	32.3	4.5
8.5	0.00	0.0	0.00	0.0	-0.5	-1.28	-11.37	3.07	127.0	2.2	37.1	28.7	0.0
7.9	0.09	0.8	-0.03	1.2	0.1	0.31	3.57	3.83	87.9	2.3	29.9	21.0	0.0
4.2	1.69	9.2	0.36	7.2	0.9	1.21	11.74	4.53	57.5	2.6	17.7	16.5	5.7
6.7	1.90	5.8	0.00	3.2	0.1	0.38	4.10	1.49	65.3	4.4	31.3	7.6	2.3
5.1	0.74	5.1	0.00	3.9	0.4	0.58	6.31	4.27	80.4	1.8	20.0	21.0	5.2
6.9	1.89	6.1	-0.06	6.0	0.6	1.46	11.53	3.38	56.4	0.8	15.7	34.9	7.8
8.5	0.13	1.0	0.00	5.2	2.6	1.23	14.70	3.27	59.1	3.8	33.1	13.6	4.6
5.1	1.25	8.0	0.04	3.8	1.0	0.66	6.50	4.11	86.4	5.3	31.0	4.1	4.0
7.1	0.98	3.3	0.19	1.9	0.0	-0.26	-1.73	3.47	108.5	2.2	28.1	20.2	5.7
8.7	0.00	0.0	0.00	4.3	0.2	0.81	6.42	3.65	70.1	4.5	49.0	13.8	5.8

Name	City	State	Weiss Safety Rating	2003 Weiss Safety Rating	2002 Weiss Safety Rating	Total Assets ($Mil)	One Year Asset Growth	Asset Mix (As a % of Total Assets) Comm- ercial Loans	Cons- umer Loans	Home Mort- gages	Secur- ities	Capital- ization Index	Leverage Ratio	Risk-based Capital Ratio
▲ CARTER COUNTY BK	ELIZABETHTON	TN	A-	B+	B+	193.6	6.39	19.1	8.8	28.2	13.5	7.0	9.0	12.9
CARTERVILLE ST & SVG BK	CARTERVILLE	IL	A-	A-	A-	46.5	1.36	4.0	7.1	18.9	37.5	5.6	7.6	15.7
CARTHAGE BK	CARTHAGE	MS	C	C+	C+	155.8	3.40	5.0	15.2	27.2	11.8	7.7	9.5	13.3
CARTHAGE FS&LA	CARTHAGE	NY	B-	C+	C+	119.1	1.55	0.0	4.2	67.6	12.4	6.7	8.7	18.4
CARVER FSB	NEW YORK CITY	NY	B+	B	C	553.6	7.19	0.8	0.2	18.2	23.3	8.0	9.7	15.7
CARVER ST BK	SAVANNAH	GA	E-	E-	E	25.8	9.33	11.0	11.7	27.4	14.1	5.6	7.6	12.4
CASCADE BK	EVERETT	WA	B-	B-	B-	1,049.6	22.68	9.8	0.9	11.1	22.8	4.3	8.3	10.6
CASEY COUNTY BK	LIBERTY	KY	B	B	C+	125.0	-1.80	3.9	9.9	25.3	27.8	9.3	10.5	17.4
▲ CASEY ST BK	CASEY	IL	B	B-	C+	123.6	8.71	8.9	6.1	22.9	30.6	6.2	8.2	12.7
CASHMERE VALLEY BK	CASHMERE	WA	B	B+	B+	636.9	22.20	4.4	8.3	13.3	41.9	4.8	6.8	12.9
▼ CASS COMMERCIAL BK	BRIDGETON	MO	B-	B	B+	341.0	13.45	25.5	0.4	1.3	1.4	5.2	9.6	11.2
CASS COUNTY BK	PLATTSMOUTH	NE	C-	C-	C	50.8	4.02	2.9	3.4	24.2	19.0	5.7	7.7	15.2
CASTLE B&TC	MERIDEN	CT	D	D	D+	74.6	-3.48	11.6	7.5	2.0	36.9	5.7	7.7	13.0
CASTLE BK NA	DE KALB	IL	C+	B-	B-	711.2	8.94	11.2	1.9	11.8	17.3	3.1	6.9	10.1
▲ CASTLE ROCK BK	CASTLE ROCK	CO	C	D+	D	93.1	2.42	5.5	3.6	12.7	5.5	5.3	8.1	11.3
▲ CASTLE ROCK BK	CASTLE ROCK	MN	A-	A-	A-	98.1	9.37	17.0	4.6	8.1	44.8	10.0	11.1	19.6
CASTROVILLE ST BK	CASTROVILLE	TX	B	B	B	66.7	5.12	2.6	6.5	11.1	41.7	7.8	9.5	20.4
CATAHOULA-LASALLE BK	JONESVILLE	LA	A-	A-	B+	75.7	2.38	5.5	8.2	10.0	32.8	10.0	12.5	25.2
▼ CATAWBA VALLEY BK	HICKORY	NC	C+	B-	B	442.4	9.76	31.3	5.2	11.6	12.9	5.0	8.0	11.0
▼ CATHAY BK	LOS ANGELES	CA	B	A-	A-	5,762.4	91.47	14.3	0.1	4.0	29.7	5.2	7.7	11.2
▲ CATTARAUGUS COUNTY BK	LITTLE VALLEY	NY	C+	C	B-	120.0	-4.25	7.8	3.9	28.9	32.7	8.7	10.1	19.5
▲ CATTLE NB&TC	SEWARD	NE	A-	B	B	118.9	1.92	4.0	1.5	16.0	21.9	9.9	10.9	15.7
CATTLEMANS NAT BK	ROUND MOUNTAIN	TX	D+	D+	D	71.0	-11.83	5.3	8.8	6.4	31.8	6.5	8.5	16.9
CAVALRY BANKING	MURFREESBORO	TN	B+	B+	B+	517.1	11.05	22.8	6.5	24.7	7.2	7.2	9.5	12.7
CAYUGA LAKE NB	UNION SPRINGS	NY	A-	A-	A-	81.6	-0.35	5.5	6.2	26.5	26.1	10.0	11.6	22.0
CB&T BK OF MIDDLE GEORGIA	WARNER ROBINS	GA	B-	B-	B	365.1	12.83	10.3	2.4	12.7	9.8	3.5	8.0	10.3
CB&T BK RUSSELL CTY	PHENIX CITY	AL	B-	B-	B	209.7	17.71	13.9	4.8	15.7	11.6	3.8	8.3	10.4
CBC BK	BOWLING GREEN	MO	D	D	D+	44.6	9.68	6.0	2.9	17.0	7.7	3.8	7.3	10.4
CECIL FEDERAL BK	ELKTON	MD	B-	B-	B-	168.2	25.28	20.5	5.5	37.0	3.4	5.7	9.3	11.5
CECILIAN BK	CECILIA	KY	B	B	B	281.0	13.02	4.8	7.6	26.5	31.4	7.2	9.2	14.7
CEDAR CREEK BK	SEVEN POINTS	TX	A-	A-	B	104.9	-1.73	9.3	2.1	11.8	27.1	9.3	10.5	19.0
▼ CEDAR HILL NB	LAWRENCEVILLE	GA	B-	B	B	8.8	-6.74	0.0	8.7	0.0	77.3	10.0	64.9	164.9
CEDAR RAPIDS B&TC	CEDAR RAPIDS	IA	C-	C-	C	187.9	46.16	34.7	1.1	3.3	14.3	7.4	10.0	12.8
▼ CEDAR RAPIDS ST BK	CEDAR RAPIDS	NE	E-	E	D-	26.9	17.33	10.6	3.8	2.2	13.9	3.4	7.5	10.2
CEDAR SECURITY BK	FORDYCE	NE	C+	C+	C+	20.4	-2.86	19.6	6.0	8.1	18.3	10.0	12.7	20.5
▲ CEDAR VALLEY B&TC	LA PORTE CITY	IA	D	C-	C-	31.4	7.43	10.5	5.1	18.7	16.6	6.0	8.0	12.9
CEDARS BK	LOS ANGELES	CA	B	B-	C	420.8	3.98	9.6	0.6	2.0	18.8	7.1	9.5	12.6
CEDARSTONE BK	LEBANON	TN	D	NR	NR	15.6	N/A	6.8	4.7	5.5	25.0	10.0	81.3	121.0
CELTIC BK CORP	SALT LAKE CITY	UT	D+	D	D	71.9	61.86	31.0	0.7	2.3	0.0	6.7	10.6	12.2
CENBANK	BUFFALO LAKE	MN	B-	B-	B-	36.4	-6.83	7.5	6.3	17.1	26.8	5.3	7.3	11.5
▲ CENLAR FSB	EWING TWP	NJ	C	E	C+	503.7	2.36	0.0	4.5	14.2	59.9	3.6	5.6	18.1
CENTENNIAL BK	FOUNTAIN VALLEY	CA	B	B-	B-	377.3	47.53	0.0	0.7	1.0	10.9	6.1	10.8	11.9
▲ CENTENNIAL BK	CENTENNIAL	CO	E+	E-	E-	57.6	-1.31	2.7	1.4	0.8	9.2	4.4	6.4	26.2
▲ CENTENNIAL BK	OMAHA	NE	E+	E-	E+	33.7	-25.61	20.8	6.1	32.1	7.9	5.8	7.8	12.6
CENTENNIAL BK	OGDEN	UT	D	D	D	108.7	2.93	4.6	2.3	3.9	3.1	6.3	10.3	12.0
▲ CENTENNIAL BK OF PUEBLO	PUEBLO	CO	B+	B	B	33.3	0.66	9.6	4.1	8.7	17.1	9.0	10.3	16.8
▲ CENTENNIAL BK WEST	FORT COLLINS	CO	D	D-	D-	691.1	-4.02	8.9	3.7	6.8	4.0	6.3	10.0	11.9
▼ CENTENNIAL NB	WALKER	MN	D+	C+	C+	41.9	-0.04	5.6	6.4	23.1	9.0	7.5	9.3	13.8
CENTER BK	LOS ANGELES	CA	B+	B+	B+	1,186.0	32.98	20.6	3.6	0.2	13.2	5.2	8.7	11.2
▲ CENTER NB	LITCHFIELD	MN	A	A-	B+	126.2	6.71	14.6	11.0	9.0	26.8	10.0	11.5	18.5
▲ CENTER POINT B&TC	CENTER POINT	IA	B+	B	B-	20.5	-3.20	6.8	2.3	18.2	31.2	9.6	10.7	16.7
CENTERA BK	SUBLETTE	KS	B-	B-	C+	145.7	4.58	8.9	2.9	7.2	31.6	5.3	7.3	11.7
CENTERBANK	MILFORD	OH	D	D	D	42.7	11.17	23.3	1.3	5.1	3.5	7.7	11.3	13.1
▲ CENTERBANK OF	JACKSONVILLE	FL	D	D-	D	117.1	46.19	27.7	2.8	7.8	0.4	3.7	8.8	10.3
CENTERSTATE BK MID	LEESBURG	FL	D	NR	NR	38.6	N/A	4.1	1.7	31.4	15.1	10.0	20.3	33.7
▲ CENTERSTATE BK OF	WINTER HAVEN	FL	C	C-	D+	133.8	35.59	10.1	13.2	4.8	20.3	5.0	7.6	11.0
▲ CENTERVILLE ST BK	CENTERVILLE	KS	E+	E	E	8.2	1.16	5.7	1.4	2.5	76.5	6.0	8.1	23.1
▲ CENTIER BK	WHITING	IN	A-	B+	B+	1,417.6	7.52	4.7	1.3	32.3	29.5	6.9	8.9	13.3
CENTINEL BK OF TAOS	TAOS	NM	B+	B+	B+	117.2	-0.38	5.8	3.3	12.2	24.2	5.9	7.9	13.4
▼ CENTRA BK	MORGANTOWN	WV	D+	C-	D+	398.9	30.27	15.4	3.7	18.9	5.4	2.9	7.6	9.9
▲ CENTRAL B&T	LANDER	WY	B	B-	B-	67.0	1.21	11.3	10.0	25.4	29.2	5.3	7.3	14.0
CENTRAL B&TC	CORDELE	GA	B-	B-	C+	53.4	-7.64	19.5	9.0	18.2	14.7	6.5	8.5	13.3
▲ CENTRAL B&TC	HUTCHINSON	KS	C-	D+	D+	213.9	-7.15	11.1	1.8	15.1	28.7	6.4	8.4	14.8
▲ CENTRAL B&TC	LEXINGTON	KY	B-	C+	B-	1,113.5	6.46	19.2	20.5	13.1	12.8	4.5	8.1	10.8

Asset Quality Index	Non-Performing Loans as a % of Total Loans	Non-Performing Loans as a % of Capital	Net Charge-offs Avg Loans	Profitability Index	Net Income ($Mil)	Return on Assets (R.O.A.)	Return on Equity (R.O.E.)	Net Interest Spread	Overhead Efficiency Ratio	Liquidity Index	Liquidity Ratio	Hot Money Ratio	Stability Index
7.8	0.12	1.0	0.33	9.3	1.7	1.80	19.98	4.60	61.3	3.2	19.4	13.2	6.6
7.1	1.00	5.6	0.01	4.1	0.2	0.69	8.49	3.51	73.5	6.3	39.2	0.8	5.9
4.3	0.81	6.0	0.46	3.0	0.2	0.26	2.69	4.58	92.4	2.4	17.5	17.0	4.4
6.5	0.30	2.6	0.01	4.3	0.3	0.55	6.40	3.02	71.0	3.1	20.3	14.3	4.7
5.7	0.51	3.3	0.01	6.3	2.8	1.04	10.13	3.77	65.6	0.8	20.6	44.9	6.2
2.5	1.64	14.3	0.03	3.9	0.1	0.36	4.62	5.98	91.1	2.5	43.3	29.2	0.0
8.0	0.11	0.8	0.00	6.5	5.8	1.22	13.99	3.51	51.0	0.6	6.8	39.3	2.9
4.6	1.25	6.9	0.47	6.0	0.6	1.01	9.43	4.42	60.4	4.3	46.6	15.2	6.5
5.2	0.99	7.5	0.40	4.5	0.7	1.19	14.65	3.49	56.9	4.9	39.0	10.4	5.1
6.1	0.55	3.1	0.10	8.1	5.3	1.69	20.54	3.97	53.6	5.9	76.7	12.7	6.3
3.1	1.11	7.9	-0.01	6.0	0.6	0.39	3.90	3.75	84.6	5.1	77.8	16.9	6.7
5.3	1.43	9.3	-0.21	5.9	0.2	0.94	12.21	4.84	70.3	4.9	113.8	22.4	3.1
8.4	0.00	0.0	0.09	1.0	0.1	0.13	1.76	2.54	101.3	6.9	66.7	3.6	2.7
4.6	0.48	2.7	0.01	5.3	2.9	0.86	7.59	3.68	68.8	6.0	116.0	16.2	6.3
3.0	1.16	10.0	-0.01	7.5	0.4	0.96	12.24	4.98	70.2	3.0	45.6	22.9	4.2
6.4	1.76	7.5	0.23	8.1	1.0	2.03	18.55	3.89	47.2	6.3	64.7	7.2	7.8
8.4	0.41	1.6	0.02	5.3	0.3	0.91	9.51	3.14	63.0	3.7	80.7	27.8	5.6
6.5	1.12	4.7	0.05	6.9	0.6	1.65	13.35	4.26	63.3	4.5	63.7	16.6	7.8
4.6	0.29	1.7	0.30	4.8	1.8	0.83	6.97	3.35	62.7	1.2	11.9	28.8	6.2
4.5	0.83	4.0	-0.01	9.5	43.5	1.54	12.96	4.06	39.3	2.7	44.9	44.1	9.8
4.9	1.84	9.2	0.56	3.2	0.3	0.42	4.09	4.79	83.0	5.6	33.0	3.1	4.5
6.5	0.50	2.9	-0.08	6.3	1.0	1.65	14.54	4.34	60.6	3.1	11.4	13.2	6.3
4.9	1.07	5.5	1.07	2.5	0.1	0.34	4.13	4.34	75.8	4.7	66.7	16.2	2.3
7.3	0.22	1.7	0.05	6.3	2.2	0.86	9.16	4.43	76.8	4.9	54.0	14.2	4.0
8.6	0.33	1.4	0.24	6.5	0.5	1.30	11.51	4.45	57.2	6.4	79.7	9.0	6.7
6.0	0.27	2.6	0.56	10.0	3.2	1.80	23.21	4.78	34.7	1.0	8.2	29.6	6.9
5.4	0.62	5.6	0.49	8.9	1.4	1.43	17.41	4.88	50.9	0.6	7.1	38.5	6.1
7.2	0.23	2.2	0.22	4.7	0.2	1.08	14.50	4.09	73.0	5.7	48.6	7.3	3.0
4.0	1.03	8.3	-0.07	7.2	0.8	1.02	9.51	4.74	64.2	2.7	18.1	15.7	2.5
7.8	0.34	2.3	0.05	6.7	1.8	1.31	14.04	4.21	56.4	1.4	12.3	25.2	5.1
8.9	0.16	0.7	-0.02	6.4	0.7	1.33	12.65	4.21	73.7	5.7	66.3	12.4	6.1
9.3	0.00	0.0	0.00	7.8	-0.1	-2.87	-4.40	1.73	95.2	5.0	N/A	0.0	5.0
8.2	0.00	0.0	0.00	1.9	0.3	0.39	4.01	3.12	72.3	2.3	30.3	21.3	1.8
1.3	2.27	20.5	-0.34	6.4	0.2	1.48	20.35	4.06	62.4	0.7	11.8	40.2	0.3
8.0	0.08	0.4	-0.92	4.0	0.1	0.67	5.19	4.41	82.0	5.8	50.3	4.6	5.5
1.7	4.99	37.6	0.92	3.3	0.0	0.15	1.73	4.61	93.9	4.3	45.1	14.4	2.7
7.4	0.00	0.0	-0.01	7.2	2.6	1.25	14.02	4.02	51.1	1.4	31.7	45.4	5.0
9.4	0.00	0.0	0.00	0.0	-0.3	-5.55	-8.50	0.47	894.6	6.1	368.0	25.5	0.0
1.8	2.78	20.7	0.14	8.7	0.5	1.43	14.14	6.02	59.5	0.4	14.8	88.3	0.0
7.3	0.11	0.9	0.42	4.3	0.2	0.89	12.44	4.62	75.3	4.3	10.4	5.9	4.7
8.0	25.54	99.0	0.30	2.7	0.6	0.23	4.25	2.82	96.2	0.4	17.6	418.8	2.6
4.4	0.67	4.7	0.04	9.7	2.8	1.71	16.09	4.34	21.8	7.1	221.7	17.2	6.6
7.4	3.20	3.6	1.52	2.0	0.1	0.42	6.69	1.24	79.1	8.1	101.5	1.2	0.0
2.6	2.45	21.1	-0.57	5.1	0.2	0.92	12.05	4.93	78.4	2.4	21.7	17.8	0.0
0.9	2.84	21.6	0.67	4.1	0.2	0.44	4.92	6.34	63.4	1.8	37.1	39.1	5.1
8.4	0.03	0.2	0.02	6.5	0.3	1.50	14.35	4.61	66.4	5.6	58.2	9.8	7.3
1.3	1.75	12.7	0.46	6.7	3.8	1.09	10.00	4.86	61.0	1.9	19.7	19.9	5.9
1.7	4.20	26.0	0.24	3.2	0.0	0.11	1.05	4.20	85.2	2.7	37.8	22.2	3.4
6.3	0.35	2.8	0.05	8.4	7.3	1.33	14.76	3.91	54.7	4.0	94.1	36.2	8.0
7.2	0.63	2.9	-0.03	8.7	0.9	1.32	11.93	4.11	48.2	7.3	84.1	5.4	7.0
9.1	0.00	0.0	-0.07	8.3	0.2	1.71	15.09	4.67	59.7	4.9	30.8	4.3	6.7
5.7	0.31	2.3	0.32	6.3	1.1	1.55	18.93	4.26	64.3	2.5	35.1	23.0	5.5
5.3	1.01	7.2	0.00	0.6	0.0	0.10	0.86	3.21	93.3	5.7	84.9	13.3	0.0
6.9	0.02	0.2	0.16	1.2	0.6	1.06	12.59	3.87	88.6	0.6	9.1	46.1	0.0
7.7	0.02	0.1	0.00	0.0	-0.2	-1.56	-4.81	2.30	172.9	2.8	51.9	28.4	0.0
6.8	0.13	0.7	-0.02	1.8	0.1	0.22	1.94	3.51	80.2	3.8	35.5	14.5	2.3
8.8	0.07	0.1	0.00	1.3	0.0	0.34	3.42	1.81	82.5	6.8	87.5	5.8	3.9
6.9	1.00	6.7	0.05	8.1	9.5	1.37	15.80	3.91	59.5	6.5	57.7	8.3	7.7
8.6	0.02	0.1	-0.01	7.8	1.0	1.66	20.98	4.82	68.7	4.7	30.2	7.4	6.3
8.0	0.02	0.2	0.10	2.9	0.8	0.41	5.47	3.28	69.8	1.8	33.1	31.3	0.0
4.5	1.15	9.2	0.25	8.0	0.6	1.89	26.04	4.42	55.1	5.6	38.8	5.4	5.6
5.9	0.19	1.3	0.62	6.1	0.3	0.93	11.33	4.25	60.1	4.4	68.2	17.8	5.3
1.7	3.97	26.5	4.63	3.3	0.5	0.42	5.08	3.90	74.1	1.7	28.9	28.9	2.6
4.2	1.33	10.6	0.17	7.2	6.6	1.19	13.42	3.97	61.1	4.0	28.5	14.1	7.4

Name	City	State	Weiss Safety Rating	2003 Weiss Safety Rating	2002 Weiss Safety Rating	Total Assets ($Mil)	One Year Asset Growth	Asset Mix (As a % of Total Assets) Commercial Loans	Consumer Loans	Home Mortgages	Securities	Capitalization Index	Leverage Ratio	Risk-based Capital Ratio
CENTRAL BANK FOR SAVINGS	WINONA	MS	E-	E-	E	33.8	-19.87	0.4	5.5	58.1	7.3	4.1	6.1	12.4
▼ CENTRAL BANK USA INC	GREENSBURG	KY	B-	B	C+	184.2	14.82	5.8	6.1	15.7	6.2	6.0	9.0	11.7
CENTRAL BK	STORM LAKE	IA	D+	C-	C	258.4	11.95	22.7	3.5	19.9	4.0	2.3	7.1	9.3
CENTRAL BK	ASHKUM	IL	B	B	B+	30.4	-5.95	9.5	13.1	22.8	26.0	9.6	10.7	17.2
▲ CENTRAL BK	RUSSIAVILLE	IN	C-	D+	D	56.3	9.86	2.0	7.4	23.7	49.8	5.7	7.7	20.2
CENTRAL BK	STILLWATER	MN	C+	C+	B-	290.3	12.16	20.0	3.9	9.9	5.8	3.4	8.4	10.2
▼ CENTRAL BK	LEBANON	MO	B+	A-	B+	193.1	9.36	8.3	6.4	23.8	10.8	9.4	10.6	15.9
▲ CENTRAL BK	CENTRAL CITY	NE	C+	C	C-	19.4	-12.07	10.2	4.7	8.6	40.5	10.0	15.1	24.3
CENTRAL BK	SAVANNAH	TN	B+	B	B	81.3	2.90	6.7	8.0	28.1	28.0	10.0	12.5	19.9
CENTRAL BK	PROVO	UT	B	B	B	394.1	0.91	20.5	4.8	2.4	25.9	10.0	17.2	23.0
CENTRAL BK FSB	NICHOLASVILLE	KY	B-	B-	B-	102.7	16.60	18.9	4.8	20.4	12.5	6.7	8.7	12.5
▲ CENTRAL BK FULTON	FULTON	IL	B	B-	C+	54.8	0.96	3.8	3.1	15.9	42.9	9.2	10.5	17.8
▲ CENTRAL BK IL	GENESEO	IL	B	B-	C+	165.3	-5.07	4.1	2.9	12.8	37.4	8.3	9.9	16.1
▲ CENTRAL BK OF GEORGIA	ELLAVILLE	GA	B	B-	B-	151.7	7.97	16.0	4.7	19.5	14.0	5.7	7.9	11.5
▲ CENTRAL BK OF HOUSTON	HOUSTON	TX	D+	D-	D+	370.7	-3.71	9.9	3.4	3.9	9.7	2.2	6.5	9.2
CENTRAL BK OF KANSAS CITY	KANSAS CITY	MO	A-	A-	B-	129.6	5.63	14.2	4.7	12.7	13.4	10.0	12.4	18.5
▲ CENTRAL BK OF MISSOURI	SEDALIA	MO	B+	B	B	63.7	9.65	2.7	5.4	36.6	13.4	6.0	8.0	12.8
CENTRAL BK OF THE SOUTH	ANNISTON	AL	B	B	B	4.8	171.98	0.0	0.0	0.0	0.0	10.0	26.3	131.7
CENTRAL BK-LK OF THE	OSAGE BEACH	MO	B-	B-	B-	384.6	1.07	6.9	6.4	17.6	17.4	5.1	7.3	11.1
CENTRAL CALIFORNIA BK	SONORA	CA	B-	B-	B-	394.6	110.16	5.6	0.5	6.1	8.1	5.0	8.5	11.0
CENTRAL CO-OP BK	SOMERVILLE	MA	B-	B-	B-	506.8	6.36	0.9	0.2	32.3	23.8	5.7	7.7	11.9
CENTRAL FLORIDA ST BK	BELLEVIEW	FL	D	D	D	50.8	82.52	9.3	3.4	16.4	14.8	7.8	10.6	13.2
CENTRAL FS&LA	CICERO	IL	B-	C+	C-	171.9	-1.76	0.0	0.1	38.0	36.6	6.7	8.8	26.2
CENTRAL FS&LA OF CHICAGO	CHICAGO	IL	B+	B+	A-	110.6	-1.17	0.0	0.1	30.3	0.0	10.0	15.5	25.6
CENTRAL FS&LA OF ROLLA	ROLLA	MO	B+	B+	A-	64.5	-4.25	0.0	1.6	46.7	34.5	10.0	18.7	44.8
CENTRAL IL BK	CHAMPAIGN	IL	E+	D	C	770.1	-25.82	18.4	0.1	5.6	18.8	2.4	6.0	9.4
CENTRAL KENTUCKY FSB	DANVILLE	KY	B-	C+	C-	150.7	7.44	2.0	2.6	61.3	6.8	7.0	9.0	15.2
CENTRAL NATIONAL BANK	WACO	TX	B-	B-	B-	388.9	2.42	26.2	3.7	15.2	16.4	6.0	8.0	12.2
CENTRAL NB	JUNCTION CITY	KS	A-	A-	B+	551.1	-7.12	7.8	2.8	7.8	24.3	9.6	10.7	16.0
CENTRAL NB	LYNCHBURG	VA	C-	C	C	114.9	-1.68	10.9	2.4	2.1	17.6	5.4	7.4	14.9
CENTRAL NB OF ALVA	ALVA	OK	A-	A-	B+	185.0	4.93	11.8	3.0	3.3	35.0	10.0	14.3	24.3
▼ CENTRAL NB OF POTEAU	POTEAU	OK	B+	A-	A-	144.8	5.38	4.7	6.8	15.1	28.3	6.1	8.1	17.0
CENTRAL NB&TC	ATTICA	IN	A-	A-	A	63.0	7.03	0.6	3.5	26.0	44.8	10.0	17.6	41.8
CENTRAL NB&TC OF ENID	ENID	OK	C+	C+	C+	352.1	-4.94	7.4	7.6	22.3	24.3	5.7	7.7	12.5
CENTRAL PACIFIC BK	HONOLULU	HI	A-	A-	A-	2,475.1	19.18	11.5	3.1	9.2	25.7	6.3	8.9	12.0
▲ CENTRAL PROGRESSIVE BK	LACOMBE	LA	B-	C+	C	435.0	32.83	6.1	5.0	11.3	6.6	5.7	8.7	11.5
▲ CENTRAL ST BK	CALERA	AL	A	A-	A-	123.0	3.53	3.4	7.1	17.9	18.4	10.0	12.8	17.7
CENTRAL ST BK	ELKADER	IA	B+	B+	A-	85.2	-0.08	8.4	3.4	13.3	23.4	10.0	21.2	22.2
▲ CENTRAL ST BK	MUSCATINE	IA	B+	B	B	267.7	-2.57	6.7	5.3	13.4	36.8	7.7	9.5	16.5
CENTRAL ST BK	STATE CENTER	IA	A-	B+	A-	65.9	9.47	15.5	6.8	9.4	21.1	10.0	16.5	21.6
▲ CENTRAL ST BK	CLAYTON	IL	C+	C	D+	67.4	-0.39	10.7	16.9	28.4	18.8	8.2	9.8	14.9
CENTRAL ST BK	BEULAH	MI	A	A	A	58.5	-3.19	25.7	2.5	23.0	6.2	10.0	12.5	17.2
CENTRAL SVG BK	SAULT STE MARIE	MI	B	B	C	181.0	-3.82	10.0	3.8	23.9	29.5	7.5	9.3	17.0
CENTRAL TRUST BK	JEFFERSON CITY	MO	B	B	B	1,415.0	0.91	9.1	8.1	12.1	35.9	5.3	7.3	15.1
▼ CENTRAL VALLEY BK	OTTUMWA	IA	D-	NR	NR	120.4	N/A	11.5	4.5	34.1	10.4	6.4	8.4	12.8
▼ CENTRAL VALLEY BK NA	TOPPENISH	WA	B-	B	B+	105.5	17.64	8.3	0.7	2.0	15.3	5.3	7.3	12.7
CENTRAL VALLEY CMNTY BK	CLOVIS	CA	B-	B-	B-	350.4	12.51	15.9	1.8	2.1	27.6	5.7	7.7	12.0
▲ CENTRAL VIRGINIA BK	POWHATAN	VA	B	B-	B-	364.3	11.05	9.5	3.0	11.9	44.0	6.4	8.4	13.1
CENTRAL WEST END BK FSB	ST LOUIS	MO	C-	C-	C-	47.4	-1.66	3.6	0.6	50.2	23.1	6.7	8.7	18.2
CENTREBANK	VEEDERSBURG	IN	C+	C+	D+	43.5	6.40	11.1	4.2	25.2	7.0	10.0	11.4	16.1
CENTREVILLE NB OF MD	CENTREVILLE	MD	A-	A-	A	271.2	3.75	4.8	2.8	27.6	22.4	7.7	9.5	15.6
CENTREVILLE SVGS BK	W WARWICK	RI	A	A	A+	773.6	5.06	0.3	0.7	25.5	63.8	10.0	21.0	67.5
▲ CENTRIX B&TC	BEDFORD	NH	B-	C+	C+	192.5	31.71	17.3	1.6	3.6	12.1	7.7	10.7	13.1
▼ CENTRUE BK	KANKAKEE	IL	C	C+	C+	604.6	515.20	7.2	1.8	37.0	17.4	5.5	7.5	12.6
CENTURY B&T	MILLEDGEVILLE	GA	A	A	A	139.0	5.77	3.9	5.6	16.4	34.2	10.0	11.3	21.8
▼ CENTURY B&T	COLDWATER	MI	A-	A	A	224.8	-1.16	14.6	4.3	15.5	24.4	10.0	12.4	18.2
CENTURY B&TC	SOMERVILLE	MA	B-	B-	B-	1,572.5	-2.29	4.1	0.3	6.6	55.9	4.6	6.6	15.3
▲ CENTURY BANK	LUCEDALE	MS	C+	C	C	165.7	-1.08	11.3	26.6	11.2	23.4	9.8	10.9	16.2
CENTURY BK	PARMA	OH	B-	B-	B-	124.9	-4.61	0.0	0.1	42.1	14.6	9.3	10.6	17.0
CENTURY BK	EUGENE	OR	D	NR	NR	17.2	N/A	9.4	2.9	0.0	23.1	10.0	81.6	122.8
CENTURY BK FSB	SARASOTA	FL	C-	D+	D	451.3	27.45	1.3	0.7	41.6	7.1	3.2	6.1	10.1
▲ CENTURY BK FSB	SANTA FE	NM	B-	C+	C+	369.0	8.10	11.5	1.1	11.6	13.6	4.8	8.2	10.9
CENTURY BK NA	NEW BOSTON	TX	C	C-	D+	565.7	39.80	14.9	4.0	11.6	31.0	4.1	6.9	10.5
CENTURY BK OF BARTOW	CARTERSVILLE	GA	C+	C	C	80.9	10.15	14.3	5.1	14.4	14.4	8.1	9.9	13.5

Asset Quality Index	Non-Performing Loans as a % of Total Loans	Non-Performing Loans as a % of Capital	Net Charge-offs Avg Loans	Profitability Index	Net Income ($Mil)	Return on Assets (R.O.A.)	Return on Equity (R.O.E.)	Net Interest Spread	Overhead Efficiency Ratio	Liquidity Index	Liquidity Ratio	Hot Money Ratio	Stability Index
1.4	4.13	38.6	-0.01	1.2	-0.3	-1.70	-30.65	2.64	120.1	1.2	28.2	37.2	0.0
3.6	0.94	7.5	0.09	8.3	1.9	2.14	21.01	4.45	45.7	1.7	10.9	20.5	6.7
4.7	0.47	5.2	-0.31	4.8	1.0	0.79	10.91	3.77	70.1	2.0	11.9	18.6	2.9
3.9	1.81	9.9	0.18	8.1	0.3	1.80	16.76	4.24	59.5	4.6	44.4	12.8	6.6
7.4	0.92	4.5	0.52	3.7	0.2	0.67	8.56	4.35	83.2	4.5	7.0	4.4	2.0
7.7	0.13	1.2	0.04	9.4	2.9	2.12	26.15	4.77	58.7	3.0	11.5	13.7	5.9
6.9	0.20	1.3	0.37	5.2	1.2	1.24	11.40	4.28	71.4	4.1	37.9	13.9	6.0
4.8	3.00	9.2	-0.06	6.0	0.2	1.62	11.01	4.47	65.2	5.8	57.8	6.5	5.0
6.4	1.18	5.5	0.07	5.6	0.4	1.02	8.25	4.43	68.4	4.0	88.3	27.6	6.0
4.6	2.72	9.5	1.82	10.0	4.2	2.08	11.97	5.59	55.1	4.9	71.7	16.7	9.3
5.4	0.38	3.2	0.83	5.2	0.4	0.88	10.38	3.74	59.0	0.9	26.7	64.5	5.6
5.1	1.23	3.9	-0.72	5.3	0.3	1.23	8.87	4.11	69.3	4.5	26.7	7.7	6.4
5.3	1.97	7.8	0.03	4.8	0.8	1.02	9.43	3.68	73.9	3.0	23.0	14.9	5.1
4.3	1.16	10.8	-0.03	8.7	1.2	1.68	23.01	4.60	39.1	1.2	18.6	30.3	5.7
4.1	1.08	9.3	0.05	3.3	1.0	0.52	7.20	4.15	74.4	2.9	40.7	22.2	3.1
4.4	2.46	11.7	0.39	9.9	1.4	2.15	15.31	5.83	62.5	4.2	40.5	13.9	7.4
7.0	0.31	2.3	0.19	9.8	0.7	2.43	24.66	4.48	47.5	4.4	25.2	7.7	7.4
10.0	0.00	0.0	0.00	2.7	0.0	0.21	0.64	0.78	41.7	8.8	136.7	0.0	5.5
3.8	1.36	11.6	0.02	10.0	3.6	1.90	26.19	4.85	51.2	4.5	63.4	17.9	6.2
6.2	0.00	0.0	-0.01	8.0	2.5	1.30	10.68	5.00	56.5	5.7	94.6	15.8	4.1
8.9	0.00	0.0	-0.01	3.5	0.8	0.34	3.98	3.23	84.3	4.0	23.7	9.9	5.1
8.5	0.14	0.9	0.00	0.6	0.0	0.07	0.57	3.62	82.9	5.6	75.9	12.7	0.0
7.7	0.11	0.4	0.00	4.2	0.2	0.23	2.12	2.76	87.1	3.5	11.3	11.2	5.4
7.2	0.26	1.5	0.00	4.4	0.3	0.45	2.95	3.69	80.2	1.3	5.2	25.1	7.6
8.7	1.14	3.3	0.00	4.6	0.2	0.62	3.22	3.13	71.2	3.9	62.7	19.4	6.6
0.0	6.48	49.8	3.13	0.6	-9.1	-2.19	-32.89	2.57	72.1	4.5	70.7	19.0	2.9
4.4	1.11	10.3	0.02	6.9	0.9	1.20	12.30	3.53	47.9	0.8	6.6	32.0	5.9
7.7	0.13	1.1	0.06	5.8	2.8	1.44	18.40	3.52	60.0	3.7	47.9	18.4	4.2
7.9	0.13	0.6	-0.06	6.0	3.4	1.19	10.65	3.95	68.5	4.3	27.8	9.1	7.1
1.9	4.23	28.3	0.00	5.2	0.5	0.92	12.35	3.42	61.6	5.0	100.0	20.5	3.3
5.4	2.44	7.7	0.51	5.8	1.4	1.49	9.33	4.96	68.7	3.0	35.9	18.6	7.6
6.2	0.43	3.2	0.11	9.5	1.5	2.07	24.86	4.67	58.3	4.3	32.2	11.0	6.7
8.9	1.10	3.0	0.21	6.9	0.5	1.48	8.54	3.51	57.6	7.3	99.3	6.5	8.6
4.3	0.94	7.4	0.19	4.4	1.6	0.88	10.99	4.08	74.2	3.6	18.9	11.2	4.3
6.1	1.28	9.8	0.06	9.5	17.2	1.50	18.43	4.43	50.3	3.8	38.3	18.3	7.8
4.6	0.52	4.3	0.05	7.7	2.6	1.22	14.43	5.13	63.1	3.7	55.1	20.6	4.3
8.2	0.35	1.8	0.09	7.2	1.1	1.74	13.29	5.39	66.4	1.6	32.3	33.3	7.4
4.7	4.43	11.2	-0.02	8.5	1.2	2.78	13.20	4.52	42.2	6.4	92.3	10.8	8.2
7.3	0.32	1.6	-0.37	7.2	1.8	1.31	13.44	4.06	59.6	4.3	42.5	14.0	6.8
5.9	0.90	3.9	0.08	9.9	0.8	2.61	15.53	4.22	35.1	1.5	22.0	27.3	8.6
3.1	1.87	13.1	0.90	8.8	0.8	2.38	23.27	4.93	50.1	2.6	29.8	18.5	5.0
7.0	0.51	2.7	0.00	7.3	0.3	0.96	7.46	4.81	71.6	6.3	97.2	12.0	8.6
5.3	1.13	5.5	-0.04	5.1	0.7	0.73	7.40	3.77	72.2	4.0	60.8	20.0	6.1
7.6	0.54	2.8	0.13	8.3	9.8	1.35	16.40	2.95	65.8	6.8	62.5	6.8	6.7
0.0	6.02	41.4	1.18	9.5	0.7	1.62	10.97	5.21	48.3	4.5	22.8	6.4	0.3
8.3	0.18	1.4	0.03	6.1	0.5	0.94	12.88	4.93	71.7	4.9	52.3	13.8	4.9
8.4	0.00	0.0	-0.11	6.3	1.8	1.07	13.82	4.66	72.1	5.9	52.7	8.4	4.1
7.0	0.39	2.1	0.14	6.0	2.2	1.18	13.62	3.95	62.5	3.8	30.0	12.6	4.9
9.6	0.00	0.0	0.00	4.0	0.1	0.52	5.75	3.61	81.1	2.1	35.9	30.1	4.3
4.9	1.29	7.9	0.00	4.2	0.2	0.71	6.50	4.50	75.6	2.5	33.0	20.6	4.4
7.7	0.29	1.8	0.00	7.1	1.7	1.24	12.57	4.05	58.7	4.6	35.0	10.1	7.4
10.0	0.01	0.0	0.00	6.8	6.8	1.76	7.08	3.08	52.0	8.1	139.9	6.4	9.9
8.4	0.00	0.0	0.00	4.1	0.5	0.58	5.44	4.09	68.7	3.2	38.6	18.4	5.1
2.6	2.04	13.9	0.28	4.5	2.5	0.83	8.61	3.59	65.4	4.2	21.3	8.1	5.1
8.7	0.36	1.6	0.28	8.3	0.9	1.26	11.05	3.71	58.2	6.1	54.6	7.7	8.0
5.7	1.48	7.0	0.03	6.8	1.4	1.23	10.18	3.84	64.7	5.5	51.0	10.1	7.6
9.3	0.17	0.8	0.03	4.9	5.5	0.68	10.02	2.89	68.4	6.8	48.6	4.1	4.8
4.0	0.69	3.5	0.48	6.9	1.0	1.17	10.78	5.59	66.5	4.1	45.9	16.0	5.4
6.7	0.76	5.1	0.00	3.6	0.2	0.35	3.39	2.75	78.7	2.5	17.2	16.6	5.7
9.2	0.00	0.0	0.00	0.0	-0.5	-6.80	-9.48	0.79	679.7	10.0	227.7	0.0	0.0
3.5	0.88	11.3	0.05	6.8	2.4	1.12	17.80	3.18	53.3	1.1	4.8	28.2	3.2
8.5	0.04	0.4	-0.02	7.4	2.0	1.12	14.04	4.73	67.7	0.7	15.7	43.6	5.0
7.2	0.32	2.7	-0.01	4.1	2.0	0.74	10.25	3.47	68.7	1.5	11.3	22.9	3.4
8.1	0.03	0.3	0.18	3.7	0.3	0.70	7.15	4.25	75.1	0.6	11.1	45.3	2.2

Name	City	State	Weiss Safety Rating	2003 Weiss Safety Rating	2002 Weiss Safety Rating	Total Assets ($Mil)	One Year Asset Growth	Asset Mix (As a % of Total Assets)				Capital-ization Index	Leverage Ratio	Risk-based Capital Ratio
								Comm-ercial Loans	Cons-umer Loans	Home Mort-gages	Secur-ities			
CENTURY BK OF FLORIDA	TAMPA	FL	B	B	B-	74.7	55.41	10.7	2.6	14.4	17.6	10.0	12.3	18.1
CENTURY BK OF KY	LAWRENCEBURG	KY	C-	C-	D+	82.5	19.70	4.4	7.5	35.1	14.0	5.2	7.2	11.4
CENTURY BK OF THE OZARKS	GAINESVILLE	MO	B+	B+	B+	149.3	-0.08	7.0	5.5	23.9	19.5	6.5	8.6	13.7
▲ CENTURY NB	ORLANDO	FL	C+	C	C-	283.8	26.18	5.2	0.3	2.1	34.0	4.7	6.7	14.9
CENTURY NB	ZANESVILLE	OH	B-	B-	B-	526.5	15.23	2.2	11.3	27.3	29.9	3.8	5.8	12.8
▲ CENTURY NB OF OKLAHOMA	PRYOR	OK	C+	C	C	17.6	5.97	10.8	15.4	33.0	6.2	10.0	12.0	18.4
CENTURY S&LA	TRINIDAD	CO	B-	C+	C+	88.2	-0.34	0.0	1.3	33.4	46.5	8.4	9.9	25.8
CENTURY SVG BK	BRIDGETON	NJ	B+	B+	A-	245.2	-0.27	0.1	0.1	23.7	61.4	10.0	18.2	55.8
CERESCOBANK	CERESCO	NE	B-	B-	B-	33.7	5.28	18.7	6.0	24.3	7.6	9.3	10.5	15.3
CFBANK	FAIRLAWN	OH	C-	C	B	128.5	15.73	4.5	6.8	31.6	17.3	10.0	11.3	16.8
CHAMBERS BK	DANVILLE	AR	B-	B-	B-	430.4	2.12	3.8	1.9	11.6	5.0	9.8	12.1	14.8
CHAMBERS ST BK	CHAMBERS	NE	A-	A-	A-	27.1	3.74	4.6	7.6	1.7	5.7	10.0	26.7	41.8
CHAMPAIGN NB	URBANA	OH	B-	B-	B-	270.1	-0.32	16.5	2.4	16.4	8.5	7.1	9.5	12.6
CHAMPION BK	PARKER	CO	D	D	D	9.4	49.42	5.6	3.7	34.5	0.0	10.0	27.9	38.9
CHAMPLAIN NB	ELIZABETHTOWN	NY	C+	C+	B-	151.9	-1.71	9.2	3.7	10.5	44.4	6.8	8.8	15.2
▼ CHAPPELL HILL BK	CHAPPELL HILL	TX	C-	C	C+	23.1	11.92	4.5	8.2	15.3	13.0	10.0	14.2	33.7
CHARLEROI FSB	CHARLEROI	PA	B-	B-	B+	359.8	-1.90	3.9	3.5	18.8	50.5	10.0	15.6	36.3
▲ CHARLES SCHWAB BK NA	RENO	NV	C	C-	NR	3,774.6	437.69	0.0	0.0	4.1	62.2	7.2	9.2	27.6
CHARLESTON FS&LA	CHARLESTON	IL	D	D	D	31.0	-3.62	0.0	1.9	15.0	68.5	6.1	8.1	44.2
CHARLEVOIX ST BK	CHARLEVOIX	MI	B	B	B-	119.7	5.63	6.0	5.7	26.3	9.2	6.3	8.3	12.4
CHARLOTTE ST BK	PORT CHARLOTTE	FL	B+	B+	A-	165.9	24.75	2.0	0.7	16.9	12.9	5.7	7.7	11.6
CHART BANK, A CO-OP BANK	WALTHAM	MA	B-	B-	C+	249.1	26.19	1.6	0.2	17.8	13.8	5.3	7.4	11.2
▲ CHART BK	PERRYVILLE	AR	B-	C+	C	113.9	-3.74	6.0	3.5	14.9	34.6	10.0	11.3	19.7
CHARTER B&TC	MARIETTA	GA	B-	B-	B	299.1	6.64	24.4	1.4	6.8	12.9	4.7	8.2	10.8
▲ CHARTER BK	JOHNSTON	IA	C	C-	D+	64.8	7.87	11.9	4.7	19.7	18.4	5.8	7.8	13.1
CHARTER BK	SANTA FE	NM	C	C	C	869.0	13.94	2.2	1.9	30.3	31.9	4.0	6.0	12.6
▲ CHARTER BK	CORPUS CHRISTI	TX	C+	C	C	110.3	-0.08	22.6	12.2	8.0	27.5	3.2	6.0	10.1
CHARTER BK	BELLEVUE	WA	C+	C+	C	205.5	20.80	22.9	1.3	8.2	24.0	4.7	7.4	10.8
CHARTER BK EAU CLAIRE	EAU CLAIRE	WI	B+	B+	A-	364.0	13.76	10.7	1.0	19.8	29.5	10.0	11.0	15.7
▲ CHARTER NB&TC	HOFFMAN ESTATES	IL	C+	C	C	124.2	-0.04	8.7	7.1	1.3	19.7	6.2	8.2	12.2
CHARTER ONE BK NA	CLEVELAND	OH	C-	C	C	42,582.5	-2.38	2.9	16.3	35.2	14.5	4.3	6.3	11.1
CHARTER WEST NB	W POINT	NE	B-	B-	B-	101.0	0.71	5.5	5.1	11.3	18.5	5.1	7.5	11.1
CHARTERBANK	W POINT	GA	C	C-	C	929.7	3.26	2.0	0.7	15.3	60.8	7.1	9.1	27.5
▲ CHASE MANHATTAN BK USA	NEWARK	DE	C	C-	C-	42,389.3	28.41	2.6	55.1	2.8	0.5	8.4	13.3	13.7
▼ CHASEWOOD BK	HOUSTON	TX	D	D+	D+	70.5	2.52	3.0	1.5	6.2	54.1	5.1	7.1	19.8
CHATTAHOOCHEE NB	ALPHARETTA	GA	C-	C-	D+	162.2	21.82	19.5	0.2	4.6	22.2	2.0	6.2	9.0
▼ CHB AMERICA BK	NEW YORK	NY	B	B+	A-	361.0	13.85	16.4	0.5	4.8	8.2	10.0	15.1	19.4
CHEAHA BK	OXFORD	AL	C	C	C	91.5	24.24	5.2	6.4	20.1	39.8	5.2	7.2	12.6
CHELSEA GROTON SVGS BK	NORWICH	CT	B+	A-	A-	648.5	4.72	2.7	2.0	42.0	25.3	10.0	13.7	20.5
CHELSEA PROVIDENT CO-OP	CHELSEA	MA	C+	C+	B-	41.9	2.95	0.0	1.1	51.0	18.7	7.0	9.0	16.0
CHELSEA ST BK	CHELSEA	MI	A+	A+	A+	189.3	4.96	8.8	1.9	21.4	29.2	10.0	15.1	24.6
CHELSEA SVG BK	BELLE PLAINE	IA	A-	B+	B+	75.5	7.27	6.1	3.9	14.4	54.0	10.0	13.7	31.2
▼ CHELTEN HILLS SVGS BK	ABINGTON	PA	C+	B-	B-	20.9	13.57	0.0	0.6	77.4	2.6	9.6	10.8	21.5
CHEMICAL B&TC	MIDLAND	MI	A	A	A	1,622.4	1.27	7.6	8.9	25.1	32.1	10.0	11.0	19.8
CHEMICAL BK SHORELINE	BENTON HARBOR	MI	A-	A-	A-	1,300.8	4.78	8.4	6.2	22.8	20.1	7.4	9.3	13.6
CHEMICAL BK WEST	WALKER	MI	A-	A-	A-	901.7	22.60	9.8	7.9	27.5	12.8	8.2	10.8	13.5
CHEMUNG CANAL TRUST CO	ELMIRA	NY	C+	C+	C	731.3	-2.74	16.5	10.0	15.8	39.9	7.6	9.4	17.5
CHEROKEE BK NA	CANTON	GA	C	C	C-	137.2	14.62	7.1	2.2	5.1	33.9	7.8	9.6	14.3
▲ CHEROKEE ST BK	CHEROKEE	IA	A	A-	A-	153.5	-2.72	3.9	2.1	8.8	41.4	8.9	10.2	18.1
CHEROKEE ST BK	ST PAUL	MN	C-	B-	C	241.9	0.60	10.5	0.9	7.0	17.5	6.7	8.7	12.5
CHERRYVILLE FS&LA	CHERRYVILLE	NC	B+	B+	B+	77.3	0.97	1.0	0.7	43.7	32.1	10.0	14.1	30.0
CHESAPEAKE B&TC	CHESTERTOWN	MD	A	A	A	81.3	7.91	10.3	5.9	39.8	18.9	9.9	10.9	17.1
CHESAPEAKE BK	KILMARNOCK	VA	B-	B-	C+	340.1	10.72	14.3	5.4	8.6	19.8	5.1	8.1	11.1
▲ CHESAPEAKE BK OF	BALTIMORE	MD	C-	D	D+	216.4	5.69	5.8	3.9	34.1	0.2	3.6	8.4	10.3
▲ CHESTATEE ST BK	DAWSONVILLE	GA	C-	D	C-	236.7	16.80	12.0	4.0	5.2	13.6	6.7	9.1	12.3
▲ CHESTER COUNTY BK	HENDERSON	TN	C	C-	C-	42.4	3.56	3.5	11.4	13.1	32.7	6.1	8.1	18.0
CHESTER NB	CHESTER	IL	B	B	B	99.9	-3.85	1.6	1.4	23.1	57.4	6.8	8.8	25.4
CHESTER NB	PERRYVILLE	MO	B	B	B	8.6	-7.71	1.2	3.5	60.5	0.0	10.0	24.6	52.3
CHESTERFIELD FS&LA OF	CHICAGO	IL	B+	B+	B+	361.8	-1.84	0.0	0.3	35.3	14.2	10.0	17.8	45.4
▲ CHESTERFIELD ST BK	CHESTERFIELD	IL	C	C-	C-	14.5	1.02	7.7	11.9	15.6	32.0	9.2	10.4	18.5
CHESTERTOWN BK OF MD	CHESTERTOWN	MD	A-	A-	A	226.7	8.11	8.5	1.7	26.7	9.9	6.9	8.9	18.6
CHETOPA ST B&TC	CHETOPA	KS	B-	B-	B-	25.8	7.24	2.2	6.1	19.5	9.4	5.4	7.4	12.7
CHEVIOT SAVINGS BANK	CHEVIOT	OH	B+	A-	A-	278.8	14.84	0.0	0.1	61.9	21.6	10.0	20.3	46.1
CHEVRON CREDIT BK NA	MURRAY	UT	B+	B+	B+	164.1	15.47	0.0	0.0	0.0	16.4	10.0	26.0	48.0

Asset Quality Index	Non-Performing Loans as a % of Total Loans	Non-Performing Loans as a % of Capital	Net Charge-offs Avg Loans	Profitability Index	Net Income ($Mil)	Return on Assets (R.O.A.)	Return on Equity (R.O.E.)	Net Interest Spread	Overhead Efficiency Ratio	Liquidity Index	Liquidity Ratio	Hot Money Ratio	Stability Index
8.8	0.31	1.5	0.00	4.8	0.3	0.77	6.12	4.64	71.2	4.1	59.9	17.9	2.8
5.7	0.39	3.9	0.04	3.8	0.3	0.83	11.42	3.77	76.1	1.5	26.9	29.4	0.9
6.5	0.32	2.2	0.07	9.1	1.5	2.05	23.63	4.77	56.8	3.0	23.0	14.7	6.7
9.6	0.00	0.0	0.00	4.0	1.0	0.69	10.91	2.54	54.7	7.5	83.8	3.7	3.4
4.7	1.03	8.6	0.00	9.7	4.3	1.71	29.35	4.20	47.7	3.9	31.7	12.7	5.4
7.7	0.00	0.0	0.23	7.6	0.2	1.82	15.29	7.45	69.6	5.2	33.7	3.1	4.0
3.8	3.13	13.0	0.37	4.3	0.3	0.59	6.00	2.53	68.3	0.8	13.6	35.2	5.3
10.0	0.17	0.3	0.00	4.8	1.0	0.77	4.24	3.34	59.9	6.6	51.3	2.8	8.3
3.9	1.46	9.2	-0.07	8.4	0.3	1.54	14.81	4.29	45.2	5.3	39.5	8.1	4.5
6.3	0.17	0.9	0.06	1.3	-0.4	-0.71	-5.52	3.53	128.0	2.6	42.0	27.2	6.1
4.3	0.83	5.3	-0.12	10.0	5.5	2.57	21.59	5.03	41.5	1.3	27.0	32.8	7.2
7.9	0.29	0.6	0.10	9.9	0.4	2.74	10.32	4.83	34.5	6.1	143.0	17.0	7.4
3.6	1.99	15.6	0.15	8.0	1.8	1.29	13.72	4.79	58.3	2.7	22.9	16.4	6.0
8.7	0.09	0.2	0.00	0.0	-0.3	-5.96	-19.21	4.94	206.1	8.0	175.0	10.3	0.0
5.6	1.22	6.2	0.33	3.6	0.5	0.61	6.98	4.59	89.2	4.1	11.0	7.3	5.0
7.0	2.02	5.6	0.00	1.6	0.0	0.04	0.30	2.22	89.7	4.9	155.1	31.1	4.0
7.0	1.65	3.3	0.04	3.4	0.6	0.33	1.98	2.39	80.8	2.1	31.3	24.1	7.2
10.0	0.00	0.0	0.00	3.5	9.6	0.59	6.45	2.01	56.2	5.1	19.0	2.8	3.0
8.8	0.00	0.0	0.00	2.1	0.0	0.16	2.01	1.74	91.6	3.1	14.1	13.3	2.3
7.2	0.02	0.2	-0.05	8.4	0.8	1.37	16.46	4.67	57.4	3.0	20.6	14.5	5.6
6.6	0.00	0.0	-0.02	7.6	1.4	1.75	21.77	4.88	68.7	5.4	27.7	2.0	6.0
8.8	0.02	0.1	-0.01	4.3	0.7	0.60	7.78	3.73	75.7	2.3	32.6	22.5	4.0
6.0	1.44	6.8	0.36	5.1	0.8	1.33	15.34	4.12	60.9	1.4	31.6	37.1	3.8
2.2	2.29	19.3	0.14	6.4	1.5	1.04	13.03	4.41	60.5	1.6	29.4	30.1	5.6
7.9	0.02	0.2	0.00	5.0	0.2	0.74	9.63	3.81	69.4	1.3	26.3	31.5	3.3
2.7	1.64	14.9	0.63	6.6	5.0	1.22	19.05	2.84	62.9	0.8	21.9	58.7	5.1
3.8	0.97	9.0	0.21	10.0	1.8	3.23	49.61	7.33	57.4	3.1	13.1	13.1	4.9
8.4	0.00	0.0	0.00	4.2	0.8	0.81	11.24	4.25	75.3	3.6	15.3	11.2	3.8
5.0	1.38	8.2	0.09	10.0	4.1	2.32	21.52	4.78	28.4	2.4	11.1	16.6	7.7
5.5	0.88	6.6	0.03	3.5	0.4	0.69	8.32	3.63	83.9	5.9	47.4	6.3	3.5
4.7	0.75	7.2	0.23	5.4	212.5	1.01	14.30	3.13	68.0	4.2	16.5	8.1	4.0
6.2	0.49	3.9	0.15	6.0	0.6	1.22	14.95	4.03	69.9	3.0	36.2	18.7	6.1
3.1	1.87	3.5	0.08	3.6	2.9	0.64	3.50	2.16	65.1	0.7	11.7	42.9	7.7
3.9	0.72	4.2	2.99	10.0	603.4	3.08	23.19	4.81	45.7	0.1	3.8	94.6	7.1
5.9	1.67	6.8	0.00	2.7	0.2	0.42	6.24	3.52	88.8	2.6	58.2	37.1	2.2
5.5	0.39	2.2	0.00	2.1	0.2	0.29	3.39	0.82	46.9	1.3	28.9	35.6	4.7
5.6	0.79	3.8	1.12	4.1	1.1	0.63	3.95	3.61	71.1	3.3	75.7	51.4	6.5
8.4	0.16	1.2	0.00	5.3	0.4	0.99	14.19	3.76	54.9	1.9	7.5	18.6	1.6
9.2	0.45	2.0	-0.03	4.4	2.0	0.63	4.46	3.76	80.7	7.0	67.8	4.4	8.8
8.9	0.00	0.0	0.00	5.1	0.1	0.60	6.43	3.95	77.8	6.3	61.2	6.3	4.3
8.8	0.65	2.6	0.00	8.6	1.3	1.40	9.18	4.77	57.1	4.6	11.9	4.2	9.4
8.2	0.13	0.4	0.21	8.8	0.9	2.47	18.16	4.30	41.9	4.6	13.3	4.6	7.4
5.6	1.03	7.8	0.00	4.8	0.1	0.88	8.24	3.48	57.9	9.3	927.9	4.6	0.0
8.3	0.14	0.7	0.03	9.7	14.3	1.78	15.81	4.32	49.5	7.6	84.1	5.1	9.2
7.1	0.48	3.0	0.09	7.2	7.4	1.20	11.47	3.74	56.9	6.8	67.6	7.9	8.5
3.9	0.75	3.8	0.10	7.8	4.9	1.24	10.74	4.04	56.9	5.0	38.1	9.1	8.1
3.3	2.94	13.4	0.18	5.6	4.0	1.08	10.50	3.77	66.2	4.7	31.4	8.4	6.8
8.8	0.03	0.2	0.02	2.8	0.2	0.24	2.95	3.68	82.7	3.8	13.3	9.9	4.5
8.8	0.03	0.1	0.00	7.7	1.2	1.55	14.01	3.95	45.0	4.4	16.6	6.1	7.7
1.7	2.74	20.9	0.11	7.2	2.2	1.80	20.15	4.93	65.3	3.8	19.2	10.5	5.8
7.3	0.55	2.2	0.00	5.8	0.5	1.33	9.54	2.97	53.7	2.7	53.1	30.8	7.3
8.6	0.03	0.2	0.04	9.5	0.8	2.10	19.27	4.28	59.5	3.8	13.1	9.9	8.0
6.2	0.47	3.7	0.12	6.3	2.0	1.17	13.90	5.02	69.6	3.5	20.5	12.1	4.5
3.5	0.56	5.2	0.49	4.5	1.0	0.93	10.85	3.88	78.9	1.3	11.4	25.9	4.7
4.2	0.73	5.3	0.15	2.8	0.7	0.61	6.80	3.95	70.5	3.4	48.9	21.1	2.7
4.5	1.75	7.3	0.20	4.8	0.2	0.87	10.67	4.64	69.9	5.7	103.1	15.6	2.8
9.7	0.37	1.2	-0.05	4.6	0.5	0.95	10.69	3.25	59.1	4.8	36.4	9.8	5.9
9.6	0.00	0.0	-0.06	6.3	0.0	0.86	3.53	4.69	69.2	5.2	186.3	43.6	7.3
9.0	0.23	0.5	0.00	4.5	1.0	0.53	3.01	2.89	74.5	3.8	69.9	26.8	8.1
5.8	0.85	4.2	-0.31	5.6	0.1	1.43	13.97	3.62	59.8	6.3	59.1	3.2	4.3
7.9	0.15	1.1	0.00	10.0	2.0	1.80	18.79	4.63	43.2	7.9	114.7	5.5	8.9
8.3	0.08	0.8	0.01	8.4	0.3	1.96	26.92	4.04	54.1	4.9	46.9	11.8	5.6
9.6	0.21	0.8	0.00	4.6	0.6	0.44	2.53	3.02	78.0	1.9	26.1	22.3	7.8
10.0	0.00	0.0	0.00	10.0	2.3	3.47	8.29	1.08	91.2	0.0	N/A	100.0	4.7

Name	City	State	Weiss Safety Rating	2003 Weiss Safety Rating	2002 Weiss Safety Rating	Total Assets ($Mil)	One Year Asset Growth	Asset Mix (As a % of Total Assets) Commercial Loans	Consumer Loans	Home Mortgages	Securities	Capitalization Index	Leverage Ratio	Risk-based Capital Ratio
▲ CHEVY CHASE BK FSB	CHEVY CHASE	MD	C+	C	C-	12,862.5	10.68	7.0	3.3	56.5	5.0	4.0	6.0	10.9
CHEYENNE MOUNTAIN BK	COLORADO SPRINGS	CO	D+	D+	D+	48.2	1.71	10.0	4.2	13.2	26.7	7.2	9.1	15.9
CHEYENNE ST BK	CHEYENNE	WY	C	C	D	19.9	42.94	16.6	3.2	5.9	5.5	10.0	17.0	15.9
CHICAGO COMMUNITY BK	CHICAGO	IL	B-	B-	B-	234.6	3.64	1.8	1.4	20.9	22.5	7.1	9.0	13.8
CHICKASHA B&TC	CHICKASHA	OK	B-	B-	C	106.8	1.83	11.4	6.3	12.7	5.9	8.4	9.9	14.2
CHICOPEE SVGS BK	CHICOPEE	MA	B-	B	B+	352.9	6.02	8.1	0.5	36.4	11.3	9.2	12.0	14.4
CHILLICOTHE ST BK	CHILLICOTHE	MO	B	B-	B-	95.0	3.72	5.3	6.3	30.5	25.1	6.6	8.6	15.2
▲ CHINATOWN FSB	NEW YORK CITY	NY	A+	A	A	131.5	-2.77	0.9	0.4	49.6	2.0	10.0	17.1	26.8
▲ CHINATRUST BK USA	TORRANCE	CA	B+	B-	B	1,863.8	6.46	7.8	0.1	0.7	36.4	9.6	10.7	16.0
▼ CHINESE AMERICAN BK	NEW YORK	NY	C-	C+	B-	367.6	0.80	6.8	0.5	0.7	40.7	7.8	9.5	14.2
CHINO COMMERCIAL BK NA	CHINO	CA	C+	C+	C	93.5	50.95	6.1	0.9	5.8	23.2	5.7	7.7	14.1
CHIPPEWA VALLEY BK	WINTER	WI	B-	B-	B-	110.9	15.65	10.1	3.0	29.4	5.5	5.9	8.3	11.6
▲ CHISHOLM TRAIL ST BK	WICHITA	KS	C-	C	C	80.4	4.39	4.5	14.5	16.1	25.5	5.9	7.9	13.1
CHITTENDEN TRUST CO	BURLINGTON	VT	B-	B-	B-	2,918.5	-0.12	10.7	7.4	14.2	27.1	4.8	7.4	10.9
▲ CHOICE BK	SCOTTSDALE	AZ	C+	C-	NR	37.6	54.10	5.1	0.2	29.8	23.2	10.0	28.2	34.4
▲ CHOICE FINANCIAL GROUP	GRAFTON	ND	C	C-	D	240.3	27.14	28.9	4.2	1.9	8.5	8.2	11.4	13.5
CHOICEONE BK	SPARTA	MI	B-	C+	C	225.3	8.73	11.4	6.1	27.8	18.0	7.4	9.3	13.4
CHRISTIANA B&TC	GREENVILLE	DE	C	C	C	142.5	16.90	11.5	4.0	13.3	12.3	6.5	10.3	12.1
CHURCH POINT B&TC	CHURCH POINT	LA	B	B	B	38.0	-4.95	4.8	7.7	13.2	50.3	10.0	12.5	29.3
CIB BK	HILLSIDE	IL	E-	D	C	1,325.7	-22.65	17.7	0.0	1.2	25.3	0.1	3.4	6.1
CIB BK	INDIANAPOLIS	IN	D-	D+	C+	144.5	-18.85	21.5	0.2	2.5	22.9	7.2	9.5	12.6
CINCINNATI FS&LA	CINCINNATI	OH	B-	C+	C	80.7	5.84	0.0	0.1	36.0	10.7	6.9	8.9	14.8
CINCINNATUS S&LC	CHEVIOT	OH	B-	B-	B-	78.6	7.33	0.9	1.6	68.2	5.6	10.0	19.6	32.8
▲ CIRCLE BK	NOVATO	CA	B	B-	C	136.8	49.35	0.9	0.2	9.3	15.6	7.9	9.6	13.5
CISSNA PARK ST BK	CISSNA PARK	IL	A-	A-	A	44.9	-0.79	16.1	1.5	5.3	40.4	9.8	10.9	19.8
CIT BANK	SALT LAKE CITY	UT	B+	B+	B	231.0	538.78	6.0	88.9	0.0	0.3	9.0	13.7	14.2
▼ CITADEL BK	COLORADO SPRINGS	CO	C	C+	B	63.0	22.82	10.7	5.4	7.6	3.2	4.7	6.7	15.0
▲ CITIBANK (WEST), FSB	SAN FRANCISCO	CA	C+	C	C-	88,814.1	22.76	1.6	6.9	66.8	3.7	5.5	7.5	14.2
CITIBANK FSB	RESTON	VA	B	B	B	26,349.3	17.15	1.8	9.6	44.2	4.8	5.8	7.8	12.9
CITIBANK NA	NEW YORK	NY	C+	C+	B-	648,243.0	23.92	2.9	10.3	0.9	15.9	4.3	6.3	12.6
▲ CITIBANK NEVADA NA	LAS VEGAS	NV	C	B-	B	19,444.6	102.42	6.6	79.1	0.0	1.7	10.0	13.8	16.1
▲ CITIBANK SOUTH DAKOTA NA	SIOUX FALLS	SD	C	C-	C+	52,910.5	47.31	0.0	77.7	0.0	2.9	10.0	13.5	15.8
▲ CITIBANK USA NA	SIOUX FALLS	SD	B	B-	C+	5,111.7	18.07	79.7	7.7	0.0	0.1	10.0	16.9	18.4
CITIBANK-DELAWARE	NEW CASTLE	DE	B	B	B+	6,272.1	5.44	0.7	0.0	0.0	19.8	10.0	18.0	27.1
CITICORP TRUST BANK, FSB	NEWARK	DE	B-	B-	C+	26,524.1	75.06	0.0	10.7	86.5	0.0	4.5	6.5	13.4
▼ CITIZENS & FARMERS BK	W POINT	VA	C	B-	B+	586.4	8.93	4.2	16.8	26.2	11.1	6.8	8.8	12.4
▼ CITIZENS & MERCHANTS ST	DOUGLASVILLE	GA	B-	B	B	198.2	23.44	12.2	1.2	6.7	7.0	3.4	8.2	10.2
▼ CITIZENS & NORTHERN BK	WELLSBORO	PA	B+	A-	A-	1,093.2	5.72	3.2	3.0	28.5	43.7	6.6	8.6	15.9
CITIZENS & PEOPLES BK NA	PENSACOLA	FL	B-	B-	B-	121.1	8.93	8.7	1.0	14.5	15.0	3.5	7.2	10.3
CITIZENS 1ST BANK	TYLER	TX	A+	A+	A+	602.2	4.30	1.2	1.3	14.3	64.9	10.0	14.0	38.6
▼ CITIZENS B&LA	GREER	SC	B-	B	B	94.8	1.04	0.0	1.0	56.4	12.3	10.0	18.8	37.6
CITIZENS B&TC	GUNTERSVILLE	AL	D	D	NR	66.2	80.67	14.2	6.2	10.0	31.9	10.0	14.8	21.1
▲ CITIZENS B&TC	VAN BUREN	AR	A	A-	A-	255.6	6.82	7.1	10.6	24.9	24.9	10.0	11.1	18.1
CITIZENS B&TC	EASTMAN	GA	B-	B-	B-	134.6	6.68	4.9	11.7	14.5	25.2	5.7	7.7	12.5
CITIZENS B&TC	CAMPBELLSVILLE	KY	A-	A-	A	138.3	11.36	1.7	8.5	18.6	43.0	9.9	10.9	20.2
CITIZENS B&TC	COVINGTON	LA	C+	C+	C	86.6	3.24	6.0	4.9	13.6	24.7	6.1	8.1	13.2
CITIZENS B&TC	PLAQUEMINE	LA	B	B	B-	122.0	1.56	3.9	5.0	24.7	6.9	10.0	12.7	17.7
CITIZENS B&TC	SPRINGHILL	LA	B-	B-	B	94.3	4.14	6.2	6.2	12.9	43.1	5.9	7.9	15.8
CITIZENS B&TC	HUTCHINSON	MN	A-	A-	A-	153.5	-4.61	11.4	2.4	14.4	34.7	10.0	11.2	17.9
▲ CITIZENS B&TC	CHILLICOTHE	MO	B	B-	B-	1,017.7	4.64	5.3	0.9	24.5	31.6	5.4	7.4	12.5
▼ CITIZENS B&TC	ROCK PORT	MO	C+	B-	C	52.0	19.94	13.3	5.7	17.3	23.3	8.7	10.1	18.4
CITIZENS B&TC	MARKS	MS	A-	A	A	105.7	-4.66	7.0	7.5	12.3	35.1	10.0	14.7	23.0
CITIZENS B&TC	BIG TIMBER	MT	B	B+	B+	44.3	4.73	6.3	4.9	8.9	29.5	10.0	14.6	25.4
CITIZENS B&TC	OKMULGEE	OK	C	C	C	147.6	9.26	7.6	9.5	22.3	20.5	4.8	6.8	11.0
CITIZENS B&TC	ATWOOD	TN	D+	D	D	19.8	12.92	4.8	18.9	13.8	34.5	5.9	7.9	16.9
CITIZENS B&TC	BLACKSTONE	VA	B	B	B	266.6	-0.97	8.8	7.0	31.2	17.3	6.8	8.8	14.7
▲ CITIZENS B&TC CHICAGO	CHICAGO	IL	C	D+	D	61.6	-0.29	8.7	0.4	12.3	4.1	6.8	8.8	12.7
CITIZENS B&TC IN ST PAUL	ST PAUL	NE	B+	B+	B+	49.0	1.91	5.7	7.5	3.3	35.6	10.0	14.8	24.2
▲ CITIZENS B&TC OF ARDMORE	ARDMORE	OK	A-	B+	B+	130.1	3.46	6.1	10.2	9.4	36.3	10.0	11.2	18.2
CITIZENS B&TC OF GRAINGER	RUTLEDGE	TN	A	A	A-	146.0	4.81	2.5	3.7	15.0	49.5	10.0	17.4	36.9
CITIZENS B&TC OF JACKSON	JACKSON	KY	C+	C+	C-	110.6	4.80	7.8	13.6	22.8	12.2	6.1	8.1	11.8
CITIZENS B&TC OF VIVIAN	VIVIAN	LA	C	C	C	75.8	2.64	8.7	16.8	22.9	31.0	6.1	8.1	15.8
CITIZENS B&TC OF WEST	CARROLLTON	GA	B	B	B	499.0	6.49	10.8	4.8	22.3	16.0	4.3	7.4	10.7
▲ CITIZENS BANK & TRUST, INC.	TRENTON	GA	C	C-	C-	68.0	-3.73	2.1	15.7	35.5	11.4	6.9	8.9	14.2

Asset Quality Index	Non-Performing Loans as a % of Total Loans	Non-Performing Loans as a % of Capital	Net Charge-offs Avg Loans	Profitability Index	Net Income ($Mil)	Return on Assets (R.O.A.)	Return on Equity (R.O.E.)	Net Interest Spread	Overhead Efficiency Ratio	Liquidity Index	Liquidity Ratio	Hot Money Ratio	Stability Index
6.8	0.12	1.8	0.01	6.1	74.1	1.17	22.78	2.64	68.3	1.0	8.0	29.9	3.8
4.5	1.49	8.9	0.10	1.6	0.0	0.04	0.45	4.09	96.7	4.9	28.3	5.8	2.9
7.1	0.00	0.0	0.00	2.8	0.1	0.71	4.18	5.36	78.2	2.3	43.6	25.2	0.0
4.4	1.15	7.0	-0.01	10.0	2.5	2.20	21.34	5.97	44.5	2.3	18.7	17.8	7.6
5.2	0.41	3.0	0.23	6.8	0.6	1.15	11.78	6.28	67.8	3.6	20.9	11.6	4.6
7.6	0.64	3.9	0.03	4.1	1.2	0.67	5.78	3.38	73.9	4.8	61.2	16.0	6.5
6.4	0.49	3.4	-0.21	8.4	1.0	2.06	23.86	4.03	52.7	3.7	26.7	11.9	6.3
7.8	0.56	2.7	0.00	10.0	1.6	2.42	14.54	6.66	41.3	4.0	15.2	8.9	10.0
5.6	1.55	6.7	0.39	7.1	10.6	1.16	10.24	3.65	49.3	5.4	202.5	44.7	8.5
6.0	0.72	2.5	0.09	2.3	0.4	0.20	1.64	2.59	84.8	5.9	123.3	17.1	6.5
9.3	0.00	0.0	0.00	4.1	0.3	0.71	9.37	4.00	74.0	7.0	68.1	2.7	0.9
3.8	1.23	11.8	0.00	7.6	0.8	1.42	16.23	5.07	70.5	3.7	28.3	12.6	6.4
4.7	0.67	5.1	1.40	3.2	0.3	0.79	9.78	4.08	82.0	4.9	58.1	13.5	2.8
6.1	0.89	6.6	0.10	8.6	22.9	1.55	20.15	4.13	58.4	6.0	38.8	6.2	6.9
9.1	0.00	0.0	0.00	3.3	0.1	0.46	1.48	4.10	86.5	5.4	113.9	18.3	1.3
2.8	1.84	12.8	0.07	7.9	1.9	1.69	14.48	4.32	60.8	1.2	14.1	28.9	6.2
5.0	0.61	4.7	0.53	5.0	1.0	0.89	9.45	3.82	70.2	1.0	6.5	29.1	4.7
8.6	0.12	0.9	0.00	3.1	0.4	0.62	6.28	3.33	83.6	4.2	17.0	7.8	5.1
8.4	1.15	3.2	-0.21	3.8	0.1	0.50	4.10	3.82	81.0	4.4	33.2	10.5	5.8
0.0	11.63	99.1	2.42	1.3	-2.8	-0.38	-7.16	2.43	91.5	5.5	152.2	24.8	1.8
1.7	9.03	43.9	0.00	1.1	-0.4	-0.53	-5.76	2.82	77.3	2.9	58.4	35.4	3.8
9.1	0.05	0.4	0.00	4.7	0.3	0.82	9.10	3.48	71.2	3.1	16.8	13.6	4.8
3.9	2.49	9.8	0.12	6.5	0.3	0.85	3.93	4.58	69.6	2.7	4.3	14.4	8.3
6.3	0.00	0.0	0.00	5.1	0.4	0.67	6.67	3.98	64.1	4.9	83.6	18.7	5.1
8.9	0.02	0.1	0.00	5.2	0.3	1.27	11.54	3.30	61.0	5.5	50.0	8.6	7.7
5.5	0.11	0.7	1.34	10.0	2.0	2.13	14.42	7.50	16.3	0.2	7.8	98.0	4.3
8.8	0.02	0.1	0.00	4.0	0.2	0.54	7.76	2.67	87.0	8.0	95.2	0.6	4.0
5.1	0.21	2.4	0.23	7.5	557.7	1.27	10.63	3.08	44.7	0.5	8.4	60.8	4.3
7.9	0.22	2.2	0.07	7.8	130.9	1.03	12.71	3.05	52.1	1.8	29.9	59.2	6.5
3.4	1.95	12.1	1.70	8.3	4,419.0	1.44	18.31	4.13	60.0	4.0	95.8	38.9	5.9
2.2	1.59	6.2	5.75	10.0	483.2	5.04	28.67	14.27	33.3	0.2	6.3	90.9	7.9
1.9	2.08	6.7	6.31	10.0	781.9	2.88	14.84	11.50	49.4	0.5	6.7	63.3	7.9
5.1	0.88	3.5	2.75	10.0	123.6	4.72	25.56	7.70	56.5	0.4	6.8	66.6	7.9
10.0	0.33	0.3	-0.01	9.3	50.0	1.61	5.84	1.72	66.4	4.8	94.7	24.1	6.3
6.0	0.34	4.7	0.54	10.0	199.9	1.95	25.17	3.71	19.3	0.4	15.5	100.0	6.4
2.4	1.84	11.4	0.32	10.0	5.1	1.79	17.20	6.21	66.7	5.2	56.6	13.2	8.1
4.7	0.53	5.0	-0.03	8.9	1.2	1.25	16.13	4.24	51.0	1.3	10.8	25.8	6.8
6.1	1.90	10.4	0.07	5.8	6.4	1.19	12.87	3.71	61.2	3.3	5.8	11.7	8.5
7.6	0.04	0.4	-0.01	7.7	0.7	1.23	17.78	4.12	53.2	1.1	7.0	28.4	5.3
9.8	0.11	0.3	0.00	9.1	7.5	2.47	17.23	3.47	26.0	1.1	23.5	33.7	10.0
3.4	4.34	15.4	0.00	8.9	0.7	1.48	7.86	3.61	41.3	2.1	37.6	31.0	8.1
8.4	0.51	2.0	0.01	0.3	-0.1	-0.26	-1.73	3.74	96.0	1.0	20.0	33.1	0.0
7.3	0.72	4.0	0.00	9.1	1.8	1.44	13.08	4.68	53.2	1.6	23.7	25.0	8.8
5.0	0.68	5.5	-0.13	7.4	1.3	1.90	25.78	4.43	53.1	4.1	89.8	29.0	4.4
8.6	0.00	0.0	-0.12	6.2	0.9	1.40	11.12	4.51	62.5	4.3	16.6	7.2	7.0
8.4	0.15	1.0	-0.01	4.6	0.2	0.54	6.47	4.39	82.9	4.2	31.9	11.5	4.0
6.3	0.92	5.1	-0.06	4.3	0.4	0.72	5.91	5.13	76.2	5.1	36.3	7.7	5.9
8.2	0.30	1.5	0.00	5.1	0.3	0.60	7.44	4.16	81.1	5.7	78.7	12.6	3.8
6.4	2.14	10.5	0.22	6.3	1.0	1.29	11.51	3.92	57.3	6.2	40.8	2.6	6.8
6.6	0.84	6.2	0.05	5.8	5.0	0.99	12.50	3.22	56.4	5.8	69.7	13.5	6.3
2.9	3.40	16.7	0.03	6.9	0.4	1.51	13.70	4.07	62.5	5.1	57.7	12.6	6.5
7.2	0.92	3.3	0.85	5.5	0.7	1.30	9.13	4.24	67.1	1.8	16.0	20.5	7.9
5.8	2.12	7.4	0.00	5.9	0.2	0.96	6.60	4.05	62.0	5.9	90.6	13.1	6.7
4.4	1.16	11.0	0.18	5.2	0.6	0.80	11.82	4.54	73.8	4.0	25.8	10.3	3.3
7.6	0.08	0.4	0.00	6.0	0.1	1.36	16.49	4.98	69.7	2.7	73.0	36.9	2.8
4.5	1.10	8.3	0.33	5.3	1.5	1.12	13.08	4.07	67.3	2.7	31.6	18.7	5.2
6.1	0.00	0.0	-0.01	3.7	0.3	0.94	10.65	4.30	80.2	5.2	155.2	28.4	1.2
7.4	0.98	3.2	-0.02	7.1	0.4	1.43	9.24	4.70	56.4	4.7	58.1	14.6	7.0
8.3	0.14	0.6	0.02	5.4	0.6	1.01	9.30	4.46	73.7	3.7	21.4	11.3	5.9
6.9	2.71	5.9	0.48	7.7	0.9	1.23	6.99	4.50	68.5	3.9	32.5	13.1	8.2
3.9	0.98	6.0	0.18	6.3	0.9	1.63	14.78	4.62	63.1	2.6	28.7	18.5	6.9
3.5	2.11	14.2	0.48	4.9	0.3	0.90	11.00	4.63	76.4	4.4	73.9	18.4	3.6
5.5	0.66	6.4	0.13	10.0	4.1	1.72	22.81	5.04	47.6	1.4	14.6	26.5	6.5
3.5	0.91	6.7	0.38	4.4	0.2	0.50	5.65	5.14	80.0	2.2	27.4	19.8	3.8

Name	City	State	Weiss Safety Rating	2003 Weiss Safety Rating	2002 Weiss Safety Rating	Total Assets ($Mil)	One Year Asset Growth	Asset Mix (As a % of Total Assets) Commercial Loans	Consumer Loans	Home Mortgages	Securities	Capitalization Index	Leverage Ratio	Risk-based Capital Ratio
CITIZENS BANK-HIGGINSPORT	HIGGINSPORT	OH	C+	C+	C	107.2	4.09	5.2	3.5	34.1	26.8	5.6	7.6	13.5
CITIZENS BK	ENTERPRISE	AL	B	B	A-	88.3	9.59	9.0	3.2	11.3	28.5	10.0	14.6	22.9
CITIZENS BK	GENEVA	AL	A	A	A	118.7	1.04	1.7	10.0	16.8	60.5	10.0	16.2	38.6
CITIZENS BK	GREENSBORO	AL	B+	B+	B+	66.8	-2.99	5.1	11.0	14.1	38.7	10.0	11.0	19.3
CITIZENS BK	MOULTON	AL	B	B	B	98.9	-4.79	3.9	5.9	5.9	63.9	10.0	15.5	33.9
CITIZENS BK	ROBERTSDALE	AL	B+	B+	B+	90.8	8.31	5.6	6.4	12.3	44.2	9.5	10.7	21.2
CITIZENS BK	VALLEY HEAD	AL	C	C	C	23.0	-0.60	3.7	11.6	34.8	26.6	10.0	15.9	32.8
CITIZENS BK	BATESVILLE	AR	C-	C-	C-	430.5	4.29	11.5	8.7	24.2	28.4	4.2	6.2	11.3
CITIZENS BK	PAGOSA SPRINGS	CO	C-	C-	D+	52.8	6.71	12.7	1.0	16.5	23.9	4.5	6.5	11.4
▲ CITIZENS BK	WILMINGTON	DE	C+	C	C-	1,275.9	28.85	3.8	1.5	38.0	27.1	4.0	6.0	12.6
CITIZENS BK	OVIEDO	FL	C+	C+	B-	140.0	4.03	9.6	2.3	8.8	21.3	6.5	8.7	12.1
CITIZENS BK	PERRY	FL	B	B-	B-	67.7	-0.98	12.8	3.6	16.4	2.9	10.0	11.4	15.5
▼ CITIZENS BK	CAIRO	GA	C+	B-	C-	49.5	12.64	8.9	18.9	18.7	24.9	10.0	11.0	17.2
CITIZENS BK	FORT VALLEY	GA	B	B	B+	102.1	-1.31	21.4	6.5	11.3	27.2	5.7	7.7	11.7
▲ CITIZENS BK	NASHVILLE	GA	B	B	B-	122.6	25.07	3.1	9.0	27.8	7.0	5.4	9.2	11.3
▼ CITIZENS BK	SWAINSBORO	GA	C+	B-	B-	84.8	9.06	10.9	14.4	17.5	14.6	5.6	8.0	11.5
CITIZENS BK	WARRENTON	GA	B	B	B-	49.7	4.13	10.2	8.2	11.1	31.9	7.0	9.0	17.3
CITIZENS BK	SAC CITY	IA	B	B	B	31.7	5.20	8.7	7.1	11.0	39.4	10.0	11.4	18.5
▼ CITIZENS BK	CHATSWORTH	IL	D	D+	D+	42.1	5.57	11.9	6.5	9.2	17.5	4.2	7.7	10.6
▲ CITIZENS BK	MOORESVILLE	IN	B+	B	A-	259.2	2.90	6.3	20.0	13.0	26.2	10.0	11.1	16.5
CITIZENS BK	GEORGETOWN	KY	C+	C+	C	75.9	-8.16	11.5	8.5	22.1	15.3	6.7	8.7	14.7
CITIZENS BK	HARTFORD	KY	C+	C+	B-	19.8	10.29	1.5	12.9	21.6	40.1	10.0	16.7	50.9
▲ CITIZENS BK	HICKMAN	KY	B	B-	B-	83.7	5.39	6.3	6.7	17.6	23.5	9.4	10.6	17.5
CITIZENS BK	MOREHEAD	KY	C+	C+	C+	81.0	7.93	7.1	7.6	19.3	39.0	6.3	8.4	16.6
▲ CITIZENS BK	MT VERNON	KY	B-	C+	B-	121.3	0.69	4.2	14.4	31.1	14.6	10.0	11.1	16.9
CITIZENS BK	NEW LIBERTY	KY	D+	D+	D+	15.7	2.08	4.4	4.7	42.4	0.0	5.8	7.8	12.5
CITIZENS BK	VILLE PLATTE	LA	B+	B+	B+	160.7	7.65	16.2	6.7	19.7	38.8	8.2	9.8	21.5
▲ CITIZENS BK	FLINT	MI	B-	C+	C+	5,592.9	2.22	16.6	17.6	8.9	22.1	5.1	7.6	11.1
▲ CITIZENS BK	AMSTERDAM	MO	D	E	D	19.3	-9.23	5.9	3.4	27.2	26.1	6.6	8.6	15.0
CITIZENS BK	CHARLESTON	MO	A-	A-	B+	75.9	6.02	9.5	9.3	5.8	24.2	10.0	13.4	18.2
CITIZENS BK	EDINA	MO	B	B-	B-	61.8	-0.87	17.3	3.6	5.1	11.4	4.8	8.1	10.9
CITIZENS BK	OREGON	MO	C+	C+	B-	21.8	2.16	5.5	1.1	2.2	32.3	10.0	13.6	29.7
▲ CITIZENS BK	ROGERSVILLE	MO	D	E+	E	50.9	8.48	12.2	7.5	18.4	27.0	5.3	7.3	12.8
CITIZENS BK	SPARTA	MO	C-	C	C	45.5	-2.16	4.5	7.9	37.2	17.5	9.6	10.7	17.8
▲ CITIZENS BK	BYHALIA	MS	C	D+	C-	53.8	-2.91	2.5	14.4	14.4	32.5	7.3	9.2	17.8
CITIZENS BK	COLUMBIA	MS	B	B-	B-	262.2	-5.53	4.9	11.0	20.1	21.3	9.3	10.5	17.1
CITIZENS BK	PHILADELPHIA	MS	B-	B-	B	567.2	1.94	7.9	11.4	16.2	24.8	7.3	9.2	14.5
CITIZENS BK	CLOVIS	NM	A-	A-	B+	186.2	2.92	10.9	5.0	5.5	32.4	10.0	12.2	21.8
CITIZENS BK	FARMINGTON	NM	B+	B+	B+	440.1	17.74	8.4	3.7	11.0	50.1	5.6	7.6	14.9
CITIZENS BK	TUCUMCARI	NM	B+	B+	B+	54.5	4.10	1.3	0.5	2.4	5.8	10.0	12.9	20.0
CITIZENS BK	ASHVILLE	OH	B-	B-	C	88.8	6.22	2.4	3.6	34.4	24.5	6.7	8.7	14.5
CITIZENS BK	VELMA	OK	C+	C+	C+	17.0	-0.97	12.1	13.2	12.4	26.3	10.0	16.0	23.0
CITIZENS BK	CORVALLIS	OR	A	A	A	335.2	5.29	6.9	0.9	7.1	28.9	10.0	11.7	17.8
CITIZENS BK	OLANTA	SC	B	B	B	211.8	6.02	18.3	14.5	20.6	8.4	8.7	10.1	14.9
CITIZENS BK	CARTHAGE	TN	A+	A+	A+	439.0	0.46	7.2	5.6	23.9	40.4	10.0	16.4	26.0
CITIZENS BK	ELIZABETHTON	TN	A-	A-	B+	512.3	-11.34	23.3	5.2	15.5	15.5	9.4	10.6	18.8
▲ CITIZENS BK	HARTSVILLE	TN	B	B-	B-	80.7	11.52	5.1	9.7	25.9	22.1	6.6	8.6	13.9
▼ CITIZENS BK	NEW TAZEWELL	TN	D+	C+	D+	124.7	-6.76	8.6	13.3	20.4	19.8	7.5	9.3	14.6
▼ CITIZENS BK	KILGORE	TX	B-	B	B+	206.7	-5.31	23.0	5.6	11.6	28.0	10.0	13.3	28.1
CITIZENS BK	SLATON	TX	C+	C+	C-	120.5	-1.18	6.8	6.4	14.1	38.9	6.5	8.6	15.8
CITIZENS BK	MUKWONAGO	WI	A-	A-	B+	448.1	6.46	8.2	1.7	8.6	24.6	9.1	10.4	15.2
CITIZENS BK	WESTON	WV	A	A	A-	141.4	9.37	22.9	6.7	20.5	31.1	9.8	10.8	16.8
CITIZENS BK & SVG CO	RUSSELLVILLE	AL	B-	B-	B-	508.3	7.67	5.0	3.4	18.1	46.2	6.4	8.4	17.7
▲ CITIZENS BK CO	BEVERLY	OH	B-	C+	C+	73.7	5.29	8.2	7.3	25.4	42.3	6.7	8.7	18.2
▲ CITIZENS BK IL NA	BERWYN	IL	C+	C	C-	180.2	-14.63	9.8	3.2	5.5	42.3	5.4	7.4	14.9
CITIZENS BK LONDON	LONDON	OH	B-	C+	B+	55.8	-0.34	7.5	2.0	27.6	0.7	7.8	9.5	13.1
CITIZENS BK MN	NEW ULM	MN	A-	A-	A-	203.7	1.40	5.5	2.5	14.8	22.1	9.4	10.6	15.2
CITIZENS BK MORGANTOWN	MORGANTOWN	WV	C+	C+	B	39.4	0.24	6.8	3.6	13.0	54.5	10.0	14.2	31.6
CITIZENS BK NA	FORT SCOTT	KS	C	C	C	243.2	3.96	15.1	2.1	8.9	28.8	5.7	7.7	12.1
CITIZENS BK NA	ABILENE	TX	B	B	B	52.1	9.20	13.4	14.0	10.0	23.7	5.9	8.2	11.7
CITIZENS BK NH	MANCHESTER	NH	C+	C+	C+	8,358.9	16.21	10.0	12.2	18.5	36.7	4.0	6.0	10.6
CITIZENS BK OF ADA	ADA	OK	A-	A-	A-	123.8	2.26	9.3	9.4	31.0	31.7	10.0	11.1	20.1
CITIZENS BK OF AMERICUS	AMERICUS	GA	B	B-	B-	157.8	4.69	7.3	6.7	14.1	34.3	6.4	8.4	13.8
CITIZENS BK OF BLOUNT CTY	MARYVILLE	TN	A	A	A-	237.2	-8.88	2.9	3.3	9.5	21.0	10.0	15.6	20.4

Asset Quality Index	Non-Performing Loans as a % of Total Loans	Non-Performing Loans as a % of Capital	Net Charge-offs Avg Loans	Profitability Index	Net Income ($Mil)	Return on Assets (R.O.A.)	Return on Equity (R.O.E.)	Net Interest Spread	Overhead Efficiency Ratio	Liquidity Index	Liquidity Ratio	Hot Money Ratio	Stability Index
5.3	0.94	7.5	0.08	4.8	0.5	0.93	12.34	3.53	58.5	4.7	34.0	9.1	4.4
8.6	0.40	1.5	-0.11	3.8	0.3	0.76	5.20	3.46	74.5	4.2	40.5	14.2	7.5
8.5	0.31	0.6	0.20	10.0	1.3	2.23	14.19	4.80	33.0	1.8	15.4	20.5	8.8
7.0	0.80	3.8	0.04	9.4	0.7	2.05	19.03	4.47	39.7	1.8	23.8	23.2	6.1
5.7	5.08	8.7	2.96	3.6	0.3	0.53	3.54	3.49	78.3	4.4	25.2	7.3	6.2
5.2	1.74	7.2	0.01	5.3	0.4	0.88	7.68	3.56	65.5	2.4	20.8	17.6	5.8
7.3	0.90	3.2	-0.13	2.1	0.0	0.28	1.82	5.49	94.9	5.7	52.7	6.3	4.9
4.1	1.29	11.7	0.08	5.3	2.2	1.00	16.58	3.47	59.0	2.9	26.0	15.8	3.0
7.9	0.39	3.1	-0.01	6.0	0.3	1.36	19.08	4.60	74.2	5.1	56.8	12.1	3.0
6.0	0.51	2.6	0.27	5.3	5.4	0.87	7.34	3.67	56.5	6.3	49.9	7.9	4.2
8.0	0.28	2.1	0.00	3.3	0.3	0.46	5.38	4.31	84.0	2.6	22.3	16.8	5.0
8.2	0.17	1.1	0.02	4.3	0.4	1.06	9.33	4.16	75.8	3.0	43.4	21.6	5.9
2.8	2.40	13.4	0.25	9.5	0.4	1.51	13.74	5.04	55.6	0.9	21.2	34.7	5.7
6.4	0.42	3.4	0.03	10.0	1.1	2.19	28.54	5.31	39.9	4.1	15.1	8.0	7.2
4.3	0.85	6.8	0.56	7.2	1.1	1.83	19.54	4.39	50.9	1.5	33.1	39.5	6.4
5.0	0.48	4.1	0.06	6.3	0.5	1.08	13.35	4.79	65.3	2.6	13.5	16.1	4.9
3.4	1.43	3.9	0.52	3.3	0.1	0.59	3.82	3.60	78.3	5.9	59.3	8.1	7.1
8.3	0.45	2.1	0.01	6.0	0.2	1.41	11.78	4.13	68.9	1.7	14.3	21.4	6.0
7.6	0.12	1.0	0.25	3.4	0.1	0.54	6.78	3.46	74.7	4.0	43.3	15.7	2.2
5.5	0.63	3.4	0.52	7.2	1.6	1.23	11.22	4.76	67.0	4.5	25.1	6.4	6.9
2.1	3.07	16.3	0.59	0.9	0.0	0.01	0.13	3.73	99.7	4.0	80.1	24.3	4.4
7.0	1.54	3.3	0.16	4.8	0.1	0.87	5.36	3.84	72.2	6.8	59.9	0.0	4.3
4.5	1.36	8.5	0.29	5.9	0.5	1.15	11.11	4.55	57.2	1.5	10.4	22.6	5.4
5.5	0.70	3.5	0.15	4.5	0.3	0.67	7.35	4.51	80.5	4.5	21.5	6.1	3.8
4.0	1.75	10.9	0.86	6.5	0.6	1.00	9.10	5.06	58.8	3.1	40.3	19.8	6.2
8.6	0.10	0.9	-0.04	7.6	0.2	1.77	23.82	4.74	62.0	4.7	40.6	9.0	3.7
7.5	0.14	0.6	0.04	5.4	0.8	1.03	10.45	3.28	56.7	4.9	143.6	30.9	6.2
4.9	0.56	4.0	0.28	6.0	31.2	1.13	12.82	4.01	60.6	3.5	12.2	11.5	6.6
6.2	0.21	1.5	-0.08	6.3	0.2	1.64	19.02	4.60	69.5	3.6	20.9	11.2	1.9
7.8	0.05	0.2	0.16	10.0	0.7	1.85	13.54	4.91	40.7	3.4	21.1	12.6	7.2
6.1	0.07	0.7	-0.01	9.4	0.5	1.47	18.39	4.31	42.3	3.6	10.7	10.5	6.0
9.3	0.00	0.0	-0.02	4.5	0.1	1.11	8.27	3.39	55.8	8.2	142.7	4.7	4.6
4.8	0.74	6.1	-1.02	4.0	0.2	0.73	10.27	4.05	86.4	5.5	36.8	5.3	1.5
2.8	3.03	17.9	0.28	2.7	0.1	0.32	2.94	4.64	89.9	3.2	34.1	17.0	3.8
4.3	1.06	5.0	0.88	5.5	0.3	1.12	12.28	5.39	65.8	3.7	61.4	19.9	3.2
4.7	1.47	8.1	0.23	6.5	1.6	1.22	11.56	4.04	61.9	2.0	25.7	20.2	5.5
3.6	1.62	9.6	0.15	7.3	3.6	1.27	12.60	4.62	58.3	4.1	48.8	16.8	7.5
6.7	1.51	7.0	0.03	6.6	1.3	1.34	11.12	4.22	62.3	4.1	60.6	19.8	7.0
7.9	0.37	1.8	0.13	9.7	5.1	2.41	29.17	4.24	52.1	7.0	97.8	9.3	5.8
7.7	0.00	0.0	0.00	4.5	0.3	1.03	8.20	3.46	70.6	8.4	159.3	6.0	6.8
8.1	0.27	2.1	-0.05	6.4	0.6	1.29	14.86	4.15	66.0	3.4	22.9	12.6	4.8
4.8	2.09	8.2	0.11	5.9	0.1	0.83	5.31	5.84	78.4	4.4	15.3	5.6	5.5
7.4	0.65	3.1	0.06	9.2	2.2	1.31	11.63	4.72	61.3	4.5	26.8	7.3	7.8
4.6	1.00	7.0	0.07	8.3	1.5	1.41	14.25	4.60	56.7	3.6	41.1	17.4	6.6
9.0	0.44	1.4	0.06	10.0	5.4	2.46	14.88	4.97	29.7	2.0	34.3	29.4	9.4
5.7	0.45	2.7	0.19	10.0	6.1	2.33	19.91	4.99	52.4	0.9	21.9	39.4	8.2
4.6	0.77	6.1	0.16	6.1	0.4	0.97	11.37	4.52	65.6	1.4	18.0	26.5	5.0
1.1	4.01	25.7	0.76	2.8	0.0	-0.06	-0.68	5.34	100.1	4.3	40.8	13.6	4.6
5.3	2.96	9.8	0.00	3.8	0.7	0.62	4.64	4.43	78.4	6.5	95.7	12.1	5.7
7.5	0.27	1.6	0.23	5.4	0.7	1.23	13.58	4.37	68.1	2.6	10.1	15.5	3.5
8.0	0.19	1.1	0.04	7.5	2.8	1.25	12.40	3.96	56.8	4.9	81.3	18.4	6.5
8.3	0.04	0.2	0.02	6.6	0.7	0.95	8.79	3.53	55.6	5.9	49.8	7.6	6.8
5.8	1.63	7.9	0.95	5.9	3.0	1.19	13.16	4.14	56.4	2.0	11.7	18.6	5.4
6.4	1.13	6.0	0.27	4.3	0.3	0.71	7.77	3.69	74.1	6.4	74.3	8.1	5.1
7.4	0.19	1.0	1.24	2.4	0.3	0.32	4.29	3.77	62.7	6.2	50.0	5.6	4.7
8.2	0.14	1.2	0.25	4.8	0.2	0.76	8.16	3.71	67.8	3.7	40.2	16.4	5.5
7.9	0.01	0.1	-0.02	7.4	1.3	1.32	11.32	4.01	60.4	5.1	49.9	11.9	7.6
9.3	0.00	0.0	1.12	3.1	0.1	0.55	3.78	3.24	78.2	4.5	63.1	16.1	4.7
5.2	0.92	6.6	0.02	3.6	0.9	0.77	9.91	3.48	75.2	3.2	26.3	14.6	3.5
6.7	0.00	0.0	0.21	6.6	0.4	1.53	14.33	4.01	67.8	1.4	9.8	24.4	7.3
7.6	0.05	0.4	0.08	9.1	62.2	1.56	20.44	3.38	40.9	4.8	28.1	9.7	6.6
6.4	1.32	6.9	-0.12	5.1	0.7	1.06	9.49	4.74	74.6	3.4	16.7	12.3	6.7
5.9	0.78	4.9	0.05	9.8	1.4	1.71	20.68	4.82	50.3	2.9	18.7	14.7	5.8
7.6	0.11	0.4	0.22	9.3	1.8	1.51	9.92	4.56	53.2	4.1	51.9	17.3	7.6

Name	City	State	Weiss Safety Rating	2003 Weiss Safety Rating	2002 Weiss Safety Rating	Total Assets ($Mil)	One Year Asset Growth	Asset Mix (As a % of Total Assets) Commercial Loans	Consumer Loans	Home Mortgages	Securities	Capitalization Index	Leverage Ratio	Risk-based Capital Ratio
▲ CITIZENS BK OF BLYTHEDALE	BLYTHEDALE	MO	B-	C	C	25.5	7.21	3.0	6.1	22.3	30.1	10.0	11.7	19.1
CITIZENS BK OF CAPE	CAPE VINCENT	NY	B	B	B	25.5	10.59	0.7	3.9	15.3	50.7	10.0	18.7	35.7
CITIZENS BK OF COCHRAN	COCHRAN	GA	C	C+	B	81.4	9.07	11.4	9.7	30.2	12.7	9.2	10.4	17.8
CITIZENS BK OF CT	NEW LONDON	CT	C+	C+	B-	3,763.5	18.41	8.8	12.0	17.3	32.4	3.4	6.1	10.2
CITIZENS BK OF CUMBERLAND	BURKESVILLE	KY	C	C	C	78.7	19.50	7.7	19.6	44.2	5.2	5.4	7.4	11.7
▲ CITIZENS BK OF DE GRAFF	DE GRAFF	OH	C+	C	C+	29.9	5.20	6.8	9.5	21.2	40.5	9.5	10.7	21.8
▲ CITIZENS BK OF EAST TN	ROGERSVILLE	TN	C-	D+	C-	106.5	-5.99	4.1	7.4	28.5	20.4	5.8	7.8	12.3
CITIZENS BK OF EDINBURG	EDINBURG	IL	D	D	D+	18.0	-0.08	12.3	10.3	15.4	10.9	7.0	9.0	13.8
▲ CITIZENS BK OF EDMOND	EDMOND	OK	B+	B-	C+	209.9	-1.89	7.6	8.4	14.0	27.3	9.0	10.3	16.6
CITIZENS BK OF EFFINGHAM	SPRINGFIELD	GA	C+	C+	C-	113.6	5.02	13.5	5.0	12.7	8.2	3.8	8.0	10.4
CITIZENS BK OF ELDON	ELDON	MO	A-	A-	A-	86.7	3.72	5.0	7.3	19.8	35.6	10.0	14.0	25.9
▲ CITIZENS BK OF FAYETTE	FAYETTE	AL	A+	A	A	164.0	-2.96	15.5	6.5	10.6	47.9	10.0	25.2	41.1
▲ CITIZENS BK OF FORSYTH	CUMMING	GA	B	C+	C+	121.1	18.38	7.9	6.0	11.8	12.5	7.1	9.6	12.6
CITIZENS BK OF	FROSTPROOF	FL	A	A	A	239.8	111.28	6.5	5.6	22.8	25.4	6.9	8.9	14.1
▼ CITIZENS BK OF KS NA	KINGMAN	KS	D+	C-	C	165.5	10.83	17.6	3.6	12.8	38.5	5.5	7.5	12.9
CITIZENS BK OF LAFAYETTE	LAFAYETTE	TN	B+	B	B	276.7	1.18	4.1	9.9	20.1	36.5	10.0	11.1	21.1
CITIZENS BK OF LAS CRUCES	LAS CRUCES	NM	B-	B-	B-	243.6	3.53	5.5	8.9	10.2	25.1	5.6	7.6	11.8
CITIZENS BK OF LOGAN	LOGAN	OH	D	D	D-	169.9	9.81	12.6	14.1	18.3	15.3	6.0	9.1	11.8
▲ CITIZENS BK OF MA	BOSTON	MA	C+	C	C	29,630.2	18.72	14.4	17.2	14.5	28.3	3.8	5.8	10.9
▲ CITIZENS BK OF NEVADA	NEVADA CITY	CA	B	B-	B-	159.3	25.67	11.2	2.6	0.6	6.9	6.7	10.3	12.2
▲ CITIZENS BK OF NEW HAVEN	NEW HAVEN	MO	B	B-	B-	152.7	5.89	10.1	2.6	26.0	4.9	7.3	9.3	12.8
CITIZENS BK OF NEWBURG	ROLLA	MO	C	C	C-	198.9	5.71	1.0	5.6	21.6	42.6	5.0	7.0	11.3
CITIZENS BK OF NORBORNE	NORBORNE	MO	B	B	B	22.2	-6.00	6.4	2.6	5.7	20.4	10.0	12.3	19.3
CITIZENS BK OF NORTHERN	NEWPORT	KY	C+	C	C	176.2	9.37	18.3	2.5	22.1	10.5	4.3	8.1	10.6
▲ CITIZENS BK OF PA	PHILADELPHIA	PA	C+	C	D+	28,374.8	18.88	9.3	15.2	21.0	28.1	3.5	5.6	10.3
CITIZENS BK OF SOUTHERN	GREENCASTLE	PA	B-	B-	B-	257.7	9.06	5.2	2.7	28.1	23.7	5.0	7.0	11.5
CITIZENS BK OF SPENCER TN	SPENCER	TN	B-	B-	B-	32.4	8.11	4.2	13.0	21.5	42.2	10.0	12.0	27.1
CITIZENS BK OF WASH CTY	SANDERSVILLE	GA	B-	B-	B-	145.2	5.33	7.5	13.2	32.9	21.0	7.3	9.2	15.6
▼ CITIZENS BK OF WEIR	WEIR	KS	E+	D-	D-	7.3	6.66	8.1	10.6	21.7	19.5	6.5	8.5	15.6
▲ CITIZENS BK OF WINFIELD	WINFIELD	AL	A+	A	A	150.6	-4.36	7.6	5.5	5.3	71.0	10.0	17.8	33.7
▲ CITIZENS BK OKLAHOMA	PAWHUSKA	OK	C+	C-	E+	30.6	3.89	18.5	3.9	21.3	5.9	10.0	12.4	19.0
▲ CITIZENS BK RI	PROVIDENCE	RI	B-	C+	C	11,194.8	16.12	5.2	27.7	16.5	19.1	5.2	7.2	11.1
CITIZENS BK WAKULLA	CRAWFORDVILLE	FL	D	D	D	58.7	8.01	7.4	8.2	12.9	43.7	5.1	7.1	15.9
CITIZENS BKG CO	SANDUSKY	OH	B	B	B	504.4	-0.41	9.4	3.1	21.2	15.2	5.9	7.9	12.0
CITIZENS BUSINESS BK	ONTARIO	CA	A-	B+	A-	4,356.1	24.08	3.6	0.6	3.2	46.2	6.1	8.2	12.8
▲ CITIZENS CITY & CTY BK	TRENTON	TN	D-	E	E	26.0	-2.09	6.2	13.1	16.7	9.8	6.3	8.3	12.7
CITIZENS CMNTY BK	POCATELLO	ID	C-	C-	D	103.9	16.37	22.4	5.3	5.5	3.4	3.6	7.5	10.3
▲ CITIZENS CMNTY BK DECATUR	DECATUR	IL	E+	E-	E-	13.8	0.91	11.5	3.2	13.6	26.7	10.0	11.7	17.8
CITIZENS CMRC NB	VERSAILLES	KY	C+	C+	C+	192.6	13.95	10.6	5.2	25.1	13.1	5.0	7.9	11.0
CITIZENS COMMUNITY BK	HAHIRA	GA	B-	B-	C+	93.3	0.03	11.6	8.9	19.8	17.8	7.1	9.0	16.3
CITIZENS COMMUNITY BK	MASCOUTAH	IL	B-	B-	B-	180.7	17.53	6.5	5.1	18.3	29.3	5.9	7.9	13.7
CITIZENS COMMUNITY BK	PILOT GROVE	MO	D	D	D+	74.8	7.35	13.6	7.4	21.5	8.3	3.6	7.0	10.3
▼ CITIZENS COMMUNITY BK	WINCHESTER	TN	B+	B+	A	106.1	15.34	14.1	8.0	17.5	17.1	9.7	10.8	14.9
CITIZENS COMMUNITY BK	S HILL	VA	C+	C+	C-	93.8	23.30	22.8	12.7	18.7	20.7	7.4	9.3	14.3
▲ CITIZENS COMMUNITY	EAU CLAIRE	WI	B-	C	C	152.0	20.77	0.1	33.9	59.3	0.0	7.9	9.6	14.7
CITIZENS DEPOSIT BK	ARLINGTON	KY	A	A-	A-	107.0	8.11	7.3	11.2	34.1	29.7	10.0	13.1	21.3
▲ CITIZENS DEPOSIT BK &	VANCEBURG	KY	B-	C+	C	86.7	0.10	5.8	8.4	24.7	26.5	10.0	13.0	22.9
▲ CITIZENS EXCHANGE BK	PEARSON	GA	B-	B-	C+	25.3	-2.03	3.1	9.6	13.6	36.0	9.0	10.4	19.8
CITIZENS EXCHANGE BK	FAIRMOUNT	IN	B-	B-	B-	49.2	1.93	4.3	7.3	24.1	33.9	10.0	12.2	23.7
▼ CITIZENS FINANCIAL BANK	GLASGOW	KY	C	B-	B	43.8	12.90	9.7	5.0	19.5	21.7	6.4	8.4	12.9
▼ CITIZENS FINANCIAL SVCS	HAMMOND	IN	C-	C	C+	1,459.3	-5.17	3.3	0.5	20.3	23.6	7.0	9.0	13.0
▲ CITIZENS FIRST BK	LADY LAKE	FL	B-	C	C	636.8	27.81	8.4	1.6	8.3	61.4	5.9	7.9	16.1
▼ CITIZENS FIRST BK	ROME	GA	B-	B	B	271.3	6.07	8.0	1.8	30.7	9.6	3.7	7.6	10.4
CITIZENS FIRST BK	CLINTON	IA	C+	C+	C-	83.0	17.10	21.3	5.4	25.0	7.3	5.6	8.8	11.4
▲ CITIZENS FIRST BK	BOWLING GREEN	KY	D	D-	C-	164.7	6.60	19.4	6.3	21.7	7.8	4.0	7.7	10.5
▲ CITIZENS FIRST BK	WARTBURG	TN	C-	D+	D-	76.3	12.27	13.0	16.6	32.5	11.5	5.8	7.8	11.7
CITIZENS FIRST BK	RAVENSWOOD	WV	C-	C-	D	50.7	17.97	12.5	18.9	35.0	0.0	6.3	8.3	12.5
CITIZENS FIRST NB	PRINCETON	IL	B-	B-	B-	614.1	1.46	15.1	2.7	11.9	27.3	5.5	7.9	11.4
CITIZENS FIRST NB STORM	STORM LAKE	IA	A-	A-	A	168.8	1.24	6.0	7.4	11.6	45.8	6.2	8.2	16.2
CITIZENS FIRST ST BK	HARTFORD CITY	IN	B-	B-	B	93.1	-5.56	8.5	17.5	20.7	11.3	6.2	8.2	12.1
CITIZENS FIRST ST BK	WALNUT	IL	D	C-	D	57.2	8.22	7.6	5.5	29.0	11.1	5.5	7.6	11.4
▼ CITIZENS FIRST SVG BK	PORT HURON	MI	B+	A	A	1,103.2	6.31	11.8	7.7	39.1	4.9	8.2	9.9	13.5
CITIZENS FS&LA	COVINGTON	KY	B	B	B	27.9	-0.91	0.0	0.2	67.0	9.6	10.0	26.8	53.8
CITIZENS FS&LA	BELLEFONTAINE	OH	C+	C	C	122.1	-4.24	0.0	0.2	51.6	20.8	5.9	7.9	17.2

Asset Quality Index	Non-Performing Loans as a % of Total Loans	as a % of Capital	Net Charge-offs Avg Loans	Profitability Index	Net Income ($Mil)	Return on Assets (R.O.A.)	Return on Equity (R.O.E.)	Net Interest Spread	Overhead Efficiency Ratio	Liquidity Index	Liquidity Ratio	Hot Money Ratio	Stability Index
7.7	0.46	2.4	0.06	6.7	0.1	1.09	9.34	4.86	64.5	5.5	40.2	6.9	5.5
10.0	0.15	0.2	0.03	6.6	0.2	1.29	6.79	5.17	62.9	8.3	127.4	3.4	6.2
2.1	1.62	4.7	9.12	2.0	-1.3	-3.03	-16.54	5.03	80.7	3.0	40.3	20.2	4.6
6.7	0.45	3.5	0.12	8.4	25.7	1.42	18.55	3.19	40.5	5.0	32.0	10.3	6.4
4.2	0.49	5.2	0.36	7.9	0.8	2.20	28.94	4.30	44.0	2.6	36.6	22.4	0.7
8.0	0.18	0.8	0.03	3.3	0.1	0.74	6.83	3.33	77.2	3.2	45.3	19.7	4.1
5.1	0.64	5.2	0.37	4.2	0.4	0.79	10.08	4.72	73.8	2.2	16.5	18.4	2.1
6.6	0.00	0.0	0.17	4.7	0.1	0.86	9.76	3.85	68.5	5.3	41.2	5.1	2.2
7.9	0.16	0.9	0.26	5.3	1.2	1.08	10.47	4.92	76.1	3.1	11.0	13.3	5.5
4.4	0.92	8.6	0.02	7.1	0.7	1.28	16.40	4.25	51.2	2.0	17.1	19.3	4.6
7.7	0.65	2.4	0.10	5.4	0.4	0.95	6.94	4.12	69.3	4.7	36.1	10.3	7.3
7.6	2.05	3.4	0.23	10.0	2.4	2.88	10.44	4.22	30.3	2.9	43.2	24.4	8.8
8.3	0.00	0.0	0.06	5.1	0.6	0.93	10.68	4.23	67.6	3.5	56.3	24.1	4.6
7.9	0.04	0.2	0.09	6.6	0.9	1.13	8.23	3.84	66.6	4.4	26.1	8.2	8.6
1.4	4.06	28.9	0.55	2.8	-0.1	-0.08	-0.97	3.66	72.6	3.9	82.9	30.8	4.7
7.1	0.70	3.0	0.16	5.9	1.4	1.02	9.26	3.98	63.6	3.7	56.6	22.5	6.4
4.7	0.99	7.4	-0.01	8.2	2.3	1.94	25.65	4.94	63.0	4.1	16.4	8.1	5.3
0.8	3.41	24.6	0.18	6.2	0.9	1.04	11.26	4.92	65.5	2.6	22.3	17.0	5.1
6.0	0.27	1.4	0.11	7.8	204.4	1.41	11.99	3.43	47.1	4.1	21.4	10.0	7.6
6.5	0.00	0.0	0.04	6.6	0.9	1.24	12.92	5.69	61.6	5.0	18.4	2.6	5.7
6.6	0.15	1.3	0.00	8.0	1.1	1.44	16.40	5.16	56.9	3.2	12.3	12.9	5.1
6.5	0.44	3.7	0.02	3.5	0.4	0.40	6.09	3.10	77.3	1.9	7.6	18.9	3.0
7.3	0.00	0.0	-0.01	4.4	0.1	0.80	6.61	4.09	73.6	4.5	46.9	11.6	5.7
4.7	0.97	8.8	0.10	5.9	0.8	0.91	11.10	4.04	67.5	3.4	13.3	12.0	3.6
5.4	0.30	1.2	0.35	4.0	116.1	0.84	5.95	3.49	64.2	5.4	33.2	8.2	4.4
5.5	0.77	6.9	0.06	5.5	1.4	1.12	16.02	3.65	60.2	3.9	6.7	8.4	5.5
4.2	5.19	16.1	0.45	5.2	0.1	0.79	5.92	4.74	69.0	5.2	76.8	15.1	5.8
4.4	1.18	8.2	0.37	4.4	0.6	0.88	9.66	4.08	62.3	3.2	45.3	21.6	4.7
5.2	1.52	10.4	-0.08	3.3	0.0	0.65	7.64	4.71	87.2	4.1	60.0	16.1	0.8
9.2	0.49	0.6	0.42	9.0	1.2	1.65	9.07	4.50	42.8	0.7	9.1	34.8	8.8
8.4	0.00	0.0	0.08	5.4	0.2	1.40	11.43	4.30	56.5	4.7	45.7	12.7	3.0
5.9	0.53	3.2	1.29	6.2	12.2	0.23	2.52	3.97	53.2	6.4	46.6	6.2	6.7
6.8	0.00	0.0	0.15	4.1	0.2	0.67	9.61	4.14	81.3	3.8	40.9	16.0	0.3
4.5	0.60	3.6	0.22	6.3	2.6	1.04	9.16	4.00	63.9	5.4	34.6	5.0	7.2
8.8	0.07	0.4	-0.09	9.3	29.4	1.44	16.26	4.15	49.3	2.9	11.5	14.3	8.1
4.5	0.57	4.6	0.41	2.6	0.1	0.61	7.64	4.70	86.4	3.1	45.2	21.7	1.2
5.4	0.59	5.2	0.10	5.3	0.4	0.82	10.79	4.33	72.7	3.1	52.8	27.3	3.3
1.2	7.88	36.9	-0.16	0.3	0.0	0.07	0.62	3.48	149.5	1.4	38.8	35.8	1.2
5.5	0.60	5.6	-0.02	6.3	1.1	1.14	14.27	4.12	65.2	1.2	8.3	27.6	4.0
6.2	0.83	4.9	0.54	5.1	0.6	1.23	12.89	4.25	70.7	5.0	60.9	13.6	4.8
6.7	0.74	4.9	0.02	7.4	1.2	1.32	17.12	3.94	41.1	1.5	21.9	26.4	4.4
4.2	0.83	8.2	0.06	5.1	0.3	0.80	11.12	3.63	65.6	4.3	70.2	18.4	2.3
4.6	1.29	7.1	-0.05	10.0	1.1	2.03	17.78	5.76	43.9	4.4	62.4	18.2	8.2
5.0	0.48	3.3	0.26	3.6	0.3	0.55	5.93	3.57	64.0	3.5	68.3	26.2	5.4
4.2	0.42	4.0	0.23	4.1	0.4	0.58	6.11	4.86	78.7	1.8	5.2	18.9	2.9
8.1	0.14	0.7	0.25	8.2	0.8	1.46	11.00	4.06	41.3	2.4	41.4	30.4	8.1
7.0	0.45	2.0	0.81	6.5	0.7	1.51	11.80	5.33	59.8	4.5	24.5	6.8	5.5
7.4	0.43	2.0	-0.07	5.8	0.2	1.54	14.16	4.44	68.1	4.2	36.1	12.9	5.5
5.4	2.03	8.3	-0.07	3.1	0.1	0.39	3.21	3.26	81.7	6.8	100.1	9.4	5.2
1.5	4.58	32.0	0.49	0.4	0.0	-0.04	-0.45	2.55	95.4	3.9	108.7	47.3	1.5
3.6	2.36	16.7	0.38	2.3	1.0	0.14	1.56	1.94	85.3	2.7	32.4	25.7	6.1
9.6	0.05	0.2	0.26	6.6	3.4	1.19	16.41	4.01	53.2	4.9	47.1	12.3	4.1
7.3	0.27	2.7	0.00	8.6	1.7	1.27	16.79	3.86	50.0	3.8	12.3	9.6	6.6
6.8	0.43	4.0	0.04	4.1	0.4	0.94	10.69	3.65	71.3	2.1	27.7	21.8	1.4
3.8	1.18	11.3	0.04	3.3	0.4	0.50	6.71	3.70	78.1	2.5	16.0	16.4	2.3
3.9	0.95	8.9	0.16	5.1	0.3	0.84	10.68	4.63	67.6	3.8	42.0	16.4	3.1
4.1	0.83	7.6	0.15	4.2	0.2	0.83	9.86	4.90	63.2	3.2	34.3	16.9	0.3
7.7	0.18	1.3	0.05	5.9	3.6	1.19	14.22	4.09	66.2	2.4	8.2	16.1	5.9
7.9	0.07	0.4	0.00	7.2	1.4	1.60	16.96	3.27	57.0	6.3	79.2	10.8	7.7
2.5	2.05	16.9	0.27	5.6	0.3	0.58	7.13	4.39	76.0	4.3	19.5	7.1	5.8
2.7	2.38	20.5	1.02	2.5	0.0	0.03	0.34	3.88	72.0	4.2	17.1	7.5	2.3
7.1	0.40	3.3	0.06	5.3	3.9	0.72	6.87	3.47	73.8	3.3	12.5	12.6	8.5
9.3	0.05	0.2	0.00	7.1	0.2	1.24	4.71	4.05	54.6	4.3	24.9	8.2	7.0
8.4	0.15	1.3	0.00	3.6	0.3	0.43	5.74	2.59	77.9	1.8	20.0	21.3	3.4

Name	City	State	Weiss Safety Rating	2003 Weiss Safety Rating	2002 Weiss Safety Rating	Total Assets ($Mil)	One Year Asset Growth	Asset Mix (As a % of Total Assets) Commercial Loans	Consumer Loans	Home Mortgages	Securities	Capitalization Index	Leverage Ratio	Risk-based Capital Ratio
CITIZENS GUARANTY BK	RICHMOND	KY	C-	D+	D-	102.8	9.59	4.6	9.0	33.1	29.1	4.7	6.7	13.3
CITIZENS HOME BK	GREENFIELD	MO	C+	C+	C+	114.6	-2.98	1.6	2.8	21.7	36.3	10.0	11.6	23.0
CITIZENS INDEPENDENT BK	ST LOUIS PARK	MN	C+	C+	C+	212.7	0.61	21.6	11.5	14.1	24.3	9.8	10.8	17.3
CITIZENS NB	PUTNAM	CT	A+	A+	A+	253.7	5.09	3.2	0.8	11.7	57.9	10.0	12.3	24.9
▲ CITIZENS NB	MACOMB	IL	B-	C+	C+	216.8	0.51	2.5	9.4	26.3	23.4	5.5	7.5	12.9
▼ CITIZENS NB	ARLINGTON	KS	D+	D+	D+	36.9	-4.62	7.8	8.1	4.9	14.6	7.5	9.3	13.3
CITIZENS NB	GREENLEAF	KS	C+	C+	C+	150.4	3.36	4.2	10.4	13.8	46.6	5.9	7.9	14.1
▼ CITIZENS NB	LAUREL	MD	B+	A-	A	1,120.8	29.08	8.7	31.5	5.5	17.5	5.3	7.3	13.8
CITIZENS NB	LOUP CITY	NE	B	B	B	7.7	16.97	5.7	7.5	5.9	45.5	10.0	25.4	44.5
▼ CITIZENS NB	SEVIERVILLE	TN	B	B+	B+	456.5	7.16	3.5	1.5	16.5	21.4	4.6	7.9	10.8
▲ CITIZENS NB	BENBROOK	TX	D+	D	D-	92.6	3.02	32.4	6.9	8.7	6.5	5.6	8.0	11.5
CITIZENS NB	CROCKETT	TX	C+	C+	C+	72.3	-0.37	7.5	11.9	7.3	39.1	6.4	8.4	16.1
▲ CITIZENS NB	HENDERSON	TX	B	B-	B-	591.9	3.22	4.5	5.6	16.3	47.3	7.7	9.5	20.8
CITIZENS NB	TEAGUE	TX	B	B	C+	53.1	23.81	2.4	7.0	11.0	11.9	7.9	13.2	13.2
CITIZENS NB	WILLS POINT	TX	B	B	B	73.2	4.41	8.1	8.8	24.1	29.2	6.7	8.7	15.9
CITIZENS NB	WINDSOR	VA	D	D	NR	20.6	146.67	10.3	7.4	8.5	41.5	10.0	20.7	33.2
CITIZENS NB AT	BROWNWOOD	TX	A	A	A+	130.8	1.27	11.2	5.3	7.7	25.5	10.0	12.1	19.9
▲ CITIZENS NB IN WAXAHACHIE	WAXAHACHIE	TX	C-	C-	C	380.3	11.26	6.9	3.7	13.4	1.7	4.1	7.5	10.6
CITIZENS NB	MC CONNELSVILLE	OH	B	B+	B+	57.6	1.52	0.4	8.4	34.7	14.3	10.0	15.5	28.3
CITIZENS NB NA	BOSSIER CITY	LA	C+	C+	B-	187.3	-6.50	6.7	5.9	14.6	17.8	6.5	8.5	12.3
CITIZENS NB OF AKRON	AKRON	CO	A-	A-	A-	45.4	-5.47	4.5	3.1	0.4	46.9	10.0	17.2	29.2
CITIZENS NB OF ALBION	ALBION	IL	A	A	A	160.7	5.63	8.8	5.8	15.8	30.6	10.0	16.9	26.4
▲ CITIZENS NB OF ATHENS	ATHENS	TN	B+	B	B	390.7	8.36	8.9	5.0	19.0	18.1	6.5	8.9	12.2
▲ CITIZENS NB OF BLUFFTON	BLUFFTON	OH	C+	C	C+	359.8	4.95	9.0	1.0	18.6	12.9	5.2	8.4	11.2
CITIZENS NB OF	BRECKENRIDGE	TX	B-	B-	B-	61.1	0.11	10.5	8.5	7.6	2.1	8.1	11.0	13.4
▼ CITIZENS NB OF CHEBOYGAN	CHEBOYGAN	MI	A-	A	A	259.9	1.38	3.4	3.5	29.3	35.0	7.8	9.6	18.1
▼ CITIZENS NB OF CHILLICOTHE	CHILLICOTHE	OH	C+	B-	B	127.7	1.30	6.8	4.5	33.8	22.3	6.8	8.8	15.4
CITIZENS NB OF CROSBYTON	CROSBYTON	TX	B+	B+	A-	28.6	-5.56	2.1	6.4	7.2	12.2	10.0	14.7	33.0
▼ CITIZENS NB OF ELKINS	ELKINS	WV	B+	A-	A-	210.9	7.37	12.1	5.8	25.4	25.5	7.7	9.5	14.3
CITIZENS NB OF EVANS CITY	EVANS CITY	PA	B-	B-	B-	444.9	0.35	11.0	5.9	15.0	11.1	5.5	7.5	11.5
▲ CITIZENS NB OF GR ST LOUIS	MAPLEWOOD	MO	B	B-	C+	350.0	10.26	17.1	5.5	10.3	16.7	5.8	9.1	11.6
CITIZENS NB OF HAMMOND	HAMMOND	NY	E+	E+	E	16.4	25.58	3.0	7.7	37.7	31.8	4.5	6.6	15.8
CITIZENS NB OF HILLSBORO	HILLSBORO	TX	A	A	A	78.1	-3.72	4.5	7.3	5.5	69.4	10.0	19.2	51.6
CITIZENS NB OF JESSAMINE	NICHOLASVILLE	KY	B-	C+	C+	141.1	-1.02	9.9	5.1	26.8	15.0	6.7	8.8	13.1
▲ CITIZENS NB OF LEBANON	LEBANON	KY	B	B-	B	109.4	11.71	6.4	6.6	16.4	56.1	6.0	8.0	15.8
CITIZENS NB OF MERIDIAN	MERIDIAN	MS	A	A-	B+	784.2	19.23	4.7	4.7	21.8	40.3	9.9	10.9	17.4
CITIZENS NB OF MEYERSDALE	MEYERSDALE	PA	B	B	B+	56.4	1.54	1.5	5.4	22.7	47.7	10.0	13.6	28.5
▲ CITIZENS NB OF NASHVILLE	NASHVILLE	AR	A	A-	A	46.2	-2.03	10.5	7.2	15.4	48.8	10.0	16.4	33.5
CITIZENS NB OF PAINTSVILLE	PAINTSVILLE	KY	C+	C+	C+	342.1	0.72	4.4	3.7	25.6	36.7	5.2	7.2	13.2
CITIZENS NB OF PARIS	PARIS	IL	C+	C+	B	195.0	4.57	12.2	1.9	9.1	31.4	7.4	9.3	14.2
▼ CITIZENS NB OF PARK RAPIDS	PARK RAPIDS	MN	B-	B	B+	167.5	3.35	5.3	18.2	23.9	19.2	4.0	7.2	10.5
▼ CITIZENS NB OF QUITMAN	QUITMAN	GA	D	C	C	81.8	13.00	3.3	17.7	16.0	19.8	3.1	7.2	10.1
▼ CITIZENS NB OF	RUSSELLVILLE	KY	C	B-	A-	177.7	0.95	3.7	3.7	16.5	47.8	3.4	5.4	11.4
▼ CITIZENS NB OF SOMERSET	SOMERSET	KY	C	C+	B	318.4	-0.72	8.6	4.7	21.5	24.6	9.9	11.0	18.4
▼ CITIZENS NB OF	DAYTON	OH	D+	C-	D-	74.9	12.12	20.1	6.1	26.8	2.2	4.6	7.9	10.8
CITIZENS NB OF URBANA	URBANA	OH	B-	B-	B-	205.5	18.71	4.9	5.1	6.9	56.5	4.3	6.3	17.6
CITIZENS NB OF WISNER	WISNER	NE	D+	D+	D+	33.9	5.64	13.2	4.0	7.1	3.7	6.6	9.7	12.2
CITIZENS NB OF WOODSFIELD	WOODSFIELD	OH	B+	B+	A-	56.0	-5.16	2.3	7.1	19.1	45.5	10.0	12.7	31.8
▼ CITIZENS NB SPRINGFIELD	SPRINGFIELD	MO	C	C+	C+	222.6	11.17	14.5	3.7	12.6	11.4	4.4	6.4	10.9
▼ CITIZENS NB-BERKELEY	BERKELEY SPRINGS	WV	B-	B	B	220.8	12.86	3.7	7.6	45.8	19.5	6.5	8.5	14.3
▼ CITIZENS NB-MILAM CTY	CAMERON	TX	B+	A-	A-	203.9	-6.52	2.5	2.5	6.3	56.3	7.2	9.2	21.8
CITIZENS PROGRESSIVE BK	COLUMBIA	LA	B	B-	C+	36.4	1.55	23.6	13.1	25.7	8.7	10.0	12.1	16.5
CITIZENS S&LA FSB	LEAVENWORTH	KS	B+	B+	B+	208.9	-1.21	0.0	0.9	46.0	43.2	10.0	12.8	32.7
▲ CITIZENS SAVINGS BANK	CLARKS SUMMIT	PA	B	B-	B-	298.4	-1.31	0.0	0.2	50.4	40.9	6.9	8.9	23.4
CITIZENS SAVINGS BK	MARSHALLTOWN	IA	C-	D+	D	36.5	-3.96	10.6	4.3	54.3	1.5	6.8	8.8	14.0
▲ CITIZENS SAVINGS BK	BLOOMINGTON	IL	B-	C+	C+	330.3	-3.59	7.8	0.5	32.0	7.0	7.4	9.3	16.0
▼ CITIZENS SECURITY B&TC	BIXBY	OK	C+	B-	B-	238.2	21.80	8.3	6.1	22.8	11.7	2.5	7.8	9.6
CITIZENS SECURITY BK	TIFTON	GA	B-	B-	C+	161.3	-1.52	7.6	6.5	16.2	13.8	5.1	8.0	11.1
CITIZENS SECURITY BK GUAM	AGANA	GU	C+	C	C-	125.9	-2.22	10.4	4.4	27.1	16.6	8.2	9.8	16.1
CITIZENS SOUTH BANK	GASTONIA	NC	B+	B+	B-	491.0	-0.39	2.4	1.0	22.8	24.8	10.0	12.4	17.8
CITIZENS ST B&TC	ELLSWORTH	KS	B-	B-	B-	58.0	4.95	3.5	7.4	19.5	29.8	7.5	9.4	16.7
CITIZENS ST B&TC	HIAWATHA	KS	B+	B+	B+	64.8	1.05	3.3	4.6	5.7	40.2	10.0	12.5	22.7
CITIZENS ST B&TC	WOODBINE	KS	D	D	D	7.7	0.76	24.2	2.3	3.5	20.0	9.5	10.7	22.7
CITIZENS ST B&TC	FORT ATKINSON	WI	B	B-	C+	80.2	25.35	3.6	4.5	22.6	23.2	9.2	10.5	17.0

Asset Quality Index	Non-Performing Loans as a % of Total Loans	Non-Performing Loans as a % of Capital	Net Charge-offs Avg Loans	Profitability Index	Net Income ($Mil)	Return on Assets (R.O.A.)	Return on Equity (R.O.E.)	Net Interest Spread	Overhead Efficiency Ratio	Liquidity Index	Liquidity Ratio	Hot Money Ratio	Stability Index
7.2	0.51	4.1	-0.03	5.0	0.5	0.87	13.27	4.18	75.2	2.7	36.3	20.8	2.2
5.9	2.68	11.6	0.03	3.2	0.3	0.54	4.80	3.14	75.8	5.1	59.1	14.3	5.8
6.1	0.46	2.6	0.38	3.6	0.7	0.67	6.25	4.64	85.1	5.7	28.3	0.0	5.3
9.2	1.18	3.0	0.31	9.4	2.0	1.63	13.38	4.61	47.9	4.8	13.3	3.2	8.8
5.8	0.27	1.8	0.18	4.4	0.8	0.72	7.77	3.67	76.3	6.1	57.6	8.3	5.3
1.4	4.32	27.7	0.05	5.5	0.3	1.40	13.64	4.18	65.8	6.5	86.0	9.2	4.7
8.2	0.12	0.7	0.39	4.2	0.6	0.82	10.39	3.99	76.3	4.7	42.4	12.0	3.2
6.8	0.00	0.0	0.02	9.6	9.1	1.65	22.40	4.32	45.3	6.1	44.2	7.2	7.9
8.6	0.00	0.0	0.14	0.3	0.0	-0.19	-0.77	3.75	104.8	5.0	157.9	30.9	3.1
7.2	0.03	0.2	0.04	7.3	3.3	1.51	18.53	4.05	63.9	1.1	11.9	28.9	6.7
4.8	0.49	4.4	0.51	3.5	0.2	0.49	5.92	5.00	82.2	2.9	44.1	23.7	1.5
8.1	0.08	0.5	0.04	4.6	0.4	1.19	15.33	4.10	76.0	5.2	55.9	11.7	3.4
8.3	0.06	0.2	0.25	4.8	3.0	1.03	10.53	3.57	71.2	5.7	112.2	17.6	6.0
6.6	0.17	1.1	-0.09	9.7	0.4	1.53	12.18	5.35	54.6	2.8	16.0	14.9	6.3
8.5	0.17	1.0	0.00	10.0	0.9	2.36	24.10	4.88	53.0	4.1	40.5	14.6	5.9
8.5	0.00	0.0	0.00	0.0	-0.3	-3.19	-13.41	2.28	199.2	7.0	256.8	17.6	0.0
5.8	1.48	6.4	0.00	9.6	1.4	2.17	17.66	4.10	54.2	4.1	43.5	15.4	9.0
2.5	1.06	9.6	0.13	7.8	3.3	1.80	21.28	5.23	72.9	4.7	42.9	12.3	6.1
5.5	2.09	8.7	0.05	3.7	0.2	0.54	3.52	3.68	77.4	6.0	109.2	14.9	7.4
7.6	0.01	0.1	0.04	6.4	1.1	1.19	14.95	5.19	71.3	2.4	34.5	23.2	3.7
8.6	0.07	0.2	-0.02	4.8	0.2	0.84	4.81	3.76	71.2	5.4	55.7	10.5	7.8
7.9	0.80	2.8	0.02	7.6	1.2	1.50	8.59	4.45	47.3	1.7	16.0	22.0	8.7
7.2	0.13	1.0	0.08	7.4	3.2	1.66	18.71	4.32	58.7	1.7	12.7	20.1	5.9
3.5	1.24	10.4	0.08	4.9	1.4	0.81	9.36	4.23	72.9	1.4	7.6	23.6	5.5
7.4	0.00	0.0	-0.33	8.8	0.6	2.12	19.96	4.15	52.1	4.3	55.9	16.0	6.3
8.4	0.34	1.9	0.14	7.7	1.5	1.19	12.15	4.04	61.4	6.8	70.1	6.5	7.3
3.7	2.25	16.1	0.07	3.5	0.3	0.53	6.02	4.17	81.4	6.4	52.2	4.8	4.9
8.8	0.01	0.0	0.02	5.4	0.1	0.87	6.10	2.62	60.7	6.1	161.7	18.7	6.3
6.7	0.70	4.7	1.32	4.8	0.7	0.66	6.72	4.40	67.8	2.7	21.5	16.3	6.0
4.6	0.68	5.5	0.00	4.6	1.9	0.86	10.15	4.15	82.3	6.0	43.8	4.5	6.2
7.4	0.14	1.1	0.01	6.2	1.9	1.11	12.46	3.99	57.3	3.5	30.6	14.5	5.0
8.9	0.00	0.0	0.10	4.8	0.1	0.84	12.03	5.25	73.2	3.6	49.4	16.6	0.1
9.2	1.46	2.0	0.84	6.0	0.6	1.42	7.06	3.46	56.3	5.3	45.3	9.3	8.3
5.9	0.59	4.8	0.40	6.2	0.7	1.00	11.68	4.26	61.1	2.2	25.7	19.2	4.3
8.2	0.24	1.1	0.18	5.3	0.9	1.63	19.74	3.34	61.1	4.2	22.1	8.6	4.8
8.3	0.29	1.4	0.05	6.9	6.1	1.65	15.30	4.01	62.1	5.2	87.8	17.6	7.3
7.6	0.91	2.8	0.06	4.0	0.2	0.72	5.16	3.78	76.7	3.9	18.0	9.9	6.9
6.9	0.56	1.5	1.04	9.5	0.4	1.60	10.10	4.21	45.5	0.9	10.9	32.2	8.8
5.7	0.86	5.7	0.05	5.1	1.7	1.04	13.12	3.71	65.9	2.3	17.5	17.9	4.2
7.0	0.26	1.6	0.03	3.1	0.3	0.35	3.59	2.76	84.9	4.3	31.6	10.5	5.3
5.5	0.33	3.3	0.04	7.2	1.5	1.84	24.21	4.03	55.6	3.9	19.0	10.0	6.1
5.3	0.33	3.2	0.06	5.7	0.4	1.15	15.88	4.34	63.3	2.4	28.2	19.3	2.3
1.4	3.00	13.5	0.00	4.1	0.9	0.96	10.04	3.16	59.5	2.3	33.8	24.7	5.1
2.6	3.22	18.2	0.12	7.9	3.5	2.18	20.21	3.93	50.2	3.8	27.4	12.0	7.4
6.6	0.31	3.0	0.00	2.8	0.1	0.40	5.14	3.58	86.1	4.6	57.5	15.0	0.0
7.2	0.77	4.2	0.23	7.7	1.4	1.39	22.71	4.00	50.8	2.6	8.2	15.1	4.8
0.4	2.38	19.3	-0.06	8.3	0.4	2.40	25.14	4.57	53.2	3.4	22.8	12.9	4.5
7.6	1.62	4.6	0.07	4.4	0.2	0.70	5.40	4.00	75.0	7.1	68.4	2.4	5.3
4.3	0.69	7.6	0.01	4.4	0.9	0.78	12.15	3.32	63.3	3.6	36.1	15.5	3.4
6.0	0.47	4.1	0.08	5.3	1.1	1.09	13.44	4.33	64.1	2.0	13.1	18.6	4.3
7.8	0.48	1.2	0.04	5.5	1.3	1.28	10.79	3.88	70.8	5.2	41.3	9.3	7.6
5.8	1.02	6.0	0.56	8.1	0.4	2.27	18.01	6.47	61.0	3.4	45.9	18.9	5.8
9.2	0.07	0.3	0.00	4.4	0.6	0.59	4.63	2.53	67.1	2.9	35.5	19.2	7.1
9.2	0.22	1.4	0.06	4.5	0.8	0.54	6.34	3.02	70.1	3.1	24.4	14.6	4.8
7.3	0.48	4.5	0.03	5.6	0.3	1.36	15.55	4.73	71.5	5.4	35.9	5.7	2.9
5.2	1.08	7.6	-0.24	4.9	1.4	0.84	9.28	3.62	68.8	5.6	58.1	11.7	4.1
4.4	0.74	7.3	0.29	7.3	1.0	0.94	11.73	4.59	69.3	1.5	21.8	26.6	4.3
4.7	0.50	3.6	-0.18	10.0	1.5	1.82	19.20	4.98	51.4	2.1	13.9	18.4	6.9
3.4	2.46	15.5	0.33	5.7	0.7	1.03	11.08	5.05	72.9	3.6	34.3	15.3	4.3
7.3	0.31	1.5	0.08	5.1	2.1	0.83	5.98	2.82	65.2	1.2	24.1	32.0	7.1
6.8	0.40	2.3	-0.61	6.3	0.5	1.63	16.75	4.16	67.3	4.0	23.9	9.7	5.4
7.8	0.62	2.1	0.01	5.4	0.4	1.24	9.60	3.66	69.7	6.2	46.5	3.8	6.9
6.1	2.27	8.0	0.06	2.7	0.0	0.56	5.18	3.48	82.8	7.5	88.6	1.5	2.3
5.4	0.80	4.2	0.10	6.1	0.3	0.78	7.03	3.92	75.6	5.3	37.3	7.1	5.8

| Name | City | State | Weiss Safety Rating | 2003 Weiss Safety Rating | 2002 Weiss Safety Rating | Total Assets ($Mil) | One Year Asset Growth | Asset Mix (As a % of Total Assets) | | | | Capital- ization Index | Leverage Ratio | Risk-based Capital Ratio |
								Comm- ercial Loans	Cons- umer Loans	Home Mort- gages	Secur- ities			
CITIZENS ST BK	VERNON	AL	B+	B+	B+	47.8	3.24	2.4	15.3	6.2	59.7	10.0	18.1	41.4
▲ CITIZENS ST BK	BALD KNOB	AR	C	D+	D+	62.3	2.16	5.8	11.6	11.1	41.8	10.0	11.0	19.0
▲ CITIZENS ST BK	CORTEZ	CO	C-	C-	C	79.1	9.75	9.4	14.7	9.1	27.9	4.9	7.0	10.9
CITIZENS ST BK	KINGSLAND	GA	B-	B-	B-	37.6	12.22	0.1	11.2	10.9	10.0	7.2	9.1	13.0
▼ CITIZENS ST BK	MONTICELLO	IA	B	B+	A-	189.6	1.64	9.2	5.0	15.4	30.7	6.2	8.2	13.6
CITIZENS ST BK	OAKLAND	IA	A-	A-	B+	64.0	7.84	12.4	2.1	25.1	20.2	9.3	10.5	17.4
▲ CITIZENS ST BK	SHELDON	IA	B+	B	B	76.5	-4.71	8.3	2.7	12.5	32.2	7.6	9.4	16.0
CITIZENS ST BK	WAUKON	IA	C	C+	C+	63.2	9.87	17.1	4.8	14.0	5.6	3.0	7.3	10.0
CITIZENS ST BK	WYOMING	IA	A-	A-	A-	69.8	0.19	7.1	5.1	6.3	43.1	10.0	18.7	33.5
CITIZENS ST BK	CROPSEY	IL	E-	E-	E-	26.1	25.84	9.8	4.2	11.9	10.2	2.9	8.0	9.9
▲ CITIZENS ST BK	LENA	IL	C+	C	C	135.0	-0.39	13.5	5.9	8.6	25.3	6.9	8.9	13.0
CITIZENS ST BK	NEW CASTLE	IN	B	B	B+	228.8	1.13	4.5	9.7	13.3	46.5	7.7	9.4	19.2
CITIZENS ST BK	PETERSBURG	IN	B-	B-	B-	129.1	1.86	8.0	8.2	12.8	20.2	5.2	8.1	11.2
CITIZENS ST BK	ASHLAND	KS	E-	E-	E-	13.9	-3.72	10.7	2.4	10.7	10.8	7.0	9.0	14.0
▼ CITIZENS ST BK	GENESEO	KS	E+	D-	D-	5.4	-1.98	4.7	5.6	0.7	7.8	5.6	7.6	22.1
▲ CITIZENS ST BK	GRAINFIELD	KS	C	C-	C-	8.0	-2.43	4.5	2.2	3.5	2.1	10.0	12.1	27.7
CITIZENS ST BK	GRIDLEY	KS	D+	D+	D+	73.3	-0.76	11.1	7.1	19.0	27.1	4.8	6.8	11.7
CITIZENS ST BK	HUGOTON	KS	A	A	A	81.8	-5.59	3.2	1.9	3.0	23.8	10.0	12.3	18.0
▲ CITIZENS ST BK	MARYSVILLE	KS	B	C+	B-	221.5	7.81	16.2	2.7	7.4	13.8	8.4	10.3	13.7
▲ CITIZENS ST BK	MILTONVALE	KS	C-	D+	D+	29.3	2.61	3.3	2.3	4.2	60.8	6.8	8.8	20.2
CITIZENS ST BK	MORLAND	KS	D-	D	D-	27.7	10.03	11.1	6.6	10.0	11.0	5.0	7.0	12.6
CITIZENS ST BK	MOUNDRIDGE	KS	A-	A-	A-	150.2	0.58	5.8	2.3	8.6	36.7	8.5	10.0	16.1
CITIZENS ST BK	PAOLA	KS	A-	A-	A	52.3	6.05	13.5	2.5	18.7	12.6	10.0	14.2	17.6
▼ CITIZENS ST BK	NEW BALTIMORE	MI	C+	B	B	177.3	4.32	11.2	1.8	15.2	18.4	2.8	7.5	9.8
▲ CITIZENS ST BK	HAYFIELD	MN	C+	C	C	47.9	3.25	12.9	6.2	10.1	8.1	4.5	8.2	10.8
CITIZENS ST BK	KELLIHER	MN	E-	E-	E-	14.1	-4.63	9.6	5.8	24.9	22.1	6.2	8.2	14.4
▼ CITIZENS ST BK	ROSEAU	MN	A-	A	A	148.0	-2.66	5.2	9.9	7.1	50.1	10.0	11.8	20.2
CITIZENS ST BK	SHAKOPEE	MN	D+	D+	C-	22.1	-4.02	12.4	6.3	18.6	29.6	7.3	9.2	20.2
▲ CITIZENS ST BK	TYLER	MN	D	D-	D	15.6	3.52	12.5	6.9	4.0	51.0	7.7	9.5	14.9
CITIZENS ST BK	WATERVILLE	MN	B	B	B	23.4	-0.95	10.3	3.5	9.4	29.3	5.8	7.8	12.4
CITIZENS ST BK	WAVERLY	MN	C	B-	B-	43.5	5.79	10.5	3.7	19.2	18.0	6.2	8.2	14.0
CITIZENS ST BK	HAMILTON	MT	C+	C+	C+	68.9	-3.86	16.8	1.6	19.5	23.3	5.7	7.7	13.2
CITIZENS ST BK	ENDERLIN	ND	A-	B+	B+	62.7	0.96	5.4	8.3	3.7	4.5	10.0	15.1	16.9
CITIZENS ST BK	LANKIN	ND	B	B	B	34.5	-0.06	4.0	7.0	5.5	32.2	10.0	11.6	17.9
CITIZENS ST BK	MOHALL	ND	C+	C+	B-	31.1	2.14	27.0	6.4	6.8	16.4	4.5	7.4	10.8
CITIZENS ST BK	CARLETON	NE	E+	E+	E+	8.0	5.36	7.4	5.2	7.4	15.6	5.7	7.7	15.6
▲ CITIZENS ST BK	CLEARWATER	NE	C-	D+	C-	15.4	7.64	6.6	6.2	0.3	0.1	5.5	9.0	11.4
▼ CITIZENS ST BK	MORRISON	OK	D	D+	D+	61.0	6.50	21.5	12.8	16.3	21.5	6.1	8.1	12.3
CITIZENS ST BK	OKEMAH	OK	E+	E	E	27.4	3.24	10.3	8.5	17.3	34.4	6.1	8.1	15.7
▼ CITIZENS ST BK	JASPER	TN	C-	C	C	58.2	5.38	15.6	10.2	27.3	21.7	5.5	7.5	12.4
CITIZENS ST BK	ANTON	TX	D-	D-	D	29.7	3.51	9.0	8.6	0.9	20.2	4.8	6.8	11.1
▲ CITIZENS ST BK	BUFFALO	TX	B	B-	B-	142.7	32.10	6.7	6.7	7.3	50.4	5.6	7.6	14.8
CITIZENS ST BK	CORRIGAN	TX	A-	A-	A-	39.8	-5.18	9.1	22.1	8.9	38.5	10.0	12.9	23.4
▲ CITIZENS ST BK	GANADO	TX	D+	D	D	40.6	0.82	4.8	3.5	8.8	65.6	5.1	7.1	21.9
▼ CITIZENS ST BK	LULING	TX	C+	B-	B-	52.5	1.76	14.1	7.6	11.3	22.7	9.7	10.8	17.8
CITIZENS ST BK	MILES	TX	D-	D-	D	37.4	-1.41	6.2	9.7	26.7	14.1	6.5	8.5	16.7
CITIZENS ST BK	PRINCETON	TX	B	B	B	71.3	5.39	3.8	5.7	8.1	56.9	5.3	7.3	20.5
CITIZENS ST BK	ROMA	TX	A-	A-	A-	59.1	3.18	3.2	15.0	6.2	62.8	10.0	14.1	44.2
▼ CITIZENS ST BK	SEALY	TX	A-	A	A	125.0	-0.31	6.1	15.3	9.8	42.6	7.2	9.1	19.5
CITIZENS ST BK	SOMERVILLE	TX	B-	B-	B	185.6	6.54	6.1	12.7	11.1	34.4	6.5	8.5	15.4
▼ CITIZENS ST BK	TENAHA	TX	D+	C-	C-	21.5	1.41	6.6	17.0	7.3	28.2	10.0	11.3	26.7
▲ CITIZENS ST BK	TYLER	TX	B+	B	B-	140.8	2.60	9.4	10.0	25.0	11.6	8.5	10.0	14.7
CITIZENS ST BK	WOODVILLE	TX	B-	B-	B-	118.5	-4.56	4.3	15.8	10.9	45.9	9.2	10.4	18.9
▲ CITIZENS ST BK	CADOTT	WI	C-	C-	D+	91.9	-0.32	5.5	2.2	22.2	32.1	7.6	9.4	15.3
▲ CITIZENS ST BK	HUDSON	WI	A	B+	B+	149.1	14.65	18.4	2.1	19.6	3.8	10.0	11.9	16.4
CITIZENS ST BK	TREMPEALEAU	WI	C+	C+	B-	26.7	2.33	5.5	10.6	25.0	24.5	7.4	9.3	15.7
▼ CITIZENS ST BK BALLARD CTY	WICKLIFFE	KY	C+	B-	A-	58.7	-6.75	5.6	7.0	24.4	36.0	3.5	5.5	11.2
CITIZENS ST BK LIBERAL KS	LIBERAL	KS	C	C	D	57.2	-3.54	8.4	2.3	5.1	49.4	8.9	10.2	20.9
CITIZENS ST BK MIDWEST	CAVALIER	ND	C	C-	D	124.9	5.02	9.2	8.0	3.8	14.8	4.7	8.1	10.8
▲ CITIZENS ST BK OF	ARLINGTON	SD	C+	C	C+	66.4	42.02	5.0	4.1	6.3	19.7	6.8	8.8	13.6
CITIZENS ST BK OF CHENEY	CHENEY	KS	A-	A-	A-	35.8	2.26	6.7	16.8	15.9	27.5	10.0	12.6	21.6
CITIZENS ST BK OF CHOTEAU	CHOTEAU	MT	A	A	A	52.1	1.77	17.4	5.0	3.9	22.5	10.0	15.3	23.4
▼ CITIZENS ST BK OF CLARA	CLARA CITY	MN	B-	B	C+	153.7	18.84	15.4	2.6	6.8	14.7	4.3	7.5	10.7
▲ CITIZENS ST BK OF CLAYTON	CLAYTON	WI	C	C-	D+	17.2	-2.64	8.8	3.0	20.7	22.2	9.5	10.7	19.2

Asset Quality Index	Non-Performing Loans as a % of Total Loans	Non-Performing Loans as a % of Capital	Net Charge-offs Avg Loans	Profitability Index	Net Income ($Mil)	Return on Assets (R.O.A.)	Return on Equity (R.O.E.)	Net Interest Spread	Overhead Efficiency Ratio	Liquidity Index	Liquidity Ratio	Hot Money Ratio	Stability Index
7.4	2.66	4.0	0.51	9.0	0.4	1.78	9.95	4.63	41.8	4.1	74.6	20.7	6.5
3.0	4.23	15.3	1.04	4.3	0.3	1.05	9.61	4.74	75.5	4.1	36.6	13.2	4.7
2.1	2.02	16.0	0.21	5.8	0.3	0.86	11.25	4.78	76.0	3.2	15.9	13.0	4.2
6.1	0.36	2.6	0.13	5.5	0.2	0.96	10.64	4.83	71.1	5.2	42.3	9.4	5.4
6.0	0.62	2.8	0.15	7.3	1.5	1.58	13.02	3.83	54.3	4.9	41.9	11.2	7.4
7.0	0.74	4.7	-0.35	9.8	0.8	2.46	23.66	4.51	41.9	2.9	30.8	17.5	7.0
6.7	0.41	2.0	0.02	6.4	0.5	1.16	10.52	4.41	62.9	6.0	42.2	3.5	6.7
2.5	0.47	3.2	0.09	3.8	0.2	0.64	5.83	3.47	74.9	6.6	69.6	5.7	6.0
7.8	1.02	2.3	0.34	8.5	0.7	1.96	9.93	4.59	48.1	5.8	50.3	7.3	8.0
6.6	0.05	0.5	0.01	3.6	0.1	0.74	9.25	3.79	72.1	4.8	48.0	12.2	0.3
5.0	0.42	2.5	0.08	5.6	0.7	1.00	9.71	3.84	59.6	2.8	26.1	16.4	6.0
8.5	0.20	0.8	0.20	5.6	1.2	1.05	11.04	4.11	66.4	4.7	31.0	7.7	5.9
5.0	0.47	2.6	0.51	9.6	1.2	1.81	15.85	4.57	67.9	4.1	15.9	8.2	5.8
4.2	1.46	10.1	-0.13	1.1	0.0	0.22	2.51	4.48	95.1	4.3	46.4	12.7	0.2
9.2	0.00	0.0	0.00	3.2	0.0	0.71	9.19	3.45	75.0	9.4	237.9	4.1	0.7
8.8	0.00	0.0	0.00	5.0	0.0	0.77	5.78	3.39	77.3	8.3	175.1	8.6	4.3
6.4	0.23	2.0	0.16	3.8	0.2	0.59	8.32	3.83	75.4	5.9	101.4	14.4	2.2
7.5	0.10	0.5	-0.04	8.8	0.5	1.28	10.48	5.06	62.6	1.2	25.5	32.4	7.7
5.5	0.42	2.9	0.17	8.2	2.2	2.02	18.34	3.78	38.0	2.4	25.7	18.2	7.4
9.2	0.00	0.0	0.02	3.6	0.2	1.12	13.29	3.49	66.2	3.0	69.3	37.7	2.4
5.8	0.22	1.8	0.90	2.7	0.0	0.18	2.44	3.85	94.0	4.6	95.7	20.9	1.5
6.2	0.82	4.1	-0.24	9.2	1.2	1.63	15.66	4.37	51.0	5.8	40.8	5.2	8.0
5.3	0.59	1.8	-0.01	7.4	0.4	1.35	5.97	4.46	51.1	1.6	15.7	23.3	8.4
8.3	0.20	1.7	0.34	4.2	0.4	0.47	6.04	4.33	74.0	3.3	31.2	15.6	4.7
4.0	0.98	9.3	0.01	5.8	0.3	1.21	15.49	4.74	76.3	4.9	17.7	3.3	4.9
1.3	6.67	40.8	0.02	2.5	0.0	0.25	3.06	4.35	73.9	5.1	32.8	3.7	0.3
6.1	1.37	4.9	0.80	5.6	0.9	1.23	10.16	3.70	61.9	4.2	72.4	22.2	8.4
4.9	2.39	9.4	0.00	2.8	0.0	0.32	3.22	3.57	87.3	6.6	88.1	7.5	2.9
5.3	2.70	8.8	-0.11	3.3	0.1	0.90	9.28	4.36	70.3	5.3	31.7	2.2	2.4
7.0	0.11	0.6	0.22	7.9	0.1	1.21	12.64	4.39	62.5	5.7	51.3	5.6	6.9
8.7	0.11	0.8	0.02	6.9	0.3	1.39	16.73	4.76	72.7	6.0	52.6	6.0	5.0
7.9	0.20	1.5	0.07	7.1	0.4	1.08	13.91	4.57	63.4	5.6	41.7	6.7	5.0
5.7	0.69	3.9	1.35	9.5	0.6	1.90	13.05	4.25	36.7	4.0	18.6	9.2	8.3
5.6	3.06	11.9	0.03	5.6	0.2	1.14	9.48	4.81	67.8	5.8	54.3	7.9	6.1
1.7	3.95	35.9	1.16	4.9	0.1	0.56	7.79	4.00	51.8	4.2	17.3	7.8	4.2
6.3	0.17	1.5	0.00	4.4	0.0	0.82	10.79	5.33	85.8	3.6	26.5	11.6	0.5
6.1	0.22	1.7	0.02	9.0	0.2	2.20	24.34	4.51	55.7	4.3	54.5	14.4	3.7
1.8	2.95	25.2	0.36	3.8	0.3	0.87	11.03	4.98	72.2	0.7	10.9	34.9	2.3
1.2	5.67	30.0	1.24	2.5	0.1	0.40	4.60	4.55	85.7	5.2	45.1	9.5	2.2
5.8	0.49	4.1	0.16	4.7	0.3	0.98	12.79	5.32	85.3	3.5	14.0	11.3	3.0
5.1	1.32	10.8	-0.03	3.7	0.1	0.59	8.89	2.76	71.2	4.7	153.4	38.4	0.2
8.0	0.02	0.1	0.08	6.5	0.9	1.41	14.51	4.25	56.9	1.5	17.5	24.9	5.6
4.7	2.13	8.7	0.22	6.9	0.3	1.40	10.95	5.12	70.5	3.1	41.4	19.8	7.3
9.3	0.69	2.2	-0.05	5.7	0.2	1.13	18.25	3.96	61.5	5.6	50.8	8.7	1.7
3.3	2.97	15.5	0.08	5.9	0.3	1.03	9.98	4.45	65.4	4.0	41.6	15.5	5.5
2.8	2.78	16.4	0.99	3.9	0.1	0.55	6.55	4.32	82.1	4.1	105.1	31.3	1.2
4.6	1.92	3.8	0.25	6.9	0.4	1.23	9.61	3.47	46.7	0.9	23.9	43.6	6.4
8.3	0.31	0.7	0.14	5.9	0.3	1.14	8.25	4.41	66.2	6.0	225.5	27.6	7.0
7.9	0.19	1.1	-0.03	7.8	0.8	1.30	12.83	3.98	60.2	5.3	52.3	11.5	6.9
5.1	0.77	4.3	0.25	4.6	0.6	0.60	7.05	4.15	78.8	4.0	32.9	12.8	4.4
2.0	8.69	26.9	0.23	3.9	0.1	0.63	5.76	3.91	77.5	5.5	117.9	17.4	2.1
7.9	0.13	0.9	-0.04	8.7	1.2	1.76	17.87	5.13	60.2	2.3	18.9	17.7	5.2
5.0	1.29	5.5	0.96	4.5	0.5	0.77	7.68	4.68	75.7	4.0	15.8	8.5	4.7
4.6	1.94	11.8	0.07	1.9	0.1	0.27	2.75	3.34	91.9	3.5	10.1	10.8	4.4
7.2	0.10	0.7	0.01	9.3	1.2	1.77	15.50	5.61	63.6	1.4	9.6	24.4	7.4
4.4	1.46	9.9	0.01	6.5	0.2	1.40	15.09	4.11	63.4	3.7	25.2	11.4	5.6
2.8	0.90	4.7	-0.35	5.7	0.4	1.20	11.78	4.34	63.6	2.4	7.6	16.3	5.0
4.3	4.58	15.6	-0.13	2.6	0.1	0.32	3.10	3.96	77.9	5.3	43.0	8.7	3.5
4.1	0.69	5.6	0.38	5.2	0.5	0.85	10.06	4.68	69.5	3.9	27.9	11.5	4.4
6.7	0.00	0.0	-0.16	5.7	0.3	0.91	9.82	3.97	64.1	4.5	42.9	12.9	4.2
7.5	0.15	0.7	0.24	10.0	0.5	2.90	23.58	5.55	47.8	5.0	69.0	15.0	7.1
5.7	1.99	7.5	-0.02	9.7	0.5	1.76	12.07	4.27	39.6	4.5	63.2	16.5	8.3
5.1	0.82	6.6	-0.97	10.0	2.3	3.07	37.90	3.87	39.3	3.4	31.0	15.1	5.7
5.8	0.95	4.9	0.02	5.8	0.1	1.03	9.91	4.05	62.7	6.9	118.6	10.3	3.2

Name	City	State	Weiss Safety Rating	2003 Weiss Safety Rating	2002 Weiss Safety Rating	Total Assets ($Mil)	One Year Asset Growth	Asset Mix (As a % of Total Assets)				Capital- ization Index	Leverage Ratio	Risk-based Capital Ratio
								Comm- ercial Loans	Cons- umer Loans	Home Mort- gages	Secur- ities			
▼ CITIZENS ST BK OF FINLEY	FINLEY	ND	D-	C-	C+	47.6	20.06	12.8	7.4	2.6	16.1	2.8	7.8	9.8
CITIZENS ST BK OF GLENVILLE	GLENVILLE	MN	B+	B+	B+	29.3	2.04	4.2	8.3	13.0	21.5	8.7	10.1	20.6
CITIZENS ST BK OF LOYAL	LOYAL	WI	B	B	B	98.4	4.24	7.0	3.2	21.1	18.1	8.5	10.0	14.8
CITIZENS ST BK OF MILFORD	MILFORD	IL	C+	C+	B-	35.3	1.68	8.7	3.5	2.8	28.4	9.2	10.5	16.3
CITIZENS ST BK OF	NORWOOD YOUNG AM	MN	C	C	C+	48.5	3.77	17.1	5.4	13.5	2.0	3.0	8.8	10.0
CITIZENS ST BK OF OLIVIA	OLIVIA	MN	B-	C+	C+	26.3	-6.26	42.7	3.4	3.4	12.1	10.0	12.4	18.1
CITIZENS ST BK OF	ONTONAGON	MI	B+	B+	B	51.8	4.08	3.9	7.7	17.4	47.3	10.0	14.6	34.1
CITIZENS ST BK OF OURAY	OURAY	CO	A-	A-	A	68.1	8.29	4.7	4.0	7.9	50.8	10.0	11.7	28.4
▼ CITIZENS ST BK OF POMONA	POMONA	KS	B	B+	B+	13.0	-4.27	6.8	18.7	24.0	26.0	10.0	12.2	21.8
▼ CITIZENS ST BK OF SHIPMAN	SHIPMAN	IL	C	B-	C+	52.2	-8.07	8.1	4.9	18.8	24.3	5.9	7.9	11.7
CITIZENS ST BK OF TAYLOR	REYNOLDS	GA	C	C	C-	40.9	5.99	10.4	20.8	16.0	19.2	10.0	13.0	20.7
CITIZENS STATE BK	POCAHONTAS	IA	B-	B-	B-	85.8	3.02	7.9	2.9	17.4	25.1	6.9	8.9	13.6
▲ CITIZENS SVG B&TC	NASHVILLE	TN	C	C-	C-	52.0	-4.13	2.0	2.4	7.8	14.3	7.4	9.4	12.9
CITIZENS SVG BK	ANAMOSA	IA	B	B	B	88.8	-0.96	7.0	1.9	18.5	48.5	5.1	7.1	14.3
CITIZENS SVG BK	HAWKEYE	IA	A-	A-	A-	20.8	-0.94	4.2	4.5	9.6	55.6	10.0	13.9	27.1
CITIZENS SVG BK	SPILLVILLE	IA	B-	B-	B-	34.2	4.82	6.0	2.0	8.5	19.3	9.5	10.7	14.5
CITIZENS SVG BK	BOGALUSA	LA	C+	C+	C+	145.2	4.47	2.2	10.6	37.3	1.8	7.0	9.0	16.7
▼ CITIZENS SVG BK	MARTINS FERRY	OH	C+	B-	B-	271.0	0.89	11.0	9.7	13.9	39.4	6.6	8.6	14.9
CITIZENS TRI-COUNTY BK	DUNLAP	TN	B	B	B	306.2	1.59	0.2	15.5	25.1	19.5	6.1	8.1	13.4
▲ CITIZENS TRUST BK	ATLANTA	GA	C+	C	C+	336.1	-7.71	4.6	1.9	21.2	26.9	6.1	8.2	14.8
CITIZENS TRUST CO	COUDERSPORT	PA	A-	A-	A-	142.5	5.35	3.4	4.0	26.2	49.7	10.0	12.0	28.1
CITIZENS UNION BK	SHELBYVILLE	KY	B	B	A-	458.9	3.36	4.3	2.2	24.9	11.8	9.6	10.7	15.4
▼ CITIZENS UNION ST B&TC	CLINTON	MO	B-	B	B	274.4	-2.43	11.5	3.0	17.9	16.2	6.0	8.0	11.9
CITIZENS-FARMERS BK	COLE CAMP	MO	A-	A-	A-	69.7	3.37	5.4	8.7	31.1	19.1	10.0	18.7	19.5
CITIZENS-UNION SVGS BK	FALL RIVER	MA	C+	C+	C+	512.7	-1.68	2.5	1.0	32.4	45.2	7.8	9.5	17.5
CITRUS & CHEMICAL BK	BARTOW	FL	C+	C+	C+	654.3	10.85	7.0	2.6	8.3	40.4	4.6	6.7	11.0
CITRUS BK NA	VERO BEACH	FL	D-	D	C-	183.6	-9.29	4.9	0.4	4.7	33.7	8.3	9.8	16.8
▲ CITY AND SUBURBAN FSB	YONKERS	NY	B	B-	B-	630.7	5.47	0.6	0.2	0.6	26.1	5.8	7.8	12.4
CITY B&TC	NATCHITOCHES	LA	B	B	B	153.1	-9.96	5.1	6.1	23.7	33.0	7.3	9.2	19.1
CITY B&TC	LINCOLN	NE	C	C	C	164.3	8.47	11.7	1.7	10.1	8.2	3.1	7.9	10.0
CITY B&TC OF MOBERLY	MOBERLY	MO	B	B	B	147.5	-3.17	4.3	16.5	6.2	42.8	6.0	8.0	15.7
▼ CITY BANK NEW MEXICO	RUIDOSO	NM	C+	B-	B-	58.2	60.38	18.7	10.6	22.9	0.0	3.6	8.4	10.3
▲ CITY BK	HONOLULU	HI	B+	B	B-	1,884.4	10.89	11.6	6.6	18.0	17.8	6.4	9.4	12.1
▼ CITY BK	LUBBOCK	TX	C+	B-	B-	848.9	27.94	17.5	9.2	4.6	4.1	4.5	9.2	10.8
▲ CITY BK	LYNNWOOD	WA	A-	B	B	631.5	-4.62	7.5	0.5	4.0	1.0	10.0	25.0	24.7
CITY BK OF HARTFORD	HARTFORD	AL	B-	B-	B-	27.9	5.72	8.3	12.7	22.6	13.3	10.0	11.4	16.5
CITY FIRST BK OF DC NA	WASHINGTON	DC	B	B-	C-	86.4	17.08	7.0	0.1	6.4	15.7	10.0	12.4	18.3
CITY NB	BEVERLY HILLS	CA	A-	B+	B	13,270.5	9.28	18.7	2.1	16.2	25.3	6.1	8.1	15.4
▼ CITY NB	CORSICANA	TX	C	C+	C+	44.3	-0.77	7.6	9.7	22.3	6.0	7.1	9.1	16.6
▼ CITY NB	WESLACO	TX	C-	C	C+	72.5	-14.42	9.0	2.8	9.0	26.7	6.0	8.0	15.0
CITY NB OF COLORADO CITY	COLORADO CITY	TX	A-	A-	A-	59.6	2.14	3.7	8.5	9.7	58.5	10.0	14.5	34.3
CITY NB OF FLORIDA	MIAMI	FL	A-	A-	B+	2,566.6	10.94	9.4	0.9	7.1	21.0	6.0	8.0	13.1
CITY NB OF GREELEY	GREELEY CENTER	NE	C-	C-	D+	17.4	-4.23	1.9	4.6	6.2	39.9	9.1	10.4	22.4
CITY NB OF KILGORE	KILGORE	TX	B-	B-	C+	147.5	2.29	15.1	11.1	11.8	30.6	5.5	7.5	12.6
CITY NB OF METROPOLIS	METROPOLIS	IL	A	A	A	153.5	5.01	5.3	7.0	27.9	38.4	10.0	15.1	25.3
CITY NB OF MINERAL WELLS	MINERAL WELLS	TX	A-	A-	A-	106.9	0.45	5.3	5.4	30.8	34.2	7.6	9.4	17.8
CITY NB OF NJ	NEWARK	NJ	C-	C-	C-	339.6	52.02	4.3	0.4	11.1	45.3	4.9	6.9	12.8
▼ CITY NB OF SAN SABA	SAN SABA	TX	B-	B	B+	47.0	3.08	2.1	2.9	1.5	60.2	10.0	14.1	39.4
CITY NB OF SHENANDOAH	SHENANDOAH	IA	C-	C-	C	56.2	-5.76	5.1	2.2	8.1	50.3	7.2	9.1	18.1
CITY NB OF SULPHUR	SULPHUR SPRINGS	TX	C+	C+	C-	238.9	27.79	7.2	9.5	18.0	32.2	5.2	7.2	12.4
CITY NB OF TAYLOR	TAYLOR	TX	C+	C	B-	164.8	4.44	8.5	1.9	8.4	62.0	8.1	9.8	23.5
CITY NB OF WV	CHARLESTON	WV	A-	B+	C+	2,197.9	11.08	2.1	2.6	26.4	30.2	7.3	9.2	14.6
CITY NB&TC	GLOVERSVILLE	NY	B-	B-	B	388.4	-1.92	3.3	17.0	16.4	46.2	6.3	8.3	17.2
CITY NB&TC OF GUYMON	GUYMON	OK	A-	A-	A-	128.8	0.01	6.0	4.4	12.7	46.9	8.3	9.9	19.8
CITY NB&TC OF LAWTON OK	LAWTON	OK	A	A	A	177.9	5.74	6.3	5.4	23.2	13.0	10.0	12.5	18.9
CITY SAVINGS BANK	MICHIGAN CITY	IN	D-	D+	C-	145.7	4.53	10.7	8.2	29.2	9.6	7.9	10.3	13.2
▲ CITY ST BK	CENTRAL CITY	IA	C+	C	C	76.0	2.74	4.0	1.7	33.4	21.7	7.3	9.2	14.3
CITY ST BK	NORWALK	IA	B	B	B	133.7	9.38	13.4	3.5	12.5	6.2	5.8	7.8	11.8
CITY ST BK	OGDEN	IA	C	C	C	98.8	10.55	9.1	2.2	15.5	20.7	5.6	7.7	11.5
CITY ST BK	FORT SCOTT	KS	C+	C+	C	27.7	2.29	2.3	6.6	25.9	24.0	6.9	9.0	15.7
CITY ST BK	SUTTON	NE	B-	C+	C+	63.8	69.27	19.7	3.8	4.6	22.1	5.2	8.1	11.2
CITY ST BK OF PALACIOS	PALACIOS	TX	D+	D	D	41.5	0.33	2.2	4.6	4.4	27.5	8.6	10.1	21.0
CITY SVG B&TC	DE RIDDER	LA	A	A	A	116.1	7.18	6.1	9.9	21.2	25.4	9.6	10.7	17.0
▼ CITYWIDE BKS	AURORA	CO	D-	D+	D+	647.7	15.22	16.1	1.4	3.5	13.8	3.2	7.7	10.1

Asset Quality Index	Non-Performing Loans		Net Charge-offs Avg Loans	Profitability Index	Net Income ($Mil)	Return on Assets (R.O.A.)	Return on Equity (R.O.E.)	Net Interest Spread	Overhead Efficiency Ratio	Liquidity Index	Liquidity Ratio	Hot Money Ratio	Stability Index
	as a % of Total Loans	as a % of Capital											
7.2	0.19	1.7	0.02	3.6	0.1	0.56	6.69	4.33	87.8	2.1	27.9	21.4	1.7
8.4	0.00	0.0	0.00	8.0	0.3	1.77	16.50	4.26	59.7	7.6	92.6	2.9	7.0
4.6	1.57	10.1	0.30	5.5	0.5	0.92	8.90	3.80	64.1	4.1	55.6	17.3	6.0
7.4	0.60	3.2	-0.06	3.3	0.1	0.53	5.11	3.95	86.5	5.3	30.4	3.8	4.0
5.1	0.07	0.4	0.26	5.6	0.3	1.43	9.51	4.73	65.1	3.9	13.5	9.2	6.7
8.0	0.42	2.1	0.09	4.0	0.1	0.51	4.06	4.97	81.7	5.6	88.4	14.5	4.2
8.5	0.75	1.8	0.39	5.7	0.3	1.10	7.29	4.65	68.3	7.7	118.1	6.1	7.3
9.2	0.00	0.0	0.01	9.9	0.7	1.96	16.72	4.88	52.8	6.3	44.3	2.5	7.5
7.6	0.28	1.4	0.19	8.7	0.1	1.45	11.42	5.00	59.3	5.6	38.1	2.1	6.3
1.9	2.65	15.2	-0.27	7.3	0.3	1.26	12.97	4.84	56.2	4.5	18.7	5.9	5.0
3.3	4.09	18.4	0.38	9.9	0.5	2.25	16.83	5.17	54.3	4.6	79.6	18.2	7.0
7.4	0.42	2.9	-0.04	4.8	0.4	0.99	11.76	3.95	66.4	4.2	22.4	8.3	5.3
4.9	0.27	2.0	-0.13	4.1	0.2	0.68	7.61	5.01	88.0	2.2	33.2	25.5	3.8
7.1	0.23	1.4	0.00	8.2	0.9	1.87	25.46	4.06	49.3	4.4	12.0	5.8	6.0
8.7	0.98	2.9	0.50	5.7	0.1	1.03	7.47	3.27	55.4	4.1	17.2	8.2	7.7
4.4	1.91	12.0	-0.01	7.2	0.2	1.40	13.19	4.61	53.5	4.8	27.2	5.8	4.5
4.4	0.87	6.1	0.24	3.7	0.3	0.43	4.82	3.56	82.4	8.5	204.4	10.2	4.6
6.2	0.59	3.6	0.07	6.6	1.6	1.22	14.93	3.86	59.3	4.1	8.5	7.1	5.0
5.6	0.31	2.1	0.48	9.8	2.5	1.62	18.85	5.39	54.3	3.0	41.8	21.6	5.4
3.6	1.32	8.5	0.43	4.5	1.5	0.86	10.11	5.26	77.1	1.7	11.8	21.1	3.7
9.3	0.24	0.8	0.02	5.2	0.8	1.10	8.89	3.52	64.2	5.9	61.5	10.7	7.6
5.0	0.90	5.5	0.01	7.7	3.3	1.45	12.63	4.39	61.3	1.4	12.4	25.4	8.6
3.8	1.08	4.9	0.04	5.5	1.5	1.06	7.75	3.88	57.6	4.2	36.5	12.9	7.0
5.5	1.76	6.4	-0.02	9.8	0.7	1.89	10.10	4.22	40.8	4.5	55.0	15.0	8.6
9.7	0.07	0.4	0.01	3.5	1.3	0.52	5.16	3.08	81.0	5.1	59.0	14.4	6.5
8.0	0.27	1.9	0.03	5.1	2.6	0.82	11.93	3.67	71.9	4.7	47.7	13.3	4.1
2.3	5.10	23.5	-0.15	0.9	0.1	0.08	0.81	3.03	96.0	5.6	158.6	23.7	3.2
5.2	0.34	2.9	0.00	9.4	6.6	2.10	29.28	3.53	50.2	1.4	11.6	25.0	7.3
6.4	0.69	3.9	0.09	6.8	1.1	1.43	15.95	4.35	69.0	5.7	45.5	7.4	4.9
6.8	0.15	1.5	-0.01	6.8	1.0	1.20	15.47	3.53	48.9	3.7	26.0	11.8	4.2
7.5	0.17	0.9	0.08	5.2	0.7	0.89	11.30	2.92	62.7	6.9	72.0	6.3	5.6
6.4	0.32	3.4	0.25	6.3	0.4	1.40	17.45	5.72	66.5	2.4	9.0	16.2	2.9
7.7	0.28	2.0	0.14	9.5	24.9	2.63	29.83	4.80	48.0	4.0	38.9	17.3	6.6
3.9	1.02	7.8	0.70	4.5	3.2	0.77	8.14	4.09	72.0	1.4	28.2	32.8	5.7
5.7	0.73	2.5	0.10	10.0	9.5	3.04	12.22	5.85	53.5	4.2	47.1	15.7	10.0
5.8	0.72	4.5	0.06	6.9	0.2	1.50	13.29	4.91	58.0	3.0	53.1	26.2	5.8
7.1	0.00	0.0	0.00	4.8	0.5	1.08	8.86	5.01	73.0	3.5	92.8	40.2	5.1
7.0	0.52	3.1	0.02	9.8	102.3	1.57	17.10	4.53	51.6	7.5	99.5	7.7	7.9
4.6	1.36	7.9	0.20	5.7	0.3	1.17	12.78	4.40	74.6	5.5	100.2	16.3	3.9
4.6	1.46	8.9	2.88	3.1	0.1	0.14	1.75	4.37	72.0	3.5	59.6	22.4	3.2
8.7	0.32	0.7	0.10	5.6	0.4	1.28	8.89	3.35	68.8	4.3	16.0	6.6	7.0
8.6	0.05	0.3	-0.02	9.8	29.6	2.43	28.58	4.17	44.5	6.4	69.2	10.4	8.2
8.7	0.20	0.8	-0.25	2.7	0.0	0.43	4.14	3.57	90.5	4.4	78.2	17.5	2.3
5.6	0.39	2.0	0.03	3.7	0.3	0.39	3.73	3.98	88.9	3.0	6.8	13.1	6.2
8.6	0.49	1.8	0.05	8.8	1.2	1.60	10.43	4.19	41.0	4.4	32.1	10.3	8.5
6.8	0.03	0.1	0.01	10.0	1.0	1.82	11.34	5.28	47.6	1.7	17.0	21.7	9.2
5.8	1.02	6.8	0.33	4.9	1.1	0.83	11.91	3.99	70.8	5.8	160.4	21.5	1.9
9.6	0.25	0.3	0.04	3.5	0.1	0.60	4.30	3.05	78.9	6.9	79.1	5.8	5.4
9.2	0.00	0.0	0.01	2.4	0.1	0.39	4.06	3.36	87.3	6.1	56.5	6.5	3.3
4.4	1.17	7.3	0.43	5.5	1.3	1.22	13.00	4.29	74.6	2.5	17.4	16.7	5.5
6.1	2.16	7.6	-0.89	5.1	1.4	1.76	19.31	4.00	75.5	3.8	31.3	12.9	3.8
9.1	0.29	1.7	0.24	10.0	25.3	2.29	24.04	4.55	46.4	5.2	27.7	7.5	7.4
5.4	0.57	2.6	0.30	6.0	2.4	1.23	13.21	3.99	56.6	4.9	32.6	7.5	5.0
7.3	1.24	4.9	0.11	9.5	1.4	2.17	20.26	4.62	52.5	2.7	28.4	17.8	6.8
7.3	0.85	4.4	0.13	6.3	1.0	1.13	9.05	4.53	75.9	4.6	35.2	10.3	8.0
0.2	3.55	26.4	0.04	5.4	0.4	0.58	5.78	3.67	70.1	0.6	12.6	49.1	5.5
5.3	0.94	7.3	0.04	4.4	0.5	1.18	12.90	3.14	61.0	2.1	16.2	18.6	4.5
6.7	0.48	3.5	0.03	5.7	0.7	1.10	13.07	3.45	70.0	7.5	117.8	8.6	5.5
5.4	0.68	5.5	0.04	6.5	0.7	1.45	18.06	3.74	46.0	0.7	10.6	36.3	5.0
8.6	0.00	0.0	0.02	5.6	0.2	1.27	14.08	4.35	68.3	3.7	54.2	18.9	5.0
3.5	0.67	3.3	-0.06	8.5	0.3	1.31	8.43	5.13	61.5	2.2	9.1	17.5	7.5
2.8	2.30	14.5	0.10	2.6	0.1	0.38	3.88	4.15	88.2	2.9	21.9	15.1	2.1
8.4	0.11	0.6	0.09	9.5	1.3	2.21	20.83	5.52	63.0	3.6	18.1	11.1	8.2
0.0	3.27	29.1	0.63	7.6	5.0	1.60	20.56	5.53	60.8	4.5	30.3	8.9	5.5

Name	City	State	Weiss Safety Rating	2003 Weiss Safety Rating	2002 Weiss Safety Rating	Total Assets ($Mil)	One Year Asset Growth	Asset Mix (As a % of Total Assets)				Capital-ization Index	Leverage Ratio	Risk-based Capital Ratio
								Comm-ercial Loans	Cons-umer Loans	Home Mort-gages	Secur-ities			
▲ CLACKAMAS COUNTY BK	SANDY	OR	A+	A	A	157.8	2.45	2.9	3.6	5.7	20.4	10.0	14.9	20.1
CLARE BK NA	PLATTEVILLE	WI	B-	B-	B-	177.5	2.58	3.2	5.3	37.3	36.0	5.3	7.3	16.7
CLAREMONT SVGS BK	CLAREMONT	NH	A	A	A	276.8	3.97	1.8	3.9	38.7	34.1	10.0	13.8	24.3
CLARENCE ST BK	CLARENCE	MO	B-	B-	B-	15.7	-0.77	4.4	5.1	15.0	50.6	10.0	21.6	47.9
CLARKE COUNTY ST BK	OSCEOLA	IA	C	C	C	108.5	3.59	14.2	2.0	20.6	18.8	6.0	8.0	12.0
CLARKSBURG COMMERCIAL	CLARKSBURG	OH	D+	D+	D+	16.7	2.04	13.9	8.5	29.5	18.0	8.1	9.8	15.4
CLARKSON BK	CLARKSON	NE	C-	D+	D-	38.1	-4.80	4.2	3.0	3.8	40.9	9.6	10.7	19.2
▲ CLARKSTON ST BK	CLARKSTON	MI	B	B-	B-	145.1	11.20	24.3	2.3	6.3	26.8	6.7	8.7	12.9
▲ CLASSIC BK CORP	ASHLAND	KY	C+	C-	C	335.3	2.22	15.4	12.9	33.9	13.0	5.5	7.5	11.6
CLAXTON BK	CLAXTON	GA	B	B	B+	100.2	3.09	5.9	4.3	10.7	30.0	9.3	10.5	18.1
▲ CLAY CITY BKG CO	CLAY CITY	IL	C+	C	C	53.4	15.29	9.7	5.1	9.8	30.1	10.0	13.0	19.0
▲ CLAY COUNTY BK	CLAY	WV	D+	D-	C-	55.4	-6.92	3.6	8.6	34.7	47.0	10.0	11.9	28.2
CLAY COUNTY SAVINGS BANK	LIBERTY	MO	C	C	D+	85.0	0.35	1.7	1.3	41.2	20.4	10.0	12.5	21.7
CLAY COUNTY ST BK	LOUISVILLE	IL	C+	C+	B-	59.9	-0.03	6.3	11.9	13.4	37.3	10.0	15.4	25.4
CLEAR CREEK NB	GEORGETOWN	CO	E-	E-	E-	21.9	-5.99	3.7	2.4	9.2	13.7	3.8	5.8	10.8
▼ CLEAR LAKE B&TC	CLEAR LAKE	IA	C	C+	C+	176.4	0.92	14.9	14.4	16.8	17.5	3.3	7.3	10.2
▼ CLEARFIELD B&TC	CLEARFIELD	PA	B-	B	B+	296.3	16.68	6.3	6.1	15.1	37.6	6.1	8.1	17.1
▲ CLEBURNE COUNTY BK	HEBER SPRINGS	AR	B	B-	C+	210.3	1.99	2.6	2.3	17.9	48.1	6.8	8.8	17.7
CLEO ST BK	CLEO SPRINGS	OK	A-	A-	A	38.7	1.67	2.9	2.6	2.2	67.4	10.0	22.7	46.7
▼ CLEVELAND BK	CLEVELAND	OK	D	D+	C	41.6	2.40	8.2	11.9	16.1	36.1	5.4	7.4	13.0
CLEVELAND CMNTY BK SSB	CLEVELAND	MS	B-	B-	B-	30.0	1.09	6.7	10.5	41.0	21.5	10.0	12.4	25.5
CLEVELAND ST BK	CLEVELAND	MS	B	B	A-	184.4	-2.13	2.3	8.6	10.6	54.2	10.0	11.2	26.2
CLEVELAND ST BK	CLEVELAND	WI	B+	B+	B+	39.8	-1.03	5.9	4.1	31.7	40.9	10.0	14.0	27.8
CLIFTON HEIGHTS S&L	CINCINNATI	OH	E-	E-	E-	14.8	-0.29	0.0	0.1	64.2	0.0	6.9	8.9	12.8
CLIFTON SAVINGS BANK, SLA	CLIFTON	NJ	B+	A-	A-	703.9	19.53	0.0	0.1	38.7	52.6	10.0	19.0	57.7
CLINTON B&TC	CLINTON	LA	B+	B+	B+	62.1	4.29	4.6	6.0	20.2	25.1	10.0	12.5	20.2
CLINTON BK	CLINTON	KY	B-	B-	B-	39.7	3.59	5.4	6.2	9.6	41.1	10.0	17.2	29.3
▼ CLINTON NB	CLINTON	IA	B+	A-	A-	253.8	0.19	10.2	2.9	11.3	41.6	10.0	11.6	21.2
CLINTON ST BK	CLINTON	MN	A-	A-	A-	56.8	5.78	11.1	4.0	3.5	36.8	10.0	12.1	17.9
CLINTON SVGS BK	CLINTON	MA	B	B-	B-	350.5	17.81	3.3	0.8	45.2	21.1	7.4	9.3	16.8
▼ CLOVER CMNTY BK	CLOVER	SC	B	B+	A-	76.7	9.47	23.5	4.4	11.3	19.3	8.1	9.9	13.4
CLOVER LEAF BK	EDWARDSVILLE	IL	C+	C	C+	105.1	2.92	4.9	2.2	26.6	23.1	9.3	10.6	16.9
CLYDE SVG BK CO	CLYDE	OH	B-	B-	B	85.9	-3.00	6.7	16.7	16.7	12.1	6.9	9.5	12.4
▼ CMMNTY BK OAK PARK RIVER	OAK PARK	IL	B-	B	C+	189.9	21.15	18.3	0.6	16.4	6.6	3.9	7.8	10.4
CNA TR CORP	COSTA MESA	CA	B+	B+	B+	194.1	-17.67	0.0	0.0	0.0	63.3	10.0	14.0	86.9
CNB COMMUNITY BK	CLARION	PA	D	NR	NR	22.8	N/A	3.6	2.9	24.2	13.1	10.0	41.2	78.2
CNB NB	LAKE CITY	FL	C	C	C	847.4	7.11	12.5	4.3	19.1	6.0	3.2	7.5	10.1
▲ CNLBANK	ORLANDO	FL	C-	D+	D	349.9	65.23	15.3	1.7	1.8	17.9	6.9	10.7	12.4
▲ COAST BK OF FLORIDA	BRADENTON	FL	D	D-	D-	334.5	59.95	11.0	5.4	14.6	14.2	6.3	8.3	12.5
COAST COMMUNITY BK	BILOXI	MS	B-	B-	C+	143.9	7.83	6.2	3.5	17.6	8.3	4.1	7.7	10.6
▲ COAST NB	SAN LUIS OBISPO	CA	B	B-	C+	154.3	15.81	19.2	2.5	1.6	5.1	6.9	9.3	12.4
COASTAL BK	MERRITT ISLAND	FL	C-	C-	C-	77.3	60.50	2.3	2.0	21.8	0.0	3.0	6.0	10.0
COASTAL BK	SAVANNAH	GA	C	C	C-	250.9	13.79	10.3	3.0	14.5	4.1	4.4	8.5	10.7
COASTAL BK OF GEORGIA	BRUNSWICK	GA	B-	B-	B	406.9	1.52	5.9	2.6	17.9	9.3	3.5	7.9	10.2
COASTAL CMNTY BK	EVERETT	WA	C+	C	C	112.4	9.54	19.3	3.9	10.9	0.9	4.6	9.4	10.8
COASTAL COMMERCE BK	HOUMA	LA	B-	C+	C-	123.4	12.41	25.0	5.1	15.1	21.6	6.5	8.5	12.2
COASTAL COMMUNITY BANK	APALACHICOLA	FL	C	C	D+	188.1	29.46	7.2	2.9	27.3	3.2	2.4	7.2	9.4
▲ COASTAL FEDERAL BANK	MYRTLE BEACH	SC	B	B-	B-	1,280.1	12.96	2.5	2.0	24.1	31.1	5.4	7.4	13.4
▼ COATESVILLE SVG BK	COATESVILLE	PA	C-	C	C	248.1	4.01	0.0	0.1	29.5	58.2	4.6	6.6	15.3
▲ COBIZ BK NA	DENVER	CO	B+	B	B	1,523.3	26.14	18.9	0.9	5.9	28.0	6.3	8.3	12.1
▲ COCONUT GROVE BK	MIAMI	FL	B	B-	A	447.1	16.48	2.9	3.0	5.5	55.1	10.0	11.7	21.8
▼ COFFEE COUNTY BK	MANCHESTER	TN	B-	B	B	67.9	35.13	26.3	16.6	27.9	11.3	7.3	9.5	12.7
COHUTTA BKG CO	CHATSWORTH	GA	B-	B-	B	253.2	13.33	13.6	1.5	8.5	15.3	3.2	8.3	10.1
COLCHESTER ST BK	COLCHESTER	IL	D-	D-	C+	34.2	-5.86	13.9	12.4	15.9	21.8	6.9	8.9	15.3
▲ COLDWATER NATIVE BK	COLDWATER	KS	C+	C	C	14.9	-4.83	1.1	2.0	1.4	63.2	10.0	21.2	64.0
COLE TAYLOR BK	ROSEMONT	IL	B-	B-	B-	2,763.5	4.92	20.1	0.8	4.8	20.4	4.2	8.1	10.6
COLEMAN COUNTY ST BK	COLEMAN	TX	B	B	B	40.9	0.62	10.5	6.5	12.6	24.6	10.0	12.1	20.8
COLERIDGE NB	COLERIDGE	NE	C-	C-	C-	33.8	7.15	6.4	4.2	5.2	44.7	6.4	8.4	15.6
COLFAX BKG CO	COLFAX	LA	B-	B-	B-	58.8	10.59	3.8	12.1	28.6	37.9	6.6	8.6	18.0
▲ COLLEGE SVGS BK	PRINCETON	NJ	D	D-	D	724.9	153.27	0.0	0.0	0.0	98.7	3.4	5.4	43.1
▲ COLLEGIATE PEAKS BK	BUENA VISTA	CO	B-	C+	C+	78.5	0.29	8.1	4.2	3.8	21.6	8.0	9.7	13.3
COLLINS ST BK	COLLINS	WI	C+	C+	B-	14.6	13.16	6.2	11.6	22.2	0.0	10.0	16.1	21.4
COLLINSVILLE B&LA	COLLINSVILLE	IL	B+	B+	B+	140.1	0.49	0.0	0.1	36.1	54.2	10.0	17.4	66.5
COLLINSVILLE SVG SOCIETY	COLLINSVILLE	CT	B	B	B	100.5	-1.68	2.1	0.4	60.0	14.1	9.3	10.5	18.6

Asset Quality Index	Non-Performing Loans as a % of Total Loans	Non-Performing Loans as a % of Capital	Net Charge-offs Avg Loans	Profitability Index	Net Income ($Mil)	Return on Assets (R.O.A.)	Return on Equity (R.O.E.)	Net Interest Spread	Overhead Efficiency Ratio	Liquidity Index	Liquidity Ratio	Hot Money Ratio	Stability Index
8.5	0.16	0.6	-0.02	9.8	1.7	2.16	14.31	5.26	65.0	6.7	79.6	8.6	9.5
7.1	0.51	3.7	-0.03	5.5	1.2	1.30	17.14	3.16	56.2	6.6	57.0	5.2	5.4
9.3	0.12	0.4	0.03	6.2	1.5	1.09	7.73	3.76	69.3	6.5	74.6	9.2	8.2
8.9	0.54	1.1	0.12	6.1	0.1	1.16	5.40	3.78	52.1	6.6	97.8	8.8	5.3
3.9	1.47	12.6	0.57	2.7	0.3	0.58	7.28	3.60	73.3	4.1	25.4	9.7	3.4
6.0	0.58	3.9	0.00	3.0	0.0	0.28	2.73	4.76	94.7	5.1	26.3	2.3	2.9
2.2	7.70	30.1	0.52	6.0	0.3	1.65	15.26	3.71	55.4	7.3	130.8	10.1	4.4
8.3	0.05	0.4	0.28	4.7	0.7	1.01	12.13	3.83	59.8	1.9	25.9	21.7	5.0
3.6	0.76	5.5	0.17	6.9	2.2	1.28	13.10	4.33	57.7	2.8	13.2	15.0	2.7
4.3	1.94	10.7	0.08	5.6	0.7	1.37	13.18	4.26	69.5	3.0	20.8	14.4	6.8
7.6	0.56	2.6	0.20	3.0	0.1	0.50	3.83	3.88	82.5	4.0	11.2	8.0	5.4
4.4	4.08	14.4	-0.15	2.2	0.2	0.85	7.44	4.12	78.4	4.0	19.8	9.5	3.0
8.8	0.06	0.3	0.00	1.9	0.0	-0.02	-0.17	3.42	98.5	2.2	13.0	18.1	4.6
2.8	6.41	22.6	-0.03	7.0	0.4	1.19	7.73	3.98	51.7	5.0	39.6	10.1	7.7
5.2	2.10	18.7	0.00	0.3	-0.1	-0.76	-13.52	4.30	115.4	6.3	53.2	2.0	0.0
3.5	0.65	5.9	2.01	4.3	0.6	0.66	8.17	4.16	55.3	3.1	15.2	13.7	3.9
5.2	1.11	7.3	0.22	5.3	1.3	0.90	10.97	3.32	62.9	3.7	24.2	11.3	4.7
8.3	0.29	1.3	0.30	4.7	1.2	1.12	11.75	3.73	64.8	2.2	23.1	18.8	5.4
9.5	0.03	0.0	-0.44	9.6	0.5	2.32	10.42	3.62	37.4	5.2	66.8	13.5	8.0
3.2	2.03	15.8	0.08	5.1	0.2	1.15	15.73	4.03	65.4	4.8	9.3	2.6	2.3
5.5	1.65	8.4	0.17	3.4	0.1	0.50	4.07	3.84	83.4	7.1	277.7	17.0	5.5
8.6	0.18	0.6	0.33	4.8	0.8	0.91	8.01	4.02	69.3	2.7	47.9	30.5	6.0
7.4	2.21	7.4	0.00	6.7	0.2	1.15	8.12	4.23	76.1	4.1	28.3	10.8	7.1
1.9	3.27	29.9	0.15	3.3	0.0	0.47	5.24	3.03	84.5	0.8	13.1	33.2	0.3
9.9	0.06	0.1	0.00	4.6	1.7	0.49	2.97	2.35	62.8	3.7	35.8	15.0	8.1
5.8	1.50	7.2	0.14	5.9	0.4	1.22	10.13	4.52	69.6	4.0	43.3	15.6	5.7
7.6	1.25	3.6	0.32	3.7	0.2	0.78	4.72	3.68	74.1	4.1	20.8	8.8	5.7
8.9	0.33	1.3	0.02	4.7	1.1	0.86	7.32	4.06	77.7	5.4	38.2	6.3	7.0
8.4	0.01	0.1	0.00	9.1	0.8	2.75	22.99	3.83	29.6	3.0	45.5	23.2	8.0
8.3	0.26	1.8	0.00	5.1	1.4	0.84	8.83	3.53	65.5	6.1	50.6	5.9	5.0
7.7	0.00	0.0	0.03	7.4	0.5	1.36	13.57	5.07	63.7	3.2	30.4	15.8	5.3
5.4	1.01	6.0	0.03	3.9	0.4	0.71	6.80	3.32	70.3	4.1	29.9	11.0	5.1
6.4	0.10	0.8	0.63	8.1	0.6	1.34	14.67	4.64	61.3	3.4	16.6	12.0	5.7
6.0	0.70	7.2	0.00	9.2	1.2	1.39	17.99	4.38	49.7	1.7	18.8	22.2	5.0
10.0	0.00	0.0	0.00	4.2	-1.0	-0.91	-5.92	3.60	96.1	4.9	N/A	0.7	3.8
9.2	0.00	0.0	0.00	0.0	-0.6	-6.76	-12.73	1.21	568.8	8.9	247.7	7.1	0.0
6.2	0.18	1.7	0.46	3.8	0.3	0.08	0.93	4.04	73.5	4.8	92.7	20.0	4.8
5.9	0.43	3.1	0.03	2.9	0.8	0.50	5.95	4.11	72.5	2.4	13.0	16.6	4.2
4.9	0.68	5.7	0.98	1.6	0.4	0.25	2.93	3.32	77.0	5.1	51.3	12.5	0.4
6.8	0.40	3.1	0.08	6.8	0.7	0.97	10.50	4.63	66.4	2.1	31.4	24.7	5.8
8.2	0.00	0.0	0.00	6.0	0.8	1.04	11.40	5.07	67.5	3.0	53.4	30.0	4.7
7.4	0.05	0.6	0.00	5.4	0.2	0.53	7.91	4.14	66.2	2.0	44.0	52.7	4.5
7.0	0.16	1.3	-0.51	3.6	0.8	0.63	7.31	3.80	78.0	2.0	26.9	22.6	4.0
5.4	0.21	2.0	0.26	8.3	2.6	1.29	16.43	3.82	44.3	1.4	8.5	24.7	6.2
6.5	0.00	0.0	0.04	5.9	0.6	1.12	12.38	4.86	63.1	3.0	17.2	14.3	5.3
6.3	0.37	2.8	0.38	5.6	0.5	0.89	10.39	4.80	67.2	2.7	37.7	22.0	4.3
6.3	0.00	0.0	0.04	3.9	1.0	1.22	13.07	4.26	69.6	0.9	20.2	36.3	5.0
6.0	0.61	4.6	0.07	7.5	7.9	1.26	17.07	3.81	53.2	0.5	5.7	47.8	6.9
6.2	1.62	10.0	0.00	3.6	0.7	0.57	9.41	2.34	65.6	2.3	29.1	19.8	2.6
8.4	0.27	2.1	0.04	7.8	8.6	1.19	15.96	4.27	54.1	4.0	52.7	21.7	7.3
9.1	0.31	1.0	0.55	4.5	2.3	1.11	9.46	4.30	69.5	3.0	11.2	13.6	5.7
3.7	1.27	10.6	-0.14	10.0	0.8	2.59	28.00	5.07	48.7	2.4	39.9	29.2	5.9
3.8	0.98	8.7	0.35	6.5	1.3	1.02	12.60	4.50	59.3	1.3	6.4	25.3	6.3
1.2	3.56	22.0	1.78	4.6	0.2	1.19	13.65	3.99	38.7	3.4	49.3	19.4	1.7
9.7	0.00	0.0	-0.16	3.1	0.0	0.35	1.70	3.55	86.0	4.9	64.5	12.9	4.7
5.0	1.10	8.2	0.29	5.6	11.9	0.88	9.88	3.89	58.8	1.2	18.4	30.7	7.2
8.4	0.18	0.8	-0.01	5.1	0.2	0.86	7.52	4.56	82.4	5.7	75.3	12.2	5.8
3.4	2.93	17.0	0.05	6.4	0.2	1.32	15.99	4.46	58.3	1.0	24.8	38.8	4.0
8.4	0.00	0.0	0.33	5.3	0.3	1.15	13.74	4.52	76.7	1.7	15.9	22.3	5.0
10.0	0.00	0.0	0.00	1.6	1.3	0.42	7.72	1.08	42.5	7.2	90.8	6.9	1.1
8.0	0.00	0.0	0.01	6.6	0.5	1.29	11.90	5.25	64.8	4.3	17.7	7.2	5.7
4.5	1.84	9.3	0.05	5.6	0.1	0.83	5.31	4.45	70.0	5.3	85.4	14.3	5.3
10.0	0.00	0.0	0.00	4.5	0.4	0.63	3.63	1.95	49.9	4.1	57.7	19.2	8.1
9.1	0.16	1.2	-0.02	5.1	0.5	0.91	8.81	3.43	61.0	4.1	20.1	8.9	5.8

Name	City	State	Weiss Safety Rating	2003 Weiss Safety Rating	2002 Weiss Safety Rating	Total Assets ($Mil)	One Year Asset Growth	Asset Mix (As a % of Total Assets)				Capital-ization Index	Leverage Ratio	Risk-based Capital Ratio
								Comm-ercial Loans	Cons-umer Loans	Home Mort-gages	Secur-ities			
COLOMBO BANK	ROCKVILLE	MD	D+	D	D+	109.3	9.67	18.1	1.3	24.0	1.8	2.6	7.1	9.6
COLONIAL BK	AURORA	CO	C+	C+	C+	175.6	13.09	5.9	4.1	3.2	28.8	4.9	6.9	11.6
COLONIAL BK FSB	BRIDGETON	NJ	C-	C-	D+	283.6	18.18	2.2	1.1	24.5	57.2	3.2	5.2	11.7
COLONIAL BK NA	MONTGOMERY	AL	B-	B-	C+	17,437.7	7.73	5.0	1.1	12.5	18.3	4.7	6.8	11.6
▼ COLONIAL CO-OP BK	GARDNER	MA	C	C+	C+	72.5	0.58	2.5	3.9	57.7	10.0	9.1	10.4	19.5
COLONIAL FSB	QUINCY	MA	B-	B-	B-	221.1	1.60	0.1	0.5	39.2	45.3	6.1	8.1	22.8
COLONIAL SVGS FA	FORT WORTH	TX	A-	A	A-	1,082.7	-23.92	0.1	0.6	51.7	13.4	10.0	13.4	29.2
COLONIAL VA BK	GLOUCESTER	VA	D	D	NR	31.7	N/A	17.7	7.2	6.5	19.0	10.0	36.8	50.6
COLONY BANK QUITMAN, FSB	QUITMAN	GA	C+	C+	C	102.3	17.28	5.4	7.2	39.0	7.5	6.3	8.5	12.0
COLONY BK OF ASHBURN	ASHBURN	GA	C	C	C-	303.9	15.74	1.1	7.3	16.5	15.5	4.1	7.3	10.5
▲ COLONY BK OF DODGE	EASTMAN	GA	C+	C	C-	69.0	4.85	0.6	10.0	16.7	16.9	4.3	7.1	10.6
COLONY BK OF FITZGERALD	FITZGERALD	GA	C+	C+	C	157.5	9.42	3.6	7.4	16.5	11.8	5.6	7.9	11.5
▲ COLONY BK SOUTHEAST	BROXTON	GA	C+	C	C	107.0	20.69	11.9	2.0	14.4	5.9	5.2	8.5	11.1
▲ COLONY BK WILCOX	ROCHELLE	GA	C+	C	C-	52.0	12.47	0.0	8.0	8.6	14.9	3.9	7.8	10.5
COLONY BK WORTH	SYLVESTER	GA	C	C	C-	146.1	19.71	1.7	15.0	16.2	8.1	3.0	7.2	10.0
COLORADO B&TC OF LA	LA JUNTA	CO	B	B	B	62.5	0.65	10.1	6.6	6.2	55.5	8.2	9.8	24.4
▲ COLORADO EAST B&T	LAMAR	CO	C	C	C	271.3	3.17	11.5	4.4	4.3	30.9	4.9	6.9	11.4
COLORADO FSB	GREENWOOD VLG	CO	C	C	C-	39.9	-26.22	0.0	0.0	72.8	0.0	3.4	11.9	10.2
▼ COLORADO MOUNTAIN BK	WESTCLIFFE	CO	D	B	B-	72.0	-3.28	6.1	4.0	30.0	8.8	4.2	6.6	10.6
▲ COLORADO NB	COLORADO SPRINGS	CO	B-	C+	B	98.7	-2.33	5.6	2.2	10.0	36.8	7.0	9.0	16.4
COLORADO ST B&TC NA	DENVER	CO	C+	C+	C-	413.9	36.29	8.3	1.7	5.7	2.3	6.8	8.8	13.6
▲ COLORADO ST BK	WALSH	CO	B	B-	B+	32.0	10.81	3.5	2.2	7.7	29.1	10.0	12.3	19.8
▲ COLORADO VALLEY BK	LA GRANGE	TX	C	D+	D+	29.7	-0.87	4.7	19.1	32.7	1.9	7.2	9.1	14.3
COLUMBIA BK	COLUMBIA	MD	C+	C+	C+	1,129.8	14.39	10.9	0.5	7.7	10.5	3.4	8.4	10.2
▲ COLUMBIA BK	FAIR LAWN	NJ	A-	B+	B+	3,300.0	11.24	2.8	0.1	45.5	25.9	7.2	9.2	16.5
▲ COLUMBIA COMMUNITY BK	HILLSBORO	OR	C+	D+	D-	120.8	34.19	21.8	0.7	1.0	13.7	5.3	9.3	11.2
▼ COLUMBIA COUNTY BK	LAKE CITY	FL	D+	C-	C	140.3	12.60	7.1	5.4	12.2	16.6	1.8	6.6	8.8
COLUMBIA COUNTY FARMERS	BLOOMSBURG	PA	B	B	B+	228.5	-0.46	6.1	2.2	32.6	26.6	10.0	11.4	19.2
COLUMBIA NB	COLUMBIA	IL	C	C	C	36.3	-0.19	3.3	8.6	39.2	24.9	8.6	10.0	18.1
▼ COLUMBIA RIVER BK	THE DALLES	OR	B-	B	B-	666.2	15.00	14.3	3.1	4.6	4.5	3.5	8.9	10.2
COLUMBIA S&LA	MILWAUKEE	WI	C-	C-	C-	19.9	5.34	0.0	0.9	48.7	2.0	10.0	13.3	23.8
COLUMBIA ST BK	TACOMA	WA	B+	B	B-	1,855.6	8.13	19.1	5.0	5.3	25.4	7.9	9.6	14.1
▲ COLUMBIA SVGS BK	CINCINNATI	OH	C-	D+	D+	64.6	6.26	0.0	0.3	48.2	14.5	6.5	8.5	12.5
COLUMBIA TR BK	PASCO	WA	B-	B-	C+	174.9	17.37	16.7	1.0	4.8	10.1	6.0	9.2	11.7
▲ COLUMBIAN B&TC	TOPEKA	KS	B	C+	C-	225.5	2.99	19.2	2.0	13.2	7.6	10.0	11.9	15.6
COLUMBUS B&TC	COLUMBUS	GA	A-	A-	A-	4,972.0	19.06	7.1	5.6	2.1	7.1	10.0	19.7	20.8
COLUMBUS B&TC	COLUMBUS	NE	C+	C+	C	76.8	-0.53	19.2	3.7	10.9	20.9	6.7	8.7	12.3
COLUMBUS JUNCTION ST BK	COLUMBUS JUNCT	IA	C	C	C	42.9	3.14	8.4	5.8	19.3	45.3	6.6	8.6	17.8
COLUMBUS ST BK	COLUMBUS	TX	B+	B+	A-	83.5	2.88	0.9	2.2	2.2	69.5	10.0	13.2	41.6
COLUMBUS SVGS BK	CHICAGO	IL	C	C	C	19.5	-4.17	0.0	0.3	25.7	61.5	10.0	16.3	49.7
COMANCHE NB	COMANCHE	TX	A	A	A	129.9	8.33	1.9	7.1	9.6	54.5	10.0	15.2	35.0
COMERICA B&T NA	ANN ARBOR	MI	B	B-	B-	12.2	21.95	0.0	0.0	0.0	0.0	10.0	90.2	295.5
COMERICA BK	DETROIT	MI	B	B-	B-	54,646.4	-7.43	37.0	1.4	3.0	7.9	7.0	10.3	12.5
COMMERCE B&TC	TOPEKA	KS	B	B	B-	952.1	8.98	8.4	12.2	9.7	40.8	4.9	7.0	13.2
COMMERCE B&TC	WORCESTER	MA	B-	C+	C+	1,003.2	7.93	8.1	2.4	22.2	34.5	6.2	8.2	13.5
▼ COMMERCE BK	AURORA	CO	B+	A-	A-	92.9	2.91	22.3	0.7	5.7	27.9	7.1	9.1	14.2
▼ COMMERCE BK	GENEVA	MN	B-	B-	C	95.8	43.47	14.1	2.6	23.8	0.7	9.3	11.9	14.5
▼ COMMERCE BK	LAREDO	TX	B+	A-	B	377.1	-15.60	6.6	3.1	4.5	59.3	5.8	7.8	18.0
▲ COMMERCE BK DE NA	WILMINGTON	DE	B-	C+	C+	349.1	26.18	1.2	1.0	7.3	50.3	4.2	6.2	13.1
COMMERCE BK HARRISBURG	CAMP HILL	PA	C	C	C	1,184.2	40.16	11.6	3.3	13.7	42.3	2.6	5.8	9.6
COMMERCE BK NA	PEORIA	IL	B	B+	B+	885.3	-6.37	14.5	2.8	12.6	28.6	7.7	9.5	15.3
COMMERCE BK NA	WICHITA	KS	B	B+	B+	1,125.0	-1.93	7.9	13.6	6.0	47.8	7.1	9.1	15.9
▼ COMMERCE BK NA	KANSAS CITY	MO	B-	B	B+	12,239.7	3.80	10.9	14.6	10.7	30.6	3.8	7.2	10.4
▲ COMMERCE BK NA	CHERRY HILL	NJ	B-	C+	B-	18,821.3	41.57	5.4	0.8	8.0	56.4	4.0	6.0	12.2
▲ COMMERCE BK NORTH	RAMSEY	NJ	B-	C+	B-	2,863.4	31.72	3.9	0.4	5.9	58.5	4.3	6.3	14.4
COMMERCE BK OF AZ	TUCSON	AZ	E	D-	D	73.4	147.25	15.2	2.1	2.7	4.9	2.7	8.3	9.8
▼ COMMERCE BK OF OMAHA NA	OMAHA	NE	B-	B	B+	4.2	-23.78	0.0	59.3	0.0	9.8	10.0	86.0	107.6
COMMERCE BK OF WA NA	SEATTLE	WA	B-	B-	B-	706.7	2.61	23.6	1.3	3.5	46.9	5.0	7.0	16.0
▲ COMMERCE BK PENN NA	PHILADELPHIA	PA	B-	C+	B-	4,982.5	21.16	2.9	0.6	7.4	63.8	4.2	6.2	14.9
COMMERCE NB	FULLERTON	CA	D	D	NR	30.8	N/A	8.6	5.1	0.0	32.7	10.0	38.3	58.6
▲ COMMERCE NB	CORINTH	MS	B	B-	B-	64.2	10.97	18.8	14.6	18.8	25.6	8.3	9.8	16.1
▲ COMMERCE NB	COLUMBUS	OH	B-	C+	C+	411.4	2.19	21.8	0.8	24.0	3.2	5.4	7.4	11.7
COMMERCE NB OF FLORIDA	WINTER PARK	FL	D	D	NR	43.2	66.24	6.4	0.5	4.8	34.4	10.0	12.5	20.7
▼ COMMERCEBANK NA	MIAMI	FL	B-	B	B	3,444.8	12.93	12.6	0.4	2.3	39.8	5.6	7.6	13.8

Asset Quality Index	Non-Performing Loans as a % of Total Loans	Non-Performing Loans as a % of Capital	Net Charge-offs Avg Loans	Profitability Index	Net Income ($Mil)	Return on Assets (R.O.A.)	Return on Equity (R.O.E.)	Net Interest Spread	Overhead Efficiency Ratio	Liquidity Index	Liquidity Ratio	Hot Money Ratio	Stability Index
2.8	1.62	16.6	-0.01	3.6	0.1	0.22	2.93	3.40	92.3	2.1	45.4	61.4	4.5
5.9	0.89	7.4	0.16	6.6	1.2	1.37	19.54	5.30	70.7	4.5	11.5	4.7	5.1
9.1	0.12	0.8	0.01	4.0	0.9	0.65	11.08	3.02	67.3	1.6	31.1	32.3	2.3
6.4	0.35	2.8	0.21	5.8	85.0	1.02	12.08	3.68	59.7	2.3	6.3	16.8	6.7
9.2	0.13	0.9	0.05	2.7	0.1	0.26	2.36	4.03	88.2	5.5	64.4	11.6	4.8
8.6	0.09	0.5	0.00	4.9	0.8	0.74	9.64	2.66	60.3	1.8	21.1	22.3	4.8
6.8	0.41	1.7	0.29	6.0	5.9	1.06	7.83	3.43	79.1	1.4	29.3	120.6	10.0
8.7	0.00	0.0	0.00	0.0	-0.6	-4.85	-11.34	3.13	233.6	7.2	118.5	9.7	0.0
4.4	0.68	6.4	0.09	7.8	0.6	1.16	12.62	3.98	54.4	1.3	8.8	25.5	5.5
3.6	1.16	9.7	0.33	5.2	1.3	0.87	10.91	3.42	54.7	3.8	45.9	17.3	4.1
7.5	0.14	1.3	0.08	5.0	0.4	1.15	16.40	4.01	60.6	2.2	33.9	25.8	4.2
3.7	0.75	6.7	0.12	5.9	0.8	1.02	12.77	3.91	55.2	3.7	62.1	25.2	4.6
4.3	0.98	8.9	0.01	5.0	0.4	0.84	10.86	3.93	63.6	3.2	47.2	22.2	4.5
4.6	1.01	9.5	-0.08	8.3	0.4	1.39	18.21	4.14	46.7	2.5	40.9	27.4	4.9
2.4	1.37	14.3	0.38	5.7	0.8	1.05	15.20	4.25	51.8	2.4	44.6	32.8	3.8
8.5	0.50	1.8	0.05	6.3	0.4	1.20	11.97	4.77	68.1	5.4	37.9	6.5	5.1
3.8	1.58	9.7	-0.60	5.2	1.3	0.96	10.68	4.79	71.1	2.0	18.7	19.5	4.2
6.9	0.51	3.2	1.69	10.0	0.6	2.67	26.87	3.79	88.3	4.8	20.6	4.1	4.8
0.3	6.88	61.8	6.14	9.5	0.5	1.42	19.99	5.11	60.1	2.1	26.3	20.2	4.8
6.4	0.49	1.3	0.04	5.9	0.4	0.79	5.21	3.86	66.1	4.6	30.0	8.0	5.7
1.3	3.56	7.6	0.06	4.6	1.2	0.58	2.81	4.69	79.7	9.3	414.4	4.5	7.2
4.5	1.89	8.2	0.10	7.4	0.2	1.25	10.35	4.03	55.0	3.6	68.4	25.1	6.2
7.2	0.22	1.8	0.08	7.1	0.2	1.43	16.02	4.90	60.5	4.8	60.1	14.4	3.7
7.5	0.10	0.9	0.02	7.3	6.3	1.16	14.48	4.26	59.3	5.9	39.0	6.8	6.9
8.6	0.21	1.5	0.00	6.6	18.6	1.16	12.59	3.16	49.1	1.2	4.8	26.6	7.6
5.4	0.00	0.0	0.45	5.9	0.6	0.97	11.16	4.84	56.8	2.6	34.3	20.0	4.7
4.6	0.25	2.7	-0.04	5.0	0.8	1.17	17.70	4.03	69.9	1.9	13.9	19.2	3.6
6.6	1.00	5.4	0.13	4.7	1.1	0.92	8.11	3.54	66.8	3.4	33.1	15.6	7.1
4.7	1.52	9.3	-0.02	4.2	0.1	0.71	7.12	3.97	75.5	6.5	71.7	6.9	4.0
5.8	0.18	1.4	0.30	9.8	4.7	1.54	15.32	6.21	53.5	2.7	23.9	16.2	7.5
2.1	4.20	20.2	0.00	6.3	0.1	1.18	8.25	4.77	61.3	2.4	28.6	17.6	5.3
6.8	0.48	2.9	0.14	6.2	11.2	1.25	13.07	4.33	65.0	5.2	48.3	13.7	7.5
4.8	1.59	14.3	0.17	3.9	0.2	0.65	7.66	3.03	71.6	1.8	22.5	22.1	2.5
5.6	0.77	6.2	0.00	4.7	0.6	0.70	7.51	4.53	70.4	1.8	19.5	21.2	4.7
7.2	0.10	0.7	0.00	8.4	2.4	2.17	20.04	5.13	51.8	2.9	18.6	15.0	4.4
8.2	0.64	1.7	0.35	9.5	84.9	3.58	20.34	3.13	79.2	3.8	57.3	26.0	8.0
6.3	0.29	2.3	0.04	4.4	0.3	0.86	10.26	3.90	73.9	3.8	9.8	9.6	3.8
5.0	1.69	9.2	0.07	5.1	0.2	1.09	12.25	3.87	73.3	4.2	37.7	13.2	4.0
9.3	0.00	0.0	0.06	4.9	0.4	0.85	6.47	2.78	56.7	2.5	49.2	31.6	7.2
10.0	0.00	0.0	0.00	2.0	0.0	0.44	2.81	3.42	93.0	3.9	116.7	35.5	4.7
8.7	0.37	0.9	0.21	7.0	0.7	1.14	7.51	3.67	58.1	1.7	31.2	30.5	8.3
10.0	0.00	0.0	0.00	8.7	1.8	30.17	35.96	1.11	55.8	10.0	1,614.7	0.0	6.0
5.2	1.09	7.1	0.62	7.4	374.6	1.39	13.50	3.62	54.1	8.1	139.7	7.0	8.6
6.0	0.39	2.8	0.25	7.8	8.9	1.87	24.24	3.42	61.4	6.6	107.6	12.4	5.3
4.6	2.98	16.7	0.53	6.3	5.8	1.08	13.30	3.50	79.4	3.2	18.9	13.9	5.7
5.9	1.12	7.6	-0.05	9.6	1.0	2.13	23.42	5.24	63.9	4.8	11.8	3.2	6.7
2.9	1.46	11.1	0.00	10.0	1.4	3.14	28.01	5.57	34.2	0.4	3.6	60.3	6.8
7.6	0.29	1.0	0.21	9.0	2.9	1.56	13.95	3.11	45.0	1.7	35.8	39.4	6.5
9.8	0.11	0.5	0.07	5.3	2.0	1.21	19.74	4.31	59.0	8.3	160.7	7.7	4.4
8.8	0.13	1.1	0.09	5.2	4.7	0.84	14.59	4.60	71.2	3.4	8.4	11.6	4.2
7.0	0.56	3.3	0.12	9.5	7.2	1.57	15.32	4.12	56.9	4.4	26.4	7.7	6.3
7.2	0.42	1.5	0.46	6.4	7.0	1.18	10.51	3.71	64.1	3.0	34.4	23.8	6.3
6.2	0.53	3.8	0.48	9.4	96.1	1.57	21.31	3.75	57.5	5.3	27.6	6.6	7.0
9.5	0.34	1.9	0.16	5.5	76.3	0.99	17.55	4.89	72.5	5.4	31.7	7.6	4.7
9.6	0.52	2.2	0.54	10.0	24.6	1.85	30.15	4.10	55.8	7.5	103.3	7.6	6.0
7.0	0.00	0.0	0.00	0.9	0.1	0.14	1.73	4.56	87.8	2.2	29.2	21.7	0.0
5.7	1.15	0.8	4.92	10.0	0.1	3.54	4.97	7.65	94.6	5.0	4,375.0	97.7	5.7
6.4	0.58	3.7	0.18	7.7	4.5	1.26	17.76	3.60	44.5	5.0	110.4	21.9	5.2
9.6	0.41	1.8	0.22	8.2	30.4	1.26	20.97	4.14	49.8	5.5	35.4	8.5	5.1
9.4	0.00	0.0	0.00	0.0	-1.6	-16.28	-32.60	1.88	987.0	9.3	159.2	0.0	0.0
7.7	0.13	0.8	0.10	7.5	0.6	1.95	19.53	4.36	57.7	4.0	30.8	12.1	5.1
6.8	0.03	0.2	-0.02	5.6	1.8	0.87	5.66	3.62	57.4	0.6	7.1	40.4	6.5
8.9	0.00	0.0	0.00	0.0	-0.3	-1.36	-9.90	2.83	148.0	8.4	141.3	4.3	0.0
4.9	2.28	13.4	0.04	5.7	13.5	0.81	10.72	3.09	60.1	5.7	88.6	16.5	5.6

Name	City	State	Weiss Safety Rating	2003 Weiss Safety Rating	2002 Weiss Safety Rating	Total Assets ($Mil)	One Year Asset Growth	Asset Mix (As a % of Total Assets)				Capital-ization Index	Leverage Ratio	Risk-based Capital Ratio
								Comm-ercial Loans	Cons-umer Loans	Home Mort-gages	Secur-ities			
▲ COMMERCEFIRST BK	ANNAPOLIS	MD	C-	D+	D-	55.9	14.85	42.6	0.0	0.0	12.5	6.8	8.8	13.8
▲ COMMERCEWEST BK NA	NEWPORT BEACH	CA	C	D+	D	108.3	34.95	36.7	1.6	1.7	35.9	10.0	17.1	20.8
COMMERCIAL & SVG BK	MILLERSBURG	OH	C+	C	C	319.9	5.06	8.0	3.7	26.3	23.7	9.2	10.5	17.1
COMMERCIAL B&TC	MONTICELLO	AR	C+	C+	C	161.4	4.64	16.3	23.6	10.2	29.7	8.0	9.6	14.7
COMMERCIAL B&TC	PARIS	TN	B-	B-	B-	429.2	13.32	12.0	7.3	17.9	21.2	5.5	7.6	11.4
COMMERCIAL B&TC-TROUP	LAGRANGE	GA	B	B	B	206.2	4.22	15.3	2.4	17.7	11.0	4.9	8.6	11.0
COMMERCIAL BK	OZARK	AL	C-	C-	C-	58.2	-3.62	6.6	18.5	29.2	13.0	6.2	8.2	13.6
COMMERCIAL BK	CRAWFORD	GA	A-	A-	A-	82.6	-1.00	6.8	8.7	35.2	29.7	10.0	12.9	25.1
▼ COMMERCIAL BK	THOMASVILLE	GA	B-	B	B	415.5	12.41	14.7	2.7	14.2	11.1	3.6	8.0	10.3
▲ COMMERCIAL BK	PARSONS	KS	A	A-	A	183.5	-4.53	6.4	14.7	12.1	40.1	10.0	16.1	30.9
COMMERCIAL BK	W LIBERTY	KY	B-	B-	B-	121.0	2.67	8.4	9.3	24.6	41.5	5.6	7.6	16.4
▲ COMMERCIAL BK	ALMA	MI	B-	C+	B-	239.8	2.78	10.9	2.6	34.8	9.8	6.5	8.5	12.6
▲ COMMERCIAL BK	MARYLAND HEIGHTS	MO	C+	C	C-	156.0	7.80	13.8	3.3	18.5	29.4	6.4	8.5	12.1
▼ COMMERCIAL BK	DE KALB	MS	C	C+	C	108.6	3.65	6.9	12.8	23.4	16.8	6.2	8.2	12.4
▲ COMMERCIAL BK	BASSETT	NE	B	B-	C+	40.2	8.02	5.3	4.7	1.6	34.6	10.0	11.4	17.4
COMMERCIAL BK	DELPHOS	OH	C-	D+	D+	208.8	-0.74	5.8	4.0	16.3	29.2	8.2	9.8	19.5
COMMERCIAL BK	HONEA PATH	SC	A	A	A	117.2	16.13	3.2	5.4	20.7	33.4	10.0	17.1	35.8
COMMERCIAL BK	MASON	TX	C+	C+	C+	18.5	4.51	5.3	4.5	13.4	30.9	10.0	11.6	19.4
COMMERCIAL BK	WHITEWATER	WI	C+	C+	B-	89.0	4.02	0.9	1.9	23.2	38.5	8.6	10.1	26.2
COMMERCIAL BK FLORIDA	MIAMI	FL	B	B	B	847.3	12.92	4.0	0.4	2.0	34.9	5.2	7.2	12.4
COMMERCIAL BK OF	COSTA MESA	CA	D	D	NR	103.2	174.66	21.9	0.3	0.0	7.6	10.0	27.4	38.4
COMMERCIAL BK OF	DEMOPOLIS	AL	B	B+	A-	82.8	-6.81	9.1	13.1	29.8	19.2	6.9	8.9	13.5
COMMERCIAL BK OF	GRAYSON	KY	A-	A	A	152.4	1.45	2.6	10.5	19.4	49.9	10.0	13.9	36.3
▼ COMMERCIAL BK OF MOTT	MOTT	ND	C-	C	C	45.4	11.35	6.3	4.0	1.5	20.7	5.6	8.7	11.4
▲ COMMERCIAL BK OF NELSON	NELSON	NE	B+	B	B-	25.0	-1.87	11.5	2.4	2.9	30.0	10.0	18.7	30.5
COMMERCIAL BK OF OAK	OAK GROVE	MO	A-	A-	A-	126.2	-6.89	4.0	2.1	12.7	64.1	10.0	12.1	41.1
COMMERCIAL BK OF PA	LATROBE	PA	A-	A	A	371.6	1.21	4.5	0.7	24.6	37.1	10.0	11.5	24.4
COMMERCIAL BK OF TX NA	NACOGDOCHES	TX	B-	C+	C	292.9	-1.73	2.8	21.5	16.4	36.0	6.3	8.3	20.4
▲ COMMERCIAL BK OF VOLUSIA	ORMOND BEACH	FL	E+	E-	E-	39.6	-18.67	34.5	2.2	15.6	6.4	6.9	9.0	13.6
COMMERCIAL BK-CLAIBORNE	HARROGATE	TN	B	B	B	399.6	8.63	5.4	4.9	29.4	16.8	8.8	10.2	16.5
COMMERCIAL BKNG COMPANY	HAHIRA	GA	B-	B-	C	121.3	4.67	10.9	7.3	32.7	9.4	7.2	9.9	12.6
COMMERCIAL CAPITAL BANK,	IRVINE	CA	B+	B+	B+	4,374.4	268.68	0.2	0.0	19.2	10.6	5.6	7.6	11.5
COMMERCIAL CAPITAL BK	DELHI	LA	D+	D+	D+	26.0	7.25	9.3	2.8	6.8	13.1	8.9	10.2	14.4
▲ COMMERCIAL FEDERAL BK	OMAHA	NE	C+	C	C	11,537.7	-9.72	3.5	6.3	34.9	18.6	4.3	6.3	11.3
COMMERCIAL NB	TEXARKANA	TX	B-	B-	B-	158.4	-0.42	14.8	13.5	17.7	18.8	6.7	8.7	12.3
▲ COMMERCIAL NB AINSWORTH	AINSWORTH	NE	A-	B+	B+	61.8	-0.83	10.1	2.7	2.3	25.5	10.0	12.4	17.2
▼ COMMERCIAL NB OF BRADY	BRADY	TX	A	A+	A+	82.4	0.32	6.0	7.0	17.1	39.7	10.0	15.4	31.3
COMMERCIAL NB OF L'ANSE	LANSE	MI	B-	B-	B	63.0	-0.80	9.1	9.5	24.6	31.5	9.2	10.5	19.5
COMMERCIAL ST BK	DONALSONVILLE	GA	C+	C+	C	73.5	-6.69	15.1	13.0	12.2	32.4	9.3	10.6	17.7
COMMERCIAL ST BK	WATERLOO	IL	B	B-	B-	92.5	-0.06	11.7	4.6	27.2	39.4	7.8	9.6	16.7
COMMERCIAL ST BK	BONNER SPRINGS	KS	B-	B-	B-	89.9	4.86	11.9	7.8	10.6	45.7	6.1	8.1	15.4
COMMERCIAL ST BK	CEDAR BLUFFS	NE	D+	D+	D	8.7	-1.64	8.2	2.8	8.4	33.8	10.0	14.3	24.9
COMMERCIAL ST BK	ELSIE	NE	C-	D+	D+	11.8	-1.04	9.4	7.0	0.8	5.1	8.4	10.6	13.7
COMMERCIAL ST BK	REPUBLIC CITY	NE	A-	A-	A-	46.2	-3.26	2.4	1.1	0.0	71.4	10.0	17.6	37.7
▲ COMMERCIAL ST BK	WAUSA	NE	C-	D+	C-	51.0	5.93	12.8	3.3	2.0	29.2	9.3	10.5	17.1
COMMERCIAL ST BK	WAGNER	SD	A	A	A	101.4	2.44	8.1	4.2	2.9	44.3	10.0	14.6	25.0
▲ COMMERCIAL ST BK	ANDREWS	TX	D+	E	E-	105.0	28.55	35.9	13.3	4.0	11.5	6.7	9.4	12.3
COMMERCIAL ST BK	PALMER	TX	C+	C+	B-	44.6	-1.21	11.0	4.3	8.5	32.9	8.0	9.7	17.1
▼ COMMERCIAL ST BK	SINTON	TX	B	B+	B+	50.3	-2.73	5.5	3.2	1.8	20.3	7.4	9.3	24.8
COMMERCIAL ST BK EL	EL CAMPO	TX	C+	C+	B-	120.5	1.12	11.2	6.8	10.8	21.1	6.3	8.4	12.5
COMMERCIAL SVG BK	CARROLL	IA	A-	A-	A-	80.2	-2.38	12.6	6.2	17.2	20.3	8.7	10.2	14.7
▲ COMMERCIAL SVG BK	UPPER SANDUSKY	OH	C	C-	C-	274.5	2.68	5.5	17.2	13.5	18.1	5.0	7.7	11.0
COMMERCIAL TC OF FAYETTE	FAYETTE	MO	A	A	A	85.2	-4.85	5.3	7.1	46.2	19.4	10.0	11.2	19.1
COMMODORE BK	SOMERSET	OH	C	C	B-	62.2	6.57	5.5	4.4	23.6	40.7	6.7	8.7	17.7
COMMONWEALTH B&TC	LOUISVILLE	KY	B	B	B	489.1	2.46	4.3	3.5	20.7	17.4	7.1	9.3	12.6
▲ COMMONWEALTH BK FSB	MT STERLING	KY	C-	D+	D	19.2	-2.46	0.0	4.6	81.9	0.2	10.0	12.0	20.5
▼ COMMONWEALTH CMNTY BK	HARTFORD	KY	B	B+	A-	161.9	4.68	0.3	5.6	32.1	43.9	8.9	10.3	21.4
COMMONWEALTH CO-OP BK	BOSTON	MA	C+	C+	C+	49.3	-2.21	0.0	0.8	52.8	30.6	10.0	12.5	25.0
COMMONWEALTH NB	MOBILE	AL	D+	D+	D+	48.7	4.32	5.3	6.8	17.0	38.8	5.7	7.7	18.9
COMMONWEALTH NB	WORCESTER	MA	D-	D-	D	172.2	53.02	17.0	0.1	16.4	16.8	7.0	9.0	13.0
COMMUNITY B&T	CORNELIA	GA	B-	B-	B-	663.7	11.75	6.9	7.3	17.4	12.9	6.3	8.4	12.0
COMMUNITY B&T	WACO	TX	B-	B-	B	262.9	3.89	27.3	6.2	23.2	17.0	8.3	9.9	14.0
▲ COMMUNITY B&TC	NEOSHO	MO	B+	B	B	280.1	-2.40	4.1	4.7	19.2	46.9	5.6	7.6	17.1
▲ COMMUNITY B&TC	WOLFEBORO	NH	C	C	B	429.6	10.10	3.8	0.5	29.4	1.6	5.0	8.7	11.0

Asset Quality Index	Non-Performing Loans as a % of Total Loans	as a % of Capital	Net Charge-offs Avg Loans	Profitability Index	Net Income ($Mil)	Return on Assets (R.O.A.)	Return on Equity (R.O.E.)	Net Interest Spread	Overhead Efficiency Ratio	Liquidity Index	Liquidity Ratio	Hot Money Ratio	Stability Index
6.4	0.19	1.3	-0.12	3.1	0.2	0.84	9.80	4.04	76.2	3.4	78.0	31.9	0.7
8.4	0.00	0.0	0.00	3.0	0.4	0.88	5.16	4.28	76.7	4.2	41.0	14.3	2.0
7.6	0.22	1.4	0.07	3.7	1.2	0.75	7.23	4.04	75.9	3.0	14.9	14.2	5.0
3.0	1.68	11.1	0.15	5.5	0.8	0.97	10.35	4.06	58.2	0.9	13.2	32.6	4.5
6.1	0.41	3.0	0.20	6.5	3.1	1.48	17.07	3.94	60.3	5.3	56.3	12.5	5.3
7.3	0.04	0.4	0.01	9.5	1.6	1.56	18.16	4.25	49.0	2.9	14.9	14.3	7.1
3.2	1.75	13.3	0.77	4.7	0.2	0.55	6.77	4.94	76.3	3.8	37.2	14.9	3.1
6.3	1.22	5.2	-1.34	7.4	0.5	1.26	9.96	4.44	60.2	4.6	40.1	11.8	7.1
8.1	0.06	0.5	0.07	9.8	3.6	1.81	22.95	4.44	38.2	1.0	7.0	30.1	7.2
6.8	1.19	3.3	0.73	7.3	1.5	1.61	9.79	3.95	57.6	5.2	79.0	16.6	8.8
4.5	1.12	5.0	-0.44	5.3	0.6	0.91	8.90	3.77	66.9	2.4	32.7	21.3	6.2
4.3	1.47	13.0	0.00	5.7	1.2	1.01	11.99	4.38	65.0	4.2	17.6	7.8	4.2
5.9	0.65	4.5	1.03	3.8	0.4	0.56	6.57	3.75	68.1	4.3	35.4	12.0	3.6
2.7	2.75	21.3	0.17	5.5	0.6	1.03	12.72	4.21	67.4	2.7	11.9	15.1	5.2
7.3	0.01	0.0	-0.03	5.9	0.2	1.18	10.18	3.92	54.5	3.4	13.0	11.6	5.2
3.8	1.92	9.7	-0.11	3.1	0.7	0.66	6.67	3.85	77.2	6.0	66.2	10.8	2.6
8.9	0.57	1.4	0.14	6.9	0.6	1.15	6.78	4.20	62.3	6.8	92.1	10.1	8.4
8.7	0.53	2.2	0.05	4.5	0.1	0.73	6.18	4.57	77.5	4.4	57.9	14.5	4.0
9.1	0.43	1.6	-0.01	3.2	0.1	0.31	3.07	2.94	82.2	6.8	99.8	9.6	5.2
8.3	0.00	0.0	-0.06	8.2	5.6	1.35	18.54	4.03	48.9	2.0	30.7	25.3	5.6
8.7	0.00	0.0	0.00	0.0	-0.6	-1.52	-5.03	3.40	112.2	4.9	143.4	32.0	0.0
4.5	0.74	5.6	0.43	6.1	0.6	1.33	14.81	4.48	56.8	1.0	14.0	31.2	6.5
8.6	0.30	0.9	0.16	5.0	0.6	0.81	5.76	4.05	74.0	6.3	46.3	3.3	8.0
3.8	1.15	8.7	0.05	5.6	0.2	0.98	10.92	4.16	60.3	3.4	7.3	11.1	3.7
7.9	1.18	3.2	-0.66	7.3	0.2	1.20	6.29	4.32	62.2	5.2	43.4	9.1	7.0
7.7	1.27	3.2	0.21	4.0	0.5	0.80	6.56	2.32	58.5	9.1	265.1	6.4	6.9
7.6	0.93	3.8	0.22	5.4	2.1	1.06	8.90	3.75	80.2	5.1	36.1	7.6	7.4
5.1	0.91	4.7	0.31	4.2	1.1	0.74	7.63	3.32	74.0	4.1	55.9	18.5	4.9
3.9	2.30	13.1	0.71	0.3	0.0	-0.12	-1.17	3.83	111.0	6.5	104.0	11.6	0.5
5.3	0.80	5.0	0.42	7.1	2.2	1.11	10.92	4.31	55.7	3.2	46.8	21.5	5.1
4.9	0.54	4.4	0.73	4.3	0.3	0.45	4.37	3.37	69.8	1.1	27.9	45.5	5.3
6.1	0.14	1.5	0.00	9.4	18.9	1.35	11.31	2.90	24.9	0.4	1.5	54.2	9.7
4.0	1.78	12.1	0.05	3.8	0.1	0.85	8.80	5.09	70.6	1.4	29.9	33.7	1.2
3.8	0.86	9.2	0.48	4.5	38.5	0.64	9.18	2.70	69.5	1.2	15.6	29.8	5.5
3.9	1.03	9.0	0.10	8.6	1.6	2.00	23.95	4.88	64.7	2.9	22.6	15.3	6.4
8.2	0.29	1.2	0.01	6.3	0.4	1.27	10.02	4.46	57.4	5.9	43.0	4.4	6.9
8.6	0.02	0.1	-0.10	9.7	1.0	2.32	15.01	5.01	53.9	2.4	31.7	20.5	9.1
5.5	0.43	2.2	0.36	4.5	0.3	0.87	8.02	4.32	73.2	6.3	54.2	4.6	6.1
4.4	1.41	6.2	0.15	9.7	0.9	2.32	19.42	4.88	51.5	4.7	36.9	10.7	4.3
8.5	0.14	0.7	0.14	6.3	0.8	1.63	16.97	4.02	65.4	3.5	9.2	11.1	5.1
6.7	0.58	3.3	0.00	6.8	0.7	1.64	19.12	3.86	60.3	2.8	13.2	14.9	5.2
6.0	1.55	5.7	0.00	2.5	0.0	0.07	0.50	4.12	95.6	4.3	20.1	7.2	4.0
3.9	1.08	7.2	0.18	7.0	0.1	1.30	12.44	4.97	61.5	3.3	48.6	17.9	3.1
9.6	1.43	1.8	-0.08	7.5	0.4	1.56	8.78	3.48	38.5	1.3	16.4	27.9	7.5
2.4	2.65	15.4	0.76	7.3	0.5	1.85	17.44	3.86	52.7	2.1	29.1	22.6	6.3
7.4	0.96	2.8	-0.11	10.0	1.0	1.94	13.52	4.88	48.5	3.4	28.2	14.1	9.6
7.3	0.07	0.5	0.06	5.7	0.5	1.07	11.06	5.14	65.1	2.0	40.3	34.9	2.7
5.1	1.81	9.4	-0.30	7.2	0.4	1.80	18.77	5.41	67.7	4.2	27.3	9.7	5.3
9.2	0.55	1.4	0.02	4.7	0.3	1.08	12.09	3.10	71.8	7.1	120.0	10.3	6.5
3.3	2.04	15.6	0.09	5.1	0.7	1.21	14.32	5.40	77.7	3.4	19.6	12.4	4.7
7.7	0.28	1.9	0.02	6.2	0.6	1.36	13.29	4.06	65.0	5.0	27.6	4.3	7.3
3.6	0.96	8.8	0.74	3.5	0.8	0.57	7.48	4.33	74.9	1.3	8.7	25.5	3.2
8.3	0.49	2.8	0.15	8.0	0.6	1.33	10.33	3.72	47.6	4.2	31.9	11.4	8.1
7.1	0.40	2.3	0.53	2.9	0.2	0.54	6.17	3.90	85.5	3.6	16.6	11.2	3.7
7.0	0.30	2.2	0.10	5.2	2.0	0.85	8.96	4.12	81.1	3.9	15.4	9.4	5.6
7.7	0.31	2.3	0.00	3.2	0.1	0.56	4.64	4.10	88.9	1.9	6.4	18.6	3.8
8.2	0.49	2.3	0.06	4.9	0.9	1.13	11.49	3.26	59.3	2.9	42.4	22.9	5.9
7.2	1.32	6.2	0.00	2.6	0.0	-0.06	-0.52	3.09	86.2	7.5	264.1	15.2	5.3
5.7	1.23	6.3	0.37	4.5	0.1	0.59	7.68	4.65	79.9	4.1	59.9	17.7	2.5
8.7	0.00	0.0	0.00	0.4	0.1	0.13	1.36	3.36	89.2	5.0	48.1	11.8	0.0
4.8	1.06	8.2	0.25	7.1	3.7	1.15	13.12	4.63	67.2	4.4	67.0	18.7	5.3
7.7	0.28	2.0	-0.05	3.9	0.8	0.62	6.36	3.46	75.9	2.6	26.5	17.5	5.4
8.0	0.42	2.0	0.16	8.8	3.3	2.36	28.54	4.01	58.4	7.9	117.2	5.6	6.3
2.9	1.42	13.1	0.03	10.0	3.8	1.79	21.16	5.24	40.5	4.8	14.8	3.5	6.8

Name	City	State	Weiss Safety Rating	2003 Weiss Safety Rating	2002 Weiss Safety Rating	Total Assets ($Mil)	One Year Asset Growth	Asset Mix (As a % of Total Assets) Comm-ercial Loans	Cons-umer Loans	Home Mort-gages	Secur-ities	Capital-ization Index	Leverage Ratio	Risk-based Capital Ratio
▲ COMMUNITY B&TC	TULSA	OK	C	D+	C+	167.9	15.89	16.4	5.4	8.2	2.4	4.0	8.3	10.5
▲ COMMUNITY B&TC	CLARKS SUMMIT	PA	B	B-	B-	516.3	0.88	8.3	4.7	24.1	19.0	6.4	8.5	12.1
COMMUNITY B&TC	SHEBOYGAN	WI	C	C	C-	369.2	20.73	18.3	2.0	12.4	13.4	4.7	8.7	10.9
COMMUNITY B&TC ALABAMA	UNION SPRINGS	AL	B-	B-	B-	55.8	-0.12	8.4	9.8	17.6	23.1	9.9	11.0	16.5
COMMUNITY B&TC OF	ASHLAND CITY	TN	B-	C+	B-	111.9	23.77	14.7	6.4	17.7	23.4	6.1	8.3	11.8
COMMUNITY B&TC OF SE	ENTERPRISE	AL	B-	B-	B	236.3	11.78	9.8	3.2	15.6	15.4	4.0	7.6	10.5
▲ COMMUNITY B&TC-TROUP	LAGRANGE	GA	B	B-	B-	101.0	19.40	2.5	2.0	15.5	12.7	6.2	8.2	12.1
▲ COMMUNITY BANK	CABOT	AR	C	D+	C-	329.1	7.94	9.8	3.1	24.4	27.4	6.3	8.3	14.4
COMMUNITY BANK OF	BRADENTON	FL	C-	C-	D+	151.1	25.78	17.3	1.5	3.8	7.5	4.5	7.4	10.5
COMMUNITY BANKERS BK	MIDLOTHIAN	VA	C-	C-	C-	107.9	1.31	5.0	1.4	0.8	16.9	5.9	7.9	19.0
▲ COMMUNITY BANKS	MILLERSBURG	PA	B	B-	B-	1,952.3	6.46	13.0	4.5	17.2	33.2	5.1	7.6	11.1
▲ COMMUNITY BANKS OF CO	CRIPPLE CREEK	CO	C+	C+	C+	567.9	31.78	11.2	1.9	23.6	3.3	4.7	9.4	10.8
▲ COMMUNITY BANKS OF	TRACY	CA	C+	C+	NR	102.0	4.65	4.3	0.5	12.0	7.8	8.9	10.3	14.2
▲ COMMUNITY BK	BLOUNTSVILLE	AL	D+	D	D+	542.1	-1.67	8.8	10.1	25.6	29.1	6.3	8.3	15.1
COMMUNITY BK	PASADENA	CA	B+	B+	B+	1,782.7	20.59	22.1	0.7	0.1	31.8	6.5	8.5	12.2
▼ COMMUNITY BK	SANTA MARIA	CA	D	D+	D	62.6	34.20	17.4	4.9	3.1	7.9	3.3	8.3	10.2
▲ COMMUNITY BK	LOGANVILLE	GA	D+	C	B-	277.7	11.96	2.9	1.1	9.5	7.8	7.2	11.9	12.7
COMMUNITY BK	ALTON	IA	C	C	C	34.6	2.31	26.5	5.1	15.2	2.8	7.4	9.5	12.8
▼ COMMUNITY BK	DUNLAP	IA	C	C+	B-	61.2	-2.22	4.2	4.2	11.5	20.9	6.9	8.9	13.8
COMMUNITY BK	MUSCATINE	IA	B+	B+	B	109.0	4.09	9.3	10.5	25.5	24.7	7.8	9.5	15.7
COMMUNITY BK	NEVADA	IA	B-	B-	B-	78.9	11.58	3.0	0.6	16.8	19.8	7.6	9.4	14.4
▲ COMMUNITY BK	GLEN ELLYN	IL	C	C-	C-	231.8	2.14	11.2	1.0	8.2	19.3	5.7	7.7	11.8
▲ COMMUNITY BK	HOOPESTON	IL	C+	C	C-	71.4	-7.49	18.1	3.5	13.9	41.6	7.8	9.5	18.7
▲ COMMUNITY BK	PITTSFIELD	IL	C-	D+	C+	30.4	-22.74	8.3	3.4	10.9	41.0	10.0	11.5	20.5
COMMUNITY BK	WINSLOW	IL	A-	A-	A-	80.6	1.58	8.5	3.0	16.8	24.2	10.0	13.1	19.0
COMMUNITY BK	NOBLESVILLE	IN	B+	B+	B+	198.0	13.25	8.6	2.3	17.6	1.9	8.6	11.8	13.9
COMMUNITY BK	LIBERAL	KS	C	C	C	58.0	14.98	14.0	3.9	1.8	35.7	6.9	8.9	15.2
COMMUNITY BK	MANSFIELD	LA	C+	C	C	108.4	4.54	5.9	6.8	12.8	37.9	6.3	8.3	15.8
▼ COMMUNITY BK	RACELAND	LA	C-	C+	C+	179.6	2.31	22.9	5.6	23.6	2.8	8.3	9.8	14.3
COMMUNITY BK	CARO	MI	C-	D+	C-	84.4	-13.25	2.9	2.6	28.0	37.8	6.2	8.3	20.6
COMMUNITY BK	AUSTIN	MN	C	NR	NR	20.7	N/A	19.3	7.5	2.0	5.3	10.0	24.5	36.1
COMMUNITY BK	MEMPHIS	MO	B-	C+	C+	29.2	-5.97	7.8	5.0	14.2	44.8	6.4	8.4	16.6
COMMUNITY BK	AMORY	MS	C+	B-	B-	143.7	-1.98	2.5	4.0	18.0	54.4	4.2	6.2	16.2
COMMUNITY BK	INDIANOLA	MS	B-	B-	C+	93.4	4.21	3.6	6.2	18.1	15.5	5.9	8.1	11.7
COMMUNITY BK	RONAN	MT	B	B	B-	97.9	5.94	23.1	6.4	6.9	24.1	8.5	10.0	15.5
▼ COMMUNITY BK	PILOT MOUNTAIN	NC	B	A	A-	319.2	32.03	5.2	4.5	12.8	23.5	8.5	10.0	15.1
COMMUNITY BK	ALMA	NE	B-	B-	C+	44.3	6.51	13.4	7.4	14.0	21.6	9.4	10.6	15.3
▲ COMMUNITY BK	SANTA FE	NM	C+	C	C-	141.7	6.82	32.3	2.4	12.0	13.0	5.6	7.8	11.5
▼ COMMUNITY BK	CROOKSVILLE	OH	C	C+	C+	133.8	10.83	3.0	20.7	34.7	23.7	5.3	7.3	12.9
COMMUNITY BK	BRISTOW	OK	B	B	B-	54.7	6.69	6.6	7.0	22.6	10.7	5.1	7.1	13.1
COMMUNITY BK	JOSEPH	OR	C+	C	C-	274.9	9.20	20.8	2.3	5.3	28.5	5.8	7.8	12.9
COMMUNITY BK	AVON	SD	B-	B-	B-	39.6	11.27	3.8	4.0	1.2	57.0	10.0	14.5	31.4
▼ COMMUNITY BK	LEXINGTON	TN	B-	B	B	57.6	2.88	10.8	11.8	19.4	38.6	9.0	10.4	19.0
COMMUNITY BK	GRANBURY	TX	B+	B+	B+	336.6	-0.10	8.7	5.3	14.2	19.3	6.7	8.7	14.7
COMMUNITY BK	LONGVIEW	TX	C+	C	C	57.8	1.05	9.9	13.0	35.1	0.0	5.0	7.0	12.5
▲ COMMUNITY BK	WELLINGTON	TX	D+	E+	D-	54.8	31.75	18.6	7.8	11.8	10.3	6.7	8.7	12.9
COMMUNITY BK	STAUNTON	VA	B-	B-	B	359.6	15.69	6.2	11.7	33.2	11.7	5.0	7.5	11.0
COMMUNITY BK	SUPERIOR	WI	C	C	C-	78.6	5.67	9.0	3.8	30.8	25.7	7.8	9.5	16.8
COMMUNITY BK BOONE	BOONE	IA	C+	C+	C	133.4	12.80	9.4	2.2	15.7	20.1	3.9	7.4	10.4
COMMUNITY BK CAMERON	CAMERON	WI	C+	C	C	65.7	21.59	21.2	3.1	47.6	4.1	5.3	7.3	11.6
▲ COMMUNITY BK CENTRAL WI	COLBY	WI	C-	C+	B-	93.0	-0.12	27.0	2.9	14.1	12.3	9.2	10.5	14.8
COMMUNITY BK CORP	CHASKA	MN	D+	D	D	68.7	30.49	9.3	6.7	9.3	7.9	2.9	10.3	9.9
▼ COMMUNITY BK DELAVAN	DELAVAN	WI	C+	B-	B-	154.6	7.72	9.6	2.1	14.0	30.9	5.3	7.3	11.9
▼ COMMUNITY BK DESOTO CTY	SOUTHAVEN	MS	C+	B-	C+	169.0	17.58	4.2	2.5	15.0	8.8	3.2	7.9	10.1
COMMUNITY BK ELLISVILLE MS	ELLISVILLE	MS	B-	B-	C+	348.6	4.41	4.6	8.8	21.8	14.5	5.6	7.6	11.4
COMMUNITY BK ELMHURST	ELMHURST	IL	C+	C+	C+	123.0	4.09	12.2	0.6	6.7	52.1	5.3	7.7	11.2
▼ COMMUNITY BK FINANCIAL	OCONTO FALLS	WI	B-	B	B	86.0	7.49	20.4	4.4	7.4	13.4	4.8	8.6	10.9
COMMUNITY BK GALESBURG	GALESBURG	IL	B-	C+	C+	42.7	-4.28	11.8	2.9	20.2	34.0	9.4	10.6	21.1
▲ COMMUNITY BK LEMONT	LEMONT	IL	C+	D+	D+	41.2	24.67	6.9	8.5	7.9	17.4	10.0	12.6	16.7
COMMUNITY BK MA CO-OP BK	BROCKTON	MA	B-	C+	C	258.3	10.91	2.4	0.4	45.7	11.2	6.8	8.8	14.8
▲ COMMUNITY BK MERIDIAN MS	MERIDIAN	MS	B-	C+	C+	124.1	12.55	3.4	4.4	23.2	25.0	5.5	7.5	12.4
COMMUNITY BK MISSOULA	MISSOULA	MT	B	B	B-	61.2	9.30	13.3	4.6	12.3	13.1	5.9	8.9	11.7
COMMUNITY BK MN VALLEY	JORDAN	MN	C-	C-	C+	107.0	25.18	26.5	7.2	13.8	12.8	2.9	7.4	9.9
▲ COMMUNITY BK MO	RICHMOND	MO	C+	C	C-	36.1	30.44	32.1	3.6	17.0	6.9	6.4	8.9	12.1

Asset Quality Index	Non-Performing Loans as a % of Total Loans	Non-Performing Loans as a % of Capital	Net Charge-offs Avg Loans	Profitability Index	Net Income ($Mil)	Return on Assets (R.O.A.)	Return on Equity (R.O.E.)	Net Interest Spread	Overhead Efficiency Ratio	Liquidity Index	Liquidity Ratio	Hot Money Ratio	Stability Index
2.8	1.43	6.1	0.04	2.8	0.2	0.19	1.76	1.30	74.1	3.5	49.2	19.8	4.8
5.8	0.49	3.9	0.08	4.9	2.3	0.90	10.17	3.79	68.9	6.1	53.3	7.0	5.8
4.7	1.28	10.3	0.06	3.1	0.7	0.42	4.66	3.33	85.1	1.0	10.5	30.1	3.6
3.2	3.00	15.8	-0.13	8.2	0.5	1.61	15.02	5.38	60.0	3.3	52.2	21.9	5.8
6.1	0.49	4.0	0.22	4.8	0.5	0.85	10.62	4.01	62.1	1.1	26.2	34.8	5.4
6.6	0.43	4.1	0.25	8.3	1.6	1.42	19.72	4.37	50.0	1.5	12.3	23.9	6.2
8.7	0.05	0.4	0.03	6.4	0.5	1.16	14.15	4.52	64.5	5.3	101.3	18.7	5.6
2.1	2.56	8.9	-0.41	3.3	1.6	0.96	6.69	4.35	72.6	1.8	23.8	22.5	5.2
2.6	1.44	13.5	0.17	4.1	0.5	0.68	9.63	3.28	59.1	5.0	73.9	16.9	3.2
9.2	0.41	1.5	0.03	3.2	0.2	0.41	5.49	2.63	79.7	7.6	63.7	0.0	2.2
6.8	0.54	3.8	0.09	5.1	10.2	1.07	13.30	3.49	64.4	5.5	36.8	8.7	6.7
6.7	0.06	0.6	0.25	7.7	2.5	1.01	11.46	3.71	60.1	2.1	28.7	21.9	5.6
5.0	0.58	2.9	0.00	4.8	0.4	0.81	5.96	4.23	76.3	4.7	96.6	23.1	3.9
1.8	3.68	20.7	2.77	2.0	0.9	0.34	4.12	4.23	88.0	6.9	151.9	14.5	2.6
7.7	0.50	3.3	0.11	7.8	9.8	1.17	13.76	4.22	54.3	3.9	52.9	22.0	7.0
8.2	0.00	0.0	0.00	2.7	0.2	0.60	7.05	4.67	85.1	4.7	57.0	14.4	0.0
2.5	0.66	4.3	0.45	10.0	3.4	2.51	21.51	6.26	36.3	1.2	12.5	28.6	7.4
6.7	0.15	1.3	0.03	5.7	0.2	1.18	12.34	4.79	73.1	3.7	8.7	9.7	4.2
3.6	1.08	5.3	1.47	2.8	0.1	0.33	2.75	4.35	70.1	5.2	35.2	6.3	5.2
6.6	0.23	1.1	0.09	5.5	0.6	1.17	8.46	3.93	62.8	4.0	40.6	15.0	7.7
7.7	0.00	0.0	0.00	7.0	0.4	1.09	12.03	2.93	40.4	5.4	61.9	11.7	5.5
5.5	0.52	4.3	-0.09	5.3	1.2	1.02	13.70	4.24	65.5	4.5	24.2	6.7	2.7
4.3	2.71	13.1	0.09	4.3	0.4	1.10	11.98	3.79	72.1	5.7	43.5	6.0	3.6
5.5	3.43	15.8	0.00	4.2	0.2	1.00	9.97	3.15	53.1	8.6	255.3	9.3	2.2
5.6	1.26	6.2	-0.07	7.9	0.6	1.45	11.13	4.18	50.5	4.1	19.1	8.6	7.2
6.1	0.29	2.0	0.01	9.8	1.6	1.58	13.90	5.36	51.5	4.0	17.5	8.7	8.0
4.3	1.59	8.5	0.05	4.6	0.2	0.80	9.14	3.61	72.4	2.5	35.7	23.5	3.7
6.3	0.43	2.6	0.12	5.7	0.8	1.34	17.17	4.69	71.8	2.8	19.9	15.4	3.7
1.6	3.63	25.8	0.19	8.8	1.3	1.41	14.57	5.41	60.5	4.6	51.7	14.7	5.9
7.7	0.72	3.5	0.14	2.9	0.2	0.56	6.60	3.39	85.3	6.4	61.7	5.7	3.0
6.9	0.00	0.0	0.00	0.0	-0.1	-1.50	-3.77	0.30	210.0	9.2	218.9	5.7	0.0
7.8	0.20	0.8	0.07	4.1	0.1	0.63	5.56	2.89	63.6	5.8	47.8	6.4	5.8
4.1	2.29	8.0	0.22	1.8	-0.2	-0.22	-2.13	1.47	89.3	2.2	32.2	24.4	5.7
7.8	0.23	1.9	0.03	5.7	0.4	0.92	10.78	4.22	65.6	2.1	26.8	20.9	5.0
3.8	2.03	11.5	-0.09	5.2	0.6	1.27	12.48	5.26	74.6	5.5	41.0	7.1	5.4
6.9	0.15	0.3	0.00	9.2	1.9	1.29	6.26	4.70	54.5	1.5	16.9	25.2	5.7
7.3	0.43	2.6	0.41	8.0	0.4	1.86	17.42	3.84	47.1	2.5	33.2	20.2	4.2
3.6	0.82	4.1	0.02	3.4	0.5	0.71	6.10	4.34	82.7	4.2	33.2	11.9	5.1
5.0	0.37	3.2	0.93	3.3	0.3	0.42	5.58	3.95	74.6	3.4	13.6	11.9	3.0
5.1	0.95	7.0	-0.07	9.8	0.4	1.58	23.17	4.79	58.4	6.3	86.1	10.6	5.3
5.2	0.50	3.8	0.22	5.3	2.0	1.45	19.93	4.26	67.7	5.7	50.2	9.0	3.6
8.5	0.78	1.9	0.03	4.9	0.2	1.10	7.64	4.06	56.0	4.8	49.1	12.3	4.9
5.1	1.47	7.7	0.04	4.9	0.3	0.95	8.96	3.87	66.8	2.1	15.2	18.7	4.8
6.7	0.25	1.8	0.15	8.9	3.5	2.08	23.97	4.82	63.8	4.8	31.2	7.6	6.5
7.9	0.05	0.4	0.15	9.2	0.6	2.23	32.01	5.62	66.3	5.0	37.0	8.5	4.1
5.3	0.55	4.3	-0.01	2.5	-0.1	-0.27	-2.82	4.09	99.0	3.5	56.6	20.4	2.5
4.6	0.73	7.1	0.20	5.6	1.7	1.00	12.42	3.91	63.1	1.6	15.0	23.6	4.8
2.9	3.09	19.2	0.85	6.1	0.5	1.18	12.45	4.24	57.1	3.0	17.2	14.0	4.2
6.7	0.67	6.1	0.20	4.3	0.6	0.94	12.58	3.30	59.5	0.7	13.2	37.5	4.3
7.8	0.23	2.5	0.00	8.3	0.6	1.94	27.88	4.43	53.9	2.7	31.0	18.5	4.0
2.9	2.36	11.6	0.22	4.6	0.4	0.83	6.27	3.54	73.8	2.4	30.4	19.7	6.5
8.4	0.00	0.0	0.00	3.3	0.1	0.44	4.45	4.77	80.4	3.1	25.0	14.5	0.0
8.3	0.24	1.8	0.00	6.2	0.8	1.05	14.22	3.80	58.8	2.0	12.7	18.9	3.4
4.3	0.61	5.8	0.03	4.6	0.7	0.84	10.77	4.31	63.9	2.5	34.5	21.7	5.2
4.1	1.12	10.1	0.04	7.7	2.1	1.25	16.10	4.09	53.9	2.9	34.0	18.7	5.4
5.8	1.58	8.8	0.22	3.4	0.4	0.66	8.70	3.27	77.7	3.9	23.9	10.3	3.8
7.2	0.18	1.6	0.09	5.3	0.4	0.81	9.37	4.44	74.5	4.1	41.8	14.7	6.5
9.0	0.17	0.7	0.02	5.5	0.2	1.09	10.38	4.34	69.6	3.8	51.0	18.1	4.8
7.8	0.31	1.6	1.13	3.5	0.1	0.45	3.45	4.88	77.7	3.4	25.4	13.2	3.0
7.0	0.28	2.5	0.04	4.4	0.8	0.68	7.59	3.84	73.6	4.8	20.7	3.9	4.1
6.6	0.57	4.7	0.03	4.0	0.4	0.69	9.10	3.60	68.9	2.2	14.2	17.7	5.0
7.2	0.00	0.0	0.22	8.8	0.6	2.19	24.63	4.90	55.7	3.4	55.7	21.4	6.4
7.5	0.13	1.2	0.02	2.9	0.2	0.45	5.61	4.53	83.9	1.9	15.1	19.5	3.7
7.9	0.13	1.2	0.00	6.7	0.3	1.80	20.82	4.58	57.5	2.6	42.1	26.4	0.5

Name	City	State	Weiss Safety Rating	2003 Weiss Safety Rating	2002 Weiss Safety Rating	Total Assets ($Mil)	One Year Asset Growth	Asset Mix (As a % of Total Assets)				Capital-ization Index	Leverage Ratio	Risk-based Capital Ratio
								Comm-ercial Loans	Cons-umer Loans	Home Mort-gages	Secur-ities			
▲ COMMUNITY BK NA	SUMMERSVILLE	MO	B-	C+	C	37.1	2.65	9.6	11.1	14.1	12.0	8.1	9.8	14.3
COMMUNITY BK NA	CANTON	NY	B	B	B	4,346.9	29.55	8.4	11.3	20.9	35.0	5.0	7.0	12.7
▼ COMMUNITY BK NA	CARMICHAELS	PA	C+	B-	B+	314.1	17.38	8.3	19.3	18.4	15.7	4.9	6.9	11.1
▼ COMMUNITY BK NORTHERN	STERLING	VA	C	C+	C+	869.9	21.58	6.4	18.7	3.3	24.2	4.9	6.9	11.4
COMMUNITY BK OELWEIN	OELWEIN	IA	B	B	B	40.0	-3.98	11.8	10.4	16.6	3.8	5.4	7.8	11.3
▼ COMMUNITY BK OF BERGEN	MAYWOOD	NJ	B+	A-	A-	235.0	4.04	0.6	1.4	42.9	28.7	9.7	10.8	19.1
▲ COMMUNITY BK OF BROWARD	DANIA	FL	D	D-	D-	179.8	63.91	5.6	1.3	2.7	15.7	7.2	11.1	12.7
▲ COMMUNITY BK OF CENTRAL	SALINAS	CA	B	B-	C+	1,043.0	10.45	13.5	1.0	2.1	16.7	5.7	8.6	11.5
COMMUNITY BK OF EAST TN	CLINTON	TN	C	C	C	69.4	6.48	9.4	19.0	10.8	31.1	6.4	8.4	13.4
COMMUNITY BK OF EASTON	EASTON	IL	B-	B-	B-	20.3	9.28	4.8	6.8	7.1	20.5	10.0	11.8	25.8
▲ COMMUNITY BK OF EL	EL DORADO SPRING	MO	A-	B+	B+	67.6	5.23	4.3	4.2	20.1	28.0	10.0	11.3	20.5
COMMUNITY BK OF FLORIDA	HOMESTEAD	FL	C	C	C-	417.9	12.31	8.3	4.0	5.1	24.2	2.9	7.9	9.9
COMMUNITY BK OF GEORGIA	BAXLEY	GA	D	NR	NR	9.6	N/A	0.4	0.7	3.4	0.0	10.0	67.7	145.3
▲ COMMUNITY BK OF	CHICAGO	IL	D	E-	E-	40.1	-20.87	14.2	5.6	7.7	8.3	6.4	8.4	13.5
▲ COMMUNITY BK OF MARION	OCALA	FL	B	B-	B-	215.4	13.82	7.7	1.6	11.7	19.0	6.0	8.0	12.2
COMMUNITY BK OF MARSHALL	MARSHALL	MO	C+	C+	C+	66.1	1.06	6.6	8.3	17.2	23.8	6.8	8.8	14.7
COMMUNITY BK OF	FOREST	MS	C+	C+	C+	522.1	10.66	6.2	4.7	13.6	17.7	3.8	7.4	10.4
▲ COMMUNITY BK OF N AR	FAYETTEVILLE	AR	B-	C+	C+	212.0	0.43	8.5	3.0	13.0	3.7	7.6	10.4	13.0
▲ COMMUNITY BK OF NAPLES	NAPLES	FL	B	B-	B-	267.1	18.34	6.6	1.4	21.9	7.5	4.6	7.6	10.8
COMMUNITY BK OF NEVADA	LAS VEGAS	NV	B	B-	D+	575.0	28.21	11.2	0.5	2.5	12.1	6.3	8.3	12.4
COMMUNITY BK OF NJ	FREEHOLD	NJ	C	C	B-	376.9	-3.16	4.2	0.6	5.1	30.5	3.9	7.2	10.5
COMMUNITY BK OF ORANGE	MIDDLETOWN	NY	D	D	D	22.3	44.49	13.9	4.4	4.8	22.2	10.0	13.9	23.8
▼ COMMUNITY BK OF PETTIS	SEDALIA	MO	C	C+	C+	117.8	-6.93	4.0	1.7	11.9	40.3	6.5	8.5	16.0
▲ COMMUNITY BK OF RAYMORE	RAYMORE	MO	C	C+	C	79.1	1.41	24.4	2.7	11.9	10.9	2.8	7.2	9.8
▲ COMMUNITY BK OF ROCKIES	LA JARA	CO	C	C	B-	180.3	4.12	9.9	6.0	11.1	3.0	6.5	9.1	12.1
▲ COMMUNITY BK OF SAN	STOCKTON	CA	B-	C+	D+	105.5	27.75	15.2	1.1	4.9	17.9	8.2	9.8	14.1
COMMUNITY BK OF SHELL	SHELL KNOB	MO	E-	E-	E-	16.4	4.97	11.5	13.8	11.7	0.0	3.7	6.6	10.4
COMMUNITY BK OF SMITH CTY	CARTHAGE	TN	B-	B-	B-	76.1	24.32	8.6	25.4	31.3	13.0	6.0	8.0	12.0
▲ COMMUNITY BK OF SULLIVAN	MONTICELLO	NY	C+	C	C	68.6	7.73	22.3	5.3	3.7	14.8	7.2	9.7	12.6
▲ COMMUNITY BK OF THE BAY	OAKLAND	CA	D-	E-	E-	38.1	-10.43	10.7	3.4	7.3	33.8	10.0	18.1	34.4
▲ COMMUNITY BK OF THE	JAMESTOWN	TN	C-	D	D-	61.8	1.04	8.3	17.4	21.0	12.8	8.2	9.8	14.3
COMMUNITY BK OF THE	GREAT BEND	KS	C-	D+	E-	53.1	-0.49	33.3	12.2	7.7	10.9	6.3	9.2	12.0
COMMUNITY BK OF THE	MERRITT ISLAND	FL	B-	C+	C	74.5	16.88	9.4	1.7	0.6	29.5	8.3	9.9	16.7
COMMUNITY BK OF THE	SMYRNA	GA	C	C	C	200.4	36.15	10.5	3.1	9.1	13.3	3.5	8.1	10.2
▼ COMMUNITY BK OF TRENTON	TRENTON	IL	B+	A-	B	53.5	0.35	5.5	3.7	29.2	27.6	10.0	14.2	21.5
▲ COMMUNITY BK OF TRI-CTY	WALDORF	MD	B-	B	B	394.8	31.27	12.0	1.0	14.0	25.2	4.2	7.5	10.6
COMMUNITY BK OF WEST	VILLA RICA	GA	D	D	NR	55.6	128.34	15.3	1.7	17.0	14.5	10.0	15.5	19.5
▲ COMMUNITY BK OF WICHITA	WICHITA	KS	D+	C-	C	29.1	9.56	15.2	14.9	11.3	9.2	7.4	9.6	12.8
▲ COMMUNITY BK OWATONNA	OWATONNA	MN	C-	D	NR	24.2	104.23	10.9	1.9	7.6	29.2	10.0	14.6	20.8
▲ COMMUNITY BK OZARKS	SUNRISE BEACH	MO	C-	D+	D+	70.2	6.31	9.1	5.2	28.7	16.1	5.2	7.2	12.5
COMMUNITY BK	PARKERSBURG	WV	B	B	B	179.2	1.74	5.2	10.4	43.7	24.8	6.8	8.8	16.4
COMMUNITY BK PICKENS	JASPER	GA	B	B	C-	139.9	43.82	13.0	5.8	24.8	17.2	6.9	9.2	12.4
COMMUNITY BK PLYMOUTH	PLYMOUTH	MN	D	D-	E-	47.1	10.28	29.2	3.1	8.1	0.1	4.1	9.4	10.5
COMMUNITY BK	CHICAGO	IL	D	D-	D-	244.4	19.95	7.9	0.4	9.8	15.8	4.3	7.9	10.6
COMMUNITY BK RED RIVER	E GRAND FORKS	MN	B+	B+	B+	218.2	96.66	14.1	8.5	7.1	21.2	5.9	8.0	11.7
COMMUNITY BK	RUSSELLVILLE	MO	B+	B+	B+	46.9	2.64	1.3	7.7	19.3	41.6	10.0	16.7	31.0
▼ COMMUNITY BK SOUTHERN IN	NEW ALBANY	IN	C+	B-	B	555.0	25.27	14.6	1.2	17.4	17.2	4.0	7.9	10.5
▲ COMMUNITY BK SPRING	SPRING GREEN	WI	C+	C	C-	72.4	0.77	9.0	9.3	24.7	4.3	6.8	8.8	12.3
COMMUNITY BK TX NA	GRAND PRAIRIE	TX	D	D	D	43.6	-3.10	18.6	4.2	5.3	24.3	10.0	12.4	17.4
COMMUNITY BK VERNON	VERNON CENTER	MN	C+	C+	C	91.7	4.48	6.1	5.4	20.3	17.7	6.6	8.6	12.7
COMMUNITY BK WINSTED	WINSTED	MN	C-	C-	C+	42.2	1.08	16.6	5.2	13.0	24.6	6.8	8.8	13.8
▲ COMMUNITY BK-DEARBORN	DEARBORN	MI	C+	C	C	472.4	23.08	5.2	0.9	14.5	2.7	4.1	9.4	10.6
COMMUNITY BK-SHELBY CTY	COWDEN	IL	B-	B-	B-	61.4	-2.25	12.0	1.4	6.9	57.0	8.0	9.6	23.0
COMMUNITY BKG CO	FITZGERALD	GA	B-	B-	B-	79.6	2.19	21.5	10.6	17.6	16.4	8.1	9.7	14.8
COMMUNITY BKS OF	ROCKY FORD	CO	C	C	C+	108.7	-13.71	7.5	3.3	21.2	10.8	5.7	7.7	13.4
COMMUNITY BUSINESS BK	SAUK CITY	WI	C	C-	C	46.5	-0.14	14.0	2.1	15.6	16.3	7.8	9.8	13.2
COMMUNITY CAPITAL BK	JONESBORO	GA	D	D	D	64.3	96.07	14.4	0.8	1.6	9.6	10.0	14.3	15.9
▼ COMMUNITY CAPITAL BK	BROOKLYN	NY	D-	D+	D+	146.2	32.69	32.0	0.0	1.0	30.1	3.2	5.2	10.5
▼ COMMUNITY CENTRAL BK	MT CLEMENS	MI	C+	B-	B-	413.2	28.03	10.2	3.1	18.4	13.7	5.5	8.0	11.4
COMMUNITY COMMERCE BK	LOS ANGELES	CA	A-	A	A-	250.1	6.44	0.0	0.1	7.2	0.0	8.8	11.5	14.0
COMMUNITY DEVELOPMENT	OGEMA	MN	D+	C-	E-	16.2	13.64	15.1	3.8	18.4	17.4	9.2	10.5	18.2
COMMUNITY FIRST B&TC	CELINA	OH	B-	B-	B-	655.1	-7.53	6.3	13.5	23.6	17.2	8.0	9.7	15.6
▲ COMMUNITY FIRST B&TC	COLUMBIA	TN	B-	C	C	243.5	35.60	10.2	4.1	22.6	12.8	6.2	9.3	11.9
▼ COMMUNITY FIRST BANK	MADISONVILLE	KY	E+	D-	E-	49.9	40.42	0.9	5.2	67.7	5.0	5.5	7.5	13.9

Asset Quality Index	Non-Performing Loans as a % of Total Loans	as a % of Capital	Net Charge-offs Avg Loans	Profitability Index	Net Income ($Mil)	Return on Assets (R.O.A.)	Return on Equity (R.O.E.)	Net Interest Spread	Overhead Efficiency Ratio	Liquidity Index	Liquidity Ratio	Hot Money Ratio	Stability Index
7.7	0.05	0.3	-0.02	7.7	0.2	1.24	12.84	6.12	69.6	3.7	31.2	13.4	4.3
5.5	0.52	2.3	0.34	6.8	25.1	1.25	10.25	4.59	59.9	4.3	9.4	6.0	8.2
4.6	0.53	3.8	0.18	3.7	0.6	0.41	4.67	3.66	80.3	5.7	44.7	6.7	4.3
2.5	1.90	18.3	0.08	5.8	4.1	1.00	14.66	3.87	49.0	3.5	41.2	17.7	3.9
4.2	1.26	11.2	0.50	4.3	0.2	0.71	9.40	3.59	63.4	2.8	47.2	26.7	4.7
7.6	0.47	2.5	0.02	5.3	1.0	0.85	7.70	4.61	71.4	6.4	56.3	6.0	7.1
7.6	0.00	0.0	0.00	0.8	0.1	0.14	1.39	4.14	87.0	4.3	12.4	6.2	0.0
5.1	1.22	9.3	0.00	7.5	6.5	1.26	15.17	4.42	52.8	4.9	93.1	22.9	7.7
5.5	0.46	3.0	1.86	4.3	0.2	0.45	5.28	4.52	65.2	7.0	105.7	9.0	3.8
8.5	0.00	0.0	0.00	6.4	0.1	1.15	10.00	2.66	38.5	8.3	153.1	5.7	4.7
8.7	0.16	0.8	0.06	8.3	0.7	2.15	18.78	3.52	37.5	4.6	43.7	12.9	7.3
4.5	0.88	7.2	0.39	6.1	2.4	1.21	15.49	4.59	68.5	3.6	37.6	16.3	4.2
10.0	0.00	0.0	0.00	0.0	-0.3	-7.29	-10.57	0.69	896.7	6.6	340.6	19.7	0.0
0.0	23.00	116.9	0.23	0.1	-0.2	-0.89	-9.95	4.76	116.7	5.2	47.2	10.1	3.5
8.6	0.00	0.0	0.00	5.6	1.1	1.01	12.75	4.03	61.8	6.0	53.6	8.2	4.6
7.4	0.28	1.8	0.22	6.5	0.4	1.15	13.04	3.83	59.3	5.2	39.0	8.5	4.2
6.6	0.35	3.2	0.31	6.0	2.5	0.98	13.45	4.06	59.7	1.8	18.6	21.1	4.9
4.1	0.35	2.3	0.33	8.2	1.6	1.43	12.33	5.11	50.4	2.1	22.8	19.2	5.9
6.6	0.27	2.6	0.07	9.5	2.0	1.56	20.45	4.00	38.1	1.1	12.6	29.6	5.8
6.7	0.72	4.9	-0.03	8.1	3.3	1.31	15.55	4.76	55.9	8.4	259.8	10.4	4.5
7.9	0.05	0.4	0.00	3.6	0.9	0.47	7.44	3.17	73.7	4.2	11.4	6.7	3.4
8.8	0.00	0.0	0.55	0.0	-0.7	-6.26	-40.46	2.96	244.8	5.7	105.8	14.7	0.0
5.3	0.98	5.6	0.46	4.7	0.7	1.14	13.58	3.42	68.4	3.9	42.0	16.1	2.9
8.3	0.01	0.1	-0.01	6.2	0.4	0.96	13.38	3.94	79.5	4.8	15.3	3.4	3.9
1.8	2.01	12.7	0.01	8.5	1.2	1.36	11.87	5.06	63.5	3.9	36.4	14.3	6.7
8.6	0.00	0.0	0.10	4.2	0.4	0.74	7.50	3.87	63.8	3.6	74.8	32.3	5.7
1.4	2.27	20.7	0.13	4.5	0.1	0.73	10.92	5.30	76.3	6.0	66.5	7.0	0.3
3.3	0.80	7.5	0.44	6.6	0.3	0.88	10.65	4.56	62.0	3.3	77.1	33.8	5.3
5.3	0.25	1.8	0.22	5.0	0.3	0.86	9.07	4.95	72.9	5.9	55.4	7.6	4.3
6.8	0.00	0.0	-0.38	0.0	-0.2	-1.08	-12.05	3.52	157.8	3.2	66.8	29.9	0.7
2.7	2.14	15.0	0.64	2.3	0.2	0.55	5.78	4.01	87.9	2.2	34.5	26.8	0.6
2.7	1.50	11.5	0.52	4.3	0.2	0.64	6.77	4.97	75.1	3.8	25.3	11.0	3.4
9.0	0.00	0.0	0.00	3.9	0.3	0.77	7.77	4.05	69.1	4.2	60.4	17.6	5.3
7.2	0.00	0.0	0.00	4.4	0.8	0.90	11.65	3.92	68.4	1.9	25.3	22.3	4.6
3.7	5.81	24.6	0.27	8.5	0.4	1.31	9.06	4.32	39.9	4.8	35.8	9.5	8.0
8.1	0.20	1.7	-0.01	4.7	1.8	0.94	12.79	3.53	66.7	3.5	11.4	11.2	4.0
8.5	0.00	0.0	0.00	0.0	-0.2	-0.90	-5.41	3.36	105.9	1.0	22.1	34.6	0.0
7.3	0.00	0.0	0.05	2.4	0.0	0.15	1.57	4.01	94.0	4.2	78.1	20.5	4.2
8.9	0.00	0.0	0.00	1.3	0.2	1.56	9.80	3.15	111.4	4.9	43.1	8.2	0.0
5.9	0.09	0.8	-0.06	6.8	0.4	1.25	17.81	4.70	61.0	2.8	38.2	20.9	2.3
8.2	0.18	1.3	0.10	7.4	1.0	1.16	13.49	4.36	61.5	4.1	26.5	9.8	5.1
7.2	0.38	3.0	0.03	7.6	0.9	1.46	15.78	4.41	44.4	1.2	16.7	29.1	3.8
8.3	0.00	0.0	0.02	4.4	0.3	1.49	16.39	4.50	62.5	0.7	11.9	42.0	0.0
1.1	2.80	23.8	0.07	6.2	1.3	1.11	13.61	4.18	53.8	0.8	16.8	42.9	4.2
4.8	0.43	2.2	0.04	9.6	1.7	1.48	12.39	4.91	57.5	4.6	22.0	5.7	7.7
7.7	0.01	0.0	0.20	8.6	0.3	1.44	8.41	4.41	48.5	4.8	23.5	4.7	7.2
5.8	0.64	5.8	0.06	4.1	2.0	0.73	9.41	2.91	62.3	2.7	18.8	15.8	4.8
5.2	0.68	4.7	0.18	4.9	0.3	0.74	7.20	3.78	72.7	2.3	34.4	25.6	4.9
5.7	1.90	10.4	0.16	0.0	0.0	-0.69	-5.54	3.09	103.0	3.5	72.8	29.1	0.0
3.9	1.56	11.7	0.18	6.3	0.8	1.63	19.10	4.03	61.9	6.7	87.1	8.0	4.2
3.7	1.80	9.2	0.02	7.6	0.3	1.59	14.60	4.26	81.6	3.3	30.6	15.2	6.1
4.8	0.40	3.6	-0.04	6.8	2.9	1.26	14.06	4.28	52.1	1.2	27.8	35.8	4.8
8.0	0.45	1.5	0.06	5.7	0.4	1.42	14.79	3.11	58.4	4.6	36.5	10.9	4.4
6.4	0.28	1.5	0.10	4.6	0.3	0.78	6.95	3.73	66.6	3.9	43.0	15.8	6.2
2.8	2.03	12.9	0.16	4.5	0.6	1.07	11.60	4.30	65.5	4.2	67.6	20.2	4.0
5.3	0.71	5.2	0.08	5.2	0.2	0.85	8.91	4.33	67.5	2.8	38.3	20.5	4.3
7.3	0.06	0.3	0.00	0.7	0.0	0.15	0.99	3.69	80.3	3.4	53.7	21.6	0.0
2.4	2.87	31.9	0.25	3.2	0.3	0.40	7.97	4.13	81.0	2.0	41.7	51.1	1.7
5.5	0.87	7.6	1.30	3.4	1.1	0.56	6.91	3.38	68.1	1.6	35.3	50.2	4.1
5.9	0.26	1.7	-0.05	9.9	2.1	1.70	14.82	7.12	59.9	5.2	138.1	24.9	8.6
3.2	4.92	28.6	0.06	2.1	-0.1	-0.57	-4.11	3.65	107.8	2.1	43.7	28.7	0.0
4.0	0.77	4.2	0.21	3.9	2.8	0.84	7.34	4.09	74.0	4.8	20.9	4.0	5.8
7.1	0.05	0.5	0.14	5.0	1.0	0.88	10.36	3.54	60.4	3.8	67.4	26.0	4.7
7.5	0.27	2.9	0.02	0.2	-0.4	-1.63	-19.58	3.07	159.5	3.3	10.3	12.1	1.2

Name	City	State	Weiss Safety Rating	2003 Weiss Safety Rating	2002 Weiss Safety Rating	Total Assets ($Mil)	One Year Asset Growth	Asset Mix (As a % of Total Assets)				Capital- ization Index	Leverage Ratio	Risk-based Capital Ratio
								Comm- ercial Loans	Cons- umer Loans	Home Mort- gages	Secur- ities			
▲ COMMUNITY FIRST BK	HARRISON	AR	C+	C	D+	299.0	17.65	13.4	12.2	27.9	12.5	5.0	7.6	11.0
COMMUNITY FIRST BK	KEOSAUQUA	IA	A-	A-	A-	108.5	3.47	8.9	5.1	19.5	25.1	9.0	10.3	15.7
▲ COMMUNITY FIRST BK	FAIRVIEW HEIGHTS	IL	B-	C+	C+	107.2	16.34	10.1	1.6	16.6	5.9	5.9	8.7	11.6
▲ COMMUNITY FIRST BK	CORYDON	IN	C+	C	C	261.2	13.95	7.5	12.5	24.4	36.8	5.0	7.0	12.5
▲ COMMUNITY FIRST BK	NEW IBERIA	LA	B-	C+	C+	80.6	-0.84	7.7	12.4	26.7	19.7	7.3	9.2	14.8
COMMUNITY FIRST BK	PIKESVILLE	MD	B-	B-	C	57.3	8.39	3.5	1.0	55.7	0.0	8.2	10.9	13.5
▲ COMMUNITY FIRST BK	BUTLER	MO	B-	C+	C+	92.4	0.12	13.5	4.1	22.1	19.2	6.2	8.2	13.1
COMMUNITY FIRST BK	GLENDIVE	MT	C+	B-	B-	36.0	3.37	1.9	2.9	2.7	31.3	8.1	9.7	18.3
▲ COMMUNITY FIRST BK	PRINEVILLE	OR	C	D+	D	104.5	18.29	11.1	2.6	7.8	15.2	6.7	8.8	12.3
COMMUNITY FIRST BK	WALHALLA	SC	B-	B-	B-	295.1	8.97	6.8	7.8	18.3	39.2	6.1	8.1	15.4
▲ COMMUNITY FIRST BK	LYNCHBURG	VA	C	C-	D	150.2	-8.33	14.4	3.3	23.6	4.8	5.4	8.7	11.3
▲ COMMUNITY FIRST BK	KENNEWICK	WA	C	C-	D	64.2	-12.71	13.3	10.7	3.7	27.6	10.0	14.7	21.4
COMMUNITY FIRST BK	BOSCOBEL	WI	C+	C+	B-	155.8	3.45	10.6	2.6	13.3	22.5	6.1	8.1	12.5
▲ COMMUNITY FIRST BK	ROSHOLT	WI	C+	B-	C	53.3	5.15	18.9	3.5	15.3	24.4	8.2	9.8	14.9
COMMUNITY FIRST BK	KOKOMO	IN	D	D	NR	57.5	93.62	22.4	0.9	7.6	14.9	10.0	20.8	26.7
▲ COMMUNITY FIRST BK NA	FOREST	OH	C	C-	C-	39.5	-3.67	8.6	5.5	45.9	8.4	8.1	9.7	15.8
▼ COMMUNITY FIRST BK NA	REYNOLDSVILLE	PA	D+	D+	C	71.7	-0.36	9.2	5.9	13.7	42.2	7.9	9.6	17.8
▼ COMMUNITY FIRST NB	MANHATTAN	KS	D	D+	D	43.0	32.86	14.3	7.1	31.0	2.3	3.0	7.6	10.0
COMMUNITY FIRST NB	W PLAINS	MO	C+	C+	C	92.6	15.17	14.3	7.3	21.7	18.3	6.0	8.0	12.0
COMMUNITY FIRST NB	FARGO	ND	B	B	B	5,528.4	-0.20	8.4	13.2	4.8	27.8	5.1	7.1	11.3
COMMUNITY FIRSTBANK	CHARLESTON	SC	C	C	C	256.4	7.19	14.3	4.2	21.7	9.9	3.9	8.0	10.5
▲ COMMUNITY FS&LA LITTLE	LITTLE FALLS	MN	B+	B-	B	75.4	0.29	12.4	3.3	33.9	15.2	9.8	10.8	19.6
▲ COMMUNITY FSB	WOODHAVEN	NY	C-	D+	D	60.9	62.21	0.0	0.2	1.8	54.4	8.1	9.7	20.9
▲ COMMUNITY GTY SVGS BK	PLYMOUTH	NH	C-	D+	D+	68.3	1.51	7.7	4.2	34.0	22.0	5.2	7.2	11.3
COMMUNITY MSB	MT VERNON	NY	C-	C-	C-	127.2	7.18	0.2	0.2	55.4	19.7	4.3	6.3	13.7
▲ COMMUNITY NB	ESCONDIDO	CA	B+	B-	C	532.5	21.15	7.9	1.7	2.5	3.4	7.2	10.8	12.6
COMMUNITY NB	BARTOW	FL	B	B+	B+	80.3	15.91	8.0	5.4	19.9	16.9	6.8	8.8	14.5
COMMUNITY NB	ASHBURN	GA	C	C	C-	137.3	-16.31	13.2	6.7	19.4	7.4	8.4	9.9	13.6
COMMUNITY NB	WATERLOO	IA	C	C	C-	248.7	6.92	26.7	4.4	13.5	7.8	3.5	7.7	10.3
COMMUNITY NB	METROPOLIS	IL	D+	D	D+	135.2	-1.59	5.9	4.1	15.3	38.2	5.6	7.6	14.1
COMMUNITY NB	MONMOUTH	IL	B-	B-	B-	51.0	-7.88	3.0	9.7	16.9	27.6	8.9	10.2	22.8
COMMUNITY NB	CHANUTE	KS	D	C-	C-	409.5	-3.16	18.4	8.7	26.4	10.9	5.7	7.7	11.6
COMMUNITY NB	SENECA	KS	C+	C+	B-	124.2	9.95	7.3	2.5	24.0	19.1	5.6	7.6	12.2
COMMUNITY NB	TOPEKA	KS	D-	D	D	71.1	10.73	17.6	3.4	27.3	4.3	3.3	7.5	10.1
COMMUNITY NB	N BRANCH	MN	B-	B-	C	115.7	8.75	15.0	2.5	10.2	2.2	4.0	9.4	10.5
COMMUNITY NB	NORTHFIELD	MN	C+	C	D+	172.7	14.48	27.1	3.6	10.4	14.0	4.7	8.9	10.9
COMMUNITY NB	MONETT	MO	D	D	D	42.2	170.12	11.9	5.7	19.6	8.1	10.0	11.4	15.4
COMMUNITY NB	FRANKLIN	OH	B	B	B-	138.0	15.47	2.8	3.6	35.2	17.4	6.9	9.0	14.6
▲ COMMUNITY NB	ALVA	OK	D	E-	E-	42.1	-5.49	17.5	4.8	6.3	32.0	7.0	9.0	13.8
▲ COMMUNITY NB	OKARCHE	OK	A-	B+	B+	42.9	8.36	11.2	7.6	8.1	35.1	10.0	13.0	18.6
COMMUNITY NB	DAYTON	TN	B+	B+	A-	91.6	7.71	20.9	8.6	22.7	27.9	8.0	9.6	16.5
COMMUNITY NB	BELLAIRE	TX	D-	D-	D	102.9	9.60	5.3	8.2	3.5	66.4	6.5	8.6	22.5
COMMUNITY NB	DETROIT	TX	C	C	C	19.4	-4.32	13.9	6.8	7.3	8.1	9.5	10.6	22.7
▲ COMMUNITY NB	HONDO	TX	C-	D+	C-	81.4	2.46	12.7	9.4	9.0	14.0	8.4	9.9	15.8
COMMUNITY NB	MIDLAND	TX	B-	B-	B-	324.7	8.16	26.6	3.1	5.4	18.9	4.6	7.0	10.8
▼ COMMUNITY NB	S BOSTON	VA	B-	B	B	244.9	0.14	2.2	5.0	6.8	28.1	6.3	8.3	15.2
COMMUNITY NB	DERBY CENTER	VT	B-	B-	B-	308.4	4.02	6.3	7.1	36.8	23.2	6.3	8.3	17.1
▼ COMMUNITY NB OF NW PA	ALBION	PA	A-	A	A	67.4	-2.42	0.8	2.8	36.3	35.4	10.0	21.0	54.9
COMMUNITY NB OF THE	MORRISTOWN	TN	D	D	NR	49.0	149.91	10.1	6.9	15.5	30.4	10.0	14.7	22.2
▲ COMMUNITY NB PASCO CTY	ZEPHYRHILLS	FL	C+	C-	C-	198.4	14.75	10.9	6.4	21.6	8.7	4.4	8.1	10.7
▲ COMMUNITY NB SARASOTA	VENICE	FL	B-	C+	C	98.7	16.49	9.1	6.5	31.3	1.8	5.1	7.8	11.0
▼ COMMUNITY PLUS SAVINGS	ROCHESTER HILLS	MI	C-	NR	NR	47.9	N/A	0.0	5.4	51.9	5.6	6.6	8.6	18.1
COMMUNITY PRIDE BK	HAM LAKE	MN	C+	C+	D+	62.0	17.42	18.4	1.2	6.2	6.8	4.9	9.5	10.9
COMMUNITY SECURITY BK	NEW PRAGUE	MN	C-	C-	D	73.5	23.70	19.5	2.4	16.2	7.6	3.0	7.9	10.0
▲ COMMUNITY SHORES BK	MUSKEGON	MI	C	C-	D+	184.4	-0.65	32.6	6.1	9.9	8.9	4.0	8.2	10.5
COMMUNITY SOUTH BK	PARSONS	TN	B-	B-	C+	257.6	12.72	9.8	7.7	21.7	22.0	8.3	9.9	15.0
COMMUNITY SPIRIT BK	RED BAY	AL	D+	D+	D	81.9	-3.07	8.8	7.1	22.7	19.0	6.3	8.3	12.8
COMMUNITY ST BK	STARKE	FL	A-	A-	A-	54.3	0.50	10.8	8.8	16.2	31.5	10.0	14.9	26.0
COMMUNITY ST BK	INDIANOLA	IA	C+	C+	C	69.3	12.30	10.1	3.2	16.5	29.7	5.9	7.9	13.9
COMMUNITY ST BK	PATON	IA	B-	B-	B-	26.3	-1.51	1.7	2.2	5.0	50.3	10.0	14.0	20.3
▲ COMMUNITY ST BK	SPENCER	IA	B-	C-	C-	81.7	19.94	16.4	3.4	7.0	27.2	7.0	9.0	13.1
COMMUNITY ST BK	W BRANCH	IA	C	C	C+	80.3	1.18	8.0	3.9	17.7	29.1	5.1	7.1	11.9
COMMUNITY ST BK	AVILLA	IN	B-	B-	B-	113.9	-1.17	22.3	4.4	30.1	25.3	7.8	9.6	17.2
COMMUNITY ST BK	BROOK	IN	B	B	B	31.8	1.71	5.8	4.2	18.7	23.5	10.0	18.7	29.8

Asset Quality Index	Non-Performing Loans as a % of Total Loans	Non-Performing Loans as a % of Capital	Net Charge-offs Avg Loans	Profitability Index	Net Income ($Mil)	Return on Assets (R.O.A.)	Return on Equity (R.O.E.)	Net Interest Spread	Overhead Efficiency Ratio	Liquidity Index	Liquidity Ratio	Hot Money Ratio	Stability Index
4.3	0.80	8.0	0.18	6.1	1.5	1.01	13.54	4.57	60.0	0.7	10.3	35.2	3.3
5.8	0.57	3.4	-0.15	9.7	1.2	2.22	20.30	4.80	53.3	4.9	25.3	3.9	8.1
6.5	0.00	0.0	0.00	6.6	0.6	1.06	12.13	3.63	47.2	3.4	32.3	15.4	5.6
4.4	1.06	8.1	0.06	4.2	0.8	0.63	8.84	3.34	68.1	6.2	56.7	7.7	3.4
5.9	0.37	2.5	0.06	5.6	0.4	1.04	11.91	4.80	66.1	2.8	30.2	17.7	5.3
6.6	0.64	4.7	-0.02	6.5	0.3	1.18	10.82	3.89	58.1	1.6	35.5	45.3	4.6
4.4	0.99	7.6	0.04	7.7	0.6	1.28	14.77	3.73	47.1	3.6	6.4	10.3	5.0
3.3	2.26	12.9	0.01	5.5	0.2	0.83	8.52	3.79	66.2	3.7	29.7	13.1	4.9
4.6	0.30	2.3	0.63	5.4	0.5	0.98	11.38	5.44	64.4	2.7	9.8	15.0	3.2
6.2	0.60	3.7	0.12	7.0	1.7	1.17	15.23	3.09	47.5	3.0	43.8	22.8	4.1
6.3	0.15	1.3	1.84	2.6	0.2	0.28	3.26	3.90	74.4	1.5	11.0	23.0	4.6
3.3	3.91	14.6	0.40	1.9	0.1	0.30	2.14	3.98	93.6	4.4	56.4	15.6	3.0
3.8	1.69	13.1	0.02	7.3	1.2	1.63	19.70	4.14	72.5	3.8	21.3	10.9	6.3
4.9	1.11	6.6	-0.10	7.2	0.4	1.55	16.26	6.49	71.3	3.8	33.3	14.0	5.0
8.4	0.69	2.6	0.00	0.0	-0.1	-0.38	-1.72	3.09	88.2	4.5	69.7	17.4	0.0
4.2	1.54	12.4	0.04	4.3	0.2	0.72	7.57	4.17	73.6	4.4	26.2	8.1	3.6
3.4	3.25	15.3	0.13	1.5	0.3	0.69	7.12	2.04	103.7	3.4	29.8	14.8	4.7
5.4	0.41	4.3	0.12	2.7	0.1	0.52	6.69	4.44	79.9	4.2	13.6	7.2	0.0
7.8	0.01	0.1	0.05	6.0	0.5	1.10	14.18	3.76	65.2	2.0	20.6	19.7	3.9
5.4	0.62	4.1	0.25	10.0	47.5	1.74	19.46	4.97	54.5	4.8	31.2	11.3	7.9
7.2	0.33	3.3	0.02	4.9	1.1	0.89	11.88	3.26	58.4	1.7	21.7	22.8	4.2
7.1	0.40	2.1	-0.01	8.1	1.4	3.70	34.53	3.09	28.1	3.9	45.5	16.3	6.7
9.8	0.00	0.0	0.00	2.7	0.2	0.52	5.10	3.10	79.6	2.3	33.4	24.3	0.5
8.9	0.09	0.8	0.01	4.4	0.3	0.80	11.21	4.72	76.3	4.4	20.6	6.6	2.0
9.8	0.02	0.2	0.01	1.9	0.0	0.03	0.38	3.11	98.7	7.9	93.3	2.8	3.1
6.8	0.16	1.2	0.00	9.4	4.2	1.68	16.04	5.34	56.7	0.9	20.4	37.5	6.1
5.6	0.49	3.5	0.03	8.4	0.4	1.14	12.26	4.60	61.0	3.5	57.4	21.4	5.3
3.6	1.55	11.4	4.16	2.8	-0.8	-1.08	-10.51	4.58	60.3	1.7	15.4	22.3	3.8
6.2	0.16	1.3	0.09	4.3	0.9	0.73	7.60	4.02	69.0	3.1	19.3	13.8	4.3
4.4	1.78	12.4	0.01	3.3	0.4	0.56	7.56	3.84	76.7	4.2	17.5	7.4	2.0
6.4	0.48	2.0	0.31	5.0	0.2	0.89	8.67	3.17	59.7	5.7	106.0	16.1	5.0
0.6	3.13	25.3	0.64	4.5	1.4	0.67	7.76	4.50	71.8	3.2	33.8	17.1	4.1
4.6	1.26	10.3	0.21	4.6	0.4	0.66	8.70	4.02	78.1	6.1	76.6	11.6	4.4
6.7	0.12	1.3	0.01	4.2	0.2	0.49	6.86	4.44	79.4	3.9	14.3	9.0	1.9
5.9	0.21	1.7	-0.01	10.0	1.4	2.51	24.83	6.04	57.9	3.7	23.6	11.2	7.2
5.2	0.36	2.4	0.20	5.7	0.9	1.11	10.33	5.08	64.9	3.3	14.0	12.2	4.9
8.1	0.00	0.0	0.02	0.0	-0.2	-1.34	-7.26	4.06	102.0	5.3	58.3	11.7	0.0
4.8	1.36	10.2	0.08	5.4	0.6	0.86	9.41	4.18	67.7	1.7	26.0	26.1	4.8
3.8	0.74	4.4	-0.07	4.9	0.3	1.51	17.53	3.98	60.1	2.3	36.1	26.0	1.1
8.1	0.00	0.0	-0.05	9.6	0.5	2.21	17.43	4.45	54.4	1.6	19.7	24.6	7.3
5.9	0.39	2.6	0.10	8.4	0.9	2.03	21.00	5.07	62.9	3.1	22.0	14.2	6.2
8.7	0.08	0.3	0.33	0.2	0.0	0.04	0.48	2.84	92.1	2.5	9.7	15.9	0.0
5.2	1.30	5.2	0.00	5.5	0.1	0.89	8.44	4.02	65.9	5.7	115.6	16.1	4.0
2.1	2.81	16.7	0.55	6.8	0.6	1.36	13.57	5.32	62.9	4.2	65.1	17.9	4.8
6.8	0.18	0.9	0.19	3.8	0.9	0.56	4.86	3.76	74.0	3.2	40.7	19.1	6.5
4.6	1.64	10.7	0.00	4.6	1.0	0.83	10.02	2.82	62.9	6.4	58.7	7.3	4.9
5.9	0.68	4.8	0.03	5.3	1.5	0.94	11.02	4.10	73.6	5.4	45.0	8.8	5.2
9.6	0.00	0.0	0.01	7.3	0.4	1.13	5.40	3.55	60.3	6.0	93.9	12.9	8.1
8.4	0.00	0.0	0.06	0.0	-0.6	-2.70	-16.10	3.45	164.5	2.4	11.2	16.6	0.0
8.1	0.13	1.2	0.04	6.7	1.8	1.83	24.91	3.65	47.0	3.1	27.2	15.3	3.9
7.8	0.12	1.2	0.03	8.6	1.0	2.07	27.06	5.37	58.0	4.7	30.2	8.0	4.2
9.1	0.02	0.2	0.03	3.3	0.0	0.33	3.90	1.53	84.3	3.3	39.9	18.5	0.0
7.2	0.00	0.0	-0.02	9.3	0.7	2.50	27.06	4.87	49.7	1.7	16.2	21.2	1.3
6.6	0.09	0.9	0.00	9.8	0.5	1.60	20.64	4.69	54.5	3.2	12.5	12.6	3.6
4.5	0.75	6.9	0.10	3.5	0.5	0.57	7.00	3.46	70.6	0.6	4.8	35.3	4.3
4.2	1.06	6.4	1.03	5.6	0.9	0.76	7.02	5.20	74.3	1.5	9.8	23.5	5.3
2.6	2.43	16.9	0.25	2.8	0.2	0.45	5.37	4.13	85.9	2.7	27.8	17.5	1.8
5.8	1.71	6.3	0.47	8.5	0.3	1.11	7.51	6.25	71.7	4.2	20.3	8.0	7.3
8.6	0.17	1.2	0.01	5.8	0.3	0.88	11.15	4.10	68.5	4.5	40.4	12.5	4.7
6.6	2.70	7.5	0.00	3.8	0.1	0.67	4.77	3.10	69.4	7.9	151.1	8.9	5.1
8.4	0.00	0.0	-0.02	7.2	0.7	1.83	20.15	3.78	57.9	4.0	34.2	12.9	4.5
2.7	3.86	31.4	0.01	4.6	0.3	0.74	9.90	3.70	73.4	5.3	44.0	9.2	3.9
6.3	0.54	3.4	-0.01	4.3	0.4	0.70	7.36	4.25	78.0	4.7	22.8	5.4	5.4
4.3	5.83	19.3	-0.03	7.6	0.2	1.51	8.20	4.67	55.7	1.9	31.8	28.1	6.6

Name	City	State	Weiss Safety Rating	2003 Weiss Safety Rating	2002 Weiss Safety Rating	Total Assets ($Mil)	One Year Asset Growth	Asset Mix (As a % of Total Assets)				Capital-ization Index	Leverage Ratio	Risk-based Capital Ratio
								Comm-ercial Loans	Cons-umer Loans	Home Mort-gages	Secur-ities			
COMMUNITY ST BK	ROYAL CENTER	IN	B	B	B	52.6	-1.41	1.8	6.4	15.7	26.0	10.0	11.3	16.9
▲ COMMUNITY ST BK	COFFEYVILLE	KS	C-	D+	D-	45.7	1.04	20.3	6.2	10.5	27.2	6.5	8.5	13.6
COMMUNITY ST BK	BOWLING GREEN	MO	A	A	A	157.5	1.27	9.4	5.1	20.4	32.9	10.0	15.8	25.8
COMMUNITY ST BK	POTEAU	OK	D+	D+	D+	129.2	-2.43	9.8	12.5	24.9	11.0	5.9	7.9	12.5
COMMUNITY ST BK	ORBISONIA	PA	B	B	B	173.7	8.67	1.1	14.0	57.3	4.7	6.6	8.7	13.7
▲ COMMUNITY ST BK	AUSTIN	TX	D+	D-	D-	56.4	14.84	6.7	4.3	5.0	65.1	5.3	7.3	17.7
COMMUNITY ST BK	BOLING	TX	C+	C+	C+	63.2	2.42	11.2	7.8	1.1	43.2	6.4	8.4	18.8
▲ COMMUNITY ST BK	NORWALK	WI	D+	D	E	20.7	2.21	3.2	10.8	29.2	3.5	7.9	9.6	15.1
COMMUNITY ST BK	PRENTICE	WI	B-	B-	C+	24.7	8.75	22.6	7.7	30.9	13.3	10.0	15.3	20.8
COMMUNITY ST BK	UNION GROVE	WI	B	B	A-	225.8	4.26	24.2	3.1	13.3	8.3	8.6	10.6	13.8
▲ COMMUNITY ST BK NA	ANKENY	IA	B	B-	B-	462.8	5.73	11.5	0.6	14.5	36.7	6.6	8.7	14.7
COMMUNITY ST BK OF	CANTON	OK	C	C-	D+	25.9	4.28	12.2	16.2	14.8	15.0	10.0	12.6	16.2
COMMUNITY ST BK	PLYMOUTH	IL	B-	B-	B-	13.1	-7.30	3.2	1.4	4.7	58.8	10.0	15.7	36.5
COMMUNITY ST BK RK FALLS	ROCK FALLS	IL	C	C	D+	130.2	4.34	17.6	5.8	17.6	13.6	4.7	6.9	10.9
COMMUNITY ST BK SHELBINA	SHELBINA	MO	C+	C+	C+	50.4	-3.49	1.0	9.1	19.8	35.6	8.1	9.8	19.4
▲ COMMUNITY ST BK ST	ST CHARLES	MI	A-	A-	A-	131.6	3.89	5.7	11.8	24.5	32.3	10.0	11.2	19.0
▲ COMMUNITY STATE BANK	GALVA	IL	C	C-	D	50.9	7.10	13.1	5.7	11.7	25.4	7.0	9.0	13.4
COMMUNITY STATE BK	BRADLEY	AR	C	C	C-	13.0	-7.29	13.4	7.4	11.6	7.7	10.0	12.2	22.0
▲ COMMUNITY STATE BK	HENNESSEY	OK	C-	D+	D-	25.9	-4.21	19.7	17.1	11.2	2.7	6.6	8.7	12.2
▲ COMMUNITY STATE BK	MILBANK	SD	B-	C+	C+	65.9	31.93	14.2	9.9	8.8	3.8	10.0	15.0	16.2
COMMUNITY SVG BK	EDGEWOOD	IA	C+	C+	C+	146.3	3.52	9.4	2.7	6.1	23.7	8.6	10.0	14.1
COMMUNITY SVG BK	ROBINS	IA	C+	C+	C+	69.1	18.42	12.2	1.8	19.4	28.8	8.3	9.9	15.1
▼ COMMUNITY SVGS BK	CHICAGO	IL	C+	B	B	405.2	-1.08	0.0	0.1	43.5	30.8	10.0	14.8	38.9
COMMUNITY T&BC	OOLTEWAH	TN	B-	B-	C	58.5	-1.35	16.4	4.0	15.5	10.4	10.0	13.4	15.4
▲ COMMUNITY TR BK	CHOUDRANT	LA	C+	C	C	395.8	16.54	17.3	6.8	14.6	10.4	4.7	8.4	10.9
COMMUNITY TR BK INC	PIKEVILLE	KY	B-	C+	C+	2,432.1	-2.64	8.8	15.8	19.4	15.6	6.9	8.9	12.7
COMMUNITY TRUST BK	HIRAM	GA	C+	C+	C+	186.3	12.99	5.4	1.5	4.1	17.8	4.3	8.5	10.7
COMMUNITY TRUST BK	IRVINGTON	IL	B-	C+	C+	62.7	1.57	7.0	3.3	23.5	28.4	7.9	9.6	17.8
COMMUNITYS BK	BRIDGEPORT	CT	D-	D-	D-	45.6	-5.36	5.5	7.3	2.7	47.6	5.3	8.0	11.3
COMPASS BK	BIRMINGHAM	AL	B	B	B	27,848.9	8.61	11.9	13.0	8.6	27.0	4.6	6.7	10.9
COMPASS BK FOR SVGS	NEW BEDFORD	MA	B	B	B	4,755.1	19.35	2.3	18.1	36.7	12.6	5.6	7.6	11.7
COMPASS FSB	WILMERDING	PA	C-	C-	C+	41.7	8.72	0.7	0.3	45.1	43.1	7.6	9.4	26.0
CONCORD BK	ST LOUIS	MO	B	B	B	129.8	9.44	15.6	1.8	14.5	4.1	5.5	9.6	11.4
CONCORD BK NA	HOUSTON	TX	B-	B-	B	114.0	45.03	7.2	0.3	2.2	6.6	5.4	9.9	11.3
CONCORDE BK	BLOMKEST	MN	C	C	C	34.3	4.96	5.1	4.3	13.3	25.7	6.9	8.9	13.3
▼ CONCORDIA B&TC	VIDALIA	LA	B	B+	A	365.0	-2.89	5.6	7.2	23.1	28.1	9.7	10.8	20.8
▼ CONCORDIA BK	CONCORDIA	MO	C+	B-	B-	49.0	-7.17	8.3	5.0	25.5	9.9	10.0	11.3	16.9
CONDON NB OF COFFEYVILLE	COFFEYVILLE	KS	C+	C+	C+	86.9	-11.36	10.2	8.3	12.0	49.7	6.1	8.1	17.6
CONGRESSIONAL BK	POTOMAC	MD	D	D	NR	33.7	N/A	15.2	0.7	31.4	0.0	10.0	30.4	46.3
CONNEAUT SVGS BK	CONNEAUT	OH	B	B	B	80.1	-1.74	0.0	1.1	63.4	21.0	8.7	10.1	23.1
CONNECTICUT B&TC	HARTFORD	CT	D	NR	NR	24.9	N/A	8.7	0.3	0.2	34.6	10.0	66.6	163.6
▲ CONNECTICUT COMMUNITY	WESTPORT	CT	B	C+	C-	256.8	75.30	15.9	0.5	10.3	9.5	8.7	11.3	13.9
CONNECTICUT RIVER BK NA	SPRINGFIELD	VT	B-	B-	B-	216.6	9.28	22.3	4.7	28.4	5.4	5.8	7.8	12.7
CONNECTICUT RIVER	WETHERSFIELD	CT	D	D	D	43.2	113.30	5.1	8.8	14.3	25.6	10.0	11.5	17.9
CONSOLIDATED B&TC	RICHMOND	VA	E-	E-	E-	77.2	-19.13	36.6	3.8	10.1	27.3	2.3	4.7	9.3
▼ CONSUMER NB	JACKSON	MS	D	D	E-	34.8	22.08	13.8	16.9	15.3	11.2	8.1	9.8	13.5
CONSUMERS NB	MINERVA	OH	B-	B-	B-	186.0	2.26	5.8	3.5	29.1	16.0	7.1	9.1	14.4
CONTINENTAL BK	SALT LAKE CITY	UT	D	D	NR	13.2	N/A	36.0	0.0	0.0	0.0	10.0	70.5	49.2
CONTINENTAL BK OF	CITY OF INDUSTR	CA	D	D	NR	37.4	N/A	7.5	2.6	0.2	18.0	10.0	19.0	29.0
CONTINENTAL COMMUNITY	AURORA	IL	E-	E-	D-	137.0	-23.43	24.0	1.8	7.3	29.6	1.3	4.4	8.3
CONTINENTAL NB	HARLOWTON	MT	B-	B	B	38.7	5.02	9.3	7.6	6.0	24.7	10.0	13.1	17.3
CONTINENTAL NB OF MIAMI	MIAMI	FL	C	C	C	209.8	10.31	4.4	14.9	8.3	10.1	5.6	7.8	11.5
CONTINENTAL SAVINGS BANK,	MILWAUKEE	WI	B	B	B-	172.1	-1.77	2.1	0.7	35.0	3.2	10.0	11.4	17.4
▼ CONVERSE COUNTY BK	DOUGLAS	WY	B+	A-	A	171.9	4.95	13.4	9.0	6.4	45.7	5.7	7.7	14.4
CONWAY BK NA	CONWAY SPRINGS	KS	B-	B-	B-	111.6	2.97	12.8	2.8	9.9	12.8	8.1	10.1	13.4
CONWAY NB	CONWAY	SC	A-	A-	A-	662.3	9.17	9.8	5.2	19.5	29.4	7.8	9.5	16.1
COOPERATIVE BK	ROSLINDALE	MA	B+	B+	B+	252.1	13.50	7.6	0.1	30.4	22.2	6.9	8.9	12.6
▲ COOPERATIVE BK	WILMINGTON	NC	B	B-	C+	527.9	1.12	3.0	1.2	42.4	9.2	6.2	8.4	11.9
COPIAH BK NA	HAZLEHURST	MS	B	B	B	90.1	3.69	9.9	9.1	13.3	35.1	7.0	9.0	14.2
▲ COPPER STAR BK	SCOTTSDALE	AZ	C	D	E+	100.2	46.18	10.6	0.5	13.0	4.5	10.0	15.5	17.2
COQUINA BK	ORMOND BEACH	FL	B+	B+	B+	114.7	15.29	22.4	3.1	12.5	9.7	7.4	10.0	12.8
CORDER BK	CORDER	MO	C-	C-	C	9.3	-1.95	9.5	6.7	26.4	7.4	10.0	15.1	23.1
CORN BELT B&TC	PITTSFIELD	IL	B	B	B-	157.2	12.60	13.1	3.5	9.8	20.7	6.5	8.5	12.1
CORN CITY ST BK	DESHLER	OH	A-	A-	A-	46.2	1.17	0.1	6.7	36.2	37.0	10.0	17.2	30.9

Asset Quality Index	Non-Performing Loans as a % of Total Loans	Non-Performing Loans as a % of Capital	Net Charge-offs Avg Loans	Profitability Index	Net Income ($Mil)	Return on Assets (R.O.A.)	Return on Equity (R.O.E.)	Net Interest Spread	Overhead Efficiency Ratio	Liquidity Index	Liquidity Ratio	Hot Money Ratio	Stability Index
5.5	1.68	8.2	-0.05	5.6	0.2	0.86	7.52	4.92	72.4	6.0	39.9	3.5	5.7
6.1	0.44	2.7	0.05	7.0	0.3	1.26	14.59	4.73	66.4	3.7	31.8	13.7	2.9
8.7	0.37	1.3	0.02	6.4	0.9	1.14	7.28	3.72	57.3	4.3	40.9	13.6	8.6
1.2	2.71	23.1	0.44	5.5	0.7	1.02	12.66	5.12	65.0	1.6	19.3	24.0	2.5
6.5	0.23	2.1	0.20	6.1	0.9	1.06	12.47	4.25	59.7	3.7	48.7	18.5	5.0
7.2	0.69	1.6	0.49	3.1	0.1	0.46	5.32	4.09	76.3	5.4	43.0	8.0	2.2
8.4	0.08	0.4	0.09	4.2	0.3	0.94	10.78	4.24	78.5	5.6	64.1	10.8	3.8
5.1	0.81	5.5	0.23	4.4	0.1	0.82	8.18	3.52	73.0	7.6	128.4	6.8	3.1
3.9	3.33	16.6	0.03	10.0	0.2	1.79	11.96	5.48	47.9	3.9	12.2	8.8	6.3
4.5	1.01	6.8	0.02	10.0	2.8	2.58	24.92	5.69	57.5	4.6	33.5	10.0	7.8
6.4	0.63	3.6	0.01	5.0	2.4	1.06	11.20	3.49	66.4	6.8	54.3	2.5	5.9
3.0	3.08	16.0	1.20	8.6	0.2	1.48	11.88	6.11	53.2	5.2	40.7	8.9	4.1
9.4	0.52	1.1	0.00	7.4	0.1	1.40	8.68	3.23	36.4	6.4	62.8	3.6	5.5
3.6	1.49	11.6	0.35	4.2	0.4	0.63	7.51	3.99	67.8	5.6	56.2	10.8	4.0
5.3	1.25	6.2	0.01	4.1	0.2	0.80	8.19	2.79	60.9	8.0	163.8	9.1	4.0
5.9	1.09	5.4	0.23	5.9	0.6	0.93	8.11	4.58	73.3	5.7	43.1	6.5	7.0
5.6	0.61	4.2	0.10	7.4	0.4	1.46	16.28	5.29	60.1	3.2	36.7	18.1	3.0
6.0	1.71	7.5	0.00	7.0	0.1	1.19	10.12	5.13	59.9	6.6	109.5	10.7	2.8
2.2	2.10	16.3	1.37	8.3	0.2	1.83	20.91	6.29	62.0	6.0	55.2	6.6	3.6
5.0	1.34	7.7	0.23	9.8	1.9	6.40	46.95	19.65	41.6	2.0	18.2	19.2	7.1
4.5	1.40	9.3	0.18	5.7	1.0	1.38	15.67	3.72	58.8	3.3	21.6	13.3	5.1
2.3	5.57	35.1	0.33	2.3	0.1	0.14	1.61	3.07	85.2	3.3	27.6	14.5	4.7
9.8	0.17	0.7	0.00	2.7	0.5	0.23	1.59	2.69	88.6	7.7	144.6	9.9	7.8
8.5	0.02	0.1	1.04	3.2	0.2	0.63	4.77	4.30	73.4	1.6	28.7	29.8	5.7
6.4	0.38	3.1	0.06	4.2	1.3	0.69	8.27	3.87	72.4	6.3	78.1	10.9	4.0
4.3	1.08	6.6	0.31	7.7	16.9	1.38	12.40	4.38	54.7	2.8	24.4	18.2	8.5
4.8	0.62	5.1	0.04	7.2	1.4	1.55	18.39	4.14	69.5	1.7	20.1	23.3	5.2
7.7	0.58	3.3	0.03	5.5	0.3	1.05	10.54	4.42	66.5	5.1	22.2	2.3	4.8
8.8	0.00	0.0	0.04	0.0	-0.3	-1.22	-14.31	3.92	110.4	5.6	50.3	8.1	0.0
6.1	0.42	3.2	0.53	8.2	178.7	1.31	17.52	3.64	56.0	3.6	12.3	11.1	7.5
5.1	0.46	3.1	0.16	5.6	17.3	0.83	8.48	3.54	58.6	5.0	28.2	8.6	6.7
5.2	2.23	12.1	0.00	4.8	0.2	0.90	9.98	2.93	58.0	3.7	31.9	13.6	4.3
7.2	0.00	0.0	0.00	9.3	1.0	1.70	17.43	4.46	36.4	0.5	5.0	41.3	5.8
7.3	0.00	0.0	0.00	5.7	0.6	1.15	12.28	4.26	52.8	0.8	25.1	60.5	5.3
8.6	0.10	0.6	-0.20	3.2	0.1	0.40	4.37	3.91	89.5	4.0	35.5	13.6	4.4
4.5	1.57	8.4	0.07	6.4	2.3	1.23	10.96	3.69	57.2	2.6	44.7	29.3	8.0
1.0	7.11	41.7	0.10	7.2	0.4	1.54	13.79	4.60	70.3	6.1	41.8	2.9	5.3
8.5	0.08	0.5	0.07	3.9	0.3	0.71	8.79	3.46	73.6	2.9	8.0	14.0	3.2
9.7	0.00	0.0	0.00	0.0	-0.6	-4.18	-11.18	3.06	227.9	5.4	155.6	24.9	0.0
8.7	0.39	2.6	0.00	4.3	0.3	0.74	7.39	3.02	64.8	6.9	107.4	9.9	3.1
9.7	0.00	0.0	0.00	0.0	-2.4	-22.36	-27.61	1.47	1,758.3	6.4	143.1	15.1	0.0
6.2	0.59	4.0	0.21	7.5	3.4	2.71	25.68	4.27	40.2	4.3	28.5	9.5	5.4
7.8	0.25	2.2	-0.04	4.4	0.7	0.61	7.97	4.20	77.9	7.2	83.6	5.9	4.0
8.1	0.02	0.1	0.01	0.0	-0.3	-1.62	-11.95	3.33	132.2	6.1	82.0	11.1	0.0
4.0	1.82	15.3	-0.44	0.0	-0.2	-0.45	-9.85	3.83	109.9	6.8	58.6	2.2	0.0
4.6	0.67	4.7	0.31	2.2	0.1	0.42	4.07	4.44	79.9	3.7	42.5	17.1	0.6
3.9	1.62	11.6	0.17	7.4	1.2	1.29	13.41	5.19	66.0	4.5	9.6	4.7	5.4
9.0	0.00	0.0	0.00	0.0	-0.4	-9.69	-13.41	4.62	211.4	1.7	4.9	19.2	0.0
9.2	0.00	0.0	0.00	0.0	-0.5	-3.26	-14.72	2.32	222.8	5.4	287.3	46.8	0.0
2.7	2.82	24.7	-0.64	0.0	-1.4	-1.84	-39.09	2.39	140.9	3.5	55.2	24.3	0.4
3.3	4.00	20.6	0.54	8.0	0.3	1.39	11.04	4.81	51.5	2.7	25.5	16.8	5.6
5.4	0.25	2.1	0.02	3.3	0.4	0.37	4.72	4.28	90.1	4.4	47.3	14.6	3.3
8.8	0.07	0.4	0.00	4.0	0.5	0.58	4.60	3.08	75.7	1.6	15.6	23.1	7.2
8.2	0.00	0.0	0.02	6.5	1.3	1.46	18.55	3.15	54.8	5.4	126.1	20.6	7.4
3.6	2.81	19.9	0.05	3.7	0.3	0.48	4.84	3.66	74.2	0.8	16.3	41.0	5.3
8.6	0.09	0.5	0.06	7.6	4.1	1.29	13.29	4.24	56.7	2.6	30.9	19.0	7.0
8.5	0.21	1.6	0.00	5.6	1.0	0.83	9.25	4.32	72.0	3.9	33.5	13.4	5.1
8.8	0.12	1.1	0.02	5.4	2.1	0.81	9.46	3.73	68.3	1.4	14.6	25.4	5.5
5.9	0.70	4.0	0.00	6.9	0.6	1.37	14.83	5.32	71.6	2.6	29.7	18.5	5.2
6.1	0.05	0.3	0.00	3.2	0.3	0.65	5.52	5.00	72.6	1.3	19.3	29.0	2.7
5.6	0.98	6.9	0.17	7.0	0.5	0.95	9.20	4.91	50.0	3.7	26.9	12.0	7.2
8.3	0.25	1.2	0.00	5.0	0.1	1.14	7.54	4.24	72.7	6.3	89.3	9.5	4.3
7.9	0.06	0.5	0.11	7.6	1.6	2.01	24.19	3.46	41.6	0.8	8.7	33.6	5.5
9.1	0.14	0.4	-0.05	9.0	0.4	1.61	9.47	3.89	40.1	5.9	78.2	11.5	8.0

Name	City	State	Weiss Safety Rating	2003 Weiss Safety Rating	2002 Weiss Safety Rating	Total Assets ($Mil)	One Year Asset Growth	Asset Mix (As a % of Total Assets)				Capital- ization Index	Leverage Ratio	Risk-based Capital Ratio
								Comm- ercial Loans	Cons- umer Loans	Home Mort- gages	Secur- ities			
▲ CORN GROWERS ST BK	MURDOCK	NE	D-	D-	D-	14.4	7.32	3.8	6.5	8.0	46.7	5.9	7.9	16.8
CORNER STONE BK	STEWARTSVILLE	MO	C+	C+	B-	100.4	0.98	9.3	16.4	25.4	18.4	10.0	12.0	18.7
▲ CORNERBANK NA	WINFIELD	KS	C	C-	C	209.0	1.32	8.0	3.1	6.9	28.0	5.0	7.2	11.0
CORNERSTONE B&T	CARROLLTON	IL	C-	D+	D	101.7	8.19	6.6	2.2	8.9	29.8	7.5	9.3	14.7
CORNERSTONE BK	STAMFORD	CT	B+	B+	B+	229.7	-1.16	6.0	0.8	14.0	24.6	7.9	9.6	15.0
CORNERSTONE BK	OVERLAND PARK	KS	D+	D	D-	97.7	23.21	16.5	1.0	9.4	8.4	5.8	9.8	11.6
CORNERSTONE BK	SENATOBIA	MS	D+	D+	C-	49.1	-7.13	8.0	10.4	29.3	2.0	7.1	9.1	15.4
▲ CORNERSTONE BK	WILSON	NC	C+	C	C-	103.3	13.09	26.1	3.8	24.2	12.0	6.8	8.8	12.9
▲ CORNERSTONE BK	MOORESTOWN	NJ	B-	C	C	109.4	3.76	16.2	0.2	11.4	25.4	10.0	13.1	18.7
CORNERSTONE BK	SPRINGFIELD	OH	B	B	B	410.7	15.27	4.9	0.2	43.5	11.6	9.2	10.4	15.3
CORNERSTONE BK NA	YORK	NE	B	C+	C+	384.4	4.89	13.1	3.8	4.6	32.0	5.5	7.5	12.5
CORNERSTONE COMMUNITY	ST PETERSBURG	FL	B	B	B-	163.8	34.68	1.1	0.9	26.1	9.0	6.3	9.1	12.0
▲ CORNERSTONE COMMUNITY	CHATTANOOGA	TN	C	C-	C-	228.1	27.19	25.3	2.5	10.4	13.2	3.1	8.1	10.1
▼ CORNERSTONE COMMUNITY	GRAFTON	WI	C	C+	C+	71.8	14.64	10.9	0.6	9.5	9.7	5.1	8.7	11.0
▲ CORNERSTONE NB	EASLEY	SC	C+	C	C-	86.1	18.08	11.8	2.9	13.9	14.5	6.2	8.9	11.9
▲ CORNERSTONE NB&TC	PALATINE	IL	C+	D+	C	218.7	27.35	16.3	1.3	7.6	14.2	8.4	12.5	13.7
▲ CORNERSTONE ST BK	LE SUEUR	MN	C+	C-	C-	78.4	-0.85	10.5	7.0	27.0	21.0	7.7	9.5	14.8
CORNERSTONEBANK	ATLANTA	GA	D	D	D-	99.7	14.50	14.6	3.0	6.1	5.6	5.1	9.3	11.1
▲ CORNHUSKER BK	LINCOLN	NE	B+	B	B-	235.3	2.29	9.7	1.9	11.8	41.3	7.2	9.2	16.7
▲ CORNING S&LA	CORNING	AR	D+	D	D-	16.6	0.83	17.3	6.0	41.5	12.5	8.5	10.0	17.4
▲ CORSICANA NB&T	CORSICANA	TX	A+	A	A+	168.0	-2.26	7.4	5.6	12.0	30.3	10.0	12.8	20.7
CORTEZ COMMUNITY BK	BROOKSVILLE	FL	D	NR	NR	23.2	N/A	0.3	1.1	4.9	8.5	10.0	55.5	75.6
CORTLAND SVG & BKG CO	CORTLAND	OH	B+	B+	B+	438.1	0.72	3.8	1.5	14.4	48.5	7.9	9.6	19.1
▲ CORTRUST BK NA	MITCHELL	SD	B-	C+	C+	376.6	5.13	10.4	13.4	15.1	24.5	6.6	8.6	13.1
▲ CORUS BK NA	CHICAGO	IL	A+	A	A	3,632.0	32.87	2.1	0.2	1.2	1.2	10.0	16.8	18.5
CORYDON ST BK	CORYDON	IA	A-	A-	B+	43.4	8.31	8.4	6.4	16.2	27.8	10.0	11.1	16.1
▼ COSMOPOLITAN B&T	CHICAGO	IL	B	B+	B-	372.4	9.42	6.4	0.3	3.6	9.2	7.3	11.5	12.7
COTTAGE SAVINGS BK	MONTGOMERY	OH	B	B	C	33.3	-1.17	3.6	0.0	42.3	0.0	10.0	19.4	31.9
▲ COTTONPORT BK	COTTONPORT	LA	D	D-	D	205.1	1.95	12.3	13.3	14.6	20.1	7.4	9.3	15.3
COTTONWOOD VALLEY BK	CEDAR POINT	KS	C	C	C	19.0	-1.71	12.9	4.0	2.3	13.3	9.3	10.6	15.5
▲ COULEE ST BK	LA CROSSE	WI	A	A-	A-	116.1	-4.61	14.6	1.7	10.3	26.2	10.0	11.6	16.5
▲ COUNTRY BK	PRESCOTT	AZ	C-	D	NR	61.9	76.32	5.1	1.5	9.9	22.3	10.0	14.7	21.1
COUNTRY BK	ALEDO	IL	D	D	D+	72.0	14.85	14.8	1.7	2.4	16.5	3.0	7.8	10.0
COUNTRY BK	NEW YORK	NY	D-	D+	B-	305.2	5.63	12.2	0.1	8.5	38.6	3.1	5.1	10.7
COUNTRY BK FOR SVGS	WARE	MA	A-	A-	A-	1,010.0	6.44	2.5	4.8	27.2	41.0	10.0	12.3	23.2
COUNTRY CLUB BK NA	SHAWNEE MISSION	KS	B-	B-	B-	426.4	8.26	19.1	6.7	5.6	28.5	4.9	7.0	11.5
COUNTRY TRUST BK	BLOOMINGTON	IL	B+	B+	B+	26.6	0.67	0.0	0.0	0.0	90.5	10.0	97.9	356.5
COUNTRYBANK USA	CANDO	ND	D-	D-	D-	36.3	1.78	10.6	17.5	11.7	13.3	3.5	7.2	10.2
COUNTRYSIDE BK	REPUBLIC	MO	D	D	D	76.8	11.55	10.1	8.3	21.5	13.7	4.6	7.2	10.8
COUNTY BK	MERCED	CA	B-	B-	C+	1,315.6	16.57	15.9	2.9	1.8	27.2	4.1	7.6	10.5
▲ COUNTY BK	REHOBOTH BEACH	DE	B+	B	B	282.4	14.20	9.8	1.8	12.9	5.7	6.2	8.8	11.9
COUNTY BK	BRUNSWICK	MO	D+	D+	C+	37.5	2.38	5.8	5.9	6.1	23.4	5.1	7.1	11.5
COUNTY BKG&TC	ELKTON	MD	A-	A-	A	414.5	7.48	19.8	8.0	27.1	15.1	7.2	9.1	18.5
▲ COUNTY COMMERCE BK	VENTURA	CA	D+	D	NR	56.1	85.15	19.0	1.0	1.0	2.7	10.0	12.7	18.4
COUNTY FIRST BK	LA PLATA	MD	B	B	B	135.6	5.64	5.5	0.6	1.9	32.2	7.1	9.2	12.6
COUNTY NB	GLEN BURNIE	MD	C+	C+	C+	130.8	19.17	15.0	3.2	12.0	22.4	6.1	8.1	13.9
COUNTY NB	CLEARFIELD	PA	B-	B-	B-	687.1	-1.48	23.5	4.3	16.6	21.3	4.5	7.2	10.8
COUNTY SVGS BK	ESSINGTON	PA	D+	D	D	51.8	2.80	1.7	0.3	50.2	18.8	5.1	7.1	18.4
▼ COUNTYBANK	GREENWOOD	SC	A-	A	A	200.0	7.07	11.5	4.1	19.6	14.1	9.7	10.8	14.8
COUPLAND ST BK	COUPLAND	TX	B-	B-	B-	57.5	7.59	6.7	3.1	1.3	54.4	5.9	7.9	17.3
COVENANT BK	LEEDS	AL	D-	E+	E	65.2	-3.94	19.1	5.4	16.3	18.8	4.3	6.9	10.6
COVENANT BK	CLARKSDALE	MS	C	C	D+	137.5	24.46	17.6	6.2	11.1	18.5	5.3	7.9	11.2
▲ COVINGTON COUNTY BK	ANDALUSIA	AL	B-	C+	C	217.7	-0.38	20.3	4.3	18.9	10.4	5.5	8.0	11.4
▲ COVINGTON COUNTY BK	COLLINS	MS	B	B-	C+	54.9	2.20	6.7	11.1	7.8	41.7	9.4	10.6	18.0
COVINGTON S&LA	COVINGTON	OH	A-	A-	A-	68.4	-4.78	0.4	1.0	51.8	6.8	10.0	16.3	40.0
COWBOY ST BK	RANCHESTER	WY	D-	D-	D	41.4	5.83	16.5	10.7	11.9	29.5	5.1	7.1	11.8
▲ COWLITZ BK	LONGVIEW	WA	B-	C	C	259.7	-12.90	16.1	1.1	6.9	22.1	10.0	12.3	17.3
COZAD ST B&TC	COZAD	NE	B+	B+	B	93.4	1.65	10.4	4.2	6.1	21.5	9.4	10.6	15.2
▼ CP BURNETT & SONS,	ELDORADO	IL	C+	B-	A-	50.7	-6.76	1.0	2.0	11.8	68.9	8.8	10.2	32.5
CRAWFORD COUNTY T&SB	DENISON	IA	B	B	B	102.8	5.10	7.1	14.3	10.7	17.9	9.7	10.8	14.9
▲ CREDICARD NB	SAN ANTONIO	TX	C+	C-	C+	8.4	8.26	3.1	81.6	0.0	0.0	10.0	28.8	36.0
▼ CREDIT FIRST NA	BROOK PARK	OH	B-	B	B	6.6	-22.20	0.0	0.0	0.0	0.0	10.0	61.3	5,653.7
▲ CRESCENT B&TC	JASPER	GA	C+	C	D	415.9	32.93	4.8	5.4	11.8	4.3	9.1	12.5	14.2
▼ CRESCENT B&TC	NEW ORLEANS	LA	C+	B-	C+	324.1	12.40	4.1	83.2	3.5	1.3	9.0	11.9	14.2

Asset Quality Index	Non-Performing Loans		Net Charge-offs Avg Loans	Profitability Index	Net Income ($Mil)	Return on Assets (R.O.A.)	Return on Equity (R.O.E.)	Net Interest Spread	Overhead Efficiency Ratio	Liquidity Index	Liquidity Ratio	Hot Money Ratio	Stability Index
	as a % of Total Loans	as a % of Capital											
5.6	1.80	9.9	0.00	3.1	0.0	0.46	5.88	3.22	82.8	4.5	10.2	4.3	1.7
3.3	1.75	10.1	0.87	10.0	1.4	2.72	22.73	5.92	49.9	4.0	43.4	15.9	9.1
5.0	0.76	6.0	0.05	3.8	0.9	0.84	11.35	4.01	73.5	0.9	19.1	34.6	3.4
1.3	3.35	13.4	-0.08	3.4	0.2	0.37	2.80	3.91	87.3	3.7	13.8	10.4	3.8
6.0	1.02	5.6	-0.73	7.3	1.6	1.44	15.48	4.23	68.5	5.7	45.9	7.3	5.9
4.7	0.81	6.7	0.00	1.9	0.2	0.52	5.68	2.86	70.4	1.4	6.7	22.9	0.1
5.1	0.78	5.2	2.26	1.6	-0.1	-0.38	-4.18	3.97	95.3	4.7	152.6	35.1	1.4
7.1	0.48	3.9	0.45	3.6	0.3	0.57	6.48	3.00	63.1	2.2	16.6	18.3	2.6
8.2	0.67	3.2	0.07	3.5	0.3	0.51	3.91	3.77	72.4	3.2	31.0	16.1	6.9
6.1	0.30	2.3	0.06	4.6	1.3	0.65	6.24	2.62	67.6	0.5	6.8	47.3	5.8
6.1	0.38	2.6	0.14	6.5	2.8	1.50	19.03	4.52	68.8	2.8	27.8	17.1	5.0
8.7	0.00	0.0	0.10	5.2	0.6	0.78	8.46	3.81	60.8	3.5	31.7	14.9	5.0
7.5	0.25	2.4	0.13	6.9	1.2	1.15	15.32	4.92	56.5	2.2	19.6	18.7	3.5
7.5	0.00	0.0	0.11	4.0	0.2	0.54	5.75	3.55	79.8	5.0	72.4	15.3	3.9
8.5	0.00	0.0	0.01	3.9	0.3	0.62	7.07	3.88	73.3	1.8	14.8	20.1	4.7
8.7	0.00	0.0	0.00	3.8	0.7	0.68	6.19	3.33	65.3	1.7	29.4	29.6	2.6
3.9	0.77	4.5	-0.10	5.1	0.4	1.08	10.06	4.63	64.3	4.5	16.0	5.6	4.6
6.6	0.29	2.6	0.69	1.4	0.0	0.00	-0.02	3.21	80.1	0.6	19.9	70.1	0.0
6.5	0.74	4.1	-0.19	7.6	2.1	1.79	19.76	4.27	63.5	4.1	16.7	8.2	5.5
4.4	1.50	10.2	-0.03	5.7	0.1	0.96	9.85	3.89	70.3	1.5	18.4	25.3	3.0
8.4	0.38	1.5	0.02	9.9	1.5	1.73	12.84	5.14	58.4	3.4	22.7	13.0	8.8
9.7	0.00	0.0	0.00	0.0	-0.8	-10.15	-16.64	1.66	815.1	8.7	360.7	8.7	0.0
6.5	1.05	4.6	0.01	5.1	2.2	1.01	10.08	3.76	70.6	4.7	34.0	9.6	5.9
6.8	0.28	1.8	3.79	5.7	1.8	0.96	10.78	6.55	57.5	3.0	11.8	13.9	4.2
7.3	0.81	2.8	-0.05	9.8	35.7	2.05	12.24	4.29	33.1	5.2	130.1	24.6	10.0
8.1	0.02	0.1	0.01	10.0	0.7	3.20	26.88	5.14	26.3	2.6	12.4	15.5	8.6
5.7	0.37	2.4	0.03	10.0	3.8	2.09	18.44	5.66	43.8	0.7	12.4	43.9	8.0
8.8	0.00	0.0	0.00	4.9	0.1	0.42	2.20	2.57	78.8	7.8	472.2	13.5	2.8
0.7	5.35	32.4	0.48	5.6	1.1	1.06	11.50	4.81	66.3	5.7	76.3	13.4	4.1
7.8	0.00	0.0	-0.14	5.0	0.1	1.10	9.32	4.68	76.0	6.2	77.9	8.1	5.0
8.6	0.14	0.8	0.00	6.7	1.0	1.62	14.16	4.25	61.9	4.3	20.2	7.6	7.3
8.9	0.00	0.0	0.00	2.0	0.2	0.57	3.85	3.21	72.8	8.1	103.8	1.3	0.5
4.9	1.88	16.6	0.09	3.7	0.2	0.63	8.11	4.08	73.9	1.8	18.1	21.1	0.0
5.3	0.50	5.0	-0.02	2.4	0.6	0.36	7.18	2.74	77.3	8.9	172.2	4.6	1.7
8.9	0.25	1.1	0.05	5.4	4.7	0.94	7.64	3.66	65.9	3.9	10.8	9.4	8.9
6.3	0.29	2.3	-0.13	5.6	2.3	1.09	15.73	3.79	78.3	5.2	29.0	3.7	4.6
6.9	0.00	0.0	0.00	10.0	1.5	11.06	11.37	3.95	67.6	0.0	0.0	100.0	3.0
4.3	0.69	5.5	0.02	3.9	0.1	0.75	8.73	4.09	81.1	3.7	30.8	13.4	1.7
5.8	0.54	5.2	0.03	3.1	0.2	0.55	7.81	3.52	72.1	3.4	56.3	22.5	2.0
6.9	0.60	4.3	0.19	6.9	7.9	1.24	16.12	4.63	60.7	5.6	76.7	15.5	6.1
7.3	0.07	0.5	0.71	10.0	3.2	2.37	26.37	9.57	50.0	4.8	33.5	8.3	5.6
7.7	0.23	1.9	0.00	3.5	0.1	0.61	8.62	2.93	82.2	6.0	63.5	8.5	3.0
7.8	0.01	0.1	0.03	10.0	3.6	1.79	17.58	4.79	47.9	4.1	30.8	11.6	8.7
8.6	0.00	0.0	0.00	1.3	0.1	0.28	2.16	3.63	80.4	7.9	106.2	3.7	0.0
8.5	0.09	0.6	0.01	4.9	0.6	0.90	10.12	3.92	66.1	5.2	16.5	1.0	5.3
8.7	0.12	0.8	0.09	3.3	0.3	0.41	4.93	3.73	82.4	4.7	45.5	13.0	3.9
5.0	0.52	3.7	0.16	6.3	3.9	1.14	12.46	3.97	62.7	5.3	68.8	14.6	6.2
6.1	0.64	4.8	0.00	3.3	0.1	0.29	4.03	3.49	87.5	3.0	35.0	18.6	2.9
5.9	0.53	3.3	0.03	10.0	2.3	2.33	20.72	4.89	63.2	3.4	14.0	12.1	8.6
4.2	2.63	7.5	-0.04	1.6	0.1	0.44	4.06	3.64	95.1	2.2	31.1	22.5	4.8
4.3	1.26	12.2	0.48	4.7	0.3	0.89	13.50	4.68	69.4	3.4	24.2	12.7	0.3
6.0	0.25	2.0	0.29	4.1	0.7	0.96	12.20	3.89	70.8	1.5	13.6	23.9	1.9
6.9	0.46	4.1	0.18	6.2	1.6	1.44	18.32	3.71	53.2	1.7	21.7	22.8	3.9
6.8	0.69	3.2	-0.18	6.2	0.4	1.58	15.19	3.86	57.9	4.1	67.8	19.0	5.0
9.5	0.34	1.2	0.00	5.1	0.3	0.74	4.71	3.06	64.8	5.3	49.6	10.1	7.2
4.3	1.07	8.0	0.13	2.1	0.0	0.19	2.62	4.42	92.7	2.8	19.3	15.3	1.7
7.6	0.29	1.4	0.21	4.4	1.0	0.73	5.82	5.10	79.6	3.3	47.6	21.2	4.4
4.5	0.84	4.9	0.09	8.4	0.8	1.71	15.91	4.60	61.7	5.4	46.5	9.1	7.1
6.8	4.55	9.6	-0.05	3.0	0.1	0.30	2.96	2.73	89.0	9.0	215.2	7.1	4.7
5.2	0.70	4.3	0.67	6.9	0.6	1.16	11.02	4.05	45.7	4.3	27.6	8.9	5.6
4.8	0.84	2.1	1.19	6.4	0.1	1.19	4.09	16.83	86.4	1.5	40.0	37.3	5.6
10.0	0.00	0.0	0.00	10.0	1.7	54.70	106.48	0.16	47.0	0.0	N/A	100.0	0.0
4.1	0.57	3.8	-0.05	6.6	1.0	0.51	4.52	3.47	65.5	1.5	25.6	28.1	4.6
1.5	2.17	12.2	1.65	10.0	5.1	3.29	26.49	13.61	57.2	5.1	108.8	20.0	7.3

Name	City	State	Weiss Safety Rating	2003 Weiss Safety Rating	2002 Weiss Safety Rating	Total Assets ($Mil)	One Year Asset Growth	Asset Mix (As a % of Total Assets)				Capital-ization Index	Leverage Ratio	Risk-based Capital Ratio
								Comm-ercial Loans	Cons-umer Loans	Home Mort-gages	Secur-ities			
▲ CRESCENT BK	MYRTLE BEACH	SC	C	C-	C	132.9	37.95	16.1	2.7	18.6	6.8	3.8	7.7	10.4
▲ CRESCENT ST BK	CARY	NC	B-	C+	C-	309.2	36.33	14.0	2.1	9.4	13.4	5.4	9.2	11.3
CRESCO UNION SVG BK	CRESCO	IA	A-	A-	A-	202.8	-0.59	8.5	4.7	17.6	31.3	10.0	11.0	17.5
CREST SVGS BK	WILDWOOD	NJ	C+	C+	C	277.3	9.34	1.3	1.1	50.3	19.1	4.8	6.8	12.1
CRESTMARK BK	TROY	MI	C-	D+	D-	114.6	36.42	83.6	0.0	0.0	2.8	4.6	8.8	10.8
CROCKETT NB	OZONA	TX	A-	A-	B+	170.8	12.26	3.0	2.4	27.6	6.2	8.7	10.1	14.2
▲ CROGHAN COLONIAL BK	FREMONT	OH	B	B-	B-	413.9	6.03	8.3	10.1	25.7	15.0	6.9	8.9	14.0
CROOKSTON NB	CROOKSTON	MN	C+	C+	C+	34.8	1.08	8.6	4.9	8.4	30.7	6.7	8.7	16.2
CROSBY ST BK	CROSBY	TX	C+	C+	B-	164.2	8.07	9.5	4.4	8.0	18.0	2.8	6.1	9.9
▲ CROSS COUNTRY BK	WILMINGTON	DE	B-	C+	C-	1,046.8	-19.69	0.0	95.7	0.0	10.5	10.0	52.8	27.3
CROSS COUNTY BK	WYNNE	AR	A-	B+	B-	161.7	0.11	9.8	3.4	12.7	22.7	10.0	11.3	17.2
▲ CROSS COUNTY FSB	NEW YORK CITY	NY	C+	C	C	358.3	6.46	0.0	0.1	28.8	36.8	4.7	6.7	14.6
▲ CROSS KEYS BK	ST JOSEPH	LA	A	A-	A-	190.3	0.78	5.8	5.5	20.6	37.6	10.0	11.2	19.2
CROSSROADS BK	EFFINGHAM	IL	A-	A-	A-	86.0	1.42	10.2	9.8	18.5	15.1	10.0	13.3	18.9
▼ CROW RIVER ST BK	DELANO	MN	C	C+	C+	56.6	14.35	12.4	10.3	4.8	40.1	6.8	8.8	15.0
▲ CROWELL ST BK	CROWELL	TX	B-	C+	C	22.0	-3.28	11.0	12.1	9.5	20.0	10.0	11.2	18.4
▲ CROWLEY B&LA	CROWLEY	LA	C-	D+	D+	38.5	-7.26	0.0	2.4	23.3	64.1	7.5	9.3	30.0
▲ CROWN BK	EDINA	MN	C	C-	D	118.4	21.77	58.5	1.8	2.2	8.6	3.2	8.2	10.1
▼ CROWN BK NA	OCEAN CITY	NJ	C	B-	C	242.1	16.45	8.9	0.5	3.5	4.2	10.0	15.7	18.6
CROYDON SVGS BK	CROYDON	PA	C	C	C-	8.1	9.68	0.0	0.0	62.9	1.2	10.0	11.5	21.5
CRYSTAL LAKE B&TC NA	CRYSTAL LAKE	IL	C+	C+	C+	454.6	27.33	25.5	7.0	1.2	24.1	5.9	8.7	11.7
CRYSTAL RIVER BK	CRYSTAL RIVER	FL	B+	B+	A-	66.4	3.95	0.0	1.2	40.0	25.0	8.1	9.7	22.7
CSB BK	CAPAC	MI	B-	B-	B-	203.8	0.74	4.8	1.7	29.1	26.5	5.7	7.7	13.7
▲ CSB BK	CLAYCOMO	MO	B-	C+	C	117.3	33.87	0.9	1.1	8.8	2.1	5.3	8.8	11.2
CSB BK	CURWENSVILLE	PA	B-	C+	D	203.7	12.72	17.2	9.4	16.3	22.2	7.6	9.4	13.5
CSB STATE BK	CYNTHIANA	IN	B	B	B	51.8	-7.74	2.2	1.2	19.3	43.8	9.1	10.4	19.8
CUERO ST BK SSB	CUERO	TX	B+	B+	B+	177.7	2.67	1.5	3.7	33.0	45.9	10.0	12.7	33.7
CULBERTSON BK	CULBERTSON	NE	C	C+	C+	16.0	0.84	8.3	1.8	1.0	48.9	10.0	16.0	31.0
CULLMAN SVGS BK	CULLMAN	AL	B	B	B	179.3	14.03	0.3	2.4	38.5	31.6	10.0	13.0	22.8
▲ CUMBERLAND B&TC	CLARKSVILLE	TN	C-	D+	D	76.1	31.96	10.5	2.4	22.4	16.6	8.0	9.7	14.9
CUMBERLAND BK	CARTHAGE	TN	C-	C-	D+	282.5	-5.34	35.6	7.8	17.9	21.5	5.7	7.7	12.7
▲ CUMBERLAND BK SOUTH	FRANKLIN	TN	C	C-	D+	311.6	34.20	10.4	0.8	6.5	35.7	5.4	7.4	13.6
CUMBERLAND COUNTY BK	CROSSVILLE	TN	B	B	B	144.6	9.15	2.3	4.8	20.4	44.2	5.8	7.8	20.4
▲ CUMBERLAND FEDERAL BK	CUMBERLAND	WI	B-	C+	C+	65.0	6.68	7.6	2.8	44.5	26.6	8.1	9.7	22.4
CUMBERLAND SECURITY BK	SOMERSET	KY	A-	A-	B+	133.9	0.46	14.3	8.6	20.2	13.5	8.2	9.9	13.5
▲ CUMBERLAND VALLEY NB&TC	E BERNSTADT	KY	D-	E-	E-	440.4	-4.71	7.4	3.8	24.4	33.4	5.5	7.5	14.6
CURRIE ST BK	CURRIE	MN	E-	E-	E-	24.6	19.77	15.5	3.9	7.7	5.5	3.4	7.4	10.2
CURTIS ST BK	CURTIS	NE	C+	C+	C+	21.6	0.69	15.9	4.5	5.9	26.8	10.0	11.9	17.8
CUSTAR ST BK	CUSTAR	OH	A	A	A	52.9	2.06	1.1	2.6	45.8	34.0	10.0	17.0	38.4
CUSTER FS&LA	BROKEN BOW	NE	C+	C+	C	52.4	2.33	13.8	8.3	16.9	34.0	7.9	9.6	16.6
CUSTODIAL TRUST CO	PRINCETON	NJ	A+	A+	A+	450.2	-24.24	39.5	0.0	0.0	4.9	10.0	35.6	43.4
CUYAMACA BK NA	SANTEE	CA	C+	C+	C	116.8	14.32	13.7	7.1	7.4	8.8	3.7	7.9	10.3
CYGNET PRIVATE BK	PONTE VEDRA BCH	FL	D	NR	NR	25.2	N/A	36.3	2.3	4.8	19.8	10.0	42.0	61.3
CYPRESS BK	PALM COAST	FL	B-	B-	B-	133.7	23.76	6.0	1.3	7.2	21.0	4.4	7.1	10.7
CYPRESS BK FSB	PITTSBURG	TX	D+	D+	D+	97.4	5.51	6.2	18.1	37.6	20.3	4.8	6.8	12.4
CYRIL ST BK	CYRIL	OK	B-	B-	B-	22.9	3.99	4.2	8.7	2.8	48.3	10.0	14.3	34.0
D L EVANS BK	BURLEY	ID	C	C	C	411.8	19.50	11.9	8.0	4.6	12.3	3.2	7.4	10.1
D'HANIS ST BK	D HANIS	TX	C+	C+	C	28.7	4.12	8.4	22.1	10.9	15.1	8.4	10.0	15.5
DACOTAH BK	ROLLA	ND	B-	B-	B-	114.5	11.84	17.0	4.1	6.6	29.8	6.7	8.7	13.4
DACOTAH BK	ABERDEEN	SD	B-	B-	B	803.6	11.77	16.0	6.4	8.1	14.3	7.0	9.4	12.5
DACOTAH BK VALLEY CITY	VALLEY CITY	ND	B-	B-	B-	95.7	10.33	15.5	8.7	6.3	26.9	8.9	10.3	16.0
DAIRY ST BK	RICE LAKE	WI	B	B	B+	236.8	0.44	10.6	3.2	10.8	48.9	7.0	9.0	17.7
DAIRYLAND ST BK	BRUCE	WI	D	D+	D+	32.6	5.85	8.7	11.4	27.3	2.3	3.8	7.6	10.4
DAIRYMANS ST BK	CLINTONVILLE	WI	B+	B+	B	95.5	-2.86	8.2	2.8	21.3	27.3	10.0	11.0	16.5
DAKOTA COMMUNITY BK	HEBRON	ND	C+	B-	C+	186.2	26.36	11.6	9.0	6.6	5.3	3.8	8.1	10.4
DAKOTA COUNTY ST BK	S SIOUX CITY	NE	B-	B-	B-	92.5	-3.14	11.5	4.5	19.4	31.8	5.9	7.9	12.6
DAKOTA HERITAGE ST BK	CHANCELLOR	SD	B-	B-	B-	30.3	1.90	11.9	7.1	10.1	21.6	10.0	11.0	16.9
DAKOTA PRAIRIE BK	PRESHO	SD	B-	B-	B-	27.6	8.89	10.3	4.2	0.9	25.9	9.2	10.7	14.4
▼ DAKOTA ST BK	BLUNT	SD	C-	C	C+	24.8	9.40	6.5	2.2	1.3	23.3	7.3	9.2	13.2
▲ DAKOTA WESTERN BK	BOWMAN	ND	D+	D	C-	101.8	3.74	10.2	6.0	2.7	16.9	6.1	8.5	11.8
▲ DALHART FS&LA	DALHART	TX	B-	C+	C	101.9	2.45	0.2	1.6	44.7	38.0	6.1	8.1	22.8
DALLAS CITY BK	DALLAS	TX	D	D	NR	30.0	N/A	8.3	3.4	6.6	18.2	10.0	32.3	53.4
DALLAS NB	DALLAS	TX	C	C	C-	85.2	-2.78	13.5	7.3	6.0	43.0	6.1	8.1	16.2
DAMARISCOTTA B&TC	DAMARISCOTTA	ME	B-	B-	B-	136.1	4.29	11.5	5.5	19.8	13.5	7.6	9.4	14.4

Asset Quality Index	Non-Performing Loans as a % of Total Loans	Non-Performing Loans as a % of Capital	Net Charge-offs Avg Loans	Profitability Index	Net Income ($Mil)	Return on Assets (R.O.A.)	Return on Equity (R.O.E.)	Net Interest Spread	Overhead Efficiency Ratio	Liquidity Index	Liquidity Ratio	Hot Money Ratio	Stability Index
7.0	0.00	0.0	0.00	4.6	0.5	0.78	9.66	3.53	55.3	2.9	44.6	24.8	1.9
7.2	0.13	0.9	0.11	4.2	1.1	0.71	7.05	3.60	67.1	0.7	8.1	34.0	5.6
6.8	0.45	2.2	0.03	6.0	1.4	1.38	11.24	4.19	61.7	4.2	7.0	6.1	7.8
8.5	0.05	0.5	0.00	5.5	1.2	0.85	11.99	3.61	64.9	0.6	6.6	35.0	3.7
2.5	1.86	11.6	-0.05	8.7	0.6	1.11	8.50	13.40	77.6	6.8	4,710.3	18.4	6.5
8.2	0.20	1.6	0.02	9.5	1.9	2.31	22.91	5.15	58.9	2.7	54.5	41.1	6.9
4.7	0.52	3.6	0.21	7.1	2.5	1.21	11.85	4.26	60.2	3.9	9.9	8.4	6.4
8.6	0.00	0.0	0.00	5.4	0.2	1.35	14.98	3.38	67.1	7.1	119.6	10.3	4.6
8.5	0.00	0.0	0.00	5.6	1.0	1.22	18.56	4.60	76.0	5.9	57.5	9.5	4.0
3.3	4.40	5.3	20.69	10.0	136.3	24.75	53.91	13.62	38.9	3.1	67.2	83.9	9.5
5.9	0.97	5.7	-0.09	9.1	1.4	1.70	15.03	4.58	52.8	2.0	7.6	18.1	6.3
9.3	0.05	0.3	0.01	4.8	1.2	0.66	9.97	3.27	68.1	1.8	23.3	22.5	3.4
8.5	0.13	0.6	-0.06	9.1	2.1	2.13	19.14	4.65	55.9	3.1	27.5	15.3	6.7
7.9	0.15	0.8	0.05	6.6	0.4	1.00	7.64	3.95	61.1	4.1	31.2	11.4	7.2
4.2	2.45	12.3	0.18	4.6	0.2	0.73	8.18	4.33	81.6	5.6	30.7	2.0	3.8
7.9	0.12	0.6	0.11	9.3	0.3	2.64	23.28	5.60	56.0	4.7	70.2	15.0	4.9
7.7	0.68	2.1	0.03	4.4	0.1	0.70	7.80	2.49	59.3	4.6	31.6	8.9	2.8
7.8	0.00	0.0	0.02	5.6	0.9	1.55	20.02	4.57	56.5	0.7	9.5	36.5	1.5
1.8	3.49	16.7	0.01	8.5	1.9	1.61	9.84	5.37	54.3	3.0	46.3	24.7	7.8
8.4	0.00	0.0	0.00	5.3	0.0	0.98	8.07	4.22	66.5	5.0	N/A	0.0	0.0
6.8	0.33	2.5	0.03	3.7	1.4	0.62	7.27	2.55	60.6	0.9	19.8	34.7	4.8
9.9	0.00	0.0	0.00	7.8	0.5	1.55	15.12	4.47	69.7	5.2	65.5	13.5	7.4
6.8	0.36	2.4	0.16	4.8	0.7	0.72	8.23	3.89	77.8	5.8	39.9	4.5	5.1
6.7	0.00	0.0	0.00	9.5	0.9	1.63	16.45	4.33	41.2	2.9	18.4	14.7	6.1
4.7	0.87	5.6	0.18	4.7	0.8	0.80	7.69	3.92	64.3	3.1	17.1	13.6	4.6
9.3	0.00	0.0	-0.01	4.4	0.2	0.72	6.62	3.74	74.9	1.8	8.5	19.5	5.3
9.1	0.51	1.8	0.09	5.0	0.7	0.80	6.43	3.67	65.3	5.9	82.4	13.4	6.7
8.7	0.68	1.7	0.09	2.6	0.0	0.53	3.38	4.41	83.5	3.4	24.1	12.3	2.9
8.9	0.24	1.1	0.05	4.6	0.7	0.78	5.76	3.24	67.4	1.5	21.2	26.9	7.7
8.2	0.06	0.4	0.10	2.1	0.2	0.43	4.29	3.44	73.8	3.3	52.3	21.1	0.0
3.3	1.94	15.0	0.35	3.6	0.6	0.43	5.57	3.60	80.4	2.0	29.2	24.0	3.3
5.3	1.22	9.9	0.26	3.7	1.0	0.67	9.69	3.22	73.7	0.8	17.2	42.8	4.0
8.7	0.15	0.8	0.19	6.3	0.9	1.23	15.62	3.28	60.7	7.0	90.8	8.5	5.7
4.9	1.34	7.3	0.02	4.9	0.2	0.65	6.17	2.72	61.1	3.3	55.4	23.9	5.0
7.5	0.17	1.1	0.27	10.0	1.3	1.96	19.64	5.70	52.9	3.7	26.6	12.0	7.7
2.2	3.77	24.7	1.04	2.2	0.9	0.38	5.21	3.56	91.9	1.9	30.3	27.2	1.8
0.9	1.93	21.2	-0.01	4.6	0.1	0.69	9.50	4.56	70.8	0.9	9.7	31.7	0.1
6.9	1.16	6.3	-0.04	7.1	0.2	1.65	14.19	5.38	61.6	1.4	11.6	23.9	4.4
8.9	0.53	1.8	0.07	10.0	0.5	1.85	10.76	4.20	35.3	5.5	79.3	13.6	8.7
4.5	1.39	8.6	-0.02	6.2	0.3	0.96	10.27	3.09	59.6	1.9	9.4	19.0	4.7
8.1	0.00	0.0	0.00	9.9	4.0	1.64	5.27	2.31	46.3	1.7	43.2	96.6	9.7
7.9	0.06	0.6	0.00	4.8	0.4	0.80	9.97	5.27	76.4	3.4	30.3	14.6	4.3
8.6	0.00	0.0	0.00	0.0	-1.2	-13.97	-25.30	1.16	1,004.4	6.3	183.1	19.6	0.0
8.4	0.00	0.0	0.00	4.1	0.4	0.64	8.15	2.98	63.6	4.6	29.9	8.5	5.8
4.2	0.52	5.1	0.37	4.5	0.3	0.69	9.76	3.79	70.1	1.7	7.5	20.0	2.7
8.7	0.00	0.0	-0.13	6.6	0.2	1.58	11.13	3.40	57.9	7.8	174.6	11.1	6.3
4.4	0.60	5.9	0.19	5.4	1.7	0.84	11.22	5.16	72.5	2.6	13.9	15.9	3.2
3.7	1.05	5.9	0.98	6.4	0.2	1.49	14.54	4.63	65.3	4.0	80.4	23.2	4.5
4.7	1.21	6.6	0.25	3.3	0.3	0.44	4.27	3.69	79.0	3.9	39.1	15.4	5.6
4.2	1.39	10.2	0.07	7.8	4.9	1.25	13.18	4.28	54.3	4.9	44.2	11.8	6.4
3.7	1.27	5.3	-0.08	6.4	0.5	1.13	8.34	4.15	57.7	3.9	17.9	9.4	6.8
8.9	0.22	1.1	0.00	5.9	1.4	1.17	13.10	3.18	53.6	2.8	30.5	18.0	6.0
0.9	2.39	24.9	0.01	9.4	0.4	2.29	29.41	5.53	57.2	4.8	19.3	4.0	4.8
7.1	0.56	2.6	0.60	5.5	0.5	1.01	8.48	4.95	72.8	4.7	24.9	5.6	6.6
6.4	0.35	3.4	-0.08	5.8	0.8	0.85	11.15	5.73	78.6	1.4	16.4	25.8	4.2
5.0	1.33	9.2	-0.21	6.5	0.7	1.48	19.01	4.09	61.9	4.2	41.5	14.3	5.6
5.0	1.29	7.2	0.12	3.7	0.1	0.79	7.19	3.66	70.2	6.1	170.3	19.3	4.4
7.3	0.09	0.5	-0.46	6.5	0.2	1.44	14.32	4.48	64.9	4.1	29.6	11.2	5.3
8.4	0.00	0.0	0.00	4.1	0.1	0.58	6.46	4.94	85.7	1.8	27.8	22.1	3.0
2.2	1.91	14.1	0.79	5.1	0.4	0.84	9.92	3.79	63.6	3.8	22.8	10.6	4.5
7.4	0.06	0.4	0.09	4.1	0.3	0.52	6.39	3.15	75.5	1.3	18.5	28.6	4.3
9.3	0.00	0.0	0.00	0.0	-0.7	-6.02	-14.68	2.65	272.2	5.2	136.0	22.8	0.0
8.0	0.18	0.9	0.51	3.1	0.2	0.39	4.61	4.35	86.9	4.5	30.3	9.0	3.0
4.2	1.88	13.0	0.02	4.6	0.6	0.83	9.01	3.88	68.9	4.1	43.4	15.4	5.9

Name	City	State	Weiss Safety Rating	2003 Weiss Safety Rating	2002 Weiss Safety Rating	Total Assets ($Mil)	One Year Asset Growth	Asset Mix (As a % of Total Assets) Commercial Loans	Consumer Loans	Home Mortgages	Securities	Capitalization Index	Leverage Ratio	Risk-based Capital Ratio
DAMASCUS COMMUNITY BK	DAMASCUS	MD	A-	A-	B	148.0	6.46	8.1	4.9	20.5	21.6	10.0	14.2	22.8
DANVERS SVGS BK	DANVERS	MA	C+	C+	B-	975.9	16.92	16.8	0.5	14.3	21.5	5.4	7.7	11.3
DANVILLE ST SVG BK	DANVILLE	IA	B+	B	B-	74.6	-0.42	4.3	5.0	23.2	44.1	9.6	10.8	21.7
DARBY B&TC	VIDALIA	GA	C-	C-	C	479.3	11.79	13.6	3.5	13.7	13.2	3.7	7.8	10.4
DARLINGTON COUNTY BK	DARLINGTON	SC	B-	B-	B-	36.2	11.85	9.8	10.6	3.5	30.5	9.9	10.9	18.0
DART BK	MASON	MI	B+	B+	B+	212.8	-3.94	6.1	4.7	29.4	26.4	8.2	9.8	16.6
DAVIDSON TRUST CO.	GREAT FALLS	MT	C	C	C+	4.7	-1.71	0.0	0.0	0.0	80.4	10.0	70.8	315.2
DAVIS COUNTY SVG BK	BLOOMFIELD	IA	B-	B-	B	68.6	2.74	6.2	5.2	8.3	20.3	7.7	9.5	14.0
DAVIS TRUST CO	ELKINS	WV	A-	A-	A	126.0	3.56	6.4	11.2	33.3	12.4	10.0	13.9	20.7
DAVISON ST BK	DAVISON	MI	C+	B-	B-	50.7	12.64	14.7	5.8	5.7	18.3	5.7	8.8	11.6
▲ DE MOTTE STATE BANK	DE MOTTE	IN	A-	B+	B+	261.8	6.05	17.9	2.8	21.4	28.8	8.4	9.9	16.1
DE SOTO ST BK	DE SOTO	KS	B	B	B+	34.5	4.56	1.6	7.9	7.3	46.0	10.0	16.8	50.7
DE WITT B&TC	DE WITT	AR	C-	C-	B+	114.1	-29.13	9.5	4.9	20.3	17.1	10.0	16.3	24.8
DE WITT B&TC	DE WITT	IA	B+	B+	B-	95.7	-4.55	7.8	2.6	11.0	41.7	10.0	12.8	21.6
▲ DE WITT ST BK	DE WITT	NE	C+	C	C-	32.2	37.27	6.1	3.5	9.8	20.2	5.0	7.0	11.3
▲ DE WITT SVGS BK	CLINTON	IL	C+	C	C-	75.8	-9.82	0.9	12.8	23.6	40.1	6.9	8.9	20.1
DEAN CO-OP BK	FRANKLIN	MA	B-	B-	B-	177.6	13.47	3.5	1.1	50.5	11.3	5.7	7.7	12.3
DEARBORN FSB	DEARBORN	MI	A+	A+	A+	270.1	-3.01	0.1	0.1	72.4	0.0	10.0	20.5	36.2
▲ DEARBORN SA	LAWRENCEBURG	IN	B+	B	B-	83.8	3.93	0.8	1.3	37.7	9.9	10.0	11.2	19.0
DECATUR B&TC NA	DECATUR	IN	B-	B-	B-	146.6	2.79	13.3	5.5	25.2	12.4	5.9	8.0	11.7
▼ DECATUR COUNTY BK	DECATURVILLE	TN	B-	B	B+	82.1	6.23	3.9	4.6	12.6	48.3	10.0	12.5	25.4
▲ DECATUR FIRST BK	DECATUR	GA	B-	C+	C+	117.2	17.69	9.1	2.2	11.7	13.2	5.3	8.7	11.2
DECATUR ST BK	DECATUR	AR	B-	B-	B-	146.1	3.80	3.1	14.4	18.2	16.6	10.0	13.0	19.0
DECORAH B&TC	DECORAH	IA	A-	A-	A	197.9	8.97	8.6	5.3	17.5	35.8	6.9	8.9	14.0
▼ DEDHAM CO-OP BK	DEDHAM	MA	B	B+	B+	80.9	5.14	0.0	0.4	38.4	49.7	10.0	15.9	32.3
▼ DEDHAM INST FOR SVGS	DEDHAM	MA	C	C+	C+	866.1	1.98	0.8	0.5	48.6	34.4	9.0	10.3	19.6
▲ DEEPGREEN BK	SEVEN HILLS	OH	D+	D-	D-	179.3	-45.97	0.0	0.0	0.0	0.0	10.0	22.4	24.7
DEFIANCE ST BK	DEFIANCE	IA	C-	C+	C+	20.6	11.80	11.8	7.5	15.8	0.8	7.7	9.5	14.4
▼ DEKALB BK	CROSSVILLE	AL	E+	D	C-	28.5	-10.37	7.0	11.8	14.0	30.4	5.7	7.7	15.7
DEKALB CMNTY BK	SMITHVILLE	TN	B-	B-	B-	106.5	13.17	5.5	12.1	52.6	12.1	4.9	6.9	12.9
DEL NORTE FS&LA	DEL NORTE	CO	D+	D	D	27.9	11.07	4.8	2.6	49.8	10.5	6.1	8.1	15.2
▼ DELANCO FSB	DELANCO	NJ	B-	B	B	70.8	6.31	0.3	0.5	38.6	43.4	9.0	10.3	23.3
▼ DELAWARE COUNTY B&TC	LEWIS CENTER	OH	C+	B-	B-	575.0	9.35	6.6	7.9	22.1	16.7	4.4	6.4	11.5
▼ DELAWARE NB	GEORGETOWN	DE	B-	B	B	376.8	10.78	4.0	3.4	21.2	26.6	3.6	6.4	10.3
▼ DELAWARE NB OF DELHI	DELHI	NY	B-	B+	B+	159.4	12.40	5.0	2.9	13.2	48.4	7.0	9.0	18.2
DELAWARE PLACE BK	CHICAGO	IL	C	C	D+	236.7	8.20	1.2	30.6	2.6	21.1	3.6	7.6	10.3
DELTA BK	VIDALIA	LA	B-	B-	B	126.3	2.09	7.3	6.5	12.4	38.7	6.4	8.4	15.4
DELTA BK	COOPER	TX	C-	C-	C-	19.0	-7.30	5.4	11.6	15.8	26.6	6.4	11.5	12.1
DELTA NB	MANTECA	CA	A-	A-	B+	146.7	10.66	2.4	0.4	0.3	24.0	10.0	11.5	17.4
DELTA NB&TC	NEW YORK	NY	C-	C-	C+	385.4	-13.19	13.8	2.3	0.0	40.2	8.4	10.0	25.0
▲ DELTA SOUTHERN BANK	RULEVILLE	MS	B-	C	D+	91.2	65.14	4.0	3.6	6.6	58.1	6.3	8.3	14.3
▲ DELTA T&B	PARKDALE	AR	D	D-	D-	185.5	9.80	29.0	4.4	13.9	15.8	7.6	9.4	13.5
DENALI ST BK	FAIRBANKS	AK	B	B	B	191.4	9.08	14.3	2.7	5.7	44.8	6.0	8.0	16.3
DENISON ST BK	HOLTON	KS	B+	B+	A+	188.5	18.79	8.2	4.7	23.7	21.6	9.7	10.8	14.9
▲ DENMARK ST BK	DENMARK	WI	C+	C	C	323.3	-2.73	10.3	2.8	31.7	15.6	8.8	10.2	14.7
DENVER SVG BK	DENVER	IA	B	B	B	58.8	13.26	4.2	3.4	23.3	39.2	5.0	7.0	13.0
DEPOSIT B&TC	GREENSBURG	KY	A	A	A	77.7	0.23	2.3	7.8	27.3	32.5	10.0	12.1	20.5
DEPOSIT BK OF CARLISLE	CARLISLE	KY	A	A	A	58.8	0.13	3.7	7.7	22.7	35.2	10.0	20.6	37.1
▲ DESERT COMMUNITY BK	VICTORVILLE	CA	B	B-	B-	453.1	21.31	14.7	9.9	3.6	14.0	6.2	9.1	11.9
DESERT COMMUNITY BK	LAS VEGAS	NV	C	C	C	59.8	3.68	12.7	0.7	1.3	2.3	8.3	11.6	13.6
▼ DESERT HILLS BK	PHOENIX	AZ	B-	B-	D+	116.9	19.77	19.5	2.6	14.0	4.8	8.5	11.0	13.8
DESJARDINS BK NA	HALLANDALE	FL	B+	NR	NR	107.8	N/A	8.7	0.2	55.9	14.2	10.0	14.2	25.9
DESTIN BK	DESTIN	FL	C+	C+	C+	449.2	26.90	11.1	2.3	22.9	22.5	5.6	7.6	11.8
▲ DETROIT COMMERCE BK	DETROIT	MI	C	C-	C-	59.2	41.67	16.0	0.3	9.3	0.0	3.0	9.2	10.0
▲ DEUEL COUNTY NB	CLEAR LAKE	SD	B	B-	B-	43.3	20.95	6.5	3.1	3.7	36.8	10.0	13.4	20.1
DEUTSCHE BK FLORIDA NA	PALM BEACH	FL	C+	B-	C	14.9	0.78	0.0	0.0	0.0	51.6	10.0	92.2	787.6
DEUTSCHE BK TC AMERICAS	NEW YORK	NY	C+	B-	C	30,969.0	-25.18	8.1	1.6	0.7	0.2	10.0	21.9	42.8
DEUTSCHE BK TR CO DE	WILMINGTON	DE	B-	B	C+	712.3	2.50	16.6	0.9	0.0	6.3	10.0	24.6	36.2
▲ DEVON BK	CHICAGO	IL	B-	C+	C	261.1	2.70	13.3	1.0	9.4	21.1	8.5	10.5	13.7
DEWEY ST BK	DEWEY	IL	D	D-	E+	18.3	-9.37	4.0	2.3	16.8	50.3	7.7	9.5	23.5
DIABLO VALLEY BK	DANVILLE	CA	D	D	NR	83.4	N/A	24.4	0.3	5.3	22.8	10.0	17.5	22.9
▲ DIAMOND STATE BK	MURFREESBORO	AR	B-	C+	C	187.7	3.02	4.5	10.4	22.0	31.4	6.2	8.2	14.8
DICKINSON COUNTY BK	ENTERPRISE	KS	C+	C+	C+	11.7	3.70	9.2	4.2	23.7	30.0	10.0	12.2	26.1
DILLARD NB	GILBERT	AZ	B	B	B-	30.2	63.84	0.0	0.0	0.0	0.0	10.0	46.7	107.9

Asset Quality Index	Non-Performing Loans as a % of Total Loans	Non-Performing Loans as a % of Capital	Net Charge-offs Avg Loans	Profitability Index	Net Income ($Mil)	Return on Assets (R.O.A.)	Return on Equity (R.O.E.)	Net Interest Spread	Overhead Efficiency Ratio	Liquidity Index	Liquidity Ratio	Hot Money Ratio	Stability Index
6.0	1.58	6.8	0.20	9.3	1.2	1.60	11.41	5.07	55.4	5.4	36.8	6.0	8.4
6.3	0.39	3.3	0.24	3.8	3.1	0.66	8.44	3.82	77.0	4.0	32.8	12.8	4.2
5.6	1.76	7.0	0.01	7.5	0.5	1.43	12.70	3.84	48.6	5.2	36.5	7.0	7.0
2.6	1.61	14.5	0.91	6.4	2.7	1.16	15.21	4.37	53.0	0.5	6.1	50.5	3.3
5.0	1.71	8.4	0.29	5.6	0.2	0.99	9.31	4.37	66.2	5.6	33.3	2.9	4.4
6.2	0.41	2.6	2.92	5.3	1.0	0.94	9.47	3.96	61.2	2.3	31.9	23.1	6.0
6.7	0.00	0.0	0.00	9.9	0.0	1.67	2.34	2.58	97.9	1.8	58.6	100.0	0.0
4.8	0.71	4.6	1.12	5.0	0.2	0.52	5.07	4.17	62.9	4.5	35.3	11.0	5.4
7.7	0.48	2.3	0.01	5.3	1.2	1.89	12.29	4.29	75.1	5.4	37.2	5.9	8.5
8.2	0.05	0.4	0.32	4.8	0.3	1.01	11.67	4.17	67.9	3.2	64.2	29.4	2.9
7.4	0.37	2.3	0.01	7.1	1.5	1.15	11.75	4.11	58.4	2.9	11.6	14.1	6.2
6.3	5.83	7.6	0.59	3.5	0.1	0.36	2.11	2.70	75.6	6.7	114.7	11.8	5.8
1.7	7.92	25.9	0.34	4.0	0.9	1.38	9.00	3.98	53.3	1.3	28.0	33.8	5.5
6.9	1.22	4.6	0.05	5.8	0.6	1.31	10.12	3.41	66.4	3.5	14.8	11.4	5.8
4.4	1.77	14.6	0.00	5.5	0.2	1.00	12.49	4.27	71.0	3.3	16.0	12.6	4.6
4.3	1.15	5.3	2.56	4.5	0.3	0.84	9.70	3.77	63.1	4.4	62.9	16.8	3.5
9.3	0.01	0.1	0.01	4.6	0.5	0.60	7.80	4.33	78.3	4.5	29.2	8.6	4.1
9.4	0.13	0.6	0.00	8.0	1.5	1.13	5.60	3.88	53.2	1.5	20.0	25.9	9.1
5.7	0.99	6.1	0.00	6.5	0.4	1.10	9.62	3.57	55.9	1.7	34.6	33.8	6.2
5.5	0.43	1.5	0.33	9.8	1.1	1.52	8.06	4.79	45.7	5.3	43.8	9.5	8.0
8.9	0.60	1.9	0.28	3.5	0.3	0.69	5.29	3.32	80.3	5.0	34.8	7.8	6.5
8.5	0.05	0.4	-0.05	3.9	0.3	0.59	6.51	4.07	75.3	2.2	27.2	19.9	4.2
4.9	1.18	6.2	0.56	9.3	1.9	2.73	21.55	5.27	43.8	0.9	19.8	39.7	6.8
7.3	0.33	1.9	0.00	8.5	1.9	1.90	19.93	3.74	49.7	4.4	19.3	6.6	7.2
10.0	0.00	0.0	0.00	4.2	0.3	0.73	4.57	2.99	65.0	2.6	43.0	27.2	7.7
9.8	0.22	1.2	0.00	2.7	1.6	0.36	3.37	2.51	86.2	4.6	39.4	11.8	6.7
8.8	0.05	0.2	0.05	1.7	7.6	8.90	40.04	2.36	23.3	1.2	35.6	2,204.0	5.7
8.0	0.00	0.0	0.23	5.2	0.1	1.10	11.52	4.57	74.2	5.0	68.9	13.2	3.0
2.6	3.42	20.2	2.54	2.9	0.0	0.28	3.72	4.53	90.8	4.4	47.5	14.1	0.8
4.6	0.81	7.8	1.86	3.7	0.0	0.01	0.11	4.30	55.5	2.9	42.9	23.9	4.5
8.4	0.06	0.6	0.00	4.5	0.1	0.61	7.40	3.31	71.6	1.0	27.1	53.4	3.7
8.9	0.01	0.0	0.02	4.1	0.2	0.49	4.66	3.42	74.4	2.1	18.9	18.7	4.9
4.5	0.81	8.6	0.27	4.5	2.0	0.71	10.62	3.65	68.2	2.7	22.2	16.3	4.4
6.6	0.30	2.1	0.11	5.6	1.7	0.93	11.17	4.01	69.2	3.7	17.7	11.0	5.7
6.7	0.77	3.4	0.18	5.5	0.8	1.05	11.36	3.87	65.0	5.0	43.3	10.9	5.0
4.9	0.37	2.8	0.25	4.9	1.0	0.88	9.94	4.67	63.7	1.8	16.8	20.3	4.1
4.0	1.98	12.2	0.03	8.4	1.2	1.91	22.55	4.56	63.2	3.0	42.1	21.1	6.1
4.0	2.66	9.5	0.38	4.0	0.1	0.61	5.21	3.69	72.2	5.3	131.7	19.5	3.7
6.2	2.36	11.0	-0.31	5.7	0.6	0.85	7.53	4.40	73.9	4.4	100.9	28.7	6.6
9.3	0.00	0.0	0.00	2.4	0.5	0.24	2.40	1.74	92.0	5.5	293.9	36.7	4.5
4.8	2.16	9.0	0.17	6.2	0.3	0.92	10.23	4.00	72.9	3.2	11.2	12.5	5.7
1.3	4.03	27.7	0.28	1.3	0.2	0.22	2.58	4.25	87.9	2.7	33.5	19.1	3.0
8.5	0.00	0.0	-0.01	5.6	0.8	0.89	11.54	4.85	76.9	4.0	37.9	14.1	5.3
5.0	1.26	7.5	-0.03	9.7	1.8	2.20	20.31	5.07	59.3	3.3	24.5	13.4	8.5
3.3	2.48	15.8	0.01	6.2	1.8	1.11	10.79	4.37	64.9	3.9	28.2	11.7	5.3
8.2	0.00	0.0	0.02	6.3	0.4	1.32	13.65	4.03	54.1	1.6	12.6	21.6	6.0
8.5	0.11	0.5	0.14	10.0	0.8	1.99	16.30	4.67	48.2	5.6	39.6	5.9	8.3
8.5	0.23	0.6	0.22	10.0	0.9	3.06	14.58	5.22	37.4	3.0	19.6	14.6	9.4
6.7	0.48	3.3	0.96	6.6	2.2	1.01	10.96	5.77	67.4	5.9	43.7	5.1	4.4
4.8	0.00	0.0	0.11	4.8	0.3	0.88	6.93	5.39	74.2	5.1	41.9	9.6	4.3
4.6	0.69	4.7	0.00	3.8	0.3	0.46	3.90	5.36	85.7	3.7	23.1	11.5	2.8
9.4	0.00	0.0	0.00	9.7	0.6	1.77	9.21	4.00	53.9	0.7	11.7	43.8	4.5
7.9	0.29	2.6	0.11	7.9	2.8	1.34	18.56	4.34	52.8	2.8	24.4	15.8	3.2
3.2	0.58	5.1	0.11	1.0	0.0	0.13	1.40	5.04	88.5	0.7	17.8	52.0	3.7
6.2	1.60	5.9	-0.01	5.6	0.2	1.17	8.31	5.24	73.7	4.6	18.2	4.9	6.6
10.0	0.00	0.0	0.00	9.5	0.2	3.34	3.64	1.47	82.6	0.0	N/A	101.0	5.0
6.1	6.77	6.5	1.90	2.3	18.0	0.11	0.50	2.79	85.3	9.0	189.1	5.7	7.9
7.7	0.46	1.4	0.00	6.4	3.6	1.01	3.79	1.08	37.6	0.3	7.7	84.6	5.0
4.3	1.58	9.5	-0.02	4.9	1.2	0.94	8.85	4.39	75.2	5.0	41.1	10.3	5.9
8.0	0.01	0.1	0.33	3.6	0.1	0.80	8.42	4.00	79.1	5.0	39.4	6.7	0.7
9.3	0.00	0.0	0.00	0.0	-1.5	-4.39	-20.27	2.22	283.3	6.6	92.3	9.5	0.0
4.0	1.77	12.6	0.07	7.9	2.0	2.13	26.55	4.07	55.1	2.1	29.1	23.3	5.2
8.9	0.07	0.3	0.04	5.6	0.1	1.33	10.48	4.29	68.2	4.7	83.5	16.7	4.4
10.0	0.00	0.0	0.00	9.5	3.3	18.67	40.57	0.58	80.5	0.0	N/A	100.0	2.1

Name	City	State	Weiss Safety Rating	2003 Weiss Safety Rating	2002 Weiss Safety Rating	Total Assets ($Mil)	One Year Asset Growth	Asset Mix (As a % of Total Assets)				Capital- ization Index	Leverage Ratio	Risk-based Capital Ratio
								Comm- ercial Loans	Cons- umer Loans	Home Mort- gages	Secur- ities			
DILLEY ST BK	DILLEY	TX	A-	A-	A-	46.2	-3.00	2.2	6.0	1.6	71.1	10.0	29.5	92.0
▼ DIME BANK	HONESDALE	PA	B-	B	B-	316.6	8.71	11.3	6.1	16.6	17.9	5.7	8.6	11.5
DIME SVGS BK	NORWICH	CT	B	B	B	476.4	5.08	4.8	0.8	26.0	32.1	7.3	9.6	12.7
DIME SVGS BK OF	BROOKLYN	NY	B+	B+	B	3,344.3	8.04	0.0	0.1	3.3	21.5	5.3	7.3	14.4
▲ DIRECT MRCH CREDIT CRD BK	PHOENIX	AZ	A	A-	C+	344.6	-65.74	0.0	20.2	0.0	54.8	10.0	70.8	127.5
DISCOVER BK	GREENWOOD	DE	C-	D+	D+	17,544.3	-9.12	0.0	93.1	0.9	0.1	10.0	17.9	15.3
▼ DISCOVERY BK	SAN MARCOS	CA	C-	C	D	86.4	39.34	25.3	1.5	2.1	2.0	7.5	12.3	12.9
DIXON BK	DIXON	KY	B+	B+	B+	60.0	4.60	7.5	5.3	11.2	55.5	10.0	16.5	33.3
▲ DMB COMMUNITY BK	DE FOREST	WI	A-	A-	B+	141.2	28.68	12.4	2.6	7.2	13.3	10.0	11.5	17.3
DNB FIRST NA	DOWNINGTOWN	PA	C	C	C+	435.0	8.68	8.9	0.3	10.5	41.4	5.1	7.1	12.5
DOLLAR BK FSB	PITTSBURGH	PA	B	B	B	5,226.6	4.69	5.0	1.7	61.3	20.4	5.6	7.6	14.5
DOLORES ST BK	DOLORES	CO	A-	A-	A-	85.1	8.47	10.8	10.4	21.4	35.9	10.0	11.2	25.1
▲ DOMESTIC BK	CRANSTON	RI	A	A-	B	207.6	0.81	5.0	27.9	30.0	6.7	10.0	13.6	20.6
DONLEY COUNTY ST BK	CLARENDON	TX	B	B	B	32.7	-0.03	4.8	5.6	0.1	66.7	10.0	19.8	43.1
▲ DOOLIN SECURITY SVGS BK	NEW MARTINSVILLE	WV	B-	C+	B-	42.2	2.13	0.0	2.9	31.6	34.7	10.0	12.3	30.0
▲ DORAL BK	SAN JUAN	PR	C+	C	B	8,650.5	39.83	0.3	0.9	21.3	52.4	4.5	6.5	19.4
▲ DORAL BK FSB	NEW YORK	NY	B	B-	B	523.8	10.45	0.8	0.1	4.1	45.9	7.0	9.0	23.4
DORSEY ST BK	ABBEVILLE	GA	D	D	D-	6.5	-5.94	7.5	17.5	18.3	10.6	10.0	14.0	24.9
▲ DOUGLAS COUNTY BK	DOUGLASVILLE	GA	B	B	B+	231.6	12.69	3.2	1.5	20.2	6.7	7.5	9.3	14.9
▼ DOUGLAS COUNTY BK	LAWRENCE	KS	B-	B+	A-	187.3	3.87	8.0	1.8	9.5	35.5	10.0	13.4	22.2
▲ DOUGLAS NB	DOUGLAS	GA	D+	D	D-	78.4	22.88	11.4	6.6	14.7	7.8	5.0	8.5	11.0
DOUGLASS NB	KANSAS CITY	MO	D+	D	D+	89.7	-3.56	22.2	6.3	17.2	19.5	5.3	7.3	12.0
DOWNERS GROVE NB	DOWNERS GROVE	IL	B-	B-	B-	225.3	5.41	17.6	1.2	22.2	10.0	4.2	7.9	10.6
DOWNEY S&LA FA	NEWPORT BEACH	CA	B	B	B-	14,209.3	19.00	0.0	0.1	88.9	4.5	4.7	6.7	13.6
DOWNS NB	DOWNS	KS	C-	D+	D	15.8	2.94	6.9	4.1	6.5	25.2	8.6	10.0	20.3
DRAKE BK	ST PAUL	MN	D-	D+	D	38.8	57.04	37.8	6.3	8.8	11.4	7.0	11.3	12.5
▲ DRAYTON ST BK	DRAYTON	ND	B	B-	B	36.8	0.43	11.2	13.7	4.3	20.0	10.0	11.2	19.5
DRUMMOND COMMUNITY BK	CHIEFLAND	FL	A	A	A-	123.1	-8.96	7.0	7.1	24.9	30.8	10.0	11.5	21.4
▲ DRYADES SVGS BK FSB	NEW ORLEANS	LA	D+	D	E	106.6	12.11	7.3	6.6	21.8	28.2	5.7	7.7	15.8
DSRM NB	ALBUQUERQUE	NM	B-	B-	B-	3.0	3.10	0.0	0.0	0.0	73.1	10.0	82.2	290.7
▲ DU QUOIN ST BK	DU QUOIN	IL	B-	C+	C+	90.0	9.00	9.0	4.1	17.4	40.5	6.3	8.3	17.0
▲ DUBLIN NB	DUBLIN	TX	C	C-	D+	27.9	-1.90	3.2	7.5	10.3	39.1	10.0	11.5	23.8
▼ DUBUQUE B&TC	DUBUQUE	IA	B-	B	B	748.8	9.05	16.7	2.3	5.7	18.2	4.5	7.8	10.8
DUKES COUNTY SVGS BK	WAYLAND	MA	B	B	B	252.3	2.15	0.1	0.9	34.4	34.1	9.9	10.9	24.8
DUNLAP BK	DUNLAP	IL	B	B-	C-	49.4	1.66	3.3	5.2	25.0	38.9	7.4	9.3	22.6
DUNNELLON ST BK	DUNNELLON	FL	B+	B+	A-	60.6	1.29	0.3	0.6	42.5	32.6	6.8	8.8	21.7
DUPAGE NB	W CHICAGO	IL	C+	B-	B	85.7	41.03	4.9	0.5	11.0	23.0	7.0	9.0	14.0
DUPONT ST BK	DUPONT	IN	B	B	A-	28.6	26.45	3.2	8.7	37.1	12.0	10.0	14.6	21.7
DURAND ST BK	DURAND	IL	D+	D+	C-	73.0	-1.91	15.5	7.6	15.6	30.9	6.0	8.0	12.4
▲ DURDEN BKG CO	TWIN CITY	GA	B	B-	B-	98.7	11.58	16.5	15.7	27.0	15.8	7.1	9.1	14.1
DUTTON ST BK	DUTTON	MT	D+	D+	C-	20.9	8.63	5.9	4.1	4.9	40.1	7.0	9.0	15.7
DWELLING HOUSE S&LA	PITTSBURGH	PA	D+	D+	D+	21.2	-1.86	0.0	1.5	29.8	49.8	10.0	16.3	70.7
DYSART ST BK	DYSART	IA	C	B-	B	11.7	-11.16	3.2	1.1	4.1	6.9	10.0	13.2	28.0
▲ E*TRADE BANK	ARLINGTON	VA	C+	C	C	22,922.2	32.29	0.0	18.7	17.1	52.4	4.0	6.0	11.8
EAGLE B&TC	LITTLE ROCK	AR	B	B	B	87.6	9.96	11.5	1.8	6.6	48.2	6.3	8.3	14.8
EAGLE B&TC OF MISSOURI	HILLSBORO	MO	B+	B	B-	518.7	5.70	13.1	1.0	8.7	23.8	7.1	9.1	12.9
▼ EAGLE BK	WILLIAMSTOWN	KY	A	A+	A+	146.2	3.09	0.7	2.9	36.2	28.0	10.0	13.0	22.5
▼ EAGLE BK	EVERETT	MA	C-	B-	B-	437.9	8.14	2.5	0.2	15.4	55.9	9.3	10.6	14.6
EAGLE BK	GLENWOOD	MN	A	A	A	84.8	1.12	10.8	9.1	25.9	7.2	10.0	12.2	16.7
▲ EAGLE BK	JARRELL	TX	E	E-	E-	14.7	-4.16	5.1	17.2	6.4	38.8	6.5	8.5	20.3
EAGLE COMMUNITY BK	MAPLE GROVE	MN	D	D	D	11.8	55.54	17.0	0.2	0.7	7.7	10.0	25.4	28.8
EAGLE NB	STOCKBRIDGE	GA	C-	C-	C	64.1	8.30	4.6	1.5	11.4	10.3	6.9	9.1	12.4
EAGLE NB	UPPER DARBY	PA	D-	D-	D-	89.8	39.45	5.6	3.2	19.4	29.9	9.7	10.8	20.5
EAGLE NB OF MIAMI	MIAMI	FL	C+	C+	C	274.7	7.56	23.1	1.0	5.6	22.8	5.6	7.6	12.5
EAGLE SAVINGS BANK	CINCINNATI	OH	B-	B-	B-	68.4	-3.41	7.0	0.2	43.5	2.8	9.3	10.9	14.4
EAGLE ST BK	EAGLE	NE	C-	C-	C-	12.0	0.51	2.7	11.3	13.2	12.5	8.6	10.1	24.0
▼ EAGLE VALLEY BK NA	ST CROIX FALLS	WI	C+	B-	B	185.4	35.97	9.8	2.6	14.0	7.1	6.2	9.6	11.9
▲ EAGLEBANK	BETHESDA	MD	B-	C+	C	476.7	25.42	19.2	0.6	2.8	12.4	5.1	9.0	11.1
▲ EAGLEMARK SVGS BK	CARSON CITY	NV	B+	B	B-	32.5	14.30	0.0	34.1	0.0	59.0	10.0	15.4	20.2
EARLHAM SVGS BK	W DES MOINES	IA	B	B-	C+	198.8	-1.43	9.9	1.9	13.6	39.6	9.0	10.3	19.3
▲ EARTHSTAR BK	SOUTHAMPTON	PA	C+	C	C-	177.2	72.94	8.0	4.3	17.0	59.7	7.6	9.4	14.5
EAST BOSTON SVG BK	BOSTON	MA	A-	A-	A-	765.1	0.77	1.1	0.2	24.6	39.3	10.0	12.4	15.1
EAST BRIDGEWATER SVGS BK	READVILLE	MA	C	C	C+	121.0	-1.46	0.1	0.3	17.0	68.2	6.8	8.8	30.3
EAST CAMBRIDGE SVGS BK	CAMBRIDGE	MA	C+	C+	B-	647.7	4.23	0.7	0.3	48.7	23.6	9.2	10.4	18.1

Asset Quality Index	Non-Performing Loans as a % of Total Loans	Non-Performing Loans as a % of Capital	Net Charge-offs Avg Loans	Profitability Index	Net Income ($Mil)	Return on Assets (R.O.A.)	Return on Equity (R.O.E.)	Net Interest Spread	Overhead Efficiency Ratio	Liquidity Index	Liquidity Ratio	Hot Money Ratio	Stability Index
8.9	1.29	0.7	1.24	6.7	0.3	1.04	3.65	3.34	61.9	3.4	42.7	18.4	7.5
4.5	0.88	7.0	0.67	6.6	1.6	1.06	12.23	3.82	53.0	6.4	94.6	12.4	5.3
7.6	0.47	2.7	0.01	4.6	2.9	1.22	12.56	3.10	72.3	4.9	36.2	9.3	6.2
6.4	0.05	0.5	0.01	9.8	26.0	1.61	17.93	3.29	33.1	1.0	3.3	29.2	8.7
7.0	6.55	1.7	40.47	10.0	40.0	22.85	32.21	7.69	59.8	8.6	26,916.0	9.5	7.7
2.0	2.51	10.7	5.96	10.0	360.3	4.12	25.23	6.86	49.4	0.3	6.4	83.4	9.4
7.0	0.00	0.0	0.00	2.0	0.1	0.23	1.85	4.63	85.0	2.2	31.5	22.9	0.3
4.9	6.01	14.5	1.02	5.4	0.3	0.93	5.93	4.01	46.8	3.8	22.5	10.6	7.1
6.9	0.13	0.7	0.35	7.1	0.9	1.26	9.00	4.31	58.0	1.1	11.4	29.1	7.0
5.3	1.07	7.1	0.08	3.9	1.5	0.72	10.24	3.52	77.3	4.6	14.4	4.6	3.1
7.6	0.44	4.1	0.05	5.1	20.2	0.79	10.40	2.78	61.1	0.8	2.5	31.1	6.9
8.3	0.01	0.1	0.06	7.9	0.8	1.85	17.08	4.36	37.0	4.3	84.8	21.4	6.5
6.8	0.34	1.8	0.09	10.0	1.9	1.79	13.24	5.60	69.2	1.5	19.7	26.2	8.4
7.4	3.65	4.2	0.25	6.1	0.3	1.57	8.05	3.44	63.1	3.8	101.3	36.1	5.5
8.6	1.12	2.6	0.57	3.1	0.1	0.35	2.34	3.05	86.9	5.7	54.1	8.2	5.2
6.9	1.39	8.7	0.10	9.6	98.6	2.53	44.36	1.99	28.0	0.7	15.0	52.2	5.8
9.3	0.04	0.1	0.07	4.7	0.7	0.25	2.80	2.02	78.8	4.2	124.6	55.1	6.4
3.0	4.42	16.9	0.59	5.1	0.1	1.27	9.97	4.88	67.3	7.2	191.8	15.7	1.0
5.4	0.05	0.4	-0.01	10.0	3.5	3.14	33.35	4.73	43.9	1.5	16.7	24.8	6.8
8.9	0.32	1.2	0.16	3.4	0.4	0.47	3.49	4.03	85.7	7.4	109.3	8.5	7.0
4.6	0.61	5.5	0.10	5.0	0.7	1.75	20.95	4.31	63.7	0.7	9.0	36.3	0.0
5.3	0.24	2.0	0.20	2.9	0.1	0.28	3.78	4.32	88.5	2.5	44.3	30.2	2.4
7.7	0.27	2.5	-0.03	5.1	0.9	0.80	9.43	4.39	73.8	4.7	24.0	5.0	5.0
7.8	0.29	3.7	0.00	5.3	40.7	0.62	8.36	2.44	60.7	0.8	12.5	40.7	5.7
8.7	0.09	0.4	0.00	3.5	0.1	0.74	7.08	4.34	82.6	7.5	111.0	5.1	3.4
4.0	2.55	19.4	0.00	0.4	-0.1	-0.33	-2.93	4.24	94.1	3.6	17.6	11.2	0.0
4.9	1.44	7.7	0.11	9.8	0.4	2.03	18.31	4.19	45.3	4.5	71.2	17.8	6.5
8.2	0.35	1.6	0.23	10.0	2.0	3.14	25.85	6.85	50.2	2.6	10.0	15.3	7.9
1.9	2.76	19.1	0.16	4.7	0.1	0.14	1.72	3.84	91.6	3.0	68.1	57.7	1.7
9.9	0.00	0.0	0.00	9.5	0.0	1.89	2.31	2.32	87.8	0.0	N/A	100.0	0.0
4.6	2.45	13.4	0.09	7.8	0.8	1.81	19.15	4.53	56.1	2.5	15.3	16.3	5.6
6.1	1.49	5.5	-0.27	2.8	0.1	0.66	5.84	3.76	85.1	5.0	39.6	9.7	3.6
8.2	0.07	0.6	0.09	8.6	5.6	1.50	18.90	3.58	55.8	4.6	19.9	5.4	6.4
9.0	0.01	0.0	0.02	4.6	1.0	0.76	6.56	3.66	68.4	6.2	66.5	9.7	7.0
7.6	0.78	4.0	0.14	4.4	0.2	0.91	9.67	3.28	75.1	6.7	73.9	6.1	5.9
9.6	0.07	0.4	0.00	8.0	0.6	1.84	19.75	4.25	59.5	6.2	51.0	4.2	7.1
8.9	0.00	0.0	0.00	3.0	0.1	0.23	2.46	4.70	94.5	2.9	32.4	18.2	4.1
5.8	0.98	4.4	0.12	3.7	0.1	0.53	3.25	4.85	79.6	1.7	15.1	21.1	6.5
3.3	2.17	15.0	1.18	2.8	0.2	0.41	5.21	4.08	74.4	3.8	24.2	10.7	3.0
4.9	0.78	5.7	0.30	9.9	0.9	1.73	19.78	5.32	49.7	2.3	14.4	17.5	5.7
3.0	2.93	16.1	0.00	4.4	0.1	0.74	8.01	3.46	62.4	3.4	59.8	19.6	3.0
1.0	14.85	30.8	0.33	3.3	0.0	0.30	1.67	3.70	78.1	4.4	63.8	15.5	4.2
9.5	0.18	0.3	0.00	1.8	0.0	-0.26	-1.99	2.80	104.4	8.9	140.8	0.0	4.9
7.5	0.18	1.5	0.29	5.3	120.1	0.84	14.50	2.09	49.8	0.8	1.9	31.0	3.5
6.9	0.56	3.1	0.01	3.9	0.3	0.64	7.72	4.13	80.3	2.9	10.4	14.0	5.4
7.4	0.40	2.5	0.02	5.9	2.4	0.96	9.74	3.48	61.9	5.4	37.4	6.5	6.3
9.3	0.07	0.4	0.00	7.9	1.0	1.41	10.78	4.38	58.7	2.9	16.4	14.4	8.5
9.7	0.15	0.5	-0.01	2.3	0.6	0.28	2.65	2.24	93.0	7.9	165.4	10.6	6.6
7.7	0.25	1.6	0.00	7.6	0.8	1.78	13.92	4.87	65.3	4.4	15.0	6.3	8.2
5.6	1.34	4.8	1.35	3.3	0.1	1.06	12.90	7.20	82.4	6.5	60.5	2.5	0.0
7.3	0.00	0.0	0.00	0.1	-0.1	-1.71	-6.00	4.81	121.1	3.8	57.7	17.1	0.0
7.3	0.00	0.0	-0.76	2.3	0.0	0.10	1.13	4.18	94.4	4.2	41.6	14.5	3.0
3.6	2.91	11.4	0.89	0.0	-0.2	-0.50	-3.85	3.06	131.7	6.7	78.4	6.6	1.7
7.4	0.00	0.0	-0.28	5.0	1.1	0.76	10.27	3.64	70.0	0.8	15.9	39.8	4.1
9.0	0.08	0.6	0.00	3.9	0.2	0.49	4.48	3.08	74.6	3.3	13.0	12.5	5.2
7.1	0.00	0.0	-0.34	3.8	0.0	0.57	5.69	3.07	79.5	7.7	196.1	13.7	2.7
5.8	0.59	5.0	0.18	3.4	0.2	0.22	2.28	4.95	88.3	2.5	18.8	17.0	4.1
8.4	0.03	0.3	-0.03	5.4	2.1	0.94	11.68	4.23	67.0	4.7	65.8	17.4	4.0
8.2	0.00	0.0	0.00	10.0	1.5	10.28	73.91	17.36	65.6	5.0	0.0	0.0	3.2
7.7	0.67	3.3	-0.23	6.2	1.3	1.26	11.94	3.64	51.9	7.4	93.4	6.4	5.2
7.1	1.13	4.7	0.09	3.5	0.6	0.74	8.31	2.80	63.4	2.9	36.4	19.1	2.4
9.5	0.11	0.4	0.01	5.8	4.0	1.05	8.15	3.79	66.8	4.5	34.1	10.6	7.9
8.1	1.41	3.1	-0.01	2.9	0.3	0.46	5.24	3.00	83.0	5.3	46.6	10.2	4.8
7.2	0.57	3.7	0.00	3.2	1.0	0.31	3.05	3.14	83.9	5.1	53.8	13.1	6.5

Name	City	State	Weiss Safety Rating	2003 Weiss Safety Rating	2002 Weiss Safety Rating	Total Assets ($Mil)	One Year Asset Growth	Asset Mix (As a % of Total Assets)				Capital-ization Index	Leverage Ratio	Risk-based Capital Ratio
								Comm-ercial Loans	Cons-umer Loans	Home Mort-gages	Secur-ities			
EAST CAROLINA BK	ENGELHARD	NC	**B**	B	B	488.7	18.01	9.6	3.3	4.7	24.1	**6.1**	8.4	11.9
▼ EAST DUBUQUE SVGS BK	DUBUQUE	IA	**C-**	C	NR	162.8	N/A	11.8	8.6	24.9	7.3	**3.1**	7.2	10.0
EAST PENN BK	EMMAUS	PA	**C**	C	C	348.1	17.50	11.3	1.6	20.9	27.2	**5.7**	7.7	11.9
EAST PROSPECT ST BK	E PROSPECT	PA	**A-**	A-	A-	60.2	3.45	0.8	5.1	15.7	72.4	**10.0**	20.7	39.1
EAST TEXAS NB OF	PALESTINE	TX	**B**	B	B	109.2	0.04	14.4	9.9	8.6	38.2	**5.6**	7.6	12.7
EAST VALLEY COMMUNITY BK	CHANDLER	AZ	**C**	C	C	41.9	1.76	9.6	0.7	7.0	0.1	**3.2**	8.7	10.1
▲ EAST WISCONSIN SAVINGS	KAUKAUNA	WI	**B-**	C+	C+	199.8	4.96	0.7	1.1	67.7	19.6	**6.0**	8.0	16.2
EAST-WEST BK	SAN MARINO	CA	**B-**	B-	B+	4,896.8	36.17	9.6	0.4	4.2	9.2	**3.9**	8.8	10.5
▲ EASTBANK	MINNEAPOLIS	MN	**C**	C-	D+	32.8	25.83	18.5	3.1	17.3	0.0	**6.6**	10.2	12.2
EASTBANK NA	NEW YORK	NY	**A**	A	A	132.9	-0.19	5.0	0.0	7.0	8.3	**10.0**	12.8	16.7
EASTERN BK	BOSTON	MA	**B**	B	B	5,063.2	11.36	11.9	19.2	14.9	22.1	**5.4**	7.9	11.3
EASTERN COLORADO BK	CHEYENNE WELLS	CO	**B**	B-	B-	103.4	12.26	12.3	2.1	8.4	13.7	**7.9**	10.1	13.3
EASTERN FEDERAL BANK	NORWICH	CT	**B-**	B-	B-	161.2	7.83	3.2	1.3	40.4	11.0	**5.9**	7.9	12.6
▼ EASTERN INTERNATIONAL BK	LOS ANGELES	CA	**B**	B+	B+	86.8	-2.99	0.0	0.2	2.3	9.3	**10.0**	12.2	17.5
EASTERN MICHIGAN BK	CROSWELL	MI	**B-**	B-	B+	228.2	0.94	6.8	4.7	28.4	15.4	**6.8**	8.8	13.8
EASTERN NB	MIAMI	FL	**C+**	C+	C+	348.1	10.90	5.8	0.9	8.5	10.6	**9.5**	10.6	14.9
EASTERN SVGS BK FSB	HUNT VALLEY	MD	**D**	D	D	706.1	0.20	0.0	0.1	66.6	1.6	**10.0**	15.0	21.8
EASTHAMPTON SVGS BK	EASTHAMPTON	MA	**A**	A	A	622.7	9.13	2.6	1.4	56.4	19.8	**10.0**	11.7	20.6
EASTLAND NB	EASTLAND	TX	**A-**	A-	A-	57.9	-0.86	9.8	14.4	12.6	37.5	**8.3**	9.8	17.3
EASTMAN NB OF NEWKIRK	NEWKIRK	OK	**B**	B	B	46.3	-4.65	1.8	4.8	10.8	56.1	**10.0**	11.9	28.7
▲ EASTON B&TC	EASTON	MD	**C+**	C	D+	105.7	5.67	16.4	5.7	18.4	6.3	**5.0**	8.3	11.0
EASTSIDE CMRL BK NA	BELLEVUE	WA	**D**	D	D	35.4	107.84	33.2	2.9	13.5	6.0	**6.5**	10.9	12.1
EASTWOOD BK	KASSON	MN	**B-**	B-	C+	251.3	6.31	6.4	7.9	8.5	21.6	**5.6**	8.3	11.5
EATON FSB	CHARLOTTE	MI	**B-**	B-	B	308.7	-6.22	0.1	0.4	64.6	4.8	**9.2**	10.4	20.1
▲ EATON NB&TC	EATON	OH	**B+**	B	B	163.3	0.72	8.9	9.7	11.3	13.0	**7.7**	9.4	14.3
▲ EBANK	ATLANTA	GA	**D-**	E-	D-	112.2	3.89	14.6	1.8	18.2	19.3	**6.7**	8.7	13.7
▲ ECONOMY CO-OP BK	MERRIMAC	MA	**D+**	D+	D-	25.9	-0.72	0.0	2.9	59.9	6.3	**5.2**	7.2	16.4
EDEN STATE BK	EDEN	TX	**C-**	C	C+	56.0	53.45	2.8	8.5	7.7	40.9	**5.1**	7.1	14.7
EDENS BK	WILMETTE	IL	**B**	B-	C+	178.1	10.03	5.9	0.3	11.7	20.1	**5.6**	8.4	11.5
▲ EDGAR COUNTY B&TC	PARIS	IL	**D+**	D	C-	162.7	3.76	14.9	1.8	9.6	23.3	**7.0**	9.0	13.4
EDGARTOWN NB	WAYLAND	MA	**C**	C	C	125.0	-3.86	5.7	0.3	52.8	16.8	**4.9**	6.9	13.0
▲ EDISON NB	FORT MYERS	FL	**D+**	D	D+	136.6	19.60	6.2	3.8	22.1	21.2	**4.7**	6.7	10.9
EDMOND B&TC	EDMOND	OK	**C-**	C-	D-	67.2	17.48	25.2	3.7	18.4	0.0	**3.6**	9.0	10.3
▲ EDMONTON ST BK	GLASGOW	KY	**A-**	B+	B+	284.0	9.37	12.2	11.6	20.0	16.7	**9.1**	10.4	15.7
EDON ST BK CO	EDON	OH	**A-**	A-	A-	61.5	-1.40	6.1	2.4	13.8	51.0	**10.0**	15.0	28.5
EFFINGHAM ST BK	EFFINGHAM	IL	**C+**	B-	B-	373.7	24.50	14.6	2.5	9.9	19.5	**4.5**	7.7	10.8
EFS BK	ELGIN	IL	**B**	B	B	946.9	10.41	3.9	0.6	50.5	10.2	**5.8**	8.1	11.6
EGYPTIAN ST BK	CARRIERS MILLS	IL	**B+**	B	B-	40.2	-0.39	13.5	8.5	14.0	49.0	**9.1**	10.4	21.5
EISENHOWER NB	SAN ANTONIO	TX	**A**	A	A	168.6	-0.96	0.1	4.1	1.3	83.0	**10.0**	13.4	47.2
EITZEN ST BK	EITZEN	MN	**B**	B	B	40.3	5.33	11.6	2.0	6.1	16.7	**6.1**	8.6	11.8
EL DORADO SVGS BK FSB	PLACERVILLE	CA	**A-**	A-	A-	1,333.4	4.88	0.0	0.1	25.2	44.7	**7.7**	9.5	33.2
▼ ELBERFELD ST BK	ELBERFELD	IN	**D**	D+	D	45.4	-7.32	5.8	6.6	22.8	21.4	**9.3**	10.5	18.2
▼ ELBERTON FS&LA	ELBERTON	GA	**C**	C+	C+	22.0	-5.29	1.2	0.5	41.8	7.1	**10.0**	24.5	60.2
ELDERTON ST BK	ELDERTON	PA	**C+**	C+	D+	131.0	-5.40	7.3	5.0	27.3	23.3	**6.4**	8.4	13.3
ELGIN BK OF TEXAS	ELGIN	TX	**B+**	B+	B+	82.6	-2.25	3.4	5.3	21.2	34.0	**10.0**	12.0	23.0
ELGIN ST BK	ELGIN	IA	**E+**	E+	D	20.0	-1.61	6.8	4.1	8.1	41.7	**6.0**	8.0	14.9
ELGIN ST BK	ELGIN	IL	**D+**	C+	B-	224.7	2.56	18.6	0.3	6.4	11.0	**4.2**	8.2	10.6
ELIZABETH ST BK	ELIZABETH	IL	**C+**	C+	C+	66.9	-9.12	4.6	2.6	17.1	41.4	**5.6**	7.6	15.8
▲ ELIZABETHTON FSB	ELIZABETHTON	TN	**A+**	A	A	333.8	-1.41	0.0	2.9	40.0	29.7	**10.0**	20.8	43.2
▲ ELK COUNTY S&LA	RIDGWAY	PA	**C**	D	D	10.5	0.36	0.2	2.9	60.1	24.5	**10.0**	22.0	44.9
▲ ELK HORN B&TC	ARKADELPHIA	AR	**C+**	C	C-	165.6	6.28	8.3	4.6	15.6	36.5	**5.3**	7.3	14.3
ELK ST BK	CLYDE	KS	**C-**	C-	D+	26.7	3.13	4.9	4.2	11.9	37.3	**6.3**	8.3	17.2
ELKHART COMMUNITY BK	ELKHART	IN	**C**	C	C	60.7	24.02	16.4	1.1	16.9	0.0	**6.3**	10.4	12.0
▲ ELKHART ST BK	ELKHART	TX	**D+**	D	D+	44.4	-6.37	5.0	17.7	2.8	56.9	**5.8**	7.8	24.4
ELKHORN VALLEY B&TC	NORFOLK	NE	**D+**	D+	E+	244.8	10.46	11.5	5.8	8.2	31.2	**6.5**	8.5	13.6
ELKTON B&TC	ELKTON	KY	**A-**	A-	A-	101.6	3.09	5.0	6.4	19.0	44.1	**10.0**	12.3	17.5
ELKVILLE ST BK	ELKVILLE	IL	**B-**	B-	B-	17.0	-9.49	1.5	3.7	3.3	79.6	**10.0**	17.0	53.9
ELLIS ST BK	ELLIS	KS	**B**	B	B	41.7	3.08	6.2	6.7	11.8	48.9	**10.0**	13.4	26.8
▲ ELMIRA S&L FA	ELMIRA	NY	**B**	B-	B-	215.8	-4.99	0.8	0.3	45.3	3.2	**6.5**	8.5	13.1
ELMIRA SVGS BK FSB	ELMIRA	NY	**C**	C	C-	313.1	11.03	10.0	9.1	27.5	32.2	**4.7**	6.8	12.5
▼ ELSA ST B&TC	ELSA	TX	**D+**	C	B-	136.9	4.21	2.1	20.6	8.8	33.4	**5.9**	7.9	12.9
▼ ELYSIAN BK	ELYSIAN	MN	**C+**	B	B	33.3	3.81	11.2	10.2	15.9	24.7	**8.0**	9.7	16.3
EMBASSY BK FOR THE LEHIGH	BETHLEHEM	PA	**D-**	D-	D-	137.1	35.24	9.2	0.5	25.7	26.6	**8.3**	9.9	14.1
EMERALD BK	DUBLIN	OH	**D**	NR	NR	7.4	N/A	0.0	0.0	0.0	0.0	**10.0**	96.6	439.4

Asset Quality Index	Non-Performing Loans		Net Charge-offs Avg Loans	Profitability Index	Net Income ($Mil)	Return on Assets (R.O.A.)	Return on Equity (R.O.E.)	Net Interest Spread	Overhead Efficiency Ratio	Liquidity Index	Liquidity Ratio	Hot Money Ratio	Stability Index
	as a % of Total Loans	as a % of Capital											
8.4	0.00	0.0	0.02	5.6	2.4	1.04	12.06	4.18	69.2	1.7	24.8	24.0	4.9
5.2	0.35	3.6	0.16	6.3	1.1	1.42	19.03	3.78	61.2	1.4	14.6	26.4	1.6
7.3	0.53	4.3	0.03	5.2	1.9	1.09	14.29	3.84	62.9	4.8	16.8	3.4	3.7
9.2	2.21	2.2	0.00	8.5	0.8	2.60	10.83	4.23	43.8	5.1	36.1	7.7	8.3
8.1	0.10	0.5	-0.04	5.4	0.6	1.09	13.01	4.62	76.0	5.3	33.0	4.8	5.5
6.8	0.02	0.2	-0.06	1.9	0.1	0.38	3.95	5.14	88.4	0.6	9.2	49.6	5.0
5.8	0.78	7.3	0.01	5.1	0.8	0.83	10.46	3.14	60.8	3.1	4.6	12.7	4.7
7.0	0.08	0.7	0.05	9.6	37.1	1.64	18.15	4.17	39.9	3.0	40.2	27.1	8.3
3.4	0.88	6.2	0.54	7.1	0.2	1.49	14.46	5.86	63.8	2.1	41.2	33.4	0.0
7.5	0.00	0.0	0.01	6.4	0.5	0.79	6.12	4.19	66.8	5.5	84.3	15.7	7.7
6.0	0.48	3.3	0.30	6.5	26.2	1.08	11.32	3.87	64.5	4.3	15.9	7.5	7.7
4.7	0.84	5.8	0.08	5.4	0.6	1.18	12.00	4.34	71.0	2.0	23.1	19.8	6.2
8.3	0.10	0.9	0.04	4.6	0.1	0.17	2.09	4.12	75.3	1.2	7.2	27.0	5.1
7.6	0.00	0.0	-0.01	3.8	0.1	0.30	2.52	3.50	95.5	7.1	124.7	10.7	6.4
4.3	1.42	11.1	0.01	6.2	1.2	1.08	12.65	3.94	61.1	4.7	26.0	6.0	5.4
3.9	1.00	6.6	0.48	3.6	0.8	0.48	4.60	3.73	76.1	2.3	31.1	22.1	4.3
0.3	19.87	105.6	0.22	10.0	21.0	6.03	41.06	8.99	38.4	1.4	9.7	25.0	10.0
9.6	0.16	1.0	-0.01	5.9	2.8	0.92	7.85	3.32	58.1	4.1	31.6	11.6	8.3
7.5	0.29	1.6	-0.05	10.0	0.5	1.82	18.10	5.35	55.7	4.5	18.7	5.7	7.9
9.1	0.74	1.9	-0.04	5.7	0.3	1.14	9.52	3.40	60.1	7.0	125.5	11.2	5.6
5.8	0.51	4.5	0.02	4.6	0.5	0.92	11.13	4.00	67.3	2.6	19.6	16.4	4.4
8.2	0.00	0.0	0.00	0.7	0.0	0.04	0.42	5.49	82.6	2.6	57.3	35.0	0.0
5.0	0.51	4.1	-0.01	7.2	2.3	1.84	22.02	3.90	65.5	2.4	6.4	16.1	5.8
8.6	0.29	2.2	0.00	4.4	1.1	0.69	6.94	2.67	60.8	0.9	21.2	35.2	5.4
5.6	0.51	3.7	0.06	7.9	1.1	1.25	13.28	4.33	64.8	4.7	34.0	9.0	6.7
1.8	2.72	22.7	0.54	2.5	0.4	0.68	9.72	3.52	74.5	2.1	47.3	63.3	2.6
8.9	0.00	0.0	0.00	4.1	0.1	0.68	8.79	3.44	64.8	6.7	112.7	11.7	3.1
6.9	0.01	0.1	-0.01	6.6	0.3	1.00	14.63	3.85	68.3	3.2	68.8	30.8	2.8
4.2	0.81	6.6	0.00	10.0	1.5	1.79	21.72	4.85	45.2	1.6	6.4	20.4	5.2
1.4	3.83	24.6	-0.04	6.4	1.8	2.17	23.65	4.00	54.2	0.8	5.8	31.6	5.0
9.5	0.10	1.0	0.01	3.3	0.2	0.33	4.82	3.64	86.9	4.3	19.2	7.0	3.0
8.9	0.00	0.0	0.00	2.5	0.3	0.38	6.19	4.11	92.7	3.9	25.5	10.6	2.2
3.7	1.00	9.3	0.13	6.4	0.5	1.46	15.26	4.79	66.6	1.2	9.4	27.6	4.8
5.9	0.40	2.5	-0.01	8.0	2.5	1.80	17.30	4.11	54.9	5.2	40.3	9.1	7.4
9.1	0.21	0.6	0.01	5.4	0.3	1.00	6.84	3.56	59.0	4.3	13.7	6.2	7.2
3.4	1.45	11.5	0.10	5.4	1.6	0.87	10.26	3.92	66.9	2.1	10.5	18.3	4.9
7.5	0.25	2.4	0.00	4.4	3.8	0.82	10.01	2.91	65.0	1.9	24.1	21.6	5.4
8.6	0.06	0.3	0.21	6.4	0.3	1.43	13.40	4.34	59.4	4.4	13.8	6.0	6.6
6.9	8.20	4.8	1.72	8.9	2.0	2.29	15.19	4.18	66.6	5.2	37.5	7.8	9.1
4.4	0.93	6.8	0.75	6.6	0.3	1.69	17.73	3.89	57.8	5.7	65.2	10.6	6.6
10.0	0.05	0.2	0.02	7.2	6.2	0.94	9.98	3.26	54.5	3.1	53.0	34.2	8.5
6.1	0.54	2.8	0.78	0.8	0.0	0.17	1.63	3.57	102.1	6.1	57.2	6.4	3.0
8.4	1.24	2.4	0.00	3.0	0.0	0.17	0.70	3.15	92.8	5.7	68.9	9.5	5.3
4.0	1.44	11.5	0.05	7.0	0.9	1.38	17.11	3.87	45.3	3.8	27.1	11.6	4.5
8.3	0.85	3.3	0.05	4.7	0.3	0.77	6.28	5.27	80.2	5.3	38.8	7.6	6.9
3.9	3.43	19.4	-0.02	3.3	0.1	0.58	7.37	4.12	86.0	5.2	41.8	6.0	1.4
2.1	2.36	18.0	-0.17	3.0	0.4	0.34	4.10	4.15	78.5	3.7	10.0	9.8	4.1
5.7	1.09	7.0	-0.01	7.2	0.5	1.47	19.79	3.22	51.6	4.2	24.7	8.9	4.9
8.6	0.60	1.8	-0.01	9.8	2.6	1.55	7.55	3.95	35.3	3.7	54.1	20.4	9.7
9.1	1.15	3.3	1.02	4.6	0.1	0.89	4.11	3.92	70.2	3.5	46.5	16.5	4.3
5.5	0.71	3.5	0.05	5.1	0.9	1.10	11.96	4.05	65.9	2.4	22.7	17.9	4.7
6.6	0.75	4.8	-0.01	4.3	0.1	0.98	11.57	4.12	75.9	4.0	83.2	25.1	3.7
6.4	0.15	1.1	0.00	6.4	0.4	1.24	9.96	4.81	64.5	0.8	15.1	38.1	4.3
3.8	1.27	4.6	9.18	4.3	0.1	0.57	7.17	5.19	80.8	6.9	53.0	0.0	2.6
4.3	1.59	10.3	-0.19	9.6	2.0	1.71	20.46	4.14	45.8	5.8	41.0	5.2	1.9
7.7	0.67	2.6	0.20	6.9	0.7	1.41	10.91	4.47	59.9	3.2	34.9	17.0	7.7
9.6	0.32	0.3	0.00	6.4	0.2	1.86	11.72	3.79	48.3	7.6	116.5	5.5	4.9
8.6	0.01	0.0	-0.09	3.9	0.2	0.74	5.39	3.25	70.3	2.4	32.8	21.6	6.2
5.1	0.60	5.3	1.28	7.0	1.2	1.08	12.21	3.59	52.3	0.6	9.4	42.2	5.7
5.2	0.31	2.7	0.69	4.9	1.3	0.84	11.63	3.64	68.6	1.0	19.6	33.5	3.2
1.3	3.17	21.1	0.50	8.1	1.3	1.96	24.19	5.48	65.9	1.3	27.4	33.4	5.7
2.3	3.68	21.0	-0.32	10.0	0.6	3.38	33.44	5.30	32.5	7.4	91.6	4.5	5.8
9.1	0.00	0.0	0.00	0.0	-0.3	-0.42	-4.21	2.41	107.3	3.3	15.6	12.6	0.0
10.0	0.00	0.0	0.00	0.0	-0.3	-8.89	-9.13	0.51	1,916.7	10.0	18,525.6	0.0	0.0

Name	City	State	Weiss Safety Rating	2003 Weiss Safety Rating	2002 Weiss Safety Rating	Total Assets ($Mil)	One Year Asset Growth	Asset Mix (As a % of Total Assets)				Capital-ization Index	Leverage Ratio	Risk-based Capital Ratio
								Comm-ercial Loans	Cons-umer Loans	Home Mort-gages	Secur-ities			
EMIGRANT SVG BK	NEW YORK	NY	A-	A	A	9,632.4	-4.57	0.5	0.1	47.5	33.7	7.7	9.5	16.3
EMINENCE SECURITY BK	EMINENCE	MO	D-	D-	D-	48.4	-0.17	4.0	12.7	16.8	26.0	4.2	6.2	10.7
EMMET COUNTY ST BK	ESTHERVILLE	IA	B	B	B	65.9	1.93	4.7	2.2	14.4	20.6	10.0	12.7	17.9
EMPIRE BK	SPRINGFIELD	MO	B-	B-	B-	615.1	5.44	18.8	13.4	8.5	16.9	3.8	7.2	10.4
▼ EMPORIA ST B&TC	EMPORIA	KS	B-	B	A-	110.1	-2.95	7.7	9.3	13.2	36.1	9.7	10.8	20.2
EMPRISE BK	IOLA	KS	B-	B-	B	94.0	-16.86	10.0	19.9	16.0	12.8	5.1	7.1	11.7
EMPRISE BK	WICHITA	KS	B-	B-	B	534.8	4.72	22.5	3.2	9.5	12.7	3.6	7.6	10.3
EMPRISE BK NA	HAYS	KS	B-	B-	B	94.5	0.54	12.7	16.3	9.7	23.3	6.5	8.5	15.0
EMPRISE BK NA	HILLSBORO	KS	B-	B-	B	95.1	0.73	7.1	16.9	18.3	9.5	7.7	9.4	13.9
ENCINO ST BK	ENCINO	CA	C	C	C+	188.9	21.95	8.9	1.9	3.8	33.9	4.0	6.0	10.9
ENCORE BK	HOUSTON	TX	C-	D+	D+	1,283.0	-3.89	5.2	9.9	31.9	42.7	4.2	6.2	13.7
ENERBANK USA	SALT LAKE CITY	UT	D	D	D	54.5	127.87	0.0	82.6	0.0	0.0	10.0	26.7	18.2
ENFIELD FS&LA	ENFIELD	CT	B	B	B	207.6	27.20	3.0	0.6	38.4	24.1	10.0	11.4	23.4
ENGLEWOOD BK	ENGLEWOOD	FL	B	B	B	171.7	15.17	1.2	0.4	10.2	38.1	4.5	6.5	13.3
ENLOE ST BK	ENLOE	TX	B-	B-	B-	16.3	-1.10	6.8	10.6	24.4	3.4	10.0	16.2	23.0
▲ ENNIS ST BK	ENNIS	TX	D+	D	D	98.3	0.15	18.6	5.1	13.8	8.8	5.0	7.0	11.4
ENTERPRISE B&T	CLAYTON	MO	C+	C+	C+	1,014.2	17.34	24.8	0.7	10.1	8.8	4.1	8.2	10.5
ENTERPRISE B&TC	LOWELL	MA	C+	C+	C+	805.8	7.42	16.3	0.5	5.2	23.7	4.3	7.3	10.7
ENTERPRISE BK	KENILWORTH	NJ	D	D	D	47.3	41.21	9.3	0.1	4.2	50.1	10.0	13.3	26.5
ENTERPRISE BK	ALLISON PARK	PA	E-	E-	E-	102.1	16.40	32.6	0.4	5.9	0.0	2.4	6.7	9.4
▲ ENTERPRISE BK	HOUSTON	TX	B	C+	D+	112.3	72.95	30.2	4.8	4.5	7.8	9.8	11.4	14.8
ENTERPRISE BK NA	OMAHA	NE	C	C	D	127.8	20.73	19.9	6.4	10.1	20.8	5.5	7.9	11.4
▲ ENTERPRISE BK S CAROLINA	EHRHARDT	SC	A+	A	A+	278.4	8.72	15.2	11.8	6.7	22.4	10.0	15.2	23.5
▲ ENTERPRISE NB	MEMPHIS	TN	C+	C-	C-	338.3	29.04	14.1	2.2	10.7	19.2	5.6	8.1	11.5
ENTERPRISE NB PALM BEACH	N PALM BEACH	FL	D-	D-	D	170.9	21.67	3.9	0.4	10.3	29.0	4.1	7.1	10.6
EPHRATA NB	EPHRATA	PA	A	A	A	534.8	6.84	5.0	2.8	21.3	38.1	10.0	11.8	20.0
▲ EQUITABLE BK	FORT LAUDERDALE	FL	B-	C	D	167.0	23.29	19.8	1.3	4.4	3.8	6.4	9.4	12.0
EQUITABLE BK SSB	WAUWATOSA	WI	B	B	B	420.6	0.24	0.0	14.7	28.1	8.7	10.0	11.1	15.1
▲ EQUITABLE CO-OP BK	LYNN	MA	B	B-	B	76.7	7.05	0.0	0.5	34.7	28.9	10.0	15.0	21.9
EQUITABLE FSB GRAND	GRAND ISLAND	NE	D+	D+	D+	145.5	-1.20	1.3	1.1	58.3	12.6	7.6	9.4	16.5
▼ EQUITABLE S&LA	STERLING	CO	C+	B-	B-	231.6	10.51	0.0	0.4	75.1	12.2	6.0	8.0	17.7
EQUITABLE S&LC	CADIZ	OH	C	C	C	13.3	-8.86	0.0	1.2	23.8	57.3	10.0	21.8	53.3
▼ EQUITY BK	DODGE CENTER	MN	C	C+	D+	44.6	56.69	24.7	5.9	14.4	8.1	8.0	11.8	13.3
▲ EQUITY BK NA	ANDOVER	KS	D+	D	E-	40.6	24.82	30.2	5.9	13.9	19.4	10.0	11.8	15.2
ERICSON ST BK	ERICSON	NE	D+	D	D-	24.5	12.76	3.3	14.1	2.0	14.6	8.4	9.9	14.0
ERIE ST BK	ERIE	IL	B-	B	B	18.7	-5.82	4.5	6.6	24.6	16.8	10.0	12.4	23.3
▼ ERWIN NB	ERWIN	TN	C	C+	C+	94.5	1.80	4.3	11.8	18.4	52.5	6.4	8.4	19.4
▼ ESB BK	ELLWOOD CITY	PA	B	NR	NR	1,319.1	N/A	1.4	1.2	13.3	65.5	5.5	7.5	16.6
ESCAMBIA COUNTY BK	FLOMATON	AL	B-	B-	B-	89.4	21.62	4.4	2.5	3.7	80.4	10.0	11.5	32.3
ESCROW BK USA	MIDVALE	UT	B+	B+	B+	22.4	-27.57	0.0	0.0	0.0	36.8	10.0	80.5	345.5
▼ ESPIRITO SANTO BK	MIAMI	FL	C-	C+	B-	589.6	6.58	22.4	0.4	15.3	32.1	4.5	6.5	16.7
ESSA B&T	STROUDSBURG	PA	B	B	B	571.0	9.81	0.5	1.7	71.7	10.1	6.6	8.6	16.4
ESSEX SVGS BK	ESSEX	CT	B+	B+	B+	212.1	8.66	2.0	0.3	62.6	6.1	8.9	10.3	18.0
EUDORA BK	EUDORA	AR	C	C	C-	32.0	6.10	10.8	6.0	4.2	45.7	6.4	8.4	15.2
EUREKA BK	PITTSBURGH	PA	A-	A-	A-	86.6	6.53	14.8	1.0	30.3	22.9	10.0	19.1	30.1
▲ EUREKA HOMESTEAD	METAIRIE	LA	B-	C+	C+	115.1	-0.84	0.0	0.5	71.9	16.9	8.3	9.9	20.1
EUREKA SVGS BK	LA SALLE	IL	A-	A-	A-	335.1	4.07	0.1	1.7	51.1	35.6	10.0	16.9	37.2
EUROBANK	BOCA RATON	FL	D	D	D	78.1	-5.20	1.6	1.0	8.0	24.5	9.0	10.3	15.7
EUROBANK	HATO REY	PR	D+	D+	C-	1,926.8	61.48	13.6	4.5	5.3	24.5	3.2	6.3	10.1
EVABANK	EVA	AL	C+	C	C-	173.7	20.88	2.7	12.8	43.5	10.1	6.5	8.5	12.9
EVANGELINE B&TC	VILLE PLATTE	LA	A	A	A+	410.7	1.43	3.6	6.4	20.0	41.2	10.0	16.3	33.7
▼ EVANS NB	ANGOLA	NY	B	B+	B+	391.2	17.85	6.3	0.8	10.2	39.6	5.4	7.4	13.3
EVERBANK	JACKSONVILLE	FL	B+	B	B	2,680.3	95.72	0.8	0.4	67.7	5.8	5.3	7.3	11.4
▲ EVERETT CO-OP BK	EVERETT	MA	A-	B+	B+	208.6	9.43	1.5	0.5	45.6	22.9	8.0	9.7	18.1
EVERGREEN BANK	SEATTLE	WA	B	B	B+	195.1	12.23	14.3	3.2	9.2	16.9	9.9	11.0	14.9
▲ EVERGREEN COMMUNITY BK	EVERGREEN PARK	IL	C	D+	D+	76.4	3.96	11.1	0.6	29.5	25.0	6.0	8.0	14.2
▼ EVERGREEN FS&LA	GRANTS PASS	OR	C+	B	B+	317.4	6.02	8.2	0.1	31.1	21.1	6.1	8.1	15.5
▲ EVERGREEN NB	EVERGREEN	CO	B-	C+	C+	78.3	8.64	7.3	4.8	6.3	33.3	6.5	8.5	15.7
EVERTRUST BK	CITY OF INDUSTR	CA	B-	B-	B	261.2	13.08	1.4	0.0	0.0	9.2	4.4	8.0	10.7
EVERTRUST BK	EVERETT	WA	B+	A-	A-	761.1	6.98	3.2	0.4	3.0	9.0	6.0	9.6	11.8
EXANTE BK	SALT LAKE CITY	UT	D	D	NR	13.3	N/A	0.0	0.0	0.0	89.4	10.0	87.6	167.7
EXCEL BK MN	MINNEAPOLIS	MN	B-	B-	B-	472.7	13.85	37.6	0.5	1.3	0.6	5.6	10.4	11.5
EXCEL BK NA	NEW YORK	NY	C-	D+	B-	263.8	-11.79	0.1	0.0	0.0	70.8	9.8	10.9	27.1
EXCHANGE B&TC	PERRY	OK	C+	C+	C+	109.1	1.80	4.5	15.0	20.2	30.6	6.3	8.3	12.8

Asset Quality Index	Non-Performing Loans as a % of Total Loans	Non-Performing Loans as a % of Capital	Net Charge-offs Avg Loans	Profitability Index	Net Income ($Mil)	Return on Assets (R.O.A.)	Return on Equity (R.O.E.)	Net Interest Spread	Overhead Efficiency Ratio	Liquidity Index	Liquidity Ratio	Hot Money Ratio	Stability Index
6.5	1.24	7.8	0.00	8.7	163.6	3.41	46.17	2.98	34.7	8.4	147.5	6.1	8.8
5.1	0.69	5.5	-0.09	5.0	0.3	1.11	14.43	4.56	69.9	2.1	7.4	17.5	2.0
8.2	0.44	2.1	0.07	4.8	0.3	0.96	7.21	4.07	73.3	5.6	42.1	6.8	6.4
3.7	0.87	7.4	0.18	6.9	3.5	1.16	14.91	3.91	58.8	5.4	60.9	13.0	5.8
8.4	0.06	0.2	0.01	4.2	0.5	0.90	8.01	3.66	78.1	5.4	42.3	8.0	6.9
5.2	0.30	2.1	0.03	5.0	0.4	0.95	8.79	3.94	75.9	4.9	23.3	3.7	6.4
4.6	0.67	5.5	0.12	4.6	3.2	1.19	14.33	3.82	73.5	7.4	99.1	7.2	5.7
6.6	0.40	2.8	0.04	4.4	0.4	0.93	11.09	3.22	75.3	6.3	56.4	5.2	6.0
7.2	0.04	0.3	-0.02	3.7	0.3	0.67	7.13	3.80	82.6	3.6	26.0	12.5	5.7
8.8	0.00	0.0	0.03	4.2	0.5	0.53	8.96	3.68	73.5	4.9	59.8	15.7	2.5
7.3	0.47	3.7	0.14	3.8	3.2	0.49	7.63	1.94	69.9	0.4	3.1	58.5	2.6
5.5	0.32	1.2	0.93	0.0	-0.5	-2.37	-8.21	8.73	137.9	0.1	0.9	90.4	0.0
7.3	0.36	1.8	0.22	3.8	0.5	0.53	4.25	3.69	75.9	2.2	28.9	21.0	6.3
8.0	0.14	0.5	-0.06	3.5	0.5	0.64	5.60	3.36	80.3	4.8	25.1	4.6	5.9
6.9	0.10	0.5	0.57	10.0	0.2	1.93	12.54	6.29	55.7	5.9	62.9	7.1	6.1
3.7	1.70	14.5	0.21	3.6	0.3	0.65	9.21	4.14	76.7	6.4	62.6	5.5	1.7
7.9	0.28	2.6	0.12	6.0	4.8	1.00	12.07	3.95	60.2	1.8	17.7	21.4	6.2
5.7	0.66	4.8	0.24	5.8	3.8	0.98	12.13	4.55	65.9	7.6	99.5	6.0	5.3
9.1	0.00	0.0	0.00	0.0	-0.3	-1.50	-10.92	2.61	145.9	6.0	67.4	9.4	0.0
1.3	2.72	30.8	-0.01	2.5	0.2	0.41	6.19	3.60	79.1	6.4	82.2	10.6	0.3
6.4	0.14	0.7	0.09	5.3	0.5	0.82	5.27	5.53	73.7	3.1	44.9	22.4	5.5
7.6	0.06	0.5	0.05	4.0	0.6	0.90	11.10	3.79	59.9	2.5	14.1	16.6	3.3
7.3	0.38	1.2	-0.75	10.0	2.5	1.81	10.81	4.97	41.7	4.2	45.0	15.5	8.9
3.3	1.40	4.6	-0.01	2.1	0.1	0.08	0.66	1.92	88.5	1.7	19.1	22.4	6.1
5.8	0.86	7.2	0.02	0.9	0.1	0.07	0.91	3.13	95.9	1.9	8.3	18.7	1.2
8.3	0.72	3.3	0.04	6.2	3.4	1.27	10.51	4.03	61.1	4.4	15.6	6.0	8.5
8.2	0.00	0.0	-0.03	5.9	0.8	1.03	11.61	4.68	64.7	6.0	68.9	10.9	4.0
7.7	0.05	0.4	-0.02	4.7	1.2	0.57	5.27	3.67	80.2	2.8	22.2	15.9	5.6
9.9	0.00	0.0	0.01	4.2	0.3	0.73	4.48	3.57	81.4	5.6	48.8	7.7	6.6
6.4	0.27	2.1	0.47	2.2	0.1	0.14	1.47	3.14	93.2	1.7	17.9	21.8	4.8
8.6	0.01	0.1	0.01	3.1	0.2	0.15	1.85	2.09	89.8	2.2	34.1	26.6	3.7
7.4	0.54	0.6	0.00	5.4	0.1	1.11	4.81	3.65	78.9	6.5	60.1	2.6	4.3
2.4	2.29	13.9	-0.09	5.7	0.3	1.32	10.27	5.13	66.7	2.6	60.2	46.4	3.3
5.8	0.44	2.6	0.44	0.7	-0.1	-0.42	-3.43	4.98	103.0	4.0	17.6	8.9	1.9
5.6	0.10	0.7	-0.01	5.9	0.1	1.05	10.75	4.52	55.9	5.0	10.8	1.1	1.5
2.1	7.41	34.7	0.06	5.6	0.1	1.16	8.96	4.30	61.5	5.3	62.8	10.7	5.8
5.4	0.83	4.2	0.41	3.7	0.3	0.64	8.07	3.33	73.8	1.6	15.6	23.2	3.3
9.6	0.50	1.6	0.16	4.8	4.9	1.08	10.08	2.33	65.4	5.0	36.9	11.7	4.8
7.9	5.21	6.6	0.00	3.8	0.4	1.04	7.83	3.26	67.6	2.1	31.0	24.3	4.8
10.0	0.00	0.0	0.00	10.0	8.9	88.35	125.79	2.13	14.0	5.0	N/A	0.0	1.9
5.3	1.76	12.1	-0.01	2.1	0.4	0.15	2.20	2.47	91.2	3.7	87.7	39.9	3.8
7.9	0.18	1.6	0.00	5.0	2.0	0.74	8.50	3.34	70.4	1.5	8.8	22.6	6.1
9.0	0.00	0.0	0.00	5.1	0.8	0.75	6.89	3.86	80.8	5.0	29.0	5.3	6.7
8.4	0.00	0.0	-0.01	6.1	0.2	1.17	14.20	4.63	67.4	1.2	17.4	29.3	3.4
8.0	0.57	1.9	0.01	5.3	0.4	0.96	4.54	3.78	67.8	1.4	18.6	27.7	8.0
8.6	0.10	0.8	0.00	4.1	0.3	0.58	6.00	2.16	65.0	3.4	2.5	10.8	5.8
8.2	1.06	3.4	0.08	5.7	1.5	0.92	5.24	3.12	49.3	7.6	133.1	9.0	8.3
3.1	2.23	12.3	-0.30	0.9	0.0	0.03	0.28	3.33	100.9	2.6	30.2	18.7	4.2
2.0	2.89	27.3	0.95	4.9	12.2	0.98	16.22	3.56	54.2	0.6	10.4	51.7	4.4
5.1	0.42	3.8	0.32	10.0	1.8	2.18	26.56	6.16	33.9	1.8	6.1	19.1	3.6
8.0	1.07	3.3	0.21	7.5	2.5	1.23	7.67	3.75	52.9	5.7	129.8	18.7	8.6
7.2	0.31	1.8	-0.05	6.4	2.3	1.20	13.41	3.91	69.8	3.5	20.3	11.9	5.8
6.7	0.39	4.3	0.01	8.7	13.9	1.26	17.08	3.63	75.0	0.7	8.9	41.7	6.8
8.9	0.00	0.0	0.02	6.3	0.9	0.93	9.67	3.28	56.2	3.8	55.7	19.8	5.9
6.8	0.44	2.7	0.06	4.8	0.7	0.76	7.08	4.97	76.9	3.0	31.1	17.1	5.5
9.3	0.00	0.0	0.01	2.8	0.2	0.59	7.20	3.38	81.6	7.3	82.9	3.2	4.5
9.3	0.00	0.0	0.00	3.5	0.1	0.07	0.85	2.96	101.4	1.7	28.0	27.2	4.7
7.6	0.78	4.0	0.15	4.7	0.3	0.70	8.45	3.91	76.4	7.2	68.5	1.8	4.2
7.5	0.00	0.0	0.00	7.6	2.0	1.59	20.49	3.62	44.5	3.5	81.5	43.1	4.6
6.8	0.09	0.8	0.01	8.1	5.2	1.37	14.28	3.99	52.1	2.2	16.2	18.3	7.4
10.0	0.00	0.0	0.00	0.0	-0.4	-4.98	-5.24	1.71	106.6	5.0	N/A	0.0	0.0
6.1	0.34	2.7	-0.09	6.1	3.3	1.46	15.12	4.19	60.2	0.7	12.4	46.6	6.2
8.9	1.40	1.9	-0.03	2.1	-0.7	-0.49	-4.53	1.29	189.9	2.0	43.3	55.7	3.5
3.6	1.49	9.7	0.17	6.9	0.9	1.69	18.91	4.74	58.0	3.1	27.1	15.3	4.6

| Name | City | State | Weiss Safety Rating | 2003 Weiss Safety Rating | 2002 Weiss Safety Rating | Total Assets ($Mil) | One Year Asset Growth | Asset Mix (As a % of Total Assets) | | | | Capital- ization Index | Risk-based | |
								Comm- ercial Loans	Cons- umer Loans	Home Mort- gages	Secur- ities		Leverage Ratio	Capital Ratio
EXCHANGE B&TC	NATCHITOCHES	LA	B	B-	B-	107.3	-1.85	3.7	3.5	20.5	44.8	8.4	10.0	21.2
▼ EXCHANGE BK	SANTA ROSA	CA	B+	A-	A-	1,238.6	13.64	12.5	9.4	3.5	18.6	5.1	9.2	11.1
EXCHANGE BK	MILLEDGEVILLE	GA	B+	B+	B+	171.1	4.58	3.4	3.3	12.7	27.1	9.2	10.5	14.6
▲ EXCHANGE BK	MOUND CITY	MO	C+	C-	B-	21.0	4.25	4.0	0.7	2.4	39.5	10.0	16.6	34.1
▼ EXCHANGE BK	GIBBON	NE	C	B-	C+	91.2	4.04	19.1	3.0	6.3	14.4	4.7	7.7	10.9
▼ EXCHANGE BK	LUCKEY	OH	D	D+	D+	98.1	-7.79	2.0	8.2	28.5	23.4	6.6	8.6	15.2
EXCHANGE BK	SKIATOOK	OK	D+	D+	D+	87.0	3.23	5.2	11.4	21.0	25.1	3.7	7.1	10.4
▼ EXCHANGE BK	ESTILL	SC	B	B+	B+	50.7	11.99	13.9	4.5	1.9	53.9	10.0	16.5	31.2
EXCHANGE BK NE MO	KAHOKA	MO	C-	C-	C-	92.4	151.55	1.7	1.9	8.5	58.1	4.7	6.7	14.7
EXCHANGE BK OF AL	ALTOONA	AL	B-	B	B+	185.4	5.60	7.6	4.5	18.4	31.3	10.0	11.1	17.6
EXCHANGE BK OF FAIRFAX	FAIRFAX	MO	B-	B-	B	16.9	-1.21	1.4	1.7	2.1	62.9	10.0	17.4	54.9
EXCHANGE BK OF MISSOURI	FAYETTE	MO	C-	C-	C-	63.9	47.66	9.2	7.0	26.1	21.8	2.3	6.0	9.3
EXCHANGE BK OF SC	KINGSTREE	SC	B	B	B	108.6	1.98	6.0	9.5	18.4	23.3	10.0	16.2	24.5
EXCHANGE NB	MOORE	OK	C+	B-	B-	76.4	16.32	4.2	10.7	9.0	37.8	5.5	7.5	13.5
EXCHANGE NB	COTTONWOOD FALLS	KS	C+	C+	B	35.8	1.66	9.0	6.0	7.2	18.0	9.0	10.3	17.4
EXCHANGE NB JEFFERSON	JEFFERSON CITY	MO	B	B	B-	536.7	10.52	18.1	4.9	13.0	24.2	6.6	8.6	12.9
EXCHANGE NB&TC OF	ATCHISON	KS	A-	A-	A-	168.1	-0.06	6.6	24.6	17.3	21.8	7.8	9.5	14.1
▲ EXCHANGE ST BK	ADAIR	IA	C-	D+	D+	41.2	16.20	10.2	4.2	24.2	22.7	4.4	6.9	10.7
EXCHANGE ST BK	COLLINS	IA	B-	C+	C	84.2	23.05	5.7	2.5	10.7	15.2	8.1	9.7	13.7
▲ EXCHANGE ST BK	SPRINGVILLE	IA	A-	B+	B	26.8	-2.78	7.6	3.5	26.4	14.1	10.0	18.7	28.5
EXCHANGE ST BK	LANARK	IL	C-	C-	C-	59.7	0.67	6.8	2.4	10.1	40.0	5.3	7.3	14.4
▲ EXCHANGE ST BK	ST PAUL	KS	D	D-	E+	57.5	5.34	10.9	5.0	21.1	33.0	4.9	6.9	14.4
EXCHANGE ST BK	CARSONVILLE	MI	B-	B-	B-	98.3	4.20	3.7	3.9	30.5	20.6	6.9	9.0	12.8
EXCHANGE ST BK	HILLS	MN	B	B	B	62.9	73.66	3.5	2.8	10.1	24.2	8.7	10.9	13.9
EXECUTIVE NB	MIAMI	FL	C+	C+	C+	246.3	4.01	9.0	3.9	4.6	49.2	8.2	9.8	17.8
EXPRESS BK OF TX	ROUND ROCK	TX	D	D	NR	32.2	N/A	16.9	2.8	3.3	44.5	10.0	18.1	28.3
▲ EXTRACO BANKS NA	TEMPLE	TX	B-	C+	B-	840.6	0.33	7.1	6.5	23.2	20.2	5.7	7.7	13.7
▲ F & M B&TC	MANCHESTER	GA	B+	B	B	58.2	-1.04	10.8	12.5	13.3	16.9	10.0	12.6	18.9
▲ F&M B&TC	TULSA	OK	B-	C+	C+	1,067.3	9.24	41.6	2.0	4.4	8.0	5.1	10.0	11.1
F&M BK NA OK CITY OK	YUKON	OK	A-	A-	B	48.0	2.93	11.1	4.2	4.2	31.8	9.6	10.7	17.6
▲ F&M BK-IA CENTRAL	MARSHALLTOWN	IA	B-	C+	C+	433.8	-12.08	8.0	2.5	16.1	29.1	6.5	8.5	15.6
▲ F&M BK-WI	KAUKAUNA	WI	C+	C-	D+	1,603.5	-8.30	11.0	2.2	13.9	29.2	9.9	10.9	16.7
▼ F&M COMMUNITY BK NA	PRESTON	MN	B	B+	B	72.0	15.95	7.7	6.6	12.8	27.5	8.4	9.9	13.9
FACTORY POINT NB	MANCHESTER CENTR	VT	B-	B-	B-	306.1	-0.07	9.8	2.9	16.4	26.4	5.2	7.2	12.1
▲ FAHEY BKG CO	MARION	OH	A	A-	B+	207.7	11.76	4.9	3.8	19.4	14.9	10.0	15.7	31.9
FAIRBANK ST BK	FAIRBANK	IA	C+	C+	C+	24.8	4.11	18.9	5.1	13.6	21.4	5.8	8.1	11.6
FAIRFAX ST SVG BK	FAIRFAX	IA	B+	B+	B	94.7	8.34	8.2	3.3	15.2	47.2	10.0	14.0	22.0
FAIRFIELD COUNTY BK CORP	RIDGEFIELD	CT	B	B	B	1,096.9	81.32	10.3	1.5	25.1	12.7	5.4	9.0	11.3
▼ FAIRFIELD FS&LA	LANCASTER	OH	C-	C	B-	256.1	-1.67	0.0	0.4	71.6	15.8	7.1	9.0	18.1
FAIRFIELD NB	FAIRFIELD	IL	A	A	A	229.3	-5.98	6.3	2.7	7.1	55.5	10.0	12.0	26.0
▼ FAIRMOUNT FSB	BALTIMORE	MD	B-	B	B	39.7	-7.66	0.5	0.3	39.3	44.0	10.0	13.2	42.4
▼ FAIRMOUNT ST BK	FAIRMOUNT	IN	B-	B	B	32.7	-1.60	1.4	7.5	22.3	20.1	10.0	14.4	24.8
FAIRPORT SVGS BK	FAIRPORT	NY	B-	B-	B-	120.3	14.44	0.0	0.3	73.4	13.5	9.2	12.5	21.8
FAIRVIEW S&LA	FAIRVIEW	OK	C	C-	C-	24.1	1.42	3.7	2.6	59.4	15.8	10.0	12.5	24.8
▲ FAIRVIEW ST BKG CO	FAIRVIEW	IL	D+	D	C-	20.0	-14.99	1.9	8.1	15.8	58.2	10.0	11.3	27.1
▲ FALCON INTERNATIONAL BK	LAREDO	TX	B	B-	C+	324.3	10.25	11.4	6.7	13.4	8.5	7.8	9.5	14.5
FALCON NB	FOLEY	MN	D	D	NR	20.9	N/A	14.1	1.6	2.9	37.7	10.0	22.3	34.2
▲ FALFURRIAS ST BK	FALFURRIAS	TX	D	D-	D-	14.5	-1.29	14.9	10.7	1.5	6.6	8.2	9.8	14.0
FALL RIVER FIVE CENTS SB	FALL RIVER	MA	B	B	B-	498.1	3.79	4.8	2.0	35.1	24.5	9.0	10.3	16.3
FALLS BK	CUYAHOGA FALLS	OH	C	C+	C+	79.8	17.30	0.5	13.9	42.6	4.7	7.7	9.5	16.5
▲ FALLS CITY NB	FALLS CITY	TX	A-	B	B+	102.5	5.01	4.5	7.4	17.3	34.2	9.7	10.8	21.2
▼ FALMOUTH CO-OP BK	FALMOUTH	MA	B-	B+	A-	154.7	-5.62	3.3	0.2	34.1	31.4	9.0	10.3	16.5
▲ FAMILY B&TC	PALOS HILLS	IL	D+	D	D-	79.4	-4.49	5.8	2.7	14.4	17.7	6.5	8.5	13.5
FAMILY BK FSB	PAINTSVILLE	KY	C	C	C-	96.3	-1.47	1.6	3.8	47.5	17.1	6.4	8.4	16.1
▲ FAMILY FEDERAL SVGS OF IL	CICERO	IL	C	C-	C-	64.0	-9.01	0.0	0.1	42.7	23.2	8.9	10.2	21.1
▼ FAMILY FS&LA	FITCHBURG	MA	C	B-	C+	88.8	-6.88	0.0	0.7	32.8	49.0	9.8	10.9	29.0
▲ FAMILY FSB	PELHAM	GA	C	C-	C-	73.0	3.96	3.4	6.3	45.1	14.5	5.6	7.6	14.3
FANNIN BK	WINDOM	TX	D-	E+	D-	42.5	-2.85	7.8	9.0	24.0	24.2	4.9	6.9	11.5
FAR EAST NB	LOS ANGELES	CA	C	C	B-	1,684.1	-1.44	10.1	0.2	3.7	20.5	5.1	7.1	11.6
FAR WEST BK	PROVO	UT	A-	A-	B+	360.1	17.26	15.0	5.4	4.0	17.1	10.0	12.2	15.6
FARLEY ST BK	PARKVILLE	MO	C-	C-	C-	33.6	0.48	2.7	2.7	19.1	44.1	6.1	8.1	17.7
FARM BUREAU BK FSB	SPARKS	NV	C	C-	D	385.1	11.49	9.4	54.7	3.8	25.7	7.0	9.4	13.5
▼ FARMER CITY ST BK	FARMER CITY	IL	C+	B-	B	65.7	8.57	11.8	6.0	6.1	55.0	6.6	8.6	18.1
FARMERS & COMMERCIAL BK	HOLDEN	MO	B-	B	B	87.0	5.37	20.6	7.5	24.7	13.4	9.0	10.3	14.7

Asset Quality Index	Non-Performing Loans as a % of Total Loans	Non-Performing Loans as a % of Capital	Net Charge-offs Avg Loans	Profitability Index	Net Income ($Mil)	Return on Assets (R.O.A.)	Return on Equity (R.O.E.)	Net Interest Spread	Overhead Efficiency Ratio	Liquidity Index	Liquidity Ratio	Hot Money Ratio	Stability Index
6.0	0.57	1.7	0.03	5.2	0.7	1.21	8.65	4.77	75.5	4.4	37.0	11.8	7.7
7.1	0.59	4.2	0.00	8.8	8.6	1.45	15.60	5.53	60.7	6.4	47.7	6.7	8.6
8.6	0.18	1.1	-0.01	4.9	0.7	0.85	8.23	3.54	71.5	4.0	25.9	10.4	6.5
3.3	8.51	17.4	0.76	7.3	0.2	1.87	11.31	3.98	57.4	7.0	68.7	0.9	6.9
0.0	14.61	87.8	3.97	3.7	-3.7	-7.69	-86.48	4.17	56.3	1.0	25.3	38.2	5.3
3.7	1.84	12.2	1.94	0.5	-0.2	-0.47	-5.30	3.81	95.3	4.6	42.3	12.4	3.6
4.9	0.49	4.3	0.33	4.4	0.3	0.78	10.79	4.65	77.6	2.6	12.1	15.7	2.2
8.7	0.26	0.6	-0.02	5.3	0.2	0.94	5.77	3.53	68.0	3.1	28.2	15.5	6.0
7.2	0.20	0.6	0.00	1.8	0.0	0.00	0.03	3.12	92.5	4.6	11.5	4.2	4.2
2.8	4.11	21.8	0.22	5.8	1.0	1.12	10.07	4.25	62.8	3.2	17.2	13.1	6.1
9.5	0.09	0.1	0.00	4.1	0.1	0.64	3.60	3.25	75.7	7.4	79.1	0.7	5.7
5.5	0.14	1.0	0.20	5.5	0.3	0.82	8.24	4.02	64.0	4.2	6.1	6.5	5.5
5.2	1.15	3.1	0.09	9.2	0.7	1.37	6.94	4.66	58.9	5.8	45.3	6.2	8.3
6.3	0.47	3.2	0.37	7.7	0.5	1.42	17.97	5.36	63.0	3.4	9.8	11.6	3.3
4.2	3.07	15.9	-0.07	4.3	0.1	0.55	5.28	4.36	70.0	5.0	69.7	15.0	3.1
4.6	1.28	8.5	0.02	6.4	2.8	1.07	11.22	3.25	55.3	5.5	76.6	14.7	6.7
7.1	0.02	0.2	0.14	9.8	1.4	1.64	16.97	4.14	45.7	3.9	17.0	9.6	7.2
8.5	0.10	1.0	-0.05	5.2	0.2	1.00	14.55	3.99	68.3	5.3	42.3	8.4	3.0
8.3	0.10	0.8	-0.22	4.5	0.4	1.04	10.63	3.65	69.5	3.1	44.2	21.3	4.8
8.7	0.01	0.0	0.00	8.4	0.3	2.48	14.54	3.88	34.3	7.5	82.0	1.9	7.8
5.1	1.62	11.5	0.02	5.5	0.4	1.43	19.27	3.78	58.7	2.8	22.8	16.0	3.0
6.5	0.49	3.1	0.17	2.9	0.2	0.65	9.64	3.69	73.5	4.5	50.5	14.4	0.5
5.4	0.69	5.1	0.04	4.3	0.4	0.78	8.52	3.73	71.1	5.8	40.9	4.7	5.0
8.2	0.00	0.0	0.01	6.4	0.2	1.06	10.66	3.91	56.9	4.4	55.2	15.5	5.8
6.5	0.35	1.5	-0.42	3.2	0.5	0.42	4.31	3.66	85.7	3.3	13.4	12.4	4.3
9.0	0.00	0.0	0.00	0.0	-0.2	-1.59	-7.85	2.63	163.3	2.5	45.0	29.6	0.0
5.3	0.53	3.2	0.03	4.7	4.2	0.99	11.45	4.00	73.6	7.3	103.3	8.2	5.3
5.9	1.25	6.1	0.75	6.7	0.3	0.98	7.88	5.93	71.7	3.9	41.9	16.0	6.3
4.5	1.14	8.8	0.06	5.1	4.4	0.85	8.70	3.59	70.2	3.3	37.0	20.5	7.8
8.4	0.29	1.2	0.07	5.6	0.3	1.29	11.57	3.78	68.6	5.6	67.9	11.4	7.5
5.1	0.81	5.3	0.74	4.3	1.7	0.78	9.24	3.52	68.2	5.4	50.9	10.9	4.9
5.1	1.92	8.4	0.80	2.5	5.5	0.68	5.75	4.17	75.8	3.5	18.8	12.6	5.1
5.9	0.82	5.3	0.13	4.3	0.3	0.73	6.91	4.46	79.0	4.8	33.5	8.3	5.8
5.7	0.67	5.0	0.08	6.5	1.7	1.15	14.42	4.12	62.2	4.5	16.4	5.7	4.5
7.9	0.02	0.1	0.11	7.0	1.3	1.30	8.24	4.72	60.0	3.6	55.5	22.3	7.7
2.1	2.03	9.9	0.00	4.4	0.1	0.83	6.39	4.42	64.5	5.6	53.2	7.0	5.8
8.7	0.87	2.7	-0.11	4.9	0.6	1.25	8.52	3.76	61.0	6.7	70.9	5.4	8.1
6.4	0.65	5.1	0.06	6.1	4.4	0.96	10.13	4.56	73.4	6.0	57.6	11.2	7.8
5.7	1.08	9.6	0.02	2.3	-0.1	-0.08	-0.84	2.48	101.6	3.2	20.2	13.8	4.3
9.3	0.19	0.6	-0.04	6.2	1.6	1.35	11.06	3.31	49.6	2.9	18.3	14.7	7.7
9.8	0.41	1.3	0.00	4.4	0.1	0.55	4.23	2.79	67.6	3.5	41.3	17.9	5.3
4.8	3.47	12.7	0.49	3.6	0.1	0.44	3.05	4.00	79.8	7.4	121.9	8.8	6.4
8.0	0.26	1.9	0.00	4.0	0.3	0.47	4.27	3.47	76.4	3.7	11.6	10.1	5.6
8.5	0.09	0.5	0.01	5.8	0.1	1.02	8.33	3.42	58.0	3.3	8.3	11.6	4.3
5.9	2.31	6.5	0.20	2.6	0.1	1.31	11.26	4.24	79.1	3.6	37.0	13.7	1.5
6.3	0.31	2.4	0.09	10.0	4.2	2.60	27.79	5.83	57.5	2.0	42.6	47.9	5.1
8.8	0.00	0.0	0.00	0.0	-0.2	-2.58	-9.64	3.24	155.9	7.3	339.3	16.3	0.0
3.1	1.03	4.8	1.70	5.9	0.1	1.29	9.67	4.65	69.2	3.6	70.4	21.6	3.0
9.2	0.01	0.1	0.00	4.7	1.2	0.48	4.60	3.50	78.1	5.3	54.9	12.3	6.3
5.5	0.27	2.3	0.02	3.0	0.1	0.27	2.80	2.77	87.0	3.3	46.9	19.7	4.7
8.6	0.23	1.0	0.17	6.8	0.8	1.52	14.45	4.10	45.6	4.5	78.8	19.8	6.3
9.5	0.00	0.0	0.00	3.6	0.0	0.05	0.47	2.90	94.0	7.8	141.4	9.0	5.8
5.4	0.65	4.1	0.03	2.9	0.2	0.57	6.64	3.81	84.8	3.4	78.9	32.0	2.7
5.5	0.99	6.9	-0.02	4.0	0.4	0.79	8.98	3.31	79.5	2.1	28.1	22.3	4.3
2.6	3.02	20.7	0.02	6.1	0.4	1.27	13.11	3.94	61.0	1.3	5.5	25.1	3.6
9.3	0.10	0.4	0.01	2.5	0.1	0.15	1.38	2.76	94.3	1.8	16.1	20.4	5.1
5.5	0.39	3.1	0.00	4.8	0.3	0.68	8.45	3.27	70.5	1.5	28.1	30.0	4.3
4.8	0.98	9.6	0.03	4.7	0.3	1.14	18.35	4.80	77.9	4.0	10.4	8.2	1.1
2.4	1.94	13.3	-0.07	4.6	5.6	0.66	7.16	3.68	61.7	0.8	13.9	36.1	7.8
6.1	0.35	1.7	1.57	9.8	2.6	1.60	12.65	6.73	62.8	7.4	106.7	7.8	7.9
9.4	0.00	0.0	0.00	3.2	0.1	0.57	6.78	4.11	88.6	4.6	46.1	12.9	3.2
3.4	0.53	3.9	2.17	2.5	0.4	0.18	1.87	4.14	68.9	0.7	19.4	52.5	4.1
8.0	0.50	2.3	0.07	4.5	0.3	0.90	10.08	3.74	77.3	3.4	18.4	12.2	4.8
3.5	1.92	13.4	0.65	8.0	0.8	1.74	16.09	5.28	67.2	3.9	15.2	9.3	6.6

| Name | City | State | Weiss Safety Rating | 2003 Weiss Safety Rating | 2002 Weiss Safety Rating | Total Assets ($Mil) | One Year Asset Growth | Asset Mix (As a % of Total Assets) | | | | Capital- ization Index | Leverage Ratio | Risk-based Capital Ratio |
								Comm- ercial Loans	Cons- umer Loans	Home Mort- gages	Secur- ities			
▲ FARMERS & DROVERS BK	COUNCIL GROVE	KS	A+	A	A+	98.1	0.92	5.5	10.3	11.0	38.6	10.0	30.2	46.0
▲ FARMERS & MECHANICS BK	GALESBURG	IL	B+	B	B-	172.6	5.99	14.7	5.3	12.9	31.7	7.8	9.5	15.1
FARMERS & MECHANICS BK	FREDERICK	MD	A-	B+	B+	1,488.2	-30.58	10.7	10.9	9.9	31.5	10.0	11.8	20.1
FARMERS & MECHANICS BK	BURLINGTON	NJ	C+	C+	C+	1,236.2	4.85	0.7	0.2	22.3	54.4	4.3	6.3	16.6
▼ FARMERS & MERCH BK HILL	HILL CITY	KS	C-	B-	B-	33.5	1.87	9.1	3.5	4.5	0.6	6.3	9.6	12.0
▲ FARMERS & MERCHANTS B&T	MT PLEASANT	IA	C+	C-	C+	12.3	-10.53	11.3	1.0	9.8	18.0	10.0	19.1	31.7
▲ FARMERS & MERCHANTS	BURLINGTON	IA	C+	C-	C+	223.4	-8.02	7.6	1.7	15.2	50.2	5.2	7.2	15.8
▼ FARMERS & MERCHANTS	BREAUX BRIDGE	LA	C+	B-	A-	203.6	5.03	20.3	3.7	10.4	47.8	7.6	9.4	19.4
FARMERS & MERCHANTS	HAGERSTOWN	MD	B-	B-	B-	919.5	8.18	9.6	3.5	17.1	23.2	4.3	6.4	11.9
FARMERS & MERCHANTS	HANNIBAL	MO	C+	C+	C	80.1	-1.62	14.2	5.0	28.8	12.7	10.0	11.2	16.6
FARMERS & MERCHANTS	MARINETTE	WI	B+	B+	B+	131.4	-3.14	8.2	3.6	25.9	32.0	8.8	10.2	18.6
▲ FARMERS & MERCHANTS BK	CENTRE	AL	B-	C+	C	58.4	-1.73	12.1	9.2	14.8	31.7	10.0	11.1	18.6
FARMERS & MERCHANTS BK	LAFAYETTE	AL	A-	B+	B+	89.0	5.41	7.6	5.0	8.5	56.2	10.0	11.5	20.4
▲ FARMERS & MERCHANTS BK	PIEDMONT	AL	B	B-	C+	141.2	3.44	10.0	8.0	19.9	27.6	7.2	9.1	14.6
FARMERS & MERCHANTS BK	WATERLOO	AL	B+	B+	B+	44.1	-0.32	8.5	6.7	5.1	59.4	10.0	18.5	38.4
FARMERS & MERCHANTS BK	STUTTGART	AR	A	A	A	298.4	25.82	8.6	6.1	12.8	25.6	10.0	12.0	17.9
FARMERS & MERCHANTS BK	LONG BEACH	CA	A+	A+	A+	2,912.2	10.03	4.0	0.3	3.1	49.7	10.0	19.5	40.9
▲ FARMERS & MERCHANTS BK	MONTICELLO	FL	B-	C+	B-	309.3	22.87	8.6	4.4	10.3	12.1	4.4	8.4	10.7
FARMERS & MERCHANTS BK	DUBLIN	GA	B+	A-	A	403.4	4.01	5.7	4.9	8.4	26.5	10.0	17.2	23.3
▼ FARMERS & MERCHANTS BK	EATONTON	GA	C-	C	B	148.4	8.91	7.4	5.0	14.2	27.4	6.3	8.3	12.6
▲ FARMERS & MERCHANTS BK	LAKELAND	GA	C	D+	D+	193.1	4.92	33.6	13.9	15.6	12.7	7.9	10.0	13.3
FARMERS & MERCHANTS BK	STATESBORO	GA	B-	B-	B-	153.4	10.28	8.2	6.8	23.3	6.2	5.3	8.0	11.2
FARMERS & MERCHANTS BK	SYLVANIA	GA	A-	A-	A-	106.8	2.38	2.8	6.5	10.5	52.6	10.0	11.6	22.7
FARMERS & MERCHANTS BK	WASHINGTON	GA	A-	A-	A	222.3	4.35	5.7	5.1	9.0	46.8	10.0	15.6	29.3
FARMERS & MERCHANTS BK	HUTSONVILLE	IL	C	C	C	36.8	1.10	4.2	3.1	8.0	21.8	10.0	15.8	46.4
FARMERS & MERCHANTS BK	BOSWELL	IN	A-	A-	A-	64.7	-1.88	8.7	6.0	16.8	25.6	10.0	14.7	21.6
FARMERS & MERCHANTS BK	LAOTTO	IN	C+	C+	C	74.5	6.08	6.9	4.0	28.8	25.1	5.9	7.9	14.3
FARMERS & MERCHANTS BK	MOUND CITY	KS	D	D	D-	32.4	1.29	4.1	5.2	13.4	44.5	3.7	5.7	11.6
FARMERS & MERCHANTS BK	HALE	MO	D-	D-	E	15.4	0.57	7.9	4.0	21.8	21.0	6.8	8.8	14.2
FARMERS & MERCHANTS BK	ST CLAIR	MO	B-	B-	B-	141.7	4.95	7.0	4.3	25.3	11.4	5.2	7.7	11.2
▲ FARMERS & MERCHANTS BK	BALDWYN	MS	A+	A	A	139.5	-0.09	4.1	11.7	18.1	22.2	10.0	14.6	21.0
FARMERS & MERCHANTS BK	GRANITE QUARRY	NC	B+	B+	B+	385.4	6.36	7.4	3.6	24.6	8.4	6.2	10.0	11.9
FARMERS & MERCHANTS BK	AXTELL	NE	D+	D+	D+	4.6	-4.05	3.4	4.8	8.1	43.9	10.0	12.9	28.5
FARMERS & MERCHANTS BK	IMPERIAL	NE	B+	B+	B+	47.1	6.68	8.0	4.3	4.9	14.9	10.0	11.3	18.6
FARMERS & MERCHANTS BK	MILFORD	NE	B+	B	B	207.8	6.00	3.7	3.2	14.8	27.6	7.2	9.1	14.9
▲ FARMERS & MERCHANTS BK	MILLIGAN	NE	C-	D+	D	27.2	4.10	3.6	1.8	8.6	0.0	4.4	8.0	10.7
FARMERS & MERCHANTS BK	CALDWELL	OH	B+	A-	A-	62.7	-0.14	10.1	6.3	26.1	24.4	10.0	11.7	24.5
FARMERS & MERCHANTS BK	MIAMISBURG	OH	C	C	C	75.4	-0.79	6.6	2.7	27.0	33.4	6.6	8.6	17.8
FARMERS & MERCHANTS BK	ARNETT	OK	B-	B-	B	24.3	-1.75	8.6	12.4	6.3	23.5	10.0	14.5	23.7
FARMERS & MERCHANTS BK	CRESCENT	OK	A-	A-	B	88.5	1.22	12.9	7.1	16.9	21.7	10.0	11.7	16.4
▲ FARMERS & MERCHANTS BK	DUKE	OK	C-	D+	C-	11.6	10.91	15.1	3.7	0.8	31.8	10.0	14.9	29.8
FARMERS & MERCHANTS BK	MAYSVILLE	OK	B-	B	B	15.1	-0.74	7.2	7.0	10.2	37.1	8.5	10.0	22.3
FARMERS & MERCHANTS BK	ADAMSVILLE	TN	C	C	C	28.5	-2.88	1.6	12.8	15.4	32.9	9.9	11.0	24.0
▲ FARMERS & MERCHANTS BK	CLARKSVILLE	TN	D+	D	D+	446.0	10.52	8.3	6.7	18.5	8.7	3.9	7.5	10.5
FARMERS & MERCHANTS BK	DYER	TN	C	C	C	53.8	-1.85	5.8	9.5	22.4	36.8	7.2	9.2	14.4
FARMERS & MERCHANTS BK	TREZEVANT	TN	C-	D+	D-	90.0	12.03	9.1	10.8	27.5	3.2	5.1	8.1	11.1
FARMERS & MERCHANTS BK	DE LEON	TX	C+	C+	C	50.2	-2.81	3.0	6.6	10.5	61.8	8.1	9.7	25.8
FARMERS & MERCHANTS B&K	NEW CASTLE	VA	B+	B+	B+	43.1	4.38	3.8	8.1	34.4	18.2	10.0	13.1	26.5
FARMERS & MERCHANTS BK	ONLEY	VA	A-	A-	A	265.9	4.91	6.0	2.6	38.2	15.7	6.5	8.5	19.3
FARMERS & MERCHANTS BK	TIMBERVILLE	VA	C+	C+	C	304.7	3.50	3.3	6.6	36.8	14.6	4.6	6.6	11.0
FARMERS & MERCHANTS BK	SPOKANE	WA	B-	B-	B-	318.6	9.36	15.9	7.1	6.1	2.1	6.0	10.1	11.8
▼ FARMERS & MERCHANTS BK	BERLIN	WI	B+	A-	A-	97.2	11.71	8.7	12.5	44.9	21.6	10.0	12.9	22.0
FARMERS & MERCHANTS BK	KENDALL	WI	C	C	C-	31.1	-1.15	3.9	7.3	11.6	5.1	6.5	8.5	12.4
▲ FARMERS & MERCHANTS BK	ORFORDVILLE	WI	C+	C	C	25.8	1.65	3.5	7.1	23.1	33.7	9.4	10.6	18.2
FARMERS & MERCHANTS BK	RUDOLPH	WI	C	C-	C	30.3	2.23	14.7	3.7	18.3	32.4	7.1	9.1	15.3
▲ FARMERS & MERCHANTS BK	TOMAH	WI	B-	C+	C+	151.9	2.00	37.5	4.5	23.6	16.1	7.8	9.5	14.5
FARMERS & MERCHANTS BK	LODI	CA	A-	A-	A-	1,184.7	8.23	11.9	1.3	9.4	21.1	6.7	10.4	12.3
FARMERS & MERCHANTS BK	HOLLY HILL	SC	A	A	A	179.4	5.62	5.3	8.0	13.5	24.6	10.0	14.3	24.8
▲ FARMERS & MERCHANTS	SENOIA	GA	D	D	E+	78.7	3.85	6.0	2.8	18.6	13.9	4.9	7.6	11.0
▼ FARMERS & MERCHANTS NB	NASHVILLE	IL	C+	B-	B-	120.1	-1.42	1.5	2.4	18.5	47.5	10.0	11.9	29.8
FARMERS & MERCHANTS NB	PAXTON	IL	A-	A-	A-	94.6	3.13	5.9	5.8	20.8	33.5	10.0	11.8	18.6
FARMERS & MERCHANTS NB	HATTON	ND	C-	C	C+	15.8	3.94	5.8	10.2	5.9	17.7	9.6	10.7	18.8
▼ FARMERS & MERCHANTS NB	ASHLAND	NE	B	B+	B+	47.5	11.16	9.1	4.0	21.3	10.5	10.0	11.9	15.7
FARMERS & MERCHANTS NB	W POINT	NE	B-	B-	B-	80.4	1.52	4.6	1.7	6.2	22.4	5.7	7.7	11.5

Asset Quality Index	Non-Performing Loans as a % of Total Loans	as a % of Capital	Net Charge-offs Avg Loans	Profitability Index	Net Income ($Mil)	Return on Assets (R.O.A.)	Return on Equity (R.O.E.)	Net Interest Spread	Overhead Efficiency Ratio	Liquidity Index	Liquidity Ratio	Hot Money Ratio	Stability Index
8.1	0.55	1.0	0.00	9.8	1.0	1.89	6.28	4.47	40.2	3.2	25.6	14.2	9.6
6.0	0.50	2.0	0.18	5.3	0.9	1.03	7.33	4.01	65.2	4.0	10.8	8.3	7.4
7.6	0.33	1.4	0.16	7.8	11.1	1.47	11.69	3.96	57.3	7.7	124.9	8.6	7.4
7.3	1.18	6.0	-0.01	5.0	4.5	0.72	11.11	3.26	65.0	2.3	26.4	25.4	4.4
1.6	4.91	37.7	0.00	9.0	0.4	2.07	20.54	4.69	54.7	3.9	22.9	10.1	5.5
8.9	0.00	0.0	0.00	1.2	0.0	0.42	2.15	3.11	86.7	7.4	178.2	13.4	5.9
6.0	0.82	3.9	0.01	3.7	0.8	0.65	7.83	3.09	75.7	5.6	39.0	5.7	4.2
3.0	4.00	20.9	0.28	10.0	3.2	3.17	34.80	5.26	41.7	1.4	15.6	26.2	7.9
7.5	0.17	1.5	0.06	5.4	4.6	1.01	14.18	3.86	65.1	4.4	17.1	6.5	5.6
5.9	0.97	6.5	0.01	3.0	0.2	0.38	3.37	3.85	91.1	4.7	27.8	6.3	4.4
5.7	1.14	5.9	0.02	6.0	0.8	1.14	10.74	4.25	59.7	3.7	42.4	16.9	6.7
7.2	0.78	3.8	1.15	7.9	0.4	1.43	13.96	4.33	60.0	3.7	20.1	10.8	4.0
8.8	0.21	0.7	3.74	6.9	0.6	1.28	11.24	4.63	56.4	2.2	8.9	17.5	6.2
4.9	0.93	5.7	0.20	7.2	1.1	1.46	16.23	5.10	62.0	4.2	18.0	7.9	5.1
7.6	0.10	0.2	1.35	9.3	0.8	3.33	18.59	5.77	28.1	2.3	50.1	39.1	7.1
7.1	0.71	3.5	0.02	9.9	2.5	1.75	13.96	4.52	48.9	1.8	16.9	20.7	8.0
9.1	1.44	2.9	0.00	9.7	24.4	1.72	8.72	4.47	34.9	6.7	65.4	8.0	10.0
6.7	0.20	1.8	0.02	8.0	2.0	1.35	16.61	4.73	58.5	5.4	81.2	15.8	4.8
4.4	1.99	7.5	0.12	9.8	5.8	2.86	16.52	4.33	35.6	3.3	44.5	19.7	9.8
1.5	5.47	38.7	-0.02	8.0	1.1	1.51	17.34	4.42	52.8	1.2	9.1	27.5	5.5
3.1	1.37	9.9	0.00	6.4	1.2	1.31	13.29	4.78	61.5	1.1	8.5	28.5	3.7
4.8	0.78	7.0	0.10	8.0	0.9	1.26	15.53	4.55	56.1	1.8	32.0	29.6	4.6
7.8	0.42	1.6	-0.04	5.7	0.7	1.22	11.44	3.53	58.8	1.3	12.5	27.0	6.4
5.9	2.62	7.6	0.16	6.3	1.4	1.27	8.22	3.56	52.2	2.5	35.4	22.4	8.6
9.8	0.00	0.0	0.00	2.8	0.1	0.63	3.99	1.26	54.6	6.4	168.9	17.7	6.0
8.3	0.16	0.7	0.05	6.9	0.3	1.01	6.90	4.75	62.5	4.1	49.1	15.8	7.3
8.9	0.00	0.0	0.01	4.6	0.4	0.97	12.49	4.15	77.0	6.2	57.3	5.9	4.1
8.2	0.28	2.3	0.00	4.1	0.2	0.92	16.13	3.33	75.6	1.5	15.6	24.6	1.4
6.4	0.44	3.1	-0.06	3.2	0.1	0.66	7.59	4.30	80.2	6.7	75.2	4.1	1.2
7.7	0.22	2.1	0.04	6.4	0.8	1.07	14.16	4.82	61.6	2.6	9.6	15.2	4.5
7.9	0.47	1.8	-0.05	10.0	1.5	2.11	14.13	5.50	52.6	2.4	22.6	18.0	9.3
6.2	0.45	3.3	0.08	7.7	2.1	1.11	10.90	4.94	68.1	2.2	19.3	18.5	6.6
7.9	0.00	0.0	-0.23	3.1	0.0	1.03	8.20	4.41	80.2	3.9	39.2	13.0	2.5
8.3	0.00	0.0	0.03	7.7	0.3	1.13	10.42	4.03	51.5	5.5	72.0	12.6	6.4
8.2	0.04	0.2	-0.04	6.0	1.1	1.07	9.98	4.12	65.6	4.7	28.9	7.3	6.7
7.2	0.00	0.0	0.00	7.1	0.1	0.97	12.14	4.67	66.0	4.2	23.3	8.2	3.6
5.7	2.17	9.1	0.15	5.8	0.3	0.95	7.89	4.60	69.2	6.8	87.7	7.5	6.6
9.1	0.11	0.6	0.06	2.9	0.2	0.54	5.90	3.66	83.2	6.1	38.4	2.0	4.3
4.5	2.02	7.8	1.18	7.6	0.2	1.77	11.94	4.42	46.5	6.0	62.7	5.9	6.4
6.0	1.21	6.6	1.04	7.7	0.8	1.68	13.68	4.69	59.6	2.3	16.2	17.8	7.9
6.0	5.39	13.4	-0.05	1.6	0.0	0.22	1.47	2.68	92.4	5.0	100.9	17.6	3.8
6.6	0.90	3.3	0.00	5.2	0.1	1.30	12.83	3.09	69.9	5.8	56.9	6.3	5.2
5.4	1.97	6.2	0.98	3.7	0.1	0.66	5.74	4.31	69.0	6.2	80.4	10.1	4.0
3.2	1.51	15.0	0.22	3.9	1.5	0.69	9.32	4.27	71.6	3.5	37.1	16.4	2.1
4.7	1.48	9.2	-0.01	4.4	0.2	0.90	10.26	4.62	75.9	2.1	5.6	17.6	3.7
2.2	1.98	17.4	0.59	5.5	0.4	0.94	11.26	5.35	68.2	2.6	20.4	16.5	3.2
8.9	0.06	0.2	0.03	3.7	0.2	0.66	6.76	3.48	79.0	5.6	45.6	7.6	4.3
8.6	0.03	0.1	0.00	7.9	0.3	1.31	10.25	4.55	52.4	7.0	108.0	9.3	6.3
6.2	0.01	0.0	0.07	9.9	2.2	1.71	16.47	4.87	50.5	4.3	23.6	7.7	8.9
4.6	0.61	5.3	0.08	6.6	1.7	1.13	14.02	3.87	59.6	5.1	39.4	9.1	4.7
3.8	0.71	5.9	0.08	7.0	1.4	0.92	9.36	4.63	72.4	2.4	25.6	18.1	6.7
4.9	1.98	11.0	0.13	9.4	1.0	2.11	16.70	4.76	30.3	1.6	25.8	26.2	7.0
2.4	1.47	13.1	-0.01	9.9	0.5	2.93	33.86	5.62	45.9	1.4	12.0	25.2	4.8
4.1	2.57	12.7	0.28	4.4	0.1	0.74	7.07	3.63	64.0	5.7	50.1	7.6	4.8
7.1	0.11	0.6	0.00	5.0	0.2	1.05	10.70	3.95	67.2	4.7	65.0	15.7	4.4
4.3	1.31	9.5	0.27	7.5	1.0	1.33	13.45	4.33	52.1	2.1	19.1	19.1	6.2
8.4	0.29	1.8	0.04	9.0	8.4	1.46	14.56	4.59	55.7	2.9	31.7	22.1	9.1
8.0	0.60	2.3	-0.17	8.2	1.3	1.34	9.27	3.98	60.0	4.8	33.5	8.4	8.6
7.2	0.09	0.8	0.27	2.3	0.1	0.16	2.13	4.18	90.3	1.6	13.0	22.0	2.4
7.9	1.42	4.1	-0.49	2.7	0.4	0.65	5.21	3.40	80.2	6.1	54.5	7.2	6.3
7.8	0.70	3.0	0.01	7.5	0.6	1.39	11.19	4.23	56.1	5.3	66.8	12.9	7.3
4.2	1.97	8.3	-0.27	3.5	0.0	0.43	3.97	4.15	87.5	7.5	93.1	2.4	4.2
7.5	0.46	2.9	0.21	5.9	0.2	0.94	7.76	5.19	71.6	4.2	25.8	8.9	5.8
7.2	0.00	0.0	-0.01	8.5	0.8	1.85	23.79	3.86	51.3	4.8	55.9	13.7	5.7

Name	City	State	Weiss Safety Rating	2003 Weiss Safety Rating	2002 Weiss Safety Rating	Total Assets ($Mil)	One Year Asset Growth	Asset Mix (As a % of Total Assets)				Capital-ization Index	Leverage Ratio	Risk-based Capital Ratio
								Comm-ercial Loans	Cons-umer Loans	Home Mort-gages	Secur-ities			
FARMERS & MERCHANTS NB	FAIRVIEW	OK	A-	A-	A-	58.6	7.15	6.6	6.5	6.8	45.0	10.0	11.6	24.4
FARMERS & MERCHANTS ST	WATERLOO	WI	A	A	A	124.8	7.65	5.9	2.9	13.6	29.1	10.0	13.5	19.5
FARMERS & MERCHANTS ST	NEOLA	IA	C+	C+	B	44.2	0.83	3.9	4.2	12.0	43.5	7.5	9.3	19.6
FARMERS & MERCHANTS ST	WINTERSET	IA	B	B	B	120.2	1.63	3.5	2.8	14.6	35.0	6.8	8.8	14.8
FARMERS & MERCHANTS ST	MERIDIAN	ID	C+	C+	C	418.9	22.47	41.3	4.3	5.0	13.6	3.2	7.6	10.1
▲ FARMERS & MERCHANTS ST	VIRDEN	IL	A-	B+	B+	70.7	0.61	4.5	4.0	12.6	35.1	9.4	10.6	19.1
▲ FARMERS & MERCHANTS ST	ARGONIA	KS	D	D	D	19.0	9.90	11.5	6.4	5.7	25.2	7.1	9.1	15.5
FARMERS & MERCHANTS ST	CAWKER CITY	KS	D	D-	D	9.4	4.22	7.9	4.7	7.7	0.1	7.4	10.0	12.8
FARMERS & MERCHANTS ST	WAKEFIELD	KS	D+	C-	B-	23.4	30.79	7.7	4.8	3.3	60.5	6.8	8.8	17.9
FARMERS & MERCHANTS ST	ALPHA	MN	C-	D+	D+	23.2	2.56	11.2	4.4	13.2	14.4	9.9	10.9	16.4
FARMERS & MERCHANTS ST	APPLETON	MN	B-	B-	B-	36.1	-0.75	4.6	3.3	3.3	41.7	10.0	12.0	21.1
▲ FARMERS & MERCHANTS ST	BLOOMING PRAIRIE	MN	C+	C	C	49.6	11.41	11.4	6.8	15.1	7.1	5.4	8.3	11.3
FARMERS & MERCHANTS ST	CLARKFIELD	MN	C+	C+	C+	31.1	-3.27	6.4	2.6	4.2	28.7	8.5	10.0	15.0
▲ FARMERS & MERCHANTS ST	NEW YORK MILLS	MN	C+	C-	B	49.5	0.79	11.4	2.7	6.4	42.0	10.0	12.7	18.3
▼ FARMERS & MERCHANTS ST	PAYNESVILLE	MN	B	B+	B+	25.8	4.95	5.5	4.8	7.0	48.8	8.8	10.2	26.6
FARMERS & MERCHANTS ST	PIERZ	MN	B+	B+	B+	148.3	2.36	11.6	4.0	10.3	24.4	6.3	8.5	12.0
FARMERS & MERCHANTS ST	SACRED HEART	MN	C	C	C-	23.5	-3.60	2.4	4.6	5.8	51.8	9.6	10.8	17.0
▲ FARMERS & MERCHANTS ST	SPRINGFIELD	MN	C+	C	C	84.8	3.68	6.0	3.7	4.9	17.7	5.2	7.5	11.1
▲ FARMERS & MERCHANTS ST	LANGDON	ND	A-	B+	B	42.4	1.87	10.0	3.4	2.5	33.0	10.0	14.2	20.6
FARMERS & MERCHANTS ST	TOLNA	ND	B	B	B	40.6	6.73	4.9	4.3	0.4	44.2	10.0	11.5	21.3
FARMERS & MERCHANTS ST	BLOOMFIELD	NE	C	C+	C+	89.0	-0.17	10.0	14.1	1.8	12.6	4.6	8.7	10.8
FARMERS & MERCHANTS ST	WAYNE	NE	B-	B-	B-	33.2	10.93	7.1	2.2	5.0	27.1	4.0	7.4	10.5
▲ FARMERS & MERCHANTS ST	ARCHBOLD	OH	C+	C	C	711.7	-1.71	14.7	5.9	14.5	24.8	6.4	8.4	15.8
FARMERS & MERCHANTS ST	IROQUOIS	SD	C	C	C+	37.4	2.50	12.8	5.0	1.3	14.1	5.3	8.5	11.2
▼ FARMERS & MERCHANTS ST	PLANKINTON	SD	B	A-	A-	56.9	8.02	12.4	8.8	5.3	14.3	9.2	11.0	14.4
FARMERS & MERCHANTS ST	SCOTLAND	SD	D+	D+	D+	22.2	1.57	8.7	4.2	3.8	39.1	7.8	9.5	17.7
FARMERS & MERCHANTS ST	KRUM	TX	B-	C+	D+	141.1	20.13	11.6	12.6	13.6	11.2	4.9	8.3	10.9
FARMERS & MERCHANTS ST	LADONIA	TX	E	E	E+	15.4	-3.81	2.9	10.5	4.6	47.0	6.0	8.0	21.0
FARMERS & MERCHANTS SVG	LONE TREE	IA	C-	C-	C-	89.6	7.52	2.1	2.2	9.4	42.0	6.5	8.5	16.1
FARMERS & MERCHANTS SVG	MANCHESTER	IA	B-	B-	B-	141.3	2.79	29.4	1.3	8.2	25.9	5.3	7.5	11.2
FARMERS & MERCHANTS SVG	WAUKON	IA	B	B	B-	78.1	-3.99	5.0	6.2	15.3	15.3	8.1	9.7	15.1
FARMERS & MERCHANTS	CHAMBERSBURG	PA	B-	B-	B-	554.7	3.90	9.3	4.4	27.0	26.5	5.5	7.5	11.9
▲ FARMERS & MERCHANTS	COLUMBUS	WI	A-	B+	B+	144.2	7.95	6.7	2.3	17.7	14.1	9.1	10.4	14.9
FARMERS & MINERS BK	PENNINGTON GAP	VA	B+	B+	B	107.3	0.89	3.8	14.6	29.7	14.7	7.8	9.5	18.2
FARMERS & MRCH BK OF	COLBY	KS	B-	B-	B-	71.2	-0.69	3.7	2.6	12.2	42.8	9.3	10.5	20.7
FARMERS & MRCH ST BK	BUSHNELL	IL	B-	B-	B-	55.7	0.33	3.8	9.5	15.1	15.6	8.8	10.2	17.5
FARMERS & STOCKMENS BK	CLAYTON	NM	B-	B-	B	51.4	5.77	8.7	6.2	4.3	18.7	5.4	7.4	11.8
▲ FARMERS & TRADERS BK	CAMPTON	KY	B-	B-	B-	43.3	15.59	0.9	6.8	22.9	28.8	6.9	8.9	15.8
▲ FARMERS & TRADERS ST BK	SHABBONA	IL	B+	B	B	31.7	4.69	2.6	2.0	15.1	33.5	10.0	15.9	29.4
FARMERS & TRADERS SVG BK	BANCROFT	IA	B	B	B	38.3	3.39	4.2	2.6	5.4	27.2	9.8	10.8	15.6
▲ FARMERS & TRADERS SVG BK	DOUDS	IA	E+	E	E+	16.7	2.76	2.7	11.3	33.3	1.2	6.0	8.0	15.7
▼ FARMERS AND MECHANICS	BLOOMFIELD	IN	C+	B-	B	61.0	-1.21	0.0	0.6	44.7	34.2	10.0	18.6	55.9
▼ FARMERS AND MERCHANTS	UPPERCO	MD	B	B+	B+	148.3	5.77	5.2	0.4	19.8	21.3	9.7	10.8	16.0
FARMERS B&T	ATWOOD	KS	C	C	C	49.6	1.22	3.1	2.2	5.6	52.5	6.2	8.2	17.1
▼ FARMERS B&TC	BLYTHEVILLE	AR	B	B+	A-	182.1	3.85	14.0	4.4	10.5	36.8	10.0	11.7	19.0
▲ FARMERS B&TC	MAGNOLIA	AR	B+	B	B	410.8	0.51	7.9	4.5	17.3	35.7	7.8	9.6	15.7
FARMERS B&TC	GEORGETOWN	KY	B-	B-	B+	205.4	1.45	15.9	2.8	11.2	27.1	4.6	6.6	11.3
▼ FARMERS B&TC	MARION	KY	B	B+	B+	107.6	5.20	5.2	9.4	30.7	24.4	10.0	11.7	18.7
FARMERS B&TC	PRINCETON	KY	A	A	A	91.2	-4.05	2.4	6.8	20.9	48.5	10.0	16.9	35.3
▼ FARMERS B&TC	NEBRASKA CITY	NE	C	C+	B-	39.3	-6.51	2.6	2.8	5.5	55.9	6.6	8.6	23.7
FARMERS B&TC NA	GREAT BEND	KS	A-	A-	A	410.4	28.51	6.0	0.9	9.3	39.6	7.3	9.2	15.2
FARMERS BK	GREENWOOD	AR	A	A	A	183.2	5.31	8.9	9.9	32.6	29.5	10.0	19.0	31.7
▲ FARMERS BK	HAMBURG	AR	E+	D-	D	37.8	-12.00	1.8	7.8	13.6	37.2	5.3	7.3	14.1
FARMERS BK	AULT	CO	C	C	C	80.9	22.82	8.8	1.7	5.7	3.1	5.2	9.2	11.1
FARMERS BK	FORSYTH	GA	B-	B-	B-	69.2	14.12	8.8	3.6	15.8	15.0	5.1	7.4	11.1
FARMERS BK	UNION POINT	GA	C+	B-	B	83.7	13.82	33.7	1.5	8.6	22.4	8.0	9.7	13.8
▲ FARMERS BK	FRANKFORT	IN	C+	C	C-	453.1	-2.16	15.0	7.2	11.6	15.1	6.2	8.6	11.9
FARMERS BK	HARDINSBURG	KY	A-	B+	B+	76.1	0.42	9.5	13.0	16.0	16.2	10.0	18.3	27.2
▲ FARMERS BK	MILTON	KY	A+	A	A	104.1	4.12	1.9	8.9	34.4	38.5	10.0	17.4	32.9
FARMERS BK	NICHOLASVILLE	KY	B-	B-	B-	91.1	-5.91	30.9	6.0	22.1	19.2	8.4	9.9	14.6
FARMERS BK	LOHMAN	MO	B+	B+	B+	43.4	1.07	2.1	8.5	13.5	59.4	10.0	14.4	34.9
FARMERS BK	COOK	NE	C	C-	C-	64.4	27.17	6.6	6.1	21.2	18.7	5.4	7.4	11.6
▲ FARMERS BK	LINCOLN	NE	C+	C	C-	18.8	3.25	10.6	4.8	22.8	19.3	4.2	6.4	10.6
FARMERS BK	OCONTO	NE	C-	C-	C	18.9	0.66	6.0	8.9	2.0	24.3	10.0	13.0	15.9

Asset Quality Index	Non-Performing Loans as a % of Total Loans	as a % of Capital	Net Charge-offs Avg Loans	Profitability Index	Net Income ($Mil)	Return on Assets (R.O.A.)	Return on Equity (R.O.E.)	Net Interest Spread	Overhead Efficiency Ratio	Liquidity Index	Liquidity Ratio	Hot Money Ratio	Stability Index
8.6	0.00	0.0	-0.03	10.0	0.8	2.57	22.34	4.78	49.1	4.2	42.0	14.3	7.5
8.6	0.03	0.1	0.02	7.6	0.7	1.20	8.74	4.35	59.6	3.1	11.4	13.2	8.9
8.2	0.52	2.4	0.13	4.3	0.3	1.13	12.16	3.25	68.4	5.7	81.7	13.1	4.5
8.7	0.05	0.3	0.06	4.8	0.5	0.86	8.96	3.60	69.3	4.7	27.9	6.4	5.8
4.8	0.46	4.4	0.56	9.5	2.8	1.41	19.26	5.17	54.6	1.7	16.3	21.6	3.8
7.7	0.43	2.1	-0.03	7.8	0.6	1.79	16.76	3.37	52.2	6.7	73.0	5.9	7.4
6.4	0.82	5.2	0.23	3.2	0.1	0.70	7.91	5.07	85.2	3.8	49.7	15.8	1.3
6.8	0.00	0.0	-0.02	7.8	0.1	2.28	23.66	4.68	55.7	2.0	9.1	18.4	3.0
7.4	1.06	4.5	-0.09	4.5	0.1	0.86	10.34	3.74	81.9	1.0	7.7	29.8	3.0
3.7	2.37	13.5	-0.01	4.0	0.1	0.67	6.07	3.95	74.7	4.3	78.9	18.1	3.1
4.4	3.75	14.5	0.05	6.3	0.3	1.67	14.18	3.81	63.9	5.1	60.1	12.6	5.9
7.6	0.15	1.4	0.15	7.6	0.5	1.91	24.83	5.10	64.9	4.1	22.8	8.9	4.6
4.7	0.73	4.1	-0.02	3.6	0.1	0.68	6.58	4.03	82.4	3.8	30.3	12.6	4.9
5.5	2.83	11.1	-0.05	4.5	0.4	1.64	13.38	4.80	62.4	4.0	22.7	9.6	4.3
7.1	1.10	3.0	0.00	8.0	0.2	1.85	17.12	4.78	59.8	7.1	82.1	4.7	6.3
5.1	0.90	7.5	-0.04	10.0	2.3	3.11	35.00	4.81	34.4	1.3	7.9	26.0	6.3
6.9	1.22	4.3	0.13	4.3	0.1	0.97	8.59	4.23	73.7	3.6	35.6	13.5	3.7
4.3	0.91	7.4	0.00	4.9	0.5	1.10	14.45	3.71	71.0	5.3	42.9	8.6	5.0
7.1	0.35	1.4	0.08	8.5	0.4	1.92	13.47	4.10	50.2	7.5	104.4	5.9	8.2
5.7	2.25	9.3	0.19	4.9	0.3	1.29	10.92	3.48	58.9	3.6	41.2	17.4	5.9
5.0	0.42	3.5	0.90	7.9	0.6	1.34	15.97	5.01	45.0	4.0	29.8	11.6	3.5
8.3	0.00	0.0	-0.01	7.0	0.3	1.74	24.29	3.98	54.0	3.3	24.1	13.6	4.9
3.9	1.40	10.3	0.12	5.7	3.9	1.09	12.90	3.98	59.4	2.7	29.3	18.0	4.8
4.4	0.57	4.8	0.00	8.3	0.3	1.45	16.82	4.22	45.9	3.2	17.3	13.4	4.9
2.3	2.89	18.6	0.44	9.8	0.7	2.39	21.20	4.91	46.1	1.7	20.3	23.3	8.4
5.9	1.51	7.4	-0.16	4.4	0.1	1.11	11.65	4.02	72.3	4.6	36.8	8.2	3.0
5.1	0.43	4.0	0.49	9.7	1.4	2.17	27.50	5.75	70.5	2.5	31.1	19.7	4.2
4.7	3.19	12.1	0.09	2.6	0.0	0.56	7.30	3.34	91.0	5.7	57.2	7.2	0.3
7.1	0.87	4.5	-0.05	2.2	0.2	0.52	6.16	2.32	82.3	6.6	81.9	7.9	4.2
8.2	0.15	1.2	0.00	5.8	0.7	1.04	13.58	3.67	57.4	3.6	31.5	14.1	4.3
7.0	0.46	3.1	0.03	7.3	0.7	1.85	19.26	4.43	56.9	5.2	58.0	12.2	5.6
7.1	0.45	3.5	-0.18	4.7	2.5	0.92	11.61	3.53	68.8	6.6	61.0	5.9	5.0
6.1	0.59	4.0	0.05	6.0	0.7	1.01	9.58	4.08	61.6	5.3	38.8	7.4	6.3
5.5	0.75	4.3	0.26	7.9	0.8	1.43	14.85	5.63	62.2	5.4	97.7	17.6	6.1
4.7	2.24	7.4	0.15	5.7	0.4	1.12	8.35	3.99	62.9	1.7	20.1	22.3	6.5
7.1	0.36	1.9	0.07	4.8	0.3	0.89	8.57	3.84	74.0	6.1	74.8	10.1	5.8
4.7	0.61	4.2	-0.05	7.3	0.3	1.06	11.59	4.75	65.7	2.8	59.0	32.5	6.1
6.2	0.27	1.2	0.54	5.7	0.2	1.22	12.74	4.74	73.5	5.4	51.9	10.1	4.9
9.1	0.02	0.1	0.41	5.3	0.2	1.26	8.18	3.93	70.4	4.6	70.1	17.1	7.1
7.0	0.25	1.3	0.32	4.8	0.2	1.14	10.24	3.58	64.4	5.1	77.0	15.4	5.8
4.6	0.35	2.6	0.00	3.1	0.1	0.68	8.35	3.22	78.3	8.3	230.0	11.2	1.7
8.9	0.58	1.4	0.06	2.8	0.1	0.16	0.82	2.64	91.1	3.8	42.3	16.2	6.3
7.7	0.52	3.0	0.02	4.3	0.5	0.74	6.87	4.01	74.0	3.6	35.8	15.7	6.2
5.4	2.04	8.9	-0.15	5.2	0.3	1.22	14.81	3.54	65.7	4.6	19.3	5.4	4.4
4.3	3.34	14.8	0.19	5.5	1.0	1.06	8.91	3.96	61.4	1.3	9.7	25.9	6.0
5.6	0.76	4.1	0.63	7.3	3.8	1.82	17.83	4.10	51.1	2.2	35.6	28.1	5.7
7.4	0.27	2.3	0.07	4.9	0.9	0.85	12.83	3.25	68.3	3.7	20.3	10.8	5.8
4.2	3.32	17.9	1.61	4.8	0.4	0.79	6.64	4.63	61.2	2.3	14.5	17.4	7.1
8.9	0.41	1.1	-0.08	7.1	0.6	1.20	7.16	4.04	60.9	6.7	78.5	7.1	8.2
9.4	0.03	0.1	-0.02	3.6	0.1	0.55	6.03	3.40	82.6	6.3	54.0	4.2	3.4
7.8	0.35	1.9	0.04	9.8	4.4	2.27	22.55	4.13	39.9	0.9	23.2	44.5	6.7
8.1	0.64	1.9	0.00	9.3	1.1	1.19	5.84	5.51	58.6	2.1	13.8	18.2	8.7
4.6	1.72	5.5	0.64	0.1	-0.2	-0.81	-6.91	3.47	107.9	4.9	44.2	11.3	1.3
4.3	1.07	7.4	0.03	9.8	0.9	2.41	19.84	4.68	44.6	2.0	29.1	24.7	0.8
6.9	0.00	0.0	0.18	7.6	0.6	1.79	13.97	4.65	61.2	3.3	33.4	16.1	7.6
4.3	1.56	9.9	0.40	9.1	0.7	1.66	16.83	4.38	53.1	1.9	21.7	20.2	6.1
4.4	0.63	5.0	1.04	5.0	1.9	0.80	9.46	3.81	60.6	2.3	17.1	17.6	3.5
6.0	1.56	5.2	0.16	8.5	0.6	1.50	8.28	4.83	59.5	5.8	43.6	5.4	8.5
8.6	0.31	1.0	-0.02	8.5	0.9	1.69	9.85	4.08	45.5	1.7	26.3	25.9	9.4
7.0	0.24	1.7	0.04	4.9	0.4	0.93	9.72	4.81	71.2	4.0	9.1	7.9	4.5
8.8	0.05	0.1	0.12	6.1	0.2	1.04	7.10	3.54	58.1	6.5	58.8	4.0	6.8
6.3	0.59	4.9	0.02	5.4	0.3	1.08	13.82	4.80	68.8	2.5	20.3	17.2	3.5
5.4	1.37	13.0	0.00	3.2	0.0	0.47	7.38	5.05	91.1	4.3	34.2	9.4	3.5
1.8	4.46	20.5	0.09	3.7	0.1	1.00	7.67	3.79	72.3	3.8	75.5	20.1	4.5

Name	City	State	Weiss Safety Rating	2003 Weiss Safety Rating	2002 Weiss Safety Rating	Total Assets ($Mil)	One Year Asset Growth	Asset Mix (As a % of Total Assets)				Capital-ization Index	Leverage Ratio	Risk-based Capital Ratio
								Comm-ercial Loans	Cons-umer Loans	Home Mort-gages	Secur-ities			
FARMERS BK	CARNEGIE	OK	B	B	B-	30.7	5.08	10.2	12.3	2.6	15.6	10.0	11.1	18.4
▼ FARMERS BK	CORNERSVILLE	TN	B-	B	B	82.7	9.25	2.9	5.2	38.3	18.1	9.0	10.3	16.6
FARMERS BK	PARSONS	TN	D+	D+	D+	37.5	-4.31	11.6	13.2	22.8	28.0	7.0	9.0	17.2
FARMERS BK	PORTLAND	TN	B	B-	B-	324.6	12.78	8.3	3.4	13.9	33.8	6.6	8.6	13.9
FARMERS BK	WOODLAND MILLS	TN	C+	C+	C+	13.5	-1.92	5.5	12.8	9.5	41.8	10.0	15.1	33.9
▼ FARMERS BK	WINDSOR	VA	A-	A	A+	220.7	24.23	5.6	2.7	13.6	25.8	8.2	9.8	14.9
FARMERS BK & CAPITAL TR	FRANKFORT	KY	C+	C+	B	534.5	-5.02	3.2	4.2	19.2	36.8	4.3	6.3	12.5
▲ FARMERS BK & SVGS CO	POMEROY	OH	B	B-	B	151.0	5.51	4.7	11.6	36.8	21.8	6.4	8.4	14.3
FARMERS BK NORTHERN MO	UNIONVILLE	MO	B-	B-	C	242.4	-1.27	8.6	3.2	8.9	35.3	7.3	9.2	16.1
▼ FARMERS BK OF	APPOMATTOX	VA	B	B+	B+	142.0	6.26	9.0	19.1	16.3	36.7	9.3	10.6	17.0
▼ FARMERS BK OF GOWER	GOWER	MO	C	C+	C	33.2	10.37	9.4	2.3	6.5	49.2	6.9	8.9	16.6
FARMERS BK OF GREEN CITY	GREEN CITY	MO	C	C-	D+	22.2	-3.07	11.0	3.2	8.6	32.4	9.1	10.4	14.8
▲ FARMERS BK OF LIBERTY	LIBERTY	IL	D	D-	E-	44.4	2.62	5.3	11.7	22.5	18.2	5.1	7.1	11.2
FARMERS BK OF LINCOLN	LINCOLN	MO	B-	B-	B-	71.1	2.47	4.5	3.6	28.8	24.7	6.6	8.6	15.0
▲ FARMERS BK OF LYNCHBURG	LYNCHBURG	TN	C+	C-	B-	59.7	-1.40	2.0	3.2	19.8	34.6	10.0	12.1	22.2
▲ FARMERS BK OF MT PULASKI	MT PULASKI	IL	C+	C-	C-	40.9	-1.04	1.7	6.9	18.5	54.8	10.0	11.7	32.1
FARMERS BK OF	PORTAGEVILLE	MO	B	B	B+	50.4	-1.18	4.2	14.6	13.0	35.8	9.7	10.8	17.7
FARMERS BK OF WILLARDS	WILLARDS	MD	B	B-	B-	174.9	8.55	10.0	4.0	41.0	10.4	6.7	8.7	14.1
FARMERS BLDG & SVG BK	ROCHESTER	PA	B+	B+	B+	48.5	-1.25	0.0	0.4	43.7	31.6	10.0	19.6	49.6
FARMERS CITIZENS BK	BUCYRUS	OH	B-	B-	B+	151.6	2.89	5.6	3.8	19.9	37.8	6.7	8.8	12.9
FARMERS DEPOSIT BK	EMINENCE	KY	C+	C+	C+	100.7	-29.85	7.4	9.3	19.2	23.6	6.3	8.4	14.5
▲ FARMERS DEPOSIT BK	MIDDLEBURG	KY	D	D-	E+	44.3	-3.19	2.7	9.9	23.0	38.1	6.1	8.1	16.5
FARMERS EXCHANGE BK	LOUISVILLE	AL	D+	D+	D-	61.7	21.13	48.4	4.8	15.6	19.1	5.5	7.9	11.4
FARMERS EXCHANGE BK	CHEROKEE	OK	C-	C-	B-	100.7	-0.04	10.0	6.5	10.5	22.5	4.2	6.3	11.0
FARMERS EXCHANGE BK	NESHKORO	WI	C+	C+	C+	49.2	9.33	11.1	4.3	30.3	16.5	6.5	8.5	14.9
FARMERS FIRST BK	LITITZ	PA	B	B	B	1,590.6	-0.71	13.5	9.3	5.3	15.4	5.9	9.2	11.7
FARMERS NB	GRIGGSVILLE	IL	C-	C-	D+	28.4	2.91	3.0	14.4	19.5	10.7	5.1	8.4	11.1
FARMERS NB	PHILLIPSBURG	KS	B	B	B	69.6	6.28	6.9	4.8	8.9	32.6	10.0	12.0	19.8
FARMERS NB	WALTON	KY	C	C-	C-	53.3	-5.17	5.8	4.1	33.2	10.4	7.5	9.4	13.6
FARMERS NB	EMLENTON	PA	C+	C+	B-	263.6	4.82	6.6	5.0	37.4	19.5	4.9	7.0	11.0
FARMERS NB OF BUHL	BUHL	ID	A-	A	A	299.4	7.62	13.6	4.8	2.8	27.6	10.0	14.3	20.1
FARMERS NB OF CANFIELD	CANFIELD	OH	B+	B+	A-	802.5	0.78	2.3	19.1	19.3	33.1	6.9	8.9	15.6
FARMERS NB OF CYNTHIANA	CYNTHIANA	KY	A	A	A	112.7	4.37	9.7	5.4	8.8	51.2	10.0	16.1	30.8
▲ FARMERS NB OF DANVILLE	DANVILLE	KY	A	A-	A	319.2	-1.46	5.7	2.4	31.3	28.3	10.0	11.5	18.5
FARMERS NB OF KANSAS	WALNUT	KS	B+	B+	B+	22.9	6.97	10.3	10.3	24.0	13.9	9.1	10.4	15.9
FARMERS NB OF KITTANNING	KITTANNING	PA	B	B	A	141.7	5.56	11.8	3.7	28.6	26.2	6.8	8.8	14.2
FARMERS NB OF LEBANON	LEBANON	KY	C	C	C	102.3	3.68	7.6	3.7	11.1	46.2	6.1	8.1	17.2
FARMERS NB OF NEWCASTLE	NEWCASTLE	TX	C+	C+	C+	18.2	15.42	4.9	11.5	7.2	16.8	10.0	13.3	25.6
FARMERS NB OF OSBORNE	OSBORNE	KS	B-	B-	B-	37.5	-6.40	4.0	5.0	8.0	27.8	10.0	11.8	20.3
▲ FARMERS NB OF	SCOTTSVILLE	KY	A-	B+	B+	186.0	-0.84	6.4	4.1	24.7	32.2	10.0	14.1	23.4
FARMERS NB OF SEYMOUR	SEYMOUR	TX	B-	B-	B-	50.1	5.30	11.2	8.8	14.0	1.2	8.5	10.4	13.7
▲ FARMERS NB OF STAFFORD	STAFFORD	KS	C-	C-	C-	74.7	16.41	5.8	2.6	6.4	50.4	5.3	7.3	14.1
▼ FARMERS NB OF WINFIELD	MT PLEASANT	IA	E-	E-	E-	20.5	-7.08	2.7	5.0	17.7	6.7	7.0	9.0	27.4
▲ FARMERS NB	PROPHETSTOWN	IL	A	A-	A-	246.2	5.47	1.9	1.4	6.2	44.1	10.0	12.0	21.4
▲ FARMERS SECURITY BK	WASHBURN	ND	C+	C	C-	27.4	-3.29	8.4	6.2	14.3	32.8	8.5	10.0	17.4
FARMERS ST B&TC	JACKSONVILLE	IL	B	B	B	152.9	1.82	9.0	8.1	18.8	33.7	10.0	12.5	21.5
▼ FARMERS ST B&TC	MT STERLING	IL	D+	D+	C+	57.1	-2.05	11.8	7.3	11.1	26.1	6.0	8.0	12.9
FARMERS ST B&TC	CHURCH POINT	LA	B	B	B-	58.1	0.02	14.0	13.1	20.5	28.7	10.0	12.2	22.0
FARMERS ST BK	BRUSH	CO	A-	A-	A-	34.6	-3.08	3.0	11.2	1.3	44.8	10.0	13.6	24.8
FARMERS ST BK	FORT MORGAN	CO	A+	A+	A+	139.9	-1.62	6.5	0.9	10.2	48.6	10.0	14.3	27.6
▲ FARMERS ST BK	DUBLIN	GA	B+	B	B-	99.4	-0.54	30.3	8.1	16.4	24.5	9.3	10.6	16.1
▲ FARMERS ST BK	LINCOLNTON	GA	A-	A	A	93.7	-2.06	5.2	6.8	21.4	42.4	10.0	11.2	22.4
FARMERS ST BK	LUMPKIN	GA	D	D	D	54.0	5.19	14.1	13.3	12.2	28.5	5.5	7.5	11.7
FARMERS ST BK	ALGONA	IA	B-	B-	B-	59.0	-0.90	14.0	3.3	10.5	18.3	6.7	8.7	13.2
▲ FARMERS ST BK	HAWARDEN	IA	C+	C	C	46.2	-1.27	9.4	5.4	4.2	36.5	6.7	8.7	14.1
FARMERS ST BK	JESUP	IA	C+	C+	C	119.8	-1.91	10.2	14.2	4.5	17.5	5.3	8.8	11.2
FARMERS ST BK	LAKE VIEW	IA	C	C	C	22.7	-0.07	10.9	8.8	13.3	34.5	8.8	10.2	25.8
FARMERS ST BK	MARCUS	IA	B+	B+	B+	48.8	-2.16	8.8	3.4	6.6	32.1	10.0	12.8	21.5
FARMERS ST BK	MARION	IA	A	A	A	437.2	3.64	12.3	3.6	11.2	28.2	10.0	11.7	17.0
FARMERS ST BK	NORTHWOOD	IA	C+	C+	C	68.6	27.54	6.3	4.7	14.9	38.3	5.9	7.9	14.4
▼ FARMERS ST BK	YALE	IA	D+	C-	C	28.7	1.11	1.1	3.5	16.5	47.1	7.2	9.2	18.5
FARMERS ST BK	ALTO PASS	IL	B	B-	C+	135.8	4.50	10.0	6.6	27.9	3.7	6.2	8.2	12.1
▲ FARMERS ST BK	DANFORTH	IL	C+	B-	B+	44.9	1.24	9.2	2.4	7.4	31.8	9.0	10.4	17.9
FARMERS ST BK	ELMWOOD	IL	B-	B-	B-	35.6	1.43	3.1	3.2	27.9	28.9	9.8	10.9	17.7

Asset Quality Index	Non-Performing Loans as a % of Total Loans	Non-Performing Loans as a % of Capital	Net Charge-offs Avg Loans	Profitability Index	Net Income ($Mil)	Return on Assets (R.O.A.)	Return on Equity (R.O.E.)	Net Interest Spread	Overhead Efficiency Ratio	Liquidity Index	Liquidity Ratio	Hot Money Ratio	Stability Index
7.4	0.12	0.7	0.06	7.2	0.3	2.08	18.97	5.22	60.7	4.0	35.3	13.3	4.7
4.4	1.94	12.7	0.00	3.8	0.2	0.50	4.89	3.51	82.1	3.0	34.4	18.2	5.6
4.6	1.50	8.6	0.18	4.5	0.2	0.78	8.63	4.84	76.0	4.9	63.7	14.3	3.0
5.5	0.61	3.8	0.28	6.7	1.7	1.11	12.03	4.20	61.3	3.7	17.2	10.5	5.5
8.2	0.00	0.0	-0.04	3.5	0.0	0.62	4.26	3.41	79.1	6.7	67.0	2.7	4.6
8.6	0.19	1.2	0.00	7.3	1.2	1.16	11.59	3.58	49.5	2.6	34.2	20.2	6.6
4.6	1.39	9.9	0.19	5.6	3.6	1.31	20.71	3.73	59.9	5.7	52.6	9.8	4.9
6.4	0.46	3.5	0.23	5.0	0.7	0.99	11.50	4.40	66.8	4.3	45.5	14.7	5.4
4.4	1.37	6.9	-0.01	6.2	1.3	1.09	10.17	3.73	58.7	4.6	14.5	4.8	6.0
5.9	0.36	1.8	0.24	4.8	0.6	0.85	8.01	4.41	73.4	4.4	39.8	13.1	6.4
6.9	0.07	0.3	0.00	4.5	0.2	1.27	11.31	3.48	60.6	7.9	115.6	4.9	3.7
9.0	0.15	0.6	-0.19	5.7	0.1	1.03	10.05	3.19	58.9	4.4	86.9	19.0	3.9
4.1	0.73	6.3	0.23	7.4	0.3	1.29	18.05	4.71	54.2	3.6	21.4	11.8	2.0
8.8	0.11	0.8	0.07	6.7	0.5	1.56	18.07	3.96	62.3	4.6	52.6	14.2	5.3
6.4	0.79	3.5	-0.76	3.3	0.2	0.68	5.64	4.03	76.2	1.8	23.9	23.2	3.7
5.7	3.29	9.1	-0.06	2.7	0.1	0.45	3.72	3.66	78.8	3.3	36.6	17.3	4.1
6.8	0.06	0.3	0.86	7.6	0.2	0.92	8.43	3.92	59.1	1.8	27.6	25.4	6.3
6.4	0.27	2.3	0.03	7.5	1.0	1.22	13.96	4.79	55.1	4.0	35.3	13.2	5.2
8.1	2.12	4.7	0.00	7.6	0.3	1.32	6.89	3.72	48.1	5.0	N/A	0.0	6.6
7.6	0.58	3.3	0.52	3.7	0.4	0.58	6.68	3.61	81.5	4.0	27.8	11.1	5.6
0.3	13.04	42.2	13.95	0.8	-0.2	-0.35	-2.79	2.95	104.0	4.6	58.5	16.5	5.0
1.7	7.08	34.6	0.11	3.9	0.2	0.75	8.34	4.48	77.6	2.6	27.4	17.8	3.0
5.3	0.64	5.7	-0.09	4.5	0.3	0.85	10.72	3.85	72.2	0.9	23.3	40.9	1.3
2.7	1.32	10.5	0.69	7.7	1.0	1.91	25.43	4.72	55.5	2.6	9.2	15.5	6.0
6.4	0.01	0.0	0.03	9.0	0.3	1.39	11.18	4.93	57.0	5.2	54.8	11.3	4.7
5.9	0.61	4.4	0.21	7.0	10.2	1.26	13.84	3.47	59.3	3.6	18.7	11.8	7.5
4.9	0.39	3.4	0.07	5.3	0.2	1.08	12.61	4.62	73.1	5.1	44.7	10.5	3.6
5.0	2.82	11.9	0.50	5.6	0.3	0.83	6.95	3.50	57.9	6.9	97.7	8.3	5.8
4.9	1.14	7.9	0.09	4.5	0.2	0.83	8.56	4.55	76.4	4.8	33.3	8.1	3.7
5.1	0.64	5.6	0.05	4.4	0.9	0.71	9.25	3.82	76.4	4.3	28.8	10.0	4.6
5.4	1.29	5.7	0.04	8.7	2.5	1.68	11.78	4.50	48.4	7.0	118.3	11.5	8.7
6.7	0.31	1.9	0.23	6.5	4.7	1.17	13.02	3.99	58.0	4.3	32.6	10.8	6.3
6.7	2.01	5.3	0.09	8.3	1.3	2.25	13.99	4.22	46.4	1.5	12.0	23.8	8.5
8.8	0.14	0.8	0.03	6.9	2.2	1.34	11.49	3.90	58.7	4.3	46.9	15.1	7.1
7.6	0.18	1.2	-0.02	6.3	0.1	0.99	9.28	4.62	69.5	3.4	48.5	17.4	6.0
4.9	2.08	13.0	2.70	7.8	0.8	1.16	11.63	4.14	35.6	4.9	27.6	5.4	8.5
9.0	0.05	0.3	0.06	2.6	0.1	0.26	3.07	2.93	83.7	5.5	71.4	14.0	3.8
8.0	1.05	2.8	-0.18	5.7	0.1	1.03	7.83	5.11	76.1	6.6	53.8	0.0	4.4
4.6	2.60	11.8	0.05	5.6	0.3	1.28	10.86	3.28	60.4	6.3	135.8	15.5	5.9
6.6	2.12	8.4	0.11	5.6	1.1	1.22	8.38	3.94	67.2	3.9	18.8	9.9	8.2
4.2	0.72	5.4	0.55	9.4	0.5	2.18	21.58	4.54	55.8	2.7	37.0	20.9	6.6
6.3	0.48	2.1	0.73	3.9	0.4	1.01	12.11	3.54	81.3	2.5	42.8	28.5	3.1
7.3	1.01	4.1	-0.07	0.8	0.0	-0.10	-1.07	3.35	104.6	9.1	239.2	6.3	0.0
7.9	0.78	2.8	0.01	6.5	1.7	1.37	11.18	3.52	42.3	2.3	30.4	21.6	7.8
1.5	4.98	26.4	-0.06	4.2	0.1	0.56	5.56	4.02	68.8	4.0	25.4	10.0	5.3
7.8	0.88	3.4	-0.01	4.4	0.8	0.99	7.92	4.07	74.9	5.6	40.9	6.2	6.7
3.7	2.06	14.1	0.37	4.1	0.2	0.61	8.63	3.74	69.9	3.4	31.6	15.0	2.6
8.1	0.23	0.9	-0.21	4.5	0.2	0.81	6.52	4.70	80.2	4.8	92.3	18.7	5.0
6.3	1.31	4.2	0.00	4.7	0.1	0.81	5.87	4.01	75.4	4.5	44.8	13.4	6.9
7.5	1.63	5.3	-0.01	9.4	1.6	2.23	15.77	4.10	54.3	3.0	7.6	13.2	9.8
5.2	0.73	4.2	0.21	6.3	0.7	1.34	12.24	4.27	59.5	2.5	32.7	20.1	6.8
6.1	2.25	9.5	0.10	7.5	0.8	1.68	14.97	4.06	58.6	3.3	48.1	19.9	8.1
3.2	2.16	16.2	0.49	3.7	0.1	0.54	7.08	4.60	79.9	2.3	35.4	25.3	1.9
8.3	0.01	0.1	-0.07	7.3	0.5	1.72	19.93	3.72	52.5	5.2	36.0	6.7	5.2
8.1	0.00	0.0	0.02	6.0	0.3	1.40	14.70	3.77	65.2	4.9	29.1	6.1	4.3
3.2	1.42	11.4	0.35	5.2	0.7	1.24	14.16	4.18	63.1	2.9	10.1	14.0	4.5
4.7	2.50	10.3	0.49	5.2	0.1	0.74	6.99	3.65	63.0	8.1	112.4	1.5	3.9
8.4	0.42	1.7	0.11	5.7	0.3	1.12	8.61	3.49	57.5	6.0	84.6	12.1	7.1
8.5	0.30	1.5	0.08	7.3	3.4	1.55	12.99	4.31	66.4	4.8	29.8	6.7	7.5
7.8	0.19	1.3	-0.02	6.5	0.4	1.26	14.98	4.40	63.5	3.0	41.1	20.4	3.3
8.9	0.17	0.8	0.29	1.1	-0.1	-0.40	-4.22	3.33	117.2	3.7	41.5	16.9	2.1
4.6	1.03	8.9	-0.12	9.1	1.5	2.22	26.87	4.72	48.1	6.6	56.9	5.3	5.3
5.8	0.00	0.0	0.02	7.6	0.3	1.50	14.10	4.28	52.2	6.0	46.5	4.9	5.6
5.7	1.08	5.9	0.31	3.8	0.1	0.77	6.98	3.92	77.6	5.6	70.4	12.1	4.6

Name	City	State	Weiss Safety Rating	2003 Weiss Safety Rating	2002 Weiss Safety Rating	Total Assets ($Mil)	One Year Asset Growth	Asset Mix (As a % of Total Assets)				Capital-ization Index	Leverage Ratio	Risk-based Capital Ratio
								Comm-ercial Loans	Cons-umer Loans	Home Mort-gages	Secur-ities			
FARMERS ST BK	MEDORA	IL	C+	C+	C+	18.4	7.05	3.7	5.4	5.2	62.4	9.5	14.5	14.6
FARMERS ST BK	PITTSFIELD	IL	B-	B	B	161.5	5.08	3.6	7.5	13.5	18.4	6.5	9.1	12.2
FARMERS ST BK	SOMONAUK	IL	B+	B+	B+	209.1	2.58	2.5	4.2	13.2	42.5	7.7	9.5	15.9
FARMERS ST BK	BROOKSTON	IN	C+	C+	C	49.7	0.75	7.7	4.8	47.9	12.4	10.0	11.6	18.4
FARMERS ST BK	LAGRANGE	IN	B+	B+	B+	321.6	2.17	6.0	4.4	37.0	14.9	7.2	9.1	14.4
FARMERS ST BK	LANESVILLE	IN	B-	B-	B	77.6	-2.99	2.1	2.9	44.9	12.9	9.9	10.9	17.3
FARMERS ST BK	MENTONE	IN	C+	C+	B-	98.6	4.50	13.6	3.4	22.2	14.5	5.7	8.6	11.5
▲ FARMERS ST BK	NEW ROSS	IN	C+	C	C-	46.4	-3.40	5.5	8.8	11.9	33.0	7.9	9.6	16.0
FARMERS ST BK	SWEETSER	IN	B-	B-	B-	17.0	4.80	6.1	9.3	16.0	28.6	10.0	16.4	35.4
▲ FARMERS ST BK	ATWOOD	KS	D+	D	D+	14.5	1.83	1.0	4.6	11.8	23.3	8.2	9.8	16.4
FARMERS ST BK	CIRCLEVILLE	KS	D+	D+	D+	40.0	0.50	4.9	5.2	18.2	39.4	6.1	8.1	16.5
FARMERS ST BK	CORNING	KS	C-	C-	C-	7.1	6.80	6.6	11.2	36.2	20.4	7.9	9.6	16.5
FARMERS ST BK	DWIGHT	KS	C	C-	C+	12.6	1.82	2.7	4.1	1.3	39.8	10.0	15.3	28.3
FARMERS ST BK	FAIRVIEW	KS	D-	D-	D-	15.1	-2.57	1.7	7.1	15.1	20.0	6.9	8.9	15.4
▼ FARMERS ST BK	HAZELTON	KS	C+	B-	B-	5.2	4.55	0.5	3.3	2.3	65.9	10.0	17.8	35.2
▼ FARMERS ST BK	MCPHERSON	KS	D	D+	D+	65.5	12.13	10.5	7.2	29.3	32.1	5.3	7.3	13.4
FARMERS ST BK	PHILLIPSBURG	KS	D-	E+	E+	22.4	2.11	11.0	5.9	12.8	32.6	5.7	7.7	12.2
FARMERS ST BK	WATHENA	KS	B+	B+	B+	48.9	8.28	11.4	9.3	16.6	24.4	10.0	19.3	32.0
FARMERS ST BK	WESTMORELAND	KS	A-	A-	A	62.8	2.36	4.8	6.1	10.6	26.9	10.0	19.3	25.6
▲ FARMERS ST BK	BOONEVILLE	KY	B	B-	B-	38.0	-2.22	16.8	5.8	17.9	44.2	6.2	8.2	15.9
FARMERS ST BK	BRECKENRIDGE	MI	B-	B-	B-	123.5	-1.53	12.6	5.4	16.5	20.8	8.6	10.1	15.3
▼ FARMERS ST BK	HARTLAND	MN	D+	C-	D+	40.8	9.92	10.7	2.9	11.5	10.7	5.2	8.3	11.1
▲ FARMERS ST BK	SHERBURN	MN	B-	C+	C	24.6	-0.83	3.2	5.3	5.7	18.7	8.5	10.0	14.6
FARMERS ST BK	UNDERWOOD	MN	C	C	C-	33.0	9.00	6.2	11.8	22.6	16.1	5.3	7.6	11.3
FARMERS ST BK	WATKINS	MN	A-	A-	B+	29.7	3.92	8.1	6.8	8.5	33.3	10.0	13.2	19.6
FARMERS ST BK	CAMERON	MO	B	B	B	151.9	2.36	1.5	4.5	62.1	1.4	7.2	9.1	14.7
FARMERS ST BK	SCHELL CITY	MO	C	C	C	57.0	6.32	7.6	5.4	24.7	13.6	9.2	10.5	17.2
FARMERS ST BK	VICTOR	MT	B-	B	B	226.9	6.02	7.9	10.3	9.6	27.3	9.7	10.8	16.2
▼ FARMERS ST BK	ELGIN	ND	D-	D	C-	27.4	2.62	8.7	3.8	0.6	23.3	8.9	10.2	14.9
FARMERS ST BK	BIG SPRINGS	NE	B-	B-	B-	19.8	0.63	1.5	2.3	0.8	55.6	10.0	21.7	58.4
FARMERS ST BK	CARROLL	NE	D	D-	E	14.1	-5.24	6.3	4.2	4.0	17.1	7.7	9.5	13.9
▲ FARMERS ST BK	DODGE	NE	C-	D+	D+	41.2	-2.99	17.9	2.1	4.5	31.8	7.1	9.1	16.0
FARMERS ST BK	EUSTIS	NE	B	B	B	29.4	2.29	7.3	4.3	1.5	34.8	10.0	11.4	18.6
FARMERS ST BK	EWING	NE	A-	A-	A-	14.6	9.68	10.5	2.8	1.6	16.2	10.0	23.5	40.4
▲ FARMERS ST BK	FAIRMONT	NE	C-	D+	D+	8.0	-1.89	3.7	4.5	5.3	11.2	10.0	14.5	21.8
FARMERS ST BK	HUMPHREY	NE	B	B	B+	18.6	2.39	6.2	3.0	1.6	28.8	10.0	13.3	22.5
FARMERS ST BK	MAYWOOD	NE	D-	D-	D	59.1	54.27	3.2	2.4	7.4	19.2	8.6	10.0	14.3
▲ FARMERS ST BK	WALLACE	NE	D-	E	D	30.9	-4.91	3.6	2.0	3.0	39.4	6.1	8.1	15.8
▼ FARMERS ST BK	NEW MADISON	OH	C-	C+	B	85.9	-13.36	6.3	15.8	34.3	12.3	10.0	14.0	23.2
FARMERS ST BK	W SALEM	OH	B-	B-	B-	61.6	5.13	6.3	4.7	58.1	5.6	6.6	8.6	14.5
FARMERS ST BK	ALLEN	OK	C+	C	D+	32.2	6.04	9.3	16.1	17.9	10.5	8.9	10.3	15.0
▲ FARMERS ST BK	QUINTON	OK	C+	C	C	54.3	1.58	5.3	9.2	19.2	37.7	7.6	9.4	17.6
FARMERS ST BK	CANTON	SD	B	B	B+	36.9	9.92	9.0	8.1	15.4	16.4	9.1	10.4	15.5
▲ FARMERS ST BK	FAITH	SD	D	D-	D	36.2	7.59	7.4	2.5	2.1	7.1	4.7	8.2	10.8
▼ FARMERS ST BK	FLANDREAU	SD	B-	B	B	91.8	12.98	9.5	2.8	21.4	46.7	5.3	7.3	15.5
FARMERS ST BK	HOSMER	SD	B-	B-	B-	14.2	-7.42	6.2	2.7	0.0	17.5	10.0	22.8	29.6
▲ FARMERS ST BK	MARION	SD	D	D-	D+	66.2	29.06	8.5	4.4	10.1	19.6	4.4	7.7	10.7
▲ FARMERS ST BK	PARKSTON	SD	A	A-	B+	99.7	2.85	9.4	4.4	0.0	35.1	10.0	15.6	24.9
FARMERS ST BK	MOUNTAIN CITY	TN	A	A	A	117.9	2.20	2.8	8.0	27.5	43.9	10.0	13.9	28.7
FARMERS ST BK	BERTRAM	TX	B+	B+	B+	26.3	-2.93	3.8	6.3	4.6	69.4	10.0	16.7	56.3
FARMERS ST BK	CENTER	TX	B	B	B	196.3	10.81	7.0	2.9	9.6	27.4	8.8	10.2	17.3
FARMERS ST BK	GROESBECK	TX	B-	B-	B	92.2	-1.50	5.3	9.8	16.1	42.7	5.7	7.7	15.7
FARMERS ST BK	WINTHROP	WA	C	C+	C+	14.9	9.80	11.5	6.3	5.2	33.5	10.0	17.0	36.3
FARMERS ST BK	BANGOR	WI	B	B	B	74.9	3.15	7.0	9.6	23.8	28.9	10.0	12.3	20.1
FARMERS ST BK	MARKESAN	WI	B+	B+	B+	80.7	-5.32	7.5	4.2	14.1	35.1	10.0	13.0	23.1
FARMERS ST BK	RIDGELAND	WI	C	C	C	31.4	2.65	8.0	6.4	30.0	14.8	6.3	8.3	15.8
FARMERS ST BK	PINE BLUFFS	WY	C+	C+	B-	15.5	-1.52	5.9	4.4	0.7	34.3	10.0	15.5	24.2
FARMERS ST BK ASTORIA	ASTORIA	IL	B	B-	D	15.3	-9.45	3.4	26.1	16.6	33.1	10.0	11.0	21.2
FARMERS ST BK HILLSBORO	HILLSBORO	WI	A	A	A	69.1	8.19	4.6	6.2	18.5	29.8	10.0	14.3	17.2
FARMERS ST BK OF ADAMS	ADAMS	MN	B	B	B-	61.5	1.33	6.5	3.3	4.0	17.9	7.1	9.1	12.7
FARMERS ST BK OF	ALICEVILLE	KS	C	C	C	48.5	5.98	4.1	5.2	12.5	46.3	7.3	9.2	17.2
FARMERS ST BK OF BLUE	BLUE MOUND	KS	B-	B+	B+	39.1	-0.43	3.0	2.5	5.5	8.1	10.0	15.6	22.6
FARMERS ST BK OF BUCKLIN	BUCKLIN	KS	D+	D+	C-	27.8	-1.97	5.4	2.9	4.1	45.0	4.6	6.6	17.7
▲ FARMERS ST BK OF CALHAN	CALHAN	CO	D+	D	C-	136.6	5.38	10.0	7.7	24.8	17.8	7.1	9.1	13.1

Arrows denote recent upgrades ▲ or downgrades ▼

www.WeissRatings.com

Asset Quality Index	Non-Performing Loans as a % of Total Loans	Non-Performing Loans as a % of Capital	Net Charge-offs Avg Loans	Profitability Index	Net Income ($Mil)	Return on Assets (R.O.A.)	Return on Equity (R.O.E.)	Net Interest Spread	Overhead Efficiency Ratio	Liquidity Index	Liquidity Ratio	Hot Money Ratio	Stability Index
9.7	0.45	0.9	0.00	5.2	0.1	0.99	6.90	3.74	61.5	5.0	39.0	6.5	5.0
8.0	0.15	1.1	-0.04	3.5	0.5	0.64	6.67	3.56	85.3	2.8	24.0	16.1	6.0
7.4	0.31	1.5	0.05	6.5	1.3	1.21	12.44	3.85	56.4	4.3	47.6	15.3	5.6
5.5	1.42	9.5	0.40	3.6	0.2	0.70	6.12	4.00	69.7	4.2	21.4	8.2	4.4
8.3	0.05	0.4	0.20	6.6	1.9	1.18	12.78	4.06	60.6	6.4	73.2	9.6	6.1
6.4	1.06	5.6	0.03	4.3	0.2	0.63	5.83	3.52	71.3	7.9	98.6	2.0	5.3
5.6	0.56	4.7	-0.01	4.2	0.3	0.52	5.89	4.23	81.4	2.1	21.1	19.0	4.3
8.3	0.05	0.3	-0.11	5.3	0.2	1.03	10.75	4.84	74.8	5.2	30.1	4.3	3.6
8.4	0.22	0.6	0.10	5.2	0.1	1.20	7.33	4.57	76.8	6.8	129.6	12.1	5.5
3.9	2.34	13.3	0.00	5.5	0.1	1.36	14.41	3.43	57.1	6.3	92.0	9.8	2.9
5.9	0.99	5.9	0.57	3.8	0.1	0.60	7.45	3.73	79.3	3.5	48.1	18.8	2.7
8.1	0.00	0.0	-0.08	8.3	0.1	1.29	13.26	3.84	53.3	4.4	33.7	8.3	3.6
7.3	0.00	0.0	0.00	3.6	0.1	1.29	8.67	3.62	65.1	4.1	20.7	8.6	4.5
2.2	3.14	21.1	0.08	3.9	0.1	0.92	10.39	4.01	77.5	5.5	63.9	9.6	1.7
9.2	0.00	0.0	0.14	7.9	0.0	1.57	9.28	3.52	55.2	1.9	45.9	32.8	5.0
4.6	1.44	11.2	0.06	5.3	0.4	1.13	15.69	3.93	62.8	3.8	50.9	18.1	0.6
4.4	1.36	9.9	-0.03	4.5	0.1	0.80	10.11	3.97	73.5	1.4	22.2	26.7	1.5
5.9	1.36	4.2	1.40	6.5	0.3	1.26	6.36	4.78	65.3	4.9	35.6	8.4	6.9
8.3	0.20	0.6	-0.70	8.8	0.5	1.60	8.04	4.55	48.7	5.3	52.4	10.4	8.0
7.8	0.05	0.3	-0.04	8.1	0.4	1.88	22.79	4.62	61.5	2.1	12.0	18.0	5.6
4.6	0.62	3.8	0.44	4.8	0.5	0.86	8.67	4.17	68.7	3.8	31.1	12.9	6.1
3.6	0.57	4.4	0.11	5.0	0.2	1.17	11.74	4.69	72.6	1.5	14.4	23.6	3.0
8.2	0.12	0.7	0.07	6.6	0.2	1.61	16.38	4.04	58.1	5.5	41.2	4.0	5.1
6.8	0.41	3.6	0.15	8.6	0.3	1.71	21.37	4.83	63.2	2.9	33.3	18.4	3.5
7.3	0.72	2.7	-0.16	9.5	0.4	2.68	20.25	4.91	49.2	5.6	85.5	14.0	8.4
4.8	0.83	7.2	0.14	8.3	0.9	1.22	12.26	4.55	59.1	3.9	11.1	8.6	5.9
7.2	0.88	4.9	0.12	2.8	0.1	0.29	2.74	3.42	82.5	4.6	83.8	18.8	4.5
4.0	1.99	10.6	0.65	5.7	1.0	0.89	8.16	4.56	69.1	4.8	55.4	14.8	6.4
0.0	10.79	65.7	0.07	7.0	0.3	2.16	20.93	4.08	47.1	3.5	28.6	13.9	3.8
9.6	0.00	0.0	0.00	4.8	0.1	1.07	4.94	3.46	58.9	5.4	83.3	13.4	5.5
6.8	0.00	0.0	-0.09	4.6	0.1	0.66	7.26	4.26	73.7	3.2	15.1	12.6	1.4
6.4	0.61	3.5	-0.03	2.8	0.1	0.32	3.62	3.50	88.8	4.1	60.5	18.1	3.7
6.3	1.58	6.7	0.02	4.5	0.1	0.81	7.06	3.44	65.5	6.3	116.0	14.1	5.2
7.1	1.81	3.8	0.00	8.0	0.1	1.33	5.71	4.32	48.2	6.5	110.6	11.2	7.0
8.4	0.00	0.0	0.00	3.3	0.0	0.62	4.36	4.33	83.2	7.2	80.0	1.9	4.1
8.5	0.00	0.0	0.00	7.9	0.2	1.96	14.88	4.25	49.9	5.5	42.4	3.8	6.3
0.0	5.77	35.8	0.56	5.4	0.3	1.20	12.10	4.95	66.0	2.3	46.6	33.8	3.4
2.3	4.53	25.4	0.09	4.0	0.1	0.71	9.16	3.71	67.2	7.6	154.2	10.7	2.0
3.7	2.77	12.5	2.60	1.0	-0.8	-1.76	-12.17	4.31	80.2	5.2	52.1	11.1	5.0
8.4	0.18	1.6	-0.01	6.2	0.3	0.97	11.26	4.03	70.6	4.9	21.6	3.9	5.0
4.0	1.07	6.9	0.04	9.9	0.4	2.23	21.91	5.54	56.1	4.6	63.3	16.0	5.2
7.9	0.12	0.7	0.12	5.1	0.4	1.40	15.29	5.33	73.6	4.5	6.5	4.4	3.5
6.8	0.55	3.5	0.04	6.5	0.2	1.11	10.50	4.57	65.5	3.8	32.9	13.9	5.5
2.0	0.89	8.1	0.05	7.6	0.3	1.51	18.42	5.55	62.9	1.2	13.6	29.0	3.4
9.0	0.00	0.0	0.00	4.1	0.3	0.74	9.79	2.53	65.4	3.3	9.7	11.9	5.4
4.5	3.86	11.0	0.00	6.6	0.1	1.42	6.31	4.62	70.5	2.4	18.7	17.3	6.9
5.8	0.23	1.9	0.12	3.6	0.1	0.43	5.77	4.58	83.9	4.7	17.4	4.1	2.4
7.3	0.62	2.1	-0.18	7.8	1.2	2.35	15.40	4.08	48.6	4.5	28.4	8.0	8.6
7.1	1.35	4.5	0.30	7.4	0.8	1.31	9.45	4.30	55.8	2.8	26.1	16.4	8.1
9.0	0.27	0.3	0.00	6.4	0.1	1.07	6.48	3.88	61.0	5.9	64.2	9.4	7.1
4.4	1.39	6.9	0.18	7.2	1.5	1.54	13.52	4.40	66.2	2.6	35.3	20.6	7.8
8.3	0.13	0.7	0.00	5.8	0.7	1.48	18.75	4.42	67.8	4.1	24.9	9.2	5.3
5.9	3.37	8.5	0.74	3.5	0.0	0.46	2.78	5.09	86.0	7.6	81.8	0.0	4.1
4.3	2.75	13.4	0.60	6.4	0.4	1.10	8.82	4.30	57.7	5.6	79.8	13.2	6.5
7.0	1.53	5.8	0.06	5.2	0.5	1.20	9.09	4.39	65.3	2.9	28.8	16.7	7.3
6.0	0.95	7.0	-0.07	6.3	0.2	1.49	18.11	3.69	58.7	6.4	92.4	10.6	4.3
8.3	0.90	2.5	0.00	5.0	0.1	0.81	4.94	5.19	80.9	6.3	53.6	2.3	5.3
7.1	0.12	0.6	0.29	4.6	0.1	0.76	6.97	4.67	78.8	6.4	84.5	8.3	5.6
8.7	0.36	1.5	0.02	9.9	0.6	1.78	12.78	4.10	39.2	5.1	83.7	16.4	8.8
4.3	1.01	7.3	0.00	10.0	0.9	2.77	28.16	4.83	38.7	3.3	24.6	13.5	6.3
6.3	0.83	4.1	-0.18	4.9	0.3	1.10	12.08	2.69	38.9	6.0	118.6	15.6	3.2
2.7	5.94	21.8	-0.82	9.2	0.4	2.24	13.89	5.84	60.0	6.5	120.0	13.3	7.9
3.7	5.35	22.7	0.21	3.6	0.1	0.52	5.18	3.54	82.3	4.2	35.5	12.3	3.0
1.5	3.67	24.7	0.93	6.7	0.7	0.97	10.42	5.43	54.2	2.6	12.3	15.5	5.8

Name	City	State	Weiss Safety Rating	2003 Weiss Safety Rating	2002 Weiss Safety Rating	Total Assets ($Mil)	One Year Asset Growth	Asset Mix (As a % of Total Assets)				Capital-ization Index	Leverage Ratio	Risk-based Capital Ratio
								Comm-ercial Loans	Cons-umer Loans	Home Mort-gages	Secur-ities			
FARMERS ST BK OF CROSBY	CROSBY	ND	B	B	B+	47.3	-2.62	2.2	1.6	2.4	60.0	10.0	16.7	34.0
▼ FARMERS ST BK OF DARWIN	DARWIN	MN	B	B+	B+	21.6	0.75	13.5	8.8	2.9	34.1	8.6	10.1	14.3
▼ FARMERS ST BK OF DENT	DENT	MN	E	D-	D-	24.6	0.03	5.4	5.8	7.0	16.7	4.9	6.9	12.0
FARMERS ST BK OF DENTON	DENTON	MT	D	D	D-	16.2	-3.70	7.6	13.9	0.0	4.1	6.7	9.8	12.3
FARMERS ST BK OF ELKTON	ELKTON	MN	B	B	B	34.3	6.82	7.4	4.0	10.4	33.5	10.0	11.1	17.1
▼ FARMERS ST BK OF EMDEN	EMDEN	IL	B	B+	B+	31.3	-0.68	3.9	1.6	1.9	74.1	10.0	24.1	60.2
FARMERS ST BK OF HAMEL	HAMEL	MN	A-	A-	A-	65.1	-0.93	22.2	0.9	4.2	33.4	10.0	12.7	19.6
▼ FARMERS ST BK OF	HIGHLAND	KS	C	B-	B-	15.1	12.15	4.2	0.9	4.7	47.0	9.6	10.7	27.0
FARMERS ST BK OF HOFFMAN	HOFFMAN	IL	B	B	B	112.1	-5.96	2.1	5.2	18.0	47.9	10.0	12.2	25.6
▲ FARMERS ST BK OF HOFFMAN	HOFFMAN	MN	C+	C	C+	22.8	3.40	14.3	5.2	3.9	41.0	10.0	11.5	17.1
FARMERS ST BK OF JETMORE	JETMORE	KS	C	C	B-	18.4	15.98	1.8	2.7	3.3	58.9	10.0	12.6	29.2
FARMERS ST BK OF MADELIA	MADELIA	MN	B	B	B	53.7	4.02	15.0	6.5	15.7	10.8	6.7	8.7	13.3
FARMERS ST BK OF MUNITH	MUNITH	MI	B-	B-	B-	59.6	-0.42	1.8	4.2	44.0	15.2	8.5	10.0	16.4
FARMERS ST BK OF	SAVANNAH	MO	C+	C+	C+	80.2	13.69	11.0	3.4	22.9	21.4	3.0	6.4	10.0
FARMERS ST BK OF OAKLEY	OAKLEY	KS	B-	B-	B	72.7	-5.38	9.2	3.9	9.4	31.5	10.0	14.0	23.5
FARMERS ST BK OF RAYMOND	RAYMOND	MN	C+	C+	C+	23.6	-3.42	11.4	1.6	0.6	28.7	10.0	13.7	24.9
FARMERS ST BK OF	SUBLETTE	IL	C	C	C-	44.4	-4.20	0.8	7.5	11.1	52.5	8.3	9.9	21.8
FARMERS ST BK OF TRIMONT	TRIMONT	MN	B	B	B-	37.3	-1.34	11.8	2.9	3.6	35.3	10.0	14.1	21.1
FARMERS ST BK OF TURTON	TURTON	SD	C	C	C+	18.3	7.33	3.9	4.4	0.8	18.0	10.0	13.2	19.6
FARMERS ST BK OF WAUPACA	WAUPACA	WI	A-	A-	B+	157.8	5.72	10.8	8.3	25.7	26.0	10.0	13.2	20.3
FARMERS ST BK STANBERRY	STANBERRY	MO	A-	A-	A-	41.2	0.87	2.4	4.7	10.6	34.1	10.0	19.2	31.3
FARMERS ST BK STICKNEY	STICKNEY	SD	C	C	C+	34.4	5.87	5.3	5.0	2.4	6.2	5.0	7.8	11.0
▲ FARMERS ST BK WESTERN IL	ALPHA	IL	B-	C+	C-	96.2	-3.51	6.1	6.6	12.4	24.6	7.5	9.3	14.5
FARMERS ST BK-CAMP POINT	CAMP POINT	IL	C-	C-	C-	34.9	-2.52	7.5	2.8	12.5	43.4	7.4	9.3	19.0
FARMERS ST BK-FULTON CTY	LEWISTOWN	IL	B	B	B+	66.9	0.73	5.7	2.8	11.4	35.4	8.5	10.0	18.4
▲ FARMERS ST BK-WEST	W CONCORD	MN	C	C-	D+	49.6	4.42	9.1	8.6	31.2	13.3	5.7	7.7	11.9
▲ FARMERS STATE BK	NEW WASHINGTON	OH	B	B-	B-	142.9	12.03	7.4	1.6	31.7	8.8	7.8	9.5	14.0
▼ FARMERS SVG B&T-TRAER	TRAER	IA	B-	B	B	62.5	-0.75	3.3	1.8	10.5	52.9	5.0	7.0	15.2
FARMERS SVG BK	BEAMAN	IA	B-	B-	B	109.1	8.08	11.9	8.3	25.5	17.9	7.3	9.2	15.2
FARMERS SVG BK	COLESBURG	IA	C+	C+	C-	65.9	20.46	7.8	5.9	12.7	39.9	7.1	9.1	15.2
▼ FARMERS SVG BK	FOSTORIA	IA	B+	A-	A-	47.0	5.39	5.5	4.4	16.1	24.2	10.0	15.1	20.6
FARMERS SVG BK	FREDERIKA	IA	B	B	B+	30.5	-1.27	9.9	4.0	9.7	40.2	10.0	15.3	24.3
▲ FARMERS SVG BK	HALBUR	IA	C	C-	C-	17.4	-4.58	15.8	3.2	22.5	10.0	6.3	8.3	13.8
FARMERS SVG BK	KEOTA	IA	B+	B	B	57.7	4.38	2.7	1.1	2.3	47.7	10.0	13.8	25.8
FARMERS SVG BK	REMSEN	IA	A-	A-	A	101.4	1.65	2.1	0.9	4.3	38.2	10.0	13.5	23.3
FARMERS SVG BK	VICTOR	IA	A-	A-	A-	28.5	-0.69	10.1	4.0	15.9	25.3	10.0	17.5	26.1
▲ FARMERS SVG BK	WALFORD	IA	D+	D-	D-	42.0	-3.75	6.9	1.5	7.3	52.2	7.0	9.0	19.4
FARMERS SVG BK	WEVER	IA	C-	C-	D+	40.2	3.56	2.8	4.3	31.2	32.0	7.1	9.1	16.5
FARMERS SVG BK	SPENCER	OH	A+	A+	A+	212.4	4.63	1.2	1.1	18.9	56.5	10.0	18.6	44.0
FARMERS SVG BK	MINERAL POINT	WI	B	B	B	143.8	2.34	10.7	7.7	14.7	22.2	5.5	7.5	11.5
▼ FARMERS SVGS B&T-VINTON	VINTON	IA	B-	B	B	58.5	0.02	5.6	2.4	33.1	27.6	5.0	7.0	12.8
▲ FARMERS T&SB	BUFFALO CENTER	IA	B	C+	C	116.4	0.23	7.6	3.2	10.4	11.7	6.6	9.6	12.2
FARMERS T&SB	EARLING	IA	D-	D	D	50.1	-2.38	16.6	4.2	14.8	3.6	5.5	8.8	11.4
FARMERS T&SB	SPENCER	IA	B-	B-	B-	191.2	13.24	5.4	7.0	11.6	18.5	3.5	7.5	10.3
FARMERS T&SB	WILLIAMSBURG	IA	A	A	A	90.4	-1.57	8.6	5.1	26.3	30.4	10.0	14.5	24.6
FARMINGTON ST BK	FARMINGTON	WA	C-	C-	C-	7.0	6.54	9.6	2.6	10.3	5.4	10.0	20.1	23.3
FARMINGTON SVGS BK	FARMINGTON	CT	B	B	B	749.8	13.33	11.4	0.7	19.2	35.1	6.9	8.9	15.4
▼ FARNAM BK	FARNAM	NE	C	C+	B-	20.5	8.77	3.8	4.6	5.4	24.9	9.5	10.7	15.1
FARWELL ST SVG BK	FARWELL	MI	A+	A+	A+	92.7	-0.59	0.8	4.4	56.5	24.9	10.0	15.6	31.9
▼ FAUQUIER BK	WARRENTON	VA	B	B+	B+	414.4	12.43	5.8	10.3	28.3	12.2	6.1	8.1	12.1
▲ FAYETTE COUNTY BK	ST ELMO	IL	B-	C+	C+	18.6	-0.51	12.5	4.3	9.3	43.6	10.0	11.9	22.6
FAYETTE COUNTY NB	FAYETTEVILLE	WV	B	B	B	66.1	-3.23	1.6	4.4	22.1	44.2	9.8	10.9	25.3
FAYETTE SVG BK SSB	LA GRANGE	TX	C-	C-	C-	61.1	-4.15	1.1	3.9	29.2	34.7	5.6	7.6	16.0
▲ FAYETTEVILLE BK	FAYETTEVILLE	TX	B-	C	D	62.5	24.08	2.2	3.9	26.9	31.0	6.1	8.1	12.9
▼ FBR NATIONAL TC	BETHESDA	MD	D+	C-	D	32.7	-64.62	0.0	0.0	0.0	57.2	10.0	52.5	139.2
▼ FCN BK NA	BROOKVILLE	IN	A-	A	A	235.5	20.12	1.8	3.4	33.9	36.2	9.2	10.5	20.4
▲ FDS BK	MASON	OH	B+	B	B	81.1	-6.55	0.0	30.2	0.0	33.5	10.0	47.3	68.9
FEDERAL MEDICAL BK FSB	BALTIMORE	MD	D	D+	D+	52.9	-23.43	1.4	1.5	55.2	18.3	6.7	8.7	20.9
FEDERAL SVGS BK	DOVER	NH	B-	B-	B-	239.6	11.08	1.5	1.6	51.3	6.2	5.3	7.3	12.1
▲ FEDERAL TRUST BANK	SANFORD	FL	C	D+	D+	510.5	18.84	2.5	0.2	62.6	7.5	4.9	6.9	11.6
FEDERATED BK	ONARGA	IL	C+	C+	C	57.7	0.48	6.2	2.0	9.7	46.9	6.8	8.8	17.9
FEDERATION BK	WASHINGTON	IA	D+	D	C-	104.2	-12.92	7.8	3.0	34.0	21.8	6.6	8.6	14.6
FELICIANA B&TC	CLINTON	LA	A-	A-	A-	70.1	5.58	6.4	7.4	25.1	27.4	10.0	14.0	22.0
▲ FELTON BK	FELTON	DE	D+	E-	E-	60.7	27.73	7.8	1.4	23.2	15.2	4.6	7.4	10.8

Asset Quality Index	Non-Performing Loans as a % of Total Loans	Non-Performing Loans as a % of Capital	Net Charge-offs Avg Loans	Profitability Index	Net Income ($Mil)	Return on Assets (R.O.A.)	Return on Equity (R.O.E.)	Net Interest Spread	Overhead Efficiency Ratio	Liquidity Index	Liquidity Ratio	Hot Money Ratio	Stability Index
5.6	3.32	5.8	1.84	4.4	0.1	0.59	3.50	3.70	59.4	4.9	45.0	11.3	6.5
5.4	0.92	4.1	0.00	10.0	0.3	2.58	24.37	5.25	52.4	4.6	47.1	11.1	6.5
4.3	1.37	11.3	0.20	3.5	0.0	0.36	4.88	5.48	80.9	3.5	40.6	15.0	0.7
4.0	0.21	1.7	2.03	5.4	0.1	1.20	11.95	6.13	60.5	1.3	12.9	26.2	2.3
5.7	2.09	9.4	0.15	7.9	0.3	1.86	16.43	4.41	50.8	5.0	42.8	10.3	6.5
9.8	0.84	0.6	0.00	4.3	0.1	0.81	3.36	2.92	58.4	4.7	115.7	26.3	6.7
8.9	0.05	0.2	0.00	6.2	0.5	1.59	12.79	4.29	62.9	4.7	30.6	8.1	7.4
9.2	0.00	0.0	0.65	2.8	0.0	0.36	3.20	2.70	87.1	6.8	82.2	5.0	4.7
5.5	2.45	8.8	1.54	4.1	0.4	0.70	5.68	3.55	70.0	6.5	46.1	2.3	6.2
4.7	3.31	14.6	0.10	5.8	0.2	1.53	12.55	3.89	61.8	3.5	27.6	12.1	5.6
8.2	1.58	2.5	0.22	1.9	0.0	0.10	0.81	2.87	96.5	6.6	119.6	12.2	4.1
5.5	0.40	3.0	-0.09	9.0	0.6	2.11	23.11	4.94	53.4	3.4	60.9	24.4	6.5
4.4	1.43	9.7	-0.12	5.1	0.2	0.66	6.62	3.96	80.2	4.9	41.1	10.5	5.1
3.2	1.46	11.1	0.04	4.0	0.2	0.59	6.77	3.63	68.9	3.7	18.9	10.9	5.3
1.2	9.32	32.8	0.07	5.5	0.3	0.78	5.50	3.70	64.4	3.3	27.1	14.4	6.4
8.7	0.62	2.0	0.12	5.7	0.2	1.55	11.82	3.50	55.2	7.3	115.4	6.9	5.4
5.7	1.41	5.5	0.09	4.6	0.2	0.77	7.49	3.56	69.5	2.3	33.4	23.2	4.1
5.8	1.64	5.9	-0.04	6.8	0.2	1.17	8.12	3.84	57.2	4.2	21.2	8.3	6.7
7.0	0.00	0.0	0.07	3.6	0.1	0.86	6.34	3.70	77.5	2.2	32.9	19.5	4.9
5.3	2.32	10.6	0.44	8.0	1.2	1.54	11.57	5.00	54.3	3.2	15.6	12.8	8.1
8.6	0.15	0.4	-0.01	7.5	0.3	1.60	8.43	3.58	51.3	4.4	14.6	6.1	8.4
7.0	0.03	0.3	-0.02	8.2	0.3	1.49	20.01	4.09	46.8	4.7	45.3	12.3	4.5
5.2	1.12	6.7	0.14	6.0	0.6	1.31	13.92	4.65	66.3	4.6	32.7	9.3	4.3
7.5	0.00	0.0	0.00	5.6	0.2	0.99	7.24	3.25	56.6	4.9	33.0	7.3	4.3
6.9	0.98	4.9	0.14	5.3	0.4	1.44	14.67	3.05	51.0	7.7	120.9	6.7	5.6
3.7	1.15	9.2	0.24	7.5	0.5	1.89	21.80	5.11	55.3	4.2	22.6	8.1	4.4
4.7	0.73	5.9	0.08	6.4	0.8	1.14	11.48	4.24	55.6	2.2	17.4	18.3	6.2
9.2	0.00	0.0	-0.02	4.7	0.5	1.47	19.17	2.87	63.7	6.2	49.7	4.4	4.6
4.0	1.22	9.0	-0.02	7.8	0.8	1.48	15.52	4.16	52.2	2.5	14.2	16.4	6.0
8.6	0.11	0.7	-0.34	4.8	0.4	1.18	13.25	4.09	64.7	3.7	15.6	10.4	3.5
7.2	1.08	4.6	-0.03	7.2	0.3	1.13	7.40	4.05	61.0	4.0	15.0	8.7	7.0
8.6	0.41	1.3	-0.05	6.3	0.2	1.26	8.37	3.47	43.5	8.0	136.7	6.4	5.8
5.6	0.95	8.0	0.00	6.1	0.1	1.00	11.92	4.12	60.9	5.4	48.8	7.1	4.4
7.7	1.44	4.5	0.20	6.3	0.3	1.19	8.71	3.77	54.0	6.4	49.1	2.7	7.2
8.5	0.00	0.0	0.32	5.4	0.5	0.99	7.32	2.35	39.2	6.0	97.4	14.8	7.5
8.6	0.00	0.0	0.00	8.3	0.3	1.86	10.53	4.03	49.9	5.6	38.3	4.9	8.0
9.3	0.14	0.6	0.00	3.1	0.2	1.06	12.39	3.39	69.8	4.3	32.6	11.2	1.7
5.2	1.18	7.8	0.00	3.7	0.1	0.60	6.59	3.52	75.4	5.4	47.2	9.2	2.9
8.9	2.48	5.3	-0.02	10.0	3.2	2.97	16.64	4.53	25.2	6.5	112.1	13.4	9.7
5.0	0.59	4.9	0.00	8.7	1.7	2.34	29.47	4.02	51.7	3.7	25.8	11.7	6.1
9.0	0.00	0.0	-0.05	6.3	0.4	1.46	20.59	3.58	62.1	4.4	35.3	11.5	5.3
5.8	0.13	0.9	0.08	7.1	1.0	1.70	18.21	3.97	56.5	5.9	54.3	8.5	6.2
1.2	2.79	25.1	0.51	3.0	0.1	0.47	5.83	3.70	80.0	3.8	13.3	9.6	1.7
5.9	0.23	2.2	0.48	7.8	1.5	1.60	20.82	3.84	47.4	4.6	15.7	4.5	5.3
8.3	0.68	2.8	-0.04	9.7	1.2	2.51	17.52	4.36	42.3	4.6	11.7	4.5	9.1
4.5	2.08	9.1	0.00	6.1	0.1	1.50	7.48	5.18	68.8	2.2	43.3	26.5	3.7
5.6	1.23	6.8	-0.46	4.7	3.1	0.87	9.63	3.82	63.9	7.6	109.1	7.0	5.0
3.1	1.71	10.5	0.03	5.7	0.1	1.18	11.04	4.54	60.2	2.1	23.6	18.9	4.4
8.5	0.42	1.7	0.04	9.7	0.8	1.74	9.89	4.24	39.4	6.1	65.4	8.5	9.5
5.6	0.35	3.1	0.05	7.4	2.3	1.17	14.37	4.73	66.7	4.2	22.4	8.1	5.7
8.6	0.29	1.1	0.25	6.0	0.1	1.51	12.87	4.24	64.4	5.0	38.0	6.1	5.4
6.3	1.41	5.4	0.16	5.6	0.4	1.05	9.37	4.71	71.0	4.6	27.0	6.7	5.5
7.3	0.76	5.0	-0.04	4.9	0.3	0.98	13.10	4.39	72.6	6.4	66.6	6.7	2.8
8.0	0.00	0.0	0.01	5.2	0.3	0.99	9.53	4.28	62.6	2.2	25.2	18.9	4.6
6.5	0.00	0.0	0.00	0.9	-0.1	-0.91	-1.18	2.74	103.8	0.1	7.0	101.0	0.0
6.4	0.78	3.7	0.04	6.6	1.3	1.12	9.66	3.78	55.5	4.9	35.6	8.5	7.1
6.5	0.00	0.0	0.00	10.0	10.5	22.66	46.09	1.56	81.2	1.9	51.2	100.0	4.7
8.5	0.04	0.3	0.62	0.7	-0.6	-2.21	-23.37	2.08	156.6	2.4	56.2	50.5	2.5
8.1	0.00	0.0	0.01	6.0	1.0	0.84	11.62	3.82	65.5	1.2	6.5	25.8	4.3
3.3	1.16	13.4	0.02	4.6	1.8	0.75	11.10	3.02	57.3	0.3	6.7	72.4	3.0
6.9	0.41	1.1	0.00	3.7	0.2	0.76	5.75	3.35	68.4	5.0	56.0	12.8	6.0
1.4	4.90	31.5	0.14	3.5	0.4	0.65	6.98	3.31	74.6	4.5	27.9	7.9	3.0
5.2	2.41	10.0	0.00	8.1	0.5	1.55	10.68	5.90	65.5	1.8	18.3	21.1	7.7
7.9	0.04	0.2	0.00	2.9	0.1	0.47	5.55	2.32	67.6	5.4	51.2	9.6	3.5

| Name | City | State | Weiss Safety Rating | 2003 Weiss Safety Rating | 2002 Weiss Safety Rating | Total Assets ($Mil) | One Year Asset Growth | Asset Mix (As a % of Total Assets) | | | | Capital- ization Index | Leverage Ratio | Risk-based Capital Ratio |
								Comm- ercial Loans	Cons- umer Loans	Home Mort- gages	Secur- ities			
FIDELITY & TR BK	BETHESDA	MD	D	D	NR	137.2	N/A	2.7	0.0	72.5	1.5	10.0	11.0	19.0
▼ FIDELITY B&TC	DYERSVILLE	IA	C	C+	C+	93.5	5.75	15.7	2.1	17.0	7.6	2.8	7.6	9.9
▲ FIDELITY B&TC	BATON ROUGE	LA	D	D+	E-	120.5	15.37	33.9	6.6	6.5	1.0	4.0	8.0	10.5
FIDELITY BK	NORCROSS	GA	C+	C+	C	1,172.8	12.19	8.0	41.6	6.7	15.2	5.8	8.4	11.6
FIDELITY BK	WICHITA	KS	C+	C+	C+	1,641.5	24.38	3.0	1.0	18.1	47.3	3.9	5.9	12.4
▼ FIDELITY BK	HAGERSTOWN	MD	B+	A-	A-	259.7	441.81	7.6	3.4	30.1	14.5	6.1	8.1	17.2
▼ FIDELITY BK	BIRMINGHAM	MI	B	A-	A-	246.3	-8.67	7.7	0.6	10.4	6.3	7.2	9.7	12.7
▲ FIDELITY BK	EDINA	MN	B+	B	B-	352.0	-49.20	30.6	0.8	45.2	8.0	8.2	9.8	16.9
FIDELITY BK	FUQUAY-VARINA	NC	B+	B+	B+	1,131.1	-0.66	7.8	2.7	13.9	17.1	6.0	8.0	12.4
FIDELITY BK	WICHITA FALLS	TX	D	D	NR	34.9	N/A	17.5	2.1	8.8	16.0	10.0	21.9	25.3
▲ FIDELITY BK OF FLORIDA NA	MERRITT ISLAND	FL	C+	C-	D	205.0	0.11	2.7	2.0	11.8	9.6	10.0	13.0	17.7
▲ FIDELITY BK TX	WACO	TX	D+	D	C+	71.5	32.30	9.9	10.2	28.8	12.2	3.9	8.1	10.5
▲ FIDELITY CO-OP BK	FITCHBURG	MA	C+	C	B-	301.7	4.39	1.3	0.6	41.7	34.3	7.0	9.0	18.5
FIDELITY DEPOSIT &	DUNMORE	PA	C-	C	C	539.9	-7.83	25.3	2.9	21.9	22.5	6.1	8.1	13.5
FIDELITY FEDERAL B&T	W PALM BEACH	FL	C+	C+	B-	3,394.3	20.04	3.7	1.3	31.8	19.9	3.5	6.8	10.2
FIDELITY FS&LA	DELAWARE	OH	A	A-	A-	83.2	0.43	1.1	1.8	58.0	12.3	10.0	18.2	39.4
FIDELITY FSB	MARION	IN	B-	B-	B-	114.6	-7.51	1.8	7.9	48.1	12.1	6.7	8.7	15.8
▼ FIDELITY HMSTD ASSN	NEW ORLEANS	LA	A-	A	A	713.7	-0.97	0.0	0.7	58.5	34.6	10.0	16.7	42.4
FIDELITY MANAGEMENT	BOSTON	MA	A-	A-	A-	112.7	16.15	0.0	0.0	0.0	5.5	10.0	60.2	62.0
FIDELITY NB	W MEMPHIS	AR	B-	B-	B-	204.7	-0.05	3.6	5.3	9.8	53.9	6.1	8.1	17.3
FIDELITY NB	MEDFORD	WI	D-	D-	D-	94.9	-6.06	18.0	4.3	17.2	17.9	5.1	7.6	11.1
FIDELITY PERSONAL TRUST	BOSTON	MA	D+	D+	D+	12.5	77.86	0.0	0.0	0.0	88.2	10.0	88.4	91.5
FIDELITY S&LA OF BUCKS CTY	BRISTOL	PA	C+	C+	B-	63.6	-13.02	0.3	0.5	37.1	46.2	10.0	16.2	36.8
FIDELITY ST B&TC	DODGE CITY	KS	A+	A+	A+	123.6	-3.68	8.2	3.1	4.7	42.1	10.0	18.6	34.1
▲ FIDELITY ST B&TC	TOPEKA	KS	B-	C+	C+	98.6	-0.10	10.2	19.1	3.4	36.6	5.9	7.9	14.3
FIDELITY SVG BK	PITTSBURGH	PA	C+	C+	C+	636.1	1.64	5.3	0.7	22.6	47.6	5.6	7.6	13.0
▼ FIDUCIARY TC INTL	NEW YORK	NY	C-	C-	D+	1,337.5	-12.57	4.6	10.2	0.0	21.0	10.0	13.1	25.6
FIFE COMMERCIAL BANK	FIFE	WA	B-	B-	C+	64.2	5.14	13.2	2.0	16.6	3.9	6.6	8.6	12.7
▲ FIFTH DISTRICT S&LA	NEW ORLEANS	LA	A-	B+	B+	331.9	-1.03	0.0	0.7	60.1	27.7	10.0	13.2	33.1
FIFTH THIRD BANK NA	FRANKLIN	TN	B-	B-	B-	1,262.4	41.67	18.7	10.3	9.1	0.2	9.5	15.3	14.6
FIFTH THIRD BK	GRAND RAPIDS	MI	B+	B+	B+	37,007.5	43.49	23.8	11.9	5.1	18.4	4.9	9.5	11.0
FIFTH THIRD BK	CINCINNATI	OH	B+	B+	B+	60,511.0	9.42	10.1	7.8	11.3	37.7	5.7	8.0	11.6
FILLEY BK	FILLEY	NE	D-	D-	D-	12.0	8.61	1.9	8.1	12.3	36.1	5.4	7.4	14.5
FINANCE & THRIFT CO	PORTERVILLE	CA	B	B	B	111.9	2.77	0.0	80.4	6.4	1.6	10.0	15.9	20.1
▲ FINANCE FACTORS	HONOLULU	HI	B	C+	C-	521.6	13.42	0.0	0.2	14.2	37.9	8.4	9.9	14.9
FINANCIAL FSB	MEMPHIS	TN	A-	A-	B	314.0	14.66	6.8	2.6	22.2	0.0	6.4	10.6	12.1
▼ FIRESIDE BK	PLEASANTON	CA	B	B+	B+	1,102.9	-0.21	0.0	89.6	0.0	10.8	10.0	14.3	17.0
▲ FIRST & CITIZENS BANK	MONTEREY	VA	C	D+	D	84.8	14.18	23.2	9.4	33.6	16.5	6.6	8.6	13.6
▲ FIRST & FARMERS BANK	PORTLAND	ND	B-	C+	C+	37.3	3.73	11.3	7.9	5.8	20.1	10.0	11.7	16.4
FIRST & FARMERS BK INC	ALBANY	KY	B-	B-	B+	227.3	154.14	6.5	9.0	16.4	34.0	5.1	7.1	12.0
FIRST & PEOPLES B&TC	RUSSELL	KY	B	B+	A-	197.2	-1.85	0.6	12.3	19.2	42.8	10.0	17.0	34.8
FIRST ADVANTAGE BK	COON RAPIDS	MN	D	D	NR	16.1	N/A	8.6	4.1	8.2	28.1	10.0	23.0	28.2
FIRST ALLIANCE BK	CORDOVA	TN	C	C	C-	77.4	15.96	14.1	2.4	15.0	5.9	7.3	9.5	12.7
FIRST AMERICA BK	BRADENTON	FL	D	NR	NR	14.7	N/A	4.6	0.0	0.5	0.0	10.0	68.7	217.5
FIRST AMERICAN B&TC	ATHENS	GA	A	A	A	242.8	6.53	1.4	2.1	10.5	36.4	10.0	11.5	18.6
FIRST AMERICAN B&TC	VACHERIE	LA	B+	B+	B+	446.8	2.63	3.0	2.9	21.5	28.7	7.8	9.5	16.6
▲ FIRST AMERICAN B&TC	MADISON	SD	B-	C+	C	148.0	7.61	30.2	6.3	8.6	6.5	5.9	9.1	11.6
▲ FIRST AMERICAN BK	DECATUR	AL	B	B-	B-	946.6	10.64	6.9	2.8	9.3	12.6	5.1	7.9	11.1
FIRST AMERICAN BK	ROSEMEAD	CA	B-	B-	A-	218.9	9.66	15.3	1.3	0.3	42.1	6.9	8.9	17.7
FIRST AMERICAN BK	FORT DODGE	IA	C+	C	C	942.9	10.05	24.8	1.1	6.4	16.2	3.7	7.8	10.4
FIRST AMERICAN BK	CARPENTERSVILLE	IL	B-	B-	B-	2,054.3	6.78	19.0	1.3	4.5	12.6	3.6	9.0	10.3
FIRST AMERICAN BK	VINCENNES	IN	C+	C+	B-	132.0	-22.55	7.6	3.5	28.9	14.1	7.4	9.3	14.4
▲ FIRST AMERICAN BK	ERICK	OK	B-	C+	C+	26.2	-3.13	3.5	6.0	5.4	48.4	6.7	8.7	18.1
▼ FIRST AMERICAN BK	PURCELL	OK	D	C-	C	244.1	8.01	12.3	9.0	11.5	9.9	4.5	7.3	10.7
▲ FIRST AMERICAN BK	STONEWALL	OK	D+	D	E+	17.6	-2.76	15.1	14.5	19.5	17.4	8.0	9.7	15.9
FIRST AMERICAN BK OF PA	EVERETT	PA	B	B	B	205.4	1.15	8.9	2.6	16.1	13.6	6.1	8.9	11.8
▲ FIRST AMERICAN BK SSB	BRYAN	TX	B	C+	C	3,491.7	6.87	21.2	6.3	9.4	9.8	5.7	9.3	11.5
FIRST AMERICAN INTL BK	BROOKLYN	NY	B-	B	B-	146.9	77.19	0.4	0.3	7.5	10.4	5.1	8.4	11.1
FIRST AMERICAN NB	IUKA	MS	A-	A-	B+	141.7	-2.24	3.5	8.2	24.7	38.3	10.0	11.5	17.3
FIRST AMERICAN ST BK	GREENWOOD VLG	CO	C-	C-	C-	137.8	14.51	7.9	0.4	5.4	38.2	3.7	5.7	10.7
FIRST AMERICAN ST BK OF MN	HANCOCK	MN	D	D	D	21.4	9.06	47.2	5.4	2.8	14.2	6.4	8.4	12.7
FIRST AMERICAN TRUST FSB	SANTA ANA	CA	B+	B+	B+	319.5	49.04	0.0	0.0	0.0	88.5	8.3	9.9	28.4
FIRST ARIZONA SVGS FSB	SCOTTSDALE	AZ	C-	C-	D+	241.0	-1.31	0.0	0.1	33.1	39.8	4.1	6.1	15.0
FIRST ARKANSAS B&T	JACKSONVILLE	AR	A+	A+	A+	262.7	0.28	10.9	2.6	12.9	26.6	10.0	14.7	22.3

Asset Quality Index	Non-Performing Loans as a % of Total Loans	as a % of Capital	Net Charge-offs Avg Loans	Profitability Index	Net Income ($Mil)	Return on Assets (R.O.A.)	Return on Equity (R.O.E.)	Net Interest Spread	Overhead Efficiency Ratio	Liquidity Index	Liquidity Ratio	Hot Money Ratio	Stability Index
9.9	0.23	2.0	0.31	0.0	-0.6	-1.22	-10.45	3.45	103.5	4.8	20.4	4.1	0.0
6.6	0.31	3.3	-0.03	6.0	0.4	0.93	12.24	3.95	62.5	4.4	23.9	7.2	4.5
1.2	2.47	19.1	0.71	3.5	0.2	0.24	2.72	6.30	91.8	3.4	48.9	20.3	3.5
6.6	0.23	2.1	0.33	3.9	3.9	0.69	8.29	3.31	67.6	1.7	16.4	22.6	4.9
5.2	1.08	7.2	0.09	5.0	5.8	0.77	11.64	2.41	62.8	0.9	19.7	48.2	4.1
7.0	0.16	1.3	0.05	4.5	0.9	0.68	7.76	4.06	74.2	6.2	51.3	5.9	5.8
4.4	1.58	11.7	0.00	8.6	2.4	1.94	20.00	4.52	56.6	7.8	89.3	3.2	7.3
8.8	0.13	1.0	0.00	9.6	3.9	2.27	19.50	3.82	42.2	6.6	47.0	1.6	6.1
7.8	0.34	2.1	0.13	5.3	4.4	0.78	8.02	3.88	70.5	6.5	76.9	11.1	8.6
8.8	0.00	0.0	0.00	0.0	-0.4	-2.68	-10.95	2.80	143.5	5.9	69.3	10.4	0.0
3.4	1.74	9.2	0.25	10.0	2.1	2.08	16.50	5.57	20.5	5.3	101.7	18.4	7.3
7.8	0.17	1.5	0.06	4.3	0.3	0.75	9.85	3.74	66.9	4.7	38.7	11.2	2.5
9.8	0.00	0.0	-0.01	3.2	0.7	0.47	5.30	3.31	81.7	3.8	11.1	9.8	4.8
2.8	2.72	21.3	0.19	3.6	1.6	0.58	7.30	3.26	66.9	1.4	21.6	27.3	3.2
7.0	0.37	3.9	0.01	5.1	12.7	0.79	11.25	3.33	64.9	0.9	20.7	52.4	4.5
9.2	0.22	0.9	0.01	9.4	0.6	1.33	7.47	3.60	44.8	1.9	22.6	20.6	9.0
2.1	2.14	17.0	0.69	4.9	0.3	0.44	5.25	3.13	67.0	1.5	28.6	31.0	5.5
9.7	0.14	0.5	0.00	5.8	3.1	0.86	5.15	2.96	57.4	2.7	5.6	14.7	9.0
10.0	0.00	0.0	0.00	10.0	7.5	13.73	22.41	1.77	92.4	0.0	N/A	100.0	4.7
8.2	0.19	1.0	0.27	7.8	2.0	1.95	25.25	4.23	52.1	1.2	13.5	28.6	4.2
2.2	1.87	16.9	0.47	1.6	0.1	0.27	3.65	3.95	83.8	1.4	16.6	26.7	1.3
6.8	0.00	0.0	0.00	2.0	-0.6	-12.16	-13.86	2.58	117.9	0.8	35.4	100.0	0.0
9.5	0.53	1.4	0.00	2.6	0.1	0.25	1.64	2.86	120.4	2.9	30.7	17.2	6.0
8.9	0.23	0.5	0.06	7.9	1.0	1.54	8.07	4.45	55.3	6.6	64.3	7.0	8.8
4.7	0.73	4.4	0.22	4.3	0.3	0.67	8.19	3.62	78.2	5.0	37.0	8.7	4.9
5.3	1.69	9.1	0.25	3.8	2.5	0.79	9.76	2.59	67.9	4.3	23.9	7.8	4.2
5.9	1.56	0.4	0.00	1.0	-6.0	-0.86	-1.59	2.48	94.1	8.9	122.0	0.0	7.6
5.9	0.59	4.8	0.00	10.0	0.9	2.64	31.23	5.87	55.1	3.8	65.6	21.5	5.1
9.5	0.16	0.8	0.00	5.3	1.4	0.84	6.32	3.19	61.5	4.1	27.7	10.6	7.4
6.9	0.17	0.4	0.02	3.7	-3.1	-0.59	-3.37	0.36	84.1	5.1	163.8	33.4	5.6
5.6	0.69	4.5	0.39	8.6	231.3	1.26	12.82	3.65	57.3	7.3	62.0	3.7	7.8
7.1	0.51	3.4	0.52	9.8	582.2	1.98	26.64	3.66	48.8	5.2	27.0	6.6	7.2
5.8	1.30	8.6	0.00	3.9	0.0	0.70	9.47	3.76	75.2	6.6	88.7	7.6	1.7
3.7	1.01	4.7	1.03	10.0	1.8	3.24	21.12	16.43	58.6	0.8	N/A	30.0	8.6
4.8	2.52	13.2	-1.44	5.1	2.6	1.04	10.54	4.36	74.2	6.7	228.3	19.0	5.0
7.1	0.37	3.1	0.01	9.8	2.3	1.55	14.01	3.02	41.5	0.6	3.3	35.3	7.4
4.3	0.78	3.6	4.23	10.0	11.6	2.11	14.91	14.51	45.6	0.5	7.9	61.5	9.8
6.0	0.26	2.1	0.15	4.8	0.3	0.80	9.66	3.72	68.0	4.9	41.1	10.9	2.8
7.2	0.63	3.6	0.44	3.3	0.1	0.57	4.79	3.61	80.6	4.0	6.2	7.5	5.2
4.6	0.72	2.9	0.30	5.1	0.1	0.15	1.18	4.16	94.0	4.8	42.4	11.4	5.4
6.4	1.97	4.9	0.69	4.3	0.7	0.67	3.93	4.34	76.7	5.8	48.8	7.3	7.4
9.1	0.00	0.0	0.00	0.0	-0.4	-6.10	-20.02	1.91	561.5	3.0	54.6	22.1	0.0
4.8	0.50	3.8	-0.02	2.9	0.1	0.29	2.90	3.98	83.6	3.4	72.2	30.5	6.5
10.0	0.00	0.0	0.00	0.0	-0.4	-6.04	-7.60	0.12	6,837.5	9.6	3,095.2	2.5	0.0
9.1	0.13	0.6	0.02	6.9	1.6	1.33	11.68	3.81	60.3	4.8	17.5	4.0	7.8
6.0	1.04	6.1	0.13	8.8	3.3	1.49	15.58	4.66	59.3	5.3	37.1	6.5	6.0
5.0	0.79	5.8	0.12	8.4	1.6	2.21	21.36	5.49	63.3	2.7	18.6	15.9	5.0
6.5	0.24	1.9	-0.01	7.8	6.2	1.37	15.22	4.32	61.3	1.6	20.5	25.3	6.5
8.8	0.00	0.0	-0.16	5.2	1.0	0.94	10.25	4.57	71.7	6.5	65.5	7.6	4.2
4.9	0.43	3.3	0.22	5.4	4.6	1.00	10.89	3.29	56.8	4.5	31.6	9.7	5.5
6.6	0.68	5.7	0.04	5.4	7.8	0.80	8.91	4.04	72.8	5.2	54.7	14.6	7.0
4.2	1.81	11.6	0.36	2.0	0.1	0.15	1.57	2.93	75.3	3.9	12.7	9.3	3.2
8.8	0.00	0.0	0.06	6.7	0.2	1.40	15.34	3.73	61.7	3.2	61.0	27.2	5.7
3.6	1.18	10.0	1.25	2.7	0.1	0.06	0.82	4.75	84.1	4.3	41.0	13.6	1.8
4.8	0.39	2.3	0.35	9.5	0.2	2.07	21.45	6.51	69.2	4.3	37.9	10.3	3.0
6.6	0.41	3.3	0.02	5.6	1.0	0.93	10.76	3.74	66.7	3.2	10.7	12.5	6.6
5.0	0.76	5.5	0.25	7.1	29.3	1.67	16.96	4.21	58.6	4.7	33.2	12.1	8.5
7.8	0.00	0.0	0.00	4.4	0.2	0.32	3.74	4.67	86.4	7.5	97.3	6.5	5.3
5.5	2.89	11.0	0.78	5.6	0.8	1.12	9.63	4.78	69.9	6.6	81.0	9.7	6.3
4.0	2.13	20.9	0.00	6.1	0.9	1.24	23.85	4.18	55.5	3.8	37.5	15.3	2.9
7.7	0.05	0.3	-0.05	5.4	0.1	0.89	10.31	4.96	66.6	3.6	52.3	17.5	2.0
9.7	0.00	0.0	0.00	8.9	1.6	1.12	11.45	2.00	80.2	5.0	213.3	94.9	4.5
9.5	0.08	0.6	0.00	2.9	0.2	0.14	2.35	2.06	91.0	1.6	31.4	31.7	2.4
8.6	0.13	0.6	0.04	10.0	3.3	2.50	16.41	5.03	60.2	3.7	29.8	13.0	9.7

| Name | City | State | Weiss Safety Rating | 2003 Weiss Safety Rating | 2002 Weiss Safety Rating | Total Assets ($Mil) | One Year Asset Growth | Asset Mix (As a % of Total Assets) | | | | Capital-ization Index | Leverage Ratio | Risk-based Capital Ratio |
								Comm-ercial Loans	Cons-umer Loans	Home Mort-gages	Secur-ities			
FIRST ARKANSAS VALLEY	RUSSELLVILLE	AR	B	B-	C+	475.3	19.02	9.3	4.9	13.3	24.2	5.4	7.4	11.4
FIRST B&T	SPIRIT LAKE	IA	B-	B	B	63.5	-3.17	7.2	4.2	23.9	14.1	8.0	9.7	15.2
FIRST B&T	EVANSTON	IL	C	C	C	344.2	4.19	20.5	34.3	5.4	6.3	3.8	9.4	10.4
FIRST B&T	NEW ORLEANS	LA	C+	C+	C+	680.7	18.35	17.4	8.6	10.3	6.9	4.6	6.6	11.0
FIRST B&T EAST TEXAS	DIBOLL	TX	B-	B-	B-	530.6	3.68	8.6	15.7	11.1	31.8	7.5	9.3	16.2
FIRST B&T OF CHILDRESS	CHILDRESS	TX	C	C	C	59.2	0.15	46.2	4.4	12.8	5.8	5.9	7.9	18.8
FIRST B&T OF MEMPHIS	MEMPHIS	TX	C-	D+	D+	40.1	4.15	42.3	5.7	2.3	1.4	6.9	8.9	15.7
FIRST B&T SB	PARIS	IL	B-	B	B	220.3	1.88	3.1	11.5	15.9	38.4	9.7	10.8	22.3
FIRST B&TC	GLIDDEN	IA	B+	B+	B	59.1	8.27	3.7	3.1	15.4	30.8	10.0	11.8	18.9
▲ FIRST B&TC	COZAD	NE	B-	C+	B-	99.5	13.92	27.1	4.4	5.1	22.1	4.4	8.6	10.7
▲ FIRST B&TC	CLINTON	OK	C+	C	C	37.2	-5.14	2.6	8.6	15.9	40.8	8.7	10.1	26.3
▲ FIRST B&TC	DUNCAN	OK	B	B	A-	277.9	1.92	9.7	10.3	21.0	17.7	9.7	10.8	16.3
FIRST B&TC	PERRY	OK	B-	B-	B-	92.1	-8.24	4.8	9.0	12.2	43.3	10.0	12.1	18.1
FIRST B&TC	WAGONER	OK	B+	A-	B+	126.8	5.62	13.3	10.9	28.8	4.3	7.8	9.6	13.2
FIRST B&TC	DAWSON	TX	E-	E-	E-	22.3	0.28	7.1	14.5	13.2	29.5	4.2	6.2	12.0
▲ FIRST B&TC	LUBBOCK	TX	C	D+	C	239.7	22.76	10.8	4.0	14.1	18.4	4.1	7.2	10.5
FIRST B&TC	LEBANON	VA	C+	C+	C+	599.9	2.82	15.1	6.4	22.6	10.7	3.5	6.9	10.2
FIRST B&TC	MENOMONIE	WI	B	B	B+	100.9	0.04	10.9	2.2	12.4	30.9	6.7	8.7	14.4
▲ FIRST B&TC OF ILLINOIS	PALATINE	IL	D	D-	D-	538.7	-19.40	0.5	0.1	2.7	11.7	10.0	11.4	18.2
FIRST B&TC OF	MURPHYSBORO	IL	B-	B-	B-	55.1	1.37	6.0	3.7	13.0	41.4	8.3	9.8	16.3
▼ FIRST B&TC OF PRINCETON	PRINCETON	KY	C+	B+	A-	87.5	-1.74	4.6	4.1	16.1	48.2	3.5	5.5	12.0
FIRST BANK & TRUST	BROKEN BOW	OK	B+	B+	B	83.7	2.61	8.5	10.5	26.6	31.5	7.6	9.4	17.1
FIRST BANKAMERICANO	ELIZABETH	NJ	B	B	B-	87.2	57.97	16.7	0.3	3.1	28.5	10.0	12.7	17.0
FIRST BANKCENTRE	BROKEN ARROW	OK	D-	D-	NR	27.0	-1.62	32.7	11.0	12.2	19.9	8.3	9.9	14.4
▲ FIRST BANKERS TC NA	QUINCY	IL	B	B-	B-	332.5	5.09	14.9	14.4	9.6	15.0	5.9	9.0	11.7
FIRST BARTLESVILLE BK	BARTLESVILLE	OK	D	D	NR	21.9	N/A	17.5	0.9	2.8	25.1	10.0	22.2	53.3
FIRST BETHANY B&T NA	BETHANY	OK	B-	B-	B	125.3	0.87	7.3	4.1	6.0	44.8	5.8	7.8	14.4
FIRST BK	KETCHIKAN	AK	B	B	B	302.2	1.82	11.3	3.2	6.5	37.6	6.7	8.7	14.0
FIRST BK	WADLEY	AL	C-	C-	C	49.4	6.63	19.3	6.9	11.6	43.7	5.8	7.8	14.9
FIRST BK	SAN LUIS OBISPO	CA	B	B	B-	269.2	-12.19	6.9	2.7	6.8	23.7	8.0	9.7	14.2
▼ FIRST BK	CORAL GABLES	FL	C	B	B	145.0	28.30	4.7	0.3	3.4	38.4	9.2	10.5	16.5
FIRST BK	W DES MOINES	IA	B-	C+	D+	115.1	7.67	23.0	3.5	15.9	17.1	7.0	9.0	12.6
▼ FIRST BK	MORGANTOWN	IN	D+	C-	C	210.7	18.95	12.4	15.4	12.4	17.1	2.7	7.6	9.7
FIRST BK	STERLING	KS	C+	C+	D+	71.8	-10.56	10.2	3.7	13.4	34.6	10.0	11.3	21.1
FIRST BK	LOUISVILLE	KY	D-	D+	D	198.7	-12.29	3.9	2.9	39.9	17.2	4.4	6.4	14.6
▲ FIRST BK	BATON ROUGE	LA	D+	D-	D	97.7	15.68	15.5	2.4	5.7	13.6	4.6	8.0	10.8
FIRST BK	CREVE COEUR	MO	B-	B-	C+	7,304.0	3.52	17.6	0.7	10.6	16.8	4.3	8.6	10.7
FIRST BK	MCCOMB	MS	A-	A-	A-	242.3	1.73	20.7	5.0	6.6	43.1	8.5	10.0	17.0
FIRST BK	TROY	NC	B+	B+	A-	1,558.3	17.52	6.8	3.9	31.0	6.8	5.2	8.1	11.2
▲ FIRST BK	LEXINGTON	TN	C	C+	B-	1,092.2	-0.94	12.1	5.6	20.5	15.5	6.8	8.8	12.7
FIRST BK	AZLE	TX	B	B	B-	151.0	-1.19	10.1	10.4	10.1	27.8	8.2	10.2	13.5
▼ FIRST BK	BURKBURNETT	TX	B	B	B-	138.8	1.74	16.9	6.7	26.4	8.2	3.9	7.3	10.5
FIRST BK	FARMERSVILLE	TX	C+	C+	C	91.4	-2.36	9.0	6.1	11.2	17.2	5.7	7.7	11.8
FIRST BK	GROVETON	TX	A-	A-	A-	34.9	-0.31	2.7	14.0	7.7	54.6	10.0	11.1	24.7
▲ FIRST BK	STRASBURG	VA	B-	B-	B-	374.1	16.86	9.4	8.7	18.6	15.8	5.8	8.7	11.6
FIRST BK	TOMAH	WI	C	C	C-	66.3	-2.71	3.6	2.7	13.0	17.5	8.7	10.1	13.9
FIRST BK BRUNSWICK	BRUNSWICK	GA	B-	C+	C-	155.3	2.40	12.5	3.6	16.5	8.4	6.3	9.9	12.0
FIRST BK FNCL CENTRE	OCONOMOWOC	WI	B-	B-	B-	343.2	13.45	14.5	2.7	13.4	8.8	3.8	8.1	10.4
FIRST BK HIGHLAND PARK	HIGHLAND PARK	IL	B+	B	B	688.9	3.28	6.2	0.6	5.2	10.0	5.9	10.0	11.7
FIRST BK JACKSONVILLE	JACKSONVILLE	FL	D	D	D	26.7	28.52	13.1	2.8	12.6	20.1	10.0	20.2	29.0
FIRST BK KS	SALINA	KS	B	B	B-	127.4	0.44	6.0	6.3	22.0	37.4	6.5	8.5	15.9
FIRST BK OF BALDWIN	BALDWIN	WI	A	A	A	105.7	-5.43	21.1	3.3	12.5	15.3	10.0	13.5	18.5
▲ FIRST BK OF BERNE	BERNE	IN	A-	B+	B+	359.5	2.77	1.7	2.6	40.1	21.0	10.0	11.2	19.2
FIRST BK OF BEVERLY HILLS	BEVERLY HILLS	CA	B-	B-	B-	1,207.0	57.21	0.1	0.0	4.5	27.8	4.9	7.5	10.9
FIRST BK OF BOAZ	BOAZ	AL	A+	A+	A	123.7	8.00	5.5	8.1	10.2	61.2	10.0	14.2	28.6
FIRST BK OF CELESTE	CELESTE	TX	C	C	C	35.7	0.57	5.6	13.6	12.6	15.4	6.7	8.7	15.7
FIRST BK OF CHANDLER	CHANDLER	OK	B+	B	B	57.4	4.25	11.2	6.8	20.8	11.7	7.9	9.7	13.2
FIRST BK OF CHARLESTON	CHARLESTON	WV	D	D	NR	53.6	343.76	37.8	2.9	19.1	11.0	10.0	12.8	18.2
FIRST BK OF CLEWISTON	CLEWISTON	FL	B-	B-	C+	161.9	10.20	6.9	6.9	16.5	12.2	5.9	7.9	13.0
FIRST BK OF COASTAL	PEMBROKE	GA	C+	B-	B	84.4	-8.23	6.1	5.7	10.1	31.6	6.9	8.9	15.7
FIRST BK OF CONROE NA	CONROE	TX	C	B-	B-	202.1	15.96	12.1	10.1	4.9	11.7	7.3	9.3	12.8
▲ FIRST BK OF DALTON	DALTON	GA	C+	C	D	103.4	13.73	10.4	6.6	12.7	21.0	8.0	9.6	14.3
FIRST BK OF DE	BRANDYWINE	DE	C	C	C-	49.0	-13.99	2.6	3.5	14.1	3.1	10.0	19.6	27.8
▲ FIRST BK OF DOTHAN	DOTHAN	AL	D+	D	D	31.4	18.82	20.9	7.6	14.8	14.0	7.8	9.5	15.4

Asset Quality Index	Non-Performing Loans as a % of Total Loans	Non-Performing Loans as a % of Capital	Net Charge-offs Avg Loans	Profitability Index	Net Income ($Mil)	Return on Assets (R.O.A.)	Return on Equity (R.O.E.)	Net Interest Spread	Overhead Efficiency Ratio	Liquidity Index	Liquidity Ratio	Hot Money Ratio	Stability Index
7.2	0.18	1.2	0.09	8.6	3.3	1.48	16.27	4.30	48.9	1.0	15.4	32.6	6.1
4.6	0.63	4.4	-0.07	7.9	0.6	1.82	18.63	4.77	59.0	5.6	35.7	4.1	6.0
3.4	0.96	8.0	0.04	5.0	1.4	0.80	8.60	3.35	63.8	4.1	16.2	7.9	4.9
3.8	0.92	8.5	0.01	6.4	4.8	1.57	21.79	5.17	64.7	5.5	47.4	9.1	4.5
4.5	0.61	3.1	0.38	8.3	3.5	1.32	12.34	4.73	62.3	5.6	68.7	12.9	6.6
6.5	0.08	0.9	0.00	4.7	0.3	1.07	13.28	3.15	68.3	1.0	24.3	38.1	3.7
4.5	0.58	4.3	0.08	4.2	0.2	1.19	13.28	2.69	66.7	2.4	35.8	25.4	3.2
4.2	2.25	10.0	0.34	3.8	0.6	0.54	5.07	3.76	75.0	3.6	32.8	14.6	5.0
8.5	0.43	2.1	-0.02	6.0	0.4	1.48	12.73	3.56	57.9	4.9	29.1	6.1	6.5
5.7	0.28	2.2	0.01	7.3	0.9	1.77	19.59	4.49	59.6	2.2	19.4	18.4	6.3
8.9	0.41	1.2	0.17	4.2	0.2	0.96	9.04	4.03	80.7	5.9	58.0	8.1	3.5
4.7	0.77	4.2	0.13	6.5	2.0	1.45	12.77	4.39	64.5	3.2	46.4	21.2	7.0
4.1	4.29	16.7	0.81	5.4	0.5	0.98	8.08	4.33	62.8	3.1	20.8	13.9	5.7
5.2	0.46	3.9	0.14	10.0	1.9	3.01	30.35	4.88	44.6	3.6	17.7	11.0	7.4
5.0	0.35	2.9	-0.55	2.8	0.0	0.34	5.22	5.50	92.3	3.3	30.3	13.6	0.0
3.1	0.80	6.7	0.33	9.0	1.8	1.59	20.29	5.82	74.0	1.1	10.9	30.0	4.1
5.8	0.33	3.2	0.06	7.5	4.1	1.37	19.45	4.15	57.8	3.6	31.6	14.1	4.2
7.8	0.31	2.0	0.14	4.5	0.4	0.75	8.52	3.38	72.9	3.3	19.9	13.0	5.8
0.0	17.47	68.3	0.60	2.6	3.9	1.39	12.85	2.75	66.3	6.0	594.5	28.1	4.7
7.0	0.39	1.7	0.38	3.6	0.2	0.68	6.99	3.93	80.4	6.3	74.2	8.4	4.9
3.6	1.55	6.4	-0.31	5.4	0.5	1.15	11.97	3.86	60.6	3.0	21.7	14.7	4.8
8.2	0.12	0.7	0.15	10.0	1.0	2.39	25.46	5.05	51.8	3.6	21.6	11.8	6.2
8.7	0.06	0.3	0.03	4.1	0.3	0.74	5.64	4.50	79.6	3.4	35.0	16.6	6.4
0.6	5.66	36.5	0.58	0.1	-0.1	-0.53	-5.30	3.89	90.3	3.4	87.7	35.6	0.0
6.0	0.66	4.9	0.38	7.1	2.1	1.33	14.90	3.76	53.6	7.0	92.9	9.0	4.8
9.7	0.00	0.0	0.00	0.0	-0.5	-6.65	-22.78	0.49	1,240.0	5.6	79.9	12.0	0.0
8.8	0.09	0.5	-0.75	5.4	0.9	1.46	18.83	3.82	77.6	3.7	16.8	10.7	4.1
7.8	0.12	0.6	0.45	4.8	1.3	0.86	9.49	4.24	81.2	3.8	45.3	17.6	5.5
4.0	2.19	11.8	0.08	8.3	0.3	1.36	15.85	4.84	54.0	2.6	11.6	15.8	4.2
6.4	0.00	0.0	-0.02	6.2	1.3	0.96	10.07	4.62	68.2	2.1	9.6	17.9	5.2
9.3	0.03	0.1	-0.02	2.6	0.1	0.20	1.91	3.25	93.5	3.9	66.9	24.0	4.2
7.6	0.27	2.1	0.06	7.6	1.0	1.86	20.30	5.23	59.3	4.0	21.8	9.8	4.4
6.2	0.16	1.6	-0.04	4.5	0.7	0.74	10.00	4.21	74.4	1.5	18.6	25.9	2.8
4.1	4.43	17.4	0.35	3.1	0.3	0.78	6.84	3.95	73.0	4.2	47.7	15.1	4.6
2.7	2.04	18.2	4.10	0.4	-1.3	-1.24	-17.52	2.62	143.2	6.6	134.6	14.4	0.9
3.2	2.41	20.8	-0.01	3.8	0.4	0.82	10.53	4.44	77.6	2.7	50.1	29.0	2.9
4.4	1.25	7.8	0.40	7.7	47.6	1.31	12.43	4.81	54.2	5.4	31.8	7.9	7.8
8.5	0.02	0.1	0.08	8.3	1.6	1.32	12.94	3.97	56.3	4.7	41.5	11.6	7.5
6.7	0.31	2.2	0.09	9.1	10.4	1.38	12.59	4.41	55.3	4.7	81.1	20.4	9.2
2.5	2.48	15.2	0.11	6.3	7.0	1.28	11.39	4.30	60.8	2.6	24.5	19.1	9.1
5.2	0.60	3.4	-0.02	9.6	1.3	1.71	16.21	5.78	60.1	4.2	21.3	8.0	5.7
8.1	0.11	1.1	0.06	9.7	1.4	2.06	26.27	6.06	65.3	2.6	14.9	16.2	5.8
6.3	0.42	3.5	0.13	5.1	0.5	1.06	13.62	4.33	77.1	4.2	57.2	17.0	4.5
8.0	0.61	2.1	0.57	6.9	0.3	1.62	14.56	4.24	63.6	2.3	28.8	19.7	7.2
7.0	0.13	1.1	0.17	6.2	2.1	1.14	14.62	3.86	60.4	3.4	24.3	12.9	4.8
3.9	1.09	7.7	-0.15	2.9	0.1	0.24	2.42	3.89	91.6	4.6	27.3	6.9	4.8
4.4	0.43	1.9	0.32	5.4	0.8	1.00	5.97	4.35	66.0	3.2	15.5	13.0	7.2
7.1	0.14	1.3	0.04	6.4	2.0	1.18	14.87	3.98	59.6	1.8	12.0	19.8	4.2
8.6	0.00	0.0	-0.01	9.0	4.9	1.46	14.82	3.47	30.4	0.8	21.8	57.9	7.2
8.4	0.00	0.0	-0.03	0.0	-0.1	-0.77	-4.27	3.61	127.9	3.8	59.5	19.3	4.3
4.2	1.69	10.1	-0.06	8.4	1.4	2.10	22.25	4.01	62.5	4.3	40.8	13.8	6.3
6.9	0.83	4.3	0.13	9.8	0.9	1.61	12.17	4.79	52.0	4.1	32.7	12.1	8.3
8.9	0.40	2.4	0.00	6.2	2.1	1.13	10.13	3.28	53.4	3.3	26.4	14.3	7.4
6.1	0.23	2.1	-0.02	6.3	5.8	1.06	13.20	2.75	36.8	0.4	7.6	71.4	7.1
8.7	0.06	0.2	0.09	10.0	1.4	2.17	15.42	4.33	38.5	3.4	10.0	11.3	9.2
7.5	0.32	1.9	-0.03	5.5	0.2	1.30	14.94	4.12	73.0	6.4	109.7	13.1	4.2
6.9	0.36	2.7	-0.24	10.0	0.9	2.90	28.67	5.10	44.0	2.3	30.5	20.7	6.4
8.7	0.00	0.0	0.00	0.0	-0.4	-1.70	-10.58	1.42	242.3	1.8	27.0	24.2	0.0
5.2	1.51	11.4	0.05	5.0	0.6	0.80	9.83	3.92	68.2	5.5	58.0	11.9	4.5
4.0	2.10	11.0	0.10	8.3	0.7	1.60	17.38	5.04	55.6	4.2	30.8	11.1	5.5
2.7	1.61	11.9	0.16	8.4	1.7	1.77	19.05	5.31	69.5	2.2	26.2	19.6	6.8
6.8	0.49	3.3	0.07	5.9	0.5	1.07	11.65	4.29	63.9	5.5	56.8	11.4	3.7
5.2	1.93	5.9	5.58	10.0	1.8	7.11	39.39	4.66	43.1	8.6	167.0	5.8	4.3
5.1	0.02	0.1	3.13	3.8	0.1	0.88	5.23	5.96	73.2	3.2	60.6	27.4	5.4

| Name | City | State | Weiss Safety Rating | 2003 Weiss Safety Rating | 2002 Weiss Safety Rating | Total Assets ($Mil) | One Year Asset Growth | Asset Mix (As a % of Total Assets) | | | | Capital-ization Index | Leverage Ratio | Risk-based Capital Ratio |
								Comm-ercial Loans	Cons-umer Loans	Home Mort-gages	Secur-ities			
FIRST BK OF FAIRLAND	FAIRLAND	OK	D+	D+	D+	9.6	0.48	5.4	8.7	19.2	17.1	7.5	9.3	16.3
FIRST BK OF GEORGIA	THOMSON	GA	B	B	B-	285.0	-6.54	9.7	4.7	20.4	12.3	5.5	8.4	11.4
FIRST BK OF HASKELL	HASKELL	OK	C+	C+	C+	23.0	-3.03	8.2	12.8	20.4	10.9	7.9	9.6	14.0
▲ FIRST BK OF HENRY COUNTY	MCDONOUGH	GA	C+	D+	D	148.3	143.12	6.5	1.1	0.7	15.5	10.0	16.4	19.4
FIRST BK OF IDAHO FSB	KETCHUM	ID	C+	C+	C	266.4	23.97	6.8	4.5	23.3	2.7	4.7	8.0	10.8
FIRST BK OF INDIANTOWN	INDIANTOWN	FL	C	C-	C-	60.3	15.89	7.6	32.0	8.7	3.8	6.1	8.1	12.1
▲ FIRST BK OF KANSAS CITY	KANSAS CITY	MO	C+	C	D+	30.5	6.12	3.6	1.8	18.9	7.1	6.5	8.6	13.1
▲ FIRST BK OF LINCOLN	LINCOLN	MT	C	C	C+	10.4	9.25	7.3	9.5	7.0	29.2	10.0	15.3	31.0
▲ FIRST BK OF LINDEN	LINDEN	AL	C+	C-	C	91.7	0.43	9.0	17.4	14.2	37.4	7.6	9.4	16.3
▲ FIRST BK OF MEDICINE LODGE	MEDICINE LODGE	KS	D+	E-	E-	132.8	13.29	23.0	3.4	5.7	16.6	9.6	11.1	14.7
FIRST BK OF MISSOURI	GLADSTONE	MO	A-	A-	A	374.2	-1.40	14.6	1.2	3.1	14.5	7.4	9.8	12.9
FIRST BK OF MULESHOE	MULESHOE	TX	B+	B+	B+	73.6	-3.43	6.3	6.1	2.4	47.8	10.0	14.8	32.4
FIRST BK OF NEWTON	NEWTON	KS	C+	C+	C	106.9	2.24	12.8	15.4	29.5	15.7	4.0	6.6	10.5
▲ FIRST BK OF NORTHERN KY	FORT MITCHELL	KY	D+	E+	E	67.2	-30.16	29.9	2.5	6.7	7.7	10.0	14.1	20.4
FIRST BK OF OAK PARK	OAK PARK	IL	B	B	C+	254.5	10.10	3.3	0.2	1.2	17.4	6.9	10.9	12.4
FIRST BK OF OH	TIFFIN	OH	A	A	A	111.3	-5.10	0.3	22.1	3.2	61.3	10.0	35.4	89.1
▲ FIRST BK OF OKARCHE	OKARCHE	OK	A-	B+	A-	43.0	-0.13	7.7	6.8	4.5	12.4	10.0	18.5	26.1
▼ FIRST BK OF OWASSO	OWASSO	OK	B-	B+	B+	184.5	11.08	10.1	2.9	8.7	30.0	3.4	7.2	10.2
FIRST BK OF PIKE	MOLENA	GA	C	C	D+	32.8	1.28	6.9	27.9	24.4	23.7	7.5	9.3	16.4
FIRST BK OF SNOOK	SNOOK	TX	D+	D+	D-	48.3	1.06	3.2	19.7	23.3	9.3	7.8	9.5	14.6
▲ FIRST BK OF SOUTH AR	CAMDEN	AR	B+	B	B-	90.6	-1.14	8.9	11.4	24.5	28.7	9.3	10.5	18.0
▼ FIRST BK OF TENNESSEE	SPRING CITY	TN	C+	C+	C	139.5	5.05	10.0	9.0	21.7	7.3	5.4	8.6	11.3
FIRST BK OF THE LAKE	OSAGE BEACH	MO	D+	D+	C	47.8	1.37	4.1	8.4	24.4	23.0	6.9	8.9	15.2
▲ FIRST BK OF THE SOUTH	RAINSVILLE	AL	D	D-	D-	68.1	-0.61	6.4	12.1	18.9	29.7	5.8	7.8	13.6
FIRST BK OF THE SOUTH	LAWRENCEVILLE	GA	B	B	B	354.1	19.24	13.8	1.3	3.7	7.9	6.4	10.4	12.0
FIRST BK OF TROY	TROY	KS	C	C	C	17.8	-1.35	1.8	9.2	10.6	43.8	9.7	10.8	21.1
FIRST BK OF TURLEY	TULSA	OK	B-	B-	B-	36.6	-5.62	8.9	5.9	31.2	22.0	10.0	14.1	26.2
FIRST BK OF WEST TX	COAHOMA	TX	C-	C	C	94.3	5.65	10.7	6.8	12.1	39.4	5.4	7.4	13.8
▲ FIRST BK OF WHITE	WHITE	SD	B-	C+	C+	38.1	5.68	24.5	8.7	14.6	16.9	5.1	8.4	11.1
FIRST BK OKLAHOMA	CLAREMORE	OK	B	B	B	146.4	8.47	9.3	7.6	11.4	37.2	5.7	7.7	13.5
FIRST BK RICHMOND NA	RICHMOND	IN	C	C	C+	556.8	-3.91	7.5	0.6	33.5	12.9	7.2	9.2	13.1
FIRST BK ROXTON TEXAS	ROXTON	TX	C	C	C	18.9	9.74	8.6	24.2	14.5	10.6	7.1	9.1	15.3
FIRST BK THE AMERICAS SSB	CHICAGO	IL	E-	E	D+	74.5	-13.43	1.0	0.8	36.8	27.9	3.9	5.9	14.0
FIRST BK UPPER MICHIGAN	GLADSTONE	MI	B-	B-	B-	150.0	9.89	8.5	14.6	26.3	12.1	8.6	10.1	14.6
FIRST BKG CTR-BURLINGTON	BURLINGTON	WI	B	B	B	564.2	10.93	6.0	0.3	22.3	12.2	6.4	8.9	12.0
▲ FIRST BOULDER VALLEY BK	BOULDER	MT	C	D-	D-	23.8	4.72	27.7	11.9	24.4	4.2	7.5	9.3	12.9
▼ FIRST BRADENTON BK	BRADENTON	FL	C+	B-	NR	63.9	N/A	3.6	4.4	23.4	3.5	4.2	7.9	10.6
▲ FIRST BRANDON NB	BRANDON	VT	B	B-	C+	89.2	5.18	3.5	5.4	37.1	25.3	8.1	9.7	18.2
▲ FIRST BREMEN BK	BREMEN	OH	B	B-	B-	272.7	3.31	2.5	8.0	27.1	21.7	7.2	9.2	13.5
▲ FIRST BUS BK - MILWAUKEE	BROOKFIELD	WI	C+	C	C	72.8	9.70	21.9	0.3	12.4	11.1	8.8	10.7	14.0
FIRST BUSINESS BK	MELBOURNE	FL	C-	C	B-	90.4	54.20	13.4	2.0	4.4	7.6	3.9	7.9	10.4
▲ FIRST BUSINESS BK	MADISON	WI	C+	C	C	467.8	6.31	25.1	0.3	3.2	11.5	4.5	9.1	10.7
▲ FIRST CA BK	CAMARILLO	CA	B-	C+	C+	275.7	23.78	14.5	0.8	5.6	29.9	6.1	8.1	12.4
FIRST CAPITAL BK	NORCROSS	GA	C	C+	C+	503.4	24.96	4.3	0.0	2.8	22.0	5.1	8.6	11.1
▲ FIRST CAPITAL BK	PEORIA	IL	C	D+	D+	254.0	17.49	25.3	0.6	12.5	22.5	3.6	6.4	10.3
FIRST CAPITAL BK	GUTHRIE	OK	D	D+	C-	77.7	7.35	23.1	4.8	11.1	0.0	6.2	8.2	12.5
FIRST CAPITAL BK	BENNETTSVILLE	SC	D+	D	E-	41.8	15.71	15.2	9.9	27.6	0.2	6.7	9.0	12.2
▲ FIRST CAPITAL BK	GLEN ALLEN	VA	C-	D+	D	147.1	31.05	9.7	1.0	16.9	26.8	4.7	6.9	10.9
▲ FIRST CAPITAL BK OF KY	LOUISVILLE	KY	B-	C+	C+	227.1	-6.80	8.8	1.0	21.3	6.9	6.8	10.0	12.4
▼ FIRST CARNEGIE DEPOSIT	CARNEGIE	PA	D+	B-	B	92.7	-37.93	4.6	0.4	11.1	3.6	3.1	5.1	17.3
▲ FIRST CAROLINA STATE BK	ROCKY MOUNT	NC	C	C-	D	65.7	14.12	8.1	1.6	21.0	9.0	7.4	9.3	13.3
FIRST CENTRAL BANK	WARRENSBURG	MO	B	B	B	109.3	21.51	6.3	4.9	11.6	29.3	5.4	7.4	13.5
FIRST CENTRAL BK	CAMBRIDGE	NE	D+	D+	D+	60.4	-0.87	13.2	3.1	3.5	17.4	5.8	8.4	11.6
FIRST CENTRAL BK	PHILIPPI	WV	C+	C+	C+	86.7	2.18	8.6	14.9	33.2	8.4	6.6	8.6	13.2
FIRST CENTRAL BK MCCOOK	MC COOK	NE	D+	D+	D+	40.2	-2.84	24.3	5.7	10.3	14.8	7.0	9.1	12.5
▼ FIRST CENTRAL NB	ST PARIS	OH	B+	A-	A-	66.4	-0.24	3.9	6.6	24.3	22.1	10.0	14.7	22.6
FIRST CENTRAL ST BK	DE WITT	IA	B+	B+	B+	159.6	7.10	8.5	5.0	9.6	22.2	7.1	9.1	13.5
FIRST CENTRAL SVGS BK	WHITESTONE	NY	B-	B-	C+	181.4	39.91	3.4	0.6	12.1	12.4	4.9	7.1	11.0
FIRST CENTURY BK	TAZEWELL	TN	B	B	B	280.0	2.65	2.4	5.2	21.5	35.7	7.1	9.1	17.0
FIRST CENTURY BK NA	BLUEFIELD	WV	C+	C+	C+	364.9	-0.38	11.6	5.4	19.7	23.6	5.9	7.9	12.0
FIRST CHARTER BK	CHARLOTTE	NC	C+	C+	B	4,329.0	9.04	4.6	2.4	13.0	35.6	4.4	6.4	10.7
FIRST CHATHAM BK	SAVANNAH	GA	D	D-	D	178.1	46.68	12.5	2.7	8.7	20.4	7.5	9.5	12.9
▼ FIRST CHEROKEE ST BK	WOODSTOCK	GA	D	D+	D+	264.3	52.60	3.0	2.2	7.1	10.4	3.6	7.8	10.3
▼ FIRST CHOICE BK	GENEVA	IL	D+	C-	D-	89.3	39.93	47.4	1.0	7.8	2.7	7.4	12.3	12.8

Asset Quality Index	Non-Performing Loans as a % of Total Loans	Non-Performing Loans as a % of Capital	Net Charge-offs Avg Loans	Profitability Index	Net Income ($Mil)	Return on Assets (R.O.A.)	Return on Equity (R.O.E.)	Net Interest Spread	Overhead Efficiency Ratio	Liquidity Index	Liquidity Ratio	Hot Money Ratio	Stability Index
7.6	0.00	0.0	0.04	6.2	0.1	1.57	13.53	4.82	71.3	8.2	123.5	2.6	3.7
4.8	0.76	6.5	0.15	8.8	1.7	1.21	14.33	4.10	70.9	1.6	10.7	21.7	5.3
4.0	1.20	8.9	0.16	10.0	0.2	1.91	20.19	6.24	56.3	2.8	27.8	15.8	5.7
6.9	0.01	0.1	-0.02	4.0	0.9	1.46	10.58	3.65	46.5	1.3	31.2	52.6	3.5
7.3	0.28	2.7	0.01	5.8	1.2	0.94	10.85	4.30	67.4	0.6	18.4	72.3	2.2
6.2	0.11	0.9	0.01	6.3	0.3	1.14	14.93	6.28	70.2	6.8	60.0	2.3	3.7
5.8	0.29	2.4	0.00	9.6	0.2	1.41	16.69	5.22	49.9	6.3	84.8	10.2	4.1
8.3	1.05	2.2	-0.06	4.1	0.0	0.53	3.46	3.59	85.9	8.9	148.7	1.2	4.8
3.6	1.34	7.4	2.01	4.3	0.4	0.83	8.80	3.94	49.0	1.7	36.1	45.0	4.3
3.9	0.87	4.7	-0.46	2.1	0.2	0.28	2.55	4.16	87.0	3.5	12.7	11.2	3.3
5.3	0.60	3.9	-0.03	8.4	2.3	1.22	11.93	4.25	58.4	3.9	21.6	10.2	8.4
7.5	0.76	2.1	0.21	5.4	0.4	0.93	6.64	4.76	75.0	5.6	83.1	13.6	6.0
6.5	0.08	0.9	0.00	6.9	0.9	1.61	24.25	4.29	61.9	4.4	30.7	9.8	4.2
1.9	4.83	19.2	-2.36	4.3	2.4	7.10	61.98	4.14	139.0	6.6	91.1	9.8	1.9
7.2	0.25	1.5	0.01	10.0	2.7	2.17	20.00	5.98	45.1	1.4	23.5	27.9	6.3
7.7	1.32	0.9	1.14	8.7	0.9	1.50	4.18	5.06	53.6	4.4	76.8	20.3	7.9
7.5	0.68	2.3	0.02	10.0	0.7	3.30	18.81	5.23	32.3	3.9	89.2	29.3	7.9
8.3	0.16	1.5	0.00	7.9	1.6	1.82	25.80	4.06	58.6	4.2	6.3	6.2	5.5
6.4	0.02	0.1	0.03	5.1	0.1	0.80	8.53	4.55	73.6	4.8	29.5	6.8	3.5
3.7	2.26	15.2	0.21	1.8	-0.1	-0.28	-3.00	5.05	91.3	3.0	68.8	34.1	2.4
5.3	0.85	4.5	0.15	8.3	0.6	1.30	12.21	4.36	55.6	3.2	12.9	12.8	6.1
3.1	1.54	13.8	0.18	7.3	1.2	1.74	20.18	5.26	65.7	3.0	18.7	14.3	6.9
3.5	1.97	14.2	-0.04	4.1	0.1	0.56	6.29	3.63	73.4	1.9	29.5	26.6	2.8
2.1	3.49	24.1	0.50	3.7	0.3	0.76	10.09	4.21	77.7	3.7	37.9	15.7	1.9
7.2	0.00	0.0	-0.02	8.2	2.3	1.33	13.02	4.39	44.3	3.9	22.5	10.4	3.9
8.5	0.00	0.0	0.05	3.4	0.1	0.51	4.59	3.30	81.4	5.4	50.3	7.2	3.8
4.4	3.64	15.5	0.28	5.0	0.2	1.05	7.42	5.08	77.4	3.1	54.3	25.9	5.3
4.0	2.00	12.3	0.31	3.9	0.3	0.61	7.99	3.81	75.7	2.7	41.9	25.6	3.7
2.8	1.89	16.3	0.57	6.4	0.2	1.17	14.29	3.61	48.4	2.5	36.5	24.7	5.5
7.3	0.30	2.1	0.31	7.9	0.8	1.09	14.96	3.77	60.9	3.4	77.4	35.9	4.5
2.7	2.51	19.1	0.90	4.2	1.9	0.65	7.23	3.89	58.1	1.2	20.9	30.3	4.2
5.7	0.70	4.5	0.14	8.9	0.2	2.09	22.63	5.33	64.4	5.1	101.4	17.0	4.3
1.6	3.68	22.9	0.33	1.1	-0.2	-0.49	-5.78	4.64	114.9	4.7	29.6	7.4	0.3
4.0	1.04	6.9	0.05	10.0	2.2	2.93	27.59	5.47	48.3	1.9	12.3	19.1	8.1
6.1	0.61	4.8	0.01	6.1	2.9	1.06	11.38	4.03	67.1	1.8	12.9	19.8	6.2
4.9	0.54	4.4	0.04	7.3	0.2	1.79	19.20	6.32	72.9	3.3	44.7	17.4	5.2
7.4	0.00	0.0	0.00	4.5	0.3	0.96	11.77	3.56	65.8	4.1	80.0	22.7	0.2
5.8	0.55	3.5	0.02	7.0	0.6	1.23	12.77	4.87	66.3	4.9	26.7	4.8	5.1
5.8	0.49	3.4	0.31	6.5	1.5	1.08	11.97	4.32	59.0	3.0	32.0	17.5	6.0
4.6	1.17	7.2	0.00	1.3	0.1	0.15	1.20	2.89	94.1	1.3	17.2	28.1	3.4
7.2	0.00	0.0	0.00	4.5	0.3	0.71	9.08	4.21	60.2	4.1	79.5	21.5	0.5
6.3	0.17	1.5	-0.06	5.7	2.6	1.15	13.65	3.39	54.8	0.4	5.1	61.9	5.2
4.4	1.38	10.2	0.00	5.9	1.2	0.89	11.98	4.90	70.1	4.6	50.0	14.4	4.1
7.5	0.06	0.5	0.00	4.1	1.5	0.62	7.92	3.17	57.3	1.2	16.3	29.7	3.9
5.4	0.70	2.5	0.12	2.6	0.2	0.13	1.25	0.53	59.6	0.7	12.3	40.9	3.4
0.7	3.67	33.7	-0.02	8.4	0.8	2.15	26.73	5.97	61.5	3.4	20.1	12.3	4.6
3.8	0.38	3.3	0.36	5.1	0.2	1.06	10.73	4.85	67.0	1.1	8.1	29.0	3.7
8.8	0.00	0.0	0.00	2.0	0.2	0.31	4.36	3.12	77.9	4.5	53.4	15.7	3.3
4.5	0.79	6.5	0.03	4.0	0.8	0.72	7.06	3.30	74.5	2.1	14.5	18.3	4.9
5.2	0.92	5.7	0.00	1.3	-13.6	-20.00	-146.21	0.85	-1,616.9	4.0	77.6	23.1	6.5
7.8	0.03	0.2	0.00	3.0	0.2	0.71	6.02	1.66	76.5	0.9	24.5	42.9	3.1
7.3	0.12	0.5	0.12	8.3	0.6	1.25	10.53	3.71	56.4	6.6	157.7	16.6	7.5
0.6	3.04	23.6	0.00	6.6	0.4	1.29	15.56	4.87	60.8	4.5	38.8	11.9	3.8
3.9	0.96	5.6	0.45	7.4	0.6	1.27	10.16	5.22	55.9	5.7	45.0	6.5	6.6
3.4	0.85	6.1	0.32	4.9	0.2	0.96	10.86	4.86	64.8	2.8	38.2	21.5	3.7
5.8	1.94	8.8	0.15	5.7	0.3	1.02	6.75	4.34	66.6	4.8	28.7	6.1	7.2
8.2	0.07	0.5	0.03	5.9	0.9	1.09	11.64	3.70	63.1	4.4	42.0	13.4	6.9
7.3	0.10	1.1	0.00	8.8	1.2	1.42	20.85	4.17	42.2	6.8	100.7	10.9	4.0
4.5	2.14	12.2	0.03	6.2	1.5	1.05	11.87	4.08	64.5	4.2	25.9	9.2	4.8
4.3	0.97	6.6	0.06	5.0	1.5	0.80	8.57	4.37	73.8	5.1	42.4	10.0	4.5
7.1	0.53	4.1	0.35	4.4	19.2	0.90	13.23	3.17	62.5	1.2	10.6	27.9	4.1
8.5	0.00	0.0	0.01	1.2	0.2	0.22	2.75	3.04	83.6	1.5	28.7	30.6	0.0
4.4	0.32	3.1	0.01	2.1	-0.8	-0.66	-8.42	3.89	89.4	1.3	17.0	27.5	3.7
4.7	0.81	5.9	0.00	1.4	0.0	0.08	0.61	4.15	89.7	0.7	9.6	36.1	0.0

Name	City	State	Weiss Safety Rating	2003 Weiss Safety Rating	2002 Weiss Safety Rating	Total Assets ($Mil)	One Year Asset Growth	Asset Mix (As a % of Total Assets)				Capital-ization Index	Leverage Ratio	Risk-based Capital Ratio
								Comm-ercial Loans	Cons-umer Loans	Home Mort-gages	Secur-ities			
FIRST CITIZENS B&TC	COLUMBIA	SC	B	B	B	4,271.6	7.40	4.9	11.6	24.9	18.6	4.8	6.9	11.3
FIRST CITIZENS BK	LUVERNE	AL	B-	B-	B-	65.3	4.22	10.9	12.1	10.6	26.4	9.5	10.7	15.8
FIRST CITIZENS BK	TALLADEGA	AL	B	B	B	107.8	8.73	2.3	5.0	18.5	47.0	5.0	7.0	15.8
FIRST CITIZENS BK	GLENNVILLE	GA	B-	B-	C+	73.6	12.85	3.9	4.7	18.4	18.6	8.7	10.6	13.9
FIRST CITIZENS BK	SHEPHERDSVILLE	KY	B-	C+	B-	156.8	-0.26	11.7	1.5	13.0	19.9	5.4	7.4	12.1
FIRST CITIZENS BK	PRESQUE ISLE	ME	C+	C	C	137.1	-3.04	12.8	11.6	21.0	26.8	6.9	8.9	15.5
FIRST CITIZENS BK	BILLINGS	MT	C	C	C	174.7	5.96	20.8	5.7	7.4	24.7	5.4	7.4	11.9
FIRST CITIZENS BK NA	COLUMBIA FALLS	MT	C+	C+	C+	49.6	8.70	22.5	3.6	9.7	2.2	4.9	7.7	11.0
▲ FIRST CITIZENS BK OF BUTTE	BUTTE	MT	C+	C	B-	60.8	7.69	30.1	3.2	6.1	17.2	7.3	9.2	13.5
▲ FIRST CITIZENS BK OF	POLSON	MT	C	D+	D-	29.7	6.64	21.7	15.0	13.6	2.6	7.8	9.5	13.2
▲ FIRST CITIZENS NB	MASON CITY	IA	A-	B+	B	748.7	-1.10	14.1	2.8	13.5	38.0	8.0	9.7	15.4
▲ FIRST CITIZENS NB	UPPER SANDUSKY	OH	A-	A-	A	215.3	-3.87	3.1	2.4	37.0	27.5	10.0	14.7	24.3
FIRST CITIZENS NB	MANSFIELD	PA	C+	C+	C+	494.4	10.75	5.6	2.6	37.6	19.9	3.6	6.2	10.3
FIRST CITIZENS NB	DYERSBURG	TN	B	B	B	738.9	2.86	7.4	5.2	20.4	20.0	6.0	8.0	12.5
FIRST CITIZENS ST BK	WHITEWATER	WI	A+	A+	A+	169.1	1.62	7.3	5.1	30.9	7.2	10.0	14.2	20.0
▲ FIRST CITRUS BK	TAMPA	FL	B-	C+	C-	130.2	30.56	13.4	1.6	8.0	11.6	10.0	13.0	15.8
FIRST CITY BK	NEW BRITAIN	CT	C	C-	C-	187.2	-4.01	9.1	1.9	13.7	37.3	5.6	7.6	14.2
▲ FIRST CITY BK	COLUMBUS	OH	D+	D	D-	53.6	1.86	0.9	1.0	26.2	12.4	5.5	7.5	14.7
FIRST CITY BK OF FLORIDA	FORT WALTON BCH	FL	C+	C+	C+	211.9	13.54	11.3	1.5	26.1	10.7	4.5	7.8	10.7
FIRST CLERMONT BK	MILFORD	OH	A	A	A	202.0	7.83	2.5	3.6	17.1	16.2	10.0	12.3	16.0
FIRST CMNTY BK	BATESVILLE	AR	C-	C-	C	316.7	9.88	22.9	7.0	20.8	19.8	4.5	7.3	10.7
FIRST CMNTY BK	KEOKUK	IA	B-	B-	B-	110.8	-1.57	13.2	2.3	21.2	25.5	6.5	8.5	13.1
FIRST CMNTY BK	HILLSBORO	IL	D+	D+	C-	48.0	13.20	10.3	14.3	19.9	26.5	5.6	7.6	12.9
FIRST CMNTY BK	HAMMOND	LA	C	C	C-	48.3	35.28	6.9	7.4	31.9	10.3	6.8	8.8	12.9
FIRST CMNTY BK	CORPUS CHRISTI	TX	C	C-	D	109.7	8.10	17.3	16.4	17.0	9.5	6.1	8.6	11.8
▲ FIRST CMNTY BK OF CENTRAL	WETUMPKA	AL	C+	C-	D	110.8	22.27	9.0	7.2	13.6	16.6	6.5	8.9	12.1
FIRST CMNTY BK OF PALM	PAHOKEE	FL	B	B	B	163.1	19.51	7.7	1.8	11.4	22.2	5.1	7.1	11.6
FIRST CMNTY BK	XENIA	IL	B+	B+	B	27.4	2.97	3.5	9.4	26.7	23.3	8.5	13.1	13.8
FIRST CMNTY BK-BEDFORD	SHELBYVILLE	TN	B+	B+	A-	202.5	6.36	13.1	7.0	17.1	23.2	9.8	10.8	16.4
▼ FIRST CMRL BK	EDMOND	OK	C+	B-	C+	139.7	7.23	23.5	4.6	22.2	3.4	5.6	9.4	11.4
▼ FIRST COAST CMNTY BK	FERNANDINA BEACH	FL	B-	B	B	166.9	14.75	41.0	2.9	10.7	12.6	4.9	7.5	11.0
FIRST COASTAL BK NA	EL SEGUNDO	CA	C+	C+	C	209.0	35.17	10.3	0.6	10.4	31.3	3.7	6.8	10.3
FIRST COLEBROOK BK	COLEBROOK	NH	B+	B+	B	126.7	8.02	15.1	2.9	15.7	22.3	7.4	9.3	13.4
FIRST COLEMAN NB	COLEMAN	TX	B-	B-	B-	53.3	-0.56	11.4	11.9	12.3	0.8	7.7	11.1	13.1
FIRST COLLINSVILLE BK	COLLINSVILLE	IL	B-	B-	B-	450.5	22.77	1.3	6.0	51.1	14.7	4.6	6.6	11.5
FIRST COLUMBIA B&TC	BLOOMSBURG	PA	B-	B-	B	227.7	1.35	7.2	2.7	32.4	27.1	5.3	7.3	12.0
FIRST COMMAND BK	FORT WORTH	TX	C	C-	C	445.8	19.43	3.9	54.1	0.7	16.5	3.7	6.6	10.4
FIRST COMMERCE BK	ENCINO	CA	B-	C+	C	196.8	39.94	17.2	0.6	1.6	5.7	6.2	9.4	11.9
▲ FIRST COMMERCE BK	MARYSVILLE	KS	C+	D+	D	24.6	38.93	11.5	7.0	38.2	4.0	10.0	12.9	18.1
▲ FIRST COMMERCE BK	LEWISBURG	TN	C-	D	D	98.3	64.29	14.8	6.3	21.1	15.7	10.0	12.8	18.1
FIRST COMMERCE BK	CORPUS CHRISTI	TX	A+	A+	A+	121.7	-0.63	5.5	6.9	20.4	22.4	10.0	11.7	16.5
▲ FIRST COMMERCE	DOUGLASVILLE	GA	C-	D	NR	85.0	238.50	5.3	2.4	7.5	7.5	7.9	12.1	13.2
FIRST COMMERCIAL BK	BIRMINGHAM	AL	B	B	B-	1,636.2	-3.00	34.9	3.5	11.9	9.6	4.2	10.5	10.6
▼ FIRST COMMERCIAL BK	HUNTSVILLE	AL	B-	B	B	453.8	6.62	14.8	1.1	9.4	15.7	3.6	8.8	10.3
▲ FIRST COMMERCIAL BK	CHICAGO	IL	B-	C+	C	217.6	25.35	1.2	0.6	14.3	20.0	3.9	7.4	10.4
▼ FIRST COMMERCIAL BK	BLOOMINGTON	MN	E+	E-	E-	47.0	69.97	9.0	2.1	16.2	7.7	6.8	8.8	12.7
FIRST COMMERCIAL BK	GIDEON	MO	C-	C-	D+	117.0	8.18	13.8	2.3	9.9	17.5	3.0	6.7	10.0
FIRST COMMERCIAL BK	JACKSON	MS	C-	D+	D-	132.7	31.25	43.3	2.7	11.0	12.8	9.8	11.8	14.8
FIRST COMMERCIAL BK	GOOD HOPE	AL	B-	B-	C	106.6	12.36	10.6	9.1	19.3	21.5	9.5	10.7	15.9
FIRST COMMERCIAL BK NA	SEGUIN	TX	C-	D+	D-	76.2	-25.94	12.4	3.6	9.0	16.7	10.0	13.9	21.0
FIRST COMMERCIAL BK OF	ORLANDO	FL	C+	C	C	277.8	19.05	6.2	1.1	2.0	1.9	3.6	6.9	10.3
▲ FIRST COMMERCIAL BK	TAMPA	FL	C-	D	C-	136.3	33.63	10.1	1.5	9.0	13.8	3.5	7.6	10.3
FIRST COMMERCIAL BK USA	ALHAMBRA	CA	C+	C+	C	300.2	10.03	9.9	0.0	1.0	20.7	9.4	11.7	14.5
▲ FIRST COMMONWEALTH BK	PRESTONSBURG	KY	A	A-	A-	164.6	-4.22	7.9	7.0	31.1	31.3	9.6	10.7	19.5
FIRST COMMONWEALTH BK	INDIANA	PA	B	B	B	6,202.1	29.17	7.0	8.9	17.5	36.4	5.4	7.9	11.3
FIRST COMMTY BK OF	PORT CHARLOTTE	FL	B-	B-	C	210.0	29.31	7.8	3.3	20.5	6.7	5.5	7.7	11.4
FIRST COMMUNITY B&T	BEECHER	IL	B	B-	B-	108.0	7.58	7.1	3.6	13.0	33.1	6.9	8.9	14.7
FIRST COMMUNITY B&TC	BARGERSVILLE	IN	D+	D+	D-	163.8	0.76	15.2	15.8	15.3	12.3	5.8	8.1	11.6
FIRST COMMUNITY BANK	SIDNEY	IA	C+	C+	B-	36.9	18.16	15.8	2.7	25.0	10.7	9.0	10.3	16.2
▲ FIRST COMMUNITY BANK	SHERRARD	IL	D	E	E+	45.0	-0.58	6.6	6.2	12.6	36.1	5.0	7.1	11.0
▲ FIRST COMMUNITY BANK NA	SAN BENITO	TX	B-	C+	C+	109.6	25.46	9.0	6.0	5.8	34.9	7.4	9.3	13.4
FIRST COMMUNITY BK	CHATOM	AL	C-	B-	B-	223.8	-3.75	8.5	4.2	12.8	25.4	6.2	8.2	12.3
▲ FIRST COMMUNITY BK	JONESBORO	AR	C+	C	C-	697.1	-3.69	9.6	3.0	20.2	36.4	5.1	7.1	12.7
▲ FIRST COMMUNITY BK	MARION	AR	B-	C-	C	49.4	10.76	5.9	7.7	15.7	26.8	10.0	15.5	24.4

Asset Quality Index	Non-Performing Loans as a % of Total Loans	Non-Performing Loans as a % of Capital	Net Charge-offs Avg Loans	Profitability Index	Net Income ($Mil)	Return on Assets (R.O.A.)	Return on Equity (R.O.E.)	Net Interest Spread	Overhead Efficiency Ratio	Liquidity Index	Liquidity Ratio	Hot Money Ratio	Stability Index
6.8	0.36	2.8	0.22	5.3	17.1	0.81	10.21	3.89	70.7	6.9	72.4	7.5	6.8
4.5	1.18	6.4	0.96	6.7	0.4	1.24	11.23	4.66	51.8	2.2	34.3	26.7	4.6
7.1	0.48	2.8	-0.01	9.8	1.0	1.80	26.35	4.30	46.9	2.2	12.6	17.8	6.4
7.8	0.26	1.6	0.06	5.6	0.4	1.16	11.04	5.34	70.8	3.3	21.3	13.2	4.2
8.8	0.07	0.6	0.06	5.0	0.8	0.95	12.94	3.06	73.6	5.0	36.2	8.4	5.7
3.7	1.86	12.2	0.23	4.4	0.4	0.58	6.56	4.61	75.8	6.7	70.9	6.9	4.4
3.9	1.48	11.1	0.28	4.5	0.5	0.61	8.62	4.23	64.9	6.1	56.9	8.2	3.5
8.1	0.00	0.0	0.02	5.4	0.2	0.88	11.47	4.71	74.3	2.2	39.3	30.7	4.9
4.4	0.69	4.6	0.00	7.6	0.7	2.45	27.81	5.82	54.3	4.9	33.8	7.9	5.3
3.7	1.24	9.6	0.03	8.1	0.2	1.36	14.96	6.76	67.1	3.0	35.7	18.7	3.3
7.6	0.32	1.8	0.33	6.3	5.3	1.39	13.90	3.34	52.6	3.1	17.9	13.7	6.5
8.9	0.42	1.7	0.08	5.4	1.1	0.99	6.26	4.21	67.1	3.3	20.7	12.9	8.6
4.7	0.73	6.0	-0.13	6.3	3.2	1.33	16.11	4.15	66.4	3.5	20.5	11.8	4.6
7.0	0.26	1.7	0.03	6.6	4.2	1.14	11.74	4.04	64.5	1.4	13.9	25.4	6.2
8.5	0.11	0.6	0.08	9.3	1.3	1.48	10.85	4.93	57.1	4.7	51.7	14.6	8.5
7.3	0.09	0.5	0.05	3.5	0.3	0.40	3.10	4.15	74.1	1.5	17.5	25.2	6.4
7.4	0.85	5.8	0.01	4.4	0.8	0.88	12.29	4.02	67.5	2.0	31.8	27.1	3.2
4.2	0.95	9.3	0.00	6.3	0.4	1.67	22.51	4.19	45.6	8.7	150.5	2.9	1.3
7.9	0.12	1.2	0.00	5.4	0.8	0.82	10.67	4.22	67.6	7.3	93.5	7.2	3.5
7.6	0.19	1.2	0.04	9.0	1.4	1.34	10.94	3.68	61.1	1.2	5.1	25.6	8.2
4.3	0.98	9.7	0.25	4.7	1.4	0.89	13.13	3.70	58.3	0.6	7.9	40.9	2.8
5.4	0.66	4.7	0.09	5.3	0.6	1.04	12.05	3.80	64.1	3.8	8.5	9.4	4.9
4.8	1.35	10.7	0.07	4.6	0.2	0.96	12.53	3.76	63.6	4.9	36.3	9.0	2.6
6.2	0.29	2.6	0.01	5.2	0.3	1.18	13.45	5.02	67.4	1.6	21.4	24.6	0.0
3.2	1.49	13.0	0.32	6.2	0.9	1.60	19.18	5.89	77.3	2.0	26.1	21.5	4.1
8.1	0.00	0.0	0.06	4.1	0.5	0.93	10.42	4.09	63.6	1.5	30.1	32.9	2.9
8.9	0.00	0.0	-0.11	6.3	1.2	1.56	21.92	4.17	64.3	5.9	41.3	4.8	4.5
7.6	0.23	1.2	-0.07	6.7	0.2	1.57	11.70	4.08	64.0	3.9	22.2	10.3	6.3
5.7	0.51	2.8	0.16	7.8	1.3	1.33	12.25	4.26	58.3	1.9	34.1	31.3	7.5
3.8	1.36	10.5	0.06	3.9	0.3	0.38	3.60	5.00	81.1	3.7	12.3	10.2	4.6
3.5	1.74	15.1	0.01	9.4	1.3	1.46	20.71	3.61	51.7	1.4	18.6	26.9	5.6
8.1	0.01	0.1	0.00	4.3	0.7	0.68	7.68	4.18	74.8	5.4	53.9	11.3	4.7
7.4	0.46	3.1	-0.01	5.3	0.5	0.85	9.01	4.82	76.8	4.2	24.1	8.4	5.8
4.2	0.69	4.9	-0.26	10.0	0.7	2.57	24.82	5.04	54.1	3.4	28.3	14.1	7.1
7.4	0.31	3.5	0.01	7.4	2.3	1.09	15.74	3.60	55.4	4.1	20.7	8.5	4.8
6.4	0.42	3.5	0.10	6.1	1.2	1.04	14.22	3.80	66.2	4.4	8.8	4.9	4.6
5.7	0.06	0.5	0.26	6.7	3.5	1.58	24.96	4.35	65.8	3.0	29.6	16.4	3.5
7.3	0.10	0.8	-0.01	5.7	0.9	0.97	11.35	4.31	59.3	7.1	97.0	8.6	4.6
8.1	0.28	1.8	0.00	4.9	0.2	1.66	13.06	4.35	58.1	4.7	3.1	2.2	0.1
8.2	0.07	0.4	0.01	2.1	0.3	0.70	5.34	3.49	70.3	1.4	30.7	37.4	1.1
8.3	0.23	1.3	0.03	10.0	1.6	2.61	22.04	5.91	65.1	4.4	22.9	7.2	8.7
7.2	0.00	0.0	0.00	2.6	0.3	0.80	6.16	3.75	61.7	0.9	23.4	41.7	0.4
7.5	0.44	3.5	0.15	9.5	12.0	1.52	14.60	3.82	53.9	1.6	12.5	23.4	8.4
5.0	0.80	6.5	0.21	8.3	2.9	1.30	14.47	3.87	46.4	1.2	11.4	28.2	6.6
5.4	0.40	3.7	-0.06	7.9	1.5	1.43	19.85	5.28	52.7	1.5	16.2	24.6	4.3
1.7	1.79	14.4	0.01	0.4	0.0	-0.18	-1.75	4.98	66.2	0.5	11.5	64.2	1.2
5.3	0.31	2.7	0.00	4.3	0.4	0.76	9.63	3.08	64.5	2.5	19.2	16.8	3.6
8.2	0.02	0.1	0.01	2.0	0.3	0.44	3.69	2.92	72.9	1.8	34.1	32.6	0.8
8.1	0.14	0.9	0.24	6.0	0.5	1.01	10.04	4.40	60.2	3.2	36.6	17.8	3.9
4.3	2.69	11.7	0.22	5.8	1.9	4.47	37.36	4.96	42.7	4.8	38.6	10.6	1.8
6.3	0.26	2.7	0.01	5.7	1.4	1.02	15.03	4.13	56.1	5.7	135.9	19.4	4.2
5.3	0.33	3.0	0.02	3.7	0.3	0.50	6.91	3.61	73.4	2.6	41.8	27.4	3.3
7.4	0.00	0.0	0.00	4.0	1.2	0.79	6.94	3.35	56.1	3.4	83.7	58.2	7.1
8.3	0.06	0.3	0.18	8.4	1.6	1.89	18.09	4.62	60.9	2.8	7.9	14.2	7.1
5.8	0.70	4.0	0.28	5.4	30.1	1.09	12.97	3.25	58.5	3.3	17.9	13.3	6.8
6.9	0.05	0.5	0.00	5.5	1.0	0.97	11.89	4.05	59.7	0.8	18.0	44.4	4.6
7.0	0.49	2.7	0.04	7.9	0.8	1.46	16.42	4.53	57.5	4.2	29.3	10.3	5.1
0.9	2.17	8.2	0.90	3.9	0.5	0.63	3.68	4.49	78.2	3.3	14.1	12.3	5.1
8.0	0.02	0.2	-0.06	4.6	0.2	0.82	7.79	3.75	70.9	1.1	19.0	31.9	1.0
8.6	0.05	0.3	0.06	4.4	0.3	1.13	14.39	3.42	65.1	3.9	75.1	23.0	1.7
8.4	0.19	1.1	0.12	4.4	0.8	1.47	15.93	4.97	76.8	1.8	17.1	20.4	4.1
2.7	2.71	21.2	-0.05	7.2	1.8	1.58	19.42	4.78	62.7	2.5	10.6	15.9	5.4
3.6	1.52	11.7	0.46	5.1	2.9	0.80	8.87	3.33	61.3	0.6	5.3	36.2	5.2
8.4	0.18	0.7	0.45	4.8	0.2	0.87	7.09	3.86	66.9	1.0	25.5	37.6	4.0

Name	City	State	Weiss Safety Rating	2003 Weiss Safety Rating	2002 Weiss Safety Rating	Total Assets ($Mil)	One Year Asset Growth	Asset Mix (As a % of Total Assets)				Capital-ization Index	Leverage Ratio	Risk-based Capital Ratio
								Comm-ercial Loans	Cons-umer Loans	Home Mort-gages	Secur-ities			
▼ FIRST COMMUNITY BK	VAN BUREN	AR	D	C-	C	52.6	-9.84	12.3	16.9	18.3	10.9	5.3	7.3	11.5
FIRST COMMUNITY BK	N MIAMI BEAC	FL	C+	C+	C+	205.6	10.83	8.9	6.8	18.6	14.1	5.2	7.2	11.4
FIRST COMMUNITY BK	NEWELL	IA	B-	B-	B-	48.0	-4.43	0.3	1.5	7.3	24.5	7.4	9.2	13.3
▲ FIRST COMMUNITY BK	ELGIN	IL	B+	B	B-	127.2	5.02	5.2	1.0	6.5	24.8	7.1	9.0	13.6
FIRST COMMUNITY BK	JOLIET	IL	D	NR	NR	19.1	N/A	0.0	1.9	0.0	0.0	10.0	533.0	408.2
▲ FIRST COMMUNITY BK	EMPORIA	KS	C-	D+	D	41.7	9.08	3.3	2.6	18.8	24.2	5.5	7.5	15.2
▼ FIRST COMMUNITY BK	KANSAS CITY	KS	C+	B-	B-	189.7	12.55	24.7	2.0	7.7	1.8	3.5	8.1	10.3
FIRST COMMUNITY BK	CLINTON	KY	B-	C+	C+	55.6	4.78	6.9	5.9	9.6	18.4	10.0	12.2	18.4
FIRST COMMUNITY BK	HARBOR SPRINGS	MI	B-	B-	B	176.1	4.07	3.9	1.9	23.4	8.5	7.3	9.5	12.8
▲ FIRST COMMUNITY BK	LESTER PRAIRIE	MN	C+	C	C-	26.7	10.97	10.5	7.7	12.4	23.6	5.5	7.7	11.4
FIRST COMMUNITY BK	SAVAGE	MN	B	B	B	92.3	19.53	29.6	3.5	3.3	13.4	5.2	8.4	11.1
FIRST COMMUNITY BK	SILVER LAKE	MN	B-	B-	B-	25.0	8.99	3.3	2.1	11.1	34.8	5.8	7.8	12.7
▲ FIRST COMMUNITY BK	BRANSON	MO	C	C-	D+	76.1	8.37	7.5	1.5	9.9	19.1	8.0	9.7	14.7
▼ FIRST COMMUNITY BK	LEE'S SUMMIT	MO	C-	C	C	370.9	14.11	5.7	6.6	25.4	1.5	5.0	7.0	11.3
FIRST COMMUNITY BK	POPLAR BLUFF	MO	C+	C+	C+	193.1	10.67	12.6	8.1	17.5	31.2	6.0	8.0	12.9
FIRST COMMUNITY BK	GLASGOW	MT	B	B	B	152.5	7.66	5.0	9.0	6.8	23.7	6.4	8.4	12.2
FIRST COMMUNITY BK	COLUMBUS	OH	B	C+	C	97.8	4.23	0.6	0.5	35.0	11.4	9.8	10.9	14.9
FIRST COMMUNITY BK	WOODSTOCK	VT	D+	D+	C	63.5	12.23	12.3	1.0	21.1	7.9	10.0	11.6	16.5
FIRST COMMUNITY BK	MILTON	WI	B	B	B	59.6	-4.83	9.3	3.9	28.3	16.1	5.1	7.4	11.1
FIRST COMMUNITY BK LEWIS	VANCEBURG	KY	C	C	C	29.5	-2.64	2.1	18.1	24.8	34.3	6.8	8.8	14.5
FIRST COMMUNITY BK NA	OLNEY	IL	B	B	B-	132.5	-5.17	7.6	6.0	18.0	17.0	10.0	14.3	24.3
FIRST COMMUNITY BK NA	LEXINGTON	SC	B-	B-	B-	231.7	12.60	5.4	2.5	12.3	26.1	5.3	7.3	11.8
▼ FIRST COMMUNITY BK NA	HOUSTON	TX	C-	C	C	543.6	23.92	15.8	4.4	5.0	18.7	3.5	7.2	10.2
▼ FIRST COMMUNITY BK NA	BLUEFIELD	VA	B+	A-	B	1,842.3	8.75	5.1	6.7	21.9	24.5	4.5	6.5	10.8
FIRST COMMUNITY BK OF	ROGERSVILLE	TN	C+	B-	B	195.4	6.41	9.6	2.6	19.8	11.2	3.5	8.0	10.2
▲ FIRST COMMUNITY BK OF	ROBERTA	GA	C+	C	D+	59.9	2.56	7.0	6.4	16.1	11.8	9.7	10.9	14.7
FIRST COMMUNITY BK OF SW	FORT MYERS	FL	C	C-	D	194.8	66.73	9.4	1.3	14.0	2.5	3.2	9.8	10.1
FIRST COMMUNITY BK OF	TIFTON	GA	B-	B-	B	232.0	4.86	20.1	8.0	16.2	16.4	3.6	7.4	10.3
▲ FIRST COMMUNITY BK SA NA	SAN ANTONIO	TX	D+	D	E+	17.3	-68.29	13.7	1.7	0.7	19.5	10.0	36.3	43.6
▲ FIRST COMMUNITY NB	CUBA	MO	B+	B	A-	131.7	1.46	1.3	4.7	27.0	28.9	8.9	10.3	15.9
FIRST COMMUNITY ST BK	STAUNTON	IL	C+	C+	D+	37.5	-1.72	16.3	3.4	16.3	7.4	7.8	9.7	13.2
FIRST CONSTITUTION BK	CRANBURY	NJ	B+	B+	B	325.2	14.94	10.4	0.9	8.5	31.1	8.2	9.8	13.9
▲ FIRST CONSUMERS NB	LAKE OSWEGO	OR	B	B-	C+	66.1	1.64	0.0	0.0	0.0	27.7	10.0	26.0	124.6
▲ FIRST CORNERSTONE BK	KING OF PRUSSIA	PA	C-	D	D	91.6	29.17	11.6	0.3	20.3	24.2	10.0	11.2	17.7
FIRST COUNTY BANK	NEW BADEN	IL	B-	B-	B-	326.6	16.79	1.0	4.8	47.0	20.9	4.9	6.9	12.6
FIRST COUNTY BK	STAMFORD	CT	A-	B+	B+	936.4	7.94	4.2	1.0	41.9	18.8	8.5	10.0	15.2
▼ FIRST CRAWFORD ST BK	ROBINSON	IL	B+	B+	B+	105.5	5.09	12.5	15.7	18.2	18.9	10.0	11.4	16.7
FIRST CREDIT BK	LOS ANGELES	CA	B-	B-	C-	367.6	6.73	0.7	0.0	3.5	7.0	10.0	16.4	19.9
FIRST DAKOTA NB	YANKTON	SD	C	C	C	487.9	8.22	15.2	5.0	6.2	5.8	4.3	8.4	10.7
FIRST DELTA BK	MARKED TREE	AR	C	C	D+	46.6	7.79	3.6	4.2	12.3	42.1	10.0	11.2	22.4
▲ FIRST DUPAGE BK	WESTMONT	IL	C-	D+	D	178.8	44.53	13.5	0.7	6.1	12.8	4.3	8.8	10.7
FIRST EAGLE NB	HANOVER PARK	IL	A	A	A-	243.1	-1.91	6.5	0.3	11.6	15.7	9.3	12.3	14.4
▼ FIRST EAST SIDE SAVINGS	CHICAGO	IL	C+	B	B	123.1	30.05	0.1	0.0	13.9	27.3	8.4	10.0	16.2
FIRST ELECTRONIC BK	DRAPER	UT	D	D	D	6.9	49.20	0.3	0.0	0.0	0.7	10.0	36.8	142.8
FIRST ENTERPRISE BK	OKLAHOMA CITY	OK	D-	D-	D-	145.7	-9.18	20.8	3.2	12.3	4.4	6.9	9.0	12.6
FIRST EXCHANGE BK	MANNINGTON	WV	C	C	D+	121.8	6.83	4.8	19.6	36.1	8.8	3.4	6.7	10.2
FIRST FARMERS & MERCH ST	BROWNSDALE	MN	B	B	B	63.6	-2.71	12.1	2.6	5.6	16.9	7.6	11.0	13.0
FIRST FARMERS & MERCH ST	GRAND MEADOW	MN	B	B	B	26.8	0.52	13.8	1.2	3.7	12.4	7.3	10.6	12.8
FIRST FARMERS &	FAIRMONT	MN	B	B	B	55.6	14.21	22.2	5.3	11.7	5.4	4.1	9.3	10.6
FIRST FARMERS &	LE SUEUR	MN	B	B	B	85.9	-0.05	14.1	3.1	9.6	15.3	7.4	10.1	12.8
FIRST FARMERS &	LUVERNE	MN	B+	B+	B+	101.2	-0.14	13.6	2.9	3.6	18.6	8.8	10.3	14.0
▲ FIRST FARMERS &	COLUMBIA	TN	B	B-	B	833.7	-3.48	4.9	2.8	19.4	39.3	9.7	10.8	19.6
FIRST FARMERS B&T	CONVERSE	IN	B	B	B	419.2	7.04	10.0	2.7	12.2	15.7	6.0	8.8	11.8
FIRST FARMERS B&TC	OWENTON	KY	B	B	A-	69.2	5.13	15.1	4.9	30.8	5.8	10.0	14.3	20.7
▲ FIRST FARMERS NB OF	WAURIKA	OK	A-	B+	B+	36.0	-8.64	4.1	4.1	6.2	34.5	10.0	20.0	47.1
▲ FIRST FARMERS ST BK	MINIER	IL	B-	C+	C	78.8	-1.45	6.9	1.0	9.9	23.7	6.9	8.9	12.4
FIRST FARMERS ST BK	SULLIVAN	IN	B	B	B	183.1	0.62	4.7	4.5	28.4	22.9	9.0	10.3	16.6
FIRST FED CMTY BK OF	BUCYRUS	OH	B	B	B	121.8	-0.56	3.4	3.7	63.5	11.6	9.7	10.8	19.7
FIRST FEDERAL BANK	DUNN	NC	B	B-	B-	169.4	6.92	7.3	5.5	32.7	5.2	8.5	10.0	15.0
▲ FIRST FEDERAL BANK FSB	TUSCALOOSA	AL	C-	D	D-	108.0	3.78	0.6	0.9	54.7	3.3	7.7	9.5	13.3
▲ FIRST FEDERAL BANK FSB	BERESFORD	SD	C-	D+	D	40.0	0.89	7.0	5.1	12.7	31.4	9.6	10.8	15.6
▼ FIRST FEDERAL BANK OF CA	SANTA MONICA	CA	B+	A-	B+	5,532.0	24.12	1.0	0.0	53.9	7.1	5.4	7.4	14.6
▲ FIRST FEDERAL BK	FORT PAYNE	AL	C-	D+	D+	77.0	2.84	7.8	6.2	24.6	26.5	5.5	7.5	17.8
FIRST FEDERAL BK	SIOUX CITY	IA	C-	D+	C-	595.0	-1.94	4.8	9.5	30.8	17.5	6.0	8.0	11.9

Asset Quality Index	Non-Performing Loans as a % of Total Loans	Non-Performing Loans as a % of Capital	Net Charge-offs Avg Loans	Profitability Index	Net Income ($Mil)	Return on Assets (R.O.A.)	Return on Equity (R.O.E.)	Net Interest Spread	Overhead Efficiency Ratio	Liquidity Index	Liquidity Ratio	Hot Money Ratio	Stability Index
4.7	0.56	4.7	1.30	1.2	-0.2	-0.64	-8.11	4.40	93.2	2.0	41.8	42.1	0.0
7.3	0.18	1.5	0.43	5.8	1.0	1.03	14.11	4.75	64.7	5.9	81.4	13.4	3.4
4.3	1.42	7.1	-0.19	6.9	0.4	1.64	13.63	3.88	57.3	4.8	29.5	6.8	6.1
7.7	0.02	0.1	0.00	8.4	1.0	1.62	17.60	4.49	51.9	4.0	31.1	12.0	5.7
10.0	0.00	0.0	0.00	0.0	-0.6	-6.91	-7.26	0.08	9,242.9	10.0	2,640.7	0.0	0.0
8.9	0.00	0.0	-0.01	5.2	0.2	1.08	13.30	3.62	66.3	5.8	107.3	15.5	2.5
6.3	0.09	0.8	0.10	6.6	1.0	1.06	12.17	3.95	49.2	3.1	43.8	21.2	5.2
7.2	0.36	1.9	-0.05	5.6	0.4	1.31	10.07	4.48	63.0	2.0	14.2	19.0	5.6
4.0	0.70	5.6	0.31	9.1	1.2	1.35	14.08	5.19	61.3	1.6	19.5	24.7	6.3
4.7	0.81	6.2	0.52	9.3	0.3	2.45	29.77	5.42	52.8	3.7	9.1	10.0	5.1
8.2	0.00	0.0	0.02	10.0	1.1	2.49	29.90	4.85	43.4	5.6	47.1	7.4	6.0
8.8	0.00	0.0	0.08	8.0	0.3	2.03	23.49	4.79	53.3	3.7	14.3	10.4	5.7
4.6	0.50	3.3	0.04	3.5	0.3	0.83	8.93	4.08	72.8	4.9	52.2	12.6	3.4
5.7	0.51	5.8	0.04	4.3	1.2	0.67	9.90	4.42	77.2	1.9	15.6	19.8	2.3
5.1	0.64	4.8	0.70	4.0	0.8	0.81	10.22	4.44	72.4	3.5	13.4	11.4	3.0
4.7	0.75	5.4	-0.09	7.6	0.9	1.22	13.76	4.68	61.2	4.0	15.1	8.6	5.7
6.1	0.00	0.0	0.09	5.2	0.6	1.26	11.55	4.43	69.8	3.9	36.9	14.6	6.4
8.6	0.00	0.0	0.00	1.2	0.0	-0.06	-0.50	3.73	99.1	4.1	38.9	14.2	5.6
4.3	1.26	11.4	-0.05	9.0	0.7	2.30	31.87	4.35	53.5	4.5	30.8	9.4	5.6
4.2	1.52	8.9	0.26	7.8	0.2	1.37	14.77	5.84	60.5	1.8	24.8	23.7	4.5
5.3	1.80	6.2	0.20	4.0	0.5	0.74	5.02	3.52	71.6	7.4	130.5	10.1	6.4
8.7	0.15	1.1	0.08	4.9	0.9	0.79	10.59	3.98	69.9	3.4	44.1	19.3	3.8
4.4	0.72	5.0	0.36	3.8	1.2	0.48	5.14	4.91	81.6	1.9	14.9	19.5	3.4
7.5	0.25	1.6	0.28	8.9	10.1	1.55	14.89	4.46	55.0	4.8	45.5	14.8	8.1
8.1	0.11	1.0	0.11	6.9	1.1	1.18	15.14	4.02	56.5	1.3	10.1	25.3	4.7
8.1	0.17	1.1	0.36	4.1	0.3	0.93	8.59	4.68	71.9	2.3	28.9	19.9	3.4
3.7	0.87	8.0	0.00	8.2	1.1	1.30	15.55	4.82	49.3	3.5	49.8	20.4	4.6
4.9	0.47	4.5	0.44	10.0	1.9	1.65	22.36	4.60	45.3	2.2	17.7	18.2	6.2
7.5	0.00	0.0	0.00	1.4	-0.1	-0.58	-4.15	0.41	356.9	5.8	247.5	30.5	2.4
8.2	0.39	2.2	0.07	6.1	1.0	1.56	15.11	4.37	62.7	3.2	26.5	14.3	6.4
8.4	0.00	0.0	0.00	5.6	0.1	0.78	8.06	4.01	70.5	6.7	103.6	10.5	4.0
8.5	0.22	1.5	0.00	7.4	1.9	1.25	13.15	4.28	60.6	4.7	9.1	3.3	5.4
10.0	0.00	0.0	0.00	4.2	0.2	0.55	2.12	4.45	53.5	7.7	187.0	13.0	6.8
8.8	0.00	0.0	0.00	2.0	0.2	0.49	4.21	3.19	80.8	3.5	46.3	18.7	1.0
8.9	0.00	0.0	-0.01	7.9	2.0	1.26	17.78	3.13	47.2	4.5	31.5	9.8	4.9
6.7	0.83	5.7	0.01	6.6	5.1	1.16	11.75	4.05	59.8	6.3	64.1	8.9	6.8
6.9	0.56	3.0	0.12	9.2	0.8	1.59	13.72	4.54	50.5	4.6	55.6	15.9	7.5
3.6	3.68	15.9	0.00	10.0	7.5	4.08	26.07	5.04	22.4	2.1	46.8	60.3	10.0
3.1	1.45	12.0	0.24	5.0	2.1	0.87	9.43	5.07	75.5	3.8	26.4	11.3	5.1
6.0	1.31	5.1	-0.04	6.2	0.3	1.44	13.21	4.87	56.5	3.5	61.7	23.5	2.7
4.9	0.73	6.4	0.23	3.0	0.5	0.55	6.28	3.72	67.3	1.6	7.0	21.3	3.3
7.2	0.70	3.9	0.00	9.1	1.9	1.62	12.32	4.96	50.5	1.3	7.2	24.8	8.5
9.0	0.00	0.0	0.07	3.0	0.1	0.09	0.86	2.64	94.3	3.5	64.2	29.6	1.8
10.0	0.00	0.0	0.00	0.0	-1.7	-54.14	-136.35	0.64	744.8	7.8	188.6	12.6	0.0
0.3	9.66	78.1	1.66	4.2	0.7	0.89	10.02	4.52	71.2	4.1	61.3	19.8	4.9
7.5	0.03	0.3	0.07	4.6	0.4	0.69	10.36	4.22	68.2	3.6	21.0	11.8	3.7
7.9	0.00	0.0	0.02	7.2	0.3	0.90	7.67	4.92	64.6	3.1	19.4	13.7	6.3
5.4	1.15	7.9	0.58	8.0	0.2	1.08	9.93	4.97	56.5	1.3	29.1	36.5	6.2
5.9	0.36	3.2	-0.06	8.5	0.4	1.57	17.46	4.80	58.8	3.7	49.8	18.1	5.6
2.5	1.93	9.1	0.65	4.0	0.2	0.48	3.40	4.74	70.5	3.9	44.7	16.2	5.8
8.0	0.00	0.0	0.00	8.0	0.6	1.22	11.31	4.62	64.3	3.4	15.7	12.0	6.8
4.7	1.64	6.3	0.32	5.2	4.6	1.12	9.12	4.00	75.6	5.7	50.8	9.1	7.5
6.5	0.32	2.3	0.17	8.5	2.9	1.43	14.32	4.46	54.6	2.2	22.7	18.7	6.1
5.1	1.88	9.6	0.41	8.6	0.4	1.26	8.63	4.69	55.3	4.0	17.5	8.9	7.7
8.1	1.53	2.8	-0.21	8.4	0.4	2.05	10.43	4.47	52.3	6.3	165.4	17.9	7.4
5.5	0.65	4.0	-0.19	6.6	0.6	1.46	14.84	4.15	70.4	3.6	7.8	10.4	4.8
4.3	1.97	11.2	0.52	6.3	1.1	1.14	10.84	3.34	54.4	4.8	36.2	9.9	6.9
5.2	1.00	7.1	0.20	5.3	0.5	0.77	7.16	3.41	65.1	2.0	24.2	20.3	6.0
6.1	0.24	1.8	0.12	4.9	0.6	0.72	7.19	4.20	72.1	0.8	13.4	36.4	6.0
8.1	0.12	1.1	0.01	2.7	0.5	0.91	9.43	3.13	87.2	0.5	10.8	62.6	4.3
3.4	2.23	12.0	0.43	3.1	0.1	0.69	6.39	3.55	74.3	1.7	17.3	22.9	4.4
8.5	0.03	0.3	-0.01	9.1	31.7	1.22	15.01	3.06	35.8	0.4	2.5	51.4	7.7
6.3	0.67	4.2	0.17	4.3	0.2	0.54	7.13	3.33	73.9	3.2	70.1	31.6	3.3
2.4	1.00	8.4	0.51	4.6	2.6	0.84	7.98	3.12	65.8	1.9	10.4	19.2	6.4

Name	City	State	Weiss Safety Rating	2003 Weiss Safety Rating	2002 Weiss Safety Rating	Total Assets ($Mil)	One Year Asset Growth	Asset Mix (As a % of Total Assets)				Capital-ization Index	Leverage Ratio	Risk-based Capital Ratio
								Comm-ercial Loans	Cons-umer Loans	Home Mort-gages	Secur-ities			
FIRST FEDERAL BK	COLCHESTER	IL	B	B	B+	301.7	-8.86	2.5	3.6	26.0	49.8	5.6	7.6	19.1
FIRST FEDERAL BK	BEMIDJI	MN	B-	B-	B-	156.8	0.24	1.4	18.7	20.2	39.8	6.1	8.1	15.2
FIRST FEDERAL BK	ROSWELL	NM	B	B	B	361.2	0.39	2.8	2.3	35.8	13.8	5.9	7.9	14.3
▲ FIRST FEDERAL BK	HAZLETON	PA	C-	D+	C	872.1	0.64	4.2	13.8	17.5	44.6	4.8	6.8	13.7
▲ FIRST FEDERAL BK FOR SVGS	COLUMBIA	MS	C-	D+	C	142.4	1.79	9.1	14.5	21.0	8.1	6.2	8.2	12.2
FIRST FEDERAL BK FSB	KANSAS CITY	MO	B	B	B	433.3	-9.08	0.0	0.6	62.2	11.6	10.0	11.8	20.5
FIRST FEDERAL BK MIDWEST	DEFIANCE	OH	A-	A-	B	1,051.9	2.35	12.4	4.0	17.7	14.4	7.3	9.2	12.9
FIRST FEDERAL BK OF AR FA	HARRISON	AR	B	B	B+	712.3	1.98	2.9	4.4	40.1	10.0	8.8	10.2	15.0
▼ FIRST FEDERAL BK OF LA	LAKE CHARLES	LA	B	A-	A-	512.0	0.10	0.3	1.8	30.9	50.5	10.0	13.4	39.5
FIRST FEDERAL BK OF N FL	PALATKA	FL	C+	C	C	249.7	7.75	1.8	5.5	44.4	10.0	6.3	8.3	13.8
FIRST FEDERAL BK OF OHIO	GALION	OH	B+	A-	A	236.0	-6.02	6.0	8.5	29.1	18.9	10.0	14.1	26.4
FIRST FEDERAL CAPITAL	LA CROSSE	WI	B-	B-	C+	3,613.8	15.05	4.9	10.7	27.9	17.5	4.1	6.1	11.3
FIRST FEDERAL COMMUNITY	DOVER	OH	B+	A-	B+	135.6	-0.11	11.5	2.0	29.7	4.0	10.0	11.7	17.4
FIRST FEDERAL COMMUNITY	PARIS	TX	C	C	C	274.1	-4.95	4.3	7.8	58.2	7.7	6.1	8.1	13.8
FIRST FEDERAL FSB	HUTCHINSON	MN	C-	C-	C-	505.0	-5.78	11.6	4.8	7.3	13.9	7.3	9.2	13.8
▼ FIRST FEDERAL OF	ALPENA	MI	C-	C+	C+	253.2	10.85	10.8	2.5	43.6	18.6	4.0	6.7	10.5
FIRST FEDERAL OF SC FSB	WALTERBORO	SC	D	D+	C	96.8	-0.16	3.2	6.3	30.2	15.3	8.0	9.7	18.0
FIRST FEDERAL OF THE	SYLACAUGA	AL	C-	C	B-	138.5	-0.89	2.0	2.7	35.3	21.3	7.4	9.2	15.3
▲ FIRST FEDERAL SB CRESTON	CRESTON	IA	B+	B	B+	50.5	-0.78	1.2	3.4	27.4	40.6	10.0	11.8	32.1
▼ FIRST FEDERAL SVGS	MIDDLETOWN	NY	A-	A	A+	182.5	-0.14	1.5	0.0	8.1	31.2	10.0	25.9	78.7
▼ FIRST FIDELITY BK	BURKE	SD	A	A+	A+	213.0	-2.69	5.7	6.9	2.3	48.4	10.0	13.7	24.1
▲ FIRST FIDELITY BK NA	OKLAHOMA CITY	OK	B	C+	C+	630.2	9.59	7.7	22.7	10.9	26.5	6.0	8.0	12.2
▲ FIRST FINANCIAL B&TC	PLAQUEMINE	LA	B-	C+	C+	51.8	23.98	0.0	6.8	26.4	54.5	10.0	14.1	34.5
FIRST FINANCIAL BK	BESSEMER	AL	C-	C	C+	208.2	10.88	3.3	3.8	20.9	11.6	5.3	8.6	11.3
▲ FIRST FINANCIAL BK	EL DORADO	AR	C+	C	C	464.0	-0.30	3.6	2.5	4.7	3.1	5.1	7.1	12.0
FIRST FINANCIAL BK	ENGLEWOOD	CO	B+	B+	B-	232.3	-28.81	0.0	0.0	0.0	70.6	10.0	38.8	72.7
▼ FIRST FINANCIAL BK	HARRODSBURG	KY	C	B-	B	132.0	3.06	2.6	0.9	46.0	19.8	10.0	11.2	18.7
FIRST FINANCIAL BK	TWIN VALLEY	MN	B-	B-	B-	12.9	-7.35	8.2	6.1	13.9	23.0	10.0	11.5	19.9
FIRST FINANCIAL BK	DOWNINGTOWN	PA	B	B	B	641.2	10.05	7.7	2.2	21.7	28.1	7.8	9.5	14.1
FIRST FINANCIAL BK NA	TERRE HAUTE	IN	B+	B+	B+	1,665.9	31.20	13.2	11.6	15.2	23.8	10.0	12.0	16.8
FIRST FINANCIAL BK NA	HAMILTON	OH	B-	B-	B+	1,760.4	8.96	10.6	11.4	23.6	15.1	3.3	6.4	10.2
FIRST FINANCIAL BK NA	CLEBURNE	TX	A-	A-	A-	213.5	5.21	12.2	7.0	4.7	43.2	6.8	8.9	15.3
FIRST FINANCIAL BK NA	SOUTHLAKE	TX	A-	A-	A-	77.0	5.24	16.5	4.0	19.2	13.9	6.2	8.5	11.9
▲ FIRST FINANCIAL BK USA	DAKOTA DUNES	SD	C+	C	C	216.7	-1.60	1.2	34.4	0.2	18.3	9.5	20.1	14.6
FIRST FLORIDA BK	NAPLES	FL	C	C	E+	219.7	57.70	8.6	0.6	2.2	3.3	3.0	10.7	10.0
FIRST FS&LA	SAN RAFAEL	CA	A	A-	B+	191.4	-0.23	0.0	0.0	7.7	0.0	10.0	13.1	16.0
▲ FIRST FS&LA	TWIN FALLS	ID	B	B-	B-	331.4	4.41	5.1	3.4	58.0	4.8	6.8	8.8	15.1
▲ FIRST FS&LA	INDEPENDENCE	KS	B	B-	B-	166.1	4.82	0.1	2.4	45.0	25.1	6.9	8.9	17.4
▼ FIRST FS&LA	HAZARD	KY	B	A-	A	139.8	2.51	0.0	2.5	21.2	62.0	10.0	22.4	82.0
FIRST FS&LA	LEXINGTON	KY	B	B	B	129.7	-4.76	0.3	0.3	57.5	9.7	10.0	18.7	30.5
FIRST FS&LA	MOREHEAD	KY	B-	B-	B-	39.0	0.04	0.0	1.8	57.9	16.6	10.0	19.7	36.8
▼ FIRST FS&LA	OPELOUSAS	LA	C-	C	C-	66.8	-8.48	0.1	3.7	63.5	18.1	8.7	10.2	17.4
FIRST FS&LA	ABERDEEN	MS	C+	C+	C+	23.8	3.30	0.0	1.5	54.1	33.9	10.0	17.7	46.1
▲ FIRST FS&LA	PASCAGOULA	MS	C-	D+	C-	231.3	0.53	0.0	0.9	70.8	11.8	5.2	7.2	14.6
FIRST FS&LA	DELTA	OH	A	A	A+	146.3	-9.36	1.4	2.0	69.2	4.8	10.0	19.0	39.7
FIRST FS&LA	LAKEWOOD	OH	B	B	B	1,070.4	-0.16	1.2	0.2	55.7	25.4	9.2	10.5	21.0
FIRST FS&LA	NEWARK	OH	A-	A-	A-	189.9	-0.48	0.0	0.3	58.0	3.3	10.0	14.0	23.9
FIRST FS&LA	TYLER	TX	C	C	C+	230.2	5.89	1.5	8.6	31.6	39.2	5.7	7.7	14.7
▲ FIRST FS&LA OF ALLEN	OAKDALE	LA	D+	D	D-	49.5	-3.47	3.7	4.1	24.7	36.9	7.5	9.3	18.3
▼ FIRST FS&LA OF BATH	BATH	ME	B-	B	B	115.8	6.01	1.8	0.8	48.9	15.5	10.0	11.7	26.8
FIRST FS&LA OF BUCKS CTY	BRISTOL	PA	B	B	B+	484.9	3.33	0.6	0.3	51.8	35.9	9.9	11.0	20.1
FIRST FS&LA OF	CENTERBURG	OH	C+	C+	C+	25.2	-5.80	0.0	0.9	50.8	22.4	10.0	12.3	29.0
FIRST FS&LA OF	CHARLESTON	SC	B-	B-	B-	2,399.7	7.06	2.4	10.1	41.4	15.8	5.0	7.0	11.5
▲ FIRST FS&LA OF CULLMAN	CULLMAN	AL	B+	B	B	66.4	8.19	4.1	2.4	33.5	21.4	10.0	11.6	25.5
▲ FIRST FS&LA OF	EDWARDSVILLE	IL	A+	A	A	135.1	15.25	0.0	0.6	66.9	6.0	10.0	19.9	41.5
FIRST FS&LA OF GREENE CTY	WAYNESBURG	PA	B+	B+	B+	589.3	0.24	0.0	2.1	65.4	21.6	10.0	14.4	29.9
FIRST FS&LA OF	GREENSBURG	IN	B-	B-	B	88.3	15.11	2.7	3.1	59.6	12.7	7.5	9.3	16.5
▼ FIRST FS&LA OF HAMMOND	HAMMOND	IN	C	C+	C+	40.4	4.91	0.0	0.1	71.4	10.1	8.7	10.2	22.4
▲ FIRST FS&LA OF KEWANEE	KEWANEE	IL	B-	C+	C	80.9	-0.55	0.0	0.4	52.8	34.8	10.0	12.2	32.7
FIRST FS&LA OF LITTLEFIELD	LITTLEFIELD	TX	B-	B-	B-	39.0	1.91	19.0	7.1	16.0	18.5	10.0	15.9	33.2
FIRST FS&LA OF LORAIN	LORAIN	OH	B+	B+	B+	390.7	1.91	0.0	0.5	53.5	14.9	10.0	13.5	26.7
FIRST FS&LA OF	MARTINSVILLE	VA	B	B	B-	53.0	-7.87	0.0	0.4	38.8	46.1	10.0	16.0	47.1
FIRST FS&LA OF MATTOON	MATTOON	IL	B+	B+	B+	73.2	-5.85	0.0	0.6	24.7	56.1	10.0	22.2	68.3
FIRST FS&LA OF MCMINNVILLE	MCMINNVILLE	OR	A	A	A	271.1	3.62	0.0	3.5	45.6	27.7	10.0	14.1	29.1

Asset Quality Index	Non-Performing Loans as a % of Total Loans	Non-Performing Loans as a % of Capital	Net Charge-offs Avg Loans	Profitability Index	Net Income ($Mil)	Return on Assets (R.O.A.)	Return on Equity (R.O.E.)	Net Interest Spread	Overhead Efficiency Ratio	Liquidity Index	Liquidity Ratio	Hot Money Ratio	Stability Index
6.2	1.14	6.8	0.06	4.9	1.1	0.67	7.57	2.72	66.0	2.9	19.7	15.1	5.8
7.2	0.15	1.0	0.20	5.1	0.6	0.83	10.18	3.06	69.2	2.2	32.7	25.2	4.3
8.0	0.07	0.6	0.02	5.8	1.4	0.76	9.72	3.47	68.6	2.4	45.2	33.5	5.1
2.5	1.84	11.7	1.06	3.6	3.3	0.76	10.04	2.74	62.2	0.7	6.1	34.3	3.7
2.3	1.87	14.2	1.00	4.4	0.4	0.61	7.61	3.59	74.5	1.5	32.0	36.3	3.9
8.1	0.18	1.2	0.00	3.7	0.9	0.42	3.59	2.76	80.9	3.9	6.7	8.4	5.8
6.7	0.35	2.7	0.06	6.0	5.4	1.04	9.34	3.43	59.0	1.1	13.5	30.9	9.4
5.0	0.47	3.7	0.14	6.6	3.8	1.08	10.46	3.73	60.1	1.5	17.7	24.6	7.0
9.4	0.23	0.7	0.03	3.9	0.8	0.32	2.44	2.64	84.2	2.0	7.5	18.3	8.7
3.7	1.13	10.4	-0.01	5.5	1.3	1.10	12.60	4.46	62.0	1.5	13.5	24.5	2.8
6.2	0.81	2.9	0.00	4.7	0.9	0.72	5.29	3.13	71.9	2.8	39.4	21.8	7.6
5.6	0.34	3.9	0.16	7.5	20.0	1.11	13.01	3.42	62.9	1.6	4.7	20.3	6.8
6.7	0.65	4.5	0.33	4.3	0.4	0.56	4.75	3.29	74.5	1.5	19.1	25.5	7.0
4.9	0.48	4.6	-0.02	4.7	1.1	0.75	9.73	3.96	67.9	1.5	2.8	20.2	2.7
2.2	2.02	16.5	0.66	6.3	2.0	0.79	8.22	3.91	65.9	1.2	13.2	28.7	5.5
3.7	1.00	10.1	0.06	2.8	0.2	0.19	2.12	3.14	90.6	1.8	24.4	22.4	4.3
1.4	5.02	30.6	0.07	4.8	0.3	0.67	6.98	3.49	76.1	3.8	33.3	13.6	4.5
3.8	0.92	6.5	2.39	1.7	-0.6	-0.87	-8.89	3.59	92.8	2.2	43.4	37.1	4.9
9.5	0.00	0.0	0.00	4.4	0.3	0.95	8.44	2.87	69.3	4.7	49.5	13.1	6.8
8.8	0.10	0.1	0.00	5.1	0.5	0.58	2.21	2.55	79.0	5.0	112.7	23.2	8.3
6.6	1.52	5.2	0.29	10.0	3.4	3.16	23.68	14.08	77.8	5.0	37.9	9.1	9.5
4.9	0.40	2.5	0.27	7.3	5.3	1.72	17.77	4.38	64.0	6.6	53.0	3.9	7.4
7.1	1.70	4.5	0.13	4.8	0.2	0.78	5.02	2.91	79.5	0.8	5.4	32.2	6.3
4.6	1.55	11.7	0.26	2.2	0.3	0.29	3.19	3.24	80.2	2.8	21.6	15.7	3.6
3.7	0.42	4.4	0.05	6.3	4.5	1.95	27.07	4.31	58.9	1.0	16.5	33.0	3.9
10.0	0.00	0.0	0.00	7.1	2.1	1.92	4.04	1.27	19.0	9.7	2,115.5	2.0	4.2
6.4	0.52	2.7	0.00	2.6	-0.4	-0.54	-4.01	3.16	125.7	2.0	7.7	18.3	7.4
7.8	1.03	4.2	0.00	4.0	0.0	0.52	4.60	4.04	79.9	7.2	74.3	0.9	5.2
5.3	1.05	6.4	0.03	4.9	3.1	1.00	10.59	3.58	65.7	7.1	77.3	5.9	4.2
4.9	1.86	9.4	0.40	8.3	14.3	1.86	15.57	3.88	52.2	4.5	32.7	13.0	7.6
5.5	0.61	7.4	0.32	9.1	12.6	1.46	27.45	3.99	53.9	2.3	16.2	18.0	5.7
8.0	0.09	0.5	0.16	9.7	1.8	1.70	18.28	4.50	56.1	4.8	32.2	7.7	7.6
5.4	0.74	6.4	-0.05	5.2	0.4	1.02	12.07	5.22	74.0	2.5	11.7	16.4	7.1
3.6	3.47	5.4	8.46	10.0	2.3	2.03	9.85	30.21	81.4	8.4	582.5	10.5	8.0
4.8	0.28	2.2	0.00	6.8	1.2	1.21	12.08	5.62	55.8	3.3	38.1	18.1	5.9
7.0	0.03	0.2	0.00	8.4	1.0	1.05	8.09	4.49	59.9	0.8	5.5	32.0	7.9
8.2	0.13	1.2	0.07	4.8	1.2	0.75	8.60	3.63	70.8	1.4	15.4	25.9	5.1
5.5	0.90	6.6	0.01	5.3	0.6	0.77	8.46	3.19	62.8	2.9	44.2	24.3	5.7
8.2	3.42	3.6	0.24	3.8	0.2	0.31	1.34	2.60	77.6	4.8	106.1	24.3	7.8
7.4	0.36	1.5	-0.02	3.9	0.4	0.55	2.87	3.96	84.9	2.3	15.6	17.6	7.8
5.1	1.62	5.1	0.00	5.7	0.2	1.02	4.63	3.88	59.2	3.1	8.8	12.9	6.6
4.6	1.00	6.8	0.44	2.1	0.0	-0.12	-1.07	2.89	94.0	1.2	2.2	25.8	4.1
8.2	0.16	0.5	0.00	7.1	0.1	1.07	5.67	3.53	51.0	4.1	51.1	14.5	5.0
5.2	0.71	7.3	0.10	2.9	0.5	0.48	6.57	2.34	81.9	1.0	14.4	32.3	2.6
9.3	0.06	0.2	0.00	7.2	0.9	1.18	6.47	4.41	60.5	3.8	31.3	13.3	8.2
6.9	0.99	6.3	0.00	4.4	2.6	0.49	4.67	2.13	67.6	1.1	5.2	28.5	7.9
6.3	1.74	9.9	0.00	6.2	0.9	0.91	6.56	3.78	65.8	1.0	21.1	34.2	7.9
3.6	1.48	10.0	0.88	4.0	0.5	0.43	4.89	2.91	68.7	1.1	5.5	27.4	3.8
2.0	7.74	35.5	-0.10	3.7	0.1	0.51	5.78	3.27	83.2	4.2	16.5	7.8	3.6
5.9	1.04	5.0	0.01	3.6	0.2	0.34	2.64	3.50	84.8	3.2	44.9	21.1	7.3
8.1	0.07	0.4	0.00	4.1	1.0	0.42	3.59	2.31	76.4	3.4	28.1	14.3	6.7
8.5	0.38	1.9	0.00	4.1	0.1	0.63	5.37	2.84	66.8	4.8	35.0	9.4	4.9
5.8	0.46	4.7	0.33	7.0	12.4	1.03	15.19	3.55	56.9	1.1	8.6	29.1	6.4
8.3	0.01	0.0	-0.16	5.1	0.3	0.83	7.20	3.35	69.5	2.7	53.3	31.7	6.2
9.0	0.12	0.4	0.00	9.7	1.0	1.50	8.81	3.63	32.1	1.7	26.1	24.9	8.4
6.6	0.71	3.1	0.00	4.6	2.4	0.80	5.05	2.89	65.6	1.6	14.6	22.2	8.7
9.2	0.03	0.3	0.00	5.0	0.3	0.74	7.90	3.43	65.3	1.1	20.8	32.9	4.7
6.4	0.37	2.6	0.00	4.0	0.1	0.54	5.04	3.50	73.0	0.9	23.0	36.1	4.7
6.2	1.80	7.9	0.00	3.4	0.2	0.50	4.21	3.27	80.1	4.6	32.5	9.5	6.0
8.4	0.31	1.0	-0.11	3.5	0.1	0.42	2.65	3.30	82.6	3.2	42.2	19.4	6.3
5.7	1.49	7.2	0.11	4.8	1.4	0.72	5.35	3.36	71.0	3.0	41.5	20.7	7.5
5.9	5.52	14.0	0.00	4.8	0.2	0.78	5.12	2.68	54.6	2.9	49.0	25.7	6.5
8.8	2.25	2.7	0.00	5.0	0.3	0.82	3.75	3.14	60.2	4.7	52.8	13.5	6.6
8.4	0.45	2.0	0.01	7.2	1.3	0.96	6.86	3.83	60.5	2.9	39.9	22.0	8.3

| Name | City | State | Weiss Safety Rating | 2003 Weiss Safety Rating | 2002 Weiss Safety Rating | Total Assets ($Mil) | One Year Asset Growth | Asset Mix (As a % of Total Assets) | | | | Capital-ization Index | Leverage Ratio | Risk-based Capital Ratio |
								Comm-ercial Loans	Cons-umer Loans	Home Mort-gages	Secur-ities			
FIRST FS&LA OF OLATHE	OLATHE	KS	A-	A-	A	46.0	-5.85	0.0	0.0	78.8	6.1	10.0	24.2	49.5
▲ FIRST FS&LA OF PEKIN	PEKIN	IL	D-	E	E-	33.1	-3.03	1.2	2.7	47.4	24.5	5.4	7.4	13.9
▲ FIRST FS&LA OF PORT	PORT ANGELES	WA	B	B-	B-	745.9	7.23	0.4	1.6	56.4	24.8	6.0	8.0	17.3
FIRST FS&LA OF	RAVENSWOOD	WV	D+	D+	D	7.0	7.23	0.0	0.4	70.7	12.7	10.0	14.8	31.3
▲ FIRST FS&LA OF SHELBYVILLE	SHELBYVILLE	IL	C-	D+	C-	25.2	5.64	1.2	8.7	43.1	27.5	9.3	10.5	24.7
FIRST FS&LA OF VALDOSTA	VALDOSTA	GA	B	B	B+	153.4	-3.15	0.1	6.4	62.1	6.7	10.0	15.7	26.0
FIRST FS&LA OF VAN WERT	VAN WERT	OH	A-	B+	B+	112.1	0.02	0.0	0.4	36.2	40.8	10.0	13.5	31.5
FIRST FS&LA OF WAKEENEY	WAKEENEY	KS	C+	C+	C+	31.5	-3.82	0.3	2.7	38.2	29.3	10.0	12.2	26.5
▲ FIRST FS&LA OF	WASHINGTON	IN	B	B-	B-	52.1	-5.47	0.0	2.0	34.5	42.4	10.0	11.7	35.5
FIRST FSB	OTTAWA	IL	C-	D+	D+	427.6	-2.10	0.4	0.8	54.9	8.3	4.7	6.7	13.3
▼ FIRST FSB	EVANSVILLE	IN	C+	B+	B	261.7	40.65	2.0	26.4	28.4	28.8	8.3	9.9	15.1
▲ FIRST FSB	HUNTINGTON	IN	B	C+	D+	224.7	2.40	6.4	6.3	42.8	15.9	10.0	11.3	18.5
▲ FIRST FSB	ROCHESTER	IN	B-	C+	C+	367.4	1.66	0.0	0.7	62.9	0.0	6.8	8.8	12.5
FIRST FSB	ELIZABETHTOWN	KY	B-	B-	NR	689.2	2.67	4.4	6.4	30.3	6.2	5.4	8.3	11.3
▼ FIRST FSB	MORRIS	MN	C	C+	C	104.6	40.34	12.7	17.4	13.5	0.1	3.4	8.8	10.2
FIRST FSB	MONESSEN	PA	D+	D+	C	309.3	4.38	0.4	1.1	37.6	39.2	4.6	6.6	16.6
▲ FIRST FSB	CLARKSVILLE	TN	B-	C	C	243.6	-1.46	1.4	1.7	19.5	21.1	10.0	11.3	20.1
FIRST FSB	DICKSON	TN	B-	B-	B-	311.0	7.91	8.3	10.0	31.0	17.8	4.4	6.4	10.9
FIRST FSB	SISTERSVILLE	WV	B	B	B	47.7	1.70	0.9	1.5	51.8	31.9	10.0	15.1	41.1
FIRST FSB	SHERIDAN	WY	A-	A-	A-	166.2	0.09	0.2	1.5	25.0	58.0	10.0	17.9	52.0
▲ FIRST FSB CHAMPAIGN	CHAMPAIGN	IL	B-	C+	C+	152.3	-6.10	7.1	4.9	36.4	2.6	5.9	7.9	15.1
FIRST FSB OF ANGOLA	ANGOLA	IN	B	B	B	122.1	-1.19	1.6	4.5	54.7	1.0	10.0	11.5	26.2
▲ FIRST FSB OF BOSTON	BOSTON	MA	B	B-	B-	70.5	-31.13	0.0	0.1	44.6	0.1	10.0	19.1	29.9
FIRST FSB OF EASTERN OHIO	ZANESVILLE	OH	C+	C+	B-	258.4	9.20	4.0	20.3	37.9	3.1	3.3	7.0	10.1
FIRST FSB OF FLORIDA	LIVE OAK	FL	B+	B+	B	377.1	5.96	17.7	5.9	31.3	12.1	9.3	10.5	16.0
FIRST FSB OF FRANKFORT	FRANKFORT	KY	A-	A-	A	138.0	-0.30	0.0	0.2	81.4	2.0	10.0	11.9	23.0
FIRST FSB OF IOWA	FORT DODGE	IA	B+	B+	B+	444.7	4.48	0.5	2.5	45.6	4.4	5.3	7.3	11.9
▲ FIRST FSB OF LAKE COUNTY	LEESBURG	FL	B	B-	B-	1,011.1	9.52	3.6	4.3	38.4	7.3	5.9	7.9	11.9
FIRST FSB OF LINCOLNTON	LINCOLNTON	NC	A	A	A	196.3	10.09	0.2	2.2	62.4	11.8	10.0	18.9	32.0
FIRST FSB OF MASCOUTAH	MASCOUTAH	IL	B	B-	C+	77.7	-3.78	0.0	4.5	33.0	56.6	10.0	11.1	27.4
FIRST FSB OF THE GLADES	CLEWISTON	FL	B+	B+	B	112.9	10.30	4.5	5.2	32.0	6.9	5.8	7.8	14.1
▲ FIRST FSB OF THE MIDWEST	STORM LAKE	IA	C+	C	C+	689.3	-1.80	12.9	2.4	6.3	39.7	5.1	7.1	11.7
▲ FIRST FSB OF VIRGINIA	PETERSBURG	VA	B+	B	B-	282.1	10.94	4.5	2.6	41.0	16.3	7.7	9.4	15.6
FIRST FSB OF WABASH	WABASH	IN	C+	C	C	237.6	-0.98	3.5	7.2	29.0	32.8	5.9	7.9	13.6
FIRST FSB OF WISCONSIN	WAUKESHA	WI	B-	B-	B	80.0	-1.16	4.9	0.9	45.7	6.0	10.0	14.4	17.3
▼ FIRST GASTON BK OF NC	GASTONIA	NC	C	C+	B-	208.4	8.94	17.0	2.7	11.1	17.2	4.4	7.8	10.7
FIRST GEORGIA COMMUNITY	JACKSON	GA	C	C	D+	174.7	12.50	7.4	1.5	4.8	11.4	4.7	8.8	10.8
FIRST GUARANTY B&TC	JACKSONVILLE	FL	A	A	A	277.8	3.88	2.9	0.9	18.3	16.3	10.0	14.9	20.6
▲ FIRST GUARANTY BK	MARTIN	KY	A-	B	B	50.0	1.14	6.2	11.1	25.0	39.0	10.0	11.4	23.0
▲ FIRST GUARANTY BK	HAMMOND	LA	B	B-	C+	530.6	12.87	12.0	4.1	14.0	15.5	5.2	9.0	11.2
FIRST GULF BK	FOLEY	AL	B-	B-	B-	306.9	22.82	10.2	2.3	21.7	12.9	4.7	6.7	10.8
▼ FIRST HARRISON BK	CORYDON	IN	C+	B-	A-	411.9	4.68	5.6	4.3	43.1	16.4	6.9	9.0	14.0
▲ FIRST HAWAIIAN BK	HONOLULU	HI	A-	B-	B-	10,016.2	6.91	10.7	8.0	12.2	20.3	9.0	10.3	15.6
▼ FIRST HEIGHTS BANK, A FSB	BLOOMFIELD HILLS	MI	D	D+	D+	0.6	0.00	0.0	0.0	0.0	0.0	3.9	5.9	29.5
▲ FIRST HERITAGE BK	SNOHOMISH	WA	A-	B	B+	110.2	6.25	9.4	2.1	10.6	13.3	10.0	13.5	16.5
FIRST HOME BK	SEMINOLE	FL	B-	B-	B-	73.0	14.96	7.9	1.9	21.2	7.6	7.2	9.2	13.5
FIRST HOME SAVINGS BANK	MOUNTAIN GROVE	MO	B-	B-	B-	260.9	-1.93	4.0	4.1	36.1	16.7	6.6	8.6	14.4
FIRST HOPE BK A NAT BKG	HOPE	NJ	B-	B-	B-	282.9	14.67	3.8	0.8	28.5	18.6	5.9	7.9	12.6
FIRST ILLINOIS BK	E ST LOUIS	IL	A	A-	B+	45.5	-13.98	4.5	9.1	5.5	64.3	9.8	10.9	47.1
▲ FIRST IN BK NA	INDIANAPOLIS	IN	C	C-	C+	2,122.5	-5.03	14.4	1.3	24.6	10.2	5.5	8.3	11.4
FIRST INDEPENDENCE NB	DETROIT	MI	C	C	C	167.7	0.18	5.6	1.2	6.9	39.9	7.1	9.0	20.4
FIRST INDEPENDENT BANK	RUSSELL	MN	C+	C+	C+	137.6	10.39	15.8	10.1	13.1	6.1	3.1	7.7	10.1
▲ FIRST INDEPENDENT BK	AURORA	MO	C+	C-	C-	82.8	8.57	17.4	7.5	17.8	31.9	6.9	8.9	15.6
FIRST INDEPENDENT BK	VANCOUVER	WA	B+	A-	A	677.9	2.53	5.3	1.0	6.2	39.2	10.0	13.6	23.0
FIRST INDEPENDENT BK OF	RENO	NV	B	B	B-	228.0	6.21	10.2	0.8	2.8	19.7	6.4	8.7	12.1
FIRST INDEPENDENT BK	WOOD LAKE	MN	C+	C+	C+	18.9	3.31	2.9	8.9	19.3	17.6	6.6	8.6	13.0
▲ FIRST INDEPENDENT NB	PLANO	TX	C	D+	D	67.9	-3.95	12.9	1.9	8.4	0.3	6.8	10.5	12.4
▼ FIRST INTEGRITY BK NA	STAPLES	MN	D+	D+	D	74.5	-21.16	20.7	4.4	10.0	5.4	6.8	8.8	12.9
▲ FIRST INTERCONTINENTAL BK	DORAVILLE	GA	C	D+	D+	85.3	12.79	4.8	2.1	0.2	11.9	5.4	8.6	11.3
FIRST INTERNATIONAL B&TC	WATFORD CITY	ND	C+	C+	C+	636.5	16.16	16.7	6.4	5.2	16.2	4.0	7.4	10.5
▲ FIRST INTERNATIONAL BK	CHULA VISTA	CA	D+	D-	E-	60.7	14.88	0.8	0.2	8.3	13.3	10.0	17.6	25.9
FIRST INTERNET BK IN	INDIANAPOLIS	IN	C	C	C+	370.7	11.09	0.2	46.7	21.2	30.1	10.0	11.0	15.7
FIRST INTERSTATE BK	BILLINGS	MT	B-	B-	B-	3,978.7	6.87	12.6	12.5	7.9	19.9	4.8	7.6	10.9
▲ FIRST INTL BK	PLANO	TX	C-	D	D	203.0	11.62	7.7	1.8	3.1	0.0	4.0	8.5	10.5

Asset Quality Index	Non-Performing Loans as a % of Total Loans	Non-Performing Loans as a % of Capital	Net Charge-offs Avg Loans	Profitability Index	Net Income ($Mil)	Return on Assets (R.O.A.)	Return on Equity (R.O.E.)	Net Interest Spread	Overhead Efficiency Ratio	Liquidity Index	Liquidity Ratio	Hot Money Ratio	Stability Index
8.6	0.14	0.5	0.00	10.0	0.6	2.65	10.57	5.15	25.1	1.0	9.6	30.3	8.0
5.5	1.93	14.9	0.00	3.3	0.1	0.50	6.88	2.80	83.3	3.7	20.1	10.8	1.3
9.2	0.11	0.9	0.01	5.0	2.3	0.63	7.86	2.57	66.0	0.9	15.4	33.5	5.3
9.7	0.00	0.0	0.00	3.7	0.0	0.64	4.31	3.53	77.7	3.1	14.2	13.1	3.0
5.3	0.50	2.5	0.50	5.3	0.2	1.27	12.24	4.04	68.2	2.5	33.5	20.5	5.0
6.9	0.68	3.4	0.00	4.1	0.4	0.54	3.50	3.10	76.8	1.6	18.2	23.5	7.6
8.6	0.34	1.2	0.00	5.4	0.5	0.84	6.30	3.01	54.4	2.3	18.4	17.7	7.3
8.5	0.50	2.4	0.00	3.7	0.1	0.54	4.49	3.10	78.0	2.4	18.4	17.6	5.0
6.3	2.55	8.6	-0.10	5.2	0.2	0.76	6.88	2.78	55.3	3.7	100.1	39.9	5.0
5.6	0.42	4.9	0.06	3.5	0.9	0.42	6.34	2.67	79.6	2.4	5.9	16.3	3.0
6.4	0.19	1.2	0.19	2.6	-0.3	-0.25	-2.12	2.83	110.7	0.6	10.8	44.1	6.1
5.0	0.81	5.2	-0.12	4.8	0.9	0.81	7.27	3.03	67.7	0.8	17.1	36.3	6.2
4.0	0.77	7.4	0.48	6.8	1.7	0.97	10.96	3.77	66.7	0.7	10.7	34.5	5.7
5.1	0.63	5.2	0.14	8.0	3.9	1.15	12.35	3.82	58.9	4.3	52.8	16.7	3.9
6.7	0.02	0.2	-0.16	4.9	0.4	0.78	5.61	4.48	83.0	1.6	9.6	21.3	5.2
6.3	0.33	2.6	0.09	2.2	0.4	0.25	3.79	1.66	84.7	4.5	32.0	9.8	2.9
6.5	0.39	1.5	-0.06	3.7	0.4	0.30	2.23	3.38	83.4	1.8	32.8	30.6	5.9
7.1	0.10	1.0	0.30	10.0	3.7	2.44	34.29	4.25	42.8	1.1	6.3	27.4	5.8
9.3	0.22	0.8	0.00	5.1	0.2	0.90	5.81	3.70	66.4	2.8	39.7	23.4	7.4
9.4	0.00	0.0	0.04	5.3	0.7	0.82	4.45	3.04	59.7	3.9	62.1	21.7	8.3
8.1	0.06	0.5	-0.03	6.1	0.7	0.85	10.55	3.47	74.4	2.7	28.0	17.4	4.2
8.7	0.11	0.6	0.02	4.5	0.4	0.60	5.11	2.69	67.1	2.7	49.6	32.1	6.8
5.0	0.75	2.9	0.00	6.6	0.1	0.30	1.52	3.40	98.4	0.7	18.9	52.9	8.4
4.6	0.41	4.6	0.11	5.3	1.0	0.80	10.94	3.71	62.4	0.8	13.7	35.2	4.5
5.6	0.42	2.7	-0.74	8.8	2.4	1.25	12.08	4.13	62.8	0.8	19.5	51.9	6.8
7.7	0.30	2.3	0.00	5.3	0.5	0.76	6.51	2.47	54.1	1.6	4.9	19.8	7.2
7.4	0.14	1.6	0.04	8.4	2.7	1.24	14.25	3.18	57.4	3.3	3.2	11.1	6.2
5.8	0.67	6.2	0.09	6.5	4.9	0.99	11.92	3.41	51.2	1.4	14.6	26.6	6.3
6.2	2.07	8.2	0.05	7.0	0.9	0.92	4.84	3.26	53.4	0.8	17.7	37.0	8.5
6.2	1.42	4.8	0.75	5.5	0.3	0.85	7.44	3.02	54.5	4.4	44.0	13.7	5.4
7.2	0.21	1.8	0.00	8.6	1.0	1.68	18.31	3.09	70.1	1.7	36.9	49.2	7.4
5.8	0.20	1.5	0.01	4.2	2.7	0.78	11.34	2.40	59.5	0.5	3.0	43.6	4.6
6.8	0.33	2.5	0.34	6.3	1.2	0.88	9.43	4.24	60.5	1.8	17.1	20.9	5.3
4.1	0.75	4.8	0.54	5.0	1.2	0.96	11.42	3.05	60.3	1.7	20.0	22.9	4.5
7.6	0.72	4.1	0.02	3.7	0.1	0.36	2.38	3.70	78.8	1.1	7.2	28.8	6.7
1.7	4.28	35.6	0.08	5.2	1.0	0.98	12.14	3.48	62.5	1.6	9.1	20.7	4.9
4.6	1.25	9.9	-0.02	3.3	0.5	0.57	6.97	3.65	77.3	2.3	39.8	30.9	3.2
6.7	1.10	5.2	0.00	7.4	1.7	1.19	8.22	4.67	63.2	8.8	307.3	8.2	8.6
7.0	0.66	3.1	0.02	9.1	0.6	2.19	19.88	3.56	43.6	6.9	98.5	8.5	7.2
4.8	0.88	6.7	0.14	8.6	4.1	1.62	17.35	5.06	52.4	1.6	26.0	27.2	6.2
8.7	0.05	0.5	0.04	6.9	1.6	1.09	16.74	3.72	60.8	3.6	23.3	11.7	5.3
3.6	1.37	11.5	0.12	6.1	1.8	0.87	8.56	3.22	60.6	1.2	19.9	30.3	5.9
6.7	0.17	0.5	0.21	9.4	70.8	1.42	7.46	4.12	48.9	6.4	84.4	12.1	8.7
10.0	0.00	0.0	0.00	2.0	0.0	0.00	0.00	0.00	100.0	5.0	2,074.1	100.0	0.0
7.5	0.38	1.9	0.30	7.7	0.7	1.35	9.80	7.98	73.7	4.8	19.2	3.9	8.2
6.2	0.26	2.1	-0.01	8.7	0.8	2.26	25.23	4.66	54.9	4.4	36.4	11.9	4.9
3.9	1.50	10.3	-0.69	5.1	1.0	0.77	8.76	3.23	67.4	2.9	40.1	20.9	5.7
9.4	0.00	0.0	0.00	4.1	0.9	0.65	8.41	3.57	77.7	6.9	80.0	7.3	4.3
9.8	0.28	0.5	-4.74	7.4	0.4	1.84	16.54	4.29	62.5	4.5	30.3	9.3	6.0
4.3	1.50	9.9	0.80	5.3	10.2	0.95	9.75	3.75	62.1	3.2	24.6	16.1	3.5
6.7	2.26	7.8	-0.35	4.6	0.5	0.66	7.50	3.82	82.0	3.4	42.7	18.8	2.8
2.6	1.14	10.0	0.32	9.4	0.9	1.32	15.08	4.97	34.3	2.6	8.6	15.4	5.1
5.3	1.14	7.1	0.09	6.1	0.4	0.94	10.50	3.72	58.2	5.1	84.9	16.1	3.8
5.0	4.28	13.8	-0.09	4.8	3.7	1.08	7.95	4.11	73.1	6.0	45.4	5.4	8.8
7.6	0.09	0.6	-0.01	6.2	1.4	1.22	14.35	5.30	59.9	4.7	24.9	5.6	5.9
1.0	3.36	25.6	0.79	5.0	0.1	0.86	9.62	4.27	52.6	3.9	18.9	9.3	4.7
4.5	0.30	2.3	0.00	3.4	0.3	0.75	7.73	5.08	87.9	0.8	16.0	38.0	4.3
1.6	3.81	25.2	2.52	3.2	0.0	-0.06	-0.68	9.18	87.0	4.0	41.1	15.1	4.2
7.2	0.08	0.7	0.10	4.2	0.5	1.14	13.50	3.54	70.3	2.5	37.2	24.3	1.4
4.1	0.90	8.0	0.06	6.2	3.2	1.05	13.67	4.53	62.6	4.9	86.9	19.0	4.6
7.6	0.05	0.2	-0.02	2.7	0.1	0.18	1.24	5.04	96.1	4.9	49.6	11.9	1.3
4.7	0.55	3.3	0.26	3.1	0.9	0.52	4.49	2.38	52.6	1.3	24.0	29.6	5.2
4.5	0.91	6.5	0.21	7.3	23.4	1.20	14.25	4.45	59.3	4.9	37.3	12.2	7.2
2.2	1.64	15.3	-0.03	5.9	1.7	1.63	18.91	4.82	63.8	2.0	15.9	19.3	4.3

Name	City	State	Weiss Safety Rating	2003 Weiss Safety Rating	2002 Weiss Safety Rating	Total Assets ($Mil)	One Year Asset Growth	Asset Mix (As a % of Total Assets)				Capital- ization Index	Leverage Ratio	Risk-based Capital Ratio
								Comm- ercial Loans	Cons- umer Loans	Home Mort- gages	Secur- ities			
▲ FIRST INVESTORS FSB	WOODBRIDGE TWP	NJ	A	A-	A	45.9	3.38	0.0	0.9	3.9	55.4	10.0	21.5	82.3
▲ FIRST IOWA ST BK	ALBIA	IA	C+	C	B+	119.4	5.31	21.2	4.4	15.7	17.9	9.1	10.4	14.5
FIRST KANSAS B&TC	GARDNER	KS	C+	C	C	92.8	5.27	12.9	2.4	17.0	33.9	4.4	6.4	12.4
FIRST KANSAS BK	HOISINGTON	KS	B	B	B-	63.0	0.15	4.8	4.4	8.9	65.0	5.2	7.2	18.5
▲ FIRST KENSINGTON BK	SPRING HILL	FL	B	C+	C	289.5	9.76	1.7	0.4	3.0	60.7	6.9	8.9	18.1
FIRST KENTUCKY BK INC	MAYFIELD	KY	B-	B-	B-	251.8	4.40	3.8	8.5	36.2	16.6	5.8	7.8	12.3
FIRST KEYSTONE BANK	MEDIA	PA	C+	C+	C+	560.4	2.18	1.9	0.3	32.2	37.6	6.1	8.1	15.5
FIRST LA BK	SHREVEPORT	LA	D+	D	B-	86.9	4.60	28.0	5.0	9.2	9.0	8.7	11.4	13.9
▼ FIRST LIBERTY NB	WASHINGTON	DC	C-	C-	B	102.8	11.66	4.5	2.3	1.5	21.2	6.2	8.2	19.4
FIRST LIBERTY NB	LIBERTY	TX	A	A	A	213.7	-5.06	6.5	6.4	8.7	60.2	10.0	12.5	31.1
FIRST LOUISIANA NB	BREAUX BRIDGE	LA	B-	B-	B	97.7	2.96	5.4	14.5	21.1	24.5	6.0	8.0	15.3
▲ FIRST LOWNDES BK	FORT DEPOSIT	AL	C+	C-	D-	118.3	40.07	14.0	17.3	23.8	11.5	5.9	7.9	12.3
▲ FIRST MADISON VALLEY BK	ENNIS	MT	B-	C+	C+	70.2	0.12	25.0	11.5	11.8	18.7	6.2	8.3	12.2
FIRST MAIN STREET BK NA	LONGMONT	CO	A-	A-	A-	384.9	-9.41	8.1	1.8	9.7	26.2	10.0	11.8	17.0
FIRST MARINER BK	BALTIMORE	MD	C	C-	C-	1,108.6	13.20	5.7	1.0	9.1	30.2	4.7	6.7	11.1
FIRST MARKET BK FSB	MEMPHIS	TN	B-	B-	B-	1,032.3	5.72	8.1	15.3	6.6	31.7	3.5	6.3	10.3
FIRST MERCHANTS BK NA	MUNCIE	IN	C+	C+	B-	834.0	7.34	17.6	7.2	19.2	15.1	5.2	7.6	11.1
▲ FIRST METRO BK	MUSCLE SHOALS	AL	A-	B+	B+	255.8	5.99	11.9	7.5	18.9	26.3	8.6	10.0	16.7
FIRST MID ILLINOIS B&T NA	MATTOON	IL	B	B	B	794.6	5.10	10.9	2.8	15.9	20.5	6.2	8.3	11.9
FIRST MIDWEST BK	ITASCA	IL	B-	B-	B-	6,801.9	5.76	14.9	6.3	5.8	30.4	3.9	7.2	10.4
FIRST MIDWEST BK	POPLAR BLUFF	MO	C	C	C	146.7	4.40	16.2	12.7	19.0	7.0	2.9	7.7	9.9
▲ FIRST MIDWEST BK	VAN BUREN	MO	B-	C+	C+	35.2	-0.44	14.3	4.8	16.0	12.0	7.8	9.8	13.2
FIRST MIDWEST BK	CENTERVILLE	SD	C-	C-	D	73.4	8.02	19.7	7.2	7.6	8.9	6.8	8.8	14.7
FIRST MIDWEST BK DEXTER	DEXTER	MO	C+	C+	C+	122.7	16.16	16.7	6.4	14.3	12.3	3.7	7.8	10.3
FIRST MIDWEST BK PIEDMONT	PIEDMONT	MO	B-	C+	C+	59.6	0.92	10.8	6.2	15.1	18.6	8.1	9.8	13.7
FIRST MINNETONKA CITY BK	MINNETONKA	MN	B	B	B	149.0	2.88	15.7	4.6	12.4	29.1	6.1	8.1	12.5
▲ FIRST MISSOURI NB	BROOKFIELD	MO	C+	C	C-	62.1	4.38	5.7	5.6	25.0	17.7	8.1	9.7	14.5
FIRST MISSOURI ST BK	POPLAR BLUFF	MO	C	C+	B-	159.6	13.54	11.9	6.7	21.0	12.5	2.9	6.9	9.9
FIRST MN BK NA	MINNETONKA	MN	B	B	B-	339.8	13.91	9.6	3.0	9.8	43.1	6.4	8.4	14.3
▼ FIRST MORRIS B&TC	MORRISTOWN	NJ	C	C+	C+	519.0	25.08	2.7	0.1	9.6	44.8	4.2	6.2	12.2
FIRST MOUNTAIN BK	BIG BEAR LAKE	CA	B-	B-	C+	118.5	10.69	5.1	1.8	4.4	12.8	6.5	9.1	12.1
▼ FIRST MOUNTAIN BK	LEADVILLE	CO	D	D+	D+	23.1	10.43	1.6	11.2	38.1	0.9	5.1	7.1	15.2
FIRST MUTUAL BK	BELLEVUE	WA	B-	B-	B-	962.7	18.73	3.4	9.5	11.6	12.6	5.5	7.6	11.4
FIRST NAT EXCH BK	ROANOKE	VA	C-	C-	D+	243.9	-12.70	3.9	0.8	5.6	28.3	5.2	7.2	12.8
FIRST NATION BK	COVINGTON	GA	B	B	B	436.1	2.11	5.9	1.5	4.4	5.6	6.1	9.7	11.8
FIRST NATIONAL BANK OF	OVERLAND PARK	KS	C	C-	C	1,090.8	0.93	11.2	32.6	0.8	7.8	3.7	5.7	11.3
FIRST NATIONAL BANKERS BK	BATON ROUGE	LA	C	C	C	227.8	31.06	4.3	0.0	0.9	7.7	7.0	9.0	17.9
FIRST NATIONAL BANKING CO	ASH FLAT	AR	B	B	B-	273.0	13.26	8.3	7.3	32.6	15.7	5.9	7.9	12.1
FIRST NATIONAL BK	OLNEY	IL	D+	D+	D+	6.7	-0.04	10.0	5.3	0.0	61.2	10.0	100.0	308.5
▲ FIRST NATIONAL BK OF CO	BOULDER	CO	C	C-	C	681.3	-8.65	11.4	17.2	9.0	4.8	3.7	7.7	10.4
FIRST NATIONAL COMMUNITY	E LIVERPOOL	OH	B-	B-	B-	93.2	3.78	17.0	6.2	17.8	33.6	7.5	9.3	17.3
FIRST NATIONAL COMMUNITY	DUNMORE	PA	B-	B-	B-	856.7	10.09	15.5	8.2	8.7	22.7	5.2	8.3	11.2
FIRST NATIONS BK	CHICAGO	IL	C	C	C	153.0	15.13	12.8	1.4	7.0	11.4	4.3	7.9	10.7
FIRST NAVY BK	PENSACOLA	FL	A-	A	A	60.0	2.40	0.0	9.7	0.0	70.4	10.0	20.9	133.6
▲ FIRST NB	ASHDOWN	AR	A	A-	A	86.7	3.19	21.0	15.1	12.7	26.8	10.0	13.6	21.0
FIRST NB	HOT SPRINGS	AR	A-	A-	A-	181.2	21.35	9.4	4.8	21.4	16.4	9.7	10.8	16.4
FIRST NB	MC GEHEE	AR	B-	B-	B-	47.3	5.20	12.1	5.9	6.2	48.1	10.0	12.7	23.8
FIRST NB	MT IDA	AR	A-	A-	A-	78.2	-4.12	17.0	6.4	11.7	32.6	10.0	11.8	23.4
FIRST NB	PARAGOULD	AR	A-	A-	A	472.8	9.99	3.3	6.4	28.6	26.5	10.0	11.9	19.3
FIRST NB	RANCHO SANTA FE	CA	B+	B	B-	1,189.9	7.01	26.6	1.5	2.4	8.8	5.6	9.7	11.5
FIRST NB	FORT COLLINS	CO	C+	C+	C+	1,223.0	1.35	8.3	22.5	11.5	8.3	3.5	5.5	10.3
▼ FIRST NB	JULESBURG	CO	C	C+	B-	91.0	46.79	7.5	4.1	8.3	11.1	3.5	7.5	10.3
▲ FIRST NB	STEAMBOAT SPRING	CO	D	D	D	54.4	12.60	13.9	4.1	4.3	18.7	4.0	8.0	10.5
▲ FIRST NB	TELLURIDE	CO	B-	B	B-	110.6	24.55	10.3	1.4	8.5	18.8	5.1	7.9	11.1
▲ FIRST NB	ORANGE PARK	FL	C+	C-	C-	81.9	22.61	8.5	3.2	12.3	6.0	7.3	10.5	12.7
FIRST NB	TARPON SPRINGS	FL	C	C	C-	25.0	-11.74	9.5	3.3	13.5	3.9	10.0	11.5	22.5
▲ FIRST NB	SAVANNAH	GA	C+	C	C+	127.4	59.60	16.6	2.6	15.5	19.1	6.2	8.2	12.8
FIRST NB	ST MARYS	GA	B-	B-	B-	151.5	15.71	8.8	5.6	28.9	7.2	8.7	10.6	13.9
▼ FIRST NB	DAVENPORT	IA	C	C+	C+	92.8	4.60	7.7	1.5	2.5	34.3	5.8	7.8	13.7
FIRST NB	FONTANELLE	IA	D+	D+	C-	149.3	41.95	6.2	2.4	6.4	22.9	3.5	10.2	10.2
▼ FIRST NB	SIOUX CITY	IA	C+	B-	B-	141.4	9.37	11.5	2.8	11.2	17.9	6.0	8.0	11.7
FIRST NB	ANTIOCH	IL	B-	B-	C+	143.4	4.66	3.9	1.8	28.8	22.4	5.4	7.4	11.4
FIRST NB	CHICAGO HEIGHTS	IL	C-	C-	C	463.7	10.23	9.9	32.5	2.6	11.4	5.1	7.1	11.3
FIRST NB	MCHENRY	IL	B	B	B+	132.7	-1.18	2.0	1.0	26.2	49.6	10.0	11.1	24.1

Asset Quality Index	Non-Performing Loans as a % of Total Loans	Non-Performing Loans as a % of Capital	Net Charge-offs Avg Loans	Profitability Index	Net Income ($Mil)	Return on Assets (R.O.A.)	Return on Equity (R.O.E.)	Net Interest Spread	Overhead Efficiency Ratio	Liquidity Index	Liquidity Ratio	Hot Money Ratio	Stability Index
9.5	2.30	0.9	0.15	10.0	0.6	2.07	11.53	1.93	73.4	2.9	80.9	86.7	9.0
3.8	1.65	10.7	0.05	8.4	1.1	1.89	17.32	4.56	45.8	1.6	16.7	22.8	7.7
8.9	0.10	0.9	0.07	7.7	0.9	2.01	32.93	3.68	53.6	1.9	24.9	20.8	3.8
9.1	0.10	0.4	-0.20	6.0	0.5	1.61	20.52	3.41	54.4	4.0	21.8	9.7	5.2
8.7	0.02	0.1	0.00	5.3	1.5	1.01	11.84	3.13	48.5	1.5	7.5	21.9	4.1
5.7	0.49	4.0	0.11	4.7	1.3	1.06	11.96	3.96	70.8	3.4	13.7	12.0	5.1
5.7	0.61	3.9	0.03	3.5	1.0	0.37	4.57	2.59	82.6	1.2	13.5	28.4	5.2
1.4	4.63	27.6	1.47	4.0	0.1	0.31	2.78	5.32	70.2	2.1	31.7	25.2	5.7
6.1	1.19	3.4	-0.06	1.3	-0.2	-0.34	-3.62	3.99	121.5	7.6	207.8	14.3	4.2
9.0	0.72	1.6	0.36	6.6	1.3	1.21	9.54	3.34	60.0	6.9	82.3	7.8	7.1
7.8	0.10	0.7	0.06	6.8	0.8	1.57	20.86	4.15	68.2	4.2	75.8	19.5	4.9
3.7	0.67	5.8	0.22	6.9	0.8	1.51	19.19	5.59	52.2	1.1	19.8	31.4	3.5
5.2	0.39	3.1	0.14	6.8	0.6	1.62	20.60	5.13	65.4	2.8	33.9	18.8	4.5
7.7	0.78	3.9	0.04	5.8	2.0	0.97	8.66	4.28	72.8	4.1	33.4	12.1	6.9
5.7	1.21	10.2	0.02	3.8	2.8	0.53	7.94	3.64	85.7	2.9	22.0	16.3	4.0
7.2	0.20	1.7	0.11	6.3	5.5	1.07	16.11	3.21	53.5	1.5	24.2	34.3	6.2
3.6	1.81	14.9	0.08	8.6	5.0	1.24	16.00	3.71	51.8	4.3	75.8	21.5	6.3
6.2	0.67	4.0	0.08	8.8	1.7	1.39	14.02	3.91	50.7	6.1	106.0	14.9	6.0
5.6	0.38	2.7	0.11	7.2	5.0	1.27	13.29	4.02	59.3	3.3	34.0	16.5	6.4
6.5	0.68	4.6	0.21	8.6	52.4	1.58	18.77	4.04	51.0	3.2	13.5	13.4	6.7
4.8	0.69	6.9	0.23	8.1	1.0	1.41	18.82	4.95	59.6	3.1	10.5	12.9	3.4
8.1	0.00	0.0	-0.01	5.6	0.2	0.98	9.85	3.89	66.9	3.8	45.8	17.0	5.5
2.7	2.01	12.5	0.19	5.4	0.3	0.92	8.74	5.07	73.2	6.3	78.7	9.6	3.7
6.4	0.38	3.5	0.02	5.5	0.5	0.90	11.37	4.39	65.5	2.0	8.7	18.3	4.4
5.6	0.37	2.6	0.07	5.5	0.3	0.90	9.34	3.85	64.6	4.2	14.3	7.1	5.5
7.2	0.38	2.6	-0.05	4.9	0.8	1.09	13.14	3.72	68.3	4.5	29.2	8.7	4.8
6.6	0.23	1.7	0.25	4.7	0.2	0.78	7.90	3.77	64.0	1.4	22.0	27.5	3.8
5.3	0.44	4.7	0.04	5.3	0.6	0.78	11.42	3.61	64.7	1.6	9.4	20.6	3.6
6.9	0.83	4.7	0.15	9.9	2.7	1.66	20.31	4.54	46.4	3.4	10.9	11.8	4.8
8.3	0.36	2.6	0.00	5.0	2.1	0.84	13.99	3.52	64.4	8.1	184.7	10.7	2.8
6.2	0.55	3.7	0.03	5.5	0.6	1.07	11.69	5.95	75.9	5.4	30.2	2.8	4.5
4.8	1.16	8.7	-0.09	9.0	0.2	1.83	26.39	5.81	69.6	6.9	89.3	5.9	2.3
5.4	0.44	4.5	0.06	6.4	4.8	1.06	14.31	4.18	58.8	0.8	5.3	32.2	4.7
2.6	4.00	28.4	0.00	4.3	1.1	0.86	12.22	3.19	62.2	6.5	76.3	9.2	2.5
4.8	0.17	0.5	0.20	6.6	2.2	1.03	4.57	4.72	63.7	2.5	35.7	23.8	7.9
2.8	1.11	12.7	3.11	5.6	4.7	0.88	14.35	5.78	38.9	5.2	48.8	13.5	5.0
9.6	0.00	0.0	0.00	2.4	0.3	0.27	3.30	2.44	91.6	7.8	70.1	0.0	3.7
4.5	0.87	7.4	0.09	9.3	3.0	2.29	26.83	5.17	59.0	3.5	8.7	10.6	6.1
4.5	53.71	8.2	-23.91	3.7	0.0	-0.03	-0.03	2.17	250.7	0.0	N/A	101.0	3.0
2.8	1.25	10.9	1.43	3.4	1.6	0.46	5.50	5.14	66.4	4.9	58.2	15.0	3.9
6.7	0.50	2.6	0.21	4.4	0.4	0.83	8.74	4.69	77.0	4.2	23.1	8.6	5.0
7.1	0.23	1.8	0.08	5.0	4.7	1.14	13.62	3.32	59.8	3.3	31.4	15.4	5.2
4.5	0.48	4.4	0.01	5.3	0.5	0.73	9.58	3.88	65.3	3.1	50.1	26.4	3.9
9.7	0.00	0.0	0.07	5.8	0.2	0.58	2.92	3.75	80.7	6.9	52.6	0.0	8.4
6.0	0.75	3.3	0.29	7.4	0.3	0.78	5.73	4.87	43.2	1.5	6.8	22.5	8.5
7.9	0.03	0.2	0.01	6.2	0.9	1.06	9.56	4.12	58.3	2.2	24.6	18.8	6.9
6.4	2.20	7.3	0.08	4.7	0.2	0.93	7.43	3.97	75.2	2.0	29.8	25.1	5.0
8.0	0.76	3.3	0.07	7.0	0.5	1.16	10.18	3.39	50.7	4.8	98.2	19.7	7.7
6.2	1.48	8.2	0.35	5.9	2.4	1.04	8.69	3.68	56.5	2.6	13.2	16.0	7.3
6.3	0.23	0.7	0.25	9.8	9.5	1.65	7.68	5.94	49.2	5.9	51.0	10.5	8.3
4.1	0.69	7.1	1.14	5.8	5.2	0.88	12.45	4.54	58.1	5.2	67.5	16.1	5.0
7.4	0.13	1.0	0.20	8.1	0.6	1.50	16.54	5.41	57.2	2.1	16.5	18.6	4.7
4.4	0.29	2.2	0.11	3.4	0.2	0.66	8.59	4.34	78.8	2.2	25.6	19.5	0.0
7.2	0.10	0.8	0.01	8.9	0.7	1.38	17.63	5.72	60.1	3.3	30.8	15.3	5.9
6.7	0.09	0.5	0.00	3.6	0.2	0.62	6.17	2.86	63.5	0.7	9.8	38.5	6.3
6.3	3.10	11.5	-0.44	1.7	0.0	0.20	1.65	3.86	105.3	6.1	113.6	14.0	4.1
5.8	0.64	4.9	0.02	3.4	0.4	0.61	7.64	3.71	69.1	5.1	65.3	15.2	3.9
7.2	0.27	2.0	0.06	7.7	1.0	1.29	14.75	5.67	58.3	0.5	7.2	60.1	5.2
3.5	2.56	17.1	0.93	4.1	0.3	0.60	7.44	4.17	71.1	5.6	59.1	10.2	3.9
1.6	1.24	8.0	0.80	5.5	0.6	1.08	11.67	5.26	65.7	3.3	25.1	13.5	4.9
1.3	2.97	19.3	0.54	2.3	0.1	0.11	1.09	3.04	85.0	4.0	33.3	12.9	5.8
7.3	0.59	5.6	0.03	6.3	0.9	1.37	18.70	4.08	69.1	4.0	21.9	9.7	4.7
2.0	1.57	14.9	0.17	8.7	4.0	1.75	23.80	4.38	53.5	2.8	38.3	21.8	5.1
8.0	1.38	5.0	-0.01	4.3	0.6	0.83	7.41	3.59	71.1	5.5	41.3	7.3	6.6

Name	City	State	Weiss Safety Rating	2003 Weiss Safety Rating	2002 Weiss Safety Rating	Total Assets ($Mil)	One Year Asset Growth	Asset Mix (As a % of Total Assets) Commercial Loans	Consumer Loans	Home Mortgages	Securities	Capitalization Index	Leverage Ratio	Risk-based Capital Ratio
FIRST NB	MULBERRY GROVE	IL	D-	D-	E+	88.1	3.83	22.1	7.9	13.6	27.5	3.2	5.9	10.1
FIRST NB	VANDALIA	IL	A	A	A	182.7	4.41	7.3	3.5	15.2	40.4	10.0	11.2	20.9
FIRST NB	CLOVERDALE	IN	C-	D+	D+	210.9	-4.00	7.1	3.1	33.9	3.4	5.7	7.7	12.8
▼ FIRST NB	ABILENE	KS	B	B+	B+	108.9	9.67	4.1	2.6	14.7	46.7	4.8	6.8	13.5
FIRST NB	GOODLAND	KS	C	C	C-	307.7	1.16	5.2	3.0	6.6	34.8	5.1	7.1	12.9
FIRST NB	HAYS	KS	D	D	D	73.6	5.22	6.6	2.9	9.9	11.5	4.9	6.9	11.5
FIRST NB	ARCADIA	LA	D	D	E	99.5	-8.26	7.3	6.7	16.3	12.3	4.6	6.6	11.7
FIRST NB	CRYSTAL FALLS	MI	B+	B+	B+	65.0	3.23	10.9	4.9	27.1	12.6	10.0	12.6	20.4
FIRST NB	CHISHOLM	MN	C-	C-	C-	57.9	4.53	15.2	10.8	17.2	33.6	5.4	7.4	13.8
▼ FIRST NB	FULDA	MN	C-	B-	B-	121.0	3.51	5.2	4.2	3.5	11.3	5.1	8.2	11.1
▲ FIRST NB	HAWLEY	MN	C-	D+	D	61.0	6.02	8.9	11.1	18.4	7.7	5.2	8.1	11.1
FIRST NB	CAMDENTON	MO	A+	A+	A+	235.4	-1.47	5.0	7.6	15.0	43.0	10.0	16.2	28.9
▲ FIRST NB	LAMAR	MO	B+	B	B-	45.8	-4.39	22.6	6.6	19.2	20.4	8.1	9.7	15.3
▲ FIRST NB	MALDEN	MO	E+	E	E	119.5	-6.42	15.2	6.9	26.2	8.7	5.3	7.3	11.4
FIRST NB	MOUNTAIN VIEW	MO	C+	C+	C+	196.9	11.29	10.1	11.5	31.0	4.1	4.3	7.5	10.6
FIRST NB	ROSEDALE	MS	B+	B+	B+	47.4	0.50	4.7	8.1	3.8	5.0	10.0	16.0	21.1
FIRST NB	MILNOR	ND	B+	B+	B+	47.5	2.06	10.5	9.8	5.3	20.9	10.0	12.9	19.6
▲ FIRST NB	BEEMER	NE	D	D-	D+	77.8	4.80	7.6	3.2	2.8	18.9	6.7	8.7	13.6
FIRST NB	N PLATTE	NE	C	C	C	482.2	-4.20	10.7	32.9	5.9	18.2	5.5	7.6	11.4
FIRST NB	SCHUYLER	NE	B-	B-	B-	90.8	0.95	7.2	3.3	10.2	21.9	6.2	8.2	12.6
FIRST NB	LEBANON	OH	A	A	A-	88.1	7.94	1.7	1.9	16.1	19.5	10.0	13.8	20.5
▼ FIRST NB	ORRVILLE	OH	B	B+	B+	298.5	2.25	7.6	2.2	33.0	24.2	6.7	8.7	12.9
FIRST NB	POWHATAN POINT	OH	C+	C+	B-	16.5	9.71	5.4	9.3	17.6	45.7	10.0	15.6	25.0
FIRST NB	HEAVENER	OK	B	B-	B-	67.1	-0.17	4.7	6.8	53.8	3.1	6.3	8.3	16.0
FIRST NB	HENRYETTA	OK	B-	C+	C+	62.2	-9.46	4.0	9.8	20.7	37.4	9.6	10.8	18.8
▲ FIRST NB	MIDWEST CITY	OK	C-	D+	C-	297.0	-3.01	6.5	5.6	12.3	41.7	7.6	9.4	17.6
FIRST NB	SALLISAW	OK	B	B	B	180.1	3.69	6.8	6.5	17.0	39.9	5.0	7.0	13.0
▲ FIRST NB	FORT PIERRE	SD	B	C+	C	477.4	41.05	13.4	11.5	5.3	18.0	10.0	11.9	16.6
▼ FIRST NB	LENOIR CITY	TN	B	B+	A-	289.6	-0.61	12.5	3.0	15.3	27.0	10.0	13.6	19.9
FIRST NB	BEDFORD	TX	C	C	C	50.4	3.62	19.1	19.8	5.5	4.9	3.3	7.2	10.2
FIRST NB	BORGER	TX	B-	B-	B-	36.8	-16.66	27.8	2.6	2.2	0.0	10.0	12.9	16.1
▲ FIRST NB	DUBLIN	TX	D+	D-	D-	58.0	0.15	13.2	10.9	5.4	22.9	6.2	8.2	14.4
FIRST NB	FABENS	TX	B	B	B+	202.7	9.71	15.1	1.2	3.4	25.9	5.6	7.6	13.0
FIRST NB	FAIRFIELD	TX	A-	A-	A-	115.7	6.12	3.9	3.9	14.1	51.4	6.7	8.7	19.8
FIRST NB	GLEN ROSE	TX	B-	B-	C+	47.3	6.12	9.5	18.5	10.7	4.7	7.7	9.5	17.4
▲ FIRST NB	GROESBECK	TX	C+	C	C-	37.4	4.93	5.1	19.4	25.8	10.6	8.8	10.2	19.1
▲ FIRST NB	JASPER	TX	B	B-	B-	190.9	0.22	1.9	7.9	5.8	61.8	7.8	9.5	31.5
FIRST NB	LUBBOCK	TX	E	E-	D-	37.7	5.75	19.6	13.4	3.9	19.6	0.0	0.3	0.8
▲ FIRST NB	ROTAN	TX	B	B-	B-	38.9	-4.24	7.8	5.6	2.3	33.6	10.0	11.0	18.7
▲ FIRST NB	SACHSE	TX	B+	B-	C	70.3	-2.96	6.9	2.5	15.6	22.5	10.0	12.0	17.4
FIRST NB	SPEARMAN	TX	D+	C	C-	72.5	-1.20	9.0	4.2	2.1	19.0	8.7	10.1	15.3
FIRST NB	SWEETWATER	TX	A-	A-	A-	127.5	8.92	7.1	5.7	8.5	52.6	6.2	8.2	16.9
▲ FIRST NB	WICHITA FALLS	TX	C+	C-	D+	143.6	-7.23	12.0	13.1	18.5	13.3	8.2	10.0	13.5
FIRST NB	CHRISTIANSBURG	VA	B	B	B-	705.8	4.49	8.0	5.9	23.7	15.3	4.7	8.2	10.8
▼ FIRST NB	ROCKY MOUNT	VA	C-	C+	C+	270.8	5.29	3.5	2.2	8.4	25.7	4.5	6.5	12.7
FIRST NB	RONCEVERTE	WV	B-	B-	B	187.8	15.80	16.6	8.2	25.0	13.7	6.7	8.7	12.4
FIRST NB	SPENCER	WV	C+	C+	C-	114.0	0.20	23.4	5.9	23.2	14.4	8.2	9.8	14.5
FIRST NB	GILLETTE	WY	B	B	B	219.3	5.79	13.0	5.6	8.0	53.0	6.9	8.9	19.6
FIRST NB - COLORADO	FOWLER	CO	D-	D-	D	67.7	-2.22	11.8	5.0	13.7	8.5	4.9	6.9	11.2
FIRST NB - SIDNEY	SIDNEY	NE	C-	C+	B-	131.2	44.86	18.1	3.6	5.1	18.2	5.1	7.2	11.0
FIRST NB ALASKA	ANCHORAGE	AK	A+	A+	A+	2,152.8	4.33	12.7	1.4	4.0	40.1	10.0	20.6	32.6
▲ FIRST NB AMERICAN	E LANSING	MI	B-	C	C-	395.9	-15.33	0.1	0.0	51.0	4.8	10.0	18.4	26.1
FIRST NB AMES, IA	AMES	IA	A-	A-	A-	403.6	-0.41	7.5	1.0	7.6	38.5	7.9	9.6	15.1
FIRST NB AT DARLINGTON	DARLINGTON	WI	B	B	B	62.3	4.93	5.4	7.0	11.8	34.3	10.0	11.7	18.1
FIRST NB AT MARIANNA	MARIANNA	AR	B-	B-	B	53.4	-1.85	7.3	5.2	8.2	41.0	10.0	11.8	26.2
FIRST NB AT PARIS	PARIS	AR	B-	B-	B-	101.5	9.44	3.9	5.1	27.4	27.5	7.4	9.3	15.3
FIRST NB AT ST JAMES	ST JAMES	MN	C-	D+	D	24.7	-4.72	7.8	4.6	16.8	26.2	6.6	8.6	14.5
FIRST NB CALUMET-LAKE	CALUMET	MI	B-	B-	B-	50.8	7.11	16.5	2.3	18.8	20.0	6.0	8.0	11.8
FIRST NB CEDAR FALLS	CEDAR FALLS	IA	B	B	B	51.7	5.86	9.4	2.1	25.5	11.2	5.8	7.9	11.6
FIRST NB CENTRAL FLORIDA	WINTER PARK	FL	D	D	D+	271.5	13.92	10.0	1.2	5.2	11.3	3.4	7.6	10.2
FIRST NB ELK CITY	ELK CITY	OK	B+	A-	A-	176.0	4.06	6.1	3.2	16.2	33.7	7.0	9.0	15.4
▲ FIRST NB FOX VALLEY	NEENAH	WI	C+	C	C-	179.2	17.89	25.7	2.7	18.7	11.5	7.4	9.5	12.9
FIRST NB FREDERICKSBURG	FREDERICKSBURG	PA	B-	B-	B	147.2	4.23	3.9	5.0	30.0	17.9	6.5	8.6	12.7
▼ FIRST NB GRAFORD	GRAFORD	TX	D-	D	C+	46.6	11.06	5.3	19.3	19.4	40.2	5.0	7.0	14.3

Asset Quality Index	Non-Performing Loans as a % of Total Loans	Non-Performing Loans as a % of Capital	Net Charge-offs Avg Loans	Profitability Index	Net Income ($Mil)	Return on Assets (R.O.A.)	Return on Equity (R.O.E.)	Net Interest Spread	Overhead Efficiency Ratio	Liquidity Index	Liquidity Ratio	Hot Money Ratio	Stability Index
6.1	0.43	4.0	0.16	2.9	0.3	0.62	10.38	3.45	76.3	4.0	34.9	13.4	1.2
8.7	0.19	0.8	-0.01	6.5	1.1	1.23	10.30	4.13	63.9	3.8	23.7	10.7	7.9
3.9	1.69	14.7	0.27	3.6	0.4	0.40	5.14	3.52	82.3	5.5	68.1	13.7	2.6
7.1	0.37	2.5	0.06	7.4	0.7	1.41	19.77	3.44	52.4	4.1	22.6	9.1	6.2
3.9	1.62	9.7	0.16	4.0	1.5	1.00	11.25	4.30	77.5	2.8	26.3	16.5	4.4
2.8	2.15	16.8	0.14	4.3	0.4	0.96	13.57	3.87	74.5	3.8	32.0	13.5	2.3
2.1	2.30	20.7	0.00	5.5	0.7	1.48	20.49	4.09	68.3	3.5	36.1	16.1	2.1
7.6	0.88	4.5	0.16	4.9	0.3	0.80	6.36	4.02	69.6	6.6	116.8	12.4	6.7
3.6	1.98	13.6	0.47	4.1	0.2	0.65	8.81	3.85	83.0	6.0	37.2	2.4	3.7
2.0	2.50	19.1	0.26	6.9	0.5	0.82	9.16	4.95	67.7	6.2	50.0	5.3	5.4
4.0	0.99	9.2	0.03	8.1	0.5	1.47	19.27	5.03	58.3	4.1	41.7	14.7	2.9
8.5	0.10	0.3	0.04	9.4	1.8	1.50	9.16	3.92	45.3	2.9	24.4	15.5	9.2
5.3	0.63	4.2	-0.44	7.7	0.4	1.84	18.67	4.27	62.3	4.8	43.8	11.8	6.0
3.1	2.02	19.3	0.10	2.1	0.3	0.43	6.14	3.39	78.2	2.8	21.9	15.8	0.0
5.7	0.29	2.9	0.18	6.1	0.9	0.93	12.37	5.09	70.9	2.4	13.2	16.8	4.2
6.2	0.39	2.1	0.23	10.0	0.6	3.02	18.92	9.14	48.5	3.2	51.5	22.4	6.5
5.8	1.32	6.5	0.11	7.4	0.4	1.66	12.75	4.82	63.9	5.1	46.5	10.7	7.3
0.9	2.72	18.0	0.21	4.9	0.3	0.88	9.48	4.39	68.9	1.7	28.8	27.9	2.6
2.3	1.78	13.8	3.58	5.0	2.0	0.83	10.92	6.24	46.2	4.2	36.2	12.7	3.9
4.9	0.75	5.8	0.24	6.4	0.7	1.51	18.46	4.28	63.6	4.9	28.6	5.9	5.4
8.8	0.02	0.1	0.01	6.9	0.6	1.49	10.38	4.79	70.9	3.0	42.0	20.8	9.3
5.4	0.72	4.2	-0.02	4.7	1.5	0.99	8.80	4.48	74.1	4.9	28.1	5.1	6.4
8.6	0.00	0.0	-0.03	4.1	0.1	0.81	5.02	4.63	80.5	6.6	66.1	3.2	5.0
4.7	1.00	9.1	-0.21	10.0	0.8	2.51	31.67	6.53	45.3	2.8	23.0	15.9	5.7
1.2	6.98	28.5	0.40	5.2	0.5	1.49	11.62	4.34	62.6	2.3	22.2	18.4	5.9
3.2	2.67	12.0	0.16	7.5	2.5	1.70	16.32	4.25	68.4	4.6	21.7	5.3	6.5
5.3	1.03	7.4	0.14	9.2	1.9	2.18	29.94	4.29	51.5	2.2	31.0	23.1	5.0
4.5	0.94	3.8	8.33	9.9	4.3	1.80	13.32	9.01	45.4	6.9	110.0	11.3	6.4
8.6	0.47	2.2	0.11	3.9	0.9	0.64	4.72	3.84	76.7	2.8	17.8	15.2	6.8
3.2	1.08	9.5	0.45	5.8	0.2	0.59	8.26	5.21	84.3	2.5	37.6	24.8	4.7
1.0	4.92	25.2	-0.03	3.5	0.2	1.10	8.84	4.45	77.4	3.3	37.1	17.4	5.2
3.5	2.03	12.2	0.17	4.2	0.2	0.72	8.90	4.48	79.1	5.5	47.2	8.2	2.9
4.4	1.56	11.1	-0.14	9.8	2.6	2.55	33.75	4.48	43.0	4.2	75.1	23.1	5.9
5.3	1.95	7.2	0.03	6.3	0.8	1.38	13.95	4.61	65.8	1.3	18.1	28.5	6.4
7.5	0.14	0.8	0.17	9.9	0.8	3.43	34.04	4.99	46.0	6.4	68.0	7.1	5.2
3.2	1.74	10.4	0.18	5.5	0.1	0.71	7.02	4.78	77.5	4.5	87.9	20.0	4.3
6.9	0.75	2.6	0.17	5.3	1.1	1.15	12.22	3.66	62.2	3.2	49.9	25.1	5.3
0.0	26.58	182.3	22.39	1.4	-2.4	-12.48	-172.05	2.69	404.0	2.1	45.2	48.5	3.0
3.9	3.50	16.3	-0.06	9.1	0.3	1.65	13.32	4.97	70.4	3.5	12.2	11.5	6.3
8.3	0.35	1.9	0.22	9.1	0.6	1.63	13.70	5.00	56.6	3.1	22.2	14.2	5.0
1.3	5.34	29.1	0.08	4.4	0.3	0.88	8.49	4.37	76.1	3.2	54.8	24.7	4.1
8.6	0.25	1.2	0.12	10.0	1.4	2.21	25.00	4.43	44.5	1.9	21.0	20.6	8.0
3.9	0.90	6.4	0.37	6.8	1.3	1.77	18.50	5.11	65.8	2.3	27.7	19.7	4.2
6.1	0.53	4.0	0.19	8.3	4.2	1.23	13.60	4.11	61.4	3.5	23.5	12.5	6.9
1.7	4.19	31.4	0.02	4.8	1.1	0.81	12.40	2.76	59.4	6.1	86.0	13.0	3.4
4.8	0.61	5.4	0.14	5.6	0.9	1.02	12.66	4.02	60.3	4.9	17.3	3.2	4.6
4.6	1.38	9.7	-0.03	3.5	0.4	0.72	7.45	4.38	73.1	3.9	27.3	11.4	5.1
4.6	3.19	13.9	0.01	6.2	1.7	1.53	16.99	3.49	54.6	2.8	27.7	16.8	5.4
4.7	0.86	7.7	0.15	3.4	0.1	0.38	5.59	5.14	85.7	6.1	65.6	8.5	2.1
1.0	2.57	17.7	1.10	7.5	0.8	1.22	13.54	4.03	55.2	3.5	21.8	12.4	4.4
8.4	0.95	2.3	0.04	10.0	19.0	1.75	8.60	5.06	56.4	7.2	80.6	7.2	10.0
3.5	4.46	19.3	0.95	10.0	5.5	2.74	15.27	8.30	50.5	0.8	10.9	34.5	7.2
6.4	1.04	4.9	0.01	9.6	3.3	1.67	16.58	3.99	40.3	5.3	32.5	4.7	7.8
6.4	1.55	6.8	-0.01	4.2	0.3	0.79	6.57	3.48	72.9	5.7	55.1	9.0	6.4
6.3	2.22	6.5	0.21	3.3	0.1	0.37	3.06	3.66	85.9	6.0	59.6	7.6	4.8
6.0	0.76	4.7	-0.15	6.2	0.6	1.11	12.15	4.04	62.1	2.4	34.8	23.6	4.8
5.4	0.84	5.2	0.09	4.8	0.1	0.81	9.55	4.66	76.6	4.7	38.7	8.3	3.6
5.9	0.31	1.7	0.04	4.5	0.2	0.74	6.43	4.10	71.2	4.5	51.3	14.6	6.2
5.0	0.98	8.6	-0.27	1.9	0.0	0.04	0.50	3.14	97.0	4.8	41.9	11.4	4.0
5.0	0.82	7.3	0.04	2.6	0.4	0.30	4.35	3.98	85.5	8.1	122.4	4.8	2.3
4.9	1.51	9.4	-0.01	6.4	1.4	1.58	16.22	3.32	56.7	1.8	19.5	21.4	7.0
5.6	0.49	3.8	0.04	7.0	1.0	1.09	12.28	4.34	56.7	0.8	10.3	33.2	3.8
5.1	1.01	7.4	0.05	3.7	0.4	0.51	5.88	4.22	83.7	6.2	43.7	3.3	4.9
1.5	3.69	24.8	1.56	4.1	0.1	0.34	4.71	4.22	63.4	3.1	50.7	24.6	2.1

Name	City	State	Weiss Safety Rating	2003 Weiss Safety Rating	2002 Weiss Safety Rating	Total Assets ($Mil)	One Year Asset Growth	Asset Mix (As a % of Total Assets)				Capital- ization Index	Leverage Ratio	Risk-based Capital Ratio
								Comm- ercial Loans	Cons- umer Loans	Home Mort- gages	Secur- ities			
FIRST NB HEREFORD	HEREFORD	TX	C+	C+	C	58.6	11.92	15.3	6.5	6.5	14.7	6.8	8.8	12.4
▲ FIRST NB HINCKLEY	HINCKLEY	MN	C-	D+	NR	6.9	N/A	12.6	3.2	19.1	0.0	10.0	54.0	69.0
▼ FIRST NB IN ALAMOGORDO	ALAMOGORDO	NM	A-	A	A-	199.2	3.79	23.3	5.7	9.3	39.9	9.0	10.3	20.4
FIRST NB IN AMBOY	AMBOY	IL	C-	C-	C	115.5	-9.16	7.9	4.3	17.7	33.6	9.1	10.4	18.5
▲ FIRST NB IN BELLEVILLE	BELLEVILLE	KS	B+	B	B+	81.0	0.53	7.6	4.3	11.2	31.6	6.7	8.7	14.6
▲ FIRST NB IN BLYTHEVILLE	BLYTHEVILLE	AR	B	C+	C	192.3	3.63	5.0	2.4	13.2	50.3	6.0	8.0	17.5
▲ FIRST NB IN BRONTE	BRONTE	TX	C-	D+	D+	25.5	9.73	14.6	5.4	9.9	55.0	10.0	11.1	25.7
▲ FIRST NB IN BROOKINGS	BROOKINGS	SD	B-	C+	C+	590.1	10.50	19.5	15.4	12.4	20.7	5.6	8.3	11.4
▲ FIRST NB IN CAMERON	CAMERON	TX	B-	C+	B-	146.0	-3.18	7.6	4.5	14.8	34.2	8.0	9.7	17.9
▲ FIRST NB IN CANNON FALLS	CANNON FALLS	MN	C+	C-	D+	116.7	6.93	15.2	5.8	7.0	18.5	6.8	9.0	12.4
▼ FIRST NB IN CARLYLE	CARLYLE	IL	B	B	B	111.6	-0.87	0.4	1.9	8.7	57.2	10.0	14.2	32.6
▲ FIRST NB IN CIMARRON	CIMARRON	KS	C	C-	C	54.0	-0.56	7.3	4.5	8.1	39.3	5.3	7.3	12.9
▼ FIRST NB IN CISCO	CISCO	TX	B-	B	B	44.4	16.27	9.1	3.4	3.7	46.0	10.0	15.3	30.5
FIRST NB IN COOPER	COOPER	TX	C-	C-	C-	18.4	-1.77	4.4	6.7	12.3	33.5	4.7	10.4	10.9
▼ FIRST NB IN CRESTON	CRESTON	IA	B-	B	B	150.0	1.15	8.2	5.5	16.6	25.5	6.1	8.1	12.4
FIRST NB IN DALHART	DALHART	TX	C	C	C+	45.6	-2.41	10.4	2.0	0.2	11.5	7.0	9.0	14.0
FIRST NB IN DURANT	DURANT	OK	B-	B-	B-	181.4	9.31	18.6	6.4	4.5	32.1	5.8	7.8	13.1
FIRST NB IN EDINBURG	EDINBURG	TX	B	B	B	2,609.4	47.54	5.4	2.9	8.6	44.8	5.3	7.3	13.2
FIRST NB IN EVANSTON	EVANSTON	WY	B-	B-	B-	234.0	15.29	11.6	10.4	4.4	52.9	4.8	6.8	15.1
▼ FIRST NB IN EXETER	EXETER	NE	C-	B-	B-	25.0	-0.69	3.2	2.4	7.1	25.9	10.0	12.8	20.3
FIRST NB IN FAIRFIELD	FAIRFIELD	IA	B	B	B	102.6	3.07	21.1	4.4	16.7	12.2	6.4	8.4	12.3
FIRST NB IN FALFURRIAS	FALFURRIAS	TX	B-	B	A-	64.6	5.95	2.0	9.7	0.0	71.3	10.0	11.2	53.3
FIRST NB IN FLEETWOOD	FLEETWOOD	PA	B-	B-	B-	153.6	4.30	13.4	2.9	25.8	29.4	8.7	10.2	20.2
FIRST NB IN FRANKFORT	FRANKFORT	KS	C+	B-	B-	28.8	2.28	20.2	4.8	9.1	41.1	7.6	9.4	16.4
▲ FIRST NB IN FREDONIA	FREDONIA	KS	A	A-	A	78.3	8.22	7.7	11.4	11.1	57.1	10.0	14.0	26.7
FIRST NB IN GEORGE WEST	GEORGE WEST	TX	B-	C+	C	100.3	3.62	15.2	8.4	10.2	20.6	7.9	9.6	14.1
▲ FIRST NB IN GEORGETOWN	GEORGETOWN	IL	C+	C	C	24.4	4.56	5.2	1.3	11.4	24.8	6.0	8.0	15.4
FIRST NB IN GRAHAM	GRAHAM	TX	B	B	B-	131.4	0.27	10.6	16.4	13.5	17.5	6.8	8.8	12.6
FIRST NB IN GREEN FOREST	GREEN FOREST	AR	A-	A-	A-	298.6	17.52	8.3	6.1	11.3	18.8	8.4	9.9	14.6
▲ FIRST NB IN HOMER	HOMER	IL	D+	D	C-	11.1	-4.95	3.8	6.0	16.6	23.8	8.6	10.1	19.0
FIRST NB IN HOMINY	HOMINY	OK	C+	C+	B-	34.8	0.28	5.0	11.3	6.4	58.4	6.7	8.7	18.3
▲ FIRST NB IN HOWELL	HOWELL	MI	C+	C	B-	449.3	5.27	7.6	6.1	12.5	14.5	7.7	9.6	13.1
FIRST NB IN LAS VEGAS	LAS VEGAS	NM	B-	B-	B+	104.4	7.01	2.4	4.6	17.0	52.2	6.1	8.1	18.8
FIRST NB IN MAHNOMEN	MAHNOMEN	MN	C+	C	C-	50.3	1.87	20.3	8.4	14.3	28.1	8.1	9.7	15.5
▲ FIRST NB IN MANITOWOC	MANITOWOC	WI	B	B-	C+	606.1	5.93	16.5	3.4	17.2	25.9	6.6	8.6	13.1
FIRST NB IN MARLOW	MARLOW	OK	B-	B-	B-	57.9	6.65	6.8	10.6	15.9	42.0	6.7	8.7	15.8
FIRST NB IN MENA	MENA	AR	A	A	A	122.3	-3.03	6.6	3.5	23.8	30.4	10.0	13.0	24.5
▲ FIRST NB IN MONTEVIDEO	MONTEVIDEO	MN	B+	B	B	135.3	-10.63	8.5	3.6	7.9	33.4	10.0	14.4	20.5
FIRST NB IN MUNDAY	MUNDAY	TX	C	C	C	70.6	10.41	6.8	5.1	5.8	44.5	4.1	6.2	12.8
FIRST NB IN NEW BREMEN	NEW BREMEN	OH	B+	B+	B+	147.3	-2.20	3.5	4.6	22.2	34.0	9.1	10.4	19.1
FIRST NB IN OKEENE	OKEENE	OK	C+	C+	B+	65.4	-2.11	5.0	1.3	0.1	73.6	10.0	22.8	62.9
FIRST NB IN OLNEY	OLNEY	IL	B-	C+	C+	209.1	-6.90	4.5	3.9	17.8	37.1	6.1	8.1	14.8
FIRST NB IN ORD	ORD	NE	A-	A-	A-	75.4	-3.54	7.6	3.4	10.6	31.9	10.0	11.5	19.1
FIRST NB IN PAWHUSKA	PAWHUSKA	OK	C	C	D	30.4	4.99	11.0	19.7	18.6	15.3	7.8	9.6	14.1
FIRST NB IN PAXTON	PAXTON	IL	A-	A-	A	65.5	-9.72	7.5	3.1	12.1	38.6	10.0	14.3	28.0
FIRST NB IN PHILIP	PHILIP	SD	A	A	A	111.8	5.65	15.8	2.9	0.0	19.8	10.0	14.6	18.0
FIRST NB IN PORT LAVACA	PORT LAVACA	TX	B+	B+	B+	128.3	-0.40	2.2	5.9	10.0	57.5	10.0	15.9	47.4
FIRST NB IN PRATT	PRATT	KS	C-	C	C-	77.1	-1.82	18.3	7.1	10.4	25.2	6.5	8.5	13.7
FIRST NB IN QUANAH	QUANAH	TX	C-	C-	C-	31.1	-5.62	2.3	9.2	7.1	53.2	7.5	9.3	20.0
▼ FIRST NB IN SIOUX FALLS	SIOUX FALLS	SD	B-	B	B	780.8	7.37	15.2	3.7	17.5	26.1	6.8	8.8	14.5
FIRST NB IN STAUNTON	STAUNTON	IL	B+	B+	A-	316.4	1.07	5.5	3.7	22.6	33.4	7.1	9.1	16.4
FIRST NB IN TIGERTON	TIGERTON	WI	C+	C+	C+	19.2	5.94	2.8	3.9	35.7	33.6	10.0	12.3	31.1
FIRST NB IN TREMONT	TREMONT	IL	B-	B-	B-	97.1	20.57	10.5	5.6	21.1	30.0	6.7	8.7	14.1
FIRST NB IN TRINIDAD	TRINIDAD	CO	B-	B-	B-	187.5	5.50	2.8	4.1	33.0	15.2	8.4	9.9	21.2
FIRST NB IN VIROQUA	VIROQUA	WI	C+	C+	B-	85.5	-4.95	12.5	7.5	17.8	10.1	7.0	9.0	13.2
FIRST NB IN WELLINGTON	WELLINGTON	KS	B-	B-	B-	72.9	4.46	14.5	7.4	9.3	10.9	8.2	10.6	13.5
FIRST NB IN WEST UNION	W UNION	WV	B+	B+	B+	67.3	4.80	4.0	4.2	21.9	51.1	10.0	13.6	30.1
FIRST NB IN WEWOKA	WEWOKA	OK	B	B	B	34.0	-0.14	7.4	11.5	17.0	46.3	10.0	15.8	32.2
FIRST NB IN WHITNEY	WHITNEY	TX	B+	B+	B+	53.2	-2.82	8.5	2.8	0.4	66.4	9.2	10.5	29.8
FIRST NB IN WINNEBAGO	WINNEBAGO	MN	B-	B-	B	36.2	-6.40	6.5	3.1	8.1	30.4	10.0	13.2	21.7
FIRST NB INDEPENDENCE KS	INDEPENDENCE	KS	C-	C-	C-	45.5	2.50	13.7	5.0	14.6	4.6	4.1	8.1	10.5
FIRST NB IZARD CTY	CALICO ROCK	AR	A+	A+	A+	117.4	5.11	2.9	5.7	19.9	25.1	10.0	24.0	41.5
FIRST NB MIDLAND	MIDLAND	TX	C-	C-	C-	111.6	12.27	26.6	4.2	9.6	37.1	5.6	7.6	12.0
FIRST NB MIDWEST	OSKALOOSA	IA	B-	C+	B-	93.8	0.09	8.3	39.3	14.9	2.8	6.0	8.9	11.7

Asset Quality Index	Non-Performing Loans as a % of Total Loans	Non-Performing Loans as a % of Capital	Net Charge-offs Avg Loans	Profitability Index	Net Income ($Mil)	Return on Assets (R.O.A.)	Return on Equity (R.O.E.)	Net Interest Spread	Overhead Efficiency Ratio	Liquidity Index	Liquidity Ratio	Hot Money Ratio	Stability Index
4.4	1.51	10.6	0.01	4.3	0.2	0.81	9.68	4.64	70.5	1.8	31.6	29.3	4.8
8.1	0.03	0.1	0.00	6.1	0.1	1.57	2.60	7.10	55.2	3.6	19.6	11.1	0.6
6.2	0.83	3.9	0.08	9.2	2.2	2.17	20.54	4.70	56.1	2.2	28.9	20.5	7.8
2.1	4.73	23.7	0.13	3.2	0.3	0.53	5.26	4.29	74.5	4.7	37.3	10.4	4.1
7.6	0.08	0.4	0.11	5.1	0.5	1.27	11.21	4.28	69.9	4.4	28.4	8.7	6.6
5.2	1.93	8.5	0.44	4.7	1.1	1.13	12.90	3.70	59.9	1.5	13.5	24.2	5.2
6.3	1.61	5.9	0.89	2.6	0.1	0.62	5.64	4.19	80.5	2.8	15.3	14.8	3.7
4.9	0.38	3.0	0.62	7.0	3.6	1.23	14.48	3.76	60.0	4.5	39.0	12.0	4.5
6.7	0.63	3.1	0.05	4.2	0.8	1.03	10.57	3.77	72.5	4.8	35.0	8.9	5.6
5.0	0.61	4.4	-0.05	4.0	0.5	0.88	10.94	4.58	78.4	3.3	15.2	12.4	4.5
9.5	0.20	0.5	0.00	3.4	0.3	0.59	4.07	2.96	73.8	7.3	73.5	3.8	8.0
6.0	0.59	4.3	-0.05	6.3	0.4	1.50	21.90	4.58	68.7	1.6	12.5	22.0	3.4
6.5	2.32	4.4	-0.42	4.2	0.2	0.97	6.11	4.19	77.4	4.4	89.8	21.2	5.5
5.0	6.71	17.8	0.00	4.1	0.1	1.12	10.09	3.02	66.8	6.7	141.8	13.6	3.7
3.6	2.03	15.3	0.01	7.8	1.2	1.62	19.41	3.65	61.4	4.7	30.1	7.7	5.8
8.3	0.00	0.0	-0.02	3.7	0.1	0.62	7.14	4.12	82.9	5.8	59.1	8.7	4.3
8.2	0.11	0.8	-0.01	6.6	1.2	1.40	17.27	4.23	67.2	3.2	33.4	16.9	4.5
8.6	0.33	2.2	0.20	8.9	31.0	2.58	37.65	4.43	44.4	0.9	13.9	34.0	4.7
4.9	1.14	6.7	0.04	6.7	1.8	1.59	22.30	4.02	62.6	3.1	45.6	22.2	4.4
1.7	11.45	45.8	0.00	3.9	0.1	0.60	4.57	3.46	84.0	6.5	67.2	6.1	6.4
4.7	0.85	6.8	0.02	4.9	0.5	0.87	10.24	3.87	64.9	5.4	40.7	7.9	4.8
8.1	3.01	4.2	2.49	3.2	0.2	0.54	4.96	2.71	71.6	6.8	70.6	4.9	3.5
6.8	0.50	2.5	0.01	4.2	0.5	0.70	7.03	3.83	78.3	7.2	71.0	3.7	5.9
8.4	0.09	0.4	-0.31	3.7	0.1	0.76	7.11	4.06	74.2	1.8	16.1	20.3	4.6
7.6	1.07	3.2	0.27	8.1	0.7	1.89	13.77	3.81	51.5	3.0	19.3	14.2	8.7
4.4	1.23	8.3	0.01	8.2	1.1	2.18	22.45	5.38	58.7	1.9	23.6	21.6	6.6
4.9	1.00	4.3	0.00	1.8	0.0	0.31	2.43	3.44	83.3	5.3	40.2	5.1	5.0
5.7	0.49	3.5	0.05	9.6	1.5	2.26	24.85	4.97	55.1	2.8	11.7	14.6	6.8
5.8	0.53	3.4	0.09	7.3	2.4	1.64	16.31	4.23	54.7	2.5	37.6	24.8	6.4
6.2	0.86	3.8	-0.61	1.7	0.0	-0.22	-2.15	4.66	104.7	5.3	50.4	8.0	4.2
5.5	1.09	5.0	0.00	7.1	0.3	1.69	20.54	3.76	62.9	5.1	54.1	12.1	4.3
4.4	1.11	7.7	0.29	8.3	2.8	1.27	13.92	4.68	59.0	5.1	66.6	15.2	5.9
6.2	0.91	4.8	0.29	4.0	0.5	0.99	12.18	3.83	73.3	3.9	17.0	9.3	5.4
4.4	1.60	10.2	1.10	4.2	0.4	1.61	16.76	4.42	65.9	4.8	39.4	10.8	4.2
4.7	0.80	4.8	0.29	6.8	4.0	1.35	13.24	3.82	57.6	3.5	21.5	12.4	6.1
5.4	0.78	4.6	0.01	8.8	0.6	2.09	22.45	4.62	56.9	5.1	40.8	9.5	5.8
8.9	0.05	0.2	0.17	6.5	0.7	1.15	8.97	3.74	54.9	5.8	84.8	14.2	7.5
7.4	1.04	4.2	-0.02	7.9	1.3	1.85	13.16	3.73	58.8	3.5	24.6	12.3	7.5
1.6	6.47	39.5	0.83	1.8	0.1	0.25	3.85	3.28	90.5	1.5	14.8	23.8	2.7
5.4	1.20	6.3	0.34	6.8	1.4	1.94	18.70	3.83	58.3	5.8	50.4	8.2	7.4
6.9	5.45	5.5	0.00	6.1	0.5	1.58	7.08	2.74	47.6	1.3	5.4	24.9	4.3
6.3	0.49	2.4	0.16	4.5	0.9	0.88	8.36	3.96	70.1	4.8	34.0	8.9	5.1
8.5	0.50	2.2	0.03	5.8	0.5	1.21	9.78	3.95	65.4	4.6	67.8	16.7	8.0
5.4	0.94	6.0	-0.11	6.2	0.2	1.11	11.79	5.66	71.7	3.7	65.8	22.2	4.2
9.3	0.02	0.1	-0.02	7.1	0.6	1.66	11.90	3.67	54.6	6.5	109.9	12.3	8.8
7.1	0.38	1.7	0.05	9.7	0.9	1.57	10.67	4.63	50.8	5.2	35.5	6.3	9.6
9.4	0.21	0.3	-0.06	4.4	0.5	0.73	4.62	3.10	67.0	4.5	90.5	24.3	7.2
6.8	0.17	1.1	0.09	2.1	0.2	0.40	4.29	3.56	89.2	5.2	34.7	6.5	4.6
5.2	2.12	8.3	0.14	2.5	0.1	0.64	6.93	3.23	94.6	4.6	55.1	14.7	3.0
6.8	0.42	2.7	-0.07	4.3	3.5	0.86	10.05	3.33	73.5	2.9	21.4	15.3	5.5
6.2	0.70	3.7	-0.03	6.1	2.5	1.53	15.09	3.46	57.2	5.2	35.7	6.6	7.1
9.3	0.11	0.4	0.00	4.4	0.0	0.33	2.75	3.30	60.7	8.6	169.7	5.4	4.7
5.4	0.60	3.8	0.02	6.8	0.5	1.16	11.84	4.27	63.7	3.0	13.8	13.8	5.6
6.5	0.85	4.3	0.19	4.0	0.5	0.57	5.72	3.85	76.5	5.8	108.2	16.8	5.1
3.0	1.82	11.5	0.18	6.1	0.6	1.38	12.97	4.43	67.1	5.5	46.6	7.8	6.3
6.2	0.39	2.9	0.07	4.8	0.5	1.26	11.95	4.30	71.5	2.2	29.7	21.4	5.4
9.3	0.14	0.4	0.02	5.9	0.4	1.33	9.67	4.33	60.9	1.4	31.1	39.5	6.8
6.6	1.31	3.6	0.81	4.5	0.2	0.88	5.28	4.79	79.5	3.0	51.9	25.8	6.6
8.6	0.01	0.0	-0.15	7.0	0.4	1.32	12.59	3.49	52.1	4.7	24.7	5.3	6.7
5.3	2.55	9.0	-0.22	4.2	0.2	0.86	6.07	3.95	78.5	6.9	74.0	4.5	5.6
4.1	1.08	10.1	0.00	7.3	0.4	1.68	19.91	5.78	67.1	1.7	11.8	20.6	3.7
8.8	0.02	0.1	-0.11	10.0	1.2	2.16	9.14	4.92	44.6	4.9	59.1	15.5	10.0
8.6	0.05	0.3	0.11	2.5	0.2	0.39	5.34	3.85	83.9	3.9	20.3	9.9	3.0
4.0	0.58	5.0	0.00	5.9	0.5	0.99	9.53	4.33	67.4	3.9	16.1	9.5	4.7

Name	City	State	Weiss Safety Rating	2003 Weiss Safety Rating	2002 Weiss Safety Rating	Total Assets ($Mil)	One Year Asset Growth	Commercial Loans	Consumer Loans	Home Mortgages	Securities	Capitalization Index	Leverage Ratio	Risk-based Capital Ratio
▲ FIRST NB MUHLENBERG	CENTRAL CITY	KY	C	C-	B	111.2	-5.46	8.7	5.3	40.7	25.9	8.1	9.7	17.6
▲ FIRST NB MUSKOGEE	MUSKOGEE	OK	C	C-	D-	95.6	20.13	21.2	4.7	11.6	33.4	6.5	8.5	13.6
▲ FIRST NB NELSONVILLE	NELSONVILLE	OH	C-	D+	D+	53.6	0.13	5.6	3.5	70.9	7.2	4.9	6.9	12.9
FIRST NB NORTHEAST	LYONS	NE	B-	B-	B-	161.4	0.12	11.3	3.5	5.3	30.9	5.9	7.9	12.1
▲ FIRST NB NORTHWEST	PANAMA CITY	FL	B	B-	B+	127.6	-9.51	3.5	1.2	10.1	10.1	9.6	10.8	18.0
▼ FIRST NB OELWEIN	OELWEIN	IA	B-	B	B	91.9	9.16	9.2	2.9	10.3	20.3	4.9	7.9	11.0
FIRST NB OF ABILENE	ABILENE	TX	A-	A-	A-	733.5	0.76	16.6	9.4	5.0	47.0	6.8	8.8	15.9
FIRST NB OF ABSECON	ABSECON	NJ	B	B	B+	151.4	-0.23	1.0	0.2	22.7	62.8	6.1	8.1	16.8
FIRST NB OF AINSWORTH	AINSWORTH	NE	C-	C-	D	39.9	1.86	4.4	4.5	3.4	5.4	9.2	11.3	14.3
FIRST NB OF AKRON	AKRON	IA	A-	A-	B+	39.6	-0.79	11.8	12.0	28.0	18.5	6.7	8.8	14.1
FIRST NB OF ALACHUA	ALACHUA	FL	B+	B+	B+	232.3	6.32	6.0	3.5	8.9	16.0	8.7	10.2	16.9
▼ FIRST NB OF ALBANY	ALBANY	TX	A	A+	A+	219.4	5.17	8.7	8.1	14.2	23.6	7.8	9.5	18.0
FIRST NB OF ALBION	ALBION	NE	B-	B-	B-	37.6	0.34	1.3	6.3	5.8	30.5	10.0	12.3	20.7
FIRST NB OF ALLENDALE	ALLENDALE	IL	B+	B+	B	84.5	2.21	11.7	10.4	18.9	29.7	10.0	11.7	19.6
FIRST NB OF ALTAVISTA	ALTAVISTA	VA	B	B	B	211.2	2.82	8.8	20.9	15.4	17.6	6.5	9.8	12.1
FIRST NB OF ALTHEIMER	ALTHEIMER	AR	C	C	C	12.8	-1.16	24.0	9.4	10.1	28.7	10.0	19.1	36.4
FIRST NB OF ALTUS	ALTUS	OK	B+	B+	B+	224.6	4.19	4.8	1.1	2.9	70.6	7.2	9.1	23.8
FIRST NB OF ALVIN	ALVIN	TX	A+	A+	A+	94.6	3.95	5.7	4.4	4.5	56.7	10.0	13.1	26.6
FIRST NB OF AMHERST	AMHERST	TX	C	C	C	16.9	-6.19	4.8	2.4	0.4	61.5	10.0	19.0	57.5
▼ FIRST NB OF ANDERSON	ANDERSON	TX	B-	B	B-	84.3	9.64	12.1	12.8	10.0	26.3	8.0	9.7	16.7
▲ FIRST NB OF ANSON	ANSON	TX	C	D	D	43.8	1.44	14.7	9.0	16.8	13.4	10.0	11.0	17.4
FIRST NB OF ANTHONY	ANTHONY	KS	C-	C-	D+	96.3	12.65	14.4	3.9	8.7	12.2	4.9	6.9	13.6
▲ FIRST NB OF ARCOLA	ARCOLA	IL	C	B-	B-	94.6	-8.61	4.4	1.1	5.1	70.0	10.0	11.0	34.7
▼ FIRST NB OF ARENZVILLE	ARENZVILLE	IL	D+	C-	D+	41.7	10.99	7.3	5.9	14.9	29.2	6.2	8.2	14.1
FIRST NB OF ARTESIA	ARTESIA	NM	B-	B-	C+	345.1	18.36	20.1	4.1	6.4	24.7	5.0	7.2	11.0
▲ FIRST NB OF ARVADA	ARVADA	CO	B	B-	B-	173.0	2.56	16.5	1.7	7.8	24.5	5.3	7.3	11.6
FIRST NB OF ASPERMONT	ASPERMONT	TX	A-	A-	A	32.0	0.65	3.5	1.9	0.8	73.3	10.0	30.7	92.6
FIRST NB OF ASSUMPTION	ASSUMPTION	IL	C+	C+	C+	19.2	-5.63	4.9	6.4	17.0	59.2	10.0	12.0	20.9
FIRST NB OF ATHENS	ATHENS	TX	B	B+	A-	213.4	-6.10	5.9	12.3	7.5	33.9	10.0	12.0	21.8
▲ FIRST NB OF ATMORE	ATMORE	AL	A-	A-	A-	101.5	10.44	12.7	7.9	13.1	34.4	10.0	14.5	24.4
FIRST NB OF AUDRAIN CTY	MEXICO	MO	B	B	B	112.3	-6.26	6.9	9.8	25.2	17.7	5.5	7.5	12.8
▼ FIRST NB OF AVA	AVA	IL	B	B+	B+	42.6	4.75	5.5	8.9	24.9	29.5	10.0	11.5	19.1
FIRST NB OF AZ	SCOTTSDALE	AZ	B-	B-	B-	1,517.1	86.49	9.6	0.7	0.7	0.3	3.0	7.7	10.0
FIRST NB OF BAGLEY	BAGLEY	MN	C	C	C+	63.5	1.66	16.3	10.7	13.3	23.0	7.4	9.3	13.1
FIRST NB OF BAIRD	BAIRD	TX	C	C	C	102.7	15.06	26.9	11.5	11.6	11.6	5.3	7.8	11.2
FIRST NB OF BALDWIN	FOLEY	AL	D-	D-	D	106.0	78.82	8.9	2.1	38.9	2.0	2.9	7.2	10.0
FIRST NB OF BALLINGER	BALLINGER	TX	B	B	B	54.0	17.84	9.5	6.2	10.1	23.3	6.1	8.1	11.9
FIRST NB OF BANCROFT	BANCROFT	NE	B-	B-	B-	14.7	3.84	6.6	5.2	8.0	13.7	10.0	19.0	28.8
FIRST NB OF BANGOR	BANGOR	WI	B+	A-	A-	165.2	1.24	9.7	4.4	16.9	29.0	10.0	15.8	23.2
▼ FIRST NB OF BAR HARBOR	BAR HARBOR	ME	D+	C-	C-	227.6	13.53	8.6	3.3	15.3	12.5	3.1	6.9	10.1
FIRST NB OF BARNESVILLE	BARNESVILLE	GA	C+	C	D+	108.6	10.43	3.9	2.7	18.0	11.7	6.1	9.2	11.9
▼ FIRST NB OF BARRON	BARRON	WI	D	D+	D+	48.0	15.65	6.9	3.6	33.9	12.4	5.2	7.2	11.2
▲ FIRST NB OF BARRY	BARRY	IL	B-	C+	C	107.7	0.58	9.1	5.3	6.6	24.4	10.0	13.6	23.6
FIRST NB OF BASTROP	BASTROP	TX	A-	A-	A-	253.4	3.73	3.7	4.2	27.4	32.2	9.8	10.9	20.0
FIRST NB OF BATTLE LAKE	BATTLE LAKE	MN	B+	B+	A-	38.3	10.77	3.9	3.2	12.8	38.7	8.4	9.9	16.7
▲ FIRST NB OF BEARDSTOWN	BEARDSTOWN	IL	A-	B+	A-	49.2	4.03	5.8	16.6	21.1	30.0	10.0	16.7	27.8
FIRST NB OF BEEVILLE	BEEVILLE	TX	B-	B-	B-	109.3	-10.31	10.5	4.2	3.0	51.3	6.6	8.6	17.6
FIRST NB OF BELDEN	BELDEN	NE	D+	D+	D+	26.5	4.03	5.9	2.4	2.4	9.4	7.0	10.3	12.5
▼ FIRST NB OF BELLEVUE	BELLEVUE	OH	B-	B	A-	97.6	-7.91	8.4	2.5	8.9	16.8	4.7	11.8	10.9
▲ FIRST NB OF BELLS/SAVOY	BELLS	TX	B-	C+	C+	40.8	-5.21	8.9	10.0	14.0	38.4	10.0	12.7	25.2
FIRST NB OF BELLVILLE	BELLVILLE	TX	B+	B+	B	111.3	6.22	7.0	6.7	24.2	30.7	6.3	8.4	14.6
FIRST NB OF BELOIT	BELOIT	KS	B	B	B	53.3	0.85	11.7	4.8	9.1	32.2	9.3	10.5	18.0
FIRST NB OF BEMIDJI	BEMIDJI	MN	A+	A+	A+	356.3	3.12	9.5	7.7	18.4	40.7	10.0	12.6	22.1
FIRST NB OF BERLIN	BERLIN	WI	B	B+	B+	219.7	5.94	14.1	5.7	18.3	33.9	5.1	8.1	11.0
FIRST NB OF BERRYVILLE	BERRYVILLE	AR	B+	A-	A-	126.6	0.34	8.4	7.8	27.5	16.0	10.0	13.6	20.9
▼ FIRST NB OF BERWICK	BERWICK	PA	B+	A-	A-	486.5	5.29	7.1	2.9	18.1	45.2	6.4	8.4	14.8
FIRST NB OF BLANCHESTER	BLANCHESTER	OH	B-	B-	B-	48.6	0.70	0.3	6.8	34.9	45.4	6.6	8.6	17.5
FIRST NB OF BLUE EARTH	BLUE EARTH	MN	B	B	A-	118.1	6.71	12.4	3.5	3.8	20.2	8.9	10.2	14.2
FIRST NB OF BOSQUE CTY	VALLEY MILLS	TX	C	C	C	79.0	-2.83	8.5	11.7	21.2	18.7	7.1	9.1	18.3
FIRST NB OF BREWSTER	BREWSTER	MN	C	C	B-	24.8	8.77	4.9	3.0	4.0	53.3	10.0	11.6	21.2
FIRST NB OF BRIDGEPORT	BRIDGEPORT	TX	B-	B-	B-	156.3	9.05	9.7	7.2	7.8	33.6	6.3	8.3	15.8
FIRST NB OF BROOKFIELD	BROOKFIELD	IL	B	B	B	212.1	22.14	6.9	1.0	28.8	26.0	7.0	9.0	15.3
FIRST NB OF BROOKSVILLE	BROOKSVILLE	KY	B+	B+	B+	58.9	-1.51	2.4	6.5	36.3	25.1	9.4	10.6	19.2
▲ FIRST NB OF BROWNFIELD	BROWNFIELD	TX	A	A-	A-	109.6	2.21	1.5	4.2	4.7	63.5	10.0	16.0	32.5

Asset Quality Index	Non-Performing Loans as a % of Total Loans	Non-Performing Loans as a % of Capital	Net Charge-offs Avg Loans	Profitability Index	Net Income ($Mil)	Return on Assets (R.O.A.)	Return on Equity (R.O.E.)	Net Interest Spread	Overhead Efficiency Ratio	Liquidity Index	Liquidity Ratio	Hot Money Ratio	Stability Index
4.6	1.74	10.7	0.19	3.4	0.3	0.61	6.24	4.28	72.3	2.0	8.7	18.6	3.8
4.6	1.31	9.3	0.09	3.6	0.6	1.27	15.49	3.85	68.0	1.1	5.6	28.0	1.1
6.0	0.41	4.9	0.02	5.0	0.3	1.16	17.02	4.42	74.2	2.4	18.0	17.3	3.1
7.1	0.41	2.6	-0.06	5.5	0.9	1.16	13.18	3.42	59.4	4.9	29.1	5.8	4.9
5.5	0.06	0.4	0.00	7.1	3.4	4.85	45.20	4.07	39.7	2.7	17.2	15.7	6.5
5.4	0.22	1.4	0.19	4.4	0.3	0.76	7.35	3.92	72.4	3.7	15.2	10.8	5.3
8.3	0.09	0.4	-0.01	10.0	9.7	2.60	29.12	4.10	41.9	4.5	28.6	8.1	8.2
10.0	0.20	0.8	0.00	4.5	0.6	0.84	10.00	4.14	72.8	5.4	32.8	4.1	5.3
1.7	3.22	17.7	0.16	6.0	0.2	1.08	9.46	4.55	66.1	5.4	54.7	10.2	5.6
6.4	0.47	3.4	0.03	8.1	0.3	1.31	15.08	3.14	52.2	3.8	20.7	10.7	7.3
4.5	2.36	11.1	-0.02	7.4	1.2	1.05	10.19	4.02	64.0	5.9	98.1	15.3	6.5
8.4	0.05	0.2	0.03	9.8	2.4	2.21	20.54	4.28	43.5	3.7	64.4	25.9	8.1
5.2	4.15	18.4	0.01	4.4	0.1	0.68	5.45	3.72	71.8	6.0	46.3	5.0	5.4
6.5	0.71	3.6	0.03	5.4	0.4	0.99	8.23	3.93	63.9	2.7	34.3	19.8	5.9
5.2	0.49	3.3	0.11	5.0	1.0	0.93	9.00	3.78	68.9	3.9	36.7	14.4	5.9
5.4	1.98	5.0	1.05	2.8	0.0	0.02	0.08	4.96	80.2	3.2	64.7	24.1	4.2
8.3	0.93	2.6	0.17	6.5	2.0	1.78	18.91	3.48	55.7	2.8	8.8	14.6	5.8
9.0	0.10	0.2	-0.01	10.0	1.4	2.91	20.65	4.86	49.7	4.8	34.2	9.1	9.4
9.7	0.00	0.0	-0.90	2.5	0.0	0.09	0.46	3.51	94.1	3.1	46.4	18.4	4.0
4.0	1.89	10.2	0.16	8.1	0.5	1.33	13.76	4.26	52.6	3.7	47.9	17.8	5.7
3.6	3.37	18.0	0.91	4.3	0.3	1.12	10.04	5.61	66.6	3.9	50.7	17.1	3.8
2.5	1.74	14.0	0.27	3.5	0.2	0.36	4.07	4.63	85.7	3.8	27.9	12.1	4.3
9.7	0.12	0.2	-0.06	2.4	0.1	0.25	2.22	2.07	89.3	3.5	33.8	15.2	5.2
7.0	0.26	1.7	0.01	2.7	0.1	0.30	3.62	3.71	90.9	2.5	45.2	30.7	2.5
5.8	0.60	4.9	0.12	9.4	3.5	2.06	27.75	5.07	60.3	3.6	22.2	11.7	5.2
7.4	0.08	0.7	-0.03	6.4	1.2	1.42	19.18	4.20	66.2	2.9	40.4	21.4	5.2
9.9	0.00	0.0	-18.52	8.9	0.8	4.62	14.70	3.76	37.1	3.5	78.7	30.7	8.0
8.0	1.50	4.5	0.31	3.9	0.1	0.60	4.99	4.09	78.9	3.4	11.0	11.2	4.0
7.9	0.14	0.5	0.08	3.5	0.7	0.67	5.39	3.45	81.7	5.0	42.3	10.7	7.6
5.5	1.97	7.3	0.05	6.9	0.8	1.54	10.47	4.41	66.4	4.1	30.9	11.6	8.7
5.1	0.51	3.9	0.00	9.5	0.8	1.49	17.97	4.04	52.4	5.5	54.6	11.3	6.4
5.6	2.73	13.9	0.15	7.2	0.3	1.19	10.39	4.73	62.6	3.1	27.8	15.4	6.4
3.6	1.09	11.7	0.21	8.0	6.7	0.98	13.47	6.02	86.3	1.5	7.0	22.5	5.9
3.9	1.17	7.7	1.19	3.3	0.1	0.30	3.24	4.96	82.0	5.7	29.9	0.7	4.2
5.3	0.62	5.5	0.10	8.9	0.9	1.71	22.47	5.11	54.5	2.0	27.7	22.1	3.9
8.6	0.00	0.0	0.01	0.4	0.1	0.17	2.06	3.57	98.5	1.9	14.0	19.5	0.0
6.8	0.28	1.9	0.09	4.9	0.2	0.95	10.12	4.22	76.2	2.5	37.0	25.0	5.9
7.0	0.28	1.0	-0.02	7.9	0.1	1.93	10.32	5.71	58.3	5.2	57.1	10.0	5.7
4.6	3.19	12.6	0.18	9.6	1.3	1.64	10.59	3.93	28.6	6.0	54.9	8.3	8.4
5.0	0.60	6.0	0.07	5.0	1.1	1.00	14.27	4.18	72.1	3.8	11.4	9.7	3.0
4.5	0.39	3.0	0.04	5.5	0.6	1.10	12.14	4.50	66.8	1.7	12.9	21.6	3.4
2.1	2.56	23.7	0.05	5.3	0.3	1.24	17.33	4.55	78.5	3.4	16.5	12.1	2.8
3.8	3.26	11.0	-0.57	7.6	1.2	2.14	13.68	4.12	45.3	4.6	117.2	30.2	7.9
6.4	0.67	3.3	0.06	8.2	1.7	1.32	11.79	4.55	60.3	3.1	19.0	14.1	8.0
8.9	0.02	0.1	-0.05	5.9	0.3	1.33	13.13	4.24	69.6	4.9	36.5	8.9	6.5
7.7	0.05	0.2	0.13	7.3	0.3	1.27	7.58	4.81	64.3	4.0	17.8	8.7	7.8
8.8	0.13	0.6	-0.01	6.9	0.7	1.30	15.76	4.02	60.7	3.4	10.0	11.7	4.0
0.0	4.48	33.4	-0.12	7.9	0.2	1.85	18.64	4.94	62.5	3.6	22.7	11.9	4.3
5.9	0.90	5.1	0.04	5.1	0.5	1.03	8.45	4.75	77.0	3.9	14.9	9.1	6.2
8.1	0.74	2.7	0.49	3.4	0.1	0.57	4.56	4.63	77.0	2.5	47.8	31.4	4.3
8.5	0.05	0.4	-0.01	10.0	1.1	1.97	23.75	4.81	44.4	2.7	14.7	15.5	6.2
8.4	0.00	0.0	-0.01	5.0	0.2	0.86	8.32	3.80	68.4	4.8	38.3	10.4	5.7
8.0	0.42	1.7	0.06	7.9	3.1	1.77	13.37	3.84	51.4	2.9	23.1	15.3	9.1
6.5	0.35	2.5	0.03	7.0	1.3	1.17	14.46	4.32	62.6	3.9	7.1	8.2	5.1
4.7	2.20	11.5	0.08	9.4	1.4	2.15	15.77	5.18	62.8	4.1	29.3	11.2	9.4
7.7	0.52	2.6	0.09	7.9	3.6	1.49	15.72	3.68	49.1	5.0	40.7	10.4	6.8
8.3	0.12	0.5	0.05	7.3	0.3	1.16	10.39	4.50	64.9	6.7	67.1	4.6	5.1
4.8	0.53	3.3	-0.01	8.3	1.2	2.01	17.54	4.19	49.4	3.8	10.9	9.4	8.2
7.1	0.41	2.2	-0.05	3.3	0.3	0.62	6.91	3.37	83.1	5.5	85.5	14.4	3.9
7.8	0.42	1.3	-0.27	2.5	0.0	0.33	2.80	3.36	90.8	4.3	64.2	16.1	3.9
4.9	1.07	5.3	0.46	4.7	0.9	1.10	11.93	3.67	69.0	4.0	69.5	23.9	5.3
6.4	0.78	5.4	0.00	4.5	0.8	0.81	9.14	3.83	68.6	4.0	29.1	11.6	5.3
5.3	0.94	5.7	0.05	7.0	0.5	1.57	14.33	4.28	64.9	5.4	40.0	7.1	6.6
9.3	0.01	0.0	-0.24	6.4	0.7	1.26	8.05	4.23	60.6	2.3	16.2	17.8	8.7

Name	City	State	Weiss Safety Rating	2003 Weiss Safety Rating	2002 Weiss Safety Rating	Total Assets ($Mil)	One Year Asset Growth	Asset Mix (As a % of Total Assets) Commercial Loans	Consumer Loans	Home Mortgages	Securities	Capitalization Index	Leverage Ratio	Risk-based Capital Ratio
▲ FIRST NB OF BROWNSTOWN	BROWNSTOWN	IL	C-	D+	D+	20.5	-3.32	3.3	10.2	16.4	31.3	9.9	10.9	19.3
▲ FIRST NB OF BRUNDIDGE	BRUNDIDGE	AL	C	C-	D+	84.6	12.23	7.1	13.2	24.8	12.8	5.9	7.9	11.7
▲ FIRST NB OF BRYAN	BRYAN	TX	A	A-	A-	348.2	0.96	14.1	14.1	19.6	23.9	9.8	10.8	19.6
FIRST NB OF BUFFALO	BUFFALO	WY	C	C+	C	124.7	8.58	12.1	6.5	8.8	27.3	7.0	9.0	14.5
FIRST NB OF BUHL	BUHL	MN	C-	C-	C-	12.7	0.04	8.6	8.2	32.0	29.7	9.6	10.7	21.2
▲ FIRST NB OF BULLARD	BULLARD	TX	D-	E	E-	43.5	7.94	5.1	26.2	18.9	22.4	5.8	7.8	15.2
FIRST NB OF BURLESON	BURLESON	TX	B+	B+	B+	112.7	6.63	15.1	3.8	2.3	44.4	5.5	7.5	15.5
▲ FIRST NB OF BYERS	BYERS	TX	B+	B	B	62.9	4.16	8.8	11.8	9.2	17.3	10.0	11.4	18.5
▲ FIRST NB OF CAINSVILLE	CAINSVILLE	MO	C	C-	C-	16.2	30.39	4.8	9.3	13.2	12.9	8.6	10.1	13.8
FIRST NB OF CALUMET	CALUMET	OK	C+	C+	B-	18.9	-5.82	1.7	2.5	1.4	56.5	10.0	17.3	47.3
FIRST NB OF CAMBRIDGE	CAMBRIDGE	NE	C-	C-	C+	38.1	-6.39	1.9	7.0	8.1	30.6	10.0	11.6	18.7
FIRST NB OF CANADIAN	CANADIAN	TX	B	B	B	61.1	6.54	3.3	5.1	3.3	45.3	7.9	9.6	19.3
FIRST NB OF CANTON	CANTON	PA	B	B	B	57.9	5.53	12.5	6.5	31.4	14.5	10.0	12.6	18.2
▼ FIRST NB OF CANTON	CANTON	TX	B	B+	B+	70.2	7.36	6.7	10.3	15.5	5.8	7.0	9.0	16.5
FIRST NB OF CARMI	CARMI	IL	C	C	C-	191.0	-1.20	16.4	10.8	13.6	20.0	5.7	7.7	11.9
FIRST NB OF CARROLLTON	CARROLLTON	KY	B+	B+	B+	63.6	4.96	2.8	5.9	27.3	37.4	10.0	11.2	19.8
FIRST NB OF CARROLLTON	CARROLLTON	MO	C	C	B-	35.2	4.67	1.9	2.5	6.7	55.4	6.7	8.7	18.5
FIRST NB OF CASS LAKE	CASS LAKE	MN	C	C	C	21.5	11.24	9.8	8.9	12.8	25.2	5.3	7.3	13.1
FIRST NB OF CATLIN	CATLIN	IL	D+	C	C+	46.0	16.84	0.6	16.3	7.6	56.7	6.0	8.0	19.3
FIRST NB OF CENTERVILLE	CENTERVILLE	TN	B	B	A-	94.9	-3.11	1.3	6.6	33.2	36.1	10.0	15.3	34.6
▲ FIRST NB OF CENTRAL	ALICEVILLE	AL	B	C+	B-	155.5	8.74	10.4	8.7	26.8	19.1	7.6	9.4	14.1
▲ FIRST NB OF CENTRAL TEXAS	WACO	TX	C	C-	D+	264.7	4.67	23.6	15.5	12.0	5.4	5.1	8.3	11.1
▲ FIRST NB OF CENTRALIA	CENTRALIA	KS	B	B-	C+	70.4	18.59	12.0	2.1	8.6	40.0	6.5	8.5	15.1
FIRST NB OF CHADRON	CHADRON	NE	B+	B+	B	46.5	4.01	10.8	2.9	3.9	23.4	8.9	10.3	15.0
FIRST NB OF CHASKA	CHASKA	MN	B+	B+	B	170.5	-3.38	13.9	2.6	6.9	30.3	8.5	10.0	14.4
FIRST NB OF CHATSWORTH	CHATSWORTH	GA	C	C-	C-	140.9	-5.48	13.7	10.4	14.5	27.4	7.3	9.2	15.5
FIRST NB OF CHATTOOGA	SUMMERVILLE	GA	B+	B+	B+	43.6	2.21	3.6	6.3	22.3	40.8	10.0	12.4	23.4
FIRST NB OF CHELSEA	CHELSEA	OK	E+	E+	E	23.6	1.77	2.8	9.8	21.0	41.4	6.6	8.6	18.7
FIRST NB OF CHESTER	W CHESTER	PA	B-	C+	C+	756.4	14.44	12.3	1.3	16.4	17.4	5.3	8.6	11.3
FIRST NB OF CHILLICOTHE	CHILLICOTHE	IL	C-	C-	C-	85.1	-6.61	2.8	15.9	17.1	50.2	6.0	8.0	16.6
▲ FIRST NB OF CHILLICOTHE	CHILLICOTHE	TX	B-	C	C	37.4	-0.22	6.0	9.7	9.4	39.3	10.0	11.5	20.3
▲ FIRST NB OF CHRISMAN	CHRISMAN	IL	B	B-	B	42.1	-4.37	8.6	7.7	4.5	45.8	9.4	10.6	18.9
▼ FIRST NB OF CLARKSDALE	CLARKSDALE	MS	B+	A-	A-	211.9	13.44	12.2	5.6	7.6	36.0	7.7	9.5	15.6
▲ FIRST NB OF CLAUDE	CLAUDE	TX	C-	C+	C	28.2	5.48	2.2	0.8	3.6	11.7	8.9	10.3	17.5
FIRST NB OF CLIFTON	CLIFTON	IL	B+	B+	B+	29.4	3.42	9.5	5.9	13.5	37.8	9.3	10.5	20.4
FIRST NB OF CLIFTON	CLIFTON	KS	C	C	C	41.0	3.10	9.0	5.4	19.9	30.4	5.9	7.9	13.9
FIRST NB OF CLINTON	CLINTON	MO	C	C	C+	72.5	5.75	23.0	7.6	15.9	8.1	5.8	8.3	11.6
FIRST NB OF CO CITY	COLORADO CITY	TX	D+	C	C+	21.5	-12.63	34.5	7.4	5.7	10.8	10.0	11.0	32.7
FIRST NB OF COFFEE CTY	DOUGLAS	GA	B	B	B-	109.5	5.92	8.6	6.1	19.8	4.0	6.3	8.3	12.2
FIRST NB OF COKATO	COKATO	MN	C	C+	C+	29.3	10.24	6.8	9.0	11.6	27.3	8.6	10.0	20.0
FIRST NB OF COLD SPRING	COLD SPRING	MN	C	C-	C	82.6	4.03	19.7	9.6	7.5	29.7	5.5	8.0	11.4
FIRST NB OF COLERAINE	COLERAINE	MN	C-	C-	C-	58.3	4.76	3.6	10.3	29.2	41.2	5.6	7.6	15.7
▼ FIRST NB OF COLORADO SPR	COLORADO SPRINGS	CO	C-	C	C-	74.9	-12.85	49.0	9.0	1.1	5.3	3.9	7.9	10.4
▼ FIRST NB OF COLUMBIA	COLUMBIA	KY	C-	C+	B+	176.3	3.93	6.7	9.0	27.6	16.3	6.7	8.7	13.4
FIRST NB OF CORTEZ	CORTEZ	CO	C+	C+	B-	69.7	3.01	2.2	4.2	8.0	68.3	6.9	8.9	22.9
FIRST NB OF COWETA	COWETA	OK	D	D	D	58.0	4.58	13.6	12.4	14.7	40.7	4.7	6.8	13.4
▲ FIRST NB OF CRESTVIEW	CRESTVIEW	FL	B+	B	B	162.1	9.67	4.4	1.1	7.8	33.8	10.0	13.9	22.4
FIRST NB OF CROCKETT	CROCKETT	TX	D	D	C+	129.5	1.98	12.8	8.3	15.7	9.9	3.9	7.9	10.5
FIRST NB OF CROSBY	CROSBY	MN	A-	A-	B+	50.3	8.52	5.4	9.3	30.1	33.9	8.4	9.9	19.2
FIRST NB OF CROSSETT	CROSSETT	AR	B+	B+	B	130.3	7.84	32.3	13.0	8.6	30.9	8.2	9.8	15.3
FIRST NB OF CUNNINGHAM	CUNNINGHAM	KS	C+	C+	B-	20.4	-1.31	3.4	5.1	10.4	35.6	9.1	10.4	20.0
FIRST NB OF DAMARISCOTTA	DAMARISCOTTA	ME	B	B	B	611.7	15.65	14.4	2.6	33.5	21.6	5.6	7.6	12.1
FIRST NB OF DANA	DANA	IN	C-	D+	D+	31.9	57.80	3.0	6.0	15.1	36.3	5.0	7.0	18.2
FIRST NB OF DANVILLE	DANVILLE	IL	C+	C+	C	160.9	4.61	9.1	1.7	11.7	38.9	4.3	6.3	12.5
FIRST NB OF DAVIS	DAVIS	OK	C	C-	C+	55.7	35.94	10.9	17.0	14.0	27.5	6.4	8.4	14.0
FIRST NB OF DE QUEEN	DE QUEEN	AR	A	A	A	116.2	4.15	5.3	3.6	8.5	53.0	10.0	17.9	33.7
FIRST NB OF DE WITT	DE WITT	AR	C-	D+	C+	101.8	3.39	6.4	4.9	10.1	32.6	6.8	8.8	15.2
▼ FIRST NB OF DECATUR	DECATUR	IL	B+	A-	A-	433.9	-0.34	14.5	5.3	7.1	30.7	5.5	7.5	11.8
FIRST NB OF DECATUR	BAINBRIDGE	GA	D	NR	NR	18.3	N/A	18.8	3.7	10.6	7.9	10.0	31.7	34.6
FIRST NB OF DEER RIVER	DEER RIVER	MN	C	C-	C+	15.8	-4.38	18.0	3.8	20.0	17.3	10.0	14.6	28.2
▲ FIRST NB OF DEERWOOD	DEERWOOD	MN	B+	B	B	149.8	1.80	12.2	3.8	9.8	25.6	7.3	9.2	12.8
FIRST NB OF DENNISON	DENNISON	OH	B+	A-	A-	152.0	3.58	8.4	24.8	20.6	18.3	7.8	9.6	14.6
▲ FIRST NB OF DIETERICH	DIETERICH	IL	B	B-	C+	153.2	5.89	9.2	4.9	14.5	30.1	6.3	8.3	13.4
▼ FIRST NB OF DIGHTON	DIGHTON	KS	B	B+	B+	48.5	-0.76	5.5	4.2	1.5	46.7	10.0	19.2	36.3

Asset Quality Index	Non-Performing Loans as a % of Total Loans	Non-Performing Loans as a % of Capital	Net Charge-offs Avg Loans	Profitability Index	Net Income ($Mil)	Return on Assets (R.O.A.)	Return on Equity (R.O.E.)	Net Interest Spread	Overhead Efficiency Ratio	Liquidity Index	Liquidity Ratio	Hot Money Ratio	Stability Index
4.4	1.88	9.1	-0.17	4.3	0.1	0.75	6.94	4.13	77.3	4.6	37.0	8.4	2.4
5.2	0.41	3.8	0.10	5.7	0.5	1.09	14.14	4.68	64.3	0.7	15.3	47.5	3.1
7.8	0.13	0.7	-0.18	7.9	2.6	1.46	13.13	4.69	64.0	6.0	65.3	10.6	7.4
3.2	2.18	14.4	0.07	6.3	0.6	1.06	11.87	4.24	58.1	2.5	24.8	17.3	5.5
5.2	1.33	6.8	0.00	4.9	0.1	1.20	11.12	4.63	74.8	4.5	74.8	16.8	2.8
3.9	1.20	7.9	0.18	3.7	0.2	0.76	9.83	4.01	77.3	6.3	72.5	8.2	0.6
8.6	0.07	0.5	0.02	10.0	1.3	2.26	31.99	4.53	57.5	4.5	31.7	9.4	5.8
6.5	1.09	5.4	1.34	5.9	0.3	0.83	7.31	4.53	71.5	5.7	76.3	12.3	5.8
6.2	0.31	2.2	-0.02	4.5	0.1	0.85	7.74	4.75	68.1	4.1	25.7	8.7	4.3
7.8	0.00	0.0	-0.81	3.4	0.1	0.53	2.56	2.56	95.2	5.7	46.7	4.1	5.1
2.9	5.01	25.3	0.22	4.4	0.1	0.71	6.28	3.77	77.8	4.3	22.0	7.7	4.0
8.9	0.00	0.0	-0.02	6.2	0.7	2.14	23.66	3.41	56.6	5.5	84.6	14.4	5.1
4.8	2.16	12.0	0.09	4.8	0.3	0.87	6.95	4.53	69.6	3.0	29.0	16.1	6.3
6.9	0.82	4.3	0.05	8.0	0.6	1.70	18.70	4.08	59.8	6.7	95.8	9.5	6.1
3.2	1.46	9.7	0.60	3.4	0.6	0.62	6.74	3.85	67.8	3.5	21.3	12.2	4.2
8.9	0.30	1.4	0.32	6.0	0.3	0.89	8.07	3.88	66.3	4.1	33.9	12.3	6.0
5.6	2.30	8.7	0.05	6.3	0.3	1.66	19.98	3.42	57.2	4.4	16.3	6.0	3.8
6.3	0.16	0.9	-0.02	0.0	0.0	-0.30	-3.17	3.47	108.1	5.1	45.9	8.1	3.2
6.2	0.68	2.5	0.45	4.6	0.2	1.05	12.24	3.60	67.5	8.1	156.4	7.6	2.2
8.1	1.09	3.9	0.07	4.0	0.3	0.56	3.63	4.40	80.5	4.3	25.1	8.1	7.0
6.4	0.25	1.8	0.09	5.5	0.9	1.15	12.16	4.18	64.9	1.7	13.5	20.5	4.7
7.1	0.01	0.1	0.04	7.2	1.6	1.21	15.62	4.34	60.7	2.8	19.4	15.4	3.7
7.4	0.37	2.5	-0.03	6.4	0.5	1.59	19.80	3.83	56.0	0.9	5.5	31.0	5.7
7.8	0.25	1.4	-0.02	8.1	0.4	1.89	18.01	4.73	58.0	5.5	47.3	8.6	7.0
4.8	2.40	12.5	-0.02	3.7	0.0	-0.02	-0.24	3.91	79.6	4.3	30.7	10.3	7.4
5.9	0.40	2.3	0.48	3.7	0.5	0.67	7.45	4.44	79.1	2.4	33.8	22.1	2.8
8.5	0.24	1.0	-0.09	8.5	0.5	2.03	17.01	5.49	55.8	2.4	18.7	17.2	6.2
4.0	2.65	12.1	1.15	2.5	0.0	0.17	1.98	4.76	94.0	3.6	23.2	11.3	1.0
6.2	0.34	2.9	-0.15	5.2	3.5	0.99	11.57	4.39	73.5	4.9	26.0	4.3	4.4
3.6	2.54	15.8	0.79	4.4	0.5	1.31	16.69	3.36	57.4	2.4	7.7	16.4	2.9
6.9	0.65	2.6	0.21	4.7	0.2	1.20	10.21	4.08	74.6	3.6	43.7	17.6	4.5
9.0	0.00	0.0	0.03	6.6	0.3	1.59	14.79	3.54	55.3	4.3	54.7	15.8	6.0
7.3	0.54	3.0	0.06	6.9	1.5	1.47	15.98	3.95	53.3	1.8	20.7	21.8	5.6
2.9	2.70	14.8	0.58	6.9	0.1	0.81	8.06	3.82	69.0	6.9	128.2	12.0	4.5
7.0	0.45	2.0	0.03	4.8	0.1	0.95	9.27	3.39	63.4	6.8	82.3	7.1	6.2
6.0	0.39	2.8	0.06	7.6	0.3	1.50	17.51	4.45	67.3	3.2	46.7	20.0	3.5
3.8	1.45	12.5	0.01	5.7	0.5	1.44	17.33	4.52	65.2	4.0	31.0	11.8	4.8
7.5	0.31	1.5	0.64	1.3	0.0	-0.28	-2.46	3.03	95.9	6.3	66.0	4.8	3.1
5.9	0.22	2.0	0.05	9.7	1.2	2.16	26.34	4.80	53.8	1.4	15.7	25.7	5.8
7.7	0.57	2.4	-0.05	2.7	0.1	0.33	3.11	3.86	92.1	7.5	85.0	2.8	3.7
5.3	0.77	5.4	0.13	4.3	0.3	0.76	9.42	3.80	74.4	4.4	36.2	11.9	3.4
4.9	1.38	9.5	1.95	3.1	0.0	-0.09	-1.09	3.18	74.2	3.0	36.0	18.8	3.4
7.7	0.00	0.0	0.00	4.9	0.3	0.83	10.23	4.81	71.0	4.0	42.3	15.2	3.2
0.5	4.03	24.0	2.26	4.2	0.4	0.46	4.21	4.30	64.3	1.9	15.3	19.4	4.8
5.0	4.90	12.3	0.01	4.7	0.3	0.85	8.85	4.00	80.4	4.0	20.8	9.8	4.6
4.6	0.96	6.3	0.16	3.9	0.2	0.83	11.86	4.36	82.9	4.3	23.7	8.0	2.6
9.1	0.01	0.0	0.03	5.4	1.0	1.08	8.69	3.69	56.0	3.5	54.2	22.6	6.3
2.8	1.61	13.6	0.09	5.1	0.9	1.45	18.61	5.01	69.6	3.8	18.8	10.2	1.9
8.5	0.00	0.0	-0.01	7.6	0.4	1.73	16.91	4.20	60.6	4.9	39.1	10.1	7.4
5.1	1.22	7.2	0.23	7.9	0.9	1.39	14.44	4.87	61.7	1.9	18.1	19.7	5.4
8.6	0.01	0.1	0.00	5.1	0.1	0.99	9.69	4.74	78.3	5.4	44.2	5.3	4.4
6.1	0.59	5.1	0.05	7.9	4.0	1.37	17.17	3.86	50.9	1.6	7.8	21.5	5.7
3.3	5.12	15.8	7.02	0.2	-0.4	-2.64	-31.13	2.97	130.3	8.8	167.9	4.3	3.8
5.0	1.29	9.4	0.00	6.9	1.0	1.22	18.91	4.43	65.3	6.8	72.4	6.6	4.8
3.4	1.07	9.0	0.69	9.8	0.6	2.21	27.87	5.50	51.8	1.1	6.4	27.9	3.5
7.8	1.41	3.5	0.02	9.6	0.9	1.62	9.32	3.84	38.4	1.2	5.3	26.0	9.3
3.1	1.67	10.3	0.72	5.0	0.6	1.10	12.81	3.52	67.8	3.4	48.6	20.7	5.1
7.6	0.29	2.1	0.05	7.6	2.5	1.17	15.37	3.48	55.5	3.7	38.9	16.0	6.9
8.3	0.00	0.0	0.00	0.0	-0.4	-6.87	-16.81	1.70	282.6	5.4	54.2	8.0	0.0
8.5	0.26	0.8	0.00	3.3	0.0	0.43	2.91	4.51	86.1	8.1	114.6	1.6	4.3
6.6	0.48	2.7	0.20	7.4	1.2	1.61	15.17	4.43	66.7	3.2	23.8	14.1	6.8
7.0	0.11	0.7	0.07	4.9	0.5	0.66	6.76	4.22	73.8	6.4	64.7	8.2	6.2
8.5	0.12	0.8	-0.01	6.0	1.0	1.26	15.05	3.76	54.5	5.2	39.0	8.5	4.6
4.2	7.35	13.8	6.02	3.2	0.0	0.14	0.75	3.79	63.3	7.5	126.4	8.6	6.4

Name	City	State	Weiss Safety Rating	2003 Weiss Safety Rating	2002 Weiss Safety Rating	Total Assets ($Mil)	One Year Asset Growth	Commercial Loans	Consumer Loans	Home Mortgages	Securities	Capitalization Index	Leverage Ratio	Risk-based Capital Ratio
								Asset Mix (As a % of Total Assets)						
FIRST NB OF DOZIER	DOZIER	AL	B+	B+	B+	32.2	-3.81	7.2	4.2	6.9	58.5	10.0	13.9	29.3
FIRST NB OF DRYDEN	DRYDEN	NY	A	A	A	85.1	4.85	4.2	13.1	10.5	47.9	10.0	12.7	33.7
▼ FIRST NB OF DURANGO	DURANGO	CO	B-	B	B	264.5	7.68	5.8	2.2	8.2	17.0	3.6	7.6	10.3
FIRST NB OF DWIGHT	DWIGHT	IL	A-	A-	A	92.0	-0.67	5.8	1.8	13.6	35.2	10.0	14.8	25.6
FIRST NB OF E ARKANSAS	FORREST CITY	AR	A-	A-	A-	230.9	-0.83	1.0	7.2	7.2	44.9	10.0	12.3	26.5
FIRST NB OF EAGLE LAKE	EAGLE LAKE	TX	D+	D+	D+	65.1	-2.83	9.2	3.6	6.2	38.6	7.4	9.3	15.3
FIRST NB OF EAGLE RIVER	EAGLE RIVER	WI	C	C	B-	150.5	12.54	1.8	3.2	40.9	25.9	5.0	7.0	13.0
▲ FIRST NB OF EDGEWOOD	EDGEWOOD	TX	C-	D+	D+	15.2	0.84	3.8	7.6	18.8	22.5	8.5	10.0	18.5
FIRST NB OF EKALAKA	EKALAKA	MT	D+	D+	C	25.0	7.61	9.6	5.5	2.0	28.8	7.4	9.3	14.0
▼ FIRST NB OF ELDORADO	ELDORADO	TX	B-	B	B+	37.6	-2.10	9.6	3.6	10.3	42.4	10.0	12.2	23.5
FIRST NB OF ELK RIVER	ELK RIVER	MN	C-	C-	C	408.3	-3.76	19.5	1.6	1.8	28.8	7.7	9.4	13.9
▲ FIRST NB OF ELKHART	ELKHART	KS	B-	C+	B	44.9	-0.74	4.6	9.0	11.7	11.9	10.0	12.1	19.0
▼ FIRST NB OF ELMER	ELMER	NJ	B+	A-	A-	189.1	9.40	5.5	4.5	28.3	7.4	6.8	8.9	12.3
FIRST NB OF ELY	ELY	NV	A-	A-	A-	49.9	4.99	11.1	3.3	4.6	57.6	10.0	19.1	28.0
FIRST NB OF EMORY	EMORY	TX	C+	C+	C+	72.5	4.58	8.4	11.0	15.0	29.5	8.8	10.2	19.7
FIRST NB OF ESTES PARK	ESTES PARK	CO	B+	B+	B	88.7	1.99	13.8	10.4	11.2	8.1	7.0	9.3	12.5
▼ FIRST NB OF EVANT	EVANT	TX	D	C-	C+	24.3	5.58	26.1	7.5	3.4	13.3	10.0	12.7	22.2
FIRST NB OF FAIRBURY	FAIRBURY	NE	A-	A-	A-	97.0	-3.60	6.1	4.7	4.9	48.8	10.0	22.5	43.6
FIRST NB OF FAIRFAX	FAIRFAX	MN	B+	B+	B+	23.8	-1.60	9.0	11.3	2.4	6.2	10.0	32.5	34.8
FIRST NB OF FAIRFIELD	FAIRFIELD	MT	A	A	A	82.2	12.85	16.2	9.6	4.2	26.4	10.0	12.6	20.2
▲ FIRST NB OF FARRAGUT	SHENANDOAH	IA	D+	D-	D	25.6	1.96	10.0	8.1	12.7	41.9	6.2	8.2	15.6
▲ FIRST NB OF FLEMING	FLEMING	CO	D	E+	E-	11.3	-4.17	5.8	7.6	24.9	9.8	8.3	9.9	16.1
▲ FIRST NB OF FLETCHER	FLETCHER	OK	B	B-	C+	18.0	1.28	4.5	3.8	5.2	62.4	10.0	11.9	26.5
FIRST NB OF FLORIDA	MILTON	FL	B-	B-	C+	352.1	-1.11	3.6	0.5	5.1	34.1	8.5	10.0	16.6
▼ FIRST NB OF FLORIDA	NAPLES	FL	C+	B-	B-	4,055.0	41.05	5.0	1.9	17.8	21.0	3.1	6.2	10.1
FIRST NB OF FLOYDADA	FLOYDADA	TX	A	A	A	71.6	-0.01	7.3	1.5	3.6	51.3	10.0	15.1	38.1
FIRST NB OF FORSYTH	CUMMING	GA	D	NR	NR	33.6	N/A	2.0	1.5	13.6	9.0	10.0	35.0	40.7
▼ FIRST NB OF FREDERICK	FREDERICK	SD	C	C+	C+	12.8	3.02	4.6	1.4	0.0	52.1	10.0	17.0	34.1
▲ FIRST NB OF FREMONT	FREMONT	IN	C-	C	C+	117.2	-1.04	4.0	17.3	22.3	4.7	3.5	7.2	10.3
FIRST NB OF FRIEND	FRIEND	NE	B	B	B	36.5	-6.15	8.2	4.2	9.4	23.5	7.4	9.2	15.2
▲ FIRST NB OF FT SMITH	FORT SMITH	AR	A	A-	A-	671.3	2.45	23.9	4.5	5.0	18.1	10.0	15.9	21.3
▼ FIRST NB OF FT STOCKTON	FORT STOCKTON	TX	B	B+	B+	43.4	-0.20	7.9	4.2	5.9	57.1	10.0	16.9	39.0
FIRST NB OF GAYLORD	GAYLORD	MI	E-	E-	D+	154.9	-26.55	7.0	8.2	34.1	17.1	2.6	5.4	9.7
FIRST NB OF GEORGIA	BUCHANAN	GA	A-	A-	A-	187.8	-0.67	3.6	5.3	27.5	23.9	8.0	9.7	16.8
FIRST NB OF GERMANTOWN	GERMANTOWN	OH	D	D	D+	44.9	-15.49	7.2	6.1	21.9	26.1	7.3	9.2	18.7
FIRST NB OF GIDDINGS	GIDDINGS	TX	B	B	B+	100.2	0.78	5.2	1.6	8.4	44.9	8.2	9.8	19.4
▼ FIRST NB OF GILBERT	GILBERT	MN	C	C+	C+	22.9	0.22	3.1	16.1	30.1	14.3	10.0	12.8	25.2
FIRST NB OF GILMAN	GILMAN	IL	C	C-	D-	46.2	2.17	9.3	10.2	5.0	39.4	3.8	5.8	11.4
FIRST NB OF GILMER	GILMER	TX	D	D	D	164.1	-6.17	8.5	22.7	11.8	30.7	6.1	8.1	16.0
FIRST NB OF GIRARD	GIRARD	KS	C+	C+	B-	67.6	-3.44	13.9	8.7	15.5	28.9	8.1	9.7	16.4
▲ FIRST NB OF GOLIAD	GOLIAD	TX	D+	E-	D	40.7	-13.96	13.4	11.6	19.3	13.4	4.9	6.9	11.4
▲ FIRST NB OF GORDON	GORDON	NE	B-	C+	B-	96.5	0.18	7.8	4.1	1.4	35.7	10.0	11.6	18.8
FIRST NB OF GRANBURY	GRANBURY	TX	B	B+	B+	268.9	5.20	3.0	5.9	7.4	49.1	8.0	9.7	19.0
▲ FIRST NB OF GRAND RIDGE	GRAND RIDGE	IL	A-	B+	B	27.2	7.23	6.2	3.7	17.1	34.5	10.0	12.0	24.1
▲ FIRST NB OF GRANT PARK	GRANT PARK	IL	B-	C+	D+	133.9	24.94	15.2	3.4	20.7	38.4	6.4	8.4	15.5
FIRST NB OF GRAYSON	GRAYSON	KY	B-	B-	B-	148.6	6.12	4.0	19.2	29.7	21.7	5.4	7.4	13.7
FIRST NB OF GREENCASTLE	GREENCASTLE	PA	B+	B+	B+	277.4	7.16	11.1	4.3	51.0	11.2	6.8	8.8	14.5
FIRST NB OF GRIFFIN	GRIFFIN	GA	C+	C+	C+	311.0	-0.44	7.1	5.0	9.1	12.6	8.1	10.4	13.4
FIRST NB OF GROTON	GROTON	NY	A-	A-	A-	96.5	1.87	6.3	14.0	21.4	35.2	10.0	11.2	22.9
FIRST NB OF GWINNETT	DULUTH	GA	D+	C	D+	103.3	29.17	8.3	1.7	6.4	9.3	3.3	8.0	10.1
FIRST NB OF HAMILTON	HAMILTON	AL	B	B	B-	223.2	0.46	10.6	13.4	22.9	35.6	6.5	8.5	15.1
▲ FIRST NB OF HAMILTON	HAMILTON	TX	C	C-	D+	33.5	1.15	8.7	7.5	13.9	10.9	6.6	8.6	17.6
FIRST NB OF HAMPTON	HAMPTON	IA	A	A	A	92.8	1.97	5.9	4.7	12.5	47.8	10.0	12.2	23.2
▲ FIRST NB OF HARTFORD	HARTFORD	AL	A-	B+	A-	77.8	1.95	3.7	11.2	10.6	55.3	10.0	14.5	32.6
▲ FIRST NB OF HARTFORD	HARTFORD	WI	B	B	B	135.3	-0.05	8.4	1.1	11.0	35.9	10.0	14.3	24.8
▲ FIRST NB OF HARVEYVILLE	HARVEYVILLE	KS	C+	C	C	10.0	3.34	6.1	5.5	29.0	29.4	10.0	11.2	23.0
FIRST NB OF HEBBRONVILLE	HEBBRONVILLE	TX	A	A	A	79.4	-2.84	3.4	10.5	2.6	67.7	10.0	15.1	39.5
FIRST NB OF HENNING	HENNING	MN	B+	B+	A-	72.9	10.28	9.4	6.7	17.1	29.3	9.1	10.4	16.3
FIRST NB OF HERMAN	HERMAN	MN	C	C	C+	18.7	9.50	6.8	3.5	2.5	48.8	8.9	10.3	19.7
FIRST NB OF HICO	HICO	TX	C+	C+	C	26.6	4.96	3.2	7.8	9.2	42.3	7.1	9.1	20.3
FIRST NB OF HOLCOMB	HOLCOMB	KS	D+	D+	D+	42.0	4.41	10.2	18.8	12.4	30.8	7.2	9.1	14.7
▼ FIRST NB OF HOLDREGE	HOLDREGE	NE	B-	B+	B	100.0	-7.45	7.5	1.7	1.1	49.9	10.0	18.8	37.6
▲ FIRST NB OF HOLLAND	HOLLAND	TX	D+	D	E+	8.5	-0.91	0.4	35.9	8.3	1.2	10.0	11.6	23.2
FIRST NB OF HOOKER	HOOKER	OK	B+	B+	B+	49.1	4.77	5.5	2.2	4.7	44.9	10.0	12.1	22.0

Asset Quality Index	Non-Performing Loans as a % of Total Loans	Non-Performing Loans as a % of Capital	Net Charge-offs Avg Loans	Profitability Index	Net Income ($Mil)	Return on Assets (R.O.A.)	Return on Equity (R.O.E.)	Net Interest Spread	Overhead Efficiency Ratio	Liquidity Index	Liquidity Ratio	Hot Money Ratio	Stability Index
9.1	0.04	0.1	-0.08	4.9	0.2	1.02	7.38	3.75	66.2	4.0	79.3	23.3	6.6
8.4	0.25	0.6	0.15	6.7	0.6	1.29	9.79	4.44	60.4	7.5	89.3	3.1	8.1
7.5	0.08	0.7	0.01	9.4	2.8	2.16	28.27	4.74	58.0	4.7	46.3	13.2	6.9
9.2	0.00	0.0	0.00	5.3	0.6	1.28	7.99	2.99	61.3	7.0	78.3	4.7	8.1
7.6	0.97	2.9	0.21	5.5	1.2	1.03	8.36	4.15	68.6	4.5	55.5	16.6	7.3
5.8	1.15	6.1	0.04	1.9	0.1	0.24	2.47	3.94	97.1	5.0	55.0	12.7	3.3
3.4	2.26	19.4	0.12	5.6	0.6	0.89	12.44	3.78	62.8	2.2	29.3	21.3	3.7
8.6	0.00	0.0	0.00	4.5	0.1	0.61	6.05	5.02	82.1	6.8	65.8	1.5	3.2
1.9	5.05	23.1	-0.10	6.0	0.1	1.01	11.04	3.68	60.5	6.4	115.1	12.2	3.9
8.9	0.00	0.0	0.04	4.1	0.2	0.88	7.34	4.27	79.3	3.8	33.4	13.7	4.5
1.8	3.82	22.9	1.45	4.7	2.0	1.01	11.36	3.87	73.6	0.8	17.2	40.7	3.6
2.2	2.86	15.5	-0.01	6.6	0.3	1.06	9.19	4.72	65.7	1.7	29.4	28.1	6.1
7.4	0.26	2.3	0.00	8.1	1.0	1.12	12.52	4.91	59.9	4.5	31.2	9.3	6.4
9.2	0.00	0.0	0.00	9.2	0.7	2.85	15.55	4.61	49.5	5.7	27.9	0.0	8.0
4.6	1.36	6.8	0.65	5.3	0.5	1.47	14.67	4.34	62.9	2.7	37.4	21.9	4.2
7.7	0.00	0.0	0.05	9.6	0.6	1.39	15.23	5.32	56.9	4.4	25.4	7.4	6.3
0.5	12.96	45.7	-0.10	0.3	-0.5	-4.02	-27.48	4.25	84.6	5.1	90.0	15.7	4.4
6.7	4.25	6.8	0.04	5.1	0.3	0.68	3.03	3.91	69.3	4.4	33.9	11.1	8.0
6.6	0.00	0.0	-0.11	10.0	0.4	2.92	8.91	4.92	40.7	7.1	81.2	3.1	6.3
7.9	0.32	1.3	0.49	7.7	0.5	1.36	11.19	3.92	48.1	4.6	98.1	21.9	7.0
7.7	0.39	2.3	0.04	4.0	0.1	0.89	10.95	3.52	77.5	4.3	29.3	9.6	3.2
1.6	4.24	27.5	0.00	3.4	0.1	0.99	10.32	4.31	75.8	3.0	62.3	26.3	2.4
6.9	3.15	5.7	0.58	6.5	0.1	1.39	11.07	4.23	72.5	5.6	37.9	2.1	4.6
5.2	0.55	3.0	0.04	4.4	1.2	0.69	7.21	3.59	76.6	4.5	28.9	8.7	5.1
7.4	0.17	1.1	0.05	6.2	19.9	1.02	10.13	3.99	60.9	2.6	14.6	16.3	7.5
9.0	0.11	0.3	-0.05	7.6	0.8	1.99	13.28	3.31	47.2	3.1	47.0	21.3	9.1
8.8	0.00	0.0	0.00	0.0	-0.5	-4.53	-10.14	1.42	201.3	4.8	86.0	18.2	0.0
9.5	1.03	1.9	-0.38	2.1	0.0	0.23	1.38	3.40	92.9	6.1	54.7	3.7	4.9
5.1	0.48	4.3	0.06	3.3	0.2	0.34	4.90	5.44	89.0	5.2	30.4	4.6	3.3
8.2	0.00	0.0	-0.01	9.2	0.4	2.20	22.34	4.32	50.4	6.0	49.3	5.6	6.0
6.4	1.03	4.2	0.16	8.6	5.3	1.58	9.68	4.12	54.8	6.5	72.9	9.1	9.3
9.0	0.15	0.3	-0.54	4.8	0.2	0.77	4.51	4.08	72.2	2.8	38.5	20.7	6.2
0.0	13.18	92.4	0.79	0.0	-0.2	-0.25	-4.83	3.24	93.6	3.9	60.3	21.6	0.0
8.2	0.15	0.9	0.06	6.0	1.0	1.08	11.22	4.22	69.5	3.3	38.5	18.2	6.3
6.4	0.58	3.2	0.27	3.7	0.3	1.02	11.05	4.48	74.4	5.7	36.0	3.4	1.6
8.0	0.62	2.8	-0.07	4.6	0.4	0.80	8.47	3.84	72.1	4.4	22.3	6.7	5.4
6.0	1.18	4.8	0.31	3.4	0.0	0.27	2.14	4.66	91.2	7.6	121.5	6.2	4.2
5.4	0.64	5.8	0.14	7.7	0.4	1.63	31.25	4.19	61.4	3.4	21.1	12.7	4.4
0.0	10.95	56.7	4.92	1.4	-0.9	-1.04	-12.20	4.50	62.7	3.7	77.6	31.2	3.4
3.0	2.37	14.6	0.02	8.6	0.7	2.04	21.25	4.01	45.0	3.9	36.5	14.3	5.8
0.3	7.18	55.9	2.30	0.7	-0.2	-0.93	-19.06	3.67	111.8	4.6	42.8	12.5	2.1
4.4	3.10	13.4	2.37	5.3	0.5	0.93	8.44	4.36	54.5	4.1	60.6	18.0	5.0
6.7	0.81	3.0	0.14	4.8	1.1	0.84	8.91	3.72	74.9	4.9	48.6	12.9	5.7
7.9	1.17	4.6	-0.04	9.6	0.2	1.49	12.18	5.10	49.0	5.1	47.1	10.6	7.2
5.7	0.83	4.7	0.04	3.8	0.4	0.61	6.41	4.16	81.4	4.0	31.8	12.3	3.9
5.3	0.43	3.5	0.09	6.8	0.8	1.12	15.74	4.65	63.9	3.1	31.3	16.6	4.0
7.9	0.12	1.0	0.25	6.4	1.4	0.99	11.07	4.05	64.4	4.5	17.3	5.8	5.7
3.2	1.10	6.5	0.12	7.6	1.8	1.18	10.01	5.10	66.7	5.6	62.7	12.6	7.1
7.3	0.81	3.6	0.43	8.6	0.7	1.45	12.58	5.23	55.4	6.1	66.7	8.9	6.7
4.5	0.99	9.3	0.06	3.9	0.3	0.65	7.98	4.22	68.5	4.4	29.0	9.2	0.5
4.7	0.97	5.7	0.24	7.2	1.4	1.31	13.54	4.43	56.5	1.4	19.7	27.3	5.3
7.1	0.64	3.3	-0.16	4.9	0.2	1.26	15.23	3.86	75.2	7.1	111.4	9.5	3.3
8.4	0.88	3.1	-0.02	7.7	0.8	1.78	13.44	3.99	56.3	4.9	27.3	4.8	8.1
8.0	0.67	1.4	0.32	6.0	0.5	1.23	8.36	4.11	58.4	4.8	118.3	24.5	7.3
7.2	1.86	6.3	0.00	4.0	0.5	0.71	4.97	3.52	77.4	6.2	57.3	7.9	7.5
8.8	0.00	0.0	-0.07	4.9	0.1	1.00	8.84	3.93	70.8	6.1	101.9	12.3	4.8
8.6	1.71	2.2	0.04	9.6	0.8	1.96	12.51	4.80	44.3	2.9	25.2	15.6	9.0
5.1	0.75	4.4	0.06	8.2	0.7	2.10	19.39	4.31	56.9	4.5	22.7	6.5	7.4
8.8	0.00	0.0	0.03	5.5	0.1	1.38	13.24	3.91	65.5	3.3	46.6	17.4	3.5
8.8	0.00	0.0	-0.32	4.4	0.1	0.99	10.67	4.04	79.4	5.7	62.9	10.4	4.4
1.1	3.34	22.1	0.20	7.0	0.3	1.23	13.32	5.27	65.0	1.1	20.5	31.7	4.1
5.4	3.91	7.8	-2.00	2.4	-1.1	-2.02	-10.11	4.09	207.7	4.4	25.5	7.7	7.7
5.5	1.32	5.9	-0.13	4.7	0.1	1.11	9.93	5.64	83.3	6.5	68.2	4.0	1.6
5.9	2.29	7.7	-0.01	6.9	0.3	1.32	10.37	5.23	68.7	4.4	23.0	7.0	6.8

Name	City	State	Weiss Safety Rating	2003 Weiss Safety Rating	2002 Weiss Safety Rating	Total Assets ($Mil)	One Year Asset Growth	Asset Mix (As a % of Total Assets)				Capital- ization Index	Leverage Ratio	Risk-based Capital Ratio
								Comm- ercial Loans	Cons- umer Loans	Home Mort- gages	Secur- ities			
FIRST NB OF HOPE	HOPE	AR	B	B	B+	124.8	-3.14	2.5	5.6	26.6	25.4	10.0	18.5	33.6
FIRST NB OF HOPE	HOPE	KS	C-	C-	B	37.0	0.51	8.6	4.8	5.4	13.7	10.0	12.0	15.0
FIRST NB OF HOWARD	HOWARD	KS	B	B	B	7.6	8.73	2.6	0.6	2.3	12.7	10.0	15.1	26.9
▲ FIRST NB OF HOWARD CTY	DIERKS	AR	A	A-	A	39.4	3.44	12.8	8.2	11.1	44.7	10.0	17.7	32.0
FIRST NB OF HOXIE	HOXIE	KS	B	B	B	62.7	-6.63	8.2	2.5	2.8	47.5	10.0	11.5	20.9
FIRST NB OF HUDSON	WOODBURY	MN	A-	A-	B+	347.6	6.13	11.7	6.1	26.6	10.3	7.4	10.0	12.9
FIRST NB OF HUGHES	HUGHES SPRINGS	TX	A-	B+	B	140.2	-4.36	15.6	6.8	12.7	31.1	7.6	9.4	16.9
FIRST NB OF HUGO	HUGO	CO	B	B	B-	52.8	4.34	5.6	2.1	3.5	16.1	9.5	10.3	14.6
FIRST NB OF HUNTSVILLE	HUNTSVILLE	TX	B+	B+	B+	225.1	1.31	5.5	12.4	10.6	48.6	7.9	9.6	24.0
FIRST NB OF HUTCHINSON	HUTCHINSON	KS	B+	B+	B+	443.6	3.82	10.6	2.6	7.4	47.3	7.8	9.5	19.1
FIRST NB OF ILLINOIS	LANSING	IL	B+	A-	A-	344.8	6.58	19.3	2.4	7.9	34.3	10.0	11.5	17.8
▼ FIRST NB OF IPSWICH	IPSWICH	MA	C-	C	C	387.3	24.80	5.3	0.5	14.6	48.8	4.7	6.7	11.8
FIRST NB OF IVESDALE	IVESDALE	IL	B	B+	B+	10.8	-0.17	3.3	19.6	5.9	29.0	10.0	14.1	24.7
FIRST NB OF JACKSBORO	JACKSBORO	TX	C+	C+	C+	113.5	11.93	9.8	7.0	11.3	35.3	5.1	7.1	12.6
▼ FIRST NB OF JACKSON	JACKSON	KY	C+	B-	B	99.8	-3.72	2.8	4.6	15.9	56.3	10.0	12.5	30.6
FIRST NB OF JASPER	JASPER	AL	B	B	B	525.8	-7.09	16.3	6.5	12.0	19.1	5.4	8.7	11.3
FIRST NB OF JEANERETTE	JEANERETTE	LA	A-	A-	A-	80.5	2.60	9.8	11.8	27.2	10.1	10.0	12.2	16.7
FIRST NB OF	JEFFERSONVILLE	NY	B+	B	B	359.5	8.33	5.2	4.1	22.9	31.3	8.4	9.9	17.1
▲ FIRST NB OF JOHNSON	JOHNSON	NE	B+	B	B	56.8	-1.85	3.1	3.5	1.9	69.2	10.0	16.8	39.1
FIRST NB OF JONESBORO	JONESBORO	IL	C-	D+	D+	60.0	6.04	8.5	6.9	38.4	23.3	6.7	8.7	16.5
FIRST NB OF KANSAS	BURLINGTON	KS	C	C	C-	54.2	-2.60	10.4	6.5	9.2	53.0	6.7	8.7	18.9
FIRST NB OF KEMP	KEMP	TX	D+	D+	D	48.7	-3.26	2.8	6.4	12.2	40.1	6.9	8.9	20.8
FIRST NB OF KINMUNDY	KINMUNDY	IL	B+	B+	A-	26.8	-1.87	4.7	11.3	16.4	38.3	10.0	16.9	35.3
▼ FIRST NB OF LA FOLLETTE	LA FOLLETTE	TN	B-	B	B	171.1	1.97	6.0	6.0	31.7	26.4	8.0	9.7	17.0
▲ FIRST NB OF LA GRANGE	LA GRANGE	IL	A-	B	A-	203.5	8.31	14.0	1.1	28.2	25.2	6.4	8.4	14.5
▼ FIRST NB OF LACON	LACON	IL	C+	B-	B-	55.2	4.46	6.8	5.0	9.5	26.4	7.8	9.6	14.8
▲ FIRST NB OF LAKE CITY	LAKE CITY	CO	C	D+	D	31.3	3.82	2.7	3.8	23.7	22.2	6.3	8.3	15.7
FIRST NB OF LAKE JACKSON	LAKE JACKSON	TX	B+	B+	A-	185.6	-1.93	1.4	2.0	1.9	77.2	5.3	7.3	22.2
FIRST NB OF LAMAR	LAMAR	CO	B-	B	B	163.4	1.21	5.9	2.6	11.7	32.0	8.0	9.7	15.2
FIRST NB OF LAMESA	LAMESA	TX	B	B	B+	109.3	0.54	4.8	2.6	2.0	45.5	8.0	9.6	25.0
FIRST NB OF LAS ANIMAS	LAS ANIMAS	CO	B	B-	B-	137.6	10.36	31.3	3.9	7.8	13.8	4.8	8.2	10.9
FIRST NB OF LAWRENCE CTY	WALNUT RIDGE	AR	B+	B+	A-	128.6	18.90	7.0	4.7	11.1	34.8	8.7	10.1	17.5
FIRST NB OF LAYTON	LAYTON	UT	B-	B	B-	243.2	6.84	9.7	2.2	2.0	16.9	9.5	10.8	14.6
FIRST NB OF LE CENTER	LE CENTER	MN	B+	B+	B+	60.9	6.49	6.6	4.6	16.5	26.2	10.0	12.4	18.2
▲ FIRST NB OF LE ROY	LE ROY	KS	C+	C-	B-	22.4	-3.14	3.7	6.0	19.4	8.4	10.0	20.8	31.9
FIRST NB OF LERNA	LERNA	IL	A	A	A-	8.7	-3.65	9.7	6.4	17.4	60.7	10.0	18.6	26.8
FIRST NB OF LEWELLEN	LEWELLEN	NE	B	B	B	20.3	-0.18	6.9	2.3	2.6	27.4	10.0	24.3	38.1
FIRST NB OF LEWISTOWN	LEWISTOWN	MT	C+	C+	C+	81.0	4.38	11.7	4.8	8.3	7.8	4.0	7.8	10.5
FIRST NB OF LEWISVILLE	LEWISVILLE	AR	B	B	B+	34.5	11.67	6.5	12.9	31.2	31.2	8.7	10.1	23.3
▲ FIRST NB OF LEXINGTON	LEXINGTON	KY	D	D-	D	66.7	55.42	2.7	2.7	29.1	19.6	7.9	9.6	15.8
▲ FIRST NB OF LIBERAL	LIBERAL	KS	B-	C+	B	166.6	6.68	5.3	2.6	2.4	57.1	7.2	9.1	19.2
FIRST NB OF LILLY	LILLY	PA	B-	B-	B-	23.4	1.18	2.1	5.1	14.5	67.2	10.0	13.9	37.6
FIRST NB OF LINDEN	LINDEN	TX	C-	C-	C+	54.4	2.13	7.2	6.9	12.0	57.1	6.9	8.9	20.4
FIRST NB OF LINDSAY	LINDSAY	OK	D	D	C	26.1	4.11	16.1	10.7	7.9	27.4	9.0	10.3	17.0
FIRST NB OF LIPAN	LIPAN	TX	C-	D+	D	12.1	3.72	7.4	17.5	11.1	10.4	9.7	10.8	19.6
FIRST NB OF LITCHFIELD	LITCHFIELD	CT	C	C	C	433.9	28.59	4.5	1.6	25.2	46.1	4.5	6.5	13.5
▼ FIRST NB OF LITCHFIELD	LITCHFIELD	IL	C	C+	C	73.8	-1.13	3.7	6.6	15.0	29.9	6.3	8.4	12.7
▲ FIRST NB OF LIVERPOOL	LIVERPOOL	PA	B+	B	B-	32.5	9.17	4.5	5.3	62.6	9.6	10.0	11.6	20.2
FIRST NB OF LIVINGSTON	LIVINGSTON	TX	A	A	A	207.4	-0.68	4.5	5.1	6.3	59.0	10.0	14.6	38.5
FIRST NB OF LOGAN	LOGAN	IA	B+	B+	B+	25.7	-0.09	4.7	2.6	5.0	26.8	10.0	12.7	20.1
▼ FIRST NB OF LONG ISLAND	HUNTINGTON	NY	A-	A	A+	953.3	13.34	5.4	0.6	16.1	57.7	7.7	9.5	27.4
FIRST NB OF LOUISBURG	LOUISBURG	KS	A	A	A	63.0	3.37	4.3	3.2	16.4	44.6	10.0	19.6	43.4
FIRST NB OF LOUISIANA	CROWLEY	LA	B	B	B	129.7	1.40	15.7	4.3	9.9	19.6	7.5	9.4	13.8
▲ FIRST NB OF LUCEDALE	LUCEDALE	MS	C	D-	E-	76.6	-8.64	4.0	10.2	17.9	22.4	6.2	8.2	13.4
FIRST NB OF MANCHESTER	MANCHESTER	KY	B+	B+	A-	143.8	-1.96	12.7	5.3	15.6	39.6	10.0	13.6	24.7
▼ FIRST NB OF MANCHESTER	MANCHESTER	TN	B+	A-	A-	146.8	2.20	20.9	9.4	21.4	21.9	9.4	10.6	17.1
FIRST NB OF MANHATTAN	MANHATTAN	IL	B+	B+	B+	93.5	1.01	3.1	1.5	17.5	35.5	9.9	10.9	23.2
FIRST NB OF MANNING	MANNING	IA	A-	A-	A-	54.6	0.27	16.0	2.4	7.7	25.1	10.0	16.2	26.0
FIRST NB OF MARENGO	MARENGO	IL	C	C	D+	241.4	1.88	10.5	4.8	27.8	14.8	5.3	7.5	11.2
FIRST NB OF MARIN	LAS VEGAS	NV	D	D	D	201.9	-9.73	0.0	112.9	4.1	2.7	10.0	30.3	50.4
FIRST NB OF MARQUETTE	MARQUETTE	NE	B-	B-	C+	25.5	-2.50	4.5	4.2	8.2	43.2	10.0	16.8	29.7
FIRST NB OF MARYSVILLE	MARYSVILLE	PA	B+	B+	A-	105.6	1.23	3.4	2.8	32.0	39.4	10.0	11.3	23.6
FIRST NB OF MAYFIELD	MAYFIELD	KY	C-	D+	C-	136.6	-15.02	6.7	6.4	15.6	36.0	8.2	9.8	17.1
FIRST NB OF MCCLUSKY	MCCLUSKY	ND	C	C	C-	24.9	1.39	3.8	5.1	3.1	27.0	10.0	11.7	15.6

Asset Quality Index	Non-Performing Loans as a % of Total Loans	Non-Performing Loans as a % of Capital	Net Charge-offs Avg Loans	Profitability Index	Net Income ($Mil)	Return on Assets (R.O.A.)	Return on Equity (R.O.E.)	Net Interest Spread	Overhead Efficiency Ratio	Liquidity Index	Liquidity Ratio	Hot Money Ratio	Stability Index
6.1	1.34	4.1	0.07	4.9	0.6	0.92	4.93	4.78	75.8	2.3	39.7	29.6	7.3
1.4	3.83	22.6	0.74	5.9	0.3	1.62	13.67	4.32	61.3	2.6	20.9	16.4	5.2
9.0	0.37	1.1	0.00	8.1	0.1	1.85	12.26	4.49	60.4	7.2	76.7	1.6	6.1
8.2	0.29	0.9	0.32	6.6	0.2	1.02	5.96	4.08	55.5	0.8	8.3	33.6	8.4
8.6	0.00	0.0	0.03	5.3	0.3	1.01	8.93	3.70	62.0	3.7	75.4	26.0	5.5
8.1	0.03	0.3	0.05	10.0	4.7	2.78	27.68	5.21	56.5	4.8	21.5	3.9	7.0
6.4	0.53	2.5	0.09	9.6	1.7	2.36	18.81	6.02	57.6	4.3	34.0	11.5	7.7
5.8	0.72	4.5	0.10	8.2	0.6	2.16	20.77	5.25	62.0	2.9	44.3	24.0	5.3
8.0	0.00	0.0	0.02	5.4	1.1	0.97	9.46	3.58	65.3	2.7	26.8	17.0	6.2
8.9	0.09	0.4	-0.03	5.2	2.4	1.05	10.74	3.48	69.2	5.1	81.6	17.4	6.4
7.3	1.47	6.3	0.06	5.0	1.6	0.96	8.00	3.93	69.3	5.0	38.8	9.1	7.2
9.3	0.01	0.1	0.02	2.4	0.5	0.29	4.40	3.57	96.4	3.4	23.3	13.0	2.5
7.5	0.19	0.6	0.91	3.5	0.0	0.30	2.20	3.81	83.3	4.4	72.8	16.8	6.2
6.8	0.10	0.7	-0.05	5.4	0.7	1.28	17.90	3.41	63.8	3.6	54.6	22.6	4.2
9.4	0.46	1.1	0.06	2.5	-0.1	-0.26	-2.08	3.23	87.6	2.9	67.7	39.4	6.3
7.9	0.08	0.7	-0.09	8.0	3.4	1.30	14.35	3.62	53.9	1.5	12.9	23.2	6.6
7.7	0.66	3.3	0.13	6.6	0.3	0.81	6.81	4.76	71.8	4.8	75.0	16.6	7.3
5.8	0.71	4.0	0.17	9.7	3.1	1.71	17.88	5.45	57.9	4.1	17.5	8.2	6.3
6.6	5.67	6.1	-3.72	6.4	0.4	1.21	6.64	3.75	53.3	4.4	25.6	7.5	6.3
2.5	2.74	20.0	0.62	4.9	0.3	0.87	10.09	4.38	69.9	4.7	45.0	12.3	3.5
4.7	2.55	11.2	-0.01	4.8	0.3	1.19	13.29	3.39	65.7	5.5	107.5	17.0	4.3
5.3	1.91	7.3	-0.29	2.4	0.0	0.18	2.02	3.70	94.6	5.7	53.3	8.7	2.4
8.0	0.88	2.5	-0.02	5.2	0.1	0.82	4.89	3.84	71.1	7.5	84.0	2.3	6.8
3.8	2.29	15.5	0.04	7.0	0.9	1.11	11.41	4.78	65.2	2.5	17.8	16.8	5.4
8.6	0.12	0.9	0.05	9.8	2.3	2.31	26.69	4.34	55.6	4.7	32.6	8.5	7.2
3.8	2.36	15.1	0.05	6.7	0.4	1.56	16.62	4.19	61.2	5.2	44.6	9.9	5.0
8.8	0.18	1.2	0.00	2.4	0.1	0.33	4.13	2.54	86.8	5.3	63.5	12.6	4.9
10.0	0.25	0.5	0.07	7.9	1.8	1.92	29.81	3.41	40.0	3.9	52.6	18.4	5.6
5.2	1.48	8.1	0.01	9.9	1.5	1.77	18.53	4.58	46.3	3.1	26.9	15.1	5.0
6.9	1.29	3.3	-0.08	4.4	0.5	0.93	9.48	2.76	63.3	4.2	105.4	33.9	5.5
7.4	0.00	0.0	0.00	9.0	1.6	2.30	27.37	4.99	51.5	2.6	12.0	15.6	6.5
5.5	0.87	4.5	0.07	5.6	0.9	1.34	13.38	4.21	58.0	1.8	14.4	20.1	5.7
3.6	1.73	10.0	0.16	9.2	1.9	1.59	14.78	5.08	57.2	3.1	57.1	31.5	6.7
5.7	1.79	8.7	-0.02	7.3	0.6	2.16	17.03	4.36	50.8	4.2	45.2	14.8	6.9
2.7	3.96	13.3	-1.08	8.1	0.3	2.28	11.11	4.49	44.5	4.1	84.0	20.6	6.3
5.9	5.24	8.8	-0.06	7.6	0.1	1.42	7.40	5.07	68.7	5.0	26.4	3.1	7.7
8.0	1.35	3.0	-0.08	9.8	0.4	4.08	17.05	5.82	43.7	5.7	49.0	4.7	6.3
4.4	0.85	8.0	0.21	9.0	0.6	1.53	20.20	4.85	48.8	2.0	20.8	19.7	3.9
2.9	2.22	12.5	0.46	4.7	0.1	0.75	7.21	4.10	82.7	0.9	20.4	35.8	5.8
8.8	0.00	0.0	0.01	0.4	0.1	0.35	3.55	3.45	85.1	8.3	115.2	2.0	0.0
3.9	4.00	14.3	-0.13	4.8	1.0	1.15	12.24	3.38	65.8	1.7	17.7	22.0	5.9
9.4	0.96	1.9	0.16	4.0	0.1	1.00	7.18	3.73	74.9	3.9	19.6	9.8	5.9
2.6	6.41	25.7	0.18	4.4	0.3	1.00	11.25	3.50	73.8	3.3	20.7	12.8	4.2
0.5	8.23	40.2	5.99	1.7	-0.1	-0.56	-5.19	5.06	63.8	4.7	35.1	9.6	4.0
4.1	1.81	8.3	0.06	4.0	0.0	0.73	6.90	5.48	86.2	5.8	87.9	11.8	2.6
7.7	0.36	2.7	0.05	4.1	1.8	0.84	13.38	3.45	66.2	4.2	27.1	9.4	2.4
6.1	0.78	5.5	0.02	4.6	0.4	1.04	11.90	3.56	67.0	3.8	28.7	12.2	3.7
7.8	0.87	5.7	0.00	9.5	0.2	1.56	13.45	4.80	51.4	4.0	56.5	17.5	7.5
8.8	0.07	0.1	0.02	7.5	1.4	1.36	8.56	4.35	65.1	5.6	41.2	6.5	8.9
8.6	0.12	0.5	0.33	6.3	0.2	1.08	8.24	4.29	61.7	4.8	28.7	6.2	7.2
9.9	0.01	0.0	0.00	7.4	6.1	1.30	13.60	4.28	59.4	5.9	39.5	3.5	7.4
9.3	0.13	0.3	0.11	9.4	0.7	2.06	10.67	4.03	56.4	5.1	81.7	16.0	9.0
7.0	0.56	3.6	0.02	6.1	0.7	1.04	11.15	4.80	70.7	4.1	23.7	9.3	5.6
3.0	1.55	9.9	0.23	3.5	0.3	0.78	9.55	3.55	78.3	2.2	20.5	18.8	2.8
6.4	1.60	5.8	0.17	5.0	0.7	0.93	6.88	4.03	67.4	2.2	43.4	37.3	6.9
5.2	0.92	5.3	0.08	9.5	1.2	1.55	14.33	4.54	47.8	2.2	26.6	19.7	7.3
9.5	0.03	0.1	0.00	5.0	0.6	1.20	10.53	4.47	71.5	6.3	115.6	13.9	6.7
7.6	0.49	1.7	-0.17	8.5	0.4	1.44	9.18	4.17	47.7	6.5	71.9	7.1	8.1
5.0	0.85	7.7	-0.06	6.8	1.4	1.17	15.96	4.07	57.3	2.7	35.4	20.4	2.6
0.5	8.95	16.9	14.63	10.0	9.1	8.78	32.39	25.88	54.3	4.6	88.0	22.0	8.2
6.4	1.69	4.5	1.98	5.3	0.1	0.65	3.80	3.88	57.7	2.9	43.6	23.9	6.4
9.2	0.59	2.7	0.01	4.5	0.4	0.79	7.04	3.20	73.6	5.0	65.3	15.7	7.1
3.9	1.88	10.3	2.04	3.0	0.5	0.77	8.18	3.62	77.8	3.6	20.4	11.7	2.6
5.1	0.81	4.4	0.25	5.7	0.1	1.13	9.55	4.88	75.5	5.2	46.4	7.3	3.6

Name	City	State	Weiss Safety Rating	2003 Weiss Safety Rating	2002 Weiss Safety Rating	Total Assets ($Mil)	One Year Asset Growth	Asset Mix (As a % of Total Assets) Commercial Loans	Consumer Loans	Home Mortgages	Securities	Capitalization Index	Leverage Ratio	Risk-based Capital Ratio
FIRST NB OF	MC CONNELLSBURG	PA	B-	B-	B-	158.3	14.57	6.2	3.7	34.2	22.7	7.6	9.4	15.4
FIRST NB OF	MC CONNELSVILLE	OH	B-	B-	B	83.4	5.81	4.1	9.0	51.2	6.4	8.0	9.7	15.4
FIRST NB OF MCGREGOR	MC GREGOR	TX	C-	C-	D+	66.4	3.89	8.0	10.4	28.2	12.7	6.6	8.6	15.0
FIRST NB OF MCINTOSH	MCINTOSH	MN	B-	B-	B	22.7	-1.90	6.4	4.5	9.3	45.5	10.0	28.6	67.6
FIRST NB OF MCMINNVILLE	MC MINNVILLE	TN	A+	A+	A+	313.4	1.11	13.7	0.9	19.3	44.9	10.0	15.8	30.2
▲ FIRST NB OF MEDFORD	MEDFORD	OK	C-	D+	D+	24.3	0.82	4.0	0.9	3.8	44.0	9.2	10.5	20.3
FIRST NB OF MENAHGA	MENAHGA	MN	B+	B+	B+	48.4	4.09	14.4	6.8	18.8	33.2	10.0	11.4	21.2
▼ FIRST NB OF MERCERSBURG	MERCERSBURG	PA	A-	A	A	118.1	1.98	6.7	8.7	28.8	16.3	10.0	11.1	15.6
▲ FIRST NB OF MERTZON	MERTZON	TX	A-	B+	A-	127.9	3.70	5.7	4.0	2.7	66.4	10.0	12.4	34.1
▲ FIRST NB OF MEXIA	MEXIA	TX	C-	D	D-	71.1	-3.06	6.9	5.8	19.1	43.3	7.6	9.4	20.0
FIRST NB OF MIFFLINTOWN	MIFFLINTOWN	PA	C+	C+	C+	235.7	11.56	4.6	1.7	41.3	27.4	6.6	8.6	16.4
FIRST NB OF MILACA	MILACA	MN	A-	A-	A-	131.5	5.72	14.8	8.9	15.0	35.3	8.8	10.2	17.9
FIRST NB OF MILLSTADT	MILLSTADT	IL	B+	A-	A-	86.9	-2.38	1.2	1.7	20.2	55.2	10.0	13.1	31.2
FIRST NB OF MINEOLA	MINEOLA	TX	D	D	D+	32.0	-5.37	1.7	7.1	12.7	68.7	5.4	7.4	26.3
FIRST NB OF MINERSVILLE	MINERSVILLE	PA	B	B	B	84.4	3.74	4.2	5.2	25.4	50.4	10.0	12.3	23.3
FIRST NB OF MISSOURI	LEE'S SUMMIT	MO	B-	B-	B-	167.3	-8.22	9.9	4.0	13.0	20.5	6.8	8.8	14.1
▲ FIRST NB OF MONAHANS	MONAHANS	TX	C+	C-	D+	194.5	68.06	12.2	5.7	14.3	12.6	5.1	7.1	11.5
FIRST NB OF MONTEREY	MONTEREY	IN	B	B	B	218.8	1.91	3.0	4.0	14.5	42.8	6.8	8.8	16.5
▲ FIRST NB OF MONTGOMERY	MONTGOMERY	MN	C+	C	C+	58.8	-2.62	11.9	6.0	27.4	20.8	9.5	10.6	17.5
▲ FIRST NB OF MOODY	MOODY	TX	A-	B+	A-	38.1	5.90	5.5	5.9	21.2	33.9	10.0	16.8	30.8
FIRST NB OF MOOSE LAKE	MOOSE LAKE	MN	B	B	B-	60.6	6.12	9.1	4.3	20.3	6.0	6.9	9.9	12.5
FIRST NB OF MORGAN	MORGAN CITY	UT	A-	A-	A-	62.5	11.13	7.5	10.2	15.8	15.7	10.0	13.7	18.3
▲ FIRST NB OF MT	LIBBY	MT	C	C-	D	228.9	27.11	18.1	17.2	11.9	12.1	4.7	8.4	10.8
FIRST NB OF MT AUBURN	MT AUBURN	IL	B	B	B	20.9	0.64	5.3	6.1	31.1	25.3	6.3	8.3	15.0
FIRST NB OF MT DORA	MT DORA	FL	A	A	A	127.9	1.07	3.6	4.3	22.9	35.8	10.0	13.1	24.8
FIRST NB OF MT PULASKI	MT PULASKI	IL	E-	E-	E-	48.6	-7.42	2.1	4.7	29.1	23.7	5.6	7.6	13.6
▼ FIRST NB OF MT VERNON	MT VERNON	IL	B+	A-	A-	38.2	-2.85	2.9	3.6	19.3	47.3	10.0	18.5	20.6
▲ FIRST NB OF MT VERNON	MT VERNON	MO	B+	B	B	87.9	-9.09	2.4	5.7	19.3	16.7	10.0	13.0	19.1
FIRST NB OF MT VERNON	MT VERNON	TX	B+	B+	A-	112.5	-6.14	2.8	5.4	19.4	55.6	7.7	9.5	25.0
FIRST NB OF MUSCATINE	MUSCATINE	IA	B	B	B	272.6	-7.23	15.8	3.9	32.2	7.9	7.5	9.4	14.5
▼ FIRST NB OF NASH	NASH	OK	E+	D-	D	8.2	9.02	2.8	12.6	6.4	0.3	8.1	9.7	18.3
FIRST NB OF NASSAU	FERNANDINA BEACH	FL	A	A-	B+	133.4	12.72	2.5	2.1	12.4	28.4	9.0	10.3	14.3
▼ FIRST NB OF NEGAUNEE	NEGAUNEE	MI	B-	B	B	136.9	12.60	37.2	1.7	18.7	21.5	4.6	7.8	10.8
FIRST NB OF NEVADA	RENO	NV	B	B	B-	1,068.0	61.00	8.2	0.4	30.5	1.3	5.7	7.7	11.9
FIRST NB OF NEVADA MO	NEVADA	MO	B	B	B	63.9	-4.82	2.1	2.8	12.6	50.5	10.0	11.3	24.9
FIRST NB OF NEW HOLLAND	NEW HOLLAND	OH	E-	E-	E-	40.7	1.85	12.5	24.4	21.3	2.0	2.4	5.2	9.4
FIRST NB OF NEW MEXICO	CLAYTON	NM	D+	D+	D	96.6	5.97	8.2	5.3	10.9	14.1	4.1	7.2	10.5
▼ FIRST NB OF NEW RICHMOND	NEW RICHMOND	WI	B-	B	C+	108.6	2.41	8.0	5.0	10.2	16.8	3.4	7.8	10.2
▼ FIRST NB OF NEWMAN GROVE	NEWMAN GROVE	NE	D+	C-	B+	30.9	-4.42	2.0	3.6	0.6	38.2	5.9	7.9	14.2
FIRST NB OF NEWPORT	NEWPORT	PA	A-	A-	A-	124.6	-0.04	3.5	1.8	32.5	38.7	8.6	10.1	20.0
FIRST NB OF NEWTON	NEWTON	TX	C-	D+	C+	110.6	-1.99	13.1	9.1	10.7	33.8	9.2	10.4	19.7
FIRST NB OF NIAGARA	NIAGARA	WI	B+	B	B	59.4	-0.79	8.3	14.4	33.4	17.2	10.0	12.6	20.2
FIRST NB OF NOKOMIS	NOKOMIS	IL	A-	A-	A	92.3	2.10	4.8	5.0	19.5	27.6	10.0	11.8	20.2
FIRST NB OF NORTH CTY	CARLSBAD	CA	B+	B+	B	88.5	21.18	22.8	0.0	3.3	26.3	6.2	8.2	13.1
▲ FIRST NB OF NORTH EAST	N EAST	MD	B+	B	B	122.0	1.71	7.8	4.3	24.2	16.5	5.7	7.7	13.1
▲ FIRST NB OF NORTHERN CA	DALY CITY	CA	C+	C	B+	470.0	14.51	10.2	0.4	0.6	16.6	9.5	11.5	14.6
FIRST NB OF NORTHFIELD	NORTHFIELD	MN	B-	B	A-	90.4	3.44	10.9	3.1	17.4	16.4	8.9	10.2	16.1
FIRST NB OF NORWAY	NORWAY	MI	B	B	B+	70.6	2.42	14.9	3.7	37.2	11.4	10.0	12.2	18.6
▲ FIRST NB OF ODON	ODON	IN	C	C-	B-	45.3	2.91	3.8	7.6	12.9	46.4	8.0	9.7	16.0
FIRST NB OF OGDEN	OGDEN	IL	C+	C+	C+	66.0	0.02	2.4	1.4	12.0	29.1	5.0	7.0	12.8
FIRST NB OF OK	PONCA CITY	OK	D	D	D	70.2	11.38	21.0	11.7	12.2	22.5	6.1	8.1	12.1
FIRST NB OF OKAWVILLE	OKAWVILLE	IL	B	B	B	41.6	7.14	6.8	3.3	17.3	42.2	10.0	12.3	23.0
FIRST NB OF OLATHE	OLATHE	KS	B-	B-	B-	560.0	12.04	13.1	1.2	2.2	28.0	3.2	7.9	10.1
FIRST NB OF OLNEY	OLNEY	TX	B-	B-	B-	41.3	-1.93	10.0	6.6	15.5	0.0	8.4	10.9	13.7
FIRST NB OF OMAHA	OMAHA	NE	C	C	C	6,670.9	16.01	12.6	9.9	4.5	24.9	4.6	7.3	10.8
▲ FIRST NB OF ONEIDA	ONEIDA	TN	B-	C-	C+	200.5	3.89	6.6	7.2	26.2	19.0	5.7	7.7	12.0
▲ FIRST NB OF ORDWAY	ORDWAY	CO	C+	C	C-	39.2	2.14	10.7	1.4	13.1	1.8	6.2	8.5	11.9
FIRST NB OF ORWELL	ORWELL	VT	C	C	C	25.7	-4.22	4.8	10.4	51.9	0.0	8.8	10.2	17.6
FIRST NB OF OSAKIS	OSAKIS	MN	A-	A-	B+	53.7	-1.03	13.1	6.2	27.5	20.7	10.0	11.2	18.2
FIRST NB OF OTTAWA	OTTAWA	IL	C+	B-	B	313.7	33.42	4.1	6.7	7.0	37.0	4.5	6.5	11.9
FIRST NB OF OXFORD	OXFORD	MS	A-	A-	A-	199.7	2.77	4.4	5.4	16.8	39.7	8.3	9.9	17.2
FIRST NB OF PADUCAH	PADUCAH	TX	B-	C+	C+	43.2	2.64	6.1	9.7	2.2	59.1	10.0	12.3	24.7
FIRST NB OF PALMERTON	PALMERTON	PA	A	A	A	447.9	1.07	4.1	1.5	30.1	37.7	10.0	13.2	23.1
FIRST NB OF PANA	PANA	IL	A-	A-	A-	93.8	6.02	9.4	6.0	26.3	20.9	10.0	11.6	19.3

Asset Quality Index	Non-Performing Loans as a % of Total Loans	Non-Performing Loans as a % of Capital	Net Charge-offs Avg Loans	Profitability Index	Net Income ($Mil)	Return on Assets (R.O.A.)	Return on Equity (R.O.E.)	Net Interest Spread	Overhead Efficiency Ratio	Liquidity Index	Liquidity Ratio	Hot Money Ratio	Stability Index
5.2	1.08	7.8	0.12	4.3	0.6	0.77	8.16	3.85	69.7	3.6	27.1	12.7	4.9
4.3	0.82	5.5	0.16	4.8	0.3	0.72	6.12	4.90	77.0	4.3	16.4	6.5	6.3
4.6	0.94	6.9	-0.02	3.8	0.2	0.44	5.11	3.81	84.4	3.6	38.6	16.3	3.5
9.0	0.01	0.0	-0.13	6.8	0.2	1.79	6.23	3.23	49.9	6.8	125.8	11.4	5.6
9.5	0.45	1.3	0.04	9.3	2.3	1.47	9.37	3.87	42.0	1.9	26.9	22.8	9.5
8.9	0.10	0.5	0.13	3.2	0.1	0.62	6.40	3.54	85.2	2.3	31.6	18.9	3.5
5.3	1.83	8.6	0.01	8.8	0.5	2.08	17.82	4.41	54.8	5.0	36.7	8.9	7.0
8.1	0.36	2.2	0.04	5.9	0.7	1.25	11.10	4.11	62.0	3.9	32.0	13.1	7.9
9.5	0.00	0.0	-0.16	5.6	0.8	1.20	9.88	3.95	57.2	2.7	44.8	27.8	7.7
7.0	0.46	2.1	0.21	5.0	0.5	1.30	13.97	4.86	79.3	3.4	16.0	12.2	2.2
7.7	0.11	0.8	0.09	4.7	1.1	0.91	10.55	3.50	68.0	1.9	21.3	20.2	3.8
6.4	0.83	4.5	0.07	5.6	0.8	1.18	11.33	4.10	66.0	6.1	44.6	4.3	7.6
9.6	0.21	0.6	0.01	4.6	0.3	0.69	5.20	2.94	67.7	5.3	50.5	10.0	7.2
8.8	0.56	1.8	-0.05	1.3	0.0	0.10	1.32	3.22	100.0	6.5	64.6	5.2	0.9
9.0	0.00	0.0	0.02	4.2	0.3	0.79	6.37	3.70	72.6	3.2	23.7	13.8	7.2
2.6	2.26	14.0	1.57	4.0	0.8	0.91	9.96	3.98	70.2	7.0	108.3	10.9	4.9
6.6	0.24	2.3	0.14	4.8	0.9	1.01	14.66	3.54	70.1	3.0	48.9	26.3	4.3
7.2	0.45	2.4	0.17	4.8	1.1	1.04	12.14	3.45	58.4	4.3	18.9	7.1	5.1
6.9	0.57	3.3	-0.04	4.0	0.2	0.79	7.65	3.96	62.2	6.2	62.6	7.3	3.7
8.7	0.32	0.9	0.06	8.2	0.4	1.89	10.88	4.57	56.1	5.7	46.5	7.0	7.5
5.6	0.73	6.0	0.00	9.6	0.6	2.14	20.81	5.17	58.3	4.0	21.4	9.7	7.2
6.7	1.02	4.9	0.15	9.8	0.5	1.55	11.49	4.74	52.3	5.7	70.9	11.5	8.4
3.1	1.05	8.0	2.22	4.4	0.4	0.35	3.75	5.37	78.8	3.4	23.1	12.7	3.9
4.3	0.98	5.5	0.00	4.7	0.1	1.03	10.05	3.37	59.7	3.2	61.5	23.3	6.0
9.0	0.00	0.0	0.03	6.3	0.6	0.93	7.01	4.06	76.0	6.5	54.0	4.4	7.9
1.9	3.50	27.2	0.77	2.2	0.1	0.19	2.51	4.43	87.5	5.3	59.8	11.7	0.0
8.7	1.45	3.0	-0.03	6.5	0.2	1.21	6.71	3.28	52.4	5.2	48.4	10.3	7.5
5.2	1.67	8.4	0.14	6.9	1.2	2.61	20.21	4.35	54.7	5.8	81.3	12.3	5.2
8.9	0.32	1.2	-0.43	5.4	0.6	1.12	11.66	3.76	60.7	3.4	19.6	12.5	6.1
5.3	0.73	5.3	0.16	6.3	1.6	1.16	12.28	3.40	53.9	5.7	47.9	8.3	5.6
7.9	0.00	0.0	0.05	0.7	0.0	-0.08	-0.76	3.45	101.9	7.7	132.7	7.1	0.0
8.8	0.00	0.0	0.15	7.2	0.5	0.87	8.18	3.87	72.0	2.5	37.7	24.7	7.4
8.0	0.17	1.5	0.04	5.3	0.6	0.94	12.07	4.06	67.7	4.0	29.4	11.5	4.9
8.4	0.31	2.3	-0.17	10.0	23.3	4.76	54.69	3.79	21.2	4.6	112.8	30.7	6.8
9.0	0.57	1.9	0.02	5.3	0.3	0.93	8.13	4.55	70.8	4.8	32.5	7.9	5.4
0.0	8.30	71.9	3.10	2.7	-0.7	-3.43	-45.57	6.42	64.3	2.0	29.7	25.5	2.5
7.2	0.20	1.9	0.11	4.2	0.3	0.59	8.12	5.59	83.7	2.1	11.5	18.1	2.1
6.6	0.39	3.5	-0.06	6.3	0.7	1.30	16.84	5.00	75.6	3.0	15.0	13.9	5.2
2.2	4.26	25.6	-0.01	3.5	0.1	0.63	8.40	3.37	80.8	5.0	38.6	9.2	5.5
8.9	0.39	2.0	-0.01	6.4	0.8	1.30	12.70	3.87	62.5	3.8	20.2	10.6	6.9
2.4	2.89	9.4	0.03	5.0	0.5	0.83	5.82	5.37	79.0	4.0	44.5	16.0	6.2
6.1	1.16	6.6	0.11	7.5	0.4	1.34	10.80	5.03	57.6	5.3	33.3	5.1	5.8
7.7	0.50	2.2	0.12	7.4	0.6	1.36	10.62	4.05	52.2	4.6	55.7	14.6	7.3
7.6	0.37	2.7	0.48	9.1	0.8	1.92	22.32	5.90	64.2	1.8	14.4	20.1	6.6
6.6	0.27	2.0	0.16	5.7	0.4	0.60	7.68	3.77	74.6	6.0	85.8	13.0	6.8
3.4	0.88	4.9	0.24	5.4	1.9	0.84	7.22	5.26	78.0	7.4	108.1	8.4	7.0
4.2	1.94	11.8	0.27	5.2	0.3	0.70	6.97	4.00	63.0	6.5	56.6	3.6	4.8
3.7	2.66	16.4	0.20	8.2	0.4	1.22	10.16	4.74	58.7	3.6	31.1	13.9	7.0
6.5	1.07	4.4	0.04	3.2	0.1	0.54	6.02	4.25	85.3	6.6	45.2	0.8	3.0
8.4	0.15	1.2	0.00	6.3	0.3	1.04	15.02	3.67	63.2	3.9	55.6	18.2	4.6
4.2	0.91	7.3	0.38	2.8	0.2	0.66	8.11	4.32	77.3	3.7	39.4	16.2	2.2
8.9	0.00	0.0	-0.02	5.4	0.2	0.96	7.71	4.18	66.9	4.7	14.0	3.7	5.7
6.4	0.17	1.3	0.19	5.7	3.2	1.17	14.05	4.18	61.0	3.0	15.3	14.2	5.6
6.5	0.23	1.6	-0.01	9.5	0.5	2.17	20.61	4.00	50.3	4.3	58.5	16.8	6.3
3.8	1.54	9.9	1.20	5.6	21.6	0.67	9.48	2.81	87.7	4.4	64.8	19.6	4.5
4.9	0.62	5.5	0.61	8.3	2.0	2.00	25.98	4.32	48.4	1.6	32.7	34.0	5.8
8.3	0.00	0.0	-0.15	3.7	0.1	0.61	7.10	4.13	78.7	1.4	31.5	35.1	4.1
3.2	1.99	14.9	0.09	5.6	0.1	0.96	9.60	5.10	71.8	6.7	62.7	3.8	4.3
8.5	0.30	1.7	0.23	9.0	0.5	1.92	17.09	4.59	53.6	6.8	92.0	8.3	7.4
4.5	2.24	12.1	0.19	4.2	1.1	0.74	9.08	3.61	76.1	5.9	55.1	8.8	4.2
6.9	0.40	2.0	0.08	9.0	1.6	1.60	15.42	4.35	50.9	1.8	19.1	21.2	7.0
5.3	4.74	9.8	0.35	4.8	0.3	1.23	10.15	3.09	59.2	4.0	69.8	20.0	5.1
8.4	0.95	3.8	0.02	7.5	3.4	1.49	11.28	4.40	54.4	4.8	36.5	9.9	8.6
8.3	0.57	3.1	-0.02	6.0	0.5	1.13	9.82	4.13	58.8	6.2	67.0	7.7	6.9

Name	City	State	Weiss Safety Rating	2003 Weiss Safety Rating	2002 Weiss Safety Rating	Total Assets ($Mil)	One Year Asset Growth	Asset Mix (As a % of Total Assets)				Capital-ization Index	Leverage Ratio	Risk-based Capital Ratio
								Comm-ercial Loans	Cons-umer Loans	Home Mort-gages	Secur-ities			
▲ FIRST NB OF PANDORA	PANDORA	OH	D+	D	C-	105.6	-10.13	7.9	1.6	17.7	27.9	6.0	8.0	14.3
▼ FIRST NB OF PAONIA	PAONIA	CO	E-	D-	D-	48.0	-0.70	11.9	5.9	6.7	23.1	4.0	6.0	10.6
FIRST NB OF PARK FALLS	PARK FALLS	WI	A-	A-	A-	72.4	-5.27	20.5	2.0	22.1	34.4	10.0	15.9	27.9
FIRST NB OF PAWNEE	PAWNEE	OK	B-	B-	B-	50.2	1.08	6.0	7.6	9.4	29.0	9.2	10.5	17.5
FIRST NB OF PENNSYLVANIA	GREENVILLE	PA	B-	B-	B-	4,590.5	3.66	8.6	10.8	23.3	23.8	4.9	6.9	11.0
FIRST NB OF PETERSTOWN	PETERSTOWN	WV	C+	C+	B-	39.5	7.75	5.9	6.4	30.9	39.2	7.8	9.6	18.7
FIRST NB OF PHILLIPS	W HELENA	AR	C+	C	D+	182.4	-3.16	13.9	4.4	7.7	39.8	7.9	9.6	17.8
▼ FIRST NB OF PICAYUNE	PICAYUNE	MS	B-	B+	A-	156.7	7.61	4.6	8.1	32.0	9.9	5.0	7.6	11.0
FIRST NB OF PIKEVILLE	PIKEVILLE	TN	A-	A-	A	66.2	0.64	1.4	15.9	15.9	26.7	10.0	13.3	18.5
FIRST NB OF PINE CITY	PINE CITY	MN	B+	B+	B-	53.1	-4.42	7.5	5.6	32.8	29.5	8.0	9.6	20.0
FIRST NB OF PINEDALE	PINEDALE	WY	A-	A-	A-	51.2	21.59	10.6	4.4	10.9	37.2	10.0	13.3	24.0
▲ FIRST NB OF PLAINVIEW	PLAINVIEW	MN	B-	C+	C+	125.8	8.34	9.3	3.8	34.0	9.5	5.9	7.9	11.8
FIRST NB OF PLATTEVILLE	PLATTEVILLE	WI	B-	B-	C+	131.2	4.77	16.6	1.9	6.5	28.1	9.7	10.8	15.4
▲ FIRST NB OF POLK CTY	WINTER HAVEN	FL	C+	C	C	165.8	32.48	4.4	5.4	18.7	46.7	5.1	7.1	19.2
FIRST NB OF POLK CTY	CEDARTOWN	GA	A	A	A	149.6	-0.80	5.3	6.7	32.8	28.8	10.0	12.5	22.4
FIRST NB OF PONTOTOC	PONTOTOC	MS	B+	B+	A-	205.8	1.49	10.3	11.9	23.2	20.6	10.0	14.5	23.3
▲ FIRST NB OF PORT ALLEGANY	PORT ALLEGANY	PA	C	C-	D+	87.7	-1.17	0.9	3.7	35.0	34.9	6.6	8.6	17.6
FIRST NB OF PORTLAND	PORTLAND	IN	B-	B-	B-	115.8	4.30	9.4	6.9	30.5	10.3	6.1	8.5	11.8
▲ FIRST NB OF PRIMGHAR	PRIMGHAR	IA	B-	C+	C+	23.3	-2.31	7.0	4.3	8.1	42.6	10.0	24.1	37.9
FIRST NB OF PROCTOR	PROCTOR	MN	D+	D+	D+	20.2	3.96	9.8	8.7	28.2	32.0	7.4	9.2	18.4
▲ FIRST NB OF PULASKI	PULASKI	TN	A-	B+	A-	421.7	4.45	4.8	5.7	13.9	36.8	8.8	10.2	16.3
FIRST NB OF QUITAQUE	QUITAQUE	TX	B-	B-	B-	34.2	4.19	6.2	5.7	0.5	33.3	10.0	13.0	25.6
▲ FIRST NB OF QUITMAN	QUITMAN	TX	A-	B+	B+	135.8	-0.99	4.5	8.5	30.2	20.9	7.6	9.4	16.4
▲ FIRST NB OF RAYMOND	RAYMOND	IL	B-	C	C	103.6	-3.54	7.2	6.6	10.4	36.5	10.0	11.6	16.1
FIRST NB OF REFUGIO	REFUGIO	TX	B	B	B+	56.4	0.32	1.0	6.1	2.2	65.1	10.0	16.8	52.2
FIRST NB OF REMBRANDT	REMBRANDT	IA	B	B	B	34.4	3.08	5.2	7.9	7.2	35.0	10.0	17.4	29.9
FIRST NB OF RIVER FALLS	RIVER FALLS	WI	B+	B+	A-	264.5	8.28	4.3	5.0	8.7	37.7	7.1	9.0	14.8
FIRST NB OF ROMNEY	ROMNEY	WV	B	B	B+	118.2	0.52	3.6	8.8	32.2	30.2	9.3	10.5	19.7
FIRST NB OF RUSSELL	RUSSELL SPRINGS	KY	A-	A-	A	130.3	8.75	5.7	4.0	10.6	43.5	10.0	11.7	21.6
FIRST NB OF S PADRE ISLAND	S PADRE ISLAND	TX	B-	C+	C+	56.7	2.00	7.6	2.1	12.2	43.1	5.9	7.9	22.1
▲ FIRST NB OF SANDOVAL	SANDOVAL	IL	B	B-	B	46.8	-7.67	3.3	6.3	16.7	52.8	10.0	11.1	25.1
FIRST NB OF SANTA FE	SANTA FE	NM	B+	B+	B+	452.6	6.75	5.6	2.7	12.0	26.4	5.2	7.6	11.2
FIRST NB OF SANTO	SANTO	TX	D	D	D	64.9	4.10	7.4	13.3	13.1	34.2	5.9	7.9	15.2
FIRST NB OF SARCOXIE	SARCOXIE	MO	B-	B-	B-	25.1	-6.12	15.2	9.9	18.7	10.7	9.7	10.8	15.5
FIRST NB OF SAUK CENTRE	SAUK CENTRE	MN	B+	B+	B+	88.2	-1.50	11.1	4.2	6.4	40.3	8.7	10.1	15.6
FIRST NB OF SC	HOLLY HILL	SC	A	A	A	132.1	4.07	6.6	6.3	14.2	18.9	10.0	15.1	25.1
FIRST NB OF SCOTIA	SCOTIA	NY	C	C	C+	265.4	6.27	5.4	40.8	6.7	16.7	3.5	6.7	10.3
▲ FIRST NB OF SCOTT CITY	SCOTT CITY	KS	C+	C-	B-	60.2	2.90	9.8	4.4	5.6	17.0	10.0	12.1	15.8
FIRST NB OF SEDAN	SEDAN	KS	B	B	B	43.1	-0.97	5.2	3.0	7.3	51.2	9.7	10.8	23.7
▲ FIRST NB OF SEILING	SEILING	OK	C+	C	C+	53.7	-5.01	3.2	2.7	4.2	63.5	10.0	15.7	37.2
FIRST NB OF SEYMOUR	SEYMOUR	TX	B+	B+	B+	29.2	-2.51	4.3	0.5	0.0	64.4	10.0	11.1	38.9
FIRST NB OF SHELBY	SHELBY	NC	A	A	A	700.2	4.90	7.0	4.1	10.6	39.4	10.0	12.1	19.5
FIRST NB OF SHELBY	SHELBY	OH	D	D-	D+	201.0	-10.74	8.0	9.4	12.8	40.3	7.0	9.0	18.1
▼ FIRST NB OF SHELBY CTY	COLUMBIANA	AL	D	D+	C-	220.6	3.12	3.5	6.8	11.6	21.4	4.8	6.8	11.5
FIRST NB OF SHINER	SHINER	TX	B+	B+	A	106.7	-1.54	3.4	3.3	3.2	58.2	10.0	13.8	30.8
FIRST NB OF SIOUX CENTER	SIOUX CENTER	IA	C+	C+	D	85.1	-2.26	7.1	2.2	4.6	16.8	8.2	9.8	14.0
▼ FIRST NB OF SLIPPERY ROCK	SLIPPERY ROCK	PA	C-	C+	C+	330.0	-3.84	5.0	5.7	25.4	26.3	6.5	8.5	15.1
FIRST NB OF SMITH CENTER	SMITH CENTER	KS	B	B	B	36.3	3.28	5.4	1.8	5.4	45.7	9.5	10.7	17.3
▲ FIRST NB OF SONORA	SONORA	TX	B+	B-	C+	122.3	1.59	9.3	12.9	16.4	19.1	7.3	9.2	14.1
FIRST NB OF SOUTH GEORGIA	ALBANY	GA	B-	B-	C+	82.9	10.79	17.4	5.2	23.6	9.0	5.6	8.2	11.4
▼ FIRST NB OF SOUTH MIAMI	S MIAMI	FL	D+	C-	B-	315.2	3.10	2.7	13.3	4.2	30.8	8.2	9.8	24.6
FIRST NB OF SOUTHERN KS	MT HOPE	KS	D-	D-	D-	58.0	1.31	20.6	5.8	12.0	20.6	5.9	7.9	11.8
FIRST NB OF SPARTA	SPARTA	IL	B-	B-	B-	61.6	1.60	4.3	10.6	22.6	38.5	9.4	10.6	18.3
FIRST NB OF SPEARVILLE	SPEARVILLE	KS	C	C	C	17.1	0.87	10.1	3.6	0.4	21.3	10.0	16.6	25.5
FIRST NB OF ST IGNACE	ST IGNACE	MI	C-	C-	C	192.7	-1.02	9.6	4.7	15.9	32.5	8.8	10.3	14.0
▲ FIRST NB OF ST JO	ST JO	TX	C-	D	C+	32.4	-1.71	5.5	4.6	16.5	30.2	9.3	10.6	21.4
▼ FIRST NB OF ST LOUIS	CLAYTON	MO	B-	B	B	1,146.9	-0.24	7.2	2.3	20.6	12.3	3.4	7.1	10.2
FIRST NB OF ST MARYS	LEONARDTOWN	MD	A-	A-	A	414.9	4.25	4.6	3.5	22.6	35.5	9.3	10.5	26.0
▼ FIRST NB OF ST MARYS	ST MARYS	WV	D-	D	E-	38.3	-3.76	6.1	11.9	28.2	20.8	8.3	9.8	17.5
▲ FIRST NB OF ST PETER	ST PETER	MN	B-	C+	C+	119.9	-2.21	10.4	4.2	9.7	21.0	6.2	8.6	11.9
FIRST NB OF STANTON	STANTON	TX	B+	B+	B+	56.7	0.67	3.7	5.1	1.3	68.4	10.0	13.9	44.9
▼ FIRST NB OF STARBUCK	STARBUCK	MN	D+	D+	D+	23.7	-12.03	2.4	4.2	7.9	39.7	8.2	9.8	20.1
FIRST NB OF STEELEVILLE	STEELEVILLE	IL	B	B-	B-	141.8	-2.43	5.0	5.2	18.3	44.7	9.6	10.8	21.5
FIRST NB OF STERLING CITY	STERLING CITY	TX	B+	A-	A-	39.1	-0.01	5.7	8.0	2.5	55.9	10.0	15.6	31.3

Asset Quality Index	Non-Performing Loans		Net Charge-offs Avg Loans	Profitability Index	Net Income ($Mil)	Return on Assets (R.O.A.)	Return on Equity (R.O.E.)	Net Interest Spread	Overhead Efficiency Ratio	Liquidity Index	Liquidity Ratio	Hot Money Ratio	Stability Index
	as a % of Total Loans	as a % of Capital											
3.5	1.95	11.3	0.33	1.3	0.0	0.08	0.94	3.23	96.7	3.5	42.2	18.1	2.9
1.2	3.75	33.4	4.08	2.8	-0.7	-2.69	-41.07	4.16	80.7	3.4	50.4	19.5	0.3
7.7	1.22	4.2	0.00	6.9	0.4	1.11	7.13	4.54	66.9	4.6	13.0	4.4	7.4
4.4	2.09	10.7	-0.09	5.0	0.3	1.08	10.14	4.44	70.0	5.8	61.5	9.8	4.6
5.4	0.75	6.4	0.33	7.2	31.8	1.42	18.79	3.73	53.4	4.1	13.5	8.5	5.1
5.3	1.83	10.4	-0.01	6.5	0.3	1.39	15.37	4.72	62.5	5.5	40.6	7.0	3.8
4.1	1.58	5.5	0.08	5.8	1.0	1.11	9.24	4.52	66.1	2.5	13.5	16.2	6.1
4.0	0.92	9.0	0.04	10.0	2.3	3.03	37.07	5.26	48.8	2.4	19.9	17.5	6.6
7.8	0.03	0.1	0.02	7.6	0.4	1.19	9.02	4.26	60.5	3.4	59.3	24.0	6.9
9.0	0.07	0.4	-0.04	7.1	0.5	1.67	17.16	4.14	60.3	7.4	107.8	7.0	6.8
7.7	0.45	1.1	0.16	10.0	0.7	3.15	22.11	5.56	44.6	6.8	49.7	0.4	7.4
5.5	0.51	4.8	-0.05	6.5	1.0	1.63	20.54	3.80	57.3	2.8	20.8	15.7	5.0
5.1	1.12	6.3	-0.18	4.5	0.6	0.84	7.81	3.50	70.0	2.1	22.0	19.1	6.5
9.0	0.00	0.0	0.00	4.3	0.5	0.63	9.70	3.34	71.0	7.0	72.4	5.2	4.4
8.3	0.55	2.6	0.08	9.6	1.2	1.60	12.50	5.20	58.7	4.4	19.3	6.8	8.2
4.5	2.52	11.0	0.74	9.1	1.5	1.47	10.03	4.83	48.1	3.0	41.3	20.5	8.5
4.4	2.32	13.9	-0.08	3.0	0.4	0.81	8.73	3.75	81.1	5.0	33.6	7.5	4.6
5.8	0.34	3.1	0.11	9.7	0.8	1.51	17.32	4.61	52.3	3.6	16.8	11.3	5.7
7.3	1.79	3.9	0.00	5.3	0.1	0.87	3.76	3.79	64.8	6.3	53.7	2.3	6.9
6.4	1.28	6.6	0.06	3.8	0.0	0.36	3.84	4.31	81.8	5.9	55.6	5.5	2.7
6.1	0.69	3.6	0.35	7.1	2.7	1.29	12.51	4.52	60.7	1.9	28.5	24.9	6.5
5.1	3.22	10.5	0.38	4.5	0.1	0.60	4.67	3.15	80.8	4.6	76.3	18.0	5.6
8.1	0.10	0.6	0.07	7.0	1.1	1.63	16.77	4.40	66.1	4.2	35.6	12.8	7.2
4.5	2.34	11.2	0.38	5.3	0.6	1.13	9.89	4.06	67.2	3.2	16.1	13.3	6.2
8.2	0.71	0.8	0.35	3.5	0.2	0.56	3.33	3.33	79.7	4.7	40.8	11.6	6.6
6.1	2.14	6.8	0.10	5.5	0.2	1.01	5.80	3.26	55.4	6.0	58.5	7.7	6.6
5.0	1.09	6.3	0.01	7.0	2.2	1.71	17.37	4.13	60.6	4.3	37.7	12.8	7.5
6.6	0.78	4.3	0.16	4.7	0.5	0.86	8.17	3.99	71.9	3.6	16.4	11.0	6.2
7.0	1.57	6.0	0.02	5.7	0.8	1.20	9.85	4.16	62.0	3.5	33.7	15.2	7.6
6.5	1.39	8.6	0.03	9.9	0.7	2.36	31.82	4.89	51.6	4.2	14.7	7.4	4.8
8.6	0.59	1.6	0.29	4.5	0.3	1.16	9.73	3.35	68.7	6.5	76.8	7.8	5.3
8.8	0.02	0.2	0.01	8.1	3.1	1.40	18.44	4.77	61.7	4.4	26.8	7.9	5.5
1.6	3.87	23.4	2.49	5.2	0.3	0.77	10.12	4.51	50.6	2.7	44.7	26.7	1.5
5.8	0.44	2.9	-0.02	10.0	0.4	2.83	26.30	5.52	49.5	3.6	28.9	13.2	6.9
7.5	0.10	0.5	0.73	5.5	0.5	1.07	9.85	3.66	63.0	3.9	54.2	17.7	6.9
7.5	0.93	3.3	0.02	6.8	0.7	1.13	7.43	4.39	68.3	5.7	49.8	8.6	8.3
4.1	0.55	5.0	0.31	3.8	0.5	0.41	6.09	4.29	80.8	6.9	57.1	2.9	3.7
4.0	1.13	6.4	-0.49	3.7	0.3	0.85	7.00	4.14	71.2	4.5	50.0	14.2	3.9
6.7	1.56	4.9	0.01	6.8	0.3	1.30	12.27	4.06	56.8	5.6	60.8	10.3	5.6
8.1	0.96	1.7	-0.21	3.1	0.2	0.62	3.79	3.48	88.3	1.7	32.8	33.0	5.5
9.3	0.00	0.0	0.00	6.4	0.2	1.10	9.89	3.52	55.7	5.5	42.3	7.4	6.5
6.1	1.44	5.4	0.26	6.9	4.5	1.30	9.90	3.66	51.7	1.0	24.3	35.8	8.3
1.2	6.40	24.2	0.39	2.0	-0.1	-0.09	-0.91	4.55	69.9	5.2	48.4	10.9	3.5
4.4	0.96	7.0	0.77	1.5	0.0	0.03	0.51	3.33	87.0	3.3	47.3	21.4	1.1
8.5	1.01	2.3	0.12	5.3	0.5	0.86	6.08	3.03	48.8	5.0	66.6	16.1	7.0
6.8	0.01	0.1	-0.02	3.9	0.3	0.60	4.23	3.51	73.7	3.7	19.4	11.0	5.5
2.5	3.74	21.9	0.20	1.9	-0.9	-0.55	-6.01	3.49	84.4	4.4	30.3	9.7	5.2
8.7	0.50	1.9	0.05	4.8	0.2	1.09	9.94	3.85	72.1	6.3	52.5	3.9	5.2
6.7	0.46	3.3	0.13	9.1	1.3	2.13	23.89	5.02	59.9	3.1	27.4	15.4	5.4
4.8	0.65	5.8	0.18	7.0	0.5	1.20	15.12	4.39	55.7	2.3	22.6	18.4	5.8
8.4	0.23	0.6	0.77	1.2	-0.4	-0.23	-2.10	2.34	104.7	6.0	75.8	11.9	3.6
1.3	3.77	30.6	0.30	4.4	0.1	0.39	5.00	4.89	78.3	2.7	52.8	31.6	1.7
4.4	1.92	8.6	0.31	5.2	0.3	0.95	8.78	4.22	65.6	4.5	29.4	8.5	4.3
2.9	3.33	11.3	0.19	6.1	0.1	1.35	8.11	4.07	59.7	5.9	108.5	14.0	5.3
2.4	3.65	18.5	0.00	5.6	1.0	0.99	9.51	4.07	64.1	5.8	52.6	8.9	6.5
8.7	0.02	0.1	-0.99	3.7	0.2	1.10	10.72	4.31	66.1	6.2	78.3	9.9	2.6
7.5	0.24	1.8	0.03	8.0	6.9	1.22	13.20	3.61	48.6	5.4	36.6	9.3	7.6
8.9	0.00	0.0	0.01	10.0	4.2	2.03	20.10	4.56	36.9	6.9	68.8	5.4	8.0
0.3	7.41	41.0	-0.12	3.2	0.1	0.31	3.19	4.91	88.5	5.7	41.7	5.6	2.9
4.3	1.43	9.9	0.10	6.8	0.7	1.12	12.84	4.01	65.7	4.4	29.2	9.3	4.4
9.4	0.02	0.0	-1.54	5.0	0.3	1.12	7.94	3.16	67.4	3.5	59.4	21.6	7.3
8.8	0.10	0.4	-0.19	3.6	0.1	0.69	7.16	4.13	79.4	5.5	45.9	5.5	1.6
7.6	0.42	1.7	0.38	4.8	0.6	0.84	7.82	3.58	65.1	6.8	106.2	11.5	5.9
8.7	0.69	1.6	0.01	5.3	0.2	0.82	4.94	4.53	78.9	5.4	42.2	7.7	6.9

Name	City	State	Weiss Safety Rating	2003 Weiss Safety Rating	2002 Weiss Safety Rating	Total Assets ($Mil)	One Year Asset Growth	Asset Mix (As a % of Total Assets)				Capital-ization Index	Leverage Ratio	Risk-based Capital Ratio
								Comm-ercial Loans	Cons-umer Loans	Home Mort-gages	Secur-ities			
FIRST NB OF STIGLER	STIGLER	OK	B	B	B	84.8	5.92	7.3	5.0	5.0	43.9	5.1	7.1	12.9
FIRST NB OF STOUGHTON	STOUGHTON	WI	B	B	C+	210.8	15.10	9.3	1.3	11.0	30.0	7.0	9.2	12.5
FIRST NB OF STRASBURG	STRASBURG	CO	B-	B-	B-	269.1	4.48	8.2	1.5	7.7	9.3	7.6	10.6	13.0
▼ FIRST NB OF STRATTON	STRATTON	CO	C-	C-	C	38.5	-0.55	6.8	3.3	2.5	10.5	6.3	8.4	14.7
FIRST NB OF STUTTGART	STUTTGART	AR	C-	D+	C+	36.0	69.94	8.0	6.1	16.1	27.6	10.0	13.9	21.5
FIRST NB OF SUFFIELD	SUFFIELD	CT	A-	A-	A-	179.5	9.58	5.4	1.1	60.4	15.0	8.2	9.8	18.4
▲ FIRST NB OF SULLIVAN	SULLIVAN	IL	C-	D+	D	66.2	-3.71	19.7	10.6	22.3	19.7	5.2	7.2	11.7
▲ FIRST NB OF SUMMERFIELD	SUMMERFIELD	KS	C+	C	C-	6.8	17.06	5.0	1.3	12.8	5.1	9.2	10.5	16.8
▲ FIRST NB OF SYCAMORE	SYCAMORE	OH	B	B-	B-	78.2	-2.13	4.1	8.7	26.7	40.5	9.7	10.8	21.0
▲ FIRST NB OF SYRACUSE	SYRACUSE	KS	B-	C+	B	89.7	3.72	5.1	2.1	11.7	11.6	7.4	9.4	12.8
FIRST NB OF TAHOKA	TAHOKA	TX	B+	B+	A-	44.6	-5.15	3.3	4.1	7.6	39.4	10.0	12.0	31.6
FIRST NB OF TALLADEGA	TALLADEGA	AL	A	A	A	258.6	4.15	4.0	5.4	13.6	52.2	10.0	11.8	17.6
FIRST NB OF TEXHOMA	TEXHOMA	OK	A-	A-	A-	63.9	3.69	4.8	7.7	5.2	39.8	10.0	11.6	20.6
▼ FIRST NB OF THE CAROLINAS	GAFFNEY	SC	C	C-	C	82.8	11.32	10.6	5.9	11.7	8.2	4.4	11.2	10.7
FIRST NB OF THE LAKES	NAVARRE	MN	C+	C+	C+	58.7	1.61	19.9	9.3	3.1	20.6	5.9	7.9	14.5
▲ FIRST NB OF THE NORTH	SANDSTONE	MN	C-	D+	D	58.1	-0.06	4.1	8.7	21.8	14.8	5.4	7.4	12.8
FIRST NB OF THE ROCKIES	GRAND JUNCTION	CO	B-	B-	B	259.5	16.90	16.0	3.0	6.9	9.5	4.1	8.0	10.6
▲ FIRST NB OF THE SOUTH	MILLEDGEVILLE	GA	C+	C	B-	156.3	25.49	6.0	2.9	12.3	10.9	4.2	8.1	10.6
▲ FIRST NB OF THE SOUTH	SPARTANBURG	SC	C+	C	C-	209.8	29.76	20.4	2.5	18.6	16.5	7.1	9.1	12.5
FIRST NB OF THOMAS	THOMAS	OK	B+	B+	B+	32.2	-4.53	11.1	8.3	4.6	42.9	10.0	16.3	30.3
▲ FIRST NB OF THREE RIVERS	THREE RIVERS	MI	B-	C+	C-	143.9	2.93	6.6	4.3	19.0	26.0	6.5	8.5	13.3
▼ FIRST NB OF	THROCKMORTON	TX	C-	C+	C+	21.8	3.87	1.8	5.2	3.3	23.5	8.6	10.1	23.0
▲ FIRST NB OF TOM BEAN	TOM BEAN	TX	C+	C	C-	39.1	1.05	13.7	10.4	10.0	35.3	10.0	11.2	24.2
FIRST NB OF TRENTON	TRENTON	TX	B-	B-	B	118.6	-0.14	3.5	2.4	31.1	28.8	6.6	8.6	16.6
▲ FIRST NB OF TRIBUNE	TRIBUNE	KS	C	C	C+	69.3	92.58	10.0	1.2	4.4	47.2	4.4	6.4	12.9
FIRST NB OF TRINITY	TRINITY	TX	B	B	B	35.8	-1.12	5.6	11.2	10.4	36.6	9.1	10.4	19.9
FIRST NB OF TULLAHOMA	TULLAHOMA	TN	D	D+	C-	70.1	-2.74	16.6	5.3	11.6	41.8	4.9	7.0	14.3
▲ FIRST NB OF UNADILLA	UNADILLA	NE	B	B-	B-	39.9	-2.11	6.2	6.2	20.8	23.6	10.0	12.1	20.5
▼ FIRST NB OF UTICA	UTICA	NE	C+	B-	B	23.9	2.61	7.9	2.6	9.5	26.7	10.0	12.2	19.0
▲ FIRST NB OF VALENTINE	VALENTINE	NE	B	B-	B+	167.9	27.48	3.7	2.6	1.3	68.9	6.7	8.8	20.1
FIRST NB OF VALPARAISO	VALPARAISO	IN	A	A-	A-	654.5	4.56	1.1	3.7	13.4	61.3	8.3	9.9	31.2
▲ FIRST NB OF VOLGA	VOLGA	SD	B-	C+	C+	27.3	3.76	4.6	12.5	22.0	25.0	7.9	9.6	16.4
FIRST NB OF WACONIA	WACONIA	MN	A-	A-	B+	188.0	-0.93	11.0	2.5	11.3	27.7	9.5	11.0	14.6
FIRST NB OF WADENA	WADENA	MN	D	C-	C-	50.8	3.43	8.5	4.3	21.5	29.5	5.1	7.1	14.0
▼ FIRST NB OF WAHOO	WAHOO	NE	B-	B	B	91.0	3.61	8.1	2.1	18.1	28.7	6.3	8.3	14.3
FIRST NB OF WAKEFIELD	WAKEFIELD	MI	C+	B-	B-	46.5	0.09	5.4	15.8	29.7	25.5	8.3	9.8	19.0
FIRST NB OF WALKER	WALKER	MN	B+	B+	B+	229.5	7.07	12.2	5.4	25.7	19.3	6.6	8.7	13.8
▲ FIRST NB OF WAMEGO	WAMEGO	KS	D+	D	D+	81.8	0.21	13.1	4.9	11.4	17.6	9.6	10.7	15.3
FIRST NB OF WASECA	WASECA	MN	B-	B-	B-	110.6	-3.42	7.5	4.0	25.6	9.2	6.3	8.3	12.0
FIRST NB OF WASHINGTON	WASHINGTON	KS	A-	A-	A	51.1	-5.56	2.9	3.6	9.9	53.7	10.0	18.6	38.4
▼ FIRST NB OF WATERLOO	WATERLOO	IL	C+	B-	B-	259.6	-0.91	3.5	2.0	19.1	40.3	6.0	8.0	15.2
FIRST NB OF WAUCHULA	WAUCHULA	FL	B	B	B+	80.5	1.34	12.5	3.6	26.3	14.6	10.0	11.4	19.0
FIRST NB OF WAVERLY	WAVERLY	IA	B	B	B	158.6	12.44	12.4	3.0	12.6	22.6	6.8	8.8	14.5
▲ FIRST NB OF WAVERLY	WAVERLY	OH	C	D+	C	163.0	7.58	0.9	3.1	20.9	31.3	6.7	8.8	16.6
FIRST NB OF WAYNE	WAYNE	NE	B-	B-	B-	32.1	-5.12	12.7	7.6	17.2	13.9	8.7	10.3	13.9
FIRST NB OF WAYNESBORO	WAYNESBORO	GA	A-	A-	A-	82.5	-0.05	5.7	14.9	18.1	29.1	10.0	13.8	24.9
▲ FIRST NB OF WELLSTON	WELLSTON	OH	A-	B+	B+	82.4	-1.06	1.6	19.0	39.8	23.3	10.0	12.6	22.6
FIRST NB OF WEST UNION	W UNION	IA	B-	B-	B-	80.1	-5.36	6.1	4.5	20.8	33.2	7.6	9.4	17.5
▲ FIRST NB OF WIGGINS	WIGGINS	MS	E	E-	E-	50.4	-4.15	7.5	19.4	16.5	37.6	5.6	7.6	13.3
FIRST NB OF WILLIAMSON	WILLIAMSON	WV	A-	A-	A	71.4	-2.85	10.1	5.9	20.1	41.8	10.0	16.5	37.3
▼ FIRST NB OF WINNSBORO	WINNSBORO	TX	B-	B	B+	122.7	-2.37	4.8	7.1	21.4	14.9	10.0	13.2	20.0
FIRST NB OF WOODSBORO	WOODSBORO	TX	B-	B-	B	29.9	4.35	4.2	7.3	7.2	53.6	10.0	18.6	45.4
FIRST NB OF WYNNE	WYNNE	AR	A-	A	A	180.6	1.08	17.5	4.0	10.2	11.8	10.0	14.5	21.2
FIRST NB OF WYOMING	WYOMING	DE	A+	A+	A	222.9	14.48	4.4	4.1	22.7	19.4	10.0	15.8	23.6
▲ FIRST NB OF WYOMING	LARAMIE	WY	B	C+	C+	155.8	13.80	11.6	1.9	7.0	18.2	7.9	9.6	14.1
▲ FIRST NB OF YUMA	YUMA	CO	B	B	B	273.7	14.82	9.8	2.8	6.9	3.7	6.2	9.6	11.9
FIRST NB OSCEOLA CTY	KISSIMMEE	FL	C	C-	C+	177.6	17.20	9.8	4.4	16.5	15.7	4.6	7.0	10.8
▲ FIRST NB PASCO	DADE CITY	FL	C+	C	C-	88.6	14.27	3.1	24.1	24.9	19.1	6.1	8.1	12.0
FIRST NB SCOTTSBORO AL	SCOTTSBORO	AL	B	B	A-	290.8	-4.96	3.8	6.7	14.1	54.1	10.0	12.3	27.1
FIRST NB SOUTH	ALMA	GA	B	B-	B-	208.9	0.55	17.7	3.0	16.6	3.7	6.9	9.7	12.4
FIRST NB SOUTH DAKOTA	YANKTON	SD	C	C	C	411.9	1.05	9.7	32.9	2.7	10.0	4.5	7.3	10.7
FIRST NB TAYLORVILLE	TAYLORVILLE	IL	B	B	B+	127.8	5.23	4.5	4.9	10.6	51.5	7.9	9.6	13.4
▲ FIRST NB TX	KILLEEN	TX	B	B-	B-	495.4	12.06	3.9	11.1	11.7	30.5	6.2	8.2	18.1
▲ FIRST NB USA	BOUTTE	LA	B	B-	B-	134.1	6.86	4.2	2.9	29.9	0.0	9.9	11.7	14.9

Asset Quality Index	Non-Performing Loans as a % of Total Loans	as a % of Capital	Net Charge-offs Avg Loans	Profitability Index	Net Income ($Mil)	Return on Assets (R.O.A.)	Return on Equity (R.O.E.)	Net Interest Spread	Overhead Efficiency Ratio	Liquidity Index	Liquidity Ratio	Hot Money Ratio	Stability Index
8.7	0.02	0.1	0.05	10.0	1.0	2.51	35.23	4.51	50.4	3.7	9.7	10.1	4.6
7.8	0.40	2.6	0.04	5.0	1.0	1.01	10.58	3.42	66.3	0.5	8.2	50.3	5.3
5.8	0.52	3.6	0.17	8.2	1.5	1.15	10.49	5.58	66.2	3.0	33.9	18.2	5.7
4.9	2.86	16.9	-0.01	5.4	0.2	1.12	12.61	5.08	74.4	4.3	87.9	21.9	3.2
4.5	2.65	11.9	0.14	0.1	0.0	-0.27	-2.11	3.59	97.4	2.3	55.4	58.0	4.4
6.8	0.43	3.3	0.00	6.3	0.8	0.93	9.64	4.00	63.3	3.6	27.7	12.8	6.7
7.9	0.00	0.0	0.17	4.1	0.3	0.97	13.53	3.56	74.2	4.3	21.5	7.5	2.7
8.7	0.00	0.0	0.00	4.0	0.0	0.59	5.49	3.88	79.0	6.4	78.9	7.1	5.1
5.0	1.10	4.4	-0.29	5.3	0.4	1.10	8.48	4.19	67.0	2.5	19.9	16.8	5.6
6.2	0.23	1.7	-0.03	7.0	0.6	1.21	13.21	4.46	55.9	0.6	5.9	43.2	5.7
8.5	1.09	3.1	0.32	6.0	0.3	1.24	10.37	3.18	66.4	3.7	81.1	28.9	6.7
5.8	2.82	9.6	1.45	10.0	2.3	1.79	14.99	4.78	32.1	1.8	26.4	24.2	8.2
8.2	0.03	0.1	0.14	7.2	0.5	1.59	13.40	4.32	61.3	3.3	58.9	24.2	7.5
5.6	0.44	1.4	-0.03	6.2	0.1	1.27	9.20	4.66	66.8	3.9	18.3	9.6	3.9
6.2	0.61	3.5	-0.04	4.9	0.4	1.31	16.61	3.42	75.2	6.8	54.0	1.4	4.4
3.5	1.82	14.6	-0.05	7.5	0.3	0.99	13.80	4.53	64.8	6.2	41.3	2.2	2.4
5.0	0.28	2.1	1.17	7.6	1.3	1.01	11.46	4.98	71.4	3.6	40.9	17.0	6.2
6.2	0.07	0.2	-0.04	5.1	0.6	0.82	3.78	4.96	73.8	2.9	19.1	15.0	6.2
8.2	0.02	0.2	0.01	3.6	0.7	0.77	9.50	3.29	63.6	1.3	12.1	26.9	2.4
7.1	0.89	2.4	0.02	7.3	0.3	1.83	11.85	4.25	61.3	4.7	70.7	16.5	7.0
6.0	0.47	3.4	0.08	4.2	0.6	0.87	10.16	3.90	76.7	3.4	22.7	13.0	3.8
5.5	3.02	9.3	-0.03	4.3	0.1	0.88	8.76	2.67	69.1	6.4	85.1	8.5	3.7
8.1	0.00	0.0	0.14	4.1	0.2	0.85	7.96	4.13	80.8	3.0	53.9	26.5	2.8
7.0	0.71	4.5	0.08	4.4	0.6	0.98	11.32	3.58	77.7	4.7	57.3	15.7	4.5
7.8	0.15	0.7	0.40	2.7	0.1	0.38	4.70	2.29	78.2	4.6	82.2	18.4	3.4
5.4	1.34	6.1	0.20	9.0	0.4	2.11	20.37	5.05	62.6	5.4	30.5	3.4	6.0
4.2	1.47	8.2	0.72	2.3	0.1	0.27	3.45	3.81	90.5	4.4	30.4	9.6	2.8
8.4	0.20	1.0	-0.10	7.1	0.3	1.52	12.75	4.33	59.0	6.5	60.7	4.5	5.1
6.8	1.24	5.6	0.03	5.5	0.1	0.80	5.45	3.94	74.9	5.6	54.1	7.1	5.0
9.5	0.07	0.2	0.03	5.5	1.1	1.31	17.15	2.81	42.7	0.7	12.3	43.6	4.7
9.3	0.25	0.8	-0.04	7.8	1.7	0.54	5.11	4.17	58.5	4.7	31.1	8.4	8.1
6.9	0.33	2.1	-0.25	10.0	0.3	1.83	19.84	4.99	45.1	5.7	56.8	8.9	5.8
8.6	0.16	1.0	0.02	10.0	2.3	2.43	22.96	4.61	53.6	4.8	29.4	7.0	8.0
3.4	2.22	16.7	0.00	4.3	0.2	0.93	12.48	3.97	74.1	6.9	83.9	6.3	2.3
6.5	0.43	3.0	-0.16	6.4	0.5	1.03	12.51	3.62	58.3	6.3	63.8	6.6	5.4
4.5	1.04	6.3	-0.06	6.4	0.3	1.23	12.65	5.14	64.8	3.9	44.7	16.4	4.4
5.0	0.93	7.0	0.03	9.2	2.6	2.29	26.42	4.25	50.4	3.8	38.0	15.2	6.5
1.4	6.95	40.6	0.76	2.8	0.1	0.19	1.82	3.82	77.3	4.7	45.6	12.3	4.5
4.1	1.33	10.1	0.08	6.6	0.9	1.59	16.69	4.63	67.1	3.7	15.5	10.6	6.1
6.7	5.12	9.1	-0.02	5.9	0.3	1.02	5.55	3.38	55.6	7.1	97.2	7.5	7.3
4.5	2.31	14.9	0.11	4.4	1.1	0.79	9.98	3.30	66.8	4.1	18.9	8.3	4.2
6.2	1.55	8.4	0.21	4.4	0.4	1.02	8.55	5.05	72.7	3.4	68.8	28.0	5.2
7.8	0.25	1.4	-0.06	6.1	0.9	1.16	11.07	4.20	63.9	6.2	50.5	5.5	6.3
3.1	2.68	14.7	0.61	5.1	0.7	0.92	10.45	3.78	68.8	4.5	46.5	13.9	5.2
7.2	0.27	1.9	0.02	7.6	0.3	1.77	17.17	4.78	63.3	5.0	30.3	6.0	5.2
6.0	1.43	5.1	0.24	6.9	0.5	1.17	8.70	5.46	63.6	3.2	50.2	21.7	6.8
7.7	0.30	1.6	0.44	6.0	0.4	1.03	7.93	4.69	68.3	4.5	42.9	13.0	6.7
6.8	0.50	2.9	0.22	4.2	0.3	0.80	8.47	3.42	80.1	6.8	70.6	5.1	5.1
0.5	6.35	33.7	3.17	0.0	-0.4	-1.36	-16.01	2.66	114.1	2.6	49.6	31.5	1.8
6.4	3.10	7.9	1.27	9.3	0.8	2.20	12.26	4.92	53.6	5.0	40.4	10.0	8.3
3.2	3.69	18.2	0.80	8.5	1.1	1.79	13.30	5.78	49.1	2.6	24.0	16.8	6.7
8.9	0.16	0.3	0.12	3.8	0.1	0.81	4.60	3.79	80.5	6.2	52.0	4.4	6.4
5.5	1.70	7.7	0.05	8.5	1.1	1.17	8.12	4.21	58.9	3.4	50.3	21.4	9.2
7.8	0.52	2.0	0.06	9.9	1.7	1.64	9.72	4.51	49.1	5.9	40.1	4.1	9.6
5.6	1.38	9.8	0.06	6.8	1.1	1.45	16.68	4.63	65.2	2.4	36.6	24.9	4.9
5.2	0.65	5.3	0.19	9.3	2.0	1.48	16.66	5.24	48.6	2.3	32.2	23.2	5.5
5.7	0.32	3.0	0.04	4.6	0.6	0.70	10.48	3.53	69.9	3.3	37.9	17.8	4.1
5.8	0.45	3.9	0.00	6.2	0.5	1.12	14.01	5.50	70.6	4.0	5.9	7.7	3.4
8.6	0.74	2.1	0.30	4.5	1.3	0.89	7.18	3.59	68.2	3.4	26.9	13.9	5.9
5.1	0.68	5.1	-0.52	8.7	1.6	1.51	15.96	5.07	45.7	2.0	31.9	27.5	5.1
2.8	1.04	7.0	1.98	4.8	1.8	0.84	7.97	5.45	56.0	6.8	86.9	9.0	5.6
6.9	0.88	3.9	0.10	6.0	0.8	1.34	13.90	3.82	49.8	4.2	24.0	8.6	6.0
8.3	0.10	0.5	0.62	6.9	1.8	0.75	8.94	4.31	96.1	5.9	41.4	4.3	5.2
5.5	0.31	2.3	0.04	9.2	0.9	1.37	13.92	5.40	69.9	4.2	25.9	8.9	6.4

| Name | City | State | Weiss Safety Rating | 2003 Weiss Safety Rating | 2002 Weiss Safety Rating | Total Assets ($Mil) | One Year Asset Growth | Asset Mix (As a % of Total Assets) | | | | Capital-ization Index | Leverage Ratio | Risk-based Capital Ratio |
								Comm-ercial Loans	Cons-umer Loans	Home Mort-gages	Secur-ities			
FIRST NB WAUPACA	WAUPACA	WI	C+	C+	C+	407.3	2.81	9.9	4.9	26.2	6.4	4.1	8.1	10.6
FIRST NB WEST METRO	DALLAS	GA	C-	D+	D	101.6	60.64	5.9	2.0	9.4	3.9	7.7	11.5	13.1
FIRST NB&T	FORT WALTON BCH	FL	B+	B+	B+	395.9	13.24	3.7	3.5	16.6	11.1	6.0	8.0	12.8
FIRST NB&T	PHILLIPSBURG	KS	A-	A-	B+	143.4	-0.51	8.1	5.5	6.4	30.3	10.0	12.6	19.6
FIRST NB&T	ST JOHN	KS	B	B	B	47.4	-4.03	6.0	2.2	3.0	25.7	10.0	14.5	23.5
FIRST NB&T	LONDON	KY	C+	C	C+	267.4	19.13	6.8	6.7	25.2	11.1	6.6	8.6	13.0
FIRST NB&T	PIPESTONE	MN	B-	B-	B-	121.2	8.05	29.2	3.3	6.6	11.1	7.8	10.2	13.2
▲ FIRST NB&T OF FULLERTON	FULLERTON	NE	B	B-	B-	43.5	-3.46	8.2	1.2	1.9	23.0	10.0	21.0	28.9
▲ FIRST NB&T OF SYRACUSE	SYRACUSE	NE	D	D-	E+	49.7	-7.73	6.2	2.6	9.3	36.1	6.1	8.1	14.0
FIRST NB&TC	LOUISVILLE	GA	B-	C+	C+	504.9	13.91	8.8	7.8	20.0	13.6	6.7	8.7	12.5
▲ FIRST NB&TC	CLINTON	IL	A-	B+	B+	68.8	4.66	4.1	4.3	20.9	44.7	10.0	12.7	27.7
FIRST NB&TC	KOKOMO	IN	D+	D	C-	1,417.2	-9.08	15.9	1.5	17.1	34.5	6.5	8.5	14.7
FIRST NB&TC	COLUMBIA	MO	B-	B-	B-	356.1	1.16	13.7	3.3	23.9	12.3	8.5	10.0	13.8
FIRST NB&TC	ASHEBORO	NC	B	B	B	651.4	5.05	29.3	2.5	12.9	17.6	6.3	9.2	12.0
FIRST NB&TC	FALLS CITY	NE	A-	A-	A-	75.9	0.15	1.6	2.9	14.3	63.2	10.0	14.0	29.7
▲ FIRST NB&TC	SHAWNEE	OK	B+	B	B-	98.1	17.69	9.3	4.3	10.4	59.3	9.0	10.3	24.2
FIRST NB&TC	BELOIT	WI	C+	C+	C+	544.7	9.22	5.6	9.2	16.3	24.4	4.1	6.8	10.6
FIRST NB&TC	POWELL	WY	C+	C	C-	209.2	1.54	13.9	5.4	6.0	22.2	4.9	7.6	11.0
▲ FIRST NB&TC CHICKASHA OK	CHICKASHA	OK	A+	A	A	233.2	1.77	14.6	8.2	11.0	29.6	10.0	12.9	18.0
▼ FIRST NB&TC IN LARNED	LARNED	KS	E-	D	D	64.7	-10.58	4.2	2.1	3.1	40.3	5.4	7.4	13.2
FIRST NB&TC OF ADA	ADA	OK	B+	B+	B+	339.8	13.09	9.2	4.5	20.2	37.2	6.9	8.9	15.5
▼ FIRST NB&TC OF ARDMORE	ARDMORE	OK	B	B+	B+	272.7	-1.09	9.0	8.4	11.4	41.0	5.7	7.7	14.4
▼ FIRST NB&TC OF BEATRICE	BEATRICE	NE	B-	B	B	157.0	6.11	7.3	4.7	10.8	43.6	6.7	8.7	16.1
▼ FIRST NB&TC OF BOTTINEAU	BOTTINEAU	ND	B	B	B	95.5	-0.48	3.3	3.1	3.2	43.9	10.0	12.9	29.1
FIRST NB&TC OF BROKEN	BROKEN ARROW	OK	C-	C-	C-	176.9	-2.49	6.5	6.5	15.7	31.5	5.1	7.1	12.1
FIRST NB&TC OF COLUMBUS	COLUMBUS	NE	C	C	C	407.0	5.70	11.9	34.7	4.9	12.0	3.7	7.9	10.4
FIRST NB&TC OF IRON	IRON MOUNTAIN	MI	B	B	B+	203.4	1.84	33.5	5.0	19.9	30.0	9.7	10.8	15.0
FIRST NB&TC OF JUNCTION	JUNCTION CITY	KS	C+	B-	C+	73.5	6.73	7.7	1.9	10.2	38.1	6.9	8.9	13.7
FIRST NB&TC OF	LEAVENWORTH	KS	A-	A-	A-	93.8	5.51	10.6	25.1	24.3	14.6	7.8	9.5	13.8
FIRST NB&TC OF MCALESTER	MCALESTER	OK	A-	A-	A	419.5	-1.68	4.1	3.0	9.3	40.1	10.0	17.2	36.4
FIRST NB&TC OF MIAMI	MIAMI	OK	C+	C	C-	119.1	4.62	9.7	10.3	14.0	28.4	5.8	7.8	13.9
FIRST NB&TC OF MINDEN	MINDEN	NE	B+	B+	B+	51.6	-3.00	5.5	2.3	10.0	38.0	10.0	11.8	19.6
▼ FIRST NB&TC OF MOUNTAIN	MOUNTAIN HOME	AR	A	A+	A+	266.0	-3.13	6.0	4.3	16.9	41.2	7.7	9.4	17.1
▲ FIRST NB&TC OF NEWTOWN	NEWTOWN	PA	A+	A	A	631.4	3.18	1.6	3.0	16.6	43.0	10.0	11.0	21.7
FIRST NB&TC OF OKMULGEE	OKMULGEE	OK	A-	A-	A	108.0	-7.26	9.9	5.0	18.9	35.2	10.0	12.9	22.0
▲ FIRST NB&TC OF VINITA	VINITA	OK	B-	C+	C+	168.8	51.64	5.5	9.2	16.4	40.0	6.0	8.0	14.1
FIRST NB&TC OF	WEATHERFORD	TX	C	C	C	108.4	7.26	6.9	8.4	8.0	26.3	5.5	7.5	12.0
FIRST NB&TC OF WILLISTON	WILLISTON	ND	C+	C+	B-	144.6	2.72	25.6	3.9	2.8	20.5	9.3	10.6	14.4
FIRST NB&TC TREASURE	STUART	FL	B	B	B	1,428.1	8.18	3.0	5.6	18.4	38.5	5.2	7.2	12.1
FIRST NB&TC-ROCHELLE	ROCHELLE	IL	B	B	B-	180.1	-1.29	4.0	4.7	12.2	42.7	6.7	8.7	15.7
FIRST NB&TC-WEATHERFORD	WEATHERFORD	OK	A-	A-	A-	86.2	-5.49	17.0	12.6	13.7	10.1	10.0	19.2	28.0
▼ FIRST NB, TORRINGTON	TORRINGTON	WY	C-	C+	B-	152.1	22.57	13.8	4.0	4.1	7.4	2.8	7.6	9.8
FIRST NB-BENTON	BENTON	LA	B	B	B+	46.2	-5.68	2.4	1.9	17.3	55.4	10.0	14.0	50.1
▲ FIRST NB-CUMBERLANDS	LIVINGSTON	TN	B	B-	C+	384.0	5.85	17.2	6.1	22.5	6.1	6.9	8.9	13.3
FIRST NB-DE RIDDER	DE RIDDER	LA	A+	A+	A+	147.4	-2.66	2.5	6.1	9.7	64.9	10.0	15.4	45.8
FIRST NB-PINCKNEYVILLE	PINCKNEYVILLE	IL	B-	B-	B	93.6	-1.16	1.3	2.0	16.2	69.1	6.7	8.7	28.6
▼ FIRST NB-RUIDOSO	RUIDOSO	NM	A-	A	A-	50.7	-1.15	6.3	6.0	10.3	25.6	10.0	11.7	18.9
FIRST NEBRASKA BK	VALLEY	NE	B-	C+	B-	147.3	-1.64	12.0	3.6	5.6	20.7	3.8	8.0	10.4
FIRST NEIGHBOR BK NA	TOLEDO	IL	D	D	D	192.3	2.54	17.4	7.6	18.3	17.4	8.3	9.9	13.7
FIRST NEODESHA BK	NEODESHA	KS	B-	B-	B-	51.2	6.05	10.2	8.0	17.5	15.8	5.3	7.3	11.8
FIRST NEW MEXICO BK	DEMING	NM	B	B	A-	215.9	17.72	5.2	7.6	6.9	23.0	6.1	8.1	12.6
FIRST NEWTON NB	NEWTON	IA	C+	B-	B-	72.9	1.75	5.5	1.2	20.1	42.9	5.9	7.9	17.3
FIRST NIAGARA BANK	LOCKPORT	NY	B+	B+	C	4,673.7	42.70	8.4	4.0	25.2	24.0	10.0	11.4	17.9
▼ FIRST NIAGARA COMMERCIAL	TROY	NY	C+	B+	B+	186.1	27.48	0.0	0.0	0.0	91.5	4.4	6.4	25.8
FIRST NM BK SILVER CITY	SILVER CITY	NM	B	B	A-	53.9	7.35	6.5	4.4	11.0	24.0	8.0	9.7	18.5
FIRST NORTHERN BK OF	DIXON	CA	B	B	B	586.2	13.22	14.3	0.8	7.3	8.9	5.1	8.1	11.1
▲ FIRST NW BK	ARLINGTON HGHTS	IL	C-	D	D-	236.0	2.21	17.5	2.0	1.6	24.1	4.9	7.5	10.9
FIRST OPTION BANK	OSAWATOMIE	KS	B-	B-	C+	120.6	7.60	4.4	3.4	42.4	18.0	5.2	7.2	12.7
▲ FIRST PACIFIC BANK OF CA	SAN DIEGO	CA	C+	C	D-	175.1	47.32	19.2	0.8	4.8	5.1	6.4	11.6	12.1
FIRST PALMETTO SVGS BK	CAMDEN	SC	C+	C+	C+	680.2	16.27	14.4	2.4	33.2	13.4	3.9	6.6	10.5
FIRST PENN BK	PHILADELPHIA	PA	C+	C+	C+	499.4	2.80	5.3	4.6	23.7	18.3	5.9	7.9	13.3
▲ FIRST PEOPLES BK	PORT ST LUCIE	FL	D	D	D	78.9	16.37	17.6	11.9	8.5	11.0	6.3	8.3	13.2
▲ FIRST PEOPLES BK	PINE MOUNTAIN	GA	B	B-	C+	66.5	8.43	10.3	14.7	15.4	30.1	8.6	10.0	15.7
▲ FIRST PEOPLES BK OF TN	JEFFERSON CITY	TN	C+	C	C	97.1	-3.03	12.6	7.0	24.0	19.4	6.1	8.1	13.5

Asset Quality Index	Non-Performing Loans as a % of Total Loans	Non-Performing Loans as a % of Capital	Net Charge-offs Avg Loans	Profitability Index	Net Income ($Mil)	Return on Assets (R.O.A.)	Return on Equity (R.O.E.)	Net Interest Spread	Overhead Efficiency Ratio	Liquidity Index	Liquidity Ratio	Hot Money Ratio	Stability Index
4.5	0.68	6.8	0.23	7.7	2.7	1.32	16.21	4.57	51.1	2.8	19.6	15.7	4.8
7.1	0.00	0.0	0.01	2.5	0.2	0.41	3.20	4.40	67.9	0.6	4.8	34.7	0.8
8.8	0.14	0.9	0.02	6.1	3.0	1.61	19.50	3.50	70.5	8.8	224.2	7.9	5.9
6.0	1.52	6.6	0.10	7.3	1.2	1.65	13.18	4.51	51.0	4.6	50.7	14.8	7.3
5.0	2.90	10.8	-0.23	7.4	0.6	2.56	18.60	4.45	62.2	3.7	56.7	19.3	6.4
5.1	0.65	5.2	-0.10	4.9	1.1	0.91	11.40	3.82	68.1	2.8	38.4	21.2	3.9
5.1	0.60	3.5	-0.05	8.6	1.5	2.44	20.25	4.34	39.2	2.7	23.7	16.4	6.4
4.1	2.35	7.0	0.48	5.8	0.2	1.04	4.92	4.15	63.4	4.7	57.5	14.2	7.2
4.8	2.18	11.9	-0.03	2.7	0.1	0.37	4.46	3.67	91.3	6.7	57.4	2.9	1.7
4.3	0.86	6.8	0.27	6.6	3.1	1.26	14.63	4.82	60.0	1.8	28.1	26.6	4.4
9.1	0.35	1.2	-0.02	7.2	0.7	1.99	14.71	4.42	55.0	3.8	28.4	11.9	7.0
2.0	4.33	23.0	0.52	1.8	1.1	0.15	1.51	2.80	80.3	4.6	20.8	6.5	5.3
4.9	0.91	6.3	0.12	6.4	1.7	0.92	9.15	4.01	74.4	4.9	34.8	8.1	5.8
4.7	1.12	8.1	0.85	5.2	2.3	0.71	7.46	3.83	67.1	2.4	32.1	21.5	6.2
9.5	0.00	0.0	0.00	5.6	0.5	1.21	8.66	3.88	59.4	4.2	45.1	15.0	8.5
5.9	1.42	4.9	0.08	6.6	0.7	1.50	15.28	3.55	66.0	1.9	16.6	19.4	6.3
6.0	0.33	2.3	0.09	4.8	2.4	0.87	10.10	3.79	70.8	4.3	28.1	9.2	5.6
4.5	1.83	14.7	0.35	4.4	1.3	1.18	14.46	4.10	78.4	4.9	36.8	9.3	3.9
7.3	0.24	0.9	0.21	9.6	2.0	1.73	11.21	5.28	55.7	4.3	30.7	10.5	9.1
1.4	6.56	36.7	1.40	0.0	-0.5	-1.41	-17.63	2.95	111.7	3.3	15.2	12.6	1.8
5.7	0.75	4.4	0.24	6.8	2.0	1.23	13.84	3.75	60.3	1.6	19.2	23.7	6.6
7.3	0.26	1.3	0.02	6.7	2.0	1.46	16.05	4.63	68.3	4.9	65.8	16.0	6.1
8.0	0.30	1.4	-0.01	3.9	0.5	0.59	6.20	3.02	79.6	4.6	30.5	8.8	5.7
7.8	1.50	4.6	-0.34	3.7	0.4	0.78	5.98	3.39	73.5	6.9	97.1	8.4	7.1
6.0	0.53	4.1	-0.10	3.2	0.5	0.52	7.25	3.04	81.6	5.7	39.5	5.2	2.6
2.4	1.79	14.9	3.32	5.7	2.0	1.01	12.77	6.19	38.5	5.8	64.4	11.6	4.6
4.3	1.70	9.0	0.30	5.4	0.9	0.93	8.09	4.16	67.0	3.1	23.9	14.5	6.8
4.4	2.38	8.9	0.83	9.6	0.9	2.50	18.96	4.94	47.8	3.3	15.7	12.7	4.3
6.4	0.05	0.4	0.07	9.6	0.7	1.49	15.71	4.75	56.5	4.8	34.2	9.0	6.9
7.5	3.09	6.4	0.22	6.1	2.4	1.12	6.35	3.13	48.5	4.8	93.3	20.0	8.3
3.5	1.82	12.6	0.63	5.5	0.6	1.05	12.81	4.13	59.5	5.2	33.2	5.5	4.7
8.7	0.00	0.0	0.00	5.7	0.3	1.22	10.45	3.83	67.4	7.1	82.7	5.0	6.5
8.8	0.17	0.9	0.13	7.9	1.9	1.46	11.70	4.12	57.4	4.5	34.3	10.4	7.5
8.1	1.13	4.6	-0.01	8.5	4.5	1.44	13.13	4.28	57.8	7.3	91.6	6.4	8.8
6.2	1.37	6.2	-0.02	9.5	1.2	2.16	17.41	4.91	60.3	3.7	11.7	10.1	7.7
5.3	0.70	4.8	0.59	6.0	0.7	0.79	10.07	4.51	68.8	2.0	7.7	18.3	4.0
4.2	1.13	8.7	0.55	4.5	0.4	0.70	9.39	3.62	72.1	2.8	21.4	15.6	4.2
3.7	1.13	6.0	0.10	7.5	1.2	1.69	14.49	3.56	53.0	2.8	22.3	15.8	6.8
8.6	0.18	1.4	0.00	7.2	7.7	1.10	15.35	4.00	65.3	4.2	18.5	8.7	6.2
7.6	0.29	1.2	0.20	5.5	1.2	1.33	12.95	4.10	68.1	2.4	20.5	17.5	6.6
7.7	0.22	0.8	0.13	7.7	0.6	1.42	7.58	4.98	64.8	4.9	46.1	11.5	6.7
3.1	1.18	12.0	0.01	6.1	0.9	1.25	16.66	4.38	53.3	0.7	11.5	36.1	4.0
6.7	3.07	7.2	0.02	7.7	0.4	1.43	11.28	4.41	54.4	5.5	51.0	9.1	4.8
7.1	0.27	2.3	0.05	6.4	2.8	1.46	16.92	3.70	60.9	4.0	42.4	15.5	4.8
9.2	0.24	0.4	0.06	7.0	1.0	1.35	8.34	4.16	57.4	5.1	62.2	14.6	9.2
9.4	0.09	0.2	0.01	3.8	0.4	0.90	9.73	3.32	72.2	5.7	64.2	10.7	4.9
8.4	0.39	1.9	0.03	7.5	0.4	1.60	13.05	4.90	70.0	2.3	28.6	19.8	8.0
5.8	0.44	3.6	0.04	7.5	1.2	1.57	19.71	4.04	60.8	3.0	29.3	16.4	6.3
1.1	3.86	25.9	0.26	5.3	0.8	0.84	8.08	3.99	60.9	2.3	21.1	18.0	5.0
7.7	0.11	1.0	0.05	6.1	0.4	1.38	19.11	3.59	63.2	2.8	16.9	15.2	5.3
5.5	0.56	3.2	0.16	8.3	1.6	1.52	19.21	4.94	50.6	8.1	98.4	2.7	5.3
9.5	0.00	0.0	0.00	3.8	0.2	0.63	8.16	3.07	78.3	5.3	32.9	5.0	4.7
6.5	0.43	2.4	0.24	5.8	25.5	1.13	6.75	3.73	56.7	1.2	13.2	29.7	5.8
8.6	0.00	0.0	0.00	1.8	0.4	0.38	3.46	1.03	128.3	8.7	583.3	9.1	0.6
5.2	1.33	5.8	-0.19	4.8	0.2	0.73	7.54	4.64	73.1	7.1	77.6	3.8	5.8
6.5	0.23	1.6	-0.08	6.8	3.0	1.07	12.81	5.19	68.1	7.5	171.2	12.9	5.8
8.1	0.10	0.9	0.01	4.9	1.1	0.94	13.26	3.76	59.0	1.7	14.2	20.9	2.5
5.2	1.01	9.7	0.05	6.7	1.0	1.57	21.47	4.41	67.3	1.9	13.6	19.2	5.2
6.9	0.19	1.4	0.02	3.5	0.5	0.61	5.94	4.98	72.0	2.6	25.5	17.4	2.3
5.8	0.25	2.4	-0.13	8.2	4.1	1.24	18.59	3.22	43.3	1.6	35.2	43.9	5.3
4.4	1.45	11.2	0.06	3.5	1.4	0.59	7.53	3.89	80.9	7.0	109.8	10.9	3.5
1.2	3.17	24.4	0.03	1.5	0.0	-0.08	-1.03	4.10	90.4	3.7	39.2	16.0	3.4
5.4	0.64	3.7	0.13	8.9	0.5	1.44	13.51	5.28	67.8	1.4	12.6	25.6	4.9
4.5	0.83	6.2	0.35	3.4	0.2	0.40	4.88	4.34	82.0	4.8	18.6	3.8	3.8

| Name | City | State | Weiss Safety Rating | 2003 Weiss Safety Rating | 2002 Weiss Safety Rating | Total Assets ($Mil) | One Year Asset Growth | Asset Mix (As a % of Total Assets) | | | | Capital-ization Index | Risk-based | |
								Comm-ercial Loans	Cons-umer Loans	Home Mort-gages	Secur-ities		Leverage Ratio	Capital Ratio
▲ FIRST PERSONAL BK	ORLAND PARK	IL	C+	C	C	128.8	36.36	19.0	0.2	21.1	16.6	7.5	9.5	12.9
FIRST PIEDMONT BK	WINDER	GA	B+	B+	B+	77.8	16.02	1.8	0.8	12.2	13.1	9.7	12.2	14.8
FIRST PIEDMONT FS&LA	GAFFNEY	SC	A+	A+	A+	234.5	1.99	2.7	8.7	43.8	2.1	10.0	20.4	29.9
FIRST PIONEER NB	WRAY	CO	A-	A-	A-	107.5	4.45	6.7	4.0	1.0	36.1	10.0	14.7	23.6
▲ FIRST PLACE BK	WARREN	OH	B-	C+	B-	1,659.9	8.70	2.7	1.2	45.6	19.2	6.0	8.0	13.3
▼ FIRST PORT CITY BK	BAINBRIDGE	GA	A-	A	A-	103.5	10.89	4.3	2.9	16.8	37.3	9.1	10.4	18.2
▲ FIRST PREMIER BK	SIOUX FALLS	SD	B-	C	D-	890.6	-5.59	5.5	45.2	5.6	31.4	10.0	24.0	42.2
FIRST PRESIDIO BK	PRESIDIO	TX	B-	B-	B-	21.6	7.02	3.4	19.6	3.5	61.0	6.4	8.5	23.3
FIRST PRIORITY BK	BRADENTON	FL	D	D	NR	42.0	N/A	10.1	1.1	2.6	11.4	10.0	20.0	30.2
FIRST PROGRESSIVE BK	BREWTON	AL	C+	C+	B-	24.0	2.45	5.1	5.6	12.6	55.1	10.0	28.9	73.6
▼ FIRST PRYORITY BK	PRYOR	OK	B	B	A-	129.4	0.44	10.3	18.2	9.2	22.0	8.7	11.6	13.9
FIRST REGIONAL BK	LOS ANGELES	CA	B-	C+	B-	978.6	69.78	12.7	0.9	1.2	0.3	5.0	9.7	11.0
FIRST RELIANCE BK	FLORENCE	SC	B-	B-	C+	217.9	44.85	16.0	6.0	21.0	11.0	5.3	8.7	11.2
FIRST REPUBLIC BK	LAS VEGAS	NV	C+	C+	C+	6,831.0	26.88	2.9	3.6	44.2	12.9	5.1	7.1	13.5
▲ FIRST ROBINSON SB NA	ROBINSON	IL	B+	B	C+	103.5	-0.62	6.2	4.5	30.6	25.7	8.3	9.8	17.5
FIRST S&LA	MEBANE	NC	B	B	B	51.4	-6.15	0.0	0.0	42.5	41.3	10.0	17.9	48.7
FIRST SAFETY BK	ST BERNARD	OH	A-	A-	A-	48.4	-8.63	2.2	1.3	31.5	29.3	10.0	14.6	25.7
▲ FIRST SAVANNA SVG BK	SAVANNA	IL	C	C-	C-	12.2	-0.90	0.0	3.2	48.0	28.5	10.0	12.2	29.4
FIRST SAVERS BK	GREENVILLE	SC	C+	C+	C+	185.4	24.11	1.1	2.0	31.7	20.7	4.9	6.9	12.2
FIRST SAVINGS BANK, FSB	CLARKSVILLE	IN	B	B	B	220.1	-2.59	3.6	5.8	49.3	8.0	10.0	12.3	22.6
FIRST SEC BK OF LEXINGTON	LEXINGTON	KY	C-	C-	C	216.6	-6.96	20.1	2.2	7.0	19.4	9.6	10.7	15.4
FIRST SECURITY B&T	ISLAND	KY	E-	E-	E-	24.0	-3.37	5.5	13.3	35.9	15.5	5.7	7.7	13.5
▲ FIRST SECURITY B&TC	CHARLES CITY	IA	B+	B	B	213.4	0.20	12.7	4.0	12.8	29.1	7.2	9.1	13.8
▲ FIRST SECURITY B&TC	NORTON	KS	D	D-	C	58.4	-1.78	10.6	4.1	2.9	44.5	4.8	6.8	14.1
FIRST SECURITY B&TC	OKLAHOMA CITY	OK	C	C	C	40.8	5.11	21.1	5.6	19.4	17.8	6.1	8.2	12.5
▲ FIRST SECURITY BK	MOUNTAIN HOME	AR	B	C+	B-	269.1	-6.96	10.3	5.6	16.8	40.6	6.0	8.0	14.4
▲ FIRST SECURITY BK	SEARCY	AR	B	B-	B-	1,130.3	47.46	7.3	8.0	14.4	27.9	5.0	7.0	11.3
▲ FIRST SECURITY BK	MACKINAW	IL	D+	D	D	48.1	-8.27	9.5	6.0	23.0	23.4	7.2	9.1	15.1
FIRST SECURITY BK	OVERBROOK	KS	C	C	C	23.9	-0.29	3.3	2.4	6.2	51.9	9.9	10.9	21.3
▲ FIRST SECURITY BK	OWENSBORO	KY	D+	D	D	110.7	23.41	14.6	6.6	13.3	26.8	5.4	7.4	11.5
FIRST SECURITY BK	BYRON	MN	C-	C-	D+	35.0	4.25	10.3	2.1	6.4	10.0	5.2	8.9	11.1
▲ FIRST SECURITY BK	UNION STAR	MO	D-	E+	D-	16.7	-1.29	9.8	7.0	33.8	18.8	6.5	8.5	14.6
FIRST SECURITY BK	BATESVILLE	MS	A	A	A-	377.2	12.18	5.0	8.5	13.1	27.0	8.6	10.1	15.5
FIRST SECURITY BK	BOZEMAN	MT	B	B	B+	420.7	13.44	18.4	4.1	8.7	28.1	5.9	7.9	13.0
FIRST SECURITY BK	UNDERWOOD	ND	D	D	D+	23.5	-1.91	5.1	7.9	2.7	42.7	6.5	8.5	19.4
FIRST SECURITY BK	BEAVER	OK	D	D	D+	64.6	4.78	11.6	4.3	10.1	23.9	2.4	6.5	9.4
▲ FIRST SECURITY BK -	SANBORN	MN	E	E-	D	12.7	7.57	8.9	2.8	4.2	17.2	5.5	7.5	12.3
FIRST SECURITY BK CANBY	CANBY	MN	B	B	B-	32.8	4.22	11.9	1.6	1.0	37.9	9.5	10.6	17.6
▲ FIRST SECURITY BK	CLARKSVILLE	AR	B	B-	B-	116.0	-9.00	8.9	3.5	8.9	51.3	6.3	8.3	12.1
FIRST SECURITY BK DEER	DEER LODGE	MT	C	C-	C-	25.6	7.24	7.7	11.1	21.9	13.1	6.8	8.9	17.1
FIRST SECURITY BK LK	LAKE BENTON	MN	C-	C-	B-	16.7	17.88	3.2	4.0	8.2	30.3	6.1	8.1	13.2
FIRST SECURITY BK	MISSOULA	MT	B	B	B-	606.3	12.47	13.3	3.7	9.0	40.6	5.8	7.8	13.3
FIRST SECURITY BK NA	FLOWER MOUND	TX	B-	B-	B-	90.6	18.75	8.2	7.5	10.0	10.1	2.9	7.6	9.9
FIRST SECURITY BK OF	CONWAY	AR	B-	C+	B-	283.8	6.92	7.6	7.8	21.0	15.7	3.7	7.5	10.4
FIRST SECURITY BK OF	HELENA	MT	D+	D+	D+	37.9	0.07	9.3	14.6	29.4	14.1	5.5	7.5	11.9
FIRST SECURITY BK OF MALTA	MALTA	MT	D+	D+	D	22.8	-5.00	9.2	15.6	2.5	22.5	8.8	10.2	16.8
FIRST SECURITY BK OF	ROUNDUP	MT	B	B-	B	39.3	1.33	13.4	5.2	5.1	24.2	9.9	10.9	16.3
▲ FIRST SECURITY BK STORDEN	STORDEN	MN	B-	C-	D	42.2	3.58	7.9	9.0	11.2	32.1	8.1	9.7	17.1
FIRST SECURITY BK WEST	BEULAH	ND	B+	B+	B+	69.3	1.34	17.8	2.6	3.8	38.2	10.0	11.3	18.3
FIRST SECURITY	HENDRICKS	MN	C-	C-	C-	15.2	10.34	9.7	3.9	12.4	10.2	6.7	8.7	13.8
FIRST SECURITY BK-SLEEPY	SLEEPY EYE	MN	B	B+	B+	123.4	4.38	14.8	3.3	7.1	31.9	5.4	7.4	12.8
FIRST SECURITY FSB	CHICAGO	IL	A	A+	A+	505.5	19.07	0.0	0.3	23.8	14.3	10.0	22.1	34.4
FIRST SECURITY NB	NORCROSS	GA	A-	B+	A-	98.0	-2.42	5.0	5.8	0.7	6.0	10.0	12.6	16.7
▼ FIRST SECURITY ST BK	EVANSDALE	IA	C+	B-	C+	81.8	11.53	17.1	43.6	9.1	3.1	5.2	9.5	11.1
FIRST SECURITY ST BK	CARUTHERSVILLE	MO	B-	B-	C	58.7	10.54	22.0	8.0	20.7	1.1	3.5	8.3	10.2
FIRST SECURITY ST BK	CHARLESTON	MO	C+	C+	C	163.0	22.73	16.9	4.1	15.4	14.4	3.3	7.3	10.1
▲ FIRST SECURITY ST BK	CRANFILLS GAP	TX	C	C-	C+	57.2	47.84	6.5	6.7	8.8	45.8	5.1	7.1	14.6
FIRST SECURITY T&SB	ELMWOOD PARK	IL	B+	B+	A-	241.0	11.95	2.3	1.6	14.2	36.8	10.0	11.6	23.8
▲ FIRST SECURITY THRIFT CO	ORANGE	CA	A+	A	A	157.3	-7.83	0.0	0.0	0.0	14.0	10.0	15.3	23.1
FIRST SECURITY TR BK	FLORENCE	KY	B	NR	NR	68.9	N/A	2.3	1.4	24.6	24.1	10.0	11.9	17.2
FIRST SENTINEL BK	RICHLANDS	VA	B	B	B	84.2	14.19	6.7	24.1	22.6	24.6	7.2	9.1	15.1
▲ FIRST SENTRY BK	HUNTINGTON	WV	C+	C-	C	189.2	10.84	25.0	3.2	17.8	10.3	7.1	9.1	12.7
▲ FIRST SERVICE BK	GREENBRIER	AR	B-	C-	C-	113.8	8.80	8.3	7.9	23.1	12.8	6.4	8.5	12.1
FIRST SHORE FS&LA	SALISBURY	MD	B	B	B	277.3	13.04	1.1	5.3	46.4	20.0	6.9	8.9	17.0

Asset Quality Index	Non-Performing Loans as a % of Total Loans	Non-Performing Loans as a % of Capital	Net Charge-offs Avg Loans	Profitability Index	Net Income ($Mil)	Return on Assets (R.O.A.)	Return on Equity (R.O.E.)	Net Interest Spread	Overhead Efficiency Ratio	Liquidity Index	Liquidity Ratio	Hot Money Ratio	Stability Index
5.9	1.21	8.5	0.36	3.7	0.3	0.50	6.15	4.24	70.0	6.4	92.2	11.8	3.2
7.0	0.30	1.9	0.00	6.6	0.4	1.14	9.17	4.42	58.0	1.7	18.8	22.5	6.5
7.8	0.03	0.1	-0.01	10.0	2.2	1.88	8.70	4.94	50.7	3.5	23.2	12.4	10.0
8.3	0.38	1.4	-0.03	6.5	0.7	1.21	8.02	3.98	60.8	3.8	23.7	10.8	8.5
4.4	0.85	7.2	0.22	5.4	7.6	0.92	9.93	3.17	58.8	0.9	15.2	36.7	7.5
9.0	0.00	0.0	0.04	6.4	0.6	1.13	9.59	3.53	55.7	5.7	46.0	7.5	7.0
3.7	4.17	7.4	16.23	8.9	47.0	10.67	44.73	24.38	54.9	4.9	145.3	31.4	7.2
6.7	0.74	2.5	0.10	4.3	0.1	0.94	10.89	4.25	73.8	2.5	47.9	25.5	4.0
9.4	0.00	0.0	0.00	0.0	-0.6	-4.37	-16.28	0.67	765.8	8.0	316.8	12.7	0.0
8.7	0.00	0.0	0.00	4.1	0.1	0.81	2.81	4.28	74.3	1.2	36.1	42.4	5.3
3.6	0.62	3.4	0.00	9.6	1.1	1.69	13.83	4.93	52.8	5.0	36.3	8.7	7.3
6.9	0.01	0.1	0.10	6.2	4.9	1.12	12.32	4.98	60.6	4.2	16.2	7.3	5.3
5.8	0.68	6.1	0.18	4.3	0.6	0.59	6.61	4.42	74.4	0.5	6.7	46.0	4.2
7.7	0.26	3.2	0.02	4.1	21.2	0.67	11.01	3.31	70.5	6.2	45.5	7.3	3.8
5.9	0.84	5.1	0.59	5.8	0.4	0.86	8.55	4.14	64.8	5.0	39.4	9.7	5.4
8.6	0.00	0.0	0.00	4.8	0.2	0.64	3.62	3.03	63.1	3.3	60.9	25.4	6.7
8.5	0.71	2.9	0.00	8.9	0.5	1.91	12.83	3.84	58.4	5.6	86.2	14.0	8.0
6.2	2.38	8.6	0.42	2.5	0.0	0.34	2.23	3.45	83.0	2.5	N/A	15.1	4.8
5.9	0.44	4.1	0.22	4.7	0.4	0.40	5.55	2.76	82.2	0.9	24.2	50.3	4.3
6.6	0.81	4.8	0.18	3.7	0.4	0.38	3.09	2.84	76.3	2.6	30.1	18.8	6.6
3.2	2.84	17.3	0.19	2.6	0.6	0.48	4.56	2.99	83.4	1.3	14.6	27.9	4.2
5.4	0.37	3.2	0.45	1.6	0.0	0.23	3.00	4.11	90.9	2.4	18.0	17.1	0.1
7.6	0.28	1.7	0.06	5.9	1.4	1.31	12.75	4.41	65.7	4.3	26.1	8.8	6.9
4.0	2.01	9.0	0.55	3.8	0.4	1.19	14.74	3.46	67.3	5.7	66.8	10.7	2.1
7.7	0.13	1.1	-0.09	8.0	0.4	1.96	24.55	5.41	69.1	2.0	22.4	19.5	3.5
5.6	0.78	4.8	0.26	7.8	2.0	1.49	18.32	4.32	45.4	6.2	90.5	12.9	6.3
5.6	0.55	3.4	0.32	6.5	6.5	1.15	12.63	4.16	57.6	4.8	53.1	16.6	6.5
4.9	1.31	8.5	0.76	4.3	0.3	1.04	11.38	5.86	74.5	2.3	30.7	21.1	1.9
9.1	0.00	0.0	0.00	3.0	0.1	0.59	5.48	2.82	76.7	5.7	107.7	15.2	3.6
5.0	0.75	6.4	-0.18	3.3	0.4	0.76	10.40	3.44	66.6	1.5	9.4	22.8	1.7
4.2	1.29	11.1	0.23	5.1	0.2	1.20	13.59	4.89	71.8	3.4	24.9	12.9	3.7
6.5	0.28	2.1	0.03	2.6	0.0	0.27	3.29	4.22	88.4	4.5	17.2	5.3	1.7
7.4	0.23	1.2	0.14	9.6	3.1	1.70	15.42	4.68	55.3	3.8	34.5	14.0	7.6
4.8	0.83	5.2	0.06	7.9	3.8	1.86	19.70	4.47	59.4	5.3	34.6	5.7	6.3
6.0	0.90	4.4	0.04	5.0	0.1	1.17	14.38	3.74	68.1	3.5	65.2	20.0	2.3
6.9	0.29	3.0	0.02	5.6	0.5	1.46	23.47	2.83	49.5	0.9	14.5	33.0	3.0
3.1	2.60	17.9	-0.02	5.1	0.1	1.36	18.52	3.66	65.6	6.8	82.4	5.4	1.7
7.3	0.00	0.0	0.10	6.9	0.4	2.28	15.10	4.20	46.6	5.0	11.3	1.4	6.3
8.0	0.10	0.4	0.03	6.2	0.9	1.45	14.67	4.50	57.4	3.6	31.8	14.4	6.7
8.1	0.01	0.0	0.00	5.9	0.1	1.03	11.27	3.74	64.6	6.7	88.6	8.3	4.0
5.4	0.92	6.3	0.00	8.9	0.2	2.01	26.07	4.64	60.3	5.6	46.3	5.0	3.2
5.0	1.26	7.3	0.12	10.0	5.7	1.91	22.40	4.74	37.3	4.1	10.8	7.7	7.0
3.1	0.36	2.4	0.00	4.0	0.4	0.95	8.75	4.42	72.5	2.2	32.3	25.0	6.3
5.3	0.36	2.8	0.17	8.1	2.1	1.46	17.87	4.33	53.6	4.3	84.2	24.0	6.2
5.2	0.69	6.1	0.14	4.9	0.2	1.02	13.55	5.22	77.8	1.7	24.3	23.8	2.9
1.1	3.79	22.5	-0.19	5.3	0.1	0.88	8.85	5.23	74.1	4.3	34.8	9.8	4.0
4.8	1.75	9.4	0.00	9.2	0.4	2.27	20.40	5.08	56.3	5.3	42.3	8.4	7.0
3.4	1.85	7.6	-1.49	5.0	0.3	1.34	10.80	4.50	66.1	5.0	15.2	2.1	5.1
6.4	1.04	5.1	-0.08	9.0	0.7	2.13	20.28	4.23	50.6	2.6	10.7	15.8	6.1
5.4	1.10	7.0	0.00	7.7	0.1	1.34	15.76	4.73	57.3	6.3	68.5	5.7	3.4
7.3	0.23	1.7	-0.02	9.2	1.4	2.28	34.25	4.42	52.8	5.0	26.0	3.5	5.7
5.7	1.98	8.1	0.00	6.8	1.1	0.45	2.59	3.95	76.4	2.6	41.5	26.8	9.3
7.1	0.29	1.4	0.00	8.3	1.0	2.07	17.96	5.38	59.5	5.8	79.4	12.0	7.0
5.8	0.30	2.6	0.06	5.5	0.4	0.91	9.49	4.30	64.6	1.0	18.9	33.0	4.5
6.6	0.36	3.7	0.03	5.7	0.3	1.07	12.62	4.16	71.2	2.1	8.4	18.0	4.7
5.9	0.56	5.8	0.12	6.4	0.9	1.19	16.99	3.97	60.5	0.8	11.5	33.4	4.0
7.4	0.37	1.5	0.10	4.6	0.3	1.09	12.63	4.22	76.6	5.1	43.1	10.3	3.5
7.4	1.02	3.6	0.22	4.8	1.0	0.81	6.75	3.44	62.7	7.0	309.3	17.4	6.8
7.6	0.04	0.2	0.00	9.4	1.2	1.38	9.45	3.64	32.7	8.8	1,579.0	8.4	8.9
8.4	0.54	2.8	0.00	4.3	0.1	0.72	3.18	3.85	83.6	2.9	12.6	14.0	3.2
7.3	0.02	0.1	0.14	7.8	0.5	1.16	12.64	4.88	60.1	5.1	88.9	17.1	5.3
7.3	0.20	1.6	0.11	4.2	0.8	0.88	9.85	3.42	53.2	1.2	19.4	30.9	3.7
5.3	0.53	4.5	0.30	7.2	0.6	1.11	13.50	5.24	61.6	1.1	15.1	30.7	4.5
8.5	0.05	0.4	0.01	4.6	0.9	0.66	7.09	2.83	61.6	1.8	20.1	21.3	5.4

Name	City	State	Weiss Safety Rating	2003 Weiss Safety Rating	2002 Weiss Safety Rating	Total Assets ($Mil)	One Year Asset Growth	Asset Mix (As a % of Total Assets)				Capital-ization Index	Leverage Ratio	Risk-based Capital Ratio
								Comm-ercial Loans	Cons-umer Loans	Home Mort-gages	Secur-ities			
▼ FIRST SIGNATURE B&TC	PORTSMOUTH	NH	D+	C	C	478.4	356.41	0.0	0.2	2.4	88.5	5.5	7.5	18.1
▲ FIRST SOURCE BK	S BEND	IN	B	B-	B-	3,243.7	0.80	40.5	1.9	5.4	22.9	8.5	10.3	13.7
FIRST SOURCE BK	GERMANTOWN	TN	D	D	NR	46.1	202.44	15.7	3.2	17.7	0.0	10.0	25.6	28.6
FIRST SOUTH BK	WASHINGTON	NC	B+	B+	B-	719.2	8.44	6.2	4.1	17.5	7.3	5.6	8.3	11.4
▲ FIRST SOUTH BK	SPARTANBURG	SC	C+	D	C+	283.3	25.46	17.0	0.2	17.5	6.5	7.4	9.3	13.8
FIRST SOUTH BK	BOLIVAR	TN	B	B-	B-	250.2	2.16	10.7	5.3	16.0	19.5	6.5	8.5	13.1
FIRST SOUTHEAST BANK	HARMONY	MN	C+	C+	D+	40.4	5.56	12.3	5.6	8.5	7.5	5.8	9.1	11.6
FIRST SOUTHERN BANK	GRAND TOWER	IL	D+	D+	D	74.1	46.97	12.4	6.6	32.1	10.2	5.4	7.8	11.3
FIRST SOUTHERN BK	FLORENCE	AL	D-	D-	E+	94.5	-1.59	10.6	4.2	32.5	14.0	6.1	8.1	13.3
FIRST SOUTHERN BK	BOCA RATON	FL	D+	D	E+	275.1	10.72	4.0	0.7	5.5	14.9	5.1	8.4	11.1
▼ FIRST SOUTHERN NATIONAL	LANCASTER	KY	C+	B-	B-	366.0	1.02	5.4	2.9	18.1	15.4	4.8	7.3	10.9
FIRST SOUTHERN NB	STEVENSON	AL	B	B	B	151.5	1.93	0.9	14.1	29.1	32.6	6.0	8.0	14.6
▲ FIRST SOUTHERN NB	STATESBORO	GA	D	D-	D-	74.3	57.37	12.0	7.4	14.2	7.0	4.5	9.4	10.7
FIRST ST B&T	BAYPORT	MN	A-	A-	A-	163.5	3.74	8.0	8.1	28.1	27.5	8.2	9.8	16.9
▼ FIRST ST B&TC	VALDOSTA	GA	B-	B-	B	356.8	11.82	14.4	2.3	14.3	7.8	3.5	8.0	10.2
FIRST ST B&TC	TONGANOXIE	KS	C+	C+	C+	240.0	6.83	4.3	8.1	16.9	12.4	4.8	6.8	11.2
FIRST ST B&TC	FREMONT	NE	B-	B	B	149.0	4.44	21.2	4.6	13.2	23.8	4.5	7.1	10.7
FIRST ST B&TC	CARTHAGE	TX	A	A	A+	267.7	-5.31	1.6	9.4	10.6	61.7	10.0	17.5	42.0
FIRST ST B&TC OF LARNED	LARNED	KS	B-	C+	C	82.8	-3.35	7.4	4.5	11.3	31.1	6.8	8.8	15.1
FIRST ST BK	CONWAY	AR	B-	B-	C	426.5	7.11	13.1	4.0	10.7	21.5	10.0	13.9	16.7
▲ FIRST ST BK	CROSSETT	AR	D	D-	D	29.4	-8.94	9.3	13.5	21.6	21.9	7.3	9.2	16.3
▲ FIRST ST BK	LONOKE	AR	B+	B	B-	213.2	19.89	6.7	1.6	16.8	20.3	7.7	9.5	14.4
FIRST ST BK	PARKIN	AR	D-	D-	E+	21.9	1.23	10.7	4.9	16.4	43.5	9.9	11.0	24.1
▲ FIRST ST BK	RUSSELLVILLE	AR	C-	D+	D+	241.4	11.88	3.9	3.7	9.4	52.6	5.9	7.9	16.1
▲ FIRST ST BK	FLAGSTAFF	AZ	C+	C-	D	55.3	38.05	11.8	2.0	3.7	10.9	8.3	11.2	13.6
FIRST ST BK	IDAHO SPRINGS	CO	D+	D	D	29.9	-1.31	0.1	0.3	3.8	5.0	10.0	12.6	17.3
▲ FIRST ST BK	SARASOTA	FL	D+	D	D	231.7	24.53	15.1	2.6	5.1	6.6	3.0	7.8	10.0
▼ FIRST ST BK	STOCKBRIDGE	GA	B	B+	B+	546.5	9.05	9.6	2.6	6.2	10.1	6.4	9.7	12.0
FIRST ST BK	WRENS	GA	C	C	C+	91.3	-2.70	7.9	10.0	20.7	19.9	6.4	8.4	13.3
▲ FIRST ST BK	BELMOND	IA	A	A-	A-	66.1	-2.17	6.9	3.0	9.8	51.2	10.0	12.2	22.9
FIRST ST BK	BRITT	IA	C+	C+	B-	73.4	19.69	7.6	3.4	10.2	45.7	6.9	8.9	16.4
FIRST ST BK	CONRAD	IA	B+	B	B	112.9	5.87	9.9	2.4	9.3	37.9	6.1	8.1	14.1
▼ FIRST ST BK	HAWARDEN	IA	D+	C-	C	29.8	0.98	16.2	6.7	14.2	13.9	5.7	8.5	11.5
FIRST ST BK	HUXLEY	IA	B-	B	B-	36.3	18.04	8.1	3.6	14.8	18.9	10.0	14.1	20.5
FIRST ST BK	IDA GROVE	IA	C	C	C	74.0	2.99	8.1	5.7	9.4	12.1	6.2	9.0	11.9
FIRST ST BK	LYNNVILLE	IA	C+	C+	C	58.8	5.11	8.1	2.6	6.8	26.4	6.5	8.5	12.1
FIRST ST BK	MANCHESTER	IA	B	B	B	100.7	-1.99	9.7	4.0	10.9	32.1	7.8	9.5	16.7
▲ FIRST ST BK	NORA SPRINGS	IA	B+	B	B	43.2	1.24	3.2	6.6	26.5	21.7	5.1	7.1	11.9
▲ FIRST ST BK	RICEVILLE	IA	B+	B	B	53.1	-3.14	5.4	2.9	9.5	33.0	6.8	8.8	14.4
FIRST ST BK	SIOUX RAPIDS	IA	B-	B-	B-	22.3	-2.64	6.8	2.3	2.8	56.2	10.0	15.6	15.6
FIRST ST BK	STUART	IA	B	B	B	83.9	-1.67	11.3	3.1	14.9	35.3	10.0	12.5	22.8
FIRST ST BK	SUMNER	IA	B+	B+	B	55.8	0.18	5.9	3.2	14.0	46.5	8.6	10.0	19.8
FIRST ST BK	TABOR	IA	D	D	D	23.1	7.27	8.8	6.7	9.3	30.3	6.8	8.8	14.5
▲ FIRST ST BK	WEBSTER CITY	IA	B	B-	B-	156.6	-0.22	12.7	4.2	15.3	25.6	6.5	8.5	12.9
▼ FIRST ST BK	BEARDSTOWN	IL	C	C+	C+	51.6	16.09	12.3	7.1	16.3	37.2	10.0	11.1	19.8
FIRST ST BK	DIX	IL	C-	C	C+	22.9	7.87	6.9	11.4	21.2	32.7	9.3	10.5	18.2
FIRST ST BK	ELDORADO	IL	C-	D+	D+	97.7	13.72	3.7	3.2	8.1	33.8	7.8	9.5	14.8
FIRST ST BK	FORREST	IL	B-	B	B	51.1	0.97	2.7	10.9	38.1	6.3	8.0	9.6	14.6
▼ FIRST ST BK	GRAND CHAIN	IL	E-	E	D-	14.3	-1.15	2.2	6.3	16.3	49.5	5.7	7.7	20.0
FIRST ST BK	MENDOTA	IL	B	B	B-	274.0	11.78	4.3	3.7	21.6	27.8	6.7	8.7	13.6
FIRST ST BK	MONTICELLO	IL	B	B-	D+	162.2	18.26	6.4	7.6	18.4	32.9	6.7	8.7	15.3
FIRST ST BK	ST PETER	IL	B-	B-	B-	22.5	2.17	3.5	7.1	10.2	53.5	10.0	14.1	27.6
FIRST ST BK	W SALEM	IL	C+	B-	B-	15.9	5.01	2.8	7.4	12.0	50.5	10.0	19.8	41.4
FIRST ST BK	WINCHESTER	IL	D	D	D+	37.0	-12.27	5.8	5.2	12.8	45.3	3.9	5.9	12.6
▼ FIRST ST BK	BOURBON	IN	A	A+	A+	83.6	0.87	2.9	2.4	19.2	45.7	10.0	29.3	73.3
FIRST ST BK	BRAZIL	IN	B+	B	B	131.3	7.47	21.7	4.9	30.3	14.3	8.1	9.7	14.9
FIRST ST BK	MIDDLEBURY	IN	B-	B-	B-	286.3	5.43	31.1	4.0	27.8	20.1	6.5	8.5	13.4
FIRST ST BK	ARMA	KS	D+	D+	D+	9.9	-10.34	5.0	5.1	12.0	52.9	8.6	10.0	17.9
FIRST ST BK	JUNCTION CITY	KS	C	C	C-	36.4	-1.66	26.2	2.6	4.4	35.9	7.2	9.1	15.0
FIRST ST BK	NESS CITY	KS	B+	B+	B+	36.1	6.51	8.7	1.9	2.1	50.1	10.0	15.5	27.6
▲ FIRST ST BK	NORTON	KS	C	D+	D+	120.3	6.55	13.8	4.7	6.2	37.8	6.4	8.4	13.9
FIRST ST BK	IRVINGTON	KY	A-	A-	A-	128.9	5.91	0.6	7.5	26.6	43.9	7.3	9.2	19.8
FIRST ST BK	BIGFORK	MN	D+	D+	D+	38.1	7.78	9.4	7.6	40.5	13.1	6.4	8.4	13.5
FIRST ST BK	CLEARBROOK	MN	C+	B-	C+	23.7	-1.42	7.1	10.1	12.8	25.0	9.7	10.8	16.4

Asset Quality Index	Non-Performing Loans as a % of Total Loans	Non-Performing Loans as a % of Capital	Net Charge-offs / Avg Loans	Profitability Index	Net Income ($Mil)	Return on Assets (R.O.A.)	Return on Equity (R.O.E.)	Net Interest Spread	Overhead Efficiency Ratio	Liquidity Index	Liquidity Ratio	Hot Money Ratio	Stability Index
10.0	0.20	0.1	0.50	2.1	0.4	0.18	2.38	1.09	78.6	0.2	9.6	94.7	1.5
5.4	1.28	7.1	0.05	5.0	15.7	0.98	9.14	3.66	71.8	4.9	34.9	11.9	6.9
7.2	0.00	0.0	0.00	0.1	-0.1	-0.49	-1.80	3.68	90.2	5.5	227.1	38.1	0.0
5.0	0.48	4.1	0.04	9.9	5.9	1.67	18.11	4.64	49.5	2.4	21.8	17.7	6.5
6.7	0.53	4.6	0.04	6.3	1.6	1.18	16.07	3.81	53.6	3.8	37.2	15.2	4.6
7.0	0.14	1.0	0.69	7.6	2.1	1.69	18.77	4.23	63.4	2.5	25.9	18.1	6.1
2.3	1.90	16.7	0.24	7.7	0.4	1.69	18.81	4.79	65.1	3.9	6.1	8.0	4.8
6.0	0.61	5.8	0.16	2.8	0.2	0.52	6.45	3.60	67.3	3.7	28.2	12.3	2.2
1.3	5.36	37.7	0.23	1.1	-0.1	-0.29	-3.46	3.79	107.4	5.5	63.2	11.5	0.3
3.4	1.08	9.4	0.00	3.8	0.8	0.61	7.75	4.09	75.0	3.4	16.3	12.0	1.8
4.5	1.17	10.1	0.00	7.2	1.9	1.04	13.36	4.43	66.9	3.4	19.7	12.7	5.5
7.8	0.04	0.3	0.07	5.9	0.8	1.01	11.55	4.51	66.4	1.7	12.0	20.7	5.2
7.4	0.24	2.0	0.09	1.9	0.5	1.57	18.34	4.10	78.7	2.7	36.7	21.4	0.0
8.6	0.03	0.2	0.20	6.1	0.9	1.06	10.98	4.41	66.8	3.7	42.1	17.1	6.0
7.2	0.02	0.2	0.03	10.0	3.1	1.81	23.02	4.32	37.1	1.1	8.0	28.9	7.2
3.8	1.13	10.1	0.05	6.2	1.2	1.02	12.79	4.86	68.3	3.6	10.3	10.5	4.4
4.6	1.21	9.7	0.02	6.9	0.9	1.19	15.92	4.65	62.0	2.9	16.1	14.7	4.9
8.8	0.60	1.0	-0.12	7.5	2.2	1.54	9.35	3.59	46.7	4.8	127.8	29.7	8.6
7.9	0.12	0.5	0.00	6.5	0.8	1.85	16.25	4.20	64.1	3.7	45.9	17.5	5.5
6.3	1.17	5.6	0.13	6.2	2.2	1.05	7.71	3.65	60.3	2.0	33.2	28.0	6.8
4.6	0.58	3.2	0.66	2.1	0.1	0.36	3.97	5.13	88.8	2.6	34.3	21.0	1.2
8.4	0.00	0.0	0.00	6.7	1.2	1.17	11.49	4.22	56.4	3.0	47.7	25.8	5.8
2.9	4.71	17.9	0.35	3.4	0.1	0.67	6.11	4.40	87.0	4.4	116.0	27.0	0.0
4.4	2.80	14.8	0.67	4.7	1.1	0.90	11.71	3.56	65.8	0.8	15.4	38.2	1.8
7.3	0.00	0.0	0.21	3.4	0.2	0.71	6.19	5.35	76.6	4.4	24.2	7.5	4.5
1.2	4.39	21.3	0.55	5.5	0.2	1.38	11.12	4.82	77.0	7.3	101.4	6.5	5.5
3.7	0.59	5.9	-0.02	4.7	1.0	0.86	11.61	4.04	64.3	2.3	24.4	18.3	2.5
4.7	0.54	4.3	0.01	9.4	4.0	1.50	15.50	3.94	45.1	4.8	76.3	18.0	7.4
4.6	0.59	4.4	0.35	4.3	0.3	0.73	8.80	5.03	71.8	3.3	32.0	15.7	4.2
8.9	0.22	0.7	-0.03	6.7	0.5	1.34	10.81	3.60	52.2	5.9	42.5	4.4	7.6
5.7	1.07	5.8	0.31	5.8	0.4	1.21	13.38	3.44	46.4	3.0	34.8	18.3	3.7
6.5	0.54	2.2	0.25	5.5	0.6	1.08	8.05	3.58	60.3	4.1	11.7	7.3	7.4
2.8	2.80	20.9	0.14	5.5	0.1	0.93	9.75	4.27	66.3	5.1	67.6	13.9	4.2
7.4	0.02	0.1	0.00	2.6	0.0	0.18	1.23	1.83	89.4	4.0	60.7	18.3	6.4
3.7	1.51	12.2	0.11	6.3	0.8	2.02	22.58	4.04	55.1	2.5	37.4	24.7	4.3
8.4	0.10	0.7	-0.13	6.3	0.3	0.99	11.41	4.13	55.7	4.4	20.5	6.8	4.8
7.8	0.02	0.1	0.05	4.8	0.6	1.11	11.51	3.40	66.7	5.5	56.1	11.4	6.0
3.6	1.56	11.5	0.00	6.1	0.3	1.39	16.42	4.24	63.2	5.5	31.8	3.2	6.3
6.5	0.82	4.2	0.15	6.5	0.4	1.44	13.50	4.22	62.8	5.0	29.8	5.7	7.3
9.1	0.39	0.8	-0.03	4.5	0.1	0.85	5.58	3.57	68.3	6.0	66.5	7.0	5.5
8.7	0.01	0.1	1.18	4.1	0.3	0.69	5.33	3.87	60.1	5.9	123.4	16.5	6.7
8.7	0.14	0.6	-0.04	6.9	0.4	1.35	13.22	4.06	58.0	4.4	15.3	6.4	6.3
4.4	1.68	10.7	0.57	5.3	0.1	0.99	11.26	3.96	65.1	4.7	35.9	7.6	2.0
5.7	0.38	2.4	0.18	6.7	1.0	1.26	12.95	3.51	65.2	4.4	17.3	6.6	6.6
0.6	8.61	38.3	-1.37	7.0	0.4	1.44	12.49	4.25	64.0	5.7	34.7	3.1	4.7
5.9	1.17	6.2	0.29	2.3	0.0	0.28	2.55	3.39	97.9	3.6	71.1	21.8	3.3
3.1	3.34	12.3	1.39	9.1	1.0	2.03	19.93	6.36	70.3	4.9	59.5	13.9	5.7
4.0	1.40	10.8	0.09	10.0	0.7	2.81	28.92	5.04	38.5	4.2	25.5	8.6	6.1
4.7	3.39	15.0	-0.04	2.4	0.0	0.21	2.80	3.35	85.7	6.8	84.8	5.4	0.1
5.9	0.44	2.7	0.03	5.1	1.3	0.95	9.32	3.46	60.5	1.8	17.9	21.4	5.3
5.6	0.77	5.0	0.00	6.9	1.2	1.57	18.11	3.58	57.8	2.2	13.3	18.1	6.3
8.8	0.12	0.3	-0.02	7.1	0.2	1.43	10.16	4.26	59.3	4.8	36.9	7.0	5.7
8.6	0.00	0.0	0.00	3.8	0.1	0.65	3.29	3.43	75.6	5.0	52.6	10.4	5.1
3.4	1.48	10.3	0.50	5.4	0.2	0.99	14.33	4.25	71.4	4.1	7.5	6.9	3.0
9.4	0.09	0.1	-0.64	8.9	0.6	1.53	5.35	3.92	54.2	5.6	69.8	11.8	9.1
4.5	1.06	7.2	0.40	5.7	0.4	0.70	7.32	3.06	62.0	4.2	70.4	20.8	6.3
4.0	1.85	14.9	0.12	6.3	1.5	1.08	13.14	4.10	62.7	3.5	24.8	12.5	5.0
9.1	0.12	0.4	0.12	2.9	0.0	0.68	6.88	3.96	83.3	6.1	42.4	0.0	1.8
8.8	0.00	0.0	-0.10	3.8	0.1	0.68	7.23	3.74	84.9	5.8	51.1	7.4	3.7
9.1	0.38	0.9	-0.12	6.3	0.3	1.54	9.90	4.49	56.7	4.6	29.5	8.3	6.7
3.4	1.51	8.1	-0.03	7.4	1.0	1.75	17.79	4.44	49.7	1.4	8.6	24.0	5.8
8.5	0.26	1.4	0.11	7.6	0.8	1.25	13.74	4.02	60.8	6.0	42.6	4.0	7.1
1.4	3.88	32.2	-0.16	5.7	0.2	1.03	12.08	4.59	60.8	5.0	37.2	8.4	3.5
4.0	1.84	10.1	-0.69	7.0	0.2	1.47	13.63	4.33	71.4	5.4	44.1	5.5	6.0

	Name	City	State	Weiss Safety Rating	2003 Weiss Safety Rating	2002 Weiss Safety Rating	Total Assets ($Mil)	One Year Asset Growth	Commercial Loans	Consumer Loans	Home Mortgages	Securities	Capitalization Index	Leverage Ratio	Risk-based Capital Ratio
	FIRST ST BK	FOUNTAIN	MN	C	C	C-	34.7	-0.47	9.4	4.2	17.6	14.2	7.9	9.6	13.8
	FIRST ST BK	GROVE CITY	MN	B-	B-	B-	15.8	8.48	10.2	6.7	6.7	30.8	10.0	20.6	31.8
▲	FIRST ST BK	LE CENTER	MN	B-	C+	C	60.1	2.96	16.3	11.0	20.4	19.0	8.0	9.6	13.7
	FIRST ST BK	RED WING	MN	B-	B-	B	50.5	1.76	14.7	4.7	8.8	47.8	10.0	12.6	22.4
▼	FIRST ST BK	ROSEMOUNT	MN	B-	B	B	56.6	-7.84	6.0	5.0	13.6	51.3	7.9	9.6	18.6
	FIRST ST BK	SAUK CENTRE	MN	B+	B+	A-	83.1	1.19	9.5	9.7	7.8	41.0	10.0	11.7	21.8
	FIRST ST BK	SWANVILLE	MN	C-	C-	C	23.8	-2.95	16.4	7.6	7.5	27.4	10.0	13.0	19.0
▼	FIRST ST BK	PURDY	MO	C-	C	C	134.3	3.97	11.6	3.5	7.9	34.8	4.9	6.9	13.3
	FIRST ST BK	ST CHARLES	MO	A+	A+	A	150.6	0.55	7.9	1.1	25.8	20.6	10.0	15.8	23.4
	FIRST ST BK	HOLLY SPRINGS	MS	B-	C+	B	104.3	-13.28	18.4	7.6	21.8	31.3	9.8	10.8	18.4
	FIRST ST BK	WAYNESBORO	MS	A	A	A-	293.2	-0.96	14.8	4.1	11.0	36.4	10.0	12.9	20.2
▲	FIRST ST BK	FORSYTH	MT	B	B-	B-	66.8	-0.21	5.6	10.0	9.3	36.4	10.0	11.5	21.5
	FIRST ST BK	SHELBY	MT	A-	A-	A-	70.7	1.07	13.1	2.4	0.1	55.5	10.0	17.1	30.2
	FIRST ST BK	THOMPSON FALLS	MT	C-	C-	C-	141.5	15.95	7.2	5.8	25.0	18.9	6.6	8.6	12.9
	FIRST ST BK	BURLINGTON	NC	A	A	A	377.4	7.27	18.5	1.3	12.7	31.5	10.0	15.2	22.8
	FIRST ST BK	GOLVA	ND	C+	C+	C+	32.6	7.46	4.3	3.4	5.1	24.9	6.7	8.7	14.5
	FIRST ST BK	HARVEY	ND	C+	C+	B	61.9	-4.41	12.6	2.9	4.5	48.0	8.3	9.9	18.6
▲	FIRST ST BK	HOPE	ND	C	C-	C-	19.2	14.69	5.4	1.7	0.5	32.5	5.3	7.3	12.7
	FIRST ST BK	LAMOURE	ND	B-	B-	C+	94.5	4.13	12.2	3.0	2.5	8.6	4.4	8.2	10.7
▼	FIRST ST BK	BEAVER CITY	NE	B	B+	A-	38.3	2.41	8.4	2.6	4.4	26.6	10.0	16.7	21.9
▲	FIRST ST BK	GOTHENBURG	NE	C-	D	C	168.5	13.05	9.9	2.4	6.2	22.9	6.5	8.5	12.4
▲	FIRST ST BK	HORDVILLE	NE	B-	C+	C-	24.6	-4.61	3.2	1.6	5.3	41.4	10.0	13.8	25.9
▲	FIRST ST BK	IMPERIAL	NE	B-	C+	B-	28.2	-1.68	5.2	3.2	4.0	31.4	6.8	8.8	15.2
	FIRST ST BK	LINCOLN	NE	C+	C+	C+	77.0	10.19	11.2	4.1	14.7	26.1	6.3	8.3	12.8
	FIRST ST BK	RANDOLPH	NE	A-	A-	A-	30.4	1.68	4.5	2.8	4.4	40.6	10.0	17.4	30.7
▲	FIRST ST BK	SCOTTSBLUFF	NE	B-	C+	C+	194.1	-0.99	10.9	4.3	5.3	10.2	5.4	8.5	11.3
▲	FIRST ST BK	SHELTON	NE	C-	D	D	38.5	11.56	11.8	5.5	6.0	9.7	6.9	10.2	12.5
▼	FIRST ST BK	SOCORRO	NM	C+	B-	B	92.7	22.46	0.9	2.1	12.7	52.5	7.0	9.0	31.3
	FIRST ST BK	CANISTEO	NY	D-	D-	D-	42.6	-2.27	16.6	6.8	22.2	22.5	6.8	8.8	15.0
	FIRST ST BK	ALTUS	OK	B-	B-	C+	103.6	24.10	25.5	4.5	10.8	32.1	6.5	8.5	17.3
▲	FIRST ST BK	ANADARKO	OK	A	A-	A-	66.8	-0.82	5.2	7.0	3.8	55.4	10.0	20.5	47.8
▲	FIRST ST BK	BOISE CITY	OK	B-	C+	C+	31.3	8.80	4.6	6.6	1.6	18.1	10.0	12.5	17.1
	FIRST ST BK	CAMARGO	OK	D-	D-	D-	15.3	13.02	14.4	15.7	3.8	5.9	5.0	7.8	11.0
	FIRST ST BK	CANUTE	OK	C+	C	C	12.1	7.26	10.1	4.5	1.3	48.1	10.0	14.5	32.3
▼	FIRST ST BK	ELMORE CITY	OK	E+	D-	D-	7.2	2.84	7.6	4.9	7.7	56.7	6.8	8.8	22.4
	FIRST ST BK	FAIRFAX	OK	C-	C-	B-	41.7	0.64	3.3	10.2	4.7	49.6	10.0	16.1	34.7
	FIRST ST BK	GRANDFIELD	OK	D-	D-	D-	23.6	-2.86	5.7	3.8	12.1	30.3	5.7	7.7	14.1
	FIRST ST BK	KETCHUM	OK	C-	D+	D	23.8	2.01	7.6	33.8	19.8	14.5	8.7	10.1	15.3
	FIRST ST BK	KEYES	OK	D-	D-	E+	44.5	20.37	2.9	3.2	2.8	36.7	5.3	7.3	13.8
	FIRST ST BK	NOBLE	OK	C-	C-	C-	60.3	1.94	6.9	7.7	8.8	37.1	7.1	9.1	15.4
▼	FIRST ST BK	PICHER	OK	D-	D	D	7.0	-5.17	11.4	17.3	14.2	32.1	7.8	9.6	17.1
▲	FIRST ST BK	RYAN	OK	D+	D	D	32.0	7.49	5.1	13.9	21.2	6.7	6.4	8.4	14.2
	FIRST ST BK	TAHLEQUAH	OK	B-	B-	D+	67.1	11.35	5.4	5.6	11.8	29.3	10.0	11.8	17.8
▼	FIRST ST BK	VALLIANT	OK	C-	C+	B	36.6	8.94	26.5	35.3	16.8	10.0	10.0	13.5	18.1
▼	FIRST ST BK	WATONGA	OK	B-	B	B-	36.0	10.56	4.7	8.3	5.8	43.6	7.6	9.4	18.8
▲	FIRST ST BK	WAUKOMIS	OK	D-	E+	E+	16.2	7.32	18.0	11.8	18.9	0.0	5.8	7.8	12.7
	FIRST ST BK	WAYNOKA	OK	C-	D+	D+	16.8	-2.38	2.7	5.7	6.0	54.2	10.0	12.5	26.9
▲	FIRST ST BK	ARMOUR	SD	C+	C	C+	66.0	-1.27	12.2	4.6	2.6	23.2	7.4	9.2	15.5
▼	FIRST ST BK	ROSCOE	SD	C	C+	C-	56.2	7.23	22.0	2.8	0.0	14.1	8.0	9.9	13.3
▼	FIRST ST BK	CHAPEL HILL	TN	B	B+	B+	37.2	3.46	4.4	9.3	23.6	35.6	10.0	16.2	30.3
	FIRST ST BK	HENDERSON	TN	B+	B+	B+	140.2	8.04	4.9	6.0	19.0	55.7	10.0	13.3	31.4
	FIRST ST BK	UNION CITY	TN	C+	C+	C	669.7	12.18	7.7	4.7	19.2	17.8	5.6	8.2	11.5
▲	FIRST ST BK	ABERNATHY	TX	E+	E-	E-	22.1	-35.57	2.5	6.6	0.4	49.8	6.6	8.6	20.2
	FIRST ST BK	ATHENS	TX	B+	A-	A-	247.9	-5.68	6.0	8.4	12.8	43.7	7.5	9.3	18.1
▲	FIRST ST BK	AVINGER	TX	C-	D+	D	14.0	-29.08	5.1	9.3	23.8	0.0	6.8	8.8	19.7
	FIRST ST BK	BEDIAS	TX	A-	A-	A-	51.7	1.31	8.2	12.7	12.2	34.6	10.0	13.8	26.3
▲	FIRST ST BK	BEN WHEELER	TX	C	C-	B-	67.5	4.39	11.8	13.1	12.7	32.3	9.8	10.9	20.5
	FIRST ST BK	BREMOND	TX	C	C-	D+	78.5	-12.38	6.7	11.8	38.5	10.4	5.9	7.9	13.8
	FIRST ST BK	BROWNSBORO	TX	D	D	E	49.9	9.30	5.8	14.7	17.6	33.4	7.0	9.0	15.8
	FIRST ST BK	BURNET	TX	A+	A+	A+	126.4	-1.35	8.8	7.0	16.6	39.7	10.0	13.3	24.0
	FIRST ST BK	CELINA	TX	C+	C+	C+	89.8	11.98	4.3	10.1	21.9	19.1	6.0	8.0	12.1
▲	FIRST ST BK	CLUTE	TX	A-	B+	B+	77.9	1.42	13.4	17.1	11.1	21.2	10.0	11.4	18.1
	FIRST ST BK	COLUMBUS	TX	A	A	A	75.7	5.49	2.2	3.8	4.5	38.5	10.0	22.5	64.5
	FIRST ST BK	FRANKSTON	TX	B	B	B	109.0	6.85	19.0	8.8	14.8	27.6	9.2	10.5	16.7

Asset Quality Index	Non-Performing Loans as a % of Total Loans	Non-Performing Loans as a % of Capital	Net Charge-offs Avg Loans	Profitability Index	Net Income ($Mil)	Return on Assets (R.O.A.)	Return on Equity (R.O.E.)	Net Interest Spread	Overhead Efficiency Ratio	Liquidity Index	Liquidity Ratio	Hot Money Ratio	Stability Index
8.5	0.00	0.0	0.02	3.8	0.1	0.52	5.51	3.77	76.9	6.9	91.6	7.9	3.6
8.2	0.24	0.7	-0.41	8.6	0.2	2.80	13.58	5.41	53.7	3.5	22.5	11.7	6.3
6.1	0.50	3.5	0.15	8.0	0.7	2.40	26.01	4.83	53.0	4.6	32.6	9.4	4.3
8.7	0.16	0.6	-0.01	4.3	0.2	0.65	5.40	2.98	67.5	5.6	40.6	6.4	4.7
6.5	1.90	8.0	0.03	4.6	0.2	0.73	7.00	4.66	75.9	4.0	13.0	8.1	4.4
5.8	1.61	6.3	0.37	5.4	0.6	1.43	11.80	3.94	58.0	5.8	58.3	8.5	6.6
4.5	2.99	12.5	3.09	3.7	0.1	0.69	5.15	5.98	89.8	3.8	28.0	11.1	4.2
2.0	4.39	26.3	0.06	4.9	0.8	1.14	15.86	3.86	70.9	5.2	56.2	13.1	3.3
8.9	0.00	0.0	-0.18	10.0	1.5	1.91	12.02	4.70	45.0	5.1	26.9	3.8	9.1
5.1	1.19	4.7	1.65	4.6	0.4	0.82	7.08	4.76	72.5	2.3	33.5	24.2	5.3
8.5	0.35	1.4	0.25	8.0	1.9	1.33	10.32	4.57	56.2	2.8	12.3	14.8	7.2
4.5	3.57	13.8	0.24	5.4	0.4	1.10	9.52	4.05	55.6	4.1	55.1	16.9	5.2
8.5	1.47	3.2	-0.12	8.1	0.5	1.39	8.38	4.39	51.2	4.5	29.3	8.3	6.9
2.1	3.10	22.7	0.14	7.2	0.7	1.10	12.95	4.78	57.0	4.1	74.1	24.2	5.3
6.1	1.70	6.5	0.07	6.1	1.8	0.98	6.14	3.26	58.8	1.6	12.0	22.3	8.4
8.4	0.05	0.3	0.00	8.1	0.4	2.37	26.63	4.39	44.6	3.7	55.6	19.0	4.9
3.1	4.65	19.6	0.24	5.5	0.4	1.16	11.52	3.50	56.4	4.6	28.1	7.7	5.5
7.4	0.00	0.0	-0.02	6.5	0.1	1.17	15.56	3.62	54.9	4.3	35.1	9.4	4.8
5.7	0.15	1.0	0.29	5.9	0.7	1.48	12.87	4.49	63.1	2.4	8.5	16.4	6.5
4.2	2.64	10.6	1.95	7.1	0.3	1.75	10.45	3.70	41.1	3.3	42.2	18.7	7.2
3.0	1.91	10.1	0.03	7.3	1.3	1.64	14.25	4.18	45.8	1.5	22.5	26.2	5.3
7.5	1.01	3.4	-0.05	4.9	0.1	0.98	7.15	3.49	56.1	5.6	75.0	11.0	5.2
3.1	1.92	10.0	0.47	3.7	0.2	1.13	11.89	4.29	68.5	2.1	28.4	21.6	4.8
7.9	0.06	0.4	0.31	5.1	0.4	0.95	11.65	4.20	69.1	4.2	26.6	9.7	4.0
8.5	0.88	2.5	0.00	9.0	0.3	2.08	11.79	4.15	51.2	6.0	38.2	2.3	8.0
4.4	1.07	8.1	0.16	10.0	2.2	2.37	27.40	4.88	50.0	4.9	42.9	11.3	6.5
2.4	1.07	8.2	1.00	8.3	0.5	2.48	23.78	5.11	44.9	1.3	10.2	26.0	5.1
7.5	1.84	4.2	0.56	3.5	0.2	0.43	4.69	4.43	83.5	6.2	62.4	7.3	3.8
3.1	1.56	10.8	2.64	2.4	0.1	0.28	3.17	4.64	78.5	5.8	49.4	6.6	2.3
4.2	2.12	12.8	0.15	5.1	0.6	1.21	13.98	3.65	72.6	4.6	37.7	11.2	5.3
9.1	1.18	1.9	0.09	10.0	1.0	2.95	14.15	4.97	44.5	5.4	34.2	4.8	8.1
6.8	0.44	2.4	-0.19	5.5	0.2	1.58	12.92	5.78	72.5	2.8	31.5	18.2	5.0
7.4	0.00	0.0	0.63	5.7	0.1	1.38	17.50	5.34	75.4	5.1	146.1	25.5	1.5
7.8	1.16	2.4	0.00	6.6	0.1	1.27	9.08	4.16	64.2	5.5	58.4	8.8	4.8
9.0	0.00	0.0	-0.09	3.5	0.0	0.60	6.59	4.83	89.9	5.0	33.3	4.6	0.7
3.7	6.51	11.6	0.57	1.7	0.0	0.14	0.84	3.67	100.8	5.2	150.5	27.7	3.8
4.0	0.80	5.0	1.11	5.0	0.2	1.31	16.56	4.15	68.1	5.4	69.2	11.4	1.7
3.2	1.26	7.8	0.49	9.0	0.3	2.25	22.25	5.75	55.5	3.4	61.7	20.2	2.5
2.3	3.41	24.6	0.53	3.7	0.1	0.60	8.17	4.59	84.8	2.4	29.6	19.7	1.0
4.6	3.16	11.3	1.24	3.9	0.3	0.85	9.26	4.20	66.5	7.2	118.1	9.8	2.7
1.9	4.41	21.6	-0.11	5.0	0.0	1.09	11.56	4.85	76.9	5.1	56.3	10.8	1.3
3.5	2.40	18.8	0.12	6.2	0.2	1.07	13.00	4.40	55.4	5.2	130.5	21.7	1.7
5.1	1.49	7.7	-0.53	4.5	0.3	0.79	6.70	4.39	74.4	4.8	51.6	13.0	4.1
1.7	7.09	37.4	0.10	8.7	0.4	2.08	14.97	7.29	61.0	2.1	13.1	18.5	7.1
4.2	2.32	10.8	0.22	9.5	0.4	2.41	24.57	5.17	57.7	4.0	39.3	14.6	6.0
7.9	0.00	0.0	0.00	3.0	0.0	0.49	6.32	4.54	89.4	5.4	97.9	15.3	0.1
5.9	3.92	8.9	1.14	1.6	0.0	-0.05	-0.36	3.45	94.5	4.8	39.3	7.6	3.0
4.0	1.16	7.6	0.01	5.5	0.4	1.18	12.41	4.36	71.5	5.4	31.7	3.7	5.2
2.5	3.28	23.4	0.27	7.8	0.4	1.32	13.72	4.42	42.8	1.8	16.7	20.2	4.5
5.7	3.57	11.1	-0.01	5.6	0.2	1.08	6.64	4.38	67.5	4.0	50.9	17.0	6.9
6.4	2.74	7.5	-0.22	7.6	1.3	1.81	14.36	3.93	51.1	1.5	18.3	24.7	6.7
5.7	0.44	3.7	0.14	4.9	2.5	0.77	9.15	4.38	77.2	2.2	14.7	17.9	4.4
1.8	8.99	34.1	-1.35	2.6	0.1	0.77	8.96	4.50	84.5	1.1	31.4	37.6	1.4
6.6	0.72	3.4	0.15	8.2	1.7	1.28	11.58	4.18	57.9	4.8	79.3	18.4	7.2
8.4	0.00	0.0	0.00	8.8	0.2	2.37	25.75	3.94	47.3	5.6	112.8	16.1	2.7
8.0	0.55	2.0	0.45	9.9	0.7	2.55	18.36	4.61	49.0	4.9	137.3	27.8	8.0
2.7	2.82	12.7	1.26	7.1	0.5	1.57	14.61	4.33	56.4	2.9	48.0	25.9	4.5
3.7	1.37	11.5	0.21	6.9	0.5	1.22	15.77	5.35	62.3	4.2	38.5	13.5	3.1
3.6	1.99	12.9	-0.10	4.1	0.3	1.14	13.72	4.47	76.8	1.7	21.3	23.0	0.5
8.5	0.06	0.2	-0.29	10.0	1.9	3.00	21.16	5.21	43.3	4.2	41.5	14.4	9.2
8.1	0.07	0.6	0.00	5.4	0.5	1.12	13.96	5.06	81.6	4.2	14.0	7.3	3.9
7.6	0.11	0.5	0.28	6.0	0.4	0.97	8.58	4.83	81.4	5.1	69.0	14.3	6.1
9.5	0.77	0.6	0.24	8.9	0.8	2.10	9.14	3.90	46.9	4.6	141.5	34.5	9.0
6.5	0.37	2.1	-0.08	4.4	0.5	0.86	8.24	3.95	70.5	3.5	10.7	11.0	6.9

Name	City	State	Weiss Safety Rating	2003 Weiss Safety Rating	2002 Weiss Safety Rating	Total Assets ($Mil)	One Year Asset Growth	Asset Mix (As a % of Total Assets)				Capital- ization Index	Leverage Ratio	Risk-based Capital Ratio
								Comm- ercial Loans	Cons- umer Loans	Home Mort- gages	Secur- ities			
FIRST ST BK	GAINESVILLE	TX	B+	B+	A-	234.6	-0.24	7.0	4.6	14.0	36.0	6.9	8.9	16.5
FIRST ST BK	GRAHAM	TX	C	C	D+	61.6	21.98	12.0	12.6	11.8	0.6	5.9	7.9	13.4
FIRST ST BK	GRANDVIEW	TX	C+	C+	C	52.2	0.10	15.7	16.9	17.0	18.3	6.3	8.3	12.8
▲ FIRST ST BK	GRANGER	TX	B-	C+	C	64.8	-3.53	17.2	5.1	3.0	31.7	10.0	11.0	16.3
▲ FIRST ST BK	GRAPELAND	TX	C-	D+	C-	65.7	16.87	5.8	11.9	18.3	39.4	6.3	8.2	21.0
FIRST ST BK	HALLSVILLE	TX	D+	D+	C	30.0	2.46	1.6	9.0	23.4	32.0	6.3	8.3	20.6
▼ FIRST ST BK	HEMPHILL	TX	C+	B-	B-	54.7	0.46	2.5	4.2	3.2	77.8	9.7	10.8	35.6
▲ FIRST ST BK	HUNTSVILLE	TX	B	B-	C	50.8	-9.11	7.6	11.0	24.2	18.7	10.0	13.2	22.8
FIRST ST BK	ITALY	TX	D-	D-	D	12.3	-6.74	5.4	10.1	9.7	17.5	6.1	8.1	16.5
▲ FIRST ST BK	JUNCTION	TX	C	C-	C	30.9	-10.93	3.1	2.0	14.2	48.3	6.3	8.3	17.6
FIRST ST BK	LIVINGSTON	TX	B+	A-	B+	210.8	-2.54	4.3	6.3	6.8	42.6	10.0	11.3	26.8
FIRST ST BK	LOUISE	TX	B	B	B	126.2	3.93	12.8	8.8	10.3	29.9	6.6	8.6	14.8
FIRST ST BK	MAYPEARL	TX	B-	B-	C+	20.8	4.31	5.8	17.5	22.9	23.5	10.0	11.0	18.9
▼ FIRST ST BK	MENARD	TX	D+	C-	C-	16.8	-6.56	7.7	8.3	13.0	17.2	9.7	10.8	17.6
▲ FIRST ST BK	MESQUITE	TX	A	A-	B+	174.9	2.56	24.4	6.4	13.2	14.7	10.0	14.9	19.7
FIRST ST BK	MINERAL WELLS	TX	B-	B-	B	55.6	6.62	7.9	8.4	12.6	15.6	8.7	10.1	18.6
FIRST ST BK	MOBEETIE	TX	D-	D-	D-	33.2	13.87	9.7	7.1	5.3	50.1	4.5	6.5	17.2
FIRST ST BK	NEW BRAUNFELS	TX	B-	B-	B-	151.5	8.94	18.1	9.8	14.0	5.3	5.1	7.6	11.1
FIRST ST BK	OVERTON	TX	C+	C+	B-	44.1	-9.42	11.5	6.2	5.1	43.9	10.0	17.2	42.4
FIRST ST BK	PAINT ROCK	TX	B-	B-	B-	42.3	3.35	6.0	5.6	9.4	33.0	10.0	13.1	21.6
▲ FIRST ST BK	RICE	TX	D	D-	D-	9.8	4.51	4.0	14.3	16.5	24.3	10.0	11.2	24.7
FIRST ST BK	SHALLOWATER	TX	C-	C-	C-	28.8	0.15	7.3	8.4	4.3	24.2	7.7	9.5	19.5
▼ FIRST ST BK	SPEARMAN	TX	B+	A-	A-	65.4	4.71	9.9	3.8	1.4	45.1	10.0	12.2	22.7
FIRST ST BK	THREE RIVERS	TX	B	B+	B+	73.9	1.30	3.3	7.7	9.2	47.0	10.0	18.0	44.8
FIRST ST BK	VAN	TX	A-	A-	A-	33.8	2.27	7.3	14.8	24.6	22.1	10.0	13.7	24.0
FIRST ST BK	YOAKUM	TX	A-	A-	A-	89.9	2.63	6.5	11.9	17.2	39.4	10.0	12.3	25.8
▲ FIRST ST BK	DANVILLE	VA	C	D+	C	41.9	3.03	1.4	10.1	32.5	16.5	10.0	16.3	25.4
▼ FIRST ST BK	FOUNTAIN CITY	WI	C-	C+	C+	21.3	2.17	18.4	8.8	10.1	21.0	6.2	8.2	14.1
▼ FIRST ST BK	NEW LONDON	WI	B-	A-	A	268.1	-4.31	4.8	4.1	21.8	19.5	8.5	10.0	14.8
FIRST ST BK	BARBOURSVILLE	WV	C+	C+	C	118.7	6.70	10.5	5.3	26.1	21.6	5.1	7.1	11.3
FIRST ST BK	WHEATLAND	WY	B-	B-	B-	143.4	12.67	11.6	5.5	6.2	13.1	4.1	7.7	10.6
FIRST ST BK & TC	CARUTHERSVILLE	MO	B	B	B+	195.2	12.62	11.8	11.3	23.3	5.6	5.0	9.2	11.0
▲ FIRST ST BK ALEXANDRIA	ALEXANDRIA	MN	B+	B	B	84.3	13.06	17.6	7.5	18.5	18.7	6.8	9.4	12.3
FIRST ST BK CAMPBELL HILL	CAMPBELL HILL	IL	C-	C-	C	63.6	47.27	5.4	6.4	20.2	45.0	3.9	6.6	10.5
▼ FIRST ST BK CENTRAL TX	TEMPLE	TX	C+	B-	B-	574.9	17.80	11.9	3.3	4.3	21.5	3.4	7.1	10.2
▲ FIRST ST BK CLAREMONT	GROTON	SD	B-	B-	B-	28.7	12.30	8.3	3.9	1.4	15.8	10.0	18.2	24.2
FIRST ST BK EAST DETROIT	EASTPOINTE	MI	B+	B+	A-	734.4	3.71	2.6	1.4	30.8	26.9	8.1	9.7	16.9
▼ FIRST ST BK FLORIDA KEYS	KEY WEST	FL	C+	B-	B	526.4	8.80	2.4	1.6	24.8	26.4	3.2	6.4	10.1
▲ FIRST ST BK FORT	FORT LAUDERDALE	FL	E	E-	D	31.5	5.80	9.0	5.2	2.1	14.4	6.6	8.8	12.2
▼ FIRST ST BK HONEY GROVE	HONEY GROVE	TX	D-	D	D	19.3	7.46	3.7	2.9	0.7	73.5	6.6	8.6	25.7
▲ FIRST ST BK IA	NEW HAMPTON	IA	D	D-	D-	45.5	-6.73	6.9	5.3	14.6	37.8	5.9	7.9	14.4
FIRST ST BK IN TEMPLE	TEMPLE	OK	C+	C+	B-	20.9	0.47	7.5	7.5	9.9	26.5	10.0	16.0	38.7
FIRST ST BK IN TUSCOLA	TUSCOLA	TX	D-	D	D+	20.8	13.22	1.6	8.3	10.6	40.6	5.5	7.5	21.5
FIRST ST BK JONES OK	JONES	OK	B	B	B	27.7	3.66	4.1	8.5	9.6	64.6	10.0	14.4	37.9
FIRST ST BK KIESTER	KIESTER	MN	D+	D	D	20.3	-1.17	13.2	2.3	5.0	22.8	9.1	10.4	18.6
FIRST ST BK KIOWA KS	KIOWA	KS	B+	B+	B+	33.0	-0.89	2.2	2.4	7.9	35.6	10.0	14.0	23.7
FIRST ST BK LAKE LILLIAN, MN	LAKE LILLIAN	MN	C+	C+	C+	128.6	-9.77	2.7	0.4	0.7	55.8	3.8	5.8	23.3
FIRST ST BK MILLER	MILLER	SD	A	A	A	95.5	2.12	19.7	4.8	1.8	17.1	10.0	12.3	15.9
FIRST ST BK NA	CANADIAN	TX	B-	B-	B-	75.2	11.54	11.3	7.4	4.1	0.5	6.2	10.9	11.9
FIRST ST BK NM	TAOS	NM	C+	C+	B-	1,709.9	17.26	9.7	1.7	15.5	15.1	3.0	7.5	10.0
FIRST ST BK OF ADAMS	WINCHESTER	OH	B-	B-	B-	118.4	0.79	2.6	11.3	26.5	29.6	6.3	8.3	14.6
FIRST ST BK OF ARCADIA	ARCADIA	FL	B+	A	A-	115.6	-4.63	3.2	2.4	19.8	23.8	6.2	8.2	14.2
FIRST ST BK OF ASHBY	ASHBY	MN	D	D	D	24.8	3.05	5.3	7.2	18.1	26.7	5.4	7.4	14.0
▲ FIRST ST BK OF AUDUBON	AUDUBON	MN	C	C-	C	10.8	0.98	20.3	11.1	9.2	48.1	10.0	11.5	22.7
FIRST ST BK OF BEECHER	BEECHER CITY	IL	B+	B+	A-	36.9	2.87	8.8	14.1	24.4	13.1	10.0	16.4	24.6
▲ FIRST ST BK OF BIGGSVILLE	BIGGSVILLE	IL	B	B-	C+	16.5	-3.60	6.5	7.7	20.6	44.0	10.0	14.1	24.4
FIRST ST BK OF BLAKELY	BLAKELY	GA	A-	A-	A-	193.9	11.00	15.3	5.4	14.6	13.6	10.0	11.6	16.1
FIRST ST BK OF	BLOOMINGTON	IL	B	B	C	70.6	2.75	4.8	2.3	25.9	39.4	6.9	8.9	18.8
FIRST ST BK OF BURLINGAME	BURLINGAME	KS	C-	C-	C-	54.8	1.09	19.1	5.7	13.2	24.9	6.6	8.6	13.4
FIRST ST BK OF BUXTON	BUXTON	ND	C+	C+	C	59.5	10.02	11.7	5.4	15.1	13.8	6.4	9.1	12.1
FIRST ST BK OF CA	GRANADA HILLS	CA	B-	B-	B-	218.5	25.34	12.4	1.1	5.0	7.8	5.8	8.8	11.6
▲ FIRST ST BK OF CHICO	CHICO	TX	B+	B-	C	80.0	11.95	15.4	12.0	10.0	15.0	8.4	9.9	14.6
FIRST ST BK OF CLAY	LINEVILLE	AL	B-	C+	C+	104.8	5.86	4.6	11.6	16.1	42.5	7.0	9.0	15.7
FIRST ST BK OF COLFAX	COLFAX	IA	A-	A-	A-	53.6	3.80	9.3	2.4	28.3	16.1	8.3	9.8	15.5

Asset Quality Index	Non-Performing Loans as a % of Total Loans	Non-Performing Loans as a % of Capital	Net Charge-offs Avg Loans	Profitability Index	Net Income ($Mil)	Return on Assets (R.O.A.)	Return on Equity (R.O.E.)	Net Interest Spread	Overhead Efficiency Ratio	Liquidity Index	Liquidity Ratio	Hot Money Ratio	Stability Index
7.1	0.67	3.3	0.11	5.7	1.4	1.21	12.07	4.69	77.3	4.6	37.4	11.3	6.7
6.5	0.66	4.1	0.17	7.0	0.5	1.58	20.27	3.78	64.3	6.2	132.9	16.0	3.4
6.0	0.27	1.9	0.20	8.5	0.4	1.33	13.88	5.59	67.5	4.2	19.8	8.0	4.8
7.8	0.00	0.0	-0.03	5.8	0.5	1.46	14.14	3.95	65.0	3.0	21.6	14.9	4.4
8.2	0.14	0.9	0.01	2.0	0.2	0.45	5.91	2.57	84.1	6.1	238.7	25.3	2.7
8.8	0.01	0.0	-0.05	3.2	0.1	0.44	5.39	4.12	86.4	6.1	133.3	16.2	2.6
8.4	1.48	2.3	0.33	3.1	0.1	0.46	4.16	2.32	71.3	7.6	192.1	13.8	4.8
7.6	0.51	2.6	0.00	7.5	0.9	3.32	28.22	4.59	53.7	5.7	112.5	17.0	4.5
4.9	1.35	9.0	0.13	1.0	0.0	-0.22	-2.95	4.47	102.6	4.4	94.2	19.8	1.4
9.4	0.00	0.0	0.00	5.7	0.3	1.75	20.14	4.17	70.8	1.5	12.9	23.5	3.6
6.1	1.70	6.9	-0.01	7.9	1.7	1.60	13.48	4.55	59.1	4.5	66.5	18.2	7.2
4.9	0.74	5.3	0.36	7.8	1.3	2.08	25.24	5.23	63.0	4.2	16.8	7.5	4.5
7.7	0.08	0.5	0.34	9.6	0.2	2.04	18.49	5.03	64.0	3.9	57.4	16.6	5.6
7.2	0.18	0.7	0.16	1.0	0.0	-0.51	-3.67	4.44	115.6	4.6	72.3	15.9	2.9
6.1	1.20	5.3	0.71	6.6	1.0	1.17	7.91	6.92	59.2	5.3	26.9	2.3	7.9
6.5	0.88	4.0	-0.03	5.3	0.4	1.34	13.21	4.10	72.1	6.1	94.0	12.3	5.9
8.3	0.46	2.1	-0.08	3.6	0.2	0.83	13.45	2.57	69.6	3.1	59.8	28.3	1.6
4.0	0.83	7.3	0.24	5.6	0.7	0.87	11.15	4.91	81.0	4.4	54.8	16.5	5.5
8.3	1.02	1.8	0.31	2.5	0.1	0.36	2.12	2.98	83.4	4.3	98.9	25.7	5.8
4.5	3.01	10.8	0.37	6.2	0.2	0.98	7.47	4.99	68.3	3.2	49.6	22.3	4.9
5.4	2.90	9.1	0.00	5.5	0.1	1.73	14.93	4.81	68.3	5.7	103.1	14.5	0.1
4.1	1.25	6.0	0.84	4.0	0.1	0.57	6.14	3.59	76.6	4.3	88.1	22.7	1.9
6.4	1.42	4.7	0.09	5.4	0.5	1.37	10.57	3.73	64.8	3.3	74.5	31.6	7.2
8.6	1.14	2.0	0.35	3.6	0.2	0.52	2.83	3.49	77.7	5.2	129.8	22.5	6.3
7.8	0.28	1.3	0.04	8.0	0.2	1.23	8.95	4.60	62.3	3.5	32.1	14.6	8.4
7.6	0.44	1.4	0.14	7.7	1.0	2.12	16.36	4.35	54.5	5.3	48.0	9.6	7.6
3.8	3.20	13.0	0.93	4.1	0.3	1.52	9.35	6.90	64.5	3.0	36.2	18.6	3.8
7.1	0.30	2.0	0.10	3.9	0.1	0.64	6.05	3.60	79.9	7.8	102.4	1.6	3.0
4.1	1.85	11.2	-0.07	7.2	1.5	1.14	9.51	4.32	63.9	2.0	24.9	19.7	7.5
4.0	0.55	4.9	0.32	6.3	0.6	1.09	14.21	4.41	77.5	3.3	10.4	12.1	5.5
8.1	0.00	0.0	0.10	8.0	0.8	1.22	16.16	4.21	52.0	2.0	26.8	21.4	4.3
5.8	0.21	1.9	0.12	6.6	1.1	1.19	13.35	4.00	56.1	0.9	9.3	32.5	5.4
6.8	0.29	2.0	0.24	9.8	0.6	1.52	16.16	4.71	41.1	5.4	32.3	3.8	6.1
3.6	2.65	14.8	0.11	5.9	0.3	1.08	13.12	4.08	63.3	3.2	17.7	13.3	3.3
5.1	0.41	3.3	-0.75	8.4	3.8	1.39	17.36	4.60	54.4	2.5	16.3	16.7	5.4
6.6	0.53	2.0	0.00	4.8	0.1	0.69	3.64	4.45	75.6	4.0	13.9	8.5	6.3
6.2	0.93	6.0	0.08	5.4	3.5	0.95	10.26	3.48	63.0	4.5	62.2	17.7	6.5
6.9	0.36	3.6	0.01	7.3	4.6	1.77	26.87	4.31	63.9	3.7	24.7	11.3	5.8
0.3	9.42	24.8	0.12	0.0	-0.1	-0.52	-4.70	0.58	233.7	5.2	24.2	1.6	2.1
9.6	0.00	0.0	-0.38	1.4	0.0	-0.04	-0.45	2.23	101.7	7.1	245.8	16.9	1.6
8.7	0.01	0.1	-0.07	2.5	0.0	0.15	2.02	3.50	95.6	4.3	10.8	5.9	0.8
8.3	0.01	0.0	0.02	6.8	0.2	2.13	12.96	5.23	48.3	5.1	156.4	28.3	4.6
7.3	0.19	0.6	0.00	4.7	0.1	0.78	10.12	3.97	75.2	6.8	86.4	6.0	1.7
8.8	0.07	0.1	-0.50	6.8	0.2	1.51	10.18	4.56	65.5	4.9	42.8	11.0	5.3
4.9	1.15	6.3	-0.55	4.4	0.2	1.48	14.13	4.41	64.9	6.0	61.7	6.1	2.5
8.4	0.06	0.2	-0.19	6.5	0.2	1.21	7.34	4.39	58.0	5.5	96.3	15.8	6.4
8.6	0.03	0.1	0.35	5.4	1.1	1.39	25.80	2.35	37.8	6.6	42.0	0.3	3.9
8.0	0.19	1.1	0.00	9.1	0.9	1.90	16.18	4.93	50.1	3.4	15.9	12.3	7.5
2.5	0.78	5.6	0.00	7.0	0.8	2.10	19.10	4.40	54.3	3.1	15.5	13.4	6.7
5.0	0.67	4.8	0.29	6.2	7.6	0.91	9.44	4.54	65.1	1.6	12.7	23.1	7.1
7.4	0.28	1.9	0.01	5.0	0.5	0.91	10.81	4.31	72.4	6.1	42.5	3.5	4.6
5.1	2.13	13.1	0.05	9.9	1.3	2.26	21.55	5.13	57.8	3.3	37.0	17.3	7.8
5.1	1.16	8.0	0.00	7.5	0.2	1.92	25.95	3.76	53.0	6.8	105.2	8.8	2.3
8.2	0.02	0.1	-0.67	3.3	0.0	0.83	7.13	3.39	96.4	6.7	71.9	3.9	3.2
5.0	1.08	4.6	-0.02	10.0	0.5	2.58	15.65	4.99	51.0	4.8	50.1	12.8	8.4
1.8	8.97	28.3	0.40	4.6	0.1	1.19	8.04	3.88	61.3	6.2	82.2	9.1	7.3
7.3	0.64	3.7	-0.02	6.2	0.8	0.85	7.02	3.84	62.1	2.4	37.5	26.2	5.9
8.0	0.16	0.9	-0.02	5.4	0.4	1.11	13.14	3.55	71.6	3.0	13.3	14.0	5.9
5.4	0.54	3.8	0.23	3.9	0.2	0.66	7.69	3.81	74.7	2.5	35.7	22.9	3.2
4.5	1.00	8.1	0.19	5.8	0.4	1.31	15.09	3.94	64.2	5.5	55.6	10.1	4.1
5.0	0.15	0.7	0.00	8.1	1.1	1.08	7.52	3.87	49.9	1.4	31.6	45.1	6.3
7.5	0.18	1.2	0.11	9.0	0.8	2.05	20.32	4.87	60.3	4.1	45.3	15.4	5.9
5.8	0.75	4.2	0.54	6.9	1.1	2.10	24.65	5.30	64.6	1.0	21.1	33.1	4.2
8.7	0.14	1.0	0.00	9.4	0.7	2.45	25.07	3.95	33.9	2.5	33.5	20.8	7.6

Name	City	State	Weiss Safety Rating	2003 Weiss Safety Rating	2002 Weiss Safety Rating	Total Assets ($Mil)	One Year Asset Growth	Asset Mix (As a % of Total Assets) Comm- ercial Loans	Cons- umer Loans	Home Mort- gages	Secur- ities	Capital- ization Index	Leverage Ratio	Risk-based Capital Ratio
FIRST ST BK OF DE QUEEN	DE QUEEN	AR	C+	C+	C+	45.1	7.51	7.6	11.0	20.9	17.3	8.2	9.8	15.5
FIRST ST BK OF DEKALB CTY	FORT PAYNE	AL	B	B-	B-	69.3	-3.24	22.7	8.0	12.2	23.4	10.0	12.5	18.7
FIRST ST BK OF DONGOLA	DONGOLA	IL	D+	D+	C-	16.9	4.44	1.5	23.6	44.7	4.1	10.0	12.3	20.5
▼ FIRST ST BK OF FERTILE	FERTILE	MN	B	B+	B+	31.4	-1.28	6.3	5.9	3.9	44.8	10.0	15.8	27.1
▲ FIRST ST BK OF GACKLE	GACKLE	ND	C+	C-	C-	27.8	5.79	1.6	1.4	1.0	33.1	6.7	8.7	14.3
FIRST ST BK OF GOFF	GOFF	KS	C	C	C	5.8	-3.45	5.0	30.4	21.0	14.8	10.0	11.6	17.1
▲ FIRST ST BK OF HEALY	HEALY	KS	A-	B+	B	38.4	3.24	12.7	1.9	3.2	32.8	10.0	24.4	38.8
FIRST ST BK OF HILL COUNTY	MT CALM	TX	D-	D-	D	16.1	-0.38	8.4	10.3	10.2	29.9	5.2	7.2	14.7
▼ FIRST ST BK OF HOTCHKISS	HOTCHKISS	CO	C-	B	B-	48.4	11.65	5.9	2.4	5.3	18.6	9.8	10.9	15.6
▲ FIRST ST BK OF IDABEL	IDABEL	OK	A	A-	A	51.6	2.65	10.7	4.8	15.3	44.1	10.0	12.1	23.5
FIRST ST BK OF JOPLIN	JOPLIN	MO	B	B-	B-	112.4	0.54	11.5	4.5	20.2	3.7	8.3	9.9	13.6
▼ FIRST ST BK OF KC KS	KANSAS CITY	KS	C-	C+	B-	83.1	11.52	20.2	3.8	6.6	28.5	3.9	6.8	10.5
FIRST ST BK OF KENSINGTON	KENSINGTON	MN	B-	B-	C+	65.6	15.88	10.8	5.7	18.1	38.5	6.4	8.4	14.9
FIRST ST BK OF LE ROY	LE ROY	MN	C+	C+	C	49.8	-0.33	13.3	4.8	7.4	28.4	6.3	8.3	12.2
▼ FIRST ST BK OF LOOMIS	LOOMIS	NE	D+	C-	C	39.9	0.70	12.0	14.7	4.5	20.1	5.2	9.0	11.2
FIRST ST BK OF MALTA	MALTA	MT	A	A	A	85.8	-1.66	5.5	5.6	2.2	39.2	10.0	16.0	26.2
FIRST ST BK OF MAPLETON	MAPLETON	IA	A-	A-	B+	31.5	-5.27	11.3	10.7	20.8	22.2	6.6	8.6	14.2
FIRST ST BK OF MATADOR	MATADOR	TX	B+	B+	B+	11.2	-0.44	13.3	2.4	0.0	65.3	9.3	10.5	27.2
FIRST ST BK OF MIAMI	MIAMI	TX	D-	E	E-	25.1	-7.81	28.1	11.9	3.6	26.0	7.0	9.0	14.7
▲ FIRST ST BK OF MUNICH	MUNICH	ND	C	D+	D	69.3	3.82	10.1	4.3	5.2	17.5	7.8	9.6	13.3
FIRST ST BK OF MURDOCK	MURDOCK	MN	C-	D+	D+	8.1	-1.65	11.3	9.3	20.7	1.3	10.0	11.7	15.9
FIRST ST BK OF ND	ARTHUR	ND	B-	B-	C+	75.5	10.98	15.8	4.3	4.7	8.9	4.6	8.4	10.8
FIRST ST BK OF NEWCASTLE	NEWCASTLE	WY	A	A	A+	95.0	-1.76	5.9	7.6	6.5	59.9	10.0	18.3	38.8
FIRST ST BK OF NW AR	HUNTSVILLE	AR	C	C-	D+	62.2	-7.85	11.3	4.2	19.8	15.9	10.0	12.3	17.7
FIRST ST BK OF ODEM	ODEM	TX	B	B	B	53.7	1.71	9.8	5.7	3.3	51.3	10.0	11.5	25.5
▼ FIRST ST BK OF OKABENA	OKABENA	MN	C+	B-	B	24.3	2.45	3.9	2.3	5.3	43.7	10.0	18.8	28.4
▲ FIRST ST BK OF OLMSTED	OLMSTED	IL	B-	C+	C+	24.1	10.82	14.8	7.8	24.3	37.1	10.0	12.9	25.1
▲ FIRST ST BK OF POND CREEK	POND CREEK	OK	D-	E-	D-	31.0	-14.00	24.8	14.1	13.8	10.8	6.5	8.8	12.1
▲ FIRST ST BK OF PORTER	PORTER	IN	B+	B	B+	108.2	6.53	2.0	1.2	22.3	34.3	10.0	13.0	25.2
FIRST ST BK OF PORTER	PORTER	OK	C	C	E	32.1	5.21	17.8	9.8	22.2	0.7	7.9	10.1	13.3
FIRST ST BK OF RANDOLPH	CUTHBERT	GA	B	B+	B+	45.9	-4.23	18.5	8.5	3.7	41.2	10.0	12.2	18.3
FIRST ST BK OF RANSOM	RANSOM	KS	B+	B+	B+	33.7	-2.20	3.8	0.7	0.7	54.7	10.0	21.9	52.0
FIRST ST BK OF RED BUD	RED BUD	IL	B+	B	C+	96.3	4.53	2.6	3.6	12.1	52.3	10.0	12.6	26.6
▲ FIRST ST BK OF SAN DIEGO	SAN DIEGO	TX	C	D+	D	44.6	-2.89	6.2	11.8	6.7	41.1	8.0	9.7	21.9
FIRST ST BK OF	SHANNON	IL	B	B	B-	123.1	-1.66	4.6	3.8	11.7	30.3	6.8	8.8	14.6
FIRST ST BK OF SHARON	SHARON	ND	D+	D	C-	58.6	3.36	7.0	7.9	1.6	28.1	4.5	8.1	10.8
FIRST ST BK OF ST JOSEPH	ST JOSEPH	MN	B	B	B	61.9	3.91	6.6	6.0	8.3	35.3	5.9	7.9	13.5
▲ FIRST ST BK OF ST ROBERT	ST ROBERT	MO	B-	C+	C+	62.9	9.22	4.3	12.3	35.3	13.3	5.5	7.5	12.4
▼ FIRST ST BK OF STRATFORD	STRATFORD	TX	B	A-	A-	144.4	-1.40	5.8	2.9	7.8	26.7	5.9	7.9	12.6
▲ FIRST ST BK OF THE SOUTH	SULLIGENT	AL	B+	B-	B-	87.5	-1.62	3.7	11.4	15.1	53.8	10.0	12.6	23.9
FIRST ST BK OF	THERMOPOLIS	WY	C-	C-	C-	57.1	40.05	27.1	5.9	14.1	21.9	5.3	7.9	11.2
FIRST ST BK OF THORNTON	THORNTON	IA	D	D	D+	23.2	0.23	3.3	3.6	6.7	59.1	7.6	9.4	21.8
FIRST ST BK OF UVALDE	UVALDE	TX	A-	A-	A-	366.4	3.84	9.0	2.7	6.8	48.5	8.2	9.8	18.5
▲ FIRST ST BK OF VAN ORIN	VAN ORIN	IL	C-	C	C+	26.6	86.51	7.3	4.5	9.3	41.6	6.5	8.5	15.3
FIRST ST BK OF WABASHA	WABASHA	MN	B+	B+	B+	89.1	-5.72	11.0	7.3	12.6	42.0	7.1	9.1	17.6
▲ FIRST ST BK OF WARNER SD	WARNER	SD	E+	E-	E-	30.4	-5.93	13.7	7.3	3.8	26.4	6.4	8.4	13.2
FIRST ST BK OF WARREN	WARREN	AR	B-	B-	C-	99.2	2.01	18.4	7.7	11.4	32.9	10.0	11.0	18.8
FIRST ST BK OF WILTON	WILTON	ND	C-	C-	C-	24.5	2.89	2.2	1.8	2.6	46.0	7.5	9.3	17.0
FIRST ST BK OF WYOMING	WYOMING	MN	A	A	A	115.1	7.90	6.2	4.7	10.5	46.9	10.0	13.4	22.7
FIRST ST BK RUSH CITY	RUSH CITY	MN	B+	B+	B+	48.9	1.23	7.3	4.6	15.3	14.8	7.7	9.5	14.2
FIRST ST BK SOUTHWEST	PIPESTONE	MN	C+	C+	B-	120.4	3.12	10.3	12.6	7.6	21.0	6.0	8.1	11.7
FIRST ST BK THAYER	THAYER	KS	B-	B-	B-	10.0	5.24	4.1	7.9	20.2	31.8	6.5	8.5	17.3
FIRST ST BK TX	KEENE	TX	B	B	B	147.9	9.32	14.0	14.8	13.4	21.1	5.5	7.5	13.3
FIRST ST BK-CANDO	CANDO	ND	C	C	C	38.2	-1.72	8.0	6.3	2.3	28.7	8.3	9.9	15.1
▲ FIRST ST BK-DECATUR	DECATUR	MI	B+	B	B+	54.4	8.60	4.1	4.6	45.6	28.5	10.0	14.5	27.9
▼ FIRST ST BK-WESTERN IL	LA HARPE	IL	C+	C+	C+	153.8	15.51	7.8	2.5	14.5	29.5	3.0	6.6	10.0
FIRST ST COMMUNITY BK	FARMINGTON	MO	B+	B+	B	534.0	7.61	5.7	3.9	31.5	14.2	6.8	8.8	13.3
FIRST STAR SVGS BK	BETHLEHEM	PA	C+	C+	C	565.3	15.88	0.3	0.6	29.9	52.0	5.1	7.1	17.1
FIRST STATE BK OF PINEVILLE	PINEVILLE	KY	B-	C+	C	210.8	3.05	15.3	3.8	23.5	13.3	6.4	8.4	12.2
FIRST STATE BK ROUND LAKE	ROUND LAKE BEACH	IL	C-	C	D+	129.8	18.09	5.2	3.3	14.0	18.8	6.0	8.0	11.8
FIRST STATE BK SOUTHWEST	TELL CITY	IN	B-	B-	B	74.9	9.70	29.6	11.2	19.9	12.3	3.7	7.7	10.3
FIRST SUBURBAN NB	MAYWOOD	IL	D	D	D-	150.9	7.03	23.0	2.2	7.0	18.3	5.0	7.7	11.0
FIRST SUMMIT BK	JOHNSTOWN	PA	B-	B-	B-	357.0	9.44	6.9	6.5	21.1	39.3	6.1	8.1	14.6
FIRST SUSQUEHANNA B&T	SUNBURY	PA	B-	B-	B	351.4	-2.23	4.1	12.0	25.0	17.5	5.4	7.9	11.3

Asset Quality Index	Non-Performing Loans as a % of Total Loans	as a % of Capital	Net Charge-offs Avg Loans	Profitability Index	Net Income ($Mil)	Return on Assets (R.O.A.)	Return on Equity (R.O.E.)	Net Interest Spread	Overhead Efficiency Ratio	Liquidity Index	Liquidity Ratio	Hot Money Ratio	Stability Index
8.1	0.16	1.0	0.12	4.3	0.2	0.91	9.27	4.26	78.2	3.1	61.0	28.6	4.5
6.9	0.63	3.3	-0.14	5.4	0.4	1.09	8.92	4.61	65.2	1.7	24.5	24.9	5.4
1.1	4.52	25.7	0.24	1.8	0.0	-0.24	-1.89	4.70	101.2	4.1	45.6	13.5	3.8
8.6	1.22	2.8	-0.04	4.4	0.1	0.90	5.65	3.64	74.8	6.5	72.0	7.3	6.3
4.7	0.08	0.3	-0.07	7.5	0.2	1.28	10.57	3.72	54.3	6.2	59.6	6.6	6.7
6.8	0.00	0.0	0.18	9.7	0.0	1.50	13.06	4.83	53.8	3.6	30.6	12.0	4.3
5.8	5.75	12.1	-4.22	10.0	1.0	4.86	19.91	6.30	40.5	2.3	29.5	19.9	8.4
4.7	1.99	10.8	-0.24	1.6	0.0	0.25	3.74	3.04	91.8	3.6	76.9	24.4	1.2
0.6	3.07	15.2	0.10	10.0	0.4	1.71	12.83	4.84	54.0	1.8	33.8	32.2	5.6
4.1	3.13	9.6	0.00	9.2	0.4	1.41	9.61	4.17	54.7	2.4	8.9	16.5	8.7
4.3	1.58	11.7	0.01	7.5	1.0	1.80	18.00	4.96	63.9	4.7	32.0	8.7	6.0
0.3	7.66	66.5	0.11	4.8	0.4	0.89	12.59	4.23	57.2	1.2	19.6	30.9	3.9
7.2	0.56	3.7	0.09	7.2	0.6	1.82	21.23	3.45	41.0	4.9	52.4	12.4	4.2
8.2	0.06	0.4	0.39	9.3	0.6	2.24	26.53	4.65	59.7	5.7	30.5	0.9	5.1
3.4	0.82	6.6	1.16	5.9	0.2	0.85	9.83	4.38	58.9	3.3	55.0	23.0	3.0
8.0	1.18	3.6	0.01	7.3	0.5	1.13	7.25	3.67	50.2	3.8	49.7	17.4	8.2
8.0	0.00	0.0	-0.04	8.8	0.2	1.46	17.59	3.78	52.5	3.8	28.0	12.1	7.3
8.8	0.00	0.0	0.00	4.7	0.1	0.89	8.49	3.89	74.4	3.4	10.2	11.4	6.1
6.5	0.11	0.5	1.04	2.1	0.0	0.18	1.60	4.82	91.3	4.5	57.5	15.2	0.8
4.6	0.72	5.3	-0.06	4.2	0.3	0.79	8.65	3.90	70.3	3.5	17.2	11.7	2.8
5.6	1.24	8.2	-0.22	7.6	0.1	1.81	16.22	5.90	71.3	5.7	52.3	5.6	2.7
6.0	0.28	2.7	-0.06	7.8	0.7	1.87	21.80	4.89	57.4	2.8	24.5	16.2	5.6
8.2	1.87	3.6	0.15	9.3	1.0	1.94	10.63	4.47	44.2	2.4	27.5	19.0	9.1
3.3	3.75	19.6	0.60	7.8	0.5	1.49	12.22	5.13	54.9	2.0	21.2	19.6	2.5
9.0	0.00	0.0	1.16	4.1	0.2	0.82	7.31	4.46	70.6	4.2	62.9	17.7	5.9
4.9	5.95	15.4	-0.19	6.2	0.2	1.32	7.08	4.32	57.5	0.9	24.0	34.5	5.7
8.0	0.21	0.9	0.00	8.2	0.2	1.73	13.65	4.51	53.7	4.4	22.4	6.5	5.3
3.5	1.22	9.4	1.34	2.5	0.2	1.02	11.90	5.69	62.5	3.6	16.9	11.4	0.7
8.3	0.69	2.6	0.65	5.1	0.7	1.27	9.28	3.92	59.9	5.8	119.8	17.6	7.5
3.7	1.34	10.5	0.19	8.3	0.3	1.96	19.65	6.24	65.7	1.3	29.0	36.1	3.9
7.1	0.76	3.0	-0.03	5.8	0.3	1.15	9.39	4.26	69.2	4.2	21.1	8.3	6.0
9.6	0.01	0.0	-0.02	5.3	0.2	1.14	5.30	3.05	51.1	7.9	118.1	5.0	7.1
9.2	0.33	1.0	-0.33	5.3	0.6	1.21	9.49	3.57	57.2	6.3	45.6	2.7	5.7
4.6	2.38	7.0	-1.29	5.4	0.4	1.62	16.57	4.13	66.4	3.9	69.3	20.5	3.2
6.2	0.56	3.1	0.00	5.6	0.9	1.47	14.59	3.28	57.4	6.8	117.0	12.3	6.1
4.1	1.68	13.1	0.32	4.3	0.3	0.98	12.02	4.03	62.8	2.7	35.7	20.7	2.9
8.2	0.07	0.4	0.05	9.2	0.6	1.88	22.11	4.02	54.6	4.4	57.7	16.2	5.5
6.0	0.38	3.4	0.10	5.8	0.3	1.06	14.05	4.67	64.3	4.2	43.5	14.4	4.0
4.3	1.40	9.8	-0.14	6.5	1.1	1.57	17.91	4.12	64.8	2.6	39.5	25.9	6.4
8.6	0.48	1.3	0.14	6.9	0.6	1.30	10.23	4.02	57.8	3.1	59.1	27.7	5.0
5.9	0.35	3.1	-0.02	8.3	0.6	2.49	31.74	5.47	49.1	1.9	3.5	18.6	2.8
8.7	0.31	1.2	0.50	2.0	0.1	0.42	4.68	3.17	89.7	4.2	15.0	7.0	1.3
8.8	0.17	0.8	-0.01	8.3	2.9	1.58	16.14	3.98	49.5	1.0	19.1	33.1	7.4
7.9	0.26	1.0	0.02	3.5	0.1	0.70	6.14	3.81	77.6	5.4	61.3	11.5	4.6
5.2	1.00	4.8	0.25	10.0	1.2	2.50	23.58	4.85	45.8	3.5	50.1	19.1	6.5
2.5	3.54	21.7	0.21	1.0	0.0	0.25	2.88	3.86	80.8	5.1	31.5	5.4	1.0
4.7	1.61	7.9	0.07	4.6	0.4	0.79	7.29	4.02	69.3	2.3	34.5	25.5	5.6
8.2	0.42	2.1	-0.02	6.5	0.1	1.12	11.67	4.22	59.5	4.3	17.0	6.5	3.0
7.6	1.71	5.8	0.07	9.1	0.9	1.66	12.74	4.21	51.3	4.5	32.4	9.9	8.7
5.5	0.73	5.0	0.00	7.6	0.4	1.77	18.46	4.67	65.1	6.6	65.1	5.1	6.7
7.5	0.15	1.1	0.03	5.2	0.6	1.05	12.42	4.27	63.9	3.6	15.1	10.9	3.3
8.6	0.00	0.0	0.13	4.7	0.1	1.14	13.30	3.52	73.9	8.0	118.4	3.3	5.6
6.1	0.19	0.9	0.22	5.2	0.6	0.85	6.27	4.86	68.7	1.6	22.7	24.8	7.8
6.6	0.85	5.0	0.03	4.0	0.2	0.77	7.61	4.11	78.6	3.4	31.4	15.1	4.1
6.0	1.38	6.0	-0.01	5.1	0.2	0.87	6.07	3.67	66.2	2.9	37.1	19.3	6.9
5.0	1.25	7.8	0.03	5.0	0.6	0.89	9.26	3.97	67.8	4.3	40.4	13.8	4.7
6.0	0.21	1.5	0.73	8.5	3.6	1.40	14.12	3.85	52.3	5.9	76.0	12.5	7.1
8.2	0.37	2.2	0.01	3.6	2.2	0.81	11.42	1.94	52.2	8.7	204.8	8.6	3.7
5.4	0.97	8.2	-0.08	6.4	1.7	1.64	18.87	4.16	60.1	4.4	57.6	17.4	4.6
3.5	1.63	5.1	0.03	3.8	0.3	0.52	3.57	3.83	82.7	5.2	86.6	17.5	4.5
5.5	0.69	5.8	0.13	5.6	0.4	0.96	11.82	4.07	59.8	4.5	16.5	5.9	5.1
2.2	2.38	20.1	-0.21	1.9	0.1	0.17	2.06	4.22	93.0	3.1	18.5	13.8	2.0
6.3	0.53	3.4	0.20	5.7	2.0	1.16	14.50	3.63	58.8	3.4	13.5	11.8	4.1
4.8	0.70	6.2	0.29	5.5	1.6	0.92	11.73	3.90	70.5	4.6	11.3	4.4	5.9

Name	City	State	Weiss Safety Rating	2003 Weiss Safety Rating	2002 Weiss Safety Rating	Total Assets ($Mil)	One Year Asset Growth	Asset Mix (As a % of Total Assets) Commercial Loans	Consumer Loans	Home Mortgages	Securities	Capitalization Index	Leverage Ratio	Risk-based Capital Ratio
FIRST SVG BK PERKASIE	PERKASIE	PA	B+	B+	A-	901.3	8.58	2.5	0.2	31.9	43.3	10.0	11.6	24.3
FIRST SVGS BK	DANVILLE	IL	B	B	B	36.3	-6.57	0.0	1.7	52.9	38.1	10.0	17.5	47.0
FIRST SVGS BK	WOODBRIDGE	NJ	B+	B+	B+	2,167.2	-3.95	0.3	0.1	36.0	36.5	8.6	10.1	20.7
FIRST SVGS BK	BERESFORD	SD	D+	D+	D+	371.4	4.64	7.0	4.6	6.4	12.7	4.0	7.8	10.5
FIRST SVGS BK FSB	MANHATTAN	KS	D-	D-	E-	119.9	-5.21	9.1	2.3	36.2	12.0	4.7	6.7	11.6
FIRST SVGS BK FSB	THREE RIVERS	MI	A-	A-	A-	116.2	-0.36	4.2	4.9	43.3	18.6	10.0	11.0	21.6
FIRST SVGS BK HEGEWISCH	CHICAGO	IL	B-	B-	B	421.2	1.14	0.0	0.2	28.4	48.4	7.2	9.1	33.0
FIRST SVGS BK RENTON	RENTON	WA	A-	A-	A	730.3	3.53	0.0	0.0	30.5	47.3	9.7	10.8	24.9
FIRST T&SB	CORALVILLE	IA	C+	B-	C+	39.9	16.79	6.0	2.3	8.2	48.6	10.0	11.8	19.9
FIRST T&SB	MARCUS	IA	C+	C+	C	36.4	-3.91	7.2	9.2	9.4	27.5	8.4	9.9	15.0
FIRST T&SB	MOVILLE	IA	B-	B-	B	71.2	0.60	1.9	2.2	5.3	49.0	10.0	21.2	42.8
FIRST T&SB	WHEATLAND	IA	D+	D+	D	69.6	2.19	11.1	5.9	9.4	14.2	5.5	8.0	11.4
FIRST T&SB	WATSEKA	IL	B+	B+	B+	130.0	5.55	9.6	5.1	8.4	36.0	7.2	9.1	15.5
FIRST T&SB OF ALBANY IL	ALBANY	IL	A-	A-	A-	58.6	-3.92	3.3	5.5	15.9	47.6	10.0	17.3	31.8
FIRST T&SB ONEIDA TN	ONEIDA	TN	B-	B-	C+	103.0	-2.48	12.6	12.3	28.3	23.7	5.4	7.4	13.3
FIRST TC	DENVER	CO	B-	B-	B	1,761.7	14.02	0.0	0.0	0.0	86.4	5.1	7.1	22.0
FIRST TENNESSEE BK NA	MEMPHIS	TN	B	B	B	27,034.9	-1.58	11.6	1.8	21.5	8.3	5.1	7.1	12.1
▼ FIRST TEXAS BK	BELTON	TX	A-	A	A	57.9	10.25	8.4	8.6	21.5	36.9	7.5	9.3	17.7
FIRST TEXAS BK	GEORGETOWN	TX	A-	A-	A-	235.2	4.92	5.5	2.3	5.2	51.4	6.2	8.2	16.0
FIRST TEXAS BK	KILLEEN	TX	A	A	A	146.9	-3.98	3.8	3.8	10.4	47.9	10.0	11.3	22.5
FIRST TEXAS BK	LAMPASAS	TX	A	A	A	94.3	4.73	6.3	4.6	9.2	54.6	10.0	12.9	30.4
FIRST TEXAS BK	ROUND ROCK	TX	A-	A-	A-	142.7	3.32	8.7	4.7	7.3	34.6	6.0	8.0	14.0
FIRST TEXOMA BK	SHERMAN	TX	B-	B-	B-	37.4	23.44	38.9	6.0	9.5	3.4	3.1	8.5	10.0
FIRST TIER B&T	SALAMANCA	NY	C-	C-	C+	259.8	19.15	7.9	6.5	11.3	46.9	3.7	5.7	11.7
FIRST TR BK	CHARLOTTE	NC	C+	C+	C+	222.5	12.10	13.4	0.8	4.3	17.9	4.2	7.8	10.6
▲ FIRST TR BK IL	KANKAKEE	IL	C+	C	C	116.8	1.15	19.5	1.6	7.7	40.0	6.0	8.1	14.0
FIRST TRADE UNION BK	BOSTON	MA	B-	B-	C+	367.5	19.30	4.9	0.4	17.0	24.5	5.1	7.1	12.2
FIRST TRI-COUNTY BK	SWANTON	NE	D-	E+	E+	33.6	7.25	5.3	10.4	17.7	7.9	4.4	7.1	10.7
FIRST TRUST BK FOR SVGS	BRENTWOOD	TN	C+	C+	C+	218.8	-8.40	1.3	0.6	45.6	8.6	7.1	9.2	12.6
▲ FIRST TUSKEGEE BK	TUSKEGEE	AL	E+	E-	D	62.3	-11.24	7.0	5.0	10.9	29.0	5.3	7.3	12.3
▼ FIRST UNION DIRECT BK NA	AUGUSTA	GA	C	B-	B	6,118.5	39.64	0.0	0.0	0.0	0.0	10.0	18.2	90.1
▲ FIRST UNITED B&T	OAKLAND	MD	B-	B-	B+	1,154.0	15.67	14.7	16.3	19.1	17.4	4.7	7.8	10.8
▲ FIRST UNITED B&TC	DURANT	OK	B+	B-	C+	1,013.4	10.12	19.4	9.0	9.9	10.5	5.7	9.1	11.6
▲ FIRST UNITED BK	SAN DIEGO	CA	C+	C	C	156.2	-0.89	0.7	0.0	1.8	2.9	5.4	7.4	12.8
▼ FIRST UNITED BK	ENGLEWOOD	CO	C+	B-	B+	165.8	14.91	8.0	0.5	3.5	0.1	6.7	11.2	12.3
▲ FIRST UNITED BK	CRETE	IL	C+	C	C-	347.0	12.71	8.5	2.4	19.5	19.1	6.4	8.8	12.0
FIRST UNITED BK	MADISONVILLE	KY	C-	D+	D+	115.2	23.32	14.4	7.8	37.3	13.0	5.9	7.9	12.5
FIRST UNITED BK	FARMERVILLE	LA	C+	B-	B+	107.4	-3.32	4.9	32.0	6.3	36.1	10.0	12.2	22.2
FIRST UNITED BK	PARK RIVER	ND	C	C	C	93.5	0.98	12.4	8.0	6.6	17.0	4.7	7.9	10.8
▲ FIRST UNITED BK	DIMMITT	TX	C+	C	C	341.2	24.47	11.8	7.2	5.5	23.5	4.8	7.5	10.9
FIRST UNITED BK NA	MIDDLETOWN	IN	C+	C+	B-	84.7	3.65	17.2	16.7	20.0	17.0	5.0	7.6	11.0
FIRST UNITED NB	FRYBURG	PA	B-	B-	B-	164.7	0.99	5.2	14.7	38.8	19.6	6.1	8.1	14.8
FIRST UNITED SECURITY	THOMASVILLE	AL	B+	B+	B-	578.3	7.09	6.1	17.0	18.1	23.4	10.0	12.2	18.3
FIRST UTAH BK	SALT LAKE CITY	UT	C-	D+	C	139.2	3.30	13.5	2.6	3.5	6.8	3.1	7.9	10.0
▼ FIRST VALLEY BK	SEELEY LAKE	MT	B-	B	C+	34.6	12.36	26.1	5.0	18.6	2.8	5.3	8.2	11.3
▲ FIRST VICTORIA NB	VICTORIA	TX	C+	C+	B	823.9	18.56	17.4	6.7	10.4	19.5	5.6	7.9	11.5
▲ FIRST VOLUNTEER BK OF TN	CHATTANOOGA	TN	B	B	B	441.6	-4.09	8.1	4.2	19.9	12.0	6.8	8.8	12.6
FIRST WASHINGTON ST BK	WINDSOR	NJ	C+	C+	C	474.4	13.90	1.0	0.8	8.3	44.0	5.6	7.6	13.5
FIRST WESTERN B&T	MINOT	ND	B	B	B	354.1	23.68	11.9	4.9	2.9	46.3	6.2	8.2	15.0
▼ FIRST WESTERN BK	BOONEVILLE	AR	C+	B-	B-	247.3	9.26	3.3	6.1	21.2	24.1	5.4	7.4	12.1
▼ FIRST WESTERN BK	STURGIS	SD	B+	A-	A-	317.8	8.55	9.7	8.4	8.5	15.2	7.6	9.6	13.0
▼ FIRST WESTERN BK CUSTER	CUSTER	SD	B+	A-	A-	98.0	6.97	10.9	3.8	10.8	24.7	7.6	9.4	13.9
▼ FIRST WESTERN BK WALL	WALL	SD	B+	A-	A-	307.5	127.61	16.1	4.7	3.3	13.8	6.5	9.7	12.1
FIRST WESTERN FSB	RAPID CITY	SD	B-	B	B+	23.7	-5.17	16.6	1.5	28.1	0.0	10.0	16.8	21.9
FIRST WESTERN TR BK	DENVER	CO	D	NR	NR	19.2	N/A	25.1	0.1	4.4	0.0	10.0	27.7	47.2
FIRST WESTROADS BK	OMAHA	NE	B-	B-	B-	186.9	2.32	12.3	1.1	5.4	20.8	6.2	8.3	11.9
FIRST WHITNEY B&T	ATLANTIC	IA	A-	A-	A-	96.8	2.50	9.7	2.3	6.2	36.5	7.7	10.3	13.1
▲ FIRST, A NATL BANKING ASSN	HATTIESBURG	MS	B	B-	C+	180.3	63.63	9.0	4.8	24.9	10.9	7.9	9.9	13.3
FIRST-CITIZENS B&TC	RALEIGH	NC	B	B	B	11,413.4	2.25	7.9	11.7	7.0	16.8	5.7	7.7	11.6
▼ FIRST-CITIZENS BK NA	ROANOKE	VA	B	B+	B+	220.0	5.63	0.0	89.6	0.0	0.0	10.0	25.0	27.9
FIRST-KNOX NB	MT VERNON	OH	B-	B-	B-	744.8	-0.85	7.6	11.7	22.8	30.3	4.5	6.5	13.6
FIRST-LOCKHART NB	LOCKHART	TX	A-	A-	B+	106.2	-1.75	15.9	5.7	13.1	19.9	9.8	10.9	15.7
FIRST-NICHOLS NB OF	KENEDY	TX	C	C-	D+	36.4	-7.30	16.1	4.8	4.3	42.7	7.5	9.3	17.8
FIRSTBANK	EVERGREEN	CO	B-	B-	B-	94.6	9.44	0.1	0.5	12.3	75.5	4.0	6.0	17.7

Asset Quality Index	Non-Performing Loans as a % of Total Loans	Non-Performing Loans as a % of Capital	Net Charge-offs Avg Loans	Profitability Index	Net Income ($Mil)	Return on Assets (R.O.A.)	Return on Equity (R.O.E.)	Net Interest Spread	Overhead Efficiency Ratio	Liquidity Index	Liquidity Ratio	Hot Money Ratio	Stability Index
9.8	0.39	1.6	0.00	4.8	4.3	0.97	7.98	2.48	57.9	4.2	37.1	13.2	8.1
9.4	0.40	1.2	0.05	4.8	0.2	0.80	4.51	3.17	60.5	8.3	1,368.5	11.0	6.0
9.7	0.05	0.3	0.00	5.9	11.4	1.05	10.44	2.83	48.2	5.8	32.2	5.7	6.3
1.7	2.01	18.1	0.78	8.1	3.2	1.71	22.61	5.19	57.9	0.7	9.7	37.1	4.7
2.5	1.83	18.9	0.03	3.3	0.4	0.70	10.52	3.74	80.6	2.5	18.0	16.9	0.7
6.2	0.39	2.3	0.05	3.7	0.3	0.46	3.60	3.57	82.7	2.9	28.9	16.6	7.3
9.9	0.22	0.7	0.00	3.6	0.9	0.41	4.28	2.41	73.0	8.0	228.9	12.5	5.3
9.8	0.15	0.7	0.00	6.9	4.7	1.29	12.15	2.50	19.2	4.8	155.1	39.7	7.3
8.8	0.59	2.1	0.03	2.8	0.1	0.25	2.03	3.39	86.7	4.6	29.0	7.8	6.1
8.0	0.10	0.6	0.00	4.7	0.1	0.73	7.52	4.23	76.2	4.1	22.7	9.3	4.6
7.8	3.28	4.2	0.01	3.0	0.2	0.43	1.95	3.01	75.1	9.0	243.3	6.9	5.3
1.4	1.99	15.5	0.16	4.8	0.4	1.22	13.89	4.12	64.8	4.7	33.9	9.2	4.0
7.1	0.28	1.6	0.07	6.5	0.7	1.16	13.17	3.85	53.8	4.4	42.6	13.5	5.4
8.8	0.83	2.2	0.00	8.2	0.6	1.89	10.50	3.80	48.5	5.8	56.5	8.6	8.9
4.6	0.66	5.0	0.61	6.6	0.8	1.43	19.25	4.09	51.3	4.5	98.3	26.2	4.7
8.6	0.00	0.0	0.00	4.2	5.3	0.63	6.68	4.01	83.4	9.2	141.5	0.0	4.0
6.4	0.41	3.4	0.25	9.8	245.2	1.88	24.05	3.79	65.4	1.3	21.6	33.1	7.8
8.4	0.12	0.7	0.11	8.0	0.4	1.21	12.45	5.39	68.2	4.5	17.3	6.0	7.4
8.7	0.53	2.5	0.09	10.0	2.1	1.75	21.87	5.02	46.0	5.8	39.7	4.6	6.8
9.4	0.04	0.2	0.11	9.8	1.1	1.54	13.53	4.70	63.1	4.5	26.5	7.2	8.3
9.4	0.04	0.1	0.04	8.8	0.6	1.33	10.26	4.51	58.3	5.9	45.5	5.1	8.0
7.5	0.32	1.8	0.17	7.0	0.7	0.95	11.56	4.90	73.0	5.1	33.4	6.2	6.3
7.4	0.00	0.0	0.04	3.3	0.1	0.61	6.92	4.19	84.3	1.8	38.2	51.7	5.1
5.7	0.76	5.5	0.22	6.4	1.2	0.98	16.54	3.85	65.0	6.2	72.7	10.5	3.3
7.5	0.00	0.0	0.04	6.0	1.1	1.03	14.04	3.80	50.8	2.0	17.1	19.3	4.6
4.3	1.92	12.0	0.07	3.9	0.4	0.73	9.29	3.03	66.9	3.0	8.9	13.5	4.0
8.2	0.15	1.3	0.01	5.0	1.4	0.79	10.77	3.46	63.4	2.3	51.2	71.5	4.0
2.9	1.41	12.2	0.04	5.5	0.2	1.27	15.69	4.20	61.9	5.8	56.0	8.2	1.7
3.4	0.96	8.2	0.01	4.1	0.3	0.29	3.15	3.14	93.3	0.7	3.5	32.3	5.0
6.6	0.06	0.6	0.68	3.3	0.3	0.85	13.48	4.52	83.2	2.7	34.6	19.9	0.0
8.3	0.00	0.0	-0.02	1.3	-4.4	-0.14	-0.74	-0.48	-8.4	10.0	1,535.8	0.0	7.9
5.5	0.63	5.0	0.11	6.1	6.6	1.16	13.46	3.73	66.5	2.1	6.0	18.0	7.7
5.5	0.60	4.1	0.08	9.5	12.3	2.47	22.72	4.96	49.2	2.4	18.5	17.8	9.3
7.4	0.00	0.0	0.00	5.2	0.8	1.02	14.08	3.47	49.7	5.5	207.6	37.1	3.1
3.3	1.14	8.1	0.00	6.2	0.7	0.92	8.29	7.22	72.8	3.7	7.8	9.6	7.8
3.6	1.79	13.6	-0.01	6.4	1.7	1.01	12.16	3.64	65.5	3.8	32.8	13.6	3.9
5.6	0.33	2.9	0.10	5.1	0.5	0.94	12.94	4.30	61.7	2.6	22.9	17.0	2.5
3.9	2.51	8.6	0.21	2.7	0.2	0.43	3.47	2.72	87.5	4.8	101.2	22.6	6.8
4.5	0.63	5.5	-0.03	5.0	0.5	1.14	14.50	4.23	68.8	4.0	28.1	11.2	3.9
3.6	1.47	11.8	0.04	5.9	2.2	1.36	16.83	4.45	69.1	1.4	12.3	24.5	4.3
3.2	1.00	8.8	0.64	9.3	0.6	1.47	18.50	4.91	53.2	3.1	30.6	16.6	6.2
5.4	0.48	3.9	0.06	6.3	0.9	1.14	13.20	4.19	59.3	5.0	38.8	9.3	5.4
4.5	2.23	10.8	0.67	10.0	6.7	2.34	18.58	7.47	48.8	3.2	46.3	21.4	8.5
5.3	0.20	1.7	0.22	7.7	0.9	1.34	17.68	6.65	67.5	3.5	26.9	13.1	1.8
8.2	0.01	0.1	0.02	9.7	0.4	2.34	31.36	4.14	43.5	4.5	64.7	16.6	5.8
3.9	0.47	3.4	0.46	7.2	5.0	1.23	12.73	4.05	60.6	2.8	28.4	17.3	5.6
5.1	0.87	6.4	0.26	6.9	2.2	0.99	10.80	5.23	71.4	3.3	23.9	13.6	5.3
9.3	0.01	0.1	-0.01	5.6	2.7	1.14	15.42	3.83	64.4	6.3	46.2	3.6	3.8
6.3	0.57	2.4	0.32	6.4	1.9	1.13	11.20	4.03	57.9	4.9	88.4	18.9	5.2
4.8	0.89	7.0	0.01	4.0	0.8	0.63	8.28	4.08	75.4	1.0	14.1	31.0	4.1
5.4	0.94	6.8	0.01	9.0	3.3	2.13	21.66	4.50	51.6	3.6	37.3	15.9	7.7
4.8	1.46	9.2	0.14	8.1	0.9	1.99	20.52	4.26	52.8	4.3	41.3	13.8	7.7
6.2	0.47	3.5	0.10	8.3	2.3	1.85	18.21	5.15	55.0	2.0	17.9	19.5	7.2
4.9	1.06	5.5	-0.01	10.0	0.3	2.53	15.39	6.91	59.3	1.2	6.2	25.6	7.2
9.4	0.00	0.0	0.00	0.0	-2.1	-33.94	-66.47	0.48	4,265.3	8.7	370.8	8.8	0.0
4.6	0.78	6.0	0.16	10.0	1.7	1.85	23.02	4.61	41.5	5.3	38.0	7.3	6.6
8.3	0.31	1.7	-0.01	9.4	1.1	2.21	20.92	4.02	42.2	3.7	16.9	10.7	8.6
6.3	0.37	2.8	0.17	5.3	0.6	0.82	8.24	5.42	72.8	1.9	22.5	21.1	4.6
7.6	0.30	2.3	0.30	4.7	40.2	0.71	8.61	3.48	73.3	7.3	108.1	9.9	6.8
5.5	0.40	1.1	3.14	10.0	2.8	2.49	10.41	4.98	70.3	0.3	15.6	98.6	8.2
4.3	1.35	12.7	0.36	10.0	6.9	1.87	35.08	4.66	42.2	3.6	11.8	10.5	5.6
7.9	0.20	1.2	0.09	6.7	0.7	1.29	12.16	4.45	67.5	2.6	14.7	15.8	6.8
8.6	0.00	0.0	0.46	3.9	0.2	1.02	11.00	3.90	79.8	4.7	22.8	5.2	3.5
10.0	0.24	0.8	-0.10	8.5	0.7	1.55	22.69	3.93	53.7	4.7	7.5	2.9	4.9

Name	City	State	Weiss Safety Rating	2003 Weiss Safety Rating	2002 Weiss Safety Rating	Total Assets ($Mil)	One Year Asset Growth	Commercial Loans	Consumer Loans	Home Mortgages	Securities	Capitalization Index	Leverage Ratio	Risk-based Capital Ratio
FIRSTBANK	LITTLETON	CO	B-	B-	B-	243.4	20.17	1.1	0.5	10.7	73.1	3.8	5.8	16.4
FIRSTBANK	MT PLEASANT	MI	B+	B+	B+	172.2	5.99	13.2	10.1	18.0	6.8	6.8	9.5	12.3
FIRSTBANK	ANTLERS	OK	B+	B+	B	100.1	-3.44	14.6	21.2	25.2	9.0	7.0	9.0	14.4
▲ FIRSTBANK ADAMS COUNTY	THORNTON	CO	B	B-	B-	110.2	7.59	0.1	0.6	14.7	72.1	4.9	6.9	19.9
FIRSTBANK ALMA	ALMA	MI	B+	B+	B+	237.8	-0.79	14.7	8.3	17.8	13.4	6.2	8.2	12.1
FIRSTBANK ARVADA	ARVADA	CO	B-	B-	B-	254.1	6.12	0.5	0.5	12.5	76.8	4.0	6.0	18.6
▲ FIRSTBANK BRECKENRIDGE	BRECKENRIDGE	CO	B	B-	B-	108.5	16.30	0.1	0.3	31.7	44.6	5.2	7.2	14.9
▼ FIRSTBANK CHERRY CREEK	DENVER	CO	B-	B	B	307.8	15.02	0.3	0.5	16.5	66.2	3.8	5.8	16.0
▼ FIRSTBANK DENVER	DENVER	CO	B-	B	B	277.5	23.43	1.1	0.6	18.4	66.1	3.9	5.8	13.8
FIRSTBANK EL PASO COUNTY	COLORADO SPRINGS	CO	B-	B-	B-	84.0	5.88	0.7	0.4	17.2	66.1	5.2	7.2	19.3
▲ FIRSTBANK LAKEVIEW	LAKEVIEW	MI	A-	B+	B	114.4	-6.20	10.2	2.7	26.2	9.0	7.4	9.3	12.9
FIRSTBANK NORTH	WESTMINSTER	CO	B-	B-	B-	288.9	7.86	0.5	0.5	12.8	76.7	4.1	6.1	18.3
FIRSTBANK NORTHERN CO	FORT COLLINS	CO	B-	B-	B-	172.1	14.82	0.4	0.7	43.0	34.3	4.0	6.0	12.9
FIRSTBANK NORTHWEST	CLARKSTON	WA	C+	C+	B-	730.9	112.59	10.1	5.8	21.1	16.2	3.9	6.7	10.5
FIRSTBANK OF ARAPAHOE	CENTENNIAL	CO	B-	B-	B-	282.0	0.13	0.9	0.6	15.3	73.1	4.4	6.4	18.6
FIRSTBANK OF AURORA	AURORA	CO	B-	B-	B-	332.6	2.51	0.6	0.5	11.7	76.8	4.1	6.1	19.1
▼ FIRSTBANK OF AVON	AVON	CO	B-	B	B	296.5	14.40	1.6	0.8	34.0	46.7	4.3	6.3	14.5
FIRSTBANK OF BOULDER	BOULDER	CO	B-	B-	B-	418.6	11.68	0.7	0.5	13.5	76.1	3.8	5.8	17.9
FIRSTBANK OF COLORADO	LAKEWOOD	CO	B	B	B-	844.5	-8.51	1.3	3.5	11.9	58.0	4.9	7.0	19.2
FIRSTBANK OF COLORADO	COLORADO SPRINGS	CO	B-	B-	B-	123.5	10.54	0.1	0.3	14.1	73.0	3.3	5.3	14.9
FIRSTBANK OF DOUGLAS	CASTLE ROCK	CO	B-	B-	B-	265.8	6.01	0.2	0.4	14.0	75.5	4.3	6.3	20.2
FIRSTBANK OF GREELEY	GREELEY	CO	B-	B-	B-	43.0	25.72	0.5	0.5	34.6	48.3	5.8	7.8	18.0
FIRSTBANK OF LAKEWOOD	LAKEWOOD	CO	B-	B-	B-	270.3	5.72	1.2	0.5	10.9	77.0	4.2	6.2	18.3
FIRSTBANK OF LITTLETON	LITTLETON	CO	B-	B-	B-	323.8	12.76	0.9	0.5	14.3	70.2	3.8	5.8	16.2
FIRSTBANK OF LONGMONT	LONGMONT	CO	B-	B-	B-	314.4	18.04	0.7	0.6	18.6	58.8	4.1	6.1	15.6
FIRSTBANK OF PARKER	PARKER	CO	B-	B-	B-	97.8	13.95	0.2	0.3	11.6	75.3	3.2	5.2	16.6
FIRSTBANK OF	SILVERTHORNE	CO	B-	B-	B-	142.4	14.95	0.5	0.7	31.9	44.0	4.2	6.2	13.8
FIRSTBANK OF SOUTH	LITTLETON	CO	B-	B-	B-	487.1	12.04	0.4	0.7	14.4	68.5	3.9	5.9	17.7
FIRSTBANK OF TECH CENTER	GREENWOOD VLG	CO	B-	B-	B-	383.8	7.38	1.1	0.3	10.5	69.2	3.8	5.8	16.2
FIRSTBANK OF VAIL	VAIL	CO	B	B	B	249.7	14.31	2.9	1.0	43.2	35.0	5.1	7.1	15.0
FIRSTBANK OF WHEAT RIDGE	WHEAT RIDGE	CO	B-	B-	B-	279.9	7.63	0.5	0.4	12.8	71.9	4.1	6.1	17.5
FIRSTBANK PR	SAN JUAN	PR	C+	C+	C	14,299.2	44.60	11.7	8.5	24.0	40.9	5.7	7.7	14.1
FIRSTBANK ST JOHNS	ST JOHNS	MI	B+	B+	B	50.0	17.75	17.4	9.0	12.8	6.5	5.3	9.3	11.3
▲ FIRSTBANK SW NA	AMARILLO	TX	A-	B+	B+	414.0	1.56	16.0	6.4	7.8	25.5	9.2	10.5	16.0
FIRSTBANK WEST BRANCH	W BRANCH	MI	B+	B+	B	205.9	7.40	8.1	7.3	31.0	4.4	5.9	8.2	11.7
FIRSTCAPITAL BK SSB	CORPUS CHRISTI	TX	C-	C-	C-	781.8	4.08	16.8	3.6	9.7	20.0	5.1	8.1	11.0
FIRSTCITY BK	STOCKBRIDGE	GA	C-	C-	D	91.2	70.83	3.1	3.5	17.3	3.2	3.4	8.5	10.2
FIRSTIER BK	LOUISVILLE	CO	D	D	NR	42.4	N/A	12.6	0.3	13.1	0.0	10.0	11.3	18.5
▲ FIRSTIER BK	KIMBALL	NE	C+	D+	D+	84.9	0.90	10.3	3.6	5.9	7.8	7.3	10.1	12.8
FIRSTMERIT BK NA	AKRON	OH	C+	C+	C+	10,355.6	-2.71	13.3	15.7	9.2	27.6	5.5	7.5	12.9
FIRSTRUST SVGS BK	CONSHOHOCKEN	PA	B-	B-	B-	1,979.4	0.89	21.2	9.0	14.3	15.1	7.4	9.3	13.9
▲ FIRSTSERVICE BK	CRESTWOOD	MO	C+	C	D	83.3	36.12	15.5	0.9	14.2	4.7	8.7	11.8	13.9
FISHER NB	FISHER	IL	B+	B	B	44.4	4.87	5.4	5.9	26.0	20.1	10.0	12.0	18.9
FITCHBURG SVGS BK FSB	FITCHBURG	MA	B+	A-	A-	279.4	3.69	3.3	1.1	36.6	33.8	10.0	11.7	20.3
FIVE POINTS BK	GRAND ISLAND	NE	B+	B+	B+	362.0	4.58	23.2	3.8	8.4	24.3	7.1	9.1	13.0
▼ FIVE POINTS BK OF HASTINGS	HASTINGS	NE	B	B+	NR	90.3	21.97	13.7	3.9	14.2	16.9	6.7	8.7	12.3
FIVE STAR BK	ROCKLIN	CA	A-	A-	B	87.9	17.15	1.8	0.3	0.7	4.3	10.0	14.2	16.7
▲ FIVE STAR BK	COLORADO SPRINGS	CO	B+	B	B	198.6	-9.16	0.0	40.1	0.7	52.8	10.0	15.3	27.2
FIVE STAR BK NATOMAS	SACRAMENTO	CA	B	NR	NR	57.4	N/A	0.5	2.8	2.8	3.2	10.0	41.3	36.8
▲ FLAG BK	ATLANTA	GA	C	C-	D+	741.9	20.04	5.3	1.9	10.6	13.1	5.2	8.1	11.1
FLAGLER BK	W PALM BEACH	FL	C+	C+	C-	66.5	23.11	10.5	0.2	3.7	6.9	7.4	9.2	14.2
FLAGSHIP B&TC	WORCESTER	MA	B-	B-	B-	488.3	-2.93	12.1	1.0	5.2	37.4	4.5	7.3	10.8
▲ FLAGSHIP NB	BRADENTON	FL	D	D-	D	113.9	28.97	12.2	6.4	21.2	17.4	2.2	6.2	9.2
FLAGSTAR BK FSB	TROY	MI	B-	C+	C	11,945.6	17.66	2.1	0.2	80.9	0.2	4.4	6.4	11.7
FLANAGAN ST BK	FLANAGAN	IL	B-	B-	B	82.9	2.92	9.1	3.0	18.6	22.8	7.9	9.6	14.3
▲ FLATBUSH FS&LA	NEW YORK CITY	NY	C-	D	C-	140.9	0.65	0.7	0.1	56.5	21.3	9.2	10.4	24.6
FLATHEAD BK OF BIGFORK	BIGFORK	MT	A-	B+	B+	159.3	13.72	12.8	4.4	13.9	27.3	7.5	9.3	14.2
▲ FLATIRONS BK	BOULDER	CO	B-	C	D	37.7	-7.75	12.8	0.9	16.7	0.0	10.0	21.6	24.9
FLEET BK RI NA	PROVIDENCE	RI	B-	B-	B-	8,567.4	37.91	0.0	74.8	0.0	0.1	10.0	23.0	23.8
FLEET ME NA	S PORTLAND	ME	B-	C+	C+	49.6	191.87	0.0	0.0	0.0	0.0	10.0	55.1	168.1
FLEET NB	PROVIDENCE	RI	B-	C+	C+	213,732.1	11.88	10.7	4.3	17.3	9.3	5.9	7.9	11.8
FLINT CREEK VALLEY BK	PHILIPSBURG	MT	C-	C-	C	43.2	9.68	27.2	6.8	11.9	9.5	7.6	9.4	13.7
▼ FLINT HILLS BK OF ESKRIDGE	ESKRIDGE	KS	C-	C	C-	40.2	20.13	8.5	6.2	18.6	37.0	6.0	8.0	15.4
▼ FLORA B&TC	FLORA	IL	E	D	E+	74.9	2.22	9.3	14.0	26.7	9.4	4.6	6.6	10.9

Asset Quality Index	Non-Performing Loans as a % of Total Loans	as a % of Capital	Net Charge-offs Avg Loans	Profitability Index	Net Income ($Mil)	Return on Assets (R.O.A.)	Return on Equity (R.O.E.)	Net Interest Spread	Overhead Efficiency Ratio	Liquidity Index	Liquidity Ratio	Hot Money Ratio	Stability Index
9.0	0.01	0.0	-0.08	7.4	2.1	1.76	27.73	4.11	51.8	4.6	10.3	4.0	4.3
5.7	0.74	5.8	0.05	9.6	1.3	1.48	15.58	4.51	56.3	3.9	13.4	9.1	7.3
7.1	0.08	0.5	0.40	10.0	1.6	2.97	31.27	6.56	56.3	3.1	40.4	19.6	6.6
10.0	0.00	0.0	0.17	7.8	0.9	1.66	22.15	4.67	65.8	4.1	11.2	7.4	5.7
7.8	0.06	0.5	0.22	9.6	2.0	1.66	18.79	4.31	53.4	4.8	30.3	6.8	7.4
10.0	0.26	0.7	0.06	9.8	2.3	1.88	27.85	4.24	48.3	4.8	20.3	3.8	6.0
9.7	0.01	0.1	0.04	10.0	1.1	2.15	27.84	5.05	45.9	4.6	8.6	3.5	6.3
8.8	0.60	2.4	0.09	8.1	2.1	1.39	22.36	3.60	52.4	4.6	19.3	5.5	5.6
10.0	0.15	0.9	0.06	9.7	2.3	1.75	27.33	4.15	50.5	5.1	12.1	1.0	5.6
10.0	0.00	0.0	0.07	4.7	0.4	1.02	13.14	4.02	78.8	4.8	11.3	2.7	5.1
8.1	0.00	0.0	0.00	7.3	0.7	1.22	12.04	4.09	63.7	4.6	24.7	5.8	7.2
10.0	0.00	0.0	0.16	9.6	2.4	1.74	25.43	4.14	56.5	4.9	15.7	3.1	5.9
8.6	0.50	4.1	0.02	9.3	1.3	1.58	24.46	4.46	62.2	4.9	16.5	2.9	5.6
5.3	0.34	2.3	0.22	4.9	3.3	0.92	9.92	4.28	69.7	2.8	15.5	15.2	5.6
9.6	0.37	1.3	0.02	9.6	2.5	1.81	26.02	4.10	49.9	5.1	21.8	2.5	6.0
10.0	0.06	0.2	0.15	9.8	3.3	1.97	29.57	4.48	55.4	4.7	11.2	3.3	5.7
9.7	0.02	0.1	0.03	10.0	2.8	1.94	27.69	4.69	48.8	4.5	11.9	5.3	5.9
10.0	0.15	0.5	0.04	10.0	4.2	2.03	30.23	4.06	42.6	4.9	12.5	2.5	5.8
9.7	0.22	0.7	0.27	9.0	6.6	1.53	21.45	3.42	50.3	6.9	55.7	2.3	5.7
10.0	0.02	0.1	0.12	2.1	0.2	0.36	6.35	3.34	96.9	4.9	16.6	3.1	4.2
9.6	0.00	0.0	0.04	9.8	2.4	1.85	21.41	3.99	43.6	4.6	20.7	5.2	6.7
8.5	0.11	0.6	0.07	6.8	0.2	1.01	11.97	4.52	79.4	4.3	10.7	6.0	5.7
10.0	0.00	0.0	0.10	9.8	2.6	1.96	28.83	4.12	46.9	4.9	23.9	4.1	5.9
10.0	0.16	0.6	0.02	8.2	2.4	1.51	23.50	4.06	58.4	4.7	12.1	3.8	5.7
10.0	0.00	0.0	0.09	9.7	2.6	1.79	27.11	4.16	49.5	5.5	32.8	3.5	5.7
10.0	0.02	0.1	0.14	5.0	0.5	1.03	17.16	3.62	69.9	4.8	13.5	2.8	4.4
9.6	0.09	0.7	0.03	9.6	1.1	1.61	24.03	4.27	53.2	4.8	10.9	2.6	5.9
10.0	0.05	0.2	0.07	9.8	4.6	1.94	29.93	4.01	44.5	5.5	31.5	2.9	5.7
10.0	0.00	0.0	0.04	10.0	3.7	1.94	30.86	4.22	36.9	4.9	18.3	2.8	5.8
9.8	0.01	0.1	0.01	10.0	2.4	1.88	25.14	4.72	49.4	4.8	7.3	2.2	6.5
10.0	0.00	0.0	0.06	9.8	2.8	2.02	29.99	3.98	38.7	4.5	21.6	6.5	6.0
4.9	1.32	8.6	0.47	5.3	75.3	1.13	14.98	2.84	42.0	0.6	12.0	65.9	4.8
5.3	0.21	1.7	0.08	5.5	0.2	0.91	9.85	4.66	72.1	2.4	10.8	16.7	5.4
6.0	0.63	3.3	0.00	6.1	2.9	1.41	13.22	3.97	68.2	7.6	315.8	14.5	7.0
6.3	0.32	3.0	0.02	9.8	1.6	1.59	18.57	4.75	63.6	3.8	12.7	9.6	7.2
2.3	1.99	12.1	0.16	3.6	2.1	0.55	5.23	3.80	83.3	6.4	96.1	12.7	5.4
5.1	0.32	3.1	-0.02	8.1	0.9	2.36	29.48	5.78	53.4	6.2	140.0	16.5	3.5
9.0	0.00	0.0	0.00	0.0	-0.3	-1.73	-12.41	3.32	133.5	6.4	240.6	22.3	0.0
5.1	0.44	2.8	0.56	5.4	0.9	1.99	18.30	4.67	44.6	4.5	59.8	16.0	3.8
4.2	0.89	6.7	1.37	5.5	42.3	0.81	10.80	3.74	58.9	2.9	12.7	14.6	5.6
5.7	0.65	3.7	0.21	3.6	6.7	0.67	5.62	4.49	80.5	4.9	41.9	13.5	9.0
7.4	0.00	0.0	0.00	3.9	0.4	0.94	7.84	3.55	47.7	3.4	55.5	21.9	2.3
8.3	0.46	2.4	0.10	9.7	0.5	2.46	20.67	4.98	49.2	3.4	42.7	18.7	6.1
8.7	0.21	1.0	0.06	4.2	0.6	0.40	3.41	3.47	83.7	1.6	22.2	25.5	7.0
7.9	0.08	0.6	0.03	6.6	2.4	1.32	14.48	3.56	63.6	3.4	20.7	12.6	6.6
8.1	0.15	1.2	0.00	3.1	0.2	0.33	3.83	3.19	72.6	3.9	33.6	13.4	5.5
7.4	0.03	0.2	0.02	7.9	1.1	1.90	16.83	3.77	41.9	1.6	34.5	37.0	7.8
6.0	1.12	2.6	3.89	5.8	1.2	1.14	7.55	4.55	71.6	8.4	195.8	10.1	5.9
8.9	0.00	0.0	0.00	0.0	-0.5	-2.99	-8.00	1.89	192.0	9.0	1,381.8	7.0	3.8
3.5	0.63	4.5	0.11	4.3	4.1	1.15	12.66	4.47	69.0	4.0	58.1	19.3	4.6
6.6	0.30	1.8	0.00	5.3	0.5	1.53	16.48	4.19	60.7	5.4	114.1	18.6	1.5
8.8	0.01	0.1	-0.01	7.7	3.1	1.27	16.61	4.34	61.4	6.5	61.0	6.8	5.8
4.9	0.46	5.0	0.29	3.0	0.4	0.69	10.97	3.37	69.7	2.8	41.4	23.5	3.4
5.1	0.55	7.5	0.02	7.9	82.0	1.42	20.94	2.39	47.2	0.3	3.3	73.1	6.1
3.7	2.23	15.4	0.38	6.2	0.6	1.54	15.80	3.82	61.7	3.8	10.5	9.7	5.5
9.5	0.12	0.8	0.01	2.4	0.1	0.10	0.96	3.61	95.3	2.5	29.8	19.3	3.3
7.3	0.16	0.8	0.15	10.0	2.1	2.65	24.23	5.73	52.3	4.1	11.0	7.2	7.3
5.2	1.52	6.1	0.02	6.1	0.5	2.37	11.25	6.36	53.7	2.3	38.6	29.6	1.9
2.5	2.40	5.0	6.14	7.4	28.6	0.69	2.44	7.02	38.7	5.1	3.2	0.0	8.2
10.0	0.00	0.0	0.00	9.5	1.5	9.78	18.72	0.70	24.4	8.9	131.5	0.0	5.7
4.3	1.01	2.4	0.20	5.6	700.5	0.70	4.91	2.02	53.9	8.0	99.3	4.1	7.0
3.1	2.94	22.4	0.05	4.8	0.2	0.75	8.13	5.44	78.2	4.3	16.9	7.2	3.8
5.9	1.13	7.7	0.05	7.0	0.3	1.78	21.33	3.59	53.2	3.4	29.5	14.5	2.9
2.8	1.80	16.5	1.61	2.1	-0.3	-0.93	-12.98	3.77	74.6	4.4	74.4	18.7	0.7

Name	City	State	Weiss Safety Rating	2003 Weiss Safety Rating	2002 Weiss Safety Rating	Total Assets ($Mil)	One Year Asset Growth	Commercial Loans	Consumer Loans	Home Mortgages	Securities	Capitalization Index	Leverage Ratio	Risk-based Capital Ratio
▼ FLORA SVGS BK	FLORA	IL	D+	C-	D+	27.8	8.33	6.6	7.9	49.5	12.3	7.6	9.4	16.0
▲ FLORENCE NB	FLORENCE	SC	B	B-	B-	62.6	12.38	17.7	3.7	15.6	1.9	6.8	9.8	12.3
FLORENCE SVGS BK	FLORENCE	MA	B	B	B	776.8	8.10	1.7	0.9	40.2	38.2	5.9	7.9	14.5
▼ FLORIDA BK NA	TAMPA	FL	C-	C+	C	1,027.0	12.01	15.3	1.5	12.0	0.3	2.9	7.8	9.9
▲ FLORIDA CHOICE BK	MT DORA	FL	C+	C-	C-	173.7	33.61	7.9	0.9	10.6	12.7	6.5	9.5	12.2
FLORIDA CITIZENS BK	GAINESVILLE	FL	C-	C-	D+	145.4	10.18	20.4	5.7	6.6	18.4	3.9	7.6	10.5
▲ FLORIDA COMMUNITY BK	IMMOKALEE	FL	C-	D	C	600.7	13.22	6.6	1.6	5.7	7.0	5.7	9.7	11.6
▲ FLORIDA GULF BK	FORT MYERS	FL	C	D+	D-	175.2	66.66	11.1	7.2	11.4	11.6	8.8	10.9	14.0
▲ FLORIDA PARISHES BK	HAMMOND	LA	C+	C	C	93.9	9.70	1.1	4.8	65.6	7.9	6.3	8.3	15.7
▲ FLORIDA SVGS BK	MIAMI	FL	C	D+	D+	116.9	25.89	3.4	3.5	24.3	20.9	4.4	6.7	10.7
FLORIDIAN COMMUNITY BK	DAVIE	FL	D	D	NR	27.3	90.04	31.0	0.7	7.7	5.5	10.0	23.9	33.2
FLUSHING SVGS BK FSB	NEW YORK CITY	NY	B+	B+	B+	2,012.7	9.11	0.6	0.0	21.7	25.3	5.3	7.3	13.5
FMB BK	WRIGHT CITY	MO	D-	D	D+	38.9	5.48	9.5	9.2	12.6	24.2	5.2	7.2	12.2
▼ FNB BK NA	DANVILLE	PA	B-	B	B+	286.6	-6.40	3.0	21.1	29.3	22.0	4.6	6.6	11.0
▲ FNB SALEM B&T NA	SALEM	VA	B	B-	B-	383.7	7.40	5.5	15.2	13.9	14.5	4.5	8.5	10.7
FNB SOUTHEAST	REIDSVILLE	NC	B-	B-	B-	786.1	1.48	11.2	7.4	12.8	16.2	5.9	8.4	11.7
FOOTHILL INDEPENDENT BK	GLENDORA	CA	A-	A-	B-	743.7	14.64	5.8	0.4	0.7	21.6	7.9	9.6	13.9
FOOTHILLS BK	YUMA	AZ	C+	C+	C+	99.9	18.85	7.1	1.2	8.0	3.7	5.3	8.3	11.2
▲ FOOTHILLS BK	WHEAT RIDGE	CO	C+	C	B	108.2	9.14	11.5	15.8	6.5	8.8	4.4	9.6	10.7
▼ FORD COUNTY ST BK	SPEARVILLE	KS	D-	C-	C+	46.4	133.77	5.1	1.8	1.8	7.0	0.9	4.2	14.3
FORDYCE B&TC	FORDYCE	AR	B-	B-	C+	91.0	7.80	14.7	15.3	29.4	22.2	6.4	8.4	13.9
FOREST HILL ST BK	BEL AIR	MD	A-	A-	A	392.9	9.74	8.8	14.0	17.2	15.7	6.6	8.6	16.3
FOREST PARK NB&TC	FOREST PARK	IL	C+	C+	C+	137.8	1.96	9.3	1.8	21.6	20.6	4.5	7.0	10.7
▼ FORETHOUGHT FSB	BATESVILLE	IN	B-	B+	B	89.9	69.55	0.0	0.0	0.0	92.3	5.2	7.2	37.8
▼ FORREST CITY BK NA	FORREST CITY	AR	D	D+	C-	70.0	-18.98	6.2	3.1	21.4	43.3	7.2	9.1	19.5
FORRESTON ST BK	FORRESTON	IL	C	C	C	109.8	4.13	12.7	1.0	6.1	19.0	5.7	9.5	11.5
▲ FORT DAVIS ST BK	FORT DAVIS	TX	D-	E-	E-	49.9	6.53	5.9	10.0	4.9	45.0	5.6	7.6	19.5
▲ FORT DES MOINES	DES MOINES	IA	C+	C	C	21.1	2.41	6.9	3.2	24.7	21.7	7.0	9.0	17.4
FORT GIBSON ST BK	FORT GIBSON	OK	C	C	C	51.0	4.98	7.2	15.6	10.9	32.8	5.9	7.9	12.5
FORT HOOD NB	FORT HOOD	TX	B-	B-	B-	189.0	14.66	0.0	6.9	1.4	50.1	4.4	6.4	18.9
FORT JENNINGS ST BK	FORT JENNINGS	OH	C	C-	D	94.4	0.66	10.0	6.0	27.9	7.6	5.6	7.8	11.5
FORT KNOX NB	RADCLIFF	KY	D+	D	D	41.5	9.53	0.1	0.5	46.4	22.0	4.3	6.3	16.9
FORT LEE FEDERAL SAVINGS	FORT LEE	NJ	C	C	D+	27.3	2.47	21.2	2.6	23.1	23.8	10.0	14.0	37.8
▲ FORT MADISON B&TC	FORT MADISON	IA	B	B-	C+	120.7	-5.16	10.9	4.8	33.2	30.6	7.3	9.2	18.4
FORT MORGAN ST BK	FORT MORGAN	CO	C	C-	D+	33.7	12.79	11.3	5.1	16.7	17.0	6.1	8.2	12.5
FORT RILEY NB	FORT RILEY	KS	B-	B-	B-	31.9	12.95	0.2	10.4	2.0	52.1	8.3	9.9	29.3
FORT SILL NB	FORT SILL	OK	A	A	A	257.2	14.96	0.5	10.6	7.5	64.6	10.0	12.6	37.2
▲ FORT WASHINGTON TRUST	CINCINNATI	OH	D+	D	NR	30.1	N/A	0.0	0.0	21.2	54.1	10.0	12.9	38.7
▲ FORT WORTH NB	FORT WORTH	TX	C	C-	D+	88.5	14.88	16.9	8.0	11.2	7.2	4.5	8.0	10.7
FORTRESS BK CRESCO	CRESCO	IA	B-	B-	B-	66.9	4.52	7.2	3.7	15.2	22.7	7.5	9.3	14.2
FORTRESS BK NA	HOUSTON	MN	B-	B-	B-	55.9	1.64	12.0	5.0	7.9	18.5	6.8	8.9	12.4
FORTRESS BK WESTBY	WESTBY	WI	B-	B-	B-	130.2	13.08	18.1	6.9	12.4	18.5	5.4	8.5	11.3
▼ FOSTER BANK	CHICAGO	IL	D+	C-	C-	338.4	9.96	20.7	0.6	9.4	15.2	1.5	6.2	8.5
▲ FOUNDATION BANK	CINCINNATI	OH	C-	D+	C+	98.3	62.57	1.5	1.2	36.5	0.1	4.6	6.6	12.7
▲ FOUNDATION BK	BELLEVUE	WA	C-	D+	D-	167.0	42.74	38.7	2.0	2.5	31.9	8.0	9.7	14.4
FOUNDERS BK	WORTH	IL	C+	C+	C	728.3	16.26	7.3	0.8	4.2	30.2	3.4	6.1	10.2
▲ FOUNDERS TR PERSONAL BK	GRAND RAPIDS	MI	C+	C	D+	252.3	15.20	13.0	2.5	27.1	11.1	8.2	10.0	13.5
▼ FOUNTAIN TRUST CO	COVINGTON	IN	B+	A	A	124.2	3.04	1.8	5.8	16.4	38.3	10.0	18.2	34.7
FOUR CORNERS CMNTY BK	FARMINGTON	NM	B-	B-	C	88.4	35.66	13.0	2.7	4.2	37.0	6.9	8.9	14.3
FOUR COUNTY BK	ALLENTOWN	GA	B-	B-	B	37.5	-5.66	24.7	8.6	11.3	31.4	10.0	13.3	21.3
▼ FOUR OAKS B&TC	FOUR OAKS	NC	B-	B	B	384.5	15.49	7.0	4.3	14.4	13.0	5.8	8.5	11.6
FOURTH FSB	NEW YORK CITY	NY	A	A	A	236.1	1.17	0.0	0.2	0.4	4.5	10.0	17.1	36.6
FOWLER ST BK	FOWLER	CO	C+	C+	C+	47.9	-2.12	17.2	7.5	6.0	50.0	10.0	12.3	21.2
FOWLER ST BK	FOWLER	IN	A-	A-	A	119.8	-10.04	5.0	5.4	18.0	36.0	10.0	12.8	21.5
▼ FOWLER ST BK	FOWLER	KS	B	B+	B+	40.6	5.34	4.1	5.1	5.1	45.1	10.0	16.3	33.6
FOX CHASE BK	HATBORO	PA	B-	B-	B-	886.5	6.65	0.0	0.2	33.6	39.1	5.3	7.3	15.4
FOX RIVER ST BK	BURLINGTON	WI	D	D	NR	37.5	N/A	25.3	1.0	10.5	8.0	10.0	27.4	25.0
FOX VALLEY SVGS BK	FOND DU LAC	WI	B	B+	B+	358.9	8.85	0.0	0.5	46.5	25.2	7.2	9.1	16.4
▲ FOXBORO FEDERAL SAVINGS	FOXBORO	MA	A	A-	A-	115.9	2.29	0.0	0.5	56.8	29.1	10.0	12.7	21.6
▲ FPC FINANCIAL FSB	MADISON	WI	B+	B	B	1,352.8	26.09	0.3	100.4	0.0	0.3	10.0	14.8	15.9
FRAMINGHAM CO-OP BK	FRAMINGHAM	MA	A+	A+	A+	301.4	3.50	5.1	0.7	16.9	27.4	10.0	19.9	27.1
▲ FRANCES SLOCUM B&TC NA	WABASH	IN	B-	C+	C+	174.6	-1.73	9.1	17.2	19.6	11.0	8.5	10.0	13.7
FRANKLIN B&TC	FRANKLIN	KY	C+	C	C	201.8	1.25	15.3	5.6	23.4	3.3	6.8	9.2	12.3
FRANKLIN BANK	SOUTHFIELD	MI	C+	NR	NR	531.8	N/A	11.6	0.4	8.0	8.8	2.0	4.9	9.0

Asset Quality Index	Non-Performing Loans as a % of Total Loans	Non-Performing Loans as a % of Capital	Net Charge-offs Avg Loans	Profitability Index	Net Income ($Mil)	Return on Assets (R.O.A.)	Return on Equity (R.O.E.)	Net Interest Spread	Overhead Efficiency Ratio	Liquidity Index	Liquidity Ratio	Hot Money Ratio	Stability Index
1.7	5.38	38.1	0.30	3.1	0.1	0.57	6.03	2.93	77.5	6.4	312.9	21.2	3.6
7.3	0.20	1.8	-0.07	4.4	0.2	0.70	7.34	3.47	72.9	1.6	21.2	25.2	5.7
8.2	0.48	3.3	0.03	5.0	3.0	0.79	10.00	3.36	69.2	5.3	44.7	9.6	5.1
7.0	0.05	0.4	2.02	2.1	-4.0	-0.81	-10.02	3.25	77.9	1.4	25.6	56.7	5.8
3.4	1.35	10.6	0.00	4.9	0.7	0.92	10.35	4.16	63.5	2.4	19.4	17.5	5.1
4.7	0.74	6.4	0.18	3.4	0.6	0.84	11.48	3.49	79.8	2.2	31.9	23.7	3.0
2.8	0.48	3.7	0.06	10.0	6.3	2.22	23.10	5.52	35.3	0.8	14.9	35.3	7.5
8.2	0.12	0.7	0.00	2.9	0.4	0.48	5.71	3.53	70.6	6.2	64.0	9.3	1.7
8.7	0.11	1.1	0.01	4.7	0.3	0.67	8.14	2.84	64.3	1.0	12.9	31.1	4.1
8.6	0.15	1.4	0.00	2.8	0.1	0.17	2.37	2.99	89.7	2.0	42.9	53.7	3.7
8.6	0.00	0.0	0.00	0.1	-0.1	-0.60	-2.20	4.83	110.1	3.0	45.1	23.1	0.0
6.6	0.31	2.9	0.00	8.0	11.7	1.19	15.57	3.47	47.2	0.8	2.6	31.5	7.2
2.5	3.15	21.0	-0.03	3.0	0.1	0.29	4.02	3.89	89.7	7.4	107.7	7.1	1.7
3.5	0.54	4.5	0.10	8.9	2.0	1.35	16.57	3.60	54.3	4.2	7.7	6.1	6.6
5.4	0.22	1.2	0.35	4.9	1.4	0.77	5.68	3.97	61.6	3.4	20.5	12.7	7.0
4.7	0.71	6.0	0.20	6.2	4.5	1.13	13.70	3.89	59.7	1.5	14.8	23.8	5.2
7.6	0.03	0.2	-0.02	9.0	4.9	1.37	14.46	4.85	60.1	7.5	86.2	4.5	6.7
5.2	0.66	5.1	-0.05	6.6	0.6	1.17	14.13	5.13	62.9	6.6	65.3	4.7	4.1
5.7	0.03	0.2	0.24	4.3	0.4	0.77	8.08	4.16	74.4	1.0	22.2	33.6	6.0
3.3	3.93	18.1	-0.08	3.0	0.1	0.19	7.00	0.89	71.2	7.0	94.7	7.7	5.0
5.1	0.70	5.4	-0.22	7.1	0.7	1.54	18.74	4.61	62.5	1.2	16.1	29.7	4.2
7.6	0.02	0.1	0.11	10.0	3.6	1.86	21.27	4.64	41.4	6.2	48.4	5.1	8.1
5.2	0.92	8.5	0.00	5.0	0.8	1.10	15.33	4.16	70.8	4.9	30.0	6.4	4.0
9.8	0.00	0.0	0.00	5.6	0.2	0.59	7.07	2.20	81.5	4.9	15.4	2.8	1.8
0.9	10.98	50.7	2.24	1.2	-0.1	-0.17	-1.86	2.82	82.5	2.6	57.7	36.7	2.4
5.5	0.69	5.5	0.06	7.4	0.9	1.58	18.14	3.26	39.1	3.1	15.7	13.4	4.8
3.9	2.80	13.1	0.20	4.0	0.5	1.90	27.00	3.98	74.7	4.5	23.8	6.2	0.3
3.2	3.01	15.8	0.11	2.0	0.0	0.18	1.83	3.60	91.0	5.8	138.4	17.8	5.1
5.7	0.41	2.9	0.03	7.1	0.3	1.33	16.96	5.31	69.1	1.1	19.8	31.6	3.6
9.0	0.01	0.0	0.73	4.7	0.5	0.55	10.02	3.69	96.4	6.7	47.7	1.1	4.7
4.7	0.94	8.3	0.05	5.4	0.4	0.96	12.00	4.38	60.5	5.9	64.4	9.7	3.8
9.9	0.00	0.0	0.03	4.5	0.2	1.07	15.01	3.69	78.4	6.5	42.0	0.6	2.0
8.0	0.69	2.8	0.00	2.3	0.0	0.18	1.22	3.27	89.9	2.7	45.3	27.7	0.8
5.9	0.53	3.3	0.16	5.4	0.8	1.31	13.68	4.05	67.7	2.9	22.3	15.4	5.3
7.2	0.00	0.0	-0.07	7.8	0.3	1.98	24.95	5.36	65.3	2.1	25.3	19.7	4.2
6.9	1.71	3.1	0.75	8.6	0.3	1.95	23.74	3.81	84.3	8.2	114.0	2.8	5.8
8.2	1.51	2.6	0.90	10.0	3.2	2.52	19.59	3.60	69.3	5.1	17.8	2.0	8.3
7.4	0.00	0.0	0.00	1.1	0.0	0.07	0.31	2.58	95.4	3.5	30.0	14.3	0.0
6.7	0.11	1.1	0.16	4.5	0.4	0.85	10.91	4.17	64.2	2.1	36.1	29.2	3.4
6.7	0.13	0.6	0.17	3.8	0.2	0.68	4.63	3.80	71.9	3.5	23.9	12.4	7.7
5.5	0.03	0.1	0.11	2.2	0.1	0.18	1.44	4.17	91.6	4.5	19.4	6.1	6.5
3.9	1.09	7.3	-0.07	5.0	0.7	1.03	9.73	4.31	62.1	1.6	12.5	21.7	6.1
6.8	0.25	3.1	0.15	6.6	2.8	1.72	27.11	4.36	64.2	1.9	20.0	20.3	3.8
1.8	1.38	17.5	0.01	4.1	0.4	0.72	6.99	3.17	75.0	1.4	6.7	23.2	6.5
8.3	0.00	0.0	0.00	2.7	0.5	0.69	8.10	3.49	69.2	3.7	16.0	10.6	1.6
8.4	0.15	1.4	0.00	5.8	3.4	0.93	15.96	4.00	63.0	5.2	105.6	19.4	4.4
8.4	0.15	1.2	-0.01	6.0	1.2	1.01	11.11	3.47	63.7	1.3	6.8	24.5	3.2
8.0	0.73	1.9	0.46	4.7	0.4	0.61	3.22	3.61	72.5	6.6	63.6	6.8	8.6
8.7	0.00	0.0	0.03	5.8	0.7	1.60	18.90	4.14	58.2	1.6	24.1	25.3	2.7
4.5	2.75	11.0	1.03	4.6	0.2	1.07	8.18	4.82	65.5	3.2	48.3	21.4	5.3
5.1	0.75	6.5	0.43	5.6	1.8	0.97	11.42	4.51	60.9	1.0	13.5	32.3	4.7
7.3	0.00	0.0	0.00	7.0	0.9	0.74	4.27	4.24	71.4	3.5	33.3	15.3	8.6
3.5	5.64	18.7	0.02	5.0	0.3	1.09	9.06	3.85	48.6	2.3	16.6	17.6	4.3
6.5	1.85	7.6	0.59	5.0	0.6	1.02	7.89	4.56	61.3	4.7	34.3	9.2	6.3
5.5	6.50	16.4	0.02	4.0	0.0	0.18	1.04	3.18	60.3	5.5	41.6	7.2	5.9
8.0	0.24	1.8	0.00	4.4	3.2	0.73	9.97	2.17	55.2	2.1	18.0	18.6	4.6
8.3	0.00	0.0	0.00	0.0	-0.3	-2.21	-6.83	2.79	160.3	1.2	9.6	27.4	0.0
6.2	0.49	3.6	0.07	5.0	1.0	0.59	6.31	2.48	61.9	1.4	19.1	27.9	4.7
8.5	0.00	0.0	0.00	6.9	0.7	1.03	7.97	3.52	55.7	1.8	24.3	22.5	7.9
5.3	0.23	1.4	1.51	10.0	18.7	3.38	19.60	12.86	47.5	0.1	2.0	99.5	5.8
8.8	0.03	0.1	0.00	9.5	2.3	1.55	7.74	4.37	42.8	3.8	46.3	17.5	9.4
4.7	0.30	1.3	0.19	4.5	0.7	0.77	4.59	4.75	68.8	4.8	39.2	10.8	6.5
3.9	1.20	10.1	0.26	4.6	0.8	0.75	8.22	3.59	65.5	1.9	25.7	22.5	4.5
4.7	0.27	3.4	1.40	0.0	-3.8	-2.30	-10.61	2.09	133.7	2.3	50.0	55.7	0.0

Name	City	State	Weiss Safety Rating	2003 Weiss Safety Rating	2002 Weiss Safety Rating	Total Assets ($Mil)	One Year Asset Growth	Asset Mix (As a % of Total Assets)				Capital-ization Index	Leverage Ratio	Risk-based Capital Ratio
								Comm-ercial Loans	Cons-umer Loans	Home Mort-gages	Secur-ities			
▲ FRANKLIN BK	FRANKLIN	IL	B-	C+	C+	22.7	10.93	3.1	10.3	14.3	38.5	9.9	10.9	19.3
▲ FRANKLIN BK	NUTLEY	NJ	C	D+	D-	78.2	39.40	2.4	1.0	3.9	6.7	10.0	12.8	16.3
▼ FRANKLIN BK OF CALIFORNIA	ORANGE	CA	D+	C-	C-	2.0	-9.50	0.0	0.2	0.0	0.0	10.0	89.4	464.0
FRANKLIN BK SSB	AUSTIN	TX	C	C	D	3,068.8	165.31	0.3	0.5	75.3	7.0	5.3	7.3	12.2
FRANKLIN COMMUNITY BK NA	ROCKY MOUNT	VA	D-	D-	D-	78.4	174.96	8.2	2.6	13.5	7.1	1.6	7.9	8.6
FRANKLIN FS&LA OF	GLEN ALLEN	VA	B+	B+	B+	884.2	-6.07	0.1	0.0	12.6	67.4	8.4	9.9	19.5
FRANKLIN GROVE BK	FRANKLIN GROVE	IL	B	B-	B-	23.9	3.95	13.5	3.8	15.9	47.1	10.0	18.8	40.9
FRANKLIN NB	MINNEAPOLIS	MN	B-	B-	C+	114.2	45.35	6.9	1.0	23.1	3.3	3.5	7.9	10.3
▲ FRANKLIN NB	MT VERNON	TX	D-	E	E-	25.8	-39.77	1.9	8.5	8.7	18.8	10.0	15.0	24.3
▲ FRANKLIN S&LC	CINCINNATI	OH	C+	C	C	269.7	-2.42	4.1	0.8	43.1	18.6	6.3	8.3	13.7
▲ FRANKLIN SAVINGS BANK, SLA	SALEM	NJ	C+	C	C+	237.7	-7.52	1.7	1.1	39.7	48.2	6.8	8.8	20.8
▲ FRANKLIN SECURITY BK, FSB	VIRGINIA BEACH	VA	C+	C	D-	43.3	-26.87	0.0	0.0	16.2	44.6	10.0	16.8	79.1
▼ FRANKLIN ST B&TC	WINNSBORO	LA	C-	C-	C+	97.7	1.45	18.6	9.1	17.4	27.3	7.5	9.3	17.9
FRANKLIN ST BK	FRANKLIN	MN	D	D	D	20.9	17.02	1.9	6.0	14.3	28.2	6.4	8.4	13.5
▲ FRANKLIN ST BK	FRANKLIN	NE	B+	B	B	39.2	2.59	2.9	3.7	2.3	55.4	10.0	17.7	36.2
FRANKLIN ST BK	FRANKLIN	WI	B-	B-	B-	92.2	4.72	23.1	1.8	9.4	3.1	4.8	9.1	10.9
FRANKLIN SVGS BK	FARMINGTON	ME	A	A	A	289.0	-0.51	7.0	8.2	33.0	15.2	10.0	20.5	30.4
FRANKLIN SVGS BK	FRANKLIN	NH	B-	B-	B	268.2	11.30	1.4	1.6	39.5	30.9	9.9	10.9	20.0
▲ FRANKLIN TEMPLETON B&T	SALT LAKE CITY	UT	C	C-	C-	151.3	-18.83	0.0	36.0	2.0	20.8	10.0	17.9	22.3
FRATERNITY FS&LA	BALTIMORE	MD	B-	B	B+	145.0	20.33	0.0	0.7	74.4	12.2	9.8	10.9	22.4
▲ FREDERICK COUNTY BK	FREDERICK	MD	C-	D	D	156.6	19.58	12.2	1.6	11.3	10.0	5.5	9.4	11.4
FREDONIA VALLEY BK	FREDONIA	KY	C	C	C+	70.3	-3.49	3.0	5.5	31.6	31.7	7.0	9.0	15.0
▲ FREEDOM BK	HUNTINGBURG	IN	B	B-	B-	158.8	13.94	10.8	10.4	45.2	0.0	5.7	8.5	11.5
▲ FREEDOM BK	CASSVILLE	MO	C+	C	C	50.6	20.98	13.0	9.5	23.2	9.9	6.3	8.3	12.5
FREEDOM BK	BELINGTON	WV	C+	C	C-	103.7	-1.29	7.4	6.4	29.2	16.8	6.6	8.7	13.9
FREEDOM BK OF GEORGIA	COMMERCE	GA	D	NR	NR	26.3	N/A	4.8	3.1	9.6	13.2	10.0	34.1	36.8
FREEDOM BK OF VIRGINIA	VIENNA	VA	D	D	D	52.9	4.32	15.6	5.3	4.8	30.4	10.0	13.7	21.3
▲ FREEDOM FINANCIAL BK	W DES MOINES	IA	C-	C-	C	84.9	44.16	14.5	0.5	3.4	0.0	6.2	11.7	11.9
▼ FREEDOM NB	GREENVILLE	RI	C+	B-	B-	45.2	52.74	17.8	0.8	14.4	26.2	10.0	15.2	22.0
▲ FREEDOM SECURITY BK	CORALVILLE	IA	B+	B	B	84.5	4.95	9.4	3.1	22.8	21.2	7.6	9.4	15.6
FREEDOM ST BK	FREEDOM	OK	E-	E-	E-	14.1	7.73	5.6	9.6	4.1	22.1	6.0	8.0	16.9
FREEHOLD S&LA	FREEHOLD	NJ	B+	B	B	212.0	-2.10	0.0	0.2	37.5	46.6	9.6	10.7	31.2
FREELAND ST BK	FREELAND	MI	B	B	B	56.1	-4.38	2.1	3.1	29.0	52.0	10.0	14.5	43.4
▼ FREEPORT ST BK	HARPER	KS	E-	E+	E+	13.9	5.24	7.0	4.5	10.7	36.8	4.6	6.7	12.1
FREEPORT ST BK	FREEPORT	MN	C-	D+	D+	59.5	6.05	12.2	7.1	8.9	15.2	5.4	8.2	11.3
FREMONT BK	FREMONT	CA	B+	B+	B	1,631.1	-8.09	5.7	0.5	7.8	2.9	5.3	8.0	11.2
▲ FREMONT INVESTMENT &	ANAHEIM	CA	B	C	D	10,189.2	44.23	0.0	0.0	52.5	0.0	8.9	10.3	15.4
FREMONT NB OF CANON CITY	CANON CITY	CO	B+	B+	B+	129.0	0.53	5.9	1.8	12.7	27.7	10.0	11.7	19.5
FREMONT NB&TC	FREMONT	NE	C	C	C	347.0	0.00	11.4	34.5	13.9	14.4	3.7	6.9	10.3
FRIENDS BK	NEW SMYRNA BEACH	FL	C+	C+	C-	95.9	45.86	3.8	2.8	7.4	25.0	10.0	13.0	20.1
▲ FRIENDSHIP BK	FRIENDSHIP	TN	D+	D	D	82.8	-14.61	10.7	8.8	22.1	20.8	9.3	10.5	16.1
▲ FRIENDSHIP ST BK	FRIENDSHIP	IN	B	B-	C+	179.9	9.04	4.4	9.8	43.2	13.0	5.6	7.6	13.3
FRIONA ST BK NA	FRIONA	TX	B-	B-	B-	75.3	-4.99	18.2	4.4	2.0	0.0	7.7	10.6	13.1
▲ FRONT RANGE BK	LAKEWOOD	CO	E+	E-	D-	81.2	18.22	18.4	2.9	14.8	23.3	2.1	7.2	9.1
FRONTENAC BK	EARTH CITY	MO	C+	C+	C	250.7	48.12	3.3	0.6	18.6	8.5	5.6	10.3	11.5
▲ FRONTIER BK	LAGRANGE	GA	C+	C-	C	305.1	1.52	6.6	4.2	24.7	15.9	5.8	7.8	11.7
FRONTIER BK	ROCK RAPIDS	IA	B-	C+	C+	134.0	19.15	15.7	1.6	4.6	32.3	6.1	8.1	13.9
▲ FRONTIER BK	HADDAM	KS	C	C-	D	14.1	-15.62	8.2	3.4	15.2	18.4	8.8	10.2	17.4
FRONTIER BK	EVERETT	WA	B-	B-	B-	2,179.3	6.79	8.1	1.2	7.4	6.3	4.4	9.7	10.7
▲ FRONTIER BK FSB	PARK CITY	UT	C+	C	D	148.9	33.17	4.1	1.0	26.4	3.7	3.8	6.3	10.4
▲ FRONTIER ST BK	OKLAHOMA CITY	OK	C+	C	C+	390.3	58.27	1.5	0.7	1.4	87.4	4.2	6.2	21.2
▼ FRONTIER SVGS BK	COUNCIL BLUFFS	IA	C+	B-	B-	25.3	10.08	4.1	0.5	6.7	2.4	7.9	9.6	20.9
FRONTIER TRUST COMPANY	FARGO	ND	B-	B-	B-	18.2	9.19	0.0	0.0	0.0	66.8	10.0	82.2	303.4
▲ FROST NB	SAN ANTONIO	TX	B+	B	B	9,595.6	-4.54	23.3	3.1	4.2	30.4	5.4	7.4	14.0
FROST ST BK	FROST	MN	D-	D-	D	15.7	13.04	9.5	6.8	9.2	11.6	6.8	8.8	12.9
FSGBANK NA	CHATTANOOGA	TN	B-	B-	C	657.8	148.80	17.9	11.0	11.4	13.1	6.6	9.3	12.2
▲ FULLERTON COMMUNITY BK	FULLERTON	CA	C+	C	C-	492.0	9.60	4.5	0.1	20.9	21.9	4.3	6.4	11.1
▼ FULLERTON FSA	BALTIMORE	MD	C-	C	C	11.5	-2.15	0.0	0.4	50.2	23.1	9.3	10.5	25.9
FULLERTON NB	FULLERTON	NE	C+	C+	C+	22.3	0.98	10.4	3.7	4.9	22.4	6.8	8.8	15.4
FULTON BK	LANCASTER	PA	B	B	B+	4,503.0	12.80	9.2	5.0	10.4	18.5	4.9	7.8	11.0
▲ FULTON COUNTY NB&TC	MC CONNELLSBURG	PA	B	B-	B+	145.3	-5.91	7.0	1.9	29.6	19.1	10.0	11.4	17.3
▲ FULTON ST BK	FULTON	SD	B-	C	C	31.6	1.17	15.8	14.7	2.9	11.8	10.0	11.0	15.3
FULTON SVGS BK	FULTON	NY	A-	A-	B	393.1	17.13	1.1	0.7	61.7	15.4	10.0	11.3	20.7
▲ FUTURUS BK NA	ALPHARETTA	GA	E	E+	D	66.3	34.23	8.7	1.2	5.3	2.5	3.2	8.2	10.1

Asset Quality Index	Non-Performing Loans as a % of Total Loans	Non-Performing Loans as a % of Capital	Net Charge-offs Avg Loans	Profitability Index	Net Income ($Mil)	Return on Assets (R.O.A.)	Return on Equity (R.O.E.)	Net Interest Spread	Overhead Efficiency Ratio	Liquidity Index	Liquidity Ratio	Hot Money Ratio	Stability Index
8.4	0.00	0.0	0.00	9.3	0.2	2.02	19.27	5.05	51.8	4.6	41.9	9.7	4.2
7.6	0.00	0.0	0.00	3.7	0.4	1.13	11.38	4.24	65.8	6.2	62.9	7.2	2.2
10.0	0.00	0.0	-286.96	0.5	-0.1	-6.85	-7.76	2.00	364.0	5.0	N/A	0.0	4.1
7.4	0.38	3.9	0.05	3.4	10.7	0.81	8.56	2.44	49.7	0.4	6.4	63.7	6.9
7.7	0.20	2.2	1.30	0.0	-0.3	-0.91	-10.93	3.51	76.4	4.5	72.9	17.7	0.0
8.5	0.31	0.8	0.00	5.0	3.0	0.69	6.86	1.82	52.8	3.7	54.8	20.3	6.0
8.6	1.27	3.2	0.00	7.1	0.2	1.23	6.73	4.28	57.5	3.3	31.0	13.8	5.7
7.4	0.11	1.1	0.00	8.5	1.0	1.90	23.77	5.72	61.8	3.0	8.5	13.4	4.9
5.6	1.05	3.8	1.95	5.7	0.6	3.56	36.74	4.84	62.1	6.3	62.1	6.1	0.0
4.1	1.60	14.0	0.03	3.3	0.5	0.37	4.53	2.38	75.4	1.7	24.2	24.8	4.1
8.7	0.31	1.6	0.01	3.2	0.3	0.28	3.23	2.83	83.7	1.6	24.4	25.6	4.3
8.5	0.00	0.0	0.00	3.0	-0.8	-3.22	-20.35	-0.11	247.5	5.4	40.9	7.7	4.3
2.0	3.67	23.4	0.27	6.8	0.6	1.14	12.66	4.55	70.8	2.8	37.0	19.9	4.6
5.7	1.52	10.7	0.00	4.9	0.1	0.84	10.28	3.38	61.1	3.5	45.4	16.5	2.0
6.0	2.52	5.2	-0.08	8.6	0.4	1.94	10.85	4.81	48.2	5.9	44.4	5.2	6.5
4.7	0.23	2.1	0.21	5.7	0.3	0.68	7.50	4.50	70.2	3.8	14.1	10.0	6.0
6.8	1.01	3.6	0.07	7.9	1.9	1.32	6.45	5.19	63.1	5.5	51.2	10.5	8.6
9.4	0.13	0.7	0.02	4.0	0.9	0.66	6.03	3.56	80.0	4.4	14.9	5.9	6.2
6.7	0.50	1.8	1.25	4.8	0.4	0.55	3.20	5.93	74.0	0.3	10.6	84.0	2.6
9.7	0.04	0.3	0.00	3.3	0.2	0.32	2.73	2.60	79.6	2.2	10.8	17.6	6.8
8.1	0.21	1.7	0.00	3.0	0.6	0.85	9.50	3.80	69.9	3.4	48.8	20.0	2.0
4.2	3.05	15.4	0.31	4.1	0.4	1.03	11.54	3.59	57.4	7.1	83.3	5.2	3.6
7.8	0.08	0.8	0.06	5.9	0.7	0.94	11.11	3.45	52.0	2.2	10.9	17.9	5.4
7.9	0.07	0.6	0.10	8.5	0.4	1.73	21.70	5.09	48.6	1.6	26.5	27.4	3.8
4.3	1.37	10.1	0.10	4.3	0.4	0.75	8.69	4.14	77.3	5.2	36.0	7.0	4.1
7.4	0.00	0.0	0.00	0.0	-0.7	-8.45	-18.41	3.51	220.7	5.6	104.5	16.2	0.0
8.3	0.00	0.0	0.00	0.5	0.0	0.01	0.06	3.43	98.9	3.1	45.9	21.3	0.0
5.6	0.00	0.0	0.00	4.2	0.3	0.92	9.72	3.21	67.7	1.0	26.7	47.6	4.4
8.8	0.10	0.4	0.00	0.0	-0.2	-1.07	-6.66	2.72	147.6	5.0	61.5	13.4	2.3
7.3	0.35	2.0	0.50	4.9	0.4	0.93	8.32	4.19	69.8	3.5	52.9	19.8	7.1
1.8	5.36	25.6	-0.20	1.8	0.0	0.17	2.14	3.35	95.0	7.6	117.3	5.7	0.3
8.5	0.03	0.1	0.00	5.6	0.9	0.88	8.32	2.82	51.5	1.3	19.8	29.1	6.3
7.2	2.83	7.9	0.03	3.9	0.2	0.68	4.71	3.24	67.0	7.5	104.1	5.4	6.7
8.6	0.00	0.0	0.00	2.7	0.0	0.48	7.01	3.94	87.6	3.4	20.3	12.4	0.3
3.2	1.48	12.6	0.51	4.8	0.2	0.72	8.91	5.08	71.6	4.5	39.2	12.2	3.3
8.2	0.42	3.5	0.00	6.5	4.4	0.53	6.56	3.35	85.3	7.4	82.6	6.1	7.3
5.2	1.65	12.2	0.33	10.0	199.6	4.10	42.87	5.47	31.4	1.4	21.7	32.3	8.2
8.4	0.46	2.2	0.17	7.5	1.1	1.62	13.52	4.61	62.8	5.5	65.4	13.0	7.7
2.4	1.62	13.4	4.04	6.6	1.9	1.13	15.24	6.92	39.8	6.5	168.5	17.6	4.2
8.7	0.00	0.0	0.00	3.0	0.2	0.38	2.73	2.78	65.5	6.5	122.0	13.6	2.0
4.0	1.38	8.2	0.46	2.5	0.5	1.09	10.69	4.40	79.4	1.1	21.3	32.1	2.0
6.9	0.14	1.2	0.12	8.2	1.1	1.25	14.90	4.60	59.7	3.6	14.9	10.9	4.8
4.7	0.34	2.1	0.25	6.4	0.6	1.62	13.27	4.64	61.2	2.0	23.8	19.8	6.6
1.7	3.38	28.9	0.43	4.3	0.3	0.75	10.32	4.54	69.4	2.4	20.3	17.4	1.7
6.2	0.47	3.8	0.01	5.2	1.1	0.96	10.76	2.98	45.1	4.2	30.2	10.7	5.1
4.0	1.07	8.7	0.05	6.6	1.7	1.14	13.96	4.24	65.0	1.7	12.6	20.5	3.9
6.6	0.04	0.3	0.05	4.9	0.7	1.11	12.39	3.48	68.5	0.8	21.3	48.3	4.6
6.8	0.00	0.0	0.00	4.4	0.1	0.70	5.65	4.03	70.2	5.3	65.2	10.9	3.9
5.4	0.83	6.5	0.00	10.0	20.7	1.95	20.12	5.05	40.0	4.5	38.6	14.5	9.2
7.5	0.24	2.7	0.03	6.0	1.1	1.57	24.82	5.24	67.6	2.1	47.1	61.9	3.7
8.3	1.85	4.5	0.49	7.8	4.8	2.73	53.96	3.56	23.6	0.3	1.0	67.0	3.4
8.3	0.00	0.0	0.00	0.0	-0.1	-1.03	-10.31	3.52	123.3	9.1	195.0	5.3	2.6
7.8	0.00	0.0	0.00	10.0	1.0	10.68	12.88	4.40	53.2	4.9	196.6	100.0	1.2
5.7	0.92	5.3	0.23	9.0	71.3	1.46	17.66	4.09	60.2	6.8	67.6	7.3	7.6
2.9	1.61	12.1	0.12	6.4	0.1	1.25	14.84	3.68	47.2	1.9	49.5	39.1	1.7
4.7	0.55	3.5	0.65	4.2	1.6	0.49	4.29	4.52	77.7	2.4	18.2	17.3	3.1
8.1	0.00	0.0	0.01	3.9	1.0	0.40	5.70	3.45	84.5	0.8	18.7	42.0	3.9
9.8	0.00	0.0	0.00	2.4	0.0	0.14	1.11	2.43	92.5	4.9	51.1	10.5	4.3
6.0	0.21	1.3	0.01	6.5	0.1	1.08	12.26	4.48	60.2	5.5	50.8	6.6	4.6
6.7	0.57	5.0	0.07	7.3	26.9	1.19	18.09	3.09	58.1	6.4	43.0	5.0	6.3
4.7	1.52	8.8	0.66	4.3	0.5	0.63	5.70	3.64	78.0	5.3	58.2	13.2	5.4
3.8	2.23	12.5	-1.26	7.3	0.2	1.26	11.85	4.91	63.7	5.8	53.9	8.0	4.7
7.4	1.08	7.1	0.05	7.0	2.3	1.16	10.44	3.84	58.5	4.1	22.5	8.9	6.8
7.4	0.01	0.1	0.00	0.0	-0.1	-0.40	-4.82	3.56	96.9	4.6	35.5	10.7	0.0

Name	City	State	Weiss Safety Rating	2003 Weiss Safety Rating	2002 Weiss Safety Rating	Total Assets ($Mil)	One Year Asset Growth	Asset Mix (As a % of Total Assets)				Capital-ization Index	Leverage Ratio	Risk-based Capital Ratio
								Comm-ercial Loans	Cons-umer Loans	Home Mort-gages	Secur-ities			
G W JONES EXCHANGE BANK	MARCELLUS	MI	D+	D	D-	54.2	1.86	8.0	4.4	37.0	10.5	5.6	7.6	14.8
GAINESVILLE BANK & TRUST	GAINESVILLE	GA	C+	C+	C+	404.9	5.82	4.2	2.6	10.5	15.4	3.8	7.0	10.4
GALENA ST B&TC	GALENA	IL	B	B	B	212.7	6.97	17.6	1.7	15.1	24.6	6.9	8.9	13.7
GALION B&LA	GALION	OH	C-	C-	C-	54.4	0.11	4.1	5.8	48.3	18.0	6.8	8.8	17.5
▲ GALLUP FSB	GALLUP	NM	C	C-	C+	231.9	1.13	11.8	1.7	33.3	26.7	5.1	7.1	13.6
▲ GARDEN CITY BK	GARDEN CITY	MO	B-	C+	C-	70.7	7.81	12.4	4.0	29.9	12.9	6.1	8.1	12.5
▼ GARDEN CITY ST BK	GARDEN CITY	KS	D+	C	C	41.0	19.32	60.0	6.3	7.5	4.4	6.6	10.7	12.2
GARDEN PLAIN ST BK	WICHITA	KS	D+	D+	D	42.9	-10.44	16.0	6.1	22.9	11.4	6.9	8.9	13.4
▲ GARDINER SVGS INSTITUTION	GARDINER	ME	B-	C+	C+	656.6	3.37	7.0	3.0	23.9	11.1	4.2	10.2	10.6
▲ GARDNER NB	GARDNER	KS	E+	D	D	82.4	15.64	11.2	6.9	20.0	14.3	3.1	6.8	10.0
GARFIELD COUNTY BK	JORDAN	MT	C	B-	B	25.4	-1.29	2.8	4.7	1.6	13.5	10.0	16.2	20.4
▼ GARNAVILLO SVG BK	GARNAVILLO	IA	C-	C+	C-	24.5	-7.46	10.1	3.7	11.2	32.0	10.0	11.0	18.0
GARNETT ST SVG BK	GARNETT	KS	B	B+	B+	74.8	16.22	7.9	2.3	6.4	65.6	10.0	11.3	33.8
GARRETT ST BK	GARRETT	IN	B-	C+	C+	122.0	-1.33	7.9	3.7	50.3	16.1	6.2	8.2	15.2
▲ GARRISON ST B&T	GARRISON	ND	C+	C	C-	56.8	2.40	5.5	3.5	3.2	40.1	9.0	10.4	19.9
GARY ST BK	GARY	MN	B-	B-	B-	10.1	3.85	11.2	6.8	2.0	13.8	10.0	13.7	18.4
GATE CITY BK	FARGO	ND	A	A	A-	743.9	5.74	0.1	26.7	58.7	1.6	10.0	12.2	19.6
GATES BKG&TC	GATES	TN	B+	B	B	29.8	-2.95	4.6	2.7	11.1	43.5	10.0	11.0	21.3
GATEWAY B&TC	RINGGOLD	GA	B-	C+	C+	165.2	14.74	23.3	6.5	11.9	15.3	6.3	9.1	12.0
▲ GATEWAY B&TC	ELIZABETH CITY	NC	C	C-	D+	393.9	42.08	18.3	2.3	10.6	9.0	6.9	10.0	12.4
GATEWAY BK	MENDOTA HEIGHTS	MN	D	NR	NR	14.8	N/A	48.7	2.6	1.9	5.1	10.0	40.0	36.1
▼ GATEWAY BK	ST LOUIS	MO	E+	D-	D	37.4	2.95	4.0	1.1	29.5	32.1	6.7	8.8	12.4
GATEWAY BK FSB	SAN FRANCISCO	CA	B-	B-	C+	337.5	11.41	0.2	0.0	85.1	0.7	5.3	7.3	13.7
GATEWAY BK OF PA	MCMURRAY	PA	D	NR	NR	20.1	N/A	0.5	0.0	0.1	79.8	10.0	223.4	947.8
▲ GATEWAY BUSINESS BK	CERRITOS	CA	A	A-	B	179.8	-5.82	9.5	0.0	55.0	0.3	10.0	14.8	17.7
▲ GATEWAY COMMUNITY BK	ROSCOE	IL	C-	D	D	44.3	50.94	23.8	3.9	11.2	8.6	10.0	16.5	20.7
GATEWAY NB	DALLAS	TX	C	C	C+	208.4	13.64	16.7	3.9	1.5	21.5	5.4	7.4	11.3
▲ GATEWAY ST BK	CLINTON	IA	A-	B+	B+	72.6	8.86	8.8	3.7	17.4	17.1	5.0	7.0	12.0
▲ GATEWAY SVGS BK	ANKENY	IA	C-	C-	C-	76.6	13.45	11.0	1.7	12.0	14.4	4.6	8.0	10.8
GE CAPITAL CONSUMER CARD	MASON	OH	C	C	NR	6,268.5	100.75	0.4	95.4	0.1	0.1	10.0	35.2	37.2
▲ GE CAPITAL FNCL	SALT LAKE CITY	UT	A-	B+	B+	1,619.5	-40.65	73.8	19.7	0.1	0.3	10.0	63.2	56.9
GEAUGA SVG BK	NEWBURY	OH	C+	C+	C+	359.2	31.94	0.1	0.2	29.8	48.2	5.5	7.5	16.4
GEDDES FS&LA	SYRACUSE	NY	A	A	A	294.3	2.17	0.0	0.4	75.1	10.9	10.0	15.2	32.5
▲ GENERATIONS BK	KANSAS CITY	MO	C+	C-	D+	81.5	29.64	0.0	1.0	22.5	71.7	8.2	9.8	32.6
▲ GENESEE REGIONAL BK	ROCHESTER	NY	E+	E-	E-	42.6	-8.20	28.5	7.3	3.4	13.0	9.6	10.7	15.7
▲ GENEVA ST BK	GENEVA	NE	D	D-	D	144.4	15.75	3.0	1.9	6.7	13.3	4.2	8.8	10.6
GENOA BKG CO	GENOA	OH	C+	C+	C+	185.9	15.91	11.7	5.9	34.3	15.3	5.8	7.7	12.2
▲ GENOA NB	GENOA	NE	C-	D+	D-	46.4	7.50	3.4	3.2	5.1	29.5	9.2	10.5	16.1
GENOA S&LC	GENOA	OH	D+	C-	C-	94.4	-17.72	4.3	4.6	39.6	5.3	5.8	7.8	11.9
▲ GEORGE D WARTHEN BK	SANDERSVILLE	GA	B-	C+	B-	120.4	-6.74	16.8	12.5	24.6	24.0	7.8	9.5	15.8
GEORGE ST BK	GEORGE	IA	C+	C+	C+	45.9	7.01	7.1	2.6	5.2	23.4	4.2	8.3	10.6
▼ GEORGE WASHINGTON BK	OAK LAWN	IL	C	C+	C+	220.8	9.33	5.7	0.2	13.3	29.4	7.7	9.5	15.2
▼ GEORGETOWN SVGS BK	GEORGETOWN	MA	C-	C+	C+	124.9	9.11	0.9	0.4	64.2	12.4	4.7	6.7	12.5
GEORGIA B&TC	AUGUSTA	GA	B-	B-	B-	677.4	11.88	6.6	6.8	13.1	23.3	5.1	7.8	11.0
GEORGIA B&TC	CALHOUN	GA	B-	B-	B	373.3	8.21	15.7	6.7	11.0	11.9	3.4	7.7	10.2
▲ GEORGIA BANKING CO	ATLANTA	GA	C-	D	D	128.0	141.37	7.8	2.1	77.0	0.4	7.5	9.3	14.7
▼ GEORGIA CENTRAL BK	SOCIAL CIRCLE	GA	D+	C	B	85.1	2.04	3.2	4.3	10.2	30.2	5.3	7.3	12.5
GEORGIA COMMERCE BK	ATLANTA	GA	D	D	NR	53.0	N/A	6.8	1.2	10.3	13.3	10.0	26.0	28.5
GEORGIA COMMUNITY BANK	DALTON	GA	E-	E-	D	48.9	-12.48	15.0	10.0	15.0	6.1	1.6	5.4	8.6
GEORGIA ST BK	MABLETON	GA	B	B	B	328.3	21.68	2.5	1.4	6.4	30.6	4.7	6.7	11.2
GEORGIAN BK	POWDER SPRINGS	GA	D	D	D	476.0	568.93	21.9	0.5	3.4	6.9	7.5	13.4	12.9
GERBER ST BK	ARGENTA	IL	B	B-	B-	51.0	5.72	2.0	2.8	12.2	58.9	10.0	16.2	16.9
GERMAN AMERICAN BK	JASPER	IN	B-	B-	B	415.1	0.93	20.2	5.0	6.9	23.4	3.5	7.7	10.2
▲ GERMAN-AMERICAN ST BK	GERMAN VALLEY	IL	B-	C+	C	115.4	6.65	13.6	4.0	16.5	20.2	6.3	8.4	12.1
GERMANTOWN T&SB	BREESE	IL	A+	A+	A+	261.0	1.83	6.3	2.5	18.1	52.0	10.0	11.9	25.2
GIBRALTAR BK FSB	CORAL GABLES	FL	B-	C+	C+	784.0	11.16	3.6	4.0	28.4	3.2	4.0	7.5	10.5
GIBRALTAR SVGS BK FSB	NEWARK	NJ	D+	D+	C+	108.3	-7.62	0.0	0.0	33.2	47.8	10.0	13.5	39.1
GIBSLAND B&TC	GIBSLAND	LA	D	D	D	90.7	5.70	11.3	15.3	19.2	24.6	6.5	8.5	14.4
GIBSONVILLE COMMUNITY SB	GIBSONVILLE	NC	E-	E-	E-	19.5	1.89	30.8	6.4	35.9	1.0	2.2	6.9	9.2
▲ GIFFORD ST BK	GIFFORD	IL	C+	C-	C-	61.8	0.19	6.1	6.8	18.6	28.4	8.9	10.3	16.5
GILMER NB	GILMER	TX	C+	C	C+	179.3	-2.60	3.6	20.4	12.4	36.2	10.0	11.2	20.6
GILMORE BK	LOS ANGELES	CA	A	A	A	101.0	6.04	8.1	5.0	19.2	39.1	10.0	15.7	32.2
GIRARD NB	GIRARD	KS	C+	B-	B-	279.8	2.11	16.0	7.4	11.5	17.3	6.7	9.2	12.3
GLACIER BK	KALISPELL	MT	B+	B+	B	638.3	15.71	9.0	4.0	15.6	32.3	6.9	8.9	14.4

Asset Quality Index	Non-Performing Loans as a % of Total Loans	Non-Performing Loans as a % of Capital	Net Charge-offs Avg Loans	Profitability Index	Net Income ($Mil)	Return on Assets (R.O.A.)	Return on Equity (R.O.E.)	Net Interest Spread	Overhead Efficiency Ratio	Liquidity Index	Liquidity Ratio	Hot Money Ratio	Stability Index
7.0	0.33	2.7	-0.02	4.0	0.2	0.77	10.56	3.87	78.4	7.1	116.3	9.8	1.8
4.7	0.46	4.4	0.03	6.0	2.1	1.04	14.67	3.90	60.1	3.2	24.6	14.1	4.3
7.7	0.31	2.2	0.01	8.8	1.6	1.46	17.03	3.61	45.6	2.2	12.1	17.9	6.3
2.1	3.11	23.0	0.23	3.4	0.1	0.43	5.01	3.85	79.2	3.4	21.9	12.6	3.3
4.0	0.82	6.7	0.91	4.4	0.8	0.64	8.87	3.03	54.3	0.8	18.7	49.6	3.6
6.6	0.01	0.1	-0.04	7.9	0.4	1.12	10.08	4.62	55.9	4.6	85.1	19.0	5.7
2.0	2.80	20.6	0.53	5.5	0.3	1.35	12.79	5.37	63.6	0.8	7.5	32.7	0.0
5.3	0.39	2.8	1.08	4.0	0.2	0.68	7.15	5.29	71.1	4.0	21.0	9.3	2.6
4.8	0.58	4.0	0.05	6.6	4.6	1.43	14.00	3.27	55.3	1.6	17.3	24.2	7.1
4.3	0.90	9.0	0.50	1.9	-0.1	-0.33	-4.60	4.29	98.6	3.9	42.3	16.0	1.0
2.0	5.16	21.3	0.11	9.2	0.2	1.36	8.62	4.80	55.4	4.4	54.7	15.6	7.7
3.3	5.02	26.7	0.05	4.1	0.1	0.96	8.85	4.14	75.9	4.8	22.4	3.6	2.5
9.3	0.93	2.1	-0.46	3.7	0.3	0.68	5.51	2.82	70.7	6.6	108.4	11.6	6.9
9.0	0.01	0.1	-0.01	6.1	0.7	1.18	14.64	4.11	57.3	3.1	23.4	14.2	4.6
4.5	1.83	8.3	0.77	4.1	0.2	0.75	7.10	3.76	70.2	4.1	18.9	8.3	5.4
6.6	0.06	0.3	0.00	10.0	0.1	2.67	19.78	5.97	55.8	2.1	10.6	17.6	5.0
6.9	0.14	1.0	0.12	6.7	3.1	0.83	6.86	3.61	66.9	3.7	7.8	9.6	8.1
8.7	0.85	3.0	0.08	4.0	0.1	0.64	5.88	3.26	75.6	2.6	48.2	30.0	6.7
6.1	0.55	4.4	0.18	7.5	1.1	1.31	15.17	4.39	55.2	2.5	7.9	15.7	4.3
5.8	0.41	2.9	-0.05	3.1	1.0	0.57	5.96	3.63	79.1	1.4	11.7	24.3	5.6
8.0	0.00	0.0	0.00	0.0	-0.3	-6.56	-12.86	2.18	321.3	4.1	47.9	13.9	0.0
2.8	4.06	27.3	0.58	0.9	0.0	-0.12	-1.28	3.68	95.8	3.7	12.1	10.3	0.5
4.8	0.80	9.4	0.00	9.7	2.4	1.48	19.81	3.88	60.7	0.6	5.6	40.7	4.8
10.0	0.00	0.0	0.00	0.0	-0.9	-9.79	-11.52	0.67	1,501.6	8.1	4,503.3	12.2	0.0
7.9	0.08	0.5	0.00	9.4	2.7	3.43	21.41	4.77	82.9	2.2	9.9	17.7	7.0
8.0	0.00	0.0	0.00	2.2	0.2	0.83	5.27	4.10	72.7	3.0	32.8	17.6	0.7
7.6	0.21	1.7	0.34	3.7	0.5	0.46	6.43	4.59	79.7	5.1	37.1	8.1	2.4
7.3	0.10	0.8	0.06	4.9	0.3	0.87	9.42	3.93	63.7	3.4	28.3	14.1	6.2
6.9	0.10	0.9	0.06	4.9	0.2	0.55	6.77	3.51	74.2	1.3	24.8	30.7	0.8
2.4	2.80	6.8	6.62	10.0	382.0	10.89	38.68	4.55	32.7	0.2	6.3	94.3	3.2
6.6	1.48	2.1	4.87	10.0	63.3	7.37	12.06	10.38	37.1	0.8	21.1	78.0	9.0
5.2	2.22	14.9	0.09	7.4	4.1	2.42	33.20	3.46	35.0	0.9	7.4	32.0	3.8
9.5	0.33	1.8	0.08	7.6	1.6	1.09	7.20	3.27	48.4	1.2	10.7	27.9	8.6
8.4	0.00	0.0	-0.03	3.6	0.2	0.49	5.05	1.90	69.0	0.8	18.3	42.3	2.0
1.1	3.60	21.3	4.35	0.0	-0.4	-1.88	-17.17	3.77	124.4	5.8	85.0	12.9	1.8
0.7	4.74	39.5	0.00	6.5	0.8	1.13	12.95	4.66	68.0	2.0	11.4	18.6	5.2
8.4	0.00	0.0	0.03	5.3	0.8	0.92	11.86	3.69	64.6	2.0	31.1	26.4	3.2
3.0	2.07	12.1	-0.12	2.2	0.1	0.56	5.50	3.22	83.8	2.8	42.4	24.8	3.5
1.1	3.39	26.5	0.78	1.6	-0.4	-0.71	-9.35	3.18	128.0	2.7	20.0	16.1	2.7
4.3	1.68	10.5	0.11	4.1	0.5	0.71	7.48	4.12	72.0	4.0	26.3	10.4	4.5
7.3	0.00	0.0	-0.05	9.2	0.5	2.01	23.88	4.18	50.7	5.3	35.9	6.4	5.2
5.9	0.51	2.8	1.72	2.5	0.4	0.32	2.96	3.32	59.5	4.5	35.0	11.0	5.6
6.0	0.78	8.7	0.00	2.7	0.1	0.13	1.97	3.23	91.9	2.2	11.6	17.6	3.1
5.4	0.56	4.4	0.22	7.5	4.2	1.28	16.43	4.13	63.4	2.6	32.2	19.5	5.1
1.9	0.86	8.5	0.12	8.8	2.2	1.24	16.61	4.04	52.2	1.2	8.4	26.3	6.5
6.6	0.26	2.9	0.00	3.8	1.2	2.53	28.93	4.53	73.5	0.6	7.0	39.4	2.1
3.9	1.89	13.9	1.87	1.3	-0.4	-0.94	-12.17	3.83	85.6	2.4	32.8	21.1	3.7
9.1	0.00	0.0	0.00	0.0	-0.4	-2.14	-7.72	3.29	131.6	5.9	60.4	8.7	0.0
0.0	15.84	128.2	0.25	0.0	-1.7	-6.69	-108.14	2.11	125.7	3.4	6.3	10.9	0.0
8.6	0.07	0.6	0.23	7.0	1.8	1.12	16.83	3.55	57.6	0.8	14.7	40.2	5.7
7.0	0.00	0.0	0.00	0.8	0.2	0.11	0.69	3.84	62.6	0.6	5.6	39.6	0.0
7.9	2.57	5.6	-0.36	4.8	0.2	0.86	5.24	3.57	74.7	5.0	44.0	10.5	6.1
8.0	0.18	1.4	0.02	7.4	2.8	1.34	16.72	3.61	48.2	4.5	30.4	9.2	5.8
6.2	0.37	3.0	0.04	5.5	0.6	1.10	13.01	4.04	58.3	2.7	16.2	15.7	5.0
9.2	0.02	0.1	0.01	8.6	2.4	1.84	14.59	2.77	32.6	3.9	22.1	10.4	8.7
4.8	0.49	5.4	-0.01	7.4	6.7	1.75	23.12	4.18	61.6	0.6	22.1	84.0	6.4
8.8	1.12	2.9	0.00	0.7	-0.2	-0.44	-3.34	1.61	144.5	2.8	23.3	16.0	5.9
3.4	1.77	12.7	1.00	5.6	0.6	1.19	15.53	5.27	63.9	2.7	46.4	28.1	1.2
3.5	0.55	6.5	0.12	4.9	0.1	1.02	14.87	5.26	84.6	2.5	37.3	19.4	0.3
4.2	1.69	10.2	0.32	5.7	0.4	1.43	13.64	3.76	61.4	2.6	22.0	16.5	5.2
3.3	3.91	16.3	1.04	5.7	1.0	1.15	10.57	3.92	48.7	3.6	77.0	33.1	6.0
8.7	0.00	0.0	-0.01	7.5	0.8	1.50	9.65	4.43	66.7	1.9	16.9	19.9	9.2
3.4	1.36	8.7	0.35	6.7	1.6	1.14	10.59	4.39	59.1	3.8	38.9	15.7	6.7
6.1	0.50	2.9	0.06	10.0	5.5	1.78	18.29	4.65	46.6	4.9	18.3	3.4	7.6

| Name | City | State | Weiss Safety Rating | 2003 Weiss Safety Rating | 2002 Weiss Safety Rating | Total Assets ($Mil) | One Year Asset Growth | Asset Mix (As a % of Total Assets) | | | | Capital-ization Index | Leverage Ratio | Risk-based Capital Ratio |
								Comm-ercial Loans	Cons-umer Loans	Home Mort-gages	Secur-ities			
GLACIER BK OF WHITEFISH	WHITEFISH	MT	B	B	B	161.8	13.99	7.1	4.2	15.3	36.8	5.6	7.6	12.8
▼ GLADEWATER NB	GLADEWATER	TX	B-	B	B+	25.8	-3.14	11.5	10.6	22.0	11.3	10.0	13.3	24.1
GLASFORD ST BK	GLASFORD	IL	B+	B+	B+	22.8	-3.23	2.1	9.8	14.9	50.2	7.0	9.0	24.6
▼ GLASGOW SVG BK	GLASGOW	MO	C+	B-	B-	30.9	-1.77	1.5	7.4	9.7	47.3	7.3	9.2	15.2
GLEN BURNIE MSB	GLEN BURNIE	MD	C-	C-	C-	56.3	3.90	0.0	0.1	62.4	17.7	8.5	10.0	22.6
GLEN ROCK SVG BK	GLEN ROCK	NJ	C-	C-	C-	115.0	-1.97	0.0	0.1	51.2	37.3	4.5	6.6	16.6
GLENCOE ST BK	GLENCOE	OK	C+	C+	C+	10.8	1.98	2.9	20.7	2.3	54.0	10.0	23.9	45.8
▲ GLENNVILLE BK	GLENNVILLE	GA	A	A-	B+	108.4	1.71	5.2	6.1	15.6	32.4	10.0	12.0	19.6
▲ GLENS FALLS NB&TC	GLENS FALLS	NY	B+	B	B	1,207.1	4.54	4.4	19.1	20.6	35.8	5.8	7.8	14.2
GLENVIEW ST BK	GLENVIEW	IL	B+	B+	B+	890.0	2.42	6.8	19.9	13.8	42.0	7.0	9.0	14.0
▼ GLENWOOD ST BK	GLENWOOD	IA	C+	B-	B-	97.7	5.02	2.7	3.3	8.4	38.1	10.0	12.1	26.9
GLENWOOD ST BK	GLENWOOD	MN	A	A-	A-	102.4	7.58	14.4	4.4	14.5	13.7	9.9	11.3	15.0
▲ GLOBAL COMMERCE BK	DORAVILLE	GA	A-	B	B	85.8	10.70	5.3	0.5	2.0	10.7	9.0	13.3	14.1
GLOBE HOMESTEAD SAVINGS	METAIRIE	LA	B-	B-	B-	29.8	-8.99	0.0	1.4	76.8	10.5	10.0	16.8	38.1
GLOUCESTER CO-OP BK	GLOUCESTER	MA	C+	C+	C+	119.6	9.03	1.9	0.9	47.6	18.3	7.8	9.5	15.8
GLOUCESTER COUNTY FSB	SEWELL	NJ	D	D	D+	311.0	2.29	4.8	13.3	28.1	37.8	5.8	7.8	12.9
GLOUSTER COMMUNITY BK	LANCASTER	OH	C+	C+	C+	120.8	4.94	5.6	9.8	21.8	36.4	4.5	6.5	11.6
▲ GMAC BK	GREENVILLE	DE	B+	B	C-	3,474.5	23.06	0.0	0.1	87.0	0.2	9.2	10.5	16.0
GMAC COMMERCIAL	MIDVALE	UT	B+	B+	NR	1,200.9	116.18	0.0	0.0	0.0	0.1	10.0	47.5	40.6
GNB FINANCIAL NA	GAINESVILLE	TX	B+	B+	B+	223.0	23.50	16.1	6.0	11.8	14.3	7.7	9.8	13.1
▲ GOGEBIC RANGE BK	BESSEMER	MI	C-	D	D	29.9	27.77	24.4	8.7	13.3	3.4	8.5	11.1	13.7
GOLD BK	BRADENTON	FL	C+	C+	C+	910.4	14.90	6.8	0.9	6.8	22.9	3.5	7.3	10.3
▲ GOLD BK	LEAWOOD	KS	B-	C+	C+	3,265.4	41.19	17.4	0.7	5.5	24.2	6.0	8.2	11.8
▲ GOLD COUNTRY BK NA	MARYSVILLE	CA	C-	D+	E	144.3	35.49	9.4	1.8	5.3	0.3	5.4	7.4	12.0
▲ GOLDEN BELT BK FSA	ELLIS	KS	B	B-	B-	122.5	8.69	7.0	3.3	20.5	36.1	5.9	7.9	19.0
GOLDEN PRAGUE FS&LA	BALTIMORE	MD	E-	E-	E-	33.3	-0.48	0.7	2.5	60.0	21.5	4.9	6.9	14.4
▼ GOLDEN SECURITY BK	ALHAMBRA	CA	B	A-	B+	135.6	28.65	0.0	0.0	1.0	4.3	3.9	7.8	10.5
GOLDEN ST BK	GOLDEN	IL	C+	C+	C+	26.3	5.62	13.4	2.3	8.2	43.0	5.6	7.6	12.4
GOLDEN ST BUSINESS BK	UPLAND	CA	D	D	NR	43.6	N/A	8.6	0.2	2.7	0.6	10.0	22.8	31.7
▲ GOLETA NB	GOLETA	CA	C+	C-	D	342.9	15.71	12.1	15.9	12.0	7.5	8.2	10.4	13.5
GOLF SAVINGS BK	MOUNTLAKE TER	WA	B+	B+	B+	211.9	14.23	0.4	0.3	16.4	0.0	9.5	13.6	14.6
GOODFIELD ST BK	GOODFIELD	IL	D+	D+	D+	44.7	15.87	12.9	8.1	23.9	16.3	5.3	8.1	11.2
GOODMAN ST BK	GOODMAN	MO	C	C	C	12.7	-2.02	0.2	2.3	55.1	25.8	10.0	12.1	28.1
GOOSE RIVER BK	MAYVILLE	ND	D+	D+	D+	64.7	4.69	15.6	8.0	3.2	15.1	4.8	6.8	10.9
▲ GORDON BK	GORDON	GA	D+	D	E-	38.4	-2.60	3.9	3.3	19.4	26.6	10.0	16.8	30.4
GORHAM ST BK	GORHAM	KS	E+	E	D	15.3	18.40	7.8	7.6	14.4	5.7	5.8	7.8	14.5
▼ GORHAM SVGS BK	GORHAM	ME	C	C+	C+	576.0	6.64	3.6	0.4	41.7	24.3	7.5	9.3	15.3
GOSHEN COMMUNITY BK	GOSHEN	IN	C	C	C	49.1	11.28	21.4	2.1	8.5	0.0	6.7	10.6	12.3
▼ GOTHAM BK OF NEW YORK	NEW YORK	NY	B	B+	A	169.1	-0.38	37.6	0.0	0.8	37.0	10.0	11.5	22.5
▲ GOTHENBURG ST B&TC	GOTHENBURG	NE	B	C+	C-	79.4	-2.09	20.9	4.3	4.2	12.4	8.7	10.4	13.9
GOUVERNEUR S&LA	GOUVERNEUR	NY	A-	A-	A-	98.4	10.24	3.8	9.2	53.0	14.5	10.0	17.7	32.1
▲ GRABILL BK	GRABILL	IN	B	B-	B-	500.1	15.84	10.0	1.7	12.7	14.9	7.4	9.5	12.8
GRAFTON ST BK	GRAFTON	WI	B	B	B	170.3	11.48	17.3	1.7	9.6	15.8	5.9	8.4	11.7
GRAHAM NB	GRAHAM	TX	B-	B-	B-	91.0	6.93	8.9	16.1	5.9	0.8	4.7	10.2	10.9
GRAHAM S&LA FA	GRAHAM	TX	C+	C+	C	81.5	0.55	0.6	2.3	58.8	2.5	6.7	8.8	17.4
▲ GRAND B&TC OF FLORIDA	W PALM BEACH	FL	C+	C	C	243.5	52.13	17.7	2.3	10.5	14.5	6.3	9.5	12.0
▲ GRAND BK	DALLAS	TX	C-	D+	D	148.5	7.25	9.1	2.6	7.2	28.9	8.4	9.9	17.7
GRAND BK FOR SVGS FSB	HATTIESBURG	MS	D+	D+	E-	45.1	-19.50	0.5	2.0	72.1	0.0	8.7	10.1	19.5
GRAND BK NA	HAMILTON	NJ	B	B+	B-	166.6	5.43	8.4	1.1	7.7	13.5	6.6	9.7	12.2
GRAND BK OF TX	GRAND PRAIRIE	TX	C-	C-	C-	73.1	3.88	13.2	4.9	6.1	11.9	4.6	7.1	10.8
GRAND HAVEN BK	GRAND HAVEN	MI	C	C	C	112.9	-14.13	21.3	2.5	12.9	0.0	3.8	8.7	10.4
▲ GRAND LAKE BK	TULSA	OK	C+	C	D	136.1	13.85	18.2	2.7	16.4	17.2	6.3	8.6	12.0
GRAND MARAIS ST BK	GRAND MARAIS	MN	B	B	B	64.8	-4.98	23.6	3.4	35.2	18.2	5.8	7.8	13.8
GRAND MARSH ST BK	GRAND MARSH	WI	A	A	A	97.0	-2.73	4.4	2.6	34.6	39.2	10.0	13.5	25.8
GRAND MOUNTAIN BANK, FSB	GRANBY	CO	D	D	NR	24.1	N/A	5.6	2.2	30.9	18.3	10.0	12.7	22.6
GRAND RAPIDS ST BK	GRAND RAPIDS	MN	B+	B+	B+	241.4	0.61	8.3	6.5	13.7	50.6	7.3	9.2	14.8
▲ GRAND SAVINGS BK	GROVE	OK	B-	C	C-	159.5	10.59	4.3	17.1	37.0	2.4	7.5	9.3	13.7
▲ GRAND SOUTH BANK	GREENVILLE	SC	D+	C-	C+	200.2	29.04	15.0	3.6	13.4	7.9	4.3	8.1	10.6
GRAND VALLEY NB	GRAND JUNCTION	CO	B-	C+	C+	140.7	9.60	5.7	1.4	6.0	44.9	5.2	7.2	12.5
▲ GRANGE BK	COLUMBUS	OH	C-	D+	D-	222.0	56.92	8.4	14.6	32.0	18.4	7.0	9.0	13.3
GRANGER NB	GRANGER	TX	C+	B-	B-	21.9	1.46	2.3	2.6	3.6	62.5	10.0	12.6	32.7
▲ GRANITE CMNTY BK NA	GRANITE BAY	CA	C-	D+	D	66.1	50.44	11.6	0.6	7.9	6.5	7.4	10.5	12.8
GRANITE FALLS BK	GRANITE FALLS	MN	D	D	D	64.4	28.28	6.6	2.8	2.9	42.2	4.5	6.5	13.2
▲ GRANITE ST BK	MONROVIA	CA	B-	C+	C+	108.7	9.58	9.5	1.6	2.4	8.8	7.2	9.1	14.9

Asset Quality Index	Non-Performing Loans as a % of Total Loans	Non-Performing Loans as a % of Capital	Net Charge-offs Avg Loans	Profitability Index	Net Income ($Mil)	Return on Assets (R.O.A.)	Return on Equity (R.O.E.)	Net Interest Spread	Overhead Efficiency Ratio	Liquidity Index	Liquidity Ratio	Hot Money Ratio	Stability Index
3.8	2.13	13.8	0.00	9.9	1.3	1.67	20.82	4.57	44.3	4.8	9.8	2.4	6.8
4.0	2.71	11.8	0.25	2.2	0.0	0.06	0.47	4.90	94.2	4.8	54.2	13.3	5.1
8.2	0.02	0.1	-0.12	3.2	0.1	0.39	4.27	3.51	87.0	7.7	91.2	0.5	5.5
5.9	0.71	2.9	0.00	6.7	0.2	1.19	11.64	4.00	54.1	7.7	118.8	6.1	5.0
8.2	0.42	2.7	0.00	2.2	0.1	0.31	3.04	1.45	73.4	5.0	N/A	0.0	4.9
9.9	0.12	0.9	0.00	2.8	0.2	0.36	5.56	2.81	76.6	8.8	281.2	8.3	2.8
7.3	0.61	0.8	0.29	5.8	0.1	1.29	5.45	5.33	66.6	3.8	54.7	16.9	4.6
8.0	0.72	3.2	-0.03	7.4	0.7	1.28	10.88	4.18	56.6	2.8	45.5	27.5	6.9
7.4	0.25	1.6	0.09	8.6	8.6	1.43	16.98	4.00	54.4	4.9	21.8	5.5	7.9
7.8	0.06	0.3	0.01	5.9	4.5	1.01	11.11	3.23	65.1	6.3	64.6	8.9	6.6
7.8	1.89	5.2	-0.49	3.9	0.4	0.79	6.16	3.20	72.8	7.4	105.5	6.3	7.0
8.0	0.06	0.4	0.00	8.2	0.9	1.84	15.47	4.06	54.7	2.8	27.7	17.1	8.9
6.5	0.39	2.3	0.00	10.0	0.7	1.75	13.57	4.58	42.8	3.3	52.6	22.5	8.3
9.5	0.00	0.0	0.00	4.3	0.1	0.67	4.17	3.10	67.5	1.5	22.3	27.3	5.9
8.5	0.00	0.0	0.00	3.6	0.3	0.52	5.36	3.44	72.7	2.7	18.1	15.7	5.5
3.6	1.39	7.6	-0.08	1.1	0.3	0.19	2.25	3.06	78.2	1.3	19.8	28.3	2.6
7.9	0.25	2.2	0.66	2.5	0.3	0.49	8.05	3.64	76.5	1.7	13.8	20.5	2.6
9.3	0.04	0.4	0.03	10.0	47.6	3.05	28.02	3.86	27.6	0.2	4.0	91.0	5.8
7.3	0.00	0.0	0.00	10.0	25.2	5.43	12.45	4.59	3.6	2.1	33.3	39.2	5.2
6.6	0.49	3.4	0.27	6.0	0.9	0.75	7.74	5.79	81.1	3.6	24.1	12.0	5.2
6.9	0.00	0.0	0.42	2.5	0.1	0.69	6.22	4.24	71.1	2.3	29.8	20.9	0.0
6.6	0.23	2.1	0.13	5.0	3.8	0.87	12.50	3.16	61.2	2.9	24.0	15.4	4.9
4.7	1.29	9.0	0.20	6.9	18.0	1.35	15.37	4.13	60.8	0.5	6.6	61.5	6.8
4.4	1.32	11.7	0.85	5.2	0.4	0.58	8.74	5.95	71.5	5.6	52.1	10.2	2.8
7.8	0.43	2.3	0.01	6.1	1.0	1.58	19.00	2.95	51.4	2.9	50.8	29.5	5.5
3.3	1.56	14.3	0.00	2.8	0.1	0.67	9.13	3.01	90.7	1.3	13.3	27.0	0.3
6.1	0.09	0.9	0.00	10.0	1.9	3.04	37.94	5.26	37.6	8.9	193.0	6.4	6.2
8.6	0.00	0.0	0.00	4.9	0.1	0.93	11.68	3.19	58.0	2.9	16.3	14.7	5.3
8.3	0.00	0.0	0.00	0.0	-0.6	-3.78	-11.56	2.92	193.1	7.8	267.4	13.4	0.0
4.2	0.54	4.0	0.45	5.6	2.0	1.22	11.92	5.76	72.6	4.0	33.4	12.7	3.5
7.4	0.00	0.0	0.03	10.0	2.9	2.98	21.19	6.22	73.0	0.5	3.2	46.8	4.7
8.2	0.00	0.0	0.11	5.9	0.3	1.20	15.48	3.96	54.0	2.3	21.9	17.9	2.6
6.0	2.97	12.9	0.00	3.0	0.0	0.22	1.85	5.65	94.9	3.2	27.8	13.8	4.9
4.6	0.63	6.1	0.06	4.2	0.1	0.23	3.40	4.27	75.8	3.5	35.6	15.9	2.4
3.2	6.32	17.7	1.50	1.3	0.0	0.18	1.02	4.53	88.3	1.7	31.5	31.2	3.0
7.8	0.07	0.5	0.03	2.0	0.0	0.42	5.42	3.82	87.9	7.1	129.9	10.4	0.8
9.1	0.14	1.0	0.01	2.8	0.9	0.31	3.13	3.25	87.4	4.8	28.4	6.3	6.3
5.9	0.05	0.3	0.09	6.3	0.3	1.22	9.18	4.55	69.2	0.6	9.8	41.4	3.1
8.9	0.00	0.0	-0.15	4.0	0.6	0.66	6.22	3.25	65.7	1.2	25.8	32.9	7.0
7.5	0.20	1.2	0.13	6.6	0.6	1.33	12.73	4.23	53.3	2.7	36.5	20.5	5.4
7.0	0.28	1.1	0.28	6.2	0.5	1.06	5.82	4.29	62.4	1.9	10.7	19.3	7.2
6.2	0.35	2.7	-0.02	6.9	2.7	1.14	13.75	3.48	53.2	3.1	40.4	19.6	5.1
5.6	0.34	3.0	0.04	8.9	1.2	1.37	16.43	4.29	55.8	3.9	25.8	10.7	6.7
6.4	0.19	1.5	0.03	6.5	0.8	1.81	17.81	3.75	59.7	4.6	32.6	9.2	6.6
5.9	0.65	5.1	0.03	5.2	0.5	1.11	12.55	3.59	72.0	2.0	29.8	25.3	5.7
8.4	0.00	0.0	0.00	3.9	0.7	0.61	7.36	4.43	72.6	4.7	22.8	5.4	4.1
8.9	0.00	0.0	0.00	2.1	0.4	0.61	6.45	2.38	69.9	7.9	85.3	1.8	1.5
5.0	0.74	6.2	0.05	9.1	0.7	3.07	35.91	6.00	71.7	0.9	9.2	31.3	1.7
5.9	0.71	5.4	0.00	5.6	1.1	1.33	14.04	3.98	67.8	4.7	57.6	15.8	3.5
4.3	2.22	18.2	0.10	6.7	0.5	1.48	21.86	6.00	77.5	5.9	42.1	4.2	3.3
0.0	4.56	38.3	0.72	3.7	-0.1	-0.20	-2.28	3.73	64.3	3.0	8.1	13.5	5.5
4.6	0.98	7.1	0.21	4.2	0.7	1.01	11.15	4.31	68.8	2.5	27.1	18.2	3.9
8.7	0.00	0.0	0.01	8.9	0.7	2.19	28.53	4.47	53.9	3.9	21.9	10.3	5.9
6.9	1.32	5.0	0.00	9.4	0.8	1.61	12.49	3.66	38.1	5.4	49.0	9.5	8.6
9.3	0.00	0.0	0.00	0.0	-0.2	-1.86	-9.36	3.31	149.5	1.1	34.1	49.8	0.0
6.5	0.82	3.9	0.10	6.6	2.0	1.64	17.09	4.05	56.9	1.1	14.1	29.9	7.0
3.9	0.71	6.0	0.52	7.4	1.4	1.83	20.33	5.05	58.6	2.4	26.4	18.2	3.4
1.7	1.76	16.6	0.76	3.6	0.5	0.56	7.13	3.48	57.8	2.8	43.6	25.1	3.3
7.0	0.43	2.6	0.09	7.9	0.9	1.25	17.72	4.55	64.3	6.8	71.0	6.2	4.5
7.8	0.15	1.3	0.05	2.0	0.1	0.14	1.46	2.24	82.1	0.4	5.9	69.0	4.7
8.3	3.10	5.5	0.64	3.3	0.0	0.38	2.99	3.51	88.4	6.2	76.2	8.1	5.2
7.4	0.00	0.0	0.00	3.1	0.2	0.73	6.50	4.93	76.1	4.4	47.1	14.0	0.9
6.8	0.69	3.3	-0.01	4.9	0.4	1.36	19.19	3.21	56.7	7.3	92.0	5.2	1.8
6.1	1.21	7.2	0.00	5.1	0.4	0.73	7.92	4.34	74.2	5.1	59.6	14.5	4.9

| Name | City | State | Weiss Safety Rating | 2003 Weiss Safety Rating | 2002 Weiss Safety Rating | Total Assets ($Mil) | One Year Asset Growth | Asset Mix (As a % of Total Assets) | | | | Capital-ization Index | Leverage Ratio | Risk-based Capital Ratio |
								Comm-ercial Loans	Cons-umer Loans	Home Mort-gages	Secur-ities			
GRANITE SVGS BK	ROCKPORT	MA	B-	B	B+	53.0	-3.91	0.0	0.7	41.2	32.4	10.0	14.8	33.7
GRANT COUNTY BK	ULYSSES	KS	B+	B+	B+	139.7	-1.38	5.9	3.5	18.4	46.0	7.8	9.6	16.9
▲ GRANT COUNTY BK	MEDFORD	OK	B+	B	B	60.5	-3.05	1.9	4.0	4.7	66.3	10.0	14.5	34.3
▲ GRANT COUNTY BK	PETERSBURG	WV	B-	C+	C+	173.3	-1.48	6.4	11.3	27.7	10.7	8.0	9.7	14.4
GRANT COUNTY DEPOSIT BK	WILLIAMSTOWN	KY	B	B	B	93.4	6.38	0.3	5.4	21.4	29.6	9.1	10.4	18.8
GRANT COUNTY ST BK	SWAYZEE	IN	B-	B-	B-	61.0	-4.87	2.7	5.6	38.2	21.3	9.5	10.7	21.1
GRANT COUNTY ST BK	CARSON	ND	B-	B-	B-	22.0	1.20	3.9	1.8	1.1	1.6	10.0	11.6	17.7
GRANTS ST BK	GRANTS	NM	C+	C+	C+	80.9	11.50	11.7	3.3	7.7	47.6	5.8	7.8	19.5
GRANVILLE NB	GRANVILLE	IL	C+	C+	B-	44.8	6.82	6.7	9.2	26.8	27.9	6.1	8.1	14.4
GRAPELAND ST BK	GRAPELAND	TX	E-	E-	E-	13.5	-26.79	4.4	17.8	0.9	57.1	5.4	7.4	16.2
GRATIOT ST BK	GRATIOT	WI	B	B	B+	33.7	9.80	1.3	1.8	4.8	56.8	10.0	15.2	31.9
GRATZ NB	GRATZ	PA	A	A	A	93.8	10.86	7.2	2.1	34.6	24.3	10.0	12.4	22.1
GRAYSON NB	INDEPENDENCE	VA	B-	B-	B-	263.8	2.29	4.1	5.1	34.0	17.6	6.2	8.2	13.5
▼ GREAT BASIN BK OF NEVADA	ELKO	NV	C-	C	D+	144.6	24.40	11.3	7.5	4.2	26.9	5.3	7.7	11.2
GREAT EASTERN BK	NEW YORK	NY	B+	B+	B	295.6	5.81	14.1	0.4	2.1	23.7	9.1	10.4	15.3
▼ GREAT EASTERN BK OF	MIAMI	FL	C-	C-	C-	65.0	7.88	17.6	1.1	3.1	12.9	9.2	10.5	14.8
GREAT FLORIDA BK	MIAMI	FL	D	NR	NR	57.9	N/A	0.0	0.0	0.0	62.2	10.0	96.3	1,022.2
GREAT LAKES BANKERS BK	GAHANNA	OH	C+	C+	C+	43.0	6.12	4.8	0.0	2.0	9.8	7.8	10.0	13.2
GREAT LAKES BK NA	BLUE ISLAND	IL	C+	C+	C+	686.3	-0.34	14.5	0.8	11.0	35.7	5.3	7.3	12.3
GREAT MIDWEST BK, SSB	BROOKFIELD	WI	A	A	A-	462.5	-6.43	0.0	0.4	73.0	10.7	10.0	16.9	21.2
GREAT NORTHERN BK	ANTIOCH	IL	C-	C-	D+	20.0	18.74	2.7	1.1	9.2	22.2	10.0	19.7	29.2
GREAT NORTHERN BK	ST MICHAEL	MN	D-	D-	E	59.9	12.73	35.1	4.3	12.6	10.4	3.0	8.2	10.0
▲ GREAT PLAINS BK	EUREKA	SD	C	D+	D-	38.8	0.67	17.3	4.4	2.3	16.7	10.0	14.2	15.0
▼ GREAT PLAINS NB	BELFIELD	ND	C-	C	C	52.7	7.49	12.0	6.0	2.9	26.7	8.4	10.0	15.6
▲ GREAT PLAINS NB	ELK CITY	OK	B	B-	C+	204.6	8.70	12.9	11.2	14.5	14.1	5.4	7.8	11.3
▲ GREAT RIVER B&T	PRINCETON	IA	C+	C-	D-	77.2	5.56	16.5	4.3	9.8	21.4	8.6	10.0	13.8
▲ GREAT SOUTHERN BK	REEDS SPRING	MO	B+	B-	C+	1,698.7	17.86	5.3	4.9	9.4	19.8	6.3	8.7	12.0
▲ GREAT SOUTHERN NB	MERIDIAN	MS	B+	B	B	227.5	0.43	11.1	11.7	14.3	28.1	7.6	9.4	16.2
GREAT WESTERN BK	CLIVE	IA	B-	B-	B-	517.8	27.94	13.8	3.4	14.7	18.0	5.9	7.9	11.7
▲ GREAT WESTERN BK	OMAHA	NE	B-	C+	B-	898.5	8.47	20.0	3.3	4.0	11.3	4.0	8.2	10.5
GREAT WESTERN BK	WATERTOWN	SD	B-	B-	B-	973.3	11.04	14.4	6.1	8.6	16.3	5.8	8.4	11.6
▲ GREATBANK	ALGONQUIN	IL	C+	C	C	270.7	7.12	10.1	32.1	5.4	6.3	4.4	6.4	11.5
▲ GREATBANK, A NA	EVANSTON	IL	C+	C	C	279.8	13.48	5.8	27.4	4.6	9.6	4.6	6.9	10.8
▼ GREATER ATLANTIC BK	RESTON	VA	D	D+	D	503.1	-4.48	10.5	0.1	18.0	40.7	3.6	5.6	11.3
▲ GREATER BAY BK NA	PALO ALTO	CA	B+	B-	B-	6,943.3	336.41	12.0	2.1	2.2	27.8	7.7	9.5	13.6
GREATER BUFFALO SVGS BK	BUFFALO	NY	C	C-	D-	493.3	67.90	2.4	2.5	39.7	40.7	9.6	10.7	19.7
▼ GREATER CHICAGO BK	BELLWOOD	IL	C-	C	C+	60.8	-6.19	21.8	0.4	23.9	10.3	9.8	10.8	18.2
GREATER COMMUNITY BK	TOTOWA	NJ	C+	C+	B-	504.2	6.72	3.8	0.6	12.3	21.4	3.5	6.9	10.3
▲ GREATER DE VALLEY SVGS	BROOMALL	PA	C+	C	C-	382.8	-0.47	1.2	0.9	23.5	32.8	7.5	9.3	16.9
▲ GREATER ROME BK	ROME	GA	B	B-	B-	147.2	19.81	11.3	7.4	16.0	25.6	6.9	8.9	12.8
▲ GREATER SOUTH TEXAS BK	FALFURRIAS	TX	E	E-	E-	28.2	-28.58	2.3	7.8	51.0	18.8	8.3	9.9	17.9
▲ GREEN BELT BANK & TRUST	IOWA FALLS	IA	A-	B+	B+	136.8	-0.93	10.0	3.5	12.3	12.5	10.0	11.2	15.2
GREEN LAKE ST BK	GREEN LAKE	WI	C+	B-	B-	63.9	11.68	22.3	2.7	25.2	11.6	7.1	9.0	12.9
GREEN RIVER BK	MORGANTOWN	KY	B-	B-	C+	49.5	1.90	3.1	10.3	37.9	7.8	6.2	8.2	12.6
GREENE COUNTY BK	STRAFFORD	MO	D+	D+	D	30.3	-3.13	4.0	3.9	11.9	59.6	7.6	9.4	21.3
▲ GREENE COUNTY BK	GREENEVILLE	TN	B	B-	B-	1,123.6	23.75	11.4	6.5	21.3	2.9	5.2	8.7	11.2
GREENE COUNTY	CATSKILL	NY	C-	NR	NR	5.2	N/A	0.0	0.0	0.0	72.0	10.0	65.8	190.2
▼ GREENEVILLE FEDERAL BK	GREENEVILLE	TN	C	C+	C	129.2	0.02	7.3	7.8	32.3	1.7	9.2	11.4	14.3
GREENFIELD BKG CO	GREENFIELD	IN	A-	A-	A-	275.2	3.67	3.5	5.0	9.7	49.4	10.0	11.7	24.4
GREENFIELD BKG CO	GREENFIELD	TN	B-	B-	B-	46.8	-1.66	8.5	12.6	25.6	24.2	10.0	12.4	16.7
GREENFIELD CO-OP	GREENFIELD	MA	A	A	A	201.6	3.54	5.1	0.3	42.4	28.7	10.0	11.6	20.5
GREENFIELD SVGS BK	GREENFIELD	MA	B	B+	A-	484.1	6.53	1.9	0.1	36.3	40.2	8.6	10.0	17.9
GREENLEAF - WAYSIDE BK	GREENLEAF	WI	C-	C-	C-	47.5	-5.31	16.5	4.4	23.8	6.5	7.4	9.2	13.6
GREENPOINT BK	BROOKLYN	NY	B	B	B-	25,955.7	14.46	0.0	0.1	54.5	26.5	6.2	8.2	13.9
GREENSBURG ST BK	GREENSBURG	KS	A-	A-	A-	36.9	0.98	3.6	6.3	6.4	66.6	10.0	15.1	38.1
▲ GREENSFORK TOWNSHIP ST	SPARTANBURG	IN	A	A-	C+	70.4	19.43	0.2	0.8	1.6	66.9	10.0	21.9	60.1
GREENVILLE BKG CO	GREENVILLE	GA	B-	B-	B-	23.7	6.02	7.7	5.0	19.8	23.5	10.0	13.3	22.5
GREENVILLE COMMUNITY BK	GREENVILLE	MI	C	C-	D+	100.1	12.61	23.7	10.3	21.8	10.3	5.7	8.2	11.5
GREENVILLE FIRST BK NA	GREENVILLE	SC	C-	C-	D	273.1	42.42	13.3	1.9	20.2	6.1	3.9	7.8	10.5
GREENVILLE FS&LA	GREENVILLE	OH	C	C	B	126.3	-7.95	1.3	3.6	46.0	29.4	9.6	10.8	22.8
GREENVILLE NB	GREENVILLE	OH	B+	B+	A-	281.4	1.05	3.8	12.3	40.5	18.5	7.6	9.4	16.2
▼ GREENVILLE SVGS BK	GREENVILLE	PA	B-	B	B+	130.7	-1.61	1.5	2.0	62.0	13.1	9.7	10.8	20.3
GREENWOODS ST BK	LAKE MILLS	WI	B-	C+	C	41.9	-3.38	4.0	2.5	23.6	42.3	6.6	8.6	13.4
GREER ST BK	GREER	SC	B	B	B	222.7	13.22	12.2	4.2	11.5	36.7	6.0	8.0	12.7

Asset Quality Index	Non-Performing Loans as a % of Total Loans	Non-Performing Loans as a % of Capital	Net Charge-offs Avg Loans	Profitability Index	Net Income ($Mil)	Return on Assets (R.O.A.)	Return on Equity (R.O.E.)	Net Interest Spread	Overhead Efficiency Ratio	Liquidity Index	Liquidity Ratio	Hot Money Ratio	Stability Index
8.8	0.84	3.0	0.01	3.2	0.1	0.36	2.37	3.20	80.6	7.1	106.4	8.9	7.0
6.2	1.97	9.6	-0.05	5.3	0.9	1.21	12.25	3.64	64.2	1.8	18.1	20.8	6.1
7.9	2.82	5.1	0.37	5.1	0.4	1.25	9.02	3.10	60.0	1.2	28.2	36.0	6.1
4.4	0.74	5.4	0.52	7.0	1.0	1.20	12.64	4.60	54.7	4.6	43.0	12.7	5.5
5.6	1.04	5.6	0.13	4.7	0.4	0.75	7.21	4.31	74.7	4.4	34.6	11.0	5.7
7.8	0.35	1.9	0.03	4.4	0.3	0.80	7.39	4.14	70.7	5.0	63.2	13.8	5.1
7.0	0.16	1.0	0.00	6.6	0.2	1.75	15.30	3.84	57.4	5.9	55.3	5.4	5.6
5.8	1.38	5.3	1.02	5.6	0.5	1.27	16.33	4.13	71.5	4.3	42.6	13.9	4.3
4.0	1.68	12.1	0.05	4.5	0.2	0.67	7.98	3.73	73.8	5.9	47.2	5.5	4.9
4.1	4.72	17.2	0.41	3.9	0.1	1.09	16.92	5.20	70.7	2.5	30.1	17.5	0.0
4.9	4.09	9.7	0.41	4.8	0.2	1.08	7.30	3.26	52.7	4.9	53.8	13.0	6.9
9.1	0.01	0.0	0.00	9.6	0.9	1.91	15.34	4.24	37.1	5.7	55.9	9.2	7.8
4.5	1.05	8.5	0.09	6.3	1.7	1.26	15.83	4.19	57.8	3.1	27.9	15.3	5.1
0.3	16.67	129.1	0.24	5.1	0.7	0.95	12.32	5.99	78.1	2.2	15.5	18.1	2.9
8.3	0.20	1.1	-0.11	6.0	1.1	0.77	7.42	4.10	70.8	5.6	52.1	10.0	5.5
1.7	3.17	19.9	0.09	2.9	0.2	0.49	4.55	4.38	74.7	3.2	76.7	36.2	4.8
10.0	0.00	0.0	0.00	0.0	-0.8	-2.93	-2.98	0.25	1,314.5	10.0	15,044.4	0.0	0.0
7.6	0.00	0.0	0.00	5.4	0.2	0.79	9.01	4.95	74.7	5.3	21.0	0.8	4.6
7.5	0.40	3.0	0.25	4.2	2.9	0.83	11.40	3.97	75.2	6.6	65.4	7.2	3.5
8.9	0.32	1.5	0.00	5.8	1.3	0.57	3.28	3.14	75.7	4.0	34.3	12.9	8.3
8.9	0.00	0.0	0.00	1.7	0.0	-0.05	-0.25	3.57	99.4	2.9	79.9	42.8	0.0
8.0	0.17	1.5	0.04	3.6	0.2	0.65	8.15	5.01	81.8	1.7	14.0	20.5	2.2
3.5	2.40	11.8	-0.01	10.0	0.6	3.21	24.72	5.08	46.0	4.7	14.9	3.9	7.2
2.1	2.97	17.6	0.43	5.7	0.3	0.99	9.80	4.29	58.9	3.2	29.6	15.3	4.3
4.6	0.58	5.2	0.24	9.2	2.5	2.48	30.66	5.37	54.1	1.5	12.5	24.3	5.8
8.3	0.00	0.0	0.04	3.4	0.3	0.66	5.99	4.28	82.2	3.9	7.5	8.2	4.1
5.5	0.54	4.1	0.21	9.6	13.3	1.65	19.17	4.03	45.6	0.8	12.2	37.9	7.5
5.9	0.53	3.1	0.21	6.8	1.3	1.13	11.76	5.56	72.4	3.6	28.7	13.1	5.6
4.0	0.97	6.3	0.30	7.2	2.9	1.17	10.80	4.67	56.9	4.5	18.8	5.8	4.4
4.8	0.59	5.0	0.12	7.5	6.7	1.54	18.63	4.50	55.3	4.3	42.9	14.2	6.3
4.6	1.02	8.4	0.25	9.5	7.7	1.63	18.26	4.01	47.5	2.0	24.0	20.1	6.4
5.1	0.41	4.8	0.16	8.5	2.8	2.03	32.40	3.95	60.1	2.9	41.6	23.4	4.5
5.8	0.04	0.5	0.09	6.3	2.2	1.56	23.21	3.94	61.6	1.7	12.7	21.0	4.5
6.7	0.45	4.2	0.03	2.6	0.3	0.11	1.95	1.57	96.1	1.5	31.4	33.6	2.3
6.4	0.91	5.8	0.57	9.6	45.8	1.75	20.93	6.49	60.1	3.8	24.9	13.6	6.0
9.6	0.17	1.0	0.00	3.2	1.4	0.65	8.07	3.00	66.4	2.1	14.0	18.5	4.4
2.0	3.70	24.3	0.07	5.8	0.3	1.04	9.56	5.39	81.8	5.8	60.6	9.5	5.9
7.2	0.16	1.1	0.13	5.7	2.3	0.92	10.70	4.14	65.2	6.9	65.0	4.7	5.1
5.6	0.76	4.2	0.32	3.4	1.4	0.71	7.63	3.59	75.3	7.9	115.0	5.8	4.8
7.4	0.12	0.9	0.32	6.0	0.7	1.00	11.47	4.06	65.0	3.9	36.0	14.3	4.6
0.3	12.70	70.9	0.58	1.8	0.0	0.20	2.06	4.68	95.9	0.9	19.8	38.3	0.0
7.4	0.70	4.5	0.06	7.9	1.3	1.88	17.40	3.86	48.7	5.8	59.8	10.9	7.2
4.7	0.87	7.2	0.06	8.6	0.5	1.54	17.47	4.06	40.5	3.4	54.9	21.0	5.6
6.1	0.24	2.1	0.27	5.7	0.4	1.40	16.77	3.98	66.0	3.0	41.5	21.1	5.0
6.0	2.49	9.0	-0.89	3.6	0.1	0.65	7.20	3.66	80.9	4.6	12.2	4.4	1.9
5.7	0.59	4.5	0.48	7.5	6.4	1.14	11.15	4.76	56.7	3.8	27.2	14.4	6.9
10.0	0.00	0.0	0.00	1.4	0.0	0.06	0.13	0.19	66.7	5.0	N/A	0.0	0.0
2.4	2.12	15.8	0.09	6.6	0.6	0.88	8.06	4.37	60.4	1.0	7.2	30.0	6.6
7.8	1.69	4.9	0.26	5.4	1.4	1.06	9.03	3.85	68.5	8.8	137.3	1.8	7.3
6.2	1.25	5.5	-0.09	4.2	0.2	0.96	8.03	3.48	71.2	3.7	65.5	22.8	4.5
9.7	0.20	1.1	0.00	6.5	1.0	1.01	8.94	3.68	59.9	4.5	23.8	6.4	7.3
9.1	0.43	2.2	0.00	4.2	1.4	0.60	5.73	3.20	75.9	4.2	49.2	16.1	6.5
4.6	0.71	4.9	-0.35	2.3	0.0	-0.01	-0.13	3.97	91.6	6.5	69.6	6.7	2.8
5.3	1.17	8.2	0.03	9.5	243.0	2.00	20.98	3.30	40.7	3.8	6.6	9.3	9.6
8.1	2.36	4.3	-0.02	8.7	0.3	1.44	9.35	3.96	47.3	3.9	38.4	15.1	7.3
6.8	0.00	0.0	0.00	9.5	2.5	6.48	30.35	1.80	35.7	9.9	648.1	0.4	8.9
8.6	0.00	0.0	-0.01	5.0	0.1	1.01	7.67	4.90	77.9	4.1	32.2	9.8	5.3
3.4	1.07	9.1	0.20	4.2	0.4	0.70	8.75	3.26	59.8	1.7	26.7	26.3	3.7
7.0	0.18	1.8	0.16	4.0	1.0	0.75	10.07	3.32	52.4	0.5	2.7	41.9	1.3
4.9	1.10	5.7	-0.01	2.4	0.0	-0.03	-0.31	2.45	103.9	4.5	35.6	11.1	5.4
5.0	0.69	5.0	0.07	7.8	2.1	1.46	15.89	4.37	52.3	4.4	24.6	7.1	6.7
7.3	0.39	2.8	0.05	4.3	0.5	0.78	7.28	3.22	58.9	4.9	48.7	12.6	6.4
9.5	0.00	0.0	0.06	9.1	0.4	1.96	23.20	3.84	53.1	6.1	68.4	9.0	4.8
5.2	1.13	7.1	0.66	6.1	1.2	1.10	12.66	3.65	66.4	1.6	14.0	22.9	5.1

Name	City	State	Weiss Safety Rating	2003 Weiss Safety Rating	2002 Weiss Safety Rating	Total Assets ($Mil)	One Year Asset Growth	Asset Mix (As a % of Total Assets)				Capital-ization Index	Leverage Ratio	Risk-based Capital Ratio
								Comm-ercial Loans	Cons-umer Loans	Home Mort-gages	Secur-ities			
▲ GREERS FERRY LAKE ST BK	HEBER SPRINGS	AR	C	C-	C+	49.2	-9.94	15.2	5.7	26.6	27.3	6.6	8.6	15.8
GRIFFITH SVGS BK	GRIFFITH	IN	C	C	C	98.3	-10.44	0.0	2.3	65.4	18.7	5.3	7.3	13.4
GRINNELL ST BK	MARENGO	IA	B+	B	B	121.5	-2.98	5.3	1.6	9.4	35.7	10.0	12.0	15.0
GRUNDY BK	MORRIS	IL	B-	C+	C	146.7	-1.98	2.8	3.9	10.2	15.1	4.3	7.5	10.7
GRUNDY NB	GRUNDY	VA	A-	A-	A-	225.6	2.56	18.9	7.0	7.9	52.9	10.0	20.9	38.0
▼ GRUNDY NB OF GRUNDY CTR	GRUNDY CENTER	IA	B	B+	B+	137.1	7.92	16.4	1.4	11.6	29.9	9.3	10.5	14.9
GRUVER ST BK	GRUVER	TX	B+	B+	A-	33.1	3.09	6.5	3.2	0.8	35.3	10.0	14.6	24.8
▲ GSL SAVINGS BANK	GUTTENBERG	NJ	B	B-	B-	114.5	-1.22	0.0	0.0	35.6	51.8	10.0	11.8	29.6
GUARANTEE ST BK	LAWTON	OK	E-	E-	D-	53.8	8.56	13.8	9.5	14.3	6.6	1.9	6.9	8.9
GUARANTY B&TC	DENVER	CO	C+	C+	C+	1,052.7	6.25	21.1	0.9	11.6	9.1	3.2	8.7	10.1
GUARANTY B&TC	CEDAR RAPIDS	IA	C	C	C	241.1	4.86	5.1	0.8	18.6	45.3	5.1	7.1	12.9
GUARANTY B&TC	NEW ROADS	LA	B-	B-	B-	53.9	11.14	11.5	4.9	20.0	13.4	7.4	9.3	16.1
GUARANTY B&TC	BELZONI	MS	B+	B+	B	251.3	7.48	14.2	4.3	7.1	31.0	10.0	11.3	17.1
GUARANTY B&TC	HUNTINGTON	WV	C	C-	C-	107.3	5.44	20.3	11.5	10.3	17.9	7.8	10.1	13.1
▲ GUARANTY B&TC-DELHI	DELHI	LA	A	A-	A-	79.3	0.46	7.5	10.0	17.0	18.6	9.9	11.0	16.4
▲ GUARANTY BANK	MILWAUKEE	WI	B+	B-	C	1,888.4	-9.28	0.1	8.0	29.8	2.7	9.9	11.0	14.9
▲ GUARANTY BK	MAMOU	LA	C+	C	C	83.8	-0.14	8.1	8.8	27.8	17.3	6.7	8.8	14.9
▼ GUARANTY BK	SPRINGFIELD	MO	B	B+	NR	409.6	4.98	10.7	1.0	31.4	4.1	6.8	8.8	13.0
GUARANTY BK	AUSTIN	TX	C+	C+	C+	16,476.5	-5.11	11.6	0.3	26.6	32.7	4.6	6.6	11.0
GUARANTY BK	CHARLOTTESVILLE	VA	B	B	B	254.8	34.09	2.9	1.3	14.2	7.0	6.4	9.0	12.0
GUARANTY BK OF CALIFORNIA	LOS ANGELES	CA	C+	C+	C	143.7	4.39	16.2	0.1	0.1	15.0	8.0	9.7	16.9
GUARANTY BOND BK	MT PLEASANT	TX	B-	C+	C+	519.2	-1.90	10.5	5.7	27.6	18.0	6.5	8.5	13.3
GUARANTY ST B&TC	BELOIT	KS	B-	B-	B	96.3	15.71	8.2	1.2	8.6	14.8	6.2	9.1	11.9
GUARANTY SVGS & HMSTD	METAIRIE	LA	B-	B-	B	207.7	-2.67	1.1	0.3	21.5	52.9	10.0	12.4	27.0
GUARD SECURITY BK	PLAINS	PA	C-	D+	D+	77.9	6.96	11.2	29.5	0.5	45.3	7.2	9.2	18.2
GUARDIAN BK	VALDOSTA	GA	B-	B-	B-	92.0	10.72	9.8	4.1	25.1	6.7	6.8	8.8	12.3
GUARDIAN SVGS BK	GRANITE CITY	IL	B	B	B	39.6	0.49	0.0	0.8	33.7	58.5	10.0	15.8	49.2
GUARDIAN SVGS BK FSB	CINCINNATI	OH	B-	C+	C-	456.9	-2.20	0.0	0.0	41.1	1.5	6.0	8.0	17.9
▲ GUARDIAN TRUST COMPANY	NEW YORK	NY	D+	D	D	5.3	9.39	0.0	0.0	0.0	59.0	10.0	69.9	170.0
GUERNSEY BK	COLUMBUS	OH	D+	D	D	63.8	20.38	2.2	1.6	36.5	0.0	10.0	11.1	16.6
GUIDE ROCK ST BK	GUIDE ROCK	NE	C-	C-	C-	23.6	7.20	14.4	10.0	3.4	12.8	9.9	11.0	15.5
GUILFORD SVGS BK	GUILFORD	CT	B+	B+	B+	381.8	-0.40	0.7	0.4	48.1	28.5	10.0	13.2	26.3
GULF COAST B&TC	NEW ORLEANS	LA	C-	C-	D	397.6	12.98	16.2	8.0	20.2	7.5	4.2	7.7	10.6
GULF COAST BK	ABBEVILLE	LA	A	A	A-	172.0	2.61	5.1	17.0	12.8	25.0	10.0	16.6	29.3
GULF COAST BK	WINNIE	TX	B+	B+	A-	59.8	3.45	9.1	5.2	10.5	31.7	9.7	10.8	17.1
GULF COAST COMMUNITY BK	PENSACOLA	FL	D	D	NR	76.0	N/A	5.1	2.3	10.7	16.4	10.0	19.7	19.5
GULF FEDERAL BK FSB	MOBILE	AL	E-	E-	E-	15.2	-6.09	9.4	5.4	27.2	15.0	5.4	7.4	14.6
GULF ST COMMUNITY BK	CARRABELLE	FL	A-	A-	B+	110.6	26.57	2.5	1.5	18.2	5.4	8.3	9.8	15.0
▲ GULFSTREAM BUSINESS BK	STUART	FL	B-	C	C+	251.1	37.23	15.0	1.9	5.7	10.8	5.3	8.6	11.2
▲ GULFSTREAM COMMUNITY BK	PORT RICHEY	FL	C+	C	D	45.2	26.60	10.5	2.8	27.4	10.7	10.0	11.2	18.6
▲ GUNNISON B&TC	GUNNISON	CO	C+	C	C-	49.7	8.75	16.1	2.4	12.1	0.0	4.7	8.8	10.9
GUNNISON S&LA	GUNNISON	CO	B-	B-	B-	85.1	0.22	0.0	1.4	66.6	9.6	7.7	9.5	19.7
GUNNISON VALLEY BK	GUNNISON	UT	B-	B+	D+	49.0	6.29	23.5	18.4	4.4	8.3	10.0	11.8	15.5
▲ GUTHRIE COUNTY ST BK	GUTHRIE CENTER	IA	C+	C	C	81.5	9.26	7.3	4.2	26.1	35.0	4.7	6.7	12.9
▼ GWINNETT BKG CO	LAWRENCEVILLE	GA	C+	B-	C+	281.1	26.44	16.8	2.4	4.8	10.2	5.0	9.0	11.0
▲ GWINNETT COMMUNITY BK	DULUTH	GA	B-	C-	C-	227.2	24.12	13.1	2.5	4.7	17.4	6.9	9.7	12.4
▲ H F GEHANT BKG CO	W BROOKLYN	IL	B-	C+	C+	30.8	-3.06	3.6	5.8	18.9	21.3	10.0	13.4	23.0
▲ HABERSHAM BK	CLARKESVILLE	GA	B	B-	C+	377.5	-5.59	4.4	3.9	5.0	19.0	10.0	11.3	15.1
HABIB AMERICAN BK	NEW YORK	NY	B	B	B	281.1	20.88	20.2	1.8	10.5	5.0	7.9	9.6	13.8
HADDON SVG BK	HADDON HEIGHTS	NJ	C+	C+	C+	260.7	8.72	0.0	0.0	29.1	65.3	9.0	10.3	30.2
HAGERSTOWN TRUST CO	HAGERSTOWN	MD	B	B	B+	454.2	0.56	6.0	6.8	17.0	29.3	4.7	6.7	11.6
HALIFAX NB	HALIFAX	PA	A-	A-	A-	58.8	1.11	0.8	1.5	36.4	39.4	10.0	16.3	25.6
▲ HALSTEAD BK	HALSTEAD	KS	C-	D+	C-	53.1	1.04	10.3	6.9	11.7	20.1	5.9	7.9	12.5
HAMILTON BK	HAMILTON	MO	B	B	B	43.7	3.46	5.7	5.0	10.5	39.1	10.0	12.4	21.9
▲ HAMILTON FS&LA	BALTIMORE	MD	B	B-	B-	240.7	-3.61	0.0	0.1	53.0	31.0	10.0	12.7	29.7
HAMLER ST BK	HAMLER	OH	A-	A-	A-	51.0	2.41	3.8	2.8	20.5	39.5	10.0	15.8	29.9
HAMLIN B&TC	SMETHPORT	PA	A	A	A	379.1	8.19	2.0	5.6	26.1	52.7	10.0	13.0	33.0
HAMLIN NB	HAMLIN	TX	B	B	B	87.3	6.49	20.3	5.4	6.0	29.9	10.0	13.7	22.2
HAMPDEN BK	SPRINGFIELD	MA	C	C	C+	410.3	0.19	4.8	0.7	21.7	32.9	5.5	7.5	11.9
▲ HAMPTON ST BK	HAMPTON	IA	B+	B	C+	47.9	-1.07	2.9	3.5	17.8	31.3	10.0	11.1	18.4
HAMPTONS ST BK	SOUTHAMPTON	NY	D-	D-	D-	55.7	33.37	13.0	2.8	0.0	30.6	5.9	7.9	13.4
HANCOCK B&TC	HAWESVILLE	KY	A-	A-	A-	116.0	12.08	5.1	7.0	18.5	57.6	10.0	14.0	28.8
HANCOCK BK	GULFPORT	MS	B+	B+	B+	2,697.1	7.20	5.4	8.6	16.7	30.4	6.2	8.2	14.2
HANCOCK BK OF FLORIDA	TALLAHASSEE	FL	B+	NR	NR	79.6	N/A	5.9	1.9	12.7	27.2	4.9	6.9	11.3

Asset Quality Index	Non-Performing Loans as a % of Total Loans	Non-Performing Loans as a % of Capital	Net Charge-offs Avg Loans	Profitability Index	Net Income ($Mil)	Return on Assets (R.O.A.)	Return on Equity (R.O.E.)	Net Interest Spread	Overhead Efficiency Ratio	Liquidity Index	Liquidity Ratio	Hot Money Ratio	Stability Index
3.8	1.82	12.0	2.19	6.9	0.3	1.27	14.32	4.48	49.4	2.1	14.9	18.6	4.6
6.1	0.77	7.5	0.00	5.2	0.5	1.03	13.88	3.34	45.1	6.5	85.5	9.5	3.3
7.8	0.35	1.4	0.00	5.5	0.8	1.31	10.01	4.37	70.4	5.0	30.3	5.8	7.6
6.4	0.26	1.7	0.08	7.1	1.1	1.52	14.37	4.92	70.7	5.7	41.7	6.2	6.5
6.0	2.86	5.5	0.08	7.4	1.5	1.36	6.32	4.07	49.4	1.2	28.7	36.8	8.9
8.4	0.00	0.0	-0.01	5.6	0.7	1.09	9.31	3.73	67.7	1.6	12.9	22.3	6.8
8.5	0.00	0.0	-0.10	4.8	0.2	1.16	8.10	4.31	71.1	2.4	43.3	31.1	7.2
9.9	0.26	0.9	0.00	4.2	0.4	0.62	5.30	3.52	72.5	6.3	88.9	12.3	6.4
5.3	0.26	2.9	0.45	2.9	0.1	0.52	7.60	5.56	90.1	2.2	14.9	17.9	0.3
4.7	0.77	6.9	0.08	6.6	5.4	1.03	12.15	5.06	68.7	3.7	34.4	17.8	6.8
5.8	1.11	8.5	0.14	4.4	1.4	1.13	17.59	3.68	74.6	2.2	11.8	17.5	2.7
4.9	1.07	7.8	-0.01	8.8	0.3	1.21	13.12	4.86	62.4	4.4	30.9	10.0	5.0
5.0	1.66	8.0	0.06	7.1	2.2	1.73	15.47	4.57	60.7	3.1	39.4	19.3	7.1
5.8	0.26	1.9	-0.05	3.2	0.2	0.38	3.80	3.80	76.8	1.6	13.8	23.4	4.6
7.9	0.29	1.7	0.22	10.0	0.9	2.26	20.02	4.96	58.8	4.3	44.3	14.3	7.5
5.5	0.53	5.4	0.07	7.2	5.8	0.63	7.50	4.18	91.3	0.5	11.0	75.2	5.8
4.5	0.68	4.9	0.09	5.6	0.5	1.12	12.43	5.59	62.3	3.2	26.3	14.4	4.6
7.2	0.29	2.5	0.09	5.9	2.1	1.06	11.09	3.14	55.3	1.5	7.3	22.7	3.8
5.8	0.73	8.1	0.12	4.9	67.4	0.79	13.47	2.67	71.2	0.6	3.7	34.8	3.5
7.5	0.10	0.3	-0.24	4.1	0.3	0.30	2.10	1.69	72.1	4.5	21.4	6.0	5.0
3.6	0.98	7.3	0.22	5.2	0.6	0.87	9.10	4.21	68.8	1.5	18.9	26.2	5.0
4.8	1.01	7.6	0.17	5.1	2.5	0.98	11.13	4.01	67.5	3.2	48.2	22.6	5.3
6.3	0.21	1.6	0.12	5.2	0.5	0.95	10.32	3.77	63.4	3.6	27.7	12.9	4.6
8.6	0.87	2.9	0.06	3.0	0.3	0.23	1.85	2.42	88.1	2.9	4.5	13.6	7.6
6.8	0.16	0.7	0.43	2.2	0.1	0.13	1.35	2.11	84.7	0.7	16.3	52.2	4.6
6.9	0.55	4.6	0.01	4.3	0.4	0.84	9.83	3.98	67.6	3.2	51.8	23.3	3.6
9.8	0.04	0.1	0.20	4.1	0.1	0.51	3.29	2.80	73.3	4.2	30.4	10.8	5.9
5.8	0.75	5.1	0.00	9.5	3.8	1.69	21.73	2.07	49.1	3.3	49.9	23.3	4.7
6.8	0.00	0.0	0.00	2.7	0.0	0.38	0.59	4.57	99.0	3.9	140.3	100.0	0.0
3.0	3.76	26.3	0.00	0.9	0.0	0.10	0.91	3.95	95.0	3.0	53.6	27.0	0.0
4.3	0.94	5.1	-0.04	4.1	0.1	0.99	9.14	4.31	67.0	4.6	47.4	11.2	2.4
9.7	0.36	1.6	-0.02	4.4	1.3	0.66	5.00	3.25	68.4	6.8	81.1	8.4	7.8
2.3	1.99	20.1	0.25	8.9	4.4	2.31	30.97	6.43	61.3	1.7	15.2	21.9	3.8
7.0	0.79	2.7	0.22	7.5	1.0	1.11	6.65	5.52	69.6	5.2	38.7	8.2	7.9
5.7	0.92	4.5	0.53	5.6	0.3	1.00	9.05	5.48	81.9	4.7	33.5	9.2	7.0
9.0	0.00	0.0	0.00	0.0	-0.5	-1.59	-8.21	2.79	126.7	8.1	107.9	2.4	0.0
1.7	4.65	21.5	0.48	0.9	0.0	-0.38	-4.13	4.19	106.9	4.8	45.3	9.6	0.3
8.7	0.00	0.0	0.04	7.3	0.5	1.05	10.32	4.53	69.8	6.8	58.0	4.0	5.7
7.3	0.01	0.1	-0.01	5.5	1.1	0.96	11.56	3.86	54.0	2.6	34.8	20.7	4.6
8.3	0.00	0.0	0.00	3.1	0.1	0.45	4.09	3.66	74.0	2.1	47.0	46.4	1.1
6.8	0.17	1.5	0.00	7.1	0.3	1.26	14.70	5.86	66.9	1.2	16.3	29.1	3.9
7.6	0.62	4.9	0.00	4.0	0.2	0.49	5.32	2.75	74.2	1.6	17.3	23.2	4.8
2.9	2.46	14.5	0.78	10.0	0.7	2.78	24.38	5.92	39.0	6.6	73.4	6.6	5.7
8.5	0.03	0.3	0.00	5.6	0.6	1.36	18.70	3.73	67.8	4.5	20.7	6.1	4.3
4.0	0.59	5.1	0.05	5.1	1.3	0.97	11.04	4.07	59.1	0.6	11.0	52.8	5.0
6.2	0.10	0.8	0.03	5.4	0.9	0.86	9.42	3.85	59.3	1.6	29.6	30.4	4.9
6.7	0.79	3.7	-0.03	4.4	0.1	0.79	5.95	3.47	61.9	6.9	216.6	18.2	5.3
5.4	0.62	3.6	0.21	5.1	1.6	0.85	7.05	4.08	73.2	1.8	20.1	20.8	4.8
4.4	1.90	10.9	-0.01	9.5	1.9	1.48	14.20	3.78	63.2	4.1	105.4	38.2	5.6
9.0	0.54	1.6	0.00	3.6	0.6	0.49	4.72	2.20	64.9	8.5	163.7	6.2	5.9
6.7	0.30	2.5	-0.01	7.6	2.8	1.19	18.75	3.70	65.2	5.9	42.3	4.5	6.3
9.6	0.14	0.4	0.02	7.3	0.4	1.41	8.71	4.33	53.6	4.8	40.5	11.1	8.0
7.5	0.31	2.2	0.05	3.3	0.2	0.65	8.08	3.94	83.1	6.3	77.8	9.1	3.0
5.0	2.87	11.1	0.06	5.7	0.3	1.23	9.34	3.77	71.7	5.9	47.8	5.7	6.3
9.5	0.29	1.3	0.00	4.0	0.6	0.47	3.64	2.06	65.0	3.6	43.8	18.0	7.1
9.3	0.00	0.0	-0.01	6.9	0.4	1.44	9.19	3.97	50.6	4.7	61.9	15.4	8.1
7.1	1.81	3.8	0.35	8.2	2.8	1.53	8.28	3.81	45.3	6.2	55.7	7.4	9.2
4.3	3.12	11.5	-0.14	8.6	0.9	2.08	15.23	4.86	53.8	4.5	53.1	14.6	8.5
9.0	0.07	0.5	0.00	2.8	0.8	0.37	4.93	2.75	82.2	1.4	14.8	26.5	3.8
8.7	0.02	0.1	-0.02	8.4	0.6	2.66	22.02	4.75	59.2	3.3	13.0	12.5	6.2
8.9	0.04	0.2	0.16	0.0	-0.1	-0.38	-4.61	3.67	103.8	4.5	63.0	16.5	4.0
8.8	1.16	3.4	0.07	5.8	0.8	1.44	10.87	3.76	58.7	5.3	65.5	14.4	7.8
8.2	0.35	2.0	0.47	6.4	15.1	1.16	12.88	4.14	64.2	5.2	52.6	14.2	7.3
2.1	1.29	2.8	-0.18	0.0	-0.4	-1.27	-4.27	2.04	132.5	4.5	32.8	10.1	6.3

Name	City	State	Weiss Safety Rating	2003 Weiss Safety Rating	2002 Weiss Safety Rating	Total Assets ($Mil)	One Year Asset Growth	Asset Mix (As a % of Total Assets) Commercial Loans	Consumer Loans	Home Mortgages	Securities	Capitalization Index	Leverage Ratio	Risk-based Capital Ratio
HANCOCK BK OF LOUISIANA	BATON ROUGE	LA	B+	B+	B+	1,798.9	10.11	7.5	14.3	12.5	28.2	6.3	8.3	12.0
HANCOCK COUNTY SVGS BK	CHESTER	WV	B+	B+	A-	269.3	2.33	0.1	2.0	60.5	24.8	10.0	13.2	29.1
▼ HANMI BK	LOS ANGELES	CA	B	B+	A-	3,085.6	87.21	18.1	2.1	3.0	14.9	5.2	9.6	11.1
HANOVER BK	MECHANICSVILLE	VA	C	C	C	114.3	25.71	10.9	10.3	17.6	15.9	4.8	6.8	12.0
▼ HANSTON ST BK	HANSTON	KS	D+	C-	C-	30.7	5.31	8.9	4.0	6.0	45.2	6.9	8.9	16.1
HAPPY ST BK	HAPPY	TX	B	B	B-	267.2	75.30	13.0	8.8	16.9	10.1	6.2	8.2	12.3
▲ HARBOR BK OF MARYLAND	BALTIMORE	MD	B-	C	C-	233.4	7.59	27.2	3.4	13.7	17.9	6.4	8.4	12.2
HARBOR COMMUNITY BK	RAYMOND	WA	D	D	D-	49.6	12.75	3.1	2.1	23.7	31.2	6.2	8.2	16.7
HARBOR FSB	FORT PIERCE	FL	A	A	A	2,588.8	14.48	2.7	1.8	43.1	23.6	8.6	10.1	18.6
HARDIN COUNTY BK	SAVANNAH	TN	B	B	B+	209.6	4.32	5.8	11.6	25.8	33.4	7.4	9.3	13.6
▲ HARDIN COUNTY SVG BK	ELDORA	IA	C+	C	C	118.9	0.85	7.8	1.8	4.0	44.3	9.3	10.6	17.2
▲ HARDWARE ST BK	LOVINGTON	IL	D	D-	D-	21.0	-0.96	13.0	4.1	8.9	18.8	6.3	8.4	12.6
HARDWICK ST BK	HARDWICK	MN	C	C	C	15.0	-9.87	4.3	7.8	2.3	64.9	10.0	15.1	17.9
HARFORD BK	ABERDEEN	MD	A	A	A	169.7	5.20	7.6	12.6	12.1	13.1	10.0	11.7	15.3
HARLEYSVILLE NB&TC	HARLEYSVILLE	PA	B	B	B-	2,829.5	64.71	7.4	4.2	16.8	32.0	5.2	8.0	11.1
HARLEYSVILLE SVG BK	HARLEYSVILLE	PA	C+	C+	C+	707.9	7.54	0.0	0.2	41.5	48.0	4.2	6.2	14.5
▲ HARRINGTON BK FSB	CHAPEL HILL	NC	C-	D+	D	126.1	41.96	5.9	0.6	30.2	25.5	6.5	8.5	12.8
▲ HARRIS BK ARGO	SUMMIT ARGO	IL	B-	C+	C+	401.6	-1.49	2.0	27.4	20.6	9.2	5.8	7.8	11.7
HARRIS BK ARLINGTON	ROLLING MEADOWS	IL	B-	B-	B-	322.1	-1.53	1.8	18.4	13.6	16.7	5.8	7.9	11.6
HARRIS BK AURORA NA	AURORA	IL	C+	C+	C+	204.3	7.23	1.6	26.2	29.9	8.9	4.8	6.8	11.2
▲ HARRIS BK BARRINGTON NA	BARRINGTON	IL	B	B-	B	1,296.5	3.89	2.7	42.6	10.8	10.9	5.0	7.0	12.0
HARRIS BK BARTLETT	BARTLETT	IL	B-	B-	B	216.3	3.03	1.6	12.7	32.0	15.7	5.8	7.8	12.1
HARRIS BK BATAVIA NA	BATAVIA	IL	C+	B-	B-	190.5	14.99	2.3	24.2	22.4	7.8	4.9	6.9	12.2
HARRIS BK CARY-GROVE	CARY	IL	B-	B-	B	213.5	4.41	7.9	6.9	33.2	14.0	5.4	7.5	11.3
HARRIS BK ELK GROVE NA	ELK GROVE VLG	IL	B-	B-	B	187.7	8.67	4.8	11.2	16.7	14.6	5.7	7.9	11.6
HARRIS BK FRANKFORT	FRANKFORT	IL	C+	C+	B-	327.3	17.44	1.8	16.8	26.4	8.5	5.0	7.0	11.3
HARRIS BK	GLENCOE	IL	B-	B-	B-	545.4	2.46	5.9	7.0	10.9	4.6	5.5	8.0	11.4
HARRIS BK HINSDALE NA	HINSDALE	IL	B-	B-	B	794.9	0.28	4.0	10.4	22.8	12.9	5.7	7.9	11.6
HARRIS BK HOFFMAN	HOFFMAN ESTATES	IL	B-	B-	B-	113.7	-5.79	1.5	4.7	35.9	15.6	6.8	8.8	14.0
HARRIS BK HUNTLEY	HUNTLEY	IL	B-	B-	B-	162.3	38.62	1.5	12.9	25.1	13.5	4.0	7.0	10.5
▲ HARRIS BK JOLIET NA	JOLIET	IL	B-	B-	B-	1,281.2	1.92	1.5	23.9	12.7	26.1	5.9	7.9	12.4
HARRIS BK LIBERTYVILLE	LIBERTYVILLE	IL	B-	B-	B-	379.7	2.53	5.0	14.2	19.8	13.5	5.3	7.3	11.7
HARRIS BK MARENGO	MARENGO	IL	B-	B-	B-	92.2	-2.36	2.0	14.3	31.2	9.0	7.1	9.1	12.5
HARRIS BK NA	SCOTTSDALE	AZ	C+	C+	B	948.7	106.53	3.7	1.2	22.1	36.1	7.6	9.4	18.8
HARRIS BK NAPERVILLE	NAPERVILLE	IL	B-	B-	B	818.9	4.11	3.9	23.0	18.0	13.7	5.5	7.5	11.4
HARRIS BK NH NA	NASHUA	NH	B-	B-	B-	11.4	0.49	0.0	0.0	0.0	0.2	10.0	95.2	486.8
HARRIS BK OAKBROOK	OAKBROOK TERRACE	IL	B-	B-	B-	146.6	0.82	3.9	6.1	25.3	16.3	5.8	8.6	11.6
HARRIS BK PALATINE NA	PALATINE	IL	B-	B-	B	573.6	-6.88	3.8	23.3	16.1	18.3	5.6	7.6	11.8
HARRIS BK ROSELLE	ROSELLE	IL	B-	B-	B	538.5	4.45	7.1	11.4	20.7	8.8	5.9	7.9	12.1
HARRIS BK WESTCHESTER	WESTCHESTER	IL	B-	B-	B	211.2	-0.49	1.4	32.9	19.4	15.2	5.4	7.4	11.7
HARRIS BK WILMETTE NA	WILMETTE	IL	C+	C+	B-	150.1	14.62	1.3	33.4	23.0	7.3	6.6	8.6	13.2
HARRIS BK WINNETKA NA	WINNETKA	IL	B-	B-	B	468.5	-4.91	7.9	8.2	19.2	14.6	5.6	7.6	11.5
HARRIS BK WOODSTOCK	WOODSTOCK	IL	B-	B-	B-	270.3	9.75	1.4	14.1	22.0	21.3	5.6	7.7	11.5
HARRIS BK-ST CHARLES	ST CHARLES	IL	B-	B-	B	519.4	12.59	1.7	14.1	17.8	18.4	5.4	7.4	11.5
HARRIS T&SB	CHICAGO	IL	B-	B-	B-	20,370.7	-3.45	17.8	7.1	14.3	26.2	6.3	8.3	12.1
HARRISON B&LA	HARRISON	OH	B	B	B	228.1	-7.51	2.3	1.1	34.7	39.5	9.7	10.8	23.8
HARRISON COUNTY BK	LOST CREEK	WV	C+	C	C-	69.4	9.94	3.7	13.9	19.2	43.2	7.6	9.4	18.0
HARRISON DEPOSIT B&TC	CYNTHIANA	KY	B	B+	B+	63.6	8.66	1.2	7.3	25.0	45.1	6.4	8.4	19.5
HART COUNTY B&TC	MUNFORDVILLE	KY	B-	B-	C	26.6	-7.28	4.6	3.1	3.4	52.1	10.0	13.9	25.2
HARTFORD ST BK	HARTFORD	KS	C+	C+	C+	52.6	86.72	11.0	3.6	18.8	26.0	8.4	10.0	14.9
▲ HARTFORD SVGS BK	HARTFORD	WI	C+	C	C	239.6	23.32	0.0	0.6	32.0	44.3	4.6	6.6	20.2
HARTSBURG ST BK	HARTSBURG	IL	C	C	C-	13.0	-0.12	4.8	4.7	15.6	15.9	10.0	11.9	16.6
HARTSVILLE COMMUNITY BK	HARTSVILLE	SC	D+	D+	C-	61.1	19.29	8.2	9.4	16.6	5.9	2.9	8.1	9.9
HARTWICK ST BK	HARTWICK	IA	D	D	D+	21.6	2.49	1.7	2.4	28.3	35.5	6.7	8.7	18.7
▼ HARVARD ST BK	HARVARD	IL	B-	B	B	159.5	-6.33	9.0	2.5	12.0	31.2	9.6	10.7	18.0
▲ HARVARD ST BK	HARVARD	NE	B-	C+	C+	30.9	-8.83	9.9	8.9	6.4	9.7	10.0	14.4	17.1
▼ HARVARD SVG BK	HARVARD	IL	D+	B	C+	121.0	1.25	1.7	12.8	37.0	12.1	5.8	7.8	14.3
▼ HARVEST COMMUNITY BK	PENNSVILLE	NJ	E+	D-	D	84.5	20.87	21.1	1.1	23.9	12.6	1.4	6.0	8.4
▲ HARWOOD ST BK	HARWOOD	ND	C	C-	D+	19.7	4.33	12.6	5.8	6.3	28.5	10.0	12.2	23.4
HASKELL NB	HASKELL	TX	C+	C+	C+	56.8	-5.11	4.5	8.4	10.4	44.4	8.3	9.9	21.1
HASTINGS CITY BK	HASTINGS	MI	B+	B+	A-	237.3	1.11	5.2	5.4	32.9	33.9	9.1	10.4	19.3
HASTINGS ST BK	HASTINGS	NE	C	C	C+	132.6	4.78	12.7	8.5	8.0	35.3	3.2	6.2	10.1
HATBORO FEDERAL SVGS FA	HATBORO	PA	A+	A+	A+	373.0	4.00	0.0	0.0	90.6	4.1	10.0	17.7	33.8
HAVANA NB	HAVANA	IL	C+	C+	B-	139.9	7.48	2.7	2.6	12.7	29.8	5.8	7.8	13.1

Asset Quality Index	Non-Performing Loans as a % of Total Loans	Non-Performing Loans as a % of Capital	Net Charge-offs Avg Loans	Profitability Index	Net Income ($Mil)	Return on Assets (R.O.A.)	Return on Equity (R.O.E.)	Net Interest Spread	Overhead Efficiency Ratio	Liquidity Index	Liquidity Ratio	Hot Money Ratio	Stability Index
6.2	0.42	2.5	0.46	9.5	16.7	1.91	18.69	4.48	50.3	3.2	7.8	12.4	7.8
6.3	1.20	5.5	0.10	4.9	0.9	0.67	4.84	3.56	71.6	2.5	21.0	16.9	7.6
4.9	0.39	1.8	0.21	8.4	14.8	1.34	12.06	4.27	51.6	1.6	20.8	27.9	7.5
7.5	0.02	0.3	0.24	2.2	0.2	0.27	3.91	3.93	86.7	3.2	21.3	13.5	2.5
2.6	4.38	22.2	0.03	3.9	0.1	0.68	7.68	4.20	79.4	3.8	39.6	15.9	3.7
7.5	0.11	0.7	0.10	4.5	0.5	0.49	3.95	5.37	84.2	2.3	28.5	19.5	5.7
5.5	0.55	3.8	0.17	4.7	0.9	0.82	8.44	5.03	73.9	4.6	41.8	12.6	4.3
4.7	2.31	13.6	-0.01	3.5	0.2	0.82	9.84	4.01	92.6	5.7	57.2	9.3	1.6
8.8	0.11	0.8	0.00	9.8	19.5	1.55	15.28	3.98	43.3	1.1	16.6	31.8	9.9
7.6	0.30	1.8	0.09	6.4	1.2	1.16	12.94	4.71	67.1	1.6	11.7	22.2	5.1
6.6	0.41	1.9	-0.07	3.2	0.4	0.66	6.42	3.26	78.0	7.2	119.1	10.2	4.5
8.3	0.00	0.0	0.07	4.2	0.1	0.87	10.52	3.58	76.4	4.6	39.1	9.2	1.3
8.7	0.36	0.7	1.02	4.1	0.1	1.02	7.00	3.54	70.7	4.2	32.2	9.1	4.2
6.8	0.53	3.3	0.33	6.8	0.9	1.15	9.74	4.83	64.4	4.7	30.9	8.3	7.5
8.5	0.25	1.6	0.21	7.0	17.8	1.49	18.40	4.00	54.9	6.1	54.6	10.3	6.1
10.0	0.08	0.6	0.00	3.9	2.5	0.72	11.77	1.95	53.6	4.3	20.6	7.5	3.9
8.0	0.08	0.5	0.15	2.6	0.2	0.38	4.18	2.91	70.1	0.5	5.4	44.7	1.5
3.7	0.47	4.8	0.24	5.3	1.9	0.93	11.95	3.79	60.9	7.0	124.6	11.7	5.3
7.4	0.06	0.6	0.05	7.1	1.9	1.19	15.38	3.76	53.9	6.7	101.6	11.5	5.8
7.0	0.05	0.6	0.11	1.7	0.2	0.21	3.13	3.04	85.2	7.2	88.3	6.8	4.6
5.9	0.35	3.3	0.21	9.0	10.4	1.51	19.71	3.57	40.8	6.7	62.9	7.7	6.9
6.0	0.30	2.8	0.09	6.6	1.0	0.87	11.07	3.81	61.3	7.3	82.8	5.1	6.5
6.9	0.11	1.3	0.06	2.5	0.0	-0.02	-0.23	3.10	85.5	7.5	127.4	9.6	4.7
5.0	0.96	9.6	0.01	7.3	1.3	1.26	17.22	3.84	55.3	6.8	77.2	7.7	5.9
8.0	0.00	0.0	0.11	7.1	0.9	1.04	13.95	3.85	57.9	6.5	401.5	20.4	6.2
3.0	0.55	5.6	0.04	6.1	1.6	1.02	13.57	3.84	56.1	6.5	77.3	9.6	5.4
6.7	0.21	2.1	-0.06	6.1	2.7	1.01	13.04	3.73	48.5	5.0	41.2	10.3	5.7
8.0	0.12	1.1	0.05	8.4	5.7	1.43	18.13	3.90	41.7	5.6	51.0	9.9	6.5
7.4	0.26	2.1	0.01	7.7	0.7	1.20	13.71	3.90	57.3	7.3	151.1	12.2	5.7
8.5	0.01	0.1	0.07	3.6	0.4	0.54	8.03	3.09	74.5	6.7	98.7	11.4	5.5
4.2	0.93	3.2	-0.27	3.4	2.5	0.39	2.27	3.81	81.3	6.2	129.3	16.5	7.8
6.5	0.19	1.9	0.08	5.2	1.8	0.93	12.49	3.69	62.1	6.5	124.1	14.3	5.7
5.9	0.21	1.8	-0.04	4.1	0.3	0.67	7.43	3.70	74.1	4.7	62.7	15.5	6.3
6.4	0.43	1.9	0.08	2.1	0.3	0.10	1.11	2.70	94.8	7.9	98.1	4.0	5.8
6.8	0.10	1.0	0.13	5.9	3.6	0.86	11.53	3.28	57.1	6.6	91.5	11.1	6.2
10.0	0.00	0.0	0.00	3.8	0.0	0.46	0.48	0.94	15.7	10.0	2,209.0	0.0	5.3
8.4	0.08	0.7	0.03	6.0	0.8	1.05	13.23	3.86	59.3	5.4	59.4	12.6	6.0
2.8	1.38	12.5	0.23	5.9	3.1	1.03	13.48	3.47	55.7	7.1	135.0	12.4	6.0
4.2	0.94	9.1	0.05	6.7	2.8	1.03	13.34	4.08	56.3	5.9	49.6	7.1	6.3
6.5	0.14	1.4	0.10	5.5	1.0	1.00	13.25	3.46	55.5	7.3	105.8	8.4	5.7
6.8	0.08	0.7	0.02	3.5	0.4	0.48	5.83	3.27	71.3	5.9	54.4	8.7	5.0
8.2	0.06	0.6	0.03	6.6	2.6	1.12	14.81	3.46	47.4	4.8	83.3	18.7	6.2
6.3	0.37	3.3	0.06	4.7	1.1	0.77	10.11	3.20	67.6	6.3	95.9	13.2	6.2
5.4	0.40	3.9	0.08	4.7	2.0	0.79	11.19	3.11	62.0	8.1	185.8	10.8	5.4
5.1	1.49	8.8	0.38	3.8	81.1	0.79	10.09	2.46	73.0	4.0	57.1	22.6	5.6
5.2	2.40	11.1	0.00	5.3	1.0	0.85	7.86	2.73	54.9	1.4	10.0	25.0	6.4
7.6	0.00	0.0	0.03	5.1	0.2	0.73	8.20	4.36	68.6	3.4	9.3	11.2	3.0
8.8	0.00	0.0	0.06	7.3	0.6	1.85	21.23	3.21	50.5	5.4	51.9	10.2	5.4
8.4	1.32	2.3	-0.82	6.6	0.2	1.75	12.69	5.42	54.5	6.8	85.4	7.3	4.3
8.5	0.00	0.0	0.00	3.8	0.2	0.76	7.38	3.28	71.3	1.3	8.9	26.0	3.6
9.3	0.13	0.4	0.01	3.2	0.6	0.48	3.19	2.51	76.9	6.3	172.1	18.8	7.2
8.4	0.14	0.7	-0.02	3.9	0.1	0.95	8.45	3.41	68.3	3.3	73.3	27.5	4.5
7.9	0.02	0.3	0.06	3.6	0.1	0.46	5.76	4.53	81.9	3.3	10.8	12.3	4.0
8.9	0.24	1.4	0.00	3.7	0.1	0.87	10.08	3.26	72.6	6.5	81.2	7.1	2.4
4.1	2.15	9.5	0.23	5.0	0.4	0.45	3.70	4.18	60.7	2.3	33.1	23.9	6.8
4.0	1.32	7.3	0.31	6.1	0.2	1.16	8.25	4.69	62.9	4.7	27.7	6.5	4.9
0.3	18.00	99.5	0.05	2.2	-3.0	-4.93	-45.61	2.69	73.3	2.9	34.3	18.6	7.4
7.1	0.39	5.0	-0.01	2.0	0.1	0.29	4.95	3.86	88.6	4.0	47.3	16.3	0.0
5.4	2.99	11.9	-0.51	6.7	0.2	2.32	20.08	4.11	67.5	6.0	64.4	6.6	3.6
8.1	0.21	0.9	0.57	3.4	0.2	0.57	5.85	3.32	81.3	3.4	46.8	19.3	4.0
8.6	0.22	1.1	0.14	5.2	1.1	0.91	8.63	3.56	67.8	5.8	42.2	5.4	6.4
3.9	1.28	12.5	0.15	5.7	0.9	1.32	23.27	3.84	62.8	1.7	16.2	21.2	3.2
9.7	0.14	0.7	-0.01	7.6	2.3	1.22	6.91	2.99	36.1	1.6	12.1	22.1	8.7
2.9	2.30	13.1	-0.01	4.1	0.6	0.85	8.64	3.31	68.4	3.7	21.6	11.1	6.0

Name	City	State	Weiss Safety Rating	2003 Weiss Safety Rating	2002 Weiss Safety Rating	Total Assets ($Mil)	One Year Asset Growth	Commercial Loans	Consumer Loans	Home Mortgages	Securities	Capitalization Index	Leverage Ratio	Risk-based Capital Ratio
HAVEN SB	HOBOKEN	NJ	B+	B+	B+	677.1	7.51	0.0	0.1	61.1	29.0	7.1	9.1	22.0
▲ HAVERFORD TC	RADNOR	PA	B+	B	B	125.2	5.17	5.0	64.3	0.2	0.0	9.9	10.9	15.7
▼ HAVERHILL CO-OP BK	HAVERHILL	MA	B-	B	B+	155.4	10.38	3.3	1.8	40.2	29.4	9.8	10.8	19.8
▲ HAVILAND ST BK	HAVILAND	KS	C-	D+	D-	19.7	0.94	2.5	2.1	9.4	9.6	9.5	10.7	20.3
HAWAII NB	HONOLULU	HI	C-	C-	D+	445.1	10.76	22.9	1.5	8.6	14.0	4.7	6.7	11.1
HBANK TEXAS	GRAPEVINE	TX	B-	C+	C-	45.9	-0.12	14.2	6.8	11.3	11.3	10.0	11.0	19.5
HCSB STATE BANKING ASSOC.	PLAINVIEW	TX	C+	C+	C	230.0	5.39	8.6	5.3	11.3	30.2	5.4	7.4	12.5
HEADLAND NB	HEADLAND	AL	A-	A-	A-	83.3	-2.50	7.6	8.2	13.2	39.8	10.0	15.3	26.0
▼ HEADWATERS ST BK	LAND O LAKES	WI	C-	B-	B-	53.6	2.67	3.1	6.4	30.3	24.4	9.3	10.5	18.5
HEARTLAND B&TC	BLOOMINGTON	IL	A-	A-	B+	724.0	8.67	13.5	1.8	15.7	8.6	6.9	9.1	12.5
▲ HEARTLAND BK	SOMERS	IA	A-	B+	B+	60.0	5.03	4.5	3.8	16.0	25.5	10.0	11.7	16.2
▲ HEARTLAND BK	LEAWOOD	KS	C+	C	D+	64.1	51.68	21.3	3.0	7.0	11.1	3.7	9.1	10.4
HEARTLAND BK	CLAYTON	MO	C+	C	D+	504.3	-19.70	20.9	1.2	18.0	6.8	7.6	9.4	13.7
HEARTLAND BK	GAHANNA	OH	B-	C+	C+	361.4	7.31	14.0	3.2	12.1	21.0	5.8	8.3	11.6
▲ HEARTLAND CMNTY BK	FRANKLIN	IN	C	D+	C	179.2	3.40	9.8	5.3	14.3	22.5	7.4	9.2	14.2
▲ HEARTLAND COMMUNITY BK	CAMDEN	AR	C	C-	C	219.4	-12.01	4.6	3.7	12.8	49.2	10.0	11.0	26.1
HEARTLAND COMMUNITY BK	BENNET	NE	D	D-	C-	50.7	4.80	16.0	5.7	13.2	35.3	5.3	7.3	12.8
HEARTLAND NB	SEBRING	FL	C	C	C-	134.9	28.26	8.4	8.6	15.6	18.4	4.2	7.0	10.6
HEARTLAND ST BK	EDGELEY	ND	C	C	C	38.0	6.13	8.7	3.6	3.1	23.2	6.8	8.8	12.5
HEARTLAND ST BK	WESSINGTON	SD	D-	E-	E-	31.2	-0.58	9.6	9.5	2.1	10.2	4.7	7.6	10.8
HEBBRONVILLE STATE BK	HEBBRONVILLE	TX	C-	C-	C+	57.6	102.56	5.7	13.6	6.6	48.8	5.5	7.5	14.2
HEBER SPRINGS ST BK	HEBER SPRINGS	AR	B	B	B	120.8	4.32	7.6	5.7	9.6	28.5	7.9	9.6	15.3
HEBER VALLEY NB	HEBER	UT	B-	C+	C+	25.0	13.33	2.3	1.8	6.2	26.4	7.2	9.2	13.7
HEBRON SVG BK	HEBRON	MD	B	B	B	254.5	19.71	8.2	2.6	29.3	6.1	5.2	7.2	11.1
▲ HEDRICK SVGS BK	OTTUMWA	IA	D+	D	D	58.4	7.04	13.4	4.4	15.8	18.6	5.0	7.0	12.7
▼ HEIGHTS BK	PEORIA HEIGHTS	IL	C+	B-	B	37.3	0.05	1.4	13.1	48.9	8.3	9.1	10.4	19.6
HELENA NB	HELENA	AR	A	A	B+	131.0	-0.29	5.7	7.1	9.4	28.8	10.0	12.1	23.0
▲ HELM BK	MIAMI	FL	B-	C+	C+	311.8	30.91	3.5	3.3	70.2	4.3	5.0	7.0	14.0
▲ HEMISPHERE NB	MIAMI	FL	C-	D	D-	188.6	10.41	28.5	0.4	0.8	28.4	9.9	11.0	25.7
HEMLOCK FEDERAL BK FOR	OAK FOREST	IL	C+	C+	B-	311.3	-1.63	0.0	0.1	36.2	41.6	4.2	6.3	14.0
▲ HENDERSON FSB	HENDERSON	TX	A-	B+	B+	76.3	-1.68	0.5	2.1	58.9	24.7	10.0	13.6	31.7
HENDERSON NB	HENDERSON	KY	D	D	D	28.8	-17.01	2.5	4.2	14.1	34.5	10.0	14.5	24.8
▼ HENDERSON ST BK	HENDERSON	NE	D	D+	C-	42.3	7.84	6.6	2.9	1.5	50.8	5.6	7.6	12.4
HENDRICKS COUNTY B&TC	BROWNSBURG	IN	B-	B	B+	138.6	-9.43	4.8	2.1	14.5	24.8	10.0	11.3	19.6
HENRY COUNTY BK	MT PLEASANT	IA	B-	B-	C+	54.0	-0.63	9.5	2.5	11.7	37.1	5.8	7.8	11.9
▼ HENRY COUNTY BK	NAPOLEON	OH	B	B+	B	195.5	9.51	12.0	7.3	19.8	32.2	8.0	9.7	15.9
HENRY ST BK	HENRY	IL	B	B	B	74.5	-1.97	2.7	2.2	12.3	44.9	10.0	15.0	29.0
HEREFORD ST BK	HEREFORD	TX	A-	A-	A-	92.4	12.59	25.7	4.4	4.4	31.4	7.0	9.0	14.1
HERGET NB OF PEKIN	PEKIN	IL	B-	B	B+	221.4	2.48	5.9	2.7	5.8	54.6	7.6	9.4	20.9
▲ HERITAGE B&TC	NORFOLK	VA	B+	B	B	146.5	13.82	12.5	4.3	21.7	12.0	6.9	8.9	12.9
HERITAGE BANK	HOPKINSVILLE	KY	B+	B+	A-	575.1	18.72	9.5	7.3	33.9	33.1	7.1	9.1	13.9
▲ HERITAGE BANK	ST GEORGE	UT	A-	B	B	523.5	10.74	0.0	0.0	0.3	92.7	8.0	9.7	38.2
▲ HERITAGE BK	DECATUR	AL	D+	D	E-	544.0	1.85	20.5	1.9	15.8	17.5	6.4	8.5	12.1
HERITAGE BK	JONESBORO	AR	D	D-	D	191.3	-4.31	13.4	5.6	21.1	14.7	7.1	9.1	12.7
HERITAGE BK	LOUISVILLE	CO	C-	C-	C	391.6	2.10	8.0	1.8	7.7	16.3	4.5	8.2	10.8
HERITAGE BK	HINESVILLE	GA	A-	A-	A	293.7	17.95	5.6	6.7	11.8	25.4	7.9	9.6	14.7
▲ HERITAGE BK	JONESBORO	GA	C-	C	C	334.5	16.84	13.4	3.9	6.9	13.3	3.8	7.8	10.4
▲ HERITAGE BK	MARION	IA	C	D+	D+	33.6	-3.65	2.4	3.1	23.0	42.8	6.5	8.5	17.3
HERITAGE BK	CHICAGO HEIGHTS	IL	B+	B+	B	237.6	7.81	16.3	0.6	18.2	22.3	6.2	8.2	12.0
HERITAGE BK	TOPEKA	KS	D	D	NR	26.9	174.29	30.2	1.4	24.0	0.0	10.0	15.6	20.2
HERITAGE BK	ERLANGER	KY	D+	D+	C	243.5	16.56	10.0	3.3	19.9	10.1	4.0	7.9	10.5
HERITAGE BK	GREAT FALLS	MT	B-	B-	B-	330.6	5.88	18.0	7.2	14.7	12.2	3.9	7.9	10.4
HERITAGE BK	LUCAMA	NC	B-	B-	B-	222.2	5.77	7.6	4.2	17.7	19.9	5.0	7.0	11.6
▲ HERITAGE BK	WOOD RIVER	NE	B-	B-	B-	438.3	-0.58	16.6	3.7	6.1	31.4	5.9	7.9	13.0
▲ HERITAGE BK	SPENCER	WI	C-	D	D	63.0	-8.28	13.2	3.7	25.0	26.2	8.0	9.7	16.1
▲ HERITAGE BK CENTRAL IL	TRIVOLI	IL	C+	C	C	277.4	14.46	16.7	2.0	9.7	29.4	5.5	7.5	11.9
HERITAGE BK NA	HOLSTEIN	IA	C+	C+	B-	109.7	1.27	12.4	3.3	8.4	9.9	5.9	8.4	11.7
HERITAGE BK NA	SPICER	MN	C+	C+	C+	118.5	6.30	19.9	6.1	20.9	8.5	3.4	8.4	10.2
▼ HERITAGE BK OF ASHLAND	ASHLAND	KY	E	D	C-	113.6	-16.72	15.1	17.3	23.6	18.5	4.9	6.9	11.3
▼ HERITAGE BK OF COMMERCE	SAN JOSE	CA	B+	A-	B	1,087.6	8.45	27.5	0.7	1.0	21.2	8.2	10.0	13.5
HERITAGE BK OF FLORIDA	LUTZ	FL	C+	C	D+	102.2	39.78	11.0	4.0	18.6	1.0	6.2	9.1	11.9
HERITAGE BK OF NEVADA	RENO	NV	B	B-	B-	178.2	33.71	15.1	0.7	1.7	13.8	6.7	8.9	12.2
HERITAGE BK OF NORTH	ORANGE PARK	FL	B	B	B	98.9	40.93	9.0	5.8	9.9	1.0	8.0	11.7	13.3
▲ HERITAGE BK OF	SCHAUMBURG	IL	C	D+	C-	105.2	4.21	1.7	0.8	27.3	21.0	5.9	7.9	13.8

Asset Quality Index	Non-Performing Loans as a % of Total Loans	Non-Performing Loans as a % of Capital	Net Charge-offs Avg Loans	Profitability Index	Net Income ($Mil)	Return on Assets (R.O.A.)	Return on Equity (R.O.E.)	Net Interest Spread	Overhead Efficiency Ratio	Liquidity Index	Liquidity Ratio	Hot Money Ratio	Stability Index
9.9	0.04	0.3	0.00	5.9	3.5	1.04	11.76	3.06	48.8	3.4	40.3	18.0	6.0
5.6	0.00	0.0	0.00	7.0	2.1	2.99	28.20	1.36	79.5	0.1	N/A	83.8	7.0
7.6	0.47	2.7	-0.18	3.5	0.3	0.36	3.35	3.40	82.8	2.4	35.4	25.0	5.6
3.7	1.04	5.9	0.20	7.1	0.1	1.44	13.73	4.93	58.6	5.5	90.4	13.7	2.3
7.5	0.43	3.3	-0.10	2.5	0.5	0.22	3.36	4.29	93.2	5.5	73.1	13.9	2.7
8.3	0.00	0.0	0.00	4.1	0.2	0.78	7.10	4.07	67.9	4.5	69.0	17.2	1.9
7.9	0.19	1.3	0.09	4.1	0.8	0.70	8.74	4.26	81.2	2.7	41.4	25.1	4.0
8.0	0.26	0.8	0.03	6.6	0.7	1.67	10.85	3.66	61.8	4.7	36.3	10.5	7.9
2.3	3.89	23.2	0.11	7.6	0.4	1.55	14.99	4.74	60.8	3.9	34.1	13.3	6.4
6.8	0.21	1.6	0.06	8.9	6.0	1.67	17.83	3.96	60.2	2.8	33.9	19.1	7.5
8.1	0.26	1.4	-0.02	6.9	0.4	1.48	11.88	4.40	65.3	3.7	19.9	11.1	7.1
7.9	0.00	0.0	0.11	1.6	0.1	0.37	3.70	4.36	82.9	2.3	39.2	30.1	4.6
3.1	1.79	12.7	0.69	4.5	1.8	0.70	7.40	4.73	73.9	0.8	19.9	46.6	4.3
5.4	0.97	8.1	0.15	6.6	2.2	1.21	14.98	4.27	64.1	2.1	13.3	18.2	4.9
4.0	1.81	11.1	-0.39	3.5	0.8	0.87	9.39	4.34	78.0	2.8	28.3	17.3	3.1
3.8	4.22	13.9	0.22	2.7	0.3	0.30	2.65	2.62	85.8	2.0	18.6	19.4	5.0
8.6	0.01	0.1	0.12	4.2	0.3	1.16	15.88	4.42	71.1	4.1	44.7	15.1	1.1
7.9	0.00	0.0	0.01	4.5	0.5	0.79	11.69	4.11	69.0	4.3	30.3	10.1	3.3
4.5	0.34	2.0	0.41	5.2	0.2	0.88	7.97	4.35	65.8	3.9	56.8	18.4	4.3
2.6	0.94	9.2	-0.01	4.7	0.2	1.41	17.61	4.77	70.9	2.4	13.1	16.9	1.7
7.7	0.19	0.8	0.58	3.9	0.2	0.67	7.29	4.58	85.7	1.8	21.1	21.9	1.7
7.6	0.45	2.6	0.02	6.0	0.6	0.97	10.31	3.98	65.7	3.4	27.5	13.8	5.9
8.6	0.03	0.2	0.01	4.2	0.1	0.87	9.48	4.90	71.3	5.0	56.8	12.9	3.2
5.5	0.43	4.2	-0.05	8.0	1.6	1.32	18.31	4.02	50.4	4.1	67.2	21.2	5.1
3.3	4.00	32.3	0.35	4.6	0.2	0.66	9.42	4.05	71.0	4.9	116.4	23.0	2.3
3.4	2.46	16.1	0.10	9.7	0.4	1.94	18.23	4.72	49.3	3.7	51.5	18.5	6.6
8.5	0.08	0.3	0.02	6.8	0.7	1.01	8.34	4.17	66.3	5.1	114.0	21.6	7.0
7.2	0.00	0.0	0.01	8.2	2.4	1.67	25.05	4.47	58.1	2.8	38.5	21.4	4.3
8.3	0.18	0.9	-0.18	2.6	0.4	0.39	4.33	3.78	90.8	4.5	87.4	22.2	2.5
7.9	0.21	1.4	0.00	3.8	0.8	0.51	7.22	2.44	74.1	3.3	20.4	12.9	3.6
7.9	1.14	5.5	0.00	6.8	0.4	1.11	8.28	4.05	56.8	1.8	8.4	19.3	7.2
8.0	0.76	2.8	0.18	0.0	-0.2	-1.05	-7.43	3.15	129.1	3.3	33.9	16.7	0.0
8.7	0.11	0.6	1.33	1.8	0.0	-0.01	-0.19	2.56	105.2	3.7	30.6	13.5	1.8
5.8	1.44	6.9	0.08	3.4	0.3	0.41	3.74	3.61	85.4	6.7	70.9	7.2	5.6
5.0	0.48	1.6	-0.01	4.4	0.2	0.75	5.19	3.85	72.5	4.5	34.8	10.8	7.0
5.4	0.92	5.5	0.56	5.0	0.9	0.92	9.38	4.15	61.1	0.7	9.0	34.3	5.7
7.3	1.50	4.7	0.42	4.6	0.4	0.99	6.41	3.68	64.7	4.3	38.4	13.0	7.5
8.2	0.06	0.4	0.02	9.5	0.8	1.68	18.14	4.79	54.4	1.4	21.5	27.8	8.0
9.1	0.06	0.2	-0.01	4.0	1.1	0.97	9.42	3.32	71.9	4.4	32.2	10.5	5.8
8.4	0.03	0.2	-0.01	7.4	1.1	1.51	16.99	4.23	59.2	2.3	24.6	18.5	5.6
7.1	0.23	1.5	0.10	5.9	2.3	0.83	8.16	2.73	54.9	2.0	36.3	31.6	6.7
6.8	0.00	0.0	0.00	6.6	3.3	1.27	6.23	1.58	19.3	4.0	129.6	98.3	9.7
2.4	2.54	18.0	1.17	2.8	2.1	0.78	8.91	3.44	82.7	2.3	17.0	17.7	2.5
3.1	2.24	16.5	1.59	2.0	0.5	0.52	6.01	3.12	76.9	2.6	9.2	15.4	1.4
3.5	1.53	12.7	0.30	4.1	1.4	0.71	8.75	5.14	79.8	1.6	12.8	21.7	2.9
6.4	0.39	2.0	-0.05	10.0	3.5	2.41	21.91	5.10	58.9	2.9	25.3	15.5	7.1
4.8	0.27	2.4	0.14	5.8	1.8	1.09	14.46	4.32	59.7	4.8	55.6	14.8	3.4
9.1	0.15	0.8	0.00	4.3	0.2	0.97	11.65	3.84	77.3	4.7	25.9	5.6	3.4
8.9	0.06	0.5	-0.01	8.3	2.1	1.83	22.22	4.25	61.2	6.3	75.6	10.4	6.3
8.2	0.00	0.0	0.00	0.1	-0.1	-0.64	-3.45	4.60	97.9	1.8	16.1	20.3	0.0
1.6	1.67	16.0	0.02	7.5	1.7	1.41	18.47	4.31	48.7	2.2	12.5	17.7	3.6
6.8	0.14	1.2	0.07	7.6	2.1	1.30	15.38	4.30	61.4	3.7	20.7	10.9	4.7
7.4	0.22	1.6	-0.08	4.5	0.9	0.84	8.89	4.42	76.7	4.9	33.4	7.4	5.1
4.1	1.37	7.9	0.03	9.5	4.6	2.08	21.10	3.74	45.0	4.0	30.6	11.7	6.7
5.2	0.97	5.6	-0.01	4.0	0.3	0.80	8.01	4.23	75.3	4.4	31.7	10.3	2.2
6.0	0.30	2.5	-0.01	6.2	1.5	1.10	14.61	3.68	50.8	1.7	24.3	24.2	3.2
3.8	0.41	3.7	0.25	6.6	0.8	1.37	15.91	4.51	70.8	3.3	16.6	12.5	5.5
4.6	0.46	4.2	0.16	8.9	1.0	1.75	20.41	4.86	66.8	2.8	11.9	14.6	5.3
1.3	5.89	42.4	3.04	0.3	-0.8	-1.39	-18.63	3.98	97.2	2.9	18.9	14.6	1.0
7.7	0.32	2.1	0.55	4.5	3.5	0.67	6.71	4.28	77.3	4.3	25.9	11.2	7.4
7.2	0.00	0.0	0.44	5.2	0.5	1.01	10.66	4.30	50.5	4.5	81.7	21.1	4.6
7.5	0.00	0.0	0.00	5.5	0.9	1.09	12.31	4.80	62.3	3.9	28.0	11.4	5.0
7.0	0.00	0.0	0.00	5.2	0.5	1.08	9.51	4.40	55.4	2.0	40.9	35.0	7.1
3.7	0.46	1.8	0.00	3.9	0.4	0.73	4.54	4.30	76.5	4.5	23.7	6.4	7.3

Name	City	State	Weiss Safety Rating	2003 Weiss Safety Rating	2002 Weiss Safety Rating	Total Assets ($Mil)	One Year Asset Growth	Asset Mix (As a % of Total Assets) Commercial Loans	Consumer Loans	Home Mortgages	Securities	Capitalization Index	Leverage Ratio	Risk-based Capital Ratio
HERITAGE BK OF THE OZARKS	LEBANON	MO	D	D	NR	10.2	N/A	5.1	6.3	31.1	0.0	10.0	39.4	46.4
▲ HERITAGE BK OF THE SOUTH	ALBANY	GA	B	C+	C	328.9	-1.55	8.2	16.7	21.9	16.6	8.8	10.2	14.3
HERITAGE BK SSB	TERRELL	TX	C	C-	C+	54.8	-5.47	5.0	4.7	19.4	0.9	10.0	12.0	17.4
▲ HERITAGE CMNTY BK	DANVILLE	KY	C-	D+	E-	106.9	41.35	11.2	4.5	24.4	2.1	7.3	9.5	12.7
HERITAGE CO-OP BK	SALEM	MA	B+	B+	B	249.3	9.10	4.4	1.3	30.5	26.0	9.3	10.5	17.1
HERITAGE COMMUNITY BK	QUITMAN	GA	B-	B-	C+	94.1	13.47	17.9	6.3	17.5	13.9	4.1	7.8	10.6
▼ HERITAGE COMMUNITY BK	GLENWOOD	IL	C+	B	B+	235.2	-3.28	6.6	0.4	12.5	13.7	5.9	9.2	11.7
HERITAGE COMMUNITY BK	COLUMBUS	IN	B-	C+	B-	255.2	-18.66	8.1	4.0	26.2	14.4	10.0	12.1	18.0
HERITAGE COMMUNITY BK	GREENEVILLE	TN	D	D	NR	30.7	N/A	8.6	11.5	17.1	2.4	10.0	28.0	37.1
▲ HERITAGE FIRST BANK	ROME	GA	D	D-	D	43.2	68.88	9.7	17.9	27.2	6.1	10.0	11.5	17.3
HERITAGE NB	GRANBURY	TX	B-	B-	B-	229.2	7.50	4.8	1.3	14.0	52.9	4.3	6.3	14.5
▲ HERITAGE OAKS BK	PASO ROBLES	CA	B-	C+	C+	462.7	32.99	8.4	1.1	1.6	13.6	5.7	8.3	11.5
HERITAGE ST BK	LAWRENCEVILLE	IL	B-	B-	B-	72.3	5.41	4.9	3.6	15.6	10.8	5.8	8.6	11.6
HERITAGE ST BK	NEVADA	MO	C	C	C	72.8	0.12	5.6	6.9	34.8	11.6	5.5	7.5	11.7
▼ HERITAGE SVGS BK	OLYMPIA	WA	B-	B	B+	559.7	12.46	5.9	2.9	10.3	6.1	3.5	7.9	10.3
HERNANDO CTY BK	BROOKSVILLE	FL	B+	B+	A-	53.4	7.16	1.2	1.6	55.5	12.7	4.9	6.9	13.7
▼ HERNDON NB	HERNDON	PA	B-	B	B+	28.3	-0.69	1.7	2.2	15.4	55.4	10.0	26.4	64.4
HERON LAKE ST BK	HERON LAKE	MN	D+	D+	D+	28.6	0.60	7.2	3.5	8.2	37.3	6.7	8.7	16.0
▲ HERRIN SECURITY BK	HERRIN	IL	B	B-	B-	142.1	6.97	6.2	9.0	13.6	56.1	6.7	8.7	19.7
HERRING NB	VERNON	TX	C+	C+	C+	339.4	3.66	18.1	6.2	5.0	8.4	4.9	8.2	11.0
▲ HERSHEY ST BK	HERSHEY	NE	C	B-	B	34.4	-4.63	19.2	9.5	21.6	6.7	10.0	14.7	21.3
HERTFORD SVGS BK, SSB	HERTFORD	NC	D+	C-	D+	15.4	-3.72	0.0	1.1	47.2	3.3	9.0	10.4	27.3
HFS BANK FSB	HOBART	IN	B-	B-	B-	234.7	2.24	2.4	1.8	50.4	14.5	6.5	8.5	14.9
▲ HIAWATHA B&TC	HIAWATHA	IA	B+	B	B-	24.1	-5.60	12.7	4.0	26.1	5.2	6.4	10.0	12.1
▲ HIAWATHA NB	HAGER CITY	WI	D	D-	D	52.8	-6.60	3.6	3.5	23.5	12.8	6.0	8.0	15.0
▼ HIBERNIA HMSTD & SA	NEW ORLEANS	LA	B	B+	B+	58.4	-2.36	0.0	0.1	26.4	55.9	10.0	25.9	66.4
▼ HIBERNIA NB	NEW ORLEANS	LA	B-	B	B	21,258.8	19.11	12.7	13.9	22.4	18.9	3.6	7.8	10.3
▲ HICKORY POINT B&T	FORSYTH	IL	C+	C	C	790.9	-0.97	4.6	11.5	8.5	51.3	6.0	8.0	15.7
▲ HICKSVILLE BK	HICKSVILLE	OH	C-	D+	D+	137.7	4.00	15.2	4.2	24.7	29.5	4.3	6.4	13.0
HICKSVILLE BLDG LOAN &	HICKSVILLE	OH	C-	C-	C-	65.1	6.57	7.1	17.7	29.4	11.7	4.8	8.7	10.9
▲ HIGH COUNTRY BK	SALIDA	CO	B-	C	C-	196.8	4.97	10.6	4.5	34.4	9.2	6.5	8.5	12.6
HIGH DESERT ST BK	ALBUQUERQUE	NM	D-	D	D-	31.4	-9.40	4.8	0.3	11.5	0.0	9.4	11.4	14.5
▲ HIGH PLAINS BK	FLAGLER	CO	C	C-	D	70.3	3.71	8.4	4.2	5.9	9.5	5.2	8.6	11.1
▼ HIGH POINT B&TC	HIGH POINT	NC	A-	A	A	644.0	4.56	13.5	4.0	14.8	20.1	10.0	12.9	18.8
HIGHLAND BK	ST MICHAEL	MN	B-	B-	B-	402.8	18.21	19.1	0.8	3.9	33.4	5.8	7.8	11.7
HIGHLAND COMMUNITY BK	CHICAGO	IL	C	C	D-	101.5	-4.15	18.3	1.0	9.5	54.0	9.5	10.7	24.1
HIGHLAND FALLS FS&LA	HIGHLAND FALLS	NY	B-	B-	B-	47.1	-3.61	0.0	1.0	42.1	26.9	10.0	14.6	37.8
HIGHLAND FS&LA	CROSSVILLE	TN	B+	B+	A-	60.0	-1.93	0.0	0.9	54.8	15.2	10.0	17.3	34.6
▲ HIGHLAND ST BK	HIGHLAND	WI	D+	D	D	23.5	1.75	15.0	8.3	49.1	6.1	5.4	7.4	13.1
HIGHLANDS BK	JACKSON	LA	B+	B+	A-	71.9	10.01	8.7	4.0	17.2	14.5	7.8	9.5	14.0
▲ HIGHLANDS COMMUNITY BK	COVINGTON	VA	C	C-	D	40.9	33.56	9.7	17.2	25.4	20.7	10.0	17.0	29.6
HIGHLANDS INDEPENDENT BK	SEBRING	FL	C	C	B-	204.4	20.87	11.5	4.5	22.8	18.2	3.6	6.6	10.3
▲ HIGHLANDS UNION BK	ABINGDON	VA	C	C-	C-	546.7	6.66	6.9	10.2	28.4	22.7	4.7	6.7	11.3
HILL B&TC	WEIMAR	TX	A-	A-	A-	93.3	-0.72	2.1	2.5	2.7	79.7	10.0	19.3	65.1
HILL-DODGE BANKING	WARSAW	IL	C+	C+	C+	31.7	2.37	12.7	9.2	24.9	20.1	6.8	8.8	14.0
HILLCREST BK	OVERLAND PARK	KS	C+	C+	C-	1,145.9	12.25	18.8	0.3	2.0	15.7	3.2	8.5	10.1
HILLS B&TC	HILLS	IA	B+	B+	B+	1,232.9	7.04	4.5	2.5	29.8	17.3	6.8	8.8	13.6
▲ HILLSBORO BK	PLANT CITY	FL	A-	B+	B+	68.2	16.65	15.0	2.6	5.1	34.8	10.0	12.7	22.8
HILLSBORO ST BK	HILLSBORO	KS	C	C	C-	11.9	3.40	9.7	6.7	28.0	2.7	10.0	11.2	15.8
HILLSDALE COUNTY NB	HILLSDALE	MI	B+	A-	B+	256.1	0.68	9.7	8.9	18.9	20.0	8.9	10.3	15.3
▲ HILLTOP CMNTY BK	SUMMIT	NJ	C-	D	D-	128.6	19.72	9.7	0.4	5.1	43.4	6.8	8.9	13.0
HILLTOP NB	CASPER	WY	B+	B+	A-	333.3	9.50	10.3	9.8	12.7	40.3	7.0	9.0	16.6
HINGHAM INST FOR SVGS	HINGHAM	MA	B+	B+	B+	526.0	14.40	0.0	0.2	34.9	15.4	6.7	8.7	14.3
HINSBROOK B&TC	WILLOWBROOK	IL	C	C-	D+	427.0	8.40	12.3	5.9	1.9	14.4	3.9	8.5	10.4
HINSDALE B&TC	HINSDALE	IL	B-	B-	B-	808.9	17.56	28.0	5.5	6.6	20.7	4.0	7.8	10.5
HNB NB	HANNIBAL	MO	B+	A-	A-	138.0	3.67	6.5	4.5	30.7	22.3	9.9	10.9	16.6
HOBLITZELL NB OF HYNDMAN	HYNDMAN	PA	C+	C	C-	65.6	3.44	3.5	6.3	48.4	9.8	9.2	10.4	17.4
HOCKING VALLEY BK OF	ATHENS	OH	B+	B+	B+	166.8	-2.21	8.3	6.8	30.9	20.4	8.1	9.7	16.6
HODGE B&TC	HODGE	LA	B	B	B	48.0	-2.25	17.9	14.1	25.7	26.6	10.0	12.7	23.5
HOISINGTON NB	HOISINGTON	KS	C+	C+	B-	22.4	-3.14	2.5	5.0	19.1	40.9	10.0	15.3	37.0
▼ HOLBROOK CO-OP BK	HOLBROOK	MA	D	C	C+	75.0	2.29	2.0	0.6	31.0	26.9	6.5	8.5	16.0
▲ HOLCOMB ST BK	HOLCOMB	IL	B+	B	B-	88.8	-0.02	9.6	4.2	10.3	23.9	9.0	10.4	15.6
HOLLADAY B&TC	SALT LAKE CITY	UT	D	D	D+	40.0	-26.56	3.2	1.2	7.1	1.7	10.0	19.1	27.3
HOLMES COUNTY B&TC	LEXINGTON	MS	B-	C+	B-	90.9	6.49	8.0	21.1	7.5	22.8	8.1	9.8	15.1

Asset Quality Index	Non-Performing Loans as a % of Total Loans	Non-Performing Loans as a % of Capital	Net Charge-offs Avg Loans	Profitability Index	Net Income ($Mil)	Return on Assets (R.O.A.)	Return on Equity (R.O.E.)	Net Interest Spread	Overhead Efficiency Ratio	Liquidity Index	Liquidity Ratio	Hot Money Ratio	Stability Index
8.8	0.00	0.0	0.00	0.0	-0.3	-6.83	-16.57	3.68	215.0	6.8	59.2	0.0	0.0
6.7	0.17	1.1	0.12	5.2	1.8	1.09	11.26	4.26	70.1	0.9	11.8	31.8	4.6
3.6	1.94	6.4	0.31	1.8	0.0	0.00	-0.02	0.06	105.9	3.5	58.9	21.6	4.8
4.3	1.41	12.0	0.08	3.4	0.4	0.77	9.54	4.30	74.3	4.0	51.1	17.6	2.8
8.8	0.08	0.5	-0.01	5.5	1.1	0.87	8.41	3.40	61.7	6.1	78.0	11.9	6.5
3.4	1.35	12.6	0.00	9.8	0.7	1.57	20.75	4.69	50.7	1.5	17.7	26.0	6.7
3.2	2.26	18.0	-0.09	8.0	2.1	1.78	19.62	4.81	64.7	5.0	26.8	4.4	6.8
4.6	1.65	7.9	0.48	5.7	0.9	0.69	5.15	4.61	81.8	4.4	28.9	8.8	5.8
8.4	0.00	0.0	0.00	0.0	-0.7	-6.08	-18.42	2.50	293.1	5.2	133.6	23.4	0.0
7.5	0.05	0.3	-0.03	0.0	-0.2	-1.03	-8.35	4.00	110.1	1.7	38.9	61.7	0.0
9.1	0.26	1.5	0.03	5.4	1.5	1.33	19.30	3.51	63.1	4.3	40.9	13.8	3.9
5.1	0.33	2.1	0.10	7.3	2.3	1.17	13.37	5.79	67.9	5.3	35.1	5.6	4.7
7.2	0.00	0.0	-0.02	7.2	0.6	1.77	19.99	4.13	51.7	1.6	7.9	20.3	5.7
8.2	0.05	0.5	0.00	5.2	0.4	1.20	14.79	4.26	73.1	3.2	10.4	12.4	3.5
6.7	0.12	1.1	0.00	9.8	4.3	1.57	17.19	5.15	58.0	1.9	21.4	20.0	7.4
9.4	0.15	1.5	0.00	9.0	0.5	1.85	26.45	4.87	67.5	5.3	44.4	8.8	6.3
7.3	5.36	5.5	0.20	3.1	0.1	0.54	2.04	3.31	79.0	9.2	149.7	0.0	5.8
1.7	4.78	24.5	0.68	6.0	0.1	0.93	10.35	3.98	58.7	2.7	29.9	18.4	4.2
6.2	0.92	4.4	0.04	6.6	1.5	2.09	23.99	4.19	47.3	4.1	9.8	7.1	5.0
4.7	0.66	5.4	0.23	5.6	1.9	1.10	12.64	4.72	65.8	2.8	29.5	17.7	4.6
3.2	3.69	18.0	2.28	4.9	0.1	0.52	3.59	5.24	55.6	3.7	66.2	23.1	4.7
9.9	0.00	0.0	0.00	1.9	0.0	0.21	1.84	1.94	95.9	8.0	819.6	12.6	3.5
5.3	0.57	5.0	0.18	4.9	0.8	0.66	7.74	2.56	63.5	2.2	33.3	25.9	4.9
3.8	1.07	8.6	0.23	7.5	0.1	1.08	10.96	5.01	63.9	3.4	13.8	11.4	6.1
1.3	4.01	25.2	0.28	3.1	0.1	0.36	4.05	4.94	92.2	7.2	72.1	2.2	2.9
9.6	0.00	0.0	0.00	4.3	0.1	0.46	1.80	2.32	74.4	3.6	36.0	15.8	7.1
6.1	0.46	3.4	0.33	9.4	138.6	1.42	16.15	4.07	52.7	3.8	24.6	13.3	7.0
7.0	0.31	1.4	0.14	3.4	1.8	0.46	5.85	2.37	76.4	3.1	58.4	32.3	4.8
4.9	0.82	7.8	0.03	4.1	0.5	0.76	12.10	3.84	69.3	1.7	15.2	22.0	2.4
6.8	0.25	2.2	0.13	4.3	0.2	0.64	7.34	3.89	74.1	2.0	23.1	19.7	3.6
6.5	0.15	1.3	1.37	5.3	0.6	0.62	7.04	3.86	70.1	1.4	10.1	24.6	4.5
0.2	5.08	31.2	0.46	0.3	-0.1	-0.60	-5.40	4.46	104.0	7.5	214.1	15.0	3.2
6.3	0.15	1.2	0.42	6.5	0.3	0.96	11.10	5.44	67.3	1.8	24.8	23.2	3.8
5.9	1.19	6.0	0.37	6.5	3.3	1.03	7.87	3.79	58.7	2.3	39.3	29.2	8.5
5.3	0.95	6.7	0.40	6.5	2.7	1.44	16.97	4.31	65.3	3.8	8.4	9.0	5.5
5.0	2.89	8.9	-0.42	2.8	0.2	0.32	2.40	4.14	89.8	4.9	86.6	18.9	3.4
8.7	0.00	0.0	0.00	3.8	0.1	0.37	2.37	2.90	77.9	2.8	35.6	19.7	6.3
8.0	0.35	1.3	0.00	4.6	0.2	0.64	3.71	3.60	72.2	4.1	35.1	12.9	6.9
8.4	0.00	0.0	0.04	7.5	0.2	1.69	23.35	4.71	64.2	5.7	59.6	7.3	2.6
7.3	0.27	1.9	0.18	8.2	0.6	1.83	18.96	4.50	60.6	3.0	44.3	22.7	6.2
7.2	1.08	3.8	0.01	1.9	0.1	0.66	3.80	3.69	73.8	4.9	85.5	17.4	1.4
6.1	0.40	3.8	0.04	5.5	0.9	0.92	14.53	4.18	64.2	3.6	30.7	13.9	3.7
3.9	1.30	12.3	0.34	4.6	2.5	0.93	13.96	3.77	66.8	4.2	42.2	14.6	3.1
9.2	0.29	0.2	-0.58	5.3	0.4	0.88	4.57	2.82	57.5	1.9	26.3	22.3	8.2
5.3	0.61	4.6	0.16	9.4	0.4	2.47	27.43	4.33	39.7	2.6	21.3	16.5	5.0
3.5	1.58	12.8	0.29	6.5	6.1	1.11	12.71	3.55	45.4	2.8	32.7	25.2	7.0
7.0	0.49	3.8	0.01	6.9	7.2	1.19	13.21	3.58	57.8	4.5	21.0	7.3	7.9
8.5	0.62	2.2	-0.23	7.1	0.4	1.17	8.95	4.39	59.3	4.4	51.1	14.9	6.5
7.7	0.46	3.2	-0.04	4.4	0.1	0.80	7.42	5.44	81.0	3.9	35.0	11.7	3.4
7.0	0.32	1.9	0.13	4.9	0.9	0.70	6.08	4.38	78.9	4.9	20.7	3.6	7.3
9.2	0.00	0.0	0.00	2.1	0.5	0.72	7.94	3.29	83.2	4.5	31.2	9.3	1.1
7.0	0.35	2.1	0.13	6.4	2.5	1.50	17.18	4.47	71.4	4.7	32.5	8.6	6.3
9.2	0.13	1.1	0.00	7.9	2.8	1.12	13.39	3.52	51.0	4.0	29.4	11.4	5.7
4.8	0.34	2.9	0.01	6.0	2.4	1.15	13.50	3.91	53.8	1.1	11.6	29.8	4.0
6.7	0.21	1.7	0.09	6.6	3.9	1.00	11.51	3.50	60.0	1.7	23.3	24.3	5.6
8.2	0.11	0.7	0.18	5.1	0.5	0.81	7.42	3.93	74.4	5.2	29.7	3.8	7.1
5.7	0.61	4.3	0.11	5.5	0.3	0.94	9.15	4.15	61.5	2.6	30.4	18.6	3.8
6.0	0.31	2.0	0.19	6.3	0.9	1.05	10.73	4.75	67.1	4.7	23.2	4.8	6.4
4.5	2.32	10.2	0.15	7.9	0.5	1.90	15.03	4.35	55.1	3.9	56.0	18.3	7.4
9.1	0.00	0.0	-0.02	4.5	0.1	0.94	6.15	3.64	84.0	6.4	77.3	7.0	5.1
9.6	0.00	0.0	0.00	0.9	-0.3	-0.73	-8.60	3.02	130.8	7.4	104.7	6.4	3.7
7.3	0.62	3.4	-0.01	5.5	0.6	1.23	12.28	4.23	69.0	4.3	72.3	19.0	6.0
0.0	14.14	42.5	0.02	7.5	0.2	0.98	5.34	5.11	66.5	7.3	148.6	11.8	6.6
4.5	0.58	3.2	0.41	7.0	0.7	1.49	14.67	4.55	62.6	3.2	54.4	24.8	6.4

Name	City	State	Weiss Safety Rating	2003 Weiss Safety Rating	2002 Weiss Safety Rating	Total Assets ($Mil)	One Year Asset Growth	Asset Mix (As a % of Total Assets) Commercial Loans	Consumer Loans	Home Mortgages	Securities	Capitalization Index	Leverage Ratio	Risk-based Capital Ratio
HOME B&LC	GREENFIELD	OH	B-	B-	B-	46.3	-4.11	0.0	0.2	42.7	17.4	10.0	13.3	38.2
HOME B&TC	EUREKA	KS	D-	D-	D+	50.3	4.14	31.1	9.8	20.6	11.3	5.8	8.1	11.6
HOME BANK OF AR	PORTLAND	AR	D	D-	E-	37.4	51.08	30.6	17.8	12.6	7.7	6.9	9.4	12.5
▼ HOME BANK SB	MARTINSVILLE	IN	B	B+	A-	186.9	-2.10	0.0	3.0	69.3	8.9	10.0	13.5	25.6
HOME BK	LAFAYETTE	LA	B+	B+	B	309.5	12.88	4.9	2.9	33.4	24.8	9.8	10.8	19.5
HOME BK FSB	DUCKTOWN	TN	B	B	B-	103.6	13.19	3.7	7.4	30.8	10.4	6.4	8.4	12.5
▲ HOME BK OF CA	SAN DIEGO	CA	B	B-	D+	153.0	17.91	0.0	0.0	4.5	0.0	6.1	10.2	11.9
HOME BK OF TENNESSEE	MARYVILLE	TN	B	B	B-	97.2	2.94	12.6	3.4	14.6	11.1	5.9	8.9	11.7
▲ HOME BKG CO	SELMER	TN	D+	D	D-	55.8	8.29	0.8	15.1	32.1	17.7	5.5	7.5	12.9
HOME BUILDERS ASSN	LYNCHBURG	OH	C	C	C	21.5	-3.82	1.5	3.5	53.1	4.3	10.0	16.9	31.1
▲ HOME BUILDING SVGS BK FSB	WASHINGTON	IN	B	B-	B-	53.8	4.31	3.1	9.4	43.9	19.5	10.0	11.4	21.7
HOME CITY FSB OF	SPRINGFIELD	OH	C+	C+	C+	153.0	3.10	9.6	1.6	41.0	6.7	5.9	7.9	12.2
HOME EXCHANGE BK	JAMESPORT	MO	B	B	B	67.2	1.18	1.7	1.7	7.6	53.6	8.6	10.1	20.3
HOME FED BK CORP	MIDDLESBORO	KY	C+	C+	C+	272.4	4.71	2.2	2.0	40.2	22.1	6.4	8.4	14.3
▼ HOME FEDERAL BANK OF TN	KNOXVILLE	TN	A-	A	A	1,593.0	1.91	3.2	2.4	17.7	54.7	10.0	14.3	31.7
▲ HOME FEDERAL BK	SIOUX FALLS	SD	C	C-	D+	840.1	6.05	21.6	13.2	15.2	14.6	4.1	8.3	10.5
▲ HOME FEDERAL BK OF	HALLANDALE	FL	B+	B	C+	108.8	7.45	1.5	0.7	29.7	2.7	6.0	8.0	11.9
HOME FS&LA	NAMPA	ID	B	B	B-	519.9	10.61	0.3	1.2	47.2	16.1	6.3	8.4	14.4
HOME FS&LA	ASHLAND	KY	B	B	C+	177.5	-1.75	0.0	0.6	39.4	44.8	10.0	11.8	28.6
HOME FS&LA	SHREVEPORT	LA	A-	A-	A-	95.7	-5.05	0.0	0.7	22.8	69.1	10.0	19.5	71.2
▲ HOME FS&LA	BAMBERG	SC	B-	C+	C-	26.2	6.06	1.1	8.6	64.8	3.1	10.0	11.2	19.7
▲ HOME FS&LA OF	COLLINSVILLE	IL	B	B-	C+	152.4	8.62	0.0	0.8	36.6	48.3	7.2	9.1	24.7
▲ HOME FS&LA OF GRAND	GRAND ISLAND	NE	B	B-	B-	162.5	2.54	6.4	5.7	28.7	33.4	6.6	8.6	15.5
HOME FS&LA OF NEBRASKA	LEXINGTON	NE	B	B	B-	62.1	-1.04	29.7	6.1	14.2	13.6	10.0	12.8	16.1
HOME FS&LA OF NILES	NILES	OH	A-	B+	B+	96.6	-2.69	0.1	0.5	31.4	51.2	10.0	14.6	38.2
▲ HOME FSB	DETROIT	MI	E+	E-	D-	26.2	-1.53	0.2	0.3	22.5	55.2	6.3	8.3	28.5
HOME FSB	ROCHESTER	MN	B-	B-	B-	907.7	16.74	18.2	2.2	17.8	12.1	5.3	8.1	11.2
HOME LOAN & INVESTMENT	WARWICK	RI	B	B	B	259.5	-5.03	1.3	0.1	38.3	8.2	10.0	23.3	41.2
HOME LOAN IND BK	GRAND JUNCTION	CO	D-	D-	D	49.1	4.24	0.8	35.2	10.4	32.8	4.5	7.2	10.7
HOME LOAN SAVINGS BANK	COSHOCTON	OH	B-	B	A-	159.9	8.33	4.7	7.6	52.9	11.0	10.0	11.0	17.8
HOME NB	RACINE	OH	D	D	D-	51.8	-4.19	4.6	17.2	37.8	21.7	9.3	10.5	18.3
▲ HOME NB	BLACKWELL	OK	B+	B-	B-	810.8	8.29	9.3	2.5	11.1	26.3	10.0	11.2	16.0
HOME NB OF THORNTOWN	THORNTOWN	IN	C+	C+	B-	46.0	4.52	6.7	6.5	20.1	25.4	8.5	10.0	15.7
HOME S&L COMPANY OF	KENTON	OH	A	A	A	105.2	-0.57	3.3	5.9	53.8	20.2	10.0	20.5	39.2
HOME S&LA FA	NORBORNE	MO	B+	B+	B+	82.7	1.46	1.3	3.8	60.7	18.0	10.0	13.4	27.2
HOME S&LC	YOUNGSTOWN	OH	C+	B-	B+	2,127.4	N/A	3.5	7.0	32.7	9.0	3.8	8.3	10.4
HOME SAVINGS BK	CHANUTE	KS	B-	B-	B+	60.0	-2.00	0.1	3.1	28.2	55.5	10.0	23.4	66.9
▲ HOME SAVINGS BK	JEFFERSON CITY	MO	C	C-	C-	28.4	-7.02	0.0	4.7	67.9	4.1	9.2	10.4	18.2
▲ HOME SAVINGS BK	SALT LAKE CITY	UT	D+	D+	D+	80.0	0.61	0.0	0.2	9.0	0.0	10.0	11.1	16.1
HOME SAVINGS BK	WAPAKONETA	OH	C	C	C-	29.1	-0.57	0.0	0.1	55.9	5.8	8.4	9.9	25.0
▲ HOME ST B&TC	MCPHERSON	KS	B-	C+	C+	94.6	4.46	14.8	12.1	19.3	27.5	6.2	8.2	13.1
▲ HOME ST BK	LOVELAND	CO	B	B-	B-	393.0	5.45	7.8	2.0	11.9	17.9	6.9	9.0	12.9
HOME ST BK	JEFFERSON	IA	B+	B	B	114.0	4.26	14.8	3.3	13.9	10.0	6.2	8.2	12.4
HOME ST BK	ROYAL	IA	A-	A-	A-	34.0	-2.50	4.5	1.1	4.0	42.2	10.0	26.7	39.6
HOME ST BK	LITCHFIELD	MN	B-	B-	B-	87.0	15.22	27.2	7.7	9.1	13.5	3.9	7.9	10.5
▲ HOME ST BK	LOUISVILLE	NE	A-	B+	B+	62.7	-1.59	7.9	6.8	17.7	12.0	9.8	10.9	15.7
HOME ST BK ERIE KS	ERIE	KS	B-	B-	B-	20.3	0.56	6.6	4.0	18.1	39.8	6.1	8.1	19.0
HOME ST BK NA	CRYSTAL LAKE	IL	B	B	B-	567.1	6.13	11.1	2.3	11.9	25.6	5.4	7.4	11.7
HOME SVG BK	KENT	OH	C-	C-	C-	100.7	-4.79	2.8	11.4	31.3	19.0	4.9	6.9	11.4
HOME SVG BK OF ALBEMARLE	ALBEMARLE	NC	C+	C+	C+	208.5	-3.23	2.1	1.0	45.2	12.6	9.8	10.9	19.0
HOME SVGS BK	MADISON	WI	C+	C+	C	132.2	7.72	0.5	1.4	40.7	15.5	6.6	8.7	15.4
▲ HOME SVGS BK FSB	LUDLOW	KY	C+	C-	D+	39.2	-3.03	0.0	0.1	54.1	11.3	10.0	11.8	26.5
HOME SVGS BK, SSB	EDEN	NC	B-	B-	B-	109.2	0.95	1.4	2.1	38.7	41.1	10.0	15.9	38.1
HOME T&SB	OSAGE	IA	A-	A-	A-	132.1	-4.48	6.4	1.4	11.1	56.1	7.2	9.2	20.3
▲ HOME TOWN BK OF VILLA	VILLA RICA	GA	C	C-	D-	179.6	18.93	6.4	2.9	13.8	8.9	3.4	7.9	10.2
HOME VALLEY BK	CAVE JUNCTION	OR	B-	C+	D+	146.4	48.69	7.7	2.2	24.5	11.1	6.9	8.9	13.4
HOMEBANK	SEAGOVILLE	TX	B	B	B	82.5	-5.16	10.6	4.9	8.1	26.0	10.0	11.1	17.9
HOMEFEDERAL BK	COLUMBUS	IN	B+	B+	B	856.0	-1.79	7.3	4.1	27.1	14.6	8.2	9.8	13.5
HOMELAND COMMUNITY BK	MC MINNVILLE	TN	D	D	NR	27.9	N/A	1.4	3.6	8.5	45.5	10.0	28.3	52.5
HOMELAND FSB	COLUMBIA	LA	C	C	D+	77.9	6.50	19.1	17.1	27.8	4.6	8.1	9.8	15.3
HOMESTAR BK	MANTENO	IL	C	C	C+	383.8	2.97	3.2	4.0	32.9	18.2	5.1	7.1	11.7
HOMESTEAD BK	SUWANEE	GA	D	D	NR	79.8	98.05	10.4	1.4	15.0	22.9	10.0	12.8	15.4
HOMESTEAD BK	PONCHATOULA	LA	C+	C+	B-	135.4	4.30	0.0	1.1	26.4	55.6	6.1	8.1	23.1
HOMESTEAD SVGS BK	ALBION	MI	C	C	C	65.8	0.04	2.8	1.0	48.9	11.7	6.2	8.2	14.4

Asset Quality Index	Non-Performing Loans as a % of Total Loans	Non-Performing Loans as a % of Capital	Net Charge-offs Avg Loans	Profitability Index	Net Income ($Mil)	Return on Assets (R.O.A.)	Return on Equity (R.O.E.)	Net Interest Spread	Overhead Efficiency Ratio	Liquidity Index	Liquidity Ratio	Hot Money Ratio	Stability Index
3.7	6.82	21.5	0.00	4.9	0.2	0.76	5.96	2.41	42.6	3.9	90.1	29.1	6.1
1.0	2.93	26.9	0.22	5.8	0.4	1.43	20.00	4.45	72.0	2.1	22.3	19.1	2.9
4.8	0.49	3.9	0.15	2.6	0.1	0.44	4.65	5.32	77.4	1.3	25.4	31.4	2.3
5.8	1.50	9.0	0.01	4.2	0.5	0.50	3.79	3.04	75.3	1.1	21.8	33.0	7.1
7.0	0.48	2.8	0.02	5.2	1.3	0.87	8.06	3.84	66.3	0.8	14.8	35.1	6.1
5.5	0.72	6.0	0.28	9.0	0.9	1.70	19.26	4.94	67.0	1.4	16.0	25.6	7.0
5.7	0.16	1.3	0.00	10.0	2.2	3.06	31.34	5.10	32.0	4.4	90.2	25.9	7.4
3.6	1.62	12.9	0.08	5.5	0.6	1.20	13.24	4.34	68.6	1.9	20.5	20.3	6.3
4.3	1.08	8.4	0.77	5.4	0.2	0.86	11.33	4.95	68.8	3.2	44.7	19.9	2.4
7.2	0.56	2.4	0.05	6.6	0.1	1.09	6.11	4.51	63.0	2.6	22.1	16.3	5.0
6.0	1.12	6.5	0.06	5.6	0.2	0.80	6.89	3.33	62.0	2.8	49.5	28.2	5.8
6.1	0.22	2.2	0.47	3.6	0.4	0.49	6.36	2.91	72.5	0.9	21.7	40.2	3.7
8.8	0.04	0.1	0.01	6.3	0.2	0.73	6.95	3.16	52.5	2.4	4.4	16.1	6.0
5.2	1.13	9.0	0.06	4.4	0.9	0.70	8.00	3.95	71.6	2.0	38.0	32.5	2.9
8.3	1.00	2.6	0.08	5.7	6.3	0.79	5.61	2.87	61.9	4.4	94.7	29.5	10.0
4.3	0.31	2.9	0.17	5.1	3.3	0.80	8.98	3.40	66.1	0.5	6.5	47.6	4.5
6.1	0.04	0.4	0.00	10.0	1.2	2.31	28.57	3.73	43.9	0.7	17.8	55.6	6.3
7.4	0.08	0.7	0.04	6.0	2.2	0.90	10.51	3.89	70.1	1.9	4.8	18.3	4.9
6.0	1.72	6.1	0.02	4.2	0.7	0.74	6.14	3.11	66.0	3.0	55.9	31.8	6.4
9.8	0.01	0.0	0.00	5.1	0.4	0.73	3.84	2.95	66.0	3.8	6.9	8.8	7.4
8.4	0.25	1.9	0.00	5.6	0.1	0.73	6.45	3.77	68.9	1.1	20.2	32.4	5.3
6.9	0.59	2.8	0.00	4.6	0.6	0.77	8.33	2.37	54.5	2.3	3.1	16.3	4.8
7.1	0.45	2.6	-0.04	4.4	0.5	0.59	6.93	2.76	74.5	1.3	23.4	29.3	5.6
6.2	1.09	5.6	0.96	3.7	0.0	0.07	0.56	4.53	70.4	4.0	14.2	8.8	6.1
6.6	2.16	6.0	0.00	6.9	0.6	1.19	7.84	3.00	48.7	3.6	71.0	26.6	8.3
6.1	0.53	1.7	0.00	4.5	0.2	1.27	15.99	5.10	80.3	2.6	54.0	32.7	1.5
5.3	0.40	3.6	0.04	5.9	4.7	1.06	12.46	3.41	52.6	1.9	41.8	66.2	5.4
4.9	2.25	4.8	0.14	9.3	2.4	1.76	7.45	6.33	84.6	3.3	48.6	21.9	9.3
3.9	1.20	8.3	-0.09	3.0	0.1	0.24	3.34	3.65	76.9	0.4	3.1	62.1	1.2
3.5	1.13	8.3	0.46	6.9	0.8	1.07	9.66	3.74	53.1	1.3	7.7	25.9	7.8
0.4	4.97	29.1	0.94	3.9	0.2	0.64	6.04	4.10	73.7	3.0	44.0	21.9	4.2
5.5	1.59	8.7	-0.03	6.8	4.9	1.19	11.43	4.21	59.7	1.4	11.8	25.1	5.9
6.6	0.36	2.3	0.36	4.8	0.2	0.86	8.95	4.63	71.0	3.2	28.0	15.0	4.3
7.5	1.07	3.7	0.09	7.8	0.7	1.28	6.40	3.52	46.0	3.8	35.0	14.2	8.8
6.8	0.92	5.1	0.12	5.0	0.4	0.84	6.40	2.51	45.8	2.6	31.7	19.2	7.0
5.1	0.73	5.9	0.07	6.8	9.6	0.94	9.57	3.80	60.5	4.0	20.6	10.5	3.5
7.8	0.16	0.2	0.00	3.5	0.1	0.45	1.82	2.72	80.2	5.1	40.9	9.4	6.6
6.0	0.31	2.5	0.04	3.4	0.1	0.37	3.55	2.95	85.8	2.7	12.9	15.5	3.7
1.2	4.86	28.7	0.26	8.6	0.5	1.15	10.67	4.35	55.9	7.1	1,677.3	16.8	6.3
9.7	0.00	0.0	0.00	3.5	0.1	0.49	4.97	2.94	78.5	3.5	44.4	18.2	3.9
7.4	0.16	1.2	0.00	4.9	0.5	1.04	12.99	4.25	76.6	4.1	43.6	14.9	4.8
4.8	1.28	9.4	0.12	7.5	2.5	1.27	14.55	4.69	63.3	2.9	20.7	14.8	5.1
8.3	0.03	0.2	0.98	6.0	0.6	1.10	12.92	3.71	51.7	6.5	69.7	8.2	6.3
8.6	0.20	0.4	-0.02	9.8	0.4	2.24	8.25	3.92	35.8	5.6	33.2	2.7	8.0
7.7	0.14	1.2	0.01	9.0	0.9	2.10	25.03	5.47	63.9	3.0	20.6	14.5	5.9
6.9	0.38	2.5	0.19	10.0	1.0	3.03	28.45	4.79	40.3	2.4	38.9	28.3	6.9
9.3	0.00	0.0	0.00	5.2	0.1	1.02	12.48	3.46	72.4	6.2	67.6	6.0	5.8
8.4	0.12	0.9	0.06	6.8	4.2	1.48	19.42	4.13	58.6	3.2	55.6	28.5	5.4
5.6	0.38	3.6	0.01	3.2	0.1	0.26	3.75	3.69	86.5	4.5	34.0	10.7	2.9
9.5	0.08	0.5	0.11	3.0	0.3	0.32	3.05	3.08	82.8	6.0	178.5	22.3	6.2
8.5	0.13	1.1	0.02	3.6	0.3	0.43	4.96	3.12	85.5	2.1	27.0	21.0	4.0
9.1	0.40	1.9	0.00	3.1	0.1	0.51	4.27	3.55	80.8	2.9	44.2	23.3	5.1
8.7	1.73	5.0	0.05	3.7	0.3	0.54	3.43	2.47	65.8	6.0	331.7	27.2	7.8
9.0	0.34	1.6	0.00	7.1	1.1	1.65	17.67	2.98	39.8	6.4	73.2	9.5	6.9
4.5	0.17	1.0	0.20	3.9	0.9	1.03	8.34	3.85	64.3	1.9	8.1	18.6	5.5
8.7	0.06	0.5	0.07	4.9	0.5	0.72	7.72	4.08	69.9	5.2	21.7	1.5	4.2
8.1	0.01	0.1	0.58	4.0	0.2	0.50	4.18	5.42	88.1	6.0	52.7	6.0	5.4
5.4	0.94	6.6	0.06	6.0	3.7	0.86	8.37	3.24	64.4	2.7	19.9	16.1	5.0
9.6	0.00	0.0	0.00	0.0	-0.5	-4.46	-13.01	2.60	222.0	3.6	47.9	18.1	0.0
2.8	1.72	12.2	-0.07	7.2	0.5	1.27	13.07	5.22	64.9	1.5	22.1	26.6	5.7
2.7	2.24	19.7	0.00	6.8	2.4	1.29	18.07	3.87	71.8	4.3	28.9	9.7	5.1
8.9	0.00	0.0	0.00	0.0	-0.5	-1.34	-9.77	2.83	121.8	2.4	54.0	43.5	0.0
6.6	0.60	2.4	0.00	3.1	0.1	0.20	2.24	2.00	86.4	2.3	15.4	17.6	4.7
8.4	0.03	0.3	0.00	3.0	0.1	0.19	2.30	3.83	91.4	6.0	67.3	9.6	3.4

Name	City	State	Weiss Safety Rating	2003 Weiss Safety Rating	2002 Weiss Safety Rating	Total Assets ($Mil)	One Year Asset Growth	Asset Mix (As a % of Total Assets)				Capital-ization Index	Risk-based	
								Comm-ercial Loans	Cons-umer Loans	Home Mort-gages	Secur-ities		Leverage Ratio	Capital Ratio
▲ HOMESTREET BK	SEATTLE	WA	A-	B+	B	1,614.7	-6.45	1.4	0.0	29.6	7.8	8.3	9.8	14.0
▲ HOMETOWN BK	REDWOOD FALLS	MN	B-	C+	C+	77.8	-4.60	10.8	3.1	34.2	24.9	10.0	11.5	20.5
▲ HOMETOWN BK	ST CLOUD	WI	B-	C+	B-	96.5	6.06	25.2	2.5	10.3	3.1	6.4	9.9	12.0
▲ HOMETOWN BK A CO-OP BK	WEBSTER	MA	B	B-	C+	127.0	3.38	3.9	2.3	33.7	16.4	6.2	8.2	12.7
▲ HOMETOWN BK NA	CARTHAGE	MO	C+	C	D+	174.1	10.86	15.2	4.8	21.3	4.6	5.0	8.5	11.0
▼ HOMETOWN BK NA	GALVESTON	TX	B+	A-	A	186.4	2.81	5.2	6.1	20.0	30.5	8.9	10.3	19.0
HOMETOWN BK OF ALABAMA	ONEONTA	AL	D	D	NR	39.0	N/A	16.0	16.1	19.7	24.0	10.0	17.0	23.2
HOMETOWN COMMUNITY BK	CYRUS	MN	E-	E-	E-	20.7	1.95	14.4	9.6	16.1	10.0	4.7	7.0	10.8
HOMETOWN NB	LONGVIEW	WA	C	C	D	34.2	7.67	13.1	1.4	22.6	10.1	8.3	9.9	14.6
HOMETRUST BANK	CLYDE	NC	A-	A-	B+	748.0	3.62	14.3	0.3	27.9	4.8	9.5	10.9	14.6
HOMEWOOD FSB	BALTIMORE	MD	B-	B-	B+	69.8	-11.51	1.9	0.1	51.5	34.5	10.0	15.1	38.2
HOMOSASSA SPRINGS BK	HOMOSASSA SPRING	FL	B+	B+	A-	65.1	0.19	0.1	0.7	53.7	25.0	6.3	8.3	18.9
HONDO NB	HONDO	TX	D+	D+	D+	67.1	2.97	6.6	3.3	7.6	33.7	5.7	7.7	13.0
▼ HONESDALE NB	HONESDALE	PA	B	B	B+	335.7	2.19	15.1	9.8	23.1	23.9	7.1	9.0	13.1
HONOR ST BK	HONOR	MI	B-	B-	B-	180.7	-2.89	6.1	11.7	20.1	10.7	6.6	8.6	12.7
HOOSAC BK	N ADAMS	MA	B-	B-	B-	302.2	-0.08	5.2	1.0	27.3	37.3	10.0	13.3	24.5
▲ HOPETON ST BK	HOPETON	OK	C+	C	C	21.2	-1.11	4.7	4.9	0.2	72.1	10.0	18.8	50.8
▲ HOPEWELL VALLEY	PENNINGTON	NJ	B-	C+	C	149.3	34.68	2.5	0.4	16.7	18.0	7.9	9.6	13.8
▲ HOPKINS FSB	BALTIMORE	MD	B+	B-	B-	213.8	-4.37	2.0	0.2	15.0	56.7	6.6	8.7	18.1
HORATIO ST BK	HORATIO	AR	B-	B-	B-	72.3	2.90	3.9	22.5	23.6	16.9	9.2	10.5	19.6
▲ HORICON BK	HORICON	WI	C+	C-	C-	323.9	4.09	9.8	4.4	33.3	6.9	7.2	9.3	12.7
HORIZON BK	FYFFE	AL	A-	B+	B+	75.0	0.93	2.8	8.6	25.4	19.9	10.0	17.7	27.1
▲ HORIZON BK	BRADENTON	FL	D	D-	E-	110.7	39.55	12.8	4.6	19.9	6.2	3.8	7.1	10.4
▲ HORIZON BK	DECATUR	GA	C	C-	D+	149.7	38.17	17.0	2.2	7.6	3.2	3.5	8.9	10.3
HORIZON BK	WAVERLY	NE	B-	B-	B-	75.8	6.56	41.7	8.4	5.1	24.3	5.5	8.2	11.4
HORIZON BK	BELLINGHAM	WA	A+	A+	A+	878.2	6.64	9.8	0.5	13.9	12.3	10.0	12.1	15.9
▲ HORIZON BK FSB	PEMBROKE PINES	FL	D-	E	E-	90.1	8.70	1.4	0.2	67.9	7.4	4.7	6.7	13.4
▲ HORIZON BK NA	LIMON	CO	B	B	B	519.1	55.83	5.0	0.3	7.2	1.4	6.0	11.0	11.8
HORIZON BK NA	MICHIGAN CITY	IN	C+	C+	C	804.8	3.47	8.1	7.0	31.7	27.3	5.2	7.2	13.2
▲ HORIZON CAPITAL BK	WEBSTER	TX	B-	C+	D-	367.3	4.09	18.7	4.0	13.2	6.7	6.5	8.7	12.1
▲ HORIZON COMMUNITY BK	LAKE HAVASU CITY	AZ	C-	D	D	68.1	93.22	10.7	2.2	13.4	0.0	10.0	13.3	17.3
▲ HORIZON FSB	OSKALOOSA	IA	D+	D	D+	97.6	9.02	22.1	8.0	37.2	12.6	8.0	9.6	13.7
▲ HORIZON ST BK	CAMERON	MO	D-	E+	D-	21.3	0.42	7.0	3.2	15.9	12.6	6.2	8.3	13.6
▼ HORRY CTY ST BK	LORIS	SC	D	C-	D+	282.6	8.46	20.2	9.5	14.3	11.2	3.2	7.6	10.1
HOUGHTON ST BK	RED OAK	IA	C+	C+	B-	118.1	-0.49	32.6	3.6	8.2	17.6	4.6	7.8	10.8
HOUSEHOLD BK SB NA	LAS VEGAS	NV	A-	A	A-	4,235.6	-4.15	0.0	0.0	0.0	65.6	10.0	60.4	226.8
HOUSTON COMMUNITY BK NA	HOUSTON	TX	B-	B-	C+	139.0	7.89	9.6	23.4	7.7	3.1	4.4	8.4	10.7
HOWARD ST BK, HOWARD KS	HOWARD	KS	D+	D+	D	33.9	-6.38	3.6	8.2	13.8	9.9	5.7	8.2	11.5
HOWARD SVGS BK	GLENVIEW	IL	D	D	D	37.9	-24.40	2.3	0.0	20.6	18.1	10.0	17.7	37.6
▼ HOYNE SVGS BK	CHICAGO	IL	C+	B-	B-	335.3	-1.88	0.0	0.0	63.8	22.4	10.0	18.6	47.9
HSBC BANK USA	BUFFALO	NY	B-	B-	B-	110,305.4	22.02	6.4	2.8	33.1	15.8	4.3	6.3	11.9
▼ HUDSON CITY SAVINGS BK	PARAMUS	NJ	B	NR	NR	18,671.2	N/A	0.0	0.0	53.6	43.8	4.7	6.7	18.9
▲ HUDSON RIVER B&TC	HUDSON	NY	B+	B	C+	2,608.6	2.64	6.2	2.8	36.9	25.5	6.0	8.0	13.9
▲ HUDSON RIVER COMMERCIAL	COHOES	NY	B-	C	C	40.8	66.76	0.0	0.0	0.0	93.9	10.0	11.6	51.3
HUDSON SVGS BK	HUDSON	MA	B-	B-	B-	557.2	12.41	3.9	1.0	39.1	16.8	6.0	8.0	12.2
HUDSON UNITED BK	MAHWAH	NJ	B-	B-	C+	8,934.6	12.32	20.4	9.6	2.1	38.0	4.1	6.1	12.7
HUDSON VALLEY BK	YONKERS	NY	A-	A-	B+	1,810.3	13.07	12.4	0.8	4.9	50.3	6.6	8.6	16.4
▼ HULETT NB	HULETT	WY	E-	E	D-	22.7	27.80	8.9	5.8	12.3	10.9	3.5	6.5	10.2
HULL FSB	BALTIMORE	MD	C+	C+	C+	14.3	12.11	0.0	0.8	95.2	0.9	10.0	13.4	27.0
HULL ST BK	HULL	TX	B+	B+	B+	36.9	-3.12	12.9	16.2	7.0	12.9	10.0	15.6	25.4
▲ HUMBOLDT BK	EUREKA	CA	B	B	B	1,459.6	38.34	11.0	3.6	2.2	15.0	6.7	10.0	12.3
HUMBOLDT T&SB	HUMBOLDT	IA	B	B	B-	129.4	1.20	13.3	3.4	11.1	36.3	5.5	7.5	12.3
HUME BK	HUME	MO	D+	D+	D+	15.2	23.74	8.2	13.2	14.3	22.6	8.2	10.1	13.5
HUNTINGDON SVG BK	HUNTINGDON	PA	C+	C+	C+	12.1	0.72	0.0	1.6	57.4	8.3	10.0	18.2	45.7
▼ HUNTINGDON VALLEY BK	HUNTINGDON VLLY	PA	C+	B	C	146.1	N/A	0.1	0.1	45.4	33.9	6.2	8.2	16.6
HUNTINGTON FSB	HUNTINGTON	WV	B+	B+	B+	414.7	1.65	0.5	0.4	27.0	55.5	10.0	12.6	37.9
HUNTINGTON NB	COLUMBUS	OH	C+	C+	C+	31,056.8	9.78	12.1	7.9	15.1	15.7	4.0	6.0	10.9
HUNTINGTON ST BK	HUNTINGTON	TX	B-	B-	C+	139.8	7.37	4.4	19.7	16.4	14.0	6.1	8.1	14.1
▼ HURON COMMUNITY BK	E TAWAS	MI	B-	B	B	164.5	-0.63	35.4	3.2	28.0	13.7	6.5	8.5	13.0
HURON NB	ROGERS CITY	MI	B-	B-	C+	46.3	3.59	6.6	6.3	35.8	10.7	8.4	9.9	14.8
HUSTISFORD ST BK	HUSTISFORD	WI	B+	B+	B+	35.8	-4.53	3.3	6.6	45.4	19.2	10.0	17.4	29.6
▼ HYDE PARK B&TC	CHICAGO	IL	B-	B	B	318.3	9.45	3.1	0.1	5.5	53.4	5.2	7.2	16.4
HYDE PARK CO-OP BK	HYDE PARK	MA	B	B	C+	121.1	4.87	0.2	0.7	30.4	41.9	6.3	8.4	15.5
▲ HYDE PARK SVGS BK	BOSTON	MA	A-	B+	B+	762.1	13.55	0.0	0.1	17.8	66.9	10.0	12.4	31.8

Asset Quality Index	Non-Performing Loans as a % of Total Loans	Non-Performing Loans as a % of Capital	Net Charge-offs Avg Loans	Profitability Index	Net Income ($Mil)	Return on Assets (R.O.A.)	Return on Equity (R.O.E.)	Net Interest Spread	Overhead Efficiency Ratio	Liquidity Index	Liquidity Ratio	Hot Money Ratio	Stability Index
7.0	0.19	1.5	0.01	7.6	10.0	1.26	12.78	4.59	63.1	1.4	15.6	27.9	7.6
7.4	0.03	0.2	0.55	4.3	0.2	0.54	4.83	3.47	68.2	2.4	31.9	20.4	3.9
5.6	0.44	2.8	0.03	4.3	0.4	0.74	6.55	4.12	82.8	5.7	50.2	7.4	6.0
8.9	0.00	0.0	0.04	9.1	0.8	1.25	15.71	4.60	52.0	2.6	22.5	16.9	4.8
5.5	0.59	5.6	0.06	4.2	0.6	0.72	8.52	4.31	72.3	1.0	8.6	30.8	3.9
8.3	0.13	0.8	0.26	8.4	1.2	1.33	12.83	4.43	56.6	5.0	69.1	16.0	7.0
8.1	0.00	0.0	0.00	0.0	-0.2	-1.43	-7.14	4.07	92.5	1.6	32.5	33.9	0.0
3.7	0.71	6.4	1.34	3.9	0.0	0.43	6.03	5.04	61.1	4.0	53.9	15.4	0.3
2.9	2.11	16.5	0.25	5.7	0.2	1.05	10.89	4.62	59.8	4.1	100.3	29.6	0.8
6.6	0.31	1.9	0.00	6.3	4.8	1.29	11.71	3.32	64.3	2.0	33.2	28.2	7.6
8.8	0.83	2.9	0.00	3.5	0.1	0.25	1.63	1.71	74.5	1.1	15.5	30.2	6.1
10.0	0.00	0.0	0.00	9.7	0.8	2.27	26.29	4.29	52.5	5.0	45.2	10.7	6.9
5.9	0.33	2.3	0.44	4.6	0.3	0.80	10.74	4.24	72.7	1.9	28.1	23.9	1.9
4.0	1.57	10.8	0.04	6.3	2.1	1.27	14.06	4.13	55.7	3.0	20.9	14.4	6.4
5.0	0.81	6.2	0.27	5.6	0.6	0.65	7.59	4.54	79.6	5.2	43.9	10.0	4.9
9.0	0.44	1.6	-0.03	4.4	1.4	0.97	7.02	2.79	73.7	2.9	14.5	14.3	6.9
7.0	4.89	5.7	-0.49	6.9	0.2	1.63	9.13	4.06	53.2	2.3	48.5	29.7	4.4
9.0	0.00	0.0	0.00	3.9	0.5	0.76	7.85	3.67	69.2	2.7	31.1	18.6	5.0
7.9	0.62	2.7	0.00	9.1	2.7	2.47	30.01	3.04	31.0	3.1	54.1	28.7	5.7
5.8	0.56	3.0	0.22	5.1	0.3	0.88	8.58	3.57	58.8	4.9	145.5	30.0	5.1
3.4	1.52	12.5	0.07	5.6	1.2	0.77	8.11	4.06	70.0	1.0	5.3	28.6	5.0
6.5	1.12	3.8	-0.16	9.6	0.7	1.81	10.13	4.81	49.2	2.1	18.4	18.9	8.4
6.7	0.16	1.7	0.09	3.0	0.3	0.64	9.50	4.39	74.0	4.1	31.9	11.9	2.7
7.1	0.07	0.6	0.00	7.4	1.0	1.47	19.95	4.09	50.1	2.9	43.5	24.4	2.0
8.0	0.00	0.0	0.00	9.9	0.9	2.50	27.28	4.04	44.5	5.3	40.7	8.5	6.0
7.5	0.02	0.1	-0.02	9.3	6.8	1.59	12.48	4.39	49.4	2.4	28.4	19.2	9.2
2.7	2.02	23.9	-0.02	3.4	0.3	0.70	10.58	2.79	80.0	0.6	18.2	67.8	2.3
7.0	0.14	1.2	0.01	8.2	3.5	1.53	14.05	5.00	39.9	2.4	44.3	33.0	5.4
6.9	0.32	2.5	0.16	5.4	3.7	0.92	11.97	3.58	69.0	3.2	29.7	15.7	3.6
7.0	0.14	1.3	0.08	4.5	1.6	0.88	9.99	4.23	63.8	4.0	30.2	11.6	4.5
7.4	0.13	0.7	0.00	2.5	0.3	1.07	7.67	4.73	77.4	5.6	67.3	11.7	1.0
1.4	3.32	26.3	0.32	8.2	0.6	1.27	13.27	4.53	55.6	1.4	4.6	23.0	4.8
5.7	0.73	5.3	-0.08	3.0	0.1	0.49	6.01	4.26	87.7	5.6	57.9	8.0	1.7
1.1	2.58	25.3	0.39	4.1	1.0	0.70	9.45	4.02	66.4	2.4	13.6	17.0	3.2
5.1	0.28	1.7	0.17	7.7	0.7	1.27	10.67	4.36	52.8	4.1	34.1	12.7	6.7
6.5	0.00	0.0	0.00	10.0	229.8	10.48	16.40	0.30	53.2	5.0	7,123.6	100.0	8.3
5.3	0.55	5.3	0.10	7.9	1.2	1.84	22.19	6.11	64.2	1.5	29.3	32.1	5.7
5.2	0.12	1.0	0.04	5.9	0.2	1.02	11.90	4.46	63.5	4.1	16.6	8.0	2.7
0.3	41.41	86.3	0.00	0.0	-2.3	-11.26	-46.17	2.60	156.7	6.3	1,172.9	23.2	4.2
10.0	0.06	0.2	0.00	2.9	0.5	0.28	1.52	3.09	85.0	8.5	311.1	9.7	7.7
6.3	0.48	3.4	0.09	6.7	657.4	1.30	16.02	3.06	50.5	4.8	99.3	24.8	6.5
10.0	0.20	1.6	0.00	10.0	113.5	1.85	24.53	2.59	24.1	1.7	24.6	31.3	5.4
5.3	1.04	5.8	0.15	7.1	16.2	1.25	12.40	3.87	48.8	7.8	87.1	4.4	8.2
10.0	0.00	0.0	0.00	4.6	0.2	1.10	9.87	2.26	21.2	5.3	12.5	0.0	2.3
5.7	0.53	4.7	0.10	5.0	2.1	0.75	9.58	3.70	68.7	2.9	28.0	16.5	5.0
5.9	0.52	3.9	0.49	9.0	68.1	1.64	23.49	4.48	57.3	3.1	12.1	13.3	4.8
8.0	0.91	4.6	0.01	8.6	12.4	1.44	17.19	4.52	48.3	5.8	43.0	9.3	7.6
8.0	0.12	1.1	-0.01	4.5	0.1	0.88	13.40	5.52	76.4	2.6	45.4	22.2	0.3
5.2	2.00	14.3	0.00	8.7	0.1	1.04	7.80	3.19	36.1	1.1	4.5	26.5	5.0
4.9	2.37	9.0	0.31	7.4	0.2	1.29	8.45	5.15	66.3	5.6	56.5	9.6	7.0
4.7	0.44	2.1	0.12	8.9	7.8	1.20	9.04	5.79	63.9	2.7	16.4	16.1	8.7
7.4	0.21	1.5	0.20	8.1	1.2	1.80	22.95	3.71	47.0	2.0	12.1	18.9	6.0
5.4	0.27	1.0	-0.22	4.9	0.1	1.22	7.03	4.28	58.1	1.4	15.1	25.6	3.0
6.2	3.39	11.2	0.00	2.9	0.0	0.33	1.82	2.58	82.5	4.0	N/A	6.4	5.5
9.8	0.18	1.2	0.00	2.9	0.2	0.34	4.16	2.98	86.3	6.8	72.4	6.9	2.2
8.2	1.35	3.7	0.00	5.2	1.9	0.91	7.37	2.89	51.2	3.2	51.9	25.6	7.3
6.0	0.43	5.2	0.37	7.4	206.9	1.35	26.82	3.26	63.1	4.3	29.7	13.1	5.0
4.9	0.87	5.8	0.54	6.8	1.1	1.62	19.25	4.54	71.4	5.7	80.2	13.9	4.7
4.0	2.07	15.3	-0.04	6.4	1.0	1.17	12.62	4.32	64.2	5.9	45.1	5.7	6.2
6.0	0.78	5.9	0.73	6.6	0.2	1.01	10.15	4.69	50.7	4.6	66.1	16.2	4.5
7.7	0.94	3.6	-0.02	7.8	0.2	1.21	7.12	4.47	53.2	6.0	69.6	9.6	6.7
9.1	0.19	1.1	0.00	5.7	1.9	1.21	16.79	3.36	64.8	4.7	27.8	6.4	4.6
8.4	0.00	0.0	0.00	4.3	0.3	0.47	5.31	3.04	80.9	2.5	49.8	35.9	5.3
10.0	0.00	0.0	0.02	6.3	5.0	1.38	9.42	2.82	41.7	6.0	159.2	19.3	9.0

Name	City	State	Weiss Safety Rating	2003 Weiss Safety Rating	2002 Weiss Safety Rating	Total Assets ($Mil)	One Year Asset Growth	Asset Mix (As a % of Total Assets)				Capital-ization Index	Leverage Ratio	Risk-based Capital Ratio
								Comm-ercial Loans	Cons-umer Loans	Home Mort-gages	Secur-ities			
▲ HYDEN CITIZENS BK	HYDEN	KY	B	B-	B-	98.6	1.50	16.2	6.0	24.0	34.7	5.9	7.9	14.0
IBERIABANK	LAFAYETTE	LA	B	B	B	2,344.9	17.53	7.5	12.6	22.5	25.2	5.0	7.0	11.7
IBERVILLE T&SB	PLAQUEMINE	LA	B	A-	B+	185.9	-0.28	3.3	5.0	17.1	18.8	9.3	10.5	15.4
IDABEL NB	IDABEL	OK	C+	C+	C+	89.2	11.29	5.4	6.0	10.3	49.6	6.1	8.1	17.8
▼ IDAHO BKG CO	BOISE	ID	D+	C-	C-	159.3	26.74	8.2	4.3	4.1	22.4	3.7	7.7	10.4
IDAHO INDEPENDENT BK	COEUR D'ALENE	ID	B+	B+	B+	389.1	10.24	19.8	3.0	2.6	5.7	6.6	10.1	12.2
▼ IDEAL FSB	BALTIMORE	MD	E+	D-	D-	8.5	4.30	0.0	0.6	25.1	18.7	8.3	9.9	22.4
ILLINI BK	SPRINGFIELD	IL	C-	C-	C-	203.6	-16.70	11.9	1.9	10.4	11.2	5.8	8.2	11.6
ILLINI ST BK	OGLESBY	IL	B+	B+	B+	68.8	1.95	5.7	4.0	14.6	41.2	10.0	12.7	25.9
ILLINOIS CMNTY BK	EFFINGHAM	IL	E-	E-	E-	42.5	-4.37	3.2	3.9	31.3	23.5	3.0	5.0	10.9
ILLINOIS NB	SPRINGFIELD	IL	D+	D+	D+	298.5	12.92	11.9	14.1	8.0	8.7	3.2	7.6	10.1
▲ ILLINOIS ST BK LAKE HILLS	LAKE IN THE HILL	IL	C+	D+	D	105.8	32.07	9.4	1.0	11.5	15.4	8.2	10.7	13.5
ILLINOIS-SERVICE FS&LA	CHICAGO	IL	C-	C-	C-	127.0	-4.85	0.4	0.6	18.8	58.2	9.9	10.9	31.4
IMPERIAL CAPITAL BK	LA JOLLA	CA	A-	A-	B-	1,839.1	25.04	7.7	0.1	0.1	4.4	10.0	13.9	15.7
▼ IMPERIAL S&LA INC	MARTINSVILLE	VA	E-	E-	E+	9.8	-6.41	2.5	9.0	36.6	19.0	6.6	8.6	19.4
INATRUST FSB	PHILADELPHIA	PA	D	D	D	2.9	-2.95	0.0	0.0	0.0	77.0	10.0	79.3	235.9
INDEPENDENCE BK	HAVRE	MT	B-	B-	B-	270.0	9.56	13.3	3.9	4.5	17.0	8.4	10.3	13.7
▲ INDEPENDENCE BK	INDEPENDENCE	OH	B-	C+	C+	150.1	-8.41	40.6	1.4	5.3	32.6	7.1	9.1	14.0
INDEPENDENCE BK	E GREENWICH	RI	D+	D	NR	42.1	61.78	37.1	0.1	16.7	15.4	10.0	13.6	21.2
▲ INDEPENDENCE BK OF KY	OWENSBORO	KY	C-	D+	C-	440.1	27.90	8.5	6.3	20.0	14.8	4.9	7.8	11.0
▼ INDEPENDENCE COMMUNITY	MARCY	NY	B-	B	B-	17,963.7	100.11	2.5	0.3	18.0	22.9	3.4	5.4	10.7
▲ INDEPENDENCE FEDERAL	INDEPENDENCE	IA	D	D-	D-	22.5	-1.72	0.1	3.0	68.9	25.6	8.7	10.1	20.1
INDEPENDENCE FSB	WASHINGTON	DC	D	D	C	194.8	-20.45	0.2	11.7	27.1	30.3	7.9	9.6	27.3
▼ INDEPENDENCE ST BK	INDEPENDENCE	WI	D+	C-	C-	47.4	0.32	9.5	2.6	17.6	22.3	2.5	10.0	9.6
INDEPENDENCE TRUST	FRANKLIN	TN	C+	NR	NR	2.6	N/A	0.0	0.0	0.0	57.0	10.0	79.4	192.5
INDEPENDENT BANK SOUTH	LESLIE	MI	B-	B-	C+	387.0	17.56	4.3	2.1	20.2	28.0	4.5	7.0	10.8
▲ INDEPENDENT BANK WEST MI	ROCKFORD	MI	B	B-	C+	477.7	-3.26	5.0	6.4	31.3	12.8	4.8	7.6	10.9
▲ INDEPENDENT BANKERS BK IL	SPRINGFIELD	IL	C	C-	C-	439.2	20.81	8.7	0.6	0.1	53.7	5.5	7.5	12.0
▲ INDEPENDENT BANKERS BK	LAKE MARY	FL	C	C	C	317.6	49.49	0.8	0.7	2.6	5.1	3.7	7.0	10.4
INDEPENDENT BK	BAY CITY	MI	B-	B-	C+	1,254.4	11.32	13.1	11.4	27.0	15.6	3.6	7.4	10.3
▲ INDEPENDENT BK	MEMPHIS	TN	C	D+	D	427.4	17.51	3.1	77.6	0.5	12.3	5.3	9.6	11.2
INDEPENDENT BK	MC KINNEY	TX	C+	C+	C-	249.3	0.79	9.0	5.3	10.7	16.2	5.3	7.3	11.3
INDEPENDENT BK	VERONA	WI	B+	B+	A-	102.8	-1.03	8.4	3.1	15.7	21.6	10.0	12.4	18.3
INDEPENDENT BK EAST MI	TROY	MI	B-	B-	C+	661.9	85.63	11.0	7.6	14.4	16.8	4.6	11.2	10.8
INDEPENDENT BK OF TX	IRVING	TX	D	D	NR	24.6	113.16	21.1	2.9	5.8	8.1	10.0	28.6	37.5
▲ INDEPENDENT COMMUNITY	TEQUESTA	FL	C-	D+	D+	85.8	24.56	7.7	1.5	3.2	17.5	5.0	7.9	11.0
INDEPENDENT FARMERS BK	MAYSVILLE	MO	C+	C+	C	59.5	11.85	6.7	7.6	10.9	32.1	6.3	8.3	12.9
INDEPENDENT NB	OCALA	FL	C+	C	C-	168.4	19.38	6.5	2.0	17.9	25.5	5.9	7.9	11.7
INDIAN RIVER NB	VERO BEACH	FL	C+	C+	C+	622.2	20.54	2.5	1.7	13.6	44.4	4.1	6.2	11.8
INDIAN VILLAGE COMMUNITY	GNADENHUTTEN	OH	D+	D+	D+	99.6	1.20	0.1	3.9	37.0	37.4	6.1	8.1	16.2
▼ INDIANA FIRST SVG BK	INDIANA	PA	B-	B	B	168.7	-0.31	1.5	0.9	35.1	29.5	10.0	11.5	21.8
INDIANA LAWRENCE BK	N MANCHESTER	IN	B-	B-	B-	131.6	-2.99	4.7	3.8	21.5	15.0	7.2	9.2	14.6
INDUSTRIAL BK NA	OXON HILL	MD	C-	C-	C-	316.7	4.57	3.2	2.7	22.4	35.6	5.5	7.5	14.7
INDUSTRIAL FSB	LEXINGTON	NC	A+	A+	A+	141.7	1.95	0.0	0.2	45.9	41.1	10.0	24.4	63.5
INDUSTRIAL ST BK	KANSAS CITY	KS	A-	A	A	149.6	-4.21	12.2	2.2	4.0	33.8	10.0	14.9	22.2
INDUSTRY ST BK	INDUSTRY	TX	B-	B-	B-	170.9	4.48	7.7	5.4	6.6	51.8	6.3	8.3	16.3
INDYMAC BK FSB	PASADENA	CA	B	B-	C+	14,872.1	40.72	0.0	0.2	56.1	16.1	5.7	7.7	13.1
INEZ DEPOSIT BK	INEZ	KY	B+	B+	B+	92.2	-3.90	2.9	7.0	30.8	46.3	8.1	9.7	22.7
INEZ DEPOSIT BK FSB	LOUISA	KY	B+	B+	B+	45.3	-6.80	2.3	4.4	30.9	43.5	10.0	11.3	27.1
INFIBANK NA	ATLANTA	GA	C	C-	C-	110.0	-1.86	0.5	59.1	0.0	11.9	10.0	21.6	21.5
▲ ING BANK FSB	WILMINGTON	DE	B-	C	C-	29,260.1	81.27	0.0	1.5	22.2	73.0	8.0	9.6	25.9
▲ INLAND COMMUNITY BK NA	RIALTO	CA	D+	D-	D	93.7	40.93	9.8	0.6	3.3	8.9	10.0	13.3	19.4
INLAND EMPIRE NB	RIVERSIDE	CA	B+	B+	B	97.5	19.35	7.4	1.0	5.8	23.4	6.4	8.4	12.9
INLAND NORTHWEST BK	SPOKANE	WA	B-	B-	C	223.7	6.50	18.3	2.5	10.1	20.8	6.6	8.6	12.8
INNOVATIVE BK	OAKLAND	CA	A-	B+	B	82.5	29.86	29.4	0.3	1.9	7.1	10.0	13.0	23.0
INSOUTH BK	BROWNSVILLE	TN	C-	C-	D	494.0	-7.78	7.0	2.1	41.9	10.0	6.3	8.3	12.5
INSTITUTION FOR SVGS	NEWBURYPORT	MA	B+	A-	A-	484.0	3.33	0.0	0.6	35.3	55.5	10.0	17.2	43.6
INSURBANC	FARMINGTON	CT	D	D	D	60.9	33.09	19.4	0.4	3.6	34.5	10.0	11.5	18.4
▲ INSURORS BK OF TENNESSEE	NASHVILLE	TN	C	C-	D+	63.1	31.22	17.5	2.4	13.1	21.5	7.2	9.1	13.0
INTEGRA BK NA	EVANSVILLE	IN	D+	C+	C+	2,688.6	-9.94	9.9	7.0	18.7	26.1	5.5	7.5	11.7
INTEGRITY B&T	MONUMENT	CO	C-	C-	NR	13.6	N/A	1.5	1.6	5.2	7.3	10.0	27.4	29.1
▲ INTEGRITY BANK PLUS	WABASSO	MN	E	E-	D	47.0	-8.33	12.8	2.0	4.6	33.6	5.5	7.5	13.0
▲ INTEGRITY BK	ALPHARETTA	GA	C	D+	D-	349.3	56.04	3.5	0.3	3.4	10.8	6.5	11.6	12.1
INTEGRITY BK	CAMP HILL	PA	D	D	NR	94.5	183.93	5.5	0.8	23.4	30.2	10.0	12.4	15.2

Asset Quality Index	Non-Performing Loans as a % of Total Loans	as a % of Capital	Net Charge-offs Avg Loans	Profitability Index	Net Income ($Mil)	Return on Assets (R.O.A.)	Return on Equity (R.O.E.)	Net Interest Spread	Overhead Efficiency Ratio	Liquidity Index	Liquidity Ratio	Hot Money Ratio	Stability Index
5.5	0.67	4.2	0.05	9.2	1.2	2.37	30.46	4.86	58.1	2.4	20.3	17.6	5.1
6.6	0.29	1.9	0.12	7.5	13.9	1.24	12.76	3.74	55.3	3.9	24.6	12.8	7.7
4.1	1.95	12.1	0.18	5.9	0.9	0.96	8.40	4.99	74.8	4.7	31.8	8.2	6.9
6.4	0.66	3.4	0.41	6.6	0.8	1.84	22.55	4.09	53.6	1.8	19.8	21.3	3.2
8.4	0.00	0.0	-0.10	2.7	0.3	0.38	4.81	3.64	84.9	0.8	18.2	36.8	3.0
7.3	0.14	0.9	-0.33	8.7	2.4	1.30	13.68	5.40	62.0	8.1	129.7	5.7	6.2
6.4	0.00	0.0	0.00	2.2	0.0	0.26	2.65	4.28	93.7	2.0	39.0	26.4	1.0
2.4	2.08	15.9	1.35	2.3	-0.9	-0.84	-9.84	4.55	105.8	3.3	31.5	15.8	3.5
8.6	0.72	2.7	-0.01	5.3	0.4	1.28	9.90	4.25	67.4	4.8	27.1	5.6	6.6
4.2	1.40	13.6	0.32	0.0	-0.2	-0.76	-14.81	3.46	119.1	7.3	73.8	2.3	0.0
5.0	0.41	3.7	-0.03	3.3	1.1	0.76	9.70	3.91	84.2	2.8	22.9	15.9	3.2
7.3	0.20	1.4	-0.03	3.5	0.3	0.51	4.74	3.11	72.4	0.9	12.9	33.5	5.3
6.9	2.00	4.8	0.02	1.9	0.2	0.26	2.36	3.55	90.3	2.6	30.7	18.9	5.6
5.5	1.05	6.1	-0.02	10.0	21.9	2.32	19.16	4.95	36.1	2.4	33.3	31.9	9.5
2.2	3.55	19.9	2.23	2.0	0.0	-0.68	-7.84	4.06	82.9	4.3	53.9	14.1	0.3
6.6	0.00	0.0	0.00	0.0	-0.2	-10.64	-13.35	2.37	338.2	5.0	685.3	100.0	0.0
4.1	1.38	9.5	0.13	9.7	2.1	1.59	14.94	4.75	45.1	1.2	8.2	26.5	6.7
4.6	1.70	8.8	-0.01	4.4	0.8	1.00	11.42	3.86	54.1	1.8	39.3	48.5	4.4
1.2	7.07	29.5	0.54	3.0	0.1	0.73	5.18	3.69	79.8	7.5	172.2	12.6	0.0
3.9	1.39	13.2	0.10	3.5	1.0	0.47	6.09	3.67	76.8	2.2	12.6	17.6	3.2
5.2	0.60	3.2	0.01	9.5	92.4	1.48	14.27	4.02	45.7	4.3	19.4	8.2	9.2
2.9	3.54	24.2	0.00	2.9	0.0	0.21	2.05	2.38	88.0	3.9	7.4	8.2	2.3
3.9	1.79	8.7	0.01	0.5	-1.2	-1.21	-12.38	2.76	122.5	3.0	45.9	24.6	3.7
2.7	3.08	20.6	0.35	4.9	0.2	0.92	9.28	4.02	72.6	4.0	25.0	10.1	1.7
7.7	0.00	0.0	0.00	10.0	0.1	3.82	4.67	1.74	87.4	5.0	689.7	100.0	0.0
6.6	0.22	2.0	0.15	9.2	3.0	1.58	22.01	4.18	58.0	1.3	4.0	24.7	5.8
5.6	0.42	4.0	0.11	10.0	5.4	2.31	30.52	5.33	53.2	1.7	5.3	19.6	6.1
9.4	0.00	0.0	0.00	4.0	1.7	0.80	11.04	2.36	74.6	2.2	48.4	58.7	2.6
8.6	0.02	0.2	-0.23	5.2	1.2	0.80	12.21	3.45	76.8	5.6	33.4	3.3	2.9
5.0	0.64	5.0	0.22	9.0	8.7	1.43	15.81	5.50	65.3	0.7	10.1	37.4	7.0
5.0	0.23	2.0	0.51	4.7	1.8	0.90	10.55	3.50	61.1	0.6	6.8	44.7	3.2
7.2	0.20	1.6	-0.02	5.3	1.4	1.15	13.90	4.43	71.9	3.6	42.7	17.5	3.9
6.2	1.45	7.3	0.66	4.4	0.4	0.75	5.97	4.33	77.6	4.0	10.3	7.9	7.5
3.7	0.99	5.4	0.11	5.7	2.5	1.08	10.32	4.41	71.3	2.1	15.1	18.3	6.2
8.6	0.00	0.0	0.00	0.0	-0.4	-4.42	-15.12	3.33	229.0	6.5	102.6	10.1	0.0
7.5	0.13	1.0	0.00	2.9	0.2	0.54	6.20	3.22	65.1	3.5	23.1	12.4	3.2
5.8	0.63	4.4	0.06	6.0	0.3	1.09	12.74	3.97	60.1	3.7	28.2	12.7	3.8
7.4	0.19	1.6	-0.06	6.1	1.0	1.20	15.49	4.72	61.6	4.3	34.7	11.6	3.7
8.8	0.06	0.4	0.02	5.6	2.4	0.80	11.39	2.67	57.3	3.8	21.5	10.5	5.1
5.4	1.12	8.4	0.33	1.7	0.2	0.33	4.22	2.47	82.1	2.0	23.0	20.0	0.5
9.7	0.25	1.1	0.04	3.1	0.3	0.35	3.03	2.79	87.4	6.3	76.6	10.3	6.5
6.8	0.33	2.3	-0.03	5.0	0.5	0.72	8.25	4.12	73.3	5.0	27.7	4.5	5.8
5.0	1.06	6.3	0.08	3.4	1.0	0.61	7.44	5.03	91.2	4.4	32.8	10.6	3.9
9.8	0.18	0.4	0.00	9.9	1.2	1.68	6.95	3.94	32.6	4.0	78.2	27.1	9.7
6.5	2.36	8.2	-0.19	9.1	1.1	1.41	9.83	4.32	54.8	5.1	38.8	8.7	8.7
8.5	0.02	0.1	0.35	6.8	1.3	1.46	16.72	3.50	55.8	2.8	43.5	26.0	4.9
4.9	0.76	7.0	0.07	8.0	70.2	1.00	12.71	3.26	65.9	0.4	7.5	66.8	7.8
8.0	0.23	0.9	0.08	4.7	0.4	0.81	7.49	3.95	75.8	3.6	53.1	19.1	6.0
8.5	0.81	2.9	0.20	6.4	0.3	1.20	10.49	4.10	66.3	2.0	41.3	35.6	6.6
3.3	2.08	4.4	7.02	10.0	5.6	10.07	47.10	21.62	81.1	1.1	33.2	99.3	7.4
9.8	0.07	0.2	0.17	4.1	74.8	0.60	6.13	1.89	45.2	0.7	8.9	37.7	4.9
8.7	0.00	0.0	-0.13	2.5	0.1	0.31	3.68	4.66	94.5	7.1	101.5	7.6	2.5
6.7	0.04	0.3	-0.03	9.9	1.1	2.29	27.32	5.97	58.3	3.7	11.3	10.3	6.9
6.9	0.64	4.6	0.23	4.6	0.9	0.81	9.37	4.33	73.3	4.7	44.1	12.3	4.0
8.0	0.23	1.2	0.63	10.0	0.7	1.94	13.78	6.51	57.5	7.4	103.7	6.2	6.5
5.5	0.84	7.6	0.17	4.6	2.2	0.93	11.24	4.77	70.1	1.8	17.4	21.2	2.1
10.0	0.06	0.1	-0.02	4.9	2.0	0.82	3.62	2.54	55.9	6.1	72.7	10.9	9.9
8.6	0.00	0.0	-0.01	0.0	-0.4	-1.20	-10.08	2.99	129.7	0.6	21.0	76.9	0.0
8.4	0.00	0.0	0.00	2.2	0.2	0.78	8.61	3.17	80.3	1.2	27.5	34.5	2.7
4.9	1.25	7.6	0.11	1.2	-19.4	-1.41	-14.68	3.48	172.5	3.2	20.3	14.3	5.6
7.6	0.00	0.0	0.00	0.0	-0.2	-4.01	-11.80	5.32	146.1	3.5	34.6	13.7	1.9
3.2	1.59	9.7	0.11	2.0	0.1	0.43	5.62	3.56	87.9	1.5	16.9	25.2	0.0
3.6	0.80	5.8	0.43	6.3	1.9	1.25	12.91	4.54	44.0	3.1	10.0	12.8	2.5
9.1	0.00	0.0	0.00	0.0	-0.1	-0.32	-2.89	2.64	82.0	5.7	174.5	25.3	0.0

Name	City	State	Weiss Safety Rating	2003 Weiss Safety Rating	2002 Weiss Safety Rating	Total Assets ($Mil)	One Year Asset Growth	Asset Mix (As a % of Total Assets) Commercial Loans	Consumer Loans	Home Mortgages	Securities	Capitalization Index	Leverage Ratio	Risk-based Capital Ratio
▲ INTER NATIONAL BANK	MCALLEN	TX	B	B-	C+	899.9	18.16	10.0	1.3	6.7	42.3	8.1	9.8	16.1
▲ INTER SVGS BK FSB	EDINA	MN	B-	C	C	647.9	15.99	1.1	0.7	58.4	6.9	6.0	8.0	12.5
INTER-STATE FS&LA	KANSAS CITY	KS	B+	B+	B+	223.0	-4.64	0.0	0.1	33.1	60.3	10.0	21.5	125.3
INTERAMERICA BK	ALBUQUERQUE	NM	B	B	B-	26.7	-0.68	18.6	5.4	1.7	21.3	6.5	8.5	13.5
▲ INTERAMERICAN BK FSB	MIAMI	FL	B+	B	B	231.4	14.28	3.4	1.3	21.7	1.4	8.0	9.7	14.6
▼ INTERAUDI BK	NEW YORK	NY	C+	B-	B-	882.7	15.96	9.7	0.1	6.2	38.3	5.9	7.9	19.1
▼ INTERBANK	ELK CITY	OK	C	C+	C+	132.3	15.93	11.2	11.9	21.1	17.3	5.4	7.7	11.3
INTERBUSINESS BK NA	LOS ANGELES	CA	C	C-	D	178.2	24.00	20.6	0.1	0.1	11.2	9.4	10.6	14.6
▼ INTERCHANGE ST BK	SADDLE BROOK	NJ	C+	B-	B+	1,404.8	7.10	7.5	0.2	18.8	26.8	3.3	6.4	10.1
INTERCITY ST BK	SCHOFIELD	WI	B+	A-	A-	118.7	-8.79	5.2	6.8	27.0	12.0	10.0	15.1	17.4
▲ INTERCONTINENTAL BK	W MIAMI	FL	C	C-	D	105.0	50.23	3.9	0.8	1.1	51.1	6.7	8.7	21.5
INTERCONTINENTAL NB	SAN ANTONIO	TX	C	C	C-	100.2	5.10	35.0	1.2	5.9	14.4	7.4	9.3	22.1
INTERCREDIT BK NA	MIAMI	FL	C-	C-	C-	377.7	19.59	8.7	0.9	34.6	9.4	5.4	7.4	12.5
INTERNATIONAL BK	TRINIDAD	CO	B-	B-	B	27.5	64.31	17.6	4.2	18.3	1.2	10.0	12.3	15.4
INTERNATIONAL BK	RATON	NM	B-	B-	B	158.5	2.68	19.9	2.4	9.0	18.4	6.8	8.8	12.4
▲ INTERNATIONAL BK CHICAGO	CHICAGO	IL	A-	B+	B-	118.1	5.33	5.0	2.7	17.0	26.0	8.1	9.8	14.5
▼ INTERNATIONAL BK OF	AMHERST	WI	B+	A-	A-	38.4	5.76	9.7	3.3	25.3	25.1	10.0	13.2	24.1
INTERNATIONAL BK OF CA	LOS ANGELES	CA	C	C	C-	186.4	-3.78	12.8	0.1	0.0	11.0	7.2	9.1	13.5
▼ INTERNATIONAL BK OF	LAREDO	TX	B+	A-	B+	7,918.5	46.17	12.5	2.9	10.6	27.4	3.5	8.2	10.2
▼ INTERNATIONAL BK OF	ZAPATA	TX	A-	A-	B+	256.4	-16.49	5.1	4.0	19.6	51.4	9.2	10.4	21.9
▲ INTERNATIONAL BK OF MIAMI	CORAL GABLES	FL	B	C+	C+	1,057.4	9.85	4.3	0.4	3.6	20.3	7.3	9.2	16.2
▼ INTERNATIONAL BK/CMMRCE	BROWNSVILLE	TX	B+	A-	B+	800.3	32.48	4.6	2.8	4.9	56.0	7.9	9.6	20.8
INTERNATIONAL CITY BK NA	LONG BEACH	CA	A	A-	B	193.6	19.29	19.2	0.1	2.2	21.1	10.0	12.6	18.0
▲ INTERNATIONAL FINANCE BK	MIAMI	FL	D+	D	D-	236.4	6.19	5.8	0.4	4.8	41.9	6.2	8.3	15.4
INTERSTATE BK	OAK FOREST	IL	B-	C+	C-	161.7	8.22	4.3	0.5	10.5	25.2	5.5	7.7	11.3
INTERSTATE BK SSB	PERRYTON	TX	C+	C	C-	75.0	6.57	15.0	2.3	21.6	19.4	5.8	7.8	13.6
INTERSTATE FS&LA OF	MC GREGOR	IA	D+	D+	D+	8.7	-3.65	0.0	0.9	69.1	0.5	10.0	16.5	35.1
▼ INTERSTATE NET BK	CHERRY HILL	NJ	D+	D+	D-	211.5	59.86	28.3	1.7	2.1	8.7	4.3	9.4	10.6
▲ INTERVEST NB	NEW YORK	NY	B+	B	B	982.2	56.67	0.1	0.0	0.0	19.8	6.3	9.7	12.0
▲ INTRUST BK NA	WICHITA	KS	B+	B	B	2,679.5	5.60	31.6	9.0	6.1	20.1	5.5	8.8	11.4
INVESTMENT SVG BK	ALTOONA	PA	C+	C+	C	102.3	4.55	7.4	2.3	44.5	29.2	10.0	14.0	29.0
INVESTORS B&TC	BOSTON	MA	C+	C+	B-	10,919.4	30.67	0.1	0.5	0.0	88.8	3.5	5.5	17.6
▲ INVESTORS CMNTY BK	MANITOWOC	WI	B-	C	C+	266.3	4.16	10.9	0.3	3.7	7.8	5.8	8.6	11.6
INVESTORS NB	CHILLICOTHE	MO	B-	B-	B-	58.1	-0.76	4.1	5.5	41.6	28.6	10.0	11.8	22.9
INVESTORS SVGS BK	SHORT HILLS	NJ	C+	C+	B-	5,324.5	-0.57	0.0	0.0	20.1	73.5	5.8	7.8	26.7
▲ INVESTORSBANK	PEWAUKEE	WI	B-	C	D+	207.8	17.55	15.5	0.1	20.9	5.8	6.7	9.3	12.3
▼ INWOOD NB OF DALLAS	DALLAS	TX	B-	B	B+	901.1	25.50	9.1	1.9	6.8	7.8	4.2	8.0	10.6
▲ IONIA COUNTY NB OF IONIA	IONIA	MI	C	D	D	233.4	3.47	12.8	8.9	34.3	14.4	6.7	8.7	13.6
IOWA BK	BELLEVUE	IA	C	C+	C+	33.4	5.31	16.3	5.1	11.4	1.7	4.0	7.9	10.5
IOWA FALLS ST BK	IOWA FALLS	IA	A-	A-	B+	93.1	14.01	3.9	2.6	12.6	38.8	9.9	10.9	18.3
IOWA PRAIRIE BK	BRUNSVILLE	IA	C+	C+	C+	42.3	-7.07	5.3	5.4	8.4	29.5	7.1	9.1	16.4
IOWA ST B&TC	FAIRFIELD	IA	C+	C+	C+	88.7	4.06	12.2	2.4	22.4	13.0	6.3	8.3	14.4
▲ IOWA ST B&TC	IOWA CITY	IA	B+	B	B	520.4	6.09	9.7	1.5	20.7	38.9	6.3	8.4	15.0
▲ IOWA ST BK	ALGONA	IA	B	B-	B-	216.7	18.32	9.7	2.7	8.9	34.3	7.3	9.2	16.3
IOWA ST BK	CLARKSVILLE	IA	D-	D-	D	104.2	20.01	9.2	2.6	2.7	20.9	2.9	7.1	9.9
IOWA ST BK	DES MOINES	IA	A	A	A	232.5	0.19	6.4	1.3	15.5	30.5	8.4	10.0	14.5
▲ IOWA ST BK	HULL	IA	B+	B	B-	212.8	4.70	10.5	3.8	13.2	28.1	7.9	9.6	14.2
IOWA ST BK	SAC CITY	IA	C	C	C	63.6	-0.18	16.9	7.7	19.2	32.6	6.1	8.1	12.6
▼ IOWA ST BK	WAPELLO	IA	D-	D	D+	32.5	0.95	5.9	3.7	20.7	4.6	3.2	7.5	10.1
IOWA ST SVG BK	CRESTON	IA	B-	B-	B-	111.2	3.31	7.6	4.4	12.8	34.5	4.8	6.8	12.8
IOWA ST SVG BK	KNOXVILLE	IA	C+	C+	C	80.0	2.05	13.8	10.5	18.1	13.5	5.8	8.2	11.6
IOWA SVG BK	DIKE	IA	A+	A+	A+	29.0	2.60	2.7	1.1	6.7	50.5	9.7	10.8	23.4
IOWA SVGS BK	CARROLL	IA	B-	B-	B-	139.3	4.70	18.1	3.8	6.9	20.4	5.2	7.2	11.5
IOWA T&SB	CENTERVILLE	IA	A	A-	A	131.8	1.68	5.2	4.4	19.5	46.5	9.8	10.9	22.8
IOWA T&SB	EMMETSBURG	IA	B	B-	B-	83.9	-0.13	7.3	5.0	9.6	26.9	7.6	9.4	13.9
IOWA-NEBRASKA STATE BK	S SIOUX CITY	NE	C+	C+	C	187.6	17.85	6.4	6.4	13.6	18.6	6.6	8.8	12.2
▲ IPAVA ST BK	IPAVA	IL	D+	E+	D+	59.4	12.48	7.9	9.6	18.2	17.9	8.8	10.2	14.1
▲ IPSWICH CO-OP BK	IPSWICH	MA	B	B-	C	157.0	17.81	1.4	0.4	52.0	26.6	6.2	8.2	14.1
IPSWICH ST BK	IPSWICH	SD	B+	B+	B+	35.5	-2.45	6.8	4.4	2.0	36.6	10.0	16.4	23.6
IRAAN ST BK	IRAAN	TX	B	B	B	19.8	1.27	22.1	9.9	12.1	42.2	6.7	8.7	16.9
IRELAND BK	MALAD CITY	ID	C	C	C	171.1	8.06	13.8	7.2	5.7	24.8	5.1	7.5	11.1
▼ IRON & GLASS BK	PITTSBURGH	PA	C+	B	B	300.8	0.28	11.0	0.8	6.1	30.9	8.6	10.0	15.5
IRON WKRS SVG BK	ASTON	PA	C+	C+	B-	131.5	2.03	0.6	0.4	42.4	27.9	5.6	7.6	14.9
IRONSTONE BANK	FORT MYERS	FL	B-	B-	B	1,325.2	18.91	5.3	0.8	15.7	2.1	10.0	14.4	16.3

Asset Quality Index	Non-Performing Loans as a % of Total Loans	as a % of Capital	Net Charge-offs Avg Loans	Profitability Index	Net Income ($Mil)	Return on Assets (R.O.A.)	Return on Equity (R.O.E.)	Net Interest Spread	Overhead Efficiency Ratio	Liquidity Index	Liquidity Ratio	Hot Money Ratio	Stability Index
6.9	0.46	2.6	0.03	10.0	7.6	1.88	24.79	4.56	42.9	0.6	8.8	47.3	5.0
4.5	0.89	9.4	0.02	10.0	6.4	2.02	25.36	3.32	30.6	1.0	1.8	28.0	5.7
9.9	0.14	0.2	0.00	4.4	0.6	0.50	2.35	2.08	59.6	2.0	7.9	18.2	8.1
1.6	2.83	20.0	-0.42	0.9	0.0	-0.27	-3.02	4.79	98.1	3.7	53.6	18.6	4.0
5.3	0.58	4.6	-0.01	9.4	1.5	1.31	13.22	4.65	59.9	1.4	31.2	40.1	6.7
9.6	0.20	0.8	0.00	3.6	2.5	0.58	7.20	1.80	70.1	5.3	387.8	57.8	4.8
2.9	1.77	16.0	0.02	7.4	1.2	1.80	23.34	5.44	70.5	1.8	7.5	19.4	4.2
7.4	0.16	1.1	0.00	3.0	0.5	0.59	5.66	3.75	73.8	3.1	55.6	29.7	1.9
4.9	0.74	4.3	0.13	7.4	8.5	1.22	11.75	4.15	58.8	5.2	19.3	1.6	8.4
4.0	2.90	13.3	0.01	9.3	0.9	1.42	9.66	3.58	42.1	6.9	100.6	10.6	7.4
10.0	0.00	0.0	1.32	3.0	0.3	0.65	7.84	2.20	60.5	5.0	111.2	22.4	1.4
8.1	0.05	0.4	0.00	3.1	0.1	0.27	2.80	3.53	90.7	5.2	46.2	10.8	4.4
5.7	0.79	8.2	0.04	3.8	1.3	0.71	9.90	3.21	67.4	0.8	21.3	44.9	2.2
8.2	0.01	0.1	0.00	5.1	0.1	0.99	7.98	6.32	72.0	2.4	48.6	33.1	3.3
4.2	0.66	5.1	0.00	9.3	1.2	1.47	16.79	5.24	57.8	2.7	21.4	16.0	6.2
8.9	0.00	0.0	-0.19	8.2	0.9	1.60	17.01	3.50	62.7	2.9	48.6	27.3	6.2
4.3	4.07	18.8	0.02	9.1	0.3	1.73	13.58	4.67	61.8	5.6	68.5	11.5	7.7
4.1	0.51	3.5	0.00	3.1	0.3	0.32	3.55	3.82	87.4	3.7	80.7	31.6	4.5
5.8	0.71	4.0	0.02	8.7	43.9	1.42	13.67	3.15	52.1	1.5	18.5	27.6	7.6
9.3	0.32	1.1	0.21	9.8	3.0	2.34	19.18	4.18	35.8	1.0	26.2	47.0	6.3
6.1	1.17	7.4	-1.14	9.0	9.8	1.87	21.50	3.79	58.3	3.5	62.0	32.4	5.2
7.5	0.75	2.4	0.07	8.5	4.7	1.29	13.89	3.04	51.6	1.0	25.8	37.2	6.3
8.5	0.28	1.3	-0.14	10.0	7.1	7.86	65.47	5.32	20.7	1.6	6.8	20.4	6.8
9.0	0.17	0.9	-0.15	2.3	0.8	0.66	8.38	3.66	88.2	2.8	51.4	31.3	1.3
3.7	1.65	14.0	0.00	10.0	2.0	2.43	32.95	5.03	55.2	2.3	30.4	20.6	5.2
7.2	0.23	1.6	0.10	7.0	0.6	1.48	16.89	3.68	70.5	3.0	58.3	29.5	4.1
9.4	0.00	0.0	0.00	3.8	0.0	0.52	3.22	3.07	76.6	4.8	27.9	4.4	3.7
5.3	0.51	4.7	0.20	2.4	0.3	0.27	2.99	4.44	80.0	1.5	18.0	25.8	0.3
5.6	0.00	0.0	0.00	8.5	5.0	1.13	11.62	3.51	29.8	6.7	251.9	19.2	6.6
7.5	0.26	1.9	0.24	7.3	15.6	1.17	12.87	3.80	61.4	4.0	22.5	11.1	7.5
9.5	0.08	0.3	0.11	2.8	0.3	0.48	3.48	3.32	78.1	5.5	77.5	14.5	7.2
10.0	0.00	0.0	0.00	7.5	71.8	1.42	23.99	2.18	65.8	6.9	69.9	7.3	4.9
3.9	1.51	13.4	0.06	6.1	1.3	1.06	12.19	3.00	43.4	0.6	10.9	44.4	5.0
6.6	1.17	6.1	0.02	3.8	0.2	0.68	6.00	3.26	73.9	4.4	70.2	17.8	5.5
10.0	0.32	0.9	-0.03	3.7	16.3	0.60	7.93	1.84	55.6	5.9	57.9	11.5	5.1
4.3	1.11	9.9	-0.12	9.0	1.7	1.75	19.17	3.22	32.9	0.4	3.7	59.2	5.5
3.9	0.41	2.6	-0.02	10.0	10.8	2.45	22.23	4.66	50.8	6.3	134.1	16.2	8.4
4.2	1.28	10.3	0.09	4.8	1.0	0.87	9.73	4.18	73.4	3.9	8.4	8.3	4.4
3.7	0.87	6.2	0.09	3.6	0.1	0.53	5.00	3.95	77.8	5.6	57.6	10.0	5.5
8.7	0.31	1.6	0.00	8.2	0.9	1.99	17.73	4.46	51.0	4.1	20.1	8.5	6.2
7.1	0.00	0.0	-0.03	4.9	0.2	0.72	7.60	4.23	79.2	6.3	54.0	4.2	4.1
6.6	0.53	3.3	0.05	4.9	0.4	0.85	9.66	4.46	72.6	6.2	56.1	5.7	4.8
8.0	0.36	2.3	0.25	6.3	2.9	1.13	13.45	3.31	60.9	3.1	18.1	13.9	6.4
5.6	0.60	3.0	0.01	5.3	1.0	0.89	8.25	3.63	67.2	4.1	24.2	9.0	5.1
1.8	1.82	17.1	0.29	4.5	0.5	1.04	14.84	3.87	66.4	6.5	51.1	3.9	1.7
8.8	0.06	0.4	-0.06	10.0	3.2	2.77	26.98	4.75	50.1	4.9	40.2	10.3	8.0
6.4	0.58	3.3	-0.04	6.6	1.1	1.01	9.99	3.93	63.4	4.7	31.4	8.0	5.5
6.1	0.41	2.9	0.16	5.0	0.4	1.25	14.92	3.19	59.8	5.0	38.2	8.9	4.2
2.6	2.28	24.1	0.01	6.4	0.2	1.09	14.80	4.78	65.9	4.2	24.3	8.4	1.7
7.7	0.34	2.3	0.01	4.0	0.4	0.65	7.79	4.11	80.1	3.1	20.9	14.0	4.7
4.1	1.14	9.3	0.16	5.3	0.5	1.19	14.50	5.36	71.8	6.1	38.8	2.4	3.4
8.9	0.00	0.0	0.00	7.2	0.2	1.59	11.76	4.24	58.6	6.7	48.7	0.8	9.2
6.7	0.26	2.1	0.06	5.6	0.8	1.16	14.13	3.67	65.8	4.1	35.7	13.1	5.3
8.9	0.03	0.1	-0.01	8.7	1.3	2.00	17.07	3.96	50.1	4.3	38.0	12.6	8.7
5.7	1.04	5.8	0.16	6.9	0.5	1.27	12.18	4.30	57.1	3.8	22.3	10.7	6.2
5.7	0.34	2.6	0.11	4.6	0.8	0.90	10.97	3.71	69.9	3.7	14.1	10.4	3.3
6.1	0.22	1.6	0.02	7.1	0.4	1.41	18.03	4.05	51.4	3.7	20.2	11.0	3.3
9.8	0.00	0.0	0.00	4.6	0.8	1.06	12.25	3.21	60.8	3.5	33.2	15.4	5.1
8.3	0.19	0.6	-0.09	6.5	0.2	1.20	7.23	4.31	60.5	3.3	21.3	13.0	7.4
7.3	0.00	0.0	0.06	8.5	0.2	2.12	18.77	4.40	58.8	3.0	45.9	18.9	5.7
3.6	1.74	14.8	0.15	4.2	0.6	0.65	9.07	4.57	80.5	4.0	11.8	8.3	3.3
3.0	3.06	16.4	0.32	6.5	1.8	1.23	12.17	4.23	54.7	5.4	42.1	8.2	5.8
9.7	0.11	0.8	0.00	3.6	0.4	0.53	7.17	3.78	77.2	5.3	43.5	8.9	3.7
6.5	0.36	2.1	0.06	0.3	-1.6	-0.25	-1.71	3.68	101.8	0.6	6.5	45.0	6.8

Name	City	State	Weiss Safety Rating	2003 Weiss Safety Rating	2002 Weiss Safety Rating	Total Assets ($Mil)	One Year Asset Growth	Asset Mix (As a % of Total Assets)				Capital-ization Index	Leverage Ratio	Risk-based Capital Ratio
								Comm-ercial Loans	Cons-umer Loans	Home Mort-gages	Secur-ities			
▼ IROQUOIS FARMERS ST BK	IROQUOIS	IL	B	B+	B+	34.3	-2.33	4.0	5.6	12.5	28.1	10.0	14.4	21.5
IROQUOIS FS&LA	WATSEKA	IL	C	C	C-	322.8	-0.05	0.9	4.2	46.7	36.1	5.4	7.4	17.7
IRWIN B&TC	IRWIN	PA	A-	A-	A-	658.3	8.37	5.9	1.7	27.5	27.4	6.4	8.4	13.9
IRWIN UNION B&TC	COLUMBUS	IN	B-	B-	B-	5,074.3	-3.36	7.5	1.1	27.3	0.3	9.2	11.7	14.3
IRWIN UNION BK FSB	LOUISVILLE	KY	B-	B-	B-	281.6	-34.02	2.6	1.9	12.2	14.6	8.0	9.7	14.9
ISABELLA B&T	MT PLEASANT	MI	B-	B-	B-	542.0	2.46	7.2	4.8	27.1	25.8	5.6	7.6	13.2
ISB COMMUNITY BK	IXONIA	WI	B	B	B	246.0	5.23	11.8	1.0	7.2	15.7	6.3	9.4	12.0
ISLANDERS BK	FRIDAY HARBOR	WA	A-	B+	B+	161.0	7.88	4.5	3.0	18.7	29.5	8.3	9.9	16.6
▲ ISLANDS COMMUNITY BK NA	BEAUFORT	SC	C-	D+	D	41.6	39.69	14.1	4.6	14.3	5.1	10.0	13.0	15.3
ISRAEL DISCOUNT BK OF NY	NEW YORK	NY	B-	B-	B	8,456.4	10.89	14.0	0.8	0.4	59.4	4.6	6.6	12.8
ITASCA B&TC	ITASCA	IL	C-	C	B-	337.3	0.74	29.0	1.5	11.1	17.0	7.3	9.5	12.7
▼ ITS BK	JOHNSTON	IA	B-	B	B	2.7	-6.75	0.0	0.0	0.0	36.5	10.0	72.9	274.3
IUKA ST BK	IUKA	IL	C+	C+	C+	13.9	-0.83	4.3	14.2	34.5	26.3	10.0	16.2	21.7
JACKSBORO NB	JACKSBORO	TX	B-	B-	B-	96.3	5.01	10.7	6.3	11.1	41.3	5.5	7.5	14.1
JACKSON B&T	GAINESBORO	TN	B	B	B-	161.8	6.07	5.1	7.0	32.0	25.1	8.6	10.1	16.9
JACKSON COUNTY BK	SEYMOUR	IN	B	B	B	319.7	0.67	7.7	4.5	34.7	20.4	7.4	9.3	15.4
JACKSON COUNTY BK	MC KEE	KY	A	A	A	110.1	1.23	2.9	14.3	21.2	40.5	10.0	18.5	34.6
▲ JACKSON COUNTY BK	BLACK RIVER FALL	WI	B	C	C	178.9	20.20	2.8	4.0	16.5	16.7	6.3	8.3	13.5
JACKSON FEDERAL BK	FULLERTON	CA	B	B-	C+	1,846.0	12.38	0.0	0.0	10.0	30.1	6.6	8.6	14.3
JACKSON FS&LA	JACKSON	MN	B-	B-	B-	29.6	1.07	0.0	2.6	32.1	48.3	10.0	18.1	42.1
JACKSON PARISH BK	JONESBORO	LA	C	C	C-	43.7	2.56	6.1	6.0	7.2	50.6	10.0	11.7	29.3
▼ JACKSON ST B&T	JACKSON	WY	B-	B	B-	586.1	12.38	16.0	1.8	22.0	5.6	5.9	8.9	11.7
▲ JACKSON SVG BK SSB	SYLVA	NC	B+	B	B	29.6	-3.08	0.0	1.3	65.3	3.5	10.0	16.7	37.0
▲ JACKSONVILLE BK	JACKSONVILLE	FL	C-	D	C-	218.6	33.07	7.1	2.1	9.0	9.2	4.6	8.7	10.8
JACKSONVILLE SB	JACKSONVILLE	IL	D+	D	D	265.8	1.80	7.4	3.9	23.8	42.7	4.6	6.6	13.3
JAMES MONROE BK	ARLINGTON	VA	B-	B-	B-	341.1	16.70	7.9	0.8	6.6	19.7	6.5	8.5	12.7
JAMESTOWN SAVINGS BANK	LAKEWOOD	NY	C-	C-	D+	385.4	11.62	5.4	0.3	28.8	32.8	3.8	5.8	10.6
JAMESTOWN ST BK	JAMESTOWN	KS	B-	B-	B-	17.5	0.74	2.0	2.9	2.9	66.3	10.0	21.7	42.6
▲ JANESVILLE ST BK	JANESVILLE	MN	C-	C	C	44.9	-5.07	3.2	5.5	17.9	24.9	4.9	9.5	10.9
JARRETTSVILLE FS&LA	JARRETTSVILLE	MD	B+	B+	B+	70.4	3.94	0.0	0.1	62.5	19.8	10.0	11.7	31.4
JASPER BKG CO	JASPER	GA	C-	C-	C-	237.8	-3.70	4.5	5.1	10.6	43.6	5.4	7.4	14.1
▲ JASPER ST BK	JASPER	MN	D-	E-	E-	16.4	-10.66	12.0	15.7	7.8	10.1	8.5	10.0	14.3
▲ JEFF DAVIS B&TC	JENNINGS	LA	B+	B	B	358.6	-0.05	7.4	11.9	17.1	35.3	7.3	9.2	16.7
▼ JEFFERSON B&TC	EUREKA	MO	C+	B-	B-	677.9	10.70	17.4	0.7	4.0	10.9	3.9	8.6	10.5
JEFFERSON BANK	FAYETTE	MS	D	D+	D+	38.6	-3.70	7.7	2.1	2.6	39.2	3.6	5.7	10.3
▼ JEFFERSON BK	DALLAS	TX	D+	D+	D+	159.2	9.98	10.3	5.1	22.6	24.7	3.3	6.2	10.1
JEFFERSON BK OF MO	JEFFERSON CITY	MO	B	B	B	402.6	3.74	15.6	19.5	9.5	19.7	4.0	7.5	10.5
JEFFERSON CTY BK	DAYKIN	NE	B	B	B-	27.7	0.50	2.9	3.2	6.0	36.9	10.0	11.7	23.7
JEFFERSON FEDERAL BANK	MORRISTOWN	TN	A	A-	A-	282.3	-22.38	4.5	2.1	30.0	26.2	10.0	22.2	38.8
▼ JEFFERSON SECURITY BK	SHEPHERDSTOWN	WV	C	C+	B-	200.0	5.69	3.2	3.4	30.4	26.7	5.3	7.3	13.5
JEFFERSON ST BK	SAN ANTONIO	TX	B	B	B	570.2	2.20	9.1	2.5	18.1	36.9	6.1	8.1	12.8
JENNINGS ST BK	SPRING GROVE	MN	D	D	D-	49.8	0.94	13.1	7.1	18.6	6.3	5.2	8.1	11.2
▼ JENNINGS ST BK	DAVENPORT	NE	C-	C+	C+	20.3	4.73	3.7	1.7	3.4	37.1	8.4	9.9	16.5
JERSEY SHORE ST BK	JERSEY SHORE	PA	A	A	A	528.6	5.09	6.0	2.6	27.5	34.8	7.6	9.4	17.7
JERSEY ST BK	JERSEYVILLE	IL	C-	C	B-	117.2	2.14	9.1	4.3	16.6	42.2	6.5	8.6	15.4
JEWETT CITY SVGS BK	JEWETT CITY	CT	A-	A-	B+	217.6	1.31	2.4	0.9	34.5	41.5	10.0	12.0	22.3
JIM THORPE NB	JIM THORPE	PA	B	B	B	103.2	-7.28	1.0	1.5	39.2	39.3	9.2	10.5	23.2
JLB SERVICE BK	NEW CASTLE	DE	B-	B-	NR	5.4	N/A	0.0	0.0	0.0	98.8	10.0	71.9	69.8
JOHN O MELBY & CO BK	WHITEHALL	WI	C+	C+	C	39.8	0.92	6.4	9.7	16.4	37.9	8.5	10.0	18.1
JOHN WARNER BK	CLINTON	IL	C	C-	B+	92.5	1.65	9.4	1.9	10.4	43.0	3.2	5.2	11.6
▲ JOHNSON BK	RACINE	WI	B-	C+	C+	2,378.6	5.75	19.8	2.5	8.5	16.1	5.4	7.4	11.3
JOHNSON BK ARIZONA NA	PHOENIX	AZ	B-	B-	B-	499.7	11.60	13.7	0.9	13.3	14.6	5.6	7.6	12.2
JOHNSON CITY BK	JOHNSON CITY	TX	A-	A-	A-	55.1	14.45	5.0	14.7	30.4	8.7	10.0	12.7	19.8
JOHNSON COUNTY BK	MOUNTAIN CITY	TN	B+	B+	B+	88.8	4.51	0.3	7.7	54.1	10.4	9.1	10.4	19.5
JOHNSON ST BK	JOHNSON CITY	KS	B-	B	B	53.4	8.55	2.3	1.2	3.8	43.4	10.0	16.1	22.0
JOHNSONVILLE ST BK	JOHNSONVILLE	SC	B-	B-	B-	22.6	5.90	2.2	28.8	15.4	31.5	10.0	14.1	28.4
▼ JONES COUNTY BK	HADDOCK	GA	E+	D-	D-	5.5	10.51	9.2	26.4	11.0	6.4	4.4	6.4	13.8
JONES NB&TC OF SEWARD	SEWARD	NE	B+	B+	B+	171.8	0.02	8.7	4.8	15.1	34.2	8.0	9.7	16.4
▼ JONESBORO ST BK	JONESBORO	LA	B+	A-	B+	75.4	-0.71	6.7	5.9	11.7	50.0	10.0	17.6	42.9
JONESBURG ST BK	JONESBURG	MO	C	C	C	44.4	3.69	3.2	6.6	38.2	10.0	5.3	7.3	13.8
JONESTOWN B&TC	JONESTOWN	PA	B	B	B-	210.5	5.93	5.1	26.5	28.5	21.7	7.2	9.1	13.7
JOURDANTON ST BK	JOURDANTON	TX	B+	B+	B+	80.2	-1.81	9.8	6.0	5.8	48.2	10.0	18.0	35.2
JOY ST BK	JOY	IL	C-	C-	B-	32.2	-1.46	2.8	4.6	14.0	34.5	6.0	8.0	13.7
▲ JP MORGAN TC NA	LOS ANGELES	CA	C	C-	C-	955.0	160.10	0.0	0.0	0.1	0.6	10.0	39.6	144.9

Asset Quality Index	Non-Performing Loans as a % of Total Loans	Non-Performing Loans as a % of Capital	Net Charge-offs Avg Loans	Profitability Index	Net Income ($Mil)	Return on Assets (R.O.A.)	Return on Equity (R.O.E.)	Net Interest Spread	Overhead Efficiency Ratio	Liquidity Index	Liquidity Ratio	Hot Money Ratio	Stability Index
6.8	0.80	3.3	0.05	5.7	0.2	1.27	8.60	4.19	67.9	4.2	81.4	22.0	7.5
6.7	0.66	4.9	0.28	4.1	0.9	0.57	7.66	2.26	67.2	1.8	20.9	22.2	2.9
8.2	0.20	1.5	0.40	8.1	4.4	1.38	15.37	3.85	55.5	3.7	13.3	10.5	6.8
4.3	0.96	6.4	0.63	9.6	33.1	1.37	11.91	5.81	74.5	1.7	15.9	22.2	8.5
8.8	0.31	1.8	0.10	6.1	2.8	1.33	15.05	2.05	55.8	5.2	220.1	80.9	5.0
5.0	0.80	5.9	-0.06	5.8	2.8	1.05	12.71	3.92	65.9	3.7	29.8	13.3	5.7
5.4	0.50	3.7	0.01	6.7	1.5	1.22	13.11	4.16	58.9	1.5	13.6	23.7	5.8
8.5	0.18	0.9	-0.03	7.2	0.8	1.10	11.30	4.71	67.2	5.6	46.8	8.4	6.2
5.7	1.17	7.3	0.13	1.1	0.0	-0.02	-0.12	4.03	89.5	3.8	65.4	20.5	0.0
8.5	1.19	4.9	0.04	3.8	28.7	0.72	10.80	1.91	61.1	3.0	53.0	50.6	4.0
2.4	2.43	17.9	0.55	6.3	1.8	1.07	11.28	4.04	59.0	1.7	25.2	24.6	6.1
10.0	0.00	0.0	0.00	10.0	0.1	4.11	5.26	1.27	14.7	0.0	N/A	101.0	0.0
7.9	0.62	2.5	1.22	5.4	0.1	0.95	5.79	4.37	65.9	5.5	39.5	3.1	5.0
8.1	0.19	1.2	-0.16	8.6	1.0	1.99	24.01	4.65	62.3	2.6	10.8	15.6	5.0
5.1	1.33	7.8	0.13	5.4	0.8	1.03	9.86	4.13	69.9	2.8	26.4	16.5	5.6
6.4	0.64	4.6	0.11	5.4	1.0	0.63	6.51	3.79	78.8	4.6	30.7	8.3	5.7
6.6	1.61	4.3	0.61	7.9	0.9	1.55	8.40	4.39	50.4	4.0	67.5	23.0	8.4
5.1	1.36	9.7	0.00	7.1	1.2	1.45	17.07	3.42	59.4	6.8	89.3	9.8	6.2
5.3	0.47	3.3	-0.09	9.6	13.1	1.39	12.15	3.78	41.1	0.4	2.3	54.8	9.7
7.5	0.94	2.1	0.00	5.2	0.2	0.99	5.35	3.51	59.3	5.9	48.5	5.9	6.3
6.0	4.12	9.7	-0.21	2.6	0.1	0.53	4.73	3.39	82.0	5.0	44.0	10.6	3.9
2.6	1.52	13.7	-0.01	9.8	8.2	2.83	32.65	4.44	39.7	2.9	16.4	14.9	5.6
7.4	0.98	3.8	0.00	6.7	0.1	0.90	4.92	3.79	61.2	3.5	N/A	10.3	7.0
4.7	0.44	3.9	0.03	4.7	0.9	0.90	12.22	3.46	57.4	5.9	81.0	13.2	3.1
3.7	1.81	11.2	0.60	2.7	0.5	0.36	4.80	3.18	78.9	1.5	14.9	25.0	2.6
8.6	0.18	1.3	0.15	5.1	1.4	0.91	11.43	3.79	57.7	5.5	59.2	12.4	4.5
8.4	0.20	2.1	0.02	4.2	1.6	0.86	15.76	2.92	60.6	5.3	47.1	10.0	2.2
9.2	0.19	0.2	0.00	6.2	0.1	1.36	5.82	4.53	59.2	4.8	22.3	3.6	5.7
3.0	3.22	18.7	-0.42	7.6	0.4	1.87	19.02	3.91	54.8	6.4	56.0	4.0	5.7
8.9	0.43	2.2	0.00	6.9	0.4	1.00	8.12	3.31	43.5	4.2	16.8	7.4	6.5
4.5	1.66	11.3	0.53	3.7	0.8	0.64	9.18	3.10	64.0	4.5	71.9	19.1	2.6
1.5	2.99	14.8	0.11	4.8	0.1	1.35	13.62	5.15	75.9	2.8	48.4	22.0	1.7
7.1	0.33	1.8	0.15	7.7	2.6	1.45	15.09	4.53	62.5	5.1	115.2	21.3	5.6
4.9	0.41	3.7	0.08	5.7	3.5	1.05	12.09	3.11	43.3	3.3	29.1	14.6	5.3
4.2	1.29	7.1	-3.36	3.7	0.1	0.29	4.24	3.83	80.3	1.4	10.9	24.6	2.9
2.6	1.41	16.1	0.75	3.7	-0.9	-1.22	-18.21	4.77	112.3	0.6	6.2	36.8	3.7
6.1	0.20	1.7	0.04	9.8	3.8	1.89	26.32	4.26	44.8	4.8	48.9	13.1	6.2
8.9	0.00	0.0	0.00	5.1	0.2	1.34	11.54	3.35	58.2	6.6	97.8	10.7	5.8
8.4	0.58	1.7	0.02	7.9	1.7	1.21	5.45	3.82	53.5	2.9	39.9	21.8	7.9
6.2	0.38	3.0	-0.13	5.2	0.9	0.88	12.34	4.11	70.9	4.3	21.5	7.5	2.7
6.2	0.58	3.8	-0.01	5.3	3.8	1.36	16.58	4.14	72.2	4.1	17.1	8.2	6.1
1.8	3.11	27.5	-0.01	9.2	0.3	1.41	17.27	6.21	64.1	2.6	42.4	26.6	1.8
3.4	4.12	22.3	0.00	5.4	0.1	1.02	9.15	4.08	72.7	4.8	21.9	3.9	3.4
7.4	0.39	2.2	0.04	9.7	4.8	1.84	17.62	4.42	51.5	4.2	23.0	8.4	8.6
1.9	4.81	26.7	0.40	3.2	0.3	0.53	6.08	2.71	77.3	5.4	41.1	7.8	3.3
8.7	0.00	0.0	0.00	6.1	1.2	1.08	8.61	4.39	67.6	4.6	22.7	5.6	7.3
7.0	0.97	4.5	-0.09	4.4	0.5	0.93	9.06	3.68	69.4	3.5	13.7	11.3	5.7
10.0	0.00	0.0	0.00	10.0	1.0	40.24	61.18	0.97	43.2	0.0	N/A	100.0	0.1
3.9	2.82	14.8	0.09	5.3	0.3	1.25	11.95	4.08	69.5	4.7	38.0	11.0	5.5
7.4	0.00	0.0	0.02	5.1	0.5	0.96	9.18	3.80	64.1	2.7	20.9	15.9	5.2
6.2	0.52	4.5	0.10	4.4	9.4	0.81	10.42	3.57	71.7	2.8	26.6	19.6	5.4
8.5	0.03	0.3	-0.02	7.8	3.0	1.25	16.61	4.53	56.6	2.9	15.9	14.4	5.6
7.8	0.04	0.2	0.15	10.0	0.6	2.34	18.96	5.41	51.8	3.1	61.1	28.9	7.7
5.4	0.85	5.4	0.02	8.1	0.5	1.11	10.72	4.69	58.6	4.0	60.3	18.6	6.2
6.4	1.84	4.8	0.06	3.9	0.3	1.01	6.46	4.38	74.7	3.6	59.0	20.3	6.6
5.5	1.62	5.4	0.29	7.1	0.1	1.27	8.80	5.12	63.2	4.3	56.6	14.8	5.7
0.9	3.50	20.0	0.00	0.8	0.0	-0.54	-8.26	5.24	110.2	6.1	69.5	7.3	0.0
5.5	0.80	4.7	-0.02	6.6	1.1	1.27	12.70	3.69	65.9	2.5	17.8	16.8	7.9
6.9	3.64	5.5	-0.59	4.8	0.2	0.44	2.47	2.13	76.5	7.5	250.0	15.0	8.9
7.1	0.27	2.4	0.09	8.1	0.4	2.02	28.05	4.25	56.3	7.2	110.9	8.8	4.3
5.8	0.30	2.2	0.20	5.5	1.1	1.00	10.83	3.85	66.8	4.6	18.8	5.5	5.7
8.7	0.04	0.1	0.57	4.8	0.4	1.02	5.71	5.11	74.8	5.5	32.0	2.9	7.0
4.1	2.08	11.6	0.09	5.6	0.2	1.23	13.63	4.17	59.1	3.2	43.7	19.6	3.7
6.5	0.03	0.0	0.00	9.5	11.8	2.42	3.10	1.32	82.0	9.6	203.0	2.4	5.0

| Name | City | State | Weiss Safety Rating | 2003 Weiss Safety Rating | 2002 Weiss Safety Rating | Total Assets ($Mil) | One Year Asset Growth | Asset Mix (As a % of Total Assets) | | | | Capital-ization Index | Leverage Ratio | Risk-based Capital Ratio |
								Comm-ercial Loans	Cons-umer Loans	Home Mort-gages	Secur-ities			
▲ JPMORGAN CHASE BK	NEW YORK	NY	C-	D	C-	654,641.0	-1.09	3.4	4.8	9.2	8.9	3.5	5.5	11.0
JUNCTION NB	JUNCTION	TX	B	B+	B+	38.7	-4.41	9.3	9.0	12.5	28.3	10.0	12.8	25.7
JUNIATA VALLEY BK	MIFFLINTOWN	PA	A	A	A	384.0	-1.80	6.8	15.8	33.1	20.4	10.0	11.5	18.7
JUNIPER BK	WILMINGTON	DE	D-	D-	D-	437.2	13.19	0.0	49.2	0.0	15.4	9.8	10.9	21.2
JUSTIN ST BK	JUSTIN	TX	A-	A-	A-	55.0	3.68	7.9	2.9	17.4	5.6	10.0	11.5	16.7
▲ K BK	OWINGS MILLS	MD	C-	D	D	482.6	13.17	12.6	7.0	3.5	9.8	6.9	8.9	13.4
▲ KAHOKA ST BK	KAHOKA	MO	C+	C	C	33.2	-0.34	10.3	8.8	25.7	15.9	8.8	10.2	16.6
▲ KAISER FEDERAL BANK	COVINA	CA	B	B-	B+	557.1	28.49	0.0	9.9	61.7	7.5	10.0	11.1	18.6
KALAMAZOO COUNTY ST BK	SCHOOLCRAFT	MI	B+	B+	B+	75.1	0.86	6.1	10.4	21.4	31.6	10.0	12.1	20.8
KANABEC ST BK	MORA	MN	A	A	A	115.8	0.65	11.2	5.1	16.8	41.4	10.0	11.7	21.1
KANSAS ST BK	MANHATTAN	KS	B-	B-	C+	402.0	12.85	11.3	4.1	19.9	13.3	5.5	7.5	12.2
KANSAS ST BK	OTTAWA	KS	B	B	B-	93.7	-3.04	5.8	4.1	15.7	39.9	6.0	8.0	17.3
KANSAS ST BK OVERBROOK	OVERBROOK	KS	C+	C+	C	38.7	-1.10	5.0	7.8	16.3	42.8	9.9	10.9	18.0
KANZA BK	KINGMAN	KS	B-	B-	B+	125.3	8.94	16.4	3.5	10.7	23.5	8.4	9.9	13.9
KAPLAN ST BK	KAPLAN	LA	A	A	A	73.2	-12.31	3.3	5.5	12.3	64.0	10.0	11.3	30.4
▲ KARNES CTY NB	KARNES CITY	TX	B+	B	B	54.7	-1.50	4.4	9.1	9.4	43.1	10.0	13.0	26.4
▲ KASSON ST BK	KASSON	MN	B-	C+	B-	60.9	-3.11	12.9	13.6	9.1	23.7	7.9	9.6	13.7
KATAHDIN TRUST CO	PATTEN	ME	C+	C+	C-	327.3	8.83	14.9	6.1	18.5	21.2	5.2	7.2	11.7
KAW VALLEY ST B&TC	TOPEKA	KS	B-	B-	B-	355.8	3.01	18.7	4.2	9.1	36.9	7.6	9.4	15.4
KAW VALLEY ST B&TC	WAMEGO	KS	A-	A-	A-	74.6	-3.60	11.2	5.6	11.3	28.3	10.0	11.1	16.0
▼ KAW VALLEY ST BK	EUDORA	KS	D+	C-	C	35.1	-10.02	9.1	20.5	13.1	39.8	5.5	7.5	13.5
KEARNEY COMMERCIAL BK	KEARNEY	MO	B	B	B-	99.4	7.99	10.9	7.2	20.5	18.6	7.2	9.1	13.5
KEARNEY ST B&TC	KEARNEY	NE	B	B	B	137.9	12.82	17.3	7.0	17.4	25.6	5.9	7.9	12.3
▲ KEARNEY TRUST CO	KEARNEY	MO	B-	C+	C+	117.6	2.94	7.6	6.4	17.9	18.8	6.7	8.8	12.6
▲ KEARNY COUNTY BK	LAKIN	KS	A+	A	A	97.7	-2.60	8.5	2.5	9.4	50.2	10.0	21.9	42.7
KEARNY FSB	KEARNY	NJ	B+	B+	A	1,853.2	23.42	0.3	0.2	20.5	64.9	9.8	10.9	32.9
KENDALL ST BK	VALLEY FALLS	KS	D	D	D	27.4	-1.18	38.4	3.2	9.3	7.8	4.4	8.3	10.7
KENNEBEC FS&LA OF	WATERVILLE	ME	C+	C+	C	64.1	16.09	1.2	1.9	59.0	12.3	6.0	8.0	12.6
KENNEBEC SVGS BK	AUGUSTA	ME	B+	B+	B+	490.2	8.16	1.1	0.9	64.9	17.5	10.0	12.0	20.0
KENNEBUNK SVGS BK	KENNEBUNK	ME	B+	B+	B+	613.8	9.07	4.6	0.4	30.4	11.5	5.7	8.6	11.5
▲ KENNETT NB	KENNETT	MO	C	C-	C	102.3	-6.26	9.2	5.3	15.5	44.8	10.0	11.1	20.1
KENT BK	KENT	IL	C	C-	C	80.5	8.63	6.8	9.6	18.9	26.3	7.1	9.1	12.8
KENT CMRC BK	KENTWOOD	MI	C	C	C	81.5	0.05	36.0	0.5	12.3	1.2	5.0	9.1	11.0
▼ KENT COUNTY ST BK	JAYTON	TX	D-	D+	D	39.3	46.43	23.4	12.3	10.9	9.0	1.9	6.1	8.9
KENT ST BK	KENT	MN	D-	D-	D	7.0	2.72	7.4	11.4	1.8	11.9	8.1	9.7	14.3
KENTLAND BK	KENTLAND	IN	A	A	A	191.7	11.97	7.0	3.9	15.2	28.2	10.0	11.7	20.2
KENTLAND FS&LA	KENTLAND	IN	D	D	D+	3.3	2.09	0.0	2.0	36.8	31.0	10.0	20.3	72.5
KENTUCKY BANKING	GLASGOW	KY	B-	B-	B	121.6	8.09	5.1	9.9	19.5	19.0	5.5	7.5	11.9
KENTUCKY BK	PARIS	KY	B	B	B+	515.5	27.62	2.8	2.1	25.5	25.6	5.4	7.4	12.8
▲ KENTUCKY FS&LA	COVINGTON	KY	D	D-	D-	37.0	-11.10	0.0	0.8	70.0	5.6	7.0	9.0	19.7
KENTUCKY HOME BK	BARDSTOWN	KY	C+	C+	C+	69.6	22.59	4.2	9.1	24.9	2.6	6.2	8.8	11.9
KENTUCKY NB	ELIZABETHTOWN	KY	C	C	C	106.5	13.01	5.9	5.8	40.7	9.5	6.4	8.4	13.5
KENTUCKY NB OF PIKEVILLE	PIKEVILLE	KY	B+	B+	B	70.7	5.09	13.8	12.0	24.9	13.8	10.0	11.2	17.7
KENTUCKY TRUST BK	BEAVER DAM	KY	D	D	D	99.4	3.48	10.3	4.9	38.5	16.9	5.1	7.1	12.2
KENTUCKY-FARMERS BK	ASHLAND	KY	A+	A+	A+	115.9	-13.84	4.1	11.4	23.2	47.4	10.0	23.3	39.7
KEOKUK COUNTY ST BK	SIGOURNEY	IA	B-	B-	C	45.6	1.13	10.6	4.4	8.4	19.5	8.2	9.8	14.7
▲ KEOKUK SVG B&TC	KEOKUK	IA	C+	C	C+	99.4	-2.65	11.8	4.2	29.4	17.6	5.0	7.3	11.0
KERNDT BROTHERS SVG BK	LANSING	IA	B-	B-	B-	143.4	67.55	7.0	3.1	11.5	13.4	5.4	8.6	11.3
KEVIL BK	KEVIL	KY	B	B	B+	33.5	-3.64	1.0	3.0	10.0	74.3	10.0	11.2	35.2
KEY BK USA NA	CLEVELAND	OH	C+	C	C	10,190.7	5.23	7.2	39.1	43.4	0.0	5.8	8.7	11.6
KEY COMMUNITY BANK	INVER GROVE HGTS	MN	C	C	D+	77.3	12.27	15.7	3.4	7.0	8.4	5.1	7.1	11.8
▲ KEY WEST BK	KEY WEST	FL	B+	B	B-	97.8	43.23	0.5	0.5	69.9	0.0	7.4	9.3	16.0
KEYBANK NA	CLEVELAND	OH	C+	C	C	74,847.1	-0.36	20.9	7.0	3.3	9.3	5.1	7.1	11.1
KEYSAVINGS BK	WISCONSIN RAPIDS	WI	B-	B-	B-	72.2	-0.85	0.0	0.8	57.1	10.2	10.0	14.8	30.1
KEYSTONE BK	NORTHWOODS	MO	C-	D+	D-	122.0	1.35	9.6	2.1	18.8	44.3	6.6	8.6	16.3
KEYSTONE CMNTY BK	KALAMAZOO	MI	C	C+	C+	135.5	16.08	35.1	1.6	4.8	1.7	3.1	8.4	10.0
▲ KEYSTONE NAZARETH B&TC	BETHLEHEM	PA	B+	B	A-	2,149.6	102.04	2.0	5.8	21.5	42.4	10.0	12.5	21.4
KEYSTONE ST SVGS BK	SHARPSBURG	PA	D	D	C-	26.8	-5.57	3.0	0.0	5.3	52.3	10.0	14.1	72.4
KEYSTONE SVG BK	KEYSTONE	IA	C-	C-	C-	48.7	3.34	3.9	6.9	12.7	34.5	5.4	7.4	12.7
▲ KILGORE NB	KILGORE	TX	C	C-	D	32.2	12.44	12.7	8.5	19.7	7.1	8.3	9.9	15.9
KILLBUCK SVG BK CO	KILLBUCK	OH	A-	A-	A	284.3	-0.24	13.9	3.0	31.9	18.7	10.0	11.6	16.9
KINDERHOOK ST BK	KINDERHOOK	IL	E+	E+	D-	27.0	-4.20	7.8	6.1	14.9	26.8	5.8	7.8	13.1
KINDRED ST BK	KINDRED	ND	D	D	D	17.8	7.79	7.9	8.2	5.6	36.7	6.9	8.9	15.5
KING SOUTHERN BK	CHAPLIN	KY	C-	D+	D	100.6	40.78	7.9	2.3	40.8	5.3	3.1	6.7	10.1

Asset Quality Index	Non-Performing Loans as a % of Total Loans	Non-Performing Loans as a % of Capital	Net Charge-offs Avg Loans	Profitability Index	Net Income ($Mil)	Return on Assets (R.O.A.)	Return on Equity (R.O.E.)	Net Interest Spread	Overhead Efficiency Ratio	Liquidity Index	Liquidity Ratio	Hot Money Ratio	Stability Index
6.4	1.21	5.7	0.32	2.4	1,072.0	0.33	5.69	1.48	89.8	5.6	144.1	22.6	4.0
6.3	1.91	6.4	1.35	5.4	0.2	1.09	8.23	4.50	68.6	3.9	62.8	19.1	6.3
7.9	0.15	0.9	0.04	7.8	2.9	1.52	12.70	4.41	58.0	5.0	39.9	10.0	7.9
2.7	1.61	4.6	4.98	0.0	-16.5	-6.46	-41.03	2.40	159.5	0.3	16.2	97.4	0.0
7.4	0.11	0.6	0.01	10.0	0.9	3.17	29.75	5.43	45.9	5.6	45.9	7.1	7.6
3.0	0.74	5.9	0.69	8.2	3.3	1.40	16.16	6.01	59.7	3.9	49.3	17.8	3.7
5.3	0.78	5.0	0.04	5.7	0.2	1.03	10.23	4.43	60.8	4.2	48.4	15.6	3.9
8.5	0.02	0.1	0.00	4.4	1.7	0.51	6.45	2.05	61.6	0.6	6.6	35.3	5.6
8.0	0.54	2.5	-0.05	4.7	0.3	0.71	6.11	4.26	75.7	4.5	30.6	8.9	6.1
8.8	0.00	0.0	0.03	8.0	1.2	2.13	18.31	3.80	44.6	7.5	98.3	6.5	8.6
8.0	0.09	0.8	-0.12	7.6	3.6	1.83	24.79	3.20	46.6	0.9	19.0	34.7	4.4
8.6	0.40	2.1	0.00	5.0	0.6	1.14	14.33	3.49	70.8	4.9	70.2	15.5	5.5
4.4	2.66	11.6	-0.05	5.8	0.2	0.95	9.23	4.30	61.8	4.4	11.8	5.7	4.0
4.1	1.44	7.7	0.05	6.2	0.8	1.37	11.92	4.87	57.8	3.9	29.2	12.0	7.9
9.2	0.07	0.2	-0.07	9.5	0.9	2.26	17.28	4.87	56.3	4.1	36.4	13.3	8.5
5.5	2.45	8.8	0.17	5.8	0.4	1.29	9.35	5.08	69.5	2.4	17.3	17.3	6.5
4.3	1.05	6.3	-0.02	6.8	0.5	1.78	17.56	4.16	56.8	4.7	47.9	12.8	5.7
5.7	0.52	4.2	0.06	6.2	1.7	1.02	12.68	4.27	64.7	2.3	12.5	17.0	4.0
5.0	1.34	8.0	0.26	3.8	1.5	0.81	8.84	2.98	62.0	1.4	29.1	33.8	4.6
8.4	0.11	0.6	0.15	9.0	0.8	2.04	15.55	4.41	58.8	4.8	39.5	10.8	7.8
1.6	4.50	31.1	0.56	7.7	0.3	1.57	20.41	4.99	68.2	5.8	39.9	4.4	3.6
5.1	0.76	5.7	0.62	5.9	0.4	0.87	9.31	4.67	67.8	2.2	10.9	17.5	5.4
7.2	0.01	0.1	0.32	9.2	1.1	1.57	20.35	4.02	50.1	3.1	31.1	16.7	4.6
4.5	0.68	5.0	0.40	5.6	0.6	0.99	11.68	4.40	60.8	4.7	29.4	7.1	4.3
8.6	1.32	2.7	0.08	9.4	1.1	2.24	10.06	3.95	39.4	4.2	30.5	10.7	9.8
7.8	0.40	1.0	0.01	5.0	6.8	0.70	4.71	2.68	62.3	2.4	25.4	21.6	9.2
7.9	0.06	0.6	0.02	5.2	0.1	0.82	9.99	5.06	76.9	3.9	29.0	12.0	2.6
6.6	0.35	3.2	0.14	4.4	0.2	0.54	5.69	3.35	77.8	1.3	20.8	29.8	4.1
9.7	0.11	0.7	0.01	4.9	2.2	0.91	7.60	3.04	59.7	3.6	33.1	14.8	7.5
7.2	0.29	2.4	0.04	7.1	3.6	1.20	13.45	4.49	65.2	4.9	20.3	3.5	6.4
3.4	6.27	23.1	1.49	2.9	0.3	0.55	5.46	3.55	81.2	3.7	22.2	11.2	3.6
1.9	2.65	17.4	0.64	8.1	0.5	1.30	13.17	4.03	48.7	3.5	18.3	11.6	5.3
4.5	0.56	4.7	0.51	6.2	0.3	0.79	7.93	4.81	62.9	0.7	9.2	38.5	4.3
3.2	1.57	14.0	1.97	1.9	-0.6	-3.57	-46.84	3.68	87.5	4.0	110.6	35.1	0.3
7.9	0.00	0.0	0.05	1.9	0.0	0.08	0.86	4.14	98.1	6.5	77.4	6.3	1.7
7.3	1.14	5.7	0.10	9.4	1.4	1.53	13.16	4.23	48.4	5.7	57.3	10.8	7.9
9.3	0.00	0.0	0.00	1.1	0.0	-0.06	-0.30	3.55	101.7	4.5	34.2	8.1	3.5
3.8	1.84	14.7	0.44	4.0	0.4	0.69	9.30	3.59	69.6	4.6	38.5	11.6	5.0
5.1	0.55	3.6	0.11	6.5	2.9	1.11	11.43	3.83	63.4	3.3	20.4	13.1	5.6
6.5	0.62	5.1	0.00	3.0	0.1	0.32	3.78	3.28	85.4	3.4	24.5	12.8	1.6
5.7	0.44	3.9	0.14	6.5	0.4	1.09	12.27	4.21	61.7	3.1	56.0	26.0	4.4
2.8	2.29	20.0	0.07	4.3	0.3	0.51	6.09	3.86	75.5	1.6	26.7	27.8	4.1
6.1	0.73	4.2	0.08	9.7	0.6	1.61	14.72	4.63	50.2	3.7	64.3	21.2	5.9
4.3	1.23	11.2	0.40	1.3	-0.1	-0.09	-1.28	3.84	74.0	1.5	11.6	23.2	1.4
8.4	0.74	1.3	0.26	10.0	2.1	3.49	15.01	8.65	43.2	4.3	37.0	12.6	9.1
8.4	0.05	0.3	0.00	6.6	0.3	1.10	11.25	4.60	66.4	5.4	46.4	9.0	5.2
5.8	0.33	2.2	0.90	4.4	0.5	0.99	10.20	4.44	74.5	4.1	12.9	7.7	5.2
4.8	0.73	6.2	-0.08	5.1	0.8	1.18	13.65	3.71	58.9	2.6	17.6	16.1	4.9
8.1	1.94	4.0	0.05	5.5	0.2	1.40	13.08	3.45	63.5	5.1	43.7	10.2	5.7
2.6	1.75	13.4	0.94	10.0	88.6	1.75	16.18	5.33	49.7	0.4	2.5	54.9	8.0
4.2	1.00	9.9	0.10	6.1	0.7	1.78	25.01	3.67	69.3	4.0	52.3	17.3	4.5
9.2	0.00	0.0	0.00	9.5	1.2	2.82	30.81	4.06	37.3	0.4	9.5	69.5	6.8
5.1	0.74	6.7	0.50	5.1	374.4	1.01	14.86	3.18	61.1	6.9	63.4	6.5	5.6
7.7	1.07	4.8	0.24	3.5	0.2	0.58	3.96	3.32	64.9	7.7	137.9	8.7	6.6
5.0	1.63	8.3	0.46	3.4	0.3	0.48	5.53	3.74	86.6	5.0	23.1	3.1	2.2
5.6	0.20	1.9	0.11	3.7	0.3	0.42	5.00	3.65	77.7	1.7	28.8	29.1	4.6
8.2	0.48	1.6	0.18	5.0	8.2	0.81	5.47	3.54	64.9	5.8	30.3	4.6	8.0
10.0	0.12	0.1	0.00	0.0	-0.1	-0.58	-4.06	1.36	157.2	9.6	1,507.6	2.4	4.6
4.7	0.82	5.9	0.05	4.4	0.2	0.69	9.06	3.97	81.2	4.5	22.0	6.3	3.7
8.3	0.04	0.2	0.10	2.7	0.1	0.59	5.62	4.56	85.4	4.7	78.1	17.6	0.2
8.7	0.11	0.7	-0.03	5.6	1.6	1.09	9.09	3.78	63.4	3.0	18.6	14.6	7.6
1.1	6.38	47.1	1.12	1.6	-0.1	-0.40	-5.17	3.50	85.0	0.8	8.4	33.6	1.0
7.1	0.52	2.6	0.03	4.9	0.1	1.09	12.68	4.92	74.0	5.1	31.4	3.4	2.2
8.6	0.09	1.1	0.05	8.4	1.0	2.18	34.30	4.50	49.1	3.0	41.2	21.1	2.8

Name	City	State	Weiss Safety Rating	2003 Weiss Safety Rating	2002 Weiss Safety Rating	Total Assets ($Mil)	One Year Asset Growth	Asset Mix (As a % of Total Assets)				Capital-ization Index	Leverage Ratio	Risk-based Capital Ratio
								Comm-ercial Loans	Cons-umer Loans	Home Mort-gages	Secur-ities			
KINGSLEY ST BK	KINGSLEY	IA	A-	A-	A-	97.1	4.95	6.4	3.4	14.7	38.8	10.0	13.5	25.2
▲ KINGSTON NB	KINGSTON	OH	A	A-	A-	127.0	3.55	18.0	5.1	17.4	20.7	10.0	11.3	16.5
KINGSTREE FS&LA	KINGSTREE	SC	C	C	C	22.9	-5.35	0.2	1.4	58.2	28.8	10.0	20.7	47.5
▼ KIRKPATRICK BK	EDMOND	OK	C	B-	B-	315.2	26.05	6.2	2.1	14.2	7.0	2.5	7.7	9.5
KIRKWOOD B&TC	BISMARCK	ND	B-	C+	C+	97.8	8.83	42.5	3.9	3.5	8.7	5.7	8.3	11.5
▼ KISHACOQUILLAS VALLEY NB	BELLEVILLE	PA	C+	B-	B-	373.6	11.74	6.2	2.2	16.7	34.0	3.8	7.8	10.4
KISLAK NB	MIAMI LAKES	FL	B	B	B+	962.1	18.57	4.3	0.1	4.8	38.7	6.4	8.4	15.4
▲ KIT CARSON ST BK	KIT CARSON	CO	C-	C-	D+	48.4	-5.43	12.4	3.0	4.3	27.8	9.4	10.6	17.3
KITSAP BK	PORT ORCHARD	WA	B+	B+	A-	536.6	5.45	9.1	4.1	8.2	8.0	6.3	9.5	12.0
KLEBERG FIRST NB	KINGSVILLE	TX	C	C	C+	177.3	6.39	7.5	38.0	9.0	22.3	6.3	8.4	14.1
▲ KLEIN BK	KLEIN	TX	B+	B	B	596.7	8.17	2.2	1.6	7.8	65.2	5.7	7.7	27.0
▲ KLEIN NB OF MADISON	MADISON	MN	A-	B+	B	54.8	-6.99	9.3	3.8	4.1	33.0	10.0	13.6	19.5
KNISELY BK	BUTLER	IN	D-	D-	D+	51.8	3.36	3.1	7.2	34.1	28.8	5.2	7.2	14.0
▲ KOPERNIK FEDERAL BK	BALTIMORE	MD	B-	C+	C	28.5	11.01	0.0	2.5	70.5	10.1	10.0	11.4	25.0
KOSCIUSZKO FSB	BALTIMORE	MD	C	C	C+	13.9	7.45	0.0	0.1	65.4	6.0	10.0	13.9	27.5
KRESS NB	KRESS	TX	B-	B-	C+	25.9	2.20	6.9	3.1	0.5	59.0	9.5	10.7	25.5
▼ KS BANK, INC	SMITHFIELD	NC	B-	B	B	217.6	13.77	6.8	1.2	36.5	15.9	6.5	8.5	13.1
LA COSTE NB	LA COSTE	TX	B-	B-	B-	26.6	0.80	2.8	4.3	6.3	64.5	10.0	14.9	46.7
LA FARGE ST BK	LA FARGE	WI	A	A	A	36.2	3.75	4.9	3.1	9.1	34.9	10.0	25.9	35.2
▼ LA JOLLA BK FSB	LA JOLLA	CA	B+	A-	B+	1,796.2	30.91	1.5	0.2	8.7	3.8	5.3	8.3	11.2
LA MONTE COMMUNITY BK	LA MONTE	MO	A-	A-	A-	25.1	-2.82	1.5	3.0	20.9	41.5	8.9	10.3	18.5
▼ LA PLATA ST BK	LA PLATA	MO	B-	B+	A-	61.8	8.91	2.0	3.9	8.8	46.0	5.8	7.8	16.6
▼ LA PORTE SVGS BK	LA PORTE	IN	C-	C	B-	254.3	-5.10	2.2	9.7	34.2	29.5	7.8	9.5	16.5
LA SALLE NB	LA SALLE	IL	D+	D	D	129.8	-2.93	11.9	2.1	13.4	46.2	4.8	6.8	12.9
LA SALLE ST BK	LA SALLE	IL	C	C	C	102.8	4.73	3.1	17.0	23.6	37.4	6.4	8.4	16.6
▲ LABE BK	CHICAGO	IL	C-	NR	NR	396.9	N/A	3.7	0.2	7.6	31.8	5.8	7.8	12.7
▲ LABETTE BK	ALTAMONT	KS	C+	C	C	171.5	32.80	4.6	6.5	24.8	20.1	5.3	7.3	11.9
LACONIA SVGS BK	LACONIA	NH	B-	B-	C+	799.2	1.69	5.3	12.9	21.8	21.8	6.8	8.8	13.4
LADYSMITH FS&LA	LADYSMITH	WI	C	C-	D	30.3	-7.53	4.7	3.6	42.1	37.3	10.0	12.2	21.5
LAFAYETTE AMBASSADOR BK	EASTON	PA	B	B	B+	1,197.1	9.79	7.8	6.2	14.8	24.2	4.9	7.1	11.0
LAFAYETTE B&TC NA	LAFAYETTE	IN	C+	C+	C+	892.0	2.37	6.4	6.0	12.7	17.7	4.9	7.7	11.0
LAFAYETTE COMMUNITY BK	LAFAYETTE	IN	C+	C+	C+	121.4	35.96	15.8	2.9	25.7	13.9	5.3	7.8	11.2
LAFAYETTE FSB	FALL RIVER	MA	B-	B-	B-	108.4	-0.30	0.3	0.8	28.9	61.0	8.3	9.9	35.8
LAFAYETTE ST BK	MAYO	FL	C+	C+	B-	50.3	8.22	8.8	5.5	12.6	10.9	8.2	10.1	13.5
LAFAYETTE SVGS BK FSB	LAFAYETTE	IN	C	C	C+	342.9	9.93	4.4	1.1	39.1	3.2	6.0	8.3	11.7
▲ LAKE AREA BK	LINDSTROM	MN	B	B-	C	204.9	5.59	21.0	2.2	9.4	11.2	5.8	8.9	11.6
LAKE AREA NB	TRINITY	TX	C+	C+	C+	20.6	-3.53	11.3	5.9	18.5	30.2	10.0	14.8	25.3
LAKE BK NA	TWO HARBORS	MN	E-	E-	E-	69.6	-3.68	7.3	2.7	28.1	27.6	5.1	7.1	14.2
LAKE CITY BK	WARSAW	IN	B+	B	B-	1,335.8	7.91	25.9	4.6	3.8	21.2	7.0	9.0	12.5
▲ LAKE CITY FS&LA	LAKE CITY	MN	B+	B	B	55.3	3.04	5.9	8.6	53.7	7.0	10.0	12.4	20.8
LAKE COMMUNITY BK	LAKEPORT	CA	B-	C+	C+	121.3	0.33	5.5	0.8	4.6	6.7	6.8	10.2	12.3
▲ LAKE COUNTRY COMMUNITY	MORRISTOWN	MN	E	E-	D-	25.6	20.43	7.5	16.8	48.2	6.4	5.1	7.1	11.3
▲ LAKE COUNTRY ST BK	LONG PRAIRIE	MN	B-	C+	C	82.3	18.16	16.3	7.8	10.9	28.3	6.7	8.7	14.3
▲ LAKE COUNTY BK	ST IGNATIUS	MT	B	B-	C+	27.1	6.08	9.8	15.2	7.0	2.3	10.0	15.8	19.2
LAKE ELMO BK	LAKE ELMO	MN	B-	B-	C+	238.9	3.72	9.7	2.9	18.9	17.9	5.6	8.0	11.5
▼ LAKE FOREST B&TC	LAKE FOREST	IL	C+	B-	B-	1,175.7	16.28	36.9	3.4	4.9	13.1	2.3	8.7	9.3
LAKE FS&LA OF HAMMOND	HAMMOND	IN	B+	B	B	69.1	7.02	0.1	1.3	63.6	12.2	10.0	16.2	32.9
▲ LAKE REGION BK	NEW LONDON	MN	C+	C	C	84.7	7.03	16.7	7.0	12.4	32.4	5.7	7.7	13.6
LAKE SHORE S&LA	DUNKIRK	NY	B-	B-	B	317.0	24.73	1.8	0.9	46.8	28.7	5.9	7.9	16.4
LAKE SUNAPEE BK FSB	NEWPORT	NH	B	B	B-	591.0	21.85	2.9	1.7	36.8	24.9	3.8	7.2	10.4
LAKE-OSCEOLA STATE BANK	BALDWIN	MI	B-	B-	B-	136.0	1.44	3.6	2.8	50.0	15.4	6.4	8.4	15.5
▲ LAKELAND BK	NEWFOUNDLAND	NJ	B-	C+	B-	1,613.2	21.82	4.0	6.2	16.3	35.6	4.4	6.4	11.7
LAKES ST BK	PEQUOT LAKES	MN	B+	B+	B+	71.7	4.81	8.1	7.5	12.7	10.4	6.7	8.8	12.3
▲ LAKESIDE BK	CHICAGO	IL	B+	B	B+	556.5	11.45	10.0	0.4	1.9	3.9	5.4	10.2	11.3
▼ LAKESIDE BK OF SALINA	SALINA	OK	B	B	A-	25.8	2.79	1.8	16.1	30.7	15.2	8.2	9.9	13.5
LAKESIDE COMMUNITY BK	STERLING HEIGHTS	MI	D	D	B+	42.8	-4.42	19.2	4.0	10.3	15.0	8.0	9.7	14.2
LAKESIDE NB	ROCKWALL	TX	B-	B-	C+	40.4	7.02	11.6	10.6	9.2	42.4	7.5	9.3	18.5
LAKESIDE ST BK	NEW TOWN	ND	A-	A-	B+	48.7	3.89	9.7	6.2	2.6	38.2	10.0	14.2	20.9
▼ LAKESIDE ST BK	OOLAGAH	OK	C	C+	C+	31.1	2.63	3.5	14.6	25.4	36.7	6.8	8.8	17.2
LAKEWOOD BK NA	BAXTER	MN	B+	B+	B+	79.8	14.36	14.6	3.8	17.8	14.5	4.9	8.7	11.0
LAMAR B&TC	LAMAR	MO	A-	A-	A-	105.3	1.66	5.4	5.7	34.6	9.0	7.0	9.0	14.8
▲ LAMAR BK	BEAUMONT	TX	A-	B+	B	109.6	-4.74	7.1	27.7	10.2	21.1	8.0	9.7	13.9
LAMAR NB	PARIS	TX	B+	B+	B	103.4	7.71	5.9	9.9	25.8	23.5	7.8	9.5	19.4
▲ LAMESA NB	LAMESA	TX	B	B-	B-	163.5	0.52	9.2	0.4	0.4	50.6	10.0	13.4	27.0

Asset Quality Index	Non-Performing Loans as a % of Total Loans	Non-Performing Loans as a % of Capital	Net Charge-offs Avg Loans	Profitability Index	Net Income ($Mil)	Return on Assets (R.O.A.)	Return on Equity (R.O.E.)	Net Interest Spread	Overhead Efficiency Ratio	Liquidity Index	Liquidity Ratio	Hot Money Ratio	Stability Index
8.8	0.57	2.0	0.28	6.5	0.8	1.56	11.18	3.06	43.5	4.0	55.9	17.5	8.2
8.1	0.11	0.7	0.09	8.6	1.0	1.61	14.57	4.67	50.3	2.0	27.7	22.3	7.1
9.7	0.00	0.0	0.00	4.9	0.1	0.69	3.40	3.45	67.9	4.1	30.4	9.2	5.0
4.2	0.59	6.1	0.00	5.4	1.6	1.10	13.56	4.56	72.2	2.9	17.7	14.8	5.2
7.4	0.00	0.0	0.03	9.1	0.9	1.87	23.14	5.17	55.5	5.6	47.7	7.6	4.6
5.0	0.80	5.4	0.24	5.0	2.0	1.12	13.56	3.57	72.6	3.8	29.0	12.3	5.1
8.8	0.03	0.3	0.09	4.6	6.1	1.37	16.66	3.45	65.2	0.5	4.2	39.6	5.6
2.5	3.37	17.7	0.18	5.6	0.3	1.16	11.01	4.79	65.2	3.9	105.0	34.7	3.0
6.8	0.10	0.8	0.01	7.2	3.8	1.45	14.29	5.09	72.2	5.1	32.4	6.3	8.6
3.3	0.63	4.7	0.24	7.9	1.6	1.79	21.31	4.35	69.1	2.2	16.3	18.3	6.9
9.4	0.10	0.4	0.50	10.0	5.1	1.75	23.12	5.07	59.4	5.2	36.0	7.1	5.5
4.9	1.33	5.4	0.20	5.0	0.4	1.28	9.82	4.00	71.0	4.6	56.9	14.7	6.5
3.8	2.43	19.6	0.10	3.7	0.2	0.78	11.13	4.28	81.4	4.9	31.0	6.6	0.1
6.9	0.89	5.7	0.03	6.0	0.1	1.03	8.93	3.63	52.6	2.1	28.5	22.3	5.7
8.4	0.00	0.0	0.00	5.5	0.1	1.19	8.56	3.83	56.8	3.8	23.3	10.6	5.0
8.1	0.23	0.8	0.92	5.8	0.2	1.37	13.48	3.82	62.0	4.8	129.8	28.7	4.6
5.1	0.76	6.7	0.13	4.4	0.6	0.59	6.79	3.86	74.0	1.5	20.9	26.1	4.6
6.5	6.20	9.9	1.25	4.3	0.1	0.99	6.70	4.20	75.7	3.8	52.3	18.1	4.9
6.2	2.32	5.3	0.00	9.6	0.3	1.68	6.76	4.08	34.4	6.6	61.5	4.0	9.6
7.1	0.20	2.1	0.01	10.0	23.1	2.74	32.87	3.76	23.2	0.4	3.4	61.8	8.2
9.0	0.00	0.0	0.04	4.4	0.1	0.76	7.30	3.25	65.0	8.5	159.3	5.5	7.1
7.7	0.50	1.3	-0.04	3.1	0.0	0.14	0.93	0.39	46.8	4.6	70.3	17.2	7.2
6.2	0.53	3.4	0.12	2.3	0.3	0.21	2.26	2.49	93.8	3.5	17.7	11.7	4.3
5.4	1.75	11.2	0.10	3.5	0.5	0.72	10.86	3.28	73.0	4.9	37.3	9.6	2.2
3.0	2.17	11.7	0.59	2.8	0.3	0.51	5.26	3.13	86.3	3.5	27.5	13.3	4.4
2.2	2.89	21.9	0.01	9.8	1.9	1.90	19.57	3.61	57.1	2.2	19.5	18.4	1.5
5.5	0.58	4.7	0.29	6.1	0.9	1.10	13.55	4.63	69.9	2.7	18.1	15.6	3.5
4.9	0.51	2.9	0.06	3.8	2.2	0.56	5.21	4.01	82.1	5.2	37.7	7.6	6.7
7.2	1.12	5.1	0.56	3.0	0.1	0.54	4.74	3.27	70.7	3.7	5.7	9.8	3.9
7.9	0.18	1.5	0.02	8.2	8.7	1.43	17.89	3.89	54.7	4.4	11.1	5.6	7.0
2.7	1.04	4.6	0.45	5.8	3.5	0.78	5.10	3.80	65.4	4.2	31.7	11.3	7.3
4.6	0.70	7.0	0.04	5.7	0.6	1.04	13.07	3.95	57.4	4.2	25.0	8.6	2.1
9.8	0.00	0.0	0.00	4.3	0.3	0.51	5.32	2.55	69.7	4.1	65.9	21.3	5.7
2.8	3.44	23.5	0.02	4.1	0.2	0.64	6.24	4.05	77.9	3.1	23.1	14.1	4.6
3.0	1.67	16.7	0.27	6.1	1.5	0.93	11.10	3.36	58.7	0.6	8.7	50.2	4.8
5.3	0.82	7.0	0.02	7.8	2.0	1.92	22.55	4.42	58.6	4.0	20.7	9.7	6.0
8.0	0.56	2.0	-0.05	5.1	0.1	0.97	6.38	5.81	79.7	3.5	30.3	12.4	4.8
2.1	3.59	24.0	0.05	0.0	-0.2	-0.44	-7.26	1.94	120.8	2.5	33.1	21.1	0.0
7.1	0.48	3.4	0.02	7.1	7.3	1.13	12.17	3.69	60.7	2.8	14.5	15.3	7.5
7.7	0.00	0.0	0.00	5.3	0.2	0.64	4.69	3.84	72.1	3.7	8.5	9.7	6.9
4.9	0.78	5.5	0.02	10.0	1.2	1.95	20.08	5.39	43.4	4.4	60.8	18.2	7.3
7.7	0.06	0.7	0.08	3.2	0.0	0.07	0.91	4.65	92.1	5.2	38.4	7.7	0.3
4.3	1.52	10.4	0.22	6.3	0.4	1.06	11.71	5.08	66.9	4.8	27.6	5.9	4.9
6.7	0.87	4.0	0.19	6.4	0.2	1.39	9.30	6.58	67.7	6.5	56.9	4.0	5.6
5.3	0.99	8.2	0.04	7.6	2.1	1.75	21.84	4.48	61.7	3.8	27.2	11.6	4.7
6.6	0.30	2.5	0.05	9.8	12.3	2.21	25.10	3.43	39.2	1.4	22.1	31.7	6.6
9.5	0.24	1.1	0.00	6.0	0.3	0.80	4.98	3.66	63.0	2.3	32.3	23.0	7.3
4.8	1.10	7.4	-0.08	5.7	0.5	1.26	15.65	4.55	77.8	5.6	33.6	3.0	3.7
6.1	0.51	3.7	0.08	4.6	0.9	0.60	7.33	3.14	72.1	1.9	8.3	19.0	4.0
7.1	0.08	0.7	0.00	8.4	3.7	1.31	13.97	4.23	53.9	0.9	20.6	37.8	6.4
5.0	1.01	7.7	0.30	6.1	0.7	1.01	11.37	4.82	65.2	4.4	22.1	6.7	5.4
4.1	1.81	11.5	0.30	5.8	8.6	1.09	13.62	4.09	59.4	6.8	57.0	5.6	6.0
6.1	0.02	0.1	0.13	10.0	0.9	2.55	22.65	5.36	54.6	5.0	62.8	13.8	7.5
6.5	0.19	1.6	0.00	10.0	6.7	2.50	24.48	4.85	48.3	0.7	13.1	37.7	8.6
6.8	0.82	4.2	0.98	10.0	0.3	2.32	19.47	6.14	44.1	6.5	83.8	9.1	6.3
1.1	5.71	36.4	-2.42	2.0	0.1	0.55	6.03	3.21	108.5	4.2	37.5	13.4	1.4
6.3	0.55	2.5	0.07	4.8	0.2	0.92	9.87	4.10	74.5	6.0	42.5	4.1	6.3
8.0	0.51	1.8	0.54	6.5	0.4	1.42	9.80	4.11	54.8	4.7	34.3	9.4	8.1
7.8	0.21	1.3	0.35	4.9	0.1	0.89	10.06	5.04	80.2	3.4	23.8	12.8	4.2
7.6	0.24	1.7	0.07	6.2	0.6	1.60	15.80	5.30	70.6	3.3	11.0	12.3	6.8
6.0	0.88	6.8	0.13	8.6	1.0	1.84	20.48	3.45	55.2	4.9	41.5	10.7	7.2
5.9	0.43	2.6	0.19	8.0	1.0	1.79	17.73	5.20	73.3	4.7	33.4	9.2	7.2
8.4	0.10	0.5	0.03	7.3	0.6	1.20	13.18	4.02	60.9	3.8	70.8	26.5	6.1
4.4	4.72	13.8	0.17	5.9	1.4	1.62	12.38	3.00	44.9	3.7	62.6	25.5	7.2

Name	City	State	Weiss Safety Rating	2003 Weiss Safety Rating	2002 Weiss Safety Rating	Total Assets ($Mil)	One Year Asset Growth	Asset Mix (As a % of Total Assets) Comm-ercial Loans	Cons-umer Loans	Home Mort-gages	Secur-ities	Capital-ization Index	Leverage Ratio	Risk-based Capital Ratio
LAMONT BK OF ST JOHN	ST JOHN	WA	C	C+	C+	22.6	5.64	2.4	2.9	0.0	68.0	10.0	14.0	37.4
LANCASTER NB	LANCASTER	NH	B+	B+	A-	57.3	0.79	6.2	5.0	38.5	26.0	9.8	10.8	20.5
LANDMANDS NB	AUDUBON	IA	B	B	B	52.0	0.64	10.0	22.3	5.0	14.6	6.1	8.8	11.9
LANDMARK BK NA	FORT LAUDERDALE	FL	A-	A-	B	238.3	20.41	2.4	0.1	4.7	7.9	8.0	10.3	13.3
▲ LANDMARK BK NA	ADA	OK	B-	C+	C+	318.2	6.71	7.3	12.4	26.3	13.3	6.2	8.2	13.0
▲ LANDMARK BK NA	DENISON	TX	B-	C+	C+	72.7	29.50	9.6	10.6	19.0	3.1	3.1	7.2	10.1
▼ LANDMARK BK OF FLORIDA	SARASOTA	FL	D+	C-	D+	151.9	50.61	7.6	2.8	8.0	15.1	2.1	6.8	9.1
▲ LANDMARK COMMUNITY BK	PITTSTON	PA	D	D-	D-	87.4	45.12	13.3	5.5	13.5	36.1	10.0	11.8	22.5
▲ LANDMARK COMMUNITY BK	ISANTI	MN	C	C-	D+	101.4	20.24	12.8	2.0	9.6	11.2	8.0	10.4	13.3
LANDMARK NB	SOLANA BEACH	CA	D	D	D	54.6	122.04	7.4	2.0	8.3	22.4	10.0	13.0	17.4
LANDMARK NB	MANHATTAN	KS	A-	A-	B+	477.9	46.86	8.5	1.9	28.7	29.5	8.3	9.9	17.8
▲ LANDMARK SVGS BK FSB	INDIANAPOLIS	IN	C+	C-	C-	72.7	-10.92	1.3	0.1	25.9	0.2	7.5	9.3	17.6
▲ LANGFORD ST BK	LANGFORD	SD	C+	C	C+	11.5	2.67	1.9	0.5	0.0	59.4	10.0	19.7	47.0
LANIER COMMUNITY BK	BUFORD	GA	D	D	NR	76.1	249.01	16.2	4.2	1.2	11.4	10.0	18.1	21.7
LAONA ST BK	LAONA	WI	C-	D+	D	102.3	0.99	19.3	5.9	22.7	32.7	6.3	8.3	14.0
LAPEER COUNTY B&TC	LAPEER	MI	A	A	A-	251.6	2.35	5.9	6.2	16.9	25.9	10.0	11.9	19.8
LAREDO NB	LAREDO	TX	B	B	B	2,688.3	-5.39	15.8	4.3	15.3	27.6	6.1	8.1	15.2
LASALLE BANK NA	CHICAGO	IL	B-	B-	B-	62,764.9	2.20	26.2	0.6	3.2	32.9	5.8	7.8	11.6
LASALLE FSB	BUCHANAN	MI	C	C	C	181.5	-0.73	2.8	0.9	47.5	12.5	6.8	8.9	12.3
▼ LATHROP BK	LATHROP	MO	C-	C+	B-	37.5	32.47	6.3	4.1	20.9	28.3	5.9	7.9	13.7
LATIMER ST BK	WILBURTON	OK	A-	A-	A-	65.4	6.25	4.7	12.6	13.4	45.9	10.0	14.7	34.0
▲ LAUDERDALE COUNTY BK	HALLS	TN	D+	D	D-	36.5	-1.25	11.8	8.5	16.1	32.5	6.3	8.3	15.7
LAURA ST BK	WILLIAMSFIELD	IL	C-	C-	C	9.5	1.30	7.4	20.3	14.8	1.8	10.0	16.4	32.2
▲ LAUREL NB	LONDON	KY	B-	C+	C+	71.4	7.69	0.9	9.1	32.0	37.9	6.3	8.3	17.4
▼ LAUREL SVGS BK	ALLISON PARK	PA	B-	B	A-	299.0	-7.30	0.2	1.0	54.5	27.1	5.8	7.8	16.9
LAURENS ST BK	LAURENS	IA	C+	C+	B-	50.8	0.52	3.8	3.7	6.2	39.3	7.3	9.2	16.8
▼ LAWRENCE BK	LAWRENCE	KS	C-	C+	C+	37.6	12.05	24.9	3.5	15.2	1.3	2.8	8.2	9.8
LAWRENCE FSB	IRONTON	OH	C+	C+	C+	124.5	-8.34	0.8	29.6	26.6	21.1	9.0	10.4	15.6
▲ LAWRENCE SVG BK	N ANDOVER	MA	A-	B+	B	476.2	11.38	2.6	0.1	13.0	49.7	10.0	11.4	20.6
LAWRENCEBURG FSB	LAWRENCEBURG	TN	B	B	B	45.5	-3.40	0.0	4.5	75.1	1.7	10.0	18.4	35.8
LAWRENCEBURG NB	HARRODSBURG	KY	B-	B-	B	144.8	5.97	5.0	14.3	26.7	20.1	5.6	7.6	12.3
LAWSON BK	LAWSON	MO	C-	C-	C-	100.0	7.71	8.4	4.0	20.9	14.7	5.2	7.3	11.2
LAYTON ST BK	MILWAUKEE	WI	C+	C+	B-	91.0	3.25	8.1	0.7	11.0	19.9	6.4	8.4	12.3
LEA COUNTY STATE BANK	HOBBS	NM	B-	B-	B	175.6	-0.15	7.4	2.1	1.4	72.6	5.4	7.4	20.8
▼ LEADER BK NA	ARLINGTON	MA	C	B-	D	122.9	20.40	0.3	0.1	41.0	2.4	8.4	10.1	13.7
▼ LEADERS BK	OAK BROOK	IL	C-	C	D	184.7	40.85	25.9	2.4	7.2	8.0	6.6	11.2	12.2
LEBANON VALLEY FARMERS	LEBANON	PA	B+	B+	B+	772.4	-2.13	8.4	5.3	14.7	28.0	5.3	7.3	12.0
LEBANON-CITIZENS NB	LEBANON	OH	B	B+	B+	497.7	-2.69	6.4	8.0	23.6	27.2	6.6	8.6	14.0
LEDYARD NB	NORWICH	VT	B-	B-	B-	256.5	3.87	26.4	3.0	16.2	23.0	6.2	8.2	13.1
LEE B&TC	PENNINGTON GAP	VA	B+	A-	A-	144.3	-1.02	12.8	6.8	30.6	11.9	10.0	12.3	17.7
▼ LEE BK	LEE	MA	C+	B-	B-	262.3	9.75	6.6	0.8	55.5	8.4	5.6	7.6	12.5
LEE COUNTY B&T NA	FORT MADISON	IA	A	A	A-	111.9	-4.93	7.4	2.2	37.6	7.3	9.3	10.5	16.5
▲ LEEDS FSB	BALTIMORE	MD	C	D+	A-	455.7	1.80	0.1	0.5	47.0	10.1	4.0	6.0	15.7
LEESBURG FSB	LEESBURG	OH	B-	B-	B-	50.0	6.32	5.9	18.8	50.9	2.4	10.0	11.6	17.1
LEESPORT BK	WYOMISSING	PA	B-	B-	B-	618.4	3.98	16.4	1.8	15.3	27.2	6.0	8.1	11.7
▲ LEGACY B&TC	PLATO	MO	B-	C-	E	37.5	72.24	4.8	8.3	28.2	9.0	4.0	7.0	10.5
▼ LEGACY BK	ALTOONA	IA	C-	C	D+	61.7	14.61	4.5	7.0	25.3	27.2	5.3	7.3	13.5
LEGACY BK	COLWICH	KS	B-	B	B-	148.9	4.91	17.3	1.8	9.9	9.4	5.1	9.6	11.1
LEGACY BK	PITTSFIELD	MA	C+	C+	C+	647.0	7.14	3.9	0.6	40.6	15.7	6.3	8.3	12.7
▲ LEGACY BK	HINTON	OK	B-	C+	D+	367.1	19.32	20.7	5.3	10.5	13.3	6.3	9.4	12.0
▲ LEGACY BK	HARRISBURG	PA	C-	D+	D-	302.1	19.87	31.0	1.9	8.6	17.2	7.7	9.5	15.6
▲ LEGACY BK	MILWAUKEE	WI	C	C-	D+	92.8	28.50	17.5	2.0	48.2	20.5	6.2	9.6	11.9
LEGACY BK NA	CAMPBELL	CA	D	D	NR	27.6	N/A	24.4	10.5	0.1	3.5	10.0	38.1	36.6
LEGACY BK NA	LA JOLLA	CA	D	D	D	30.3	81.94	7.7	0.1	3.4	22.4	10.0	23.0	31.9
▼ LEGACY BK OF TX	PLANO	TX	D	D+	D+	876.5	1.64	9.1	3.1	3.9	11.6	5.6	8.7	11.5
LEGEND BK NA	BOWIE	TX	B-	B-	B	305.0	10.35	10.9	7.3	3.8	28.6	7.1	9.1	14.4
▲ LEGENDS BK	CLARKSVILLE	TN	B-	C+	C	173.5	32.94	10.9	3.0	12.9	20.1	6.9	9.1	12.5
LEGG MASON TRUST FSB	BALTIMORE	MD	D	D	D	7.5	-3.61	0.0	0.0	0.0	76.3	10.0	76.8	114.7
▲ LEHMAN BROTHERS BK FSB	WILMINGTON	DE	C-	D+	C-	20,471.9	37.38	1.4	0.1	76.0	0.0	3.5	6.2	10.3
▲ LEIGHTON ST BK	PELLA	IA	C	C-	D+	60.8	9.84	9.5	3.5	17.9	22.2	6.0	8.0	12.6
LEITCHFIELD DEP B&TC	LEITCHFIELD	KY	A-	B+	A-	81.7	-3.80	7.1	4.7	19.3	15.6	10.0	13.4	19.1
LEMONT NB	LEMONT	IL	D-	D+	C-	71.0	-0.40	0.1	0.2	11.2	32.2	5.8	7.8	23.6
▲ LENA ST BK	LENA	IL	B-	C+	C	61.3	-1.14	11.2	2.7	7.1	29.9	9.2	10.5	16.1
LENOX NB	LENOX	MA	B+	B+	B+	47.4	-6.71	2.7	1.9	28.5	40.9	10.0	12.0	28.0

Asset Quality Index	Non-Performing Loans as a % of Total Loans	Non-Performing Loans as a % of Capital	Net Charge-offs Avg Loans	Profitability Index	Net Income ($Mil)	Return on Assets (R.O.A.)	Return on Equity (R.O.E.)	Net Interest Spread	Overhead Efficiency Ratio	Liquidity Index	Liquidity Ratio	Hot Money Ratio	Stability Index
7.6	3.99	7.0	2.33	1.8	0.0	0.23	1.67	2.27	88.0	10.0	245.3	0.0	4.3
8.3	0.24	1.3	0.01	5.2	0.2	0.74	6.88	4.26	72.3	6.2	48.5	4.1	6.2
3.4	0.81	6.6	1.90	7.1	0.3	1.09	12.51	5.32	44.0	3.4	32.0	15.4	4.9
7.3	0.00	0.0	0.00	8.9	1.6	1.41	14.22	4.31	45.1	3.5	52.7	22.6	6.0
5.0	0.58	4.4	0.30	4.3	1.0	0.65	7.86	4.38	78.9	4.9	85.4	18.7	4.5
5.6	0.47	3.6	0.67	0.0	-0.2	-0.70	-7.77	4.39	106.7	3.3	46.0	19.5	4.1
8.5	0.00	0.0	0.00	3.2	0.3	0.48	7.18	3.49	72.3	2.2	29.9	21.3	0.2
8.4	0.00	0.0	0.27	0.0	-0.2	-0.39	-3.29	2.88	103.9	4.0	71.2	20.6	0.0
3.2	1.41	10.5	0.04	7.9	0.9	1.81	21.38	4.94	62.7	4.2	60.8	19.2	3.0
8.9	0.00	0.0	0.00	0.0	-1.1	-4.44	-28.28	3.27	210.2	4.2	65.2	18.3	0.0
6.2	0.57	2.8	0.01	7.3	2.1	1.11	9.54	3.77	60.9	5.9	52.8	8.0	6.5
3.5	2.29	15.3	0.01	5.5	0.3	0.80	8.81	2.83	66.1	2.7	37.3	21.1	4.8
9.3	0.00	0.0	0.00	2.9	0.0	0.49	2.52	3.88	83.8	5.4	48.3	6.5	4.8
8.5	0.00	0.0	0.00	0.0	-0.1	-0.26	-1.70	3.20	89.9	3.2	58.0	25.3	0.0
2.0	3.69	24.3	0.10	5.1	0.6	1.09	13.22	3.46	54.7	3.7	28.6	12.9	4.6
6.8	0.87	4.1	0.14	8.2	1.7	1.39	10.88	4.59	64.8	4.5	24.6	6.7	8.5
5.4	1.55	10.6	0.34	6.9	14.1	1.06	13.56	8.16	77.8	3.7	81.5	47.3	6.1
6.1	1.05	6.7	0.30	4.4	329.2	1.04	13.58	3.32	58.8	1.8	19.8	23.5	5.3
3.9	1.54	13.5	0.29	2.7	0.1	0.15	1.65	2.92	85.8	2.2	6.6	17.4	4.9
7.7	0.02	0.1	0.24	4.1	0.1	0.53	6.58	3.72	82.1	5.1	68.3	14.0	3.2
6.0	2.39	6.0	0.93	10.0	0.9	2.93	19.12	4.62	35.9	4.4	96.7	23.3	7.9
6.4	0.44	2.8	-0.34	3.0	0.1	0.28	3.69	4.25	84.3	4.8	124.4	26.9	1.6
7.4	0.00	0.0	0.21	2.9	0.0	0.37	2.22	3.90	90.2	7.9	111.6	2.6	3.6
8.6	0.03	0.2	0.11	7.8	0.5	1.45	16.81	3.85	58.9	5.7	70.7	11.4	4.8
5.7	1.22	7.5	-0.05	4.3	0.9	0.61	6.85	2.56	70.1	6.8	80.2	7.8	5.3
8.1	0.37	1.8	0.14	6.8	0.5	1.99	21.20	4.01	67.3	3.0	34.4	18.2	4.4
6.0	0.16	1.6	0.01	2.7	0.1	0.51	5.97	4.26	83.4	3.1	46.2	21.0	0.0
3.2	1.51	9.6	0.97	3.4	0.2	0.39	3.85	3.71	73.2	1.5	19.6	25.5	4.2
9.3	0.05	0.2	-0.23	6.7	3.2	1.36	11.76	3.09	52.0	5.3	40.8	8.3	6.9
7.0	0.66	2.9	0.11	9.3	0.3	1.31	7.18	4.63	56.8	3.1	15.7	13.7	7.0
3.5	1.96	17.3	0.30	6.7	0.9	1.25	16.67	4.01	55.6	3.0	9.3	13.3	5.9
4.9	0.69	6.5	0.18	5.6	0.7	1.42	19.68	4.94	67.6	4.4	29.8	9.3	2.4
6.0	0.13	1.0	0.00	4.0	0.3	0.65	7.65	4.26	75.8	4.1	24.9	9.6	3.5
7.2	1.93	4.8	-0.13	3.7	1.0	1.07	14.07	3.04	79.8	3.6	12.7	10.9	5.0
9.4	0.00	0.0	0.00	2.5	0.3	0.44	4.41	1.91	64.3	7.0	85.3	7.4	1.4
8.1	0.00	0.0	0.00	2.2	0.2	0.21	1.94	2.92	74.8	1.3	4.9	24.9	1.0
8.0	0.14	1.2	0.01	9.6	6.6	1.68	23.97	3.69	48.3	6.3	43.7	2.8	6.8
5.0	0.72	5.1	0.19	6.6	3.1	1.21	13.22	4.01	63.6	5.8	50.1	7.9	5.8
6.2	0.43	3.1	0.03	6.8	1.4	1.12	13.75	4.35	69.2	4.9	25.9	4.3	4.3
4.5	1.95	11.6	0.29	6.5	0.8	1.14	9.33	4.52	58.6	2.2	33.4	25.5	7.3
7.0	0.36	3.8	0.00	4.7	0.9	0.66	8.67	3.41	68.9	3.0	10.2	13.3	4.5
8.7	0.11	0.8	-0.04	8.7	1.1	1.86	17.32	4.53	57.9	5.5	41.3	7.3	8.2
7.7	0.07	0.5	0.00	3.2	1.5	0.64	7.43	1.61	45.9	2.9	58.9	37.1	4.4
7.0	0.22	1.6	0.30	6.1	0.2	1.00	8.53	4.86	61.1	1.4	10.6	24.9	5.7
7.7	0.33	2.5	0.12	4.2	2.2	0.74	9.22	3.48	72.4	3.6	9.3	10.2	4.7
6.5	0.17	1.2	0.03	4.1	0.1	0.50	4.44	5.81	79.7	2.0	12.6	18.7	4.9
3.9	2.27	16.2	0.06	5.5	0.4	1.26	17.14	4.22	68.8	6.6	59.2	3.3	3.0
4.6	1.35	9.9	0.52	4.7	0.5	0.74	7.61	4.41	73.7	1.8	24.2	22.0	6.0
8.5	0.12	1.1	-0.01	3.4	1.7	0.54	6.22	3.27	76.1	4.9	45.2	11.6	5.3
6.7	0.21	1.7	-0.09	5.6	2.2	1.28	13.63	4.80	71.4	3.6	27.7	12.7	4.5
5.8	0.30	1.8	0.33	2.1	0.9	0.60	5.31	3.75	83.2	3.7	16.9	10.7	5.2
7.0	0.39	2.7	0.07	8.2	0.8	1.69	20.93	4.92	53.4	2.2	50.3	48.3	3.8
8.5	0.00	0.0	0.00	0.0	-1.2	-12.87	-28.67	3.25	460.5	8.2	141.6	5.4	0.0
8.9	0.00	0.0	0.00	0.0	-0.7	-5.04	-20.74	3.11	257.6	2.5	44.2	29.9	0.0
1.0	3.10	20.5	0.20	4.6	3.3	0.75	7.74	4.43	80.7	4.3	38.3	12.9	6.8
7.2	0.21	1.3	-0.03	5.6	1.7	1.13	12.66	4.05	62.3	3.4	33.9	15.7	4.0
6.7	0.56	4.2	0.02	4.2	0.7	0.92	10.33	4.44	69.3	1.4	24.3	28.1	5.4
6.7	0.00	0.0	0.00	0.0	-0.2	-6.21	-7.72	3.22	106.8	0.9	38.6	100.0	0.0
2.9	1.32	18.3	0.02	10.0	236.5	2.82	37.45	4.64	27.2	0.5	17.4	97.2	6.5
6.0	0.46	3.6	0.08	4.7	0.3	1.03	12.97	3.27	67.7	4.9	69.5	15.5	3.6
5.8	0.77	4.1	0.07	8.1	0.7	1.59	12.39	4.72	58.1	3.7	10.8	10.2	7.8
9.7	0.60	1.4	-0.02	0.1	-0.4	-1.03	-12.49	2.43	138.7	8.7	174.2	5.8	2.5
8.6	0.00	0.0	-0.14	6.9	0.3	1.04	10.06	3.54	63.1	5.7	52.7	7.9	6.3
8.9	0.12	0.5	0.00	6.3	0.3	1.09	9.35	4.06	57.2	4.6	30.0	8.3	5.5

| Name | City | State | Weiss Safety Rating | 2003 Weiss Safety Rating | 2002 Weiss Safety Rating | Total Assets ($Mil) | One Year Asset Growth | Asset Mix (As a % of Total Assets) | | | | Capital- ization Index | Leverage Ratio | Risk-based Capital Ratio |
								Comm- ercial Loans	Cons- umer Loans	Home Mort- gages	Secur- ities			
LEONARDVILLE ST BK	LEONARDVILLE	KS	D	D+	C	6.0	-4.42	0.7	0.9	0.0	62.4	10.0	34.1	189.8
▼ LEWISBURG BKG CO	LEWISBURG	KY	B+	A-	A-	59.6	-0.97	8.7	4.9	23.7	36.3	10.0	12.8	25.4
LEWISTON ST BK	LEWISTON	UT	C	C-	D+	135.7	10.21	16.6	6.1	6.5	13.9	3.1	8.4	10.1
LEWISTON STATE BK OF	PRESTON	ID	C	C-	D+	17.8	11.24	5.6	11.1	13.9	47.7	10.0	18.9	37.1
LEXINGTON BK FSB	LEXINGTON	KY	C-	C-	D+	148.3	9.47	18.0	4.4	29.1	1.4	2.7	7.4	9.7
▼ LEXINGTON ST BK	LEXINGTON	NC	B+	A-	A-	899.4	0.62	10.4	6.3	22.4	14.6	7.9	9.9	13.3
LIBERTY B&TC	TOCCOA	GA	C	C+	C+	24.3	-4.62	14.7	5.9	17.0	14.6	10.0	13.2	21.0
▼ LIBERTY B&TC	NEW ORLEANS	LA	C-	C	C-	336.1	20.26	3.2	8.5	15.8	52.2	5.0	7.0	16.0
LIBERTY BANK OF ARKANSAS	JONESBORO	AR	C+	C+	C+	810.3	140.52	15.6	3.5	13.6	21.2	5.9	8.3	11.7
LIBERTY BELL BK	CHERRY HILL	NJ	D	D	NR	56.4	N/A	2.9	0.2	1.6	49.6	10.0	17.8	42.5
LIBERTY BK	GERALDINE	AL	A-	A-	A-	80.4	7.23	2.2	14.3	19.1	38.2	10.0	12.6	24.7
▼ LIBERTY BK	S SAN FRANCISCO	CA	C+	B-	B	141.9	13.17	8.0	0.5	1.7	20.5	3.5	9.1	10.3
LIBERTY BK	MIDDLETOWN	CT	A+	A+	A+	2,184.0	3.19	13.5	6.4	28.3	15.3	10.0	13.7	19.0
▲ LIBERTY BK	ALTON	IL	B-	C+	C	151.6	-0.52	9.1	3.3	18.6	30.8	6.6	8.6	14.1
▲ LIBERTY BK	SPRINGFIELD	MO	B-	C+	C+	457.6	2.31	11.1	6.0	20.1	1.2	5.3	8.4	11.2
LIBERTY BK	N RICHLAND HILLS	TX	B	B-	C+	83.4	1.85	8.3	8.5	5.9	38.1	6.8	8.8	14.9
LIBERTY BK	SALT LAKE CITY	UT	C	C	C	9.7	23.42	0.0	0.4	28.7	2.6	10.0	26.8	41.0
LIBERTY BK FOR SVG	CHICAGO	IL	A-	A-	A-	770.4	-0.42	0.0	0.1	24.8	61.2	10.0	16.8	46.9
▲ LIBERTY BK FSB	W DES MOINES	IA	C-	C-	D	610.0	33.26	20.0	1.7	15.6	1.5	4.5	8.3	10.8
▼ LIBERTY BK NA	TWINSBURG	OH	C	B-	B-	59.1	13.45	27.6	2.7	12.5	6.9	10.0	11.4	15.8
LIBERTY BK OF NY	NEW YORK	NY	B-	B-	B-	67.2	-11.35	14.1	1.3	2.4	28.4	10.0	13.1	23.8
LIBERTY BK SSB	AUSTIN	TX	B	B	B-	175.1	0.56	23.5	2.4	5.3	0.1	6.9	8.9	13.9
LIBERTY FIRST BK	LIBERTY	MO	D	D	NR	22.3	N/A	4.1	1.7	7.0	46.9	10.0	25.2	56.9
▲ LIBERTY FS&LA	BALTIMORE	MD	B	B-	B	59.4	3.06	0.0	0.1	66.2	28.0	10.0	16.7	45.7
LIBERTY FSB	IRONTON	OH	B-	B-	B-	46.8	0.98	0.0	3.7	36.0	39.1	10.0	16.6	36.8
▲ LIBERTY FSB	ENID	OK	B-	C+	C+	129.9	8.30	0.1	1.3	47.4	14.0	10.0	11.1	18.1
LIBERTY NATIONAL BK	LAWTON	OK	C	C	C	110.6	22.10	10.6	10.0	21.7	5.2	3.5	7.4	10.3
LIBERTY NB	LONGWOOD	FL	D+	D+	C-	74.1	-6.37	26.3	0.7	1.7	11.2	7.7	9.5	13.8
LIBERTY NB	CONYERS	GA	C+	C+	C	178.8	27.35	6.1	1.3	2.9	9.0	4.2	8.1	10.6
LIBERTY NB	SIOUX CITY	IA	D	D	NR	64.5	45.74	31.5	1.5	13.9	14.3	10.0	20.2	20.6
▲ LIBERTY NB	ADA	OH	B	B-	C	153.9	0.91	20.9	5.0	16.6	17.2	8.9	10.3	15.1
▲ LIBERTY NB	GRANBURY	TX	C-	D+	C-	60.5	-10.04	9.0	2.5	13.9	12.3	9.3	10.5	14.4
LIBERTY NB IN PARIS	PARIS	TX	A+	A+	A+	225.5	-3.98	3.8	4.4	18.6	57.6	10.0	16.8	47.7
LIBERTY SA FSA	FORT SCOTT	KS	B-	B-	B-	39.6	-2.49	0.2	3.5	22.9	60.6	10.0	14.5	55.8
▲ LIBERTY ST BK	POWERS LAKE	ND	A-	B+	B+	29.8	9.85	6.3	6.9	3.5	39.1	10.0	16.0	25.8
▲ LIBERTY ST BK	LIBERTY	TN	B+	B	B	92.5	3.85	8.3	13.5	28.7	30.2	8.2	9.8	17.7
▼ LIBERTY SVGS BK FSB	WHITING	IN	C+	B-	C+	70.8	4.51	0.0	0.3	51.3	24.6	8.3	9.9	23.8
▲ LIBERTY SVGS BK FSB	ST CLOUD	MN	B	C+	D+	127.0	9.92	0.0	1.7	36.6	3.9	6.2	8.2	13.2
▲ LIBERTY SVGS BK FSB	LIBERTY	MO	C+	C	C	215.1	12.00	2.1	0.9	26.2	18.1	7.6	9.4	14.3
LIBERTY SVGS BK FSB	WILMINGTON	OH	C	C-	D+	1,853.4	4.86	1.1	1.3	34.3	34.0	5.1	7.1	14.6
▲ LIBERTY SVGS BK FSB	POTTSVILLE	PA	C+	C	C	25.7	1.97	0.2	4.1	69.0	4.9	10.0	11.1	23.4
LIBERTY T&SB	DURANT	IA	A-	A-	A-	112.5	-5.69	3.2	3.7	10.1	47.1	10.0	12.7	25.8
LIBERTYBANK	EUGENE	OR	B	B	NR	546.0	10.73	8.1	1.8	1.4	3.7	6.6	8.6	12.3
▼ LIBERTYVILLE B&TC	LIBERTYVILLE	IL	C+	B-	C+	639.6	18.32	20.4	1.9	6.4	16.7	4.2	9.2	10.6
▲ LIBERTYVILLE SVG BK	FAIRFIELD	IA	B-	C+	C+	112.4	5.06	8.4	5.6	16.9	22.3	10.0	11.0	17.3
LINCOLN BANK	PLAINFIELD	IN	B	B	B+	580.0	4.80	4.5	1.0	35.6	18.1	10.0	11.2	16.0
LINCOLN COUNTY BK	MERRILL	WI	C+	C+	C+	63.0	2.69	12.6	6.4	26.5	14.3	5.8	7.8	12.2
▲ LINCOLN FSB OF NEBRASKA	LINCOLN	NE	B-	C	C-	316.7	-7.64	0.4	0.1	39.9	0.1	9.8	10.9	16.7
▲ LINCOLN NB OF HODGENVILLE	HODGENVILLE	KY	A+	A	A	126.7	5.70	2.5	14.4	34.3	21.2	10.0	15.5	23.6
LINCOLN PARK S&LA	LINCOLN PARK	NJ	D+	D+	C-	78.8	14.61	0.0	0.5	54.5	25.5	4.8	6.8	13.0
LINCOLN PARK SVGS BK	CHICAGO	IL	C	C	C	245.2	4.47	0.8	0.6	31.3	16.0	6.1	8.1	12.5
LINCOLN ST BK	HANKINSON	ND	C-	C	B-	32.9	2.23	10.5	6.7	4.2	41.0	6.4	8.4	14.3
LINCOLN ST BK	MILWAUKEE	WI	B-	B-	B-	399.8	7.39	22.1	4.6	6.7	9.8	4.7	8.8	10.9
LINCOLN ST BK SB	ROCHELLE	IL	E-	E-	E-	40.8	4.70	16.7	17.8	17.3	1.3	0.2	4.3	6.5
▲ LINCOLN SVG BK	REINBECK	IA	C+	C	C	343.0	6.34	19.1	4.3	7.7	7.0	4.5	8.4	10.7
LINCOLN TRUST CO	ENGLEWOOD	CO	A-	A-	A-	358.7	7.89	0.0	0.0	0.0	82.1	10.0	11.1	36.9
LINDALE ST BK	LINDALE	TX	B-	B-	B	73.0	0.34	12.6	10.2	18.8	22.7	8.7	10.2	15.8
LINDELL B&TC	ST LOUIS	MO	A	A-	B+	275.4	1.18	11.5	1.2	14.7	30.2	10.0	12.0	21.9
▲ LINDEN ST BK	LINDEN	IN	B	B-	B-	54.9	7.76	3.2	6.1	16.7	28.7	10.0	12.3	23.6
LINN COUNTY ST BK	COGGON	IA	C+	C+	C+	21.9	-2.69	5.7	3.0	27.1	11.1	5.9	7.9	13.5
LINN ST BK	LINN	MO	A	A	A	188.1	-0.10	3.7	7.6	30.2	25.0	10.0	12.4	20.5
LINO LAKES ST BK	LINO LAKES	MN	C+	C	C-	85.4	11.80	22.8	2.1	3.7	7.5	5.4	10.2	11.3
LISCO ST BK	LISCO	NE	C+	C+	C+	16.0	4.39	7.4	0.6	2.9	13.2	5.8	8.9	11.6
LISLE SVGS BK	LISLE	IL	A-	A-	B+	493.1	12.15	0.0	0.0	72.9	8.0	10.0	15.9	27.1

Asset Quality Index	Non-Performing Loans as a % of Total Loans	Non-Performing Loans as a % of Capital	Net Charge-offs Avg Loans	Profitability Index	Net Income ($Mil)	Return on Assets (R.O.A.)	Return on Equity (R.O.E.)	Net Interest Spread	Overhead Efficiency Ratio	Liquidity Index	Liquidity Ratio	Hot Money Ratio	Stability Index
10.0	5.26	0.6	0.00	0.0	0.0	-0.95	-2.72	1.73	151.8	9.6	178.0	0.0	3.3
8.0	0.92	3.6	3.21	3.7	0.0	-0.02	-0.13	3.68	59.5	4.2	32.3	11.6	6.6
4.3	0.51	4.6	-0.01	6.6	0.8	1.20	14.25	4.41	57.0	3.4	11.0	11.4	4.4
8.4	0.00	0.0	-0.05	3.4	0.1	0.80	4.04	2.76	62.5	2.2	28.0	18.8	2.1
3.2	1.30	15.2	0.12	3.6	0.4	0.48	6.40	3.49	76.8	0.7	4.8	34.1	3.7
5.9	0.67	4.8	0.30	6.4	4.5	1.03	10.26	4.76	70.1	3.7	29.1	12.8	6.4
6.4	1.40	6.3	0.15	2.2	0.0	-0.04	-0.31	4.84	98.8	4.8	56.1	12.1	4.3
6.7	0.95	4.9	0.44	4.7	1.3	0.82	11.48	4.55	77.1	3.7	13.9	10.6	2.0
1.3	3.16	20.5	0.64	4.5	3.3	0.88	9.46	3.45	63.6	1.5	22.4	26.5	5.0
10.0	0.00	0.0	0.00	0.0	-1.1	-6.04	-24.19	-0.18	**,***.*	10.0	469.8	0.0	0.0
7.5	0.83	3.2	0.35	8.9	0.6	1.46	11.83	4.74	53.2	5.2	67.9	13.4	6.7
7.5	0.00	0.0	0.00	4.3	0.4	0.59	6.57	4.43	75.4	6.9	72.0	6.0	4.9
8.2	0.08	0.4	-0.01	7.8	15.9	1.49	10.46	3.73	57.8	6.8	83.7	10.3	10.0
4.5	1.79	11.3	0.10	6.8	0.8	1.03	11.70	3.43	53.3	4.7	46.2	13.3	4.0
7.8	0.10	0.9	0.15	5.6	2.4	1.06	12.44	3.49	56.1	4.7	38.8	11.2	4.4
8.2	0.00	0.0	0.01	7.5	0.7	1.65	17.16	5.30	71.0	3.3	15.8	12.6	6.3
7.7	0.00	0.0	-0.05	6.7	0.0	0.89	3.25	5.66	80.7	2.9	81.2	47.2	4.3
10.0	0.37	0.7	0.00	5.5	3.7	0.95	5.44	3.31	59.2	7.2	110.4	9.6	9.0
2.2	1.17	11.3	0.03	6.2	3.7	1.25	12.11	3.75	64.2	0.6	6.1	39.4	7.7
4.3	2.56	14.6	0.02	0.8	-0.2	-0.57	-4.73	3.41	118.2	6.1	79.2	10.8	5.9
6.1	2.74	8.8	1.19	3.0	0.1	0.25	1.93	4.24	87.8	3.7	55.7	19.0	5.1
7.4	0.34	2.3	0.02	5.7	0.9	0.94	10.76	3.71	67.1	4.7	76.8	18.5	5.5
9.5	0.00	0.0	0.00	0.0	-0.2	-1.86	-6.46	4.44	122.8	3.8	27.0	10.7	0.0
9.7	0.08	0.3	0.00	4.0	0.2	0.53	3.12	3.17	74.0	2.7	10.4	15.1	6.6
6.0	0.75	2.0	-0.26	5.0	0.2	0.91	5.05	3.84	65.7	3.7	23.1	11.1	6.4
8.9	0.13	0.9	0.01	4.2	0.4	0.70	6.22	2.86	70.5	3.8	1.7	8.3	6.2
2.7	1.41	13.7	0.55	7.2	0.8	1.61	21.18	5.71	64.2	2.6	30.9	19.1	5.1
2.1	2.38	16.2	0.74	1.4	0.0	0.03	0.26	3.64	96.5	5.9	55.1	7.0	2.8
6.0	0.42	3.7	0.01	6.5	0.9	1.09	13.63	3.95	59.2	5.4	59.0	12.6	4.6
6.2	1.41	5.1	0.03	0.0	-0.3	-1.00	-4.93	2.63	108.0	2.4	23.9	17.7	0.0
5.0	0.59	4.0	0.09	5.6	0.8	1.07	10.01	4.75	68.3	3.3	10.4	12.0	5.5
2.2	1.92	13.0	0.00	7.6	0.6	1.92	18.82	4.99	64.5	1.6	22.3	25.9	5.8
9.6	0.43	0.7	0.30	9.3	1.8	1.62	9.34	4.20	44.7	5.8	62.2	11.4	8.4
8.5	2.12	4.6	0.14	3.2	0.1	0.37	2.60	2.60	78.0	4.8	30.5	7.4	5.9
8.1	0.42	1.4	0.00	7.9	0.2	1.29	7.55	4.05	52.9	7.1	105.9	8.8	8.0
6.1	0.45	2.5	0.31	6.5	0.6	1.21	12.38	4.49	60.0	2.5	34.3	21.0	5.8
9.7	0.00	0.0	-0.01	3.4	0.1	0.32	3.10	2.53	78.9	2.7	57.7	34.0	4.9
7.1	0.16	1.2	0.01	9.2	1.5	2.46	27.27	3.87	56.2	1.7	35.5	40.4	5.4
7.7	0.39	2.9	0.01	4.0	0.7	0.70	7.20	3.27	69.5	1.5	21.2	26.6	4.8
5.6	1.21	9.9	0.41	3.3	5.9	0.65	8.79	2.56	77.5	3.2	56.1	34.8	4.1
6.2	1.39	9.2	-0.03	4.0	0.1	0.56	5.11	3.78	76.3	3.4	20.3	12.6	3.9
8.6	0.66	2.1	0.21	5.4	0.6	0.95	7.40	3.53	59.8	6.6	67.9	7.1	6.3
6.8	0.14	1.3	0.33	9.4	3.7	1.40	16.75	5.84	55.2	2.3	19.2	17.8	4.9
7.0	0.11	0.9	0.11	5.8	3.2	1.04	11.81	3.24	50.6	1.8	24.0	22.5	5.1
4.3	2.56	14.7	0.11	6.2	0.9	1.53	15.03	4.11	55.6	3.5	53.4	22.2	5.0
6.1	0.95	5.9	0.05	4.4	1.9	0.64	5.59	2.84	69.7	0.8	17.6	38.4	8.8
4.7	0.79	6.9	0.28	8.0	0.4	1.21	15.93	4.42	59.4	3.1	31.3	16.8	4.5
5.2	0.56	3.7	0.00	7.4	2.7	1.68	15.02	3.99	48.9	3.7	13.4	10.1	7.2
8.0	0.00	0.0	0.01	10.0	1.1	1.82	11.90	4.45	43.5	4.1	32.6	11.9	9.2
7.8	0.17	1.7	-0.03	4.6	0.3	0.70	10.12	3.12	65.3	3.4	38.6	17.7	2.7
5.5	0.84	6.3	0.01	2.9	0.5	0.44	4.72	3.38	85.4	4.2	50.6	16.7	5.3
5.2	1.26	7.6	-0.04	5.2	0.2	1.11	13.44	4.23	75.5	3.5	10.0	10.9	3.2
3.6	0.79	6.9	0.03	6.0	1.7	0.84	9.53	4.25	66.2	5.2	32.3	5.3	6.2
0.0	13.80	152.7	0.01	1.8	-1.1	-5.49	-88.01	4.40	101.1	2.2	28.7	20.9	1.5
4.2	0.50	3.5	0.18	4.8	1.2	0.68	6.31	4.26	72.6	3.7	14.3	10.2	5.8
8.8	0.00	0.0	0.00	8.6	2.1	1.14	10.60	4.06	68.3	4.8	N/A	1.6	5.0
6.1	1.15	6.4	0.14	5.1	0.4	1.02	10.12	3.63	62.2	3.8	37.1	15.1	4.9
7.9	0.00	0.0	-0.37	10.0	4.0	2.87	19.18	4.62	37.6	3.7	10.7	10.0	8.6
6.4	1.38	5.0	-0.24	4.5	0.3	0.90	7.23	4.19	68.4	5.2	62.9	12.9	5.1
1.5	6.88	24.2	0.15	5.0	0.1	0.95	6.07	4.41	66.8	8.1	109.9	1.2	6.5
6.5	0.85	4.2	0.15	9.2	1.4	1.47	11.35	4.40	55.0	6.0	52.7	7.6	8.2
7.1	0.00	0.0	0.12	5.6	0.4	0.85	8.50	4.61	63.0	2.6	28.2	18.2	4.9
8.2	0.00	0.0	0.09	7.9	0.1	1.76	18.14	4.17	58.8	4.2	71.3	17.3	5.0
5.7	2.14	11.9	0.49	9.7	4.1	1.71	11.10	3.99	31.6	2.1	9.1	17.9	9.4

Name	City	State	Weiss Safety Rating	2003 Weiss Safety Rating	2002 Weiss Safety Rating	Total Assets ($Mil)	One Year Asset Growth	Asset Mix (As a % of Total Assets)				Capital-ization Index	Leverage Ratio	Risk-based Capital Ratio
								Comm-ercial Loans	Cons-umer Loans	Home Mort-gages	Secur-ities			
LITCHFIELD BANCORP	LITCHFIELD	CT	C+	C+	C+	165.7	0.69	1.8	1.0	37.3	37.5	5.7	7.7	15.1
▼ LITCHFIELD NB	LITCHFIELD	IL	C	C+	C	75.8	-9.74	2.9	8.0	18.9	31.5	4.7	6.7	13.1
LITTLE BK	KINSTON	NC	B	B	B	138.9	18.30	35.1	3.3	7.9	10.5	10.0	11.8	15.5
LITTLE HORN ST BK	HARDIN	MT	C	C-	D	64.5	18.43	22.1	20.4	7.0	15.3	6.8	8.9	12.3
LITTLE RIVER BK	LEPANTO	AR	B	B	A-	52.1	-0.26	3.0	5.3	13.8	56.5	10.0	11.3	30.0
▲ LIVE OAK ST BK	DALLAS	TX	C-	D+	D-	71.9	22.47	8.4	2.3	18.0	2.8	4.2	8.5	10.6
LIVINGSTON ST BK	LIVINGSTON	WI	A-	A-	A-	99.3	7.37	9.1	4.5	23.4	20.0	10.0	11.3	17.1
▼ LLANO NB	LLANO	TX	B	B+	B+	68.8	8.55	7.1	8.0	9.5	19.1	10.0	11.0	18.1
LLEWELLYN-EDISON SVGS BK	W ORANGE	NJ	B-	B	B+	146.7	-4.08	0.8	0.1	17.6	57.3	10.0	12.8	45.0
▲ LOGAN B&TC	LOGAN	WV	B	B-	C+	183.1	6.17	8.2	8.5	28.7	31.6	7.0	9.0	18.4
▲ LOGAN COUNTY BK	SCRANTON	AR	A-	B+	B+	55.8	4.20	4.7	7.6	18.5	51.0	10.0	15.9	29.0
LOGAN COUNTY BK	LINCOLN	IL	B-	B-	C+	75.4	13.46	8.4	9.6	15.3	39.9	5.3	7.3	12.9
LOGANSPORT SVGS BK FSB	LOGANSPORT	IN	B	B-	B-	163.3	2.00	12.0	5.4	30.4	17.2	8.3	9.9	16.8
LONE STAR BK	MOULTON	TX	C-	C-	C-	95.3	-3.76	10.5	12.2	23.9	12.3	5.5	7.5	11.6
LONE STAR CAPITAL BK NA	SAN ANTONIO	TX	D+	D	D	79.6	-19.12	17.8	4.6	4.3	22.1	8.8	10.2	16.6
▲ LONE STAR NB	PHARR	TX	C+	C	C	968.0	33.69	13.5	4.7	5.7	33.7	5.8	7.8	12.9
▲ LONE STAR ST BK	LONE STAR	TX	C+	C	C-	25.9	-21.74	5.9	11.8	15.6	0.0	6.6	8.6	16.0
▼ LONG ISLAND COMMERCIAL	ISLANDIA	NY	C-	C	C-	545.1	8.95	16.6	0.2	0.4	49.5	3.4	5.4	10.8
LONGLEAF COMMUNITY BK	ROCKINGHAM	NC	D	D	NR	21.7	N/A	24.8	3.5	26.3	2.0	10.0	33.8	41.2
▲ LONGVIEW ST BK	LONGVIEW	IL	C+	C	C	37.6	5.88	14.9	3.7	16.8	14.6	3.3	6.6	10.1
LOOMIS FS&LA	CHICAGO	IL	B+	A-	A-	89.9	-0.84	0.0	0.1	40.6	54.3	10.0	14.5	48.7
▼ LORAIN NB	LORAIN	OH	B-	B	B	757.5	1.06	8.1	7.1	15.7	19.6	5.8	8.0	11.6
LORRAINE ST BK	LORRAINE	KS	C+	C+	C+	13.8	7.27	5.4	8.5	2.7	34.3	10.0	11.6	17.3
▲ LOS ALAMOS NB	LOS ALAMOS	NM	B+	B	B-	1,018.3	4.79	7.6	4.8	20.9	10.9	6.3	8.8	12.0
LOS ANGELES NB	BUENA PARK	CA	B+	B+	B+	197.8	9.21	7.0	0.1	2.5	12.9	7.3	9.6	12.8
LOS PADRES BK	SOLVANG	CA	C+	C+	C	1,044.3	21.51	5.3	0.1	10.7	41.0	3.9	6.1	10.4
LOTT ST BK	LOTT	TX	C-	C-	C-	35.9	7.54	4.4	6.6	46.5	14.2	6.1	8.1	14.1
LOUISVILLE CMNTY DEVELOP	LOUISVILLE	KY	D	D	D	35.4	-9.76	14.7	0.1	12.6	48.1	10.0	13.1	24.9
LOVELADY ST BK	LOVELADY	TX	C+	C+	C+	26.9	0.71	17.9	25.1	14.5	13.3	10.0	11.3	16.8
▲ LOWCOUNTRY NB	BEAUFORT	SC	B-	C+	C+	128.4	35.16	5.3	2.1	18.5	24.9	7.2	9.3	12.7
▲ LOWELL CO-OP BK	LOWELL	MA	B-	C+	C+	111.4	15.17	0.0	2.5	23.3	35.6	5.7	7.7	13.0
LOWELL FIVE CENTS SB	LOWELL	MA	B+	B+	B+	674.8	6.75	0.6	0.5	19.9	53.8	10.0	12.8	27.8
LOWRY ST BK	LOWRY	MN	B-	C+	C	25.4	4.62	12.6	14.5	17.0	6.6	8.9	10.7	14.1
LUANA SVG BK	LUANA	IA	A-	B+	B+	124.8	14.58	10.9	5.9	23.2	18.7	7.5	9.4	13.5
LUBBOCK NB	LUBBOCK	TX	B-	B-	B-	404.9	6.62	13.2	2.7	11.6	28.3	5.6	7.6	11.9
LUMBEE GUARANTY BK	PEMBROKE	NC	A-	B+	B+	158.8	3.23	4.4	10.4	22.0	17.0	10.0	11.7	17.8
LUMPKIN COUNTY BK	DAHLONEGA	GA	E-	E-	D+	68.9	-8.50	6.5	5.2	27.4	6.8	2.6	5.9	9.6
▲ LUSITANIA SVGS BK FSB	NEWARK	NJ	A	A-	A-	163.6	5.38	0.1	1.4	31.3	30.5	9.5	10.7	29.0
LUSK ST BK	LUSK	WY	C-	C-	D	31.7	2.95	9.0	7.0	6.7	5.2	3.4	7.8	10.2
▲ LUTHER BURBANK SVGS	SANTA ROSA	CA	A-	B+	B+	1,424.2	5.60	0.0	0.1	12.8	1.3	6.9	8.9	12.5
LUZERNE NB	LUZERNE	PA	C	C	C+	183.5	5.08	10.6	4.6	21.5	37.4	6.2	8.2	15.9
LUZO COMMUNITY BK	NEW BEDFORD	MA	C+	C+	C+	73.9	1.74	11.1	2.4	23.1	10.7	7.6	9.4	19.4
LYDIAN PRIVATE BANK	PALM BEACH	FL	C+	C+	C+	1,274.4	58.70	0.3	5.9	82.7	0.9	4.8	6.8	12.2
LYNDON ST BK	LYNDON	KS	C+	C	C	70.2	1.45	10.3	8.2	28.5	26.7	5.6	7.6	12.5
LYNDONVILLE SVG B&TC	LYNDONVILLE	VT	B-	C+	C	149.9	8.12	6.3	2.6	22.4	21.4	6.8	8.8	13.6
LYNNVILLE NB	LYNNVILLE	IN	B	B	B-	97.6	41.70	1.8	5.3	33.7	7.2	6.9	8.9	13.5
LYON COUNTY ST BK	EMPORIA	KS	B	B	B-	67.0	3.63	8.7	4.3	14.8	32.0	5.5	7.5	15.4
▲ LYONS FSA	LYONS	KS	C+	C-	C-	52.3	5.44	12.2	4.6	30.1	11.4	8.2	9.8	16.9
LYONS NB	LYONS	NY	C-	C-	C-	250.4	20.67	11.4	7.6	11.9	30.0	4.4	6.7	10.7
▲ LYONS ST BK	LYONS	KS	D-	E	E-	79.8	-1.33	11.1	4.6	8.1	19.5	5.5	7.6	11.3
LYTLE ST BK	LYTLE	TX	B+	B+	B+	64.0	-4.64	2.7	19.9	8.0	47.8	10.0	14.0	22.6
▼ M & I BK FSB	LAS VEGAS	NV	B-	B	B	1,225.3	28.38	1.3	23.2	25.3	7.5	7.0	10.7	12.5
▲ M C BANK & TRUST COMPANY	MORGAN CITY	LA	A-	A-	B	183.5	3.58	19.3	6.0	8.0	41.8	10.0	13.1	23.2
▼ M&I BK MAYVILLE	MAYVILLE	WI	B-	B	B	3.3	17.84	0.0	0.0	0.0	0.0	10.0	59.2	319.2
▼ M&I MARSHALL & ILSLEY BK	MILWAUKEE	WI	B-	B	B	32,042.1	7.63	18.6	2.8	18.5	15.9	4.1	6.1	10.6
M&T BK NA	OAKFIELD	NY	B	B-	B-	387.0	-28.71	0.0	0.0	55.0	24.4	10.0	19.0	28.8
MACATAWA BK	HOLLAND	MI	C+	C+	C+	1,525.8	21.39	18.3	2.2	11.8	8.4	3.2	7.9	10.1
MACHIAS SVGS BK	MACHIAS	ME	A-	B+	B+	461.8	17.18	17.5	2.2	16.6	9.7	10.0	13.0	15.6
MACKINAC SVGS BK FSB	BOYNTON BEACH	FL	C+	C+	C-	128.6	7.35	0.0	0.0	59.5	0.0	4.6	6.6	16.1
MACOMB CMNTY BK	CLINTON TWP	MI	C	C	C	91.4	-4.22	9.0	1.1	17.7	0.0	4.3	8.9	10.6
MACON B&TC	LAFAYETTE	TN	A-	A-	A-	214.7	1.82	3.7	9.9	18.4	42.4	9.7	10.8	21.1
▲ MACON BK	FRANKLIN	NC	B-	C+	C+	782.3	40.72	2.3	1.9	21.5	20.4	5.8	7.8	11.7
MACON-ATLANTA STATE	MACON	MO	A-	A-	A	133.8	-4.14	5.5	4.5	20.5	28.9	10.0	13.0	20.5
▼ MADISON B&TC	MADISON	IN	C	C+	B-	210.5	4.42	1.5	0.2	2.5	0.0	10.0	12.9	46.2

Asset Quality Index	Non-Performing Loans as a % of Total Loans	as a % of Capital	Net Charge-offs Avg Loans	Profitability Index	Net Income ($Mil)	Return on Assets (R.O.A.)	Return on Equity (R.O.E.)	Net Interest Spread	Overhead Efficiency Ratio	Liquidity Index	Liquidity Ratio	Hot Money Ratio	Stability Index
8.3	0.23	1.7	0.00	3.7	0.5	0.57	7.54	3.73	79.6	5.6	42.7	6.9	4.0
6.5	0.14	1.0	1.05	3.7	0.2	0.51	6.09	3.57	74.8	6.6	68.9	6.1	3.3
6.6	0.42	2.6	0.86	3.9	0.4	0.64	5.42	3.42	63.3	2.2	36.9	28.3	7.0
4.2	0.83	5.9	0.23	5.3	0.2	0.76	7.57	5.02	68.8	3.6	10.7	10.5	4.2
6.8	2.84	8.3	-0.73	5.9	0.5	1.89	16.84	3.26	47.9	4.2	105.5	30.8	5.2
7.4	0.00	0.0	0.00	5.6	0.6	1.74	20.91	4.76	58.4	4.1	41.7	15.0	0.0
7.4	0.13	0.8	0.09	8.5	0.7	1.43	12.86	3.55	40.6	4.6	65.7	16.2	6.9
5.5	1.61	7.9	0.09	5.5	0.3	0.95	8.71	4.56	71.0	5.0	70.5	15.1	5.8
8.3	1.39	3.9	0.00	3.2	0.2	0.21	1.66	2.63	94.2	1.8	3.9	18.7	6.7
5.0	1.19	6.7	0.05	6.5	0.9	1.01	11.35	3.77	61.4	4.9	40.7	10.5	6.2
8.7	0.95	2.2	-0.06	7.2	0.4	1.48	9.35	4.34	44.4	5.0	61.5	13.4	7.1
5.2	0.73	5.0	0.02	5.8	0.4	0.99	13.32	3.37	62.9	3.3	26.5	14.2	4.7
4.1	1.62	10.4	0.14	4.9	0.6	0.72	6.70	2.51	58.6	1.9	35.1	31.7	6.4
2.8	0.94	8.8	1.49	3.8	0.2	0.41	5.53	5.19	73.5	3.4	34.6	16.0	3.0
5.6	0.52	1.3	0.63	1.6	-0.1	-0.20	-1.13	3.79	98.4	3.0	48.2	23.8	4.8
4.3	1.26	9.8	0.30	6.6	5.2	1.12	15.92	3.81	52.5	0.7	13.4	40.7	3.7
8.0	0.01	0.0	0.00	7.2	0.2	1.78	20.49	4.19	59.7	6.3	106.0	12.9	3.6
9.1	0.02	0.2	0.91	2.5	0.3	0.11	1.98	3.58	74.3	4.8	12.3	3.2	3.3
8.6	0.00	0.0	0.00	0.0	-0.2	-2.41	-6.02	4.09	106.7	5.4	122.7	18.2	0.0
7.1	0.21	2.1	0.00	4.2	0.1	0.63	9.52	3.70	75.2	5.3	90.6	16.2	4.0
8.7	1.53	4.3	0.00	4.9	0.3	0.69	4.80	2.97	65.1	3.3	47.6	19.7	7.7
4.6	0.88	7.1	0.26	6.4	4.2	1.13	13.85	3.97	64.5	3.3	12.9	12.3	5.3
8.0	0.14	0.7	-0.08	5.7	0.1	1.06	9.24	4.39	64.2	3.6	37.7	13.8	4.5
6.9	0.45	3.7	0.07	8.6	6.4	1.26	15.41	4.09	52.2	4.3	64.6	21.2	7.2
7.3	0.00	0.0	0.00	6.9	1.0	1.04	10.99	3.61	52.7	2.9	60.1	44.0	5.7
8.5	0.00	0.0	-0.02	6.0	4.5	0.89	14.22	3.04	54.7	0.5	4.0	46.3	3.9
6.5	0.39	3.0	-0.01	4.2	0.1	0.44	5.45	3.75	83.6	6.5	87.3	9.7	3.3
2.7	6.92	21.3	3.62	0.0	-0.1	-0.38	-2.88	3.08	112.0	0.1	N/A	81.4	3.2
3.0	2.64	13.9	1.02	5.8	0.2	1.08	9.60	5.44	65.1	4.8	73.3	16.5	4.8
6.4	0.50	3.6	0.00	5.4	0.5	0.93	11.95	3.86	60.7	0.8	11.5	33.3	3.3
8.1	0.19	1.3	0.00	5.2	0.3	0.61	7.62	3.68	74.8	3.3	56.8	28.8	4.4
9.9	0.22	0.6	-0.03	4.4	2.8	0.85	6.40	3.45	70.5	8.3	172.4	8.6	8.5
5.8	0.00	0.0	0.12	10.0	0.4	2.84	27.03	5.03	42.8	3.8	29.9	12.5	5.0
8.2	0.11	0.8	-0.08	9.5	1.4	2.39	24.20	4.10	33.8	0.5	4.6	45.6	7.2
7.7	0.24	1.9	0.27	5.2	1.8	0.92	12.37	4.22	68.6	2.6	16.7	16.4	4.0
7.0	0.61	3.3	0.28	6.3	1.0	1.23	10.99	5.20	69.6	4.4	30.8	10.1	6.8
1.7	2.16	22.9	3.29	1.4	0.0	-0.02	-0.29	3.98	86.3	3.5	49.8	19.0	0.0
9.0	0.00	0.0	-0.01	7.4	0.9	1.07	10.03	3.43	46.3	3.0	27.1	16.0	6.9
4.8	0.45	4.1	0.24	9.7	0.4	2.27	27.29	5.20	55.3	4.7	46.1	12.7	4.5
6.3	0.17	1.6	-0.21	9.0	16.4	2.31	25.87	3.02	22.0	0.2	0.7	73.4	9.3
5.5	1.53	8.9	0.62	3.5	0.6	0.63	7.67	4.09	76.3	5.2	34.0	6.3	3.4
7.6	0.38	2.0	-0.21	3.6	0.2	0.47	4.94	3.27	77.0	7.5	156.7	11.3	4.0
7.4	0.02	0.3	0.05	5.3	4.6	0.75	13.25	2.67	64.5	0.6	2.5	34.5	3.5
6.1	0.36	2.7	0.03	8.3	0.7	2.09	24.39	5.33	59.1	2.3	17.2	17.6	5.0
6.9	0.64	4.7	0.17	4.2	0.7	0.88	10.28	4.07	73.4	4.7	31.0	8.2	4.5
6.9	0.41	3.4	-0.05	6.6	0.6	1.46	17.15	4.22	65.3	4.6	71.8	17.1	4.5
8.4	0.04	0.2	-0.06	5.2	0.4	1.26	15.54	4.23	79.1	4.5	43.7	13.2	5.8
6.4	0.24	1.6	0.00	6.4	0.5	1.98	20.91	2.72	57.8	2.9	41.6	22.4	4.3
4.9	0.98	8.7	0.03	4.1	0.9	0.79	11.82	4.19	73.2	1.9	14.9	19.5	2.5
1.7	2.74	20.9	-0.80	3.3	0.2	0.53	6.96	4.27	81.6	3.6	22.3	11.7	1.6
7.6	0.86	2.1	0.73	7.2	0.5	1.44	9.95	4.98	63.2	3.1	48.1	22.0	6.7
4.1	1.13	8.8	0.72	10.0	10.3	1.93	15.51	4.63	60.6	0.4	14.1	91.2	7.8
5.3	2.38	8.2	-0.01	5.5	1.0	1.04	7.65	4.27	67.1	3.0	42.4	22.4	7.2
10.0	0.00	0.0	0.00	3.8	0.0	0.46	0.77	0.91	97.7	10.0	590.3	0.0	5.1
5.7	0.48	4.4	0.04	8.6	225.2	1.45	19.06	3.69	47.8	2.9	32.8	23.0	7.4
8.4	1.14	4.0	0.27	7.2	5.2	2.44	11.69	1.87	59.7	6.1	683.8	26.2	6.3
7.3	0.21	1.7	0.14	5.8	6.9	0.95	10.11	3.70	56.2	1.5	10.9	23.4	7.1
6.1	0.74	4.3	0.28	6.9	3.2	1.44	10.65	4.44	61.3	1.7	11.0	20.5	7.5
7.0	0.36	3.2	0.00	6.7	0.3	0.41	6.25	2.77	83.8	3.2	42.3	19.5	3.7
0.7	2.36	20.6	0.12	4.2	0.3	0.70	7.12	4.42	65.2	1.1	9.2	28.5	4.9
7.5	0.39	1.6	0.07	5.7	1.1	1.07	9.53	4.13	66.3	2.3	35.3	25.1	7.1
6.5	0.58	5.2	0.04	5.3	3.0	0.83	10.95	3.46	61.9	2.3	38.9	29.5	4.3
5.3	2.54	11.4	0.07	6.2	0.8	1.11	8.81	3.67	60.7	4.2	19.6	8.1	7.5
10.0	0.77	0.6	0.54	1.1	-0.3	-0.28	-2.17	0.65	127.6	7.6	449.8	14.5	7.0

Name	City	State	Weiss Safety Rating	2003 Weiss Safety Rating	2002 Weiss Safety Rating	Total Assets ($Mil)	One Year Asset Growth	Asset Mix (As a % of Total Assets)				Capital-ization Index	Leverage Ratio	Risk-based Capital Ratio
								Comm-ercial Loans	Cons-umer Loans	Home Mort-gages	Secur-ities			
▲ MADISON BK	PALM HARBOR	FL	B-	C+	C-	225.8	14.69	5.3	0.6	9.7	8.4	4.9	9.2	11.0
▲ MADISON BK	RICHMOND	KY	C	C	C-	127.8	14.65	5.3	6.5	25.9	14.8	3.6	6.7	10.3
MADISON BK	BLUE BELL	PA	C	C	C-	215.3	-5.37	15.4	1.0	48.9	1.2	6.3	9.1	12.0
▲ MADISON BOHEMIAN SAVINGS	FOREST HILL	MD	C	C-	D+	195.3	5.37	0.1	2.2	55.4	22.3	8.6	10.1	20.8
MADISON COMMUNITY BK NA	ANDERSON	IN	B-	B-	B-	259.7	13.02	31.0	3.3	21.9	4.9	3.7	8.2	10.3
MADISON COUNTY BK	MADISON	MS	D-	D-	D	26.2	18.62	12.0	1.1	10.5	13.2	6.2	8.2	12.2
MADISON COUNTY BK	MADISON	NE	A	A	A-	119.1	11.10	7.4	2.5	30.3	16.5	10.0	12.2	19.0
▲ MADISON COUNTY	MADISON	FL	B	B-	B-	44.7	18.28	12.5	9.1	6.1	28.7	10.0	12.4	19.9
▲ MADISON SQUARE FSB	BALTIMORE	MD	C	C-	C-	114.8	4.46	0.3	7.9	54.4	27.1	8.6	10.1	20.9
MADISONVILLE ST BK	MADISONVILLE	TX	B	B	C+	217.9	35.82	1.7	3.1	5.0	15.4	5.1	10.0	11.1
MAGIC VALLEY BK	TWIN FALLS	ID	C+	C	C	78.1	13.64	31.5	6.5	8.1	9.0	6.2	9.4	11.9
MAGNOLIA ST BK	BAY SPRINGS	MS	A-	A-	A-	133.5	-0.03	2.3	10.7	13.7	42.3	8.6	10.1	19.6
▼ MAGYAR SVGS BK	NEW BRUNSWICK	NJ	C	C+	B-	277.2	2.30	4.7	9.2	39.6	27.7	6.3	8.3	14.5
MAHOPAC NB	MAHOPAC	NY	B	B	B	410.4	12.80	8.4	1.0	20.1	33.8	4.6	6.6	11.8
MAIN ST BK	NORTHVILLE	MI	D	NR	NR	17.1	N/A	3.7	0.1	6.0	25.9	10.0	57.7	93.7
MAIN ST NB	CLEVELAND	TX	D-	D-	D-	37.0	10.85	8.9	10.7	7.0	29.1	5.2	7.2	12.6
MAIN STREET BK	COVINGTON	GA	B-	B	A-	2,135.7	14.49	4.8	1.8	8.2	13.7	3.8	8.0	10.4
▲ MAIN STREET BK CORP	WHEELING	WV	C+	C-	D-	110.8	28.82	10.3	4.5	41.3	18.6	5.8	7.8	13.1
▲ MAINE B&TC	PORTLAND	ME	B-	B-	B	306.7	13.16	12.2	0.5	5.9	12.0	3.7	9.3	10.3
MAINLAND BK	TEXAS CITY	TX	C	C	C	59.6	-0.63	6.2	11.6	11.7	48.2	6.9	8.9	17.5
MAINSOURCE BK	GREENSBURG	IN	C-	C-	D+	813.2	-2.56	8.3	7.1	16.4	27.7	5.4	7.4	12.2
▲ MAINSTREET BK	FOREST LAKE	MN	C-	C+	C	272.0	30.01	16.8	2.0	6.0	7.9	3.1	7.8	10.0
▲ MAINSTREET BK	ASHLAND	MO	D-	E-	E-	27.5	26.11	27.8	7.2	18.4	15.5	3.2	6.9	10.1
MAINSTREET BK	HERNDON	VA	D	NR	NR	15.1	N/A	18.2	0.5	2.8	64.5	10.0	221.9	214.3
MAINSTREET COMMUNITY BK	DELAND	FL	D	D	NR	22.9	N/A	21.9	3.3	8.4	18.3	10.0	30.9	39.4
MAINSTREET SVGS BK FSB	HASTINGS	MI	D-	D-	E-	87.4	-1.75	1.8	5.9	61.5	4.5	3.7	5.7	10.9
MALAGA BANK FSB	PALOS VERDES EST	CA	B	B	B-	484.9	37.18	0.7	0.1	11.5	0.0	5.9	7.9	13.1
MALVERN FSB	PAOLI	PA	C+	C+	C+	469.2	0.34	3.9	0.3	49.0	17.9	5.6	7.6	12.9
▲ MALVERN NB	MALVERN	AR	B+	B	B	383.2	1.99	5.9	4.3	11.8	44.5	7.9	9.6	17.2
MALVERN T&SB	MALVERN	IA	B+	B+	B+	34.1	-1.06	4.3	6.0	12.0	26.2	10.0	17.5	25.2
▼ MANASQUAN SVG BK	WALL	NJ	A-	A	A	500.7	9.67	1.8	0.3	56.7	28.7	9.9	10.9	24.0
MANATEE RIVER COMMUNITY	PALMETTO	FL	C	C	C	108.4	27.45	2.9	5.4	48.5	0.0	5.3	7.3	12.1
MANCOS VALLEY BK	MANCOS	CO	D+	D+	D+	39.2	-0.12	7.4	1.9	4.9	26.0	4.8	6.8	13.5
MANHATTAN ST BK	MANHATTAN	MT	C	C-	C+	75.8	16.44	6.8	5.7	9.4	29.6	6.0	8.1	13.1
MANOR NB	MANOR	PA	C+	C+	C+	18.2	-6.37	0.1	0.4	26.3	56.4	10.0	13.0	39.8
▲ MANSFIELD CO-OP BK	MANSFIELD	MA	B	B-	B+	231.4	0.59	2.1	1.0	41.4	31.8	10.0	11.8	22.8
MANSFIELD ST BK	MANSFIELD	SD	C-	C-	C-	9.3	-6.29	2.9	1.3	0.9	47.0	10.0	20.0	40.3
▲ MANSON ST BK	MANSON	IA	C+	C+	C+	36.4	75.20	9.8	2.1	8.1	46.0	6.8	8.8	15.3
MANUFACTURERS & TRADERS	BUFFALO	NY	B-	B-	B-	51,497.4	3.44	15.9	11.3	8.2	14.9	4.4	6.6	10.7
MANUFACTURERS B&TC	FOREST CITY	IA	B	B	B	205.2	-2.56	7.3	5.7	17.1	24.7	6.1	8.1	12.1
MANUFACTURERS BK	LOS ANGELES	CA	B+	B+	B+	1,641.7	37.30	26.6	0.1	0.1	40.3	10.0	12.9	16.8
MAPLE BK	CHAMPLIN	MN	D	D	NR	16.5	N/A	28.0	6.4	11.6	4.0	10.0	22.4	26.4
MAPLE CITY SVGS BK FSB	HORNELL	NY	B-	B-	B-	43.8	0.28	0.0	1.8	65.5	15.9	10.0	13.7	23.5
MAQUOKETA ST BK	MAQUOKETA	IA	A-	A-	A-	225.2	4.13	11.7	5.0	8.8	31.6	9.9	10.9	16.5
MARATHON BK	WINCHESTER	VA	B-	B-	B-	341.1	37.12	9.2	6.5	23.0	4.5	4.1	8.2	10.5
▼ MARATHON NB-NY	NEW YORK CITY	NY	B-	B	B	674.8	116.46	13.0	0.3	3.9	29.6	3.7	5.7	10.6
MARATHON ST BK	MARATHON CITY	WI	B+	B+	A-	105.9	8.63	7.9	2.4	13.9	54.0	10.0	16.9	16.8
MARATHON SVGS BK	WAUSAU	WI	B-	B-	B-	144.2	-1.29	3.9	2.3	45.4	27.9	8.5	10.0	17.2
▼ MARBLEHEAD BK	LAKESIDE MARBLEH	OH	B-	B	B	25.6	-6.12	3.1	1.0	23.4	61.5	10.0	11.1	20.1
MARBLEHEAD SVGS BK	MARBLEHEAD	MA	C+	C+	C+	191.3	10.60	0.3	1.1	60.8	16.4	7.3	9.2	18.5
▼ MARCO COMMUNITY BK	MARCO ISLAND	FL	D-	D	NR	81.5	N/A	4.9	1.7	10.1	0.0	5.4	8.0	11.3
▼ MARFA NB	MARFA	TX	B-	B	B	34.6	0.43	2.7	8.5	12.9	52.8	10.0	11.9	26.7
MARIES COUNTY BK	VIENNA	MO	B-	B-	B-	228.1	6.71	4.4	7.2	23.4	24.2	6.6	8.7	13.0
▲ MARINE B&TC	VERO BEACH	FL	D-	E	E-	63.1	-0.46	8.7	1.5	10.0	24.5	10.0	11.1	18.0
MARINE BANK	SCOTTSDALE	AZ	D+	D+	C	95.9	-6.46	11.8	0.2	11.5	17.7	7.1	9.0	12.7
▲ MARINE BK	WAUWATOSA	WI	D-	D	C	333.1	-19.24	20.2	0.2	2.1	25.9	4.8	7.7	10.9
MARINE BK OF THE FLORIDA	MARATHON	FL	C	C	D+	190.7	33.65	5.0	1.3	22.8	10.4	2.9	6.9	9.9
▲ MARINE BK-SPRINGFIELD	SPRINGFIELD	IL	B+	B	B-	613.5	-4.04	12.9	1.1	10.3	16.3	5.9	8.3	11.7
MARINE TC OF CARTHAGE	CARTHAGE	IL	C+	C+	C+	82.2	5.94	9.7	8.7	22.8	8.2	5.6	8.2	11.4
▲ MARINERBANK	PORT TOWNSEND	WA	D+	D	D	31.6	88.26	8.1	1.3	9.9	4.7	10.0	20.7	25.3
▲ MARINERS BANK	EDGEWATER	NJ	C+	C-	D	91.3	40.53	13.7	0.5	7.4	8.3	7.4	9.3	13.1
MARION B&TC	MARION	AL	A	A	A-	111.0	9.32	3.9	10.5	15.1	38.6	10.0	13.3	19.8
▲ MARION BK	MARION	OH	C	C-	D+	117.2	9.22	10.1	19.4	17.9	23.9	6.7	8.8	13.5
▼ MARION CENTER NB	MARION CENTER	PA	C+	B-	B-	187.4	0.22	8.3	5.2	21.9	35.1	6.2	8.2	14.7

Asset Quality Index	Non-Performing Loans as a % of Total Loans	Non-Performing Loans as a % of Capital	Net Charge-offs Avg Loans	Profitability Index	Net Income ($Mil)	Return on Assets (R.O.A.)	Return on Equity (R.O.E.)	Net Interest Spread	Overhead Efficiency Ratio	Liquidity Index	Liquidity Ratio	Hot Money Ratio	Stability Index
7.4	0.10	0.9	0.01	6.7	1.1	1.06	11.87	4.08	61.1	2.7	28.4	17.9	5.1
7.8	0.07	0.7	0.01	4.2	0.4	0.60	9.19	4.18	76.7	1.4	13.3	25.2	3.1
4.0	1.19	11.9	0.21	3.8	0.5	0.51	5.79	4.97	88.5	1.7	12.0	20.4	4.3
8.4	0.30	2.0	0.03	2.8	0.3	0.29	2.91	2.38	77.3	1.8	20.7	21.5	5.2
4.3	0.72	7.4	0.85	9.8	2.0	1.59	19.60	4.55	47.9	2.1	22.9	19.4	6.4
8.3	0.00	0.0	0.27	0.0	-0.4	-2.68	-27.06	3.26	183.8	1.8	26.8	24.6	0.0
7.4	0.28	1.6	0.00	9.1	0.8	1.33	10.59	3.67	48.4	1.2	18.0	30.7	8.0
8.2	0.10	0.5	0.26	4.2	0.2	0.73	6.01	3.43	67.0	3.6	64.9	23.3	5.7
7.2	0.50	3.1	0.01	2.6	0.1	0.21	2.07	2.86	89.5	2.4	9.5	16.7	5.2
7.1	0.00	0.0	-0.09	9.8	1.6	1.59	16.14	4.93	35.8	1.1	8.0	28.0	7.1
7.5	0.20	1.6	-0.04	5.1	0.4	0.92	10.04	5.21	75.3	2.8	21.8	15.6	3.7
7.9	0.39	2.0	0.08	6.3	0.8	1.25	13.08	4.40	60.3	3.0	14.2	14.1	5.8
8.6	0.08	0.6	0.00	2.4	0.3	0.20	2.35	3.21	90.2	7.0	94.1	9.0	4.7
4.7	1.33	8.7	0.23	6.5	2.1	1.05	13.12	4.24	61.8	6.0	54.6	8.5	5.9
10.0	0.00	0.0	0.00	0.0	-0.4	-7.14	-11.36	1.27	291.8	9.6	202.6	2.5	0.0
4.6	1.33	9.0	0.21	2.6	0.0	0.03	0.39	4.82	88.2	4.6	44.7	12.8	1.7
4.0	0.46	2.8	0.12	9.3	15.5	1.52	12.57	4.61	53.2	1.8	13.8	20.8	9.6
5.5	0.62	5.5	-0.01	4.2	0.5	0.93	11.89	3.89	56.3	4.8	41.4	11.1	2.2
6.8	0.00	0.0	-0.07	5.5	1.5	0.97	6.39	4.81	74.4	5.3	23.7	1.1	7.9
4.9	0.96	4.8	1.82	5.0	0.4	1.25	14.23	4.76	71.6	3.6	20.1	11.4	3.3
1.5	3.35	21.4	0.14	9.1	6.3	1.56	16.89	4.10	60.6	3.4	17.3	12.1	5.9
3.6	0.82	7.7	0.14	7.0	2.3	1.72	19.94	5.12	61.3	2.9	17.7	14.7	4.8
6.3	0.27	2.1	0.03	3.1	0.1	0.49	5.46	4.26	80.9	1.6	7.3	20.5	2.3
9.7	0.00	0.0	0.00	0.0	-0.9	-13.59	-15.67	0.20	6,492.9	8.3	626.4	10.8	0.0
9.1	0.00	0.0	0.00	0.0	-0.6	-5.70	-17.18	2.97	233.9	2.5	54.3	30.0	0.0
7.2	0.18	2.2	-0.02	2.1	0.0	0.04	0.58	3.86	95.1	2.2	15.3	18.2	2.3
7.1	0.00	0.0	0.00	9.2	2.7	1.21	14.86	3.17	37.8	1.2	29.9	54.1	5.0
4.8	0.68	6.1	0.02	3.5	0.9	0.37	4.91	2.10	75.0	1.4	9.6	24.5	4.4
6.6	0.62	3.1	0.17	6.6	2.2	1.14	12.09	4.06	57.6	3.1	20.5	14.3	5.5
7.6	1.19	3.5	-0.03	5.4	0.2	1.00	5.53	4.07	72.2	7.4	87.7	3.7	6.7
9.9	0.09	0.5	0.00	6.3	2.3	0.95	8.54	3.36	50.8	6.1	58.3	8.7	7.3
7.4	0.39	3.9	0.00	4.1	0.4	0.81	11.14	3.12	73.7	1.7	28.7	27.8	3.3
2.2	4.05	27.7	-0.04	4.2	0.3	1.33	18.30	3.69	77.8	4.4	86.9	20.1	2.8
4.7	1.67	11.1	0.40	7.2	0.6	1.68	21.17	5.29	64.5	4.4	31.9	10.3	3.4
10.0	0.00	0.0	0.00	2.8	0.0	0.30	2.40	4.00	90.9	5.4	38.7	3.7	4.2
9.3	0.00	0.0	0.01	4.2	0.7	0.60	5.13	3.32	70.3	3.7	16.5	10.4	6.5
8.9	0.00	0.0	0.12	3.7	0.1	1.39	7.01	3.41	58.0	3.0	34.3	16.1	3.4
7.7	0.37	1.5	0.00	5.3	0.2	0.94	8.65	3.58	65.1	5.7	41.1	5.6	5.0
4.7	0.50	2.7	0.21	8.8	354.4	1.41	11.23	4.02	55.1	4.5	24.4	9.4	10.0
6.2	0.55	3.5	0.13	6.7	1.5	1.48	15.60	3.96	62.3	4.3	30.9	10.6	6.9
7.4	0.77	3.0	0.72	4.7	9.6	1.28	9.62	3.27	59.4	5.4	219.6	42.1	8.3
7.7	0.00	0.0	0.02	0.0	-0.2	-2.98	-11.93	4.12	151.5	1.0	31.1	41.7	0.0
4.6	2.50	12.9	0.00	4.7	0.2	0.77	5.40	4.45	73.0	3.5	8.7	10.7	6.0
7.5	0.34	1.8	-0.01	7.1	1.6	1.45	12.88	3.91	54.5	3.6	21.8	11.6	7.7
7.3	0.10	0.9	0.05	8.0	2.0	1.28	16.96	5.01	59.6	4.0	40.9	15.0	4.8
5.1	0.79	4.4	0.22	8.2	3.3	1.17	12.77	4.48	55.0	4.5	45.4	13.8	6.0
9.3	0.06	0.1	0.08	4.9	0.4	0.86	5.09	2.67	46.7	5.4	128.7	21.0	8.5
5.7	0.91	5.4	0.59	4.4	0.6	0.78	7.99	3.15	58.4	3.8	20.1	10.3	5.3
10.0	0.00	0.0	0.00	4.2	0.1	0.88	8.12	3.85	79.7	5.1	19.4	1.8	4.6
9.5	0.16	1.3	0.03	3.3	0.3	0.33	3.61	3.63	91.2	4.6	14.8	4.5	4.5
9.1	0.00	0.0	0.00	0.0	-0.3	-1.08	-10.02	2.66	97.1	3.1	58.9	27.3	0.0
4.5	4.70	14.2	-0.50	6.8	0.3	1.45	12.32	4.69	72.0	3.9	15.3	9.6	7.0
7.4	0.37	2.8	0.09	6.6	1.5	1.30	14.94	4.17	56.4	3.8	10.6	9.2	5.3
6.6	0.52	2.3	2.54	0.0	-0.2	-0.61	-5.53	2.55	137.1	1.6	19.6	24.2	2.6
4.5	0.73	4.9	0.00	3.2	0.3	0.62	6.48	3.64	79.1	0.7	18.0	60.1	1.0
1.3	4.66	29.9	1.41	1.5	0.4	0.19	2.32	2.59	78.3	3.0	49.8	26.7	2.6
8.2	0.17	1.9	0.05	4.5	0.7	0.73	10.21	4.13	70.5	1.7	19.9	23.3	3.3
6.5	0.30	2.5	0.47	8.4	5.6	1.78	21.75	3.54	49.1	4.5	37.5	11.5	6.7
4.8	0.47	4.2	-0.03	9.0	0.6	1.39	17.09	4.28	51.8	2.9	21.0	15.1	6.4
7.5	0.00	0.0	0.00	1.1	0.1	0.32	1.64	4.63	87.8	6.7	76.4	6.2	0.0
7.3	0.00	0.0	0.13	5.1	0.8	1.78	20.15	4.37	49.6	1.8	30.3	28.1	2.5
7.1	0.06	0.3	0.47	9.1	1.2	2.18	16.18	4.89	43.8	1.2	9.3	26.5	8.0
4.1	0.69	5.0	0.34	4.3	0.4	0.62	7.28	4.21	74.8	2.2	17.4	18.4	2.6
3.4	2.82	18.7	0.84	4.7	0.5	0.58	6.83	4.08	61.7	3.7	29.6	12.9	5.7

Name	City	State	Weiss Safety Rating	2003 Weiss Safety Rating	2002 Weiss Safety Rating	Total Assets ($Mil)	One Year Asset Growth	Asset Mix (As a % of Total Assets) Commercial Loans	Consumer Loans	Home Mortgages	Securities	Capitalization Index	Leverage Ratio	Risk-based Capital Ratio
▲ MARION COUNTY SB	SALEM	IL	C	C-	C	79.4	-1.78	1.0	12.1	38.4	25.8	7.3	9.2	20.4
MARION COUNTY ST BK	PELLA	IA	B+	B	C+	147.0	3.07	12.3	2.1	13.3	34.2	7.3	9.2	14.3
MARION NB	MARION	KS	D+	D+	D+	21.1	4.32	4.9	2.7	14.8	48.1	6.3	8.3	21.9
MARION ST BK	MARION	LA	C	C-	C-	75.1	1.69	6.8	15.8	16.5	32.2	7.7	9.4	15.5
MARION ST BK	MARION	TX	B+	B+	B+	41.0	3.24	7.5	11.0	3.7	44.4	10.0	13.8	30.4
MARITIME SVGS BK	W ALLIS	WI	C+	C+	C	298.9	9.82	0.2	0.2	46.9	5.7	7.2	9.3	12.6
MARKESAN ST BK	MARKESAN	WI	A-	A-	A-	70.1	1.97	5.6	4.7	9.0	29.9	10.0	15.5	16.4
▼ MARKLEBANK	MARKLE	IN	B+	A-	B+	219.3	14.07	6.4	12.5	23.9	16.1	8.3	9.9	13.6
▼ MARLBOROUGH CO-OP BK	MARLBOROUGH	MA	C+	B-	B	83.8	4.55	1.4	2.5	37.1	36.0	10.0	11.0	19.1
MARLBOROUGH SVGS BK	MARLBOROUGH	MA	B+	B+	B+	265.2	3.56	0.5	1.6	45.9	37.4	10.0	12.0	23.3
MAROA FORSYTH	MAROA	IL	B+	B	B+	22.7	13.95	10.4	5.4	10.4	31.9	10.0	11.4	19.2
MARQUETTE BK	CHICAGO	IL	C+	C+	B-	1,383.1	4.87	4.0	0.8	19.6	34.3	3.7	5.7	10.7
▼ MARQUETTE FARMERS ST BK	MARQUETTE	KS	C-	C+	C+	22.7	5.25	6.0	8.3	19.6	18.3	10.0	14.8	22.6
MARQUETTE SVGS BK	ERIE	PA	A	A	A	475.1	-0.46	0.0	0.7	39.3	49.8	10.0	15.7	33.2
MARS NB	MARS	PA	B	B	A-	284.2	3.81	8.8	3.1	21.5	39.3	9.4	10.6	19.3
MARSEILLES BK	MARSEILLES	IL	C+	C	C	30.5	2.94	1.6	13.1	33.3	35.7	5.9	7.9	15.8
MARSHALL BK NA	HALLOCK	MN	B+	B+	B+	68.4	24.93	26.3	2.9	5.4	18.6	10.0	12.3	16.7
MARSHALL COUNTY ST BK	VARNA	IL	D	C-	C	19.9	5.19	5.7	6.1	10.3	54.7	9.3	10.5	22.5
MARSHALL COUNTY ST BK	NEWFOLDEN	MN	B	B	B	21.2	3.11	10.7	9.9	9.9	30.9	10.0	25.0	53.5
MARSHALL NB&TC	MARSHALL	VA	A-	A-	A	145.8	11.26	10.7	2.7	29.6	6.2	6.3	8.3	16.5
MARSHFIELD SVGS BK	MARSHFIELD	WI	A	A	A	143.5	9.86	10.0	9.2	53.2	4.2	10.0	17.9	24.3
MARTHAS VINEYARD CO-OP	VINEYARD HAVEN	MA	B-	B-	C	124.0	15.62	1.0	0.8	70.0	2.7	6.0	8.0	13.9
MARTINSBURG B&TC	MEXICO	MO	B	B	C	135.4	10.54	5.8	2.7	19.4	22.5	8.9	10.3	15.0
MARYLAND B&TC NA	LEXINGTON PARK	MD	C+	C+	B-	306.4	3.18	12.2	2.6	21.5	29.3	6.0	8.0	14.0
MARYLAND PERMANENT B&TC	OWINGS MILLS	MD	D	D-	E	75.3	-11.31	17.8	1.4	6.5	10.6	8.2	10.0	13.5
▲ MASCOMA SVGS BK	LEBANON	NH	B	B-	B-	707.9	8.39	6.0	4.7	44.8	13.1	6.1	8.1	13.9
MASON CITY NB	MASON CITY	IL	A-	A-	A-	59.6	-0.39	1.2	3.3	20.6	48.2	10.0	14.5	32.0
MASON NB	MASON	TX	C	B-	B-	61.7	12.25	6.3	8.7	13.2	27.7	10.0	13.5	21.4
MASON ST BK	MASON	MI	A	A+	A+	126.0	2.14	3.1	0.7	66.8	6.7	10.0	11.1	19.5
MASPETH FS&LA	MASPETH	NY	A+	A+	A+	1,313.7	2.97	0.0	0.0	54.5	10.2	10.0	21.7	37.5
MASSBANK	READING	MA	B	B	B+	980.2	-2.84	0.0	0.3	23.8	48.0	9.2	10.4	38.6
MASSENA S&LA	MASSENA	NY	B	B	B-	91.0	18.64	0.0	11.2	72.2	0.0	8.3	9.8	17.0
▲ MASSMUTUAL TRUST	HARTFORD	CT	C-	D	D	13.2	1.63	0.0	0.0	0.0	84.7	10.0	90.9	3,159.0
MATRIX CAPITAL BANK	DENVER	CO	D	C-	D-	1,656.5	-0.72	8.5	0.0	49.2	12.3	4.6	6.6	13.7
▼ MAUCH CHUNK TRUST CO	JIM THORPE	PA	B-	B	B	282.2	13.11	2.7	2.2	20.3	54.6	5.6	7.6	14.6
MAXWELL ST BK	MAXWELL	IA	A-	A-	B+	19.5	2.92	2.4	2.6	13.8	46.1	8.3	9.9	17.7
MAY NB OHIO	LORAIN	OH	B+	B+	B+	30.3	6.82	0.0	0.0	0.0	90.3	10.0	100.1	368.2
MAYFLOWER CO-OP BK	MIDDLEBORO	MA	B	B	B	214.1	1.95	2.4	1.3	26.1	35.4	6.4	8.4	14.7
MAYNARD SVG BK	MAYNARD	IA	A-	A-	A-	38.8	0.74	5.1	4.8	12.6	47.6	10.0	12.1	21.9
MAYVILLE ST BK	MAYVILLE	MI	B	B	B	82.6	-3.39	3.8	3.6	55.4	19.4	7.5	9.4	18.3
MAYVILLE SVGS BK	MAYVILLE	WI	C+	C	C-	47.0	-0.91	1.4	3.6	44.2	0.2	7.1	9.1	22.3
MAZON ST BK	MAZON	IL	C	C	C	75.9	-2.16	3.6	3.2	21.8	27.2	6.8	8.8	14.6
MB FINANCIAL BK NA	CHICAGO	IL	B+	B+	B	4,169.2	5.27	19.9	0.4	10.5	24.1	5.9	7.9	11.7
▲ MBANK	GRESHAM	OR	B+	B-	B-	184.4	6.00	14.0	2.2	8.3	10.3	9.4	11.7	14.5
MBNA AMERICA BK NA	WILMINGTON	DE	B	B	B	57,380.0	4.98	0.0	32.9	0.0	9.2	10.0	19.5	22.6
▲ MBNA AMERICA DE NA	WILMINGTON	DE	A-	B+	B	3,328.1	66.79	72.3	6.8	1.5	5.6	10.0	16.5	18.6
MCALLEN NB	MCALLEN	TX	B	B	C+	146.9	19.24	10.8	4.0	8.0	16.5	7.1	9.1	12.7
MCCLAIN BK NA	PURCELL	OK	D+	D+	C-	143.7	-0.63	4.7	8.9	19.5	21.1	9.0	10.3	16.2
MCCLAVE ST BK	MC CLAVE	CO	D-	E+	E-	15.7	1.50	6.1	8.9	6.7	19.0	8.3	9.9	14.1
MCCOOK NB	MC COOK	NE	A-	A-	A	200.4	17.59	5.3	3.8	6.1	29.7	10.0	14.7	19.8
▲ MCCURTAIN COUNTY NB	BROKEN BOW	OK	D+	D	D-	92.0	6.63	13.0	10.7	21.1	21.6	5.5	7.5	13.9
▲ MCFARLAND ST BK	MC FARLAND	WI	B-	B-	B-	158.0	15.05	10.1	2.2	13.4	3.2	3.9	9.6	10.4
MCGEHEE BK	MC GEHEE	AR	A	A	A	109.7	15.71	12.7	1.7	5.0	36.7	9.2	13.7	14.3
MCHENRY SVGS BK	MCHENRY	IL	D+	D+	D-	214.9	7.86	5.1	14.2	49.8	7.3	4.7	6.7	11.0
▲ MCINTOSH COMMERCIAL BK	CARROLLTON	GA	C-	D	D	125.6	57.43	16.8	2.0	14.1	6.6	6.7	9.9	12.3
▲ MCINTOSH COUNTY BK	ASHLEY	ND	B	B-	C+	58.1	1.61	6.8	3.9	3.1	27.7	9.6	10.7	16.7
MCINTOSH ST BK	JACKSON	GA	B+	B+	B+	300.6	16.82	8.9	4.7	16.6	16.2	7.0	9.1	12.5
▲ MCKENZIE BKG CO	MC KENZIE	TN	B+	B	B-	85.7	-4.55	4.0	7.3	24.8	9.0	9.3	10.5	25.8
▲ MCKENZIE COUNTY BK	WATFORD CITY	ND	A-	B+	B	31.8	6.09	7.8	10.5	11.9	31.0	10.0	11.2	15.5
MCM SVGS BANK FSB	HANNIBAL	MO	D-	D-	D-	78.0	22.53	1.8	5.0	29.2	46.8	4.4	6.4	15.1
▲ MCMULLEN BK	TILDEN	TX	E+	E-	E-	37.6	-4.44	7.1	3.1	6.0	41.3	6.6	8.6	16.4
MCNB B&TC	WELCH	WV	C+	C+	A-	235.4	3.62	1.0	4.3	14.2	43.9	8.4	10.0	17.6
▼ MCVILLE ST BK	MCVILLE	ND	D	D+	C-	22.2	20.13	13.4	4.8	5.0	22.7	4.7	8.2	10.9
MEADE COUNTY BK	BRANDENBURG	KY	B	B	B	100.9	-1.71	0.0	5.3	37.4	37.5	6.5	8.5	18.2

Asset Quality Index	Non-Performing Loans as a % of Total Loans	Non-Performing Loans as a % of Capital	Net Charge-offs Avg Loans	Profitability Index	Net Income ($Mil)	Return on Assets (R.O.A.)	Return on Equity (R.O.E.)	Net Interest Spread	Overhead Efficiency Ratio	Liquidity Index	Liquidity Ratio	Hot Money Ratio	Stability Index
3.0	2.71	15.2	0.21	4.7	0.3	0.75	7.97	3.23	62.2	7.3	149.5	11.8	4.5
8.3	0.22	1.4	0.02	8.2	1.5	2.06	22.15	3.35	41.1	1.9	27.7	24.5	6.0
7.2	0.47	1.2	0.00	4.0	0.1	0.53	4.14	3.60	78.0	6.2	74.7	7.5	3.7
4.1	1.30	7.8	0.32	3.9	0.3	0.74	8.29	4.02	74.0	5.0	143.6	27.8	3.2
8.4	0.00	0.0	0.46	6.6	0.2	1.08	7.83	4.05	58.9	7.1	90.6	6.1	6.7
7.7	0.07	0.6	0.07	3.6	0.9	0.63	6.82	2.94	73.7	3.6	28.5	13.2	4.7
6.2	1.52	5.6	0.28	9.8	0.6	1.57	9.93	4.78	51.2	4.6	30.3	8.2	8.3
5.4	0.52	4.0	0.13	8.0	1.4	1.27	12.62	4.42	58.1	1.1	6.2	27.9	6.4
9.7	0.00	0.0	-0.01	2.8	0.1	0.21	1.88	2.76	101.8	3.6	57.0	20.0	5.9
9.8	0.49	2.2	0.00	5.0	1.0	0.80	6.74	3.46	64.4	5.3	47.0	10.2	7.0
3.7	3.93	16.8	0.02	4.3	0.1	0.86	7.30	4.99	84.6	5.3	45.2	6.7	5.9
6.8	0.93	7.8	0.06	3.9	4.4	0.64	10.55	3.40	78.1	5.7	64.9	13.1	4.4
1.6	8.92	37.9	0.00	5.3	0.1	1.07	7.24	3.89	62.3	4.6	70.0	15.4	5.2
10.0	0.27	0.7	0.01	6.1	2.3	0.95	6.11	2.70	42.7	8.8	687.4	7.8	8.6
6.9	0.79	3.5	0.03	4.6	1.1	0.79	7.25	3.60	71.2	6.3	47.7	3.7	6.5
7.1	0.55	3.6	0.28	9.4	0.4	2.51	28.72	5.27	53.4	4.0	25.1	9.9	4.5
5.0	1.74	7.6	0.02	6.6	0.5	1.65	10.20	5.16	55.4	3.4	23.8	13.1	7.1
2.4	6.09	23.7	-0.02	4.2	0.1	1.36	13.29	3.97	64.0	2.2	10.5	17.5	1.2
6.2	5.03	7.9	0.02	9.7	0.2	2.23	8.54	3.61	40.8	8.6	195.5	8.5	7.1
6.8	0.00	0.0	-0.04	8.7	0.9	1.28	8.18	5.03	60.9	3.9	19.1	9.9	8.9
7.2	0.75	3.4	0.20	9.4	1.0	1.45	8.23	4.25	45.9	3.4	25.3	13.2	9.0
9.5	0.00	0.1	0.01	5.5	0.4	0.69	8.79	4.31	70.1	3.7	16.2	10.6	4.0
7.9	0.26	1.7	0.14	5.6	0.8	1.17	11.47	4.38	65.2	3.6	28.7	13.4	4.9
4.8	1.73	12.1	-0.13	4.0	1.0	0.69	8.72	4.35	78.0	6.5	81.6	10.0	4.4
2.3	2.55	13.2	-0.02	1.2	0.0	0.01	0.11	4.05	99.8	6.4	117.4	13.5	2.7
6.8	0.21	1.8	-0.03	4.9	2.8	0.80	9.12	3.98	73.1	1.4	14.6	26.4	6.0
8.9	0.76	2.3	0.22	5.3	0.3	1.09	7.54	3.23	53.4	3.6	35.1	15.3	7.4
2.8	3.85	17.2	0.04	9.6	0.7	2.28	16.74	5.19	55.4	3.7	25.7	11.9	7.9
9.4	0.05	0.3	0.00	7.5	0.8	1.18	10.75	3.35	53.9	4.5	22.5	6.2	8.1
8.8	0.51	1.8	0.00	9.8	10.5	1.60	7.46	4.61	32.9	2.7	30.7	24.6	10.0
10.0	0.15	0.4	0.00	4.2	3.7	0.74	7.00	2.15	56.8	9.2	411.6	5.6	7.8
6.6	0.23	2.2	0.09	6.6	0.5	1.16	11.53	3.93	50.4	1.0	7.4	29.4	5.3
8.1	0.00	0.0	0.00	4.3	0.1	1.54	1.69	3.70	80.4	4.5	173.2	100.0	0.0
0.7	3.31	35.4	0.14	4.0	6.6	0.79	12.08	3.01	64.6	0.5	10.5	74.1	3.9
7.0	0.75	3.7	0.27	4.3	1.3	1.01	12.06	2.86	63.4	3.2	15.4	13.1	4.4
8.7	0.00	0.0	0.00	9.8	0.2	2.04	17.82	4.60	42.6	3.2	40.4	16.8	8.4
10.0	0.00	0.0	0.00	9.5	15.2	95.17	96.84	0.73	47.9	0.0	N/A	100.0	3.0
9.2	0.00	0.0	-0.01	5.1	0.9	0.85	10.12	3.69	68.9	3.1	14.0	13.4	4.9
6.4	1.98	7.1	0.11	8.4	0.3	1.68	13.49	4.30	46.4	4.2	15.3	7.7	7.5
7.0	0.66	4.5	0.03	6.0	0.4	1.04	10.94	3.74	64.1	6.7	72.1	5.9	5.5
9.5	0.14	0.8	0.24	6.9	0.3	1.10	12.54	5.85	51.2	3.1	32.9	17.3	4.0
7.0	0.66	3.3	-0.06	3.2	0.2	0.48	5.54	4.30	86.2	5.7	50.9	7.8	3.4
6.0	0.86	5.4	0.24	8.1	29.6	1.44	14.00	3.84	60.3	2.0	15.8	19.2	7.7
6.1	0.43	2.7	0.02	7.4	0.9	0.98	8.38	5.14	73.5	3.3	29.6	15.1	6.7
4.9	1.80	4.1	4.51	10.0	1,104.7	3.86	19.77	5.85	54.8	4.4	121.3	34.9	9.3
5.9	0.95	3.9	1.75	10.0	44.3	3.10	15.84	5.02	51.6	0.9	21.8	65.1	8.6
4.6	1.11	8.2	0.03	5.3	0.6	0.92	9.93	4.59	75.4	0.8	14.4	34.7	5.0
1.8	3.62	20.3	0.87	4.2	0.2	0.32	3.04	4.87	82.8	4.3	29.0	9.9	5.2
0.0	16.31	90.5	2.33	2.4	0.1	0.76	7.21	5.58	69.1	1.7	20.8	22.5	0.7
6.3	0.58	2.3	0.30	6.9	1.3	1.32	8.80	3.93	53.9	3.2	20.8	13.5	8.4
3.8	0.90	6.2	0.24	4.3	0.4	0.83	10.97	3.59	63.7	2.2	36.2	27.7	1.1
7.2	0.00	0.0	0.01	9.1	1.1	1.47	15.75	4.04	49.6	1.5	5.5	21.7	5.9
8.8	0.00	0.0	-0.10	7.0	0.6	1.10	8.16	3.23	55.6	4.1	73.5	24.3	8.5
4.8	0.45	5.2	0.02	3.3	0.6	0.57	8.49	3.83	80.6	1.9	20.1	20.1	2.2
7.2	0.09	0.7	0.00	2.7	0.3	0.59	5.85	3.55	63.4	0.5	9.7	61.8	1.5
4.6	1.36	6.9	-0.11	8.1	0.5	1.78	17.26	4.35	54.3	5.2	23.2	1.8	7.4
5.6	0.66	4.9	0.01	7.7	1.9	1.29	13.97	4.36	61.0	2.2	30.6	22.9	5.7
6.2	1.24	3.6	-0.21	9.0	0.7	1.53	14.57	4.74	60.3	7.5	166.9	12.1	5.6
7.4	0.39	2.1	0.04	6.7	0.3	1.60	14.57	4.16	57.9	1.9	36.9	32.9	7.0
6.3	0.55	3.8	0.27	2.5	0.1	0.22	3.45	2.63	88.3	2.5	22.9	17.5	1.1
6.9	0.53	2.9	-0.19	1.6	0.0	0.22	2.70	3.73	121.3	4.6	39.4	11.7	1.0
8.5	0.50	1.9	0.33	3.2	0.7	0.55	5.71	2.78	72.9	7.6	160.8	11.4	6.2
3.5	1.69	14.7	0.15	5.3	0.1	1.05	12.98	4.10	70.7	2.1	5.4	17.3	1.0
6.5	0.64	4.3	0.03	6.9	0.6	1.21	14.59	3.30	54.1	4.4	28.3	8.7	5.6

Name	City	State	Weiss Safety Rating	2003 Weiss Safety Rating	2002 Weiss Safety Rating	Total Assets ($Mil)	One Year Asset Growth	Asset Mix (As a % of Total Assets) Commercial Loans	Consumer Loans	Home Mortgages	Securities	Capitalization Index	Leverage Ratio	Risk-based Capital Ratio
MECHANICS & FARMERS BK	DURHAM	NC	B-	B-	B-	218.3	5.62	2.9	2.9	16.3	12.7	6.6	8.9	12.2
MECHANICS BK	RICHMOND	CA	A	A	A	2,293.9	8.80	8.2	14.5	3.1	19.3	8.3	10.2	13.6
▲ MECHANICS BK	WATER VALLEY	MS	B-	C-	B	132.4	4.68	9.9	8.4	28.5	20.2	10.0	12.8	20.0
MECHANICS CO-OP BK	TAUNTON	MA	B-	B	C+	154.8	33.49	2.4	10.9	15.9	50.7	5.8	7.8	17.4
▲ MECHANICS SVGS BK	MANSFIELD	OH	B-	C+	C+	309.8	0.05	11.3	2.4	56.0	8.5	5.9	7.9	16.2
▲ MECHANICS SVGS BK	PICKENS	SC	C	C-	D+	71.0	0.58	1.2	3.5	59.8	13.9	5.6	7.6	13.4
MECHANICS' SVGS BK	AUBURN	ME	A	A	A-	214.5	6.77	3.9	10.3	49.9	9.2	10.0	12.7	18.8
▲ MEDALLION BK	SALT LAKE CITY	UT	C-	D	NR	193.3	N/A	46.4	42.2	0.0	3.2	10.0	19.3	17.1
MEDFORD CO-OP BK	MEDFORD	MA	C+	C	C	437.8	2.40	4.9	0.2	38.3	22.8	6.6	8.6	15.1
▲ MEDIAPOLIS SVG BK	MEDIAPOLIS	IA	B	B+	C-	102.2	-0.70	5.5	3.6	13.2	49.8	6.4	8.4	17.1
MEDINA BKG CO	MEDINA	TN	B	B-	B-	28.1	-2.13	14.3	7.7	7.9	48.9	10.0	17.7	35.9
▲ MEDINA S&LA	MEDINA	NY	C	C-	D+	34.2	-3.43	2.2	12.5	40.6	7.9	9.4	10.6	21.1
MEDINA VALLEY ST BK	DEVINE	TX	B	B	B	65.0	-4.00	8.0	13.1	4.1	41.8	10.0	11.5	27.9
▼ MEDWAY CO-OP BK	MEDWAY	MA	B-	B	B-	120.1	10.37	0.1	0.6	48.2	25.6	6.7	8.7	17.4
▼ MEETING HOUSE CO-OP BK	NEWTON CENTER	MA	C-	C	C	41.5	7.41	0.0	0.5	40.3	19.7	6.7	8.8	13.9
MELLON 1ST BUSINESS BK NA	LOS ANGELES	CA	B+	B+	B+	2,697.7	9.59	11.4	0.6	0.1	25.7	4.6	6.7	13.0
MELLON BK NA	PITTSBURGH	PA	A-	A-	B+	23,663.5	-19.95	5.9	2.3	0.5	36.0	6.6	9.3	12.2
▲ MELLON TR OF NEW	BOSTON	MA	A-	B	B+	7,527.5	0.61	2.1	5.6	6.7	22.0	5.3	7.3	17.4
MELLON UNITED NB	MIAMI	FL	A-	A-	A-	2,088.5	20.85	9.4	2.8	2.7	18.2	8.7	10.4	13.9
MELROSE CO-OP BK	MELROSE	MA	B-	B	B	117.5	7.91	0.0	0.6	45.2	27.7	10.0	11.6	19.7
MELVIN SVG BK	MELVIN	IA	B+	B+	B+	43.4	-0.82	5.2	3.0	5.3	57.5	10.0	20.0	31.5
MEMBERS TRUST COMPANY	TAMPA	FL	D	D	NR	19.4	N/A	0.0	0.0	0.0	71.8	10.0	96.1	546.5
MEMPHIS ST BK	MEMPHIS	TX	B+	B+	B+	38.1	56.61	3.7	2.8	2.0	65.4	6.8	8.8	19.1
MEMPHISFIRST COMMUNITY	MEMPHIS	TN	D-	D-	C-	26.0	-14.56	11.4	6.2	18.4	21.4	8.2	9.8	15.8
MENARD NB	MENARD	TX	B+	B+	B	29.2	7.87	5.2	2.7	8.8	51.8	10.0	12.2	26.0
MENNO ST BK	MENNO	SD	B	B	B	28.2	-1.00	3.3	2.1	3.3	46.8	9.9	10.9	21.5
▲ MENO GUARANTY BK	MENO	OK	A-	B+	B+	26.4	-3.66	3.3	2.1	0.2	77.0	10.0	20.8	68.8
MER ROUGE ST BK	MER ROUGE	LA	B	B	B+	34.0	-2.72	7.4	6.5	5.2	32.0	10.0	12.5	22.8
MERAMEC VALLEY BK	VALLEY PARK	MO	C	C	C	124.8	8.33	15.8	6.3	21.9	8.1	3.7	7.8	10.4
▲ MERCANTILE B&T FSB	DALLAS	TX	C+	C	C	176.9	-6.10	2.4	1.7	38.9	16.1	6.1	8.1	14.7
MERCANTILE B&TC	BOSTON	MA	C-	C-	C-	107.5	4.92	16.1	0.2	11.2	21.4	4.7	6.7	11.4
▲ MERCANTILE BK	ORLANDO	FL	B-	C+	C	2,829.9	31.89	8.2	16.4	3.0	28.8	4.7	6.7	10.8
MERCANTILE BK	LOUISIANA	MO	A+	A+	A+	115.1	7.88	1.5	3.9	23.1	34.4	10.0	21.6	33.7
MERCANTILE BK TX	FORT WORTH	TX	B-	B-	B	212.7	-10.27	21.9	4.0	7.1	9.8	5.4	7.9	11.3
MERCANTILE BK W MI	GRAND RAPIDS	MI	B+	B	B	1,375.6	33.23	23.9	0.4	5.4	8.6	7.0	11.1	12.5
▲ MERCANTILE NB	LOS ANGELES	CA	C+	C-	C-	224.2	17.08	23.1	0.4	1.8	17.7	5.6	7.8	11.4
MERCANTILE NB OF INDIANA	HAMMOND	IN	C+	C	D+	780.6	4.73	21.4	1.8	14.4	17.4	6.2	8.9	11.9
MERCANTILE SAFE DEPOSIT &	BALTIMORE	MD	A-	A-	A	4,525.8	-6.63	24.1	0.8	4.4	17.8	6.8	9.1	12.4
MERCANTILE SAVINGS BANK	CINCINNATI	OH	C-	C-	C-	63.4	-14.37	0.1	0.9	37.7	17.1	7.8	9.5	17.4
MERCANTILE T&SB	QUINCY	IL	C+	C+	C+	502.4	4.65	18.7	13.6	17.3	18.2	4.4	7.8	10.7
MERCEDES NB	MERCEDES	TX	E-	E-	D	39.5	-0.83	5.3	9.7	24.9	0.6	5.5	7.5	14.7
MERCER COUNTY ST BK	SANDY LAKE	PA	C+	C+	C+	244.8	-1.12	4.7	3.9	19.0	39.8	5.7	7.7	14.4
MERCER SAVINGS BANK	CELINA	OH	C+	C+	B-	130.6	-1.60	1.6	2.1	51.3	32.7	8.8	10.2	24.9
▲ MERCHANTS & CITIZENS BK	MC RAE	GA	C-	D+	C-	106.3	3.85	8.6	12.5	12.8	26.4	6.1	8.1	12.5
MERCHANTS & FARMERS	LEESVILLE	LA	A-	B+	B+	155.6	12.10	6.6	5.0	8.6	50.3	10.0	15.4	30.7
▼ MERCHANTS & FARMERS BK	EUTAW	AL	C	C+	C+	50.1	16.57	5.3	7.6	12.0	53.8	7.3	9.2	14.1
MERCHANTS & FARMERS BK	MILLPORT	AL	B	B	B	63.6	-6.33	7.8	4.4	15.1	26.0	10.0	12.8	20.3
MERCHANTS & FARMERS BK	DUMAS	AR	B	B	B+	76.2	2.97	10.2	5.1	4.4	29.4	10.0	11.0	19.1
MERCHANTS & FARMERS BK	COMER	GA	A+	A+	A+	118.2	-0.92	13.5	9.3	18.1	32.2	10.0	14.0	24.0
MERCHANTS & FARMERS BK	DONALSONVILLE	GA	B-	B-	C+	88.6	-2.94	6.4	5.4	17.7	20.4	6.5	8.5	13.5
▲ MERCHANTS & FARMERS BK	MELVILLE	LA	D	D-	D-	8.4	-6.94	2.3	8.4	17.3	27.2	10.0	11.8	19.7
MERCHANTS & FARMERS BK	SALISBURY	MO	C	C	C	87.6	20.16	6.9	3.6	16.8	25.6	5.0	7.4	11.0
MERCHANTS & FARMERS BK	HOLLY SPRINGS	MS	D+	C-	B-	63.8	7.53	6.9	11.0	18.0	28.7	8.1	9.8	16.6
MERCHANTS & FARMERS BK	KOSCIUSKO	MS	B+	B+	B	1,090.6	3.01	10.9	5.3	18.8	17.8	7.0	9.0	12.9
MERCHANTS &	JOLIET	IL	D+	D	D+	90.2	4.24	30.5	5.3	2.7	14.3	4.4	7.1	10.7
▲ MERCHANTS & MARINE BK	PASCAGOULA	MS	B+	B-	B-	309.1	-0.26	26.5	15.2	1.4	35.5	10.0	11.2	20.4
MERCHANTS & PLANTERS BK	CLARENDON	AR	B-	B-	B	29.6	1.51	8.7	9.2	5.6	57.2	10.0	13.3	28.0
▲ MERCHANTS & PLANTERS BK	NEWPORT	AR	C	C-	C+	146.5	1.10	10.6	8.7	13.0	31.2	6.3	8.3	14.2
MERCHANTS & PLANTERS BK	RAYMOND	MS	B+	B+	B+	66.7	-0.10	2.6	11.1	12.7	44.1	10.0	11.6	23.1
▲ MERCHANTS & PLANTERS BK	TOONE	TN	D	D-	D	96.0	-10.38	12.4	16.6	13.1	32.8	6.1	8.2	13.5
▼ MERCHANTS & SOUTHERN BK	GAINESVILLE	FL	B-	B	B	220.6	12.14	7.5	1.4	13.8	34.1	5.0	7.0	11.4
MERCHANTS B&TC	W HARRISON	IN	B-	B-	B-	139.4	14.19	14.2	2.9	21.8	13.9	8.7	10.3	13.9
▲ MERCHANTS BK	HANCEVILLE	AL	C+	C	C-	135.6	1.51	17.9	6.0	20.0	19.5	6.2	8.3	12.3
MERCHANTS BK	JACKSON	AL	B	B	B	136.8	-1.23	10.4	7.5	24.2	18.5	7.7	10.3	13.0

Asset Quality Index	Non-Performing Loans as a % of Total Loans	Non-Performing Loans as a % of Capital	Net Charge-offs Avg Loans	Profitability Index	Net Income ($Mil)	Return on Assets (R.O.A.)	Return on Equity (R.O.E.)	Net Interest Spread	Overhead Efficiency Ratio	Liquidity Index	Liquidity Ratio	Hot Money Ratio	Stability Index
3.7	1.18	9.1	-0.05	4.5	0.9	0.82	9.52	4.68	74.9	4.7	34.6	9.5	5.0
7.5	0.27	1.8	-0.02	6.9	12.0	1.06	10.57	4.42	63.7	5.2	105.4	20.8	9.0
4.7	1.14	5.7	0.13	7.6	0.9	1.42	13.77	4.79	55.1	3.4	22.2	12.5	5.7
7.1	0.51	2.9	-0.02	5.5	0.5	0.77	9.85	3.72	68.5	6.3	106.3	13.9	3.5
5.8	0.71	6.3	0.03	5.8	1.6	1.05	13.56	3.82	58.4	6.7	71.0	7.0	4.0
8.4	0.16	1.7	0.01	5.2	0.3	0.80	10.56	2.96	62.3	1.7	10.9	20.8	3.0
7.8	0.44	2.8	0.13	7.7	1.2	1.10	8.47	4.20	59.6	1.6	27.4	28.3	7.8
8.1	0.19	1.0	1.29	6.0	1.5	2.98	12.69	8.53	36.7	0.3	14.1	100.0	4.5
6.5	0.58	4.8	0.27	3.9	1.6	0.74	8.88	3.46	70.1	2.7	16.7	15.6	4.4
7.5	0.66	3.1	-0.01	6.2	1.0	1.91	22.02	3.62	39.0	5.9	72.5	12.2	5.0
8.8	0.23	0.4	0.02	5.9	0.2	1.39	7.90	4.77	62.0	6.1	56.5	6.3	5.9
5.4	0.39	2.2	0.42	3.5	0.1	0.32	3.00	4.25	82.8	4.4	40.6	13.2	3.9
8.2	0.48	1.4	0.74	5.1	0.4	1.24	10.81	3.95	69.5	4.7	75.8	17.5	5.0
7.1	0.63	4.4	0.00	4.2	0.4	0.60	6.75	3.20	75.0	4.7	38.6	11.2	5.3
6.8	1.45	10.7	-0.01	2.8	0.0	0.20	2.34	3.86	94.3	6.6	85.0	8.6	4.1
7.2	0.01	0.0	-0.10	6.9	12.4	0.95	7.59	2.98	46.4	9.0	407.1	6.6	9.0
9.2	0.29	0.6	-0.01	9.5	239.4	2.16	25.60	2.46	66.3	8.2	100.3	2.8	7.4
8.1	0.14	0.3	0.00	8.5	75.1	2.25	25.55	1.33	56.2	8.0	342.5	12.4	8.4
6.7	0.17	0.5	0.12	7.1	9.6	0.98	4.51	3.89	49.9	6.4	43.5	4.9	9.0
10.0	0.29	1.4	0.00	3.4	0.3	0.46	3.88	2.53	72.8	8.4	158.2	6.6	6.9
8.8	0.53	0.9	-0.01	5.3	0.3	1.15	5.66	3.26	55.4	4.6	64.5	16.0	6.5
10.0	0.00	0.0	0.00	0.0	-0.5	-5.59	-5.86	2.04	206.4	5.0	7,096.7	100.0	0.0
8.3	0.39	0.8	0.00	3.3	0.1	0.52	5.22	2.59	77.2	4.5	46.7	13.7	5.5
2.0	4.29	22.0	-0.24	0.5	-0.2	-1.53	-15.53	3.67	130.8	2.8	66.0	49.6	3.2
9.2	0.00	0.0	0.48	6.0	0.2	1.44	11.81	3.82	63.5	2.4	46.7	32.5	7.5
8.9	0.04	0.2	0.15	6.7	0.2	1.25	11.72	3.99	53.9	7.0	79.1	5.2	6.0
9.8	0.00	0.0	-0.06	8.7	0.3	2.04	9.67	3.17	38.7	5.1	35.9	7.5	8.0
8.7	0.16	0.6	-0.06	4.8	0.2	0.84	6.65	4.34	72.7	4.2	88.0	24.5	6.0
5.5	0.47	4.7	0.03	5.8	1.0	1.71	21.22	4.24	66.5	4.2	8.8	6.3	4.4
9.2	0.01	0.1	0.00	3.4	0.3	0.34	4.20	2.48	83.2	1.5	35.1	58.1	3.1
8.7	0.00	0.0	-0.13	2.5	0.1	0.22	3.30	3.66	94.3	2.6	33.4	19.7	3.8
6.8	0.19	1.0	0.28	4.6	12.1	0.96	8.89	3.57	53.7	1.8	19.5	22.8	6.1
8.2	0.08	0.2	0.43	10.0	1.5	2.77	12.33	4.54	34.2	0.7	9.3	36.1	9.4
7.6	0.09	0.7	0.16	5.3	0.8	0.79	10.09	5.23	63.4	5.2	38.2	7.7	4.5
7.0	0.31	2.3	0.10	5.7	6.9	1.06	9.47	3.39	45.9	0.3	4.1	70.9	8.8
7.5	0.19	1.1	-0.05	3.7	0.5	0.47	4.55	4.51	82.0	4.9	35.6	8.8	4.3
3.7	1.48	11.2	1.68	3.4	0.8	0.21	2.33	3.78	73.6	6.5	59.9	6.7	5.3
5.4	1.04	6.5	0.01	8.8	31.8	1.40	14.29	3.51	61.5	3.1	39.2	24.9	8.4
1.7	3.45	18.8	0.16	4.5	0.1	0.36	3.57	3.23	91.4	1.6	16.1	24.0	5.7
4.7	0.51	4.3	0.17	4.7	2.3	0.94	11.63	3.20	62.5	1.4	27.8	31.1	5.1
0.6	3.25	32.9	0.42	4.7	0.2	0.84	11.19	6.24	72.0	0.8	15.3	38.0	0.3
4.9	1.35	8.1	0.11	3.5	0.8	0.68	7.96	3.12	76.6	3.2	11.9	12.9	4.6
3.0	2.66	13.1	0.45	3.0	0.0	0.03	0.29	2.57	97.7	4.6	16.8	4.8	6.8
2.2	1.07	6.2	0.79	7.0	0.8	1.46	14.03	4.72	54.0	1.3	16.9	27.5	4.6
8.7	0.67	2.0	0.21	6.0	1.0	1.38	9.11	4.89	70.8	3.1	9.4	13.2	7.6
4.8	2.09	7.1	0.90	4.3	0.2	0.80	8.23	5.02	74.3	5.0	27.1	4.5	3.9
5.3	1.59	7.6	-0.27	5.9	0.4	1.15	9.20	5.17	64.1	1.1	26.7	37.4	4.9
4.9	2.50	10.9	0.45	4.4	0.3	0.78	6.94	4.20	76.5	3.6	40.4	17.1	6.0
8.3	0.06	0.2	0.06	10.0	1.8	2.98	21.04	5.00	50.6	4.7	33.6	9.4	9.6
5.5	0.40	1.9	0.77	6.7	0.6	1.19	10.21	3.86	60.4	4.8	39.9	10.8	6.7
4.0	6.31	15.4	1.98	3.8	0.0	0.69	5.60	4.51	79.6	5.7	86.3	12.5	1.6
6.3	0.41	4.0	0.00	4.2	0.4	0.85	11.93	3.51	74.7	3.0	12.4	14.0	3.2
1.4	4.48	25.7	0.35	4.5	0.4	1.18	12.33	4.44	74.8	1.8	18.3	20.2	3.5
5.9	0.66	4.2	0.65	5.7	5.5	1.00	9.66	4.25	59.8	4.2	52.7	19.2	8.0
6.4	0.01	0.1	-0.04	3.2	0.2	0.36	4.93	4.08	85.1	3.8	21.7	10.5	2.8
5.9	0.71	3.0	0.01	5.7	1.5	1.00	8.61	4.25	73.1	5.2	45.8	10.6	6.4
7.4	0.76	2.0	0.00	5.0	0.2	1.01	8.28	4.83	71.4	1.7	18.5	22.8	4.5
2.7	2.76	17.4	2.09	4.9	0.6	0.80	9.85	4.92	62.0	2.3	21.7	17.9	3.9
8.1	0.10	0.4	0.06	5.4	0.4	1.08	9.48	4.45	67.2	3.2	37.4	18.3	5.7
3.8	1.69	9.0	1.05	1.6	0.2	0.37	4.70	4.31	78.2	3.1	41.1	19.7	1.3
8.8	0.11	1.1	0.00	5.2	1.2	1.12	17.10	4.29	77.8	4.5	18.7	5.7	4.4
4.5	1.33	9.9	0.73	5.9	0.6	0.88	8.60	4.00	71.3	1.7	6.4	19.8	6.3
5.8	0.50	4.0	0.02	4.1	0.5	0.81	9.78	4.24	74.5	3.1	11.7	13.3	3.3
4.4	1.16	7.3	0.11	6.7	0.9	1.22	11.39	5.10	63.7	1.8	25.0	22.6	6.1

Name	City	State	Weiss Safety Rating	2003 Weiss Safety Rating	2002 Weiss Safety Rating	Total Assets ($Mil)	One Year Asset Growth	Asset Mix (As a % of Total Assets)				Capital- ization Index	Leverage Ratio	Risk-based Capital Ratio
								Comm- ercial Loans	Cons- umer Loans	Home Mort- gages	Secur- ities			
MERCHANTS BK	RUGBY	ND	B-	B-	B	38.8	-8.39	3.8	3.1	3.1	69.1	6.9	8.9	18.1
MERCHANTS BK	BURLINGTON	VT	A-	A-	A-	1,036.2	15.13	7.3	0.7	23.1	36.5	6.7	8.7	14.1
▲ MERCHANTS BK NA	CALEDONIA	MN	B	B-	B-	39.6	-5.50	9.6	5.5	6.9	28.4	5.8	7.8	12.6
▲ MERCHANTS BK NA	HAMPTON	MN	B	B-	B-	95.7	2.24	17.3	2.7	9.5	13.3	7.6	9.7	13.0
MERCHANTS BK NA	LA CRESCENT	MN	B	B	NR	47.4	N/A	15.4	9.8	13.2	15.1	5.9	8.7	11.7
▲ MERCHANTS BK NA	WINONA	MN	B	B-	B-	467.7	8.58	18.7	5.9	7.6	14.5	8.9	10.2	15.0
▲ MERCHANTS BK NA	ONALASKA	WI	B	B-	B-	21.4	-55.91	11.7	2.5	4.6	13.9	10.0	18.4	18.2
MERCHANTS BK OF CA NA	CARSON	CA	A-	A-	A-	56.3	38.23	22.1	0.4	10.2	15.8	10.0	15.9	23.4
▲ MERCHANTS NB	HILLSBORO	OH	C+	C	B	352.1	4.86	7.2	7.6	32.7	9.2	5.2	7.7	11.1
MERCHANTS NB KITTANNING	KITTANNING	PA	B+	A-	A-	160.4	6.24	3.9	9.4	18.6	40.1	7.0	9.0	17.0
▲ MERCHANTS NB OF BANGOR	BANGOR	PA	B-	C+	B-	264.1	7.66	6.8	1.2	25.8	45.7	8.6	10.0	19.1
MERCHANTS NB OF	SACRAMENTO	CA	A-	A-	A-	116.2	8.61	1.8	0.4	9.1	72.1	8.9	10.2	31.3
MERCHANTS ST BK	FREEMAN	SD	D	D-	E-	88.6	3.65	8.5	3.5	3.8	15.2	5.0	8.3	11.0
MEREDITH VILLAGE SVGS BK	MEREDITH	NH	A-	A-	A-	449.5	9.15	3.0	2.5	37.4	20.1	9.4	10.6	16.9
MERIDIAN BANK NA	WICKENBURG	AZ	A	A	B+	618.2	40.21	24.7	1.5	3.1	22.2	10.0	15.6	20.1
▲ MERRICK BK	S JORDAN	UT	C-	D+	D+	458.8	25.65	0.0	110.1	0.0	0.7	10.0	21.5	23.6
MERRILL FS&LA	MERRILL	WI	C-	C-	C	23.4	-2.66	0.0	3.9	64.8	1.4	10.0	15.9	31.8
MERRILL LYNCH B&TC	PLAINSBORO	NJ	B-	B-	B-	12,992.8	-8.20	0.0	1.7	21.0	65.1	4.3	6.3	20.2
MERRILL LYNCH BK USA	SALT LAKE CITY	UT	B-	C+	C+	66,421.6	2.85	17.7	4.4	17.0	42.0	5.2	7.2	11.3
MERRILL LYNCH TRUST	PENNINGTON	NJ	B+	B+	B+	207.5	-6.77	0.0	0.0	0.0	67.8	10.0	40.6	107.5
MERRILL MERCHANTS BK	BANGOR	ME	B	B	B	357.6	12.80	15.8	4.4	23.5	17.3	5.7	7.7	12.2
MERRIMAC SVGS BK	MERRIMAC	MA	C	C-	C-	37.8	3.87	0.5	9.4	38.0	32.2	8.1	9.7	20.4
MERRIMACK COUNTY SVGS	CONCORD	NH	B	B	B	341.4	6.19	3.0	6.8	33.0	21.5	10.0	11.7	19.3
MESA BK	MESA	AZ	C	C	C	87.6	30.28	8.3	0.5	2.3	0.0	3.3	7.5	10.1
MESILLA VALLEY BK	LAS CRUCES	NM	C	C-	D	26.4	13.41	19.1	3.5	10.8	11.2	9.3	12.9	14.4
METAIRIE B&TC	METAIRIE	LA	A-	A	A	266.4	0.71	1.9	8.6	28.4	23.3	10.0	12.7	21.6
METAMORA ST BK	METAMORA	OH	D	D	D	47.4	0.37	6.7	3.7	41.7	10.5	6.2	8.2	13.3
METCALF BK	OVERLAND PARK	KS	B-	B-	B-	249.0	1.45	4.8	2.7	4.5	31.6	6.0	8.1	13.1
METHUEN CO-OP BK	METHUEN	MA	B-	B-	B-	74.6	5.83	0.0	1.9	45.3	32.3	8.2	9.8	18.8
▲ METLIFE BK NA	BRIDGEWATER	NJ	D	D-	D-	2,485.8	163.40	13.0	0.0	16.5	47.9	10.0	14.4	21.1
▲ METRO BANK, FSB	ORLANDO	FL	D	D-	E	11.4	5.75	0.5	0.3	14.2	7.0	10.0	31.8	97.0
METRO BK	PELL CITY	AL	B-	B-	C+	387.1	19.97	7.4	6.5	19.4	15.5	4.4	7.3	10.7
▼ METRO BK OF DADE COUNTY	MIAMI	FL	C+	B-	B-	203.9	-10.60	14.5	2.6	3.2	13.7	7.3	9.3	12.8
METROBANK	FARMINGTON HILLS	MI	B-	B-	C+	174.4	9.66	14.0	0.6	5.7	20.0	8.6	10.7	13.9
METROBANK NA	DAVENPORT	IA	B	B	B	561.6	1.83	4.1	7.3	8.4	51.0	6.7	8.7	17.5
METROBANK NA	HOUSTON	TX	D	D	C	880.8	1.71	11.6	1.1	0.9	31.8	7.4	9.3	14.2
METROPOLITAN B&TC	CHICAGO	IL	B-	B-	B	234.2	23.25	3.8	0.4	10.1	14.8	3.3	7.5	10.2
METROPOLITAN BK	OAKLAND	CA	B-	B-	C+	91.1	14.07	4.9	0.3	19.3	17.6	6.7	8.8	13.6
METROPOLITAN NB	LITTLE ROCK	AR	C	C-	C-	1,010.7	21.82	16.8	3.4	8.5	28.3	3.3	6.6	10.1
▲ METROPOLITAN NB	SPRINGFIELD	MO	B+	B	B-	289.4	3.29	11.5	2.7	26.8	7.2	7.9	9.6	13.4
METROPOLITAN NB	NEW YORK	NY	B-	C+	D-	239.0	22.83	32.8	0.0	0.7	5.3	6.1	10.5	11.8
▲ METROPOLITAN SB	PITTSBURGH	PA	D-	E+	E+	13.6	8.43	0.5	4.6	57.0	0.0	4.6	6.6	13.0
METUCHEN SB	METUCHEN	NJ	B-	B-	B-	277.0	7.11	1.1	0.0	43.8	34.1	5.2	7.2	17.2
METZ BKG CO	METZ	MO	B-	C+	C	41.9	4.44	6.6	3.6	13.8	17.1	8.3	9.9	14.0
▲ MFB FINANCIAL	MISHAWAKA	IN	C+	C	C	427.6	0.51	13.2	1.2	33.0	7.1	5.8	8.0	11.6
MIAMI SAVINGS BANK	MIAMITOWN	OH	C+	C+	C+	98.2	4.59	3.7	2.1	48.9	0.5	7.0	9.0	14.7
MIAMI VALLEY BK	QUINCY	OH	A-	B+	B+	131.9	-19.89	2.2	0.7	46.9	11.8	9.2	10.4	25.7
MICHIGAN HERITAGE BK	FARMINGTON HILLS	MI	B-	C+	C+	157.6	7.68	29.0	0.2	11.0	15.2	7.1	10.0	12.6
▲ MID AMERICA B&TC	DIXON	MO	B-	C+	C+	89.6	-1.81	4.7	7.4	26.3	8.0	6.7	8.7	12.3
▲ MID AMERICA BK	LINN	MO	B-	C+	C	68.7	23.28	5.9	7.0	26.4	20.5	6.5	8.5	12.3
MID AMERICA BK	FOOTVILLE	WI	D-	D-	E-	46.1	12.95	19.4	2.9	23.4	9.7	5.1	7.8	11.1
MID AMERICA BK FSB	CLARENDON HILLS	IL	B	B-	B-	9,051.5	56.98	1.5	0.1	45.2	14.2	4.2	6.7	10.6
▲ MID CAROLINA BANK	BURLINGTON	NC	B	B-	C-	252.6	25.52	11.7	2.0	13.0	10.6	6.5	9.7	12.1
MID CITY BK	OMAHA	NE	B	B	A-	213.9	4.42	29.7	5.1	2.9	26.6	10.0	17.1	27.5
▼ MID PENN BK	MILLERSBURG	PA	C	B-	B-	390.0	10.33	5.0	2.1	10.9	8.4	2.4	6.4	9.4
▲ MID ST BK	WATERVILLE	WA	D-	E	E-	44.3	7.79	2.9	3.3	11.8	6.2	4.4	6.8	10.7
▲ MID-AMERICA BK	BALDWIN CITY	KS	D+	C-	D-	32.8	-6.69	4.9	3.1	24.8	2.8	7.4	9.3	13.1
MID-CENTRAL FSB	WADENA	MN	C	C	C-	84.9	18.06	5.5	29.8	53.1	5.0	3.7	6.2	10.4
MID-MISSOURI BK	SPRINGFIELD	MO	B-	B-	B-	334.9	1.59	16.2	3.2	25.3	9.5	8.1	9.7	14.1
▼ MID-SOUTHERN SVGS BK FSB	SALEM	IN	B-	B	B+	152.2	7.58	8.6	3.8	37.4	27.9	8.0	9.7	18.3
MID-STATE B&TC	ARROYO GRANDE	CA	B+	B+	A-	2,252.0	11.25	7.4	1.2	6.5	29.6	8.0	9.6	13.9
MID-VALLEY BK	WOODBURN	OR	B	B-	D+	87.0	12.81	15.4	2.7	1.1	22.5	7.6	10.1	13.0
▲ MID-WISCONSIN BK-MEDFORD	MEDFORD	WI	B	B-	B-	381.6	3.26	8.3	2.4	20.8	20.6	6.1	8.1	12.0
MIDAMERICA NB	CANTON	IL	B	B+	A-	339.0	16.58	12.3	7.4	9.1	26.1	6.5	8.5	12.9

Asset Quality Index	Non-Performing Loans as a % of Total Loans	Non-Performing Loans as a % of Capital	Net Charge-offs as a % of Avg Loans	Profitability Index	Net Income ($Mil)	Return on Assets (R.O.A.)	Return on Equity (R.O.E.)	Net Interest Spread	Overhead Efficiency Ratio	Liquidity Index	Liquidity Ratio	Hot Money Ratio	Stability Index
9.6	0.37	0.9	0.51	6.2	0.3	1.24	12.66	4.84	61.7	5.2	33.5	5.8	4.5
9.1	0.14	0.9	-0.02	6.8	5.7	1.16	13.18	4.28	68.7	4.9	20.6	4.5	7.8
7.9	0.20	1.4	0.00	9.0	0.3	1.57	17.92	4.27	62.8	4.4	10.6	5.5	6.3
4.1	1.12	5.5	0.50	7.0	0.7	1.43	11.02	4.94	63.6	4.2	18.5	7.6	6.6
3.7	1.35	11.3	0.06	7.5	0.4	1.75	22.29	4.91	59.5	3.9	6.6	8.2	5.1
5.4	0.48	2.7	-0.01	8.9	3.1	1.37	11.49	4.40	61.7	3.8	25.1	11.3	7.8
8.5	0.00	0.0	0.00	3.4	-0.2	-2.03	-10.12	3.64	177.2	1.4	1.4	22.0	6.2
8.7	0.14	0.5	0.01	10.0	0.7	2.56	16.08	6.67	77.0	1.6	32.7	33.2	8.2
4.6	0.54	5.2	0.19	7.6	2.2	1.27	17.49	4.20	52.7	3.7	20.8	11.1	3.5
5.8	1.40	7.3	0.02	6.2	0.9	1.17	12.68	3.69	58.4	5.9	46.9	6.4	6.6
7.2	1.25	5.6	0.02	4.2	1.1	0.83	8.12	3.18	67.1	5.6	49.3	9.1	5.8
10.0	0.00	0.0	0.00	5.7	0.6	1.10	11.11	3.87	63.3	3.8	62.9	23.8	6.2
1.3	3.35	27.8	0.08	4.7	0.4	0.93	11.45	5.11	69.1	4.0	15.8	9.0	2.8
6.8	0.57	3.6	0.01	5.6	2.3	1.08	9.91	3.97	68.6	3.5	19.9	11.9	7.1
6.9	0.43	1.6	0.03	10.0	8.2	2.71	15.12	7.34	61.7	0.9	15.3	33.4	9.7
1.8	4.65	12.0	9.94	9.7	7.7	3.53	17.36	19.90	40.7	0.5	13.7	71.6	8.0
4.7	2.44	11.9	0.00	1.8	0.0	-0.14	-0.88	3.11	102.5	3.6	19.5	10.9	5.2
10.0	0.04	0.2	0.00	9.8	158.3	2.23	36.82	1.33	21.6	2.5	42.0	48.4	5.5
7.0	0.64	4.2	0.42	7.2	422.4	1.27	18.24	2.27	24.1	1.4	26.6	68.7	5.4
6.6	0.00	0.0	0.00	10.0	8.0	7.79	19.32	4.37	74.9	1.3	31.6	47.4	4.2
8.1	0.03	0.3	0.04	8.2	2.3	1.33	16.95	3.99	59.8	2.0	12.2	18.7	4.8
8.8	0.00	0.0	0.00	3.2	0.1	0.55	5.73	3.98	83.8	6.5	82.7	8.5	3.6
8.5	0.01	0.1	0.02	3.8	0.9	0.55	4.22	3.56	82.0	6.4	52.1	4.9	7.8
5.4	0.00	0.0	0.00	10.0	0.7	1.76	20.07	6.67	55.8	2.1	30.9	24.7	6.0
8.2	0.00	0.0	0.00	3.1	0.1	0.54	4.57	5.38	83.3	1.4	27.4	32.0	0.0
8.4	0.01	0.0	0.04	5.4	1.3	0.94	6.70	4.38	75.1	5.1	25.9	3.1	8.5
5.4	0.74	6.3	0.19	3.4	0.2	0.69	8.59	4.80	80.7	3.8	15.1	9.9	2.6
8.7	0.00	0.0	0.14	4.5	1.0	0.84	10.11	3.80	81.4	7.3	72.3	3.4	5.4
9.9	0.02	0.1	0.21	3.6	0.2	0.47	4.83	3.49	77.1	6.4	65.5	6.3	4.6
9.3	0.00	0.0	0.00	0.0	-1.7	-0.17	-1.62	1.89	79.8	8.2	186.0	10.6	7.3
7.6	3.09	2.1	0.00	0.0	-0.5	-7.79	-20.43	2.20	286.2	6.2	109.9	12.6	3.8
4.9	0.74	6.5	0.18	9.1	2.8	1.51	21.16	4.32	41.0	7.7	133.9	8.4	5.3
3.6	2.20	15.6	0.15	4.3	0.6	0.56	6.12	4.59	79.1	4.2	20.8	7.9	4.2
1.3	3.41	11.8	-0.21	3.7	0.3	0.31	1.99	4.37	88.0	4.0	20.0	9.6	6.5
6.2	0.67	2.4	0.02	6.3	3.2	1.09	10.06	3.68	63.9	3.1	24.4	14.6	6.1
0.9	3.28	20.6	0.09	5.7	4.7	1.08	12.55	4.16	65.7	2.2	34.4	26.7	3.9
3.4	1.22	11.4	0.00	9.7	1.7	1.54	20.56	5.85	60.5	4.5	44.9	13.8	6.7
7.8	0.02	0.2	0.00	6.5	0.7	1.51	17.98	4.11	57.2	5.8	187.0	26.7	5.0
4.6	1.38	13.0	0.27	5.3	4.2	0.89	13.51	3.67	69.0	1.9	18.0	20.9	4.0
5.5	0.33	2.2	0.08	7.6	2.5	1.72	15.14	4.25	57.9	3.8	18.3	10.1	7.1
5.9	0.02	0.1	0.00	4.7	1.4	1.21	8.38	3.66	76.1	2.5	28.2	18.6	6.2
7.8	0.00	0.0	0.00	5.1	0.1	1.05	16.39	3.62	54.2	9.4	393.1	4.0	1.3
9.9	0.00	0.0	0.00	4.1	0.8	0.59	8.34	3.48	70.0	4.6	11.4	4.3	3.9
7.5	0.07	0.5	0.14	9.6	0.5	2.41	25.34	5.12	53.1	3.6	25.2	12.0	5.1
6.3	0.40	3.7	0.11	3.3	1.2	0.54	6.81	2.87	79.6	0.9	10.6	31.7	4.0
6.0	0.67	6.2	-0.60	6.5	0.6	1.26	14.30	3.32	57.2	1.0	19.2	33.0	4.6
6.9	0.46	2.5	0.00	8.6	2.0	2.81	28.19	3.92	36.9	5.4	73.1	14.7	7.6
4.2	1.35	10.0	0.09	5.0	0.6	0.78	7.81	4.22	75.0	0.6	10.5	47.7	5.1
5.5	0.30	2.0	0.17	6.2	0.6	1.23	11.31	4.41	59.2	1.0	17.9	33.7	5.7
7.8	0.17	1.4	-0.01	8.5	0.5	1.57	18.46	4.36	48.8	4.8	30.0	7.0	4.1
2.7	1.98	18.3	0.13	3.4	0.1	0.54	6.95	4.84	85.4	4.4	41.5	13.2	0.8
5.6	0.43	4.6	0.01	7.0	49.7	1.09	11.13	3.09	54.3	2.0	9.7	18.5	7.6
7.4	0.19	1.5	0.06	4.5	1.0	0.85	8.57	3.47	67.6	1.6	10.9	21.3	5.0
4.5	4.09	10.5	0.31	4.8	1.3	1.18	7.03	4.42	71.4	5.9	69.5	11.5	7.5
4.5	0.55	5.2	0.03	5.1	1.9	1.02	14.53	3.38	63.5	7.7	124.3	8.0	3.9
6.1	0.02	0.2	-0.01	4.6	0.2	0.80	11.20	5.13	78.3	1.6	7.9	21.1	0.9
1.2	3.02	23.2	0.08	6.1	0.2	1.01	10.71	4.70	65.1	3.7	80.8	28.6	2.8
4.7	0.27	3.6	0.03	6.8	0.6	1.49	23.19	4.15	64.4	4.2	7.2	6.6	4.3
7.7	0.19	1.4	0.06	5.2	1.6	0.94	9.43	4.03	76.4	6.0	59.2	10.0	5.1
5.6	0.78	5.3	0.07	3.5	0.3	0.39	4.10	2.38	72.1	0.8	15.4	34.9	5.8
5.8	0.88	4.1	-0.09	9.8	17.3	1.55	12.74	5.21	63.5	6.2	49.4	8.4	10.0
8.2	0.00	0.0	0.00	5.9	0.4	0.97	9.75	5.67	67.8	6.3	71.1	8.0	4.5
6.6	0.61	5.0	-0.01	6.9	2.3	1.23	14.67	4.06	59.4	1.7	15.5	21.2	5.2
5.7	0.40	2.5	0.53	4.2	1.4	0.85	7.98	4.08	75.7	1.6	20.7	25.0	6.5

Name	City	State	Weiss Safety Rating	2003 Weiss Safety Rating	2002 Weiss Safety Rating	Total Assets ($Mil)	One Year Asset Growth	Asset Mix (As a % of Total Assets)				Capital-ization Index	Leverage Ratio	Risk-based Capital Ratio
								Comm-ercial Loans	Cons-umer Loans	Home Mort-gages	Secur-ities			
MIDAMERICAN B&TC NA	LEAVENWORTH	KS	B	B	B	101.3	-0.71	12.2	3.8	16.6	24.7	7.7	9.5	14.5
MIDDLEBURG BK	MIDDLEBURG	VA	A-	A-	A-	538.0	14.38	4.0	2.3	21.0	32.4	8.6	10.0	15.7
MIDDLEFIELD BKG CO	MIDDLEFIELD	OH	B+	B+	A-	279.8	12.10	16.6	1.9	44.0	19.9	6.6	8.6	14.9
MIDDLESEX FS&LA	SOMERVILLE	MA	A-	A	A-	369.4	1.50	0.0	0.1	35.6	19.1	10.0	12.1	20.4
MIDDLESEX SVGS BK	NATICK	MA	B	B	B+	3,044.8	-1.63	4.0	0.4	26.0	39.0	7.1	9.1	18.1
MIDDLETON COMM BK	MIDDLETON	WI	A-	B+	B-	123.6	2.34	16.0	3.1	10.9	18.7	8.9	10.7	14.1
MIDDLETOWN ST BK	MIDDLETOWN	IL	D	D+	D+	17.5	6.25	8.0	5.3	17.5	24.7	6.0	8.0	13.4
MIDDLETOWN VALLEY BK	MIDDLETOWN	MD	A+	A+	A+	148.7	10.59	2.1	0.6	30.0	48.1	10.0	20.1	57.9
▲ MIDFIRST BK	OKLAHOMA CITY	OK	B	B-	B-	9,234.2	0.76	3.7	0.4	41.0	30.9	5.0	7.0	16.7
MIDLAND COMMUNITY BK	KINCAID	IL	C	C	C	32.5	-1.18	10.5	6.6	28.6	39.3	7.3	9.2	19.5
▲ MIDLAND FS&LA	BRIDGEVIEW	IL	C	C-	C-	154.0	-4.03	0.0	1.0	57.5	31.2	4.8	6.8	13.4
MIDLAND NB OF NEWTON	NEWTON	KS	B-	B-	B-	117.6	0.59	10.6	4.0	5.1	34.6	6.4	8.4	12.9
MIDSOUTH BK	MURFREESBORO	TN	D	NR	NR	55.4	N/A	12.5	2.6	12.0	31.1	10.0	53.0	91.2
MIDSOUTH BK NA	DOTHAN	AL	A-	A-	B+	186.8	2.26	12.2	6.2	16.6	28.5	9.6	10.7	15.8
MIDSOUTH BK NA	LAFAYETTE	LA	B-	C+	C	477.0	18.79	17.2	6.4	9.8	32.7	6.1	8.1	12.9
▲ MIDSTATE FS&LA	BALTIMORE	MD	B+	B	B+	114.8	-8.84	0.0	0.7	39.7	33.9	10.0	13.8	32.8
MIDSTATES BK NA	COUNCIL BLUFFS	IA	C	C-	C-	282.9	19.95	4.4	1.8	16.0	36.4	6.3	8.3	14.8
MIDTOWN B&TC	ATLANTA	GA	D	D	NR	31.2	N/A	13.3	1.2	4.6	18.4	10.0	42.4	50.8
MIDWEST B&TC	ELMWOOD PARK	IL	B	B	B	1,973.5	0.11	7.2	0.3	6.0	33.2	6.7	8.7	13.5
MIDWEST BANKCENTRE	LEMAY	MO	B-	B-	B-	975.2	6.30	12.0	1.8	6.5	33.9	7.0	9.0	13.6
MIDWEST BK	DETROIT LAKES	MN	C+	C+	B-	108.4	12.74	17.4	6.7	15.8	1.1	3.7	8.6	10.4
MIDWEST BK NA	PARKERS PRAIRIE	MN	B-	B-	B-	80.4	28.90	13.5	5.1	13.9	2.6	3.8	8.9	10.4
▲ MIDWEST BK NA	PIERCE	NE	A	A-	A-	242.4	8.01	11.1	2.7	2.8	26.1	10.0	11.8	17.5
MIDWEST BK WESTERN IL	MONMOUTH	IL	B-	B-	B-	307.3	3.63	8.4	2.3	2.9	43.4	5.4	7.4	12.3
▼ MIDWEST COMMUNITY BK	FREEPORT	IL	C	C+	C+	136.0	12.28	12.2	1.9	19.0	1.4	2.4	7.8	9.4
MIDWEST COMMUNITY BK	PLAINVILLE	KS	C+	C	C	80.1	102.22	12.2	5.3	29.2	16.3	6.0	8.0	12.2
MIDWEST FS&LA OF ST	ST JOSEPH	MO	C+	C+	C+	19.3	-2.64	0.0	0.3	17.0	65.3	10.0	28.2	108.0
▲ MIDWEST HERITAGE BK, FSB	CHARITON	IA	C	C-	C-	116.0	-1.47	5.9	29.1	30.3	14.5	4.6	6.9	10.8
MIDWEST INDEPENDENT BK	JEFFERSON CITY	MO	B-	B-	B-	207.1	58.16	6.1	0.9	4.9	0.8	4.1	8.6	10.6
▼ MIDWESTONE B&TC	OSKALOOSA	IA	D-	D	D+	262.2	2.73	18.7	1.5	11.9	8.1	4.3	8.3	10.6
▼ MIDWESTONE BK	BURLINGTON	IA	D-	NR	NR	177.9	N/A	7.4	1.3	36.0	18.9	5.9	7.9	14.3
MIFFLIN CNTY SB	LEWISTOWN	PA	B+	B+	B+	77.7	7.13	4.1	4.6	63.4	3.0	10.0	12.4	18.9
MIFFLINBURG B&TC	MIFFLINBURG	PA	B+	B+	B+	263.3	3.77	6.3	3.3	18.8	36.7	6.7	8.7	15.4
MILFORD B&LA	MILFORD	IL	D-	D-	E+	14.7	13.91	0.0	0.3	0.0	7.3	6.7	8.7	18.7
MILFORD BK	MILFORD	CT	B	B	B	334.7	8.14	4.5	0.5	55.4	12.5	6.6	8.6	15.1
MILFORD FS&LA	MILFORD	MA	B+	B+	B+	346.7	4.12	0.0	0.9	76.8	5.6	7.6	9.4	16.8
MILFORD NB&TC	MILFORD	MA	C+	C+	C+	307.9	14.29	5.4	1.9	26.3	28.4	5.7	7.7	11.8
▼ MILLBURY NB	MILLBURY	MA	C+	B-	B	63.7	8.59	15.3	2.7	13.9	17.6	7.6	9.4	14.3
MILLBURY SVGS BK	MILLBURY	MA	B	B	B	160.9	6.09	3.7	1.9	30.7	41.7	9.0	10.3	16.4
▲ MILLEDGEVILLE ST BK	MILLEDGEVILLE	IL	A-	B+	B+	55.2	-1.09	7.1	3.0	11.3	27.3	10.0	12.5	18.3
▲ MILLENNIA COMMUNITY BK	GREENVILLE	NC	D	D-	D	25.5	10.00	16.0	8.7	26.8	4.4	10.0	20.0	31.5
MILLENNIUM BK	EDWARDS	CO	D-	D-	D	43.8	21.88	9.4	5.2	20.2	39.9	6.9	8.9	14.6
MILLENNIUM BK	GAINESVILLE	FL	B-	C+	C+	145.2	11.67	4.4	1.9	14.3	21.6	5.5	7.5	12.3
MILLENNIUM BK NA	RESTON	VA	C-	C-	D	344.4	9.29	5.1	1.3	27.1	21.8	6.9	8.9	13.1
MILLENNIUM ST BK OF TX	DALLAS	TX	D	D	NR	30.8	N/A	47.3	4.7	1.4	0.0	10.0	15.5	21.2
MILLINGTON SVGS BK	MILLINGTON	NJ	B-	B-	B-	216.1	9.70	1.2	0.8	55.2	14.3	5.7	7.7	12.4
▼ MILLS COUNTY BK NA	GLENWOOD	IA	C-	C	C-	35.3	-0.95	10.5	6.1	22.9	31.1	5.9	7.9	14.8
MILLS COUNTY ST BK	GOLDTHWAITE	TX	B	B	B	135.5	-2.64	9.4	11.4	18.0	30.7	8.9	10.3	18.8
▲ MILLVILLE S&LA	MILLVILLE	NJ	B+	B	B	96.6	11.10	0.3	0.0	27.9	63.1	10.0	11.8	38.0
MILTON BKG CO	WELLSTON	OH	C-	C-	C-	69.3	-0.36	7.4	19.8	35.8	11.2	6.4	8.4	12.8
MILTON SAVINGS BANK	MILTON	PA	B	B	B	49.8	-7.82	0.0	0.7	67.5	7.5	10.0	16.0	33.6
▲ MILTON SVG BK	MILTON	WI	D+	D-	D-	18.3	-1.34	3.4	3.9	54.6	20.2	7.1	9.0	18.3
MILWAUKEE WESTERN BK	MILWAUKEE	WI	C	C	C-	153.0	-15.43	24.5	1.6	17.2	13.4	5.8	8.7	11.6
▲ MINDEN B&LA	MINDEN	LA	A	A-	B+	108.4	20.03	9.6	4.2	33.5	37.9	10.0	14.4	31.1
MINDEN EXCHANGE B&TC	MINDEN	NE	B-	B-	B	131.0	-4.48	16.8	4.5	6.3	23.7	10.0	15.6	22.5
MINEOLA CMNTY BK SSB	MINEOLA	TX	B	B-	B-	127.0	-3.40	0.3	1.9	18.5	66.7	10.0	14.3	41.1
MINER COUNTY BK	HOWARD	SD	B-	B-	B-	30.9	5.07	4.5	3.9	2.8	35.5	10.0	11.1	17.4
MINERS & MERCHANTS B&TC	GRUNDY	VA	B-	B-	B-	390.6	1.90	8.9	16.5	22.0	25.9	5.7	7.7	13.3
▲ MINERS & MERCHANTS BK	THOMAS	WV	B	B-	B-	41.8	0.22	0.8	6.5	31.9	41.9	10.0	12.1	29.3
MINERS EXCHANGE BK	COEBURN	VA	B	B	B	70.1	6.26	1.3	12.9	29.9	25.4	9.2	10.5	20.1
▲ MINERS NB OF EVELETH	EVELETH	MN	D+	C	B-	39.5	1.45	3.9	5.7	31.3	28.2	9.5	10.7	21.6
MINERS ST BK	IRON RIVER	MI	C+	C	C-	73.6	6.66	30.1	1.7	14.3	15.3	7.5	9.3	13.7
MINERS ST BK OF	FRONTENAC	KS	A-	A-	A	43.8	0.97	6.9	4.4	22.3	58.0	10.0	27.4	50.4
MINERSVILLE SAFE DEPOSIT	MINERSVILLE	PA	C	C+	B-	101.6	26.31	9.8	9.1	28.5	38.1	5.5	7.5	16.1

Asset Quality Index	Non-Performing Loans as a % of Total Loans	Non-Performing Loans as a % of Capital	Net Charge-offs / Avg Loans	Profitability Index	Net Income ($Mil)	Return on Assets (R.O.A.)	Return on Equity (R.O.E.)	Net Interest Spread	Overhead Efficiency Ratio	Liquidity Index	Liquidity Ratio	Hot Money Ratio	Stability Index
6.9	0.42	2.5	0.07	7.9	0.7	1.37	14.31	4.61	61.8	4.3	17.5	7.1	6.3
9.0	0.12	0.7	-0.06	9.2	3.9	1.49	15.21	4.41	54.4	4.1	39.9	14.6	7.3
7.4	0.51	4.0	-0.01	6.7	1.7	1.22	14.34	3.94	58.4	6.4	67.2	8.6	5.9
7.7	0.10	0.6	0.32	7.4	2.0	1.09	9.02	3.25	44.9	0.9	17.0	34.8	7.8
9.2	0.44	2.5	0.01	4.5	13.0	0.87	9.79	2.69	58.9	7.0	485.8	17.3	6.9
7.7	0.30	1.9	-0.05	9.3	0.9	1.53	14.38	4.06	51.3	1.4	16.4	27.0	6.7
5.4	0.90	6.4	-0.04	5.7	0.1	1.22	14.80	3.65	67.4	4.0	67.9	18.0	2.3
10.0	0.38	0.7	0.00	10.0	1.5	2.11	10.60	4.79	36.7	6.8	52.9	2.1	9.6
7.0	0.44	3.0	0.02	10.0	187.2	4.09	57.23	4.24	27.1	0.4	7.4	74.4	7.5
5.2	1.52	8.2	0.11	4.6	0.1	0.67	7.39	3.43	65.6	2.7	25.6	16.9	3.5
8.4	0.06	0.5	0.00	3.8	0.4	0.51	7.46	3.11	77.5	1.9	7.0	18.5	3.0
6.8	0.21	1.2	0.22	5.6	0.8	1.34	14.64	3.99	66.3	4.0	36.3	13.9	4.7
9.4	0.00	0.0	0.00	0.0	-1.6	-7.28	-11.45	1.39	432.5	6.1	190.5	23.4	0.0
8.5	0.11	0.6	0.00	6.7	1.5	1.56	13.74	4.24	59.6	3.9	39.6	15.3	6.9
6.2	0.55	3.8	0.18	9.0	3.7	1.61	19.30	5.17	61.7	5.9	69.7	11.7	4.5
9.2	0.61	2.3	0.00	5.2	0.6	0.93	7.04	2.83	46.5	3.8	70.7	27.2	6.9
5.4	0.94	6.4	0.07	7.0	2.6	1.93	23.89	4.13	54.6	4.8	42.3	11.6	3.1
9.4	0.00	0.0	0.00	0.0	-1.0	-8.56	-18.43	2.23	461.3	8.3	179.2	9.1	0.0
6.3	1.19	6.9	0.19	5.7	9.0	0.92	11.36	2.99	59.2	4.3	22.9	10.1	6.0
6.7	0.48	3.0	0.35	4.0	3.5	0.74	8.34	3.25	68.3	4.4	16.7	6.2	5.2
6.6	0.04	0.4	0.07	8.1	0.6	1.07	12.71	4.77	62.6	4.0	16.9	9.1	5.0
5.0	0.41	3.7	0.04	7.6	0.5	1.20	12.92	4.98	56.8	2.7	9.0	15.1	5.1
6.9	0.39	2.0	-0.02	6.9	1.3	1.12	8.97	4.09	61.2	3.6	18.2	11.2	7.3
5.6	1.23	6.4	0.33	4.4	1.3	0.90	10.73	2.93	60.4	1.4	7.2	23.9	5.3
4.5	0.74	7.7	0.00	5.7	0.9	1.31	17.07	4.01	65.1	4.5	14.3	5.5	4.7
4.8	0.97	8.7	0.91	4.8	0.3	0.86	10.32	5.49	66.6	1.6	15.8	23.3	4.2
10.0	0.00	0.0	0.00	3.6	0.1	0.64	2.29	2.66	74.1	6.0	61.4	5.6	5.4
4.6	0.41	4.4	0.18	4.3	0.2	0.39	5.77	4.20	87.9	2.5	20.8	17.2	3.2
8.3	0.00	0.0	0.01	9.0	1.3	1.46	18.84	4.00	62.4	6.9	51.1	1.0	4.5
0.2	6.23	47.3	0.37	9.7	1.9	1.50	15.05	5.23	49.2	4.5	23.9	6.7	5.0
0.3	6.62	40.5	0.22	6.4	0.8	1.27	8.12	4.04	66.1	4.5	18.8	6.1	0.3
6.4	0.93	6.3	0.12	4.8	0.3	0.73	5.81	3.89	67.8	5.0	37.0	9.0	6.6
6.3	0.76	4.4	0.00	5.6	1.6	1.20	13.41	3.26	61.7	4.6	49.1	14.4	6.1
4.0	2.02	16.7	0.00	4.6	0.1	0.98	11.32	3.23	58.9	1.3	26.1	29.5	1.7
7.3	0.41	3.3	0.05	4.8	1.0	0.62	7.34	3.77	75.3	6.1	45.4	4.8	4.7
8.7	0.00	0.0	0.00	5.9	0.8	0.45	4.83	2.99	78.3	1.6	3.4	19.8	5.8
8.4	0.18	1.5	0.12	4.6	1.0	0.68	9.64	3.78	75.7	5.1	33.9	6.9	3.4
5.9	1.15	7.9	-0.02	3.9	0.2	0.52	5.46	4.27	80.3	7.1	91.2	6.5	4.9
9.6	0.00	0.0	0.00	4.5	0.7	0.85	8.07	3.32	66.5	5.6	55.9	10.8	6.3
8.5	0.25	1.2	0.00	6.3	0.4	1.52	11.44	3.93	60.0	3.4	55.2	21.0	7.3
4.6	1.81	5.9	0.88	0.0	-0.5	-4.08	-23.99	3.37	174.6	6.5	218.5	20.7	0.0
8.9	0.00	0.0	0.00	0.0	-0.2	-0.70	-8.54	2.77	125.9	1.2	15.6	29.9	0.0
5.5	0.47	1.5	0.04	4.6	0.5	0.64	3.51	3.78	69.5	3.4	20.3	12.5	7.5
8.8	0.11	0.9	0.17	2.4	0.8	0.51	6.79	3.29	83.5	1.1	15.4	30.4	2.4
8.2	0.00	0.0	0.00	0.0	-0.4	-3.51	-17.50	2.82	140.8	5.2	128.7	21.8	0.0
5.6	0.87	8.7	0.05	4.8	0.8	0.73	9.44	3.58	67.9	2.9	13.2	14.6	4.2
4.8	1.44	9.4	0.10	4.5	0.1	0.74	8.41	4.91	87.9	4.5	30.7	9.3	3.7
4.7	1.06	5.8	0.22	5.6	1.0	1.45	13.94	3.95	65.6	3.3	34.8	16.9	6.5
9.3	0.85	2.1	0.00	5.1	0.4	0.93	7.73	3.07	55.4	3.3	48.2	20.1	6.4
4.4	0.79	7.2	0.17	5.9	0.4	1.02	12.68	5.02	68.6	4.5	36.0	11.0	2.8
7.2	0.50	2.4	0.04	8.6	0.4	1.39	8.30	4.17	46.3	3.8	17.4	10.3	6.3
9.4	0.10	0.6	0.02	2.5	0.0	0.24	2.52	4.29	91.4	4.3	35.8	10.2	2.3
2.5	2.77	21.4	1.82	3.5	0.4	0.49	5.48	4.26	77.3	2.6	20.9	16.8	3.7
8.4	0.57	2.1	0.00	7.4	0.6	1.14	6.86	3.70	56.3	1.3	5.5	24.1	8.3
3.0	5.36	20.1	-0.26	7.1	0.7	1.03	6.50	4.61	41.7	5.5	47.8	9.0	7.9
9.8	0.41	0.8	0.03	4.5	0.5	0.85	6.01	3.06	63.1	2.8	40.6	23.4	7.9
7.5	0.71	3.2	-0.01	3.4	0.1	0.31	2.80	4.01	78.7	6.4	56.9	4.6	4.6
5.9	0.27	1.8	0.33	5.3	2.2	1.14	12.47	3.96	61.3	3.7	21.3	11.2	5.2
8.7	0.79	3.0	-0.03	5.7	0.2	1.14	9.55	4.09	61.5	4.0	43.4	15.6	4.9
6.7	0.48	2.1	0.23	6.0	0.4	1.00	9.41	5.88	68.5	6.6	86.6	8.9	4.9
3.0	3.75	17.9	0.14	1.8	0.0	0.08	0.74	3.93	96.2	5.4	36.9	5.9	4.0
5.2	0.76	5.4	0.08	3.8	0.3	0.69	7.48	3.36	75.8	7.1	72.7	3.0	4.4
9.2	0.62	0.8	0.00	9.2	0.5	2.13	7.76	3.83	40.6	5.3	35.5	5.9	8.0
3.5	1.74	10.8	0.18	3.3	0.3	0.58	6.46	4.36	83.9	2.6	26.6	17.4	4.9

Name	City	State	Weiss Safety Rating	2003 Weiss Safety Rating	2002 Weiss Safety Rating	Total Assets ($Mil)	One Year Asset Growth	Commercial Loans	Consumer Loans	Home Mortgages	Securities	Capitalization Index	Leverage Ratio	Risk-based Capital Ratio
MINNESOTA FIRST CREDIT &	ROCHESTER	MN	C-	C-	C	24.3	1.89	1.1	13.8	83.7	0.0	7.8	9.5	15.8
MINNSTAR BK NA	LAKE CRYSTAL	MN	B	B	B	81.5	1.84	12.6	7.3	15.3	16.6	7.7	9.5	13.3
MINNWEST BK CENTRAL	MONTEVIDEO	MN	C+	C+	B-	176.4	3.97	11.3	5.1	6.3	8.7	6.3	8.9	12.0
▲ MINNWEST BK M.V.	REDWOOD FALLS	MN	B-	C+	C+	307.3	18.01	10.3	2.5	4.5	6.6	4.7	8.6	10.9
MINNWEST BK SIOUX FALLS	SIOUX FALLS	SD	C+	C+	B-	44.0	36.17	12.0	2.2	11.3	2.3	7.2	10.4	12.7
▼ MINNWEST BK SOUTH	TRACY	MN	C+	B-	B-	175.4	4.60	18.0	2.3	3.1	7.7	6.4	9.2	12.0
▲ MINNWEST BK-LUVERNE	LUVERNE	MN	B-	C+	B-	131.2	15.41	12.1	3.1	7.7	18.7	5.9	7.9	12.2
MINNWEST BK-ORTONVILLE	ORTONVILLE	MN	C+	C+	B-	77.9	9.72	9.1	4.9	8.3	5.5	4.2	8.4	10.6
MINOTOLA NB	VINELAND	NJ	A-	A-	A	592.7	3.31	9.7	1.0	10.3	16.0	10.0	13.0	15.9
MINSTER BK	MINSTER	OH	B-	B	B	212.5	-0.89	8.7	2.1	18.0	18.8	7.3	9.2	13.1
▲ MIRAE BK	LOS ANGELES	CA	D+	D-	D	90.2	52.42	16.8	0.3	2.9	7.3	10.0	17.9	24.9
▲ MISSION BK	KINGMAN	AZ	C+	C-	D	33.5	20.23	7.2	2.4	5.5	4.2	10.0	15.9	19.7
MISSION BK	BAKERSFIELD	CA	C+	C+	C+	105.0	24.65	18.4	0.2	1.1	6.1	4.2	7.4	10.6
MISSION BK	MISSION	KS	A-	A-	A-	440.3	0.22	16.9	0.8	1.2	29.1	10.0	13.0	17.0
MISSION COMMUNITY BK	SAN LUIS OBISPO	CA	B-	B-	C	129.5	34.73	12.8	1.0	3.2	13.4	4.9	8.5	10.9
MISSION NB	SAN FRANCISCO	CA	D	C-	C-	96.2	58.93	3.1	0.6	3.3	12.5	3.3	6.8	10.2
▲ MISSION OAKS NB	TEMECULA	CA	B+	B	C-	100.0	33.64	10.0	1.5	2.4	18.3	9.4	10.6	15.1
MISSION VALLEY BK	SUN VALLEY	CA	C+	C+	D	94.6	41.82	26.0	1.2	0.0	18.3	8.6	10.1	13.9
MISSISSIPPI COUNTY S&LA	CHARLESTON	MO	C-	C-	C-	11.5	-2.33	0.0	0.8	53.3	21.7	10.0	22.6	48.6
MISSISSIPPI NATIONAL	RIDGELAND	MS	C	C	C-	55.1	6.39	0.4	0.0	0.3	21.2	10.0	14.1	43.7
MISSISSIPPI RIVER BK	BELLE CHASSE	LA	A	A-	A-	96.8	9.76	28.5	4.3	8.5	20.1	10.0	12.0	17.6
MISSOURI B&TC	KANSAS CITY	MO	C+	C+	C+	227.7	4.48	28.4	3.0	8.7	10.2	3.3	7.5	10.1
▲ MISSOURI BK	WARRENTON	MO	B+	B	B	116.7	11.41	8.2	3.2	23.8	27.3	5.3	7.3	11.7
▲ MISSOURI FSB	CAMERON	MO	D+	D-	D-	52.2	-14.10	2.7	4.4	52.0	11.8	5.7	7.7	15.1
MISSOURI ST B&TC	ST LOUIS	MO	C	C	C-	625.3	15.86	18.6	0.7	7.2	6.4	3.7	8.7	10.3
▼ MITCHELL BANK	MILWAUKEE	WI	B-	B	B	79.8	11.71	19.4	1.8	13.1	7.8	9.9	10.9	16.1
MITSUBISHI TR & BKG CORP	NEW YORK	NY	A+	A+	A+	693.2	43.30	0.2	0.0	0.0	15.2	10.0	20.3	102.5
▼ MIZUHO CORPORATE BK OF	LOS ANGELES	CA	C	C+	C	433.3	6.94	3.8	0.0	0.2	75.6	10.0	14.1	63.8
▼ MIZUHO CORPORATE BK USA	NEW YORK	NY	C+	B-	B	2,592.6	-19.93	24.1	0.0	2.8	32.4	10.0	35.8	42.9
▼ MIZUHO TRUST & BANKING CO	NEW YORK	NY	C+	B-	C	63.0	-54.63	0.0	0.0	0.0	0.0	10.0	62.5	166.9
MMA TRUST COMPANY	GOSHEN	IN	D	D	D	2.3	-8.39	0.0	0.0	0.0	69.8	10.0	76.9	195.1
MOHAVE ST BK	LAKE HAVASU CITY	AZ	A-	A-	B+	248.5	18.16	7.3	1.2	7.0	28.5	6.6	8.7	12.6
MOJAVE DESERT BK NA	MOJAVE	CA	C-	C-	D+	60.7	22.03	8.4	5.8	1.1	29.4	5.9	7.9	14.0
▲ MONADNOCK COMMUNITY BK	PETERBOROUGH	NH	E+	E-	E-	54.4	29.31	5.2	0.7	33.8	35.8	7.9	9.6	22.5
MONARCH BK	CHESAPEAKE	VA	C-	C-	D+	206.0	21.97	21.5	1.6	8.1	15.3	5.9	11.1	11.6
▼ MONARCH COMMUNITY BANK	COLDWATER	MI	C+	B-	B-	277.3	38.80	1.6	3.4	49.9	6.3	7.6	9.4	15.3
MONITOR BK	BIG PRAIRIE	OH	C	C+	B-	26.1	11.31	15.1	7.3	14.3	2.5	10.0	13.4	22.4
▲ MONMOUTH COMMUNITY BK	LONG BRANCH	NJ	C+	C-	C	255.3	25.23	8.9	0.3	4.3	37.4	6.3	8.3	13.4
MONOGRAM CREDIT CARD BK	ALPHARETTA	GA	C-	D+	C-	3,721.8	-61.19	0.0	83.6	0.0	0.0	10.0	16.1	22.6
MONONA STATE BK	MONONA	WI	A-	A-	B+	231.3	9.59	13.0	1.9	22.5	15.7	8.3	10.1	13.6
MONONGAHELA VALLEY BK	FAIRMONT	WV	C+	C	D	102.8	9.87	8.6	13.4	16.9	21.8	6.1	8.1	12.1
MONROE B&T	MONROE	MI	C+	B-	B+	1,524.9	6.72	6.1	5.4	18.9	32.7	8.6	10.0	15.2
▲ MONROE BK	BLOOMINGTON	IN	B-	C+	B	603.9	5.82	14.5	3.1	18.1	17.5	5.6	7.6	11.7
▲ MONROE COUNTY BK	FORSYTH	GA	C	C-	C+	78.9	7.38	21.4	2.9	15.8	30.6	5.0	7.0	14.9
MONROE FS&LA	TIPP CITY	OH	C	C	C	81.7	5.34	2.2	1.1	47.8	20.3	6.1	8.1	14.2
MONROE SAVINGS BANK SLA	WILLIAMSTOWN	NJ	C+	C	C-	72.4	3.39	1.3	10.1	46.1	18.5	7.0	9.0	17.1
MONROE ST BK	MONROE	IA	B-	B-	B	20.8	3.30	7.1	8.0	14.7	34.0	10.0	17.6	30.9
MONSON SVGS BK	MONSON	MA	B-	B-	C+	162.9	8.82	8.0	1.4	27.3	22.2	6.3	8.3	12.6
▲ MONTANA ST BK	PLENTYWOOD	MT	B-	C+	C+	43.1	0.45	5.2	4.4	1.2	16.0	8.3	9.9	17.6
▲ MONTECITO B&T	SANTA BARBARA	CA	B+	B-	B-	611.0	11.97	11.8	3.9	2.9	29.2	6.0	8.8	11.8
▲ MONTEREY COUNTY BK	MONTEREY	CA	B-	C	D+	119.3	25.46	15.0	0.7	5.4	10.7	7.8	10.2	13.1
MONTEZUMA ST BK	MONTEZUMA	IA	B	B	B	32.3	-8.00	17.3	7.1	10.4	14.5	10.0	19.6	28.9
MONTEZUMA ST BK	MONTEZUMA	KS	C+	C+	C	54.2	11.83	3.4	1.6	2.9	32.3	6.6	8.6	13.5
MONTGOMERY B&TC	AILEY	GA	B	B	B-	148.9	6.55	9.4	7.5	20.0	10.1	6.9	8.9	12.4
▲ MONTGOMERY FIRST NB	SIKESTON	MO	C+	C+	C	649.5	11.82	17.5	4.4	20.1	8.7	8.6	12.0	13.9
▼ MONTICELLO BK	JACKSONVILLE	FL	C	C	D	179.4	30.23	5.1	1.4	32.2	4.6	5.3	7.3	11.4
▲ MONTICELLO BKG CO	MONTICELLO	KY	C	D+	D+	336.6	8.83	9.5	12.8	20.4	16.3	5.8	8.1	11.6
MONTROSE ST BK	MONTROSE	MI	A-	A-	A	60.6	0.81	1.4	4.2	40.6	34.1	10.0	17.3	32.2
MONTROSE SVG BK	MONTROSE	MO	B+	B+	B	33.1	-3.53	7.3	6.5	17.5	33.2	10.0	12.3	22.9
MONTROSEBANK	MONTROSE	CO	B	B	B-	103.1	12.98	20.8	5.0	15.5	12.6	4.7	7.9	10.9
▼ MOODY NB OF GALVESTON	GALVESTON	TX	B	A-	A	926.4	30.90	3.8	1.5	2.6	69.0	5.2	7.2	18.3
MOORESVILLE SVGS BK SSB	MOORESVILLE	NC	B	B	B	132.9	-4.34	2.7	1.9	65.2	1.7	10.0	13.2	22.6
▼ MOORHEAD ST BK	MOORHEAD	IA	C+	B-	B-	14.8	9.32	3.2	1.8	4.7	0.0	10.0	15.8	20.0
MOREHEAD BK	MOREHEAD	KY	C+	B-	B-	50.6	-4.06	4.0	9.0	48.8	15.6	5.1	7.1	13.6

Asset Quality Index	Non-Performing Loans as a % of Total Loans	Non-Performing Loans as a % of Capital	Net Charge-offs Avg Loans	Profitability Index	Net Income ($Mil)	Return on Assets (R.O.A.)	Return on Equity (R.O.E.)	Net Interest Spread	Overhead Efficiency Ratio	Liquidity Index	Liquidity Ratio	Hot Money Ratio	Stability Index
5.8	0.69	6.3	0.19	7.2	0.1	0.99	10.70	6.37	72.7	5.2	21.6	1.2	3.5
5.0	0.87	6.4	0.11	8.5	0.8	1.93	21.18	5.45	63.7	3.7	15.1	10.7	6.2
5.1	0.28	2.3	0.07	6.8	1.2	1.34	15.14	4.47	51.0	1.7	6.8	19.8	4.8
4.5	0.52	4.8	-0.03	10.0	2.4	1.66	19.17	4.65	41.9	1.9	6.8	18.6	6.0
8.2	0.00	0.0	-0.09	4.9	0.2	1.07	10.98	4.52	56.7	0.5	5.1	47.6	3.4
2.6	1.07	8.5	-0.02	7.9	1.3	1.43	14.54	4.16	48.2	2.6	4.8	15.0	6.0
4.5	0.69	5.2	0.01	6.6	0.7	1.06	12.23	3.72	55.1	4.0	11.6	8.2	5.4
2.3	1.10	10.3	-0.08	8.9	0.5	1.41	16.26	4.45	47.5	1.1	5.5	27.1	6.1
6.0	0.30	1.7	0.03	8.1	3.6	1.24	9.48	4.94	65.4	5.1	29.6	5.0	8.9
4.1	1.65	11.3	-0.07	6.5	1.0	0.93	9.97	3.86	70.3	4.3	22.5	7.8	6.3
6.9	0.89	3.3	0.54	1.7	0.2	0.40	2.12	4.25	76.3	4.5	105.1	25.7	0.7
7.5	0.00	0.0	-0.01	3.2	0.2	1.23	7.76	4.09	71.0	6.6	76.2	6.9	1.2
7.7	0.00	0.0	0.00	5.7	0.5	0.96	14.11	4.04	58.6	6.0	81.8	13.0	3.6
6.0	2.49	11.0	-0.11	9.7	3.7	1.69	12.88	4.16	39.2	6.3	69.6	9.4	8.7
6.8	0.24	1.9	0.00	5.3	0.5	0.79	8.96	4.77	72.6	2.5	39.7	27.8	4.5
7.4	0.05	0.5	0.00	3.9	0.2	0.51	7.01	4.70	81.4	5.1	70.6	14.5	2.8
7.3	0.00	0.0	0.00	7.5	0.7	1.43	13.73	4.87	64.6	2.8	30.2	17.6	4.0
8.4	0.00	0.0	0.00	3.1	0.3	0.71	6.81	4.33	74.7	2.2	45.4	38.5	1.4
6.6	2.23	5.8	0.00	3.7	0.0	0.68	3.00	4.43	80.8	4.1	23.8	8.4	4.8
9.7	0.00	0.0	0.00	1.8	0.1	0.29	2.21	1.91	81.4	7.3	65.4	0.0	1.8
7.1	0.81	4.1	0.14	10.0	0.8	1.78	14.86	5.37	56.2	6.2	67.2	7.9	8.2
7.7	0.16	1.6	0.01	6.8	1.7	1.58	20.85	3.92	59.6	6.7	94.3	10.8	5.2
8.8	0.07	0.6	0.01	9.4	1.3	2.16	29.00	4.32	50.6	4.6	18.7	5.2	5.9
6.6	0.20	1.9	0.37	3.1	0.1	0.30	3.91	3.17	84.4	2.0	40.8	36.0	1.9
4.3	0.39	3.2	-0.05	5.6	3.1	1.01	10.85	3.86	53.6	2.7	33.7	19.2	5.1
3.1	2.76	17.7	-0.01	3.8	0.2	0.48	4.21	4.49	81.7	5.7	58.7	9.3	4.8
10.0	86.40	1.0	0.00	7.8	2.4	0.96	3.20	1.09	60.2	10.0	4,328.7	0.0	7.5
10.0	0.00	0.0	0.00	1.8	0.4	0.16	1.09	1.59	89.6	4.6	125.2	32.0	6.3
8.7	0.73	1.1	0.05	2.6	8.4	0.60	1.85	1.71	77.9	9.9	412.2	0.5	6.5
10.0	0.00	0.0	0.00	7.6	2.0	5.81	8.63	1.35	75.3	9.4	395.6	4.3	5.0
6.5	0.00	0.0	0.00	0.0	-0.1	-3.50	-4.39	1.25	106.6	5.0	1,668.0	100.0	0.0
7.7	0.01	0.1	0.01	9.9	2.0	1.69	19.10	5.07	47.3	4.4	12.9	5.5	6.9
3.2	1.33	9.8	-0.03	6.8	0.3	1.10	13.91	5.64	68.1	3.7	8.8	9.6	2.6
7.3	0.27	1.6	-0.01	1.9	0.0	0.05	0.71	2.81	96.8	2.1	2.1	17.1	1.8
8.5	0.00	0.0	0.00	2.3	0.3	0.29	2.81	3.05	87.1	2.5	44.9	30.5	4.9
3.8	0.69	5.2	1.67	3.1	0.3	0.23	1.68	3.28	83.1	1.3	19.6	28.1	5.8
6.8	0.86	3.5	0.07	3.7	0.1	0.63	4.67	3.30	73.0	5.8	151.4	19.5	3.7
8.6	0.26	1.7	0.00	3.7	0.7	0.56	7.32	3.72	74.4	1.8	21.1	21.5	3.7
1.2	4.41	15.0	7.98	10.0	333.4	16.25	62.25	23.04	31.3	5.0	457.7	95.3	9.0
7.1	0.37	2.8	0.04	7.6	1.2	1.02	10.43	3.58	56.4	2.2	9.0	17.4	6.4
7.8	0.00	0.0	0.08	5.2	0.5	0.97	11.86	4.07	57.9	3.2	18.7	13.5	4.1
3.2	3.73	21.9	0.16	8.2	11.1	1.52	15.37	3.98	49.0	5.0	45.5	13.8	8.6
4.3	1.23	11.1	0.19	6.1	3.3	1.09	14.53	3.67	61.1	3.3	37.0	17.6	4.7
3.4	2.74	17.2	0.00	4.4	0.6	1.59	22.80	2.74	74.6	4.1	77.7	20.7	4.0
7.8	0.15	1.3	0.01	2.7	0.1	0.15	1.84	2.85	91.7	2.0	23.0	19.9	3.1
6.4	0.23	1.8	0.00	6.2	0.4	1.01	11.13	4.20	60.6	2.1	7.4	18.0	4.2
4.2	4.70	12.7	0.00	8.4	0.2	1.64	9.39	4.38	53.0	5.9	55.5	5.2	6.5
6.5	0.44	3.3	0.03	5.4	0.6	0.78	9.48	3.65	74.9	3.2	16.0	13.2	4.9
6.7	0.12	0.7	-0.04	6.8	0.4	1.62	16.00	4.25	62.4	6.9	80.3	5.7	5.7
7.0	0.14	0.8	0.03	8.7	6.1	2.05	21.38	4.75	67.6	7.0	91.5	8.3	6.6
6.3	0.43	3.0	0.00	6.1	0.6	1.02	10.07	4.71	76.6	1.2	23.2	31.8	4.4
5.4	2.88	8.5	0.11	4.9	0.1	0.83	4.16	4.59	69.0	6.3	71.0	7.9	5.8
7.0	0.22	1.5	0.10	5.1	0.3	1.12	13.24	4.23	69.9	2.5	7.6	15.8	4.6
4.7	0.96	7.4	0.07	7.7	0.8	1.13	12.55	5.14	65.8	1.4	31.0	39.0	5.8
6.4	0.33	2.4	0.00	3.9	3.0	0.97	11.19	3.42	66.9	1.4	18.4	26.5	3.8
1.5	2.01	22.7	0.00	9.8	1.6	2.06	25.75	3.20	61.4	0.5	7.3	49.0	3.9
3.3	1.52	13.2	0.43	5.0	1.8	1.07	13.08	4.49	62.7	1.5	12.9	23.7	3.6
6.8	2.34	7.3	0.03	7.3	0.3	1.09	6.37	4.54	64.2	6.7	78.5	6.6	8.1
4.7	3.29	13.2	0.03	8.9	0.2	1.30	10.14	4.09	49.4	5.0	57.5	13.1	6.9
7.6	0.01	0.1	0.00	10.0	1.4	2.83	32.17	6.64	54.0	4.5	15.5	5.6	6.4
7.2	1.49	5.1	0.64	4.5	2.8	0.61	8.67	2.38	70.2	4.2	33.1	11.5	5.7
4.6	3.35	20.0	0.00	4.0	0.4	0.53	3.93	3.81	78.4	5.8	129.4	18.1	8.0
2.2	4.09	18.5	-0.44	9.8	0.2	2.63	16.19	4.00	35.8	5.5	60.4	8.7	7.1
2.2	4.05	35.2	0.19	4.7	0.2	0.89	12.80	3.97	74.0	4.2	36.8	12.9	4.5

| Name | City | State | Weiss Safety Rating | 2003 Weiss Safety Rating | 2002 Weiss Safety Rating | Total Assets ($Mil) | One Year Asset Growth | Asset Mix (As a % of Total Assets) | | | | Capital-ization Index | Leverage Ratio | Risk-based Capital Ratio |
								Comm-ercial Loans	Cons-umer Loans	Home Mort-gages	Secur-ities			
MORGAN BK NA	HUDSON	OH	C	C	C-	131.9	28.51	14.2	35.7	7.3	27.0	4.2	7.6	10.6
MORGAN FEDERAL BK	FORT MORGAN	CO	B	B	B	92.2	-1.68	0.8	0.9	39.3	33.2	8.7	10.1	18.7
MORGAN STANLEY BK	W VALLEY CITY	UT	A	A	A-	3,832.3	31.31	9.0	0.0	0.0	17.8	10.0	36.3	26.1
MORGAN STANLEY TRUST	JERSEY CITY	NJ	B+	B+	B+	67.9	14.08	0.0	0.0	0.0	74.6	10.0	56.6	167.9
MORGANTON FS&LA	MORGANTON	NC	B+	B+	A	72.5	-1.53	0.0	0.8	14.9	20.6	10.0	28.6	39.1
MORGANTOWN B&TC	MORGANTOWN	KY	C	C	B-	129.9	8.12	3.1	8.0	31.8	38.7	8.7	10.1	18.8
▲ MORNINGSIDE B&TC	SIOUX CITY	IA	B+	B	B	35.1	-3.59	11.6	6.2	25.6	40.0	6.6	8.6	14.6
MORRILL & JANES B&TC	MERRIAM	KS	B	B	B-	371.6	1.02	17.2	1.4	4.3	35.3	6.2	8.2	12.8
MORRIS BLDG LOAN SB	MORRIS	IL	D+	D+	D	39.2	-3.95	0.0	3.2	44.0	16.3	7.2	9.1	20.1
▲ MORRIS COUNTY NB OF	NAPLES	TX	C-	D+	D+	73.8	4.46	10.8	18.4	17.9	22.4	5.7	8.0	11.5
MORRIS PLAN CO-TERRE	TERRE HAUTE	IN	B+	B	D+	47.1	-0.86	2.2	48.2	37.1	3.3	9.7	10.8	14.8
MORRIS ST BK	DUBLIN	GA	B-	B-	B-	112.9	-7.78	7.6	4.8	17.8	31.2	8.8	10.2	16.1
MORRIS ST BK	MORRIS	OK	C+	C+	C+	44.6	3.55	6.0	27.8	31.1	4.5	6.6	8.6	12.3
▲ MORTON COMMUNITY BK	MORTON	IL	B	B-	B-	1,046.0	10.96	8.3	3.0	23.0	30.0	5.2	7.2	12.2
MORTON SVGS BK	MORTON	PA	E-	E-	E-	19.1	-5.10	0.0	0.8	50.4	37.3	4.2	6.2	15.8
MOUND CITY BK	PLATTEVILLE	WI	B-	B-	C+	187.4	-5.28	9.2	3.5	26.1	17.7	7.3	9.2	14.0
MOUNT GILEAD S&LA	MT GILEAD	NC	D+	D+	D+	8.7	1.98	0.0	0.1	74.7	3.1	10.0	17.1	37.6
MOUNT MCKINLEY BK	FAIRBANKS	AK	A	A	A	204.5	3.43	9.6	1.0	13.9	30.9	10.0	17.5	27.4
MOUNT PROSPECT NB	MT PROSPECT	IL	D+	C	C	334.7	19.51	22.7	1.3	1.7	24.9	3.2	7.2	10.1
MOUNT RAINIER NB	ENUMCLAW	WA	B+	A-	A-	167.9	14.04	13.0	3.1	5.5	21.8	9.0	10.7	14.1
MOUNT STERLING BK	MT STERLING	KY	C+	B-	B-	100.6	2.32	2.7	6.9	30.6	20.1	8.0	9.6	17.8
MOUNT VERNON B&TC	MT VERNON	IA	A-	A-	A-	60.5	0.10	5.6	4.1	40.9	25.5	10.0	14.3	25.7
▲ MOUNT VERNON BK	MT VERNON	GA	C+	C+	C+	72.9	5.09	3.7	7.6	20.0	23.8	6.7	8.7	14.0
MOUNTAIN 1ST B&T	HENDERSONVILLE	NC	D	NR	NR	70.4	N/A	4.9	1.1	14.1	7.6	10.0	51.9	35.0
MOUNTAIN HERITAGE BK	CLAYTON	GA	D	D	NR	39.5	N/A	7.8	6.3	19.8	17.6	10.0	28.7	39.5
MOUNTAIN NB	TUCKER	GA	B	B	B	248.1	-1.31	36.0	1.6	2.0	3.2	4.8	9.3	10.9
▼ MOUNTAIN NB	SEVIERVILLE	TN	C+	B-	B-	249.2	17.49	3.7	3.1	11.1	14.4	5.2	8.6	11.2
MOUNTAIN NB	GALAX	VA	D+	C+	C+	224.3	-0.19	1.4	3.9	8.2	30.6	4.6	6.6	13.8
▲ MOUNTAIN ST BK	DAWSONVILLE	GA	D+	D	NR	62.4	174.73	6.7	1.8	4.1	12.9	10.0	17.2	19.3
MOUNTAIN STATES BK	DENVER	CO	A	A	A	279.5	-0.88	8.2	2.9	9.3	46.4	10.0	14.1	26.7
MOUNTAIN VALLEY BK	WALDEN	CO	E+	D-	D	15.7	30.42	6.7	3.5	7.9	30.4	10.0	23.6	57.8
MOUNTAIN VALLEY BK	DUNLAP	TN	B-	B-	B-	67.0	9.53	4.6	23.1	28.8	14.6	10.0	12.2	18.1
MOUNTAIN VALLEY BK NA	ELKINS	WV	B+	A-	A-	88.3	-0.97	6.9	3.9	26.7	37.3	10.0	13.4	25.5
MOUNTAIN VALLEY	CLEVELAND	GA	D	NR	NR	21.8	N/A	1.1	2.4	2.2	11.3	10.0	111.0	104.1
▲ MOUNTAIN WEST BK	COEUR D'ALENE	ID	B-	B-	C	583.1	29.34	7.3	1.4	11.0	30.9	5.3	7.3	11.6
MOUNTAIN WEST BK NA	HELENA	MT	C+	C+	C+	424.6	7.60	19.4	3.4	9.6	3.4	3.9	8.6	10.4
MOUNTAIN WEST BK NA	KALISPELL	MT	C+	C+	C	73.6	19.86	24.1	6.2	5.6	8.5	5.4	8.7	11.3
MT MORRIS S&LA	MT MORRIS	IL	E-	E-	E-	45.8	8.56	0.0	3.1	35.8	26.2	3.7	5.7	14.3
MT VICTORY ST BK	MT VICTORY	OH	C+	C+	C+	11.3	-4.68	4.6	17.3	9.9	37.8	10.0	13.5	28.8
MT WASHINGTON CO-OP BK	S BOSTON	MA	B	B	B	359.1	15.00	0.1	0.4	45.8	25.7	6.3	8.3	16.4
MT WASHINGTON S&LC	CINCINNATI	OH	C+	B-	B-	60.4	-8.14	0.0	0.7	73.6	7.1	10.0	21.2	39.2
MT. TROY BANK	PITTSBURGH	PA	B+	B	B	74.7	7.33	0.0	0.7	31.7	42.8	10.0	11.6	23.9
MUENSTER ST BK	MUENSTER	TX	A	A	A	73.6	3.47	2.4	3.5	7.4	67.3	10.0	16.6	43.7
MULESHOE ST BK	MULESHOE	TX	C	C	C	75.9	2.18	8.1	7.0	6.2	26.9	6.9	8.9	12.6
MULVANE ST BK	MULVANE	KS	B+	B+	B+	68.0	9.63	11.7	10.5	5.5	36.2	10.0	11.2	20.1
MUNCY B&TC	MUNCY	PA	A	A	A	139.6	5.75	4.2	6.7	45.9	22.3	10.0	11.6	17.4
▲ MUNICIPAL T&SB	BOURBONNAIS	IL	A+	A	A	283.6	2.59	0.6	5.5	18.7	23.7	10.0	12.3	26.5
MURPHY BK	FRESNO	CA	B-	B-	A-	97.9	11.04	6.5	66.9	4.1	3.6	9.0	12.0	14.1
MURPHY WALL ST B&TC	PINCKNEYVILLE	IL	B+	B	B	68.4	-0.87	10.5	3.8	19.7	33.1	10.0	14.7	29.0
▲ MURRAY BK	MURRAY	KY	C	C-	D+	148.2	30.73	4.7	6.8	20.8	41.2	5.9	7.9	17.1
MURRAY ST BK	MURRAY	NE	B	B	B+	35.6	-0.49	9.3	6.1	22.4	21.3	10.0	12.5	20.8
MUSKEGON CMRC BK	MUSKEGON	MI	C	C	C	94.1	10.90	16.4	1.1	17.2	0.1	5.9	10.0	11.7
▼ MUTUAL BK	HARVEY	IL	D+	C-	C	429.1	89.08	7.9	0.3	6.1	11.0	2.9	8.0	9.9
▲ MUTUAL COMMUNITY SVGS	DURHAM	NC	D+	D-	D	94.8	-3.26	2.9	1.3	36.5	16.1	6.0	8.1	13.9
MUTUAL FS&LA OF CHICAGO	CHICAGO	IL	A-	B+	B+	68.6	-0.50	0.0	0.0	30.7	42.5	10.0	26.4	72.9
▼ MUTUAL FSB	MUNCIE	IN	B+	A-	B+	815.9	2.58	6.1	18.3	49.0	4.5	9.4	10.6	15.9
MUTUAL FSB OF PLYMOUTH	WHITMAN	MA	B+	B+	A-	108.8	-0.17	0.0	0.8	45.9	43.0	10.0	12.0	28.6
MUTUAL FSB, A FSB	SIDNEY	OH	B	B	B-	94.3	8.79	2.8	27.5	47.6	2.0	8.9	10.5	14.1
MUTUAL S&LA	METAIRIE	LA	B+	B+	B+	48.9	-5.69	0.0	3.2	75.8	1.7	10.0	16.6	33.3
MUTUAL S&LA FA	HARTSVILLE	SC	C+	C+	B-	63.5	-6.58	1.1	5.3	32.1	20.4	10.0	18.4	39.5
▼ MUTUAL SA FSA	LEAVENWORTH	KS	B+	A-	A	256.9	-2.63	2.2	1.6	39.5	33.5	10.0	16.8	32.6
▲ MUTUAL SVGS BK	FRANKLIN	IN	B-	C+	C	120.1	17.04	5.8	5.2	44.6	0.0	10.0	13.6	20.3
MWABANK	ROCK ISLAND	IL	D	D	NR	19.5	66.97	0.0	0.4	76.9	3.0	10.0	35.6	63.2
▲ N.J.M. BK FSB	W TRENTON	NJ	B-	C+	C	297.2	28.92	0.1	0.2	56.1	30.9	10.0	12.8	33.4

Asset Quality Index	Non-Performing Loans as a % of Total Loans	Non-Performing Loans as a % of Capital	Net Charge-offs Avg Loans	Profitability Index	Net Income ($Mil)	Return on Assets (R.O.A.)	Return on Equity (R.O.E.)	Net Interest Spread	Overhead Efficiency Ratio	Liquidity Index	Liquidity Ratio	Hot Money Ratio	Stability Index
3.6	1.56	14.1	0.23	4.4	0.4	0.71	9.31	3.58	71.1	3.8	5.9	9.0	3.3
8.6	0.03	0.2	0.01	6.5	0.5	1.04	10.48	2.91	53.5	0.8	12.2	33.9	5.9
8.4	0.00	0.0	0.00	7.9	26.7	1.32	3.40	1.26	16.5	3.3	69.7	56.6	10.0
6.6	0.00	0.0	0.00	10.0	31.0	86.06	151.04	1.70	44.2	1.7	44.7	100.0	3.7
6.7	1.21	2.2	0.00	4.3	0.2	0.52	1.84	3.11	81.3	3.6	37.0	16.2	7.3
4.1	1.68	9.0	0.85	3.1	0.3	0.53	5.21	3.25	79.5	3.3	47.2	21.3	5.3
7.1	0.08	0.5	0.00	6.0	0.2	0.95	10.15	3.62	75.6	4.8	24.8	4.9	7.8
7.7	0.03	0.1	0.00	6.1	1.8	0.96	9.89	3.19	56.5	1.5	4.3	21.5	6.0
7.6	0.16	1.0	-0.02	1.3	-0.1	-0.27	-2.87	3.92	106.8	7.1	64.0	1.5	2.5
2.5	1.85	15.5	0.78	6.7	0.6	1.75	21.65	5.15	61.8	1.9	14.3	19.6	3.3
1.9	1.79	11.0	3.23	7.6	0.4	1.71	16.30	8.45	29.6	1.6	6.5	20.3	6.5
3.7	4.73	25.2	0.01	5.3	0.9	1.57	15.07	4.33	64.8	3.3	29.3	15.0	4.2
4.6	0.45	4.1	0.60	9.7	0.3	1.50	17.68	6.02	50.7	1.6	22.4	25.4	4.3
7.0	0.60	4.5	0.02	5.8	7.4	1.44	19.54	2.54	44.4	2.3	38.2	44.8	6.7
9.3	0.24	2.1	0.00	2.3	0.0	0.06	1.03	2.74	97.8	2.0	19.8	19.3	0.0
4.4	1.68	12.7	0.41	4.1	0.7	0.68	7.47	3.22	68.2	2.3	17.6	17.8	4.2
8.5	0.00	0.0	0.00	3.8	0.0	0.58	3.13	3.82	80.8	4.1	22.5	8.7	3.0
8.9	0.18	0.6	0.00	7.7	1.2	1.21	7.02	4.86	66.0	5.4	40.3	7.3	9.0
3.0	1.47	13.4	0.48	4.0	1.0	0.62	9.17	3.38	60.9	2.2	35.9	27.6	2.8
8.4	0.02	0.1	0.02	5.7	0.8	0.94	9.02	4.66	70.2	3.1	26.7	14.8	6.2
5.7	0.69	3.0	-0.04	6.8	0.6	1.27	8.80	4.76	59.4	4.2	42.5	14.6	5.0
8.8	0.46	2.0	0.00	6.2	0.3	0.96	6.75	4.04	66.9	5.5	32.9	3.5	7.2
4.4	1.04	6.9	-0.07	6.2	0.5	1.36	15.03	4.30	68.4	3.1	73.1	36.8	5.2
7.7	0.00	0.0	0.00	0.0	-0.8	-3.75	-9.84	0.59	121.0	4.8	117.5	25.1	0.0
9.0	0.00	0.0	0.00	0.0	-0.6	-4.19	-12.53	2.54	210.1	4.5	132.6	33.1	0.0
6.7	0.08	0.7	0.06	6.7	1.2	0.97	9.83	4.99	65.2	1.2	9.4	27.0	7.5
3.8	0.87	7.4	0.32	4.9	1.0	0.88	10.40	4.39	68.4	0.9	8.5	31.1	4.4
2.5	3.09	20.5	0.03	4.5	0.8	0.71	10.88	2.42	60.0	7.0	106.3	10.4	2.8
7.4	0.00	0.0	0.00	1.0	0.0	0.01	0.04	4.63	86.5	5.2	38.5	7.7	0.0
8.8	0.46	1.4	0.10	6.9	1.6	1.16	8.39	3.74	59.0	6.7	64.1	6.1	8.2
6.4	2.45	3.1	0.00	0.9	0.0	-0.16	-1.04	0.09	383.3	7.8	139.9	7.3	3.0
3.2	2.42	14.0	0.34	7.1	0.4	1.13	9.12	5.88	63.2	3.0	21.8	14.9	6.2
8.9	0.00	0.0	0.01	5.0	0.4	0.92	6.86	4.52	71.5	5.0	34.2	7.5	7.6
9.8	0.00	0.0	0.00	0.0	-0.8	-10.88	-18.62	0.20	3,390.9	6.5	144.2	14.6	0.0
4.7	0.73	3.7	0.12	7.0	3.6	1.28	11.66	4.87	64.2	4.4	20.3	6.8	7.1
3.1	1.26	11.4	0.10	7.6	2.5	1.21	14.21	4.88	57.2	1.7	20.2	23.2	4.7
7.9	0.03	0.3	0.06	4.2	0.2	0.50	5.69	4.40	82.7	2.6	32.3	19.6	5.0
4.1	0.85	7.4	0.13	1.9	0.0	-0.01	-0.15	3.20	96.3	3.7	4.4	9.4	0.3
7.6	0.44	1.4	-0.04	5.3	0.1	1.12	8.25	4.66	70.4	5.2	41.1	5.9	5.0
8.3	0.41	3.2	0.04	4.5	1.3	0.74	9.11	3.97	74.2	1.1	10.2	28.4	4.6
2.6	4.48	15.2	0.12	5.9	0.4	1.12	5.13	3.62	50.4	2.6	12.1	15.6	6.7
9.2	0.22	1.0	0.06	6.6	0.4	1.03	8.71	3.17	52.5	1.7	24.6	24.9	6.3
9.5	0.00	0.0	-0.13	9.8	0.8	2.15	13.05	4.04	27.9	3.4	46.2	19.1	9.0
6.9	0.58	3.6	0.06	3.3	0.1	0.37	4.29	4.25	87.8	3.5	23.7	12.5	3.9
8.0	0.03	0.1	0.19	5.0	0.4	1.15	9.87	4.26	69.2	4.7	51.9	13.7	5.5
7.3	0.69	4.1	0.06	7.6	1.0	1.44	12.70	4.45	55.5	3.2	15.7	13.0	8.3
8.7	0.40	1.5	0.00	8.5	2.6	1.85	15.09	2.93	40.3	7.9	152.2	9.4	9.0
3.6	0.55	3.9	0.14	10.0	1.9	3.96	33.85	7.06	38.2	3.1	79.5	48.6	7.6
6.7	1.37	4.6	0.19	6.0	0.4	1.09	7.39	4.20	65.4	3.6	25.4	12.2	6.6
7.4	0.47	2.7	0.01	4.6	0.5	0.75	9.35	2.90	62.9	2.7	55.4	49.7	5.0
8.3	0.00	0.0	0.00	6.4	0.2	1.06	8.77	4.06	62.5	5.5	53.9	10.1	6.0
0.6	2.19	18.3	0.07	9.5	0.6	1.42	13.79	4.59	55.4	1.2	18.8	29.8	6.4
2.2	1.77	15.9	0.90	4.8	1.7	0.92	11.32	4.72	51.5	2.2	33.4	25.0	3.7
4.3	1.79	14.9	0.17	1.6	0.1	0.26	3.25	3.63	86.3	3.0	41.9	21.1	3.3
8.4	1.30	2.0	0.00	9.4	0.7	1.90	6.89	3.50	42.6	3.9	56.0	18.1	7.3
4.4	0.64	4.8	-0.09	5.5	3.9	0.95	8.46	3.61	62.1	1.4	4.7	23.0	8.4
9.2	0.12	0.5	0.24	5.0	0.4	0.69	5.71	3.72	74.2	3.6	15.4	11.0	7.1
4.7	0.43	3.6	0.12	8.2	0.7	1.40	13.49	4.54	56.0	2.9	3.9	13.6	5.8
9.0	0.00	0.0	0.00	6.6	0.3	1.02	6.27	3.36	57.4	1.1	3.9	27.1	6.3
5.0	2.47	6.7	0.11	2.7	0.3	0.91	4.57	3.61	69.7	2.0	28.1	22.8	5.6
6.4	1.16	3.9	0.03	4.5	0.6	0.48	2.94	2.08	66.9	3.1	26.9	15.2	7.8
7.7	0.33	2.0	0.15	4.3	0.4	0.67	7.09	3.90	74.7	6.6	70.3	7.7	3.9
8.3	0.00	0.0	0.00	0.0	-1.0	-11.73	-27.80	2.84	526.5	0.8	15.7	34.5	0.0
10.0	0.00	0.0	0.00	3.7	0.6	0.45	3.44	2.56	70.0	1.1	24.0	33.8	6.9

Name	City	State	Weiss Safety Rating	2003 Weiss Safety Rating	2002 Weiss Safety Rating	Total Assets ($Mil)	One Year Asset Growth	Asset Mix (As a % of Total Assets)				Capital- ization Index	Leverage Ratio	Risk-based Capital Ratio
								Comm- ercial Loans	Cons- umer Loans	Home Mort- gages	Secur- ities			
▼ NAB BK	CHICAGO	IL	D-	D	D+	139.9	-15.20	7.1	0.7	34.1	12.2	5.0	7.0	13.2
NANTUCKET BK	NANTUCKET	MA	B+	B+	B+	571.4	19.10	6.2	0.4	44.3	5.9	6.4	8.4	12.5
NAPA COMMUNITY BK	NAPA	CA	C	C	C	66.0	36.76	8.6	0.1	4.6	0.0	10.0	13.2	16.4
NAPOLEON BK	NAPOLEON	MO	B+	B+	B+	37.2	0.15	6.1	6.9	16.8	43.2	10.0	15.5	33.0
▲ NAPOLEON ST BK	NAPOLEON	IN	A-	B+	B+	88.9	5.12	6.9	13.3	29.7	10.4	9.6	10.7	16.2
▲ NARA BK NA	LOS ANGELES	CA	B+	B	B-	1,395.2	30.81	20.5	3.7	1.8	9.1	5.6	9.1	11.4
NASHVILLE SVGS BK	NASHVILLE	IL	B-	B	C+	31.9	18.84	0.0	2.3	25.4	46.7	7.6	9.4	26.6
NATBANK NA	HOLLYWOOD	FL	B+	B+	B+	72.7	-15.83	20.9	5.0	44.3	20.9	10.0	18.9	33.9
NATICK FSB	NATICK	MA	C	C	B-	176.1	-8.84	0.0	0.5	27.3	46.9	8.9	10.2	26.8
NATIONAL ADVISORS TRUST	OVERLAND PARK	KS	D	D	D	2.9	3.02	0.0	0.0	0.0	54.6	10.0	69.0	215.4
▲ NATIONAL AMERICAN BK	SAN FRANCISCO	CA	C+	C-	C-	84.9	3.98	0.1	0.0	2.2	14.7	10.0	11.7	18.3
▲ NATIONAL AMERICAN BK	UVALDE	TX	D	D-	D-	43.8	-34.43	7.0	1.9	2.4	26.5	10.0	11.1	21.3
▲ NATIONAL B&T	LA GRANGE	TX	B+	B	B	90.4	-1.29	2.8	8.6	16.8	54.6	10.0	11.6	28.8
▲ NATIONAL B&TC	WILMINGTON	OH	C+	C	C	649.2	-6.05	14.1	12.9	18.3	27.8	6.2	8.2	13.5
▼ NATIONAL B&TC OF	SYCAMORE	IL	B+	A-	B+	485.8	14.19	11.5	15.6	4.9	21.6	8.8	11.2	14.0
NATIONAL BANK	HILLSBORO	IL	C+	C+	C	194.6	-9.32	5.0	2.4	17.4	20.9	7.9	9.6	14.4
▲ NATIONAL BANK OF	MONTPELIER	OH	A-	A-	A-	113.4	-1.40	1.5	3.2	30.4	46.1	10.0	14.5	37.2
NATIONAL BK	BETTENDORF	IA	C+	C+	C-	371.8	23.77	20.0	12.6	7.4	16.8	5.9	9.2	11.7
NATIONAL BK	GATESVILLE	TX	B-	B-	B-	318.8	6.25	7.6	11.1	16.0	21.1	7.4	9.3	15.1
NATIONAL BK OF ADAMS	W UNION	OH	A-	A-	A-	66.4	10.16	2.8	8.5	29.5	16.0	10.0	14.2	31.0
NATIONAL BK OF ANDREWS	ANDREWS	TX	B-	B-	B-	71.0	7.86	20.5	10.1	11.8	16.9	6.7	8.7	14.2
NATIONAL BK OF ARIZONA	TUCSON	AZ	B-	B-	B-	3,324.3	10.08	9.3	1.0	17.7	6.8	3.5	5.5	10.6
▼ NATIONAL BK OF ARKANSAS	N LITTLE ROCK	AR	D	D+	D+	135.6	0.40	10.6	2.7	18.2	12.4	6.9	8.9	12.6
▼ NATIONAL BK OF	BLACKSBURG	VA	B+	A-	B+	476.5	19.67	8.1	6.5	14.7	27.3	4.3	8.0	10.7
NATIONAL BK OF CALIFORNIA	LOS ANGELES	CA	B-	B-	C+	221.9	23.49	41.8	0.7	0.0	6.1	7.7	9.6	13.1
▼ NATIONAL BK OF CAMBRIDGE	CAMBRIDGE	MD	A-	A	A	196.3	0.16	7.0	3.3	12.6	43.0	10.0	16.3	29.1
▲ NATIONAL BK OF COMMERCE	BIRMINGHAM	AL	B	B-	B-	1,403.6	0.96	7.1	1.0	9.8	23.2	5.0	7.3	11.0
▲ NATIONAL BK OF COMMERCE	BERKELEY	IL	C	C-	C-	359.3	-11.75	5.8	0.7	3.2	45.5	5.2	7.2	11.9
NATIONAL BK OF COMMERCE	STARKVILLE	MS	B+	A-	A-	1,056.7	-1.45	7.9	4.9	17.4	35.1	6.1	8.1	14.1
NATIONAL BK OF COMMERCE	MEMPHIS	TN	B	B	B	23,696.9	5.05	8.8	6.4	14.8	25.2	4.8	7.5	10.9
NATIONAL BK OF COMMERCE	SUPERIOR	WI	A-	A-	B	322.9	15.46	15.7	1.7	10.5	17.6	9.5	11.8	14.5
NATIONAL BK OF COXSACKIE	COXSACKIE	NY	A	A	A	149.0	-2.63	5.6	8.0	30.0	31.0	9.7	10.8	21.0
NATIONAL BK OF	DAINGERFIELD	TX	D+	D+	D	74.4	4.16	6.8	11.7	25.1	20.4	6.0	8.0	14.5
▲ NATIONAL BK OF DAVIS	DAVIS	WV	E+	E-	E-	24.4	-1.15	12.5	6.9	13.7	46.9	4.8	6.8	16.4
NATIONAL BK OF DELAWARE	WALTON	NY	A	A	A	153.7	0.98	6.5	4.0	17.7	49.4	10.0	13.4	28.0
NATIONAL BK OF EARLVILLE	EARLVILLE	IL	A-	A-	A-	49.2	-2.26	4.9	5.5	16.8	35.1	10.0	15.6	27.1
▼ NATIONAL BK OF GAINESVILLE	GAINESVILLE	GA	D+	D+	D-	58.4	23.12	11.8	16.9	22.7	4.4	6.1	8.1	12.2
NATIONAL BK OF GENEVA	GENEVA	NY	D+	D+	C-	688.4	-9.33	9.6	6.4	5.4	32.7	6.5	8.5	13.6
▼ NATIONAL BK OF GEORGIA	ATHENS	GA	C+	B-	C+	148.3	27.97	9.1	2.3	28.3	1.1	5.1	8.3	11.1
NATIONAL BK OF HARVEY	HARVEY	ND	C	C	C+	53.7	7.74	24.5	1.4	7.3	32.7	9.2	10.5	15.5
NATIONAL BK OF	INDIANAPOLIS	IN	C	C	C	847.4	9.04	28.0	3.4	13.6	15.1	4.0	6.4	10.5
NATIONAL BK OF KANSAS	LEAWOOD	KS	A	A-	B	310.3	62.85	8.5	0.3	25.0	19.0	8.1	11.6	13.5
NATIONAL BK OF	MADISONVILLE	TX	C+	C+	C	39.6	2.73	9.7	8.5	12.1	24.6	10.0	11.3	20.3
NATIONAL BK OF MALVERN	MALVERN	PA	A-	A-	B+	103.7	16.14	25.4	2.7	49.2	17.3	10.0	11.5	18.7
NATIONAL BK OF MIDDLEBURY	MIDDLEBURY	VT	B-	B-	B-	179.6	4.66	3.7	0.9	41.4	20.7	6.5	8.5	14.0
▼ NATIONAL BK OF NEW YORK	NEW YORK CITY	NY	A-	A	A+	159.0	2.95	2.2	0.0	0.0	14.4	10.0	14.9	18.3
NATIONAL BK OF NORTH EAST	N EAST	PA	D	D	C-	75.2	-7.82	13.9	3.5	11.3	9.2	7.6	9.4	14.1
NATIONAL BK OF OAK	OAK HARBOR	OH	B-	C+	B-	146.9	14.79	7.3	8.0	25.3	15.1	6.8	8.8	13.0
NATIONAL BK OF	PETERSBURG	IL	C+	B-	B-	132.8	-3.41	4.4	5.3	21.0	37.9	9.2	10.5	18.4
▲ NATIONAL BK OF SALLISAW	SALLISAW	OK	A	A-	A-	82.4	11.71	22.1	7.2	5.8	32.8	10.0	13.7	21.3
▲ NATIONAL BK OF SC	SUMTER	SC	B	B-	B	3,054.4	14.26	18.8	2.3	7.9	9.9	4.4	8.5	10.7
NATIONAL BK OF ST ANNE	ST ANNE	IL	B-	B-	B-	28.2	-0.93	8.9	6.5	8.3	38.6	9.9	10.9	24.7
NATIONAL BK OF STAMFORD	STAMFORD	NY	B-	B-	B	103.1	-2.54	8.5	2.4	7.9	53.9	10.0	14.1	30.5
NATIONAL BK OF TENNESSEE	NEWPORT	TN	C+	C+	C+	157.4	0.65	6.1	7.0	15.3	31.0	5.7	7.7	12.8
NATIONAL BK OF TEXAS	FORT WORTH	TX	B	B+	B+	92.0	13.51	9.6	11.0	0.6	37.1	6.2	8.2	16.7
NATIONAL BK OF THE	SANTA ROSA	CA	B	B-	B-	511.7	-2.49	6.0	0.1	15.9	9.8	4.9	8.2	11.0
▼ NATIONAL BK OF VERNON	VERNON	NY	C+	B-	B-	66.7	1.11	8.1	3.5	23.2	37.1	9.2	10.5	22.4
▼ NATIONAL BK OF WALTON	MONROE	GA	B-	B	B	240.1	2.09	6.4	4.3	12.6	22.1	3.7	7.1	10.4
NATIONAL BK OF WAUPUN	WAUPUN	WI	B+	B+	A-	103.7	2.33	15.4	6.9	20.1	14.4	6.5	9.3	12.1
NATIONAL CAPITAL BK OF WA	WASHINGTON	DC	A+	A+	A+	207.9	11.69	12.1	1.4	41.7	17.0	10.0	13.4	23.3
▼ NATIONAL CITY BK	NEW ALBANY	IN	C	B-	B-	377.5	5.92	7.2	0.3	2.6	0.0	8.0	9.7	27.4
NATIONAL CITY BK	CLEVELAND	OH	C+	C+	C+	47,666.7	2.16	18.0	14.4	12.4	4.4	3.7	6.6	10.3
NATIONAL CITY BK INDIANA	INDIANAPOLIS	IN	C+	C+	C	40,988.9	-22.11	4.1	0.6	76.5	1.6	4.3	6.3	11.9
NATIONAL CITY BK KY	LOUISVILLE	KY	C+	C+	C+	8,404.1	-10.08	19.2	1.7	6.4	7.3	3.3	5.3	12.8

Asset Quality Index	Non-Performing Loans as a % of Total Loans	as a % of Capital	Net Charge-offs Avg Loans	Profitability Index	Net Income ($Mil)	Return on Assets (R.O.A.)	Return on Equity (R.O.E.)	Net Interest Spread	Overhead Efficiency Ratio	Liquidity Index	Liquidity Ratio	Hot Money Ratio	Stability Index
2.7	2.42	21.6	0.99	0.7	-0.6	-0.85	-11.88	3.65	122.4	6.6	77.5	9.3	1.6
7.2	0.00	0.0	-0.03	9.5	3.9	1.49	10.29	4.23	41.0	3.9	30.8	12.3	8.1
5.5	1.27	6.7	0.00	3.2	0.2	0.60	4.29	5.62	75.4	6.9	75.4	5.2	2.9
8.7	0.00	0.0	0.09	5.3	0.2	1.24	8.07	4.04	67.0	6.9	150.9	13.9	6.7
6.9	0.32	2.2	0.05	7.9	0.5	1.07	9.94	4.19	59.7	3.6	38.0	16.5	6.2
6.1	0.36	2.9	0.18	9.6	9.5	1.46	16.12	4.69	54.2	2.8	40.7	30.5	7.8
9.7	0.00	0.0	0.00	4.3	0.1	0.74	6.83	3.01	64.5	6.1	246.7	26.5	4.4
6.8	0.70	2.4	-0.02	4.7	0.3	0.74	3.94	4.10	75.4	4.2	14.7	7.3	6.6
8.3	0.42	1.3	0.03	3.2	0.3	0.33	3.32	2.07	86.6	3.2	47.0	22.1	4.9
7.1	0.00	0.0	0.00	0.0	-0.8	-49.55	-73.75	0.09	177.4	5.0	250.0	100.0	0.0
4.3	1.94	9.0	0.00	2.8	0.1	0.25	2.51	2.91	89.4	5.6	164.2	25.0	5.6
3.7	5.45	21.5	0.56	0.1	-0.7	-2.74	-23.96	2.58	102.9	4.7	131.6	29.8	1.8
7.2	0.53	1.8	0.16	6.1	0.5	1.10	9.65	3.87	62.4	5.3	40.6	7.8	5.3
3.7	1.51	9.7	0.51	4.2	2.7	0.83	9.27	3.64	73.0	4.2	11.1	7.0	3.9
4.8	0.51	3.0	0.06	7.3	2.7	1.25	10.17	3.57	60.7	3.1	44.1	21.9	6.8
5.0	1.07	7.0	0.05	3.9	0.6	0.64	6.72	3.89	74.2	6.5	46.5	2.4	3.8
8.7	0.89	2.7	0.24	5.4	0.6	1.03	7.04	4.00	63.0	6.4	52.1	4.7	8.1
5.2	0.43	2.9	0.58	4.5	1.5	0.81	8.27	5.09	72.8	4.0	13.3	8.2	2.2
4.5	1.00	6.5	0.54	8.2	1.9	1.23	13.08	4.52	67.0	3.9	32.6	13.1	5.9
5.8	2.31	8.5	0.08	8.4	0.6	1.74	12.72	3.67	50.5	7.9	119.6	5.1	8.5
5.0	0.67	4.0	0.84	7.5	0.6	1.69	18.34	5.43	68.4	5.1	51.3	11.2	5.9
3.9	0.68	6.6	0.02	8.8	19.2	1.21	15.97	4.57	55.2	7.8	98.7	5.3	7.1
0.9	3.32	26.2	0.23	6.4	1.3	1.90	23.19	4.36	66.6	1.2	7.8	26.9	3.8
7.9	0.03	0.2	0.12	10.0	4.1	1.93	18.75	4.75	51.3	4.6	41.4	12.2	7.0
8.1	0.04	0.3	-0.03	6.7	1.2	1.17	12.83	5.01	65.1	3.9	32.9	13.0	4.6
8.3	1.04	3.1	0.07	5.5	0.9	0.94	5.83	3.45	60.7	2.0	23.2	19.6	8.7
8.2	0.10	0.8	0.18	6.1	7.1	1.03	14.45	2.82	70.9	1.4	16.6	27.2	6.3
6.8	0.34	1.4	-0.24	2.9	1.5	0.81	8.95	2.20	75.3	1.9	29.9	27.0	4.2
8.0	0.55	3.7	0.27	6.5	6.2	1.16	13.35	3.76	62.9	3.7	35.7	18.0	7.3
4.9	0.71	3.5	0.24	9.0	179.0	1.55	12.79	3.79	51.5	1.6	16.2	24.4	10.0
5.4	0.90	5.5	0.05	8.2	2.3	1.54	12.88	4.54	53.9	1.2	14.4	29.2	8.3
8.4	0.20	0.9	0.23	8.1	1.0	1.30	11.69	4.43	52.4	7.6	76.6	2.4	7.6
4.8	1.23	9.5	0.01	4.2	0.4	1.01	11.99	4.45	76.4	2.9	23.8	15.2	2.9
6.0	1.71	8.7	-0.07	3.3	0.1	0.58	9.17	4.37	84.2	5.1	49.3	9.1	1.4
9.1	0.65	1.8	0.51	5.9	0.8	1.06	7.47	4.44	64.5	4.4	27.1	8.4	7.9
8.6	0.37	1.2	-0.04	5.5	0.3	1.15	7.29	4.23	64.5	3.4	50.5	19.8	7.4
1.8	3.18	20.9	2.91	0.9	-0.6	-2.07	-20.06	4.85	72.6	5.8	176.8	24.4	0.0
1.2	4.78	28.1	1.85	3.4	1.1	0.31	3.56	3.90	61.2	3.9	35.8	14.0	3.6
7.3	0.12	1.2	0.00	5.1	0.7	0.95	11.40	3.89	54.2	1.9	22.6	20.6	2.3
3.4	2.73	14.2	-0.24	6.9	0.4	1.44	13.67	3.61	51.5	3.6	54.6	19.3	5.7
4.8	0.60	6.0	0.17	4.5	3.0	0.71	11.31	3.17	66.5	7.4	100.2	7.6	3.5
6.6	0.77	4.0	0.00	9.8	5.9	4.76	39.51	4.40	77.9	3.8	75.8	28.4	7.3
6.3	1.70	6.8	0.17	2.9	0.0	0.21	1.77	4.17	93.4	5.5	56.9	10.2	3.5
6.1	1.24	7.8	0.00	8.3	0.6	1.15	9.92	4.52	55.3	4.3	12.5	6.4	7.0
6.5	0.64	4.8	0.00	5.5	0.9	0.97	11.48	4.61	72.3	5.2	28.6	3.9	5.0
5.5	1.37	6.6	0.00	7.1	1.3	1.56	10.72	3.52	51.8	2.1	37.6	31.5	9.3
1.2	7.14	42.4	0.62	0.4	-0.5	-1.24	-12.86	3.91	112.5	5.3	65.1	12.5	3.7
5.3	0.46	3.7	0.20	4.8	0.4	0.51	5.75	4.27	76.0	4.3	22.9	7.4	5.1
3.9	2.03	8.5	2.21	3.6	0.3	0.44	3.81	3.82	70.9	4.7	36.4	10.4	6.4
8.1	0.00	0.0	0.00	6.0	0.4	1.07	7.57	3.60	61.7	2.1	24.7	19.4	9.0
7.0	0.24	2.1	0.16	9.7	26.6	1.77	21.39	4.18	35.7	1.5	15.3	25.6	7.8
8.2	0.19	0.6	-2.22	4.2	0.1	0.79	6.95	3.42	72.6	7.4	71.5	0.9	3.9
9.5	0.14	0.4	0.07	3.4	0.3	0.67	4.57	3.09	84.9	5.3	36.4	6.7	7.7
6.4	0.10	0.8	2.21	4.9	0.6	0.80	10.38	4.52	64.6	4.0	21.3	9.5	4.3
6.6	0.43	2.2	1.48	4.9	0.5	1.15	14.12	4.27	77.1	4.2	55.6	16.4	5.8
5.6	0.41	3.5	0.06	9.8	4.2	1.62	19.68	4.94	54.9	4.3	51.1	16.3	7.0
7.0	0.65	2.9	0.09	3.6	0.2	0.53	4.90	4.31	82.3	5.6	60.3	10.3	5.3
4.5	0.60	5.7	0.01	10.0	2.2	1.85	26.08	4.79	46.2	3.2	12.7	13.0	7.0
5.3	0.62	4.7	-0.01	7.4	0.6	1.13	11.42	4.59	62.3	3.7	25.2	11.4	6.6
9.1	0.00	0.0	0.00	9.2	1.3	1.28	9.53	4.57	54.6	5.2	24.4	1.7	9.1
6.6	2.60	5.0	0.22	2.2	0.1	0.03	0.33	0.87	95.6	9.1	492.9	6.3	6.8
4.8	0.62	6.7	0.49	8.7	390.1	1.66	25.62	4.01	45.8	5.2	25.7	5.7	5.3
3.0	1.47	14.3	0.16	10.0	656.7	3.19	33.92	4.68	40.4	3.5	3.7	10.3	6.8
5.4	0.86	6.5	-0.01	5.8	49.6	1.21	14.58	2.70	56.7	7.3	83.7	6.6	4.3

Name	City	State	Weiss Safety Rating	2003 Weiss Safety Rating	2002 Weiss Safety Rating	Total Assets ($Mil)	One Year Asset Growth	Asset Mix (As a % of Total Assets)				Capital-ization Index	Leverage Ratio	Risk-based Capital Ratio
								Comm-ercial Loans	Cons-umer Loans	Home Mort-gages	Secur-ities			
NATIONAL CITY BK MIDWEST	BANNOCKBURN	IL	C+	C+	B-	19,651.3	3.44	16.3	3.6	4.8	6.7	5.2	7.2	11.3
NATIONAL CITY BK OF PA	PITTSBURGH	PA	C-	C-	C-	14,296.3	5.01	11.5	1.1	6.2	4.8	3.3	5.3	14.1
▲ NATIONAL EXCHANGE B&TC	FOND DU LAC	WI	A+	A	A	784.8	-3.61	16.3	4.4	13.8	21.7	10.0	13.1	18.5
NATIONAL FAMILY BK	MUNDEN	KS	C+	C+	C	16.9	-4.79	2.2	3.7	.10.4	55.4	8.8	10.2	24.7
NATIONAL GRAND	MARBLEHEAD	MA	A-	A-	A-	208.4	1.15	2.4	4.1	45.2	25.3	7.2	9.1	17.9
NATIONAL IRON BK	SALISBURY	CT	C-	C-	C-	92.2	-2.73	1.1	1.0	25.7	52.3	4.8	6.8	15.0
NATIONAL PENN BK	BOYERTOWN	PA	C+	C+	B-	4,118.7	32.54	11.1	1.5	14.4	23.0	4.0	7.9	10.5
NATIONAL REPUBLIC BK	CHICAGO	IL	C	D+	D+	492.8	18.72	3.2	0.3	4.1	1.7	9.7	10.8	16.8
NATIONAL UNION	KINDERHOOK	NY	C	C	B	127.9	-2.51	6.6	2.4	20.9	44.4	6.1	8.1	18.1
▲ NATIONWIDE TRUST	COLUMBUS	OH	B-	C-	C	31.7	75.47	0.0	0.0	0.0	38.4	10.0	11.1	24.0
▲ NATIVE AMERICAN BK NA	BROWNING	MT	D	D-	D-	45.9	37.48	37.0	4.8	8.8	10.0	10.0	11.5	21.3
NAUGATUCK SVGS BK	NAUGATUCK	CT	A-	A-	A-	611.1	5.18	4.5	0.9	39.7	18.0	10.0	12.6	19.3
▼ NAUGATUCK VALLEY S&L SB	NAUGATUCK	CT	B-	B	NR	253.7	6.48	1.7	0.4	55.6	12.3	6.7	8.7	15.7
NB OF FREDERICKSBURG	FREDERICKSBURG	VA	A-	A-	A	397.0	12.42	6.3	2.7	11.2	30.5	6.4	8.4	15.7
NBANC	OKLAHOMA CITY	OK	C	C	D	135.7	4.67	21.9	4.5	19.2	7.5	3.9	7.7	10.4
▼ NBANC	TULSA	OK	C-	C	D	140.4	-0.40	24.6	7.1	8.6	2.8	3.4	8.5	10.2
▼ NBANK NA	COMMERCE	GA	D+	C	C	362.6	19.25	0.6	1.5	66.4	1.8	3.6	5.6	11.3
NBC BK FSB	BELZONI	MS	B	B	B	25.3	-1.21	0.0	4.1	16.2	38.7	10.0	21.0	67.9
NBRS FNCL	RISING SUN	MD	B-	B-	B-	119.1	2.96	22.8	2.4	17.4	10.1	6.1	9.7	11.8
NBT BANK NA	NORWICH	NY	B-	B-	B-	4,097.7	5.39	10.9	10.1	20.8	25.5	4.0	6.5	10.5
NCB FSB	HILLSBORO	OH	A-	B+	B	677.4	25.01	13.9	1.3	38.1	3.6	8.6	10.8	13.8
▲ NCW COMMUNITY BK	WENATCHEE	WA	C	C-	D+	55.3	27.51	18.2	3.9	3.9	8.4	6.6	8.7	12.2
NEBRASKA BANKERS BK NA	LINCOLN	NE	B-	B-	B	19.8	36.93	8.3	0.0	3.7	0.0	10.0	17.9	19.4
NEBRASKA NB	KEARNEY	NE	C+	B-	C+	85.2	23.69	13.1	2.7	7.3	32.6	6.0	8.0	12.2
NEBRASKA ST B&TC	BROKEN BOW	NE	A	A	A	83.7	0.03	8.5	5.9	6.5	10.9	10.0	13.2	17.9
NEBRASKA ST BK	BRISTOW	NE	C-	C-	C-	9.3	-9.24	11.1	4.5	3.6	32.4	10.0	18.2	29.0
▼ NEBRASKA ST BK	LYNCH	NE	C-	C	C-	9.4	-6.50	3.7	2.7	3.7	56.2	10.0	19.1	44.1
NEBRASKA ST BK	OSHKOSH	NE	B-	B-	B+	32.3	10.65	1.4	0.2	0.6	15.7	5.7	9.2	11.5
NEBRASKA ST BK OF OMAHA	OMAHA	NE	D-	D-	D	203.9	8.35	24.1	3.4	12.0	4.1	3.1	8.2	10.1
NEBRASKALAND NB	N PLATTE	NE	C+	C+	C+	127.2	34.04	17.0	1.7	10.7	6.1	4.3	8.6	10.6
NECEDAH BK	NECEDAH	WI	B	B	C+	36.9	5.40	6.7	5.7	14.1	26.1	10.0	11.4	15.5
▲ NEEDHAM CO-OP BK	NEEDHAM	MA	A+	A	A+	428.3	2.95	0.0	0.4	35.3	35.7	10.0	32.7	54.3
NEFFS NB	NEFFS	PA	A+	A+	A+	205.8	7.48	1.1	3.4	21.9	58.7	10.0	17.5	41.0
NEHAWKA BK	NEHAWKA	NE	C+	C+	C	13.7	-1.81	2.9	8.4	49.1	1.8	10.0	13.6	23.9
NEIGHBORHOOD NB	SAN DIEGO	CA	C+	C+	D+	79.1	30.49	32.1	3.7	4.3	12.7	6.8	8.8	13.1
NEIGHBORHOOD NB	ALEXANDRIA	MN	D-	D	D	36.4	28.11	12.1	5.5	21.7	19.0	6.6	8.6	12.4
NEIGHBORS BK	ALPHARETTA	GA	D	D	NR	28.9	N/A	10.4	2.4	2.4	11.5	10.0	35.0	37.6
▲ NEKOMA ST BK	LA CROSSE	KS	D	D	D-	26.5	5.24	6.0	2.5	6.9	54.0	6.7	8.7	20.6
NEKOOSA PORT EDWARDS ST	NEKOOSA	WI	B	B	B	169.1	2.18	4.5	2.5	34.8	29.8	6.9	8.9	17.3
NELSONVILLE HOME &	NELSONVILLE	OH	C+	B-	NR	16.7	-6.66	0.0	1.2	60.1	21.9	10.0	12.2	27.4
▲ NEOSHO S&LA FA	NEOSHO	MO	C	D+	B-	68.4	2.19	0.9	1.9	34.1	41.5	10.0	11.1	27.9
▲ NESQUEHONING SVG BK	NESQUEHONING	PA	B	B-	C+	26.1	4.03	1.2	1.4	55.3	25.3	10.0	12.0	24.1
NETBANK	ALPHARETTA	GA	D-	D-	D-	4,748.5	13.27	7.7	5.8	63.2	9.1	4.9	6.9	12.4
▲ NETWORK BK	ONTARIO	CA	A-	B+	B-	280.5	79.00	6.2	0.1	0.8	3.5	8.4	10.4	13.7
NEVADA B&TC	CALIENTE	NV	C+	C+	C+	72.5	-5.93	1.9	5.7	11.3	60.3	7.6	9.4	25.4
NEVADA CMRC BK	LAS VEGAS	NV	C-	D+	D	99.8	22.22	9.4	0.8	4.1	29.5	4.8	6.8	12.3
▲ NEVADA FIRST BK	LAS VEGAS	NV	B	C+	C	328.1	32.58	20.7	0.4	0.9	5.1	6.5	10.9	12.1
NEVADA SECURITY BK	RENO	NV	D	D-	D	237.6	115.03	10.3	1.5	0.4	42.9	7.7	9.5	17.8
NEVADA ST BK	LAS VEGAS	NV	B-	B-	B-	3,193.0	11.12	9.5	1.3	17.6	14.5	3.6	5.8	10.3
▲ NEW ALBIN SVG BK	NEW ALBIN	IA	B-	C+	B-	119.5	4.37	2.3	1.3	11.5	65.3	4.8	10.4	10.9
▲ NEW BUFFALO SVGS BK FSB	NEW BUFFALO	MI	B	B-	B-	124.9	3.24	1.0	1.1	33.4	0.5	10.0	12.9	17.6
▼ NEW CARLISLE FSB	NEW CARLISLE	OH	C	C+	C+	83.1	5.11	8.4	5.4	31.0	17.3	7.9	9.6	14.7
▲ NEW CENTURY BK	CHICAGO	IL	D+	C-	D	232.9	45.67	11.6	0.6	8.5	5.7	4.8	8.2	10.9
▼ NEW CENTURY BK	DUNN	NC	B-	B	B-	247.0	53.93	20.0	5.9	11.3	5.9	4.8	8.8	10.9
▲ NEW CENTURY BK	PHOENIXVILLE	PA	C-	D	D	133.8	21.53	8.5	1.9	21.5	12.7	5.9	7.9	12.4
▼ NEW CENTURY	FAYETTEVILLE	NC	C+	NR	NR	42.3	N/A	21.1	9.5	11.0	1.2	10.0	21.8	24.2
NEW CITY BK	CHICAGO	IL	D	D	NR	30.5	N/A	7.5	0.5	8.3	12.8	10.0	29.4	43.8
NEW COMMERCE BK NA	GREENVILLE	SC	D+	D+	D+	92.7	34.37	13.2	2.7	9.2	17.9	6.9	9.5	12.5
NEW ERA BK	FREDERICKTOWN	MO	A	A	A-	209.4	0.18	1.3	3.4	44.1	17.2	10.0	11.5	19.1
NEW FOUNDATION L&BC	CINCINNATI	OH	D-	D	D-	15.8	0.06	0.0	0.3	61.0	4.9	8.0	9.6	17.5
NEW FRONTIER BK	GREELEY	CO	C	C	C	453.6	33.07	10.7	2.9	7.4	6.8	4.0	8.6	10.5
▲ NEW FRONTIER BK	ST CHARLES	MO	C+	C	D+	92.2	28.89	6.9	1.0	23.7	8.8	6.3	9.3	12.0
NEW HORIZONS BK	E ELLIJAY	GA	D	NR	NR	16.1	N/A	3.0	1.4	5.0	48.0	10.0	54.5	103.7
NEW LIBERTY BK	PLYMOUTH	MI	D	D	D	59.9	13.08	18.7	1.2	6.2	3.4	5.5	10.1	11.4

Asset Quality Index	Non-Performing Loans as a % of Total Loans	as a % of Capital	Net Charge-offs Avg Loans	Profitability Index	Net Income ($Mil)	Return on Assets (R.O.A.)	Return on Equity (R.O.E.)	Net Interest Spread	Overhead Efficiency Ratio	Liquidity Index	Liquidity Ratio	Hot Money Ratio	Stability Index
6.4	0.95	5.7	0.08	3.8	66.2	0.67	9.52	2.10	76.2	9.2	234.7	5.5	5.2
6.5	1.37	6.9	0.40	1.4	15.4	0.22	4.19	1.36	80.2	9.1	409.5	6.2	4.1
8.0	0.37	1.6	0.02	9.7	6.7	1.71	12.14	4.40	49.4	5.4	43.8	8.7	9.5
3.7	4.16	12.0	-0.12	1.5	0.0	-0.01	-0.11	3.46	100.3	5.5	46.2	5.4	4.6
9.2	0.05	0.4	0.03	8.9	1.4	1.30	14.41	4.06	56.3	5.2	32.8	5.6	6.3
10.0	0.00	0.0	-0.01	3.2	0.2	0.46	6.79	3.67	90.4	3.7	16.2	10.6	2.6
6.4	0.39	2.4	0.08	6.9	24.2	1.31	12.97	4.14	58.2	4.6	16.0	5.6	7.1
2.7	1.52	12.4	-0.17	10.0	9.0	3.82	35.84	5.26	22.0	0.4	6.6	61.9	6.0
7.8	0.80	4.2	0.31	4.0	0.5	0.70	9.20	3.90	75.2	5.9	51.4	7.7	4.2
6.5	0.00	0.0	0.00	10.0	4.6	16.63	30.29	4.52	85.3	0.1	7.0	100.0	2.4
4.5	1.47	8.0	-0.22	0.0	-0.4	-1.86	-13.30	4.96	128.9	4.4	91.0	21.8	3.4
7.3	1.11	6.2	0.03	5.0	2.9	0.98	7.36	4.12	72.3	7.1	83.4	6.3	8.8
7.1	0.48	3.9	-0.02	4.1	0.8	0.63	7.24	3.69	77.4	5.7	50.3	9.0	3.5
8.3	0.10	0.7	-0.02	10.0	3.4	1.78	20.35	4.56	50.3	5.3	38.5	7.4	7.6
4.2	0.79	6.7	0.02	5.3	1.0	1.36	14.77	4.41	67.9	4.2	14.2	7.2	4.5
1.6	2.66	24.7	0.68	4.3	0.5	0.67	7.03	5.12	80.7	2.9	15.0	14.5	3.9
5.3	0.87	11.4	0.03	3.7	0.1	0.05	0.82	7.69	99.5	0.9	17.2	34.7	2.1
5.6	4.04	5.3	2.43	8.6	0.2	1.85	8.81	4.42	43.3	5.3	76.6	14.6	7.3
4.3	1.26	9.6	0.00	5.1	0.5	0.88	9.23	4.43	70.0	3.6	21.1	11.7	5.4
6.3	0.45	3.6	0.28	7.3	26.1	1.29	16.75	4.02	54.0	3.2	12.4	13.1	6.0
6.8	0.51	4.0	0.03	9.6	15.2	4.57	45.39	2.29	38.7	0.9	27.8	76.3	8.4
7.1	0.06	0.4	0.00	3.1	0.2	0.57	6.55	3.84	79.4	3.7	80.5	29.0	4.2
8.3	0.00	0.0	0.00	2.3	0.0	0.31	1.54	3.95	87.1	5.5	30.8	0.0	2.8
5.5	1.23	8.4	0.05	7.1	0.8	1.85	20.25	4.08	51.1	1.9	17.5	19.8	4.1
7.0	0.00	0.0	-0.01	8.1	0.7	1.73	12.75	4.16	55.5	5.0	58.9	13.1	8.9
6.8	1.67	5.0	1.13	5.1	0.1	1.20	6.99	5.20	64.9	4.6	56.8	13.1	3.7
6.5	6.02	10.0	0.06	4.0	0.0	0.91	4.93	4.25	72.0	5.4	50.0	7.7	3.7
7.5	0.12	0.9	0.00	8.8	0.4	2.51	27.22	3.76	55.6	3.5	26.4	13.0	5.0
2.5	0.92	9.2	0.38	6.4	1.6	1.63	19.98	4.92	57.6	2.7	12.7	15.3	1.7
7.2	0.21	1.9	0.05	5.8	0.6	0.97	11.47	4.15	60.3	1.4	22.7	28.6	5.3
1.1	6.41	20.2	-0.20	4.3	0.2	0.95	5.63	3.99	68.7	4.8	43.8	11.9	6.1
7.7	3.26	6.1	0.00	9.4	3.1	1.47	4.52	4.23	38.9	5.9	87.8	14.0	10.0
9.8	0.31	0.6	0.01	7.6	1.6	1.56	9.02	3.61	37.3	4.2	38.8	13.4	9.8
7.8	0.69	3.7	0.07	4.9	0.1	0.92	6.76	5.05	77.4	7.7	104.4	3.1	5.1
5.3	1.08	7.5	-0.01	3.8	0.1	0.30	3.49	5.14	91.8	3.8	86.7	29.9	3.7
8.3	0.03	0.2	0.06	0.4	0.0	-0.18	-2.01	3.97	97.2	0.6	5.3	37.9	0.0
7.8	0.00	0.0	0.00	0.0	-0.5	-4.51	-10.67	4.00	186.6	5.7	70.9	11.6	0.0
4.7	3.93	13.1	0.09	3.5	0.1	0.45	5.32	3.96	87.3	7.3	77.9	2.9	1.8
4.6	1.77	11.2	0.00	5.0	1.1	1.25	14.04	2.78	47.0	4.5	113.1	30.8	6.0
9.6	0.00	0.0	0.00	3.7	0.1	0.67	5.55	2.80	69.5	5.3	90.1	15.0	0.3
9.1	0.47	2.0	-0.09	3.0	0.1	0.43	3.68	2.50	79.1	4.2	67.2	18.6	4.6
8.1	0.62	3.3	0.00	4.2	0.1	0.86	6.96	3.44	67.7	3.4	25.0	13.2	5.7
0.5	2.93	31.6	0.07	3.5	12.1	0.55	6.83	3.01	82.8	1.0	15.0	32.9	6.8
7.3	0.00	0.0	0.02	6.8	2.1	1.68	16.33	5.17	53.4	6.0	105.4	15.5	6.7
9.2	0.03	0.1	-0.28	3.6	0.2	0.57	6.08	4.01	84.8	5.2	29.3	3.8	3.7
9.2	0.00	0.0	0.00	3.2	0.3	0.66	10.15	4.13	80.3	4.9	64.2	14.3	1.1
7.2	0.03	0.2	0.07	6.1	1.7	1.14	12.01	5.12	54.3	7.4	108.9	8.1	5.1
8.6	0.00	0.0	0.00	0.8	0.4	0.37	4.13	2.96	76.5	3.9	31.5	12.6	0.0
8.3	0.11	1.2	0.09	9.2	21.5	1.39	21.40	4.74	56.9	8.2	120.4	4.7	5.6
8.1	0.80	2.1	0.28	6.1	0.8	1.39	11.98	2.90	31.9	6.7	161.7	16.2	7.0
5.0	1.11	7.1	-0.01	5.4	0.8	1.32	9.96	3.34	59.7	0.7	12.1	43.1	7.3
2.4	2.42	17.2	0.05	4.0	0.2	0.41	4.15	3.37	84.5	2.5	30.9	19.2	4.8
4.0	1.00	8.9	0.46	2.7	0.3	0.22	2.81	4.05	76.3	1.2	15.5	29.6	3.5
6.7	0.42	3.7	0.10	4.8	0.9	0.81	7.83	3.84	58.1	4.5	53.2	15.6	1.6
5.5	0.57	5.6	0.00	3.2	0.4	0.59	8.22	3.61	81.8	5.3	42.9	8.9	2.8
7.7	0.00	0.0	0.00	0.0	-0.5	-3.65	-12.36	3.12	133.2	6.5	67.7	5.9	2.1
9.3	0.00	0.0	0.00	0.0	-0.1	-1.06	-3.03	4.04	99.3	5.5	224.8	34.4	0.0
5.1	0.82	5.9	0.36	1.5	0.1	0.21	2.41	3.33	85.6	0.8	18.5	47.5	4.6
7.9	0.57	3.2	0.00	9.1	2.6	2.47	19.18	3.85	41.1	4.2	17.6	7.8	8.8
3.7	3.32	24.8	0.00	3.1	0.0	0.29	3.05	2.37	88.0	2.3	25.1	17.9	2.3
4.8	0.40	3.6	0.17	7.2	2.6	1.26	15.44	4.30	47.0	1.8	38.3	42.8	3.9
7.6	0.00	0.0	0.17	2.4	0.2	0.48	5.04	3.58	76.1	4.4	34.9	11.4	3.5
9.7	0.00	0.0	0.00	0.0	-0.5	-7.93	-12.43	0.78	896.4	3.3	58.1	19.9	0.0
7.6	0.14	1.0	0.20	1.2	0.1	0.18	1.51	4.02	93.0	1.6	28.5	29.0	0.0

Name	City	State	Weiss Safety Rating	2003 Weiss Safety Rating	2002 Weiss Safety Rating	Total Assets ($Mil)	One Year Asset Growth	Asset Mix (As a % of Total Assets) Commercial Loans	Consumer Loans	Home Mortgages	Securities	Capitalization Index	Leverage Ratio	Risk-based Capital Ratio
NEW MARKET BK	NEW MARKET	MN	C+	C+	C+	60.6	19.60	7.0	3.6	13.4	8.5	5.4	8.9	11.3
▲ NEW MEXICO B&TC	ALBUQUERQUE	NM	B	B-	B-	395.6	11.75	13.2	1.8	4.9	17.0	5.6	7.9	11.5
▲ NEW MILLENNIUM BK	NEW BRUNSWICK	NJ	B	B	B-	98.6	12.24	12.6	8.5	3.4	10.3	10.0	13.2	16.5
NEW PEOPLES BK	HONAKER	VA	B-	B-	B-	394.0	20.08	9.0	11.4	30.6	1.5	4.7	8.3	10.9
NEW REPUBLIC SVGS BK	ROCKY MOUNT	NC	B-	B-	C	33.5	21.43	2.3	0.5	45.3	0.0	10.0	11.2	18.7
▼ NEW RICHMOND NB	NEW RICHMOND	OH	C-	C+	C+	74.1	-0.96	6.7	3.0	25.8	5.0	5.9	8.3	11.7
▼ NEW SOUTH FSB	IRONDALE	AL	C	C	C-	1,403.4	-3.71	3.8	10.2	31.2	15.1	6.4	8.4	12.5
▲ NEW SOUTHERN BK	MACON	GA	C	D+	D-	191.0	62.32	21.4	1.9	11.7	6.9	6.7	11.0	12.3
NEW TRIPOLI NB	NEW TRIPOLI	PA	A	A	A-	222.8	8.16	2.8	2.4	24.8	41.0	10.0	13.0	22.2
▼ NEW VIENNA SVG BK	NEW VIENNA	IA	B	B+	B+	26.0	-3.22	12.7	2.5	9.0	16.1	10.0	15.0	19.8
NEW WASHINGTON ST BK	NEW WASHINGTON	IN	B+	B+	B+	189.7	8.83	6.1	6.1	37.3	7.2	6.3	8.3	12.0
▼ NEW WEST BK	GREELEY	CO	D-	D	NR	39.2	104.49	4.2	1.9	6.9	0.5	9.9	13.3	14.9
NEW WINDSOR ST BK	NEW WINDSOR	MD	B-	B-	B-	139.4	16.23	9.7	3.2	27.0	14.8	5.8	8.4	11.6
NEW YORK COMMUNITY BK	NEW YORK CITY	NY	A-	A-	B+	24,203.2	94.09	0.5	0.0	2.5	34.2	5.4	7.4	17.3
NEW YORK LIFE TRUST CO	PARSIPPANY	NJ	D	D	D	21.4	228.88	0.0	0.0	0.0	97.7	10.0	89.7	265.2
NEW YORK NB	NEW YORK CITY	NY	D	D	D+	138.6	-2.93	11.2	0.9	8.3	26.7	4.0	6.0	12.0
▼ NEWALLIANCE BK	NEW HAVEN	CT	B	A-	A-	6,369.9	159.69	4.3	0.7	29.5	36.4	9.6	10.8	18.7
▼ NEWBERRY FSB	NEWBERRY	SC	B+	A-	A-	203.0	-4.68	3.1	3.0	11.5	67.6	10.0	16.1	20.7
NEWBURYPORT FIVE CNTS SB	NEWBURYPORT	MA	A	A	A	462.1	8.91	1.8	0.9	43.2	25.7	10.0	14.7	23.0
NEWFIELD NB	NEWFIELD	NJ	C	C	B-	410.7	-5.33	8.3	1.5	15.9	31.4	6.5	8.5	14.0
NEWFIRST NB	EL CAMPO	TX	B	B	B+	155.3	9.11	12.6	5.3	3.2	32.7	7.2	9.2	14.3
NEWMIL BK	NEW MILFORD	CT	B	B	B	730.8	7.29	2.9	0.3	40.3	25.7	5.3	7.3	13.3
NEWNAN COWETA BK	NEWNAN	GA	C+	C+	C	125.9	25.21	13.4	2.6	6.6	3.4	4.0	8.6	10.5
NEWPORT FEDERAL SVGS BK	NEWPORT	RI	C+	C+	C+	173.9	4.40	9.0	0.1	58.6	5.3	4.9	7.0	11.7
NEWPORT FS&LA	NEWPORT	TN	A	A	A-	121.8	7.65	0.0	2.7	51.4	30.6	10.0	12.0	27.0
▲ NEWTON COUNTY BK	NEWTON	MS	A	A-	A-	139.6	-0.80	3.1	11.2	16.6	31.0	10.0	11.1	15.8
▼ NEWTON CTY LOAN & SVGS	GOODLAND	IN	D+	C-	C-	8.1	-4.16	0.0	0.0	91.8	0.0	10.0	16.9	34.1
NEWTON FEDERAL BK	COVINGTON	GA	A+	A+	A+	226.0	6.31	0.0	0.8	64.3	4.3	10.0	18.0	34.2
NEWTON TRUST CO	NEWTON	NJ	B+	B+	B+	314.4	-1.39	5.3	1.0	14.1	26.5	9.1	10.4	15.4
NEWTOWN SVGS BK	NEWTOWN	CT	B-	B-	C+	601.3	6.85	5.6	5.5	42.1	14.9	7.3	9.2	13.0
▲ NEXITY BK	BIRMINGHAM	AL	C+	C	D	568.8	13.49	3.3	1.0	3.4	33.5	4.7	7.6	10.8
▲ NICOLET NB	GREEN BAY	WI	C-	D+	D	374.7	24.27	32.1	1.4	9.9	8.2	6.5	9.6	12.1
NICOLLET COUNTY BK	ST PETER	MN	B	B	B	103.9	-1.97	7.0	8.3	7.4	37.9	6.1	8.1	13.7
▲ NITTANY BK	STATE COLLEGE	PA	C+	C	C-	276.1	26.00	2.5	0.6	52.0	19.0	4.5	6.5	12.9
NIXON ST BK	NIXON	TX	D+	D+	D+	54.6	1.10	11.8	12.0	4.3	30.8	5.3	7.3	14.1
NLSB	PLAINFIELD	IL	B	B	B	982.7	0.79	8.1	1.1	19.2	30.4	6.3	8.3	14.6
▲ NODAWAY VALLEY BK	MARYVILLE	MO	B+	B	B	535.7	-1.22	9.6	3.2	14.2	15.0	5.3	8.5	11.2
NOKOMIS SB	NOKOMIS	IL	C	C	C-	28.9	4.04	16.5	0.8	2.2	54.7	8.8	10.2	76.5
NORBANK	N KANSAS CITY	MO	C+	C+	C+	35.4	-4.74	14.8	3.8	6.3	55.1	6.7	8.7	22.1
▲ NORCROWN BK OF	LIVINGSTON	NJ	C+	C	C	622.0	3.93	4.5	0.1	9.1	7.8	5.3	7.3	11.8
▲ NORDSTROM FSB	SCOTTSDALE	AZ	B+	B	B	140.3	-37.22	0.0	50.0	0.3	9.9	10.0	65.9	53.7
NORMANGEE ST BK	NORMANGEE	TX	A-	A-	A-	51.0	0.26	0.6	14.3	8.9	53.3	10.0	15.3	34.6
NORTH ABINGTON CO-OP BK	N ABINGTON	MA	D	C-	C-	75.0	-6.43	0.0	1.7	36.1	42.3	8.6	10.1	23.1
NORTH ADAMS ST BK	URSA	IL	C-	C	C-	24.5	-5.65	11.8	7.0	17.9	24.4	8.0	9.7	15.3
NORTH AKRON SVG BK	AKRON	OH	B-	B-	B-	170.0	3.61	0.0	0.7	69.0	8.5	6.9	8.9	21.2
NORTH ALABAMA BK	HAZEL GREEN	AL	D+	D+	C-	80.3	-2.84	10.7	9.8	18.1	10.2	8.9	10.3	14.1
▲ NORTH AMERICAN BKG CO	ROSEVILLE	MN	C+	C-	C-	112.6	24.39	26.2	5.3	4.5	11.2	4.7	9.2	10.9
▼ NORTH AMERICAN ST BK	BELGRADE	MN	B	B+	A-	99.0	18.58	9.3	4.9	18.7	15.6	9.4	11.2	14.5
NORTH AMERICAN SVGS BK	GRANDVIEW	MO	B	B	B-	1,334.9	19.42	1.9	0.3	32.4	13.6	6.8	8.8	12.7
▲ NORTH ARUNDEL SVGS BK	PASADENA	MD	B-	C+	C+	27.0	-3.23	0.0	1.5	52.8	29.5	10.0	13.1	32.3
▼ NORTH ATLANTA NB	ALPHARETTA	GA	E	D+	D	89.0	45.47	21.3	3.1	5.0	8.6	2.3	6.0	9.3
▼ NORTH BK	CHICAGO	IL	C+	B-	B-	97.1	2.61	10.1	0.7	9.5	34.8	6.4	8.5	14.8
NORTH BROOKFIELD SVGS BK	N BROOKFIELD	MA	A-	A-	A-	156.3	1.85	0.2	1.5	45.4	35.7	10.0	11.5	24.5
NORTH CAMBRIDGE CO-OP BK	CAMBRIDGE	MA	B+	B+	A-	89.9	0.73	0.0	0.4	41.5	34.9	10.0	16.0	34.4
▲ NORTH CASCADES NB	CHELAN	WA	C	C-	D+	200.0	0.54	7.9	1.1	2.9	37.2	5.7	7.8	11.5
NORTH CENTRAL BK	HENNEPIN	IL	B	B	B	94.2	-2.88	2.9	6.0	24.6	47.5	8.0	9.7	22.3
NORTH COMMUNITY BK	CHICAGO	IL	B	B-	B-	387.2	7.65	3.4	0.2	13.6	17.2	5.8	8.1	11.6
NORTH COUNTRY B&TC	MANISTIQUE	MI	E-	E-	D-	343.8	-27.44	30.7	0.8	12.9	18.8	2.0	5.2	9.1
NORTH COUNTRY SVGS BK	CANTON	NY	B-	B-	B-	212.6	1.62	0.4	6.6	62.5	19.3	10.0	13.2	25.5
▲ NORTH COUNTY BK	ARLINGTON	WA	D+	D	D+	84.3	49.47	11.2	1.8	5.3	4.7	8.2	11.8	13.5
▲ NORTH COUNTY SB	RED BUD	IL	C-	D+	D+	30.1	6.28	1.2	9.3	46.4	22.8	5.9	7.9	16.2
▼ NORTH DALLAS B&TC	DALLAS	TX	B	B+	A-	875.6	3.35	7.0	2.3	6.2	54.1	9.9	10.9	31.5
▲ NORTH EASTON SVGS BK	N EASTON	MA	B	B-	B-	393.9	1.24	0.8	1.4	40.4	35.8	6.3	8.3	14.8
▼ NORTH FORK BK	MATTITUCK	NY	B	B	B	25,963.4	18.23	8.9	6.2	11.7	33.3	4.5	6.7	10.8

Asset Quality Index	Non-Performing Loans as a % of Total Loans	as a % of Capital	Net Charge-offs Avg Loans	Profitability Index	Net Income ($Mil)	Return on Assets (R.O.A.)	Return on Equity (R.O.E.)	Net Interest Spread	Overhead Efficiency Ratio	Liquidity Index	Liquidity Ratio	Hot Money Ratio	Stability Index
5.7	0.00	0.0	0.01	9.0	0.4	1.42	16.26	5.69	57.7	4.8	25.0	4.4	4.4
6.1	0.19	1.1	0.39	6.2	2.3	1.16	11.13	5.07	66.3	3.0	17.0	14.0	6.2
4.5	0.69	3.7	0.18	10.0	0.9	1.92	14.87	7.24	71.7	6.3	57.7	5.2	6.0
6.7	0.23	2.3	0.06	6.2	2.0	1.07	13.02	5.22	65.3	2.3	25.2	18.7	4.8
6.2	1.72	12.5	0.00	7.9	0.2	0.95	7.94	5.08	75.3	1.3	14.1	27.0	5.5
1.4	2.99	26.3	2.88	3.7	-0.1	-0.18	-1.98	5.26	71.7	3.3	27.0	14.2	6.0
2.6	2.24	19.7	0.21	5.0	6.5	0.96	11.70	3.59	77.1	0.6	14.6	67.0	6.9
7.1	0.00	0.0	0.00	3.5	0.7	0.77	8.23	3.59	54.8	0.6	9.3	40.7	2.4
7.6	0.88	3.1	0.01	8.0	1.8	1.59	11.24	3.90	46.1	4.3	26.0	8.7	9.0
8.2	0.00	0.0	-0.34	8.8	0.3	2.07	13.40	4.25	48.4	6.2	67.1	8.3	6.3
6.8	0.46	4.0	0.09	9.9	1.5	1.63	19.92	6.35	61.0	4.0	21.2	9.8	6.2
8.3	0.00	0.0	0.00	0.2	-0.1	-0.41	-2.95	3.83	95.9	3.9	56.8	18.4	0.0
4.9	1.67	13.5	0.01	3.6	0.3	0.49	5.70	4.12	79.6	5.3	51.0	11.2	4.7
5.8	0.20	0.6	0.00	9.8	190.4	1.54	10.48	4.51	18.9	3.8	4.7	9.0	10.0
9.2	0.00	0.0	0.00	0.0	-0.1	-1.10	-1.20	4.53	136.4	0.1	8.4	100.0	0.0
4.0	2.37	18.4	0.22	2.2	0.0	0.05	0.77	4.88	93.1	3.1	54.0	28.5	1.8
8.0	0.43	1.3	0.22	3.8	17.3	0.79	5.44	2.99	79.5	7.0	57.5	4.8	9.1
8.8	0.32	0.6	1.38	4.0	0.5	0.49	3.48	2.62	75.2	1.4	13.8	25.6	8.0
6.9	1.30	5.6	0.01	6.6	2.8	1.21	7.57	3.77	63.1	2.3	21.5	18.2	8.9
4.8	1.33	8.7	0.50	4.6	2.1	0.99	11.61	4.36	66.3	4.4	25.2	7.2	3.1
6.4	0.36	2.2	0.02	5.5	0.8	1.05	10.81	5.13	69.8	3.9	14.8	9.3	5.5
7.4	0.31	2.3	0.01	6.8	4.6	1.29	15.44	4.04	57.6	7.4	91.5	6.1	5.8
7.1	0.00	0.0	-0.01	5.8	0.6	1.07	12.35	4.32	58.5	2.3	31.4	22.0	1.8
8.5	0.00	0.0	0.00	3.9	0.4	0.44	6.21	3.57	82.5	1.3	6.6	24.6	4.2
7.6	0.36	1.7	0.07	9.6	0.9	1.50	11.14	4.57	53.2	1.3	30.1	39.1	8.7
7.3	0.87	4.3	-0.02	7.2	1.2	1.65	13.53	4.62	66.2	5.1	57.5	14.1	8.8
5.4	1.91	10.4	0.00	5.1	0.0	1.06	6.36	5.28	82.5	4.8	9.9	2.7	3.0
9.3	0.23	1.0	0.01	8.9	1.4	1.22	6.84	3.10	42.8	1.3	21.6	30.1	9.0
7.0	0.55	3.2	0.34	5.9	1.7	1.09	10.47	4.53	59.7	5.9	38.5	3.1	6.3
6.4	0.38	3.2	0.03	4.3	2.1	0.72	7.79	3.52	72.6	4.6	29.8	8.1	6.2
7.2	0.57	4.4	0.13	4.2	3.7	1.35	17.94	3.05	61.4	3.8	52.8	19.1	3.5
5.0	0.62	5.0	0.92	2.4	0.6	0.35	3.81	2.95	63.7	0.6	14.3	60.5	1.2
6.0	0.61	3.8	-0.02	5.3	0.7	1.27	14.68	3.65	62.6	4.2	20.5	8.2	5.7
9.0	0.04	0.4	0.06	4.8	1.1	0.81	12.48	3.03	56.7	0.7	12.2	44.1	3.7
5.1	0.57	3.5	0.20	5.5	0.4	1.32	18.17	4.42	71.8	5.5	60.5	11.2	2.3
9.1	0.00	0.0	0.00	4.7	0.6	0.11	1.43	0.46	54.5	9.3	266.8	4.5	5.8
7.0	0.17	1.1	0.05	6.7	4.1	1.52	13.24	3.64	61.2	5.5	53.0	10.8	7.3
8.9	0.04	0.1	0.00	2.4	0.0	0.21	2.03	1.90	81.8	8.7	187.0	7.6	4.2
8.9	0.00	0.0	-0.03	6.2	0.7	3.87	42.55	4.10	61.2	3.9	39.1	15.4	4.3
4.7	0.61	5.8	0.05	5.6	3.0	0.96	13.58	4.50	62.9	4.8	39.0	10.7	3.9
5.7	0.77	0.5	5.90	10.0	2.9	11.65	30.78	16.20	64.2	2.1	47.4	70.2	4.7
8.5	1.00	2.3	0.01	7.3	0.4	1.66	11.05	4.40	51.7	4.5	43.2	13.0	7.8
9.7	0.01	0.1	0.10	1.1	-0.1	-0.21	-2.23	3.23	105.9	4.9	33.2	7.3	4.0
1.8	4.73	28.1	0.54	6.1	0.1	1.16	11.23	5.16	65.5	5.2	41.6	5.9	3.4
6.3	1.07	8.3	0.00	3.8	0.5	0.54	5.98	3.16	73.9	8.6	484.2	9.6	5.3
1.7	3.04	19.6	0.23	8.5	0.8	1.96	20.25	6.32	47.6	1.3	30.5	37.6	4.2
6.9	0.36	3.0	0.01	5.1	0.5	0.86	9.81	5.07	74.6	0.9	7.5	31.2	4.2
4.1	1.64	10.3	0.03	6.0	0.6	1.30	10.92	4.86	68.7	1.3	25.6	31.6	6.7
5.3	1.17	10.0	-0.10	10.0	13.1	2.03	21.49	4.29	47.9	1.5	3.6	22.1	9.0
5.4	1.79	8.0	0.00	4.2	0.1	0.67	4.86	3.70	71.6	3.6	38.9	16.4	5.9
8.1	0.02	0.3	0.09	1.6	0.0	-0.12	-1.88	3.67	98.4	2.2	35.4	26.8	0.7
5.6	1.46	8.8	0.01	4.4	0.4	0.76	9.15	4.24	76.0	3.0	44.5	21.6	4.3
9.5	0.35	1.7	0.27	5.6	0.8	0.97	8.78	3.76	62.5	5.8	46.0	6.9	6.8
10.0	0.00	0.0	0.00	4.2	0.3	0.67	3.78	2.69	58.3	6.9	352.4	17.9	7.7
5.3	0.89	5.0	-0.03	3.1	0.4	0.37	4.36	3.69	81.8	2.8	25.1	16.0	3.5
7.4	0.22	0.8	0.10	4.7	0.5	0.99	8.25	3.27	54.9	5.2	57.5	11.8	6.4
7.4	0.23	1.8	-0.02	10.0	3.9	2.02	26.79	6.32	58.8	4.4	19.8	6.6	6.1
1.1	5.76	44.7	8.54	0.0	-2.4	-1.23	-22.42	2.77	141.6	6.6	66.2	6.9	1.6
8.0	0.66	3.5	-0.03	3.6	0.5	0.50	3.75	3.96	78.4	5.8	47.2	7.0	6.4
4.4	0.45	3.1	0.04	5.7	0.4	1.06	12.13	5.38	59.0	1.7	30.3	29.4	5.7
8.5	0.18	1.4	0.06	3.7	0.1	0.66	8.32	3.36	72.3	5.8	97.6	14.7	2.8
9.5	0.08	0.2	0.30	4.7	3.1	0.70	6.53	2.95	64.2	7.6	320.3	14.5	7.3
9.8	0.00	0.0	0.01	4.5	1.6	0.83	10.15	3.28	71.0	5.6	47.8	8.7	4.8
7.5	0.10	0.6	0.12	9.8	212.9	1.89	19.86	4.29	34.4	5.1	27.6	7.7	9.2

Name	City	State	Weiss Safety Rating	2003 Weiss Safety Rating	2002 Weiss Safety Rating	Total Assets ($Mil)	One Year Asset Growth	Asset Mix (As a % of Total Assets)				Capital-ization Index	Leverage Ratio	Risk-based Capital Ratio
								Comm-ercial Loans	Cons-umer Loans	Home Mort-gages	Secur-ities			
NORTH FSB	CHICAGO	IL	C+	C+	B-	133.9	0.68	1.5	0.1	35.9	8.6	8.1	9.7	15.5
NORTH GEORGIA BK	WATKINSVILLE	GA	C	C	C+	92.5	23.18	2.2	1.1	15.1	10.6	4.0	8.0	10.5
▲ NORTH GEORGIA NB	CALHOUN	GA	B	C+	C	114.5	16.90	12.8	4.0	12.7	23.6	9.8	10.9	15.8
NORTH HOUSTON BK	HOUSTON	TX	B-	B-	B-	380.3	24.27	1.1	1.3	18.4	26.3	4.1	9.4	10.5
NORTH JACKSON BK	STEVENSON	AL	B+	B	B-	118.9	8.86	7.3	13.6	18.4	26.3	8.4	9.9	14.4
▼ NORTH LOUP VALLEY BK	N LOUP	NE	E+	D-	E	17.5	5.86	4.5	4.2	3.0	43.4	6.7	8.7	14.7
NORTH MIDDLESEX SVGS BK	AYER	MA	B	B	B	307.7	6.03	5.4	0.5	34.4	29.9	6.6	8.6	16.4
NORTH MILWAUKEE ST BK	MILWAUKEE	WI	C-	C-	D+	57.4	5.88	4.6	5.2	21.7	15.4	6.1	8.7	11.8
NORTH PENN BK	SCRANTON	PA	C	C	NR	93.8	N/A	15.8	8.4	32.0	32.2	6.1	8.1	13.8
NORTH SALEM ST BK	N SALEM	IN	C	C-	D+	106.9	7.80	12.0	8.6	11.7	24.9	4.0	7.8	10.5
NORTH SHORE BK A CO-OP	PEABODY	MA	B-	B-	B-	375.6	9.29	4.4	0.6	23.6	23.6	6.9	8.9	14.0
NORTH SHORE BK FSB	BROOKFIELD	WI	B-	B-	B-	1,819.9	13.80	1.6	10.8	23.7	33.6	8.0	9.7	20.8
NORTH SHORE BK OF	DULUTH	MN	B-	B-	C+	164.1	-0.90	9.2	0.9	37.5	15.5	5.1	7.1	11.2
NORTH SHORE CMNTY B&T	WILMETTE	IL	C+	C+	C+	869.2	6.29	16.6	4.6	11.3	14.2	4.4	8.5	10.7
NORTH SHORE TRUST &	WAUKEGAN	IL	B	B	B	247.9	-2.89	0.0	0.1	41.8	48.3	10.0	15.8	51.2
▼ NORTH SIDE B&TC	CINCINNATI	OH	A-	A	A	395.7	-2.50	32.1	2.8	14.7	20.6	10.0	13.4	19.8
NORTH SIDE FS&LA OF	CHICAGO	IL	C+	C+	B-	40.9	6.88	1.7	0.2	62.0	8.6	10.0	13.0	30.4
NORTH SIDE ST BK	ROCK SPRINGS	WY	B	B	B+	114.8	2.12	3.2	2.6	14.0	59.2	10.0	17.0	46.7
NORTH ST BK	RALEIGH	NC	C	C-	C-	284.5	14.75	9.3	0.7	14.3	12.9	6.6	8.8	12.2
▼ NORTH STAR BK	ROSEVILLE	MN	B	A-	A-	256.0	-3.04	23.4	1.7	6.5	19.3	7.7	9.5	13.1
▲ NORTH VALLEY BANK	ZANESVILLE	OH	C+	C-	C-	126.5	32.09	12.4	10.0	30.7	0.5	6.6	9.9	12.2
NORTH VALLEY BK	REDDING	CA	B+	B+	B+	728.0	56.05	5.1	7.6	8.4	28.8	6.1	8.1	13.1
▲ NORTH VALLEY BK	THORNTON	CO	C+	C	C-	107.0	13.31	12.2	5.4	11.6	15.8	3.6	7.7	10.3
NORTHAMPTON CO-OP BK	NORTHAMPTON	MA	B+	B+	A	148.4	13.53	0.3	0.4	30.3	41.9	10.0	12.4	23.4
NORTHBROOK B&TC	NORTHBROOK	IL	C+	C+	C	308.7	42.18	27.0	5.3	5.6	21.4	4.8	8.7	10.9
NORTHEAST BK	MINNEAPOLIS	MN	C+	C+	C	311.5	17.60	25.5	1.0	1.4	18.4	3.3	7.9	10.2
▼ NORTHEAST BK FSB	AUBURN	ME	C+	B-	C+	537.2	15.16	12.0	17.4	22.2	12.6	4.4	7.9	10.7
NORTHEAST GEORGIA BK	LAVONIA	GA	B+	B+	B+	267.8	4.81	5.6	5.0	7.6	24.4	7.7	9.5	14.0
NORTHEAST MISSOURI ST BK	KIRKSVILLE	MO	B-	B-	B-	24.1	8.23	1.4	9.9	15.4	50.8	10.0	12.4	25.7
NORTHEAST NB	MESQUITE	TX	D-	D-	D-	43.9	21.60	14.3	2.8	20.0	25.9	5.9	7.9	16.6
▲ NORTHEAST SECURITY BK	SUMNER	IA	B-	C+	C+	54.2	0.72	10.3	2.4	15.1	24.4	5.5	7.5	11.4
NORTHERN B&TC	WOBURN	MA	B+	B	B	346.9	4.47	12.0	0.6	20.6	10.9	6.0	9.1	11.8
NORTHERN HANCOCK B&TC	NEWELL	WV	C	C	C	24.6	4.88	27.0	22.2	27.5	8.2	10.0	11.9	16.9
▲ NORTHERN MICHIGAN B&T	ESCANABA	MI	C-	C	C-	160.5	-1.55	17.4	4.6	12.0	8.8	3.7	8.0	10.4
NORTHERN NB	NISSWA	MN	B-	B-	C+	92.3	4.52	14.3	2.8	23.0	6.6	6.1	9.2	11.8
▼ NORTHERN NECK ST BK	WARSAW	VA	B-	B	B-	291.1	2.02	3.1	11.3	29.3	29.2	6.2	8.2	13.2
NORTHERN NV BK	RENO	NV	B	B	C-	97.8	32.00	10.1	0.4	1.4	5.6	6.9	9.7	12.4
NORTHERN S&LC	ELYRIA	OH	A-	A-	A	314.1	-3.01	0.1	0.1	60.7	12.9	10.0	13.5	27.6
▲ NORTHERN ST BK	GONVICK	MN	B-	C	C+	30.2	-4.67	3.0	4.0	4.3	54.1	10.0	20.4	62.0
NORTHERN ST BK	THIEF RIVER FALL	MN	A-	A-	A-	168.2	-2.11	9.3	8.4	18.4	27.4	10.0	15.2	28.4
NORTHERN ST BK	VIRGINIA	MN	C-	C-	C	43.8	6.22	21.7	9.8	16.3	27.0	6.7	8.7	14.4
NORTHERN ST BK	ASHLAND	WI	B+	B+	B	146.2	2.67	8.2	3.1	35.9	22.0	5.9	7.9	13.0
NORTHERN STAR BK	MANKATO	MN	D-	E	E	44.9	-12.38	13.6	13.2	8.7	12.9	6.1	8.7	11.8
NORTHERN TR BK CA NA	SANTA BARBARA	CA	B	B	B	1,356.0	11.77	9.9	11.4	54.9	0.9	5.8	8.3	11.6
NORTHERN TRUST BK FSB	BLOOMFIELD HILLS	MI	B-	B-	B-	529.1	19.61	4.7	12.8	42.4	1.4	8.2	9.9	13.5
NORTHERN TRUST BK NA	PHOENIX	AZ	B	B	B	1,169.7	-0.14	8.2	4.8	49.6	4.5	7.0	9.0	13.2
▼ NORTHERN TRUST BK OF FL	MIAMI	FL	B	B	B-	4,935.3	8.31	11.1	4.9	34.0	5.0	5.4	7.9	11.3
NORTHERN TRUST BK TX NA	DALLAS	TX	B	B	B	1,014.3	9.87	7.9	8.0	56.5	0.9	5.8	8.3	11.6
NORTHERN TRUST CO	CHICAGO	IL	B-	B-	B-	35,218.2	11.61	7.1	2.5	7.4	22.9	4.2	6.2	12.2
NORTHFIELD SVGS BK	NEW YORK CITY	NY	A-	A-	A-	1,495.1	4.09	0.1	0.2	10.7	73.2	6.8	8.8	25.8
▼ NORTHFIELD SVGS BK	NORTHFIELD	VT	B	B+	B+	473.5	14.81	2.1	0.6	40.7	32.4	10.0	12.5	23.2
▲ NORTHLAND COMMUNITY BK	NORTHOME	MN	C-	D+	D	49.8	8.73	10.7	5.6	27.9	5.5	5.6	8.2	11.5
▼ NORTHLAND FINANCIAL	STEELE	ND	D+	C	C-	75.2	19.66	16.1	3.3	3.5	18.0	3.4	7.7	10.2
NORTHLAND NB	GLADSTONE	MO	B+	B	B	59.9	1.54	13.0	4.9	21.7	17.7	10.0	11.5	17.5
NORTHMARK BK	N ANDOVER	MA	B+	A-	A-	253.1	-2.44	6.5	0.7	31.8	14.7	8.9	10.3	18.4
▼ NORTHPOINTE BK	GRAND RAPIDS	MI	C-	C	C+	211.3	27.79	0.2	0.0	49.7	8.7	7.9	9.6	14.9
▲ NORTHRIM BK	ANCHORAGE	AK	C	C-	B-	738.5	3.36	21.3	1.0	4.8	8.1	5.7	9.4	11.6
NORTHSIDE BK	PITTSBURGH	PA	D	D+	C+	530.8	2.90	5.7	22.1	11.3	32.5	5.1	7.1	11.1
▲ NORTHSIDE CMNTY BK	GURNEE	IL	B+	B	B	448.8	13.34	12.6	0.6	9.8	2.5	7.9	11.7	13.2
NORTHSTAR BANK OF TEXAS	DENTON	TX	C	C	C-	266.1	13.13	14.0	4.2	8.2	4.4	3.1	7.9	10.1
▲ NORTHSTAR BK	ESTHERVILLE	IA	C	C-	C-	62.4	13.87	11.1	7.7	16.9	0.5	5.3	8.5	11.2
NORTHSTAR BK	BAD AXE	MI	D+	D+	D-	95.4	20.76	9.2	7.1	16.8	9.3	5.3	8.5	11.2
NORTHSTAR BK	SEATTLE	WA	C+	C+	B-	149.8	44.36	16.3	2.3	17.5	3.5	4.9	8.2	10.9
NORTHSTAR BK NA	KANSAS CITY	MO	D+	D+	D+	148.1	37.10	20.5	0.5	8.8	6.7	5.6	11.2	11.4

Asset Quality Index	Non-Performing Loans as a % of Total Loans	Non-Performing Loans as a % of Capital	Net Charge-offs Avg Loans	Profitability Index	Net Income ($Mil)	Return on Assets (R.O.A.)	Return on Equity (R.O.E.)	Net Interest Spread	Overhead Efficiency Ratio	Liquidity Index	Liquidity Ratio	Hot Money Ratio	Stability Index
8.7	0.00	0.0	0.00	3.3	0.2	0.23	2.42	2.65	86.3	1.9	39.1	39.2	5.0
6.9	0.14	1.3	0.11	8.1	0.6	1.39	17.77	4.71	41.9	2.4	23.8	18.0	1.3
8.5	0.09	0.5	0.11	5.2	0.6	1.06	11.56	3.92	60.3	1.9	28.1	24.7	5.1
7.1	0.00	0.0	-0.07	10.0	3.4	1.83	19.93	5.35	44.7	0.5	5.3	45.5	7.0
7.2	0.26	1.8	0.24	10.0	1.4	2.43	26.44	5.41	39.6	1.3	19.2	28.1	5.7
1.8	5.34	26.3	0.37	3.3	0.1	0.63	7.27	3.09	72.2	3.9	88.6	24.1	1.0
6.9	1.20	7.5	0.13	4.6	1.1	0.73	8.11	3.50	73.6	3.1	20.7	13.9	5.3
3.2	2.15	16.6	-0.30	4.8	0.2	0.73	8.52	5.40	78.1	2.5	14.8	16.3	3.7
4.2	2.13	14.2	0.24	3.4	0.2	0.43	5.19	3.16	84.5	7.0	118.1	10.5	1.4
3.8	1.23	9.8	0.63	4.1	0.4	0.69	8.50	3.95	72.2	3.2	20.5	13.3	3.9
8.9	0.07	0.6	-0.03	3.9	1.0	0.54	6.03	3.66	78.4	4.3	26.6	9.0	4.8
6.3	0.59	3.5	0.06	4.2	4.7	0.53	5.08	3.02	75.5	2.5	10.8	16.2	7.5
7.6	0.40	3.8	0.00	4.7	0.5	0.63	8.12	4.33	88.9	5.7	35.2	3.3	4.9
4.3	0.99	7.8	0.13	4.0	2.9	0.66	7.49	2.58	82.3	1.3	25.3	30.8	5.1
9.0	0.36	1.0	0.01	3.8	0.6	0.47	2.85	2.30	74.8	3.1	51.2	26.7	7.8
5.4	1.91	10.0	0.00	6.3	1.5	0.78	5.81	3.54	55.0	3.0	39.0	19.6	7.6
3.6	1.68	6.9	0.00	3.7	0.1	0.41	2.37	4.22	86.8	2.3	22.3	18.3	6.3
9.6	0.10	0.2	0.09	4.5	0.5	0.80	4.77	3.53	65.7	5.1	44.2	10.6	8.1
6.0	0.48	4.0	0.14	3.1	0.6	0.45	5.87	3.03	68.4	5.6	64.9	12.8	2.1
4.0	2.19	14.9	-0.05	3.6	0.4	0.29	2.97	4.47	75.6	5.5	29.4	1.7	6.6
4.1	0.64	5.9	0.15	9.8	0.9	1.57	19.80	5.19	49.0	1.1	6.2	27.6	5.3
5.8	0.72	4.6	0.17	9.7	4.9	1.53	18.18	5.42	63.6	6.3	59.2	7.5	6.8
6.9	0.17	1.6	0.13	8.7	1.2	2.43	31.56	5.97	62.1	4.1	10.0	7.2	4.1
10.0	0.00	0.0	0.00	4.4	0.6	0.83	6.69	3.18	70.0	4.9	63.8	15.9	7.4
6.9	0.26	2.3	0.04	4.5	1.3	0.92	11.56	3.01	49.6	1.3	7.2	25.8	3.5
5.3	0.64	5.7	0.06	6.6	2.4	1.65	20.46	4.69	61.2	5.5	43.0	7.6	4.7
4.7	0.39	3.7	0.02	5.2	2.2	0.84	10.39	3.56	67.1	0.6	15.8	67.9	5.1
5.5	0.48	2.9	0.36	8.4	1.7	1.29	13.08	4.64	60.1	3.1	24.2	14.4	6.2
8.5	0.28	0.9	0.14	6.3	0.2	1.38	11.09	4.13	59.5	4.2	35.8	10.7	5.3
6.2	0.41	2.8	0.06	2.0	0.1	0.22	2.93	4.31	96.0	3.8	36.0	14.4	0.5
7.8	0.00	0.0	0.00	5.0	0.2	0.76	7.73	3.73	72.3	4.0	21.7	9.3	4.7
8.3	0.00	0.0	0.01	9.1	2.6	1.52	16.92	5.20	57.7	3.9	16.0	9.6	6.0
3.5	1.63	9.8	0.73	8.6	0.3	2.49	21.25	7.25	63.3	2.9	38.1	17.7	3.9
2.1	2.44	20.8	0.05	5.9	0.7	0.89	10.96	4.64	77.2	2.1	24.9	19.7	5.8
8.3	0.00	0.0	0.00	5.6	0.6	1.30	14.37	4.51	70.2	2.4	22.8	17.8	4.6
7.7	0.03	0.2	-0.13	6.6	2.0	1.33	13.16	4.14	60.2	5.3	65.1	14.0	5.7
7.3	0.00	0.0	0.69	7.2	0.6	1.35	13.53	5.70	51.9	6.6	94.7	10.1	2.8
9.4	0.32	1.7	0.00	6.1	1.6	1.00	7.51	3.43	56.3	2.4	26.1	18.5	7.7
7.4	5.62	5.4	-0.37	3.8	0.2	1.10	5.33	2.70	54.9	7.2	137.4	11.5	4.7
5.2	3.02	9.8	-0.23	7.9	1.5	1.68	10.37	3.57	51.8	7.2	67.6	3.4	9.4
4.4	1.14	8.1	0.04	4.1	0.1	0.66	7.55	4.77	84.7	4.4	21.2	7.0	3.3
8.8	0.00	0.0	-0.05	8.4	1.4	1.97	23.84	4.48	56.9	3.7	19.9	11.0	6.4
2.2	1.24	9.6	2.77	0.5	-0.2	-0.67	-7.87	4.41	103.2	4.5	62.5	16.2	2.1
8.0	0.11	1.1	0.00	6.0	6.5	0.98	10.98	2.13	73.7	3.2	20.1	14.3	6.6
6.1	0.02	0.2	0.13	0.8	-0.8	-0.30	-2.50	1.92	103.7	4.6	169.7	88.5	6.2
8.4	0.16	1.4	-0.01	8.9	8.2	1.41	15.17	2.85	59.3	6.3	127.0	15.9	6.3
8.4	0.16	1.7	-0.01	9.4	41.7	1.68	21.55	2.64	49.3	6.4	49.5	7.3	7.2
8.0	0.04	0.3	0.00	8.1	6.0	1.24	12.84	3.34	60.4	4.2	23.8	11.1	8.0
8.1	0.70	3.2	0.01	5.7	182.2	1.08	17.03	1.14	68.0	7.1	234.6	16.9	5.5
9.2	0.91	1.8	0.00	6.5	8.3	1.13	11.83	2.98	42.5	4.5	25.5	10.2	8.0
9.6	0.28	1.3	0.02	4.1	1.6	0.71	5.53	3.50	80.4	4.8	51.0	13.7	7.1
8.3	0.07	0.7	-0.03	6.3	0.3	1.39	18.55	5.35	71.7	3.7	24.8	11.2	2.7
3.0	1.83	17.0	-0.03	4.8	0.2	0.47	6.12	4.58	81.7	1.8	22.9	22.7	3.0
8.2	0.10	0.6	0.03	6.3	0.4	1.20	10.51	4.00	52.8	3.2	37.7	18.4	6.2
9.1	0.00	0.0	0.00	5.3	1.0	0.80	7.95	3.26	59.5	3.7	63.3	26.1	6.2
2.3	3.30	29.0	-0.15	10.0	2.8	2.77	29.78	5.86	49.8	1.6	5.8	20.9	7.0
2.7	1.40	10.0	0.25	9.6	5.6	1.51	14.95	6.00	57.4	4.4	42.7	13.5	7.0
0.6	3.21	24.3	0.19	4.2	2.0	0.77	10.42	3.20	69.3	6.6	87.7	10.4	4.4
5.6	0.36	2.5	0.51	8.3	3.0	1.36	12.02	4.18	36.2	0.9	21.9	39.7	7.0
4.8	0.35	3.3	1.36	5.5	1.4	1.04	13.10	4.87	65.4	2.4	33.3	21.9	4.1
6.9	0.01	0.1	0.19	4.6	0.2	0.67	7.27	3.55	72.9	4.3	64.8	17.5	3.4
8.0	0.03	0.3	0.03	1.3	0.1	0.10	1.25	3.13	89.5	0.9	21.5	40.0	0.3
3.6	1.30	12.6	0.09	6.8	0.8	1.13	14.12	4.68	51.6	4.6	37.7	11.1	4.6
4.0	0.86	6.4	-0.03	0.7	-0.2	-0.28	-2.36	3.61	98.5	0.5	4.6	50.5	1.2

Name	City	State	Weiss Safety Rating	2003 Weiss Safety Rating	2002 Weiss Safety Rating	Total Assets ($Mil)	One Year Asset Growth	Commercial Loans	Consumer Loans	Home Mortgages	Securities	Capitalization Index	Leverage Ratio	Risk-based Capital Ratio
NORTHUMBERLAND NB	NORTHUMBERLAND	PA	B	B	B+	271.2	20.50	3.3	2.2	43.2	39.6	5.9	7.9	18.4
▲ NORTHVIEW B&TC	NORTHFIELD	IL	C	C-	C-	337.9	1.50	18.1	2.0	15.3	9.3	5.3	7.8	11.3
▲ NORTHVIEW BK	FINLAYSON	MN	B-	C+	B-	117.4	39.37	7.5	6.4	31.5	6.2	6.5	8.9	12.1
▲ NORTHWAY ST BK	GRAYSLAKE	IL	D	D-	D-	49.5	19.83	22.4	1.3	7.0	5.5	4.4	8.8	10.7
NORTHWEST B&TC	ACWORTH	GA	D	NR	NR	28.3	N/A	1.8	0.5	0.7	31.0	10.0	59.3	106.1
▲ NORTHWEST B&TC	DAVENPORT	IA	C	D+	D-	178.7	-5.44	14.1	3.3	21.6	14.0	4.6	6.6	12.3
NORTHWEST BK	ROANOKE	TX	B-	C+	C+	108.4	4.88	12.6	5.8	8.7	15.3	6.6	8.9	12.2
▲ NORTHWEST BK OF	ROCKFORD	IL	B-	C+	C+	168.9	3.84	20.1	2.4	10.9	16.7	5.5	8.4	11.4
NORTHWEST BUSINESS BK	SEATTLE	WA	B+	B+	B-	144.2	48.28	19.7	2.3	4.1	4.8	9.4	10.6	15.0
NORTHWEST COMMERCIAL	LAKEWOOD	WA	D	D	D	18.9	210.42	13.5	2.2	1.6	11.8	10.0	19.4	28.1
▼ NORTHWEST COMMUNITY BK	WINSTED	CT	C+	B-	B-	275.3	5.11	1.7	1.9	40.4	33.4	8.9	10.2	18.6
▲ NORTHWEST COMMUNITY BK	CHAMPLIN	MN	D	E	E	28.1	27.23	34.7	0.9	8.2	6.8	6.3	8.9	12.0
NORTHWEST FSB	SPENCER	IA	B	B	B	416.8	8.29	13.7	4.9	28.1	7.6	5.3	8.0	11.2
NORTHWEST GEORGIA BK	RINGGOLD	GA	B-	B-	B-	478.6	20.93	11.8	2.9	7.1	30.2	5.2	7.2	15.7
NORTHWEST NB OF	ARLINGTON	TX	D-	D-	D-	49.2	-17.68	26.1	4.8	7.9	28.1	8.7	10.1	18.4
NORTHWEST SVGS BK	WARREN	PA	B-	C+	C+	5,396.2	10.22	1.8	6.2	49.2	23.9	5.6	7.6	15.0
▼ NORTHWESTERN BK	CHIPPEWA FALLS	WI	B+	A	A	271.7	5.08	4.9	1.4	15.1	34.7	10.0	12.3	19.9
NORTHWESTERN BK NA	DILWORTH	MN	C+	C+	C	115.5	4.55	21.1	12.2	11.1	9.9	2.7	7.4	9.7
NORTHWESTERN MUTUAL	MILWAUKEE	WI	D	D	D	12.0	11.89	0.0	0.0	0.0	82.7	10.0	82.8	239.1
NORTHWESTERN ST BK	ORANGE CITY	IA	A-	A-	B+	87.5	7.59	12.9	7.3	11.1	6.7	8.0	10.0	13.3
NORTHWESTERN SVG B&TC	TRAVERSE CITY	MI	B-	B-	C-	577.7	0.81	7.3	3.2	20.2	0.1	4.3	8.1	10.6
NORTHWOOD SVG BK	PHILADELPHIA	PA	D	D	D-	9.1	3.77	0.0	0.0	59.1	29.8	8.4	10.0	19.9
▲ NORTHWOODS BK OF MN	PARK RAPIDS	MN	C+	C	C-	91.7	2.60	7.7	4.4	22.2	14.9	6.3	8.4	11.9
▲ NORTHWOODS ST BK	NORTHWOOD	IA	B-	C+	C	80.3	5.56	13.5	4.1	11.1	25.3	5.9	7.9	11.9
NORTHWOODS ST BK	RHINELANDER	WI	C+	C+	C+	84.0	11.77	8.7	3.2	40.7	1.3	5.5	7.7	11.4
▲ NORWAY SVGS BK	NORWAY	ME	B-	C+	B-	655.5	4.40	7.6	6.3	25.0	11.6	7.0	9.0	12.5
NORWOOD CO-OP BK	NORWOOD	MA	A+	A+	A+	349.2	16.48	1.8	0.6	25.1	15.8	10.0	13.0	19.3
NOVA SAVINGS BK	PHILADELPHIA	PA	D-	E	E-	391.5	20.28	1.8	1.4	7.9	52.9	3.1	5.1	10.4
NVE BK	ENGLEWOOD	NJ	B-	B-	B	631.4	3.42	0.4	0.1	22.0	50.1	9.0	10.3	23.8
O'BANNON BANKING CO	BUFFALO	MO	B-	B-	B-	125.6	9.44	6.7	3.8	28.1	17.4	6.4	8.4	13.1
OAK BK	CHICAGO	IL	B-	B-	B-	136.9	9.63	6.2	0.5	22.5	9.6	8.9	10.3	14.3
OAK BK	FITCHBURG	WI	B-	B-	D+	110.0	19.81	22.0	2.8	16.1	10.2	6.5	10.9	12.1
OAK BROOK BK	OAK BROOK	IL	B-	B-	B-	2,067.1	23.49	4.9	14.4	5.6	38.0	5.0	7.0	11.5
OAK CREEK VALLEY BK	VALPARAISO	NE	B-	B-	B+	42.7	4.53	6.2	1.6	9.9	39.0	6.3	8.3	14.6
OAK HILL BANKS	JACKSON	OH	C+	C+	C+	970.3	13.20	16.0	6.9	18.1	8.0	4.0	7.8	10.5
▼ OAK LAWN BK	OAK LAWN	IL	D+	C-	D+	63.1	12.40	13.8	0.4	9.1	14.0	4.5	8.2	10.8
▲ OAK VALLEY COMMUNITY	OAKDALE	CA	B+	B-	B+	277.7	29.67	6.0	0.5	2.8	12.7	7.8	10.3	13.2
▼ OAKDALE ST BK	OAKDALE	IL	E	E+	D-	18.3	12.15	3.1	2.1	19.8	40.5	4.4	6.4	13.1
OAKLAND COMMERCE BK	FARMINGTON HILLS	MI	C	C	C	128.9	-0.93	10.5	0.5	25.2	0.0	3.7	7.5	10.3
▲ OAKLAND DEPOSIT BK	OAKLAND	TN	C-	D+	D+	83.6	4.51	5.5	6.1	31.1	14.1	5.8	7.8	11.8
▼ OAKLAND ST BK	OAKLAND	IA	D	D+	C-	28.5	-20.31	22.0	2.4	9.0	3.1	7.0	9.0	15.4
OAKLEY NB OF BUFFALO	BUFFALO	MN	B+	B+	B	164.5	7.56	10.5	2.5	12.2	25.8	7.1	9.1	13.0
OAKS B&TC	DALLAS	TX	A	A	A	104.9	3.12	12.3	11.6	8.7	12.4	9.4	10.6	15.3
OAKWOOD ST BK	OAKWOOD	TX	D	D+	D+	2.3	2.92	0.1	2.4	0.0	49.5	10.0	13.8	85.5
OBA FSB	GERMANTOWN	MD	C+	C+	B-	433.4	-1.32	2.6	0.0	52.3	16.9	6.0	8.0	13.4
▲ OCALA NB	OCALA	FL	C	C-	D+	93.6	21.83	3.7	2.2	27.2	9.7	4.5	7.3	10.7
▲ OCEAN BK	MIAMI	FL	C	D	D	4,486.2	7.00	10.2	0.6	6.2	17.8	7.0	9.0	12.7
OCEAN CITY HOME BK	OCEAN CITY	NJ	C+	C	C	478.9	8.41	0.8	0.2	55.2	20.4	5.0	7.0	13.7
OCEAN NB	KENNEBUNK	ME	B-	B-	B-	1,629.6	179.02	6.4	0.4	13.1	22.1	4.4	7.4	10.7
OCEANFIRST BK	BRICK	NJ	B	B	B	1,852.2	5.52	3.3	0.1	62.4	12.1	4.3	6.3	11.0
OCEANIC BK	SAN FRANCISCO	CA	B+	B+	A-	166.9	2.96	2.9	0.2	3.1	10.3	10.0	12.7	16.6
OCEANSIDE BK	JACKSONVILLE BCH	FL	C+	C+	C+	170.7	21.49	9.3	3.4	6.7	16.4	5.1	8.4	11.1
OCONEE FS&LA	SENECA	SC	A-	A-	A	316.9	4.78	0.0	0.5	55.4	27.8	10.0	14.5	39.6
OCONEE ST BK	WATKINSVILLE	GA	B-	B-	B-	247.1	-9.03	9.3	4.4	13.3	20.5	6.6	8.7	13.0
OCULINA BANK	FORT PIERCE	FL	D	NR	NR	12.4	N/A	5.2	3.4	42.0	20.7	10.0	39.2	91.1
▲ OCWEN FEDERAL BK FSB	FORT LEE	NJ	B-	D+	D	1,000.8	1.95	0.0	0.0	0.1	0.6	10.0	16.2	18.3
ODEBOLT ST BK	ODEBOLT	IA	D	D+	C-	8.4	-1.59	3.9	0.4	0.0	83.2	10.0	38.3	462.3
ODIN ST BK	ODIN	MN	C	C	B	39.3	10.41	10.1	3.1	4.5	31.1	8.7	10.1	16.8
▼ OGLESBY ST BK	OGLESBY	TX	E+	D-	D-	7.7	3.37	3.8	27.0	33.0	9.1	6.4	8.4	13.6
▼ OGLETHORPE BK	BRUNSWICK	GA	D-	D	NR	58.6	N/A	11.5	4.9	27.2	8.4	10.0	12.9	15.0
OHIO CENTRAL SVGS	DUBLIN	OH	B-	B-	C+	56.3	14.67	0.2	33.8	12.3	42.7	4.7	6.7	13.6
OHIO HERITAGE BK	COSHOCTON	OH	C	C	C	175.5	1.30	4.6	11.0	47.1	12.5	5.2	7.2	12.0
OHIO LEGACY BK NA	WOOSTER	OH	C	D+	D-	172.6	21.20	6.4	0.9	28.3	19.2	9.8	10.9	16.5
OHIO RIVER BK	IRONTON	OH	C+	C+	C+	78.3	3.75	5.5	4.6	26.5	37.0	5.8	7.8	15.1

Asset Quality Index	Non-Performing Loans as a % of Total Loans	Non-Performing Loans as a % of Capital	Net Charge-offs Avg Loans	Profitability Index	Net Income ($Mil)	Return on Assets (R.O.A.)	Return on Equity (R.O.E.)	Net Interest Spread	Overhead Efficiency Ratio	Liquidity Index	Liquidity Ratio	Hot Money Ratio	Stability Index
9.5	0.11	0.7	0.03	5.3	1.3	1.00	13.08	3.07	49.4	5.4	48.1	10.1	4.6
4.7	0.90	7.8	0.05	4.5	1.1	0.68	8.89	3.74	65.9	2.5	39.5	27.4	3.2
4.8	0.75	6.4	0.11	10.0	1.0	1.77	20.02	5.79	46.3	1.1	11.8	29.2	5.4
7.2	0.00	0.0	0.03	2.2	0.1	0.30	3.03	3.30	81.8	5.2	93.1	16.9	4.6
9.9	0.00	0.0	0.00	0.0	-0.9	-9.75	-14.15	1.01	846.0	6.4	511.7	20.8	0.0
3.2	1.02	8.1	0.56	7.2	0.9	1.06	15.64	3.81	69.0	3.2	47.7	22.9	4.2
5.4	0.54	4.2	0.21	5.9	0.5	0.94	10.76	5.99	75.8	3.6	20.1	11.5	4.1
5.0	0.73	5.9	0.65	7.4	1.1	1.29	15.36	4.38	56.7	1.8	27.6	25.3	5.6
7.3	0.07	0.5	0.46	7.1	0.9	1.29	12.01	4.71	50.2	5.2	51.6	11.9	5.7
8.6	0.00	0.0	0.00	0.0	-0.5	-7.16	-28.33	3.32	296.0	5.8	213.8	30.6	0.0
5.9	1.40	7.3	-0.03	3.6	0.7	0.48	4.69	3.44	80.8	4.8	30.5	7.2	5.5
5.8	0.38	3.3	0.00	4.5	0.1	0.98	11.44	5.93	71.8	4.0	15.7	8.5	2.6
4.1	1.29	12.2	0.00	7.3	3.0	1.48	17.94	3.84	62.6	1.3	16.8	27.7	6.3
4.2	1.44	11.7	0.25	7.0	2.5	1.13	14.80	4.17	60.3	0.7	7.8	33.8	4.4
3.3	2.82	15.0	0.03	2.0	0.1	0.31	3.08	4.12	90.1	3.3	38.9	17.9	1.1
5.5	0.85	5.3	0.12	5.3	27.0	1.00	10.16	3.59	59.7	7.9	112.8	6.4	6.8
5.0	2.63	11.9	0.14	8.3	2.0	1.49	11.22	4.92	51.4	4.0	12.7	8.1	8.2
3.9	0.72	6.5	0.05	6.1	0.8	1.44	16.58	5.16	72.2	3.5	7.2	10.7	5.2
7.7	0.00	0.0	0.00	0.0	-1.1	-17.72	-20.99	0.68	227.5	1.5	50.8	100.0	0.0
6.3	0.57	4.2	-0.01	9.7	0.8	1.75	18.02	3.89	39.6	2.0	20.7	19.7	8.1
5.8	0.26	2.3	0.10	6.1	2.6	0.92	10.24	3.78	75.3	4.5	29.0	8.4	6.0
8.2	0.77	4.5	0.00	4.2	0.0	0.88	8.62	4.02	77.5	5.0	N/A	0.0	1.9
3.4	1.43	12.4	0.04	9.2	0.9	2.01	22.92	4.37	61.9	0.7	13.1	42.6	6.3
7.6	0.30	2.1	-0.55	6.2	0.6	1.49	17.12	4.23	67.0	2.6	8.4	15.2	4.4
2.6	1.13	8.7	0.41	7.5	0.5	1.26	12.79	4.78	46.0	1.2	15.9	29.3	5.9
6.2	0.37	2.6	0.01	4.3	3.1	0.97	9.31	4.10	77.6	4.4	28.5	8.9	7.0
8.8	0.00	0.0	-0.10	8.6	2.1	1.26	9.64	3.82	51.6	4.3	61.7	18.8	8.6
4.6	1.17	7.3	2.32	0.7	-0.1	-0.03	-0.38	2.39	78.5	3.3	17.0	12.6	1.7
7.8	0.76	2.8	0.00	4.1	1.6	0.52	4.97	2.94	74.0	4.4	26.4	8.0	6.8
6.8	0.22	1.8	0.06	4.4	0.5	0.83	10.07	3.76	70.1	4.1	27.0	10.3	4.7
8.9	0.10	0.8	0.00	4.3	0.4	0.61	5.96	4.30	76.2	1.5	20.0	25.4	6.4
5.8	0.94	6.8	0.01	5.0	0.4	0.82	7.61	3.51	63.8	2.4	31.7	20.5	2.9
8.0	0.03	0.3	0.03	5.9	10.8	1.11	16.23	3.07	54.7	3.8	82.2	37.7	4.6
8.7	0.16	1.0	0.00	7.5	0.4	1.86	22.04	4.23	54.5	3.8	6.3	8.8	5.4
4.3	0.65	6.4	0.15	8.8	6.6	1.38	17.70	4.04	50.5	1.6	10.0	20.9	5.4
5.2	0.72	6.0	0.01	2.6	0.1	0.33	3.80	3.61	81.2	3.4	45.6	19.1	4.1
7.3	0.02	0.2	0.00	7.0	1.5	1.13	12.23	5.07	57.3	1.8	16.1	20.4	5.4
5.7	2.39	18.5	0.02	4.5	0.1	1.11	18.37	3.63	68.4	5.4	73.9	12.0	0.1
1.4	1.72	17.6	0.91	4.9	0.1	0.17	2.19	3.93	51.4	0.9	21.2	37.3	5.3
6.6	0.39	2.9	0.29	4.0	0.3	0.78	10.07	4.52	79.9	3.7	58.5	19.3	1.9
0.3	11.74	54.5	0.43	2.5	0.1	0.41	4.59	3.53	88.4	6.4	132.5	14.8	1.9
5.4	0.66	4.4	0.01	7.3	1.2	1.53	16.58	3.90	61.9	4.1	26.3	9.7	7.7
7.9	0.00	0.0	-0.03	9.4	0.7	1.44	14.05	5.62	63.1	6.1	58.3	8.7	7.1
10.0	0.00	0.0	0.00	0.0	0.0	-1.42	-9.87	3.37	131.4	6.8	59.4	0.0	1.7
9.4	0.05	0.5	0.02	3.3	1.0	0.46	5.85	2.09	81.8	0.6	16.3	68.3	4.5
8.2	0.13	1.3	-0.06	8.4	0.8	1.88	26.38	4.41	65.6	3.9	14.2	9.4	2.7
3.5	2.00	13.8	-0.22	8.7	36.2	1.66	18.79	4.32	45.4	5.1	136.2	27.9	6.2
8.7	0.00	0.0	0.00	4.8	1.6	0.69	9.63	3.16	65.2	0.9	24.8	41.5	3.8
6.3	0.40	1.2	0.07	7.7	6.8	1.45	8.79	6.85	68.7	5.9	37.7	6.6	7.8
8.0	0.24	2.9	0.00	6.3	8.3	0.93	14.33	3.12	64.0	1.3	4.8	24.9	6.0
7.5	0.42	2.2	0.00	4.9	0.7	0.87	6.79	3.22	54.8	3.8	97.2	50.5	7.7
8.4	0.00	0.0	0.02	4.5	0.6	0.69	9.43	4.12	71.4	4.1	40.1	14.7	4.3
8.9	0.25	1.0	0.00	5.7	1.3	0.85	5.67	2.51	46.2	4.0	47.6	16.9	8.2
5.4	0.48	3.5	-0.04	5.8	1.2	0.99	11.67	4.36	69.1	4.4	25.2	7.8	4.6
9.3	0.00	0.0	0.00	0.0	-0.1	-3.16	-5.38	4.22	115.7	3.3	79.9	31.0	0.0
3.9	151.95	4.4	19.60	5.6	8.4	1.64	8.92	-56.11	90.2	2.9	56.8	69.5	7.3
10.0	1.74	0.4	0.00	0.0	0.0	-0.97	-2.45	1.24	182.0	10.0	431.3	0.0	2.5
4.9	1.38	7.0	0.69	4.5	0.2	1.20	11.73	3.76	47.9	3.0	42.2	21.4	3.1
2.8	0.52	4.2	0.39	3.7	0.0	0.74	9.01	4.73	88.9	3.6	39.6	14.5	1.0
8.4	0.00	0.0	0.01	0.0	-0.6	-3.00	-18.46	3.84	132.6	0.9	16.5	34.4	0.0
6.0	0.14	0.9	0.04	2.6	0.0	0.09	1.32	2.26	95.1	3.1	18.0	13.8	4.8
8.1	0.04	0.5	0.23	5.3	0.9	1.02	14.40	3.29	61.0	3.7	23.8	11.5	2.8
8.8	0.17	1.1	0.22	3.0	0.6	0.74	6.70	3.47	69.9	2.2	27.4	20.1	1.8
7.0	0.23	1.6	0.49	6.8	0.5	1.19	15.16	4.06	59.1	4.7	26.9	6.4	5.3

Name	City	State	Weiss Safety Rating	2003 Weiss Safety Rating	2002 Weiss Safety Rating	Total Assets ($Mil)	One Year Asset Growth	Comm-ercial Loans	Cons-umer Loans	Home Mort-gages	Secur-ities	Capital-ization Index	Leverage Ratio	Risk-based Capital Ratio
▲ OHIO SVGS BK FSB	CLEVELAND	OH	B-	C+	C+	12,323.0	-7.76	0.3	7.0	65.4	0.1	5.9	7.9	12.2
▲ OHIO VALLEY BK CO	GALLIPOLIS	OH	B-	C+	C+	708.1	2.90	30.6	16.9	31.7	11.1	6.7	8.7	12.4
OHIO VALLEY NB OF	HENDERSON	KY	B+	B	B	165.8	1.92	7.0	4.7	29.9	24.0	7.1	9.1	16.3
▲ OKAW B&LA SVGS BK	MATTOON	IL	C+	C	C	15.8	-6.31	0.0	0.2	55.5	6.3	10.0	19.3	44.9
OKEMAH NB	OKEMAH	OK	A-	A-	A-	57.1	-1.36	0.1	13.4	25.6	35.8	10.0	13.0	27.4
▲ OKEY-VERNON FIRST NB	CORNING	IA	B+	B	B+	43.5	-1.30	5.5	2.1	3.9	55.2	10.0	13.3	29.3
OKLAHOMA B&TC	CLINTON	OK	A+	A+	A+	100.0	-1.32	2.3	3.2	6.8	68.1	10.0	17.2	43.7
OKLAHOMA NB&TC	TULSA	OK	D+	D	D+	252.3	22.48	22.1	3.5	22.0	0.0	4.0	8.1	10.5
OKLAHOMA ST BK	BUFFALO	OK	C+	C+	C+	33.6	-3.88	2.0	9.0	4.3	44.8	6.0	8.0	16.6
OKLAHOMA ST BK	OKLAHOMA CITY	OK	E	E	E+	39.2	-10.18	4.4	9.7	14.4	31.7	6.0	8.0	14.9
OKLAHOMA ST BK	VINITA	OK	B+	A-	A-	64.6	17.35	8.9	6.9	19.0	24.7	8.7	10.1	15.4
OLATHE STATE BANK	OLATHE	CO	D-	D-	E+	38.6	14.69	7.2	2.9	7.2	11.9	4.3	7.2	10.6
OLD EXCHANGE NB OF	OKAWVILLE	IL	D+	D+	D+	38.2	3.09	2.9	1.7	9.3	31.9	6.9	8.9	16.3
OLD FARMERS & MERCNTS ST	HILLSDALE	IL	D+	D+	D+	39.9	11.66	8.8	6.7	15.7	39.1	5.3	7.3	13.9
OLD FLORIDA BK	FORT MYERS	FL	C	C	C-	202.9	89.15	4.1	2.0	8.2	7.7	5.5	9.6	11.4
▲ OLD FORGE BK	OLD FORGE	PA	A-	B+	B+	214.4	4.22	9.1	10.6	27.2	21.7	10.0	13.1	18.5
OLD FORT BKG CO	OLD FORT	OH	B-	B-	B-	310.9	9.28	11.8	17.1	12.0	22.7	5.5	8.2	11.4
OLD HARBOR BK	CLEARWATER	FL	D	D	NR	55.4	N/A	10.4	0.2	2.1	28.2	10.0	14.4	19.8
▲ OLD LINE BK	WALDORF	MD	B	C+	C-	98.9	6.04	7.5	19.9	2.5	19.1	10.0	12.6	17.3
OLD MISSION BK	SAULT STE MARIE	MI	B-	B-	C	64.2	3.10	13.4	3.2	14.6	20.7	8.2	9.8	14.6
OLD MISSOURI NB	SPRINGFIELD	MO	C-	C-	D	68.3	11.29	13.0	6.8	22.5	2.2	6.4	9.0	12.1
OLD NB	EVANSVILLE	IN	C+	B-	B-	8,815.4	-7.68	10.9	8.0	9.9	30.5	5.1	7.1	14.6
▲ OLD POINT NB OF PHOEBUS	HAMPTON	VA	B+	B	B	670.5	12.61	7.9	10.4	13.0	29.1	6.9	8.9	13.8
OLD SECOND BK KANE CITY	ELBURN	IL	B	B	B	316.5	18.00	5.2	0.7	18.4	19.2	3.7	7.5	10.3
OLD SECOND BK YORKVILLE	YORKVILLE	IL	B	B	B	324.4	22.86	5.1	4.9	15.2	17.1	4.0	7.7	10.5
OLD SECOND NB OF AURORA	AURORA	IL	B+	B+	B+	1,369.0	14.11	8.6	1.2	13.8	21.6	5.6	7.8	11.5
OLMSTED NB	ROCHESTER	MN	C-	C+	C+	41.0	35.11	25.7	4.9	14.4	0.2	5.5	9.2	11.4
OLPE ST BK	OLPE	KS	B+	B+	B+	30.5	0.14	9.2	4.9	20.9	35.0	10.0	14.6	26.7
▲ OLYMPIA FS&LA	OLYMPIA	WA	A	A-	A-	393.2	1.37	0.0	0.0	68.1	17.7	10.0	13.8	29.1
▼ OLYMPIC SA	REFUGIO	TX	B-	B	B	17.9	-9.41	0.0	0.3	54.7	11.3	10.0	12.8	28.1
▼ OMAHA ST BK	OMAHA	NE	A-	A	B+	198.6	-0.23	25.3	2.1	8.7	4.3	6.8	10.9	12.4
OMEGA BK NA	STATE COLLEGE	PA	A+	A+	A+	1,130.9	-1.75	6.7	2.4	24.3	19.8	10.0	13.0	20.6
▲ OMNI BK	METAIRIE	LA	C+	C	C	463.7	20.81	7.5	2.8	27.3	8.6	5.8	7.8	11.8
OMNI BK NA	ALHAMBRA	CA	B	B	B	210.0	5.94	1.6	1.8	1.9	12.7	9.4	10.6	14.6
▲ OMNI NB	FAYETTEVILLE	NC	C	C-	D	269.8	47.91	13.3	0.7	12.7	19.8	4.4	10.7	10.7
▼ OMNIBANK	MANTEE	MS	B-	B	B+	82.7	0.61	14.6	9.7	22.7	1.2	10.0	13.5	17.5
▲ OMNIBANK NA	HOUSTON	TX	D	D-	D-	315.3	2.78	14.1	1.1	3.5	0.1	5.2	8.9	11.1
▲ ONE B&T NA	LITTLE ROCK	AR	C	D+	C	274.7	10.36	27.2	6.3	27.4	0.5	4.1	8.4	10.5
ONE UNITED BK	BOSTON	MA	D	D-	D-	446.3	-2.28	1.9	0.4	19.9	27.3	4.3	6.3	11.1
ONEIDA SVGS BK	ONEIDA	NY	B-	B	B	429.2	2.09	8.6	8.8	22.7	38.5	6.0	8.0	13.4
ONSTED ST BK	ONSTED	MI	B	B	B-	64.5	1.93	5.6	3.8	25.6	13.6	8.9	10.6	14.1
ONTARIO NB	CLIFTON SPRINGS	NY	C+	C+	C+	102.6	0.67	8.3	3.7	27.1	21.7	5.7	7.7	12.1
▲ OOSTBURG ST BK	OOSTBURG	WI	A+	A	A	107.0	6.13	12.4	3.5	17.2	29.8	10.0	15.5	24.0
▲ OPTIMUMBANK.COM	PLANTATION	FL	B+	B	C-	153.7	46.67	0.4	0.1	37.8	12.9	10.0	11.1	16.7
ORANGE COMMUNITY BK	ORANGE	CA	B+	B+	C	119.1	30.52	16.6	0.9	1.6	20.8	8.8	10.2	14.9
ORANGE COUNTY TRUST CO	MIDDLETOWN	NY	A	A	A	386.3	10.22	10.7	0.6	13.3	48.6	10.0	14.2	27.7
ORANGE CTY BUS BK NA	NEWPORT BEACH	CA	D	D	D	71.1	97.04	10.9	0.3	0.0	24.0	10.0	27.2	42.5
▲ ORANGE SVG BK TX	MAURICEVILLE	TX	C+	C-	E-	41.7	26.45	3.8	15.9	13.8	20.2	6.0	8.0	13.1
ORANGE SVGS BK SSB	ORANGE	TX	B-	B-	B-	200.8	2.43	9.1	6.3	27.9	25.5	5.2	7.2	13.1
ORANGEBURG NB	ORANGEBURG	SC	B	B-	B-	183.7	6.91	14.7	9.3	20.3	14.3	7.6	9.4	13.9
▲ OREGON COAST BK	NEWPORT	OR	C+	C-	D	50.2	57.43	11.9	7.0	12.5	28.6	10.0	11.1	15.2
OREGON COMMUNITY B&TC	OREGON	WI	A	A	A	138.6	8.02	9.7	1.8	18.8	16.7	10.0	12.8	19.1
OREGON PACIFIC BKG CO	FLORENCE	OR	B	B-	C+	132.1	13.97	9.5	2.3	12.4	10.8	7.1	9.5	12.6
OREGON TRAIL BK	GUERNSEY	WY	C	C	C	18.9	-1.54	5.9	2.4	9.1	27.1	8.0	9.6	14.8
ORIENTAL B&TC	SAN JUAN	PR	C+	C+	C+	3,686.2	23.06	2.0	0.5	17.5	75.4	4.5	6.5	23.9
ORION BK	NAPLES	FL	C+	B-	C+	1,115.6	34.92	2.8	0.9	18.4	7.6	3.5	9.4	10.3
ORITANI SVG BK	HACKENSACK	NJ	A	A	A	1,018.0	2.85	0.0	0.1	18.0	59.2	10.0	11.4	31.9
ORMSBY ST BK	ORMSBY	MN	B	B	B	21.8	4.27	8.6	3.3	4.2	53.9	10.0	14.4	24.4
ORRSTOWN BK	SHIPPENSBURG	PA	B+	B+	B+	489.4	9.52	6.9	1.5	32.2	14.9	6.5	8.5	12.7
▲ OSAGE FEDERAL BK	PAWHUSKA	OK	B	C+	C+	89.0	13.34	0.2	6.1	50.3	30.6	10.0	12.4	26.8
OSAGE VALLEY BK	WARSAW	MO	B	B	B	89.3	6.21	4.7	2.6	37.9	37.0	5.2	7.2	13.8
OSGOOD ST BK	OSGOOD	OH	B-	B	B+	97.0	24.35	8.2	3.0	20.5	23.8	6.5	8.5	13.4
OSSIAN ST BK	OSSIAN	IN	B-	B-	B-	93.8	-0.32	6.2	4.8	18.8	34.1	7.1	9.0	13.9
▲ OSWEGO COMMUNITY BK	OSWEGO	IL	B+	B	B+	158.4	6.05	3.9	4.0	10.7	64.6	6.5	8.5	24.3

Asset Quality Index	Non-Performing Loans as a % of Total Loans	as a % of Capital	Net Charge-offs Avg Loans	Profitability Index	Net Income ($Mil)	Return on Assets (R.O.A.)	Return on Equity (R.O.E.)	Net Interest Spread	Overhead Efficiency Ratio	Liquidity Index	Liquidity Ratio	Hot Money Ratio	Stability Index
4.1	1.23	12.9	0.19	4.9	34.9	0.59	7.23	3.13	62.4	1.0	3.0	28.4	6.3
4.4	0.59	4.9	0.52	5.5	3.4	0.97	11.01	4.08	61.7	1.8	17.7	20.7	4.8
8.4	0.23	1.5	0.03	6.5	1.3	1.48	16.81	4.00	68.4	4.7	21.2	4.9	6.0
8.1	1.25	3.7	0.00	4.2	0.1	0.57	2.99	4.72	78.6	6.8	30,085.7	18.6	4.5
7.2	0.95	3.4	0.32	8.6	0.5	1.84	14.41	4.80	62.2	4.9	68.3	15.1	8.1
9.5	0.20	0.5	0.94	4.6	0.2	1.07	8.22	4.12	68.0	5.9	46.7	5.3	7.3
9.3	1.48	2.2	-0.01	8.2	0.9	1.77	10.41	3.38	53.6	3.5	50.8	20.3	9.6
3.8	1.28	12.6	0.07	3.5	0.6	0.52	6.62	4.26	69.9	0.9	15.1	33.5	0.6
6.7	0.45	2.6	0.04	10.0	0.4	2.33	29.38	4.71	53.8	1.5	10.6	23.6	4.4
0.3	9.84	44.0	3.24	0.6	-0.1	-0.52	-5.22	3.97	98.1	3.7	41.5	17.0	1.5
5.1	2.13	13.7	-0.02	6.0	0.4	1.38	13.46	5.08	74.0	3.1	11.7	13.1	6.5
5.9	0.56	5.8	0.04	6.1	0.2	1.21	17.82	5.95	68.3	2.7	27.8	17.3	0.7
4.1	1.85	12.2	0.03	5.2	0.3	1.30	14.78	3.99	66.1	3.7	30.1	13.5	2.0
7.0	0.60	4.1	0.15	5.1	0.3	1.27	17.57	3.88	67.4	3.2	36.6	17.7	2.2
5.5	0.11	0.8	0.00	2.8	0.2	0.23	2.00	4.13	86.0	1.6	20.8	24.5	5.8
5.7	0.99	5.0	0.15	8.4	1.7	1.56	12.01	4.52	49.5	3.5	26.9	13.3	7.9
5.1	0.28	2.3	0.49	4.7	1.4	0.95	11.30	3.90	67.4	1.0	17.0	32.6	4.3
8.8	0.00	0.0	0.00	0.0	-0.2	-0.97	-5.79	2.78	123.0	6.0	69.3	9.7	0.0
7.1	0.00	0.0	0.01	4.2	0.4	0.76	5.81	3.73	67.2	3.5	33.6	15.2	5.3
5.2	0.59	3.9	0.00	5.5	0.3	0.96	9.91	4.37	68.0	2.7	33.1	19.1	2.1
5.4	0.48	4.3	-0.05	2.4	0.2	0.50	5.67	3.81	78.1	3.4	52.0	20.5	3.5
4.1	1.90	12.5	0.59	4.8	39.8	0.89	11.16	3.50	66.8	3.2	26.5	17.3	4.6
6.8	0.42	2.9	0.21	6.7	4.2	1.27	14.32	4.07	61.0	3.4	18.8	12.2	5.8
5.7	0.66	5.6	0.00	6.7	1.8	1.20	15.33	3.81	54.5	4.8	53.8	14.6	6.3
7.9	0.08	0.7	0.09	5.2	0.9	0.63	8.04	4.18	81.7	3.2	35.6	17.6	6.1
8.7	0.07	0.6	-0.03	9.3	9.8	1.48	18.93	3.90	57.8	4.8	35.1	12.4	7.5
3.6	0.77	4.0	0.05	6.6	0.2	0.98	6.13	4.99	64.1	1.0	19.7	33.6	4.8
8.5	0.06	0.2	0.01	5.5	0.2	1.33	9.06	3.49	57.8	4.5	57.2	15.3	6.5
9.7	0.00	0.0	0.00	6.3	1.9	0.97	7.10	3.37	56.7	1.6	27.0	27.6	8.0
9.8	0.00	0.0	0.00	8.2	0.1	1.09	6.22	4.41	61.0	1.8	41.9	32.6	5.7
8.3	0.00	0.0	0.01	9.3	1.3	1.37	12.49	5.41	68.3	6.2	38.1	1.0	7.7
8.6	0.37	2.1	0.09	7.7	7.4	1.31	11.70	3.97	63.5	6.8	58.7	6.0	9.9
4.6	0.92	8.5	0.05	6.5	2.2	1.01	13.37	5.28	67.5	2.9	29.7	17.3	3.3
4.8	0.51	3.5	0.15	6.3	1.0	0.98	9.26	4.13	61.5	1.6	33.4	33.9	6.1
3.9	0.55	5.0	0.10	4.9	1.5	1.24	17.04	6.05	73.8	0.3	2.5	63.4	3.4
5.4	0.72	4.4	0.17	3.5	0.2	0.54	4.04	5.68	89.6	4.0	16.7	9.0	6.4
1.0	2.96	26.7	0.13	4.4	1.1	0.73	8.33	4.50	71.8	1.9	27.0	22.8	3.9
5.3	0.41	4.0	0.20	3.3	0.6	0.44	5.30	4.57	79.8	0.7	8.8	37.4	4.6
4.8	0.67	6.6	0.31	4.1	2.0	0.92	14.64	4.26	73.1	1.6	22.3	25.1	1.3
7.2	0.30	1.4	0.13	4.4	1.6	0.76	7.14	3.71	78.6	5.7	53.5	9.6	6.0
7.6	0.48	2.9	0.13	6.1	0.3	0.93	8.72	4.60	69.5	6.1	59.5	7.1	5.0
2.8	3.42	27.9	0.82	3.0	0.0	0.03	0.37	4.19	79.8	4.9	38.0	10.0	4.6
8.8	0.44	1.7	0.00	8.6	0.9	1.61	10.64	4.43	53.1	4.9	29.0	5.9	9.0
9.0	0.00	0.0	0.00	6.5	0.8	1.15	10.78	3.95	49.6	1.4	30.8	34.1	4.5
8.4	0.00	0.0	0.00	5.8	0.5	0.92	8.76	4.92	69.5	5.8	74.4	12.8	4.5
8.5	1.01	3.0	-0.02	7.5	2.8	1.48	10.45	4.32	54.0	4.8	15.8	3.2	7.9
9.2	0.00	0.0	0.00	0.0	-0.9	-3.25	-11.54	2.98	171.9	6.0	82.4	11.4	0.0
2.6	0.93	3.3	0.53	2.4	0.0	0.07	0.50	5.14	87.7	4.4	41.7	13.2	4.6
5.9	0.29	2.3	0.44	5.2	1.0	1.01	13.40	3.98	72.7	2.4	41.5	30.9	5.3
6.3	0.11	0.8	0.07	10.0	1.6	1.76	19.45	4.20	43.3	2.5	20.0	16.8	6.3
8.2	0.00	0.0	0.15	3.1	0.2	0.85	8.24	4.91	77.9	4.6	41.0	12.2	1.1
6.4	1.31	7.0	0.02	9.1	1.0	1.40	11.06	3.57	46.2	2.5	28.7	18.5	8.4
7.2	0.00	0.0	-1.46	4.6	0.5	0.71	7.20	6.00	93.7	4.3	20.3	7.1	5.3
8.2	0.08	0.5	0.00	6.5	0.1	1.50	15.95	5.16	77.2	4.4	42.3	11.3	4.3
6.3	4.09	16.4	0.19	7.1	35.6	2.05	39.90	2.80	42.0	0.5	0.6	34.9	4.7
7.6	0.00	0.0	0.01	9.4	7.5	1.47	17.77	4.25	48.7	2.2	28.2	28.9	7.5
9.4	0.14	0.4	0.00	6.5	5.1	1.02	9.12	2.71	44.3	7.3	95.5	8.8	9.8
8.9	0.04	0.1	-0.39	8.8	0.2	1.95	13.33	3.77	49.7	3.0	56.0	22.3	6.3
5.4	0.88	7.1	-0.01	8.8	3.7	1.54	17.89	4.19	56.8	4.5	25.8	6.9	5.9
8.1	0.02	0.1	-0.05	4.1	0.2	0.46	4.07	2.92	80.1	0.8	3.5	31.8	5.1
7.5	0.12	0.6	0.00	6.1	0.5	1.04	9.35	3.54	55.4	3.2	23.4	13.8	6.9
4.2	1.62	11.0	0.22	4.6	0.5	0.94	9.62	3.63	69.5	4.0	13.3	8.3	5.0
5.5	1.53	8.9	0.01	4.8	0.4	0.84	9.17	3.73	71.0	3.2	44.5	19.7	4.9
9.5	0.30	0.9	0.11	6.5	1.1	1.44	16.66	4.23	57.1	5.2	35.4	6.7	5.6

Name	City	State	Weiss Safety Rating	2003 Weiss Safety Rating	2002 Weiss Safety Rating	Total Assets ($Mil)	One Year Asset Growth	Asset Mix (As a % of Total Assets) Comm- ercial Loans	Cons- umer Loans	Home Mort- gages	Secur- ities	Capital- ization Index	Leverage Ratio	Risk-based Capital Ratio
OSWEGO COUNTY NB	OSWEGO	NY	C+	C+	C+	216.5	7.89	5.2	6.0	23.5	27.7	10.0	11.0	19.2
OTOE CTY B&TC	NEBRASKA CITY	NE	B	B	B-	69.1	3.59	12.0	3.0	4.8	43.9	10.0	11.0	19.6
▼ OTTAWA SVGS BK	OTTAWA	IL	D+	B+	B-	163.8	13.16	0.0	5.1	41.7	16.5	5.8	7.8	12.8
OTTOVILLE BK CO	OTTOVILLE	OH	A-	A-	A-	55.5	-2.89	4.3	1.8	13.4	48.7	10.0	19.6	35.4
OUACHITA INDEPENDENT	MONROE	LA	C+	C	C	236.7	10.85	12.0	4.7	15.6	11.5	3.8	7.7	10.4
OWEN COMMUNITY BK SB	SPENCER	IN	C	C	D+	62.9	2.48	0.6	12.5	51.1	3.7	7.7	9.5	15.0
OWEN COUNTY ST BK	SPENCER	IN	B-	B-	B-	179.4	4.62	3.7	9.9	26.1	37.5	6.8	8.8	16.9
OWINGSVILLE BKG CO	OWINGSVILLE	KY	B-	B-	B-	58.4	9.39	0.0	18.3	32.0	26.1	7.5	9.3	15.3
OXFORD B&T	ADDISON	IL	B-	B-	B-	428.7	9.70	10.5	14.3	2.4	10.8	5.9	8.3	11.7
OXFORD BK	OXFORD	MI	B	B	B	494.7	7.26	6.2	12.5	16.1	20.6	6.8	8.8	13.9
▲ OXFORD UNIVERSITY BK	OXFORD	MS	C+	C	C	51.0	11.36	11.0	9.2	21.4	27.6	8.9	10.2	15.4
▼ OZARK BK	OZARK	MO	B	B+	A-	187.1	2.78	3.3	2.6	19.5	29.7	9.6	10.7	17.7
▼ OZARK MOUNTAIN BK	BRANSON	MO	B-	B	B	252.4	-5.03	5.5	3.9	15.9	31.3	5.7	7.7	13.0
OZARKS FS&LA	FARMINGTON	MO	B-	B-	B-	191.0	2.69	0.0	2.1	69.7	5.9	9.5	10.7	18.3
OZAUKEE BK	CEDARBURG	WI	B-	B-	C+	585.4	8.84	12.1	1.8	13.0	20.4	3.6	6.8	10.3
OZONA NB	OZONA	TX	B+	B+	A-	140.6	5.43	9.6	4.8	3.1	35.5	10.0	12.8	23.5
PACESETTER BK-HARTFORD	HARTFORD CITY	IN	B	B	B	100.0	-4.32	9.8	10.8	38.0	15.1	9.2	10.5	18.9
PACIFIC CAPITAL BK NA	SANTA BARBARA	CA	B	B	B	5,678.2	25.23	9.3	5.5	14.5	26.3	4.8	6.8	11.9
PACIFIC CITY BK	LOS ANGELES	CA	D	D	NR	85.1	N/A	14.7	8.3	0.4	0.0	10.0	20.8	24.3
PACIFIC COAST BKR BK	SAN FRANCISCO	CA	B	B-	B-	283.6	58.44	3.3	0.4	5.7	18.0	6.3	8.3	14.1
▼ PACIFIC COMMERCE BK NA	LOS ANGELES	CA	D-	D	D	39.8	97.79	9.2	0.2	20.9	39.5	9.9	11.0	23.3
▲ PACIFIC CONTINENTAL BK	EUGENE	OR	B-	C	D+	460.7	12.17	19.8	2.2	6.6	6.0	6.1	9.9	11.8
▲ PACIFIC GLOBAL BK	CHICAGO	IL	B	B-	C-	95.9	17.32	0.5	0.6	34.1	10.8	7.5	9.3	15.3
▲ PACIFIC INTERNATIONAL BK	SEATTLE	WA	C	C-	D	78.4	73.86	10.9	0.3	0.6	3.8	10.0	13.0	15.2
▲ PACIFIC LIBERTY BK	HUNTINGTON BEACH	CA	A-	B	C	123.5	50.37	18.7	1.8	0.5	19.4	9.7	12.0	14.7
PACIFIC MERCANTILE BK	COSTA MESA	CA	C	C	C-	789.9	22.10	12.9	0.6	12.7	30.1	4.2	7.1	10.6
▼ PACIFIC NB	MIAMI	FL	C-	C	C	359.3	31.19	2.5	0.1	2.0	49.5	5.7	7.7	19.1
▲ PACIFIC PREMIER BANK	SAN BERNARDINO	CA	D+	D-	E	419.1	73.12	0.0	0.0	6.6	11.6	7.2	9.1	13.6
▲ PACIFIC ST BK	STOCKTON	CA	B	C+	C	233.0	25.99	15.8	3.5	6.6	6.9	7.2	9.6	12.7
PACIFIC TRUST BK	CHULA VISTA	CA	B	B	B	664.1	24.88	0.1	0.7	80.6	0.8	8.4	10.0	17.0
PACIFIC WESTERN NB	SANTA MONICA	CA	B	B	C+	1,529.8	45.76	18.5	1.2	1.8	11.6	3.2	8.2	10.1
PACIFICA BK	BELLEVUE	WA	C+	C+	D+	177.9	12.32	12.6	0.4	2.0	15.1	5.9	8.7	11.7
PADUCAH B&TC	PADUCAH	KY	B-	B-	C+	363.1	4.09	4.3	4.8	34.6	19.1	5.6	7.6	12.7
▼ PAGE COUNTY FSA	CLARINDA	IA	B-	B	B	29.8	-4.55	1.9	5.0	77.6	0.1	10.0	14.9	26.8
▲ PAGE COUNTY ST BK	CLARINDA	IA	B+	B	A-	53.7	-2.71	9.9	6.6	7.9	52.2	10.0	13.0	25.2
PAGE VALLEY BK	LURAY	VA	D+	D+	D+	85.9	13.47	3.0	4.1	28.3	45.3	4.4	6.4	14.8
PALISADES NB	PALISADE	CO	D+	D+	C-	36.0	8.57	2.2	5.1	6.8	5.9	4.8	6.8	13.6
PALM BEACH COUNTY BK	W PALM BEACH	FL	B-	B-	B-	236.0	44.14	17.8	2.1	13.8	15.3	4.2	7.3	10.6
PALM BK	TAMPA	FL	D	D	NR	63.3	121.16	18.0	2.6	4.9	31.2	10.0	17.7	23.9
▲ PALM DESERT NB	PALM DESERT	CA	C+	C	C	333.8	55.54	8.0	1.1	1.7	1.6	5.6	7.6	20.3
▼ PALMER ST BK	TAYLORVILLE	IL	C	B-	C+	49.2	-0.90	15.6	7.2	9.7	24.8	7.4	9.7	12.8
PALMETTO BK	LAURENS	SC	C+	C+	C+	941.1	9.47	18.5	5.6	13.7	16.2	3.9	7.7	10.5
PALMETTO ST BK	HAMPTON	SC	A	A	A	225.8	6.90	4.3	7.4	13.5	27.0	10.0	11.6	18.3
▲ PALMYRA ST BK	PALMYRA	MO	B+	B	B	83.2	0.08	8.3	3.8	9.6	16.0	8.1	9.7	13.5
PALMYRA ST BK	PALMYRA	WI	A+	A+	A+	32.2	8.93	16.7	4.2	23.8	19.1	10.0	16.6	25.5
▼ PALO SVG BK	PALO	IA	B-	B	B	29.0	0.83	6.5	5.1	33.1	29.1	8.2	9.8	18.5
PALOS B&TC	PALOS HEIGHTS	IL	B-	B-	B-	415.3	8.89	6.2	2.3	7.4	43.2	5.8	7.8	12.8
PAMPLICO B&TC	PAMPLICO	SC	C	C+	C+	19.4	-0.85	1.7	7.4	24.6	39.9	10.0	16.4	42.7
PAMRAPO SAVINGS BANK, SLA	BAYONNE	NJ	B	B	B	646.6	1.43	0.0	0.4	40.3	36.7	5.8	7.8	16.2
PAN AMERICAN BK	LOS ANGELES	CA	B+	B+	B+	42.2	1.74	5.8	0.4	45.8	26.1	10.0	14.0	31.9
▲ PAN AMERICAN BK	CHICAGO	IL	D	D-	D-	29.0	-2.14	14.6	1.6	2.5	6.1	9.0	10.3	14.7
▲ PAN AMERICAN BK FSB	BURLINGAME	CA	B	B-	B-	1,669.1	23.56	1.8	27.7	0.0	67.3	5.3	7.3	18.3
▲ PANAMERICAN BK	HOLLYWOOD	FL	E+	D-	E	156.1	56.44	12.7	1.7	5.8	13.1	6.7	8.9	12.3
PANHANDLE ST BK	SANDPOINT	ID	B-	B-	B-	462.9	20.46	14.3	4.0	10.2	19.6	4.7	7.7	10.9
PANOLA NB	CARTHAGE	TX	B+	B+	B+	74.0	0.75	8.9	18.2	27.0	7.3	10.0	12.1	18.3
PANORA ST BK	PANORA	IA	D	D+	D+	45.6	-1.51	3.1	7.1	24.0	43.4	5.7	7.7	16.1
▲ PAONIA ST BK	PAONIA	CO	C-	D	D	45.7	8.38	4.0	4.4	20.8	28.4	7.2	9.1	17.0
PAPER CITY SA	WISCONSIN RAPIDS	WI	C	C-	C-	144.5	-4.35	0.0	2.9	67.1	2.5	5.6	7.6	11.7
PARAGON B&TC	HOLLAND	MI	C	C	C	107.2	-0.26	26.0	1.0	14.8	4.1	5.9	9.4	11.7
PARAGON BK	WELLS	MN	D-	D-	E	40.6	18.09	22.3	16.8	21.4	0.0	4.6	7.9	10.8
▲ PARAGON COMMERCIAL BK	RALEIGH	NC	B-	C	C	307.8	25.18	12.0	0.6	6.9	14.2	7.8	10.6	13.2
▲ PARAMOUNT BK	FARMINGTON HILLS	MI	B-	C	C-	173.4	-0.82	10.7	1.3	19.1	0.4	9.3	12.1	14.4
PARIS NB	PARIS	MO	B+	B+	B+	55.7	-1.66	8.4	2.5	8.4	39.1	10.0	11.4	19.7
▲ PARISH NB	BOGALUSA	LA	B-	B-	B-	499.2	20.71	10.1	4.4	14.9	8.1	5.5	8.8	11.4

Asset Quality Index	Non-Performing Loans as a % of Total Loans	Non-Performing Loans as a % of Capital	Net Charge-offs Avg Loans	Profitability Index	Net Income ($Mil)	Return on Assets (R.O.A.)	Return on Equity (R.O.E.)	Net Interest Spread	Overhead Efficiency Ratio	Liquidity Index	Liquidity Ratio	Hot Money Ratio	Stability Index
6.0	1.03	5.0	0.28	3.4	0.7	0.62	5.40	3.90	81.3	4.4	29.5	9.5	5.1
7.1	1.64	7.0	0.58	5.2	0.3	0.88	7.72	4.18	73.1	3.5	8.6	10.6	5.3
0.3	12.99	91.0	0.01	2.4	-3.0	-3.70	-38.46	2.96	55.5	3.9	61.7	21.8	6.1
8.8	0.41	0.8	0.95	8.0	0.5	1.66	8.13	4.72	45.7	4.0	24.1	9.9	7.3
6.6	0.22	1.9	-0.07	5.7	1.0	0.89	10.54	4.39	73.7	2.8	8.1	14.4	4.3
3.3	1.25	9.2	0.42	4.7	0.2	0.79	7.42	5.54	71.7	0.7	15.1	44.0	4.8
7.3	0.40	2.5	0.09	4.9	0.9	1.02	11.63	4.00	63.7	4.3	20.2	7.6	4.6
6.1	0.34	2.2	0.20	6.7	0.4	1.26	13.37	4.98	62.7	3.2	27.8	15.0	5.0
6.9	0.20	1.6	0.02	4.4	2.1	1.01	11.77	4.29	74.8	5.7	59.3	11.2	4.7
4.2	1.40	9.7	0.28	5.4	2.4	0.97	10.98	3.80	63.0	4.5	72.4	19.1	5.4
4.6	2.38	14.4	0.00	4.2	0.2	0.69	6.72	3.93	67.9	2.5	40.0	27.7	0.7
8.7	0.00	0.0	0.06	4.9	0.9	0.90	8.24	3.58	72.9	1.5	13.0	23.3	7.1
5.4	0.51	3.7	0.13	7.4	1.6	1.22	16.30	3.74	56.3	4.2	33.0	11.5	5.3
6.1	0.72	5.1	0.06	4.5	0.6	0.67	5.98	3.03	63.8	3.2	15.8	13.2	6.6
4.9	0.76	7.0	0.04	8.4	3.8	1.30	19.05	3.85	57.5	3.5	15.9	11.7	5.1
8.3	0.73	2.6	0.20	4.8	0.6	0.87	6.83	4.19	75.1	6.1	66.0	10.1	7.2
6.4	0.45	2.6	0.42	4.5	0.4	0.77	7.30	4.53	71.3	6.2	61.3	6.7	6.0
5.2	0.63	4.5	0.88	10.0	60.8	2.26	26.29	5.91	45.9	3.1	33.6	21.2	7.3
7.0	0.00	0.0	0.00	0.4	-0.1	-0.17	-0.72	3.99	86.1	5.4	102.1	16.9	0.0
8.9	0.00	0.0	0.04	7.4	1.7	1.33	16.86	4.63	46.3	5.2	32.3	5.3	4.4
9.6	0.00	0.0	0.00	0.0	-0.5	-2.74	-23.17	3.43	166.0	2.5	36.1	24.1	0.0
4.1	0.83	6.8	0.14	9.1	3.8	1.71	17.44	5.72	55.1	3.8	15.9	10.2	6.5
8.9	0.08	0.6	-0.01	6.5	0.5	0.98	10.40	4.56	62.4	5.6	58.3	9.8	4.6
7.3	0.00	0.0	0.00	2.4	0.2	0.66	5.07	4.09	71.8	2.8	38.8	21.5	0.9
8.2	0.00	0.0	-0.05	8.5	0.9	1.56	13.07	4.88	53.4	3.8	24.8	10.9	6.3
6.7	0.32	2.7	0.38	3.4	2.1	0.55	8.16	2.97	67.5	3.5	37.6	16.6	4.3
10.0	0.00	0.0	-2.50	5.7	2.4	1.44	19.90	3.11	61.2	6.4	128.1	15.2	2.1
3.9	0.56	4.9	0.05	3.3	1.3	0.74	8.27	3.58	73.8	0.5	3.8	38.3	1.3
8.0	0.00	0.0	0.01	8.5	1.6	1.48	15.32	5.30	55.1	2.5	41.5	28.9	4.7
9.1	0.00	0.0	0.00	5.1	2.6	0.79	7.94	3.19	56.0	0.6	5.1	36.5	4.6
5.1	0.39	1.9	-0.11	9.9	11.8	1.70	12.16	5.63	45.6	6.7	56.2	6.3	7.6
7.4	0.10	0.7	-0.95	6.4	1.7	2.03	22.70	4.90	77.7	4.3	119.4	40.3	3.4
5.5	0.68	5.3	-0.02	8.1	3.3	1.82	21.93	4.18	61.2	3.8	26.4	11.5	5.1
5.0	1.94	11.1	0.12	6.7	0.1	0.87	6.05	3.86	50.8	4.4	9.3	5.5	6.4
8.1	0.81	2.2	1.28	5.7	0.4	1.51	11.87	4.25	65.4	5.6	68.2	11.7	6.7
8.5	0.15	1.0	0.05	3.1	0.2	0.39	6.65	3.95	89.2	4.3	19.6	7.6	1.8
8.9	0.06	0.3	-0.03	5.9	0.2	1.22	18.89	3.84	65.9	8.0	98.8	1.6	2.3
8.3	0.08	0.9	0.00	5.1	1.3	1.17	16.11	4.23	67.8	3.9	34.4	13.7	4.6
8.6	0.00	0.0	0.00	0.0	-0.1	-0.34	-1.76	3.39	93.5	2.2	7.5	17.1	0.0
6.1	0.99	4.7	0.45	7.4	1.8	1.14	15.61	4.09	78.4	3.9	98.9	41.4	3.5
7.4	0.06	0.3	-0.11	6.7	0.3	1.01	8.14	4.46	64.4	4.4	28.3	9.0	4.3
5.2	0.43	3.8	0.28	7.4	5.8	1.28	15.99	4.74	63.2	3.0	17.9	14.5	4.8
8.1	0.16	0.8	-0.19	10.0	2.0	1.77	15.79	4.59	51.8	2.8	25.3	16.0	8.3
6.6	0.23	1.5	0.17	6.2	0.5	1.27	12.56	4.16	68.5	5.7	46.5	6.8	6.7
8.5	0.11	0.4	0.19	8.1	0.2	1.17	7.41	3.68	55.7	7.2	136.3	11.2	9.1
4.1	2.18	14.0	0.00	8.7	0.3	1.99	20.20	4.13	53.9	3.5	27.9	13.3	6.4
5.2	1.49	9.9	0.15	6.6	3.3	1.62	21.25	4.26	65.6	5.1	65.4	15.4	4.4
3.9	7.73	18.5	0.05	3.9	0.1	0.59	3.57	4.15	79.3	3.4	43.8	16.4	4.8
7.4	0.35	2.5	0.03	8.8	4.1	1.27	16.72	3.90	49.2	1.2	2.7	26.0	6.1
9.0	0.00	0.0	0.00	5.2	0.2	0.71	5.00	5.37	77.8	4.6	74.1	17.3	6.5
1.7	1.83	10.5	4.20	3.6	0.3	1.69	16.86	4.80	83.0	4.1	84.6	24.1	3.0
7.0	0.11	0.4	4.75	9.2	10.7	1.28	19.45	6.56	44.3	0.5	6.2	54.1	5.3
3.9	0.30	1.7	1.04	0.3	-0.4	-0.60	-5.64	4.17	91.6	1.8	15.6	20.7	3.0
6.3	0.43	3.4	0.00	6.5	2.6	1.18	14.69	4.73	64.1	5.5	66.5	13.5	4.4
5.1	1.27	6.5	0.27	6.0	0.4	0.97	8.15	4.81	69.8	4.6	91.1	19.7	6.2
4.7	1.91	12.6	0.12	4.5	0.2	0.92	12.06	4.00	78.4	6.9	83.4	6.2	1.7
3.0	3.23	18.9	0.75	5.8	0.2	0.91	10.40	4.56	71.5	5.7	72.0	11.7	2.9
3.3	1.64	16.5	0.27	4.9	0.5	0.67	8.85	2.88	57.4	2.3	18.6	18.0	3.5
3.9	1.01	7.4	0.35	5.2	0.5	0.97	9.33	3.96	71.7	0.8	15.0	41.2	5.7
1.3	2.57	24.4	0.94	5.1	0.1	0.55	7.02	5.86	65.6	5.6	39.7	6.2	2.2
7.3	0.00	0.0	0.00	5.6	1.3	0.87	10.16	3.61	54.4	0.4	5.5	58.0	6.0
4.8	1.16	8.8	0.09	5.2	0.7	0.81	7.41	3.10	85.4	1.2	7.4	27.2	6.2
8.0	0.76	3.4	-0.05	5.8	0.3	1.04	9.08	3.83	64.2	3.9	31.4	12.5	6.4
7.1	0.05	0.4	-0.02	6.5	2.2	0.92	11.56	4.72	78.1	6.6	76.3	8.9	4.9

Name	City	State	Weiss Safety Rating	2003 Weiss Safety Rating	2002 Weiss Safety Rating	Total Assets ($Mil)	One Year Asset Growth	Commercial Loans	Consumer Loans	Home Mortgages	Securities	Capitalization Index	Leverage Ratio	Risk-based Capital Ratio
▲ PARK AVENUE BANK	NEW YORK	NY	D	D-	D	87.9	-48.85	6.3	0.0	0.0	35.1	10.0	13.7	23.5
PARK AVENUE BK	VALDOSTA	GA	B	B-	C+	738.1	-1.03	6.8	2.6	15.6	14.0	9.4	10.8	14.5
PARK BK	PARKVILLE	MO	B+	A-	A	75.2	5.33	5.3	1.2	5.2	54.5	10.0	11.8	23.4
PARK BK	HOLMEN	WI	D+	D+	D-	42.5	-7.30	27.4	5.6	36.5	12.3	9.2	10.4	18.2
PARK BK	MADISON	WI	C+	C+	C+	364.6	19.45	15.3	2.2	19.8	4.3	3.5	8.1	10.3
PARK BK	MILWAUKEE	WI	B+	B+	B+	591.0	5.52	33.2	1.0	3.7	11.9	6.4	9.7	12.0
▲ PARK CITIES BK	DALLAS	TX	C-	D+	D-	206.7	42.19	16.6	1.7	9.4	5.3	3.7	8.4	10.4
PARK FEDERAL SVGS BK	CHICAGO	IL	B	B	B	268.9	0.33	2.6	3.2	0.0	23.6	8.4	9.9	16.3
PARK NB	NEWARK	OH	B-	B-	B-	1,639.1	-5.66	9.1	9.0	11.9	31.3	4.4	6.4	12.9
▼ PARK NB&T	CHICAGO	IL	B-	B	A	266.0	21.71	5.2	0.2	4.3	15.0	6.3	10.0	12.0
PARK RIDGE COMMUNITY BK	PARK RIDGE	IL	A-	B+	B	176.7	4.83	2.6	0.3	21.9	15.8	7.6	9.4	14.5
PARK ST BK	DULUTH	MN	D	D	D-	29.0	3.27	17.6	8.1	31.8	14.5	5.3	7.3	11.7
PARK ST BK	NICOMA PARK	OK	A-	A-	A-	45.7	-0.37	4.6	9.2	10.9	61.8	10.0	17.0	39.6
PARK ST BK & TR	WOODLAND PARK	CO	C+	C+	C+	76.7	0.32	4.2	3.0	9.5	33.7	7.1	9.1	14.8
▼ PARK VIEW FSB	CLEVELAND	OH	C-	C	C+	761.4	2.33	0.7	1.1	18.3	8.5	3.4	8.0	10.2
PARKE BK	SEWELL	NJ	B	B	B	198.1	30.83	2.2	0.2	16.5	8.6	8.9	11.3	14.1
PARKVALE SVGS BK	MONROEVILLE	PA	B-	B-	B-	1,611.8	-1.92	2.4	1.0	49.4	30.7	5.4	7.4	14.3
▲ PARKWAY B&TC	HARWOOD HEIGHTS	IL	D	D-	B-	1,584.9	4.28	3.6	0.6	1.8	16.1	6.2	8.2	12.0
PARKWAY BK	LENOIR	NC	D	D	D	66.5	39.86	17.3	2.8	14.4	14.5	6.6	8.6	12.7
▲ PARKWAY BK NA	PLANO	TX	D+	D	D-	62.4	15.07	17.1	2.8	16.9	22.6	6.9	8.9	13.0
PARTNERS BK	GLEN CARBON	IL	C-	C-	D	130.5	43.46	16.1	0.3	9.7	47.5	4.6	6.6	13.8
PARTNERS BK OF TX	HUMBLE	TX	D	D	NR	60.8	N/A	19.6	2.1	8.5	8.1	10.0	27.5	29.5
PASCACK COMMUNITY BK	WESTWOOD	NJ	D	D	D	47.9	25.71	14.2	1.0	0.3	10.2	10.0	18.4	20.3
PASSUMPSIC SVGS BK	ST JOHNSBURY	VT	B	B	B-	368.6	6.47	8.5	11.5	31.1	15.7	10.0	11.8	15.6
PATAPSCO BK	DUNDALK	MD	B-	B-	B-	209.8	33.29	10.4	4.9	37.3	13.9	4.8	6.8	12.1
▲ PATASKALA BKG CO	PATASKALA	OH	C-	D+	D+	34.0	-0.16	0.0	2.8	45.2	23.2	6.5	8.6	22.6
PATHFINDER BK	OSWEGO	NY	C	C	C	299.1	5.82	4.7	1.2	43.0	24.8	4.9	6.9	12.7
▲ PATHFINDER COMMERCIAL BK	OSWEGO	NY	D+	D	D	36.9	151.16	0.0	0.0	0.0	88.4	5.6	7.6	34.3
▼ PATRICK HENRY NB	BASSETT	VA	D+	C-	C	387.2	1.91	7.2	3.1	9.6	30.2	3.9	5.9	11.6
▲ PATRIOT BK	BROOKLYN	IA	C	C-	D+	75.7	74.03	7.5	4.4	19.6	20.7	5.8	7.8	12.6
▲ PATRIOT BK	MILLINGTON	TN	B+	B	B+	83.0	44.40	4.9	3.5	20.7	10.9	6.8	9.7	12.4
▼ PATRIOT BK NA	FREDERICKSBURG	VA	C+	B	B	239.2	7.34	0.7	1.7	7.1	28.5	5.6	7.6	14.6
▼ PATRIOT NB	STAMFORD	CT	C	C+	C+	353.1	16.97	2.5	0.4	10.6	26.7	5.6	7.6	11.6
PATRIOTS BK	GARNETT	KS	C-	C-	C	66.5	3.55	15.2	4.9	19.2	26.0	6.3	8.3	13.0
▲ PATTERSON BK	PATTERSON	GA	D-	E-	E-	92.2	-2.66	15.6	5.0	12.1	15.5	4.6	7.8	10.8
PATTERSON ST BK	PATTERSON	LA	C+	C+	C+	127.4	3.22	16.4	8.4	35.1	22.7	4.6	6.6	11.7
PAULS VALLEY NB	PAULS VALLEY	OK	A-	A-	A-	106.7	-0.25	14.2	16.4	11.7	30.9	10.0	12.7	17.8
PAVILLION BK	DALLAS	TX	C	C-	C+	51.1	-12.81	4.7	3.7	7.1	7.1	10.0	11.1	17.2
▲ PAYNE COUNTY BK	PERKINS	OK	A	A-	A	83.4	-2.04	15.8	16.1	14.7	26.8	10.0	16.6	25.2
PBK BK	STANFORD	KY	D-	D-	E+	94.5	-8.24	4.2	4.1	17.0	31.3	6.4	8.4	15.1
▲ PCB, THE COMMUNITY BANK	MALONE	FL	C	C-	D+	58.7	12.99	7.6	2.5	17.0	14.3	3.7	7.1	10.3
▲ PCSB CMRL BK	BREWSTER	NY	B-	C+	C+	20.9	28.31	0.0	0.0	0.0	98.5	10.0	20.8	169.6
PEABODY ST BK	PEABODY	KS	C+	C+	C+	38.3	3.91	9.0	3.7	14.0	42.5	8.8	10.2	19.7
▲ PEACHTREE BANK	MAPLESVILLE	AL	A	A-	A-	59.3	2.25	4.4	10.3	14.2	29.7	10.0	15.2	24.3
PEACHTREE BK	DULUTH	GA	C+	C+	C	316.7	50.25	11.5	3.2	3.7	6.1	4.8	9.1	10.9
PEACHTREE NB	PEACHTREE CITY	GA	B-	B-	B	281.5	-3.63	25.7	2.3	8.7	10.5	5.7	9.6	11.5
PEAK NB	NEDERLAND	CO	D	D	D+	193.8	2.53	0.9	1.3	7.0	14.6	6.9	8.9	13.6
PEAPACK-GLADSTONE BK	GLADSTONE	NJ	B+	B+	A-	999.8	5.45	1.8	0.9	25.7	46.6	5.4	7.4	17.7
▲ PEARLAND ST BK	PEARLAND	TX	A+	A	A	113.0	-5.59	6.2	3.8	8.3	56.5	10.0	12.9	23.5
PECOS COUNTY ST BK	FORT STOCKTON	TX	B	B	B	83.8	4.48	8.2	10.3	9.9	42.7	6.5	8.5	17.2
PEE DEE FSB	MARION	SC	B-	B-	C+	45.5	-7.49	9.9	8.8	26.3	1.8	10.0	18.8	33.1
PEKIN NB	PEKIN	IL	C+	C+	C+	22.4	-4.47	5.6	3.4	15.8	50.2	10.0	16.1	33.9
PEKIN SVG BK	PEKIN	IL	C+	C+	C+	113.7	-0.30	8.0	2.9	23.4	27.9	6.5	8.6	14.0
▲ PELHAM BKG CO	PELHAM	GA	A-	B+	B+	49.6	1.31	7.1	6.3	9.0	46.1	10.0	14.6	24.7
PELICAN NB	NAPLES	FL	D+	C	C+	258.3	10.67	0.7	7.2	15.5	41.6	4.0	6.0	14.3
▼ PELLA ST BK	PELLA	IA	D-	D	D+	63.5	10.88	9.0	1.3	9.5	40.3	6.6	8.6	13.6
PEMIGEWASSET NB OF	PLYMOUTH	NH	C	C+	C+	237.8	8.15	3.0	24.7	22.1	16.6	5.6	7.6	11.6
PENDER ST BK	PENDER	NE	C+	C+	C-	74.5	20.09	7.2	1.1	1.5	1.4	5.9	8.6	11.7
PENDLETON COUNTY BK	FRANKLIN	WV	A	A-	A-	157.6	0.60	3.8	7.2	30.5	20.4	10.0	14.9	22.6
▲ PENINSULA BK	ENGLEWOOD	FL	C+	C	C	352.9	23.56	5.1	1.0	1.4	16.2	3.6	8.3	10.3
PENINSULA BK	PRINCESS ANNE	MD	A-	A-	A	867.1	8.13	13.3	4.5	14.6	11.8	6.4	8.4	14.3
PENINSULA BK	ISHPEMING	MI	B	B	B	120.3	5.39	6.8	8.4	38.1	4.5	7.2	9.1	15.2
PENN FSB	NEWARK	NJ	B+	B+	B+	1,900.7	4.98	1.3	0.2	56.2	27.3	6.6	8.6	16.9
▼ PENN SECURITY B&TC	SCRANTON	PA	B	A-	A-	579.3	-0.87	5.9	4.5	19.6	50.9	8.8	10.2	20.8

Asset Quality Index	Non-Performing Loans as a % of Total Loans	Non-Performing Loans as a % of Capital	Net Charge-offs Avg Loans	Profitability Index	Net Income ($Mil)	Return on Assets (R.O.A.)	Return on Equity (R.O.E.)	Net Interest Spread	Overhead Efficiency Ratio	Liquidity Index	Liquidity Ratio	Hot Money Ratio	Stability Index
1.7	47.52	39.7	1.37	0.0	-1.5	-2.91	-20.55	-0.12	1,588.2	2.9	79.1	76.3	2.6
4.7	1.03	6.1	0.19	6.8	4.6	1.25	11.02	4.39	62.0	3.1	24.5	14.3	5.9
9.7	0.08	0.2	0.25	4.4	0.2	0.41	3.40	2.96	88.6	7.6	82.8	1.7	6.9
1.9	3.30	21.9	1.29	7.7	0.3	1.47	14.60	5.56	69.0	6.7	59.6	3.1	2.3
5.9	0.37	3.6	0.02	7.2	2.2	1.26	15.74	3.91	63.5	2.4	13.4	16.7	4.1
6.9	0.40	3.0	0.00	6.9	4.9	1.65	17.18	3.80	59.6	6.5	118.3	14.1	7.7
5.3	0.03	0.3	0.05	5.1	1.1	1.18	14.32	4.22	50.4	1.3	30.8	46.0	1.1
4.3	1.98	12.2	-0.02	5.3	1.2	0.91	9.14	3.49	60.7	0.9	18.9	35.2	5.8
6.6	0.48	4.3	0.21	9.8	15.5	1.89	35.99	4.15	43.5	4.8	29.1	10.4	5.4
3.1	1.12	7.1	0.00	9.6	2.6	1.94	17.18	5.06	40.8	2.2	32.5	23.9	8.3
9.0	0.00	0.0	0.00	9.8	2.1	2.34	25.04	3.94	38.2	7.0	70.4	5.2	6.8
3.6	1.41	13.7	0.20	3.2	0.1	0.32	4.45	4.71	92.5	4.3	29.3	10.0	1.9
8.7	0.73	1.2	0.32	8.2	0.4	1.70	9.68	4.89	65.1	5.3	84.3	15.1	8.0
4.3	2.09	11.2	0.03	5.4	0.4	0.99	10.90	5.28	76.5	4.1	18.2	8.1	4.3
2.8	1.78	17.2	-0.01	5.9	2.5	0.69	8.39	3.20	66.1	1.1	13.5	30.3	5.8
5.3	0.45	3.1	0.00	8.1	1.3	1.37	12.42	4.39	42.0	0.7	12.5	36.1	7.4
8.3	0.42	3.0	0.16	3.6	5.3	0.66	8.19	1.95	60.0	6.8	71.8	8.6	5.5
0.5	3.48	26.1	0.22	7.6	10.1	1.30	15.00	3.93	44.6	4.0	66.9	27.0	8.0
6.7	0.31	2.3	0.10	1.2	0.0	0.10	1.07	2.84	95.1	4.5	103.1	24.1	0.0
3.2	2.07	15.5	0.18	2.5	0.2	0.60	7.07	4.34	82.7	1.2	11.5	27.3	3.1
7.1	0.42	2.8	-0.01	3.5	0.4	0.72	11.13	2.98	60.7	1.0	12.5	30.8	1.5
8.7	0.00	0.0	0.00	0.0	-0.4	-1.95	-6.00	3.46	143.5	3.2	62.1	27.5	0.0
7.6	0.00	0.0	0.00	0.6	0.1	0.21	1.18	4.07	90.7	3.8	19.9	10.3	0.0
7.3	0.54	3.3	0.19	4.5	1.7	0.90	7.74	4.13	72.1	4.2	27.2	9.5	6.5
7.3	0.21	1.7	0.28	5.1	0.8	0.87	9.60	4.34	70.5	6.9	76.2	6.8	4.2
7.4	0.84	4.8	0.02	3.7	0.1	0.54	6.26	4.35	85.7	6.7	63.9	4.1	3.1
4.2	1.62	11.5	0.19	3.5	0.7	0.50	5.83	3.61	79.1	4.5	23.0	6.7	4.0
9.4	0.00	0.0	0.00	1.7	0.1	0.56	7.05	1.60	49.8	5.3	13.9	0.0	0.0
2.5	3.92	31.9	0.10	3.8	1.1	0.56	9.48	2.59	70.0	6.4	69.5	8.9	2.6
4.1	1.27	9.2	0.03	5.4	0.3	0.81	10.04	5.25	76.6	6.1	53.2	5.6	2.8
8.6	0.00	0.0	0.03	6.1	0.5	1.22	12.90	3.92	60.1	3.5	14.8	11.6	4.6
2.7	4.23	26.4	0.01	5.2	1.0	0.88	11.75	3.58	66.5	6.2	47.3	4.4	4.3
5.6	1.78	13.9	0.00	2.9	0.6	0.36	4.75	3.27	83.8	3.3	35.6	16.9	3.6
4.6	1.00	7.3	0.13	3.7	0.3	0.75	8.78	4.03	84.3	3.2	21.1	13.8	2.8
3.3	1.58	12.4	0.55	3.1	0.4	0.82	10.71	5.06	76.7	2.2	18.4	18.2	0.9
5.9	0.50	4.7	0.46	4.6	0.5	0.78	11.65	4.19	67.1	3.0	34.0	18.2	3.6
5.3	1.75	7.7	0.24	6.5	0.6	1.12	8.64	5.10	63.5	4.0	24.6	9.7	7.5
5.2	2.41	11.6	0.14	2.0	0.0	0.03	0.28	3.89	99.4	6.7	69.8	5.5	4.6
6.2	0.86	3.1	0.57	10.0	0.8	1.84	10.50	5.71	51.5	5.4	50.9	9.7	9.1
2.8	3.07	17.8	0.44	1.1	0.1	0.24	2.94	3.95	94.8	2.9	14.2	14.5	0.1
5.7	1.07	10.2	-0.05	4.8	0.3	0.87	12.24	4.14	60.6	2.6	18.2	16.3	3.5
10.0	0.00	0.0	0.00	3.8	0.1	0.56	2.38	1.18	20.7	4.5	43.2	10.6	0.2
5.4	2.04	8.2	-0.14	3.6	0.1	0.73	6.28	3.43	74.5	4.9	43.1	11.1	5.3
8.2	0.00	0.0	-0.16	9.2	0.4	1.44	9.35	4.90	64.2	5.0	52.2	12.2	8.8
7.1	0.00	0.0	0.10	4.4	1.1	0.77	8.39	4.02	66.8	2.9	43.4	23.8	4.6
1.7	2.21	16.3	1.32	6.2	1.1	0.73	7.58	4.62	51.6	0.8	10.3	33.8	6.8
0.8	3.14	21.0	0.02	10.0	3.4	3.45	39.99	6.31	48.9	6.5	69.9	8.5	6.4
9.4	0.26	1.6	0.03	7.8	6.2	1.28	17.18	3.72	57.9	6.7	67.9	6.8	6.0
9.1	0.16	0.5	0.14	10.0	1.7	2.95	21.88	5.08	46.4	1.9	29.1	26.1	8.1
7.4	0.52	3.0	0.21	8.8	0.9	2.08	25.17	4.71	63.5	1.7	15.9	22.1	5.3
6.3	1.18	3.5	0.01	5.3	0.1	0.34	1.87	4.39	78.2	3.8	50.2	17.9	6.2
9.0	1.19	2.8	0.00	4.4	0.1	0.90	5.70	5.33	77.7	2.9	38.5	17.8	5.4
5.6	0.79	5.5	-0.03	3.7	0.3	0.50	5.90	2.99	75.7	4.2	30.2	10.6	4.3
8.7	0.17	0.5	0.01	8.2	0.4	1.52	10.11	4.41	53.9	4.9	50.8	12.5	7.7
7.8	0.20	1.3	0.32	2.3	0.0	-0.03	-0.54	2.66	99.7	6.9	87.6	8.7	1.9
1.3	7.90	45.7	0.80	5.0	0.3	0.94	10.08	4.35	55.8	4.3	66.2	17.7	3.8
5.6	0.23	1.5	0.13	2.1	0.2	0.16	1.54	4.06	97.0	5.1	21.8	2.5	5.1
3.4	0.79	7.4	-0.01	6.5	0.4	1.09	13.04	4.13	56.0	0.9	8.0	31.5	5.7
7.2	0.79	3.8	0.18	8.6	1.2	1.48	9.96	4.98	54.4	2.8	14.7	15.0	9.0
5.3	0.27	1.9	0.11	7.3	2.1	1.24	15.47	3.46	50.1	5.3	146.6	25.3	4.4
5.6	0.30	1.9	-0.04	10.0	7.7	1.83	15.42	4.88	43.8	5.8	43.7	5.9	8.9
4.3	1.03	8.0	0.32	6.7	0.6	1.04	11.23	4.45	62.8	6.2	70.1	10.5	6.1
9.0	0.17	1.3	0.00	5.1	6.7	0.73	8.20	2.43	57.7	2.9	42.9	30.6	7.6
7.2	0.84	3.4	0.02	4.6	2.5	0.86	8.35	3.45	78.0	4.3	21.5	7.5	7.6

Name	City	State	Weiss Safety Rating	2003 Weiss Safety Rating	2002 Weiss Safety Rating	Total Assets ($Mil)	One Year Asset Growth	Comm-ercial Loans	Cons-umer Loans	Home Mort-gages	Secur-ities	Capital-ization Index	Leverage Ratio	Risk-based Capital Ratio
PENNSVILLE NB	PENNSVILLE	NJ	C+	C+	C+	165.5	-3.83	1.2	0.9	25.9	59.1	4.0	6.0	14.8
PENNSYLVANIA BUSINESS BK	PHILADELPHIA	PA	D	D	D+	162.7	3.56	17.5	0.1	1.8	38.0	5.2	7.2	11.4
PENNSYLVANIA ST BK	CAMP HILL	PA	C-	C-	C-	209.2	14.91	7.3	0.8	11.6	18.4	4.5	7.5	10.8
PENTUCKET BK	HAVERHILL	MA	B+	B+	B+	398.3	6.77	5.2	0.2	32.7	39.0	10.0	11.7	18.3
▲ PEOPLES B&T	PANA	IL	B-	C+	C	112.5	0.56	14.1	3.0	16.1	26.5	6.7	8.7	13.3
PEOPLES B&TC	SELMA	AL	B-	B-	B-	761.2	-0.71	10.4	7.0	10.4	29.7	6.6	8.6	14.0
PEOPLES B&TC	BUFORD	GA	B-	B-	B-	319.2	5.35	6.4	3.6	11.9	17.3	5.3	8.1	11.2
PEOPLES B&TC	MCPHERSON	KS	C+	C+	B	200.6	3.20	32.6	4.2	8.5	26.9	8.1	9.7	15.4
PEOPLES B&TC	HAZARD	KY	C-	C-	D+	239.1	5.59	24.2	15.5	22.1	11.7	4.2	7.6	10.6
▲ PEOPLES B&TC	OWENTON	KY	B+	C+	C+	57.7	-4.92	5.1	6.9	31.0	9.5	10.0	11.7	16.8
PEOPLES B&TC	TROY	MO	C-	C-	C-	320.4	6.49	8.2	1.6	10.2	34.5	2.5	6.2	9.5
PEOPLES B&TC	N CARROLLTON	MS	B	B	B	42.9	8.58	0.3	8.7	16.1	63.6	10.0	11.4	31.2
PEOPLES B&TC	TUPELO	MS	B+	B+	B+	1,416.5	2.26	8.2	5.8	20.8	24.5	6.4	8.5	14.0
PEOPLES B&TC	PARSHALL	ND	B+	B+	B+	42.0	4.32	3.1	2.8	2.0	25.6	10.0	14.5	24.1
PEOPLES B&TC	RYAN	OK	C-	C-	D+	16.1	-3.40	1.6	5.9	14.3	22.9	10.0	14.7	31.3
PEOPLES B&TC	MANCHESTER	TN	B-	B-	B-	59.1	2.69	8.0	5.5	12.6	44.5	7.7	9.5	14.1
▼ PEOPLES B&TC OF MADISON	BEREA	KY	C+	B-	B-	223.1	8.40	3.1	4.4	38.2	16.8	4.9	6.9	12.2
PEOPLES B&TC PICKETT CTY	BYRDSTOWN	TN	B-	B-	C+	80.6	3.78	14.9	21.8	13.7	11.7	10.0	12.1	16.1
▼ PEOPLES B&TC POINTE	NEW ROADS	LA	B+	A-	A-	57.8	5.59	38.6	10.2	10.9	7.9	10.0	12.3	17.7
PEOPLES BK	MAGNOLIA	AR	C	C	D+	45.8	-7.27	15.0	12.1	30.6	23.5	9.8	10.9	19.7
▲ PEOPLES BK	SHERIDAN	AR	B+	B	B-	63.1	6.91	29.3	14.8	6.8	24.8	10.0	11.2	17.5
▼ PEOPLES BK	BRIDGEPORT	CT	D+	B-	B-	10,677.6	-9.83	12.6	1.1	28.9	23.6	8.6	10.0	17.5
PEOPLES BK	PALM HARBOR	FL	B-	C+	C+	344.7	39.09	8.4	1.1	6.6	10.1	5.6	8.1	11.5
▲ PEOPLES BK	BLACKSHEAR	GA	B	B-	C+	165.2	6.10	11.5	4.4	13.7	18.1	8.9	10.2	14.8
PEOPLES BK	EATONTON	GA	B	B	B	122.1	11.26	4.0	6.9	19.7	18.8	6.2	8.2	13.3
PEOPLES BK	LITHONIA	GA	C+	C+	B-	154.7	12.57	3.4	2.4	11.3	16.2	3.8	7.4	10.4
PEOPLES BK	LYONS	GA	D	D+	C-	61.7	-7.30	13.8	5.7	7.1	16.3	6.2	8.5	11.9
PEOPLES BK	WILLACOOCHEE	GA	B-	B-	B-	43.9	0.22	6.0	7.5	17.4	25.9	9.5	10.6	18.3
PEOPLES BK	WINDER	GA	B	B+	B+	238.5	9.91	5.5	4.9	11.2	31.5	9.3	10.5	16.8
▼ PEOPLES BK	ROCK VALLEY	IA	C+	B-	C+	161.8	4.90	12.3	5.2	11.9	15.4	3.6	7.5	10.3
PEOPLES BK	BROWNSTOWN	IN	B	B	B	100.8	7.90	3.3	14.6	16.7	33.7	7.4	9.3	19.8
▼ PEOPLES BK	WASHINGTON	IN	B-	B	B	190.6	6.61	8.1	3.5	10.3	28.2	5.4	7.4	11.3
▲ PEOPLES BK	COLDWATER	KS	C-	D+	D+	35.4	1.37	9.4	9.3	4.5	36.1	7.3	9.2	14.6
▼ PEOPLES BK	LAWRENCE	KS	D	C-	C	319.6	1.80	9.9	2.5	14.3	11.2	3.4	7.4	10.2
▲ PEOPLES BK	PRATT	KS	B+	B	B	193.2	-2.07	12.6	4.9	6.6	35.4	10.0	13.1	25.6
▲ PEOPLES BK	LEBANON	KY	C-	D	D-	43.6	-1.99	18.2	6.7	10.8	10.4	5.8	8.5	11.6
PEOPLES BK	MARION	KY	C-	C-	C-	25.2	9.17	5.7	13.3	23.3	23.4	10.0	11.9	18.2
PEOPLES BK	MOREHEAD	KY	B	B-	C+	81.4	10.98	25.0	5.1	15.1	34.2	8.0	9.7	14.8
▼ PEOPLES BK	MT WASHINGTON	KY	C	C+	C+	95.8	-2.14	3.9	6.5	11.6	18.9	8.9	10.3	15.5
PEOPLES BK	TAYLORSVILLE	KY	B-	C+	C+	86.4	1.38	5.2	5.1	22.8	17.6	6.6	8.6	12.9
PEOPLES BK	CHATHAM	LA	C+	C+	C+	17.6	0.22	3.7	20.2	26.8	10.1	10.0	13.6	25.0
▼ PEOPLES BK	ELKTON	MD	B-	B	B	107.7	2.19	5.7	7.3	26.6	23.1	4.7	6.7	12.1
▲ PEOPLES BK	KAHOKA	MO	B	B-	C+	59.7	6.76	3.6	4.3	12.2	40.4	8.0	9.7	19.1
▼ PEOPLES BK	SENECA	MO	E+	D-	D+	30.4	-2.42	5.4	14.2	30.3	23.8	5.7	7.7	14.3
PEOPLES BK	MENDENHALL	MS	B-	C+	D+	131.7	-3.05	2.9	6.4	14.1	23.2	8.8	10.2	15.6
PEOPLES BK	RIPLEY	MS	B	B	B+	298.1	-0.93	7.5	6.9	15.2	48.4	7.1	9.1	19.9
PEOPLES BK	NEWTON	NC	C+	C+	C+	684.3	3.10	11.2	2.2	14.3	13.4	5.5	8.8	11.4
PEOPLES BK	GAMBIER	OH	C-	C-	D+	40.1	9.69	1.9	4.9	40.3	19.7	6.6	8.6	15.2
▲ PEOPLES BK	OKLAHOMA CITY	OK	E	E-	E-	24.3	-3.14	5.9	11.6	14.5	7.1	4.6	8.0	10.8
▲ PEOPLES BK	WESTVILLE	OK	A	A-	B+	45.2	-0.75	3.8	8.4	19.8	16.2	10.0	11.9	19.6
PEOPLES BK	IVA	SC	B	B	B	150.9	5.12	3.7	6.0	21.8	25.8	8.4	9.9	16.4
PEOPLES BK	CLIFTON	TN	C	C-	C-	97.1	2.39	11.4	13.7	22.4	16.2	6.3	8.3	12.9
▼ PEOPLES BK	SARDIS	TN	C+	B-	B-	37.1	3.86	4.2	11.1	28.8	31.8	10.0	12.6	26.0
▲ PEOPLES BK	COLLEYVILLE	TX	D+	D	D	30.0	59.84	7.5	1.8	8.8	15.9	10.0	16.9	23.2
PEOPLES BK	LUBBOCK	TX	B	B	B	96.0	7.69	15.8	9.9	10.2	9.5	8.9	10.4	14.0
PEOPLES BK	PARIS	TX	A-	A-	B	90.5	-10.08	10.3	7.7	37.7	12.9	10.0	14.2	23.2
PEOPLES BK	EWING	VA	B-	B	B	41.8	5.48	1.0	14.8	41.4	4.3	10.0	13.5	25.5
▲ PEOPLES BK	LYNDEN	WA	B	B-	B-	563.6	8.50	11.0	8.7	16.6	4.9	5.1	8.3	11.1
PEOPLES BK	ELKHORN	WI	D	D-	D-	90.6	35.23	5.2	2.4	17.2	0.6	5.7	9.9	11.5
▲ PEOPLES BK A CODORUS	GLEN ROCK	PA	C+	C	C	385.3	7.18	2.9	1.8	18.9	17.5	3.3	7.7	10.1
PEOPLES BK ARLINGTON	ARLINGTON HGHTS	IL	C-	D+	D	81.0	11.32	18.4	1.5	5.0	26.0	7.0	9.3	12.5
▲ PEOPLES BK CO	COLDWATER	OH	A	A-	B+	264.0	6.30	7.3	5.3	23.9	28.5	8.4	9.9	18.1
PEOPLES BK MARYCREST	BOURBONNAIS	IL	B+	B+	A-	108.3	3.83	4.6	8.1	17.8	22.8	6.1	8.2	15.1
PEOPLES BK NA	MARIETTA	OH	B+	B+	B+	1,758.8	-5.02	5.6	3.7	16.7	34.6	6.3	8.3	13.8

Asset Quality Index	Non-Performing Loans as a % of Total Loans	as a % of Capital	Net Charge-offs / Avg Loans	Profitability Index	Net Income ($Mil)	Return on Assets (R.O.A.)	Return on Equity (R.O.E.)	Net Interest Spread	Overhead Efficiency Ratio	Liquidity Index	Liquidity Ratio	Hot Money Ratio	Stability Index
9.2	0.41	2.4	0.08	6.3	0.9	1.06	16.76	3.65	64.3	5.6	33.2	3.1	3.8
4.2	1.80	12.2	2.40	1.2	0.1	0.09	1.29	4.23	92.2	1.6	14.6	22.9	2.3
5.1	0.97	8.2	0.03	3.2	0.3	0.34	4.36	3.75	86.5	4.8	29.4	6.5	2.8
9.7	0.05	0.2	-0.04	4.8	2.1	1.05	8.48	3.29	60.7	3.2	31.1	16.1	8.1
4.6	1.40	9.8	0.17	3.9	0.3	0.59	6.68	4.20	80.8	3.9	11.2	9.2	4.7
5.3	1.19	6.6	0.51	4.6	3.8	0.97	10.40	3.65	75.1	2.4	34.7	23.9	5.7
7.3	0.05	0.4	-0.10	6.1	1.7	1.08	13.04	4.32	62.1	1.4	21.3	27.8	4.8
4.1	1.11	6.1	0.58	6.0	1.1	1.09	10.51	4.16	64.5	4.7	32.0	8.5	5.5
3.2	1.58	13.6	0.52	4.4	1.3	1.11	14.13	4.28	65.5	2.7	32.2	19.0	3.8
5.7	0.90	5.3	0.14	10.0	0.8	2.80	23.25	6.25	52.5	4.0	11.6	8.5	7.6
4.6	1.26	11.7	0.01	5.0	1.5	0.95	15.55	3.37	63.7	4.2	23.4	8.3	4.0
8.8	0.82	2.1	0.06	7.1	0.3	1.20	10.47	3.24	47.7	1.6	19.9	24.0	6.2
5.7	1.35	9.0	0.24	7.7	10.3	1.45	15.69	4.29	65.1	5.0	49.6	14.8	8.0
4.6	1.77	6.6	-0.13	6.8	0.3	1.55	10.61	3.78	52.3	6.8	91.1	8.4	7.7
5.0	4.92	13.4	-0.03	4.4	0.1	1.13	7.59	3.53	69.4	6.6	170.7	16.9	2.5
7.3	0.98	4.2	0.01	4.6	0.3	0.89	8.54	4.38	73.9	4.6	38.8	11.6	5.1
8.5	0.03	0.3	0.02	7.3	1.3	1.19	16.05	4.51	60.7	1.8	15.3	19.9	5.4
3.8	1.61	9.0	0.49	9.6	0.8	2.06	16.96	5.81	46.7	3.0	47.0	23.9	7.4
4.9	1.40	8.9	-0.06	9.2	0.4	1.54	12.80	4.16	58.8	2.6	14.5	16.2	8.1
5.3	1.40	7.6	-0.28	5.8	0.4	1.78	16.68	3.87	68.6	5.2	40.0	8.4	3.4
7.7	0.27	1.3	0.00	7.8	0.4	1.34	12.43	4.49	46.4	4.5	62.3	16.1	4.0
7.3	0.47	2.8	0.12	1.3	144.3	-1.01	-10.07	3.09	134.4	5.8	28.9	4.2	5.2
7.4	0.12	0.3	-0.02	6.5	1.2	0.79	4.15	3.96	61.8	3.5	27.0	13.2	6.0
4.9	0.46	2.7	0.03	7.4	1.1	1.29	11.29	5.07	58.3	2.1	14.1	18.4	6.8
6.4	0.35	2.6	0.05	5.7	0.6	0.94	11.33	4.51	69.5	4.7	33.8	9.2	4.5
6.7	0.13	1.2	0.00	6.9	1.4	1.87	25.06	4.43	59.7	3.5	39.2	17.4	5.0
0.4	4.77	38.5	0.00	4.8	0.3	0.86	11.07	4.10	70.0	2.4	11.7	16.7	3.2
7.5	0.39	1.9	-0.33	5.4	0.3	1.37	12.87	4.37	71.0	3.4	61.0	24.1	5.6
7.9	0.38	2.0	0.10	4.4	1.0	0.86	8.08	4.33	80.2	3.0	21.5	14.8	6.4
6.6	0.40	3.7	0.00	7.1	1.3	1.66	20.86	4.19	56.8	2.3	10.2	16.8	2.4
5.9	0.90	4.0	0.19	4.9	0.5	0.96	9.53	4.07	67.2	6.0	49.3	6.5	5.2
6.0	0.59	4.7	0.19	9.2	1.4	1.48	19.30	4.18	45.3	4.5	8.7	4.5	5.7
5.7	0.46	2.3	-0.02	7.7	0.3	1.40	12.77	4.70	53.7	3.4	46.3	19.2	4.3
0.2	2.91	28.2	0.57	5.6	1.7	1.07	14.20	5.27	81.4	4.4	30.0	9.3	4.3
5.0	2.05	7.6	0.25	7.4	1.3	1.34	9.93	4.96	60.0	3.4	60.0	29.0	7.7
7.9	0.00	0.0	0.01	6.4	0.3	1.26	14.80	4.09	57.1	3.0	28.7	16.2	3.2
4.9	1.69	8.3	0.66	2.5	0.0	0.15	1.33	4.54	80.8	4.9	31.3	7.0	3.6
4.4	2.14	12.6	0.07	6.8	0.6	1.47	14.70	4.63	68.4	2.4	22.6	17.8	5.4
2.5	4.23	25.3	0.02	5.8	0.6	1.33	12.40	4.35	72.7	3.4	25.7	13.5	6.3
7.3	0.05	0.4	0.09	7.9	0.9	2.11	23.67	4.80	57.0	3.8	16.2	10.2	5.2
4.6	1.50	5.8	0.08	8.6	0.1	1.64	12.39	5.66	58.7	5.9	108.6	14.2	4.9
2.3	2.48	20.1	-0.01	7.8	0.7	1.25	18.52	3.91	64.6	3.3	34.6	16.8	6.1
8.9	0.01	0.1	-0.03	6.5	0.4	1.28	13.46	3.42	46.4	3.5	36.6	16.4	5.4
2.9	2.50	16.5	1.40	2.5	0.0	0.04	0.48	4.79	84.2	3.5	70.2	28.0	1.0
4.3	1.72	9.5	-0.03	6.0	1.0	1.53	14.34	4.34	69.9	4.6	31.5	8.9	6.0
8.4	0.17	0.8	0.38	5.7	1.7	1.12	11.89	3.50	60.6	3.7	54.8	21.3	5.3
4.9	0.82	6.7	0.83	4.4	2.6	0.75	8.64	3.78	62.9	1.4	19.0	27.9	4.7
7.2	0.22	1.6	0.06	4.2	0.2	0.76	8.58	4.23	73.1	4.3	61.4	16.9	3.0
4.2	0.69	6.5	0.08	4.5	0.2	1.30	16.78	5.65	78.5	1.0	12.2	30.5	0.7
7.8	0.47	2.5	0.15	9.9	0.5	2.42	19.73	5.21	56.8	4.0	62.7	18.6	8.9
4.7	1.19	7.0	0.26	6.7	0.9	1.26	12.59	4.57	62.8	2.5	27.8	18.4	6.0
6.8	0.34	2.6	0.03	4.8	0.5	0.94	11.58	4.92	71.9	1.6	24.7	26.0	3.2
2.3	6.91	26.5	0.30	5.4	0.2	0.94	7.46	3.76	53.3	4.2	85.0	22.3	4.7
7.4	0.09	0.4	0.24	0.7	0.0	0.03	0.16	4.54	88.4	5.1	50.0	11.0	0.0
5.9	0.02	0.1	0.08	5.3	0.4	0.83	7.09	4.80	69.6	2.8	39.7	22.7	5.9
8.0	0.51	2.7	0.30	9.8	0.7	1.56	11.29	4.68	65.7	2.8	22.9	15.5	6.3
3.9	3.22	15.3	1.15	6.2	0.2	0.83	6.30	4.45	57.9	4.7	100.6	20.6	5.3
7.4	0.15	1.3	0.01	7.0	3.0	1.09	13.21	4.66	70.9	6.0	57.8	9.5	5.7
8.4	0.00	0.0	0.00	1.1	0.0	0.09	0.84	3.22	83.9	3.0	29.5	16.5	0.0
7.0	0.42	3.7	0.11	4.9	1.8	0.96	12.21	3.89	69.9	4.6	28.7	7.8	4.3
8.5	0.00	0.0	0.93	2.4	0.2	0.47	4.78	2.58	74.0	3.2	18.5	13.3	4.9
8.5	0.04	0.3	0.03	8.9	1.7	1.33	13.43	3.51	46.0	6.6	57.8	5.5	7.4
8.3	0.07	0.5	0.00	5.1	0.5	0.88	10.29	3.27	75.2	5.3	39.8	7.9	6.6
6.4	0.62	2.9	0.28	7.5	11.2	1.29	12.37	3.57	55.7	3.4	12.6	12.2	7.6

Name	City	State	Weiss Safety Rating	2003 Weiss Safety Rating	2002 Weiss Safety Rating	Total Assets ($Mil)	One Year Asset Growth	Asset Mix (As a % of Total Assets) Comm-ercial Loans	Cons-umer Loans	Home Mort-gages	Secur-ities	Capital-ization Index	Leverage Ratio	Risk-based Capital Ratio
PEOPLES BK OF ALTENBURG	ALTENBURG	MO	C-	C-	C-	39.7	-1.04	2.4	2.2	17.5	46.5	6.4	8.4	14.5
PEOPLES BK OF BEDFORD	SHELBYVILLE	TN	B-	C+	D+	47.2	33.39	6.5	11.9	17.0	19.9	9.6	10.7	15.9
PEOPLES BK OF BILOXI	BILOXI	MS	B	B	B	580.8	-0.54	9.4	1.6	10.1	33.3	10.0	14.5	24.5
PEOPLES BK OF BULLITT CTY	SHEPHERDSVILLE	KY	A	A-	A-	169.6	-0.97	0.3	4.7	30.2	24.5	10.0	14.9	34.4
▲ PEOPLES BK OF CMRC	MEDFORD	OR	A-	B+	B	58.0	12.51	15.3	1.7	9.7	9.8	10.0	15.1	19.1
▲ PEOPLES BK OF COFFEE CTY	ELBA	AL	C+	C	C	103.6	4.65	11.7	6.3	16.3	20.8	8.4	10.0	15.3
PEOPLES BK OF COMMERCE	CAMBRIDGE	MN	B+	B+	B	248.2	23.76	21.6	3.8	7.2	14.5	4.8	8.2	10.9
PEOPLES BK OF CUBA	CUBA	MO	B-	B-	B	123.7	3.53	21.5	11.0	27.3	11.5	7.6	9.7	13.0
PEOPLES BK OF EAST TN	MADISONVILLE	TN	C+	C+	C+	102.9	7.62	11.5	12.7	31.4	13.4	6.2	8.4	11.9
PEOPLES BK OF FLEMING CTY	FLEMINGSBURG	KY	A-	A-	A-	153.3	6.78	9.8	11.0	23.1	13.3	10.0	11.6	16.6
PEOPLES BK OF FRANKLIN	BUDE	MS	D+	D+	D+	56.3	15.22	7.4	27.9	25.8	11.3	6.2	8.3	11.9
▲ PEOPLES BK OF GRACEVILLE	GRACEVILLE	FL	A	A-	A-	51.5	4.79	4.1	4.1	13.9	51.4	10.0	19.9	44.4
▼ PEOPLES BK OF	GREENSBORO	AL	B+	A-	A-	66.2	7.41	9.0	11.0	9.5	31.0	10.0	11.9	18.7
▲ PEOPLES BK OF JAMESTOWN	JAMESTOWN	MO	C+	C	C-	28.6	7.93	6.0	6.4	22.2	34.6	8.5	10.0	17.4
PEOPLES BK OF KENT CTY MD	CHESTERTOWN	MD	A	A	A	187.8	11.86	12.4	4.0	24.3	11.9	9.5	10.9	14.6
PEOPLES BK OF LOUISIANA	AMITE	LA	C+	C+	C+	72.9	25.14	8.5	10.2	17.7	10.6	5.3	7.9	11.2
▼ PEOPLES BK OF MACON	MACON	IL	C+	B-	B-	16.7	1.10	11.6	5.7	18.2	44.7	10.0	16.0	31.7
PEOPLES BK OF MARYLAND	DENTON	MD	A-	A-	A	109.8	-0.04	12.3	3.8	28.7	17.2	7.8	9.6	18.3
▼ PEOPLES BK OF MULLENS	MULLENS	WV	A	A+	A+	119.6	-1.62	3.3	3.9	9.2	66.2	10.0	16.0	38.6
▲ PEOPLES BK OF NORTH	CULLMAN	AL	B	B-	C	344.0	18.87	7.6	5.5	17.2	28.3	10.0	11.2	16.9
PEOPLES BK OF POLK CTY	BENTON	TN	C	C	C	22.3	0.47	20.5	8.6	17.3	23.8	10.0	12.3	19.3
PEOPLES BK OF RED LEVEL	RED LEVEL	AL	C+	C+	B-	13.1	2.49	3.0	10.2	8.4	61.0	10.0	16.3	39.9
▲ PEOPLES BK OF TALBOTTON	TALBOTTON	GA	C+	C	C	17.7	2.20	4.3	15.6	12.0	40.8	10.0	15.4	29.6
▼ PEOPLES BK OF THE OZARKS	NIXA	MO	B-	B	B	249.8	8.42	3.6	3.8	27.6	9.1	4.4	7.5	10.7
▲ PEOPLES BK OF VA	RICHMOND	VA	C+	C-	D	162.1	66.23	9.4	2.2	5.4	36.6	10.0	11.1	15.7
PEOPLES BK SB	MUNSTER	IN	B	B	B	539.9	8.23	7.1	1.1	41.9	15.2	6.0	8.0	12.6
▲ PEOPLES BK WI	HAYWARD	WI	A	A-	A	252.2	11.87	6.5	1.6	9.6	22.2	10.0	11.5	15.5
PEOPLES BK-DEER LODGE	DEER LODGE	MT	D+	D+	C-	21.1	-1.98	5.9	5.2	14.1	42.8	9.5	10.7	23.0
▲ PEOPLES BL&SC	MASON	OH	B-	C+	B-	32.9	-3.87	0.0	0.8	37.8	39.0	10.0	18.4	53.1
PEOPLES CMNTY BK OF SC	AIKEN	SC	B-	B-	C+	117.7	11.30	7.1	1.7	8.6	33.4	5.6	7.6	11.7
▲ PEOPLES CMNTY BK OF THE	SARASOTA	FL	C	C-	D	171.5	68.55	4.5	2.7	10.3	7.0	6.6	10.4	12.2
PEOPLES COMMUNITY BANK	W CHESTER	OH	C+	B-	B	846.5	35.82	3.7	2.2	20.3	24.8	6.6	8.6	14.2
▲ PEOPLES COMMUNITY BK	COLUMBIA	AL	C	D+	D	154.5	-7.58	6.8	9.6	15.7	13.3	6.2	8.5	11.9
PEOPLES COMMUNITY BK	COLQUITT	GA	C	C-	C-	122.3	8.25	6.6	4.8	17.1	12.6	3.2	7.0	10.1
PEOPLES COMMUNITY BK	TELL CITY	IN	C+	C+	B-	33.4	-1.09	4.2	8.3	67.4	0.0	10.0	13.9	22.3
▲ PEOPLES COMMUNITY BK	GREENVILLE	MO	A-	B-	B-	65.8	-1.20	9.2	11.1	33.4	10.7	10.0	13.1	21.2
▲ PEOPLES COMMUNITY BK	MONTROSS	VA	B	B-	C+	100.6	2.27	4.8	6.9	40.8	3.0	7.1	9.4	14.1
PEOPLES COMMUNITY STATE	DONIPHAN	MO	B+	B	B-	82.6	6.58	3.1	9.4	40.0	15.0	7.1	9.1	14.5
PEOPLES EXC BK OF MONROE	BEATRICE	AL	B-	C+	B-	57.0	-13.19	13.0	7.7	22.6	12.0	8.4	9.9	15.0
PEOPLES EXCHANGE BK	BELLEVILLE	KS	B	B	B	51.5	1.82	9.4	2.3	9.9	28.1	9.1	10.4	15.5
PEOPLES EXCHANGE BK	BEATTYVILLE	KY	C	C	D+	195.7	-0.63	9.1	6.0	32.8	2.3	4.0	7.0	10.5
▲ PEOPLES FEDERAL SVGS BK	AURORA	IN	A-	B+	B+	120.7	6.69	3.5	2.3	63.3	4.4	10.0	17.6	29.4
PEOPLES FIRST COMMUNITY	PANAMA CITY	FL	B	B	B	1,409.7	8.41	2.3	2.5	21.5	5.3	3.6	8.0	10.3
PEOPLES FS&LA	SIDNEY	OH	B	B	B	135.8	-5.42	3.3	3.1	65.6	3.9	9.9	10.9	20.0
▲ PEOPLES FSB	BRIGHTON	MA	A	A-	A-	277.3	4.71	0.5	0.8	41.3	13.7	9.7	10.8	17.0
PEOPLES FSB OF DEKALB	AUBURN	IN	A-	A-	A-	370.3	-2.02	2.5	1.1	63.8	18.8	10.0	11.9	22.0
PEOPLES HOME SVGS BK	BEAVER FALLS	PA	B-	B-	B	315.7	0.71	0.4	17.4	17.9	51.8	10.0	11.4	27.0
PEOPLES INDEPENDENT	BOAZ	AL	C-	C-	C	119.4	18.09	8.4	5.4	13.6	43.3	4.9	6.9	12.6
PEOPLES NB	NICEVILLE	FL	B	B	B	130.6	39.03	8.6	4.9	13.7	17.1	5.8	7.9	11.6
PEOPLES NB	COUNCIL BLUFFS	IA	B-	C+	C+	355.0	10.92	7.8	2.3	20.1	28.0	4.5	6.5	11.8
PEOPLES NB	MORA	MN	B+	B+	B+	165.0	4.52	18.8	3.9	11.0	31.4	7.5	9.4	14.1
PEOPLES NB	HALLSTEAD	PA	A-	A-	A-	384.1	5.72	7.2	4.8	26.4	29.2	8.4	9.9	15.4
PEOPLES NB	EASLEY	SC	B-	B-	B-	248.5	-3.16	9.5	3.9	13.6	14.4	6.9	8.9	12.4
PEOPLES NB	DANVILLE	VA	B	B+	B+	371.6	0.84	3.8	3.6	8.6	32.6	8.4	10.0	17.7
PEOPLES NB COLORADO	COLORADO SPRINGS	CO	C-	C-	C-	248.3	9.66	8.6	2.2	5.5	2.9	4.4	8.9	10.7
PEOPLES NB MONUMENT	MONUMENT	CO	C-	C+	C	104.9	-12.68	7.2	0.8	12.4	4.9	3.9	7.6	10.4
PEOPLES NB OF CHECOTAH	CHECOTAH	OK	A	A	A	102.4	-1.83	4.7	13.3	11.6	41.8	10.0	16.4	33.1
PEOPLES NB OF KEWANEE	KEWANEE	IL	B+	A-	A-	206.7	0.60	13.8	3.6	7.3	32.0	10.0	15.2	21.5
▼ PEOPLES NB OF LA FOLLETTE	LA FOLLETTE	TN	A-	A	A	109.4	3.26	2.0	4.3	26.7	19.9	10.0	15.3	23.8
PEOPLES NB OF	MC LEANSBORO	IL	C	C	C	448.3	4.74	10.8	1.3	14.6	13.8	3.6	7.6	10.3
PEOPLES NB OF MT	MT PLEASANT	OH	C+	C+	B-	42.6	-2.53	0.2	11.9	23.7	43.6	10.0	16.2	40.5
▼ PEOPLES NB OF NEW	NEW LEXINGTON	OH	B-	B	B+	85.3	3.03	6.2	13.3	41.6	11.7	9.2	10.5	16.5
PEOPLES S&LA OF	MONTICELLO	IN	B	B	B	37.8	-8.74	0.0	0.3	82.2	0.0	10.0	29.9	64.8
PEOPLES S&LC	BUCYRUS	OH	B+	B+	A-	114.1	3.10	0.0	1.2	53.1	12.3	10.0	17.1	36.1

Asset Quality Index	Non-Performing Loans as a % of Total Loans	as a % of Capital	Net Charge-offs Avg Loans	Profitability Index	Net Income ($Mil)	Return on Assets (R.O.A.)	Return on Equity (R.O.E.)	Net Interest Spread	Overhead Efficiency Ratio	Liquidity Index	Liquidity Ratio	Hot Money Ratio	Stability Index
7.7	0.02	0.1	1.09	4.6	0.2	0.77	9.42	3.94	72.0	4.9	18.4	3.4	3.9
7.9	0.00	0.0	0.11	5.6	0.3	1.39	13.37	4.82	67.0	2.5	39.4	27.3	1.9
4.9	3.08	11.1	0.08	5.3	3.1	1.06	7.44	3.70	67.3	2.3	27.8	19.5	7.9
5.9	3.94	11.6	-0.01	7.2	0.5	0.64	4.16	4.55	58.2	8.2	108.7	2.7	8.8
7.2	0.06	0.3	0.15	9.5	0.4	1.43	9.68	5.61	70.9	2.3	32.1	21.9	7.7
3.7	1.95	9.0	0.24	4.5	0.6	1.16	9.09	4.13	54.3	2.5	41.0	27.8	5.8
8.1	0.14	1.2	-0.01	8.6	2.4	2.05	24.93	5.04	60.8	1.9	11.1	19.2	6.3
3.9	0.62	4.7	0.05	8.4	1.2	1.98	19.69	4.88	59.1	3.4	15.6	11.9	7.1
6.8	0.34	2.9	0.23	4.1	0.3	0.62	7.53	4.08	80.3	1.7	16.2	22.3	4.3
5.2	1.49	9.0	0.22	7.2	0.9	1.21	10.30	4.46	55.4	2.4	33.0	21.4	7.1
2.0	1.76	15.5	0.09	5.7	0.3	0.96	11.70	4.94	70.2	3.4	77.9	32.0	3.0
9.3	0.11	0.2	0.33	10.0	0.8	3.22	16.46	4.13	38.9	5.6	47.8	7.9	8.9
4.5	2.63	11.1	0.03	9.5	0.7	1.98	16.09	4.24	54.1	4.4	51.4	15.1	8.3
4.7	3.25	18.6	0.37	5.1	0.2	1.45	14.31	4.26	64.5	4.1	11.6	7.3	4.1
8.1	0.12	0.9	0.03	9.2	1.3	1.45	13.35	4.32	49.2	3.5	21.1	12.0	7.5
6.3	0.16	1.4	0.13	8.2	0.7	2.12	26.15	5.29	60.6	2.9	13.4	14.4	5.0
8.8	0.00	0.0	0.00	4.4	0.1	0.85	5.43	3.73	73.2	4.6	32.3	6.7	5.5
8.3	0.12	0.9	0.16	10.0	1.0	1.86	18.79	4.84	48.4	7.3	87.9	5.7	8.6
9.9	0.64	0.7	0.12	6.4	0.7	1.12	6.87	2.95	51.0	7.2	117.9	10.3	8.9
4.9	1.53	6.8	0.20	6.0	1.6	1.01	7.80	4.39	68.7	3.4	17.6	12.4	6.9
8.1	0.00	0.0	-0.03	3.1	0.0	0.38	3.01	4.30	90.0	2.8	55.0	26.0	4.3
8.0	1.21	1.8	-0.12	6.3	0.1	1.42	8.78	4.66	70.3	5.1	41.0	6.4	4.7
5.9	3.34	7.7	-0.15	6.3	0.1	1.57	9.94	5.74	62.3	5.5	52.2	7.1	4.4
7.4	0.06	0.6	0.03	5.1	0.9	0.75	9.81	4.38	67.5	3.2	12.6	12.8	4.8
8.7	0.00	0.0	0.00	3.3	0.6	0.84	7.78	3.35	57.3	3.9	58.8	21.0	2.8
6.6	0.42	3.9	0.02	7.2	3.1	1.17	14.56	4.05	58.5	2.8	16.4	14.9	6.0
6.5	0.28	1.7	0.02	9.8	2.4	1.89	16.75	4.39	41.5	0.5	4.9	48.6	8.0
5.3	1.74	6.4	0.12	3.2	0.1	0.45	4.41	4.40	87.2	4.8	44.8	9.3	2.6
7.5	0.69	1.3	0.00	3.5	0.1	0.40	1.92	2.66	79.7	4.7	50.2	13.3	6.0
8.8	0.00	0.0	0.08	6.3	0.7	1.17	14.63	4.17	57.4	1.6	11.4	22.3	4.3
7.5	0.00	0.0	0.03	2.9	0.3	0.37	4.04	3.70	66.0	3.6	45.2	18.1	4.3
4.4	1.10	7.8	0.74	3.7	1.7	0.41	5.12	2.64	60.6	0.8	3.9	31.8	5.3
2.5	1.90	15.5	0.22	5.4	1.0	1.23	14.35	4.36	54.7	1.4	14.3	26.2	3.7
6.8	0.17	1.8	-0.08	7.4	0.7	1.25	17.32	4.15	51.4	1.2	9.7	27.9	4.3
4.7	1.51	9.3	0.63	3.4	0.1	0.38	2.81	3.96	82.3	1.5	11.3	23.7	4.8
8.1	0.24	1.1	0.00	10.0	0.9	2.70	19.43	5.62	53.0	4.8	41.9	11.4	8.1
8.3	0.09	0.7	-0.01	6.5	0.6	1.23	13.41	4.80	65.6	5.0	43.0	11.0	4.5
7.2	0.35	2.6	0.06	10.0	1.1	2.65	27.00	5.14	51.3	4.0	21.9	9.7	7.1
7.9	0.20	1.4	-0.09	6.4	0.3	1.13	11.32	5.23	63.5	2.2	29.4	21.4	5.1
8.3	0.17	1.0	-0.06	6.4	0.4	1.41	13.04	3.76	65.7	2.3	13.3	17.1	6.0
5.3	0.42	4.2	0.04	4.9	0.8	0.84	11.27	4.38	74.7	2.9	11.1	14.0	4.0
8.1	0.43	2.1	0.07	5.2	0.5	0.79	4.28	3.40	62.8	1.1	8.3	28.7	7.9
5.3	0.83	8.0	0.07	6.9	7.3	1.05	13.24	4.20	64.3	8.0	15.9	52.1	7.3
4.9	0.92	7.0	0.28	4.6	0.5	0.73	6.35	3.39	64.6	2.8	20.3	15.6	6.1
8.6	0.00	0.0	0.01	7.9	1.5	1.09	9.94	3.78	55.0	1.4	26.3	29.8	7.2
9.2	0.14	0.9	0.00	7.3	2.0	1.05	9.13	3.47	55.0	2.1	27.5	20.5	7.5
7.9	0.24	0.8	0.37	3.1	0.9	0.53	4.57	2.88	78.4	7.1	94.1	8.6	6.2
5.0	0.79	5.1	0.29	4.5	0.5	0.82	11.62	3.52	64.6	2.9	7.0	13.8	2.4
8.3	0.03	0.2	0.10	5.6	0.5	0.79	9.93	4.92	71.7	3.4	52.2	23.3	4.2
4.7	0.88	4.8	-0.16	5.1	2.0	1.18	10.33	3.45	65.0	4.2	30.0	10.8	7.1
6.4	0.79	4.8	0.51	7.9	1.0	1.25	12.58	4.35	48.5	1.7	15.4	20.8	6.7
5.8	1.11	6.4	0.32	6.9	2.2	1.18	10.97	3.88	53.0	4.4	22.7	7.1	7.6
6.4	0.50	3.9	0.12	7.0	0.9	0.71	8.07	3.58	79.0	1.7	22.1	23.2	5.3
3.9	2.86	14.2	0.02	4.7	1.6	0.86	8.54	3.22	61.2	6.4	68.4	9.1	5.9
2.2	1.78	15.1	0.22	7.8	2.0	1.64	18.06	5.89	69.9	3.8	12.4	9.9	5.4
3.7	1.83	16.6	0.02	6.3	0.1	0.22	2.59	5.93	92.8	5.0	12.9	1.5	3.7
7.6	0.74	2.0	0.62	6.9	0.8	1.53	9.31	4.34	64.3	4.6	37.3	11.1	9.0
5.5	3.18	9.4	2.03	5.2	0.7	0.64	3.98	5.34	45.2	5.6	57.7	11.2	7.1
5.7	1.84	7.9	0.06	8.7	0.8	1.43	9.05	5.57	58.9	4.5	52.2	15.4	8.5
5.4	0.58	5.5	0.13	4.2	1.8	0.80	10.52	3.91	77.4	1.6	7.8	21.0	3.8
8.8	0.67	1.7	0.46	2.8	0.1	0.28	1.74	3.44	80.5	7.4	85.0	3.3	5.8
4.6	1.43	10.3	0.06	3.8	0.2	0.54	5.10	4.30	81.9	4.4	20.3	6.6	5.6
9.4	0.11	0.3	0.00	6.2	0.2	1.02	3.51	3.84	59.7	3.7	20.2	11.0	6.3
8.3	0.54	1.8	0.00	4.4	0.4	0.61	3.35	3.15	71.3	4.0	30.6	12.0	7.8

Name	City	State	Weiss Safety Rating	2003 Weiss Safety Rating	2002 Weiss Safety Rating	Total Assets ($Mil)	One Year Asset Growth	Asset Mix (As a % of Total Assets)				Capital-ization Index	Leverage Ratio	Risk-based Capital Ratio
								Comm-ercial Loans	Cons-umer Loans	Home Mort-gages	Secur-ities			
▲ PEOPLES S&LC	W LIBERTY	OH	C	C-	C-	39.3	-0.47	2.1	3.6	54.5	1.1	8.0	9.6	17.4
▲ PEOPLES SAVING BK	INDIANOLA	IA	C	C-	C	81.1	7.75	5.8	4.0	22.0	31.9	4.8	6.9	11.5
PEOPLES SAVINGS BANK	MONTEZUMA	IA	B-	B-	B-	32.1	2.72	12.1	5.3	6.7	47.1	9.1	10.4	20.5
PEOPLES SECURITY BK	LOUISA	KY	B-	B-	C+	45.5	1.51	3.3	9.1	31.7	29.5	9.8	10.9	21.2
PEOPLES SOUTHERN BK	CLANTON	AL	A	A	A+	122.0	-1.44	7.4	5.5	8.0	53.2	10.0	16.2	30.3
PEOPLES ST B&TC	BAXLEY	GA	B-	B-	B-	59.7	2.00	5.4	7.1	7.1	6.1	10.0	13.2	15.7
▲ PEOPLES ST BK	LAKE CITY	FL	E+	E-	D+	50.2	10.01	10.8	7.1	13.4	9.7	6.3	9.2	12.0
▲ PEOPLES ST BK	JEFFERSONVILLE	GA	C	C-	C	21.1	-15.08	10.2	22.9	14.0	28.7	6.7	8.7	15.6
▲ PEOPLES ST BK	ALBIA	IA	B-	C+	B-	63.2	-2.92	8.4	5.3	17.4	35.1	8.5	10.0	16.9
PEOPLES ST BK	ELKADER	IA	B+	B+	B+	65.3	5.01	6.7	3.0	14.5	39.4	8.3	9.9	16.7
PEOPLES ST BK	WINFIELD	IA	C+	C+	C+	21.1	8.58	5.4	3.4	19.4	42.8	10.0	12.0	24.4
PEOPLES ST BK	CHANDLERVILLE	IL	D+	D+	D	40.8	2.01	11.3	14.3	19.0	22.8	6.5	8.5	14.0
PEOPLES ST BK	MANITO	IL	B	B+	B	53.7	-1.39	2.6	1.1	7.8	29.7	9.9	10.9	17.5
PEOPLES ST BK	MANSFIELD	IL	A-	A-	B+	118.5	1.54	6.2	4.2	12.7	47.2	10.0	11.4	24.7
▲ PEOPLES ST BK	NEWTON	IL	C-	D+	C	212.4	5.31	4.8	3.1	10.5	38.4	5.6	7.6	14.0
▲ PEOPLES ST BK	ELLETTSVILLE	IN	C+	C-	C	186.8	-0.47	8.6	2.5	12.0	41.3	6.6	8.6	14.1
PEOPLES ST BK	CHERRYVALE	KS	B	B	B+	13.6	-13.04	2.9	18.9	18.3	5.9	10.0	21.6	28.0
PEOPLES ST BK	MC DONALD	KS	D+	D+	D+	43.7	4.29	15.0	4.2	2.6	10.8	6.7	8.9	12.2
PEOPLES ST BK	MANY	LA	C+	C+	C	275.5	14.89	6.9	3.6	6.5	34.1	5.6	7.6	11.6
PEOPLES ST BK	HAMTRAMCK	MI	B-	B-	B	429.6	3.04	11.5	5.5	26.3	12.5	6.8	8.8	12.4
PEOPLES ST BK	WELLS	MN	C-	C-	C-	20.4	0.23	5.0	5.0	9.7	28.3	8.6	10.1	18.4
PEOPLES ST BK	FAIRMOUNT	ND	D-	D	D	14.8	6.43	25.4	11.9	3.9	17.3	5.9	7.9	13.0
PEOPLES ST BK	VELVA	ND	B	B	B+	26.0	-1.08	3.4	7.2	3.9	36.8	10.0	17.1	28.5
PEOPLES ST BK	WESTHOPE	ND	B	B	B-	36.3	6.39	5.0	3.3	3.3	44.9	7.6	9.4	17.9
PEOPLES ST BK	BLAIR	OK	C+	B-	B-	15.8	-10.73	9.7	16.1	7.2	36.1	7.4	9.2	16.9
PEOPLES ST BK	TULSA	OK	B	B	B	64.0	15.43	16.1	16.5	9.9	20.6	2.0	6.5	9.0
▼ PEOPLES ST BK	DE SMET	SD	B	B+	A-	51.1	-3.61	33.0	5.1	9.5	14.2	10.0	16.7	22.0
PEOPLES ST BK	SUMMIT	SD	C+	C+	C+	34.5	15.81	14.9	7.1	8.5	26.1	5.2	7.7	11.2
PEOPLES ST BK	CLYDE	TX	B-	B-	B-	113.3	-0.75	10.2	9.1	7.7	41.9	10.0	11.4	23.7
PEOPLES ST BK	HALLETTSVILLE	TX	B+	B+	B+	133.5	2.73	1.9	3.7	5.5	63.4	10.0	13.1	39.8
PEOPLES ST BK	ROCKSPRINGS	TX	B+	B+	A-	39.6	-3.43	4.3	3.9	4.6	60.4	7.2	11.5	12.6
PEOPLES ST BK	SHEPHERD	TX	C	C-	C	57.8	11.31	2.5	10.8	6.3	52.5	4.5	6.6	14.4
▲ PEOPLES ST BK	AUGUSTA	WI	B	B-	B	45.6	0.42	6.2	4.1	14.8	21.0	10.0	12.4	20.0
PEOPLES ST BK	MAZOMANIE	WI	B-	B-	C+	94.5	11.38	11.3	6.1	18.7	7.8	5.2	8.8	11.2
PEOPLES ST BK	PRAIRIE DU CHIEN	WI	B	B	B-	243.7	0.74	8.5	2.1	11.1	8.9	6.5	9.3	12.2
PEOPLES ST BK	WAUSAU	WI	C+	B-	B-	431.2	13.47	13.5	1.5	24.5	16.6	4.1	7.4	10.6
PEOPLES ST BK	FRANCESVILLE	IN	B	B	B	133.4	5.40	10.1	2.8	8.5	30.2	6.9	8.9	12.8
▼ PEOPLES ST BK MADISON	MADISON LAKE	MN	C	C	C-	24.3	-6.15	18.8	12.8	6.5	22.5	6.9	8.9	13.9
PEOPLES ST BK OF BLOOMER	BLOOMER	WI	B+	B+	B+	97.5	4.32	9.8	5.2	23.6	26.2	9.5	10.6	18.1
▲ PEOPLES ST BK OF COLFAX	COLFAX	IL	B-	C+	C+	23.0	1.06	3.6	9.2	18.9	20.6	9.8	10.8	20.3
PEOPLES ST BK OF COMFREY	COMFREY	MN	D-	D-	D-	13.5	3.71	6.1	4.6	5.6	26.9	6.0	8.0	13.5
PEOPLES ST BK OF	TRENTON	TN	B-	B-	C	82.6	0.31	4.1	10.4	26.6	9.0	6.2	8.2	13.5
PEOPLES ST BK OF MINNEOLA	MINNEOLA	KS	C+	C+	C	13.8	11.95	1.4	1.6	7.6	64.1	8.3	9.8	18.6
PEOPLES ST BK OF MUNISING	MUNISING	MI	C+	C+	C+	100.6	6.75	31.2	8.5	28.5	18.4	8.7	10.2	14.5
▲ PEOPLES ST BK OF	PLAINVIEW	MN	B	B-	B	98.1	3.35	11.1	3.9	9.8	24.9	7.5	9.4	14.0
▼ PEOPLES ST BK OF	WYALUSING	PA	C-	NR	NR	167.5	3.23	13.4	4.1	28.9	26.5	4.4	7.1	10.7
▲ PEOPLES SVG BK	CRAWFORDSVILLE	IA	B+	B	B-	21.8	9.42	4.0	5.0	23.2	41.9	5.2	7.2	11.7
PEOPLES SVG BK	WELLSBURG	IA	B	B	B	52.0	12.12	1.5	2.1	7.6	44.6	6.2	8.2	13.8
PEOPLES SVG BK	NEW MATAMORAS	OH	B	B	B	37.2	-3.82	23.7	4.6	21.1	27.2	10.0	12.9	21.2
PEOPLES SVG BK OF	RHINELAND	MO	B	B	B	119.3	4.80	4.0	4.8	42.9	16.8	7.3	9.2	14.7
PEOPLES SVGS BK	CHARLES CITY	IA	C+	C	D+	83.4	6.46	6.1	3.6	6.9	15.2	6.3	8.3	12.9
▲ PEOPLES SVGS BK	CHESTERFIELD	NJ	C-	D+	D+	96.4	8.75	1.1	4.2	38.1	20.9	4.8	6.8	13.1
PEOPLES SVGS BK	URBANA	OH	C+	C+	C-	83.5	4.89	0.0	3.3	57.4	7.9	10.0	11.4	21.6
▲ PEOPLES SVGS BK OF TROY	TROY	OH	A-	B+	B+	190.6	-7.62	3.5	4.3	51.4	8.6	10.0	11.6	18.9
PEOPLES T&SB	ADEL	IA	C+	C	C	141.2	6.23	7.3	4.2	18.8	12.5	5.6	7.8	11.5
▲ PEOPLES T&SB	RIVERSIDE	IA	B+	B	B-	15.2	-3.97	4.0	4.4	22.3	53.0	10.0	11.2	22.0
▼ PEOPLES T&SB	BOONVILLE	IN	B-	B	A-	100.5	1.97	7.0	4.1	21.9	31.1	10.0	23.0	42.4
PEOPLES TR CO OF ST	ST ALBANS	VT	B+	A-	A-	202.0	-0.73	4.7	3.9	23.7	28.0	10.0	12.7	22.0
▼ PEOPLES TRUST CO	LINTON	IN	C-	C-	C-	118.0	-1.84	5.6	10.6	26.6	16.4	5.7	7.7	11.6
PEOPLES WEBSTER COUNTY	RED CLOUD	NE	A-	A-	A-	54.3	1.94	6.8	2.4	5.9	37.1	10.0	27.3	34.6
PEOPLESBANK	HOLYOKE	MA	B+	B+	B	950.1	7.27	6.1	0.3	32.7	27.4	8.3	9.9	16.1
PEOTONE B&TC	PEOTONE	IL	C+	C+	C+	106.3	5.27	18.0	6.3	8.4	26.0	5.4	7.4	11.4
PEPPERELL B&T	BIDDEFORD	ME	D+	D+	D	100.8	-1.19	5.0	2.7	15.5	32.6	5.2	7.2	12.6
▼ PERKINS ST BK	WILLISTON	FL	C	B-	B-	159.5	1.00	4.4	12.9	23.9	19.0	5.8	7.8	12.8

Asset Quality Index	Non-Performing Loans as a % of Total Loans	as a % of Capital	Net Charge-offs Avg Loans	Profitability Index	Net Income ($Mil)	Return on Assets (R.O.A.)	Return on Equity (R.O.E.)	Net Interest Spread	Overhead Efficiency Ratio	Liquidity Index	Liquidity Ratio	Hot Money Ratio	Stability Index
7.8	0.00	0.0	-0.04	5.6	0.2	0.89	9.24	3.59	62.4	1.5	19.1	25.9	4.2
8.7	0.04	0.2	0.00	3.7	0.3	0.59	7.88	3.61	80.7	5.2	39.2	8.5	3.3
6.5	0.62	2.5	0.35	7.2	0.3	1.77	17.39	4.64	59.6	5.4	39.6	7.2	4.7
5.2	1.42	6.8	0.23	5.1	0.2	0.94	8.50	5.35	78.3	4.9	34.7	8.4	4.9
8.9	0.57	1.3	0.00	7.3	1.0	1.68	10.13	3.93	61.4	4.1	45.6	15.7	9.8
6.9	0.05	0.3	-0.01	10.0	0.6	1.93	15.42	5.91	52.6	3.0	24.0	14.9	6.3
2.2	2.07	15.5	0.00	3.9	0.2	0.88	9.72	4.32	63.1	2.5	33.9	21.5	3.4
0.7	5.45	25.9	2.44	1.0	0.0	0.34	4.08	5.63	84.5	2.3	51.3	30.5	3.2
8.1	0.23	1.3	0.60	5.0	0.4	1.07	10.79	3.91	63.1	3.6	33.6	14.7	4.7
6.1	0.53	3.0	0.02	7.5	0.5	1.64	17.17	3.69	52.2	4.2	22.1	8.2	6.8
6.8	2.00	7.6	0.02	4.2	0.1	0.70	5.59	4.27	81.1	3.9	21.1	9.7	4.9
3.6	1.51	11.2	0.37	4.9	0.2	0.80	9.62	4.38	66.7	4.4	56.8	15.7	3.0
7.8	0.56	2.8	0.00	4.4	0.3	0.92	8.04	3.42	63.4	4.2	99.2	28.6	6.2
7.9	1.18	3.9	0.08	6.0	0.7	1.14	9.92	3.56	56.4	6.1	87.3	12.9	6.6
2.4	3.24	19.1	0.06	6.3	1.3	1.24	14.70	3.74	49.3	6.0	63.0	10.4	4.7
4.5	2.05	10.5	0.83	3.9	0.8	0.85	9.17	3.83	78.6	3.0	14.2	13.9	5.0
6.0	1.09	4.0	0.14	10.0	0.4	5.00	24.01	7.32	42.9	4.3	34.5	9.2	6.6
4.0	1.05	8.9	-0.14	6.6	0.2	1.13	13.74	5.46	64.9	1.2	19.6	29.8	2.8
4.4	0.93	6.1	0.14	4.7	1.3	0.97	11.99	4.05	69.0	3.4	18.1	12.2	3.7
4.1	1.25	9.8	0.46	6.1	1.9	0.92	9.54	4.58	70.9	2.7	25.6	16.8	5.9
5.7	0.65	3.6	0.33	4.0	0.1	0.67	6.72	3.92	82.2	5.3	43.7	6.1	3.3
5.3	0.75	5.8	0.37	4.1	0.1	0.70	8.89	4.25	73.6	4.0	34.7	11.2	1.7
7.3	1.18	3.5	0.06	4.5	0.1	1.04	5.92	4.34	71.2	5.2	41.3	9.0	6.7
8.2	0.01	0.0	0.00	7.8	0.3	1.60	16.86	3.97	55.4	3.2	18.4	13.3	6.2
5.1	1.73	8.9	-0.10	5.8	0.1	1.56	16.94	4.27	69.7	4.5	32.4	7.7	3.6
1.4	2.08	24.0	0.09	2.2	0.1	0.44	6.30	2.38	78.6	3.0	10.9	13.5	4.4
4.0	2.69	12.0	-0.17	10.0	0.8	2.94	18.13	4.75	37.9	4.4	30.5	10.1	8.8
5.0	0.77	5.7	0.22	6.3	0.2	1.29	16.25	3.86	61.7	1.7	25.3	24.3	5.0
7.0	1.52	6.0	0.42	4.0	0.5	0.84	7.43	4.10	75.1	2.4	30.7	19.8	5.2
9.4	1.40	2.0	-0.05	4.9	0.7	1.01	7.60	2.93	51.4	5.1	100.2	19.4	7.2
9.2	0.06	0.2	0.00	8.7	0.4	2.09	17.87	3.54	44.2	1.8	22.1	21.6	6.3
8.4	0.05	0.3	-0.01	5.5	0.3	1.04	15.33	4.26	67.4	1.6	17.0	24.1	3.3
8.4	0.22	1.1	0.13	5.2	0.3	1.18	9.57	3.98	71.2	7.4	85.6	3.1	5.7
4.8	0.62	5.2	0.04	8.4	0.6	1.31	14.19	4.43	60.5	3.6	17.9	11.2	5.3
6.2	0.36	2.8	0.01	6.9	1.9	1.54	16.54	3.37	52.5	1.0	24.9	39.4	6.7
4.8	0.89	8.2	0.07	5.9	1.8	0.85	11.13	3.68	64.1	0.8	12.1	33.8	4.1
8.6	0.12	0.8	0.21	5.8	0.7	1.05	11.59	4.07	65.7	3.3	11.7	12.0	5.4
2.4	2.80	13.0	0.03	8.0	0.4	2.82	22.77	4.36	52.4	6.5	68.6	4.1	4.7
6.2	0.39	2.2	0.10	5.7	0.5	1.02	9.69	4.11	56.0	6.0	65.7	9.0	6.0
8.3	0.05	0.3	-0.11	7.8	0.2	1.30	11.28	4.37	57.8	6.2	78.4	8.2	4.5
4.0	2.23	12.5	0.00	1.7	0.0	0.09	1.10	3.17	92.9	6.4	79.5	7.4	1.8
4.8	0.56	2.7	-0.15	5.3	0.4	0.90	7.12	5.12	83.3	5.2	50.1	10.6	6.9
9.9	0.18	0.5	-1.08	7.0	0.1	1.83	18.85	4.30	54.4	7.2	147.6	11.4	4.0
3.6	1.66	10.5	0.08	6.6	0.6	1.16	11.10	4.96	65.2	3.6	32.5	14.7	6.7
5.2	1.28	8.0	0.17	6.4	0.8	1.52	15.74	4.17	66.4	4.2	22.8	8.4	5.8
3.7	1.39	12.0	1.69	4.8	0.6	0.71	9.37	4.18	71.2	3.1	17.7	13.7	1.6
5.1	1.51	9.5	0.00	4.9	0.1	1.10	15.21	4.25	68.6	3.9	40.1	12.9	5.1
3.3	2.32	13.6	1.16	6.9	0.3	1.30	15.56	3.94	58.4	2.7	5.6	14.5	5.6
5.9	1.45	6.5	0.84	6.4	0.2	1.19	9.36	5.05	66.7	5.8	44.0	5.4	6.3
6.3	0.33	2.6	-0.01	5.4	0.5	0.92	10.14	3.66	64.2	3.5	27.2	13.3	5.3
6.7	0.27	2.1	0.15	5.3	0.6	1.47	17.96	3.07	56.8	2.9	53.3	28.6	4.0
6.7	0.23	2.3	0.00	5.0	0.4	0.81	12.35	4.39	66.5	2.1	25.5	19.9	2.8
5.5	1.66	10.4	0.51	2.2	0.2	0.42	3.41	3.62	87.4	6.7	193.4	18.3	5.8
5.6	0.65	4.2	0.11	5.6	0.7	0.72	6.11	3.92	72.3	0.9	22.3	36.6	7.1
6.8	0.31	2.6	0.18	5.3	0.7	1.01	11.50	4.24	61.8	2.9	25.9	15.7	4.4
9.4	0.02	0.1	0.00	9.5	0.2	2.14	18.10	4.75	49.6	5.3	32.5	2.3	7.0
8.7	0.26	0.5	-0.01	1.9	-0.1	-0.17	-0.70	2.99	104.4	6.1	68.3	10.3	7.8
5.1	2.82	12.8	0.34	5.4	1.0	0.94	7.26	5.24	67.2	5.0	33.8	7.0	7.5
3.6	0.66	3.3	0.13	1.9	0.1	0.08	0.73	0.50	79.3	4.0	22.3	9.6	4.2
6.5	2.48	4.7	0.07	9.7	0.5	1.79	6.86	4.37	42.0	6.9	62.8	2.4	8.5
9.4	0.06	0.4	0.02	5.2	4.2	0.91	9.11	3.37	63.4	4.4	24.2	7.3	6.9
1.9	2.69	22.8	0.11	8.8	1.1	2.06	29.22	4.56	53.6	4.8	13.4	3.0	5.3
5.4	0.95	7.8	0.15	2.5	0.0	0.08	1.21	3.12	82.4	1.8	16.1	20.4	2.0
1.8	4.03	30.5	0.09	5.4	1.0	1.23	15.12	4.98	70.9	2.6	23.6	16.8	4.7

Name	City	State	Weiss Safety Rating	2003 Weiss Safety Rating	2002 Weiss Safety Rating	Total Assets ($Mil)	One Year Asset Growth	Asset Mix (As a % of Total Assets)				Capital-ization Index	Leverage Ratio	Risk-based Capital Ratio
								Comm-ercial Loans	Cons-umer Loans	Home Mort-gages	Secur-ities			
PERPETUAL FSB	URBANA	OH	A-	A-	A-	323.7	6.50	3.3	1.4	29.0	0.0	10.0	16.1	20.6
PERPETUAL SVG BK	WELLSVILLE	OH	B-	B-	C+	65.9	5.61	0.5	3.8	25.7	31.8	6.9	8.9	13.9
PERRY ST BK	PERRY	MO	C+	C+	C+	132.1	5.62	8.5	9.1	12.1	13.4	4.9	8.1	11.0
PERRYTON NB	PERRYTON	TX	A-	A-	A-	69.8	7.85	7.9	9.9	2.9	45.6	10.0	11.7	22.3
PERU FSB	PERU	IL	B	B	B	108.9	5.61	0.8	2.6	48.3	29.5	10.0	11.2	18.8
▲ PESHTIGO NB	PESHTIGO	WI	B	B-	B-	58.3	-0.10	8.4	4.1	18.5	35.6	8.1	9.8	17.3
PETEFISH SKILES & CO	VIRGINIA	IL	A-	A-	A-	95.9	8.93	8.2	9.6	16.5	36.4	8.9	10.3	16.3
▲ PETERSBURG ST BK	PETERSBURG	NE	C-	D+	D	22.2	-0.06	4.1	5.2	1.1	17.0	8.4	9.9	15.6
PETIT JEAN ST BK	MORRILTON	AR	D	D	D	92.6	-6.87	7.7	18.4	34.6	9.8	9.2	10.5	16.2
PFF B&T	POMONA	CA	B+	B+	A-	3,606.9	16.87	4.7	1.1	43.6	8.6	5.3	7.9	11.2
PHELPS COUNTY BK	ROLLA	MO	B	B	B	206.4	9.48	6.0	3.5	39.7	24.6	5.3	7.3	13.7
▲ PHENIX-GIRARD BK	PHENIX CITY	AL	A+	A	A	121.2	8.27	7.4	2.5	9.4	29.4	10.0	13.3	21.8
▲ PHILADELPHIA TRUST CO	PHILADELPHIA	PA	B	B-	B-	23.0	-0.73	14.6	8.3	15.6	28.8	10.0	37.2	58.8
PHILO EXCHANGE BK	PHILO	IL	B	B	B	35.7	4.92	9.7	5.5	17.7	22.6	10.0	14.0	19.2
PHOENIX SVG BK	LYNNWOOD	WA	B+	A-	B	84.8	-43.63	0.0	13.0	41.6	0.0	10.0	15.5	24.0
PHOENIXVILLE FEDERAL BANK	PHOENIXVILLE	PA	B-	B-	B-	316.2	7.93	3.9	0.8	35.3	35.9	8.3	9.8	18.6
▲ PIEDMONT BK OF GEORGIA	ATLANTA	GA	C-	D+	D-	137.8	14.54	24.6	0.7	0.6	14.9	5.7	8.6	11.5
PIEDMONT COMMUNITY BK	GRAY	GA	D	D	D	45.1	101.03	22.1	2.9	15.6	9.9	10.0	15.0	17.3
PIEDMONT FS&LA	WINSTON-SALEM	NC	A	A	A	849.0	-0.03	0.0	0.1	51.6	22.4	10.0	19.9	55.2
PIER 1 NB	OMAHA	NE	C+	C+	C+	2.7	1.98	0.0	0.0	0.0	94.2	10.0	79.5	368.0
PIERCE CMRL BK	TACOMA	WA	B-	C+	C-	140.4	26.93	21.3	3.4	19.0	0.7	5.4	8.2	11.3
PIGEON FALLS ST BK	PIGEON FALLS	WI	D	D-	E+	40.8	7.77	10.0	5.0	18.1	20.9	5.8	8.3	11.6
PIGGOTT ST BK	PIGGOTT	AR	B-	B-	B-	62.3	-1.50	10.8	5.6	18.8	37.5	7.3	9.2	18.2
▲ PIKE COUNTY NB	MCCOMB	MS	A-	B	B	139.1	-2.54	12.1	14.2	15.1	15.6	10.0	11.3	18.0
PIKES PEAK NB	COLORADO SPRINGS	CO	B+	B+	A-	84.0	-0.46	5.6	10.0	3.6	1.3	7.6	9.4	16.3
▲ PILGRIM BK	PITTSBURG	TX	D+	D	D-	238.1	3.15	11.8	7.4	21.8	11.6	4.6	7.4	10.8
PILGRIM CO-OP BK	HALIFAX	MA	C+	C+	C+	128.3	7.99	0.0	0.9	48.5	28.1	6.1	8.1	14.2
PILOT GROVE SVG BK	PILOT GROVE	IA	B	B-	B-	198.8	2.90	5.8	4.0	31.0	17.1	6.9	8.9	13.0
▲ PILSEN ST BK	LINCOLNVILLE	KS	D+	D	D	10.4	8.65	5.3	3.5	9.1	2.9	10.0	14.3	17.8
▲ PINE BLUFF NB	PINE BLUFF	AR	B-	C	C	259.9	10.65	8.4	8.7	8.0	21.3	7.5	10.2	12.9
▼ PINE CITY ST BK	PINE CITY	MN	D	D+	D+	62.7	2.44	7.9	6.5	25.4	5.5	5.9	8.2	11.7
▲ PINE COUNTRY BK	ROYALTON	MN	B-	C+	C	65.1	12.15	12.1	4.1	11.8	36.0	5.7	7.7	12.1
PINE ISLAND BK	PINE ISLAND	MN	B	B	B+	42.6	-0.90	5.4	2.0	5.7	30.7	6.6	8.6	13.4
PINE RIVER ST BK	PINE RIVER	MN	B-	C+	C-	74.7	4.00	8.3	3.7	17.7	21.6	6.0	8.0	13.6
PINE RIVER VALLEY BK	BAYFIELD	CO	B	A-	B+	105.8	28.25	3.9	4.3	15.4	39.3	5.1	7.1	11.6
▲ PINE ST BK	KINGSLAND	AR	E+	E	E-	17.9	-0.01	11.4	10.4	32.9	18.2	6.2	8.2	16.1
PINEBANK NA	MIAMI	FL	B	B	B	387.3	8.16	6.2	0.6	41.7	6.3	6.4	8.4	29.7
PINEHURST BK	ST PAUL	MN	D	NR	NR	10.4	N/A	2.9	0.5	26.4	0.0	10.0	176.7	149.5
PINELAND ST BK	METTER	GA	B-	B-	B-	61.5	-3.89	33.9	11.0	8.1	11.5	7.8	9.6	13.6
▲ PINERIES BK	STEVENS POINT	WI	C	C-	D+	40.2	4.51	1.6	4.1	43.9	3.0	6.4	8.4	14.3
▲ PINNACLE BK	JASPER	AL	B-	C+	C	210.4	-4.78	4.6	6.4	13.8	41.3	7.5	9.3	17.7
▲ PINNACLE BK	ORANGE CITY	FL	D+	D-	D	70.6	15.61	10.9	9.5	2.9	12.5	5.4	8.6	11.3
PINNACLE BK	ELBERTON	GA	A	A	A	373.5	7.27	4.4	5.5	12.7	23.9	10.0	11.5	16.0
PINNACLE BK	PAPILLION	NE	B	B	B	1,682.1	2.44	10.6	3.9	12.8	15.2	5.6	8.5	11.5
PINNACLE BK	BEAVERTON	OR	D	D	D	34.6	179.55	32.4	1.9	2.3	0.0	8.3	13.3	13.6
▼ PINNACLE BK WY	TORRINGTON	WY	B	B+	B+	338.0	0.82	11.4	6.1	11.4	19.3	4.9	7.7	11.0
▲ PINNACLE NB	NASHVILLE	TN	C	D+	D+	585.8	45.31	25.8	2.3	10.2	28.1	4.5	8.1	10.8
▲ PIONEER B&T	PONCA CITY	OK	B+	B	B-	171.0	1.20	26.0	6.3	12.0	14.8	8.0	9.6	15.4
▼ PIONEER B&TC	MAPLEWOOD	MO	C+	B-	B-	388.7	42.09	3.2	0.4	11.3	21.7	4.7	7.6	10.8
PIONEER B&TC	BELLE FOURCHE	SD	A	A	A-	284.0	1.33	9.9	3.7	5.5	46.7	9.1	10.4	18.6
▲ PIONEER BK	SERGEANT BLUFF	IA	B	B-	B-	95.8	2.98	26.1	5.8	13.6	28.4	7.9	9.6	15.3
PIONEER BK	CANMER	KY	B-	B-	C+	66.5	-4.05	7.0	5.3	21.0	8.8	7.6	9.4	13.8
▲ PIONEER BK	MAPLETON	MN	B	B-	B-	155.5	2.65	18.7	2.8	9.8	3.2	5.2	9.3	11.1
PIONEER BK	ROSWELL	NM	C+	C+	C+	458.1	5.81	1.2	1.5	50.1	32.4	5.1	7.1	17.5
PIONEER BK	STANLEY	VA	B-	B-	B-	120.5	5.87	4.1	11.4	33.9	11.7	6.6	8.6	14.6
PIONEER BK	AUBURNDALE	WI	C-	C-	C+	99.8	-2.58	8.6	4.7	19.3	33.8	8.9	10.3	18.3
PIONEER CMNTY BK	IAEGER	WV	B	B	B-	56.1	8.18	6.0	12.6	48.9	8.3	10.0	12.5	19.2
PIONEER FS&LA	DEER LODGE	MT	B+	B+	B+	69.5	1.26	0.0	6.0	62.6	19.1	10.0	14.3	29.3
PIONEER NB OF DULUTH	DULUTH	MN	C+	C+	C	69.7	-2.52	24.9	1.5	18.9	14.4	7.5	9.3	13.7
PIONEER NB OF LADYSMITH	LADYSMITH	WI	B-	B-	B	60.3	-1.76	7.8	3.0	3.9	52.0	6.5	8.5	13.8
PIONEER SAVINGS BK	CLEVELAND	OH	B	B	B	25.5	4.59	0.0	0.5	47.0	21.0	10.0	20.9	57.2
PIONEER SVGS BK	TROY	NY	C+	C+	C+	667.6	5.20	1.5	2.2	39.3	33.9	8.9	10.3	22.7
PIONEER TR BK NA	SALEM	OR	A+	A+	A+	214.0	-0.01	10.1	1.0	8.9	29.4	10.0	12.5	19.1
▲ PIQUA ST BK	PIQUA	KS	C-	D+	D+	22.1	4.06	3.0	10.3	7.6	46.2	8.5	10.0	19.4

Asset Quality Index	Non-Performing Loans as a % of Total Loans	Non-Performing Loans as a % of Capital	Net Charge-offs Avg Loans	Profitability Index	Net Income ($Mil)	Return on Assets (R.O.A.)	Return on Equity (R.O.E.)	Net Interest Spread	Overhead Efficiency Ratio	Liquidity Index	Liquidity Ratio	Hot Money Ratio	Stability Index
5.6	0.72	3.9	0.00	9.7	2.5	1.60	9.73	3.38	28.7	1.3	8.2	25.6	9.3
5.4	0.64	4.3	0.02	6.5	0.5	1.47	15.86	3.90	65.3	6.6	88.4	8.9	6.0
3.7	1.27	9.9	0.13	4.2	0.4	0.64	6.88	3.96	69.5	1.7	11.7	20.8	5.6
8.2	0.19	0.7	0.02	8.9	0.7	2.07	17.61	4.23	51.7	1.4	26.8	30.4	7.5
6.3	1.13	5.7	0.07	4.1	0.3	0.64	5.61	2.70	66.3	2.4	34.1	22.5	6.5
6.4	0.85	4.7	0.09	8.0	0.5	1.73	17.75	4.43	55.9	3.5	39.4	17.1	5.7
7.7	0.24	1.2	0.08	7.0	0.5	1.00	8.87	4.88	51.6	4.2	11.5	6.8	7.0
4.9	0.67	4.5	-0.11	6.9	0.1	1.25	12.97	3.92	52.2	2.8	32.1	16.5	3.1
0.6	3.88	26.0	2.52	5.4	0.4	0.89	8.64	5.14	48.7	1.8	25.6	23.0	3.3
7.7	0.30	3.0	-0.08	8.7	22.4	1.26	16.07	4.00	49.0	0.5	3.5	46.4	7.4
8.9	0.03	0.3	0.17	6.0	1.4	1.37	18.91	3.98	68.6	6.5	67.9	8.2	5.0
8.8	0.36	1.4	0.43	9.4	1.4	2.28	17.63	4.18	58.3	5.1	45.2	10.6	9.2
7.9	0.00	0.0	0.00	10.0	0.7	6.46	17.15	3.08	64.1	5.2	31,730.0	71.0	6.3
7.1	0.01	0.0	-0.01	6.3	0.3	1.45	8.04	4.07	64.1	5.7	68.1	11.4	7.6
5.0	1.16	5.8	0.02	7.4	0.4	0.99	5.84	5.19	91.3	3.2	50.8	22.0	9.2
5.4	0.76	3.5	-0.01	4.1	0.9	0.59	5.34	3.18	74.6	1.5	14.0	24.4	7.0
7.7	0.00	0.0	-0.03	2.5	0.5	0.74	8.59	3.63	74.2	2.9	39.8	20.6	1.5
8.2	0.00	0.0	0.00	0.3	0.0	0.07	0.45	3.44	84.5	3.7	48.4	18.1	0.0
9.1	0.21	0.5	0.00	6.0	3.5	0.82	4.02	2.72	50.3	3.3	57.7	28.1	9.2
10.0	0.00	0.0	0.00	7.0	0.0	2.20	2.80	1.11	90.2	5.0	N/A	0.0	0.0
8.3	0.00	0.0	-0.04	5.8	0.6	0.88	11.05	4.16	63.4	4.5	86.2	22.2	4.3
3.9	1.42	10.7	-0.01	3.5	0.1	0.57	6.86	4.43	77.9	7.0	69.8	3.3	2.3
7.1	0.00	0.0	0.12	6.4	0.3	1.04	11.39	4.05	59.2	3.6	40.1	16.8	4.3
7.5	0.43	2.3	0.37	7.0	0.8	1.14	10.24	7.07	67.8	4.4	49.2	15.4	5.8
4.7	1.31	6.7	0.40	10.0	1.0	2.43	25.39	5.05	58.2	7.4	113.1	7.9	6.9
4.3	0.89	8.9	0.31	4.1	1.0	0.81	11.28	4.34	64.7	1.2	12.5	28.4	2.4
6.9	0.56	4.4	0.00	3.2	0.3	0.46	5.75	2.82	73.4	3.5	48.9	19.9	4.4
5.4	0.58	4.0	0.06	7.8	1.3	1.28	12.67	4.00	50.6	4.4	19.8	6.6	6.2
3.3	2.19	11.3	0.41	2.5	0.0	0.75	5.21	4.72	84.6	5.1	77.6	13.9	3.0
5.2	0.58	3.7	0.30	4.7	1.0	0.78	7.49	4.38	75.6	2.7	19.2	16.1	4.5
1.0	3.98	37.6	0.03	7.7	0.6	1.87	22.49	4.57	58.2	4.0	21.6	9.6	3.7
4.7	1.27	8.9	0.06	9.1	0.5	1.62	20.96	5.35	53.8	3.6	12.7	10.8	4.5
0.0	9.63	34.2	1.49	4.1	0.2	1.05	8.28	4.42	71.9	5.9	38.6	3.2	5.6
6.2	0.57	4.0	0.11	5.9	0.5	1.18	14.16	4.31	72.2	6.3	66.7	7.1	5.7
9.0	0.00	0.0	0.02	7.6	0.6	1.22	15.72	4.44	60.5	2.3	31.4	21.3	5.5
4.5	1.16	7.4	1.38	4.2	0.1	1.06	12.89	5.54	73.4	3.4	76.4	26.5	0.0
7.6	0.32	2.9	-0.03	5.1	1.3	0.67	8.08	3.27	71.5	0.9	20.5	37.8	4.7
10.0	0.00	0.0	0.00	0.0	-0.3	-7.28	-9.38	0.92	642.6	9.6	1,111.6	2.8	0.0
2.5	1.03	5.9	0.55	3.8	0.2	0.68	6.19	4.75	71.9	3.7	51.5	18.4	5.0
4.5	1.15	8.6	0.21	8.3	0.2	1.16	12.94	4.57	61.6	6.1	85.4	11.6	3.6
7.4	0.30	1.6	0.23	5.8	1.0	0.96	10.57	3.88	60.3	0.9	23.6	37.8	4.2
3.9	1.43	10.6	-0.01	2.1	0.1	0.31	3.09	3.50	83.0	1.2	23.0	31.9	4.0
7.2	0.55	2.9	0.30	9.5	4.4	2.38	19.83	4.84	52.1	2.9	20.5	15.0	9.1
5.5	0.77	5.6	-0.01	9.0	12.7	1.54	16.43	4.30	53.2	6.0	52.1	10.0	7.5
6.9	0.00	0.0	0.00	1.2	0.1	0.39	2.64	5.19	75.5	4.6	59.3	15.2	0.0
4.3	1.10	9.3	0.10	8.6	2.2	1.32	16.52	4.55	61.3	5.3	55.5	12.5	6.7
8.3	0.01	0.1	0.03	4.2	2.4	0.87	11.96	3.51	63.6	1.3	24.3	29.7	2.6
7.3	0.21	1.3	0.25	7.0	0.9	1.07	11.20	4.24	63.6	3.5	47.9	19.4	6.4
7.8	0.00	0.0	0.00	4.7	1.8	1.02	13.98	3.32	64.4	5.3	38.2	7.1	3.7
8.5	0.35	1.5	0.00	9.3	2.4	1.67	14.83	4.34	50.4	6.6	95.2	11.6	7.7
8.3	0.13	0.8	-0.22	6.9	0.7	1.49	16.54	4.50	64.9	3.4	15.6	12.2	6.1
3.6	1.25	8.4	-0.01	8.0	0.7	2.12	20.10	4.40	66.0	2.4	17.9	17.2	6.6
4.9	0.46	4.0	0.02	9.9	1.7	2.24	23.10	4.80	49.7	1.3	6.2	24.3	6.5
5.4	0.70	5.9	0.00	7.6	2.5	1.10	15.88	3.02	54.8	0.8	14.5	36.3	3.8
5.8	0.38	2.8	0.19	6.4	0.8	1.25	14.12	5.35	68.8	5.8	51.4	8.4	4.6
1.9	4.58	23.3	0.04	3.7	0.2	0.45	4.44	4.47	83.0	3.8	21.0	10.8	5.3
4.8	1.52	8.8	0.01	8.7	0.4	1.37	10.16	5.84	63.5	4.1	23.2	9.3	6.8
8.8	0.12	0.6	0.03	5.1	0.3	0.79	5.60	3.45	66.0	1.8	14.4	19.9	7.0
6.3	0.45	3.2	0.03	5.4	0.4	1.24	12.90	5.00	76.3	5.7	33.7	2.3	4.6
5.6	1.32	5.5	0.06	7.2	0.5	1.60	17.13	4.61	59.0	5.7	42.6	5.9	5.9
10.0	0.32	0.8	0.00	5.5	0.1	1.05	5.07	4.83	69.5	2.5	N/A	15.1	3.0
9.6	0.16	0.8	0.05	3.5	1.6	0.50	4.87	3.10	76.6	7.1	86.2	6.8	6.5
8.2	0.53	2.3	0.01	10.0	2.9	2.67	20.05	5.03	35.8	5.8	34.7	2.2	9.6
3.1	5.22	20.4	0.65	4.3	0.1	0.78	7.72	4.30	77.8	5.6	67.9	9.8	3.6

Name	City	State	Weiss Safety Rating	2003 Weiss Safety Rating	2002 Weiss Safety Rating	Total Assets ($Mil)	One Year Asset Growth	Asset Mix (As a % of Total Assets)				Capital-ization Index	Leverage Ratio	Risk-based Capital Ratio
								Comm-ercial Loans	Cons-umer Loans	Home Mort-gages	Secur-ities			
PISCATAQUA SVGS BK	PORTSMOUTH	NH	A-	A-	A	173.0	-2.14	0.0	0.9	43.0	43.3	10.0	17.1	44.7
PITNEY BOWES BK	SALT LAKE CITY	UT	B	B+	B+	542.1	7.57	61.1	0.0	0.0	31.8	5.7	7.7	11.8
PITTSFIELD CO-OP BK	PITTSFIELD	MA	B	B	B	203.7	-0.52	4.2	0.5	37.7	31.9	10.0	15.1	28.5
PLACER SIERRA BK	AUBURN	CA	B+	B	B-	986.3	1.93	5.8	0.7	10.2	12.1	6.9	8.9	12.6
▲ PLAINS COMMERCE BK	HOVEN	SD	B-	C	B	206.7	4.03	11.0	6.1	3.8	24.4	10.0	11.9	16.5
PLAINS ST BK	PLAINS CITY	KS	A-	A-	A-	47.3	1.96	10.8	4.2	3.7	16.3	10.0	13.6	18.4
▲ PLAINS ST BK	PLAINS	TX	C+	C	C	18.1	-4.35	3.0	4.3	3.8	34.2	10.0	13.3	29.2
PLAINSCAPITAL BK	LUBBOCK	TX	C+	B-	B-	2,176.8	4.73	21.1	2.1	11.3	8.7	3.8	7.8	10.4
PLANTATION FEDERAL BANK	PAWLEY'S ISLAND	SC	C+	C+	C+	286.2	12.68	2.5	3.1	41.1	16.8	5.0	7.0	12.1
PLANTERS & CITIZENS BK	CAMILLA	GA	A-	A-	B+	81.7	6.95	7.9	4.6	5.4	33.2	10.0	12.7	18.5
PLANTERS & MERCHANTS BK	GILLETT	AR	C+	C+	C+	28.3	2.91	5.4	7.9	9.6	41.5	10.0	12.2	22.9
▼ PLANTERS & MERCHANTS ST	HEARNE	TX	A-	A	A	181.5	7.24	4.8	10.6	16.2	18.9	10.0	11.0	19.9
PLANTERS B&TC	INDIANOLA	MS	B	B	B	421.9	4.18	12.1	7.8	16.9	27.7	7.5	9.4	15.1
PLANTERS B&TC OF VA	STAUNTON	VA	B-	B-	B	770.0	37.51	4.8	2.4	18.7	22.3	5.4	7.4	11.4
PLANTERS BK	HOPKINSVILLE	KY	C	C	D+	210.4	17.58	14.2	4.2	20.3	5.4	4.9	8.8	10.9
▲ PLANTERS BK OF MAURY CITY	MAURY CITY	TN	D	D-	D	25.4	-12.20	3.3	12.1	26.9	7.0	9.1	10.4	17.7
PLANTERSFIRST	CORDELE	GA	C+	C+	B-	304.8	8.77	13.5	6.7	14.8	15.2	7.0	9.0	12.7
PLAQUEMINE B&TC	PLAQUEMINE	LA	A-	A-	B+	82.2	-2.70	9.3	8.8	15.2	24.4	10.0	14.3	22.2
PLATINUM BK	BRANDON	FL	C+	C+	C+	212.4	20.19	15.3	1.2	6.0	24.5	3.5	7.2	10.3
▲ PLATINUM COMMUNITY BK	ROLLING MEADOWS	IL	D	D-	D-	134.3	15.52	0.1	0.7	34.0	30.3	6.2	8.3	17.2
PLATTE CENTER BK	PLATTE CENTER	NE	D+	D	D	5.5	-2.85	7.0	6.7	9.1	9.6	9.9	10.9	17.0
PLATTE VALLEY BK	N BEND	NE	B+	B+	B+	43.6	-1.59	18.0	3.3	4.6	29.3	10.0	21.6	28.6
▲ PLATTE VALLEY BK OF MO	PLATTE CITY	MO	B	C+	B	217.1	15.75	10.3	3.2	23.0	14.1	6.2	8.5	11.9
PLATTE VALLEY NB	SCOTTSBLUFF	NE	B-	B-	B-	261.7	7.97	18.8	5.7	29.6	5.6	6.8	8.8	12.4
PLATTE VALLEY NB	TORRINGTON	WY	B-	B-	B-	90.5	5.40	6.0	3.3	24.2	10.3	3.9	7.7	10.5
PLATTE VALLEY ST B&TC	KEARNEY	NE	C	C	C	386.2	2.58	14.6	31.7	3.3	14.4	5.0	7.8	11.0
PLATTSMOUTH ST BK	PLATTSMOUTH	NE	B-	B-	C+	75.7	-1.51	10.2	3.0	8.6	39.3	6.7	8.7	14.4
PLAZA BK	NORRIDGE	IL	B-	B-	B-	350.5	19.96	3.2	0.4	15.7	18.3	7.0	9.0	12.7
PLAZA PARK ST BK	WAITE PARK	MN	B+	B+	B	116.3	0.48	7.8	5.5	16.8	17.7	6.8	8.8	12.6
PLEASANT HILL BK	PLEASANT HILL	MO	B-	B	B	71.0	0.17	1.4	4.5	18.8	48.7	10.0	11.4	29.2
PLEASANTS COUNTY BK	ST MARYS	WV	B	B	B	46.9	-2.77	6.0	13.7	19.1	37.8	10.0	12.4	23.0
PLEASANTVILLE ST BK	PLEASANTVILLE	IA	B+	B+	B+	28.3	-0.11	3.2	6.1	8.4	61.7	10.0	15.7	39.3
PLUMAS BK	QUINCY	CA	B-	B-	C+	403.9	24.08	11.8	6.4	4.5	28.2	5.1	7.6	11.1
PLUS INTERNATIONAL BK	MIAMI	FL	C	C-	D	63.3	32.30	65.0	1.2	0.0	26.5	10.0	14.6	116.1
▼ PLYMOUTH SVGS BK	WAREHAM	MA	B	A-	A-	1,470.8	-4.91	3.2	2.4	19.2	46.2	7.8	9.5	18.5
PMI BK GREAT FALLS	GREAT FALLS	MT	D	D	D	16.7	68.39	14.3	18.6	5.3	8.9	10.0	17.4	18.8
PNC BK NA	PITTSBURGH	PA	B	B	B	67,526.8	11.26	18.8	4.6	15.5	20.7	5.8	7.8	11.9
▼ PNC BK, DELAWARE	WILMINGTON	DE	B	B+	B+	2,602.2	2.59	10.9	2.0	30.6	29.2	5.0	7.0	15.0
▲ POCA VALLEY BK	WALTON	WV	C+	C	C-	201.5	0.02	8.8	11.9	32.2	12.9	5.8	7.8	12.8
▲ POCAHONTAS ST BK	POCAHONTAS	IA	A	A-	B+	57.9	4.04	4.1	2.2	6.9	39.2	9.3	10.5	16.9
POCONO CMNTY BK	STROUDSBURG	PA	B+	B	B	121.9	8.51	6.6	0.1	26.6	21.2	7.8	9.5	16.5
POINTBANK	PILOT POINT	TX	C+	C+	C+	213.1	14.79	6.8	5.1	7.3	24.5	4.8	6.8	11.6
POINTE BANK	BOCA RATON	FL	B-	B-	C+	373.6	13.91	10.8	2.0	21.8	18.7	6.1	8.3	11.8
POINTPATHBANK NA	COLUMBUS	GA	B	B	B	6.2	1.14	0.0	0.0	0.0	0.0	10.0	94.9	340.1
▲ POLK COUNTY BK	JOHNSTON	IA	D+	D-	D-	108.5	12.18	18.9	2.7	14.4	5.1	3.5	7.7	10.2
▲ POLONIA BK	PHILADELPHIA	PA	C-	D	D	179.8	-4.75	0.1	1.9	46.6	36.1	5.5	7.5	16.5
▲ PONCE DE LEON FEDERAL BK	NEW YORK CITY	NY	D+	D-	D	557.1	12.34	4.9	1.1	32.9	1.7	5.6	7.6	11.6
▲ PONTIAC NB	PONTIAC	IL	B-	C+	C+	243.7	8.43	6.3	2.6	15.7	30.4	5.9	7.9	13.4
▲ PONTOTOC COUNTY BK	ROFF	OK	C-	C-	C	28.2	-0.48	16.2	16.0	19.7	24.8	9.3	10.5	19.1
PONY EXPRESS BK	BRAYMER	MO	C+	C+	B	103.0	18.22	12.9	4.7	18.7	8.6	3.7	7.6	10.4
PONY EXPRESS COMMUNITY	ST JOSEPH	MO	C-	C-	D+	33.7	3.82	8.2	5.6	28.6	25.8	5.7	7.7	13.9
POPLAR GROVE ST BK	POPLAR GROVE	IL	A-	A-	A-	61.2	8.35	7.8	1.6	12.8	40.5	10.0	17.2	35.2
▼ PORT AUSTIN ST BK	PORT AUSTIN	MI	B+	A-	A-	32.8	5.22	4.8	6.7	42.7	9.2	10.0	17.1	29.3
PORT BYRON ST BK	PORT BYRON	IL	B-	B-	B-	72.2	2.46	10.0	4.3	12.7	17.7	9.4	10.6	15.4
▲ PORT CITY CAPITAL BK	WILMINGTON	NC	D	D-	D	91.1	76.89	6.0	0.1	7.8	9.9	6.8	9.6	12.3
PORT RICHMOND SVGS	PHILADELPHIA	PA	B	B	B	45.7	8.53	4.8	0.0	83.5	0.2	10.0	13.5	25.1
▲ PORT WASHINGTON ST BK	PORT WASHINGTON	WI	B-	C+	C+	239.0	0.97	19.8	3.0	22.1	18.2	5.1	7.6	11.0
PORTAGE COMMERCE BK	PORTAGE	MI	C-	C-	C-	173.5	17.29	18.9	1.9	15.7	1.2	3.1	8.2	10.1
PORTAGE COMMUNITY BK	RAVENNA	OH	C	C-	D+	118.3	18.21	18.4	4.0	28.0	2.7	3.7	8.2	10.3
PORTAGE COUNTY BK	ALMOND	WI	B+	B	B	56.2	-5.14	9.5	2.7	25.0	14.7	10.0	11.2	16.8
PORTAGE NB	PORTAGE	PA	C+	C+	C	211.4	5.18	6.7	4.5	22.5	43.4	6.2	8.2	15.9
▼ PORTALES NB	PORTALES	NM	B-	B	B+	102.4	14.02	4.4	11.3	11.3	31.1	7.4	9.3	18.2
PORTLAND BK	PORTLAND	AR	C-	C-	D+	65.6	2.23	6.5	5.0	17.7	24.7	6.0	8.0	13.8
▲ POSTVILLE ST BK	POSTVILLE	IA	B+	B	B	60.7	-2.96	6.9	3.5	10.2	52.9	10.0	12.0	22.9

Asset Quality Index	Non-Performing Loans as a % of Total Loans	Non-Performing Loans as a % of Capital	Net Charge-offs Avg Loans	Profitability Index	Net Income ($Mil)	Return on Assets (R.O.A.)	Return on Equity (R.O.E.)	Net Interest Spread	Overhead Efficiency Ratio	Liquidity Index	Liquidity Ratio	Hot Money Ratio	Stability Index
9.9	0.24	0.7	0.00	5.1	0.6	0.73	4.30	2.77	67.1	6.0	106.0	15.4	8.6
4.4	1.76	10.8	4.78	10.0	40.1	15.35	190.95	26.05	1.2	10.0	296.4	0.0	6.7
9.6	0.46	1.7	0.01	3.7	0.6	0.60	4.01	3.32	72.3	3.4	32.7	15.3	8.0
5.6	0.24	1.2	0.22	7.9	6.6	1.38	10.12	4.94	57.9	6.6	74.7	8.8	8.3
4.3	0.96	4.0	0.98	8.2	2.2	2.09	13.88	4.58	52.8	3.0	17.1	14.3	8.5
7.2	0.21	0.9	0.00	7.3	0.4	1.51	10.57	3.59	58.2	2.5	38.6	26.5	8.4
8.7	0.21	0.7	-0.08	5.1	0.1	1.21	9.87	3.59	69.6	4.5	53.4	13.3	4.4
6.3	0.22	1.8	0.12	7.5	12.3	1.16	13.41	4.38	79.2	1.2	17.5	31.2	6.9
8.1	0.02	0.2	0.02	5.3	1.0	0.72	10.43	2.69	62.0	0.7	17.3	49.5	4.2
7.5	1.14	4.6	-0.04	6.0	0.4	1.02	7.92	4.89	68.0	4.3	30.6	10.3	6.9
6.1	1.92	6.2	-0.39	3.5	0.1	0.67	5.68	3.80	72.4	3.0	71.5	34.9	4.5
7.9	0.40	1.9	0.38	5.9	1.1	1.25	10.36	4.09	63.9	4.7	74.0	18.3	8.3
4.5	1.21	7.5	0.32	7.3	2.7	1.27	13.25	4.11	58.1	2.2	29.8	22.0	5.8
4.8	1.02	6.7	0.08	5.6	4.0	1.02	10.64	3.78	60.2	4.0	19.2	9.2	6.2
4.8	0.54	4.9	0.26	3.7	0.5	0.52	6.06	3.71	74.1	1.6	6.7	21.0	3.1
6.2	0.49	2.4	0.73	0.7	0.0	0.20	2.00	4.16	84.0	4.5	101.5	24.7	0.7
3.8	1.24	9.2	0.11	7.6	2.7	1.83	19.78	5.09	64.2	1.6	12.1	22.4	5.1
6.0	1.31	5.5	0.02	6.0	0.4	0.97	6.97	4.36	69.3	4.5	59.6	15.8	7.5
7.4	0.00	0.0	0.00	4.9	1.3	1.26	17.49	3.51	61.8	3.5	45.5	19.1	4.2
5.2	1.43	10.0	0.00	0.8	0.0	-0.04	-0.52	2.60	100.8	1.9	27.7	24.4	2.8
5.5	1.45	7.5	0.00	4.5	0.0	1.00	9.30	3.99	68.8	6.1	72.8	7.4	3.0
8.2	0.06	0.2	-0.08	6.8	0.3	1.28	6.04	4.67	63.4	5.0	25.8	3.6	7.0
6.0	0.75	5.9	0.05	6.9	1.6	1.46	16.98	4.90	72.0	3.5	21.9	11.9	6.2
5.8	0.34	3.0	0.31	7.5	1.6	1.24	13.95	4.63	57.1	2.4	13.4	16.8	5.2
7.8	0.18	1.8	0.31	5.7	0.4	0.96	11.13	3.81	60.5	2.0	14.7	18.8	5.0
2.4	1.46	11.8	2.80	6.9	2.5	1.30	15.67	5.68	45.2	4.1	84.4	27.4	4.6
8.6	0.00	0.0	0.00	4.7	0.2	0.63	7.11	4.05	75.3	3.6	12.7	10.7	4.0
4.2	1.00	7.3	0.04	10.0	3.6	2.14	25.03	5.86	42.5	3.4	42.8	18.7	6.7
6.7	0.22	1.8	-0.12	8.7	1.3	2.15	23.74	4.50	52.4	6.0	37.6	2.0	6.8
5.3	3.55	12.0	0.17	3.0	0.1	0.36	3.11	3.05	85.7	7.7	109.0	5.0	4.9
5.4	2.09	8.4	-0.01	5.0	0.2	0.79	6.18	4.33	68.7	4.3	18.8	7.3	5.5
8.9	0.00	0.0	-0.16	6.2	0.2	1.27	7.77	3.59	57.1	5.8	108.4	15.9	7.5
5.5	0.89	6.1	0.21	6.1	1.8	0.88	11.09	4.82	72.0	7.0	84.0	7.7	4.0
6.2	1.27	5.9	0.86	2.6	0.2	0.68	4.60	4.03	75.3	1.0	28.1	57.2	1.1
8.7	0.49	2.2	0.21	4.6	5.5	0.75	7.87	3.13	73.5	3.5	15.6	11.7	8.1
7.5	0.00	0.0	0.00	0.0	-0.2	-3.09	-17.76	3.47	181.2	2.1	48.7	31.9	0.0
6.0	0.61	3.7	0.42	8.6	456.0	1.39	15.37	3.43	66.9	6.5	46.7	5.4	7.8
8.7	0.18	1.5	0.45	9.8	29.9	2.44	32.52	3.89	50.9	7.4	64.3	3.3	7.1
4.5	0.74	6.4	0.20	5.3	1.0	0.97	12.13	4.48	68.4	3.6	37.0	16.2	3.7
5.6	1.08	3.9	0.15	9.3	0.7	2.33	16.76	4.03	36.4	3.8	14.5	10.0	8.5
6.8	0.87	5.4	0.11	5.7	0.7	1.22	13.01	3.18	57.3	6.8	87.3	9.0	5.9
8.0	0.06	0.5	0.13	6.5	1.4	1.30	18.91	5.22	67.8	3.5	25.9	12.6	3.4
6.9	0.29	2.2	0.27	5.5	2.0	1.07	11.96	4.53	68.2	3.7	11.9	10.2	4.8
10.0	0.00	0.0	0.00	2.8	0.0	1.10	1.19	1.03	87.8	0.0	N/A	100.0	5.9
1.4	2.35	22.8	0.24	8.6	0.7	1.31	17.20	5.60	56.4	2.6	27.8	17.9	3.1
6.0	0.61	4.2	-0.01	2.6	0.3	0.35	4.75	2.83	82.8	2.3	12.8	17.5	2.4
2.1	1.83	18.5	0.01	10.0	3.5	1.30	16.97	5.34	51.1	1.1	16.0	30.7	5.5
4.9	0.85	5.9	0.29	5.8	1.3	1.06	12.77	3.88	68.6	3.7	12.1	10.4	4.8
3.5	1.89	9.7	0.87	3.4	0.1	0.88	8.79	4.11	75.4	3.8	82.4	28.3	2.1
5.9	0.34	2.3	0.26	7.5	1.0	2.06	17.86	4.70	52.0	1.8	7.5	19.3	5.1
5.9	1.16	8.5	0.25	4.6	0.1	0.77	9.82	4.63	78.7	5.6	35.0	3.7	3.1
6.5	3.16	7.2	-0.02	7.5	0.5	1.78	10.14	3.83	48.9	7.9	206.8	13.2	8.9
8.6	0.04	0.2	-0.02	7.1	0.2	1.26	7.14	4.19	55.2	5.5	82.1	14.2	7.0
4.6	1.26	8.3	0.02	4.4	0.3	0.71	7.16	3.97	69.0	3.7	25.4	11.7	4.8
7.5	0.00	0.0	0.00	1.6	0.3	0.73	7.79	3.27	65.4	1.4	30.6	35.9	0.0
8.7	0.50	3.4	0.00	6.2	0.4	1.55	11.66	4.62	66.2	2.9	19.0	14.8	6.4
6.6	0.21	1.9	0.12	5.9	0.9	0.72	9.32	4.05	75.4	3.6	16.7	11.0	4.0
2.0	1.37	13.6	0.36	9.8	1.3	1.52	18.97	4.63	48.0	2.0	26.9	22.5	5.3
5.8	0.50	4.6	0.01	4.3	0.4	0.68	8.17	4.24	63.0	5.3	24.2	1.1	3.7
7.6	0.68	4.1	0.11	6.5	0.4	1.45	13.46	4.24	64.7	5.6	73.6	12.7	6.6
7.9	0.32	1.8	0.06	3.4	0.7	0.65	7.68	3.24	76.6	4.1	14.0	7.8	4.1
8.3	0.06	0.3	0.29	3.9	0.3	0.56	5.75	5.67	90.1	5.5	39.0	6.5	4.8
7.6	0.47	3.1	0.02	3.2	0.0	0.02	0.30	4.09	103.8	3.8	90.6	30.8	3.0
7.0	1.24	4.2	-0.01	6.2	0.4	1.27	10.76	3.46	43.9	6.6	65.5	5.1	5.7

Name	City	State	Weiss Safety Rating	2003 Weiss Safety Rating	2002 Weiss Safety Rating	Total Assets ($Mil)	One Year Asset Growth	Comm-ercial Loans	Cons-umer Loans	Home Mort-gages	Secur-ities	Capital-ization Index	Leverage Ratio	Risk-based Capital Ratio
POTOMAC BK OF VA	FAIRFAX	VA	C+	C+	C+	201.7	35.76	16.0	2.8	5.8	14.2	10.0	13.4	16.9
POTOMAC VALLEY BK	GAITHERSBURG	MD	A-	A-	A-	862.9	34.46	6.4	0.6	14.1	14.3	6.1	8.1	15.6
POTTER ST BK	POTTER	NE	C-	C-	C	17.8	4.42	8.1	5.6	2.5	21.5	10.0	12.8	17.2
▲ POWELL ST BK	POWELL	TX	C+	C-	C-	18.3	-2.44	7.2	18.7	8.9	29.9	10.0	11.0	17.6
▼ POWELL VALLEY NB	JONESVILLE	VA	A-	A	A	214.4	7.93	18.4	7.5	20.5	19.3	10.0	12.6	18.9
PRAIRIE B&TC	BRIDGEVIEW	IL	C	C-	C-	380.4	16.11	9.6	0.8	5.7	14.2	3.4	8.2	10.2
▲ PRAIRIE COMMUNITY BK	MARENGO	IL	C	D+	C	49.7	15.23	5.2	2.7	35.1	21.3	8.0	9.7	15.2
PRAIRIE ST B&TC	MT ZION	IL	B+	B+	B+	181.8	3.74	9.8	1.8	18.9	18.0	6.3	8.7	12.0
PRAIRIE ST BK	AUGUSTA	KS	D+	D+	C-	317.4	-4.99	9.1	7.4	6.6	33.9	4.1	6.2	10.5
PRAIRIE SUN BK	MILAN	MN	C-	C-	D-	29.5	5.21	4.6	3.9	6.2	41.8	5.5	7.5	13.2
PREFERRED BK	LOS ANGELES	CA	C+	C+	B-	849.1	8.11	17.4	0.0	1.4	19.9	3.3	8.5	10.1
▲ PREFERRED BK	CASEY	IL	D+	D	D+	46.0	-2.54	11.6	13.9	28.0	2.3	7.9	9.6	15.2
▲ PREFERRED BK	BIG LAKE	MN	A-	B+	B	60.7	19.90	9.7	3.9	19.3	12.9	6.9	10.2	12.5
PREFERRED BK	HOUSTON	TX	B-	B	B	158.1	-8.35	3.2	1.8	29.4	21.5	7.1	9.1	18.1
▲ PREMIER AMERICAN BK	MIAMI	FL	D	D-	D	106.1	45.14	14.4	0.9	0.8	37.9	6.3	8.4	14.3
▲ PREMIER BANK	FORT ATKINSON	WI	A+	A	A	215.1	3.76	10.9	2.7	10.7	30.7	10.0	12.7	16.2
PREMIER BK	DENVER	CO	C	C+	B-	123.2	-2.49	28.8	0.6	1.9	12.0	7.2	9.1	13.2
PREMIER BK	TALLAHASSEE	FL	C-	C-	C-	208.8	37.14	9.3	2.6	11.1	13.7	3.5	7.4	10.3
PREMIER BK	DUBUQUE	IA	B-	B-	C	141.6	37.30	19.5	2.2	15.4	12.1	4.9	8.3	10.9
PREMIER BK	ROCK VALLEY	IA	C+	C+	C+	96.5	10.57	11.8	6.3	8.8	9.2	4.1	8.0	10.6
▲ PREMIER BK	WILMETTE	IL	C-	D+	D-	95.6	29.44	40.4	0.2	1.6	22.7	5.3	7.3	11.8
▼ PREMIER BK	LENEXA	KS	C+	B-	B+	167.6	8.77	17.0	0.6	4.9	9.2	6.6	9.0	12.2
PREMIER BK	ROCHESTER	MN	C	C	C	118.2	-0.16	10.2	3.4	7.4	10.0	4.9	8.9	11.0
PREMIER BK	JEFFERSON CITY	MO	C+	C+	C-	382.0	64.07	7.1	0.9	12.2	10.4	3.9	8.5	10.5
▲ PREMIER BK	DOYLESTOWN	PA	B-	C+	C	524.1	-13.22	7.6	0.2	5.4	24.3	5.9	7.9	12.2
▲ PREMIER BK MN	FARMINGTON	MN	D+	D-	E	135.7	7.81	10.2	0.4	5.1	9.1	2.0	7.3	9.0
PREMIER BK OF BRENTWOOD	BRENTWOOD	TN	C+	C+	C	150.8	15.92	18.7	1.9	8.2	8.4	4.1	8.1	10.5
PREMIER BK OF	JACKSONVILLE	IL	B-	B-	B-	55.3	6.56	4.8	28.3	15.3	22.7	7.2	9.2	14.1
▲ PREMIER BK-MAPLEWOOD	MAPLEWOOD	MN	C	C-	C	402.0	9.17	9.3	0.9	6.8	16.0	2.7	7.5	9.7
▲ PREMIER CMNTY BK OF	FORT LAUDERDALE	FL	C+	C	D+	114.1	5.15	15.7	1.3	1.2	4.4	5.7	7.7	12.4
▲ PREMIER COMMERCIAL BK NA	ANAHEIM	CA	C	C-	D-	128.0	33.93	14.4	0.3	0.1	17.7	5.8	8.5	11.6
▲ PREMIER COMMUNITY BK	MARION	WI	A	A-	A-	149.7	4.82	4.5	3.4	22.4	18.6	9.9	10.9	15.9
▲ PREMIER COMMUNITY BK OF	FORT MYERS	FL	C+	C	C+	58.3	6.71	9.1	0.8	7.6	17.8	5.3	7.9	11.2
PREMIER SERVICE BK	RIVERSIDE	CA	D-	D-	D	84.6	58.81	11.2	1.9	7.4	19.4	6.4	8.4	13.7
PREMIER VALLEY BK	FRESNO	CA	C	C-	D	182.3	74.06	9.3	5.4	4.8	26.3	8.0	9.7	15.6
PREMIER WEST BK	MEDFORD	OR	C+	C+	C-	774.8	43.64	13.7	1.9	3.8	3.0	3.2	8.3	10.1
▲ PRESCOTT ST BK	PRESCOTT	KS	D	D-	E+	12.9	9.81	5.3	6.6	21.0	32.6	7.4	9.3	18.3
PRESIDENTIAL BK FSB	BETHESDA	MD	C-	C-	C-	419.5	14.29	2.7	0.3	9.3	1.8	4.8	6.8	11.6
PRESTON NB	DALLAS	TX	C-	C-	C-	48.4	14.03	20.9	8.2	26.9	0.0	7.7	9.5	13.8
PRIME BK	ORANGE	CT	B	B	B	40.3	1.40	30.7	1.3	1.5	33.5	10.0	15.6	27.9
▲ PRIME PACIFIC BK NA	LYNNWOOD	WA	C	D+	D	60.0	32.21	12.1	0.9	4.2	5.9	10.0	14.1	18.5
PRIME SECURITY BK	KARLSTAD	MN	C-	C-	C	65.4	18.95	21.0	3.1	20.7	0.5	3.9	9.4	10.4
▼ PRIMEBANK	LE MARS	IA	B+	A-	A	204.6	16.70	13.2	2.3	14.9	11.9	7.7	9.6	13.1
▲ PRIMESOUTH BK	TALLASSEE	AL	B	B-	B-	78.4	9.01	13.6	12.8	21.1	24.0	7.4	9.2	14.7
▲ PRIMESOUTH BK	BLACKSHEAR	GA	C+	C	C	224.7	18.12	6.5	6.2	20.1	11.1	5.9	8.1	11.7
PRIMETRUST BK	NASHVILLE	TN	D-	D-	D-	248.6	51.75	16.3	3.7	11.8	15.7	4.1	9.0	10.5
PRINCE GEORGE'S FSB	UPPER MARLBORO	MD	A-	A-	A-	97.0	11.48	0.0	0.6	48.4	12.6	10.0	11.7	24.5
PRINCEVILLE ST BK	PRINCEVILLE	IL	C-	C-	C-	42.4	9.70	26.1	3.1	16.2	30.7	6.9	8.9	14.2
PRINCIPAL BK	DES MOINES	IA	B-	B-	B-	2,340.7	18.98	0.0	0.2	42.0	2.8	3.9	5.9	13.8
PRINSBURG ST BK	PRINSBURG	MN	B	B	B	37.6	6.90	9.1	2.6	4.0	20.0	10.0	13.9	16.0
PRIOR LAKE ST BK	PRIOR LAKE	MN	A	A	A	149.3	13.73	16.2	3.5	3.2	22.7	8.9	10.3	14.1
PRIORITY BK	OZARK	AR	C	C	C	34.9	-3.61	1.5	0.6	75.7	0.3	5.3	7.3	14.8
PRIORITYONE BK	MAGEE	MS	B	B	B-	305.0	5.25	8.2	11.2	17.8	17.1	7.4	9.2	13.2
▲ PRIVATE BK	BLOOMFIELD HILLS	MI	B-	C	B-	288.1	18.30	15.6	2.4	28.6	1.8	5.5	8.2	11.3
PRIVATE BK MN	MINNEAPOLIS	MN	C+	C+	C	126.5	18.38	28.9	10.7	11.7	3.6	3.0	9.4	10.0
PRIVATE BK OF THE	PALO ALTO	CA	D	D	NR	43.1	N/A	5.3	0.0	7.3	32.7	10.0	39.3	68.4
PRIVATEBANK	ST LOUIS	MO	C+	C+	C	240.0	35.47	15.1	1.0	16.4	25.6	3.7	6.8	10.3
PRIVATEBANK & TC	CHICAGO	IL	B-	B-	C+	1,955.0	23.74	9.1	3.4	10.6	23.2	4.5	6.7	10.8
PRODUCE ST BK	HOLLANDALE	MN	B	B	B-	28.1	1.18	18.9	8.4	15.5	8.2	10.0	12.5	18.0
PROFESSIONAL BK NA	DALLAS	TX	D	NR	NR	16.8	N/A	17.1	0.2	33.9	23.4	10.0	54.1	77.2
▲ PROFESSIONAL BUSINESS BK	PASADENA	CA	D	D-	D	116.2	64.57	5.1	1.8	5.4	8.1	6.5	10.1	12.1
PROFILE BK FSB	ROCHESTER	NH	A	A	A	126.7	7.60	2.8	0.3	33.1	42.4	10.0	13.9	32.4
▲ PROFINIUM FINANCIAL	TRUMAN	MN	C	D+	C+	190.0	267.25	10.2	12.1	5.3	10.7	7.0	10.2	12.5
PROGRESS BK	SULLIVAN	MO	B-	B-	B-	119.3	23.26	6.4	11.3	40.0	3.7	5.6	8.2	11.4

Asset Quality Index	Non-Performing Loans as a % of Total Loans	Non-Performing Loans as a % of Capital	Net Charge-offs Avg Loans	Profitability Index	Net Income ($Mil)	Return on Assets (R.O.A.)	Return on Equity (R.O.E.)	Net Interest Spread	Overhead Efficiency Ratio	Liquidity Index	Liquidity Ratio	Hot Money Ratio	Stability Index
8.5	0.00	0.0	-0.06	3.4	0.4	0.47	5.10	3.61	79.4	5.2	52.9	12.0	5.6
7.4	0.00	0.0	0.00	10.0	6.8	1.64	19.70	4.62	47.4	4.0	38.3	14.6	7.1
2.4	1.66	8.3	1.16	3.2	0.0	0.47	3.67	4.21	78.8	4.1	54.2	15.4	4.1
6.0	0.21	1.1	0.22	9.7	0.2	1.83	17.10	5.91	57.1	3.9	33.1	11.5	3.5
5.3	1.58	7.9	-0.16	8.7	1.7	1.59	11.94	5.20	52.9	2.8	50.9	31.3	8.2
4.9	0.46	4.0	0.09	6.5	3.3	1.80	21.85	4.29	53.8	2.0	10.1	18.4	4.0
9.1	0.00	0.0	0.00	2.9	0.1	0.31	3.43	3.43	84.7	2.6	28.7	18.2	3.1
7.2	0.48	4.1	0.04	7.7	1.6	1.83	21.24	3.84	55.7	3.3	31.7	15.9	6.2
4.8	0.76	5.7	0.59	3.1	0.5	0.31	4.58	3.79	83.8	2.7	13.6	15.2	2.8
8.7	0.04	0.3	-0.01	5.4	0.2	1.15	15.57	3.71	77.4	6.5	47.0	1.8	2.8
8.4	0.02	0.1	0.44	7.1	5.2	1.28	14.85	4.14	48.2	3.4	79.2	45.0	5.0
1.3	4.03	26.9	1.28	3.1	0.1	0.50	5.33	3.70	77.1	6.4	256.7	22.2	2.7
5.0	0.75	4.2	0.26	7.1	0.4	1.46	10.88	5.70	68.4	4.6	19.2	5.5	8.1
4.8	1.41	8.4	0.06	4.8	0.5	0.67	7.65	3.18	68.4	3.4	87.9	76.9	5.2
7.5	0.00	0.0	0.00	0.7	0.2	0.30	3.58	2.66	86.9	3.3	48.6	22.2	0.0
7.8	0.15	0.5	0.00	9.7	2.0	1.76	12.31	4.24	46.7	5.9	43.6	5.3	9.3
3.0	2.29	17.3	0.25	6.8	0.7	1.07	12.50	3.98	72.4	4.1	30.5	11.4	4.0
5.2	0.37	3.5	0.07	4.8	0.7	0.69	9.66	4.03	72.7	4.8	32.6	8.3	3.0
8.3	0.00	0.0	0.01	5.4	0.6	0.93	10.93	3.80	61.6	1.8	15.0	20.6	4.7
5.6	0.42	3.9	-0.01	8.1	0.8	1.76	21.77	3.93	53.5	1.2	13.3	28.2	5.6
3.7	3.14	22.6	0.23	4.3	0.6	1.36	18.80	3.84	57.6	7.6	159.4	11.0	0.6
3.7	0.78	6.3	0.00	6.8	1.1	1.36	15.23	4.07	71.2	4.0	12.1	8.4	6.5
3.6	0.77	6.2	0.02	9.3	0.9	1.54	17.58	5.28	53.1	4.8	33.8	8.4	6.1
7.4	0.06	0.6	0.00	6.1	1.7	1.00	12.06	3.67	50.8	0.7	12.9	43.9	4.6
3.5	0.44	1.5	0.00	5.1	2.7	1.01	5.69	4.04	58.9	2.5	11.3	16.3	5.7
4.0	0.00	0.0	0.16	8.4	1.0	1.42	18.79	5.65	55.6	4.0	31.2	12.1	4.1
5.0	0.55	5.2	0.28	5.3	0.6	0.82	9.88	3.94	61.2	1.3	16.9	28.1	4.3
5.1	0.39	2.4	0.28	7.7	0.3	1.03	10.71	4.32	68.1	3.6	50.8	19.0	5.4
3.5	0.51	4.5	-0.01	10.0	3.5	1.76	24.02	5.23	41.9	6.3	68.5	9.3	4.9
6.3	0.00	0.0	-0.02	3.6	0.2	0.37	3.05	4.32	80.2	5.4	99.0	17.9	6.0
8.6	0.00	0.0	0.00	3.1	0.4	0.72	8.41	3.75	79.4	6.2	70.2	10.1	1.9
6.9	0.27	1.6	0.03	7.0	0.9	1.20	11.14	4.54	60.8	4.5	42.3	13.3	7.4
8.7	0.04	0.3	2.74	1.1	-0.2	-0.58	-6.64	4.45	72.8	4.2	32.9	11.7	4.3
8.9	0.00	0.0	0.00	0.4	-0.2	-0.48	-5.69	4.53	98.7	6.6	58.6	3.4	0.0
8.5	0.00	0.0	0.00	2.9	0.7	0.86	8.61	3.57	66.7	6.9	80.0	7.3	1.8
5.3	0.40	2.6	1.23	6.4	4.0	1.14	10.36	5.49	68.0	7.0	93.9	9.0	6.1
8.6	0.00	0.0	0.00	3.6	0.0	0.51	5.65	4.24	87.2	2.8	38.7	18.3	2.3
2.8	1.25	12.1	0.77	5.9	0.8	0.40	5.79	3.07	80.9	2.8	44.4	27.0	3.0
2.7	1.44	11.6	0.40	7.0	0.5	2.15	23.05	5.88	64.9	2.9	19.8	14.8	4.1
8.6	0.38	1.2	-1.85	7.7	0.3	1.36	8.39	4.99	55.8	5.2	97.5	17.5	6.0
6.5	0.72	3.8	0.16	4.4	0.2	0.85	5.74	5.68	70.7	2.6	57.3	33.9	5.3
5.9	0.44	4.1	0.03	6.0	0.3	0.81	9.26	5.55	71.5	3.9	19.8	10.0	3.2
5.0	0.97	7.4	-0.09	8.1	1.8	1.78	17.30	3.59	51.3	3.6	16.6	11.3	7.5
7.9	0.13	0.9	-0.06	8.7	0.9	2.38	28.20	4.29	46.2	3.4	16.3	12.3	5.6
4.6	0.77	6.6	0.03	7.7	1.4	1.26	16.23	4.47	46.2	2.6	37.5	23.1	3.4
8.3	0.05	0.4	0.00	0.6	0.3	0.27	3.21	3.34	84.1	1.4	30.5	35.2	0.0
9.1	0.53	2.8	0.00	7.9	0.6	1.27	10.69	3.46	43.8	2.6	61.8	45.4	7.3
6.4	0.47	3.1	0.00	4.3	0.2	1.07	11.68	3.90	73.0	4.3	9.6	6.1	3.3
9.9	0.14	1.2	0.01	3.7	-3.5	-0.32	-4.93	1.87	155.8	5.0	180.5	71.8	4.9
7.2	0.81	3.6	-0.07	6.6	0.3	1.75	13.64	4.03	50.1	6.4	79.6	8.8	6.7
8.2	0.18	1.1	-0.03	9.9	1.7	2.22	21.32	4.55	52.2	5.9	45.5	5.8	7.8
6.0	0.30	2.9	0.04	10.0	0.8	4.24	56.17	5.08	54.2	1.7	25.2	25.2	4.3
5.8	0.45	3.2	0.14	6.8	1.9	1.29	13.76	4.74	62.6	6.9	191.4	17.3	5.2
8.4	0.00	0.0	0.15	7.8	1.7	1.24	16.24	4.34	58.6	1.3	31.2	47.0	5.0
7.7	0.03	0.3	0.26	5.5	0.6	0.95	10.32	4.36	59.3	2.2	12.0	17.7	4.7
9.8	0.00	0.0	0.00	0.0	-1.2	-6.97	-14.75	1.75	400.6	9.1	274.7	6.0	0.0
8.6	0.03	0.3	0.00	6.0	1.2	1.07	14.17	3.22	58.5	0.3	5.9	79.7	4.2
8.2	0.06	0.4	-0.03	7.3	13.1	1.39	17.33	4.25	45.4	0.8	14.9	39.0	6.7
5.2	1.81	9.7	0.68	6.7	0.3	1.85	15.13	4.47	56.8	6.3	64.1	6.9	6.2
9.1	0.00	0.0	0.00	0.0	-0.6	-10.03	-15.29	2.96	358.9	1.3	22.3	29.3	0.0
7.3	0.00	0.0	0.00	1.1	0.3	0.57	5.60	3.99	84.2	5.4	34.8	4.9	0.0
9.3	0.00	0.0	0.00	7.3	0.6	0.97	6.98	3.73	56.3	1.3	19.0	28.7	8.8
2.9	1.18	7.4	-0.07	6.8	1.4	1.46	12.02	4.50	65.5	3.1	12.9	13.2	7.6
5.1	0.78	7.8	0.16	6.7	0.6	1.08	13.18	4.85	60.5	1.9	9.3	19.1	4.7

Name	City	State	Weiss Safety Rating	2003 Weiss Safety Rating	2002 Weiss Safety Rating	Total Assets ($Mil)	One Year Asset Growth	Asset Mix (As a % of Total Assets) Comm- ercial Loans	Cons- umer Loans	Home Mort- gages	Secur- ities	Capital- ization Index	Leverage Ratio	Risk-based Capital Ratio
▼ PROGRESSIVE BK NA	WHEELING	WV	C+	B-	B-	282.8	3.48	6.3	6.6	14.7	37.9	4.9	6.9	12.5
PROGRESSIVE NB DESOTO	MANSFIELD	LA	E-	E-	E-	17.5	-2.30	3.8	14.1	18.8	32.2	6.0	8.0	16.5
PROGRESSIVE OZARK BK FSB	SALEM	MO	C-	C-	C-	97.0	5.86	9.6	6.4	46.9	12.0	5.2	7.2	11.8
PROGRESSIVE ST B&TC	WINNSBORO	LA	C	C	C+	253.9	-2.62	13.1	3.8	13.1	12.8	6.8	9.5	12.4
PROGRESSIVE ST BK	LUMBERTON	NC	B	B	B-	60.7	-1.07	17.5	14.8	17.2	23.6	10.0	11.0	20.8
▲ PROGRESSIVE SVGS BANK	JAMESTOWN	TN	B	B-	C+	168.0	9.22	2.4	5.1	35.1	25.4	5.2	7.2	11.9
PROGRESSIVE-HOME FS&LA	PITTSBURGH	PA	D+	D+	C-	81.5	-7.15	0.2	1.2	45.8	32.9	9.9	10.9	26.1
▲ PROGROWTH BK	NICOLLET	MN	D+	D	D-	102.3	-5.10	6.2	9.0	10.9	18.9	6.1	8.5	11.9
▲ PROSPECT BK	COLUMBUS	OH	B-	C+	C+	202.1	21.25	6.5	0.5	46.2	0.0	4.7	8.0	10.9
PROSPECT FSB	WORTH	IL	B+	B+	A	244.9	-5.00	0.0	0.0	16.6	58.8	10.0	14.6	59.6
PROSPER ST BK	PROSPER	TX	E	E	E	10.5	12.74	1.8	1.8	0.9	55.8	6.0	8.0	24.4
▲ PROSPERITY B&TC	SPRINGFIELD	VA	B	B-	C+	113.9	3.06	14.3	3.4	5.7	22.8	7.0	9.0	12.7
PROSPERITY BK	ST AUGUSTINE	FL	C	C	C	633.2	22.82	2.4	8.5	25.1	23.8	2.9	6.5	9.9
▲ PROSPERITY BK	EL CAMPO	TX	B	B-	B-	2,432.2	22.94	3.6	2.0	11.1	57.4	4.7	6.7	17.4
PROVIDENT BK	AMESBURY	MA	B-	B-	B-	272.2	18.91	3.6	0.6	28.2	23.0	9.0	10.4	19.3
▲ PROVIDENT BK	JERSEY CITY	NJ	A-	B+	B	4,139.6	4.94	8.1	3.7	28.8	33.5	10.0	13.6	21.9
▲ PROVIDENT BK	MONTEBELLO	NY	A-	B+	B+	1,673.2	56.92	5.8	1.5	23.4	34.7	10.0	11.9	18.9
PROVIDENT BK	CINCINNATI	OH	C-	C-	C+	16,616.5	-6.85	18.2	1.2	3.0	25.0	5.1	7.1	12.3
PROVIDENT BK OF MARYLAND	BALTIMORE	MD	B-	B-	C+	6,164.0	21.34	5.5	8.1	17.0	34.7	6.2	8.2	12.9
PROVIDENT COMMUNITY BK	UNION	SC	C+	C+	C+	353.4	N/A	3.6	1.6	17.6	45.1	6.0	8.0	15.6
▲ PROVIDENT MUNICIPAL BK	MONTEBELLO	NY	A-	B	B-	91.0	128.91	0.0	0.0	0.0	97.3	8.8	10.2	49.9
▼ PROVIDENT ST BK	PRESTON	MD	B-	B	B	156.0	4.75	9.9	2.3	23.6	11.5	5.5	8.4	11.4
PROVIDENT SVGS BK FSB	RIVERSIDE	CA	B	B	B	1,320.6	4.57	1.0	0.1	47.6	19.2	4.9	6.9	12.4
PROVIDIAN NB	TILTON	NH	B-	B-	C+	12,754.1	-10.22	0.0	54.0	0.0	24.3	10.0	25.3	22.4
PROVINCE BK FSB	MARIETTA	PA	D	D	D	50.8	12.29	1.7	2.0	14.2	52.8	10.0	21.9	55.2
PROVINCIAL BK	LAKEVILLE	MN	C	B-	C+	57.2	24.52	14.7	6.8	29.1	2.7	4.8	8.8	10.9
PRP NB	PLEASURE RIDG PK	KY	C	C	C	58.1	-5.16	1.8	6.6	21.2	38.9	7.1	9.1	18.6
PRUDENTIAL BANK & TRUST	HARTFORD	CT	B	B-	C	225.9	-67.14	0.0	0.0	0.0	85.1	10.0	15.4	48.2
PRUDENTIAL SAVINGS BANK	PHILADELPHIA	PA	B	B	B+	409.9	6.41	0.8	0.1	26.1	57.9	7.3	9.2	24.9
PUBLIC BK	ST CLOUD	FL	B-	B-	B	313.9	80.06	5.2	1.4	15.2	23.1	6.0	8.0	12.6
PUBLIC SVGS BK	WILLOW GROVE	PA	E-	E-	E-	24.4	1.68	0.0	0.0	83.8	2.0	6.0	8.1	15.3
▲ PUEBLO B&TC	PUEBLO	CO	B-	B-	D+	348.1	2.17	4.9	1.0	6.5	12.8	5.6	9.1	11.5
PULASKI B&TC	LITTLE ROCK	AR	B+	B+	B-	367.1	-9.32	8.9	15.2	19.0	11.4	6.8	8.8	14.9
PULASKI BK	ST LOUIS	MO	B-	B-	B-	564.5	22.09	2.6	0.6	48.2	11.8	6.7	8.7	12.7
▼ PULASKI SVGS BK	CHICAGO	IL	B-	B	B	44.7	7.52	0.0	0.5	60.3	14.1	10.0	14.7	38.4
PULLMAN B&TC	CHICAGO	IL	B	B	C+	1,140.5	3.97	4.2	0.3	2.1	9.0	7.2	15.0	12.7
PURDUM ST BK	PURDUM	NE	E-	E-	E-	20.3	-9.48	7.3	3.0	1.8	5.9	6.6	9.0	12.2
▲ PUTNAM COUNTY BK	HURRICANE	WV	B+	B	B-	469.0	-1.44	2.4	2.8	20.0	30.1	9.3	10.6	25.7
PUTNAM COUNTY NB OF	CARMEL	NY	B	B	A	175.4	-0.91	18.0	1.1	15.5	25.0	10.0	20.9	38.5
PUTNAM COUNTY ST BK	UNIONVILLE	MO	B-	B-	B-	67.7	-1.94	10.2	5.8	13.8	8.0	8.1	9.8	14.2
PUTNAM COUNTY SVGS BK	BREWSTER	NY	B	B	B	884.1	4.62	2.4	1.1	19.5	49.6	6.7	8.7	21.2
▼ PUTNAM FIDUCIARY TC	BOSTON	MA	B	B+	B+	286.5	2.93	0.0	0.0	0.0	0.0	10.0	13.9	17.2
PUTNAM ST BK	PALATKA	FL	B	B-	D	107.4	5.19	15.6	2.9	2.6	11.8	6.3	9.6	12.0
PUTNAM SVGS BK	PUTNAM	CT	C+	C+	C+	279.3	14.56	1.1	0.4	36.3	44.4	6.9	8.9	15.7
PYRAMAX BANK, FSB	GREENFIELD	WI	B-	B	NR	436.3	4.04	3.0	0.8	46.3	6.5	8.0	9.9	13.4
QUAD CITY B&TC	BETTENDORF	IA	C	C	C	632.3	16.48	28.9	3.3	12.0	17.2	3.4	7.5	10.2
▲ QUAIL CREEK BK NA	OKLAHOMA CITY	OK	B+	B-	C+	266.6	2.46	9.0	3.7	13.9	9.2	6.6	9.6	12.2
QUAINT OAK SB	SOUTHAMPTON	PA	B-	B-	B-	44.4	19.23	0.0	0.1	72.3	0.4	5.9	7.9	15.2
QUAKER CITY BK	WHITTIER	CA	B+	B+	B+	1,871.3	15.31	0.0	0.5	18.5	15.3	6.0	8.0	12.4
QUAKERTOWN NB	QUAKERTOWN	PA	B-	B-	B-	554.5	5.54	8.8	1.0	14.0	45.4	5.2	7.2	12.2
▼ QUALITY BK	FINGAL	ND	E	D	C	22.5	63.38	6.5	6.2	0.9	30.0	6.0	8.0	12.3
QUANTUM NB	SUWANEE	GA	C+	C+	C+	180.1	18.49	9.6	0.7	0.3	7.9	3.1	8.3	10.1
QUARRY CITY S&LA	WARRENSBURG	MO	C+	C+	C+	17.0	-1.66	0.0	1.6	60.1	3.6	10.0	18.7	32.2
QUEEN CITY FSB	VIRGINIA	MN	A-	A	A	178.8	6.05	9.0	7.8	21.8	57.7	7.6	9.4	22.3
QUEENSTOWN BK OF MD	QUEENSTOWN	MD	B+	B+	B+	313.4	12.96	6.1	5.2	24.3	18.3	8.3	9.9	14.3
▲ R-G CROWN BANK	CASSELBERRY	FL	B-	C	C-	1,432.5	57.12	3.2	0.4	31.7	17.4	5.4	7.4	12.1
▲ R-G PREMIER BK OF PR	SAN JUAN	PR	B-	C+	C	6,674.1	20.09	3.6	2.3	35.2	39.2	5.1	7.1	13.3
RABUN COUNTY BK	CLAYTON	GA	C	C	C-	170.3	11.57	3.4	4.4	40.1	9.8	5.5	7.5	11.7
RACCOON VALLEY BK	PERRY	IA	B-	B-	B	155.6	70.76	13.6	4.2	13.7	29.7	6.5	8.5	12.1
RAHWAY SVGS INST	RAHWAY	NJ	A-	A-	A-	428.3	-0.49	0.0	0.3	30.6	56.4	10.0	13.8	31.4
▲ RAINIER PACIFIC SVGS BK	FIFE	WA	B-	C	C+	759.2	6.47	0.3	12.2	16.4	29.2	10.0	11.1	17.5
▲ RALLS COUNTY ST BK	NEW LONDON	MO	D+	D-	D-	53.3	-0.74	10.2	12.2	14.9	13.0	7.0	9.0	12.5
RAMONA NB	RAMONA	CA	D	D	D	30.7	32.37	16.1	2.9	6.1	4.6	10.0	17.9	23.7
RAMSEY NB&TC OF DEVILS	DEVILS LAKE	ND	B	B	C+	145.7	0.22	12.5	2.5	6.5	17.1	10.0	11.3	17.0

Asset Quality Index	Non-Performing Loans as a % of Total Loans	Non-Performing Loans as a % of Capital	Net Charge-offs Avg Loans	Profitability Index	Net Income ($Mil)	Return on Assets (R.O.A.)	Return on Equity (R.O.E.)	Net Interest Spread	Overhead Efficiency Ratio	Liquidity Index	Liquidity Ratio	Hot Money Ratio	Stability Index
4.4	1.39	8.6	0.18	5.2	1.3	0.92	11.48	3.58	63.8	4.7	31.9	8.1	4.7
5.0	0.49	2.9	0.16	2.4	0.0	0.09	1.16	4.79	97.1	3.9	92.4	25.8	0.0
3.6	1.33	13.7	0.18	4.9	0.5	0.94	12.04	4.02	78.7	0.9	6.2	30.3	3.7
5.0	0.76	5.4	0.03	3.3	0.9	0.70	7.59	4.08	78.9	2.3	23.9	18.6	4.4
5.6	0.84	3.7	-0.05	6.7	0.3	0.99	8.99	5.06	73.1	6.0	65.9	9.1	3.6
7.5	0.04	0.3	0.03	7.7	1.4	1.70	21.68	3.42	63.5	0.7	2.5	33.5	5.5
1.8	6.32	27.7	0.03	2.6	0.1	0.12	1.00	2.34	77.0	4.2	27.2	9.7	5.6
2.1	2.85	21.3	1.37	2.8	0.1	0.18	2.12	3.82	89.7	4.5	30.8	9.3	2.1
7.4	0.20	2.1	0.00	5.5	0.9	0.94	12.47	3.43	58.7	3.9	30.1	12.4	5.0
9.7	0.78	1.1	0.00	4.7	0.6	0.49	3.41	2.32	70.9	4.4	62.2	18.2	7.5
9.8	0.00	0.0	0.00	0.6	0.0	0.04	0.54	4.17	106.0	6.7	59.9	1.1	0.0
8.5	0.00	0.0	-0.02	6.3	0.6	1.19	14.23	4.73	65.1	5.3	38.9	7.6	4.9
5.4	0.43	4.2	0.00	6.7	3.4	1.12	17.65	4.27	63.6	2.7	18.5	15.8	3.7
7.6	0.19	0.5	0.06	8.9	17.8	1.47	13.33	3.75	47.6	4.5	55.9	18.0	8.8
9.2	0.04	0.2	0.01	3.9	0.7	0.57	4.27	3.86	81.7	4.1	21.0	8.7	7.7
8.8	0.15	0.6	0.12	5.3	20.7	1.00	7.24	3.59	59.3	7.9	113.2	5.8	8.7
6.5	0.56	2.6	0.02	5.6	6.5	0.81	5.95	4.37	72.1	1.7	23.8	30.8	8.4
6.2	0.66	5.6	1.53	2.1	-20.9	-0.25	-4.23	2.16	88.4	0.8	15.1	42.1	2.5
6.0	1.01	6.7	0.22	5.4	25.4	0.92	10.83	3.41	64.5	3.7	23.4	13.3	5.1
5.7	0.68	3.4	1.11	3.6	1.3	0.76	8.15	3.17	65.0	4.6	92.5	23.3	2.7
10.0	0.00	0.0	0.00	6.1	0.5	1.21	11.36	2.60	11.9	0.7	14.7	49.3	6.3
7.5	0.25	2.2	0.01	4.6	0.6	0.82	9.79	3.94	70.1	4.0	20.9	9.5	5.0
7.4	0.12	1.0	0.05	8.9	8.5	1.28	17.53	3.19	47.6	1.2	22.2	39.7	7.4
3.8	2.49	4.6	9.03	9.8	179.0	2.74	11.61	5.54	47.2	3.2	70.8	74.6	9.2
9.6	0.00	0.0	0.00	0.0	-0.3	-1.34	-6.00	2.00	140.4	2.9	67.8	35.8	0.0
7.0	0.09	0.8	0.02	8.7	0.3	0.96	10.50	5.11	69.9	3.8	12.5	9.6	4.9
6.6	0.30	1.6	0.16	3.3	0.2	0.66	7.22	4.15	83.9	6.7	61.5	3.6	3.7
9.3	0.00	0.0	-0.15	4.1	1.1	0.70	5.29	2.07	96.2	3.3	80.1	63.0	5.2
9.1	0.25	0.9	0.00	4.4	1.0	0.49	5.26	2.61	70.7	3.1	50.5	26.2	5.4
4.9	1.52	11.5	-0.01	9.3	2.2	2.03	25.83	6.20	53.8	2.2	11.2	17.7	5.6
2.6	2.69	29.1	0.13	1.3	0.0	0.02	0.20	3.45	99.8	1.8	N/A	18.7	0.3
4.0	1.06	8.2	0.07	10.0	7.1	4.09	47.36	7.44	49.6	6.4	76.6	10.2	7.0
7.6	0.09	0.8	0.13	9.6	2.5	1.38	16.06	5.15	81.2	3.7	28.4	12.6	5.7
4.7	0.68	6.5	0.04	8.3	2.8	1.11	12.60	3.33	54.6	0.6	5.7	37.4	5.7
10.0	0.00	0.0	0.00	3.5	0.1	0.31	1.84	3.95	86.3	7.8	258.0	13.5	6.2
4.1	2.42	12.2	-0.01	10.0	13.6	2.40	16.12	6.01	33.1	2.4	23.4	19.6	8.3
0.0	21.08	129.2	0.02	3.3	0.1	0.93	9.82	3.71	74.3	2.4	51.7	29.4	0.7
8.3	0.53	2.2	-0.06	5.9	2.5	1.07	9.94	3.13	44.3	4.5	99.5	26.7	5.3
4.2	6.02	16.0	-0.02	6.0	1.1	1.24	5.86	4.69	63.3	5.7	37.0	4.2	6.9
5.1	0.78	5.7	-0.10	8.5	0.4	1.24	12.50	4.02	49.6	3.0	36.3	18.7	5.3
8.6	0.44	1.9	-0.01	5.6	3.8	0.88	10.12	3.02	52.4	8.1	122.7	4.8	5.6
10.0	0.00	0.0	0.00	3.7	-1.4	-0.86	-6.41	-0.67	100.9	3.5	100.8	100.0	3.7
5.7	0.68	4.8	0.00	5.9	0.6	1.11	11.83	4.46	62.8	3.6	64.2	27.1	5.9
7.7	0.48	2.7	0.04	3.6	0.8	0.61	6.79	3.23	73.9	3.8	28.6	12.2	4.7
5.1	0.53	4.3	-0.07	3.6	0.9	0.44	4.35	2.72	76.7	1.4	5.7	23.5	3.0
4.0	1.49	12.5	0.08	6.5	3.3	1.11	14.97	3.76	56.5	2.0	21.1	19.9	4.0
6.6	0.12	1.0	-0.01	10.0	3.6	2.72	28.14	4.54	45.6	3.6	38.4	16.6	6.8
9.7	0.00	0.0	0.00	8.4	0.3	1.30	17.08	3.80	37.6	8.1	466.1	11.8	1.3
7.1	0.26	2.5	0.04	9.1	10.2	1.12	14.10	3.53	47.9	0.6	4.1	35.4	7.7
8.7	0.18	1.1	0.03	5.2	2.9	1.07	14.62	3.36	63.2	3.9	16.8	9.4	5.2
2.8	1.06	6.2	0.65	3.0	0.0	0.11	1.06	3.72	89.4	4.8	65.7	13.5	0.7
5.9	0.42	3.9	0.02	5.5	0.9	1.07	13.04	4.26	60.8	3.2	45.3	20.5	4.2
9.1	0.00	0.0	0.00	4.6	0.1	0.98	5.37	3.81	73.2	4.2	17.3	7.2	5.0
7.7	0.56	2.3	0.06	8.9	1.2	1.33	13.26	3.32	40.6	3.2	15.9	13.0	6.3
5.1	0.86	6.3	0.08	8.2	2.2	1.46	14.95	4.41	47.0	2.7	15.2	15.4	6.5
4.8	0.67	5.9	0.07	5.6	11.0	1.62	14.43	2.91	52.3	0.7	13.1	49.7	6.3
5.1	1.85	14.0	0.18	7.9	54.4	1.69	24.00	2.83	33.6	0.5	5.3	50.1	5.1
5.1	0.83	8.3	0.03	5.9	0.8	0.99	13.52	4.26	66.7	2.5	22.8	17.3	3.0
4.7	0.57	3.7	0.21	4.1	0.6	0.70	8.19	3.44	75.8	5.2	34.7	6.5	4.9
10.0	0.49	1.2	0.00	5.5	2.0	0.94	6.96	3.14	54.6	7.3	106.9	8.6	7.6
7.9	0.08	0.4	0.46	3.8	1.9	0.52	4.59	4.35	76.9	3.1	9.8	12.8	4.5
4.8	0.85	6.4	-0.29	3.7	0.2	0.62	7.00	4.21	78.0	5.2	39.6	8.7	2.1
8.5	0.00	0.0	0.01	0.0	-0.1	-0.81	-4.36	3.83	113.9	6.8	89.8	8.0	0.0
4.9	1.44	7.7	0.12	5.5	0.7	0.97	8.00	4.13	69.9	5.8	45.4	6.5	6.6

Name	City	State	Weiss Safety Rating	2003 Weiss Safety Rating	2002 Weiss Safety Rating	Total Assets ($Mil)	One Year Asset Growth	Asset Mix (As a % of Total Assets) Comm- ercial Loans	Cons- umer Loans	Home Mort- gages	Secur- ities	Capital- ization Index	Leverage Ratio	Risk-based Capital Ratio
▲ RANCHERS BANKS	BELEN	NM	D	D	C-	118.6	1.16	10.0	1.2	5.7	48.2	10.0	11.2	22.4
▲ RANCHO BERNARDO CMNTY	SAN DIEGO	CA	B-	C	C	107.7	22.96	13.3	0.4	2.3	14.8	5.6	8.7	11.5
▲ RANCHO BK	SAN DIMAS	CA	C-	C-	C+	222.8	5.87	12.8	2.3	1.6	26.5	5.0	7.0	11.6
RANCHO SANTA FE T&LA	SAN MARCOS	CA	B	B	B-	96.9	-23.33	0.0	98.9	0.0	0.0	10.0	25.6	27.6
RANDALL ST BK	RANDALL	MN	C+	C+	B-	31.6	14.26	7.5	5.2	30.9	9.3	7.3	9.7	12.8
RANDALL-STORY ST BK	STORY CITY	IA	A-	A-	A-	70.5	1.02	3.5	1.4	18.4	35.0	9.1	10.4	16.2
RANDOLPH B&TC	ASHEBORO	NC	C-	C-	C	256.0	0.44	20.1	2.9	24.6	20.9	5.4	7.4	12.4
RANDOLPH COUNTY BK NA	WINCHESTER	IN	B-	B-	B-	94.0	3.58	10.9	10.0	28.4	5.0	5.1	8.1	11.1
RANDOLPH NB	RANDOLPH CEN	VT	B	B	B	123.6	9.92	29.1	5.0	37.6	9.3	7.0	9.0	14.0
▼ RANDOLPH ST BK	RANDOLPH	IA	B	B+	B+	43.4	17.17	17.9	6.4	8.9	24.4	10.0	13.6	19.5
RANDOLPH SVGS BK	RANDOLPH	MA	B	B	B	341.6	4.99	0.7	0.7	36.7	33.8	7.0	9.0	16.7
▲ RANTOUL FIRST BK SB	RANTOUL	IL	E+	E-	E-	31.7	-2.41	1.2	3.2	32.5	39.1	5.3	7.3	17.9
▼ RAPPAHANNOCK NB	WASHINGTON	VA	B-	B	B-	50.6	24.16	2.0	3.0	45.1	19.2	7.1	9.1	13.6
▲ RARITAN ST BK	RARITAN	IL	C+	C	C	90.6	-0.41	4.3	6.1	18.6	32.4	7.6	9.4	16.5
RAVALLI COUNTY BK	HAMILTON	MT	B-	B-	B	143.2	5.87	14.4	2.8	26.6	19.9	9.5	10.6	16.5
RAWLINS NB	RAWLINS	WY	B+	B+	B+	117.2	-7.98	12.4	5.5	3.1	23.7	8.6	10.0	14.0
RAYMOND FEDERAL BANK	RAYMOND	WA	C-	C-	C-	50.0	3.84	0.0	2.8	69.2	16.2	6.9	8.9	19.5
RAYMOND JAMES BK FSB	ST PETERSBURG	FL	B-	B-	C+	911.5	-4.00	13.6	0.2	42.6	20.0	6.4	8.4	18.6
RAYNE B&LA	RAYNE	LA	B+	B+	B	53.0	-3.94	0.0	1.5	43.4	42.4	10.0	15.0	40.0
▲ RAYNE ST B&TC	RAYNE	LA	B	B-	B-	159.5	6.07	14.6	3.9	11.6	24.2	6.5	8.5	13.6
▼ RBC CENTURA BK	ROCKY MOUNT	NC	C-	C	B-	21,482.1	12.57	11.1	2.1	22.1	23.6	6.2	8.3	15.2
▼ RBC CENTURA CARD BK	ATLANTA	GA	C-	C	B-	9.9	2.60	0.0	44.5	0.0	19.0	10.0	93.2	169.4
RCB BK	CLAREMORE	OK	A	A	A-	671.8	0.05	4.6	9.3	10.8	48.8	10.0	11.5	24.3
READING CO-OP BK	READING	MA	B-	B-	B	213.6	9.04	1.5	0.5	48.8	25.9	6.6	8.6	14.0
READING ST BK	READING	KS	C-	C-	D+	12.3	9.47	27.8	7.1	11.5	11.0	9.4	11.2	14.5
READLYN SVG BK	READLYN	IA	A-	A-	A-	36.8	1.21	5.9	1.8	21.7	40.1	10.0	12.7	21.7
RED CEDAR BK NA	BOYCEVILLE	WI	C	C	C-	27.2	0.28	14.9	4.3	15.7	12.7	8.1	9.7	13.9
RED LAKE COUNTY ST BK	RED LAKE FALLS	MN	B+	B+	A-	43.2	1.40	9.7	16.3	25.5	16.0	10.0	11.8	18.6
RED MOUNTAIN BK NA	HOOVER	AL	D	NR	NR	8.5	N/A	2.4	0.0	0.0	35.4	10.0	96.0	352.8
RED OAK BK	HANOVER TWP	NJ	C-	D+	D-	97.1	23.97	8.1	0.5	33.4	8.9	9.3	11.9	14.4
RED RIVER BK	ALEXANDRIA	LA	B-	B-	B-	372.4	24.82	17.0	6.2	19.5	19.1	5.6	7.6	11.8
▲ RED RIVER ST BK	HALSTAD	MN	C+	C-	D	29.8	-2.50	25.2	39.9	4.9	6.4	6.4	9.6	12.1
▲ RED ROCK COMMUNITY BK	LAS VEGAS	NV	C	C-	C	108.8	0.31	16.0	0.9	2.7	0.6	6.9	8.9	13.9
REDDING BK OF COMMERCE	REDDING	CA	B-	B-	C	409.7	5.97	24.2	0.7	1.6	18.3	6.7	9.3	12.3
▲ REDMOND NB	REDMOND	WA	B	B-	C+	99.6	15.87	10.1	2.7	8.1	2.8	9.4	13.0	14.5
REDSTONE BK NA	HOUSTON	TX	B-	B-	B-	107.4	136.35	18.8	2.7	7.2	38.8	10.0	22.6	43.5
REDWOOD BK	WATERTOWN	NY	C+	C+	C+	90.8	3.77	12.3	3.2	12.7	33.4	6.0	8.0	14.0
REDWOOD CAP BK	EUREKA	CA	D	NR	NR	33.8	N/A	3.6	1.3	0.1	27.8	10.0	52.7	83.8
▼ REEDSBURG BK	REEDSBURG	WI	B	A-	A-	163.1	14.13	5.6	4.0	15.5	17.2	6.6	8.6	12.6
▼ REELFOOT BK	UNION CITY	TN	C-	C-	C-	136.8	-6.74	22.0	10.7	20.4	9.0	7.2	9.1	12.8
REGAL B&TC	OWINGS MILLS	MD	C+	C+	C	100.9	18.21	20.6	0.6	16.2	12.7	6.1	8.1	11.8
▲ REGAL FNCL BK	SEATTLE	WA	D+	D	D	94.6	42.51	24.8	0.4	2.5	8.9	10.0	16.7	22.9
REGENCY SVGS BK FSB	NAPERVILLE	IL	B-	B-	C+	1,354.1	3.78	0.0	0.1	12.6	9.9	9.2	12.4	14.4
▼ REGENT B&TC NA	NOWATA	OK	D	C-	C-	80.7	17.90	24.7	3.7	10.3	32.4	6.1	8.2	15.3
REGENT BK	DAVIE	FL	C+	C+	C+	170.2	10.07	11.2	0.5	9.2	1.1	3.7	7.2	10.4
REGENTS BK NA	LA JOLLA	CA	D+	D	D-	162.1	50.45	14.9	1.7	2.6	2.0	5.7	8.1	11.5
REGIONAL BK	NEW ALBANY	IN	C-	C-	C-	250.9	7.93	13.9	3.1	17.9	27.3	5.0	7.0	11.0
REGIONAL MISSOURI BK	MARCELINE	MO	C+	C+	C	66.8	9.32	9.6	6.4	34.0	10.4	5.5	7.5	11.5
▼ REGIONS BANK	BIRMINGHAM	AL	B	B	B	46,170.7	1.57	11.4	5.0	21.7	18.2	5.4	7.6	11.3
▲ REGIONS MORGAN KEEGAN	BIRMINGHAM	AL	C+	C	D+	11.7	0.25	0.0	0.0	0.0	50.8	10.0	93.4	578.1
▲ RELIABANK DAKOTA	ESTELLINE	SD	B-	C	C-	105.3	4.16	12.4	6.2	7.8	14.5	5.9	8.6	11.7
▲ RELIANCE BK	ATHENS	AL	C-	D+	D+	71.2	4.40	16.7	9.5	13.5	18.5	6.0	8.1	11.8
RELIANCE BK	DES PERES	MO	C+	C+	C	348.9	39.87	12.9	0.7	11.5	31.2	10.0	12.2	17.4
▼ RELIANCE SVGS BK	ALTOONA	PA	B-	B+	B-	268.1	11.10	5.0	1.6	43.7	15.2	9.3	10.8	14.4
▼ RENASANT BK	GERMANTOWN	TN	C-	C	C-	220.7	-3.08	16.2	2.9	9.5	13.2	3.7	8.2	10.4
REPUBLIC B&T	NORMAN	OK	B-	C+	C	184.2	22.77	13.4	3.5	19.4	6.8	7.7	9.5	13.1
REPUBLIC B&TC	LOUISVILLE	KY	B	B+	B	2,177.8	19.33	1.4	2.2	36.8	16.9	4.9	6.9	12.9
REPUBLIC B&TC OF INDIANA	JEFFERSONVILLE	IN	B	B+	B	48.1	49.22	0.8	0.1	30.4	6.8	10.0	12.1	16.7
REPUBLIC BK	LANSING	MI	B	B	B	5,692.0	13.51	0.7	0.6	39.0	17.4	5.5	7.5	12.4
REPUBLIC BK	DULUTH	MN	B-	B-	C+	193.3	11.73	22.6	3.1	17.0	6.5	6.1	9.7	11.8
▲ REPUBLIC BK	W BOUNTIFUL	UT	B	B-	B+	271.9	20.60	0.0	0.0	0.0	11.0	7.6	11.0	13.0
REPUBLIC BK OF CHICAGO	DARIEN	IL	B+	B+	B-	611.8	21.42	12.4	5.8	13.9	19.9	6.6	9.8	12.2
▲ REPUBLIC BKG CO	REPUBLIC	OH	B+	B	B	26.3	3.50	11.8	7.6	36.5	12.9	10.0	15.5	22.8
REPUBLIC FIRST BK	PHILADELPHIA	PA	C	C	C-	636.0	4.56	8.5	0.2	24.4	8.8	6.2	8.4	11.9

Asset Quality Index	Non-Performing Loans as a % of Total Loans	Non-Performing Loans as a % of Capital	Net Charge-offs Avg Loans	Profitability Index	Net Income ($Mil)	Return on Assets (R.O.A.)	Return on Equity (R.O.E.)	Net Interest Spread	Overhead Efficiency Ratio	Liquidity Index	Liquidity Ratio	Hot Money Ratio	Stability Index
1.7	13.32	42.7	4.01	0.0	-0.4	-0.72	-6.38	3.74	107.8	4.6	27.8	7.3	4.5
5.5	0.40	3.4	0.07	7.9	0.8	1.48	17.35	5.33	53.4	2.2	31.3	22.8	4.2
8.5	0.00	0.0	-0.09	3.9	0.5	0.40	5.77	4.85	81.0	5.2	44.5	10.2	2.2
4.4	0.84	2.8	2.94	8.9	2.0	3.85	17.00	12.22	43.7	0.5	10.8	62.9	7.3
3.3	1.84	15.1	-0.02	10.0	0.5	3.42	34.10	5.70	36.9	3.4	14.6	12.0	5.6
9.0	0.11	0.5	0.03	7.0	0.5	1.29	11.99	3.76	51.2	5.3	44.4	9.0	7.4
1.9	3.52	26.0	-0.04	3.4	0.7	0.53	6.57	4.05	76.5	3.6	34.7	15.2	3.0
4.8	0.59	5.8	0.11	10.0	0.8	1.72	21.01	5.09	48.6	1.3	12.7	26.5	6.3
5.8	0.42	3.5	0.01	5.0	0.4	0.75	8.22	5.22	75.9	4.9	24.8	4.0	5.4
6.1	1.33	6.2	-0.20	6.0	0.2	1.01	7.08	4.61	65.8	3.8	37.8	15.3	6.5
9.6	0.13	0.8	0.00	4.5	1.1	0.67	7.48	3.66	73.2	5.7	47.4	7.8	5.3
7.6	0.31	1.9	0.49	0.0	-0.2	-1.17	-16.21	3.18	131.3	6.2	83.4	10.6	0.0
9.2	0.00	0.0	0.00	9.0	0.4	1.52	15.90	5.04	54.8	3.3	9.1	11.9	5.0
4.3	0.91	5.5	0.33	5.8	0.5	1.08	11.77	3.83	52.4	4.0	49.8	16.6	4.1
4.0	2.27	14.4	0.25	8.7	1.0	1.37	13.11	5.11	55.1	4.5	24.0	6.4	6.7
5.2	0.49	3.1	0.02	7.2	0.9	1.53	15.38	5.05	69.3	1.8	15.5	20.4	7.1
7.7	0.55	4.6	0.13	4.0	0.1	0.45	5.11	3.84	80.8	1.0	5.0	29.0	3.7
7.6	0.65	5.1	0.00	4.6	3.2	0.72	8.65	1.96	39.0	0.7	15.2	47.9	4.6
5.9	2.02	5.5	0.04	6.4	0.3	1.13	6.88	3.57	49.0	2.5	36.6	24.3	7.2
7.9	0.07	0.5	-0.06	5.9	0.9	1.16	13.48	5.01	67.4	3.5	20.0	12.2	4.9
4.4	0.79	3.0	0.30	2.0	6.1	0.06	0.38	3.18	92.5	5.6	35.4	7.7	8.7
6.8	0.91	0.4	3.23	9.6	0.2	3.00	3.23	7.24	31.0	0.0	N/A	100.0	3.4
7.8	0.79	2.8	0.10	8.6	4.9	1.48	12.60	4.21	56.5	3.3	19.0	13.1	8.4
9.7	0.04	0.3	0.02	4.2	0.7	0.70	7.93	3.72	71.9	3.6	25.5	12.1	5.0
5.2	2.13	13.8	0.00	3.5	0.0	0.62	5.57	3.27	80.9	3.4	67.2	22.5	4.1
9.0	0.00	0.0	0.00	7.6	0.3	1.74	13.33	3.55	48.8	3.9	25.2	10.5	8.0
3.1	4.71	31.6	-0.07	4.9	0.1	0.85	8.82	4.59	76.6	5.1	44.9	10.1	3.8
7.6	0.05	0.3	-0.01	7.2	0.4	1.63	13.81	5.01	66.3	4.6	35.8	10.4	6.3
10.0	0.00	0.0	0.00	0.0	-0.4	-9.21	-9.61	-0.05	**, *** *	7.0	789.5	17.7	0.0
8.2	0.32	2.1	0.00	2.4	0.3	0.56	4.66	3.49	74.9	2.4	20.6	17.8	4.9
8.2	0.01	0.1	0.04	6.0	1.9	1.05	13.85	3.62	64.1	1.8	25.1	22.5	4.7
5.7	0.38	3.1	0.01	9.0	0.4	2.34	23.95	4.58	46.8	1.7	18.2	22.6	4.7
2.8	1.43	6.9	1.17	2.0	0.1	0.21	1.85	4.28	76.9	4.1	79.7	25.1	5.4
4.3	1.17	8.5	0.24	7.0	2.6	1.28	14.35	4.47	53.8	3.4	52.4	23.0	5.8
5.5	0.29	1.8	0.03	7.9	0.7	1.49	11.85	6.15	57.0	2.4	31.7	20.2	6.5
9.0	0.00	0.0	0.00	0.0	-0.4	-0.75	-2.98	2.70	119.4	6.0	49.0	6.1	6.9
6.0	0.82	5.1	0.01	3.8	0.2	0.54	6.79	3.91	81.5	7.8	114.2	5.0	4.1
9.9	0.00	0.0	0.00	0.0	-1.1	-11.19	-22.07	0.77	1,536.0	9.3	191.0	3.5	0.0
3.7	0.52	1.7	0.22	5.6	0.8	0.97	5.07	4.58	69.2	3.6	14.8	11.2	7.2
2.8	1.01	7.5	0.60	2.2	-0.1	-0.16	-1.70	4.88	95.5	2.7	22.8	16.3	3.4
5.1	0.42	3.8	0.03	5.9	0.5	0.99	12.57	4.53	66.4	1.6	14.5	22.8	1.7
8.7	0.00	0.0	0.00	1.1	0.1	0.24	1.56	3.35	84.2	4.7	112.6	25.4	0.1
4.0	1.09	5.6	0.01	10.0	15.8	2.37	19.28	4.46	25.5	1.3	21.0	31.7	8.3
2.4	3.03	19.3	0.00	3.6	0.2	0.45	4.96	4.85	86.9	3.5	6.2	10.4	1.3
5.2	0.40	4.2	0.00	5.4	0.6	0.80	11.50	5.22	76.0	5.1	28.1	4.0	3.6
8.6	0.00	0.0	0.00	1.9	0.5	0.68	8.62	3.55	84.9	7.5	98.3	6.6	0.7
3.9	1.41	10.1	0.13	6.5	1.4	1.08	12.75	3.21	56.2	2.9	17.0	14.7	2.9
7.8	0.12	1.3	0.11	7.5	0.5	1.66	22.40	3.80	56.9	3.6	13.7	11.1	4.4
5.8	0.65	5.6	0.26	7.1	299.1	1.31	15.69	3.73	61.3	3.7	27.4	15.2	7.3
9.8	0.00	0.0	0.00	7.2	0.1	2.21	2.37	2.56	92.2	5.0	3,034.5	100.0	0.9
6.5	0.15	1.2	-0.04	7.0	1.0	1.90	22.26	5.27	58.2	2.5	12.7	16.5	5.1
3.9	0.73	6.0	0.32	4.1	0.2	0.52	6.63	3.80	67.8	0.7	11.6	37.0	3.2
8.8	0.18	0.9	0.00	2.9	0.6	0.40	3.71	2.57	71.3	2.7	42.5	26.4	5.6
7.2	0.28	1.9	0.09	4.0	0.8	0.64	5.79	3.43	73.7	2.8	8.2	14.3	6.2
7.2	0.09	0.8	-0.04	2.3	-0.1	-0.05	-0.62	3.66	91.5	1.8	21.7	22.0	4.8
4.6	0.87	6.2	0.04	5.0	0.9	1.07	11.08	4.79	78.9	4.3	27.9	9.1	4.9
6.1	0.80	8.2	0.25	9.6	18.3	1.70	24.18	4.59	51.9	5.1	37.5	11.5	6.1
9.2	0.00	0.0	0.09	4.4	0.1	0.26	2.05	4.10	83.8	3.7	6.5	9.8	5.0
6.1	0.80	7.8	0.08	7.1	35.2	1.28	17.13	2.92	43.9	1.8	16.5	21.4	6.6
5.3	1.31	11.1	-0.19	6.2	1.3	1.39	15.51	4.66	68.3	1.2	13.0	28.3	4.9
5.1	0.59	4.5	1.25	10.0	5.2	3.90	38.80	5.00	12.7	0.4	15.5	86.0	6.8
4.6	1.60	12.3	0.04	5.6	3.8	1.34	13.84	3.66	59.8	2.7	38.2	23.3	6.8
7.2	0.30	1.6	0.00	9.9	0.2	1.84	12.22	5.01	45.9	3.2	18.3	13.4	8.0
4.6	1.05	8.5	0.33	3.1	1.7	0.53	6.30	2.95	71.8	3.1	30.1	16.3	3.2

Name	City	State	Weiss Safety Rating	2003 Weiss Safety Rating	2002 Weiss Safety Rating	Total Assets ($Mil)	One Year Asset Growth	Asset Mix (As a % of Total Assets) Comm- ercial Loans	Cons- umer Loans	Home Mort- gages	Secur- ities	Capital- ization Index	Leverage Ratio	Risk-based Capital Ratio
▲ REPUBLIC NB	HOUSTON	TX	B-	C+	C+	473.5	6.93	25.2	5.4	4.9	17.9	5.8	8.5	11.6
▲ RESOURCE BK	MANDEVILLE	LA	C	C-	D+	180.7	16.12	49.6	3.5	9.7	6.6	4.8	8.8	10.9
▲ RESOURCE BK	VIRGINIA BEACH	VA	B-	C+	C	1,061.3	29.11	10.0	0.3	14.3	10.4	5.4	8.3	11.3
RESOURCE BK NA	DE KALB	IL	D+	D+	C-	215.2	0.24	7.6	1.1	5.9	26.0	9.7	10.8	15.8
RETAILERS NB	SIOUX FALLS	SD	B+	B+	A	227.2	16.82	0.0	49.6	0.0	33.0	10.0	45.8	63.5
▲ REYNOLDS ST BK	REYNOLDS	IL	A	A-	B+	63.4	9.38	0.5	0.2	0.4	86.7	10.0	18.6	57.4
RHINEBECK SVGS BK	RHINEBECK	NY	C	C	C	363.1	6.30	4.5	27.6	13.5	15.3	3.7	7.4	10.4
RICHARDSON CTY B&TC	FALLS CITY	NE	A-	A-	A-	76.0	3.81	9.1	3.8	9.1	47.0	10.0	12.0	24.9
RICHLAND COUNTY BK	RICHLAND CENTER	WI	B+	A-	A-	106.7	0.88	5.4	6.4	16.0	45.0	10.0	17.5	34.7
RICHLAND ST BK	RAYVILLE	LA	A-	A-	A-	134.0	7.20	14.4	8.5	11.5	27.6	10.0	12.1	18.2
RICHLAND ST BK	BRUCE	SD	B	B	B	21.7	-33.82	1.5	4.7	3.5	41.6	10.0	18.1	40.5
RICHLAND TRUST CO	MANSFIELD	OH	B-	B-	B-	575.8	7.99	7.4	7.2	15.0	37.7	4.4	6.4	12.5
▼ RICHTON B&TC	RICHTON	MS	C-	C+	D	72.4	1.31	9.0	18.3	17.1	32.9	7.6	9.4	14.8
RICHWOOD BKG CO	RICHWOOD	OH	B	B	B	157.3	-0.78	14.0	5.1	11.3	35.0	6.9	8.9	14.3
RIDDELL NB	BRAZIL	IN	B	B	B+	130.5	-4.02	3.3	15.0	25.1	32.5	9.0	10.3	17.6
RIDGEDALE ST BK	MINNETONKA	MN	C	C-	C-	107.1	5.60	20.9	5.3	24.8	24.4	5.0	7.0	11.5
RIDGESTONE BK	BROOKFIELD	WI	C	C	C-	89.7	-2.03	24.1	0.5	7.2	5.6	5.1	9.9	11.1
RIDGEWOOD SVGS BK	NEW YORK CITY	NY	B+	B+	A-	3,290.6	6.06	0.0	0.1	39.0	46.5	10.0	14.8	28.7
▼ RIGGS BK NA	MC LEAN	VA	D+	C	B-	6,453.3	-7.12	5.3	1.0	19.7	33.3	4.4	6.5	10.7
▲ RIGHT BK TX NA	HOUSTON	TX	D+	D	D	70.5	105.64	29.6	4.3	5.8	9.3	10.0	18.7	21.2
▼ RILEY ST BK	RILEY	KS	B	B+	B+	31.2	5.75	8.5	8.9	8.3	18.4	9.8	10.8	16.0
▲ RIO BK	MCALLEN	TX	D	E+	E+	70.7	14.36	9.3	7.3	8.6	16.9	5.4	7.8	11.3
RIO GRANDE S&LA	MONTE VISTA	CO	C+	C+	C+	88.6	-3.05	0.2	4.0	66.5	0.0	6.8	8.8	15.5
▼ RIPLEY FS&LA	RIPLEY	OH	C+	B-	B	79.8	-0.22	5.0	2.6	40.7	9.4	10.0	13.2	22.7
▲ RIPLEY NB	RIPLEY	OH	E	E	E	56.2	-16.57	7.0	1.5	30.0	14.6	5.6	7.6	12.9
▲ RIVER BANK	STODDARD	WI	B+	B	B-	216.0	3.16	7.9	1.2	9.6	18.7	7.8	9.6	13.4
RIVER CITIES BK	WISCONSIN RAPIDS	WI	B+	B+	B+	142.0	10.53	9.7	0.7	9.8	26.3	6.2	8.7	11.9
RIVER CITY BK	SACRAMENTO	CA	B	B	B	725.3	7.02	11.9	5.1	6.5	35.7	6.3	8.4	12.3
▲ RIVER CITY BK	LOUISVILLE	KY	A	A-	A-	196.3	-10.09	2.2	4.0	54.0	20.2	10.0	13.4	25.3
RIVER FALLS ST BK	RIVER FALLS	WI	A-	A-	A-	74.0	-1.11	5.0	3.2	26.6	20.2	10.0	15.1	24.7
▲ RIVER VALLEY FINANCIAL BK	MADISON	IN	A-	B	B	257.5	9.01	12.6	3.1	32.6	10.2	9.0	10.3	14.3
▲ RIVER VALLEY ST BK	ROTHSCHILD	WI	B	B-	B-	387.4	11.69	20.6	2.8	15.7	10.4	7.3	10.1	12.7
RIVERBANK	CHISAGO CITY	MN	C	C-	C+	77.0	13.81	14.9	3.1	14.1	11.6	5.8	8.7	11.6
▲ RIVERBANK	OSCEOLA	WI	C	C-	C+	215.5	19.05	17.9	7.9	7.4	4.6	3.1	7.9	10.1
RIVERBEND BK	FORT WORTH	TX	C	C-	C-	35.5	-6.46	17.4	10.6	8.5	8.7	6.2	8.2	13.6
RIVERGREEN BK	KENNEBUNK	ME	D	D	NR	43.3	124.58	14.1	1.5	2.9	4.5	10.0	15.5	19.1
RIVERHILLS BANK	PORT GIBSON	MS	B-	B-	B	150.1	10.95	13.3	7.3	17.8	23.2	6.0	8.0	12.8
▼ RIVERSIDE BK	SPARKMAN	AR	D+	C-	D+	42.8	-1.92	9.8	15.0	48.1	8.6	2.6	7.4	9.6
RIVERSIDE BK	MARIETTA	GA	B-	B-	C+	495.8	10.93	9.5	1.3	8.2	16.8	5.2	9.0	11.2
RIVERSIDE BK	POUGHKEEPSIE	NY	B-	C+	B-	122.0	5.90	34.9	1.5	1.9	8.6	5.5	8.2	11.4
RIVERSIDE BK OF CENTRAL	WINTER PARK	FL	D-	D-	D	67.8	55.60	3.6	6.8	19.3	20.0	7.0	9.0	12.8
RIVERSIDE BK OF GULF	CAPE CORAL	FL	B-	B-	C+	323.1	47.98	3.2	1.5	23.0	17.9	5.4	9.2	11.3
RIVERSIDE COMMUNITY BK	ROCKFORD	IL	B-	B-	C+	180.1	8.89	12.9	3.0	16.4	19.3	5.2	7.7	11.2
▲ RIVERSIDE NB OF FLORIDA	FORT PIERCE	FL	A-	B+	B+	2,123.4	6.75	3.5	19.1	23.0	26.8	7.5	9.3	13.5
RIVERTON COMMUNITY BK	RIVERTON	IL	C+	C+	B-	34.3	0.83	4.6	8.5	26.4	36.3	7.8	9.5	21.7
RIVERVIEW COMMUNITY BK	OTSEGO	MN	D	D	NR	63.1	204.91	17.3	2.7	22.5	7.5	6.7	9.1	12.3
▼ RIVERVIEW COMMUNITY BK	CAMAS	WA	B+	A-	A	500.2	17.43	11.5	1.0	10.1	9.6	8.0	10.4	13.3
▲ RIVOLI B&TC	MACON	GA	B	B-	C+	160.0	11.35	7.6	6.0	11.8	15.1	6.5	8.8	12.1
ROANOKE RAPIDS SVG BK	ROANOKE RAPIDS	NC	C+	B-	D+	57.7	-3.10	0.0	7.0	20.9	33.9	10.0	13.3	23.3
ROANOKE VALLEY SVGS BK	ROANOKE RAPIDS	NC	B	B	B+	43.6	-0.24	0.0	0.5	43.9	19.3	10.0	19.2	45.2
▲ ROBERT LEE ST BK	ROBERT LEE	TX	C+	C	C-	37.9	-4.80	10.0	14.3	12.6	32.4	10.0	11.1	20.5
ROBERTS CTY NB OF	SISSETON	SD	A-	A-	A-	43.9	3.14	1.9	2.2	5.2	67.6	10.0	19.0	44.0
▼ ROBERTSON BKG CO	DEMOPOLIS	AL	D	C-	C	211.9	-0.51	8.8	9.6	31.6	19.4	8.9	10.2	16.8
ROCHELLE ST BK	ROCHELLE	GA	C	C	C	19.7	1.99	3.2	10.8	9.3	39.9	10.0	14.0	28.6
ROCHESTER B&TC	ROCHESTER	MN	C+	C+	B-	48.3	-6.96	9.9	4.5	4.9	55.8	8.5	12.6	13.7
ROCHESTER ST BK	ROCHESTER	IL	A-	A-	B+	56.3	6.46	5.3	7.2	15.5	50.0	10.0	15.2	29.8
ROCK BR CMNTY BK	NITRO	WV	C-	D+	D+	42.4	-1.05	7.7	11.5	22.0	29.5	7.3	9.2	16.2
ROCK COMMUNITY BK	GLEN ROCK	NJ	C+	C+	B-	35.5	-14.23	5.2	1.5	27.3	8.5	10.0	15.0	19.3
ROCK RIVER BK	OREGON	IL	C+	C+	C	67.2	-8.47	4.2	2.6	9.9	36.7	8.3	9.9	18.4
ROCK SPRINGS NB	ROCK SPRINGS	WY	A-	A-	A	244.7	3.55	9.2	4.6	13.1	48.5	7.0	9.0	18.4
▼ ROCKHOLD BROWN & CO BK	BAINBRIDGE	OH	C+	B-	B-	33.0	14.50	6.6	6.8	50.4	8.7	8.5	10.0	16.3
ROCKINGHAM HERITAGE BK	HARRISONBURG	VA	B	B	B-	197.6	9.25	15.1	2.2	15.5	3.9	6.8	9.9	12.3
ROCKLAND S&LA	ROCKLAND	ME	B	B-	B-	72.2	2.55	4.5	13.3	51.4	7.9	10.0	11.9	18.7
ROCKLAND TRUST CO	ROCKLAND	MA	B	B	B	2,673.3	10.24	7.2	12.0	16.4	28.8	5.0	7.0	11.3

Asset Quality Index	Non-Performing Loans as a % of Total Loans	as a % of Capital	Net Charge-offs Avg Loans	Profitability Index	Net Income ($Mil)	Return on Assets (R.O.A.)	Return on Equity (R.O.E.)	Net Interest Spread	Overhead Efficiency Ratio	Liquidity Index	Liquidity Ratio	Hot Money Ratio	Stability Index
8.0	0.01	0.1	0.15	6.0	2.4	1.05	12.57	4.64	60.7	1.8	27.2	24.6	4.2
7.9	0.01	0.1	0.06	3.8	0.6	0.65	7.76	4.38	70.6	2.0	22.8	20.0	3.6
7.5	0.13	0.4	-0.01	6.2	3.5	0.75	5.94	3.77	71.1	0.4	3.7	54.7	5.5
1.5	5.51	29.3	0.16	4.5	1.0	0.92	7.98	4.38	75.9	3.3	29.1	14.7	6.5
5.1	2.54	2.5	8.40	10.0	17.8	15.39	36.97	12.89	81.9	5.0	33,921.5	99.7	8.2
9.3	0.87	0.3	-0.09	9.3	0.6	1.86	10.04	3.89	21.0	6.8	91.7	8.1	8.7
6.0	0.13	1.2	0.11	5.1	1.3	0.74	10.19	5.01	78.0	6.1	42.5	3.7	3.2
8.6	0.95	2.8	0.01	5.9	0.4	0.98	7.69	3.28	59.2	5.8	65.9	10.3	7.8
8.8	0.30	0.7	0.24	4.6	0.6	1.04	5.75	3.86	68.7	6.5	79.3	9.7	8.6
8.0	0.50	2.4	0.14	6.3	0.8	1.20	10.01	4.95	71.5	3.2	21.7	13.6	6.7
8.7	1.16	2.1	0.19	9.5	0.4	3.03	16.31	3.03	69.0	6.6	188.3	18.7	4.8
7.3	0.34	2.4	0.13	9.7	4.8	1.71	29.21	3.99	43.4	2.9	37.4	19.6	5.4
2.3	3.54	18.3	0.13	6.6	0.6	1.57	16.79	5.60	73.3	4.6	44.8	12.6	5.0
7.7	0.29	1.8	-0.15	5.7	0.9	1.17	13.06	4.28	67.9	4.0	22.9	9.6	5.6
5.0	0.99	5.4	0.32	4.5	0.4	0.52	5.13	3.62	76.4	4.1	18.9	8.4	5.5
7.9	0.01	0.1	0.08	4.9	0.7	1.34	19.36	4.16	65.4	5.1	46.9	11.2	3.3
5.8	0.67	5.1	0.08	3.7	0.2	0.46	4.71	3.86	84.3	2.6	35.0	21.6	4.6
10.0	0.06	0.2	0.00	4.9	14.0	0.87	5.79	3.10	59.1	9.2	423.5	5.6	10.0
9.3	0.21	1.6	0.06	1.3	-19.9	-0.54	-7.77	3.38	111.5	4.6	39.1	14.1	3.5
7.9	0.03	0.1	0.07	0.7	0.0	0.00	-0.02	4.99	91.9	2.1	30.7	23.7	0.0
5.9	0.97	6.1	0.01	7.1	0.2	1.55	14.38	3.89	57.4	4.1	44.1	15.2	6.8
4.2	0.99	8.4	0.22	3.6	0.3	0.77	10.72	5.39	86.6	1.2	12.5	28.1	1.0
6.4	0.24	2.3	0.03	3.8	0.3	0.55	6.42	3.73	78.7	1.5	11.6	23.4	4.3
6.4	0.59	2.6	-0.01	2.6	0.0	0.08	0.56	2.82	94.2	2.2	21.1	18.4	6.9
2.7	3.23	24.2	3.18	1.5	-0.7	-2.12	-33.36	4.02	101.8	4.0	40.4	15.0	1.0
5.5	0.26	1.9	0.00	7.6	2.1	1.89	19.19	3.68	42.6	1.9	26.4	23.5	6.1
8.6	0.14	1.0	0.00	6.9	0.7	1.07	12.06	3.29	51.9	3.4	21.6	12.8	5.7
8.4	0.24	1.5	-0.04	4.8	3.2	0.91	11.04	3.68	72.3	5.2	41.8	9.0	5.8
8.7	0.40	2.1	0.94	10.0	2.7	2.70	21.44	5.73	42.2	7.9	92.1	2.9	7.7
7.5	1.16	4.5	0.06	5.4	0.3	0.75	4.96	4.10	68.4	5.7	59.7	9.4	7.4
6.0	0.53	3.8	0.02	7.7	1.3	1.05	9.82	3.48	55.7	1.2	29.0	38.1	6.6
4.5	1.19	9.0	0.10	8.8	3.7	1.96	19.32	4.57	54.9	2.1	17.8	19.0	6.8
5.3	0.14	0.8	0.45	8.4	0.4	1.20	8.82	4.71	51.9	2.8	38.2	20.4	5.0
2.4	1.68	15.6	0.02	9.5	1.5	1.40	17.25	4.58	60.4	1.8	19.9	21.9	5.7
4.8	1.59	11.6	0.04	8.0	0.4	2.23	27.18	5.15	69.6	5.3	47.7	9.6	3.5
7.3	0.03	0.1	0.00	0.0	-0.2	-0.82	-4.52	3.68	115.0	5.8	91.8	14.0	0.0
6.5	0.12	0.9	-0.01	5.1	0.8	1.06	13.13	3.92	61.8	3.2	51.4	25.9	4.6
4.2	0.90	8.8	0.07	10.0	0.6	2.86	37.54	6.06	48.5	0.9	8,9	31.9	3.9
6.8	0.01	0.1	0.14	6.2	2.7	1.07	12.29	3.80	60.2	1.7	22.6	23.5	4.6
7.5	0.31	2.5	0.00	6.3	0.7	1.20	16.05	4.86	62.5	5.4	34.2	5.0	4.1
8.5	0.01	0.1	0.05	0.1	-0.1	-0.24	-3.04	3.87	101.3	3.8	4.1	8.8	0.0
7.1	0.39	3.2	0.17	6.7	1.4	0.92	11.50	4.23	69.0	1.7	10.8	20.6	4.3
8.5	0.15	1.2	0.06	5.0	0.9	1.01	13.38	3.68	67.6	2.2	21.8	18.6	5.0
6.6	0.45	3.0	0.27	9.1	19.0	1.79	19.78	4.57	59.7	5.8	62.3	12.5	7.4
8.6	0.00	0.0	0.00	3.5	0.1	0.55	6.00	2.95	77.0	6.6	71.2	6.5	3.8
8.3	0.16	1.4	0.04	1.3	0.1	0.31	3.58	4.15	85.9	4.0	111.0	36.6	0.0
5.1	0.33	2.3	0.36	8.5	3.8	1.49	12.50	4.85	60.8	0.8	19.3	48.7	8.0
6.8	0.52	4.3	0.35	6.2	0.9	1.10	12.94	4.55	67.4	3.1	15.6	13.7	4.6
7.9	0.31	1.2	0.38	2.6	0.1	0.41	3.02	3.05	84.9	5.4	76.6	14.1	4.9
10.0	0.69	1.9	0.00	4.1	0.1	0.53	2.79	2.73	61.5	5.9	9,657.4	28.6	6.6
7.1	0.47	1.9	0.44	3.3	0.1	0.55	4.86	4.43	82.8	5.8	103.5	15.1	3.2
9.8	0.00	0.0	0.02	6.3	0.3	1.31	6.83	3.63	62.8	6.8	81.9	7.0	8.1
1.0	4.13	26.5	0.45	5.2	1.2	1.11	10.46	3.93	56.7	1.9	29.8	26.2	5.6
8.1	0.96	2.7	0.10	3.5	0.1	0.53	3.70	3.84	81.1	3.5	49.9	17.2	4.2
8.7	0.02	0.1	0.42	4.0	0.3	1.02	8.24	3.21	69.7	4.4	6.8	4.7	5.0
9.1	0.29	0.7	0.25	5.8	0.4	1.43	9.65	3.66	59.5	7.3	86.3	4.0	8.0
3.8	1.46	9.4	0.04	5.6	0.2	0.92	10.24	4.79	68.7	5.7	56.3	8.7	3.5
9.0	0.38	1.8	-0.01	3.8	0.1	0.54	3.72	4.22	74.8	3.6	32.8	14.4	6.7
7.8	0.25	1.3	0.44	6.4	0.3	0.95	9.82	4.24	66.7	3.9	23.6	10.2	5.0
7.5	0.68	3.6	-0.01	8.8	2.0	1.65	18.14	4.23	48.3	4.1	52.2	17.5	6.1
1.7	4.88	37.1	0.51	4.7	0.1	0.74	7.35	4.84	73.3	4.8	14.8	3.6	4.6
4.9	0.39	3.2	0.00	8.0	1.2	1.27	13.17	4.32	55.6	2.9	29.3	16.9	6.0
4.8	1.42	9.8	0.05	7.6	0.4	1.19	10.01	4.22	56.8	1.5	5.2	22.1	6.1
7.6	0.20	1.4	0.09	7.3	14.8	1.16	13.82	4.24	62.4	5.1	25.0	6.3	7.2

| Name | City | State | Weiss Safety Rating | 2003 Weiss Safety Rating | 2002 Weiss Safety Rating | Total Assets ($Mil) | One Year Asset Growth | Asset Mix (As a % of Total Assets) | | | | Capital- ization Index | Leverage Ratio | Risk-based Capital Ratio |
								Comm- ercial Loans	Cons- umer Loans	Home Mort- gages	Secur- ities			
ROCKPORT NB	ROCKPORT	MA	C+	C+	C+	109.6	13.04	4.0	3.4	24.1	25.6	5.2	7.2	11.9
ROCKVILLE BK	S WINDSOR	CT	B-	B	B	800.7	9.80	9.0	0.4	43.5	17.0	6.2	8.2	13.0
ROCKWOOD BK	EUREKA	MO	B	B	B	297.3	9.99	6.7	2.5	16.8	1.6	6.2	9.8	11.9
▲ ROCKY MOUNTAIN B&T	FLORENCE	CO	C-	C-	D-	92.8	18.99	5.8	0.6	11.0	38.9	5.2	7.2	13.3
ROCKY MOUNTAIN BK	BILLINGS	MT	C+	C+	C+	382.7	6.83	15.7	3.5	9.3	11.9	5.1	7.9	11.1
ROEBLING BK	ROEBLING	NJ	C+	C+	C+	89.9	2.90	1.7	0.4	46.6	24.2	6.2	8.2	14.5
▲ ROLETTE ST BK	ROLETTE	ND	C	C-	D+	29.0	5.12	5.8	3.5	3.1	21.9	8.1	9.7	15.9
▲ ROLFE ST BK	ROLFE	IA	B+	B	B	30.7	-3.41	7.9	3.9	9.1	24.7	7.5	9.3	14.2
ROLLING HILLS B&T	ATLANTIC	IA	B+	A-	A-	89.8	18.66	18.4	3.9	5.5	11.2	7.9	10.0	13.2
ROMA BANK	TRENTON	NJ	A+	A+	A+	687.4	5.51	0.1	0.3	38.0	46.1	10.0	18.5	39.8
▼ ROME SAVINGS BANK	ROME	NY	B-	NR	NR	265.3	N/A	7.8	10.9	40.5	8.6	5.5	10.6	11.4
RONDOUT SVGS BK	KINGSTON	NY	B	B	A-	186.5	6.13	3.8	0.4	24.1	48.2	10.0	12.2	24.5
ROOT RIVER ST BK	CHATFIELD	MN	C+	C+	C+	62.2	1.62	8.3	1.8	19.4	20.3	7.9	9.6	14.8
ROSCOE ST BK	ROSCOE	TX	B	B	B-	53.2	2.82	6.6	4.7	6.8	41.0	9.0	10.4	18.6
▲ ROSE HILL BK	ROSE HILL	KS	A-	A-	A-	111.1	7.10	6.7	20.2	19.4	21.8	10.0	11.9	16.8
ROSEDALE FS&LA	BALTIMORE	MD	A+	A+	A+	575.8	3.60	0.0	0.1	65.5	11.3	10.0	18.6	35.8
▲ ROSELLE SB	ROSELLE	NJ	B	B-	B	407.4	2.37	0.0	0.2	12.0	83.2	10.0	13.3	61.4
ROSEMOUNT NB	ROSEMOUNT	MN	C	C	C-	51.7	-2.10	16.8	15.3	15.9	13.5	6.1	9.5	11.8
▲ ROSSVILLE BK	ROSSVILLE	GA	A-	B+	B+	93.0	-4.54	10.7	2.6	11.7	28.7	10.0	11.0	17.7
▲ ROUND TOP ST BK	ROUND TOP	TX	B+	B	B-	130.5	4.81	5.3	10.2	21.6	21.0	6.9	8.9	15.4
▲ ROUNDBANK	WASECA	MN	B	B-	B-	186.5	1.79	12.5	3.2	13.5	28.8	6.3	8.3	13.6
ROWAN SVGS BK	CHINA GROVE	NC	B-	C+	C+	162.2	16.49	0.6	1.8	26.4	5.6	4.5	7.5	10.8
ROWLEY SVG BK	ROWLEY	IA	C+	B-	B	13.4	2.80	12.1	9.0	22.7	1.1	9.2	10.4	18.9
ROXBORO SVGS BK	ROXBORO	NC	A-	B+	B	146.2	-0.23	1.0	2.4	31.8	49.6	10.0	16.4	35.9
▲ ROXBURY BK	ROXBURY	KS	D-	E	E-	12.2	-7.52	11.8	7.6	15.7	16.3	9.2	10.5	16.5
ROXBURY HIGHLAND CO-OP	BOSTON	MA	C-	C-	C-	28.2	-2.16	0.0	1.5	35.1	26.9	8.7	10.1	19.7
ROYAL AMERICAN BK	INVERNESS	IL	B	B	A-	371.4	15.67	30.5	1.5	4.4	8.9	4.8	9.0	10.9
ROYAL BK	ELROY	WI	C+	C+	C	141.1	8.41	14.1	7.3	18.4	19.5	5.2	7.4	11.1
▲ ROYAL BK AMERICA	NARBERTH	PA	A-	B+	B	1,183.1	-0.24	1.6	0.1	3.8	48.0	7.4	9.2	14.3
ROYAL BKS OF MO	UNIVERSITY CITY	MO	B-	B-	B-	295.5	6.22	6.6	1.0	7.3	14.5	6.7	9.4	12.3
▲ ROYAL OAKS BK SSB	HOUSTON	TX	C+	C	D-	108.1	43.85	14.2	6.0	18.9	2.7	7.8	9.5	13.6
ROYAL PALM BK OF FLORIDA	NAPLES	FL	D	D	D	73.3	22.09	1.3	0.6	30.5	12.1	9.2	10.5	14.8
▼ ROYAL SVGS BK	CHICAGO	IL	C-	B-	B+	92.8	6.78	9.0	0.2	21.8	48.0	10.0	13.9	28.1
▼ RUBY VALLEY NB	TWIN BRIDGES	MT	D+	C-	D+	52.0	3.12	25.4	6.5	11.4	4.1	8.8	11.1	14.0
▲ RUMSON FAIR HAVEN B&TC	FAIR HAVEN	NJ	D	D-	D-	100.8	40.45	5.9	0.2	26.3	33.1	10.0	11.2	17.5
RURAL AMER BK	HECTOR	MN	B	B	B	60.1	-2.04	15.7	4.0	3.0	24.5	6.0	8.0	11.7
RURAL AMERICAN BANK	LONSDALE	MN	B	B	B	68.9	0.10	13.9	3.9	14.6	22.7	5.9	7.9	11.7
RURAL AMERICAN BK - LUCK	LUCK	WI	B	B	B	58.0	-2.05	2.4	4.3	19.9	18.5	5.2	7.6	11.2
RURAL AMERICAN BK FOLEY	FOLEY	MN	B	B	B	68.8	-7.60	9.2	3.2	13.1	22.3	5.5	8.0	11.4
RURAL AMERICAN BK-ADA	ADA	MN	B	B	B	33.3	-6.46	5.7	10.0	6.9	18.8	6.2	8.3	11.9
RURAL AMERICAN BK-BRAHAM	BRAHAM	MN	B	B	B	36.5	-2.04	7.1	6.1	17.7	11.9	5.8	7.8	11.7
▼ RUSHFORD ST BK	RUSHFORD	MN	D+	C-	C	36.6	15.82	3.9	10.5	19.7	13.6	4.9	8.3	10.9
RUSHVILLE ST BK	RUSHVILLE	IL	A-	A-	A-	67.2	2.49	8.6	4.4	7.0	58.4	10.0	14.7	33.0
▼ RUSHVILLE ST BK	RUSHVILLE	MO	D-	D	D	22.9	1.15	4.6	5.5	22.8	41.9	7.5	9.4	18.2
▲ RUSTON B&LA	RUSTON	LA	B-	C+	C-	63.3	-3.73	2.4	10.4	42.8	14.6	8.5	10.0	16.2
RUTH ST BK	RUTH	MI	B	B	B	28.9	-1.75	3.0	2.9	13.4	53.7	10.0	12.1	25.5
S&C BK	NEW RICHMOND	WI	B	B	B+	357.9	5.41	8.3	3.7	13.9	18.7	8.2	9.8	13.6
S&T BK	INDIANA	PA	B	B	B-	2,953.5	2.80	17.4	2.4	14.2	17.4	4.3	8.1	10.6
SABINE ST B&TC	MANY	LA	C	C	C	397.0	17.57	17.5	5.8	9.8	30.0	4.4	6.4	11.9
SACO & BIDDEFORD SVGS IN	SACO	ME	B	B	B	555.5	7.71	0.5	0.8	55.7	23.6	9.6	10.8	19.6
SACRAMENTO DEPOSIT BK	SACRAMENTO	KY	A-	B+	B+	51.8	5.64	4.6	15.8	23.4	27.9	10.0	17.3	30.0
SAEHAN BK	LOS ANGELES	CA	B-	C+	C+	306.6	11.99	24.6	0.5	0.2	12.4	7.1	10.0	12.6
▲ SAFRA NB	NEW YORK	NY	B+	B	B-	4,040.9	-1.64	22.7	5.0	3.3	31.9	10.0	11.8	25.4
SAINT CASIMIRS SVG BK	BALTIMORE	MD	B-	B-	B+	120.7	-1.47	0.0	0.1	4.7	66.1	10.0	17.2	73.5
SAINTE MARIE ST BK	STE. MARIE	IL	D	D	D+	21.6	-1.57	1.0	1.0	2.5	58.3	10.0	18.7	51.9
▼ SALEM CO-OP BK	SALEM	NH	B+	A	A	233.0	4.68	0.0	0.1	41.8	47.8	10.0	19.1	37.0
▼ SALEM FIVE CENTS SVGS BK	SALEM	MA	B	B+	B	1,695.7	9.63	3.5	1.4	24.9	41.2	7.7	9.5	16.2
SALIN B&TC	INDIANAPOLIS	IN	B-	B-	D+	997.9	10.07	21.1	9.5	7.9	9.3	4.9	9.1	11.0
SALINE ST BK	WILBER	NE	C+	C+	C	93.1	11.83	14.6	4.5	17.6	10.1	4.7	7.0	10.9
SALISBURY B&TC	LAKEVILLE	CT	B	B	B	324.0	6.36	2.7	1.8	26.0	47.4	5.9	7.9	16.3
SALT CREEK VALLEY BK	LAURELVILLE	OH	B	B	B+	34.5	-2.20	1.8	5.2	31.5	36.3	10.0	12.4	26.2
▲ SALT LICK DEPOSIT BK	OWINGSVILLE	KY	B-	C+	C+	58.3	2.28	15.4	7.8	38.5	15.5	4.8	6.9	11.7
▲ SALYERSVILLE NB	SALYERSVILLE	KY	A	A-	A-	85.4	1.86	6.2	5.9	17.1	39.3	10.0	14.4	29.8
SAMSON BKG CO	SAMSON	AL	B+	B+	B+	41.3	1.54	3.4	7.8	14.0	47.4	10.0	15.4	29.9

Asset Quality Index	Non-Performing Loans as a % of Total Loans	Non-Performing Loans as a % of Capital	Net Charge-offs Avg Loans	Profitability Index	Net Income ($Mil)	Return on Assets (R.O.A.)	Return on Equity (R.O.E.)	Net Interest Spread	Overhead Efficiency Ratio	Liquidity Index	Liquidity Ratio	Hot Money Ratio	Stability Index
8.8	0.04	0.4	0.06	6.3	0.5	1.02	14.21	4.99	67.9	4.9	7.4	1.6	3.8
7.6	0.29	2.4	0.13	3.4	1.4	0.36	4.07	3.41	78.2	6.3	65.6	9.0	5.3
6.5	0.00	0.0	-0.08	6.7	1.6	1.14	11.63	3.31	57.4	3.0	23.3	14.6	5.8
2.2	5.10	30.8	1.42	6.6	0.6	1.39	18.48	4.07	61.4	0.5	4.3	43.5	3.1
3.1	1.16	6.8	-0.01	3.5	0.3	0.14	1.55	0.69	68.3	2.2	17.6	18.3	5.0
8.0	0.29	2.3	-0.04	4.6	0.3	0.60	7.27	4.01	75.1	2.9	27.3	16.4	4.5
4.2	2.17	10.9	0.14	5.6	0.2	1.52	16.21	4.08	70.3	4.8	45.6	11.9	3.6
5.9	0.99	6.5	-0.05	5.4	0.2	1.03	11.00	4.67	67.0	4.3	28.1	9.2	6.5
7.5	0.00	0.0	0.03	6.7	0.5	1.13	9.39	4.14	61.5	5.6	39.3	5.9	6.9
8.8	0.27	0.7	0.00	7.6	3.7	1.09	5.90	3.63	53.4	3.3	36.4	17.4	9.6
5.1	0.51	3.7	0.06	6.5	0.8	1.12	9.12	2.18	64.1	1.5	8.9	23.2	2.9
9.8	0.14	0.5	-0.04	3.9	0.4	0.48	3.93	3.52	78.6	5.5	41.7	7.0	6.9
8.5	0.23	1.6	0.09	3.1	0.1	0.26	2.71	3.65	86.1	6.4	72.9	8.2	4.0
8.5	0.10	0.5	0.15	6.1	0.4	1.47	13.99	4.65	73.0	3.7	34.7	14.8	5.5
5.3	0.49	2.8	0.06	8.8	0.7	1.23	10.19	5.53	65.6	3.3	11.7	12.3	7.6
9.2	0.27	1.1	-0.16	9.1	4.2	1.46	7.83	3.79	34.1	2.2	14.8	18.0	9.3
10.0	0.53	0.5	0.00	4.0	1.6	0.79	5.96	2.42	51.5	7.8	158.7	10.5	7.3
4.9	0.59	4.1	0.20	5.3	0.3	1.08	11.06	5.38	75.1	4.9	44.1	11.0	4.7
7.6	1.02	5.8	0.11	5.8	0.6	1.33	12.54	4.95	74.3	3.4	21.8	12.6	5.7
8.2	0.04	0.3	0.01	9.1	1.0	1.56	18.09	4.40	52.0	5.1	109.3	21.1	5.2
5.6	0.67	4.5	0.00	7.3	1.8	1.90	21.88	3.80	49.1	0.9	21.5	34.8	6.0
3.8	0.27	1.4	1.22	3.5	0.1	0.16	1.05	3.75	67.0	1.7	25.5	24.6	7.0
8.2	0.00	0.0	-0.02	4.5	0.1	0.87	8.09	4.87	81.3	8.5	132.2	1.8	5.3
7.5	2.24	5.4	0.06	6.5	1.0	1.42	8.31	3.75	52.5	5.3	77.6	15.7	8.1
1.5	3.18	19.7	0.34	3.6	0.1	1.24	12.23	4.91	72.4	6.5	92.1	8.8	0.3
9.3	0.02	0.1	0.15	1.9	0.0	0.01	0.14	3.65	98.7	7.5	129.6	9.1	3.9
7.7	0.03	0.3	0.00	6.6	1.8	1.00	11.17	4.09	62.1	3.4	55.1	25.3	6.1
4.5	0.84	7.3	0.07	5.2	0.7	0.94	11.89	4.61	71.1	3.5	15.3	11.4	4.5
6.5	1.55	5.6	-0.04	9.1	9.4	1.63	17.09	3.80	50.0	4.2	26.9	12.2	9.0
6.9	0.18	1.3	0.00	4.9	1.3	0.87	9.46	3.33	62.2	3.3	20.3	13.0	5.2
7.2	0.12	1.0	0.22	3.8	0.4	0.74	7.46	5.07	72.5	3.2	69.6	35.8	2.6
9.0	0.00	0.0	0.00	0.4	0.0	-0.01	-0.05	3.92	97.7	4.3	69.3	18.4	0.0
9.7	0.32	0.9	0.00	1.5	-0.2	-0.41	-2.85	2.68	122.1	7.3	112.8	8.1	6.9
1.4	3.22	21.2	-0.24	10.0	0.7	2.83	25.53	6.26	54.5	3.7	27.5	12.6	6.6
9.7	0.00	0.0	0.04	0.1	-0.1	-0.28	-2.44	2.72	98.8	4.6	38.3	11.4	0.0
6.8	0.00	0.0	0.03	6.5	0.3	0.99	7.19	3.98	60.8	5.4	34.3	4.6	7.9
5.1	0.93	5.9	0.01	9.8	0.6	1.58	16.16	4.54	48.3	4.6	32.3	9.0	7.0
5.4	0.80	7.1	0.06	10.0	0.5	1.75	23.31	4.85	53.0	3.9	22.3	10.1	6.3
7.5	0.23	1.8	0.06	9.0	0.5	1.37	16.16	4.66	56.8	4.7	15.0	3.8	6.8
6.4	0.45	3.3	0.01	9.7	0.3	1.47	16.71	4.78	52.3	4.1	6.3	7.1	7.0
3.9	1.65	14.4	0.12	9.5	0.3	1.52	19.04	4.68	52.5	4.4	27.7	8.4	6.8
8.0	0.03	0.3	-0.47	5.0	0.2	1.04	13.38	5.13	79.4	5.2	30.6	4.4	2.1
8.9	0.18	0.4	0.02	8.0	0.5	1.54	9.95	4.28	50.6	3.4	16.1	11.9	7.9
2.0	5.77	30.5	0.28	1.0	0.0	-0.12	-1.29	3.44	100.2	4.8	40.1	8.0	2.5
7.4	0.01	0.1	0.13	4.7	0.3	0.85	8.68	4.33	73.6	1.6	16.5	23.3	4.2
9.4	0.16	0.4	-0.06	4.4	0.1	0.80	6.61	3.02	65.2	6.6	103.1	10.9	6.0
5.1	0.57	3.5	0.37	7.4	2.2	1.24	11.62	4.85	67.2	4.1	16.6	8.3	6.2
6.3	0.60	4.2	0.19	9.6	24.7	1.70	16.24	3.95	44.5	3.8	11.6	9.9	9.0
6.3	0.24	1.9	0.09	5.4	2.8	1.45	19.23	4.39	72.0	1.9	26.4	23.2	3.2
9.5	0.19	1.2	-0.01	4.9	2.6	0.95	8.56	2.88	61.4	5.9	93.7	14.8	7.3
6.4	1.57	5.4	0.65	9.3	0.6	2.46	14.61	4.38	44.6	4.4	95.9	23.2	8.1
4.7	0.51	3.7	0.10	9.4	2.4	1.58	16.51	4.49	59.1	2.3	20.1	17.8	5.3
8.9	0.06	0.2	-0.12	5.3	17.4	0.83	7.53	2.28	59.0	4.4	131.6	60.1	7.3
10.0	0.00	0.0	0.00	3.8	0.4	0.61	3.55	2.46	63.4	9.1	1,097.7	5.9	7.7
9.9	0.59	0.6	0.00	0.5	0.0	-0.18	-0.95	1.52	112.4	7.9	248.8	12.8	4.6
8.0	0.00	0.0	0.00	4.9	0.9	0.77	4.02	2.72	70.8	1.5	19.2	25.1	8.8
8.9	0.09	0.5	0.00	4.5	5.6	0.69	7.20	2.70	68.3	2.4	23.5	19.7	7.9
6.5	0.26	2.1	0.03	5.2	5.2	1.08	10.75	3.49	68.4	1.7	10.4	20.2	6.9
4.2	0.53	3.2	-0.15	5.8	0.4	0.96	8.34	3.97	61.7	6.4	75.3	8.4	6.2
7.3	0.60	3.1	0.02	5.6	2.2	1.37	15.45	3.74	65.3	6.9	102.2	10.7	5.7
7.1	1.32	5.2	0.00	5.2	0.1	0.79	6.18	4.71	77.0	4.9	60.5	13.9	5.9
3.9	1.23	8.7	-0.01	2.9	0.2	0.56	6.20	3.04	73.3	3.8	69.5	22.7	5.2
8.8	0.00	0.0	0.93	6.9	0.6	1.40	9.62	4.15	59.5	3.8	78.3	26.6	8.6
8.6	0.99	2.5	-0.03	6.1	0.3	1.48	9.57	3.45	60.2	4.5	56.5	15.4	6.2

Name	City	State	Weiss Safety Rating	2003 Weiss Safety Rating	2002 Weiss Safety Rating	Total Assets ($Mil)	One Year Asset Growth	Asset Mix (As a % of Total Assets) Commercial Loans	Consumer Loans	Home Mortgages	Securities	Capitalization Index	Leverage Ratio	Risk-based Capital Ratio
▲ SAN ANGELO NB	SAN ANGELO	TX	A	A-	A-	305.4	-5.16	8.8	4.1	5.5	50.3	8.7	10.1	20.1
SAN DIEGO NB	SAN DIEGO	CA	B	B	C+	2,106.0	9.12	4.9	0.1	0.3	17.6	4.8	10.6	10.9
SAN DIEGO TR BK	SAN DIEGO	CA	D	D	NR	40.4	N/A	5.0	0.1	2.3	8.4	10.0	31.1	35.6
SAN JOAQUIN BK	BAKERSFIELD	CA	C+	C+	C+	442.9	17.03	13.2	0.6	0.9	22.4	4.9	7.0	12.2
▲ SAN JOSE TRI COUNTY BK	SAN JOSE	IL	C-	C	C+	7.4	3.27	17.2	10.3	36.1	5.3	8.1	9.7	15.8
▲ SAN LUIS TRUST BK FSB	SAN LUIS OBISPO	CA	B	C+	C	130.5	59.78	4.8	1.8	24.5	9.4	5.3	8.0	11.2
▼ SAN LUIS VALLEY FEDERAL BK	ALAMOSA	CO	A-	A	A-	156.3	4.13	1.6	1.6	57.3	17.6	10.0	14.5	28.5
SANBORN SVG BK	SANBORN	IA	C	C	C-	39.1	0.67	10.4	6.8	16.9	22.2	6.9	8.9	12.7
SAND RIDGE BK	HIGHLAND	IN	B-	B	B	865.9	0.97	5.8	5.1	33.1	26.2	5.3	7.3	13.0
SANDERSON ST BK	SANDERSON	TX	B-	B-	C+	30.4	9.56	2.9	2.0	39.7	25.7	10.0	13.1	29.5
SANDHILLS BK	BETHUNE	SC	B-	C	D+	55.6	-12.43	10.4	6.5	22.5	14.4	8.7	10.1	15.5
SANDY SPRING BK	OLNEY	MD	B	B-	B-	2,419.4	2.63	4.0	4.4	17.1	36.6	5.0	7.0	14.0
SANFORD INST FOR SVGS	SANFORD	ME	C+	C+	C+	334.8	5.75	1.2	2.6	50.4	23.7	8.2	9.8	18.2
SANGER BK	SANGER	TX	B	B	C+	61.7	4.12	19.2	5.6	14.4	22.1	10.0	11.3	17.9
▲ SANIBEL CAPTIVA COMMUNITY	SANIBEL	FL	C+	C	NR	83.8	69.33	9.8	0.8	32.3	6.0	6.6	8.7	12.2
SANTA ANNA NB	SANTA ANNA	TX	B-	B-	B-	35.5	34.15	5.3	4.8	3.6	56.0	10.0	13.6	34.9
SANTA CLARA VALLEY BK NA	SANTA PAULA	CA	D+	C-	C-	58.4	23.01	11.2	2.1	7.8	19.6	6.6	8.6	13.7
SANTA CRUZ CNTY BK	SANTA CRUZ	CA	D	NR	NR	32.9	N/A	13.9	1.3	1.5	20.5	10.0	41.3	50.9
SANTA LUCIA BK	ATASCADERO	CA	C+	C+	B-	200.4	18.18	15.7	0.7	0.1	28.3	4.7	6.7	11.5
SAPELO NB	DARIEN	GA	C-	D+	D+	56.7	9.25	15.0	6.3	19.1	9.8	6.1	8.1	12.9
SARATOGA NB&TC	SARATOGA SPRINGS	NY	B	B	B	175.5	4.51	3.6	45.7	25.6	8.4	7.0	9.0	14.2
SARGENT COUNTY BK	FORMAN	ND	A	A	A	62.2	-1.01	5.3	3.1	1.6	40.6	10.0	17.1	27.0
SATILLA COMMUNITY BK	ST MARYS	GA	D-	D-	D	55.2	63.44	12.7	8.2	11.4	18.6	5.6	9.2	11.4
SAUGUSBANK A CO-OP BK	SAUGUS	MA	B-	B-	B-	147.1	7.76	2.3	1.7	29.7	26.8	6.1	8.1	12.5
SAUK VALLEY B&TC	STERLING	IL	D+	D+	D	159.0	23.62	21.9	3.0	12.1	10.3	4.6	7.3	10.8
▲ SAVANNA-THOMSON ST BK	THOMSON	IL	C	D+	D+	54.0	-2.34	17.1	3.5	18.1	16.6	7.7	9.4	13.8
SAVANNAH BK NA	SAVANNAH	GA	C+	B-	B	427.1	30.83	5.1	2.4	20.3	6.8	4.0	7.7	10.5
SAVANNAH BK NA	SAVANNAH	NY	C	C	C	91.0	10.36	15.6	2.9	9.0	36.2	5.1	7.1	15.5
SAVERS CO-OP BK	SOUTHBRIDGE	MA	C+	B-	B-	302.8	-2.29	1.3	7.9	39.5	26.8	9.2	10.5	20.2
SAVINGS B&T	WADSWORTH	OH	B	B	B+	373.9	113.69	8.6	9.2	8.9	39.6	6.0	8.0	14.7
▲ SAVINGS BANK	PRIMGHAR	IA	B-	C+	C-	51.9	10.42	7.1	5.1	10.7	24.5	5.3	7.9	11.2
▼ SAVINGS BK	WAKEFIELD	MA	B-	B	B	394.8	-3.67	0.3	0.3	22.3	58.6	10.0	13.1	26.6
▼ SAVINGS BK	CIRCLEVILLE	OH	A	A+	A+	201.7	-0.53	9.3	7.6	32.8	39.8	10.0	12.4	26.6
SAVINGS BK OF DANBURY	DANBURY	CT	B-	B-	B-	521.3	0.03	2.3	0.2	34.3	31.0	10.0	11.5	20.4
SAVINGS BK OF MENDOCINO	UKIAH	CA	A+	A+	A+	651.7	4.36	5.3	4.2	6.1	49.3	10.0	14.3	21.3
SAVINGS BK OF WALPOLE	WALPOLE	NH	C+	C+	C+	225.4	7.66	3.8	1.0	46.2	24.3	6.1	8.1	13.6
SAVINGS INSTITUTE	WILLIMANTIC	CT	C	C	C-	549.3	7.86	3.4	0.5	44.6	16.8	4.7	6.7	12.4
SAWYER SVGS BK	SAUGERTIES	NY	C	C	C	154.7	-1.66	8.6	0.6	26.2	52.4	6.6	8.6	19.7
SBU BANK	UTICA	NY	B	B-	B	1,300.9	2.41	4.4	4.9	38.2	25.2	7.5	9.4	17.5
SBU MUNICIPAL BK	UTICA	NY	A	A-	C+	111.5	1.45	0.0	0.0	0.0	86.2	10.0	53.8	165.9
SCANDIA AMERICAN B&TC	STANLEY	ND	A	A	A	60.0	1.26	3.4	1.5	2.2	45.9	10.0	20.4	35.6
▲ SCANDIA ST BK OF SCANDIA	SCANDIA	KS	B+	B	B+	22.4	2.64	5.1	3.7	6.1	25.0	10.0	12.9	18.4
SCHERTZ B&TC	SCHERTZ	TX	A-	A-	A-	103.5	-0.32	6.7	2.5	9.5	33.0	10.0	14.0	22.5
▲ SCHUYLER ST BK	RUSHVILLE	IL	B+	B	B-	43.2	2.96	3.3	9.6	8.6	52.5	9.8	10.9	22.7
▲ SCHUYLER SVG BK	KEARNY	NJ	B	B-	C	120.2	1.44	0.0	0.2	49.8	40.6	10.0	11.6	32.9
SCHWERTNER ST BK	SCHWERTNER	TX	C	C-	C-	19.7	-1.42	4.2	8.8	2.1	20.4	10.0	14.8	33.0
SCITUATE FSB	SCITUATE	MA	B-	B-	B-	198.3	2.39	0.0	0.5	47.1	31.7	5.4	7.4	19.0
▲ SCOTIABANK DE PR	HATO REY	PR	D	D-	D-	1,276.8	-4.53	13.1	36.5	19.4	0.3	10.0	13.7	15.8
SCOTT COUNTY ST BK	SCOTTSBURG	IN	A-	A-	B+	123.2	11.89	4.9	6.6	45.2	16.9	9.9	10.9	18.9
SCOTT ST BK	BETHANY	IL	B+	B+	A-	55.3	2.60	11.7	11.1	23.3	25.7	10.0	14.3	22.6
SCOTT VALLEY BK	YREKA	CA	B	B	A-	312.3	10.46	16.1	1.0	1.5	28.4	8.6	10.8	13.8
▼ SCOTTDALE B&TC	SCOTTDALE	PA	B+	A-	A	183.1	5.24	1.9	4.3	13.5	57.4	10.0	18.1	32.3
▲ SCOTTISH BK	CHARLOTTE	NC	C+	C	C	139.2	4.08	18.0	1.9	7.1	17.5	5.0	9.0	11.0
▼ SCOTTSBURG B&LA	SCOTTSBURG	IN	B	B+	B+	83.5	1.45	0.0	0.2	35.2	52.7	10.0	13.7	34.9
SCRIBNER BK	SCRIBNER	NE	B	B	B	39.7	-5.84	6.3	2.8	5.5	23.1	8.3	9.9	18.7
▼ SEA ISLAND BK	STATESBORO	GA	B-	B	B	289.5	10.57	18.1	4.1	13.3	8.2	2.4	7.8	9.4
SEACOAST COMMERCE BK	CHULA VISTA	CA	D	D	NR	25.3	126.97	6.7	0.5	4.2	7.8	10.0	32.4	41.7
SEAMANS BK	PROVINCETOWN	MA	B	B	B+	231.0	10.67	1.9	0.6	24.9	33.2	9.3	10.6	17.8
SEAPORT BK	SEADRIFT	TX	B+	B+	B+	25.6	-1.89	4.2	9.1	7.4	52.8	10.0	17.7	38.2
SEASONS BK	BLAIRSVILLE	GA	D	D	NR	43.8	77.10	23.8	3.6	14.4	15.5	10.0	14.8	18.6
SEATTLE SB	SEATTLE	WA	A-	A-	C+	143.4	-31.22	0.0	0.0	25.2	0.0	10.0	16.1	21.0
▲ SEAWAY COMMUNITY BK	ST CLAIR	MI	D+	D-	D-	93.3	31.70	5.4	3.3	24.8	9.4	4.9	8.7	10.9
▲ SEAWAY NB OF CHICAGO	CHICAGO	IL	C+	C	C	317.1	4.02	8.1	1.0	24.1	43.8	6.5	8.5	18.0
▼ SEBREE DEPOSIT BK	SEBREE	KY	D-	D+	D	24.0	-10.57	5.5	9.2	26.1	34.1	6.8	8.8	18.6

Asset Quality Index	Non-Performing Loans as a % of Total Loans	Non-Performing Loans as a % of Capital	Net Charge-offs Avg Loans	Profitability Index	Net Income ($Mil)	Return on Assets (R.O.A.)	Return on Equity (R.O.E.)	Net Interest Spread	Overhead Efficiency Ratio	Liquidity Index	Liquidity Ratio	Hot Money Ratio	Stability Index
7.5	0.02	0.1	0.13	10.0	3.4	2.12	15.17	4.52	43.2	3.8	34.5	13.9	8.7
4.4	2.47	16.3	0.00	10.0	19.7	1.90	18.06	5.16	40.3	5.7	229.0	31.6	8.1
8.3	0.00	0.0	0.00	0.0	-0.8	-5.43	-15.26	2.68	232.4	7.5	162.8	12.1	0.0
5.6	0.87	6.9	-0.04	7.3	2.7	1.23	18.27	4.45	53.3	9.4	397.4	4.4	3.6
1.7	3.70	26.0	0.12	3.9	0.0	0.65	6.66	5.39	85.0	5.2	36.6	3.9	3.5
7.0	0.51	4.9	0.01	10.0	1.6	2.73	33.00	6.78	31.9	1.8	45.6	115.9	5.9
8.5	0.14	0.7	0.00	5.9	0.7	0.95	6.65	4.16	70.7	1.2	6.3	26.2	8.4
7.9	0.04	0.3	0.00	4.9	0.2	1.11	11.26	3.85	68.4	3.7	15.9	10.7	4.1
4.8	1.13	9.1	0.41	7.7	5.4	1.24	16.54	4.13	57.9	3.9	25.9	10.8	5.9
8.6	0.25	0.8	0.00	4.3	0.2	1.13	7.59	3.49	68.0	3.1	79.5	48.1	6.7
4.0	2.25	12.3	0.51	2.8	-0.1	-0.30	-2.82	4.81	97.8	3.3	55.0	22.4	3.1
8.7	0.23	1.5	0.02	6.4	13.5	1.14	14.75	3.66	66.5	6.0	50.9	10.1	6.6
6.9	0.47	2.9	-0.02	3.7	1.1	0.67	6.16	3.47	77.7	4.9	30.3	6.2	6.5
7.8	0.36	1.6	0.03	6.7	0.3	0.94	8.55	4.72	67.7	4.5	88.5	20.1	4.5
9.0	0.00	0.0	0.00	3.4	0.3	0.81	9.29	3.86	54.3	4.1	84.4	23.3	2.2
8.6	1.59	3.1	0.40	5.0	0.2	1.07	7.99	3.47	56.3	5.0	39.4	9.9	4.6
8.5	0.00	0.0	0.07	3.2	0.2	0.60	6.81	4.53	84.3	4.7	37.9	10.8	1.5
8.8	0.00	0.0	0.00	0.0	-1.5	-13.65	-24.47	2.28	566.0	5.7	107.6	16.3	0.0
5.4	0.72	5.7	0.00	5.3	0.8	0.82	12.13	4.87	72.8	5.4	47.6	9.8	3.9
4.2	1.24	8.6	0.02	4.0	0.3	0.71	9.03	3.45	72.9	5.2	54.4	11.3	3.4
3.8	0.48	4.1	0.11	9.4	1.3	1.46	16.50	3.90	38.6	3.6	5.3	10.3	6.9
8.5	0.13	0.4	0.15	9.7	0.8	2.37	12.90	4.34	33.9	5.9	70.4	10.4	9.0
3.5	1.82	15.7	0.09	1.7	0.2	0.61	7.03	4.21	84.8	0.7	12.2	39.8	0.0
8.7	0.00	0.0	0.01	4.1	0.6	0.75	9.31	3.35	67.1	3.9	17.4	9.9	5.0
2.5	2.22	23.0	0.26	4.0	0.5	0.67	9.53	3.93	66.0	1.8	17.2	20.4	2.6
3.8	1.13	5.3	0.02	4.4	0.4	1.48	10.25	3.76	57.8	4.5	24.8	6.4	4.5
7.1	0.03	0.3	0.06	5.2	1.6	0.82	11.49	3.68	61.3	2.1	33.8	27.3	4.9
8.8	0.19	1.0	0.12	3.8	0.2	0.54	7.19	3.54	73.9	5.9	85.6	12.3	3.2
9.0	0.14	0.8	-0.04	2.8	0.4	0.30	2.85	3.41	88.8	5.2	40.7	9.1	5.9
3.7	1.30	3.9	0.09	5.8	1.8	0.97	6.40	4.19	69.3	4.8	26.4	5.6	6.8
6.8	0.46	4.0	0.00	6.2	0.4	1.58	21.20	3.78	51.3	2.0	17.2	19.4	5.2
9.9	0.23	0.5	0.00	3.4	0.7	0.37	2.67	2.95	82.0	5.8	52.6	8.9	7.5
8.6	0.35	1.5	0.20	7.0	1.2	1.24	9.84	4.16	62.1	4.6	30.5	8.6	8.5
9.5	0.06	0.3	0.00	3.2	1.6	0.63	5.21	3.19	86.2	6.4	87.2	11.6	7.6
9.0	0.27	0.8	0.09	9.1	4.9	1.49	10.25	4.45	50.0	4.6	41.0	12.4	10.0
7.4	0.32	2.6	-0.17	3.6	0.6	0.54	6.50	3.58	80.7	4.5	27.2	7.7	4.4
6.9	0.38	4.0	0.01	3.5	1.3	0.48	7.13	3.74	82.1	4.7	36.7	10.4	3.3
9.6	0.13	0.7	0.04	3.1	0.5	0.62	7.12	3.48	80.1	4.0	16.9	9.2	4.8
6.6	0.38	2.4	0.17	6.5	6.7	1.02	8.50	3.59	64.4	2.4	29.7	29.1	5.6
10.0	0.00	0.0	0.00	6.7	0.8	1.33	2.78	3.01	10.6	6.8	87.4	9.4	7.8
8.9	0.47	1.0	-0.03	8.3	0.5	1.51	7.34	3.67	39.4	5.0	79.1	16.0	8.8
7.0	0.06	0.3	0.00	8.0	0.2	1.75	13.18	4.70	62.9	3.6	12.3	10.5	8.6
8.7	0.29	1.2	0.01	5.9	0.6	1.18	8.36	4.95	71.2	3.5	13.7	11.6	8.2
8.7	0.00	0.0	0.00	6.8	0.4	1.76	16.06	3.19	47.8	5.6	58.6	10.0	6.0
8.9	0.22	1.0	0.00	4.4	0.5	0.81	6.93	3.25	64.5	7.6	287.9	14.4	6.8
8.6	0.00	0.0	0.03	4.1	0.1	1.18	8.36	3.31	63.8	6.9	135.0	11.9	4.5
8.7	0.00	0.0	0.01	4.2	0.6	0.63	8.52	2.85	67.7	1.7	27.9	27.4	4.2
0.5	4.62	29.8	1.22	2.4	-0.3	-0.05	-0.38	4.81	80.0	0.5	7.9	65.2	8.0
7.5	0.43	2.8	0.05	6.6	0.7	1.13	10.31	4.26	60.5	5.0	56.5	14.3	6.5
3.9	2.98	12.2	-0.03	6.4	0.4	1.30	9.14	4.74	63.1	3.4	29.9	14.4	7.7
4.9	1.20	6.5	0.01	5.7	1.2	0.80	7.19	4.67	74.4	6.2	97.1	13.7	6.6
7.1	4.28	6.9	0.00	4.8	0.8	0.83	4.15	3.23	65.8	7.8	73.9	0.6	8.5
4.6	0.76	6.1	-0.10	3.5	0.4	0.54	6.10	3.75	81.6	1.3	9.3	26.5	4.4
7.5	0.23	0.6	0.00	4.0	0.2	0.44	3.09	2.19	66.8	1.4	27.2	30.6	7.6
4.8	1.96	8.8	0.00	6.6	0.2	0.98	8.57	4.42	70.8	7.0	72.2	3.7	6.1
7.7	0.16	1.6	0.00	9.1	1.7	1.26	16.06	4.56	55.8	1.8	23.2	22.1	7.0
7.8	0.00	0.0	0.00	0.0	-0.6	-5.13	-15.08	3.54	218.9	7.3	145.5	11.7	0.0
8.3	0.06	0.4	0.02	5.0	0.9	0.82	7.92	3.53	61.1	3.5	22.3	12.5	6.4
8.5	1.21	2.2	0.00	4.8	0.1	0.72	4.02	3.62	69.4	2.8	62.1	33.6	7.3
8.4	0.42	2.2	0.13	0.0	-0.4	-1.79	-11.50	3.72	124.9	1.1	11.6	28.9	0.0
6.6	0.14	0.6	1.00	10.0	1.5	2.13	14.71	5.99	89.0	1.0	25.8	43.7	8.4
6.0	0.78	6.9	0.03	1.7	0.1	0.23	2.81	4.33	90.2	1.5	11.2	23.0	0.3
4.0	3.35	19.3	0.18	3.6	1.4	0.90	10.52	4.09	84.2	1.4	17.2	27.3	4.2
3.0	4.33	20.2	-0.53	0.8	0.0	-0.05	-0.53	3.25	100.2	4.9	87.1	16.5	0.7

Name	City	State	Weiss Safety Rating	2003 Weiss Safety Rating	2002 Weiss Safety Rating	Total Assets ($Mil)	One Year Asset Growth	Asset Mix (As a % of Total Assets)				Capital- ization Index	Leverage Ratio	Risk-based Capital Ratio
								Comm- ercial Loans	Cons- umer Loans	Home Mort- gages	Secur- ities			
▲ SECOND B&T	CULPEPER	VA	B	B-	A-	403.0	11.21	7.4	4.9	14.5	19.7	5.5	8.0	11.4
▲ SECOND FS&LA OF CHICAGO	CHICAGO	IL	C	D+	C	235.5	-5.80	0.0	0.0	62.9	19.7	9.9	10.9	17.7
SECOND FS&LA OF	PHILADELPHIA	PA	C	C	C	15.4	-7.79	0.0	0.0	24.9	47.0	10.0	41.4	82.7
SECOND NB	GREENVILLE	OH	B-	B-	B-	387.8	4.62	3.6	6.6	15.4	46.5	4.0	6.0	13.9
▼ SECOND NB OF WARREN	WARREN	OH	C+	B-	B-	2,015.6	4.84	8.0	9.8	21.2	25.4	5.1	7.1	12.0
SECURITY B&TC	ALBANY	GA	B-	B-	B	312.7	10.03	16.6	3.9	17.3	14.3	4.0	7.6	10.5
SECURITY B&TC	MAYSVILLE	KY	A-	A-	A-	48.1	-4.05	5.2	4.0	28.7	27.9	10.0	20.8	21.7
SECURITY B&TC	SCOTT CITY	MO	C+	C+	C+	64.9	1.92	2.2	5.4	35.7	37.7	5.9	7.9	16.7
▲ SECURITY B&TC	MIAMI	OK	A-	B+	B	81.4	-5.12	15.1	3.5	9.6	42.0	10.0	11.7	19.2
▲ SECURITY B&TC	PARIS	TN	B+	B	B	129.6	3.90	9.0	4.6	25.7	15.2	6.9	8.9	13.2
SECURITY B&TC OF GLENCOE	GLENCOE	MN	B+	A-	A	179.5	9.62	8.5	1.9	5.9	31.2	7.8	9.5	14.2
SECURITY BANK OF BIBB	MACON	GA	C+	C+	C+	543.4	14.85	8.2	2.5	6.9	6.9	3.3	9.2	10.2
SECURITY BANK USA	BEMIDJI	MN	C-	C-	D+	76.9	2.03	23.3	6.2	24.3	5.7	3.2	8.0	10.1
▼ SECURITY BK	TUSCALOOSA	AL	B	B+	B+	79.3	-0.55	19.0	2.2	42.2	7.0	10.0	12.9	18.1
SECURITY BK	RICH HILL	MO	C-	C	B	52.2	1.44	8.6	12.6	27.2	22.6	5.4	7.4	14.5
▲ SECURITY BK	PAWNEE	OK	B	B-	C+	226.4	6.58	22.9	3.4	15.1	4.2	7.3	9.2	14.0
SECURITY BK	MADISON	SD	C+	C+	C	127.8	-9.89	6.9	3.7	24.4	1.6	7.4	10.1	12.8
▲ SECURITY BK	NEWBERN	TN	B+	B	B	135.7	-6.08	5.6	6.1	20.0	24.8	9.3	10.6	17.2
▼ SECURITY BK	RALLS	TX	C+	B-	B	118.7	3.39	12.6	6.2	6.1	37.6	6.9	8.9	15.5
▲ SECURITY BK	NEW AUBURN	WI	B-	C	C+	33.6	18.18	9.6	5.1	19.1	26.2	10.0	12.6	17.0
▲ SECURITY BK MN	ALBERT LEA	MN	B	B-	C	71.8	-8.53	34.8	17.3	5.4	23.7	10.0	13.0	20.7
▲ SECURITY BK NA	N LAUDERDALE	FL	C-	D	D+	96.0	0.98	5.3	0.3	28.3	5.4	6.6	8.6	13.9
SECURITY BK OF HOUSTON	PERRY	GA	C+	C+	C	195.4	29.72	7.1	4.6	12.2	8.6	4.2	8.3	10.6
SECURITY BK OF JONES	GRAY	GA	B-	B	A-	252.2	-2.70	3.3	5.4	16.8	19.2	6.7	8.7	13.1
▼ SECURITY BK OF KANSAS	KANSAS CITY	KS	B+	A-	A	512.8	1.08	21.3	3.5	1.3	15.4	8.9	11.0	14.0
SECURITY BK OF SW MO	CASSVILLE	MO	C	C	B-	58.1	11.72	8.7	6.7	19.5	23.8	7.9	9.6	14.8
▲ SECURITY BK SB	SPRINGFIELD	IL	D	D-	D	181.9	-10.64	0.6	3.6	28.3	38.6	9.5	10.7	22.2
SECURITY BK WACONIA	WACONIA	MN	B	B	A-	132.2	6.68	7.3	1.4	5.6	33.3	7.3	9.2	13.9
▼ SECURITY BK-PULASKI CTY	WAYNESVILLE	MO	D-	D	D	66.1	-12.31	6.5	7.8	20.5	20.1	8.2	9.8	15.5
SECURITY BK-WHITESBORO	WHITESBORO	TX	C+	C+	C+	73.6	-4.45	5.4	6.0	32.7	18.6	5.8	7.8	14.2
▲ SECURITY BUS BK OF SAN	SAN DIEGO	CA	D	D	D	71.8	69.82	18.1	1.2	1.4	14.6	10.0	23.5	25.2
▲ SECURITY EXCHANGE BK	MARIETTA	GA	B+	B	C+	84.5	26.66	16.0	0.9	2.2	30.3	9.9	10.9	15.2
SECURITY FEDERAL BK	AIKEN	SC	C	C-	C	552.7	21.47	3.0	2.7	19.7	47.6	3.9	5.9	12.8
SECURITY FIRST BANK OF ND	NEW SALEM	ND	C+	C+	C	71.1	7.75	19.1	6.9	5.8	6.4	7.0	9.5	12.5
SECURITY FIRST BK	SIDNEY	NE	D+	D	D	467.6	7.62	18.5	5.1	9.7	13.7	3.9	7.5	10.4
▲ SECURITY FIRST BK	CHEYENNE	WY	B-	C+	C+	61.8	-5.50	11.0	4.6	11.5	6.8	7.9	9.9	13.3
SECURITY FIRST NB OF HUGO	HUGO	OK	B	B	B-	79.1	-1.99	14.0	6.7	21.7	11.3	5.5	7.9	12.2
SECURITY FS	LINCOLN	NE	B-	B-	B-	102.3	-10.17	3.4	1.6	40.9	3.0	8.0	9.7	13.3
SECURITY FSB	JASPER	AL	B-	B-	B	42.4	1.17	0.0	3.0	7.7	44.8	10.0	12.2	62.3
▲ SECURITY FSB	LOGANSPORT	IN	B-	C+	C+	160.1	-7.13	2.7	6.1	53.7	18.2	8.4	9.9	17.6
SECURITY FSB	BROCKTON	MA	C+	C+	C+	109.9	11.36	0.0	1.2	72.7	9.9	10.0	11.3	20.7
SECURITY FSB	ELIZABETHTON	TN	A-	A-	A-	57.8	2.34	6.8	3.6	48.6	14.8	10.0	21.8	26.3
▲ SECURITY FSB OF	MC MINNVILLE	TN	B+	B	B	107.3	7.75	10.2	8.8	28.7	9.8	7.5	9.3	15.6
▼ SECURITY HOME BK	MALMO	NE	D	D+	D	21.9	4.01	6.8	4.5	32.8	6.5	6.0	8.0	12.2
SECURITY NB	WITT	IL	B	B	B	49.8	2.82	6.2	6.9	22.8	37.1	10.0	12.7	22.0
SECURITY NB	LAUREL	NE	B	B-	B-	97.3	-2.14	12.1	3.5	5.7	30.4	8.7	10.1	14.9
SECURITY NB OF DURAND	DURAND	WI	A+	A+	A+	242.9	16.73	5.6	2.4	7.5	50.3	10.0	11.1	19.3
SECURITY NB OF ENID	ENID	OK	B	B+	B+	167.4	0.71	10.5	3.2	13.7	39.3	5.8	7.8	13.6
SECURITY NB OF OMAHA	OMAHA	NE	B	B	B-	443.6	9.17	18.1	7.6	13.9	17.1	4.8	8.0	10.9
SECURITY NB OF SD	DAKOTA DUNES	SD	A-	A-	B+	19.9	-28.01	13.9	3.9	6.8	27.8	10.0	15.5	24.2
SECURITY NB OF SIOUX CITY	SIOUX CITY	IA	A-	A-	B+	537.5	-1.46	18.0	5.2	14.4	25.8	7.0	9.0	15.3
SECURITY NB&TC	SPRINGFIELD	OH	B-	B-	B-	897.3	3.94	9.7	5.6	11.5	40.5	3.9	5.9	13.3
▼ SECURITY ST B&TC	FREDERICKSBURG	TX	C+	B	A-	507.6	8.13	8.6	7.4	17.1	19.6	10.0	11.0	16.1
SECURITY ST BK	MC RAE	GA	B+	B+	B-	40.5	9.53	29.2	4.7	11.3	40.4	10.0	11.1	18.4
▲ SECURITY ST BK	ALGONA	IA	C	C-	D+	46.6	5.74	18.1	9.5	5.7	12.4	7.3	9.2	14.6
▼ SECURITY ST BK	ANAMOSA	IA	C	C+	C+	91.0	9.53	18.2	4.4	23.4	19.1	5.0	7.1	11.0
SECURITY ST BK	GUTTENBERG	IA	A-	A-	A-	66.4	3.12	6.7	4.8	15.0	44.0	10.0	13.9	24.3
SECURITY ST BK	HUBBARD	IA	B+	B+	A-	37.6	-2.95	2.2	6.7	30.6	17.5	10.0	12.3	20.8
SECURITY ST BK	INDEPENDENCE	IA	C+	C+	C+	63.3	-0.51	7.9	3.2	13.7	33.3	5.5	7.5	12.5
SECURITY ST BK	NEW HAMPTON	IA	B	B	B	130.3	-2.71	5.4	4.7	17.4	31.6	7.4	9.3	15.3
▲ SECURITY ST BK	RADCLIFFE	IA	D+	D	D+	32.6	5.38	10.1	3.0	4.9	54.8	6.8	8.8	16.1
▼ SECURITY ST BK	RED OAK	IA	D	D+	C-	62.3	4.27	13.5	8.4	8.6	22.9	5.3	7.3	11.3
▲ SECURITY ST BK	STUART	IA	C+	C	C+	65.3	-7.45	9.7	1.7	5.7	53.4	4.7	6.7	13.8
SECURITY ST BK	SUTHERLAND	IA	C-	C-	C-	49.3	5.23	9.6	6.8	6.2	10.8	5.0	8.3	11.0

Asset Quality Index	Non-Performing Loans as a % of Total Loans	Non-Performing Loans as a % of Capital	Net Charge-offs Avg Loans	Profitability Index	Net Income ($Mil)	Return on Assets (R.O.A.)	Return on Equity (R.O.E.)	Net Interest Spread	Overhead Efficiency Ratio	Liquidity Index	Liquidity Ratio	Hot Money Ratio	Stability Index
6.3	0.36	2.9	0.02	7.1	2.4	1.16	14.62	4.23	60.3	4.4	26.7	7.8	6.8
5.1	1.89	11.9	-0.01	2.6	0.4	0.35	3.15	4.82	86.2	3.2	30.7	16.1	4.7
7.4	0.00	0.0	0.00	6.0	0.1	1.17	2.82	3.03	58.0	4.3	53.3	14.1	5.0
8.3	0.26	1.8	-0.03	9.7	3.4	1.74	29.28	4.28	43.8	2.0	7.7	18.3	5.3
4.0	1.66	13.7	1.12	3.0	-3.3	-0.32	-4.48	2.86	86.1	2.5	12.6	16.5	6.3
4.8	0.77	6.9	0.31	6.2	1.8	1.21	15.91	4.39	47.9	1.8	13.9	19.7	5.7
7.8	1.45	4.1	-0.08	9.0	0.5	2.00	9.65	4.40	54.0	4.9	42.9	11.0	8.3
8.4	0.12	0.9	0.00	4.8	0.3	0.96	12.01	3.86	78.5	4.3	25.6	8.6	4.6
8.7	0.00	0.0	0.02	5.5	0.6	1.53	13.89	3.59	62.0	4.0	8.5	7.5	6.1
6.4	0.23	1.7	0.21	9.4	1.0	1.49	16.14	4.27	52.3	4.6	40.7	12.0	6.0
8.3	0.17	1.1	-0.14	9.5	2.1	2.42	24.08	3.95	41.5	4.4	38.7	12.7	7.5
3.7	0.64	5.0	0.21	7.9	3.1	1.21	12.41	4.24	63.8	1.3	11.3	25.7	5.5
4.3	0.94	9.2	0.01	5.2	0.5	1.24	14.95	3.72	69.3	4.2	6.8	6.1	4.3
7.6	0.41	2.6	0.00	3.7	0.1	0.20	1.48	3.60	75.4	0.7	10.5	35.4	7.2
3.9	0.94	4.7	0.06	4.3	0.2	0.71	7.06	4.16	77.3	5.3	51.1	10.5	3.7
5.6	0.73	5.4	-0.03	8.7	2.8	2.52	27.82	4.01	33.1	4.5	94.9	24.9	4.9
3.2	1.18	9.0	0.68	6.0	0.8	1.25	12.19	5.27	78.6	3.0	14.4	13.9	5.3
5.7	1.10	5.7	0.06	6.1	0.8	1.18	11.01	4.20	67.4	4.2	35.5	12.5	6.1
4.2	1.04	4.7	0.44	2.9	0.3	0.43	3.94	4.18	88.3	2.9	14.6	14.5	4.8
4.0	3.42	17.5	-0.02	9.6	0.3	1.77	13.73	4.71	42.3	3.1	16.7	13.8	7.1
5.2	1.78	8.1	0.90	7.2	1.0	2.51	20.41	5.05	49.4	4.2	15.6	7.4	4.4
8.9	0.01	0.1	-0.06	2.5	0.0	0.08	0.93	4.14	88.0	3.4	43.6	18.8	2.5
4.7	0.39	3.6	0.10	8.7	1.4	1.52	19.21	4.70	50.8	2.8	27.7	17.0	4.7
3.7	0.72	2.8	0.19	8.9	2.3	1.82	11.28	5.01	36.2	1.4	17.1	25.9	6.5
3.3	0.95	5.3	0.00	9.4	3.6	1.42	12.26	4.05	52.8	2.6	31.4	19.1	8.7
3.0	2.71	18.8	0.02	10.0	0.9	3.33	34.69	5.70	45.1	4.0	24.8	10.0	6.0
8.5	0.23	1.1	0.05	0.7	0.1	0.09	0.79	2.76	99.0	4.6	20.4	5.1	4.6
4.7	1.55	9.1	0.00	8.5	1.4	2.10	22.16	3.46	44.9	4.1	41.5	14.7	7.2
0.3	8.76	50.9	0.10	4.4	0.2	0.70	7.14	4.49	75.9	3.7	33.6	14.5	2.8
7.7	0.35	2.8	0.65	3.2	0.2	0.49	6.28	4.16	86.0	5.4	49.5	9.6	3.5
8.4	0.00	0.0	0.00	0.0	-0.2	-0.67	-4.18	4.34	102.4	5.1	64.4	13.8	0.0
7.5	0.00	0.0	0.07	7.0	0.5	1.25	11.40	4.17	50.0	1.0	6.5	29.2	4.0
5.4	0.86	6.1	0.11	4.5	2.4	0.88	14.67	2.61	57.6	2.1	43.4	45.1	3.4
4.5	1.42	10.3	-0.01	8.1	0.4	1.23	12.69	4.79	61.9	3.4	30.2	14.8	4.8
2.6	1.79	12.5	0.61	3.6	1.3	0.56	5.89	4.19	80.4	2.2	19.5	18.2	3.6
2.1	4.35	27.9	0.15	4.0	0.2	0.77	7.98	4.14	78.4	5.4	56.9	10.7	5.0
4.6	1.00	8.9	0.06	10.0	1.0	2.45	32.97	6.08	41.9	2.4	45.9	31.9	5.5
4.0	1.18	10.0	0.00	10.0	1.2	2.30	23.94	3.75	60.9	1.7	8.6	20.1	7.1
8.5	1.69	1.4	0.00	3.4	0.1	0.33	2.44	2.25	80.2	4.0	93.5	28.2	5.4
3.9	1.16	7.5	0.08	4.1	0.4	0.53	5.54	3.00	71.4	2.3	21.4	18.0	4.7
9.1	0.02	0.2	0.00	2.5	0.1	0.15	1.27	3.14	93.7	2.2	20.2	18.3	6.5
8.0	0.91	3.0	0.01	9.2	0.4	1.30	5.88	4.48	51.5	2.3	26.9	19.0	7.8
6.5	0.26	1.9	0.08	5.6	0.4	0.84	8.64	4.05	71.2	1.7	27.3	26.5	6.2
3.4	1.94	16.7	0.05	6.4	0.1	1.20	13.65	4.35	56.3	3.0	21.1	14.3	2.3
8.4	0.27	1.1	0.51	5.8	0.2	0.93	7.21	3.85	64.2	4.1	33.1	12.1	6.2
5.2	1.26	7.6	0.03	5.2	0.6	1.29	12.38	4.30	67.4	2.9	14.2	14.5	5.5
7.9	1.34	5.1	-0.01	9.7	2.3	1.91	17.28	4.02	32.7	1.6	18.9	24.6	8.7
6.9	0.37	2.2	0.42	6.1	1.3	1.54	18.09	3.81	62.5	4.2	24.9	8.8	5.6
7.8	0.05	0.4	-0.48	9.1	4.4	2.07	24.25	4.60	57.9	5.2	52.8	12.0	6.1
9.1	0.00	0.0	0.00	9.4	0.2	2.32	14.80	3.56	59.8	3.7	50.7	16.9	8.0
8.4	0.16	1.0	0.00	9.6	4.6	1.67	19.33	3.95	54.4	5.1	31.3	5.2	7.4
4.2	1.61	11.0	0.07	8.9	6.4	1.42	24.13	3.78	50.5	4.3	20.4	7.6	5.3
1.9	3.28	20.6	0.12	7.8	2.3	0.94	8.04	4.67	54.9	5.5	63.6	13.1	8.3
7.8	0.36	1.5	-0.01	5.2	0.3	1.29	10.66	4.29	70.6	2.5	30.0	19.1	6.5
4.2	0.95	7.3	0.03	7.1	0.3	1.13	12.30	4.51	57.8	4.1	42.6	14.8	3.7
5.1	0.64	6.1	0.11	5.9	0.4	0.90	12.63	3.82	59.0	4.6	27.4	7.1	4.0
8.7	0.08	0.3	0.02	7.2	0.6	1.68	11.87	3.59	45.5	4.6	36.2	10.7	8.2
6.0	1.27	7.0	0.01	4.9	0.2	0.96	8.04	3.79	74.8	6.3	55.5	5.1	7.3
5.8	1.07	6.9	0.01	3.7	0.2	0.60	7.17	3.61	82.0	5.9	40.1	4.0	4.6
4.4	1.22	5.9	-0.03	8.6	1.3	1.91	16.73	4.36	49.8	6.2	52.8	6.0	7.6
5.0	0.62	2.8	-0.08	5.6	0.3	1.52	17.97	3.35	53.2	3.1	52.4	24.5	2.2
1.0	3.39	24.4	0.00	6.3	0.3	0.97	11.50	4.53	60.4	4.3	17.4	6.7	3.7
7.5	0.35	1.3	0.00	3.8	0.2	0.55	6.00	2.12	65.0	3.1	7.2	12.8	5.2
5.2	0.45	4.0	0.01	8.0	0.5	1.88	21.36	4.58	53.9	5.0	28.5	5.2	3.8

Name	City	State	Weiss Safety Rating	2003 Weiss Safety Rating	2002 Weiss Safety Rating	Total Assets ($Mil)	One Year Asset Growth	Asset Mix (As a % of Total Assets)				Capital- ization Index	Leverage Ratio	Risk-based Capital Ratio
								Comm- ercial Loans	Cons- umer Loans	Home Mort- gages	Secur- ities			
SECURITY ST BK	WAVERLY	IA	A-	A-	B+	64.5	9.16	4.1	3.7	12.5	54.4	5.9	7.9	15.1
SECURITY ST BK	HAMILTON	IL	C+	C+	C+	48.4	1.63	11.4	9.6	37.2	15.1	6.1	8.1	13.4
SECURITY ST BK	SCOTT CITY	KS	B-	B-	B-	138.6	-15.14	13.3	1.3	2.9	44.1	10.0	13.6	22.7
SECURITY ST BK	WELLINGTON	KS	B-	C+	B-	39.3	-1.95	12.9	3.5	5.5	45.8	10.0	14.3	26.4
▲ SECURITY ST BK	AITKIN	MN	B+	A-	A-	91.5	2.91	10.8	3.8	13.5	21.1	8.1	9.7	13.7
▲ SECURITY ST BK	FERGUS FALLS	MN	B-	C+	C+	68.4	-2.11	11.0	1.4	13.2	30.7	6.4	8.5	13.3
▼ SECURITY ST BK	HIBBING	MN	B-	B+	B	81.9	-0.12	22.6	5.2	14.1	23.0	8.0	9.7	13.9
▼ SECURITY ST BK	HOWARD LAKE	MN	B-	B	B-	66.8	6.46	9.7	2.4	5.5	18.7	4.7	8.1	10.8
SECURITY ST BK	LEWISTON	MN	B+	B	B	86.2	0.26	10.2	6.0	9.7	16.0	8.4	9.9	14.0
▼ SECURITY ST BK	MANKATO	MN	C-	C	C	97.9	-4.51	24.9	6.0	4.5	24.7	4.8	7.9	10.9
SECURITY ST BK	OKLEE	MN	B-	B-	A-	26.1	4.96	2.2	2.9	3.7	45.2	10.0	17.8	51.9
▼ SECURITY ST BK	SEBEKA	MN	D-	D	D-	25.0	2.36	20.2	4.3	6.6	30.6	6.7	8.7	19.1
SECURITY ST BK	WANAMINGO	MN	B	B	B	54.6	6.80	3.9	3.7	10.2	27.5	8.6	10.1	14.8
SECURITY ST BK	DUNSEITH	ND	C+	C+	C+	38.8	-2.67	7.4	10.0	8.1	22.2	8.2	9.8	16.3
▲ SECURITY ST BK	HUNTER	ND	C	C-	D+	34.8	15.30	9.2	6.7	5.5	16.8	5.0	7.6	11.0
SECURITY ST BK	WISHEK	ND	C+	C+	B-	47.1	6.72	7.6	4.7	1.8	32.8	6.8	8.8	13.2
SECURITY ST BK	ANSLEY	NE	E-	E-	D-	13.1	10.39	1.3	12.4	10.7	15.5	3.0	6.7	10.0
SECURITY ST BK	CHEYENNE	OK	A-	A-	A-	78.0	0.82	4.6	5.2	10.0	38.5	10.0	13.2	22.6
SECURITY ST BK	WEWOKA	OK	B-	B-	B-	37.8	2.95	6.3	17.7	17.2	45.7	10.0	14.2	27.4
SECURITY ST BK	ALEXANDRIA	SD	B	B	B	50.4	1.79	4.2	6.3	7.1	33.3	10.0	12.4	19.8
▲ SECURITY ST BK	EMERY	SD	B	B-	B-	29.0	-3.65	7.6	6.6	4.1	30.5	10.0	14.9	15.6
SECURITY ST BK	TYNDALL	SD	B+	B+	B+	31.4	-2.33	14.4	2.4	2.8	5.4	10.0	18.3	21.3
▼ SECURITY ST BK	ANAHUAC	TX	B	B+	A-	64.2	-8.58	2.9	10.0	8.1	64.4	10.0	12.5	25.4
SECURITY ST BK	FARWELL	TX	A	A	A-	98.8	-5.90	1.3	0.4	1.5	79.0	10.0	15.7	53.6
▼ SECURITY ST BK	LITTLEFIELD	TX	C+	B-	B-	69.0	-3.62	6.3	4.8	9.2	31.7	8.6	10.1	15.3
SECURITY ST BK	ODESSA	TX	C+	C+	C+	161.3	7.32	27.7	9.5	9.0	20.9	4.9	7.8	10.9
SECURITY ST BK	PEARSALL	TX	B+	B+	B+	337.7	7.44	3.1	0.7	0.8	74.9	4.9	6.9	21.6
SECURITY ST BK	STOCKDALE	TX	B	B	B	28.3	-6.06	6.7	9.9	7.7	38.0	10.0	14.6	27.1
▲ SECURITY ST BK	WINGATE	TX	D-	E+	E+	23.7	9.13	8.8	13.1	10.6	35.1	5.4	7.4	15.5
▼ SECURITY ST BK	CENTRALIA	WA	B	B+	B+	263.9	6.63	19.9	4.0	4.1	13.4	9.4	11.3	14.5
▲ SECURITY ST BK	IRON RIVER	WI	B-	C	C	96.9	14.88	17.3	3.0	11.7	18.5	10.0	15.2	19.7
SECURITY ST BK	BASIN	WY	B-	B-	C+	118.0	3.17	17.5	8.8	8.0	25.9	6.8	8.8	13.0
SECURITY ST BK ND	HANNAFORD	ND	C-	C-	C+	276.2	24.86	19.1	5.3	9.8	13.3	3.8	7.7	10.4
SECURITY ST BK OF KENYON	KENYON	MN	B-	C+	B-	56.0	4.93	11.3	3.9	7.8	6.5	6.5	10.6	12.1
SECURITY ST BK OF MAPLE	MAPLE LAKE	MN	B	B	B-	62.1	2.41	6.3	2.4	20.5	16.8	8.1	9.7	13.8
SECURITY ST BK OF MARINE	MARINE ON ST CRX	MN	B+	B+	B+	82.3	8.48	5.4	3.8	37.7	9.6	9.3	10.5	15.5
SECURITY ST BK OF PECOS	PECOS	TX	B	B	B	95.9	8.66	17.3	6.6	6.9	28.9	5.9	7.9	13.1
SECURITY ST BK OF STAPLES	STAPLES	MN	B+	B+	B+	34.3	4.89	12.6	12.2	32.9	25.8	5.3	7.3	13.5
SECURITY ST BK OF	WARROAD	MN	B+	B+	B+	66.0	-5.85	10.4	10.5	9.6	48.0	10.0	18.4	19.4
SECURITY ST BK SHELDON	SHELDON	IA	A-	A-	B+	58.7	-5.39	20.7	3.5	16.1	10.5	8.1	10.0	13.5
▲ SECURITY ST SAVINGS BK	LAS VEGAS	NV	D+	D	D	52.2	12.14	4.1	0.0	39.7	17.8	6.3	8.3	14.1
SECURITY STATE BANK NA	ORE CITY	TX	D	D	D	41.7	-16.64	5.7	18.9	17.0	31.7	9.7	10.8	21.1
SECURITY SVG BK	EAGLE GROVE	IA	B	B	B	86.9	13.07	16.9	4.1	8.2	36.7	6.4	8.4	15.0
▲ SECURITY SVG BK	GOWRIE	IA	C-	D+	D+	56.1	3.24	5.0	6.9	18.9	31.5	5.4	7.4	12.7
SECURITY SVG BK	LARCHWOOD	IA	B	B+	B+	54.3	3.45	8.5	2.7	14.6	7.5	7.6	10.8	13.0
▼ SECURITY SVG BK SSB	SOUTHPORT	NC	B-	B	B	313.7	-0.89	1.0	1.6	45.0	8.0	10.0	13.3	18.0
▲ SECURITY SVGS BK	MONMOUTH	IL	B-	C+	C+	127.6	2.79	2.3	5.3	29.2	23.3	7.3	9.2	16.3
SECURITY SVGS BK FSB	SALINA	KS	C+	C	C	792.6	11.71	9.3	0.9	22.8	24.1	5.0	7.0	11.5
▼ SECURITY T&SB	STORM LAKE	IA	B-	B	B	95.9	4.03	4.2	3.1	9.4	58.1	9.6	10.7	25.8
▲ SEI PRIVATE TRUST COMPANY	OAKS	PA	B	B-	B-	38.1	8.08	0.0	0.0	0.0	65.1	10.0	51.4	110.1
SELECT BK	GRAND RAPIDS	MI	B-	B-	B-	98.1	11.46	19.1	1.4	22.1	4.5	5.8	9.1	11.6
SELECT BK	EGG HARBOR CITY	NJ	C	C-	D	82.9	30.65	1.9	0.1	26.3	27.1	6.4	8.4	18.2
▲ SENATH ST BK	SENATH	MO	A-	B+	B+	43.4	7.70	7.4	18.5	45.9	0.5	10.0	14.6	22.7
SENATOBIA BK	SENATOBIA	MS	B+	B+	B	162.5	19.02	4.8	5.0	13.6	43.1	6.7	8.7	15.9
SENATOR BANK	TOWSON	MD	E-	E-	E-	19.7	-10.98	2.4	0.3	24.4	34.0	5.5	7.5	30.8
▼ SENECA FALLS SVGS BK	SENECA FALLS	NY	D-	NR	NR	138.4	N/A	0.0	1.4	40.1	41.0	4.8	6.8	14.7
SENECA FS&LA	BALDWINSVILLE	NY	C+	C+	C+	123.1	2.28	2.7	0.8	53.8	9.1	6.4	8.4	19.7
SENECA NB	SENECA	SC	B-	B-	B-	47.3	-2.67	7.4	2.8	14.6	21.1	6.5	8.5	13.0
SENTRY BANK & TRUST	CHERAW	SC	B	B	B+	154.6	9.66	5.7	4.4	40.7	17.7	10.0	14.3	22.3
▲ SEQUOIA NB	SAN FRANCISCO	CA	D	D-	D+	65.7	4.90	6.1	0.2	7.4	12.5	8.5	10.0	17.5
▲ SERVICE 1ST BK	STOCKTON	CA	C+	C-	D	124.7	34.17	11.3	0.7	2.9	38.8	5.3	7.3	11.7
SETTLERS BK	MARIETTA	OH	B-	B-	C-	67.5	16.00	8.5	8.6	33.6	10.6	8.5	10.1	13.8
SEVERN SVGS BK FSB	ANNAPOLIS	MD	A-	A-	B+	619.3	22.96	1.0	0.2	32.8	1.7	6.9	8.9	12.6
SEVIER COUNTY BK	SEVIERVILLE	TN	A-	A-	A	297.2	9.05	0.6	1.7	9.0	32.9	10.0	12.3	22.4

Asset Quality Index	Non-Performing Loans as a % of Total Loans	Non-Performing Loans as a % of Capital	Net Charge-offs Avg Loans	Profitability Index	Net Income ($Mil)	Return on Assets (R.O.A.)	Return on Equity (R.O.E.)	Net Interest Spread	Overhead Efficiency Ratio	Liquidity Index	Liquidity Ratio	Hot Money Ratio	Stability Index
7.4	0.64	3.0	0.25	8.6	0.5	1.60	18.59	3.45	45.1	2.9	12.2	14.2	6.5
5.3	0.47	4.0	-0.32	7.2	0.3	1.15	14.23	4.15	60.7	2.7	22.4	16.5	5.0
4.8	3.81	11.3	1.77	4.0	0.7	1.00	7.20	3.83	70.3	2.8	25.8	16.3	5.1
3.7	8.59	25.4	4.58	5.2	0.1	0.53	3.72	4.56	73.5	4.1	16.3	8.5	7.3
5.6	0.32	2.1	0.05	10.0	1.3	2.98	27.54	5.66	44.4	5.2	31.2	4.8	7.6
7.6	0.50	3.7	-0.03	7.5	0.6	1.92	23.59	4.63	60.2	6.2	82.4	10.3	5.1
3.4	2.24	13.8	-0.07	6.9	0.4	1.03	10.58	4.61	60.9	5.6	47.0	7.7	6.9
5.1	1.11	8.3	0.02	7.6	0.5	1.73	19.39	4.47	53.7	1.3	25.9	31.5	6.2
6.6	0.53	3.8	0.84	7.3	0.7	1.54	15.54	4.86	58.8	3.2	18.5	13.2	6.2
0.9	4.61	33.0	1.50	2.7	0.1	0.11	1.32	3.38	64.2	2.3	8.9	16.8	3.9
9.5	0.18	0.2	-0.04	3.4	0.1	0.67	3.62	2.26	63.7	7.8	157.6	9.8	6.5
2.3	4.45	25.6	0.00	4.2	0.1	0.92	10.25	3.76	73.4	5.7	67.3	9.4	1.7
5.4	0.69	4.0	0.36	5.6	0.3	1.05	9.90	3.71	53.2	6.1	59.9	7.4	5.2
4.6	1.27	6.6	0.05	4.9	0.2	0.93	9.18	4.85	76.8	5.7	51.5	8.1	4.8
4.3	0.46	4.0	0.03	5.9	0.2	1.25	15.82	4.59	62.7	4.5	30.0	8.9	4.3
7.2	0.56	3.1	0.11	5.5	0.3	1.20	13.20	3.67	61.9	5.9	50.3	6.4	5.0
4.4	0.05	0.5	1.29	2.5	0.0	-0.14	-1.90	5.00	83.5	1.4	23.2	26.8	0.3
7.6	1.24	4.7	0.46	7.4	0.5	1.19	8.82	4.20	56.6	2.7	36.8	21.5	7.3
7.5	0.87	2.8	0.38	3.6	0.1	0.45	3.23	4.24	84.9	1.6	11.8	21.4	4.0
6.7	1.16	5.4	0.01	4.5	0.3	1.04	8.54	3.73	68.8	5.4	48.8	9.5	6.3
8.4	0.00	0.0	0.00	4.8	0.2	1.03	7.09	3.62	59.9	7.8	142.1	8.2	6.3
8.3	0.33	1.0	0.00	7.8	0.2	1.32	7.11	4.67	58.7	7.5	82.7	2.1	6.6
8.6	0.83	1.7	0.08	3.2	0.0	0.03	0.21	3.85	92.5	2.3	44.1	32.8	6.4
9.4	0.01	0.0	0.00	6.1	0.5	1.06	7.00	3.08	43.9	2.2	49.5	51.6	8.1
8.4	0.05	0.3	0.00	3.2	0.1	0.28	2.46	4.37	93.4	3.5	7.7	11.0	5.6
5.0	0.43	3.7	0.51	4.4	0.6	0.70	8.91	5.00	76.7	2.1	9.0	18.0	3.1
7.8	1.22	3.0	0.00	9.8	3.4	2.07	30.39	3.76	23.1	0.4	4.5	58.3	6.3
8.3	0.51	1.3	0.05	5.4	0.2	1.06	7.43	4.09	68.3	5.8	65.1	10.2	5.5
6.6	0.72	3.9	-0.27	4.4	0.1	0.78	10.66	4.65	79.9	4.9	46.9	9.5	1.1
4.8	1.18	6.4	0.03	8.8	2.7	2.06	18.63	5.13	59.0	8.8	203.2	7.8	8.3
3.2	4.55	20.5	0.00	10.0	1.0	2.13	13.95	5.18	33.0	1.2	26.0	33.6	8.1
4.6	1.37	10.0	0.03	6.3	0.7	1.24	14.83	4.02	59.0	2.5	14.8	16.5	4.6
3.6	1.14	11.2	0.04	3.9	0.9	0.69	9.37	4.19	79.8	2.8	17.7	15.4	3.6
7.0	0.00	0.0	0.00	8.3	0.6	2.10	19.02	5.04	57.8	3.7	29.8	13.2	6.3
8.8	0.00	0.0	0.02	6.6	0.5	1.47	15.35	4.46	67.9	5.6	40.5	6.4	5.3
5.3	0.93	6.3	-0.02	9.9	0.7	1.71	16.67	5.04	49.8	4.5	73.4	18.0	7.2
5.1	0.34	1.9	0.24	5.0	0.4	0.89	8.77	4.51	77.2	3.7	38.0	15.8	5.1
6.0	0.41	3.2	0.23	5.9	0.2	1.38	18.12	4.20	71.1	4.3	52.7	15.6	5.5
4.6	4.76	10.5	-0.01	5.7	0.3	0.85	4.66	4.00	66.0	4.6	41.2	12.1	6.3
7.3	0.00	0.0	0.01	7.4	0.4	1.28	10.73	4.00	57.1	4.2	10.2	6.6	8.1
4.2	1.88	16.6	0.00	2.6	0.1	0.44	5.48	2.88	85.5	1.7	34.2	34.4	0.0
3.8	0.92	2.5	2.14	3.4	0.2	0.70	4.04	5.05	72.2	3.7	76.2	27.0	3.0
8.4	0.00	0.0	0.14	5.2	0.4	0.87	10.14	3.32	62.3	6.7	64.3	4.1	4.8
6.9	0.59	4.5	-0.05	5.2	0.4	1.29	17.23	3.74	64.6	3.7	17.2	10.6	2.2
7.0	0.55	4.2	0.00	5.6	0.3	0.95	9.92	4.09	64.4	1.8	23.0	22.8	6.1
6.8	1.24	5.9	0.18	3.5	0.8	0.54	3.85	3.26	71.9	5.6	114.4	17.9	7.5
4.2	2.04	13.0	0.14	3.9	0.4	0.56	5.99	3.54	73.9	4.8	85.2	19.2	4.8
6.7	0.28	2.8	0.03	5.7	4.8	1.22	18.23	2.45	55.4	0.8	9.8	32.8	4.7
5.6	1.83	6.0	0.42	4.2	0.4	0.90	8.35	3.33	64.5	1.7	25.5	25.7	6.0
6.5	0.00	0.0	0.00	10.0	0.4	2.26	4.35	4.88	98.5	0.0	1.8	100.0	2.9
5.9	0.35	3.1	0.23	6.1	0.3	0.69	7.54	4.14	68.0	0.3	3.3	67.4	5.2
9.4	0.00	0.0	0.00	3.2	0.3	0.71	8.06	3.13	72.2	2.0	39.9	34.7	1.5
6.5	0.48	2.5	-0.12	10.0	0.7	3.26	22.73	5.51	45.1	5.3	32.8	4.6	7.9
6.2	0.71	3.9	0.55	8.2	1.0	1.23	13.98	4.23	56.7	3.1	15.5	13.4	5.5
10.0	0.00	0.0	0.00	2.9	0.0	0.37	5.24	2.37	83.3	4.4	64.0	15.5	0.4
7.1	0.57	3.9	0.10	0.1	-0.3	-0.40	-5.74	3.23	110.2	3.9	12.0	9.2	0.0
8.2	0.25	1.8	0.02	3.7	0.3	0.42	5.03	3.10	80.0	4.0	42.3	15.3	4.2
8.0	0.00	0.0	0.10	4.3	0.2	0.71	8.64	3.51	73.5	1.1	10.9	29.3	5.1
4.8	1.89	9.5	0.10	5.1	0.7	0.91	6.27	3.32	64.4	0.8	16.9	45.0	7.8
7.7	0.00	0.0	0.00	0.5	-0.1	-0.22	-2.15	3.62	105.7	4.3	49.2	15.1	3.8
7.2	0.14	0.9	0.00	4.3	0.8	1.36	19.31	3.66	67.1	2.5	9.3	16.1	5.2
5.1	0.68	5.1	0.19	5.3	0.3	0.95	9.38	4.09	60.5	3.6	37.8	16.4	4.1
7.6	0.03	0.3	0.04	10.0	6.3	2.14	24.66	4.94	29.9	0.5	2.3	46.7	7.3
8.9	0.01	0.1	-0.05	5.4	1.4	0.94	7.62	3.33	56.8	4.1	85.5	28.3	7.7

| Name | City | State | Weiss Safety Rating | 2003 Weiss Safety Rating | 2002 Weiss Safety Rating | Total Assets ($Mil) | One Year Asset Growth | Asset Mix (As a % of Total Assets) | | | | Capital- ization Index | Leverage Ratio | Risk-based Capital Ratio |
								Comm- ercial Loans	Cons- umer Loans	Home Mort- gages	Secur- ities			
SEWICKLEY SVGS BK	SEWICKLEY	PA	A+	A+	A+	240.9	1.48	0.0	0.2	8.2	65.6	10.0	23.4	66.7
SEYMOUR BK	SEYMOUR	MO	B	B	B+	116.6	-2.10	1.5	9.2	22.8	35.2	10.0	11.6	19.9
▼ SHAMROCK BK NA	COALGATE	OK	B-	B	A-	160.3	10.54	7.0	8.4	14.5	38.8	8.0	9.7	17.6
SHARON CO-OP BK	SHARON	MA	C+	C+	C+	66.7	0.68	1.0	1.5	58.2	26.2	9.8	10.9	22.0
▲ SHARON SVG BK	DARBY	PA	C+	C	C+	192.1	6.61	0.0	0.5	50.6	39.8	6.0	8.0	21.3
SHATTUCK NB	SHATTUCK	OK	B-	B-	B-	32.1	-6.61	8.4	6.1	6.3	37.1	10.0	12.0	29.9
SHELBY COUNTY BK	SHELBYVILLE	IN	D-	E	E-	121.2	14.49	13.0	3.0	19.9	19.5	3.3	6.2	10.2
SHELBY COUNTY ST BK	HARLAN	IA	C+	C+	C+	198.3	-3.69	8.6	18.4	7.0	13.1	5.5	8.3	11.4
SHELBY COUNTY ST BK	SHELBYVILLE	IL	A-	A-	B+	130.0	-1.18	7.3	5.3	11.9	40.4	10.0	12.0	21.1
▲ SHELBY ST BK	SHELBY	MI	A-	B+	B+	141.8	-7.01	3.3	7.0	18.8	32.5	9.0	10.3	16.0
SHELBY SVG BK SSB	CENTER	TX	B-	B-	B	143.4	1.50	7.5	10.4	23.5	22.2	6.0	8.0	13.9
SHELL LAKE ST BK	SHELL LAKE	WI	A+	A+	A+	117.4	4.07	12.3	3.8	23.0	37.2	10.0	15.8	25.7
SHELTER FINANCIAL BK	COLUMBIA	MO	C+	C+	C+	101.5	14.51	5.2	31.2	54.5	0.0	8.0	9.8	13.3
SHENANDOAH NB	STAUNTON	VA	D+	D+	D+	118.6	2.15	1.0	3.4	7.4	17.0	4.0	6.0	12.3
SHENANDOAH VALLEY NB	WINCHESTER	VA	C+	C+	C+	253.3	29.60	4.8	0.9	23.5	19.7	3.3	7.6	10.2
▲ SHERBURNE ST BK	BECKER	MN	D+	D+	D-	53.0	6.48	5.9	3.4	14.7	11.7	2.7	7.1	9.7
SHERIDAN ST BK	SHERIDAN	IL	C+	B-	B-	21.2	-0.52	4.5	7.0	29.2	30.8	7.4	9.3	18.5
▼ SHERIDAN ST BK	SHERIDAN	WY	B-	B	B-	89.2	12.62	9.6	1.5	11.1	23.8	5.5	7.5	12.6
SHERMAN COUNTY BK	LOUP CITY	NE	C+	C	C	83.9	5.17	7.3	3.6	3.9	28.5	7.2	9.1	14.6
SHERWOOD COMMUNITY	CREIGHTON	MO	B-	B-	B-	31.9	6.09	2.0	6.9	9.8	41.4	8.3	9.9	17.3
SHERWOOD ST BK	SHERWOOD	OH	D-	D-	D+	35.9	10.77	8.3	11.0	28.0	18.4	5.5	7.5	12.8
SHORE BK	ONLEY	VA	B-	B-	B-	218.1	17.70	3.2	1.1	36.3	16.3	5.7	7.7	12.3
▲ SHORE CMNTY BK	TOMS RIVER	NJ	C+	C	C	116.9	25.10	17.0	0.8	13.2	29.6	5.2	7.2	11.4
SHOREBANK	CHICAGO	IL	C	C	C	1,378.7	9.15	17.0	0.3	15.0	28.5	4.3	6.7	10.7
SHOREBANK	CLEVELAND	OH	C	C	C	68.2	6.28	14.5	0.0	4.0	49.2	8.8	10.2	19.6
SHOREBANK PACIFIC	ILWACO	WA	C	C-	C	91.5	9.62	12.6	6.2	0.4	53.3	6.2	8.2	16.0
▲ SHORELINE BK	SHORELINE	WA	B-	C+	C-	57.2	26.99	14.2	3.0	10.4	7.1	10.0	13.1	15.7
▼ SHOSHONE FIRST BK	CODY	WY	B-	B	B-	235.2	16.76	11.4	2.6	12.7	12.7	5.4	8.0	11.3
SHREWSBURY ST BK	SHREWSBURY	NJ	A+	A+	A+	425.0	4.76	4.5	0.4	24.1	31.2	10.0	14.0	22.2
SIBLEY ST BK	SIBLEY	IA	B+	B+	B-	67.3	-2.00	6.0	11.9	7.2	16.7	10.0	13.4	16.8
SICILY ISLAND ST BK	SICILY ISLAND	LA	C+	C	C+	27.7	10.89	22.3	11.0	24.3	16.1	10.0	11.2	17.8
SIDELL ST BK	SIDELL	IL	C-	C-	D	16.4	-0.82	3.3	10.2	2.3	21.4	8.1	9.7	20.1
▲ SIDNEY FS&LA	SIDNEY	NE	E+	E+	D-	27.3	-3.08	0.0	13.3	47.7	21.9	6.5	8.5	16.6
SIDNEY ST BK	SIDNEY	MI	B+	B+	B	49.2	-6.86	2.6	8.0	62.8	8.0	10.0	11.7	21.6
▲ SIGNATURE BANK	NEW YORK	NY	C-	D-	D-	2,680.6	78.82	11.7	0.3	3.0	72.6	10.0	11.4	29.9
▲ SIGNATURE BK	ST PETERSBURG	FL	C+	C	C-	133.9	30.78	17.3	4.3	10.9	15.0	5.5	7.9	11.4
▲ SIGNATURE BK	BAD AXE	MI	B-	C+	C+	241.1	0.56	9.7	3.9	23.7	12.1	4.6	7.6	10.8
SIGNATURE BK	MINNETONKA	MN	D	D	NR	32.1	N/A	34.3	3.2	3.5	4.7	10.0	24.7	22.6
SIGNATURE BK	SPRINGFIELD	MO	C	C	C-	354.3	16.05	20.9	1.6	10.2	3.8	6.6	8.6	12.4
▲ SIGNATURE BK	DALLAS	TX	C	C-	D+	61.4	16.53	9.5	6.9	20.9	14.1	7.5	9.5	12.9
▲ SIGNATURE BK NA	TOLEDO	OH	C-	D+	D	187.0	27.63	19.9	1.5	16.6	4.3	8.0	10.7	13.3
SILEX BKG CO	SILEX	MO	B	B	B	54.4	2.62	2.7	1.1	13.7	44.3	10.0	15.1	29.0
▲ SILICON VALLEY BK	SANTA CLARA	CA	A	A-	A-	4,571.6	13.21	32.9	3.0	1.0	40.0	9.1	10.6	14.3
▼ SILVER FALLS BK	SILVERTON	OR	B-	B	B	54.9	16.37	9.7	0.1	5.2	13.3	10.0	12.3	18.1
SILVER LAKE BK	TOPEKA	KS	B	B	B	152.2	8.17	20.5	1.7	18.2	13.6	5.9	9.2	11.7
▲ SILVER ST BK	HENDERSON	NV	C	D+	D+	597.1	39.17	9.2	0.5	4.5	15.0	6.1	8.9	11.8
SILVERGATE BK	LA JOLLA	CA	D+	C-	C-	486.6	18.49	0.0	0.0	43.8	31.6	4.1	6.1	11.7
SIMMESPORT ST BK	SIMMESPORT	LA	B	B	B	40.2	3.55	7.9	21.9	32.5	14.6	10.0	14.6	25.6
SIMMONS FIRST BANK HOT	HOT SPRINGS	AR	B-	B-	B-	157.7	13.80	3.9	2.7	15.4	37.4	4.8	6.8	14.1
SIMMONS FIRST BK	RUSSELLVILLE	AR	B-	B	B-	197.4	-7.98	10.8	3.6	13.2	16.2	9.8	10.8	17.0
SIMMONS FIRST BK	SEARCY	AR	B-	B-	B-	122.3	4.35	8.4	6.0	24.3	19.2	8.9	10.3	16.5
SIMMONS FIRST BK	JONESBORO	AR	B-	B-	B-	215.8	14.38	8.4	8.3	27.6	7.7	4.4	7.9	10.7
SIMMONS FIRST BK NW AR	ROGERS	AR	B-	C+	C+	240.4	11.48	6.4	6.5	12.9	17.6	5.3	7.3	11.4
SIMMONS FIRST BK OF	EL DORADO	AR	B	B	B-	196.5	7.22	10.8	8.2	9.4	45.7	6.0	8.0	15.4
SIMMONS FIRST BK OF SE AR	LAKE VILLAGE	AR	B-	B-	B-	126.0	11.77	8.8	9.8	8.1	24.7	6.6	8.6	14.1
SIMMONS FIRST NB	PINE BLUFF	AR	B-	B-	B-	1,140.3	14.63	7.1	24.6	7.8	19.9	5.4	7.4	12.2
▼ SIMSBURY B&TC	SIMSBURY	CT	C	C+	C+	196.6	7.73	4.8	5.4	42.3	19.4	4.9	7.0	14.1
▲ SINCERE FSB	SAN FRANCISCO	CA	C	C-	C	53.3	-7.40	0.0	0.4	9.1	0.0	10.0	12.7	19.0
SIOUXLAND NB	S SIOUX CITY	NE	C-	C-	D+	36.3	9.46	14.3	5.7	19.9	11.5	6.8	8.8	16.3
▲ SIUSLAW VALLEY BK	FLORENCE	OR	A	A-	A-	255.2	17.61	8.8	2.5	5.9	25.5	10.0	12.4	17.0
SIWOOGANOCK BK	LANCASTER	NH	C+	C+	C	81.8	6.61	2.2	20.9	35.5	6.8	5.5	7.5	11.9
SKAGIT ST BK	BURLINGTON	WA	A-	A-	A-	476.0	1.65	15.8	3.3	7.6	10.7	10.0	11.5	15.7
▲ SKOWHEGAN SVGS BK	SKOWHEGAN	ME	C+	C	D+	386.0	-5.77	2.3	13.2	39.7	17.4	10.0	11.2	17.5
SKY BK	SALINEVILLE	OH	B-	B-	B-	12,049.1	1.90	18.0	5.8	10.7	19.9	5.4	7.4	11.3

Asset Quality Index	Non-Performing Loans as a % of Total Loans	Non-Performing Loans as a % of Capital	Net Charge-offs Avg Loans	Profitability Index	Net Income ($Mil)	Return on Assets (R.O.A.)	Return on Equity (R.O.E.)	Net Interest Spread	Overhead Efficiency Ratio	Liquidity Index	Liquidity Ratio	Hot Money Ratio	Stability Index
10.0	0.06	0.0	0.00	8.3	1.7	1.39	5.71	3.07	34.8	7.8	185.9	12.5	9.5
7.4	1.01	4.7	1.44	3.5	0.2	0.37	3.07	3.98	67.0	3.5	39.6	17.1	6.7
3.6	2.46	12.1	0.45	6.1	0.6	0.80	7.68	4.81	70.6	2.7	21.1	16.0	5.1
9.9	0.00	0.0	0.01	3.0	0.1	0.29	2.85	3.08	84.0	5.2	54.7	11.4	4.7
9.9	0.04	0.3	0.02	3.6	0.6	0.60	7.79	3.26	69.9	4.9	26.5	5.0	4.1
8.6	0.86	2.5	-0.07	3.4	0.1	0.51	4.27	3.83	84.6	6.3	73.2	8.9	5.1
2.3	1.60	14.1	0.09	2.7	0.3	0.58	7.50	3.42	79.0	1.9	22.7	21.2	2.3
3.0	0.98	6.8	1.56	8.2	1.5	1.43	14.72	5.18	40.9	3.7	29.6	12.9	5.7
8.6	0.18	0.8	0.03	5.9	1.1	1.59	13.01	3.88	66.1	4.5	27.0	7.5	7.0
6.9	0.46	2.3	0.07	6.7	0.9	1.23	10.87	4.81	71.5	4.7	26.5	5.7	6.6
4.6	0.92	7.2	-0.11	6.4	1.1	1.53	19.86	3.76	56.2	4.2	67.8	20.1	5.2
8.8	0.17	0.6	0.06	9.4	1.0	1.75	11.01	4.45	49.5	3.6	16.0	11.2	9.6
6.3	0.17	1.5	0.03	3.3	0.1	0.24	2.30	2.63	79.8	0.9	1.7	28.8	4.9
1.2	3.83	34.2	0.00	4.6	0.5	0.89	15.18	3.20	59.8	6.1	91.0	13.6	2.7
8.8	0.00	0.0	0.02	6.9	1.9	1.60	21.51	3.58	81.0	1.6	12.9	22.5	4.8
7.4	0.00	0.0	0.05	7.5	0.5	1.80	24.14	5.64	64.8	3.3	19.0	13.0	3.3
6.5	0.48	2.1	-0.02	4.9	0.1	0.74	5.80	3.78	70.6	6.5	63.1	2.8	6.3
5.2	1.51	10.5	0.00	6.0	0.7	1.41	15.76	3.11	61.8	3.7	21.5	11.3	5.0
3.2	3.14	17.3	-0.04	5.0	0.4	0.95	10.14	3.83	68.1	3.7	38.8	16.3	5.9
6.0	0.98	4.1	-0.04	4.8	0.1	0.81	8.16	3.29	68.3	8.0	151.6	8.1	5.5
6.2	0.40	3.8	0.13	2.6	0.1	0.28	3.67	4.58	87.2	1.8	23.5	22.5	1.8
6.7	0.49	4.2	-0.01	6.1	1.1	1.08	13.43	3.73	57.1	4.0	22.8	9.5	4.8
7.1	0.60	5.1	0.04	4.0	0.3	0.64	8.56	4.07	68.4	3.6	24.9	11.7	4.0
3.1	2.78	23.7	0.27	6.3	7.7	1.12	15.55	4.11	56.0	0.7	13.1	48.7	5.1
2.2	5.37	25.5	1.12	1.7	0.0	0.10	0.94	3.84	92.6	0.1	3.3	89.2	5.0
5.7	2.17	11.4	0.33	1.2	0.1	0.13	1.83	3.11	88.2	0.5	9.8	61.0	3.9
7.2	0.00	0.0	0.00	3.5	0.2	0.59	5.20	4.56	81.6	2.7	59.5	34.3	5.5
7.4	0.31	2.9	-0.01	9.2	2.5	2.16	28.06	3.92	48.8	3.6	38.0	16.4	5.2
9.3	0.19	0.8	0.07	8.9	2.9	1.39	9.96	4.05	55.8	5.3	30.5	3.8	9.3
6.8	0.60	3.1	0.97	8.5	0.4	1.21	9.12	4.55	45.2	4.8	32.9	8.0	6.1
4.4	2.27	13.1	-0.04	5.4	0.2	1.04	9.45	4.95	70.6	0.9	24.8	42.1	4.5
8.1	0.00	0.0	0.03	2.7	0.0	0.33	3.15	3.72	92.3	7.6	127.0	6.6	2.9
2.1	2.50	18.9	0.00	2.9	0.0	0.26	3.22	2.92	90.0	3.3	27.9	14.4	1.0
7.7	0.14	0.9	0.23	7.3	0.3	1.24	10.50	5.20	61.8	5.9	47.2	5.8	6.1
9.3	1.08	2.0	0.01	2.4	20.9	1.85	18.77	2.63	87.0	7.9	91.9	4.3	3.2
8.2	0.03	0.2	0.01	3.5	0.3	0.40	4.85	3.84	73.3	1.6	19.9	24.7	4.7
7.4	0.14	1.2	0.11	4.8	1.2	0.94	11.03	4.31	68.9	3.2	13.3	12.7	5.0
6.4	1.97	7.1	0.00	0.0	-0.6	-4.58	-15.81	5.22	149.3	5.1	52.4	11.3	0.0
7.1	0.09	0.8	0.03	5.0	1.6	0.93	10.80	3.09	51.4	3.7	29.7	13.3	4.0
8.3	0.00	0.0	-0.01	2.9	0.1	0.50	5.54	4.24	84.3	5.5	81.7	13.9	2.9
8.4	0.09	0.7	0.00	2.2	0.4	0.46	4.35	3.19	69.8	2.0	33.8	28.7	1.1
9.4	0.00	0.0	-0.01	4.9	0.3	1.19	7.92	3.37	52.3	8.9	374.8	7.5	7.4
8.2	0.60	2.6	-0.01	9.1	29.4	1.35	12.88	5.32	70.3	8.0	129.5	6.7	7.9
2.7	3.67	20.6	0.05	9.7	0.4	1.42	11.68	4.91	51.6	7.1	154.3	13.1	1.3
8.4	0.12	0.9	-0.01	4.4	0.4	0.55	5.96	3.57	68.6	4.6	31.9	9.4	6.0
3.9	0.68	5.2	0.12	6.1	3.2	1.14	14.44	4.33	55.7	6.4	79.5	10.6	4.3
8.9	0.14	1.6	0.00	1.9	0.1	0.03	0.55	1.59	97.5	2.4	52.4	65.2	2.1
3.5	2.61	12.7	0.51	9.1	0.4	2.15	15.39	5.29	42.5	3.0	50.1	25.4	6.5
4.9	0.89	2.3	-0.01	3.9	0.4	0.48	3.58	1.82	65.0	4.0	22.1	9.5	6.0
3.7	1.15	3.9	0.05	5.4	0.8	0.85	4.70	4.02	66.3	2.5	33.2	21.3	7.4
3.7	1.25	5.8	0.23	5.0	0.6	0.99	7.26	3.98	63.5	1.3	20.7	28.9	6.6
4.9	0.40	4.1	0.43	8.4	1.4	1.35	16.56	4.24	47.7	1.5	7.6	22.8	5.8
4.2	0.65	4.4	0.10	5.5	1.2	1.02	10.73	4.18	60.8	2.6	41.8	26.9	5.6
5.2	1.02	5.8	0.07	6.9	1.3	1.32	16.89	3.69	51.3	1.7	17.9	22.8	6.2
4.0	1.75	9.6	0.34	7.3	0.7	1.11	11.80	4.31	52.5	2.5	32.6	20.3	6.7
4.7	0.66	4.1	0.71	7.7	7.0	1.19	13.42	4.47	66.5	5.3	43.6	11.8	6.4
8.9	0.00	0.0	0.00	5.6	0.9	0.92	13.55	3.84	64.4	5.6	40.7	6.1	3.0
7.5	0.00	0.0	0.00	2.4	0.1	0.25	1.99	3.96	91.5	4.7	41.3	12.0	4.7
4.3	1.42	9.7	0.03	4.2	0.1	0.73	7.96	3.73	73.6	4.5	98.0	23.2	3.7
8.3	0.17	0.8	0.01	10.0	2.1	1.79	16.54	5.02	53.5	5.5	30.9	2.3	7.5
7.3	0.09	0.9	0.10	4.6	0.7	1.62	18.27	4.32	81.2	5.4	40.1	7.3	4.5
5.4	1.54	9.0	0.34	6.2	2.6	1.08	9.49	4.37	58.0	4.5	33.1	10.1	7.3
5.6	0.95	5.1	0.19	3.0	1.2	0.62	5.19	4.21	77.0	6.4	61.9	8.0	5.5
4.2	1.21	10.1	0.39	8.4	76.4	1.28	16.07	3.80	52.0	3.0	11.6	13.8	6.6

Name	City	State	Weiss Safety Rating	2003 Weiss Safety Rating	2002 Weiss Safety Rating	Total Assets ($Mil)	One Year Asset Growth	Asset Mix (As a % of Total Assets)				Capital-ization Index	Leverage Ratio	Risk-based Capital Ratio
								Comm-ercial Loans	Cons-umer Loans	Home Mort-gages	Secur-ities			
▼ SKY TRUST NA	PEPPER PIKE	OH	B-	B	B	18.2	8.37	0.0	0.0	0.0	0.6	10.0	95.2	248.4
▼ SKYLANDS CMNTY BK	HACKETTSTOWN	NJ	B-	B	B	441.5	17.69	13.0	1.6	15.5	19.1	3.6	7.2	10.3
SLADES FERRY TRUST	SOMERSET	MA	B-	B-	B-	518.6	24.33	6.3	0.7	17.6	15.3	6.6	8.6	13.2
SLAVIE FSB	BEL AIR	MD	C-	C-	C-	146.9	28.60	0.0	0.5	72.1	13.9	5.5	7.5	15.3
▼ SLEEPY HOLLOW BK	SLEEPY HOLLOW	NY	C-	C	B-	237.3	30.91	1.5	1.0	35.2	33.2	4.4	6.4	12.1
SLOAN ST BK	SLOAN	IA	B	B	B	34.8	1.88	6.9	4.9	20.7	39.5	10.0	11.8	22.2
SLOCOMB NB	SLOCOMB	AL	B-	B-	B	49.0	0.25	4.3	2.2	11.1	59.6	8.6	10.0	21.9
SLOVAK SVGS BK	PITTSBURGH	PA	B	B	B	50.3	17.55	0.0	0.4	43.1	25.2	10.0	12.2	25.3
SLOVENIAN S&LA OF	STRABANE	PA	A	A	A	169.2	8.02	0.0	0.3	45.0	45.1	10.0	13.4	33.5
▲ SLOVENIAN S&LA OF	E CONEMAUGH	PA	B-	C+	C+	95.4	3.79	0.3	1.5	47.9	16.8	7.2	9.1	24.5
SMACKOVER ST BK	SMACKOVER	AR	C+	C+	C	127.7	-3.07	8.4	12.1	24.6	45.8	9.1	10.4	21.6
SMALL TOWN BK	WEDOWEE	AL	B+	B	B	159.9	7.75	6.6	9.6	18.2	29.9	6.2	8.2	12.3
▼ SMITH CTY ST B&TC	SMITH CENTER	KS	B	B+	A-	62.3	2.63	3.7	3.6	6.3	51.3	9.9	10.9	23.4
SMITH RIVER COMMUNITY BK	MARTINSVILLE	VA	D-	D-	D-	60.8	25.98	21.4	4.6	18.5	13.3	2.6	6.8	9.6
SMITHFIELD ST BK	SMITHFIELD	PA	D+	D+	D+	343.8	-7.01	0.9	4.0	8.4	76.9	3.9	5.9	12.8
SNB BANK OF WICHITA	WICHITA	KS	D	D	NR	29.1	N/A	14.9	30.5	11.4	8.6	10.0	19.1	25.8
SNYDER NB	SNYDER	TX	B-	B-	B-	108.2	-0.91	5.0	4.4	5.3	60.9	7.5	9.3	20.2
SOBIESKI BK	S BEND	IN	E-	E-	E+	105.1	-12.46	5.3	1.4	34.0	33.2	0.0	3.0	7.4
SOFISA BK OF FLORIDA	MIAMI	FL	D+	D	C	85.4	62.84	6.9	0.7	13.3	33.2	10.0	22.3	33.0
▲ SOLANO BK	VACAVILLE	CA	B	B-	B-	106.0	39.30	40.8	0.7	5.2	6.5	3.3	8.8	10.2
▲ SOLOMON ST BK	SOLOMON	KS	A-	B+	B+	118.8	6.05	5.2	6.4	49.7	11.5	8.7	10.2	17.2
SOLON ST BK	SOLON	IA	B+	B	B	65.5	-4.73	9.4	3.1	9.9	30.6	10.0	17.0	24.4
▲ SOLVAY BK	SOLVAY	NY	B	B-	B-	437.2	1.93	13.8	3.9	36.9	21.4	6.8	8.8	16.3
▲ SOMERSET HILLS BK	BERNARDSVILLE	NJ	C	D+	D	175.8	8.25	29.3	1.0	16.3	16.1	6.0	9.9	11.8
▲ SOMERSET NB	SOMERSET	KY	B+	B	C+	133.7	32.88	2.1	7.2	35.1	23.8	7.0	9.0	15.8
SOMERSET SVGS BK, SLA	BOUND BROOK	NJ	A-	B+	A	595.5	-1.81	0.0	0.0	38.1	53.0	10.0	12.2	32.4
SOMERSET TRUST CO	SOMERSET	PA	C-	C-	C-	406.2	2.53	14.2	3.8	15.4	29.3	6.5	8.5	14.4
SOMERSET VALLEY BK	SOMERVILLE	NJ	C	C	C	481.3	13.41	3.9	1.8	10.6	25.6	4.1	6.9	10.6
SOMERVILLE B&TC	SOMERVILLE	TN	B	B+	B+	178.6	2.48	3.6	8.2	44.2	0.0	5.9	7.9	16.0
▲ SOMERVILLE NB	SOMERVILLE	OH	B	B-	B-	116.6	-3.32	2.8	7.8	34.1	12.4	7.3	9.2	15.1
▲ SONOMA NB	SANTA ROSA	CA	B+	B	B	959.7	26.80	1.3	0.1	3.9	0.1	5.6	8.0	11.5
SONOMA VALLEY BK	SONOMA	CA	B+	B+	A-	209.7	8.77	5.0	1.1	2.9	20.1	4.7	8.4	10.8
▲ SOONER ST BK	TUTTLE	OK	A	A-	A-	108.4	7.10	4.2	6.6	8.6	35.9	10.0	11.4	20.1
▲ SOUND BANKING COMPANY	MOREHEAD CITY	NC	C-	D+	D	54.9	35.39	12.5	7.1	19.2	14.3	10.0	12.2	16.8
▲ SOUND BKG CO	TACOMA	WA	C	D+	D	60.0	-32.89	9.6	1.3	10.6	5.7	5.8	7.8	13.3
SOUND COMMUNITY BANK	SEATTLE	WA	C	C	NR	156.2	12.02	2.8	22.6	46.6	2.0	6.5	8.5	13.6
SOUND FEDERAL SAVINGS	MAMARONECK	NY	A-	A-	B-	900.3	12.25	0.1	0.2	43.8	37.6	9.6	10.7	24.8
SOUTH ADAMS SVGS BK	ADAMS	MA	C+	C+	B-	197.8	-1.25	1.9	2.2	46.8	32.8	9.8	10.9	20.3
▲ SOUTH BAY BK NA	TORRANCE	CA	C+	C-	D	178.8	1.77	16.7	0.5	1.9	6.1	5.2	9.6	11.2
SOUTH CAROLINA B&T NA	ORANGEBURG	SC	B+	B+	B	1,171.8	14.14	8.8	8.3	23.2	12.3	6.1	8.4	11.8
SOUTH CAROLINA B&T	ROCK HILL	SC	B	B	B	157.4	7.14	10.0	3.7	22.0	13.6	5.4	8.1	11.3
▼ SOUTH CAROLINA	COLUMBIA	SC	D+	C-	C-	34.7	13.46	11.4	6.2	14.8	9.9	5.1	8.8	11.1
SOUTH CENTRAL BK DAVIESS	OWENSBORO	KY	C+	C+	C+	165.5	4.49	12.6	12.7	20.8	5.2	4.6	7.9	10.8
SOUTH CENTRAL BK NA	CHICAGO	IL	C+	C+	C+	170.7	13.85	11.0	7.3	20.5	24.4	5.6	7.6	12.8
SOUTH CENTRAL BK OF	BOWLING GREEN	KY	B-	C+	C+	169.3	6.50	5.0	5.8	36.3	5.6	8.5	10.0	14.0
SOUTH CENTRAL BK-BARREN	GLASGOW	KY	B-	C+	C+	236.9	5.74	6.6	5.7	15.1	15.8	8.3	9.8	14.2
SOUTH CENTRAL ST BK	CAMPBELL	NE	C+	C+	D	77.4	-1.70	2.2	3.1	5.5	24.3	5.9	7.9	12.3
SOUTH CENTRAL SVGS BK	ELIZABETHTOWN	KY	C+	C+	C+	79.6	-8.26	13.5	6.6	23.5	2.5	6.7	9.0	12.2
SOUTH COAST CMRL BK	IRVINE	CA	A	A	A-	140.0	3.26	0.0	0.0	0.1	2.9	10.0	11.5	15.6
SOUTH COASTAL BK	ROCKLAND	MA	D+	D+	D	268.6	7.70	2.9	0.3	33.8	29.6	4.3	6.3	11.6
▲ SOUTH COUNTY BK NA	RANCHO SANTA MAR	CA	C+	C-	C-	124.9	4.80	14.1	1.8	10.1	16.1	7.9	9.6	13.5
SOUTH CTRL BK OF MONROE	TOMPKINSVILLE	KY	C+	C+	C+	109.5	2.36	2.8	6.8	11.8	13.0	6.9	8.9	13.6
SOUTH END SVGS BK	HOMEWOOD	IL	C+	B-	B-	38.9	1.24	0.0	0.0	24.4	62.5	10.0	13.8	59.1
▲ SOUTH GEORGIA BANKING CO	OMEGA	GA	A-	B+	B+	172.3	0.95	13.7	13.4	13.1	21.0	10.0	11.0	16.7
SOUTH GEORGIA BK	GLENNVILLE	GA	C	C	C+	75.3	19.34	35.6	9.7	11.4	13.9	5.2	7.9	11.2
▼ SOUTH LAFOURCHE B&TC	LAROSE	LA	D	C-	C+	74.8	9.92	13.6	9.2	36.4	7.7	6.7	8.7	14.2
SOUTH LOUISIANA BK	HOUMA	LA	B+	A-	B	205.6	8.37	21.0	7.1	13.2	24.5	9.0	10.3	16.5
SOUTH OTTUMWA SVG BK	OTTUMWA	IA	B+	B+	A-	260.7	2.67	5.7	0.9	14.1	51.5	6.9	8.9	17.7
▲ SOUTH PADRE BK NA	S PADRE ISLAND	TX	B	B-	C+	30.1	8.15	2.5	4.0	35.2	17.7	10.0	15.7	25.2
SOUTH POINTE BK	CARBONDALE	IL	C+	C	C	185.4	23.92	5.3	2.3	26.5	31.7	5.9	7.9	14.7
SOUTH SHORE CO-OP BK	WEYMOUTH	MA	C	C	C	152.7	22.41	11.3	0.2	53.5	12.6	6.5	8.5	14.6
SOUTH SHORE SVGS BK	WEYMOUTH	MA	B	B	B	881.3	15.83	4.5	0.6	22.4	35.6	6.0	8.0	13.4
SOUTH SIDE T&SB	PEORIA	IL	B	B	B	489.5	6.10	7.4	3.6	27.7	18.3	7.2	9.1	15.4
▲ SOUTH SOUND BK	OLYMPIA	WA	B	C	C	73.2	2.78	18.1	3.8	4.8	10.2	10.0	13.7	17.0

Asset Quality Index	Non-Performing Loans as a % of Total Loans	Non-Performing Loans as a % of Capital	Net Charge-offs Avg Loans	Profitability Index	Net Income ($Mil)	Return on Assets (R.O.A.)	Return on Equity (R.O.E.)	Net Interest Spread	Overhead Efficiency Ratio	Liquidity Index	Liquidity Ratio	Hot Money Ratio	Stability Index
7.4	0.00	0.0	0.00	7.5	0.4	4.48	5.01	1.22	92.0	10.0	2,732.2	0.0	4.8
5.8	0.46	3.0	0.03	10.0	4.0	1.90	18.18	4.84	42.2	4.3	34.6	11.6	7.7
5.9	1.17	8.5	-0.04	4.1	1.4	0.59	6.76	3.55	71.7	6.6	73.9	8.2	5.3
8.6	0.26	2.7	0.00	2.0	0.1	0.10	1.19	2.56	91.8	1.6	9.2	21.6	4.2
7.9	0.26	2.5	0.04	2.6	0.4	0.38	5.95	3.05	85.6	3.3	37.4	17.4	2.6
3.9	4.66	19.8	0.00	7.1	0.3	1.62	13.64	3.97	58.0	5.6	49.0	8.3	6.9
9.0	0.13	0.5	-0.04	5.3	0.3	1.25	12.03	3.83	65.9	1.7	19.9	22.8	5.1
7.4	0.61	3.0	0.00	4.6	0.2	0.76	5.98	2.38	48.6	8.1	509.7	12.1	5.9
7.8	1.21	3.9	0.00	6.5	0.8	0.95	6.53	2.63	38.5	1.9	26.7	23.8	8.6
6.0	1.26	7.4	0.74	5.6	0.3	0.58	6.22	2.71	53.9	4.6	41.9	12.1	4.8
3.5	3.44	15.2	0.54	6.3	0.8	1.17	11.33	3.88	49.8	1.3	17.5	27.7	5.6
6.5	0.18	1.2	0.11	10.0	1.5	1.95	21.22	4.92	41.1	1.8	17.1	21.3	6.9
9.0	0.04	0.2	0.09	4.6	0.3	1.07	9.55	3.11	78.4	6.8	93.3	8.9	6.3
7.2	0.33	3.4	1.46	0.0	-0.2	-0.71	-9.64	3.37	77.7	3.5	71.0	28.3	0.0
6.1	2.57	6.2	0.24	5.0	1.7	0.96	14.43	3.09	46.7	6.2	62.4	8.8	1.6
7.4	0.08	0.3	0.00	0.0	-0.3	-2.58	-9.72	5.67	125.1	1.7	39.9	75.4	0.0
9.3	0.11	0.3	0.20	4.5	0.5	0.84	8.71	3.79	65.4	2.0	37.0	32.3	5.4
0.3	5.54	78.2	1.66	0.0	-1.2	-2.16	-62.82	1.40	228.9	1.1	16.0	30.2	0.1
6.7	3.66	8.1	0.11	1.0	0.0	0.01	0.06	3.37	99.3	3.8	44.2	16.5	5.5
8.2	0.00	0.0	0.00	1.5	0.1	0.22	2.64	5.13	85.8	7.8	148.2	9.6	3.5
8.6	0.08	0.6	0.06	8.8	0.9	1.45	14.86	3.67	39.1	6.6	146.6	15.3	6.0
5.3	2.50	8.3	0.00	10.0	1.0	2.92	16.53	5.58	41.6	4.5	17.2	5.8	8.4
5.5	1.07	7.3	-0.09	6.4	2.4	1.08	12.55	3.88	55.1	5.4	51.2	11.0	5.0
8.5	0.00	0.0	0.01	3.3	0.5	0.62	5.98	3.55	84.2	4.7	19.8	4.9	5.5
6.2	0.79	5.6	0.19	9.0	1.0	1.69	19.93	5.12	61.5	5.8	37.6	3.7	5.2
9.9	0.03	0.1	0.00	5.7	2.7	0.89	7.52	2.66	56.4	3.1	7.4	12.7	7.5
1.8	4.36	28.3	0.23	3.7	1.5	0.72	8.73	3.66	79.0	3.9	24.2	10.6	4.8
7.6	0.19	1.5	0.05	4.5	1.8	0.78	10.90	3.72	69.1	6.2	60.3	8.9	3.2
3.4	1.59	8.6	-0.02	7.9	1.0	1.12	10.34	4.01	50.9	5.3	121.7	20.6	7.4
5.5	0.52	4.0	0.17	7.3	0.7	1.25	14.47	3.82	55.1	6.8	78.7	7.9	4.9
6.9	0.10	1.0	0.03	9.8	7.2	1.60	20.70	4.29	37.0	2.6	43.4	28.2	5.8
4.6	0.75	5.3	0.42	9.2	1.4	1.35	14.15	5.29	62.3	3.3	23.6	13.2	6.9
8.5	0.13	0.6	0.03	8.1	1.0	1.93	16.34	4.64	62.5	3.8	26.1	11.4	8.1
8.3	0.06	0.3	0.20	2.1	0.1	0.48	3.98	3.88	84.2	2.8	42.3	24.7	0.6
9.2	0.03	0.2	-0.31	5.5	0.3	1.14	16.99	3.55	55.7	6.3	62.2	6.1	1.9
6.6	0.08	0.9	0.58	2.9	0.2	0.29	3.36	3.92	82.8	1.2	4.8	26.3	1.9
8.0	0.34	1.8	0.00	5.7	3.1	0.69	5.77	3.11	63.1	1.4	15.9	25.9	6.9
9.7	0.00	0.0	0.08	3.4	0.5	0.49	4.15	2.97	73.6	6.0	78.0	12.3	6.2
6.4	0.02	0.1	-0.03	4.0	0.5	0.57	4.59	4.54	78.7	3.8	9.8	9.1	5.1
6.3	0.44	3.7	0.14	7.0	6.2	1.10	12.71	4.42	66.6	3.2	14.7	13.1	7.4
5.9	0.47	4.5	0.02	7.4	0.8	1.04	13.28	4.58	68.6	1.4	10.7	24.8	6.1
4.4	0.67	4.3	1.14	2.5	0.0	0.20	1.86	5.22	93.3	3.2	65.0	28.9	4.0
5.4	0.32	3.0	0.49	3.9	0.5	0.61	8.10	4.30	70.3	3.6	33.5	15.1	4.3
6.5	0.42	2.7	-0.18	4.6	0.7	0.82	10.37	4.90	78.2	4.1	41.5	14.8	3.8
5.2	0.57	4.5	0.04	5.9	0.8	0.99	9.89	4.15	67.9	3.8	19.3	10.6	5.8
4.5	0.94	6.8	0.23	7.5	1.4	1.15	11.90	3.78	58.4	1.4	13.2	25.5	6.1
6.6	0.43	2.4	0.03	5.1	0.3	0.82	7.91	3.78	61.9	5.9	46.0	5.3	4.7
2.7	1.42	12.6	0.64	4.5	0.3	0.70	8.06	4.15	59.3	0.6	7.7	37.9	4.2
7.2	0.33	2.2	-0.05	10.0	1.5	2.19	19.53	4.79	53.1	6.2	639.2	24.0	8.5
9.7	0.00	0.0	0.00	2.1	0.3	0.22	3.71	3.07	87.7	1.8	7.4	19.2	2.1
8.1	0.31	1.9	0.02	4.0	0.5	0.76	8.25	4.61	83.2	6.0	47.2	5.5	3.9
2.1	3.43	24.2	0.19	4.5	0.4	0.69	7.73	3.07	66.7	4.0	47.9	17.0	5.4
9.9	0.33	0.6	0.00	2.2	0.0	0.10	0.71	2.63	94.5	7.8	489.7	13.3	5.6
6.1	0.44	2.4	0.34	8.6	1.2	1.38	12.62	4.89	57.6	4.7	41.3	11.9	6.8
6.6	0.03	0.3	-0.01	7.0	0.4	1.07	13.83	4.61	64.3	2.9	52.4	27.0	0.9
0.4	4.72	38.8	1.29	6.8	0.3	0.93	10.69	5.02	62.9	2.6	41.4	26.8	4.7
5.0	1.31	6.0	0.17	9.5	1.5	1.43	13.22	5.25	62.4	3.4	51.0	22.6	7.7
8.0	0.83	3.7	-0.06	6.6	2.2	1.65	16.51	3.63	55.5	3.6	45.3	18.6	7.1
7.6	0.00	0.0	0.00	5.8	0.2	1.03	6.75	4.57	61.5	3.8	18.4	10.2	6.5
4.2	1.71	11.6	0.16	4.7	0.8	0.84	9.99	3.98	70.4	3.8	19.0	10.6	4.1
9.3	0.05	0.5	0.08	4.1	0.5	0.61	7.88	4.04	79.8	3.4	12.1	11.7	2.7
9.2	0.14	0.9	-0.16	4.7	3.3	0.78	8.27	3.47	70.4	3.7	23.6	11.4	5.4
4.2	1.88	12.0	0.27	6.8	2.8	1.18	12.88	3.81	56.9	5.8	57.3	10.1	5.8
7.1	0.12	0.7	0.27	8.9	0.6	1.63	14.55	5.94	54.1	3.3	11.8	12.1	4.0

Name	City	State	Weiss Safety Rating	2003 Weiss Safety Rating	2002 Weiss Safety Rating	Total Assets ($Mil)	One Year Asset Growth	Commercial Loans	Consumer Loans	Home Mortgages	Securities	Capitalization Index	Leverage Ratio	Risk-based Capital Ratio
SOUTH STORY B&TC	SLATER	IA	A-	A-	A-	49.2	0.31	5.8	7.0	20.6	38.0	10.0	15.0	25.4
SOUTH TEXAS NB OF LAREDO	LAREDO	TX	B	B	B	643.8	1.43	9.9	6.9	8.7	37.2	5.5	7.5	15.5
▲ SOUTH VALLEY B&TC	KLAMATH FALLS	OR	C+	C-	D-	364.5	6.71	18.6	4.0	4.4	22.5	6.9	8.9	12.8
▲ SOUTHBANK	WOODSTOCK	GA	D	D-	D	87.6	73.10	12.5	1.2	2.1	12.0	10.0	15.3	16.5
SOUTHBANK FSB	PALM BCH GARDENS	FL	C-	C-	D	21.4	-18.75	0.8	0.0	8.8	18.8	9.1	10.4	37.4
SOUTHBANK FSB	CORINTH	MS	C-	C-	D	428.8	-4.85	3.7	2.0	21.9	34.0	6.0	8.0	13.7
▲ SOUTHBRIDGE SVGS BK	SOUTHBRIDGE	MA	B-	B-	B-	350.0	3.61	1.2	1.8	53.2	18.1	10.0	11.0	18.9
SOUTHCOAST COMMUNITY BK	MT PLEASANT	SC	B+	B	C+	303.9	40.14	41.1	1.1	26.3	12.8	8.4	9.9	14.4
SOUTHEAST BK & TR	ATHENS	TN	D-	D-	D	98.2	62.82	12.5	8.8	17.6	12.0	7.0	9.6	12.5
▲ SOUTHEAST NB	DAVENPORT	IA	B	B-	B-	128.0	-4.68	5.9	7.8	11.0	45.9	10.0	11.0	20.1
▲ SOUTHEASTERN BK	DARIEN	GA	A	A-	A-	384.4	3.93	6.0	5.0	12.6	35.4	10.0	11.9	20.0
SOUTHERN AZ COMMUNITY	TUCSON	AZ	C	C	C	80.5	-6.31	11.3	0.8	3.8	0.1	4.5	9.0	10.8
SOUTHERN B&TC	MT OLIVE	NC	B-	B-	B-	995.9	7.57	7.4	3.1	13.1	24.7	5.6	7.6	13.1
SOUTHERN BK	SARDIS	GA	D+	D+	D	67.4	7.18	2.4	17.2	23.8	7.9	5.5	7.8	11.4
SOUTHERN BK COMPANY	GADSDEN	AL	B+	B+	B+	106.9	-4.83	0.5	5.8	25.9	56.3	10.0	15.5	45.0
SOUTHERN BK OF COMMERCE	PARAGOULD	AR	B-	B-	B-	35.2	8.98	10.3	32.2	34.3	2.8	10.0	12.2	17.8
SOUTHERN CMNTY B&TC	WINSTON-SALEM	NC	B-	B-	B-	852.9	17.66	11.7	2.3	9.5	26.7	2.6	7.0	9.6
▲ SOUTHERN CMNTY BK OF	ORLANDO	FL	C	C-	D-	663.6	60.73	13.4	1.5	5.4	13.7	4.5	6.7	10.8
▲ SOUTHERN CMNTY BK OF	BOCA RATON	FL	C-	D+	D	187.0	70.04	2.3	0.3	8.8	6.3	4.0	9.3	10.5
SOUTHERN CO NB	PUEBLO	CO	D-	D-	D	25.8	17.03	10.1	19.7	17.9	11.6	6.4	9.3	12.0
▲ SOUTHERN COMMERCE BK	TAMPA	FL	D+	D-	E-	57.5	29.05	31.9	4.6	19.7	0.0	10.0	16.5	21.6
SOUTHERN COMMERCIAL BK	ST LOUIS	MO	D	D	D+	455.3	-7.34	13.8	1.7	11.8	19.6	5.3	7.7	11.2
▲ SOUTHERN COMMUNITY B&T	MIDLOTHIAN	VA	D+	D	D	135.3	34.68	27.4	2.4	10.6	6.1	5.4	9.6	11.3
SOUTHERN COMMUNITY BK	FAYETTEVILLE	GA	C	C	B-	233.5	46.45	10.8	2.1	12.3	21.4	3.5	7.2	10.3
▲ SOUTHERN COMMUNITY BK	BONITA SPRINGS	FL	C	C-	D-	192.5	36.02	2.1	1.9	3.7	8.3	3.6	9.2	10.3
▲ SOUTHERN HERITAGE BK	OAKWOOD	GA	B	B-	B	117.8	-0.01	6.9	4.6	21.7	3.0	9.1	11.1	14.3
▲ SOUTHERN HERITAGE BK	JONESVILLE	LA	B+	B	A	161.4	-7.45	5.9	9.0	21.5	40.9	10.0	11.3	24.0
SOUTHERN HERITAGE BK	CLEVELAND	TN	C+	C+	C	143.4	20.03	22.3	3.8	6.5	10.6	4.1	8.3	10.6
SOUTHERN HORIZON BK	LEARY	GA	C	C	D+	17.4	20.07	5.6	5.6	48.5	4.0	7.6	9.4	15.5
SOUTHERN ILLINOIS BK	JOHNSTON CITY	IL	C	C	C	42.2	22.13	5.4	7.0	20.9	37.5	6.2	8.2	14.2
▲ SOUTHERN MICHIGAN B&T	COLDWATER	MI	B-	C	C	309.2	-1.47	12.6	5.4	22.4	13.3	6.7	8.7	12.8
▼ SOUTHERN MISSOURI BK	MARSHFIELD	MO	C-	C	D	86.4	0.45	15.4	5.9	25.1	6.8	4.8	6.9	10.9
SOUTHERN MO B&TC	POPLAR BLUFF	MO	B-	B-	B-	305.9	9.50	12.8	4.9	39.7	11.3	5.8	7.8	11.8
▼ SOUTHERN NB	MARIETTA	GA	C	C+	B-	207.0	29.78	13.4	2.3	5.3	21.4	4.3	7.7	10.6
SOUTHERN NB OF TX	SUGAR LAND	TX	C+	C+	C+	1,090.3	45.50	5.8	1.2	5.5	47.9	4.9	6.9	12.6
SOUTHERN NH B&TC	SALEM	NH	C+	C+	C+	341.8	11.23	12.8	0.5	1.4	4.3	3.3	8.0	10.2
SOUTHERN STATE BK	MALVERN	AR	D+	C	C-	69.2	9.70	12.2	4.5	21.0	30.4	6.4	8.4	13.6
SOUTHLAND BK	DOTHAN	AL	B-	B-	C+	211.3	-1.25	7.5	3.9	17.2	11.3	6.0	8.0	13.8
▲ SOUTHPORT BK	KENOSHA	WI	B+	B	C+	295.2	22.63	5.6	0.6	20.3	16.0	9.3	10.6	14.4
▲ SOUTHSIDE BANK	TYLER	TX	B	B-	B-	1,514.8	9.76	5.3	5.7	10.8	51.0	5.8	7.8	18.3
SOUTHSIDE BK	TAPPAHANNOCK	VA	C+	C+	C	379.9	33.54	5.3	8.9	34.1	20.7	4.2	6.2	11.6
SOUTHTRUST BK	BIRMINGHAM	AL	B	B	B	52,825.5	2.34	23.9	2.2	8.2	21.0	4.8	6.9	10.9
SOUTHWEST BK	FORT WORTH	TX	B-	B-	B-	260.5	5.63	8.3	3.1	4.2	43.1	6.1	8.1	17.1
▲ SOUTHWEST BK	ODESSA	TX	C	C-	C-	81.4	16.61	36.0	11.6	6.4	21.6	4.2	6.9	10.6
SOUTHWEST BK OF ALABAMA	MC INTOSH	AL	A-	A-	A-	71.6	7.33	3.2	7.4	4.4	58.9	10.0	15.4	31.1
▲ SOUTHWEST BK OF ST LOUIS	ST LOUIS	MO	B-	B-	B-	2,424.7	7.97	26.0	0.5	4.2	17.6	3.2	8.0	10.1
▼ SOUTHWEST BK OF TEXAS NA	HOUSTON	TX	B-	B	B	6,332.2	16.70	25.0	2.1	10.4	25.2	3.5	8.3	10.3
SOUTHWEST CMNTY BK	ENCINITAS	CA	C+	C+	C+	411.6	46.01	15.9	0.3	0.2	10.9	4.4	6.8	10.7
▲ SOUTHWEST CMNTY BK	OZARK	MO	D+	D	E	45.0	32.38	4.2	3.7	21.7	16.4	6.0	8.0	11.7
SOUTHWEST GEORGIA BK	MOULTRIE	GA	A	A	A	292.1	22.86	2.4	3.3	10.9	54.9	10.0	12.0	26.4
▲ SOUTHWEST MISSOURI BK	CARTHAGE	MO	C+	C	C	419.3	1.79	12.3	11.7	24.9	17.0	6.1	8.1	12.5
▼ SOUTHWEST NB	WEATHERFORD	OK	C+	B-	B	38.1	-5.44	13.0	13.1	8.1	36.5	10.0	12.5	20.6
SOUTHWEST NB OF WICHITA	WICHITA	KS	C+	C+	C+	142.7	1.00	7.7	23.1	3.4	16.5	3.9	7.9	10.5
▲ SOUTHWEST SECURITIES	ARLINGTON	TX	C	D+	D+	620.3	-3.70	6.7	11.3	21.9	0.1	6.5	9.5	12.1
SOUTHWEST ST BK	SENTINEL	OK	D-	D-	C+	36.8	6.70	10.5	7.8	10.6	6.8	2.7	6.9	9.7
▲ SOUTHWESTERN BK	OKLAHOMA CITY	OK	D+	D	D+	127.7	-0.77	23.4	2.2	9.9	16.5	5.2	8.0	11.1
SOUTHWESTERN NB	HOUSTON	TX	B-	C+	C+	157.7	13.53	14.0	1.4	3.6	12.7	6.6	8.8	12.2
▲ SOUTHWESTUSA BK	LAS VEGAS	NV	D	D-	D-	85.4	20.87	30.5	0.8	0.6	12.6	7.1	9.1	13.6
SOVEREIGN BK	WYOMISSING	PA	B-	C+	C+	47,177.0	17.34	14.6	9.0	20.7	28.5	4.8	6.9	12.1
SOY CAPITAL B&TC	DECATUR	IL	A	A	A-	237.3	10.52	16.8	14.1	4.5	30.8	10.0	13.5	16.3
▲ SPALDING CITY BK	SPALDING	NE	C	C-	D+	28.1	5.82	1.8	1.3	3.8	47.8	6.8	8.8	20.5
▲ SPECTRUM BK	MONTEBELLO	CA	C	C-	C-	130.0	8.35	7.6	1.6	2.3	29.5	4.6	6.6	12.6
SPENCER COUNTY BK	SANTA CLAUS	IN	C	C	C+	72.8	10.11	8.5	5.0	15.7	32.4	7.8	9.6	17.0
SPENCER SAVINGS BANK, SLA	ELMWOOD PARK	NJ	A	A	A	1,527.5	8.99	0.0	0.1	34.6	44.3	10.0	12.6	26.7

Asset Quality Index	Non-Performing Loans as a % of Total Loans	as a % of Capital	Net Charge-offs / Avg Loans	Profitability Index	Net Income ($Mil)	Return on Assets (R.O.A.)	Return on Equity (R.O.E.)	Net Interest Spread	Overhead Efficiency Ratio	Liquidity Index	Liquidity Ratio	Hot Money Ratio	Stability Index
8.2	1.27	3.7	0.06	6.7	0.3	1.12	7.46	3.61	56.6	7.7	96.6	2.8	7.7
6.6	0.23	1.0	0.09	5.9	3.3	1.03	9.69	3.98	61.3	1.7	32.0	31.9	6.5
4.0	1.46	9.7	0.17	4.1	1.6	0.88	9.49	4.10	74.2	2.4	38.2	26.8	4.8
5.9	0.00	0.0	0.82	0.0	-0.3	-0.71	-5.47	3.76	89.2	1.2	12.9	28.5	0.0
7.0	8.17	7.5	0.00	2.5	-0.1	-0.45	-4.55	4.69	118.1	4.1	105.8	28.5	3.8
4.1	2.24	13.8	0.14	1.7	-1.3	-0.58	-7.19	2.04	106.7	1.2	29.3	49.4	3.5
8.1	0.60	3.5	0.04	4.2	1.6	0.91	7.71	3.73	77.5	5.5	51.3	10.3	7.1
7.2	0.47	3.6	0.01	5.3	1.4	1.02	9.96	3.82	59.2	3.3	40.0	18.7	5.6
8.1	0.07	0.5	0.07	0.2	-0.1	-0.14	-1.37	3.76	90.2	2.8	16.3	15.1	0.0
8.6	0.04	0.2	0.04	3.8	0.4	0.65	5.75	3.68	82.6	4.7	24.5	4.9	6.5
6.9	0.99	4.2	0.24	8.3	2.8	1.48	12.10	5.02	57.3	4.2	27.2	9.9	7.1
6.9	0.00	0.0	0.04	9.1	0.7	1.57	16.10	5.72	53.9	4.9	32.6	7.4	4.3
6.2	0.46	2.9	0.13	4.6	3.1	0.62	6.81	3.78	78.1	5.3	69.6	14.6	6.2
2.8	1.44	12.8	1.15	5.1	0.4	1.21	16.09	5.17	64.4	3.7	44.2	17.1	2.5
8.8	0.38	0.9	0.00	4.9	0.4	0.64	4.17	2.86	63.4	2.2	20.2	18.5	8.0
4.4	0.71	4.4	0.45	7.0	0.2	1.27	10.60	6.48	63.6	2.4	49.5	34.1	5.4
7.5	0.31	2.8	0.19	3.6	2.1	0.52	7.41	3.19	68.0	0.6	7.3	36.5	4.7
4.9	0.33	3.3	0.13	6.2	3.6	1.09	16.63	3.57	48.1	4.0	52.7	18.3	4.3
7.3	0.00	0.0	0.00	1.1	0.1	0.14	1.55	3.63	76.9	2.5	15.3	16.4	2.8
5.1	0.40	3.4	0.38	0.7	0.0	-0.09	-0.96	5.73	96.7	1.0	23.8	37.0	0.0
4.6	1.69	7.9	0.07	1.6	0.1	0.20	1.22	3.91	88.0	3.7	52.9	18.7	2.5
2.2	2.77	20.0	0.11	4.6	2.3	1.00	13.13	3.96	64.4	7.4	83.6	4.9	1.3
3.9	1.30	9.7	0.15	2.2	0.3	0.41	3.81	3.86	85.5	2.9	43.5	24.4	6.4
6.1	0.51	4.8	0.08	5.9	1.1	1.00	14.96	4.29	55.3	1.8	27.7	26.4	1.4
7.2	0.00	0.0	0.00	4.7	0.8	0.94	10.43	3.91	54.5	2.9	44.6	24.6	3.1
7.2	0.12	0.8	0.07	5.7	0.7	1.11	10.12	4.33	59.9	4.5	59.7	17.5	5.8
7.7	0.30	1.3	-0.01	5.3	0.9	1.13	9.95	4.29	69.6	3.7	59.3	23.2	6.8
8.1	0.10	0.9	0.02	5.5	0.7	1.01	12.27	4.28	61.7	1.6	21.9	25.5	5.3
8.2	0.03	0.2	0.09	7.5	0.3	4.03	41.28	5.76	70.5	3.0	16.0	13.7	4.3
7.2	0.38	2.5	0.48	4.1	0.2	0.76	9.24	3.67	68.6	4.8	42.4	11.5	4.1
4.3	1.05	8.0	-0.05	5.2	1.8	1.14	12.93	4.46	69.9	3.5	25.3	12.7	4.2
4.2	1.09	11.3	2.96	3.7	-0.1	-0.27	-3.76	4.78	55.0	0.9	15.8	34.3	3.5
8.2	0.05	0.5	0.04	5.9	1.6	1.05	12.22	3.35	56.0	3.4	8.6	11.3	4.9
4.6	1.04	9.1	0.01	3.9	0.9	0.83	11.19	3.69	73.7	1.4	15.5	25.5	4.1
7.4	0.88	6.5	0.16	3.9	3.5	0.72	10.23	3.04	56.4	1.0	10.1	31.9	3.3
7.2	0.00	0.0	-0.12	7.6	1.9	1.15	14.23	4.52	49.5	3.6	56.3	23.0	4.2
3.1	2.68	17.8	0.37	4.5	0.4	1.02	12.20	4.26	60.3	1.0	16.8	32.2	2.1
5.8	0.44	2.6	0.05	4.8	1.2	1.02	11.83	3.14	54.9	3.8	72.1	27.0	5.8
6.9	0.38	2.5	0.00	8.1	2.0	1.43	13.65	4.37	53.4	1.7	13.3	20.6	5.5
8.7	0.29	1.5	0.08	4.6	8.7	1.17	14.78	3.16	67.5	3.4	25.5	15.6	6.3
3.7	1.20	9.4	0.23	7.0	2.1	1.08	13.49	5.09	69.0	4.1	24.3	9.3	4.1
5.7	0.63	4.8	0.31	8.2	375.9	1.43	17.15	3.50	49.6	2.3	16.8	18.0	8.0
7.2	0.86	5.1	0.11	3.9	1.2	0.95	11.44	4.26	83.8	3.4	17.5	12.4	4.2
4.4	1.04	9.2	0.49	6.6	0.6	1.38	19.86	4.60	67.8	3.0	27.4	15.7	3.4
8.3	0.76	1.4	0.20	6.3	0.5	1.45	9.09	4.78	65.7	3.7	39.2	16.3	7.6
4.2	0.78	2.5	0.11	3.2	6.3	0.53	2.68	3.43	64.6	3.8	18.5	11.0	8.2
8.0	0.21	1.4	0.13	6.5	32.8	1.07	12.21	4.17	65.8	3.9	19.2	10.4	7.1
7.4	0.28	2.1	-0.06	8.1	2.4	1.31	19.36	5.94	58.5	6.9	54.3	2.1	3.4
8.4	0.00	0.0	0.15	4.6	0.2	1.07	13.21	4.47	64.5	2.1	14.3	18.6	1.4
8.7	0.57	1.5	0.04	8.1	2.2	1.57	12.50	4.25	67.7	3.1	25.8	14.6	6.8
5.2	0.81	6.4	0.33	5.4	2.2	1.01	12.82	4.71	69.4	4.2	38.4	13.5	3.3
2.8	3.95	14.6	-0.20	8.7	0.3	1.50	12.32	5.26	57.9	4.8	47.8	12.3	5.3
6.8	0.04	0.4	0.07	7.5	1.1	1.53	19.28	3.76	64.9	3.8	33.0	13.5	5.9
3.5	0.95	8.3	0.59	7.8	4.1	1.30	14.12	5.15	57.5	0.4	13.0	76.6	7.1
2.3	2.80	30.8	0.01	7.4	0.4	1.85	27.12	4.61	59.5	1.7	28.9	29.1	1.7
3.7	3.35	27.6	-0.02	2.7	0.4	0.55	6.92	3.95	83.1	3.4	16.6	12.4	3.0
7.1	0.11	0.9	0.22	5.3	1.1	1.42	16.05	4.09	59.9	0.9	25.3	50.9	5.0
3.7	3.33	25.7	0.00	1.1	0.1	0.29	3.38	4.51	94.1	1.9	39.4	37.5	0.0
4.5	0.63	5.6	0.47	6.6	262.7	1.13	12.24	3.36	53.7	0.6	6.2	41.9	8.0
6.8	0.04	0.1	0.07	9.5	2.1	1.84	10.74	4.42	73.2	3.8	22.2	10.8	8.6
7.9	1.05	4.0	0.00	4.0	0.1	0.83	9.88	2.93	60.9	4.5	51.9	14.5	3.2
8.6	0.00	0.0	-0.01	3.7	0.4	0.58	8.97	3.98	79.8	3.9	59.9	20.7	3.1
4.8	1.86	10.4	0.13	3.9	0.2	0.53	5.56	3.79	77.4	5.4	70.0	12.9	4.0
8.8	0.09	0.4	-0.01	6.4	6.9	0.93	7.18	2.87	54.8	2.2	11.5	17.7	10.0

Name	City	State	Weiss Safety Rating	2003 Weiss Safety Rating	2002 Weiss Safety Rating	Total Assets ($Mil)	One Year Asset Growth	Asset Mix (As a % of Total Assets)				Capital-ization Index	Leverage Ratio	Risk-based Capital Ratio
								Comm-ercial Loans	Cons-umer Loans	Home Mort-gages	Secur-ities			
SPENCER ST BK	SPENCER	NE	C	C	C	17.8	9.84	1.6	7.7	2.2	59.2	10.0	13.6	30.1
▼ SPENCER SVGS BK	SPENCER	MA	A-	A	A	263.8	3.02	4.2	6.1	41.3	20.6	10.0	15.0	23.1
SPIRIT BK	BELMONT	MS	D+	D+	D	20.2	3.62	11.1	6.5	14.6	41.0	10.0	12.0	21.0
SPIRIT OF AMERICA NB	MILFORD	OH	B+	B+	B+	29.7	3.65	0.0	0.0	0.0	96.8	10.0	78.8	407.3
▲ SPIRITBANK	TULSA	OK	C+	C	D+	596.9	4.61	23.8	5.5	20.5	15.5	5.4	7.4	11.8
SPIRO ST BK	SPIRO	OK	B-	B-	B-	47.5	-1.14	4.6	7.1	10.0	46.3	10.0	11.7	31.4
SPIVEY ST BK	SWAINSBORO	GA	B-	B-	B-	94.5	2.34	6.2	6.6	14.0	24.2	5.6	7.7	11.5
SPRATT S&LA	CHESTER	SC	A	A	A	97.4	-4.94	1.9	0.4	19.0	40.5	10.0	21.3	47.6
SPRING HILL ST BK	LONGVIEW	TX	C-	C-	C	95.9	6.58	10.9	14.2	31.6	1.2	5.5	7.5	11.9
SPRING VALLEY BANK	WYOMING	OH	A-	A-	B+	50.7	9.89	1.9	0.7	28.9	9.9	10.0	25.3	32.7
SPRING VALLEY CITY BK	SPRING VALLEY	IL	A	A	A	139.6	-1.07	7.2	11.2	42.6	19.0	10.0	14.4	25.4
SPRINGFIELD ST BK	SPRINGFIELD	KY	A	A	A	190.4	4.28	2.8	3.5	23.8	34.6	10.0	11.5	20.8
SPRINGFIELD ST BK	SPRINGFIELD	NE	C	C	C	27.9	5.35	6.1	7.2	20.9	19.8	5.6	7.6	13.9
SPRINGS VALLEY B&TC	FRENCH LICK	IN	D+	D	D+	222.5	-7.77	6.0	6.0	30.2	11.7	6.9	8.9	13.4
SPUR SECURITY BK	SPUR	TX	D+	D+	D+	28.0	-3.22	4.6	10.2	9.9	47.2	5.9	7.9	22.2
SSBBANK	STOCKBRIDGE	MI	B-	B-	B-	79.6	3.12	8.1	12.7	29.1	27.5	6.9	8.9	14.6
ST ANSGAR ST BK	ST ANSGAR	IA	A-	A-	A-	88.8	-2.39	5.3	2.4	9.4	26.3	10.0	12.4	20.0
ST ANTHONY PARK BK	ST PAUL	MN	B-	B-	C+	174.9	9.98	35.0	1.5	5.6	9.1	3.4	7.9	10.2
▲ ST CLAIR COUNTY ST BK	OSCEOLA	MO	B-	C+	C+	92.7	-3.55	7.2	5.9	31.7	12.9	7.5	9.3	15.8
ST CLAIR ST BK	ST CLAIR	MN	B+	B+	B+	48.9	2.15	7.1	9.6	12.6	6.0	10.0	12.6	19.8
▲ ST EDMONDS FSB	PHILADELPHIA	PA	C+	C-	D+	113.4	30.41	0.1	0.5	40.8	34.7	10.0	18.2	43.3
▲ ST HENRY BK	ST HENRY	OH	A+	A	A	155.1	5.02	8.8	1.9	18.8	41.9	10.0	17.7	32.5
ST JAMES FS&LA	ST JAMES	MN	E-	E-	E-	22.1	12.65	4.6	8.4	60.9	6.6	5.5	7.5	14.4
ST JOHN NB	ST JOHN	KS	B	B	B	32.0	2.08	10.7	3.1	5.0	34.5	10.0	16.4	27.0
ST JOHNS B&TC	ST JOHN	MO	C	C-	D+	307.7	6.38	4.7	2.1	10.7	17.6	5.1	8.2	11.1
ST JOSEPH CAP BK	MISHAWAKA	IN	B-	B-	C+	312.7	15.00	18.4	1.7	20.1	15.4	5.8	8.7	11.6
ST LANDRY B&TC	OPELOUSAS	LA	B	B+	A-	225.9	-5.03	12.2	3.0	3.1	47.4	10.0	13.6	26.7
ST LANDRY HOMESTEAD FSB	OPELOUSAS	LA	A-	A-	A-	196.4	7.29	3.8	3.8	61.4	1.8	10.0	12.5	20.6
▲ ST MARTIN B&TC	ST MARTINVILLE	LA	B	B-	B-	154.0	1.17	9.9	5.8	15.2	20.7	6.4	8.4	14.2
ST MARTIN NB	ST MARTIN	MN	C+	C+	C+	16.2	8.05	6.4	5.5	19.3	36.4	10.0	11.6	21.1
ST MARYS ST BK	ST MARYS	KS	B-	B-	B-	63.9	2.52	18.9	5.7	15.5	23.2	8.1	9.8	14.2
ST MICHAELS BK	ST MICHAELS	MD	A-	A-	A	261.8	17.08	18.8	6.1	27.2	5.3	6.0	8.0	15.2
ST STEPHEN ST BK	ST STEPHEN	MN	E-	E-	D	20.9	2.93	37.4	17.5	8.9	0.0	3.8	8.3	10.4
ST TAMMANY HOMESTEAD	COVINGTON	LA	B	B	B-	72.3	4.13	0.0	0.4	38.4	30.0	10.0	11.0	22.2
STAFFORD SVGS BK	STAFFORD SPRINGS	CT	B	B	B+	203.8	3.30	0.0	0.5	36.5	47.0	10.0	21.4	35.3
STANDARD B&TC	HICKORY HILLS	IL	B-	B-	B-	1,446.5	-0.28	12.5	2.9	7.0	11.4	6.1	8.9	11.8
STANDARD BANK	MONTEREY PARK	CA	B	B	B+	984.9	5.53	0.1	0.3	7.4	31.3	7.9	9.6	14.5
STANDARD BK PASB	MURRYSVILLE	PA	C+	C+	B	255.4	-7.57	0.9	0.4	33.6	44.2	10.0	12.8	27.5
▲ STANDARD FEDERAL BK NA	TROY	MI	B-	C+	C+	44,253.1	-10.99	8.8	0.6	19.4	27.1	6.4	8.4	20.1
STANDING STONE NB	LANCASTER	OH	C+	C+	C+	68.1	7.62	2.7	21.4	16.9	38.4	6.6	8.6	16.1
STANLEY BK	STANLEY	KS	A	A	A	111.8	0.82	29.1	5.1	8.7	21.4	10.0	18.2	27.8
STANTON NB	STANTON	NE	C-	C-	D+	27.9	5.67	3.9	4.9	24.6	24.6	7.8	9.5	16.9
STAR BK	LAKE WORTH	TX	C+	C+	C+	59.1	6.03	22.3	8.0	20.6	23.9	7.0	9.0	16.7
STAR BK NA	BERTHA	MN	C+	C-	D+	88.6	0.74	8.6	7.6	12.5	21.6	4.9	8.2	10.9
STAR FINANCIAL BK	FORT WAYNE	IN	B-	B-	B-	1,347.2	-1.56	9.5	18.6	19.6	13.8	6.9	8.9	12.6
STARION FINANCIAL	BISMARCK	ND	B+	B+	B	402.7	9.37	9.1	5.4	11.0	28.4	6.6	8.6	12.5
STATE B&T	WINFIELD	AL	A	A	A	155.1	1.37	0.9	9.2	15.7	51.9	10.0	12.4	28.2
STATE B&T	FARGO	ND	C+	C+	C+	1,076.9	56.97	23.1	16.3	12.2	6.0	3.4	8.7	10.2
▼ STATE B&T	SEGUIN	TX	B+	A-	A-	256.3	-2.80	4.4	2.6	15.9	41.6	10.0	15.0	26.7
STATE B&T OF KENMARE	KENMARE	ND	C+	C+	B-	65.9	3.31	21.4	4.8	6.4	15.8	3.1	7.5	10.1
STATE B&TC	NEVADA	IA	A-	A-	A-	108.4	8.65	6.4	1.1	7.7	50.3	8.9	10.3	16.3
▲ STATE B&TC	HARRODSBURG	KY	B-	C+	C+	121.1	0.79	6.5	5.0	27.9	30.2	6.3	8.3	13.9
STATE B&TC	GOLDEN MEADOW	LA	A-	A-	A-	79.9	0.56	27.9	8.4	29.2	13.8	9.7	10.8	17.4
STATE B&TC	CLEVELAND	MS	B-	B-	C+	640.0	4.02	13.3	6.5	19.3	9.9	5.6	9.0	11.5
STATE B&TC	DILLON	MT	B	B	B+	75.5	7.73	12.7	5.3	7.7	15.1	7.4	9.3	13.0
STATE B&TC	DEFIANCE	OH	D	D-	E+	393.1	-12.15	17.3	4.9	15.0	24.9	7.0	9.0	14.4
▼ STATE B&TC	BEEVILLE	TX	B+	A-	A-	60.0	2.84	6.0	6.1	6.0	8.3	6.4	8.4	19.4
STATE B&TC	DALLAS	TX	C-	C-	D	140.7	9.60	21.3	1.0	13.9	5.0	7.3	10.1	12.7
▲ STATE BANK	ROCKY FORD	CO	B	B-	B-	18.7	-7.32	6.0	3.4	3.5	18.3	10.0	13.3	21.4
STATE BANK	LA GRANGE	TX	C+	C+	C+	746.8	22.34	8.6	6.9	15.0	31.7	5.3	7.3	11.7
▲ STATE BANK - LA JUNTA	LA JUNTA	CO	B	B-	B-	53.2	-0.78	6.7	5.6	9.9	23.3	9.1	10.4	16.1
STATE BANK OF LA CROSSE	LA CROSSE	WI	B-	B-	B-	279.3	4.60	11.6	1.9	7.8	29.4	6.4	8.4	13.5
▼ STATE BK	SPENCER	IA	E-	E-	E-	37.5	-2.10	7.8	7.8	24.1	3.9	3.1	7.7	10.0
STATE BK	SPIRIT LAKE	IA	B-	B-	B-	45.9	-1.77	7.6	2.5	20.6	29.0	9.0	10.4	18.0

Asset Quality Index	Non-Performing Loans		Net Charge-offs Avg Loans	Profitability Index	Net Income ($Mil)	Return on Assets (R.O.A.)	Return on Equity (R.O.E.)	Net Interest Spread	Overhead Efficiency Ratio	Liquidity Index	Liquidity Ratio	Hot Money Ratio	Stability Index
	as a % of Total Loans	as a % of Capital											
8.5	0.14	0.3	0.19	3.3	0.1	0.68	5.01	3.10	75.4	6.0	71.4	8.3	4.0
8.8	0.00	0.0	0.09	5.5	1.0	0.76	5.11	4.07	69.4	5.7	46.2	7.1	8.3
8.7	0.00	0.0	-0.02	4.0	0.1	0.54	4.53	3.36	74.8	1.3	33.2	33.6	3.7
10.0	0.00	0.0	0.00	9.5	2.9	19.61	24.13	1.07	28.2	5.0	N/A	0.0	3.5
3.9	1.38	12.8	0.27	5.4	2.6	0.89	11.55	4.83	71.9	1.6	20.4	24.5	3.3
7.1	1.52	3.6	0.43	4.2	0.2	0.87	7.32	4.83	76.2	7.7	93.8	2.9	4.5
3.9	0.94	5.6	0.05	7.1	0.8	1.72	15.19	4.79	62.3	1.7	27.3	27.2	6.6
9.5	1.55	2.4	0.06	8.5	0.7	1.32	6.37	3.32	42.9	3.0	61.1	30.5	9.0
3.0	1.62	15.3	0.33	4.0	0.3	0.60	8.17	3.98	71.2	5.7	81.3	12.9	3.1
8.8	0.63	2.0	0.00	10.0	1.3	5.45	22.78	5.95	22.2	5.0	55.4	12.5	8.0
6.2	1.02	5.0	0.14	6.8	0.8	1.11	7.83	3.80	52.4	6.3	68.3	9.5	8.5
8.5	0.56	2.7	0.16	7.4	1.4	1.43	12.75	3.95	51.2	3.2	24.6	13.8	7.4
8.3	0.00	0.0	0.01	6.0	0.2	1.43	18.80	4.03	64.0	6.4	49.6	2.9	4.2
3.1	1.63	12.3	0.37	1.5	0.2	0.21	2.33	3.11	87.2	4.4	32.9	10.8	3.0
6.6	0.70	3.4	1.11	3.9	0.1	0.52	6.74	4.08	81.4	2.7	37.5	21.8	2.1
7.8	0.19	1.3	0.11	3.9	0.3	0.62	6.96	3.87	77.4	5.0	35.3	8.2	4.8
7.7	0.89	4.3	-0.12	6.0	0.6	1.32	10.92	3.58	60.1	5.6	65.3	11.3	7.1
4.8	0.69	6.3	0.78	10.0	2.1	2.51	31.19	5.06	53.9	3.7	15.5	10.7	5.3
5.1	0.81	6.2	0.01	5.1	0.4	0.93	10.15	3.34	56.8	4.1	31.5	11.7	5.1
8.2	0.01	0.0	-0.03	7.5	0.4	1.69	13.90	3.68	42.9	8.2	218.9	11.6	6.0
8.1	0.21	0.6	-0.04	4.4	0.3	0.64	5.08	3.25	70.8	3.0	48.2	26.5	4.0
9.1	0.71	1.8	-0.01	9.0	1.3	1.64	8.83	3.96	40.5	5.3	39.8	7.9	9.1
6.6	0.03	0.3	-0.14	2.4	0.0	0.30	3.78	5.38	94.7	0.8	22.1	39.0	0.3
8.6	0.04	0.1	0.09	6.9	0.2	1.44	8.89	4.47	58.2	3.6	58.3	19.9	6.3
3.8	0.76	6.5	0.06	5.0	1.2	0.80	9.68	4.36	73.1	4.7	16.7	4.6	3.9
8.5	0.00	0.0	0.00	4.2	1.2	0.78	9.11	3.23	60.2	1.6	22.4	24.5	4.7
8.8	0.63	1.8	0.09	4.0	0.9	0.76	5.72	2.88	69.9	7.9	156.6	9.7	7.2
6.3	0.59	4.1	0.08	8.1	1.1	1.19	9.44	3.88	52.7	1.0	9.8	30.2	7.9
4.9	0.78	4.9	0.62	8.3	1.6	2.05	23.43	5.30	54.0	3.6	32.4	14.6	6.2
5.1	2.34	10.4	-0.07	8.3	0.2	2.27	19.96	4.06	56.4	4.5	47.5	12.0	4.9
6.4	0.30	1.9	0.04	4.4	0.3	0.89	9.01	3.91	69.4	4.3	24.4	8.0	5.2
7.0	0.00	0.0	0.46	10.0	2.7	2.13	25.66	4.82	34.5	2.6	14.5	16.0	7.8
3.2	1.07	9.7	0.02	2.0	0.0	-0.04	-0.45	5.49	100.6	5.6	42.3	3.8	0.3
6.3	1.34	7.4	0.00	5.3	0.3	0.76	7.02	2.99	63.1	2.6	3.8	14.8	5.4
9.8	0.75	1.2	0.00	4.0	0.9	0.93	3.76	2.57	69.0	7.5	113.6	7.9	8.4
4.0	1.91	11.7	0.01	4.8	5.2	0.73	6.91	4.06	71.9	5.3	28.9	7.5	7.6
5.2	0.54	3.6	0.00	7.9	5.2	1.08	11.34	2.58	30.7	1.8	39.6	54.6	6.9
9.8	0.25	0.7	-0.02	2.3	0.4	0.30	2.18	2.26	92.2	8.2	140.7	6.3	6.4
3.5	1.78	5.8	0.13	6.1	83.2	0.37	2.59	3.16	83.1	5.2	28.8	7.9	8.1
7.3	0.29	1.6	0.28	4.2	0.3	0.79	8.64	4.25	73.9	3.5	48.2	19.0	4.0
8.1	0.01	0.0	0.08	7.2	0.9	1.72	9.39	4.16	62.6	7.9	94.4	3.2	9.8
7.8	0.00	0.0	0.42	3.9	0.1	0.83	8.79	3.89	79.5	6.2	60.7	6.9	2.4
8.3	0.00	0.0	0.02	5.8	0.3	1.05	11.97	5.12	71.4	3.5	50.1	19.0	3.8
4.3	1.35	9.0	0.23	8.1	0.8	1.84	20.33	4.67	62.7	4.4	25.8	7.7	5.8
4.2	1.22	8.9	0.49	4.8	5.2	0.77	8.38	3.87	72.3	5.4	47.2	12.2	7.2
7.5	0.23	1.6	0.02	8.9	3.9	1.97	22.02	4.27	50.9	3.4	32.3	15.4	6.6
8.6	0.57	1.4	0.16	8.2	1.4	1.82	13.64	4.59	51.3	3.9	78.4	28.3	8.0
7.1	0.11	1.0	-0.04	6.9	5.3	1.03	12.33	3.77	60.4	2.0	16.6	19.8	7.1
9.1	0.02	0.1	0.10	4.5	1.2	0.90	5.77	4.16	76.4	4.3	25.0	8.2	8.4
4.4	0.45	4.6	0.79	5.2	0.4	1.35	18.80	3.22	57.3	2.3	11.4	17.1	4.1
9.1	0.15	0.6	0.02	8.3	0.8	1.52	14.80	3.65	43.9	2.5	20.9	17.3	7.6
4.5	2.19	13.9	0.07	7.1	1.0	1.64	19.33	4.72	54.8	2.0	14.9	18.8	4.2
5.6	0.79	5.3	0.06	5.7	0.5	1.20	10.92	4.74	75.9	3.7	43.8	17.3	7.2
5.9	0.37	3.1	0.74	7.2	3.8	1.20	13.65	4.87	62.0	2.2	27.7	20.4	4.6
8.1	0.14	1.0	0.02	6.4	0.6	1.55	16.94	4.87	66.4	4.5	40.2	12.6	6.0
0.9	4.53	27.9	0.62	2.5	1.0	0.48	5.15	3.50	78.1	2.7	23.3	16.5	2.6
7.2	0.10	0.4	0.03	9.5	0.7	2.15	25.39	3.58	57.4	6.6	128.1	13.8	6.9
2.6	1.77	14.3	0.22	5.6	0.9	1.29	12.61	4.80	72.8	2.0	25.7	20.9	5.4
7.2	0.00	0.0	0.00	5.5	0.1	1.12	8.32	4.29	69.4	4.3	61.4	15.5	6.0
6.2	0.24	1.8	0.11	6.1	3.8	1.13	14.87	4.77	74.0	4.9	47.0	12.1	4.3
8.4	0.10	0.5	0.07	4.5	0.2	0.87	8.17	4.71	73.7	2.1	31.5	25.7	5.2
4.5	1.90	11.4	-0.01	5.2	1.5	1.03	11.50	3.88	70.2	4.2	21.5	8.5	5.3
2.4	1.97	19.8	0.18	6.1	0.3	1.48	18.10	5.06	70.3	3.7	11.8	10.0	0.3
4.9	1.66	9.6	-0.09	7.7	0.4	1.77	17.02	3.99	54.8	4.7	36.3	10.4	5.9

Name	City	State	Weiss Safety Rating	2003 Weiss Safety Rating	2002 Weiss Safety Rating	Total Assets ($Mil)	One Year Asset Growth	Commercial Loans	Consumer Loans	Home Mortgages	Securities	Capitalization Index	Leverage Ratio	Risk-based Capital Ratio
STATE BK	WORTHINGTON	IA	C	C	D+	48.0	18.86	18.2	2.7	11.2	3.5	1.7	7.2	8.7
▲ STATE BK	FREEPORT	IL	B-	C+	C	93.9	11.01	15.8	1.3	3.7	17.4	3.2	7.5	10.1
STATE BK	WONDER LAKE	IL	B	B-	B-	159.7	6.73	0.7	1.2	44.4	11.2	7.1	9.1	14.8
STATE BK	HOXIE	KS	B	B+	B	83.3	6.97	8.9	2.9	1.7	8.8	7.7	9.5	13.1
▼ STATE BK	WINFIELD	KS	B	B+	A-	97.6	2.93	15.9	4.2	18.5	35.1	6.6	8.6	15.7
▼ STATE BK	FENTON	MI	C+	B	B	368.8	5.32	13.6	6.7	6.7	22.1	4.3	7.9	10.6
STATE BK	NEW PRAGUE	MN	B+	B+	B	91.6	19.24	11.6	2.2	18.4	37.7	5.6	7.6	12.8
STATE BK	TOWER	MN	C-	C-	C-	44.5	1.76	2.9	12.3	26.7	0.0	3.3	7.7	10.1
STATE BK	RICHMOND	MO	B	B-	B-	25.1	10.96	5.6	5.8	14.1	38.5	6.6	8.6	16.3
▲ STATE BK	BENKELMAN	NE	B-	C	C	34.5	-13.80	3.1	3.0	1.0	25.0	10.0	11.4	15.6
STATE BK	GRESHAM	WI	B+	B+	B+	20.0	9.08	4.7	2.2	9.2	23.2	10.0	24.2	64.2
STATE BK CERRO GORDO	CERRO GORDO	IL	B	B+	B+	25.2	-5.08	2.8	5.9	29.9	27.8	10.0	13.7	27.3
STATE BK GREEN RIVER	GREEN RIVER	WY	C+	C	C-	26.1	7.53	11.2	11.0	12.2	24.8	10.0	11.6	16.3
▲ STATE BK ILLINOIS	W CHICAGO	IL	B+	C	A-	181.4	-1.38	11.6	1.2	30.7	14.2	7.0	9.0	14.3
STATE BK IN EDEN VALLEY	EDEN VALLEY	MN	B	B	A-	34.6	5.95	21.7	3.6	6.9	37.4	7.4	9.3	15.8
STATE BK LAWLER	NEW HAMPTON	IA	A-	A-	A-	152.4	1.49	36.9	2.7	12.5	12.2	10.0	12.2	15.6
STATE BK OF ALCESTER	ALCESTER	SD	B-	B-	B	70.2	-5.54	7.3	7.3	7.4	15.3	9.4	10.6	17.1
STATE BK OF ALLERTON	ALLERTON	IL	B	B	B	22.6	14.52	2.3	2.9	6.3	28.4	5.8	7.8	13.1
STATE BK OF ANNAWAN	ANNAWAN	IL	D	D+	D+	37.6	13.50	11.7	1.1	7.3	36.1	5.9	7.9	14.0
▼ STATE BK OF ARCADIA	ARCADIA	WI	B	B+	B+	94.4	1.42	4.2	3.2	12.9	32.9	7.7	9.5	22.4
STATE BK OF ARTHUR	ARTHUR	IL	B	B	B-	75.5	8.06	10.2	11.4	11.3	42.0	10.0	13.9	23.8
STATE BK OF ASHLAND	ASHLAND	IL	B+	B+	B+	51.3	-1.96	5.3	9.4	24.2	28.5	10.0	12.9	19.1
STATE BK OF AUBURN	AUBURN	IL	B+	B+	B	88.9	1.42	2.2	2.0	13.7	53.0	8.9	10.3	24.6
STATE BK OF AUGUSTA	AUGUSTA	IL	C+	C+	C+	27.5	8.18	11.2	3.5	8.2	21.9	5.5	7.5	11.7
▲ STATE BK OF AURORA	AURORA	MN	E+	E-	E-	28.8	-3.06	40.5	4.9	18.1	10.3	5.1	7.6	11.1
▲ STATE BK OF BARTLEY	BARTLEY	NE	C	C-	C-	14.3	18.96	5.7	4.7	13.6	25.3	9.2	10.5	18.1
STATE BK OF BELLE PLAINE	BELLE PLAINE	MN	D+	C-	B-	90.8	-6.78	7.1	3.1	7.2	37.5	6.3	8.3	15.4
STATE BK OF BELLINGHAM	BELLINGHAM	MN	D	D+	D+	18.8	8.35	4.7	3.1	0.7	11.6	5.7	7.7	13.1
STATE BK OF BEMENT	BEMENT	IL	B	B+	B+	49.8	0.61	12.7	6.1	16.7	24.5	10.0	14.4	22.2
▲ STATE BK OF BERN	BERN	KS	B+	B	B+	45.8	74.13	10.3	3.7	3.5	45.5	10.0	11.6	21.7
STATE BK OF BIRD ISLAND	BIRD ISLAND	MN	B	B	B	34.5	0.81	12.3	6.0	2.7	30.2	10.0	13.2	20.7
STATE BK OF BLUE MOUND	BLUE MOUND	IL	D	D	D	25.8	-4.73	18.1	5.4	7.1	13.4	6.0	8.1	14.4
▲ STATE BK OF BLUE RAPIDS	BLUE RAPIDS	KS	B-	C+	C+	32.2	4.80	11.5	10.7	20.5	33.0	10.0	12.2	22.4
STATE BK OF BOTTINEAU	BOTTINEAU	ND	D+	C-	C-	40.4	-3.03	9.0	6.4	6.8	18.3	5.9	8.4	11.7
STATE BK OF BRICELYN	BRICELYN	MN	C+	C+	C+	23.6	-4.58	2.3	3.0	10.2	19.6	10.0	13.4	18.2
STATE BK OF BROOKS	CORNING	IA	C	C	C	12.2	-1.85	6.8	5.3	5.4	60.8	10.0	13.3	40.8
▲ STATE BK OF BURDEN	BURDEN	KS	E+	E	E-	8.9	-3.21	5.1	7.9	41.4	7.8	7.5	9.3	16.4
▲ STATE BK OF BURNETTSVILLE	BURNETTSVILLE	IN	B-	C+	C+	24.5	-6.62	3.4	22.2	16.4	37.6	10.0	11.8	18.5
▼ STATE BK OF BURRTON	BURRTON	KS	D-	D	D	9.5	15.79	8.6	7.5	19.8	21.6	9.4	12.3	14.5
STATE BK OF BUSSEY	BUSSEY	IA	C+	C+	B-	23.9	6.93	6.3	12.9	3.4	44.6	10.0	12.6	26.2
STATE BK OF CAIRO	CAIRO	NE	B-	B-	B	72.9	-1.47	7.7	3.4	1.0	31.3	10.0	18.7	29.3
STATE BK OF CANTON	CANTON	KS	B-	B	B	21.7	4.76	4.9	2.5	5.6	47.0	10.0	17.8	38.0
STATE BK OF CARBONDALE	CARBONDALE	KS	D	D	D	15.4	0.06	7.5	6.2	24.1	30.2	6.7	8.8	16.2
STATE BK OF CAZENOVIA	CAZENOVIA	WI	B	B	B+	31.9	4.41	1.6	6.4	28.9	13.7	10.0	13.8	25.8
▲ STATE BK OF CEYLON	CEYLON	MN	C-	D	D	10.1	-2.58	4.8	9.3	9.0	39.4	10.0	11.0	21.6
STATE BK OF CHANDLER	CHANDLER	MN	B	B	B	28.1	-4.07	11.0	4.7	2.1	33.1	10.0	11.5	19.7
STATE BK OF CHANHASSEN	CHANHASSEN	MN	A-	A-	B+	110.9	-12.68	14.1	1.1	6.5	29.6	9.4	10.8	14.5
STATE BK OF CHERRY	CHERRY	IL	B+	B+	B+	62.1	1.39	3.9	7.0	22.6	44.0	9.8	10.9	22.1
STATE BK OF CHESTER	CHESTER	NE	C-	C-	C	19.7	4.57	3.6	5.5	4.6	24.1	7.8	9.6	14.9
▼ STATE BK OF CHILTON	CHILTON	WI	B+	A-	A+	98.8	-0.10	14.5	2.6	4.4	14.3	10.0	21.2	27.4
▲ STATE BK OF CHITTENANGO	CHITTENANGO	NY	C+	C	C+	14.1	58.02	0.0	0.0	0.0	55.5	10.0	18.6	76.6
▲ STATE BK OF CHRISMAN	CHRISMAN	IL	C+	C	C	53.8	9.77	9.6	4.0	9.0	35.6	5.1	7.1	12.6
STATE BK OF CLARKS GROVE	CLARKS GROVE	MN	C	C	B-	17.7	30.61	23.9	2.0	8.8	22.0	10.0	14.4	21.4
▲ STATE BK OF COCHRAN	COCHRAN	GA	D+	D	C-	154.2	-3.43	5.0	10.5	28.0	8.2	9.8	10.9	15.8
STATE BK OF COKATO	COKATO	MN	C-	C-	D+	69.8	23.74	18.7	6.1	18.4	11.8	4.0	7.4	10.5
STATE BK OF COLD SPRING	COLD SPRING	MN	C	C	C-	38.3	11.07	5.2	19.4	26.8	11.3	5.7	8.1	11.5
STATE BK OF COLON	COLON	NE	C	C	C	13.7	7.41	6.6	1.1	8.4	30.6	10.0	12.0	19.7
▼ STATE BK OF COLONY	COLONY	KS	B	B+	B+	13.1	4.70	7.8	9.7	17.5	39.7	10.0	11.4	22.8
STATE BK OF COLUSA	COLUSA	IL	B	B	B+	16.0	5.48	1.9	5.3	12.3	53.0	10.0	18.2	36.5
STATE BK OF CONCRETE	CONCRETE	WA	C-	C-	C-	22.3	4.45	5.6	3.8	28.8	35.0	9.4	10.6	22.3
▲ STATE BK OF CONWAY	CONWAY SPRINGS	KS	E+	D-	D+	17.0	6.97	6.4	8.4	7.3	49.3	7.8	9.5	17.9
STATE BK OF COUNTRYSIDE	COUNTRYSIDE	IL	C+	B-	B+	799.2	10.86	4.5	0.0	3.8	19.8	5.6	9.1	11.5
STATE BK OF CROSS PLAINS	CROSS PLAINS	WI	C	C	C	409.2	6.32	15.7	4.0	14.7	13.0	3.7	7.6	10.4
STATE BK OF DANVERS	DANVERS	MN	C+	C+	C	38.0	-1.68	10.2	2.2	1.7	29.6	9.3	10.5	15.8

Asset Quality Index	Non-Performing Loans as a % of Total Loans	as a % of Capital	Net Charge-offs Avg Loans	Profitability Index	Net Income ($Mil)	Return on Assets (R.O.A.)	Return on Equity (R.O.E.)	Net Interest Spread	Overhead Efficiency Ratio	Liquidity Index	Liquidity Ratio	Hot Money Ratio	Stability Index
3.7	0.86	4.7	0.13	4.8	0.2	0.88	5.81	4.13	61.8	1.4	8.9	23.8	5.8
7.3	0.19	1.7	0.01	5.8	0.5	1.01	13.36	3.51	52.8	4.0	40.6	15.4	5.1
8.6	0.18	1.5	-0.01	7.3	1.3	1.67	19.99	4.49	62.9	4.1	38.5	13.9	4.9
4.2	1.49	9.9	0.23	6.9	0.5	1.25	12.84	4.57	53.5	5.1	92.7	17.2	7.4
6.5	0.64	3.4	0.27	6.2	0.8	1.64	15.40	4.06	61.5	3.8	21.5	10.9	6.1
6.7	0.64	5.2	0.04	5.6	1.7	0.91	11.88	3.73	69.6	5.3	35.3	5.8	5.3
7.4	0.48	3.5	0.00	10.0	1.3	2.98	38.41	4.80	43.1	0.9	10.8	32.2	6.7
4.4	0.75	7.4	0.08	9.9	0.5	2.26	30.18	5.48	63.5	6.4	43.5	1.6	3.7
7.6	0.14	0.9	0.06	4.8	0.1	1.13	13.30	3.71	69.9	3.2	28.5	15.1	4.2
5.0	1.32	6.7	0.22	9.1	0.3	1.80	15.52	4.16	54.0	4.7	29.7	7.3	6.4
9.7	0.00	0.0	0.00	8.5	0.2	1.69	7.02	4.27	55.6	6.2	292.0	24.6	7.0
7.8	0.14	0.5	-0.03	3.3	0.1	0.49	3.18	3.58	84.0	5.9	67.8	10.0	6.1
7.9	0.00	0.0	0.07	4.8	0.1	0.62	5.19	4.34	79.7	6.4	62.7	6.0	3.0
8.0	0.20	1.4	0.24	9.5	2.1	2.28	22.32	5.08	57.3	3.5	29.2	13.9	7.3
8.4	0.08	0.5	0.06	9.6	0.5	2.61	27.25	4.74	43.4	1.5	13.8	23.5	5.4
5.1	1.53	8.9	0.00	6.7	0.9	1.17	9.75	3.57	44.0	7.5	96.4	6.1	7.0
4.3	2.44	13.1	0.09	3.8	0.3	0.75	7.10	3.31	77.4	7.5	112.4	7.2	5.2
6.1	1.97	11.5	0.00	3.7	0.1	0.62	7.87	3.02	77.9	7.7	133.4	7.1	6.3
6.2	1.34	8.7	0.00	2.0	0.0	0.06	0.76	2.69	93.9	4.0	70.7	20.3	2.2
9.0	0.10	0.5	0.01	4.9	0.6	1.17	12.26	3.14	59.3	7.7	114.4	5.7	6.1
5.1	2.34	8.0	0.04	7.1	0.5	1.22	8.70	4.94	61.1	5.2	31.0	4.7	6.5
8.1	0.00	0.0	-0.05	7.0	0.4	1.33	10.48	3.96	60.5	2.2	16.4	17.9	6.8
6.7	0.57	1.9	0.19	5.9	0.7	1.61	14.48	2.60	46.1	2.7	22.4	16.1	7.4
5.9	0.00	0.0	0.05	4.8	0.1	0.60	8.00	3.46	72.1	4.2	32.8	11.7	5.5
0.9	4.04	37.6	0.35	3.8	0.1	0.54	6.91	4.53	75.7	4.5	23.2	6.5	1.9
8.2	0.00	0.0	0.60	6.4	0.1	2.16	21.42	4.03	52.4	3.2	61.2	21.9	3.3
1.5	9.62	41.3	4.91	2.4	0.0	-0.07	-0.76	3.95	65.0	6.0	51.6	6.1	3.5
7.0	0.00	0.0	0.00	6.8	0.1	1.24	16.29	4.45	54.2	3.1	9.4	12.8	3.0
4.9	2.65	11.0	0.01	4.8	0.2	0.79	5.63	3.97	75.0	5.3	64.7	12.4	6.9
7.5	1.60	5.8	1.08	5.1	0.1	0.70	5.57	4.49	65.8	3.9	26.4	10.9	8.0
8.2	0.40	1.4	0.00	4.1	0.1	0.43	3.12	4.19	80.7	7.6	76.5	0.4	6.1
5.1	0.75	4.2	0.08	2.1	0.1	0.39	4.57	3.85	86.3	5.5	45.3	7.6	2.9
5.8	1.30	6.0	0.13	4.4	0.1	0.78	6.54	3.34	73.6	6.4	87.9	10.3	4.5
2.7	0.98	6.7	0.53	6.0	0.3	1.29	13.86	4.80	68.1	4.6	60.3	15.2	4.5
7.4	0.24	1.2	-0.02	5.7	0.2	1.41	10.71	4.39	67.1	5.1	46.1	8.0	5.0
6.3	3.44	7.1	0.12	3.8	0.1	1.15	8.76	2.71	54.2	6.8	82.0	4.7	3.8
5.2	1.64	10.9	1.16	2.6	0.0	0.16	1.72	5.35	97.5	4.7	39.1	8.2	0.5
7.4	0.27	1.2	0.27	4.5	0.1	0.80	6.70	4.52	70.4	2.1	40.9	26.8	3.8
2.1	6.90	26.9	0.36	0.6	-0.1	-1.80	-14.13	5.63	108.9	6.0	70.4	7.7	2.4
5.0	3.61	11.2	0.28	6.6	0.2	1.75	14.19	3.71	53.6	6.8	83.6	5.4	5.0
4.0	4.59	12.4	-0.47	4.4	0.3	0.77	4.26	4.07	46.2	6.2	146.7	17.1	5.1
7.8	2.70	5.6	-0.05	5.6	0.1	0.85	4.68	3.78	67.0	6.8	65.6	1.8	6.1
8.6	0.17	1.0	0.00	3.4	0.0	0.49	5.70	4.10	87.9	6.9	74.7	2.9	1.9
7.7	1.00	4.4	0.07	4.9	0.1	0.72	5.43	3.95	65.4	7.6	98.0	4.2	5.8
5.4	1.84	7.3	0.35	3.8	0.0	0.77	7.16	3.91	79.3	2.5	32.9	18.0	3.4
5.9	1.94	8.8	0.26	7.4	0.2	1.32	11.09	4.53	50.8	4.0	44.3	15.5	5.9
8.5	0.03	0.1	0.08	6.3	0.5	0.97	8.33	4.12	75.7	4.7	21.5	5.0	8.0
8.8	0.06	0.3	0.03	5.0	0.3	0.85	7.68	3.27	59.8	6.0	81.5	11.4	6.0
6.8	0.18	1.2	0.51	5.9	0.1	1.43	14.79	3.47	56.8	3.1	54.3	20.8	3.7
4.0	2.27	8.2	-0.06	8.5	1.0	2.01	9.81	4.58	57.1	4.6	29.7	8.0	9.5
10.0	0.00	0.0	0.00	4.4	0.1	0.95	4.93	2.51	8.6	9.3	324.5	4.8	0.5
5.9	0.61	5.0	-0.01	5.9	0.3	1.05	15.03	3.52	60.1	5.1	97.0	18.1	4.2
8.5	0.04	0.1	0.04	2.7	0.0	0.32	2.07	4.57	92.1	4.5	43.7	10.8	4.2
1.3	3.80	23.6	0.79	7.7	1.1	1.37	12.47	4.98	44.1	2.7	26.5	17.2	6.3
7.4	0.12	1.1	-0.21	6.2	0.5	1.54	20.78	4.91	68.3	4.3	19.4	7.5	2.9
7.1	0.17	1.5	0.07	6.1	0.3	1.52	18.99	4.67	64.1	4.5	16.2	5.2	3.7
6.1	1.63	7.6	0.00	3.4	0.0	0.54	4.49	3.50	80.2	4.5	39.0	9.9	3.9
6.0	1.61	7.5	0.00	2.4	0.0	0.31	2.71	2.81	90.5	6.3	75.4	7.2	5.6
9.1	0.00	0.0	0.00	8.3	0.1	1.57	8.65	3.99	50.2	7.2	98.8	4.9	6.3
3.4	5.02	19.6	0.12	3.3	0.0	0.38	3.67	5.26	89.4	4.6	107.0	20.8	3.3
3.6	4.35	17.3	-0.45	0.3	0.0	-0.06	-0.66	3.98	100.0	3.3	25.0	13.0	0.9
3.1	1.48	10.4	-0.01	10.0	11.7	3.00	30.69	4.82	32.7	4.9	75.0	17.4	7.7
5.6	0.27	2.5	0.11	5.9	2.1	1.04	13.25	4.09	69.0	2.1	17.6	18.5	3.8
7.3	0.00	0.0	-0.03	6.1	0.3	1.42	14.09	4.99	55.7	3.8	28.2	11.9	3.4

Name	City	State	Weiss Safety Rating	2003 Weiss Safety Rating	2002 Weiss Safety Rating	Total Assets ($Mil)	One Year Asset Growth	Asset Mix (As a % of Total Assets)				Capital- ization Index	Leverage Ratio	Risk-based Capital Ratio
								Comm- ercial Loans	Cons- umer Loans	Home Mort- gages	Secur- ities			
▲ STATE BK OF DAVIS	DAVIS	IL	B-	C+	C	76.0	7.59	16.7	4.6	11.5	31.3	6.0	8.0	11.9
STATE BK OF DE KALB	DE KALB	TX	B+	B+	B+	112.4	2.13	10.2	5.1	7.8	39.4	10.0	15.0	24.3
STATE BK OF DELANO	DELANO	MN	A-	A-	A-	94.4	32.42	22.7	5.0	17.3	9.2	8.6	12.1	13.9
STATE BK OF DELPHOS	DELPHOS	KS	C	C	C-	27.5	2.94	9.9	5.8	16.0	19.9	6.7	8.7	13.3
▼ STATE BK OF DOWNS	DOWNS	KS	B	B+	B+	54.7	1.03	4.2	1.3	3.5	6.7	10.0	14.5	17.0
STATE BK OF DRUMMOND	DRUMMOND	WI	B	B	B	35.5	6.37	6.3	5.4	32.8	28.8	10.0	12.6	22.7
STATE BK OF EAGLE BUTTE	EAGLE BUTTE	SD	C+	C+	C+	28.2	2.72	6.0	12.0	2.2	49.0	10.0	11.7	20.5
STATE BK OF EASTON	EASTON	MN	C+	C+	C+	16.1	-0.69	12.9	7.3	7.7	17.0	10.0	13.5	18.4
▲ STATE BK OF ELDRED	ELDRED	IL	D-	E+	E+	8.4	27.91	5.6	19.2	26.0	16.2	10.0	19.4	31.7
▼ STATE BK OF ESCANABA	ESCANABA	MI	A-	A	A	109.1	0.29	6.3	7.2	23.3	24.8	10.0	19.3	30.6
STATE BK OF EWEN	EWEN	MI	B+	B+	B+	39.5	-2.26	9.8	9.9	32.1	32.2	10.0	17.0	30.8
STATE BK OF FAIRMONT	FAIRMONT	MN	B	B	B-	67.3	4.54	17.1	9.3	5.3	26.6	10.0	11.4	16.4
STATE BK OF FARIBAULT	FARIBAULT	MN	A-	A-	A-	155.9	5.42	7.6	5.5	10.5	29.9	8.4	9.9	15.0
STATE BK OF FLORENCE	FLORENCE	WI	C	C	C-	44.2	0.42	27.9	6.7	32.4	8.8	8.3	9.9	13.6
STATE BK OF GENEVA	GENEVA	IL	B+	B+	B+	81.1	-3.84	3.1	1.4	10.8	40.5	7.5	9.3	16.3
▲ STATE BK OF GIBBON	GIBBON	MN	E+	E-	E-	21.5	4.46	3.7	2.8	8.2	5.8	4.1	7.9	10.6
STATE BK OF GILMAN	GILMAN	WI	C	C	B-	50.3	9.90	8.5	5.7	19.3	16.1	5.6	7.9	11.5
▲ STATE BK OF GRAYMONT	GRAYMONT	IL	B-	C+	C+	89.1	-2.79	6.5	7.6	15.1	43.8	6.5	8.5	18.2
STATE BK OF HAMBURG	HAMBURG	MN	E-	E-	D-	20.4	0.93	5.9	3.6	11.7	43.8	5.2	7.2	13.9
▲ STATE BK OF HAWLEY	HAWLEY	MN	B-	C+	C	61.3	-0.63	12.5	9.1	12.1	27.7	6.0	8.0	12.5
STATE BK OF HERSCHER	HERSCHER	IL	A-	A-	A-	105.2	13.57	22.7	2.5	12.4	29.2	10.0	11.3	17.3
STATE BK OF HILDRETH	HILDRETH	NE	C-	C-	C-	13.4	2.08	7.1	1.0	3.4	19.8	10.0	21.7	29.9
STATE BK OF HOWARDS	HOWARDS GROVE	WI	B-	B-	C	156.8	42.13	7.2	4.2	16.6	28.0	5.1	7.2	11.1
▲ STATE BK OF HUDSON	HUDSON	SD	B-	C+	C+	19.0	6.95	7.9	5.5	6.8	0.0	10.0	14.9	24.5
▼ STATE BK OF INDIA (CALIF)	LOS ANGELES	CA	C	C+	C-	147.1	40.46	23.1	0.2	0.0	45.3	10.0	11.0	20.1
STATE BK OF INDUSTRY	INDUSTRY	IL	B+	B+	B	27.8	-2.02	11.5	19.2	16.0	34.2	10.0	13.1	21.3
STATE BK OF JEFFERS	JEFFERS	MN	C+	C+	C+	17.9	7.40	6.6	3.8	3.0	44.3	10.0	12.6	25.6
STATE BK OF JEWETT	JEWETT	TX	B	B+	B+	39.3	-2.57	2.8	7.0	5.7	43.7	10.0	14.1	28.6
▲ STATE BK OF KERKHOVEN	KERKHOVEN	MN	C-	D+	D+	19.7	-6.54	10.2	3.3	9.2	27.8	6.5	8.5	13.6
STATE BK OF KIMBALL	KIMBALL	MN	C+	C	C	55.6	10.79	9.7	7.5	26.7	15.1	5.6	7.6	12.0
STATE BK OF KS	FREDONIA	KS	B-	B-	B-	83.0	-4.43	3.6	1.7	7.9	15.8	6.7	8.7	12.3
▼ STATE BK OF LAKE PARK	LAKE PARK	MN	D+	D+	C-	25.9	8.98	11.8	11.9	28.1	24.7	5.9	7.9	14.1
STATE BK OF LAKOTA	LAKOTA	ND	B-	B-	B	35.5	1.48	7.2	4.8	3.7	54.7	10.0	12.3	27.8
STATE BK OF LEBO	LEBO	KS	C	C-	C	17.0	-5.74	1.5	2.9	20.3	15.8	10.0	11.8	18.1
▼ STATE BK OF LEDYARD	LEDYARD	IA	B-	B	B	24.3	0.76	9.3	4.5	3.8	18.1	10.0	17.4	23.8
STATE BK OF LEON	LEON	KS	D	D+	D+	10.3	0.63	9.2	4.7	8.3	46.8	6.6	8.6	20.3
STATE BK OF LIMA	LIMA	IL	C+	C+	C+	29.0	1.46	25.4	2.5	6.7	13.9	3.3	7.8	10.2
STATE BK OF LINCOLN	LINCOLN	IL	A+	A+	A+	171.4	4.34	9.5	2.2	12.4	32.2	10.0	13.5	23.1
▲ STATE BK OF LISMORE	LISMORE	MN	B-	C+	B-	27.2	6.85	13.2	2.0	1.1	3.4	8.9	12.7	14.1
STATE BK OF LIZTON	LIZTON	IN	A-	A	A	197.0	4.63	7.7	4.4	18.5	31.2	10.0	13.2	21.5
STATE BK OF LONG ISLAND	NEW HYDE PARK	NY	B-	B-	B-	1,497.0	5.20	18.0	0.6	3.5	42.7	5.6	7.6	13.1
▲ STATE BK OF LONG LAKE	LONG LAKE	MN	B-	C+	C	137.4	-0.63	15.9	2.5	14.6	12.9	6.4	9.0	12.1
▼ STATE BK OF LORETTO	LORETTO	MN	D	C+	C	98.9	-13.64	15.3	1.2	19.7	2.4	7.1	9.1	12.6
▼ STATE BK OF LUCAN	LUCAN	MN	C-	C	C	25.8	-2.99	7.2	3.8	4.7	27.6	10.0	12.6	20.4
STATE BK OF MARIETTA	MARIETTA	MN	C-	C-	C	6.7	-12.88	9.2	6.4	3.4	34.5	8.7	10.1	17.7
▼ STATE BK OF MCGREGOR	MCGREGOR	MN	C-	C	C	42.6	2.38	10.9	9.0	21.8	2.5	6.6	9.0	12.2
STATE BK OF MEDORA	MEDORA	IN	B	B	B	54.1	-0.66	6.6	12.2	30.3	28.3	10.0	13.1	23.3
STATE BK OF MISSOURI	CONCORDIA	MO	B	B	B	55.1	12.80	5.8	5.3	32.0	18.3	6.4	8.4	14.4
STATE BK OF NAUVOO	NAUVOO	IL	D	D	D	23.7	1.95	6.5	9.0	41.2	9.9	8.3	9.9	17.2
▲ STATE BK OF NEW RICHLAND	NEW RICHLAND	MN	C+	C-	C	41.6	3.74	5.7	5.5	22.6	11.2	7.1	9.0	13.1
STATE BK OF NEWBURG	NEWBURG	WI	C-	C-	C-	100.7	18.52	4.4	2.8	34.9	14.7	10.0	11.0	16.9
STATE BK OF NIANTIC	NIANTIC	IL	B+	B+	B+	46.1	2.41	4.1	15.0	27.1	19.8	10.0	15.2	22.7
STATE BK OF ODELL	ODELL	NE	D-	D	C-	20.5	1.25	3.9	15.5	13.4	5.4	8.4	9.9	15.4
STATE BK OF OSKALOOSA	OSKALOOSA	KS	D-	D-	D-	30.3	-2.65	1.1	2.9	18.8	53.7	4.2	6.2	28.0
▲ STATE BK OF OXFORD	OXFORD	IN	B	B-	B-	69.9	-0.65	8.3	2.3	16.2	28.2	9.6	10.7	16.3
▲ STATE BK OF PARK RAPIDS	PARK RAPIDS	MN	C+	C	C-	87.4	5.68	22.4	7.2	14.0	26.3	6.3	8.3	13.2
STATE BK OF PAW PAW	PAW PAW	IL	A-	A-	A-	24.0	4.52	7.0	3.8	13.4	29.5	10.0	14.1	23.6
▲ STATE BK OF PEARL CITY	PEARL CITY	IL	B	B-	C	33.8	-7.30	4.7	9.0	15.6	43.1	10.0	11.8	24.4
STATE BK OF PRAIRIE DU	PRAIRIE DU ROCHE	IL	D	D	D	40.9	8.12	1.9	13.8	29.0	33.6	4.9	6.9	13.1
STATE BK OF REESEVILLE	REESEVILLE	WI	B	B	C+	40.1	6.28	1.6	2.4	23.5	31.3	10.0	11.7	23.4
STATE BK OF RICHMOND	RICHMOND	MN	A-	A-	A-	64.0	8.46	3.1	4.8	23.7	35.0	10.0	12.3	23.2
STATE BK OF RIVERDALE	RIVERDALE	NE	A-	A-	A-	31.0	2.21	5.0	4.8	2.7	24.5	10.0	23.7	35.6
▼ STATE BK OF ROGERS	ROGERS	MN	C	C+	C+	76.6	-1.84	19.5	4.0	15.5	16.3	7.4	9.3	13.3
STATE BK OF SAUNEMIN	SAUNEMIN	IL	D	D	D	21.7	3.91	11.5	6.3	10.8	32.8	6.5	8.5	14.8

Asset Quality Index	Non-Performing Loans as a % of Total Loans	Non-Performing Loans as a % of Capital	Net Charge-offs Avg Loans	Profitability Index	Net Income ($Mil)	Return on Assets (R.O.A.)	Return on Equity (R.O.E.)	Net Interest Spread	Overhead Efficiency Ratio	Liquidity Index	Liquidity Ratio	Hot Money Ratio	Stability Index
6.1	0.50	3.8	-0.02	7.5	0.6	1.45	18.44	4.03	46.1	2.8	25.3	15.9	5.1
5.2	1.68	6.0	-0.04	9.5	1.3	2.29	15.24	4.11	48.0	3.6	47.3	18.8	9.1
6.9	0.33	2.2	-0.01	10.0	1.4	3.08	24.42	5.94	48.0	4.1	16.5	8.3	8.8
4.4	1.27	8.5	0.07	5.4	0.2	1.09	12.30	4.46	74.4	4.3	41.6	14.0	4.3
3.3	3.58	18.8	0.26	9.6	0.6	2.32	16.00	4.89	49.7	5.8	68.4	10.7	7.8
7.8	0.24	1.0	0.06	4.9	0.2	0.99	7.74	4.62	76.7	5.6	39.8	6.2	5.8
6.8	0.79	2.5	2.08	4.4	0.1	0.85	7.65	5.19	71.9	1.7	29.3	29.5	3.6
6.3	1.00	4.7	0.18	5.2	0.1	1.23	9.31	4.28	69.5	5.2	50.7	9.0	5.0
2.6	4.10	12.6	-0.09	4.4	0.1	1.26	8.01	5.27	70.2	6.2	49.0	1.5	0.0
5.7	2.45	7.7	0.24	10.0	1.1	2.03	10.46	5.34	41.2	5.3	45.2	9.7	9.4
6.2	1.61	5.3	0.03	8.2	0.3	1.63	9.53	5.52	57.1	4.2	29.3	10.5	7.3
4.5	1.79	9.9	0.09	5.5	0.4	1.27	11.43	3.80	53.3	3.1	17.1	13.8	4.3
8.6	0.16	0.9	0.04	7.8	1.4	1.80	17.55	4.59	62.6	5.6	43.2	7.2	7.6
3.1	2.14	15.1	0.22	7.3	0.3	1.30	13.26	5.76	62.0	5.0	43.6	10.7	3.6
9.2	0.00	0.0	-0.03	5.8	0.5	1.29	14.44	4.09	68.6	3.6	24.0	11.7	6.2
6.3	0.05	0.4	0.00	5.7	0.1	1.32	16.43	3.80	65.1	5.4	55.7	8.4	1.7
2.1	2.39	18.1	0.05	5.4	0.3	1.01	12.19	5.28	73.5	4.4	38.9	12.6	4.5
4.9	1.21	5.2	-0.08	5.0	0.5	1.12	9.66	3.75	64.1	3.5	10.4	11.2	6.3
2.6	4.35	18.9	0.00	3.0	0.1	0.80	10.81	3.70	79.3	6.5	89.7	8.5	0.0
8.0	0.06	0.5	-0.01	7.8	0.6	1.84	22.58	4.94	64.4	4.9	26.4	4.6	5.0
5.2	2.17	11.1	-0.03	5.9	0.6	1.06	9.51	3.92	61.2	2.7	39.4	23.8	6.4
4.1	3.06	9.3	-0.27	2.9	0.0	0.43	1.99	4.55	90.2	4.8	31.0	5.0	4.4
6.7	0.25	2.0	0.01	4.8	0.6	0.80	10.44	3.70	74.3	8.1	93.6	1.4	4.3
8.2	0.07	0.3	-0.61	7.6	0.2	1.88	12.76	3.57	52.2	8.2	152.2	6.0	5.7
5.3	1.49	6.8	0.30	2.4	0.5	0.69	6.32	2.57	79.1	3.2	60.8	32.2	5.7
7.6	0.25	1.0	-1.07	8.1	0.2	1.32	9.96	4.04	49.4	3.9	45.2	16.6	6.9
8.6	0.04	0.1	0.05	3.0	0.0	0.42	3.33	3.08	82.1	8.4	118.8	0.6	4.6
6.8	2.43	5.4	-0.15	3.7	0.2	0.87	5.70	4.02	86.8	5.3	36.6	6.7	7.6
7.3	0.05	0.4	0.00	6.5	0.1	1.38	15.31	4.80	71.5	4.4	21.5	6.3	3.7
4.7	0.95	7.9	0.01	9.2	0.5	1.89	24.64	3.91	55.5	6.2	49.4	4.4	4.8
7.1	0.00	0.0	0.01	4.8	0.4	0.99	9.67	3.48	62.0	5.3	76.3	14.2	5.9
4.7	0.83	6.5	0.00	7.6	0.2	1.78	23.15	4.72	58.7	3.8	27.7	11.7	3.0
7.8	0.91	3.1	0.00	5.2	0.2	1.34	11.13	3.70	59.2	4.5	29.3	8.8	4.5
7.2	0.58	3.1	-0.18	5.6	0.2	1.65	14.14	4.46	64.3	3.8	35.0	12.4	4.3
7.0	0.06	0.2	0.33	7.5	0.2	1.67	9.81	3.87	58.9	4.1	88.7	22.2	5.7
9.0	0.09	0.4	0.65	1.5	-0.1	-1.98	-22.40	3.57	85.6	8.0	105.0	1.1	2.6
4.4	1.00	8.9	-0.01	7.0	0.3	1.72	21.61	3.61	49.3	3.8	29.7	12.4	5.3
8.5	0.17	0.7	0.10	9.8	2.5	2.83	20.92	4.30	49.8	4.1	32.1	12.0	9.2
6.5	0.05	0.3	0.00	4.3	0.1	0.69	5.50	4.49	75.0	6.8	83.7	6.7	5.6
8.8	0.18	0.7	-0.01	5.3	0.9	0.93	7.00	4.05	71.2	5.5	43.9	8.1	8.2
7.1	0.54	3.3	0.52	4.8	7.8	1.07	13.62	4.24	66.2	3.7	30.2	16.8	5.3
4.6	1.02	8.5	0.01	8.0	0.8	1.15	13.42	5.42	59.9	1.0	10.2	30.0	4.6
1.0	4.57	38.7	0.02	6.7	0.4	0.67	7.83	4.22	66.6	2.3	31.7	21.5	5.9
4.8	2.88	11.5	-0.73	1.6	0.0	0.18	1.50	3.50	83.8	7.0	90.9	7.0	3.7
8.3	0.00	0.0	0.06	9.3	0.1	2.28	24.48	5.56	48.9	4.1	22.9	8.3	3.3
1.8	3.42	29.9	0.01	10.0	0.8	3.56	37.55	5.28	37.0	4.1	35.2	13.0	6.0
4.8	2.22	9.8	0.19	5.8	0.3	1.16	9.04	3.70	57.5	4.8	57.1	13.6	6.5
6.1	0.69	5.3	0.23	8.0	0.5	1.97	22.91	4.32	56.8	5.1	35.4	7.2	5.9
3.3	2.22	15.1	-0.07	4.2	0.1	1.20	12.34	4.54	71.5	5.5	69.1	10.5	1.8
5.9	0.52	4.6	0.09	7.4	0.4	1.93	23.80	4.27	47.3	4.5	22.5	6.1	4.7
1.9	3.68	24.5	-0.12	10.0	0.9	1.86	17.37	4.23	28.8	4.5	73.8	19.4	6.3
5.0	1.53	7.0	0.40	10.0	0.7	2.90	18.98	4.97	44.2	3.2	36.9	18.1	8.1
1.3	5.28	34.1	0.57	0.7	0.0	-0.38	-3.78	3.88	100.2	4.8	54.8	11.6	2.3
9.7	0.00	0.0	-0.05	2.5	0.1	0.41	6.44	2.47	85.4	8.2	212.7	11.6	0.8
8.2	0.23	1.2	-0.03	4.9	0.3	0.78	7.07	4.59	76.2	5.0	35.2	7.6	5.1
4.0	1.64	11.3	0.33	6.1	0.8	1.75	20.38	4.23	56.7	4.4	20.8	6.8	4.1
8.4	0.00	0.0	-0.03	6.1	0.1	1.22	8.34	4.49	62.4	3.3	18.3	12.3	7.0
7.1	0.90	4.3	0.18	6.1	0.3	1.52	14.18	4.17	59.3	3.8	43.4	16.4	4.9
8.1	0.01	0.1	-0.22	3.7	0.1	0.63	9.31	3.23	73.0	5.4	38.0	6.3	1.7
9.2	0.42	1.6	-0.04	5.1	0.2	0.96	8.10	4.10	66.5	7.0	98.0	7.9	5.6
9.0	0.01	0.0	-0.01	6.9	0.4	1.22	10.05	3.72	52.5	4.9	38.1	9.5	6.6
7.0	0.00	0.0	0.01	10.0	0.4	2.24	9.58	4.89	32.3	5.4	17.8	0.0	8.5
2.5	2.93	19.9	-0.19	5.5	0.5	1.18	13.20	4.66	68.1	6.2	44.6	3.1	4.5
7.3	0.49	2.9	-0.02	4.8	0.1	1.05	12.58	3.78	67.5	4.5	42.2	10.3	2.3

Name	City	State	Weiss Safety Rating	2003 Weiss Safety Rating	2002 Weiss Safety Rating	Total Assets ($Mil)	One Year Asset Growth	Asset Mix (As a % of Total Assets)				Capital-ization Index	Leverage Ratio	Risk-based Capital Ratio
								Comm-ercial Loans	Cons-umer Loans	Home Mort-gages	Secur-ities			
STATE BK OF SCHALLER	SCHALLER	IA	C+	C+	C+	17.4	-3.34	4.4	2.4	4.9	42.3	10.0	11.8	22.4
STATE BK OF SCOTIA	SCOTIA	NE	C	C	C	23.2	3.52	4.2	3.1	0.9	35.8	10.0	20.6	31.3
▼ STATE BK OF SEATON	SEATON	IL	C-	C	C-	33.3	91.01	13.0	1.4	6.4	31.6	6.3	8.3	13.8
STATE BK OF SLATER	SLATER	MO	B-	B-	B-	32.7	-0.93	16.8	10.3	16.5	15.1	9.9	11.0	15.8
STATE BK OF SOUTHERN	CEDAR CITY	UT	A-	B+	B+	375.1	12.68	8.2	6.1	4.9	27.7	10.0	12.0	16.7
▼ STATE BK OF SPEER	SPEER	IL	C	C+	C+	97.5	7.56	4.7	2.3	15.1	43.1	5.4	7.4	13.6
STATE BK OF SPRING HILL	SPRING HILL	KS	C	C	C+	42.0	6.33	5.2	3.5	10.9	51.8	5.9	11.4	11.7
STATE BK OF ST JACOB	ST JACOB	IL	A-	A-	A-	36.9	2.79	5.3	8.8	25.1	25.2	10.0	14.4	26.1
STATE BK OF STREETER	STREETER	ND	D	D	D+	7.8	-5.84	7.7	5.4	0.4	3.9	10.0	15.9	21.4
▼ STATE BK OF SW MISSOURI	SPRINGFIELD	MO	D+	C-	C-	80.2	-3.49	2.9	10.3	34.4	8.1	1.4	6.3	8.4
▲ STATE BK OF TABLE ROCK	TABLE ROCK	NE	D+	D	D	21.8	-6.30	7.8	6.0	12.8	11.6	9.1	10.4	15.7
STATE BK OF TAUNTON	TAUNTON	MN	C+	C+	C	31.6	20.69	9.9	10.8	4.2	39.2	10.0	14.0	15.3
STATE BK OF TEXAS	HOUSTON	TX	C-	C-	C-	96.1	4.51	23.2	3.3	5.2	30.5	5.9	7.9	14.9
STATE BK OF THE LAKES	ANTIOCH	IL	B	B	B	437.1	6.00	7.4	8.3	8.6	34.0	7.2	9.1	13.7
STATE BK OF TOLEDO	TOLEDO	IA	B	B	B	77.1	4.47	6.0	6.3	30.9	10.9	5.9	7.9	12.1
▲ STATE BK OF TOULON	TOULON	IL	C+	C	C	134.1	3.92	2.4	3.5	5.1	46.0	4.6	6.6	13.5
STATE BK OF TOWNSEND	TOWNSEND	MT	C	C	C	34.7	3.35	6.0	5.2	4.4	16.5	7.6	9.4	19.2
STATE BK OF VIROQUA	VIROQUA	WI	C+	B-	B-	74.1	-0.66	25.3	8.4	13.9	16.3	6.9	8.9	12.5
STATE BK OF WAPELLO	WAPELLO	IA	B+	B+	B+	31.6	-3.04	3.1	5.2	17.1	46.0	10.0	15.0	30.5
STATE BK OF WATERLOO	WATERLOO	IL	B-	B-	B-	76.1	8.56	1.3	2.0	43.3	16.8	9.2	10.4	16.3
STATE BK OF WAVERLY	WAVERLY	IA	A+	A+	A+	114.5	-2.88	3.5	2.1	14.4	44.5	10.0	15.3	29.1
STATE BK OF WHEATON	WHEATON	MN	A	A	A	58.4	-10.05	21.4	2.2	6.5	15.3	10.0	21.3	26.9
STATE BK OF WHITTINGTON	BENTON	IL	C+	C+	C+	70.2	-0.31	4.1	22.3	25.6	24.1	6.5	8.6	15.0
STATE BK OF WILEY	WILEY	CO	A-	A-	A-	70.9	10.41	15.0	4.9	15.5	36.2	10.0	27.3	38.4
STATE BK OF WITHEE	WITHEE	WI	C	C-	D+	57.8	0.13	3.6	3.2	20.0	30.2	8.3	9.9	19.1
STATE BK OF WYNNEWOOD	WYNNEWOOD	OK	B-	B-	C+	40.1	5.98	13.0	9.6	23.9	19.5	8.1	9.8	14.2
STATE BK OF YOUNG	NORWOOD YOUNG AM	MN	B+	B+	B	109.3	-1.38	6.4	3.6	9.5	16.7	9.3	10.6	14.8
STATE BK TEXAS	IRVING	TX	C+	C+	C+	148.5	-4.70	5.8	1.1	0.2	1.2	7.8	10.3	13.2
▲ STATE CENTRAL BK	KEOKUK	IA	B	C+	C-	180.5	1.45	22.9	3.5	15.1	24.4	10.0	14.7	23.1
STATE EXCHANGE BK	MANKATO	KS	B-	B-	B-	26.7	0.72	15.3	8.2	5.8	31.2	9.2	10.5	18.3
STATE EXCHANGE BK	LAMONT	OK	E-	E-	E-	26.7	5.31	11.6	7.7	8.2	17.4	3.8	7.0	10.4
▲ STATE FARM BK, FSB	BLOOMINGTON	IL	D	D-	D-	9,057.3	47.80	0.1	26.1	22.2	39.9	7.7	9.4	16.5
▲ STATE FINANCIAL BK NA	HALES CORNERS	WI	B	B-	B-	1,590.7	22.00	9.7	1.9	6.3	32.1	5.6	7.6	11.5
▲ STATE GUARANTY BK	OKEENE	OK	B	B-	B-	29.0	-5.36	7.8	6.4	4.3	45.2	10.0	12.6	22.0
STATE NB	LUBBOCK	TX	B	B-	C+	1,136.4	1.14	18.5	3.1	7.4	16.4	5.3	7.8	11.2
STATE NB IN WEST	WEST	TX	C+	C+	C+	48.0	1.52	8.6	6.7	2.3	61.1	8.8	10.2	28.6
STATE NB OF BIG SPRING	BIG SPRING	TX	B+	B+	A	179.3	14.94	6.8	2.3	1.5	65.1	10.0	12.8	34.4
STATE NB OF GARFIELD	GARFIELD	WA	C	C	D	57.0	5.68	28.9	5.2	7.3	9.9	8.7	10.4	13.9
▲ STATE NB OF GROOM	GROOM	TX	E	E	C-	23.2	70.43	10.1	3.6	2.1	10.9	6.4	8.4	12.4
STATE NB TX	IOWA PARK	TX	B-	B-	C+	139.5	5.09	5.5	5.5	11.2	38.2	6.8	8.8	16.9
STATE NB&TC	WAYNE	NE	A-	A-	A-	75.1	5.26	6.1	3.5	10.3	26.6	10.0	14.7	24.5
STATE OF FRANKLIN SVG BK	JOHNSON CITY	TN	C+	C+	C+	307.2	8.33	9.7	1.3	19.6	33.8	5.4	7.4	12.1
STATE STREET B&TC	QUINCY	IL	B+	B+	B+	109.0	2.60	4.7	23.6	14.9	30.7	9.4	11.6	14.5
STATE STREET B&TC	BOSTON	MA	C+	C+	C+	90,895.6	20.74	0.1	0.1	0.0	39.3	3.3	5.3	13.6
STATE SVG BK	BAXTER	IA	C+	C	C	79.0	4.05	13.3	5.0	25.9	5.5	4.7	7.9	10.9
▼ STATE SVG BK	RAKE	IA	D+	C-	C-	29.0	7.53	12.0	2.4	4.6	4.1	6.7	10.1	12.3
STATE SVG BK OF	MANISTIQUE	MI	B	B	B+	102.3	7.51	17.4	7.5	20.0	36.9	6.4	8.4	14.1
STATE SVG BK-FRANKFORT	FRANKFORT	MI	A	A	A	65.2	-0.44	4.2	4.7	21.3	13.8	10.0	15.1	20.8
STATE SVGS BK	CRESTON	IA	D+	D	D	30.1	1.08	18.4	12.1	17.0	2.8	6.5	8.9	12.1
STATE-INVESTORS BK	METAIRIE	LA	B	B	B	143.1	-2.08	0.0	0.8	60.9	17.5	10.0	11.7	23.8
▲ STATEWIDE BANK	TERRYTOWN	LA	D	D	D+	77.8	52.37	11.0	9.5	26.7	16.0	10.0	11.1	19.2
▲ STEARNS BK ARIZONA NA	SCOTTSDALE	AZ	B+	B	B-	100.5	24.10	14.1	0.8	0.7	4.6	10.0	13.6	16.0
STEARNS BK NA	EVANSVILLE	MN	A-	B	C+	37.9	15.53	10.5	1.3	1.8	5.1	10.0	12.3	15.0
STEARNS BK NA	HOLDINGFORD	MN	A-	B	C+	51.5	16.58	8.7	2.8	3.9	6.2	9.5	12.6	14.6
STEARNS BK NA	ST CLOUD	MN	A-	B	C+	874.7	17.82	5.6	0.4	0.9	9.3	8.0	12.6	13.3
STEARNS BK NA	UPSALA	MN	A-	B	C+	38.0	19.39	8.7	1.0	1.2	11.3	9.5	11.9	14.6
STEEL VALLEY BK NA	DILLONVALE	OH	D	D	D+	55.8	-2.39	7.8	2.5	11.8	0.1	8.8	10.2	16.3
STEELE STREET STATE BK	DENVER	CO	D	D	NR	45.4	N/A	16.3	0.0	4.2	29.8	10.0	21.0	28.2
▼ STEPHENS FEDERAL BK	TOCCOA	GA	B-	B	B	181.3	19.92	2.5	1.6	51.0	3.8	7.4	9.3	15.5
▲ STEPHENS SECURITY BK	STEPHENS	AR	C	C-	C+	34.5	12.85	26.3	14.9	20.5	12.5	6.0	8.1	11.7
STEPHENSON NB&T	MARINETTE	WI	B	B+	B+	201.8	3.33	19.4	3.3	15.4	17.7	8.3	9.9	14.2
STEPHENVILLE B&TC	STEPHENVILLE	TX	A-	A-	A-	145.1	4.40	14.1	6.2	12.8	41.3	6.7	8.7	16.4
▲ STERLING B&T FSB	SOUTHFIELD	MI	C-	D-	D-	870.9	-8.89	1.0	1.5	19.1	5.4	6.2	8.2	15.5
▼ STERLING BK	MONTGOMERY	AL	B-	B	B	446.3	25.53	13.8	4.6	9.2	7.7	3.3	7.6	10.2

Asset Quality Index	Non-Performing Loans as a % of Total Loans	Non-Performing Loans as a % of Capital	Net Charge-offs Avg Loans	Profitability Index	Net Income ($Mil)	Return on Assets (R.O.A.)	Return on Equity (R.O.E.)	Net Interest Spread	Overhead Efficiency Ratio	Liquidity Index	Liquidity Ratio	Hot Money Ratio	Stability Index
6.6	2.01	7.0	0.63	8.4	0.1	1.58	12.90	4.46	64.4	6.1	56.6	4.0	4.6
4.7	3.68	8.8	1.31	5.2	0.1	1.16	5.53	4.64	55.9	6.3	69.6	5.4	4.3
6.1	0.19	1.4	0.43	6.7	0.2	1.54	17.71	3.21	23.9	1.5	35.7	65.6	3.7
4.4	0.95	6.1	-0.01	6.4	0.2	0.94	8.53	4.44	66.7	4.6	28.8	7.5	5.0
5.6	1.36	6.6	0.14	9.5	2.9	1.62	13.66	4.88	59.2	5.5	39.0	6.1	8.1
8.5	0.24	2.2	0.15	3.8	0.4	0.87	13.75	3.00	67.5	2.6	19.0	16.3	2.8
8.9	0.07	0.2	0.06	3.7	0.1	0.59	5.22	3.33	78.9	6.2	58.3	6.0	5.2
8.5	0.06	0.2	0.02	7.5	0.3	1.72	12.22	3.83	56.5	6.0	62.8	8.4	8.4
3.3	1.09	4.5	0.11	3.5	0.0	0.68	4.32	4.29	79.3	7.6	110.1	4.5	2.3
6.6	0.19	2.3	0.00	8.9	0.7	1.71	25.45	3.91	60.8	2.8	38.5	21.9	4.8
5.4	0.77	5.2	0.64	2.0	0.0	0.02	0.17	3.74	97.6	5.3	45.8	6.3	1.9
2.9	5.76	19.0	0.14	3.8	0.1	0.53	3.65	3.53	77.5	4.8	54.2	13.3	4.8
6.4	0.33	2.1	0.03	3.0	0.1	0.30	3.75	3.98	85.4	2.0	40.4	40.5	2.8
4.4	0.99	6.0	0.06	5.9	2.1	0.99	10.70	3.91	75.2	1.7	15.0	20.9	6.3
7.4	0.33	3.0	0.02	7.1	0.6	1.55	19.76	4.07	57.6	2.8	15.1	15.0	5.6
4.5	1.33	6.8	0.12	5.4	0.8	1.12	12.91	3.67	58.1	4.3	11.5	6.4	4.5
4.2	1.73	10.3	0.67	7.0	0.3	1.51	16.24	4.97	64.2	6.3	55.8	5.2	4.3
4.5	0.73	5.7	0.07	6.1	0.4	1.12	12.34	4.04	58.6	4.7	42.4	11.7	6.0
8.0	0.83	2.1	-0.09	5.8	0.2	1.29	8.25	4.03	67.2	7.1	65.4	1.5	7.7
5.1	2.01	13.0	-0.01	6.4	0.5	1.27	12.66	3.31	55.0	5.4	52.5	10.3	5.1
9.1	0.00	0.0	0.06	8.9	1.2	1.95	12.61	4.57	56.1	4.5	30.2	8.7	9.9
8.0	0.12	0.4	0.78	9.2	0.5	1.70	8.22	4.67	51.1	4.1	33.7	12.3	8.0
4.0	0.90	6.2	0.83	6.6	0.5	1.34	15.59	4.77	63.3	5.2	45.7	9.7	4.5
6.6	2.55	5.3	-0.36	10.0	0.9	2.53	8.97	5.23	45.4	1.0	8.6	30.5	8.6
5.4	0.94	4.9	-0.10	4.2	0.2	0.80	7.74	3.73	68.8	5.8	68.6	10.6	3.2
5.2	0.53	3.8	0.03	8.2	0.3	1.75	16.99	4.85	66.2	2.1	17.1	18.9	5.9
5.1	1.44	9.9	-0.01	9.3	1.1	2.07	20.05	4.07	56.5	3.3	33.1	16.1	8.1
3.4	2.40	17.5	0.06	8.7	2.5	3.22	32.44	5.41	42.4	1.3	29.3	35.3	6.0
4.6	3.47	12.9	0.02	4.0	0.4	0.47	3.11	3.79	77.5	5.1	29.2	4.7	6.6
7.1	0.28	1.3	0.17	6.7	0.3	1.76	16.42	3.73	52.2	6.4	75.6	8.3	5.4
1.0	2.75	24.3	0.62	3.4	0.0	0.34	4.71	5.02	51.9	1.2	13.4	28.8	0.7
6.9	0.21	1.2	0.61	1.0	2.8	0.07	0.69	2.69	81.6	1.1	14.5	31.7	5.0
5.1	0.97	5.3	0.02	5.6	7.4	0.98	9.48	3.60	59.4	4.0	52.9	21.4	7.5
8.6	0.00	0.0	0.29	5.0	0.1	0.94	7.48	3.65	67.3	3.1	45.3	20.6	5.3
4.8	0.73	3.9	0.07	7.1	7.2	1.27	10.30	4.99	65.8	7.1	125.6	12.0	7.0
6.9	1.33	2.9	-0.10	4.7	0.1	0.52	5.11	3.86	75.6	6.8	66.3	4.0	3.0
7.1	2.74	4.9	0.83	4.6	1.2	1.32	11.28	3.07	68.3	3.5	40.9	17.5	7.0
4.4	1.07	7.0	1.35	3.8	0.1	0.43	4.07	5.06	79.9	4.3	59.5	16.5	3.4
8.2	0.00	0.0	0.01	0.4	0.0	-0.25	-3.24	4.18	106.3	4.6	71.2	15.5	0.9
6.9	0.63	2.9	-0.08	4.1	0.7	1.06	11.00	3.88	73.3	4.2	55.3	18.0	4.8
8.4	0.10	0.4	0.01	6.6	0.4	1.16	7.82	3.87	58.1	6.3	51.8	3.7	8.1
5.1	1.42	8.9	0.11	4.8	1.3	0.84	10.97	2.93	62.9	7.6	130.0	8.8	3.8
7.3	0.12	0.6	0.11	6.6	0.8	1.53	13.21	4.30	68.1	6.8	76.3	7.1	6.8
9.3	0.00	0.0	0.00	6.0	413.5	0.98	13.59	1.25	75.2	5.1	213.0	81.8	5.4
5.5	1.02	9.7	-0.18	5.2	0.4	1.11	14.33	3.94	57.0	2.4	10.3	16.5	4.3
1.4	2.25	17.9	0.12	7.3	0.2	1.26	12.74	3.78	46.9	1.0	25.7	37.1	4.2
5.9	1.16	6.9	0.14	7.2	0.6	1.24	13.92	4.29	52.3	4.1	19.6	8.4	5.8
8.5	0.11	0.5	-0.01	9.7	0.6	1.71	11.40	4.87	49.2	4.3	28.7	9.4	9.5
2.9	1.92	16.1	0.33	7.2	0.3	2.03	23.70	4.65	63.5	4.6	26.5	6.8	2.3
6.9	1.26	7.9	0.00	4.5	0.4	0.58	5.03	3.06	70.1	3.0	3.6	12.9	6.4
5.3	0.11	0.6	1.10	0.0	-0.8	-2.34	-16.60	3.19	146.7	1.7	19.3	22.6	4.4
7.1	0.15	0.9	0.36	10.0	2.8	5.62	44.70	9.38	34.0	1.1	15.1	30.8	8.1
4.7	0.49	2.9	-0.21	9.8	0.5	2.45	17.94	4.87	46.0	0.8	17.7	41.3	7.8
7.1	0.07	0.5	0.00	10.0	0.8	3.21	22.70	5.05	29.4	0.5	4.6	43.1	8.4
5.4	0.48	3.1	0.08	10.0	16.3	3.83	31.28	6.78	35.7	0.3	2.7	64.0	8.6
7.4	0.00	0.0	0.01	10.0	0.5	2.83	21.85	5.02	37.3	0.9	20.3	39.2	7.9
2.9	3.17	17.0	0.55	0.8	-0.1	-0.34	-3.14	3.89	101.6	5.5	106.8	17.3	2.2
9.0	0.00	0.0	0.00	0.0	-0.3	-1.34	-5.99	3.23	114.5	5.7	37.1	4.3	0.0
4.3	1.27	10.7	0.05	3.8	0.4	0.42	4.19	3.16	77.4	1.3	14.8	27.4	5.6
3.7	1.32	11.2	1.17	5.3	0.2	1.26	14.86	4.88	64.8	2.6	44.9	28.9	3.5
4.5	1.18	8.0	0.00	7.5	1.2	1.16	11.83	4.01	61.8	1.8	19.0	20.7	7.0
8.5	0.04	0.2	-0.01	10.0	1.6	2.11	23.57	4.58	46.2	3.3	19.1	12.8	7.5
3.2	2.33	13.3	0.10	2.0	-1.4	-0.32	-3.85	1.70	119.6	3.7	74.7	30.5	3.9
5.4	0.91	7.6	-0.03	9.5	3.0	1.54	19.96	3.50	38.1	7.6	182.4	13.2	6.3

Name	City	State	Weiss Safety Rating	2003 Weiss Safety Rating	2002 Weiss Safety Rating	Total Assets ($Mil)	One Year Asset Growth	Commercial Loans	Consumer Loans	Home Mortgages	Securities	Capitalization Index	Leverage Ratio	Risk-based Capital Ratio
▼ STERLING BK	LANTANA	FL	C+	NR	NR	213.4	N/A	3.5	0.6	16.1	6.4	5.0	8.5	11.0
▲ STERLING BK	MT LAUREL	NJ	C-	D+	D-	283.7	25.30	9.5	16.9	6.8	26.0	5.3	7.3	11.3
▲ STERLING BK	HOUSTON	TX	B+	B	C+	3,085.6	-10.38	19.9	2.6	5.0	16.3	8.7	10.1	15.3
STERLING BK	BARRON	WI	C+	B-	C+	149.1	-0.54	4.7	1.8	24.7	25.5	6.5	8.5	14.1
STERLING FEDERAL BK FSB	STERLING	IL	C+	C+	C+	405.4	-9.35	0.2	4.5	25.7	37.8	7.7	9.4	18.4
STERLING NB	NEW YORK	NY	B	B	B	1,719.3	13.35	29.7	0.9	7.1	39.8	4.7	6.8	12.2
STERLING SAVINGS BANK	SPOKANE	WA	B-	B-	B-	6,103.9	52.77	19.2	3.0	14.9	30.9	4.7	6.7	10.9
STERLING ST BK	AUSTIN	MN	C-	C-	D+	276.2	-9.66	12.4	3.1	12.8	11.3	4.3	8.0	10.6
STERLINGSOUTH B&TC	GREENSBORO	NC	D-	D-	D-	106.0	19.72	13.0	4.5	7.2	11.3	9.3	11.0	14.4
STEUBEN TRUST CO	HORNELL	NY	C	C+	C+	290.7	-2.03	9.6	11.6	23.3	29.3	5.5	7.5	14.0
▲ STEWARDSON NB	STEWARDSON	IL	C+	C-	C-	44.1	-1.37	9.9	3.5	23.0	28.6	8.7	10.2	17.9
▼ STILLMAN BANCCORP N.A.	STILLMAN VALLEY	IL	B+	A-	B	277.0	-1.22	6.6	2.1	8.2	25.8	10.0	11.7	19.3
STILLWATER NB&TC	STILLWATER	OK	B-	B-	B	1,746.7	15.20	19.7	17.7	3.8	11.6	5.6	8.5	11.4
STISSING NB OF PINE PLAINS	PINE PLAINS	NY	C-	C	C+	40.9	4.78	1.9	3.2	24.6	37.2	5.6	7.6	17.2
▲ STOCK EXCHANGE BK	CALDWELL	KS	B-	C+	C+	28.6	-2.33	4.0	5.9	4.2	38.6	10.0	11.3	20.6
STOCK EXCHANGE BK	WOODWARD	OK	A	A	A	126.0	6.47	7.6	4.8	5.7	46.8	10.0	15.5	32.1
▼ STOCK GROWERS BK	NAPOLEON	ND	C+	B-	B-	34.8	0.64	3.2	2.7	1.8	32.9	8.7	10.1	15.9
▲ STOCK YARDS B&TC	LOUISVILLE	KY	A	A-	B+	1,122.3	3.06	14.4	3.5	18.4	13.5	9.0	10.3	14.3
STOCKGROWERS ST BK	MAPLE HILL	KS	C-	C-	D-	57.3	10.42	7.0	3.3	16.4	39.7	5.5	7.5	14.0
▲ STOCKGROWERS STATE	ASHLAND	KS	C-	D+	D+	103.5	0.17	9.1	2.3	2.6	29.5	9.1	10.4	15.1
STOCKMAN BK OF MT	MILES CITY	MT	C+	C	C-	935.4	9.30	9.5	3.5	3.9	16.1	4.4	7.8	10.7
▲ STOCKMANS BANK	ALTUS	OK	E+	E-	E-	99.7	6.25	9.9	8.0	7.9	0.8	5.1	7.7	11.1
STOCKMANS BK	ELK GROVE	CA	B	B	B	282.7	17.55	8.3	0.5	2.9	9.4	6.3	9.1	12.0
STOCKMENS BK	KINGMAN	AZ	C+	C+	C+	866.3	20.11	4.6	0.8	3.2	39.8	3.0	6.1	10.0
▲ STOCKMENS BK	CASCADE	MT	C+	C	C+	24.3	8.40	9.3	5.9	6.4	30.6	10.0	13.8	19.9
STOCKMENS NB IN COTULLA	COTULLA	TX	B+	B+	B+	33.8	0.80	10.4	6.7	4.6	36.9	10.0	11.6	22.3
▼ STOCKTON NB	STOCKTON	KS	C-	B-	B-	59.8	-1.34	15.8	3.8	6.5	1.5	9.1	11.8	14.2
▼ STONE CITY BK OF BEDFORD	BEDFORD	IN	C-	C	C-	58.1	9.58	15.2	3.7	20.2	13.6	6.1	8.1	12.2
STONE CTY NB	CRANE	MO	B-	B-	B	73.8	3.75	6.8	7.4	17.3	45.8	7.0	9.0	18.5
▼ STONEBRIDGE BK	W CHESTER	PA	D-	D+	C-	365.3	35.82	7.7	0.6	41.4	25.8	3.5	6.4	10.3
▲ STONEHAM CO-OP BK	STONEHAM	MA	B-	C+	C+	350.3	7.45	0.0	0.5	50.7	14.9	5.8	7.8	12.6
STONEHAM SVGS BK	STONEHAM	MA	B	B-	B-	301.3	-6.07	3.9	0.1	25.8	26.2	7.7	9.5	13.8
▲ STOUGHTON CO-OP BK	STOUGHTON	MA	C	C-	D+	75.7	3.01	0.0	2.8	60.1	25.4	6.7	8.7	18.4
STRASBURG ST BK	STRASBURG	ND	C+	C+	C+	41.7	-3.99	5.2	1.7	0.6	33.2	7.5	10.2	12.9
▲ STRASBURG SVG	STRASBURG	OH	A-	B+	B+	39.1	0.84	0.0	4.9	68.5	0.0	10.0	15.1	26.7
STRATA BK	MEDWAY	MA	C-	C-	D+	318.4	6.20	6.6	0.4	43.8	17.8	5.0	7.3	11.0
▼ STRATEGIC CAP BK	CHAMPAIGN	IL	C+	B-	B+	190.4	24.18	25.9	2.0	2.8	22.9	4.5	7.2	10.7
▲ STRATFORD ST BK	STRATFORD	WI	B+	B	B	98.4	3.20	5.5	3.0	8.1	41.2	10.0	12.2	20.2
STREATOR HOME B&LA	STREATOR	IL	A	A	A	124.5	1.67	0.0	1.8	45.5	48.3	10.0	18.9	51.6
STROUD NB	STROUD	OK	C+	C+	C+	40.3	-1.18	9.9	7.4	24.7	30.4	9.8	10.8	18.2
STURDY SVGS BK	STONE HARBOR	NJ	B	B	A-	427.5	9.00	2.1	0.2	33.6	10.9	9.7	10.8	15.9
STURGIS B&TC	STURGIS	MI	C-	C	C	313.4	6.33	3.8	3.0	29.7	9.0	4.0	7.2	10.5
▲ STUTSMAN COUNTY ST BK	JAMESTOWN	ND	B	B-	C+	128.4	5.65	13.3	15.3	12.1	21.5	6.9	8.9	12.8
▲ SUBURBAN B&TC	ELMHURST	IL	D+	D-	D-	521.9	3.54	6.5	0.1	3.2	31.6	6.2	8.2	12.4
SUBURBAN BK BARRINGTON	BARRINGTON	IL	B-	B-	B	266.3	-3.42	1.7	47.0	11.5	8.3	5.6	9.4	11.5
▼ SUBURBAN FSB	CROFTON	MD	D	D+	C-	262.6	2.25	0.0	1.1	52.2	4.8	3.5	6.3	10.3
▲ SUFFOLK CTY NB OF	RIVERHEAD	NY	B+	B	B+	1,422.2	3.87	11.5	13.6	8.1	27.3	5.2	7.2	11.4
SUFFOLKFIRST BK	SUFFOLK	VA	D	D	NR	59.6	120.68	3.8	2.4	16.4	31.0	10.0	16.2	28.3
SUGAR RIVER SVGS BK	NEWPORT	NH	A	A	A	187.0	2.58	0.5	3.4	51.2	22.4	10.0	13.6	22.2
▲ SULPHUR COMMUNITY BK	SULPHUR	OK	C+	C	C	52.3	1.42	8.0	10.0	5.9	38.1	7.6	9.4	17.5
▲ SUMITOMO TR & BKG CO USA	HOBOKEN	NJ	A+	A	A+	357.8	-1.78	0.0	0.0	0.0	16.1	10.0	18.7	81.3
SUMMIT BK	ARKADELPHIA	AR	B-	B-	C	598.4	9.58	10.3	8.9	19.4	18.4	6.6	8.6	12.6
SUMMIT BK	PRESCOTT	AZ	C-	C-	D+	31.7	34.57	8.3	1.3	0.0	0.0	10.0	24.9	29.3
SUMMIT BK	OAKLAND	CA	B+	B+	B+	149.0	9.58	26.5	1.6	1.8	1.0	6.5	9.6	12.1
SUMMIT BK	TULSA	OK	D-	D-	D	65.6	50.98	31.3	1.6	16.4	7.0	4.7	8.5	10.9
SUMMIT BK	EUGENE	OR	D	NR	NR	15.1	N/A	3.6	1.0	1.1	44.8	10.0	70.9	147.3
SUMMIT BK NA	FORT WORTH	TX	B+	B+	B	969.3	31.18	25.6	4.4	7.9	21.5	5.8	8.2	11.6
SUMMIT COMMUNITY BK	E LANSING	MI	D	D	C-	62.9	138.81	2.6	3.7	62.1	3.0	10.0	11.6	17.3
SUMMIT COMMUNITY BK	MOOREFIELD	WV	B-	B-	C+	397.8	11.72	5.9	6.7	28.3	24.4	4.6	6.9	10.8
SUMMIT FSB	SUMMIT	NJ	C-	C-	C-	161.3	0.65	0.0	0.1	14.4	60.6	8.0	9.6	30.0
SUMMIT NB	ATLANTA	GA	B-	B-	C+	505.6	20.00	13.8	0.2	1.3	26.9	6.2	8.2	13.2
▲ SUMMIT NB	GREENVILLE	SC	B	B-	B-	331.9	3.57	10.3	1.8	12.7	19.5	6.9	8.9	13.0
▲ SUMMIT ST BK	SANTA ROSA	CA	B	B-	B-	238.6	3.25	8.7	0.3	14.9	5.5	6.9	9.0	12.5
SUMNER NB OF SHELDON	SHELDON	IL	C+	C+	C-	12.1	16.96	9.5	13.4	29.7	15.9	10.0	11.2	18.1

Asset Quality Index	Non-Performing Loans as a % of Total Loans	as a % of Capital	Net Charge-offs Avg Loans	Profitability Index	Net Income ($Mil)	Return on Assets (R.O.A.)	Return on Equity (R.O.E.)	Net Interest Spread	Overhead Efficiency Ratio	Liquidity Index	Liquidity Ratio	Hot Money Ratio	Stability Index
2.9	0.98	9.6	0.06	9.8	1.6	2.27	21.02	4.21	53.7	1.3	12.4	26.1	2.2
7.4	0.16	1.4	0.00	2.5	0.4	0.32	4.35	3.65	87.0	3.7	16.5	10.5	2.1
5.4	0.64	3.5	0.91	6.8	14.9	0.96	8.17	4.91	66.4	4.4	53.8	18.4	7.5
2.7	2.90	20.9	0.02	6.9	1.2	1.60	19.29	4.06	60.0	4.5	28.9	8.5	5.9
4.6	1.07	4.7	0.22	4.1	1.4	0.66	6.45	3.29	74.3	1.7	13.0	20.7	5.3
8.6	0.27	1.9	0.57	9.9	13.9	1.64	24.20	4.80	57.1	1.9	18.3	21.5	4.9
6.3	0.29	2.6	0.16	6.4	28.9	1.04	12.29	3.84	59.4	0.6	4.0	40.2	6.8
5.2	0.64	5.5	0.51	3.2	0.4	0.28	3.63	4.53	94.4	3.3	26.2	14.1	3.0
8.2	0.00	0.0	0.01	0.6	0.0	0.06	0.64	2.73	93.4	2.4	34.1	22.5	0.0
2.8	2.38	16.3	0.18	4.3	1.1	0.73	8.99	4.48	75.4	4.8	18.2	3.6	4.2
8.6	0.27	1.5	0.00	3.6	0.2	0.99	9.56	2.92	71.6	3.5	37.8	16.7	4.7
7.1	0.71	3.1	-0.02	4.9	1.2	0.89	7.27	3.87	76.2	5.0	91.9	18.8	7.9
3.9	1.11	10.0	0.32	7.4	10.6	1.28	14.73	4.31	49.1	0.9	7.3	32.1	6.9
9.1	0.35	2.1	-0.04	3.7	0.1	0.67	8.58	3.69	85.4	5.8	35.0	2.3	3.5
8.6	0.43	1.7	-0.02	3.7	0.1	0.70	6.13	3.79	78.4	4.0	77.4	22.1	4.5
8.4	1.42	3.3	0.13	6.5	0.7	1.17	7.60	4.04	63.8	4.5	33.5	10.2	8.3
3.6	1.91	10.3	0.03	8.2	0.4	1.96	19.56	4.25	42.8	5.8	53.7	7.8	5.3
7.6	0.39	2.7	0.11	9.7	9.7	1.74	16.96	4.43	55.7	4.1	21.9	10.4	8.6
5.4	0.98	5.8	-0.07	6.5	0.4	1.31	15.01	4.14	55.2	3.6	8.9	10.4	3.2
1.3	2.97	16.3	1.41	2.6	0.2	0.34	3.18	4.18	72.0	1.7	12.0	20.6	4.5
3.7	1.33	10.3	0.11	7.8	9.5	2.08	22.97	4.14	53.2	5.6	56.3	11.3	7.3
0.2	2.00	20.3	0.65	5.4	0.7	1.39	18.71	5.49	66.4	2.1	25.1	19.8	1.6
5.0	0.61	4.4	0.00	10.0	3.5	2.55	28.50	4.59	42.8	4.0	56.8	19.4	6.9
7.2	0.27	2.2	0.05	6.6	4.5	1.12	17.96	4.29	65.0	6.5	64.4	7.5	4.0
8.1	1.11	3.5	0.12	5.3	0.2	1.43	10.76	4.46	71.5	5.5	101.8	15.4	4.7
8.6	0.07	0.3	-0.33	9.7	0.4	2.26	19.61	4.18	57.3	4.8	79.9	17.4	6.4
1.6	3.69	25.5	0.01	8.5	0.6	1.95	16.92	4.57	54.2	1.9	28.3	25.1	6.5
4.5	1.27	9.7	0.29	2.7	0.1	0.23	2.57	4.83	88.4	4.1	33.0	12.3	4.1
7.2	0.51	2.7	0.24	6.2	0.6	1.53	16.68	4.11	60.8	4.4	28.1	8.5	4.8
5.5	0.58	7.0	0.27	2.7	0.7	0.42	7.74	2.63	70.1	1.7	14.1	21.3	1.0
9.4	0.13	1.2	0.01	4.1	0.9	0.50	6.44	3.72	85.1	4.3	25.6	8.1	3.9
8.6	0.17	1.0	0.00	4.9	1.4	0.89	8.58	3.83	72.1	4.4	37.3	12.0	5.7
9.0	0.32	2.4	-0.09	3.1	0.2	0.42	4.85	3.55	80.0	5.0	57.4	12.7	4.0
4.1	1.08	5.9	0.63	5.8	0.2	1.09	10.79	4.46	61.2	4.4	18.7	6.8	4.1
6.9	1.20	6.8	0.01	9.4	0.4	2.06	13.81	4.90	54.8	6.9	147.5	13.8	8.4
9.4	0.00	0.0	0.00	3.9	0.9	0.60	8.14	3.67	76.5	3.7	26.2	11.7	2.6
4.4	1.81	8.4	0.00	2.8	-0.9	-0.93	-10.20	0.57	96.6	0.4	6.1	57.7	7.0
5.4	3.14	12.2	0.95	5.2	0.6	1.21	10.26	3.48	51.4	1.0	21.5	33.7	6.2
8.5	0.61	1.5	0.13	7.7	0.8	1.35	6.82	3.09	37.8	3.4	17.6	12.2	8.6
3.8	2.91	15.7	0.28	5.7	0.3	1.22	11.18	5.28	76.1	3.3	20.7	13.3	5.1
6.5	0.56	3.7	0.00	4.5	1.2	0.58	5.19	3.95	76.7	5.0	23.7	3.0	6.6
2.1	2.26	18.0	0.23	4.1	0.9	0.61	6.52	3.28	73.0	3.5	29.3	14.1	5.2
6.1	0.34	1.9	0.06	4.8	0.5	0.84	7.15	4.05	61.2	3.1	16.6	13.5	6.1
2.2	1.37	6.1	1.14	6.0	3.6	1.43	11.01	3.95	57.2	4.7	92.4	21.4	8.1
5.7	0.02	0.2	0.20	6.5	1.3	0.91	10.12	3.51	58.9	7.0	89.3	8.0	6.7
7.2	0.28	4.0	0.09	2.6	0.7	0.51	7.99	3.53	78.9	0.5	3.3	41.5	2.3
6.0	0.97	7.3	0.05	9.7	10.0	1.48	19.71	4.84	52.0	7.4	70.5	4.0	8.1
9.2	0.00	0.0	0.01	0.0	-0.1	-0.44	-2.51	2.87	115.3	5.2	86.0	16.0	0.0
8.0	0.65	3.3	0.02	6.4	1.0	1.06	8.11	4.53	69.1	3.9	22.5	10.1	7.7
5.4	0.47	2.8	0.08	6.4	0.3	1.30	14.50	5.08	71.9	2.1	11.5	18.4	3.5
10.0	0.00	0.0	0.00	8.6	3.1	1.95	7.21	0.95	81.6	10.0	509.4	0.0	9.3
5.9	0.47	3.5	0.05	5.2	3.3	1.13	13.14	4.23	61.0	1.8	17.7	20.1	5.3
7.4	0.00	0.0	0.00	0.0	-0.3	-2.17	-11.96	3.95	138.6	8.5	166.5	6.3	1.4
6.6	0.47	3.4	0.04	6.7	0.7	0.88	9.69	5.34	69.9	3.8	56.9	20.1	6.2
5.3	1.33	11.9	0.00	1.5	0.1	0.41	4.69	3.10	82.1	2.8	40.6	23.0	0.0
9.6	0.00	0.0	0.00	0.0	-0.7	-13.81	-18.40	1.38	976.0	7.8	132.3	6.4	0.0
6.5	0.42	3.1	0.07	7.9	5.2	1.19	14.06	4.28	56.7	4.0	25.5	10.3	6.4
8.8	0.00	0.0	0.00	0.2	-0.1	-0.37	-2.82	3.04	87.1	2.1	4.4	17.5	0.0
7.1	0.29	2.7	0.11	8.9	2.8	1.45	20.53	3.93	44.7	1.7	9.2	20.2	5.4
9.8	0.00	0.0	0.00	1.7	0.1	0.08	0.83	2.55	95.1	2.2	24.8	18.8	5.0
7.4	0.04	0.3	0.21	6.5	2.9	1.19	13.88	4.17	56.9	0.9	15.0	33.1	4.3
8.2	0.08	0.6	-0.10	6.2	2.0	1.19	14.19	3.62	55.7	2.7	35.9	20.1	5.0
6.3	0.20	1.3	0.11	6.7	1.2	1.05	10.17	4.35	52.7	5.0	64.0	15.7	6.3
3.8	2.96	17.0	-0.05	7.8	0.1	2.01	18.68	5.12	62.3	7.3	124.1	8.5	5.3

Name	City	State	Weiss Safety Rating	2003 Weiss Safety Rating	2002 Weiss Safety Rating	Total Assets ($Mil)	One Year Asset Growth	Asset Mix (As a % of Total Assets)				Capitalization Index	Leverage Ratio	Risk-based Capital Ratio
								Commercial Loans	Consumer Loans	Home Mortgages	Securities			
SUMTER B&TC	AMERICUS	GA	B	B	B	166.6	-3.98	16.1	4.5	12.6	15.6	4.7	8.1	10.9
▲ SUMTER NB	SUMTER	SC	B	C+	B-	128.3	10.34	36.3	7.5	18.1	2.9	6.3	9.3	12.0
▼ SUN COUNTRY BK	UPLAND	CA	C+	B	B	327.1	72.91	12.5	1.6	3.6	16.7	5.1	7.5	11.1
SUN NB	VINELAND	NJ	C+	C+	C	2,576.6	15.68	10.0	1.4	4.1	31.4	4.6	7.1	10.8
▼ SUN SOCIETY BK	ELLINGTON	MO	B	A-	E	258.1	1080.63	9.6	4.1	15.2	25.3	10.0	12.6	18.7
SUN WEST BK	LAS VEGAS	NV	B	B-	C+	258.6	23.22	25.8	1.8	0.0	5.9	6.6	8.9	12.2
SUNBANK	LEWISBURG	PA	C+	C+	B-	1,053.7	2.90	12.9	9.9	11.9	20.5	5.1	7.6	11.1
SUNBANK NA	MURRELLS INLET	SC	D-	D-	D	77.8	54.20	26.6	5.1	8.9	5.9	7.2	10.8	12.7
▼ SUNCOAST BK	SARASOTA	FL	D	D+	D-	91.2	33.44	4.0	3.2	6.9	10.9	2.9	8.1	9.9
▼ SUNDANCE ST BK	SUNDANCE	WY	C-	C	C	85.4	7.13	14.7	9.0	3.2	36.4	6.4	8.4	13.8
SUNDOWN ST BK	SUNDOWN	TX	D+	C-	C-	60.4	9.92	12.8	5.5	7.8	25.6	5.4	8.1	11.3
▲ SUNFIRST BANK	ST GEORGE	UT	B-	C+	D-	83.6	42.96	16.2	5.5	9.3	8.9	8.3	10.1	13.5
SUNFLOWER BK NA	SALINA	KS	C+	C+	B-	1,034.0	5.26	11.2	4.4	17.8	24.3	6.9	8.9	13.8
SUNMARK CMNTY BK	HAWKINSVILLE	GA	C	C-	C	138.1	-1.89	8.1	9.2	34.6	9.0	7.6	9.4	13.8
▲ SUNNYSIDE FS&LA OF	IRVINGTON	NY	C+	C	C-	105.2	1.11	0.0	0.3	16.3	72.9	5.2	7.2	29.6
SUNRISE BK ALBUQUERQUE	ALBUQUERQUE	NM	C	C	C	76.0	27.50	10.8	0.8	8.0	0.1	4.0	7.5	10.5
SUNRISE BK AZ	PHOENIX	AZ	C	C	C	133.3	41.40	6.3	0.9	2.6	0.0	3.6	8.6	10.3
SUNRISE BK DAKOTA	ONIDA	SD	C-	D+	D+	25.0	9.68	5.5	3.7	3.3	26.9	8.3	9.9	18.0
SUNRISE BK SAN DIEGO	SAN DIEGO	CA	C	C	C	72.2	24.44	4.9	0.9	1.0	0.0	10.0	12.5	15.1
SUNSET BK & SVG	WAUKESHA	WI	C	C	D+	106.9	23.81	15.0	0.7	32.5	10.2	4.3	7.5	10.7
SUNSHINE ST COMMUNITY BK	PORT ORANGE	FL	B-	B-	B-	91.5	30.84	7.2	3.7	19.4	24.4	5.7	7.7	11.8
▲ SUNSHINE STATE FS&LA	PLANT CITY	FL	B	B-	B-	183.9	2.72	8.4	1.1	38.1	15.0	10.0	11.3	19.3
▲ SUNSOUTH BK	DOTHAN	AL	C-	D+	D-	82.8	24.23	17.7	5.3	22.3	8.4	6.1	9.5	11.9
SUNSTATE BK	CASA GRANDE	AZ	C	B-	C+	150.0	23.59	15.0	2.0	6.6	31.0	6.7	8.7	14.5
▲ SUNTRUST BANCARD NA	ORLANDO	FL	B+	B	B	191.0	-2.89	78.4	0.8	0.0	0.1	10.0	14.9	15.9
SUNTRUST BK	ATLANTA	GA	B	B	B	125,880.6	6.01	16.0	10.1	19.4	18.3	5.3	7.6	11.2
SUNWEST BK	TUSTIN	CA	A-	A-	B	303.4	6.41	18.6	1.8	0.5	33.1	9.1	10.8	14.3
SUPERIOR NB	SUPERIOR	WI	B	B	B	32.5	5.29	3.6	2.8	29.7	50.3	10.0	12.1	27.1
SUPERIOR NB&TC	HANCOCK	MI	B-	B-	B	291.5	3.18	9.1	7.0	29.0	30.7	5.7	7.7	13.7
SUPERIOR SVG OF NEW	BRANFORD	CT	B	B	B-	446.8	-11.33	0.0	11.5	36.8	23.2	5.6	7.6	19.0
SUPERIOR SVGS BK	SUPERIOR	WI	A-	A-	B+	55.1	0.46	1.2	3.8	56.3	13.3	10.0	15.4	29.9
▲ SURETY BK	DE LAND	FL	B-	C	D	72.9	-1.34	0.7	0.3	11.0	18.6	10.0	11.8	17.1
▲ SURETY BK NA	FORT WORTH	TX	E+	E-	E+	58.4	-40.70	21.3	9.2	23.8	0.0	10.0	14.0	18.6
SURREY B&T	MT AIRY	NC	C+	C+	C+	154.1	32.98	46.4	4.8	17.3	1.9	3.6	7.8	10.3
SUSQUEHANNA BK	BALTIMORE	MD	C+	C+	B-	1,387.1	11.82	5.9	4.6	23.7	12.7	4.8	6.8	10.9
SUSQUEHANNA PATRIOT BK	MARLTON	NJ	B-	B-	B-	2,130.6	165.30	7.2	1.6	13.5	24.4	4.1	12.6	10.6
SUSSEX BK	FRANKLIN	NJ	C	C-	D-	250.6	6.56	5.7	0.6	14.1	29.8	5.0	7.0	11.7
▲ SUTTON BK	ATTICA	OH	C+	D+	C-	263.1	18.51	7.7	6.4	9.9	22.4	6.2	8.2	12.7
SUTTON ST BK	SUTTON	NE	C	C	C	21.0	7.92	7.4	1.6	7.4	12.5	8.9	11.1	14.1
SWEDISH AMERICAN ST BK	COURTLAND	KS	C-	C-	C-	28.6	-0.76	9.4	5.7	11.3	18.7	7.4	9.3	14.6
SWEET WATER ST BK	SWEET WATER	AL	B	B+	A-	53.5	-3.76	15.7	10.7	12.8	14.6	6.6	8.6	12.3
SWINEFORD NB	MIDDLEBURG	PA	B	B	B+	263.8	-4.63	4.9	10.6	24.4	32.8	4.5	6.9	11.5
SWISHER T&SB	SWISHER	IA	B	B	B	35.2	0.94	4.2	6.2	33.4	37.1	10.0	12.4	17.6
SYCAMORE NB	CINCINNATI	OH	D	D	D-	40.8	-7.11	15.5	16.9	10.0	5.6	5.7	8.9	11.5
SYKESVILLE FSA	SYKESVILLE	MD	D+	D+	C-	82.5	18.92	0.0	0.5	46.9	31.8	3.9	5.9	12.5
▲ SYNERGY BANK	CRANFORD	NJ	C+	C	C	788.0	40.41	1.1	15.7	27.2	33.2	10.0	11.0	18.7
SYNERGY BK	HOUMA	LA	B	B	B	96.4	11.89	18.8	4.0	13.1	16.6	7.4	9.3	13.8
▲ SYNERGY BK SSB	WACO	TX	D-	E+	E-	65.2	-39.38	8.1	1.5	36.7	4.6	6.7	8.7	13.1
SYNOVUS BK OF	JACKSONVILLE	FL	B	NR	NR	24.8	N/A	15.4	0.5	2.0	0.0	10.0	82.6	33.9
▲ SYRINGA BK	BOISE	ID	D+	D-	D+	120.7	43.89	15.7	9.0	5.8	5.4	7.1	10.1	12.6
▲ SYSTEMATIC S&LA	SPRINGFIELD	MO	B	B-	B-	51.1	-3.99	0.0	0.1	75.1	0.0	10.0	13.4	25.4
▲ T. ROWE PRICE SVGS BK	BALTIMORE	MD	C-	D+	D+	105.2	5.08	0.0	0.0	0.0	99.2	10.0	13.8	52.9
TABLE GROVE ST BK	TABLE GROVE	IL	B-	B-	B	38.4	12.73	1.9	3.7	8.0	50.9	10.0	11.9	25.6
▼ TALBOT BK OF EASTON MD	EASTON	MD	A-	A	A	437.7	8.37	10.9	2.1	17.1	14.8	8.2	10.3	13.5
▲ TALBOT ST BK	WOODLAND	GA	C+	C	C-	76.5	13.13	1.4	0.8	69.5	18.3	6.2	8.2	17.2
TALBOTS CLASSICS NB	LINCOLN	RI	B	B	C+	9.9	3.37	0.0	0.0	0.0	2.4	10.0	36.1	125.0
TALLAHASSEE ST BK	TALLAHASSEE	FL	B-	B-	B	236.1	10.76	13.5	4.0	10.9	5.0	3.3	9.5	10.2
TALLAHATCHIE COUNTY BK	CHARLESTON	MS	C+	C+	C+	34.3	6.23	3.3	9.4	10.6	39.3	9.6	10.8	22.0
TAMA STATE BANK	MARSHALLTOWN	IA	C-	C-	C-	98.0	7.08	4.1	3.5	33.3	24.9	5.1	7.1	13.4
TAMALPAIS BANK	SAN RAFAEL	CA	B-	C+	C+	406.6	42.28	2.7	0.7	2.3	21.4	5.0	7.9	11.0
TAMPA ST BK	TAMPA	KS	B	B	B	36.7	-0.55	11.4	7.8	27.7	9.6	10.0	11.8	17.2
TARBORO SVG BK SSB	TARBORO	NC	B	B	B-	31.6	-12.18	0.0	0.3	58.2	8.3	10.0	14.4	21.8
TARPON COAST NB	PORT CHARLOTTE	FL	C	C	D	129.9	12.20	3.7	3.1	33.8	13.5	5.3	7.9	11.2
▲ TATTNALL BK	REIDSVILLE	GA	D-	E	E-	53.0	1.40	7.3	7.1	14.1	18.0	6.2	8.2	12.3

Asset Quality Index	Non-Performing Loans as a % of Total Loans	Non-Performing Loans as a % of Capital	Net Charge-offs Avg Loans	Profitability Index	Net Income ($Mil)	Return on Assets (R.O.A.)	Return on Equity (R.O.E.)	Net Interest Spread	Overhead Efficiency Ratio	Liquidity Index	Liquidity Ratio	Hot Money Ratio	Stability Index
6.5	0.50	4.4	0.09	9.2	1.2	1.44	17.54	4.32	54.8	1.7	12.6	20.3	6.8
5.6	0.42	3.7	0.22	8.9	0.9	1.50	17.35	4.04	43.2	2.7	37.9	22.3	5.3
2.7	1.18	6.5	0.01	6.1	1.7	1.20	10.25	5.08	74.3	4.6	28.0	7.4	5.2
4.2	1.49	8.5	0.04	4.0	9.5	0.73	7.80	3.68	73.2	6.7	58.5	6.6	6.3
8.4	0.04	0.2	0.07	6.9	2.4	2.71	22.34	5.95	49.5	2.5	14.6	16.2	2.6
4.4	1.25	9.4	-0.14	7.8	2.5	2.04	22.92	5.26	59.3	6.7	90.8	10.4	6.0
5.5	0.50	2.8	-0.03	3.5	3.6	0.68	6.52	2.99	75.1	4.7	26.4	9.9	7.9
7.9	0.00	0.0	-0.02	0.5	0.0	-0.01	-0.08	3.92	88.0	1.0	13.2	31.4	0.0
5.1	0.42	3.7	0.00	2.3	0.2	0.33	3.94	3.39	73.3	1.9	30.6	26.4	3.7
2.3	3.52	22.1	0.40	7.0	0.5	1.23	15.19	3.96	49.8	3.7	32.9	13.9	4.1
5.1	0.26	2.1	0.29	5.1	0.3	1.02	13.37	5.56	78.0	3.0	15.1	14.2	2.7
5.8	0.47	3.3	0.02	6.5	0.5	1.21	11.60	4.69	55.6	3.3	35.7	17.1	3.0
3.6	2.38	14.7	0.06	7.7	8.5	1.70	16.22	3.98	68.8	4.3	22.0	9.6	7.5
3.1	1.49	11.5	0.28	6.7	0.8	1.23	13.38	5.02	60.4	2.8	11.9	14.7	5.4
8.8	0.02	0.1	0.03	3.5	0.2	0.31	4.45	2.67	82.7	1.6	18.0	23.4	3.4
4.1	1.18	10.3	0.29	6.2	0.4	1.23	14.62	5.47	54.1	4.9	72.1	15.8	2.9
7.1	0.05	0.5	0.00	7.5	1.1	1.73	21.04	5.94	59.4	1.9	12.6	19.2	5.1
4.9	0.92	5.5	0.17	6.0	0.2	1.58	15.75	5.08	64.1	4.2	22.5	8.4	3.0
5.9	0.00	0.0	0.00	7.5	0.6	1.73	13.66	5.20	65.6	6.5	53.6	3.2	3.0
6.0	0.67	6.9	-0.01	3.8	0.2	0.48	6.22	4.28	81.0	2.8	19.6	15.5	3.6
8.6	0.00	0.0	0.07	5.0	0.5	1.12	14.21	4.09	71.3	4.7	33.6	9.3	1.9
8.1	0.20	1.2	0.35	4.1	0.5	0.55	4.82	4.01	73.9	2.4	41.0	29.9	6.7
8.0	0.12	1.0	0.00	4.2	0.3	0.88	11.06	3.82	72.6	2.3	34.4	24.8	4.0
8.5	0.18	1.2	-0.08	6.5	1.1	1.58	19.42	4.47	65.5	4.4	25.4	7.5	2.4
5.4	1.24	6.2	1.12	9.2	2.8	3.12	21.04	5.41	79.2	5.0	2.0	0.0	8.3
6.3	0.42	3.3	0.22	5.9	725.4	1.16	14.45	3.11	60.7	5.6	40.7	9.6	7.3
8.5	0.00	0.0	-0.02	7.3	1.3	0.88	7.89	5.60	71.8	5.2	37.7	7.8	6.9
5.4	3.66	12.3	0.00	5.8	0.2	1.24	10.36	4.10	72.0	4.7	27.6	6.9	6.4
6.1	0.57	4.2	0.13	6.7	1.8	1.22	16.19	3.89	56.7	5.0	41.1	10.0	5.2
8.4	0.01	0.1	0.08	6.1	2.2	0.95	13.21	2.23	22.0	7.8	1,361.5	13.6	5.6
6.7	1.36	5.8	0.00	9.6	0.4	1.38	9.09	4.81	55.1	6.5	104.1	11.6	7.1
7.1	0.00	0.0	0.00	8.4	0.9	2.37	19.28	4.35	44.3	4.8	91.2	18.5	7.9
3.7	1.72	8.4	3.96	2.7	0.4	1.06	8.30	5.37	74.9	1.7	20.9	23.4	3.6
6.6	0.26	2.2	0.14	8.2	1.1	1.46	17.79	4.23	57.3	4.3	51.3	16.5	5.0
7.6	0.25	2.4	0.05	4.2	5.0	0.75	9.06	2.87	66.5	4.0	6.0	7.8	4.1
5.5	0.54	2.1	0.13	6.4	7.1	1.08	10.35	3.45	56.7	3.9	10.7	9.1	5.5
5.2	0.99	6.7	0.04	4.1	0.9	0.71	8.84	4.12	78.1	5.2	32.3	5.3	3.2
6.0	0.24	1.8	0.22	5.4	1.3	1.00	11.48	4.02	70.2	0.6	5.0	35.9	4.4
6.6	0.43	2.6	0.14	5.1	0.1	1.21	11.17	4.41	74.6	4.0	44.7	13.6	4.2
3.3	2.32	16.5	0.46	4.5	0.1	0.80	8.85	4.73	71.6	2.8	38.4	22.1	3.3
3.7	1.14	8.8	0.08	6.3	0.3	1.17	13.87	4.76	62.9	2.4	31.7	21.4	6.0
5.9	0.36	3.0	0.10	9.5	2.2	1.56	23.25	3.83	52.5	4.4	4.6	4.8	6.6
8.9	0.47	1.9	0.00	4.2	0.1	0.78	6.22	3.86	74.7	6.7	54.3	1.6	5.7
6.0	0.19	1.6	0.35	3.2	0.1	0.30	3.44	4.77	84.8	5.1	37.1	7.9	2.4
8.5	0.00	0.0	0.00	4.3	0.2	0.55	9.52	2.18	57.6	3.2	61.3	27.2	2.0
7.5	0.09	0.5	0.08	4.3	1.9	0.53	5.19	3.29	68.7	1.0	2.4	28.3	4.6
8.3	0.09	0.6	-0.01	7.8	0.7	1.40	16.55	4.20	54.4	3.1	44.8	20.7	4.9
0.3	6.90	38.3	0.64	0.3	-0.2	-0.57	-4.84	7.11	102.7	0.8	21.5	48.0	2.0
7.0	0.00	0.0	0.00	0.0	-0.4	-4.04	-7.15	1.09	314.0	3.0	6.4	13.0	1.4
6.9	0.04	0.3	0.03	1.9	0.1	0.13	1.35	4.64	83.8	3.2	34.7	17.3	4.3
6.9	0.74	4.9	0.00	5.0	0.2	0.72	5.57	3.40	62.1	3.5	9.8	11.1	6.4
10.0	0.00	0.0	0.00	1.2	-0.1	-0.14	-1.01	0.61	130.7	0.5	7.8	52.8	1.2
5.4	2.52	9.2	0.08	3.7	0.2	0.78	6.44	4.30	73.7	3.7	4.5	9.2	4.7
6.7	0.50	3.6	0.22	8.8	2.9	1.32	12.68	3.84	45.6	2.6	25.0	16.7	7.8
3.7	2.57	24.1	0.07	6.3	0.6	1.60	19.55	6.33	76.1	3.1	12.8	13.1	4.4
10.0	0.00	0.0	0.00	9.5	0.5	10.22	30.57	0.57	76.4	5.0	N/A	0.0	0.1
4.2	0.41	3.6	0.39	10.0	2.6	2.25	25.13	5.29	29.0	1.0	10.1	29.9	7.1
7.5	0.22	0.7	0.24	4.2	0.1	0.79	7.58	4.19	73.1	4.2	42.1	14.3	3.7
7.7	0.29	2.7	-0.02	2.7	0.2	0.37	5.50	2.67	86.9	4.2	34.2	12.3	2.5
6.2	0.37	3.3	0.00	6.3	1.8	0.98	12.52	3.98	53.3	0.9	6.6	30.9	4.5
6.8	0.57	3.4	-0.04	7.6	0.3	1.85	15.97	4.54	60.8	3.5	76.2	29.6	5.8
10.0	0.00	0.0	0.00	3.8	0.1	0.64	4.17	3.31	69.5	7.9	287.7	12.9	5.9
8.1	0.15	1.4	-0.09	3.4	0.3	0.54	7.09	4.68	80.6	3.9	12.3	9.0	3.1
2.7	1.64	11.9	1.07	2.3	0.2	0.55	6.65	4.40	81.9	4.1	23.1	9.4	0.2

Name	City	State	Weiss Safety Rating	2003 Weiss Safety Rating	2002 Weiss Safety Rating	Total Assets ($Mil)	One Year Asset Growth	Asset Mix (As a % of Total Assets)				Capital-ization Index	Leverage Ratio	Risk-based Capital Ratio
								Comm-ercial Loans	Cons-umer Loans	Home Mort-gages	Secur-ities			
TAYLOR COUNTY BK	CAMPBELLSVILLE	KY	B-	C+	C+	107.2	-1.73	7.8	5.2	28.0	33.5	7.7	9.5	17.7
TAYLORSVILLE SVG BK SSB	TAYLORSVILLE	NC	D	D	D+	86.8	-1.59	1.3	3.8	35.3	24.5	8.5	10.0	18.9
TCF NB	WAYZATA	MN	B-	B-	B-	12,046.9	1.10	5.7	2.6	32.7	13.2	4.3	6.3	10.8
TCM BK NA	TAMPA	FL	D	D	D-	97.9	24.79	0.0	85.9	0.0	1.0	6.1	10.1	11.8
▼ TD BK USA FSB	JERSEY CITY	NJ	D	D+	D+	10.3	138.13	0.0	0.0	2.9	55.7	10.0	86.7	322.4
▼ TD WATERHOUSE BK NA	JERSEY CITY	NJ	D	D+	D+	9,296.1	39.14	0.2	0.2	0.0	98.5	3.6	5.6	60.2
TEAMBANK NA	PAOLA	KS	C+	C+	B-	546.5	-0.02	12.2	2.4	13.5	29.6	5.3	7.3	12.3
▲ TECHE B&TC	ST MARTINVILLE	LA	B	C	C+	68.2	-3.17	7.2	4.2	22.2	48.9	6.2	8.2	20.1
TECHE FEDERAL SAVINGS	FRANKLIN	LA	B	B	B+	578.7	12.26	1.3	6.1	50.9	21.0	6.9	8.9	16.0
TECUMSEH B&LA	TECUMSEH	NE	C	C	C+	64.3	-2.54	0.0	0.4	44.6	47.9	8.0	9.6	30.9
TELECOM CO-OP BK	MALDEN	MA	D+	D+	D	44.6	-0.55	1.2	0.8	55.0	24.8	7.0	9.0	18.4
TEMECULA VALLEY BK NA	TEMECULA	CA	B-	B-	C+	527.2	35.99	6.6	0.5	5.7	0.0	4.2	9.6	10.6
▲ TEMPLETON SVG BK	TEMPLETON	IA	A-	B+	B+	54.0	3.87	10.7	4.7	10.1	36.6	10.0	15.8	25.5
TEMPO BK FSB	TRENTON	IL	C-	D+	C-	65.8	-4.07	0.0	3.4	80.6	0.0	5.9	7.9	16.2
▲ TENNESSEE COMMERCE BK	FRANKLIN	TN	C-	D+	D	199.9	50.21	56.0	1.8	6.5	8.7	6.8	10.4	12.4
▲ TENNESSEE ST BK	PIGEON FORGE	TN	B	B-	C+	456.6	6.52	2.2	2.3	21.2	20.6	5.5	7.8	11.4
TENSAS ST BK	NEWELLTON	LA	A-	A-	A-	71.0	7.97	14.5	3.5	11.4	36.8	10.0	14.1	23.5
TERRA ALTA BK	TERRA ALTA	WV	B+	B	B-	70.6	4.31	8.5	7.1	38.1	20.8	9.2	10.5	18.6
▲ TERRABANK NA	MIAMI	FL	C+	C	D+	341.6	20.78	9.9	1.5	7.9	18.7	5.7	7.7	12.4
TERRACE BK	TAMPA	FL	C	C	C	137.6	6.02	13.9	8.8	2.3	24.0	3.7	7.3	10.4
▼ TERRE HAUTE SVGS BK	TERRE HAUTE	IN	C-	C	C+	180.4	23.47	3.5	1.9	32.2	41.1	7.2	9.1	19.2
TERRITORIAL SAVINGS BANK	HONOLULU	HI	B	B-	C	1,144.7	25.35	0.1	0.2	38.8	54.7	5.2	7.2	21.7
▲ TERRITORY BK	MUSKOGEE	OK	C-	D+	D	8.6	1.51	3.1	30.4	20.9	0.0	10.0	13.4	18.6
TEUTOPOLIS ST BK	TEUTOPOLIS	IL	A+	A+	A+	124.1	3.03	4.0	3.9	19.3	34.0	10.0	15.2	29.2
TEXAS B&TC	LONGVIEW	TX	A-	A-	A-	572.0	3.33	17.5	6.9	29.0	14.7	8.6	10.1	15.3
TEXAS BANK	FORT WORTH	TX	B-	B-	B-	1,442.8	18.78	8.8	3.1	8.7	11.3	3.9	8.0	10.5
TEXAS BK	BROWNWOOD	TX	B-	B	B	159.5	-3.61	13.4	4.5	15.8	15.8	8.0	9.7	14.5
▲ TEXAS BK OF TATUM	HENDERSON	TX	C+	C-	D+	120.0	12.88	9.4	15.8	13.0	40.1	6.0	8.0	14.3
TEXAS CAPITAL BK NA	DALLAS	TX	C	C	C-	2,399.9	19.77	27.2	0.6	5.1	32.1	3.8	7.0	10.4
TEXAS COASTAL BK	PASADENA	TX	C	C-	D	28.6	-0.28	10.2	3.6	6.1	41.3	8.4	10.0	18.1
TEXAS COMMUNITY B&T NA	DALLAS	TX	B-	B-	B-	137.5	-4.86	10.8	1.9	25.1	31.8	4.8	6.8	13.9
▼ TEXAS COMMUNITY BK NA	SOMERSET	TX	C	B-	B	79.3	323.51	21.5	8.2	6.4	25.1	10.0	11.1	19.8
▲ TEXAS COMMUNITY BK NA	THE WOODLANDS	TX	C	D+	D	73.3	89.82	11.6	2.4	14.1	0.0	6.3	9.5	11.9
TEXAS FIRST BK	GALVESTON	TX	B+	B+	B+	151.2	5.47	7.6	10.1	5.4	47.4	8.9	10.3	20.8
TEXAS FIRST BK	SANTA FE	TX	B+	B+	B+	199.0	5.40	8.5	12.1	3.9	48.1	10.0	11.1	21.3
TEXAS FIRST BK	TEXAS CITY	TX	B+	B+	B+	131.8	1.40	7.5	8.4	1.9	53.3	8.4	10.0	21.6
TEXAS FIRST NB	HOUSTON	TX	B-	B-	B-	319.5	-0.38	10.9	1.6	1.0	32.0	10.0	12.9	20.4
TEXAS FIRST ST BK	RIESEL	TX	C	C	C	162.1	12.32	13.3	18.9	14.7	20.2	3.4	6.9	10.2
TEXAS GULF BK NA	FREEPORT	TX	B+	B+	B+	196.7	-12.30	9.6	4.1	13.9	40.9	7.1	9.1	16.2
TEXAS HERITAGE BK	CROSS PLAINS	TX	C+	C+	C+	49.4	5.69	7.7	8.5	21.8	32.0	4.4	6.4	15.8
▲ TEXAS NB	JACKSONVILLE	TX	C-	D+	D-	62.7	7.77	30.0	6.9	15.3	10.9	5.8	7.8	11.6
▲ TEXAS NB	SWEETWATER	TX	B+	B-	B-	66.0	-5.37	11.9	14.3	7.0	40.8	10.0	11.1	19.4
▼ TEXAS NB	TOMBALL	TX	C+	B-	C	98.8	36.04	16.4	42.5	7.1	1.9	5.6	9.3	11.5
TEXAS PREMIER BK NA	BROOKSHIRE	TX	C	C	C	69.6	2.78	24.2	8.5	10.6	0.3	6.4	8.4	12.5
TEXAS REPUBLIC BK NA	QUANAH	TX	E-	E-	D	22.6	4.81	9.8	10.8	4.0	21.7	4.3	7.3	10.6
TEXAS ST BK	JOAQUIN	TX	D	D+	D+	70.9	-7.61	7.8	18.3	20.2	4.6	6.0	8.0	13.8
TEXAS ST BK	MCALLEN	TX	B+	B+	B+	5,430.8	33.45	17.9	3.4	5.7	26.5	5.2	7.4	11.1
TEXAS ST BK	SAN ANGELO	TX	B+	B+	A-	147.9	3.33	6.5	4.7	15.8	32.3	9.7	10.8	21.5
TEXAS STAR BK	VAN ALSTYNE	TX	B-	B-	B-	151.6	5.24	14.3	11.5	13.8	4.1	6.1	8.1	12.3
TEXAS SVG BK SSB	SNYDER	TX	B	B	B	46.5	5.01	4.6	6.6	57.9	2.8	9.8	10.9	19.8
TEXICO ST BK	TEXICO	IL	E+	E+	E+	7.8	-2.27	1.1	3.1	20.7	49.4	6.0	8.0	25.5
▲ TEXLINE ST BK	TEXLINE	TX	D	E-	E-	12.1	3.57	7.4	4.3	20.7	4.0	10.0	11.9	17.0
TEXSTAR NB	UNIVERSAL CITY	TX	D-	NR	NR	47.9	N/A	14.8	4.3	4.1	18.7	6.6	8.6	14.3
THAYER COUNTY BK	HEBRON	NE	D+	D	D	54.7	-0.05	10.1	4.5	11.0	30.1	5.4	7.4	13.4
THE BANK	BIRMINGHAM	AL	C	C-	C	1,276.6	-10.73	11.2	3.0	17.9	15.7	7.2	9.2	13.1
THE BANK	CHARLESTON	IL	B	B	B+	102.6	7.77	3.9	2.1	20.9	27.0	7.2	9.1	15.3
▲ THE BANK	OBERLIN	KS	D+	D	C-	130.1	-4.41	7.3	1.5	2.1	7.8	6.6	8.6	15.3
▲ THE BANK	SPRINGFIELD	MO	C-	D+	D+	291.8	6.16	28.4	1.4	13.3	5.6	2.2	7.1	9.2
THE BANK	WOODBURY	NJ	B	B	B	1,048.3	-0.23	12.9	2.5	17.9	23.2	5.0	7.3	11.0
▲ THE BANK	WEATHERFORD	TX	B-	C	C-	37.5	-14.29	15.8	4.3	3.5	25.6	10.0	12.2	21.4
THE BANK-OLDHAM COUNTY	LA GRANGE	KY	C	C	C-	120.3	0.01	3.0	2.7	10.5	39.8	6.0	8.1	14.7
THIRD FS&LA OF CLEVELAND	CLEVELAND	OH	B-	B-	B-	8,313.9	1.83	1.5	0.7	60.4	4.3	7.5	9.3	13.5
▲ THIRD FSB	NEWTOWN	PA	C	D+	C+	620.9	-12.33	1.4	0.9	49.0	25.5	5.6	7.6	15.1
THIRD NB OF SEDALIA	SEDALIA	MO	B	B	B	239.4	-1.81	8.1	11.6	13.2	21.3	6.5	8.5	13.9

Asset Quality Index	Non-Performing Loans as a % of Total Loans	Non-Performing Loans as a % of Capital	Net Charge-offs Avg Loans	Profitability Index	Net Income ($Mil)	Return on Assets (R.O.A.)	Return on Equity (R.O.E.)	Net Interest Spread	Overhead Efficiency Ratio	Liquidity Index	Liquidity Ratio	Hot Money Ratio	Stability Index
4.3	2.28	14.2	0.14	7.0	1.3	2.28	25.32	3.93	56.3	4.1	10.1	7.6	5.5
6.1	0.70	4.2	0.38	0.8	0.0	-0.05	-0.48	3.34	102.2	4.4	53.1	15.1	4.3
6.5	0.42	4.1	0.06	10.0	125.4	2.13	27.29	4.66	61.2	4.8	6.9	2.6	7.1
1.2	1.91	10.2	4.65	2.9	0.2	0.52	4.47	9.24	64.9	2.6	74.0	99.7	4.0
7.7	0.00	0.0	0.00	0.0	-1.7	-28.49	-33.37	1.50	3,405.1	5.0	443.5	97.6	5.3
10.0	0.24	0.0	2.05	1.9	3.5	0.08	1.60	0.96	86.2	10.0	3,682.2	0.0	1.8
3.7	1.49	8.7	0.19	4.6	1.8	0.67	6.86	3.77	79.6	5.1	55.6	13.2	5.5
8.2	0.30	1.5	0.00	3.8	0.3	0.86	10.50	3.07	73.5	3.2	55.7	25.4	5.6
5.8	0.49	3.7	0.03	7.4	3.0	1.05	11.94	3.22	64.4	1.3	5.5	24.1	6.1
4.6	2.35	9.0	0.00	3.0	0.1	0.19	1.72	1.82	87.0	3.7	12.5	10.0	5.3
8.9	0.41	2.9	0.08	1.3	-0.1	-0.26	-2.89	2.84	91.3	4.7	87.9	18.7	3.1
5.2	0.42	3.7	0.16	10.0	5.5	2.32	25.02	5.87	60.9	1.6	17.9	23.1	6.3
8.3	0.57	2.1	0.00	6.9	0.4	1.39	8.78	4.33	55.7	1.9	15.8	19.6	7.2
4.7	0.87	9.2	0.00	4.3	0.2	0.61	7.98	3.48	70.0	2.2	6.1	17.1	3.2
3.1	1.71	13.6	0.77	4.0	0.6	0.68	7.59	4.26	53.4	1.4	29.4	32.7	1.9
6.3	0.51	4.2	0.05	6.7	3.2	1.45	18.70	4.08	64.8	2.0	15.3	19.0	5.7
7.3	1.35	4.8	0.04	6.1	0.4	1.17	8.58	4.10	65.8	2.0	33.9	29.4	7.2
6.5	0.84	5.3	0.07	6.5	0.4	1.10	10.65	4.01	57.3	4.9	52.0	12.4	6.1
3.9	0.91	7.7	0.11	8.1	2.0	1.23	15.87	4.25	56.2	1.8	28.2	26.2	5.1
6.7	0.44	3.4	-0.08	4.7	0.6	0.83	11.02	4.67	70.1	4.4	31.9	10.2	3.5
8.5	0.38	2.0	0.06	2.0	0.1	0.15	1.52	2.79	91.8	4.8	18.4	4.1	4.8
9.1	0.00	0.0	0.10	9.3	7.3	1.35	18.25	3.74	43.1	0.5	4.9	45.6	5.3
6.8	0.16	0.8	0.31	7.5	0.1	2.22	16.79	8.11	72.4	5.2	68.9	12.0	3.0
8.9	0.18	0.6	0.00	7.4	0.8	1.29	8.51	3.18	41.5	8.2	125.3	4.8	8.8
6.9	0.37	2.5	0.18	6.8	3.4	1.18	11.95	3.84	65.1	5.7	56.4	10.8	7.0
4.7	0.65	5.6	0.21	6.7	7.0	1.03	12.68	4.81	68.8	4.5	59.1	18.7	6.5
4.2	1.07	7.0	0.12	9.7	1.8	2.28	21.69	5.08	60.5	3.6	11.0	10.4	6.9
4.5	1.19	6.9	0.46	5.7	0.9	1.54	18.38	4.42	65.2	2.2	24.2	19.0	3.7
6.3	0.69	5.5	0.08	4.2	9.3	0.81	11.53	3.22	63.5	1.5	13.4	25.4	4.4
8.6	0.08	0.4	-0.01	7.4	0.2	1.26	13.88	4.69	65.3	1.7	15.9	21.5	3.2
9.0	0.11	0.9	-0.02	6.7	0.5	0.76	10.85	4.02	75.8	4.6	26.3	6.9	4.3
7.5	0.06	0.2	0.16	1.7	-0.4	-1.44	-8.83	2.28	152.7	3.3	85.1	39.9	4.4
7.1	0.00	0.0	0.03	3.9	0.4	1.25	12.75	5.91	62.3	2.3	41.6	31.7	0.6
5.7	0.96	3.6	0.86	6.7	0.8	1.13	11.17	3.92	54.1	1.9	23.0	21.6	6.2
5.5	1.54	5.7	1.65	6.1	1.0	0.98	8.86	4.31	57.4	1.7	15.8	22.3	5.6
8.1	0.22	0.7	0.19	7.5	0.9	1.32	13.72	3.87	52.6	2.9	19.6	14.9	6.2
6.0	0.62	2.8	-0.28	3.5	0.9	0.56	4.24	3.92	83.8	5.0	137.3	28.9	6.0
7.2	0.03	0.3	0.04	4.5	0.5	0.65	8.85	3.57	72.3	2.0	21.6	19.7	3.3
6.0	0.70	3.8	0.67	7.4	1.5	1.47	15.88	4.17	61.3	7.4	94.1	6.4	5.5
6.6	0.17	1.5	0.01	7.0	0.4	1.73	25.88	4.77	64.3	2.0	24.7	19.7	5.0
6.1	0.39	3.1	0.11	4.0	0.2	0.77	9.92	3.92	72.5	3.7	73.3	25.3	2.3
6.5	0.86	3.1	0.46	7.8	0.6	1.84	14.54	4.74	63.0	3.2	37.4	18.4	5.9
4.0	0.60	4.9	0.23	5.5	0.2	0.36	3.60	5.47	63.9	3.2	9.1	12.5	4.9
4.4	0.70	5.6	0.55	4.4	0.2	0.65	7.57	5.27	78.7	5.3	48.4	10.1	4.2
2.9	1.51	10.6	0.00	0.3	-0.1	-0.73	-8.10	4.51	114.6	3.8	68.5	19.3	0.9
2.4	1.98	14.5	0.12	4.6	0.5	1.24	14.58	5.03	78.6	3.8	60.1	19.3	1.2
5.9	0.56	3.2	0.43	8.9	37.0	1.47	14.09	4.31	50.9	1.9	26.3	31.5	8.5
5.6	1.32	5.6	0.01	5.4	1.0	1.32	12.41	3.62	70.2	5.2	45.9	10.7	6.7
6.5	0.14	1.1	0.25	4.9	0.6	0.81	10.14	5.08	74.6	5.5	65.6	13.3	4.3
7.4	0.31	2.2	0.21	4.5	0.3	1.36	12.46	3.42	63.4	6.5	197.4	20.0	5.6
9.4	0.00	0.0	0.13	3.8	0.0	0.44	5.56	5.11	86.3	5.4	25.2	0.0	0.5
4.5	1.80	5.4	-0.07	0.5	-0.4	-3.76	-21.54	4.03	199.1	1.7	31.9	25.9	0.2
7.7	0.00	0.0	0.06	0.0	-0.4	-2.61	-16.69	2.73	159.8	4.2	53.3	16.5	0.0
4.9	1.12	8.0	0.07	5.1	0.4	1.36	18.60	3.20	58.2	4.9	48.5	11.8	2.2
3.2	2.58	15.9	1.15	5.7	3.4	0.56	5.43	3.66	84.0	2.6	38.0	32.8	6.2
5.8	1.49	9.8	-0.17	6.4	0.8	1.67	18.64	3.56	57.5	5.8	74.3	12.9	5.4
2.8	1.13	6.9	0.10	7.9	1.3	1.98	19.11	4.15	47.2	5.0	40.2	9.9	6.9
5.2	0.17	1.1	0.24	3.4	0.8	0.54	5.22	2.44	67.3	2.4	20.6	17.6	3.8
6.3	0.47	3.5	0.06	9.3	7.9	1.50	17.25	4.36	54.4	4.1	11.8	7.9	7.0
7.3	0.41	1.2	1.36	4.9	0.1	0.50	3.47	3.75	82.5	5.4	156.8	25.5	4.5
5.2	1.50	8.4	0.05	4.5	0.5	0.88	11.17	3.86	68.2	2.4	28.9	19.2	2.8
7.5	0.42	4.0	0.02	4.3	24.1	0.59	6.26	2.02	59.1	1.3	2.1	24.1	7.1
5.3	0.49	4.3	0.10	4.1	3.5	1.13	13.86	3.87	59.5	1.5	2.4	20.7	3.2
5.7	0.45	3.1	0.11	9.0	1.8	1.51	17.11	4.11	51.8	7.3	103.2	8.5	6.6

Name	City	State	Weiss Safety Rating	2003 Weiss Safety Rating	2002 Weiss Safety Rating	Total Assets ($Mil)	One Year Asset Growth	Asset Mix (As a % of Total Assets)				Capital-ization Index	Leverage Ratio	Risk-based Capital Ratio
								Comm-ercial Loans	Cons-umer Loans	Home Mort-gages	Secur-ities			
THOMAS COUNTY FS&LA	THOMASVILLE	GA	B+	B+	B+	310.4	1.74	0.0	3.2	32.0	29.0	10.0	12.2	28.9
THOMASTON SVGS BK	THOMASTON	CT	A-	A	A	431.1	0.60	1.9	0.8	41.1	29.6	10.0	16.2	32.2
THOMASVILLE NB	THOMASVILLE	GA	B-	B-	B-	213.8	10.73	17.0	5.0	30.1	5.0	5.6	8.2	11.5
THREE RIVERS BK OF MT	KALISPELL	MT	B-	C+	C	84.1	10.61	28.0	5.1	10.5	23.3	7.3	9.2	13.3
▲ THRIVENT FINANCIAL BANK	APPLETON	WI	C	C-	B-	375.7	7.00	0.2	8.9	41.4	21.8	9.2	10.4	16.6
THUMB NB&TC	PIGEON	MI	C-	C+	C+	174.8	14.67	13.4	4.5	23.8	11.6	3.3	6.9	10.2
THUNDER BK	SYLVAN GROVE	KS	C+	C	C	20.2	34.57	11.4	2.9	9.9	0.0	5.6	7.6	11.7
TIAA-CREF TRUST COMPANY	ST LOUIS	MO	D	D	D	17.4	-14.20	0.0	0.0	0.0	87.2	10.0	83.0	161.8
▲ TIB BANK OF THE KEYS	KEY LARGO	FL	B	B-	B-	758.7	20.58	7.5	11.8	10.2	10.8	8.3	11.1	13.5
TIB INDEPENDENT	IRVING	TX	C+	C+	C	1,268.4	16.34	2.4	7.4	3.2	27.6	4.4	6.4	12.2
TIDELANDS BK	MT PLEASANT	SC	D	D	NR	54.7	N/A	8.3	1.9	10.9	24.2	10.0	15.8	19.1
▲ TIERONE BK	LINCOLN	NE	A	A-	B+	2,248.2	-1.37	3.5	3.9	43.0	2.1	8.9	11.5	14.1
▼ TILDEN BK	TILDEN	NE	E+	D	D+	30.8	-1.99	8.7	3.5	3.7	27.8	4.8	6.8	11.1
TIMBERLAND BK	EL DORADO	AR	C+	C+	C-	112.2	16.24	44.0	20.8	15.2	8.4	5.5	10.2	11.4
▲ TIMBERLAND BK	HOQUIAM	WA	A-	A-	A-	435.9	-0.72	3.0	2.1	24.8	11.9	10.0	14.5	20.3
TIMBERWOOD BK	WABENO	WI	D	D	D-	57.0	309.11	17.7	3.2	17.4	7.0	5.4	9.4	11.3
▲ TIME FSB	MEDFORD	WI	A+	A	A	425.4	9.54	0.0	0.4	50.7	44.3	10.0	14.6	43.5
▼ TIMEWELL ST BK	TIMEWELL	IL	D	C-	C-	7.1	-2.77	5.8	6.0	0.1	49.0	10.0	15.8	45.3
TIOGA ST BK	SPENCER	NY	B	B	A-	270.8	14.01	8.6	3.5	20.7	49.6	6.1	8.1	16.8
TIOGA-FRANKLIN SAVINGS	PHILADELPHIA	PA	C	C+	B-	15.6	-2.12	0.0	0.0	61.9	24.4	10.0	17.0	38.0
▼ TIPPINS B&TC	CLAXTON	GA	C-	C	C	50.5	-4.30	8.3	9.6	13.5	23.6	8.6	10.0	16.3
TIPTON LATHAM BK NA	TIPTON	MO	B-	B-	B-	64.6	2.97	11.2	8.2	18.5	16.9	8.1	9.7	14.5
TITONKA SVG BK	TITONKA	IA	C+	C+	C+	108.3	3.54	2.0	2.5	6.6	58.6	6.2	8.2	22.3
TNBANK	OAK RIDGE	TN	C+	C+	C-	119.2	9.20	10.4	7.5	21.3	12.9	4.1	7.5	10.6
TOLLESON PRIVATE BK	DALLAS	TX	D	D	NR	96.5	161.54	9.5	2.7	38.3	12.4	10.0	17.4	24.0
TOMAHAWK CMNTY BK, SSB	TOMAHAWK	WI	B	B	B	74.8	1.05	2.8	3.7	29.3	26.6	10.0	12.0	21.6
▲ TOMPKINS ST BK	AVON	IL	A-	B+	B-	92.4	0.57	6.8	4.9	13.3	36.3	10.0	11.2	19.3
TOMPKINS TRUST CO	ITHACA	NY	B	B	B+	1,049.1	4.73	6.5	6.9	22.4	39.9	5.7	7.7	14.3
▼ TORREY PINES BK	SAN DIEGO	CA	C	C+	NR	212.6	294.57	14.1	1.6	2.6	34.3	10.0	12.3	18.1
TORRINGTON SVGS BK	TORRINGTON	CT	A	A	A-	623.2	-1.46	0.0	0.2	45.1	43.4	10.0	15.0	48.9
▲ TOTALBANK	MIAMI	FL	C	D	E-	601.8	9.20	7.3	0.5	3.0	21.2	4.2	7.5	10.6
TOWANDA ST BK	TOWANDA	KS	D-	D-	D-	8.0	-2.07	3.4	10.5	38.5	16.2	9.6	10.7	20.2
TOWER B&TC	FORT WAYNE	IN	C	C	C	474.3	16.37	27.1	2.0	9.3	8.5	4.6	8.5	10.8
TOWN & COUNTRY B&TC	BARDSTOWN	KY	A-	A	A	235.4	8.38	3.4	4.1	30.7	23.9	10.0	12.3	20.2
TOWN & COUNTRY BANK	STEPHENVILLE	TX	B	B	B	103.0	12.29	5.7	12.7	12.2	37.1	5.7	7.7	17.8
TOWN & COUNTRY BK	BUFFALO	IL	B-	B-	C+	58.6	34.83	7.7	23.1	22.4	25.2	5.5	7.5	11.7
TOWN & COUNTRY BK	SPRINGFIELD	IL	B-	B-	C+	226.3	2.52	6.4	14.4	13.7	31.4	5.9	7.9	15.6
TOWN & COUNTRY BK	LEAWOOD	KS	D	D	D	68.0	21.45	11.1	1.5	13.7	6.2	8.4	9.9	14.4
TOWN & COUNTRY BK	SALEM	MO	B+	B+	B	368.6	40.35	3.7	5.4	40.7	17.4	6.3	8.4	14.8
▼ TOWN & COUNTRY BK	RAVENNA	NE	B+	A-	A-	75.1	42.51	7.3	4.3	4.2	25.8	10.0	12.3	18.7
TOWN & COUNTRY BK	LAS VEGAS	NV	B-	B-	B-	117.3	130.86	1.0	0.5	2.1	26.4	7.6	9.4	14.5
TOWN & COUNTRY BK	WATERTOWN	WI	D	D	E+	26.9	6.46	10.1	3.2	20.5	23.5	6.0	8.0	12.5
TOWN & COUNTRY BK	LA BELLE	MO	B	B-	B-	22.2	6.01	13.5	5.4	5.4	11.1	5.8	8.4	11.6
TOWN & COUNTRY BK	LA GRANGE	MO	B	B-	B-	21.0	-4.49	18.6	5.8	14.9	8.1	3.9	8.5	10.5
▲ TOWN & COUNTRY BK OF	QUINCY	IL	B	C+	C+	92.9	4.68	21.0	3.5	22.5	5.2	6.4	8.6	12.0
▲ TOWN AND COUNTRY BK	REPUBLIC	MO	C+	D+	D+	59.3	22.36	7.9	5.7	22.2	16.1	7.1	9.1	15.9
▲ TOWN BK	DELAFIELD	WI	C	D+	D+	234.2	18.69	26.4	1.1	7.6	5.0	4.3	8.6	10.6
TOWN BK OF WESTFIELD	WESTFIELD	NJ	C+	C	D-	122.9	31.51	22.4	0.3	10.3	15.5	9.8	11.9	14.8
▲ TOWN CTR BK	PORTLAND	OR	B	C+	B-	81.0	34.62	11.2	1.4	8.2	5.4	7.1	11.7	12.6
▼ TOWN NORTH BK NA	FARMERS BRANCH	TX	B-	B+	A-	485.2	20.24	5.5	12.5	8.3	40.8	5.7	7.7	13.6
▲ TOWN SQUARE BK	ASHLAND	KY	C-	D	D	121.4	31.05	14.5	11.0	22.3	5.8	5.6	8.6	11.4
TOWN-COUNTRY NB	CAMDEN	AL	C	C-	C-	76.1	2.80	7.4	27.1	11.7	19.5	9.3	10.5	15.5
TOWNE BANK	PORTSMOUTH	VA	B-	B-	B-	1,364.7	57.92	16.2	3.9	12.6	12.2	5.5	7.5	12.3
TOWNE BK OF AZ	MESA	AZ	D	NR	NR	13.1	N/A	7.3	0.0	0.0	38.4	10.0	81.8	162.1
▼ TOWNE CENTER BANK	LODI	NJ	C+	B	B	46.1	0.23	12.4	0.2	2.7	3.5	10.0	19.8	24.5
TRADERS & FARMERS BK	HALEYVILLE	AL	A-	B+	B-	325.3	0.53	2.9	7.9	22.8	46.9	10.0	12.4	21.8
▼ TRADERS BK	SPENCER	WV	D	C-	B-	115.8	-4.10	13.8	3.9	22.9	15.8	10.0	12.2	17.9
▲ TRADERS NB OF TULLAHOMA	TULLAHOMA	TN	C	C-	C-	117.3	-1.74	11.0	5.3	31.9	4.3	6.4	8.4	13.3
▲ TRADITION BK	HOUSTON	TX	C+	D-	D	215.3	220.10	6.5	4.1	10.2	19.7	7.6	9.4	13.1
TRADITIONAL BK	MT STERLING	KY	C+	C+	C+	569.2	11.98	9.1	2.3	22.1	18.6	4.5	8.0	10.8
TRADITIONS BK	CULLMAN	AL	D	D	NR	46.1	N/A	11.1	9.3	17.9	20.1	10.0	20.2	25.3
TRADITIONS FIRST BK	ERIN	TN	B-	C+	C	53.7	54.20	14.5	7.9	23.7	41.2	10.0	11.0	20.6
▲ TRANS-PACIFIC NB	SAN FRANCISCO	CA	B-	C	B	147.8	1.65	15.5	0.1	2.2	20.7	5.2	8.4	11.1
▲ TRANSATLANTIC BK	MIAMI	FL	C-	D	D+	449.7	19.45	12.4	0.5	4.4	9.3	3.4	7.4	10.2

Asset Quality Index	Non-Performing Loans as a % of Total Loans	Non-Performing Loans as a % of Capital	Net Charge-offs Avg Loans	Profitability Index	Net Income ($Mil)	Return on Assets (R.O.A.)	Return on Equity (R.O.E.)	Net Interest Spread	Overhead Efficiency Ratio	Liquidity Index	Liquidity Ratio	Hot Money Ratio	Stability Index
7.3	1.01	4.0	0.04	4.8	1.2	0.74	5.86	2.24	51.6	3.7	58.6	23.5	7.5
9.7	0.26	0.8	0.04	5.7	1.9	0.89	5.27	3.66	66.0	8.2	137.3	5.5	8.6
6.5	0.46	4.6	0.15	7.1	1.3	1.29	16.09	3.96	51.2	4.0	13.3	8.5	4.9
7.8	0.16	1.2	0.01	6.7	0.6	1.35	15.09	5.25	61.6	1.9	12.4	19.1	4.5
6.2	0.31	1.7	0.32	3.3	2.9	1.56	13.39	3.70	61.6	1.2	10.1	27.1	5.1
3.9	1.49	15.6	0.28	3.9	0.6	0.74	10.32	4.06	79.3	2.5	15.3	16.4	3.6
7.1	0.18	1.1	0.28	7.6	0.1	1.10	10.87	3.55	58.5	4.5	78.3	17.4	5.0
7.2	0.00	0.0	0.00	0.0	-1.8	-20.32	-23.77	3.84	137.0	0.2	11.8	100.0	0.0
5.2	0.68	4.6	0.15	5.8	3.3	0.92	9.89	4.66	72.4	2.8	30.5	17.9	5.4
5.4	1.50	9.3	1.09	4.6	6.1	0.98	14.70	3.18	71.5	3.2	38.6	23.1	4.0
8.9	0.00	0.0	0.00	0.0	-0.5	-2.24	-11.21	2.68	155.0	5.9	67.7	9.9	0.0
7.7	0.14	1.0	0.07	6.8	11.7	1.04	9.22	3.25	55.6	1.3	4.9	24.5	8.7
4.3	1.02	6.5	2.17	2.1	-0.1	-0.48	-6.13	4.83	78.1	5.7	40.5	5.2	1.0
3.1	1.23	9.4	0.16	5.9	0.5	0.95	9.55	4.50	50.0	0.9	24.9	52.5	2.0
5.8	0.62	3.1	0.03	8.4	2.9	1.28	8.69	4.85	64.8	4.2	12.5	7.1	8.8
6.6	0.00	0.0	0.01	0.6	-0.1	-0.49	-3.90	3.20	112.9	6.0	64.6	8.9	2.7
9.3	0.03	0.1	0.00	9.8	3.4	1.61	10.75	3.25	22.0	2.0	29.9	24.4	9.0
9.0	0.22	0.3	0.00	0.2	0.0	-0.54	-3.45	2.35	123.5	6.9	85.7	5.1	3.5
9.0	0.21	1.2	0.02	4.2	1.0	0.72	8.74	3.48	75.6	2.7	23.6	16.3	4.3
5.2	5.30	19.4	0.00	3.0	0.0	0.28	1.66	3.54	92.5	3.4	N/A	10.7	0.0
4.1	1.83	11.1	0.50	2.2	-0.1	-0.39	-3.92	5.23	97.8	2.8	38.0	21.6	4.0
4.8	1.15	8.0	0.51	6.8	0.5	1.64	16.92	3.90	57.5	5.3	40.6	8.2	6.2
7.7	0.53	2.1	0.06	3.6	0.4	0.74	7.98	3.45	73.7	7.2	157.0	13.1	4.7
4.0	1.33	12.8	0.22	5.0	0.5	0.84	10.98	4.37	71.8	2.8	18.8	15.5	4.0
8.6	0.00	0.0	0.00	0.0	-0.4	-0.95	-5.22	2.65	146.5	4.4	16.2	6.3	0.0
8.6	0.45	2.1	0.14	4.5	0.2	0.51	4.41	3.96	80.3	6.1	39.4	2.4	5.7
7.5	0.84	3.8	0.21	6.3	0.7	1.38	11.75	4.18	56.3	4.0	39.4	14.8	6.5
7.7	0.62	4.0	0.03	8.9	7.5	1.42	18.91	3.96	56.4	3.9	15.9	9.7	7.6
8.9	0.00	0.0	0.00	2.1	0.4	0.42	3.81	4.08	71.8	5.0	17.3	2.3	3.1
10.0	0.33	1.0	0.00	5.9	2.7	0.86	5.79	2.49	43.2	9.1	541.9	6.0	8.9
6.2	0.18	1.3	-0.11	4.6	3.5	1.21	12.88	4.55	76.1	2.8	10.3	14.3	4.5
2.0	4.61	23.6	0.25	3.8	0.0	0.68	6.40	6.33	91.2	5.9	51.3	4.6	1.7
5.4	0.57	5.0	0.47	3.5	1.1	0.50	5.94	3.14	69.2	1.3	28.1	34.3	4.3
7.1	1.11	5.5	-0.05	5.2	1.0	0.87	6.94	4.00	73.4	5.8	41.0	5.3	7.7
8.1	0.00	0.0	0.08	5.9	0.7	1.30	16.07	3.89	71.0	5.6	52.0	9.9	5.9
5.9	0.35	2.9	0.05	7.3	0.2	0.86	10.52	3.60	67.6	1.6	9.3	20.7	5.4
4.0	0.79	3.9	0.39	4.2	1.0	0.85	7.25	3.34	67.7	2.9	20.2	14.9	6.1
7.4	0.00	0.0	0.04	1.3	0.1	0.17	1.68	3.26	81.5	6.2	85.6	10.9	0.0
6.4	0.30	2.0	0.04	8.2	2.6	1.52	14.59	3.92	54.4	3.6	33.1	14.5	6.1
4.7	2.07	10.2	-0.02	8.0	0.5	1.43	11.32	4.52	58.8	2.8	20.9	15.5	6.8
7.8	0.00	0.0	0.00	3.5	0.7	1.29	13.08	3.06	47.4	7.7	167.5	11.8	2.8
8.6	0.13	1.1	0.15	2.8	0.0	0.32	4.12	3.77	87.2	4.8	33.0	8.5	1.8
8.0	0.00	0.0	0.00	7.3	0.2	1.69	18.83	3.94	55.8	2.7	25.2	16.1	6.9
4.5	0.76	6.3	-0.34	7.5	0.2	1.57	17.58	3.84	61.6	2.7	14.4	15.2	6.6
5.6	0.47	4.2	0.11	8.9	1.0	2.29	26.90	4.24	40.3	2.4	35.2	23.6	6.2
3.3	1.35	5.3	0.91	2.4	0.0	0.02	0.12	3.53	74.2	7.3	111.7	8.1	5.7
5.3	0.00	0.0	0.02	5.1	1.1	0.98	11.51	3.83	58.2	0.6	9.0	39.0	4.5
8.6	0.00	0.0	0.00	3.7	0.5	0.95	8.11	3.66	65.5	4.2	58.8	18.6	5.2
7.2	0.01	0.1	0.00	8.3	0.5	1.32	11.94	5.50	69.2	0.8	7.3	32.6	6.6
7.5	0.24	1.4	0.35	5.3	1.5	0.63	8.41	3.55	92.8	4.0	98.8	34.5	3.9
4.1	0.83	7.1	0.36	2.6	0.2	0.40	4.89	4.05	69.6	4.1	40.3	14.7	1.0
2.8	2.30	13.4	0.53	6.4	0.5	1.17	11.56	4.94	56.7	3.9	72.5	22.9	5.6
7.7	0.19	1.2	0.05	4.5	4.4	0.73	7.16	3.51	74.9	3.4	18.1	12.8	7.2
9.8	0.00	0.0	0.00	0.0	-0.3	-5.84	-6.86	0.76	818.2	10.0	495.4	0.0	0.0
7.1	0.00	0.0	0.00	4.7	0.2	0.88	4.51	6.02	72.2	4.5	8.7	4.9	6.3
6.6	1.30	4.9	0.30	7.0	2.1	1.30	10.64	4.81	56.1	1.2	10.1	27.8	6.3
0.1	10.56	54.8	0.36	4.2	0.0	0.00	0.00	4.50	77.6	5.4	45.3	8.8	6.7
3.1	1.37	11.1	-0.43	7.1	1.1	1.94	22.79	4.31	56.7	3.6	40.8	17.4	5.2
6.3	0.39	2.7	0.27	3.9	0.6	0.64	6.64	4.48	77.6	2.8	14.8	15.0	4.7
4.3	1.47	12.6	0.19	6.0	4.2	1.51	18.08	3.57	52.3	1.1	10.7	29.7	5.4
8.1	0.00	0.0	0.01	0.2	-0.1	-0.27	-1.15	4.49	88.4	1.3	29.8	39.6	0.0
8.4	0.00	0.0	0.09	3.8	0.2	0.62	5.31	3.73	71.2	5.0	127.8	24.5	1.8
8.1	0.00	0.0	0.00	5.5	0.9	1.27	12.35	4.33	71.7	1.3	21.1	29.5	6.3
5.4	1.69	13.9	0.03	6.8	2.7	1.28	17.19	4.22	56.6	2.5	43.9	31.0	3.2

Name	City	State	Weiss Safety Rating	2003 Weiss Safety Rating	2002 Weiss Safety Rating	Total Assets ($Mil)	One Year Asset Growth	Asset Mix (As a % of Total Assets) Commercial Loans	Consumer Loans	Home Mortgages	Securities	Capitalization Index	Leverage Ratio	Risk-based Capital Ratio
▲ TRANSCAPITAL BK	HALLANDALE	FL	A	B	C+	136.2	27.30	0.9	0.5	4.9	5.1	9.8	12.8	14.8
▲ TRANSPORTATION ALLIANCE	OGDEN	UT	B-	C+	C	160.2	33.62	80.2	1.4	0.5	0.0	7.1	10.9	12.6
TRAVERSE CITY ST BK	TRAVERSE CITY	MI	C-	C-	D-	129.4	32.26	15.5	8.6	13.5	8.6	4.3	8.3	10.7
TREASURY BK NA	ALEXANDRIA	VA	B+	B	B-	27,179.2	107.61	0.0	0.0	56.3	9.4	6.2	8.2	12.2
▼ TREGO-WAKEENEY STATE	WAKEENEY	KS	C-	B-	B-	45.0	7.06	18.4	2.0	11.4	13.8	6.6	8.6	12.3
TREMONT SVGS BK	TREMONT	IL	C-	C-	C	40.7	1.77	2.0	2.0	37.5	22.3	6.3	8.3	17.1
TREYNOR ST BK	TREYNOR	IA	D	D	D	51.4	5.67	3.0	7.0	13.7	21.7	4.4	6.5	11.2
TRI CITY NB	OAK CREEK	WI	A	A	A-	675.4	8.77	3.8	4.0	22.8	25.1	10.0	12.8	19.1
▲ TRI COUNTIES BK	CHICO	CA	B+	B	B	1,544.7	13.46	5.8	5.8	11.5	19.6	6.6	9.8	12.2
▲ TRI-COUNTY B&TC	CASCADE	IA	A-	B+	B	80.2	5.32	5.5	5.2	5.9	23.1	8.0	9.7	14.4
▲ TRI-COUNTY B&TC	ROACHDALE	IN	B+	B+	A-	146.7	11.80	7.6	6.4	12.7	24.2	10.0	12.0	21.7
TRI-COUNTY BANK	TRENTON	FL	B-	B-	C+	65.9	-3.61	13.4	5.0	19.5	21.9	9.7	10.8	17.8
▼ TRI-COUNTY BK	BROWN CITY	MI	B-	B	B	169.6	-2.96	5.9	2.8	15.0	24.3	8.2	9.8	16.0
▲ TRI-COUNTY BK	STUART	NE	C	C-	C	46.6	-2.74	5.0	2.9	4.2	38.6	8.0	9.7	17.6
▲ TRI-COUNTY NB	CORBIN	KY	B	B-	C+	91.0	-1.93	3.8	8.9	42.3	24.0	6.8	8.8	17.5
▼ TRI-COUNTY TRUST	GLASGOW	MO	B-	B	B-	30.6	1.55	9.6	8.1	20.2	24.8	9.4	12.2	14.5
TRI-CTY BK NA	CHEYENNE	WY	B	B	B	27.4	25.28	9.3	3.5	32.7	5.2	6.6	8.6	12.3
TRI-PARISH BANK	EUNICE	LA	A	A	A	104.8	3.70	7.6	3.9	7.3	54.5	8.7	10.1	19.3
▼ TRI-STATE BANK OF MEMPHIS	MEMPHIS	TN	C-	C-	C	133.4	9.23	4.1	2.2	9.4	32.0	10.0	11.0	18.7
▼ TRI-STATE BK&TR	HAUGHTON	LA	A	A	A	43.5	-31.79	6.5	1.3	1.7	72.8	10.0	21.9	49.1
TRIAD BK NA	TULSA	OK	B-	B-	C+	84.8	-6.44	15.2	17.4	38.7	0.0	10.0	11.8	17.2
▲ TRICENTURY BK	SIMPSON	KS	C+	C	C-	2.7	-5.37	5.7	9.0	15.5	45.0	9.6	10.7	22.9
▲ TRINITY BK	MONROE	NC	C-	D+	E+	138.1	21.82	12.4	1.4	7.5	23.7	6.8	8.8	14.1
TRINITY BK NA	FORT WORTH	TX	D	D	NR	48.6	126.92	17.1	2.0	3.7	30.2	10.0	20.5	37.6
TRISTAR BK	DICKSON	TN	B	B	C	81.7	28.24	10.0	6.2	18.4	29.0	9.0	10.3	14.6
TRIUMPH ST BK	TRIMONT	MN	D+	D+	C-	38.2	6.69	9.6	4.7	4.8	40.0	5.9	7.9	15.2
TROY B&TC	TROY	AL	C+	C+	C+	329.3	6.65	12.7	7.1	14.6	27.5	4.7	7.2	10.9
TROY ST BK	TROY	KS	D	D-	E+	20.6	-0.15	6.8	9.1	15.6	31.6	7.2	9.2	15.5
▲ TRUMAN BK	ST LOUIS	MO	C-	D+	C-	275.9	34.26	2.1	2.0	24.8	4.3	4.6	7.4	10.8
▲ TRUST BK	MONTEREY PARK	CA	B-	C+	C+	229.0	-2.16	0.6	0.1	3.0	22.4	5.4	7.9	11.3
TRUST COMPANY OF	ENGLEWOOD	CO	B+	B+	B+	221.7	-9.31	0.0	0.0	0.0	95.2	8.7	10.1	27.7
TRUST INDUSTRIAL BK	DENVER	CO	D	C-	C	2.5	0.04	0.0	0.0	0.0	99.7	10.0	79.3	79.4
▲ TRUST ONE BK	MEMPHIS	TN	C+	C	C-	493.0	16.40	11.4	1.3	15.0	14.0	4.9	7.7	10.9
TRUSTBANC	MOUNTAIN HOME	AR	B	B	B	113.2	19.35	3.3	3.1	26.7	22.3	6.4	8.4	13.3
▲ TRUSTBANK	OLNEY	IL	B-	C	C-	122.2	-2.04	8.3	7.2	15.2	26.9	9.2	10.4	16.2
TRUSTCO BANK	GLENVILLE	NY	B-	B-	C+	2,842.4	6.95	1.1	0.5	27.2	39.3	4.4	6.4	15.8
▼ TRUSTMARK NB	JACKSON	MS	B	B+	B+	8,084.9	11.83	10.9	9.3	19.4	25.8	4.9	6.9	11.3
▲ TSB BK	LOMIRA	WI	C-	D+	D	54.4	6.18	9.4	9.1	19.3	8.7	5.7	8.9	11.5
TUCUMCARI FS&LA	TUCUMCARI	NM	C-	D+	D+	21.9	14.88	0.0	1.3	45.0	25.5	10.0	12.5	25.9
TULSA NB	TULSA	OK	C-	B-	B-	154.6	9.95	11.7	2.5	16.2	23.9	5.8	7.8	11.9
TUPPER LAKE NB	TUPPER LAKE	NY	B-	B-	B-	85.7	17.79	8.9	5.3	19.2	36.4	6.6	8.6	16.7
TURBOTVILLE NB	TURBOTVILLE	PA	A-	A-	A-	84.2	0.29	5.4	4.5	27.1	34.0	10.0	12.9	23.1
▲ TURNBERRY BK	AVENTURA	FL	B+	B	B-	230.0	4.68	1.7	1.8	51.2	10.8	6.3	8.3	14.5
▲ TUSCOLA NB	TUSCOLA	IL	C-	C	D	86.1	-6.99	6.7	4.4	9.4	47.0	10.0	13.1	28.6
▲ TUSTIN COMMUNITY BK	TUSTIN	CA	B-	C+	C	38.3	46.59	2.3	28.8	3.5	8.8	7.7	10.6	13.1
▲ TWIN CITY BK	N LITTLE ROCK	AR	B-	C+	C	491.4	44.58	13.1	1.8	3.9	47.5	9.5	10.6	17.1
TWIN CITY BK	LONGVIEW	WA	C	C-	D+	30.3	12.63	10.9	1.0	3.6	5.4	9.6	10.8	15.4
TWIN LAKES NB	WICHITA	KS	C+	C+	C+	143.9	0.84	7.7	73.4	1.9	5.8	3.1	8.8	10.1
▼ TWIN OAKS SVGS BK	MARSEILLES	IL	C-	C+	C	54.0	1.22	0.8	3.1	33.3	33.6	6.5	8.5	14.7
TWIN RIVER NB	CLARKSTON	WA	D+	D+	D+	51.6	6.13	18.7	4.0	12.8	7.0	5.8	7.8	13.6
▼ TWIN VALLEY BK	W ALEXANDRIA	OH	C+	B-	B	32.8	-5.06	5.7	7.7	24.8	26.5	10.0	14.1	23.3
▼ TWO RIVER COMMUNITY BK	MIDDLETOWN	NJ	D+	C	C	218.0	42.30	18.6	0.9	2.5	17.7	2.1	6.9	9.1
▲ TWO RIVERS ST BK	BLAIR	NE	B+	B	C+	82.6	11.63	12.5	5.4	13.0	25.6	10.0	11.0	16.3
▲ UBS BK USA	SALT LAKE CITY	UT	C+	C	NR	15,615.2	N/A	18.3	20.6	0.0	0.1	10.0	11.4	26.2
UINTA COUNTY ST BK	MOUNTAIN VIEW	WY	B-	B-	B-	11.6	-2.22	0.1	0.0	0.0	27.7	10.0	27.5	128.5
ULSTER SVGS BK	KINGSTON	NY	C-	C-	B-	563.4	2.54	1.3	0.5	40.7	15.2	10.0	12.8	18.9
ULTIMA BANK MN	WINGER	MN	D	D	E	47.9	8.38	24.0	3.8	7.2	0.4	5.6	7.9	11.4
UMB BK COLORADO NA	DENVER	CO	C+	C+	C+	415.3	6.60	16.9	19.2	1.1	32.8	4.9	7.1	11.0
UMB BK NA	KANSAS CITY	MO	C+	B-	B-	5,834.8	-4.20	18.1	11.1	1.4	35.5	6.4	8.4	15.5
▼ UMB BK OMAHA NA	OMAHA	NE	C+	B-	B-	88.4	-3.66	9.0	60.0	1.5	0.2	3.0	7.5	10.0
▼ UMB BK WARSAW NA	WARSAW	MO	C+	B-	B-	83.7	-9.15	2.3	14.2	4.6	62.9	4.9	6.9	14.1
UMB NB OF AMERICA	SALINA	KS	B-	B	B	535.5	-4.48	4.6	6.9	5.1	64.3	10.0	12.6	39.2
UMB USA NA	FALLS CITY	NE	C+	C+	B-	120.6	-26.72	0.0	96.3	0.0	0.0	10.0	21.5	22.8
▼ UMBRELLABANK FSB	CHICAGO	IL	E-	E	E-	178.2	-20.96	2.8	0.7	15.6	35.4	4.3	6.3	18.3

Arrows denote recent upgrades ▲ or downgrades ▼

www.WeissRatings.com

Asset Quality Index	Non-Performing Loans as a % of Total Loans	Non-Performing Loans as a % of Capital	Net Charge-offs Avg Loans	Profitability Index	Net Income ($Mil)	Return on Assets (R.O.A.)	Return on Equity (R.O.E.)	Net Interest Spread	Overhead Efficiency Ratio	Liquidity Index	Liquidity Ratio	Hot Money Ratio	Stability Index
7.4	0.00	0.0	0.00	10.0	2.4	3.89	30.50	5.46	27.4	6.0	164.7	19.8	8.6
4.0	0.86	5.9	1.52	10.0	2.3	3.02	29.10	9.45	61.6	0.5	16.7	80.4	6.9
6.3	0.51	4.8	0.08	2.9	0.3	0.48	5.91	3.76	72.3	1.3	18.7	28.9	0.6
10.0	0.04	0.5	0.00	6.4	123.9	1.06	13.58	2.26	23.8	3.8	54.3	24.7	7.4
2.1	4.00	29.7	-0.04	8.9	0.5	1.97	22.42	3.94	45.0	5.4	65.6	12.2	5.5
5.3	1.42	8.7	0.33	3.8	0.1	0.47	5.22	3.50	81.0	6.0	78.2	10.9	3.1
7.2	0.40	3.1	0.05	3.3	0.1	0.39	5.68	3.55	89.8	6.2	70.6	8.8	1.8
8.7	0.40	2.0	0.02	6.8	3.9	1.18	9.36	4.72	67.2	5.6	37.6	5.2	8.6
7.3	0.36	2.2	0.04	8.9	10.1	1.36	13.34	5.33	61.9	4.6	22.3	7.8	7.8
6.2	0.02	0.1	0.02	8.0	0.5	1.23	11.48	4.08	58.2	4.9	36.1	8.8	7.1
4.7	2.48	10.3	0.22	7.0	0.7	1.04	8.11	4.17	59.8	7.5	119.9	8.8	7.2
7.5	0.00	0.0	-0.01	4.9	0.3	1.01	8.06	3.83	62.8	2.9	38.5	20.4	7.2
4.0	2.17	12.5	0.15	5.6	0.8	0.94	9.32	3.92	72.3	5.8	47.7	7.0	6.2
5.3	2.11	9.7	-0.21	4.0	0.2	0.68	6.97	3.59	77.4	5.6	96.0	15.4	3.9
8.5	0.02	0.2	0.08	8.0	0.7	1.46	16.26	4.55	60.4	5.5	39.7	6.8	4.9
3.6	2.74	14.1	-0.20	9.0	0.3	2.26	17.75	5.19	49.6	3.9	35.0	13.9	6.9
7.0	0.22	1.9	0.30	3.5	0.1	0.52	6.10	4.09	76.4	3.7	56.6	19.2	3.2
9.0	0.01	0.0	0.16	9.7	1.2	2.22	19.71	4.41	54.9	4.2	38.9	13.6	7.7
2.0	5.99	25.2	0.11	4.4	0.4	0.62	5.68	4.75	80.6	5.0	45.0	11.3	5.4
9.9	0.00	0.0	0.00	10.0	1.0	4.50	20.06	5.65	37.7	5.6	112.1	17.2	8.0
3.2	3.86	27.3	0.32	3.8	0.2	0.45	3.95	4.20	74.6	1.8	32.9	31.2	4.0
6.5	1.00	3.5	0.00	7.0	0.0	1.39	12.96	5.00	75.5	5.4	25.3	0.0	4.5
6.0	0.30	2.3	0.30	2.5	0.4	0.57	6.48	3.09	80.3	1.5	10.7	23.9	3.7
8.9	0.00	0.0	0.00	0.0	-0.3	-1.15	-5.02	2.61	128.2	6.3	74.6	8.8	0.0
7.2	0.05	0.3	0.22	4.4	0.3	0.70	6.15	3.82	72.0	1.7	15.4	21.6	2.2
5.2	1.12	5.4	0.06	3.5	0.1	0.61	6.75	3.97	74.6	5.5	49.5	8.6	2.5
4.4	1.09	9.0	0.06	6.3	1.9	1.15	16.06	4.01	58.5	1.1	14.4	30.1	4.4
2.4	5.50	34.8	0.06	4.8	0.1	0.90	10.18	4.06	74.2	3.4	23.2	12.6	2.1
3.1	1.53	16.5	0.14	4.3	1.0	0.82	11.05	3.19	50.4	2.1	32.8	26.3	2.8
7.4	0.00	0.0	0.00	5.2	0.9	0.74	9.58	2.95	60.5	1.2	29.9	55.9	4.7
10.0	0.00	0.0	0.00	6.3	1.5	1.33	13.77	4.32	81.0	5.0	N/A	0.3	4.2
10.0	0.00	0.0	0.00	0.2	0.0	-0.32	-0.40	0.56	125.0	0.0	N/A	100.0	0.0
4.4	0.42	1.2	0.00	4.4	0.5	0.20	1.54	0.63	49.0	2.5	33.6	21.6	4.1
8.7	0.00	0.0	-0.01	5.5	0.5	0.88	10.13	3.47	60.2	3.1	39.1	19.2	4.9
5.2	0.76	4.2	0.14	4.4	0.5	0.86	7.83	4.23	70.7	3.6	20.6	11.6	5.1
8.9	0.00	0.0	0.12	9.2	19.8	1.40	20.98	3.60	46.1	5.4	55.6	13.8	7.3
6.3	0.48	3.4	0.11	9.4	59.0	1.49	17.70	3.88	53.9	3.6	8.0	10.7	8.2
3.3	1.67	12.9	0.09	4.4	0.2	0.58	6.63	4.24	72.3	5.7	55.2	8.8	3.4
8.3	0.53	2.7	0.14	4.7	0.1	0.75	5.88	3.49	61.7	2.7	8.2	14.6	3.5
2.1	2.46	20.3	0.39	4.6	0.8	1.07	14.11	3.46	65.8	0.6	7.6	40.1	3.7
5.0	2.66	14.8	0.06	4.5	0.4	0.93	9.62	4.36	68.9	5.4	73.2	13.5	4.7
6.1	2.13	8.9	0.06	5.7	0.5	1.18	9.06	3.52	54.6	4.7	34.9	9.8	7.6
7.8	0.00	0.0	0.00	7.6	1.8	1.64	19.16	3.46	57.6	1.4	31.9	47.1	6.4
4.6	4.13	10.7	1.56	1.6	0.0	0.04	0.30	2.52	98.5	3.8	62.9	19.8	4.9
5.4	0.00	0.0	1.35	9.5	0.4	1.92	18.86	8.26	52.3	9.1	28,500.0	6.2	4.2
8.8	0.02	0.1	-0.10	3.0	1.2	0.50	4.56	3.02	72.9	0.8	11.7	34.3	5.8
2.6	2.04	13.1	0.00	2.7	0.1	0.51	4.46	4.28	83.0	3.0	55.6	28.3	0.1
5.5	0.08	0.8	0.12	8.7	1.3	1.75	19.92	4.22	62.7	3.1	18.5	14.1	5.7
6.9	0.90	4.7	0.00	1.9	-0.3	-1.16	-12.65	3.19	76.1	4.7	40.4	11.8	4.5
6.0	0.77	4.9	0.00	3.3	0.1	0.31	3.88	3.38	81.9	7.5	85.2	2.7	2.7
6.2	1.57	6.3	-0.25	2.7	0.0	0.25	1.77	4.43	83.2	5.4	29.8	2.5	5.2
7.3	0.06	0.6	0.00	3.7	0.5	0.49	7.04	4.27	76.3	4.4	24.7	7.4	0.2
5.8	0.89	5.1	0.05	7.0	0.5	1.33	12.19	4.35	54.6	2.5	40.2	27.3	5.2
7.5	0.00	0.0	0.00	3.4	37.8	0.55	4.37	1.22	17.5	7.9	66.5	0.0	4.8
10.0	12.07	0.4	0.00	3.4	0.0	0.07	0.22	1.45	81.0	10.0	271.8	0.0	5.3
1.7	6.58	33.3	0.01	4.3	1.0	0.37	2.87	4.00	92.2	7.9	124.4	6.8	8.3
2.3	1.24	12.5	-0.02	7.2	0.5	1.96	24.44	5.27	61.5	2.0	18.6	19.3	2.5
4.6	0.60	4.2	-0.53	3.7	1.6	0.79	10.58	3.81	78.9	6.4	55.3	5.8	4.9
7.9	0.54	2.3	0.07	3.0	13.3	0.44	5.10	2.76	89.6	7.6	71.2	3.0	4.9
4.1	0.26	3.1	0.02	5.9	0.3	0.79	10.90	3.22	65.0	1.9	3.4	18.5	5.0
8.0	0.30	1.4	-0.04	4.2	0.3	0.72	10.42	2.57	61.3	4.8	28.9	6.3	4.3
8.6	0.28	0.6	0.10	5.0	2.1	0.73	5.73	2.55	64.0	6.4	52.1	4.8	6.8
2.5	2.11	8.6	3.33	10.0	2.9	4.62	22.31	11.60	32.7	5.0	1.9	0.0	7.5
1.1	10.81	42.0	1.47	0.0	-4.1	-4.06	-43.05	1.42	283.2	3.4	79.0	44.3	0.4

Name	City	State	Weiss Safety Rating	2003 Weiss Safety Rating	2002 Weiss Safety Rating	Total Assets ($Mil)	One Year Asset Growth	Asset Mix (As a % of Total Assets)				Capital-ization Index	Leverage Ratio	Risk-based Capital Ratio
								Comm-ercial Loans	Cons-umer Loans	Home Mort-gages	Secur-ities			
▲ UMPQUA BK	ROSEBURG	OR	B	C+	B-	3,137.8	14.83	16.4	1.3	4.6	18.3	4.9	8.7	10.9
▼ UNIBANK	MIAMI	FL	C	C+	C+	479.1	6.27	1.4	3.0	35.0	7.0	6.7	8.7	12.3
▼ UNIBANK FOR SVGS	WHITINSVILLE	MA	C+	B-	B-	643.2	1.86	2.7	6.4	20.4	41.8	5.1	7.1	11.2
▲ UNICO BK	IRONDALE	MO	B	B-	C+	160.3	9.48	6.9	4.2	33.0	37.4	6.0	8.1	15.6
▼ UNIFIED BANKING COMPANY	LEXINGTON	KY	D	D+	D-	79.0	2.39	18.7	5.8	19.8	15.1	4.4	7.9	10.7
UNION B&L SVG BK	W BRIDGEWATER	PA	B-	B	B	36.8	-5.64	0.0	0.4	57.8	4.2	10.0	14.5	27.9
▼ UNION B&TC	MONTICELLO	AR	C	C+	C+	195.8	8.09	26.7	10.0	16.5	19.2	6.4	8.6	12.0
UNION B&TC	MINNEAPOLIS	MN	A	A	A	67.7	-0.12	4.5	0.9	2.9	47.5	10.0	12.8	28.6
UNION B&TC	LINCOLN	NE	B+	B+	B	1,382.3	7.42	12.3	28.6	6.4	6.3	5.3	9.2	11.2
UNION B&TC	POTTSVILLE	PA	C+	C+	C+	126.6	0.28	6.5	3.7	20.2	31.7	6.3	8.3	13.6
UNION B&TC	LIVINGSTON	TN	B-	B-	B-	72.1	0.85	2.2	8.3	14.9	58.0	7.0	9.0	21.4
▼ UNION B&TC	BOWLING GREEN	VA	B-	B	B-	943.9	15.90	12.1	8.4	14.8	12.8	2.4	7.5	9.5
UNION B&TC	EVANSVILLE	WI	B	B	B-	110.7	9.10	8.8	2.6	16.1	25.8	6.6	8.6	13.6
UNION BANK	KANSAS CITY	MO	B-	B-	C+	522.2	-7.52	14.9	1.5	6.2	3.4	8.9	10.4	14.1
▼ UNION BK	MARKSVILLE	LA	C+	B-	B	146.6	-0.51	6.8	14.8	23.5	18.1	4.5	8.4	10.8
UNION BK	LAKE ODESSA	MI	B-	B-	B-	160.1	3.54	22.0	2.5	9.6	9.6	3.9	8.1	10.5
▲ UNION BK	BEULAH	ND	C-	D+	D	37.1	1.70	9.3	16.7	11.7	12.6	6.2	8.6	11.9
UNION BK	JAMESTOWN	TN	A	A	A	126.4	-0.90	5.4	15.1	22.1	31.7	10.0	12.6	21.8
▲ UNION BK	JELLICO	TN	A-	B+	B+	52.2	5.38	8.8	11.1	23.7	31.9	10.0	11.4	19.8
UNION BK	MORRISVILLE	VT	A-	A-	B+	343.6	2.36	5.2	2.7	27.1	13.5	10.0	11.4	18.1
UNION BK	MIDDLEBOURNE	WV	C+	C+	B-	72.0	5.07	9.2	9.9	18.1	22.4	4.8	6.8	11.7
▲ UNION BK AZ NA	GILBERT	AZ	C+	C	D+	63.2	20.61	13.2	10.3	6.2	3.4	9.8	13.1	14.8
UNION BK CO	COLUMBUS GROVE	OH	C	C	C-	554.5	11.89	7.4	3.2	13.8	40.2	6.2	8.2	13.1
UNION BK NA	OKLAHOMA CITY	OK	B+	B+	B+	324.5	5.44	12.3	1.5	4.2	41.5	5.6	7.6	11.7
▲ UNION BK OF BENTON	BENTON	AR	C	D+	D	217.6	0.21	3.0	2.1	6.5	56.7	5.1	7.1	18.1
▲ UNION BK OF BLAIR	BLAIR	WI	C+	C	C	47.9	1.10	8.1	7.9	12.3	23.7	8.6	10.1	15.3
▲ UNION BK OF CA NA	SAN FRANCISCO	CA	A-	B+	B	45,841.0	8.90	17.3	0.9	19.3	26.7	6.3	8.5	12.0
UNION BK OF CHANDLER	CHANDLER	OK	C	C	C	66.9	11.52	25.7	6.8	13.9	15.0	7.1	9.1	12.6
▲ UNION BK OF FLORIDA	LAUDERHILL	FL	B	B-	B	1,052.5	24.27	2.4	0.5	9.8	33.7	6.0	8.1	11.8
UNION BK OF MENA	MENA	AR	B+	B+	B+	141.6	-5.68	5.6	11.3	34.2	28.5	8.7	10.1	18.5
▲ UNION BKG CO	W MANSFIELD	OH	C+	C	C	81.4	-6.29	0.9	1.4	10.0	75.9	5.7	7.7	21.7
UNION CENTER NB	UNION	NJ	B-	B-	B-	933.1	5.70	3.5	0.6	17.1	53.7	5.2	7.2	13.6
UNION COLONY BK	GREELEY	CO	C	C	C	478.9	15.93	7.5	18.1	10.7	15.9	4.1	7.2	10.5
UNION COUNTY NB OF	LIBERTY	IN	B-	B-	B	194.4	-1.69	6.4	6.0	34.8	14.5	5.5	7.5	11.6
UNION COUNTY SVGS BK	ELIZABETH	NJ	A	A	A	1,037.2	6.24	0.0	0.2	6.1	87.7	10.0	16.3	51.4
▼ UNION CREDIT BK	MIAMI	FL	C	C+	D	143.6	30.90	3.9	0.2	13.1	31.0	6.2	8.2	22.1
UNION FB OF INDIANAPOLIS	INDIANAPOLIS	IN	D-	D-	D-	3,537.2	4.17	5.9	0.4	45.9	21.6	4.8	6.8	12.2
▼ UNION FEDERAL SVGS BK	N PROVIDENCE	RI	D+	C-	C	37.4	32.01	0.0	0.0	65.5	23.2	8.5	10.0	23.3
▲ UNION FS&LA	KEWANEE	IL	C	C-	D+	120.0	-2.08	0.0	0.3	47.4	8.1	5.9	7.9	14.1
▼ UNION FS&LA	CRAWFORDSVILLE	IN	B-	B+	A-	259.0	-4.67	4.3	0.6	57.6	2.8	9.6	10.7	16.7
UNION NATIONAL COMMUNITY	MT JOY	PA	C+	C+	B-	372.4	11.46	3.8	2.8	24.1	24.9	4.3	8.3	10.6
▼ UNION NB	ELGIN	IL	C+	B-	B	235.3	23.99	20.7	0.5	1.8	2.4	3.0	9.5	10.0
UNION NB OF MT CARMEL	MT CARMEL	PA	C-	C-	C-	95.4	-6.25	5.8	4.2	35.1	31.7	7.2	9.2	16.8
UNION NB&TC	SPARTA	WI	A	A-	A-	78.8	-0.24	6.2	6.2	19.2	39.7	10.0	13.9	25.3
UNION NB&TC-BARBOURVILLE	BARBOURVILLE	KY	B-	B-	B-	180.9	4.49	8.7	6.9	28.3	15.8	8.1	9.8	14.9
▲ UNION PLANTERS	MORRISTOWN	TN	B-	C+	C+	135.3	-15.03	7.9	2.2	6.8	3.2	10.0	11.3	19.0
▲ UNION PLANTERS NA	MEMPHIS	TN	B-	C+	C+	31,944.8	-8.13	13.5	5.2	12.2	15.5	5.9	7.9	12.0
▲ UNION S&LA	CONNERSVILLE	IN	C+	C-	D+	103.8	6.65	1.2	8.7	55.3	2.7	7.2	9.2	15.7
UNION S&LA	NEW ORLEANS	LA	A-	A-	A-	76.0	-0.19	1.0	0.4	44.3	42.4	10.0	35.5	103.7
▲ UNION SAFE DEPOSIT BK	STOCKTON	CA	B+	B	B	1,128.2	1.67	12.4	0.6	12.8	31.4	5.9	8.3	11.7
UNION SAVINGS BANK	ALBUQUERQUE	NM	C+	C+	C-	63.2	23.43	0.5	1.4	15.0	42.6	6.1	8.1	16.2
▲ UNION SAVINGS BANK	CINCINNATI	OH	B+	B	C+	1,262.6	4.96	0.0	0.1	42.9	1.6	5.4	7.4	13.5
▼ UNION ST BK	PELL CITY	AL	D+	B-	B	251.9	-6.38	6.8	3.1	8.7	41.4	9.9	10.9	19.7
UNION ST BK	GREENFIELD	IA	B+	B+	B+	42.6	3.57	4.1	3.5	21.3	32.3	10.0	12.3	19.9
UNION ST BK	MONONA	IA	B+	B+	B+	66.4	2.11	4.2	4.4	21.2	26.1	9.2	10.5	16.8
UNION ST BK	ROCKWELL CITY	IA	B	B	B-	34.6	-0.76	6.6	7.7	6.8	41.4	10.0	11.3	21.4
▲ UNION ST BK	WINTERSET	IA	C+	C	C	76.8	3.06	4.8	2.5	17.3	41.6	5.7	7.7	13.9
UNION ST BK	ARKANSAS CITY	KS	B-	B-	B-	73.3	2.26	20.8	3.3	18.8	19.7	7.7	9.5	14.3
UNION ST BK	CLAY CENTER	KS	B+	B+	A-	120.5	3.45	8.1	2.7	7.3	55.5	9.1	10.4	22.2
▲ UNION ST BK	EVEREST	KS	D+	D	D	76.1	6.62	9.4	7.7	22.1	14.1	5.6	7.6	11.9
▼ UNION ST BK	OLSBURG	KS	B-	B	B	17.6	3.68	4.6	6.6	7.6	45.9	10.0	17.2	33.8
UNION ST BK	UNIONTOWN	KS	D	D	D	29.6	-0.08	5.6	5.6	22.2	18.1	5.9	7.9	13.7
UNION ST BK	BROWNS VALLEY	MN	C+	C+	C+	17.6	5.51	11.3	3.4	3.2	46.1	10.0	13.2	26.4
UNION ST BK	HAZEN	ND	B-	B-	B-	59.1	2.71	7.7	13.3	7.9	38.5	9.1	10.4	19.3

Asset Quality Index	Non-Performing Loans as a % of Total Loans	Non-Performing Loans as a % of Capital	Net Charge-offs / Avg Loans	Profitability Index	Net Income ($Mil)	Return on Assets (R.O.A.)	Return on Equity (R.O.E.)	Net Interest Spread	Overhead Efficiency Ratio	Liquidity Index	Liquidity Ratio	Hot Money Ratio	Stability Index
4.7	1.03	5.3	0.02	8.3	18.7	1.24	9.30	4.77	58.0	4.0	23.2	11.8	9.5
2.6	2.10	19.8	0.00	9.6	3.5	1.51	17.39	4.09	44.5	1.0	9.8	31.1	5.3
9.0	0.11	0.6	0.00	3.5	1.5	0.49	6.45	3.08	82.9	9.6	250.1	2.8	4.5
5.7	0.97	7.4	0.04	7.8	1.5	1.90	23.87	4.11	55.4	1.2	8.5	27.7	4.8
4.1	0.92	8.5	0.53	2.5	0.2	0.41	3.58	3.04	81.7	0.5	5.6	45.2	2.3
5.2	3.41	15.7	0.15	3.3	0.0	0.21	1.48	2.73	81.6	6.6	899.6	19.4	5.7
2.5	2.09	16.7	3.64	3.7	0.1	0.05	0.59	3.66	60.5	1.0	25.0	38.4	5.0
9.1	0.00	0.0	0.13	10.0	0.6	1.94	14.57	4.17	66.3	5.3	37.2	6.6	8.2
6.8	0.11	1.0	0.06	8.7	9.3	1.42	16.37	3.17	67.4	4.2	20.4	9.2	8.2
7.7	0.19	1.1	0.02	3.7	0.4	0.64	7.24	4.22	79.9	5.0	34.1	7.4	4.7
6.8	1.13	4.0	-0.01	9.4	0.9	2.39	28.14	5.24	54.6	3.2	18.2	13.2	4.7
3.2	1.56	14.6	-0.06	7.9	5.5	1.24	15.35	3.83	65.4	2.4	20.9	17.6	5.7
5.9	0.39	2.5	0.02	4.9	0.5	0.85	8.98	4.23	74.5	4.2	18.1	7.9	6.1
4.3	0.49	3.3	0.04	9.0	5.6	2.10	18.13	4.35	41.7	1.4	9.2	24.7	6.1
5.6	0.36	3.0	0.13	5.4	0.8	1.03	12.36	4.85	73.0	3.7	32.5	13.8	4.8
6.0	0.09	0.8	0.00	8.9	1.0	1.23	14.26	4.52	60.8	3.6	26.4	12.4	6.3
5.2	0.31	2.6	0.17	5.5	0.2	0.82	9.48	4.76	70.1	4.2	35.1	12.1	3.1
7.2	0.71	3.2	0.46	7.3	0.8	1.25	9.94	4.45	58.3	1.5	18.9	25.7	8.0
7.7	0.26	1.2	0.20	8.9	0.5	1.96	17.33	5.15	59.4	3.7	37.3	15.6	7.6
5.9	1.24	7.6	0.00	9.6	2.7	1.53	13.27	5.15	61.9	4.9	28.9	6.0	8.4
3.1	1.36	6.4	0.02	5.9	0.5	1.42	11.48	4.66	65.2	5.2	31.7	5.1	7.3
7.7	0.00	0.0	-0.02	4.0	0.2	0.60	5.00	5.84	80.9	5.0	35.3	8.2	3.9
4.3	1.45	8.7	0.33	4.0	2.0	0.76	8.07	3.58	74.5	4.0	8.2	7.7	3.9
8.8	0.05	0.3	-0.11	7.9	2.2	1.36	18.27	3.92	54.9	3.8	20.0	10.7	6.5
5.4	1.46	5.9	0.23	4.4	1.0	0.96	11.52	3.98	70.1	6.8	83.2	8.7	3.0
3.5	2.17	13.5	0.09	9.4	0.4	1.57	15.81	4.53	51.0	2.5	23.4	17.3	5.1
7.0	0.56	3.4	0.16	9.8	379.2	1.71	19.39	3.98	56.1	7.5	85.2	5.7	8.4
5.6	0.47	3.7	0.00	5.3	0.3	0.88	9.84	4.68	71.0	1.4	12.0	25.8	3.3
8.9	0.19	1.3	0.01	6.1	7.6	1.56	21.41	3.67	62.1	3.1	38.9	25.0	6.5
5.6	0.73	4.4	0.22	7.5	1.3	1.74	17.64	4.63	61.2	3.2	4.9	11.8	6.8
8.5	0.46	1.3	0.00	4.3	0.5	1.17	15.00	2.17	45.8	0.8	18.8	39.1	3.3
9.8	0.01	0.0	-0.01	4.5	3.9	0.85	11.94	3.29	65.3	2.3	26.3	19.2	4.1
3.2	1.19	7.1	1.34	4.0	1.0	0.43	4.14	4.57	65.0	5.5	155.0	25.4	5.2
6.0	0.36	3.4	-0.02	7.4	1.3	1.32	17.34	3.84	56.2	3.0	36.8	18.8	5.5
10.0	0.27	0.1	0.00	7.2	7.1	1.38	8.46	2.52	20.1	5.1	167.1	34.6	10.0
10.0	0.00	0.0	0.00	2.7	0.3	0.40	4.82	2.39	76.8	6.0	512.8	28.1	1.5
0.3	5.23	40.8	0.22	9.1	45.7	2.53	37.11	3.81	69.5	0.4	13.8	94.8	7.3
9.8	0.00	0.0	0.00	1.3	-0.3	-1.79	-15.25	2.87	117.6	3.6	27.4	12.8	0.0
4.4	0.87	8.2	0.04	3.4	0.2	0.39	5.02	3.09	77.2	3.6	14.8	11.1	2.8
3.4	1.90	14.7	0.16	5.4	0.9	0.71	5.68	3.15	65.8	0.9	14.3	32.8	7.9
6.0	0.71	5.6	0.01	4.6	1.7	0.93	11.09	4.13	74.5	2.9	11.1	14.1	4.2
6.0	0.04	0.5	-0.03	10.0	3.3	3.04	32.47	4.14	27.8	1.7	22.8	23.9	6.6
4.4	2.18	14.2	-0.08	2.5	0.2	0.33	3.77	3.36	83.3	3.5	19.9	11.9	3.0
8.6	0.02	0.1	-0.14	8.6	0.6	1.57	10.75	4.38	52.7	6.0	52.3	6.1	8.0
5.0	0.89	6.5	0.09	4.2	0.7	0.78	8.08	4.24	69.0	2.3	20.3	18.0	4.8
6.4	1.19	4.8	0.55	6.7	0.6	0.93	8.02	3.40	60.1	8.1	137.9	6.4	7.4
4.1	0.94	6.3	0.97	6.4	104.5	0.66	6.47	3.86	65.2	4.6	21.1	6.7	7.5
5.2	0.62	5.5	-0.03	4.4	0.3	0.61	6.59	4.04	73.9	2.0	5.2	17.9	4.9
9.6	0.35	0.5	0.00	6.2	0.4	0.95	2.69	3.13	53.4	4.1	14.2	7.9	8.1
9.0	0.05	0.3	0.08	5.5	6.3	1.11	13.30	4.09	69.0	3.7	36.7	18.2	7.0
8.9	0.05	0.3	0.00	5.0	0.2	0.75	9.05	3.59	64.6	0.7	20.1	57.9	3.5
6.1	0.84	7.3	0.01	10.0	15.6	2.51	34.56	2.67	52.1	2.9	37.8	27.7	6.7
5.5	1.33	5.7	2.21	1.6	-0.1	-0.05	-0.43	3.11	79.1	3.0	42.1	21.8	4.8
8.5	0.25	1.2	-0.20	7.8	0.3	1.44	11.86	4.40	51.7	4.7	55.0	13.9	5.8
6.1	0.88	5.5	0.32	5.7	0.4	1.17	11.15	3.58	60.6	2.9	16.7	14.6	7.2
8.5	0.14	0.6	0.00	5.9	0.2	1.39	12.43	3.55	60.6	5.6	40.6	6.0	6.0
5.1	1.67	10.8	0.05	5.7	0.5	1.37	17.27	3.73	63.3	2.0	21.8	19.7	4.2
6.0	0.92	6.0	-0.01	5.3	0.5	1.30	12.36	3.89	67.6	1.8	15.9	20.0	5.4
7.5	1.39	5.1	0.91	5.0	0.6	0.97	9.26	3.29	54.8	1.5	23.1	26.4	6.3
2.8	1.39	12.8	-0.01	5.2	0.3	0.77	10.08	4.15	70.6	3.1	20.6	13.9	3.0
8.6	0.24	0.6	-0.12	5.6	0.1	1.28	7.47	4.09	66.9	4.5	20.3	5.6	6.7
6.5	0.21	1.5	0.19	4.0	0.1	0.86	11.14	4.30	79.6	3.1	44.6	21.2	1.5
8.9	0.00	0.0	0.00	3.9	0.1	1.04	8.07	3.04	63.7	4.9	35.9	6.0	4.9
4.4	1.21	6.0	0.81	5.2	0.4	1.19	11.04	4.43	70.2	4.0	11.6	8.4	6.0

Name	City	State	Weiss Safety Rating	2003 Weiss Safety Rating	2002 Weiss Safety Rating	Total Assets ($Mil)	One Year Asset Growth	Asset Mix (As a % of Total Assets) Comm-ercial Loans	Cons-umer Loans	Home Mort-gages	Secur-ities	Capital-ization Index	Leverage Ratio	Risk-based Capital Ratio
UNION ST BK	NANUET	NY	B	B	B	2,972.3	9.27	5.8	0.3	8.7	42.7	5.6	7.6	13.6
UNION ST BK	CARRIZO SPRINGS	TX	D	D	D	30.9	-3.83	8.2	29.2	21.0	13.7	5.1	7.1	12.7
▼ UNION ST BK	FLORENCE	TX	C+	B-	B-	254.1	4.58	8.9	7.7	4.8	35.6	6.5	8.5	15.1
▲ UNION ST BK	KEWAUNEE	WI	C+	C-	B	67.2	-4.00	9.3	6.1	29.3	25.3	8.6	10.1	17.1
UNION ST BK	W SALEM	WI	B	B	B	46.4	2.83	7.9	8.5	23.1	44.7	10.0	13.2	23.3
▲ UNION ST BK	UPTON	WY	B-	C+	C+	21.2	-1.33	8.8	5.9	3.3	52.9	10.0	11.5	25.8
▼ UNION ST BK OF FARGO	FARGO	ND	E-	E+	E	34.6	13.07	15.8	34.3	21.6	0.1	3.1	7.8	10.0
UNION SVG BK	SEDALIA	MO	C	C	C	107.2	0.67	7.2	3.2	10.4	48.0	10.0	12.4	26.0
UNION SVGS BK	DANBURY	CT	B+	B+	B+	1,420.6	10.84	4.2	0.8	40.3	25.9	6.9	8.9	15.3
UNION SVGS BK	FREEPORT	IL	D	D-	D-	151.3	-1.03	1.3	2.7	43.6	22.7	4.7	6.7	11.8
UNION TRUST COMPANY	ELLSWORTH	ME	B-	B-	B-	466.8	18.12	2.3	2.3	35.1	28.6	5.5	7.5	13.9
UNIONBANK	STREATOR	IL	B-	B-	C+	732.0	24.61	12.1	4.3	9.2	28.0	6.8	8.8	13.3
▲ UNITED AMER BK NA	ATLANTA	GA	B	B-	D	98.6	19.62	25.6	5.8	43.1	0.1	10.0	11.5	15.3
UNITED AMERICAN BK	SAN MATEO	CA	B-	B-	NR	65.2	235.89	14.6	0.8	0.6	6.2	10.0	20.0	24.0
▼ UNITED AZ BK NA	CAVE CREEK	AZ	B-	B	B	23.1	-6.92	4.1	3.1	2.1	32.9	10.0	11.0	18.8
▼ UNITED B&T	TECUMSEH	MI	C+	B-	B	474.1	0.00	12.6	5.7	19.9	18.8	7.1	9.0	13.5
UNITED B&T WASHTENAW	ANN ARBOR	MI	C+	B-	B	167.6	19.25	14.7	2.2	13.1	9.5	3.7	8.5	10.4
UNITED B&TC	ST PETERSBURG	FL	B-	B-	C+	494.1	17.67	13.6	1.1	2.4	7.2	3.6	8.2	10.3
UNITED B&TC	ROCKMART	GA	C+	C+	C+	81.3	11.91	4.2	2.5	23.2	21.3	6.2	8.2	12.8
UNITED B&TC	HAMPTON	IA	B	B	B	76.0	-3.12	2.9	4.0	16.0	44.3	10.0	13.6	24.6
▲ UNITED B&TC	MARYSVILLE	KS	B-	B-	B+	365.4	1739.43	8.7	2.0	11.3	29.1	6.0	8.0	13.6
▲ UNITED B&TC	VERSAILLES	KY	B-	C+	B-	154.4	7.44	4.5	4.1	23.2	21.5	5.4	7.4	12.1
UNITED B&TC	NEW ORLEANS	LA	E-	E-	E+	25.3	-10.03	6.5	17.7	26.6	8.0	2.8	5.2	9.8
UNITED B&TC NA	MARSHALLTOWN	IA	B+	B	B	81.6	37.58	5.7	5.5	18.9	41.3	6.2	8.3	13.3
▼ UNITED BANKERS BK	BLOOMINGTON	MN	B-	B	B	323.5	53.13	6.0	1.7	1.0	17.6	5.7	7.7	12.3
UNITED BK	ATMORE	AL	B	B	B	275.4	10.94	14.4	4.5	8.4	21.0	7.6	9.4	13.2
UNITED BK	SPRINGDALE	AR	C+	C+	C-	148.9	26.11	4.5	2.7	41.7	0.1	3.6	9.6	10.3
UNITED BK	ZEBULON	GA	B	B-	B-	534.8	1.80	4.7	10.7	23.7	18.8	8.8	10.2	15.5
▼ UNITED BK	W SPRINGFIELD	MA	B-	NR	NR	759.4	N/A	5.6	2.7	35.0	24.2	5.8	7.8	12.9
▼ UNITED BK	FAIRFAX	VA	B	B+	B	2,925.0	20.66	7.2	0.4	15.7	21.4	4.5	8.4	10.8
▲ UNITED BK	OSSEO	WI	B-	C+	C+	140.3	2.40	11.2	3.4	15.1	13.5	4.9	7.6	11.0
▼ UNITED BK	PARKERSBURG	WV	B	B+	B	3,632.0	5.23	12.7	11.0	22.8	19.4	5.4	7.7	11.3
UNITED BK IA	IDA GROVE	IA	C	C	C	400.7	4.89	9.8	5.2	10.1	6.8	3.7	8.0	10.3
UNITED BK MI	GRAND RAPIDS	MI	B-	C+	C+	361.3	7.72	18.1	3.8	21.8	3.3	5.0	8.2	11.0
▲ UNITED BK NA	ABSAROKEE	MT	B-	C+	C+	51.6	7.57	14.5	5.4	15.9	18.2	7.3	9.2	13.4
UNITED BK NA	BUCYRUS	OH	B-	B-	B-	242.9	4.77	4.2	5.5	13.7	52.0	4.1	6.1	13.1
UNITED BK OF CHAMOIS	CHAMOIS	MO	C+	C+	C+	20.3	-2.00	7.6	6.0	17.1	29.0	10.0	13.3	22.0
UNITED BK OF EL PASO DEL	EL PASO	TX	D-	D+	D	45.2	18.83	22.5	4.6	0.0	17.0	7.8	9.5	15.3
▲ UNITED BK OF KS	WHITING	KS	C-	D+	D-	53.3	6.03	24.5	3.8	8.5	19.8	4.8	6.9	10.9
▲ UNITED BK OF PHILADELPHIA	PHILADELPHIA	PA	D-	E+	E+	71.7	-14.76	7.7	4.5	29.8	16.0	5.6	7.6	14.2
UNITED BK OF THE GULF	SARASOTA	FL	B-	B-	C	106.1	11.26	10.5	0.9	4.8	7.6	3.4	8.1	10.2
▲ UNITED BK OF UNION	UNION	MO	B	B-	C+	203.8	0.33	12.9	2.4	19.7	20.1	6.5	8.5	12.7
▲ UNITED CENTRAL BK	GARLAND	TX	C-	D+	D	312.5	5.52	9.1	1.4	0.3	6.6	7.8	10.7	13.1
▼ UNITED CITIZENS B&TC	CAMPBELLSBURG	KY	B+	A-	A-	82.8	3.87	1.0	2.7	16.4	40.0	9.8	10.8	20.7
UNITED CMNTY BK	OAKWOOD	IL	C-	C-	D	44.4	-13.47	10.5	5.8	15.5	31.9	7.7	9.5	17.6
▲ UNITED CMNTY BK	GONZALES	LA	C	C+	C	70.2	15.73	11.6	7.3	14.0	10.9	7.3	9.2	13.3
▼ UNITED CMNTY BK NA	HIGHLAND VILLAGE	TX	C	C+	C	91.7	16.37	34.8	2.4	4.5	8.9	5.6	7.6	11.7
▲ UNITED CMNTY BK OF WEST	MORGANFIELD	KY	C+	C-	D	74.0	26.60	14.6	14.3	26.8	17.1	8.2	9.8	14.5
UNITED COMMERCE BK	BLOOMINGTON	IN	B-	B-	D	108.4	13.56	17.1	4.5	33.7	7.3	7.0	9.0	13.1
UNITED COMMERCIAL BK	SAN FRANCISCO	CA	B+	B	B	6,057.1	17.61	5.8	0.0	6.0	27.1	6.2	8.2	12.6
▲ UNITED COMMERCIAL BK	ATLANTA	GA	D+	D	D	118.4	155.43	7.5	0.2	1.7	24.9	7.5	9.3	13.3
UNITED COMMUNITY BANK	BLAIRSVILLE	GA	B	B	B	3,443.5	15.93	3.9	3.2	19.5	14.7	5.5	7.9	11.4
UNITED COMMUNITY BANK	MURPHY	NC	B	B	B	877.1	6.71	2.6	2.9	20.8	22.4	4.0	6.0	10.8
UNITED COMMUNITY BK	MILFORD	IA	B	B	B	196.8	3.09	12.5	4.2	19.7	2.1	4.2	8.2	10.6
UNITED COMMUNITY BK	CHATHAM	IL	B+	B+	B-	483.9	8.99	4.5	5.0	16.4	40.1	8.3	9.9	18.6
UNITED COMMUNITY BK	LAWRENCEBURG	IN	B+	B+	B	257.0	-3.83	0.8	2.8	40.2	22.7	9.2	10.5	17.3
UNITED COMMUNITY BK	GLASGOW	KY	E-	E-	D-	34.5	-15.62	20.0	13.9	27.6	13.7	4.9	6.9	11.5
UNITED COMMUNITY BK	PERHAM	MN	C+	B-	B-	137.3	2.72	10.6	4.2	12.1	36.4	6.9	8.9	15.2
UNITED COMMUNITY BK LISLE	LISLE	IL	C-	C-	D	248.7	23.70	18.6	0.8	2.5	25.5	7.0	9.2	12.5
UNITED COMMUNITY BK OF	LEEDS	ND	C-	C-	D+	100.7	8.25	18.0	6.9	5.1	15.4	2.8	7.2	9.8
UNITED COMMUNITY BK TN	LENOIR CITY	TN	B-	B-	B-	231.8	12.95	3.4	2.9	10.4	16.2	3.8	7.8	10.4
▼ UNITED FARMERS & MERCH	MORRIS	MN	D+	C-	C-	27.2	4.22	11.0	5.3	7.6	18.7	5.1	8.4	11.1
▲ UNITED FIDELITY BK FSB	EVANSVILLE	IN	C-	D	D	189.8	30.55	2.1	22.1	24.8	33.0	5.1	7.1	13.9
▲ UNITED HERITAGE BK	ORLANDO	FL	C	C-	D	366.7	115.22	11.2	1.5	3.0	13.1	6.4	8.4	12.1

Asset Quality Index	Non-Performing Loans as a % of Total Loans	Non-Performing Loans as a % of Capital	Net Charge-offs Avg Loans	Profitability Index	Net Income ($Mil)	Return on Assets (R.O.A.)	Return on Equity (R.O.E.)	Net Interest Spread	Overhead Efficiency Ratio	Liquidity Index	Liquidity Ratio	Hot Money Ratio	Stability Index
8.7	0.28	1.9	0.02	6.0	16.0	1.09	14.89	3.22	50.8	4.1	37.4	16.4	6.4
6.3	0.24	1.8	-0.10	3.9	0.1	0.63	8.70	5.63	87.9	5.7	60.0	10.0	1.8
4.9	1.04	6.5	0.79	5.9	1.6	1.23	15.65	4.12	66.8	3.4	24.6	12.7	3.3
5.5	0.84	4.8	0.28	4.9	0.3	0.74	7.34	4.18	81.8	5.5	52.0	9.1	5.0
8.1	1.09	3.6	0.38	4.8	0.2	0.88	6.58	5.00	75.3	5.7	46.0	6.4	5.7
5.2	3.50	10.5	0.05	7.7	0.2	1.62	14.53	3.90	62.1	4.7	26.7	5.3	5.8
2.5	1.43	14.9	0.05	4.4	0.1	0.71	9.23	5.17	82.0	4.7	9.0	3.5	0.3
8.4	0.50	1.6	0.08	2.1	0.1	0.18	1.42	3.07	90.9	7.1	76.9	5.7	6.2
9.0	0.39	2.7	-0.02	5.5	6.4	0.94	10.22	3.65	63.5	7.6	108.7	7.5	7.5
3.8	1.98	18.1	0.08	1.2	0.1	0.17	2.63	3.30	94.6	4.5	31.7	9.7	2.3
6.7	0.47	3.7	0.02	6.0	2.6	1.13	14.82	3.90	67.1	4.3	16.8	6.6	4.8
4.6	1.58	8.4	0.02	4.7	2.7	0.75	7.68	3.69	71.8	1.6	18.9	23.5	5.0
5.5	1.04	7.8	0.03	5.3	0.5	0.97	8.35	4.93	63.3	2.0	8.0	18.2	6.1
7.6	0.00	0.0	0.00	0.0	-0.7	-2.45	-11.08	3.46	134.2	8.5	214.4	9.7	3.4
6.5	0.06	0.2	0.19	0.4	0.0	-0.02	-0.14	4.23	100.6	2.2	35.5	21.8	3.9
4.3	1.17	8.3	0.20	8.0	3.2	1.36	14.88	4.07	64.9	6.4	68.5	8.9	6.2
7.0	0.00	0.0	0.01	2.7	0.4	0.49	5.02	4.19	81.1	5.2	26.2	2.5	3.0
3.5	0.72	2.4	0.00	7.8	2.5	1.09	5.93	4.83	60.2	4.6	50.0	14.3	7.7
7.7	0.22	1.9	0.26	4.1	0.2	0.52	6.57	3.95	80.9	2.8	24.9	16.0	4.8
8.7	0.11	0.4	0.05	4.6	0.3	0.87	6.09	3.88	68.4	6.2	49.8	4.5	6.7
4.1	0.29	1.5	0.00	4.4	0.9	0.69	6.27	2.80	62.3	2.9	25.9	15.7	7.5
6.0	0.32	2.8	0.07	6.6	1.1	1.33	18.36	3.94	54.4	2.8	10.7	14.5	5.8
1.5	2.95	26.3	0.74	1.1	-0.1	-0.39	-7.19	5.82	98.0	7.5	138.1	9.9	0.0
8.7	0.00	0.0	0.05	0.1	0.0	0.08	1.09	2.29	97.8	2.6	21.6	16.8	5.4
6.8	0.22	1.5	0.05	6.0	1.1	0.75	10.39	3.96	80.8	6.3	37.4	0.0	3.8
4.7	0.88	6.0	0.16	4.6	1.2	0.91	9.33	4.47	73.2	1.9	23.1	20.5	4.8
3.4	1.59	11.8	0.17	6.2	1.1	1.51	15.07	3.74	68.7	0.7	12.8	35.7	8.1
4.8	0.81	5.1	0.15	9.2	3.5	1.33	12.54	5.04	62.4	3.8	16.9	10.2	8.0
6.3	0.46	3.9	-0.01	6.5	2.6	1.04	13.33	3.32	68.5	1.0	16.1	31.7	3.9
7.2	0.15	0.7	0.01	8.8	21.4	1.47	11.53	3.89	57.8	3.6	24.1	14.0	7.8
5.5	0.35	3.0	0.26	8.6	1.0	1.42	18.15	4.64	56.9	2.4	38.3	27.3	4.8
6.3	0.51	4.7	0.14	8.2	26.6	1.45	20.87	3.38	47.0	4.0	19.3	9.8	6.4
3.2	0.84	7.8	0.05	8.9	4.3	2.16	25.58	4.04	47.8	2.5	27.1	18.0	6.2
8.1	0.05	0.5	0.06	6.0	1.8	1.01	12.08	4.55	67.4	1.4	12.8	25.0	4.4
8.2	0.00	0.0	0.00	8.7	0.3	1.31	14.70	5.29	59.8	4.1	33.6	12.4	4.7
7.7	0.23	1.3	0.08	9.7	1.9	1.58	23.39	4.57	50.2	2.5	12.3	16.3	5.5
7.6	0.13	0.6	0.03	6.4	0.1	1.38	10.60	3.89	53.6	4.2	18.7	7.5	5.1
8.2	0.02	0.1	0.00	0.0	-0.3	-1.62	-11.92	4.27	139.3	2.9	28.0	16.7	0.0
7.8	0.11	0.9	0.02	3.9	0.2	0.58	7.19	3.76	76.9	2.9	43.4	23.6	3.1
2.9	1.67	10.0	-1.13	2.3	0.3	0.71	7.30	5.03	93.2	4.2	50.2	15.4	1.1
4.8	0.30	1.2	0.00	2.1	0.1	0.13	0.69	3.77	82.3	1.8	22.1	21.7	7.4
7.0	0.25	2.0	0.03	5.8	1.5	1.46	17.44	4.01	54.6	5.1	30.6	4.9	4.6
2.6	1.97	13.5	0.50	7.6	2.3	1.52	14.55	5.10	63.5	2.7	53.5	36.5	5.3
7.6	0.76	3.4	0.02	5.0	0.4	0.89	8.12	3.46	66.8	6.9	97.9	8.4	6.5
5.8	0.48	2.6	1.19	3.0	0.1	0.39	4.16	3.88	81.9	6.6	128.7	13.5	2.6
5.2	0.24	1.8	0.27	6.7	0.4	1.14	12.64	5.05	65.6	3.9	51.5	17.3	3.9
5.8	0.30	2.8	0.31	3.6	0.3	0.56	7.41	5.69	82.6	2.6	36.7	22.0	3.4
7.7	0.11	0.8	0.14	4.0	0.3	0.95	9.70	4.30	60.2	3.5	11.6	11.3	1.8
7.5	0.30	2.7	0.10	3.6	0.3	0.52	5.87	3.79	76.3	1.7	36.0	40.6	2.6
7.1	0.23	1.5	0.07	8.6	43.7	1.51	16.19	3.84	39.4	1.7	26.6	33.8	7.2
7.6	0.08	0.5	0.00	1.6	0.2	0.48	4.74	3.34	69.8	3.1	68.4	53.8	0.4
7.9	0.23	1.8	0.10	8.0	20.9	1.30	14.74	4.18	56.9	1.2	12.6	29.8	7.1
8.1	0.15	1.3	0.06	6.4	4.3	0.96	13.33	3.60	59.0	2.6	17.5	16.0	5.6
6.0	0.24	2.0	0.01	7.5	1.7	1.75	17.41	4.41	58.9	2.9	23.6	15.5	6.4
5.8	0.62	3.3	0.19	9.0	4.4	1.87	18.31	3.20	51.4	3.2	44.9	20.2	7.5
5.7	0.62	3.9	0.17	5.8	1.1	0.85	8.05	3.42	65.0	0.6	11.6	51.9	6.4
5.9	0.36	2.4	0.18	1.5	0.0	-0.05	-0.64	5.37	99.0	1.8	22.6	21.9	0.0
5.9	1.13	6.5	-0.01	3.5	0.6	0.88	9.81	3.44	77.0	3.8	34.0	14.1	5.0
7.4	0.46	3.1	0.90	2.4	0.4	0.35	3.94	3.47	70.0	3.1	14.5	13.7	1.2
4.0	0.93	8.7	0.12	6.5	0.6	1.18	15.85	4.66	61.1	1.9	20.2	20.6	3.7
6.1	0.23	0.9	0.00	2.8	0.2	0.17	1.11	3.54	89.9	4.3	50.1	16.0	6.6
8.2	0.00	0.0	0.00	3.5	0.1	0.53	6.58	4.46	84.6	4.9	8.9	1.7	3.0
3.2	0.73	4.6	0.42	2.3	0.4	0.41	4.79	2.74	83.8	0.7	2.8	33.4	3.1
8.5	0.17	1.2	0.05	3.2	0.9	0.62	6.86	3.59	64.0	4.7	92.4	21.8	2.0

Name	City	State	Weiss Safety Rating	2003 Weiss Safety Rating	2002 Weiss Safety Rating	Total Assets ($Mil)	One Year Asset Growth	Asset Mix (As a % of Total Assets) Comm-ercial Loans	Cons-umer Loans	Home Mort-gages	Secur-ities	Capital-ization Index	Leverage Ratio	Risk-based Capital Ratio
UNITED HERITAGE BK	EDISON	NJ	D-	D-	D+	56.1	21.61	11.0	0.4	15.7	42.8	5.3	7.3	15.7
UNITED KY BK-PENDLETON	FALMOUTH	KY	C	C	C	30.2	-6.17	14.2	11.4	12.9	23.8	9.6	10.8	18.0
UNITED LABOR BK FSB	OAKLAND	CA	B	B	B	133.5	4.18	1.9	0.2	4.6	9.7	6.6	9.5	12.2
▲ UNITED MIDWEST SAVINGS	DE GRAFF	OH	C-	D	D-	220.8	5.06	0.1	5.4	51.1	1.6	10.0	12.1	20.8
▲ UNITED MINNESOTA BK	NEW LONDON	MN	D	D-	D-	21.6	-13.59	13.4	6.1	15.6	22.1	6.1	8.1	12.8
UNITED MISSISSIPPI BK	NATCHEZ	MS	A-	A-	A	175.5	40.92	9.5	9.7	18.9	20.6	7.8	9.5	15.6
▲ UNITED NB	SAN MARINO	CA	C	C-	C	891.8	10.68	8.1	0.0	0.5	14.3	2.6	7.4	9.6
▲ UNITED NB	CAIRO	GA	C+	C	C+	103.4	13.68	20.1	7.8	14.1	0.3	4.8	8.8	10.9
UNITED NB	NATOMA	KS	C-	C-	D+	65.4	2.16	10.0	5.5	9.3	40.3	6.5	8.5	13.4
UNITED NE BK	GRAND ISLAND	NE	B	B	B+	503.3	-2.70	5.8	3.8	5.5	30.1	6.4	8.4	12.3
UNITED ORIENT BK	NEW YORK	NY	C-	C	C+	91.3	-5.72	9.5	0.2	15.0	12.9	7.2	9.1	14.5
▲ UNITED PACIFIC BK	CITY OF INDUSTR	CA	D	D-	D-	84.3	-27.19	1.4	0.0	1.5	21.6	10.0	14.8	26.2
UNITED PRAIRIE BK	MOUNTAIN LAKE	MN	B-	B-	C+	126.5	5.46	9.9	3.3	4.6	20.8	5.8	7.8	12.5
UNITED PRAIRIE BK MADISON	MADISON	MN	B-	B-	B-	33.6	-2.61	6.9	3.9	7.6	21.6	7.2	9.1	14.2
UNITED PRAIRIE BK NEW ULM	NEW ULM	MN	B-	B-	B-	29.5	9.33	21.3	5.8	7.3	23.4	7.2	9.1	12.9
UNITED PRAIRIE BK	OWATONNA	MN	B-	B-	C+	100.3	16.58	12.5	1.9	10.0	14.0	5.1	7.8	11.1
UNITED PRAIRIE BK SPICER	SPICER	MN	B-	B-	B-	60.9	17.37	12.7	3.2	9.1	15.7	4.1	8.2	10.6
UNITED PRAIRIE BK-JACKSON	JACKSON	MN	B-	B-	B-	35.8	-4.33	7.5	4.8	5.2	20.4	6.0	8.0	11.8
UNITED PRAIRIE BK-SLAYTON	SLAYTON	MN	B-	B-	B-	33.8	-5.73	12.0	6.5	3.9	22.6	10.0	15.1	23.1
▲ UNITED ROOSEVELT SB	CARTERET	NJ	B-	C+	B-	103.2	-1.57	0.0	0.1	18.4	71.3	10.0	12.9	50.8
▲ UNITED SECURITY BANK	FRESNO	CA	D+	D	D+	557.5	9.20	14.2	1.5	6.2	17.0	7.5	10.5	12.9
UNITED SECURITY BK	SPARTA	GA	D	D-	D-	61.0	44.29	6.1	8.3	18.3	11.2	3.3	7.4	10.2
UNITED SECURITY BK	FULTON	MO	B+	B+	B+	32.2	1.74	4.9	10.9	34.0	17.6	10.0	14.1	24.1
▲ UNITED SECURITY SVGS BK	MARION	IA	D	D-	D-	42.2	-7.78	8.4	14.0	35.9	10.9	6.6	8.6	14.1
UNITED SOUTHERN BK	UMATILLA	FL	B	B	B	313.8	6.01	6.2	3.0	17.0	22.5	6.7	8.7	14.1
▲ UNITED SOUTHERN BK	HOPKINSVILLE	KY	C+	C	C	124.1	5.43	5.4	4.6	28.4	24.0	7.2	9.1	13.7
▲ UNITED SOUTHWEST BK	COTTONWOOD	MN	E	E-	D+	41.0	-3.06	7.4	6.4	5.1	22.8	5.7	8.1	11.5
UNITED ST BK	LEWISTOWN	MO	B-	B-	B-	60.9	10.22	6.3	8.1	10.8	21.9	8.0	9.7	14.7
UNITED STATES TC OF NY	NEW YORK	NY	D+	D+	C-	6,691.6	14.39	0.0	7.5	68.4	10.8	3.6	5.6	10.8
UNITED SVG BK	PHILADELPHIA	PA	A-	A	A	218.5	5.65	0.9	0.1	47.4	35.6	10.0	14.8	34.4
UNITED TEXAS BK	DALLAS	TX	D-	D-	C-	87.2	-20.85	7.7	4.2	0.6	1.2	9.6	10.7	15.6
▲ UNITED TRUST BANK	BRIDGEVIEW	IL	E+	E-	E-	38.3	-1.16	0.3	3.2	33.7	10.1	6.9	8.9	14.5
▲ UNITED VALLEY BK	ARGYLE	MN	D-	E+	D-	16.8	10.30	14.3	5.6	2.0	19.4	10.0	12.9	16.2
UNITED VALLEY BK	CAVALIER	ND	C	C	D+	83.5	7.56	22.3	11.8	8.6	12.8	6.3	8.8	12.0
▲ UNITED-AMERICAN SVGS BK	PITTSBURGH	PA	E+	E	E-	36.1	-14.13	0.0	0.7	52.9	21.9	6.2	8.2	17.2
UNITEDKINGFIELD BK	BANGOR	ME	B-	B-	B-	422.4	8.19	9.0	1.6	22.3	21.6	4.9	6.9	11.8
▲ UNITI BK	BUENA PARK	CA	C	D+	D	102.7	94.79	26.3	1.7	0.1	6.7	10.0	17.3	21.2
▲ UNITY BK	CLINTON	NJ	C-	D+	D+	490.2	9.51	9.0	0.6	12.6	22.3	5.2	7.2	12.2
UNITY NB	CARTERSVILLE	GA	C+	C+	C+	172.3	16.16	5.2	4.5	16.7	7.2	4.7	8.5	10.8
UNITY NB OF HOUSTON	HOUSTON	TX	D	D	D+	55.9	-4.39	15.5	7.6	16.9	6.8	6.3	8.3	13.1
UNIVERSAL BANK	W COVINA	CA	C+	C+	C+	407.6	18.75	4.2	0.1	2.3	3.1	6.5	10.0	12.2
▲ UNIVERSAL FINANCIAL CORP.	SALT LAKE CITY	UT	B-	C+	C+	519.3	-39.50	97.8	0.0	0.0	0.6	10.0	21.8	23.4
UNIVERSAL SVGS BK FA	MILWAUKEE	WI	B+	B+	B+	166.3	113.30	0.0	72.5	7.4	6.0	4.5	8.8	10.8
▼ UNIVERSITY BK	ANN ARBOR	MI	E	D-	E-	45.7	6.47	12.4	0.7	41.1	2.9	5.5	7.9	11.4
UNIVERSITY NB	CHICAGO	IL	B	B+	B+	111.7	1.61	3.1	2.6	8.6	73.8	5.4	7.4	22.9
▼ UNIVERSITY NB	PITTSBURG	KS	D+	C-	C	84.3	5.55	15.4	6.4	45.0	0.0	3.5	6.7	10.3
▲ UNIVERSITY NB	ST PAUL	MN	B-	C	C	106.8	12.67	13.0	1.3	24.0	6.0	7.7	9.7	13.1
UNIVERSITY NB LAWRENCE	LAWRENCE	KS	A	A	A-	91.0	4.15	9.4	2.2	31.7	0.4	10.0	11.9	15.5
UNIVEST NB&TC	SOUDERTON	PA	A-	A-	A-	1,627.2	7.41	20.0	3.6	16.5	21.5	6.4	8.6	12.0
UNIZAN BANK NA	CANTON	OH	B-	B-	B-	2,663.7	-3.35	12.8	6.4	22.6	15.0	5.9	7.9	13.1
UPSTATE NB	LISBON	NY	D-	D-	D-	99.4	-1.51	11.3	0.5	3.8	28.5	7.5	9.4	15.6
US BK NA	CINCINNATI	OH	C+	C+	B-	189,736.6	-0.93	14.4	10.4	9.9	21.1	4.8	6.8	11.1
US BK NA ND	FARGO	ND	B	B-	B-	3,428.5	14.79	42.7	17.7	15.0	0.0	10.0	11.5	17.0
▲ US CENTURY BK	MIAMI	FL	C+	C	D	296.0	158.68	10.4	0.4	4.1	5.2	10.0	30.1	39.9
▲ US TC NA	GREENWICH	CT	B-	C	C	3,068.2	171.87	2.9	9.9	5.4	38.5	9.6	10.7	27.6
▼ USAA FSB	SAN ANTONIO	TX	B-	B-	B-	15,511.6	17.52	0.0	63.2	12.0	5.1	3.6	8.5	10.3
▲ USAA SAVINGS BANK	LAS VEGAS	NV	B+	B-	B-	6,241.8	60.30	0.0	97.9	0.0	0.2	10.0	32.5	32.3
UTAH COMMUNITY BK	SANDY	UT	B+	B+	B	37.7	-19.20	2.2	7.0	4.8	0.0	10.0	17.1	22.0
▲ UTAH INDEPENDENT BK	SALINA	UT	A-	B+	B+	35.2	-11.79	24.2	12.9	6.7	9.3	10.0	16.5	22.9
VALLEY B&T	MAPLETON	IA	A-	A-	B	53.4	1.43	11.9	4.8	4.6	36.7	10.0	11.1	16.9
▲ VALLEY B&T	NEW ULM	MN	B+	B	B	84.6	-0.97	11.3	6.5	14.1	20.2	6.2	8.7	11.9
VALLEY B&TC	BRIGHTON	CO	C+	C	C	234.4	10.16	5.6	2.1	6.8	20.0	5.5	8.0	11.4
▲ VALLEY B&TC	CHEROKEE	IA	D	D-	E+	17.8	-3.70	17.2	5.1	17.6	12.9	7.9	9.6	14.1
▲ VALLEY B&TC	SCOTTSBLUFF	NE	D+	D-	E	238.0	-1.99	20.6	6.6	10.6	14.1	4.5	7.7	10.7

Asset Quality Index	Non-Performing Loans as a % of Total Loans	as a % of Capital	Net Charge-offs Avg Loans	Profitability Index	Net Income ($Mil)	Return on Assets (R.O.A.)	Return on Equity (R.O.E.)	Net Interest Spread	Overhead Efficiency Ratio	Liquidity Index	Liquidity Ratio	Hot Money Ratio	Stability Index
6.9	0.60	3.0	0.00	0.0	-0.6	-2.23	-27.27	1.87	209.2	9.2	225.8	5.7	3.8
5.7	0.59	3.1	-0.05	2.5	0.0	0.23	2.18	3.70	86.6	5.6	64.9	11.3	3.2
6.8	0.00	0.0	0.00	5.8	0.5	0.83	8.75	4.68	71.0	1.7	38.8	66.2	6.1
2.0	2.97	19.2	0.34	6.4	1.3	0.91	7.06	4.27	74.9	0.8	18.6	41.3	7.3
6.8	0.39	2.9	0.00	4.1	0.1	0.72	9.17	4.12	76.4	4.6	31.9	6.5	1.8
5.6	0.34	2.0	0.31	6.3	1.1	1.26	12.54	4.42	77.6	3.5	31.1	14.3	8.2
5.8	0.22	2.1	0.01	5.6	4.4	1.03	14.01	3.85	53.0	5.2	180.5	36.7	4.4
5.1	0.48	4.8	0.09	7.7	0.6	1.19	13.80	4.37	50.6	2.6	5.8	15.2	2.5
3.5	2.73	14.9	-0.09	3.6	0.2	0.58	6.71	3.74	76.8	4.2	41.8	14.4	3.1
4.4	0.98	5.7	0.21	8.2	3.6	1.40	15.03	4.26	59.9	5.4	39.0	6.7	6.8
3.5	1.61	12.3	0.27	2.1	0.1	0.15	1.68	4.70	104.1	4.9	23.9	4.1	4.0
7.0	1.32	4.1	-1.57	0.8	0.1	0.30	2.30	3.12	161.8	5.5	226.9	38.1	2.2
4.6	0.79	5.2	0.13	5.4	0.6	0.99	10.99	4.78	72.3	4.7	35.9	9.9	5.1
5.1	0.60	2.8	0.68	6.4	0.3	1.66	13.97	4.48	57.7	3.4	61.7	25.3	6.0
6.7	0.16	0.7	-0.10	6.0	0.4	2.62	19.19	4.67	63.9	3.1	18.0	13.8	6.1
4.0	0.34	1.8	0.00	8.2	1.0	2.13	17.30	4.44	55.5	4.6	20.7	5.3	6.3
7.9	0.03	0.2	0.00	7.6	0.4	1.54	15.55	4.77	64.4	2.2	14.8	18.2	6.3
8.3	0.00	0.0	0.00	4.7	0.1	0.31	3.74	4.82	74.7	5.3	61.7	11.9	4.7
7.1	0.00	0.0	0.22	5.7	0.1	0.77	4.98	4.43	67.1	5.3	57.5	11.2	6.0
10.0	1.01	1.3	0.00	3.7	0.3	0.55	3.92	2.92	68.7	8.6	162.4	5.9	7.2
2.3	2.53	14.6	3.24	7.3	2.0	0.75	6.71	4.86	47.6	1.9	31.0	27.5	8.0
2.7	1.31	14.4	0.09	7.3	0.6	1.98	26.34	4.86	51.4	0.7	8.8	36.7	2.3
7.9	0.00	0.0	0.07	8.2	0.2	1.45	10.33	5.78	63.6	5.2	52.8	11.3	6.6
1.3	2.20	18.4	0.73	3.3	0.1	0.25	2.99	3.40	87.8	2.3	8.5	16.8	3.1
6.2	0.62	4.1	-0.16	5.5	1.2	0.79	9.16	4.22	70.0	6.6	77.4	9.1	4.8
8.5	0.16	1.2	-0.02	3.5	0.5	0.88	9.34	3.41	67.9	2.0	18.5	19.2	5.1
1.6	3.67	23.7	0.17	3.0	0.2	0.86	10.70	4.92	86.8	5.9	42.5	4.7	1.0
5.5	1.10	7.4	0.02	5.8	0.5	1.51	15.49	4.00	60.6	4.5	32.8	10.1	4.3
8.8	0.02	0.2	0.00	0.9	2.4	0.07	1.30	2.60	100.5	1.2	13.1	29.1	3.6
9.9	0.00	0.0	0.00	5.1	0.8	0.73	4.78	2.92	66.0	5.4	69.0	13.9	8.5
2.0	5.02	22.8	-0.52	0.0	-0.4	-0.72	-6.91	2.72	139.2	5.0	126.6	24.4	4.1
4.3	1.70	14.3	0.93	0.0	-0.2	-1.23	-13.71	3.25	119.0	1.3	29.8	37.6	0.0
7.1	0.80	3.9	0.17	2.1	0.0	0.29	3.01	1.40	78.3	4.4	18.6	5.9	2.5
4.6	0.55	4.3	0.07	5.6	0.6	1.40	15.75	4.48	64.9	4.9	63.7	14.7	4.4
3.7	2.79	23.1	0.19	2.3	0.1	0.30	3.67	3.40	87.3	3.8	81.3	27.1	0.4
5.4	0.58	4.5	-0.25	6.4	2.4	1.12	14.06	4.09	61.9	2.3	10.3	16.9	5.8
8.1	0.00	0.0	0.00	4.5	0.7	1.55	8.74	3.97	64.9	3.8	78.2	30.0	3.3
4.1	1.49	13.2	0.15	6.1	2.5	1.05	15.34	3.96	65.8	6.2	51.8	5.9	1.8
4.2	0.45	4.3	0.18	5.9	0.9	1.13	13.64	4.45	58.6	0.9	8.9	31.2	4.7
0.9	5.17	40.0	2.51	3.7	0.1	0.32	3.79	6.40	80.4	2.6	36.5	22.2	3.4
3.4	0.63	5.3	0.49	9.0	2.6	1.35	13.48	4.29	48.6	0.5	9.3	55.2	4.9
4.1	2.33	7.9	7.31	10.0	11.7	4.49	21.82	11.19	17.1	0.1	4.3	99.6	7.9
3.7	0.29	2.7	0.11	2.0	-3.1	-5.43	-44.41	4.94	213.1	1.6	41.4	97.6	8.4
2.9	1.68	17.3	0.15	1.2	-0.2	-1.02	-13.30	4.76	106.7	3.0	10.3	13.6	0.5
9.8	0.14	0.4	0.00	4.6	0.5	0.91	12.20	3.23	75.2	5.9	49.7	7.1	4.9
2.4	1.60	18.9	0.31	6.1	0.4	0.89	12.80	3.79	57.5	2.8	55.0	30.3	3.2
4.8	0.49	3.8	0.09	10.0	1.0	2.51	26.51	5.30	53.1	1.7	26.4	25.4	6.1
8.4	0.26	2.0	-0.03	10.0	1.5	3.57	30.28	5.56	45.2	3.0	43.2	22.1	8.1
5.3	0.76	4.8	0.09	8.4	11.3	1.39	13.98	4.09	60.1	4.7	21.7	6.4	9.2
4.0	1.24	7.9	0.37	4.0	7.1	0.52	4.98	3.06	70.8	3.2	20.2	14.0	6.9
3.4	1.33	7.3	3.06	0.5	0.0	0.07	0.85	3.65	97.8	4.5	53.9	14.8	3.3
3.8	0.87	5.1	0.70	10.0	1,983.3	2.09	21.20	4.34	43.5	6.1	41.7	6.7	8.8
6.3	0.49	2.6	1.37	9.8	44.7	2.66	22.60	3.85	39.4	5.2	6.6	0.0	8.1
8.8	0.00	0.0	0.00	2.9	0.8	0.67	2.14	3.83	48.8	4.5	104.8	28.0	2.4
6.6	0.02	0.0	0.00	7.0	17.6	1.25	4.58	2.65	83.8	7.8	86.4	4.1	5.7
5.4	0.21	2.0	0.80	9.1	93.5	1.29	14.88	3.87	62.4	0.9	16.2	34.9	7.8
5.5	0.46	1.4	1.51	10.0	94.1	3.18	9.94	6.30	38.3	0.1	1.8	90.0	9.4
7.1	0.00	0.0	0.11	10.0	0.4	2.19	13.49	6.80	49.1	5.6	159.4	23.6	3.2
6.3	0.91	3.5	0.10	10.0	0.4	2.17	13.21	5.53	48.8	5.9	72.7	10.7	7.9
8.3	0.00	0.0	-0.01	7.8	0.5	1.91	16.99	4.09	60.9	4.3	12.3	6.3	7.0
5.8	0.05	0.2	0.21	9.2	0.6	1.40	9.06	4.77	62.0	4.8	26.1	5.1	8.3
7.1	0.60	4.1	-0.11	5.9	1.9	1.65	18.16	6.16	76.1	3.2	21.9	13.6	4.1
4.4	1.59	10.7	-0.14	5.2	0.1	0.91	8.73	4.01	77.2	5.5	35.5	2.0	2.0
2.1	1.61	12.8	0.56	4.1	0.8	0.65	7.72	4.09	66.5	1.7	22.9	24.2	3.1

Name	City	State	Weiss Safety Rating	2003 Weiss Safety Rating	2002 Weiss Safety Rating	Total Assets ($Mil)	One Year Asset Growth	Commercial Loans	Consumer Loans	Home Mortgages	Securities	Capitalization Index	Leverage Ratio	Risk-based Capital Ratio
▲ VALLEY BK	MORENO VALLEY	CA	D+	D	D-	91.9	8.76	2.8	0.2	18.8	3.8	4.1	8.3	10.6
▲ VALLEY BK	BRISTOL	CT	C	C-	D+	117.1	36.47	14.9	1.1	11.6	27.5	5.9	7.9	12.7
▼ VALLEY BK	MOLINE	IL	C-	C+	B-	361.5	12.02	10.2	0.7	10.0	18.1	2.9	7.1	9.9
VALLEY BK	N MANKATO	MN	B+	B+	B+	106.3	-5.57	17.3	4.9	7.0	25.1	5.3	7.6	11.2
VALLEY BK	HENDERSON	NV	C	C	D	227.0	34.92	14.0	0.6	1.3	5.6	2.6	7.6	9.7
VALLEY BK	ROANOKE	VA	C+	C+	C+	346.6	20.99	17.6	2.2	9.1	20.4	3.8	7.9	10.4
VALLEY BK	PUYALLUP	WA	A	A-	A-	179.9	2.22	17.4	1.2	4.4	18.9	10.0	12.3	17.3
VALLEY BK DUNDAS	DUNDAS	MN	B	B	B	27.4	4.67	9.7	4.2	18.8	13.4	6.7	8.7	13.4
VALLEY BK MN	JORDAN	MN	B	B	B	47.6	-4.53	11.2	3.7	14.2	24.4	6.0	8.3	11.8
VALLEY BK NA	ELK POINT	SD	C+	C+	C	70.5	-0.13	15.7	2.0	3.8	24.6	10.0	12.1	17.6
VALLEY BK OF COMMERCE	ROSWELL	NM	B-	B-	B-	73.2	-4.16	26.1	3.1	4.4	12.0	6.8	9.3	12.4
VALLEY BK OF HELENA	HELENA	MT	B	B	B	230.6	15.29	7.3	3.6	17.3	44.8	5.5	7.5	13.8
VALLEY BK OF KALISPELL	KALISPELL	MT	A	A	A	101.9	-4.12	18.8	7.0	12.1	31.0	7.8	9.6	17.1
VALLEY BK OF MARYLAND	PIKESVILLE	MD	C	C-	D+	43.9	3.89	1.6	5.3	28.0	16.6	9.5	10.7	16.8
▲ VALLEY BK OF RONAN	RONAN	MT	C	D+	C-	44.7	8.71	11.7	9.0	15.4	1.8	6.1	9.6	11.9
▲ VALLEY BK-GLASGOW	GLASGOW	MT	C-	D+	D	27.7	-3.02	6.5	6.6	4.4	14.3	7.4	9.2	14.9
VALLEY CENTRAL SB	READING	OH	A	A	A	80.3	-3.99	0.0	0.7	47.7	17.6	10.0	26.4	59.5
VALLEY CMNTY BK	ST CHARLES	IL	D	D	D	123.9	7.63	11.0	4.0	12.7	18.4	2.9	7.3	9.9
VALLEY COMMERCE BK	PHOENIX	AZ	A-	A-	A-	152.2	-0.60	12.7	1.0	7.2	30.6	10.0	11.7	16.5
▼ VALLEY COMMUNITY BK	PLEASANTON	CA	C	C+	C+	119.2	19.59	14.3	0.4	8.8	14.8	8.7	10.8	13.9
VALLEY EXCHANGE BK	LENNOX	SD	B-	B	B	58.7	8.61	10.1	4.6	4.2	42.7	10.0	14.8	30.1
VALLEY FIRST CMNTY BK	SCOTTSDALE	AZ	C	C	C	53.0	22.72	9.1	0.9	2.3	0.1	5.1	11.3	11.1
▲ VALLEY INDEPENDENT BK	EL CENTRO	CA	C	C-	C-	2,423.4	28.79	3.2	0.9	6.7	21.9	4.8	8.1	10.9
VALLEY NB	PASSAIC	NJ	C+	B-	B+	10,445.3	11.29	11.1	11.2	17.1	29.9	3.1	7.0	10.1
▼ VALLEY NB	ESPANOLA	NM	C+	B-	B-	251.7	10.39	13.6	4.7	9.6	31.9	9.0	10.3	17.5
▼ VALLEY NB	TULSA	OK	D	D+	D+	160.1	22.87	27.9	1.2	6.2	1.6	1.4	7.0	8.4
VALLEY RIDGE BK	KENT CITY	MI	B+	B+	B	197.6	1.97	11.1	3.7	15.1	22.6	7.8	9.5	14.1
VALLEY ST BK	RUSSELLVILLE	AL	B+	B	C+	113.3	5.45	3.4	4.4	6.8	52.3	10.0	11.5	20.8
VALLEY ST BK	LAMAR	CO	B+	B+	B+	102.7	1.12	10.9	8.8	14.6	23.5	8.8	10.2	16.2
VALLEY ST BK	GUTTENBERG	IA	C	C+	C+	28.0	10.38	8.4	5.6	29.5	23.6	5.6	7.6	13.4
VALLEY ST BK	BELLE PLAINE	KS	B+	B+	B+	80.8	-0.79	15.3	11.9	19.2	27.7	10.0	11.5	19.0
VALLEY ST BK	ROELAND PARK	KS	D	D	E-	37.3	-8.27	9.8	11.1	22.2	17.7	5.2	7.9	11.2
VALLEY ST BK	SYRACUSE	KS	C	C-	C	44.9	-4.33	9.6	2.3	4.7	31.1	7.9	9.6	15.9
▼ VALLEY SVGS BK	CUYAHOGA FALLS	OH	D+	C	C	107.8	18.23	2.4	0.0	55.4	2.6	4.6	6.6	10.9
VALLEY VIEW ST BK	OVERLAND PARK	KS	A-	A	A	626.8	-1.03	14.5	2.0	5.3	30.0	10.0	12.7	17.3
▲ VALRICO ST BK	VALRICO	FL	B-	C+	C-	127.1	0.86	4.3	2.9	8.2	19.1	6.1	8.3	11.8
VALUEBANK TX	CORPUS CHRISTI	TX	B-	C+	C	141.8	2.80	11.5	5.4	9.5	12.3	7.0	9.0	12.8
VAN HORN ST BK	VAN HORN	TX	C-	C	C	25.2	4.09	12.5	13.4	17.9	21.6	8.5	10.0	16.6
VAN WERT FSB	VAN WERT	OH	A	A	A-	108.1	1.05	0.0	1.0	61.9	22.9	10.0	15.3	33.0
▼ VANGUARD B&TC	VALPARAISO	FL	B-	B-	B	523.2	8.72	10.3	1.4	7.6	7.2	3.4	9.7	10.2
▲ VARTAN NB	HARRISBURG	PA	B	B	C-	67.2	10.60	9.7	2.3	34.3	8.2	6.1	8.1	11.9
VECTRA BK COLORADO NA	FARMINGTON	NM	C+	C	B-	2,448.4	-11.18	10.4	1.7	9.9	17.3	6.0	8.0	13.0
VENTURA COUNTY BUSINESS	OXNARD	CA	D	D	NR	64.3	159.41	28.8	0.3	0.3	1.6	10.0	15.0	15.6
VENTURE BK	BLOOMINGTON	MN	C+	C	D-	94.5	36.00	31.8	2.3	9.2	12.5	6.3	8.6	11.9
▲ VENTURE BK	LACEY	WA	B-	C-	D+	527.0	10.81	7.8	1.8	1.8	14.3	6.3	10.5	12.0
▼ VERGAS ST BK	VERGAS	MN	B	B+	B+	35.2	3.81	14.0	6.8	7.9	44.3	10.0	14.3	25.9
VERMILLION B&TC	KAPLAN	LA	C+	C+	B-	65.2	-5.64	23.7	10.0	18.0	21.0	7.4	9.2	16.4
VERMILLION ST BK	VERMILLION	KS	B	B	B	16.9	8.25	3.0	6.6	16.2	47.5	10.0	17.2	37.9
VERMILLION ST BK	VERMILLION	MN	A	A	A	292.4	10.56	25.0	3.3	11.5	22.0	8.6	10.0	15.0
VERMILLION VALLEY BK	PIPER CITY	IL	B	B	B	88.3	6.01	4.5	5.1	13.0	37.1	7.5	9.4	15.5
VERMONT ST BK	VERMONT	IL	C	C	C	5.8	7.96	2.2	32.5	33.8	18.2	10.0	15.3	23.4
VERNON BK	LEESVILLE	LA	C-	C-	C+	38.4	2.51	7.6	12.7	18.5	32.4	7.4	9.2	16.7
VERSAILLES S&LC	VERSAILLES	OH	B	B	B	37.4	0.47	0.5	2.2	66.3	10.8	10.0	16.5	31.5
▲ VERUS BK NA	DERBY	KS	B+	B	B	77.7	2.69	3.0	8.3	20.4	27.8	7.9	9.6	15.2
VICTOR ST BK	VICTOR	IA	A-	A-	B+	34.9	1.60	8.0	3.9	20.1	46.3	10.0	11.9	18.3
▲ VICTORIA ST BK	VICTORIA	MN	A-	B+	B	57.9	7.42	4.9	2.4	13.0	33.8	7.7	9.5	14.1
VICTORY COMMUNITY BANK	FORT MITCHELL	KY	B	B-	D	53.0	69.91	0.0	0.6	45.6	0.0	10.0	12.0	18.8
VICTORY ST BK	STATEN ISLAND	NY	B-	B-	B-	209.3	18.97	5.4	0.4	0.6	45.1	6.6	8.6	17.7
VIDALIA FEDERAL SAVINGS	VIDALIA	GA	B-	B-	B-	204.8	5.96	0.2	1.4	27.0	51.0	8.7	10.1	28.0
▼ VIGILANT FSB	BALTIMORE	MD	E+	D	D	45.5	20.94	0.0	0.2	42.0	24.5	4.7	6.7	17.7
▲ VIKING COMMUNITY BK	SEATTLE	WA	B+	B	B-	280.2	13.26	12.1	1.4	8.0	7.8	7.0	9.5	12.5
VIKING ST B&T	DECORAH	IA	B+	B	B	62.3	22.98	11.6	4.7	20.4	5.1	7.1	10.1	12.6
▲ VIKING SVGS ASSOC FA	ALEXANDRIA	MN	B-	C+	C+	98.2	9.86	4.9	3.5	40.7	8.6	6.2	8.3	12.2
VILLA GROVE ST BK	VILLA GROVE	IL	C	C	C	48.6	1.96	12.5	5.1	33.1	17.5	7.2	9.1	16.2

Asset Quality Index	Non-Performing Loans as a % of Total Loans	as a % of Capital	Net Charge-offs Avg Loans	Profitability Index	Net Income ($Mil)	Return on Assets (R.O.A.)	Return on Equity (R.O.E.)	Net Interest Spread	Overhead Efficiency Ratio	Liquidity Index	Liquidity Ratio	Hot Money Ratio	Stability Index
5.7	0.25	2.2	-0.06	4.4	0.7	1.66	20.49	5.86	85.4	4.8	9.7	2.8	1.5
8.0	0.20	1.6	0.07	3.2	0.2	0.44	5.56	3.72	77.3	6.1	65.7	10.2	5.0
5.4	0.55	4.9	0.23	4.6	1.4	0.83	11.40	3.88	72.9	2.5	35.2	22.5	3.3
6.7	0.02	0.1	0.15	6.2	0.6	1.01	7.73	4.50	63.6	4.8	22.2	4.5	7.4
6.0	0.00	0.0	0.01	5.9	1.3	1.26	16.08	4.77	51.4	4.6	57.3	16.4	3.6
7.0	0.17	1.5	0.01	4.7	1.4	0.85	10.88	3.49	63.4	2.6	9.0	15.5	4.1
8.5	0.00	0.0	0.00	6.9	1.0	1.05	8.61	4.75	69.9	4.6	49.8	14.2	7.8
3.8	1.05	5.6	0.32	6.9	0.1	0.82	6.49	4.25	69.0	3.3	37.8	18.0	5.8
7.4	0.00	0.0	0.34	8.3	0.3	1.34	10.46	4.83	59.4	6.0	35.0	1.4	7.8
4.0	3.02	13.6	0.23	2.6	0.1	0.41	3.46	3.82	90.5	3.5	34.5	15.9	5.0
8.3	0.00	0.0	0.00	6.8	0.6	1.61	18.24	4.34	62.5	4.8	58.3	14.1	4.8
7.2	0.36	2.1	0.08	9.2	1.8	1.64	19.87	4.67	49.7	4.4	5.5	4.7	6.4
7.6	0.23	1.2	0.07	9.8	0.9	1.68	15.02	5.07	51.9	4.6	31.9	8.8	7.9
6.0	0.62	4.1	-0.02	3.3	0.1	0.45	4.09	3.52	81.2	1.6	24.9	25.8	4.2
3.6	1.38	10.2	0.08	8.6	0.3	1.41	14.95	6.56	64.1	5.1	42.6	9.7	4.2
3.4	1.48	10.0	1.35	5.7	0.1	0.92	10.11	4.67	63.6	6.6	96.8	10.6	3.4
9.7	0.31	0.7	0.04	7.9	0.6	1.37	5.08	3.90	45.5	8.1	537.0	12.3	8.7
6.3	0.53	5.0	0.01	2.6	0.2	0.29	4.07	3.99	85.3	3.3	16.4	12.8	2.3
8.9	0.17	0.9	0.19	5.2	0.5	0.66	6.02	3.98	76.6	5.2	24.5	2.1	6.8
2.9	0.91	6.1	-0.01	5.1	0.5	0.82	7.67	4.66	71.4	3.0	21.7	14.7	5.6
7.9	0.72	2.5	0.09	2.9	0.1	0.33	2.18	2.61	82.5	8.4	177.0	8.2	6.7
6.7	0.00	0.0	-0.03	3.3	0.1	0.31	2.49	4.83	93.4	1.2	20.6	31.1	5.5
4.4	1.07	5.6	-0.05	3.3	8.1	0.70	5.41	3.59	68.6	2.1	8.6	18.3	7.6
7.4	0.24	2.0	0.10	9.6	80.8	1.61	22.56	4.12	46.7	3.6	22.8	13.4	6.7
3.1	3.32	17.9	0.26	7.3	1.8	1.42	13.85	4.27	47.8	1.2	21.9	30.7	6.2
6.2	0.53	5.9	0.00	3.5	0.3	0.47	6.84	3.30	76.8	3.1	49.6	26.4	2.8
7.3	0.23	1.5	0.01	5.2	0.9	0.90	9.54	4.07	78.1	4.4	18.3	6.7	5.8
4.9	3.04	11.0	0.15	6.3	0.9	1.48	12.90	3.38	44.6	0.7	9.8	38.1	6.2
7.1	0.21	1.1	-0.39	5.8	0.7	1.32	12.74	4.45	60.8	3.5	38.3	17.2	6.7
4.4	0.47	3.8	0.36	2.5	0.0	0.07	0.86	2.78	66.2	6.4	118.7	13.6	3.8
7.4	0.58	3.2	-0.06	4.9	0.3	0.83	7.30	3.54	63.1	4.3	66.7	17.9	6.4
7.7	0.05	0.4	-0.04	4.2	0.2	1.08	12.78	4.33	76.7	3.6	16.4	11.0	2.6
4.7	1.80	10.5	0.01	4.8	0.3	1.16	12.74	3.57	66.3	4.2	44.7	14.8	3.7
6.8	0.52	6.3	-0.01	1.3	-0.3	-0.46	-6.83	3.39	116.6	4.0	26.2	10.3	0.3
5.7	1.77	8.3	0.01	9.5	4.7	1.51	12.27	4.02	44.7	4.1	23.4	8.9	8.7
7.0	0.22	1.7	-0.03	7.1	0.8	1.26	15.26	5.31	62.2	3.9	15.4	9.3	4.4
6.2	0.25	1.8	0.10	7.2	1.0	1.38	15.98	6.03	70.4	4.3	24.0	7.8	4.5
3.6	2.11	12.8	0.45	8.4	0.2	1.75	17.69	6.03	64.8	1.6	12.0	21.4	4.8
9.4	0.50	2.3	0.08	6.7	0.6	1.15	7.70	3.10	42.6	3.2	26.3	14.4	8.4
5.9	0.28	2.1	0.17	9.8	4.3	1.69	16.68	4.75	43.6	1.9	12.5	19.1	7.4
6.3	0.38	3.0	0.33	5.9	0.6	1.82	22.99	4.04	63.9	5.0	32.7	6.6	6.0
4.1	1.07	4.7	0.31	3.3	6.1	0.49	3.33	4.10	80.7	7.7	122.7	8.5	6.7
8.4	0.02	0.1	0.00	0.0	-0.4	-1.58	-9.75	3.73	127.6	6.2	49.8	4.4	0.0
8.2	0.00	0.0	0.00	5.1	0.5	1.07	12.62	4.52	59.2	1.6	18.0	23.5	2.1
4.7	0.42	2.2	0.19	9.8	4.2	1.62	13.16	5.49	60.7	3.8	19.1	10.5	8.2
4.7	4.53	15.0	0.07	7.7	0.2	1.35	9.76	3.96	49.6	4.8	43.2	11.5	6.7
3.6	2.50	14.8	0.04	6.7	0.5	1.46	15.97	5.14	72.6	4.1	52.7	16.8	4.6
8.6	0.63	1.7	0.00	6.6	0.1	1.27	7.27	4.10	57.6	3.7	15.2	10.2	5.7
6.6	0.89	5.6	0.00	10.0	4.7	3.30	32.17	4.52	31.4	8.1	158.8	8.9	7.5
4.5	1.64	8.5	0.55	7.9	0.7	1.71	16.46	3.99	49.7	3.1	23.8	14.1	6.7
3.4	2.01	9.4	0.05	9.8	0.1	3.72	24.97	7.14	48.8	4.4	39.6	10.2	6.1
5.4	1.20	8.0	0.25	3.0	0.1	0.40	4.49	4.53	89.6	4.5	17.8	5.8	3.1
8.6	0.53	2.6	0.00	4.7	0.1	0.73	4.47	2.89	61.8	4.3	13.7	6.3	6.6
8.4	0.10	0.6	0.10	6.8	0.5	1.31	13.82	4.85	75.7	4.6	23.8	5.7	6.1
7.2	1.61	6.3	0.00	10.0	0.6	3.53	29.90	4.92	21.5	2.6	35.3	22.1	8.2
7.3	0.57	3.3	0.03	6.2	0.4	1.34	14.53	4.10	68.8	6.5	64.5	5.8	6.7
9.4	0.00	0.0	0.00	7.4	0.5	2.24	17.25	3.48	46.4	0.9	18.8	37.7	2.4
5.9	1.95	8.6	0.15	8.0	1.1	1.15	14.72	4.49	56.1	3.9	38.5	14.9	3.7
9.4	0.59	1.8	0.00	4.5	0.7	0.70	7.09	2.27	55.7	4.3	126.6	42.4	5.8
6.0	1.77	11.7	0.00	3.0	0.0	0.12	1.70	2.88	93.7	3.2	54.1	24.3	0.7
6.2	0.28	2.1	0.08	8.5	1.9	1.42	15.59	5.62	60.4	3.2	41.1	19.2	5.5
7.8	0.19	1.5	-0.02	10.0	0.8	2.52	25.20	4.54	43.3	4.4	26.3	8.0	7.0
6.0	0.35	3.3	0.03	9.0	0.8	1.75	20.63	3.80	43.1	1.2	14.1	28.0	5.2
5.4	0.69	5.0	-0.02	4.8	0.3	1.19	12.82	3.61	65.9	5.0	37.0	8.5	3.6

Name	City	State	Weiss Safety Rating	2003 Weiss Safety Rating	2002 Weiss Safety Rating	Total Assets ($Mil)	One Year Asset Growth	Asset Mix (As a % of Total Assets) Commercial Loans	Consumer Loans	Home Mortgages	Securities	Capitalization Index	Leverage Ratio	Risk-based Capital Ratio
▲ VILLA PARK T&SB	VILLA PARK	IL	C+	C+	C+	260.7	3.60	5.0	5.6	36.5	18.1	4.0	7.2	10.5
VILLAGE B&T	N BARRINGTON	IL	D+	D+	C	134.3	13.00	11.5	1.6	5.6	15.3	4.7	7.3	10.9
▼ VILLAGE B&T SSB	LAKEWAY	TX	C+	B-	C+	110.9	3.27	11.3	1.7	12.1	11.2	7.6	9.4	13.4
▲ VILLAGE B&TC	MARTELLE	IA	B+	B	B	27.1	16.86	4.3	1.6	16.7	4.1	10.0	18.3	22.5
VILLAGE B&TC	GILFORD	NH	B	B	B+	79.8	2.43	4.6	1.3	15.2	31.1	9.9	10.9	20.8
▲ VILLAGE B&TC ARLINGTON	PROSPECT HEIGHTS	IL	D+	E-	E-	162.3	119.49	34.4	1.0	7.5	28.2	4.6	7.2	10.9
▼ VILLAGE BK	ST LIBORY	IL	C+	B-	B-	54.1	-1.31	8.7	17.7	28.8	11.5	8.6	10.1	15.5
▲ VILLAGE BK	NEWTON	MA	B+	B	B	482.3	50.87	2.4	1.1	34.8	24.8	9.7	10.8	19.4
▲ VILLAGE BK	ST FRANCIS	MN	B-	C+	C	133.9	21.04	17.1	3.8	4.6	12.8	4.2	8.4	10.6
▼ VILLAGE BK	SPRINGFIELD	MO	D+	C	C	94.0	15.05	22.5	4.2	19.1	8.3	3.7	8.2	10.3
▲ VILLAGE BK	ST GEORGE	UT	B-	C+	C+	108.7	35.12	23.6	6.9	2.6	12.3	4.4	7.4	10.7
▲ VINEYARD BK	RANCHO CUCAMONGA	CA	A-	B+	B	1,151.0	88.69	3.1	0.3	4.0	13.7	7.6	11.3	13.0
▲ VINTAGE BK	NAPA	CA	B	B-	B-	411.2	16.21	10.1	0.6	6.5	20.8	5.8	8.6	11.6
▲ VINTAGE BK	WAXAHACHIE	TX	C	C-	D+	66.7	7.53	13.4	12.0	13.5	6.2	4.7	9.1	10.8
▲ VINTON COUNTY NB OF	MC ARTHUR	OH	B	B-	B-	258.3	0.51	6.1	16.4	31.8	22.4	8.5	10.0	16.2
VIRGIN ISLANDS CMNTY BK	CHRISTIANSTED	VI	E-	E-	E-	78.4	17.50	6.1	3.2	21.9	34.6	4.0	6.0	16.1
VIRGINIA B&TC	DANVILLE	VA	A	A-	A-	147.0	-0.72	4.8	19.3	12.5	24.9	10.0	15.8	23.9
▲ VIRGINIA COMMERCE BK NA	ARLINGTON	VA	B-	C+	C	1,049.9	31.32	7.3	0.6	5.6	16.0	6.4	8.4	12.5
VIRGINIA COMMUNITY BK	LOUISA	VA	B-	C+	C	173.0	10.75	8.7	5.3	13.2	17.6	6.0	8.4	11.8
VIRGINIA HEARTLAND BK	FREDERICKSBURG	VA	B	B	B+	228.2	9.08	4.4	3.5	21.5	14.4	4.6	7.9	10.8
VIRGINIA NB	CHARLOTTESVILLE	VA	B-	B-	C+	229.1	15.19	13.7	1.9	11.1	18.4	8.3	9.8	13.7
VIRGINIA SVGS BK FSB	FRONT ROYAL	VA	B-	B-	B-	143.6	4.52	11.4	9.0	19.8	23.9	4.5	7.2	10.7
VISALIA COMMUNITY BK	VISALIA	CA	B-	B-	B-	148.5	7.85	13.7	7.9	4.6	12.4	5.7	8.4	11.5
VISION BANK, FSB	PANAMA CITY	FL	D+	D+	NR	62.3	130.49	7.7	1.1	9.1	10.2	9.7	11.1	14.8
VISION BK	GULF SHORES	AL	D+	D+	D+	250.0	67.50	17.2	3.0	14.0	6.3	4.0	9.2	10.5
VOLKSWAGEN BK USA	SALT LAKE CITY	UT	B+	B+	B+	564.4	48.39	0.0	86.1	0.0	0.5	10.0	17.6	18.2
VOLUNTEER FS&LA	MADISONVILLE	TN	B-	C+	C	132.5	-1.15	1.0	12.0	49.2	1.2	7.6	9.4	15.4
VOLUNTEER ST BK	PORTLAND	TN	B+	B+	B	172.7	-6.44	11.0	3.8	20.7	19.9	7.2	9.1	13.9
▼ VOLVO COMMERCIAL CR	SALT LAKE CITY	UT	C-	C	D	24.6	-20.24	84.8	0.0	0.0	0.0	10.0	51.9	56.6
VOYAGER BK	EDEN PRAIRIE	MN	C	C	C	471.3	32.37	24.8	2.7	8.9	24.5	3.6	6.8	10.3
WABASH SVGS BK	MT CARMEL	IL	C-	D+	D	11.8	-6.91	0.4	3.9	27.5	55.4	10.0	11.3	34.1
WACCAMAW BK	WHITEVILLE	NC	B-	B-	C+	215.3	16.89	24.9	3.7	14.7	12.7	7.2	10.0	12.7
WACHOVIA BK NA	CHARLOTTE	NC	B-	B-	C+	368,871.0	11.23	10.8	4.6	14.3	27.1	4.0	6.0	11.7
WACHOVIA BK OF DE NA	WILMINGTON	DE	B+	B+	B	3,682.2	93.71	3.0	17.7	9.0	3.2	8.0	9.7	17.6
▲ WADENA ST BK	WADENA	MN	B-	B-	B	94.5	-0.76	14.5	3.6	19.1	27.5	6.5	8.6	13.8
WAGGONER NB OF VERNON	VERNON	TX	A	A	A	201.7	4.91	6.1	12.0	13.9	26.8	10.0	13.6	20.9
WAHOO ST BK	WAHOO	NE	D+	D+	C-	47.9	10.12	7.5	5.6	37.8	5.7	5.4	7.4	11.7
WAINWRIGHT B&TC	BOSTON	MA	C+	C+	C+	676.8	17.05	6.4	0.2	26.6	19.4	6.8	9.2	12.3
▼ WAKE FOREST FS&LA	WAKE FOREST	NC	B+	A-	A-	86.3	-1.61	0.0	0.1	21.3	0.6	10.0	18.3	26.3
WAKEFIELD CO-OP BK	WAKEFIELD	MA	C	C	C	104.9	-5.44	0.2	10.1	23.8	45.7	5.2	7.2	15.4
WAKULLA BK	CRAWFORDVILLE	FL	B-	B-	B	318.2	24.97	8.9	9.2	13.0	17.3	6.6	8.8	12.2
WALCOTT T&SB	WALCOTT	IA	A-	A-	A-	58.5	1.33	12.4	2.8	21.8	15.6	10.0	21.7	34.8
WALDEN FS&LA	WALDEN	NY	C	C	C	86.3	3.40	10.3	0.6	41.0	8.3	5.8	7.8	12.5
▼ WALDEN SVGS BK	WALDEN	NY	B-	B	B	228.6	11.24	7.4	1.2	29.2	36.4	6.4	8.4	12.8
WALDO ST BK	WALDO	WI	B-	B-	C+	26.3	3.41	22.2	5.2	35.1	17.9	10.0	17.0	28.4
▲ WALKER ST BK	WALKER	IA	B+	B	B-	22.1	-4.93	6.4	5.1	13.5	35.3	8.9	10.2	17.8
▲ WALLIS STATE BK	WALLIS	TX	B-	C	C	145.9	6.30	14.7	4.8	5.1	17.0	7.4	9.4	12.9
WALLKILL VALLEY FS&LA	WALLKILL	NY	A	A	A	107.0	6.36	0.0	2.4	49.7	17.1	10.0	19.3	37.8
WALPOLE CO-OP BK	WALPOLE	MA	A+	A+	A+	294.3	7.30	4.9	0.1	13.0	23.1	10.0	16.4	20.4
WALTERS B&TC	WALTERS	OK	A-	A-	A-	50.7	-5.37	2.9	9.3	8.0	51.3	10.0	22.7	84.9
WALTON ST BK	WALTON	KS	E+	E+	E+	6.0	8.48	9.2	8.8	21.7	26.2	5.3	7.3	13.8
WALWORTH ST BK	WALWORTH	WI	C	C	C+	158.2	2.34	16.9	2.6	25.6	30.5	9.0	10.3	16.5
WANDA ST BK	WANDA	MN	B	B	B	83.8	3.46	3.4	1.3	4.2	40.8	10.0	14.6	21.8
WARE CO-OP BK	WARE	MA	C-	C-	C-	61.5	8.06	0.9	3.8	47.3	28.2	7.2	9.1	18.9
▲ WARREN B&TC	WARREN	AR	A	A-	A-	122.9	-1.05	11.5	7.6	18.5	38.3	10.0	13.9	19.7
▲ WARREN BK	WARREN	MI	C-	C	C-	467.2	8.23	3.2	1.9	4.6	12.2	6.4	9.9	12.0
▲ WARREN BOYNTON ST BK	NEW BERLIN	IL	A-	B+	B	88.7	2.29	12.6	3.9	15.1	21.2	10.0	11.9	16.9
WARRINGTON BK	PENSACOLA	FL	A-	A-	A	74.0	2.65	0.0	0.6	0.8	70.6	10.0	15.5	54.4
▲ WARSAW FS&LA	CINCINNATI	OH	B+	B	B	55.3	-2.26	0.0	0.1	76.6	7.5	10.0	16.4	26.3
▼ WARWICK COMMERCIAL BK	WARWICK	NY	C+	B	B	12.1	-49.16	0.0	0.0	0.0	69.8	10.0	24.0	71.4
▼ WARWICK SVGS BK	WARWICK	NY	C+	B	B	678.9	-12.88	3.0	0.3	12.2	45.8	5.7	7.7	17.2
WASHINGTON BUSINESS BK	OLYMPIA	WA	D	D	D	33.8	53.64	20.0	1.2	5.7	29.0	10.0	11.7	15.1
WASHINGTON COUNTY BK	BLAIR	NE	C+	B-	B-	185.2	3.35	12.5	8.2	2.4	19.2	4.0	8.3	10.5
WASHINGTON COUNTY BK NA	OAKDALE	MN	C	C	D	140.4	7.17	17.1	2.2	7.9	7.0	3.6	8.7	10.3

Asset Quality Index	Non-Performing Loans as a % of Total Loans	Non-Performing Loans as a % of Capital	Net Charge-offs Avg Loans	Profitability Index	Net Income ($Mil)	Return on Assets (R.O.A.)	Return on Equity (R.O.E.)	Net Interest Spread	Overhead Efficiency Ratio	Liquidity Index	Liquidity Ratio	Hot Money Ratio	Stability Index
7.1	0.47	4.6	0.01	7.3	1.7	1.33	17.57	4.20	56.0	4.4	11.2	5.5	4.7
8.2	0.03	0.3	0.06	3.7	0.4	0.62	7.65	3.36	70.2	1.5	32.1	35.4	3.5
3.2	1.81	12.9	0.04	4.3	0.3	0.60	6.37	4.13	82.8	3.6	23.3	11.8	5.8
6.6	0.61	2.6	0.00	8.6	0.2	1.41	7.82	4.23	43.4	5.6	46.1	7.6	7.4
6.4	1.05	4.6	0.21	4.4	0.4	0.90	8.46	4.18	75.2	5.7	42.7	6.2	6.2
4.4	0.94	5.6	0.06	3.6	0.4	0.59	5.57	3.02	68.9	3.9	76.7	27.6	4.8
3.2	1.80	12.5	0.00	4.1	0.2	0.73	7.04	4.11	75.6	5.7	67.3	10.9	5.2
6.6	0.76	4.2	0.01	5.5	1.7	0.74	6.93	3.47	63.1	7.0	122.6	11.5	5.4
7.1	0.04	0.3	0.00	10.0	1.4	2.21	27.64	5.81	56.5	3.5	21.7	12.3	5.1
5.5	0.49	4.8	0.21	2.9	0.2	0.33	4.04	3.22	82.4	2.0	23.7	19.8	3.3
8.0	0.05	0.4	0.07	7.4	0.6	1.24	16.51	5.10	59.6	3.8	43.6	17.2	4.5
7.4	0.03	0.2	0.06	9.1	7.5	1.43	14.73	5.09	44.7	1.6	6.0	20.9	8.7
8.7	0.00	0.0	0.07	9.9	3.1	1.62	18.74	5.14	52.8	7.5	124.7	9.4	6.1
6.1	0.13	1.0	0.45	6.1	0.5	1.54	15.25	5.60	65.5	1.7	14.2	21.5	4.3
4.2	1.19	7.7	0.36	5.3	1.2	0.90	9.09	4.06	63.2	4.1	58.2	19.0	5.9
0.3	8.62	70.6	1.45	1.7	0.1	0.35	6.80	5.05	93.4	6.2	47.8	3.9	0.8
7.4	0.19	0.8	0.06	9.6	1.1	1.46	9.23	4.65	57.2	4.6	22.8	6.0	9.3
7.5	0.03	0.3	0.00	8.7	6.6	1.38	20.51	4.05	47.2	4.3	60.5	19.7	5.1
5.6	0.41	3.0	0.22	7.0	1.0	1.25	14.92	4.96	59.7	5.1	39.4	9.1	4.2
6.2	0.19	1.7	0.03	6.9	1.5	1.28	16.20	4.41	60.8	2.6	8.8	15.4	6.2
8.5	0.00	0.0	0.01	4.1	0.7	0.62	6.09	4.55	76.9	4.5	31.2	9.4	5.5
5.0	0.41	3.8	0.06	6.5	0.6	0.89	12.03	4.20	69.0	2.8	40.7	23.2	4.6
7.8	0.21	1.5	-0.05	5.3	0.6	0.78	9.53	4.76	78.6	5.5	45.6	8.8	4.8
8.1	0.00	0.0	0.00	0.0	-0.3	-0.94	-7.03	2.80	134.3	3.2	85.9	64.5	0.5
4.3	1.12	9.4	0.04	4.0	0.7	0.65	7.71	3.98	63.2	2.8	34.9	19.4	0.5
5.5	0.34	1.8	0.29	10.0	4.7	1.81	10.11	4.93	32.0	0.1	2.8	100.0	5.2
4.0	0.91	7.9	0.09	5.3	0.5	0.76	8.30	3.68	70.4	1.8	18.3	21.1	5.2
6.6	0.84	5.7	0.25	7.2	1.2	1.40	14.87	4.89	77.1	3.9	18.5	9.7	6.2
7.8	0.39	0.6	0.61	1.4	-0.1	-0.49	-0.98	4.86	105.0	0.9	31.6	63.6	0.0
7.1	0.21	2.0	0.03	5.8	3.5	1.63	24.14	3.92	60.7	1.2	12.9	28.6	3.2
7.5	2.79	7.9	-0.73	2.6	0.0	0.54	4.83	3.30	81.0	9.0	247.1	7.0	2.0
4.1	1.53	10.8	0.10	6.5	1.2	1.16	11.16	3.89	56.7	2.6	37.9	23.2	5.4
6.0	0.56	3.1	0.12	6.8	2,229.0	1.23	14.32	3.52	60.8	6.0	46.2	8.9	7.0
5.8	0.39	3.5	1.16	10.0	41.0	2.75	29.06	2.24	25.1	5.6	25.5	3.1	7.0
6.8	0.13	0.9	-0.01	6.8	0.8	1.63	17.07	4.37	61.9	4.7	30.9	7.8	6.3
7.9	0.42	1.8	0.08	9.0	1.7	1.72	12.54	4.44	54.1	1.5	18.0	25.3	9.1
4.7	1.00	9.6	0.34	5.7	0.2	0.88	12.10	4.61	68.5	5.4	35.7	5.2	2.4
8.9	0.01	0.1	-0.01	4.8	3.0	0.93	11.77	3.94	69.9	3.3	14.7	12.7	3.9
4.6	2.08	9.2	0.00	8.1	0.5	1.20	6.67	3.30	39.3	0.9	21.8	36.6	8.6
8.2	0.00	0.0	-0.06	3.4	0.3	0.51	7.17	3.00	77.5	4.8	29.3	6.7	2.8
7.0	0.13	1.0	0.20	8.0	2.0	1.32	17.08	5.11	59.2	2.7	31.9	18.9	4.7
8.8	0.06	0.2	0.01	5.6	0.3	0.85	3.89	3.99	65.9	7.4	131.1	9.4	7.2
5.3	0.46	4.3	0.00	3.4	0.1	0.28	3.42	4.39	92.0	1.6	19.0	24.8	4.1
6.7	0.73	4.1	0.05	4.4	0.5	0.50	5.84	4.03	78.6	6.4	43.4	1.5	4.3
4.2	4.16	15.7	0.05	5.3	0.1	0.77	4.67	4.37	64.0	4.6	52.7	14.3	6.5
8.6	0.00	0.0	0.00	9.7	0.2	2.09	19.91	4.88	49.3	5.5	48.7	6.3	6.9
7.4	0.34	2.2	-0.04	7.4	0.9	1.19	12.31	5.06	72.4	3.2	28.4	15.2	4.7
8.4	0.19	0.7	0.00	7.2	0.6	1.13	5.90	3.82	51.1	1.7	19.0	22.3	8.8
7.7	0.51	2.0	-0.13	9.5	2.2	1.47	9.04	4.29	42.6	4.7	26.9	6.1	9.6
8.7	0.10	0.1	0.20	5.9	0.4	1.40	5.76	3.60	63.2	6.3	75.2	8.7	7.6
4.3	1.41	10.3	0.18	4.0	0.0	0.71	9.76	4.23	81.9	6.5	56.9	1.8	0.3
3.3	2.25	13.0	-0.02	8.7	1.7	2.14	20.47	4.21	51.1	2.8	15.5	15.3	8.0
5.6	2.85	8.3	-0.03	4.1	0.3	0.73	4.88	3.28	57.3	5.4	65.7	12.4	6.8
7.3	0.32	2.1	0.04	1.8	0.0	0.10	1.09	3.48	94.5	4.5	66.1	16.9	4.1
8.4	0.56	2.1	0.17	6.4	0.7	1.15	8.33	4.04	57.0	3.7	59.2	23.7	8.2
1.8	1.60	12.0	0.03	6.0	2.8	1.22	12.56	3.13	44.0	1.0	9.9	30.5	5.1
8.3	0.14	0.7	0.01	6.2	0.5	1.16	9.76	4.09	60.3	3.9	39.3	15.2	5.8
10.0	0.03	0.0	0.03	4.6	0.2	0.62	4.08	3.80	76.2	5.9	35.4	2.0	7.9
9.6	0.26	1.4	0.02	5.1	0.3	0.90	5.63	3.88	65.0	2.7	19.3	15.9	6.9
10.0	0.00	0.0	0.00	5.1	0.1	1.03	4.70	2.51	35.5	9.2	224.2	5.7	2.7
7.9	0.43	2.0	5.39	2.9	-2.2	-0.62	-7.76	2.88	77.1	9.6	287.7	2.8	5.0
8.5	0.00	0.0	-0.01	0.1	-0.1	-0.40	-3.23	4.01	95.1	6.7	79.4	6.8	0.0
4.7	0.62	5.3	0.68	6.2	0.9	1.03	12.67	4.36	54.5	3.7	36.8	15.6	5.1
6.0	0.20	1.8	0.30	5.0	0.9	1.26	14.70	4.45	73.0	3.0	22.1	14.5	4.4

Name	City	State	Weiss Safety Rating	2003 Weiss Safety Rating	2002 Weiss Safety Rating	Total Assets ($Mil)	One Year Asset Growth	Comm-ercial Loans	Cons-umer Loans	Home Mort-gages	Secur-ities	Capital-ization Index	Leverage Ratio	Risk-based Capital Ratio
▲ WASHINGTON FED BK FOR	CHICAGO	IL	B-	C+	D+	54.2	4.06	0.0	0.4	62.5	0.2	7.1	9.1	16.0
▲ WASHINGTON FIRST INTL BK	SEATTLE	WA	B	B-	C+	446.5	6.19	9.6	0.2	4.8	20.3	8.0	10.1	13.4
WASHINGTON FS&LA	SEATTLE	WA	A+	A+	A+	7,223.7	0.58	0.0	0.0	52.5	15.1	10.0	14.1	26.9
▼ WASHINGTON FSB	WASHINGTON	PA	C-	C+	B	664.0	-1.78	4.0	8.2	13.7	50.7	9.4	10.6	24.3
WASHINGTON MSB	SEATTLE	WA	B-	B-	C+	28,799.0	-14.85	4.5	1.9	45.7	4.9	4.5	6.6	11.4
▲ WASHINGTON MUTUAL BK FA	STOCKTON	CA	B-	C+	C+	240,433.6	2.32	1.4	0.2	58.4	7.4	4.0	6.0	10.9
▲ WASHINGTON MUTUAL BK	SALT LAKE CITY	UT	B	C	C	25,255.5	2781.75	0.0	0.0	1.2	64.0	10.0	97.1	493.8
WASHINGTON SA	PHILADELPHIA	PA	C	C	C	156.4	-1.61	0.0	0.7	75.8	13.2	6.0	8.0	16.4
WASHINGTON SB	EFFINGHAM	IL	B-	B-	B-	176.6	8.74	2.6	3.4	37.8	40.1	8.9	10.3	21.7
WASHINGTON ST BK	WASHINGTON	IA	A	A	A	166.9	-0.25	8.4	4.1	29.5	26.8	10.0	12.9	23.2
▲ WASHINGTON ST BK	WASHINGTON	IL	B-	C+	C+	41.9	2.18	3.4	9.0	24.9	36.8	8.5	10.0	21.0
▲ WASHINGTON ST BK	WASHINGTON	LA	C+	C	B	89.1	1.56	7.0	2.0	4.2	38.1	9.8	10.8	16.4
▲ WASHINGTON ST BK NA	FEDERAL WAY	WA	D	D-	E-	56.2	0.70	24.6	4.3	7.3	13.9	6.9	8.9	13.4
WASHINGTON SVGS BK	LOWELL	MA	C+	C+	C+	153.1	2.12	0.0	0.8	31.5	54.5	9.1	10.4	23.1
▲ WASHINGTON SVGS BK FSB	BOWIE	MD	B-	B+	A-	498.2	22.89	0.3	0.1	55.3	1.6	8.0	9.6	13.9
WASHINGTON TRUST BK	SPOKANE	WA	B+	B+	B+	2,333.9	14.31	26.1	3.0	7.8	13.6	5.1	9.4	11.1
▼ WASHINGTON TRUST CO	WESTERLY	RI	C+	B-	B-	2,179.3	18.44	2.6	0.9	22.3	41.5	3.4	5.4	10.8
WASHINGTONFIRST BK	WASHINGTON	DC	D	NR	NR	20.2	N/A	14.2	0.3	11.5	33.8	10.0	65.6	109.6
▲ WASHITA ST BK	BURNS FLAT	OK	C-	D-	D-	208.0	415.33	1.2	0.5	1.2	92.9	4.2	6.2	23.8
▲ WASHITA VALLEY BK	FORT COBB	OK	B	B-	B-	29.1	-0.50	3.8	8.8	0.8	38.9	10.0	17.6	29.7
WATERFORD CMMRCL & SVG	WATERFORD	OH	B-	B	B	27.0	-7.43	4.6	11.4	48.2	7.1	10.0	13.2	24.0
WATERMAN ST BK	WATERMAN	IL	B	B	B	26.3	-3.62	4.2	3.3	16.7	53.4	10.0	11.3	25.4
WATERTOWN SVGS BK	WATERTOWN	MA	B-	B-	B-	1,132.0	3.47	0.4	0.2	25.2	59.9	5.1	7.1	17.3
▼ WATERTOWN SVGS BK	WATERTOWN	NY	B	B+	B+	292.9	2.91	5.0	2.6	14.6	42.4	10.0	13.4	23.8
▼ WATKINS SVG BK	WATKINS	IA	B+	A-	A-	39.9	1.22	3.1	2.5	16.7	34.4	10.0	15.5	25.4
▲ WATONGA ST BK	WATONGA	OK	C	C-	C	62.4	-0.11	3.4	8.4	2.9	47.6	9.4	10.6	21.7
WAUCHULA ST BK	WAUCHULA	FL	B+	A-	A-	393.7	5.75	4.3	2.4	19.1	26.2	5.4	7.4	12.5
WAUKEE ST BK	WAUKEE	IA	C-	C-	D+	55.5	3.34	13.0	4.3	35.5	19.9	6.5	8.5	14.9
▼ WAUKEGAN S&LA SB	WAUKEGAN	IL	D+	C	C+	125.0	-5.97	0.1	1.6	54.8	27.0	8.0	9.7	23.1
WAUKESHA ST BK	WAUKESHA	WI	A	A	A	574.3	2.41	4.8	3.8	21.6	21.6	10.0	14.6	22.2
▲ WAUKON ST BK	WAUKON	IA	B+	B-	B-	77.4	4.80	18.5	2.9	17.8	14.9	8.3	10.2	13.5
WAUMANDEE ST BK	WAUMANDEE	WI	A-	A-	A-	40.9	6.17	11.0	8.9	22.4	18.6	10.0	13.7	19.9
WAURIKA NB	WAURIKA	OK	C-	D+	C-	14.4	0.15	2.7	10.3	3.5	49.5	9.4	10.6	22.0
WAUWATOSA SVG BK	WAUWATOSA	WI	B-	B-	B+	1,241.3	12.12	0.0	0.0	47.3	8.0	8.8	10.2	15.0
▲ WAWEL SAVINGS BANK	WALLINGTON	NJ	B	C+	C	73.7	15.50	1.4	0.7	31.3	43.9	10.0	17.8	43.9
WAYCROSS B&TC	WAYCROSS	GA	B+	B+	A-	96.7	-0.73	7.8	3.3	14.0	27.1	8.2	9.8	14.8
WAYLAND ST BK	MT PLEASANT	IA	A-	A-	A-	60.5	3.55	9.0	3.8	17.8	35.9	10.0	12.2	21.4
▼ WAYNE B&TC	CAMBRIDGE CITY	IN	A-	A-	A-	120.1	4.28	10.7	4.7	15.7	11.8	9.9	10.9	16.8
WAYNE BK	HONESDALE	PA	A-	A-	B+	401.3	4.96	4.0	8.0	20.3	30.3	9.5	10.6	16.8
WAYNE COUNTY BK	WAYNESBORO	TN	B+	B+	B+	147.3	4.04	8.3	24.2	27.7	13.7	10.0	13.4	19.3
WAYNE COUNTY NB OF	WOOSTER	OH	B+	B+	A-	427.4	-1.80	18.4	4.2	12.0	28.0	6.5	8.6	13.3
WAYNE SAVINGS COMMUNITY	WOOSTER	OH	B-	B-	C+	381.8	3.26	1.9	1.6	39.2	33.4	9.4	10.6	19.8
WAYPOINT BK	HARRISBURG	PA	B-	B-	B-	5,397.9	-3.59	7.0	7.9	12.0	46.6	5.4	7.4	12.6
WEATHERFORD NB	WEATHERFORD	TX	A	A	A-	222.6	9.92	5.6	3.5	12.6	40.1	6.7	8.7	16.4
▲ WEBB CITY BK	WEBB CITY	MO	B	C+	C	212.4	14.85	23.6	9.1	26.4	14.0	9.5	10.6	15.3
WEBBANK	SALT LAKE CITY	UT	C-	D+	D	18.3	-6.19	39.9	0.3	0.0	0.5	10.0	35.0	42.9
▼ WEBSTER BK NA	WATERBURY	CT	C+	NR	NR	16,981.0	N/A	13.3	0.2	32.7	22.5	4.9	6.9	11.5
WEBSTER CITY FSB	WEBSTER CITY	IA	A	A	A	101.8	-3.71	0.8	3.1	59.2	14.1	10.0	19.5	43.0
WEBSTER FIVE CENTS SB	WEBSTER	MA	B+	B+	A-	433.2	6.40	5.3	4.2	29.0	31.5	10.0	12.1	19.4
▼ WELCH ST BK	WELCH	OK	B-	B	B-	127.2	14.92	16.2	6.1	15.6	16.1	5.4	7.9	11.3
▲ WELCOME ST BK	WELCOME	MN	C	C-	C-	16.9	-0.87	21.3	8.0	5.4	12.2	7.7	9.7	13.1
WELD CTY BK	EVANS	CO	C+	C+	D+	230.5	57.32	26.2	2.8	3.3	7.5	3.2	9.5	10.1
▼ WELLESLEY CO-OP BK	WELLESLEY	MA	B-	B	B	145.5	11.75	6.1	0.3	28.8	15.4	6.1	8.2	11.9
WELLINGTON ST BK	WELLINGTON	TX	C-	C-	D	95.8	0.94	12.6	9.0	9.5	16.4	5.4	7.4	12.2
WELLS BK OF PLATTE CITY	PLATTE CITY	MO	C+	C+	C+	47.4	-3.45	2.7	3.4	8.5	56.7	8.7	10.2	25.6
WELLS FARGO BK	LOS ANGELES	CA	B	B-	B-	165.0	14.78	0.0	0.0	0.0	0.0	10.0	87.2	213.5
WELLS FARGO BK GRAND	GRAND JUNCTION	CO	B-	B-	B-	3.1	0.10	0.0	0.0	0.0	0.0	10.0	79.1	406.3
WELLS FARGO BK GRAND	GRAND JUNCTION	CO	B-	B-	B-	3.2	-4.33	0.0	0.0	0.0	0.0	10.0	79.9	193.6
WELLS FARGO BK NA	SIOUX FALLS	SD	B-	B-	B-	364,698.0	79.24	9.5	7.4	22.4	8.7	4.7	6.7	11.0
WELLS FARGO BK	OGDEN	UT	B-	C+	C+	40,574.0	118.78	5.7	19.8	70.5	0.0	3.6	5.6	10.8
WELLS FARGO CENTRAL BK	CALABASAS	CA	B-	B-	B-	6.0	0.62	0.0	0.0	0.0	0.0	10.0	89.6	442.9
WELLS FARGO FINANCIAL BK	SIOUX FALLS	SD	B-	B-	B-	1,816.7	25.83	0.0	47.9	0.0	15.7	10.0	20.4	28.7
WELLS FARGO FINANCIAL NB	LAS VEGAS	NV	B-	B-	B-	857.5	40.58	0.0	101.8	0.1	0.2	8.5	13.1	13.8
WELLS FARGO HSBC TRADE	SAN FRANCISCO	CA	B	B-	C+	967.2	28.03	57.4	0.0	0.0	0.0	4.8	9.6	10.9

Asset Quality Index	Non-Performing Loans as a % of Total Loans	Non-Performing Loans as a % of Capital	Net Charge-offs Avg Loans	Profitability Index	Net Income ($Mil)	Return on Assets (R.O.A.)	Return on Equity (R.O.E.)	Net Interest Spread	Overhead Efficiency Ratio	Liquidity Index	Liquidity Ratio	Hot Money Ratio	Stability Index
8.7	0.00	0.0	0.00	8.5	0.4	1.45	16.45	4.79	52.2	2.4	7.3	16.2	4.6
5.5	0.15	1.0	0.51	8.3	3.5	1.60	16.43	3.72	33.1	4.3	129.5	55.8	5.5
8.7	0.26	1.2	-0.01	10.0	67.8	1.82	12.51	3.41	17.6	2.8	34.4	26.1	10.0
7.7	0.31	1.1	0.07	1.9	-0.6	-0.19	-1.73	2.31	116.5	1.8	29.8	27.7	6.7
6.0	0.66	7.0	0.11	5.5	116.0	0.80	12.21	3.18	72.6	3.7	26.8	14.8	6.0
3.7	0.69	8.6	0.07	7.2	1,011.2	0.83	10.19	2.89	69.1	0.7	13.1	55.4	7.2
6.6	1.09	0.0	0.57	10.0	146.4	1.70	1.78	3.45	12.8	5.5	3,561.2	36.2	7.4
9.3	0.06	0.5	0.01	3.1	0.2	0.26	2.79	2.96	84.8	3.8	8.4	9.2	4.8
8.5	0.37	1.8	0.01	4.2	0.7	0.75	7.16	2.73	58.7	6.7	99.6	11.6	6.1
8.5	0.24	1.2	0.05	9.3	1.5	1.78	14.00	4.24	36.4	4.4	29.8	9.7	8.0
8.6	0.16	0.8	-0.01	6.9	0.3	1.30	13.13	4.31	54.0	5.3	75.0	14.1	4.4
4.9	1.48	6.9	0.75	4.1	0.3	0.73	6.56	4.36	73.0	1.3	17.8	28.2	4.2
3.8	1.72	12.0	0.10	1.4	-0.2	-0.60	-6.83	4.51	78.4	4.6	53.5	14.2	2.4
9.9	0.00	0.0	-0.03	3.2	0.3	0.44	4.19	3.20	80.9	5.0	56.1	13.8	5.6
5.2	0.61	5.5	0.03	10.0	4.9	2.18	21.78	4.93	38.8	0.2	3.9	84.2	7.0
5.8	0.68	5.1	0.29	7.0	13.5	1.19	12.16	4.60	63.0	2.8	16.4	15.8	8.2
8.3	0.45	3.2	-0.01	5.4	10.0	0.97	14.40	2.76	61.7	3.3	33.5	19.4	5.4
9.8	0.00	0.0	0.00	0.0	-0.6	-8.05	-13.34	0.92	717.2	8.2	220.9	11.6	0.0
8.2	2.10	2.2	0.03	6.8	3.5	4.23	78.40	4.59	8.5	0.1	0.2	85.6	2.7
4.1	8.73	15.3	0.11	6.1	0.2	1.15	6.52	4.41	65.1	7.2	107.9	8.3	6.8
4.4	2.39	12.9	0.07	4.4	0.1	0.77	5.93	4.68	74.1	6.1	53.6	5.6	5.0
8.2	1.21	4.7	1.10	6.2	0.2	1.54	13.80	3.84	62.4	3.7	17.4	10.8	5.7
10.0	0.08	0.4	0.00	3.8	3.4	0.62	8.87	2.35	67.3	3.2	28.2	18.2	4.9
7.4	2.10	6.5	0.13	4.1	1.0	0.71	5.28	3.40	73.5	6.1	42.1	3.6	7.8
8.8	0.30	1.2	0.15	6.3	0.2	1.11	7.36	3.41	47.8	9.6	260.5	3.0	7.2
2.8	7.92	24.6	-0.68	6.6	0.4	1.23	11.96	4.29	65.0	4.6	38.5	11.5	4.5
6.7	0.38	3.0	0.03	9.7	4.3	2.22	29.07	4.59	47.0	2.1	28.1	21.3	6.6
6.7	0.41	2.9	0.28	3.3	0.2	0.60	6.80	3.24	73.6	2.8	37.5	20.1	3.2
9.4	0.25	1.4	0.01	1.5	-0.2	-0.35	-3.37	2.60	123.2	4.8	50.0	13.5	5.2
7.9	0.87	3.6	0.49	6.4	2.4	0.82	5.73	4.32	71.1	5.2	41.0	9.2	9.3
4.4	1.19	8.6	0.00	8.7	0.8	2.13	20.88	4.27	50.6	4.7	15.7	3.8	6.9
7.6	0.36	1.6	0.10	8.1	0.3	1.30	8.58	4.85	61.7	5.9	60.5	8.3	7.0
8.2	0.00	0.0	0.00	3.6	0.1	1.03	10.01	3.76	87.4	5.0	47.4	8.9	2.6
4.3	1.12	9.5	0.07	5.4	5.2	0.86	8.63	3.14	54.9	1.3	7.8	26.6	7.9
7.3	1.21	3.1	0.00	7.8	0.5	1.27	8.61	4.47	55.5	3.4	34.7	16.1	5.2
8.5	0.20	1.1	0.00	5.9	0.5	1.01	10.32	3.68	60.1	3.7	49.9	18.0	6.3
8.7	0.31	1.3	0.01	7.8	0.4	1.36	10.82	3.98	47.8	5.8	37.1	3.3	7.1
5.6	0.78	4.7	0.01	8.3	1.0	1.63	14.76	4.04	61.8	7.1	73.0	5.2	8.7
8.3	0.12	0.7	0.16	6.1	2.4	1.21	11.31	3.88	60.4	4.3	23.0	7.5	6.2
5.2	1.28	5.8	0.13	8.7	1.2	1.58	11.44	5.20	46.5	2.6	39.4	25.7	7.6
8.4	0.12	0.8	0.05	8.4	3.0	1.38	15.50	4.04	57.5	4.1	21.3	8.5	6.3
6.1	0.58	3.3	0.00	4.6	1.4	0.74	6.90	3.25	68.3	2.2	17.4	18.4	5.2
6.2	0.75	4.6	0.13	4.7	19.3	0.72	9.50	2.18	60.2	1.5	24.8	34.9	5.6
7.6	0.43	2.1	-0.06	10.0	2.2	1.96	18.93	4.71	50.2	3.8	19.5	10.3	8.8
7.3	0.27	2.0	0.05	5.7	1.3	1.22	12.29	4.20	57.0	1.6	22.6	25.2	4.9
2.0	10.37	17.6	1.19	10.0	0.3	3.47	9.22	19.01	83.3	0.4	20.9	93.0	2.9
6.9	0.39	2.5	0.09	5.7	91.8	1.08	11.11	3.11	53.8	4.1	9.4	7.7	4.1
8.6	0.77	2.7	0.08	7.9	0.6	1.08	5.53	3.46	51.3	4.2	47.6	16.0	9.0
8.9	0.21	1.0	0.00	4.8	1.9	0.88	7.16	4.16	72.8	4.4	15.3	5.8	7.3
4.9	0.65	5.7	0.14	7.7	1.1	1.75	22.36	4.86	59.4	0.8	13.7	36.1	5.3
3.6	3.45	23.5	0.00	9.3	0.2	2.49	25.61	5.03	52.2	4.6	40.3	9.3	4.9
7.0	0.34	2.8	0.17	5.9	1.1	1.03	10.90	4.96	56.4	0.7	13.0	46.0	4.2
6.4	0.93	8.6	0.00	4.5	0.6	0.80	9.89	4.02	67.0	1.5	20.2	26.1	4.7
7.2	0.25	1.8	-0.04	3.5	0.3	0.64	8.41	4.42	80.3	3.4	43.1	18.6	2.9
7.8	0.58	1.7	-0.43	3.7	0.2	0.60	5.24	3.90	77.0	4.7	20.5	4.5	3.8
6.6	0.00	0.0	0.00	9.5	2.2	2.65	3.16	0.71	87.8	5.0	1,422.4	100.0	5.6
10.0	0.00	0.0	0.00	1.9	0.0	0.06	0.08	0.87	84.6	0.0	N/A	100.0	5.8
9.6	0.00	0.0	0.00	3.4	0.0	0.51	0.63	1.12	29.4	5.0	27,950.0	98.4	8.3
4.8	0.48	3.7	0.31	9.6	2,575.0	1.60	17.30	4.40	59.3	4.2	31.4	14.3	8.5
6.5	0.12	1.9	0.50	6.3	314.0	2.32	33.29	4.44	23.8	1.0	1.5	27.6	4.6
6.7	0.00	0.0	0.00	3.2	0.0	0.37	0.40	0.80	0.0	5.0	30,900.0	100.0	5.8
3.6	1.52	5.3	4.48	10.0	44.0	5.20	28.65	11.70	22.5	0.2	5.6	92.1	8.3
1.9	1.34	8.3	3.53	10.0	22.6	5.50	46.67	13.80	16.2	5.0	0.1	0.0	8.3
5.5	0.32	2.7	0.00	9.5	8.9	1.99	19.22	2.47	54.6	0.0	0.2	96.7	8.3

| Name | City | State | Weiss Safety Rating | 2003 Weiss Safety Rating | 2002 Weiss Safety Rating | Total Assets ($Mil) | One Year Asset Growth | Asset Mix (As a % of Total Assets) | | | | Capital-ization Index | Leverage Ratio | Risk-based Capital Ratio |
								Comm-ercial Loans	Cons-umer Loans	Home Mort-gages	Secur-ities			
WELLS FEDERAL BK FSB	WELLS	MN	B	B	B	223.2	0.89	4.0	7.2	21.3	9.8	6.2	9.1	11.9
WELLS RIVER SVGS BK	WELLS RIVER	VT	B-	B-	B-	112.8	0.19	7.6	5.0	29.9	33.8	9.9	10.9	20.4
WELLSVILLE BK	WELLSVILLE	KS	D	D-	D	26.2	7.69	10.0	8.1	18.3	35.8	6.7	8.7	16.6
WEMPLE ST BK	WAVERLY	IL	C+	C+	C+	39.1	2.79	18.4	6.1	10.9	8.1	5.2	8.7	11.2
WENONA ST BK	WENONA	IL	B-	C+	B-	27.3	-5.15	9.4	7.4	12.0	36.6	10.0	14.7	28.3
WESBANCO BK	WHEELING	WV	B+	B+	B+	3,477.2	2.38	11.9	7.1	18.7	32.5	6.4	8.4	13.7
WEST ALABAMA B&TC	REFORM	AL	C+	C+	B-	342.9	-1.15	8.9	6.0	16.9	32.1	6.5	8.5	13.7
▲ WEST B&TC	WEST	TX	A-	B+	B+	52.7	-1.03	1.7	4.6	2.5	12.1	10.0	14.5	48.5
WEST BEND SVGS BK	W BEND	WI	C+	C+	C+	355.7	3.03	8.5	2.0	22.8	18.9	6.8	8.8	14.8
▼ WEST BK	W DES MOINES	IA	B+	A-	A-	1,024.8	18.81	23.9	1.1	6.2	30.3	4.9	7.0	11.9
WEST CARROLL COMMUNITY	OAK GROVE	LA	C	C	C-	16.5	-2.64	11.9	9.4	7.9	32.3	10.0	12.9	21.1
▲ WEST CENTRAL GEORGIA BK	THOMASTON	GA	A	A-	A-	85.4	-1.05	1.5	14.1	17.7	42.2	10.0	16.1	31.2
▲ WEST CHESTER SVG BK	WASHINGTON	IA	B+	B	B	37.8	4.17	12.7	4.6	16.8	34.3	8.8	10.2	17.5
▲ WEST COAST BK	LAKE OSWEGO	OR	B+	B	B	1,714.4	7.65	12.8	2.1	2.7	17.4	5.5	9.2	11.3
▲ WEST END SVGS BK	RICHMOND	IN	C	C-	C+	145.0	2.59	1.1	4.5	60.0	17.2	8.8	10.2	18.3
WEST GATE BK	LINCOLN	NE	C+	C+	C+	222.8	2.06	9.1	2.4	23.0	11.3	6.8	8.8	12.9
WEST GEORGIA NB	CARROLLTON	GA	B	B	B	422.0	9.74	7.1	4.2	13.4	13.7	6.3	8.9	12.0
WEST IA BK	W BEND	IA	B-	B-	B-	61.9	8.47	9.1	2.6	4.2	36.8	7.8	9.5	14.7
WEST LIBERTY ST BK	W LIBERTY	IA	B	B	A-	97.3	-10.70	2.1	1.1	6.9	64.4	10.0	11.0	27.6
▲ WEST MI COMMUNITY BK	HUDSONVILLE	MI	C	D+	D+	139.9	11.50	8.7	4.0	10.7	15.9	3.0	7.3	10.0
WEST MI NB	FRANKFORT	MI	A-	A-	A-	30.0	3.39	0.5	1.5	12.6	50.7	10.0	24.7	59.8
▲ WEST MICHIGAN SVG BK	BANGOR	MI	B-	C	C+	28.5	-6.09	2.5	4.0	21.6	40.1	10.0	15.4	32.5
WEST MILTON ST BK	W MILTON	PA	B-	B-	B-	224.7	3.17	6.3	1.7	18.4	49.1	4.9	6.9	12.9
WEST ONE BK	KALISPELL	MT	B-	B-	NR	18.8	99.46	15.1	8.1	15.2	0.0	10.0	19.1	24.4
WEST PLAINS B&TC	W PLAINS	MO	B+	A-	A-	196.3	5.79	5.9	4.2	15.6	34.0	6.1	8.1	13.6
WEST PLAINS S&LA	W PLAINS	MO	B+	B+	B	64.8	2.84	0.0	0.2	64.3	22.6	10.0	14.1	33.8
WEST POINT BK	RADCLIFF	KY	A-	A-	A-	87.8	4.69	0.5	2.5	32.2	42.4	6.7	8.7	20.1
▲ WEST POINTE B&TC	BELLEVILLE	IL	C	C-	C-	424.1	2.07	13.6	2.4	11.1	35.2	5.4	7.4	13.3
WEST POINTE BK	OSHKOSH	WI	C+	C+	C+	220.8	3.65	21.4	2.8	26.1	5.5	5.4	8.6	11.3
▼ WEST SHORE BK	LUDINGTON	MI	B-	B	B	297.8	10.14	7.4	8.3	29.4	27.6	5.8	7.8	13.4
▲ WEST SIDE ST SVG BK	WESTSIDE	IA	C+	C	C	26.2	10.52	8.8	5.8	19.5	14.8	9.9	10.9	17.5
WEST SUBURBAN BK	LOMBARD	IL	B-	B-	B-	1,742.0	4.07	13.6	4.3	15.7	30.9	4.0	7.6	10.5
WEST TEXAS ST BK	SNYDER	TX	D+	D+	D	80.9	-5.78	5.7	6.8	11.1	49.9	5.6	7.6	15.5
▼ WEST TOWN SVGS BK	CICERO	IL	E	D	D	58.6	0.85	2.4	0.6	23.2	42.5	3.3	5.3	16.1
WEST TX NB	MIDLAND	TX	B-	B-	B-	321.3	8.84	20.6	5.1	6.3	20.2	4.4	7.7	10.7
WEST TX ST BK	ODESSA	TX	A-	A-	A-	165.1	5.41	39.2	5.5	5.3	16.2	10.0	12.3	15.0
WEST UNION BK	W UNION	WV	B	B	B	92.6	2.28	7.8	6.1	25.1	41.6	9.8	10.9	20.1
WEST VIEW SVG BK	PITTSBURGH	PA	C	C+	C+	431.9	18.86	0.2	0.2	7.6	80.8	4.3	6.3	18.0
▲ WESTAMERICA BK	SAN RAFAEL	CA	B	B-	B-	4,584.7	1.09	7.9	9.8	8.4	42.9	4.6	6.6	11.4
WESTBANK	WESTCHESTER	IL	C-	C-	B	179.9	8.27	0.6	9.1	7.5	12.3	8.7	10.1	15.4
WESTBANK	W SPRINGFIELD	MA	B-	B-	C+	764.0	17.80	8.1	5.9	22.2	36.4	5.1	7.1	12.6
WESTBOROUGH SVGS BK	WESTBOROUGH	MA	C+	C+	C+	262.9	4.18	1.1	0.3	46.5	35.1	9.2	10.4	20.8
WESTERLY SAVINGS BANK	WESTERLY	RI	D	D	D-	68.2	-1.88	0.9	1.8	49.1	0.1	4.9	6.9	12.3
WESTERN BK	ST PAUL	MN	B	B	B	341.4	0.14	18.5	1.0	9.1	8.3	4.8	9.3	10.9
▲ WESTERN BK	ALAMOGORDO	NM	B-	C+	C-	67.1	-4.35	6.6	6.0	21.3	21.5	10.0	12.9	22.2
WESTERN BK	ARTESIA	NM	A	A	A	98.5	5.68	25.2	7.1	5.7	32.8	10.0	11.1	16.4
WESTERN BK	LORDSBURG	NM	B	A-	A-	74.2	29.69	11.9	7.1	7.1	30.3	8.3	9.8	16.0
WESTERN BK GALLUP NM	GALLUP	NM	B	B	B	109.5	14.42	6.2	4.5	8.1	45.6	4.8	6.8	13.6
WESTERN BK OF CHINOOK NA	CHINOOK	MT	C+	C+	C+	30.2	-0.06	8.9	3.9	4.4	11.5	6.9	8.9	12.6
▲ WESTERN BK OF CLOVIS	CLOVIS	NM	C+	C	D+	43.9	-4.85	12.8	11.3	10.5	20.4	10.0	11.9	16.6
WESTERN BK OF WOLF POINT	WOLF POINT	MT	B-	B-	B-	53.3	6.74	3.0	4.7	5.5	44.7	6.8	8.8	16.0
WESTERN BK-CHEYENNE	CHEYENNE	WY	B-	B-	B	70.9	11.95	6.6	3.3	12.5	0.0	6.8	8.8	16.0
WESTERN COMMERCE BK	CARLSBAD	NM	A	A	A-	254.8	-0.57	22.3	2.0	17.4	28.4	10.0	11.4	18.5
WESTERN COMMUNITY BK	OREM	UT	C	C	D+	75.9	0.36	9.8	4.3	5.2	0.5	5.8	9.1	11.6
▼ WESTERN DAKOTA BK	TIMBER LAKE	SD	C+	B-	B	16.3	2.38	7.2	3.0	2.0	47.0	10.0	12.0	27.2
WESTERN FINANCIAL BK FSB	IRVINE	CA	C+	C+	C+	12,075.7	-6.72	0.7	69.3	0.4	26.5	6.2	8.2	16.0
WESTERN NB	LENEXA	KS	D	D+	C	86.8	-15.97	11.7	1.6	5.6	25.2	6.0	8.0	13.1
WESTERN NB	DULUTH	MN	C	C	C	116.1	12.74	8.6	15.3	10.2	27.9	4.3	7.2	10.7
▲ WESTERN NB	AMARILLO	TX	B-	C+	C+	34.8	-0.99	5.0	20.4	4.2	51.9	7.9	9.6	21.8
▲ WESTERN NB	ODESSA	TX	B-	C+	B-	511.5	25.81	38.7	1.1	1.6	22.8	8.8	10.5	14.0
WESTERN RESERVE BK	MEDINA	OH	C-	C-	C	115.2	25.58	20.2	1.1	9.6	1.4	4.0	7.1	10.5
WESTERN SECURITY BANK	BILLINGS	MT	B	B	B	454.8	3.44	9.1	4.6	8.4	43.5	7.5	9.4	16.0
▲ WESTERN SECURITY BK	SCOTTSDALE	AZ	B-	C	C-	178.7	5.26	29.6	2.4	4.5	7.8	6.8	9.7	12.4
▲ WESTERN SIERRA NB	CAMERON PARK	CA	B-	C+	C+	545.2	24.92	9.7	0.3	4.3	8.0	3.8	8.5	10.4

Asset Quality Index	Non-Performing Loans as a % of Total Loans	Non-Performing Loans as a % of Capital	Net Charge-offs Avg Loans	Profitability Index	Net Income ($Mil)	Return on Assets (R.O.A.)	Return on Equity (R.O.E.)	Net Interest Spread	Overhead Efficiency Ratio	Liquidity Index	Liquidity Ratio	Hot Money Ratio	Stability Index
6.1	0.09	0.7	0.05	7.9	1.1	0.98	9.43	3.84	69.0	2.5	6.2	15.7	7.2
6.2	1.13	5.2	0.19	4.3	0.4	0.78	6.77	4.59	79.7	4.7	18.7	4.7	6.3
2.8	3.41	21.2	-0.04	6.1	0.2	1.82	22.68	4.71	71.5	4.2	27.6	9.7	2.6
7.9	0.07	0.6	-0.01	9.0	0.5	2.36	27.03	4.29	48.0	1.6	15.1	22.5	5.0
4.6	3.93	12.1	0.36	5.2	0.2	1.50	10.32	4.36	63.0	6.1	68.3	9.2	5.3
6.6	0.59	3.4	0.23	5.7	20.1	1.18	12.06	3.77	59.9	5.0	29.5	9.6	7.9
3.6	1.92	12.1	0.52	5.1	2.0	1.20	13.56	3.87	64.0	1.6	19.0	23.8	4.6
9.5	0.08	0.1	-0.11	6.1	0.3	1.21	8.56	3.59	60.9	9.2	202.8	5.2	6.7
6.9	0.32	2.4	0.10	3.8	0.9	0.51	6.13	3.42	85.4	2.9	16.1	14.4	3.1
7.4	0.43	3.0	0.13	9.8	9.1	1.83	21.11	3.85	33.3	5.3	63.5	15.0	7.8
8.3	0.00	0.0	0.00	3.0	0.0	0.38	2.72	4.39	88.4	3.7	75.2	21.5	5.0
8.1	0.02	0.1	-0.17	6.7	0.5	1.20	7.14	4.25	62.0	3.6	26.0	12.5	8.7
8.3	0.08	0.4	-0.01	4.8	0.2	0.93	8.69	3.89	66.9	4.8	30.8	7.1	6.9
6.9	0.39	2.9	0.14	7.7	10.9	1.30	14.26	4.84	62.1	3.9	18.1	10.1	7.9
5.1	1.40	10.2	0.24	2.6	0.3	0.34	3.35	3.03	83.0	3.6	14.6	10.8	5.5
6.7	0.23	1.9	0.30	3.6	-0.1	-0.13	-1.43	4.11	80.1	1.2	11.5	27.4	3.8
4.6	0.70	5.7	0.02	8.9	2.7	1.33	14.48	4.55	62.2	3.8	41.7	16.2	6.6
5.9	0.68	3.6	0.81	4.9	0.3	0.82	7.83	4.15	69.0	3.5	41.4	17.8	4.4
9.7	0.23	0.7	0.01	5.2	0.4	0.69	6.80	2.90	47.7	5.4	47.3	9.3	6.1
4.6	0.46	2.3	2.04	1.8	0.1	0.07	0.64	2.30	87.8	3.7	22.0	11.0	4.0
9.6	0.00	0.0	-0.04	6.1	0.2	1.26	5.32	4.29	70.8	4.2	40.3	14.1	8.4
8.3	1.38	3.5	-0.16	3.6	0.1	0.58	3.71	4.57	85.1	7.5	78.6	1.4	5.1
8.3	0.33	2.0	-0.16	5.0	1.2	1.06	15.27	3.06	56.2	7.4	106.5	8.0	4.3
8.0	0.00	0.0	0.00	3.8	0.1	1.00	4.92	4.76	52.2	1.2	36.6	52.4	2.9
8.6	0.09	0.6	0.09	6.8	1.4	1.39	17.06	3.56	63.5	3.7	24.1	11.3	6.8
8.5	1.35	6.4	0.00	5.4	0.3	0.92	6.53	2.52	46.3	4.1	32.6	12.0	6.6
6.5	0.83	4.9	0.00	7.2	0.5	1.23	14.28	3.69	51.5	4.7	18.0	4.3	6.4
3.6	2.58	17.6	0.30	4.4	1.7	0.80	10.93	3.78	71.3	2.2	11.5	17.8	2.8
5.6	0.48	4.3	0.00	7.6	1.5	1.33	16.05	3.41	39.8	0.4	3.6	53.9	3.8
8.4	0.04	0.3	0.08	5.2	1.3	0.92	11.84	3.73	65.0	2.9	23.4	15.1	4.3
5.5	0.77	4.9	-0.02	7.2	0.1	1.00	9.15	4.42	65.5	3.3	14.5	12.7	5.4
5.3	1.22	9.5	0.25	7.9	11.8	1.37	17.98	3.72	56.0	5.2	26.6	6.4	7.5
4.9	2.17	9.9	0.53	2.5	0.2	0.46	5.99	3.52	87.3	4.1	59.4	17.5	2.1
8.4	0.00	0.0	2.40	0.8	-0.6	-2.04	-34.05	2.07	82.2	7.7	249.7	14.3	0.7
7.3	0.11	0.6	0.13	5.1	2.0	1.25	12.73	4.01	70.1	3.4	24.9	12.8	6.0
7.5	0.38	2.1	0.01	5.5	1.1	1.39	11.52	4.00	68.5	5.0	37.4	8.6	6.7
7.8	0.38	1.7	0.22	4.8	0.5	0.98	8.90	4.63	76.0	4.6	11.3	4.3	5.0
8.3	1.14	2.9	-0.34	3.6	1.2	0.56	8.89	1.58	56.5	7.3	79.3	4.4	2.5
8.0	0.27	1.7	0.13	10.0	47.9	2.13	29.41	5.13	44.3	4.0	14.1	9.3	7.6
2.1	1.77	13.2	0.11	6.1	1.1	1.18	12.25	3.98	50.1	3.3	34.2	16.6	6.5
6.1	0.27	1.8	0.09	5.8	3.6	0.98	11.98	3.56	63.9	4.4	35.1	11.3	5.2
9.3	0.21	1.1	0.04	3.0	0.6	0.43	3.98	3.46	84.7	5.6	37.5	5.1	6.0
6.5	0.32	3.6	0.00	3.0	0.1	0.23	3.40	3.17	87.9	1.7	22.0	24.1	2.1
7.3	0.08	0.7	0.01	10.0	4.5	2.73	28.66	5.98	54.6	5.3	29.8	3.4	7.3
4.1	3.70	16.6	0.47	4.4	0.3	0.98	7.79	5.34	72.9	4.2	76.8	19.9	5.0
8.1	0.61	2.7	0.01	10.0	1.2	2.41	22.07	4.87	51.1	2.5	27.9	18.5	8.2
3.9	2.16	10.8	0.01	7.8	0.6	1.61	15.24	5.18	69.8	3.7	46.0	17.7	6.7
7.2	0.28	1.2	0.00	5.7	0.6	1.09	11.17	3.71	63.8	5.0	103.8	21.3	6.7
3.7	1.97	14.5	0.11	6.4	0.2	1.32	15.02	4.41	62.4	5.8	47.2	6.6	5.1
7.8	0.29	1.4	0.02	5.2	0.2	0.99	8.44	5.22	68.0	5.0	55.4	12.8	3.2
7.9	0.02	0.1	-0.02	6.7	0.4	1.58	16.93	4.33	63.9	2.9	15.0	14.3	5.7
5.7	0.90	5.3	-0.01	5.7	0.3	0.91	10.25	3.79	65.7	6.8	146.0	14.2	4.9
8.5	0.30	1.5	0.06	9.6	2.9	2.21	19.08	4.99	55.7	3.2	41.4	19.1	7.6
3.1	1.43	11.6	0.13	7.0	0.4	1.17	13.34	5.95	68.6	4.3	59.1	16.6	4.0
9.0	0.00	0.0	0.11	4.3	0.1	0.55	4.55	4.01	76.5	5.7	69.7	9.8	5.1
3.6	0.66	5.7	1.94	8.9	91.6	1.52	24.76	5.12	38.6	0.6	14.5	64.1	4.3
6.3	0.21	1.1	0.53	0.4	-0.2	-0.50	-4.80	3.25	104.1	2.0	32.4	28.0	4.2
6.2	0.56	4.9	0.09	4.8	0.6	1.11	15.74	4.20	74.0	1.5	30.7	32.8	3.9
7.1	0.22	0.7	0.66	8.0	0.2	1.33	14.25	5.46	70.4	6.6	60.6	4.1	4.5
5.1	1.29	7.9	0.16	8.9	4.8	1.96	23.16	3.90	54.2	3.6	60.1	26.3	7.8
2.9	1.22	13.0	0.00	4.4	0.4	0.67	9.51	3.57	68.7	1.5	32.2	34.1	4.0
5.6	0.89	3.8	0.03	8.5	3.4	1.51	14.33	4.12	48.4	3.9	7.4	8.3	5.8
4.8	1.12	8.3	0.06	6.0	1.3	1.50	16.37	5.20	62.3	3.4	23.4	12.9	4.8
7.3	0.11	1.0	0.09	10.0	4.6	1.85	22.15	5.37	47.6	3.4	55.1	25.0	6.5

Name	City	State	Weiss Safety Rating	2003 Weiss Safety Rating	2002 Weiss Safety Rating	Total Assets ($Mil)	One Year Asset Growth	Asset Mix (As a % of Total Assets) Commercial Loans	Consumer Loans	Home Mortgages	Securities	Capitalization Index	Leverage Ratio	Risk-based Capital Ratio
WESTERN SPRINGS NB&T	WESTERN SPRINGS	IL	C+	B-	C+	178.3	1.19	8.7	3.6	10.4	16.0	3.9	7.9	10.5
WESTERN ST BK	DUARTE	CA	D-	D-	D-	72.6	-7.64	17.1	0.4	3.0	7.4	8.7	10.1	15.8
▼ WESTERN ST BK	GARDEN CITY	KS	C+	B	B	306.0	-8.72	11.5	2.3	6.8	13.3	7.3	9.3	12.8
▲ WESTERN ST BK	DEVILS LAKE	ND	C	D+	D-	241.2	-8.01	8.5	9.1	12.1	13.7	6.9	9.5	12.4
WESTERN ST BK	WATERLOO	NE	E-	E-	E-	12.9	-11.83	12.1	15.0	25.2	14.4	4.5	6.5	11.1
WESTERNBANK PUERTO RICO	MAYAGUEZ	PR	B-	B-	B-	13,080.4	38.57	4.3	2.8	11.6	49.4	5.1	7.1	13.5
WESTFIELD BK	WESTFIELD	MA	C+	C	C+	753.5	-1.24	13.1	2.0	13.5	40.1	9.6	10.7	20.1
WESTFIELD BK FSB	WESTFIELD CENTER	OH	D-	D	D-	147.6	23.63	19.7	1.3	15.2	26.3	6.6	8.6	13.2
▼ WESTMINSTER UNION BK	WESTMINSTER	MD	B+	A-	A	861.8	40.07	9.4	5.5	19.5	31.2	4.4	6.4	16.4
WESTMORELAND FS&LA	LATROBE	PA	A-	A-	B+	151.6	9.27	0.0	0.0	50.0	38.4	10.0	19.8	45.9
WESTSIDE COMMUNITY BK	UNIVERSITY PLACE	WA	B	B-	C+	64.0	10.89	23.0	2.9	7.8	10.6	8.2	10.4	13.5
WESTSOUND BK	BREMERTON	WA	B	B-	C-	89.7	43.12	9.5	2.6	16.4	5.7	8.8	11.2	14.0
▲ WESTSTAR BK	VAIL	CO	B	C+	C	587.2	-0.77	4.4	0.8	10.3	23.5	5.7	7.7	12.2
WESTVIEW SVGS BK	BALTIMORE	MD	C+	C+	C	67.3	-10.73	0.0	4.3	14.2	49.4	10.0	16.7	40.3
WEYMOUTH BK	STOW	MA	B-	B-	B-	149.8	7.34	0.9	1.0	40.4	26.3	6.1	8.1	15.0
WF NB SOUTH CENTRAL	FARIBAULT	MN	B-	B-	B-	9.5	1.05	0.0	0.0	0.0	0.0	10.0	58.1	293.7
WHAPLES & FARMERS ST BK	NEPONSET	IL	C+	C+	B-	9.9	4.88	5.7	10.1	13.8	29.0	9.7	10.8	20.7
WHEATLAND BK	DAVENPORT	WA	C+	C+	C-	145.9	3.61	11.4	2.6	6.2	11.5	8.3	11.1	13.5
WHEELER COUNTY ST BK	ALAMO	GA	B-	B-	B	47.9	8.95	2.6	25.4	18.4	12.6	8.3	9.8	15.3
WHIDBEY ISLAND BK	OAK HARBOR	WA	C+	C+	C+	632.1	10.50	7.9	22.4	9.6	3.1	4.7	9.5	10.8
WHITAKER BK	LEXINGTON	KY	C+	C+	C+	939.8	72.33	7.3	7.7	20.6	21.9	4.9	6.9	11.2
▼ WHITE HALL BK	WHITE HALL	IL	C	C+	C	42.1	5.08	14.8	2.9	14.8	22.9	2.0	6.7	9.0
WHITE OAK ST BK	WHITE OAK	TX	D-	D-	E+	42.8	12.31	8.5	14.1	21.8	0.0	3.3	6.2	10.2
▲ WHITE ROCK BK	CANNON FALLS	MN	C-	C+	C+	97.2	10.89	11.3	9.2	12.1	9.9	3.0	7.7	10.0
WHITE ST BK	S ENGLISH	IA	B	B	B	25.9	-14.57	5.2	4.7	13.7	50.1	10.0	20.7	46.4
WHITESVILLE ST BK	WHITESVILLE	WV	B-	B-	B-	59.1	-2.73	0.4	12.5	20.7	46.0	10.0	11.3	21.8
WHITNEY NB OF NEW	NEW ORLEANS	LA	B	B	B+	7,781.2	6.89	27.5	2.8	8.7	26.1	5.1	8.0	11.1
WILBER NB	ONEONTA	NY	B	B	B	725.6	-0.44	8.6	8.5	12.3	40.8	6.2	8.2	14.0
WILBURTON ST BK	WILBURTON	OK	D	D	D+	52.8	10.04	7.2	10.2	13.5	20.7	3.1	5.1	11.0
WILCOX CTY ST BK	ABBEVILLE	GA	B	B	B	50.4	7.31	2.9	23.1	21.7	36.6	10.0	11.5	21.3
WILKINSON COUNTY BK	IRWINTON	GA	B+	B+	A-	35.2	1.90	4.9	4.6	11.6	54.4	10.0	14.7	33.5
WILLAMETTE COMMUNITY BK	ALBANY	OR	D	D	NR	18.3	142.86	12.4	0.5	7.6	8.2	10.0	28.1	32.1
▲ WILLAMETTE VALLEY BK	SALEM	OR	C	D+	D	50.4	30.83	8.5	0.8	8.5	4.4	10.0	11.1	15.3
WILLIAM PENN S&LA	LEVITTOWN	PA	A-	A-	A-	259.6	-2.16	1.7	0.7	50.1	21.9	9.9	10.9	21.0
WILLIAMSBURG FIRST NB	KINGSTREE	SC	A-	B+	B+	82.2	3.21	18.2	9.2	10.0	42.4	10.0	14.1	26.4
WILLIAMSBURG NB	WILLIAMSBURG	KY	B	B	B+	64.3	-2.33	2.4	15.2	43.1	24.9	7.0	9.0	16.8
▲ WILLIAMSTOWN NB	WILLIAMSTOWN	WV	B	B-	C+	82.8	-2.80	3.5	17.8	20.8	17.4	10.0	11.2	15.7
WILLIAMSTOWN SVGS BK	WILLIAMSTOWN	MA	B-	B-	B-	207.9	11.26	6.4	0.3	30.5	40.7	5.1	7.1	14.5
WILLIAMSVILLE ST B&T	WILLIAMSVILLE	IL	C-	D+	D	100.4	12.55	8.7	4.3	37.7	32.6	5.1	7.1	14.4
WILLOW GROVE BK	MAPLE GLEN	PA	B	B	B	920.8	8.99	2.0	0.9	27.2	34.9	7.8	9.5	17.7
WILMINGTON SVGS BK	WILMINGTON	OH	A	A	A	156.9	8.99	3.1	2.9	56.6	1.4	10.0	16.6	27.6
WILMINGTON SVGS FUND	WILMINGTON	DE	A	A	B+	2,397.6	18.77	14.4	1.0	25.5	27.2	7.7	9.5	15.8
WILMINGTON TR OF PA	VILLANOVA	PA	B-	B-	C+	875.1	21.54	32.0	11.8	9.2	16.8	5.7	8.0	11.5
▲ WILMINGTON TRUST CO	WILMINGTON	DE	B	B-	C+	8,458.0	2.56	24.5	12.0	7.0	18.2	5.1	8.1	11.1
WILMINGTON TRUST FSB	BALTIMORE	MD	B-	C+	C+	209.9	12.06	11.9	34.3	21.7	1.4	5.8	8.5	11.6
WILMOT ST BK	WILMOT	SD	B-	B-	B-	30.6	23.20	10.2	3.6	2.7	35.6	7.7	9.5	13.3
WILSHIRE ST BK	LOS ANGELES	CA	B-	C+	C	1,202.5	48.54	11.7	1.4	2.3	8.4	4.9	6.9	11.7
WILSON & MUIR B&TC	BARDSTOWN	KY	A	A	A	264.7	0.70	12.6	4.9	21.7	24.5	10.0	11.9	18.2
WILSON B&TC	LEBANON	TN	B-	B-	B-	688.6	-1.17	12.4	6.5	28.2	15.8	6.8	8.8	12.9
WILSON ST BK	WILSON	KS	D+	D+	C	34.7	29.54	18.0	6.4	16.3	30.6	3.9	6.6	10.5
WILSON ST BK	WILSON	TX	C+	C+	B-	42.7	-0.94	7.8	7.6	4.0	57.5	10.0	13.5	35.2
▲ WILTON BK	WILTON	CT	C-	D+	B	104.2	4.53	7.1	2.1	2.0	12.5	10.0	12.9	16.6
▲ WILTON SVG BK	WILTON	IA	B+	B	B	76.8	5.01	3.6	2.2	7.3	45.8	7.4	9.3	17.8
WINCHESTER BK	WINCHESTER	KY	D	D	NR	25.3	73.96	12.6	2.3	23.9	24.6	10.0	27.1	40.2
WINCHESTER CO-OP BK	WINCHESTER	MA	B+	B+	B+	341.8	0.16	0.0	0.9	45.7	39.0	7.8	9.6	22.0
▲ WINCHESTER FSB	WINCHESTER	KY	B	B-	C+	130.3	15.42	0.9	1.2	63.9	0.8	6.0	8.1	13.6
WINCHESTER SVGS BK	WINCHESTER	MA	B-	B-	B-	443.4	-0.04	0.8	0.6	35.6	35.0	7.6	9.4	18.9
▲ WINDSOR FS&LA	WINDSOR	CT	B+	B	B	224.1	2.43	1.6	0.4	40.6	31.2	7.7	9.5	19.3
WINFIELD COMMUNITY BK	WINFIELD	IL	D-	D-	D-	51.8	11.17	49.0	1.6	4.5	9.8	4.3	8.5	10.7
▲ WINNSBORO ST B&TC	WINNSBORO	LA	B	B-	B	84.8	2.27	3.9	14.1	12.4	33.2	8.0	9.7	16.2
▲ WINONA NB	WINONA	MN	B+	B	B	243.6	3.51	16.2	7.1	13.9	34.1	10.0	11.0	17.4
WINSIDE ST BK	WINSIDE	NE	B-	B-	B-	20.7	1.13	3.2	5.3	8.5	39.3	10.0	16.9	27.6
WINTER HILL FSB	SOMERVILLE	MA	C+	C+	C+	227.4	-1.13	0.0	0.3	26.4	29.0	6.3	8.3	15.3
WINTHROP ST BK	WINTHROP	MN	C+	C+	B-	20.4	0.40	7.1	4.7	7.6	49.9	9.2	10.5	25.0

Asset Quality Index	Non-Performing Loans as a % of Total Loans	Non-Performing Loans as a % of Capital	Net Charge-offs Avg Loans	Profitability Index	Net Income ($Mil)	Return on Assets (R.O.A.)	Return on Equity (R.O.E.)	Net Interest Spread	Overhead Efficiency Ratio	Liquidity Index	Liquidity Ratio	Hot Money Ratio	Stability Index
4.6	0.77	6.9	0.01	7.4	1.5	1.67	19.35	4.06	54.7	5.5	71.8	14.1	5.9
4.5	0.48	2.7	0.25	0.2	-0.2	-0.60	-5.79	3.48	106.0	6.8	155.1	14.8	1.8
2.1	3.23	20.5	0.43	7.2	1.8	1.14	12.04	4.38	52.1	2.9	40.8	22.5	4.4
3.2	1.63	10.6	0.53	6.3	1.7	1.39	15.19	6.05	62.4	1.3	19.2	28.8	3.4
0.6	3.93	30.5	1.83	0.8	0.0	-0.19	-2.59	5.82	93.3	5.7	40.8	2.6	0.0
7.4	0.68	3.9	0.35	5.9	82.1	1.34	19.35	2.49	29.8	0.5	9.5	69.6	4.9
7.3	0.72	3.0	0.07	4.0	3.2	0.86	8.14	3.10	68.2	8.4	264.9	10.6	5.8
8.0	0.25	1.8	0.04	0.1	-0.3	-0.41	-4.93	2.93	106.4	1.9	40.7	56.1	0.0
7.1	0.08	0.4	0.00	8.6	5.6	1.29	11.92	3.88	51.6	7.3	90.5	6.7	8.7
5.9	2.19	5.2	0.00	5.8	0.5	0.72	3.33	2.33	52.1	3.2	28.2	15.2	8.7
7.1	0.00	0.0	0.09	9.2	0.5	1.67	16.72	5.43	53.5	2.6	41.8	27.7	5.2
7.0	0.18	1.3	0.03	5.8	0.4	1.01	9.44	5.91	76.3	2.9	20.0	15.2	5.7
4.6	0.45	2.0	0.20	7.2	3.4	1.16	9.05	4.91	69.1	6.1	91.8	13.4	7.4
8.4	0.07	0.1	0.52	2.4	0.1	0.04	0.27	2.83	97.1	3.3	59.0	24.2	5.1
9.5	0.01	0.1	0.01	4.0	0.4	0.52	6.42	3.54	73.2	6.2	70.2	10.4	4.6
10.0	0.00	0.0	0.00	6.5	0.0	0.46	0.80	0.94	13.6	0.0	N/A	100.0	5.5
8.3	0.00	0.0	0.00	1.9	0.0	-0.06	-0.56	2.88	100.7	7.9	161.0	9.4	4.9
4.9	0.93	6.2	0.58	3.7	0.4	0.55	5.13	4.35	75.9	3.3	15.4	12.8	5.3
4.5	0.50	3.2	0.18	8.6	0.5	1.99	19.78	4.50	51.2	3.5	76.9	29.9	5.7
3.5	0.80	6.7	0.30	6.7	3.2	1.06	11.14	5.18	64.6	2.2	23.9	19.0	5.5
5.1	0.70	5.0	0.14	5.8	4.2	1.15	13.75	5.15	67.0	2.0	20.2	19.5	4.3
2.7	3.24	29.8	-0.36	7.8	0.5	2.28	34.02	4.53	49.3	4.6	38.6	11.3	5.4
7.8	0.00	0.0	0.09	5.9	0.2	1.04	16.92	5.21	73.0	5.0	64.3	13.8	1.0
7.8	0.09	0.8	-0.04	6.1	0.6	1.24	16.54	5.21	74.3	3.0	17.1	14.3	3.9
8.9	0.45	0.8	0.04	4.7	0.1	0.75	3.61	3.79	74.4	6.1	71.0	9.4	6.0
8.0	1.04	3.5	0.11	4.0	0.2	0.55	4.83	4.40	77.5	4.7	34.0	9.1	4.4
6.1	0.68	5.3	0.12	7.2	45.7	1.17	15.12	4.31	66.2	4.7	29.8	11.2	7.5
6.3	0.43	2.4	0.17	6.1	4.2	1.14	13.30	3.63	58.8	3.4	34.3	16.0	6.0
7.0	0.34	2.6	0.28	8.4	0.4	1.34	23.47	4.19	51.5	4.7	76.9	17.6	2.3
4.9	1.54	7.1	2.20	5.4	0.3	1.05	8.68	4.94	59.1	2.4	32.7	21.9	5.9
9.5	0.00	0.0	0.00	6.2	0.2	1.10	7.80	3.57	56.4	6.1	72.1	9.5	6.3
8.8	0.00	0.0	0.00	0.0	-0.2	-2.59	-8.10	3.97	162.3	7.5	154.2	10.8	0.0
7.4	0.38	2.4	0.00	2.8	0.1	0.43	3.88	4.07	76.2	6.3	190.6	20.4	0.8
8.7	0.10	0.6	-0.01	5.9	1.2	0.92	8.69	2.50	40.5	2.0	34.3	28.8	6.7
5.3	2.96	10.0	-0.56	7.6	0.5	1.27	9.32	4.44	58.9	5.7	72.2	11.8	7.1
5.9	0.30	2.0	0.10	10.0	0.7	2.12	23.67	5.54	52.5	5.9	47.8	5.8	6.4
4.9	1.11	6.7	0.21	6.3	0.5	1.28	11.51	5.25	63.9	5.3	36.5	6.6	5.6
9.7	0.00	0.0	0.14	3.4	0.5	0.52	7.57	2.67	76.1	2.3	6.6	16.8	4.1
4.4	1.92	16.3	0.05	4.0	0.4	0.87	12.24	3.37	65.5	3.2	24.9	13.9	2.6
7.0	0.36	2.1	0.23	4.8	3.0	0.69	6.97	3.05	69.0	1.9	27.9	25.0	5.7
6.3	1.28	6.5	0.07	9.7	1.4	1.80	10.53	5.02	42.9	3.0	10.6	13.8	9.3
7.8	0.39	2.2	0.09	7.8	13.1	1.14	11.28	3.21	54.6	2.1	32.8	36.9	9.2
4.6	0.54	4.4	0.00	6.0	4.0	0.95	11.08	3.18	54.6	4.6	16.7	4.8	6.0
5.4	0.65	5.2	0.21	9.1	60.9	1.47	18.50	3.41	57.6	2.1	26.8	28.2	6.9
5.0	0.29	2.6	0.06	2.0	0.4	0.40	5.07	2.82	92.4	0.4	14.3	79.4	4.9
4.5	2.23	10.6	-0.01	6.2	0.2	1.46	14.36	3.30	56.1	2.0	34.9	30.6	5.4
5.3	0.39	4.2	-0.01	9.9	9.2	1.69	26.36	3.73	43.4	3.8	84.2	38.3	5.0
8.2	0.47	2.5	0.07	7.4	2.1	1.55	12.49	4.07	67.5	7.6	91.2	4.6	8.4
8.1	0.19	1.5	0.07	7.8	4.2	1.18	14.34	3.79	56.0	3.3	37.8	17.9	4.8
6.0	0.00	0.0	0.87	6.7	0.2	1.26	14.13	4.45	58.9	1.8	32.1	29.5	3.0
6.0	3.10	7.5	0.20	3.4	0.1	0.59	4.67	4.03	79.6	2.2	28.8	20.4	4.7
2.3	1.97	9.5	0.21	10.0	1.1	2.21	17.10	6.89	46.6	6.6	57.1	4.8	8.9
8.4	0.00	0.0	0.04	5.6	0.5	1.40	14.92	3.79	58.9	6.4	68.5	7.3	6.3
8.8	0.00	0.0	0.34	0.0	-0.3	-2.94	-10.87	3.42	151.0	3.1	65.2	31.1	0.0
9.0	0.22	1.3	0.00	5.1	1.4	0.84	8.93	2.85	50.2	2.8	47.9	29.4	5.4
4.6	1.08	11.7	-0.02	9.0	1.3	2.08	25.55	3.64	38.7	0.9	4.8	30.9	6.8
9.4	0.06	0.4	0.11	4.2	1.5	0.66	7.14	2.79	65.4	6.8	99.2	11.1	5.5
7.1	0.38	2.3	0.00	5.8	0.9	0.86	9.26	3.19	64.0	1.2	13.2	28.5	6.0
6.7	0.49	4.4	0.00	0.6	0.0	-0.03	-0.33	3.66	95.1	3.6	70.3	26.3	0.0
4.6	1.34	7.4	0.44	7.6	0.6	1.49	15.12	5.79	60.8	2.7	28.9	17.8	4.8
6.9	0.61	3.2	-0.01	5.3	1.6	1.36	12.36	4.20	73.0	3.5	7.7	10.6	7.2
8.6	0.00	0.0	0.00	6.7	0.2	1.71	10.22	3.66	56.0	4.9	69.3	13.6	5.7
9.0	0.00	0.0	-0.07	3.4	0.5	0.43	5.23	3.59	83.0	3.1	42.5	20.7	5.2
6.9	0.64	2.0	1.42	6.1	0.2	1.52	14.76	4.50	60.3	6.0	44.1	1.1	4.4

Name	City	State	Weiss Safety Rating	2003 Weiss Safety Rating	2002 Weiss Safety Rating	Total Assets ($Mil)	One Year Asset Growth	Asset Mix (As a % of Total Assets)				Capital-ization Index	Leverage Ratio	Risk-based Capital Ratio
								Comm-ercial Loans	Cons-umer Loans	Home Mort-gages	Secur-ities			
WINTON S&LC	CINCINNATI	OH	B-	C+	C+	555.0	7.03	2.0	0.5	48.8	4.2	6.9	8.9	12.6
WISCONSIN COMMUNITY	COTTAGE GROVE	WI	B-	B-	C+	376.7	18.26	42.4	1.1	8.8	17.8	4.9	7.1	10.9
▲ WISCONSIN ST BK	RANDOM LAKE	WI	C	C-	C-	94.2	0.96	16.3	5.7	24.1	12.4	6.2	8.7	11.9
WNB BK	WILLIAMSPORT	PA	B-	B-	B-	312.8	-0.59	5.7	5.1	27.6	9.3	8.2	9.9	13.5
WOLF RIVER CMNTY SVGS BK	HORTONVILLE	WI	B-	B-	B-	73.6	22.94	13.4	5.3	43.4	12.8	7.0	9.0	13.7
WOLVERINE BK FSB	MIDLAND	MI	A	A	A-	227.5	-1.88	7.4	2.5	40.4	5.9	10.0	16.3	26.8
WOOD & HUSTON BK	MARSHALL	MO	B+	B+	B+	348.5	5.23	7.9	4.6	27.9	11.0	6.9	9.1	12.5
WOOD COUNTY NB	QUITMAN	TX	D	D	D	64.5	-0.35	1.1	21.1	17.3	24.3	6.0	8.1	18.6
WOOD COUNTY NB	WISCONSIN RAPIDS	WI	A	A	A-	243.3	1.17	12.0	2.0	11.0	24.5	10.0	12.7	18.2
▲ WOODBURY BKG CO	WOODBURY	GA	C-	D+	D	19.6	-6.88	6.3	8.6	27.8	26.0	8.8	10.2	17.9
▲ WOODFORD ST BK	WOODFORD	WI	B-	C+	C+	108.9	8.62	11.5	9.7	31.5	5.7	5.1	8.0	11.1
▲ WOODFOREST NB	HOUSTON	TX	B+	B+	B+	1,409.0	6.98	8.1	2.6	6.8	19.8	6.0	8.1	11.8
WOODHAVEN NB	FORT WORTH	TX	B-	B-	B-	175.0	16.30	7.9	5.2	13.4	14.5	6.1	8.2	12.2
WOODHOUSE & BARTLEY BK	BLOOMINGTON	WI	B+	B	B-	25.3	-2.13	7.0	3.0	7.4	28.3	10.0	11.6	22.8
▲ WOODLAND BK	REMER	MN	C-	D+	D+	79.3	10.67	27.1	7.7	30.6	8.9	6.0	8.0	11.8
WOODLANDS BK	WILLIAMSPORT	PA	C+	C+	C+	165.1	4.37	9.5	0.7	23.9	30.0	5.0	7.2	11.0
WOODLANDS NB	HINCKLEY	MN	A-	A-	A-	100.4	10.28	13.0	5.1	13.5	15.2	7.7	9.5	14.3
WOODRUFF FS&LA	WOODRUFF	SC	B+	B+	A-	99.8	-1.35	0.0	0.0	33.3	32.3	10.0	27.7	63.1
WOODSBORO BK	WOODSBORO	MD	B-	B-	B-	159.6	13.56	20.9	2.5	14.7	24.9	6.3	8.4	14.0
WOODSFIELD SVG BK	WOODSFIELD	OH	C-	C	C	34.1	13.29	0.0	2.3	42.5	34.2	6.2	8.2	21.5
WOODSVILLE GUARANTY SB	WOODSVILLE	NH	B-	B-	B-	265.0	4.88	7.4	6.7	40.5	16.0	5.9	7.9	13.0
▼ WOORI AMER BK	NEW YORK	NY	B-	B	A	660.7	73.17	10.0	0.3	13.2	19.5	3.3	6.8	10.2
WORLD FINANCIAL CAP BK	SALT LAKE CITY	UT	D	D	NR	10.3	N/A	0.0	0.0	0.0	97.3	10.0	93.5	96.0
WORLD FINANCIAL NETWORK	GAHANNA	OH	A	A	A	616.1	16.37	0.0	31.8	0.0	16.4	10.0	55.2	47.8
WORLD SVGS BK FSB	OAKLAND	CA	B+	B+	B+	92,696.7	28.30	0.0	0.0	84.9	3.3	5.3	7.3	13.9
WORLD SVGS BK FSB TEXAS	HOUSTON	TX	D+	D+	D+	11,920.6	47.36	0.0	0.0	5.4	0.1	3.2	5.2	23.7
WORLDS FOREMOST BK	SIDNEY	NE	B+	B+	B+	174.1	21.99	0.0	46.9	0.0	0.6	10.0	34.6	24.1
WORONOCO SVGS BK	WESTFIELD	MA	B-	B-	C+	881.9	10.11	1.8	1.0	41.4	26.8	6.0	8.0	13.2
WORTH NB	LAKE WORTH	TX	B	B	B	292.2	13.64	16.1	6.2	18.4	13.5	6.6	8.8	12.2
WORTHINGTON FSB	WORTHINGTON	MN	B-	B-	B-	46.4	-2.53	0.3	3.3	61.7	17.5	10.0	12.6	27.5
WORTHINGTON NB	ARLINGTON	TX	D	D	D	37.6	50.23	35.2	8.0	4.9	0.0	10.0	17.0	20.3
▲ WRAY ST BK	WRAY	CO	B	B	B	43.0	10.32	9.4	6.2	4.5	24.5	6.4	8.4	13.2
▼ WRENTHAM CO-OP BK	WRENTHAM	MA	B	B+	B+	91.4	-4.57	0.6	0.7	39.4	22.6	9.2	10.5	25.2
WRIGHT EXPRESS FIN SVCS	SALT LAKE CITY	UT	A	A	A-	437.9	37.65	91.9	0.0	0.0	4.2	10.0	17.8	18.1
WYOMING B&TC	WYOMING	IL	B+	B+	B+	17.7	-0.70	3.9	0.9	10.1	54.0	6.6	8.6	27.5
▲ WYOMING B&TC	CHEYENNE	WY	C+	C	D+	68.0	7.53	14.1	3.2	8.1	14.3	5.3	8.3	11.2
▼ WYOMING COUNTY BK	WARSAW	NY	D+	C-	C+	774.4	9.41	9.0	5.8	13.3	27.5	4.1	6.5	10.5
WYOMING NB	RIVERTON	WY	D-	D-	D	51.3	19.46	14.9	5.7	6.8	9.9	4.2	7.4	10.6
YADKIN VALLEY B&TC	ELKIN	NC	B+	A-	A-	874.1	33.19	13.5	5.3	10.1	13.9	5.0	8.4	11.0
▲ YAKIMA FS&LA	YAKIMA	WA	A+	A	A	1,223.7	4.90	0.0	0.1	46.7	40.5	10.0	16.0	37.9
YAKIMA NB NA	YAKIMA	WA	D+	D	D+	44.5	8.95	30.2	4.6	6.2	9.5	5.9	9.2	11.7
▼ YARDVILLE NB	YARDVILLE	NJ	C	C+	C+	2,650.9	12.82	12.3	1.5	7.6	31.9	3.6	6.7	10.3
YELLOW MEDICINE COUNTY	GRANITE FALLS	MN	B	B	C+	79.0	3.09	13.5	6.1	9.9	44.6	7.1	9.1	16.4
YELLOWSTONE BK	LAUREL	MT	A+	A+	A+	294.5	11.02	22.5	3.0	8.7	21.0	10.0	16.7	21.8
▼ YOAKUM NB	YOAKUM	TX	A-	A	A	112.9	-1.97	4.0	8.8	17.9	44.0	10.0	12.7	28.5
YOLO COMMUNITY BK	WOODLAND	CA	B-	C+	D+	111.5	27.30	20.5	0.2	6.7	21.3	5.4	8.5	11.3
YORK ST B&TC	YORK	NE	C+	C+	C+	188.9	3.29	19.2	5.6	3.4	15.3	3.9	7.8	10.5
YORK TRADITIONS BK	YORK	PA	D	D	D	47.3	20.90	17.8	0.9	20.1	29.9	10.0	15.9	24.3
YOSEMITE BK	MARIPOSA	CA	B+	B+	B+	155.9	6.62	2.2	1.0	5.5	56.4	6.3	8.3	17.4
YOUNG AMERICANS BK	DENVER	CO	E-	E-	E	14.4	-0.22	0.0	0.9	0.0	83.7	5.5	7.5	36.5
YUKON NB	YUKON	OK	C+	C+	C+	158.1	11.81	3.4	3.5	19.9	45.8	5.1	7.1	14.1
YUMA COMMUNITY BK	YUMA	AZ	C	C	C	55.0	22.60	10.9	1.0	14.3	0.1	5.5	9.2	11.4
ZAPATA NB	ZAPATA	TX	B-	B-	B-	63.5	13.02	3.0	5.5	18.7	50.2	5.9	7.9	21.0
ZAVALA COUNTY BK	CRYSTAL CITY	TX	C+	C+	C	65.9	4.79	4.4	21.7	3.9	48.5	7.4	9.3	16.1
ZIONS FIRST NB	SALT LAKE CITY	UT	B-	B-	B-	11,830.8	9.69	13.5	5.8	11.4	11.4	3.6	5.6	10.8

Asset Quality Index	Non-Performing Loans as a % of Total Loans	Non-Performing Loans as a % of Capital	Net Charge-offs Avg Loans	Profitability Index	Net Income ($Mil)	Return on Assets (R.O.A.)	Return on Equity (R.O.E.)	Net Interest Spread	Overhead Efficiency Ratio	Liquidity Index	Liquidity Ratio	Hot Money Ratio	Stability Index
4.6	0.86	8.4	0.04	5.9	2.4	0.87	10.15	2.99	57.9	1.2	5.1	26.8	5.7
5.4	0.42	3.0	0.04	4.6	0.9	0.47	4.76	3.48	71.9	1.1	9.2	28.1	6.1
4.0	1.15	9.3	0.02	5.7	0.5	1.06	12.39	4.53	65.4	3.1	24.8	14.7	2.8
4.0	1.74	13.4	0.08	10.0	2.8	1.77	17.41	4.76	50.2	4.4	5.8	4.9	7.7
7.9	0.25	2.0	0.01	6.4	0.4	1.10	12.07	4.12	58.5	4.5	65.4	16.9	4.6
8.0	0.08	0.4	-0.25	7.1	1.1	0.97	6.16	3.01	62.4	1.9	39.9	45.0	8.9
5.5	0.69	5.4	0.15	8.6	3.1	1.83	19.25	4.39	58.3	4.2	25.5	9.1	6.9
3.1	2.08	8.0	1.40	2.7	0.1	0.28	2.67	4.74	83.4	5.8	61.9	9.6	4.0
6.6	1.42	6.8	0.01	9.4	2.6	2.15	16.43	3.66	48.4	4.5	26.5	7.3	9.8
8.2	0.20	1.2	0.05	4.3	0.1	1.00	9.90	4.76	78.4	4.8	65.2	13.4	2.2
5.5	0.44	4.2	0.14	7.1	0.6	1.16	14.60	4.26	57.4	4.5	34.4	10.9	3.8
5.7	0.46	3.4	0.17	7.7	13.5	1.97	23.44	4.36	73.0	4.2	21.6	9.5	7.8
3.9	0.60	5.1	0.25	8.7	1.5	1.75	20.80	5.01	61.7	2.8	30.7	18.1	4.8
8.6	0.00	0.0	0.00	6.9	0.2	1.82	16.25	3.54	44.4	8.4	186.4	8.9	7.1
3.4	1.24	11.7	0.34	6.2	0.4	1.01	13.13	4.52	64.0	2.4	19.4	17.6	3.0
5.1	1.28	9.5	0.00	4.2	0.7	0.85	11.01	3.66	73.2	6.8	64.7	5.6	3.8
7.7	0.01	0.1	0.50	8.3	0.7	1.35	11.61	4.32	58.8	5.1	31.3	5.7	7.5
5.8	3.00	4.6	0.07	4.6	0.3	0.67	2.45	3.04	64.6	3.3	42.0	18.6	8.0
6.4	1.03	6.8	0.05	4.2	0.5	0.65	7.64	3.91	76.2	5.5	49.5	9.8	4.8
6.7	0.70	4.1	-0.08	4.2	0.1	0.76	9.32	3.31	64.1	6.7	81.1	6.9	2.9
6.0	0.53	4.6	0.02	5.4	1.2	0.94	11.91	4.18	66.1	4.7	31.6	8.5	4.2
6.4	0.20	1.2	0.02	6.2	3.3	1.04	10.46	4.26	64.3	4.3	51.9	16.3	6.5
10.0	0.00	0.0	0.00	0.0	-0.3	-5.85	-6.20	1.00	708.0	5.0	1,250.4	100.0	0.0
6.7	2.09	1.1	3.32	10.0	65.9	20.36	40.17	10.51	63.2	4.3	150.1	100.0	8.8
6.5	0.43	5.1	0.00	9.7	627.2	1.44	18.99	3.04	27.7	0.5	3.1	42.4	8.0
9.4	0.82	1.0	-0.02	2.6	9.5	0.17	3.26	0.35	18.9	5.3	2,973.1	57.9	1.8
6.3	0.19	0.3	1.63	10.0	7.0	8.10	26.73	7.92	79.0	2.2	53.6	100.0	4.5
9.4	0.09	0.7	-0.01	4.1	2.9	0.70	8.44	2.66	67.2	1.6	10.0	21.5	5.3
7.9	0.07	0.5	0.20	5.0	1.3	0.93	9.85	4.18	69.8	7.2	139.1	12.2	5.4
9.0	0.51	2.8	0.01	5.8	0.2	0.91	7.46	3.51	62.0	4.9	27.5	4.8	5.5
7.7	0.00	0.0	0.00	0.0	-0.1	-0.41	-2.28	4.43	100.1	2.6	57.0	35.9	0.0
8.1	0.06	0.4	0.61	5.9	0.2	1.09	13.23	3.67	52.4	4.5	127.4	32.4	5.3
9.9	0.00	0.0	0.00	4.8	0.3	0.60	5.62	3.39	72.7	7.3	103.6	6.6	5.7
7.4	0.44	2.3	1.96	10.0	14.7	7.69	42.34	26.66	59.8	9.5	433.2	3.1	8.0
8.4	0.89	3.3	0.00	2.0	0.0	0.08	0.89	2.86	96.2	6.9	91.1	6.0	5.5
7.0	0.57	4.5	0.00	8.9	0.5	1.54	19.30	4.59	57.8	4.4	26.8	8.3	4.1
1.5	2.95	25.8	0.26	7.8	4.6	1.18	17.98	3.93	52.4	3.1	25.9	14.8	4.3
6.6	0.02	0.2	0.00	3.2	0.1	0.56	7.70	4.57	84.4	4.4	56.3	15.5	1.9
5.4	0.49	2.9	0.26	7.4	4.4	1.10	9.48	4.16	60.3	2.7	16.5	15.4	8.0
8.2	0.20	0.6	-0.01	8.8	8.0	1.32	8.14	3.27	38.5	2.2	33.5	38.2	10.0
4.9	0.69	5.1	-0.04	4.0	0.2	0.71	7.80	5.44	80.2	3.5	28.9	13.6	3.4
6.4	0.73	6.3	0.41	4.0	9.7	0.76	11.06	2.91	54.1	4.7	26.0	9.6	3.7
8.1	0.24	1.3	0.56	7.9	0.9	2.16	22.85	4.36	50.1	4.4	18.7	6.7	5.8
8.4	0.41	1.7	0.01	10.0	5.4	3.77	23.18	5.45	34.9	4.2	17.5	7.8	9.7
8.6	0.11	0.4	-0.03	5.8	0.6	1.04	8.03	3.68	59.7	4.0	69.4	23.1	7.9
8.5	0.00	0.0	0.00	5.1	0.5	1.02	12.20	4.89	77.8	4.0	18.5	9.4	4.6
5.1	0.26	1.8	0.22	5.8	1.0	1.04	10.26	3.98	58.7	3.6	35.3	15.4	6.1
9.1	0.00	0.0	0.00	0.0	-0.4	-1.77	-11.78	2.13	158.7	4.0	4.9	7.3	0.0
9.7	0.02	0.1	0.05	8.8	1.3	1.76	19.16	4.28	61.1	4.2	19.9	8.0	5.9
10.0	0.00	0.0	5.52	0.0	-0.2	-2.75	-37.97	3.18	178.5	9.9	268.9	0.8	0.0
3.9	2.34	17.9	0.02	4.4	0.8	1.07	15.65	4.27	74.5	2.1	5.5	17.8	3.1
6.2	0.22	1.6	-0.02	7.4	0.4	1.42	13.04	5.58	60.3	2.0	34.0	29.1	2.9
9.2	0.00	0.0	0.00	7.4	0.5	1.69	21.28	3.51	57.8	3.6	84.3	31.2	4.6
3.5	2.53	10.0	0.76	5.9	0.4	1.36	14.82	4.49	64.8	2.0	29.5	25.1	4.0
6.7	0.39	3.5	0.30	8.3	88.8	1.56	23.79	3.58	54.8	5.7	81.4	15.3	5.8

Section II

Weiss Recommended Companies

A compilation of those

U.S. Commercial Banks, Savings Banks,

and Savings and Loans

receiving a Weiss Safety Rating of A+, A, A-, or B+.

Institutions are ranked by Weiss Safety Rating
in each state where they have a branch location.

Section II Contents

This section provides a list of Weiss Recommended companies and contains all financial institutions receiving a Weiss Safety Rating of A+, A, A-, or B+. Recommended institutions are listed in each state in which they currently operate one or more branches. If a company is not on this list, it should not be automatically assumed that the firm is weak. Indeed, there are many firms that have not achieved a B+ or better rating but are in good condition with adequate resources to weather an average recession. Not being included in this list should not be construed as a recommendation to immediately withdraw deposits or cancel existing financial arrangements.

Institutions are ranked within each state by their Weiss Safety Rating, and then listed alphabetically by city. Companies with the same rating should be viewed as having the same relative safety regardless of their ranking in this table.

1. **Institution Name**   The name under which the institution was chartered. A company's name can be very similar to, or the same as, the name of other companies which may not be on our Recommended List, so make sure you note the exact name, city, and state of the main branch listed here before acting on this recommendation.

2. **City**   The city in which the institution's headquarters or main office is located. With the adoption of intrastate and interstate branching laws, many institutions operating in your area may actually be headquartered elsewhere. So, don't be surprised if the location cited is not in your particular city.

3. **State**   The state in which the institution's headquarters or main office is located. With the adoption of interstate branching laws, some institutions operating in your area may actually be headquartered in another state. Even so, there are no restrictions on your ability to do business with an out-of-state institution.

4. **Telephone**   The telephone number for the institution's headquarters, or main office. If the number listed is not in your area, or a local phone call, consult your local phone directory for the number of a location near you.

5. **Weiss Safety Rating**   The Weiss rating assigned to the institution at the time of publication. Our ratings are designed to distinguish levels of insolvency risk and are measured on a scale from A to F based upon a wide range of factors. Highly rated companies are, in our opinion, less likely to experience financial difficulties than lower rated firms. See *About the Weiss Safety Ratings* on page 7 for more information and a description of what each rating means.

The Weiss Safety Ratings are not deemed to be a recommendation concerning the purchase or sale of the securities of any bank or thrift that is publicly owned.

Alabama

City	Name	Telephone	City	Name	Telephone

Weiss Safety Rating: A+

City	Name	Telephone
BOAZ	FIRST BK OF BOAZ	(256) 593-8670
FAYETTE	CITIZENS BK OF FAYETTE	(205) 932-8911
PHENIX CITY	PHENIX-GIRARD BK	(334) 298-0691
WINFIELD	CITIZENS BK OF WINFIELD	(205) 487-4277

Weiss Safety Rating: A

City	Name	Telephone
CALERA	CENTRAL ST BK	(205) 668-0711
CLANTON	PEOPLES SOUTHERN BK	(205) 755-2240
GENEVA	AMERICAN BK	(334) 684-2247
GENEVA	CITIZENS BK	(334) 684-2222
MAPLESVILLE	PEACHTREE BANK	(334) 366-2921
MARION	MARION B&TC	(334) 683-6131
TALLADEGA	FIRST NB OF TALLADEGA	(256) 362-2334
WINFIELD	STATE B&T	(205) 487-4265

Weiss Safety Rating: A-

City	Name	Telephone
ATMORE	FIRST NB OF ATMORE	(251) 368-3148
DOTHAN	BANKSOUTH	(334) 677-2265
DOTHAN	MIDSOUTH BK NA	(334) 702-7774
FYFFE	HORIZON BK	(256) 623-2275
GERALDINE	LIBERTY BK	(256) 659-2175
HALEYVILLE	TRADERS & FARMERS BK	(205) 486-5263
HARTFORD	FIRST NB OF HARTFORD	(334) 588-2211
HEADLAND	HEADLAND NB	(334) 693-3352
LAFAYETTE	FARMERS & MERCHANTS BK	(334) 864-9941
MC INTOSH	SOUTHWEST BK OF ALABAMA	(251) 944-2211
MUSCLE SHOALS	FIRST METRO BK	(256) 386-0600

Weiss Safety Rating: B+

City	Name	Telephone
BIRMINGHAM	AMSOUTH BK	(205) 326-5300
BRANTLEY	BRANTLEY B&TC	(334) 527-3206
BREWTON	BANK OF BREWTON	(251) 867-5431
CAMDEN	CAMDEN NB	(334) 682-4215
CULLMAN	FIRST FS&LA OF CULLMAN	(256) 734-4863
DOZIER	FIRST NB OF DOZIER	(334) 496-3592
GADSDEN	SOUTHERN BK COMPANY	(256) 543-3860
GREENSBORO	CITIZENS BK	(334) 624-8888
GREENSBORO	PEOPLES BK OF GREENSBORO	(334) 624-8804
ROBERTSDALE	CITIZENS BK	(251) 947-1981
RUSSELLVILLE	VALLEY ST BK	(256) 332-3600
SAMSON	SAMSON BKG CO	(334) 898-7107
STEVENSON	NORTH JACKSON BK	(256) 437-2107
SULLIGENT	FIRST ST BK OF THE SOUTH	(205) 698-8116
THOMASVILLE	FIRST UNITED SECURITY BANK	(334) 636-5424
VERNON	CITIZENS ST BK	(205) 695-9162
WATERLOO	FARMERS & MERCHANTS BK	(256) 766-2579
WEDOWEE	SMALL TOWN BK	(256) 357-4936
YORK	BANK OF YORK	(205) 392-5205

Alaska

City	Name	Telephone	City	Name	Telephone
Weiss Safety Rating: A+					
ANCHORAGE	FIRST NB ALASKA	(907) 276-6300			
Weiss Safety Rating: A					
FAIRBANKS	MOUNT MCKINLEY BK	(907) 452-1751			

American Samoa: Under U.S. Regulatory Supervision

City	Name	Telephone	City	Name	Telephone

Weiss Safety Rating: A-

City	Name	Telephone
PAGO PAGO	AMERIKA SAMOA BK	(684) 633-1151

Weiss Safety Rating: B+

City	Name	Telephone
HONOLULU, HI	† BANK OF HAWAII	(888) 643-3888

† Out-of-State Institution with branches in

Arizona

City	Name	Telephone	City	Name	Telephone

Weiss Safety Rating: A

City	Name	Telephone
PHOENIX	DIRECT MRCH CREDIT CRD BK NA	(480) 718-4600
WICKENBURG	MERIDIAN BANK NA	(928) 684-7881

Weiss Safety Rating: A-

City	Name	Telephone
FORT	† ARMED FORCES BK NA	(913) 682-9090
LAKE HAVASU CITY	MOHAVE ST BK	(928) 855-0000
PHOENIX	VALLEY COMMERCE BK	(602) 840-5550

Weiss Safety Rating: B+

City	Name	Telephone
SCOTTSDALE	NORDSTROM FSB	(480) 596-3459
SCOTTSDALE	STEARNS BK ARIZONA NA	(480) 314-4200

† Out-of-State Institution with branches in Arizona

Arkansas

City	Name	Telephone	City	Name	Telephone

Weiss Safety Rating: A+

City	Name	Telephone
CALICO ROCK	FIRST NB IZARD CTY	(870) 297-3711
JACKSONVILLE	FIRST ARKANSAS B&T	(501) 982-4511
MOUNTAIN VIEW	BANK OF MOUNTAIN VIEW	(870) 269-3815

Weiss Safety Rating: A

City	Name	Telephone
ASHDOWN	FIRST NB	(870) 898-2761
BRINKLEY	BANK OF BRINKLEY	(870) 734-3133
DE QUEEN	FIRST NB OF DE QUEEN	(870) 642-2212
DELIGHT	BANK OF DELIGHT	(870) 379-2293
DIERKS	FIRST NB OF HOWARD CTY	(870) 286-2121
FORT SMITH	FIRST NB OF FT SMITH	(479) 782-2041
GREENWOOD	FARMERS BK	(479) 996-4171
HELENA	HELENA NB	(870) 338-6451
MC GEHEE	MCGEHEE BK	(870) 222-3151
MENA	FIRST NB IN MENA	(479) 394-3552
MOUNTAIN HOME	FIRST NB&TC OF MOUNTAIN HOME	(870) 425-2101
NASHVILLE	CITIZENS NB OF NASHVILLE	(870) 845-3323
STUTTGART	FARMERS & MERCHANTS BK	(870) 673-6911
VAN BUREN	CITIZENS B&TC	(479) 474-1201
WALDRON	BANK OF WALDRON	(479) 637-2161
WARREN	WARREN B&TC	(870) 226-2621

Weiss Safety Rating: A-

City	Name	Telephone
FORREST CITY	FIRST NB OF E ARKANSAS	(870) 633-3112
GREEN FOREST	FIRST NB IN GREEN FOREST	(870) 438-5214
HOT SPRINGS	FIRST NB	(501) 525-7999
LITTLE ROCK	BANK OF THE OZARKS	(501) 978-2265
MT IDA	FIRST NB	(870) 867-3148
PARAGOULD	FIRST NB	(870) 239-8521
PRESCOTT	BANK OF PRESCOTT	(870) 887-2688
SCRANTON	LOGAN COUNTY BK	(479) 938-2511
WYNNE	CROSS COUNTY BK	(870) 238-8171
WYNNE	FIRST NB OF WYNNE	(870) 238-2361

Weiss Safety Rating: B+

City	Name	Telephone
BEARDEN	BANK OF BEARDEN	(870) 687-2233
BERRYVILLE	FIRST NB OF BERRYVILLE	(870) 423-6601
CAMDEN	FIRST BK OF SOUTH AR	(870) 837-8300
CROSSETT	FIRST NB OF CROSSETT	(870) 364-1300
EUREKA SPRINGS	BANK OF EUREKA SPRINGS	(479) 253-8241
HAMPTON	CALHOUN COUNTY BK	(870) 798-2207
LITTLE ROCK	PULASKI B&TC	(501) 661-7700
LONOKE	FIRST ST BK	(501) 676-3106
MAGNOLIA	FARMERS B&TC	(870) 235-7000
MALVERN	MALVERN NB	(501) 332-6955
MC CRORY	BANK OF MCCRORY	(870) 731-2521
MENA	UNION BK OF MENA	(479) 394-1888
RISON	BANK OF RISON	(870) 325-6251
SHERIDAN	PEOPLES BK	(870) 942-5707
STAMPS	BODCAW BK	(870) 533-4486
WALNUT RIDGE	FIRST NB OF LAWRENCE CTY	(870) 886-5959

California

City	Name	Telephone

Weiss Safety Rating: A+

City	Name	Telephone
LONG BEACH	FARMERS & MERCHANTS BK	(562) 437-0011
ORANGE	FIRST SECURITY THRIFT CO	(714) 538-3481
UKIAH	SAVINGS BK OF MENDOCINO CTY	(707) 462-6613
WILLITS	BANK OF WILLITS	(707) 459-5533

Weiss Safety Rating: A

City	Name	Telephone
CERRITOS	GATEWAY BUSINESS BK	(562) 809-1473
IRVINE	SOUTH COAST CMRL BK	(949) 852-2500
JACKSON	BANK OF AMADOR	(209) 223-2431
LONG BEACH	INTERNATIONAL CITY BK NA	(562) 436-9800
LOS ANGELES	GILMORE BK	(323) 549-2100
RICHMOND	MECHANICS BK	(510) 262-7200
SAN RAFAEL	FIRST FS&LA	(415) 456-6231
SANTA CLARA	SILICON VALLEY BK	(408) 654-7400

Weiss Safety Rating: A-

City		Name	Telephone
BEVERLY HILLS		CITY NB	(310) 888-6000
CARSON		MERCHANTS BK OF CA NA	(310) 549-4350
FORT	†	ARMED FORCES BK NA	(913) 682-9090
GLENDORA		FOOTHILL INDEPENDENT BK	(626) 963-8551
HUNTINGTON		PACIFIC LIBERTY BK	(714) 429-2100
LA JOLLA		IMPERIAL CAPITAL BK	(858) 551-0511
LODI		FARMERS & MERCHANTS BK CTRL	(209) 367-2300
LOS ANGELES		COMMUNITY COMMERCE BK	(323) 888-8777
MANTECA		DELTA NB	(209) 824-4050
OAKLAND		INNOVATIVE BK	(510) 899-6800
ONTARIO		CITIZENS BUSINESS BK	(909) 980-4030
ONTARIO		NETWORK BK	(909) 983-4600
PLACERVILLE		EL DORADO SVGS BK FSB	(530) 622-1492
RANCHO		VINEYARD BK	(909) 987-0177
ROCKLIN		FIVE STAR BK	(916) 626-5000
SACRAMENTO		AMERICAN RIVER BK	(916) 368-3400
SACRAMENTO		MERCHANTS NB OF SACRAMENTO	(916) 442-3883
SAN DIEGO		ARMED FORCES BK OF CA NA	(619) 231-0018
SAN FRANCISCO		CALIFORNIA PACIFIC BK	(415) 399-8000
SAN FRANCISCO		UNION BK OF CA NA	(800) 238-4486
SANTA ROSA		LUTHER BURBANK SVGS	(707) 578-9216
TUSTIN		SUNWEST BK	(714) 730-4444

Weiss Safety Rating: B+

City		Name	Telephone
ARROYO GRANDE		MID-STATE B&TC	(805) 473-6855
AUBURN		PLACER SIERRA BK	(530) 823-7777
BREA		CAPITAL B&TC FSB	(800) 421-0180
BUENA PARK		LOS ANGELES NB	(714) 670-2400
CARLSBAD		FIRST NB OF NORTH CTY	(760) 471-1051
CHICO		BUTTE CMNTY BK	(530) 877-0857
CHICO		TRI COUNTIES BK	(530) 898-0300
COSTA MESA		CNA TR CORP	(714) 437-1012
ESCONDIDO		COMMUNITY NB	(760) 432-1100
FREMONT		FREMONT BK	(510) 792-2300
HAMPTON, VA	†	HOME SVG OF AMERICA	(757) 728-1200
IRVINE		COMMERCIAL CAPITAL BANK, FSB	(949) 585-7500
LA JOLLA		LA JOLLA BK FSB	(858) 454-8800
LOS ANGELES		CENTER BK	(213) 251-2222
LOS ANGELES		MANUFACTURERS BK	(213) 489-6200
LOS ANGELES		MELLON 1ST BUSINESS BK NA	(213) 489-1000
LOS ANGELES		NARA BK NA	(213) 639-1700
LOS ANGELES		PAN AMERICAN BK	(323) 264-3310

City	Name	Telephone
MARIPOSA	YOSEMITE BK	(209) 966-3777
OAKDALE	OAK VALLEY COMMUNITY BANK	(209) 848-2265
OAKLAND	WORLD SVGS BK FSB	(510) 446-4000
OAKLAND	SUMMIT BK	(510) 839-8800
ORANGE	BANK OF ORANGE COUNTY	(714) 940-8752
ORANGE	ORANGE COMMUNITY BK	(714) 532-0700
PALO ALTO	GREATER BAY BK NA	(650) 323-5150
PASADENA	COMMUNITY BK	(626) 577-1700
POMONA	PFF B&T	(909) 623-2323
RANCHO SANTA FE	FIRST NB	(858) 756-3023
REDDING	NORTH VALLEY BK	(530) 226-2900
RIVERSIDE	INLAND EMPIRE NB	(909) 788-2265
SAN FRANCISCO	OCEANIC BK	(415) 392-0642
SAN FRANCISCO	UNITED COMMERCIAL BK	(415) 928-0700
SAN JOSE	HERITAGE BK OF COMMERCE	(408) 947-6900
SANTA ANA	FIRST AMERICAN TRUST FSB	(714) 647-2777
SANTA BARBARA	MONTECITO B&T	(805) 963-7511
SANTA MONICA	FIRST FEDERAL BANK OF CA FSB	(310) 319-6000
SANTA ROSA	EXCHANGE BK	(707) 524-3000
SANTA ROSA	SONOMA NB	(707) 579-2265
SONOMA	SONOMA VALLEY BK	(707) 935-3200
STOCKTON	UNION SAFE DEPOSIT BK	(209) 946-5011
TEMECULA	MISSION OAKS NB	(909) 719-1200
TORRANCE	CHINATRUST BK USA	(310) 791-2828
WHITTIER	QUAKER CITY BK	(562) 907-2200

† Out-of-State Institution with branches in California

Colorado

City	Name	Telephone	City	Name	Telephone

Weiss Safety Rating: A+

FORT MORGAN	FARMERS ST BK	(970) 867-5661

Weiss Safety Rating: A

DENVER	MOUNTAIN STATES BK	(303) 388-3641

Weiss Safety Rating: A-

AKRON	CITIZENS NB OF AKRON	(970) 345-2226
ALAMOSA	SAN LUIS VALLEY FEDERAL BK	(719) 589-6653
BRUSH	FARMERS ST BK	(970) 842-5101
DOLORES	DOLORES ST BK	(970) 882-7600
ENGLEWOOD	LINCOLN TRUST CO	(303) 771-1000
FORT †	ARMED FORCES BK NA	(913) 682-9090
LONGMONT	FIRST MAIN STREET BK NA	(303) 776-5800
OURAY	CITIZENS ST BK OF OURAY	(970) 325-4478
US AIR FORCE ACA	AIR ACADEMY NB	(719) 472-1090
WILEY	STATE BK OF WILEY	(719) 829-4811
WRAY	FIRST PIONEER NB	(970) 332-4824

Weiss Safety Rating: B+

ALAMOSA	ALAMOSA NB	(719) 589-2564
AURORA	COMMERCE BK	(303) 344-5202
CANON CITY	FREMONT NB OF CANON CITY	(719) 275-3344
COLORADO	FIVE STAR BK	(719) 574-2777
COLORADO	PIKES PEAK NB	(719) 473-5310
DENVER	BANK OF DENVER	(303) 572-3600
DENVER	COBIZ BK NA	(303) 293-2265
ENGLEWOOD	FIRST FINANCIAL BK	(303) 967-7442
ENGLEWOOD	TRUST COMPANY OF AMERICA	(303) 705-6000
ESTES PARK	FIRST NB OF ESTES PARK	(970) 586-4485
FORT COLLINS	BANK OF COLORADO	(970) 206-1160
GLENWOOD	ALPINE BK	(970) 945-2424
LAMAR	VALLEY ST BK	(719) 336-4381
PUEBLO	CENTENNIAL BK OF PUEBLO	(719) 543-0763

† Out-of-State Institution with branches in Colorado

Connecticut

City	Name	Telephone	City	Name	Telephone

Weiss Safety Rating: A+

City	Name	Telephone
MIDDLETOWN	LIBERTY BK	(860) 344-7200
PUTNAM	CITIZENS NB	(860) 928-7921

Weiss Safety Rating: A

City	Name	Telephone
TORRINGTON	TORRINGTON SVGS BK	(860) 496-2152

Weiss Safety Rating: A-

City	Name	Telephone
JEWETT CITY	JEWETT CITY SVGS BK	(860) 376-4444
NAUGATUCK	NAUGATUCK SVGS BK	(203) 729-5291
STAMFORD	FIRST COUNTY BK	(203) 462-4200
SUFFIELD	FIRST NB OF SUFFIELD	(860) 668-3950
THOMASTON	THOMASTON SVGS BK	(860) 283-4373

Weiss Safety Rating: B+

City	Name	Telephone
DANBURY	UNION SVGS BK	(203) 830-4200
ESSEX	ESSEX SVGS BK	(860) 767-4414
GUILFORD	GUILFORD SVGS BK	(203) 453-2721
NORWICH	CHELSEA GROTON SVGS BK	(860) 823-4800
STAMFORD	CORNERSTONE BK	(203) 356-0111
WINDSOR	WINDSOR FS&LA	(860) 688-8511

Delaware

City	Name	Telephone	City	Name	Telephone

Weiss Safety Rating: A+

City	Name	Telephone
WYOMING	FIRST NB OF WYOMING	(302) 697-2666

Weiss Safety Rating: A

City	Name	Telephone
FORT SILL, OK	† FORT SILL NB	(580) 357-9880
WILMINGTON	WILMINGTON SVGS FUND SOCIETY	(302) 792-6000

Weiss Safety Rating: A-

City	Name	Telephone
SELBYVILLE	BALTIMORE TRUST CO	(302) 436-8236
WILMINGTON	MBNA AMERICA DE NA	(302) 453-9930

Weiss Safety Rating: B+

City	Name	Telephone
GREENVILLE	GMAC BK	(302) 428-3000
REHOBOTH BEACH	COUNTY BK	(302) 226-9800
WILMINGTON	WACHOVIA BK OF DE NA	(302) 888-7548

† Out-of-State Institution with branches in Delaware

District Of Columbia

City	Name	Telephone	City	Name	Telephone

Weiss Safety Rating: A+

City	Name	Telephone
WASHINGTON	NATIONAL CAPITAL BK OF WA	(202) 546-8000

Weiss Safety Rating: B+

City	Name	Telephone
ALEXANDRIA, VA †	TREASURY BK	(703) 518-6000

† Out-of-State Institution with branches in District Of Columbia

Florida

City	Name	Telephone	City	Name	Telephone

Weiss Safety Rating: A

City	Name	Telephone
CHIEFLAND	DRUMMOND COMMUNITY BK	(352) 493-2277
FERNANDINA	FIRST NB OF NASSAU COUNTY	(904) 321-0400
FORT PIERCE	HARBOR FSB	(772) 461-2414
FROSTPROOF	CITIZENS BK OF FROSTPROOF	(863) 635-2244
GRACEVILLE	PEOPLES BK OF GRACEVILLE	(850) 263-3267
HALLANDALE	TRANSCAPITAL BK	(954) 456-3325
JACKSONVILLE	FIRST GUARANTY B&TC	(904) 301-2000
MT DORA	FIRST NB OF MT DORA	(352) 383-2111

Weiss Safety Rating: A-

City	Name	Telephone
CARRABELLE	GULF ST COMMUNITY BK	(850) 697-3395
FORT	LANDMARK BK NA	(954) 771-5525
FORT PIERCE	RIVERSIDE NB OF FLORIDA	(772) 466-1200
MIAMI	CITY NB OF FLORIDA	(305) 577-7333
MIAMI	MELLON UNITED NB	(305) 825-9132
PENSACOLA	BANK OF THE SOUTH	(850) 456-5722
PENSACOLA	FIRST NAVY BK	(850) 453-3411
PENSACOLA	WARRINGTON BK	(850) 455-7351
PLANT CITY	HILLSBORO BK	(813) 707-6506
STARKE	COMMUNITY ST BK	(904) 964-7830

Weiss Safety Rating: B+

City	Name	Telephone
ALACHUA	FIRST NB OF ALACHUA	(386) 462-1041
ARCADIA	FIRST ST BK OF ARCADIA	(863) 494-2220
AVENTURA	TURNBERRY BK	(305) 931-7100
BIRMINGHAM, AL †	AMSOUTH BK	(205) 326-5300
BONIFAY	BANK OF BONIFAY	(850) 547-3624
BROOKSVILLE	HERNANDO CTY BK	(352) 799-2265
CLEWISTON	FIRST FSB OF THE GLADES	(863) 983-6181
CRESTVIEW	FIRST NB OF CRESTVIEW	(850) 682-5111
CRYSTAL RIVER	CRYSTAL RIVER BK	(352) 795-3451
DUNNELLON	DUNNELLON ST BK	(352) 489-2466
FORT WALTON	FIRST NB&T	(850) 796-2000
HALLANDALE	HOME FEDERAL BK OF HOLLYWOOD	(954) 458-2626
HALLANDALE	DESJARDINS BK NA	(954) 454-1001
HOLLYWOOD	NATBANK NA	(954) 923-4933
HOMOSASSA	HOMOSASSA SPRINGS BK	(352) 628-3812
INVERNESS	BANK OF INVERNESS	(352) 726-1221
JACKSONVILLE	EVERBANK	(904) 281-6177
KEY WEST	KEY WEST BK	(305) 294-3540
LIVE OAK	FIRST FSB OF FLORIDA	(386) 362-3433
MIAMI	INTERAMERICAN BK FSB	(305) 223-1434
ORLANDO	SUNTRUST BANCARD NA	(407) 858-7041
ORMOND BEACH	COQUINA BK	(386) 677-6966
PLANTATION	OPTIMUMBANK.COM	(954) 452-9501
PORT CHARLOTTE	CHARLOTTE ST BK	(941) 624-5400
TALLAHASSEE	CAPITAL CITY BK	(850) 671-0300
TALLAHASSEE	HANCOCK BK OF FLORIDA	N/A
WAUCHULA	WAUCHULA ST BK	(863) 773-4151

† Out-of-State Institution with branches in Florida

Georgia

City	Name	Telephone
WAYCROSS	WAYCROSS B&TC	(912) 283-0001
WINDER	FIRST PIEDMONT BK	(770) 307-1212

Weiss Safety Rating: A+

City	Name	Telephone
COMER	MERCHANTS & FARMERS BK	(706) 783-5161
COVINGTON	NEWTON FEDERAL BK	(770) 786-7088
LA FAYETTE	BANK OF LA FAYETTE	(706) 638-2520

Weiss Safety Rating: A

City	Name	Telephone
ATHENS	FIRST AMERICAN B&TC	(706) 354-5000
CEDARTOWN	FIRST NB OF POLK CTY	(770) 748-1750
DARIEN	SOUTHEASTERN BK	(912) 437-4141
ELBERTON	PINNACLE BK	(706) 283-2854
GLENNVILLE	GLENNVILLE BK	(912) 654-3471
MILLEDGEVILLE	CENTURY B&T	(478) 453-3571
MOULTRIE	SOUTHWEST GEORGIA BK	(229) 985-1120
THOMASTON	WEST CENTRAL GEORGIA BK	(706) 647-8951

Weiss Safety Rating: A-

City	Name	Telephone
BAINBRIDGE	FIRST PORT CITY BK	(229) 246-6200
BLAKELY	FIRST ST BK OF BLAKELY	(229) 723-3711
BUCHANAN	FIRST NB OF GEORGIA	(770) 646-6000
CAMILLA	PLANTERS & CITIZENS BK	(229) 336-5271
CHICKAMAUGA	BANK OF CHICKAMAUGA	(706) 375-3112
COLUMBUS	COLUMBUS B&TC	(706) 649-2311
CRAWFORD	COMMERCIAL BK	(706) 743-8184
DAWSON	BANK OF DAWSON	(229) 995-2141
DORAVILLE	GLOBAL COMMERCE BK	(770) 457-5858
HINESVILLE	HERITAGE BK	(912) 368-3332
LINCOLNTON	FARMERS ST BK	(706) 359-3131
NORCROSS	FIRST SECURITY NB	(770) 662-5050
OMEGA	SOUTH GEORGIA BANKING CO	(229) 528-4211
PELHAM	PELHAM BKG CO	(229) 294-2341
ROSSVILLE	ROSSVILLE BK	(706) 866-7932
SPARTA	BANK OF HANCOCK CTY	(706) 444-5781
SYLVANIA	FARMERS & MERCHANTS BK	(912) 564-7436
THOMASTON	BANK OF UPSON	(706) 647-5426
VIENNA	BANK OF DOOLY	(229) 268-4707
WASHINGTON	FARMERS & MERCHANTS BK	(706) 678-2187
WAYNESBORO	FIRST NB OF WAYNESBORO	(706) 554-8100

Weiss Safety Rating: B+

City	Name	Telephone
ADEL	ADEL BKG CO	(229) 896-7402
ALAPAHA	BANK OF ALAPAHA	(229) 532-6115
ATLANTA	AMVESCAP NATIONAL TRUST CO	N/A
BIRMINGHAM, AL †	AMSOUTH BK	(205) 326-5300
BLAKELY	BANK OF EARLY	(229) 723-3101
COLUMBUS	BB&T BANKCARD CORP	(706) 221-4171
DUBLIN	FARMERS & MERCHANTS BK	(478) 272-3100
DUBLIN	FARMERS ST BK	(478) 689-4303
IRWINTON	WILKINSON COUNTY BK	(478) 946-5531
JACKSON	MCINTOSH ST BK	(770) 775-8300
LAVONIA	NORTHEAST GEORGIA BK	(706) 356-4444
LAWRENCEVILLE	BRAND BKG CO	(770) 963-9225
MADISON	BANK OF MADISON	(706) 342-1953
MANCHESTER	F & M B&TC	(706) 846-8415
MARIETTA	SECURITY EXCHANGE BK	(770) 419-3337
MC RAE	SECURITY ST BK	(229) 868-6431
MILLEDGEVILLE	EXCHANGE BK	(478) 452-4531
SUMMERVILLE	FIRST NB OF CHATTOOGA	(706) 857-3473
THOMASVILLE	THOMAS COUNTY FS&LA	(229) 226-3221
TYNDALL, SD †	CARROLLTON FEDERAL BANK, FSB	(605) 589-3313

† Out-of-State Institution with branches in Georgia

Guam: Under U.S. Regulatory Supervision

City	Name	Telephone	City	Name	Telephone

Weiss Safety Rating: A-

City	Name	Telephone
HONOLULU, HI	† FIRST HAWAIIAN BK	(808) 525-7000
SAN FRANCISCO,	† UNION BK OF CA NA	(800) 238-4486

Weiss Safety Rating: B+

City	Name	Telephone
HONOLULU, HI	† BANK OF HAWAII	(888) 643-3888
SAN FRANCISCO,	† OCEANIC BK	(415) 392-0642

† Out-of-State Institution with branches in

Hawaii

City	Name	Telephone	City	Name	Telephone
Weiss Safety Rating: A-					
HONOLULU	CENTRAL PACIFIC BK	(808) 544-0500			
HONOLULU	FIRST HAWAIIAN BK	(808) 525-7000			
PAGO PAGO, AS	† AMERIKA SAMOA BK	(684) 633-1151			
Weiss Safety Rating: B+					
HONOLULU	BANK OF HAWAII	(888) 643-3888			
HONOLULU	CITY BK	(808) 535-2500			

† Out-of-State Institution with branches in Hawaii

Idaho

City	Name	Telephone	City	Name	Telephone

Weiss Safety Rating: A+

IDAHO FALLS	BANK OF COMMERCE	(208) 523-2020

Weiss Safety Rating: A-

BUHL	FARMERS NB OF BUHL	(208) 543-4351

Weiss Safety Rating: B+

COEUR D'ALENE	IDAHO INDEPENDENT BK	(208) 765-3619
SPOKANE, WA	† WASHINGTON TRUST BK	(509) 353-2265

† Out-of-State Institution with branches in Idaho

Illinois

City	Name	Telephone

Weiss Safety Rating: A+

City	Name	Telephone
BOURBONNAIS	MUNICIPAL T&SB	(815) 935-8000
BREESE	GERMANTOWN T&SB	(618) 526-4202
CHICAGO	CORUS BK NA	(773) 549-7100
EDWARDSVILLE	FIRST FS&LA OF EDWARDSVILLE	(618) 656-6200
LINCOLN	STATE BK OF LINCOLN	(217) 735-5551
TEUTOPOLIS	TEUTOPOLIS ST BK	(217) 857-3166

Weiss Safety Rating: A

City	Name	Telephone
ALBION	CITIZENS NB OF ALBION	(618) 445-2344
ANNA	ANNA NB	(618) 833-8506
BOWEN	BOWEN ST BK	(217) 842-5234
CHICAGO	FIRST SECURITY FSB	(773) 772-4500
CHICAGO	ALBANY B&TC NA	(773) 267-7300
DECATUR	SOY CAPITAL B&TC	(217) 428-7781
E ST LOUIS	FIRST ILLINOIS BK	(618) 271-8700
FAIRFIELD	FAIRFIELD NB	(618) 842-2107
HANOVER PARK	FIRST EAGLE NB	(630) 893-3800
LERNA	FIRST NB OF LERNA	(217) 234-9200
METROPOLIS	CITY NB OF METROPOLIS	(618) 524-2161
O'FALLON	BANK OF O'FALLON	(618) 632-3595
PROPHETSTOWN	FARMERS NB PROPHETSTOWN	(815) 537-2348
RANTOUL	BANK OF RANTOUL	(217) 892-2143
REYNOLDS	REYNOLDS ST BK	(309) 372-4242
SPRING VALLEY	SPRING VALLEY CITY BK	(815) 663-2211
STREATOR	STREATOR HOME B&LA	(815) 673-5566
VANDALIA	FIRST NB	(618) 283-1141

Weiss Safety Rating: A-

City	Name	Telephone
ALBANY	FIRST T&SB OF ALBANY IL	(309) 887-4335
AVON	TOMPKINS ST BK	(309) 465-3834
BEARDSTOWN	FIRST NB OF BEARDSTOWN	(217) 323-4105
BLOOMINGTON	HEARTLAND B&TC	(309) 662-4444
CARTERVILLE	CARTERVILLE ST & SVG BK	(618) 985-4848
CHESTER	BUENA VISTA NB	(618) 826-2331
CHICAGO	MUTUAL FS&LA OF CHICAGO	(773) 847-7747
CHICAGO	INTERNATIONAL BK CHICAGO	(773) 769-2899
CHICAGO	LIBERTY BK FOR SVG	(773) 384-4000
CISSNA PARK	CISSNA PARK ST BK	(815) 457-2111
CLINTON	FIRST NB&TC	(217) 935-2148
DWIGHT	BANK OF DWIGHT	(815) 584-1855
DWIGHT	FIRST NB OF DWIGHT	(815) 584-1212
EARLVILLE	NATIONAL BK OF EARLVILLE	(815) 246-8411
EFFINGHAM	CROSSROADS BK	(217) 347-7751
FORT †	ARMED FORCES BK NA	(913) 682-9090
GRAND RIDGE	FIRST NB OF GRAND RIDGE	(815) 249-6414
HAMMOND, IN †	BANK CALUMET	(219) 932-6900
HERRIN	BANK OF HERRIN	(618) 942-6666
HERSCHER	STATE BK OF HERSCHER	(815) 426-2156
LA GRANGE	FIRST NB OF LA GRANGE	(708) 482-7700
LA SALLE	EUREKA SVGS BK	(815) 223-0700
LISLE	LISLE SVGS BK	(630) 852-3710
MANSFIELD	PEOPLES ST BK	(217) 489-2271
MASON CITY	MASON CITY NB	(217) 482-3246
MILLEDGEVILLE	MILLEDGEVILLE ST BK	(815) 225-7171
NEW BERLIN	WARREN BOYNTON ST BK	(217) 488-6091
NOKOMIS	FIRST NB OF NOKOMIS	(217) 563-8311
PANA	FIRST NB OF PANA	(217) 562-3961
PARK RIDGE	PARK RIDGE COMMUNITY BK	(847) 384-9200

City	Name	Telephone
PAW PAW	STATE BK OF PAW PAW	(815) 627-2651
PAXTON	FARMERS & MERCHANTS NB	(217) 379-4343
PAXTON	FIRST NB IN PAXTON	(217) 379-2336
PONTIAC	BANK OF PONTIAC	(815) 844-6155
POPLAR GROVE	POPLAR GROVE ST BK	(815) 765-3333
ROCHESTER	ROCHESTER ST BK	(217) 498-7111
RUSHVILLE	RUSHVILLE ST BK	(217) 322-3323
SHELBYVILLE	SHELBY COUNTY ST BK	(217) 774-3911
SKOKIE	1ST EQUITY BANK	(847) 676-9200
ST JACOB	STATE BK OF ST JACOB	(618) 644-5555
VIRDEN	FARMERS & MERCHANTS ST BK	(217) 965-5496
VIRGINIA	PETEFISH SKILES & CO	(217) 452-3041
WINSLOW	COMMUNITY BK	(815) 367-5011

Weiss Safety Rating: B+

City	Name	Telephone
ALLENDALE	FIRST NB OF ALLENDALE	(618) 299-4411
ANNA	ANNA ST BK	(618) 833-2151
ASHLAND	STATE BK OF ASHLAND	(217) 476-3325
AUBURN	STATE BK OF AUBURN	(217) 438-6114
AURORA	OLD SECOND NB OF AURORA	(630) 892-0202
BEECHER CITY	FIRST ST BK OF BEECHER CITY	(618) 487-5161
BETHANY	SCOTT ST BK	(217) 665-3321
BLOOMINGTON	COUNTRY TRUST BK	(309) 821-4600
BOURBONNAIS	PEOPLES BK MARYCREST	(815) 936-7600
CARRIERS MILLS	EGYPTIAN ST BK	(618) 994-2319
CHAMPAIGN	BANKILLINOIS	(217) 351-6500
CHATHAM	UNITED COMMUNITY BK	(217) 483-2491
CHERRY	STATE BK OF CHERRY	(815) 894-2345
CHICAGO	CENTRAL FS&LA OF CHICAGO	(773) 528-0200
CHICAGO	CHESTERFIELD FS&LA OF CHICAG	(773) 239-6000
CHICAGO	LOOMIS FS&LA	(773) 586-6900
CHICAGO	BURLING BK	(312) 408-8400
CHICAGO	LAKESIDE BK	(312) 435-5100
CHICAGO	MB FINANCIAL BK NA	(773) 645-3333
CHICAGO HEIGHTS	HERITAGE BK	(708) 755-7400
CLIFTON	FIRST NB OF CLIFTON	(815) 694-2329
COLLINSVILLE	COLLINSVILLE B&LA	(618) 344-3172
DARIEN	REPUBLIC BK OF CHICAGO	(773) 581-4500
DECATUR	FIRST NB OF DECATUR	(217) 424-1111
ELGIN	FIRST COMMUNITY BK	(847) 622-8800
ELMWOOD PARK	FIRST SECURITY T&SB	(708) 453-3131
FARMINGTON	BANK OF FARMINGTON	(309) 245-2441
FISHER	FISHER NB	(217) 897-1136
GALESBURG	FARMERS & MECHANICS BK	(309) 343-7141
GENEVA	STATE BK OF GENEVA	(630) 232-3200
GLASFORD	GLASFORD ST BK	(309) 389-2551
GLENVIEW	GLENVIEW ST BK	(847) 729-1900
GURNEE	NORTHSIDE CMNTY BK	(847) 244-5100
HIGHLAND PARK	FIRST BK HIGHLAND PARK	(847) 432-7800
HOLCOMB	HOLCOMB ST BK	(815) 393-4413
INDUSTRY	STATE BK OF INDUSTRY	(309) 254-3434
KEWANEE	PEOPLES NB OF KEWANEE	(309) 853-3333
KINMUNDY	FIRST NB OF KINMUNDY	(618) 547-3533
LANSING	FIRST NB OF ILLINOIS	(708) 474-1300
MANHATTAN	FIRST NB OF MANHATTAN	(815) 478-4611
MARION	BANK OF MARION	(618) 997-4341
MAROA	MAROA FORSYTH COMMUNITY BK	(217) 794-2227
MATTOON	FIRST FS&LA OF MATTOON	(217) 235-5411
MIDLOTHIAN	A J SMITH FSB	(708) 687-7400
MILLSTADT	FIRST NB OF MILLSTADT	(618) 476-1351

† Out-of-State Institution with branches in Illinois

Illinois (Continued)

City	Name	Telephone	City	Name	Telephone

Weiss Safety Rating: B+ (Continued)

City	Name	Telephone
MT VERNON	FIRST NB OF MT VERNON	(618) 244-3000
MT ZION	PRAIRIE ST B&TC	(217) 864-2353
NIANTIC	STATE BK OF NIANTIC	(217) 668-2334
OGLESBY	ILLINI ST BK	(815) 883-8400
OSWEGO	OSWEGO COMMUNITY BK	(630) 554-3411
PINCKNEYVILLE	MURPHY WALL ST B&TC	(618) 357-5373
QUINCY	STATE STREET B&TC	(217) 223-6480
RED BUD	FIRST ST BK OF RED BUD	(618) 282-3861
ROBINSON	FIRST CRAWFORD ST BK	(618) 544-8666
ROBINSON	FIRST ROBINSON SB NA	(618) 544-8621
RUSHVILLE	SCHUYLER ST BK	(217) 322-4387
SHABBONA	FARMERS & TRADERS ST BK	(815) 824-2111
SOMONAUK	FARMERS ST BK	(815) 498-2396
SPRINGFIELD	MARINE BK-SPRINGFIELD	(217) 726-0600
STAUNTON	FIRST NB IN STAUNTON	(618) 635-2234
STILLMAN VALLEY	STILLMAN BANCCORP N.A.	(815) 645-2266
SYCAMORE	NATIONAL B&TC OF SYCAMORE	(815) 895-2125
TRENTON	COMMUNITY BK OF TRENTON	(618) 224-9258
W CHICAGO	STATE BK ILLINOIS	(630) 231-1800
WATSEKA	FIRST T&SB	(815) 432-2494
WORTH	PROSPECT FSB	(708) 361-8000
WYOMING	WYOMING B&TC	(309) 695-2831
XENIA	FIRST CMNTY BK XENIA-FLORA	(618) 678-2202

Indiana

City	Name	Telephone

Weiss Safety Rating:　A

City	Name	Telephone
BOURBON	FIRST ST BK	(574) 342-2415
KENTLAND	KENTLAND BK	(219) 474-5155
SPARTANBURG	GREENSFORK TOWNSHIP ST BK	(765) 874-2511
VALPARAISO	FIRST NB OF VALPARAISO	(219) 462-4161

Weiss Safety Rating:　A-

City	Name	Telephone
ATTICA	CENTRAL NB&TC	(765) 762-2414
AUBURN	PEOPLES FSB OF DEKALB COUNTY	(260) 925-2500
AURORA	PEOPLES FEDERAL SVGS BK	(812) 926-0631
BERNE	FIRST BK OF BERNE	(260) 589-2151
BOSWELL	FARMERS & MERCHANTS BK	(765) 869-5513
BROOKVILLE	FCN BK NA	(765) 647-4116
CAMBRIDGE CITY	WAYNE B&TC	(765) 478-3561
DE MOTTE	DE MOTTE STATE BANK	(219) 987-4141
FOWLER	FOWLER ST BK	(765) 884-1200
GREENFIELD	GREENFIELD BKG CO	(317) 462-1431
HAMMOND	BANK CALUMET	(219) 932-6900
LIZTON	STATE BK OF LIZTON	(317) 994-5115
MADISON	RIVER VALLEY FINANCIAL BK	(812) 273-4949
NAPOLEON	NAPOLEON ST BK	(812) 852-4242
SCOTTSBURG	SCOTT COUNTY ST BK	(812) 752-4501
WHITING	CENTIER BK	(219) 659-0043

Weiss Safety Rating:　B+

City	Name	Telephone
BRAZIL	FIRST ST BK	(812) 443-4481
COLUMBUS	HOMEFEDERAL BK	(812) 522-1592
COVINGTON	FOUNTAIN TRUST CO	(765) 793-2237
HAMMOND	LAKE FS&LA OF HAMMOND	(219) 845-0220
KENDALLVILLE	CAMPBELL & FETTER BKRS	(260) 347-1500
LAGRANGE	FARMERS ST BK	(260) 463-7111
LAWRENCEBURG	DEARBORN SA	(812) 537-0940
LAWRENCEBURG	UNITED COMMUNITY BK	(812) 537-1016
MARKLE	MARKLEBANK	(260) 758-3111
MOORESVILLE	CITIZENS BK	(317) 831-0110
MUNCIE	MUTUAL FSB	(765) 747-2800
NEW	NEW WASHINGTON ST BK	(812) 256-7100
NOBLESVILLE	COMMUNITY BK	(317) 773-0800
PORTER	FIRST ST BK OF PORTER	(219) 926-2136
ROACHDALE	TRI-COUNTY B&TC	(765) 522-1000
TERRE HAUTE	FIRST FINANCIAL BK NA	(812) 238-6000
TERRE HAUTE	MORRIS PLAN CO-TERRE HAUTE	(812) 238-6063
WARSAW	LAKE CITY BK	(574) 267-6144
WOLCOTT	BANK OF WOLCOTT	(219) 279-2185

Iowa

City	Name	Telephone	City	Name	Telephone
			SLATER	SOUTH STORY B&TC	(515) 228-3566
			SOMERS	HEARTLAND BK	(515) 467-5561

Weiss Safety Rating: A+

City	Name	Telephone
DIKE	IOWA SVG BK	(319) 989-2474
WAVERLY	STATE BK OF WAVERLY	(319) 352-6000

Weiss Safety Rating: A

City	Name	Telephone
BELMOND	FIRST ST BK	(641) 444-3226
CENTERVILLE	IOWA T&SB	(641) 437-4500
CHEROKEE	CHEROKEE ST BK	(712) 225-3000
DES MOINES	IOWA ST BK	(515) 288-0111
FORT MADISON	LEE COUNTY B&T NA	(319) 372-2243
HAMPTON	FIRST NB OF HAMPTON	(641) 456-4793
MARION	FARMERS ST BK	(319) 377-4891
POCAHONTAS	POCAHONTAS ST BK	(712) 335-3567
WASHINGTON	WASHINGTON ST BK	(319) 653-2151
WEBSTER CITY	WEBSTER CITY FSB	(515) 832-3071
WILLIAMSBURG	FARMERS T&SB	(319) 668-2525

Weiss Safety Rating: A-

City	Name	Telephone
AKRON	FIRST NB OF AKRON	(712) 568-2472
AMES	FIRST NB AMES, IA	(515) 232-5561
ATLANTIC	FIRST WHITNEY B&T	(712) 243-3195
BELLE PLAINE	CHELSEA SVG BK	(319) 444-3144
BLAIRSTOWN	BENTON COUNTY ST BK	(319) 454-6230
BLUE GRASS	BLUE GRASS SVG BK	(563) 381-1732
BOONE	BOONE B&TC	(515) 432-6200
CARROLL	COMMERCIAL SVG BK	(712) 792-4346
CASCADE	TRI-COUNTY B&TC	(563) 852-7696
CLINTON	GATEWAY ST BK	(563) 242-2265
COLFAX	FIRST ST BK OF COLFAX	(515) 674-3533
CORYDON	CORYDON ST BK	(641) 872-2212
CRESCO	CRESCO UNION SVG BK	(563) 547-2040
DECORAH	DECORAH B&TC	(563) 382-9661
DURANT	LIBERTY T&SB	(563) 785-4441
GUTTENBERG	SECURITY ST BK	(563) 252-2211
HAWKEYE	CITIZENS SVG BK	(563) 427-3255
IOWA FALLS	GREEN BELT BANK & TRUST	(641) 648-2544
IOWA FALLS	IOWA FALLS ST BK	(641) 648-5171
KEOSAUQUA	COMMUNITY FIRST BK	(319) 293-3794
KINGSLEY	KINGSLEY ST BK	(712) 378-2341
LUANA	LUANA SVG BK	(563) 539-2166
MANNING	FIRST NB OF MANNING	(712) 655-3557
MAPLETON	FIRST ST BK OF MAPLETON	(712) 882-1343
MAPLETON	VALLEY B&T	(712) 881-1131
MAQUOKETA	MAQUOKETA ST BK	(563) 652-2491
MASON CITY	FIRST CITIZENS NB	(641) 423-1600
MAXWELL	MAXWELL ST BK	(515) 387-1175
MAYNARD	MAYNARD SVG BK	(563) 637-2289
MT PLEASANT	WAYLAND ST BK	(319) 385-8189
MT VERNON	MOUNT VERNON B&TC	(319) 895-8835
NEVADA	STATE B&TC	(515) 382-2191
NEW HAMPTON	STATE BK LAWLER	(563) 238-2054
OAKLAND	CITIZENS ST BK	(712) 482-6431
ORANGE CITY	NORTHWESTERN ST BK	(712) 737-4911
OSAGE	HOME T&SB	(641) 732-3763
READLYN	READLYN SVG BK	(319) 279-3321
REMSEN	FARMERS SVG BK	(712) 786-1143
ROYAL	HOME ST BK	(712) 933-5511
SHELDON	SECURITY ST BK SHELDON	(712) 324-5141
SIOUX CITY	SECURITY NB OF SIOUX CITY IA	(712) 277-6500

City	Name	Telephone
SLATER	SOUTH STORY B&TC	(515) 228-3566
SOMERS	HEARTLAND BK	(515) 467-5561
SPRINGVILLE	EXCHANGE ST BK	(319) 854-6104
ST ANSGAR	ST ANSGAR ST BK	(641) 713-4501
STATE CENTER	CENTRAL ST BK	(641) 483-2505
STORM LAKE	CITIZENS FIRST NB STORM LAKE	(712) 732-5440
STORY CITY	RANDALL-STORY ST BK	(515) 733-4396
TEMPLETON	TEMPLETON SVG BK	(712) 669-3322
VICTOR	FARMERS SVG BK	(319) 647-3141
VICTOR	VICTOR ST BK	(319) 647-2231
WALCOTT	WALCOTT T&SB	(563) 284-6202
WAVERLY	SECURITY ST BK	(319) 352-3500
WYOMING	CITIZENS ST BK	(563) 488-2211

Weiss Safety Rating: B+

City	Name	Telephone
ASHTON	ASHTON ST BK	(712) 724-6326
ATLANTIC	ROLLING HILLS B&T	(712) 243-2244
CENTER POINT	CENTER POINT B&TC	(319) 849-1838
CHARLES CITY	FIRST SECURITY B&TC	(641) 228-2343
CLARINDA	PAGE COUNTY ST BK	(712) 542-5661
CLINTON	CLINTON NB	(563) 243-1243
CONRAD	FIRST ST BK	(641) 366-2165
CORALVILLE	FREEDOM SECURITY BK	(319) 688-9005
CORNING	OKEY-VERNON FIRST NB	(641) 322-3101
CRAWFORDSVILLE	PEOPLES SVG BK	(319) 658-2131
CRESTON	FIRST FEDERAL SB CRESTON FSB	(641) 782-8482
DANVILLE	DANVILLE ST SVG BK	(319) 392-4261
DE WITT	DE WITT B&TC	(563) 659-3211
DE WITT	FIRST CENTRAL ST BK	(563) 659-3141
DECORAH	VIKING ST B&T	(563) 387-0191
ELKADER	CENTRAL ST BK	(563) 245-2110
ELKADER	PEOPLES ST BK	(563) 245-2522
FAIRFAX	FAIRFAX ST SVG BK	(319) 846-2300
FORT DODGE	FIRST FSB OF IOWA	(515) 576-7531
FOSTORIA	FARMERS SVG BK	(712) 262-2708
GLIDDEN	FIRST B&TC	(712) 659-3611
GREENFIELD	UNION ST BK	(641) 343-7310
HAMPTON	HAMPTON ST BK	(641) 456-2559
HIAWATHA	HIAWATHA B&TC	(319) 378-5979
HILLS	HILLS B&TC	(319) 679-2291
HUBBARD	SECURITY ST BK	(641) 864-2244
HULL	IOWA ST BK	(712) 439-1025
IOWA CITY	IOWA ST B&TC	(319) 356-5800
JEFFERSON	HOME ST BK	(515) 386-2131
KEOTA	FARMERS SVG BK	(641) 636-2193
LE MARS	PRIMEBANK	(712) 546-4175
LOGAN	FIRST NB OF LOGAN	(712) 644-2310
MALVERN	MALVERN T&SB	(712) 624-8686
MARCUS	FARMERS ST BK	(712) 376-4154
MARENGO	GRINNELL ST BK	(641) 236-3174
MARSHALLTOWN	UNITED B&TC NA	(641) 753-5900
MARTELLE	VILLAGE B&TC	(319) 482-2371
MELVIN	MELVIN SVG BK	(712) 736-2420
MONONA	UNION ST BK	(563) 539-2015
MUSCATINE	CENTRAL ST BK	(563) 263-3131
MUSCATINE	COMMUNITY BK	(563) 263-1122
NORA SPRINGS	FIRST ST BK	(641) 749-5356
OTTUMWA	SOUTH OTTUMWA SVG BK	(641) 682-7541
PELLA	MARION COUNTY ST BK	(641) 628-2191
PLEASANTVILLE	PLEASANTVILLE ST BK	(515) 848-5741

Iowa (Continued)

City	Name	Telephone	City	Name	Telephone
Weiss Safety Rating: B+ (Continued)					
POSTVILLE	POSTVILLE ST BK	(563) 864-7441			
RICEVILLE	FIRST ST BK	(641) 985-2442			
RIVERSIDE	PEOPLES T&SB	(319) 648-2221			
ROLFE	ROLFE ST BK	(712) 848-3480			
SHELDON	CITIZENS ST BK	(712) 324-2519			
SIBLEY	SIBLEY ST BK	(712) 754-2561			
SIOUX CITY	MORNINGSIDE B&TC	(712) 276-5331			
SOLON	SOLON ST BK	(319) 624-3405			
SUMNER	FIRST ST BK	(563) 578-3312			
TRIPOLI	AMERICAN SVG BK	(319) 882-4279			
W DES MOINES	WEST BK	(515) 222-2300			
WALKER	WALKER ST BK	(319) 448-4317			
WAPELLO	STATE BK OF WAPELLO	(319) 523-2131			
WASHINGTON	WEST CHESTER SVG BK	(319) 653-2265			
WATKINS	WATKINS SVG BK	(319) 227-7773			
WAUKON	WAUKON ST BK	(563) 568-3451			
WILTON	WILTON SVG BK	(563) 732-2077			

Kansas

City	Name	Telephone
OLPE	OLPE ST BK	(620) 475-3213
PRATT	PEOPLES BK	(620) 672-5611
RANSOM	FIRST ST BK OF RANSOM	(785) 731-2261
SCANDIA	SCANDIA ST BK OF SCANDIA	(785) 335-2243
ULYSSES	GRANT COUNTY BK	(620) 356-4142
WALNUT	FARMERS NB OF KANSAS	(620) 354-6435
WATHENA	FARMERS ST BK	(785) 989-4431
WICHITA	INTRUST BK NA	(316) 383-1111

Weiss Safety Rating: A+

City	Name	Telephone
COUNCIL GROVE	FARMERS & DROVERS BK	(620) 767-5138
DODGE CITY	FIDELITY ST B&TC	(620) 227-8586
LAKIN	KEARNY COUNTY BK	(620) 355-6222

Weiss Safety Rating: A

City	Name	Telephone
FREDONIA	FIRST NB IN FREDONIA	(620) 378-2151
HUGOTON	CITIZENS ST BK	(620) 544-4331
LAWRENCE	UNIVERSITY NB LAWRENCE	(785) 841-1988
LEAWOOD	NATIONAL BK OF KANSAS CITY	(913) 341-1144
LOUISBURG	FIRST NB OF LOUISBURG	(913) 837-5191
PARSONS	COMMERCIAL BK	(620) 421-1000
STANLEY	STANLEY BK	(913) 681-8800

Weiss Safety Rating: A-

City	Name	Telephone
ATCHISON	EXCHANGE NB&TC OF ATCHISON	(913) 367-6000
CHENEY	CITIZENS ST BK OF CHENEY	(316) 542-3142
FORT	ARMED FORCES BK NA	(913) 682-9090
FRONTENAC	MINERS ST BK OF FRONTENAC	(621) 231-9280
GREAT BEND	FARMERS B&TC NA	(620) 792-2411
GREENSBURG	GREENSBURG ST BK	(620) 723-2131
HEALY	FIRST ST BK OF HEALY	(620) 398-2215
JUNCTION CITY	CENTRAL NB	(785) 238-4114
KANSAS CITY	INDUSTRIAL ST BK	(913) 831-2000
KANSAS CITY, MO †	BANK MIDWEST NA	(816) 471-9800
LEAVENWORTH	FIRST NB&TC OF LEAVENWORTH	(913) 682-2265
MANHATTAN	LANDMARK NB	(785) 565-2000
MILACA, MN †	COMMERCIAL FEDERAL BK, A FSB	(320) 983-3101
MISSION	MISSION BK	(913) 831-2400
MOUNDRIDGE	CITIZENS ST BK	(620) 345-6317
OLATHE	FIRST FS&LA OF OLATHE	(913) 782-0026
OVERLAND PARK	VALLEY VIEW ST BK	(913) 381-3311
PAOLA	CITIZENS ST BK	(913) 294-2321
PHILLIPSBURG	FIRST NB&T	(785) 543-6511
PLAINS CITY	PLAINS ST BK	(620) 563-7242
ROSE HILL	ROSE HILL BK	(316) 776-2131
SOLOMON	SOLOMON ST BK	(785) 655-2941
TESCOTT	BANK OF TESCOTT	(785) 283-4217
WAMEGO	KAW VALLEY ST B&TC	(785) 456-2021
WASHINGTON	FIRST NB OF WASHINGTON	(785) 325-2221
WESTMORELAND	FARMERS ST BK	(785) 457-3316

Weiss Safety Rating: B+

City	Name	Telephone
BELLE PLAINE	VALLEY ST BK	(620) 488-2211
BELLEVILLE	FIRST NB IN BELLEVILLE	(785) 527-2268
BERN	STATE BK OF BERN	(785) 336-6121
CLAY CENTER	UNION ST BK	(785) 632-3122
DERBY	VERUS BK NA	(316) 788-1111
GREELEY	BANK OF GREELEY	(785) 867-2010
HIAWATHA	CITIZENS ST B&TC	(785) 742-2101
HOLTON	DENISON ST BK	(785) 364-3131
HUTCHINSON	FIRST NB OF HUTCHINSON	(620) 663-1521
KANSAS CITY	INTER-STATE FS&LA	(913) 371-1083
KANSAS CITY	SECURITY BK OF KANSAS CITY	(913) 281-3165
KIOWA	FIRST ST BK KIOWA KS	(620) 825-4147
LEAVENWORTH	CITIZENS S&LA FSB	(913) 727-1040
LEAVENWORTH	MUTUAL SA FSA	(913) 682-3491
MULVANE	MULVANE ST BK	(316) 777-1171
NESS CITY	FIRST ST BK	(785) 798-3347

† Out-of-State Institution with branches in Kansas

Kentucky

City	Name	Telephone

Weiss Safety Rating: A+

City	Name	Telephone
ASHLAND	KENTUCKY-FARMERS BK	(606) 929-5000
HODGENVILLE	LINCOLN NB OF HODGENVILLE	(270) 358-4116
MILTON	FARMERS BK	(502) 268-5256

Weiss Safety Rating: A

City	Name	Telephone
ARLINGTON	CITIZENS DEPOSIT BK	(270) 655-6921
BARDSTOWN	WILSON & MUIR B&TC	(502) 348-5996
CARLISLE	DEPOSIT BK OF CARLISLE	(859) 289-2205
CYNTHIANA	FARMERS NB OF CYNTHIANA	(859) 234-3100
DANVILLE	FARMERS NB OF DANVILLE	(859) 236-2926
GREENSBURG	DEPOSIT B&TC	(270) 932-7491
HINDMAN	BANK OF HINDMAN	(606) 785-3158
JAMESTOWN	BANK OF JAMESTOWN	(270) 343-3186
LOUISVILLE	RIVER CITY BK	(502) 585-4600
LOUISVILLE	STOCK YARDS B&TC	(502) 582-2571
MAYSVILLE	BANK OF MAYSVILLE	(606) 564-4001
MC KEE	JACKSON COUNTY BK	(606) 287-8484
PRESTONSBURG	FIRST COMMONWEALTH BK	(606) 886-2321
PRINCETON	FARMERS B&TC	(270) 365-5526
SALYERSVILLE	SALYERSVILLE NB	(606) 349-3131
SHEPHERDSVILLE	PEOPLES BK OF BULLITT CTY	(502) 543-2226
SPRINGFIELD	SPRINGFIELD ST BK	(859) 336-3939
WILLIAMSTOWN	EAGLE BK	(859) 824-4436

Weiss Safety Rating: A-

City	Name	Telephone
BARDSTOWN	TOWN & COUNTRY B&TC	(502) 348-3911
BROWNSVILLE	BANK OF EDMONSON CTY	(270) 597-2175
CAMPBELLSVILLE	CITIZENS B&TC	(270) 465-8193
CLARKSON	BANK OF CLARKSON	(270) 242-2111
CLOVERPORT	BRECKINRIDGE BK	(270) 788-3749
COLUMBIA	BANK OF COLUMBIA	(270) 384-6433
DUNDEE	BANK OF OHIO CTY	(270) 274-5678
ELKTON	ELKTON B&TC	(270) 265-9841
FLEMINGSBURG	PEOPLES BK OF FLEMING CTY	(606) 845-2461
FORT	† ARMED FORCES BK NA	(913) 682-9090
FRANKFORT	FIRST FSB OF FRANKFORT	(502) 223-1638
FRANKFORT	BANKERS BANK OF KY INC	(502) 695-3000
GLASGOW	EDMONTON ST BK	(270) 659-0171
GRAYSON	COMMERCIAL BK OF GRAYSON	(606) 474-7811
HARDINSBURG	FARMERS BK	(270) 756-2166
HAWESVILLE	HANCOCK B&TC	(270) 927-8855
IRVINGTON	FIRST ST BK	(270) 547-2271
LEITCHFIELD	LEITCHFIELD DEP B&TC	(270) 259-5611
LEXINGTON	BANK OF THE BLUEGRASS & TC	(859) 233-4500
MARTIN	FIRST GUARANTY BK	(606) 285-3294
MAYSVILLE	SECURITY B&TC	(606) 564-3304
RADCLIFF	WEST POINT BK	(270) 351-1414
RUSSELL SPRINGS	FIRST NB OF RUSSELL SPRINGS	(270) 866-4343
SACRAMENTO	SACRAMENTO DEPOSIT BK	(270) 736-2212
SCOTTSVILLE	FARMERS NB OF SCOTTSVILLE	(270) 237-3141
SOMERSET	CUMBERLAND SECURITY BK	(606) 679-9361

Weiss Safety Rating: B+

City	Name	Telephone
BROOKSVILLE	FIRST NB OF BROOKSVILLE	(606) 735-2125
CAMPBELLSBURG	UNITED CITIZENS B&TC	(502) 532-7392
CARROLLTON	FIRST NB OF CARROLLTON	(502) 732-4406
DIXON	DIXON BK	(270) 639-5815
FRANKFORT	AMERICAN FOUNDERS BK INC	(502) 875-4500

City	Name	Telephone
HARLAN	BANK OF HARLAN	(606) 573-1202
HENDERSON	OHIO VALLEY NB OF HENDERSON	(270) 831-1500
HOPKINSVILLE	HERITAGE BANK	(270) 885-1171
INEZ	INEZ DEPOSIT BK	(606) 298-3511
LEWISBURG	LEWISBURG BKG CO	(270) 755-4818
LOUISA	INEZ DEPOSIT BK FSB	(606) 638-9461
MANCHESTER	FIRST NB OF MANCHESTER	(606) 598-6111
OWENTON	PEOPLES B&TC	(502) 484-3466
PIKEVILLE	KENTUCKY NB OF PIKEVILLE	(606) 437-4000
SOMERSET	SOMERSET NB	(606) 676-9500

† Out-of-State Institution with branches in Kentucky

Louisiana

City	Name	Telephone	City	Name	Telephone

Weiss Safety Rating: A+

City	Name	Telephone
DE RIDDER	FIRST NB-DE RIDDER	(337) 463-6231

Weiss Safety Rating: A

City	Name	Telephone
ABBEVILLE	GULF COAST BK	(337) 893-7733
BELLE CHASSE	MISSISSIPPI RIVER BK	(504) 392-1111
DE RIDDER	CITY SVG B&TC	(337) 463-8661
DELHI	GUARANTY B&TC-DELHI	(318) 878-3703
EUNICE	TRI-PARISH BANK	(337) 457-7341
GUEYDAN	BANK OF GUEYDAN	(337) 536-9206
HAUGHTON	TRI-STATE BK&TR	(318) 949-4173
KAPLAN	KAPLAN ST BK	(337) 643-7110
MINDEN	MINDEN B&LA	(318) 377-0523
ST JOSEPH	CROSS KEYS BK	(318) 766-3246
VILLE PLATTE	EVANGELINE B&TC	(337) 363-5541

Weiss Safety Rating: A-

City	Name	Telephone
ABBEVILLE	BANK OF ABBEVILLE & TRUST CO	(337) 893-0257
CLINTON	FELICIANA B&TC	(225) 683-8565
GOLDEN MEADOW	STATE B&TC	(985) 475-5826
JEANERETTE	FIRST NB OF JEANERETTE	(337) 276-3692
JONESVILLE	CATAHOULA-LASALLE BK	(318) 339-8571
LAKE CHARLES	CAMERON ST BK	(337) 433-7244
LEESVILLE	MERCHANTS & FARMERS B&TC	(337) 239-6504
METAIRIE	METAIRIE B&TC	(504) 834-6330
MORGAN CITY	M C BANK & TRUST COMPANY	(985) 384-2100
NEW ORLEANS	FIDELITY HMSTD ASSN	(504) 529-5011
NEW ORLEANS	FIFTH DISTRICT S&LA	(504) 362-7544
NEW ORLEANS	UNION S&LA	(504) 522-5581
NEWELLTON	TENSAS ST BK	(318) 467-5401
OPELOUSAS	ST LANDRY HOMESTEAD FSB	(337) 948-3033
OPELOUSAS	AMERICAN B&TC	(337) 948-3056
PLAQUEMINE	PLAQUEMINE B&TC	(225) 687-6388
RAYVILLE	RICHLAND ST BK	(318) 728-2024
SHREVEPORT	HOME FS&LA	(318) 222-1145
SUNSET	BANK OF SUNSET & TRUST CO	(337) 662-5222
WINNFIELD	BANK OF WINNFIELD & TRUST CO	(318) 628-4677

Weiss Safety Rating: B+

City	Name	Telephone
ABBEVILLE	ABBEVILLE B&L ST CHARTERED	(337) 893-1170
BATON ROUGE	HANCOCK BK OF LOUISIANA	(225) 248-7100
CLINTON	CLINTON B&TC	(225) 683-3371
COUSHATTA	BANK OF COUSHATTA	(318) 932-3491
CROWLEY	BANK OF COMMERCE & TRUST CO	(337) 783-2201
DE RIDDER	BEAUREGARD FSB	(337) 463-4493
ERATH	BANK OF ERATH	(337) 937-5816
HOUMA	SOUTH LOUISIANA BK	(985) 851-3434
JACKSON	HIGHLANDS BK	(225) 634-7741
JENNINGS	JEFF DAVIS B&TC	(337) 824-1422
JONESBORO	JONESBORO ST BK	(318) 259-4411
JONESVILLE	SOUTHERN HERITAGE BK	(318) 339-8505
LAFAYETTE	HOME BK	(337) 237-1960
METAIRIE	MUTUAL S&LA	(504) 455-2444
NEW ROADS	PEOPLES B&TC POINTE COUPEE	(225) 638-3713
RAYNE	RAYNE B&LA	(337) 334-7535
VACHERIE	FIRST AMERICAN B&TC	(225) 265-4061
VILLE PLATTE	CITIZENS BK	(337) 363-5643

Maine

City	Name	Telephone	City	Name	Telephone

Weiss Safety Rating: A

City	Name	Telephone
AUBURN	MECHANICS' SVGS BK	(207) 786-5700
FARMINGTON	FRANKLIN SVGS BK	(207) 778-3339

Weiss Safety Rating: A-

City	Name	Telephone
MACHIAS	MACHIAS SVGS BK	(207) 255-3347

Weiss Safety Rating: B+

City	Name	Telephone
AUGUSTA	KENNEBEC SVGS BK	(207) 622-5801
KENNEBUNK	KENNEBUNK SVGS BK	(207) 985-4903
LEWISTON	ANDROSCOGGIN SVGS BK	(207) 784-9164

Maryland

City	Name	Telephone	City	Name	Telephone

Weiss Safety Rating: A+

City	Name	Telephone
BALTIMORE	ROSEDALE FS&LA	(410) 668-4400
BERLIN	CALVIN B TAYLOR BKG CO	(410) 641-1700
MIDDLETOWN	MIDDLETOWN VALLEY BK	(301) 371-6700

Weiss Safety Rating: A

City	Name	Telephone
ABERDEEN	HARFORD BK	(410) 272-5000
CHESTERTOWN	CHESAPEAKE B&TC	(410) 778-1600
CHESTERTOWN	PEOPLES BK OF KENT CTY MD	(410) 778-3500
OCEAN CITY	BANK OF OCEAN CITY	(410) 213-0173

Weiss Safety Rating: A-

City	Name	Telephone
ANNAPOLIS	SEVERN SVGS BK FSB	(410) 268-4554
ANNAPOLIS	ANNAPOLIS BKG&TC	(410) 268-4285
BALTIMORE	MERCANTILE SAFE DEPOSIT & TC	(410) 237-5900
BEL AIR	FOREST HILL ST BK	(410) 838-6131
CAMBRIDGE	BANK OF THE EASTERN SHORE	(410) 228-5800
CAMBRIDGE	NATIONAL BK OF CAMBRIDGE	(410) 228-5600
CENTREVILLE	CENTREVILLE NB OF MD	(410) 758-1600
CHESTERTOWN	CHESTERTOWN BK OF MD	(410) 778-2400
DAMASCUS	DAMASCUS COMMUNITY BK	(301) 253-1000
DENTON	PEOPLES BK OF MARYLAND	(410) 479-2600
EASTON	TALBOT BK OF EASTON MD	(410) 822-1400
ELKTON	COUNTY BKG&TC	(410) 398-2600
FREDERICK	FARMERS & MECHANICS BK	(301) 694-4050
GAITHERSBURG	POTOMAC VALLEY BK	(301) 963-7600
LA PLATA	BANK OF SOUTHERN MARYLAND	(301) 934-1000
LEONARDTOWN	FIRST NB OF ST MARYS	(301) 475-8081
PRINCE	CALVERT B&TC	(410) 286-5901
PRINCESS ANNE	PENINSULA BK	(410) 651-4304
ST MICHAELS	ST MICHAELS BK	(410) 745-5091
UPPER MARLBORO	PRINCE GEORGE'S FSB	(301) 627-3504

Weiss Safety Rating: B+

City	Name	Telephone
BALTIMORE	HOPKINS FSB	(410) 675-2828
BALTIMORE	MIDSTATE FS&LA	(410) 377-4330
HAGERSTOWN	FIDELITY BK	(301) 733-6300
JARRETTSVILLE	JARRETTSVILLE FS&LA	(410) 692-5151
LAUREL	CITIZENS NB	(410) 725-3100
N EAST	FIRST NB OF NORTH EAST	(410) 287-5000
QUEENSTOWN	QUEENSTOWN BK OF MD	(410) 827-8881
WESTMINSTER	WESTMINSTER UNION BK	(410) 848-9300

Massachusetts

City	Name	Telephone	City	Name	Telephone

Weiss Safety Rating: A+

City	Name	Telephone
FRAMINGHAM	FRAMINGHAM CO-OP BK	(508) 820-4000
NEEDHAM	NEEDHAM CO-OP BK	(781) 444-2100
NORWOOD	NORWOOD CO-OP BK	(781) 762-1800
WALPOLE	WALPOLE CO-OP BK	(508) 668-1080

Weiss Safety Rating: A

City	Name	Telephone
BRIGHTON	PEOPLES FSB	(617) 254-0707
EASTHAMPTON	EASTHAMPTON SVGS BK	(413) 527-4111
FOXBORO	FOXBORO FEDERAL SAVINGS	(508) 543-5321
GREENFIELD	GREENFIELD CO-OP	(413) 772-0293
NEWBURYPORT	NEWBURYPORT FIVE CNTS SB	(978) 462-3136
TAUNTON	BRISTOL COUNTY SVGS BK	(508) 824-6626

Weiss Safety Rating: A-

City	Name	Telephone
BOSTON	EAST BOSTON SVG BK	(617) 567-1500
BOSTON	FIDELITY MANAGEMENT TRUST CO	(617) 563-7000
BOSTON	HYDE PARK SVGS BK	(617) 361-6900
BOSTON	MELLON TR OF NEW ENGLAND NA	(617) 722-7000
EVERETT	EVERETT CO-OP BK	(617) 387-1110
MARBLEHEAD	NATIONAL GRAND BK-MARBLEHEAD	(781) 631-6000
N ANDOVER	LAWRENCE SVG BK	(978) 725-7500
N BROOKFIELD	NORTH BROOKFIELD SVGS BK	(508) 867-7442
SOMERVILLE	MIDDLESEX FS&LA	(617) 666-4700
SPENCER	SPENCER SVGS BK	(508) 885-5313
WARE	COUNTRY BK FOR SVGS	(413) 967-6221

Weiss Safety Rating: B+

City	Name	Telephone
BROOKLINE	BROOKLINE BANK	(617) 730-3500
BROOKLINE	BROOKLINE CO-OP BK	(617) 277-4743
CAMBRIDGE	NORTH CAMBRIDGE CO-OP BK	(617) 876-5730
FITCHBURG	FITCHBURG SVGS BK FSB	(978) 345-1061
GLOUCESTER	CAPE ANN SVGS BK	(978) 283-0245
HAVERHILL	PENTUCKET BK	(978) 372-7731
HINGHAM	HINGHAM INST FOR SVGS	(781) 749-2200
HOLYOKE	PEOPLESBANK	(413) 538-9500
LENOX	LENOX NB	(413) 637-0017
LOWELL	LOWELL FIVE CENTS SB	(978) 452-1300
MARLBOROUGH	MARLBOROUGH SVGS BK	(508) 481-8300
MILFORD	MILFORD FS&LA	(508) 634-2500
N ANDOVER	NORTHMARK BK	(978) 686-9100
NANTUCKET	NANTUCKET BK	(508) 228-0580
NEWBURYPORT	INSTITUTION FOR SVGS	(978) 462-3106
NEWTON	VILLAGE BK	(617) 527-6090
NORTHAMPTON	NORTHAMPTON CO-OP BK	(413) 584-4474
ROSLINDALE	COOPERATIVE BK	(617) 325-2900
SALEM	HERITAGE CO-OP BK	(978) 744-5450
WEBSTER	WEBSTER FIVE CENTS SB	(508) 943-9401
WHITMAN	MUTUAL FSB OF PLYMOUTH CTY	(781) 447-4488
WINCHESTER	WINCHESTER CO-OP BK	(781) 729-3620
WOBURN	NORTHERN B&TC	(781) 937-5400

Michigan

City	Name	Telephone	City	Name	Telephone

Weiss Safety Rating: A+

City	Name	Telephone
CHELSEA	CHELSEA ST BK	(734) 475-1355
DEARBORN	DEARBORN FSB	(313) 565-3100
FARWELL	FARWELL ST SVG BK	(989) 588-9945

Weiss Safety Rating: A

City	Name	Telephone
BEULAH	CENTRAL ST BK	(231) 882-4462
FRANKFORT	STATE SVG BK-FRANKFORT	(231) 352-9691
LAPEER	LAPEER COUNTY B&TC	(810) 664-2977
MASON	MASON ST BK	(517) 676-0500
MIDLAND	WOLVERINE BK FSB	(989) 631-4280
MIDLAND	CHEMICAL B&TC	(989) 631-9200

Weiss Safety Rating: A-

City	Name	Telephone
BENTON HARBOR	CHEMICAL BK SHORELINE	(269) 927-2251
CHEBOYGAN	CITIZENS NB OF CHEBOYGAN	(231) 627-7111
COLDWATER	CENTURY B&T	(517) 278-1534
ESCANABA	STATE BK OF ESCANABA	(906) 786-1331
FRANKFORT	WEST MI NB	(231) 352-9655
LAKEVIEW	FIRSTBANK LAKEVIEW	(989) 352-7271
MONTROSE	MONTROSE ST BK	(810) 639-6101
SHELBY	SHELBY ST BK	(231) 861-2123
ST CHARLES	COMMUNITY ST BK ST CHARLES	(989) 865-9945
THREE RIVERS	FIRST SVGS BK FSB	(269) 279-5117
WALKER	CHEMICAL BK WEST	(616) 785-3400

Weiss Safety Rating: B+

City	Name	Telephone
ALMA	FIRSTBANK ALMA	(989) 463-3131
BLISSFIELD	BLISSFIELD ST BK	(517) 486-2151
CRYSTAL FALLS	FIRST NB	(906) 875-4505
DECATUR	FIRST ST BK-DECATUR	(269) 423-7014
EASTPOINTE	FIRST ST BK EAST DETROIT	(586) 775-5000
EWEN	STATE BK OF EWEN	(906) 988-2821
GRAND RAPIDS	FIFTH THIRD BK	(800) 972-3030
GRAND RAPIDS	MERCANTILE BK W MI	(616) 406-3000
HASTINGS	HASTINGS CITY BK	(269) 945-2401
HILLSDALE	HILLSDALE COUNTY NB	(517) 439-4300
KENT CITY	VALLEY RIDGE BK	(616) 678-5911
MASON	DART BK	(517) 676-3661
MT PLEASANT	FIRSTBANK	(989) 773-2600
ONTONAGON	CITIZENS ST BK OF ONTONAGON	(906) 884-4165
PORT AUSTIN	PORT AUSTIN ST BK	(989) 738-5235
PORT HURON	CITIZENS FIRST SVG BK	(810) 987-8300
SCHOOLCRAFT	KALAMAZOO COUNTY ST BK	(269) 679-5291
SIDNEY	SIDNEY ST BK	(989) 328-2501
ST JOHNS	FIRSTBANK ST JOHNS	(989) 227-8383
W BRANCH	FIRSTBANK WEST BRANCH	(989) 345-7900

Micronesia, Federated States: Under U.S. Regulatory Supervision

City	Name	Telephone	City	Name	Telephone
Weiss Safety Rating: B+					
HONOLULU, HI	† BANK OF HAWAII	(888) 643-3888			

† Out-of-State Institution with branches in

Minnesota

City	Name	Telephone

Weiss Safety Rating: A+

City	Name	Telephone
BEMIDJI	FIRST NB OF BEMIDJI	(218) 751-2430

Weiss Safety Rating: A

City	Name	Telephone
GLENWOOD	EAGLE BK	(320) 634-4545
GLENWOOD	GLENWOOD ST BK	(320) 634-5111
LITCHFIELD	CENTER NB	(320) 693-3255
MINNEAPOLIS	UNION B&TC	(612) 379-3222
MORA	KANABEC ST BK	(320) 679-3131
PRIOR LAKE	PRIOR LAKE ST BK	(952) 447-2101
VERMILLION	VERMILLION ST BK	(651) 437-4433
WHEATON	STATE BK OF WHEATON	(320) 563-8142
WYOMING	FIRST ST BK OF WYOMING	(651) 462-7611

Weiss Safety Rating: A-

City	Name	Telephone
ANNANDALE	ANNANDALE ST BK	(320) 274-8216
BAYPORT	FIRST ST B&T	(651) 439-5195
BIG LAKE	PREFERRED BK	(763) 427-4350
CASTLE ROCK	CASTLE ROCK BK	(651) 463-7590
CHANHASSEN	STATE BK OF CHANHASSEN	(952) 937-2265
CLINTON	CLINTON ST BK	(320) 325-5401
CROSBY	FIRST NB OF CROSBY	(218) 546-5153
DELANO	STATE BK OF DELANO	(763) 972-2935
EVANSVILLE	STEARNS BK NA	(218) 948-2259
FARIBAULT	STATE BK OF FARIBAULT	(507) 332-7401
HAMEL	FARMERS ST BK OF HAMEL	(763) 478-6611
HINCKLEY	WOODLANDS NB	(320) 532-4142
HOLDINGFORD	STEARNS BK NA	(320) 746-2261
HUTCHINSON	CITIZENS B&TC	(320) 587-2233
MADISON	KLEIN NB OF MADISON	(320) 598-7591
MAPLE PLAIN	BANK OF MAPLE PLAIN	(763) 479-1931
MILACA	FIRST NB OF MILACA	(320) 983-3101
NEW ULM	CITIZENS BK MN	(507) 354-3165
OLIVIA	AMERICAN ST BK OF OLIVIA	(320) 523-1111
OSAKIS	FIRST NB OF OSAKIS	(320) 859-2101
RICHMOND	STATE BK OF RICHMOND	(320) 597-2145
ROSEAU	CITIZENS ST BK	(218) 463-2135
ST CLOUD	STEARNS BK NA	(320) 253-6607
ST PAUL	AMERICAN BK	(651) 634-6402
THIEF RIVER FALL	NORTHERN ST BK	(218) 681-4020
UPSALA	STEARNS BK NA	(320) 573-2111
VICTORIA	VICTORIA ST BK	(952) 443-2491
VIRGINIA	QUEEN CITY FSB	(218) 741-2040
WACONIA	FIRST NB OF WACONIA	(952) 442-2265
WATKINS	FARMERS ST BK	(320) 764-2600
WOODBURY	FIRST NB OF HUDSON	(715) 386-5511
ZUMBROTA	BANK OF ZUMBROTA	(507) 732-7555

Weiss Safety Rating: B+

City	Name	Telephone
AITKIN	SECURITY ST BK	(218) 927-3765
ALEXANDRIA	FIRST ST BK ALEXANDRIA	(320) 763-7700
ALTURA	ALTURA ST BK	(507) 796-6761
BATTLE LAKE	FIRST NB OF BATTLE LAKE	(218) 864-5275
BAXTER	LAKEWOOD BK NA	(218) 829-8712
BUFFALO	OAKLEY NB OF BUFFALO	(763) 682-1142
CAMBRIDGE	PEOPLES BK OF COMMERCE	(763) 689-1212
CHASKA	FIRST NB OF CHASKA	(952) 448-2350
DEERWOOD	FIRST NB OF DEERWOOD	(218) 534-3111
E GRAND FORKS	COMMUNITY BK RED RIVER VLY	(218) 773-2451

City	Name	Telephone
EDINA	FIDELITY BK	(952) 831-6600
FAIRFAX	FIRST NB OF FAIRFAX	(507) 426-7242
GLENCOE	SECURITY B&TC OF GLENCOE	(320) 864-3171
GLENVILLE	CITIZENS ST BK OF GLENVILLE	(507) 448-3981
GRAND RAPIDS	GRAND RAPIDS ST BK	(218) 326-9414
HALLOCK	MARSHALL BK NA	(218) 843-3641
HENNING	FIRST NB OF HENNING	(218) 583-2933
LAKE CITY	LAKE CITY FS&LA	(651) 345-3373
LE CENTER	FIRST NB OF LE CENTER	(507) 357-2273
LEWISTON	SECURITY ST BK	(507) 523-2161
LITTLE FALLS	COMMUNITY FS&LA LITTLE FALLS	(320) 632-5461
LONG PRAIRIE	AMERICAN HERITAGE NB	(320) 732-6131
LUVERNE	FIRST FARMERS & MERCHANTS NB	(507) 283-4463
MARINE ON ST CRX	SECURITY ST BK OF MARINE	(651) 433-2424
MENAHGA	FIRST NB OF MENAHGA	(218) 564-4171
MONTEVIDEO	FIRST NB IN MONTEVIDEO	(320) 269-6454
MORA	PEOPLES NB	(320) 679-3100
N MANKATO	VALLEY BK	(507) 345-5043
NEW PRAGUE	STATE BK	(952) 758-4491
NEW ULM	VALLEY B&T	(507) 233-4700
NORWOOD YOUNG	STATE BK OF YOUNG AMERICA	(952) 467-2313
PEQUOT LAKES	LAKES ST BK	(218) 568-4473
PIERZ	FARMERS & MERCHANTS ST BK	(320) 468-6422
PINE CITY	FIRST NB OF PINE CITY	(320) 629-2561
RED LAKE FALLS	RED LAKE COUNTY ST BK	(218) 253-2143
RUSH CITY	FIRST ST BK RUSH CITY	(320) 358-4786
SAUK CENTRE	FIRST NB OF SAUK CENTRE	(320) 352-5211
SAUK CENTRE	FIRST ST BK	(320) 352-5771
ST CLAIR	ST CLAIR ST BK	(507) 245-3636
STAPLES	SECURITY ST BK OF STAPLES	(218) 894-2084
WABASHA	FIRST ST BK OF WABASHA	(651) 565-3331
WAITE PARK	PLAZA PARK ST BK	(320) 252-4200
WALKER	FIRST NB OF WALKER	(218) 547-1160
WARROAD	SECURITY ST BK OF WARROAD	(218) 386-1818
WINONA	WINONA NB	(507) 454-4320

Mississippi

City	Name	Telephone	City	Name	Telephone

Weiss Safety Rating: A+

City	Name	Telephone
BALDWYN	FARMERS & MERCHANTS BK	(662) 365-1200

Weiss Safety Rating: A

City	Name	Telephone
BATESVILLE	FIRST SECURITY BK	(662) 563-9311
FOREST	BANK OF FOREST	(601) 469-3663
GREENWOOD	BANK OF COMMERCE	(662) 453-4142
HOLLY SPRINGS	BANK OF HOLLY SPRINGS	(662) 252-2511
MERIDIAN	CITIZENS NB OF MERIDIAN	(601) 693-1331
NEW ALBANY	BANK OF NEW ALBANY	(662) 534-8171
NEWTON	NEWTON COUNTY BK	(601) 683-3101
WAYNESBORO	FIRST ST BK	(601) 735-3124

Weiss Safety Rating: A-

City	Name	Telephone
BAY SPRINGS	MAGNOLIA ST BK	(601) 764-2265
BELZONI	BANKPLUS	(601) 898-8300
IUKA	FIRST AMERICAN NB	(662) 423-3656
LAUREL	BANK OF JONES COUNTY	(601) 649-4700
MARKS	CITIZENS B&TC	(662) 326-8047
MCCOMB	FIRST BK	(601) 684-2231
MCCOMB	PIKE COUNTY NB	(601) 684-7575
NATCHEZ	UNITED MISSISSIPPI BK	(601) 445-7000
OXFORD	FIRST NB OF OXFORD	(662) 234-2821
WIGGINS	BANK OF WIGGINS	(601) 928-5233
WINONA	BANK OF WINONA	(662) 283-3231

Weiss Safety Rating: B+

City	Name	Telephone
BELZONI	GUARANTY B&TC	(662) 247-1454
CLARKSDALE	FIRST NB OF CLARKSDALE	(662) 627-3261
CRYSTAL SPRINGS	BANK OF THE SOUTH	(601) 892-3232
GULFPORT	HANCOCK BK	(228) 868-4000
KOSCIUSKO	MERCHANTS & FARMERS BK	(662) 289-5121
MERIDIAN	GREAT SOUTHERN NB	(601) 693-5141
MORTON	BANK OF MORTON	(601) 732-8944
PASCAGOULA	MERCHANTS & MARINE BK	(228) 762-3311
PONTOTOC	FIRST NB OF PONTOTOC	(662) 489-1631
RAYMOND	MERCHANTS & PLANTERS BK	(601) 857-8044
ROSEDALE	FIRST NB	(662) 759-3544
SENATOBIA	SENATOBIA BK	(662) 562-8201
STARKVILLE	NATIONAL BK OF COMMERCE	(662) 323-1341
TUPELO	BANCORPSOUTH BK	(662) 680-2000
TUPELO	PEOPLES B&TC	(662) 680-1001
WALNUT GROVE	BANK OF WALNUT GROVE	(601) 253-2411

Missouri

City	Name	Telephone	City	Name	Telephone
			MARSHALL	WOOD & HUSTON BK	(660) 886-6825
Weiss Safety Rating: A+			MARYVILLE	NODAWAY VALLEY BK	(660) 562-3232
CAMDENTON	FIRST NB	(573) 346-3311	MOBERLY	BANK OF CAIRO & MOBERLY	(660) 263-2280
LOUISIANA	MERCANTILE BK	(573) 754-6221	MONTROSE	MONTROSE SVG BK	(660) 693-4424
ST CHARLES	FIRST ST BK	(636) 940-5555	MT VERNON	FIRST NB OF MT VERNON	(417) 466-2163
			NAPOLEON	NAPOLEON BK	(816) 934-8231
Weiss Safety Rating: A			NEOSHO	COMMUNITY B&TC	(417) 451-1040
ADVANCE	BANK OF ADVANCE	(573) 722-3517	NORBORNE	HOME S&LA FA	(660) 593-3313
BETHANY	BTC BK	(660) 425-7285	PALMYRA	PALMYRA ST BK	(573) 769-2001
BOWLING GREEN	COMMUNITY ST BK	(573) 324-2233	PARIS	PARIS NB	(660) 327-4181
FAYETTE	COMMERCIAL TC OF FAYETTE	(660) 248-2222	PARKVILLE	PARK BK	(816) 741-0371
FREDERICKTOWN	NEW ERA BK	(573) 783-3336	REEDS SPRING	GREAT SOUTHERN BK	(417) 739-4818
GRAIN VALLEY	BANK OF GRAIN VALLEY	(816) 229-2000	ROLLA	CENTRAL FS&LA OF ROLLA	(573) 364-1024
LINN	LINN ST BK	(573) 897-2205	RUSSELLVILLE	COMMUNITY BK RUSSELLVILLE	(573) 782-4511
ODESSA	BANK OF ODESSA	(816) 633-5331	SALEM	BANK OF SALEM	(573) 729-3137
ST LOUIS	LINDELL B&TC	(314) 645-7700	SALEM	TOWN & COUNTRY BK	(573) 729-3155
WASHINGTON	BANK OF WASHINGTON	(636) 239-7831	SEDALIA	CENTRAL BK OF MISSOURI	(660) 827-5520
			SPRINGFIELD	METROPOLITAN NB	(417) 862-2022
Weiss Safety Rating: A-			ST ELIZABETH	BANK OF ST ELIZABETH	(573) 493-2313
ALTON	ALTON BK	(417) 778-7211	ST LOUIS	A.G. EDWARDS TRUST CO FSB	(314) 955-4200
CARROLLTON	CARROLL COUNTY TC CARROLLTON	(660) 542-2050	W PLAINS	WEST PLAINS S&LA	(417) 256-3042
CHARLESTON	CITIZENS BK	(573) 683-3373	W PLAINS	WEST PLAINS B&TC	(417) 256-2147
COLE CAMP	CITIZENS-FARMERS BK	(660) 668-4416	WARRENTON	MISSOURI BK	(636) 456-3441
EL DORADO	COMMUNITY BK OF EL DORADO	(417) 876-6811			
ELDON	CITIZENS BK OF ELDON	(573) 392-3381			
FORT †	ARMED FORCES BK NA	(913) 682-9090			
GLADSTONE	FIRST BK OF MISSOURI	(816) 436-1900			
GRANDIN	BANK OF GRANDIN	(573) 593-4211			
GREENVILLE	PEOPLES COMMUNITY BK	(573) 224-3267			
KANSAS CITY	BANK MIDWEST NA	(816) 471-9800			
KANSAS CITY	CENTRAL BK OF KANSAS CITY	(816) 483-1210			
KIMBERLING CITY	BANK OF KIMBERLING CITY	(417) 739-2201			
LA MONTE	LA MONTE COMMUNITY BK	(660) 347-5656			
LAMAR	LAMAR B&TC	(417) 682-3348			
MACON	MACON-ATLANTA STATE BANK	(660) 385-3161			
OAK GROVE	COMMERCIAL BK OF OAK GROVE	(816) 690-4416			
OLD MONROE	BANK OF OLD MONROE	(636) 665-5601			
SENATH	SENATH ST BK	(573) 738-2808			
STANBERRY	FARMERS ST BK STANBERRY	(660) 783-2820			
URBANA	BANK OF URBANA	(417) 993-4242			
VERSAILLES	BANK OF VERSAILLES	(573) 378-4626			
Weiss Safety Rating: B+					
BLOOMSDALE	BANK OF BLOOMSDALE	(573) 483-2515			
BROOKFIELD	BANK OF BROOKFIELD-PURDIN NA	(660) 258-3394			
CUBA	FIRST COMMUNITY NB CRAWFORD	(573) 885-3500			
DONIPHAN	PEOPLES COMMUNITY STATE BK	(573) 996-2114			
ELSBERRY	BANK OF LINCOLN CTY	(573) 898-5511			
FARMINGTON	FIRST ST COMMUNITY BK	(573) 756-4547			
FREEBURG	BANK OF FREEBURG	(573) 744-5231			
FULTON	UNITED SECURITY BK	(573) 592-0100			
GAINESVILLE	CENTURY BK OF THE OZARKS	(417) 679-3321			
GLADSTONE	NORTHLAND NB	(816) 436-3500			
HANNIBAL	HNB NB	(573) 221-0050			
HERMANN	BAY-HERMANN-BERGER BK	(573) 486-3134			
HILLSBORO	EAGLE B&TC OF MISSOURI	(636) 797-4040			
LAMAR	FIRST NB	(417) 682-6066			
LEBANON	CENTRAL BK	(417) 532-2151			
LEE'S SUMMIT	BANK OF LEE'S SUMMIT	(816) 524-1800			
LOHMAN	FARMERS BK	(573) 782-4431			

† Out-of-State Institution with branches in Missouri

Montana

City	Name	Telephone	City	Name	Telephone

Weiss Safety Rating: A+

City	Name	Telephone
LAUREL	YELLOWSTONE BK	(406) 628-7951

Weiss Safety Rating: A

City	Name	Telephone
CHOTEAU	CITIZENS ST BK OF CHOTEAU	(406) 466-5743
FAIRFIELD	FIRST NB OF FAIRFIELD	(406) 467-2531
KALISPELL	VALLEY BK OF KALISPELL	(406) 752-7123
MALTA	FIRST ST BK OF MALTA	(406) 654-2340

Weiss Safety Rating: A-

City	Name	Telephone
BIGFORK	FLATHEAD BK OF BIGFORK	(406) 837-1600
HELENA	AMERICAN FSB	(406) 442-3080
SHELBY	FIRST ST BK	(406) 434-5567

Weiss Safety Rating: B+

City	Name	Telephone
BOZEMAN	AMERICAN BK OF MT	(406) 587-1234
DEER LODGE	PIONEER FS&LA	(406) 846-2202
KALISPELL	GLACIER BK	(406) 756-4200
SIDNEY	1ST BK	(406) 433-3212

Nebraska

City	Name	Telephone	City	Name	Telephone

Weiss Safety Rating: A

City	Name	Telephone
BROKEN BOW	NEBRASKA ST B&TC	(308) 872-2466
LINCOLN	TIERONE BK	(402) 475-0521
MADISON	MADISON COUNTY BK	(402) 454-6511
PIERCE	MIDWEST BK NA	(402) 329-6221

Weiss Safety Rating: A-

City	Name	Telephone
ADAMS	ADAMS ST BK	(402) 988-2255
AINSWORTH	COMMERCIAL NB AINSWORTH	(402) 387-2381
AUBURN	AUBURN ST BK	(402) 274-4342
BRUNING	BRUNING ST BK	(402) 353-2555
CHAMBERS	CHAMBERS ST BK	(402) 482-5222
EWING	FARMERS ST BK	(402) 626-7272
FAIRBURY	FIRST NB OF FAIRBURY	(402) 729-3344
FALLS CITY	FIRST NB&TC	(402) 245-2491
FALLS CITY	RICHARDSON CTY B&TC	(402) 245-2486
LOUISVILLE	HOME ST BK	(402) 234-2155
MC COOK	MCCOOK NB	(308) 345-4055
OMAHA	OMAHA ST BK	(402) 333-9100
ORD	FIRST NB IN ORD	(308) 728-3201
RANDOLPH	FIRST ST BK	(402) 337-0323
RED CLOUD	PEOPLES WEBSTER COUNTY BK	(402) 746-2251
REPUBLICAN CITY	COMMERCIAL ST BK	(308) 799-2885
RIVERDALE	STATE BK OF RIVERDALE	(308) 893-2351
SEWARD	CATTLE NB&TC	(402) 643-3636
ST EDWARD	BANK OF ST EDWARD	(402) 678-2244
WAYNE	STATE NB&TC	(402) 375-1130

Weiss Safety Rating: B+

City	Name	Telephone
BLAIR	TWO RIVERS ST BK	(402) 426-9500
CHADRON	FIRST NB OF CHADRON	(308) 432-5552
COZAD	COZAD ST B&TC	(308) 784-2000
FRANKLIN	FRANKLIN ST BK	(308) 425-6225
GRAND ISLAND	FIVE POINTS BK	(308) 384-5350
IMPERIAL	FARMERS & MERCHANTS BK	(308) 882-4297
JOHNSON	FIRST NB OF JOHNSON	(402) 868-3785
LA VISTA	BANK OF NEBRASKA	(402) 331-8550
LINCOLN	CORNHUSKER BK	(402) 434-2265
LINCOLN	UNION B&TC	(402) 323-1828
MILFORD	FARMERS & MERCHANTS BK	(402) 761-7600
MINDEN	FIRST NB&TC OF MINDEN	(308) 832-2030
N BEND	PLATTE VALLEY BK	(402) 652-3221
NELSON	COMMERCIAL BK OF NELSON	(402) 225-3381
RAVENNA	TOWN & COUNTRY BK	(308) 452-3225
SEWARD	JONES NB&TC OF SEWARD	(402) 643-3602
SIDNEY	AMERICAN NB OF SIDNEY	(308) 254-5536
SIDNEY	WORLDS FOREMOST BK	(402) 323-4300
ST PAUL	CITIZENS B&TC IN ST PAUL	(308) 754-4426

Nevada

City	Name	Telephone	City	Name	Telephone
Weiss Safety Rating: A-					
ELY	FIRST NB OF ELY	(775) 289-4441			
LAS VEGAS	HOUSEHOLD BK SB NA	(831) 755-6551			
Weiss Safety Rating: B+					
CARSON CITY	EAGLEMARK SVGS BK	(775) 886-3000			
LAS VEGAS	USAA SAVINGS BANK	(702) 862-8891			

New Hampshire

City	Name	Telephone	City	Name	Telephone

Weiss Safety Rating: A

City	Name	Telephone
CLAREMONT	CLAREMONT SVGS BK	(603) 542-7711
NEWPORT	SUGAR RIVER SVGS BK	(603) 863-3000
ROCHESTER	PROFILE BK FSB	(603) 332-2610

Weiss Safety Rating: A-

City	Name	Telephone
MEREDITH	MEREDITH VILLAGE SVGS BK	(603) 279-7986
PORTSMOUTH	PISCATAQUA SVGS BK	(603) 436-5250

Weiss Safety Rating: B+

City	Name	Telephone
COLEBROOK	FIRST COLEBROOK BK	(603) 237-5551
LANCASTER	LANCASTER NB	(603) 788-4973
SALEM	SALEM CO-OP BK	(603) 898-2153

New Jersey

City	Name	Telephone	City	Name	Telephone

Weiss Safety Rating: A+

City	Name	Telephone
BOGOTA	BOGOTA SVG BK	(201) 489-3666
HOBOKEN	SUMITOMO TR & BKG CO USA	(201) 420-9470
NEW BRUNSWICK	BRUNSWICK B&TC	(732) 247-5800
PRINCETON	CUSTODIAL TRUST CO	(609) 951-2300
SHREWSBURY	SHREWSBURY ST BK	(732) 842-7700
TRENTON	ROMA BANK	(609) 599-9301

Weiss Safety Rating: A

City	Name	Telephone
ELIZABETH	UNION COUNTY SVGS BK	(908) 354-4600
ELMWOOD PARK	SPENCER SAVINGS BANK, SLA	(201) 703-3800
HACKENSACK	ORITANI SVG BK	(201) 343-3800
NEWARK	LUSITANIA SVGS BK FSB	(973) 344-5125
WOODBRIDGE	FIRST INVESTORS FSB	(732) 855-3033

Weiss Safety Rating: A-

City	Name	Telephone
BOUND BROOK	SOMERSET SVGS BK, SLA	(732) 560-1700
CAPE MAY	CAPE SVGS BK	(609) 465-5600
FAIR LAWN	COLUMBIA BK	(201) 796-3600
JERSEY CITY	PROVIDENT BK	(201) 333-1000
PITTSBURGH, PA †	MELLON BK NA	(412) 234-5000
RAHWAY	RAHWAY SVGS INST	(732) 388-1800
VINELAND	MINOTOLA NB	(856) 696-8100
WALL	MANASQUAN SVG BK	(732) 223-4450
WOODBRIDGE	BESSEMER TC	(732) 694-5500

Weiss Safety Rating: B+

City	Name	Telephone
BRIDGETON	CENTURY SVG BK	(856) 451-3300
CLIFTON	CLIFTON SAVINGS BANK, SLA	(973) 473-2200
CRANBURY	FIRST CONSTITUTION BK	(609) 655-4500
ELMER	FIRST NB OF ELMER	(856) 358-8141
FREEHOLD	FREEHOLD S&LA	(732) 462-6700
GLADSTONE	PEAPACK-GLADSTONE BK	(908) 234-0700
HOBOKEN	HAVEN SB	(201) 659-3600
JERSEY CITY	MORGAN STANLEY TRUST	(201) 938-6000
KEARNY	KEARNY FSB	(201) 991-4100
MAYWOOD	COMMUNITY BK OF BERGEN CTY	(201) 587-1221
MILLVILLE	MILLVILLE S&LA	(856) 825-0809
NEWARK	PENN FSB	(973) 589-8616
NEWTON	NEWTON TRUST CO	(973) 383-2400
OLD BRIDGE	AMBOY NB	(732) 591-8700
PENNINGTON	MERRILL LYNCH TRUST COMPANY	(609) 274-2511
WOODBRIDGE	FIRST SVGS BK	(732) 726-9700

† Out-of-State Institution with branches in New Jersey

New Mexico

City	Name	Telephone	City	Name	Telephone

Weiss Safety Rating: A

City	Name	Telephone
ARTESIA	WESTERN BK	(505) 748-1345
CARLSBAD	WESTERN COMMERCE BK	(505) 887-6686

Weiss Safety Rating: A-

City	Name	Telephone
ALAMOGORDO	FIRST NB IN ALAMOGORDO	(505) 437-4880
CARLSBAD	CARLSBAD NB	(505) 234-2500
CLOVIS	CITIZENS BK	(505) 769-1911
RUIDOSO	FIRST NB-RUIDOSO	(505) 257-4033

Weiss Safety Rating: B+

City	Name	Telephone
FARMINGTON	CITIZENS BK	(505) 599-0100
LOS ALAMOS	LOS ALAMOS NB	(505) 662-5171
ROSWELL	BANK OF THE SOUTHWEST	(505) 625-1122
SANTA FE	FIRST NB OF SANTA FE	(505) 992-2000
TAOS	CENTINEL BK OF TAOS	(505) 758-6700
TUCUMCARI	CITIZENS BK	(505) 461-1261

New York

City	Name	Telephone	City	Name	Telephone
			NEW YORK CITY	RIDGEWOOD SVGS BK	(718) 240-4800
			RIVERHEAD	SUFFOLK CTY NB OF RIVERHEAD	(631) 727-2700
			SMITHTOWN	BANK OF SMITHTOWN	(631) 360-9300

Weiss Safety Rating: A+

City	Name	Telephone
HOBOKEN, NJ †	SUMITOMO TR & BKNG CO USA	(201) 420-9470
MASPETH	MASPETH FS&LA	(718) 335-1300
NEW YORK	MITSUBISHI TR & BKG CORP USA	(212) 891-8577
NEW YORK CITY	CHINATOWN FSB	(212) 334-9191

Weiss Safety Rating: A

City	Name	Telephone
AKRON	BANK OF AKRON	(716) 542-5401
COXSACKIE	NATIONAL BK OF COXSACKIE	(518) 731-6161
DRYDEN	FIRST NB OF DRYDEN	(607) 844-8141
MIDDLETOWN	ORANGE COUNTY TRUST CO	(845) 341-5000
MILLBROOK	BANK OF MILLBROOK	(845) 677-5321
NEW YORK	EASTBANK NA	(212) 219-9000
NEW YORK CITY	BROOKLYN FSB	(718) 855-8500
NEW YORK CITY	FOURTH FSB	(212) 288-2005
SYRACUSE	GEDDES FS&LA	(315) 468-6281
UTICA	SBU MUNICIPAL BK	(315) 823-0300
WALLKILL	WALLKILL VALLEY FS&LA	(845) 895-2051
WALTON	NATIONAL BK OF DELAWARE CNTY	(607) 865-4126

Weiss Safety Rating: A-

City	Name	Telephone
BRIDGEHAMPTON	BRIDGEHAMPTON NB	(631) 537-1000
FULTON	FULTON SVGS BK	(315) 592-4201
GOUVERNEUR	GOUVERNEUR S&LA	(315) 287-2600
GROTON	FIRST NB OF GROTON	(607) 898-5871
HUNTINGTON	FIRST NB OF LONG ISLAND	(631) 427-4143
MAMARONECK	SOUND FEDERAL SAVINGS	(914) 698-6400
MIDDLETOWN	FIRST FEDERAL SVGS	(845) 343-1401
MONTEBELLO	PROVIDENT BK	(845) 369-8040
MONTEBELLO	PROVIDENT MUNICIPAL BK	(845) 357-0444
NEW YORK	BANK OF TOKYO MITSUBISHI TC	(212) 782-4000
NEW YORK	BESSEMER TRUST CO NA	(212) 708-9100
NEW YORK	EMIGRANT SVG BK	(212) 850-4000
NEW YORK CITY	ABACUS FSB	(212) 285-4770
NEW YORK CITY	AMERASIA BK	(718) 463-3600
NEW YORK CITY	ASIA BK NA	(718) 961-9700
NEW YORK CITY	NATIONAL BK OF NEW YORK CITY	(718) 358-4400
NEW YORK CITY	NEW YORK COMMUNITY BK	(718) 460-4800
NEW YORK CITY	NORTHFIELD SVGS BK	(718) 448-1000
SARATOGA	ADIRONDACK TRUST CO	(518) 584-5844
UNION SPRINGS	CAYUGA LAKE NB	(315) 889-7358
YONKERS	HUDSON VALLEY BK	(914) 961-6100

Weiss Safety Rating: B+

City	Name	Telephone
ALDEN	ALDEN ST BK	(716) 937-3381
BROOKLYN	DIME SVGS BK OF WILLIAMSBURG	(718) 782-6200
CATSKILL	BANK OF GREENE COUNTY	(518) 943-2600
GLENS FALLS	GLENS FALLS NB&TC	(518) 793-4121
HOLLAND	BANK OF HOLLAND	(716) 537-2264
HUDSON	HUDSON RIVER B&TC	(518) 828-4600
JEFFERSONVILLE	FIRST NB OF JEFFERSONVILLE	(845) 482-4000
LOCKPORT	FIRST NIAGARA BANK	(716) 625-7600
NEW YORK	GREAT EASTERN BK	(212) 725-3800
NEW YORK	INTERVEST NB	(212) 218-8383
NEW YORK	SAFRA NB	(212) 704-5500
NEW YORK CITY	ATLANTIC LIBERTY SVGS FA	(718) 855-3555
NEW YORK CITY	ATLAS S&LA	(718) 768-4800
NEW YORK CITY	CARVER FSB	(212) 876-4747
NEW YORK CITY	FLUSHING SVGS BK FSB	(718) 961-5400

† Out-of-State Institution with branches in New York

North Carolina

City	Name	Telephone	City	Name	Telephone

Weiss Safety Rating: A+

City	Name	Telephone
LEXINGTON	INDUSTRIAL FSB	(336) 243-2766

Weiss Safety Rating: A

City	Name	Telephone
BURLINGTON	FIRST ST BK	(336) 227-8861
LINCOLNTON	FIRST FSB OF LINCOLNTON	(704) 735-0416
MOYOCK	BANK OF CURRITUCK	(252) 435-6331
SHELBY	FIRST NB OF SHELBY	(704) 484-6200
WINSTON-SALEM	PIEDMONT FS&LA	(336) 770-1000

Weiss Safety Rating: A-

City	Name	Telephone
CLYDE	HOMETRUST BANK	(828) 259-3939
DANVILLE, VA †	AMERICAN NB&TC	(434) 792-5111
GRANITE FALLS	BANK OF GRANITE	(828) 496-2000
HIGH POINT	HIGH POINT B&TC	(336) 881-3300
PEMBROKE	LUMBEE GUARANTY BK	(910) 521-9707
ROXBORO	ROXBORO SVGS BK	(336) 599-2137

Weiss Safety Rating: B+

City	Name	Telephone
ASHEVILLE	ASHEVILLE SVG BK SSB	(828) 254-7411
CHERRYVILLE	CHERRYVILLE FS&LA	(704) 435-3737
ELKIN	YADKIN VALLEY B&TC	(336) 526-6300
FUQUAY-VARINA	FIDELITY BK	(919) 552-2242
GASTONIA	CITIZENS SOUTH BANK	(704) 868-5200
GRANITE QUARRY	FARMERS & MERCHANTS BK	(704) 279-7291
LEXINGTON	LEXINGTON ST BK	(336) 248-6500
MORGANTON	MORGANTON FS&LA	(828) 437-1426
SYLVA	JACKSON SVG BK SSB	(828) 586-2451
TROY	FIRST BK	(910) 576-6171
WAKE FOREST	WAKE FOREST FS&LA	(919) 556-5146
WASHINGTON	FIRST SOUTH BK	(252) 946-4178
WILMINGTON, DE †	FIRST UNION HOME EQ BK NA	(302) 888-7548

† Out-of-State Institution with branches in North Carolina

North Dakota

City	Name	Telephone	City	Name	Telephone

Weiss Safety Rating: A

City	Name	Telephone
FARGO	GATE CITY BK	(701) 293-2400
FORMAN	SARGENT COUNTY BK	(701) 724-3216
STANLEY	SCANDIA AMERICAN B&TC	(701) 628-3131

Weiss Safety Rating: A-

City	Name	Telephone
ENDERLIN	CITIZENS ST BK	(701) 437-2100
LANGDON	FARMERS & MERCHANTS ST BK	(701) 256-5431
NEW TOWN	LAKESIDE ST BK	(701) 627-4717
POWERS LAKE	LIBERTY ST BK	(701) 464-5421
TIOGA	BANK OF TIOGA	(701) 664-3388
WATFORD CITY	MCKENZIE COUNTY BK	(701) 444-6411

Weiss Safety Rating: B+

City		Name	Telephone
BEULAH		FIRST SECURITY BK WEST	(701) 873-4301
BISMARCK		STARION FINANCIAL	(701) 223-6050
COZAD, NE	†	COZAD ST B&TC	(308) 784-2000
GLEN ULLIN		BANK OF GLEN ULLIN	(701) 348-3613
MILNOR		FIRST NB	(701) 427-5212
PARSHALL		PEOPLES B&TC	(701) 862-3131

† Out-of-State Institution with branches in North Dakota

Ohio

City	Name	Telephone
EATON	EATON NB&TC	(937) 456-5544
GALION	FIRST FEDERAL BK OF OHIO	(419) 468-1518
GREENVILLE	GREENVILLE NB	(937) 548-1114
LORAIN	FIRST FS&LA OF LORAIN	(440) 282-6188
LORAIN	MAY NB OHIO	(440) 884-2108
MARIETTA	PEOPLES BK NA	(740) 373-3155
MASON	FDS BK	(513) 573-2265
MIDDLEFIELD	MIDDLEFIELD BKG CO	(440) 632-1666
MILFORD	SPIRIT OF AMERICA NB	(513) 576-5300
NEW BREMEN	FIRST NB IN NEW BREMEN	(419) 629-2761
REPUBLIC	REPUBLIC BKG CO	(419) 585-4111
ST PARIS	FIRST CENTRAL NB	(937) 663-4186
WOODSFIELD	CITIZENS NB OF WOODSFIELD	(740) 472-1696
WOOSTER	WAYNE COUNTY NB OF WOOSTER	(330) 264-1222

Weiss Safety Rating: A+

City	Name	Telephone
SPENCER	FARMERS SVG BK	(330) 648-2441
ST HENRY	ST HENRY BK	(419) 678-2358

Weiss Safety Rating: A

City	Name	Telephone
CIRCLEVILLE	SAVINGS BK	(740) 474-3191
COLDWATER	PEOPLES BK CO	(419) 678-2385
CUSTAR	CUSTAR ST BK	(419) 669-2801
DELAWARE	FIDELITY FS&LA	(740) 363-1284
DELTA	FIRST FS&LA	(419) 822-3131
GAHANNA	WORLD FINANCIAL NETWORK NB	(614) 729-4000
KENTON	HOME S&L COMPANY OF KENTON	(419) 673-1117
KINGSTON	KINGSTON NB	(740) 642-2191
LEBANON	FIRST NB	(513) 932-3221
MARION	FAHEY BKG CO	(740) 382-8231
MILFORD	FIRST CLERMONT BK	(513) 576-0600
READING	VALLEY CENTRAL SB	(513) 821-3335
TIFFIN	FIRST BK OF OH	(419) 448-9740
VAN WERT	VAN WERT FSB	(419) 238-9662
WILMINGTON	WILMINGTON SVGS BK	(937) 382-1659

Weiss Safety Rating: A-

City	Name	Telephone
CINCINNATI	NORTH SIDE B&TC	(513) 542-7800
COVINGTON	COVINGTON S&LA	(937) 473-2021
DEFIANCE	FIRST FEDERAL BK MIDWEST	(419) 782-5015
DESHLER	CORN CITY ST BK	(419) 278-0015
EDON	EDON ST BK CO	(419) 272-2521
ELYRIA	NORTHERN S&LC	(440) 323-7451
HAMLER	HAMLER ST BK	(419) 274-3955
HILLSBORO	NCB FSB	(937) 393-4246
KILLBUCK	KILLBUCK SVG BK CO	(330) 276-4881
MONTPELIER	NATIONAL BANK OF MONTPELIER	(419) 485-5521
NEWARK	FIRST FS&LA	(740) 345-3494
NILES	HOME FS&LA OF NILES	(330) 652-2539
OTTOVILLE	OTTOVILLE BK CO	(419) 453-3313
QUINCY	MIAMI VALLEY BK	(937) 843-4000
ST BERNARD	FIRST SAFETY BK	(513) 641-1765
STRASBURG	STRASBURG SVG	(330) 878-5555
TROY	PEOPLES SVGS BK OF TROY	(937) 339-5000
UPPER SANDUSKY	FIRST CITIZENS NB	(419) 294-2351
URBANA	PERPETUAL FSB	(937) 653-1700
VAN WERT	FIRST FS&LA OF VAN WERT	(419) 238-1463
W UNION	NATIONAL BK OF ADAMS COUNTY	(937) 544-2361
WELLSTON	FIRST NB OF WELLSTON	(740) 384-2146
WYOMING	SPRING VALLEY BANK	(513) 761-6688

Weiss Safety Rating: B+

City	Name	Telephone
ANDOVER	ANDOVER BK	(440) 293-7605
ATHENS	HOCKING VALLEY BK OF ATHENS	(740) 592-4441
BUCYRUS	PEOPLES S&LC	(419) 562-6896
CALDWELL	FARMERS & MERCHANTS BK	(740) 732-5621
CANFIELD	FARMERS NB OF CANFIELD	(330) 533-3341
CHEVIOT	CHEVIOT SAVINGS BANK	(513) 661-0457
CINCINNATI	UNION SAVINGS BANK	(513) 247-0300
CINCINNATI	WARSAW FS&LA	(513) 244-6900
CINCINNATI	FIFTH THIRD BK	(937) 227-6500
CORTLAND	CORTLAND SVG & BKG CO	(330) 637-8040
DENNISON	FIRST NB OF DENNISON	(740) 922-2532
DOVER	FIRST FEDERAL COMMUNITY BK	(330) 364-7777

Oklahoma

City	Name	Telephone

Weiss Safety Rating: A+

City	Name	Telephone
CHICKASHA	FIRST NB&TC CHICKASHA OK	(405) 222-2200
CLINTON	OKLAHOMA B&TC	(580) 323-2345

Weiss Safety Rating: A

City	Name	Telephone
ANADARKO	FIRST ST BK	(405) 247-2471
BROKEN ARROW	ARKANSAS VALLEY ST BK	(918) 251-9611
BROKEN BOW	AMERICAN ST BK	(580) 584-9135
CHECOTAH	PEOPLES NB OF CHECOTAH	(918) 473-2237
CLAREMORE	RCB BK	(918) 341-6150
FORT SILL	FORT SILL NB	(580) 357-9880
IDABEL	FIRST ST BK OF IDABEL	(580) 286-3357
LAWTON	CITY NB&TC OF LAWTON OK	(580) 355-3580
PERKINS	PAYNE COUNTY BK	(405) 547-2436
SALLISAW	NATIONAL BK OF SALLISAW	(918) 775-5501
TUTTLE	SOONER ST BK	(405) 381-2326
WESTVILLE	PEOPLES BK	(918) 723-5453
WOODWARD	STOCK EXCHANGE BK	(580) 256-3314

Weiss Safety Rating: A-

City	Name	Telephone
ADA	CITIZENS BK OF ADA	(580) 332-6100
ALVA	CENTRAL NB OF ALVA	(580) 327-1122
ARDMORE	CITIZENS B&TC OF ARDMORE	(580) 226-4610
ATOKA	AMERISTATE BK	(580) 889-3376
CHEYENNE	SECURITY ST BK	(580) 497-3354
CLEO SPRINGS	CLEO ST BK	(580) 438-2223
CRESCENT	FARMERS & MERCHANTS BK	(405) 969-2814
FAIRVIEW	FARMERS & MERCHANTS NB	(580) 227-3773
GUYMON	CITY NB&TC OF GUYMON	(580) 338-6561
MCALESTER	FIRST NB&TC OF MCALESTER	(918) 426-0211
MENO	MENO GUARANTY BK	(580) 776-2257
MIAMI	SECURITY B&TC	(918) 542-6661
NICOMA PARK	PARK ST BK	(405) 769-5611
OKARCHE	COMMUNITY NB	(405) 263-7491
OKARCHE	FIRST BK OF OKARCHE	(405) 263-7215
OKEMAH	OKEMAH NB	(918) 623-1211
OKMULGEE	FIRST NB&TC OF OKMULGEE	(918) 756-8440
PAULS VALLEY	PAULS VALLEY NB	(405) 238-9321
STILWELL	BANK OF COMMERCE	(918) 696-7745
TEXHOMA	FIRST NB OF TEXHOMA	(580) 423-7541
WALTERS	WALTERS B&TC	(580) 875-3396
WAURIKA	FIRST FARMERS NB OF WAURIKA	(580) 228-2326
WEATHERFORD	FIRST NB&TC-WEATHERFORD	(580) 772-5575
WILBURTON	LATIMER ST BK	(918) 465-2327
YUKON	F&M BK NA OK CITY OK	(405) 373-1900

Weiss Safety Rating: B+

City	Name	Telephone
ADA	FIRST NB&TC OF ADA	(580) 332-5132
ALTUS	FIRST NB OF ALTUS	(580) 482-7700
ANTLERS	FIRSTBANK	(580) 298-3368
BLACKWELL	HOME NB	(580) 363-0005
BROKEN BOW	FIRST BANK & TRUST	(580) 584-9123
CHANDLER	FIRST BK OF CHANDLER	(405) 258-1210
CUSHING	BANK OF CUSHING & TRUST CO	(918) 225-2010
DURANT	FIRST UNITED B&TC	(580) 924-2211
EDMOND	CITIZENS BK OF EDMOND	(405) 341-6650
ELK CITY	FIRST NB ELK CITY	(580) 225-2580
HENRYETTA	AMERICAN EXCHANGE BK	(918) 652-3321
HOOKER	FIRST NB OF HOOKER	(580) 652-2448

City	Name	Telephone
LAVERNE	BANK OF LAVERNE	(580) 921-3321
MEDFORD	GRANT COUNTY BK	(580) 395-3335
OKLAHOMA CITY	QUAIL CREEK BK NA	(405) 755-1000
OKLAHOMA CITY	UNION BK NA	(405) 782-4200
PONCA CITY	PIONEER B&T	(580) 762-5651
POTEAU	CENTRAL NB OF POTEAU	(918) 647-2233
SAPULPA	AMERICAN HERITAGE BK	(918) 224-3210
SHAWNEE	FIRST NB&TC	(405) 275-8830
THOMAS	FIRST NB OF THOMAS	(580) 661-3515
VINITA	OKLAHOMA ST BK	(918) 256-5585
WAGONER	FIRST B&TC	(918) 485-2173

Oregon

City	Name	Telephone	City	Name	Telephone
Weiss Safety Rating: A+					
SALEM	BANK OF SALEM	(503) 585-5290			
SALEM	PIONEER TR BK NA	(503) 363-3136			
SANDY	CLACKAMAS COUNTY BK	(503) 668-5501			
Weiss Safety Rating: A					
CORVALLIS	CITIZENS BK	(541) 752-5161			
FLORENCE	SIUSLAW VALLEY BK	(541) 997-3486			
MCMINNVILLE	FIRST FS&LA OF MCMINNVILLE	(503) 472-6171			
Weiss Safety Rating: A-					
MEDFORD	PEOPLES BK OF CMRC	(541) 776-5350			
SAN FRANCISCO, †	UNION BK OF CA NA	(800) 238-4486			
SEATTLE, WA †	CONTINENTAL SVG BK	(206) 623-3050			
Weiss Safety Rating: B+					
GRESHAM	MBANK	(503) 661-8688			
LAKE OSWEGO	WEST COAST BK	(541) 265-6666			
PORTLAND	AMERICAN PACIFIC BK	(503) 221-5801			

† Out-of-State Institution with branches in Oregon

Pennsylvania

City	Name	Telephone
RADNOR	HAVERFORD TC	(610) 995-8700
ROCHESTER	FARMERS BLDG & SVG BK	(724) 774-4970
SCOTTDALE	SCOTTDALE B&TC	(724) 887-8330
SHIPPENSBURG	ORRSTOWN BK	(717) 532-6114
STRASBURG	BANK OF LANCASTER CTY NA	(717) 581-6010
STROUDSBURG	POCONO CMNTY BK	(570) 424-9700
WAYNESBURG	FIRST FS&LA OF GREENE CTY	(724) 627-6116
WELLSBORO	CITIZENS & NORTHERN BK	(570) 724-3411

Weiss Safety Rating: A+

City	Name	Telephone
HATBORO	HATBORO FEDERAL SVGS FA	(215) 675-4000
NEFFS	NEFFS NB	(610) 767-3875
NEWTOWN	FIRST NB&TC OF NEWTOWN	(215) 968-4203
SEWICKLEY	SEWICKLEY SVGS BK	(412) 741-5000
STATE COLLEGE	OMEGA BK NA	(814) 237-7641

Weiss Safety Rating: A

City	Name	Telephone
EPHRATA	EPHRATA NB	(717) 733-4181
ERIE	MARQUETTE SVGS BK	(814) 455-4481
GRATZ	GRATZ NB	(717) 365-3181
JERSEY SHORE	JERSEY SHORE ST BK	(570) 398-2213
LANDISBURG	BANK OF LANDISBURG	(717) 789-3213
MIFFLINTOWN	JUNIATA VALLEY BK	(717) 436-8211
MUNCY	MUNCY B&TC	(570) 546-2211
NEW TRIPOLI	NEW TRIPOLI NB	(610) 298-8811
PALMERTON	FIRST NB OF PALMERTON	(610) 826-2239
SMETHPORT	HAMLIN B&TC	(814) 887-5555
STRABANE	SLOVENIAN S&LA OF CANONSBURG	(724) 745-5000

Weiss Safety Rating: A-

City	Name	Telephone
ALBION	COMMUNITY NB OF NW PA	(814) 756-4138
APOLLO	APOLLO TRUST CO	(724) 478-3151
BALTIMORE, MD †	MERCANTILE SAFE DEPOSIT & TC	(410) 237-5900
CAMP HILL	ATLANTIC CENTRAL BANKERS BK	(717) 737-9335
COUDERSPORT	CITIZENS TRUST CO	(814) 274-9150
E PROSPECT	EAST PROSPECT ST BK	(717) 252-1511
HALIFAX	HALIFAX NB	(717) 896-3433
HALLSTEAD	PEOPLES NB	(570) 879-2175
HONESDALE	WAYNE BK	(570) 253-1455
IRWIN	IRWIN B&TC	(724) 863-3100
LATROBE	WESTMORELAND FS&LA	(724) 539-9755
LATROBE	COMMERCIAL BK OF PA	(724) 539-3501
LEVITTOWN	WILLIAM PENN S&LA	(215) 945-1200
MALVERN	NATIONAL BK OF MALVERN	(610) 647-0100
MERCERSBURG	FIRST NB OF MERCERSBURG	(717) 328-3121
NARBERTH	ROYAL BK AMERICA	(610) 668-4700
NEWPORT	FIRST NB OF NEWPORT	(717) 567-3414
OLD FORGE	OLD FORGE BK	(570) 457-8345
PHILADELPHIA	UNITED SVG BK	(215) 467-4300
PITTSBURGH	EUREKA BK	(412) 681-8400
PITTSBURGH	ALLEGHENY VALLEY BK	(412) 781-0318
PITTSBURGH	MELLON BK NA	(412) 234-5000
SOUDERTON	UNIVEST NB&TC	(215) 721-2400
TURBOTVILLE	TURBOTVILLE NB	(570) 649-5118

Weiss Safety Rating: B+

City	Name	Telephone
BERWICK	FIRST NB OF BERWICK	(570) 752-3671
BETHLEHEM	KEYSTONE NAZARETH B&TC	(610) 861-5000
BLUE BALL	BLUE BALL NB	(717) 354-4541
GREENCASTLE	FIRST NB OF GREENCASTLE	(717) 597-2137
KITTANNING	MERCHANTS NB KITTANNING	(724) 543-1125
LEBANON	LEBANON VALLEY FARMERS BK	(717) 274-6800
LEWISTOWN	MIFFLIN CNTY SB	(717) 248-5445
LIVERPOOL	FIRST NB OF LIVERPOOL	(717) 444-3714
MARYSVILLE	FIRST NB OF MARYSVILLE	(717) 957-2196
MIFFLINBURG	MIFFLINBURG B&TC	(570) 966-1041
PERKASIE	FIRST SVG BK PERKASIE	(215) 257-5035
PITTSBURGH	MT. TROY BANK	(412) 322-6107

† Out-of-State Institution with branches in Pennsylvania

Rhode Island

City	Name	Telephone	City	Name	Telephone
Weiss Safety Rating: A					
CRANSTON	DOMESTIC BK	(401) 943-1600			
W WARWICK	CENTREVILLE SVGS BK	(401) 821-9100			

South Carolina

City	Name	Telephone	City	Name	Telephone

Weiss Safety Rating: A+

City	Name	Telephone
EHRHARDT	ENTERPRISE BK S CAROLINA	(803) 267-3191
GAFFNEY	FIRST PIEDMONT FS&LA GAFFNEY	(864) 489-6046
YORK	BANK OF YORK	(803) 684-4249

Weiss Safety Rating: A

City	Name	Telephone
CHESTER	SPRATT S&LA	(803) 385-5102
FORT SILL, OK	† FORT SILL NB	(580) 357-9880
HAMPTON	PALMETTO ST BK	(803) 943-2671
HOLLY HILL	FARMERS & MERCHANTS BK OF SC	(803) 496-1440
HOLLY HILL	FIRST NB OF SC	(803) 496-5011
HONEA PATH	COMMERCIAL BK	(864) 369-7326
MANNING	BANK OF CLARENDON	(803) 435-4451

Weiss Safety Rating: A-

City	Name	Telephone
CHARLESTON	BANK OF SOUTH CAROLINA	(843) 724-1500
CONWAY	CONWAY NB	(843) 248-5721
GREENWOOD	COUNTYBANK	(864) 942-1500
KINGSTREE	WILLIAMSBURG FIRST NB	(843) 355-6101
SENECA	OCONEE FS&LA	(864) 882-2765
WALHALLA	BLUE RIDGE BK OF WALHALLA	(864) 638-5444

Weiss Safety Rating: B+

City	Name	Telephone
MT PLEASANT	SOUTHCOAST COMMUNITY BK	(843) 884-0504
NEWBERRY	NEWBERRY FSB	(803) 321-3200
ORANGEBURG	SOUTH CAROLINA B&T NA	(803) 534-2175
UNION	ARTHUR ST BK	(864) 427-1213
WOODRUFF	WOODRUFF FS&LA	(864) 476-8144

† Out-of-State Institution with branches in South Carolina

South Dakota

City	Name	Telephone	City	Name	Telephone

Weiss Safety Rating: A

City	Name	Telephone
BELLE FOURCHE	PIONEER B&TC	(605) 892-2536
BURKE	FIRST FIDELITY BK	(605) 775-2641
MILLER	FIRST ST BK MILLER	(605) 853-2473
PARKSTON	FARMERS ST BK	(605) 928-7991
PHILIP	FIRST NB IN PHILIP	(605) 859-2525
WAGNER	COMMERCIAL ST BK	(605) 384-3646

Weiss Safety Rating: A-

City	Name	Telephone
DAKOTA DUNES	SECURITY NB OF SD	(605) 232-6060
HERREID	CAMPBELL COUNTY BK	(605) 437-2294
SISSETON	ROBERTS CTY NB OF SISSETON	(605) 698-7621

Weiss Safety Rating: B+

City	Name	Telephone
CUSTER	FIRST WESTERN BK CUSTER	(605) 673-2215
IPSWICH	IPSWICH ST BK	(605) 426-6031
SIOUX FALLS	AXSYS NB	(605) 362-2380
SIOUX FALLS	RETAILERS NB	(605) 323-2000
STURGIS	FIRST WESTERN BK	(605) 347-2562
TYNDALL	SECURITY ST BK	(605) 589-3313
WALL	FIRST WESTERN BK WALL	(605) 279-2141

Tennessee

City	Name	Telephone	City	Name	Telephone
			WINCHESTER	CITIZENS COMMUNITY BK	(931) 967-3342

Weiss Safety Rating: A+

City	Name	Telephone
CARTHAGE	CITIZENS BK	(615) 735-1490
ELIZABETHTON	ELIZABETHTON FSB	(423) 543-5050
MC MINNVILLE	FIRST NB OF MCMINNVILLE	(931) 473-4402

Weiss Safety Rating: A

City	Name	Telephone
DICKSON	BANK OF DICKSON	(615) 446-3732
GLEASON	BANK OF GLEASON	(731) 648-5506
JAMESTOWN	UNION BK	(931) 879-8111
MARYVILLE	CITIZENS BK OF BLOUNT CTY	(865) 977-5900
MORRISTOWN	JEFFERSON FEDERAL BANK	(423) 586-8421
MOUNTAIN CITY	FARMERS ST BK	(423) 727-8121
NEWPORT	NEWPORT FS&LA	(423) 623-6088
RUTLEDGE	CITIZENS B&TC OF GRAINGER CTY	(865) 828-5237

Weiss Safety Rating: A-

City	Name	Telephone
CAMDEN	BANK OF CAMDEN	(731) 584-3678
CLEVELAND	BANK OF CLEVELAND	(423) 478-5656
ELIZABETHTON	SECURITY FSB	(423) 543-1000
ELIZABETHTON	CARTER COUNTY BK	(423) 543-2131
ELIZABETHTON	CITIZENS BK	(423) 543-2265
JELLICO	UNION BK	(423) 784-9446
KNOXVILLE	HOME FEDERAL BANK OF TN	(865) 546-0330
LA FOLLETTE	PEOPLES NB OF LA FOLLETTE	(423) 562-4921
LAFAYETTE	MACON B&TC	(615) 666-2121
LOBELVILLE	BANK OF PERRY CTY	(931) 593-2265
MEMPHIS	FINANCIAL FSB	(901) 756-2848
PIKEVILLE	FIRST NB OF PIKEVILLE	(423) 447-2931
PULASKI	FIRST NB OF PULASKI	(931) 363-2585
RIPLEY	BANK OF RIPLEY	(731) 635-1230
SEVIERVILLE	SEVIER COUNTY BK	(865) 453-6101
WAYNESBORO	BANK OF WAYNESBORO	(931) 722-2265

Weiss Safety Rating: B+

City	Name	Telephone
ATHENS	CITIZENS NB OF ATHENS	(423) 745-0261
BELLS	BANK OF CROCKETT	(731) 663-2031
BIRMINGHAM, AL †	AMSOUTH BK	(205) 326-5300
CROSSVILLE	HIGHLAND FS&LA	(931) 484-6178
DAYTON	COMMUNITY NB	(423) 570-0280
FRANKEWING	BANK OF FRANKEWING	(931) 363-1796
GATES	GATES BKG&TC	(731) 836-7741
HALLS	BANK OF HALLS	(731) 836-7515
HENDERSON	FIRST ST BK	(731) 989-2161
JACKSON	BANK OF JACKSON	(731) 660-8000
LAFAYETTE	CITIZENS BK OF LAFAYETTE	(615) 666-2195
LIBERTY	LIBERTY ST BK	(615) 536-5101
MANCHESTER	FIRST NB OF MANCHESTER	(931) 728-3518
MC KENZIE	MCKENZIE BKG CO	(731) 352-2262
MC MINNVILLE	SECURITY FSB OF MCMINNVILLE	(931) 473-4483
MILLINGTON	PATRIOT BK	(901) 872-2265
MOUNTAIN CITY	JOHNSON COUNTY BK	(423) 727-7701
MURFREESBORO	CAVALRY BANKING	(615) 893-1234
NEWBERN	SECURITY BK	(731) 287-4907
PARIS	SECURITY B&TC	(731) 642-6644
PORTLAND	VOLUNTEER ST BK	(615) 325-9257
SAVANNAH	CENTRAL BK	(731) 925-9046
SHELBYVILLE	FIRST CMNTY BK-BEDFORD CTY	(931) 684-5800
TUPELO, MS †	BANCORPSOUTH BK	(662) 680-2000
WAYNESBORO	WAYNE COUNTY BK	(931) 722-5438

† Out-of-State Institution with branches in Tennessee

Texas

City	Name	Telephone	City	Name	Telephone
			HENDERSON	HENDERSON FSB	(903) 657-2577
			HEREFORD	HEREFORD ST BK	(806) 364-3456

Weiss Safety Rating: A+

City	Name	Telephone
ALVIN	FIRST NB OF ALVIN	(281) 331-3151
BURNET	FIRST ST BK	(512) 756-2191
CORPUS CHRISTI	FIRST COMMERCE BK	(361) 850-6800
CORSICANA	CORSICANA NB&T	(903) 654-4500
PARIS	LIBERTY NB IN PARIS	(903) 785-7651
PEARLAND	PEARLAND ST BK	(281) 485-3211
TYLER	CITIZENS 1ST BANK	(903) 581-1900

Weiss Safety Rating: A

City	Name	Telephone
ALBANY	FIRST NB OF ALBANY	(325) 762-2221
BRADY	COMMERCIAL NB OF BRADY	(325) 597-2961
BROWNFIELD	FIRST NB OF BROWNFIELD	(806) 637-2531
BROWNWOOD	CITIZENS NB AT BROWNWOOD	(325) 643-3545
BRYAN	FIRST NB OF BRYAN	(979) 779-1111
CARTHAGE	FIRST ST B&TC	(903) 693-6606
COLUMBUS	FIRST ST BK	(979) 732-2332
COMANCHE	COMANCHE NB	(325) 356-2577
DALLAS	OAKS B&TC	(214) 361-7400
FARWELL	SECURITY ST BK	(806) 481-3327
FLOYDADA	FIRST NB OF FLOYDADA	(806) 983-3717
FORT SILL, OK	† FORT SILL NB	(580) 357-9880
HEBBRONVILLE	FIRST NB OF HEBBRONVILLE	(361) 527-3221
HILLSBORO	CITIZENS NB OF HILLSBORO	(254) 582-2531
KILLEEN	FIRST TEXAS BK	(254) 634-2132
LAMPASAS	FIRST TEXAS BK	(512) 556-3691
LIBERTY	FIRST LIBERTY NB	(936) 336-6471
LIVINGSTON	FIRST NB OF LIVINGSTON	(936) 327-1234
MESQUITE	FIRST ST BK	(972) 285-6311
MUENSTER	MUENSTER ST BK	(940) 759-2257
SAN ANGELO	SAN ANGELO NB	(325) 659-5900
SAN ANTONIO	BROADWAY NB	(210) 283-6500
SAN ANTONIO	EISENHOWER NB	(210) 227-7131
VERNON	WAGGONER NB OF VERNON	(940) 552-2511
WEATHERFORD	WEATHERFORD NB	(817) 598-2500

Weiss Safety Rating: A-

City	Name	Telephone
ABILENE	FIRST NB OF ABILENE	(325) 627-7000
AMARILLO	AMARILLO NB	(806) 378-8000
AMARILLO	FIRSTBANK SW NA	(806) 355-9661
ARP	ARP ST BK	(903) 859-2211
ASPERMONT	FIRST NB OF ASPERMONT	(940) 989-3505
BASTROP	FIRST NB OF BASTROP	(512) 321-2561
BEAUMONT	LAMAR BK	(409) 838-4781
BEDIAS	FIRST ST BK	(936) 395-2141
BELTON	FIRST TEXAS BK	(254) 939-3701
CLEBURNE	FIRST FINANCIAL BK NA	(817) 556-5000
CLUTE	FIRST ST BK	(979) 265-2511
COLORADO CITY	CITY NB OF COLORADO CITY	(325) 728-5221
CORRIGAN	CITIZENS ST BK	(936) 398-2566
DILLEY	DILLEY ST BK	(830) 965-1511
EASTLAND	EASTLAND NB	(254) 629-6100
FAIRFIELD	FIRST NB	(903) 389-4111
FALLS CITY	FALLS CITY NB	(830) 254-3573
FORT	† ARMED FORCES BK NA	(913) 682-9090
FORT WORTH	COLONIAL SVGS FA	(817) 390-2366
GEORGETOWN	FIRST TEXAS BK	(512) 863-2567
GROVETON	FIRST BK	(936) 642-1444
HEARNE	PLANTERS & MERCHANTS ST BK	(979) 279-3438

City	Name	Telephone
HUGHES SPRINGS	FIRST NB OF HUGHES SPRINGS	(903) 639-2521
JOHNSON CITY	JOHNSON CITY BK	(830) 868-7131
JUSTIN	JUSTIN ST BK	(940) 648-2753
LOCKHART	FIRST-LOCKHART NB	(512) 398-3416
LONGVIEW	TEXAS B&TC	(903) 237-5500
LUBBOCK	AMERICAN ST BK	(806) 767-7000
MERTZON	FIRST NB OF MERTZON	(325) 835-4321
MINERAL WELLS	CITY NB OF MINERAL WELLS	(940) 325-0761
MOODY	FIRST NB OF MOODY	(254) 853-2115
NORMANGEE	NORMANGEE ST BK	(936) 396-3611
ODESSA	WEST TX ST BK	(432) 337-2851
OZONA	CROCKETT NB	(325) 392-3745
PARIS	PEOPLES BK	(903) 783-3800
PERRYTON	PERRYTON NB	(806) 435-9641
QUITMAN	FIRST NB OF QUITMAN	(903) 763-2264
ROMA	CITIZENS ST BK	(956) 849-2311
ROUND ROCK	FIRST TEXAS BK	(512) 255-2501
SCHERTZ	SCHERTZ B&TC	(210) 945-7400
SEALY	CITIZENS ST BK	(979) 885-3571
SEVEN POINTS	CEDAR CREEK BK	(903) 432-3611
SOUTHLAKE	FIRST FINANCIAL BK NA	(817) 488-5544
STEPHENVILLE	STEPHENVILLE B&TC	(254) 965-5036
SWEETWATER	FIRST NB	(325) 235-6600
UVALDE	FIRST ST BK OF UVALDE	(830) 278-6231
VAN	FIRST ST BK	(903) 963-8651
WEIMAR	HILL B&TC	(979) 725-9575
WEST	WEST B&TC	(254) 826-5333
YOAKUM	FIRST ST BK	(361) 293-3572
YOAKUM	YOAKUM NB	(361) 293-5225
ZAPATA	INTERNATIONAL BK OF COMMERCE	(956) 765-8361

Weiss Safety Rating: B+

City	Name	Telephone
ATHENS	FIRST ST BK	(903) 675-5165
BANDERA	BANDERA BK	(830) 796-3711
BEEVILLE	STATE B&TC	(361) 358-8700
BELLVILLE	FIRST NB OF BELLVILLE	(979) 865-3181
BERTRAM	FARMERS ST BK	(512) 355-2121
BIG SPRING	STATE NB OF BIG SPRING	(432) 264-2100
BRENHAM	BANK OF BRENHAM NA	(979) 836-3332
BRENHAM	BRENHAM NB	(979) 836-4571
BROWNSVILLE	INTERNATIONAL BK/CMMRCE NA	(956) 547-1000
BURLESON	FIRST NB OF BURLESON	(817) 295-0461
BYERS	FIRST NB OF BYERS	(940) 529-6161
CAMERON	CITIZENS NB-MILAM CTY	(254) 697-6653
CARMINE	CARMINE ST BK	(979) 278-3244
CARTHAGE	PANOLA NB	(903) 693-2335
CHICO	FIRST ST BK OF CHICO	(940) 644-2218
COLUMBUS	COLUMBUS ST BK	(979) 732-5786
COTULLA	STOCKMENS NB IN COTULLA	(830) 879-2331
CROSBYTON	CITIZENS NB OF CROSBYTON	(806) 675-2376
CUERO	CUERO ST BK SSB	(361) 275-2345
DE KALB	STATE BK OF DE KALB	(903) 667-2553
DEL RIO	BANK & TRUST SSB	(830) 774-2555
EL PASO	BANK OF THE WEST	(915) 532-1000
ELGIN	ELGIN BK OF TEXAS	(512) 285-3311
FORT WORTH	SUMMIT BK NA	(817) 336-8383
FREEPORT	TEXAS GULF BK NA	(979) 233-4401
GAINESVILLE	FIRST ST BK	(940) 665-1711

† Out-of-State Institution with branches in Texas

Texas (Continued)

City	Name	Telephone	City	Name	Telephone

Weiss Safety Rating: B+ (Continued)

City	Name	Telephone
GAINESVILLE	GNB FINANCIAL NA	(940) 668-8531
GALVESTON	HOMETOWN BK NA	(409) 763-1271
GALVESTON	TEXAS FIRST BK	(409) 744-6353
GRANBURY	COMMUNITY BK	(817) 573-2265
GRUVER	GRUVER ST BK	(806) 733-5061
HALLETTSVILLE	PEOPLES ST BK	(361) 798-3237
HOUSTON	STERLING BK	(713) 466-8300
HOUSTON	WOODFOREST NB	(713) 455-7000
HULL	HULL ST BK	(936) 536-6726
HUNTSVILLE	FIRST NB OF HUNTSVILLE	(936) 295-5701
JOURDANTON	JOURDANTON ST BK	(830) 769-3557
KARNES CITY	KARNES CTY NB	(830) 780-3317
KLEIN	KLEIN BK	(281) 376-7160
LA GRANGE	NATIONAL B&T	(979) 968-3136
LAKE JACKSON	FIRST NB OF LAKE JACKSON	(979) 297-4012
LAREDO	COMMERCE BK	(956) 724-1616
LAREDO	INTERNATIONAL BK OF COMMERCE	(956) 722-7611
LIVINGSTON	FIRST ST BK	(936) 327-5211
LYTLE	LYTLE ST BK	(830) 709-3601
MARION	MARION ST BK	(830) 420-2331
MATADOR	FIRST ST BK OF MATADOR	(806) 347-2661
MCALLEN	TEXAS ST BK	(956) 631-5401
MEMPHIS	MEMPHIS ST BK	(806) 259-3561
MENARD	MENARD NB	(325) 396-4524
MT VERNON	FIRST NB OF MT VERNON	(903) 537-2201
MULESHOE	FIRST BK OF MULESHOE	(806) 272-4515
OZONA	OZONA NB	(325) 392-1300
PARIS	LAMAR NB	(903) 785-0701
PEARSALL	SECURITY ST BK	(830) 334-3606
PORT LAVACA	FIRST NB IN PORT LAVACA	(361) 552-6726
ROCKSPRINGS	PEOPLES ST BK	(830) 683-2119
ROUND TOP	ROUND TOP ST BK	(979) 249-3151
SACHSE	FIRST NB	(972) 530-7999
SAN ANGELO	TEXAS ST BK	(325) 949-3721
SAN ANTONIO	FROST NB	(210) 220-4011
SANTA FE	TEXAS FIRST BK	(409) 925-2582
SEADRIFT	SEAPORT BK	(361) 785-5321
SEGUIN	STATE B&T	(830) 379-5236
SEYMOUR	FIRST NB OF SEYMOUR	(940) 889-3113
SHINER	FIRST NB OF SHINER	(361) 594-3317
SONORA	FIRST NB OF SONORA	(325) 387-3861
SPEARMAN	FIRST ST BK	(806) 659-5565
STANTON	FIRST NB OF STANTON	(432) 756-3361
STERLING CITY	FIRST NB OF STERLING CITY	(325) 378-2191
SWEETWATER	TEXAS NB	(325) 235-4997
TAHOKA	FIRST NB OF TAHOKA	(806) 561-4511
TEXAS CITY	TEXAS FIRST BK	(409) 948-1990
TYLER	CITIZENS ST BK	(903) 849-3551
WHITNEY	FIRST NB IN WHITNEY	(254) 694-2209
WINNIE	GULF COAST BK	(409) 296-2111

Utah

City	Name	Telephone	City	Name	Telephone

Weiss Safety Rating: A+

City	Name	Telephone
SALT LAKE CITY	BRIGHTON BK	(801) 943-6500

Weiss Safety Rating: A

City	Name	Telephone
AMERICAN FORK	BANK OF AMERICAN FORK	(801) 756-7681
PHOENIX, AZ	† DIRECT MRCH CREDIT CRD BK NA	(480) 718-4600
SALT LAKE CITY	WRIGHT EXPRESS FIN SVCS CORP	(801) 270-8166
W VALLEY CITY	MORGAN STANLEY BK	(801) 902-4700

Weiss Safety Rating: A-

City	Name	Telephone
CEDAR CITY	STATE BK OF SOUTHERN UTAH	(435) 865-2300
DRAPER	ADVANTA BK CORP	(801) 523-0858
MORGAN CITY	FIRST NB OF MORGAN	(801) 829-3402
PROVO	FAR WEST BK	(801) 342-6000
SALINA	UTAH INDEPENDENT BK	(435) 529-7459
SALT LAKE CITY	GE CAPITAL FNCL	(801) 517-5000
ST GEORGE	HERITAGE BANK	(435) 628-0433

Weiss Safety Rating: B+

City	Name	Telephone
MIDVALE	ESCROW BK USA	(801) 304-2900
MIDVALE	GMAC COMMERCIAL MORTGAGE BK	(801) 567-2680
MURRAY	CHEVRON CREDIT BK NA	(801) 261-6730
SALT LAKE CITY	CIT BANK	(801) 947-7563
SALT LAKE CITY	VOLKSWAGEN BK USA	(801) 743-6315
SANDY	UTAH COMMUNITY BK	(801) 545-6000

† Out-of-State Institution with branches in Utah

Vermont

City	Name	Telephone	City	Name	Telephone

Weiss Safety Rating: A-

City	Name	Telephone
BURLINGTON	MERCHANTS BK	(802) 658-3400
MORRISVILLE	UNION BK	(802) 888-6600

Weiss Safety Rating: B+

City	Name	Telephone
ST ALBANS	PEOPLES TR CO OF ST ALBANS	(802) 524-2196

Virginia

City	Name	Telephone	City	Name	Telephone

Weiss Safety Rating: A+

City	Name	Telephone
ALEXANDRIA	BURKE & HERBERT B&TC	(703) 549-6600

Weiss Safety Rating: A

City	Name	Telephone
CHESAPEAKE	BANK OF HAMPTON ROADS	(757) 436-1000
DANVILLE	VIRGINIA B&TC	(434) 793-6411
PHENIX	BANK OF CHARLOTTE CTY	(434) 542-5111

Weiss Safety Rating: A-

City	Name	Telephone
DANVILLE	AMERICAN NB&TC	(434) 792-5111
FINCASTLE	BANK OF FINCASTLE	(540) 473-2761
FORT	† ARMED FORCES BK NA	(913) 682-9090
FREDERICKSBURG	NB OF FREDERICKSBURG	(540) 899-3200
GRUNDY	GRUNDY NB	(276) 935-8111
JONESVILLE	POWELL VALLEY NB	(276) 346-1414
MARSHALL	MARSHALL NB&TC	(540) 364-1555
MC KENNEY	BANK OF MCKENNEY	(804) 478-4434
MIDDLEBURG	MIDDLEBURG BK	(540) 687-4812
ONLEY	FARMERS & MERCHANTS BK	(757) 787-4111
WINDSOR	FARMERS BK	(757) 242-6111

Weiss Safety Rating: B+

City	Name	Telephone
ALEXANDRIA	TREASURY BK NA	(703) 518-6000
BERRYVILLE	BANK OF CLARKE CTY	(540) 955-2510
BLACKSBURG	NATIONAL BK OF BLACKSBURG	(540) 552-2011
BLUEFIELD	FIRST COMMUNITY BK NA	(276) 326-9000
GLEN ALLEN	FRANKLIN FS&LA OF RICHMOND	(804) 967-7000
HAMPTON	OLD POINT NB OF PHOEBUS	(757) 728-1200
KENBRIDGE	BENCHMARK COMMUNITY	(434) 676-9054
NEW CASTLE	FARMERS & MERCHANTS BK	(540) 864-5156
NORFOLK	HERITAGE B&TC	(757) 523-2656
PENNINGTON GAP	FARMERS & MINERS BK	(276) 546-4692
PENNINGTON GAP	LEE B&TC	(276) 546-2211
PETERSBURG	FIRST FSB OF VIRGINIA	(804) 732-2350
TAZEWELL	BANK OF TAZEWELL CTY	(276) 988-5566
VIRGINIA BEACH	BANK @LANTEC	(757) 671-7900

† Out-of-State Institution with branches in Virginia

Washington

City	Name	Telephone	City	Name	Telephone

Weiss Safety Rating: A+

City	Name	Telephone
BELLINGHAM	HORIZON BK	(360) 733-3050
SEATTLE	WASHINGTON FS&LA	(206) 624-7930
YAKIMA	YAKIMA FS&LA	(509) 248-2634

Weiss Safety Rating: A

City	Name	Telephone
OLYMPIA	OLYMPIA FS&LA	(360) 754-3400
PUYALLUP	VALLEY BK	(253) 848-2316

Weiss Safety Rating: A-

City	Name	Telephone
BURLINGTON	SKAGIT ST BK	(360) 755-0411
FRIDAY HARBOR	ISLANDERS BK	(360) 378-2265
HOQUIAM	TIMBERLAND BK	(360) 533-4747
LYNNWOOD	CITY BK	(425) 745-5933
RENTON	FIRST SVGS BK RENTON	(425) 255-4400
SAN FRANCISCO, †	UNION BK OF CA NA	(800) 238-4486
SEATTLE	HOMESTREET BK	(206) 623-3050
SEATTLE	SEATTLE SB	(206) 568-7800
SNOHOMISH	FIRST HERITAGE BK	(360) 568-0536

Weiss Safety Rating: B+

City	Name	Telephone
CAMAS	RIVERVIEW COMMUNITY BK	(360) 693-6650
ENUMCLAW	MOUNT RAINIER NB	(360) 825-0100
EVERETT	EVERTRUST BK	(425) 258-3645
LYNNWOOD	PHOENIX SVG BK	(425) 778-7988
MOUNTLAKE TER	GOLF SAVINGS BK	(425) 775-9968
PORT ORCHARD	KITSAP BK	(360) 876-7800
SEATTLE	NORTHWEST BUSINESS BK	(206) 676-8880
SEATTLE	VIKING COMMUNITY BK	(206) 784-2200
SPOKANE	WASHINGTON TRUST BK	(509) 353-2265
TACOMA	COLUMBIA ST BK	(253) 305-1900
VANCOUVER	FIRST INDEPENDENT BK	(360) 699-4242

† Out-of-State Institution with branches in Washington

West Virginia

City	Name	Telephone	City	Name	Telephone

Weiss Safety Rating: A

City	Name	Telephone
FRANKLIN	PENDLETON COUNTY BK	(304) 358-2311
MULLENS	PEOPLES BK OF MULLENS	(304) 294-7115
WESTON	CITIZENS BK	(304) 269-2862

Weiss Safety Rating: A-

City	Name	Telephone
CHARLES TOWN	BANK OF CHARLES TOWN	(304) 725-8431
CHARLESTON	CITY NB OF WV	(304) 926-3301
ELKINS	DAVIS TRUST CO	(304) 636-0991
WILLIAMSON	FIRST NB OF WILLIAMSON	(304) 235-5300

Weiss Safety Rating: B+

City	Name	Telephone
BLUEFIELD, VA †	FIRST COMMUNITY BK	(276) 326-9000
BRUCETON MILLS	BRUCETON BK	(304) 379-2111
CHESTER	HANCOCK COUNTY SVGS BK FSB	(304) 387-1620
ELKINS	CITIZENS NB OF ELKINS	(304) 636-4095
ELKINS	MOUNTAIN VALLEY BK NA	(304) 637-2265
HUNTINGTON	HUNTINGTON FSB	(304) 528-6215
HURRICANE	PUTNAM COUNTY BK	(304) 562-9931
NAUGATUCK	BANK OF MINGO	(304) 235-6700
ROMNEY	BANK OF ROMNEY	(304) 822-3541
TERRA ALTA	TERRA ALTA BK	(304) 789-2436
UNION	BANK OF MONROE	(304) 772-3034
W UNION	FIRST NB IN WEST UNION	(304) 873-2401
WHEELING	WESBANCO BK	(304) 234-9000

† Out-of-State Institution with branches in West Virginia

Wisconsin

City	Name	Telephone

Weiss Safety Rating: A+

City	Name	Telephone
DURAND	SECURITY NB OF DURAND	(715) 672-4237
FOND DU LAC	NATIONAL EXCHANGE B&TC	(920) 921-7700
FORT ATKINSON	PREMIER BANK	(920) 563-6616
MEDFORD	TIME FSB	(715) 748-2231
OOSTBURG	OOSTBURG ST BK	(920) 564-2336
PALMYRA	PALMYRA ST BK	(262) 495-2101
PRAIRIE DU SAC	BANK OF PRAIRIE DU SAC	(608) 643-3393
SHELL LAKE	SHELL LAKE ST BK	(715) 468-7858
WHITEWATER	FIRST CITIZENS ST BK	(262) 473-2112

Weiss Safety Rating: A

City	Name	Telephone
ALMA	BANK OF ALMA	(608) 685-4461
BALDWIN	FIRST BK OF BALDWIN	(715) 684-3366
BROOKFIELD	GREAT MIDWEST BK, SSB	(262) 784-4400
FOND DU LAC	AMERICAN BK	(920) 922-9292
GRAND MARSH	GRAND MARSH ST BK	(608) 339-3351
HAYWARD	PEOPLES BK WI	(715) 634-2674
HILLSBORO	FARMERS ST BK HILLSBORO	(608) 489-2621
HUDSON	CITIZENS ST BK	(715) 386-9050
LA CROSSE	COULEE ST BK	(608) 784-9550
LA FARGE	LA FARGE ST BK	(608) 625-2480
LITTLE CHUTE	BLC COMMUNITY BK	(920) 788-4141
MADISON	BANKERS BK	(608) 833-5550
MARION	PREMIER COMMUNITY BK	(715) 754-2535
MARSHFIELD	MARSHFIELD SVGS BK	(715) 387-1122
OAK CREEK	TRI CITY NB	(414) 761-1610
OREGON	OREGON COMMUNITY B&TC	(608) 835-3168
SPARTA	UNION NB&TC	(608) 269-6737
SPRING VALLEY	BANK OF SPRING VALLEY	(715) 778-5537
SUN PRAIRIE	BANK OF SUN PRAIRIE	(608) 837-4511
WATERLOO	FARMERS & MERCHANTS ST	(920) 478-2181
WAUKESHA	WAUKESHA ST BK	(262) 549-8500
WISCONSIN	WOOD COUNTY NB	(715) 423-7600

Weiss Safety Rating: A-

City	Name	Telephone
BONDUEL	BONDUEL ST BK	(715) 758-2141
COLUMBUS	FARMERS & MERCHANTS UNION	(920) 623-4000
DE FOREST	DMB COMMUNITY BK	(608) 846-3711
LIVINGSTON	LIVINGSTON ST BK	(608) 943-6351
MARKESAN	MARKESAN ST BK	(920) 398-2358
MIDDLETON	MIDDLETON COMM BK	(608) 824-3200
MONONA	MONONA STATE BK	(608) 223-3000
MUKWONAGO	CITIZENS BK	(262) 363-6500
PARK FALLS	FIRST NB OF PARK FALLS	(715) 762-2411
RIVER FALLS	RIVER FALLS ST BK	(715) 425-6782
SUPERIOR	NATIONAL BK OF COMMERCE	(715) 394-5531
SUPERIOR	SUPERIOR SVGS BK	(715) 394-7778
WAUMANDEE	WAUMANDEE ST BK	(608) 626-3131
WAUPACA	FARMERS ST BK OF WAUPACA	(715) 258-1400
WOODBURY, MN †	FIRST NB OF HUDSON	(715) 386-5511

Weiss Safety Rating: B+

City	Name	Telephone
ALMOND	PORTAGE COUNTY BK	(715) 366-4311
AMHERST	INTERNATIONAL BK OF AMHERST	(715) 824-3325
ASHLAND	NORTHERN ST BK	(715) 682-2772
BANGOR	FIRST NB OF BANGOR	(608) 486-2386
BERLIN	FARMERS & MERCHANTS BK	(920) 361-1454
BIRNAMWOOD	BANNER BANKS	(715) 449-2556

City	Name	Telephone
BLOOMER	PEOPLES ST BK OF BLOOMER	(715) 568-1100
BLOOMINGTON	WOODHOUSE & BARTLEY BK	(608) 994-2759
CHILTON	STATE BK OF CHILTON	(920) 849-9371
CHIPPEWA FALLS	NORTHWESTERN BK	(715) 723-4461
CLEVELAND	CLEVELAND ST BK	(920) 693-8256
CLINTONVILLE	DAIRYMANS ST BK	(715) 823-3131
CRIVITZ	BANK NORTH	(715) 854-2541
EAU CLAIRE	CHARTER BK EAU CLAIRE	(715) 832-4254
GREEN BAY	BAY BK	(920) 490-7600
GRESHAM	STATE BK	(715) 787-3201
HUSTISFORD	HUSTISFORD ST BK	(920) 349-3241
KENOSHA	SOUTHPORT BK	(262) 942-1111
MADISON	FPC FINANCIAL FSB	(608) 821-2000
MARATHON CITY	MARATHON ST BK	(715) 443-2229
MARINETTE	FARMERS & MERCHANTS B&TC	(715) 735-6617
MARKESAN	FARMERS ST BK	(920) 398-2336
MILWAUKEE	BANK MUTUAL	(414) 354-1500
MILWAUKEE	BAY VIEW FS&LA	(414) 744-1831
MILWAUKEE	GUARANTY BANK	(414) 362-4000
MILWAUKEE	UNIVERSAL SVGS BK FA	(414) 220-8800
MILWAUKEE	PARK BK	(414) 466-8000
NIAGARA	FIRST NB OF NIAGARA	(715) 251-3113
RICHLAND CENTER	RICHLAND COUNTY BK	(608) 647-6306
RIVER FALLS	FIRST NB OF RIVER FALLS	(715) 425-2401
SCHOFIELD	INTERCITY ST BK	(715) 359-4231
STARKVILLE, MS †	FIRST FB OF EAU CLAIRE, FSB	(662) 323-1341
STODDARD	RIVER BANK	(608) 457-2100
STRATFORD	STRATFORD ST BK	(715) 687-2411
VERONA	INDEPENDENT BK	(608) 845-6486
WAUPUN	NATIONAL BK OF WAUPUN	(920) 324-5551
WISCONSIN	RIVER CITIES BK	(715) 422-1100

†   Out-of-State Institution with branches in Wisconsin

Wyoming

City	Name	Telephone	City	Name	Telephone

Weiss Safety Rating: A

City	Name	Telephone
NEWCASTLE	FIRST ST BK OF NEWCASTLE	(307) 746-4411

Weiss Safety Rating: A-

City	Name	Telephone
JACKSON	BANK OF JACKSON HOLE	(307) 733-8064
PINEDALE	FIRST NB OF PINEDALE	(307) 367-4384
ROCK SPRINGS	ROCK SPRINGS NB	(307) 362-8801
SHERIDAN	FIRST FSB	(307) 672-0464

Weiss Safety Rating: B+

City	Name	Telephone
CASPER	HILLTOP NB	(307) 265-2740
DOUGLAS	CONVERSE COUNTY BK	(307) 358-5300
RAWLINS	RAWLINS NB	(307) 324-1100
ROCK SPRINGS	AMERICAN NB OF ROCK SPRINGS	(307) 362-1234

Section III

Rating Upgrades
and Downgrades

A list of all

U.S. Commercial Banks, Savings Banks,

and Savings and Loans

receiving a rating upgrade or downgrade
during the current quarter.

Section III Contents

This section identifies those institutions receiving a rating change since the previous edition of this publication, whether it be a rating upgrade, rating downgrade, newly-rated company or the withdrawal of a rating. A rating upgrade or downgrade may entail a change from one letter grade to another, or it may mean the addition or deletion of a plus or minus sign within the same letter grade previously assigned to the company. Ratings are normally updated once each quarter of the year. In some instances, however, an institution's rating may be downgraded outside of the normal updates due to overriding circumstances.

1. **Institution Name**   The name under which the institution was chartered. A company's name can be very similar to, or the same as, that of another, so verify the company's exact name, city, and state to make sure you are looking at the correct company.

2. **New Weiss Safety Rating**   The Weiss rating assigned to the institution at the time of publication. Our ratings are designed to distinguish levels of insolvency risk and are measured on a scale from A to F based upon a wide range of factors. Highly rated companies are, in our opinion, less likely to experience financial difficulties than lower rated firms. See *About the Weiss Safety Ratings* on page 7 for more information and a description of what each rating means.

3. **State**   The state in which the institution's headquarters or main office is located.

4. **Date of Change**   Date that rating was finalized.

New Ratings

BANK NAME	STATE	PREVIOUS WEISS SAFETY RATING	DATE OF CHANGE	BANK NAME	STATE	PREVIOUS WEISS SAFETY RATING	DATE OF CHANGE
Weiss Safety Rating:		**B**					
SYNOVUS BK OF JACKSONVILLE	FL		11/02/04				
Weiss Safety Rating:		**B-**					
1ST SECURITY BK OF WA	WA		11/02/04				
Weiss Safety Rating:		**C+**					
BEVERLY B&TC NA	IL		11/02/04				
Weiss Safety Rating:		**C**					
BANK OF LOUISA NA	VA		11/02/04				
COMMUNITY BK	MN		11/02/04				
Weiss Safety Rating:		**C-**					
GREENE COUNTY COMMERCIAL BK	NY		11/02/04				
Weiss Safety Rating:		**D**					
1ST ST BK	MI		11/02/04				
AMERICAN SECURITY B&TC	TN		11/02/04				
BEACH BUSINESS BK	CA		11/02/04				
BRICKWELL COMMUNITY BK	MN		11/02/04				
CAROLINA COMMERCE BK	NC		11/02/04				
CEDARSTONE BK	TN		11/02/04				
CENTURY BK	OR		11/02/04				
COMMUNITY BK OF GEORGIA	GA		11/02/04				
EMERALD BK	OH		11/02/04				
FIRST AMERICA BK	FL		11/02/04				
FIRST COMMUNITY BK	IL		11/02/04				
FIRST NB OF DECATUR COUNTY	GA		11/02/04				
FIRST NB OF FORSYTH COUNTY	GA		11/02/04				
GATEWAY BK OF PA	PA		11/02/04				
GREAT FLORIDA BK	FL		11/02/04				
MAINSTREET BK	VA		11/02/04				
MOUNTAIN 1ST B&T	NC		11/02/04				
MOUNTAIN VALLEY COMMUNITY BK	GA		11/02/04				
NEW HORIZONS BK	GA		11/02/04				
PINEHURST BK	MN		11/02/04				
RED MOUNTAIN BK NA	AL		11/02/04				
TOWNE BK OF AZ	AZ		11/02/04				
WASHINGTONFIRST BK	DC		11/02/04				

Rating Upgrades

BANK NAME	STATE	PREVIOUS WEISS SAFETY RATING	DATE OF CHANGE		BANK NAME	STATE	PREVIOUS WEISS SAFETY RATING	DATE OF CHANGE
Weiss Safety Rating: A+					FIRST NB IN FREDONIA	KS	A-	11/02/04
					FIRST NB OF BROWNFIELD	TX	A-	11/02/04
BANK OF PRAIRIE DU SAC	WI	A	11/02/04		FIRST NB OF BRYAN	TX	A-	11/02/04
BANK OF SALEM	OR	A	11/02/04		FIRST NB OF FT SMITH	AR	A-	11/02/04
BANK OF WILLITS	CA	A	11/02/04		FIRST NB OF HOWARD CTY	AR	A-	11/02/04
BRIGHTON BK	UT	A	11/02/04		FIRST ST BK	IA	A-	11/02/04
CHINATOWN FSB	NY	A	11/02/04		FIRST ST BK	OK	A-	11/02/04
CITIZENS BK OF FAYETTE	AL	A	11/02/04		FIRST ST BK	TX	A-	11/02/04
CITIZENS BK OF WINFIELD	AL	A	11/02/04		FIRST ST BK OF IDABEL	OK	A-	11/02/04
CLACKAMAS COUNTY BK	OR	A	11/02/04		FOXBORO FEDERAL SAVINGS	MA	A-	11/02/04
CORSICANA NB&T	TX	A	11/02/04		GATEWAY BUSINESS BK	CA	A-	11/02/04
CORUS BK NA	IL	A	11/02/04		GLENNVILLE BK	GA	A-	11/02/04
ELIZABETHTON FSB	TN	A	11/02/04		GREENSFORK TOWNSHIP ST BK	IN	A-	11/02/04
ENTERPRISE BK S CAROLINA	SC	A	11/02/04		GUARANTY B&TC-DELHI	LA	A-	11/02/04
FARMERS & DROVERS BK	KS	A	11/02/04		KINGSTON NB	OH	A-	11/02/04
FARMERS & MERCHANTS BK	MS	A	11/02/04		LUSITANIA SVGS BK FSB	NJ	A-	11/02/04
FARMERS BK	KY	A	11/02/04		MIDWEST BK NA	NE	A-	11/02/04
FIRST FS&LA OF EDWARDSVILLE	IL	A	11/02/04		MINDEN B&LA	LA	A-	11/02/04
FIRST NB&TC CHICKASHA OK	OK	A	11/02/04		NATIONAL BK OF SALLISAW	OK	A-	11/02/04
FIRST NB&TC OF NEWTOWN	PA	A	11/02/04		NEWTON COUNTY BK	MS	A-	11/02/04
FIRST SECURITY THRIFT CO	CA	A	11/02/04		OLYMPIA FS&LA	WA	A-	11/02/04
KEARNY COUNTY BK	KS	A	11/02/04		PAYNE COUNTY BK	OK	A-	11/02/04
LINCOLN NB OF HODGENVILLE	KY	A	11/02/04		PEACHTREE BANK	AL	A-	11/02/04
MUNICIPAL T&SB	IL	A	11/02/04		PEOPLES BK	OK	A-	11/02/04
NATIONAL EXCHANGE B&TC	WI	A	11/02/04		PEOPLES BK CO	OH	A-	11/02/04
NEEDHAM CO-OP BK	MA	A	11/02/04		PEOPLES BK OF GRACEVILLE	FL	A-	11/02/04
OOSTBURG ST BK	WI	A	11/02/04		PEOPLES BK WI	WI	A-	11/02/04
PEARLAND ST BK	TX	A	11/02/04		PEOPLES FSB	MA	A-	11/02/04
PHENIX-GIRARD BK	AL	A	11/02/04		POCAHONTAS ST BK	IA	A-	11/02/04
PREMIER BANK	WI	A	11/02/04		PREMIER COMMUNITY BK	WI	A-	11/02/04
ST HENRY BK	OH	A	11/02/04		REYNOLDS ST BK	IL	A-	11/02/04
SUMITOMO TR & BKG CO USA	NJ	A	11/02/04		RIVER CITY BK	KY	A-	11/02/04
TIME FSB	WI	A	11/02/04		SALYERSVILLE NB	KY	A-	11/02/04
YAKIMA FS&LA	WA	A	11/02/04		SAN ANGELO NB	TX	A-	11/02/04
					SILICON VALLEY BK	CA	A-	11/02/04
Weiss Safety Rating: A					SIUSLAW VALLEY BK	OR	A-	11/02/04
					SOONER ST BK	OK	A-	11/02/04
ALBANY B&TC NA	IL	A-	11/02/04		SOUTHEASTERN BK	GA	A-	11/02/04
AMERICAN BK	AL	A-	11/02/04		STOCK YARDS B&TC	KY	A-	11/02/04
AMERICAN ST BK	OK	A-	11/02/04		TIERONE BK	NE	A-	11/02/04
ANNA NB	IL	A-	11/02/04		TRANSCAPITAL BK	FL	A-	11/02/04
ARKANSAS VALLEY ST BK	OK	A-	11/02/04		WARREN B&TC	AR	A-	11/02/04
BANK OF CHARLOTTE CTY	VA	A-	11/02/04		WEST CENTRAL GEORGIA BK	GA	A-	11/02/04
BANK OF CURRITUCK	NC	A-	11/02/04					
BANK OF DELIGHT	AR	A-	11/02/04		**Weiss Safety Rating: A-**			
BANK OF HOLLY SPRINGS	MS	A-	11/02/04					
BANK OF RANTOUL	IL	A-	11/02/04		ADAMS ST BK	NE	B+	11/02/04
BANK OF SPRING VALLEY	WI	A-	11/02/04		AIR ACADEMY NB	CO	B+	11/02/04
BROADWAY NB	TX	A-	11/02/04		AMERICAN RIVER BK	CA	B+	11/02/04
BROOKLYN FSB	NY	A-	11/02/04		AMERIKA SAMOA BK	AS	B+	11/02/04
CENTER NB	MN	A-	11/02/04		ARMED FORCES BK NA	KS	B+	11/02/04
CENTRAL ST BK	AL	A-	11/02/04		ARMED FORCES BK OF CA NA	CA	B+	11/02/04
CHEROKEE ST BK	IA	A-	11/02/04		ARP ST BK	TX	B+	11/02/04
CITIZENS B&TC	AR	A-	11/02/04		ASIA BK NA	NY	B+	11/02/04
CITIZENS NB OF NASHVILLE	AR	A-	11/02/04		ATLANTIC CENTRAL BANKERS BK	PA	B+	11/02/04
CITIZENS ST BK	WI	A-	11/02/04		BANK CALUMET	IN	B+	11/02/04
COMMERCIAL BK	KS	A-	11/02/04		BANK MIDWEST NA	MO	B+	11/02/04
COULEE ST BK	WI	A-	11/02/04		BANK OF COLUMBIA	KY	B+	11/02/04
CROSS KEYS BK	LA	A-	11/02/04		BANK OF COMMERCE	OK	B+	11/02/04
DIRECT MRCH CREDIT CRD BK NA	AZ	A-	11/02/04		BANK OF JONES COUNTY	MS	B+	11/02/04
DOMESTIC BK	RI	A-	11/02/04		BANK OF KIMBERLING CITY	MO	B+	11/02/04
FAHEY BKG CO	OH	A-	11/02/04		BANK OF MAPLE PLAIN	MN	B+	11/02/04
FARMERS NB OF DANVILLE	KY	A-	11/02/04		BANK OF PRESCOTT	AR	B+	11/02/04
FARMERS NB PROPHETSTOWN	IL	A-	11/02/04		BANK OF TESCOTT	KS	B+	11/02/04
FARMERS ST BK	SD	A-	11/02/04		BANK OF THE OZARKS	AR	B+	11/02/04
FIRST COMMONWEALTH BK	KY	A-	11/02/04		BANK OF TIOGA	ND	B+	11/02/04
FIRST INVESTORS FSB	NJ	A-	11/02/04		BANK OF TOKYO MITSUBISHI TC	NY	B+	11/02/04
FIRST NB	AR	A-	11/02/04		BANK OF UPSON	GA	B+	11/02/04

Rating Upgrades (Continued)

BANK NAME	STATE	PREVIOUS WEISS SAFETY RATING	DATE OF CHANGE
Weiss Safety Rating: A- (Continued)			
BANK OF URBANA	MO	B+	11/02/04
BANK OF VERSAILLES	MO	B+	11/02/04
BANK OF WIGGINS	MS	B+	11/02/04
BANK OF WINONA	MS	B+	11/02/04
BANK OF ZUMBROTA	MN	B+	11/02/04
BANKERS BANK OF KY INC	KY	B+	11/02/04
BRIDGEHAMPTON NB	NY	B+	11/02/04
CALIFORNIA PACIFIC BK	CA	B+	11/02/04
CAMERON ST BK	LA	B+	11/02/04
CAMPBELL COUNTY BK	SD	B+	11/02/04
CAPE SVGS BK	NJ	B+	11/02/04
CARTER COUNTY BK	TN	B+	11/02/04
CATTLE NB&TC	NE	B+	11/02/04
CENTIER BK	IN	B+	11/02/04
CITIZENS B&TC OF ARDMORE	OK	B+	11/02/04
CITY BK	WA	B+	11/02/04
COLUMBIA BK	NJ	B+	11/02/04
COMMERCIAL NB AINSWORTH	NE	B+	11/02/04
COMMUNITY BK OF EL DORADO	MO	B+	11/02/04
COMMUNITY NB	OK	B+	11/02/04
COMMUNITY ST BK ST CHARLES	MI	B+	11/02/04
DE MOTTE STATE BANK	IN	B+	11/02/04
DMB COMMUNITY BK	WI	B+	11/02/04
EDMONTON ST BK	KY	B+	11/02/04
EVERETT CO-OP BK	MA	B+	11/02/04
EXCHANGE ST BK	IA	B+	11/02/04
FALLS CITY NB	TX	B+	11/02/04
FARMERS & MERCHANTS ST BK	IL	B+	11/02/04
FARMERS & MERCHANTS ST BK	ND	B+	11/02/04
FARMERS & MERCHANTS UNION	WI	B+	11/02/04
FARMERS NB OF SCOTTSVILLE	KY	B+	11/02/04
FARMERS ST BK	GA	B+	11/02/04
FIFTH DISTRICT S&LA	LA	B+	11/02/04
FIRST BK OF BERNE	IN	B+	11/02/04
FIRST BK OF OKARCHE	OK	B+	11/02/04
FIRST CITIZENS NB	IA	B+	11/02/04
FIRST CITIZENS NB	OH	B+	11/02/04
FIRST FARMERS NB OF WAURIKA	OK	B+	11/02/04
FIRST GUARANTY BK	KY	B+	11/02/04
FIRST HAWAIIAN BK	HI	B+	11/02/04
FIRST HERITAGE BK	WA	B+	11/02/04
FIRST METRO BK	AL	B+	11/02/04
FIRST NB OF ATMORE	AL	B+	11/02/04
FIRST NB OF BEARDSTOWN	IL	B+	11/02/04
FIRST NB OF GRAND RIDGE	IL	B+	11/02/04
FIRST NB OF HARTFORD	AL	B+	11/02/04
FIRST NB OF LA GRANGE	IL	B+	11/02/04
FIRST NB OF MERTZON	TX	B+	11/02/04
FIRST NB OF MOODY	TX	B+	11/02/04
FIRST NB OF PULASKI	TN	B+	11/02/04
FIRST NB OF QUITMAN	TX	B+	11/02/04
FIRST NB OF WELLSTON	OH	B+	11/02/04
FIRST NB&TC	IL	B+	11/02/04
FIRST ST BK	TX	B+	11/02/04
FIRST ST BK OF HEALY	KS	B+	11/02/04
FIRSTBANK LAKEVIEW	MI	B+	11/02/04
FIRSTBANK SW NA	TX	B+	11/02/04
GATEWAY ST BK	IA	B+	11/02/04
GE CAPITAL FNCL	UT	B+	11/02/04
GLOBAL COMMERCE BK	GA	B	11/02/04
GREEN BELT BANK & TRUST	IA	B+	11/02/04
HEARTLAND BK	IA	B+	11/02/04
HENDERSON FSB	TX	B+	11/02/04
HERITAGE BANK	UT	B	11/02/04
HILLSBORO BK	FL	B+	11/02/04

BANK NAME	STATE	PREVIOUS WEISS SAFETY RATING	DATE OF CHANGE
HOME ST BK	NE	B+	11/02/04
HOMESTREET BK	WA	B+	11/02/04
HYDE PARK SVGS BK	MA	B+	11/02/04
INTERNATIONAL BK CHICAGO	IL	B+	11/02/04
KLEIN NB OF MADISON	MN	B+	11/02/04
LAMAR BK	TX	B+	11/02/04
LAWRENCE SVG BK	MA	B+	11/02/04
LIBERTY ST BK	ND	B+	11/02/04
LOGAN COUNTY BK	AR	B+	11/02/04
LUTHER BURBANK SVGS	CA	B+	11/02/04
M C BANK & TRUST COMPANY	LA	B+	11/02/04
MBNA AMERICA DE NA	DE	B+	11/02/04
MCKENZIE COUNTY BK	ND	B+	11/02/04
MELLON TR OF NEW ENGLAND NA	MA	B+	11/02/04
MENO GUARANTY BK	OK	B+	11/02/04
MILLEDGEVILLE ST BK	IL	B+	11/02/04
NAPOLEON ST BK	IN	B+	11/02/04
NATIONAL BANK OF MONTPELIER	OH	B+	11/02/04
NETWORK BK	CA	B+	11/02/04
OLD FORGE BK	PA	B+	11/02/04
PACIFIC LIBERTY BK	CA	B+	11/02/04
PELHAM BKG CO	GA	B+	11/02/04
PEOPLES BK OF CMRC	OR	B+	11/02/04
PEOPLES COMMUNITY BK	MO	B+	11/02/04
PEOPLES FEDERAL SVGS BK	IN	B+	11/02/04
PEOPLES SVGS BK OF TROY	OH	B+	11/02/04
PIKE COUNTY NB	MS	B+	11/02/04
PREFERRED BK	MN	B+	11/02/04
PROVIDENT BK	NY	B+	11/02/04
PROVIDENT BK	NJ	B+	11/02/04
PROVIDENT MUNICIPAL BK	NY	B+	11/02/04
RIVER VALLEY FINANCIAL BK	IN	B+	11/02/04
RIVERSIDE NB OF FLORIDA	FL	B+	11/02/04
ROSE HILL BK	KS	B+	11/02/04
ROSSVILLE BK	GA	B+	11/02/04
ROYAL BK AMERICA	PA	B+	11/02/04
SECURITY B&TC	OK	B+	11/02/04
SENATH ST BK	MO	B+	11/02/04
SHELBY ST BK	MI	B+	11/02/04
SOLOMON ST BK	KS	B+	11/02/04
SOUTH GEORGIA BANKING CO	GA	B+	11/02/04
STRASBURG SVG	OH	B+	11/02/04
TEMPLETON SVG BK	IA	B+	11/02/04
TIMBERLAND BK	WA	B+	11/02/04
TOMPKINS ST BK	IL	B+	11/02/04
TRI-COUNTY B&TC	IA	B+	11/02/04
UNION BK	TN	B+	11/02/04
UNION BK OF CA NA	CA	B+	11/02/04
UTAH INDEPENDENT BK	UT	B+	11/02/04
VICTORIA ST BK	MN	B+	11/02/04
VINEYARD BK	CA	B+	11/02/04
WARREN BOYNTON ST BK	IL	B+	11/02/04
WEST B&TC	TX	B+	11/02/04
Weiss Safety Rating: B+			
1ST BK	MT	B	11/02/04
AMERICAN BK OF MT	MT	B	11/02/04
AMERICAN FOUNDERS BK INC	KY	B	11/02/04
AMERICAN PACIFIC BK	OR	B	11/02/04
ANDROSCOGGIN SVGS BK	ME	B	11/02/04
BANK & TRUST SSB	TX	B	11/02/04
BANK MUTUAL	WI	B	11/02/04
BANK OF BONIFAY	FL	B	11/02/04
BANK OF BRENHAM NA	TX	B	11/02/04
BANK OF CAIRO & MOBERLY	MO	B	11/02/04
BANK OF CLARKE CTY	VA	B	11/02/04
BANK OF GREELEY	KS	B	11/02/04

Rating Upgrades　　(Continued)

BANK NAME	STATE	PREVIOUS WEISS SAFETY RATING	DATE OF CHANGE
Weiss Safety Rating:	**B+**	**(Continued)**	
BANK OF GREENE COUNTY	NY	B	11/02/04
BANK OF LANCASTER CTY NA	PA	B	11/02/04
BANK OF MCCRORY	AR	B	11/02/04
BANK OF MORTON	MS	B	11/02/04
BANK OF RISON	AR	B	11/02/04
BANK OF SALEM	MO	B	11/02/04
BANK OF SMITHTOWN	NY	B	11/02/04
BANK OF THE SOUTHWEST	NM	B	11/02/04
BAY BK	WI	B	11/02/04
BAY-HERMANN-BERGER BK	MO	B	11/02/04
BRENHAM NB	TX	B	11/02/04
BROOKLINE CO-OP BK	MA	B	11/02/04
CENTENNIAL BK OF PUEBLO	CO	B	11/02/04
CENTER POINT B&TC	IA	B	11/02/04
CENTRAL BK OF MISSOURI	MO	B	11/02/04
CENTRAL ST BK	IA	B	11/02/04
CHINATRUST BK USA	CA	B	11/02/04
CITIZENS BK	IN	B	11/02/04
CITIZENS BK OF EDMOND	OK	B	11/02/04
CITIZENS NB OF ATHENS	TN	B	11/02/04
CITIZENS ST BK	IA	B	11/02/04
CITIZENS ST BK	TX	B	11/02/04
CITY BK	HI	B	11/02/04
COBIZ BK NA	CO	B	11/02/04
COMMERCIAL BK OF NELSON	NE	B	11/02/04
COMMUNITY B&TC	MO	B	11/02/04
COMMUNITY FS&LA LITTLE FALLS	MN	B-	11/02/04
COMMUNITY NB	CA	B	11/02/04
CORNHUSKER BK	NE	B	11/02/04
COUNTY BK	DE	B	11/02/04
DEARBORN SA	IN	B	11/02/04
EAGLE B&TC OF MISSOURI	MO	B	11/02/04
EAGLEMARK SVGS BK	NV	B	11/02/04
EATON NB&TC	OH	B	11/02/04
F & M B&TC	GA	B	11/02/04
FARMERS & MECHANICS BK	IL	B	11/02/04
FARMERS & TRADERS ST BK	IL	B	11/02/04
FARMERS B&TC	AR	B	11/02/04
FARMERS ST BK	GA	B	11/02/04
FDS BK	OH	B	11/02/04
FIDELITY BK	MN	B	11/02/04
FIRST BK OF SOUTH AR	AR	B	11/02/04
FIRST COMMUNITY BK	IL	B	11/02/04
FIRST COMMUNITY NB CRAWFORD	MO	B	11/02/04
FIRST FEDERAL SB CRESTON FSB	IA	B	11/02/04
FIRST FS&LA OF CULLMAN	AL	B	11/02/04
FIRST FSB OF VIRGINIA	VA	B	11/02/04
FIRST NB	MO	B	11/02/04
FIRST NB	TX	B	11/02/04
FIRST NB IN BELLEVILLE	KS	B	11/02/04
FIRST NB IN MONTEVIDEO	MN	B	11/02/04
FIRST NB OF BYERS	TX	B	11/02/04
FIRST NB OF CRESTVIEW	FL	B	11/02/04
FIRST NB OF DEERWOOD	MN	B	11/02/04
FIRST NB OF JOHNSON	NE	B	11/02/04
FIRST NB OF LIVERPOOL	PA	B	11/02/04
FIRST NB OF MT VERNON	MO	B	11/02/04
FIRST NB OF NORTH EAST	MD	B	11/02/04
FIRST NB OF SONORA	TX	B	11/02/04
FIRST NB&TC	OK	B	11/02/04
FIRST ROBINSON SB NA	IL	B	11/02/04
FIRST SECURITY B&TC	IA	B	11/02/04
FIRST ST BK	AR	B	11/02/04
FIRST ST BK	IA	B	11/02/04
FIRST ST BK	IA	B	11/02/04
FIRST ST BK ALEXANDRIA	MN	B	11/02/04
FIRST ST BK OF CHICO	TX	B	11/02/04
FIRST ST BK OF PORTER	IN	B	11/02/04
FIRST ST BK OF THE SOUTH	AL	B	11/02/04
FIRST ST BK-DECATUR	MI	B	11/02/04
FIRST UNITED B&TC	OK	B	11/02/04
FIVE STAR BK	CO	B	11/02/04
FPC FINANCIAL FSB	WI	B	11/02/04
FRANKLIN ST BK	NE	B	11/02/04
FREEDOM SECURITY BK	IA	B	11/02/04
FROST NB	TX	B	11/02/04
GLENS FALLS NB&TC	NY	B	11/02/04
GMAC BK	DE	B	11/02/04
GRANT COUNTY BK	OK	B	11/02/04
GREAT SOUTHERN BK	MO	B	11/02/04
GREAT SOUTHERN NB	MS	B	11/02/04
GREATER BAY BK NA	CA	B	11/02/04
GUARANTY BANK	WI	B	11/02/04
HAMPTON ST BK	IA	B	11/02/04
HAVERFORD TC	PA	B	11/02/04
HERITAGE B&TC	VA	B	11/02/04
HIAWATHA B&TC	IA	B	11/02/04
HOLCOMB ST BK	IL	B	11/02/04
HOME FEDERAL BK OF HOLLYWOOD	FL	B	11/02/04
HOME NB	OK	B-	11/02/04
HOPKINS FSB	MD	B	11/02/04
HUDSON RIVER B&TC	NY	B	11/02/04
INTERAMERICAN BK FSB	FL	B	11/02/04
INTERVEST NB	NY	B	11/02/04
INTRUST BK NA	KS	B	11/02/04
IOWA ST B&TC	IA	B	11/02/04
IOWA ST BK	IA	B	11/02/04
JACKSON SVG BK SSB	NC	B	11/02/04
JEFF DAVIS B&TC	LA	B	11/02/04
KARNES CTY NB	TX	B	11/02/04
KEY WEST BK	FL	B	11/02/04
KEYSTONE NAZARETH B&TC	PA	B	11/02/04
KLEIN BK	TX	B	11/02/04
LAKE CITY FS&LA	MN	B	11/02/04
LAKESIDE BK	IL	B	11/02/04
LIBERTY ST BK	TN	B	11/02/04
LOS ALAMOS NB	NM	B	11/02/04
MALVERN NB	AR	B	11/02/04
MARINE BK-SPRINGFIELD	IL	B	11/02/04
MBANK	OR	B	11/02/04
MCKENZIE BKG CO	TN	B	11/02/04
MERCHANTS & MARINE BK	MS	B-	11/02/04
METROPOLITAN NB	MO	B	11/02/04
MIDSTATE FS&LA	MD	B	11/02/04
MILLVILLE S&LA	NJ	B	11/02/04
MISSION OAKS NB	CA	B	11/02/04
MISSOURI BK	MO	B	11/02/04
MONTECITO B&T	CA	B	11/02/04
MORNINGSIDE B&TC	IA	B	11/02/04
NARA BK NA	CA	B	11/02/04
NATIONAL B&T	TX	B	11/02/04
NODAWAY VALLEY BK	MO	B	11/02/04
NORDSTROM FSB	AZ	B	11/02/04
NORTHSIDE CMNTY BK	IL	B	11/02/04
OAK VALLEY COMMUNITY BANK	CA	B	11/02/04
OKEY-VERNON FIRST NB	IA	B	11/02/04
OLD POINT NB OF PHOEBUS	VA	B	11/02/04
OPTIMUMBANK.COM	FL	B	11/02/04
OSWEGO COMMUNITY BK	IL	B	11/02/04
PAGE COUNTY ST BK	IA	B	11/02/04
PALMYRA ST BK	MO	B	11/02/04
PATRIOT BK	TN	B	11/02/04

Rating Upgrades (Continued)

BANK NAME	STATE	PREVIOUS WEISS SAFETY RATING	DATE OF CHANGE
Weiss Safety Rating: B+ (Continued)			
PEOPLES B&TC	KY	B	11/02/04
PEOPLES BK	AR	B	11/02/04
PEOPLES BK	KS	B	11/02/04
PEOPLES SVG BK	IA	B	11/02/04
PEOPLES T&SB	IA	B	11/02/04
PIONEER B&T	OK	B	11/02/04
POSTVILLE ST BK	IA	B	11/02/04
PUTNAM COUNTY BK	WV	B	11/02/04
QUAIL CREEK BK NA	OK	B	11/02/04
REPUBLIC BKG CO	OH	B	11/02/04
RIVER BANK	WI	B	11/02/04
ROLFE ST BK	IA	B	11/02/04
ROUND TOP ST BK	TX	B	11/02/04
SAFRA NB	NY	B	11/02/04
SCANDIA ST BK OF SCANDIA	KS	B	11/02/04
SCHUYLER ST BK	IL	B	11/02/04
SECURITY B&TC	TN	B	11/02/04
SECURITY BK	TN	B	11/02/04
SECURITY EXCHANGE BK	GA	B	11/02/04
SECURITY FSB OF MCMINNVILLE	TN	B	11/02/04
SECURITY ST BK	MN	B	11/02/04
SOMERSET NB	KY	B	11/02/04
SONOMA NB	CA	B	11/02/04
SOUTHERN HERITAGE BK	LA	B	11/02/04
SOUTHPORT BK	WI	B	11/02/04
STATE BK ILLINOIS	IL	B-	11/02/04
STATE BK OF BERN	KS	B	11/02/04
STEARNS BK ARIZONA NA	AZ	B	11/02/04
STERLING BK	TX	B	11/02/04
STRATFORD ST BK	WI	B	11/02/04
SUFFOLK CTY NB OF RIVERHEAD	NY	B	11/02/04
SUNTRUST BANCARD NA	FL	B	11/02/04
TEXAS NB	TX	B	11/02/04
TRI COUNTIES BK	CA	B	11/02/04
TURNBERRY BK	FL	B	11/02/04
TWO RIVERS ST BK	NE	B	11/02/04
UNION SAFE DEPOSIT BK	CA	B	11/02/04
UNION SAVINGS BANK	OH	B	11/02/04
USAA SAVINGS BANK	NV	B	11/02/04
VALLEY B&T	MN	B	11/02/04
VERUS BK NA	KS	B	11/02/04
VIKING COMMUNITY BK	WA	B	11/02/04
VILLAGE B&TC	IA	B	11/02/04
VILLAGE BK	MA	B	11/02/04
WALKER ST BK	IA	B	11/02/04
WARSAW FS&LA	OH	B	11/02/04
WAUKON ST BK	IA	B	11/02/04
WEST CHESTER SVG BK	IA	B	11/02/04
WEST COAST BK	OR	B	11/02/04
WILTON SVG BK	IA	B	11/02/04
WINDSOR FS&LA	CT	B	11/02/04
WINONA NB	MN	B	11/02/04
Weiss Safety Rating: B			
ACADEMY BK	TN	B-	11/02/04
ACCESS NB	VA	B-	11/02/04
AFFINITY BK	CA	B-	11/02/04
ALABAMA EXCHANGE BK	AL	B-	11/02/04
ALAMERICA BK	AL	B-	11/02/04
ALAMO BK OF TEXAS	TX	B-	11/02/04
ALLIANCE BK	MN	B-	11/02/04
AMERICAN BKG CO	GA	B-	11/02/04
AMERICAN INTERSTATE BK	NE	B-	11/02/04
AMERICAN INVESTMENT BK NA	UT	B-	11/02/04

BANK NAME	STATE	PREVIOUS WEISS SAFETY RATING	DATE OF CHANGE
AMERICAN NB-FOX CITIES	WI	B-	11/02/04
AMERICAN STERLING BK	MO	B-	11/02/04
AMERICAN SVG	MN	B-	11/02/04
ARCHER BK	IL	B-	11/02/04
ATHOL SVGS BK	MA	B-	11/02/04
AVON ST BK	MN	B-	11/02/04
BANK 21	MO	B-	11/02/04
BANK IOWA	IA	B-	11/02/04
BANK IOWA	IA	B-	11/02/04
BANK OF ASHEVILLE	NC	B-	11/02/04
BANK OF COMMERCE	NV	B-	11/02/04
BANK OF CROCKER	MO	B-	11/02/04
BANK OF DADEVILLE	AL	B-	11/02/04
BANK OF DEERFIELD	WI	B-	11/02/04
BANK OF ESSEX	VA	B-	11/02/04
BANK OF HARRISBURG	AR	B-	11/02/04
BANK OF MINDEN	MO	B-	11/02/04
BANK OF NAVASOTA NA	TX	B-	11/02/04
BANK OF NICHOLS HILLS	OK	B-	11/02/04
BANK OF RIDGEWAY	SC	B-	11/02/04
BANK OF SULLIVAN	MO	B-	11/02/04
BANK OF THE WEST	TX	B-	11/02/04
BANK OF TRUMANN	AR	B-	11/02/04
BANK OF UTAH	UT	B-	11/02/04
BANK OF WASHINGTON	WA	B-	11/02/04
BANKANNAPOLIS	MD	B-	11/02/04
BAY FINANCIAL SVGS BK FSB	FL	B-	11/02/04
BEVERLY CO-OP BK	MA	B-	11/02/04
BMW BK OF NORTH AMERICA	UT	C+	11/02/04
BREMER BK NA	MN	B-	11/02/04
BROADWAY BK	IL	B-	11/02/04
BRYANT ST BK	SD	B-	11/02/04
CALAIS FS&LA	ME	B-	11/02/04
CAPITAL ONE BK	VA	B-	11/02/04
CARROLLTON BK	IL	B-	11/02/04
CARSON NB OF AUBURN	NE	B-	11/02/04
CASEY ST BK	IL	B-	11/02/04
CENTRAL B&T	WY	B-	11/02/04
CENTRAL BK FULTON	IL	B-	11/02/04
CENTRAL BK IL	IL	B-	11/02/04
CENTRAL BK OF GEORGIA	GA	B-	11/02/04
CENTRAL VIRGINIA BK	VA	B-	11/02/04
CIRCLE BK	CA	B-	11/02/04
CITIBANK USA NA	SD	B-	11/02/04
CITIZENS B&TC	MO	B-	11/02/04
CITIZENS BK	GA	B-	11/02/04
CITIZENS BK	KY	B-	11/02/04
CITIZENS BK	TN	B-	11/02/04
CITIZENS BK OF FORSYTH CTY	GA	B-	11/02/04
CITIZENS BK OF NEVADA COUNTY	CA	B-	11/02/04
CITIZENS BK OF NEW HAVEN	MO	B-	11/02/04
CITIZENS NB	TX	B-	11/02/04
CITIZENS NB OF GR ST LOUIS	MO	B-	11/02/04
CITIZENS NB OF LEBANON	KY	B-	11/02/04
CITIZENS SAVINGS BANK	PA	B-	11/02/04
CITIZENS ST BK	KS	B-	11/02/04
CITIZENS ST BK	TX	B-	11/02/04
CITY AND SUBURBAN FSB	NY	B-	11/02/04
CLARKSTON ST BK	MI	B-	11/02/04
CLEBURNE COUNTY BK	AR	B-	11/02/04
COAST NB	CA	B-	11/02/04
COASTAL FEDERAL BANK	SC	B-	11/02/04
COCONUT GROVE BK	FL	B-	11/02/04
COLORADO ST BK	CO	B-	11/02/04
COLUMBIAN B&TC	KS	B-	11/02/04
COMMERCE NB	MS	B-	11/02/04
COMMERCIAL BK	NE	B-	11/02/04

Rating Upgrades (Continued)

BANK NAME	STATE	PREVIOUS WEISS SAFETY RATING	DATE OF CHANGE
Weiss Safety Rating: B (Continued)			
COMMUNITY B&TC	PA	B-	11/02/04
COMMUNITY B&TC-TROUP	GA	B-	11/02/04
COMMUNITY BANKS	PA	B-	11/02/04
COMMUNITY BK OF CENTRAL CALIF	CA	B-	11/02/04
COMMUNITY BK OF MARION CTY	FL	B-	11/02/04
COMMUNITY BK OF NAPLES NA	FL	B-	11/02/04
COMMUNITY ST BK NA	IA	B-	11/02/04
CONNECTICUT COMMUNITY BK NA	CT	C+	11/02/04
COOPERATIVE BK	NC	B-	11/02/04
COVINGTON COUNTY BK	MS	B-	11/02/04
CROGHAN COLONIAL BK	OH	B-	11/02/04
DESERT COMMUNITY BK	CA	B-	11/02/04
DEUEL COUNTY NB	SD	B-	11/02/04
DORAL BK FSB	NY	B-	11/02/04
DOUGLAS COUNTY BK	GA	B-	11/02/04
DRAYTON ST BK	ND	B-	11/02/04
DURDEN BKG CO	GA	B-	11/02/04
ELMIRA S&L FA	NY	B-	11/02/04
ENTERPRISE BK	TX	B-	11/02/04
EQUITABLE CO-OP BK	MA	B-	11/02/04
FALCON INTERNATIONAL BK	TX	B-	11/02/04
FARMERS & MERCHANTS BK	AL	B-	11/02/04
FARMERS & TRADERS BK CAMPTON	KY	B-	11/02/04
FARMERS BK & SVGS CO POMEROY	OH	B-	11/02/04
FARMERS ST BK	KY	B-	11/02/04
FARMERS STATE BK	OH	B-	11/02/04
FARMERS T&SB	IA	B-	11/02/04
FINANCE FACTORS	HI	B-	11/02/04
FIRST AMERICAN BK	AL	B-	11/02/04
FIRST AMERICAN BK SSB	TX	B-	11/02/04
FIRST BANKERS TC NA	IL	B-	11/02/04
FIRST BRANDON NB	VT	B-	11/02/04
FIRST BREMEN BK	OH	B-	11/02/04
FIRST CONSUMERS NB	OR	B-	11/02/04
FIRST FARMERS & MERCHANTS NB	TN	B-	11/02/04
FIRST FIDELITY BK NA	OK	B-	11/02/04
FIRST FS&LA	ID	B-	11/02/04
FIRST FS&LA	KS	B-	11/02/04
FIRST FS&LA OF PORT ANGELES	WA	B-	11/02/04
FIRST FS&LA OF WASHINGTON	IN	B-	11/02/04
FIRST FSB	IN	B-	11/02/04
FIRST FSB OF BOSTON	MA	B-	11/02/04
FIRST FSB OF LAKE COUNTY	FL	B-	11/02/04
FIRST GUARANTY BK	LA	B-	11/02/04
FIRST KENSINGTON BK	FL	B-	11/02/04
FIRST NB	SD	B-	11/02/04
FIRST NB	TX	B-	11/02/04
FIRST NB	TX	B-	11/02/04
FIRST NB IN BLYTHEVILLE	AR	B-	11/02/04
FIRST NB IN MANITOWOC	WI	B-	11/02/04
FIRST NB NORTHWEST FLORIDA	FL	B-	11/02/04
FIRST NB OF ARVADA	CO	B-	11/02/04
FIRST NB OF CENTRAL ALABAMA	AL	B-	11/02/04
FIRST NB OF CENTRALIA	KS	B-	11/02/04
FIRST NB OF CHRISMAN	IL	B-	11/02/04
FIRST NB OF DIETERICH	IL	B-	11/02/04
FIRST NB OF FLETCHER	OK	B-	11/02/04
FIRST NB OF HARTFORD	WI	B-	11/02/04
FIRST NB OF SANDOVAL	IL	B-	11/02/04
FIRST NB OF SYCAMORE	OH	B-	11/02/04
FIRST NB OF UNADILLA	NE	B-	11/02/04
FIRST NB OF VALENTINE	NE	B-	11/02/04
FIRST NB OF WYOMING	WY	B-	11/02/04
FIRST NB OF YUMA	CO	B-	11/02/04
FIRST NB TX	TX	B-	11/02/04

BANK NAME	STATE	PREVIOUS WEISS SAFETY RATING	DATE OF CHANGE
FIRST NB USA	LA	B-	11/02/04
FIRST NB&T OF FULLERTON	NE	B-	11/02/04
FIRST NB-CUMBERLANDS	TN	B-	11/02/04
FIRST PEOPLES BK	GA	B-	11/02/04
FIRST SECURITY BK	AR	B-	11/02/04
FIRST SECURITY BK	AR	B-	11/02/04
FIRST SECURITY BK CLARKSVILLE	AR	B-	11/02/04
FIRST SOURCE BK	IN	B-	11/02/04
FIRST ST BK	IA	B-	11/02/04
FIRST ST BK	MT	B-	11/02/04
FIRST ST BK	TX	B-	11/02/04
FIRST ST BK CLAREMONT	SD	B-	11/02/04
FIRST ST BK OF BIGGSVILLE	IL	B-	11/02/04
FIRST VOLUNTEER BK OF TN	TN	B-	11/02/04
FIRST, A NATL BANKING ASSN	MS	B-	11/02/04
FIRSTBANK ADAMS COUNTY	CO	B-	11/02/04
FIRSTBANK BRECKENRIDGE	CO	B-	11/02/04
FLORENCE NB	SC	B-	11/02/04
FNB SALEM B&T NA	VA	B-	11/02/04
FORT MADISON B&TC	IA	B-	11/02/04
FREEDOM BK	IN	B-	11/02/04
FREMONT INVESTMENT & LOAN	CA	B-	11/02/04
FRIENDSHIP ST BK	IN	B-	11/02/04
FULTON COUNTY NB&TC	PA	B-	11/02/04
GOLDEN BELT BK FSA	KS	B-	11/02/04
GOTHENBURG ST B&TC	NE	B-	11/02/04
GRABILL BK	IN	B-	11/02/04
GREAT PLAINS NB	OK	B-	11/02/04
GREATER ROME BK	GA	B-	11/02/04
GREENE COUNTY BK	TN	B-	11/02/04
GSL SAVINGS BANK	NJ	B-	11/02/04
HABERSHAM BK	GA	B-	11/02/04
HAMILTON FS&LA	MD	B-	11/02/04
HARRIS BK BARRINGTON NA	IL	B-	11/02/04
HERITAGE BK OF THE SOUTH	GA	B-	11/02/04
HERRIN SECURITY BK	IL	B-	11/02/04
HOME BK OF CA	CA	B-	11/02/04
HOME BUILDING SVGS BK FSB	IN	B-	11/02/04
HOME FS&LA OF COLLINSVILLE	IL	B-	11/02/04
HOME FS&LA OF GRAND ISLAND	NE	B-	11/02/04
HOME ST BK	CO	B-	11/02/04
HOMETOWN BK A CO-OP BK	MA	B-	11/02/04
HUMBOLDT BK	CA	B-	11/02/04
HYDEN CITIZENS BK	KY	B-	11/02/04
INDEPENDENT BANK WEST MI	MI	B-	11/02/04
INTER NATIONAL BANK	TX	B-	11/02/04
INTERNATIONAL BK OF MIAMI NA	FL	B-	11/02/04
IOWA ST BK	IA	B-	11/02/04
IPSWICH CO-OP BK	MA	B-	11/02/04
JACKSON COUNTY BK	WI	B-	11/02/04
KAISER FEDERAL BANK	CA	B-	11/02/04
LAKE AREA BK	MN	B-	11/02/04
LAKE COUNTY BK	MT	B-	11/02/04
LAMESA NB	TX	B-	11/02/04
LIBERTY FS&LA	MD	B-	11/02/04
LIBERTY NB	OH	B-	11/02/04
LIBERTY SVGS BK FSB	MN	B-	11/02/04
LINDEN ST BK	IN	B-	11/02/04
LOGAN B&TC	WV	B-	11/02/04
MADISON COUNTY COMMUNITY BK	FL	B-	11/02/04
MANSFIELD CO-OP BK	MA	B-	11/02/04
MASCOMA SVGS BK	NH	B-	11/02/04
MCINTOSH COUNTY BK	ND	B-	11/02/04
MEDIAPOLIS SVG BK	IA	B-	11/02/04
MERCHANTS BK NA	MN	B-	11/02/04
MERCHANTS BK NA	MN	B-	11/02/04
MERCHANTS BK NA	MN	B-	11/02/04

Rating Upgrades (Continued)

BANK NAME	STATE	PREVIOUS WEISS SAFETY RATING	DATE OF CHANGE	BANK NAME	STATE	PREVIOUS WEISS SAFETY RATING	DATE OF CHANGE
Weiss Safety Rating: B		**(Continued)**		STATE CENTRAL BK	IA	B-	11/02/04
				STATE FINANCIAL BK NA	WI	B-	11/02/04
				STATE GUARANTY BK	OK	B-	11/02/04
MERCHANTS BK NA	WI	B-	11/02/04	STUTSMAN COUNTY ST BK	ND	B-	11/02/04
MID CAROLINA BANK	NC	B-	11/02/04	SUMMIT NB	SC	B-	11/02/04
MID-WISCONSIN BK-MEDFORD	WI	B-	11/02/04	SUMMIT ST BK	CA	B-	11/02/04
MIDFIRST BK	OK	B-	11/02/04	SUMTER NB	SC	B-	11/02/04
MINERS & MERCHANTS BK	WV	B-	11/02/04	SUNSHINE STATE FS&LA	FL	B-	11/02/04
MORTON COMMUNITY BK	IL	B-	11/02/04	SYSTEMATIC S&LA	MO	B-	11/02/04
MOUNTAIN WEST BK	ID	B-	11/02/04	TECHE B&TC	LA	C+	11/02/04
NATIONAL BK OF COMMERCE	AL	B-	11/02/04	TENNESSEE ST BK	TN	B-	11/02/04
NATIONAL BK OF SC	SC	B-	11/02/04	TIB BANK OF THE KEYS	FL	B-	11/02/04
NESQUEHONING SVG BK	PA	B-	11/02/04	TOWN & COUNTRY BK OF QUINCY	IL	B-	11/02/04
NEVADA FIRST BK	NV	B-	11/02/04	TOWN CTR BK	OR	B-	11/02/04
NEW BUFFALO SVGS BK FSB	MI	B-	11/02/04	TRI-COUNTY NB	KY	B-	11/02/04
NEW MEXICO B&TC	NM	B-	11/02/04	UMPQUA BK	OR	B-	11/02/04
NEW MILLENNIUM BK	NJ	B-	11/02/04	UNICO BK	MO	B-	11/02/04
NORTH EASTON SVGS BK	MA	B-	11/02/04	UNION BK OF FLORIDA	FL	B-	11/02/04
NORTH GEORGIA NB	GA	B-	11/02/04	UNITED AMER BK NA	GA	B-	11/02/04
OLD LINE BK	MD	B-	11/02/04	UNITED BK OF UNION	MO	B-	11/02/04
OSAGE FEDERAL BK	OK	B-	11/02/04	VARTAN NB	PA	B-	11/02/04
PACIFIC GLOBAL BK	IL	B-	11/02/04	VINTAGE BK	CA	B-	11/02/04
PACIFIC ST BK	CA	B-	11/02/04	VINTON COUNTY NB OF MCARTHUR	OH	B-	11/02/04
PAN AMERICAN BK FSB	CA	B-	11/02/04	WADENA ST BK	MN	B-	11/02/04
PEOPLES BK	GA	B-	11/02/04	WASHINGTON FIRST INTL BK	WA	B-	11/02/04
PEOPLES BK	MO	B-	11/02/04	WASHINGTON MUTUAL BK FSB	UT	B-	11/02/04
PEOPLES BK	WA	B-	11/02/04	WASHITA VALLEY BK	OK	B-	11/02/04
PEOPLES BK OF NORTH ALABAMA	AL	B-	11/02/04	WAWEL SAVINGS BANK	NJ	B-	11/02/04
PEOPLES COMMUNITY BK	VA	B-	11/02/04	WEBB CITY BK	MO	B-	11/02/04
PEOPLES ST BK	WI	B-	11/02/04	WESTAMERICA BK	CA	B-	11/02/04
PEOPLES ST BK OF PLAINVIEW	MN	B-	11/02/04	WESTSTAR BK	CO	B-	11/02/04
PESHTIGO NB	WI	B-	11/02/04	WILLIAMSTOWN NB	WV	B-	11/02/04
PHILADELPHIA TRUST CO	PA	B-	11/02/04	WILMINGTON TRUST CO	DE	B-	11/02/04
PIONEER BK	IA	B-	11/02/04	WINCHESTER FSB	KY	B-	11/02/04
PIONEER BK	MN	B-	11/02/04	WINNSBORO ST B&TC	LA	B-	11/02/04
PLATTE VALLEY BK OF MO	MO	B-	11/02/04	WRAY ST BK	CO	B-	11/02/04
PRIMESOUTH BK	AL	B-	11/02/04				
PROGRESSIVE SVGS BANK FSB	TN	B-	11/02/04	**Weiss Safety Rating: B-**			
PROSPERITY B&TC	VA	B-	11/02/04				
PROSPERITY BK	TX	B-	11/02/04	21ST CENTURY BK	MN	C+	11/02/04
RAYNE ST B&TC	LA	B-	11/02/04	ADVANTA NB	DE	C	11/02/04
REDMOND NB	WA	B-	11/02/04	ALASKA PACIFIC BK	AK	C+	11/02/04
REPUBLIC BK	UT	B-	11/02/04	ALLIANCE BK	CA	C+	11/02/04
RIVER VALLEY ST BK	WI	B-	11/02/04	ALLIANCE BK	TX	C+	11/02/04
RIVOLI B&TC	GA	B-	11/02/04	ALLIANCE FSB	IL	C+	11/02/04
ROSELLE SB	NJ	B-	11/02/04	ALLIED FIRST BK SB	IL	C+	11/02/04
ROUNDBANK	MN	B-	11/02/04	ALPHA COMMUNITY BK	IL	C+	11/02/04
SAN LUIS TRUST BK FSB	CA	B-	11/02/04	ALPINE BK OF ILLINOIS	IL	C+	11/02/04
SCHUYLER SVG BK	NJ	B-	11/02/04	ALTAMAHA B&TC	GA	C+	11/02/04
SECOND B&T	VA	B-	11/02/04	AMERICA CALIFORNIA BK	CA	C+	11/02/04
SECURITY BK	OK	B-	11/02/04	AMERICAN EXCHANGE BK	NE	C+	11/02/04
SECURITY BK MN	MN	B-	11/02/04	AMERICAN FEDERAL BK	ND	C+	11/02/04
SECURITY ST BK	SD	B-	11/02/04	AMERICAN METRO BK	IL	C+	11/02/04
SEI PRIVATE TRUST COMPANY	PA	B-	11/02/04	AMERICAN NB	NE	C+	11/02/04
SOLANO BK	CA	B-	11/02/04	AMERICAN SVGS FSB	IN	C+	11/02/04
SOLVAY BK	NY	B-	11/02/04	AMFIRST BK NA	NE	C+	11/02/04
SOMERVILLE NB	OH	B-	11/02/04	ANCHOR MSB	WA	C+	11/02/04
SOUTH PADRE BK NA	TX	B-	11/02/04	ANTWERP EXCHANGE BK CO	OH	C+	11/02/04
SOUTH SOUND BK	WA	C+	11/02/04	ARKANSAS NB	AR	C+	11/02/04
SOUTHBRIDGE SVGS BK	MA	B-	11/02/04	ARMSTRONG BK	OK	C+	11/02/04
SOUTHEAST NB	IA	B-	11/02/04	AROOSTOOK COUNTY FS&LA	ME	C+	11/02/04
SOUTHERN HERITAGE BK	GA	B-	11/02/04	ASIAN PACIFIC NB	CA	C+	11/02/04
SOUTHSIDE BANK	TX	B-	11/02/04	AUSTIN BK OF CHICAGO	IL	C+	11/02/04
ST MARTIN B&TC	LA	B-	11/02/04	BANK OF ALBUQUERQUE NA	NM	C+	11/02/04
STATE BANK	CO	B-	11/02/04	BANK OF AR NA	AR	C+	11/02/04
STATE BANK - LA JUNTA	CO	B-	11/02/04	BANK OF CAMILLA	GA	C+	11/02/04
STATE BK OF OXFORD	IN	B-	11/02/04	BANK OF DARDANELLE	AR	C+	11/02/04
STATE BK OF PEARL CITY	IL	B-	11/02/04	BANK OF DELMARVA	DE	C+	11/02/04

Rating Upgrades   (Continued)

BANK NAME	STATE	PREVIOUS WEISS SAFETY RATING	DATE OF CHANGE	BANK NAME	STATE	PREVIOUS WEISS SAFETY RATING	DATE OF CHANGE
Weiss Safety Rating: B- (Continued)				COMMUNITY ST BK	IA	C+	11/02/04
				COMMUNITY STATE BK	SD	C+	11/02/04
BANK OF EASTON, A CO-OP BANK	MA	C+	11/02/04	CORNERSTONE BK	NJ	C+	11/02/04
BANK OF HAZELTON	ND	C+	11/02/04	CORTRUST BK NA	SD	C+	11/02/04
BANK OF HAZLEHURST	GA	C+	11/02/04	COVINGTON COUNTY BK	AL	C+	11/02/04
BANK OF IDAHO	ID	C+	11/02/04	COWLITZ BK	WA	C+	11/02/04
BANK OF LENAWEE	MI	C+	11/02/04	CRESCENT ST BK	NC	C+	11/02/04
BANK OF LINCOLN CITY	TN	C+	11/02/04	CROSS COUNTRY BK	DE	C+	11/02/04
BANK OF MAUSTON	WI	C	11/02/04	CROWELL ST BK	TX	C+	11/02/04
BANK OF MT HOPE	WV	C+	11/02/04	CSB BK	MO	C+	11/02/04
BANK OF NEWPORT	RI	C+	11/02/04	CUMBERLAND FEDERAL BK FSB	WI	C+	11/02/04
BANK OF ORCHARD	NE	C+	11/02/04	DALHART FS&LA	TX	C+	11/02/04
BANK OF RICHMONDVILLE	NY	C+	11/02/04	DECATUR FIRST BK	GA	C+	11/02/04
BANK OF VERDEN	OK	C+	11/02/04	DELTA SOUTHERN BANK	MS	C+	11/02/04
BANK OF VISALIA	CA	C+	11/02/04	DEVON BK	IL	C+	11/02/04
BANK OF WAUSAU	WI	C+	11/02/04	DIAMOND STATE BK	AR	C+	11/02/04
BANK ONE NA	IL	C+	11/02/04	DOOLIN SECURITY SVGS BK	WV	C+	11/02/04
BANK PLUS	IA	C+	11/02/04	DU QUOIN ST BK	IL	C+	11/02/04
BANKIOWA	IA	C+	11/02/04	EAGLEBANK	MD	C+	11/02/04
BAYBANK	MI	C+	11/02/04	EAST WISCONSIN SAVINGS BANK	WI	C+	11/02/04
BELT VALLEY BK	MT	C	11/02/04	EQUITABLE BK	FL	C+	11/02/04
BLOOMFIELD ST BK	IN	C+	11/02/04	EUREKA HOMESTEAD	LA	C+	11/02/04
BOONE CTY BK	WV	C+	11/02/04	EVERGREEN NB	CO	C+	11/02/04
BOONE NATIONAL S&LA FA	MO	C+	11/02/04	EXTRACO BANKS NA	TX	C+	11/02/04
BRIMFIELD BK	IL	C+	11/02/04	F&M B&TC	OK	C+	11/02/04
BRUNSWICK ST BK	NE	C+	11/02/04	F&M BK-IA CENTRAL	IA	C+	11/02/04
BRYAN B&TC	GA	C+	11/02/04	FARMERS & MERCHANTS BK	AL	C+	11/02/04
BSB B&TC	NY	C+	11/02/04	FARMERS & MERCHANTS BK	FL	C+	11/02/04
BUCS FEDERAL BANK	MD	C+	11/02/04	FARMERS & MERCHANTS BK	WI	C+	11/02/04
BYRON CENTER ST BK	MI	C+	11/02/04	FARMERS ST BK	MN	C+	11/02/04
BYRON ST BK	NE	C	11/02/04	FARMERS ST BK WESTERN IL	IL	C+	11/02/04
CAMBRIA COUNTY FS&LA	PA	C+	11/02/04	FAYETTE COUNTY BK	IL	C+	11/02/04
CAROLINA FIRST BK	SC	C+	11/02/04	FAYETTEVILLE BK	TX	C+	11/02/04
CENTRAL B&TC	KY	C+	11/02/04	FIDELITY ST B&TC	KS	C+	11/02/04
CENTRAL PROGRESSIVE BK	LA	C+	11/02/04	FIRST & FARMERS BANK	ND	C+	11/02/04
CENTRIX B&TC	NH	C+	11/02/04	FIRST AMERICAN B&TC	SD	C+	11/02/04
CENTURY BK FSB	NM	C+	11/02/04	FIRST AMERICAN BK	OK	C+	11/02/04
CHART BK	AR	C+	11/02/04	FIRST B&TC	NE	C+	11/02/04
CITIZENS BK	KY	C+	11/02/04	FIRST BK	VA	C+	11/02/04
CITIZENS BK	MI	C+	11/02/04	FIRST BK OF WHITE	SD	C+	11/02/04
CITIZENS BK CO	OH	C+	11/02/04	FIRST CA BK	CA	C+	11/02/04
CITIZENS BK OF BLYTHEDALE	MO	C+	11/02/04	FIRST CAPITAL BK OF KY	KY	C+	11/02/04
CITIZENS BK RI	RI	C+	11/02/04	FIRST CITRUS BK	FL	C+	11/02/04
CITIZENS COMMUNITY FEDERAL	WI	C+	11/02/04	FIRST COMMERCIAL BK	IL	C+	11/02/04
CITIZENS DEPOSIT BK & TRUST	KY	C+	11/02/04	FIRST COMMUNITY BANK NA	TX	C+	11/02/04
CITIZENS EXCHANGE BK	GA	C+	11/02/04	FIRST COMMUNITY BK	AR	C+	11/02/04
CITIZENS FIRST BK	FL	C+	11/02/04	FIRST FARMERS ST BK	IL	C+	11/02/04
CITIZENS NB	IL	C+	11/02/04	FIRST FINANCIAL B&TC	LA	C+	11/02/04
CITIZENS SAVINGS BK	IL	C+	11/02/04	FIRST FS&LA OF KEWANEE	IL	C+	11/02/04
COLLEGIATE PEAKS BK	CO	C+	11/02/04	FIRST FSB	IN	C+	11/02/04
COLORADO NB	CO	C+	11/02/04	FIRST FSB	TN	C+	11/02/04
COMMERCE BK DE NA	DE	C+	11/02/04	FIRST FSB CHAMPAIGN URBANA	IL	C+	11/02/04
COMMERCE BK NA	NJ	C+	11/02/04	FIRST MADISON VALLEY BK	MT	C+	11/02/04
COMMERCE BK NORTH	NJ	C+	11/02/04	FIRST MIDWEST BK	MO	C+	11/02/04
COMMERCE BK PENN NA	PA	C+	11/02/04	FIRST NB	CO	C	11/02/04
COMMERCE NB	OH	C+	11/02/04	FIRST NB AMERICAN	MI	C+	11/02/04
COMMERCIAL BK	MI	C+	11/02/04	FIRST NB IN BROOKINGS	SD	C+	11/02/04
COMMUNITY BK MERIDIAN MS	MS	C+	11/02/04	FIRST NB IN CAMERON	TX	C+	11/02/04
COMMUNITY BK NA	MO	C+	11/02/04	FIRST NB OF BARRY	IL	C+	11/02/04
COMMUNITY BK OF N AR	AR	C+	11/02/04	FIRST NB OF BELLS/SAVOY	TX	C+	11/02/04
COMMUNITY BK OF SAN JOAQUIN	CA	C+	11/02/04	FIRST NB OF CHILLICOTHE	TX	C+	11/02/04
COMMUNITY BK OF THE SOUTH	FL	C+	11/02/04	FIRST NB OF ELKHART	KS	C+	11/02/04
COMMUNITY FIRST B&TC	TN	C+	11/02/04	FIRST NB OF GORDON	NE	C+	11/02/04
COMMUNITY FIRST BK	IL	C+	11/02/04	FIRST NB OF GRANT PARK	IL	C+	11/02/04
COMMUNITY FIRST BK	LA	C+	11/02/04	FIRST NB OF LIBERAL	KS	C+	11/02/04
COMMUNITY FIRST BK	MO	C+	11/02/04	FIRST NB OF ONEIDA	TN	C+	11/02/04
COMMUNITY NB SARASOTA CTY	FL	C+	11/02/04	FIRST NB OF PLAINVIEW	MN	C+	11/02/04

Rating Upgrades (Continued)

BANK NAME	STATE	PREVIOUS WEISS SAFETY RATING	DATE OF CHANGE
Weiss Safety Rating:	**B-**		**(Continued)**
FIRST NB OF PRIMGHAR	IA	C+	11/02/04
FIRST NB OF RAYMOND	IL	C	11/02/04
FIRST NB OF ST PETER	MN	C+	11/02/04
FIRST NB OF SYRACUSE	KS	C+	11/02/04
FIRST NB OF THREE RIVERS	MI	C+	11/02/04
FIRST NB OF VOLGA	SD	C+	11/02/04
FIRST NB&TC OF VINITA	OK	C+	11/02/04
FIRST PLACE BK	OH	C+	11/02/04
FIRST PREMIER BK	SD	C+	11/02/04
FIRST SECURITY BK STORDEN	MN	C+	11/02/04
FIRST SERVICE BK	AR	C+	11/02/04
FIRST ST BK	MN	C+	11/02/04
FIRST ST BK	NE	C+	11/02/04
FIRST ST BK	NE	C+	11/02/04
FIRST ST BK	NE	C+	11/02/04
FIRST ST BK	OK	C+	11/02/04
FIRST ST BK	TX	C+	11/02/04
FIRST ST BK OF OLMSTED	IL	C+	11/02/04
FIRST ST BK OF ST ROBERT	MO	C+	11/02/04
FIRST UNITED B&T	MD	C+	11/02/04
FLATIRONS BK	CO	C+	11/02/04
FRANCES SLOCUM B&TC NA	IN	C+	11/02/04
FRANKLIN BK	IL	C+	11/02/04
FULTON ST BK	SD	C+	11/02/04
GARDEN CITY BK	MO	C+	11/02/04
GARDINER SVGS INSTITUTION	ME	C+	11/02/04
GEORGE D WARTHEN BK	GA	C+	11/02/04
GERMAN-AMERICAN ST BK	IL	C+	11/02/04
GOLD BK	KS	C+	11/02/04
GRAND SAVINGS BK	OK	C+	11/02/04
GRANITE ST BK	CA	C+	11/02/04
GRANT COUNTY BK	WV	C+	11/02/04
GREAT WESTERN BK	NE	C+	11/02/04
GULFSTREAM BUSINESS BK	FL	C+	11/02/04
GWINNETT COMMUNITY BK	GA	C+	11/02/04
H F GEHANT BKG CO	IL	C+	11/02/04
HARBOR BK OF MARYLAND	MD	C+	11/02/04
HARRIS BK ARGO	IL	C+	11/02/04
HARRIS BK JOLIET NA	IL	C+	11/02/04
HARVARD ST BK	NE	C+	11/02/04
HELM BK	FL	C+	11/02/04
HERITAGE BK	NE	C+	11/02/04
HERITAGE OAKS BK	CA	C+	11/02/04
HIGH COUNTRY BK	CO	C+	11/02/04
HOME FS&LA	SC	C+	11/02/04
HOME ST B&TC	KS	C+	11/02/04
HOMETOWN BK	MN	C+	11/02/04
HOMETOWN BK	WI	C+	11/02/04
HOPEWELL VALLEY COMMUNITY BK	NJ	C+	11/02/04
HORIZON CAPITAL BK	TX	C+	11/02/04
HUDSON RIVER COMMERCIAL BK	NY	C+	11/02/04
INDEPENDENCE BK	OH	C+	11/02/04
ING BANK FSB	DE	C+	11/02/04
INTER SVGS BK FSB	MN	C	11/02/04
INVESTORS CMNTY BK	WI	C+	11/02/04
INVESTORSBANK	WI	C+	11/02/04
JOHNSON BK	WI	C+	11/02/04
KASSON ST BK	MN	C+	11/02/04
KEARNEY TRUST CO	MO	C+	11/02/04
KOPERNIK FEDERAL BK	MD	C+	11/02/04
LAKE COUNTRY ST BK	MN	C+	11/02/04
LAKELAND BK	NJ	C+	11/02/04
LANDMARK BK NA	OK	C+	11/02/04
LANDMARK BK NA	TX	C+	11/02/04
LAUREL NB	KY	C+	11/02/04
LEGACY B&TC	MO	C+	11/02/04
LEGACY BK	OK	C+	11/02/04
LEGENDS BK	TN	C+	11/02/04
LENA ST BK	IL	C+	11/02/04
LIBERTY BK	IL	C+	11/02/04
LIBERTY BK	MO	C+	11/02/04
LIBERTY FSB	OK	C+	11/02/04
LIBERTYVILLE SVG BK	IA	C+	11/02/04
LINCOLN FSB OF NEBRASKA	NE	C	11/02/04
LOWCOUNTRY NB	SC	C+	11/02/04
LOWELL CO-OP BK	MA	C+	11/02/04
MACON BK	NC	C+	11/02/04
MADISON BK	FL	C+	11/02/04
MECHANICS BK	MS	C	11/02/04
MECHANICS SVGS BK	OH	C+	11/02/04
MERCANTILE BK	FL	C+	11/02/04
MERCHANTS NB OF BANGOR	PA	C+	11/02/04
MID AMERICA B&TC	MO	C+	11/02/04
MID AMERICA BK	MO	C+	11/02/04
MINNWEST BK M.V.	MN	C+	11/02/04
MINNWEST BK-LUVERNE	MN	C+	11/02/04
MONROE BK	IN	C+	11/02/04
MONTANA ST BK	MT	C+	11/02/04
MONTEREY COUNTY BK	CA	C+	11/02/04
MUTUAL SVGS BK	IN	C+	11/02/04
N.J.M. BK FSB	NJ	C+	11/02/04
NATIONWIDE TRUST COMPANY FSB	OH	C	11/02/04
NEW ALBIN SVG BK	IA	C+	11/02/04
NORTH ARUNDEL SVGS BK FSB	MD	C+	11/02/04
NORTHEAST SECURITY BK	IA	C+	11/02/04
NORTHERN ST BK	MN	C+	11/02/04
NORTHVIEW BK	MN	C+	11/02/04
NORTHWEST BK OF ROCKFORD	IL	C+	11/02/04
NORTHWOODS ST BK	IA	C+	11/02/04
NORWAY SVGS BK	ME	C+	11/02/04
OCWEN FEDERAL BK FSB	NJ	C	11/02/04
OHIO SVGS BK FSB	OH	C+	11/02/04
OHIO VALLEY BK CO	OH	C+	11/02/04
PACIFIC CONTINENTAL BK	OR	C+	11/02/04
PARAGON COMMERCIAL BK	NC	C+	11/02/04
PARAMOUNT BK	MI	C	11/02/04
PARISH NB	LA	C+	11/02/04
PCSB CMRL BK	NY	C+	11/02/04
PEOPLES B&T	IL	C+	11/02/04
PEOPLES BL&SC	OH	C+	11/02/04
PEOPLES ST BK	IA	C+	11/02/04
PEOPLES ST BK OF COLFAX	IL	C+	11/02/04
PINE BLUFF NB	AR	C+	11/02/04
PINE COUNTRY BK	MN	C+	11/02/04
PINNACLE BK	AL	C+	11/02/04
PLAINS COMMERCE BK	SD	C	11/02/04
PONTIAC NB	IL	C+	11/02/04
PORT WASHINGTON ST BK	WI	C+	11/02/04
PREMIER BK	PA	C+	11/02/04
PRIVATE BK	MI	C	11/02/04
PROSPECT BK	OH	C+	11/02/04
PUEBLO B&TC	CO	C+	11/02/04
R-G CROWN BANK	FL	C+	11/02/04
R-G PREMIER BK OF PR	PR	C+	11/02/04
RAINIER PACIFIC SVGS BK	WA	C+	11/02/04
RANCHO BERNARDO CMNTY BK	CA	C+	11/02/04
RELIABANK DAKOTA	SD	C+	11/02/04
REPUBLIC NB	TX	C+	11/02/04
RESOURCE BK	VA	C+	11/02/04
RUSTON B&LA	LA	C+	11/02/04
SALT LICK DEPOSIT BK	KY	C+	11/02/04
SAVINGS BANK	IA	C+	11/02/04

Rating Upgrades (Continued)

BANK NAME	STATE	PREVIOUS WEISS SAFETY RATING	DATE OF CHANGE

Weiss Safety Rating: B- (Continued)

BANK NAME	STATE	PREVIOUS WEISS SAFETY RATING	DATE OF CHANGE
SECURITY BK	WI	C+	11/02/04
SECURITY FIRST BK	WY	C+	11/02/04
SECURITY FSB	IN	C+	11/02/04
SECURITY ST BK	MN	C+	11/02/04
SECURITY ST BK	WI	C+	11/02/04
SECURITY SVGS BK	IL	C+	11/02/04
SHORELINE BK	WA	C+	11/02/04
SIGNATURE BK	MI	C+	11/02/04
SLOVENIAN S&LA OF FRANKLIN	PA	C+	11/02/04
SOUTHERN MICHIGAN B&T	MI	C+	11/02/04
SOUTHWEST BK OF ST LOUIS	MO	C+	11/02/04
ST CLAIR COUNTY ST BK	MO	C+	11/02/04
STANDARD FEDERAL BK NA	MI	C+	11/02/04
STATE B&TC	KY	C+	11/02/04
STATE BK	IL	C+	11/02/04
STATE BK	NE	C+	11/02/04
STATE BK OF BLUE RAPIDS	KS	C+	11/02/04
STATE BK OF BURNETTSVILLE	IN	C+	11/02/04
STATE BK OF DAVIS	IL	C+	11/02/04
STATE BK OF GRAYMONT	IL	C+	11/02/04
STATE BK OF HAWLEY	MN	C+	11/02/04
STATE BK OF HUDSON	SD	C+	11/02/04
STATE BK OF LISMORE	MN	C+	11/02/04
STATE BK OF LONG LAKE	MN	C+	11/02/04
STOCK EXCHANGE BK	KS	C+	11/02/04
STONEHAM CO-OP BK	MA	C+	11/02/04
SUNFIRST BANK	UT	C+	11/02/04
SURETY BK	FL	C	11/02/04
THE BANK	TX	C+	11/02/04
TRANS-PACIFIC NB	CA	C+	11/02/04
TRANSPORTATION ALLIANCE BK	UT	C+	11/02/04
TRUST BK	CA	C+	11/02/04
TRUSTBANK	IL	C+	11/02/04
TUSTIN COMMUNITY BK	CA	C+	11/02/04
TWIN CITY BK	AR	C+	11/02/04
UNION PLANTERS BK-LAKEWAY AREA	TN	C+	11/02/04
UNION PLANTERS NA	TN	C+	11/02/04
UNION ST BK	WY	C+	11/02/04
UNITED B&TC	KS	C+	11/02/04
UNITED B&TC	KY	C+	11/02/04
UNITED BK	WI	C+	11/02/04
UNITED BK NA	MT	C+	11/02/04
UNITED ROOSEVELT SB	NJ	C+	11/02/04
UNIVERSAL FINANCIAL CORP.	UT	C+	11/02/04
UNIVERSITY NB	MN	C+	11/02/04
US TC NA	CT	C+	11/02/04
VALRICO ST BK	FL	C+	11/02/04
VENTURE BK	WA	C+	11/02/04
VIKING SVGS ASSOC FA	MN	C+	11/02/04
VILLAGE BK	MN	C+	11/02/04
VILLAGE BK	UT	C+	11/02/04
VIRGINIA COMMERCE BK NA	VA	C+	11/02/04
WALLIS STATE BK	TX	C	11/02/04
WASHINGTON FED BK FOR SVGS	IL	C+	11/02/04
WASHINGTON MUTUAL BK FA	CA	C+	11/02/04
WASHINGTON ST BK	IL	C+	11/02/04
WASHINGTON SVGS BK FSB	MD	C	11/02/04
WEST MICHIGAN SVG BK	MI	C+	11/02/04
WESTERN BK	NM	C+	11/02/04
WESTERN NB	TX	C+	11/02/04
WESTERN NB	TX	C+	11/02/04
WESTERN SECURITY BK	AZ	C+	11/02/04
WESTERN SIERRA NB	CA	C+	11/02/04
WOODFORD ST BK	WI	C+	11/02/04

Weiss Safety Rating: C+

BANK NAME	STATE	PREVIOUS WEISS SAFETY RATING	DATE OF CHANGE
1ST BANK OF SEA ISLE CITY	NJ	C	11/02/04
1ST BK YUMA	AZ	C-	11/02/04
1ST COLONIAL NB	NJ	C	11/02/04
ABBEVILLE S&LA SSB	SC	C	11/02/04
ACUITY BANK	WI	C	11/02/04
ADAMS COUNTY B&LC	OH	C	11/02/04
ADVANTAGE BK	NJ	C	11/02/04
ALLEGIANCE COMMUNITY BK	NJ	C	11/02/04
ALLIANCE BK	WI	C	11/02/04
ALLIANCE NB	GA	C	11/02/04
AMERICAN COMMUNITY B&T	IL	C	11/02/04
AMERICAN FNB	TX	C	11/02/04
AMERICAN NB	OH	C	11/02/04
AMERICAN NB	TX	C	11/02/04
AMERICAN ST B&TC NA	KS	C	11/02/04
AMERICAN SVG BK DANVILLE	IL	C	11/02/04
APPLE RIVER ST BK	IL	C	11/02/04
ATLANTIC BK OF NEW YORK	NY	C	11/02/04
AUBURN COMMUNITY BK	CA	C	11/02/04
AUBURNBANK	AL	C	11/02/04
BANCO POPULAR NORTH AMERICA	NY	C	11/02/04
BANK OF BELEN	NM	C	11/02/04
BANK OF BOLIVAR	MO	C	11/02/04
BANK OF BOLIVAR	TN	C-	11/02/04
BANK OF CANTON	MA	C	11/02/04
BANK OF CLARK COUNTY	WA	C	11/02/04
BANK OF EASTMAN	GA	C	11/02/04
BANK OF GALESVILLE	WI	C	11/02/04
BANK OF GIBSON CITY	IL	C	11/02/04
BANK OF KILMICHAEL	MS	C	11/02/04
BANK OF KREMLIN	OK	C	11/02/04
BANK OF MANSFIELD	MO	C	11/02/04
BANK OF PROTECTION	KS	C	11/02/04
BANK OF SOPERTON	GA	C	11/02/04
BANK OF SPRINGFIELD	IL	C	11/02/04
BANK OF ST. AUGUSTINE	FL	C	11/02/04
BANK OF STAR VALLEY	WY	C	11/02/04
BANK OF TUCSON	AZ	C	11/02/04
BANK OF TURTLE LAKE	ND	C	11/02/04
BANK OF UNION	OK	C	11/02/04
BANK STAR	MO	C	11/02/04
BANK STAR OF THE BOOTHEEL	MO	C	11/02/04
BANK STAR OF THE LEADBELT	MO	C	11/02/04
BANK STAR ONE	MO	C	11/02/04
BANKFINANCIAL FSB	IL	C	11/02/04
BATH ST BK	IN	C	11/02/04
BENJAMIN FRANKLIN SVG BK	MA	C	11/02/04
BLUE RIDGE SVGS BK INC	NC	C	11/02/04
BOELUS ST BK	NE	C	11/02/04
BOSTON TR & INVESTMENT MGMT	MA	C	11/02/04
BRAINTREE CO-OP BK	MA	C	11/02/04
BUTLER BK A CO-OP BK	MA	C	11/02/04
CALIFORNIA COMMERCE BK	CA	C	11/02/04
CALIFORNIA FIRST NB	CA	C	11/02/04
CANANDAIGUA NB&TC	NY	C	11/02/04
CANTON CO-OP BK	MA	C	11/02/04
CAPITOL NATIONAL BANK	MI	C	11/02/04
CARROLLTON BK	MD	C	11/02/04
CATTARAUGUS COUNTY BK	NY	C	11/02/04
CENTRAL BK	NE	C	11/02/04
CENTRAL ST BK	IL	C	11/02/04
CENTURY BANK	MS	C	11/02/04
CENTURY NB	FL	C	11/02/04
CENTURY NB OF OKLAHOMA	OK	C	11/02/04
CHARTER BK	TX	C	11/02/04

Rating Upgrades　(Continued)

BANK NAME	STATE	PREVIOUS WEISS SAFETY RATING	DATE OF CHANGE
Weiss Safety Rating:　C+　(Continued)			
CHARTER NB&TC	IL	C	11/02/04
CHEVY CHASE BK FSB	MD	C	11/02/04
CHOICE BK	AZ	C	11/02/04
CITIBANK (WEST), FSB	CA	C	11/02/04
CITIZENS BK	DE	C	11/02/04
CITIZENS BK IL NA	IL	C	11/02/04
CITIZENS BK OF DE GRAFF	OH	C	11/02/04
CITIZENS BK OF MA	MA	C	11/02/04
CITIZENS BK OF PA	PA	C	11/02/04
CITIZENS BK OKLAHOMA	OK	C	11/02/04
CITIZENS NB OF BLUFFTON	OH	C	11/02/04
CITIZENS ST BK	IL	C-	11/02/04
CITIZENS ST BK	MN	C	11/02/04
CITIZENS ST BK OF ARLINGTON	SD	C	11/02/04
CITIZENS TRUST BK	GA	C	11/02/04
CITY ST BK	IA	C	11/02/04
CLASSIC BK CORP	KY	C	11/02/04
CLAY CITY BKG CO	IL	C	11/02/04
COLDWATER NATIVE BK	KS	C	11/02/04
COLONY BK OF DODGE COUNTY	GA	C	11/02/04
COLONY BK SOUTHEAST	GA	C	11/02/04
COLONY BK WILCOX	GA	C	11/02/04
COLUMBIA COMMUNITY BK	OR	C-	11/02/04
COMMERCIAL BK	MO	C	11/02/04
COMMERCIAL FEDERAL BK FSB	NE	C	11/02/04
COMMUNITY BANKS OF CO	CO	C	11/02/04
COMMUNITY BANKS OF TRACY	CA	C	11/02/04
COMMUNITY BK	IL	C	11/02/04
COMMUNITY BK	NM	C	11/02/04
COMMUNITY BK LEMONT	IL	C-	11/02/04
COMMUNITY BK MO	MO	C	11/02/04
COMMUNITY BK OF SULLIVAN CTY	NY	C	11/02/04
COMMUNITY BK SPRING GREEN	WI	C	11/02/04
COMMUNITY BK-DEARBORN	MI	C	11/02/04
COMMUNITY FIRST BK	AR	C	11/02/04
COMMUNITY FIRST BK	IN	C	11/02/04
COMMUNITY FIRST BK	WI	C	11/02/04
COMMUNITY NB PASCO CTY	FL	C	11/02/04
COMMUNITY TR BK	LA	C	11/02/04
CORNERSTONE BK	NC	C	11/02/04
CORNERSTONE NB	SC	C	11/02/04
CORNERSTONE NB&TC	IL	C	11/02/04
CORNERSTONE ST BK	MN	C	11/02/04
CREDICARD NB	TX	C	11/02/04
CRESCENT B&TC	GA	C	11/02/04
CROSS COUNTY FSB	NY	C	11/02/04
DE WITT ST BK	NE	C	11/02/04
DE WITT SVGS BK	IL	C	11/02/04
DENMARK ST BK	WI	C	11/02/04
DORAL BK	PR	C	11/02/04
E*TRADE BANK	VA	C	11/02/04
EARTHSTAR BK	PA	C	11/02/04
EASTON B&TC	MD	C	11/02/04
ELK HORN B&TC	AR	C	11/02/04
ENTERPRISE NB	TN	C-	11/02/04
EXCHANGE BK	MO	C	11/02/04
F&M BK-WI	WI	C	11/02/04
FARMERS & MERCHANTS B&T	IA	C	11/02/04
FARMERS & MERCHANTS B&TC	IA	C	11/02/04
FARMERS & MERCHANTS BK	WI	C	11/02/04
FARMERS & MERCHANTS ST BK	MN	C	11/02/04
FARMERS & MERCHANTS ST BK	MN	C	11/02/04
FARMERS & MERCHANTS ST BK	MN	C	11/02/04
FARMERS & MERCHANTS ST BK	OH	C	11/02/04
FARMERS BK	IN	C	11/02/04
FARMERS BK	NE	C	11/02/04
FARMERS BK OF LYNCHBURG	TN	C	11/02/04
FARMERS BK OF MT PULASKI	IL	C	11/02/04
FARMERS SECURITY BK	ND	C	11/02/04
FARMERS ST BK	IA	C	11/02/04
FARMERS ST BK	IL	C	11/02/04
FARMERS ST BK	IN	C	11/02/04
FARMERS ST BK	OK	C	11/02/04
FARMERS ST BK OF HOFFMAN	MN	C	11/02/04
FIDELITY BK OF FLORIDA NA	FL	C	11/02/04
FIDELITY CO-OP BK	MA	C	11/02/04
FIRST AMERICAN BK	IA	C	11/02/04
FIRST B&TC	OK	C	11/02/04
FIRST BK OF DALTON	GA	C	11/02/04
FIRST BK OF HENRY COUNTY	GA	C	11/02/04
FIRST BK OF KANSAS CITY	MO	C	11/02/04
FIRST BK OF LINDEN	AL	C	11/02/04
FIRST BUS BK - MILWAUKEE	WI	C	11/02/04
FIRST BUSINESS BK	WI	C	11/02/04
FIRST CITIZENS BK OF BUTTE	MT	C	11/02/04
FIRST CMNTY BK OF CENTRAL	AL	C	11/02/04
FIRST COMMERCE BK	KS	C	11/02/04
FIRST COMMUNITY BK	AR	C	11/02/04
FIRST COMMUNITY BK	MN	C	11/02/04
FIRST COMMUNITY BK OF GEORGIA	GA	C	11/02/04
FIRST FINANCIAL BK	AR	C	11/02/04
FIRST FINANCIAL BK USA	SD	C	11/02/04
FIRST FSB OF THE MIDWEST	IA	C	11/02/04
FIRST INDEPENDENT BK	MO	C	11/02/04
FIRST IOWA ST BK	IA	C	11/02/04
FIRST LOWNDES BK	AL	C	11/02/04
FIRST MISSOURI NB	MO	C	11/02/04
FIRST NB	FL	C	11/02/04
FIRST NB	GA	C	11/02/04
FIRST NB	TX	C	11/02/04
FIRST NB	TX	C	11/02/04
FIRST NB FOX VALLEY	WI	C	11/02/04
FIRST NB IN CANNON FALLS	MN	C-	11/02/04
FIRST NB IN GEORGETOWN	IL	C	11/02/04
FIRST NB IN HOWELL	MI	C	11/02/04
FIRST NB OF HARVEYVILLE	KS	C	11/02/04
FIRST NB OF LE ROY	KS	C	11/02/04
FIRST NB OF MONAHANS	TX	C	11/02/04
FIRST NB OF MONTGOMERY	MN	C	11/02/04
FIRST NB OF NORTHERN CA	CA	C	11/02/04
FIRST NB OF ORDWAY	CO	C	11/02/04
FIRST NB OF POLK CTY	FL	C	11/02/04
FIRST NB OF SCOTT CITY	KS	C-	11/02/04
FIRST NB OF SEILING	OK	C	11/02/04
FIRST NB OF SUMMERFIELD	KS	C	11/02/04
FIRST NB OF THE SOUTH	GA	C	11/02/04
FIRST NB OF THE SOUTH	SC	C	11/02/04
FIRST NB OF TOM BEAN	TX	C	11/02/04
FIRST NB PASCO	FL	C	11/02/04
FIRST PACIFIC BANK OF CA	CA	C	11/02/04
FIRST PEOPLES BK OF TN	TN	C	11/02/04
FIRST PERSONAL BK	IL	C	11/02/04
FIRST SENTRY BK	WV	C	11/02/04
FIRST SOUTH BK	SC	C-	11/02/04
FIRST ST BK	AZ	C	11/02/04
FIRST ST BK	SD	C	11/02/04
FIRST ST BK OF GACKLE	ND	C-	11/02/04
FIRST TR BK IL	IL	C	11/02/04
FIRST UNITED BK	CA	C	11/02/04
FIRST UNITED BK	IL	C	11/02/04
FIRST UNITED BK	TX	C	11/02/04
FIRST VICTORIA NB	TX	C-	11/02/04

Rating Upgrades (Continued)

BANK NAME	STATE	PREVIOUS WEISS SAFETY RATING	DATE OF CHANGE	BANK NAME	STATE	PREVIOUS WEISS SAFETY RATING	DATE OF CHANGE
Weiss Safety Rating: C+ (Continued)				NATIONAL B&TC	OH	C	11/02/04
				NEW FRONTIER BK	MO	C	11/02/04
FIRSTIER BK	NE	C-	11/02/04	NEXITY BK	AL	C	11/02/04
FIRSTSERVICE BK	MO	C	11/02/04	NITTANY BK	PA	C	11/02/04
FLORIDA CHOICE BK	FL	C	11/02/04	NORCROWN BK OF ROSELAND	NJ	C	11/02/04
FLORIDA PARISHES BK	LA	C	11/02/04	NORTH AMERICAN BKG CO	MN	C	11/02/04
FOOTHILLS BK	CO	C	11/02/04	NORTH VALLEY BANK	OH	C	11/02/04
FORT DES MOINES COMMUNITY BK	IA	C	11/02/04	NORTH VALLEY BK	CO	C	11/02/04
FOUNDERS TR PERSONAL BK	MI	C	11/02/04	NORTHWOODS BK OF MN	MN	C	11/02/04
FRANKLIN S&LC	OH	C	11/02/04	OKAW B&LA SVGS BK	IL	C	11/02/04
FRANKLIN SAVINGS BANK, SLA	NJ	C	11/02/04	OMNI BK	LA	C	11/02/04
FRANKLIN SECURITY BK, FSB	VA	C	11/02/04	ORANGE SVG BK TX	TX	C	11/02/04
FREEDOM BK	MO	C	11/02/04	OREGON COAST BK	OR	C	11/02/04
FRONTIER BK	GA	C	11/02/04	OXFORD UNIVERSITY BK	MS	C	11/02/04
FRONTIER BK FSB	UT	C	11/02/04	PALM DESERT NB	CA	C	11/02/04
FRONTIER ST BK	OK	C	11/02/04	PENINSULA BK	FL	C	11/02/04
FULLERTON COMMUNITY BK FSB	CA	C	11/02/04	PEOPLES BK A CODORUS VALLEY	PA	C	11/02/04
GARRISON ST B&T	ND	C	11/02/04	PEOPLES BK OF COFFEE CTY	AL	C	11/02/04
GENERATIONS BK	MO	C	11/02/04	PEOPLES BK OF JAMESTOWN	MO	C	11/02/04
GIFFORD ST BK	IL	C-	11/02/04	PEOPLES BK OF TALBOTTON	GA	C	11/02/04
GOLETA NB	CA	C	11/02/04	PEOPLES BK OF VA	VA	C	11/02/04
GRAND B&TC OF FLORIDA	FL	C	11/02/04	PEOPLES ST BK	IN	C	11/02/04
GRAND LAKE BK	OK	C	11/02/04	PLAINS ST BK	TX	C	11/02/04
GREAT RIVER B&T	IA	C	11/02/04	POCA VALLEY BK	WV	C	11/02/04
GREATBANK	IL	C	11/02/04	POWELL ST BK	TX	C	11/02/04
GREATBANK, A NA	IL	C	11/02/04	PREMIER CMNTY BK OF SOUTH FL	FL	C	11/02/04
GREATER DE VALLEY SVGS BK	PA	C	11/02/04	PREMIER COMMUNITY BK OF SW FL	FL	C	11/02/04
GUARANTY BK	LA	C	11/02/04	PRIMESOUTH BK	GA	C	11/02/04
GULFSTREAM COMMUNITY BK	FL	C	11/02/04	RARITAN ST BK	IL	C	11/02/04
GUNNISON B&TC	CO	C	11/02/04	RED RIVER ST BK	MN	C	11/02/04
GUTHRIE COUNTY ST BK	IA	C	11/02/04	REGIONS MORGAN KEEGAN TRUST	AL	C	11/02/04
HARDIN COUNTY SVG BK	IA	C	11/02/04	ROBERT LEE ST BK	TX	C	11/02/04
HARTFORD SVGS BK	WI	C	11/02/04	ROYAL OAKS BK SSB	TX	C	11/02/04
HEARTLAND BK	KS	C	11/02/04	SANIBEL CAPTIVA COMMUNITY BK	FL	C	11/02/04
HERITAGE BK CENTRAL IL	IL	C	11/02/04	SCOTTISH BK	NC	C	11/02/04
HICKORY POINT B&T	IL	C	11/02/04	SEAWAY NB OF CHICAGO	IL	C	11/02/04
HOME SVGS BK FSB	KY	C	11/02/04	SECURITY ST BK	IA	C	11/02/04
HOMETOWN BK NA	MO	C	11/02/04	SERVICE 1ST BK	CA	C	11/02/04
HOPETON ST BK	OK	C	11/02/04	SHARON SVG BK	PA	C	11/02/04
HORICON BK	WI	C	11/02/04	SHORE CMNTY BK	NJ	C	11/02/04
ILLINOIS ST BK LAKE HILLS	IL	C	11/02/04	SIGNATURE BK	FL	C	11/02/04
KAHOKA ST BK	MO	C	11/02/04	SKOWHEGAN SVGS BK	ME	C	11/02/04
KEOKUK SVG B&TC	IA	C	11/02/04	SOUTH BAY BK NA	CA	C	11/02/04
LABETTE BK	KS	C	11/02/04	SOUTH COUNTY BK NA	CA	C	11/02/04
LAKE REGION BK	MN	C	11/02/04	SOUTH VALLEY B&TC	OR	C	11/02/04
LANDMARK SVGS BK FSB	IN	C	11/02/04	SOUTHWEST MISSOURI BK	MO	C	11/02/04
LANGFORD ST BK	SD	C	11/02/04	SPIRITBANK	OK	C	11/02/04
LIBERTY SVGS BK FSB	MO	C	11/02/04	ST EDMONDS FSB	PA	C	11/02/04
LIBERTY SVGS BK FSB	PA	C	11/02/04	STATE BK OF CHITTENANGO	NY	C	11/02/04
LINCOLN SVG BK	IA	C	11/02/04	STATE BK OF CHRISMAN	IL	C	11/02/04
LONE STAR NB	TX	C	11/02/04	STATE BK OF NEW RICHLAND	MN	C	11/02/04
LONE STAR ST BK	TX	C	11/02/04	STATE BK OF PARK RAPIDS	MN	C	11/02/04
LONGVIEW ST BK	IL	C	11/02/04	STATE BK OF TOULON	IL	C	11/02/04
LYONS FSA	KS	C	11/02/04	STEWARDSON NB	IL	C	11/02/04
MAIN STREET BK CORP	WV	C	11/02/04	STOCKMENS BK	MT	C	11/02/04
MANSON ST BK	IA	C	11/02/04	SULPHUR COMMUNITY BK	OK	C	11/02/04
MARINERS BANK	NJ	C	11/02/04	SUNNYSIDE FS&LA OF IRVINGTON	NY	C	11/02/04
MERCANTILE B&T FSB	TX	C	11/02/04	SUTTON BK	OH	C	11/02/04
MERCANTILE NB	CA	C	11/02/04	SYNERGY BANK	NJ	C	11/02/04
MERCHANTS BK	AL	C	11/02/04	TALBOT ST BK	GA	C	11/02/04
MERCHANTS NB	OH	C	11/02/04	TERRABANK NA	FL	C	11/02/04
MFB FINANCIAL	IN	C	11/02/04	TEXAS BK OF TATUM	TX	C	11/02/04
MISSION BK	AZ	C	11/02/04	TOWN AND COUNTRY BK	MO	C	11/02/04
MONMOUTH COMMUNITY BK NA	NJ	C	11/02/04	TRADITION BK	TX	C-	11/02/04
MONTGOMERY FIRST NB	MO	C	11/02/04	TRICENTURY BK	KS	C	11/02/04
MOUNT VERNON BK	GA	C	11/02/04	TRUST ONE BK	TN	C	11/02/04
NATIONAL AMERICAN BK	CA	C	11/02/04	UBS BK USA	UT	C	11/02/04

Rating Upgrades (Continued)

BANK NAME	STATE	PREVIOUS WEISS SAFETY RATING	DATE OF CHANGE
Weiss Safety Rating: C+ (Continued)			
UNION BK AZ NA	AZ	C	11/02/04
UNION BK OF BLAIR	WI	C	11/02/04
UNION BKG CO	OH	C	11/02/04
UNION S&LA	IN	C	11/02/04
UNION ST BK	IA	C	11/02/04
UNION ST BK	WI	C	11/02/04
UNITED CMNTY BK OF WEST KY	KY	C-	11/02/04
UNITED NB	GA	C	11/02/04
UNITED SOUTHERN BK	KY	C	11/02/04
US CENTURY BK	FL	C	11/02/04
VILLA PARK T&SB	IL	C	11/02/04
WASHINGTON ST BK	LA	C	11/02/04
WEST SIDE ST SVG BK	IA	C	11/02/04
WESTERN BK OF CLOVIS	NM	C	11/02/04
WYOMING B&TC	WY	C	11/02/04
Weiss Safety Rating: C			
ADIRONDACK BK	NY	C-	11/02/04
ADVANTAGE BK	OK	C-	11/02/04
ALBINA COMMUNITY BK	OR	C-	11/02/04
ALLEGIANCE BK OF NORTH AMERICA	PA	C-	11/02/04
AMERICAN HEARTLAND B&TC	IL	C-	11/02/04
AMERICAN NB OF MT PLEASANT	TX	C-	11/02/04
AMERICANWEST	WA	C-	11/02/04
AMERICAUNITED B&TC USA	IL	C-	11/02/04
AMES COMMUNITY BK	IA	C-	11/02/04
ARGENTINE FEDERAL SVGS	KS	C-	11/02/04
BANK 1ST	NM	C-	11/02/04
BANK 2	OK	C-	11/02/04
BANK OF COMMERCE	TX	C-	11/02/04
BANK OF DYER	TN	C-	11/02/04
BANK OF FAIRFIELD	WA	C-	11/02/04
BANK OF FAYETTEVILLE NA	AR	C-	11/02/04
BANK OF GEORGIA	GA	C-	11/02/04
BANK OF GREENEVILLE	TN	C-	11/02/04
BANK OF HIAWASSEE	GA	C-	11/02/04
BANK OF LODI NA	CA	C-	11/02/04
BANK OF MADERA COUNTY	CA	C-	11/02/04
BANK OF MASON	TN	C-	11/02/04
BANK OF MONTGOMERY CTY	MO	C-	11/02/04
BANK OF MONTICELLO	WI	D+	11/02/04
BANK OF POWHATAN NA	VA	C-	11/02/04
BANK OF QUINCY	IL	C-	11/02/04
BANK OF RICHMOND NA	VA	C-	11/02/04
BANK OF SALEM	AR	C-	11/02/04
BANK OF THE SOUTH	TN	C-	11/02/04
BANK OF WARRENSBURG	IL	C-	11/02/04
BANK OF WESTON	MO	C-	11/02/04
BANKCDA	ID	C-	11/02/04
BARTOW COUNTY BK	GA	C-	11/02/04
BAYLAKE BK	WI	D+	11/02/04
BEACH FIRST NB	SC	C-	11/02/04
BENCHMARK BK	TX	C-	11/02/04
BERKSHIRE BK	PA	C-	11/02/04
BLACKHAWK ST BK	WI	C-	11/02/04
BLOOMBURG ST BK	TX	C-	11/02/04
BRIDGE BK NA	CA	C-	11/02/04
BRIDGE COMMUNITY BK	IA	C-	11/02/04
BRIGHTON BK	TN	C-	11/02/04
BUFFALO SVG BK	IA	C-	11/02/04
BUSINESS BK	MN	C-	11/02/04
BUSINESS BK	MO	D+	11/02/04
BUSINESS BK FOX RIVER VALLEY	WI	C-	11/02/04
CAPAHA BK SB	IL	C-	11/02/04

BANK NAME	STATE	PREVIOUS WEISS SAFETY RATING	DATE OF CHANGE
CAPITAL BK	NC	C-	11/02/04
CAPITAL COMMUNITY BK	UT	C-	11/02/04
CASTLE ROCK BK	CO	C-	11/02/04
CENLAR FSB	NJ	E-	11/02/04
CENTERSTATE BK OF FLORIDA	FL	C-	11/02/04
CHARLES SCHWAB BK NA	NV	C-	11/02/04
CHARTER BK	IA	C-	11/02/04
CHASE MANHATTAN BK USA NA	DE	C-	11/02/04
CHESTER COUNTY BK	TN	C-	11/02/04
CHESTERFIELD ST BK	IL	C-	11/02/04
CHOICE FINANCIAL GROUP	ND	C-	11/02/04
CITIBANK NEVADA NA	NV	C-	11/02/04
CITIBANK SOUTH DAKOTA NA	SD	C-	11/02/04
CITIZENS B&TC CHICAGO	IL	C-	11/02/04
CITIZENS BANK & TRUST, INC.	GA	C-	11/02/04
CITIZENS BK	MS	C-	11/02/04
CITIZENS ST BK	AR	C-	11/02/04
CITIZENS ST BK	KS	C-	11/02/04
CITIZENS ST BK OF CLAYTON	WI	C-	11/02/04
CITIZENS SVG B&TC	TN	C-	11/02/04
COLORADO EAST B&T	CO	C-	11/02/04
COLORADO VALLEY BK	TX	C-	11/02/04
COMMERCEWEST BK NA	CA	D+	11/02/04
COMMERCIAL SVG BK	OH	C-	11/02/04
COMMUNITY B&TC	NH	C-	11/02/04
COMMUNITY B&TC	OK	D+	11/02/04
COMMUNITY BANK	AR	D+	11/02/04
COMMUNITY BK	IL	C-	11/02/04
COMMUNITY BK OF RAYMORE	MO	C-	11/02/04
COMMUNITY BK OF ROCKIES	CO	C-	11/02/04
COMMUNITY FIRST BK	OR	D+	11/02/04
COMMUNITY FIRST BK	VA	C-	11/02/04
COMMUNITY FIRST BK	WA	C-	11/02/04
COMMUNITY FIRST BK NA	OH	C-	11/02/04
COMMUNITY SHORES BK	MI	C-	11/02/04
COMMUNITY STATE BANK	IL	C-	11/02/04
COPPER STAR BK	AZ	D+	11/02/04
CORNERBANK NA	KS	C-	11/02/04
CORNERSTONE COMMUNITY BK	TN	C-	11/02/04
CRESCENT BK	SC	C-	11/02/04
CROWN BK	MN	C-	11/02/04
CUMBERLAND BK SOUTH	TN	C-	11/02/04
DETROIT COMMERCE BK	MI	C-	11/02/04
DUBLIN NB	TX	C-	11/02/04
EASTBANK	MN	C-	11/02/04
ELK COUNTY S&LA	PA	C-	11/02/04
EVERGREEN COMMUNITY BK	IL	C-	11/02/04
FAMILY FEDERAL SVGS OF IL	IL	C-	11/02/04
FAMILY FSB	GA	C-	11/02/04
FARMERS & MERCHANTS BK	GA	C-	11/02/04
FARMERS ST BK-WEST CONCORD	MN	C-	11/02/04
FARMERS SVG BK	IA	C-	11/02/04
FEDERAL TRUST BANK	FL	C-	11/02/04
FIRST & CITIZENS BANK	VA	C-	11/02/04
FIRST B&TC	TX	C-	11/02/04
FIRST BK	TN	C-	11/02/04
FIRST BOULDER VALLEY BK	MT	D+	11/02/04
FIRST CAPITAL BK	IL	C-	11/02/04
FIRST CAROLINA STATE BK	NC	C-	11/02/04
FIRST CITIZENS BK OF POLSON	MT	C-	11/02/04
FIRST COMMUNITY BK	MO	C-	11/02/04
FIRST IN BK NA	IN	C-	11/02/04
FIRST INDEPENDENT NB	TX	C-	11/02/04
FIRST INTERCONTINENTAL BK	GA	C-	11/02/04
FIRST NATIONAL BK OF CO	CO	C-	11/02/04
FIRST NB IN CIMARRON	KS	C-	11/02/04
FIRST NB MUHLENBERG COUNTY	KY	C-	11/02/04

Rating Upgrades   (Continued)

BANK NAME	STATE	PREVIOUS WEISS SAFETY RATING	DATE OF CHANGE
Weiss Safety Rating: C			**(Continued)**
FIRST NB MUSKOGEE	OK	C-	11/02/04
FIRST NB OF ANSON	TX	C-	11/02/04
FIRST NB OF ARCOLA	IL	C-	11/02/04
FIRST NB OF BRUNDIDGE	AL	C-	11/02/04
FIRST NB OF CAINSVILLE	MO	C-	11/02/04
FIRST NB OF CENTRAL TEXAS	TX	C-	11/02/04
FIRST NB OF HAMILTON	TX	C-	11/02/04
FIRST NB OF LAKE CITY	CO	D+	11/02/04
FIRST NB OF LUCEDALE	MS	D+	11/02/04
FIRST NB OF MT	MT	C-	11/02/04
FIRST NB OF ODON	IN	C-	11/02/04
FIRST NB OF PORT ALLEGANY	PA	C-	11/02/04
FIRST NB OF TRIBUNE	KS	C-	11/02/04
FIRST NB OF WAVERLY	OH	D+	11/02/04
FIRST SAVANNA SVG BK	IL	C-	11/02/04
FIRST SECURITY ST BK	TX	C-	11/02/04
FIRST ST BK	KS	D+	11/02/04
FIRST ST BK	ND	C-	11/02/04
FIRST ST BK	TX	C-	11/02/04
FIRST ST BK	TX	C-	11/02/04
FIRST ST BK	VA	C-	11/02/04
FIRST ST BK OF AUDUBON	MN	C-	11/02/04
FIRST ST BK OF MUNICH	ND	C-	11/02/04
FIRST ST BK OF SAN DIEGO	TX	C-	11/02/04
FLAG BK	GA	C-	11/02/04
FLORIDA GULF BK	FL	C-	11/02/04
FLORIDA SVGS BK	FL	C-	11/02/04
FORT WORTH NB	TX	C-	11/02/04
FRANKLIN BK	NJ	D+	11/02/04
FRANKLIN TEMPLETON B&T FSB	UT	C-	11/02/04
FRONTIER BK	KS	C-	11/02/04
GALLUP FSB	NM	C-	11/02/04
GATEWAY B&TC	NC	C-	11/02/04
GREAT PLAINS BK	SD	D+	11/02/04
GREERS FERRY LAKE ST BK	AR	C-	11/02/04
HARWOOD ST BK	ND	C-	11/02/04
HEARTLAND CMNTY BK	IN	C-	11/02/04
HEARTLAND COMMUNITY BK	AR	C-	11/02/04
HERITAGE BK	IA	C-	11/02/04
HERITAGE BK OF SCHAUMBURG	IL	D+	11/02/04
HERSHEY ST BK	NE	C-	11/02/04
HIGH PLAINS BK	CO	C-	11/02/04
HIGHLANDS COMMUNITY BK	VA	C-	11/02/04
HIGHLANDS UNION BK	VA	C-	11/02/04
HOME FEDERAL BK	SD	C-	11/02/04
HOME SAVINGS BK	MO	C-	11/02/04
HOME TOWN BK OF VILLA RICA	GA	C-	11/02/04
HORIZON BK	GA	C-	11/02/04
INDEPENDENT BANKERS BK IL	IL	C-	11/02/04
INDEPENDENT BANKERS BK OF FL	FL	C-	11/02/04
INDEPENDENT BK	TN	C-	11/02/04
INSURORS BK OF TENNESSEE	TN	C-	11/02/04
INTEGRITY BK	GA	C-	11/02/04
INTERCONTINENTAL BK	FL	C-	11/02/04
IONIA COUNTY NB OF IONIA	MI	D	11/02/04
JP MORGAN TC NA	CA	C-	11/02/04
KENNETT NB	MO	C-	11/02/04
KILGORE NB	TX	C-	11/02/04
LANDMARK COMMUNITY BK NA	MN	C-	11/02/04
LEEDS FSB	MD	C-	11/02/04
LEGACY BK	WI	C-	11/02/04
LEIGHTON ST BK	IA	C-	11/02/04
MADISON BK	KY	C-	11/02/04
MADISON BOHEMIAN SAVINGS BANK	MD	C-	11/02/04
MADISON SQUARE FSB	MD	C-	11/02/04
MARION BK	OH	C-	11/02/04
MARION COUNTY SB	IL	C-	11/02/04
MECHANICS SVGS BK	SC	C-	11/02/04
MEDINA S&LA	NY	C-	11/02/04
MERCHANTS & PLANTERS BK	AR	C-	11/02/04
MIDLAND FS&LA	IL	C-	11/02/04
MIDWEST HERITAGE BK, FSB	IA	C-	11/02/04
MONROE COUNTY BK	GA	C-	11/02/04
MONTICELLO BKG CO	KY	C-	11/02/04
MURRAY BK	KY	C-	11/02/04
NATIONAL BK OF COMMERCE	IL	C-	11/02/04
NCW COMMUNITY BK	WA	C-	11/02/04
NEOSHO S&LA FA	MO	C-	11/02/04
NEW SOUTHERN BK	GA	D+	11/02/04
NORTH CASCADES NB	WA	C-	11/02/04
NORTHRIM BK	AK	C-	11/02/04
NORTHSTAR BK	IA	C-	11/02/04
NORTHVIEW B&TC	IL	C-	11/02/04
NORTHWEST B&TC	IA	C-	11/02/04
OCALA NB	FL	C-	11/02/04
OCEAN BK	FL	D+	11/02/04
OMNI NB	NC	C-	11/02/04
ONE B&T NA	AR	C-	11/02/04
PACIFIC INTERNATIONAL BK	WA	C-	11/02/04
PATRIOT BK	IA	C-	11/02/04
PCB, THE COMMUNITY BANK	FL	C-	11/02/04
PEOPLES CMNTY BK OF THE WEST	FL	C-	11/02/04
PEOPLES COMMUNITY BK	AL	C-	11/02/04
PEOPLES S&LC	OH	C-	11/02/04
PEOPLES SAVING BK	IA	C-	11/02/04
PEOPLES ST BK	GA	C-	11/02/04
PINERIES BK	WI	C-	11/02/04
PINNACLE NB	TN	C-	11/02/04
PRAIRIE COMMUNITY BK	IL	C-	11/02/04
PREMIER BK-MAPLEWOOD	MN	C-	11/02/04
PREMIER COMMERCIAL BK NA	CA	C-	11/02/04
PRIME PACIFIC BK NA	WA	D+	11/02/04
PROFINIUM FINANCIAL	MN	C-	11/02/04
RED ROCK COMMUNITY BK	NV	C-	11/02/04
RESOURCE BK	LA	C-	11/02/04
RIVERBANK	WI	C-	11/02/04
ROLETTE ST BK	ND	C-	11/02/04
SAVANNA-THOMSON ST BK	IL	C-	11/02/04
SECOND FS&LA OF CHICAGO	IL	C-	11/02/04
SECURITY ST BK	IA	C-	11/02/04
SECURITY ST BK	ND	C-	11/02/04
SIGNATURE BK	TX	C-	11/02/04
SILVER ST BK	NV	D+	11/02/04
SINCERE FSB	CA	C-	11/02/04
SOMERSET HILLS BK	NJ	C-	11/02/04
SOUTHERN CMNTY BK OF CTRL FL	FL	C-	11/02/04
SOUTHERN COMMUNITY BK OF SW FL	FL	C-	11/02/04
SOUTHWEST BK	TX	C-	11/02/04
SOUTHWEST SECURITIES BANK	TX	D+	11/02/04
SPALDING CITY BK	NE	C-	11/02/04
SPECTRUM BK	CA	C-	11/02/04
STATE BK OF BARTLEY	NE	C-	11/02/04
STEPHENS SECURITY BK	AR	C-	11/02/04
STOUGHTON CO-OP BK	MA	C-	11/02/04
TEXAS COMMUNITY BK NA	TX	C-	11/02/04
THIRD FSB	PA	C-	11/02/04
THRIVENT FINANCIAL BANK	WI	C-	11/02/04
TOTALBANK	FL	C-	11/02/04
TOWN BK	WI	C-	11/02/04
TRADERS NB OF TULLAHOMA	TN	C-	11/02/04
TRI-COUNTY BK	NE	C-	11/02/04
UNION BK OF BENTON	AR	C-	11/02/04

Rating Upgrades (Continued)

BANK NAME	STATE	PREVIOUS WEISS SAFETY RATING	DATE OF CHANGE	BANK NAME	STATE	PREVIOUS WEISS SAFETY RATING	DATE OF CHANGE
Weiss Safety Rating: C (Continued)				COMMUNITY BK OWATONNA	MN	D+	11/02/04
UNION FS&LA	IL	C-	11/02/04	COMMUNITY BK OZARKS	MO	D+	11/02/04
UNITED CMNTY BK	LA	D+	11/02/04	COMMUNITY FSB	NY	D+	11/02/04
UNITED HERITAGE BK	FL	C-	11/02/04	COMMUNITY GTY SVGS BK	NH	D+	11/02/04
UNITED NB	CA	C-	11/02/04	COMMUNITY NB	TX	D+	11/02/04
UNITI BK	CA	D+	11/02/04	COMMUNITY ST BK	KS	D+	11/02/04
VALLEY BK	CT	C-	11/02/04	COMMUNITY STATE BK	OK	D+	11/02/04
VALLEY BK OF RONAN	MT	C-	11/02/04	COUNTRY BK	AZ	D+	11/02/04
VALLEY INDEPENDENT BK	CA	C-	11/02/04	CROWLEY B&LA	LA	D+	11/02/04
VINTAGE BK	TX	C-	11/02/04	CUMBERLAND B&TC	TN	D+	11/02/04
WATONGA ST BK	OK	C-	11/02/04	EXCHANGE ST BK	IA	D+	11/02/04
WELCOME ST BK	MN	C-	11/02/04	FARMERS & MERCHANTS BK	NE	D+	11/02/04
WEST END SVGS BK	IN	C-	11/02/04	FARMERS & MERCHANTS BK	OK	D+	11/02/04
WEST MI COMMUNITY BK	MI	C-	11/02/04	FARMERS NB OF STAFFORD	KS	D+	11/02/04
WEST POINTE B&TC	IL	C-	11/02/04	FARMERS ST BK	NE	D+	11/02/04
WESTERN ST BK	ND	C-	11/02/04	FARMERS ST BK	NE	D+	11/02/04
WILLAMETTE VALLEY BK	OR	D+	11/02/04	FIRST CAPITAL BK	VA	D+	11/02/04
WISCONSIN ST BK	WI	C-	11/02/04	FIRST COMMERCE BK	TN	D+	11/02/04
Weiss Safety Rating: C-				FIRST COMMERCE COMMUNITY BK	GA	D+	11/02/04
ADVANTAGE NB	IL	D+	11/02/04	FIRST COMMERCIAL BK TAMPA	FL	D+	11/02/04
AMERIANA B&TC SB	IN	D+	11/02/04	FIRST COMMUNITY BK	KS	D+	11/02/04
AMERICAN B&TC	KY	D+	11/02/04	FIRST CORNERSTONE BK	PA	D+	11/02/04
AMERICAN ENTERPRISE BK	IL	D+	11/02/04	FIRST DUPAGE BK	IL	D+	11/02/04
AMERICAN EXPRESS BK, FSB	UT	D	11/02/04	FIRST FEDERAL BANK FSB	AL	D+	11/02/04
BANK	LA	D+	11/02/04	FIRST FEDERAL BANK FSB	SD	D+	11/02/04
BANK OF BARTLETT	TN	D+	11/02/04	FIRST FEDERAL BK	AL	D+	11/02/04
BANK OF BENOIT	MS	D+	11/02/04	FIRST FEDERAL BK	PA	D+	11/02/04
BANK OF CAMDEN	SC	D+	11/02/04	FIRST FEDERAL BK FOR SVGS	MS	D+	11/02/04
BANK OF ELGIN	NE	D+	11/02/04	FIRST FS&LA	MS	D+	11/02/04
BANK OF EVANSVILLE NA	IN	D+	11/02/04	FIRST FS&LA OF SHELBYVILLE	IL	D+	11/02/04
BANK OF KENNEY	IL	D+	11/02/04	FIRST INTL BK	TX	D+	11/02/04
BANK OF KENOSHA	WI	D+	11/02/04	FIRST NB	MN	D+	11/02/04
BANK OF LOUISIANA	LA	D+	11/02/04	FIRST NB	OK	D+	11/02/04
BANK OF NAPLES	FL	D+	11/02/04	FIRST NB HINCKLEY	MN	D+	11/02/04
BANK OF SOUTHERN CT	CT	D+	11/02/04	FIRST NB IN BRONTE	TX	D+	11/02/04
BANK OF THE PRAIRIE	KS	D+	11/02/04	FIRST NB NELSONVILLE	OH	D+	11/02/04
BANK OF THE VALLEY	NE	D+	11/02/04	FIRST NB OF BROWNSTOWN	IL	D+	11/02/04
BANK OF WRIGHTSVILLE	GA	D+	11/02/04	FIRST NB OF CLAUDE	TX	D+	11/02/04
BANK OF WYANDOTTE	OK	D+	11/02/04	FIRST NB OF EDGEWOOD	TX	D+	11/02/04
BANKFIRST	SD	D+	11/02/04	FIRST NB OF FREMONT	IN	D+	11/02/04
BANKTENNESSEE	TN	D+	11/02/04	FIRST NB OF MEDFORD	OK	D+	11/02/04
BAY NET A COMMUNITY BANK	MD	D+	11/02/04	FIRST NB OF MEXIA	TX	D+	11/02/04
BRATTLEBORO S&LA FA	VT	D+	11/02/04	FIRST NB OF ST JO	TX	D	11/02/04
CANADIAN ST BK	OK	D+	11/02/04	FIRST NB OF SULLIVAN	IL	D+	11/02/04
CENTRAL B&TC	KS	D+	11/02/04	FIRST NB OF THE NORTH	MN	D+	11/02/04
CENTRAL BK	IN	D+	11/02/04	FIRST NW BK	IL	D+	11/02/04
CHESAPEAKE BK OF MARYLAND	MD	D+	11/02/04	FIRST ST BK	AR	D+	11/02/04
CHESTATEE ST BK	GA	D+	11/02/04	FIRST ST BK	NE	D	11/02/04
CHISHOLM TRAIL ST BK	KS	D+	11/02/04	FIRST ST BK	NE	D+	11/02/04
CITIZENS BK OF EAST TN	TN	D+	11/02/04	FIRST ST BK	TX	D+	11/02/04
CITIZENS FIRST BK	TN	D+	11/02/04	FIRST ST BK	TX	D+	11/02/04
CITIZENS NB IN WAXAHACHIE	TX	D+	11/02/04	FIRST ST BK OF VAN ORIN	IL	D+	11/02/04
CITIZENS ST BK	CO	D+	11/02/04	FLATBUSH FS&LA	NY	D+	11/02/04
CITIZENS ST BK	KS	D+	11/02/04	FLORIDA COMMUNITY BK	FL	D	11/02/04
CITIZENS ST BK	NE	D+	11/02/04	FOUNDATION BANK	OH	D+	11/02/04
CITIZENS ST BK	WI	D+	11/02/04	FOUNDATION BK	WA	D+	11/02/04
CNLBANK	FL	D+	11/02/04	FREDERICK COUNTY BK	MD	D+	11/02/04
COLUMBIA SVGS BK	OH	D+	11/02/04	FREEDOM FINANCIAL BK	IA	D	11/02/04
COMMERCEFIRST BK	MD	D+	11/02/04	GATEWAY COMMUNITY BK	IL	D+	11/02/04
COMMERCIAL ST BK	NE	D+	11/02/04	GATEWAY SVGS BK	IA	D+	11/02/04
COMMONWEALTH BK FSB	KY	D+	11/02/04	GENOA NB	NE	D+	11/02/04
COMMUNITY BK	IL	D+	11/02/04	GEORGIA BANKING CO	GA	D	11/02/04
COMMUNITY BK CENTRAL WI	WI	D+	11/02/04	GOGEBIC RANGE BK	MI	D	11/02/04
COMMUNITY BK OF THE CUMBERLAND	TN	D+	11/02/04	GOLD COUNTRY BK NA	CA	D+	11/02/04
				GRAND BK	TX	D+	11/02/04
				GRANGE BK	OH	D+	11/02/04
				GRANITE CMNTY BK NA	CA	D+	11/02/04

Rating Upgrades (Continued)

BANK NAME	STATE	PREVIOUS WEISS SAFETY RATING	DATE OF CHANGE

Weiss Safety Rating: C- (Continued)

BANK NAME	STATE	PREVIOUS WEISS SAFETY RATING	DATE OF CHANGE
HALSTEAD BK	KS	D+	11/02/04
HARRINGTON BK FSB	NC	D+	11/02/04
HAVILAND ST BK	KS	D+	11/02/04
HEMISPHERE NB	FL	D+	11/02/04
HERITAGE BK	GA	D+	11/02/04
HERITAGE BK	WI	D+	11/02/04
HERITAGE CMNTY BK	KY	D	11/02/04
HICKSVILLE BK	OH	D+	11/02/04
HILLTOP CMNTY BK	NJ	D+	11/02/04
HORIZON COMMUNITY BK	AZ	D+	11/02/04
INDEPENDENCE BK OF KY	KY	D+	11/02/04
INDEPENDENT COMMUNITY BK	FL	D+	11/02/04
ISLANDS COMMUNITY BK NA	SC	D+	11/02/04
JACKSONVILLE BK	FL	D	11/02/04
JANESVILLE ST BK	MN	D+	11/02/04
JPMORGAN CHASE BK	NY	D+	11/02/04
K BK	MD	D+	11/02/04
KIT CARSON ST BK	CO	D+	11/02/04
LABE BK	IL	D+	11/02/04
LEGACY BK	PA	D+	11/02/04
LEHMAN BROTHERS BK FSB	DE	D+	11/02/04
LIBERTY BK FSB	IA	D+	11/02/04
LIBERTY NB	TX	D+	11/02/04
LIVE OAK ST BK	TX	D+	11/02/04
MAINSTREET BK	MN	D+	11/02/04
MASSMUTUAL TRUST COMPANY FSB	CT	D	11/02/04
MCINTOSH COMMERCIAL BK	GA	D+	11/02/04
MEDALLION BK	UT	D	11/02/04
MERCHANTS & CITIZENS BK	GA	D+	11/02/04
MERRICK BK	UT	D+	11/02/04
MORRIS COUNTY NB OF NAPLES	TX	D+	11/02/04
NEW CENTURY BK	PA	D	11/02/04
NICOLET NB	WI	D+	11/02/04
NORTH COUNTY SB	IL	D+	11/02/04
NORTHERN MICHIGAN B&T	MI	D+	11/02/04
NORTHLAND COMMUNITY BK	MN	D+	11/02/04
OAKLAND DEPOSIT BK	TN	D+	11/02/04
PAONIA ST BK	CO	D+	11/02/04
PARK CITIES BK	TX	D+	11/02/04
PATASKALA BKG CO	OH	D+	11/02/04
PEOPLES BK	KS	D+	11/02/04
PEOPLES BK	KY	D+	11/02/04
PEOPLES ST BK	IL	D+	11/02/04
PEOPLES SVGS BK	NJ	D+	11/02/04
PETERSBURG ST BK	NE	D+	11/02/04
PIEDMONT BK OF GEORGIA	GA	D+	11/02/04
PIQUA ST BK	KS	D+	11/02/04
POLONIA BK	PA	D+	11/02/04
PONTOTOC COUNTY BK	OK	D+	11/02/04
PREMIER BK	IL	D+	11/02/04
RANCHO BK	CA	D+	11/02/04
RELIANCE BK	AL	D+	11/02/04
ROCKY MOUNTAIN B&T FLORENCE	CO	D+	11/02/04
SAN JOSE TRI COUNTY BK	IL	D+	11/02/04
SECURITY BK NA	FL	D+	11/02/04
SECURITY SVG BK	IA	D+	11/02/04
SIGNATURE BANK	NY	D+	11/02/04
SIGNATURE BK NA	OH	D+	11/02/04
SOUND BANKING COMPANY	NC	D+	11/02/04
SOUND BKG CO	WA	D+	11/02/04
SOUTHERN CMNTY BK OF SOUTH	FL	D+	11/02/04
STATE BK OF CEYLON	MN	D+	11/02/04
STATE BK OF KERKHOVEN	MN	D+	11/02/04
STERLING B&T FSB	MI	D+	11/02/04
STERLING BK	NJ	D+	11/02/04
STOCKGROWERS STATE BANK	KS	D+	11/02/04
SUNSOUTH BK	AL	D	11/02/04
T. ROWE PRICE SVGS BK	MD	D+	11/02/04
TENNESSEE COMMERCE BK	TN	D+	11/02/04
TERRITORY BK	OK	D+	11/02/04
TEXAS NB	TX	D+	11/02/04
THE BANK	MO	D+	11/02/04
TOWN SQUARE BK	KY	D+	11/02/04
TRANSATLANTIC BK	FL	D+	11/02/04
TRINITY BK	NC	D+	11/02/04
TRUMAN BK	MO	D+	11/02/04
TSB BK	WI	D+	11/02/04
UNION BK	ND	D+	11/02/04
UNITED BK OF KS	KS	D+	11/02/04
UNITED CENTRAL BK	TX	D+	11/02/04
UNITED FIDELITY BK FSB	IN	D+	11/02/04
UNITED MIDWEST SAVINGS BANK	OH	D	11/02/04
UNITY BK	NJ	D+	11/02/04
VALLEY BK-GLASGOW	MT	D+	11/02/04
WARREN BK	MI	D+	11/02/04
WASHITA ST BK	OK	D+	11/02/04
WHITE ROCK BK	MN	D+	11/02/04
WILTON BK	CT	D+	11/02/04
WOODBURY BKG CO	GA	D+	11/02/04
WOODLAND BK	MN	D+	11/02/04

Weiss Safety Rating: D+

BANK NAME	STATE	PREVIOUS WEISS SAFETY RATING	DATE OF CHANGE
ADVANCE BK	MD	D	11/02/04
ADVANTAGE COMMUNITY BK	WI	D	11/02/04
ALDEN ST BK	MI	D	11/02/04
ALLSTATE BK	IL	D	11/02/04
AMERICAN EAGLE BK	IL	D	11/02/04
AMERICAN NB OF MN	MN	D	11/02/04
ANAHUAC NB	TX	D	11/02/04
BANK OF CAVE CITY	AR	D	11/02/04
BANK OF COMMERCE	OK	D	11/02/04
BANK OF COMMERCE & TRUST CO	KS	D	11/02/04
BANK OF GOOCHLAND NA	VA	D	11/02/04
BANK OF HYDRO	OK	D	11/02/04
BANK OF LUXEMBURG	WI	D	11/02/04
BANK OF MOUNDVILLE	AL	D	11/02/04
BANK OF OAK RIDGE	NC	D-	11/02/04
BANK OF WHITTIER NA	CA	D	11/02/04
BEACH COMMUNITY BK	FL	D	11/02/04
BENCHMARK BK	IL	D	11/02/04
BONANZA VALLEY ST BK	MN	D	11/02/04
BORDER TRUST CO	ME	D	11/02/04
BRAINERD S&LA FA	MN	D	11/02/04
BUTTE ST BK	NE	D	11/02/04
CAPITAL BANK NA	MD	D	11/02/04
CARDINAL BK NA	VA	D	11/02/04
CENTRAL BK OF HOUSTON	TX	D	11/02/04
CITIZENS NB	TX	D	11/02/04
CITIZENS ST BK	TX	D	11/02/04
CLAY COUNTY BK	WV	D-	11/02/04
COMMERCIAL ST BK	TX	D-	11/02/04
COMMUNITY BK	AL	D	11/02/04
COMMUNITY BK	GA	D-	11/02/04
COMMUNITY BK	TX	D	11/02/04
COMMUNITY BK OF WICHITA	KS	D-	11/02/04
COMMUNITY ST BK	TX	D	11/02/04
COMMUNITY ST BK	WI	D	11/02/04
CORNING S&LA	AR	D	11/02/04
COUNTY COMMERCE BK	CA	D	11/02/04
DAKOTA WESTERN BK	ND	D	11/02/04
DEEPGREEN BK	OH	D	11/02/04
DOUGLAS NB	GA	D	11/02/04

Rating Upgrades (Continued)

BANK NAME	STATE	PREVIOUS WEISS SAFETY RATING	DATE OF CHANGE
Weiss Safety Rating:		**D+**	**(Continued)**
DRYADES SVGS BK FSB	LA	D	11/02/04
ECONOMY CO-OP BK	MA	D	11/02/04
EDGAR COUNTY B&TC	IL	D	11/02/04
EDISON NB	FL	D	11/02/04
ELKHART ST BK	TX	D	11/02/04
ENNIS ST BK	TX	D	11/02/04
EQUITY BK NA	KS	D	11/02/04
FAIRVIEW ST BKG CO	IL	D	11/02/04
FAMILY B&TC	IL	D	11/02/04
FARMERS & MERCHANTS BK	TN	D	11/02/04
FARMERS ST BK	KS	D	11/02/04
FARMERS ST BK OF CALHAN	CO	D	11/02/04
FARMERS SVG BK	IA	D	11/02/04
FELTON BK	DE	D-	11/02/04
FIDELITY BK TX	TX	D	11/02/04
FIRST AMERICAN BK	OK	D	11/02/04
FIRST BK	LA	D	11/02/04
FIRST BK OF DOTHAN	AL	D	11/02/04
FIRST BK OF MEDICINE LODGE	KS	D-	11/02/04
FIRST BK OF NORTHERN KY	KY	D-	11/02/04
FIRST CITY BK	OH	D	11/02/04
FIRST COMMUNITY BK SA NA	TX	D	11/02/04
FIRST FS&LA OF ALLEN PARISH	LA	D	11/02/04
FIRST INTERNATIONAL BK	CA	D	11/02/04
FIRST NB	TX	D	11/02/04
FIRST NB IN HOMER	IL	D	11/02/04
FIRST NB OF FARRAGUT	IA	D-	11/02/04
FIRST NB OF GOLIAD	TX	D-	11/02/04
FIRST NB OF HOLLAND	TX	D	11/02/04
FIRST NB OF PANDORA	OH	D	11/02/04
FIRST NB OF WAMEGO	KS	D	11/02/04
FIRST SECURITY BK	IL	D	11/02/04
FIRST SECURITY BK	KY	D	11/02/04
FIRST ST BK	FL	D	11/02/04
FIRST ST BK	OK	D	11/02/04
FORT WASHINGTON TRUST CO	OH	D	11/02/04
FRIENDSHIP BK	TN	D	11/02/04
GORDON BK	GA	D	11/02/04
GRAND SOUTH BANK	SC	D	11/02/04
GUARDIAN TRUST COMPANY FSB	NY	D	11/02/04
HEDRICK SVGS BK	IA	D	11/02/04
HERITAGE BK	AL	D	11/02/04
HIGHLAND ST BK	WI	D	11/02/04
HOME BKG CO	TN	D	11/02/04
HOME SAVINGS BK	UT	D	11/02/04
HORIZON FSB	IA	D	11/02/04
INLAND COMMUNITY BK NA	CA	D-	11/02/04
INTERNATIONAL FINANCE BK	FL	D	11/02/04
IPAVA ST BK	IL	D-	11/02/04
LAUDERDALE COUNTY BK	TN	D	11/02/04
MARINERBANK	WA	D	11/02/04
MCCURTAIN COUNTY NB	OK	D	11/02/04
MILTON SVG BK	WI	D	11/02/04
MINERS NB OF EVELETH	MN	D	11/02/04
MIRAE BK	CA	D	11/02/04
MISSOURI FSB	MO	D	11/02/04
MOUNTAIN ST BK	GA	D	11/02/04
MUTUAL COMMUNITY SVGS BK	NC	D	11/02/04
NEW CENTURY BK	IL	D	11/02/04
NORTH COUNTY BK	WA	D	11/02/04
PACIFIC PREMIER BANK	CA	D	11/02/04
PARKWAY BK NA	TX	D	11/02/04
PATHFINDER COMMERCIAL BK	NY	D	11/02/04
PEOPLES BK	TX	D	11/02/04
PILGRIM BK	TX	D	11/02/04

BANK NAME	STATE	PREVIOUS WEISS SAFETY RATING	DATE OF CHANGE
PILSEN ST BK	KS	D	11/02/04
PINNACLE BK	FL	D	11/02/04
POLK COUNTY BK	IA	D	11/02/04
PONCE DE LEON FEDERAL BK	NY	D	11/02/04
PREFERRED BK	IL	D	11/02/04
PREMIER BK MN	MN	D	11/02/04
PROGROWTH BK	MN	D	11/02/04
RALLS COUNTY ST BK	MO	D	11/02/04
REGAL FNCL BK	WA	D	11/02/04
RIGHT BK TX NA	TX	D	11/02/04
SEAWAY COMMUNITY BK	MI	D	11/02/04
SECURITY ST BK	IA	D	11/02/04
SECURITY ST SAVINGS BK	NV	D	11/02/04
SHERBURNE ST BK	MN	D	11/02/04
SOUTHERN COMMERCE BK	FL	D-	11/02/04
SOUTHERN COMMUNITY B&T	VA	D	11/02/04
SOUTHWEST CMNTY BK	MO	D	11/02/04
SOUTHWESTERN BK	OK	D	11/02/04
STATE BK OF COCHRAN	GA	D	11/02/04
STATE BK OF TABLE ROCK	NE	D	11/02/04
SUBURBAN B&TC	IL	D-	11/02/04
SYRINGA BK	ID	D	11/02/04
THE BANK	KS	D	11/02/04
UNION ST BK	KS	D	11/02/04
UNITED COMMERCIAL BK	GA	D	11/02/04
UNITED SECURITY BANK	CA	D	11/02/04
VALLEY B&TC	NE	D	11/02/04
VALLEY BK	CA	D	11/02/04
VILLAGE B&TC ARLINGTON HGTS	IL	D-	11/02/04
Weiss Safety Rating:		**D**	
1ST FINANCIAL BK	KS	D-	11/02/04
ALBEMARLE FIRST BK	VA	D-	11/02/04
ALDEN ST BK	KS	D-	11/02/04
ALLIANT BANK	KS	D-	11/02/04
AMERICAN B&TC	LA	D-	11/02/04
BANK OF ALICE	TX	D-	11/02/04
BANK OF FLORIDA A NA	FL	D-	11/02/04
BANK OF NEW CANAAN	CT	D-	11/02/04
BANK OF ONTARIO	WI	D-	11/02/04
BANK OF STAPLETON	NE	D-	11/02/04
BANK OF STEINAUER	NE	D-	11/02/04
BANK OF THE SOUTHWEST	AZ	D-	11/02/04
BAY BK	AL	D-	11/02/04
BLAINE ST BK	MN	D-	11/02/04
BUILDERS BK	IL	D-	11/02/04
CALNET BUSINESS BANK NA	CA	D-	11/02/04
CARDINAL ST BK	NC	D-	11/02/04
CAROLINA TRUST BK	NC	D-	11/02/04
CEDAR VALLEY B&TC	IA	D-	11/02/04
CENTENNIAL BK WEST	CO	D-	11/02/04
CENTERBANK OF JACKSONVILLE N	FL	D-	11/02/04
CITIZENS BK	MO	D-	11/02/04
CITIZENS BK	MO	D-	11/02/04
CITIZENS FIRST BK	KY	D-	11/02/04
CITIZENS ST BK	MN	D-	11/02/04
COAST BK OF FLORIDA	FL	D-	11/02/04
COLLEGE SVGS BK	NJ	D-	11/02/04
COMMUNITY BK OF BROWARD	FL	D-	11/02/04
COMMUNITY BK OF LAWNDALE	IL	D-	11/02/04
COMMUNITY NB	OK	D-	11/02/04
COTTONPORT BK	LA	D-	11/02/04
DELTA T&B	AR	D-	11/02/04
EXCHANGE ST BK	KS	D-	11/02/04
FALFURRIAS ST BK	TX	D-	11/02/04
FARMERS & MERCHANTS CMNTY BK	GA	D-	11/02/04
FARMERS & MERCHANTS ST BK	KS	D-	11/02/04

Rating Upgrades (Continued)

BANK NAME	STATE	PREVIOUS WEISS SAFETY RATING	DATE OF CHANGE
Weiss Safety Rating: D (Continued)			
FARMERS BK OF LIBERTY	IL	D-	11/02/04
FARMERS DEPOSIT BK	KY	D-	11/02/04
FARMERS ST BK	SD	D-	11/02/04
FARMERS ST BK	SD	D-	11/02/04
FIDELITY B&TC	LA	D-	11/02/04
FIRST B&TC OF ILLINOIS	IL	D-	11/02/04
FIRST BK OF THE SOUTH	AL	D-	11/02/04
FIRST COMMUNITY BANK	IL	D-	11/02/04
FIRST NB	CO	D-	11/02/04
FIRST NB	NE	D-	11/02/04
FIRST NB OF FLEMING	CO	D-	11/02/04
FIRST NB OF LEXINGTON	KY	D-	11/02/04
FIRST NB&T OF SYRACUSE	NE	D-	11/02/04
FIRST PEOPLES BK	FL	D-	11/02/04
FIRST SECURITY B&TC	KS	D-	11/02/04
FIRST SOUTHERN NB	GA	D-	11/02/04
FIRST ST BK	AR	D-	11/02/04
FIRST ST BK	TX	D-	11/02/04
FIRST ST BK IA	IA	D-	11/02/04
FLAGSHIP NB	FL	D-	11/02/04
GENEVA ST BK	NE	D-	11/02/04
HARDWARE ST BK	IL	D-	11/02/04
HERITAGE FIRST BANK	GA	D-	11/02/04
HIAWATHA NB	WI	D-	11/02/04
HORIZON BK	FL	D-	11/02/04
INDEPENDENCE FEDERAL BANK	IA	D-	11/02/04
KENTUCKY FS&LA	KY	D-	11/02/04
LANDMARK COMMUNITY BK	PA	D-	11/02/04
MERCHANTS & FARMERS BK	LA	D-	11/02/04
MERCHANTS & PLANTERS BK	TN	D-	11/02/04
METLIFE BK NA	NJ	D-	11/02/04
METRO BANK, FSB	FL	D-	11/02/04
MILLENNIA COMMUNITY BK	NC	D-	11/02/04
NATIONAL AMERICAN BK	TX	D-	11/02/04
NATIVE AMERICAN BK NA	MT	D-	11/02/04
NEKOMA ST BK	KS	D-	11/02/04
NORTHWAY ST BK	IL	D-	11/02/04
NORTHWEST COMMUNITY BK	MN	D-	11/02/04
OMNIBANK NA	TX	D-	11/02/04
PAN AMERICAN BK	IL	D-	11/02/04
PARK AVENUE BANK	NY	D-	11/02/04
PARKWAY B&TC	IL	D-	11/02/04
PLANTERS BK OF MAURY CITY	TN	D-	11/02/04
PLATINUM COMMUNITY BK	IL	D-	11/02/04
PORT CITY CAPITAL BK	NC	D-	11/02/04
PREMIER AMERICAN BK	FL	D-	11/02/04
PRESCOTT ST BK	KS	D-	11/02/04
PROFESSIONAL BUSINESS BK	CA	D-	11/02/04
RANCHERS BANKS	NM	D-	11/02/04
RIO BK	TX	D-	11/02/04
RUMSON FAIR HAVEN B&TC	NJ	D-	11/02/04
SCOTIABANK DE PR	PR	D-	11/02/04
SECURITY BK SB	IL	D-	11/02/04
SECURITY BUS BK OF SAN DIEGO	CA	D-	11/02/04
SEQUOIA NB	CA	D-	11/02/04
SOUTHBANK	GA	D-	11/02/04
SOUTHWESTUSA BK	NV	D-	11/02/04
STATE FARM BK, FSB	IL	D-	11/02/04
STATEWIDE BANK	LA	D-	11/02/04
TEXLINE ST BK	TX	D-	11/02/04
UNITED MINNESOTA BK	MN	D-	11/02/04
UNITED PACIFIC BK	CA	D-	11/02/04
UNITED SECURITY SVGS BK FSB	IA	D-	11/02/04
VALLEY B&TC	IA	D-	11/02/04
WASHINGTON ST BK NA	WA	D-	11/02/04

BANK NAME	STATE	PREVIOUS WEISS SAFETY RATING	DATE OF CHANGE
Weiss Safety Rating: D-			
AMERICANA COMMUNITY BK	MN	E	11/02/04
AMERICASBANK	MD	E-	11/02/04
BANK OF BOLIVAR CTY	MS	E	11/02/04
BANK OF PALMER	KS	E+	11/02/04
BAYTREE NB&TC	IL	E+	11/02/04
CALIFORNIA OAKS ST BK	CA	E-	11/02/04
CAPITAL BK&TC	NY	E-	11/02/04
CITIZENS CITY & CTY BK	TN	E+	11/02/04
COMMUNITY BK OF THE BAY	CA	E-	11/02/04
CORN GROWERS ST BK	NE	E+	11/02/04
CUMBERLAND VALLEY NB&TC	KY	E+	11/02/04
EBANK	GA	E-	11/02/04
FARMERS ST BK	NE	E+	11/02/04
FIRST FS&LA OF PEKIN	IL	E	11/02/04
FIRST NB OF BULLARD	TX	E	11/02/04
FIRST SECURITY BK	MO	E+	11/02/04
FIRST ST BK	OK	E+	11/02/04
FIRST ST BK OF POND CREEK	OK	E	11/02/04
FORT DAVIS ST BK	TX	E	11/02/04
FRANKLIN NB	TX	E+	11/02/04
HORIZON BK FSB	FL	E	11/02/04
HORIZON ST BK	MO	E+	11/02/04
JASPER ST BK	MN	E	11/02/04
LYONS ST BK	KS	E	11/02/04
MAINSTREET BK	MO	E-	11/02/04
MARINE B&TC	FL	E+	11/02/04
MARINE BK	WI	E+	11/02/04
METROPOLITAN SB	PA	E+	11/02/04
MID ST BK	WA	E	11/02/04
PATTERSON BK	GA	E	11/02/04
ROXBURY BK	KS	E+	11/02/04
SECURITY ST BK	TX	E+	11/02/04
STATE BK OF ELDRED	IL	E+	11/02/04
SYNERGY BK SSB	TX	E+	11/02/04
TATTNALL BK	GA	E+	11/02/04
UNITED BK OF PHILADELPHIA	PA	E+	11/02/04
UNITED VALLEY BK	MN	E+	11/02/04
Weiss Safety Rating: E+			
1ST UNITED BK	FL	E-	11/02/04
AIMBANK	TX	E-	11/02/04
BAILEYVILLE ST BK	KS	E-	11/02/04
BANK OF COMMERCE	IL	E-	11/02/04
BANK OF JACKSON CTY	FL	E	11/02/04
BANK OF MILAN	TN	E-	11/02/04
CENTENNIAL BK	CO	E	11/02/04
CENTENNIAL BK	NE	E	11/02/04
CENTERVILLE ST BK	KS	E	11/02/04
CITIZENS CMNTY BK DECATUR	IL	E	11/02/04
COMMERCIAL BK OF VOLUSIA CTY	FL	E	11/02/04
FARMERS & TRADERS SVG BK	IA	E	11/02/04
FARMERS BK	AR	E	11/02/04
FIRST NB	MO	E	11/02/04
FIRST ST BK	TX	E	11/02/04
FIRST ST BK OF WARNER SD	SD	E	11/02/04
FIRST TUSKEGEE BK	AL	E-	11/02/04
FRONT RANGE BK	CO	E-	11/02/04
GARDNER NB	KS	E	11/02/04
GENESEE REGIONAL BK	NY	E-	11/02/04
HOME FSB	MI	E-	11/02/04
MCMULLEN BK	TX	E-	11/02/04
MONADNOCK COMMUNITY BK	NH	E-	11/02/04
NATIONAL BK OF DAVIS	WV	E-	11/02/04
PANAMERICAN BK	FL	E-	11/02/04
PEOPLES ST BK	FL	E-	11/02/04

Rating Upgrades (Continued)

BANK NAME	STATE	PREVIOUS WEISS SAFETY RATING	DATE OF CHANGE	BANK NAME	STATE	PREVIOUS WEISS SAFETY RATING	DATE OF CHANGE

Weiss Safety Rating: E+ (Continued)

BANK NAME	STATE	PREVIOUS WEISS SAFETY RATING	DATE OF CHANGE
PINE ST BK	AR	E	11/02/04
RANTOUL FIRST BK SB	IL	E	11/02/04
SIDNEY FS&LA	NE	E	11/02/04
STATE BK OF AURORA	MN	E-	11/02/04
STATE BK OF BURDEN	KS	E	11/02/04
STATE BK OF CONWAY SPRINGS	KS	E	11/02/04
STATE BK OF GIBBON	MN	E-	11/02/04
STOCKMANS BANK	OK	E-	11/02/04
SURETY BK NA	TX	E-	11/02/04
UNITED TRUST BANK	IL	E-	11/02/04
UNITED-AMERICAN SVGS BK	PA	E	11/02/04

Weiss Safety Rating: E

BANK NAME	STATE	PREVIOUS WEISS SAFETY RATING	DATE OF CHANGE
AMERICAN ST BK	OK	E-	11/02/04
BAY PORT ST BK	MI	E-	11/02/04
EAGLE BK	TX	E-	11/02/04
FIRST NB OF WIGGINS	MS	E-	11/02/04
FIRST SECURITY BK - SANBORN	MN	E-	11/02/04
FIRST ST BK FORT LAUDERDALE	FL	E-	11/02/04
FUTURUS BK NA	GA	E-	11/02/04
GREATER SOUTH TEXAS BK FSB	TX	E-	11/02/04
INTEGRITY BANK PLUS	MN	E-	11/02/04
LAKE COUNTRY COMMUNITY BK	MN	E-	11/02/04
PEOPLES BK	OK	E-	11/02/04
RIPLEY NB	OH	E-	11/02/04
STATE NB OF GROOM	TX	E-	11/02/04
UNITED SOUTHWEST BK	MN	E-	11/02/04

Rating Downgrades

BANK NAME	STATE	PREVIOUS WEISS SAFETY RATING	DATE OF CHANGE
Weiss Safety Rating: A			
BANK OF LANDISBURG	PA	A+	11/02/04
BANK OF MILLBROOK	NY	A+	11/02/04
COMMERCIAL NB OF BRADY	TX	A+	11/02/04
EAGLE BK	KY	A+	11/02/04
FIRST FIDELITY BK	SD	A+	11/02/04
FIRST NB OF ALBANY	TX	A+	11/02/04
FIRST NB&TC OF MOUNTAIN HOME	AR	A+	11/02/04
FIRST ST BK	IN	A+	11/02/04
PEOPLES BK OF MULLENS	WV	A+	11/02/04
SAVINGS BK	OH	A+	11/02/04
Weiss Safety Rating: A-			
ABACUS FSB	NY	A	11/02/04
BANK OF CHARLES TOWN	WV	A	11/02/04
BANK OF GRANITE	NC	A	11/02/04
CENTURY B&T	MI	A	11/02/04
CITIZENS NB OF CHEBOYGAN	MI	A	11/02/04
CITIZENS ST BK	MN	A	11/02/04
CITIZENS ST BK	TX	A	11/02/04
COMMUNITY NB OF NW PA	PA	A	11/02/04
COUNTYBANK	SC	A	11/02/04
FARMERS BK	VA	A	11/02/04
FCN BK NA	IN	A	11/02/04
FIDELITY HMSTD ASSN	LA	A	11/02/04
FIRST FEDERAL SVGS	NY	A	11/02/04
FIRST NB IN ALAMOGORDO	NM	A	11/02/04
FIRST NB OF LONG ISLAND	NY	A	11/02/04
FIRST NB OF MERCERSBURG	PA	A	11/02/04
FIRST NB-RUIDOSO	NM	A	11/02/04
FIRST PORT CITY BK	GA	A	11/02/04
FIRST TEXAS BK	TX	A	11/02/04
HIGH POINT B&TC	NC	A	11/02/04
HOME FEDERAL BANK OF TN	TN	A	11/02/04
INTERNATIONAL BK OF COMMERCE	TX	A	11/02/04
MANASQUAN SVG BK	NJ	A	11/02/04
NATIONAL BK OF CAMBRIDGE	MD	A	11/02/04
NATIONAL BK OF NEW YORK CITY	NY	A	11/02/04
NORTH SIDE B&TC	OH	A	11/02/04
OMAHA ST BK	NE	A	11/02/04
PEOPLES NB OF LA FOLLETTE	TN	A	11/02/04
PLANTERS & MERCHANTS ST BK	TX	A	11/02/04
POWELL VALLEY NB	VA	A	11/02/04
SAN LUIS VALLEY FEDERAL BK	CO	A	11/02/04
SPENCER SVGS BK	MA	A	11/02/04
STATE BK OF ESCANABA	MI	A	11/02/04
TALBOT BK OF EASTON MD	MD	A	11/02/04
WAYNE B&TC	IN	A	11/02/04
YOAKUM NB	TX	A	11/02/04
Weiss Safety Rating: B+			
AMERICAN NB OF SIDNEY	NE	A-	11/02/04
AMERICAN SVG BK	IA	A-	11/02/04
ANNA ST BK	IL	A-	11/02/04
ARTHUR ST BK	SC	A-	11/02/04
ATLANTIC LIBERTY SVGS FA	NY	A-	11/02/04
BANK OF BEARDEN	AR	A-	11/02/04
BANK OF BLOOMSDALE	MO	A-	11/02/04
BANK OF LEE'S SUMMIT	MO	A-	11/02/04
BANK OF NEBRASKA	NE	A-	11/02/04
BANK OF THE SOUTH	MS	A-	11/02/04
BANK OF THE WEST	TX	A-	11/02/04
BANKILLINOIS	IL	A-	11/02/04
BODCAW BK	AR	A-	11/02/04
CAMPBELL & FETTER BKRS	IN	A-	11/02/04

BANK NAME	STATE	PREVIOUS WEISS SAFETY RATING	DATE OF CHANGE
CENTRAL BK	MO	A-	11/02/04
CENTRAL NB OF POTEAU	OK	A-	11/02/04
CITIZENS & NORTHERN BK	PA	A-	11/02/04
CITIZENS COMMUNITY BK	TN	A-	11/02/04
CITIZENS FIRST SVG BK	MI	A-	11/02/04
CITIZENS NB	MD	A-	11/02/04
CITIZENS NB OF ELKINS	WV	A-	11/02/04
CITIZENS NB-MILAM CTY	TX	A-	11/02/04
CLINTON NB	IA	A-	11/02/04
COMMERCE BK	CO	A-	11/02/04
COMMERCE BK	TX	A-	11/02/04
COMMUNITY BK OF BERGEN CTY	NJ	A-	11/02/04
COMMUNITY BK OF TRENTON	IL	A-	11/02/04
CONVERSE COUNTY BK	WY	A-	11/02/04
EXCHANGE BK	CA	A-	11/02/04
FARMERS & MERCHANTS BK	WI	A-	11/02/04
FARMERS SVG BK	IA	A-	11/02/04
FIDELITY BK	MD	A-	11/02/04
FIRST CENTRAL NB	OH	A-	11/02/04
FIRST COMMUNITY BK NA	VA	A-	11/02/04
FIRST CRAWFORD ST BK	IL	A-	11/02/04
FIRST FEDERAL BANK OF CA FSB	CA	A-	11/02/04
FIRST NB OF BERWICK	PA	A-	11/02/04
FIRST NB OF CLARKSDALE	MS	A-	11/02/04
FIRST NB OF DECATUR	IL	A-	11/02/04
FIRST NB OF ELMER	NJ	A-	11/02/04
FIRST NB OF MANCHESTER	TN	A-	11/02/04
FIRST NB OF MT VERNON	IL	A-	11/02/04
FIRST ST BK	TX	A-	11/02/04
FIRST WESTERN BK	SD	A-	11/02/04
FIRST WESTERN BK CUSTER	SD	A-	11/02/04
FIRST WESTERN BK WALL	SD	A-	11/02/04
FOUNTAIN TRUST CO	IN	A-	11/02/04
HERITAGE BK OF COMMERCE	CA	A-	11/02/04
HOMETOWN BK NA	TX	A-	11/02/04
INTERNATIONAL BK OF AMHERST	WI	A-	11/02/04
INTERNATIONAL BK OF COMMERCE	TX	A-	11/02/04
INTERNATIONAL BK/CMMRCE NA	TX	A-	11/02/04
JONESBORO ST BK	LA	A-	11/02/04
LA JOLLA BK FSB	CA	A-	11/02/04
LEWISBURG BKG CO	KY	A-	11/02/04
LEXINGTON ST BK	NC	A-	11/02/04
MARKLEBANK	IN	A-	11/02/04
MUTUAL FSB	IN	A-	11/02/04
MUTUAL SA FSA	KS	A-	11/02/04
NATIONAL B&TC OF SYCAMORE	IL	A-	11/02/04
NATIONAL BK OF BLACKSBURG	VA	A-	11/02/04
NEWBERRY FSB	SC	A-	11/02/04
NORTHWESTERN BK	WI	A-	11/02/04
PEOPLES B&TC POINTE COUPEE	LA	A-	11/02/04
PEOPLES BK OF GREENSBORO	AL	A-	11/02/04
PORT AUSTIN ST BK	MI	A-	11/02/04
PRIMEBANK	IA	A-	11/02/04
RIVERVIEW COMMUNITY BK	WA	A-	11/02/04
SALEM CO-OP BK	NH	A-	11/02/04
SCOTTDALE B&TC	PA	A-	11/02/04
SECURITY BK OF KANSAS CITY	KS	A-	11/02/04
STATE B&T	TX	A-	11/02/04
STATE B&TC	TX	A-	11/02/04
STATE BK OF CHILTON	WI	A-	11/02/04
STILLMAN BANCCORP N.A.	IL	A-	11/02/04
TOWN & COUNTRY BK	NE	A-	11/02/04
UNITED CITIZENS B&TC	KY	A-	11/02/04
WAKE FOREST FS&LA	NC	A-	11/02/04
WATKINS SVG BK	IA	A-	11/02/04
WEST BK	IA	A-	11/02/04
WESTMINSTER UNION BK	MD	A-	11/02/04

Rating Downgrades (Continued)

BANK NAME	STATE	PREVIOUS WEISS SAFETY RATING	DATE OF CHANGE
Weiss Safety Rating:	**B**		**(Continued)**
ALERUS FINANCIAL NA	ND	A-	11/02/04
ALGONQUIN ST BK	IL	B+	11/02/04
AMERICAN BK NA	TX	B+	11/02/04
APPLE BK FOR SVGS	NY	B+	11/02/04
AVON CO-OP BK	MA	B+	11/02/04
BANK OF GRAVETT	AR	B+	11/02/04
BANK OF LOCUST GROVE	OK	B+	11/02/04
BANK OF MARINGOUIN	LA	B+	11/02/04
BANK OF STOCKTON	CA	B+	11/02/04
BATH SVGS INSTITUTION	ME	B+	11/02/04
BLUE GRASS FS&LA	KY	B+	11/02/04
BYRON BK	IL	B+	11/02/04
CALLAWAY BK	MO	B+	11/02/04
CAPE COD CO-OP BK	MA	B+	11/02/04
CAPITAL BK	TX	B+	11/02/04
CAPITALBANK	SC	B+	11/02/04
CAPITOL FEDERAL SVGS BK	KS	B+	11/02/04
CATHAY BK	CA	B+	11/02/04
CHB AMERICA BK	NY	B+	11/02/04
CITIZENS NB	TN	B+	11/02/04
CITIZENS ST BK	IA	B+	11/02/04
CITIZENS ST BK OF POMONA	KS	B+	11/02/04
CLOVER CMNTY BK	SC	B+	11/02/04
COMMERCIAL ST BK	TX	B+	11/02/04
COMMONWEALTH CMNTY BK	KY	B+	11/02/04
COMMUNITY BK	NC	A-	11/02/04
CONCORDIA B&TC	LA	B+	11/02/04
COSMOPOLITAN B&T	IL	B+	11/02/04
DEDHAM CO-OP BK	MA	B+	11/02/04
DELAWARE NB OF DELHI	NY	B+	11/02/04
EASTERN INTERNATIONAL BK	CA	B+	11/02/04
ESB BK	PA	B+	11/02/04
EVANS NB	NY	B+	11/02/04
EXCHANGE BK	SC	B+	11/02/04
F&M COMMUNITY BK NA	MN	B+	11/02/04
FARMERS & MERCHANTS NB	NE	B+	11/02/04
FARMERS & MERCHANTS ST BK	MN	B+	11/02/04
FARMERS & MERCHANTS ST BK	SD	A-	11/02/04
FARMERS AND MERCHANTS BK	MD	B+	11/02/04
FARMERS B&TC	AR	B+	11/02/04
FARMERS B&TC	KY	B+	11/02/04
FARMERS BK OF APPOMATTOX	VA	B+	11/02/04
FARMERS ST BK OF DARWIN	MN	B+	11/02/04
FARMERS ST BK OF EMDEN	IL	B+	11/02/04
FAUQUIER BK	VA	B+	11/02/04
FIDELITY BK	MI	B+	11/02/04
FIRESIDE BK	CA	B+	11/02/04
FIRST BK	TX	B+	11/02/04
FIRST FEDERAL BK OF LA	LA	B+	11/02/04
FIRST FS&LA	KY	B+	11/02/04
FIRST NB	KS	B+	11/02/04
FIRST NB	OH	B+	11/02/04
FIRST NB	TN	B+	11/02/04
FIRST NB OF AVA	IL	B+	11/02/04
FIRST NB OF CANTON	TX	B+	11/02/04
FIRST NB OF DIGHTON	KS	B+	11/02/04
FIRST NB OF FT STOCKTON	TX	B+	11/02/04
FIRST NB&TC OF ARDMORE	OK	B+	11/02/04
FIRST PRYORITY BK	OK	B+	11/02/04
FIRST ST BK	GA	B+	11/02/04
FIRST ST BK	NE	B+	11/02/04
FIRST ST BK	TN	B+	11/02/04
FIRST ST BK OF FERTILE	MN	B+	11/02/04

BANK NAME	STATE	PREVIOUS WEISS SAFETY RATING	DATE OF CHANGE
FIRST ST BK OF STRATFORD	TX	B+	11/02/04
FIRST-CITIZENS BK NA	VA	B+	11/02/04
FIVE POINTS BK OF HASTINGS	NE	B+	11/02/04
FOWLER ST BK	KS	B+	11/02/04
GOLDEN SECURITY BK	CA	B+	11/02/04
GOTHAM BK OF NEW YORK	NY	B+	11/02/04
GRUNDY NB OF GRUNDY CTR	IA	B+	11/02/04
GUARANTY BK	MO	B+	11/02/04
HANMI BK	CA	B+	11/02/04
HENRY COUNTY BK	OH	B+	11/02/04
HIBERNIA HMSTD & SA	LA	B+	11/02/04
HOME BANK SB	IN	B+	11/02/04
HUDSON CITY SAVINGS BK	NJ	B+	11/02/04
IROQUOIS FARMERS ST BK	IL	B+	11/02/04
LAKESIDE BK OF SALINA	OK	B+	11/02/04
LLANO NB	TX	B+	11/02/04
MOODY NB OF GALVESTON	TX	B+	11/02/04
NEW VIENNA SVG BK	IA	B+	11/02/04
NEWALLIANCE BK	CT	A-	11/02/04
NORTH AMERICAN ST BK	MN	B+	11/02/04
NORTH DALLAS B&TC	TX	B+	11/02/04
NORTH FORK BK	NY	B+	11/02/04
NORTH STAR BK	MN	B+	11/02/04
NORTHERN TRUST BK OF FL NA	FL	B+	11/02/04
NORTHFIELD SVGS BK	VT	B+	11/02/04
OZARK BK	MO	B+	11/02/04
PENN SECURITY B&TC	PA	B+	11/02/04
PEOPLES ST BK	SD	B+	11/02/04
PINNACLE BK WY	WY	B+	11/02/04
PLYMOUTH SVGS BK	MA	B+	11/02/04
PNC BK, DELAWARE	DE	B+	11/02/04
PUTNAM FIDUCIARY TC	MA	B+	11/02/04
RANDOLPH ST BK	IA	B+	11/02/04
REEDSBURG BK	WI	B+	11/02/04
REGIONS BANK	AL	B+	11/02/04
RILEY ST BK	KS	B+	11/02/04
SALEM FIVE CENTS SVGS BK	MA	B+	11/02/04
SCOTTSBURG B&LA	IN	B+	11/02/04
SECURITY BK	AL	B+	11/02/04
SECURITY ST BK	TX	B+	11/02/04
SECURITY ST BK	WA	B+	11/02/04
SMITH CTY ST B&TC	KS	B+	11/02/04
STATE BK	KS	B+	11/02/04
STATE BK OF ARCADIA	WI	B+	11/02/04
STATE BK OF COLONY	KS	B+	11/02/04
STATE BK OF DOWNS	KS	B+	11/02/04
SUN SOCIETY BK	MO	A-	11/02/04
TRUSTMARK NB	MS	B+	11/02/04
UNITED BK	VA	B+	11/02/04
UNITED BK	WV	B+	11/02/04
VERGAS ST BK	MN	B+	11/02/04
WATERTOWN SVGS BK	NY	B+	11/02/04
WRENTHAM CO-OP BK	MA	B+	11/02/04
Weiss Safety Rating:	**B-**		
1ST CENTENNIAL BK	CA	B	11/02/04
ACCESSBANK	NM	B	11/02/04
ADAMS CO-OP BK	MA	B	11/02/04
ANADARKO B&TC	OK	B	11/02/04
ANDERSON ST BK	IL	B	11/02/04
ARIZONA B&T	AZ	B	11/02/04
ARKANSAS ST BK	AR	B	11/02/04
ARMSTRONG COUNTY B&LA	PA	B	11/02/04
ATHENS FIRST B&TC	GA	B	11/02/04
ATHOL-CLINTON CO-OP BK	MA	B	11/02/04
B&L BK	MO	B	11/02/04
BANK OF BRADFORD	TN	B	11/02/04

Rating Downgrades (Continued)

BANK NAME	STATE	PREVIOUS WEISS SAFETY RATING	DATE OF CHANGE
Weiss Safety Rating: B- (Continued)			
BANK OF CASTILE	NY	B	11/02/04
BANK OF COMMERCE	WY	B	11/02/04
BANK OF COWETA	GA	B	11/02/04
BANK OF NEW YORK-DELAWARE	DE	B	11/02/04
BANK OF THE CASCADES	OR	B	11/02/04
BANK OF WESTMINSTER	SC	B	11/02/04
BANK OF WILLIAMSBURG	VA	B	11/02/04
BANK OF YAZOO CITY	MS	B	11/02/04
BANKEAST	TN	B	11/02/04
BNY WESTERN TC	CA	B	11/02/04
BRIDGEWATER SVGS BK	MA	B	11/02/04
BULLITT COUNTY BK	KY	B	11/02/04
CASS COMMERCIAL BK	MO	B	11/02/04
CEDAR HILL NB	GA	B	11/02/04
CENTRAL BANK USA INC	KY	B	11/02/04
CENTRAL VALLEY BK NA	WA	B	11/02/04
CITIZENS & MERCHANTS ST BK	GA	B	11/02/04
CITIZENS B&LA	SC	B	11/02/04
CITIZENS BK	TX	B	11/02/04
CITIZENS FIRST BK	GA	B	11/02/04
CITIZENS NB OF PARK RAPIDS	MN	B	11/02/04
CITIZENS NB-BERKELEY SPRGS	WV	B	11/02/04
CITIZENS ST BK OF CLARA CITY	MN	B	11/02/04
CITIZENS UNION ST B&TC	MO	B	11/02/04
CITY NB OF SAN SABA	TX	B	11/02/04
CLEARFIELD B&TC	PA	B	11/02/04
CMMNTY BK OAK PARK RIVER FORE	IL	B	11/02/04
COFFEE COUNTY BK	TN	B	11/02/04
COLUMBIA RIVER BK	OR	B	11/02/04
COMMERCE BK	MN	B	11/02/04
COMMERCE BK NA	MO	B	11/02/04
COMMERCE BK OF OMAHA NA	NE	B	11/02/04
COMMERCEBANK NA	FL	B	11/02/04
COMMERCIAL BK	GA	B	11/02/04
COMMUNITY BK	TN	B	11/02/04
COMMUNITY BK FINANCIAL	WI	B	11/02/04
COMMUNITY NB	VA	B	11/02/04
CREDIT FIRST NA	OH	B	11/02/04
DECATUR COUNTY BK	TN	B	11/02/04
DELANCO FSB	NJ	B	11/02/04
DELAWARE NB	DE	B	11/02/04
DESERT HILLS BK	AZ	B	11/02/04
DIME BANK	PA	B	11/02/04
DOUGLAS COUNTY BK	KS	B	11/02/04
DUBUQUE B&TC	IA	B	11/02/04
EMPORIA ST B&TC	KS	B	11/02/04
FAIRMOUNT FSB	MD	B	11/02/04
FAIRMOUNT ST BK	IN	B	11/02/04
FALMOUTH CO-OP BK	MA	B	11/02/04
FARMERS BK	TN	B	11/02/04
FARMERS ST BK	SD	B	11/02/04
FARMERS SVG B&T-TRAER	IA	B	11/02/04
FARMERS SVGS B&T-VINTON	IA	B	11/02/04
FIRST BK OF OWASSO	OK	B+	11/02/04
FIRST COAST CMNTY BK	FL	B	11/02/04
FIRST COMMERCIAL BK	AL	B	11/02/04
FIRST FS&LA OF BATH	ME	B	11/02/04
FIRST NB IN CARLYLE	IL	B	11/02/04
FIRST NB IN CISCO	TX	B	11/02/04
FIRST NB IN CRESTON	IA	B	11/02/04
FIRST NB IN SIOUX FALLS	SD	B	11/02/04
FIRST NB OELWEIN	IA	B	11/02/04
FIRST NB OF ANDERSON	TX	B	11/02/04
FIRST NB OF BELLEVUE	OH	B	11/02/04
FIRST NB OF DURANGO	CO	B	11/02/04

BANK NAME	STATE	PREVIOUS WEISS SAFETY RATING	DATE OF CHANGE
FIRST NB OF ELDORADO	TX	B	11/02/04
FIRST NB OF HOLDREGE	NE	B+	11/02/04
FIRST NB OF LA FOLLETTE	TN	B	11/02/04
FIRST NB OF NEGAUNEE	MI	B	11/02/04
FIRST NB OF NEW RICHMOND	WI	B	11/02/04
FIRST NB OF PICAYUNE	MS	B	11/02/04
FIRST NB OF ST LOUIS	MO	B	11/02/04
FIRST NB OF WAHOO	NE	B	11/02/04
FIRST NB OF WINNSBORO	TX	B	11/02/04
FIRST NB&TC OF BEATRICE	NE	B	11/02/04
FIRST ST B&TC	GA	B	11/02/04
FIRST ST BK	MN	B	11/02/04
FIRST ST BK	OK	B	11/02/04
FIRST ST BK	WI	B	11/02/04
FIRST VALLEY BK	MT	B	11/02/04
FIRSTBANK CHERRY CREEK	CO	B	11/02/04
FIRSTBANK DENVER	CO	B	11/02/04
FIRSTBANK OF AVON	CO	B	11/02/04
FNB BK NA	PA	B	11/02/04
FORETHOUGHT FSB	IN	B+	11/02/04
FOUR OAKS B&TC	NC	B	11/02/04
GLADEWATER NB	TX	B	11/02/04
GREENVILLE SVGS BK	PA	B	11/02/04
HARVARD ST BK	IL	B	11/02/04
HAVERHILL CO-OP BK	MA	B	11/02/04
HERITAGE SVGS BK	WA	B	11/02/04
HERNDON NB	PA	B	11/02/04
HIBERNIA NB	LA	B	11/02/04
HONESDALE NB	PA	B	11/02/04
HURON COMMUNITY BK	MI	B	11/02/04
HYDE PARK B&TC	IL	B	11/02/04
INDEPENDENCE COMMUNITY BK	NY	B	11/02/04
INDIANA FIRST SVG BK	PA	B	11/02/04
INWOOD NB OF DALLAS	TX	B	11/02/04
ITS BK	IA	B	11/02/04
JACKSON ST B&T	WY	B	11/02/04
KS BANK, INC	NC	B	11/02/04
LA PLATA ST BK	MO	B+	11/02/04
LAUREL SVGS BK	PA	B	11/02/04
LORAIN NB	OH	B	11/02/04
M & I BK FSB	NV	B	11/02/04
M&I BK MAYVILLE	WI	B	11/02/04
M&I MARSHALL & ILSLEY BK	WI	B	11/02/04
MARATHON NB-NY	NY	B	11/02/04
MARBLEHEAD BK	OH	B	11/02/04
MARFA NB	TX	B	11/02/04
MAUCH CHUNK TRUST CO	PA	B	11/02/04
MEDWAY CO-OP BK	MA	B	11/02/04
MERCHANTS & SOUTHERN BK	FL	B	11/02/04
MID-SOUTHERN SVGS BK FSB	IN	B	11/02/04
MITCHELL BANK	WI	B	11/02/04
NATIONAL BK OF WALTON CTY	GA	B	11/02/04
NAUGATUCK VALLEY S&L SB	CT	B	11/02/04
NEW CENTURY BK	NC	B	11/02/04
NORTHERN NECK ST BK	VA	B	11/02/04
OLYMPIC SA	TX	B	11/02/04
OMNIBANK	MS	B	11/02/04
OZARK MOUNTAIN BK	MO	B	11/02/04
PAGE COUNTY FSA	IA	B	11/02/04
PALO SVG BK	IA	B	11/02/04
PARK NB&T	IL	B	11/02/04
PEOPLES BK	IN	B	11/02/04
PEOPLES BK	MD	B	11/02/04
PEOPLES BK OF THE OZARKS	MO	B	11/02/04
PEOPLES NB OF NEW LEXINGTON	OH	B	11/02/04
PEOPLES T&SB	IN	B	11/02/04
PORTALES NB	NM	B	11/02/04

Rating Downgrades (Continued)

BANK NAME	STATE	PREVIOUS WEISS SAFETY RATING	DATE OF CHANGE
Weiss Safety Rating:	**B-**		**(Continued)**
PROVIDENT ST BK	MD	B	11/02/04
PULASKI SVGS BK	IL	B	11/02/04
RAPPAHANNOCK NB WASHINGTON	VA	B	11/02/04
RELIANCE SVGS BK	PA	B	11/02/04
ROME SAVINGS BANK	NY	B+	11/02/04
SAVINGS BK	MA	B	11/02/04
SEA ISLAND BK	GA	B	11/02/04
SECURITY ST BK	MN	B+	11/02/04
SECURITY ST BK	MN	B	11/02/04
SECURITY SVG BK SSB	NC	B	11/02/04
SECURITY T&SB	IA	B	11/02/04
SHAMROCK BK NA	OK	B	11/02/04
SHERIDAN ST BK	WY	B	11/02/04
SHOSHONE FIRST BK	WY	B	11/02/04
SILVER FALLS BK	OR	B	11/02/04
SKY TRUST NA	OH	B	11/02/04
SKYLANDS CMNTY BK	NJ	B	11/02/04
SOUTHWEST BK OF TEXAS NA	TX	B	11/02/04
STATE BK OF LEDYARD	IA	B	11/02/04
STEPHENS FEDERAL BK	GA	B	11/02/04
STERLING BK	AL	B	11/02/04
TOWN NORTH BK NA	TX	B	11/02/04
TRI-COUNTY BK	MI	B	11/02/04
TRI-COUNTY TRUST COMPANY	MO	B	11/02/04
UNION B&TC	VA	B	11/02/04
UNION FS&LA CRAWFORDSVILLE	IN	B+	11/02/04
UNION ST BK	KS	B	11/02/04
UNITED AZ BK NA	AZ	B	11/02/04
UNITED BANKERS BK	MN	B	11/02/04
UNITED BK	MA	B	11/02/04
USAA FSB	TX	B	11/02/04
VANGUARD B&TC	FL	B	11/02/04
WALDEN SVGS BK	NY	B	11/02/04
WELCH ST BK	OK	B	11/02/04
WELLESLEY CO-OP BK	MA	B	11/02/04
WEST SHORE BK	MI	B	11/02/04
WOORI AMER BK	NY	B	11/02/04
Weiss Safety Rating:	**C+**		
1ST INDEPENDENCE BK	IN	B-	11/02/04
1ST NB&TC	FL	B-	11/02/04
ADRIAN BK	MO	B-	11/02/04
AMBLER SVG BK	PA	B-	11/02/04
AMERICAN BK NA	TX	B-	11/02/04
ASCENCIA BK INC	KY	B-	11/02/04
AUDUBON ST BK	IA	B-	11/02/04
BALTIC ST BK	OH	B-	11/02/04
BANK LEUMI USA	NY	B-	11/02/04
BANK OF FRANKLIN	MS	B-	11/02/04
BANK OF HOUSTON	MO	B-	11/02/04
BANK OF KENTUCKY	KY	B-	11/02/04
BANK OF NEW CASTLE	DE	B-	11/02/04
BANK OF RIO VISTA	CA	B-	11/02/04
BANK ONE TC NA	OH	B-	11/02/04
BANKERS TRUST COMPANY NA	IA	B-	11/02/04
BILTMORE BK OF ARIZONA	AZ	B-	11/02/04
BRENTWOOD BK	PA	B-	11/02/04
BUSINESS BK	VA	B-	11/02/04
CAMBRIDGE ST BK	MN	B	11/02/04
CAMP GROVE ST BK	IL	B-	11/02/04
CATAWBA VALLEY BK	NC	B-	11/02/04
CHELTEN HILLS SVGS BK	PA	B-	11/02/04
CITIZENS B&TC	MO	B-	11/02/04
CITIZENS BK	GA	B-	11/02/04

BANK NAME	STATE	PREVIOUS WEISS SAFETY RATING	DATE OF CHANGE
CITIZENS BK	GA	B-	11/02/04
CITIZENS NB OF CHILLICOTHE	OH	B-	11/02/04
CITIZENS SECURITY B&TC	OK	B-	11/02/04
CITIZENS ST BK	MI	B-	11/02/04
CITIZENS ST BK	TX	B-	11/02/04
CITIZENS ST BK BALLARD CTY	KY	B-	11/02/04
CITIZENS SVG BK	OH	B-	11/02/04
CITY BANK NEW MEXICO	NM	B-	11/02/04
CITY BK	TX	B-	11/02/04
COMMUNITY BK DELAVAN	WI	B-	11/02/04
COMMUNITY BK DESOTO CTY	MS	B-	11/02/04
COMMUNITY BK NA	PA	B-	11/02/04
COMMUNITY BK SOUTHERN IN	IN	B-	11/02/04
COMMUNITY CENTRAL BK	MI	B-	11/02/04
COMMUNITY SVGS BK	IL	B-	11/02/04
CONCORDIA BK	MO	B-	11/02/04
CP BURNETT & SONS, BANKERS	IL	B-	11/02/04
CRESCENT B&TC	LA	B-	11/02/04
DELAWARE COUNTY B&TC	OH	B-	11/02/04
EAGLE VALLEY BK NA	WI	B-	11/02/04
ELYSIAN BK	MN	B	11/02/04
EQUITABLE S&LA	CO	B-	11/02/04
EVERGREEN FS&LA	OR	B-	11/02/04
FARMER CITY ST BK	IL	B-	11/02/04
FARMERS & MERCHANTS B&TC	LA	B-	11/02/04
FARMERS & MERCHANTS NB	IL	B-	11/02/04
FARMERS AND MECHANICS FS&LA	IN	B-	11/02/04
FARMERS ST BK	KS	B-	11/02/04
FIRST B&TC OF PRINCETON	KY	B-	11/02/04
FIRST BK OF TENNESSEE	TN	B-	11/02/04
FIRST BRADENTON BK	FL	B-	11/02/04
FIRST CMRL BK	OK	B-	11/02/04
FIRST COMMUNITY BK	KS	B-	11/02/04
FIRST EAST SIDE SAVINGS BANK	IL	B-	11/02/04
FIRST FSB	IN	B	11/02/04
FIRST HARRISON BK	IN	B-	11/02/04
FIRST NB	IA	B-	11/02/04
FIRST NB OF FLORIDA	FL	B-	11/02/04
FIRST NB OF JACKSON	KY	B-	11/02/04
FIRST NB OF LACON	IL	B-	11/02/04
FIRST NB OF UTICA	NE	B-	11/02/04
FIRST NB OF WATERLOO	IL	B-	11/02/04
FIRST NIAGARA COMMERCIAL BK	NY	B-	11/02/04
FIRST SECURITY ST BK	IA	B-	11/02/04
FIRST SOUTHERN NATIONAL	KY	B-	11/02/04
FIRST ST BK	NM	B-	11/02/04
FIRST ST BK	TX	B-	11/02/04
FIRST ST BK CENTRAL TX	TX	B-	11/02/04
FIRST ST BK FLORIDA KEYS	FL	B-	11/02/04
FIRST ST BK OF OKABENA	MN	B-	11/02/04
FIRST ST BK-WESTERN IL	IL	B-	11/02/04
FIRST UNITED BK	CO	B-	11/02/04
FIRST WESTERN BK	AR	B-	11/02/04
FREEDOM NB	RI	B-	11/02/04
FRONTIER SVGS BK	IA	B-	11/02/04
GLASGOW SVG BK	MO	B-	11/02/04
GLENWOOD ST BK	IA	B-	11/02/04
GWINNETT BKG CO	GA	B-	11/02/04
HEIGHTS BK	IL	B-	11/02/04
HERITAGE COMMUNITY BK	IL	B-	11/02/04
HOYNE SVGS BK	IL	B-	11/02/04
HUNTINGDON VALLEY BK	PA	B-	11/02/04
INTERAUDI BK	NY	B-	11/02/04
INTERCHANGE ST BK	NJ	B-	11/02/04
IRON & GLASS BK	PA	B-	11/02/04
JEFFERSON B&TC	MO	B-	11/02/04
KISHACOQUILLAS VALLEY NB	PA	B-	11/02/04

Rating Downgrades (Continued)

BANK NAME	STATE	PREVIOUS WEISS SAFETY RATING	DATE OF CHANGE
Weiss Safety Rating: C+			**(Continued)**
LAKE FOREST B&TC	IL	B-	11/02/04
LEE BK	MA	B-	11/02/04
LIBERTY BK	CA	B-	11/02/04
LIBERTY SVGS BK FSB	IN	B-	11/02/04
LIBERTYVILLE B&TC	IL	B-	11/02/04
MARION CENTER NB	PA	B-	11/02/04
MARLBOROUGH CO-OP BK	MA	B-	11/02/04
METRO BK OF DADE COUNTY	FL	B-	11/02/04
MILLBURY NB	MA	B-	11/02/04
MINNWEST BK SOUTH	MN	B-	11/02/04
MIZUHO CORPORATE BK USA	NY	B-	11/02/04
MIZUHO TRUST & BANKING CO USA	NY	B-	11/02/04
MONARCH COMMUNITY BANK	MI	B-	11/02/04
MOORHEAD ST BK	IA	B-	11/02/04
MOUNTAIN NB	TN	B-	11/02/04
NATIONAL BK OF GEORGIA	GA	B-	11/02/04
NATIONAL BK OF VERNON	NY	B-	11/02/04
NEW CENTURY BK-FAYETTEVILLE	NC	B-	11/02/04
NORTH BK	IL	B-	11/02/04
NORTHEAST BK FSB	ME	B-	11/02/04
NORTHWEST COMMUNITY BK	CT	B-	11/02/04
PATRIOT BK NA	VA	B-	11/02/04
PEOPLES B&TC OF MADISON CTY	KY	B-	11/02/04
PEOPLES BK	IA	B-	11/02/04
PEOPLES BK	TN	B-	11/02/04
PEOPLES BK OF MACON	IL	B-	11/02/04
PIONEER B&TC	MO	B-	11/02/04
PREMIER BK	KS	B-	11/02/04
PROGRESSIVE BK NA	WV	B-	11/02/04
RIPLEY FS&LA	OH	B-	11/02/04
ROCKHOLD BROWN & CO BK	OH	B-	11/02/04
SECOND NB OF WARREN	OH	B-	11/02/04
SECURITY BK	TX	B-	11/02/04
SECURITY ST B&TC	TX	B-	11/02/04
SECURITY ST BK	TX	B-	11/02/04
SOUTHWEST NB	OK	B-	11/02/04
STATE BK	MI	B-	11/02/04
STERLING BK	FL	B-	11/02/04
STOCK GROWERS BK	ND	B-	11/02/04
STRATEGIC CAP BK	IL	B-	11/02/04
SUN COUNTRY BK	CA	B-	11/02/04
TEXAS NB	TX	B-	11/02/04
TOWNE CENTER BANK	NJ	B-	11/02/04
TWIN VALLEY BK	OH	B-	11/02/04
UMB BK OMAHA NA	NE	B-	11/02/04
UMB BK WARSAW NA	MO	B-	11/02/04
UNIBANK FOR SVGS	MA	B-	11/02/04
UNION BK	LA	B-	11/02/04
UNION NB	IL	B-	11/02/04
UNION ST BK	TX	B-	11/02/04
UNITED B&T	MI	B-	11/02/04
VALLEY NB	NM	B-	11/02/04
VILLAGE B&T SSB	TX	B-	11/02/04
VILLAGE BK	IL	B-	11/02/04
WARWICK COMMERCIAL BK	NY	B-	11/02/04
WARWICK SVGS BK	NY	B-	11/02/04
WASHINGTON TRUST CO	RI	B-	11/02/04
WEBSTER BK NA	CT	B-	11/02/04
WESTERN DAKOTA BK	SD	B-	11/02/04
WESTERN ST BK	KS	B-	11/02/04
Weiss Safety Rating: C			
ALLIANCE BK OF ARIZONA	AZ	C+	11/02/04
AMERICAN BK	MD	C+	11/02/04
ARKANSAS BANKERS BK	AR	C+	11/02/04
BANK OF AMERICA NA USA	AZ	C+	11/02/04
BANK OF EASTERN OREGON	OR	C+	11/02/04
BANK OF VERNON	TX	C+	11/02/04
BANK ONE DEARBORN NA	MI	C+	11/02/04
BANKFIRST FINANCIAL SVC	MS	C+	11/02/04
BREDA SVG BK	IA	C+	11/02/04
BUSINESS BK	LA	C+	11/02/04
CAPITAL B&TC	TN	C+	11/02/04
CARLINVILLE NB	IL	B-	11/02/04
CARROLLTON FEDERAL BANK	KY	C+	11/02/04
CENTRUE BK	IL	C+	11/02/04
CITADEL BK	CO	C+	11/02/04
CITIZENS & FARMERS BK	VA	B-	11/02/04
CITIZENS FINANCIAL BANK	KY	B-	11/02/04
CITIZENS NB OF RUSSELLVILLE	KY	C+	11/02/04
CITIZENS NB OF SOMERSET	KY	C+	11/02/04
CITIZENS NB SPRINGFIELD	MO	C+	11/02/04
CITIZENS ST BK OF SHIPMAN	IL	C+	11/02/04
CITY NB	TX	C+	11/02/04
CLEAR LAKE B&TC	IA	C+	11/02/04
COLONIAL CO-OP BK	MA	C+	11/02/04
COMMERCIAL BK	MS	C+	11/02/04
COMMUNITY BK	IA	C+	11/02/04
COMMUNITY BK	OH	C+	11/02/04
COMMUNITY BK NORTHERN VA	VA	C+	11/02/04
COMMUNITY BK OF PETTIS CTY	MO	C+	11/02/04
CORNERSTONE COMMUNITY BK	WI	C+	11/02/04
CROW RIVER ST BK	MN	C+	11/02/04
CROWN BK NA	NJ	B-	11/02/04
DEDHAM INST FOR SVGS	MA	C+	11/02/04
ELBERTON FS&LA	GA	C+	11/02/04
EQUITY BK	MN	C+	11/02/04
ERWIN NB	TN	C+	11/02/04
EXCHANGE BK	NE	B-	11/02/04
FAMILY FS&LA	MA	B-	11/02/04
FARMERS B&TC	NE	C+	11/02/04
FARMERS BK OF GOWER	MO	C+	11/02/04
FARMERS ST BK OF HIGHLAND	KS	C+	11/02/04
FARNAM BK	NE	C+	11/02/04
FIDELITY B&TC	IA	C+	11/02/04
FIRST BK	FL	B-	11/02/04
FIRST FINANCIAL BK	KY	B-	11/02/04
FIRST FS&LA OF HAMMOND	IN	C+	11/02/04
FIRST FSB	MN	C+	11/02/04
FIRST GASTON BK OF NC	NC	C+	11/02/04
FIRST MORRIS B&TC	NJ	C+	11/02/04
FIRST NB	CO	C+	11/02/04
FIRST NB	IA	C+	11/02/04
FIRST NB OF FREDERICK	SD	C+	11/02/04
FIRST NB OF GILBERT	MN	C+	11/02/04
FIRST NB OF LITCHFIELD	IL	C+	11/02/04
FIRST NB OF THE CAROLINAS	SC	C+	11/02/04
FIRST ST BK	IL	C+	11/02/04
FIRST ST BK	SD	C+	11/02/04
FIRST UNION DIRECT BK NA	GA	C+	11/02/04
GEORGE WASHINGTON BK	IL	C+	11/02/04
GORHAM SVGS BK	ME	C+	11/02/04
GREENEVILLE FEDERAL BK FSB	TN	C+	11/02/04
INTERBANK	OK	C+	11/02/04
JEFFERSON SECURITY BK	WV	C+	11/02/04
KIRKPATRICK BK	OK	B-	11/02/04
LAKESIDE ST BK	OK	C+	11/02/04
LEADER BK NA	MA	C+	11/02/04
LIBERTY BK NA	OH	B-	11/02/04
LITCHFIELD NB	IL	C+	11/02/04
MADISON B&TC	IN	C+	11/02/04

Rating Downgrades (Continued)

BANK NAME	STATE	PREVIOUS WEISS SAFETY RATING	DATE OF CHANGE	BANK NAME	STATE	PREVIOUS WEISS SAFETY RATING	DATE OF CHANGE
Weiss Safety Rating: **C**		**(Continued)**		FIRST LIBERTY NB	DC	C+	11/02/04
				FIRST NB	MN	C+	11/02/04
MAGYAR SVGS BK	NJ	C+	11/02/04	FIRST NB	VA	C	11/02/04
MERCHANTS & FARMERS BK	AL	C+	11/02/04	FIRST NB IN EXETER	NE	B-	11/02/04
MID PENN BK	PA	C+	11/02/04	FIRST NB OF COLORADO SPR	CO	C	11/02/04
MIDWEST COMMUNITY BK	IL	C+	11/02/04	FIRST NB OF COLUMBIA	KY	C	11/02/04
MIZUHO CORPORATE BK OF CA	CA	C+	11/02/04	FIRST NB OF IPSWICH	MA	C	11/02/04
MONTICELLO BK	FL	C+	11/02/04	FIRST NB OF SLIPPERY ROCK	PA	C+	11/02/04
NATIONAL CITY BK	IN	C+	11/02/04	FIRST NB OF STRATTON	CO	C	11/02/04
NEW CARLISLE FSB	OH	C+	11/02/04	FIRST NB OF THROCKMORTON	TX	C	11/02/04
NEW SOUTH FSB	AL	C+	11/02/04	FIRST NB, TORRINGTON	WY	C	11/02/04
PALMER ST BK	IL	C+	11/02/04	FIRST ST BK	MO	C	11/02/04
PATRIOT NB	CT	C+	11/02/04	FIRST ST BK	OK	C+	11/02/04
PEOPLES BK	KY	B-	11/02/04	FIRST ST BK	WI	C+	11/02/04
PEOPLES ST BK MADISON LAKE	MN	C+	11/02/04	FIRST ST BK OF HOTCHKISS	CO	C	11/02/04
PERKINS ST BK	FL	B-	11/02/04	FIRST ST BK OF KC KS	KS	C+	11/02/04
SECURITY ST BK	IA	C+	11/02/04	FLINT HILLS BK OF ESKRIDGE	KS	C	11/02/04
SIMSBURY B&TC	CT	C+	11/02/04	FLORIDA BK NA	FL	C+	11/02/04
SOUTHERN NB	GA	C+	11/02/04	FRANKLIN ST B&TC	LA	C	11/02/04
STATE BK OF INDIA (CALIF)	CA	C+	11/02/04	FULLERTON FSA	MD	C	11/02/04
STATE BK OF ROGERS	MN	C+	11/02/04	GARNAVILLO SVG BK	IA	C+	11/02/04
STATE BK OF SPEER	IL	C+	11/02/04	GEORGETOWN SVGS BK	MA	C+	11/02/04
TEXAS COMMUNITY BK NA	TX	C+	11/02/04	GREAT BASIN BK OF NEVADA	NV	C	11/02/04
TORREY PINES BK	CA	C+	11/02/04	GREAT EASTERN BK OF FLORIDA	FL	C	11/02/04
UNIBANK	FL	C+	11/02/04	GREAT PLAINS NB	ND	C	11/02/04
UNION B&TC	AR	C+	11/02/04	GREATER CHICAGO BK	IL	C	11/02/04
UNION CREDIT BK	FL	C+	11/02/04	HEADWATERS ST BK	WI	B-	11/02/04
UNITED CMNTY BK NA	TX	C+	11/02/04	JENNINGS ST BK	NE	C+	11/02/04
VALLEY COMMUNITY BK	CA	C+	11/02/04	LA PORTE SVGS BK	IN	C	11/02/04
WHITE HALL BK	IL	C+	11/02/04	LATHROP BK	MO	C+	11/02/04
YARDVILLE NB	NJ	C+	11/02/04	LAWRENCE BK	KS	C+	11/02/04
				LEADERS BK	IL	C	11/02/04
Weiss Safety Rating: **C-**				LEGACY BK	IA	C	11/02/04
				LIBERTY B&TC	LA	C	11/02/04
ALAMANCE NB	NC	C	11/02/04	LONG ISLAND COMMERCIAL BK	NY	C	11/02/04
AMERICAN BK	LA	C+	11/02/04	MARQUETTE FARMERS ST BK	KS	C	11/02/04
ANDERSON BK	OH	C	11/02/04	MEETING HOUSE CO-OP BK	MA	C	11/02/04
ANN ARBOR COMMERCE BK	MI	C	11/02/04	MILLS COUNTY BK NA	IA	C	11/02/04
BANK OF NORTHERN MI	MI	C	11/02/04	NBANC	OK	C	11/02/04
BANK OF PINE HILL	AL	C	11/02/04	NEBRASKA ST BK	NE	C+	11/02/04
BANK OF ST PETERSBURG	FL	C+	11/02/04	NEW RICHMOND NB	OH	C+	11/02/04
BEACON BANK	MN	C+	11/02/04	NORTHPOINTE BK	MI	C	11/02/04
BELMONT SVGS BK	MA	C	11/02/04	PACIFIC NB	FL	C	11/02/04
BORREGO SPRINGS BK NA	CA	C	11/02/04	PARK VIEW FSB	OH	C	11/02/04
CHAPPELL HILL BK	TX	C	11/02/04	PEOPLES ST BK OF WYALUSING	PA	C	11/02/04
CHINESE AMERICAN BK	NY	C+	11/02/04	PEOPLES TRUST CO	IN	C	11/02/04
CITIZENS FINANCIAL SVCS FSB	IN	C	11/02/04	RBC CENTURA BK	NC	C	11/02/04
CITIZENS ST BK	TN	C	11/02/04	RBC CENTURA CARD BK	GA	C	11/02/04
CITY NB	TX	C	11/02/04	RENASANT BK	TN	C	11/02/04
COATESVILLE SVG BK	PA	C	11/02/04	RICHTON B&TC	MS	C	11/02/04
COMMERCIAL BK OF MOTT	ND	C	11/02/04	ROYAL SVGS BK	IL	C+	11/02/04
COMMUNITY BK	LA	C+	11/02/04	SECURITY ST BK	MN	C	11/02/04
COMMUNITY PLUS SAVINGS BANK	MI	C+	11/02/04	SLEEPY HOLLOW BK	NY	C	11/02/04
DAKOTA ST BK	SD	C	11/02/04	SOUTHERN MISSOURI BK	MO	C	11/02/04
DISCOVERY BK	CA	C	11/02/04	STATE BK OF LUCAN	MN	C	11/02/04
EAGLE BK	MA	C	11/02/04	STATE BK OF MCGREGOR	MN	C+	11/02/04
EAST DUBUQUE SVGS BK	IA	C	11/02/04	STATE BK OF SEATON	IL	C	11/02/04
ESPIRITO SANTO BK	FL	C	11/02/04	STOCKTON NB	KS	C	11/02/04
FAIRFIELD FS&LA	OH	C	11/02/04	STONE CITY BK OF BEDFORD IN	IN	C	11/02/04
FARMERS & MERCH BK HILL CITY	KS	C	11/02/04	SUNDANCE ST BK	WY	C	11/02/04
FARMERS & MERCHANTS BK	GA	C	11/02/04	TERRE HAUTE SVGS BK	IN	C	11/02/04
FARMERS ST BK	OH	C+	11/02/04	TIPPINS B&TC	GA	C	11/02/04
FIDUCIARY TC INTL	NY	C	11/02/04	TREGO-WAKEENEY STATE BANK	KS	C	11/02/04
FIRST COMMUNITY BK	MO	C	11/02/04	TRI-STATE BANK OF MEMPHIS	TN	C	11/02/04
FIRST COMMUNITY BK NA	TX	C	11/02/04	TWIN OAKS SVGS BK	IL	C+	11/02/04
FIRST FEDERAL OF NORTHERN MI	MI	C	11/02/04	VALLEY BK	IL	C	11/02/04
FIRST FS&LA	LA	C	11/02/04	VOLVO COMMERCIAL CR CORP UTAH	UT	C	11/02/04

Rating Downgrades (Continued)

BANK NAME	STATE	PREVIOUS WEISS SAFETY RATING	DATE OF CHANGE	BANK NAME	STATE	PREVIOUS WEISS SAFETY RATING	DATE OF CHANGE
Weiss Safety Rating: C- (Continued)				PATRICK HENRY NB	VA	C-	11/02/04
				PEOPLES BK	CT	C	11/02/04
WASHINGTON FSB	PA	C+	11/02/04	RIGGS BK NA	VA	C	11/02/04
				RIVERSIDE BK	AR	C-	11/02/04
Weiss Safety Rating: D+				RUBY VALLEY NB	MT	C-	11/02/04
				RUSHFORD ST BK	MN	C-	11/02/04
ASIA-EUROPE-AMERICAS BK	WA	C	11/02/04	SOUTH CAROLINA COMMUNITY BK	SC	C-	11/02/04
BAKER-BOYER NATIONAL BANK	WA	C-	11/02/04	STATE BK OF LAKE PARK	MN	C-	11/02/04
BANK OF BENNINGTON	NE	C-	11/02/04	STATE BK OF SW MISSOURI	MO	C-	11/02/04
BANK OF LINCOLNWOOD	IL	C-	11/02/04	STATE SVG BK	IA	C-	11/02/04
BANK OF POCAHONTAS	AR	C-	11/02/04	TWO RIVER COMMUNITY BK	NJ	C-	11/02/04
BANK OF TERRELL	GA	C-	11/02/04	UNION FEDERAL SVGS BK	RI	C-	11/02/04
BANK OF THE ROCKIES NA	MT	C-	11/02/04	UNION ST BK	AL	C	11/02/04
BANK OF WAUKEGAN	IL	C-	11/02/04	UNITED FARMERS & MERCH ST BK	MN	C-	11/02/04
BANKVISTA	MN	C	11/02/04	UNIVERSITY NB	KS	C-	11/02/04
BEACH BK	FL	C-	11/02/04	VALLEY SVGS BK	OH	C-	11/02/04
BLUE RIDGE BK NA	VA	C-	11/02/04	VILLAGE BK	MO	C	11/02/04
BRAMBLE SAVINGS BK	OH	C	11/02/04	WAUKEGAN S&LA SB	IL	C	11/02/04
CAPITOL CITY B&TC	GA	C-	11/02/04	WYOMING COUNTY BK	NY	C-	11/02/04
CENTENNIAL NB	MN	C-	11/02/04				
CENTRA BK	WV	C-	11/02/04	**Weiss Safety Rating: D**			
CITIZENS BK	TN	C+	11/02/04				
CITIZENS BK OF KS NA	KS	C-	11/02/04	AMERIBANK INC	WV	C-	11/02/04
CITIZENS NB	KS	C-	11/02/04	AMERICAN BK NA	TX	C-	11/02/04
CITIZENS NB OF SOUTHWESTERN	OH	C-	11/02/04	CHASEWOOD BK	TX	D+	11/02/04
CITIZENS ST BK	TX	C-	11/02/04	CITIZENS BK	IL	D+	11/02/04
COLUMBIA COUNTY BK	FL	C-	11/02/04	CITIZENS NB OF QUITMAN	GA	C-	11/02/04
COMMUNITY FIRST BK NA	PA	C-	11/02/04	CITIZENS ST BK	OK	D+	11/02/04
ELSA ST B&TC	TX	C	11/02/04	CLEVELAND BK	OK	D+	11/02/04
FARMERS ST B&TC	IL	C-	11/02/04	COLORADO MOUNTAIN BK	CO	D+	11/02/04
FARMERS ST BK	IA	C-	11/02/04	COMMUNITY BK	CA	D+	11/02/04
FARMERS ST BK	MN	C-	11/02/04	COMMUNITY FIRST NB	KS	D+	11/02/04
FBR NATIONAL TC	MD	C-	11/02/04	CONSUMER NB	MS	D+	11/02/04
FIRST BK	IN	C-	11/02/04	ELBERFELD ST BK	IN	D+	11/02/04
FIRST CARNEGIE DEPOSIT	PA	C-	11/02/04	EXCHANGE BK	OH	D+	11/02/04
FIRST CHOICE BK	IL	C-	11/02/04	FARMERS ST BK	KS	D+	11/02/04
FIRST INTEGRITY BK NA	MN	C-	11/02/04	FIRST AMERICAN BK	OK	C-	11/02/04
FIRST NB OF ARENZVILLE	IL	C-	11/02/04	FIRST CHEROKEE ST BK	GA	D+	11/02/04
FIRST NB OF BAR HARBOR	ME	C-	11/02/04	FIRST COMMUNITY BK	AR	C-	11/02/04
FIRST NB OF NEWMAN GROVE	NE	C-	11/02/04	FIRST HEIGHTS BANK, A FSB	MI	D+	11/02/04
FIRST NB OF SOUTH MIAMI	FL	C-	11/02/04	FIRST MOUNTAIN BK	CO	D+	11/02/04
FIRST NB OF STARBUCK	MN	C-	11/02/04	FIRST NB OF BARRON	WI	D+	11/02/04
FIRST SIGNATURE B&TC	NH	C-	11/02/04	FIRST NB OF EVANT	TX	C-	11/02/04
FIRST ST BK	IA	C-	11/02/04	FIRST NB OF SHELBY CTY	AL	D+	11/02/04
FIRST ST BK	TX	C-	11/02/04	FORREST CITY BK NA	AR	D+	11/02/04
FIRST ST BK OF LOOMIS	NE	C-	11/02/04	GREATER ATLANTIC BK	VA	D+	11/02/04
FLORA SVGS BK	IL	C-	11/02/04	HENDERSON ST BK	NE	D+	11/02/04
FOSTER BANK	IL	C-	11/02/04	HOLBROOK CO-OP BK	MA	D+	11/02/04
FRANKLIN BK OF CALIFORNIA	CA	C-	11/02/04	HORRY CTY ST BK	SC	C-	11/02/04
GARDEN CITY ST BK	KS	C	11/02/04	LEGACY BK OF TX	TX	C-	11/02/04
GEORGIA CENTRAL BK	GA	C	11/02/04	MCVILLE ST BK	ND	D+	11/02/04
HANSTON ST BK	KS	C-	11/02/04	NATIONAL BK OF ARKANSAS	AR	D+	11/02/04
HARVARD SVG BK	IL	B	11/02/04	OAKLAND ST BK	IA	D+	11/02/04
IDAHO BKG CO	ID	C-	11/02/04	PEOPLES BK	KS	C-	11/02/04
INDEPENDENCE ST BK	WI	C	11/02/04	PINE CITY ST BK	MN	D+	11/02/04
INTERSTATE NET BK	NJ	C-	11/02/04	REGENT B&TC NA	OK	C-	11/02/04
JEFFERSON BK	TX	C-	11/02/04	ROBERTSON BKG CO	AL	C-	11/02/04
KAW VALLEY ST BK	KS	C-	11/02/04	SECURITY HOME BK	NE	D+	11/02/04
LANDMARK BK OF FLORIDA	FL	C-	11/02/04	SECURITY ST BK	IA	D+	11/02/04
MID-AMERICA BK	KS	C-	11/02/04	SOUTH LAFOURCHE B&TC	LA	C-	11/02/04
MUTUAL BK	IL	C	11/02/04	STATE BK OF LORETTO	MN	C-	11/02/04
NATIONAL BK OF GAINESVILLE	GA	C	11/02/04	SUBURBAN FSB	MD	D+	11/02/04
NBANK NA	GA	C-	11/02/04	SUNCOAST BK	FL	D+	11/02/04
NEWTON CTY LOAN & SVGS FSB	IN	C-	11/02/04	TD BK USA FSB	NJ	D+	11/02/04
NORTHLAND FINANCIAL	ND	C-	11/02/04	TD WATERHOUSE BK NA	NJ	D+	11/02/04
OAK LAWN BK	IL	C-	11/02/04	TIMEWELL ST BK	IL	C-	11/02/04
OTTAWA SVGS BK	IL	B+	11/02/04	TRADERS BK	WV	D+	11/02/04
				UNIFIED BANKING COMPANY	KY	D+	11/02/04

Rating Downgrades (Continued)

BANK NAME	STATE	PREVIOUS WEISS SAFETY RATING	DATE OF CHANGE
Weiss Safety Rating: D (Continued)			
VALLEY NB	OK	D+	11/02/04
Weiss Safety Rating: D-			
AMERICAN HERITAGE BK	NM	D	11/02/04
BANK OF CLARKS	NE	D	11/02/04
BANK OF DURANGO	CO	D	11/02/04
BANK OF WESTERN OKLAHOMA	OK	D+	11/02/04
BISON ST BK	KS	D	11/02/04
CENTRAL VALLEY BK	IA	D	11/02/04
CITIZENS ST BK OF FINLEY	ND	D+	11/02/04
CITYWIDE BKS	CO	D+	11/02/04
COMMUNITY CAPITAL BK	NY	D+	11/02/04
FARMERS ST BK	ND	D	11/02/04
FIRST NB GRAFORD	TX	D	11/02/04
FIRST NB OF ST MARYS	WV	D	11/02/04
FIRST ST BK	OK	D	11/02/04
FIRST ST BK HONEY GROVE TX	TX	D	11/02/04
FORD COUNTY ST BK	KS	D+	11/02/04
IOWA ST BK	IA	D	11/02/04
KENT COUNTY ST BK	TX	D	11/02/04
MARCO COMMUNITY BK	FL	D	11/02/04
MIDWESTONE B&TC	IA	D	11/02/04
MIDWESTONE BK	IA	D	11/02/04
NAB BK	IL	D	11/02/04
NEW WEST BK	CO	D	11/02/04
OGLETHORPE BK	GA	D	11/02/04
PACIFIC COMMERCE BK NA	CA	D	11/02/04
PELLA ST BK	IA	D	11/02/04
RUSHVILLE ST BK	MO	D	11/02/04
SEBREE DEPOSIT BK	KY	D+	11/02/04
SECURITY BK-PULASKI CTY	MO	D	11/02/04
SECURITY ST BK	MN	D	11/02/04
SENECA FALLS SVGS BK	NY	D	11/02/04
STATE BK OF BURRTON	KS	D	11/02/04
STONEBRIDGE BK	PA	D+	11/02/04
Weiss Safety Rating: E+			
AMERICAN UNION S&LA	IL	D-	11/02/04
CITIZENS BK OF WEIR	KS	D-	11/02/04
CITIZENS ST BK	KS	D-	11/02/04
COMMUNITY FIRST BANK	KY	D-	11/02/04
DEKALB BK	AL	D-	11/02/04
FIRST COMMERCIAL BK	MN	D-	11/02/04
FIRST NB OF NASH	OK	D-	11/02/04
FIRST ST BK	OK	D-	11/02/04
GATEWAY BK	MO	D-	11/02/04
HARVEST COMMUNITY BK	NJ	D+	11/02/04
IDEAL FSB	MD	D-	11/02/04
JONES COUNTY BK	GA	D-	11/02/04
NORTH LOUP VALLEY BK	NE	D-	11/02/04
OGLESBY ST BK	TX	D-	11/02/04
PEOPLES BK	MO	D-	11/02/04
TILDEN BK	NE	D-	11/02/04
VIGILANT FSB	MD	D	11/02/04
Weiss Safety Rating: E			
BANK OF CORBIN	KY	D-	11/02/04
FARMERS ST BK OF DENT	MN	D-	11/02/04
FLORA B&TC	IL	D	11/02/04
HERITAGE BK OF ASHLAND	KY	D	11/02/04
NORTH ATLANTA NB	GA	D	11/02/04
OAKDALE ST BK	IL	E+	11/02/04
QUALITY BK	ND	D	11/02/04

BANK NAME	STATE	PREVIOUS WEISS SAFETY RATING	DATE OF CHANGE
UNIVERSITY BK	MI	E+	11/02/04
WEST TOWN SVGS BK	IL	D	11/02/04
Weiss Safety Rating: E-			
ALLENDALE COUNTY BK	SC	E	11/02/04
CEDAR RAPIDS ST BK	NE	E	11/02/04
FARMERS NB OF WINFIELD	IA	E	11/02/04
FIRST NB OF PAONIA	CO	D-	11/02/04
FIRST NB&TC IN LARNED	KS	E	11/02/04
FIRST ST BK	IL	E	11/02/04
FREEPORT ST BK	KS	E+	11/02/04
HULETT NB	WY	E	11/02/04
IMPERIAL S&LA INC	VA	E	11/02/04
STATE BK	IA	E	11/02/04
UMBRELLABANK FSB	IL	E	11/02/04
UNION ST BK OF FARGO	ND	E	11/02/04

Appendix

RECENT BANK AND THRIFT FAILURES

2004

Institution	Headquarters	Date of Failure	Total Assets ($Mil)	Weiss Safety Rating
Bank of Ephraim	Ephraim, UT	06/25/04	46.4	D- (Weak)
Reliance Bank	White Plains, NY	03/19/04	30.3	E- (Very Weak)
Guaranty National Bank of	Tallahassee, FL	03/12/04	104.6	D- (Weak)
Dollar Savings Bank	Newark, NJ	02/13/04	11.4	C+ (Fair)

2003

Institution	Headquarters	Date of Failure	Total Assets ($Mil)	Weiss Safety Rating
Pulaski Savings Bank	Philadelphia, PA	11/14/03	9.8	E (Very Weak)
First NB Blanchardville	Blanchardville, WI	05/09/03	35.0	C (Fair)
Southern Pacific Bank	Los Angeles, CA	02/07/03	1095.0	E- (Very Weak)

2002

Institution	Headquarters	Date of Failure	Total Assets ($Mil)	Weiss Safety Rating
Farmers Bank & Trust	Cheneyville, LA	12/17/02	37.0	C+ (Fair)
Bank of Alamo	Alamo, TN	11/08/02	69.4	E- (Very Weak)
Amtrade Intl Bk of Georgia	Atlanta, GA	09/30/02	12.0	E- (Very Weak)
Universal FSB	Chicago, IL	06/27/02	52.0	C (Fair)
Connecticut Bank of Commerce	Stamford, CT	06/26/02	398.6	E- (Very Weak)
New Century Bk	Southfield, MI	03/28/02	19.0	E- (Very Weak)
Net First NB	Boca Raton, FL	03/01/02	34.7	D- (Weak)
Nextbank, NA	Phoenix, AZ	02/07/02	700.0	E- (Very Weak)
Oakwood Deposit Bk Co.	Oakwood, OH	02/01/02	72.3	C (Fair)
Bank of Sierra Blanca	Sierra Blanca, TX	01/18/02	10.8	E- (Very Weak)
Hamilton Bk NA	Miami, FL	01/11/02	1,400.0	E- (Very Weak)

2001

Institution	Headquarters	Date of Failure	At Date of Failure	
			Total Assets ($Mil)	Weiss Safety Rating
Sinclair NB	Gravette, AR	09/07/01	9.7	E- (Very Weak)
Superior Bank, FSB	Oakbrook Terrace, IL	07/27/01	2,300.0	E- (Very Weak)
Malta NB	Malta, OH	05/03/01	9.5	E+ (Very Weak)
First Alliance B & TC	Manchester, NH	02/02/01	18.4	E- (Very Weak)

2000

Institution	Headquarters	Date of Failure	At Date of Failure	
			Total Assets ($Mil)	Weiss Safety Rating
National State Bank	Metropolis, IL	12/14/00	91.7	A- (Excellent)
Bank of Honolulu	Honolulu, HI	10/16/00	66.9	D- (Weak)
Bank of Falkner	Falkner, MS	10/02/00	77.1	C+ (Fair)
Town and Country Bk	Almelund, MN	07/14/00	30.1	C- (Fair)
Monument NB	Ridgecrest, CA	06/02/00	10.0	E- (Very Weak)
Mutual Federal Svgs Bk	Atlanta, GA	03/10/00	33.8	E- (Very Weak)
Hartford-Carlisle Svgs Bk	Carlisle, IA	01/14/00	113.8	D+ (Weak)

1999

Institution	Headquarters	Date of Failure	At Date of Failure	
			Total Assets ($Mil)	Weiss Safety Rating
Golden City Commercial Bank	New York, NY	12/10/99	89.3	E- (Very Weak)
Pacific Thrift & Loan Co.	Woodland Hills, CA	11/19/99	117.6	E- (Very Weak)
Peoples NB of Commerce	Miami Beach, FL	09/10/99	37.6	E- (Very Weak)
First NB of Keystone	Keystone, WV	09/01/99	1,117.7	D+ (Weak)
East Texas National Bank	Marshall, TX	07/09/99	127.3	E- (Very Weak)
OceanMark Bank	N. Miami Beach, FL	07/09/99	70.6	E- (Very Weak)
Zia New Mexico Bank	Tucumcari, NM	04/23/99	16.8	E- (Very Weak)
Victory State Bank	Columbia, SC	03/26/99	13.9	E- (Very Weak)

1998

Institution	Headquarters	Date of Failure	At Date of Failure	
			Total Assets ($Mil)	Weiss Safety Rating
Q Bank	Fort Benton, MT	08/07/98	15.1	C- (Fair)
BestBank	Boulder, CO	07/23/98	314.1	C (Fair)
Omnibank	River Rouge, MI	04/09/98	42.2	D- (Weak)

1997

Institution	Headquarters	Date of Failure	At Date of Failure	
			Total Assets ($Mil)	Weiss Safety Rating
Southwest Bank	Jennings, LA	11/21/97	27.4	E (Very Weak)

How Do Banks and Credit Unions Differ?

Since credit unions first appeared in 1946, they have been touted as a low-cost, friendly alternative to banks. But with tightening margins, pressure to compete in technology, branch closures, and the introduction of a host of service fees — some even higher than those charged by banks — the distinction between banks and credit unions has been gradually narrowing. Following are the key differences between today's banks and credit unions.

	Banks	**Credit Unions**
Access	Practically anyone is free to open an account or request a loan from any bank or thrift. There are no membership requirements.	Credit unions are set up to serve the needs of a specific group who share a "common bond." In order to open an account or request a loan, you must demonstrate that you meet the credit union's common bond requirements.
Ownership	Banks are owned by one or more investors who determine the bank's policies and procedures. A bank's customers do not have direct input into how the bank is operated.	Although they may be sponsored by a corporation or other entity, credit unions are owned by their members through their funds on deposit. Therefore, each depositor has a voice in how the credit union is operated.
Dividends and Fees	Banks and thrifts are for-profit organizations where the profits are used to pay dividends to the bank's investors or are reinvested in an effort to increase the bank's value to investors. In an effort to generate more profits, bank services and fees are typically more costly.	Credit unions are not-for-profit organizations. Any profits generated are returned to the credit union's members in the form of higher interest rates on deposits, lower loan rates, and free or low-cost services.
Management and Staffing	A bank's management and other staff are employees of the bank, hired directly or indirectly by its investors.	Credit unions are frequently run using elected members, volunteer staff, and staff provided by the credit union's sponsor. This helps to hold down costs.
Insurance	Banks and thrifts are insured by the Federal Deposit Insurance Corporation, an agency of the federal government.	Credit unions are insured by the National Credit Union Share Insurance Fund, which is managed by the National Credit Union Administration, an agency of the federal government.

Glossary

This glossary contains the most important terms used in this publication.

ARM	Adjustable-Rate Mortgage. This is a loan whose interest rate is tied to an index and is adjusted at a predetermined frequency. An ARM is subject to credit risk if interest rates rise and the borrower is unable to make the mortgage payment.
Average Recession	A recession involving a decline in real GDP that is approximately equivalent to the average of the postwar recessions of 1957-58, 1960, 1970, 1974-75, 1980 and 1981-82. It is assumed, however, that in today's market, the financial losses suffered from a recession of that magnitude would be greater than those experienced in previous decades. (See also "Severe Recession.")
Bank Holding Company	A company that holds stock in one or more banks and possibly other companies.
Brokered Deposits	Deposits that are brought into an institution through a broker. They are relatively costly, volatile funds that are more readily withdrawn from the institution if there is a loss of confidence or intense interest rate competition. Reliance on brokered deposits is usually a sign that the institution is having difficulty attracting deposits from its local geographic markets and could be a warning signal if other institutions in the same areas are not experiencing similar difficulties.
Capital	The cushion an institution has of its own resources to help withstand losses. The basic component of capital is stockholder's equity which consists of common and preferred stock and retained earnings. (See also "Core Capital")
Cash & Equivalents	Cash plus highly liquid assets which can be readily converted to cash.
Core (Tier 1) Capital	A measurement of capital defined by the federal regulatory agencies for evaluating an institution's degree of leverage. Core capital consists of the following: common stockholder's equity, preferred stockholder's equity up to certain limits, and retained earnings net of any intangible assets.
Critical Ranges	Guidelines developed to help you evaluate the levels of each index contributing to a company's Weiss Safety Rating. The sum or average of these grades does not necessarily have a one-to-one correspondence with the final rating for an institution because the rating is derived from a wider range of more complex calculations.
Equity	Total assets minus total liabilities. This is the "capital cushion" the institution has to fall back on in times of trouble. (See also "Capital.")
FDIC	Federal Deposit Insurance Corporation. The provider of insurance on deposits. This agency also plays an active role when banks and thrifts are found to be insolvent or in need of federal assistance. It is the governing body of both the Bank Insurance Fund (BIF) and the Savings Association Insurance Fund (SAIF).

Federal Home Loan Bank (FHLB)

A quasi-governmental agency (reporting to the Federal Housing Finance Board) whose chartered purpose is to promote the issuance of mortgage loans by providing increased liquidity to lenders. This agency raises money by issuing notes and bonds and then lends the money to thrifts and other mortgage lenders.

Federal Reserve

America's central bank, regulating all banks that offer transaction accounts. It works hand-in-hand with the FDIC, providing examination and regulation of its member banks.

Federal Savings and Loan Insurance Corporation (FSLIC)

The now-defunct agency of the Federal Home Loan Bank Board that provided deposit insurance to savings and loans until it was replaced by the Savings Association Insurance Fund (SAIF) in 1989. The FSLIC was also responsible for examining thrifts and liquidating insolvent institutions. Savings and loans are now examined by the Office of Thrift Supervision and liquidated by the FDIC.

FSB

Federal Savings Bank. A thrift institution operating under a federal charter.

Goodwill

The value of an institution as a going concern, meaning the value which exceeds book value on a balance sheet. It generally represents the value of a well-respected business name, good customer relations, high employee morale and other intangible factors which would be expected to translate into greater than normal earning power. In a bank or thrift acquisition, goodwill is the value paid by a buyer of the institution in excess of the value of the institution's equity because of these intangible factors.

Hot Money

Individual deposits of $100,000 or more plus those deposits received through a broker. These types of deposits are considered "hot money" because they tend to chase whoever is offering the best interest rates at the time and are thus relatively costly and fairly volatile sources of funds.

Loan Loss Reserves

The amount of capital an institution sets aside to cover any potential losses due to the nonrepayment of loans.

N.A.

National Association. A commercial bank operating under a federal charter.

Net Charge-offs

The amount of foreclosed loans written off the institution's books since the beginning of the year, less any previous write-offs that were recovered during the year.

Net Interest Spread

The difference between the interest income earned on the institution's loans and investments and the interest expense paid on its interest-bearing deposits and borrowings. This "spread" is most commonly analyzed as a percentage of average earning assets to show the institution's net return on income-generating assets.

Since the margin between interest earned and interest paid is generally where the company generates the majority of its income, this figure provides insight into the company's ability to effectively manage interest spreads. A low Net Interest Spread can be the result of poor loan and deposit pricing, high levels of nonaccruing loans, or poor asset/liability management.

Net Profit or Loss	The bottom line income or loss the institution has sustained in its most recent reporting period.
Nonaccruing Loans	Loans for which payments are past due and full repayment is doubtful. Interest income on these loans is no longer recorded on the income statement. (See also "Past Due Loans.")
Nonperform- ing Loans	The sum of loans past due 90 days or more and nonaccruing loans. These are loans the institution made where full repaytuion is now doubtful. (See also "Past Due Loans" and "Nonaccruing Loans.")
Past Due Loans	Loans for which payments are at least 90 days in arears. The institution continues to record income on these loans, even though none is actually being received, because it is expected that the borrower will eventually repay the loan in full. It is likely, however, that at least a portion of these loans will move into nonaccruing status. (See also "Nonaccruing Loans.")
OCC	Office of the Comptroller of the Currency. This agency of the U.S. Treasury Department is the primary regulator of national banks.
OTS	Office of Thrift Supervision. This regulatory agency of the U.S. Treasury Department is responsible for chartering, examining, and supervising savings and loan institutions.
Overhead Expense	Expenses of the institution other than interest expense, such as salaries and benefits of employees, rent and utility expenses, and data processing expenses. A certain amount of "fixed" overhead is required to operate a bank or thrift, so it is important that the institution leverage that overhead to the fullest extent in supporting its revenue-generating activities.
RBCR	See "Risk-Based Capital Ratio."
Resolution Trust Corporation (RTC)	The now-defunct federal agency that was formed to handle the liquidation of insolvent savings and loans.
Restructured Loans	Loans whose terms have been modified in order to enable the borrower to make payments which he otherwise would be unable to make. Modifications could include a reduction in the interest rate or a lengthening of the time to maturity.
Risk-Based Capital Ratio	A ratio originally developed by the International Committee on Banking as a means of assessing the adequacy of an institutuion's capital in relation to the amount of credit risk on and off its balance sheet. (See also "Risk-weighted Assets.")
Risk- Weighted Assets	The sum of assets and certain off-balance sheet items after they have been individually adjusted for the level of credit risk they pose to the institution. Assets with close to no risk are weighted 0%; those with minor risk are weighted 20%; those with low risk, 50%; and those with normal or high risk, 100%.
R.O.A	Return on Assets calculated as net profit or loss as a percentage of average assets. This is the most commonly used measure of bank profitability.

R.O.E.	Return on Equity calculated as net profit or loss as a percentage of average equity. This represents the rate of return on the shareholders' investment.
S.A.	Savings Association.
Savings and Loan (S&L)	A financial institution that traditionally offered primarily home mortgages to individuals and served small depositors. However, in 1980, savings and loans were given power to diversify into other areas of lending. Also known as a thrift.
Savings and Loan Holding Company	A company that holds stock in one or more savings and loans and possibly other companies.
Savings Association Insurance Fund (SAIF)	Fund created in 1989 by Congress to replace the FSLIC as the provider of deposit insurance to thrifts. This fund is administered by the Federal Deposit Insurance Corporation (FDIC). (See also "Bank Insurance Fund.")
Savings Bank	A financial institution created to serve primarily the small saver and to lend mortgage money to individuals. Though savings banks have expanded their services, they are still primarily engaged in providing consumer mortgages and accepting consumer deposits. Also known as a thrift.
Severe Recession	A drop in real GDP which is significantly greater than that of an average postwar recession. (See also "Average Recession.")
Stockholder's Equity	See "Equity."
Thrift	Generic term for an institution formed primarily as a depository for consumer savings and a lender for home mortgages, such as a savings and loan or a savings bank.
Total Assets	Total resources of an institution, primarily composed of cash, securities (such as municipal and treasury bonds), loans, and fixed assets (such as real estate, buildings, and equipment).
Total Equity	See "Equity."
Total Liabilities	All debts owed by an institution. Normally, the largest liability of a bank or thrift is its deposits.
Trust Company	A financial institution chartered to provide trust services (legal agreements to act for the benefit of another party), which may also be authorized to provide banking services.
Weiss Safety Rating	Weiss Safety Ratings, which grade institutions on a scale from A (Excellent) to F (Failed). Ratings are based on many factors, emphasizing capitalization, asset quality, profitability, liquidity, and stability.

Weiss Ratings'

WEISS RATINGS' SAFETY GUIDES

Weiss Ratings' comprehensive industry-wide guides provide the most accurate, complete source of safety ratings on more than 15,000 financial institutions including banks and insurance companies.

Issued Quarterly. Price: $499 + $19.95 s/h for 4 quarterly issues, or $249 + $8.95 s/h for a single edition.

Guide to Life, Health, and Annuity Insurers covers more than 1,500 U.S. life, health and annuity insurers.

Guide to Property and Casualty Insurers covers more than 2,500 property and casualty insurers in the U.S.

Guide to HMOs and Health Insurers is the only source covering more than 1,200 U.S. health insurers including all Blue Cross/Blue Shield plans and over 500 HMOs.

Guide to Banks and Thrifts covers more than 9,000 banks and thrifts in the U.S.

WEISS RATINGS' INVESTMENT GUIDES

Weiss Ratings' comprehensive investment guides provide the most accurate, complete information for more than 20,000 investment choices.

Issued Quarterly. Price: $499 + $19.95 s/h for 4 quarterly issues , or $249 + $8.95 s/h for a single edition.

☆ **NEW!** *Ultimate Guided Tour of Stock Investing* is a must-have, easy-to-understand guide presented in a friendly, fun format complete with our "Wise Guide" who leads you on an informative safari through the stock market jungle. Complete with how-to information on stock investing, useful worksheets, examples on common topics such as diversification, the Weiss Performance and Risk Ratings, and much more! This guide will help you learn to invest and successfully manage your stock portfolio. Covers every stock on the American Stock Exchange, New York Stock Exchange, and the NASDAQ.

Guide to Stock Mutual Funds covers more than 7,000 equity mutual funds, including balanced funds, international funds, and individual sector funds.

Guide to Bond and Money Market Mutual Funds covers more than 4,200 fixed-income mutual funds, including government bond funds, municipal bond funds, and corporate bond funds.

Guide to Closed-End Mutual Funds covers more than 600 closed-end mutual funds, including growth funds, sector funds, international funds, municipal bond funds and other closed-end funds.

Guide to Common Stocks covers stocks on the American Stock Exchange, New York Stock Exchange, and the NASDAQ, plus more.

WEISS RATINGS' SHOPPER'S GUIDES

Weiss Ratings' Shopper's Guides come packed with customized information needed to make sound purchasing decisions.

Fully Customized Reports. Price: $49 + $4.95 s/h

Shopper's Guide to Long-Term Care Insurance gives price comparisons for long-term care insurance based on your age, gender, and location. Long-term care policies are grouped based on comparable benefit features, followed by a complete list of each policy's benefits.

Shopper's Guide to Medicare Supplement Insurance has price comparisons for Medigap insurance based on your age, gender, and zip code. Insurance companies are listed by Weiss rating to provide price and safety comparisons.

Shopper's Guide to Term Life Insurance has price comparisons for term life insurance based on your age, gender, zip code and other unique information. You'll find the insurers who are currently offering the best rates.

WEISS RATINGS' CONSUMER GUIDES

Weiss Ratings' Consumer Guides provide the critical information needed to make sound financial decisions including step-by-step instructions, worksheets, sample rates and more.

Price: $119 + $7.95 s/h for 4 quarterly issues, or $49 + $4.95 s/h for a single edition.
Consumer Guide Box Set Price: $399 + $19.95 s/h includes one full year of updates.

Consumer Guide to Variable Annuities leads you step by step through understanding when variable annuities make sense and how they actually work. This easy-to-use guide looks at the 20 best and worst variable annuities on the market today, all the costs to look for, and the advantages and disadvantages of variable annuities versus other investments.

Consumer Guide to Elder Care Choices is designed to educate you on the many care options available and to provide you with the necessary tools to make informed decisions on Continuing Care Retirement Communities, Assisted Living Facilities, Home Health Care Agencies, Adult Day Care, Nursing Homes, and more.

Consumer Guide to Long-Term Care Insurance gives you how-to information on how to select the right long-term care policy for you, with worksheets, definitions and sample policy information.

Consumer Guide to Medicare Supplement Insurance is a must have for anyone considering the purchase of Medigap insurance. This how-to guide leads you through the process showing where the gaps are, how to fill them, and how you determine what type of policy is best for you.

Consumer Guide to Auto Insurance can help you save hundreds of dollars on auto insurance. The guide can help you understand the coverage required in your state, get the right insurance for your vehicle, save money on your premiums, and so much more.

Consumer Guide to Homeowners Insurance provides a complete how-to guide on purchasing homeowner's insurance including types of coverage, how to save money, choosing the right company, and more.

For a consumer-friendly guide on Stock Investing, see the "Weiss Ratings' Investment Guides" category on the previous page for our **NEW** *Ultimate Guided Tour of Stock Investing*.

WEISS RATINGS' REPORTS AND SERVICES

See pricing below for each report and service.

Ratings Online — An on-line summary covering an individual company's Weiss Safety Rating or an investment's unique Weiss Investment Rating with the factors contributing to that rating; available 24 hours a day by visiting www.WeissRatings.com. Price: $14.99 each.

Ratings Over the Phone — Call our customer hotline at 1-800-289-9222 to receive a rating over the telephone. Price: $19 each.

Unlimited Ratings Research — The ultimate research tool providing fast, easy online access to the very latest Weiss Safety Ratings and Weiss Investment Ratings (includes 4 quarterly editions of one guide). Price: $559 per industry, + $19.95 s/h.

Rating Analysis Report — A detailed report on an individual company or investment including the rating and an in-depth analysis of each of the factors contributing to the rating. Price: $49 + $4.95 s/h.

Weiss Watchdog Service — An immediate notification service announcing any changes in a company's rating, plus a quarterly rating update. Price: $59 for first company, and $49 for each additional company.

Top-Rated Stocks Service — This monthly service highlights the cream of the investment crop with a complete list of those stocks receiving our highest Weiss Investment Ratings. Weiss' top-rated stocks averaged a positive 8.63% return in 2002, beating the broad market loss of -22.15. Price: $169 + $14.95 s/h for a monthly subscription (12 issues) or $69 + $4.95 s/h for a single issue.

WEISS RATINGS' CUSTOM REPORTS

Weiss Ratings is pleased to offer two customized options for receiving our data. Each taps into our vast data repositories and is designed to provide exactly the data you need. Choose from a variety of industries, companies, data variables, and delivery formats including print, Excel, SQL, Text or Access.

Call 1-800-289-9222 today for pricing.

Customized Reports - get right to the heart of your company's research and data needs with a report customized with just the data you need.

Complete Database Download - we design and deliver the database; you're then free to sort it, recalculate it, and format your results to suit your specific needs.

2 EASY WAYS TO ORDER

❶ Call our Customer Hotline at 1-800-289-9222

❷ Order Online at www.WeissRatings.com